BIBLE *in a* YEAR

Your Daily Encounter with God

BIBLE *in a* YEAR

Your Daily Encounter with God

Revised Standard Version of the Bible
Second Catholic Edition
Ignatius Edition

Augustine Institute
Greenwood Village, Colorado

General Editor: Dr. Tim Gray

Writers: Dr. Mark Giszczak, Dr. Tim Gray, Dr. Elizabeth Klein, Ms. Debora Holiday, Dr. Michael Morris, Dr. Scott Powell, Dr. John Sehorn

Print Production: Jeff Cole, Brenda Kraft, Grace Hagan, Jane Myers, Devin Schadt, Kris Gray, Kenzie Key, Emily Lehman, Ann Diaz, Mary Pollice, Anna Lenshek, Denise Fath, Bryan Johnson

Cover Design: Ben Dybas, Christina Gray

Augustine Institute
6160 South Syracuse Way, Suite 310
Greenwood Village, CO 80111
Information: 303-937-4420
AugustineInstitute.org

Printed in the United States of America
ISBN: 978-0-9991778-9-1 [P]
978-0-9991778-8-4 [L]

The Augustine Institute gratefully acknowledges
that this *Bible in a Year*
was made possible through the generosity of
Peter and Marilyn Coors
and Richard and Peggy McClintock

TABLE OF CONTENTS

ABBREVIATIONS FOR THE BOOKS OF THE BIBLE

The Old Testament

Gn ... Genesis
Ex ... Exodus
Lv ... Leviticus
Nm ... Numbers
Dt ... Deuteronomy
Jos ... Joshua
Jgs ... Judges
Ru ... Ruth
1 Sm ... 1 Samuel
2 Sm ... 2 Samuel
1 Kgs ... 1 Kings
2 Kgs ... 2 Kings
1 Chr ... 1 Chronicles
2 Chr ... 2 Chronicles
Ezr ... Ezra
Neh ... Nehemiah
Tb ... Tobit
Jdt ... Judith
Est ... Esther
Jb ... Job
Ps ... Psalms
Prv ... Proverbs
Eccl ... Ecclesiastes
Sg ... Song of Solomon
Wis ... Wisdom
Sir ... Sirach
Is ... Isaiah
Jer ... Jeremiah
Lam ... Lamentations
Bar ... Baruch
Ez ... Ezekiel
Dn ... Daniel
Hos ... Hosea
Jl ... Joel
Am ... Amos
Ob ... Obadiah
Jon ... Jonah
Mi ... Micah
Na ... Nahum
Hb ... Habakkuk
Zep ... Zephaniah
Hg ... Haggai
Zec ... Zechariah
Mal ... Malachi
1 Mc ... 1 Maccabees
2 Mc ... 2 Maccabees

The New Testament

Mt ... Matthew
Mk ... Mark
Lk ... Luke
Jn ... John
Acts ... Acts of the Apostles
Rom ... Romans
1 Cor ... 1 Corinthians
2 Cor ... 2 Corinthians
Gal ... Galatians
Eph ... Ephesians
Phil ... Philippians
Col ... Colossians
1 Thes ... 1 Thessalonians
2 Thes ... 2 Thessalonians
1 Tm ... 1 Timothy
2 Tm ... 2 Timothy
Ti ... Titus
Phlm ... Philemon
Heb ... Hebrews
Jas ... James
1 Pt ... 1 Peter
2 Pt ... 2 Peter
1 Jn ... 1 John
2 Jn ... 2 John
3 Jn ... 3 John
Jude ... Jude
Rev ... Revelation

ALPHABETICAL INDEX TO THE BOOKS OF THE BIBLE

WELCOME TO BIBLE IN A YEAR

There is no other book like the Bible. It is old by any standard, reaching back into the millennia. Yet, it is still very much in demand and by far the most translated book in human history, continuously translated into new languages and regularly translated afresh where it has been read for generations. Jesus himself spoke to the perennial power of the Word when he observed, "Heaven and earth will pass away, but my words will not pass away" (Mt 24:35). No matter how often God is declared dead, his Word is found to be living and active.

In the first century, Saint Paul wrote to the newly baptized Christians in Colossae: "The word of the truth, the gospel which has come to you, as indeed in the whole world it is bearing fruit and growing—so among yourselves…" (Col 1:5–6). God's Word continues, even today, to bear fruit throughout the world, whether in Africa or Asia, in Russia, or in new green shoots in the West. It is a word that not only brings inspiration, encouragement, and hope, but it changes lives. Why? There is simply no substitute for the Word of God. Other authors can be inspiring, but none can claim, as Scripture can, to be inspired by God himself. It is this divine authorship of Scripture that makes it not only precious, but a mediator of God's presence. Thus, reading the Word of God is an encounter with God. As the Second Vatican Council put it, citing Saint Augustine, "In the sacred books, the Father who is in heaven comes lovingly to meet his children, and talks with them" *(Dei Verbum,* 21). How often do people seeking God close their eyes and try to hear his voice? But God invites us to first open our eyes and read: "Blessed is he who reads" and "blessed are those who hear, and who keep what is written therein" (Rev 1:3). You don't have to be a mystic to hear God speak to you; all you need to do, as Saint Augustine discovered in his conversion, is take and read!

Comprised of seventy-three distinct books from numerous authors and genres, the Bible is more like a library than a single book. Many have picked up the Bible determined to read it in its entirety, only to put it down discouraged, and so the Word remains unheard. The Augustine Institute has published this *Bible in a Year* to provide a simple daily plan that not only makes reading the entire Bible in a single year an attainable goal, but will also help you develop the habit of daily encountering God in his Word.

Rather than simply reading sequentially from Genesis to Revelation, each day the reader is given readings from three distinct parts of the Bible—from the Old Testament, the Wisdom literature, and the New Testament. Thus, there is never a day where your only reading will be a genealogical list of names or detailed instructions on Israel's sacrificial practices, but such readings will be supplemented with passages from other parts of the Bible. In addition to Scripture passages, each day's reading includes a short reflection, providing insight as a "jumping-off point" from the Scriptures into your own prayer and helping to put the Word into action in your life.

Each day you will pick up where you left off the day before, so if you continue in these readings every day for a year, you will read through the entire Bible! Start any day of the year and keep reading each calendar day. It does not matter if you start on January 1, June 29, or September 8… just start on that day and work your way through for the next twelve months.

Many people who read through the entire Bible find it so rewarding that they repeat the journey over and over again. Once you get in the habit of reading and praying with God's Word each day, you will want to keep up your conversation with God.

Why read the Bible? "Faith comes from what is heard," as Saint Paul observed (Rom 10:17). To daily take time to listen to God is to grow daily in faith. Reading God's Word brings us understanding, and with deeper faith comes hope. As Paul reminds us, "For whatever was written in former days was written for our instruction, that by steadfastness and by the encouragement of the Scriptures we might have hope" (Rom 15:4). The greatest motive to persevere in reading Scripture? Love of God. Jesus taught, "If you continue in my word, you are truly my disciples, and you will know the truth, and the truth will make you free" (Jn 8:31). Abiding in God's Word is the way of a disciple of Jesus Christ.

Dr. Tim Gray
President, Augustine Institute

WAYS TO USE BIBLE IN A YEAR

There are several ways you might like to use the daily readings:

1) Bible in one year, once a day: Follow the plan. Read each day's readings during your daily Bible reading time to finish the whole Bible in a year.

2) Bible in one year, twice a day: Read each day's readings, but in two sittings. Read the Old Testament passage in the morning and the Wisdom literature and New Testament readings in the evening, followed by the reflection.

3) Bible in two years: Read the Old Testament readings in the first year, then the Wisdom literature and New Testament readings the second year.

KEY TO SUCCESS: APPOINT A TIME AND PLACE

The *Bible in a Year* gives you a simple-to-use reading plan. All you need to do is choose the time and place each day that you will prayerfully read God's Word. Select a time you know you can make each day. The wisdom of God's Word is that you put first things first in the day, ideally praying and reading in the morning: "Those who rise early to seek him will find favor" (Sir 32:14). Abraham, Moses, and Isaiah were each known to arise early to pray: "Morning by morning he wakens, he wakens my ear to hear as those who are taught" (Is 50:4). Indeed, Jesus himself prayed in the early hours of the morning (see Mk 1:35). But whatever time you choose, put it into your calendar as an appointment, and stick with it. Choose a place to read—one that is comfortable, and most importantly, quiet and free from distractions.

January 1

GENESIS 1

In the beginning God created the heavens and the earth. 2The earth was without form and void, and darkness was upon the face of the deep; and the Spirit of God was moving over the face of the waters.

3And God said, "Let there be light"; and there was light. 4And God saw that the light was good; and God separated the light from the darkness. 5God called the light Day, and the darkness he called Night. And there was evening and there was morning, one day.

6And God said, "Let there be a firmament in the midst of the waters, and let it separate the waters from the waters." 7And God made the firmament and separated the waters which were under the firmament from the waters which were above the firmament. And it was so. 8And God called the firmament Heaven. And there was evening and there was morning, a second day.

9And God said, "Let the waters under the heavens be gathered together into one place, and let the dry land appear." And it was so. 10God called the dry land Earth, and the waters that were gathered together he called Seas. And God saw that it was good. 11And God said, "Let the earth put forth vegetation, plants yielding seed, and fruit trees bearing fruit in which is their seed, each according to its kind, upon the earth." And it was so. 12The earth brought forth vegetation, plants yielding seed according to their own kinds, and trees bearing fruit in which is their seed, each according to its kind. And God saw that it was good. 13And there was evening and there was morning, a third day.

14And God said, "Let there be lights in the firmament of the heavens to separate the day from the night; and let them be for signs and for seasons and for days and years, 15and let them be lights in the firmament of the heavens to give light upon the earth." And it was so. 16And God made the two great lights, the greater light to rule the day, and the lesser light to rule the night; he made the stars also. 17And God set them in the firmament of the heavens to give light upon the earth, 18to rule over the day and over the night, and to separate the light from the darkness. And God saw that it was good. 19And there was evening and there was morning, a fourth day.

20And God said, "Let the waters bring forth swarms of living creatures, and let birds fly above the earth across the firmament of the heavens." 21So God created the great sea monsters and every living creature that moves, with which the waters swarm, according to their kinds, and every winged bird according to its kind. And God saw that it was good. 22And God blessed them, saying, "Be fruitful and multiply and fill the waters in the seas, and let birds multiply on the earth." 23And there was evening and there was morning, a fifth day.

24And God said, "Let the earth bring forth living creatures according to their kinds: cattle and creeping things and beasts of the earth according to their kinds." And it was so. 25And God made the beasts of the earth according to their kinds and the cattle according to their kinds, and everything that creeps upon the ground according to its kind. And God saw that it was good.

26Then God said, "Let us make man in our image, after our likeness; and let them have dominion over the fish of the sea, and over the birds of the air, and over the cattle, and over all the earth, and over every creeping thing that creeps upon the earth." 27So God created man in his own image, in the image of God he created him; male and female he created them. 28And God blessed them, and God said to them, "Be fruitful and multiply, and fill the earth and subdue it; and have dominion over the fish of the sea and over the birds of the air and over every living thing that moves upon the earth." 29And God said, "Behold, I have given you every plant yielding seed which is upon the face of all the earth, and every tree with seed in its fruit; you shall have them for food. 30And to every beast of the earth, and to every bird of the air, and to everything that creeps on the earth, everything that has the breath of life, I have given every green plant for food." And it was so. 31And God saw everything that he had made, and behold, it was very good. And there was evening and there was morning, a sixth day.

2 Thus the heavens and the earth were finished, and all the host of them. 2And on the seventh day God finished his work which he had done, and he rested on the seventh day from all his work which he had done. 3So God blessed the seventh day and hallowed it, because on it God rested from all his work which he had done in creation.

4 These are the generations of the heavens and the earth when they were created.

In the day that the LORD God made the earth and the heavens, 5when no plant of the field was yet in the earth and no herb of the field had yet sprung up—for the LORD God had not caused it to rain upon the earth, and there was no man to till the ground; 6but a mist went up from the earth and watered the whole face of the ground—7then the LORD God formed man of dust from the ground, and breathed into his nostrils the breath of life; and man became a living soul. 8And the LORD God planted a garden in Eden, in the east; and there he put the man whom he had formed. 9And out of the ground the LORD God made to grow every tree that is pleasant to the sight and good for food, the tree of life also in the midst of the garden, and the tree of the knowledge of good and evil.

10A river flowed out of Eden to water the garden, and there it divided and became four rivers. 11The name of the first is Pi′shon; it is the one which flows around the whole land of Hav′ilah, where there is gold; 12and the gold of that land is good; bdellium and onyx stone are there. 13The name of the second river is Gi′hon; it is the one which flows around the whole land of Cush. 14And the name of the third river is Tigris, which flows east of Assyria. And the fourth river is the Euphra′tes.

15The LORD God took the man and put him in the garden of Eden to till it and keep it. 16And the LORD God commanded the man, saying, "You may freely eat of every tree of the garden; 17but of the tree of the knowledge of good and evil you shall not eat, for in the day that you eat of it you shall die."

18Then the LORD God said, "It is not good that the man should be alone; I will make him a helper fit for him." 19So out of the ground the LORD God formed every beast of the field and every bird of the air, and brought them to the man to see what he would call them; and whatever the man called every living creature, that was its name. 20The man gave names to all cattle, and to the birds of the air, and to every beast of the field; but for the man there was not found a helper fit for him. 21So the LORD God caused a deep sleep to fall upon the man, and while he slept took one of his ribs and closed up its place with flesh; 22and the rib which the LORD God had taken from the man he made into a woman and brought her to the man. 23Then the man said,

"This at last is bone of my bones
  and flesh of my flesh;
she shall be called Woman,
  because she was taken out of Man."

24Therefore a man leaves his father and his mother and clings to his wife, and they become one flesh. 25And the man and his wife were both naked, and were not ashamed.

PSALM 1

Blessed is the man
  who walks not in the counsel of the wicked,
nor stands in the way of sinners,
  nor sits in the seat of scoffers;
2but his delight is in the law of the LORD,
  and on his law he meditates day and night.
3He is like a tree
  planted by streams of water,
that yields its fruit in its season,
  and its leaf does not wither.
In all that he does, he prospers.

4The wicked are not so,
  but are like chaff which the wind
    drives away.

5Therefore the wicked will not stand in
the judgment,
nor sinners in the congregation of
the righteous;
6for the LORD knows the way of
the righteous,
but the way of the wicked will perish.

MATTHEW 1

The book of the genealogy of Jesus Christ, the son of David, the son of Abraham.

2Abraham was the father of Isaac, and Isaac the father of Jacob, and Jacob the father of Judah and his brothers, 3and Judah the father of Per′ez and Ze′rah by Ta′mar, and Perez the father of Hezron, and Hezron the father of Ram, 4and Ram the father of Ammin′adab, and Ammin′adab the father of Nahshon, and Nahshon the father of Salmon, 5and Salmon the father of Boaz by Ra′hab, and Boaz the father of O′bed by Ruth, and Obed the father of Jesse, 6and Jesse the father of David the king.

And David was the father of Solomon by the wife of Uri′ah, 7and Solomon the father of Rehobo′am, and Rehoboam the father of Abi′jah, and Abijah the father of Asa, 8and Asa the father of Jehosh′aphat, and Jehoshaphat the father of Jo′ram, and Joram the father of Uzzi′ah, 9and Uzzi′ah the father of Jo′tham, and Jotham the father of A′haz, and Ahaz the father of Hezeki′ah, 10and Hezeki′ah the father of Manas′seh, and Manasseh the father of Amos, and Amos the father of Josi′ah, 11and Josi′ah the father of Jechoni′ah and his brothers, at the time of the deportation to Babylon.

12And after the deportation to Babylon: Jechoni′ah was the father of She-al′ti-el, and She-alti-el the father of Zerub′babel, 13and Zerub′babel the father of Abi′ud, and Abiud the father of Eli′akim, and Eliakim the father of A′zor, 14and A′zor the father of Za′dok, and Zadok the father of A′chim, and Achim the father of Eli′ud, 15and Eli′ud the father of Elea′zar, and Eleazar the father of Matthan, and Matthan the father of Jacob, 16and Jacob the father of Joseph the husband of Mary, of whom Jesus was born, who is called Christ.

17So all the generations from Abraham to David were fourteen generations, and from David to the deportation to Babylon fourteen generations, and from the deportation to Babylon to the Christ fourteen generations.

18Now the birth of Jesus Christ took place in this way. When his mother Mary had been betrothed to Joseph, before they came together she was found to be with child of the Holy Spirit; 19and her husband Joseph, being a just man and unwilling to put her to shame, resolved to send her away quietly. 20But as he considered this, behold, an angel of the Lord appeared to him in a dream, saying, "Joseph, son of David, do not fear to take Mary your wife, for that which is conceived in her is of the Holy Spirit; 21she will bear a son, and you shall call his name Jesus, for he will save his people from their sins." 22All this took place to fulfil what the Lord had spoken by the prophet:

23"Behold, a virgin shall conceive and bear
a son,
and his name shall be called Emmanuel"

(which means, God with us). 24When Joseph woke from sleep, he did as the angel of the Lord commanded him; he took his wife, 25but knew her not until she had borne a son; and he called his name Jesus.

2 Now when Jesus was born in Bethlehem of Judea in the days of Herod the king, behold, Wise Men from the East came to Jerusalem, saying, 2"Where is he who has been born king of the Jews? For we have seen his star in the East, and have come to worship him." 3When Herod the king heard this, he was troubled, and all Jerusalem with him; 4and assembling all the chief priests and scribes of the people, he inquired of them where the Christ was to be born. 5They told him, "In Bethlehem of Judea; for so it is written by the prophet:

6'And you, O Bethlehem, in the land of Judah,
are by no means least among the rulers
of Judah;
for from you shall come a ruler
who will govern my people Israel.'"

7Then Herod summoned the Wise Men
secretly and ascertained from them what
time the star appeared; 8and he sent them to
Bethlehem, saying, "Go and search diligently
for the child, and when you have found him
bring me word, that I too may come and
worship him." 9When they had heard the
king they went their way; and behold, the star
which they had seen in the East went before
them, till it came to rest over the place where
the child was. 10When they saw the star, they
rejoiced exceedingly with great joy; 11and
going into the house they saw the child with
Mary his mother, and they fell down and
worshiped him. Then, opening their treasures,
they offered him gifts, gold and frankincense
and myrrh. 12And being warned in a dream
not to return to Herod, they departed to their
own country by another way.

REFLECTION

Scripture begins with God creating everything out of nothing. God's word is creative, and from it ushers a world filled with beauty, truth, and goodness. Much like his Creator, the author of Genesis employs his own creativity in shaping his words to tell with beauty and brevity the story of the Lord's creation. With beguiling simplicity he employs patterns of repetition, illustrating God's order and design from day to day. The author is no mere chronicler, and the reader of Scripture is challenged to read with care, as the series of days follows a deeper pattern: the first three days give the earth form, and the next three fill the void with content (solving the problems of formlessness and void in Genesis 1:2). The seventh day has no parallel, as well as no literal sunset, and, therefore, no end. Far from primitive prose, this account rises up to a poem of high praise—simple, but deeply sublime. As a wise scribe would later say, "It is the glory of God to conceal things, but the glory of kings is to search things out" (Prv 25:2). Reading Scripture is thus a kind of royal exploration. In science, man explores the "what" and the "how" of the world, but in the quest of Scripture, we take on the greater task of discovering the "why." What is a practical way to make the daily reading of Scripture an integral part of your spiritual life?

January 2

GENESIS 3

Now the serpent was more subtle than any other wild creature that the LORD God had made. He said to the woman, "Did God say, 'You shall not eat of any tree of the garden'?" 2And the woman said to the
serpent, "We may eat of the fruit of the
trees of the garden; 3but God said, 'You
shall not eat of the fruit of the tree which
is in the midst of the garden, neither shall
you touch it, lest you die.'" 4But the serpent
said to the woman, "You will not die. 5For
God knows that when you eat of it your
eyes will be opened, and you will be like
God, knowing good and evil." 6So when
the woman saw that the tree was good for
food, and that it was a delight to the eyes,
and that the tree was to be desired to make
one wise, she took of its fruit and ate; and
she also gave some to her husband, and he
ate. 7Then the eyes of both were opened,
and they knew that they were naked; and
they sewed fig leaves together and made
themselves aprons.

8And they heard the sound of the LORD
God walking in the garden in the cool of
the day, and the man and his wife hid
themselves from the presence of the LORD
God among the trees of the garden. 9But
the LORD God called to the man, and said
to him, "Where are you?" 10And he said, "I
heard the sound of you in the garden, and
I was afraid, because I was naked; and I hid
myself." 11He said, "Who told you that you
were naked? Have you eaten of the tree of
which I commanded you not to eat?" 12The
man said, "The woman whom you gave to
be with me, she gave me fruit of the tree,
and I ate." 13Then the LORD God said to the
woman, "What is this that you have done?"
The woman said, "The serpent beguiled
me, and I ate." 14The LORD God said to
the serpent,

"Because you have done this,
cursed are you above all cattle,
and above all wild animals;
upon your belly you shall go,
and dust you shall eat
all the days of your life.
15 I will put enmity between you
and the woman,
and between your seed and her seed;
he shall bruise your head,
and you shall bruise his heel."
16 To the woman he said,
"I will greatly multiply your pain
in childbearing;
in pain you shall bring forth children,
yet your desire shall be for your husband,
and he shall rule over you."
17 And to Adam he said,
"Because you have listened to the voice of
your wife,
and have eaten of the tree
of which I commanded you,
'You shall not eat of it,'
cursed is the ground because of you;
in toil you shall eat of it all the days of
your life;
18 thorns and thistles it shall bring forth
to you;
and you shall eat the plants of the field.
19 In the sweat of your face
you shall eat bread
till you return to the ground,
for out of it you were taken;
you are dust,
and to dust you shall return."

20 The man called his wife's name Eve, because she was the mother of all living. 21 And
the LORD God made for Adam and for his
wife garments of skins, and clothed them.
22 Then the LORD God said, "Behold, the
man has become like one of us, knowing
good and evil; and now, lest he put forth his
hand and take also of the tree of life, and eat,
and live for ever"—23 therefore the LORD God
sent him forth from the garden of Eden, to
till the ground from which he was taken.
24 He drove out the man; and at the east of the
garden of Eden he placed the cherubim, and
a flaming sword which turned every way, to
guard the way to the tree of life.

4 Now Adam knew Eve his wife, and she
conceived and bore Cain, saying, "I
have gotten a man with the help of the
LORD." 2 And again, she bore his brother
Abel. Now Abel was a keeper of sheep, and
Cain a tiller of the ground. 3 In the course of
time Cain brought to the LORD an offering
of the fruit of the ground, 4 and Abel brought
some of the firstlings of his flock and of
their fat portions. And the LORD had regard
for Abel and his offering, 5 but for Cain and
his offering he had no regard. So Cain was
very angry, and his countenance fell. 6 The
LORD said to Cain, "Why are you angry, and
why has your countenance fallen? 7 If you do
well, will you not be accepted? And if you
do not do well, sin is lurking at the door; its
desire is for you, but you must master it."

8 Cain said to Abel his brother, "Let us go
out to the field." And when they were in the
field, Cain rose up against his brother Abel,
and killed him. 9 Then the LORD said to Cain,
"Where is Abel your brother?" He said, "I do
not know; am I my brother's keeper?" 10 And
the LORD said, "What have you done? The
voice of your brother's blood is crying to me
from the ground. 11 And now you are cursed
from the ground, which has opened its
mouth to receive your brother's blood from
your hand. 12 When you till the ground, it shall
no longer yield to you its strength; you shall
be a fugitive and a wanderer on the earth."
13 Cain said to the LORD, "My punishment is
greater than I can bear. 14 Behold, you have
driven me this day away from the ground;
and from your face I shall be hidden; and
I shall be a fugitive and a wanderer on the
earth, and whoever finds me will slay me."
15 Then the LORD said to him, "Not so! If any
one slays Cain, vengeance shall be taken on
him sevenfold." And the LORD put a mark on
Cain, lest any who came upon him should
kill him. 16 Then Cain went away from the
presence of the LORD, and dwelt in the land
of Nod, east of Eden.

17 Cain knew his wife, and she conceived
and bore E′noch; and he built a city, and
called the name of the city after the name of
his son, Enoch. 18 To E′noch was born I′rad;
and Irad was the father of Mehu′ja-el, and

Mehuja-el the father of Methu′sha-el, and
Methusha-el the father of La′mech. 19And
La′mech took two wives; the name of the
one was A′dah, and the name of the other
Zillah. 20A′dah bore Ja′bal; he was the
father of those who dwell in tents and have
cattle. 21His brother's name was Ju′bal; he
was the father of all those who play the lyre
and pipe. 22Zillah bore Tu′bal-cain; he was
the forger of all instruments of bronze and
iron. The sister of Tubal-cain was Na′amah.
23La′mech said to his wives:

"A′dah and Zillah, hear my voice;
you wives of Lamech, hearken to
what I say:
I have slain a man for wounding me,
a young man for striking me.
24If Cain is avenged sevenfold,
truly La′mech seventy-sevenfold."

25And Adam knew his wife again, and she
bore a son and called his name Seth, for she
said, "God has appointed for me another
child instead of Abel, for Cain slew him."
26To Seth also a son was born, and he called
his name E′nosh. At that time men began to
call upon the name of the LORD.

5 This is the book of the generations of
Adam. When God created man, he
made him in the likeness of God. 2Male
and female he created them, and he blessed
them and named them Man when they were
created. 3When Adam had lived a hundred
and thirty years, he became the father of a
son in his own likeness, after his image, and
named him Seth. 4The days of Adam after
he became the father of Seth were eight
hundred years; and he had other sons and
daughters. 5Thus all the days that Adam
lived were nine hundred and thirty years;
and he died.

6When Seth had lived a hundred and five
years, he became the father of E′nosh. 7Seth
lived after the birth of E′nosh eight hundred
and seven years, and had other sons and
daughters. 8Thus all the days of Seth were
nine hundred and twelve years; and he
died.

9When E′nosh had lived ninety years, he
became the father of Ke′nan. 10 E′nosh lived
after the birth of Ke′nan eight hundred
and fifteen years, and had other sons and
daughters. 11Thus all the days of E′nosh were
nine hundred and five years; and he died.

12When Ke′nan had lived seventy years, he
became the father of Ma-hal′alel. 13Ke′nan
lived after the birth of Ma-hal′alel eight
hundred and forty years, and had other sons
and daughters. 14Thus all the days of Ke′nan
were nine hundred and ten years; and
he died.

15When Ma-hal′alel had lived sixty-five
years, he became the father of Jar′ed. 16Ma-
hal′alel lived after the birth of Jar′ed eight
hundred and thirty years, and had other
sons and daughters. 17Thus all the days of
Ma-hal′alel were eight hundred and ninety-
five years; and he died.

18When Jar′ed had lived a hundred and
sixty-two years he became the father of
E′noch. 19Jared lived after the birth of
E′noch eight hundred years, and had other
sons and daughters. 20Thus all the days of
Jar′ed were nine hundred and sixty-two
years; and he died.

21When E′noch had lived sixty-five years,
he became the father of Methu′selah.
22E′noch walked with God after the birth
of Methu′selah three hundred years, and
had other sons and daughters. 23Thus all
the days of E′noch were three hundred and
sixty-five years. 24E′noch walked with God;
and he was not, for God took him.

25When Methu′selah had lived a hundred
and eighty-seven years, he became the father
of La′mech. 26Methu′selah lived after the
birth of La′mech seven hundred and eighty-
two years, and had other sons and daughters.
27Thus all the days of Methu′selah were nine
hundred and sixty-nine years; and he died.
28When La′mech had lived a hundred and
eighty-two years, he became the father of
a son, 29and called his name Noah, saying,
"Out of the ground which the LORD has
cursed this one shall bring us relief from
our work and from the toil of our hands."
30La′mech lived after the birth of Noah five
hundred and ninety-five years, and had
other sons and daughters. 31Thus all the
days of La′mech were seven hundred and
seventy-seven years; and he died.

[32]After Noah was five hundred years old, Noah became the father of Shem, Ham, and Ja′pheth.

PSALM 2

Why do the nations conspire
and the peoples plot in vain?
[2]The kings of the earth set themselves,
and the rulers take counsel together,
against the LORD and his anointed, saying,
[3]"Let us burst their bonds asunder,
and cast their cords from us."

[4]He who sits in the heavens laughs;
the LORD has them in derision.
[5]Then he will speak to them in his wrath,
and terrify them in his fury, saying,
[6]"I have set my king
on Zion, my holy mountain."

[7]I will tell of the decree of the LORD:
He said to me, "You are my son,
today I have begotten you.
[8]Ask of me, and I will make the nations
your heritage,
and the ends of the earth your possession.
[9]You shall break them with a rod of iron,
and dash them in pieces like a potter's
vessel."

[10]Now therefore, O kings, be wise;
be warned, O rulers of the earth.
[11]Serve the LORD with fear,
with trembling [12]rejoice,
lest he be angry, and you perish in the way;
for his wrath is quickly kindled.

Blessed are all who take refuge in him.

MATTHEW 2

[13]Now when they had departed, behold, an angel of the Lord appeared to Joseph in a dream and said, "Rise, take the child and his mother, and flee to Egypt, and remain there till
I tell you; for Herod is about to search for
the child, to destroy him." [14]And he rose and
took the child and his mother by night, and
departed to Egypt, [15]and remained there
until the death of Herod. This was to fulfil
what the Lord had spoken by the prophet,
"Out of Egypt have I called my son."
[16]Then Herod, when he saw that he had been
tricked by the Wise Men, was in a furious
rage, and he sent and killed all the male
children in Bethlehem and in all that region
who were two years old or under, according
to the time which he had ascertained from
the Wise Men. [17]Then was fulfilled what was
spoken by the prophet Jeremiah:
[18]"A voice was heard in Ra′mah,
wailing and loud lamentation,
Rachel weeping for her children;
she refused to be consoled,
because they were no more."
[19]But when Herod died, behold, an angel
of the Lord appeared in a dream to Joseph
in Egypt, saying, [20]"Rise, take the child and
his mother, and go to the land of Israel, for
those who sought the child's life are dead."
[21]And he rose and took the child and his
mother, and went to the land of Israel. [22]But
when he heard that Archela′us reigned
over Judea in place of his father Herod, he
was afraid to go there, and being warned
in a dream he withdrew to the district of
Galilee. [23]And he went and dwelt in a city
called Nazareth, that what was spoken by
the prophets might be fulfilled. "He shall
be called a Nazarene."

REFLECTION

Every great story needs a villain. In the midst of the paradise of Eden, he enters—the primordial villain, the serpent, the devil himself. All other evil antagonists in every other story are but a shadow and echo of this original evil. In Revelation 12 we are told that he is a fallen angel who rebelled against God. His three most common titles in Scripture—the deceiver, the accuser, and the destroyer—unmask his tools and his goal. In his first encounter with humanity, his words seek to weave a web of deceit about God the Father, suggesting that he is a tyrant and his law is arbitrary. Here, and in all his efforts throughout history, Satan attempts to deceive those made in the image of God, robbing them of their divine likeness. The curse upon the serpent reveals that there will be enmity between the serpent and the seed of the woman (see Gn 3:15). Unfortunately, some descendants of the woman will fall under the influence of the serpent, as Cain does in killing Abel, and later as Herod will in seeking the life of the Child born of the Virgin—the long awaited "seed" that will crush the serpent's head. The serpent brings a great division within humanity, starting with Cain, to Herod, to the end of time. The question to ask yourself is, as St. Ignatius of Loyola describes in his *Spiritual Exercises*, under whose banner will you march?

January 3

GENESIS 6

When men began to multiply
on the face of the ground, and
daughters were born to them,
2the sons of God saw that the daughters
of men were fair; and they took to wife
such of them as they chose. 3Then the
LORD said, "My spirit shall not abide in man
for ever, for he is flesh, but his days shall be a
hundred and twenty years." 4The Neph′ilim
were on the earth in those days, and also
afterward, when the sons of God came
in to the daughters of men, and they bore
children to them. These were the mighty
men that were of old, the men of renown.
5The LORD saw that the wickedness of
man was great in the earth, and that every
imagination of the thoughts of his heart was
only evil continually. 6And the LORD was
sorry that he had made man on the earth,
and it grieved him to his heart. 7So the
LORD said, "I will blot out man whom I have
created from the face of the ground, man
and beast and creeping things and birds
of the air, for I am sorry that I have made
them." 8But Noah found favor in the eyes of
the LORD.
9These are the generations of Noah. Noah
was a righteous man, blameless in his
generation; Noah walked with God. 10And
Noah had three sons, Shem, Ham, and
Ja′pheth.
11Now the earth was corrupt in God's
sight, and the earth was filled with violence.
12And God saw the earth, and behold, it was
corrupt; for all flesh had corrupted their way
upon the earth. 13And God said to Noah, "I
have determined to make an end of all flesh;
for the earth is filled with violence through
them; behold, I will destroy them with the
earth. 14Make yourself an ark of gopher
wood; make rooms in the ark, and cover it
inside and out with pitch. 15This is how you
are to make it: the length of the ark three
hundred cubits, its breadth fifty cubits, and
its height thirty cubits. 16Make a roof for the
ark, and finish it to a cubit above; and set
the door of the ark in its side; make it with
lower, second, and third decks. 17For behold,
I will bring a flood of waters upon the earth,
to destroy all flesh in which is the breath of
life from under heaven; everything that is
on the earth shall die. 18But I will establish
my covenant with you; and you shall come
into the ark, you, your sons, your wife, and
your sons' wives with you. 19And of every
living thing of all flesh, you shall bring two
of every sort into the ark, to keep them alive
with you; they shall be male and female. 20Of
the birds according to their kinds, and of the
animals according to their kinds, of every
creeping thing of the ground according to
its kind, two of every sort shall come in to
you, to keep them alive. 21Also take with you
every sort of food that is eaten, and store it
up; and it shall serve as food for you and for
them." 22Noah did this; he did all that God
commanded him.

7 Then the LORD said to Noah, "Go into
the ark, you and all your household, for
I have seen that you are righteous before
me in this generation. 2Take with you seven
pairs of all clean animals, the male and his

mate; and a pair of the animals that are not
clean, the male and his mate; 3and seven
pairs of the birds of the air also, male and
female, to keep their kind alive upon the
face of all the earth. 4For in seven days I
will send rain upon the earth forty days and
forty nights; and every living thing that I
have made I will blot out from the face of
the ground." 5And Noah did all that the
LORD had commanded him.

6Noah was six hundred years old when
the flood of waters came upon the earth.
7And Noah and his sons and his wife and
his sons' wives with him went into the
ark, to escape the waters of the flood. 8Of
clean animals, and of animals that are not
clean, and of birds, and of everything that
creeps on the ground, 9two and two, male
and female, went into the ark with Noah,
as God had commanded Noah. 10And after
seven days the waters of the flood came
upon the earth.

11In the six hundredth year of Noah's life,
in the second month, on the seventeenth day
of the month, on that day all the fountains
of the great deep burst forth, and the
windows of the heavens were opened. 12And
rain fell upon the earth forty days and forty
nights. 13On the very same day Noah and
his sons, Shem and Ham and Ja´pheth, and
Noah's wife and the three wives of his sons
with them entered the ark, 14they and every
beast according to its kind, and all the cattle
according to their kinds, and every creeping
thing that creeps on the earth according
to its kind, and every bird according to its
kind, every bird of every sort. 15They went
into the ark with Noah, two and two of all
flesh in which there was the breath of life.
16And they that entered, male and female of
all flesh, went in as God had commanded
him; and the LORD shut him in.

17The flood continued forty days upon
the earth; and the waters increased, and
bore up the ark, and it rose high above the
earth. 18The waters prevailed and increased
greatly upon the earth; and the ark floated
on the face of the waters. 19And the waters
prevailed so mightily upon the earth that all
the high mountains under the whole heaven
were covered; 20the waters prevailed above
the mountains, covering them fifteen cubits
deep. 21And all flesh died that moved upon
the earth, birds, cattle, beasts, all swarming
creatures that swarm upon the earth, and
every man; 22everything on the dry land in
whose nostrils was the breath of life died.
23He blotted out every living thing that
was upon the face of the ground, man and
animals and creeping things and birds of the
air; they were blotted out from the earth.
Only Noah was left, and those that were with
him in the ark. 24And the waters prevailed
upon the earth a hundred and fifty days.

8 But God remembered Noah and all the
beasts and all the cattle that were with
him in the ark. And God made a wind blow
over the earth, and the waters subsided; 2the
fountains of the deep and the windows of
the heavens were closed, the rain from the
heavens was restrained, 3and the waters
receded from the earth continually. At the
end of a hundred and fifty days the waters
had abated; 4and in the seventh month, on
the seventeenth day of the month, the ark
came to rest upon the mountains of Ar´arat.
5And the waters continued to abate until
the tenth month; in the tenth month, on
the first day of the month, the tops of the
mountains were seen.

6At the end of forty days Noah opened
the window of the ark which he had made,
7and sent forth a raven; and it went to and
fro until the waters were dried up from the
earth. 8Then he sent forth a dove from him,
to see if the waters had subsided from the
face of the ground; 9but the dove found no
place to set her foot, and she returned to
him to the ark, for the waters were still on
the face of the whole earth. So he put forth
his hand and took her and brought her into
the ark with him. 10He waited another seven
days, and again he sent forth the dove out
of the ark; 11and the dove came back to him
in the evening, and behold, in her mouth
a freshly plucked olive leaf; so Noah knew
that the waters had subsided from the earth.
12Then he waited another seven days, and
sent forth the dove; and she did not return
to him any more.

[13]In the six hundred and first year, in the first month, the first day of the month, the waters were dried from off the earth; and Noah removed the covering of the ark, and looked, and behold, the face of the ground was dry. [14]In the second month, on the twenty-seventh day of the month, the earth was dry. [15]Then God said to Noah, [16]"Go forth from the ark, you and your wife, and your sons and your sons' wives with you. [17]Bring forth with you every living thing that is with you of all flesh—birds and animals and every creeping thing that creeps on the earth—that they may breed abundantly on the earth, and be fruitful and multiply upon the earth." [18]So Noah went forth, and his sons and his wife and his sons' wives with him. [19]And every beast, every creeping thing, and every bird, everything that moves upon the earth, went forth by families out of the ark.

[20]Then Noah built an altar to the LORD, and took of every clean animal and of every clean bird, and offered burnt offerings on the altar. [21]And when the LORD smelled the pleasing odor, the LORD said in his heart, "I will never again curse the ground because of man, for the imagination of man's heart is evil from his youth; neither will I ever again destroy every living creature as I have done. [22]While the earth remains, seedtime and harvest, cold and heat, summer and winter, day and night, shall not cease."

9 And God blessed Noah and his sons, and said to them, "Be fruitful and multiply, and fill the earth. [2]The fear of you and the dread of you shall be upon every beast of the earth, and upon every bird of the air, upon everything that creeps on the ground and all the fish of the sea; into your hand they are delivered. [3]Every moving thing that lives shall be food for you; and as I gave you the green plants, I give you everything. [4]Only you shall not eat flesh with its life, that is, its blood. [5]For your lifeblood I will surely require a reckoning; of every beast I will require it and of man; of every man's brother I will require the life of man. [6]Whoever sheds the blood of man, by man shall his blood be shed; for God made man in his own image. [7]And you, be fruitful and multiply, bring forth abundantly on the earth and multiply in it."

[8]Then God said to Noah and to his sons with him, [9]"Behold, I establish my covenant with you and your descendants after you, [10]and with every living creature that is with you, the birds, the cattle, and every beast of the earth with you, as many as came out of the ark. [11]I establish my covenant with you, that never again shall all flesh be cut off by the waters of a flood, and never again shall there be a flood to destroy the earth." [12]And God said, "This is the sign of the covenant which I make between me and you and every living creature that is with you, for all future generations: [13]I set my bow in the cloud, and it shall be a sign of the covenant between me and the earth. [14]When I bring clouds over the earth and the bow is seen in the clouds, [15]I will remember my covenant which is between me and you and every living creature of all flesh; and the waters shall never again become a flood to destroy all flesh. [16]When the bow is in the clouds, I will look upon it and remember the everlasting covenant between God and every living creature of all flesh that is upon the earth." [17]God said to Noah, "This is the sign of the covenant which I have established between me and all flesh that is upon the earth."

A Psalm of David, when he fled from Absalom his son.

PSALM 3

O LORD, how many are my foes!
Many are rising against me;
[2]many are saying of me,
there is no help for him in God. *Selah*
[3]But you, O LORD, are a shield about me,
my glory, and the lifter of my head.
[4]I cry aloud to the LORD,
and he answers me from his
holy mountain. *Selah*

[5]I lie down and sleep;
I wake again, for the LORD sustains me.

6I am not afraid of ten thousands of people
who have set themselves against me
round about.
7Arise, O LORD!
Deliver me, O my God!
For you strike all my enemies on the cheek,
you break the teeth of the wicked.
8Deliverance belongs to the LORD;
your blessing be upon your people! *Selah*

MATTHEW 3

In those days came John the Baptist, preaching in the wilderness of Judea, 2"Repent, for the kingdom of heaven is at hand."
3For this is he who was spoken of by the prophet Isaiah when he said,

"The voice of one crying in the wilderness:
Prepare the way of the Lord,
make his paths straight."

4Now John wore a garment of camel's hair,
and a leather belt around his waist; and his
food was locusts and wild honey. 5Then
went out to him Jerusalem and all Judea and
all the region about the Jordan, 6and they
were baptized by him in the river Jordan,
confessing their sins.

7But when he saw many of the Pharisees
and Sad′ducees coming for baptism, he
said to them, "You brood of vipers! Who
warned you to flee from the wrath to
come? 8Bear fruit that befits repentance,
9and do not presume to say to yourselves,
'We have Abraham as our father'; for I tell
you, God is able from these stones to raise
up children to Abraham. 10Even now the
axe is laid to the root of the trees; every tree
therefore that does not bear good fruit is
cut down and thrown into the fire.

11"I baptize you with water for repentance, but he who is coming after me
is mightier than I, whose sandals I am
not worthy to carry; he will baptize you
with the Holy Spirit and with fire. 12His
winnowing fork is in his hand, and he
will clear his threshing floor and gather
his wheat into the granary, but the chaff
he will burn with unquenchable fire."

13Then Jesus came from Galilee to the
Jordan to John, to be baptized by him.
14John would have prevented him, saying,
"I need to be baptized by you, and do
you come to me?" 15But Jesus answered
him, "Let it be so now; for thus it is
fitting for us to fulfil all righteousness."
Then he consented. 16And when Jesus
was baptized, he went up immediately
from the water, and behold, the heavens
were opened and he saw the Spirit of God
descending like a dove, and alighting on
him; 17and behold, a voice from heaven,
saying, "This is my beloved Son, with
whom I am well pleased."

REFLECTION

The biblical story of Genesis traces out two competing family lines from Adam and Eve. The line of Cain, with descendants like Lamech, illustrates the continued corruption of Cain's family. In contrast, the descendants of Seth call upon the name of the Lord (see Gn 4:26) and are noted as being in the image and likeness of God (see 5:1–3). Keeping these two lines in mind helps us understand a key problem that leads to the Flood: the marriage between the "sons of God" and the "daughters of men" (6:2). The men mentioned are from the line of Seth, and the women are from the line of Cain, and their intermarriage means there is no longer a faithful family line. The Sethites, with the exception of Noah, become corrupted like the Cainites. Noah, a worshipper of God, conformed to him who he worshipped, alone with his family will be saved and receive a covenant with a remarkable sign, the rainbow. But more remarkable, the New Covenant of Jesus Christ will surpass the old; for whereas in the waters of the flood, sinners are wiped out, in the waters of Baptism, sins are wiped out and sinners saved. What is one resolution that you can make today to live more fully the promises made at your Baptism?

January 4

GENESIS 9

[18]The sons of Noah who went forth from the ark were Shem, Ham, and Ja′pheth. Ham was the father of Canaan. [19]These three were the sons of Noah; and from these the whole earth was peopled.

[20]Noah was the first tiller of the soil. He planted a vineyard; [21]and he drank of the wine, and became drunk, and lay uncovered in his tent. [22]And Ham, the father of Canaan, saw the nakedness of his father, and told his two brothers outside. [23]Then Shem and Ja′pheth took a garment, laid it upon both their shoulders, and walked backward and covered the nakedness of their father; their faces were turned away, and they did not see their father's nakedness. [24]When Noah awoke from his wine and knew what his youngest son had done to him, [25]he said,

"Cursed be Canaan;
  a slave of slaves shall he be to
    his brothers."

[26]He also said,

"Blessed by the LORD my God be Shem;
  and let Canaan be his slave.
[27]God enlarge Ja′pheth,
  and let him dwell in the tents of Shem;
  and let Canaan be his slave."

[28]After the flood Noah lived three hundred and fifty years. [29]All the days of Noah were nine hundred and fifty years; and he died.

10 These are the generations of the sons of Noah, Shem, Ham, and Ja′pheth; sons were born to them after the flood.

[2]The sons of Ja′pheth: Gomer, Ma′gog, Ma′dai, Ja′van, Tu′bal, Me′shech, and Ti′ras. [3]The sons of Gomer: Ash′kenaz, Ri′phath, and Togar′mah. [4]The sons of Ja′van: Eli′shah, Tar′shish, Kittim, and Do′danim. [5]From these the coastland peoples spread. These are the sons of Ja′pheth in their lands, each with his own language, by their families, in their nations.

[6]The sons of Ham: Cush, Egypt, Put, and Canaan. [7]The sons of Cush: Seba, Hav′ilah, Sabtah, Ra′amah, and Sab′teca. The sons of Raamah: Sheba and De′dan. [8]Cush became the father of Nimrod; he was the first on earth to be a mighty man. [9]He was a mighty hunter before the LORD; therefore it is said, "Like Nimrod a mighty hunter before the LORD." [10]The beginning of his kingdom was Ba′bel, E′rech, and Accad, all of them in the land of Shi′nar. [11]From that land he went into Assyria, and built Nin′eveh, Reho′both-Ir, Ca′lah, and [12]Re′sen between Nin′eveh and Ca′lah; that is the great city. [13]Egypt became the father of Lu′dim, An′amim, Leha′bim, Naph′tuhim, [14]Pathru′sim, Caslu′him (whence came the Philis′tines), and Caph′torim.

[15]Canaan became the father of Si′don his first-born, and Heth, [16]and the Jeb′usites, the Am′orites, the Gir′gashites, [17]the Hi′vites, the Arkites, the Si′nites, [18]the Ar′vadites, the Zem′arites, and the Ha′mathites. Afterward the families of the Canaanites spread abroad. [19]And the territory of the Canaanites extended from Si′don, in the direction of Ge′rar, as far as Gaza, and in the direction of Sodom, Gomor′rah, Admah, and Zeboi′im, as far as La′sha. [20]These are the sons of Ham, by their families, their languages, their lands, and their nations.

[21]To Shem also, the father of all the children of E′ber, the elder brother of Ja′pheth, children were born. [22]The sons of Shem: E′lam, Asshur, Arpach′shad, Lud, and Ar′am. [23]The sons of Ar′am: Uz, Hul, Ge′ther, and Mash. [24]Arpach′shad became the father of She′lah; and Shelah became the father of E′ber. [25]To E′ber were born two sons: the name of the one was Pe′leg, for in his days the earth was divided, and his brother's name was Joktan. [26]Joktan became the father of Almo′dad, She′leph, Haz″arma′veth, Je′rah, [27]Hador′am, U′zal, Diklah, [28]O′bal, Abim′a-el, Sheba, [29]O′phir, Hav′ilah, and Jo′bab; all these were the sons of Joktan. [30]The territory in which they lived

extended from Me´sha in the direction
of Se´phar to the hill country of the east.
[31]These are the sons of Shem, by their
families, their languages, their lands, and
their nations.
[32]These are the families of the sons of
Noah, according to their genealogies, in
their nations; and from these the nations
spread abroad on the earth after the
flood.

11 Now the whole earth had one language and few words. [2]And as men
migrated from the east, they found a
plain in the land of Shinar and settled
there. [3]And they said to one another,
"Come, let us make bricks, and burn
them thoroughly." And they had brick for
stone, and bitumen for mortar. [4]Then they
said, "Come, let us build ourselves a city,
and a tower with its top in the heavens,
and let us make a name for ourselves,
lest we be scattered abroad upon the
face of the whole earth." [5]And the LORD
came down to see the city and the tower,
which the sons of men had built. [6]And the
LORD said, "Behold, they are one people,
and they have all one language; and this
is only the beginning of what they will
do; and nothing that they propose to do
will now be impossible for them. [7]Come,
let us go down, and there confuse their
language, that they may not understand
one another's speech." [8]So the LORD
scattered them abroad from there over
the face of all the earth, and they left off
building the city. [9]Therefore its name was
called Ba´bel, because there the LORD
confused the language of all the earth;
and from there the LORD scattered them
abroad over the face of all the earth.
[10]These are the descendants of Shem.
When Shem was a hundred years old,
he became the father of Arpach´shad
two years after the flood; [11]and Shem
lived after the birth of Arpach´shad five
hundred years, and had other sons and
daughters.
[12]When Arpach´shad had lived thirty-
five years, he became the father of She´lah;
[13]and Arpach´shad lived after the birth of
She´lah four hundred and three years, and
had other sons and daughters.
[14]When She´lah had lived thirty years, he
became the father of E´ber; [15]and She´lah
lived after the birth of E´ber four hundred
and three years, and had other sons and
daughters.
[16]When E´ber had lived thirty-four years,
he became the father of Pe´leg; [17]and E´ber
lived after the birth of Pe´leg four hundred
and thirty years, and had other sons and
daughters.
[18]When Pe´leg had lived thirty years, he
became the father of Re´u; [19]and Pe´leg lived
after the birth of Re´u two hundred and nine
years, and had other sons and daughters.
[20]When Re´u had lived thirty-two years,
he became the father of Se´rug; [21]and Re´u
lived after the birth of Se´rug two hundred
and seven years, and had other sons and
daughters.
[22]When Se´rug had lived thirty years, he
became the father of Na´hor; [23]and Se´rug
lived after the birth of Na´hor two hundred
years, and had other sons and daughters.
[24]When Na´hor had lived twenty-nine
years, he became the father of Te´rah; [25]and
Na´hor lived after the birth of Te´rah a
hundred and nineteen years, and had other
sons and daughters.
[26]When Te´rah had lived seventy years, he became the father of Abram, Na´hor, and Haran.
[27]Now these are the descendants of
Te´rah. Terah was the father of Abram,
Na´hor, and Haran; and Haran was the
father of Lot. [28]Haran died before his
father Te´rah in the land of his birth, in
Ur of the Chalde´ans. [29]And Abram and
Na´hor took wives; the name of Abram's
wife was Sar´ai, and the name of Na´hor's
wife, Milcah, the daughter of Haran the
father of Milcah and Is´cah. [30]Now Sar´ai
was barren; she had no child.
[31]Te´rah took Abram his son and Lot the
son of Haran, his grandson, and Sar´ai his
daughter-in-law, his son Abram's wife, and
they went forth together from Ur of the
Chalde´ans to go into the land of Canaan;
but when they came to Haran, they settled
there. [32]The days of Te´rah were two

hundred and five years; and Terah died in Haran.

To the choirmaster: with stringed instruments.
A Psalm of David.

PSALM 4

Answer me when I call, O God of my right!
You have given me room when I was in distress.
Be gracious to me, and hear my prayer.

2O sons of men, how long will you be dull of heart?
How long will you love vain words, and seek after lies? *Selah*
3But know that the LORD has set apart the godly for himself;
the LORD hears when I call to him.

4Be angry, but sin not;
commune with your own hearts on your beds, and be silent. *Selah*
5Offer right sacrifices,
and put your trust in the LORD.

6There are many who say, "O that we might see some good!
Lift up the light of your countenance upon us, O LORD!"
7You have put more joy in my heart
than they have when their grain and wine abound.

8In peace I will both lie down and sleep;
for you alone, O LORD, make me dwell in safety.

MATTHEW 4

Then Jesus was led up by the Spirit into the wilderness to be tempted by the devil. 2And he fasted forty days and forty nights, and afterward he was hungry. 3And the tempter came and said to him, "If you are
the Son of God, command these stones to become loaves of bread." 4But he answered, "It is written,
'Man shall not live by bread alone,
but by every word that proceeds from the mouth of God.'"
5Then the devil took him to the holy city, and set him on the pinnacle of the temple,
6and said to him, "If you are the Son of God, throw yourself down; for it is written,
'He will give his angels charge of you,'
and
'On their hands they will bear you up,
lest you strike your foot against a stone.'"
7Jesus said to him, "Again it is written, 'You shall not tempt the Lord your God.'"
8Again, the devil took him to a very high mountain, and showed him all the kingdoms of the world and the glory of
them; 9and he said to him, "All these I will give you, if you will fall down and worship
me." 10Then Jesus said to him, "Begone, Satan! for it is written,
'You shall worship the Lord your God
and him only shall you serve.'"
11Then the devil left him, and behold, angels came and ministered to him.
12Now when he heard that John had been arrested, he withdrew into Galilee; 13and
leaving Nazareth he went and dwelt in Caper′na-um by the sea, in the territory of Zeb′ulun and Naph′tali, 14that what was
spoken by the prophet Isaiah might be fulfilled:
15"The land of Zeb′ulun and the land of Naph′tali,
toward the sea, across the Jordan,
Galilee of the Gentiles—
16the people who sat in darkness
have seen a great light,
and for those who sat in the region and shadow of death
light has dawned."
17From that time Jesus began to preach, saying, "Repent, for the kingdom of heaven is at hand."

18As he walked by the Sea of Galilee, he saw two brothers, Simon who is called Peter and Andrew his brother, casting a net into the sea; for they were fishermen.

[19]And he said to them, "Follow me,
and I will make you fishers of men."
[20]Immediately they left their nets and
followed him. [21]And going on from there
he saw two other brothers, James the
son of Zeb′edee and John his brother,
in the boat with Zebedee their father,
mending their nets, and he called them.
[22]Immediately they left the boat and their
father, and followed him.
[23]And he went about all Galilee, teaching
in their synagogues and preaching the
gospel of the kingdom and healing every
disease and every infirmity among the
people. [24]So his fame spread throughout
all Syria, and they brought him all the
sick, those afflicted with various diseases
and pains, demoniacs, epileptics, and
paralytics, and he healed them. [25]And great
crowds followed him from Galilee and the
Decap′olis and Jerusalem and Judea and
from beyond the Jordan.

REFLECTION

The Tower of Babel is a striking image of human pride, an attempt to rise up to the heavens by one's own ability. God, in a rather humorous way, "comes down" to see what his rebellious people are up to, showing how far from the heavens their futile efforts leave them (see Gn 11:5). Seeking to "make a name" for themselves rather than calling upon God's name, they end up scattered. The fruit of pride and sin is always isolation and disunity. In contrast, Jesus puts aside all selfishness and self-seeking, and withstands the temptations of the devil. Quoting Moses's reflection at the end of Israel's forty years of wilderness wanderings, Jesus tells the devil, and teaches us, that the meaning of life is not measured by the accumulation of material comforts and possessions, but rather by love and service of God: "Man does not live by bread alone, but by every word that proceeds from the mouth of God" (Mt 4:4, citing Dt 8:3). In the midst of his trial, Jesus's prayer unites him to God, and in this unity lies the secret to happiness. In what ways do you attempt to achieve things through your own efforts instead of relying on God?

January 5

GENESIS 12

Now the LORD said to Abram,
"Go from your country and
your kindred and your father's
house to the land that I will show you.
[2]And I will make of you a great nation,
and I will bless you, and make your
name great, so that you will be a blessing. [3]I
will bless those who bless you, and him who
curses you I will curse; and by you all the
families of the earth shall bless themselves."
[4]So Abram went, as the LORD had told
him; and Lot went with him. Abram was
seventy-five years old when he departed
from Haran. [5]And Abram took Sar′ai his
wife, and Lot his brother's son, and all their
possessions which they had gathered, and
the persons that they had gotten in Haran;
and they set forth to go to the land of
Canaan. When they had come to the land of
Canaan, [6]Abram passed through the land to
the place at She′chem, to the Oak of Mo′reh.
At that time the Canaanites were in the
land. [7]Then the LORD appeared to Abram,
and said, "To your descendants I will give
this land." So he built there an altar to the
LORD, who had appeared to him. [8]Thence
he removed to the mountain on the east of
Bethel, and pitched his tent, with Bethel on
the west and Ai on the east; and there he
built an altar to the LORD and called on the
name of the LORD. [9]And Abram journeyed
on, still going toward the Neg′eb.
[10]Now there was a famine in the land.
So Abram went down to Egypt to sojourn
there, for the famine was severe in the land.
[11]When he was about to enter Egypt, he said
to Sar′ai his wife, "I know that you are a
woman beautiful to behold; [12]and when the
Egyptians see you, they will say, 'This is his
wife'; then they will kill me, but they will let
you live. [13]Say you are my sister, that it may
go well with me because of you, and that my
life may be spared on your account." [14]When

Abram entered Egypt the Egyptians saw
that the woman was very beautiful. [15]And
when the princes of Pharaoh saw her, they
praised her to Pharaoh. And the woman
was taken into Pharaoh's house. [16]And for
her sake he dealt well with Abram; and he
had sheep, oxen, he-donkeys, menservants,
maidservants, she-donkeys, and camels.

[17]But the LORD afflicted Pharaoh and
his house with great plagues because of
Sar′ai, Abram's wife. [18]So Pharaoh called
Abram, and said, "What is this you have
done to me? Why did you not tell me that
she was your wife? [19]Why did you say,
'She is my sister,' so that I took her for my
wife? Now then, here is your wife, take
her, and be gone." [20]And Pharaoh gave
men orders concerning him; and they set
him on the way, with his wife and all that
he had.

13 So Abram went up from Egypt, he
and his wife, and all that he had, and
Lot with him, into the Neg′eb.

[2]Now Abram was very rich in cattle, in
silver, and in gold. [3]And he journeyed
on from the Neg′eb as far as Bethel, to
the place where his tent had been at the
beginning, between Bethel and Ai, [4]to
the place where he had made an altar at
the first; and there Abram called on the
name of the LORD. [5]And Lot, who went
with Abram, also had flocks and herds and
tents, [6]so that the land could not support
both of them dwelling together; for their
possessions were so great that they could
not dwell together, [7]and there was strife
between the herdsmen of Abram's cattle
and the herdsmen of Lot's cattle. At that
time the Canaanites and the Per′izzites
dwelt in the land.

[8]Then Abram said to Lot, "Let there
be no strife between you and me,
and between your herdsmen and my
herdsmen; for we are kinsmen. [9]Is not the
whole land before you? Separate yourself
from me. If you take the left hand, then
I will go to the right; or if you take the
right hand, then I will go to the left."
[10]And Lot lifted up his eyes, and saw
that the Jordan valley was well watered
everywhere like the garden of the LORD,
like the land of Egypt, in the direction of
Zoar; this was before the LORD destroyed
Sodom and Gomor′rah. [11]So Lot chose
for himself all the Jordan valley, and Lot
journeyed east; thus they separated from
each other. [12]Abram dwelt in the land of
Canaan, while Lot dwelt among the cities
of the valley and moved his tent as far as
Sodom. [13]Now the men of Sodom were
wicked, great sinners against the LORD.

[14]The LORD said to Abram, after Lot had
separated from him, "Lift up your eyes,
and look from the place where you are,
northward and southward and eastward
and westward; [15]for all the land which
you see I will give to you and to your
descendants for ever. [16]I will make your
descendants as the dust of the earth; so that
if one can count the dust of the earth, your
descendants also can be counted. [17]Arise,
walk through the length and the breadth
of the land, for I will give it to you." [18]So
Abram moved his tent, and came and
dwelt by the Oaks of Mamre, which are at
He′bron; and there he built an altar to the
LORD.

14 In the days of Am′raphel king of
Shi′nar, Ar′ioch king of Ella′sar,
Ched″-or-lao′mer king of E′lam, and Ti′dal
king of Goi′im, [2]these kings made war with
Be′ra king of Sodom, Birsha king of Go-
mor′rah, Shi′nab king of Admah, Shem-
e′ber king of Zeboi′im, and the king of
Be′la (that is, Zoar). [3]And all these joined
forces in the Valley of Siddim (that is, the
Salt Sea). [4]Twelve years they had served
Ched″-or-lao′mer, but in the thirteenth
year they rebelled. [5]In the fourteenth year
Ched″-or-lao′mer and the kings who were
with him came and subdued the Reph′aim
in Ash′teroth-karna′im, the Zu′zim in
Ham, the E′mim in Sha′veh-kir″iatha′im,
[6]and the Horites in their Mount Se′ir as
far as El-par′an on the border of the wilderness; [7]then they turned back and came
to Enmish′pat (that is, Ka′desh), and subdued all the country of the Amal′ekites,
and also the Am′orites who dwelt in Haz′a-
zon-ta′mar. [8]Then the king of Sodom, the

king of Gomor′rah, the king of Admah, the king of Zeboi′im, and the king of Be′-la (that is, Zoar) went out, and they joined battle in the Valley of Siddim [9]with Ched″-or-lao′mer king of E′lam, Ti′dal king of Goi′im, Am′raphel king of Shi′nar, and Ar′ioch king of Ella′sar, four kings against five. [10]Now the Valley of Siddim was full of bitumen pits; and as the kings of Sodom and Gomor′rah fled, some fell into them, and the rest fled to the mountain. [11]So the enemy took all the goods of Sodom and Gomor′rah, and all their provisions, and went their way; [12]they also took Lot, the son of Abram's brother, who dwelt in Sodom, and his goods, and departed.

[13]Then one who had escaped came, and told Abram the Hebrew, who was living by the Oaks of Mamre the Am′orite, brother of Eshcol and of A′ner; these were allies of Abram. [14]When Abram heard that his kinsman had been taken captive, he led forth his trained men, born in his house, three hundred and eighteen of them, and went in pursuit as far as Dan. [15]And he divided his forces against them by night, he and his servants, and routed them and pursued them to Ho′bah, north of Damascus. [16]Then he brought back all the goods, and also brought back his kinsman Lot with his goods, and the women and the people.

[17]After his return from the defeat of Ched″-or-lao′mer and the kings who were with him, the king of Sodom went out to meet him at the Valley of Sha′veh (that is, the King's Valley). [18]And Mel-chiz′edek king of Salem brought out bread and wine; he was priest of God Most High. [19]And he blessed him and said,

"Blessed be Abram by God Most High,
  maker of heaven and earth;
[20]and blessed be God Most High,
  who has delivered your enemies into
    your hand!"

And Abram gave him a tenth of everything. [21]And the king of Sodom said to Abram, "Give me the persons, but take the goods for yourself." [22]But Abram said to the king of Sodom, "I have sworn to the LORD God Most High, maker of heaven and earth, [23]that I would not take a thread or a sandal-thong or anything that is yours, lest you should say, 'I have made Abram rich.' [24]I will take nothing but what the young men have eaten, and the share of the men who went with me; let A′ner, Eshcol, and Mamre take their share."

To the choirmaster: for the flutes.
A Psalm of David.

PSALM 5

Give ear to my words, O LORD;
  give heed to my groaning.
[2]Listen to the sound of my cry,
  my King and my God,
  for to you do I pray.
[3]O LORD, in the morning you hear my voice;
  in the morning I prepare a sacrifice for
    you, and watch.

[4]For you are not a God who delights
  in wickedness;
  evil may not sojourn with you.
[5]The boastful may not stand before your eyes;
  you hate all evildoers.
[6]You destroy those who speak lies;
  the LORD abhors bloodthirsty and
    deceitful men.

[7]But I through the abundance of your
    merciful love
  will enter your house,
I will worship toward your holy temple
  in the fear of you.
[8]Lead me, O LORD, in your righteousness
  because of my enemies;
  make your way straight before me.

[9]For there is no truth in their mouth;
  their heart is destruction,
their throat is an open sepulchre,
  they flatter with their tongue.
[10]Make them bear their guilt, O God;
  let them fall by their own counsels;
because of their many transgressions cast
    them out,
  for they have rebelled against you.

11But let all who take refuge in you rejoice,
let them ever sing for joy;
and do defend them,
that those who love your name may exult
in you.
12For you bless the righteous, O LORD;
you cover him with favor as with a shield.

MATTHEW 5

Seeing the crowds, he went up on the mountain, and when he sat down his disciples came to him. 2And he opened his mouth and taught them, saying:

3"Blessed are the poor in spirit, for theirs is the kingdom of heaven.

4"Blessed are those who mourn, for they shall be comforted.

5"Blessed are the meek, for they shall inherit the earth.

6"Blessed are those who hunger and thirst for righteousness, for they shall be satisfied.

7"Blessed are the merciful, for they shall obtain mercy.

8"Blessed are the pure in heart, for they shall see God.

9"Blessed are the peacemakers, for they shall be called sons of God.

10"Blessed are those who are persecuted for righteousness' sake, for theirs is the kingdom of heaven.

11"Blessed are you when men revile you and persecute you and utter all kinds of evil
against you falsely on my account. 12Rejoice
and be glad, for your reward is great in heaven, for so men persecuted the prophets who were before you.

13"You are the salt of the earth; but if salt has lost its taste, how shall its saltiness be restored? It is no longer good for anything except to be thrown out and trodden under foot by men.

14"You are the light of the world. A city
set on a hill cannot be hidden. 15Nor
do men light a lamp and put it under a bushel, but on a stand, and it gives light to
all in the house. 16Let your light so shine
before men, that they may see your good works and give glory to your Father who is in heaven.

17"Do not think that I have come to abolish the law and the prophets; I have come not to abolish them but to fulfil
them. 18For truly, I say to you, till heaven and earth pass away, not an iota, not a dot, will pass from the law until all is
accomplished. 19Whoever then relaxes one of the least of these commandments and teaches men so, shall be called least in the kingdom of heaven; but he who does them and teaches them shall be called
great in the kingdom of heaven. 20For I tell
you, unless your righteousness exceeds that of the scribes and Pharisees, you will never enter the kingdom of heaven."

REFLECTION

God calls Abram, not in spite of the other nations, but that he might be a source of blessing for all the families of the earth (see Gn 12:3). But following a calling often means leaving some things behind, and for Abram this includes leaving behind his father's house and kindred. The fact that Abram brings his nephew Lot along on his journey points out Abram's only partial obedience. Childless, Abram takes Lot as an insurance policy in case God's promise of descendants comes up short. How hard it is to trust God, especially when we lack what we desire most. But Abram will slowly learn the tough lessons of trusting God. The Beatitudes are the blessings for those who trust in the midst of their troubles. When we trust God in the face of the world's challenges, we become the "light of the world" and the "salt of the earth" (Mt 5:13–16). Jesus's twofold image for a faithful disciple is striking. In ancient times, light came from burning costly oil. Salt, mined from the Dead Sea, was vital for transporting fish to far-away markets. What costly sacrifice are you willing to make to be a disciple? What vital discipline are you willing to practice to follow the Lord more closely?

January 6

GENESIS 15

After these things the word of the LORD came to Abram in a vision, "Fear not, Abram, I am your shield; your reward shall be very great." 2But Abram said, "O Lord GOD, what will you give me, for I continue childless, and the heir of my house is Elie′zer of Damascus?" 3And Abram said, "Behold, you have given me no offspring; and a slave born in my house will be my heir." 4And behold, the word of the LORD came to him, "This man shall not be your heir; your own son shall be your heir." 5And he brought him outside and said, "Look toward heaven, and number the stars, if you are able to number them." Then he said to him, "So shall your descendants be." 6And he believed the LORD; and he reckoned it to him as righteousness.

7And he said to him, "I am the LORD who brought you from Ur of the Chalde′ans, to give you this land to possess." 8But he said, "O Lord GOD, how am I to know that I shall possess it?" 9He said to him, "Bring me a heifer three years old, a she-goat three years old, a ram three years old, a turtledove, and a young pigeon." 10And he brought him all these, cut them in two, and laid each half over against the other; but he did not cut the birds in two. 11And when birds of prey came down upon the carcasses, Abram drove them away.

12As the sun was going down, a deep sleep fell on Abram; and behold, a dread and great darkness fell upon him. 13Then the LORD said to Abram, "Know of a surety that your descendants will be sojourners in a land that is not theirs, and will be slaves there, and they will be oppressed for four hundred years; 14but I will bring judgment on the nation which they serve, and afterward they shall come out with great possessions. 15As for yourself, you shall go to your fathers in peace; you shall be buried in a good old age. 16And they shall come back here in the fourth generation; for the iniquity of the Am′orites is not yet complete."

17When the sun had gone down and it was dark, behold, a smoking fire pot and a flaming torch passed between these pieces. 18On that day the LORD made a covenant with Abram, saying, "To your descendants I give this land, from the river of Egypt to the great river, the river Euphra′tes, 19the land of the Kenites, the Ken′izzites, the Kad′monites, 20the Hittites, the Per′izzites, the Reph′aim, 21the Am′orites, the Canaanites, the Gir′gashites and the Jeb′usites."

16 Now Sar′ai, Abram's wife, bore him no children. She had an Egyptian maid whose name was Hagar; 2and Sar′ai said to Abram, "Behold now, the LORD has prevented me from bearing children; go in to my maid; it may be that I shall obtain children by her." And Abram listened to the voice of Sar′ai. 3So, after Abram had dwelt ten years in the land of Canaan, Sar′ai, Abram's wife, took Hagar the Egyptian, her maid, and gave her to Abram her husband as a wife. 4And he went in to Hagar, and she conceived; and when she saw that she had conceived, she looked with contempt on her mistress. 5And Sar′ai said to Abram, "May the wrong done to me be on you! I gave my maid to your embrace, and when she saw that she had conceived, she looked on me with contempt. May the LORD judge between you and me!" 6But Abram said to Sar′ai, "Behold, your maid is in your power; do to her as you please." Then Sarai dealt harshly with her, and she fled from her.

7The angel of the LORD found her by a spring of water in the wilderness, the spring on the way to Shur. 8And he said, "Hagar, maid of Sar′ai, where have you come from and where are you going?" She said, "I am fleeing from my mistress Sarai." 9The angel of the LORD said to her, "Return to your mistress, and submit to her." 10The angel of the LORD also said to her, "I will so greatly multiply your descendants that they cannot be numbered for multitude." 11And the angel

of the LORD said to her, "Behold, you
are with child, and shall bear a son; you
shall call his name Ish′mael; because the
LORD has given heed to your affliction.
[12]He shall be a wild donkey of a man, his
hand against every man and every man's
hand against him; and he shall dwell over
against all his kinsmen." [13]So she called
the name of the LORD who spoke to her,
"You are a God of seeing"; for she said,
"Have I really seen God and remained
alive after seeing him?" [14]Therefore the
well was called Be′er-la′hai-roi; it lies
between Ka′desh and Be′red.
[15]And Hagar bore Abram a son; and
Abram called the name of his son, whom
Hagar bore, Ish′mael. [16]Abram was eighty-
six years old when Hagar bore Ish′mael
to Abram.

17 When Abram was ninety-nine years
old the LORD appeared to Abram,
and said to him, "I am God Almighty;
walk before me, and be blameless. [2]And I
will make my covenant between me and
you, and will multiply you exceedingly."
[3]Then Abram fell on his face; and God
said to him, [4]"Behold, my covenant is
with you, and you shall be the father of
a multitude of nations. [5]No longer shall
your name be Abram, but your name
shall be Abraham; for I have made you
the father of a multitude of nations. [6]I will
make you exceedingly fruitful; and I will
make nations of you, and kings shall come
forth from you. [7]And I will establish my
covenant between me and you and your
descendants after you throughout their
generations for an everlasting covenant,
to be God to you and to your descendants
after you. [8]And I will give to you, and to
your descendants after you, the land of
your sojournings, all the land of Canaan,
for an everlasting possession; and I will be
their God."
[9]And God said to Abraham, "As for you,
you shall keep my covenant, you and your
descendants after you throughout their
generations. [10]This is my covenant, which
you shall keep, between me and you
and your descendants after you: Every
male among you shall be circumcised.
[11]You shall be circumcised in the flesh of
your foreskins, and it shall be a sign of
the covenant between me and you. [12]He
that is eight days old among you shall be
circumcised; every male throughout your
generations, whether born in your house,
or bought with your money from any
foreigner who is not of your offspring,
[13]both he that is born in your house and
he that is bought with your money, shall
be circumcised. So shall my covenant be
in your flesh an everlasting covenant.
[14]Any uncircumcised male who is not
circumcised in the flesh of his foreskin
shall be cut off from his people; he has
broken my covenant."
[15]And God said to Abraham, "As for
Sar′ai your wife, you shall not call her
name Sarai, but Sarah shall be her name.
[16]I will bless her, and moreover I will give
you a son by her; I will bless her, and
she shall be a mother of nations; kings
of peoples shall come from her." [17]Then
Abraham fell on his face and laughed, and
said to himself, "Shall a child be born to
a man who is a hundred years old? Shall
Sarah, who is ninety years old, bear a
child?" [18]And Abraham said to God, "O
that Ish′mael might live in your sight!"
[19]God said, "No, but Sarah your wife shall
bear you a son, and you shall call his
name Isaac. I will establish my covenant
with him as an everlasting covenant
for his descendants after him. [20]As for
Ish′mael, I have heard you; behold, I will
bless him and make him fruitful and
multiply him exceedingly; he shall be the
father of twelve princes, and I will make
him a great nation. [21]But I will establish
my covenant with Isaac, whom Sarah
shall bear to you at this season next year."
[22]When he had finished talking with
him, God went up from Abraham. [23]Then
Abraham took Ish′mael his son and all the
slaves born in his house or bought with
his money, every male among the men
of Abraham's house, and he circumcised
the flesh of their foreskins that very
day, as God had said to him. [24]Abraham

was ninety-nine years old when he was circumcised in the flesh of his foreskin.
25And Ish′mael his son was thirteen years
old when he was circumcised in the flesh
of his foreskin. 26That very day Abraham
and his son Ish′mael were circumcised;
27and all the men of his house, those
born in the house and those bought
with money from a foreigner, were
circumcised with him.

To the choirmaster: with stringed instruments; according to The Sheminith.

A Psalm of David.

PSALM 6

O LORD, rebuke me not in your anger,
nor chasten me in your wrath.
2Have mercy on me, O LORD, for I
am languishing;
O LORD, heal me, for my bones
are troubled.
3My soul also is sorely troubled.
But you, O LORD—how long?

4Turn, O LORD, save my life;
deliver me for the sake of your
merciful love.
5For in death there is no remembrance
of you;
in Sheol who can give you praise?

6I am weary with my moaning;
every night I flood my bed with tears;
I drench my couch with my weeping.
7My eye wastes away because of grief,
it grows weak because of all my foes.

8Depart from me, all you workers
of evil;
for the LORD has heard the sound of my
weeping.
9The LORD has heard my supplication;
the LORD accepts my prayer.
10All my enemies shall be ashamed and
sorely troubled;
they shall turn back, and be put to shame
in a moment.

MATTHEW 5

21"You have heard that it was said to the men of old, 'You shall not kill; and whoever kills shall be liable to judgment.' 22But I say to you that every one who is angry with his brother shall be liable to judgment; whoever insults his brother shall be liable to the council, and whoever says, 'You fool!' shall be liable to the hell of fire.
23So if you are offering your gift at the altar, and there remember that your brother has something against you,
24leave your gift there before the altar and go; first be reconciled to your brother, and then come and offer your gift.
25Make friends quickly with your accuser, while you are going with him to court, lest your accuser hand you over to the judge, and the judge to the guard, and you be put in prison;
26truly, I say to you, you will never get out till you have paid the last penny.
27"You have heard that it was said, 'You shall not commit adultery.'
28But I say to you that every one who looks at a woman lustfully has already committed adultery with her in his heart.
29If your right eye causes you to sin, pluck it out and throw it away; it is better that you lose one of your members than that your whole body be thrown into hell.
30And if your right hand causes you to sin, cut it off and throw it away; it is better that you lose one of your members than that your whole body go into hell.
31"It was also said, 'Whoever divorces his wife, let him give her a certificate of divorce.'
32But I say to you that every one who divorces his wife, except on the ground of unchastity, makes her an adulteress; and whoever marries a divorced woman commits adultery.
33"Again you have heard that it was said to the men of old, 'You shall not swear falsely, but shall perform to the Lord what you have sworn.'
34But I say to you, Do not swear at all, either by heaven, for it is the throne of God,
35or by the earth, for it is

his footstool, or by Jerusalem, for it is the
city of the great King. 36And do not swear
by your head, for you cannot make one
hair white or black. 37Let what you say be
simply 'Yes' or 'No'; anything more than
this comes from the Evil One.
38"You have heard that it was said, 'An
eye for an eye and a tooth for a tooth.'
39But I say to you, Do not resist one who
is evil. But if any one strikes you on the
right cheek, turn to him the other also;
40and if any one would sue you and take
your coat, let him have your cloak as well;
41and if any one forces you to go one mile,
go with him two miles. 42Give to him who
begs from you, and do not refuse him
who would borrow from you.
43"You have heard that it was said, 'You
shall love your neighbor and hate your
enemy.' 44But I say to you, Love your
enemies and pray for those who persecute
you, 45so that you may be sons of your
Father who is in heaven; for he makes his
sun rise on the evil and on the good, and
sends rain on the just and on the unjust.
46For if you love those who love you,
what reward have you? Do not even the
tax collectors do the same? 47And if you
salute only your brethren, what more are
you doing than others? Do not even the
Gentiles do the same? 48You, therefore,
must be perfect, as your heavenly Father
is perfect."

REFLECTION

At the start of Genesis 15, God challenges Abram to look to the heavens and count the stars, if he can. We imagine Abram looking into a clear, dark sky with a myriad of stars. A careful reading of the rest of the chapter, however, shows that Abram's problem is not an innumerable host in the night sky but rather the bright light of day blocking his view of any stars whatsoever (note that the suns sets much later, in verse 12). Just as he cannot see a solitary star, even though he knows they exist, Abram must trust that God will provide the heir he does not yet see but whom God has promised to give him.

Faith includes trusting God to provide what we cannot yet see. Abram's faith in God's provision is soon tested, when he harkens to Sarai's voice and takes the forbidden fruit of her handmaid Hagar to bear a surrogate son. God makes it clear in the following chapter (see Gn 17) that it will be through Sarai, Abram's wife, that he will bless him with a son. It is also clear that Abram's faith will need to deepen if he is to become perfect like the God who has called him. Are you striving to live out God's call to holiness in your life?

January 7

GENESIS 18

**And the LORD appeared to him
by the Oaks of Mamre, as he sat
at the door of his tent in the heat
of the day. 2He lifted up his eyes and
looked, and behold, three men stood
in front of him. When he saw them,**
he ran from the tent door to meet them,
and bowed himself to the earth, 3and
said, "My lord, if I have found favor in
your sight, do not pass by your servant.
4Let a little water be brought, and wash
your feet, and rest yourselves under the
tree, 5while I fetch a morsel of bread, that
you may refresh yourselves, and after that
you may pass on—since you have come
to your servant." So they said, "Do as you
have said." 6And Abraham hastened into
the tent to Sarah, and said, "Make ready
quickly three measures of fine meal,
knead it, and make cakes." 7And Abraham
ran to the herd, and took a calf, tender
and good, and gave it to the servant, who
hastened to prepare it. 8Then he took
curds, and milk, and the calf which he
had prepared, and set it before them; and
he stood by them under the tree while
they ate.

9They said to him, "Where is Sarah your
wife?" And he said, "She is in the tent." 10The
LORD said, "I will surely return to you in the
spring, and Sarah your wife shall have a son."
And Sarah was listening at the tent door
behind him. 11Now Abraham and Sarah
were old, advanced in age; it had ceased to
be with Sarah after the manner of women.
12So Sarah laughed to herself, saying, "After
I have grown old, and my husband is old,
shall I have pleasure?" 13The LORD said to
Abraham, "Why did Sarah laugh, and say,
'Shall I indeed bear a child, now that I am
old?' 14Is anything too hard for the LORD?
At the appointed time I will return to you,
in the spring, and Sarah shall have a son."
15But Sarah denied, saying, "I did not laugh";
for she was afraid. He said, "No, but you
did laugh."

16Then the men set out from there, and
they looked toward Sodom; and Abraham
went with them to set them on their way.
17The LORD said, "Shall I hide from Abraham
what I am about to do, 18seeing that Abraham
shall become a great and mighty nation,
and all the nations of the earth shall bless
themselves by him? 19No, for I have chosen
him, that he may charge his children and his
household after him to keep the way of the
LORD by doing righteousness and justice; so
that the LORD may bring to Abraham what
he has promised him." 20Then the LORD
said, "Because the outcry against Sodom
and Gomor′rah is great and their sin is
very grave, 21I will go down to see whether
they have done altogether according to the
outcry which has come to me; and if not, I
will know."

22So the men turned from there, and
went toward Sodom; but Abraham still
stood before the LORD. 23Then Abraham
drew near, and said, "Will you indeed
destroy the righteous with the wicked?
24Suppose there are fifty righteous within
the city; will you then destroy the place
and not spare it for the fifty righteous
who are in it? 25Far be it from you to do
such a thing, to slay the righteous with
the wicked, so that the righteous fare as
the wicked! Far be that from you! Shall
not the Judge of all the earth do right?"
26And the LORD said, "If I find at Sodom
fifty righteous in the city, I will spare the
whole place for their sake." 27Abraham
answered, "Behold, I have taken upon
myself to speak to the Lord, I who am but
dust and ashes. 28Suppose five of the fifty
righteous are lacking? Will you destroy
the whole city for lack of five?" And he
said, "I will not destroy it if I find forty-
five there." 29Again he spoke to him, and
said, "Suppose forty are found there." He
answered, "For the sake of forty I will
not do it." 30Then he said, "Oh let not the
Lord be angry, and I will speak. Suppose
thirty are found there." He answered, "I
will not do it, if I find thirty there." 31He
said, "Behold, I have taken upon myself
to speak to the Lord. Suppose twenty are
found there." He answered, "For the sake
of twenty I will not destroy it." 32Then he
said, "Oh let not the Lord be angry, and
I will speak again but this once. Suppose
ten are found there." He answered, "For
the sake of ten I will not destroy it."
33And the LORD went his way, when he
had finished speaking to Abraham; and
Abraham returned to his place.

19 The two angels came to Sodom in
the evening; and Lot was sitting
in the gate of Sodom. When Lot saw
them, he rose to meet them, and bowed
himself with his face to the earth, 2and
said, "My lords, turn aside, I pray you,
to your servant's house and spend the
night, and wash your feet; then you may
rise up early and go on your way." They
said, "No; we will spend the night in the
street." 3But he urged them strongly; so
they turned aside to him and entered his
house; and he made them a feast, and
baked unleavened bread, and they ate.
4But before they lay down, the men of
the city, the men of Sodom, both young
and old, all the people to the last man,
surrounded the house; 5and they called
to Lot, "Where are the men who came to
you tonight? Bring them out to us, that
we may know them." 6Lot went out of
the door to the men, shut the door after

him, 7and said, "I beg you, my brothers,
do not act so wickedly. 8Behold, I have
two daughters who have not known man;
let me bring them out to you, and do to
them as you please; only do nothing to
these men, for they have come under
the shelter of my roof." 9But they said,
"Stand back!" And they said, "This fellow
came to sojourn, and he would play the
judge! Now we will deal worse with you
than with them." Then they pressed hard
against the man Lot, and drew near to
break the door. 10But the men put forth
their hands and brought Lot into the
house to them, and shut the door. 11And
they struck with blindness the men
who were at the door of the house, both
small and great, so that they wearied
themselves groping for the door.

12Then the men said to Lot, "Have you any
one else here? Sons-in-law, sons, daughters,
or any one you have in the city, bring them
out of the place; 13for we are about to destroy
this place, because the outcry against its
people has become great before the LORD,
and the LORD has sent us to destroy it." 14So
Lot went out and said to his sons-in-law,
who were to marry his daughters, "Up, get
out of this place; for the LORD is about to
destroy the city." But he seemed to his sons-
in-law to be jesting.

15When morning dawned, the angels
urged Lot, saying, "Arise, take your wife
and your two daughters who are here, lest
you be consumed in the punishment of the
city." 16But he lingered; so the men seized
him and his wife and his two daughters
by the hand, the LORD being merciful to
him, and they brought him forth and set
him outside the city. 17And when they
had brought them forth, they said, "Flee
for your life; do not look back or stop
anywhere in the valley; flee to the hills,
lest you be consumed." 18And Lot said to
them, "Oh, no, my lords; 19behold, your
servant has found favor in your sight,
and you have shown me great kindness
in saving my life; but I cannot flee to the
hills, lest the disaster overtake me, and I
die. 20Behold, yonder city is near enough
to flee to, and it is a little one. Let me
escape there—is it not a little one?—and
my life will be saved!" 21He said to him,
"Behold, I grant you this favor also, that I
will not overthrow the city of which you
have spoken. 22Make haste, escape there;
for I can do nothing till you arrive there."
Therefore the name of the city was called
Zoar. 23The sun had risen on the earth
when Lot came to Zoar.

24Then the LORD rained on Sodom and
Gomor′rah brimstone and fire from the
LORD out of heaven; 25and he overthrew
those cities, and all the valley, and all the
inhabitants of the cities, and what grew
on the ground. 26But Lot's wife behind
him looked back, and she became a pillar
of salt. 27And Abraham went early in
the morning to the place where he had
stood before the LORD; 28and he looked
down toward Sodom and Gomor′rah
and toward all the land of the valley, and
beheld, and behold, the smoke of the land
went up like the smoke of a furnace.

29So it was that, when God destroyed
the cities of the valley, God remembered
Abraham, and sent Lot out of the midst
of the overthrow, when he overthrew the
cities in which Lot dwelt.

A Shiggaion of David, which he sang to the LORD concerning Cush a Benjaminite.

PSALM 7

O LORD my God, in you I take refuge;
save me from all my pursuers, and
deliver me,
2lest like a lion they rend me,
dragging me away, with none to rescue.

3O LORD my God, if I have done this,
if there is wrong in my hands,
4if I have repaid my friend with evil
or plundered my enemy without cause,
5let the enemy pursue me and overtake me,
and let him trample my life to the ground,
and lay my soul in the dust. *Selah*

6Arise, O LORD, in your anger,
lift yourself up against the fury of
my enemies;
awake, O my God; you have appointed
a judgment.
7Let the assembly of the peoples be gathered
about you;
and over it take your seat on high.
8The LORD judges the peoples;
judge me, O LORD, according to my
righteousness
and according to the integrity that is
in me.
9O let the evil of the wicked come to an end,
but establish the righteous,
you who try the minds and hearts,
O righteous God.
10My shield is with God,
who saves the upright in heart.
11God is a righteous judge,
and a God who has indignation every day.
12If a man does not repent, God will whet
his sword;
he has bent and strung his bow;
13he has prepared his deadly weapons,
making his arrows fiery shafts.
14Behold, the wicked man conceives evil,
and is pregnant with mischief,
and brings forth lies.
15He makes a pit, digging it out,
and falls into the hole which he has made.
16His mischief returns upon his own head,
and on his own skull his violence descends.
17I will give to the LORD the thanks due to
his righteousness,
and I will sing praise to the name of the
LORD, the Most High.

MATTHEW 6

"Beware of practicing your piety before men in order to be seen by them; for then you will have no reward from your Father who is in heaven.

2"Thus, when you give alms, sound no
trumpet before you, as the hypocrites do in
the synagogues and in the streets, that they
may be praised by men. Truly, I say to you,
they have their reward. 3But when you give
alms, do not let your left hand know what
your right hand is doing, 4so that your alms
may be in secret; and your Father who sees
in secret will reward you.
5"And when you pray, you must not be
like the hypocrites; for they love to stand
and pray in the synagogues and at the street
corners, that they may be seen by men.
Truly, I say to you, they have their reward.
6But when you pray, go into your room and
shut the door and pray to your Father who is
in secret; and your Father who sees in secret
will reward you.
7"And in praying do not heap up empty
phrases as the Gentiles do; for they think
that they will be heard for their many words.
8Do not be like them, for your Father knows
what you need before you ask him. 9Pray
then like this:
Our Father who art in heaven,
Hallowed be thy name.
10Thy kingdom come.
Thy will be done
On earth as it is in heaven.
11Give us this day our daily bread;
12And forgive us our trespasses
As we forgive those who trespass
against us;
13And lead us not into temptation,
But deliver us from evil.
14For if you forgive men their trespasses,
your heavenly Father also will forgive
you; 15but if you do not forgive men their
trespasses, neither will your Father forgive
your trespasses.
16"And when you fast, do not look
dismal, like the hypocrites, for they
disfigure their faces that their fasting may
be seen by men. Truly, I say to you, they
have their reward. 17But when you fast,
anoint your head and wash your face,
18that your fasting may not be seen by
men but by your Father who is in secret;
and your Father who sees in secret will
reward you."

REFLECTION

At the heart of the Sermon on the Mount (Mt 5–7) is Jesus's teaching on spiritual works; namely almsgiving, prayer, and fasting. These works require the virtue of faith. A person does not give away his or her money (alms), spend time in prayer, and give up good things (fasting), without faith and a supernatural motive. And for the person who perseveres in these works, Jesus promises a reward from the Father in Heaven. Yes, God rewards deeds done out of charity and love! Of course, to receive a heavenly reward from our Father, our motives must be for the service of God alone, not for human respect and honor. In his teaching on spiritual works, Jesus frames prayer with alms and fasting, thereby instructing us that if we want intimacy with his Father, we must frame our lives with generosity to others (alms) and sacrifice of our selves (fasting), which create the conditions for deep and successful prayer. Without generosity to others and sacrifice of self, we cannot know in depth the Father, whose love gives us his very Son. How might you begin to incorporate fasting and almsgiving into your own life so as to deepen your intimacy with God?

January 8

GENESIS 19

[30]Now Lot went up out of Zoar,
and dwelt in the hills with
his two daughters, for he was
afraid to dwell in Zoar; so he dwelt in
a cave with his two daughters. [31]And
the first-born said to the younger,
"Our father is old, and there is not a man on
earth to come in to us after the manner of
all the earth. [32]Come, let us make our father
drink wine, and we will lie with him, that we
may preserve offspring through our father."
[33]So they made their father drink wine that
night; and the first-born went in, and lay
with her father; he did not know when she
lay down or when she arose. [34]And on the
next day, the first-born said to the younger,
"Behold, I lay last night with my father; let us
make him drink wine tonight also; then you
go in and lie with him, that we may preserve
offspring through our father." [35]So they
made their father drink wine that night also;
and the younger arose, and lay with him; and
he did not know when she lay down or when
she arose. [36]Thus both the daughters of Lot
were with child by their father. [37]The first-
born bore a son, and called his name Moab;
he is the father of the Moabites to this day.
[38]The younger also bore a son, and called
his name Ben-am′mi; he is the father of the
Am′monites to this day.

20 From there Abraham journeyed toward the territory of the Neg′eb, and
dwelt between Ka′desh and Shur; and he
sojourned in Ge′rar. [2]And Abraham said
of Sarah his wife, "She is my sister." And
Abim′elech king of Ge′rar sent and took
Sarah. [3]But God came to Abim′elech in a
dream by night, and said to him, "Behold,
you are a dead man, because of the woman
whom you have taken; for she is a man's wife."
[4]Now Abim′elech had not approached her;
so he said, "Lord, will you slay an innocent
people? [5]Did he not himself say to me, 'She
is my sister'? And she herself said, 'He is my
brother.' In the integrity of my heart and the
innocence of my hands I have done this."
[6]Then God said to him in the dream, "Yes, I
know that you have done this in the integrity
of your heart, and it was I who kept you from
sinning against me; therefore I did not let
you touch her. [7]Now then restore the man's
wife; for he is a prophet, and he will pray
for you, and you shall live. But if you do not
restore her, know that you shall surely die,
you, and all that are yours."

[8]So Abim′elech rose early in the morning,
and called all his servants, and told them all
these things; and the men were very much
afraid. [9]Then Abim′elech called Abraham,
and said to him, "What have you done to
us? And how have I sinned against you, that
you have brought on me and my kingdom a
great sin? You have done to me things that

ought not to be done." 10And Abim′elech
said to Abraham, "What were you thinking
of, that you did this thing?" 11Abraham said,
"I did it because I thought, There is no fear
of God at all in this place, and they will
kill me because of my wife. 12Besides she is
indeed my sister, the daughter of my father
but not the daughter of my mother; and she
became my wife. 13And when God caused me
to wander from my father's house, I said to
her, 'This is the kindness you must do me:
at every place to which we come, say of me,
He is my brother.'" 14Then Abim′elech took
sheep and oxen, and male and female slaves,
and gave them to Abraham, and restored
Sarah his wife to him. 15And Abim′elech said,
"Behold, my land is before you; dwell where
it pleases you." 16To Sarah he said, "Behold, I
have given your brother a thousand pieces of
silver; it is your vindication in the eyes of all
who are with you; and before every one you
are righted." 17Then Abraham prayed to God;
and God healed Abim′elech, and also healed
his wife and female slaves so that they bore
children. 18For the LORD had closed all the
wombs of the house of Abim′elech because
of Sarah, Abraham's wife.

21 The LORD visited Sarah as he had
said, and the LORD did to Sarah as
he had promised. 2And Sarah conceived,
and bore Abraham a son in his old age at
the time of which God had spoken to him.
3Abraham called the name of his son who
was born to him, whom Sarah bore him,
Isaac. 4And Abraham circumcised his son
Isaac when he was eight days old, as God
had commanded him. 5Abraham was a
hundred years old when his son Isaac was
born to him. 6And Sarah said, "God has
made laughter for me; every one who hears
will laugh over me." 7And she said, "Who
would have said to Abraham that Sarah
would suckle children? Yet I have borne him
a son in his old age."

8And the child grew, and was weaned; and
Abraham made a great feast on the day that
Isaac was weaned. 9But Sarah saw the son of
Hagar the Egyptian, whom she had borne to
Abraham, playing with her son Isaac. 10So
she said to Abraham, "Cast out this slave
woman with her son; for the son of this
slave woman shall not be heir with my son
Isaac." 11And the thing was very displeasing
to Abraham on account of his son. 12But God
said to Abraham, "Be not displeased because
of the lad and because of your slave woman;
whatever Sarah says to you, do as she tells
you, for through Isaac shall your descendants
be named. 13And I will make a nation of the
son of the slave woman also, because he is
your offspring." 14So Abraham rose early in
the morning, and took bread and a skin of
water, and gave it to Hagar, putting it on her
shoulder, along with the child, and sent her
away. And she departed, and wandered in
the wilderness of Be′er-she′ba.

15When the water in the skin was gone, she
cast the child under one of the bushes. 16Then
she went, and sat down over against him a
good way off, about the distance of a bowshot;
for she said, "Let me not look upon the death
of the child." And as she sat over against him,
the child lifted up his voice and wept. 17And
God heard the voice of the lad; and the angel
of God called to Hagar from heaven, and said
to her, "What troubles you, Hagar? Fear not;
for God has heard the voice of the lad where
he is. 18Arise, lift up the lad, and hold him fast
with your hand; for I will make him a great
nation." 19Then God opened her eyes, and she
saw a well of water; and she went, and filled the
skin with water, and gave the lad a drink. 20And
God was with the lad, and he grew up; he lived
in the wilderness, and became an expert with
the bow. 21He lived in the wilderness of Par′an;
and his mother took a wife for him from the
land of Egypt.

22At that time Abim′elech and Phi′col the
commander of his army said to Abraham,
"God is with you in all that you do; 23now
therefore swear to me here by God that you
will not deal falsely with me or with my
offspring or with my posterity, but as I have
dealt loyally with you, you will deal with me
and with the land where you have sojourned."
24And Abraham said, "I will swear."

25When Abraham complained to
Abim′e-lech about a well of water
which Abim′elech's servants had seized,
26Abim′elech said, "I do not know who

has done this thing; you did not tell me,
and I have not heard of it until today."
27So Abraham took sheep and oxen and
gave them to Abim′elech, and the two
men made a covenant. 28Abraham set
seven ewe lambs of the flock apart. 29And
Abim′elech said to Abraham, "What is the
meaning of these seven ewe lambs which
you have set apart?" 30He said, "These sev-
en ewe lambs you will take from my hand,
that you may be a witness for me that I
dug this well." 31Therefore that place was
called Be′er-she′ba; because there both
of them swore an oath. 32So they made a
covenant at Be′er-she′ba. Then Abim′el-
ech and Phi′col the commander of his
army rose up and returned to the land of
the Philis′tines. 33Abraham planted a tamarisk tree in Be′er-she′ba, and called there
on the name of the LORD, the Everlasting
God. 34And Abraham sojourned many
days in the land of the Philis′tines.

To the choirmaster: according to The Gittith.
A Psalm of David.

PSALM 8

O LORD, our Lord,
how majestic is your name in all the earth!

You whose glory above the heavens
is chanted
2 by the mouth of babies and infants,
you have founded a bulwark because of
your foes,
to still the enemy and the avenger.

3When I look at your heavens, the work of
your fingers,
the moon and the stars which you have
established;
4what is man that you are mindful of him,
and the son of man that you care for him?

5Yet you have made him little less than
the angels,
and you have crowned him with glory
and honor.
6You have given him dominion over the
works of your hands;
you have put all things under his feet,
7all sheep and oxen,
and also the beasts of the field,
8the birds of the air, and the fish of the sea,
whatever passes along the paths of
the sea.

9O LORD, our Lord,
how majestic is your name in all
the earth!

MATTHEW 6

**19"Do not lay up for yourselves
treasures on earth, where moth
and rust consume and where
thieves break in and steal, 20but lay up
for yourselves treasures in heaven,
where neither moth nor rust consumes**
and where thieves do not break in and steal.
21For where your treasure is, there will your
heart be also.

22"The eye is the lamp of the body. So, if
your eye is sound, your whole body will be
full of light; 23but if your eye is not sound,
your whole body will be full of darkness. If
then the light in you is darkness, how great
is the darkness!

24"No one can serve two masters; for
either he will hate the one and love the
other, or he will be devoted to the one and
despise the other. You cannot serve God
and mammon.

25"Therefore I tell you, do not be anxious
about your life, what you shall eat or what
you shall drink, nor about your body, what
you shall put on. Is not life more than
food, and the body more than clothing?
26Look at the birds of the air: they neither
sow nor reap nor gather into barns, and
yet your heavenly Father feeds them. Are
you not of more value than they? 27And
which of you by being anxious can add
one cubit to his span of life? 28And why
are you anxious about clothing? Consider

the lilies of the field, how they grow; they neither toil nor spin; 29yet I tell you, even Solomon in all his glory was not clothed like one of these. 30But if God so clothes the grass of the field, which today is alive and tomorrow is thrown into the oven, will he not much more clothe you, O you of little faith? 31Therefore do not be anxious, saying, 'What shall we eat?' or 'What shall we drink?' or 'What shall we wear?' 32For the Gentiles seek all these things; and your heavenly Father knows that you need them all. 33But seek first his kingdom and his righteousness, and all these things shall be yours as well.

34"Therefore do not be anxious about tomorrow, for tomorrow will be anxious for itself. Let the day's own trouble be sufficient for the day."

REFLECTION

In this section of his Sermon on the Mount, Jesus contrasts storing up earthly versus heavenly treasure, and then parallels it with the statement that you cannot serve two masters, God and mammon. These contrasts, earthly treasure and mammon pitted against heavenly treasure and God as master, frame the central parable that the eye is the lamp of the body. In Israel's tradition the eye is the key to charity, as a hostile eye means refusing charity to others and a good eye is one that looks with compassion at the neediness of others (see Dt 15:9; Prv 22:9). Thus, the eye—the ability to look upon the needs of others—is the lamp of the body, the light by which we walk in God's ways, serving him and storing up treasure in Heaven. At the beginning of the Sermon on the Mount, Jesus calls those who follow him to be a lamp giving light by good works (see Mt 5:14–16). The key to doing good works of charity is seeing the needs of others. Finally, Jesus's exhortation to charity concludes with a warning against anxiety, because anxiety and fear for the future can keep us from giving freely today. Do you look upon others with an eye of charity, seeking ways to serve their needs?

January 9

GENESIS 22

After these things God tested Abraham, and said to him, "Abraham!" And he said, "Here am I." 2He said, "Take your son, your only-begotten son Isaac, whom you love, and go to the land of Mori′ah, and offer him there as a burnt offering upon one of the mountains of which I shall tell you." 3So Abraham rose early in the morning, saddled his donkey, and took two of his young men with him, and his son Isaac; and he cut the wood for the burnt offering, and arose and went to the place of which God had told him. 4On the third day Abraham lifted up his eyes and saw the place afar off. 5Then Abraham said to his young men, "Stay here with the donkey; I and the lad will go yonder and worship, and come again to you." 6And Abraham took the wood of the burnt offering, and laid it on Isaac his son; and he took in his hand the fire and the knife. So they went both of them together. 7And Isaac said to his father Abraham, "My father!" And he said, "Here am I, my son." He said, "Behold, the fire and the wood; but where is the lamb for a burnt offering?" 8Abraham said, "God will provide himself the lamb for a burnt offering, my son." So they went both of them together.

9When they came to the place of which God had told him, Abraham built an altar there, and laid the wood in order, and bound Isaac his son, and laid him on the altar, upon the wood. 10Then Abraham put forth his hand, and took the knife to slay his son. 11But the angel of the LORD called to him from heaven, and said, "Abraham, Abraham!" And he said, "Here am I." 12He said, "Do not lay your hand on the lad or do anything to him; for now I know that you fear God, seeing you have not withheld your son,

your only-begotten son, from me." [13]And
Abraham lifted up his eyes and looked,
and behold, behind him was a ram,
caught in a thicket by his horns; and
Abraham went and took the ram, and
offered it up as a burnt offering instead
of his son. [14]So Abraham called the name
of that place The LORD will provide; as it
is said to this day, "On the mount of the
LORD it shall be provided."

[15]And the angel of the LORD called to
Abraham a second time from heaven,
[16]and said, "By myself I have sworn, says
the LORD, because you have done this, and
have not withheld your son, your only-
begotten son, [17]I will indeed bless you, and
I will multiply your descendants as the
stars of heaven and as the sand which is on
the seashore. And your descendants shall
possess the gate of their enemies, [18]and by
your descendants shall all the nations of the
earth bless themselves, because you have
obeyed my voice." [19]So Abraham returned
to his young men, and they arose and went
together to Be′er-she′ba; and Abraham
dwelt at Beer-sheba.

[20]Now after these things it was told
Abraham, "Behold, Milcah also has borne
children to your brother Na′hor: [21]Uz
the first-born, Buz his brother, Ke′muel
the father of Ar′am, [22]Che′sed, Ha′zo,
Pildash, Jidlaph, and Bethu′el." [23]Bethu′el
became the father of Rebekah. These
eight Milcah bore to Na′hor, Abraham's
brother. [24]Moreover, his concubine, whose
name was Reu′mah, bore Te′bah, Ga′ham,
Ta′hash, and Ma′acah.

23 Sarah lived a hundred and twenty-
seven years; these were the years
of the life of Sarah. [2]And Sarah died at
Kir′iath-ar′ba (that is, He′bron) in the
land of Canaan; and Abraham went
in to mourn for Sarah and to weep for
her. [3]And Abraham rose up from before
his dead, and said to the Hittites, [4]"I
am a stranger and a sojourner among
you; give me property among you for a
burying place, that I may bury my dead
out of my sight." [5]The Hittites answered
Abraham, [6]"Hear us, my lord; you are
a mighty prince among us. Bury your
dead in the choicest of our sepulchres;
none of us will withhold from you his
sepulchre, or hinder you from burying
your dead." [7]Abraham rose and bowed to
the Hittites, the people of the land. [8]And
he said to them, "If you are willing that
I should bury my dead out of my sight,
hear me, and entreat for me E′phron the
son of Zo′har, [9]that he may give me the
cave of Mach-pe′lah, which he owns; it is
at the end of his field. For the full price
let him give it to me in your presence
as a possession for a burying place."
[10]Now E′phron was sitting among the
Hittites; and Ephron the Hittite answered
Abraham in the hearing of the Hittites,
of all who went in at the gate of his city,
[11]"No, my lord, hear me; I give you the
field, and I give you the cave that is in it;
in the presence of the sons of my people
I give it to you; bury your dead." [12]Then
Abraham bowed down before the people
of the land. [13]And he said to E′phron in
the hearing of the people of the land,
"But if you will, hear me; I will give the
price of the field; accept it from me, that
I may bury my dead there." [14]E′phron
answered Abraham, [15]"My lord, listen to
me; a piece of land worth four hundred
shekels of silver, what is that between
you and me? Bury your dead." [16]Abraham
agreed with E′phron; and Abraham
weighed out for Ephron the silver which
he had named in the hearing of the
Hittites, four hundred shekels of silver,
according to the weights current among
the merchants.

[17]So the field of E′phron in Mach-pe′lah,
which was to the east of Mamre, the field
with the cave which was in it and all the
trees that were in the field, throughout its
whole area, was made over [18]to Abraham
as a possession in the presence of the
Hittites, before all who went in at the
gate of his city. [19]After this, Abraham
buried Sarah his wife in the cave of the
field of Mach-pe′lah east of Mamre (that
is, He′bron) in the land of Canaan. [20]The
field and the cave that is in it were made

over to Abraham as a possession for a burying place by the Hittites.

To the choirmaster: according to Muth-labben.
A Psalm of David.

PSALM 9

I will give thanks to the LORD with my
whole heart;
I will tell of all your wonderful deeds.
2 I will be glad and exult in you,
I will sing praise to your name,
O Most High.

3 When my enemies turned back,
they stumbled and perished before you.
4 For you have maintained my just cause;
you have sat on the throne giving
righteous judgment.

5 You have rebuked the nations, you have
destroyed the wicked;
you have blotted out their name for ever
and ever.
6 The enemies have vanished in everlasting
ruins;
their cities you have rooted out;
the very memory of them has perished.

7 But the LORD sits enthroned for ever,
he has established his throne for judgment;
8 and he judges the world with righteousness,
he judges the peoples with equity.

9 The LORD is a stronghold for the oppressed,
a stronghold in times of trouble.
10 And those who know your name put their
trust in you,
for you, O LORD, have not forsaken those
who seek you.

11 Sing praises to the LORD, who dwells
in Zion!
Tell among the peoples his deeds!
12 For he who avenges blood is mindful
of them;
he does not forget the cry of the poor.

13 Be gracious to me, O LORD!
Behold what I suffer from those
who hate me,
O you who lift me up from the gates
of death,
14 that I may recount all your praises,
that in the gates of the daughter of Zion
I may rejoice in your deliverance.

15 The nations have sunk in the pit which
they made;
in the net which they hid has their own
foot been caught.
16 The LORD has made himself known, he
has executed judgment;
the wicked are snared in the work of their
own hands. *Higgaion. Selah*

17 The wicked shall depart to Sheol,
all the nations that forget God.

18 For the needy shall not always be forgotten,
and the hope of the poor shall not perish
for ever.

19 Arise, O LORD! Let not man prevail;
let the nations be judged before you!
20 Put them in fear, O LORD!
Let the nations know that they are
but men! *Selah*

MATTHEW 7

"Judge not, that you be not judged. 2 For with the judgment you pronounce you will be judged, and the measure you give will be the measure you get. 3 Why do you see the speck that is in your brother's eye, but do not notice the log that is in your own eye? 4 Or how can you say to your brother, 'Let me take the speck out of your eye,' when there is the log in your own eye? 5 You hypocrite, first take the log out of your own eye, and then you will see clearly to take the speck out of your brother's eye.

6“Do not give dogs what is holy; and do not throw your pearls before swine, lest they trample them under foot and turn to attack you.

7“Ask, and it will be given you; seek, and you will find; knock, and it will be opened to you. 8For every one who asks receives, and he who seeks finds, and to him who knocks it will be opened. 9Or what man of you, if his son asks him for bread, will give him a stone? 10Or if he asks for a fish, will give him a serpent? 11If you then, who are evil, know how to give good gifts to your children, how much more will your Father who is in heaven give good things to those who ask him! 12So whatever you wish that men would do to you, do so to them; for this is the law and the prophets.

13“Enter by the narrow gate; for the gate is wide and the way is easy, that leads to destruction, and those who enter by it are many. 14For the gate is narrow and the way is hard, that leads to life, and those who find it are few.

15“Beware of false prophets, who come to you in sheep's clothing but inwardly are ravenous wolves. 16You will know them by their fruits. Are grapes gathered from thorns, or figs from thistles? 17So, every sound tree bears good fruit, but the bad tree bears evil fruit. 18A sound tree cannot bear evil fruit, nor can a bad tree bear good fruit. 19Every tree that does not bear good fruit is cut down and thrown into the fire. 20Thus you will know them by their fruits.

21“Not every one who says to me, ‘Lord, Lord,’ shall enter the kingdom of heaven, but he who does the will of my Father who is in heaven. 22On that day many will say to me, ‘Lord, Lord, did we not prophesy in your name, and cast out demons in your name, and do many mighty works in your name?’ 23And then will I declare to them, ‘I never knew you; depart from me, you evildoers.’

24“Every one then who hears these words of mine and does them will be like a wise man who built his house upon the rock; 25and the rain fell, and the floods came, and the winds blew and beat upon that house, but it did not fall, because it had been founded on the rock. 26And every one who hears these words of mine and does not do them will be like a foolish man who built his house upon the sand; 27and the rain fell, and the floods came, and the winds blew and beat against that house, and it fell; and great was the fall of it.”

28And when Jesus finished these sayings, the crowds were astonished at his teaching, 29for he taught them as one who had authority, and not as their scribes.

REFLECTION

God commands Abraham to take his son, Isaac, up Mt. Moriah and offer him as a burnt offering. How can a loving God pose such a cruel test? The first clue is the kind of sacrifice Isaac is to be—burnt offerings are made to atone for sin. What sin? Perhaps for Abraham it was sending his son Ishmael out into the wilderness, where he most certainly would have died without divine intervention. God allows Abraham to heed Sarah's request to send away Hagar and Ishmael, but Abraham, whom God blessed with riches, sends them out with only a single water skin. Now as he walks with Isaac, Abraham shares Hagar's experience, walking out of the camp with a beloved only son who is doomed to die. The redemption of Ishmael in Genesis 21 is paralleled by the redemption of Isaac in Genesis 22. God is merciful to Abraham, in spite of his guilt, and so the story is ultimately of God's mercy. Even more, Isaac carrying the wood up Moriah and his willing sacrifice foreshadows an even greater mercy, as God will not spare his Son, Jesus, as he spared Ishmael and Isaac. Jesus will carry the wood of his Cross and offer himself as the atoning sacrifice for sin, the lamb that God promised he himself would provide. Are you truly thankful for God's tremendous mercy in your own life?

January 10

GENESIS 24

Now Abraham was old, well advanced in years; and the LORD had blessed Abraham in all things. 2And Abraham said to his servant, the

oldest of his house, who had charge of all that he had, "Put your hand under my thigh, 3and I will make you swear by the LORD, the God of heaven and of the earth, that you will not take a wife for my son from the daughters of the Canaanites, among whom I dwell, 4but will go to my country and to my kindred, and take a wife for my son Isaac." 5The servant said to him, "Perhaps the woman may not be willing to follow me to this land; must I then take your son back to the land from which you came?" 6Abraham said to him, "See to it that you do not take my son back there. 7The LORD, the God of heaven, who took me from my father's house and from the land of my birth, and who spoke to me and swore to me, 'To your descendants I will give this land,' he will send his angel before you, and you shall take a wife for my son from there. 8But if the woman is not willing to follow you, then you will be free from this oath of mine; only you must not take my son back there." 9So the servant put his hand under the thigh of Abraham his master, and swore to him concerning this matter.

10Then the servant took ten of his master's camels and departed, taking all sorts of choice gifts from his master; and he arose, and went to Mesopota´mia, to the city of Na´hor. 11And he made the camels kneel down outside the city by the well of water at the time of evening, the time when women go out to draw water. 12And he said, "O LORD, God of my master Abraham, grant me success today, I beg you, and show mercy to my master Abraham. 13Behold, I am standing by the spring of water, and the daughters of the men of the city are coming out to draw water. 14Let the maiden to whom I shall say, 'Please let down your jar that I may drink,' and who shall say, 'Drink, and I will water your camels'—let her be the one whom you have appointed for your servant Isaac. By this I shall know that you have shown mercy to my master."

15Before he had done speaking, behold, Rebekah, who was born to Bethu´el the son of Milcah, the wife of Na´hor, Abraham's brother, came out with her water jar upon her shoulder. 16The maiden was very fair to look upon, a virgin, whom no man had known. She went down to the spring, and filled her jar, and came up. 17Then the servant ran to meet her, and said, "Please give me a little water to drink from your jar." 18She said, "Drink, my lord"; and she quickly let down her jar upon her hand, and gave him a drink. 19When she had finished giving him a drink, she said, "I will draw for your camels also, until they have done drinking." 20So she quickly emptied her jar into the trough and ran again to the well to draw, and she drew for all his camels. 21The man gazed at her in silence to learn whether the LORD had prospered his journey or not.

22When the camels had done drinking, the man took a gold ring weighing a half shekel, and two bracelets for her arms weighing ten gold shekels, 23and said, "Tell me whose daughter you are. Is there room in your father's house for us to lodge in?" 24She said to him, "I am the daughter of Bethu´el the son of Milcah, whom she bore to Na´hor." 25She added, "We have both straw and food enough, and room to lodge in." 26The man bowed his head and worshiped the LORD, 27and said, "Blessed be the LORD, the God of my master Abraham, who has not forsaken his mercy and his faithfulness toward my master. As for me, the LORD has led me in the way to the house of my master's kinsmen."

28Then the maiden ran and told her mother's household about these things. 29Rebekah had a brother whose name was La´ban; and Laban ran out to the man, to the spring. 30When he saw the ring, and the bracelets on his sister's arms, and when he heard the words of Rebekah his sister, "Thus the man spoke to me," he went to the man; and behold, he was standing by the camels at the spring. 31He said, "Come in, O blessed of the LORD; why do you stand outside? For I have prepared the house and a place for the camels." 32So the man came into the house; and La´ban ungirded the camels, and gave him straw and food for the camels, and water to wash his feet and the feet of the men who were with him. 33Then food was set before him to eat; but he said, "I will

not eat until I have told my errand." He said,
"Speak on."
34So he said, "I am Abraham's servant.
35The LORD has greatly blessed my
master, and he has become great; he has
given him flocks and herds, silver and
gold, menservants and maidservants,
camels and donkeys. 36And Sarah my
master's wife bore a son to my master
when she was old; and to him he has
given all that he has. 37My master made
me swear, saying, 'You shall not take a
wife for my son from the daughters of the
Canaanites, in whose land I dwell; 38but
you shall go to my father's house and to
my kindred, and take a wife for my son.'
39I said to my master, 'Perhaps the woman
will not follow me.' 40But he said to me,
'The LORD, before whom I walk, will send
his angel with you and prosper your way;
and you shall take a wife for my son from
my kindred and from my father's house;
41then you will be free from my oath,
when you come to my kindred; and if
they will not give her to you, you will be
free from my oath.'

42"I came today to the spring, and said, 'O
LORD, the God of my master Abraham, if
now you will prosper the way which I go,
43behold, I am standing by the spring of water;
let the young woman who comes out to draw,
to whom I shall say, "Please give me a little
water from your jar to drink," 44and who will
say to me, "Drink, and I will draw for your
camels also," let her be the woman whom the
LORD has appointed for my master's son.'

45"Before I had done speaking in my
heart, behold, Rebekah came out with her
water jar on her shoulder; and she went
down to the spring, and drew. I said to her,
'Please let me drink.' 46She quickly let down
her jar from her shoulder, and said, 'Drink,
and I will give your camels drink also.' So I
drank, and she gave the camels drink also.
47Then I asked her, 'Whose daughter are
you?' She said, 'The daughter of Bethu'el,
Na'hor's son, whom Milcah bore to him.'
So I put the ring on her nose, and the
bracelets on her arms. 48Then I bowed my
head and worshiped the LORD, and blessed
the LORD, the God of my master Abraham,
who had led me by the right way to take the
daughter of my master's kinsman for his
son. 49Now then, if you will deal loyally and
truly with my master, tell me; and if not,
tell me; that I may turn to the right hand or
to the left."

50Then La'ban and Bethu'el answered,
"The thing comes from the LORD; we cannot
speak to you bad or good. 51Behold, Rebekah
is before you, take her and go, and let her be
the wife of your master's son, as the LORD
has spoken."

52When Abraham's servant heard their
words, he bowed himself to the earth before
the LORD. 53And the servant brought forth
jewelry of silver and of gold, and raiment,
and gave them to Rebekah; he also gave
to her brother and to her mother costly
ornaments. 54And he and the men who
were with him ate and drank, and they
spent the night there. When they arose in
the morning, he said, "Send me back to my
master." 55Her brother and her mother said,
"Let the maiden remain with us a while,
at least ten days; after that she may go."
56But he said to them, "Do not delay me,
since the LORD has prospered my way; let
me go that I may go to my master." 57They
said, "We will call the maiden, and ask her."
58And they called Rebekah, and said to her,
"Will you go with this man?" She said, "I
will go." 59So they sent away Rebekah their
sister and her nurse, and Abraham's servant
and his men. 60And they blessed Rebekah,
and said to her, "Our sister, be the mother
of thousands of ten thousands; and may
your descendants possess the gate of those
who hate them!" 61Then Rebekah and her
maids arose, and rode upon the camels and
followed the man; thus the servant took
Rebekah, and went his way.

62Now Isaac had come from Be'er-la'hai-
roi, and was dwelling in the Neg'eb. 63And
Isaac went out to meditate in the field in
the evening; and he lifted up his eyes and
looked, and behold, there were camels
coming. 64And Rebekah lifted up her eyes,
and when she saw Isaac, she alighted from
the camel, 65and said to the servant, "Who is

the man yonder, walking in the field to meet us?" The servant said, "It is my master." So she took her veil and covered herself. 66And the servant told Isaac all the things that he had done. 67Then Isaac brought her into the tent, and took Rebekah, and she became his wife; and he loved her. So Isaac was comforted after his mother's death.

PSALM 10

Why do you stand afar off, O LORD?
Why do you hide yourself in times of trouble?
2In arrogance the wicked hotly pursue the poor;
let them be caught in the schemes which they have devised.

3For the wicked boasts of the desires of his heart,
and the man greedy for gain curses and renounces the LORD.
4In the pride of his countenance the wicked does not seek him;
all his thoughts are, "There is no God."

5His ways prosper at all times;
your judgments are on high, out of his sight;
as for all his foes, he puffs at them.
6He thinks in his heart, "I shall not be moved;
throughout all generations I shall not meet adversity."

7His mouth is filled with cursing and deceit and oppression;
under his tongue are mischief and iniquity.
8He sits in ambush in the villages;
in hiding places he murders the innocent.

His eyes stealthily watch for the hapless,
9 he lurks in secret like a lion in his den;
he lurks that he may seize the poor,
he seizes the poor when he draws him into his net.
10The hapless is crushed, sinks down,
and falls by his might.
11He thinks in his heart, "God has forgotten,
he has hidden his face, he will never see it."

12Arise, O LORD; O God, lift up your hand;
forget not the poor.
13Why does the wicked renounce God,
and say in his heart, "You will not call to account"?

14You see; yes, you note trouble and vexation,
that you may take it into your hands;
the hapless commits himself to you;
you have been the helper of the fatherless.

15Break the arm of the wicked and evildoer;
seek out his wickedness till you find none.
16The LORD is king for ever and ever;
the nations shall perish from his land.

17O LORD, you will hear the desire of the meek;
you will strengthen their heart, you will incline your ear
18to do justice to the fatherless and the oppressed,
so that man who is of the earth may strike terror no more.

MATTHEW 8

When he came down from the mountain, great crowds followed him; 2and behold, a leper came to him and knelt before him, saying, "Lord, if you will, you can make me clean." 3And he stretched out his hand and touched him, saying, "I will; be clean." And immediately his leprosy was cleansed. 4And Jesus said to him, "See that you say nothing to any one; but go, show yourself to the priest, and offer the gift that Moses commanded, for a proof to the people."

5As he entered Caper′na-um, a centurion came forward to him, begging him 6and saying, "Lord, my servant is lying paralyzed at home, in terrible distress." 7And he said to him, "I will come and heal him." 8But the centurion answered him, "Lord, I am not worthy to have you come under my roof; but only say the word, and my servant will be healed. 9For I am a man under authority, with soldiers under me; and I say to one, 'Go,' and he goes, and to another, 'Come,' and he comes, and to my slave, 'Do this,' and he does it." 10When Jesus heard him, he marveled, and said to those who followed him, "Truly, I say to you, not even in Israel have I found such faith. 11I tell you, many will come from east and west and sit at table with Abraham, Isaac, and Jacob in the kingdom of heaven, 12while the sons of the kingdom will be thrown into the outer darkness; there men will weep and gnash their teeth." 13And to the centurion Jesus said, "Go; let it be done for you as you have believed." And the servant was healed at that very moment.

14And when Jesus entered Peter's house, he saw his mother-in-law lying sick with a fever; 15he touched her hand, and the fever left her, and she rose and served him. 16That evening they brought to him many who were possessed with demons; and he cast out the spirits with a word, and healed all who were sick. 17This was to fulfil what was spoken by the prophet Isaiah, "He took our infirmities and bore our diseases."

18Now when Jesus saw great crowds around him, he gave orders to go over to the other side. 19And a scribe came up and said to him, "Teacher, I will follow you wherever you go." 20And Jesus said to him, "Foxes have holes, and birds of the air have nests; but the Son of man has nowhere to lay his head." 21Another of the disciples said to him, "Lord, let me first go and bury my father." 22But Jesus said to him, "Follow me, and leave the dead to bury their own dead."

REFLECTION

In Matthew 8–9 Jesus performs ten mighty deeds, all of which exemplify the authority he commands. Ten is a symbolic number for authority, thus God gives ten commandments (see Ex 20:1–17), and the beast's ten diadems signify his total temporal authority (see Rev 13:1). The leper recognizes Jesus's authority to will him clean. The centurion, a man of notable earthly authority, recognizes Jesus's authority to simply say the word of healing for his servant, and astonishes Jesus with his proclamation of faith. The Church has us recite the centurion's words before we encounter Jesus in the Eucharist each liturgy, making his proclamation of faith our own: "Lord, I am not worthy that you should enter under my roof, but only say the word and I shall be healed." If we approach Jesus with the faith of the leper and the centurion, he can heal our uncleanness by the authority he alone possesses. Indeed, his authority is such that even the winds and the waves—the two most chaotic and untamable elements in nature—obey him. To recognize Jesus's authority is to know he is worthy of our faith and trust. Do you recognize and accept Jesus's authority and lordship over your own life?

January 11

GENESIS 25

Abraham took another wife, whose name was Ketu´rah. 2She bore him Zimran, Jokshan, Me´dan, Mid´ian, Ishbak, and Shuah. 3Jokshan was the father of Sheba and De´dan. The sons of Dedan were Asshu´rim, Letu´shim, and Le-um´mim. 4The sons of Mid´ian were E´phah, E´pher, Ha´noch, Abi´da, and Elda´ah. All these were the children of Ketu´rah. 5Abraham gave all he had to Isaac. 6But to the sons of his concubines Abraham gave gifts, and while he was still living he sent them away from his son Isaac, eastward to the east country.

7These are the days of the years of Abraham's life, a hundred and seventy-five years. 8Abraham breathed his last and died in a good old age, an old man and full of years, and was gathered to his people. 9Isaac and

Ish′mael his sons buried him in the cave of Mach-pe′lah, in the field of E′phron the son of Zo′har the Hittite, east of Mamre, 10the field which Abraham purchased from the Hittites. There Abraham was buried, with Sarah his wife. 11After the death of Abraham God blessed Isaac his son. And Isaac dwelt at Be′er-la′hai-roi.

12These are the descendants of Ish′mael, Abraham's son, whom Hagar the Egyptian, Sarah's maid, bore to Abraham. 13These are the names of the sons of Ish′mael, named in the order of their birth: Neba′ioth, the first-born of Ishmael; and Ke′dar, Ad′beel, Mibsam, 14Mishma, Du′mah, Massa, 15Ha′dad, Te′ma, Je′tur, Na′phish, and Ked′emah. 16These are the sons of Ish′mael and these are their names, by their villages and by their encampments, twelve princes according to their tribes. 17(These are the years of the life of Ish′mael, a hundred and thirty-seven years; he breathed his last and died, and was gathered to his kindred.) 18They dwelt from Hav′ilah to Shur, which is opposite Egypt in the direction of Assyria; he settled over against all his people.

19These are the descendants of Isaac, Abraham's son: Abraham was the father of Isaac, 20and Isaac was forty years old when he took to wife Rebekah, the daughter of Bethu′el the Arame′an of Pad′dan-ar′am, the sister of La′ban the Aramean. 21And Isaac prayed to the LORD for his wife, because she was barren; and the LORD granted his prayer, and Rebekah his wife conceived. 22The children struggled together within her; and she said, "If it is thus, why do I live?" So she went to inquire of the LORD. 23And the LORD said to her,

"Two nations are in your womb,
 and two peoples, born of you, shall
  be divided;
the one shall be stronger than the other,
 the elder shall serve the younger."

24When her days to be delivered were fulfilled, behold, there were twins in her womb. 25The first came forth red, all his body like a hairy mantle; so they called his name Esau. 26Afterward his brother came forth, and his hand had taken hold of Esau's heel; so his name was called Jacob. Isaac was sixty years old when she bore them.

27When the boys grew up, Esau was a skilful hunter, a man of the field, while Jacob was a quiet man, dwelling in tents. 28Isaac loved Esau, because he ate of his game; but Rebekah loved Jacob.

29Once when Jacob was boiling pottage, Esau came in from the field, and he was famished. 30And Esau said to Jacob, "Let me eat some of that red pottage, for I am famished!" (Therefore his name was called E′dom.) 31Jacob said, "First sell me your birthright." 32Esau said, "I am about to die; of what use is a birthright to me?" 33Jacob said, "Swear to me first." So he swore to him, and sold his birthright to Jacob. 34Then Jacob gave Esau bread and pottage of lentils, and he ate and drank, and rose and went his way. Thus Esau despised his birthright.

26 Now there was a famine in the land, besides the former famine that was in the days of Abraham. And Isaac went to Ge′rar, to Abim′elech king of the Philis′tines. 2And the LORD appeared to him, and said, "Do not go down to Egypt; dwell in the land of which I shall tell you. 3Sojourn in this land, and I will be with you, and will bless you; for to you and to your descendants I will give all these lands, and I will fulfil the oath which I swore to Abraham your father. 4I will multiply your descendants as the stars of heaven, and will give to your descendants all these lands; and by your descendants all the nations of the earth shall bless themselves: 5because Abraham obeyed my voice and kept my charge, my commandments, my statutes, and my laws."

6So Isaac dwelt in Ge′rar. 7When the men of the place asked him about his wife, he said, "She is my sister"; for he feared to say, "My wife," thinking, "lest the men of the place should kill me for the sake of Rebekah"; because she was fair to look upon. 8When he had been there a long time, Abim′elech king of the Philis′tines looked out of a window and saw Isaac fondling

Rebekah his wife. 9So Abim′elech called
Isaac, and said, "Behold, she is your wife;
how then could you say, 'She is my sister'?"
Isaac said to him, "Because I thought, 'Lest
I die because of her.'" Abim′elech said,
"What is this you have done to us? One of
the people might easily have lain with your
wife, and you would have brought guilt
upon us." 11So Abim′elech warned all the
people, saying, "Whoever touches this man
or his wife shall be put to death."

12And Isaac sowed in that land, and
reaped in the same year a hundredfold. The
LORD blessed him, 13and the man became
rich, and gained more and more until he
became very wealthy. 14He had possessions
of flocks and herds, and a great household,
so that the Philis′tines envied him. 15(Now
the Philis′tines had stopped and filled with
earth all the wells which his father's servants
had dug in the days of Abraham his father.)
16And Abim′elech said to Isaac, "Go away
from us; for you are much mightier than we."

17So Isaac departed from there, and encamped in the valley of Ge′rar and dwelt
there. 18And Isaac dug again the wells of
water which had been dug in the days of
Abraham his father; for the Philis′tines
had stopped them after the death of
Abraham; and he gave them the names
which his father had given them. 19But
when Isaac's servants dug in the valley
and found there a well of springing water,
20the herdsmen of Ge′rar quarreled with
Isaac's herdsmen, saying, "The water is
ours." So he called the name of the well
E′sek, because they contended with him.
21Then they dug another well, and they
quarreled over that also; so he called its
name Sitnah. 22And he moved from there
and dug another well, and over that they
did not quarrel; so he called its name
Reho′both, saying, "For now the LORD
has made room for us, and we shall be
fruitful in the land."

23From there he went up to Be′er-she′ba.
24And the LORD appeared to him the same
night and said, "I am the God of Abraham
your father; fear not, for I am with you
and will bless you and multiply your
descendants for my servant Abraham's
sake." 25So he built an altar there and called
upon the name of the LORD, and pitched
his tent there. And there Isaac's servants
dug a well.

26Then Abim′elech went to him from
Ge′rar with Ahuz′zath his adviser and
Phi′col the commander of his army.
27Isaac said to them, "Why have you
come to me, seeing that you hate me and
have sent me away from you?" 28They
said, "We see plainly that the LORD is
with you; so we say, let there be an oath
between you and us, and let us make a
covenant with you, 29that you will do us
no harm, just as we have not touched
you and have done to you nothing but
good and have sent you away in peace.
You are now the blessed of the LORD."
30So he made them a feast, and they ate
and drank. 31In the morning they rose
early and took oath with one another;
and Isaac set them on their way, and they
departed from him in peace. 32That same
day Isaac's servants came and told him
about the well which they had dug, and
said to him, "We have found water." 33He
called it Shi′bah; therefore the name of
the city is Be′er-she′ba to this day.

34When Esau was forty years old, he
took to wife Judith the daughter of Bee′ri
the Hittite, and Bas′emath the daughter
of E′lon the Hittite; 35and they made life
bitter for Isaac and Rebekah.

To the choirmaster. Of David.

PSALM 11 [10]

In the LORD I take refuge;
  how can you say to me,
"Flee like a bird to the mountains;
2for behold, the wicked bend the bow,
  they have fitted their arrow to the string,
  to shoot in the dark at the upright
    in heart;
3if the foundations are destroyed,
  what can the righteous do?"

4The LORD is in his holy temple,
the LORD's throne is in heaven;
his eyes behold, his eyelids test,
the children of men.
5The LORD tests the righteous and
the wicked,
and his soul hates him that loves violence.
6On the wicked he will rain coals of fire
and brimstone;
a scorching wind shall be the portion of
their cup.
7For the LORD is righteous, he loves
righteous deeds;
the upright shall behold his face.

MATTHEW 8

23And when he got into the boat,
his disciples followed him. 24And
behold, there arose a great storm
on the sea, so that the boat was being
swamped by the waves; but he was
asleep. 25And they went and woke him,
saying, "Save us, Lord; we are perishing."
26And he said to them, "Why are you afraid,
O men of little faith?" Then he rose and
rebuked the winds and the sea; and there
was a great calm. 27And the men marveled,
saying, "What sort of man is this, that even
winds and sea obey him?"
28And when he came to the other side, to
the country of the Gad′arenes, two demoniacs met him, coming out of the tombs, so
fierce that no one could pass that way. 29And
behold, they cried out, "What have you to do
with us, O Son of God? Have you come here
to torment us before the time?" 30Now a herd
of many swine was feeding at some distance
from them. 31And the demons begged him,
"If you cast us out, send us away into the
herd of swine." 32And he said to them, "Go."
So they came out and went into the swine;
and behold, the whole herd rushed down the
steep bank into the sea, and perished in the
waters. 33The herdsmen fled, and going into
the city they told everything, and what had
happened to the demoniacs. 34And behold,
all the city came out to meet Jesus; and when
they saw him, they begged him to leave their
neighborhood.

9 And getting into a boat he crossed over
and came to his own city. 2And behold,
they brought to him a paralytic, lying on
his bed; and when Jesus saw their faith, he
said to the paralytic, "Take heart, my son;
your sins are forgiven." 3And behold, some
of the scribes said to themselves, "This man
is blaspheming." 4But Jesus, knowing their
thoughts, said, "Why do you think evil in
your hearts? 5For which is easier, to say,
'Your sins are forgiven,' or to say, 'Rise and
walk'? 6But that you may know that the Son
of man has authority on earth to forgive
sins"—he then said to the paralytic—"Rise,
take up your bed and go home." 7And he
rose and went home. 8When the crowds saw
it, they were afraid, and they glorified God,
who had given such authority to men.

REFLECTION

Unlike his father Abraham and his son Jacob, Isaac never leaves the Promised Land. Why does Isaac, alone among the patriarchs, never experience exile? Could it be because he alone remained faithful and chaste to his spouse? If, as the Church Fathers suggest, the Promised Land represents Heaven, perhaps Isaac's purity of life and fidelity to marriage represent the road to Heaven. Isaac remains faithful to Rebekah and does not experience exile, which in Scripture is the punishment for sin. Indeed, after Abraham disobeys God's command to leave behind his kin by taking Lot with him, a famine hits the Promised Land, forcing a brief exile for Abraham in Egypt. Likewise, immediately following Jacob's deception of his father, Jacob must flee eastward in exile. Isaac's stability is striking. Perhaps he foreshadows that beatitude promised by our Lord: "Blessed are the pure in heart, for they shall see God" (Mt 5:8). Of course, even for the Abrahams and Jacobs there is hope, as Jesus illustrates in healing the paralytic, saying those words of new creation: "Your sins are forgiven." Do you respond like the crowds, who give praise to God for giving such authority to men? Do you make use of the Sacrament of Reconciliation to often hear those words, "Your sins are forgiven"?

January 12

GENESIS 27

When Isaac was old and his eyes were dim so that he could not see, he called Esau his older son, and said to him, "My son"; and he answered, "Here I am." 2He said, "Behold, I am old; I do not know the day of my death. 3Now then, take your weapons, your quiver and your bow, and go out to the field, and hunt game for me, 4and prepare for me savory food, such as I love, and bring it to me that I may eat; that I may bless you before I die."

5Now Rebekah was listening when Isaac spoke to his son Esau. So when Esau went to the field to hunt for game and bring it, 6Rebekah said to her son Jacob, "I heard your father speak to your brother Esau, 7'Bring me game, and prepare for me savory food, that I may eat it, and bless you before the LORD before I die.' 8Now therefore, my son, obey my word as I command you. 9Go to the flock, and fetch me two good kids, that I may prepare from them savory food for your father, such as he loves; 10and you shall bring it to your father to eat, so that he may bless you before he dies." 11But Jacob said to Rebekah his mother, "Behold, my brother Esau is a hairy man, and I am a smooth man. 12Perhaps my father will feel me, and I shall seem to be mocking him, and bring a curse upon myself and not a blessing." 13His mother said to him, "Upon me be your curse, my son; only obey my word, and go, fetch them to me." 14So he went and took them and brought them to his mother; and his mother prepared savory food, such as his father loved. 15Then Rebekah took the best garments of Esau her older son, which were with her in the house, and put them on Jacob her younger son; 16and the skins of the kids she put upon his hands and upon the smooth part of his neck; 17and she gave the savory food and the bread, which she had prepared, into the hand of her son Jacob.

18So he went in to his father, and said, "My father"; and he said, "Here I am; who are you, my son?" 19Jacob said to his father, "I am Esau your first-born. I have done as you told me; now sit up and eat of my game, that you may bless me." 20But Isaac said to his son, "How is it that you have found it so quickly, my son?" He answered, "Because the LORD your God granted me success." 21Then Isaac said to Jacob, "Come near, that I may feel you, my son, to know whether you are really my son Esau or not." 22So Jacob went near to Isaac his father, who felt him and said, "The voice is Jacob's voice, but the hands are the hands of Esau." 23And he did not recognize him, because his hands were hairy like his brother Esau's hands; so he blessed him. 24He said, "Are you really my son Esau?" He answered, "I am." 25Then he said, "Bring it to me, that I may eat of my son's game and bless you." So he brought it to him, and he ate; and he brought him wine, and he drank. 26Then his father Isaac said to him, "Come near and kiss me, my son." 27So he came near and kissed him; and he smelled the smell of his garments, and blessed him, and said,

"See, the smell of my son
is as the smell of a field which the LORD
has blessed!
28May God give you of the dew of heaven,
and of the fatness of the earth,
and plenty of grain and wine.
29Let peoples serve you,
and nations bow down to you.
Be lord over your brothers,
and may your mother's sons bow down
to you.
Cursed be every one who curses you,
and blessed be every one who
blesses you!"

30As soon as Isaac had finished blessing Jacob, when Jacob had scarcely gone out from the presence of Isaac his father, Esau his brother came in from his hunting. 31He also prepared savory food, and brought it to his father. And he said to his father, "Let my father arise, and eat of his son's game, that you may bless me." 32His father Isaac said to him, "Who are you?" He answered, "I am your son, your first-born, Esau." 33Then Isaac trembled violently, and said, "Who was it then that hunted game and brought it to me, and I ate it all before you came, and I have blessed him?—yes, and he shall be blessed." 34When Esau heard the words of his father, he cried out with an exceedingly great and bitter cry, and said to his father, "Bless me, even me also, O my father!" 35But he said, "Your brother came with guile, and he has taken away your blessing." 36Esau said, "Is he not rightly named Jacob? For he has supplanted me these two times. He took away my birthright; and behold, now he has taken away my blessing." Then he said, "Have you not reserved a blessing for me?" 37Isaac answered Esau, "Behold, I have made him your lord, and all his brothers I have given to him for servants, and with grain and wine I have sustained him. What then can I do for you, my son?" 38Esau said to his father, "Have you but one blessing, my father? Bless me, even me also, O my father." And Esau lifted up his voice and wept.

39Then Isaac his father answered him:
"Behold, away from the fatness of the
earth shall your dwelling be,
and away from the dew of heaven
on high.
40By your sword you shall live,
and you shall serve your brother;
but when you break loose
you shall break his yoke from your neck."

41Now Esau hated Jacob because of the blessing with which his father had blessed him, and Esau said to himself, "The days of mourning for my father are approaching; then I will kill my brother Jacob." 42But the words of Esau her older son were told to Rebekah; so she sent and called Jacob her younger son, and said to him, "Behold, your brother Esau comforts himself by planning to kill you. 43Now therefore, my son, obey my voice; arise, flee to La'ban my brother in Haran, 44and stay with him a while, until your brother's fury turns away; 45until your brother's anger turns away, and he forgets what you have done to him; then I will send, and fetch you from there. Why should I be bereft of you both in one day?"

46Then Rebekah said to Isaac, "I am weary of my life because of the Hittite women. If Jacob marries one of the Hittite women such as these, one of the women of the land, what good will my life be to me?"

28 Then Isaac called Jacob and blessed him, and charged him, "You shall not marry one of the Canaanite women. 2Arise, go to Pad'dan-ar'am to the house of Bethu'el your mother's father; and take as wife from there one of the daughters of La'ban your mother's brother. 3God Almighty bless you and make you fruitful and multiply you, that you may become a company of peoples. 4May he give the blessing of Abraham to you and to your descendants with you, that you may take possession of the land of your sojournings which God gave to Abraham!" 5Thus Isaac sent Jacob away; and he went to Pad'dan-ar'am to La'ban, the son of Bethu'el the Arame'an, the brother of Rebekah, Jacob's and Esau's mother.

6Now Esau saw that Isaac had blessed Jacob and sent him away to Padd'an-ar'am to take a wife from there, and that as he blessed him he charged him, "You shall not marry one of the Canaanite women," 7and that Jacob had obeyed his father and his mother and gone to Pad'dan-ar'am. 8So when Esau saw that the Canaanite women did not please Isaac his father, 9Esau went to Ish'mael and took to wife, besides the wives he had, Maha'lath the daughter of Ishmael Abraham's son, the sister of Neba'ioth.

10Jacob left Be'er-she'ba, and went toward Haran. 11And he came to a certain place, and stayed there that night, because the sun had set. Taking one of the stones of the place, he put it under his head and lay down in that place to sleep. 12And he dreamed that there was a ladder set up on the earth, and the top of it reached to heaven; and behold, the angels of God were ascending and descending on it! 13And behold, the LORD stood above it and said, "I am the LORD, the God of Abraham your father and the God of Isaac; the land on which you lie I will give to you and to your

descendants; 14 and your descendants shall be
like the dust of the earth, and you shall spread
abroad to the west and to the east and to the
north and to the south; and by you and your
descendants shall all the families of the earth
bless themselves. 15 Behold, I am with you and
will keep you wherever you go, and will bring
you back to this land; for I will not leave you
until I have done that of which I have spoken
to you." 16 Then Jacob awoke from his sleep
and said, "Surely the LORD is in this place;
and I did not know it." 17 And he was afraid,
and said, "How awesome is this place! This is
none other than the house of God, and this is
the gate of heaven."

18 So Jacob rose early in the morning, and
he took the stone which he had put under
his head and set it up for a pillar and poured
oil on the top of it. 19 He called the name of
that place Bethel; but the name of the city
was Luz at the first. 20 Then Jacob made a
vow, saying, "If God will be with me, and
will keep me in this way that I go, and will
give me bread to eat and clothing to wear,
21 so that I come again to my father's house in
peace, then the LORD shall be my God, 22 and
this stone, which I have set up for a pillar,
shall be God's house; and of all that you give
me I will give the tenth to you."

To the choirmaster: according to The Sheminith.
A Psalm of David.

PSALM 12 [11]

Help, LORD; for there is no longer any one
that is godly;
for the faithful have vanished from
among the sons of men.
2 Every one utters lies to his neighbor;
with flattering lips and a double heart
they speak.

3 May the LORD cut off all flattering lips,
the tongue that makes great boasts,
4 those who say, "With our tongue we
will prevail,
our lips are with us; who is our master?"

5 "Because the poor are despoiled, because
the needy groan,
I will now arise," says the LORD;
"I will place him in the safety for which
he longs."
6 The promises of the LORD are promises
that are pure,
silver refined in a furnace on the ground,
purified seven times.

7 Do, O LORD, protect us,
guard us for ever from this generation.
8 On every side the wicked prowl,
as vileness is exalted among the sons
of men.

MATTHEW 9

**9 As Jesus passed on from there,
he saw a man called Matthew
sitting at the tax office; and he said to
him, "Follow me." And he rose and
followed him.**

10 And as he sat at table in the house, behold,
many tax collectors and sinners came and
sat down with Jesus and his disciples. 11 And
when the Pharisees saw this, they said to his
disciples, "Why does your teacher eat with
tax collectors and sinners?" 12 But when he
heard it, he said, "Those who are well have
no need of a physician, but those who are
sick. 13 Go and learn what this means, 'I
desire mercy, and not sacrifice.' For I came
not to call the righteous, but sinners."

14 Then the disciples of John came
to him, saying, "Why do we and the
Pharisees fast, but your disciples do not
fast?" 15 And Jesus said to them, "Can
the wedding guests mourn as long as
the bridegroom is with them? The days
will come, when the bridegroom is taken
away from them, and then they will fast.
16 And no one puts a piece of unshrunk
cloth on an old garment, for the patch
tears away from the garment, and a worse
tear is made. 17 Neither is new wine put
into old wineskins; if it is, the skins burst,

and the wine is spilled, and the skins are destroyed; but new wine is put into fresh wineskins, and so both are preserved."

[18]While he was thus speaking to them, behold, a ruler came in and knelt before him, saying, "My daughter has just died; but come and lay your hand on her, and she will live." [19]And Jesus rose and followed him, with his disciples. [20]And behold, a woman who had suffered from a hemorrhage for twelve years came up behind him and touched the fringe of his garment; [21]for she said to herself, "If I only touch his garment, I shall be made well." [22]Jesus turned, and seeing her he said, "Take heart, daughter; your faith has made you well." And instantly the woman was made well. [23]And when Jesus came to the ruler's house, and saw the flute players, and the crowd making a tumult, [24]he said, "Depart; for the girl is not dead but sleeping." And they laughed at him. [25]But when the crowd had been put outside, he went in and took her by the hand, and the girl arose. [26]And the report of this went through all that district.

[27]And as Jesus passed on from there, two blind men followed him, crying aloud, "Have mercy on us, Son of David." [28]When he entered the house, the blind men came to him; and Jesus said to them, "Do you believe that I am able to do this?" They said to him, "Yes, Lord." [29]Then he touched their eyes, saying, "According to your faith let it be done to you." [30]And their eyes were opened. And Jesus sternly charged them, "See that no one knows it." [31]But they went away and spread his fame through all that district.

[32]As they were going away, behold, a mute demoniac was brought to him. [33]And when the demon had been cast out, the mute man spoke; and the crowds marveled, saying, "Never was anything like this seen in Israel." [34]But the Pharisees said, "He casts out demons by the prince of demons."

REFLECTION

If all observant Jews fasted a couple of days each week, why didn't Jesus and his disciples fast? Why did Jews fast? This practice started with the destruction of Solomon's Temple by the Babylonians, and so throughout the time of exile Jews fasted on particular months and weekdays (see Zec 7:3–5). Fasting was a sign of mourning, and, with the destruction of the Temple, Jews mourned the absence of God's presence that dwelt in the Temple. Israel's sin led to the Spirit of God departing from the Temple, and so fasting was both mourning and reparation that sought God's return to his dwelling place. So why didn't Jesus's disciples fast? Jesus gives a profound answer: while the bridegroom is with them, the wedding guests cannot fast. Here Jesus alludes to the practice that, during the seven days of a wedding feast, a pious Jew is exempt from the two days of weekly fasting. As long as the disciples have Jesus with them, they have the divine Bridegroom. But once the Bridegroom ascends into Heaven, Jesus's disciples begin the practice of fasting, recalling the sacrifice Jesus their Bridegroom offered on Good Friday, just as the Jews mourned the loss of the Temple. Do you fast and practice abstinence on those days prescribed by the Church?

January 13

GENESIS 29

Then Jacob went on his journey, and came to the land of the people of the east. [2]As he looked, he saw a well in the field, and behold, three flocks of sheep lying beside it; for out of that well the flocks were watered. The stone on the well's mouth was large, [3]and when all the flocks were gathered there, the shepherds would roll the stone from the mouth of the well, and water the sheep, and put the stone back in its place upon the mouth of the well.

[4]Jacob said to them, "My brothers, where do you come from?" They said, "We are from Haran." [5]He said to them, "Do you know La'ban the son of Na'hor?" They said, "We know him." [6]He said to them, "Is

it well with him?" They said, "It is well; and see, Rachel his daughter is coming with the sheep!" [7]He said, "Behold, it is still high day, it is not time for the animals to be gathered together; water the sheep, and go, pasture them." [8]But they said, "We cannot until all the flocks are gathered together, and the stone is rolled from the mouth of the well; then we water the sheep."

[9]While he was still speaking with them, Rachel came with her father's sheep; for she kept them. [10]Now when Jacob saw Rachel the daughter of La'ban his mother's brother, and the sheep of Laban his mother's brother, Jacob went up and rolled the stone from the well's mouth, and watered the flock of Laban his mother's brother. [11]Then Jacob kissed Rachel, and wept aloud. [12]And Jacob told Rachel that he was her father's kinsman, and that he was Rebekah's son; and she ran and told her father.

[13]When La'ban heard the tidings of Jacob his sister's son, he ran to meet him, and embraced him and kissed him, and brought him to his house. Jacob told Laban all these things, [14]and La'ban said to him, "Surely you are my bone and my flesh!" And he stayed with him a month.

[15]Then La'ban said to Jacob, "Because you are my kinsman, should you therefore serve me for nothing? Tell me, what shall your wages be?" [16]Now La'ban had two daughters; the name of the older was Leah, and the name of the younger was Rachel. [17]Leah's eyes were weak, but Rachel was beautiful and lovely. [18]Jacob loved Rachel; and he said, "I will serve you seven years for your younger daughter Rachel." [19]La'ban said, "It is better that I give her to you than that I should give her to any other man; stay with me." [20]So Jacob served seven years for Rachel, and they seemed to him but a few days because of the love he had for her.

[21]Then Jacob said to La'ban, "Give me my wife that I may go in to her, for my time is completed." [22]So La'ban gathered together all the men of the place, and made a feast. [23]But in the evening he took his daughter Leah and brought her to Jacob; and he went in to her. [24](La'ban gave his maid Zilpah to his daughter Leah to be her maid.) [25]And in the morning, behold, it was Leah; and Jacob said to La'ban, "What is this you have done to me? Did I not serve with you for Rachel? Why then have you deceived me?" [26]La'ban said, "It is not so done in our country, to give the younger before the first-born. [27]Complete the week of this one, and we will give you the other also in return for serving me another seven years." [28]Jacob did so, and completed her week; then La'ban gave him his daughter Rachel to wife. [29](La'ban gave his maid Bilhah to his daughter Rachel to be her maid.) [30]So Jacob went in to Rachel also, and he loved Rachel more than Leah, and served La'ban for another seven years.

[31]When the LORD saw that Leah was hated, he opened her womb; but Rachel was barren. [32]And Leah conceived and bore a son, and she called his name Reuben; for she said, "Because the LORD has looked upon my affliction; surely now my husband will love me." [33]She conceived again and bore a son, and said, "Because the LORD has heard that I am hated, he has given me this son also"; and she called his name Simeon. [34]Again she conceived and bore a son, and said, "Now this time my husband will be joined to me, because I have borne him three sons"; therefore his name was called Levi. [35]And she conceived again and bore a son, and said, "This time I will praise the LORD"; therefore she called his name Judah; then she ceased bearing.

30 When Rachel saw that she bore Jacob no children, she envied her sister; and she said to Jacob, "Give me children, or I shall die!" [2]Jacob's anger was kindled against Rachel, and he said, "Am I in the place of God, who has withheld from you the fruit of the womb?" [3]Then she said, "Here is my maid Bilhah; go in to her, that she may bear upon my knees, and even I may have children through her." [4]So she gave him her maid Bilhah as a wife; and Jacob went in to her. [5]And Bilhah conceived and bore Jacob a son. [6]Then Rachel said, "God has judged me, and has also heard my voice

and given me a son"; therefore she called his
name Dan. 7Rachel's maid Bilhah conceived
again and bore Jacob a second son. 8Then
Rachel said, "With mighty wrestlings I have
wrestled with my sister, and have prevailed";
so she called his name Naph′tali.

9When Leah saw that she had ceased
bearing children, she took her maid Zilpah
and gave her to Jacob as a wife. 10Then
Leah's maid Zilpah bore Jacob a son. 11And
Leah said, "Good fortune!" so she called his
name Gad. 12Leah's maid Zilpah bore Jacob a
second son. 13And Leah said, "Blessed am I!
For the women will call me blessed"; so she
called his name Asher.

14In the days of wheat harvest Reuben
went and found mandrakes in the field,
and brought them to his mother Leah.
Then Rachel said to Leah, "Give me, I
pray, some of your son's mandrakes." 15But
she said to her, "Is it a small matter that
you have taken away my husband? Would
you take away my son's mandrakes also?"
Rachel said, "Then he may lie with you
tonight for your son's mandrakes." 16When
Jacob came from the field in the evening,
Leah went out to meet him, and said, "You
must come in to me; for I have hired you
with my son's mandrakes." So he lay with
her that night. 17And God hearkened to
Leah, and she conceived and bore Jacob a
fifth son. 18Leah said, "God has given me
my hire because I gave my maid to my
husband"; so she called his name Is′sachar.
19And Leah conceived again, and she bore
Jacob a sixth son. 20Then Leah said, "God
has endowed me with a good dowry;
now my husband will honor me, because
I have borne him six sons"; so she called
his name Zeb′ulun. 21Afterwards she bore
a daughter, and called her name Dinah.
22Then God remembered Rachel, and God
hearkened to her and opened her womb.
23She conceived and bore a son, and said,
"God has taken away my reproach"; 24and
she called his name Joseph, saying, "May
the LORD add to me another son!"

25When Rachel had borne Joseph, Jacob
said to La′ban, "Send me away, that I may
go to my own home and country. 26Give me
my wives and my children for whom I have
served you, and let me go; for you know
the service which I have given you." 27But
La′ban said to him, "If you will allow me to
say so, I have learned by divination that the
LORD has blessed me because of you; 28name
your wages, and I will give it." 29Jacob said to
him, "You yourself know how I have served
you, and how your cattle have fared with
me. 30For you had little before I came, and
it has increased abundantly; and the LORD
has blessed you wherever I turned. But now
when shall I provide for my own household
also?" 31He said, "What shall I give you?"
Jacob said, "You shall not give me anything;
if you will do this for me, I will again feed
your flock and keep it: 32let me pass through
all your flock today, removing from it every
speckled and spotted sheep and every black
lamb, and the spotted and speckled among
the goats; and such shall be my wages. 33So
my honesty will answer for me later, when
you come to look into my wages with you.
Every one that is not speckled and spotted
among the goats and black among the
lambs, if found with me, shall be counted
stolen." 34La′ban said, "Good! Let it be as you
have said."

To the choirmaster.
A Psalm of David.

PSALM 13 [12]

How long, O LORD? Will you forget me
for ever?
How long will you hide your face from me?
2How long must I bear pain in my soul,
and have sorrow in my heart all the day?
How long shall my enemy be exalted
over me?

3Consider and answer me, O LORD my God;
lighten my eyes, lest I sleep the sleep
of death;
4lest my enemy say, "I have prevailed
over him";
lest my foes rejoice because I am shaken.

[5]But I have trusted in your merciful love;
my heart shall rejoice in your salvation.
[6]I will sing to the LORD,
because he has dealt bountifully with me.

MATTHEW 9

[35]And Jesus went about all the cities and villages, teaching in their synagogues and preaching the gospel of the kingdom, and healing every disease and every infirmity. [36]When he saw the crowds, he had compassion for them, because they were harassed and helpless, like sheep without a shepherd. [37]Then he said to his disciples, "The harvest is plentiful, but the laborers are few; [38]pray therefore the Lord of the harvest to send out laborers into his harvest."

10 And he called to him his twelve disciples and gave them authority over unclean spirits, to cast them out, and to heal every disease and every infirmity. [2]The names of the twelve apostles are these: first, Simon, who is called Peter, and Andrew his brother; James the son of Zeb′edee, and John his brother; [3]Philip and Bartholomew; Thomas and Matthew the tax collector; James the son of Alphae′us, and Thaddae′us; [4]Simon the Cananaean, and Judas Iscariot, who betrayed him.

[5]These Twelve Jesus sent out, charging them, "Go nowhere among the Gentiles, and enter no town of the Samaritans, [6]but go rather to the lost sheep of the house of Israel. [7]And preach as you go, saying, 'The kingdom of heaven is at hand.' [8]Heal the sick, raise the dead, cleanse lepers, cast out demons. You received without pay, give without pay. [9]Take no gold, nor silver, nor copper in your belts, [10]no bag for your journey, nor two tunics, nor sandals, nor a staff; for the laborer deserves his food. [11]And whatever town or village you enter, find out who is worthy in it, and stay with him until you depart. [12]As you enter the house, salute it. [13]And if the house is worthy, let your peace come upon it; but if it is not worthy, let your peace return to you. [14]And if any one will not receive you or listen to your words, shake off the dust from your feet as you leave that house or town. [15]Truly, I say to you, it shall be more tolerable on the day of judgment for the land of Sodom and Gomor′rah than for that town.

[16]"Behold, I send you out as sheep in the midst of wolves; so be wise as serpents and innocent as doves. [17]Beware of men; for they will deliver you up to councils, and flog you in their synagogues, [18]and you will be dragged before governors and kings for my sake, to bear testimony before them and the Gentiles. [19]When they deliver you up, do not be anxious about how you are to speak or what you are to say; for what you are to say will be given to you in that hour; [20]for it is not you who speak, but the Spirit of your Father speaking through you. [21]Brother will deliver up brother to death, and the father his child, and children will rise against parents and have them put to death; [22]and you will be hated by all for my name's sake. But he who endures to the end will be saved. [23]When they persecute you in one town, flee to the next; for truly, I say to you, you will not have gone through all the towns of Israel, before the Son of man comes.

REFLECTION

In the Hebrew Scriptures there is a tradition of honoring one's father and mother (codified in the Fourth Commandment), which extends to one's ancestors. As a result, the Old Testament writers prefer not to explicitly state the sins of the patriarchs, choosing instead to show the many negative consequences of such sins, leaving it to the reader to connect the consequences with the sin. Thus, rather than blatantly telling us Abraham sinned in hearkening to Sarah's voice and sleeping with her handmaid Hagar, we see the growing conflict in the relationships. Similarly, the writer never specifically says Jacob sinned when he deceived his father while Isaac's eyes were dark, but the narrative makes it clear in the consequences that follow. After working seven years to pay the dowry for

Rachel, Jacob is deceived by his father-in-law Laban, who in the dark of the night gives Jacob his eldest daughter Leah instead. Jacob reaps what he sows; the deceiver is deceived. In the darkness there is a mix-up of birth order, the older for the younger, just as Jacob, the younger, usurped the place of his older brother Esau. The power of Hebrew narrative is much more compelling than any simple moralizing; it shows that if one sows sin, a bitter harvest will be reaped. Do you include a daily examination of conscience as part of your spiritual life?

January 14

GENESIS 30

35**But that day La'ban removed
the he-goats that were striped
and spotted, and all the she-goats that
were speckled and spotted, every one**
that had white on it, and every lamb that
was black, and put them in charge of his
sons; 36and he set a distance of three days'
journey between himself and Jacob; and
Jacob fed the rest of La'ban's flock.
37Then Jacob took fresh rods of poplar
and almond and plane, and peeled white
streaks in them, exposing the white of the
rods. 38He set the rods which he had peeled
in front of the flocks in the runnels, that
is, the watering troughs, where the flocks
came to drink. And since they bred when
they came to drink, 39the flocks bred in
front of the rods and so the flocks brought
forth striped, speckled, and spotted. 40And
Jacob separated the lambs, and set the
faces of the flocks toward the striped and
all the black in the flock of La'ban; and he
put his own droves apart, and did not put
them with Laban's flock. 41Whenever the
stronger of the flock were breeding Jacob
laid the rods in the runnels before the eyes
of the flock, that they might breed among
the rods, 42but for the feebler of the flock he
did not lay them there; so the feebler were
La'ban's, and the stronger Jacob's. 43Thus the
man grew exceedingly rich, and had large
flocks, maidservants and menservants, and
camels and donkeys.

31 Now Jacob heard that the sons of
La'ban were saying, "Jacob has taken
all that was our father's; and from what was
our father's he has gained all this wealth."
2And Jacob saw that La'ban did not regard
him with favor as before. 3Then the LORD
said to Jacob, "Return to the land of your
fathers and to your kindred, and I will be
with you." 4So Jacob sent and called Rachel
and Leah into the field where his flock was,
5and said to them, "I see that your father
does not regard me with favor as he did
before. But the God of my father has been
with me. 6You know that I have served your
father with all my strength; 7yet your father
has cheated me and changed my wages ten
times, but God did not permit him to harm
me. 8If he said, 'The spotted shall be your
wages,' then all the flock bore spotted; and
if he said, 'The striped shall be your wages,'
then all the flock bore striped. 9Thus God
has taken away the cattle of your father, and
given them to me. 10In the mating season of
the flock I lifted up my eyes, and saw in
a dream that the he-goats which leaped
upon the flock were striped, spotted, and
mottled. 11Then the angel of God said to
me in the dream, 'Jacob,' and I said, 'Here
I am!' 12And he said, 'Lift up your eyes and
see, all the goats that leap upon the flock
are striped, spotted, and mottled; for I have
seen all that La'ban is doing to you. 13I am
the God of Bethel, where you anointed a
pillar and made a vow to me. Now arise,
go forth from this land, and return to the
land of your birth.'" 14Then Rachel and
Leah answered him, "Is there any portion
or inheritance left to us in our father's
house? 15Are we not regarded by him as
foreigners? For he has sold us, and he has
been using up the money given for us. 16All
the property which God has taken away
from our father belongs to us and to our
children; now then, whatever God has said
to you, do."

[17]So Jacob arose, and set his sons and his wives on camels; [18]and he drove away all his cattle, all his livestock which he had gained, the cattle in his possession which he had acquired in Pad´dan-ar´am, to go to the land of Canaan to his father Isaac. [19]La´ban had gone to shear his sheep, and Rachel stole her father's household gods. [20]And Jacob outwitted La´ban the Arame´an, in that he did not tell him that he intended to flee. [21]He fled with all that he had, and arose and crossed the Euphra´tes, and set his face toward the hill country of Gilead.

[22]When it was told La´ban on the third day that Jacob had fled, [23]he took his kinsmen with him and pursued him for seven days and followed close after him into the hill country of Gilead. [24]But God came to La´ban the Arame´an in a dream by night, and said to him, "Take heed that you say not a word to Jacob, either good or bad."

[25]And La´ban overtook Jacob. Now Jacob had pitched his tent in the hill country, and Laban with his kinsmen encamped in the hill country of Gilead. [26]And La´ban said to Jacob, "What have you done, that you have cheated me, and carried away my daughters like captives of the sword? [27]Why did you flee secretly, and cheat me, and did not tell me, so that I might have sent you away with mirth and songs, with tambourine and lyre? [28]And why did you not permit me to kiss my sons and my daughters farewell? Now you have done foolishly. [29]It is in my power to do you harm; but the God of your father spoke to me last night, saying, 'Take heed that you speak to Jacob neither good nor bad.' [30]And now you have gone away because you longed greatly for your father's house, but why did you steal my gods?" [31]Jacob answered La´ban, "Because I was afraid, for I thought that you would take your daughters from me by force. [32]Any one with whom you find your gods shall not live. In the presence of our kinsmen point out what I have that is yours, and take it." Now Jacob did not know that Rachel had stolen them.

[33]So La´ban went into Jacob's tent, and into Leah's tent, and into the tent of the two maidservants, but he did not find them. And he went out of Leah's tent, and entered Rachel's. [34]Now Rachel had taken the household gods and put them in the camel's saddle, and sat upon them. La´ban felt all about the tent, but did not find them. [35]And she said to her father, "Let not my lord be angry that I cannot rise before you, for the way of women is upon me." So he searched, but did not find the household gods.

[36]Then Jacob became angry, and upbraided La´ban; Jacob said to Laban, "What is my offense? What is my sin, that you have hotly pursued me? [37]Although you have felt through all my goods, what have you found of all your household goods? Set it here before my kinsmen and your kinsmen, that they may decide between us two. [38]These twenty years I have been with you; your ewes and your she-goats have not miscarried, and I have not eaten the rams of your flocks. [39]That which was torn by wild beasts I did not bring to you; I bore the loss of it myself; of my hand you required it, whether stolen by day or stolen by night. [40]Thus I was; by day the heat consumed me, and the cold by night, and my sleep fled from my eyes. [41]These twenty years I have been in your house; I served you fourteen years for your two daughters, and six years for your flock, and you have changed my wages ten times. [42]If the God of my father, the God of Abraham and the Fear of Isaac, had not been on my side, surely now you would have sent me away empty-handed. God saw my affliction and the labor of my hands, and rebuked you last night."

[43]Then La´ban answered and said to Jacob, "The daughters are my daughters, the children are my children, the flocks are my flocks, and all that you see is mine. But what can I do this day to these my daughters, or to their children whom they have borne? [44]Come now, let us make a covenant, you and I; and let it be a witness between you and me." [45]So Jacob took a stone, and set it up as a pillar. [46]And Jacob said to his kinsmen, "Gather stones," and they took stones, and made a heap; and they ate there by the heap. [47]La´ban called it Je´gar-sahadu´tha: but Jacob called it Gale´ed. [48]La´ban said, "This heap is a witness between you and me today." Therefore he named it

Gale´ed, 49and the pillar Mizpah, for he said,
"The LORD watch between you and me, when
we are absent one from the other. 50If you ill-
treat my daughters, or if you take wives besides
my daughters, although no man is with us,
remember, God is witness between you
and me."

51Then La´ban said to Jacob, "See this heap
and the pillar, which I have set between
you and me. 52This heap is a witness, and
the pillar is a witness, that I will not pass
over this heap to you, and you will not
pass over this heap and this pillar to me,
for harm. 53The God of Abraham and the
God of Na´hor, the God of their father,
judge between us." So Jacob swore by the
Fear of his father Isaac, 54and Jacob offered
a sacrifice on the mountain and called his
kinsmen to eat bread; and they ate bread
and tarried all night on the mountain.

55Early in the morning La´ban arose, and
kissed his grandchildren and his daughters
and blessed them; then he departed and
returned home.

32 Jacob went on his way and the angels
of God met him; 2and when Jacob
saw them he said, "This is God's army!" So
he called the name of that place Ma´´hana´im.

3And Jacob sent messengers before him
to Esau his brother in the land of Se´ir,
the country of Edom, 4instructing them,
"Thus you shall say to my lord Esau: Thus
says your servant Jacob, 'I have sojourned
with La´ban, and stayed until now; 5and I
have oxen, donkeys, flocks, menservants,
and maidservants; and I have sent to tell
my lord, in order that I may find favor in
your sight.'"

6And the messengers returned to Jacob,
saying, "We came to your brother Esau, and
he is coming to meet you, and four hundred
men with him." 7Then Jacob was greatly afraid
and distressed; and he divided the people that
were with him, and the flocks and herds and
camels, into two companies, 8thinking, "If
Esau comes to the one company and destroys
it, then the company which is left will escape."

9And Jacob said, "O God of my father
Abraham and God of my father Isaac, O LORD
who said to me, 'Return to your country and
to your kindred, and I will do you good,' 10I
am not worthy of the least of all the mercy and
all the faithfulness which you have shown to
your servant, for with only my staff I crossed
this Jordan; and now I have become two
companies. 11Deliver me, I beg you, from the
hand of my brother, from the hand of Esau,
for I fear him, lest he come and slay us all, the
mothers with the children. 12But you said, 'I will
do you good, and make your descendants as
the sand of the sea, which cannot be numbered
for multitude.'"

To the choirmaster.
Of David.

PSALM 14 [13]

The fool says in his heart, "There is no God."
They are corrupt, they do abominable
deeds,
there is none that does good.

2The LORD looks down from heaven upon
the children of men,
to see if there are any that act wisely,
that seek after God.

3They have all gone astray, they are all
alike corrupt;
there is none that does good,
no, not one.

4Have they no knowledge, all the evildoers
who eat up my people as they eat bread,
and do not call upon the LORD?

5There they shall be in great terror,
for God is with the generation of
the righteous.

6You would confound the plans of the poor,
but the LORD is his refuge.

7O that deliverance for Israel would come
out of Zion!
When the LORD restores the fortunes of
his people,
Jacob shall rejoice, Israel shall be glad.

MATTHEW 10

24"A disciple is not above his teacher, nor a servant above his master; 25it is enough for the disciple to be like his teacher, and the servant like his master. If they have called the master of the house Be-el′zebul, how much more will they malign those of his household.

26"So have no fear of them; for nothing is covered that will not be revealed, or hidden that will not be known. 27What I tell you in the dark, utter in the light; and what you hear whispered, proclaim upon the housetops. 28And do not fear those who kill the body but cannot kill the soul; rather fear him who can destroy both soul and body in hell. 29Are not two sparrows sold for a penny? And not one of them will fall to the ground without your Father's will. 30But even the hairs of your head are all numbered. 31Fear not, therefore; you are of more value than many sparrows. 32So every one who acknowledges me before men, I also will acknowledge before my Father who is in heaven; 33but whoever denies me before men, I also will deny before my Father who is in heaven.

34"Do not think that I have come to bring peace on earth; I have not come to bring peace, but a sword. 35For I have come to set a man against his father, and a daughter against her mother, and a daughter-in-law against her mother-in-law; 36and a man's foes will be those of his own household. 37He who loves father or mother more than me is not worthy of me; and he who loves son or daughter more than me is not worthy of me; 38and he who does not take his cross and follow me is not worthy of me. 39He who finds his life will lose it, and he who loses his life for my sake will find it.

40"He who receives you receives me, and he who receives me receives him who sent me. 41He who receives a prophet because he is a prophet shall receive a prophet's reward, and he who receives a righteous man because he is a righteous man shall receive a righteous man's reward. 42And whoever gives to one of these little ones even a cup of cold water because he is a disciple, truly, I say to you, he shall not lose his reward."

REFLECTION

To what do you give first priority in your life? Many would say their families. Such an answer seems as noble as it is natural. However, even pagans and the wicked could make such a claim, while pursuing selfishness and cruelty to others. Was not Pharaoh good to his own family? Jesus overturns our thinking with his teaching on discipleship. He warns that loyalty to him may lead one to be in conflict with the most intense of family bonds, even those between parents and children. For a follower of Jesus, the first priority must be to do the will of our heavenly Father. God demands our deepest love and loyalty. Even love of self must submit to Christ: "He who loses his life for my sake will find it" (Mt 10:39). Paradoxically, unless God is put in the first place, nothing else will be in its right place in our lives. There is no St. Francis if he obeys his earthly father rather than Christ. Many a saint would not have fulfilled their divine call if they had heeded the voices of family members. However, by putting God first, we learn the humility, discipline, and charity to truly love our families. Do you truly love your family by putting God first in your life?

January 15

GENESIS 32

13So he lodged there that night, and took from what he had with him a present for his brother Esau, 14two hundred she-goats and twenty he-goats, two hundred ewes and twenty rams, 15thirty milch camels and their colts, forty cows and ten bulls, twenty she-donkeys and ten he-donkeys. 16These he delivered into the hand of his servants, every drove by itself, and said to his servants, "Pass on before me, and put a space between drove and drove." 17He instructed the foremost, "When Esau my brother meets you, and asks you, 'To whom do you belong? Where are you going? And whose are these before you?' [18]then you shall say, 'They belong to your servant Jacob; they are a present sent to my lord Esau; and moreover he is behind us.'" [19]He likewise instructed the second and the third and all who followed the droves, "You shall say the same thing to Esau when you meet him, [20]and you shall say, 'Moreover your servant Jacob is behind us.'" For he thought, "I may appease him with the present that goes before me, and afterwards I shall see his face; perhaps he will accept me." [21]So the present passed on before him; and he himself lodged that night in the camp.

[22]The same night he arose and took his two wives, his two maids, and his eleven children, and crossed the ford of the Jabbok. [23]He took them and sent them across the stream, and likewise everything that he had. [24]And Jacob was left alone; and a man wrestled with him until the breaking of the day. [25]When the man saw that he did not prevail against Jacob, he touched the hollow of his thigh; and Jacob's thigh was put out of joint as he wrestled with him. [26]Then he said, "Let me go, for the day is breaking." But Jacob said, "I will not let you go, unless you bless me." [27]And he said to him, "What is your name?" And he said, "Jacob." [28]Then he said, "Your name shall no more be called Jacob, but Israel, for you have striven with God and with men, and have prevailed." [29]Then Jacob asked him, "Tell me, I pray, your name." But he said, "Why is it that you ask my name?" And there he blessed him. [30]So Jacob called the name of the place Peni′el, saying, "For I have seen God face to face, and yet my life is preserved." [31]The sun rose upon him as he passed Penu′el, limping because of his thigh. [32]Therefore to this day the Israelites do not eat the sinew of the hip which is upon the hollow of the thigh, because he touched the hollow of Jacob's thigh on the sinew of the hip.

33 And Jacob lifted up his eyes and looked, and behold, Esau was coming, and four hundred men with him. So he divided the children among Leah and Rachel and the two maids. [2]And he put the maids with their children in front, then Leah with her children, and Rachel and Joseph last of all. [3]He himself went on before them, bowing himself to the ground seven times, until he came near to his brother.

[4]But Esau ran to meet him, and embraced him, and fell on his neck and kissed him, and they wept. [5]And when Esau raised his eyes and saw the women and children, he said, "Who are these with you?" Jacob said, "The children whom God has graciously given your servant." [6]Then the maids drew near, they and their children, and bowed down; [7]Leah likewise and her children drew near and bowed down; and last Joseph and Rachel drew near, and they bowed down. [8]Esau said, "What do you mean by all this company which I met?" Jacob answered, "To find favor in the sight of my lord." [9]But Esau said, "I have enough, my brother; keep what you have for yourself." [10]Jacob said, "No, I beg you, if I have found favor in your sight, then accept my present from my hand; for truly to see your face is like seeing the face of God, with such favor have you received me. [11]Accept, I beg you, my gift that is brought to you, because God has dealt graciously with me, and because I have enough." Thus he urged him, and he took it.

[12]Then Esau said, "Let us journey on our way, and I will go before you." [13]But Jacob said to him, "My lord knows that the children are frail, and that the flocks and herds giving suck are a care to me; and if they are overdriven for one day, all the flocks will die. [14]Let my lord pass on before his servant, and I will lead on slowly, according to the pace of the cattle which are before me and according to the pace of the children, until I come to my lord in Se′ir."

[15]So Esau said, "Let me leave with you some of the men who are with me." But he said, "What need is there? Let me find favor in the sight of my lord." [16]So Esau returned that day on his way to Se′ir. [17]But Jacob journeyed to Succoth, and built himself a house, and made booths for his cattle; therefore the name of the place is called Succoth.

[18]And Jacob came safely to the city of She′chem, which is in the land of Canaan,

on his way from Pad′dan-ar′am; and he camped before the city. 19And from the sons of Ha′mor, She′chem's father, he bought for a hundred pieces of money the piece of land on which he had pitched his tent. 20There he erected an altar and called it El-El′ohe-Israel.

34 Now Dinah the daughter of Leah, whom she had borne to Jacob, went out to visit the women of the land; 2and when She′chem the son of Ha′mor the Hi′vite, the prince of the land, saw her, he seized her and lay with her and humbled her. 3And his soul was drawn to Dinah the daughter of Jacob; he loved the maiden and spoke tenderly to her. 4So She′chem spoke to his father Ha′mor, saying, "Get me this maiden for my wife." 5Now Jacob heard that he had defiled his daughter Dinah; but his sons were with his cattle in the field, so Jacob held his peace until they came. 6And Ha′mor the father of She′chem went out to Jacob to speak with him. 7The sons of Jacob came in from the field when they heard of it; and the men were indignant and very angry, because he had wrought folly in Israel by lying with Jacob's daughter, for such a thing ought not to be done.

8But Ha′mor spoke with them, saying, "The soul of my son She′chem longs for your daughter; I beg you, give her to him in marriage. 9Make marriages with us; give your daughters to us, and take our daughters for yourselves. 10You shall dwell with us; and the land shall be open to you; dwell and trade in it, and get property in it." 11She′chem also said to her father and to her brothers, "Let me find favor in your eyes, and whatever you say to me I will give. 12Ask of me ever so much as marriage present and gift, and I will give according as you say to me; only give me the maiden to be my wife."

13The sons of Jacob answered She′chem and his father Ha′mor deceitfully, because he had defiled their sister Dinah. 14They said to them, "We cannot do this thing, to give our sister to one who is uncircumcised, for that would be a disgrace to us. 15Only on this condition will we consent to you: that you will become as we are and every male of you be circumcised. 16Then we will give our daughters to you, and we will take your daughters to ourselves, and we will dwell with you and become one people. 17But if you will not listen to us and be circumcised, then we will take our daughter, and we will be gone."

18Their words pleased Ha′mor and Ha′mor's son She′chem. 19And the young man did not delay to do the thing, because he had delight in Jacob's daughter. Now he was the most honored of all his family. 20So Ha′mor and his son She′chem came to the gate of their city and spoke to the men of their city, saying, 21"These men are friendly with us; let them dwell in the land and trade in it, for behold, the land is large enough for them; let us take their daughters in marriage, and let us give them our daughters. 22Only on this condition will the men agree to dwell with us, to become one people: that every male among us be circumcised as they are circumcised. 23Will not their cattle, their property and all their beasts be ours? Only let us agree with them, and they will dwell with us." 24And all who went out of the gate of his city hearkened to Ha′mor and his son She′chem; and every male was circumcised, all who went out of the gate of his city.

25On the third day, when they were sore, two of the sons of Jacob, Simeon and Levi, Dinah's brothers, took their swords and came upon the city unawares, and killed all the males. 26They slew Ha′mor and his son She′chem with the sword, and took Dinah out of She′chem's house, and went away. 27And the sons of Jacob came upon the slain, and plundered the city, because their sister had been defiled; 28they took their flocks and their herds, their donkeys, and whatever was in the city and in the field; 29all their wealth, all their little ones and their wives, all that was in the houses, they captured and made their prey. 30Then Jacob said to Simeon and Levi, "You have brought trouble on me by making me odious to the inhabitants of the land, the Canaanites and the

Per′izzites; my numbers are few, and if
they gather themselves against me and
attack me, I shall be destroyed, both I and
my household." 31But they said, "Should
he treat our sister as a harlot?"

A Psalm of David.

PSALM 15 [14]

O LORD, who shall sojourn in your tent?
  Who shall dwell on your holy mountain?

2He who walks blamelessly, and does what
    is right,
  and speaks truth from his heart;
3who does not slander with his tongue,
  and does no evil to his friend,
  nor takes up a reproach against
    his neighbor;
4in whose eyes a reprobate is despised,
  but who honors those who fear the LORD;
who swears to his own hurt and does
    not change;
5who does not put out his money at interest,
  and does not take a bribe against
    the innocent.

He who does these things shall never
    be moved.

MATTHEW 11

And when Jesus had finished instructing his twelve disciples, he went on from there to teach and preach in their cities.
2Now when John heard in prison about
the deeds of the Christ, he sent word by his
disciples 3and said to him, "Are you he who is
to come, or shall we look for another?" 4And
Jesus answered them, "Go and tell John what
you hear and see: 5the blind receive their sight
and the lame walk, lepers are cleansed and the
deaf hear, and the dead are raised up, and the
poor have good news preached to them. 6And
blessed is he who takes no offense at me."

7As they went away, Jesus began to speak
to the crowds concerning John: "What did
you go out into the wilderness to behold?
A reed shaken by the wind? 8Why then did
you go out? To see a man dressed in soft
robes? Behold, those who wear soft robes
are in kings' houses. 9Why then did you go
out? To see a prophet? Yes, I tell you, and
more than a prophet. 10This is he of whom it
is written,

'Behold, I send my messenger before
    your face,
  who shall prepare your way before you.'

11Truly, I say to you, among those born
of women there has arisen no one greater
than John the Baptist; yet he who is least
in the kingdom of heaven is greater than
he. 12From the days of John the Baptist
until now the kingdom of heaven has
suffered violence, and men of violence
take it by force. 13For all the prophets and
the law prophesied until John; 14and if
you are willing to accept it, he is Eli′jah
who is to come. 15He who has ears to hear,
let him hear.

16"But to what shall I compare this generation? It is like children sitting in the
market places and calling to their playmates,
17'We piped to you, and you did not dance;
we wailed, and you did not mourn.'
18For John came neither eating nor drinking,
and they say, 'He has a demon'; 19the Son of
man came eating and drinking, and they say,
'Behold, a glutton and a drunkard, a friend
of tax collectors and sinners!' Yet wisdom is
justified by her deeds."

20Then he began to upbraid the cities where
most of his mighty works had been done,
because they did not repent. 21"Woe to you,
Chora′zin! woe to you, Beth-sa′ida! for if the
mighty works done in you had been done in
Tyre and Si′don, they would have repented
long ago in sackcloth and ashes. 22But I tell
you, it shall be more tolerable on the day
of judgment for Tyre and Si′don than for
you. 23And you, Caper′na-um, will you be
exalted to heaven? You shall be brought
down to Hades. For if the mighty works
done in you had been done in Sodom, it
would have remained until this day. 24But I

tell you that it shall be more tolerable on the
day of judgment for the land of Sodom than
for you."
[25]At that time Jesus declared, "I thank
you, Father, Lord of heaven and earth,
that you have hidden these things from
the wise and understanding and revealed
them to infants; [26]yes, Father, for such
was your gracious will. [27]All things have
been delivered to me by my Father; and
no one knows the Son except the Father,
and no one knows the Father except
the Son and any one to whom the Son
chooses to reveal him. [28]Come to me, all
who labor and are heavy laden, and I will
give you rest. [29]Take my yoke upon you,
and learn from me; for I am gentle and
lowly in heart, and you will find rest for
your souls. [30]For my yoke is easy, and my
burden is light."

REFLECTION

John's disciples ask Jesus if he is "the one to come." In other words, is Jesus the Messiah, the King of Israel? Jesus sends them back to John as eyewitnesses, reporting that the blind see, the lame walk, and the deaf hear, all of which fulfill the prophetic vision of a new exodus in Isaiah 35. John's messengers come with a question in biblical code: "Are you he who is to come" (Mt 11:3), taken from messianic passages like Psalm 118, to which Jesus in turn answers with biblical echoes of Isaiah 35, basically saying "yes!" To recognize the King and his Kingdom requires a deeper vision and hearing, one which will allow us to arise from our moral leprosy and lameness, and begin to walk in the way of Jesus the Christ. Unfortunately, Jesus upbraids the cities for hearing him but not putting his words into action. He concludes by inviting us to take up his yoke, which, by his grace, is easy and light (see Mt 11:29–30). Is it not true that we are often afraid to do God's will, thinking it will rob us of pleasure, peace, and joy, only to find that submitting to God's will is the only way to really achieve the rest we desire? Do you recognize Christ as King in your own life and strive to put his words into action?

January 16

GENESIS 35

**God said to Jacob, "Arise, go
up to Bethel, and dwell there;
and make there an altar to the God
who appeared to you when you fled**
from your brother Esau." [2]So Jacob said to
his household and to all who were with him,
"Put away the foreign gods that are among
you, and purify yourselves, and change
your garments; [3]then let us arise and go up
to Bethel, that I may make there an altar
to the God who answered me in the day of
my distress and has been with me wherever
I have gone." [4]So they gave to Jacob all the
foreign gods that they had, and the rings
that were in their ears; and Jacob hid them
under the oak which was near She′chem.
[5]And as they journeyed, a terror from God
fell upon the cities that were round about
them, so that they did not pursue the sons
of Jacob. [6]And Jacob came to Luz (that is,
Bethel), which is in the land of Canaan, he
and all the people who were with him, [7]and
there he built an altar, and called the place
El-beth′el, because there God had revealed
himself to him when he fled from his brother.
[8]And Deborah, Rebekah's nurse, died, and
she was buried under an oak below Bethel;
so the name of it was called Al′lon-bac′uth.
[9]God appeared to Jacob again, when he
came from Pad′dan-ar′am, and blessed
him. [10]And God said to him, "Your name is
Jacob; no longer shall your name be called
Jacob, but Israel shall be your name." So his
name was called Israel. [11]And God said to
him, "I am God Almighty: be fruitful and
multiply; a nation and a company of nations
shall come from you, and kings shall spring
from you. [12]The land which I gave to Abraham and Isaac I will give to you, and I will
give the land to your descendants after
you." [13]Then God went up from him in the
place where he had spoken with him. [14]And
Jacob set up a pillar in the place where he

had spoken with him, a pillar of stone; and
he poured out a drink offering on it, and
poured oil on it. 15So Jacob called the name
of the place where God had spoken with
him, Bethel.

16Then they journeyed from Bethel; and
when they were still some distance from
Eph´rath, Rachel went into labor, and she
had hard labor. 17And when she was in her
hard labor, the midwife said to her, "Fear
not; for now you will have another son."
18And as her soul was departing (for she
died), she called his name Ben-o´ni; but
his father called his name Benjamin. 19So
Rachel died, and she was buried on the way
to Eph´rath (that is, Bethlehem), 20and Jacob
set up a pillar upon her grave; it is the pillar
of Rachel's tomb, which is there to this day.
21Israel journeyed on, and pitched his tent
beyond the tower of E´der.

22While Israel dwelt in that land Reuben
went and lay with Bilhah his father's
concubine; and Israel heard of it.

Now the sons of Jacob were twelve. 23The
sons of Leah: Reuben (Jacob's first-born),
Simeon, Levi, Judah, Is´sachar, and Zeb´ulun.
24The sons of Rachel: Joseph and Benjamin.
25The sons of Bilhah, Rachel's maid: Dan and
Naph´tali. 26The sons of Zilpah, Leah's maid:
Gad and Asher. These were the sons of Jacob
who were born to him in Pad´dan-ar´am.

27And Jacob came to his father Isaac at
Mamre, or Kir´iath-ar´ba (that is, He´bron),
where Abraham and Isaac had sojourned.
28Now the days of Isaac were a hundred and
eighty years. 29And Isaac breathed his last;
and he died and was gathered to his people,
old and full of days; and his sons Esau and
Jacob buried him.

36 These are the descendants of Esau
(that is, E´dom). 2Esau took his wives
from the Canaanites: A´dah the daughter of
E´lon the Hittite, Oholiba´mah the daughter
of An´ah the son of Zib´eon the Hi´vite, 3and
Bas´emath, Ish´mael's daughter, the sister of
Neba´ioth. 4And A´dah bore to Esau, Eli´phaz;
Bas´emath bore Reu´el; 5and Oholiba´mah
bore Je´ush, Ja´lam, and Ko´rah. These are the
sons of Esau who were born to him in the land
of Canaan.

6Then Esau took his wives, his sons,
his daughters, and all the members of his
household, his cattle, all his beasts, and all
his property which he had acquired in the
land of Canaan; and he went into a land away
from his brother Jacob. 7For their possessions
were too great for them to dwell together; the
land of their sojournings could not support
them because of their cattle. 8So Esau dwelt
in the hill country of Se´ir; Esau is E´dom.

9These are the descendants of Esau the father
of the E´domites in the hill country of Se´ir.
10These are the names of Esau's sons: Eli´phaz
the son of A´dah the wife of Esau, Reu´el the
son of Bas´emath the wife of Esau. 11The
sons of Eli´phaz were Te´man, Omar, Ze´pho,
Ga´tam, and Ke´naz. 12(Timna was a concubine
of Eli´phaz, Esau's son; she bore Am´alek to
Eliphaz.) These are the sons of A´dah, Esau's
wife. 13These are the sons of Reu´el: Na´hath,
Ze´rah, Shammah, and Mizzah. These are the
sons of Bas´emath, Esau's wife. 14These are the
sons of Oholiba´mah the daughter of An´ah
the son of Zib´eon, Esau's wife: she bore to Esau
Je´ush, Ja´lam, and Ko´rah.

15These are the chiefs of the sons of Esau.
The sons of Eli´phaz the first-born of Esau:
the chiefs Te´man, Omar, Ze´pho, Ke´naz,
16Ko´rah, Ga´tam, and Am´alek; these are the
chiefs of Eli´phaz in the land of E´dom; they
are the sons of A´dah. 17These are the sons of
Reu´el, Esau's son: the chiefs Na´hath, Ze´rah,
Shammah, and Mizzah; these are the chiefs
of Reu´el in the land of E´dom; they are the
sons of Bas´emath, Esau's wife. 18These are the
sons of Oholiba´mah, Esau's wife: the chiefs
Je´ush, Ja´lam, and Ko´rah; these are the chiefs
born of Oholiba´mah the daughter of An´ah,
Esau's wife. 19These are the sons of Esau (that
is, E´dom), and these are their chiefs.

20These are the sons of Se´ir the Horite,
the inhabitants of the land: Lo´tan, Sho´bal,
Zib´eon, An´ah, 21Di´shon, E´zer, and Di´shan;
these are the chiefs of the Horites, the sons of
Se´ir in the land of E´dom. 22The sons of Lo´tan
were Ho´ri and He´man; and Lo´tan's sister was
Timna. 23These are the sons of Sho´bal: Alvan,
Man´ahath, E´bal, She´pho, and Onam. 24These
are the sons of Zib´eon: A´iah and An´ah; he
is the Anah who found the hot springs in the

wilderness, as he pastured the donkeys of
Zibeon his father. 25 These are the children of
An′ah: Di′shon and Oholiba′mah the daughter
of Anah. 26 These are the sons of Di′shon:
Hemdan, Eshban, Ithran, and Che′ran. 27 These
are the sons of E′zer: Bilhan, Za′avan, and
A′kan. 28 These are the sons of Di′shan: Uz and
Ar′an. 29 These are the chiefs of the Horites:
the chiefs Lo′tan, Sho′bal, Zib′eon, An′ah,
30 Di′shon, E′zer, and Di′shan; these are the
chiefs of the Horites, according to their clans in
the land of Se′ir.
31 These are the kings who reigned in the
land of E′dom, before any king reigned over
the Israelites. 32 Be′la the son of Beor reigned in
E′dom, the name of his city being Din′habah.
33 Be′la died, and Jo′bab the son of Ze′rah of
Bozrah reigned in his stead. 34 Jo′bab died,
and Hu′sham of the land of the Te′manites
reigned in his stead. 35 Hu′sham died, and
Ha′dad the son of Be′dad, who defeated
Mid′ian in the country of Moab, reigned in
his stead, the name of his city being A′vith.
36 Ha′dad died, and Samlah of Masre′kah
reigned in his stead. 37 Samlah died, and Sha′ul
of Reho′both on the Euphra′tes reigned in his
stead. 38 Sha′ul died, and Ba′al-ha′nan the son
of Achbor reigned in his stead. 39 Ba′al-ha′nan
the son of Achbor died, and Hadar reigned in
his stead, the name of his city being Pa′u; his
wife's name was Mehet′abel, the daughter of
Ma′tred, daughter of Me′zahab.
40 These are the names of the chiefs of Esau,
according to their families and their dwelling
places, by their names: the chiefs Timna,
Alvah, Je′theth, 41 Oholiba′mah, E′lah, Pi′non,
42 Ke′naz, Te′man, Mibzar, 43 Mag′diel, and
I′ram; these are the chiefs of E′dom (that is,
Esau, the father of Edom), according to their
dwelling places in the land of their possession.

A Miktam of David.

PSALM 16 [15]

Preserve me, O God, for in you I take refuge.
2 I say to the Lord, "You are my Lord;
I have no good apart from you."
3 As for the saints in the land, they are
the noble,
in whom is all my delight.

4 Those who choose another god multiply
their sorrows;
their libations of blood I will not pour out
or take their names upon my lips.

5 The Lord is my chosen portion and my cup;
you hold my lot.
6 The lines have fallen for me in
pleasant places;
yes, I have a goodly heritage.

7 I bless the Lord who gives me counsel;
in the night also my heart instructs me.
8 I keep the Lord always before me;
because he is at my right hand, I shall not
be moved.

9 Therefore my heart is glad, and my
soul rejoices;
my body also dwells secure.
10 For you do not give me up to Sheol,
or let your godly one see the Pit.

11 You show me the path of life;
in your presence there is fulness of joy,
in your right hand are pleasures
for evermore.

MATTHEW 12

At that time Jesus went through
the grainfields on the sabbath;
his disciples were hungry, and they be-
gan to pluck heads of grain and to eat.
2 But when the Pharisees saw it, they said to
him, "Look, your disciples are doing what
is not lawful to do on the sabbath." 3 He
said to them, "Have you not read what
David did, when he was hungry, and those
who were with him: 4 how he entered the
house of God and ate the showbread,
which it was not lawful for him to eat nor
for those who were with him, but only
for the priests? 5 Or have you not read in

the law how on the sabbath the priests in the temple profane the sabbath, and are guiltless? [6]I tell you, something greater than the temple is here. [7]And if you had known what this means, 'I desire mercy, and not sacrifice,' you would not have condemned the guiltless. [8]For the Son of man is lord of the sabbath."

[9]And he went on from there, and entered their synagogue. [10]And behold, there was a man with a withered hand. And they asked him, "Is it lawful to heal on the sabbath?" so that they might accuse him. [11]He said to them, "What man of you, if he has one sheep and it falls into a pit on the sabbath, will not lay hold of it and lift it out? [12]Of how much more value is a man than a sheep! So it is lawful to do good on the sabbath." [13]Then he said to the man, "Stretch out your hand." And the man stretched it out, and it was restored, whole like the other. [14]But the Pharisees went out and took counsel against him, how to destroy him.

[15]Jesus, aware of this, withdrew from there. And many followed him, and he healed them all, [16]and ordered them not to make him known. [17]This was to fulfil what was spoken by the prophet Isaiah:

[18]"Behold, my servant whom I have chosen,
my beloved with whom my soul is
well pleased.
I will put my Spirit upon him,
and he shall proclaim justice to
the Gentiles.
[19]He will not wrangle or cry aloud,
nor will any one hear his voice in
the streets;
[20]he will not break a bruised reed
or quench a smoldering wick,
till he brings justice to victory;
[21] and in his name will the Gentiles hope."

REFLECTION

While fleeing from his brother Esau after stealing his blessing, Jacob stopped in Bethel and vowed that if God would protect him and bring him back to his homeland, then "the LORD shall be my God" (Gn 28:21). Now as he returns to the Promised Land and reconciles with Esau, Jacob fulfills his vow by summoning his family to fidelity to the Lord, calling them to put away all foreign idols and gods, and gathering at Bethel to worship the Lord. We know that Rachel had stolen Laban's household gods, and so here we are told that Jacob gathers up the idols his family now forfeits and hides them under the oak tree at Shechem (see 35:4). Such small narrative details are little threads that often interweave the stories of Israel from various generations. Thus later, when he is bringing Israel back into the Promised Land, Joshua, like Jacob here, will summon Israel to religious fidelity, commanding that they put away foreign gods and serve the Lord alone. Like Jacob, have you made promises to God that you have yet to fulfill?

January 17

GENESIS 37

Jacob dwelt in the land of his father's sojournings, in the land of Canaan. [2]This is the history of the family of Jacob.

Joseph, being seventeen years old, was shepherding the flock with his brothers; he was a lad with the sons of Bilhah and Zilpah, his father's wives; and Joseph brought an ill report of them to their father. [3]Now Israel loved Joseph more than any other of his children, because he was the son of his old age; and he made him a long robe with sleeves. [4]But when his brothers saw that their father loved him more than all his brothers, they hated him, and could not speak peaceably to him.

[5]Now Joseph had a dream, and when he told it to his brothers they only hated him the more. [6]He said to them, "Hear this

dream which I have dreamed: [7]behold, we were binding sheaves in the field, and behold, my sheaf arose and stood upright; and behold, your sheaves gathered round it, and bowed down to my sheaf." [8]His brothers said to him, "Are you indeed to reign over us? Or are you indeed to have dominion over us?" So they hated him yet more for his dreams and for his words. [9]Then he dreamed another dream, and told it to his brothers, and said, "Behold, I have dreamed another dream; and behold, the sun, the moon, and eleven stars were bowing down to me." [10]But when he told it to his father and to his brothers, his father rebuked him, and said to him, "What is this dream that you have dreamed? Shall I and your mother and your brothers indeed come to bow ourselves to the ground before you?" [11]And his brothers were jealous of him, but his father kept the saying in mind.

[12]Now his brothers went to pasture their father's flock near She′chem. [13]And Israel said to Joseph, "Are not your brothers pasturing the flock at She′chem? Come, I will send you to them." And he said to him, "Here I am." [14]So he said to him, "Go now, see if it is well with your brothers, and with the flock; and bring me word again." So he sent him from the valley of He′bron, and he came to She′chem. [15]And a man found him wandering in the fields; and the man asked him, "What are you seeking?" [16]"I am seeking my brothers," he said, "tell me, I beg you, where they are pasturing the flock." [17]And the man said, "They have gone away, for I heard them say, 'Let us go to Do′than.'" So Joseph went after his brothers, and found them at Dothan. [18]They saw him afar off, and before he came near to them they conspired against him to kill him. [19]They said to one another, "Here comes this dreamer. [20]Come now, let us kill him and throw him into one of the pits; then we shall say that a wild beast has devoured him, and we shall see what will become of his dreams." [21]But when Reuben heard it, he delivered him out of their hands, saying, "Let us not take his life." [22]And Reuben said to them, "Shed no blood; cast him into this pit here in the wilderness, but lay no hand upon him"—that he might rescue him out of their hand, to restore him to his father. [23]So when Joseph came to his brothers, they stripped him of his robe, the long robe with sleeves that he wore; [24]and they took him and cast him into a pit. The pit was empty, there was no water in it.

[25]Then they sat down to eat; and looking up they saw a caravan of Ish′maelites coming from Gilead, with their camels bearing gum, balm, and myrrh, on their way to carry it down to Egypt. [26]Then Judah said to his brothers, "What profit is it if we slay our brother and conceal his blood? [27]Come, let us sell him to the Ish′maelites, and let not our hand be upon him, for he is our brother, our own flesh." And his brothers heeded him. [28]Then Mid′ianite traders passed by; and they drew Joseph up and lifted him out of the pit, and sold him to the Ish′maelites for twenty shekels of silver; and they took Joseph to Egypt.

[29]When Reuben returned to the pit and saw that Joseph was not in the pit, he tore his clothes [30]and returned to his brothers, and said, "The lad is gone; and I, where shall I go?" [31]Then they took Joseph's robe, and killed a goat, and dipped the robe in the blood; [32]and they sent the long robe with sleeves and brought it to their father, and said, "This we have found; see now whether it is your son's robe or not." [33]And he recognized it, and said, "It is my son's robe; a wild beast has devoured him; Joseph is without doubt torn to pieces." [34]Then Jacob tore his garments, and put sackcloth upon his loins, and mourned for his son many days. [35]All his sons and all his daughters rose up to comfort him; but he refused to be comforted, and said, "No, I shall go down to Sheol to my son, mourning." Thus his father wept for him. [36]Meanwhile the Mid′ianites had sold him in Egypt to Pot′iphar, an officer of Pharaoh, the captain of the guard.

38 It happened at that time that Judah went down from his brothers, and turned in to a certain Adul′lamite, whose name was Hi′rah. 2There Judah saw the daughter of a certain Canaanite whose name was Shua; he married her and went in to her, 3and she conceived and bore a son, and he called his name Er. 4Again she conceived and bore a son, and she called his name O′nan. 5Yet again she bore a son, and she called his name She′lah. She was in Che′zib when she bore him. 6And Judah took a wife for Er his first-born, and her name was Ta′mar. 7But Er, Judah's first-born, was wicked in the sight of the LORD; and the LORD slew him. 8Then Judah said to O′nan, "Go in to your brother's wife, and perform the duty of a brother-in-law to her, and raise up offspring for your brother." 9But O′nan knew that the offspring would not be his; so when he went in to his brother's wife he spilled the semen on the ground, lest he should give offspring to his brother. 10And what he did was displeasing in the sight of the LORD, and he slew him also. 11Then Judah said to Ta′mar his daughter-in-law, "Remain a widow in your father's house, till She′lah my son grows up"—for he feared that he would die, like his brothers. So Ta′mar went and dwelt in her father's house.

12In course of time the wife of Judah, Shua's daughter, died; and when Judah was comforted, he went up to Timnah to his sheepshearers, he and his friend Hi′rah the Adul′lamite. 13And when Tamar was told, "Your father-in-law is going up to Timnah to shear his sheep," 14she put off her widow's garments, and put on a veil, wrapping herself up, and sat at the entrance to Enaim, which is on the road to Timnah; for she saw that She′lah was grown up, and she had not been given to him in marriage. 15When Judah saw her, he thought her to be a harlot, for she had covered her face. 16He went over to her at the road side, and said, "Come, let me come in to you," for he did not know that she was his daughter-in-law. She said, "What will you give me, that you may come in to me?" 17He answered, "I will send you a kid from the flock." And she said, "Will you give me a pledge, till you send it?" 18He said, "What pledge shall I give you?" She replied, "Your signet and your cord, and your staff that is in your hand." So he gave them to her, and went in to her, and she conceived by him. 19Then she arose and went away, and taking off her veil she put on the garments of her widowhood.

20When Judah sent the kid by his friend the Adul′lamite, to receive the pledge from the woman's hand, he could not find her. 21And he asked the men of the place, "Where is the harlot who was at Ena′im by the wayside?" And they said, "No harlot has been here." 22So he returned to Judah, and said, "I have not found her; and also the men of the place said, 'No harlot has been here.'" 23And Judah replied, "Let her keep the things as her own, lest we be laughed at; you see, I sent this kid, and you could not find her."

24About three months later Judah was told, "Ta′mar your daughter-in-law has played the harlot; and moreover she is with child by harlotry." And Judah said, "Bring her out, and let her be burned." 25As she was being brought out, she sent word to her father-in-law, "By the man to whom these belong, I am with child." And she said, "Mark, I beg you, whose these are, the signet and the cord and the staff." 26Then Judah acknowledged them and said, "She is more righteous than I, inasmuch as I did not give her to my son She′lah." And he did not lie with her again.

27When the time of her delivery came, there were twins in her womb. 28And when she was in labor, one put out a hand; and the midwife took and bound on his hand a scarlet thread, saying, "This came out first." 29But as he drew back his hand, behold, his brother came out; and she said, "What a breach you have made for yourself!" Therefore his name was called Per′ez. 30Afterward his brother came out with the scarlet thread upon his hand; and his name was called Ze′rah.

A Prayer of David.

PSALM 17 [16]

Hear a just cause, O LORD;
attend to my cry!
Give ear to my prayer from lips free
of deceit!
2From you let my vindication come!
Let your eyes see the right!

3If you try my heart, if you visit me by night,
if you test me, you will find no wickedness
in me;
my mouth does not transgress.
4With regard to the works of men, by the
word of your lips
I have avoided the ways of the violent.
5My steps have held fast to your paths,
my feet have not slipped.

6I call upon you, for you will answer me,
O God;
incline your ear to me, hear my words.
7Wondrously show your mercies,
O savior of those who seek refuge
from their adversaries at your
right hand.

8Keep me as the apple of the eye;
hide me in the shadow of your wings,
9from the wicked who despoil me,
my deadly enemies who surround me.

10They close their hearts to pity;
with their mouths they speak arrogantly.
11They track me down; now they
surround me;
they set their eyes to cast me to
the ground.
12They are like a lion eager to tear,
as a young lion lurking in ambush.

13Arise, O LORD! confront them,
overthrow them!
Deliver my life from the wicked by
your sword,
14from men by your hand, O LORD,
from men whose portion in life is
of the world.
May their belly be filled with what you
have stored up for them;
may their children have more than
enough;
may they leave something over to
their babies.
15As for me, I shall behold your face
in righteousness;
when I awake, I shall be satisfied with
beholding your form.

MATTHEW 12

**22Then a blind and mute demo-
niac was brought to him, and
he healed him, so that the mute
man spoke and saw. 23And all the people
were amazed, and said, "Can this be**
the Son of David?" 24But when the Pharisees
heard it they said, "It is only by Be-el′zebul,
the prince of demons, that this man casts out
demons." 25Knowing their thoughts, he said
to them, "Every kingdom divided against
itself is laid waste, and no city or house divided against itself will stand; 26and if Satan
casts out Satan, he is divided against himself;
how then will his kingdom stand? 27And if
I cast out demons by Be-el′zebul, by whom
do your sons cast them out? Therefore they
shall be your judges. 28But if it is by the Spirit
of God that I cast out demons, then the kingdom of God has come upon you. 29Or how
can one enter a strong man's house and plunder his goods, unless he first binds the strong
man? Then indeed he may plunder his
house. 30He who is not with me is against me,
and he who does not gather with me scatters.
31Therefore I tell you, every sin and blasphemy will be forgiven men, but the blasphemy
against the Spirit will not be forgiven. 32And
whoever says a word against the Son of man
will be forgiven; but whoever speaks against
the Holy Spirit will not be forgiven, either in
this age or in the age to come.
33"Either make the tree good, and its fruit
good; or make the tree bad, and its fruit bad;
for the tree is known by its fruit. 34You brood

of vipers! how can you speak good things, when you are evil? For out of the abundance of the heart the mouth speaks. 35The good man out of his good treasure brings forth good, and the evil man out of his evil treasure brings forth evil. 36I tell you, on the day of judgment men will render account for every careless word they utter; 37for by your words you will be justified, and by your words you will be condemned."

38Then some of the scribes and Pharisees said to him, "Teacher, we wish to see a sign from you." 39But he answered them, "An evil and adulterous generation seeks for a sign; but no sign shall be given to it except the sign of the prophet Jonah. 40For as Jonah was three days and three nights in the belly of the whale, so will the Son of man be three days and three nights in the heart of the earth. 41The men of Nin′eveh will arise at the judgment with this generation and condemn it; for they repented at the preaching of Jonah, and behold, something greater than Jonah is here. 42The queen of the South will arise at the judgment with this generation and condemn it; for she came from the ends of the earth to hear the wisdom of Solomon, and behold, something greater than Solomon is here."

REFLECTION

Jesus heals a man who was blind and mute. In response to this good work, the Pharisees speak evil about Jesus. Jesus sums up the lesson well: "For out of the abundance of the heart the mouth speaks" (Mt 12:34). The Pharisees' words reflect the malice in their hearts. Jesus's words are true and deeply challenging. How often do we speak words that are negative, that are the fruit of bad thoughts? Jesus warns that we will have to render an account for "every careless word," so how much more for words we have pondered deeply? In the healthcare profession, some of the most powerful tools are those that help a doctor to see below the surface, such as X-rays, MRIs, or scopes. Jesus, the divine physician, gives us a method of examining ourselves below the surface, in the depths of our hearts: evaluate the words you use about others and you will have a measure of your heart, your spiritual condition. With this test we can flag problems in our hearts and go to God and the Sacrament of Reconciliation to find the healing we need. What do your words reflect about the health of your heart?

January 18

GENESIS 39

Now Joseph was taken down to Egypt, and Pot′iphar, an officer of Pharaoh, the captain of the guard, an Egyptian, bought him from the Ish′maelites who had brought him down there. 2The LORD was with Joseph, and he became a successful man; and he was in the house of his master the Egyptian, 3and his master saw that the LORD was with him, and that the LORD caused all that he did to prosper in his hands. 4So Joseph found favor in his sight and attended him, and he made him overseer of his house and put him in charge of all that he had. 5From the time that he made him overseer in his house and over all that he had the LORD blessed the Egyptian's house for Joseph's sake; the blessing of the LORD was upon all that he had, in house and field. 6So he left all that he had in Joseph's charge; and having him he had no concern for anything but the food which he ate.

Now Joseph was handsome and good-looking. 7And after a time his master's wife cast her eyes upon Joseph, and said, "Lie with me." 8But he refused and said to his master's wife, "Behold, having me my master has no concern about anything in the house, and he has put everything that he has in my hand; 9he is not greater in this house than

I am; nor has he kept back anything from me except yourself, because you are his wife; how then can I do this great wickedness, and sin against God?” [10]And although she spoke to Joseph day after day, he would not listen to her, to lie with her or to be with her. [11]But one day, when he went into the house to do his work and none of the men of the house was there in the house, [12]she caught him by his garment, saying, “Lie with me.” But he left his garment in her hand, and fled and got out of the house. [13]And when she saw that he had left his garment in her hand, and had fled out of the house, [14]she called to the men of her household and said to them, “See, he has brought among us a Hebrew to insult us; he came in to me to lie with me, and I cried out with a loud voice; [15]and when he heard that I lifted up my voice and cried, he left his garment with me, and fled and got out of the house.” [16]Then she laid up his garment by her until his master came home, [17]and she told him the same story, saying, “The Hebrew servant, whom you have brought among us, came in to me to insult me; [18]but as soon as I lifted up my voice and cried, he left his garment with me, and fled out of the house.”

[19]When his master heard the words which his wife spoke to him, “This is the way your servant treated me,” his anger was kindled. [20]And Joseph’s master took him and put him into the prison, the place where the king’s prisoners were confined, and he was there in prison. [21]But the LORD was with Joseph and showed him mercy, and gave him favor in the sight of the keeper of the prison. [22]And the keeper of the prison committed to Joseph’s care all the prisoners who were in the prison; and whatever was done there, he was the doer of it; [23]the keeper of the prison paid no heed to anything that was in Joseph’s care, because the LORD was with him; and whatever he did, the LORD made it prosper.

40 Some time after this, the butler of the king of Egypt and his baker offended their lord the king of Egypt. [2]And Pharaoh was angry with his two officers, the chief butler and the chief baker, [3]and he put them in custody in the house of the captain of the guard, in the prison where Joseph was confined. [4]The captain of the guard charged Joseph with them, and he waited on them; and they continued for some time in custody. [5]And one night they both dreamed—the butler and the baker of the king of Egypt, who were confined in the prison—each his own dream, and each dream with its own meaning. [6]When Joseph came to them in the morning and saw them, they were troubled. [7]So he asked Pharaoh’s officers who were with him in custody in his master’s house, “Why are your faces downcast today?” [8]They said to him, “We have had dreams, and there is no one to interpret them.” And Joseph said to them, “Do not interpretations belong to God? Tell them to me, I beg you.”

[9]So the chief butler told his dream to Joseph, and said to him, “In my dream there was a vine before me, [10]and on the vine there were three branches; as soon as it budded, its blossoms shot forth, and the clusters ripened into grapes. [11]Pharaoh’s cup was in my hand; and I took the grapes and pressed them into Pharaoh’s cup, and placed the cup in Pharaoh’s hand.” [12]Then Joseph said to him, “This is its interpretation: the three branches are three days; [13]within three days Pharaoh will lift up your head and restore you to your office; and you shall place Pharaoh’s cup in his hand as formerly, when you were his butler. [14]But remember me, when it is well with you, and do me the kindness, I beg you, to make mention of me to Pharaoh, and so get me out of this house. [15]For I was indeed stolen out of the land of the Hebrews; and here also I have done nothing that they should put me into the dungeon.”

[16]When the chief baker saw that the interpretation was favorable, he said to Joseph, “I also had a dream: there were three cake baskets on my head, [17]and in the uppermost basket there were all sorts of baked food for Pharaoh, but the birds were eating it out of the basket on my head.” [18]And Joseph answered, “This is its interpretation: the three baskets are three days; [19]within

three days Pharaoh will lift up your head—
from you!—and hang you on a tree; and the
birds will eat the flesh from you.”
20 On the third day, which was Pharaoh’s
birthday, he made a feast for all his servants,
and lifted up the head of the chief butler
and the head of the chief baker among his
servants. 21 He restored the chief butler to
his butlership, and he placed the cup in
Pharaoh’s hand; 22 but he hanged the chief
baker, as Joseph had interpreted to them.
23 Yet the chief butler did not remember
Joseph, but forgot him.

To the choirmaster.

A Psalm of David the servant of the LORD,
who addressed the words of this song to the LORD
on the day when the LORD delivered him
from the hands of all his enemies,
and from the hand of Saul.
He said:

PSALM 18 [17]

I love you, O LORD, my strength.
2 The LORD is my rock, and my fortress, and
my deliverer,
my God, my rock, in whom I take refuge,
my shield, and the horn of my salvation,
my stronghold.
3 I call upon the LORD, who is worthy to
be praised,
and I am saved from my enemies.

4 The cords of death encompassed me,
the torrents of perdition assailed me;
5 the cords of Sheol entangled me,
the snares of death confronted me.

6 In my distress I called upon the LORD;
to my God I cried for help.
From his temple he heard my voice,
and my cry to him reached his ears.

7 Then the earth reeled and rocked;
the foundations also of the mountains
trembled
and quaked, because he was angry.
8 Smoke went up from his nostrils,
and devouring fire from his mouth;
glowing coals flamed forth from him.
9 He bowed the heavens, and came down;
thick darkness was under his feet.
10 He rode on a cherub, and flew;
he came swiftly upon the wings of
the wind.
11 He made darkness his covering around him,
his canopy thick clouds dark
with water.
12 Out of the brightness before him
there broke through his clouds
hailstones and coals of fire.
13 The LORD also thundered in the heavens,
and the Most High uttered his voice,
hailstones and coals of fire.
14 And he sent out his arrows, and
scattered them;
he flashed forth lightnings, and
routed them.
15 Then the channels of the sea were seen,
and the foundations of the world were
laid bare,
at your rebuke, O LORD,
at the blast of the breath of your nostrils.

16 He reached from on high, he took me,
he drew me out of many waters.
17 He delivered me from my strong enemy,
and from those who hated me;
for they were too mighty for me.
18 They came upon me in the day of
my calamity;
but the LORD was my stay.
19 He brought me forth into a broad place;
he delivered me, because he delighted
in me.

MATTHEW 12

**43 “When the unclean spirit has
gone out of a man, he passes
through waterless places seeking rest,
but he finds none. 44 Then he says, ‘I will**
return to my house from which I came.’
And when he comes he finds it empty,

swept, and put in order. 45Then he goes
and brings with him seven other spirits
more evil than himself, and they enter
and dwell there; and the last state of that
man becomes worse than the first. So
shall it be also with this evil generation."
46While he was still speaking to the
people, behold, his mother and his
brethren stood outside, asking to speak
to him. 48But he replied to the man who
told him, "Who is my mother, and who
are my brethren?" 49And stretching out
his hand toward his disciples, he said,
"Here are my mother and my brethren!
50For whoever does the will of my Father
in heaven is my brother, and sister, and
mother."

13 That same day Jesus went out of the
house and sat beside the sea. 2And
great crowds gathered about him, so that
he got into a boat and sat there; and the
whole crowd stood on the beach. 3And
he told them many things in parables,
saying: "A sower went out to sow. 4And as
he sowed, some seeds fell along the path,
and the birds came and devoured them.
5Other seeds fell on rocky ground, where
they had not much soil, and immediately
they sprang up, since they had no depth
of soil, 6but when the sun rose they were
scorched; and since they had no root
they withered away. 7Other seeds fell
upon thorns, and the thorns grew up and
choked them. 8Other seeds fell on good
soil and brought forth grain, some a
hundredfold, some sixty, some thirty. 9He
who has ears, let him hear."
10Then the disciples came and said
to him, "Why do you speak to them in
parables?" 11And he answered them,
"To you it has been given to know the
secrets of the kingdom of heaven, but
to them it has not been given. 12For to
him who has will more be given, and he
will have abundance; but from him who
has not, even what he has will be taken
away. 13This is why I speak to them in
parables, because seeing they do not
see, and hearing they do not hear, nor
do they understand. 14With them indeed
is fulfilled the prophecy of Isaiah which
says:

'You shall indeed hear but never
understand,
and you shall indeed see but never
perceive.
15For this people's heart has grown dull,
and their ears are heavy of hearing,
and their eyes they have closed,
lest they should perceive with their eyes,
and hear with their ears,
and understand with their heart,
and turn for me to heal them.'
16But blessed are your eyes, for they see,
and your ears, for they hear. 17Truly, I say
to you, many prophets and righteous men
longed to see what you see, and did not
see it, and to hear what you hear, and did
not hear it."

REFLECTION

When Joseph is sold as a slave to the Egyptian general Potiphar, it would seem that he had hit rock bottom. When things could seemingly get no worse, Joseph goes from being a slave to being a prisoner. Betrayed by his own brothers, sold as a slave, living far from his homeland, and a prisoner in a foreign land, the world turned hard against Joseph. And yet, God was still with him, in the midst of his sufferings. Both at Potiphar's house and again in Joseph's imprisonment, the beautiful line is repeated: "The LORD was with him" (Gn 39:3, 23). Joseph teaches us that contrary to appearances, God's blessing may be upon us precisely in the midst of heartbreaking troubles. The temptation is to see evils and hardships as coming from God, and to see one's success as one's own. Yet Joseph never blames God. Rather, he acknowledges God as his source of success, claiming that his ability to understand dreams needs to be credited to God alone: "Do not interpretations belong to God?" (40:8). Do you imitate Joseph's integrity of heart, turning to the One who wants to be with you in your suffering, and attributing success to its ultimate source—God?

January 19

GENESIS 41

After two whole years, Pharaoh dreamed that he was standing by the Nile, 2and behold, there came up out of the Nile seven cows sleek and fat, and they fed in the reed grass. 3And behold, seven other cows, gaunt and thin, came up out of the Nile after them, and stood by the other cows on the bank of the Nile. 4And the gaunt and thin cows ate up the seven sleek and fat cows. And Pharaoh awoke. 5And he fell asleep and dreamed a second time; and behold, seven ears of grain, plump and good, were growing on one stalk. 6And behold, after them sprouted seven ears, thin and blighted by the east wind. 7And the thin ears swallowed up the seven plump and full ears. And Pharaoh awoke, and behold, it was a dream. 8So in the morning his spirit was troubled; and he sent and called for all the magicians of Egypt and all its wise men; and Pharaoh told them his dream, but there was none who could interpret it to Pharaoh.

9Then the chief butler said to Pharaoh, "I remember my faults today. 10When Pharaoh was angry with his servants, and put me and the chief baker in custody in the house of the captain of the guard, 11we dreamed on the same night, he and I, each having a dream with its own meaning. 12A young Hebrew was there with us, a servant of the captain of the guard; and when we told him, he interpreted our dreams to us, giving an interpretation to each man according to his dream. 13And as he interpreted to us, so it came to pass; I was restored to my office, and the baker was hanged."

14Then Pharaoh sent and called Joseph, and they brought him hastily out of the dungeon; and when he had shaved himself and changed his clothes, he came in before Pharaoh. 15And Pharaoh said to Joseph, "I have had a dream, and there is no one who can interpret it; and I have heard it said of you that when you hear a dream you can interpret it." 16Joseph answered Pharaoh, "It is not in me; God will give Pharaoh a favorable answer." 17Then Pharaoh said to Joseph, "Behold, in my dream I was standing on the banks of the Nile; 18and seven cows, fat and sleek, came up out of the Nile and fed in the reed grass; 19and seven other cows came up after them, poor and very gaunt and thin, such as I had never seen in all the land of Egypt. 20And the thin and gaunt cows ate up the first seven fat cows, 21but when they had eaten them no one would have known that they had eaten them, for they were still as gaunt as at the beginning. Then I awoke. 22I also saw in my dream seven ears growing on one stalk, full and good; 23and seven ears, withered, thin, and blighted by the east wind, sprouted after them, 24and the thin ears swallowed up the seven good ears. And I told it to the magicians, but there was no one who could explain it to me."

25Then Joseph said to Pharaoh, "The dream of Pharaoh is one; God has revealed to Pharaoh what he is about to do. 26The seven good cows are seven years, and the seven good ears are seven years; the dream is one. 27The seven lean and gaunt cows that came up after them are seven years, and the seven empty ears blighted by the east wind are also seven years of famine. 28It is as I told Pharaoh, God has shown to Pharaoh what he is about to do. 29There will come seven years of great plenty throughout all the land of Egypt, 30but after them there will arise seven years of famine, and all the plenty will be forgotten in the land of Egypt; the famine will consume the land, 31and the plenty will be unknown in the land by reason of that famine which will follow, for it will be very grievous. 32And the doubling of Pharaoh's dream means that the thing is fixed by God, and God will shortly bring it to pass. 33Now therefore let Pharaoh select a man discreet and wise, and set him over the land of Egypt. 34Let Pharaoh proceed to appoint overseers over the land, and take the fifth part of the produce of the land of Egypt during the seven plenteous years. 35And let them gather all the food of

these good years that are coming, and lay
up grain under the authority of Pharaoh
for food in the cities, and let them keep it.
[36]That food shall be a reserve for the land
against the seven years of famine which are
to befall the land of Egypt, so that the land
may not perish through the famine."
[37]This proposal seemed good to Pharaoh and
to all his servants. [38]And Pharaoh said to his
servants, "Can we find such a man as this, in
whom is the Spirit of God?" [39]So Pharaoh said
to Joseph, "Since God has shown you all this,
there is none so discreet and wise as you are;
[40]you shall be over my house, and all my people
shall order themselves as you command; only
as regards the throne will I be greater than
you." [41]And Pharaoh said to Joseph, "Behold, I
have set you over all the land of Egypt." [42]Then
Pharaoh took his signet ring from his hand
and put it on Joseph's hand, and arrayed him
in garments of fine linen, and put a gold chain
about his neck; [43]and he made him to ride in
his second chariot; and they cried before him,
"Bow the knee!" Thus he set him over all the
land of Egypt. [44]Moreover Pharaoh said to
Joseph, "I am Pharaoh, and without your
consent no man shall lift up hand or foot in
all the land of Egypt." [45]And Pharaoh called
Joseph's name Zaph′enath-pane′ah; and he
gave him in marriage As′enath, the daughter
of Poti′phera priest of On. So Joseph went out
over the land of Egypt.
[46]Joseph was thirty years old when he
entered the service of Pharaoh king of
Egypt. And Joseph went out from the
presence of Pharaoh, and went through
all the land of Egypt. [47]During the seven
plenteous years the earth brought forth
abundantly, [48]and he gathered up all the
food of the seven years when there was
plenty in the land of Egypt, and stored up
food in the cities; he stored up in every
city the food from the fields around it.
[49]And Joseph stored up grain in great
abundance, like the sand of the sea, until
he ceased to measure it, for it could not
be measured.
[50]Before the year of famine came,
Joseph had two sons, whom As′enath, the
daughter of Poti′phera priest of On, bore to
him. [51]Joseph called the name of the first-
born Manas′seh, "For," he said, "God has
made me forget all my hardship and all my
father's house." [52]The name of the second
he called E′phraim, "For God has made me
fruitful in the land of my affliction."
[53]The seven years of plenty that prevailed in
the land of Egypt came to an end; [54]and the
seven years of famine began to come, as Joseph
had said. There was famine in all lands; but in
all the land of Egypt there was bread. [55]When
all the land of Egypt was famished, the people
cried to Pharaoh for bread; and Pharaoh said
to all the Egyptians, "Go to Joseph; what he
says to you, do." [56]So when the famine had
spread over all the land, Joseph opened all
the storehouses, and sold to the Egyptians, for
the famine was severe in the land of Egypt.
[57]Moreover, all the earth came to Egypt to
Joseph to buy grain, because the famine was
severe over all the earth.

To the choirmaster.

A Psalm of David the servant of the LORD,
who addressed the words of this song to the LORD
on the day when the LORD delivered him
from the hands of all his enemies,
and from the hand of Saul.
He said:

PSALM 18 [17]

[20]The LORD rewarded me according to
my righteousness;
according to the cleanness of my hands
he recompensed me.
[21]For I have kept the ways of the LORD,
and have not wickedly departed from
my God.
[22]For all his ordinances were before me,
and his statutes I did not put away
from me.
[23]I was blameless before him,
and I kept myself from guilt.
[24]Therefore the LORD has recompensed me
according to my righteousness,
according to the cleanness of my hands
in his sight.

[25]With the loyal you show yourself loyal;
with the blameless man you show
yourself blameless;
[26]with the pure you show yourself pure;
and with the crooked you show
yourself perverse.
[27]For you deliver a humble people;
but the haughty eyes you bring down.
[28]Yes, you light my lamp;
the LORD my God lightens my darkness.
[29]Yes, by you I can crush a troop;
and by my God I can leap over a wall.
[30]This God—his way is perfect;
the promise of the LORD proves true;
he is a shield for all those who take refuge
in him.

[31]For who is God, but the LORD?
And who is a rock, except our God?—
[32]the God who girded me with strength,
and made my way safe.
[33]He made my feet like deer's feet,
and set me secure on the heights.
[34]He trains my hands for war,
so that my arms can bend a bow of bronze.
[35]You have given me the shield of your
salvation,
and your right hand supported me,
and your help made me great.
[36]You gave a wide place for my steps
under me,
and my feet did not slip.
[37]I pursued my enemies and overtook them;
and did not turn back till they were
consumed.
[38]I thrust them through, so that they were
not able to rise;
they fell under my feet.
[39]For you girded me with strength for
the battle;
you made my assailants sink under me.
[40]You made my enemies turn their backs
to me,
and those who hated me I destroyed.
[41]They cried for help, but there was none
to save,
they cried to the LORD, but he did not
answer them.
[42]I beat them fine as dust before the wind;
I cast them out like the mire of the streets.

MATTHEW 13

[18]"Hear then the parable of the sower. [19]When any one hears the word of the kingdom and does not understand it, the Evil One comes and snatches away what is sown in his heart; this is what was sown along
the path. [20]As for what was sown on rocky
ground, this is he who hears the word and
immediately receives it with joy; [21]yet he has
no root in himself, but endures for a while,
and when tribulation or persecution arises
on account of the word, immediately he falls
away. [22]As for what was sown among thorns,
this is he who hears the word, but the cares of
the world and the delight in riches choke the
word, and it proves unfruitful. [23]As for what
was sown on good soil, this is he who hears
the word and understands it; he indeed bears
fruit, and yields, in one case a hundredfold,
in another sixty, and in another thirty."

[24]Another parable he put before them,
saying, "The kingdom of heaven may be
compared to a man who sowed good seed in
his field; [25]but while men were sleeping, his
enemy came and sowed weeds among the
wheat, and went away. [26]So when the plants
came up and bore grain, then the weeds
appeared also. [27]And the servants of the
householder came and said to him, 'Sir, did
you not sow good seed in your field? How
then has it weeds?' [28]He said to them, 'An
enemy has done this.' The servants said to
him, 'Then do you want us to go and gather
them?' [29]But he said, 'No; lest in gathering
the weeds you root up the wheat along with
them. [30]Let both grow together until the
harvest; and at harvest time I will tell the
reapers, Gather the weeds first and bind
them in bundles to be burned, but gather
the wheat into my barn.'"

[31]Another parable he put before them,
saying, "The kingdom of heaven is like a grain
of mustard seed which a man took and sowed
in his field; [32]it is the smallest of all seeds, but
when it has grown it is the greatest of shrubs
and becomes a tree, so that the birds of the air
come and make nests in its branches."

33He told them another parable. "The kingdom of heaven is like leaven which a woman took and hid in three measures of meal, till it was all leavened."

34All this Jesus said to the crowds in parables; indeed he said nothing to them without a parable. 35This was to fulfil what was spoken by the prophet:

"I will open my mouth in parables,
I will utter what has been hidden since the
foundation of the world."

36Then he left the crowds and went into the house. And his disciples came to him, saying, "Explain to us the parable of the weeds of the field." 37He answered, "He who sows the good seed is the Son of man; 38the field is the world, and the good seed means the sons of the kingdom; the weeds are the sons of the evil one, 39and the enemy who sowed them is the devil; the harvest is the close of the age, and the reapers are angels. 40Just as the weeds are gathered and burned with fire, so will it be at the close of the age. 41The Son of man will send his angels, and they will gather out of his kingdom all causes of sin and all evildoers, 42and throw them into the furnace of fire, where there will be weeping and gnashing of teeth. 43Then the righteous will shine like the sun in the kingdom of their Father. He who has ears, let him hear."

REFLECTION

Jesus tells a story about a rather eccentric sower. This sower sows generously, if not indiscriminately, casting his seed not only upon the rich fields but also upon the path, the rocky ground, and amidst the thorns and thistles. Precious and costly, this seed is not sown sparingly. Why such extravagance? Jesus of course is the sower, and the seed is special indeed—it is his Word. He casts the seed everywhere, because Jesus is generous and he wants all to hear and receive. Sowing is the metaphor for evangelizing, and no ground is too poor, and no soul is too hard, to have God's good seed shared upon it. Who knows where the seed will take root and bear an abundance of fruit? Do we lack Jesus's generosity, holding back sharing the truth and Good News about Jesus from those we think will not accept it? Jesus teaches us here that if we want to imitate him, we should not be miserly with his Word but share it with all. Who among your friends and family are you afraid to share the faith with? Who among those closest to you are the ripe field that simply awaits the planting of a small suggestion or invitation?

January 20

GENESIS 42

When Jacob learned that there was grain in Egypt, he said to his sons, "Why do you look at one another?" 2And he said, "Behold, I have heard that there is grain in Egypt; go down and buy grain for us there, that we may live, and not die." 3So ten of Joseph's brothers went down to buy grain in Egypt. 4But Jacob did not send Benjamin, Joseph's brother, with his brothers, for he feared that harm might befall him. 5Thus the sons of Israel came to buy among the others who came, for the famine was in the land of Canaan.

6Now Joseph was governor over the land; he it was who sold to all the people of the land. And Joseph's brothers came, and bowed themselves before him with their faces to the ground. 7Joseph saw his brothers, and knew them, but he treated them like strangers and spoke roughly to them. "Where do you come from?" he said. They said, "From the land of Canaan, to buy food." 8Thus Joseph knew his brothers, but they did not know him. 9And Joseph remembered the dreams which he had dreamed of them; and he said to them, "You are spies, you have come to see the weakness of the land." 10They said to him, "No, my lord, but to buy food have your servants come. 11We are all sons of one man, we are honest men, your servants are not spies." 12He said to them, "No, it is the weakness of the land that you have come to see." [13]And they said, "We, your servants, are twelve brothers, the sons of one man in the land of Canaan; and behold, the youngest is this day with our father, and one is no more." [14]But Joseph said to them, "It is as I said to you, you are spies. [15]By this you shall be tested: by the life of Pharaoh, you shall not go from this place unless your youngest brother comes here. [16]Send one of you, and let him bring your brother, while you remain in prison, that your words may be tested, whether there is truth in you; or else, by the life of Pharaoh, surely you are spies." [17]And he put them all together in prison for three days.

[18]On the third day Joseph said to them, "Do this and you will live, for I fear God: [19]if you are honest men, let one of your brothers remain confined in your prison, and let the rest go and carry grain for the famine of your households, [20]and bring your youngest brother to me; so your words will be verified, and you shall not die." And they did so. [21]Then they said to one another, "In truth we are guilty concerning our brother, in that we saw the distress of his soul, when he begged us and we would not listen; therefore is this distress come upon us." [22]And Reuben answered them, "Did I not tell you not to sin against the lad? But you would not listen. So now there comes a reckoning for his blood." [23]They did not know that Joseph understood them, for there was an interpreter between them. [24]Then he turned away from them and wept; and he returned to them and spoke to them. And he took Simeon from them and bound him before their eyes. [25]And Joseph gave orders to fill their bags with grain, and to replace every man's money in his sack, and to give them provisions for the journey. This was done for them.

[26]Then they loaded their donkeys with their grain, and departed. [27]And as one of them opened his sack to give his donkey food at the lodging place, he saw his money in the mouth of his sack; [28]and he said to his brothers, "My money has been put back; here it is in the mouth of my sack!" At this their hearts failed them, and they turned trembling to one another, saying, "What is this that God has done to us?"

[29]When they came to Jacob their father in the land of Canaan, they told him all that had befallen them, saying, [30]"The man, the lord of the land, spoke roughly to us, and took us to be spies of the land. [31]But we said to him, 'We are honest men, we are not spies; [32]we are twelve brothers, sons of our father; one is no more, and the youngest is this day with our father in the land of Canaan.' [33]Then the man, the lord of the land, said to us, 'By this I shall know that you are honest men: leave one of your brothers with me, and take grain for the famine of your households, and go your way. [34]Bring your youngest brother to me; then I shall know that you are not spies but honest men, and I will deliver to you your brother, and you shall trade in the land.'"

[35]As they emptied their sacks, behold, every man's bundle of money was in his sack; and when they and their father saw their bundles of money, they were dismayed. [36]And Jacob their father said to them, "You have bereaved me of my children: Joseph is no more, and Simeon is no more, and now you would take Benjamin; all this has come upon me." [37]Then Reuben said to his father, "Slay my two sons if I do not bring him back to you; put him in my hands, and I will bring him back to you." [38]But he said, "My son shall not go down with you, for his brother is dead, and he only is left. If harm should befall him on the journey that you are to make, you would bring down my gray hairs with sorrow to Sheol."

43 Now the famine was severe in the land. [2]And when they had eaten the grain which they had brought from Egypt, their father said to them, "Go again, buy us a little food." [3]But Judah said to him, "The man solemnly warned us, saying, 'You shall not see my face, unless your brother is with you.' [4]If you will send our brother with us, we will go down and buy you food; [5]but if you will not send him, we will not go down, for the man said to us, 'You shall not see my face, unless your brother is with you.'" [6]Israel said, "Why did you treat me so ill as to tell the man that you had another brother?" [7]They replied, "The man questioned us carefully about ourselves and our kindred, saying, 'Is your father still alive? Have you another brother?' What we told him was in answer to these questions; could we in any way know that he would say, 'Bring your brother down'?" [8]And Judah said to Israel his father, "Send the lad with me, and we will arise and go, that we may live and not die, both we and you and also our little ones. [9]I will be surety for him; of my hand you shall require him. If I do not bring him back to you and set him before you, then let me bear the blame for ever; [10]for if we had not delayed, we would now have returned twice."

[11]Then their father Israel said to them, "If it must be so, then do this: take some of the choice fruits of the land in your bags, and carry down to the man a present, a little balm and a little honey, gum, myrrh, pistachio nuts, and almonds. [12]Take double the money with you; carry back with you the money that was returned in the mouth of your sacks; perhaps it was an oversight. [13]Take also your brother, and arise, go again to the man; [14]may God Almighty grant you mercy before the man, that he may send back your other brother and Benjamin. If I am bereaved of my children, I am bereaved." [15]So the men took the present, and they took double the money with them, and Benjamin; and they arose and went down to Egypt, and stood before Joseph.

[16]When Joseph saw Benjamin with them, he said to the steward of his house, "Bring the men into the house, and slaughter an animal and make ready, for the men are to dine with me at noon." [17]The man did as Joseph bade him, and brought the men to Joseph's house. [18]And the men were afraid because they were brought to Joseph's house, and they said, "It is because of the money, which was replaced in our sacks the first time, that we are brought in, so that he may seek occasion against us and fall upon us, to make slaves of us and seize our donkeys." [19]So they went up to the steward of Joseph's house, and spoke with him at the door of the house, [20]and said, "Oh, my lord, we came down the first time to buy food; [21]and when we came to the lodging place we opened our sacks, and there was every man's money in the mouth of his sack, our money in full weight; so we have brought it again with us, [22]and we have brought other money down in our hand to buy food. We do not know who put our money in our sacks." [23]He replied, "Rest assured, do not be afraid; your God and the God of your father must have put treasure in your sacks for you; I received your money." Then he brought Simeon out to them. [24]And when the man had brought the men into Joseph's house, and given them water, and they had washed their feet, and when he had given their donkeys food, [25]they made ready the present for Joseph's coming at noon, for they heard that they should eat bread there.

[26]When Joseph came home, they brought into the house to him the present which they had with them, and bowed down to him to the ground. [27]And he inquired about their welfare, and said, "Is your father well, the old man of whom you spoke? Is he still alive?" [28]They said, "Your servant our father is well, he is still alive." And they bowed their heads and made obeisance. [29]And he lifted up his eyes, and saw his brother Benjamin, his mother's son, and said, "Is this your youngest brother, of whom you spoke to me? God be gracious to you, my son!" [30]Then Joseph made haste, for his heart yearned for his brother, and he sought a place to weep. And he entered his chamber and wept there. [31]Then he washed his face and came out; and controlling himself he said, "Let food be served." [32]They served him by himself, and them by themselves, and the Egyptians who ate with him by themselves, because the Egyptians might not eat bread with the Hebrews, for that is an abomination to the Egyptians. [33]And they sat before him, the first-born according to his birthright and the youngest according to his youth; and the men looked at one another in amazement. [34]Portions were taken to them from Joseph's table, but Benjamin's portion was five times

as much as any of theirs. So they drank and were merry with him.

To the choirmaster.
A Psalm of David the servant of the LORD,
who addressed the words of this song to the LORD
on the day when the LORD delivered him
from the hands of all his enemies,
and from the hand of Saul.
He said:

PSALM 18 [17]

43You delivered me from strife with
the peoples;
you made me the head of the nations;
people whom I had not known
served me.
44As soon as they heard of me they
obeyed me;
foreigners came cringing to me.
45Foreigners lost heart,
and came trembling out of their
strongholds.
46The LORD lives; and blessed be my rock,
and exalted be the God of my salvation,
47the God who gave me vengeance
and subdued peoples under me;
48who delivered me from my enemies;
yes, you exalted me above my adversaries;
you delivered me from men of violence.

49For this I will extol you, O LORD, among
the nations,
and sing praises to your name.
50Great triumphs he gives to his king,
and shows mercy to his anointed,
to David and his descendants for ever.

MATTHEW 13

44"The kingdom of heaven is like treasure hidden in a field, which a man found and covered up; then in his joy he goes and sells all that he has and buys that field.

45"Again, the kingdom of heaven is like a
merchant in search of fine pearls, 46who, on
finding one pearl of great value, went and
sold all that he had and bought it.
47"Again, the kingdom of heaven is like
a net which was thrown into the sea and
gathered fish of every kind; 48when it was
full, men drew it ashore and sat down and
sorted the good into vessels but threw away
the bad. 49So it will be at the close of the age.
The angels will come out and separate the
evil from the righteous, 50and throw them
into the furnace of fire, where there will be
weeping and gnashing of teeth.
51"Have you understood all this?" They
said to him, "Yes." 52And he said to them,
"Therefore every scribe who has been
trained for the kingdom of heaven is like a
householder who brings out of his treasure
what is new and what is old."
53And when Jesus had finished these parables, he went away from there, 54and coming
to his own country he taught them in their
synagogue, so that they were astonished,
and said, "Where did this man get this wisdom and these mighty works? 55Is not this
the carpenter's son? Is not his mother called
Mary? And are not his brethren James and
Joseph and Simon and Judas? 56And are not
all his sisters with us? Where then did this
man get all this?" 57And they took offense at
him. But Jesus said to them, "A prophet is not
without honor except in his own country and
in his own house." 58And he did not do many
mighty works there, because of their unbelief.

14 At that time Herod the tetrarch heard
about the fame of Jesus; 2and he said
to his servants, "This is John the Baptist;
he has been raised from the dead; that is
why these powers are at work in him." 3For
Herod had seized John and bound him and
put him in prison, for the sake of Hero′di-as,
his brother Philip's wife; 4because John said
to him, "It is not lawful for you to have her."
5And though he wanted to put him to death,
he feared the people, because they held him
to be a prophet. 6But when Herod's birthday
came, the daughter of Hero′di-as danced
before the company, and pleased Herod, 7so
that he promised with an oath to give her

whatever she might ask. [8]Prompted by her mother, she said, "Give me the head of John the Baptist here on a platter." [9]And the king was sorry, but because of his oaths and his guests he commanded it to be given; [10]he sent and had John beheaded in the prison, [11]and his head was brought on a platter and given to the girl, and she brought it to her mother. [12]And his disciples came and took the body and buried it; and they went and told Jesus.

REFLECTION

Jesus never tells a parable about the messiah. Instead, his parables focus on a recurring theme: the Kingdom of Heaven. In these three parables, which bring his discourse of seven parables to a conclusion, he describes how obtaining the kingdom requires arduous work. A man on a treasure hunt, a merchant in search of the priceless pearl, and a fisherman fishing for a great catch. All require relentless effort, but all are rewarded richly. The treasure in a field and the pearl of great price, like the Kingdom of Heaven, demand the same cost—all that we have. Jesus challenges us to up our effort, while also promising to reward our search for his kingdom. Most often those who are successful in the world are those few who seek success, who are willing to put in the work and effort. Even fewer are those who actively seek the treasure that lasts forever. "But seek first his kingdom and his righteousness, and all these things shall be yours as well" (Mt 6:33). How willing are you to seek after our Lord and his kingdom? Are you willing to give all that you have?

January 21

GENESIS 44

Then he commanded the steward of his house, "Fill the men's sacks with food, as much as they can carry, and put each man's money in the mouth of his sack, [2]and put my cup, the silver cup, in the mouth of the sack of the youngest, with his money for the grain." And he did as Joseph told him. [3]As soon as the morning was light, the men were sent away with their donkeys. [4]When they had gone but a short distance from the city, Joseph said to his steward, "Up, follow after the men; and when you overtake them, say to them, 'Why have you returned evil for good? Why have you stolen my silver cup? [5]Is it not from this that my lord drinks, and by this that he divines? You have done wrong in so doing.' "

[6]When he overtook them, he spoke to them these words. [7]They said to him, "Why does my lord speak such words as these? Far be it from your servants that they should do such a thing! [8]Behold, the money which we found in the mouth of our sacks, we brought back to you from the land of Canaan; how then should we steal silver or gold from your lord's house? [9]With whomever of your servants it be found, let him die, and we also will be my lord's slaves." [10]He said, "Let it be as you say: he with whom it is found shall be my slave, and the rest of you shall be blameless." [11]Then every man quickly lowered his sack to the ground, and every man opened his sack. [12]And he searched, beginning with the eldest and ending with the youngest; and the cup was found in Benjamin's sack. [13]Then they tore their clothes, and every man loaded his donkey, and they returned to the city.

[14]When Judah and his brothers came to Joseph's house, he was still there; and they fell before him to the ground. [15]Joseph said to them, "What deed is this that you have done? Do you not know that such a man as I can indeed divine?" [16]And Judah said, "What shall we say to my lord? What shall we speak? Or how can we clear ourselves? God has found out the guilt of your servants; behold, we are my lord's slaves, both we and he also in whose hand the cup has been found." [17]But he said, "Far be it from me that I should do so! Only the man in whose hand the cup was found shall be my slave; but as for you, go up in peace to your father."

[18]Then Judah went up to him and said, "O my lord, let your servant, I beg you, speak a

word in my lord's ears, and let not your anger burn against your servant; for you are like Pharaoh himself. [19]My lord asked his servants, saying, 'Have you a father, or a brother?' [20]And we said to my lord, 'We have a father, an old man, and a young brother, the child of his old age; and his brother is dead, and he alone is left of his mother's children; and his father loves him.' [21]Then you said to your servants, 'Bring him down to me, that I may set my eyes upon him.' [22]We said to my lord, 'The lad cannot leave his father, for if he should leave his father, his father would die.' [23]Then you said to your servants, 'Unless your youngest brother comes down with you, you shall see my face no more.' [24]When we went back to your servant my father we told him the words of my lord. [25]And when our father said, 'Go again, buy us a little food,' [26]we said, 'We cannot go down. If our youngest brother goes with us, then we will go down; for we cannot see the man's face unless our youngest brother is with us.' [27]Then your servant my father said to us, 'You know that my wife bore me two sons; [28]one left me, and I said, Surely he has been torn to pieces; and I have never seen him since. [29]If you take this one also from me, and harm befalls him, you will bring down my gray hairs in sorrow to Sheol.' [30]Now therefore, when I come to your servant my father, and the lad is not with us, then, as his life is bound up in the lad's life, [31]when he sees that the lad is not with us, he will die; and your servants will bring down the gray hairs of your servant our father with sorrow to Sheol. [32]For your servant became surety for the lad to my father, saying, 'If I do not bring him back to you, then I shall bear the blame in the sight of my father all my life.' [33]Now therefore, let your servant, I beg you, remain instead of the lad as a slave to my lord; and let the lad go back with his brothers. [34]For how can I go back to my father if the lad is not with me? I fear to see the evil that would come upon my father."

45 Then Joseph could not control himself before all those who stood by him; and he cried, "Make every one go out from me." So no one stayed with him when Joseph made himself known to his brothers. [2]And he wept aloud, so that the Egyptians heard it, and the household of Pharaoh heard it. [3]And Joseph said to his brothers, "I am Joseph; is my father still alive?" But his brothers could not answer him, for they were dismayed at his presence.

[4]So Joseph said to his brothers, "Come near to me, I beg you." And they came near. And he said, "I am your brother, Joseph, whom you sold into Egypt. [5]And now do not be distressed, or angry with yourselves, because you sold me here; for God sent me before you to preserve life. [6]For the famine has been in the land these two years; and there are yet five years in which there will be neither plowing nor harvest. [7]And God sent me before you to preserve for you a remnant on earth, and to keep alive for you many survivors. [8]So it was not you who sent me here, but God; and he has made me a father to Pharaoh, and lord of all his house and ruler over all the land of Egypt. [9]Make haste and go up to my father and say to him, 'Thus says your son Joseph, God has made me lord of all Egypt; come down to me, do not tarry; [10]you shall dwell in the land of Go′shen, and you shall be near me, you and your children and your children's children, and your flocks, your herds, and all that you have; [11]and there I will provide for you, for there are yet five years of famine to come; lest you and your household, and all that you have, come to poverty.' [12]And now your eyes see, and the eyes of my brother Benjamin see, that it is my mouth that speaks to you. [13]You must tell my father of all my splendor in Egypt, and of all that you have seen. Make haste and bring my father down here." [14]Then he fell upon his brother Benjamin's neck and wept; and Benjamin wept upon his neck. [15]And he kissed all his brothers and wept upon them; and after that his brothers talked with him.

[16]When the report was heard in Pharaoh's house, "Joseph's brothers have come," it pleased Pharaoh and his servants well. [17]And Pharaoh said to Joseph, "Say to your brothers, 'Do this: load your beasts and go back to the land of Canaan; [18]and take your father and your households, and come to me, and I will give you the best of the land of Egypt, and you shall eat the fat of the land.' [19]Command them also,

'Do this: take wagons from the land of Egypt
for your little ones and for your wives, and
bring your father, and come. [20]Give no thought
to your goods, for the best of all the land of
Egypt is yours.'"
[21]The sons of Israel did so; and Joseph gave
them wagons, according to the command of
Pharaoh, and gave them provisions for the
journey. [22]To each and all of them he gave
festal garments; but to Benjamin he gave
three hundred shekels of silver and five festal
garments. [23]To his father he sent as follows: ten
donkeys loaded with the good things of Egypt,
and ten she-donkeys loaded with grain, bread,
and provision for his father on the journey.
[24]Then he sent his brothers away, and as they
departed, he said to them, "Do not quarrel on
the way." [25]So they went up out of Egypt, and
came to the land of Canaan to their father Jacob.
[26]And they told him, "Joseph is still alive, and he
is ruler over all the land of Egypt." And his heart
fainted, for he did not believe them. [27]But when
they told him all the words of Joseph, which he
had said to them, and when he saw the wagons
which Joseph had sent to carry him, the spirit
of their father Jacob revived; [28]and Israel said,
"It is enough; Joseph my son is still alive; I will
go and see him before I die."

To the choirmaster.
A Psalm of David.

PSALM 19 [18]

The heavens are telling the glory of God;
and the firmament proclaims his
handiwork.
[2]Day to day pours forth speech,
and night to night declares knowledge.
[3]There is no speech, nor are there words;
their voice is not heard;
[4]yet their voice goes out through all the earth,
and their words to the end of the world.

In them he has set a tent for the sun,
[5]which comes forth like a bridegroom
leaving his chamber,
and like a strong man runs its course
with joy.
[6]Its rising is from the end of the heavens,
and its circuit to the end of them;
and there is nothing hidden from its heat.

[7]The law of the LORD is perfect,
reviving the soul;
the testimony of the LORD is sure,
making wise the simple;
[8]the precepts of the LORD are right,
rejoicing the heart;
the commandment of the LORD is pure,
enlightening the eyes;
[9]the fear of the LORD is clean,
enduring for ever;
the ordinances of the LORD are true,
and righteous altogether.
[10]More to be desired are they than gold,
even much fine gold;
sweeter also than honey
and drippings of the honeycomb.

[11]Moreover by them is your servant warned;
in keeping them there is great reward.
[12]But who can discern his errors?
Clear me from hidden faults.
[13]Keep back your servant also from
presumptuous sins;
let them not have dominion over me!
Then I shall be blameless,
and innocent of great transgression.

[14]Let the words of my mouth and the
meditation of my heart
be acceptable in your sight,
O LORD, my rock and my redeemer.

MATTHEW 14

**[13]Now when Jesus heard this, he
withdrew from there in a boat
to a lonely place apart. But when
the crowds heard it, they followed him
on foot from the towns. [14]As he went**
ashore he saw a great throng; and he had compassion on them, and healed their sick. [15]When
it was evening, the disciples came to him and
said, "This is a lonely place, and the day is
now over; send the crowds away to go into the

villages and buy food for themselves." [16]Jesus said, "They need not go away; you give them something to eat." [17]They said to him, "We have only five loaves here and two fish." [18]And he said, "Bring them here to me." [19]Then he ordered the crowds to sit down on the grass; and taking the five loaves and the two fish he looked up to heaven, and blessed, and broke and gave the loaves to the disciples, and the disciples gave them to the crowds. [20]And they all ate and were satisfied. And they took up twelve baskets full of the broken pieces left over. [21]And those who ate were about five thousand men, besides women and children.

[22]Then he made the disciples get into the boat and go before him to the other side, while he dismissed the crowds. [23]And after he had dismissed the crowds, he went up into the hills by himself to pray. When evening came, he was there alone, [24]but the boat by this time was many furlongs distant from the land, beaten by the waves; for the wind was against them. [25]And in the fourth watch of the night he came to them, walking on the sea. [26]But when the disciples saw him walking on the sea, they were terrified, saying, "It is a ghost!" And they cried out for fear. [27]But immediately he spoke to them, saying, "Take heart, it is I; have no fear."

[28]And Peter answered him, "Lord, if it is you, bid me come to you on the water." [29]He said, "Come." So Peter got out of the boat and walked on the water and came to Jesus; [30]but when he saw the wind, he was afraid, and beginning to sink he cried out, "Lord, save me." [31]Jesus immediately reached out his hand and caught him, saying to him, "O you of little faith, why did you doubt?" [32]And when they got into the boat, the wind ceased. [33]And those in the boat worshiped him, saying, "Truly you are the Son of God."

[34]And when they had crossed over, they came to land at Gennes′aret. [35]And when the men of that place recognized him, they sent round to all that region and brought to him all that were sick, [36]and begged him that they might only touch the fringe of his garment; and as many as touched it were made well.

REFLECTION

As the sons of Jacob gather and bow down before the prime minister of Egypt, ignorant that he is their brother, the dreams of Joseph's youth find fulfillment. Although Joseph's dreams foretold this moment, how could anyone have anticipated that betrayal and slavery would have a part to play? Or that from a prison cell Joseph would be raised to a position second only to Pharaoh himself? Joseph now recognizes the twisting road that God allowed to bring about the fulfillment of those dreams. But before he reveals this to his brothers, he must first discern their hearts. Joseph plants the silver cup in Benjamin's sack to see if they would once again betray and abandon a son of Rachel to Egyptian slavery. But time has brought humility and a change of heart to Joseph's brothers. Judah rises to the challenge, offering himself in order to free Benjamin, and for such self-sacrifice Judah's lineage will be blessed with the honor of being the tribe from whom the messiah will one day come (see Gn 49:10). Joseph's patience and forbearance, and his willingness to give his brothers a second chance, allow for fraternal reconciliation. To whom could you patiently extend a second chance?

January 22

GENESIS 46

So Israel took his journey with all that he had, and came to Be′er-she′ba, and offered sacrifices to the God of his father Isaac. [2]And God spoke to Israel in visions of the night, and said, "Jacob, Jacob." And he said, "Here am I." [3]Then he said, "I am God, the God of your father; do not be afraid to go down to Egypt; for I will there make of you a great nation. [4]I will go down with you to Egypt, and I will also bring you up again; and Joseph's hand shall close your eyes." [5]Then Jacob set out from Be′er-she′ba; and the sons of Israel carried Jacob their father, their little ones, and their wives, in the wagons which Pharaoh had sent to carry him. [6]They also took their cattle and their goods, which they had gained in the land of Canaan, and came into Egypt, Jacob and all his offspring with him, [7]his sons, and his sons' sons with him, his daughters, and his sons' daughters; all his offspring he brought with him into Egypt.

[8]Now these are the names of the descendants of Israel, who came into Egypt, Jacob and his sons. Reuben, Jacob's first-born, [9]and the sons of Reuben: Ha´noch, Pallu, Hezron, and Carmi. [10]The sons of Simeon: Jemu´el, Ja´min, O´had, Ja´chin, Zo´har, and Sha´ul, the son of a Canaanitish woman. [11]The sons of Levi: Gershon, Ko´hath, and Merar´i. [12]The sons of Judah: Er, O´nan, She´lah, Per´ez, and Ze´rah (but Er and Onan died in the land of Canaan); and the sons of Perez were Hezron and Ha´mul. [13]The sons of Is´sachar: To´la, Pu´vah, I´ob, and Shimron. [14]The sons of Zeb´ulun: Se´red, E´lon, and Jah´leel [15](these are the sons of Leah, whom she bore to Jacob in Pad´dan-ar´am, together with his daughter Dinah; altogether his sons and his daughters numbered thirty-three). [16]The sons of Gad: Ziph´ion, Haggi, Shu´ni, Ezbon, E´ri, Aro´di, and Are´li. [17]The sons of Asher: Imnah, Ishvah, Ishvi, Beri´ah, with Se´rah their sister. And the sons of Beriah: He´ber and Mal´chi-el [18](these are the sons of Zilpah, whom La´ban gave to Leah his daughter; and these she bore to Jacob—sixteen persons). [19]The sons of Rachel, Jacob's wife: Joseph and Benjamin. [20]And to Joseph in the land of Egypt were born Manas´seh and E´phraim, whom As´enath, the daughter of Poti´phera the priest of On, bore to him. [21]And the sons of Benjamin: Be´la, Be´cher, Ashbel, Ge´ra, Na´aman, E´hi, Rosh, Muppim, Huppim, and Ard [22](these are the sons of Rachel, who were born to Jacob—fourteen persons in all). [23]The sons of Dan: Hu´shim. [24]The sons of Naph´tali: Jah´zeel, Gu´ni, Je´zer, and Shillem [25](these are the sons of Bilhah, whom La´ban gave to Rachel his daughter, and these she bore to Jacob—seven persons in all). [26]All the persons belonging to Jacob who came into Egypt, who were his own offspring, not including Jacob's sons' wives, were sixty-six persons in all; [27]and the sons of Joseph, who were born to him in Egypt, were two; all the persons of the house of Jacob, that came into Egypt, were seventy.

[28]He sent Judah before him to Joseph, to appear before him in Go´shen; and they came into the land of Goshen. [29]Then Joseph made ready his chariot and went up to meet Israel his father in Go´shen; and he presented himself to him, and fell on his neck, and wept on his neck a good while. [30]Israel said to Joseph, "Now let me die, since I have seen your face and know that you are still alive." [31]Joseph said to his brothers and to his father's household, "I will go up and tell Pharaoh, and will say to him, 'My brothers and my father's household, who were in the land of Canaan, have come to me; [32]and the men are shepherds, for they have been keepers of cattle; and they have brought their flocks, and their herds, and all that they have.' [33]When Pharaoh calls you, and says, 'What is your occupation?' [34]you shall say, 'Your servants have been keepers of cattle from our youth even until now, both we and our fathers,' in order that you may dwell in the land of Go´shen; for every shepherd is an abomination to the Egyptians."

47 So Joseph went in and told Pharaoh, "My father and my brothers, with their flocks and herds and all that they possess, have come from the land of Canaan; they are now in the land of Go´shen." [2]And from among his brothers he took five men and presented them to Pharaoh. [3]Pharaoh said to his brothers, "What is your occupation?" And they said to Pharaoh, "Your servants are shepherds, as our fathers were." [4]They said to Pharaoh, "We have come to sojourn in the land; for there is no pasture for your servants' flocks, for the famine is severe in the land of Canaan; and now, we pray you, let your servants dwell in the land of Go´shen." [5]Then Pharaoh said to Joseph, "Your father and your brothers have come to you. [6]The land of Egypt is before you; settle your father and your brothers in the best of the land; let them dwell in the land of Go´shen; and if you know any able men among them, put them in charge of my cattle."

7Then Joseph brought in Jacob his father,
and set him before Pharaoh, and Jacob
blessed Pharaoh. 8And Pharaoh said to Jacob, "How many are the days of the years
of your life?" 9And Jacob said to Pharaoh,
"The days of the years of my sojourning
are a hundred and thirty years; few and
evil have been the days of the years of my
life, and they have not attained to the days
of the years of the life of my fathers in the
days of their sojourning." 10And Jacob blessed Pharaoh, and went out from the presence
of Pharaoh. 11Then Joseph settled his father
and his brothers, and gave them a possession in the land of Egypt, in the best of the
land, in the land of Ram′eses, as Pharaoh
had commanded. 12And Joseph provided
his father, his brothers, and all his father's
household with food, according to the number of their dependents.

13Now there was no food in all the land;
for the famine was very severe, so that
the land of Egypt and the land of Canaan
languished by reason of the famine. 14And
Joseph gathered up all the money that
was found in the land of Egypt and in the
land of Canaan, for the grain which they
bought; and Joseph brought the money into
Pharaoh's house. 15And when the money
was all spent in the land of Egypt and in the
land of Canaan, all the Egyptians came to
Joseph, and said, "Give us food; why should
we die before your eyes? For our money is
gone." 16And Joseph answered, "Give your
cattle, and I will give you food in exchange
for your cattle, if your money is gone." 17So
they brought their cattle to Joseph; and
Joseph gave them food in exchange for
the horses, the flocks, the herds, and the
donkeys: and he supplied them with food in
exchange for all their cattle that year. 18And
when that year was ended, they came to him
the following year, and said to him, "We will
not hide from my lord that our money is all
spent; and the herds of cattle are my lord's;
there is nothing left in the sight of my lord
but our bodies and our lands. 19Why should
we die before your eyes, both we and our
land? Buy us and our land for food, and we
with our land will be slaves to Pharaoh; and
give us seed, that we may live, and not die,
and that the land may not be desolate."

20So Joseph bought all the land of Egypt
for Pharaoh; for all the Egyptians sold their
fields, because the famine was severe upon
them. The land became Pharaoh's; 21and as
for the people, he made slaves of them from
one end of Egypt to the other. 22Only the land
of the priests he did not buy; for the priests
had a fixed allowance from Pharaoh, and
lived on the allowance which Pharaoh gave
them; therefore they did not sell their land.
23Then Joseph said to the people, "Behold, I
have this day bought you and your land for
Pharaoh. Now here is seed for you, and you
shall sow the land. 24And at the harvests you
shall give a fifth to Pharaoh, and four fifths
shall be your own, as seed for the field and
as food for yourselves and your households,
and as food for your little ones." 25And they
said, "You have saved our lives; may it please
my lord, we will be slaves to Pharaoh." 26So
Joseph made it a statute concerning the
land of Egypt, and it stands to this day, that
Pharaoh should have the fifth; the land of
the priests alone did not become Pharaoh's.

27Thus Israel dwelt in the land of Egypt,
in the land of Go′shen; and they gained
possessions in it, and were fruitful and
multiplied exceedingly. 28And Jacob lived
in the land of Egypt seventeen years; so the
days of Jacob, the years of his life, were a
hundred and forty-seven years.

29And when the time drew near that Israel
must die, he called his son Joseph and said
to him, "If now I have found favor in your
sight, put your hand under my thigh, and
promise to deal loyally and truly with me.
Do not bury me in Egypt, 30but let me lie
with my fathers; carry me out of Egypt
and bury me in their burying place." He
answered, "I will do as you have said." 31And
he said, "Swear to me"; and he swore to him.
Then Israel bowed himself upon the head of
his bed.

48 After this Joseph was told, "Behold,
your father is ill"; so he took
with him his two sons, Manas′seh and
E′phraim. 2And it was told to Jacob,
"Your son Joseph has come to you"; then

Israel summoned his strength, and sat up in bed. 3And Jacob said to Joseph, "God Almighty appeared to me at Luz in the land of Canaan and blessed me, 4and said to me, 'Behold, I will make you fruitful, and multiply you, and I will make of you a company of peoples, and will give this land to your descendants after you for an everlasting possession.' 5And now your two sons, who were born to you in the land of Egypt before I came to you in Egypt, are mine; E′phraim and Manas′seh shall be mine, as Reuben and Simeon are. 6And the offspring born to you after them shall be yours; they shall be called by the name of their brothers in their inheritance. 7For when I came from Paddan, Rachel to my sorrow died in the land of Canaan on the way, when there was still some distance to go to Eph′rath; and I buried her there on the way to Ephrath (that is, Bethlehem)."

To the choirmaster.
A Psalm of David.

PSALM 20 [19]

The Lord answer you in the day
of trouble!
The name of the God of Jacob
protect you!
2May he send you help from the sanctuary,
and give you support from Zion!
3May he remember all your offerings,
and regard with favor your
burnt sacrifices! *Selah*

4May he grant you your heart's desire,
and fulfil all your plans!
5May we shout for joy over your victory,
and in the name of our God set up
our banners!
May the Lord fulfil all your petitions!

6Now I know that the Lord will help
his anointed;
he will answer him from his holy heaven
with mighty victories by his right hand.
7Some boast of chariots, and some of horses;
but we boast of the name of the Lord
our God.
8They will collapse and fall;
but we shall rise and stand upright.

9Give victory to the king, O Lord;
answer us when we call.

MATTHEW 15

Then Pharisees and scribes came to Jesus from Jerusalem and said,
2"Why do your disciples transgress the tradition of the elders? For they do
not wash their hands when they eat." 3He
answered them, "And why do you transgress the commandment of God for the sake of your tradition? 4For God commanded, 'Honor your father and your mother,' and, 'He who speaks evil of father or mother, let him surely die.' 5But you say, 'If any one tells his father or his mother, What you would have gained from me is given to God, he need not honor his father.' 6So, for the sake of your tradition, you have made void the word of God. 7You hypocrites! Well did Isaiah prophesy of you, when he said:
8'This people honors me with their lips,
but their heart is far from me;
9in vain do they worship me,
teaching as doctrines the precepts of men.'"
10And he called the people to him and said to them, "Hear and understand: 11not
what goes into the mouth defiles a man, but what comes out of the mouth, this defiles a man." 12Then the disciples came and said to
him, "Do you know that the Pharisees were offended when they heard this saying?" 13He
answered, "Every plant which my heavenly Father has not planted will be rooted up. 14Let
them alone; they are blind guides. And if a blind man leads a blind man, both will fall into a pit." 15But Peter said to him, "Explain
the parable to us." 16And he said, "Are you also
still without understanding? 17Do you not see
that whatever goes into the mouth passes into the stomach, and so passes on? 18But what

comes out of the mouth proceeds from the heart, and this defiles a man. [19]For out of the heart come evil thoughts, murder, adultery, fornication, theft, false witness, slander. [20]These are what defile a man; but to eat with unwashed hands does not defile a man."

REFLECTION

The Fourth Commandment, "Honor your father and mother," was understood to mean, among other things, that children were to support their parents in their old age. The Pharisees, however, had devised a loophole, saying that if someone declared their estate as dedicated to God, they would then be exempt from using its proceeds to provide care for their parents. This clever alternative meant that individuals could selfishly ignore their duty to their parents in the name of giving their estate to God, and, since the estate would not be given until one's death, there was plenty of time to enjoy the spoils. Jesus is not impressed by such hypocrisy, and makes it known that serving God requires obeying God's commandments and serving others as God's Word directs us. To be a disciple of Jesus, we cannot look solely to our own well-being. Instead, Jesus calls us to a life of self-giving, of looking to the needs of those around us, starting with those he has placed closest to us in our own families. Such thinking flies in the face of the rampant individualism that we often see around us, but we are called not to be conformed to the world, but rather to be transformed by the renewal of our minds to the Gospel of Jesus Christ (see Rom 12:2). Do you constantly seek to serve God by serving others, especially your own family?

January 23

GENESIS 48

[8]When Israel saw Joseph's sons,
he said, "Who are these?" [9]Joseph
said to his father, "They are my
sons, whom God has given me here."
And he said, "Bring them to me, I pray
you, that I may bless them." [10]Now the eyes
of Israel were dim with age, so that he could
not see. So Joseph brought them near him;
and he kissed them and embraced them.
[11]And Israel said to Joseph, "I had not
thought to see your face; and behold, God
has let me see your children also." [12]Then
Joseph removed them from his knees, and
he bowed himself with his face to the earth.
[13]And Joseph took them both, E′phraim in
his right hand toward Israel's left hand, and
Manas′seh in his left hand toward Israel's
right hand, and brought them near him.
[14]And Israel stretched out his right hand
and laid it upon the head of E′phraim, who
was the younger, and his left hand upon
the head of Manas′seh, crossing his hands,
for Manasseh was the first-born. [15]And he
blessed Joseph, and said,

"The God before whom my fathers
    Abraham and Isaac walked,
the God who has led me all my life long to
    this day,
[16]the angel who has redeemed me from all
    evil, bless the lads;
and in them let my name be perpetuated,
    and the name of my fathers Abraham
    and Isaac;
and let them grow into a multitude in the
    midst of the earth."

[17]When Joseph saw that his father laid
his right hand upon the head of E′phraim,
it displeased him; and he took his father's
hand, to remove it from E′phraim's head
to Manas′seh's head. [18]And Joseph said to
his father, "Not so, my father; for this one
is the first-born; put your right hand upon
his head." [19]But his father refused, and
said, "I know, my son, I know; he also shall
become a people, and he also shall be great;
nevertheless his younger brother shall be
greater than he, and his descendants shall
become a multitude of nations." [20]So he
blessed them that day, saying,

"By you Israel will pronounce blessings,
    saying,
'God make you as E′phraim and as
    Manas′seh'";

and thus he put Ephraim before Manasseh.
[21]Then Israel said to Joseph, "Behold, I am

about to die, but God will be with you, and
will bring you again to the land of your
fathers. 22Moreover I have given to you
rather than to your brothers one mountain
slope which I took from the hand of the
Am′orites with my sword and with my bow."

49 Then Jacob called his sons, and said,
"Gather yourselves together, that I may
tell you what shall befall you in days to come.

2Assemble and hear, O sons of Jacob,
and hearken to Israel your father.

3Reuben, you are my first-born,
my might, and the first fruits of
my strength,
pre-eminent in pride and pre-eminent
in power.
4Unstable as water, you shall not have
pre-eminence
because you went up to your father's bed;
then you defiled it—you went up to
my couch!

5Simeon and Levi are brothers;
weapons of violence are their swords.
6O my soul, come not into their council;
O my spirit, be not joined to their
company;
for in their anger they slay men,
and in their wantonness they
hamstring oxen.
7Cursed be their anger, for it is fierce;
and their wrath, for it is cruel!
I will divide them in Jacob
and scatter them in Israel.

8Judah, your brothers shall praise you;
your hand shall be on the neck of
your enemies;
your father's sons shall bow down
before you.
9Judah is a lion's whelp;
from the prey, my son, you have gone up.
He stooped down, he lurked as a lion,
and as a lioness; who dares rouse him up?
10The scepter shall not depart from Judah,
nor the ruler's staff from between his feet,
until he comes to whom it belongs;
and to him shall be the obedience of
the peoples.
11Binding his foal to the vine
and his donkey's colt to the choice vine,
he washes his garments in wine
and his vesture in the blood of grapes;
12his eyes shall be red with wine,
and his teeth white with milk.

13Zeb′ulun shall dwell at the shore of the sea;
he shall become a haven for ships,
and his border shall be at Si′don.

14Is′sachar is a strong donkey,
crouching between the sheepfolds;
15he saw that a resting place was good,
and that the land was pleasant;
so he bowed his shoulder to bear,
and became a slave at forced labor.

16Dan shall judge his people
as one of the tribes of Israel.
17Dan shall be a serpent in the way,
a viper by the path,
that bites the horse's heels
so that his rider falls backward.
18I wait for your salvation, O LORD.

19Raiders shall raid Gad,
but he shall raid at their heels.

20Asher's food shall be rich,
and he shall yield royal dainties.

21Naph′tali is a deer let loose,
that bears comely fawns.

22Joseph is a fruitful bough,
a fruitful bough by a spring;
his branches run over the wall.
23The archers fiercely attacked him,
shot at him, and harassed him sorely;
24yet his bow remained unmoved,
his arms were made agile
by the hands of the Mighty One of Jacob
(by the name of the Shepherd, the Rock
of Israel),
25by the God of your father who will help you,
by God Almighty who will bless you
with blessings of heaven above,
blessings of the deep that lies beneath,
blessings of the breasts and of the womb.

26 The blessings of your father
are mighty beyond the blessings of the
eternal mountains,
the bounties of the everlasting hills;
may they be on the head of Joseph,
and on the brow of him who was
separate from his brothers.

27 Benjamin is a ravenous wolf,
in the morning devouring the prey,
and at evening dividing the spoil."

28 All these are the twelve tribes of Israel;
and this is what their father said to them
as he blessed them, blessing each with the
blessing suitable to him. 29 Then he charged
them, and said to them, "I am to be gathered
to my people; bury me with my fathers in
the cave that is in the field of E′phron the
Hittite, 30 in the cave that is in the field at
Mach-pe′lah, to the east of Mamre, in the
land of Canaan, which Abraham bought
with the field from E′phron the Hittite to
possess as a burying place. 31 There they
buried Abraham and Sarah his wife; there
they buried Isaac and Rebekah his wife;
and there I buried Leah— 32 the field and the
cave that is in it were purchased from the
Hittites." 33 When Jacob finished charging
his sons, he drew up his feet into the bed,
and breathed his last, and was gathered to
his people.

50 Then Joseph fell on his father's face,
and wept over him, and kissed him.
2 And Joseph commanded his servants the
physicians to embalm his father. So the
physicians embalmed Israel; 3 forty days
were required for it, for so many are required for embalming. And the Egyptians
wept for him seventy days.

4 And when the days of weeping for him
were past, Joseph spoke to the household
of Pharaoh, saying, "If now I have found
favor in your eyes, speak, I beg you, in
the ears of Pharaoh, saying, 5 My father
made me swear, saying, 'I am about to
die: in my tomb which I hewed out for
myself in the land of Canaan, there shall
you bury me.' Now therefore let me go
up, I beg you, and bury my father; then
I will return." 6 And Pharaoh answered,
"Go up, and bury your father, as he made
you swear." 7 So Joseph went up to bury
his father; and with him went up all the
servants of Pharaoh, the elders of his
household, and all the elders of the land
of Egypt, 8 as well as all the household
of Joseph, his brothers, and his father's
household; only their children, their
flocks, and their herds were left in the
land of Go′shen. 9 And there went up with
him both chariots and horsemen; it was
a very great company. 10 When they came
to the threshing floor of Atad, which
is beyond the Jordan, they lamented
there with a very great and sorrowful
lamentation; and he made a mourning
for his father seven days. 11 When the
inhabitants of the land, the Canaanites,
saw the mourning on the threshing floor
of Atad, they said, "This is a grievous
mourning to the Egyptians." Therefore
the place was named A′bel-miz′raim;
it is beyond the Jordan. 12 Thus his sons
did for him as he had commanded them;
13 for his sons carried him to the land of
Canaan, and buried him in the cave of
the field at Mach-pe′lah, to the east of
Mamre, which Abraham bought with the
field from E′phron the Hittite, to possess
as a burying place. 14 After he had buried
his father, Joseph returned to Egypt with
his brothers and all who had gone up with
him to bury his father.

15 When Joseph's brothers saw that their
father was dead, they said, "It may be that
Joseph will hate us and pay us back for all
the evil which we did to him." 16 So they sent
a message to Joseph, saying, "Your father
gave this command before he died, 17 'Say to
Joseph, Forgive, I beg you, the transgression
of your brothers and their sin, because they
did evil to you.' And now, we pray you,
forgive the transgression of the servants of
the God of your father." Joseph wept when
they spoke to him. 18 His brothers also came
and fell down before him, and said, "Behold,
we are your servants." 19 But Joseph said to
them, "Fear not, for am I in the place of God?
20 As for you, you meant evil against me; but

God meant it for good, to bring it about that many people should be kept alive, as they are today. 21So do not fear; I will provide for you and your little ones." Thus he reassured them and comforted them.

22So Joseph dwelt in Egypt, he and his father's house; and Joseph lived a hundred and ten years. 23And Joseph saw E′phraim's children of the third generation; the children also of Ma′chir the son of Manas′seh were born upon Joseph's knees. 24And Joseph said to his brothers, "I am about to die; but God will visit you, and bring you up out of this land to the land which he swore to Abraham, to Isaac, and to Jacob." 25Then Joseph took an oath of the sons of Israel, saying, "God will visit you, and you shall carry up my bones from here." 26So Joseph died, being a hundred and ten years old; and they embalmed him, and he was put in a coffin in Egypt.

To the choirmaster.
A Psalm of David.

PSALM 21 [20]

In your strength the king rejoices, O LORD;
and in your help how greatly he exults!
2You have given him his heart's desire,
and have not withheld the request of
his lips. *Selah*
3For you meet him with goodly blessings;
you set a crown of fine gold upon
his head.
4He asked life of you; you gave it to him,
length of days for ever and ever.
5His glory is great through your help;
splendor and majesty you bestow
upon him.
6Yes, you make him most blessed for ever;
you make him glad with the joy of
your face.
7For the king trusts in the LORD;
and through the steadfast love of the
Most High he shall not be moved.

8Your hand will find out all your enemies;
your right hand will find out those who
hate you.
9You will make them as a blazing oven
when you appear.
The LORD will swallow them up in
his wrath;
and fire will consume them.
10You will destroy their offspring from
the earth,
and their children from among the sons
of men.
11If they plan evil against you,
if they devise mischief, they will
not succeed.
12For you will put them to flight;
you will aim at their faces with
your bows.

13Be exalted, O LORD, in your strength!
We will sing and praise your power.

MATTHEW 15

21And Jesus went away from there and withdrew to the district of Tyre and Si′don. 22And behold, a Canaanite woman from that region came
out and cried, "Have mercy on me, O Lord, Son of David; my daughter is severely possessed by a demon." 23But he did not answer her a word. And his disciples came and begged him, saying, "Send her away, for she is crying after us." 24He answered, "I was sent only to the lost sheep of the house of Israel." 25But she came and knelt before him, saying, "Lord, help me." 26And he answered, "It is not fair to take the children's bread and throw it to the dogs." 27She said, "Yes, Lord, yet even the dogs eat the crumbs that fall from their masters' table." 28Then Jesus answered her, "O woman, great is your faith! Let it be done for you as you desire." And her daughter was healed instantly.

29And Jesus went on from there and passed along the Sea of Galilee. And he went up on the mountain, and sat down there. 30And great crowds came to him, bringing with them the lame, the maimed, the blind, the mute, and many others, and they put them at his feet, and he healed them, 31so that

the throng wondered, when they saw the
mute speaking, the maimed whole, the lame
walking, and the blind seeing; and they
glorified the God of Israel.
32Then Jesus called his disciples to him
and said, "I have compassion on the crowd,
because they have been with me now three
days, and have nothing to eat; and I am
unwilling to send them away hungry, lest
they faint on the way." 33And the disciples
said to him, "Where are we to get bread
enough in the desert to feed so great a
crowd?" 34And Jesus said to them, "How
many loaves have you?" They said, "Seven,
and a few small fish." 35And commanding
the crowd to sit down on the ground, 36he
took the seven loaves and the fish, and
having given thanks he broke them and
gave them to the disciples, and the disciples
gave them to the crowds. 37And they all
ate and were satisfied; and they took up
seven baskets full of the broken pieces left
over. 38Those who ate were four thousand
men, besides women and children. 39And
sending away the crowds, he got into the
boat and went to the region of Mag′adan.

REFLECTION

With the death of Jacob, Joseph's brothers fear he will turn against them and exact vengeance for all the evil they had caused him. Joseph shows extraordinary magnanimity, forgiving his brothers. Joseph refuses vengeance, saying, "Am I in the place of God?" (Gn 50:19). The Book of Genesis, which began with Cain killing his brother Abel, now ends with Joseph forgiving his brothers. With forgiveness there lies hope for humanity and the people of God. Joseph, reflecting on the rugged road of suffering and hardship that marked his life, reveals a deep insight when he tells his brothers, "As for you, you meant evil against me; but God meant it for good" (v. 20). St. Paul's exhortation to trust in God's providential hand sums up Joseph's wisdom well: "We know that in everything God works for good with those who love him, who are called according to his purpose" (Rom 8:28). Can you look back on the twists and turns of your life and see, like Joseph, God's merciful providence?

January 24

EXODUS 1

**These are the names of the sons
of Israel who came to Egypt with
Jacob, each with his household:
2Reuben, Simeon, Levi, and Judah,
3Is′sachar, Zeb′ulun, and Benjamin,
4Dan and Naph′tali, Gad and Asher.**
5All the offspring of Jacob were seventy
persons; Joseph was already in Egypt. 6Then
Joseph died, and all his brothers, and all that
generation. 7But the descendants of Israel
were fruitful and increased greatly; they
multiplied and grew exceedingly strong; so
that the land was filled with them.
8Now there arose a new king over Egypt,
who did not know Joseph. 9And he said to
his people, "Behold, the sons of Israel are too
many and too mighty for us. 10Come, let us
deal shrewdly with them, lest they multiply,
and, if war befall us, they join our enemies
and fight against us and escape from the
land." 11Therefore they set taskmasters over
them to afflict them with heavy burdens;
and they built for Pharaoh store-cities,
Pithom and Ra-am′ses. 12But the more they
were oppressed, the more they multiplied
and the more they spread abroad. And the
Egyptians were in dread of the sons of Israel.
13So they made the sons of Israel serve with
rigor, 14and made their lives bitter with hard
service, in mortar and brick, and in all kinds
of work in the field; in all their work they
made them serve with rigor.
15Then the king of Egypt said to the
Hebrew midwives, one of whom was named
Shiphrah and the other Puah, 16"When you
serve as midwife to the Hebrew women, and
see them upon the birthstool, if it is a son, you
shall kill him; but if it is a daughter, she shall
live." 17But the midwives feared God, and
did not do as the king of Egypt commanded
them, but let the male children live. 18So the
king of Egypt called the midwives, and said
to them, "Why have you done this, and let

the male children live?" [19]The midwives said to Pharaoh, "Because the Hebrew women are not like the Egyptian women; for they are vigorous and are delivered before the midwife comes to them." [20]So God dealt well with the midwives; and the people multiplied and grew very strong. [21]And because the midwives feared God he gave them families. [22]Then Pharaoh commanded all his people, "Every son that is born to the Hebrews you shall cast into the Nile, but you shall let every daughter live."

2 Now a man from the house of Levi went and took to wife a daughter of Levi. [2]The woman conceived and bore a son; and when she saw that he was a goodly child, she hid him three months. [3]And when she could hide him no longer she took for him a basket made of bulrushes, and daubed it with bitumen and pitch; and she put the child in it and placed it among the reeds at the river's brink. [4]And his sister stood at a distance, to know what would be done to him. [5]Now the daughter of Pharaoh came down to bathe at the river, and her maidens walked beside the river; she saw the basket among the reeds and sent her maid to fetch it. [6]When she opened it she saw the child; and behold, the baby was crying. She took pity on him and said, "This is one of the Hebrews' children." [7]Then his sister said to Pharaoh's daughter, "Shall I go and call you a nurse from the Hebrew women to nurse the child for you?" [8]And Pharaoh's daughter said to her, "Go." So the girl went and called the child's mother. [9]And Pharaoh's daughter said to her, "Take this child away, and nurse him for me, and I will give you your wages." So the woman took the child and nursed him. [10]And the child grew, and she brought him to Pharaoh's daughter, and he became her son; and she named him Moses, for she said, "Because I drew him out of the water."

[11]One day, when Moses had grown up, he went out to his people and looked on their burdens; and he saw an Egyptian beating a Hebrew, one of his people. [12]He looked this way and that, and seeing no one he killed the Egyptian and hid him in the sand. [13]When he went out the next day, behold, two Hebrews were struggling together; and he said to the man that did the wrong, "Why do you strike your fellow?" [14]He answered, "Who made you a prince and a judge over us? Do you mean to kill me as you killed the Egyptian?" Then Moses was afraid, and thought, "Surely the thing is known." [15]When Pharaoh heard of it, he sought to kill Moses.

But Moses fled from Pharaoh, and stayed in the land of Mid′ian; and he sat down by a well. [16]Now the priest of Mid′ian had seven daughters; and they came and drew water, and filled the troughs to water their father's flock. [17]The shepherds came and drove them away; but Moses stood up and helped them, and watered their flock. [18]When they came to their father Reu′el, he said, "How is it that you have come so soon today?" [19]They said, "An Egyptian delivered us out of the hand of the shepherds, and even drew water for us and watered the flock." [20]He said to his daughters, "And where is he? Why have you left the man? Call him, that he may eat bread." [21]And Moses was content to dwell with the man, and he gave Moses his daughter Zippo′rah. [22]She bore a son, and he called his name Gershom; for he said, "I have been a sojourner in a foreign land."

[23]In the course of those many days the king of Egypt died. And the sons of Israel groaned under their bondage, and cried out for help, and their cry under bondage came up to God. [24]And God heard their groaning, and God remembered his covenant with Abraham, with Isaac, and with Jacob. [25]And God saw the sons of Israel, and God knew their condition.

3 Now Moses was keeping the flock of his father-in-law, Jethro, the priest of Mid′ian; and he led his flock to the west side of the wilderness, and came to Horeb, the mountain of God. [2]And the angel of the LORD appeared to him in a flame of fire out of the midst of a bush; and he looked, and behold, the bush was burning, yet it was not consumed. [3]And Moses said, "I will turn aside and see this great sight, why the bush is not burnt."

4When the LORD saw that he turned aside to see, God called to him out of the bush, "Moses, Moses!" And he said, "Here am I." 5Then he said, "Do not come near; put off your shoes from your feet, for the place on which you are standing is holy ground." 6And he said, "I am the God of your father, the God of Abraham, the God of Isaac, and the God of Jacob." And Moses hid his face, for he was afraid to look at God.

7Then the LORD said, "I have seen the affliction of my people who are in Egypt, and have heard their cry because of their taskmasters; I know their sufferings, 8and I have come down to deliver them out of the hand of the Egyptians, and to bring them up out of that land to a good and broad land, a land flowing with milk and honey, to the place of the Canaanites, the Hittites, the Am′orites, the Per′izzites, the Hi′vites, and the Jeb′usites. 9And now, behold, the cry of the sons of Israel has come to me, and I have seen the oppression with which the Egyptians oppress them. 10Come, I will send you to Pharaoh that you may bring forth my people, the sons of Israel, out of Egypt." 11But Moses said to God, "Who am I that I should go to Pharaoh, and bring the sons of Israel out of Egypt?" 12He said, "But I will be with you; and this shall be the sign for you, that I have sent you: when you have brought forth the people out of Egypt, you shall serve God upon this mountain."

13Then Moses said to God, "If I come to the sons of Israel and say to them, 'The God of your fathers has sent me to you,' and they ask me, 'What is his name?' what shall I say to them?" 14God said to Moses, "I AM WHO I AM." And he said, "Say this to the sons of Israel, 'I AM has sent me to you.'" 15God also said to Moses, "Say this to the sons of Israel, 'The LORD, the God of your fathers, the God of Abraham, the God of Isaac, and the God of Jacob, has sent me to you': this is my name for ever, and thus I am to be remembered throughout all generations. 16Go and gather the elders of Israel together, and say to them, 'The LORD, the God of your fathers, the God of Abraham, of Isaac, and of Jacob, has appeared to me, saying, "I have observed you and what has been done to you in Egypt; 17and I promise that I will bring you up out of the affliction of Egypt, to the land of the Canaanites, the Hittites, the Am′orites, the Per′izzites, the Hi′vites, and the Jeb′usites, a land flowing with milk and honey."' 18And they will listen to your voice; and you and the elders of Israel shall go to the king of Egypt and say to him, 'The LORD, the God of the Hebrews, has met with us; and now, we beg you, let us go a three days' journey into the wilderness, that we may sacrifice to the LORD our God.' 19I know that the king of Egypt will not let you go unless compelled by a mighty hand. 20So I will stretch out my hand and strike Egypt with all the wonders which I will do in it; after that he will let you go. 21And I will give this people favor in the sight of the Egyptians; and when you go, you shall not go empty, 22but each woman shall ask of her neighbor, and of her who sojourns in her house, jewelry of silver and of gold, and clothing, and you shall put them on your sons and on your daughters; thus you shall despoil the Egyptians."

To the choirmaster: according to The Hind of the Dawn.
A Psalm of David.

PSALM 22 [21]

My God, my God, why have you
forsaken me?
Why are you so far from helping me,
from the words of my groaning?
2O my God, I cry by day, but you
do not answer;
and by night, but find no rest.

3Yet you are holy,
enthroned on the praises of Israel.
4In you our fathers trusted;
they trusted, and you delivered them.

5To you they cried, and were saved;
in you they trusted, and were
not disappointed.

6But I am a worm, and no man;
scorned by men, and despised by
the people.
7All who see me mock at me,
they make mouths at me, they wag
their heads;
8"He committed his cause to the LORD; let
him deliver him,
let him rescue him, for he delights in him!"

9Yet you are he who took me from the womb;
you kept me safe upon my mother's
breasts.
10Upon you was I cast from my birth,
and since my mother bore me you have
been my God.
11Be not far from me,
for trouble is near
and there is none to help.

MATTHEW 16

**And the Pharisees and Sad′du-
cees came, and to test him they
asked him to show them a sign from
heaven. 2He answered them, "When it is**
evening, you say, 'It will be fair weather;
for the sky is red.' 3And in the morning, 'It
will be stormy today, for the sky is red and
threatening.' You know how to interpret
the appearance of the sky, but you cannot
interpret the signs of the times. 4An evil and
adulterous generation seeks for a sign, but
no sign shall be given to it except the sign of
Jonah." So he left them and departed.
5When the disciples reached the other side,
they had forgotten to bring any bread. 6Jesus
said to them, "Take heed and beware of the
leaven of the Pharisees and Sad′ducees." 7And
they discussed it among themselves, saying,
"We brought no bread." 8But Jesus, aware of
this, said, "O men of little faith, why do you
discuss among yourselves the fact that you
have no bread? 9Do you not yet perceive?
Do you not remember the five loaves of
the five thousand, and how many baskets
you gathered? 10Or the seven loaves of the
four thousand, and how many baskets you
gathered? 11How is it that you fail to perceive
that I did not speak about bread? Beware of
the leaven of the Pharisees and Sad′ducees."
12Then they understood that he did not tell
them to beware of the leaven of bread, but of
the teaching of the Pharisees and Sad′ducees.
13Now when Jesus came into the district
of Caesare′a Philip′pi, he asked his disciples,
"Who do men say that the Son of man is?"
14And they said, "Some say John the Baptist,
others say Eli′jah, and others Jeremiah or
one of the prophets." 15He said to them,
"But who do you say that I am?" 16Simon
Peter replied, "You are the Christ, the Son of
the living God." 17And Jesus answered him,
"Blessed are you, Simon Bar-Jona! For flesh
and blood has not revealed this to you, but
my Father who is in heaven. 18And I tell you,
you are Peter, and on this rock I will build
my Church, and the gates of Hades shall not
prevail against it. 19I will give you the keys
of the kingdom of heaven, and whatever you
bind on earth shall be bound in heaven, and
whatever you loose on earth shall be loosed
in heaven." 20Then he strictly charged the
disciples to tell no one that he was the Christ.
21From that time Jesus began to show his
disciples that he must go to Jerusalem and
suffer many things from the elders and chief
priests and scribes, and be killed, and on the
third day be raised. 22And Peter took him and
began to rebuke him, saying, "God forbid,
Lord! This shall never happen to you." 23But
he turned and said to Peter, "Get behind me,
Satan! You are a hindrance to me; for you are
not on the side of God, but of men."
24Then Jesus told his disciples, "If any man
would come after me, let him deny himself
and take up his cross and follow me. 25For
whoever would save his life will lose it,
and whoever loses his life for my sake will
find it. 26For what will it profit a man, if he
gains the whole world and forfeits his life?
Or what shall a man give in return for his
life? 27For the Son of man is to come with his
angels in the glory of his Father, and then he

will repay every man for what he has done.
28Truly, I say to you, there are some standing
here who will not taste death before they see
the Son of man coming in his kingdom."

REFLECTION

The events of Caesarea Philippi are a turning point for both Jesus and Simon. Indeed, Simon's name and vocation will change, as his profession of faith wins him the name "rock," that is, Peter. What is less recognized is that not only is Simon's name changed, but Jesus here goes so far as to also change his surname, calling him Simon bar Jonah. "Bar" means "son" in Aramaic, and Jonah is an extraordinarily rare name among Jews (who wants to name their child after the prophet who rebelled against God?). We know that Peter's father's name was actually John (see Jn 21). So what does "bar Jonah" mean? Peter's vocation will echo the prophet Jonah, who was sent to preach to the capital of Israel's enemy, Nineveh. Likewise, Peter will be sent to the capital of Israel's enemy, Rome. Just as Jonah found a hearing, so too will Peter, so much so that the Christian movement will be centered in Rome, where both Peter and Paul will be martyred. Peter and his successors are cast in the role of Jonah. Could this be why Michelangelo made the prophet Jonah the largest figure in the Sistine Chapel, and placed him right above the chair of the pope? Do you witness Christ to others in those situations where he places you?

January 25

EXODUS 4

**Then Moses answered, "But
behold, they will not believe
me or listen to my voice, for they will
say, 'The LORD did not appear to you.'"**
2The LORD said to him, "What is that in
your hand?" He said, "A rod." 3And he said,
"Cast it on the ground." So he cast it on
the ground, and it became a serpent; and
Moses fled from it. 4But the LORD said to
Moses, "Put out your hand, and take it
by the tail"—so he put out his hand and
caught it, and it became a rod in his hand—
5"that they may believe that the LORD, the
God of their fathers, the God of Abraham,
the God of Isaac, and the God of Jacob, has
appeared to you." 6Again, the LORD said
to him, "Put your hand into your bosom."
And he put his hand into his bosom; and
when he took it out, behold, his hand was
leprous, as white as snow. 7Then God said,
"Put your hand back into your bosom." So
he put his hand back into his bosom; and
when he took it out, behold, it was restored
like the rest of his flesh. 8"If they will not
believe you," God said, "or heed the first
sign, they may believe the latter sign. 9If
they will not believe even these two signs
or heed your voice, you shall take some
water from the Nile and pour it upon the
dry ground; and the water which you shall
take from the Nile will become blood upon
the dry ground."
10But Moses said to the LORD, "Oh, my
Lord, I am not eloquent, either heretofore or
since you have spoken to your servant; but
I am slow of speech and of tongue." 11Then
the LORD said to him, "Who has made man's
mouth? Who makes him mute, or deaf, or
seeing, or blind? Is it not I, the LORD? 12Now
therefore go, and I will be with your mouth
and teach you what you shall speak." 13But
he said, "Oh, my Lord, send, I pray, some
other person." 14Then the anger of the LORD
was kindled against Moses and he said, "Is
there not Aaron, your brother, the Levite?
I know that he can speak well; and behold,
he is coming out to meet you, and when he
sees you he will be glad in his heart. 15And
you shall speak to him and put the words in
his mouth; and I will be with your mouth
and with his mouth, and will teach you what
you shall do. 16He shall speak for you to the
people; and he shall be a mouth for you, and
you shall be to him as God. 17And you shall
take in your hand this rod, with which you
shall do the signs."
18Moses went back to Jethro his father-in-
law and said to him, "Let me go back, I beg,
to my kinsmen in Egypt and see whether

they are still alive." And Jethro said to
Moses, "Go in peace." 19And the LORD said
to Moses in Mid′ian, "Go back to Egypt; for
all the men who were seeking your life are
dead." 20So Moses took his wife and his sons
and set them on a donkey, and went back
to the land of Egypt; and in his hand Moses
took the rod of God.

21And the LORD said to Moses, "When
you go back to Egypt, see that you do before
Pharaoh all the miracles which I have put in
your power; but I will harden his heart, so
that he will not let the people go. 22And you
shall say to Pharaoh, 'Thus says the LORD,
Israel is my first-born son, 23and I say to
you, "Let my son go that he may serve me";
if you refuse to let him go, behold, I will slay
your first-born son.'"

24At a lodging place on the way the LORD
met him and sought to kill him. 25Then
Zippo′rah took a flint and cut off her son's
foreskin, and touched Moses' feet with it,
and said, "Surely you are a bridegroom of
blood to me!" 26So he let him alone. Then it
was that she said, "You are a bridegroom of
blood," because of the circumcision.

27The LORD said to Aaron, "Go into the
wilderness to meet Moses." So he went, and
met him at the mountain of God and kissed
him. 28And Moses told Aaron all the words
of the LORD with which he had sent him,
and all the signs which he had charged him
to do. 29Then Moses and Aaron went and
gathered together all the elders of the sons
of Israel. 30And Aaron spoke all the words
which the LORD had spoken to Moses, and
did the signs in the sight of the people.
31And the people believed; and when they
heard that the LORD had visited the sons of
Israel and that he had seen their affliction,
they bowed their heads and worshiped.

5 Afterward Moses and Aaron went to
Pharaoh and said, "Thus says the LORD,
the God of Israel, 'Let my people go, that they
may hold a feast to me in the wilderness.'" 2But
Pharaoh said, "Who is the LORD, that I should
heed his voice and let Israel go? I do not know
the LORD, and moreover I will not let Israel
go." 3Then they said, "The God of the Hebrews
has met with us; let us go, we beg, a three days'
journey into the wilderness, and sacrifice to
the LORD our God, lest he fall upon us with
pestilence or with the sword." 4But the king of
Egypt said to them, "Moses and Aaron, why
do you take the people away from their work?
Get to your burdens." 5And Pharaoh said,
"Behold, the people of the land are now many
and you make them rest from their burdens!"
6The same day Pharaoh commanded the
taskmasters of the people and their foremen,
7"You shall no longer give the people straw to
make bricks, as heretofore; let them go and
gather straw for themselves. 8But the number
of bricks which they made heretofore you
shall lay upon them, you shall by no means
lessen it; for they are idle; therefore they cry,
'Let us go and offer sacrifice to our God.'
9Let heavier work be laid upon the men that
they may labor at it and pay no regard to
lying words."

10So the taskmasters and the foremen of
the people went out and said to the people,
"Thus says Pharaoh, 'I will not give you straw.
11Go yourselves, get your straw wherever
you can find it; but your work will not be
lessened in the least.'" 12So the people were
scattered abroad throughout all the land
of Egypt, to gather stubble for straw. 13The
taskmasters were urgent, saying, "Complete
your work, your daily task, as when there
was straw." 14And the foremen of the sons
of Israel, whom Pharaoh's taskmasters had
set over them, were beaten, and were asked,
"Why have you not done all your task of
making bricks today, as before?"

15Then the foremen of the sons of Israel
came and cried to Pharaoh, "Why do you
deal thus with your servants? 16No straw is
given to your servants, yet they say to us,
'Make bricks!' And behold, your servants
are beaten; but the fault is in your own
people." 17But he said, "You are idle, you
are idle; therefore you say, 'Let us go and
sacrifice to the LORD.' 18Go now, and work;
for no straw shall be given you, yet you
shall deliver the same number of bricks."
19The foremen of the sons of Israel saw that
they were in evil plight, when they said,
"You shall by no means lessen your daily
number of bricks." 20They met Moses and

Aaron, who were waiting for them, as they
came forth from Pharaoh; 21 and they said to
them, "The LORD look upon you and judge,
because you have made us offensive in the
sight of Pharaoh and his servants, and have
put a sword in their hand to kill us."
22 Then Moses turned again to the LORD
and said, "O LORD, why have you done evil
to this people? Why did you ever send me?
23 For since I came to Pharaoh to speak in
your name, he has done evil to this people,
and you have not delivered your people at
6 all." 1 But the Lord said to Moses, "Now
you shall see what I will do to Pharaoh;
for with a strong hand he will send them
out, yes, with a strong hand he will drive
them out of his land."
2 And God said to Moses, "I am the LORD.
3 I appeared to Abraham, to Isaac, and to
Jacob, as God Almighty, but by my name the
LORD I did not make myself known to them.
4 I also established my covenant with them,
to give them the land of Canaan, the land in
which they dwelt as sojourners. 5 Moreover
I have heard the groaning of the sons of
Israel whom the Egyptians hold in bondage
and I have remembered my covenant. 6 Say
therefore to the sons of Israel, 'I am the LORD,
and I will bring you out from under the
burdens of the Egyptians, and I will deliver
you from their bondage, and I will redeem
you with an outstretched arm and with great
acts of judgment, 7 and I will take you for my
people, and I will be your God; and you shall
know that I am the LORD your God, who has
brought you out from under the burdens of
the Egyptians. 8 And I will bring you into the
land which I swore to give to Abraham, to
Isaac, and to Jacob; I will give it to you for
a possession. I am the LORD.'" 9 Moses spoke
thus to the sons of Israel; but they did not
listen to Moses, because of their broken spirit
and their cruel bondage.
10 And the LORD said to Moses, 11 "Go in,
tell Pharaoh king of Egypt to let the sons of
Israel go out of his land." 12 But Moses said
to the LORD, "Behold, the sons of Israel have
not listened to me; how then shall Pharaoh
listen to me, who am a man of uncircumcised
lips?" 13 But the LORD spoke to Moses and
Aaron, and gave them a charge to the sons of
Israel and to Pharaoh king of Egypt to bring
the sons of Israel out of the land of Egypt.

To the choirmaster: according to The Hind of the Dawn.
A Psalm of David.

PSALM 22 [21]

12 Many bulls encompass me,
strong bulls of Bashan surround me;
13 they open wide their mouths at me,
like a ravening and roaring lion.

14 I am poured out like water,
and all my bones are out of joint;
my heart is like wax,
it is melted within my breast;
15 my strength is dried up like a potsherd,
and my tongue cleaves to my jaws;
you lay me in the dust of death.

16 Yes, dogs are round about me;
a company of evildoers encircle me;
they have pierced my hands and feet—
17 I can count all my bones—
they stare and gloat over me;
18 they divide my garments among them,
and for my clothing they cast lots.

19 But you, O LORD, be not far off!
O my help, hasten to my aid!
20 Deliver my soul from the sword,
my life from the power of the dog!
21 Save me from the mouth of the lion,
my afflicted soul from the horns of the
wild oxen!

22 I will tell of your name to my brethren;
in the midst of the congregation I will
praise you:
23 You who fear the LORD, praise him!
all you sons of Jacob, glorify him,
and stand in awe of him, all you sons
of Israel!
24 For he has not despised or abhorred
the affliction of the afflicted;
and he has not hidden his face from him,
but has heard, when he cried to him.

25 From you comes my praise in the great
congregation;
my vows I will pay before those who
fear him.
26 The afflicted shall eat and be satisfied;
those who seek him shall praise the LORD!
May your hearts live for ever!
27 All the ends of the earth shall remember
and turn to the LORD;
and all the families of the nations
shall worship before him.
28 For dominion belongs to the LORD,
and he rules over the nations.

29 Yes, to him shall all the proud of the earth
bow down;
before him shall bow all who go down to
the dust,
and he who cannot keep himself alive.
30 Posterity shall serve him;
men shall tell of the Lord to the coming
generation,
31 and proclaim his deliverance to a people
yet unborn,
that he has wrought it.

MATTHEW 17

And after six days Jesus took with him Peter and James and John his brother, and led them up a high mountain apart.
2 And he
was transfigured before them, and his face shone like the sun, and his garments became white as light.
3 And behold, there appeared to them Moses and Eli′jah, talking with him.
4 And Peter said to Jesus, "Lord, it is well that we are here; if you wish, I will make three booths here, one for you and one for Moses and one for Eli′jah."
5 He was still speaking, when behold, a bright cloud overshadowed them, and a voice from the cloud said, "This is my beloved Son, with whom I am well pleased; listen to him."
6 When the disciples heard this, they fell on their faces, and were filled with awe.
7 But Jesus came and touched them, saying, "Rise, and have no fear."
8 And when they lifted up their eyes, they saw no one but Jesus only.
9 And as they were coming down the mountain, Jesus commanded them, "Tell no one the vision, until the Son of man is raised from the dead."
10 And the disciples asked him, "Then why do the scribes say that first Eli′jah must come?"
11 He replied, "Eli′jah does come, and he is to restore all things;
12 but I tell you that Eli′jah has already come, and they did not know him, but did to him whatever they pleased. So also the Son of man will suffer at their hands."
13 Then the disciples understood that he was speaking to them of John the Baptist.
14 And when they came to the crowd, a man came up to him and kneeling before him said,
15 "Lord, have mercy on my son, for he is an epileptic and he suffers terribly; for often he falls into the fire, and often into the water.
16 And I brought him to your disciples, and they could not heal him."
17 And Jesus answered, "O faithless and perverse generation, how long am I to be with you? How long am I to bear with you? Bring him here to me."
18 And Jesus rebuked him, and the demon came out of him, and the boy was cured instantly.
19 Then the disciples came to Jesus privately and said, "Why could we not cast it out?"
20 He said to them, "Because of your little faith. For truly, I say to you, if you have faith as a grain of mustard seed, you will say to this mountain, 'Move from here to there,' and it will move; and nothing will be impossible to you."
22 As they were gathering in Galilee, Jesus said to them, "The Son of man is to be delivered into the hands of men,
23 and they will kill him, and he will be raised on the third day." And they were greatly distressed.

REFLECTION

Pharaoh seeks to control not only the work Israel does, but their worship as well. Moses requests a rest from their work to go a short journey into the wilderness in order to worship the God of their fathers. Not only does Pharaoh refuse them this opportunity to worship, but he increases their work so they have no time to rest—no time, that is, to worship the God of Jacob. The enemy of God's people plots to rob them of their God by taking away all rest by incessant work. After being liberated, the first command God will give to Israel is to honor the Sabbath (see Ex 16), so that they will be free to rest, and in that rest know and serve the Lord. Work is an important part of life, and God reminds Israel that he allows them six days in which to do their work, but the seventh day is a day of rest, a day set aside for worship and the service of God. Are we not in danger today of working frenetically, always too busy for prayer and worship, that is, for God? Perhaps you need to take a personal exodus, and resolve to set aside Sundays from work, and for divine rest?

January 26

EXODUS 6

**14These are the heads of their
fathers' houses: the sons of
Reuben, the first-born of Israel:
Ha'noch, Pallu, Hezron, and Carmi;**
these are the families of Reuben. 15The sons
of Simeon: Jemu'el, Ja'min, O'had, Ja'chin,
Zo'har, and Sha'ul, the son of a Canaanite
woman; these are the families of Simeon.
16These are the names of the sons of Levi
according to their generations: Gershon,
Ko'hath, and Merar'i, the years of the life of
Levi being a hundred and thirty-seven years.
17The sons of Gershon: Libni and Shim'e-i,
by their families. 18The sons of Ko'hath:
Amram, Izhar, He'bron, and Uz'ziel, the
years of the life of Kohath being a hundred
and thirty-three years. 19The sons of Merar'i:
Mah'li and Mu'shi. These are the families of
the Levites according to their generations.
20Amram took to wife Joch'ebed his father's
sister and she bore him Aaron and Moses,
the years of the life of Amram being one
hundred and thirty-seven years. 21The sons
of Izhar: Ko'rah, Ne'pheg, and Zich'ri. 22And
the sons of Uz'ziel: Mish'a-el, El'zaphan, and
Sithri. 23Aaron took to wife Eli'sheba, the
daughter of Ammin'adab and the sister of
Nahshon; and she bore him Na'dab, Abi'hu,
Elea'zar, and Ith'amar. 24The sons of Ko'rah:
Assir, Elka'nah, and Abi'asaph; these are the
families of the Ko'rahites. 25Elea'zar, Aaron's
son, took to wife one of the daughters of
Pu'ti-el; and she bore him Phin'ehas. These
are the heads of the fathers' houses of the
Levites by their families.

26These are the Aaron and Moses to whom
the LORD said: "Bring out the sons of Israel
from the land of Egypt by their hosts." 27It
was they who spoke to Pharaoh king of
Egypt about bringing out the sons of Israel
from Egypt, this Moses and this Aaron.

28On the day when the LORD spoke to
Moses in the land of Egypt, 29the LORD said
to Moses, "I am the LORD; tell Pharaoh
king of Egypt all that I say to you." 30But
Moses said to the LORD, "Behold, I am of
uncircumcised lips; how then shall Pharaoh
listen to me?"
7 1And the LORD said
to Moses, "See, I make you as God to
Pharaoh; and Aaron your brother shall be
your prophet. 2You shall speak all that I
command you; and Aaron your brother
shall tell Pharaoh to let the sons of Israel go
out of his land. 3But I will harden Pharaoh's
heart, and though I multiply my signs and
wonders in the land of Egypt, 4Pharaoh will
not listen to you; then I will lay my hand
upon Egypt and bring forth my hosts, my
people the sons of Israel, out of the land of
Egypt by great acts of judgment. 5And the
Egyptians shall know that I am the LORD,
when I stretch forth my hand upon Egypt
and bring out the sons of Israel from among
them." 6And Moses and Aaron did so; they
did as the LORD commanded them. 7Now
Moses was eighty years old, and Aaron
eighty-three years old, when they spoke
to Pharaoh.

8And the LORD said to Moses and Aaron,
9"When Pharaoh says to you, 'Prove yourselves by working a miracle,' then you shall
say to Aaron, 'Take your rod and cast it
down before Pharaoh, that it may become

a serpent.'" [10]So Moses and Aaron went to Pharaoh and did as the LORD commanded; Aaron cast down his rod before Pharaoh and his servants, and it became a serpent. [11]Then Pharaoh summoned the wise men and the sorcerers; and they also, the magicians of Egypt, did the same by their secret arts. [12]For every man cast down his rod, and they became serpents. But Aaron's rod swallowed up their rods. [13]Still Pharaoh's heart was hardened, and he would not listen to them; as the LORD had said.

[14]Then the LORD said to Moses, "Pharaoh's heart is hardened, he refuses to let the people go. [15]Go to Pharaoh in the morning, as he is going out to the water; wait for him by the river's brink, and take in your hand the rod which was turned into a serpent. [16]And you shall say to him, 'The LORD, the God of the Hebrews, sent me to you, saying, "Let my people go, that they may serve me in the wilderness; and behold, you have not yet obeyed." [17]Thus says the LORD, "By this you shall know that I am the LORD: behold, I will strike the water that is in the Nile with the rod that is in my hand, and it shall be turned to blood, [18]and the fish in the Nile shall die, and the Nile shall become foul, and the Egyptians will loathe to drink water from the Nile."'" [19]And the LORD said to Moses, "Say to Aaron, 'Take your rod and stretch out your hand over the waters of Egypt, over their rivers, their canals, and their ponds, and all their pools of water, that they may become blood; and there shall be blood throughout all the land of Egypt, both in vessels of wood and in vessels of stone.'"

[20]Moses and Aaron did as the LORD commanded; in the sight of Pharaoh and in the sight of his servants, he lifted up the rod and struck the water that was in the Nile, and all the water that was in the Nile turned to blood. [21]And the fish in the Nile died; and the Nile became foul, so that the Egyptians could not drink water from the Nile; and there was blood throughout all the land of Egypt. [22]But the magicians of Egypt did the same by their secret arts; so Pharaoh's heart remained hardened, and he would not listen to them; as the LORD had said. [23]Pharaoh turned and went into his house, and he did not lay even this to heart. [24]And all the Egyptians dug round about the Nile for water to drink, for they could not drink the water of the Nile.

[25]Seven days passed after the LORD had
8 struck the Nile. [1]Then the LORD said to Moses, "Go in to Pharaoh and say to him, 'Thus says the LORD, "Let my people go, that they may serve me. [2]But if you refuse to let them go, behold, I will plague all your country with frogs; [3]the Nile shall swarm with frogs which shall come up into your house, and into your bedchamber and on your bed, and into the houses of your servants and of your people, and into your ovens and your kneading bowls; [4]the frogs shall come up on you and on your people and on all your servants."'" [5]And the LORD said to Moses, "Say to Aaron, 'Stretch out your hand with your rod over the rivers, over the canals, and over the pools, and cause frogs to come upon the land of Egypt!'" [6]So Aaron stretched out his hand over the waters of Egypt; and the frogs came up and covered the land of Egypt. [7]But the magicians did the same by their secret arts, and brought frogs upon the land of Egypt.

[8]Then Pharaoh called Moses and Aaron, and said, "Entreat the LORD to take away the frogs from me and from my people; and I will let the people go to sacrifice to the LORD." [9]Moses said to Pharaoh, "Be pleased to command me when I am to entreat, for you and for your servants and for your people, that the frogs be destroyed from you and your houses and be left only in the Nile." [10]And he said, "Tomorrow." Moses said, "Be it as you say, that you may know that there is no one like the LORD our God. [11]The frogs shall depart from you and your houses and your servants and your people; they shall be left only in the Nile." [12]So Moses and Aaron went out from Pharaoh; and Moses cried to the LORD concerning the frogs, as he had agreed with Pharaoh. [13]And the LORD did according to the word of Moses; the frogs died out of the houses and courtyards and out of the fields. [14]And they gathered them together in heaps, and the land stank. [15]But when Pharaoh saw that there was a respite, he hardened his heart, and would not listen to them; as the LORD had said.

[16]Then the LORD said to Moses, "Say to
Aaron, 'Stretch out your rod and strike
the dust of the earth, that it may become
gnats throughout all the land of Egypt.'"
[17]And they did so; Aaron stretched out his
hand with his rod, and struck the dust of
the earth, and there came gnats on man
and beast; all the dust of the earth became
gnats throughout all the land of Egypt.
[18]The magicians tried by their secret arts
to bring forth gnats, but they could not. So
there were gnats on man and beast. [19]And
the magicians said to Pharaoh, "This is the
finger of God." But Pharaoh's heart was
hardened, and he would not listen to them;
as the LORD had said.

[20]Then the LORD said to Moses, "Rise up
early in the morning and wait for Pharaoh, as
he goes out to the water, and say to him, 'Thus
says the LORD, "Let my people go, that they
may serve me. [21]Else, if you will not let my
people go, behold, I will send swarms of flies
on you and your servants and your people,
and into your houses; and the houses of the
Egyptians shall be filled with swarms of flies,
and also the ground on which they stand.
[22]But on that day I will set apart the land of
Goshen, where my people dwell, so that no
swarms of flies shall be there; that you may
know that I am the LORD in the midst of the
earth. [23]Thus I will put a division between my
people and your people. By tomorrow shall
this sign be."'" [24]And the LORD did so; there
came great swarms of flies into the house of
Pharaoh and into his servants' houses, and in
all the land of Egypt the land was ruined by
reason of the flies.

[25]Then Pharaoh called Moses and Aaron,
and said, "Go, sacrifice to your God within the
land." [26]But Moses said, "It would not be right
to do so; for we shall sacrifice to the LORD our
God offerings abominable to the Egyptians.
If we sacrifice offerings abominable to the
Egyptians before their eyes, will they not stone
us? [27]We must go three days' journey into the
wilderness and sacrifice to the LORD our God
as he will command us." [28]So Pharaoh said, "I
will let you go, to sacrifice to the LORD your
God in the wilderness; only you shall not go
very far away. Make entreaty for me." [29]Then
Moses said, "Behold, I am going out from you
and I will pray to the LORD that the swarms
of flies may depart from Pharaoh, from his
servants, and from his people, tomorrow; only
let not Pharaoh deal falsely again by not letting
the people go to sacrifice to the LORD." [30]So
Moses went out from Pharaoh and prayed to
the LORD. [31]And the LORD did as Moses asked,
and removed the swarms of flies from Pharaoh,
from his servants, and from his people; not one
remained. [32]But Pharaoh hardened his heart
this time also, and did not let the people go.

A Psalm of David.

PSALM 23 [22]

The LORD is my shepherd, I shall not want;
[2] he makes me lie down in green pastures.
He leads me beside still waters;
[3] he restores my soul.
He leads me in paths of righteousness
for his name's sake.

[4]Even though I walk through the valley of
the shadow of death,
I fear no evil;
for you are with me;
your rod and your staff,
they comfort me.

[5]You prepare a table before me
in the presence of my enemies;
you anoint my head with oil,
my cup overflows.
[6]Surely goodness and mercy shall follow me
all the days of my life;
and I shall dwell in the house of the LORD
for ever.

MATTHEW 17

[24]When they came to Ca·per′·na·um, the collectors of the half-shekel tax went up to Peter and said, "Does not your teacher pay the tax?" [25]He said, "Yes." And when he came

home, Jesus spoke to him first, saying, "What
do you think, Simon? From whom do kings of
the earth take toll or tribute? From their sons
or from others?" 26And when he said, "From
others," Jesus said to him, "Then the sons are
free. 27However, not to give offense to them,
go to the sea and cast a hook, and take the
first fish that comes up, and when you open
its mouth you will find a shekel; take that and
give it to them for me and for yourself."

18 At that time the disciples came to
Jesus, saying, "Who is the greatest
in the kingdom of heaven?" 2And calling
to him a child, he put him in the midst of
them, 3and said, "Truly, I say to you, unless
you turn and become like children, you
will never enter the kingdom of heaven.
4Whoever humbles himself like this child,
he is the greatest in the kingdom of heaven.

5"Whoever receives one such child in my
name receives me; 6but whoever causes one
of these little ones who believe in me to sin,
it would be better for him to have a great
millstone fastened round his neck and to be
drowned in the depth of the sea.

7"Woe to the world for temptations to sin!
For it is necessary that temptations come,
but woe to the man by whom the temptation
comes! 8And if your hand or your foot
causes you to sin, cut it off and throw it from
you; it is better for you to enter life maimed
or lame than with two hands or two feet to
be thrown into the eternal fire. 9And if your
eye causes you to sin, pluck it out and throw
it from you; it is better for you to enter
life with one eye than with two eyes to be
thrown into the hell of fire.

10"See that you do not despise one of these
little ones; for I tell you that in heaven their
angels always behold the face of my Father
who is in heaven. 12What do you think?
If a man has a hundred sheep, and one of
them has gone astray, does he not leave the
ninety-nine on the hills and go in search of
the one that went astray? 13And if he finds it,
truly, I say to you, he rejoices over it more
than over the ninety-nine that never went
astray. 14So it is not the will of my Father
who is in heaven that one of these little ones
should perish."

REFLECTION

In the catacombs can be found a plethora of the earliest Christian art, all images depicting characters and stories from Sacred Scripture. One of the most popular is the depiction of Jesus as the Good Shepherd, as the earliest Christians had a fondness for connecting Psalm 23 with their prayers for the dead and their hope for life everlasting. Indeed, the story line of Psalm 23 captures the Jewish and Christian hope of Resurrection beautifully. The psalm begins with the Lord as "my shepherd," who leads us to still waters (eternal rest) and makes us lie down in green pastures (in the peaceful sleep of death). Such life-giving water and pastures "restore the soul." Then even more clearly the shepherd leads the soul through the "valley of the shadow of death," where we fear no evil. Finally, the Lord brings us to a banquet table, which Christians understand as a reference to the wedding supper of the Lamb (see Rev 19), where the heavenly banquet is celebrated and by the mercy and goodness of the Lord we "shall dwell in the house of the LORD for ever" (Ps 23:6). Is there a better prayer to know by heart, to share with someone preparing to die, or to have ready at hand when your own death approaches?

January 27

EXODUS 9

**Then the LORD said to Moses,
"Go in to Pharaoh, and say to
him, 'Thus says the LORD, the God of
the Hebrews, "Let my people go, that**
they may serve me. 2For if you refuse to let
them go and still hold them, 3behold, the
hand of the LORD will fall with a very severe
plague upon your cattle which are in the
field, the horses, the donkeys, the camels,
the herds, and the flocks. 4But the LORD
will make a distinction between the cattle of

Israel and the cattle of Egypt, so that nothing shall die of all that belongs to the sons of Israel.'" [5]And the LORD set a time, saying, "Tomorrow the LORD will do this thing in the land." [6]And the next day the LORD did this thing; all the cattle of the Egyptians died, but of the cattle of the sons of Israel not one died. [7]And Pharaoh sent, and behold, not one of the cattle of the Israelites was dead. But the heart of Pharaoh was hardened, and he did not let the people go.

[8]And the LORD said to Moses and Aaron, "Take handfuls of ashes from the kiln, and let Moses throw them toward heaven in the sight of Pharaoh. [9]And it shall become fine dust over all the land of Egypt, and become boils breaking out in sores on man and beast throughout all the land of Egypt." [10]So they took ashes from the kiln, and stood before Pharaoh, and Moses threw them toward heaven, and it became boils breaking out in sores on man and beast. [11]And the magicians could not stand before Moses because of the boils, for the boils were upon the magicians and upon all the Egyptians. [12]But the LORD hardened the heart of Pharaoh, and he did not listen to them; as the LORD had spoken to Moses.

[13]Then the LORD said to Moses, "Rise up early in the morning and stand before Pharaoh, and say to him, 'Thus says the LORD, the God of the Hebrews, "Let my people go, that they may serve me. [14]For this time I will send all my plagues upon your heart, and upon your servants and your people, that you may know that there is none like me in all the earth. [15]For by now I could have put forth my hand and struck you and your people with pestilence, and you would have been cut off from the earth; [16]but for this purpose have I let you live, to show you my power, so that my name may be declared throughout all the earth. [17]You are still exalting yourself against my people, and will not let them go. [18]Behold, tomorrow about this time I will cause very heavy hail to fall, such as never has been in Egypt from the day it was founded until now. [19]Now therefore send, get your cattle and all that you have in the field into safe shelter; for the hail shall come down upon every man and beast that is in the field and is not brought home, and they shall die."'" [20]Then he who feared the word of the LORD among the servants of Pharaoh made his slaves and his cattle flee into the houses; [21]but he who did not regard the word of the LORD left his slaves and his cattle in the field.

[22]And the LORD said to Moses, "Stretch forth your hand toward heaven, that there may be hail in all the land of Egypt, upon man and beast and every plant of the field, throughout the land of Egypt." [23]Then Moses stretched forth his rod toward heaven; and the LORD sent thunder and hail, and fire ran down to the earth. And the LORD rained hail upon the land of Egypt; [24]there was hail, and fire flashing continually in the midst of the hail, very heavy hail, such as had never been in all the land of Egypt since it became a nation. [25]The hail struck down everything that was in the field throughout all the land of Egypt, both man and beast; and the hail struck down every plant of the field, and shattered every tree of the field. [26]Only in the land of Goshen, where the sons of Israel were, there was no hail.

[27]Then Pharaoh sent, and called Moses and Aaron, and said to them, "I have sinned this time; the LORD is in the right, and I and my people are in the wrong. [28]Entreat the LORD; for there has been enough of this thunder and hail; I will let you go, and you shall stay no longer." [29]Moses said to him, "As soon as I have gone out of the city, I will stretch out my hands to the LORD; the thunder will cease, and there will be no more hail, that you may know that the earth is the LORD's. [30]But as for you and your servants, I know that you do not yet fear the LORD God." [31](The flax and the barley were ruined, for the barley was in the ear and the flax was in bud. [32]But the wheat and the spelt were not ruined, for they are late in coming up.) [33]So Moses went out of the city from Pharaoh, and stretched out his hands to the LORD; and the thunder and the hail ceased, and the rain no longer poured upon the earth. [34]But when Pharaoh saw that the rain and the hail and the thunder had

ceased, he sinned yet again, and hardened his heart, he and his servants. 35So the heart of Pharaoh was hardened, and he did not let the sons of Israel go; as the LORD had spoken through Moses.

10 Then the LORD said to Moses, "Go in to Pharaoh; for I have hardened his heart and the heart of his servants, that I may show these signs of mine among them, 2and that you may tell in the hearing of your son and of your son's son how I have made sport of the Egyptians and what signs I have done among them; that you may know that I am the LORD."

3So Moses and Aaron went in to Pharaoh, and said to him, "Thus says the LORD, the God of the Hebrews, 'How long will you refuse to humble yourself before me? Let my people go, that they may serve me. 4For if you refuse to let my people go, behold, tomorrow I will bring locusts into your country, 5and they shall cover the face of the land, so that no one can see the land; and they shall eat what is left to you after the hail, and they shall eat every tree of yours which grows in the field, 6and they shall fill your houses, and the houses of all your servants and of all the Egyptians; as neither your fathers nor your grandfathers have seen, from the day they came on earth to this day.'" Then he turned and went out from Pharaoh.

7And Pharaoh's servants said to him, "How long shall this man be a snare to us? Let the men go, that they may serve the LORD their God; do you not yet understand that Egypt is ruined?" 8So Moses and Aaron were brought back to Pharaoh; and he said to them, "Go, serve the LORD your God; but who are to go?" 9And Moses said, "We will go with our young and our old; we will go with our sons and daughters and with our flocks and herds, for we must hold a feast to the LORD." 10And he said to them, "The LORD be with you, if ever I let you and your little ones go! Look, you have some evil purpose in mind. 11No! Go, the men among you, and serve the LORD, for that is what you desire." And they were driven out from Pharaoh's presence.

12Then the LORD said to Moses, "Stretch out your hand over the land of Egypt for the locusts, that they may come upon the land of Egypt, and eat every plant in the land, all that the hail has left." 13So Moses stretched forth his rod over the land of Egypt, and the LORD brought an east wind upon the land all that day and all that night; and when it was morning the east wind had brought the locusts. 14And the locusts came up over all the land of Egypt, and settled on the whole country of Egypt, such a dense swarm of locusts as had never been before, nor ever shall be again. 15For they covered the face of the whole land, so that the land was darkened, and they ate all the plants in the land and all the fruit of the trees which the hail had left; not a green thing remained, neither tree nor plant of the field, through all the land of Egypt. 16Then Pharaoh called Moses and Aaron in haste, and said, "I have sinned against the LORD your God, and against you. 17Now therefore, forgive my sin, I beg you, only this once, and entreat the LORD your God only to remove this death from me." 18So he went out from Pharaoh, and entreated the LORD. 19And the LORD turned a very strong west wind, which lifted the locusts and drove them into the Red Sea; not a single locust was left in all the country of Egypt. 20But the LORD hardened Pharaoh's heart, and he did not let the children of Israel go.

21Then the LORD said to Moses, "Stretch out your hand toward heaven that there may be darkness over the land of Egypt, a darkness to be felt." 22So Moses stretched out his hand toward heaven, and there was thick darkness in all the land of Egypt three days; 23they did not see one another, nor did any rise from his place for three days; but all the sons of Israel had light where they dwelt. 24Then Pharaoh called Moses, and said, "Go, serve the LORD; your children also may go with you; only let your flocks and your herds remain behind." 25But Moses said, "You must also let us have sacrifices and burnt offerings, that we may sacrifice to the LORD our

God. 26Our cattle also must go with us; not a hoof shall be left behind, for we must take of them to serve the LORD our God, and we do not know with what we must serve the LORD until we arrive there." 27But the LORD hardened Pharaoh's heart, and he would not let them go. 28Then Pharaoh said to him, "Get away from me; take heed to yourself; never see my face again; for in the day you see my face you shall die." 29Moses said, "As you say! I will not see your face again."

A Psalm of David.

PSALM 24 [23]

The earth is the LORD's and the
 fulness thereof,
 the world and those who dwell therein;
2for he has founded it upon the seas,
 and established it upon the rivers.

3Who shall ascend the hill of the LORD?
 And who shall stand in his holy place?
4He who has clean hands and a pure heart,
 who does not lift up his soul to what
 is false,
 and does not swear deceitfully.
5He will receive blessing from the LORD,
 and vindication from the God of
 his salvation.
6Such is the generation of those who
 seek him,
 who seek the face of the God of Jacob.
Selah

7Lift up your heads, O gates!
 and be lifted up, O ancient doors!
 that the King of glory may come in.
8Who is the King of glory?
 The LORD, strong and mighty,
 the LORD, mighty in battle!
9Lift up your heads, O gates!
 and be lifted up, O ancient doors!
 that the King of glory may come in.
10Who is this King of glory?
 The LORD of hosts,
 he is the King of glory! *Selah*

MATTHEW 18

15"If your brother sins against you, go and tell him his fault, between you and him alone. If he listens to you, you have gained your brother. 16But if he does not listen, take one or two others along with you, that every word may be confirmed by the evidence of two or three witnesses. 17If he refuses to listen to them, tell it to the Church; and if he refuses to listen even to the Church, let him be to you as a Gentile and a tax collector. 18Truly, I say to you, whatever you bind on earth shall be bound in heaven, and whatever you loose on earth shall be loosed in heaven. 19Again I say to you, if two of you agree on earth about anything they ask, it will be done for them by my Father in heaven. 20For where two or three are gathered in my name, there am I in the midst of them."

21Then Peter came up and said to him, "Lord, how often shall my brother sin against me, and I forgive him? As many as seven times?" 22Jesus said to him, "I do not say to you seven times, but seventy times seven.

23"Therefore the kingdom of heaven may be compared to a king who wished to settle accounts with his servants. 24When he began the reckoning, one was brought to him who owed him ten thousand talents; 25and as he could not pay, his lord ordered him to be sold, with his wife and children and all that he had, and payment to be made. 26So the servant fell on his knees, imploring him, 'Lord, have patience with me, and I will pay you everything.' 27And out of pity for him the lord of that servant released him and forgave him the debt. 28But that same servant, as he went out, came upon one of his fellow servants who owed him a hundred denarii; and seizing him by the throat he said, 'Pay what you owe.' 29So his fellow servant fell down and pleaded with him, 'Have patience with me, and I will pay you.' 30He refused and went and put him in prison till he should pay the debt. 31When his fellow servants saw what had taken place, they were greatly distressed, and they went and reported to their lord all that had taken place. [32]Then his lord summoned him and said to him, 'You wicked servant! I forgave you all that debt because you pleaded with me; [33]and should not you have had mercy on your fellow servant, as I had mercy on you?' [34]And in anger his lord delivered him to the jailers, till he should pay all his debt. [35]So also my heavenly Father will do to every one of you, if you do not forgive your brother from your heart."

REFLECTION

In his model prayer, Jesus taught his disciples to ask for God's forgiveness, but with a condition—"as we forgive our debtors" (Mt 6:12; NAB). Peter wants to know how often he must forgive his brother (what might Peter's brother Andrew have been thinking at such a question?). Jesus tells a story about a debtor and his creditor. In the language of the Jews, the word for *debt* was the same as the word for *sin*, so financial debt became the perfect metaphor for sins accumulating on a divine balance sheet. The debtor, who owes a fortune, begs for patience and receives remarkable mercy, but then he soon refuses to give mercy to another who owes him much less than he himself was forgiven. The point is clear: the merciful receive mercy. When it comes to our own balance sheet before God, we need to practice all the mercy we can, for we will all need God's mercy. In practicing mercy to others, we will learn anew the great depth of God's merciful love. With whom can you share God's great mercy and forgiveness today?

January 28

EXODUS 11

The LORD said to Moses, "Yet one plague more I will bring upon Pharaoh and upon Egypt; afterwards he will let you go from here; when he lets you go, he will drive you away completely. [2]Speak now in the hearing of the people, that they ask, every man of his neighbor and every woman of her neighbor, jewelry of silver and of gold." [3]And the LORD gave the people favor in the sight of the Egyptians. Moreover, the man Moses was very great in the land of Egypt, in the sight of Pharaoh's servants and in the sight of the people.

[4]And Moses said, "Thus says the LORD: About midnight I will go forth in the midst of Egypt; [5]and all the first-born in the land of Egypt shall die, from the first-born of Pharaoh who sits upon his throne, even to the first-born of the maidservant who is behind the mill; and all the first-born of the cattle. [6]And there shall be a great cry throughout all the land of Egypt, such as there has never been, nor ever shall be again. [7]But against any of the sons of Israel, either man or beast, not a dog shall growl; that you may know that the LORD makes a distinction between the Egyptians and Israel. [8]And all these your servants shall come down to me, and bow down to me, saying, 'Get you out, and all the people who follow you.' And after that I will go out." And he went out from Pharaoh in hot anger. [9]Then the LORD said to Moses, "Pharaoh will not listen to you; that my wonders may be multiplied in the land of Egypt."

[10]Moses and Aaron did all these wonders before Pharaoh; and the LORD hardened Pharaoh's heart, and he did not let the sons of Israel go out of his land.

12 The LORD said to Moses and Aaron in the land of Egypt, [2]"This month shall be for you the beginning of months; it shall be the first month of the year for you. [3]Tell all the congregation of Israel that on the tenth day of this month they shall take every man a lamb according to their fathers' houses, a lamb for a household; [4]and if the household is too small for a lamb, then a man and his neighbor next to his house shall take according to the number of persons; according to what each can eat you shall make your count for the lamb. [5]Your lamb shall be without blemish, a male a year old; you shall take it from the sheep or from the goats; 6and you shall keep it until the fourteenth day of this month, when the whole assembly of the congregation of Israel shall kill their lambs in the evening. 7Then they shall take some of the blood, and put it on the two doorposts and the lintel of the houses in which they eat them. 8They shall eat the flesh that night, roasted; with unleavened bread and bitter herbs they shall eat it. 9Do not eat any of it raw or boiled with water, but roasted, its head with its legs and its inner parts. 10And you shall let none of it remain until the morning, anything that remains until the morning you shall burn. 11In this manner you shall eat it: your loins girded, your sandals on your feet, and your staff in your hand; and you shall eat it in haste. It is the LORD's Passover. 12For I will pass through the land of Egypt that night, and I will strike all the first-born in the land of Egypt, both man and beast; and on all the gods of Egypt I will execute judgments: I am the LORD. 13The blood shall be a sign for you, upon the houses where you are; and when I see the blood, I will pass over you, and no plague shall fall upon you to destroy you, when I strike the land of Egypt.

14"This day shall be for you a memorial day, and you shall keep it as a feast to the LORD; throughout your generations you shall observe it as an ordinance for ever. 15Seven days you shall eat unleavened bread; on the first day you shall put away leaven out of your houses, for if any one eats what is leavened, from the first day until the seventh day, that person shall be cut off from Israel. 16On the first day you shall hold a holy assembly, and on the seventh day a holy assembly; no work shall be done on those days; but what every one must eat, that only may be prepared by you. 17And you shall observe the feast of unleavened bread, for on this very day I brought your hosts out of the land of Egypt: therefore you shall observe this day, throughout your generations, as an ordinance for ever. 18In the first month, on the fourteenth day of the month at evening, you shall eat unleavened bread, and so until the twenty-first day of the month at evening. 19For seven days no leaven shall be found in your houses; for if any one eats what is leavened, that person shall be cut off from the congregation of Israel, whether he is a sojourner or a native of the land. 20You shall eat nothing leavened; in all your dwellings you shall eat unleavened bread."

21Then Moses called all the elders of Israel, and said to them, "Select lambs for yourselves according to your families, and kill the Passover lamb. 22Take a bunch of hyssop and dip it in the blood which is in the basin, and touch the lintel and the two doorposts with the blood which is in the basin; and none of you shall go out of the door of his house until the morning. 23For the LORD will pass through to slay the Egyptians; and when he sees the blood on the lintel and on the two doorposts, the LORD will pass over the door, and will not allow the destroyer to enter your houses to slay you. 24You shall observe this rite as an ordinance for you and for your sons for ever. 25And when you come to the land which the LORD will give you, as he has promised, you shall keep this service. 26And when your children say to you, 'What do you mean by this service?' 27you shall say, 'It is the sacrifice of the LORD's Passover, for he passed over the houses of the sons of Israel in Egypt, when he slew the Egyptians but spared our houses.'" And the people bowed their heads and worshiped.

28Then the sons of Israel went and did so; as the LORD had commanded Moses and Aaron, so they did.

29At midnight the LORD struck all the first-born in the land of Egypt, from the first-born of Pharaoh who sat on his throne to the first-born of the captive who was in the dungeon, and all the first-born of the cattle. 30And Pharaoh rose up in the night, he, and all his servants, and all the Egyptians; and there was a great cry in Egypt, for there was not a house where one was not dead. 31And he summoned Moses and Aaron by night, and said, "Rise up, go forth from among my people, both you and the sons of Israel; and

go, serve the LORD, as you have said. 32Take
your flocks and your herds, as you have said,
and be gone; and bless me also!"
33And the Egyptians were urgent with the
people, to send them out of the land in haste;
for they said, "We are all dead men." 34So
the people took their dough before it was
leavened, their kneading bowls being bound
up in their mantles on their shoulders. 35The
sons of Israel had also done as Moses told
them, for they had asked of the Egyptians
jewelry of silver and of gold, and clothing;
36and the LORD had given the people favor
in the sight of the Egyptians, so that they
let them have what they asked. Thus they
despoiled the Egyptians.
37And the sons of Israel journeyed from
Ram′eses to Succoth, about six hundred
thousand men on foot, besides women and
children. 38A mixed multitude also went
up with them, and very many cattle, both
flocks and herds. 39And they baked unleavened cakes of the dough which they
had brought out of Egypt, for it was not
leavened, because they were thrust out of
Egypt and could not tarry, neither had they
prepared for themselves any provisions.
40The time that the sons of Israel dwelt in
Egypt was four hundred and thirty years.
41And at the end of four hundred and thirty
years, on that very day, all the hosts of the
LORD went out from the land of Egypt. 42It
was a night of watching by the LORD, to
bring them out of the land of Egypt; so this
same night is a night of watching kept to the
LORD by all the sons of Israel throughout
their generations.
43And the LORD said to Moses and Aaron,
"This is the ordinance of the Passover: no
foreigner shall eat of it; 44but every slave
that is bought for money may eat of it after
you have circumcised him. 45No sojourner
or hired servant may eat of it. 46In one
house shall it be eaten; you shall not carry
forth any of the flesh outside the house; and
you shall not break a bone of it. 47All the
congregation of Israel shall keep it. 48And
when a stranger shall sojourn with you
and would keep the Passover to the LORD,
let all his males be circumcised, then he
may come near and keep it; he shall be as
a native of the land. But no uncircumcised
person shall eat of it. 49There shall be one
law for the native and for the stranger who
sojourns among you."
50Thus did all the sons of Israel; as the
LORD commanded Moses and Aaron, so
they did. 51And on that very day the LORD
brought the sons of Israel out of the land of
Egypt by their hosts.

A Psalm of David.

PSALM 25 [24]

To you, O LORD, I lift up my soul.
2O my God, in you I trust,
let me not be put to shame;
let not my enemies exult over me.
3Yes, let none that wait for you be put
to shame;
let them be ashamed who are wantonly
treacherous.

4Make me to know your ways, O LORD;
teach me your paths.
5Lead me in your truth, and teach me,
for you are the God of my salvation;
for you I wait all the day long.

6Be mindful of your compassion, O LORD,
and of your merciful love,
for they have been from of old.
7Remember not the sins of my youth, or
my transgressions;
according to your mercy remember me,
for your goodness' sake, O LORD!

8Good and upright is the LORD;
therefore he instructs sinners in the way.
9He leads the humble in what is right,
and teaches the humble his way.
10All the paths of the LORD are mercy
and faithfulness,
for those who keep his covenant and
his testimonies.

11For your name's sake, O LORD,
pardon my guilt, for it is great.

12Who is the man that fears the LORD?
Him will he instruct in the way that he should choose.
13He himself shall abide in prosperity,
and his children shall possess the land.
14The friendship of the LORD is for those who fear him,
and he makes known to them his covenant.
15My eyes are ever toward the LORD,
for he will pluck my feet out of the net.

16Turn to me, and be gracious to me;
for I am lonely and afflicted.
17Relieve the troubles of my heart,
and bring me out of my distresses.
18Consider my affliction and my trouble,
and forgive all my sins.

19Consider how many are my foes,
and with what violent hatred they hate me.
20Oh, guard my life, and deliver me;
let me not be put to shame, for I take refuge in you.
21May integrity and uprightness preserve me,
for I wait for you.

22Redeem Israel, O God,
out of all his troubles.

MATTHEW 19

Now when Jesus had finished these sayings, he went away from Galilee and entered the region of Judea beyond the Jordan;
2and large crowds followed him, and he healed them there.

3And Pharisees came up to him and tested him by asking, "Is it lawful to divorce one's wife for any cause?" 4He answered, "Have you not read that he who made them from the beginning made them male and female,
5and said, 'For this reason a man shall leave his father and mother and be joined to his wife, and the two shall become one'? 6So they are no longer two but one. What therefore God has joined together, let no man put asunder." 7They said to him, "Why then did Moses command one to give a certificate of divorce, and to put her away?" 8He said to them, "For your hardness of heart Moses allowed you to divorce your wives, but from the beginning it was not so. 9And I say to you: whoever divorces his wife, except for unchastity, and marries another, commits adultery; and he who marries a divorced woman, commits adultery."

10The disciples said to him, "If such is the case of a man with his wife, it is not expedient to marry." 11But he said to them, "Not all men can receive this precept, but only those to whom it is given. 12For there are eunuchs who have been so from birth, and there are eunuchs who have been made eunuchs by men, and there are eunuchs who have made themselves eunuchs for the sake of the kingdom of heaven. He who is able to receive this, let him receive it."

13Then children were brought to him that he might lay his hands on them and pray. The disciples rebuked the people; 14but Jesus said, "Let the children come to me, and do not hinder them; for to such belongs the kingdom of heaven." 15And he laid his hands on them and went away.

REFLECTION

In order to be delivered from the angel of death and to make their exodus out of Egypt, Israel must offer up a lamb for the Passover. Why does a good, holy, and spiritual God demand bloody animal sacrifice, especially of a gentle lamb? Moses Maimonides, the greatest Jewish sage of the Middle Ages, noted that the key backdrop for the Lord's Passover liturgy is Egypt's idolatry. Among the many gods of their pantheon, the Egyptians worshipped sheep as gods. Thus for the Israelites to break from Egypt, God demanded them to sacrifice a lamb in order to show that the so-called gods of Egypt are no gods at all. More than an act of loyalty, it was an act of liberation, as Israel learned to trust the Lord, and not the Egyptian superstition that had held them in chains as binding as their physical bonds. Putting the blood on the doorposts made their loyalty and worship of the God of Jacob public. God is not satisfied simply with private worship, but also calls for a public profession of faith in him. What keeps you from giving public witness to God?

January 29

EXODUS 13

The LORD said to Moses, [2]"Con-
secrate to me all the first-born; whatever is the first to open the womb among the sons of Israel, both of man and of beast, is mine."
[3]And Moses said to the people, "Remember
this day, in which you came out from Egypt, out of the house of bondage, for by strength of hand the LORD brought you out from this place; no leavened bread shall be eaten.
[4]This day you are to go forth, in the month of
Abib. [5]And when the LORD brings you into
the land of the Canaanites, the Hittites, the Am'orites, the Hi'vites, and the Jeb'usites, which he swore to your fathers to give you, a land flowing with milk and honey, you
shall keep this service in this month. [6]Seven
days you shall eat unleavened bread, and on the seventh day there shall be a feast to
the LORD. [7]Unleavened bread shall be eaten
for seven days; no leavened bread shall be seen with you, and no leaven shall be seen
with you in all your territory. [8]And you shall
tell your son on that day, 'It is because of what the LORD did for me when I came out
of Egypt.' [9]And it shall be to you as a sign
on your hand and as a memorial between your eyes, that the law of the LORD may be in your mouth; for with a strong hand the
LORD has brought you out of Egypt. [10]You
shall therefore keep this ordinance at its appointed time from year to year.

[11]"And when the LORD brings you into the
land of the Canaanites, as he swore to you and
your fathers, and shall give it to you, [12]you
shall set apart to the LORD all that first opens the womb. All the firstlings of your cattle that
are males shall be the LORD's. [13]Every firstling
of a donkey you shall redeem with a lamb, or if you will not redeem it you shall break its neck. Every first-born of man among your
sons you shall redeem. [14]And when in time
to come your son asks you, 'What does this mean?' you shall say to him, 'By strength of hand the LORD brought us out of Egypt, from
the house of bondage. [15]For when Pharaoh
stubbornly refused to let us go, the LORD slew all the first-born in the land of Egypt, both the first-born of man and the first-born of cattle. Therefore I sacrifice to the LORD all the males that first open the womb; but
all the first-born of my sons I redeem.' [16]It
shall be as a mark on your hand or frontlets between your eyes; for by a strong hand the LORD brought us out of Egypt."
[17]When Pharaoh let the people go, God
did not lead them by way of the land of the Philis'tines, although that was near; for God said, "Lest the people repent when they see
war, and return to Egypt." [18]But God led the
people round by the way of the wilderness toward the Red Sea. And the sons of Israel went up out of the land of Egypt equipped
for battle. [19]And Moses took the bones of
Joseph with him; for Joseph had solemnly sworn the sons of Israel, saying, "God will visit you; then you must carry my bones
with you from here." [20]And they moved on
from Succoth, and encamped at Etham, on
the edge of the wilderness. [21]And the LORD
went before them by day in a pillar of cloud to lead them along the way, and by night in a pillar of fire to give them light, that they
might travel by day and by night; [22]the pillar
of cloud by day and the pillar of fire by night did not depart from before the people.
14 Then the LORD said to Moses, [2]"Tell
the sons of Israel to turn back and encamp in front of Piha-hi'roth, between Migdol and the sea, in front of Ba'al-ze'phon; you shall encamp over against it,
by the sea. [3]For Pharaoh will say of the sons

of Israel, 'They are entangled in the land;
the wilderness has shut them in.' 4And I will
harden Pharaoh's heart, and he will pursue
them and I will get glory over Pharaoh and
all his host; and the Egyptians shall know
that I am the LORD." And they did so.

5When the king of Egypt was told that the
people had fled, the mind of Pharaoh and his
servants was changed toward the people, and
they said, "What is this we have done, that
we have let Israel go from serving us?" 6So
he made ready his chariot and took his army
with him, 7and took six hundred picked
chariots and all the other chariots of Egypt
with officers over all of them. 8And the LORD
hardened the heart of Pharaoh king of Egypt
and he pursued the sons of Israel as they
went forth defiantly. 9The Egyptians pursued
them, all Pharaoh's horses and chariots and
his horsemen and his army, and overtook
them encamped at the sea, by Piha-hi′roth,
in front of Ba′al-ze′phon.

10When Pharaoh drew near, the sons of
Israel lifted up their eyes, and behold, the
Egyptians were marching after them; and
they were in great fear. And the sons of
Israel cried out to the LORD; 11and they said
to Moses, "Is it because there are no graves
in Egypt that you have taken us away to
die in the wilderness? What have you done
to us, in bringing us out of Egypt? 12Is not
this what we said to you in Egypt, 'Let us
alone and let us serve the Egyptians'? For it
would have been better for us to serve the
Egyptians than to die in the wilderness."
13And Moses said to the people, "Fear not,
stand firm, and see the salvation of the
LORD, which he will work for you today;
for the Egyptians whom you see today,
you shall never see again. 14The LORD
will fight for you, and you have only to be
still." 15The LORD said to Moses, "Why do
you cry to me? Tell the sons of Israel to go
forward. 16Lift up your rod, and stretch out
your hand over the sea and divide it, that
the sons of Israel may go on dry ground
through the sea. 17And I will harden the
hearts of the Egyptians so that they shall
go in after them, and I will get glory over
Pharaoh and all his host, his chariots, and
his horsemen. 18And the Egyptians shall
know that I am the LORD, when I have
gotten glory over Pharaoh, his chariots,
and his horsemen."

19Then the angel of God who went before
the host of Israel moved and went behind
them; and the pillar of cloud moved from
before them and stood behind them,
20coming between the host of Egypt and the
host of Israel. And there was the cloud and
the darkness; and the night passed without
one coming near the other all night.

21Then Moses stretched out his hand over
the sea; and the LORD drove the sea back by a
strong east wind all night, and made the sea
dry land, and the waters were divided. 22And
the sons of Israel went into the midst of the
sea on dry ground, the waters being a wall to
them on their right hand and on their left.
23The Egyptians pursued, and went in after
them into the midst of the sea, all Pharaoh's
horses, his chariots, and his horsemen.
24And in the morning watch the LORD in the
pillar of fire and of cloud looked down upon
the host of the Egyptians, and discomfited
the host of the Egyptians, 25clogging their
chariot wheels so that they drove heavily;
and the Egyptians said, "Let us flee from
before Israel; for the LORD fights for them
against the Egyptians."

26Then the LORD said to Moses, "Stretch
out your hand over the sea, that the water
may come back upon the Egyptians, upon
their chariots, and upon their horsemen."
27So Moses stretched forth his hand over
the sea, and the sea returned to its usual
flow when the morning appeared; and
the Egyptians fled into it, and the LORD
routed the Egyptians in the midst of the
sea. 28The waters returned and covered the
chariots and the horsemen and all the host
of Pharaoh that had followed them into the
sea; not so much as one of them remained.
29But the sons of Israel walked on dry
ground through the sea, the waters being
a wall to them on their right hand and on
their left.

30Thus the LORD saved Israel that day
from the hand of the Egyptians; and Israel
saw the Egyptians dead upon the seashore.

31 And Israel saw the great work which the LORD did against the Egyptians, and the people feared the LORD; and they believed in the LORD and in his servant Moses.

15 Then Moses and the sons of Israel sang this song to the LORD, saying,
"I will sing to the Lord, for he has
triumphed gloriously;
the horse and his rider he has thrown
into the sea.
2 The Lord is my strength and my song,
and he has become my salvation;
this is my God, and I will praise him,
my father's God, and I will exalt him.
3 The LORD is a man of war;
the LORD is his name.
4 "Pharaoh's chariots and his host he cast into
the sea;
and his picked officers are sunk in the
Red Sea.
5 The floods cover them;
they went down into the depths like
a stone.
6 Your right hand, O LORD, glorious
in power,
your right hand, O LORD, shatters
the enemy.
7 In the greatness of your majesty you
overthrow your adversaries;
you send forth your fury, it consumes
them like stubble.
8 At the blast of your nostrils the waters
piled up,
the floods stood up in a heap;
the deeps congealed in the heart of the sea.
9 The enemy said, 'I will pursue, I will overtake,
I will divide the spoil, my desire shall
have its fill of them.
I will draw my sword, my hand shall
destroy them.'
10 You blew with your wind, the sea
covered them;
they sank as lead in the mighty waters.

11 "Who is like you, O LORD, among the gods?
Who is like you, majestic in holiness,
terrible in glorious deeds, doing wonders?
12 You stretched out your right hand,
the earth swallowed them.
13 "You have led in your merciful love the
people whom you have redeemed,
you have guided them by your strength
to your holy abode.
14 The peoples have heard, they tremble;
pangs have seized on the inhabitants
of Philistia.
15 Now are the chiefs of Edom dismayed;
the leaders of Moab, trembling seizes them;
all the inhabitants of Canaan have
melted away.
16 Terror and dread fall upon them;
because of the greatness of your arm,
they are as still as a stone,
till your people, O LORD, pass by,
till the people pass by whom you have
purchased.
17 You will bring them in, and plant them on
your own mountain,
the place, O LORD, which you have made
for your abode,
the sanctuary, O LORD, which your hands
have established.
18 The LORD will reign for ever and ever."
19 For when the horses of Pharaoh with
his chariots and his horsemen went into
the sea, the LORD brought back the waters
of the sea upon them; but the sons of
Israel walked on dry ground in the midst
of the sea. 20 Then Miriam, the prophetess,
the sister of Aaron, took a timbrel in her
hand; and all the women went out after
her with timbrels and dancing. 21 And
Miriam sang to them:
"Sing to the Lord, for he has triumphed
gloriously;
the horse and his rider he has thrown into
the sea."

A Psalm of David.

PSALM 26 [25]

Vindicate me, O LORD,
for I have walked in my integrity,
and I have trusted in the LORD
without wavering.
2 Prove me, O LORD, and try me;
test my heart and my mind.

3For your mercy is before my eyes,
and I walk in faithfulness to you.
4I do not sit with false men,
nor do I consort with dissemblers;
5I hate the company of evildoers,
and I will not sit with the wicked.
6I wash my hands in innocence,
and go about your altar, O LORD,
7singing aloud a song of thanksgiving,
and telling all your wondrous deeds.
8O LORD, I love the habitation of your house,
and the place where your glory dwells.
9Sweep me not away with sinners,
nor my life with bloodthirsty men,
10men in whose hands are evil devices,
and whose right hands are full of bribes.
11But as for me, I walk in my integrity;
redeem me, and have mercy on me.
12My foot stands on level ground;
in the great congregation I will bless
the LORD.

MATTHEW 19

16And behold, one came up to
him, saying, "Teacher, what
good deed must I do, to have
eternal life?" 17And he said to him,
"Why do you ask me about what is
good? One there is who is good. If you would
enter life, keep the commandments." 18He
said to him, "Which?" And Jesus said, "You
shall not kill, You shall not commit adultery,
You shall not steal, You shall not bear false
witness, 19Honor your father and mother,
and, You shall love your neighbor as yourself."
20The young man said to him, "All these I have
observed; what do I still lack?" 21Jesus said to
him, "If you would be perfect, go, sell what
you possess and give to the poor, and you will
have treasure in heaven; and come, follow me."
22When the young man heard this he went
away sorrowful; for he had great possessions.
23And Jesus said to his disciples, "Truly, I
say to you, it will be hard for a rich man to
enter the kingdom of heaven. 24Again I tell
you, it is easier for a camel to go through
the eye of a needle than for a rich man
to enter the kingdom of God." 25When
the disciples heard this they were greatly
astonished, saying, "Who then can be
saved?" 26But Jesus looked at them and said
to them, "With men this is impossible, but
with God all things are possible." 27Then
Peter said in reply, "Behold, we have left
everything and followed you. What then
shall we have?" 28Jesus said to them, "Truly,
I say to you, in the new world, when the
Son of man shall sit on his glorious throne,
you who have followed me will also sit on
twelve thrones, judging the twelve tribes of
Israel. 29And every one who has left houses
or brothers or sisters or father or mother or
children or lands, for my name's sake, will
receive a hundredfold, and inherit eternal
life. 30But many that are first will be last,
and the last first."

REFLECTION

Jesus is asked the most important question anyone could ask: What must we do to enter into eternal life? Notice that he does not say all one has to do is believe. Indeed he never mentions faith. Rather, it is the observance of the commandments that stands alone here in Jesus's teaching on salvation. The Jews held that the Ten Commandments were divided in the two tablets Moses gave: the commandments regarding God were on the first tablet, and those commandments regarding justice to neighbor were on the second tablet. The rich man had fulfilled the commandments regarding his neighbor, the second tablet. When he asks what he still lacks, Jesus tells him to sell his possessions and come follow him. In other words, Jesus is saying that his lack of following the first tablet—the justice owed God—can be fulfilled if he follows Jesus. Clearly Jesus sees service to him as service to God. That we too may enter into eternal life, we need to ask ourselves: What must I do to enter into the life God wants for me?

January 30

EXODUS 15

22Then Moses led Israel onward
from the Red Sea, and they went
into the wilderness of Shur; they went
three days in the wilderness and found
no water. 23When they came to Marah, they
could not drink the water of Marah because
it was bitter; therefore it was named Marah.
24And the people murmured against Moses,
saying, "What shall we drink?" 25And he
cried to the LORD; and the LORD showed
him a tree, and he threw it into the water,
and the water became sweet.

There the LORD made for them a statute
and an ordinance and there he tested them,
26saying, "If you will diligently listen to the
voice of the LORD your God, and do that
which is right in his eyes, and give heed
to his commandments and keep all his
statutes, I will put none of the diseases upon
you which I put upon the Egyptians; for I
am the LORD, your healer."

27Then they came to E'lim, where there
were twelve springs of water and seventy
palm trees; and they encamped there by
the water.

16 They set out from E'lim, and all the
congregation of the sons of Israel
came to the wilderness of Sin, which is
between Elim and Sinai, on the fifteenth
day of the second month after they had
departed from the land of Egypt. 2And the
whole congregation of the sons of Israel
murmured against Moses and Aaron in
the wilderness, 3and said to them, "Would
that we had died by the hand of the LORD
in the land of Egypt, when we sat by the
fleshpots and ate bread to the full; for you
have brought us out into this wilderness
to kill this whole assembly with hunger."

4Then the LORD said to Moses, "Behold,
I will rain bread from heaven for you; and
the people shall go out and gather a day's
portion every day, that I may test them,
whether they will walk in my law or not.
5On the sixth day, when they prepare what
they bring in, it will be twice as much as
they gather daily." 6So Moses and Aaron
said to all the sons of Israel, "At evening
you shall know that it was the LORD who
brought you out of the land of Egypt, 7and
in the morning you shall see the glory
of the LORD, because he has heard your
murmurings against the LORD. For what
are we, that you murmur against us?"
8And Moses said, "When the LORD gives
you in the evening flesh to eat and in the
morning bread to the full, because the
LORD has heard your murmurings which
you murmur against him—what are we?
Your murmurings are not against us but
against the LORD."

9And Moses said to Aaron, "Say to the
whole congregation of the sons of Israel,
'Come near before the LORD, for he has
heard your murmurings.'" 10And as Aaron
spoke to the whole congregation of the sons
of Israel, they looked toward the wilderness,
and behold, the glory of the LORD appeared
in the cloud. 11And the LORD said to Moses,
12"I have heard the murmurings of the sons
of Israel; say to them, 'At twilight you shall
eat flesh, and in the morning you shall be
filled with bread; then you shall know that I
am the LORD your God.'"

13In the evening quails came up and
covered the camp; and in the morning
dew lay round about the camp. 14And
when the dew had gone up, there was on
the face of the wilderness a fine, flake-like
thing, fine as hoarfrost on the ground.
15When the sons of Israel saw it, they said
to one another, "What is it?" For they did
not know what it was. And Moses said to
them, "It is the bread which the LORD has
given you to eat. 16This is what the LORD
has commanded: 'Gather of it, every man
of you, as much as he can eat; you shall take
an omer apiece, according to the number
of the persons whom each of you has in
his tent.'" 17And the sons of Israel did so;
they gathered, some more, some less. 18But
when they measured it with an omer, he
that gathered much had nothing over, and
he that gathered little had no lack; each

gathered according to what he could eat.
[19]And Moses said to them, "Let no man
leave any of it till the morning." [20]But they
did not listen to Moses; some left part of
it till the morning, and it bred worms and
became foul; and Moses was angry with
them. [21]Morning by morning they gathered
it, each as much as he could eat; but when
the sun grew hot, it melted.

[22]On the sixth day they gathered twice
as much bread, two omers apiece; and
when all the leaders of the congregation
came and told Moses, [23]he said to them,
"This is what the LORD has commanded:
'Tomorrow is a day of solemn rest, a holy
sabbath to the LORD; bake what you will
bake and boil what you will boil, and all
that is left over lay by to be kept till the
morning.'" [24]So they laid it by till the
morning, as Moses bade them; and it did
not become foul, and there were no worms
in it. [25]Moses said, "Eat it today, for today
is a sabbath to the LORD; today you will
not find it in the field. [26]Six days you shall
gather it; but on the seventh day, which
is a sabbath, there will be none." [27]On the
seventh day some of the people went out
to gather, and they found none. [28]And the
LORD said to Moses, "How long do you
refuse to keep my commandments and
my laws? [29]See! The LORD has given you
the sabbath, therefore on the sixth day he
gives you bread for two days; remain every
man of you in his place, let no man go out
of his place on the seventh day." [30]So the
people rested on the seventh day.

[31]Now the house of Israel called its name
manna; it was like coriander seed, white,
and the taste of it was like wafers made with
honey. [32]And Moses said, "This is what the
LORD has commanded: 'Let an omer of it
be kept throughout your generations, that
they may see the bread with which I fed
you in the wilderness, when I brought you
out of the land of Egypt.'" [33]And Moses said
to Aaron, "Take a jar, and put an omer of
manna in it, and place it before the LORD,
to be kept throughout your generations."
[34]As the LORD commanded Moses, so
Aaron placed it before the covenant, to be
kept. [35]And the sons of Israel ate the manna
forty years, till they came to a habitable
land; they ate the manna, till they came
to the border of the land of Canaan. [36](An
omer is the tenth part of an ephah.)

17 All the congregation of the sons of
Israel moved on from the wilderness of Sin by stages, according to the
commandment of the LORD, and camped
at Reph′idim; but there was no water for
the people to drink. [2]Therefore the people
found fault with Moses, and said, "Give us
water to drink." And Moses said to them,
"Why do you find fault with me? Why do
you put the LORD to the test?" [3]But the
people thirsted there for water, and the
people murmured against Moses, and said,
"Why did you bring us up out of Egypt, to
kill us and our children and our cattle with
thirst?" [4]So Moses cried to the LORD, "What
shall I do with this people? They are almost
ready to stone me." [5]And the LORD said to
Moses, "Pass on before the people, taking
with you some of the elders of Israel; and
take in your hand the rod with which you
struck the Nile, and go. [6]Behold, I will stand
before you there on the rock at Horeb; and
you shall strike the rock, and water shall
come out of it, that the people may drink."
And Moses did so, in the sight of the elders
of Israel. [7]And he called the name of the
place Massah and Mer′ibah, because of
the fault-finding of the sons of Israel, and
because they put the LORD to the test by
saying, "Is the LORD among us or not?"

[8]Then came Am′alek and fought with
Israel at Reph′idim. [9]And Moses said to
Joshua, "Choose for us men, and go out,
fight with Am′alek; tomorrow I will stand
on the top of the hill with the rod of God
in my hand." [10]So Joshua did as Moses told
him, and fought with Am′alek; and Moses,
Aaron, and Hur went up to the top of the
hill. [11]Whenever Moses held up his hand,
Israel prevailed; and whenever he lowered
his hand, Am′alek prevailed. [12]But Moses'
hands grew weary; so they took a stone and
put it under him, and he sat upon it, and
Aaron and Hur held up his hands, one on
one side, and the other on the other side; so

his hands were steady until the going down
of the sun. 13And Joshua mowed down
Am′alek and his people with the edge of
the sword.
14And the LORD said to Moses, "Write
this as a memorial in a book and recite
it in the ears of Joshua, that I will utterly
blot out the remembrance of Am′alek
from under heaven." 15And Moses built an
altar and called the name of it, The LORD
is my banner, 16saying, "A hand upon the
banner of the LORD! The LORD will have
war with Am′alek from generation to
generation."

A Psalm of David.

PSALM 27 [26]

The LORD is my light and my salvation;
whom shall I fear?
The LORD is the stronghold of my life;
of whom shall I be afraid?

2When evildoers assail me,
to devour my flesh,
my adversaries and foes,
they shall stumble and fall.

3Though a host encamp against me,
my heart shall not fear;
though war arise against me,
yet I will be confident.

4One thing have I asked of the LORD,
that will I seek after;
that I may dwell in the house of the LORD
all the days of my life,
to behold the beauty of the LORD,
and to inquire in his temple.

5For he will hide me in his shelter
in the day of trouble;
he will conceal me under the cover of
his tent,
he will set me high upon a rock.

6And now my head shall be lifted up
above my enemies round about me;
and I will offer in his tent
sacrifices with shouts of joy;
I will sing and make melody to the LORD.

7Hear, O LORD, when I cry aloud,
be gracious to me and answer me!
8You have said, "Seek my face."
My heart says to you,
"Your face, LORD, do I seek."
9 Hide not your face from me.

Turn not your servant away in anger,
you who have been my help.
Cast me not off, forsake me not,
O God of my salvation!
10For my father and my mother have
forsaken me,
but the LORD will take me up.

11Teach me your way, O LORD;
and lead me on a level path
because of my enemies.
12Give me not up to the will of my
adversaries;
for false witnesses have risen against me,
and they breathe out violence.

13I believe that I shall see the goodness of
the LORD
in the land of the living!
14Wait for the LORD;
be strong, and let your heart take courage;
yes, wait for the LORD!

MATTHEW 20

"For the kingdom of heaven is
like a householder who went
out early in the morning to hire
laborers for his vineyard. 2After agree-
ing with the laborers for a denarius a
day, he sent them into his vineyard.
3And going out about the third hour he saw
others standing idle in the market place;
4and to them he said, 'You go into the vineyard too, and whatever is right I will give
you.' So they went. 5Going out again about
the sixth hour and the ninth hour, he did

the same. 6And about the eleventh hour he
went out and found others standing; and he
said to them, 'Why do you stand here idle all
day?' 7They said to him, 'Because no one has
hired us.' He said to them, 'You go into the
vineyard too.' 8And when evening came, the
owner of the vineyard said to his steward,
'Call the laborers and pay them their wages, beginning with the last, up to the first.'
9And when those hired about the eleventh
hour came, each of them received a denarius. 10Now when the first came, they thought
they would receive more; but each of them
also received a denarius. 11And on receiving it they grumbled at the householder,
12saying, 'These last worked only one hour,
and you have made them equal to us who
have borne the burden of the day and the
scorching heat.' 13But he replied to one of
them, 'Friend, I am doing you no wrong;
did you not agree with me for a denarius?
14Take what belongs to you, and go; I choose
to give to this last as I give to you. 15Am I
not allowed to do what I choose with what
belongs to me? Or do you begrudge my generosity?' 16So the last will be first, and the
first last."

REFLECTION

After the multitude of great signs and wonders that Israel witnesses in Egypt, they come into the wilderness and experience a shortage of food (see Ex 16) and drink (see Ex 17). Surely, in the midst of these trials they will trust in the Lord and call upon him for help? No. Instead they blame and impute bad motives upon Moses and God. Thus begins a long tradition of murmuring and dissenting among God's people. Forty years later God will tell Moses the purpose of these tests: "that [the LORD your God] might make you know that man does not live by bread alone, but that man lives by everything that proceeds out of the mouth of the LORD" (Dt 8:3). After seeing the awesome power of God, the people thought they had found the divine sugar daddy, but God is a wise father who seeks not simply to give his children good things, but, even more, to make them good, humble, and holy. Parenting that aims at building character is far more difficult, and

God knows that Israel must learn some hard lessons and even suffer along the way to maturity. Do you see the challenges of your life as opportunities our Father provides for your growth?

January 31

EXODUS 18

Jethro, the priest of Mid′ian, Moses' father-in-law, heard of all that God had done for Moses and for Israel his people, how the LORD had brought Israel out of Egypt. 2Now
Jethro, Moses' father-in-law, had taken
Zippo′rah, Moses' wife, after he had sent her
away, 3and her two sons, of whom the name
of the one was Gershom (for he said, "I have
been a sojourner in a foreign land"), 4and the
name of the other, Elie′zer (for he said, "The
God of my father was my help, and delivered
me from the sword of Pharaoh"). 5And Jethro,
Moses' father-in-law, came with his sons and
his wife to Moses in the wilderness where he
was encamped at the mountain of God. 6And
when one told Moses, "Behold, your father-
in-law Jethro is coming to you with your wife
and her two sons with her," 7Moses went out
to meet his father-in-law, and did obeisance
and kissed him; and they asked each other of
their welfare, and went into the tent. 8Then
Moses told his father-in-law all that the LORD
had done to Pharaoh and to the Egyptians for
Israel's sake, all the hardship that had come
upon them in the way, and how the LORD
had delivered them. 9And Jethro rejoiced
for all the good which the LORD had done to
Israel, in that he had delivered them out of
the hand of the Egyptians.
10And Jethro said, "Blessed be the LORD,
who has delivered you out of the hand of the
Egyptians and out of the hand of Pharaoh.
11Now I know that the LORD is greater than

all gods, because he delivered the people from under the hand of the Egyptians, when they dealt arrogantly with them." [12]And Jethro, Moses' father-in-law, offered a burnt offering and sacrifices to God; and Aaron came with all the elders of Israel to eat bread with Moses' father-in-law before God.

[13]The next day Moses sat to judge the people, and the people stood about Moses from morning till evening. [14]When Moses' father-in-law saw all that he was doing for the people, he said, "What is this that you are doing for the people? Why do you sit alone, and all the people stand about you from morning till evening?" [15]And Moses said to his father-in-law, "Because the people come to me to inquire of God; [16]when they have a dispute, they come to me and I decide between a man and his neighbor, and I make them know the statutes of God and his decisions." [17]Moses' father-in-law said to him, "What you are doing is not good. [18]You and the people with you will wear yourselves out, for the thing is too heavy for you; you are not able to perform it alone. [19]Listen now to my voice; I will give you counsel, and God be with you! You shall represent the people before God, and bring their cases to God; [20]and you shall teach them the statutes and the decisions, and make them know the way in which they must walk and what they must do. [21]Moreover choose able men from all the people, such as fear God, men who are trustworthy and who hate a bribe; and place such men over the people as rulers of thousands, of hundreds, of fifties, and of tens. [22]And let them judge the people at all times; every great matter they shall bring to you, but any small matter they shall decide themselves; so it will be easier for you, and they will bear the burden with you. [23]If you do this, and God so commands you, then you will be able to endure, and all this people also will go to their place in peace."

[24]So Moses gave heed to the voice of his father-in-law and did all that he had said. [25]Moses chose able men out of all Israel, and made them heads over the people, rulers of thousands, of hundreds, of fifties, and of tens. [26]And they judged the people at all times; hard cases they brought to Moses, but any small matter they decided themselves. [27]Then Moses let his father-in-law depart, and he went his way to his own country.

19 On the third new moon after the sons of Israel had gone forth out of the land of Egypt, on that day they came into the wilderness of Sinai. [2]And when they set out from Reph′idim and came into the wilderness of Sinai, they encamped in the wilderness; and there Israel encamped before the mountain. [3]And Moses went up to God, and the LORD called to him out of the mountain, saying, "Thus you shall say to the house of Jacob, and tell the sons of Israel: [4]You have seen what I did to the Egyptians, and how I bore you on eagles' wings and brought you to myself. [5]Now therefore, if you will obey my voice and keep my covenant, you shall be my own possession among all peoples; for all the earth is mine, [6]and you shall be to me a kingdom of priests and a holy nation. These are the words which you shall speak to the children of Israel."

[7]So Moses came and called the elders of the people, and set before them all these words which the LORD had commanded him. [8]And all the people answered together and said, "All that the LORD has spoken we will do." And Moses reported the words of the people to the LORD. [9]And the LORD said to Moses, "Behold, I am coming to you in a thick cloud, that the people may hear when I speak with you, and may also believe you for ever."

Then Moses told the words of the people to the LORD. [10]And the LORD said to Moses, "Go to the people and consecrate them today and tomorrow, and let them wash their garments, [11]and be ready by the third day; for on the third day the LORD will come down upon Mount Sinai in the sight of all the people. [12]And you shall set bounds for the people round about, saying, 'Take heed that you do not go up into the mountain or touch the border of it; whoever touches the mountain shall be put to death; [13]no hand shall touch him, but he shall be stoned or shot; whether beast or man, he shall not live.' When the trumpet sounds a long blast, they shall come up to the mountain." [14]So Moses went down from the mountain to the people, and consecrated the people; and they washed their garments. [15]And he said to the

people, "Be ready by the third day; do not go
near a woman."
16 On the morning of the third day there was
thunder and lightning, and a thick cloud upon
the mountain, and a very loud trumpet blast,
so that all the people who were in the camp
trembled. 17 Then Moses brought the people
out of the camp to meet God; and they took
their stand at the foot of the mountain. 18 And
Mount Sinai was wrapped in smoke, because
the LORD descended upon it in fire; and the
smoke of it went up like the smoke of a kiln,
and the whole mountain quaked greatly.
19 And as the sound of the trumpet grew louder
and louder, Moses spoke, and God answered
him in thunder. 20 And the LORD came down
upon Mount Sinai, to the top of the mountain;
and the LORD called Moses to the top of the
mountain, and Moses went up. 21 And the
LORD said to Moses, "Go down and warn
the people, lest they break through to the
LORD to gaze and many of them perish.
22 And also let the priests who come near
to the LORD consecrate themselves, lest the
LORD break out upon them." 23 And Moses
said to the LORD, "The people cannot come
up to Mount Sinai; for you yourself charged
us, saying, 'Set bounds about the mountain,
and consecrate it.'" 24 And the LORD said
to him, "Go down, and come up bringing
Aaron with you; but do not let the priests
and the people break through to come up
to the LORD, lest he break out against them."
25 So Moses went down to the people and
told them.

20 And God spoke all these words,
saying,
2 "I am the LORD your God, who brought
you out of the land of Egypt, out of the
house of bondage.
3 "You shall have no other gods before me.
4 "You shall not make for yourself a graven
image, or any likeness of anything that
is in heaven above, or that is in the earth
beneath, or that is in the water under the
earth; 5 you shall not bow down to them or
serve them; for I the LORD your God am
a jealous God, visiting the iniquity of the
fathers upon the children to the third and
the fourth generation of those who hate me,
6 but showing mercy to thousands of those
who love me and keep my commandments.
7 "You shall not take the name of the LORD
your God in vain; for the LORD will not hold
him guiltless who takes his name in vain.
8 "Remember the sabbath day, to keep it
holy. 9 Six days you shall labor, and do all your
work; 10 but the seventh day is a sabbath to the
LORD your God; in it you shall not do any
work, you, or your son, or your daughter, your
manservant, or your maidservant, or your
cattle, or the sojourner who is within your
gates; 11 for in six days the LORD made heaven
and earth, the sea, and all that is in them, and
rested the seventh day; therefore the LORD
blessed the sabbath day and hallowed it.
12 "Honor your father and your mother,
that your days may be long in the land
which the LORD your God gives you.
13 "You shall not kill.
14 "You shall not commit adultery.
15 "You shall not steal.
16 "You shall not bear false witness against
your neighbor.
17 "You shall not covet your neighbor's
house; you shall not covet your neighbor's
wife, or his manservant, or his maidservant,
or his ox, or his donkey, or anything that is
your neighbor's."

A Psalm of David.

PSALM 28 [27]

To you, O LORD, I call;
  my rock, be not deaf to me,
lest, if you be silent to me,
  I become like those who go down to the Pit.
2 Hear the voice of my supplication,
  as I cry to you for help,
as I lift up my hands
  toward your most holy sanctuary.

3 Take me not off with the wicked,
  with those who are workers of evil,
who speak peace with their neighbors,
  while mischief is in their hearts.
4 Repay them according to their work,
  and according to the evil of their deeds;

repay them according to the work of
  their hands;
 render them their due reward.
5Because they do not regard the works
  of the LORD,
 or the work of his hands,
he will break them down and build them
  up no more.

6Blessed be the LORD!
 for he has heard the voice of
  my supplications.
7The LORD is my strength and my shield;
 in him my heart trusts;
so I am helped, and my heart exults,
 and with my song I give thanks to him.

8The LORD is the strength of his people,
 he is the saving refuge of his anointed.
9O save your people, and bless your heritage;
 be their shepherd, and carry them for ever.

MATTHEW 20

17And as Jesus was going up to Jerusalem, he took the twelve disciples aside, and on the way he said to them, 18"Behold, we are going up to Jerusalem; and the Son of man will be delivered to the chief priests and scribes, and they will condemn him to death, 19and deliver him to the Gentiles to be mocked and scourged and crucified, and he will be raised on the third day."

20Then the mother of the sons of Zeb′edee came up to him, with her sons, and kneeling before him she asked him for something. 21And he said to her, "What do you want?" She said to him, "Command that these two sons of mine may sit, one at your right hand and one at your left, in your kingdom." 22But Jesus answered, "You do not know what you are asking. Are you able to drink the chalice that I am to drink?" They said to him, "We are able." 23He said to them, "You will drink my chalice, but to sit at my right hand and at my left is not mine to grant, but it is for those for whom it has been prepared by my Father." 24And when the Ten heard it, they were indignant at the two brothers. 25But Jesus called them to him and said, "You know that the rulers of the Gentiles lord it over them, and their great men exercise authority over them. 26It shall not be so among you; but whoever would be great among you must be your servant, 27and whoever would be first among you must be your slave; 28even as the Son of man came not to be served but to serve, and to give his life as a ransom for many."

29And as they went out of Jericho, a great crowd followed him. 30And behold, two blind men sitting by the roadside, when they heard that Jesus was passing by, cried out, "Have mercy on us, Son of David!" 31The crowd rebuked them, telling them to be silent; but they cried out the more, "Lord, have mercy on us, Son of David!" 32And Jesus stopped and called them, saying, "What do you want me to do for you?" 33They said to him, "Lord, let our eyes be opened." 34And Jesus in pity touched their eyes, and immediately they received their sight and followed him.

REFLECTION

The mother of John and James intercedes for them to Jesus, asking that they be given the two top positions in his coming kingdom. Jesus is on his way to Jerusalem, and his disciples have a growing conviction that he is the messiah, the king who will restore the glory of the Davidic kingdom. They expect that when Jesus comes to Jerusalem, the capital of Israel, a regime change will occur. Like a good mother she seeks the best for her sons. Of course, things will turn out far differently than what they all expect, which is what Jesus says in reference to the cup he must drink. Least expected of all is that Jesus will be enthroned upon the Cross, and on his left and right will be two crucified thieves. Jesus explains that in his kingdom, power is exercised far differently than it is in the world, for if the king makes himself a slave and gives his life as a ransom, those who seek to be his closest associates must be willing to become cruciform in their service to others. Whom do you serve for Christ's sake? What cup does Christ want you to drink that you may join him in glory?

February 1

EXODUS 20

18Now when all the people perceived the thunder and the lightning and the sound of the trumpet and the mountain smoking, the people were afraid and trembled; and they stood afar off, 19and said to Moses, "You speak to us, and we will hear; but let not God speak to us, lest we die." 20And Moses said to the people, "Do not fear; for God has come to test you, and that the fear of him may be before your eyes, that you may not sin."

21And the people stood afar off, while Moses drew near to the thick darkness where God was. 22And the LORD said to Moses, "Thus you shall say to the people of Israel: 'You have seen for yourselves that I have talked with you from heaven. 23You shall not make gods of silver to be with me, nor shall you make for yourselves gods of gold. 24An altar of earth you shall make for me and sacrifice on it your burnt offerings and your peace offerings, your sheep and your oxen; in every place where I cause my name to be remembered I will come to you and bless you. 25And if you make me an altar of stone, you shall not build it of hewn stones; for if you wield your tool upon it you profane it. 26And you shall not go up by steps to my altar, that your nakedness be not exposed on it.'

21 "Now these are the ordinances which you shall set before them. 2When you buy a Hebrew slave, he shall serve six years, and in the seventh he shall go out free, for nothing. 3If he comes in single, he shall go out single; if he comes in married, then his wife shall go out with him. 4If his master gives him a wife and she bears him sons or daughters, the wife and her children shall be her master's and he shall go out alone. 5But if the slave plainly says, 'I love my master, my wife, and my children; I will not go out free,' 6then his master shall bring him to God, and he shall bring him to the door or the doorpost; and his master shall bore his ear through with an awl; and he shall serve him for life.

7"When a man sells his daughter as a slave, she shall not go out as the male slaves do. 8If she does not please her master, who has designated her for himself, then he shall let her be redeemed; he shall have no right to sell her to a foreign people, since he has dealt faithlessly with her. 9If he designates her for his son, he shall deal with her as with a daughter. 10If he takes another wife to himself, he shall not diminish her food, her clothing, or her marital rights. 11And if he does not do these three things for her, she shall go out for nothing, without payment of money.

12"Whoever strikes a man so that he dies shall be put to death. 13But if he did not lie in wait for him, but God let him fall into his hand, then I will appoint for you a place to which he may flee. 14But if a man willfully attacks another to kill him treacherously, you shall take him from my altar, that he may die.

15"Whoever strikes his father or his mother shall be put to death.

16"Whoever steals a man, whether he sells him or is found in possession of him, shall be put to death.

17"Whoever curses his father or his mother shall be put to death.

18"When men quarrel and one strikes the other with a stone or with his fist and the man does not die but keeps his bed, 19then if the man rises again and walks abroad with his staff, he that struck him shall be clear; only he shall pay for the loss of his time, and shall have him thoroughly healed.

20"When a man strikes his slave, male or female, with a rod and the slave dies under his hand, he shall be punished. 21But if the slave survives a day or two, he is not to be punished; for the slave is his money.

22"When men strive together, and hurt a woman with child, so that there is a miscarriage, and yet no harm follows, the one who hurt her shall be fined, according as the woman's husband shall lay upon him; and he shall pay as the judges determine. 23If any harm follows, then you shall give life for life, [24]eye for eye, tooth for tooth, hand for hand, foot for foot, [25]burn for burn, wound for wound, stripe for stripe.

[26]"When a man strikes the eye of his slave, male or female, and destroys it, he shall let the slave go free for the eye's sake. [27]If he knocks out the tooth of his slave, male or female, he shall let the slave go free for the tooth's sake.

[28]"When an ox gores a man or a woman to death, the ox shall be stoned, and its flesh shall not be eaten; but the owner of the ox shall be clear. [29]But if the ox has been accustomed to gore in the past, and its owner has been warned but has not kept it in, and it kills a man or a woman, the ox shall be stoned, and its owner also shall be put to death. [30]If a ransom is laid on him, then he shall give for the redemption of his life whatever is laid upon him. [31]If it gores a man's son or daughter, he shall be dealt with according to this same rule. [32]If the ox gores a slave, male or female, the owner shall give to their master thirty shekels of silver, and the ox shall be stoned.

[33]"When a man leaves a pit open, or when a man digs a pit and does not cover it, and an ox or a donkey falls into it, [34]the owner of the pit shall make it good; he shall give money to its owner, and the dead beast shall be his.

[35]"When one man's ox hurts another's, so that it dies, then they shall sell the live ox and divide the price of it; and the dead beast also they shall divide. [36]Or if it is known that the ox has been accustomed to gore in the past, and its owner has not kept it in, he shall pay ox for ox, and the dead beast shall be his.

22 "If a man steals an ox or a sheep, and kills it or sells it, he shall pay five oxen for an ox, and four sheep for a sheep.* He shall make restitution; if he has nothing, then he shall be sold for his theft. [4]If the stolen beast is found alive in his possession, whether it is an ox or a donkey or a sheep, he shall pay double.

[2]"If a thief is found breaking in, and is struck so that he dies, there shall be no bloodguilt for him; [3]but if the sun has risen upon him, there shall be bloodguilt for him.

[5]"When a man causes a field or vineyard to be grazed over, or lets his beast loose and it feeds in another man's field, he shall make restitution from the best in his own field and in his own vineyard.

[6]"When fire breaks out and catches in thorns so that the stacked grain or the standing grain or the field is consumed, he that kindled the fire shall make full restitution.

[7]"If a man delivers to his neighbor money or goods to keep, and it is stolen out of the man's house, then, if the thief is found, he shall pay double. [8]If the thief is not found, the owner of the house shall come near to God, to show whether or not he has put his hand to his neighbor's goods.

[9]"For every breach of trust, whether it is for ox, for donkey, for sheep, for clothing, or for any kind of lost thing, of which one says, 'This is it,' the case of both parties shall come before God; he whom God shall condemn shall pay double to his neighbor.

[10]"If a man delivers to his neighbor a donkey or an ox or a sheep or any beast to keep, and it dies or is hurt or is driven away, without any one seeing it, [11]an oath by the LORD shall be between them both to see whether he has not put his hand to his neighbor's property; and the owner shall accept the oath, and he shall not make restitution. [12]But if it is stolen from him, he shall make restitution to its owner. [13]If it is torn by beasts, let him bring it as evidence; he shall not make restitution for what has been torn.

[14]"If a man borrows anything of his neighbor, and it is hurt or dies, the owner not being with it, he shall make full restitution. [15]If the owner was with it, he shall not make restitution; if it was hired, it came for its hire.

[16]"If a man seduces a virgin who is not betrothed, and lies with her, he shall give the marriage present for her, and make her his wife. [17]If her father utterly refuses to give her to him, he shall pay money equivalent to the marriage present for virgins.

---

* Restoring the second half of verse 3 and the whole of verse 4 to their place immediately following verse 1.

18“You shall not permit a sorceress to live.

19“Whoever lies with a beast shall be put to death.

20“Whoever sacrifices to any god, save to the LORD only, shall be utterly destroyed.

21“You shall not wrong a stranger or oppress him, for you were strangers in the land of Egypt. 22You shall not afflict any widow or orphan. 23If you do afflict them, and they cry out to me, I will surely hear their cry; 24and my wrath will burn, and I will kill you with the sword, and your wives shall become widows and your children fatherless.

25“If you lend money to any of my people with you who is poor, you shall not be to him as a creditor, and you shall not exact interest from him. 26If ever you take your neighbor’s garment in pledge, you shall restore it to him before the sun goes down; 27for that is his only covering, it is his mantle for his body; in what else shall he sleep? And if he cries to me, I will hear, for I am compassionate.

28“You shall not revile God, nor curse a ruler of your people.

29“You shall not delay to offer from the fulness of your harvest and from the outflow of your presses.

“The first-born of your sons you shall give to me. 30You shall do likewise with your oxen and with your sheep: seven days it shall be with its dam; on the eighth day you shall give it to me.

31“You shall be men consecrated to me; therefore you shall not eat any flesh that is torn by beasts in the field; you shall cast it to the dogs.”

A Psalm of David.

PSALM 29 [28]

Ascribe to the LORD, O sons of God,
ascribe to the LORD glory and strength.
2Ascribe to the LORD the glory of his name;
worship the LORD in holy attire.

3The voice of the LORD is upon the waters;
the God of glory thunders,
the LORD, upon many waters.
4The voice of the LORD is powerful,
the voice of the LORD is full of majesty.

5The voice of the LORD breaks the cedars,
the LORD breaks the cedars of Lebanon.
6He makes Lebanon to skip like a calf,
and Sir′ion like a young wild ox.

7The voice of the LORD flashes forth
flames of fire.
8The voice of the LORD shakes
the wilderness,
the LORD shakes the wilderness
of Kadesh.

9The voice of the LORD makes the oaks
to whirl,
and strips the forests bare;
and in his temple all cry, “Glory!”

10The LORD sits enthroned over the flood;
the LORD sits enthroned as king for ever.
11May the LORD give strength to his people!
May the LORD bless his people with
peace!

MATTHEW 21

And when they drew near to Jerusalem and came to Beth′phage, to the Mount of Olives, then Jesus sent two disciples, 2saying to them, “Go into the village opposite you, and immediately you will find a donkey tied, and a colt with her; untie them and bring them to me. 3If any one says anything to you, you shall say, ‘The Lord has need of them,’ and he will send them immediately.” 4This took place to fulfil what was spoken by the prophet, saying,

5“Tell the daughter of Zion,
Behold, your king is coming to you,
humble, and mounted on a donkey,
and on a colt, the foal of a donkey.”

6The disciples went and did as Jesus had directed them; 7they brought the donkey and the colt, and put their garments on them, and he sat on them. 8Most of the crowd spread their garments on the road, and others cut branches from the trees and spread them on the road. 9And the crowds that went before him and that followed him shouted, "Hosanna to the Son of David! Blessed is he who comes in the name of the Lord! Hosanna in the highest!" 10And when he entered Jerusalem, all the city was stirred, saying, "Who is this?" 11And the crowds said, "This is the prophet Jesus from Nazareth of Galilee."

12And Jesus entered the temple of God and drove out all who sold and bought in the temple, and he overturned the tables of the money-changers and the seats of those who sold pigeons. 13He said to them, "It is written, 'My house shall be called a house of prayer'; but you make it a den of robbers."

14And the blind and the lame came to him in the temple, and he healed them. 15But when the chief priests and the scribes saw the wonderful things that he did, and the children crying out in the temple, "Hosanna to the Son of David!" they were indignant; 16and they said to him, "Do you hear what these are saying?" And Jesus said to them, "Yes; have you never read,

> 'Out of the mouths of babies and infants
> you have brought perfect praise'?"

17And leaving them, he went out of the city to Beth′any and lodged there.

REFLECTION

When they hear the dramatic sounds and see the smoke and lightning upon Mt. Sinai, the Israelites are terrified of what might happen if they were to hear the voice of God. So they plead with Moses, "Let not God speak to us, lest we die" (Ex 20:19). God's voice can be frightening, because his voice brings law and justice. His voice is the ultimate moral authority in the universe, and when we truly hear it, we are convicted to the core. It is the powerful voice that "breaks the cedars of Lebanon" (Ps 29:5) and rebukes the money-changers in the Temple, accusing them of turning God's house of prayer into a robbers' den. But it is also the voice of the humble king who comes to his people, riding on a donkey. The voice of the Lord calls us to faithful obedience, to go and do as we are directed (see Mt 21:6). Just as the voice of God gave the Law to the Israelites, directing them to take responsibility for their social actions—caring for others' property, paying restitution, guarding the rights of one another, and so on—so we ought to listen for the Lord's voice and do what he tells us. What is he saying to you today?

February 2

EXODUS 23

"You shall not utter a false report. You shall not join hands with a wicked man, to be a malicious witness. 2You shall not follow a multitude to do evil; nor shall you bear witness in a suit, turning aside after a multitude, so as to pervert justice; 3nor shall you be partial to a poor man in his suit.

4"If you meet your enemy's ox or his donkey going astray, you shall bring it back to him. 5If you see the donkey of one who hates you lying under its burden, you shall refrain from leaving him with it, you shall help him to lift it up.

6"You shall not pervert the justice due to your poor in his suit. 7Keep far from a false charge, and do not slay the innocent and righteous, for I will not acquit the wicked. 8And you shall take no bribe, for a bribe blinds the officials, and subverts the cause of those who are in the right.

9"You shall not oppress a stranger; you know the heart of a stranger, for you were strangers in the land of Egypt.

10"For six years you shall sow your land and gather in its yield; 11but the seventh year you shall let it rest and lie fallow, that the poor of your people may eat; and what they leave the wild beasts may eat. You shall do likewise with your vineyard, and with your olive orchard.

12“Six days you shall do your work, but on
the seventh day you shall rest; that your ox
and your donkey may have rest, and the son
of your maidservant, and the alien, may be
refreshed. 13Take heed to all that I have said
to you; and make no mention of the names
of other gods, nor let such be heard out of
your mouth.

14“Three times in the year you shall keep
a feast to me. 15You shall keep the feast of
unleavened bread; as I commanded you,
you shall eat unleavened bread for seven
days at the appointed time in the month of
Abib, for in it you came out of Egypt. None
shall appear before me empty-handed. 16You
shall keep the feast of harvest, of the first
fruits of your labor, of what you sow in the
field. You shall keep the feast of ingathering
at the end of the year, when you gather in
from the field the fruit of your labor. 17Three
times in the year shall all your males appear
before the Lord GOD.

18“You shall not offer the blood of my
sacrifice with leavened bread, or let the fat
of my feast remain until the morning.

19“The first of the first fruits of your
ground you shall bring into the house of the
LORD your God.

“You shall not boil a kid in its mother’s
milk.

20“Behold, I send an angel before you, to
guard you on the way and to bring you to
the place which I have prepared. 21Give heed
to him and listen to his voice, do not rebel
against him, for he will not pardon your
transgression; for my name is in him.

22“But if you listen attentively to his voice
and do all that I say, then I will be an enemy
to your enemies and an adversary to your
adversaries.

23“When my angel goes before you,
and brings you in to the Am′orites, and
the Hittites, and the Per′izzites, and the
Canaanites, the Hi′vites, and the Jeb′usites,
and I blot them out, 24you shall not bow
down to their gods, nor serve them, nor
do according to their works, but you shall
utterly overthrow them and break their
pillars in pieces. 25You shall serve the LORD
your God, and I will bless your bread and
your water; and I will take sickness away
from the midst of you. 26None shall cast
her young or be barren in your land; I will
fulfil the number of your days. 27I will send
my terror before you, and will throw into
confusion all the people against whom
you shall come, and I will make all your
enemies turn their backs to you. 28And I
will send hornets before you, which shall
drive out Hi′vite, Canaanite, and Hittite
from before you. 29I will not drive them
out from before you in one year, lest the
land become desolate and the wild beasts
multiply against you. 30Little by little I will
drive them out from before you, until you
are increased and possess the land. 31And
I will set your bounds from the Red Sea
to the sea of the Philis′tines, and from the
wilderness to the Euphra′tes; for I will
deliver the inhabitants of the land into your
hand, and you shall drive them out before
you. 32You shall make no covenant with
them or with their gods. 33They shall not
dwell in your land, lest they make you sin
against me; for if you serve their gods, it
will surely be a snare to you.”

24 And he said to Moses, “Come up to
the LORD, you and Aaron, Na′dab,
and Abi′hu, and seventy of the elders of
Israel, and worship afar off. 2Moses alone
shall come near to the LORD; but the others
shall not come near, and the people shall not
come up with him.”

3Moses came and told the people all the
words of the LORD and all the ordinances;
and all the people answered with one voice,
and said, “All the words which the LORD has
spoken we will do.” 4And Moses wrote all
the words of the LORD. And he rose early
in the morning, and built an altar at the
foot of the mountain, and twelve pillars,
according to the twelve tribes of Israel. 5And
he sent young men of the sons of Israel,
who offered burnt offerings and sacrificed
peace offerings of oxen to the LORD. 6And
Moses took half of the blood and put it
in basins, and half of the blood he threw
against the altar. 7Then he took the book
of the covenant, and read it in the hearing
of the people; and they said, “All that the

LORD has spoken we will do, and we will be
obedient." 8And Moses took the blood and
threw it upon the people, and said, "Behold
the blood of the covenant which the LORD
has made with you in accordance with all
these words."
9Then Moses and Aaron, Na′dab, and
Abi′hu, and seventy of the elders of Israel
went up, 10and they saw the God of Israel;
and there was under his feet as it were
a pavement of sapphire stone, like the
very heaven for clearness. 11And he did
not lay his hand on the chief men of the
people of Israel; they beheld God, and ate
and drank.
12The LORD said to Moses, "Come up to
me on the mountain, and wait there; and
I will give you the tables of stone, with the
law and the commandment, which I have
written for their instruction." 13So Moses
rose with his servant Joshua, and Moses
went up into the mountain of God. 14And he
said to the elders, "Wait here for us, until we
come to you again; and, behold, Aaron and
Hur are with you; whoever has a cause, let
him go to them."
15Then Moses went up on the mountain,
and the cloud covered the mountain. 16The
glory of the LORD settled on Mount Sinai,
and the cloud covered it six days; and on the
seventh day he called to Moses out of the
midst of the cloud. 17Now the appearance of
the glory of the LORD was like a devouring
fire on the top of the mountain in the sight
of the sons of Israel. 18And Moses entered
the cloud, and went up on the mountain.
And Moses was on the mountain forty days
and forty nights.

A Psalm of David.
A Song at the dedication of the Temple.

PSALM 30 [29]

I will extol you, O LORD, for you have drawn
me up,
and have not let my foes rejoice over me.
2O LORD my God, I cried to you for help,
and you have healed me.
3O LORD, you have brought up my soul
from Sheol,
restored me to life from among those
gone down to the Pit.

4Sing praises to the LORD, O you his saints,
and give thanks to his holy name.
5For his anger is but for a moment,
and his favor is for a lifetime.
Weeping may last for the night,
but joy comes with the morning.

6As for me, I said in my prosperity,
"I shall never be moved."
7By your favor, O LORD,
you had established me as a
strong mountain;
you hid your face,
I was dismayed.

8To you, O LORD, I cried;
and to the LORD I made supplication:
9"What profit is there in my death,
if I go down to the Pit?
Will the dust praise you?
Will it tell of your faithfulness?
10Hear, O LORD, and be gracious to me!
O LORD, be my helper!"

11You have turned my mourning
into dancing;
you have loosed my sackcloth
and clothed me with gladness,
12that my soul may praise you and not
be silent.
O LORD my God, I will give thanks to
you for ever.

MATTHEW 21

**18In the morning, as he was re-
turning to the city, he was hungry. 19And seeing a fig tree by the
wayside he went to it, and found nothing on it but leaves only. And he said to**
it, "May no fruit ever come from you again!"
And the fig tree withered at once. 20When
the disciples saw it they marveled, saying,

"How did the fig tree wither at once?" 21And Jesus answered them, "Truly, I say to you, if you have faith and never doubt, you will not only do what has been done to the fig tree, but even if you say to this mountain, 'Be taken up and cast into the sea,' it will be done. 22And whatever you ask in prayer, you will receive, if you have faith."

23And when he entered the temple, the chief priests and the elders of the people came up to him as he was teaching, and said, "By what authority are you doing these things, and who gave you this authority?" 24Jesus answered them, "I also will ask you a question; and if you tell me the answer, then I also will tell you by what authority I do these things. 25The baptism of John, where was it from? From heaven or from men?" And they argued with one another, "If we say, 'From heaven,' he will say to us, 'Why then did you not believe him?' 26But if we say, 'From men,' we are afraid of the multitude; for all hold that John was a prophet." 27So they answered Jesus, "We do not know." And he said to them, "Neither will I tell you by what authority I do these things.

28"What do you think? A man had two sons; and he went to the first and said, 'Son, go and work in the vineyard today.' 29And he answered, 'I will not'; but afterward he repented and went. 30And he went to the second and said the same; and he answered, 'I go, sir,' but did not go. 31Which of the two did the will of his father?" They said, "The first." Jesus said to them, "Truly, I say to you, the tax collectors and the harlots go into the kingdom of God before you. 32For John came to you in the way of righteousness, and you did not believe him, but the tax collectors and the harlots believed him; and even when you saw it, you did not afterward repent and believe him.

33"Hear another parable. There was a householder who planted a vineyard, and set a hedge around it, and dug a wine press in it, and built a tower, and leased it to tenants, and went into another country. 34When the season of fruit drew near, he sent his servants to the tenants, to get his fruit; 35and the tenants took his servants and beat one, killed another, and stoned another. 36Again he sent other servants, more than the first; and they did the same to them. 37Afterward he sent his son to them, saying, 'They will respect my son.' 38But when the tenants saw the son, they said to themselves, 'This is the heir; come, let us kill him and have his inheritance.' 39And they took him and cast him out of the vineyard, and killed him. 40When therefore the owner of the vineyard comes, what will he do to those tenants?" 41They said to him, "He will put those wretches to a miserable death, and lease the vineyard to other tenants who will give him the fruits in their seasons."

42Jesus said to them, "Have you never read in the Scriptures:

'The very stone which the builders rejected
has become the cornerstone;
this was the Lord's doing,
and it is marvelous in our eyes'?

43Therefore I tell you, the kingdom of God will be taken away from you and given to a nation producing the fruits of it. 44And he who falls on this stone will be broken to pieces; but when it falls on any one, it will crush him."

45When the chief priests and the Pharisees heard his parables, they perceived that he was speaking about them. 46But when they tried to arrest him, they feared the multitudes, because they held him to be a prophet.

REFLECTION

It is very easy to seek our own interests rather than looking out for others. Exodus warns us against lying to gain advantage or following the crowd to the point of sinning (see Ex 23:1–2). Not only that, it also mandates that we help our enemy (see v. 5). When we ignore God's direction on how to live well, we end up like the wicked tenants in Jesus's parable. Looking only to their own interests and gain, they seek to wrest control of the profitable vineyard from its rightful owner by murdering his servants and eventually his son. Their self-seeking disobedience brings upon them the same kind of wrath with which Jesus cursed the fig tree. If we reject our Lord, as the chief priests did, and if we act solely for our own interests, as the wicked tenants did, God's blessings, presence, and kingdom will be taken from us. Whose welfare can you put before your own interests today?

February 3

EXODUS 25

**The LORD said to Moses, 2“Speak
to the sons of Israel, that they
take for me an offering; from
every man whose heart makes him
willing you shall receive the offering
for me. 3And this is the offering which**
you shall receive from them: gold, silver, and
bronze, 4blue and purple and scarlet stuff
and fine twined linen, goats' hair, 5tanned
rams' skins, goatskins, acacia wood, 6oil for
the lamps, spices for the anointing oil and
for the fragrant incense, 7onyx stones, and
stones for setting, for the ephod and for
the breastpiece. 8And let them make me a
sanctuary, that I may dwell in their midst.
9According to all that I show you concerning
the pattern of the tabernacle, and of all its
furniture, so you shall make it.

10“They shall make an ark of acacia wood;
two cubits and a half shall be its length, a
cubit and a half its breadth, and a cubit and
a half its height. 11And you shall overlay it
with pure gold, within and without shall
you overlay it, and you shall make upon
it a molding of gold round about. 12And
you shall cast four rings of gold for it and
put them on its four feet, two rings on the
one side of it, and two rings on the other
side of it. 13You shall make poles of acacia
wood, and overlay them with gold. 14And
you shall put the poles into the rings on the
sides of the ark, to carry the ark by them.
15The poles shall remain in the rings of the
ark; they shall not be taken from it. 16And
you shall put into the ark the covenant
which I shall give you. 17Then you shall
make a mercy seat of pure gold; two cubits
and a half shall be its length, and a cubit
and a half its breadth. 18And you shall make
two cherubim of gold; of hammered work
shall you make them, on the two ends of
the mercy seat. 19Make one cherub on the
one end, and one cherub on the other end;
of one piece with the mercy seat shall you
make the cherubim on its two ends. 20The
cherubim shall spread out their wings
above, overshadowing the mercy seat with
their wings, their faces one to another;
toward the mercy seat shall the faces of
the cherubim be. 21And you shall put the
mercy seat on the top of the ark; and in the
ark you shall put the covenant that I shall
give you. 22There I will meet with you, and
from above the mercy seat, from between
the two cherubim that are upon the ark of
the covenant, I will speak with you of all
that I will give you in commandment for
the sons of Israel.

23“And you shall make a table of acacia
wood; two cubits shall be its length, a
cubit its breadth, and a cubit and a half
its height. 24You shall overlay it with pure
gold, and make a molding of gold around
it. 25And you shall make around it a frame
a handbreadth wide, and a molding of gold
around the frame. 26And you shall make for
it four rings of gold, and fasten the rings to
the four corners at its four legs. 27Close to
the frame the rings shall lie, as holders for
the poles to carry the table. 28You shall make
the poles of acacia wood, and overlay them
with gold, and the table shall be carried with
these. 29And you shall make its plates and
dishes for incense, and its flagons and bowls
with which to pour libations; of pure gold
you shall make them. 30And you shall set the
bread of the Presence on the table before
me always.

31“And you shall make a lampstand of
pure gold. The base and the shaft of the
lampstand shall be made of hammered
work; its cups, its capitals, and its flowers

shall be of one piece with it; 32and there
shall be six branches going out of its sides,
three branches of the lampstand out of
one side of it and three branches of the
lampstand out of the other side of it; 33three
cups made like almonds, each with capital
and flower, on one branch, and three cups
made like almonds, each with capital and
flower, on the other branch—so for the six
branches going out of the lampstand; 34and
on the lampstand itself four cups made like
almonds, with their capitals and flowers,
35and a capital of one piece with it under
each pair of the six branches going out from
the lampstand. 36Their capitals and their
branches shall be of one piece with it, the
whole of it one piece of hammered work of
pure gold. 37And you shall make the seven
lamps for it; and the lamps shall be set up
so as to give light upon the space in front
of it. 38Its snuffers and their trays shall be
of pure gold. 39Of a talent of pure gold shall
it be made, with all these utensils. 40And
see that you make them after the pattern
for them, which is being shown you on
the mountain.

26 "Moreover you shall make the
tabernacle with ten curtains of fine
twined linen and blue and purple and
scarlet stuff; with cherubim skilfully worked
shall you make them. 2The length of each
curtain shall be twenty-eight cubits, and
the breadth of each curtain four cubits; all
the curtains shall have one measure. 3Five
curtains shall be coupled to one another;
and the other five curtains shall be coupled
to one another. 4And you shall make loops
of blue on the edge of the outmost curtain
in the first set; and likewise you shall make
loops on the edge of the outmost curtain
in the second set. 5Fifty loops you shall
make on the one curtain, and fifty loops
you shall make on the edge of the curtain
that is in the second set; the loops shall be
opposite one another. 6And you shall make
fifty clasps of gold, and couple the curtains
one to the other with the clasps, that the
tabernacle may be one whole.

7"You shall also make curtains of goats'
hair for a tent over the tabernacle; eleven
curtains shall you make. 8The length of each
curtain shall be thirty cubits, and the breadth
of each curtain four cubits; the eleven
curtains shall have the same measure. 9And
you shall couple five curtains by themselves,
and six curtains by themselves, and the sixth
curtain you shall double over at the front of
the tent. 10And you shall make fifty loops
on the edge of the curtain that is outmost
in one set, and fifty loops on the edge of the
curtain which is outmost in the second set.

11"And you shall make fifty clasps of bronze,
and put the clasps into the loops, and couple
the tent together that it may be one whole.
12And the part that remains of the curtains
of the tent, the half curtain that remains,
shall hang over the back of the tabernacle.
13And the cubit on the one side, and the
cubit on the other side, of what remains in
the length of the curtains of the tent shall
hang over the sides of the tabernacle, on
this side and that side, to cover it. 14And you
shall make for the tent a covering of tanned
rams' skins and goatskins.

15"And you shall make upright frames
for the tabernacle of acacia wood. 16Ten
cubits shall be the length of a frame,
and a cubit and a half the breadth of
each frame. 17There shall be two tenons
in each frame, for fitting together; so
shall you do for all the frames of the
tabernacle. 18You shall make the frames
for the tabernacle: twenty frames for the
south side; 19and forty bases of silver you
shall make under the twenty frames, two
bases under one frame for its two tenons,
and two bases under another frame for its
two tenons; 20and for the second side of
the tabernacle, on the north side twenty
frames, 21and their forty bases of silver,
two bases under one frame, and two bases
under another frame; 22and for the rear of
the tabernacle westward you shall make
six frames. 23And you shall make two
frames for corners of the tabernacle in
the rear; 24they shall be separate beneath,
but joined at the top, at the first ring; thus
shall it be with both of them; they shall
form the two corners. 25And there shall
be eight frames, with their bases of silver,

sixteen bases; two bases under one frame,
and two bases under another frame.
26"And you shall make bars of acacia wood,
five for the frames of the one side of the
tabernacle, 27and five bars for the frames of
the other side of the tabernacle, and five bars
for the frames of the side of the tabernacle at
the rear westward. 28The middle bar, halfway
up the frames, shall pass through from end
to end. 29You shall overlay the frames with
gold, and shall make their rings of gold for
holders for the bars; and you shall overlay
the bars with gold. 30And you shall erect the
tabernacle according to the plan for it which
has been shown you on the mountain."

To the choirmaster.
A Psalm of David.

PSALM 31 [30]

In you, O LORD, I seek refuge;
let me never be put to shame;
in your righteousness deliver me!
2Incline your ear to me,
rescue me speedily!
Be a rock of refuge for me,
a strong fortress to save me!
3Yes, you are my rock and my fortress;
for your name's sake lead me and
guide me,
4take me out of the net which is hidden
for me,
for you are my refuge.
5Into your hand I commit my spirit;
you have redeemed me, O LORD,
faithful God.

6You hate those who pay regard to
vain idols;
but I trust in the LORD.
7I will rejoice and be glad for your
merciful love,
because you have seen my lowliness,
you have taken heed of my adversities,
8and have not delivered me into the hand of
the enemy;
you have set my feet in a broad place.
9Be gracious to me, O LORD, for I am
in distress;
my eye is wasted from grief,
my soul and my body also.
10For my life is spent with sorrow,
and my years with sighing;
my strength fails because of my misery,
and my bones waste away.

11I am the scorn of all my adversaries,
a horror to my neighbors,
an object of dread to my acquaintances;
those who see me in the street flee from me.
12I have passed out of mind like one who
is dead;
I have become like a broken vessel.

MATTHEW 22

**And again Jesus spoke to them in
parables, saying, 2"The kingdom
of heaven may be compared to a
king who gave a marriage feast for his son,
3and sent his servants to call those who
were invited to the marriage feast; but**
they would not come. 4Again he sent other
servants, saying, 'Tell those who are invited,
Behold, I have made ready my dinner, my oxen
and my fat calves are killed, and everything is
ready; come to the marriage feast.' 5But they
made light of it and went off, one to his farm,
another to his business, 6while the rest seized
his servants, treated them shamefully, and
killed them. 7The king was angry, and he sent
his troops and destroyed those murderers and
burned their city. 8Then he said to his servants,
'The wedding is ready, but those invited were
not worthy. 9Go therefore to the streets, and
invite to the marriage feast as many as you
find.' 10And those servants went out into the
streets and gathered all whom they found,
both bad and good; so the wedding hall was
filled with guests.
11"But when the king came in to look at the
guests, he saw there a man who had no wedding
garment; 12and he said to him, 'Friend, how did
you get in here without a wedding garment?'
And he was speechless. 13Then the king said to

the attendants, 'Bind him hand and foot, and
cast him into the outer darkness, where there
will be weeping and gnashing of teeth.' 14For
many are called, but few are chosen."
15Then the Pharisees went and took counsel
how to entangle him in his talk. 16And they
sent their disciples to him, along with the
Hero'di-ans, saying, "Teacher, we know
that you are true, and teach the way of God
truthfully, and care for no man; for you do not
regard the position of men. 17Tell us, then, what
you think. Is it lawful to pay taxes to Caesar,
or not?" 18But Jesus, aware of their malice,
said, "Why put me to the test, you hypocrites?
19Show me the money for the tax." And they
brought him a coin. 20And Jesus said to them,
"Whose likeness and inscription is this?"
21They said, "Caesar's." Then he said to them,
"Render therefore to Caesar the things that are
Caesar's, and to God the things that are God's."
22When they heard it, they marveled; and they
left him and went away.

REFLECTION

Sometimes we're just too busy for God. That is the image presented to us of those who turn down the wedding invitation of the king's son: "They made light of it and went off, one to his farm, another to his business" (Mt 22:5). The Israelites could have done the same. They could have ignored God's laws and instructions, especially when it got down to the small details of goat skin curtains and acacia poles. Yet God gave a particular "pattern" and "plan" for worship in order to teach us about himself. The Tabernacle instructions begin in Exodus 25 with the initial plan and the basic designs of key sacred objects to be present within it, the Ark of the Covenant and the table of the bread of the presence. The Ark, overlayed with pure gold and placed in the inner room of the Tabernacle, was where God's presence dwelt amongst his people, prefiguring the Virgin Mary, a pure vessel without sin, who carried God himself in her womb. The table for the bread prefigured the Christian altar from which we receive the Real Presence. The Israelites built this mysterious sanctuary in obedience to God's plan. Take a few minutes today from your busy schedule to thank God for his plan of salvation, and for his plan for you and your life.

February 4

EXODUS 26

31"And you shall make a veil
of blue and purple and scarlet
stuff and fine twined linen; in
skilled work shall it be made, with che-
rubim; 32and you shall hang it upon
four pillars of acacia overlaid with gold, with
hooks of gold, upon four bases of silver. 33And
you shall hang the veil from the clasps, and
bring the ark of the covenant in there within
the veil; and the veil shall separate for you the
holy place from the most holy. 34You shall put
the mercy seat upon the ark of the covenant
in the most holy place. 35And you shall set the
table outside the veil, and the lampstand on the
south side of the tabernacle opposite the table;
and you shall put the table on the north side.
36"And you shall make a screen for the door
of the tent, of blue and purple and scarlet
stuff and fine twined linen, embroidered
with needlework. 37And you shall make for
the screen five pillars of acacia, and overlay
them with gold; their hooks shall be of
gold, and you shall cast five bases of bronze
for them.

27 "You shall make the altar of acacia
wood, five cubits long and five cubits
broad; the altar shall be square, and its height
shall be three cubits. 2And you shall make
horns for it on its four corners; its horns shall
be of one piece with it, and you shall overlay
it with bronze. 3You shall make pots for it to
receive its ashes, and shovels and basins and
forks and firepans; all its utensils you shall
make of bronze. 4You shall also make for it a
grating, a network of bronze; and upon the
net you shall make four bronze rings at its
four corners. 5And you shall set it under the
ledge of the altar so that the net shall extend
half way down the altar. 6And you shall make
poles for the altar, poles of acacia wood, and
overlay them with bronze; 7and the poles shall
be put through the rings, so that the poles shall
be upon the two sides of the altar, when it is

carried. 8You shall make it hollow, with boards; as it has been shown you on the mountain, so shall it be made.

9“You shall make the court of the tabernacle. On the south side the court shall have hangings of fine twined linen a hundred cubits long for one side; 10their pillars shall be twenty and their bases twenty, of bronze, but the hooks of the pillars and their fillets shall be of silver. 11And likewise for its length on the north side there shall be hangings a hundred cubits long, their pillars twenty and their bases twenty, of bronze, but the hooks of the pillars and their fillets shall be of silver. 12And for the breadth of the court on the west side there shall be hangings for fifty cubits, with ten pillars and ten bases. 13The breadth of the court on the front to the east shall be fifty cubits. 14The hangings for the one side of the gate shall be fifteen cubits, with three pillars and three bases. 15On the other side the hangings shall be fifteen cubits, with three pillars and three bases. 16For the gate of the court there shall be a screen twenty cubits long, of blue and purple and scarlet stuff and fine twined linen, embroidered with needlework; it shall have four pillars and with them four bases. 17All the pillars around the court shall be filleted with silver; their hooks shall be of silver, and their bases of bronze. 18The length of the court shall be a hundred cubits, the breadth fifty, and the height five cubits, with hangings of fine twined linen and bases of bronze. 19All the utensils of the tabernacle for every use, and all its pegs and all the pegs of the court, shall be of bronze.

20“And you shall command the sons of Israel that they bring to you pure beaten olive oil for the light, that a lamp may be set up to burn continually. 21In the tent of meeting, outside the veil which is before the covenant, Aaron and his sons shall tend it from evening to morning before the LORD. It shall be a statute for ever to be observed throughout their generations by the sons of Israel.

28 “Then bring near to you Aaron your brother, and his sons with him, from among the sons of Israel, to serve me as priests—Aaron and Aaron's sons, Na′dab and Abi′hu, Elea′zar and Ith′amar. 2And you shall make holy garments for Aaron your brother, for glory and for beauty. 3And you shall speak to all who have ability, whom I have endowed with an able mind, that they make Aaron's garments to consecrate him for my priesthood. 4These are the garments which they shall make: a breastpiece, an ephod, a robe, a coat of checker work, a turban, and a sash; they shall make holy garments for Aaron your brother and his sons to serve me as priests.

5“They shall receive gold, blue and purple and scarlet stuff, and fine twined linen. 6And they shall make the ephod of gold, of blue and purple and scarlet stuff, and of fine twined linen, skilfully worked. 7It shall have two shoulder-pieces attached to its two edges, that it may be joined together. 8And the skilfully woven band upon it, to belt it on, shall be of the same workmanship and materials, of gold, blue and purple and scarlet stuff, and fine twined linen. 9And you shall take two onyx stones, and engrave on them the names of the sons of Israel, 10six of their names on the one stone, and the names of the remaining six on the other stone, in the order of their birth. 11As a jeweler engraves signets, so shall you engrave the two stones with the names of the sons of Israel; you shall enclose them in settings of gold filigree. 12And you shall set the two stones upon the shoulder-pieces of the ephod, as stones of remembrance for the sons of Israel; and Aaron shall bear their names before the LORD upon his two shoulders for remembrance. 13And you shall make settings of gold filigree, 14and two chains of pure gold, twisted like cords; and you shall attach the corded chains to the settings.

15“And you shall make a breastpiece of judgment, in skilled work; like the work of the ephod you shall make it; of gold, blue and purple and scarlet stuff, and fine twined linen shall you make it. 16It shall be square and double, a span its length and a span its breadth. 17And you shall set in it four rows of stones. A row of sardius, topaz, and carbuncle shall be the first row; 18and the second row an emerald, a sapphire, and a diamond; 19and the third row a jacinth, an agate, and an amethyst; 20and the fourth row a beryl, an onyx, and a jasper; they shall be set in gold filigree. 21There shall be twelve stones with their names according to the names of the sons of Israel; they shall be

like signets, each engraved with its name, for
the twelve tribes. 22And you shall make for the
breastpiece twisted chains like cords, of pure
gold; 23and you shall make for the breastpiece
two rings of gold, and put the two rings on the
two edges of the breastpiece. 24And you shall
put the two cords of gold in the two rings at
the edges of the breastpiece; 25the two ends
of the two cords you shall attach to the two
settings of filigree, and so attach it in front to
the shoulder-pieces of the ephod. 26And you
shall make two rings of gold, and put them at
the two ends of the breastpiece, on its inside
edge next to the ephod. 27And you shall make
two rings of gold, and attach them in front to
the lower part of the two shoulder-pieces of
the ephod, at its joining above the skilfully
woven band of the ephod. 28And they shall
bind the breastpiece by its rings to the rings
of the ephod with a lace of blue, that it may lie
upon the skilfully woven band of the ephod,
and that the breastpiece shall not come loose
from the ephod. 29So Aaron shall bear the
names of the sons of Israel in the breastpiece
of judgment upon his heart, when he goes
into the holy place, to bring them to continual
remembrance before the LORD. 30And in the
breastpiece of judgment you shall put the
U´rim and the Thummim, and they shall be
upon Aaron's heart, when he goes in before
the LORD; thus Aaron shall bear the judgment
of the sons of Israel upon his heart before the
LORD continually."

To the choirmaster.
A Psalm of David.

PSALM 31 [30]

13Yes, I hear the whispering of many—
terror on every side!—
as they scheme together against me,
as they plot to take my life.

14But I trust in you, O LORD,
I say, "You are my God."
15My times are in your hand;
deliver me from the hand of my enemies
and persecutors!
16Let your face shine on your servant;
save me in your merciful love!
17Let me not be put to shame, O LORD,
for I call on you;
let the wicked be put to shame,
let them go dumbfounded to Sheol.
18Let the lying lips be silent,
which speak insolently against
the righteous
in pride and contempt.

19O how abundant is your goodness,
which you have laid up for those who
fear you,
and wrought for those who take refuge in you,
in the sight of the sons of men!
20In the shelter of your presence you
hide them
from the plots of men;
you hold them safe under your shelter
from the strife of tongues.

21Blessed be the LORD,
for he has wondrously shown me his
merciful love
when I was beset as in a besieged city.
22I had said in my alarm,
"I am driven far from your sight."
But you heard my supplications,
when I cried to you for help.

23Love the LORD, all you his saints!
The LORD preserves the faithful,
but abundantly repays him who
acts haughtily.
24Be strong, and let your heart take courage,
all you who wait for the LORD!

MATTHEW 22

23The same day Sad´ducees came
to him, who say that there is no
resurrection; and they asked him
a question, 24saying, "Teacher, Moses said,
'If a man dies, having no children, his
brother must marry the widow, and raise
up children for his brother.' 25Now there were
seven brothers among us; the first married,

and died, and having no children left his
wife to his brother. 26So too the second and
third, down to the seventh. 27After them
all, the woman died. 28In the resurrection,
therefore, to which of the seven will she be
wife? For they all had her."

29But Jesus answered them, "You are wrong,
because you know neither the Scriptures nor
the power of God. 30For in the resurrection
they neither marry nor are given in marriage,
but are like angels in heaven. 31And as for the
resurrection of the dead, have you not read
what was said to you by God, 32'I am the God of
Abraham, and the God of Isaac, and the God
of Jacob'? He is not God of the dead, but of the
living." 33And when the crowd heard it, they
were astonished at his teaching.

34But when the Pharisees heard that he had
silenced the Sad′ducees, they came together.
35And one of them, a lawyer, asked him a
question, to test him. 36"Teacher, which is the
great commandment in the law?" 37And he
said to him, "You shall love the Lord your God
with all your heart, and with all your soul, and
with all your mind. 38This is the great and first
commandment. 39And a second is like it, You
shall love your neighbor as yourself. 40On these
two commandments depend all the law and
the prophets."

41Now while the Pharisees were gathered
together, Jesus asked them a question,
42saying, "What do you think of the Christ?
Whose son is he?" They said to him, "The
son of David." 43He said to them, "How is it
then that David, inspired by the Spirit, calls
him Lord, saying,

44'The Lord said to my Lord,
Sit at my right hand,
till I put your enemies under your feet'?

45If David thus calls him Lord, how is he his
son?" 46And no one was able to answer him
a word, nor from that day did any one dare
to ask him any more questions.

REFLECTION

The Lord knows our weaknesses before they come to the fore. He knows that most of us would like to settle down, find a comfortable spot, and just coast through life, each day easier than the last. Yet from the beginning, he set up a religion that militates against that tendency in us. He commissions a portable altar (see Ex 27:1–8) in a portable sanctuary where his presence dwells on the portable Ark of the Covenant. He is not a stagnant deity, but a God on the move. He invites us to find safety and refuge not in routines or customs, but in him alone. The psalmist speaks of "those who take refuge in you," that "in the shelter of your presence you hide them" (Ps 31:19–20). God wants us to be safe, but not comfortable. He wants us to be on the move with him, following him bravely wherever he leads us. "Be strong, and let your heart take courage!" (v. 31:24). That is the calling he issues. Jesus's teaching here shows us how the Lord wants us to direct all that dynamic courage when he tells us the two most important commandments, which are all about going out of ourselves: love God and love your neighbor. In what ways has God given you courage to go out of yourself in love?

February 5

EXODUS 28

**31"And you shall make the robe
of the ephod all of blue. 32It shall
have in it an opening for the
head, with a woven binding around
the opening, like the opening in a
garment, that it may not be torn. 33On**
its skirts you shall make pomegranates of
blue and purple and scarlet stuff, around
its skirts, with bells of gold between them,
34a golden bell and a pomegranate, a golden
bell and a pomegranate, round about on
the skirts of the robe. 35And it shall be upon
Aaron when he ministers, and its sound
shall be heard when he goes into the holy
place before the LORD, and when he comes
out, lest he die.

36"And you shall make a plate of pure gold,
and engrave on it, like the engraving of a

signet, ‘Holy to the LORD.’ 37And you shall
fasten it on the turban by a lace of blue; it
shall be on the front of the turban. 38It shall
be upon Aaron’s forehead, and Aaron shall
take upon himself any guilt incurred in the
holy offering which the sons of Israel hallow
as their holy gifts; it shall always be upon his
forehead, that they may be accepted before
the LORD.
39“And you shall weave the coat in checker
work of fine linen, and you shall make a
turban of fine linen, and you shall make a
sash embroidered with needlework.
40“And for Aaron’s sons you shall make
coats and sashes and caps; you shall make
them for glory and beauty. 41And you shall
put them upon Aaron your brother, and
upon his sons with him, and shall anoint
them and ordain them and consecrate them,
that they may serve me as priests. 42And
you shall make for them linen breeches to
cover their naked flesh; from the loins to the
thighs they shall reach; 43and they shall be
upon Aaron, and upon his sons, when they
go into the tent of meeting, or when they
come near the altar to minister in the holy
place; lest they bring guilt upon themselves
and die. This shall be a perpetual statute for
him and for his descendants after him.

29 “Now this is what you shall do to
them to consecrate them, that they
may serve me as priests. Take one young
bull and two rams without blemish, 2and
unleavened bread, unleavened cakes mixed
with oil, and unleavened wafers spread with
oil. You shall make them of fine wheat flour.
3And you shall put them in one basket and
bring them in the basket, and bring the bull
and the two rams. 4You shall bring Aaron and
his sons to the door of the tent of meeting,
and wash them with water. 5And you shall
take the garments, and put on Aaron the
coat and the robe of the ephod, and the
ephod, and the breastpiece, and belt him
with the skilfully woven band of the ephod;
6and you shall set the turban on his head,
and put the holy crown upon the turban.
7And you shall take the anointing oil, and
pour it on his head and anoint him. 8Then
you shall bring his sons, and put coats on
them, 9and you shall belt them with sashes
and bind caps on them; and the priesthood
shall be theirs by a perpetual statute. Thus
you shall ordain Aaron and his sons.
10“Then you shall bring the bull before the
tent of meeting. Aaron and his sons shall lay
their hands upon the head of the bull, 11and
you shall kill the bull before the LORD, at the
door of the tent of meeting, 12and shall take
part of the blood of the bull and put it upon
the horns of the altar with your finger, and
the rest of the blood you shall pour out at
the base of the altar. 13And you shall take
all the fat that covers the entrails, and the
appendage of the liver, and the two kidneys
with the fat that is on them, and burn them
upon the altar. 14But the flesh of the bull, and
its skin, and its dung, you shall burn with
fire outside the camp; it is a sin offering.
15“Then you shall take one of the rams,
and Aaron and his sons shall lay their hands
upon the head of the ram, 16and you shall
slaughter the ram, and shall take its blood
and throw it against the altar round about.
17Then you shall cut the ram into pieces,
and wash its entrails and its legs, and put
them with its pieces and its head, 18and burn
the whole ram upon the altar; it is a burnt
offering to the LORD; it is a pleasing odor, an
offering by fire to the LORD.
19“You shall take the other ram; and Aaron
and his sons shall lay their hands upon the
head of the ram, 20and you shall kill the
ram, and take part of its blood and put it
upon the tip of the right ear of Aaron and
upon the tips of the right ears of his sons,
and upon the thumbs of their right hands,
and upon the great toes of their right feet,
and throw the rest of the blood against the
altar round about. 21Then you shall take part
of the blood that is on the altar, and of the
anointing oil, and sprinkle it upon Aaron
and his garments, and upon his sons and
his sons’ garments with him; and he and his
garments shall be holy, and his sons and his
sons’ garments with him.
22“You shall also take the fat of the ram,
and the fat tail, and the fat that covers the
entrails, and the appendage of the liver,
and the two kidneys with the fat that is on

them, and the right thigh (for it is a ram of
ordination), 23and one loaf of bread, and one
cake of bread with oil, and one wafer, out of
the basket of unleavened bread that is before
the LORD; 24and you shall put all these in the
hands of Aaron and in the hands of his sons,
and wave them for a wave offering before
the LORD. 25Then you shall take them from
their hands, and burn them on the altar in
addition to the burnt offering, as a pleasing
odor before the LORD; it is an offering by
fire to the LORD.
26"And you shall take the breast of the
ram of Aaron's ordination and wave it
for a wave offering before the LORD; and
it shall be your portion. 27And you shall
consecrate the breast of the wave offering,
and the thigh of the priests' portion, which
is waved, and which is offered from the ram
of ordination, since it is for Aaron and for
his sons. 28It shall be for Aaron and his sons
as a perpetual debt from the sons of Israel,
for it is the priests' portion to be offered by
the sons of Israel from their peace offerings;
it is their offering to the LORD.
29"The holy garments of Aaron shall be
for his sons after him, to be anointed in
them and ordained in them. 30The son who
is priest in his place shall wear them seven
days, when he comes into the tent of meeting
to minister in the holy place.
31"You shall take the ram of ordination,
and boil its flesh in a holy place; 32and Aaron
and his sons shall eat the flesh of the ram and
the bread that is in the basket, at the door
of the tent of meeting. 33They shall eat those
things with which atonement was made, to
ordain and consecrate them, but an outsider
shall not eat of them, because they are holy.
34And if any of the flesh for the ordination,
or of the bread, remain until the morning,
then you shall burn the remainder with fire;
it shall not be eaten, because it is holy.
35"Thus you shall do to Aaron and to
his sons, according to all that I have commanded you; through seven days shall you
ordain them, 36and every day you shall offer a
bull as a sin offering for atonement. Also you
shall offer a sin offering for the altar, when
you make atonement for it, and shall anoint
it, to consecrate it. 37Seven days you shall
make atonement for the altar, and consecrate
it, and the altar shall be most holy; whatever
touches the altar shall become holy.
38"Now this is what you shall offer upon
the altar: two lambs a year old day by day
continually. 39One lamb you shall offer in the
morning, and the other lamb you shall offer in
the evening; 40and with the first lamb a tenth
measure of fine flour mingled with a fourth
of a hin of beaten oil, and a fourth of a hin
of wine for a libation. 41And the other lamb
you shall offer in the evening, and shall offer
with it a cereal offering and its libation, as in
the morning, for a pleasing odor, an offering
by fire to the LORD. 42It shall be a continual
burnt offering throughout your generations
at the door of the tent of meeting before the
LORD, where I will meet with you, to speak
there to you. 43There I will meet with the
sons of Israel, and it shall be sanctified by my
glory; 44I will consecrate the tent of meeting
and the altar; Aaron also and his sons I will
consecrate, to serve me as priests. 45And I will
dwell among the sons of Israel, and will be
their God. 46And they shall know that I am
the LORD their God, who brought them forth
out of the land of Egypt that I might dwell
among them; I am the LORD their God."

A Psalm of David.

A Maskil.

PSALM 32 [31]

Blessed is he whose transgression is forgiven,
  whose sin is covered.
2Blessed is the man to whom the LORD
    imputes no iniquity,
  and in whose spirit there is no deceit.

3When I declared not my sin, my body
    wasted away
  through my groaning all day long.
4For day and night your hand was heavy
    upon me;
  my strength was dried up as by the heat
    of summer. *Selah*

5I acknowledged my sin to you,
and I did not hide my iniquity;
I said, "I will confess my transgressions to
the LORD";
then you forgave the guilt of my sin.
Selah

6Therefore let every one who is godly
offer prayer to you;
at a time of distress, in the rush of
great waters,
they shall not reach him.
7You are a hiding place for me,
you preserve me from trouble;
you surround me with deliverance.
Selah

8I will instruct you and teach you
the way you should go;
I will counsel you with my eye upon you.
9Be not like a horse or a mule, without
understanding,
which must be curbed with bit and bridle,
else it will not keep with you.
10Many are the pangs of the wicked;
but steadfast love surrounds him who
trusts in the LORD.
11Be glad in the LORD, and rejoice, O righteous,
and shout for joy, all you upright in heart!

MATTHEW 23

Then said Jesus to the crowds and to his disciples, 2"The scribes and the Pharisees sit on Moses' seat; 3so practice and observe whatever they tell you, but not what they do; for they preach, but do not practice. 4They bind heavy burdens, hard to bear, and lay them on men's shoulders; but they themselves will not move them with their finger.
5They do all their deeds to be seen by men; for they make their phylacteries broad and their fringes long, 6and they love the place of honor at feasts and the best seats in the synagogues, 7and salutations in the market places, and being called rabbi by men. 8But you are not to be called rabbi, for you have one teacher, and you are all brethren. 9And call no man your father on earth, for you have one Father, who is in heaven. 10Neither be called masters, for you have one master, the Christ. 11He who is greatest among you shall be your servant; 12whoever exalts himself will be humbled, and whoever humbles himself will be exalted.

13"But woe to you, scribes and Pharisees, hypocrites! because you shut the kingdom of heaven against men; for you neither enter yourselves, nor allow those who would enter to go in. 15Woe to you, scribes and Pharisees, hypocrites! for you traverse sea and land to make a single proselyte, and when he becomes a proselyte, you make him twice as much a child of hell as yourselves.

16"Woe to you, blind guides, who say, 'If any one swears by the temple, it is nothing; but if any one swears by the gold of the temple, he is bound by his oath.'
17You blind fools! For which is greater, the gold or the temple that has made the gold sacred? 18And you say, 'If any one swears by the altar, it is nothing; but if any one swears by the gift that is on the altar, he is bound by his oath.' 19You blind men! For which is greater, the gift or the altar that makes the gift sacred? 20So he who swears by the altar, swears by it and by everything on it; 21and he who swears by the temple, swears by it and by him who dwells in it; 22and he who swears by heaven, swears by the throne of God and by him who sits upon it.

23"Woe to you, scribes and Pharisees, hypocrites! for you tithe mint and dill and cummin, and have neglected the weightier matters of the law, justice and mercy and faith; these you ought to have done, without neglecting the others. 24You blind guides, straining out a gnat and swallowing a camel!

25"Woe to you, scribes and Pharisees, hypocrites! for you cleanse the outside of the cup and of the plate, but inside they are full of extortion and rapacity. 26You blind Pharisee! first cleanse the inside of the cup and of the plate, that the outside also may be clean.

27“Woe to you, scribes and Pharisees,
hypocrites! for you are like whitewashed
tombs, which outwardly appear beautiful,
but within they are full of dead men’s bones
and all uncleanness. 28So you also outwardly
appear righteous to men, but within you are
full of hypocrisy and iniquity.
29“Woe to you, scribes and Pharisees,
hypocrites! for you build the tombs of the
prophets and adorn the monuments of
the righteous, 30saying, ‘If we had lived in
the days of our fathers, we would not have
taken part with them in shedding the blood
of the prophets.’ 31Thus you witness against
yourselves, that you are sons of those who
murdered the prophets. 32Fill up, then, the
measure of your fathers. 33You serpents,
you brood of vipers, how are you to escape
being sentenced to hell? 34Therefore I send
you prophets and wise men and scribes,
some of whom you will kill and crucify, and
some you will scourge in your synagogues
and persecute from town to town, 35that
upon you may come all the righteous blood
shed on earth, from the blood of innocent
Abel to the blood of Zechari´ah the son of
Barachi´ah, whom you murdered between
the sanctuary and the altar. 36Truly, I say to
you, all this will come upon this generation.”

REFLECTION

When we stand before God, we find out how much we lack. Even though the Old Covenant priests are adorned in expensive and symbolic clothing “for glory and beauty” (Ex 28:40), that does not make them holy. They still have to be consecrated or “made sacred” in order to serve in the original Tabernacle. During their ordination ceremonies, sacrificial animals are offered for them: a bull and two rams. Aaron, the high priest, and his sons place their hands on the head of each victim animal as a sign of transferring their guilt onto it before it is ritually slaughtered. We too need to get rid of our sins—“When I declared not my sin, my body wasted away” (Ps 32:3). That is one reason going to Confession regularly is so important. Sadly, the scribes and Pharisees of Jesus’s time do not embody this lesson. Jesus saves his harshest invective for them, calling them hypocrites, blind guides, whitewashed tombs, and murderers. He endorses their teaching, but not their practice instructing the crowds to do what they say “but not what they do; for they preach, but do not practice” (Mt 23:3). Make some time this week to receive the Sacrament of Reconciliation, and then with God’s grace live the faith you confess.

February 6

EXODUS 30

“You shall make an altar to burn
incense upon; of acacia wood
shall you make it. 2A cubit shall
be its length, and a cubit its breadth; it
shall be square, and two cubits shall be
its height; its horns shall be of one piece
with it. 3And you shall overlay it with pure
gold, its top and its sides round about
and its horns; and you shall make for it a
molding of gold round about. 4And two
golden rings shall you make for it; under
its molding on two opposite sides of it shall
you make them, and they shall be holders
for poles with which to carry it. 5You
shall make the poles of acacia wood, and
overlay them with gold. 6And you shall put
it before the veil that is by the ark of the
covenant, before the mercy seat that is over
the covenant, where I will meet with you.
7And Aaron shall burn fragrant incense
on it; every morning when he dresses the
lamps he shall burn it, 8and when Aaron
sets up the lamps in the evening, he shall
burn it, a perpetual incense before the
LORD throughout your generations. 9You
shall offer no unholy incense thereon, nor
burnt offering, nor cereal offering; and you
shall pour no libation thereon. 10Aaron
shall make atonement upon its horns once
a year; with the blood of the sin offering

of atonement he shall make atonement for it once in the year throughout your generations; it is most holy to the LORD."

11 The LORD said to Moses, 12 "When you take the census of the sons of Israel, then each shall give a ransom for himself to the LORD when you number them, that there be no plague among them when you number them. 13 Each who is numbered in the census shall give this: half a shekel according to the shekel of the sanctuary (the shekel is twenty gerahs), half a shekel as an offering to the LORD. 14 Every one who is numbered in the census, from twenty years old and upward, shall give the LORD's offering. 15 The rich shall not give more, and the poor shall not give less, than the half shekel, when you give the LORD's offering to make atonement for yourselves. 16 And you shall take the atonement money from the sons of Israel, and shall appoint it for the service of the tent of meeting; that it may bring the sons of Israel to remembrance before the LORD, so as to make atonement for yourselves."

17 The LORD said to Moses, 18 "You shall also make a laver of bronze, with its base of bronze, for washing. And you shall put it between the tent of meeting and the altar, and you shall put water in it, 19 with which Aaron and his sons shall wash their hands and their feet. 20 When they go into the tent of meeting, or when they come near the altar to minister, to burn an offering by fire to the LORD, they shall wash with water, lest they die. 21 They shall wash their hands and their feet, lest they die: it shall be a statute for ever to them, even to him and to his descendants throughout their generations."

22 Moreover, the LORD said to Moses, 23 "Take the finest spices: of liquid myrrh five hundred shekels, and of sweet-smelling cinnamon half as much, that is, two hundred and fifty, and of aromatic cane two hundred and fifty, 24 and of cassia five hundred, according to the shekel of the sanctuary, and of olive oil a hin; 25 and you shall make of these a sacred anointing oil blended as by the perfumer; a holy anointing oil it shall be. 26 And you shall anoint with it the tent of meeting and the ark of the covenant, 27 and the table and all its utensils, and the lampstand and its utensils, and the altar of incense, 28 and the altar of burnt offering with all its utensils and the laver and its base; 29 you shall consecrate them, that they may be most holy; whatever touches them will become holy. 30 And you shall anoint Aaron and his sons, and consecrate them, that they may serve me as priests. 31 And you shall say to the sons of Israel, 'This shall be my holy anointing oil throughout your generations. 32 It shall not be poured upon the bodies of ordinary men, and you shall make no other like it in composition; it is holy, and it shall be holy to you. 33 Whoever compounds any like it or whoever puts any of it on an outsider shall be cut off from his people.' "

34 And the LORD said to Moses, "Take sweet spices, stacte, and onycha, and galbanum, sweet spices with pure frankincense (of each shall there be an equal part), 35 and make an incense blended as by the perfumer, seasoned with salt, pure and holy; 36 and you shall beat some of it very small, and put part of it before the covenant in the tent of meeting where I shall meet with you; it shall be for you most holy. 37 And the incense which you shall make according to its composition, you shall not make for yourselves; it shall be for you holy to the LORD. 38 Whoever makes any like it to use as perfume shall be cut off from his people."

31 The LORD said to Moses, 2 "See, I have called by name Bez′alel the son of Uri, son of Hur, of the tribe of Judah: 3 and I have filled him with the Spirit of God, with ability and intelligence, with knowledge and all craftsmanship, 4 to devise artistic designs, to work in gold, silver, and bronze, 5 in cutting stones for setting, and in carving wood, for work in every craft. 6 And behold, I have appointed with him Oho′liab, the son of Ahis′amach, of the tribe of Dan; and I have given to all able men ability, that they may make all that I have commanded you: 7 the tent of meeting, and the ark of the covenant, and the mercy seat that is thereon, and all the furnishings of the tent, 8 the

table and its utensils, and the pure lampstand
with all its utensils, and the altar of incense,
[9]and the altar of burnt offering with all its
utensils, and the laver and its base, [10]and the
finely worked garments, the holy garments
for Aaron the priest and the garments of his
sons, for their service as priests, [11]and the
anointing oil and the fragrant incense for
the holy place. According to all that I have
commanded you they shall do."
[12]And the LORD said to Moses, [13]"Say
to the sons of Israel, 'You shall keep my
sabbaths, for this is a sign between me and
you throughout your generations, that you
may know that I, the LORD, sanctify you.
[14]You shall keep the sabbath, because it is
holy for you; every one who profanes it shall
be put to death; whoever does any work on
it, that soul shall be cut off from among his
people. [15]Six days shall work be done, but
the seventh day is a sabbath of solemn rest,
holy to the LORD; whoever does any work
on the sabbath day shall be put to death.
[16]Therefore the sons of Israel shall keep the
sabbath, observing the sabbath throughout
their generations, as a perpetual covenant.
[17]It is a sign for ever between me and the
sons of Israel that in six days the LORD made
heaven and earth, and on the seventh day he
rested, and was refreshed.'"
[18]And he gave to Moses, when he had
made an end of speaking with him upon
Mount Sinai, the two tables of the covenant,
tables of stone, written with the finger
of God.

PSALM 33 [32]

Rejoice in the LORD, O you righteous!
Praise befits the upright.
[2]Praise the LORD with the lyre,
make melody to him with the harp of
ten strings!
[3]Sing to him a new song,
play skillfully on the strings, with
loud shouts.

[4]For the word of the LORD is upright;
and all his work is done in faithfulness.
[5]He loves righteousness and justice;
the earth is full of the mercy of the LORD.

[6]By the word of the LORD the heavens
were made,
and all their host by the breath of his mouth.
[7]He gathered the waters of the sea as
in a bottle;
he put the deeps in storehouses.

[8]Let all the earth fear the LORD,
let all the inhabitants of the world stand
in awe of him!
[9]For he spoke, and it came to be;
he commanded, and it stood forth.

[10]The LORD brings the counsel of the nations
to nought;
he frustrates the plans of the peoples.
[11]The counsel of the LORD stands for ever,
the thoughts of his heart to all generations.
[12]Blessed is the nation whose God is the LORD,
the people whom he has chosen as
his heritage!

[13]The LORD looks down from heaven,
he sees all the sons of men;
[14]from where he sits enthroned he
looks forth
on all the inhabitants of the earth,
[15]he who fashions the hearts of them all,
and observes all their deeds.
[16]A king is not saved by his great army;
a warrior is not delivered by his
great strength.
[17]The war horse is a vain hope for victory,
and by its great might it cannot save.

[18]Behold, the eye of the LORD is on those
who fear him,
on those who hope in his merciful love,
[19]that he may deliver their soul from death,
and keep them alive in famine.

[20]Our soul waits for the LORD;
he is our help and shield.
[21]Yes, our heart is glad in him,
because we trust in his holy name.
[22]Let your mercy, O LORD, be upon us,
even as we hope in you.

MATTHEW 23

37 "O Jerusalem, Jerusalem, killing the prophets and stoning those who are sent to you! How often would I have gathered your children together as a hen gathers her brood under her wings, and you would not! 38 Behold, your house is forsaken and desolate. 39 For I tell you, you will not see me again, until you say, 'Blessed is he who comes in the name of the Lord.'"

24 Jesus left the temple and was going away, when his disciples came to point out to him the buildings of the temple. 2 But he answered them, "You see all these, do you not? Truly, I say to you, there will not be left here one stone upon another, that will not be thrown down."

3 As he sat on the Mount of Olives, the disciples came to him privately, saying, "Tell us, when will this be, and what will be the sign of your coming and of the close of the age?" 4 And Jesus answered them, "Take heed that no one leads you astray. 5 For many will come in my name, saying, 'I am the Christ,' and they will lead many astray. 6 And you will hear of wars and rumors of wars; see that you are not alarmed; for this must take place, but the end is not yet. 7 For nation will rise against nation, and kingdom against kingdom, and there will be famines and earthquakes in various places: 8 all this is but the beginning of the sufferings.

9 "Then they will deliver you up to tribulation, and put you to death; and you will be hated by all nations for my name's sake. 10 And then many will fall away, and betray one another, and hate one another. 11 And many false prophets will arise and lead many astray. 12 And because wickedness is multiplied, most men's love will grow cold. 13 But he who endures to the end will be saved. 14 And this gospel of the kingdom will be preached throughout the whole world, as a testimony to all nations; and then the end will come."

REFLECTION

We are so busy working to perfect our lives and take care of necessities that God gives us a weekly day of rest so we can keep our priorities in order. The Sabbath is a strong reminder that something—or rather, someone—should take precedence in our lives. The psalmist reminds us that "the war horse is a vain hope for victory" (Ps 33:17). He might as well have said "the bank account" or "the military" or "career success." While these things are important in their place, final victory rests in the Lord's hands alone. That is why the psalm's message stands out: "Our soul waits for the Lord; he is our help and shield" (v. 20). In the end, he alone is what will satisfy. In today's gospel passage, Jesus forecasts the Temple's downfall and destruction: "There will not be left here one stone upon another" (Mt 24:2). Indeed, the Roman army destroyed the Temple in 70 AD. The Temple was temporary, intended to point to God's ultimate desire to dwell amongst his people, to indwell in their very souls, and to bring them to an eternal Sabbath rest in Heaven. What can you do this Sunday to keep holy the Lord's Day and make God and Heaven your first priority?

February 7

EXODUS 32

When the people saw that Moses delayed to come down from the mountain, the people gathered themselves together to Aaron, and said to him, "Up, make us gods, who shall go before us; as for this Moses, the man who brought us up out of the land of Egypt, we do not know what has become of him." 2 And Aaron said to them, "Take off the rings of gold which are in the ears of your wives, your sons, and your daughters, and bring them to me." 3 So all the people took off the rings of gold which were in their ears, and brought them to Aaron. 4 And he received the gold at their hand, and fashioned it with a graving tool, and made a molten calf; and they said, "These are your gods, O Israel, who brought you up out of the land of Egypt!" [5]When Aaron saw this, he built an altar before it; and Aaron made proclamation and said, "Tomorrow shall be a feast to the LORD." [6]And they rose up early the next day, and offered burnt offerings and brought peace offerings; and the people sat down to eat and drink, and rose up to play.

[7]And the LORD said to Moses, "Go down; for your people, whom you brought up out of the land of Egypt, have corrupted themselves; [8]they have turned aside quickly out of the way which I commanded them; they have made for themselves a molten calf, and have worshiped it and sacrificed to it, and said, 'These are your gods, O Israel, who brought you up out of the land of Egypt!'" [9]And the LORD said to Moses, "I have seen this people, and behold, it is a stiff-necked people; [10]now therefore let me alone, that my wrath may burn hot against them and I may consume them; but of you I will make a great nation."

[11]But Moses begged the LORD his God, and said, "O LORD, why does your wrath burn hot against your people, whom you have brought forth out of the land of Egypt with great power and with a mighty hand? [12]Why should the Egyptians say, 'With evil intent he brought them forth, to slay them in the mountains, and to consume them from the face of the earth'? Turn from your fierce wrath, and repent of this evil against your people. [13]Remember Abraham, Isaac, and Israel, your servants, to whom you swore by your own self, and said to them, 'I will multiply your descendants as the stars of heaven, and all this land that I have promised I will give to your descendants, and they shall inherit it for ever.'" [14]And the LORD repented of the evil which he thought to do to his people.

[15]And Moses turned, and went down from the mountain with the two tables of the covenant in his hands, tables that were written on both sides; on the one side and on the other were they written. [16]And the tables were the work of God, and the writing was the writing of God, graven upon the tables. [17]When Joshua heard the noise of the people as they shouted, he said to Moses, "There is a noise of war in the camp." [18]But he said, "It is not the sound of shouting for victory, or the sound of the cry of defeat, but the sound of singing that I hear." [19]And as soon as he came near the camp and saw the calf and the dancing, Moses' anger burned hot, and he threw the tables out of his hands and broke them at the foot of the mountain. [20]And he took the calf which they had made, and burnt it with fire, and ground it to powder, and scattered it upon the water, and made the sons of Israel drink it.

[21]And Moses said to Aaron, "What did this people do to you that you have brought a great sin upon them?" [22]And Aaron said, "Let not the anger of my lord burn hot; you know the people, that they are set on evil. [23]For they said to me, 'Make us gods, who shall go before us; as for this Moses, the man who brought us up out of the land of Egypt, we do not know what has become of him.' [24]And I said to them, 'Let any who have gold take it off'; so they gave it to me, and I threw it into the fire, and there came out this calf."

[25]And when Moses saw that the people had broken loose (for Aaron had let them break loose, to their shame among their enemies), [26]then Moses stood in the gate of the camp, and said, "Who is on the LORD's side? Come to me." And all the sons of Levi gathered themselves together to him. [27]And he said to them, "Thus says the LORD God of Israel, 'Put every man his sword on his side, and go back and forth from gate to gate throughout the camp, and slay every man his brother, and every man his companion, and every man his neighbor.'" [28]And the sons of Levi did according to the word of Moses; and there fell of the people that day about three thousand men. [29]And Moses said, "Today you have ordained yourselves for the service of the LORD, each one at the cost of his son and of his brother, that he may bestow a blessing upon you this day."

30 The next day Moses said to the people, "You have sinned a great sin. And now I will go up to the LORD; perhaps I can make atonement for your sin." 31 So Moses returned to the LORD and said, "Alas, this people have sinned a great sin; they have made for themselves gods of gold. 32 But now, if you will forgive their sin—and if not, blot me, I beg you, out of your book which you have written." 33 But the LORD said to Moses, "Whoever has sinned against me, him will I blot out of my book. 34 But now go, lead the people to the place of which I have spoken to you; behold, my angel shall go before you. Nevertheless, in the day when I visit, I will visit their sin upon them."

35 And the LORD sent a plague upon the people, because they made the calf which Aaron made.

33 The LORD said to Moses, "Depart, go up from here, you and the people whom you have brought up out of the land of Egypt, to the land of which I swore to Abraham, Isaac, and Jacob, saying, 'To your descendants I will give it.' 2 And I will send an angel before you, and I will drive out the Canaanites, the Am′orites, the Hittites, the Per′izzites, the Hi′vites, and the Jeb′usites. 3 Go up to a land flowing with milk and honey; but I will not go up among you, lest I consume you in the way, for you are a stiff-necked people."

4 When the people heard these evil tidings, they mourned; and no man put on his ornaments. 5 For the LORD had said to Moses, "Say to the sons of Israel, 'You are a stiff-necked people; if for a single moment I should go up among you, I would consume you. So now put off your ornaments from you, that I may know what to do with you.' " 6 Therefore the sons of Israel stripped themselves of their ornaments, from Mount Horeb onward.

7 Now Moses used to take the tent and pitch it outside the camp, far off from the camp; and he called it the tent of meeting. And every one who sought the LORD would go out to the tent of meeting, which was outside the camp. 8 Whenever Moses went out to the tent, all the people rose up, and every man stood at his tent door, and looked after Moses, until he had gone into the tent. 9 When Moses entered the tent, the pillar of cloud would descend and stand at the door of the tent, and the LORD would speak with Moses. 10 And when all the people saw the pillar of cloud standing at the door of the tent, all the people would rise up and worship, every man at his tent door. 11 Thus the LORD used to speak to Moses face to face, as a man speaks to his friend. When Moses turned again into the camp, his servant Joshua the son of Nun, a young man, did not depart from the tent.

12 Moses said to the LORD, "See, you say to me, 'Bring up this people'; but you have not let me know whom you will send with me. Yet you have said, 'I know you by name, and you have also found favor in my sight.' 13 Now therefore, I beg you, if I have found favor in your sight, show me now your ways, that I may know you and find favor in your sight. Consider too that this nation is your people." 14 And he said, "My presence will go with you, and I will give you rest." 15 And he said to him, "If your presence will not go with me, do not carry us up from here. 16 For how shall it be known that I have found favor in your sight, I and your people? Is it not in your going with us, so that we are distinct, I and your people, from all other people that are upon the face of the earth?"

17 And the LORD said to Moses, "This very thing that you have spoken I will do; for you have found favor in my sight, and I know you by name." 18 Moses said, "I beg you, show me your glory." 19 And he said, "I will make all my goodness pass before you, and will proclaim before you my name 'The LORD'; and I will be gracious to whom I will be gracious, and will show mercy on whom I will show mercy. 20 But," he said, "you cannot see my face; for man shall not see me and live." 21 And the LORD said, "Behold, there is a place by me where you shall stand upon the rock; 22 and while my glory passes by I will put

you in a cleft of the rock, and I will cover you with my hand until I have passed by; [23]then I will take away my hand, and you shall see my back; but my face shall not be seen."

A Psalm of David,
when he feigned madness before Abimelech,
so that he drove him out, and he went away.

PSALM 34 [33]

I will bless the LORD at all times;
his praise shall continually be in
my mouth.
[2]My soul makes its boast in the LORD;
let the humble hear and be glad.
[3]O magnify the LORD with me,
and let us exalt his name together!

[4]I sought the LORD, and he answered me,
and delivered me from all my fears.
[5]Look to him, and be radiant;
so your faces shall never be ashamed.
[6]This poor man cried, and the LORD
heard him,
and saved him out of all his troubles.
[7]The angel of the LORD encamps
around those who fear him, and
delivers them.
[8]O taste and see that the LORD is good!
Blessed is the man who takes refuge
in him!
[9]O fear the LORD, you his saints,
for those who fear him have no want!
[10]The young lions suffer want and hunger;
but those who seek the LORD lack no
good thing.

[11]Come, O sons, listen to me,
I will teach you the fear of the LORD.
[12]What man is there who desires life,
and covets many days, that he may
enjoy good?
[13]Keep your tongue from evil,
and your lips from speaking deceit.
[14]Depart from evil, and do good;
seek peace, and pursue it.
[15]The eyes of the LORD are toward
the righteous,
and his ears toward their cry.
[16]The face of the LORD is against evildoers,
to cut off the remembrance of them from
the earth.
[17]When the righteous cry for help,
the LORD hears,
and delivers them out of all their troubles.
[18]The LORD is near to the brokenhearted,
and saves the crushed in spirit.

[19]Many are the afflictions of the righteous;
but the LORD delivers him out of
them all.
[20]He keeps all his bones;
not one of them is broken.
[21]Evil shall slay the wicked;
and those who hate the righteous
will be condemned.
[22]The LORD redeems the life of his servants;
none of those who take refuge in him will
be condemned.

MATTHEW 24

**[15]"So when you see the desolat-
ing sacrilege spoken of by the
prophet Daniel, standing in the
holy place (let the reader understand),
[16]then let those who are in Judea flee**
to the mountains; [17]let him who is on the
housetop not go down to take what is in
his house; [18]and let him who is in the field
not turn back to get a coat. [19]And alas for
those who are with child and for those who
are nursing in those days! [20]Pray that your
flight may not be in winter or on a sabbath.
[21]For then there will be great tribulation,
such as has not been from the beginning
of the world until now, no, and never will
be. [22]And if those days had not been shortened, no human being would be saved; but
for the sake of the elect those days will be
shortened. [23]Then if any one says to you,
'Behold, here is the Christ!' or 'There he is!'
do not believe it. [24]For false Christs and false
prophets will arise and show great signs and

wonders, so as to lead astray, if possible, even the elect. [25]Behold, I have told you beforehand. [26]So, if they say to you, 'Behold, he is in the wilderness,' do not go out; if they say, 'Behold, he is in the inner rooms,' do not believe it. [27]For as the lightning comes from the east and shines as far as the west, so will be the coming of the Son of man. [28]Wherever the body is, there the eagles will be gathered together.

[29]"Immediately after the tribulation of those days the sun will be darkened, and the moon will not give its light, and the stars will fall from heaven, and the powers of the heavens will be shaken; [30]then will appear the sign of the Son of man in heaven, and then all the tribes of the earth will mourn, and they will see the Son of man coming on the clouds of heaven with power and great glory; [31]and he will send out his angels with a loud trumpet call, and they will gather his elect from the four winds, from one end of heaven to the other.

[32]"From the fig tree learn its lesson: as soon as its branch becomes tender and puts forth its leaves, you know that summer is near. [33]So also, when you see all these things, you know that he is near, at the very gates. [34]Truly, I say to you, this generation will not pass away till all these things take place. [35]Heaven and earth will pass away, but my words will not pass away."

REFLECTION

Duplicity destroys relationships. When we say one thing and do another, we forfeit the privilege of being trusted and seriously damage what remains of friendship. Only forty days after hearing the Ten Commandants and responding with one voice, "All the words which the Lord has spoken we will do" (Ex 24:3), the people of Israel turn away from God and break the covenant relationship they have just entered into by worshipping a golden calf instead of the one true God. When Moses returns from the mountaintop, Aaron downplays his own idol-making role in the people's apostasy. Aaron and God's people prove themselves duplicitous and unfaithful. In contrast, Moses, even in his wrath, is faithful to the people, leading them back to the truth and praying to the Lord for them. Indeed, Moses's sincerity makes way for intimacy with God, where he can speak with God face to face, as the psalmist tells us, "Look to him, and be radiant" (Ps 34:5). But while Moses's intercession wins God's continued presence with his sinful people, it comes at a cost—Moses will no longer be able to see God's face. Moses is a type of Jesus Christ, who willingly wins our salvation at great cost to himself, the cost of his life. Do you have any relationships in which you have been duplicitous? How can you make amends and begin to repair that relationship?

February 8

EXODUS 34

The Lord said to Moses, "Cut two tables of stone like the first; and I will write upon the tables the words that were on the first tables, which you broke. [2]Be ready in the morning, and come up in the morning to Mount Sinai, and present yourself there to me on the top of the mountain. [3]No man shall come up with you, and let no man be seen throughout all the mountain; let no flocks or herds feed before that mountain." [4]So Moses cut two tables of stone like the first; and he rose early in the morning and went up on Mount Sinai, as the Lord had commanded him, and took in his hand two tables of stone. [5]And the Lord descended in the cloud and stood with him there, and proclaimed the name of the Lord. [6]The Lord passed before him, and proclaimed, "The Lord, the Lord, a God merciful and gracious, slow to anger, and abounding in mercy and faithfulness, [7]keeping merciful love for thousands, forgiving iniquity and transgression and sin, but who will by no means clear the guilty, visiting the iniquity of the fathers upon the children and the children's children, to the third and the fourth generation." 8And Moses made haste to bow his head toward the earth, and worshiped. 9And he said, "If now I have found favor in your sight, O Lord, let the Lord, I beg you, go in the midst of us, although it is a stiff-necked people; and pardon our iniquity and our sin, and take us for your inheritance."

10And he said, "Behold, I make a covenant. Before all your people I will do marvels, such as have not been wrought in all the earth or in any nation; and all the people among whom you are shall see the work of the LORD; for it is a terrible thing that I will do with you.

11"Observe what I command you this day. Behold, I will drive out before you the Am′orites, the Canaanites, the Hittites, the Per′izzites, the Hi′vites, and the Jeb′usites. 12Take heed to yourself, lest you make a covenant with the inhabitants of the land where you go, lest it become a snare in your midst. 13You shall tear down their altars, and break their pillars, and cut down their Ashe′rim 14(for you shall worship no other god, for the LORD, whose name is Jealous, is a jealous God), 15lest you make a covenant with the inhabitants of the land, and when they play the harlot after their gods and sacrifice to their gods and one invites you, you eat of his sacrifice, 16and you take of their daughters for your sons, and their daughters play the harlot after their gods and make your sons play the harlot after their gods.

17"You shall make for yourself no molten gods.

18"The feast of unleavened bread you shall keep. Seven days you shall eat unleavened bread, as I commanded you, at the time appointed in the month Abib; for in the month of Abib you came out from Egypt. 19All that opens the womb is mine, all your male cattle, the firstlings of cow and sheep. 20The firstling of a donkey you shall redeem with a lamb, or if you will not redeem it you shall break its neck. All the first-born of your sons you shall redeem. And none shall appear before me empty.

21"Six days you shall work, but on the seventh day you shall rest; in plowing time and in harvest you shall rest. 22And you shall observe the feast of weeks, the first fruits of wheat harvest, and the feast of ingathering at the year's end. 23Three times in the year shall all your males appear before the LORD God, the God of Israel. 24For I will cast out nations before you, and enlarge your borders; neither shall any man desire your land, when you go up to appear before the LORD your God three times in the year.

25"You shall not offer the blood of my sacrifice with leaven; neither shall the sacrifice of the feast of the Passover be left until the morning. 26The first of the first fruits of your ground you shall bring to the house of the LORD your God. You shall not boil a kid in its mother's milk."

27And the LORD said to Moses, "Write these words; in accordance with these words I have made a covenant with you and with Israel." 28And he was there with the LORD forty days and forty nights; he neither ate bread nor drank water. And he wrote upon the tables the words of the covenant, the ten commandments.

29When Moses came down from Mount Sinai, with the two tables of the covenant in his hand as he came down from the mountain, Moses did not know that the skin of his face shone because he had been talking with God. 30And when Aaron and all the sons of Israel saw Moses, behold, the skin of his face shone, and they were afraid to come near him. 31But Moses called to them; and Aaron and all the leaders of the congregation returned to him, and Moses talked with them. 32And afterward all the sons of Israel came near, and he gave them in commandment all that the LORD had spoken with him in Mount Sinai. 33And when Moses had finished speaking with them, he put a veil on his face; 34but whenever Moses went in before the LORD to speak with him, he took the veil off, until he came out; and when he came out, and told the sons of Israel what he was commanded, 35the sons of Israel saw the face of Moses, that the skin of Moses' face shone; and Moses would put the veil upon his face again, until he went in to speak with him.

35 Moses assembled all the congregation of the sons of Israel, and said to them, "These are the things which the LORD has commanded you to do. [2]Six days shall work be done, but on the seventh day you shall have a holy sabbath of solemn rest to the LORD; whoever does any work on it shall be put to death; [3]you shall kindle no fire in all your habitations on the sabbath day."

[4]Moses said to all the congregation of the sons of Israel, "This is the thing which the LORD has commanded. [5]Take from among you an offering to the LORD; whoever is of a generous heart, let him bring the LORD's offering: gold, silver, and bronze; [6]blue and purple and scarlet stuff and fine twined linen; goats' hair, [7]tanned rams' skins, and goatskins; acacia wood, [8]oil for the light, spices for the anointing oil and for the fragrant incense, [9]and onyx stones and stones for setting, for the ephod and for the breastpiece.

[10]"And let every able man among you come and make all that the LORD has commanded: the tabernacle, [11]its tent and its covering, its hooks and its frames, its bars, its pillars, and its bases; [12]the ark with its poles, the mercy seat, and the veil of the screen; [13]the table with its poles and all its utensils, and the bread of the Presence; [14]the lampstand also for the light, with its utensils and its lamps, and the oil for the light; [15]and the altar of incense, with its poles, and the anointing oil and the fragrant incense, and the screen for the door, at the door of the tabernacle; [16]the altar of burnt offering, with its grating of bronze, its poles, and all its utensils, the laver and its base; [17]the hangings of the court, its pillars and its bases, and the screen for the gate of the court; [18]the pegs of the tabernacle and the pegs of the court, and their cords; [19]the finely wrought garments for ministering in the holy place, the holy garments for Aaron the priest, and the garments of his sons, for their service as priests."

[20]Then all the congregation of the sons of Israel departed from the presence of Moses. [21]And they came, every one whose heart stirred him, and every one whose spirit moved him, and brought the LORD's offering to be used for the tent of meeting, and for all its service, and for the holy garments. [22]So they came, both men and women; all who were of a willing heart brought brooches and earrings and signet rings and armlets, all sorts of gold objects, every man dedicating an offering of gold to the LORD. [23]And every man with whom was found blue or purple or scarlet stuff or fine linen or goats' hair or tanned rams' skins or goatskins, brought them. [24]Every one who could make an offering of silver or bronze brought it as the LORD's offering; and every man with whom was found acacia wood of any use in the work, brought it. [25]And all women who had ability spun with their hands, and brought what they had spun in blue and purple and scarlet stuff and fine twined linen; [26]all the women whose hearts were moved with ability spun the goats' hair. [27]And the leaders brought onyx stones and stones to be set, for the ephod and for the breastpiece, [28]and spices and oil for the light, and for the anointing oil, and for the fragrant incense. [29]All the men and women, the sons of Israel, whose heart moved them to bring anything for the work which the LORD had commanded by Moses to be done, brought it as their freewill offering to the LORD.

A Psalm of David.

PSALM 35 [34]

Contend, O LORD, with those who contend
with me;
fight against those who fight against me!
[2]Take hold of shield and buckler,
and rise for my help!
[3]Draw the spear and javelin
against my pursuers!
Say to my soul,
"I am your deliverance!"

[4]Let them be put to shame and dishonor
who seek after my life!
Let them be turned back and confounded
who devise evil against me!
[5]Let them be like chaff before the wind,
with the angel of the LORD driving
them on!
[6]Let their way be dark and slippery,
with the angel of the LORD pursuing them!

[7]For without cause they hid their net for me;
without cause they dug a pit for my life.
[8]Let ruin come upon them unawares!
And let the net which they hid ensnare them;
let them fall therein to ruin!

[9]Then my soul shall rejoice in the LORD,
exulting in his deliverance.
[10]All my bones shall say,
"O LORD, who is like you,
you who deliver the weak
from him who is too strong for him,
the weak and needy from him who
despoils him?"

[11]Malicious witnesses rise up;
they ask me of things that I do not know.
[12]They repay me evil for good;
my soul is forlorn.
[13]But I, when they were sick—
I wore sackcloth,
I afflicted myself with fasting.
I prayed with head bowed on my bosom,
[14] as though I grieved for my friend or
my brother;
I went about as one who laments his mother,
bowed down and in mourning.

MATTHEW 24

[36]**"But of that day and hour no one knows, not even the angels of heaven, nor the Son, but the Father only.** [37]**As were the days of Noah, so**
will be the coming of the Son of man. [38]For
as in those days before the flood they were
eating and drinking, marrying and giving in
marriage, until the day when Noah entered
the ark, [39]and they did not know until the
flood came and swept them all away, so will
be the coming of the Son of man. [40]Then two
men will be in the field; one is taken and one
is left. [41]Two women will be grinding at the
mill; one is taken and one is left. [42]Watch
therefore, for you do not know on what day
your Lord is coming. [43]But know this, that
if the householder had known in what part
of the night the thief was coming, he would
have watched and would not have let his
house be broken into. [44]Therefore you also
must be ready; for the Son of man is coming
at an hour you do not expect.
[45]"Who then is the faithful and wise
servant, whom his master has set over his
household, to give them their food at the
proper time? [46]Blessed is that servant whom
his master when he comes will find so doing.
[47]Truly, I say to you, he will set him over all
his possessions. [48]But if that wicked servant
says to himself, 'My master is delayed,' [49]and
begins to beat his fellow servants, and eats
and drinks with the drunken, [50]the master
of that servant will come on a day when
he does not expect him and at an hour he
does not know, [51]and will punish him, and
put him with the hypocrites; there men will
weep and gnash their teeth.

25 "Then the kingdom of heaven shall
be compared to ten maidens who
took their lamps and went to meet the
bridegroom. [2]Five of them were foolish,
and five were wise. [3]For when the foolish
took their lamps, they took no oil with
them; [4]but the wise took flasks of oil
with their lamps. [5]As the bridegroom was
delayed, they all slumbered and slept. [6]But
at midnight there was a cry, 'Behold, the
bridegroom! Come out to meet him.' [7]Then
all those maidens rose and trimmed their
lamps. [8]And the foolish said to the wise,
'Give us some of your oil, for our lamps are
going out.' [9]But the wise replied, 'Perhaps
there will not be enough for us and for
you; go rather to the dealers and buy for
yourselves.' [10]And while they went to buy,
the bridegroom came, and those who were
ready went in with him to the marriage
feast; and the door was shut. [11]Afterward

the other maidens came also, saying, 'Lord,
lord, open to us.' 12But he replied, 'Truly,
I say to you, I do not know you.' 13Watch
therefore, for you know neither the day nor
the hour."

REFLECTION

Vigilance and radiance go hand in hand—whether it be a night watchman or a lighthouse keeper, anyone who has to stay awake at night needs light. Moses's awesome example contains a lesson for us. He encounters the Lord on Mt. Sinai in a special vision and then comes down from that literal "mountain top experience" to be with the people again. But because of his vigilance in the Lord's presence and his willingness to seek God, Moses's face begins to shine like the sun. It is so bright that the people ask him to veil himself because they cannot stand the brightness. The lesson is simple: vigilance in prayer leads to radiance in life. When we spend time building a deep relationship with God, it pays off in the rest of our lives with radiant joy, hope, and charity. The virgins in Jesus's parable are similar. They are alert, keeping vigil, keeping watch for the return of the bridegroom. They are ready, oil lamps in hand, when he comes. Jesus encourages us to follow their example in waiting for the Second Coming: "Watch therefore, for you know neither the day nor the hour" (Mt 25:13). Are you willing to keep vigil for the Lord and wait for his presence?

February 9

EXODUS 35

**30And Moses said to the sons
of Israel, "See, the LORD has
called by name Bez'alel the son
of Uri, son of Hur, of the tribe of Judah;
31and he has filled him with the Spirit
of God, with ability, with intelligence,**
with knowledge, and with all craftsmanship,
32to devise artistic designs, to work in gold
and silver and bronze, 33in cutting stones
for setting, and in carving wood, for work
in every skilled craft. 34And he has inspired
him to teach, both him and Oho'liab the son
of Ahis'amach of the tribe of Dan. 35He has
filled them with ability to do every sort of
work done by a craftsman or by a designer
or by an embroiderer in blue and purple
and scarlet stuff and fine twined linen, or
by a weaver—by any sort of workman or
skilled designer.

36 Bez'alel and Oho'liab and every able
man in whom the LORD has put
ability and intelligence to know how to
do any work in the construction of the
sanctuary shall work in accordance with all
that the LORD has commanded."

2And Moses called Bez'alel and Oho'liab
and every able man in whose mind the
LORD had put ability, every one whose heart
stirred him up to come to do the work; 3and
they received from Moses all the freewill
offering which the sons of Israel had brought
for doing the work on the sanctuary. They
still kept bringing him freewill offerings
every morning, 4so that all the able men
who were doing every sort of task on the
sanctuary came, each from the task that he
was doing, 5and said to Moses, "The people
bring much more than enough for doing the
work which the LORD has commanded us
to do." 6So Moses gave command, and word
was proclaimed throughout the camp, "Let
neither man nor woman do anything more
for the offering for the sanctuary." So the
people were restrained from bringing; 7for
the stuff they had was sufficient to do all the
work, and more.

8And all the able men among the workmen
made the tabernacle with ten curtains; they
were made of fine twined linen and blue
and purple and scarlet stuff, with cherubim
skilfully worked. 9The length of each curtain
was twenty-eight cubits, and the breadth of
each curtain four cubits; all the curtains had
the same measure.

10And he coupled five curtains to one
another, and the other five curtains he

coupled to one another. 11And he made
loops of blue on the edge of the outmost
curtain of the first set; likewise he made
them on the edge of the outmost curtain of
the second set; 12he made fifty loops on the
one curtain, and he made fifty loops on the
edge of the curtain that was in the second
set; the loops were opposite one another.
13And he made fifty clasps of gold, and
coupled the curtains one to the other with
clasps; so the tabernacle was one whole.

14He also made curtains of goats' hair for
a tent over the tabernacle; he made eleven
curtains. 15The length of each curtain
was thirty cubits, and the breadth of each
curtain four cubits; the eleven curtains
had the same measure. 16He coupled five
curtains by themselves, and six curtains by
themselves. 17And he made fifty loops on
the edge of the outmost curtain of the one
set, and fifty loops on the edge of the other
connecting curtain. 18And he made fifty
clasps of bronze to couple the tent together
that it might be one whole. 19And he made
for the tent a covering of tanned rams' skins
and goatskins.

20Then he made the upright frames for the
tabernacle of acacia wood. 21Ten cubits was
the length of a frame, and a cubit and a half
the breadth of each frame. 22Each frame had
two tenons, for fitting together; he did this
for all the frames of the tabernacle. 23The
frames for the tabernacle he made thus:
twenty frames for the south side; 24and he
made forty bases of silver under the twenty
frames, two bases under one frame for its two
tenons, and two bases under another frame
for its two tenons. 25And for the second
side of the tabernacle, on the north side, he
made twenty frames 26and their forty bases
of silver, two bases under one frame and
two bases under another frame. 27And for
the rear of the tabernacle westward he made
six frames. 28And he made two frames for
corners of the tabernacle in the rear. 29And
they were separate beneath, but joined at the
top, at the first ring; he made two of them
thus, for the two corners. 30There were eight
frames with their bases of silver: sixteen
bases, under every frame two bases.

31And he made bars of acacia wood, five for
the frames of the one side of the tabernacle,
32and five bars for the frames of the other side
of the tabernacle, and five bars for the frames
of the tabernacle at the rear westward. 33And
he made the middle bar to pass through from
end to end halfway up the frames. 34And he
overlaid the frames with gold, and made
their rings of gold for holders for the bars,
and overlaid the bars with gold.

35And he made the veil of blue and purple
and scarlet stuff and fine twined linen; with
cherubim skilfully worked he made it. 36And
for it he made four pillars of acacia, and
overlaid them with gold; their hooks were
of gold, and he cast for them four bases of
silver. 37He also made a screen for the door
of the tent, of blue and purple and scarlet
stuff and fine twined linen, embroidered
with needlework; 38and its five pillars with
their hooks. He overlaid their capitals, and
their fillets were of gold, but their five bases
were of bronze.

37 Bez′alel made the ark of acacia
wood; two cubits and a half was its
length, a cubit and a half its breadth, and a
cubit and a half its height. 2And he overlaid
it with pure gold within and without, and
made a molding of gold around it. 3And
he cast for it four rings of gold for its four
corners, two rings on its one side and two
rings on its other side. 4And he made poles
of acacia wood, and overlaid them with
gold, 5and put the poles into the rings on
the sides of the ark, to carry the ark. 6And
he made a mercy seat of pure gold; two
cubits and a half was its length, and a cubit
and a half its breadth. 7And he made two
cherubim of hammered gold; on the two
ends of the mercy seat he made them, 8one
cherub on the one end, and one cherub on
the other end; of one piece with the mercy
seat he made the cherubim on its two ends.
9The cherubim spread out their wings
above, overshadowing the mercy seat with
their wings, with their faces one to another;
toward the mercy seat were the faces of
the cherubim.

10He also made the table of acacia wood;
two cubits was its length, a cubit its breadth,

and a cubit and a half its height; [11]and he
overlaid it with pure gold, and made a
molding of gold around it. [12]And he made
around it a frame a handbreadth wide,
and made a molding of gold around the
frame. [13]He cast for it four rings of gold,
and fastened the rings to the four corners
at its four legs. [14]Close to the frame were the
rings, as holders for the poles to carry the
table. [15]He made the poles of acacia wood
to carry the table, and overlaid them with
gold. [16]And he made the vessels of pure gold
which were to be upon the table, its plates
and dishes for incense, and its bowls and
flagons with which to pour libations.

[17]He also made the lampstand of pure gold.
The base and the shaft of the lampstand
were made of hammered work; its cups, its
capitals, and its flowers were of one piece with
it. [18]And there were six branches going out of
its sides, three branches of the lampstand out
of one side of it and three branches of the
lampstand out of the other side of it; [19]three
cups made like almonds, each with capital
and flower, on one branch, and three cups
made like almonds, each with capital and
flower, on the other branch—so for the six
branches going out of the lampstand. [20]And
on the lampstand itself were four cups made
like almonds, with their capitals and flowers,
[21]and a capital of one piece with it under
each pair of the six branches going out of
it. [22]Their capitals and their branches were
of one piece with it; the whole of it was one
piece of hammered work of pure gold. [23]And
he made its seven lamps and its snuffers and
its trays of pure gold. [24]He made it and all its
utensils of a talent of pure gold.

[25]He made the altar of incense of acacia
wood; its length was a cubit, and its breadth
was a cubit; it was square, and two cubits
was its height; its horns were of one piece
with it. [26]He overlaid it with pure gold, its
top, and its sides round about, and its horns;
and he made a molding of gold round about
it, [27]and made two rings of gold on it under
its molding, on two opposite sides of it, as
holders for the poles with which to carry
it. [28]And he made the poles of acacia wood,
and overlaid them with gold.

[29]He made the holy anointing oil also, and
the pure fragrant incense, blended as by
the perfumer.

A Psalm of David.

PSALM 35 [34]

[15]But at my stumbling they gathered in glee,
they gathered together against me;
cripples whom I did not know
slandered me without ceasing;
[16]they impiously mocked more and more,
gnashing at me with their teeth.

[17]How long, O LORD, will you look on?
Rescue me from their ravages,
my life from the lions!
[18]Then I will thank you in the great
congregation;
in the mighty throng I will praise you.

[19]Let not those rejoice over me
who are wrongfully my foes,
and let not those wink the eye
who hate me without cause.
[20]For they do not speak peace,
but against those who are quiet in the land
they conceive words of deceit.
[21]They open wide their mouths against me;
they say, "Aha, Aha!
our eyes have seen it!"

[22]You have seen, O LORD; be not silent!
O LORD, be not far from me!
[23]Bestir yourself, and awake for my right,
for my cause, my God and my Lord!
[24]Vindicate me, O LORD, my God, according
to your righteousness;
and let them not rejoice over me!
[25]Let them not say to themselves,
"Aha, we have our heart's desire!"
Let them not say, "We have swallowed
him up."

[26]Let them be put to shame and confusion
altogether
who rejoice at my calamity!

Let them be clothed with shame
and dishonor
who magnify themselves against me!

27Let those who desire my vindication
shout for joy and be glad,
and say evermore,
"Great is the LORD,
who delights in the welfare of
his servant!"
28Then my tongue shall tell of your
righteousness
and of your praise all the day long.

MATTHEW 25

14"For it will be as when a man
going on a journey called his
servants and entrusted to them
his property; 15to one he gave five
talents, to another two, to another one,
to each according to his ability. Then
he went away. 16He who had received the
five talents went at once and traded with
them; and he made five talents more. 17So
also, he who had the two talents made two
talents more. 18But he who had received the
one talent went and dug in the ground and
hid his master's money. 19Now after a long
time the master of those servants came
and settled accounts with them. 20And he
who had received the five talents came
forward, bringing five talents more, saying,
'Master, you delivered to me five talents;
here I have made five talents more.' 21His
master said to him, 'Well done, good and
faithful servant; you have been faithful over
a little, I will set you over much; enter into
the joy of your master.' 22And he also who
had the two talents came forward, saying,
'Master, you delivered to me two talents;
here I have made two talents more.' 23His
master said to him, 'Well done, good and
faithful servant; you have been faithful
over a little, I will set you over much; enter
into the joy of your master.' 24He also who
had received the one talent came forward,
saying, 'Master, I knew you to be a hard
man, reaping where you did not sow, and
gathering where you did not winnow; 25so
I was afraid, and I went and hid your talent
in the ground. Here you have what is yours.'
26But his master answered him, 'You wicked
and slothful servant! You knew that I reap
where I have not sowed, and gather where
I have not winnowed? 27Then you ought to
have invested my money with the bankers,
and at my coming I should have received
what was my own with interest. 28So take
the talent from him, and give it to him who
has the ten talents. 29For to every one who
has will more be given, and he will have
abundance; but from him who has not,
even what he has will be taken away. 30And
cast the worthless servant into the outer
darkness, where there will be weeping and
gnashing of teeth.'"

REFLECTION

We are in a state of constant tension between being generous and being miserly. Everyone wants our money and most ask for it: businesses, charities, family members. The Israelites set a great example of generosity. After their apostasy at the golden calf incident, they have a change of heart, renew the covenant with the Lord, and make personal freewill offerings for the construction of the Tabernacle. In fact, they offer so much that workmen have to ask that they stop bringing offerings (see Ex 36:6). We see the counter-example in the psalm, where the psalmist's generosity and friendship have been repaid by betrayal and derision. His former friends now "hate [him] without cause" (Ps 35:19), showing themselves to be ungenerous and stingy. Jesus similarly, in the Parable of the Talents, shows us the difference between people who act out of fear and greed and those who act out of generosity and faith. The fearful, miserly servant buries the money entrusted to him in the ground and is judged "wicked and slothful" (Mt 25:26). The faithful servants, however, have diligently invested their master's money to make substantial profit. Their generosity to their master in working hard for him has paid off. Who needs your generosity (in time, talent, or treasure) today?

February 10

EXODUS 38

He made the altar of burnt offering also of acacia wood; five cubits was its length, and five cubits its breadth; it was square, and three cubits was its height. 2He made horns for it on its four corners; its horns were of one piece with it, and he overlaid it with bronze. 3And he made all the utensils of the altar, the pots, the shovels, the basins, the forks, and the firepans: all its utensils he made of bronze. 4And he made for the altar a grating, a network of bronze, under its ledge, extending halfway down. 5He cast four rings on the four corners of the bronze grating as holders for the poles; 6he made the poles of acacia wood, and overlaid them with bronze. 7And he put the poles through the rings on the sides of the altar, to carry it with them; he made it hollow, with boards.

8And he made the laver of bronze and its base of bronze, from the mirrors of the ministering women who ministered at the door of the tent of meeting.

9And he made the court; for the south side the hangings of the court were of fine twined linen, a hundred cubits; 10their pillars were twenty and their bases twenty, of bronze, but the hooks of the pillars and their fillets were of silver. 11And for the north side a hundred cubits, their pillars twenty, their bases twenty, of bronze, but the hooks of the pillars and their fillets were of silver. 12And for the west side were hangings of fifty cubits, their pillars ten, and their sockets ten; the hooks of the pillars and their fillets were of silver. 13And for the front to the east, fifty cubits. 14The hangings for one side of the gate were fifteen cubits, with three pillars and three bases. 15And so for the other side; on this hand and that hand by the gate of the court were hangings of fifteen cubits, with three pillars and three bases. 16All the hangings round about the court were of fine twined linen. 17And the bases for the pillars were of bronze, but the hooks of the pillars and their fillets were of silver; the overlaying of their capitals was also of silver, and all the pillars of the court were filleted with silver. 18And the screen for the gate of the court was embroidered with needlework in blue and purple and scarlet stuff and fine twined linen; it was twenty cubits long and five cubits high in its breadth, corresponding to the hangings of the court. 19And their pillars were four; their four bases were of bronze, their hooks of silver, and the overlaying of their capitals and their fillets of silver. 20And all the pegs for the tabernacle and for the court round about were of bronze.

21This is the sum of the things for the tabernacle, the tabernacle of the covenant, as they were counted at the commandment of Moses, for the work of the Levites under the direction of Ith′amar the son of Aaron the priest. 22Bez′alel the son of Uri, son of Hur, of the tribe of Judah, made all that the LORD commanded Moses; 23and with him was Oho′liab the son of Ahis′amach, of the tribe of Dan, a craftsman and designer and embroiderer in blue and purple and scarlet stuff and fine twined linen.

24All the gold that was used for the work, in all the construction of the sanctuary, the gold from the offering, was twenty-nine talents and seven hundred and thirty shekels, by the shekel of the sanctuary. 25And the silver from those of the congregation who were numbered was a hundred talents and a thousand seven hundred and seventy-five shekels, by the shekel of the sanctuary: 26a beka a head (that is, half a shekel, by the shekel of the sanctuary), for every one who was numbered in the census, from twenty years old and upward, for six hundred and three thousand, five hundred and fifty men. 27The hundred talents of silver were for casting the bases of the sanctuary, and the bases of the veil; a hundred bases for the hundred talents, a talent for a base. 28And of the thousand seven hundred and seventy-five shekels he made hooks for the pillars, and overlaid their capitals and made fillets for them. [29]And the bronze that was contributed was seventy talents, and two thousand and four hundred shekels; [30]with it he made the bases for the door of the tent of meeting, the bronze altar and the bronze grating for it and all the utensils of the altar, [31]the bases round about the court, and the bases of the gate of the court, all the pegs of the tabernacle, and all the pegs round about the court.

39 And of the blue and purple and scarlet stuff they made finely wrought garments, for ministering in the holy place; they made the holy garments for Aaron; as the LORD had commanded Moses.

[2]And he made the ephod of gold, blue and purple and scarlet stuff, and fine twined linen. [3]And gold leaf was hammered out and cut into threads to work into the blue and purple and the scarlet stuff, and into the fine twined linen, in skilled design. [4]They made for the ephod shoulder-pieces, joined to it at its two edges. [5]And the skilfully woven band upon it, to belt it on, was of the same materials and workmanship, of gold, blue and purple and scarlet stuff, and fine twined linen; as the LORD had commanded Moses.

[6]The onyx stones were prepared, enclosed in settings of gold filigree and engraved like the engravings of a signet, according to the names of the sons of Israel. [7]And he set them on the shoulder-pieces of the ephod, to be stones of remembrance for the sons of Israel; as the LORD had commanded Moses.

[8]He made the breastpiece, in skilled work, like the work of the ephod, of gold, blue and purple and scarlet stuff, and fine twined linen. [9]It was square; the breastpiece was made double, a span its length and a span its breadth when doubled. [10]And they set in it four rows of stones. A row of sardius, topaz, and carbuncle was the first row; [11]and the second row, an emerald, a sapphire, and a diamond; [12]and the third row, a jacinth, an agate, and an amethyst; [13]and the fourth row, a beryl, an onyx, and a jasper; they were enclosed in settings of gold filigree. [14]There were twelve stones with their names according to the names of the sons of Israel; they were like signets, each engraved with its name, for the twelve tribes. [15]And they made on the breastpiece twisted chains like cords, of pure gold; [16]and they made two settings of gold filigree and two gold rings, and put the two rings on the two edges of the breastpiece; [17]and they put the two cords of gold in the two rings at the edges of the breastpiece. [18]Two ends of the two cords they had attached to the two settings of filigree; thus they attached it in front to the shoulder-pieces of the ephod. [19]Then they made two rings of gold, and put them at the two ends of the breastpiece, on its inside edge next to the ephod. [20]And they made two rings of gold, and attached them in front to the lower part of the two shoulder-pieces of the ephod, at its joining above the skilfully woven band of the ephod. [21]And they bound the breastpiece by its rings to the rings of the ephod with a lace of blue, so that it should lie upon the skilfully woven band of the ephod, and that the breastpiece should not come loose from the ephod; as the LORD had commanded Moses.

[22]He also made the robe of the ephod woven all of blue; [23]and the opening of the robe in it was like the opening in a garment, with a binding around the opening, that it might not be torn. [24]On the skirts of the robe they made pomegranates of blue and purple and scarlet stuff and fine twined linen. [25]They also made bells of pure gold, and put the bells between the pomegranates upon the skirts of the robe round about, between the pomegranates; [26]a bell and a pomegranate, a bell and a pomegranate round about upon the skirts of the robe for ministering; as the LORD had commanded Moses.

[27]They also made the coats, woven of fine linen, for Aaron and his sons, [28]and the turban of fine linen, and the caps of fine linen, and the linen breeches of fine twined linen, [29]and the sash of fine twined linen and of blue and purple and scarlet stuff, embroidered with needlework; as the LORD had commanded Moses.

[30]And they made the plate of the holy crown of pure gold, and wrote upon it an inscription, like the engraving of a signet, "Holy to the LORD." [31]And they tied to it a

lace of blue, to fasten it on the turban above; as the LORD had commanded Moses.
32Thus all the work of the tabernacle of the
tent of meeting was finished; and the sons of Israel had done according to all that the LORD had commanded Moses; so had they
done. 33And they brought the tabernacle
to Moses, the tent and all its utensils, its hooks, its frames, its bars, its pillars, and
its bases; 34the covering of tanned rams'
skins and goatskins, and the veil of the
screen; 35the ark of the covenant with its
poles and the mercy seat; 36the table with all
its utensils, and the bread of the Presence;
37the lampstand of pure gold and its lamps
with the lamps set and all its utensils, and
the oil for the light; 38the golden altar, the
anointing oil and the fragrant incense, and
the screen for the door of the tent; 39the
bronze altar, and its grating of bronze, its poles, and all its utensils; the laver and its
base; 40the hangings of the court, its pillars,
and its bases, and the screen for the gate of the court, its cords, and its pegs; and all the utensils for the service of the tabernacle,
for the tent of meeting; 41the finely worked
garments for ministering in the holy place, the holy garments for Aaron the priest, and the garments of his sons to serve as
priests. 42According to all that the LORD had
commanded Moses, so the sons of Israel
had done all the work. 43And Moses saw
all the work, and behold, they had done it; as the LORD had commanded, so had they done it. And Moses blessed them.

To the choirmaster.
A Psalm of David, the servant of the LORD.

PSALM 36 [35]

Transgression speaks to the wicked deep in
his heart;
there is no fear of God
before his eyes.
2For he flatters himself in his own eyes
that his iniquity cannot be found out
and hated.
3The words of his mouth are mischief
and deceit;
he has ceased to act wisely and do good.
4He plots mischief while on his bed;
he sets himself in a way that is not good;
he spurns not evil.

5Your mercy, O LORD, extends to the
heavens,
your faithfulness to the clouds.
6Your righteousness is like the mountains
of God,
your judgments are like the great deep;
man and beast you save, O LORD.

7How precious is your mercy, O God!
The children of men take refuge in the
shadow of your wings.
8They feast on the abundance of your house,
and you give them drink from the river of
your delights.
9For with you is the fountain of life;
in your light do we see light.

10O continue your steadfast love to those
who know you,
and your salvation to the upright
of heart!
11Let not the foot of arrogance come
upon me,
nor the hand of the wicked drive
me away.
12There the evildoers lie prostrate,
they are thrust down, unable to rise.

MATTHEW 25

31**"When the Son of man comes in his glory, and all the angels with him, then he will sit on his glorious throne. 32Before him will be gathered all the nations, and he** will separate them one from another as a shepherd separates the sheep from the goats, 33and he will place the sheep at his right hand, but the goats at the left. 34Then the King will say to those at his right hand, 'Come, O blessed of my Father,

inherit the kingdom prepared for you
from the foundation of the world; 35for I was
hungry and you gave me food, I was thirsty
and you gave me drink, I was a stranger and
you welcomed me, 36I was naked and you
clothed me, I was sick and you visited me, I
was in prison and you came to me.' 37Then
the righteous will answer him, 'Lord, when
did we see you hungry and feed you, or
thirsty and give you drink? 38And when did
we see you a stranger and welcome you,
or naked and clothe you? 39And when did
we see you sick or in prison and visit you?'
40And the King will answer them, 'Truly, I
say to you, as you did it to one of the least of
these my brethren, you did it to me.' 41Then
he will say to those at his left hand, 'Depart
from me, you cursed, into the eternal fire
prepared for the devil and his angels; 42for I
was hungry and you gave me no food, I was
thirsty and you gave me no drink, 43I was
a stranger and you did not welcome me,
naked and you did not clothe me, sick and
in prison and you did not visit me.' 44Then
they also will answer, 'Lord, when did we
see you hungry or thirsty or a stranger or
naked or sick or in prison, and did not
minister to you?' 45Then he will answer them,
'Truly, I say to you, as you did it not to one of
the least of these, you did it not to me.' 46And
they will go away into eternal punishment, but
the righteous into eternal life."

26 When Jesus had finished all these
sayings, he said to his disciples,
2"You know that after two days the Passover
is coming, and the Son of man will be
delivered up to be crucified."

3Then the chief priests and the elders of the
people gathered in the palace of the high priest,
who was called Cai'aphas, 4and took counsel
together in order to arrest Jesus by stealth and
kill him. 5But they said, "Not during the feast,
lest there be a tumult among the people."

REFLECTION

The devil is in the details. Normally, we use that phrase to describe how a seemingly simple task ends up being far more complicated than we expected. Yet the same is true in our relationship with God. The Lord's call to repentance and faith seems simple enough, yet our fulfillment of that call depends on the details of our daily conduct. The ancient Israelites' commitment to God is tested by the detailed instructions he gave them about making the Tabernacle furniture and the exquisitely extravagant garments of the high priest. Their duty to God is to be faithful to him even down to the tiniest detail of construction. In our gospel passage, we see a different kind of detail—rather than focusing on the minutiae of religious ceremonies, the Lord enthroned in judgment drills down on how we treat other people, especially those who are weakest and least important: the hungry, the thirsty, the stranger, the naked, the sick, and the imprisoned (see Mt 25:35–36). Jesus identifies himself with the least among us and shows that our fidelity to him depends upon the particulars of our response to other people, especially people in need of our help. Do you faithfully help Jesus by helping those in need?

February 11

EXODUS 40

**The LORD said to Moses, 2"On
the first day of the first month
you shall erect the tabernacle
of the tent of meeting. 3And you shall
put in it the ark of the covenant, and
you shall screen the ark with the veil.**
4And you shall bring in the table, and set its
arrangements in order; and you shall bring
in the lampstand, and set up its lamps. 5And
you shall put the golden altar for incense
before the ark of the covenant, and set up
the screen for the door of the tabernacle.
6You shall set the altar of burnt offering
before the door of the tabernacle of the tent
of meeting, 7and place the laver between the
tent of meeting and the altar, and put water

in it. 8And you shall set up the court round
about, and hang up the screen for the gate of
the court. 9Then you shall take the anointing
oil, and anoint the tabernacle and all that is
in it, and consecrate it and all its furniture;
and it shall become holy. 10You shall also
anoint the altar of burnt offering and all
its utensils, and consecrate the altar; and
the altar shall be most holy. 11You shall also
anoint the laver and its base, and consecrate
it. 12Then you shall bring Aaron and his
sons to the door of the tent of meeting, and
shall wash them with water, 13and put upon
Aaron the holy garments, and you shall
anoint him and consecrate him, that he may
serve me as priest. 14You shall bring his sons
also and put coats on them, 15and anoint
them, as you anointed their father, that they
may serve me as priests: and their anointing
shall admit them to a perpetual priesthood
throughout their generations."

16Thus did Moses; according to all that the
LORD commanded him, so he did. 17And in
the first month in the second year, on the
first day of the month, the tabernacle was
erected. 18Moses erected the tabernacle; he
laid its bases, and set up its frames, and put
in its poles, and raised up its pillars; 19and he
spread the tent over the tabernacle, and put
the covering of the tent over it, as the LORD
had commanded Moses. 20And he took the
covenant and put it into the ark, and put
the poles on the ark, and set the mercy seat
above on the ark; 21and he brought the ark
into the tabernacle, and set up the veil of the
screen, and screened the ark of the covenant;
as the LORD had commanded Moses. 22And
he put the table in the tent of meeting, on
the north side of the tabernacle, outside the
veil, 23and set the bread in order on it before
the LORD; as the LORD had commanded
Moses. 24And he put the lampstand in the
tent of meeting, opposite the table on the
south side of the tabernacle, 25and set up
the lamps before the LORD; as the LORD
had commanded Moses. 26And he put the
golden altar in the tent of meeting before
the veil, 27and burnt fragrant incense upon
it; as the LORD had commanded Moses.
28And he put in place the screen for the door
of the tabernacle. 29And he set the altar of
burnt offering at the door of the tabernacle
of the tent of meeting, and offered upon it
the burnt offering and the cereal offering;
as the LORD had commanded Moses. 30And
he set the laver between the tent of meeting
and the altar, and put water in it for washing,
31with which Moses and Aaron and his sons
washed their hands and their feet; 32when
they went into the tent of meeting, and when
they approached the altar, they washed;
as the LORD commanded Moses. 33And he
erected the court round the tabernacle and
the altar, and set up the screen of the gate of
the court. So Moses finished the work.

34Then the cloud covered the tent of
meeting, and the glory of the LORD filled
the tabernacle. 35And Moses was not able to
enter the tent of meeting, because the cloud
abode upon it, and the glory of the LORD
filled the tabernacle. 36Throughout all their
journeys, whenever the cloud was taken up
from over the tabernacle, the sons of Israel
would go onward; 37but if the cloud was not
taken up, then they did not go onward till the
day that it was taken up. 38For throughout
all their journeys the cloud of the LORD was
upon the tabernacle by day, and fire was
in it by night, in the sight of all the house
of Israel.

A Psalm of David.

PSALM 37 [36]

Do not fret because of the wicked,
be not envious of wrongdoers!
2For they will soon fade like the grass,
and wither like the green herb.

3Trust in the LORD, and do good;
so you will dwell in the land, and be
nourished in safety.
4Take delight in the LORD,
and he will give you the desires of
your heart.

5Commit your way to the LORD;
trust in him, and he will act.

6He will bring forth your vindication
as the light,
and your right as the noonday.

7Be still before the LORD, and wait patiently
for him;
do not fret over him who prospers
in his way,
over the man who carries out
evil devices!

8Refrain from anger, and forsake wrath!
Do not fret; it tends only to evil.
9For the wicked shall be cut off;
but those who wait for the LORD shall
possess the land.

10Yet a little while, and the wicked
will be no more;
though you look well at his place,
he will not be there.
11But the meek shall possess the land,
and delight themselves in abundant
prosperity.

12The wicked plots against the righteous,
and gnashes his teeth at him;
13but the LORD laughs at the wicked,
for he sees that his day is coming.

14The wicked draw the sword and bend
their bows,
to bring down the poor and needy,
to slay those who walk uprightly;
15their sword shall enter their own heart,
and their bows shall be broken.

16Better is a little that the righteous has
than the abundance of many wicked.
17For the arms of the wicked shall be broken;
but the LORD upholds the righteous.

MATTHEW 26

6Now when Jesus was at Beth′any
in the house of Simon the leper,
7a woman came up to him with an ala-
baster jar of very expensive ointment,
and she poured it on his head, as he sat at
table. 8But when the disciples saw it, they
were indignant, saying, "Why this waste?
9For this ointment might have been sold for
a large sum, and given to the poor." 10But
Jesus, aware of this, said to them, "Why do
you trouble the woman? For she has done
a beautiful thing to me. 11For you always
have the poor with you, but you will not
always have me. 12In pouring this ointment
on my body she has done it to prepare me
for burial. 13Truly, I say to you, wherever
this gospel is preached in the whole world,
what she has done will be told in memory
of her."

14Then one of the Twelve, who was called
Judas Iscariot, went to the chief priests 15and
said, "What will you give me if I deliver him
to you?" And they paid him thirty pieces of
silver. 16And from that moment he sought
an opportunity to betray him.

17Now on the first day of Unleavened Bread
the disciples came to Jesus, saying, "Where
will you have us prepare for you to eat the
Passover?" 18He said, "Go into the city to
such a one, and say to him, 'The Teacher
says, My time is at hand; I will keep the
Passover at your house with my disciples.'"
19And the disciples did as Jesus had directed
them, and they prepared the Passover.

20When it was evening, he sat at table
with the twelve disciples; 21and as they were
eating, he said, "Truly, I say to you, one of
you will betray me." 22And they were very
sorrowful, and began to say to him one after
another, "Is it I, Lord?" 23He answered, "He
who has dipped his hand in the dish with
me, will betray me. 24The Son of man goes as
it is written of him, but woe to that man by
whom the Son of man is betrayed! It would
have been better for that man if he had not
been born." 25Judas, who betrayed him, said,
"Is it I, Master?" He said to him, "You have
said so."

26Now as they were eating, Jesus took
bread, and blessed, and broke it, and gave
it to the disciples and said, "Take, eat; this is
my body." 27And he took a chalice, and when
he had given thanks he gave it to them,
saying, "Drink of it, all of you; 28for this is

my blood of the covenant, which is poured
out for many for the forgiveness of sins. 29I
tell you I shall not drink again of this fruit of
the vine until that day when I drink it new
with you in my Father's kingdom."
30And when they had sung a hymn,
they went out to the Mount of Olives.
31Then Jesus said to them, "You will all
fall away because of me this night; for it
is written, 'I will strike the shepherd, and
the sheep of the flock will be scattered.'
32But after I am raised up, I will go before
you to Galilee." 33Peter declared to him,
"Though they all fall away because of
you, I will never fall away." 34Jesus said to
him, "Truly, I say to you, this very night,
before the cock crows, you will deny me
three times." 35Peter said to him, "Even if
I must die with you, I will not deny you."
And so said all the disciples.
36Then Jesus went with them to a place
called Gethsem′ane, and he said to his
disciples, "Sit here, while I go over there
and pray." 37And taking with him Peter and
the two sons of Zeb′edee, he began to be
sorrowful and troubled. 38Then he said to
them, "My soul is very sorrowful, even to
death; remain here, and watch with me."
39And going a little farther he fell on his face
and prayed, "My Father, if it be possible, let
this chalice pass from me; nevertheless, not
as I will, but as you will." 40And he came to
the disciples and found them sleeping; and
he said to Peter, "So, could you not watch
with me one hour? 41Watch and pray that
you may not enter into temptation; the spirit
indeed is willing, but the flesh is weak."
42Again, for the second time, he went away
and prayed, "My Father, if this cannot pass
unless I drink it, your will be done." 43And
again he came and found them sleeping,
for their eyes were heavy. 44So, leaving them
again, he went away and prayed for the
third time, saying the same words. 45Then
he came to the disciples and said to them,
"Are you still sleeping and taking your rest?
Behold, the hour is at hand, and the Son of
man is betrayed into the hands of sinners.
46Rise, let us be going; see, my betrayer is
at hand."

REFLECTION

Not everyone is allowed into the inner sanctum. You would not let a complete stranger browse through your closet or skim through your journal. When God's people set up the Tabernacle, here in the Book of Exodus, we can finally see it as a complete whole. All of the goat skins, purple threads, and bronze and gold workings have come together to make a sanctuary with gradations of holiness. As one proceeds from the Outer Court to the Inner Court to the Holy Place to the Holy of Holies, one gets closer and closer to the Divine Presence resting on the Ark of the Covenant. This series of steps sets up an order in our relationship with God. We do not start out as intimate friends but as master and servant or lawgiver and subject. Spiritually we can proceed from an arms-length relationship of servitude to a father-son relationship and finally to a more intimate, spousal-type relationship. It does not happen all at once, but gradually by stages. In the same way, not all of Jesus's thousands of disciples are invited to the Last Supper, but only his closest friends and followers, the Apostles. How has the intimacy of your relationship with the Lord grown over time?

February 12

LEVITICUS 1

The LORD called Moses, and
spoke to him from the tent of
meeting, saying, 2"Speak to the sons of
Israel, and say to them, When any man
of you brings an offering to the LORD, you
shall bring your offering of cattle from the
herd or from the flock.
3"If his offering is a burnt offering from the
herd, he shall offer a male without blemish; he
shall offer it at the door of the tent of meeting,
that he may be accepted before the LORD; 4he
shall lay his hand upon the head of the burnt
offering, and it shall be accepted for him to

make atonement for him. [5]Then he shall kill the bull before the LORD; and Aaron's sons the priests shall present the blood, and throw the blood round about against the altar that is at the door of the tent of meeting. [6]And he shall flay the burnt offering and cut it into pieces; [7]and the sons of Aaron the priest shall put fire on the altar, and lay wood in order upon the fire; [8]and Aaron's sons the priests shall lay the pieces, the head, and the fat, in order upon the wood that is on the fire upon the altar; [9]but its entrails and its legs he shall wash with water. And the priest shall burn the whole on the altar, as a burnt offering, an offering by fire, a pleasing odor to the LORD.

[10]"If his gift for a burnt offering is from the flock, from the sheep or goats, he shall offer a male without blemish; [11]and he shall kill it on the north side of the altar before the LORD, and Aaron's sons the priests shall throw its blood against the altar round about. [12]And he shall cut it into pieces, with its head and its fat, and the priest shall lay them in order upon the wood that is on the fire upon the altar; [13]but the entrails and the legs he shall wash with water. And the priest shall offer the whole, and burn it on the altar; it is a burnt offering, an offering by fire, a pleasing odor to the LORD.

[14]"If his offering to the LORD is a burnt offering of birds, then he shall bring his offering of turtledoves or of young pigeons. [15]And the priest shall bring it to the altar and wring off its head, and burn it on the altar; and its blood shall be drained out on the side of the altar; [16]and he shall take away its crop with the feathers, and cast it beside the altar on the east side, in the place for ashes; [17]he shall tear it by its wings, but shall not divide it asunder. And the priest shall burn it on the altar, upon the wood that is on the fire; it is a burnt offering, an offering by fire, a pleasing odor to the LORD.

2 "When any one brings a cereal offering as an offering to the LORD, his offering shall be of fine flour; he shall pour oil upon it, and put frankincense on it, [2]and bring it to Aaron's sons the priests. And he shall take from it a handful of the fine flour and oil, with all of its frankincense; and the priest shall burn this as its memorial portion upon the altar, an offering by fire, a pleasing odor to the LORD. [3]And what is left of the cereal offering shall be for Aaron and his sons; it is a most holy part of the offerings by fire to the LORD.

[4]"When you bring a cereal offering baked in the oven as an offering, it shall be unleavened cakes of fine flour mixed with oil, or unleavened wafers spread with oil. [5]And if your offering is a cereal offering baked on a griddle, it shall be of fine flour unleavened, mixed with oil; [6]you shall break it in pieces, and pour oil on it; it is a cereal offering. [7]And if your offering is a cereal offering cooked in a pan, it shall be made of fine flour with oil. [8]And you shall bring the cereal offering that is made of these things to the LORD; and when it is presented to the priest, he shall bring it to the altar. [9]And the priest shall take from the cereal offering its memorial portion and burn this on the altar, an offering by fire, a pleasing odor to the LORD. [10]And what is left of the cereal offering shall be for Aaron and his sons; it is a most holy part of the offerings by fire to the LORD.

[11]"No cereal offering which you bring to the LORD shall be made with leaven; for you shall burn no leaven nor any honey as an offering by fire to the LORD. [12]As an offering of first fruits you may bring them to the LORD, but they shall not be offered on the altar for a pleasing odor. [13]You shall season all your cereal offerings with salt; you shall not let the salt of the covenant with your God be lacking from your cereal offering; with all your offerings you shall offer salt.

[14]"If you offer a cereal offering of first fruits to the LORD, you shall offer for the cereal offering of your first fruits crushed new grain from fresh ears, parched with fire. [15]And you shall put oil upon it, and lay frankincense on it; it is a cereal offering. [16]And the priest shall burn as its memorial portion part of the crushed grain and of the oil with all of its frankincense; it is an offering by fire to the LORD.

3 "If a man's offering is a sacrifice of peace offering, if he offers an animal from

the herd, male or female, he shall offer it
without blemish before the LORD. 2And
he shall lay his hand upon the head of his
offering and kill it at the door of the tent of
meeting; and Aaron's sons the priests shall
throw the blood against the altar round
about. 3And from the sacrifice of the peace
offering, as an offering by fire to the LORD,
he shall offer the fat covering the entrails
and all the fat that is on the entrails, 4and
the two kidneys with the fat that is on them
at the loins, and the appendage of the liver
which he shall take away with the kidneys.
5Then Aaron's sons shall burn it on the altar
upon the burnt offering, which is upon the
wood on the fire; it is an offering by fire, a
pleasing odor to the LORD.

6"If his offering for a sacrifice of peace
offering to the LORD is an animal from
the flock, male or female, he shall offer it
without blemish. 7If he offers a lamb for
his offering, then he shall offer it before
the LORD, 8laying his hand upon the head
of his offering and killing it before the tent
of meeting; and Aaron's sons shall throw its
blood against the altar round about. 9Then
from the sacrifice of the peace offering as
an offering by fire to the LORD he shall offer
its fat, the fat tail entire, taking it away close
by the backbone, and the fat that covers the
entrails, and all the fat that is on the entrails,
10and the two kidneys with the fat that is
on them at the loins, and the appendage of
the liver which he shall take away with the
kidneys. 11And the priest shall burn it on the
altar as food offered by fire to the LORD.

12"If his offering is a goat, then he shall
offer it before the LORD, 13and lay his hand
upon its head, and kill it before the tent of
meeting; and the sons of Aaron shall throw
its blood against the altar round about.
14Then he shall offer from it, as his offering
for an offering by fire to the LORD, the fat
covering the entrails, and all the fat that is
on the entrails, 15and the two kidneys with
the fat that is on them at the loins, and the
appendage of the liver which he shall take
away with the kidneys. 16And the priest shall
burn them on the altar as food offered by fire
for a pleasing odor. All fat is the LORD's. 17It
shall be a perpetual statute throughout your
generations, in all your dwelling places, that
you eat neither fat nor blood."

A Psalm of David.

PSALM 37 [36]

18The LORD knows the days of the blameless,
and their heritage will abide for ever;
19they are not put to shame in evil times,
in the days of famine they have abundance.

20But the wicked perish;
the enemies of the LORD are like the glory
of the pastures,
they vanish—like smoke they vanish away.

21The wicked borrows, and cannot pay back,
but the righteous is generous and gives;
22for those blessed by the LORD shall possess
the land,
but those cursed by him shall be cut off.

23The steps of a man are from the LORD,
and he establishes him in whose way
he delights;
24though he fall, he shall not be cast
headlong,
for the LORD is the stay of his hand.

25I have been young, and now am old;
yet I have not seen the righteous forsaken
or his children begging bread.
26He is ever giving liberally and lending,
and his children become a blessing.

27Depart from evil, and do good;
so shall you abide for ever.
28For the LORD loves justice;
he will not forsake his saints.

The righteous shall be preserved for ever,
but the children of the wicked shall be cut off.
29The righteous shall possess the land,
and dwell upon it for ever.

30The mouth of the righteous utters wisdom,
and his tongue speaks justice.

31 The law of his God is in his heart;
his steps do not slip.

32 The wicked watches the righteous,
and seeks to slay him.
33 The LORD will not abandon him to
his power,
or let him be condemned when
he is brought to trial.

34 Wait for the LORD, and keep to his way,
and he will exalt you to possess the land;
you will look on the destruction of
the wicked.

35 I have seen a wicked man overbearing,
and towering like a cedar of Lebanon.
36 Again I passed by, and, behold, he was
no more;
though I sought him, he could not
be found.

37 Mark the blameless man, and behold
the upright,
for there is posterity for the man of peace.
38 But transgressors shall be altogether
destroyed;
the posterity of the wicked shall be cut off.

39 The salvation of the righteous is from
the LORD;
he is their refuge in the time of trouble.
40 The LORD helps them and delivers them;
he delivers them from the wicked, and
saves them,
because they take refuge in him.

MATTHEW 26

**47 While he was still speaking,
Judas came, one of the Twelve,
and with him a great crowd with swords
and clubs, from the chief priests and**
the elders of the people. 48 Now the betrayer
had given them a sign, saying, "The one
I shall kiss is the man; seize him." 49 And he
came up to Jesus at once and said, "Hail,
Master!" And he kissed him. 50 Jesus said to
him, "Friend, why are you here?" Then they
came up and laid hands on Jesus and seized
him. 51 And behold, one of those who were
with Jesus stretched out his hand and drew
his sword, and struck the slave of the high
priest, and cut off his ear. 52 Then Jesus said
to him, "Put your sword back into its place;
for all who take the sword will perish by the
sword. 53 Do you think that I cannot appeal to
my Father, and he will at once send me more
than twelve legions of angels? 54 But how then
should the Scriptures be fulfilled, that it must
be so?" 55 At that hour Jesus said to the crowds,
"Have you come out as against a robber, with
swords and clubs to capture me? Day after day
I sat in the temple teaching, and you did not
seize me. 56 But all this has taken place, that the
Scriptures of the prophets might be fulfilled."
Then all the disciples deserted him and fled.
57 Then those who had seized Jesus led
him to Cai′aphas the high priest, where the
scribes and the elders had gathered. 58 But
Peter followed him at a distance, as far as
the courtyard of the high priest, and going
inside he sat with the guards to see the
end. 59 Now the chief priests and the whole
council sought false testimony against Jesus
that they might put him to death, 60 but they
found none, though many false witnesses
came forward. At last two came forward
61 and said, "This fellow said, 'I am able to
destroy the temple of God, and to build it
in three days.'" 62 And the high priest stood
up and said, "Have you no answer to make?
What is it that these men testify against
you?" 63 But Jesus was silent. And the high
priest said to him, "I adjure you by the living
God, tell us if you are the Christ, the Son of
God." 64 Jesus said to him, "You have said so.
But I tell you, hereafter you will see the Son
of man seated at the right hand of Power,
and coming on the clouds of heaven."
65 Then the high priest tore his robes, and
said, "He has uttered blasphemy. Why do we
still need witnesses? You have now heard his
blasphemy. 66 What is your judgment?" They
answered, "He deserves death." 67 Then they
spat in his face, and struck him; and some
slapped him, 68 saying, "Prophesy to us, you
Christ! Who is it that struck you?"

69Now Peter was sitting outside in the
courtyard. And a maid came up to him, and
said, "You also were with Jesus the Galilean."
70But he denied it before them all, saying, "I
do not know what you mean." 71And when
he went out to the porch, another maid
saw him, and she said to the bystanders,
"This man was with Jesus of Nazareth."
72And again he denied it with an oath, "I
do not know the man." 73After a little while
the bystanders came up and said to Peter,
"Certainly you are also one of them, for
your accent betrays you." 74Then he began
to invoke a curse on himself and to swear,
"I do not know the man." And immediately
the cock crowed. 75And Peter remembered
the saying of Jesus, "Before the cock crows,
you will deny me three times." And he went
out and wept bitterly.

REFLECTION

Leviticus begins without introduction, immediately launching into complex ritual procedures for animal sacrifice. Here we encounter the burnt offering, the cereal offering, and the peace offering. Respectively, these offerings atone for sin, express gratitude to God, and celebrate peace with God in a sacred meal (see "food" in Lv. 3:11, 16). These offerings set the stage for intimacy with God. In the drama of Holy Thursday, we see intimacy broken. Judas, a "friend" (Mt 26:50) of Jesus, betrays his master with the greatest symbolic act of friendship—a kiss. He uses the most intimate expression of love to commit murder—a deeply ironic and twisted sin. Peter, too, who had professed his loyalty, forsakes Jesus and denies him publicly. Judas and Peter show in themselves the lesson of the psalm about the wicked: "Like smoke they vanish away" (Ps 37:20). But while both Apostles deny their Lord, only one finds, and shows us, the way back to intimacy: Peter, his heart full of sorrow, repents. Through the forgiveness of his sins, he is made righteous, and instead of vanishing away he will "possess the land, and dwell upon it for ever" (v. 29). When we sin, we have a choice to make. Will you despair, or will you, like Peter, repent and run to our merciful Lord?

February 13

LEVITICUS 4

And the LORD said to Moses,
2"Say to the sons of Israel, If any
one sins unwittingly in any of the things
which the LORD has commanded not
to be done, and does any one of them, 3if it is
the anointed priest who sins, thus bringing
guilt on the people, then let him offer for
the sin which he has committed a young
bull without blemish to the LORD for a sin
offering. 4He shall bring the bull to the door
of the tent of meeting before the LORD, and
lay his hand on the head of the bull, and kill
the bull before the LORD. 5And the anointed
priest shall take some of the blood of the
bull and bring it to the tent of meeting; 6and
the priest shall dip his finger in the blood
and sprinkle part of the blood seven times
before the LORD in front of the veil of the
sanctuary. 7And the priest shall put some
of the blood on the horns of the altar of
fragrant incense before the LORD which is
in the tent of meeting, and the rest of the
blood of the bull he shall pour out at the
base of the altar of burnt offering which is at
the door of the tent of meeting. 8And all the
fat of the bull of the sin offering he shall take
from it, the fat that covers the entrails and
all the fat that is on the entrails, 9and the two
kidneys with the fat that is on them at the
loins, and the appendage of the liver which
he shall take away with the kidneys 10(just as
these are taken from the ox of the sacrifice
of the peace offerings), and the priest shall
burn them upon the altar of burnt offering.
11But the skin of the bull and all its flesh,
with its head, its legs, its entrails, and its
dung, 12the whole bull he shall carry forth
outside the camp to a clean place, where the
ashes are poured out, and shall burn it on a
fire of wood; where the ashes are poured out
it shall be burned.

13"If the whole congregation of Israel
commits a sin unwittingly and the thing is

hidden from the eyes of the assembly, and they do any one of the things which the LORD has commanded not to be done and are guilty; [14]when the sin which they have committed becomes known, the assembly shall offer a young bull for a sin offering and bring it before the tent of meeting; [15]and the elders of the congregation shall lay their hands upon the head of the bull before the LORD, and the bull shall be killed before the LORD. [16]Then the anointed priest shall bring some of the blood of the bull to the tent of meeting, [17]and the priest shall dip his finger in the blood and sprinkle it seven times before the LORD in front of the veil. [18]And he shall put some of the blood on the horns of the altar which is in the tent of meeting before the LORD; and the rest of the blood he shall pour out at the base of the altar of burnt offering which is at the door of the tent of meeting. [19]And all its fat he shall take from it and burn upon the altar. [20]Thus shall he do with the bull; as he did with the bull of the sin offering, so shall he do with this; and the priest shall make atonement for them, and they shall be forgiven. [21]And he shall carry forth the bull outside the camp, and burn it as he burned the first bull; it is the sin offering for the assembly.

[22]"When a ruler sins, doing unwittingly any one of all the things which the LORD his God has commanded not to be done, and is guilty, [23]if the sin which he has committed is made known to him, he shall bring as his offering a goat, a male without blemish, [24]and shall lay his hand upon the head of the goat, and kill it in the place where they kill the burnt offering before the LORD; it is a sin offering. [25]Then the priest shall take some of the blood of the sin offering with his finger and put it on the horns of the altar of burnt offering, and pour out the rest of its blood at the base of the altar of burnt offering. [26]And all its fat he shall burn on the altar, like the fat of the sacrifice of peace offerings; so the priest shall make atonement for him for his sin, and he shall be forgiven.

[27]"If any one of the common people sins unwittingly in doing any one of the things which the LORD has commanded not to be done, and is guilty, [28]when the sin which he has committed is made known to him he shall bring for his offering a goat, a female without blemish, for his sin which he has committed. [29]And he shall lay his hand on the head of the sin offering, and kill the sin offering in the place of burnt offering. [30]And the priest shall take some of its blood with his finger and put it on the horns of the altar of burnt offering, and pour out the rest of its blood at the base of the altar. [31]And all its fat he shall remove, as the fat is removed from the peace offerings, and the priest shall burn it upon the altar for a pleasing odor to the LORD; and the priest shall make atonement for him, and he shall be forgiven.

[32]"If he brings a lamb as his offering for a sin offering, he shall bring a female without blemish, [33]and lay his hand upon the head of the sin offering, and kill it for a sin offering in the place where they kill the burnt offering. [34]Then the priest shall take some of the blood of the sin offering with his finger and put it on the horns of the altar of burnt offering, and pour out the rest of its blood at the base of the altar. [35]And all its fat he shall remove as the fat of the lamb is removed from the sacrifice of peace offerings, and the priest shall burn it on the altar, upon the offerings by fire to the LORD; and the priest shall make atonement for him for the sin which he has committed, and he shall be forgiven.

5 "If any one sins in that he hears a public adjuration to testify and though he is a witness, whether he has seen or come to know the matter, yet does not speak, he shall bear his iniquity. [2]Or if any one touches an unclean thing, whether the carcass of an unclean beast or a carcass of unclean cattle or a carcass of unclean swarming things, and it is hidden from him, and he has become unclean, he shall be guilty. [3]Or if he touches human uncleanness, of whatever sort the uncleanness may be with which one becomes unclean, and it is hidden from him, when he comes to know it he shall be guilty. [4]Or if any one utters with his lips a rash oath to do evil or to do good, any sort of rash oath that men swear, and it is hidden

from him, when he comes to know it he
shall in any of these be guilty. 5 When a man
is guilty in any of these, he shall confess the
sin he has committed, 6 and he shall bring
his guilt offering to the LORD for the sin
which he has committed, a female from the
flock, a lamb or a goat, for a sin offering; and
the priest shall make atonement for him for
his sin.
7 "But if he cannot afford a lamb, then
he shall bring, as his guilt offering to the
LORD for the sin which he has committed,
two turtledoves or two young pigeons,
one for a sin offering and the other for a
burnt offering. 8 He shall bring them to
the priest, who shall offer first the one for
the sin offering; he shall wring its head
from its neck, but shall not sever it, 9 and
he shall sprinkle some of the blood of the
sin offering on the side of the altar, while
the rest of the blood shall be drained out
at the base of the altar; it is a sin offering.
10 Then he shall offer the second for a burnt
offering according to the ordinance; and
the priest shall make atonement for him
for the sin which he has committed, and he
shall be forgiven.
11 "But if he cannot afford two turtledoves
or two young pigeons, then he shall bring,
as his offering for the sin which he has committed, a tenth of an ephah of fine flour for
a sin offering; he shall put no oil upon it,
and shall put no frankincense on it, for it is
a sin offering. 12 And he shall bring it to the
priest, and the priest shall take a handful of
it as its memorial portion and burn this on
the altar, upon the offerings by fire to the
LORD; it is a sin offering. 13 Thus the priest
shall make atonement for him for the sin
which he has committed in any one of
these things, and he shall be forgiven. And
the remainder shall be for the priest, as in
the cereal offering."
14 The LORD said to Moses, 15 "If any one
commits a breach of faith and sins unwittingly in any of the holy things of the
LORD, he shall bring, as his guilt offering
to the LORD, a ram without blemish out of
the flock, valued by you in shekels of silver,
according to the shekel of the sanctuary;
it is a guilt offering. 16 He shall also make
restitution for what he has done amiss in
the holy thing, and shall add a fifth to it and
give it to the priest; and the priest shall make
atonement for him with the ram of the guilt
offering, and he shall be forgiven.
17 "If any one sins, doing any of the things
which the LORD has commanded not to be
done, though he does not know it, yet he is
guilty and shall bear his iniquity. 18 He shall
bring to the priest a ram without blemish
out of the flock, valued by you at the price
for a guilt offering, and the priest shall make
atonement for him for the error which he
committed unwittingly, and he shall be
forgiven. 19 It is a guilt offering; he is guilty
before the LORD."

A Psalm of David, for the memorial offering.

PSALM 38 [37]

O LORD, rebuke me not in your anger,
nor chasten me in your wrath!
2 For your arrows have sunk into me,
and your hand has come down on me.

3 There is no soundness in my flesh
because of your indignation;
there is no health in my bones
because of my sin.
4 For my iniquities have gone over my head;
they weigh like a burden too heavy for me.

5 My wounds grow foul and fester
because of my foolishness,
6 I am utterly bowed down and prostrate;
all the day I go about mourning.
7 For my loins are filled with burning,
and there is no soundness in my flesh.
8 I am utterly spent and crushed;
I groan because of the tumult of my heart.

9 Lord, all my longing is known to you,
my sighing is not hidden from you.
10 My heart throbs, my strength fails me;
and the light of my eyes—it also has gone
from me.

[11]My friends and companions stand aloof
from my plague,
and my kinsmen stand afar off.

[12]Those who seek my life lay their snares,
those who seek my hurt speak of ruin,
and meditate treachery all the day long.

[13]But I am like a deaf man, I do not hear,
like a mute man who does not open
his mouth.
[14]Yes, I am like a man who does not hear,
and in whose mouth are no rebukes.

[15]But for you, O LORD, do I wait;
it is you, O LORD my God, who
will answer.
[16]For I pray, "Only let them not rejoice
over me,
who boast against me when my
foot slips!"

[17]For I am ready to fall,
and my pain is ever with me.
[18]I confess my iniquity,
I am sorry for my sin.
[19]Those who are my foes without
cause are mighty,
and many are those who hate me
wrongfully.
[20]Those who render me evil for good
are my adversaries because I follow
after good.

[21]Do not forsake me, O LORD!
O my God, be not far from me!
[22]Make haste to help me,
O Lord, my salvation!

MATTHEW 27

**When morning came, all the
chief priests and the elders of
the people took counsel against
Jesus to put him to death; [2]and they
bound him and led him away and
delivered him to Pilate the governor.**

[3]When Judas, his betrayer, saw that he
was condemned, he repented and brought
back the thirty pieces of silver to the chief
priests and the elders, [4]saying, "I have
sinned in betraying innocent blood." They
said, "What is that to us? See to it yourself."
[5]And throwing down the pieces of silver
in the temple, he departed; and he went
and hanged himself. [6]But the chief priests,
taking the pieces of silver, said, "It is not
lawful to put them into the treasury, since
they are blood money." [7]So they took
counsel, and bought with them the potter's
field, to bury strangers in. [8]Therefore that
field has been called the Field of Blood to
this day. [9]Then was fulfilled what had been
spoken by the prophet Jeremiah, saying,
"And they took the thirty pieces of silver,
the price of him on whom a price had been
set by some of the sons of Israel, [10]and they
gave them for the potter's field, as the Lord
directed me."
[11]Now Jesus stood before the governor;
and the governor asked him, "Are you the
King of the Jews?" Jesus said to him, "You
have said so." [12]But when he was accused
by the chief priests and elders, he made
no answer. [13]Then Pilate said to him, "Do
you not hear how many things they testify
against you?" [14]But he gave him no answer,
not even to a single charge; so that the
governor wondered greatly.

REFLECTION

Sin is destructive. Sinful acts not only harm people and our relationship with God, they also bring about great interior damage. The guilt of sin can hang over our heads (see Ps 38:4) and cause our spiritual wounds to "grow foul and fester" (v. 5). Guilt needs to be expiated, to be dealt with. That is why the Lord instructs his people in the Old Testament to expiate sin through animal sacrifice. In this segment of Leviticus, we find the sin offering and the guilt offering, which address our sinfulness, though these sacrifices are incomplete (see Heb 10:4). Indeed our sins can "weigh like a burden too heavy for me" (Ps 38:4), dragging us down and causing inner turmoil. We see the danger of bottled-up guilt in the life of Judas. After betraying Jesus, he is struck with the pangs of conscience and returns the blood money, but though he acknowledges his sin (see Mt 27:4) and regrets it (see v. 3), he cannot bring himself to true penitence, to hope in God's forgiveness. Instead, he self-destructs and commits suicide. He should have followed the example of the psalmist: "I confess my iniquity, I am sorry for my sin" (Ps 38:18). Do you let guilt consume you, or do you hope in God's forgiveness?

February 14

LEVITICUS 6

The LORD said to Moses, 2"If any one sins and commits a breach of faith against the LORD by deceiving his neighbor in a matter of deposit or security, or through robbery, or if he has oppressed his neighbor 3or has found what was lost and lied about it, swearing falsely—in any of all the things which men do and sin therein, 4when one has sinned and become guilty, he shall restore what he took by robbery, or what he got by oppression, or the deposit which was committed to him, or the lost thing which he found, 5or anything about which he has sworn falsely; he shall restore it in full, and shall add a fifth to it, and give it to him to whom it belongs, on the day of his guilt offering. 6And he shall bring to the priest his guilt offering to the LORD, a ram without blemish out of the flock, valued by you at the price for a guilt offering; 7and the priest shall make atonement for him before the LORD, and he shall be forgiven for any of the things which one may do and thereby become guilty."

8The LORD said to Moses, 9"Command Aaron and his sons, saying, This is the law of the burnt offering. The burnt offering shall be on the hearth upon the altar all night until the morning, and the fire of the altar shall be kept burning on it. 10And the priest shall put on his linen garment, and put his linen breeches upon his body, and he shall take up the ashes to which the fire has consumed the burnt offering on the altar, and put them beside the altar. 11Then he shall put off his garments, and put on other garments, and carry forth the ashes outside the camp to a clean place. 12The fire on the altar shall be kept burning on it, it shall not go out; the priest shall burn wood on it every morning, and he shall lay the burnt offering in order upon it, and shall burn on it the fat of the peace offerings. 13Fire shall be kept burning upon the altar continually; it shall not go out.

14"And this is the law of the cereal offering. The sons of Aaron shall offer it before the LORD, in front of the altar. 15And one shall take from it a handful of the fine flour of the cereal offering with its oil and all the frankincense which is on the cereal offering, and burn this as its memorial portion on the altar, a pleasing odor to the LORD. 16And the rest of it Aaron and his sons shall eat; it shall be eaten unleavened in a holy place; in the court of the tent of meeting they shall eat it. 17It shall not be baked with leaven. I have given it as their portion of my offerings by fire; it is a thing most holy, like the sin offering and the guilt offering. 18Every male among the children of Aaron may eat of it, as decreed for ever throughout your generations, from the LORD's offerings by fire; whoever touches them shall become holy."

19The LORD said to Moses, 20"This is the offering which Aaron and his sons shall offer to the LORD on the day when he is anointed: a tenth of an ephah of fine flour as a regular cereal offering, half of it in the morning and half in the evening. 21It shall be made with oil on a griddle; you shall bring it well mixed, in baked pieces like a cereal offering, and offer it for a pleasing odor to the LORD. 22The priest from among Aaron's sons, who is anointed to succeed him, shall offer it to the LORD as decreed for ever; the whole of it shall be burned. [23]Every cereal offering of a priest shall be wholly burned; it shall not be eaten.”

[24]The LORD said to Moses, [25]“Say to Aaron and his sons, This is the law of the sin offering. In the place where the burnt offering is killed shall the sin offering be killed before the LORD; it is most holy. [26]The priest who offers it for sin shall eat it; in a holy place it shall be eaten, in the court of the tent of meeting. [27]Whatever touches its flesh shall be holy; and when any of its blood is sprinkled on a garment, you shall wash that on which it was sprinkled in a holy place. [28]And the earthen vessel in which it is boiled shall be broken; but if it is boiled in a bronze vessel, that shall be scoured, and rinsed in water. [29]Every male among the priests may eat of it; it is most holy. [30]But no sin offering shall be eaten from which any blood is brought into the tent of meeting to make atonement in the holy place; it shall be burned with fire.

7 “This is the law of the guilt offering. It is most holy; [2]in the place where they kill the burnt offering they shall kill the guilt offering, and its blood shall be thrown on the altar round about. [3]And all its fat shall be offered, the fat tail, the fat that covers the entrails, [4]the two kidneys with the fat that is on them at the loins, and the appendage of the liver which he shall take away with the kidneys; [5]the priest shall burn them on the altar as an offering by fire to the LORD; it is a guilt offering. [6]Every male among the priests may eat of it; it shall be eaten in a holy place; it is most holy. [7]The guilt offering is like the sin offering, there is one law for them; the priest who makes atonement with it shall have it. [8]And the priest who offers any man’s burnt offering shall have for himself the skin of the burnt offering which he has offered. [9]And every cereal offering baked in the oven and all that is prepared on a pan or a griddle shall belong to the priest who offers it. [10]And every cereal offering, mixed with oil or dry, shall be for all the sons of Aaron, one as well as another.

[11]“And this is the law of the sacrifice of peace offerings which one may offer to the LORD. [12]If he offers it for a thanksgiving, then he shall offer with the thank offering unleavened cakes mixed with oil, unleavened wafers spread with oil, and cakes of fine flour well mixed with oil. [13]With the sacrifice of his peace offerings for thanksgiving he shall bring his offering with cakes of leavened bread. [14]And of such he shall offer one cake from each offering, as an offering to the LORD; it shall belong to the priest who throws the blood of the peace offerings. [15]And the flesh of the sacrifice of his peace offerings for thanksgiving shall be eaten on the day of his offering; he shall not leave any of it until the morning. [16]But if the sacrifice of his offering is a votive offering or a freewill offering, it shall be eaten on the day that he offers his sacrifice, and the next day what remains of it shall be eaten, [17]but what remains of the flesh of the sacrifice on the third day shall be burned with fire. [18]If any of the flesh of the sacrifice of his peace offering is eaten on the third day, he who offers it shall not be accepted, neither shall it be credited to him; it shall be an abomination, and he who eats of it shall bear his iniquity.

[19]“Flesh that touches any unclean thing shall not be eaten; it shall be burned with fire. All who are clean may eat flesh, [20]but the person who eats of the flesh of the sacrifice of the LORD’s peace offerings while an uncleanness is on him, that person shall be cut off from his people. [21]And if any one touches an unclean thing, whether the uncleanness of man or an unclean beast or any unclean abomination, and then eats of the flesh of the sacrifice of the LORD’s peace offerings, that person shall be cut off from his people.”

[22]The LORD said to Moses, [23]“Say to the people of Israel, You shall eat no fat, of ox, or sheep, or goat. [24]The fat of an animal that dies of itself, and the fat of one that is torn by beasts, may be put to any other use, but on no account shall you eat it. [25]For every person who eats of the fat of an animal of which an offering by fire is made to the LORD shall be cut off from his people. [26]Moreover you shall eat no blood whatever, whether of fowl or of animal, in any of your dwellings. [27]Whoever eats any

blood, that person shall be cut off from his
people."
28The LORD said to Moses, 29"Say to the
sons of Israel, He that offers the sacrifice of
his peace offerings to the LORD shall bring
his offering to the LORD; from the sacrifice
of his peace offerings 30he shall bring with his
own hands the offerings by fire to the LORD;
he shall bring the fat with the breast, that
the breast may be waved as a wave offering
before the LORD. 31The priest shall burn the
fat on the altar, but the breast shall be for
Aaron and his sons. 32And the right thigh
you shall give to the priest as an offering
from the sacrifice of your peace offerings;
33he among the sons of Aaron who offers
the blood of the peace offerings and the fat
shall have the right thigh for a portion. 34For
the breast that is waved and the thigh that is
offered I have taken from the sons of Israel,
out of the sacrifices of their peace offerings,
and have given them to Aaron the priest
and to his sons, as a perpetual debt from the
sons of Israel. 35This is the portion of Aaron
and of his sons from the offerings made by
fire to the LORD, consecrated to them on the
day they were presented to serve as priests
of the LORD; 36the LORD commanded this to
be given them by the sons of Israel, on the
day that they were anointed; it is a perpetual
debt throughout their generations."
37This is the law of the burnt offering, of
the cereal offering, of the sin offering, of
the guilt offering, of the consecration, and
of the peace offerings, 38which the LORD
commanded Moses on Mount Sinai, on the
day that he commanded the sons of Israel
to bring their offerings to the LORD, in the
wilderness of Sinai.

To the choirmaster: to Jeduthun.
A Psalm of David.

PSALM 39 [38]

I said, "I will guard my ways,
that I may not sin with my tongue;
I will bridle my mouth,
so long as the wicked are in my presence."
2I was mute and silent,
I held my peace to no avail;
my distress grew worse,
3 my heart became hot within me.
As I mused, the fire burned;
then I spoke with my tongue:

4"LORD, let me know my end,
and what is the measure of my days;
let me know how fleeting my life is!
5Behold, you have made my days
a few handbreadths,
and my lifetime is as nothing in your sight.
Surely every man stands as a mere breath!
Selah
6 Surely man goes about as a shadow!
Surely for nought are they in turmoil;
man heaps up, and knows not who
will gather!

7"And now, Lord, for what do I wait?
My hope is in you.
8Deliver me from all my transgressions.
Make me not the scorn of the fool!
9I am silent, I do not open my mouth;
for it is you who have done it.
10Remove your stroke from me;
I am spent by the blows of your hand.
11When you chasten man
with rebukes for sin,
you consume like a moth what is dear to him;
surely every man is a mere breath! *Selah*

12"Hear my prayer, O LORD,
and give ear to my cry;
hold not your peace at my tears!
For I am your passing guest,
a sojourner, like all my fathers.
13Look away from me, that I may
know gladness,
before I depart and be no more!"

MATTHEW 27

**15Now at the feast the governor
was accustomed to release for
the crowd any one prisoner whom they
wanted. 16And they had then a notorious**

prisoner, called Barab′bas. 17 So when they had gathered, Pilate said to them, "Whom do you want me to release for you, Barab′bas or Jesus who is called Christ?" 18 For he knew that it was out of envy that they had delivered him up. 19 Besides, while he was sitting on the judgment seat, his wife sent word to him, "Have nothing to do with that righteous man, for I have suffered much over him today in a dream." 20 Now the chief priests and the elders persuaded the people to ask for Barab′bas and destroy Jesus. 21 The governor again said to them, "Which of the two do you want me to release for you?" And they said, "Barab′bas." 22 Pilate said to them, "Then what shall I do with Jesus who is called Christ?" They all said, "Let him be crucified." 23 And he said, "Why, what evil has he done?" But they shouted all the more, "Let him be crucified."

24 So when Pilate saw that he was gaining nothing, but rather that a riot was beginning, he took water and washed his hands before the crowd, saying, "I am innocent of this righteous man's blood; see to it yourselves." 25 And all the people answered, "His blood be on us and on our children!" 26 Then he released for them Barab′bas, and having scourged Jesus, delivered him to be crucified.

REFLECTION

Leviticus acknowledges the brokenness of earthly life by listing off the evils, "which men do and sin therein" (Lv 6:3). Though the world is a morally corrupt place, Leviticus also emphasizes the ultimate seriousness of human acts, that a betrayal of another person is "a breach of faith against the LORD" (v. 2). The Lord takes our actions very seriously. He even requires that if a person has stolen, he is to offer restitution with interest (see v. 5). He is the one who holds us accountable at the final judgment. In this life, everything is tenuous. The psalmist acknowledges that we might save but not profit from it: "Man heaps up, and knows not who will gather!" (Ps 39:6). Wealth can be stolen or taxed or wasted. Though we might put forth great lifelong effort to accumulate money, we are but "a mere breath" (v. 5). Even though Jesus is sinless, he is sentenced to death. The point is that we cannot control our circumstances but only our actions. We are responsible for living uprightly and treating others with dignity, respect, and honesty, but we cannot expect that earthly life will be easy, fair, or predictable. What imperfections in this life cause you to look forward to Heaven?

February 15

LEVITICUS 8

The LORD said to Moses, 2 "Take Aaron and his sons with him, and the garments, and the anointing oil, and the bull of the sin offering, and the two rams, and the basket of unleavened bread; 3 and assemble all the congregation at the door of the tent of meeting." 4 And Moses did as the LORD commanded him; and the congregation was assembled at the door of the tent of meeting.

5 And Moses said to the congregation, "This is the thing which the LORD has commanded to be done." 6 And Moses brought Aaron and his sons, and washed them with water. 7 And he put on him the coat, and girded him with the sash, and clothed him with the robe, and put the ephod upon him, and girded him with the skilfully woven band of the ephod, binding it to him therewith. 8 And he placed the breastpiece on him, and in the breastpiece he put the U′rim and the Thummim. 9 And he set the turban upon his head, and on the turban, in front, he set the golden plate, the holy crown, as the LORD commanded Moses.

10 Then Moses took the anointing oil, and anointed the tabernacle and all that was in it, and consecrated them. 11 And he sprinkled some of it on the altar seven times, and anointed the altar and all its utensils, and the laver and its base, to consecrate them. 12 And he poured some

of the anointing oil on Aaron's head, and anointed him, to consecrate him. 13And Moses brought Aaron's sons, and clothed them with coats, and girded them with sashes, and bound caps on them, as the LORD commanded Moses.

14Then he brought the bull of the sin offering; and Aaron and his sons laid their hands upon the head of the bull of the sin offering. 15And Moses killed it, and took the blood, and with his finger put it on the horns of the altar round about, and purified the altar, and poured out the blood at the base of the altar, and consecrated it, to make atonement for it. 16And he took all the fat that was on the entrails, and the appendage of the liver, and the two kidneys with their fat, and Moses burned them on the altar. 17But the bull, and its skin, and its flesh, and its dung, he burned with fire outside the camp, as the LORD commanded Moses.

18Then he presented the ram of the burnt offering; and Aaron and his sons laid their hands on the head of the ram. 19And Moses killed it, and threw the blood upon the altar round about. 20And when the ram was cut into pieces, Moses burned the head and the pieces and the fat. 21And when the entrails and the legs were washed with water, Moses burned the whole ram on the altar, as a burnt offering, a pleasing odor, an offering by fire to the LORD, as the LORD commanded Moses.

22Then he presented the other ram, the ram of ordination; and Aaron and his sons laid their hands on the head of the ram. 23And Moses killed it, and took some of its blood and put it on the tip of Aaron's right ear and on the thumb of his right hand and on the great toe of his right foot. 24And Aaron's sons were brought, and Moses put some of the blood on the tips of their right ears and on the thumbs of their right hands and on the great toes of their right feet; and Moses threw the blood upon the altar round about. 25Then he took the fat, and the fat tail, and all the fat that was on the entrails, and the appendage of the liver, and the two kidneys with their fat, and the right thigh; 26and out of the basket of unleavened bread which was before the LORD he took one unleavened cake, and one cake of bread with oil, and one wafer, and placed them on the fat and on the right thigh; 27and he put all these in the hands of Aaron and in the hands of his sons, and waved them as a wave offering before the LORD. 28Then Moses took them from their hands, and burned them on the altar with the burnt offering, as an ordination offering, a pleasing odor, an offering by fire to the LORD. 29And Moses took the breast, and waved it for a wave offering before the LORD; it was Moses' portion of the ram of ordination, as the LORD commanded Moses.

30Then Moses took some of the anointing oil and of the blood which was on the altar, and sprinkled it upon Aaron and his garments, and also upon his sons and his sons' garments; so he consecrated Aaron and his garments, and his sons and his sons' garments with him.

31And Moses said to Aaron and his sons, "Boil the flesh at the door of the tent of meeting, and there eat it and the bread that is in the basket of ordination offerings, as I commanded, saying, 'Aaron and his sons shall eat it'; 32and what remains of the flesh and the bread you shall burn with fire. 33And you shall not go out from the door of the tent of meeting for seven days, until the days of your ordination are completed, for it will take seven days to ordain you. 34As has been done today, the LORD has commanded to be done to make atonement for you. 35At the door of the tent of meeting you shall remain day and night for seven days, performing what the LORD has charged, lest you die; for so I am commanded." 36And Aaron and his sons did all the things which the LORD commanded by Moses.

9 On the eighth day Moses called Aaron and his sons and the elders of Israel; 2and he said to Aaron, "Take a bull calf for a sin offering, and a ram for a burnt offering, both without blemish, and offer them before the LORD. 3And say to the sons of Israel, 'Take a male goat for a sin offering, and a calf and a lamb, both a year old without blemish, for a burnt offering, 4and an ox and a ram for peace offerings, to sacrifice before

the LORD, and a cereal offering mixed with
oil; for today the LORD will appear to you.'"
5And they brought what Moses commanded
before the tent of meeting; and all the
congregation drew near and stood before the
LORD. 6And Moses said, "This is the thing
which the LORD commanded you to do; and
the glory of the LORD will appear to you."
7Then Moses said to Aaron, "Draw near to
the altar, and offer your sin offering and
your burnt offering, and make atonement
for yourself and for the people; and bring the
offering of the people, and make atonement
for them; as the LORD has commanded."
8So Aaron drew near to the altar, and
killed the calf of the sin offering, which
was for himself. 9And the sons of Aaron
presented the blood to him, and he dipped
his finger in the blood and put it on the
horns of the altar, and poured out the blood
at the base of the altar; 10but the fat and the
kidneys and the appendage of the liver from
the sin offering he burned upon the altar, as
the LORD commanded Moses. 11The flesh
and the skin he burned with fire outside
the camp.
12And he killed the burnt offering; and
Aaron's sons delivered to him the blood, and
he threw it on the altar round about. 13And
they delivered the burnt offering to him,
piece by piece, and the head; and he burned
them upon the altar. 14And he washed the
entrails and the legs, and burned them with
the burnt offering on the altar.
15Then he presented the people's offering,
and took the goat of the sin offering which
was for the people, and killed it, and offered
it for sin, like the first sin offering. 16And he
presented the burnt offering, and offered
it according to the ordinance. 17And he
presented the cereal offering, and filled his
hand from it, and burned it upon the altar,
besides the burnt offering of the morning.
18He killed the ox also and the ram, the
sacrifice of peace offerings for the people;
and Aaron's sons delivered to him the blood,
which he threw upon the altar round about,
19and the fat of the ox and of the ram, the fat
tail, and that which covers the entrails, and
the kidneys, and the appendage of the liver;
20and they put the fat upon the breasts, and
he burned the fat upon the altar, 21but the
breasts and the right thigh Aaron waved for
a wave offering before the LORD; as Moses
commanded.
22Then Aaron lifted up his hands toward
the people and blessed them; and he came
down from offering the sin offering and
the burnt offering and the peace offerings.
23And Moses and Aaron went into the tent
of meeting; and when they came out they
blessed the people, and the glory of the
LORD appeared to all the people. 24And
fire came forth from before the LORD and
consumed the burnt offering and the fat
upon the altar; and when all the people saw
it, they shouted, and fell on their faces.

To the choirmaster.
A Psalm of David.

PSALM 40 [39]

I waited patiently for the LORD;
he inclined to me and heard my cry.
2He drew me up from the desolate pit,
out of the miry bog,
and set my feet upon a rock,
making my steps secure.
3He put a new song in my mouth,
a song of praise to our God.
Many will see and fear,
and put their trust in the LORD.

4Blessed is the man who makes
the LORD his trust,
who does not turn to the proud,
to those who go astray after false gods!
5You have multiplied, O LORD my God,
your wondrous deeds and your thoughts
toward us;
none can compare with you!
Were I to proclaim and tell of them,
they would be more than can be
numbered.

6Sacrifice and offering you do not desire;
but you have given me an open ear.

Burnt offering and sin offering
you have not required.
[7]Then I said, "Behold, I come;
in the roll of the book it is written of me;
[8]I delight to do your will, O my God;
your law is within my heart."

[9]I have told the glad news of deliverance
in the great congregation;
behold, I have not restrained my lips,
as you know, O LORD.
[10]I have not hidden your saving help within
my heart,
I have spoken of your faithfulness and
your salvation;
I have not concealed your mercy and
your faithfulness
from the great congregation.

[11]Do not, O LORD, withhold
your compassion from me,
let your mercy and your faithfulness
ever preserve me!
[12]For evils have encompassed me
without number;
my iniquities have overtaken me,
till I cannot see;
they are more than the hairs of my head;
my heart fails me.

[13]Be pleased, O LORD, to deliver me!
O LORD, make haste to help me!
[14]Let them be put to shame and confusion
altogether
who seek to snatch away my life;
let them be turned back and brought
to dishonor
who desire my hurt!
[15]Let them be appalled because of
their shame
who say to me, "Aha, Aha!"

[16]But may all who seek you
rejoice and be glad in you;
may those who love your salvation
say continually, "Great is the LORD!"
[17]As for me, I am poor and needy;
but the Lord takes thought for me.
You are my help and my deliverer;
do not delay, O my God!

MATTHEW 27

[27]Then the soldiers of the governor
took Jesus into the praetorium,
and they gathered the whole battalion
before him. [28]And they stripped him and
put a scarlet robe upon him, [29]and plaiting a
crown of thorns they put it on his head, and put
a reed in his right hand. And kneeling before
him they mocked him, saying, "Hail, King of
the Jews!" [30]And they spat upon him, and took
the reed and struck him on the head. [31]And
when they had mocked him, they stripped him
of the robe, and put his own clothes on him,
and led him away to crucify him.
[32]As they were marching out, they came
upon a man of Cyre′ne, Simon by name; this
man they compelled to carry his cross. [33]And
when they came to a place called Gol′gotha
(which means the place of a skull), [34]they
offered him wine to drink, mingled with gall;
but when he tasted it, he would not drink
it. [35]And when they had crucified him, they
divided his garments among them by casting
lots; [36]then they sat down and kept watch over
him there. [37]And over his head they put the
charge against him, which read, "This is Jesus
the King of the Jews." [38]Then two robbers
were crucified with him, one on the right
and one on the left. [39]And those who passed
by derided him, wagging their heads [40]and
saying, "You who would destroy the temple
and build it in three days, save yourself! If
you are the Son of God, come down from
the cross." [41]So also the chief priests, with the
scribes and elders, mocked him, saying, [42]"He
saved others; he cannot save himself. He is
the King of Israel; let him come down now
from the cross, and we will believe in him.
[43]He trusts in God; let God deliver him now,
if he desires him; for he said, 'I am the Son of
God.'" [44]And the robbers who were crucified
with him also reviled him in the same way.

REFLECTION

Nobody likes to wait. Waiting is awkward because it places us between the past and future, where we are sitting still, looking forward to the next step yet without fulfillment. Leviticus here depicts an ordination ceremony where Aaron and his sons are clothed in special priestly garments and sacrifices are made on their behalf. After the initial sacrifices, they have to wait at the door of the Tent of Meeting for seven days and nights for the presence of God. As the psalm says, "I waited patiently for the Lord" (Ps 40:1). Finally, on the eighth day, Aaron offers his first post-ordination sacrifices: a calf, a goat, an ox, and two rams. He then blesses the people. As soon as he is finished with these inaugural priestly acts, "the glory of the Lord appeared to all the people" and fire came out from the sanctuary to burn up the sacrificial offerings (Lv 9:23–24). Aaron's patience pays off. Likewise, Jesus on the Cross is taunted to become impatient. The chief priests, the scribes, and the elders say, "Let God deliver him now" (Mt 27:42–43). Little do they realize that Jesus is patiently waiting for his Father to deliver him from death: "He drew me up from the desolate pit" (Ps 40:2). In what ways can you wait for the Lord?

February 16

LEVITICUS 10

Now Na′dab and Abi′hu, the
sons of Aaron, each took his
censer, and put fire in it, and
laid incense on it, and offered unholy
fire before the LORD, such as he had
not commanded them. 2And fire came
forth from the presence of the LORD and
devoured them, and they died before the
LORD. 3Then Moses said to Aaron, "This is
what the LORD has said, 'I will show myself
holy among those who are near me, and
before all the people I will be glorified.'"
And Aaron held his peace.
4And Moses called Mish′a-el and El′zaphan,
the sons of Uz′ziel the uncle of Aaron,
and said to them, "Draw near, carry your
brethren from before the sanctuary out of
the camp." 5So they drew near, and carried
them in their coats out of the camp, as Moses
had said. 6And Moses said to Aaron and to
Elea′zar and Ith′amar, his sons, "Do not let
the hair of your heads hang loose, and do
not rend your clothes, lest you die, and lest
wrath come upon all the congregation; but
your brethren, the whole house of Israel,
may bewail the burning which the LORD has
kindled. 7And do not go out from the door
of the tent of meeting, lest you die; for the
anointing oil of the LORD is upon you." And
they did according to the word of Moses.
8And the LORD spoke to Aaron, saying,
9"Drink no wine nor strong drink, you nor
your sons with you, when you go into the tent
of meeting, lest you die; it shall be a statute
for ever throughout your generations. 10You
are to distinguish between the holy and the
common, and between the unclean and the
clean; 11and you are to teach the sons of
Israel all the statutes which the LORD has
spoken to them by Moses."
12And Moses said to Aaron and to
Elea′zar and Ith′amar, his sons who were
left, "Take the cereal offering that remains
of the offerings by fire to the LORD, and
eat it unleavened beside the altar, for it is
most holy; 13you shall eat it in a holy place,
because it is your due and your sons' due,
from the offerings by fire to the LORD; for
so I am commanded. 14But the breast that
is waved and the thigh that is offered you
shall eat in any clean place, you and your
sons and your daughters with you; for they
are given as your due and your sons' due,
from the sacrifices of the peace offerings of
the sons of Israel. 15The thigh that is offered
and the breast that is waved they shall bring
with the offerings by fire of the fat, to wave
for a wave offering before the LORD, and it
shall be yours, and your sons' with you, as a
debt for ever; as the LORD has commanded."
16Now Moses diligently inquired about the
goat of the sin offering, and behold, it was
burned! And he was angry with Elea′zar
and Ith′amar, the sons of Aaron who were
left, saying, 17"Why have you not eaten the
sin offering in the place of the sanctuary,
since it is a thing most holy and has been

given to you that you may bear the iniquity of the congregation, to make atonement for them before the LORD? 18Behold, its blood was not brought into the inner part of the sanctuary. You certainly ought to have eaten it in the sanctuary, as I commanded." 19And Aaron said to Moses, "Behold, today they have offered their sin offering and their burnt offering before the LORD; and yet such things as these have befallen me! If I had eaten the sin offering today, would it have been acceptable in the sight of the LORD?" 20And when Moses heard that, he was content.

11 And the LORD said to Moses and Aaron, 2"Say to the sons of Israel, These are the living things which you may eat among all the beasts that are on the earth. 3Whatever parts the hoof and is cloven-footed and chews the cud, among the animals, you may eat. 4Nevertheless among those that chew the cud or part the hoof, you shall not eat these: The camel, because it chews the cud but does not part the hoof, is unclean to you. 5And the rock badger, because it chews the cud but does not part the hoof, is unclean to you. 6And the hare, because it chews the cud but does not part the hoof, is unclean to you. 7And the swine, because it parts the hoof and is cloven-footed but does not chew the cud, is unclean to you. 8Of their flesh you shall not eat, and their carcasses you shall not touch; they are unclean to you.

9"These you may eat, of all that are in the waters. Everything in the waters that has fins and scales, whether in the seas or in the rivers, you may eat. 10But anything in the seas or the rivers that has not fins and scales, of the swarming creatures in the waters and of the living creatures that are in the waters, is an abomination to you. 11They shall remain an abomination to you; of their flesh you shall not eat, and their carcasses you shall have in abomination. 12Everything in the waters that has not fins and scales is an abomination to you.

13"And these you shall have in abomination among the birds, they shall not be eaten, they are an abomination: the eagle, the vulture, the osprey, 14the kite, the falcon according to its kind, 15every raven according to its kind, 16the ostrich, the nighthawk, the sea gull, the hawk according to its kind, 17the owl, the cormorant, the ibis, 18the water hen, the pelican, the carrion vulture, 19the stork, the heron according to its kind, the hoopoe, and the bat.

20"All winged insects that go upon all fours are an abomination to you. 21Yet among the winged insects that go on all fours you may eat those which have legs above their feet, with which to leap on the earth. 22Of them you may eat: the locust according to its kind, the bald locust according to its kind, the cricket according to its kind, and the grasshopper according to its kind. 23But all other winged insects which have four feet are an abomination to you.

24"And by these you shall become unclean; whoever touches their carcass shall be unclean until the evening, 25and whoever carries any part of their carcass shall wash his clothes and be unclean until the evening. 26Every animal which parts the hoof but is not cloven-footed or does not chew the cud is unclean to you; every one who touches them shall be unclean. 27And all that go on their paws, among the animals that go on all fours, are unclean to you; whoever touches their carcass shall be unclean until the evening, 28and he who carries their carcass shall wash his clothes and be unclean until the evening; they are unclean to you.

29"And these are unclean to you among the swarming things that swarm upon the earth: the weasel, the mouse, the great lizard according to its kind, 30the gecko, the land crocodile, the lizard, the sand lizard, and the chameleon. 31These are unclean to you among all that swarm; whoever touches them when they are dead shall be unclean until the evening. 32And anything upon which any of them falls when they are dead shall be unclean, whether it is an article of wood or a garment or a skin or a sack, any vessel that is used for any purpose; it must be put into water, and it shall be unclean until the evening; then it shall be clean. 33And if any of them falls into any earthen vessel, all that is in it shall be unclean, and you shall break it. 34Any food in it which may be eaten, upon which water may come, shall be unclean; and all drink which may be drunk from every such vessel shall be unclean. 35And everything upon which any part of their carcass falls shall be unclean; whether oven or stove, it shall be broken in pieces; they are unclean, and shall be unclean to you. 36Nevertheless a spring or a cistern holding water shall be clean; but whatever touches their carcass shall be unclean. 37And if any part of their carcass falls upon any seed for sowing that is to be sown, it is clean; 38but if water is put on the seed and any part of their carcass falls on it, it is unclean to you.

39"And if any animal of which you may eat dies, he who touches its carcass shall be unclean until the evening, 40and he who eats of its carcass shall wash his clothes and be unclean until the evening; he also who carries the carcass shall wash his clothes and be unclean until the evening.

41"Every swarming thing that swarms upon the earth is an abomination; it shall not be eaten. 42Whatever goes on its belly, and whatever goes on all fours, or whatever has many feet, all the swarming things that swarm upon the earth, you shall not eat; for they are an abomination. 43You shall not make yourselves abominable with any swarming thing that swarms; and you shall not defile yourselves with them, lest you become unclean. 44For I am the LORD your God; consecrate yourselves therefore, and be holy, for I am holy. You shall not defile yourselves with any swarming thing that crawls upon the earth. 45For I am the LORD who brought you up out of the land of Egypt, to be your God; you shall therefore be holy, for I am holy."

46This is the law pertaining to beast and bird and every living creature that moves through the waters and every creature that swarms upon the earth, 47to make a distinction between the unclean and the clean and between the living creature that may be eaten and the living creature that may not be eaten.

12 The LORD said to Moses, 2"Say to the sons of Israel, If a woman conceives, and bears a male child, then she shall be unclean seven days; as at the time of her menstruation, she shall be unclean. 3And on the eighth day the flesh of his foreskin shall be circumcised. 4Then she shall continue for thirty-three days in the blood of her purifying; she shall not touch any hallowed thing, nor come into the sanctuary, until the days of her purifying are completed. 5But if she bears a female child, then she shall be unclean two weeks, as in her menstruation; and she shall continue in the blood of her purifying for sixty-six days.

6"And when the days of her purifying are completed, whether for a son or for a daughter, she shall bring to the priest at the door of the tent of meeting a lamb a year old for a burnt offering, and a young pigeon or a turtledove for a sin offering, 7and he shall offer it before the LORD, and make atonement for her; then she shall be clean from the flow of her blood. This is the law for her who bears a child, either male or female. 8And if she cannot afford a lamb, then she shall take two turtledoves or two young pigeons, one for a burnt offering and the other for a sin offering; and the priest shall make atonement for her, and she shall be clean."

To the choirmaster.
A Psalm of David.

PSALM 41 [40]

Blessed is he who considers the poor!
The LORD delivers him in the day
of trouble;
2the LORD protects him and keeps him alive;
he is called blessed in the land;
you do not give him up to the will of
his enemies.
3The LORD sustains him on his sickbed;
in his illness you heal all his infirmities.

4As for me, I said, "O LORD, be gracious to me;
heal me, for I have sinned against you!"

5 My enemies say of me in malice:
"When will he die, and his name perish?"
6 And when one comes to see me, he utters
empty words,
while his heart gathers mischief;
when he goes out, he tells it abroad.
7 All who hate me whisper together about me;
they imagine the worst for me.

8 They say, "A deadly thing has fastened
upon him;
he will not rise again from where he lies."
9 Even my bosom friend in whom I trusted,
who ate of my bread, has lifted his heel
against me.
10 But you, O LORD, be gracious to me,
and raise me up, that I may repay them!

11 By this I know that you are pleased
with me,
in that my enemy has not triumphed
over me.
12 But you have upheld me because of
my integrity,
and set me in your presence for ever.

13 Blessed be the LORD, the God of Israel,
from everlasting to everlasting!
Amen and Amen.

MATTHEW 27

45 Now from the sixth hour there
was darkness over all the land
until the ninth hour. 46 And about
the ninth hour Jesus cried with a loud
voice, "Eli, Eli, la′ma sabach-tha′ni?" that
is, "My God, my God, why have you
forsaken me?" 47 And some of the bystanders
hearing it said, "This man is calling Eli′jah."
48 And one of them at once ran and took a
sponge, filled it with vinegar, and put it on
a reed, and gave it to him to drink. 49 But the
others said, "Wait, let us see whether Eli′jah
will come to save him." 50 And Jesus cried again
with a loud voice and yielded up his spirit.
51 And behold, the curtain of the temple
was torn in two, from top to bottom; and
the earth shook, and the rocks were split;
52 the tombs also were opened, and many
bodies of the saints who had fallen asleep
were raised, 53 and coming out of the tombs
after his resurrection they went into the
holy city and appeared to many. 54 When
the centurion and those who were with
him, keeping watch over Jesus, saw the
earthquake and what took place, they were
filled with awe, and said, "Truly this was the
Son of God!"
55 There were also many women there,
looking on from afar, who had followed
Jesus from Galilee, ministering to him;
56 among whom were Mary Mag′dalene, and
Mary the mother of James and Joseph, and
the mother of the sons of Zeb′edee.
57 When it was evening, there came a rich
man from Arimathe′a, named Joseph,
who also was a disciple of Jesus. 58 He went
to Pilate and asked for the body of Jesus.
Then Pilate ordered it to be given to him.
59 And Joseph took the body, and wrapped
it in a clean linen shroud, 60 and laid it in
his own new tomb, which he had hewn
in the rock; and he rolled a great stone
to the door of the tomb, and departed.
61 Mary Mag′dalene and the other Mary
were there, sitting opposite the tomb.
62 Next day, that is, after the day of
Preparation, the chief priests and the
Pharisees gathered before Pilate 63 and said,
"Sir, we remember how that impostor said,
while he was still alive, 'After three days I
will rise again.' 64 Therefore order the tomb
to be made secure until the third day, lest
his disciples go and steal him away, and tell
the people, 'He has risen from the dead,' and
the last fraud will be worse than the first."
65 Pilate said to them, "You have a guard of
soldiers; go, make it as secure as you can."
66 So they went and made the tomb secure by
sealing the stone and setting a guard.

REFLECTION

God is holy, that is, separate, different, set apart. His Holy Presence is fearsome, even dangerous. Nadab and Abihu, who have just been ordained, sin greatly against the Lord's holiness. They offer "unholy fire" (Lv 10:1) in their censers before the Lord. Scholars disagree about exactly what this means, but it is clear that they gravely violated the ritual procedure for the worship of the Lord. Immediately, they are punished by holy divine fire coming out from the sanctuary. Soon after, the Lord gives stringent new rules for the priests to follow in order to maintain their safety in his presence. The priests' holiness and separateness needs to correspond to the Lord's. In addition, the Lord institutes rules for clean and unclean foods. Some animals like snakes and most insects are forbidden because they represent impurity or even sin. Carnivores, for example, are forbidden because they are murderous animals. The strong division between the holy and the unholy, the clean and the unclean is highlighted by the curtain, which separates the Holy of Holies from the Holy Place. At the moment of Jesus's Death on the Cross, that curtain is torn asunder. We are granted a new level of access to God's presence. How have you experienced the difference between the holy and the unholy?

February 17

LEVITICUS 13

The LORD said to Moses and Aaron, [2]"When a man has on the skin of his body a swelling or an eruption or a spot, and it turns into a leprous disease on the skin of his body, then he shall be brought to Aaron the priest or to one of his sons the priests, [3]and the priest shall examine the diseased spot on the skin of his body; and if the hair in the diseased spot has turned white and the disease appears to be deeper than the skin of his body, it is a leprous disease; when the priest has examined him he shall pronounce him unclean. [4]But if the spot is white in the skin of his body, and appears no deeper than the skin, and the hair in it has not turned white, the priest shall shut up the diseased person for seven days; [5]and the priest shall examine him on the seventh day, and if in his eyes the disease is checked and the disease has not spread in the skin, then the priest shall shut him up seven days more; [6]and the priest shall examine him again on the seventh day, and if the diseased spot is dim and the disease has not spread in the skin, then the priest shall pronounce him clean; it is only an eruption; and he shall wash his clothes, and be clean. [7]But if the eruption spreads in the skin, after he has shown himself to the priest for his cleansing, he shall appear again before the priest; [8]and the priest shall make an examination, and if the eruption has spread in the skin, then the priest shall pronounce him unclean; it is leprosy.

[9]"When a man is afflicted with leprosy, he shall be brought to the priest; [10]and the priest shall make an examination, and if there is a white swelling in the skin, which has turned the hair white, and there is quick raw flesh in the swelling, [11]it is a chronic leprosy in the skin of his body, and the priest shall pronounce him unclean; he shall not shut him up, for he is unclean. [12]And if the leprosy breaks out in the skin, so that the leprosy covers all the skin of the diseased person from head to foot, so far as the priest can see, [13]then the priest shall make an examination, and if the leprosy has covered all his body, he shall pronounce him clean of the disease; it has all turned white, and he is clean. [14]But when raw flesh appears on him, he shall be unclean. [15]And the priest shall examine the raw flesh, and pronounce him unclean; raw flesh is unclean, for it is leprosy. [16]But if the raw flesh turns again and is changed to white, then he shall come to the priest, [17]and the priest shall examine him, and if the disease has turned white, then the priest shall pronounce the diseased person clean; he is clean.

18“And when there is in the skin of one’s body a boil that has healed, 19and in the place of the boil there comes a white swelling or a reddish-white spot, then it shall be shown to the priest; 20and the priest shall make an examination, and if it appears deeper than the skin and its hair has turned white, then the priest shall pronounce him unclean; it is the disease of leprosy, it has broken out in the boil. 21But if the priest examines it, and the hair on it is not white and it is not deeper than the skin, but is dim, then the priest shall shut him up seven days; 22and if it spreads in the skin, then the priest shall pronounce him unclean; it is diseased. 23But if the spot remains in one place and does not spread, it is the scar of the boil; and the priest shall pronounce him clean.

24“Or, when the body has a burn on its skin and the raw flesh of the burn becomes a spot, reddish-white or white, 25the priest shall examine it, and if the hair in the spot has turned white and it appears deeper than the skin, then it is leprosy; it has broken out in the burn, and the priest shall pronounce him unclean; it is a leprous disease. 26But if the priest examines it, and the hair in the spot is not white and it is no deeper than the skin, but is dim, the priest shall shut him up seven days, 27and the priest shall examine him the seventh day; if it is spreading in the skin, then the priest shall pronounce him unclean; it is a leprous disease. 28But if the spot remains in one place and does not spread in the skin, but is dim, it is a swelling from the burn, and the priest shall pronounce him clean; for it is the scar of the burn.

29“When a man or woman has a disease on the head or the beard, 30the priest shall examine the disease; and if it appears deeper than the skin, and the hair in it is yellow and thin, then the priest shall pronounce him unclean; it is an itch, a leprosy of the head or the beard. 31And if the priest examines the itching disease, and it appears no deeper than the skin and there is no black hair in it, then the priest shall shut up the person with the itching disease for seven days, 32and on the seventh day the priest shall examine the disease; and if the itch has not spread, and there is in it no yellow hair, and the itch appears to be no deeper than the skin, 33then he shall shave himself, but the itch he shall not shave; and the priest shall shut up the person with the itching disease for seven days more; 34and on the seventh day the priest shall examine the itch, and if the itch has not spread in the skin and it appears to be no deeper than the skin, then the priest shall pronounce him clean; and he shall wash his clothes, and be clean. 35But if the itch spreads in the skin after his cleansing, 36then the priest shall examine him, and if the itch has spread in the skin, the priest need not seek for the yellow hair; he is unclean. 37But if in his eyes the itch is checked, and black hair has grown in it, the itch is healed, he is clean; and the priest shall pronounce him clean.

38“When a man or a woman has spots on the skin of the body, white spots, 39the priest shall make an examination, and if the spots on the skin of the body are of a dull white, it is tetter that has broken out in the skin; he is clean.

40“If a man’s hair has fallen from his head, he is bald but he is clean. 41And if a man’s hair has fallen from his forehead and temples, he has baldness of the forehead but he is clean. 42But if there is on the bald head or the bald forehead a reddish-white diseased spot, it is leprosy breaking out on his bald head or his bald forehead. 43Then the priest shall examine him, and if the diseased swelling is reddish-white on his bald head or on his bald forehead, like the appearance of leprosy in the skin of the body, 44he is a leprous man, he is unclean; the priest must pronounce him unclean; his disease is on his head.

45“The leper who has the disease shall wear torn clothes and let the hair of his head hang loose, and he shall cover his upper lip and cry, ‘Unclean, unclean.’ 46He shall remain unclean as long as he has the disease; he is

unclean; he shall dwell alone in a habitation outside the camp.
47"When there is a leprous disease in a garment, whether a woolen or a linen garment,
48in warp or woof of linen or wool, or in a skin or in anything made of skin,
49if the disease shows greenish or reddish in the garment, whether in warp or woof or in skin or in anything made of skin, it is a leprous disease and shall be shown to the priest.
50And the priest shall examine the disease, and shut up that which has the disease for seven days;
51then he shall examine the disease on the seventh day. If the disease has spread in the garment, in warp or woof, or in the skin, whatever be the use of the skin, the disease is a malignant leprosy; it is unclean.
52And he shall burn the garment, whether diseased in warp or woof, woolen or linen, or anything of skin, for it is a malignant leprosy; it shall be burned in the fire.
53"And if the priest examines, and the disease has not spread in the garment in warp or woof or in anything of skin,
54then the priest shall command that they wash the thing in which is the disease, and he shall shut it up seven days more;
55and the priest shall examine the diseased thing after it has been washed. And if the diseased spot has not changed color, though the disease has not spread, it is unclean; you shall burn it in the fire, whether the leprous spot is on the back or on the front.
56"But if the priest examines, and the disease is dim after it is washed, he shall tear the spot out of the garment or the skin or the warp or woof;
57then if it appears again in the garment, in warp or woof, or in anything of skin, it is spreading; you shall burn with fire that in which is the disease.
58But the garment, warp or woof, or anything of skin from which the disease departs when you have washed it, shall then be washed a second time, and be clean."
59This is the law for a leprous disease in a garment of wool or linen, either in warp or woof, or in anything of skin, to decide whether it is clean or unclean.

To the choirmaster.
A Maskil of the Sons of Korah.

PSALM 42 [41]

As a deer longs
  for flowing streams,
so longs my soul
  for you, O God.
2My soul thirsts for God,
  for the living God.
When shall I come and behold
  the face of God?
3My tears have been my food
  day and night,
while men say to me continually,
  "Where is your God?"

4These things I remember,
  as I pour out my soul:
how I went with the throng,
  and led them in procession to the house of God,
with glad shouts and songs of thanksgiving,
  a multitude keeping festival.
5Why are you cast down, O my soul,
  and why are you disquieted within me?
Hope in God; for I shall again praise him,
  my savior 6and my God.

My soul is cast down within me,
  therefore I remember you
from the land of Jordan and of Hermon,
  from Mount Mizar.
7Deep calls to deep
  at the thunder of your cataracts;
all your waves and your billows
  have gone over me.
8By day the LORD commands his steadfast love;
  and at night his song is with me,
  a prayer to the God of my life.

9I say to God, my rock:
  "Why have you forgotten me?

Why do I go mourning
because of the oppression of the enemy?"
10 As with a deadly wound in my body,
my adversaries taunt me,
while they say to me continually,
"Where is your God?"

11 Why are you cast down, O my soul,
and why are you disquieted within me?
Hope in God; for I shall again praise him,
my help and my God.

MATTHEW 28

**Now after the sabbath, toward
the dawn of the first day of the
week, Mary Mag′dalene and the
other Mary went to see the tomb. 2 And
behold, there was a great earthquake;
for an angel of the Lord descended from**
heaven and came and rolled back the stone,
and sat upon it. 3 His appearance was like
lightning, and his clothing white as snow.
4 And for fear of him the guards trembled
and became like dead men. 5 But the angel
said to the women, "Do not be afraid;
for I know that you seek Jesus who was
crucified. 6 He is not here; for he has risen,
as he said. Come, see the place where he
lay. 7 Then go quickly and tell his disciples
that he has risen from the dead, and
behold, he is going before you to Galilee;
there you will see him. Behold, I have told
you." 8 So they departed quickly from the
tomb with fear and great joy, and ran to
tell his disciples. 9 And behold, Jesus met
them and said, "Hail!" And they came up
and took hold of his feet and worshiped
him. 10 Then Jesus said to them, "Do not
be afraid; go and tell my brethren to go to
Galilee, and there they will see me."
11 While they were going, behold, some
of the guard went into the city and told
the chief priests all that had taken place.
12 And when they had assembled with the
elders and taken counsel, they gave a sum
of money to the soldiers 13 and said, "Tell
people, 'His disciples came by night and
stole him away while we were asleep.'
14 And if this comes to the governor's ears,
we will satisfy him and keep you out of
trouble." 15 So they took the money and did
as they were directed; and this story has
been spread among the Jews to this day.
16 Now the eleven disciples went to
Galilee, to the mountain to which Jesus
had directed them. 17 And when they
saw him they worshiped him; but some
doubted. 18 And Jesus came and said
to them, "All authority in heaven and
on earth has been given to me. 19 Go
therefore and make disciples of all
nations, baptizing them in the name of
the Father and of the Son and of the Holy
Spirit, 20 teaching them to observe all that
I have commanded you; and behold, I am
with you always, to the close of the age."

REFLECTION

Skin disease diagnosis is not the first thing that we think of when it comes to devotional Bible reading. The main point to take away from this section of Leviticus is that some factors would make a person unclean, that is, ineligible to worship the Lord in the Tabernacle. A "clean" person would be allowed to enter the sanctuary and worship. Through the procedure established here, God allows one who recovered from a skin infection to be declared "clean" and thus able once again to come into God's presence in the Tabernacle. This being made "clean" is the central metaphor underlying the Sacrament of Baptism. Jesus, after his glorious Resurrection, commissions his followers to make new disciples, to baptize them, and to teach them. Baptism addresses the leprosy of sin, washing an "unclean" or sinful person in the grace of Christ's victory over death in order that he or she might be spiritually "clean" and free of sin. The Church teaches that at the moment of Baptism, a person not only becomes justified before God, but he or she actually becomes holy, and the Holy Trinity dwells in that person's soul. Like the deer who longs for water in Psalm 42, how do you long for greater intimacy with the God who dwells in your soul?

February 18

LEVITICUS 14

The LORD said to Moses, 2“This shall be the law of the leper for the day of his cleansing. He shall be brought to the priest; 3and the priest shall go out of the camp, and the priest shall make an examination. Then, if the leprous disease is healed in the leper, 4the priest shall command them to take for him who is to be cleansed two living clean birds and cedarwood and scarlet stuff and hyssop; 5and the priest shall command them to kill one of the birds in an earthen vessel over running water. 6He shall take the living bird with the cedarwood and the scarlet stuff and the hyssop, and dip them and the living bird in the blood of the bird that was killed over the running water; 7and he shall sprinkle it seven times upon him who is to be cleansed of leprosy; then he shall pronounce him clean, and shall let the living bird go into the open field. 8And he who is to be cleansed shall wash his clothes, and shave off all his hair, and bathe himself in water, and he shall be clean; and after that he shall come into the camp, but shall dwell outside his tent seven days. 9And on the seventh day he shall shave all his hair off his head; he shall shave off his beard and his eyebrows, all his hair. Then he shall wash his clothes, and bathe his body in water, and he shall be clean.

10“And on the eighth day he shall take two male lambs without blemish, and one ewe lamb a year old without blemish, and a cereal offering of three tenths of an ephah of fine flour mixed with oil, and one log of oil. 11And the priest who cleanses him shall set the man who is to be cleansed and these things before the LORD, at the door of the tent of meeting. 12And the priest shall take one of the male lambs, and offer it for a guilt offering, along with the log of oil, and wave them for a wave offering before the LORD; 13and he shall kill the lamb in the place where they kill the sin offering and the burnt offering, in the holy place; for the guilt offering, like the sin offering, belongs to the priest; it is most holy. 14The priest shall take some of the blood of the guilt offering, and the priest shall put it on the tip of the right ear of him who is to be cleansed, and on the thumb of his right hand, and on the great toe of his right foot. 15Then the priest shall take some of the log of oil, and pour it into the palm of his own left hand, 16and dip his right finger in the oil that is in his left hand, and sprinkle some oil with his finger seven times before the LORD. 17And some of the oil that remains in his hand the priest shall put on the tip of the right ear of him who is to be cleansed, and on the thumb of his right hand, and on the great toe of his right foot, upon the blood of the guilt offering; 18and the rest of the oil that is in the priest’s hand he shall put on the head of him who is to be cleansed. Then the priest shall make atonement for him before the LORD. 19The priest shall offer the sin offering, to make atonement for him who is to be cleansed from his uncleanness. And afterward he shall kill the burnt offering; 20and the priest shall offer the burnt offering and the cereal offering on the altar. Thus the priest shall make atonement for him, and he shall be clean.

21“But if he is poor and cannot afford so much, then he shall take one male lamb for a guilt offering to be waved, to make atonement for him, and a tenth of an ephah of fine flour mixed with oil for a cereal offering, and a log of oil; 22also two turtledoves or two young pigeons, such as he can afford; the one shall be a sin offering and the other a burnt offering. 23And on the eighth day he shall bring them for his cleansing to the priest, to the door of the tent of meeting, before the LORD; 24and the priest shall take the lamb of the guilt offering, and the log of oil, and the priest shall wave them for a wave offering before the LORD. 25And he shall kill the lamb of the guilt offering; and the priest shall take some of the blood of the guilt offering, and put it on the tip of the right ear of him who

is to be cleansed, and on the thumb of his
right hand, and on the great toe of his right
foot. 26And the priest shall pour some of
the oil into the palm of his own left hand;
27and shall sprinkle with his right finger
some of the oil that is in his left hand seven
times before the LORD; 28and the priest
shall put some of the oil that is in his hand
on the tip of the right ear of him who is to
be cleansed, and on the thumb of his right
hand, and the great toe of his right foot,
in the place where the blood of the guilt
offering was put; 29and the rest of the oil
that is in the priest's hand he shall put on
the head of him who is to be cleansed, to
make atonement for him before the LORD.
30And he shall offer, of the turtledoves or
young pigeons such as he can afford, 31one
for a sin offering and the other for a burnt
offering, along with a cereal offering; and
the priest shall make atonement before the
LORD for him who is being cleansed. 32This
is the law for him in whom is a leprous
disease, who cannot afford the offerings
for his cleansing."

33The LORD said to Moses and Aaron,
34"When you come into the land of Canaan,
which I give you for a possession, and I put
a leprous disease in a house in the land of
your possession, 35then he who owns the
house shall come and tell the priest, 'There
seems to me to be some sort of disease in my
house.' 36Then the priest shall command that
they empty the house before the priest goes
to examine the disease, lest all that is in the
house be declared unclean; and afterward
the priest shall go in to see the house.
37And he shall examine the disease; and if
the disease is in the walls of the house with
greenish or reddish spots, and if it appears
to be deeper than the surface, 38then the
priest shall go out of the house to the door
of the house, and shut up the house seven
days. 39And the priest shall come again on
the seventh day, and look; and if the disease
has spread in the walls of the house, 40then
the priest shall command that they take out
the stones in which is the disease and throw
them into an unclean place outside the city;
41and he shall cause the inside of the house
to be scraped round about, and the plaster
that they scrape off they shall pour into an
unclean place outside the city; 42then they
shall take other stones and put them in the
place of those stones, and he shall take other
plaster and plaster the house.

43"If the disease breaks out again in the
house, after he has taken out the stones and
scraped the house and plastered it, 44then the
priest shall go and look; and if the disease
has spread in the house, it is a malignant
leprosy in the house; it is unclean. 45And he
shall break down the house, its stones and
timber and all the plaster of the house; and
he shall carry them forth out of the city to
an unclean place. 46Moreover he who enters
the house while it is shut up shall be unclean
until the evening; 47and he who lies down in
the house shall wash his clothes; and he who
eats in the house shall wash his clothes.

48"But if the priest comes and makes
an examination, and the disease has not
spread in the house after the house was
plastered, then the priest shall pronounce
the house clean, for the disease is healed.
49And for the cleansing of the house he
shall take two small birds, with cedarwood
and scarlet stuff and hyssop, 50and shall
kill one of the birds in an earthen vessel
over running water, 51and shall take the
cedarwood and the hyssop and the scarlet
stuff, along with the living bird, and dip
them in the blood of the bird that was killed
and in the running water, and sprinkle the
house seven times. 52Thus he shall cleanse
the house with the blood of the bird, and
with the running water, and with the living
bird, and with the cedarwood and hyssop
and scarlet stuff; 53and he shall let the living
bird go out of the city into the open field;
so he shall make atonement for the house,
and it shall be clean."

54This is the law for any leprous disease:
for an itch, 55for leprosy in a garment or in
a house, 56and for a swelling or an eruption
or a spot, 57to show when it is unclean and
when it is clean. This is the law for leprosy.

15 The LORD said to Moses and Aaron,
2"Say to the sons of Israel, When
any man has a discharge from his body, his

discharge is unclean. 3And this is the law of
his uncleanness for a discharge: whether his
body runs with his discharge, or his body is
stopped from discharge, it is uncleanness
in him. 4Every bed on which he who has
the discharge lies shall be unclean; and
everything on which he sits shall be unclean.
5And any one who touches his bed shall wash
his clothes, and bathe himself in water, and
be unclean until the evening. 6And whoever
sits on anything on which he who has the
discharge has sat shall wash his clothes, and
bathe himself in water, and be unclean until
the evening. 7And whoever touches the body
of him who has the discharge shall wash his
clothes, and bathe himself in water, and be
unclean until the evening. 8And if he who has
the discharge spits on one who is clean, then
he shall wash his clothes, and bathe himself
in water, and be unclean until the evening.
9And any saddle on which he who has the
discharge rides shall be unclean. 10And
whoever touches anything that was under
him shall be unclean until the evening; and
he who carries such a thing shall wash his
clothes, and bathe himself in water, and be
unclean until the evening. 11Any one whom
he that has the discharge touches without
having rinsed his hands in water shall wash
his clothes, and bathe himself in water,
and be unclean until the evening. 12And
the earthen vessel which he who has the
discharge touches shall be broken; and every
vessel of wood shall be rinsed in water.

13"And when he who has a discharge is
cleansed of his discharge, then he shall count
for himself seven days for his cleansing,
and wash his clothes; and he shall bathe his
body in running water, and shall be clean.
14And on the eighth day he shall take two
turtledoves or two young pigeons, and come
before the Lord to the door of the tent of
meeting, and give them to the priest; 15and
the priest shall offer them, one for a sin
offering and the other for a burnt offering;
and the priest shall make atonement for him
before the Lord for his discharge.

16"And if a man has an emission of semen,
he shall bathe his whole body in water,
and be unclean until the evening. 17And
every garment and every skin on which the
semen comes shall be washed with water,
and be unclean until the evening. 18If a man
lies with a woman and has an emission of
semen, both of them shall bathe themselves
in water, and be unclean until the evening."

PSALM 43 [42]

Vindicate me, O God, and defend my cause
against an ungodly people;
from deceitful and unjust men
deliver me!
2For you are the God in whom I take refuge;
why have you cast me off?
Why do I go mourning
because of the oppression of the enemy?

3Oh, send out your light and your truth;
let them lead me,
let them bring me to your holy hill
and to your dwelling!
4Then I will go to the altar of God,
to God my exceeding joy;
and I will praise you with the lyre,
O God, my God.

5Why are you cast down, O my soul,
and why are you disquieted within me?
Hope in God; for I shall again praise him,
my savior and my God.

MARK 1

The beginning of the gospel of Jesus Christ, the Son of God.
2As it is written in Isaiah the prophet,
"Behold, I send my messenger before
your face,
who shall prepare your way;
3the voice of one crying in the wilderness:
Prepare the way of the Lord,
make his paths straight—"
4John the Baptist appeared in the wilderness,
preaching a baptism of repentance for the
forgiveness of sins. 5And there went out to
him all the country of Judea, and all the

people of Jerusalem; and they were baptized by him in the river Jordan, confessing their sins. 6Now John was clothed with camel's hair, and had a leather belt around his waist, and ate locusts and wild honey. 7And he preached, saying, "After me comes he who is mightier than I, the thong of whose sandals I am not worthy to stoop down and untie. 8I have baptized you with water; but he will baptize you with the Holy Spirit."

9In those days Jesus came from Nazareth of Galilee and was baptized by John in the Jordan. 10And when he came up out of the water, immediately he saw the heavens opened and the Spirit descending upon him like a dove; 11and a voice came from heaven, "You are my beloved Son; with you I am well pleased."

12The Spirit immediately drove him out into the wilderness. 13And he was in the wilderness forty days, tempted by Satan; and he was with the wild beasts; and the angels ministered to him.

14Now after John was arrested, Jesus came into Galilee, preaching the gospel of God, 15and saying, "The time is fulfilled, and the kingdom of God is at hand; repent, and believe in the gospel."

16And passing along by the Sea of Galilee, he saw Simon and Andrew the brother of Simon casting a net in the sea; for they were fishermen. 17And Jesus said to them, "Follow me and I will make you become fishers of men." 18And immediately they left their nets and followed him. 19And going on a little farther, he saw James the son of Zeb′edee and John his brother, who were in their boat mending the nets. 20And immediately he called them; and they left their father Zeb′edee in the boat with the hired servants, and followed him.

REFLECTION

We are all in need of cleansing. Leviticus today outlines the ceremonies for reincorporating lepers into the people of God. After recovering from his illness, the healed person has to be inspected by the priest. Once the priest verifies the recovery, the cleansing ceremonies begin. They involve sacrifices and washings, which are common in Leviticus, but they also include a unique symbolic act: the priest releases a living bird into the wild on behalf of the leper. This ceremony might indicate that the bird is carrying away the ritual impurity of the leper or that the bird's freedom signifies the newfound freedom of the leper, released from the "prison" of his disease. When Jesus arrives on the scene at the beginning of Mark, he and John the Baptist preach a different kind of cleansing. Instead of a physical cleansing from literal leprosy, they preach repentance from the spiritual leprosy of sin and spiritual cleansing in Baptism. People come to be baptized by John, "confessing their sins" (Mk 1:5). Indeed, Jesus's first line in the Gospel includes a call to repentance: "Repent, and believe in the gospel" (v. 15). In addition, Jesus invites men to follow him, and they do. How does repentance bring about cleansing and freedom in your life?

February 19

LEVITICUS 15

19"**When a woman has a discharge of blood which is her regular discharge from her body, she shall be in her impurity for seven days,** and whoever touches her shall be unclean until the evening. 20And everything upon which she lies during her impurity shall be unclean; everything also upon which she sits shall be unclean. 21And whoever touches her bed shall wash his clothes, and bathe himself in water, and be unclean until the evening. 22And whoever touches anything upon which she sits shall wash his clothes, and bathe himself in water, and be unclean until the evening; 23whether it is the bed or anything upon which she sits, when he touches it he shall be unclean until the evening. 24And if any man lies with her, and her impurity is on him, he shall be unclean seven days; and every bed on which he lies shall be unclean.

25“If a woman has a discharge of blood for many days, not at the time of her impurity, or if she has a discharge beyond the time of her impurity, all the days of the discharge she shall continue in uncleanness; as in the days of her impurity, she shall be unclean. 26Every bed on which she lies, all the days of her discharge, shall be to her as the bed of her impurity; and everything on which she sits shall be unclean, as in the uncleanness of her impurity. 27And whoever touches these things shall be unclean, and shall wash his clothes, and bathe himself in water, and be unclean until the evening. 28But if she is cleansed of her discharge, she shall count for herself seven days, and after that she shall be clean. 29And on the eighth day she shall take two turtledoves or two young pigeons, and bring them to the priest, to the door of the tent of meeting. 30And the priest shall offer one for a sin offering and the other for a burnt offering; and the priest shall make atonement for her before the LORD for her unclean discharge.

31“Thus you shall keep the sons of Israel separate from their uncleanness, lest they die in their uncleanness by defiling my tabernacle that is in their midst.”

32This is the law for him who has a discharge and for him who has an emission of semen, becoming unclean thereby; 33also for her who is sick with her impurity; that is, for any one, male or female, who has a discharge, and for the man who lies with a woman who is unclean.

16 The LORD spoke to Moses, after the death of the two sons of Aaron, when they drew near before the LORD and died; 2and the LORD said to Moses, “Tell Aaron your brother not to come at all times into the holy place within the veil, before the mercy seat which is upon the ark, lest he die; for I will appear in the cloud upon the mercy seat. 3But thus shall Aaron come into the holy place: with a young bull for a sin offering and a ram for a burnt offering. 4He shall put on the holy linen coat, and shall have the linen breeches on his body, be girded with the linen sash, and wear the linen turban; these are the holy garments. He shall bathe his body in water, and then put them on. 5And he shall take from the congregation of the sons of Israel two male goats for a sin offering, and one ram for a burnt offering.

6“And Aaron shall offer the bull as a sin offering for himself, and shall make atonement for himself and for his house. 7Then he shall take the two goats, and set them before the LORD at the door of the tent of meeting; 8and Aaron shall cast lots upon the two goats, one lot for the LORD and the other lot for Aza′zel. 9And Aaron shall present the goat on which the lot fell for the LORD, and offer it as a sin offering; 10but the goat on which the lot fell for Aza′zel shall be presented alive before the LORD to make atonement over it, that it may be sent away into the wilderness to Azazel.

11“Aaron shall present the bull as a sin offering for himself, and shall make atonement for himself and for his house; he shall kill the bull as a sin offering for himself. 12And he shall take a censer full of coals of fire from the altar before the LORD, and two handfuls of sweet incense beaten small; and he shall bring it within the veil 13and put the incense on the fire before the LORD, that the cloud of the incense may cover the mercy seat which is upon the covenant, lest he die; 14and he shall take some of the blood of the bull, and sprinkle it with his finger on the front of the mercy seat, and before the mercy seat he shall sprinkle the blood with his finger seven times.

15“Then he shall kill the goat of the sin offering which is for the people, and bring its blood within the veil, and do with its blood as he did with the blood of the bull, sprinkling it upon the mercy seat and before the mercy seat; 16thus he shall make atonement for the holy place, because of the uncleannesses of the sons of Israel, and because of their transgressions, all their sins; and so he shall do for the tent of meeting, which abides with them in the midst of their uncleannesses. 17There shall be no man in the tent of meeting when he enters to make atonement in the holy place until he comes out and has made atonement

for himself and for his house and for all the
assembly of Israel. 18Then he shall go out
to the altar which is before the LORD and
make atonement for it, and shall take some
of the blood of the bull and of the blood of
the goat, and put it on the horns of the altar
round about. 19And he shall sprinkle some
of the blood upon it with his finger seven
times, and cleanse it and hallow it from the
uncleannesses of the sons of Israel.
20"And when he has made an end of atoning
for the holy place and the tent of meeting
and the altar, he shall present the live goat;
21and Aaron shall lay both his hands upon
the head of the live goat, and confess over
him all the iniquities of the sons of Israel,
and all their transgressions, all their sins;
and he shall put them upon the head of the
goat, and send him away into the wilderness
by the hand of a man who is in readiness.
22The goat shall bear all their iniquities upon
him to a solitary land; and he shall let the
goat go in the wilderness.
23"Then Aaron shall come into the tent of
meeting, and shall put off the linen garments
which he put on when he went into the holy
place, and shall leave them there; 24and he
shall bathe his body in water in a holy place,
and put on his garments, and come forth,
and offer his burnt offering and the burnt
offering of the people, and make atonement
for himself and for the people. 25And the fat
of the sin offering he shall burn upon the
altar. 26And he who lets the goat go to Aza′zel
shall wash his clothes and bathe his body in
water, and afterward he may come into the
camp. 27And the bull for the sin offering and
the goat for the sin offering, whose blood
was brought in to make atonement in the
holy place, shall be carried forth outside the
camp; their skin and their flesh and their
dung shall be burned with fire. 28And he
who burns them shall wash his clothes and
bathe his body in water, and afterward he
may come into the camp.
29"And it shall be a statute to you for ever
that in the seventh month, on the tenth day
of the month, you shall afflict yourselves,
and shall do no work, either the native
or the stranger who sojourns among you;
30for on this day shall atonement be made
for you, to cleanse you; from all your sins
you shall be clean before the LORD. 31It is
a sabbath of solemn rest to you, and you
shall afflict yourselves; it is a statute for
ever. 32And the priest who is anointed and
consecrated as priest in his father's place
shall make atonement, wearing the holy
linen garments; 33he shall make atonement
for the sanctuary, and he shall make
atonement for the tent of meeting and for
the altar, and he shall make atonement
for the priests and for all the people of the
assembly. 34And this shall be an everlasting
statute for you, that atonement may be
made for the sons of Israel once in the year
because of all their sins." And Moses did as
the LORD commanded him.

To the choirmaster.
A Maskil of the Sons of Korah.

PSALM 44 [43]

We have heard with our ears, O God,
our fathers have told us,
what deeds you performed in their days,
in the days of old:

2you with your own hand drove out
the nations,
but you planted them;
you afflicted the peoples,
but you set them free;
3for not by their own sword did they win
the land,
nor did their own arm give them victory;
but your right hand, and your arm,
and the light of your countenance;
for you delighted in them.

4You are my King and my God,
who ordain victories for Jacob.
5Through you we push down our foes;
through your name we tread down
our assailants.
6For not in my bow do I trust,
nor can my sword save me.

[7]But you have saved us from our foes,
and have put to confusion those who
hate us.
[8]In God we have boasted continually,
and we will give thanks to your name
for ever. *Selah*

[9]Yet you have cast us off and abased us,
and have not gone out with our armies.
[10]You have made us turn back from the foe;
and our enemies have gotten spoil.
[11]You have made us like sheep for slaughter,
and have scattered us among the nations.
[12]You have sold your people for a trifle,
demanding no high price for them.

[13]You have made us the taunt of our
neighbors,
the derision and scorn of those about us.
[14]You have made us a byword among
the nations,
a laughingstock among the peoples.
[15]All day long my disgrace is before me,
and shame has covered my face,
[16]at the words of the taunters and revilers,
at the sight of the enemy and the avenger.

MARK 1

[21]And they went into Caper′-
na-um; and immediately on the
sabbath he entered the syna-
gogue and taught. [22]And they were as-
tonished at his teaching, for he taught
them as one who had authority, and not
as the scribes. [23]And immediately there was
in their synagogue a man with an unclean
spirit; [24]and he cried out, "What have you
to do with us, Jesus of Nazareth? Have
you come to destroy us? I know who
you are, the Holy One of God." [25]But Jesus rebuked him, saying, "Be silent, and
come out of him!" [26]And the unclean
spirit, convulsing him and crying with a
loud voice, came out of him. [27]And they
were all amazed, so that they questioned
among themselves, saying, "What is this?
A new teaching! With authority he commands even the unclean spirits, and they
obey him." [28]And at once his fame spread
everywhere throughout all the surrounding region of Galilee.
[29]And immediately he left the synagogue, and entered the house of Simon
and Andrew, with James and John. [30]Now
Simon's mother-in-law lay sick with a fever, and immediately they told him of her.
[31]And he came and took her by the hand
and lifted her up, and the fever left her;
and she served them.
[32]That evening, at sundown, they
brought to him all who were sick or
possessed with demons. [33]And the whole
city was gathered together about the
door. [34]And he healed many who were
sick with various diseases, and cast out
many demons; and he would not permit
the demons to speak, because they knew
him.
[35]And in the morning, a great while
before day, he rose and went out to a
lonely place, and there he prayed. [36]And
Simon and those who were with him
followed him, [37]and they found him and
said to him, "Every one is searching for
you." [38]And he said to them, "Let us go on
to the next towns, that I may preach there
also; for that is why I came out." [39]And he
went throughout all Galilee, preaching in
their synagogues and casting out demons.
[40]And a leper came to him begging him,
and kneeling said to him, "If you will, you
can make me clean." [41]Moved with pity, he
stretched out his hand and touched him,
and said to him, "I will; be clean." [42]And
immediately the leprosy left him, and he
was made clean. [43]And he sternly charged
him, and sent him away at once, [44]and said
to him, "See that you say nothing to any
one; but go, show yourself to the priest,
and offer for your cleansing what Moses
commanded, for a proof to the people."
[45]But he went out and began to talk freely
about it, and to spread the news, so that
Jesus could no longer openly enter a
town, but was out in the country; and
people came to him from every quarter.

REFLECTION

It is not always easy to bridge the holiness gap between us and God. Though he invites us and even delights in us (see Ps 44:3), we can't escape the fact that we are contingent creatures and he is the Almighty God. However, the Lord sets up liturgical means of approaching his Holy Presence on the Day of Atonement (Yom Kippur), the holiest day of the Jewish liturgical calendar. It was the only day of the year that the high priest was admitted into the Holy of Holies, the place where God's presence dwelt most intensely. The Lord's Holy Presence would rest above the mercy seat, the wings of the golden cherubim on the lid of the Ark of the Covenant (see Lv 16:2). When the high priest entered, he would bring a cloud of incense to screen himself off from the fearsome sacred presence of God, and he would bring the blood of the sacrifice to sprinkle on the Ark in atonement for the sins of the people. Then the priest would place his hands on the head of a goat, symbolically imparting the guilt of the people onto the animal, which would be driven out into the desert to die as the scapegoat. How can you recognize and approach God's Holy Presence with greater reverence?

February 20

LEVITICUS 17

And the LORD said to Moses, 2"Say to Aaron and his sons, and to all the sons of Israel, This is the thing which the LORD has commanded. 3If any man of the house of Israel kills an ox or a lamb or a goat in the camp, or kills it outside the camp, 4and does not bring it to the door of the tent of meeting, to offer it as a gift to the LORD before the tabernacle of the LORD, bloodguilt shall be imputed to that man; he has shed blood; and that man shall be cut off from among his people. 5This is to the end that the sons of Israel may bring their sacrifices which they slay in the open field, that they may bring them to the LORD, to the priest at the door of the tent of meeting, and slay them as sacrifices of peace offerings to the LORD; 6and the priest shall sprinkle the blood on the altar of the LORD at the door of the tent of meeting, and burn the fat for a pleasing odor to the LORD. 7So they shall no more slay their sacrifices for satyrs, after whom they play the harlot. This shall be a statute for ever to them throughout their generations.

8"And you shall say to them, Any man of the house of Israel, or of the strangers that sojourn among them, who offers a burnt offering or sacrifice, 9and does not bring it to the door of the tent of meeting, to sacrifice it to the LORD; that man shall be cut off from his people.

10"If any man of the house of Israel or of the strangers that sojourn among them eats any blood, I will set my face against that person who eats blood, and will cut him off from among his people. 11For the life of the flesh is in the blood; and I have given it for you upon the altar to make atonement for your souls; for it is the blood that makes atonement, by reason of the life. 12Therefore I have said to the sons of Israel, No person among you shall eat blood, neither shall any stranger who sojourns among you eat blood. 13Any man also of the sons of Israel, or of the strangers that sojourn among them, who takes in hunting any beast or bird that may be eaten shall pour out its blood and cover it with dust.

14"For the life of every creature is the blood of it; therefore I have said to the sons of Israel, You shall not eat the blood of any creature, for the life of every creature is its blood; whoever eats it shall be cut off. 15And every person that eats what dies of itself or what is torn by beasts, whether he is a native or a sojourner, shall wash his clothes, and bathe himself in water, and be unclean until the evening; then he shall be clean. 16But if he does not wash them or bathe his flesh, he shall bear his iniquity."

18 And the LORD said to Moses, 2"Say to the sons of Israel, I am the LORD your God. 3You shall not do as they do in the land of Egypt, where you dwelt, and you shall not do as they do in the land of Canaan, to which I am bringing you. You shall not walk in their statutes. 4You shall do my ordinances and keep my statutes and walk in them. I am the LORD your God. 5You shall therefore keep my statutes and my ordinances, by doing which a man shall live: I am the LORD.

6"None of you shall approach any one near of kin to him to uncover nakedness. I am the LORD. 7You shall not uncover the nakedness of your father, which is the nakedness of your mother; she is your mother, you shall not uncover her nakedness. 8You shall not uncover the nakedness of your father's wife; it is your father's nakedness. 9You shall not uncover the nakedness of your sister, the daughter of your father or the daughter of your mother, whether born at home or born abroad. 10You shall not uncover the nakedness of your son's daughter or of your daughter's daughter, for their nakedness is your own nakedness. 11You shall not uncover the nakedness of your father's wife's daughter, begotten by your father, since she is your sister. 12You shall not uncover the nakedness of your father's sister; she is your father's near kinswoman. 13You shall not uncover the nakedness of your mother's sister, for she is your mother's near kinswoman. 14You shall not uncover the nakedness of your father's brother, that is, you shall not approach his wife; she is your aunt. 15You shall not uncover the nakedness of your daughter-in-law; she is your son's wife, you shall not uncover her nakedness. 16You shall not uncover the nakedness of your brother's wife; she is your brother's nakedness. 17You shall not uncover the nakedness of a woman and of her daughter, and you shall not take her son's daughter or her daughter's daughter to uncover her nakedness; they are your near kinswomen; it is wickedness. 18And you shall not take a woman as a rival wife to her sister, uncovering her nakedness while her sister is yet alive.

19"You shall not approach a woman to uncover her nakedness while she is in her menstrual uncleanness. 20And you shall not lie carnally with your neighbor's wife, and defile yourself with her. 21You shall not give any of your children to devote them by fire to Mo'lech, and so profane the name of your God: I am the LORD. 22You shall not lie with a male as with a woman; it is an abomination. 23And you shall not lie with any beast and defile yourself with it, neither shall any woman give herself to a beast to lie with it: it is perversion.

24"Do not defile yourselves by any of these things, for by all these the nations I am casting out before you defiled themselves; 25and the land became defiled, so that I punished its iniquity, and the land vomited out its inhabitants. 26But you shall keep my statutes and my ordinances and do none of these abominations, either the native or the stranger who sojourns among you 27(for all of these abominations the men of the land did, who were before you, so that the land became defiled); 28lest the land vomit you out, when you defile it, as it vomited out the nation that was before you. 29For whoever shall do any of these abominations, the persons that do them shall be cut off from among their people. 30So keep my charge never to practice any of these abominable customs which were practiced before you, and never to defile yourselves by them: I am the LORD your God."

19 And the LORD said to Moses, 2"Say to all the congregation of the sons of Israel, You shall be holy; for I the LORD your God am holy. 3Every one of you shall revere his mother and his father, and you shall keep my sabbaths: I am the LORD your God. 4Do not turn to idols or make for yourselves molten gods: I am the LORD your God.

5"When you offer a sacrifice of peace offerings to the LORD, you shall offer it so that you may be accepted. 6It shall be eaten the same day you offer it, or on the next day; and anything left over until the third day shall be burned with fire. 7If it is eaten at all on the third day, it is an abomination;

it will not be accepted, [8]and every one who
eats it shall bear his iniquity, because he has
profaned a holy thing of the LORD; and that
person shall be cut off from his people.
[9]"When you reap the harvest of your land,
you shall not reap your field to its very border,
neither shall you gather the gleanings after
your harvest. [10]And you shall not strip your
vineyard bare, neither shall you gather the
fallen grapes of your vineyard; you shall leave
them for the poor and for the sojourner: I am
the LORD your God.
[11]"You shall not steal, nor deal falsely, nor
lie to one another. [12]And you shall not swear
by my name falsely, and so profane the name
of your God: I am the LORD.
[13]"You shall not oppress your neighbor
or rob him. The wages of a hired servant
shall not remain with you all night until the
morning. [14]You shall not curse the deaf or
put a stumbling block before the blind, but
you shall fear your God: I am the LORD.
[15]"You shall do no injustice in judgment;
you shall not be partial to the poor or defer
to the great, but in righteousness shall you
judge your neighbor. [16]You shall not go up
and down as a slanderer among your people,
and you shall not stand forth against the life
of your neighbor: I am the LORD.
[17]"You shall not hate your brother in
your heart, but you shall reason with your
neighbor, lest you bear sin because of him.
[18]You shall not take vengeance or bear any
grudge against the sons of your own people,
but you shall love your neighbor as yourself:
I am the LORD."

To the choirmaster.
A Maskil of the Sons of Korah.

PSALM 44 [43]

[17]All this has come upon us,
though we have not forgotten you,
or been false to your covenant.
[18]Our heart has not turned back,
nor have our steps departed from
your way,
[19]that you should have broken us in the
place of jackals,
and covered us with deep darkness.
[20]If we had forgotten the name of our God,
or spread forth our hands to a
strange god,
[21]would not God discover this?
For he knows the secrets of the heart.
[22]No, for your sake we are slain all the
day long,
and accounted as sheep for the slaughter.

[23]Rouse yourself! Why do you sleep,
O Lord?
Awake! Do not cast us off for ever!
[24]Why do you hide your face?
Why do you forget our affliction
and oppression?
[25]For our soul is bowed down to the dust;
our body clings to the ground.
[26]Rise up, come to our help!
Deliver us for the sake of your
merciful love!

MARK 2

And when he returned to Caper′na-um after some days, it was reported that he was at home. [2]And many were gathered together, so that there was no longer room for them, not even about the
door; and he was preaching the word
to them. [3]And they came, bringing to
him a paralytic carried by four men.
[4]And when they could not get near him
because of the crowd, they removed the
roof above him; and when they had made
an opening, they let down the pallet on
which the paralytic lay. [5]And when Jesus
saw their faith, he said to the paralytic,
"Child, your sins are forgiven." [6]Now
some of the scribes were sitting there,
questioning in their hearts, [7]"Why does
this man speak like this? It is blasphemy!
Who can forgive sins but God alone?"

8 And immediately Jesus, perceiving in his spirit that they questioned like this within themselves, said to them, "Why do you question like this in your hearts? 9 Which is easier, to say to the paralytic, 'Your sins are forgiven,' or to say, 'Rise, take up your pallet and walk'? 10 But that you may know that the Son of man has authority on earth to forgive sins"—he said to the paralytic—11 "I say to you, rise, take up your pallet and go home." 12 And he rose, and immediately took up the pallet and went out before them all; so that they were all amazed and glorified God, saying, "We never saw anything like this!"

13 He went out again beside the sea; and all the crowd gathered about him, and he taught them. 14 And as he passed on, he saw Levi the son of Alphae′us sitting at the tax office, and he said to him, "Follow me." And he rose and followed him.

15 And as he sat at table in his house, many tax collectors and sinners were sitting with Jesus and his disciples; for there were many who followed him. 16 And the scribes of the Pharisees, when they saw that he was eating with sinners and tax collectors, said to his disciples, "Why does he eat with tax collectors and sinners?" 17 And when Jesus heard it, he said to them, "Those who are well have no need of a physician, but those who are sick; I came not to call the righteous, but sinners."

18 Now John's disciples and the Pharisees were fasting; and people came and said to him, "Why do John's disciples and the disciples of the Pharisees fast, but your disciples do not fast?" 19 And Jesus said to them, "Can the wedding guests fast while the bridegroom is with them? As long as they have the bridegroom with them, they cannot fast. 20 The days will come, when the bridegroom is taken away from them, and then they will fast in that day. 21 No one sews a piece of unshrunk cloth on an old garment; if he does, the patch tears away from it, the new from the old, and a worse tear is made. 22 And no one puts new wine into old wineskins; if he does, the wine will burst the skins, and the wine is lost, and so are the skins; but new wine is for fresh skins."

23 One sabbath he was going through the grainfields; and as they made their way his disciples began to pluck heads of grain. 24 And the Pharisees said to him, "Look, why are they doing what is not lawful on the sabbath?" 25 And he said to them, "Have you never read what David did, when he was in need and was hungry, he and those who were with him: 26 how he entered the house of God, when Abi′athar was high priest, and ate the showbread, which it is not lawful for any but the priests to eat, and also gave it to those who were with him?" 27 And he said to them, "The sabbath was made for man, not man for the sabbath; 28 so the Son of man is lord even of the sabbath."

REFLECTION

Everything belongs to the Lord. That's why Leviticus forbids sacrificing animals away from the Tabernacle. All sacrifices are to be made to the Lord. Leviticus also forbids drinking blood—a practice found in other sacrificial religions—because "the life . . . is in the blood" (Lv 17:11). God desires us to partake of his life, not the life of the beasts. Leviticus also lays down very specific rules governing sexual acts: forbidding incest, homosexual acts, bestiality, and other problematic sexual practices. These rules, together with the following ones that cover honest dealing, show how holiness is meant to infuse every area of life. No realm is cut off from God's sight, and, in fact, it is in the seemingly mundane parts of life that our commitment to him is tested. Jesus, too, shows how everything belongs to him. He has the power to forgive sins (see Mk 2:5) and to heal. He is "lord of the sabbath" (v. 28). Nothing is outside his purview. He can dispense from fasting and even call sinners to be his followers. Jesus is in control of the situation and of his own mission as Messiah. How can you more fully acknowledge Jesus's lordship of everything, and of your life in particular?

February 21

LEVITICUS 19

19"You shall keep my statutes. You shall not let your cattle breed with a different kind; you shall not sow your field with two kinds of seed; nor shall there come upon you a garment of cloth made of two kinds of stuff.

20"If a man lies carnally with a woman who is a slave, betrothed to another man and not yet ransomed or given her freedom, an inquiry shall be held. They shall not be put to death, because she was not free; 21but he shall bring a guilt offering for himself to the LORD, to the door of the tent of meeting, a ram for a guilt offering. 22And the priest shall make atonement for him with the ram of the guilt offering before the LORD for his sin which he has committed; and the sin which he has committed shall be forgiven him.

23"When you come into the land and plant all kinds of trees for food, then you shall count their fruit as forbidden; three years it shall be forbidden to you, it must not be eaten. 24And in the fourth year all their fruit shall be holy, an offering of praise to the LORD. 25But in the fifth year you may eat of their fruit, that they may yield more richly for you: I am the LORD your God.

26"You shall not eat any flesh with the blood in it. You shall not practice augury or witchcraft. 27You shall not round off the hair on your temples or mar the edges of your beard. 28You shall not make any cuttings in your flesh on account of the dead or tattoo any marks upon you: I am the LORD.

29"Do not profane your daughter by making her a harlot, lest the land fall into harlotry and the land become full of wickedness. 30You shall keep my sabbaths and reverence my sanctuary: I am the LORD.

31"Do not turn to mediums or wizards; do not seek them out, to be defiled by them: I am the LORD your God.

32"You shall rise up before the hoary head, and honor the face of an old man, and you shall fear your God: I am the LORD.

33"When a stranger sojourns with you in your land, you shall not do him wrong. 34The stranger who sojourns with you shall be to you as the native among you, and you shall love him as yourself; for you were strangers in the land of Egypt: I am the LORD your God.

35"You shall do no wrong in judgment, in measures of length or weight or quantity. 36You shall have just balances, just weights, a just ephah, and a just hin: I am the LORD your God, who brought you out of the land of Egypt. 37And you shall observe all my statutes and all my ordinances, and do them: I am the LORD."

20 The LORD said to Moses, 2"Say to the sons of Israel, Any man of the sons of Israel, or of the strangers that sojourn in Israel, who gives any of his children to Mo'lech shall be put to death; the people of the land shall stone him with stones. 3I myself will set my face against that man, and will cut him off from among his people, because he has given one of his children to Mo'lech, defiling my sanctuary and profaning my holy name. 4And if the people of the land do at all hide their eyes from that man, when he gives one of his children to Mo'lech, and do not put him to death, 5then I will set my face against that man and against his family, and will cut them off from among their people, him and all who follow him in playing the harlot after Mo'lech.

6"If a person turns to mediums and wizards, playing the harlot after them, I will set my face against that person, and will cut him off from among his people. 7Consecrate yourselves therefore, and be holy; for I am the LORD your God. 8Keep my statutes, and do them; I am the LORD who sanctify you. 9For every one who curses his father or his mother shall be put to death; he has cursed his father or his mother, his blood is upon him.

10"If a man commits adultery with the wife of his neighbor, both the adulterer and the adulteress shall be put to death. 11The man

who lies with his father's wife has uncovered
his father's nakedness; both of them shall
be put to death, their blood is upon them.
[12]If a man lies with his daughter-in-law,
both of them shall be put to death; they
have committed incest, their blood is upon
them. [13]If a man lies with a male as with a
woman, both of them have committed an
abomination; they shall be put to death,
their blood is upon them. [14]If a man takes
a wife and her mother also, it is wickedness;
they shall be burned with fire, both he
and they, that there may be no wickedness
among you. [15]If a man lies with a beast, he
shall be put to death; and you shall kill the
beast. [16]If a woman approaches any beast
and lies with it, you shall kill the woman and
the beast; they shall be put to death, their
blood is upon them.

[17]"If a man takes his sister, a daughter of his
father or a daughter of his mother, and sees
her nakedness, and she sees his nakedness, it
is a shameful thing, and they shall be cut off
in the sight of the children of their people; he
has uncovered his sister's nakedness, he shall
bear his iniquity. [18]If a man lies with a woman
having her sickness, and uncovers her
nakedness, he has made naked her fountain,
and she has uncovered the fountain of her
blood; both of them shall be cut off from
among their people. [19]You shall not uncover
the nakedness of your mother's sister or of
your father's sister, for that is to make naked
one's near kin; they shall bear their iniquity.
[20]If a man lies with his uncle's wife, he has
uncovered his uncle's nakedness; they shall
bear their sin, they shall die childless. [21]If a
man takes his brother's wife, it is impurity; he
has uncovered his brother's nakedness, they
shall be childless.

[22]"You shall therefore keep all my statutes
and all my ordinances, and do them; that the
land where I am bringing you to dwell may not
vomit you out. [23]And you shall not walk in the
customs of the nation which I am casting out
before you; for they did all these things, and
therefore I abhorred them. [24]But I have said
to you, 'You shall inherit their land, and I will
give it to you to possess, a land flowing with
milk and honey.' I am the LORD your God, who
have separated you from the peoples. [25]You
shall therefore make a distinction between the
clean beast and the unclean, and between the
unclean bird and the clean; you shall not make
yourselves abominable by beast or by bird or
by anything with which the ground teems,
which I have set apart for you to hold unclean.
[26]You shall be holy to me; for I the LORD am
holy, and have separated you from the peoples,
that you should be mine.

[27]"A man or a woman who is a medium
or a wizard shall be put to death; they shall
be stoned with stones, their blood shall be
upon them."

21 And the LORD said to Moses, "Speak
to the priests, the sons of Aaron, and
say to them that none of them shall defile
himself for the dead among his people,
[2]except for his nearest of kin, his mother, his
father, his son, his daughter, his brother, [3]or
his virgin sister (who is near to him because
she has had no husband; for her he may
defile himself). [4]He shall not defile himself as
a husband among his people and so profane
himself. [5]They shall not make tonsures upon
their heads, nor shave off the edges of their
beards, nor make any cuttings in their flesh.
[6]They shall be holy to their God, and not
profane the name of their God; for they offer
the offerings by fire to the LORD, the bread
of their God; therefore they shall be holy.
[7]They shall not marry a harlot or a woman
who has been defiled; neither shall they
marry a woman divorced from her husband;
for the priest is holy to his God. [8]You shall
consecrate him, for he offers the bread of
your God; he shall be holy to you; for I the
LORD, who sanctify you, am holy. [9]And the
daughter of any priest, if she profanes herself
by playing the harlot, profanes her father; she
shall be burned with fire.

[10]"The priest who is chief among his
brethren, upon whose head the anointing
oil is poured, and who has been consecrated
to wear the garments, shall not let the hair
of his head hang loose, nor tear his clothes;
[11]he shall not go in to any dead body, nor
defile himself, even for his father or for
his mother; [12]neither shall he go out of the
sanctuary, nor profane the sanctuary of his

God; for the consecration of the anointing
oil of his God is upon him: I am the LORD.
13And he shall take a wife in her virginity.
14A widow, or one divorced, or a woman
who has been defiled, or a harlot, these he
shall not marry; but he shall take to wife a
virgin of his own people, 15that he may not
profane his children among his people; for I
am the LORD who sanctify him."
16And the LORD said to Moses, 17"Say to
Aaron, None of your descendants throughout their generations who has a blemish may
approach to offer the bread of his God. 18For
no one who has a blemish shall draw near, a
man blind or lame, or one who has a mutilated
face or a limb too long, 19or a man who has
an injured foot or an injured hand, 20or a
hunchback, or a dwarf, or a man with a defect
in his sight or an itching disease or scabs or
crushed testicles; 21no man of the descendants
of Aaron the priest who has a blemish shall
come near to offer the LORD's offerings by fire;
since he has a blemish, he shall not come near
to offer the bread of his God. 22He may eat the
bread of his God, both of the most holy and
of the holy things, 23but he shall not come
near the veil or approach the altar, because
he has a blemish, that he may not profane my
sanctuaries; for I am the LORD who sanctify
them." 24So Moses spoke to Aaron and to his
sons and to all the sons of Israel.

To the choirmaster: according to Lilies.
A Maskil of the Sons of Korah; a love song.

PSALM 45 [44]

My heart overflows with a goodly theme;
I address my verses to the king;
my tongue is like the pen of a
ready scribe.

2You are the fairest of the sons of men;
grace is poured upon your lips;
therefore God has blessed you for ever.
3Gird your sword upon your thigh, O
mighty one,
in your glory and majesty!

4In your majesty ride forth victoriously
for the cause of truth and to defend
the right;
let your right hand teach you
dread deeds!
5Your arrows are sharp
in the heart of the king's enemies;
the peoples fall under you.

6Your divine throne endures for ever
and ever.
Your royal scepter is a scepter of equity;
7 you love righteousness and hate
wickedness.
Therefore God, your God, has anointed you
with the oil of gladness above
your fellows;
8 your robes are all fragrant with myrrh
and aloes and cassia.
From ivory palaces stringed instruments
make you glad;
9 daughters of kings are among your ladies
of honor;
at your right hand stands the queen in
gold of Ophir.

10Hear, O daughter, consider, and incline
your ear;
forget your people and your
father's house;
11 and the king will desire your beauty.
Since he is your lord, bow to him;
12 the people of Tyre will court your favor
with gifts,
the richest of the people 13with all kinds
of wealth.

The daughter of the king is decked in her
chamber with gold-woven robes;
14 in many-colored robes she is led to
the king,
with her virgin companions, her escort,
in her train.
15With joy and gladness they are led along
as they enter the palace of the king.

16Instead of your fathers shall be
your sons;
you will make them princes in
all the earth.

17I will cause your name to be celebrated in
all generations;
therefore the peoples will praise you for
ever and ever.

MARK 3

Again he entered the synagogue, and a man was there who had a withered hand. 2And they watched him, to see whether he would heal him on the sabbath, so that they might accuse him. 3And he said to the man who had the withered hand, "Come here." 4And he said to them, "Is it lawful on the sabbath to do good or to do harm, to save life or to kill?" But they were silent. 5And he looked around at them with anger, grieved at their hardness of heart, and said to the man, "Stretch out your hand." He stretched it out, and his hand was restored. 6The Pharisees went out, and immediately held counsel with the Hero′dians against him, how to destroy him.

7Jesus withdrew with his disciples to the sea, and a great multitude from Galilee followed; also from Judea 8and Jerusalem and Idume′a and from beyond the Jordan and from about Tyre and Si′don a great multitude, hearing all that he did, came to him. 9And he told his disciples to have a boat ready for him because of the crowd, lest they should crush him; 10for he had healed many, so that all who had diseases pressed upon him to touch him. 11And whenever the unclean spirits saw him, they fell down before him and cried out, "You are the Son of God." 12And he strictly ordered them not to make him known.

13And he went up on the mountain, and called to him those whom he desired; and they came to him. 14And he appointed twelve, to be with him, and to be sent out to preach 15and have authority to cast out demons: 16Simon whom he surnamed Peter; 17James the son of Zeb′edee and John the brother of James, whom he surnamed Bo-aner′ges, that is, sons of thunder; 18Andrew, and Philip, and Bartholomew, and Matthew, and Thomas, and James the son of Alphae′us, and Thaddae′us, and Simon the Cananaean, 19and Judas Iscariot, who betrayed him.

REFLECTION

The laws in this segment of Leviticus prohibit mixing cattle, seeds, and cloth, but they extend further to forbid witchcraft, blood drinking, and tattoos. Some of these practices are clearly moral violations of God's order, but others point to the ritual purity system and the division of creation into the categories "clean" and "unclean." These ritual rules come in between two commands to love: first, in regard to one's fellow Israelite, "You shall love your neighbor as yourself" (Lv 19:18) and, second, in regard to sojourners, "You shall love him as yourself" (v. 34). These laws and those that follow, which protect the rights of children and other vulnerable people, show a concern for giving each person his due. They are about enacting love in practical ways, which include protecting others from harm. In the end, all of these rules point to God: "You shall be holy to me; for I the LORD am holy" (20:26). Psalm 45 is about the Israelite king, but early on it was interpreted in terms of Christ (see Heb 1:8–9). Jesus is the true king who is "the fairest of the sons of men" (Ps 45:2). He has been eternally anointed to reign over all. How can you enact love toward your neighbor in practical ways?

February 22

LEVITICUS 22

And the LORD said to Moses, 2"Tell Aaron and his sons to keep away from the holy things of the sons of Israel, which they dedicate to me, so that they may not profane my holy name: I am the LORD. 3Say to them, 'If any one of all your descendants throughout your generations approaches the holy things, which the sons of Israel dedicate to the LORD, while he has an uncleanness, that person shall be cut off from my presence: I am the LORD. 4None of the line of Aaron who is a leper or suffers a discharge may eat of the holy things until he is clean. Whoever touches anything that is unclean through contact with the dead or a man who has had an emission of semen, 5and whoever touches a creeping thing by which he may be made unclean or a man from whom he may take uncleanness, whatever his uncleanness may be—6the person who touches any such shall be unclean until the evening and shall not eat of the holy things unless he has bathed his body in water. 7When the sun is down he shall be clean; and afterward he may eat of the holy things, because such are his food. 8That which dies of itself or is torn by beasts he shall not eat, defiling himself by it: I am the LORD.' 9They shall therefore keep my charge, lest they bear sin for it and die thereby when they profane it: I am the LORD who sanctify them.

10"An outsider shall not eat of a holy thing. A sojourner of the priest's or a hired servant shall not eat of a holy thing; 11but if a priest buys a slave as his property for money, the slave may eat of it; and those that are born in his house may eat of his food. 12If a priest's daughter is married to an outsider she shall not eat of the offering of the holy things. 13But if a priest's daughter is a widow or divorced, and has no child, and returns to her father's house, as in her youth, she may eat of her father's food; yet no outsider shall eat of it. 14And if a man eats of a holy thing unwittingly, he shall add the fifth of its value to it, and give the holy thing to the priest. 15The priests shall not profane the holy things of the sons of Israel, which they offer to the LORD, 16and so cause them to bear iniquity and guilt, by eating their holy things: for I am the LORD who sanctify them."

17And the LORD said to Moses, 18"Say to Aaron and his sons and all the people of Israel, When any one of the house of Israel or of the sojourners in Israel presents his offering, whether in payment of a vow or as a freewill offering which is offered to the LORD as a burnt offering, 19to be accepted you shall offer a male without blemish, of the bulls or the sheep or the goats. 20You shall not offer anything that has a blemish, for it will not be acceptable for you. 21And when any one offers a sacrifice of peace offerings to the LORD, to fulfil a vow or as a freewill offering, from the herd or from the flock, to be accepted it must be perfect; there shall be no blemish in it. 22Animals blind or disabled or mutilated or having a discharge or an itch or scabs, you shall not offer to the LORD or make of them an offering by fire upon the altar to the LORD. 23A bull or a lamb which has a part too long or too short you may present for a freewill offering; but for a votive offering it cannot be accepted. 24Any animal which has its testicles bruised or crushed or torn or cut, you shall not offer to the LORD or sacrifice within your land; 25neither shall you offer as the bread of your God any such animals gotten from a foreigner. Since there is a blemish in them, because of their mutilation, they will not be accepted for you."

26And the LORD said to Moses, 27"When a bull or sheep or goat is born, it shall remain seven days with its mother; and from the eighth day on it shall be acceptable as an offering by fire to the LORD. 28And whether the mother is a cow or a ewe, you shall not kill both her and her young in one day. 29And when you sacrifice a sacrifice of thanksgiving to the LORD, you shall sacrifice it so that you may be accepted. 30It shall be eaten on the same day, you shall leave none of it until morning: I am the LORD.

31"So you shall keep my commandments and do them: I am the LORD. 32And you shall not profane my holy name, but I will be hallowed among the sons of Israel; I am the LORD who sanctify you, 33who brought you out of the land of Egypt to be your God: I am the LORD."

23 The LORD said to Moses, 2"Say to the sons of Israel, The appointed feasts of the LORD which you shall proclaim as holy convocations, my appointed feasts, are these. 3Six days shall work be done; but on the seventh day is a sabbath of solemn rest, a

holy convocation; you shall do no work; it is
a sabbath to the LORD in all your dwellings.
4"These are the appointed feasts of the
LORD, the holy convocations, which you shall
proclaim at the time appointed for them. 5In
the first month, on the fourteenth day of the
month in the evening, is the LORD's Passover.
6And on the fifteenth day of the same month
is the feast of unleavened bread to the LORD;
seven days you shall eat unleavened bread. 7On
the first day you shall have a holy convocation;
you shall do no laborious work. 8But you shall
present an offering by fire to the LORD seven
days; on the seventh day is a holy convocation;
you shall do no laborious work."
9And the LORD said to Moses, 10"Say to the
sons of Israel, When you come into the land
which I give you and reap its harvest, you shall
bring the sheaf of the first fruits of your harvest
to the priest; 11and he shall wave the sheaf before
the LORD, that you may find acceptance; on
the day after the sabbath the priest shall wave
it. 12And on the day when you wave the sheaf,
you shall offer a male lamb a year old without
blemish as a burnt offering to the LORD. 13And
the cereal offering with it shall be two tenths
of an ephah of fine flour mixed with oil, to be
offered by fire to the LORD, a pleasing odor;
and the drink offering with it shall be of wine,
a fourth of a hin. 14And you shall eat neither
bread nor grain parched or fresh until this
same day, until you have brought the offering
of your God: it is a statute for ever throughout
your generations in all your dwellings.
15"And you shall count from the day after the
sabbath, from the day that you brought the
sheaf of the wave offering; seven full weeks
shall they be, 16counting fifty days to the day
after the seventh sabbath; then you shall
present a cereal offering of new grain to the
LORD. 17You shall bring from your dwellings
two loaves of bread to be waved, made of two
tenths of an ephah; they shall be of fine flour,
they shall be baked with leaven, as first fruits
to the LORD. 18And you shall present with the
bread seven lambs a year old without blemish,
and one young bull, and two rams; they shall be
a burnt offering to the LORD, with their cereal
offering and their drink offerings, an offering
by fire, a pleasing odor to the LORD. 19And
you shall offer one male goat for a sin offering,
and two male lambs a year old as a sacrifice
of peace offerings. 20And the priest shall wave
them with the bread of the first fruits as a wave
offering before the LORD, with the two lambs;
they shall be holy to the LORD for the priest.
21And you shall make proclamation on the
same day; you shall hold a holy convocation;
you shall do no laborious work: it is a statute
for ever in all your dwellings throughout your
generations.
22"And when you reap the harvest of your
land, you shall not reap your field to its very
border, nor shall you gather the gleanings
after your harvest; you shall leave them for
the poor and for the stranger: I am the LORD
your God."
23And the LORD said to Moses, 24"Say to
the sons of Israel, In the seventh month, on
the first day of the month, you shall observe
a day of solemn rest, a memorial proclaimed
with blast of trumpets, a holy convocation.
25You shall do no laborious work; and you
shall present an offering by fire to the LORD."
26And the LORD said to Moses, 27"On the
tenth day of this seventh month is the day of
atonement; it shall be for you a time of holy
convocation, and you shall afflict yourselves
and present an offering by fire to the LORD.
28And you shall do no work on this same day;
for it is a day of atonement, to make atonement
for you before the LORD your God. 29For
whoever is not afflicted on this same day shall
be cut off from his people. 30And whoever does
any work on this same day, that person I will
destroy from among his people. 31You shall
do no work: it is a statute for ever throughout
your generations in all your dwellings. 32It shall
be to you a sabbath of solemn rest, and you
shall afflict yourselves; on the ninth day of the
month beginning at evening, from evening to
evening shall you keep your sabbath."
33And the LORD said to Moses, 34"Say to
the sons of Israel, On the fifteenth day of
this seventh month and for seven days is the
feast of booths to the LORD. 35On the first
day shall be a holy convocation; you shall
do no laborious work. 36Seven days you shall
present offerings by fire to the LORD; on the
eighth day you shall hold a holy convocation

and present an offering by fire to the LORD;
it is a solemn assembly; you shall do no
laborious work.
37 “These are the appointed feasts of the
LORD, which you shall proclaim as times
of holy convocation, for presenting to the
LORD offerings by fire, burnt offerings
and cereal offerings, sacrifices and drink
offerings, each on its proper day; 38 besides
the sabbaths of the LORD, and besides your
gifts, and besides all your votive offerings,
and besides all your freewill offerings,
which you give to the LORD.
39 “On the fifteenth day of the seventh
month, when you have gathered in the
produce of the land, you shall keep the feast
of the LORD seven days; on the first day shall
be a solemn rest, and on the eighth day shall
be a solemn rest. 40 And you shall take on the
first day the fruit of goodly trees, branches
of palm trees, and boughs of leafy trees, and
willows of the brook; and you shall rejoice
before the LORD your God seven days. 41 You
shall keep it as a feast to the LORD seven days
in the year; it is a statute for ever throughout
your generations; you shall keep it in the
seventh month. 42 You shall dwell in booths
for seven days; all that are native in Israel
shall dwell in booths, 43 that your generations
may know that I made the sons of Israel dwell
in booths when I brought them out of the
land of Egypt: I am the LORD your God.”
44 Thus Moses declared to the sons of Israel
the appointed feasts of the LORD.

To the choirmaster.
A Psalm of the Sons of Korah.
According to Alamoth.
A Song.

PSALM 46 [45]

God is our refuge and strength,
a very present help in trouble.
2 Therefore we will not fear though the earth
should change,
though the mountains shake in the heart
of the sea;
3 though its waters roar and foam,
though the mountains tremble with
its tumult. *Selah*
4 There is a river whose streams make glad
the city of God,
the holy habitation of the Most High.
5 God is in the midst of her, she shall not
be moved;
God will help her when morning dawns.
6 The nations rage, the kingdoms totter;
he utters his voice, the earth melts.
7 The LORD of hosts is with us;
the God of Jacob is our refuge. *Selah*
8 Come, behold the works of the LORD,
how he has wrought desolations in
the earth.
9 He makes wars cease to the end of the earth;
he breaks the bow, and shatters the spear,
he burns the chariots with fire!
10 “Be still, and know that I am God.
I am exalted among the nations,
I am exalted in the earth!”
11 The LORD of hosts is with us;
the God of Jacob is our refuge. *Selah*

MARK 3

**Then he went home; 20 and the
crowd came together again, so
that they could not even eat. 21 And
when his friends heard it, they went**
out to seize him, for they said, “He is beside
himself.” 22 And the scribes who came down
from Jerusalem said, “He is possessed by
Be-el′zebul, and by the prince of demons he
casts out the demons.” 23 And he called them
to him, and said to them in parables, “How
can Satan cast out Satan? 24 If a kingdom is
divided against itself, that kingdom cannot
stand. 25 And if a house is divided against
itself, that house will not be able to stand.
26 And if Satan has risen up against himself
and is divided, he cannot stand, but is
coming to an end. 27 But no one can enter a
strong man’s house and plunder his goods,

unless he first binds the strong man; then indeed he may plunder his house.

28“Truly, I say to you, all sins will be forgiven the sons of men, and whatever blasphemies they utter; 29but whoever blasphemes against the Holy Spirit never has forgiveness, but is guilty of an eternal sin”—30for they had said, “He has an unclean spirit.”

31And his mother and his brethren came; and standing outside they sent to him and called him. 32And a crowd was sitting about him; and they said to him, “Your mother and your brethren are outside, asking for you.” 33And he replied, “Who are my mother and my brethren?” 34And looking around on those who sat about him, he said, “Here are my mother and my brethren! 35Whoever does the will of God is my brother, and sister, and mother.”

REFLECTION

Business can dominate life. Getting things done, especially profitable and practical things, can itself become an idol in our lives. We can become so busy, so goal-oriented, so committed, that we forget about sitting still, about resting in the presence of God and in his merciful love. This is part of the reason that God establishes not only the weekly Sabbath but a whole calendar of feasts and holy days. These days would be set apart from normal business, and, like the Sabbath, would form a “temple in time” wherein one could find rest. Holidays are set apart and truly made holy by God’s command to keep the feast, to rejoice, and to engage in special rituals that commemorate moments in salvation history. For example, Passover recalls the night of deliverance from Egypt, and the Feast of Booths recalls the wilderness wanderings. These holidays remind us that “God is our refuge and strength” (Ps 46:1) and that our role is not always to work constantly, but sometimes to pause and “be still, and know that I am God” (v. 10). When we regularly allow the Lord to interrupt our business with his presence, we get back in touch with his call on our lives. How can you be still and make time for the Lord?

February 23

LEVITICUS 24

The LORD said to Moses, 2“Command the sons of Israel to bring you pure oil from beaten olives for the lamp, that a light may be kept burning continually. 3Outside the veil of the covenant, in the tent of meeting, Aaron shall keep it in order from evening to morning before the LORD continually; it shall be a statute for ever throughout your generations. 4He shall keep the lamps in order upon the lampstand of pure gold before the LORD continually.

5“And you shall take fine flour, and bake twelve cakes of it; two tenths of an ephah shall be in each cake. 6And you shall set them in two rows, six in a row, upon the table of pure gold. 7And you shall put pure frankincense with each row, that it may go with the bread as a memorial portion to be offered by fire to the LORD. 8Every sabbath day Aaron shall set it in order before the LORD continually on behalf of the sons of Israel as a covenant for ever. 9And it shall be for Aaron and his sons, and they shall eat it in a holy place, since it is for him a most holy portion out of the offerings by fire to the LORD, a perpetual debt.”

10Now an Israelite woman’s son, whose father was an Egyptian, went out among the sons of Israel; and the Israelite woman’s son and a man of Israel quarreled in the camp, 11and the Israelite woman’s son blasphemed the Name, and cursed. And they brought him to Moses. His mother’s name was Shelo′mith, the daughter of Dibri, of the tribe of Dan. 12And they put him in custody, till the will of the LORD should be declared to them.

13And the LORD said to Moses, 14“Bring out of the camp him who cursed; and let all who heard him lay their hands upon his head, and let all the congregation stone him. 15And say to the sons of Israel, Whoever curses his God shall bear his sin. 16He who blasphemes the name of the LORD shall be put to death; all the congregation shall stone him; the sojourner as well as the native, when he blasphemes the Name, shall be put to death. 17He who kills a man shall be put to death. 18He who kills a beast shall make it good, life for life. 19When a man causes a disfigurement in his neighbor, as he has done it shall be done to him, 20fracture for fracture, eye for eye, tooth for tooth; as he has disfigured a man, he shall be disfigured. 21He who kills a beast shall make it good; and he who kills a man shall be put to death. 22You shall have one law for the sojourner and for the native; for I am the LORD your God." 23So Moses spoke to the sons of Israel; and they brought him who had cursed out of the camp, and stoned him with stones. Thus the sons of Israel did as the LORD commanded Moses.

25 The LORD said to Moses on Mount Sinai, 2"Say to the sons of Israel, When you come into the land which I give you, the land shall keep a sabbath to the LORD. 3Six years you shall sow your field, and six years you shall prune your vineyard, and gather in its fruits; 4but in the seventh year there shall be a sabbath of solemn rest for the land, a sabbath to the LORD; you shall not sow your field or prune your vineyard. 5What grows of itself in your harvest you shall not reap, and the grapes of your undressed vine you shall not gather; it shall be a year of solemn rest for the land. 6The sabbath of the land shall provide food for you, for yourself and for your male and female slaves and for your hired servant and the sojourner who lives with you; 7for your cattle also and for the beasts that are in your land all its yield shall be for food.

8"And you shall count seven weeks of years, seven times seven years, so that the time of the seven weeks of years shall be to you forty-nine years. 9Then you shall send abroad the loud trumpet on the tenth day of the seventh month; on the day of atonement you shall send abroad the trumpet throughout all your land. 10And you shall hallow the fiftieth year, and proclaim liberty throughout the land to all its inhabitants; it shall be a jubilee for you, when each of you shall return to his property and each of you shall return to his family. 11A jubilee shall that fiftieth year be to you; in it you shall neither sow, nor reap what grows of itself, nor gather the grapes from the undressed vines. 12For it is a jubilee; it shall be holy to you; you shall eat what it yields out of the field.

13"In this year of jubilee each of you shall return to his property. 14And if you sell to your neighbor or buy from your neighbor, you shall not wrong one another. 15According to the number of years after the jubilee, you shall buy from your neighbor, and according to the number of years for crops he shall sell to you. 16If the years are many you shall increase the price, and if the years are few you shall diminish the price, for it is the number of the crops that he is selling to you. 17You shall not wrong one another, but you shall fear your God; for I am the LORD your God.

18"Therefore you shall do my statutes, and keep my ordinances and perform them; so you will dwell in the land securely. 19The land will yield its fruit, and you will eat your fill, and dwell in it securely. 20And if you say, 'What shall we eat in the seventh year, if we may not sow or gather in our crop?' 21I will command my blessing upon you in the sixth year, so that it will bring forth fruit for three years. 22When you sow in the eighth year, you will be eating old produce; until the ninth year, when its produce comes in, you shall eat the old. 23The land shall not be sold in perpetuity, for the land is mine; for you are strangers and sojourners with me. 24And in all the country you possess, you shall grant a redemption of the land.

25"If your brother becomes poor, and sells part of his property, then his next of kin shall come and redeem what his brother has sold. 26If a man has no one to redeem it, and then himself becomes prosperous and finds sufficient means to redeem it, 27let him reckon the years since he sold it and pay back the overpayment to the man to whom he sold it; and he shall return to his property. 28But if he has not sufficient means to get it back for himself, then what he sold shall remain in the hand of him who bought it until the year of jubilee; in the jubilee it shall be released, and he shall return to his property.

29"If a man sells a dwelling house in a walled city, he may redeem it within a whole year after its sale; for a full year he shall have the right of redemption. [30]If it is not redeemed within a full year, then the house that is in the walled city shall be made sure in perpetuity to him who bought it, throughout his generations; it shall not be released in the jubilee. [31]But the houses of the villages which have no wall around them shall be reckoned with the fields of the country; they may be redeemed, and they shall be released in the jubilee. [32]Nevertheless the cities of the Levites, the houses in the cities of their possession, the Levites may redeem at any time. [33]And if one of the Levites does not exercise his right of redemption, then the house that was sold in a city of their possession shall be released in the jubilee; for the houses in the cities of the Levites are their possession among the sons of Israel. [34]But the fields of common land belonging to their cities may not be sold; for that is their perpetual possession.

[35]"And if your brother becomes poor, and cannot maintain himself with you, you shall maintain him; as a stranger and a sojourner he shall live with you. [36]Take no interest from him or increase, but fear your God; that your brother may live beside you. [37]You shall not lend him your money at interest, nor give him your food for profit. [38]I am the Lord your God, who brought you forth out of the land of Egypt to give you the land of Canaan, and to be your God.

[39]"And if your brother becomes poor beside you, and sells himself to you, you shall not make him serve as a slave: [40]he shall be with you as a hired servant and as a sojourner. He shall serve with you until the year of the jubilee; [41]then he shall go out from you, he and his children with him, and go back to his own family, and return to the possession of his fathers. [42]For they are my servants, whom I brought forth out of the land of Egypt; they shall not be sold as slaves. [43]You shall not rule over him with harshness, but shall fear your God. [44]As for your male and female slaves whom you may have: you may buy male and female slaves from among the nations that are round about you. [45]You may also buy from among the strangers who sojourn with you and their families that are with you, who have been born in your land; and they may be your property. [46]You may bequeath them to your sons after you, to inherit as a possession for ever; you may make slaves of them, but over your brethren the sons of Israel you shall not rule, one over another, with harshness.

[47]"If a stranger or sojourner with you becomes rich, and your brother beside him becomes poor and sells himself to the stranger or sojourner with you, or to a member of the stranger's family, [48]then after he is sold he may be redeemed; one of his brothers may redeem him, [49]or his uncle, or his cousin may redeem him, or a near kinsman belonging to his family may redeem him; or if he grows rich he may redeem himself. [50]He shall reckon with him who bought him from the year when he sold himself to him until the year of jubilee, and the price of his release shall be according to the number of years; the time he was with his owner shall be rated as the time of a hired servant. [51]If there are still many years, according to them he shall refund out of the price paid for him the price for his redemption. [52]If there remain but a few years until the year of jubilee, he shall make a reckoning with him; according to the years of service due from him he shall refund the money for his redemption. [53]As a servant hired year by year shall he be with him; he shall not rule with harshness over him in your sight. [54]And if he is not redeemed by these means, then he shall be released in the year of jubilee, he and his children with him. [55]For to me the sons of Israel are servants, they are my servants whom I brought forth out of the land of Egypt: I am the Lord your God."

To the choirmaster.
A Psalm of the Sons of Korah.

PSALM 47 [46]

Clap your hands, all peoples!
  Shout to God with loud songs of joy!
[2]For the Lord, the Most High, is awesome,
  a great king over all the earth.

3He subdued peoples under us,
and nations under our feet.
4He chose our heritage for us,
the pride of Jacob whom he loves. *Selah*

5God has gone up with a shout,
the LORD with the sound of a trumpet.
6Sing praises to God, sing praises!
Sing praises to our King, sing praises!
7For God is the king of all the earth;
sing praises with a psalm!

8God reigns over the nations;
God sits on his holy throne.
9The princes of the peoples gather
as the people of the God of Abraham.
For the shields of the earth belong to God;
he is highly exalted!

MARK 4

Again he began to teach beside the sea. And a very large crowd gathered about him, so that he got into a boat and sat in it on the sea; and the whole crowd was beside the
sea on the land. 2And he taught them many
things in parables, and in his teaching he said
to them: 3"Listen! A sower went out to sow.
4And as he sowed, some seed fell along the
path, and the birds came and devoured it.
5Other seed fell on rocky ground, where it had
not much soil, and immediately it sprang up,
since it had no depth of soil; 6and when the sun
rose it was scorched, and since it had no root it
withered away. 7Other seed fell among thorns
and the thorns grew up and choked it, and it
yielded no grain. 8And other seeds fell into
good soil and brought forth grain, growing
up and increasing and yielding thirtyfold and
sixtyfold and a hundredfold." 9And he said,
"He who has ears to hear, let him hear."
10And when he was alone, those who
were about him with the Twelve asked him
concerning the parables. 11And he said to
them, "To you has been given the secret of
the kingdom of God, but for those outside
everything is in parables; 12so that they
may indeed see but not perceive, and may
indeed hear but not understand; lest they
should turn again, and be forgiven." 13And
he said to them, "Do you not understand
this parable? How then will you understand
all the parables? 14The sower sows the word.
15And these are the ones along the path,
where the word is sown; when they hear,
Satan immediately comes and takes away the
word which is sown in them. 16And these in
like manner are the ones sown upon rocky
ground, who, when they hear the word,
immediately receive it with joy; 17and they
have no root in themselves, but endure for a
while; then, when tribulation or persecution
arises on account of the word, immediately
they fall away. 18And others are the ones sown
among thorns; they are those who hear the
word, 19but the cares of the world, and the
delight in riches, and the desire for other
things, enter in and choke the word, and it
proves unfruitful. 20But those that were sown
upon the good soil are the ones who hear the
word and accept it and bear fruit, thirtyfold
and sixtyfold and a hundredfold."

REFLECTION

The Old Testament is famous for its ruthless form of justice: "Eye for eye, tooth for tooth" (Lv 24:20). And, in human terms, it is simply fair. However, the strict exactitude of this law is belied by certain elements like the sabbath year and the Jubilee year. Once every seven years, the land would lie fallow as a way of allowing the soil to regenerate. In addition, once every fifty years, not only would the land lie fallow, but all sorts of gratuitous mercies would be given out. In this Jubilee year, debts would be forgiven, slaves would be set free, and Israelites who had lost their ancestral property would be allowed to return home. This Jubilee time of liberty for all is at odds with strict justice and severe punishment. In fact, it is a way of wiping the slate clean. In his jubilee-shaped ministry, Jesus points to those who hear and respond to the word of God. The "seed" of the word might be stolen by Satan, have no root in repentance, or get choked out by worldly cares, yet the seeds in good soil are those "who hear the word and accept it and bear fruit" (Mk 4:20). How can you more fully accept God's word to you?

February 24

LEVITICUS 26

**“You shall make for yourselves
no idols and erect no graven
image or pillar, and you shall
not set up a figured stone in your land,
to bow down to them; for I am the LORD
your God. 2You shall keep my sabbaths**
and reverence my sanctuary: I am the LORD.
3“If you walk in my statutes and observe
my commandments and do them, 4then I
will give you your rains in their season, and
the land shall yield its increase, and the trees
of the field shall yield their fruit. 5And your
threshing shall last to the time of vintage,
and the vintage shall last to the time for
sowing; and you shall eat your bread to the
full, and dwell in your land securely. 6And I
will give peace in the land, and you shall lie
down, and none shall make you afraid; and
I will remove evil beasts from the land, and
the sword shall not go through your land.
7And you shall chase your enemies, and
they shall fall before you by the sword. 8Five
of you shall chase a hundred, and a hundred
of you shall chase ten thousand; and your
enemies shall fall before you by the sword.
9And I will have regard for you and make
you fruitful and multiply you, and will
confirm my covenant with you. 10And you
shall eat old store long kept, and you shall
clear out the old to make way for the new.
11And I will make my abode among you,
and my soul shall not abhor you. 12And I
will walk among you, and will be your God,
and you shall be my people. 13I am the LORD
your God, who brought you forth out of the
land of Egypt, that you should not be their
slaves; and I have broken the bars of your
yoke and made you walk erect.

14“But if you will not listen to me, and will
not do all these commandments, 15if you
spurn my statutes, and if your soul abhors
my ordinances, so that you will not do all my
commandments, but break my covenant, 16I
will do this to you: I will appoint over you
sudden terror, consumption and fever that
waste the eyes and cause life to pine away.
And you shall sow your seed in vain, for
your enemies shall eat it; 17I will set my face
against you, and you shall be struck down
before your enemies; those who hate you
shall rule over you, and you shall flee when
none pursues you. 18And if in spite of this
you will not listen to me, then I will chastise
you again sevenfold for your sins, 19and I
will break the pride of your power, and I
will make your heavens like iron and your
earth like brass; 20and your strength shall be
spent in vain, for your land shall not yield its
increase, and the trees of the land shall not
yield their fruit.

21“Then if you walk contrary to me, and
will not listen to me, I will bring more
plagues upon you, sevenfold as many as
your sins. 22And I will let loose the wild
beasts among you, which shall rob you of
your children, and destroy your cattle, and
make you few in number, so that your ways
shall become desolate.

23“And if by this discipline you are not
turned to me, but walk contrary to me,
24then I also will walk contrary to you, and I
myself will strike you sevenfold for your sins.
25And I will bring a sword upon you, that
shall execute vengeance for the covenant;
and if you gather within your cities I will
send pestilence among you, and you shall
be delivered into the hand of the enemy.
26When I break your staff of bread, ten
women shall bake your bread in one oven,
and shall deliver your bread again by weight;
and you shall eat, and not be satisfied.

27“And if in spite of this you will not listen
to me, but walk contrary to me, 28then I will
walk contrary to you in fury, and chastise
you myself sevenfold for your sins. 29You
shall eat the flesh of your sons, and you shall
eat the flesh of your daughters. 30And I will
destroy your high places, and cut down your
incense altars, and cast your dead bodies
upon the dead bodies of your idols; and my
soul will abhor you. 31And I will lay your
cities waste, and will make your sanctuaries
desolate, and I will not smell your pleasing

odors. [32]And I will devastate the land, so that your enemies who settle in it shall be astonished at it. [33]And I will scatter you among the nations, and I will unsheathe the sword after you; and your land shall be a desolation, and your cities shall be a waste.

[34]"Then the land shall enjoy its sabbaths as long as it lies desolate, while you are in your enemies' land; then the land shall rest, and enjoy its sabbaths. [35]As long as it lies desolate it shall have rest, the rest which it had not in your sabbaths when you dwelt upon it. [36]And as for those of you that are left, I will send faintness into their hearts in the lands of their enemies; the sound of a driven leaf shall put them to flight, and they shall flee as one flees from the sword, and they shall fall when none pursues. [37]They shall stumble over one another, as if to escape a sword, though none pursues; and you shall have no power to stand before your enemies. [38]And you shall perish among the nations, and the land of your enemies shall eat you up. [39]And those of you that are left shall pine away in your enemies' lands because of their iniquity; and also because of the iniquities of their fathers they shall pine away like them.

[40]"But if they confess their iniquity and the iniquity of their fathers in their treachery which they committed against me, and also in walking contrary to me, [41]so that I walked contrary to them and brought them into the land of their enemies; if then their uncircumcised heart is humbled and they make amends for their iniquity; [42]then I will remember my covenant with Jacob, and I will remember my covenant with Isaac and my covenant with Abraham, and I will remember the land. [43]But the land shall be left by them, and enjoy its sabbaths while it lies desolate without them; and they shall make amends for their iniquity, because they spurned my ordinances, and their soul abhorred my statutes. [44]Yet for all that, when they are in the land of their enemies, I will not spurn them, neither will I abhor them so as to destroy them utterly and break my covenant with them; for I am the LORD their God; [45]but I will for their sake remember the covenant with their forefathers, whom I brought forth out of the land of Egypt in the sight of the nations, that I might be their God: I am the LORD."

[46]These are the statutes and ordinances and laws which the LORD made between him and the sons of Israel on Mount Sinai by Moses.

27 The LORD said to Moses, [2]"Say to the sons of Israel, When a man makes a special vow of persons to the LORD at your valuation, [3]then your valuation of a male from twenty years old up to sixty years old shall be fifty shekels of silver, according to the shekel of the sanctuary. [4]If the person is a female, your valuation shall be thirty shekels. [5]If the person is from five years old up to twenty years old, your valuation shall be for a male twenty shekels, and for a female ten shekels. [6]If the person is from a month old up to five years old, your valuation shall be for a male five shekels of silver, and for a female your valuation shall be three shekels of silver. [7]And if the person is sixty years old and upward, then your valuation for a male shall be fifteen shekels, and for a female ten shekels. [8]And if a man is too poor to pay your valuation, then he shall bring the person before the priest, and the priest shall value him; according to the ability of him who vowed the priest shall value him.

[9]"If it is an animal such as men offer as an offering to the LORD, all of such that any man gives to the LORD is holy. [10]He shall not substitute anything for it or exchange it, a good for a bad, or a bad for a good; and if he makes any exchange of beast for beast, then both it and that for which it is exchanged shall be holy. [11]And if it is an unclean animal such as is not offered as an offering to the LORD, then the man shall bring the animal before the priest, [12]and the priest shall value it as either good or bad; as you, the priest, value it, so it shall be. [13]But if he wishes to redeem it, he shall add a fifth to the valuation.

[14]"When a man dedicates his house to be holy to the LORD, the priest shall value it as either good or bad; as the priest values it, so it shall stand. [15]And if he who dedicates it wishes to redeem his house, he shall add a

fifth of the valuation in money to it, and it shall be his.

[16]“If a man dedicates to the LORD part of the land which is his by inheritance, then your valuation shall be according to the seed for it; a sowing of a homer of barley shall be valued at fifty shekels of silver. [17]If he dedicates his field from the year of jubilee, it shall stand at your full valuation; [18]but if he dedicates his field after the jubilee, then the priest shall compute the money-value for it according to the years that remain until the year of jubilee, and a deduction shall be made from your valuation. [19]And if he who dedicates the field wishes to redeem it, then he shall add a fifth of the valuation in money to it, and it shall remain his. [20]But if he does not wish to redeem the field, or if he has sold the field to another man, it shall not be redeemed any more; [21]but the field, when it is released in the jubilee, shall be holy to the LORD, as a field that has been devoted; the priest shall be in possession of it. [22]If he dedicates to the LORD a field which he has bought, which is not a part of his possession by inheritance, [23]then the priest shall compute the valuation for it up to the year of jubilee, and the man shall give the amount of the valuation on that day as a holy thing to the LORD. [24]In the year of jubilee the field shall return to him from whom it was bought, to whom the land belongs as a possession by inheritance. [25]Every valuation shall be according to the shekel of the sanctuary: twenty gerahs shall make a shekel.

[26]“But a firstling of animals, which as a firstling belongs to the LORD, no man may dedicate; whether ox or sheep, it is the LORD’s. [27]And if it is an unclean animal, then he shall buy it back at your valuation, and add a fifth to it; or, if it is not redeemed, it shall be sold at your valuation.

[28]“But no devoted thing that a man devotes to the LORD, of anything that he has, whether of man or beast, or of his inherited field, shall be sold or redeemed; every devoted thing is most holy to the LORD. [29]No one devoted, who is to be utterly destroyed from among men, shall be ransomed; he shall be put to death.

[30]“All the tithe of the land, whether of the seed of the land or of the fruit of the trees, is the LORD’s; it is holy to the LORD. [31]If a man wishes to redeem any of his tithe, he shall add a fifth to it. [32]And all the tithe of herds and flocks, every tenth animal of all that pass under the herdsman’s staff, shall be holy to the LORD. [33]A man shall not inquire whether it is good or bad, neither shall he exchange it; and if he exchanges it, then both it and that for which it is exchanged shall be holy; it shall not be redeemed.”

[34]These are the commandments which the LORD commanded Moses for the sons of Israel on Mount Sinai.

A Song.
A Psalm of the Sons of Korah.

PSALM 48 [47]

Great is the LORD and greatly to be praised
in the city of our God!
His holy mountain, [2]beautiful in elevation,
is the joy of all the earth,
Mount Zion, in the far north,
the city of the great King.
[3]Within her citadels God
has shown himself a sure defense.

[4]For behold, the kings assembled,
they came on together.
[5]As soon as they saw it, they were astounded,
they were in panic, they took to flight;
[6]trembling took hold of them there,
anguish as of a woman with labor pains.
[7]By the east wind you shattered
the ships of Tarshish.
[8]As we have heard, so have we seen
in the city of the LORD of hosts,
in the city of our God,
which God establishes for ever. *Selah*

[9]We have thought on your mercy, O God,
in the midst of your temple.
[10]As your name, O God,
so your praise reaches to the ends
of the earth.

Your right hand is filled with victory;
11 let Mount Zion be glad!
Let the daughters of Judah rejoice
because of your judgments!

12Walk about Zion, go round about her,
number her towers,
13consider well her ramparts,
go through her citadels;
that you may tell the next generation
14 that this is God,
our God for ever and ever.
He will be our guide for ever.

MARK 4

21And he said to them, "Is a lamp brought in to be put under a bushel, or under a bed, and not on a stand? 22For there is nothing hidden, except to be made manifest; nor
is anything secret, except to come to light.
23If any man has ears to hear, let him hear."
24And he said to them, "Take heed what
you hear; the measure you give will be the
measure you get, and still more will be
given you. 25For to him who has will more
be given; and from him who has not, even
what he has will be taken away."
26And he said, "The kingdom of God is as if
a man should scatter seed upon the ground,
27and should sleep and rise night and day,
and the seed should sprout and grow, he
knows not how. 28The earth produces of
itself, first the blade, then the ear, then the
full grain in the ear. 29But when the grain is
ripe, at once he puts in the sickle, because
the harvest has come."
30And he said, "With what can we compare
the kingdom of God, or what parable shall
we use for it? 31It is like a grain of mustard
seed, which, when sown upon the ground,
is the smallest of all the seeds on earth; 32yet
when it is sown it grows up and becomes the
greatest of all shrubs, and puts forth large
branches, so that the birds of the air can
make nests in its shade."
33With many such parables he spoke the
word to them, as they were able to hear
it; 34he did not speak to them without a
parable, but privately to his own disciples he
explained everything.

REFLECTION

Here at the end of the Book of Leviticus, the Lord gives a list of blessings for obedience and punishments for disobedience. The main purpose of all the complicated laws finally becomes clear. "I will give peace in the land, and you shall lie down, and none shall make you afraid" (Lv 26:6). Obedience is about security— security from enemies and security in one's relationship with God. He goes on to say, "I will walk among you, and will be your God, and you shall be my people" (v. 12). These are incredible promises of his fidelity to us, his people. When we walk in his ways, we experience his blessings. And though Israel would have many difficult years in its relationship with the Lord, the nation would eventually play host to the King of kings in the flesh. If obedience leads to security, security counteracts fear. Jesus reveals the hidden security of faith when he sleeps in the disciples' boat during a storm. They are overwhelmed by fear and rouse Jesus, who again conquers fear with his words: "Peace! Be still!" (Mk 4:39). These words are as much for our hearts as for the waves. How have you experienced the security of obedience to God?

February 25

NUMBERS 1

The Lord spoke to Moses in the wilderness of Sinai, in the tent of meeting, on the first day of the second month, in the second year after they had
come out of the land of Egypt, saying, 2"Take
a census of all the congregation of the sons
of Israel, by families, by fathers' houses,

according to the number of names, every male, head by head; [3]from twenty years old and upward, all in Israel who are able to go forth to war, you and Aaron shall number them, company by company. [4]And there shall be with you a man from each tribe, each man being the head of the house of his fathers. [5]And these are the names of the men who shall attend you. From Reuben, Eli′zur the son of Shed′eur; [6]from Simeon, Shelu′mi-el the son of Zurishad′dai; [7]from Judah, Nahshon the son of Ammin′adab; [8]from Is′sachar, Nethan′el the son of Zu′ar; [9]from Zeb′ulun, Eli′ab the son of He′lon; [10]from the sons of Joseph, from E′phraim, Elish′ama the son of Ammi′hud, and from Manas′seh, Gama′liel the son of Pedah′zur; [11]from Benjamin, Abi′dan the son of Gideo′ni; [12]from Dan, Ahie′zer the son of Ammishad′dai; [13]from Asher, Pa′giel the son of Ochran; [14]from Gad, Eli′asaph the son of Deu′el; [15]from Naph′tali, Ahi′ra the son of E′nan." [16]These were the ones chosen from the congregation, the leaders of their ancestral tribes, the heads of the clans of Israel.

[17]Moses and Aaron took these men who have been named, [18]and on the first day of the second month, they assembled the whole congregation together, who registered themselves by families, by fathers' houses, according to the number of names from twenty years old and upward, head by head, [19]as the LORD commanded Moses. So he numbered them in the wilderness of Sinai.

[20]The people of Reuben, Israel's first-born, their generations, by their families, by their fathers' houses, according to the number of names, head by head, every male from twenty years old and upward, all who were able to go forth to war: [21]the number of the tribe of Reuben was forty-six thousand five hundred.

[22]Of the people of Simeon, their generations, by their families, by their fathers' houses, those of them that were numbered, according to the number of names, head by head, every male from twenty years old and upward, all who were able to go forth to war: [23]the number of the tribe of Simeon was fifty-nine thousand three hundred.

[24]Of the people of Gad, their generations, by their families, by their fathers' houses, according to the number of the names, from twenty years old and upward, all who were able to go forth to war: [25]the number of the tribe of Gad was forty-five thousand six hundred and fifty.

[26]Of the people of Judah, their generations, by their families, by their fathers' houses, according to the number of names, from twenty years old and upward, every man able to go forth to war: [27]the number of the tribe of Judah was seventy-four thousand six hundred.

[28]Of the people of Is′sachar, their generations, by their families, by their fathers' houses, according to the number of names, from twenty years old and upward, every man able to go forth to war: [29]the number of the tribe of Is′sachar was fifty-four thousand four hundred.

[30]Of the people of Zeb′ulun, their generations, by their families, by their fathers' houses, according to the number of names, from twenty years old and upward, every man able to go forth to war: [31]the number of the tribe of Zeb′ulun was fifty-seven thousand four hundred.

[32]Of the people of Joseph, namely, of the people of E′phraim, their generations, by their families, by their fathers' houses, according to the number of names, from twenty years old and upward, every man able to go forth to war: [33]the number of the tribe of E′phraim was forty thousand five hundred.

[34]Of the people of Manas′seh, their generations, by their families, by their fathers' houses, according to the number of names, from twenty years old and upward, every man able to go forth to war: [35]the number of the tribe of Manas′seh was thirty-two thousand two hundred.

[36]Of the people of Benjamin, their generations, by their families, by their fathers' houses, according to the number of names, from twenty years old and upward, every man able to go forth to war: [37]the number of the tribe of Benjamin was thirty-five thousand four hundred.

[38]Of the people of Dan, their generations,
by their families, by their fathers' houses,
according to the number of names, from
twenty years old and upward, every man
able to go forth to war: [39]the number of the
tribe of Dan was sixty-two thousand seven
hundred.
[40]Of the people of Asher, their generations,
by their families, by their fathers' houses,
according to the number of names, from
twenty years old and upward, every man
able to go forth to war: [41]the number of the
tribe of Asher was forty-one thousand five
hundred.
[42]Of the people of Naph′tali, their generations, by their families, by their fathers'
houses, according to the number of names,
from twenty years old and upward, every
man able to go forth to war: [43]the number
of the tribe of Naph′tali was fifty-three
thousand four hundred.
[44]These are those who were numbered,
whom Moses and Aaron numbered with the
help of the leaders of Israel, twelve men, each
representing his fathers' house. [45]So the whole
number of the sons of Israel, by their fathers'
houses, from twenty years old and upward,
every man able to go forth to war in Israel—
[46]their whole number was six hundred and
three thousand five hundred and fifty.
[47]But the Levites were not numbered by
their ancestral tribe along with them. [48]For
the LORD said to Moses, [49]"Only the tribe
of Levi you shall not number, and you shall
not take a census of them among the sons
of Israel; [50]but appoint the Levites over the
tabernacle of the covenant, and over all its
furnishings, and over all that belongs to it;
they are to carry the tabernacle and all its
furnishings, and they shall tend it, and shall
encamp around the tabernacle. [51]When the
tabernacle is to set out, the Levites shall take
it down; and when the tabernacle is to be
pitched, the Levites shall set it up. And if any
one else comes near, he shall be put to death.
[52]The sons of Israel shall pitch their tents
by their companies, every man by his own
camp and every man by his own standard;
[53]but the Levites shall encamp around the
tabernacle of the covenant, that there may be
no wrath upon the congregation of the sons
of Israel; and the Levites shall keep charge of
the tabernacle of the covenant." [54]Thus did
the sons of Israel; they did according to all
that the LORD commanded Moses.

To the choirmaster.
A Psalm of the Sons of Korah.

PSALM 49 [48]

Hear this, all peoples!
  Give ear, all inhabitants of the world,
[2]both low and high,
  rich and poor together!
[3]My mouth shall speak wisdom;
  the meditation of my heart shall
    be understanding.
[4]I will incline my ear to a proverb;
  I will solve my riddle to the music of
    the lyre.

[5]Why should I fear in times of trouble,
  when the iniquity of my persecutors
    surrounds me,
[6]men who trust in their wealth
  and boast of the abundance of their riches?
[7]Truly no man can ransom himself,
  or give to God the price of his life,
[8]for the ransom of his life is costly,
  and can never suffice,
[9]that he should continue to live on for ever,
  and never see the Pit.

[10]Yes, he shall see that even the wise die,
  the fool and the stupid alike must perish
  and leave their wealth to others.
[11]Their graves are their homes for ever,
  their dwelling places to all generations,
  though they named lands their own.
[12]Man cannot abide in his pomp,
  he is like the beasts that perish.

[13]This is the fate of those who have
    foolish confidence,
  the end of those who are pleased
    with their portion. *Selah*
[14]Like sheep they are appointed for Sheol;
  Death shall be their shepherd;

straight to the grave they descend,
and their form shall waste away;
Sheol shall be their home.
[15]But God will ransom my soul from the
power of Sheol,
for he will receive me. *Selah*

[16]Be not afraid when one becomes rich,
when the glory of his house increases.
[17]For when he dies he will carry nothing away;
his glory will not go down after him.
[18]Though, while he lives, he counts
himself happy,
and though a man gets praise when he
does well for himself,
[19]he will go to the generation of his fathers,
who will never more see the light.
[20]Man cannot abide in his pomp,
he is like the beasts that perish.

MARK 4

[35]On that day, when evening had
come, he said to them, "Let us go
across to the other side." [36]And leaving
the crowd, they took him with them, just
as he was, in the boat. And other boats were
with him. [37]And a great storm of wind arose,
and the waves beat into the boat, so that
the boat was already filling. [38]But he was in
the stern, asleep on the cushion; and they
woke him and said to him, "Teacher, do
you not care if we perish?" [39]And he awoke
and rebuked the wind, and said to the sea,
"Peace! Be still!" And the wind ceased, and
there was a great calm. [40]He said to them,
"Why are you afraid? Have you no faith?"
[41]And they were filled with awe, and said to
one another, "Who then is this, that even
wind and sea obey him?"
5 They came to the other side of the sea,
to the country of the Ger′asenes. [2]And
when he had come out of the boat, there
met him out of the tombs a man with an
unclean spirit, [3]who lived among the tombs;
and no one could bind him any more, even
with a chain; [4]for he had often been bound
with shackles and chains, but the chains he
wrenched apart, and the shackles he broke
in pieces; and no one had the strength to
subdue him. [5]Night and day among the
tombs and on the mountains he was always
crying out, and bruising himself with stones.
[6]And when he saw Jesus from afar, he ran
and worshiped him; [7]and crying out with a
loud voice, he said, "What have you to do
with me, Jesus, Son of the Most High God?
I adjure you by God, do not torment me."
[8]For he had said to him, "Come out of the
man, you unclean spirit!" [9]And Jesus asked
him, "What is your name?" He replied, "My
name is Legion; for we are many." [10]And he
begged him eagerly not to send them out
of the country. [11]Now a great herd of swine
was feeding there on the hillside; [12]and they
begged him, "Send us to the swine, let us
enter them." [13]So he gave them leave. And
the unclean spirits came out, and entered
the swine; and the herd, numbering about
two thousand, rushed down the steep bank
into the sea, and were drowned in the sea.
[14]The herdsmen fled, and told it in the city
and in the country. And people came to see
what it was that had happened. [15]And they
came to Jesus, and saw the demoniac sitting
there, clothed and in his right mind, the
man who had had the legion; and they were
afraid. [16]And those who had seen it told
what had happened to the demoniac and to
the swine. [17]And they began to beg Jesus to
depart from their neighborhood. [18]And as
he was getting into the boat, the man who
had been possessed with demons begged
him that he might be with him. [19]But he
refused, and said to him, "Go home to your
friends, and tell them how much the Lord
has done for you, and how he has had mercy
on you." [20]And he went away and began to
proclaim in the Decap′olis how much Jesus
had done for him; and all men marveled.

REFLECTION

In the Book of Numbers, God has already brought his people out of Egypt and given them the gifts of the Law and the Tabernacle. Now they need to go to the Promised

Land, so they must get organized for mobility. The census recorded here is part of that organization. According to Jewish tradition, it also hints at God's concern for every last member of his people. But the tribe-by-tribe numbering ends with a twist. The Levites are not numbered with the others. Why not? Censuses were often used to assess military capability and for tax purposes. But the Levites are entrusted with something that surpasses such human calculations: the Tabernacle, where the Lord is present in Israel's midst. God, not human resourcefulness, will guide his people. This point also appears in different ways in today's Psalm and Gospel. Financial planning is prudent, but Scripture often warns against trusting in wealth (see Ps 49:6). God alone provides true security (see v. 15). In Mark, Jesus chides the disciples for their understandable fear of the storm (see Mk 4:40). They have not yet fully realized who is among them: the "Mightier One" (see 1:7) who has power over chaos (see 4:39, 41) and over evil spirits (see 5:18–43). Do you trust that, with Christ at the center of your life, you need not "fear in times of trouble" (Ps 49:5)?

February 26

NUMBERS 2

The Lord said to Moses and
Aaron, [2]"The sons of Israel shall
encamp each by his own standard,
with the ensigns of their fathers' houses;
they shall encamp facing the tent of meeting on
every side. [3]Those to encamp on the east side
toward the sunrise shall be of the standard
of the camp of Judah by their companies, the
leader of the people of Judah being Nahshon
the son of Ammin'adab, [4]his host as numbered
being seventy-four thousand six hundred.
[5]Those to encamp next to him shall be the
tribe of Is'sachar, the leader of the people of
Issachar being Nethan'el the son of Zu'ar, [6]his
host as numbered being fifty-four thousand
four hundred. [7]Then the tribe of Zeb'ulun,
the leader of the people of Zebulun being
Eli'ab the son of He'lon, [8]his host as numbered
being fifty-seven thousand four hundred.
[9]The whole number of the camp of Judah, by
their companies, is a hundred and eighty-six
thousand four hundred. They shall set out first
on the march.

[10]"On the south side shall be the standard
of the camp of Reuben by their companies,
the leader of the people of Reuben being
Eli'zur the son of Shed'eur, [11]his host as
numbered being forty-six thousand five
hundred. [12]And those to encamp next to him
shall be the tribe of Simeon, the leader of the
people of Simeon being Shelu'mi-el the son
of Zurishad'dai, [13]his host as numbered being
fifty-nine thousand three hundred. [14]Then
the tribe of Gad, the leader of the people of
Gad being Eli'asaph the son of Reu'el, [15]his
host as numbered being forty-five thousand
six hundred and fifty. [16]The whole number
of the camp of Reuben, by their companies,
is a hundred and fifty-one thousand four
hundred and fifty. They shall set out second.

[17]"Then the tent of meeting shall set out,
with the camp of the Levites in the midst
of the camps; as they encamp, so shall
they set out, each in position, standard by
standard.

[18]"On the west side shall be the standard of
the camp of E'phraim by their companies,
the leader of the people of Ephraim being
Elish'ama the son of Ammi'hud, [19]his host
as numbered being forty thousand five
hundred. [20]And next to him shall be the
tribe of Manas'seh, the leader of the people
of Manasseh being Gama'liel the son of
Pedah'zur, [21]his host as numbered being
thirty-two thousand two hundred. [22]Then
the tribe of Benjamin, the leader of the
people of Benjamin being Abi'dan the son
of Gideo'ni, [23]his host as numbered being
thirty-five thousand four hundred. [24]The
whole number of the camp of E'phraim,
by their companies, is a hundred and eight
thousand one hundred. They shall set out
third on the march.

25 “On the north side shall be the standard
of the camp of Dan by their companies, the
leader of the people of Dan being Ahie′zer the
son of Ammishad′dai, 26 his host as numbered
being sixty-two thousand seven hundred.
27 And those to encamp next to him shall be
the tribe of Asher, the leader of the people of
Asher being Pa′giel the son of Ochran, 28 his
host as numbered being forty-one thousand
five hundred. 29 Then the tribe of Naph′tali, the
leader of the people of Naphtali being Ahi′ra
the son of E′nan, 30 his host as numbered being
fifty-three thousand four hundred. 31 The whole
number of the camp of Dan is a hundred and
fifty-seven thousand six hundred. They shall
set out last, standard by standard.”

32 These are the sons of Israel as numbered
by their fathers’ houses; all in the camps
who were numbered by their companies
were six hundred and three thousand five
hundred and fifty. 33 But the Levites were not
numbered among the sons of Israel, as the
LORD commanded Moses.

34 Thus did the sons of Israel. According
to all that the LORD commanded Moses,
so they encamped by their standards, and
so they set out, every one in his family,
according to his fathers’ house.

3 These are the generations of Aaron and
Moses at the time when the LORD
spoke with Moses on Mount Sinai. 2 These
are the names of the sons of Aaron: Na′dab
the first-born, and Abi′hu, Elea′zar, and
Ith′amar; 3 these are the names of the sons
of Aaron, the anointed priests, whom he
ordained to minister in the priest’s office.
4 But Na′dab and Abi′hu died before the
LORD when they offered unholy fire before
the LORD in the wilderness of Sinai; and
they had no children. So Elea′zar and
Ith′amar served as priests in the lifetime of
Aaron their father.

5 And the LORD said to Moses, 6 “Bring
the tribe of Levi near, and set them before
Aaron the priest, that they may minister
to him. 7 They shall perform duties for him
and for the whole congregation before
the tent of meeting, as they minister at
the tabernacle; 8 they shall have charge of
all the furnishings of the tent of meeting,
and attend to the duties for the sons of
Israel as they minister at the tabernacle.
9 And you shall give the Levites to Aaron
and his sons; they are wholly given to him
from among the sons of Israel. 10 And you
shall appoint Aaron and his sons, and
they shall attend to their priesthood; but
if any one else comes near, he shall be put
to death.”

11 And the LORD said to Moses, 12 “Behold,
I have taken the Levites from among the
sons of Israel instead of every first-born that
opens the womb among the sons of Israel.
The Levites shall be mine, 13 for all the first-
born are mine; on the day that I slew all the
first-born in the land of Egypt, I consecrated
for my own all the first-born in Israel, both
of man and of beast; they shall be mine: I am
the LORD.”

A Psalm of Asaph.

PSALM 50 [49]

The Mighty One, God the LORD,
speaks and summons the earth
from the rising of the sun to its setting.
2 Out of Zion, the perfection of beauty,
God shines forth.

3 Our God comes, he does not keep silence,
before him is a devouring fire,
round about him a mighty tempest.
4 He calls to the heavens above
and to the earth, that he may judge his
people:
5 “Gather to me my faithful ones,
who made a covenant with me by sacrifice!”
6 The heavens declare his righteousness,
for God himself is judge! *Selah*

7 “Hear, O my people, and I will speak,
O Israel, I will testify against you.
I am God, your God.
8 I do not reprove you for your sacrifices;
your burnt offerings are continually
before me.
9 I will accept no bull from your house,
nor he-goat from your folds.

10 For every beast of the forest is mine,
the cattle on a thousand hills.
11 I know all the birds of the air,
and all that moves in the field is mine.

12 "If I were hungry, I would not tell you;
for the world and all that is in it is mine.
13 Do I eat the flesh of bulls,
or drink the blood of goats?
14 Offer to God a sacrifice of thanksgiving,
and pay your vows to the Most High;
15 and call upon me in the day of trouble;
I will deliver you, and you shall glorify me."

16 But to the wicked God says:
"What right have you to recite my statutes,
or take my covenant on your lips?
17 For you hate discipline,
and you cast my words behind you.
18 If you see a thief, you are a friend of his;
and you keep company with adulterers.

19 "You give your mouth free rein for evil,
and your tongue frames deceit.
20 You sit and speak against your brother;
you slander your own mother's son.
21 These things you have done and I have
been silent;
you thought that I was one like yourself.
But now I rebuke you, and lay the charge
before you.

22 "Mark this, then, you who forget God,
lest I tear, and there be none to deliver!
23 He who brings thanksgiving as his sacrifice
honors me;
to him who orders his way aright
I will show the salvation of God!"

MARK 5

**21 And when Jesus had crossed
again in the boat to the other
side, a great crowd gathered about him;
and he was beside the sea. 22 Then came**
one of the rulers of the synagogue, Ja´irus by
name; and seeing him, he fell at his feet, 23 and
begged him, saying, "My little daughter is at
the point of death. Come and lay your hands
on her, so that she may be made well, and
live." 24 And he went with him.
And a great crowd followed him and
thronged about him. 25 And there was a
woman who had had a flow of blood for
twelve years, 26 and who had suffered much
under many physicians, and had spent all
that she had, and was no better but rather
grew worse. 27 She had heard the reports
about Jesus, and came up behind him in
the crowd and touched his garment. 28 For
she said, "If I touch even his garments, I
shall be made well." 29 And immediately the
hemorrhage ceased; and she felt in her body
that she was healed of her disease. 30 And
Jesus, perceiving in himself that power had
gone forth from him, immediately turned
about in the crowd, and said, "Who touched
my garments?" 31 And his disciples said to
him, "You see the crowd pressing around
you, and yet you say, 'Who touched me?' "
32 And he looked around to see who had
done it. 33 But the woman, knowing what
had been done to her, came in fear and
trembling and fell down before him, and
told him the whole truth. 34 And he said to
her, "Daughter, your faith has made you
well; go in peace, and be healed of your
disease."
35 While he was still speaking, there came
from the ruler's house some who said, "Your
daughter is dead. Why trouble the Teacher
any further?" 36 But ignoring what they said,
Jesus said to the ruler of the synagogue, "Do
not fear, only believe." 37 And he allowed no
one to follow him except Peter and James and
John the brother of James. 38 When they came
to the house of the ruler of the synagogue, he
saw a tumult, and people weeping and wailing
loudly. 39 And when he had entered, he said to
them, "Why do you make a tumult and weep?
The child is not dead but sleeping." 40 And they
laughed at him. But he put them all outside,
and took the child's father and mother and
those who were with him, and went in where
the child was. 41 Taking her by the hand he said
to her, "Tal´itha cu´mi"; which means, "Little
girl, I say to you, arise." 42 And immediately
the girl got up and walked; for she was

twelve years old. And immediately they were
overcome with amazement. 43And he strictly
charged them that no one should know this,
and told them to give her something to eat.

REFLECTION

The very end of the Book of Exodus says that Israel's journey to the Promised Land proceeds at the Lord's prompting (see Ex 40:36–38). When the cloud of his presence rises from the Tabernacle, Israel goes. When it stays, Israel stays. In Numbers 2, Israel's camp is rigorously organized so that the people might follow God's direction efficiently. Now as then, the Church's institutional organization should help God's people more readily discern and respond to the guidance of the Holy Spirit. What's more, we see again the centrality of the Tabernacle and its liturgy (see Nm 2:17). This too is reflected in the Church. Vatican II tells us that the source and summit of Christian life is found in worship—specifically, in the Eucharist. There, we are invited like the hemorrhaging woman to touch Jesus in faith and receive his healing (see Mk 5:27–29). The story of Jairus's daughter reminds us that Jesus's life-giving power can reach us even if we've spiritually "died" through mortal sin. The grace of the Sacrament of Reconciliation can revive us. But none of this is mere magic: worship demands conversion. Psalm 50 proclaims that liturgy without personal transformation is empty. Meeting Jesus should change us. Even *after* healing the woman, Jesus exhorts her to *stay* healed: "Go in peace, and be healed of your disease" (Mk 5:34). What disease do you need Jesus to heal?

February 27

NUMBERS 3

**14And the LORD said to Moses
in the wilderness of Sinai,
15"Number the sons of Levi, by fathers'
houses and by families; every male
from a month old and upward you**
shall number." 16So Moses numbered them
according to the word of the LORD, as he
was commanded. 17And these were the
sons of Levi by their names: Gershon and
Ko'hath and Merar'i. 18And these are the
names of the sons of Gershon by their
families: Libni and Shim'e-i. 19And the
sons of Ko'hath by their families: Amram,
Izhar, He'bron, and Uz'ziel. 20And the
sons of Merar'i by their families: Mah'li
and Mu'shi. These are the families of the
Levites, by their fathers' houses.
21Of Gershon were the family of the
Libnites and the family of the Shim'eites;
these were the families of the Ger'shonites.
22Their number according to the number
of all the males from a month old and
upward was seven thousand five hundred.
23The families of the Ger'shonites were to
encamp behind the tabernacle on the west,
24with Eli'asaph, the son of La'el as head
of the fathers' house of the Ger'shonites.
25And the charge of the sons of Gershon
in the tent of meeting was to be the
tabernacle, the tent with its covering, the
screen for the door of the tent of meeting,
26the hangings of the court, the screen for
the door of the court which is around the
tabernacle and the altar, and its cords; all
the service pertaining to these.
27Of Ko'hath were the family of the Am'ra-
mites, and the family of the Iz'harites, and the
family of the He'bronites, and the family of
the Uz'zielites; these are the families of the
Ko'hathites. 28According to the number of
all the males, from a month old and upward,
there were eight thousand six hundred,
attending to the duties of the sanctuary.
29The families of the sons of Ko'hath were to
encamp on the south side of the tabernacle,
30with Eliza'phan the son of Uz'ziel as head
of the fathers' house of the families of the
Ko'hathites. 31And their charge was to be
the ark, the table, the lampstand, the altars,
the vessels of the sanctuary with which the
priests minister, and the screen; all the service
pertaining to these. 32And Elea'zar the son
of Aaron the priest was to be chief over the
leaders of the Levites, and to have oversight
of those who had charge of the sanctuary.

33 Of Merar'i were the family of the
Mah'lites and the family of the Mu'shites:
these are the families of Merari. 34 Their
number according to the number of all
the males from a month old and upward
was six thousand two hundred. 35 And the
head of the fathers' house of the families
of Merar'i was Zu'riel the son of Abiha'il;
they were to encamp on the north side of
the tabernacle. 36 And the appointed charge
of the sons of Merar'i was to be the frames
of the tabernacle, the bars, the pillars,
the bases, and all their accessories; all the
service pertaining to these; 37 also the pillars
of the court round about, with their bases
and pegs and cords.

38 And those to encamp before the tabernacle on the east, before the tent of
meeting toward the sunrise, were Moses
and Aaron and his sons, having charge of
the rites within the sanctuary, whatever had
to be done for the sons of Israel; and any one
else who came near was to be put to death.
39 All who were numbered of the Levites,
whom Moses and Aaron numbered at the
commandment of the LORD, by families, all
the males from a month old and upward,
were twenty-two thousand.

40 And the LORD said to Moses, "Number
all the first-born males of the sons of Israel,
from a month old and upward, taking their
number by names. 41 And you shall take the
Levites for me—I am the LORD—instead of
all the first-born among the sons of Israel,
and the cattle of the Levites instead of all
the firstlings among the cattle of the sons
of Israel." 42 So Moses numbered all the first-
born among the sons of Israel, as the LORD
commanded him. 43 And all the first-born
males, according to the number of names,
from a month old and upward as numbered
were twenty-two thousand two hundred
and seventy-three.

44 And the LORD said to Moses, 45 "Take
the Levites instead of all the first-born
among the sons of Israel, and the cattle of
the Levites instead of their cattle; and the
Levites shall be mine: I am the LORD. 46 And
for the redemption of the two hundred and
seventy-three of the first-born of the sons of
Israel, over and above the number of the male
Levites, 47 you shall take five shekels apiece;
reckoning by the shekel of the sanctuary, the
shekel of twenty gerahs, you shall take them,
48 and give the money by which the excess
number of them is redeemed to Aaron and
his sons." 49 So Moses took the redemption
money from those who were over and above
those redeemed by the Levites; 50 from the
first-born of the sons of Israel he took the
money, one thousand three hundred and
sixty-five shekels, reckoned by the shekel
of the sanctuary; 51 and Moses gave the
redemption money to Aaron and his sons,
according to the word of the LORD, as the
LORD commanded Moses.

4 The LORD said to Moses and Aaron,
2 "Take a census of the sons of Ko'hath
from among the sons of Levi, by their families and their fathers' houses, 3 from thirty
years old up to fifty years old, all who can
enter the service, to do the work in the tent
of meeting. 4 This is the service of the sons
of Ko'hath in the tent of meeting: the most
holy things. 5 When the camp is to set out,
Aaron and his sons shall go in and take
down the veil of the screen, and cover the
ark of the covenant with it; 6 then they shall
put on it a covering of goatskin, and spread
over that a cloth all of blue, and shall put in
its poles. 7 And over the table of the bread
of the Presence they shall spread a cloth of
blue, and put upon it the plates, the dishes
for incense, the bowls, and the flagons for
the drink offering; the continual bread also
shall be on it; 8 then they shall spread over
them a cloth of scarlet, and cover the same
with a covering of goatskin, and shall put
in its poles. 9 And they shall take a cloth of
blue, and cover the lampstand for the light,
with its lamps, its snuffers, its trays, and all
the vessels for oil with which it is supplied:
10 and they shall put it with all its utensils in
a covering of goatskin and put it upon the
carrying frame. 11 And over the golden altar
they shall spread a cloth of blue, and cover it
with a covering of goatskin, and shall put in
its poles; 12 and they shall take all the vessels of
the service which are used in the sanctuary,
and put them in a cloth of blue, and cover

them with a covering of goatskin, and put
them on the carrying frame. 13And they
shall take away the ashes from the altar, and
spread a purple cloth over it; 14and they shall
put on it all the utensils of the altar, which
are used for the service there, the firepans,
the forks, the shovels, and the basins, all the
utensils of the altar; and they shall spread
upon it a covering of goatskin, and shall put
in its poles. 15And when Aaron and his sons
have finished covering the sanctuary and all
the furnishings of the sanctuary, as the camp
sets out, after that the sons of Ko′hath shall
come to carry these, but they must not touch
the holy things, lest they die. These are the
things of the tent of meeting which the sons
of Kohath are to carry.

16"And Elea′zar the son of Aaron the priest
shall have charge of the oil for the light,
the fragrant incense, the continual cereal
offering, and the anointing oil, with the
oversight of all the tabernacle and all that is
in it, of the sanctuary and its vessels."

17The LORD said to Moses and Aaron,
18"Let not the tribe of the families of the
Ko′hathites be destroyed from among the
Levites; 19but deal thus with them, that they
may live and not die when they come near
to the most holy things: Aaron and his sons
shall go in and appoint them each to his
task and to his burden, 20but they shall not
go in to look upon the holy things even for a
moment, lest they die."

To the choirmaster.
A Psalm of David, when Nathan the prophet came to him,
after he had gone in to Bathsheba.

PSALM 51 [50]

Have mercy on me, O God,
according to your merciful love;
according to your abundant mercy blot
out my transgressions.
2Wash me thoroughly from my iniquity,
and cleanse me from my sin!

3For I know my transgressions,
and my sin is ever before me.
4Against you, you only, have I sinned,
and done that which is evil in your sight,
so that you are justified in your sentence
and blameless in your judgment.
5Behold, I was brought forth in iniquity,
and in sin did my mother conceive me.

6Behold, you desire truth in the inward being;
therefore teach me wisdom in my
secret heart.
7Purge me with hyssop, and I shall be clean;
wash me, and I shall be whiter
than snow.
8Make me hear joy and gladness;
let the bones which you have
broken rejoice.
9Hide your face from my sins,
and blot out all my iniquities.

10Create in me a clean heart, O God,
and put a new and right spirit within me.
11Cast me not away from your presence,
and take not your holy Spirit from me.
12Restore to me the joy of your salvation,
and uphold me with a willing spirit.

13Then I will teach transgressors your ways,
and sinners will return to you.
14Deliver me from bloodguilt, O God,
O God of my salvation,
and my tongue will sing aloud of your
deliverance.

15O Lord, open my lips,
and my mouth shall show forth
your praise.
16For you take no delight in sacrifice;
were I to give a burnt offering, you would
not be pleased.
17The sacrifice acceptable to God is a
broken spirit;
a broken and contrite heart, O God, you
will not despise.

18Do good to Zion in your good pleasure;
rebuild the walls of Jerusalem,
19then will you delight in right sacrifices,
in burnt offerings and whole burnt
offerings;
then bulls will be offered on your altar.

MARK 6

He went away from there and came to his own country; and his disciples followed him. 2And on the sabbath he began to teach in the synagogue; and many who heard him were astonished, saying, "Where did this man get all this? What is the wisdom given to him? What mighty works are wrought by his hands! 3Is not this the carpenter, the son of Mary and brother of James and Joses and Judas and Simon, and are not his sisters here with us?" And they took offense at him. 4And Jesus said to them, "A prophet is not without honor, except in his own country, and among his own kin, and in his own house." 5And he could do no mighty work there, except that he laid his hands upon a few sick people and healed them. 6And he marveled because of their unbelief.

And he went about among the villages teaching.

7And he called to him the Twelve, and began to send them out two by two, and gave them authority over the unclean spirits. 8He charged them to take nothing for their journey except a staff; no bread, no bag, no money in their belts; 9but to wear sandals and not put on two tunics. 10And he said to them, "Where you enter a house, stay there until you leave the place. 11And if any place will not receive you and they refuse to hear you, when you leave, shake off the dust that is on your feet for a testimony against them." 12So they went out and preached that men should repent. 13And they cast out many demons, and anointed with oil many that were sick and healed them.

14King Herod heard of it; for Jesus' name had become known. Some said, "John the Baptist has been raised from the dead; that is why these powers are at work in him." 15But others said, "It is Eli′jah." And others said, "It is a prophet, like one of the prophets of old." 16But when Herod heard of it he said, "John, whom I beheaded, has been raised." 17For Herod had sent and seized John, and bound him in prison for the sake of Hero′di-as, his brother Philip's wife; because he had married her. 18For John said to Herod, "It is not lawful for you to have your brother's wife." 19And Hero′di-as had a grudge against him, and wanted to kill him. But she could not, 20for Herod feared John, knowing that he was a righteous and holy man, and kept him safe. When he heard him, he was much perplexed; and yet he heard him gladly. 21But an opportunity came when Herod on his birthday gave a banquet for his courtiers and officers and the leading men of Galilee. 22For when Hero′di-as' daughter came in and danced, she pleased Herod and his guests; and the king said to the girl, "Ask me for whatever you wish, and I will grant it." 23And he vowed to her, "Whatever you ask me, I will give you, even half of my kingdom." 24And she went out, and said to her mother, "What shall I ask?" And she said, "The head of John the Baptist." 25And she came in immediately with haste to the king, and asked, saying, "I want you to give me at once the head of John the Baptist on a platter." 26And the king was exceedingly sorry; but because of his oaths and his guests he did not want to break his word to her. 27And immediately the king sent a soldier of the guard and gave orders to bring his head. He went and beheaded him in the prison, 28and brought his head on a platter, and gave it to the girl; and the girl gave it to her mother. 29When his disciples heard of it, they came and took his body, and laid it in a tomb.

REFLECTION

In Mark 3:13–15, Jesus called the Twelve "to be sent out to preach and have authority to cast out demons." That purpose is realized in today's reading (see Mk 6:7, 12–13). Yet just before this, Jesus is rejected by his fellow Nazarenes, despite his "wisdom" and "mighty works" (v. 6:2). Jesus's miracles are not meant for spectacle but to elicit faith and repentance (see 1:15), so it would be contrary to his mission to perform them in the face of unbelief (see 6:5). Additionally, the sending of the disciples is immediately followed by the story of John the Baptist's imprisonment and execution. The disciples are thus sandwiched between the rejection of their Master and of his forerunner John. The cost of discipleship is steep! It requires total dependence on God. This is reflected in Jesus's instructions for the journey. If we wish to be disciples, we will need to travel light. We may need to give up possessions. We may suffer ridicule and contempt. We'll certainly need to "lay aside every weight, and sin which clings so closely" (Heb 12:1). For that, frequent prayer of Psalm 51 is a great help. And when we've been set free, we'll find ourselves prepared like the Kohathites to bear God's sacred presence on our shoulders (see Nm 4:15, 17–20). What is God asking of you to prepare you for mission?

February 28

NUMBERS 4

[21]The LORD said to Moses, [22]"Take a census of the sons of Gershon also, by their families and their fathers' houses; [23]from thirty years old up to fifty years old, you shall number them, all who can enter for service, to do the work in the tent of meeting. [24]This is the service of the families of the Ger′shonites, in serving and bearing burdens: [25]they shall carry the curtains of the tabernacle, and the tent of meeting with its covering, and the covering of goatskin that is on top of it, and the screen for the door of the tent of meeting, [26]and the hangings of the court, and the screen for the entrance of the gate of the court which is around the tabernacle and the altar, and their cords, and all the equipment for their service; and they shall do all that needs to be done with regard to them. [27]All the service of the sons of the Ger′shonites shall be at the command of Aaron and his sons, in all that they are to carry, and in all that they have to do; and you shall assign to their charge all that they are to carry. [28]This is the service of the families of the sons of the Ger′shonites in the tent of meeting, and their work is to be under the oversight of Ith′amar the son of Aaron the priest.

[29]"As for the sons of Merar′i, you shall number them by their families and their fathers' houses; [30]from thirty years old up to fifty years old, you shall number them, every one that can enter the service, to do the work of the tent of meeting. [31]And this is what they are charged to carry, as the whole of their service in the tent of meeting: the frames of the tabernacle, with its bars, pillars, and bases, [32]and the pillars of the court round about with their bases, pegs, and cords, with all their equipment and all their accessories; and you shall assign by name the objects which they are required to carry. [33]This is the service of the families of the sons of Merar′i, the whole of their service in the tent of meeting, under the hand of Ith′amar the son of Aaron the priest."

[34]And Moses and Aaron and the leaders of the congregation numbered the sons of the Ko′hathites, by their families and their fathers' houses, [35]from thirty years old up to fifty years old, every one that could enter the service, for work in the tent of meeting; [36]and their number by families was two thousand seven hundred and fifty. [37]This was the number of the families of the Ko′hathites, all who served in the tent of meeting, whom Moses and Aaron numbered according to the commandment of the LORD by Moses.

[38]The number of the sons of Gershon, by their families and their fathers' houses, [39]from thirty years old up to fifty years old, every one that could enter the service for work in the tent of meeting—[40]their number by their families and their fathers' houses was two thousand six hundred and thirty. [41]This was the number of the families of the sons of Gershon, all who served in the tent of meeting, whom Moses and Aaron numbered according to the commandment of the LORD.

[42]The number of the families of the sons of Merar′i, by their families and their fathers' houses, [43]from thirty years old up to fifty years old, every one that could enter the service, for work in the tent of meeting—[44]their number by families was three thousand two hundred. [45]These are those who were numbered of the families of the sons of Merar′i, whom Moses and Aaron numbered according to the commandment of the LORD by Moses.

[46]All those who were numbered of the Levites, whom Moses and Aaron and the

leaders of Israel numbered, by their families and their fathers' houses, 47from thirty years old up to fifty years old, every one that could enter to do the work of service and the work of bearing burdens in the tent of meeting, 48those who were numbered of them were eight thousand five hundred and eighty. 49According to the commandment of the LORD through Moses they were appointed, each to his task of serving or carrying; thus they were numbered by him, as the LORD commanded Moses.

5 The LORD said to Moses, 2"Command the sons of Israel that they put out of the camp every leper, and every one having a discharge, and every one that is unclean through contact with the dead; 3you shall put out both male and female, putting them outside the camp, that they may not defile their camp, in the midst of which I dwell." 4And the sons of Israel did so, and drove them outside the camp; as the LORD said to Moses, so the sons of Israel did.

5And the LORD said to Moses, 6"Say to the sons of Israel, When a man or woman commits any of the sins that men commit by breaking faith with the LORD, and that person is guilty, 7he shall confess his sin which he has committed; and he shall make full restitution for his wrong, adding a fifth to it, and giving it to him to whom he did the wrong. 8But if the man has no kinsman to whom restitution may be made for the wrong, the restitution for wrong shall go to the LORD for the priest, in addition to the ram of atonement with which atonement is made for him. 9And every offering, all the holy things of the sons of Israel, which they bring to the priest, shall be his; 10and every man's holy things shall be his; whatever any man gives to the priest shall be his."

11And the LORD said to Moses, 12"Say to the sons of Israel, If any man's wife goes astray and acts unfaithfully against him, 13if a man lies with her carnally, and it is hidden from the eyes of her husband, and she is undetected though she has defiled herself, and there is no witness against her, since she was not taken in the act; 14and if the spirit of jealousy comes upon him, and he is jealous of his wife who has defiled herself; or if the spirit of jealousy comes upon him, and he is jealous of his wife, though she has not defiled herself; 15then the man shall bring his wife to the priest, and bring the offering required of her, a tenth of an ephah of barley meal; he shall pour no oil upon it and put no frankincense on it, for it is a cereal offering of jealousy, a cereal offering of remembrance, bringing iniquity to remembrance.

16"And the priest shall bring her near, and set her before the LORD; 17and the priest shall take holy water in an earthen vessel, and take some of the dust that is on the floor of the tabernacle and put it into the water. 18And the priest shall set the woman before the LORD, and unbind the hair of the woman's head, and place in her hands the cereal offering of remembrance, which is the cereal offering of jealousy. And in his hand the priest shall have the water of bitterness that brings the curse. 19Then the priest shall make her take an oath, saying, 'If no man has lain with you, and if you have not turned aside to uncleanness, while you were under your husband's authority, be free from this water of bitterness that brings the curse. 20But if you have gone astray, though you are under your husband's authority, and if you have defiled yourself, and some man other than your husband has lain with you, 21then' (let the priest make the woman take the oath of the curse, and say to the woman) 'the LORD make you an execration and an oath among your people, when the LORD makes your thigh fall away and your body swell; 22may this water that brings the curse pass into your bowels and make your body swell and your thigh fall away.' And the woman shall say, 'Amen, Amen.'

23"Then the priest shall write these curses in a book, and wash them off into the water of bitterness; 24and he shall make the woman drink the water of bitterness that brings the curse, and the water that brings the curse shall enter into her and cause bitter pain. 25And the priest shall take the cereal offering of jealousy out of the woman's hand, and shall wave the cereal offering before the LORD and bring it to the altar; 26and the priest shall take a handful of the cereal offering, as its memorial portion, and burn it upon the altar, and afterward shall make the woman

drink the water. 27And when he has made
her drink the water, then, if she has defiled
herself and has acted unfaithfully against her
husband, the water that brings the curse shall
enter into her and cause bitter pain, and her
body shall swell, and her thigh shall fall away,
and the woman shall become an execration
among her people. 28But if the woman has
not defiled herself and is clean, then she shall
be free and shall conceive children.
29"This is the law in cases of jealousy, when
a wife, though under her husband's authority,
goes astray and defiles herself, 30or when the
spirit of jealousy comes upon a man and he
is jealous of his wife; then he shall set the
woman before the LORD, and the priest shall
execute upon her all this law. 31The man shall
be free from iniquity, but the woman shall
bear her iniquity."

To the choirmaster.
A Maskil of David, when Doeg, the Edomite,
came and told Saul,
"David has come to the house of Ahimelech."

PSALM 52 [51]

Why do you boast, O mighty man,
of mischief done against the godly?
All the day 2you are plotting destruction.
Your tongue is like a sharp razor,
you worker of treachery.
3You love evil more than good,
and lying more than speaking the truth.
Selah

4You love all words that devour,
O deceitful tongue.

5But God will break you down for ever;
he will snatch and tear you from your tent;
he will uproot you from the land of
the living. *Selah*
6The righteous shall see, and fear,
and shall laugh at him, saying,
7"See the man who would not make God
his refuge,
but trusted in the abundance of his riches,
and sought refuge in his wealth!"

8But I am like a green olive tree
in the house of God.
I trust in the mercy of God
for ever and ever.
9I will thank you for ever,
because you have done it.
I will proclaim your name, for it is good,
in the presence of the godly.

MARK 6

**30The apostles returned to Jesus,
and told him all that they had
done and taught. 31And he said
to them, "Come away by yourselves to
a lonely place, and rest a while." For**
many were coming and going, and they had
no leisure even to eat. 32And they went away
in the boat to a lonely place by themselves.
33Now many saw them going, and knew them,
and they ran there on foot from all the towns,
and got there ahead of them. 34As he landed he
saw a great throng, and he had compassion on
them, because they were like sheep without a
shepherd; and he began to teach them many
things. 35And when it grew late, his disciples
came to him and said, "This is a lonely place,
and the hour is now late; 36send them away, to
go into the country and villages round about
and buy themselves something to eat." 37But
he answered them, "You give them something
to eat." And they said to him, "Shall we go and
buy two hundred denarii worth of bread, and
give it to them to eat?" 38And he said to them,
"How many loaves have you? Go and see." And
when they had found out, they said, "Five, and
two fish." 39Then he commanded them all to sit
down by companies upon the green grass. 40So
they sat down in groups, by hundreds and by
fifties. 41And taking the five loaves and the two
fish he looked up to heaven, and blessed, and
broke the loaves, and gave them to the disciples
to set before the people; and he divided the two
fish among them all. 42And they all ate and were
satisfied. 43And they took up twelve baskets full
of broken pieces and of the fish. 44And those
who ate the loaves were five thousand men.

[45]Immediately he made his disciples get into
the boat and go before him to the other side,
to Beth-sa′ida, while he dismissed the crowd.
[46]And after he had taken leave of them, he
went up on the mountain to pray. [47]And when
evening came, the boat was out on the sea, and
he was alone on the land. [48]And he saw that
they were distressed in rowing, for the wind
was against them. And about the fourth watch
of the night he came to them, walking on the
sea. He meant to pass by them, [49]but when they
saw him walking on the sea they thought it was
a ghost, and cried out; [50]for they all saw him,
and were terrified. But immediately he spoke
to them and said, "Take heart, it is I; have no
fear." [51]And he got into the boat with them
and the wind ceased. And they were utterly
astounded, [52]for they did not understand about
the loaves, but their hearts were hardened.
[53]And when they had crossed over, they
came to land at Gennes′aret, and moored
to the shore. [54]And when they got out of the
boat, immediately the people recognized
him, [55]and ran about the whole neighborhood
and began to bring sick people on their
pallets to any place where they heard he was.
[56]And wherever he came, in villages, cities,
or country, they laid the sick in the market
places, and begged him that they might
touch even the fringe of his garment; and as
many as touched it were made well.

REFLECTION

Numbers 5:2 lists the types of uncleanness that bring (usually temporary) exclusion from Israel's camp. Significantly, they all relate to death. Leprosy gives a deathlike appearance (see Nm 12:12), "discharge" involves the loss of bodily fluids associated with life, and contact with a corpse is contact with death. It isn't sinful to contract leprosy or to undergo normal discharge. Burying the dead is even a work of mercy (see Tb 1:16–20)! But death is a constant reminder of its cause, which is sin. This is already suggested by the sequence of Numbers 5, which links uncleanness with "breaking faith" with the Lord and the community, whether by wronging a neighbor or one's spouse (see Nm 5:6, 12). Unchecked, these infidelities can lead us to "love evil more than good," rejoicing in selfish conniving (see Ps 52:1–4). Such deception eventually comes to naught (see vv. 5–7). Only the Lord's provision can finally satisfy us (see Mk 6:42) and make us flourish "like a green olive tree in the house of God." Can you confess, "I trust in the mercy of God for ever and ever" (Ps 52:8)?

February 29

ISAIAH 55

"Ho, every one who thirsts,
come to the waters;
and he who has no money,
come, buy and eat!
Come, buy wine and milk
without money and without price.
[2]Why do you spend your money for that
which is not bread,
and your labor for that which does
not satisfy?
Listen diligently to me, and eat what is good,
and delight yourselves in rich food.
[3]Incline your ear, and come to me;
hear, that your soul may live;
and I will make with you an everlasting
covenant,
my steadfast, merciful love for David.
[4]Behold, I made him a witness to the peoples,
a leader and commander for the peoples.
[5]Behold, you shall call nations that you
know not,
and nations that knew you not shall run
to you,
because of the LORD your God, and of the
Holy One of Israel,
for he has glorified you.

[6]"Seek the LORD while he may be found,
call upon him while he is near;
[7]let the wicked forsake his way,
and the unrighteous man his thoughts;

let him return to the LORD, that he may
have mercy on him,
and to our God, for he will
abundantly pardon.
8For my thoughts are not your thoughts,
neither are your ways my ways,
says the LORD.
9For as the heavens are higher than the earth,
so are my ways higher than your ways
and my thoughts than your thoughts.

10"For as the rain and the snow come down
from heaven,
and do not return there but water
the earth,
making it bring forth and sprout,
giving seed to the sower and bread
to the eater,
11so shall my word be that goes forth from
my mouth;
it shall not return to me empty,
but it shall accomplish that which I intend,
and prosper in the thing for which I sent it.

PSALM 119 [118]

Blessed are those whose way is blameless,
who walk in the law of the LORD!
2Blessed are those who keep his testimonies,
who seek him with their whole heart,
3who also do no wrong,
but walk in his ways!
4You have commanded your precepts
to be kept diligently.
5O that my ways may be steadfast
in keeping your statutes!
6Then I shall not be put to shame,
having my eyes fixed on all your
commandments.
7I will praise you with an upright heart,
when I learn your righteous ordinances.
8I will observe your statutes;
O forsake me not utterly!

9How can a young man keep his way pure?
By guarding it according to your word.
10With my whole heart I seek you;
let me not wander from your
commandments!
11I have laid up your word in my heart,
that I might not sin against you.
12Blessed are you, O LORD;
teach me your statutes!
13With my lips I declare
all the ordinances of your mouth.
14In the way of your testimonies I delight
as much as in all riches.
15I will meditate on your precepts,
and fix my eyes on your ways.
16I will delight in your statutes;
I will not forget your word.

17Deal bountifully with your servant,
that I may live and observe your word.
18Open my eyes, that I may behold
wondrous things out of your law.
19I am a sojourner on earth;
hide not your commandments
20My soul is consumed with longing
for your ordinances at all times.
21You rebuke the insolent, accursed ones,
who wander from your commandments;
22take away from me their scorn and contempt,
for I have kept your testimonies.
23Even though princes sit plotting
against me,
your servant will meditate on
your statutes.
24Your testimonies are my delight,
they are my counselors.

25My soul clings to the dust;
revive me according to your word!
26When I told of my ways, you answered me;
teach me your statutes!
27Make me understand the way of
your precepts,
and I will meditate on your
wondrous works.
28My soul melts away for sorrow;
strengthen me according to your word!
29Put false ways far from me;
and graciously teach me your law!
30I have chosen the way of faithfulness,
I set your ordinances before me.
31I cling to your testimonies, O LORD;
let me not be put to shame!
32I will run in the way of your commandments
when you enlarge my understanding!

33Teach me, O LORD, the way of your statutes;
and I will keep it to the end.
34Give me understanding, that I may keep your law
and observe it with my whole heart.
35Lead me in the path of your commandments,
for I delight in it.
36Incline my heart to your testimonies,
and not to gain!
37Turn my eyes from looking at vanities;
and give me life in your ways.
38Confirm to your servant your promise,
which is for those who fear you.
39Turn away the reproach which I dread;
for your ordinances are good.
40Behold, I long for your precepts;
in your righteousness give me life!

41Let your mercy come to me, O LORD,
your salvation according to your promise;
42then shall I have an answer for those who taunt me,
for I trust in your word.
43And take not the word of truth utterly out of my mouth,
for my hope is in your ordinances.
44I will keep your law continually,
for ever and ever;
45and I shall walk at liberty,
for I have sought your precepts.
46I will also speak of your testimonies before kings,
and shall not be put to shame;
47for I find my delight in your commandments,
which I love.
48I revere your commandments, which I love,
and I will meditate on your statutes.

49Remember your word to your servant,
in which you have made me hope.
50This is my comfort in my affliction
that your promise gives me life.
51Godless men utterly deride me,
but I do not turn away from your law.
52When I think of your ordinances from of old,
I take comfort, O LORD.
53Hot indignation seizes me because of the wicked,
who forsake your law.
54Your statutes have been my songs
in the house of my pilgrimage.
55I remember your name in the night, O LORD,
and keep your law.
56This blessing has fallen to me,
that I have kept your precepts.

57The LORD is my portion;
I promise to keep your words.
58I entreat your favor with all my heart;
be gracious to me according to your promise.
59When I think of your ways,
I turn my feet to your testimonies;
60I hasten and do not delay
to keep your commandments.
61Though the cords of the wicked ensnare me,
I do not forget your law.
62At midnight I rise to praise you,
because of your righteous ordinances.
63I am a companion of all who fear you,
of those who keep your precepts.
64The earth, O LORD, is full of your steadfast love;
teach me your statutes!

65You have dealt well with your servant,
O LORD, according to your word.
66Teach me good judgment and knowledge,
for I believe in your commandments.
67Before I was afflicted I went astray;
but now I keep your word.
68You are good and do good;
teach me your statutes.
69The godless besmear me with lies,
but with my whole heart I keep your precepts;
70their heart is gross like fat,
but I delight in your law.
71It is good for me that I was afflicted,
that I might learn your statutes.
72The law of your mouth is better to me
than thousands of gold and silver pieces.

73Your hands have made and fashioned me;
give me understanding that I may learn your commandments.
74Those who fear you shall see me and rejoice,
because I have hoped in your word.

75I know, O Lord, that your judgments
are right,
and that in faithfulness you have
afflicted me.
76Let your mercy be ready to comfort me
according to your promise to your servant.
77Let your compassion come to me,
that I may live;
for your law is my delight.
78Let the godless be put to shame,
because they have subverted me with guile;
as for me, I will meditate on your precepts.
79Let those who fear you turn to me,
that they may know your testimonies.
80May my heart be blameless in your statutes,
that I may not be put to shame!

81My soul languishes for your salvation;
I hope in your word.
82My eyes fail with watching for your promise;
I ask, "When will you comfort me?"
83For I have become like a wineskin
in the smoke,
yet I have not forgotten your statutes.
84How long must your servant endure?
When will you judge those who
persecute me?
85Godless men have dug pitfalls for me,
men who do not conform to your law.
86All your commandments are sure;
they persecute me with falsehood; help me!
87They have almost made an end of me
on earth;
but I have not forsaken your precepts.
88In your mercy spare my life,
that I may keep the testimonies of
your mouth.

89For ever, O Lord, your word
is firmly fixed in the heavens.
90Your faithfulness endures to
all generations;
you have established the earth, and it
stands fast.
91By your appointment they stand this day;
for all things are your servants.
92If your law had not been my delight,
I should have perished in my affliction.
93I will never forget your precepts;
for by them you have given me life.
94I am yours, save me;
for I have sought your precepts.
95The wicked lie in wait to destroy me;
but I consider your testimonies.
96I have seen a limit to all perfection,
but your commandment is
exceedingly broad.

97Oh, how I love your law!
It is my meditation all the day.
98Your commandment makes me wiser than
my enemies,
for it is ever with me.
99I have more understanding than all
my teachers,
for your testimonies are my meditation.
100I understand more than the aged,
for I keep your precepts.
101I hold back my feet from every evil way,
in order to keep your word.
102I do not turn aside from your ordinances,
for you have taught me.
103How sweet are your words to my taste,
sweeter than honey to my mouth!
104Through your precepts I get
understanding;
therefore I hate every false way.

105Your word is a lamp to my feet
and a light to my path.

JAMES 1

James, a servant of God and of the Lord Jesus Christ,

To the twelve tribes in the Dispersion: Greeting.

2Count it all joy, my brethren, when you
meet various trials, 3for you know that the
testing of your faith produces steadfastness.
4And let steadfastness have its full effect,
that you may be perfect and complete,
lacking in nothing.

5If any of you lacks wisdom, let him ask
God, who gives to all men generously and
without reproaching, and it will be given
him. 6But let him ask in faith, with no
doubting, for he who doubts is like a wave

of the sea that is driven and tossed by the wind.
7, 8For that person must not suppose that a
double-minded man, unstable in all his ways,
will receive anything from the Lord.
9Let the lowly brother boast in his exaltation,
10and the rich in his humiliation, because
like the flower of the grass he will pass away.
11For the sun rises with its scorching heat
and withers the grass; its flower falls, and its
beauty perishes. So will the rich man fade
away in the midst of his pursuits.
12Blessed is the man who endures trial, for
when he has stood the test he will receive
the crown of life which God has promised to
those who love him. 13Let no one say when
he is tempted, "I am tempted by God"; for
God cannot be tempted with evil and he
himself tempts no one; 14but each person
is tempted when he is lured and enticed by
his own desire. 15Then desire when it has
conceived gives birth to sin; and sin when it
is full-grown brings forth death.
16Do not be deceived, my beloved brethren.
17Every good endowment and every perfect
gift is from above, coming down from the
Father of lights with whom there is no
variation or shadow due to change. 18Of his
own will he brought us forth by the word of
truth that we should be a kind of first fruits
of his creatures.
19Know this, my beloved brethren. Let
every man be quick to hear, slow to speak,
slow to anger, 20for the anger of man
does not work the righteousness of God.
21Therefore put away all filthiness and rank
growth of wickedness and receive with
meekness the implanted word, which is
able to save your souls.
22But be doers of the word, and not hearers
only, deceiving yourselves. 23For if any one
is a hearer of the word and not a doer, he
is like a man who observes his natural face
in a mirror; 24for he observes himself and
goes away and at once forgets what he was
like. 25But he who looks into the perfect law,
the law of liberty, and perseveres, being no
hearer that forgets but a doer that acts, he
shall be blessed in his doing.

REFLECTION

"Those divinely revealed realities which are contained and presented in Sacred Scripture have been committed to writing under the inspiration of the Holy Spirit. For holy mother Church, relying on the belief of the Apostles (see John 20:31; 2 Tim. 3:16; 2 Peter 1:19–20, 3:15–16), holds that the books of both the Old and New Testaments in their entirety, with all their parts, are sacred and canonical because written under the inspiration of the Holy Spirit, they have God as their author and have been handed on as such to the Church herself. In composing the sacred books, God chose men and while employed by Him they made use of their powers and abilities, so that with Him acting in them and through them, they, as true authors, consigned to writing everything and only those things which He wanted. Therefore, since everything asserted by the inspired authors or sacred writers must be held to be asserted by the Holy Spirit, it follows that the books of Scripture must be acknowledged as teaching solidly, faithfully and without error that truth which God wanted to put into sacred writings for the sake of salvation. Therefore 'all Scripture is divinely inspired and has its use for teaching the truth and refuting error, for reformation of manners and discipline in right living, so that the man who belongs to God may be efficient and equipped for good work of every kind' (2 Tim. 3:16–17, Greek text)."

—Reflection from *Dei Verbum*,
Vatican II Dogmatic Constitution on
Divine Revelation

March 1

NUMBERS 6

And the LORD said to Moses, 2"Say to the sons of Israel, When either a man or a woman makes a special vow, the vow of a Naz′irite, to separate himself to the LORD, 3he shall separate himself from wine and strong drink; he shall drink no vinegar made from wine or strong drink, and shall not drink any juice of grapes or eat grapes, fresh or dried. 4All the days of his separation he shall eat nothing that is produced by the grapevine, not even the seeds or the skins.

5"All the days of his vow of separation no razor shall come upon his head; until the time is completed for which he separates himself to the LORD, he shall be holy; he shall let the locks of hair of his head grow long.

6"All the days that he separates himself to the LORD he shall not go near a dead body. 7Neither for his father nor for his mother, nor for brother or sister, if they die, shall he make himself unclean; because his separation to God is upon his head. 8All the days of his separation he is holy to the LORD.

9"And if any man dies very suddenly beside him, and he defiles his consecrated head, then he shall shave his head on the day of his cleansing; on the seventh day he shall shave it. 10On the eighth day he shall bring two turtledoves or two young pigeons to the priest to the door of the tent of meeting, 11and the priest shall offer one for a sin offering and the other for a burnt offering, and make atonement for him, because he sinned by reason of the dead body. And he shall consecrate his head that same day, 12and separate himself to the LORD for the days of his separation, and bring a male lamb a year old for a guilt offering; but the former time shall be void, because his separation was defiled.

13"And this is the law for the Naz′irite, when the time of his separation has been completed: he shall be brought to the door of the tent of meeting, 14and he shall offer his gift to the LORD, one male lamb a year old without blemish for a burnt offering, and one ewe lamb a year old without blemish as a sin offering, and one ram without blemish as a peace offering, 15and a basket of unleavened bread, cakes of fine flour mixed with oil, and unleavened wafers spread with oil, and their cereal offering and their drink offerings. 16And the priest shall present them before the LORD and offer his sin offering and his burnt offering, 17and he shall offer the ram as a sacrifice of peace offering to the LORD, with the basket of unleavened bread; the priest shall offer also its cereal offering and its drink offering. 18And the Naz′irite shall shave his consecrated head at the door of the tent of meeting, and shall take the hair from his consecrated head and put it on the fire which is under the sacrifice of the peace offering. 19And the priest shall take the shoulder of the ram, when it is boiled, and one unleavened cake out of the basket, and one unleavened wafer, and shall put them upon the hands of the Naz′irite, after he has shaven the hair of his consecration, 20and the priest shall wave them for a wave offering before the LORD; they are a holy portion for the priest, together with the breast that is waved and the thigh that is offered; and after that the Naz′irite may drink wine.

21"This is the law for the Naz′irite who takes a vow. His offering to the LORD shall be according to his vow as a Nazirite, apart from what else he can afford; in accordance with the vow which he takes, so shall he do according to the law for his separation as a Nazirite."

22The LORD said to Moses, 23"Say to Aaron and his sons, Thus you shall bless the sons of Israel: you shall say to them,

24The LORD bless you and keep you:
25The LORD make his face to shine upon you, and be gracious to you:
26The LORD lift up his countenance upon you, and give you peace.

27"So shall they put my name upon the sons of Israel, and I will bless them."

7

On the day when Moses had finished setting up the tabernacle, and had anointed and consecrated it with all its furnishings, and had anointed and consecrated the altar with all its utensils, 2the leaders of Israel, heads of their fathers' houses, the leaders of the tribes, who were over those who were numbered, 3offered and brought their offerings before the LORD, six covered wagons and twelve oxen, a wagon for every two of the leaders, and for each one an ox; they offered them before the tabernacle. 4Then the LORD said to Moses, 5"Accept these from them, that they may be used in doing the service of the tent of meeting, and give them to the Levites, to each man according to his service." 6So Moses took the wagons and the oxen, and gave them to the Levites. 7Two wagons and four oxen he gave to the sons of Gershon, according to their service; 8and four wagons and eight oxen he gave to the sons of Merar′i, according to their service, under the direction of Ith′amar the son of Aaron the priest. 9But to the sons of Ko′hath he gave none, because they were charged with the care of the holy things which had to be carried on the shoulder. 10And the leaders offered offerings for the dedication of the altar on the day it was anointed; and the leaders offered their offering before the altar. 11And the LORD said to Moses, "They shall offer their offerings, one leader each day, for the dedication of the altar."

12He who offered his offering the first day was Nahshon the son of Ammin′adab, of the tribe of Judah; 13and his offering was one silver plate whose weight was a hundred and thirty shekels, one silver basin of seventy shekels, according to the shekel of the sanctuary, both of them full of fine flour mixed with oil for a cereal offering; 14one golden dish of ten shekels, full of incense; 15one young bull, one ram, one male lamb a year old, for a burnt offering; 16one male goat for a sin offering; 17and for the sacrifice of peace offerings, two oxen, five rams, five male goats, and five male lambs a year old. This was the offering of Nahshon the son of Ammin′adab.

18On the second day Nethan′el the son of Zu′ar, the leader of Is′sachar, made an offering; 19he offered for his offering one silver plate, whose weight was a hundred and thirty shekels, one silver basin of seventy shekels, according to the shekel of the sanctuary, both of them full of fine flour mixed with oil for a cereal offering; 20one golden dish of ten shekels, full of incense; 21one young bull, one ram, one male lamb a year old, for a burnt offering; 22one male goat for a sin offering; 23and for the sacrifice of peace offerings, two oxen, five rams, five male goats, and five male lambs a year old. This was the offering of Nethan′el the son of Zu′ar.

24On the third day Eli′ab the son of He′lon, the leader of the men of Zeb′ulun: 25his offering was one silver plate, whose weight was a hundred and thirty shekels, one silver basin of seventy shekels, according to the shekel of the sanctuary, both of them full of fine flour mixed with oil for a cereal offering; 26one golden dish of ten shekels, full of incense; 27one young bull, one ram, one male lamb a year old, for a burnt offering; 28one male goat for a sin offering; 29and for the sacrifice of peace offerings, two oxen, five rams, five male goats, and five male lambs a year old. This was the offering of Eli′ab the son of He′lon.

30On the fourth day Eli′zur the son of Shed′eur, the leader of the men of Reuben: 31his offering was one silver plate whose weight was a hundred and thirty shekels, one silver basin of seventy shekels, according to the shekel of the sanctuary, both of them full of fine flour mixed with oil for a cereal offering; 32one golden dish of ten shekels, full of incense; 33one young bull, one ram, one male lamb a year old, for a burnt offering; 34one male goat for a sin offering; 35and for the sacrifice of peace offerings, two oxen, five rams, five male goats, and five male lambs a year old. This was the offering of Eli′zur the son of Shed′eur.

[36]On the fifth day Shelu′mi-el the son of Zurishad′dai, the leader of the men of Simeon: [37]his offering was one silver plate, whose weight was a hundred and thirty shekels, one silver basin of seventy shekels, according to the shekel of the sanctuary, both of them full of fine flour mixed with oil for a cereal offering; [38]one golden dish of ten shekels, full of incense; [39]one young bull, one ram, one male lamb a year old, for a burnt offering; [40]one male goat for a sin offering; [41]and for the sacrifice of peace offerings, two oxen, five rams, five male goats, and five male lambs a year old. This was the offering of Shelu′mi-el the son of Zurishad′dai.

To the choirmaster: according to Mahalath.
A Maskil of David.

PSALM 53 [52]

The fool says in his heart,
"There is no God."
They are corrupt, doing abominable
iniquity;
there is none that does good.

[2]God looks down from heaven
upon the sons of men
to see if there are any that are wise,
that seek after God.

[3]They have all fallen away;
they are all alike depraved;
there is none that does good,
no, not one.

[4]Have those who work evil no understanding,
who eat up my people as they eat bread,
and do not call upon God?

[5]There they are, in great terror,
in terror such as has not been!
For God will scatter the bones of the ungodly;
they will be put to shame, for God has
rejected them.

[6]O that deliverance for Israel would come
from Zion!
When God restores the fortunes of
his people,
Jacob will rejoice and Israel be glad.

MARK 7

Now when the Pharisees gathered together to him, with some of the scribes, who had come from Jerusalem, [2]they saw that some of his disciples ate with hands defiled, that is, unwashed. [3](For the Pharisees,
and all the Jews, do not eat unless they wash their hands, observing the tradition of the elders; [4]and when they come from the market place, they do not eat unless they purify themselves; and there are many other traditions which they observe, the washing of cups and pots and vessels of bronze.) [5]And the Pharisees and the scribes asked him, "Why do your disciples not live according to the tradition of the elders, but eat with hands defiled?" [6]And he said to them, "Well did Isaiah prophesy of you hypocrites, as it is written,

'This people honors me with their lips,
but their heart is far from me;
[7]in vain do they worship me,
teaching as doctrines the precepts of men.'

[8]You leave the commandment of God, and hold fast the tradition of men."

[9]And he said to them, "You have a fine way of rejecting the commandment of God, in order to keep your tradition! [10]For Moses said, 'Honor your father and your mother'; and, 'He who speaks evil of father or mother, let him surely die'; [11]but you say, 'If a man tells his father or his mother, What you would have gained from me is Corban' (that is, given to God)—[12]then you no longer permit him to do anything for his father or mother, [13]thus making void the word of God through your tradition which you hand on. And many such things you do."

[14]And he called the people to him again, and said to them, "Hear me, all of you, and

understand: 15there is nothing outside a
man which by going into him can defile
him; but the things which come out of a
man are what defile him." 17And when he
had entered the house, and left the people,
his disciples asked him about the parable.
18And he said to them, "Then are you also
without understanding? Do you not see
that whatever goes into a man from outside
cannot defile him, 19since it enters, not his
heart but his stomach, and so passes on?"
(Thus he declared all foods clean.) 20And he
said, "What comes out of a man is what defiles
a man. 21For from within, out of the heart of
man, come evil thoughts, fornication, theft,
murder, adultery, 22coveting, wickedness,
deceit, licentiousness, envy, slander, pride,
foolishness. 23All these evil things come
from within, and they defile a man."

REFLECTION

These readings present starkly contrasting relationships with God. The fool in Psalm 53 refuses to heed God and believes his wickedness will go unnoticed and unpunished, while Numbers 6 gives instructions for Nazirites who wish to be specially set apart for the Lord. This involves an extraordinary commitment to ritual cleanness, which must be maintained even if a family member dies (see Nm 6:7). Surprisingly, Jesus teaches that the "fool" and the "Nazirite" can coincide in people who are scrupulous about external practices but whose hearts are far from God (see Mk 7:6). Jesus doesn't thereby sweep aside ritual purity. He has come to fulfill the law, not abolish it (see Mt 5:17). Nor does he criticize it as mere human invention, for it derives from God-given law. But he points out the senselessness of worrying about uncleanness while ignoring the "evil things" to which uncleanness ultimately points (see Mk 7:20–23). This lays the groundwork for the apostolic decision not to require Mosaic ritual purity of Gentile believers (see Acts 15), which is why St. Mark recognizes in hindsight that Jesus "declared all foods clean" (Mk 7:19). The purpose of all this is beautifully expressed in the priestly blessing given by God: "So shall they put my name upon the sons of Israel, and I will bless them" (Nm 6:27). Is your heart open to receive that blessing?

March 2

NUMBERS 7

**42On the sixth day Eli´asaph the
son of Deu´el, the leader of the
men of Gad: 43his offering was
one silver plate, whose weight was a hundred and thirty shekels, one silver basin of
seventy shekels, according to the shekel of**
the sanctuary, both of them full of fine flour
mixed with oil for a cereal offering; 44one
golden dish of ten shekels, full of incense;
45one young bull, one ram, one male lamb
a year old, for a burnt offering; 46one male
goat for a sin offering; 47and for the sacrifice
of peace offerings, two oxen, five rams, five
male goats, and five male lambs a year old.
This was the offering of Eli´asaph the son
of Deu´el.

48On the seventh day Elish´ama the son
of Ammi´hud, the leader of the men of
E´phraim: 49his offering was one silver plate,
whose weight was a hundred and thirty
shekels, one silver basin of seventy shekels,
according to the shekel of the sanctuary,
both of them full of fine flour mixed with oil
for a cereal offering; 50one golden dish of ten
shekels, full of incense; 51one young bull, one
ram, one male lamb a year old, for a burnt
offering; 52one male goat for a sin offering;
53and for the sacrifice of peace offerings, two
oxen, five rams, five male goats, and five
male lambs a year old. This was the offering
of Elish´ama the son of Ammi´hud.

54On the eighth day Gama´liel the son
of Pedah´zur, the leader of the men of
Manas´seh: 55his offering was one silver plate,
whose weight was a hundred and thirty
shekels, one silver basin of seventy shekels,
according to the shekel of the sanctuary,
both of them full of fine flour mixed with oil
for a cereal offering; 56one golden dish of ten
shekels, full of incense; 57one young bull, one
ram, one male lamb a year old, for a burnt
offering; 58one male goat for a sin offering;
59and for the sacrifice of peace offerings, two

oxen, five rams, five male goats, and five
male lambs a year old. This was the offering
of Gama´liel the son of Pedah´zur.
60 On the ninth day Abi´dan the son of
Gideo´ni, the leader of the men of Benjamin: 61 his offering was one silver plate,
whose weight was a hundred and thirty
shekels, one silver basin of seventy shekels,
according to the shekel of the sanctuary,
both of them full of fine flour mixed with oil
for a cereal offering; 62 one golden dish of ten
shekels, full of incense; 63 one young bull, one
ram, one male lamb a year old, for a burnt
offering; 64 one male goat for a sin offering;
65 and for the sacrifice of peace offerings, two
oxen, five rams, five male goats, and five
male lambs a year old. This was the offering
of Abi´dan the son of Gideo´ni.
66 On the tenth day Ahie´zer the son of
Ammishad´dai, the leader of the men of
Dan: 67 his offering was one silver plate,
whose weight was a hundred and thirty
shekels, one silver basin of seventy shekels,
according to the shekel of the sanctuary,
both of them full of fine flour mixed with oil
for a cereal offering; 68 one golden dish of ten
shekels, full of incense; 69 one young bull, one
ram, one male lamb a year old, for a burnt
offering; 70 one male goat for a sin offering;
71 and for the sacrifice of peace offerings, two
oxen, five rams, five male goats, and five
male lambs a year old. This was the offering
of Ahie´zer the son of Ammishad´dai.
72 On the eleventh day Pa´giel the son of
Ochran, the leader of the men of Asher: 73 his
offering was one silver plate, whose weight
was a hundred and thirty shekels, one silver
basin of seventy shekels, according to the
shekel of the sanctuary, both of them full
of fine flour mixed with oil for a cereal
offering; 74 one golden dish of ten shekels,
full of incense; 75 one young bull, one ram,
one male lamb a year old, for a burnt
offering; 76 one male goat for a sin offering;
77 and for the sacrifice of peace offerings, two
oxen, five rams, five male goats, and five
male lambs a year old. This was the offering
of Pa´giel the son of Ochran.
78 On the twelfth day Ahi´ra the son of
E´nan, the leader of the men of Naph´tali:
79 his offering was one silver plate, whose
weight was a hundred and thirty shekels, one
silver basin of seventy shekels, according to
the shekel of the sanctuary, both of them
full of fine flour mixed with oil for a cereal
offering; 80 one golden dish of ten shekels,
full of incense; 81 one young bull, one ram,
one male lamb a year old, for a burnt
offering; 82 one male goat for a sin offering;
83 and for the sacrifice of peace offerings, two
oxen, five rams, five male goats, and five
male lambs a year old. This was the offering
of Ahi´ra the son of E´nan.
84 This was the dedication offering for the
altar, on the day when it was anointed, from
the leaders of Israel: twelve silver plates,
twelve silver basins, twelve golden dishes,
85 each silver plate weighing a hundred and
thirty shekels and each basin seventy, all
the silver of the vessels two thousand four
hundred shekels according to the shekel of
the sanctuary, 86 the twelve golden dishes,
full of incense, weighing ten shekels apiece
according to the shekel of the sanctuary,
all the gold of the dishes being a hundred
and twenty shekels; 87 all the cattle for the
burnt offering twelve bulls, twelve rams,
twelve male lambs a year old, with their
cereal offering; and twelve male goats for
a sin offering; 88 and all the cattle for the
sacrifice of peace offerings twenty-four
bulls, the rams sixty, the male goats sixty,
the male lambs a year old sixty. This was
the dedication offering for the altar, after it
was anointed.
89 And when Moses went into the tent of
meeting to speak with the Lord, he heard
the voice speaking to him from above the
mercy seat that was upon the ark of the
covenant, from between the two cherubim;
and it spoke to him.

8 Now the Lord said to Moses, 2 "Say to
Aaron, When you set up the lamps, the
seven lamps shall give light in front of the
lampstand." 3 And Aaron did so; he set up its
lamps to give light in front of the lampstand,
as the Lord commanded Moses. 4 And this
was the workmanship of the lampstand,
hammered work of gold; from its base to its
flowers, it was hammered work; according

to the pattern which the LORD had shown
Moses, so he made the lampstand.
5And the LORD said to Moses, 6"Take the
Levites from among the sons of Israel, and
cleanse them. 7And thus you shall do to
them, to cleanse them: sprinkle the water
of expiation upon them, and let them go
with a razor over all their body, and wash
their clothes and cleanse themselves.
8Then let them take a young bull and its
cereal offering of fine flour mixed with
oil, and you shall take another young bull
for a sin offering. 9And you shall present
the Levites before the tent of meeting,
and assemble the whole congregation of
the sons of Israel. 10When you present the
Levites before the LORD, the sons of Israel
shall lay their hands upon the Levites,
11and Aaron shall offer the Levites before
the LORD as a wave offering from the sons
of Israel, that it may be theirs to do the
service of the LORD. 12Then the Levites
shall lay their hands upon the heads of the
bulls; and you shall offer the one for a sin
offering and the other for a burnt offering
to the LORD, to make atonement for the
Levites. 13And you shall cause the Levites
to attend Aaron and his sons, and shall
offer them as a wave offering to the LORD.
14"Thus you shall separate the Levites
from among the sons of Israel, and the
Levites shall be mine. 15And after that the
Levites shall go in to do service at the tent
of meeting, when you have cleansed them
and offered them as a wave offering. 16For
they are wholly given to me from among
the sons of Israel; instead of all that open
the womb, the first-born of all the sons
of Israel, I have taken them for myself.
17For all the first-born among the sons of
Israel are mine, both of man and of beast;
on the day that I slew all the first-born
in the land of Egypt I consecrated them
for myself, 18and I have taken the Levites
instead of all the first-born among the
sons of Israel. 19And I have given the
Levites as a gift to Aaron and his sons
from among the sons of Israel, to do the
service for the sons of Israel at the tent of
meeting, and to make atonement for the
sons of Israel, that there may be no plague
among the sons of Israel in case the sons
of Israel should come near the sanctuary."
20Thus did Moses and Aaron and all the
congregation of the sons of Israel to the
Levites; according to all that the LORD
commanded Moses concerning the Levites,
the sons of Israel did to them. 21And the
Levites purified themselves from sin, and
washed their clothes; and Aaron offered
them as a wave offering before the LORD,
and Aaron made atonement for them to
cleanse them. 22And after that the Levites
went in to do their service in the tent of
meeting in attendance upon Aaron and his
sons; as the LORD had commanded Moses
concerning the Levites, so they did to them.
23And the LORD said to Moses, 24"This is
what pertains to the Levites: from twenty-
five years old and upward they shall go in to
perform the work in the service of the tent
of meeting; 25and from the age of fifty years
they shall withdraw from the work of the
service and serve no more, 26but minister
to their brethren in the tent of meeting,
to keep the charge, and they shall do no
service. Thus shall you do to the Levites in
assigning their duties."

To the choirmaster: with stringed instruments.

A Maskil of David, when the Ziphites went and told Saul, "David is in hiding among us."

PSALM 54 [53]

Save me, O God, by your name,
and vindicate me by your might.
2Hear my prayer, O God;
give ear to the words of my mouth.

3For insolent men have risen against me,
ruthless men seek my life;
they do not set God before them. *Selah*

4Behold, God is my helper;
the Lord is the upholder of my life.
5He will repay my enemies with evil;
in your faithfulness put an end to them.

[6]With a freewill offering I will sacrifice
to you;
I will give thanks to your name, O LORD,
for it is good.
[7]For you have delivered me from every trouble,
and my eye has looked in triumph on
my enemies.

MARK 7

[24]And from there he arose and went away to the region of Tyre and Sidon. And he entered a house, and would not have any one know it; yet he could not be hidden. [25]But immediately a woman, whose little daughter was possessed by an unclean spirit, heard of him, and came and fell down at his feet. [26]Now the woman was a Greek, a Syrophoeni′cian by birth. And she begged him to cast the demon out of her daughter. [27]And he said to her, "Let the children first be fed, for it is not right to take the children's bread and throw it to the dogs." [28]But she answered him, "Yes, Lord; yet even the dogs under the table eat the children's crumbs." [29]And he said to her, "For this saying you may go your way; the demon has left your daughter." [30]And she went home, and found the child lying in bed, and the demon gone.

[31]Then he returned from the region of Tyre, and went through Sidon to the Sea of Galilee, through the region of the Decap′olis. [32]And they brought to him a man who was deaf and had an impediment in his speech; and they begged him to lay his hand upon him. [33]And taking him aside from the multitude privately, he put his fingers into his ears, and he spat and touched his tongue; [34]and looking up to heaven, he sighed, and said to him, "Eph′phatha," that is, "Be opened." [35]And his ears were opened, his tongue was released, and he spoke plainly. [36]And he charged them to tell no one; but the more he charged them, the more zealously they proclaimed it. [37]And they were astonished beyond measure, saying, "He has done all things well; he even makes the deaf hear and the mute speak."

REFLECTION

Today's reading from Numbers completes the report of each tribe's gifts for the dedication of the altar. This can seem tedious, but perhaps we can learn to see such detailed lists as expressions of love—for the altar where the Levites serve is a place of relationship between God and Israel. This love between God and his people is the basis of the intimacy and trust in the cry for divine help that we see in Psalm 54. The Gentile woman in today's Gospel asks for a share in that relationship. Jesus's interaction with her is challenging, even upsetting, so it's worth making a few observations about it. First, Jesus's insistence that the children of Israel be fed first implies that Gentiles will be fed as well. Second, note that the children of Israel have just been miraculously fed. Third, this woman is the only person in Mark's Gospel who directly calls Jesus "Lord," hinting that she recognizes Jesus in a way his disciples still do not. Finally, those of us who are non-Jewish believers should consider the woman's humility before Israel's unique place in God's plan, something St. Paul will recommend in Romans 11:13–36. Do you take your share in Israel's intimacy with God for granted? Or are you "astonished beyond measure" (Mk 7:37) at what he has done for us?

March 3

NUMBERS 9

And the LORD spoke to Moses in the wilderness of Sinai, in the first month of the second year after they had come out of the land of Egypt, saying, [2]"Let the sons of Israel keep the Passover at its appointed time. [3]On the fourteenth day of this month,

in the evening, you shall keep it at its
appointed time; according to all its statutes
and all its ordinances you shall keep it."
4So Moses told the sons of Israel that they
should keep the Passover. 5And they kept
the Passover in the first month, on the
fourteenth day of the month, in the evening,
in the wilderness of Sinai; according to all
that the LORD commanded Moses, so the
sons of Israel did. 6And there were certain
men who were unclean through touching
the dead body of a man, so that they could
not keep the Passover on that day; and they
came before Moses and Aaron on that day;
7and those men said to him, "We are unclean
through touching the dead body of a man;
why are we kept from offering the LORD's
offering at its appointed time among the
sons of Israel?" 8And Moses said to them,
"Wait, that I may hear what the LORD will
command concerning you."

9The LORD said to Moses, 10"Say to the
sons of Israel, If any man of you or of your
descendants is unclean through touching
a dead body, or is afar off on a journey, he
shall still keep the Passover to the LORD.
11In the second month on the fourteenth
day in the evening they shall keep it; they
shall eat it with unleavened bread and bitter
herbs. 12They shall leave none of it until the
morning, nor break a bone of it; according
to all the statute for the Passover they shall
keep it. 13But the man who is clean and is not
on a journey, yet refrains from keeping the
Passover, that person shall be cut off from his
people, because he did not offer the LORD's
offering at its appointed time; that man shall
bear his sin. 14And if a stranger sojourns
among you, and will keep the Passover to
the LORD, according to the statute of the
Passover and according to its ordinance, so
shall he do; you shall have one statute, both
for the sojourner and for the native."

15On the day that the tabernacle was set up,
the cloud covered the tabernacle, the tent of
the covenant; and at evening it was over the
tabernacle like the appearance of fire until
morning. 16So it was continually; the cloud
covered it by day, and the appearance of fire
by night. 17And whenever the cloud was
taken up from over the tent, after that the
sons of Israel set out; and in the place where
the cloud settled down, there the sons of
Israel encamped. 18At the command of the
LORD the sons of Israel set out, and at the
command of the LORD they encamped; as
long as the cloud rested over the tabernacle,
they remained in camp. 19Even when the
cloud continued over the tabernacle many
days, the sons of Israel kept the charge of the
LORD, and did not set out. 20Sometimes the
cloud was a few days over the tabernacle,
and according to the command of the LORD
they remained in camp; then according to
the command of the LORD they set out.
21And sometimes the cloud remained from
evening until morning; and when the cloud
was taken up in the morning, they set out,
or if it continued for a day and a night,
when the cloud was taken up they set out.
22Whether it was two days, or a month, or a
longer time, that the cloud continued over
the tabernacle, abiding there, the sons of
Israel remained in camp and did not set out;
but when it was taken up they set out. 23At
the command of the LORD they encamped,
and at the command of the LORD they set
out; they kept the charge of the LORD, at the
command of the LORD by Moses.

10 The LORD said to Moses, 2"Make
two silver trumpets; of hammered
work you shall make them; and you shall
use them for summoning the congregation,
and for breaking camp. 3And when both
are blown, all the congregation shall gather
themselves to you at the entrance of the tent
of meeting. 4But if they blow only one, then
the leaders, the heads of the tribes of Israel,
shall gather themselves to you. 5When you
blow an alarm, the camps that are on the
east side shall set out. 6And when you blow
an alarm the second time, the camps that
are on the south side shall set out. An alarm
is to be blown whenever they are to set out.
7But when the assembly is to be gathered
together, you shall blow, but you shall not
sound an alarm. 8And the sons of Aaron,
the priests, shall blow the trumpets. The
trumpets shall be to you for a perpetual
statute throughout your generations. 9And

when you go to war in your land against the adversary who oppresses you, then you shall sound an alarm with the trumpets, that you may be remembered before the LORD your God, and you shall be saved from your enemies. [10]On the day of your gladness also, and at your appointed feasts, and at the beginnings of your months, you shall blow the trumpets over your burnt offerings and over the sacrifices of your peace offerings; they shall serve you for remembrance before your God; I am the LORD your God."

[11]In the second year, in the second month, on the twentieth day of the month, the cloud was taken up from over the tabernacle of the covenant, [12]and the sons of Israel set out by stages from the wilderness of Sinai; and the cloud settled down in the wilderness of Par′an. [13]They set out for the first time at the command of the LORD by Moses. [14]The standard of the camp of the men of Judah set out first by their companies; and over their host was Nahshon the son of Ammin′adab. [15]And over the host of the tribe of the men of Is′sachar was Nethan′el the son of Zu′ar. [16]And over the host of the tribe of the men of Zeb′ulun was Eli′ab the son of He′lon.

[17]And when the tabernacle was taken down, the sons of Gershon and the sons of Merar′i, who carried the tabernacle, set out. [18]And the standard of the camp of Reuben set out by their companies; and over their host was Eli′zur the son of Shed′eur. [19]And over the host of the tribe of the men of Simeon was Shelu′mi-el the son of Zurishad′dai. [20]And over the host of the tribe of the men of Gad was Eli′asaph the son of Deu′el.

[21]Then the Ko′hathites set out, carrying the holy things, and the tabernacle was set up before their arrival. [22]And the standard of the camp of the men of E′phraim set out by their companies; and over their host was Elish′ama the son of Ammi′hud. [23]And over the host of the tribe of the men of Manas′seh was Gama′liel the son of Pedah′zur. [24]And over the host of the tribe of the men of Benjamin was Abi′dan the son of Gideo′ni.

[25]Then the standard of the camp of the men of Dan, acting as the rear guard of all the camps, set out by their companies; and over their host was Ahie′zer the son of Ammishad′dai. [26]And over the host of the tribe of the men of Asher was Pa′giel the son of Ochran. [27]And over the host of the tribe of the men of Naph′tali was Ahi′ra the son of E′nan. [28]This was the order of march of the sons of Israel according to their hosts, when they set out.

[29]And Moses said to Ho′bab the son of Reu′el the Mid′ianite, Moses' father-in-law, "We are setting out for the place of which the LORD said, 'I will give it to you'; come with us, and we will do you good; for the LORD has promised good to Israel." [30]But he said to him, "I will not go; I will depart to my own land and to my kindred." [31]And he said, "Do not leave us, I beg you, for you know how we are to encamp in the wilderness, and you will serve as eyes for us. [32]And if you go with us, whatever good the LORD will do to us, the same will we do to you."

[33]So they set out from the mount of the LORD three days' journey; and the ark of the covenant of the LORD went before them three days' journey, to seek out a resting place for them. [34]And the cloud of the LORD was over them by day, whenever they set out from the camp.

[35]And whenever the ark set out, Moses said, "Arise, O LORD, and let your enemies be scattered; and let them who hate you flee before you." [36]And when it rested, he said, "Return, O LORD, to the ten thousand thousands of Israel."

To the choirmaster: with stringed instruments.
A Maskil of David.

PSALM 55 [54]

Give ear to my prayer, O God;
and hide not yourself from my supplication!
[2]Attend to me, and answer me;
I am overcome by my trouble.

I am distraught [3]by the noise of the enemy,
because of the oppression of the wicked.
For they bring trouble upon me,
and in anger they cherish enmity
against me.

[4]My heart is in anguish within me,
the terrors of death have fallen upon me.
[5]Fear and trembling come upon me,
and horror overwhelms me.
[6]And I say, "O that I had wings like a dove!
I would fly away and be at rest;
[7]yes, I would wander afar,
I would lodge in the wilderness, *Selah*
[8]I would wait for him who saves me
from the raging wind and tempest."

[9]Destroy their plans, O Lord, confuse
their tongues;
for I see violence and strife in the city.
[10]Day and night they go around it
on its walls;
and mischief and trouble are within it,
[11] ruin is in its midst;
oppression and fraud
do not depart from its market place.

[12]It is not an enemy who taunts me—
then I could bear it;
it is not an adversary who deals insolently
with me—
then I could hide from him.
[13]But it is you, my equal,
my companion, my familiar friend.
[14]We used to hold sweet converse together;
within God's house we walked in
fellowship.
[15]Let death come upon them;
let them go down to Sheol alive;
let them go away in terror into
their graves.

[16]But I call upon God;
and the LORD will save me.
[17]Evening and morning and at noon
I utter my complaint and moan,
and he will hear my voice.
[18]He will deliver my soul in safety
from the battle that I wage,
for many are arrayed against me.
[19]God will give ear, and humble them,
he who is enthroned from of old;
because they keep no law,
and do not fear God. *Selah*

[20]My companion stretched out his hand
against his friends,
he violated his covenant.
[21]His speech was smoother than butter,
yet war was in his heart;
his words were softer than oil,
yet they were drawn swords.

[22]Cast your burden on the LORD,
and he will sustain you;
he will never permit
the righteous to be moved.

[23]But you, O God, will cast them down
into the lowest pit;
men of blood and treachery
shall not live out half their days.
But I will trust in you.

MARK 8

**In those days, when again a
great crowd had gathered, and
they had nothing to eat, he called his disciples to him, and said to them, [2]"I have**
compassion on the crowd, because they have
been with me now three days, and have nothing to eat; [3]and if I send them away hungry to
their homes, they will faint on the way; and
some of them have come a long way." [4]And his
disciples answered him, "How can one feed
these men with bread here in the desert?" [5]And
he asked them, "How many loaves have you?"
They said, "Seven." [6]And he commanded the
crowd to sit down on the ground; and he took
the seven loaves, and having given thanks he
broke them and gave them to his disciples to
set before the people; and they set them before the crowd. [7]And they had a few small fish;
and having blessed them, he commanded that
these also should be set before them. [8]And
they ate, and were satisfied; and they took up
the broken pieces left over, seven baskets full.

9And there were about four thousand people.
10And he sent them away; and immediately he
got into the boat with his disciples, and went
to the district of Dalmanu′tha.
11The Pharisees came and began to argue
with him, seeking from him a sign from
heaven, to test him. 12And he sighed deeply
in his spirit, and said, "Why does this
generation seek a sign? Truly, I say to you,
no sign shall be given to this generation."
13And he left them, and getting into the boat
again he departed to the other side.
14Now they had forgotten to bring bread; and
they had only one loaf with them in the boat.
15And he cautioned them, saying, "Take heed,
beware of the leaven of the Pharisees and the
leaven of Herod." 16And they discussed it with
one another, saying, "We have no bread." 17And
being aware of it, Jesus said to them, "Why do
you discuss the fact that you have no bread?
Do you not yet perceive or understand? Are
your hearts hardened? 18Having eyes do you
not see, and having ears do you not hear? And
do you not remember? 19When I broke the
five loaves for the five thousand, how many
baskets full of broken pieces did you take up?"
They said to him, "Twelve." 20"And the seven
for the four thousand, how many baskets full
of broken pieces did you take up?" And they
said to him, "Seven." 21And he said to them,
"Do you not yet understand?"

REFLECTION

The cloud rises from the Tabernacle, and Israel departs at last from Sinai. It is time to follow the Lord through the wilderness. Jesus also prepares a "way" for the people by again multiplying loaves (see Mk 8:6). Later, Jesus seems frustrated when the disciples fail to solve what looks like an odd riddle (see vv. 19–21). What do these numbers mean? Five and twelve point to Israel: *twelve* tribes nourished by the *five* books of Moses. Seven, on the other hand, hints at universality: *seven* days in a week and the *seventy* nations listed in Genesis 10. The bread Jesus provides for his "way" is for all peoples. Gentiles will receive not only the "crumbs," as the Syrophoenician woman requests, but enough bread to be satisfied with plenty left over. There's another twist. St. Mark says the disciples "had only one loaf with them in the boat," but two verses later they say they "have no bread" (8:14, 16). They don't yet understand that Jesus himself *is* the bread that will feed all nations. Psalm 55 paints a vivid picture of the pain of betrayal, a pain Jesus endures at Judas's hands so that he can become our Bread of Life. Do you trust Jesus to sustain you as bread for your way, even amid deep pain?

March 4

NUMBERS 11

**And the people complained in
the hearing of the LORD about
their misfortunes; and when the
LORD heard it, his anger was kindled,
and the fire of the LORD burned among
them, and consumed some outlying parts**
of the camp. 2Then the people cried to Moses; and Moses prayed to the LORD, and
the fire abated. 3So the name of that place
was called Tab′erah, because the fire of the
LORD burned among them.
4Now the rabble that was among them
had a strong craving; and the people of
Israel also wept again, and said, "O that we
had meat to eat! 5We remember the fish we
ate in Egypt for nothing, the cucumbers,
the melons, the leeks, the onions, and the
garlic; 6but now our strength is dried up,
and there is nothing at all but this manna to
look at."
7Now the manna was like coriander seed,
and its appearance like that of gum resin.
8The people went about and gathered it,
and ground it in mills or beat it in mortars,
and boiled it in pots, and made cakes of it;
and the taste of it was like the taste of cakes
baked with oil. 9When the dew fell upon the
camp in the night, the manna fell with it.

[10]Moses heard the people weeping throughout their families, every man at the door of his tent; and the anger of the LORD blazed hotly, and Moses was displeased. [11]Moses said to the LORD, "Why have you dealt ill with your servant? And why have I not found favor in your sight, that you lay the burden of all this people upon me? [12]Did I conceive all this people? Did I bring them forth, that you should say to me, 'Carry them in your bosom, as a nurse carries the sucking child,' to the land which you swore to give their fathers? [13]Where am I to get meat to give to all this people? For they weep before me and say, 'Give us meat, that we may eat.' [14]I am not able to carry all this people alone, the burden is too heavy for me. [15]If you will deal thus with me, kill me at once, if I find favor in your sight, that I may not see my wretchedness."

[16]And the LORD said to Moses, "Gather for me seventy men of the elders of Israel, whom you know to be the elders of the people and officers over them; and bring them to the tent of meeting, and let them take their stand there with you. [17]And I will come down and talk with you there; and I will take some of the spirit which is upon you and put it upon them; and they shall bear the burden of the people with you, that you may not bear it yourself alone. [18]And say to the people, 'Consecrate yourselves for tomorrow, and you shall eat meat; for you have wept in the hearing of the LORD, saying, "Who will give us meat to eat? For it was well with us in Egypt." Therefore the LORD will give you meat, and you shall eat. [19]You shall not eat one day, or two days, or five days, or ten days, or twenty days, [20]but a whole month, until it comes out at your nostrils and becomes loathsome to you, because you have rejected the LORD who is among you, and have wept before him, saying, "Why did we come forth out of Egypt?"'" [21]But Moses said, "The people among whom I am number six hundred thousand on foot; and you have said, 'I will give them meat, that they may eat a whole month!' [22]Shall flocks and herds be slaughtered for them, to satisfy them? Or shall all the fish of the sea be gathered together for them, to satisfy them?" [23]And the LORD said to Moses, "Is the LORD's hand shortened? Now you shall see whether my word will come true for you or not."

[24]So Moses went out and told the people the words of the LORD; and he gathered seventy men of the elders of the people, and placed them round about the tent. [25]Then the LORD came down in the cloud and spoke to him, and took some of the spirit that was upon him and put it upon the seventy elders; and when the spirit rested upon them, they prophesied. But they did so no more.

[26]Now two men remained in the camp, one named Eldad, and the other named Medad, and the spirit rested upon them; they were among those registered, but they had not gone out to the tent, and so they prophesied in the camp. [27]And a young man ran and told Moses, "Eldad and Medad are prophesying in the camp." [28]And Joshua the son of Nun, the minister of Moses, one of his chosen men, said, "My lord Moses, forbid them." [29]But Moses said to him, "Are you jealous for my sake? Would that all the LORD's people were prophets, that the LORD would put his spirit upon them!" [30]And Moses and the elders of Israel returned to the camp.

[31]And there went forth a wind from the LORD, and it brought quails from the sea, and let them fall beside the camp, about a day's journey on this side and a day's journey on the other side, round about the camp, and about two cubits above the face of the earth. [32]And the people rose all that day, and all night, and all the next day, and gathered the quails; he who gathered least gathered ten homers; and they spread them out for themselves all around the camp. [33]While the meat was yet between their teeth, before it was consumed, the anger of the LORD was kindled against the people, and the LORD struck the people with a very great plague. [34]Therefore the name of that place was called Kib′roth-hatta′avah, because there they buried the people who had the craving. [35]From Kib′roth-hatta′avah the people journeyed to Haze′roth; and they remained at Hazeroth.

12 Miriam and Aaron spoke against Moses because of the Cushite woman whom he had married, for he had married a Cushite woman; [2]and they said, "Has the LORD indeed spoken only through Moses? Has he

not spoken through us also?" And the LORD
heard it. [3]Now the man Moses was very meek,
more than all men that were on the face of the
earth. [4]And suddenly the LORD said to Moses
and to Aaron and Miriam, "Come out, you
three, to the tent of meeting." And the three of
them came out. [5]And the LORD came down in
a pillar of cloud, and stood at the door of the
tent, and called Aaron and Miriam; and they
both came forward. [6]And he said, "Hear my
words: If there is a prophet among you, I the
LORD make myself known to him in a vision,
I speak with him in a dream. [7]Not so with my
servant Moses; he is entrusted with all my
house. [8]With him I speak mouth to mouth,
clearly, and not in dark speech; and he beholds
the form of the LORD. Why then were you not
afraid to speak against my servant Moses?"

[9]And the anger of the LORD was kindled
against them, and he departed; [10]and when
the cloud removed from over the tent, behold,
Miriam was leprous, as white as snow. And
Aaron turned towards Miriam, and behold,
she was leprous. [11]And Aaron said to Moses,
"Oh, my lord, do not punish us because we
have done foolishly and have sinned. [12]Let her
not be as one dead, of whom the flesh is half
consumed when he comes out of his mother's
womb." [13]And Moses cried to the LORD, "Heal
her, O God, I beg you." [14]But the LORD said
to Moses, "If her father had but spit in her
face, should she not be shamed seven days?
Let her be shut up outside the camp seven
days, and after that she may be brought in
again." [15]So Miriam was shut up outside the
camp seven days; and the people did not set
out on the march till Miriam was brought in
again. [16]After that the people set out from
Haze′roth, and encamped in the wilderness
of Par′an.

13 The LORD said to Moses, [2]"Send men
to spy out the land of Canaan, which
I give to the sons of Israel; from each tribe of
their fathers shall you send a man, every one
a leader among them." [3]So Moses sent them
from the wilderness of Par′an, according
to the command of the LORD, all of them
men who were heads of the sons of Israel.
[4]And these were their names: From the tribe
of Reuben, Sham′mu-a the son of Zaccur;
[5]from the tribe of Simeon, Sha′phat the son of
Ho′ri; [6]from the tribe of Judah, Caleb the son
of Jephun′neh; [7]from the tribe of Is′sachar,
I′gal the son of Joseph; [8]from the tribe of
E′phraim, Hoshe′a the son of Nun; [9]from the
tribe of Benjamin, Palti the son of Ra′phu;
[10]from the tribe of Zeb′ulun, Gad′diel the
son of Sodi; [11]from the tribe of Joseph (that
is from the tribe of Manas′seh), Gaddi the
son of Susi; [12]from the tribe of Dan, Am′miel
the son of Gemal′li; [13]from the tribe of Asher,
Seth′ur the son of Michael; [14]from the tribe
of Naph′tali, Nahbi the son of Voph′si; [15]from
the tribe of Gad, Geu′el the son of Machi.
[16]These were the names of the men whom
Moses sent to spy out the land. And Moses
called Hoshe′a the son of Nun Joshua.

[17]Moses sent them to spy out the land
of Canaan, and said to them, "Go up into
the Neg′eb yonder, and go up into the hill
country, [18]and see what the land is, and
whether the people who dwell in it are strong
or weak, whether they are few or many, [19]and
whether the land that they dwell in is good
or bad, and whether the cities that they dwell
in are camps or strongholds, [20]and whether
the land is rich or poor, and whether there
is wood in it or not. Be of good courage, and
bring some of the fruit of the land." Now the
time was the season of the first ripe grapes.

To the choirmaster:
according to The Dove on Far-off Terebinths.
A Miktam of David, when the Philistines
seized him in Gath.

PSALM 56 [55]

Have mercy on me, O God, for men trample
upon me;
all day long foes oppress me;
[2]my enemies trample upon me all day long,
for many fight against me proudly.
[3]When I am afraid,
I put my trust in you.
[4]In God, whose word I praise,
in God I trust without a fear.
What can flesh do to me?

[5]All day long they seek to injure my cause;
all their thoughts are against me for evil.
[6]They band themselves together, they lurk,
they watch my steps.
As they have waited for my life,
[7] so recompense them for their crime;
in wrath cast down the peoples, O God!

[8]You have kept count of my tossings;
put my tears in your bottle!
Are they not in your book?
[9]Then my enemies will be turned back
in the day when I call.
This I know, that God is for me.
[10]In God, whose word I praise,
in the LORD, whose word I praise,
[11]in God I trust without a fear.
What can man do to me?

[12]My vows to you I must perform, O God;
I will render thank offerings to you.
[13]For you have delivered my soul from death,
yes, my feet from falling,
that I may walk before God
in the light of life.

MARK 8

[22]And they came to Beth-sa′ida. And some people brought to him a blind man, and begged him to touch him. [23]And he took the blind man by the hand, and led him out of the village; and when he had spit on his eyes and laid his hands upon him, he asked him, "Do you see anything?" [24]And he looked up and said, "I see men; but they look like trees, walking."
[25]Then again he laid his hands upon his eyes; and he looked intently and was restored, and saw everything clearly. [26]And he sent him away to his home, saying, "Do not even enter the village."

[27]And Jesus went on with his disciples, to the villages of Caesare′a Philip′pi; and on the way he asked his disciples, "Who do men say that I am?" [28]And they told him, "John the Baptist; and others say, Eli′jah; and others one of the prophets." [29]And he asked them, "But who do you say that I am?" Peter answered him, "You are the Christ." [30]And he charged them to tell no one about him.

[31]And he began to teach them that the Son of man must suffer many things, and be rejected by the elders and the chief priests and the scribes, and be killed, and after three days rise again. [32]And he said this plainly. And Peter took him, and began to rebuke him. [33]But turning and seeing his disciples, he rebuked Peter, and said, "Get behind me, Satan! For you are not on the side of God, but of men."

[34]And he called to him the multitude with his disciples, and said to them, "If any man would come after me, let him deny himself and take up his cross and follow me. [35]For whoever would save his life will lose it; and whoever loses his life for my sake and the gospel's will save it. [36]For what does it profit a man, to gain the whole world and forfeit his life? [37]For what can a man give in return for his life? [38]For whoever is ashamed of me and of my words in this adulterous and sinful generation, of him will the Son of man also be ashamed, when he comes in the glory of his Father with the holy angels."

REFLECTION

Often we're all too ready to tell God how we think he should do things. We become dissatisfied, and we rebel against his plan. This is just what happens several times in Numbers 11–12. The people complain about their woes (see Nm 11:1–3), the "rabble" weep because they're sick of manna (see vv. 4–6), a young man tattles on Eldad and Medad for prophesying (see v. 27), and Aaron and Miriam object to Moses's unique authority (see 12:2, 6–8). It's no different in the Gospel. When Jesus reveals that his "way" leads to suffering and death, Peter tries to correct him! If Jesus's response seems harsh, we should consider what is at stake: God's plan for the world's salvation. For St. Peter to oppose Jesus is to "reject the LORD who is among [us]" (Nm 11:20). It is to take on the role of Satan (see Mk 8:33). Jesus demands that we "get behind [him]" by denying ourselves, taking up our cross, and following him. We can only do that by trusting God so deeply that fear is overcome. God will be faithful. He pays loving attention to our suffering, and he will deliver our souls from death. What in your life do you need to "deny" to give yourself more fully to God's plan?

March 5

NUMBERS 13

**[21]So they went up and spied out
the land from the wilderness
of Zin to Re′hob, near the entrance of
Ha′math. [22]They went up into the Ne-
g′eb, and came to He′bron; and Ahi′man,**
Sheshai, and Talmai, the descendants of A′nak,
were there. (Hebron was built seven years
before Zoan in Egypt.) [23]And they came to
the Valley of Eshcol, and cut down from
there a branch with a single cluster of grapes,
and they carried it on a pole between two of
them; they brought also some pomegranates
and figs. [24]That place was called the Valley of
Eshcol, because of the cluster which the men
of Israel cut down from there.

[25]At the end of forty days they returned
from spying out the land. [26]And they came to
Moses and Aaron and to all the congregation
of the sons of Israel in the wilderness of
Par′an, at Ka′desh; they brought back word
to them and to all the congregation, and
showed them the fruit of the land. [27]And
they told him, "We came to the land to which
you sent us; it flows with milk and honey,
and this is its fruit. [28]Yet the people who
dwell in the land are strong, and the cities
are fortified and very large; and besides, we
saw the descendants of A′nak there. [29]The
Amal′ekites dwell in the land of the Neg′eb;
the Hittites, the Jeb′usites, and the Am′orites
dwell in the hill country; and the Canaanites
dwell by the sea, and along the Jordan."

[30]But Caleb quieted the people before
Moses, and said, "Let us go up at once, and
occupy it; for we are well able to overcome
it." [31]Then the men who had gone up with
him said, "We are not able to go up against
the people; for they are stronger than we."
[32]So they brought to the sons of Israel an evil
report of the land which they had spied out,
saying, "The land, through which we have
gone to spy it out, is a land that devours its
inhabitants; and all the people that we saw
in it are men of great stature. [33]And there we
saw the Neph′ilim (the sons of A′nak, who
come from the Nephilim); and we seemed
to ourselves like grasshoppers, and so we
seemed to them."

14 Then all the congregation raised a
loud cry; and the people wept that
night. [2]And all the sons of Israel murmured
against Moses and Aaron; the whole congregation said to them, "Would that we had
died in the land of Egypt! Or would that we
had died in this wilderness! [3]Why does the
Lord bring us into this land, to fall by the
sword? Our wives and our little ones will
become a prey; would it not be better for us
to go back to Egypt?"

[4]And they said to one another, "Let us
choose a captain, and go back to Egypt."
[5]Then Moses and Aaron fell on their faces
before all the assembly of the congregation
of the sons of Israel. [6]And Joshua the son
of Nun and Caleb the son of Jephun′neh,
who were among those who had spied
out the land, tore their clothes, [7]and
said to all the congregation of the sons
of Israel, "The land, which we passed
through to spy it out, is an exceedingly
good land. [8]If the Lord delights in us,
he will bring us into this land and give
it to us, a land which flows with milk
and honey. [9]Only, do not rebel against
the Lord; and do not fear the people of
the land, for they are bread for us; their
protection is removed from them, and the
Lord is with us; do not fear them." [10]But
all the congregation said to stone them
with stones.

Then the glory of the LORD appeared at
the tent of meeting to all the sons of Israel.
11And the LORD said to Moses, "How long
will this people despise me? And how long
will they not believe in me, in spite of all the
signs which I have wrought among them?
12I will strike them with the pestilence and
disinherit them, and I will make of you a
nation greater and mightier than they."

13But Moses said to the LORD, "Then the
Egyptians will hear of it, for you brought up
this people in your might from among them,
14and they will tell the inhabitants of this land.
They have heard that you, O LORD, are in the
midst of this people; for you, O LORD, are seen
face to face, and your cloud stands over them
and you go before them, in a pillar of cloud by
day and in a pillar of fire by night. 15Now if you
kill this people as one man, then the nations
who have heard your fame will say, 16'Because
the LORD was not able to bring this people
into the land which he swore to give to them,
therefore he has slain them in the wilderness.'
17And now, I beg you, let the power of the
LORD be great as you have promised, saying,
18'The LORD is slow to anger, and abounding
in mercy, forgiving iniquity and transgression,
but he will by no means clear the guilty, visiting
the iniquity of fathers upon children, upon the
third and upon the fourth generation.' 19Pardon
the iniquity of this people, I beg you, according
to the greatness of your mercy, and according
as you have forgiven this people, from Egypt
even until now."

20Then the LORD said, "I have pardoned,
according to your word; 21but truly, as I live,
and as all the earth shall be filled with the
glory of the LORD, 22none of the men who
have seen my glory and my signs which I
wrought in Egypt and in the wilderness, and
yet have put me to the proof these ten times
and have not hearkened to my voice, 23shall
see the land which I swore to give to their
fathers; and none of those who despised me
shall see it. 24But my servant Caleb, because
he has a different spirit and has followed
me fully, I will bring into the land into
which he went, and his descendants shall
possess it. 25Now, since the Amal'ekites and
the Canaanites dwell in the valleys, turn
tomorrow and set out for the wilderness by
the way to the Red Sea."

26And the LORD said to Moses and to
Aaron, 27"How long shall this wicked congregation murmur against me? I have heard the
murmurings of the sons of Israel, which they
murmur against me. 28Say to them, 'As I live,'
says the LORD, 'what you have said in my
hearing I will do to you: 29your dead bodies
shall fall in this wilderness; and of all your
number, numbered from twenty years old and
upward, who have murmured against me, 30not
one shall come into the land where I swore that
I would make you dwell, except Caleb the son
of Jephun'neh and Joshua the son of Nun. 31But
your little ones, who you said would become a
prey, I will bring in, and they shall know the
land which you have despised. 32But as for you,
your dead bodies shall fall in this wilderness.
33And your children shall be shepherds in the
wilderness forty years, and shall suffer for
your faithlessness, until the last of your dead
bodies lies in the wilderness. 34According to
the number of the days in which you spied out
the land, forty days, for every day a year, you
shall bear your iniquity, forty years, and you
shall know my displeasure.' 35I, the LORD, have
spoken; surely this will I do to all this wicked
congregation that are gathered together against
me: in this wilderness they shall come to a full
end, and there they shall die."

36And the men whom Moses sent to spy
out the land, and who returned and made all
the congregation to murmur against him by
bringing up an evil report against the land,
37the men who brought up an evil report of
the land, died by plague before the LORD.
38But Joshua the son of Nun and Caleb the
son of Jephun'neh remained alive, of those
men who went to spy out the land.

39And Moses told these words to all the
sons of Israel, and the people mourned greatly. 40And they rose early in the morning, and
went up to the heights of the hill country,
saying, "See, we are here, we will go up to the
place which the LORD has promised; for we
have sinned." 41But Moses said, "Why now are
you transgressing the command of the LORD,
for that will not succeed? 42Do not go up lest
you be struck down before your enemies, for

the LORD is not among you. 43For there the Amal′ekites and the Canaanites are before you, and you shall fall by the sword; because you have turned back from following the LORD, the LORD will not be with you." 44But they presumed to go up to the heights of the hill country, although neither the ark of the covenant of the LORD, nor Moses, departed out of the camp. 45Then the Amal′ekites and the Canaanites who dwelt in that hill country came down, and defeated them and pursued them, even to Hormah.

To the choirmaster: according to Do Not Destroy.
A Miktam of David, when he fled from Saul, in the cave.

PSALM 57 [56]

Be merciful to me, O God, be merciful to me,
for in you my soul takes refuge;
in the shadow of your wings I will
take refuge,
till the storms of destruction pass by.
2I cry to God Most High,
to God who fulfils his purpose for me.
3He will send from heaven and save me,
he will put to shame those who trample
upon me. *Selah*
God will send forth his mercy and his
faithfulness!

4I lie in the midst of lions
that greedily devour the sons of men;
their teeth are spears and arrows,
their tongues sharp swords.

5Be exalted, O God, above the heavens!
Let your glory be over all the earth!

6They set a net for my steps;
my soul was bowed down.
They dug a pit in my way,
but they have fallen into it themselves
Selah

7My heart is steadfast, O God,
my heart is steadfast!
I will sing and make melody!
8 Awake, my soul!
Awake, O harp and lyre!
I will awake the dawn!
9I will give thanks to you, O Lord, among
the peoples;
I will sing praises to you among
the nations.
10For your mercy is great to the heavens,
your faithfulness to the clouds.

11Be exalted, O God, above the heavens!
Let your glory be over all the earth!

MARK 9

And he said to them, "Truly, I say to you, there are some standing here who will not taste death before they see the kingdom of God come with power."

2And after six days Jesus took with him
Peter and James and John, and led them
up a high mountain apart by themselves;
and he was transfigured before them, 3and
his garments became glistening, intensely
white, as no fuller on earth could bleach
them. 4And there appeared to them Eli′jah
with Moses; and they were talking to Jesus.
5And Peter said to Jesus, "Master, it is well
that we are here; let us make three booths,
one for you and one for Moses and one for
Eli′jah." 6For he did not know what to say, for
they were exceedingly afraid. 7And a cloud
overshadowed them, and a voice came out
of the cloud, "This is my beloved Son; listen
to him." 8And suddenly looking around
they no longer saw any one with them but
Jesus only.
9And as they were coming down the
mountain, he charged them to tell no one
what they had seen, until the Son of man
should have risen from the dead. 10So they
kept the matter to themselves, questioning
what the rising from the dead meant. 11And
they asked him, "Why do the scribes say
that first Eli′jah must come?" 12And he said
to them, "Eli′jah does come first to restore

all things; and how is it written of the Son of man, that he should suffer many things and be treated with contempt? [13]But I tell you that Eli′jah has come, and they did to him whatever they pleased, as it is written of him."

[14]And when they came to the disciples, they saw a great crowd about them, and scribes arguing with them. [15]And immediately all the crowd, when they saw him, were greatly amazed, and ran up to him and greeted him. [16]And he asked them, "What are you discussing with them?" [17]And one of the crowd answered him, "Teacher, I brought my son to you, for he has a mute spirit; [18]and wherever it seizes him, it dashes him down; and he foams and grinds his teeth and becomes rigid; and I asked your disciples to cast it out, and they were not able." [19]And he answered them, "O faithless generation, how long am I to be with you? How long am I to bear with you? Bring him to me." [20]And they brought the boy to him; and when the spirit saw him, immediately it convulsed the boy, and he fell on the ground and rolled about, foaming at the mouth. [21]And Jesus asked his father, "How long has he had this?" And he said, "From childhood. [22]And it has often cast him into the fire and into the water, to destroy him; but if you can do anything, have pity on us and help us." [23]And Jesus said to him, "If you can! All things are possible to him who believes." [24]Immediately the father of the child cried out and said, "I believe; help my unbelief!" [25]And when Jesus saw that a crowd came running together, he rebuked the unclean spirit, saying to it, "You mute and deaf spirit, I command you, come out of him, and never enter him again." [26]And after crying out and convulsing him terribly, it came out, and the boy was like a corpse; so that most of them said, "He is dead." [27]But Jesus took him by the hand and lifted him up, and he arose. [28]And when he had entered the house, his disciples asked him privately, "Why could we not cast it out?" [29]And he said to them, "This kind cannot be driven out by anything but prayer and fasting."

REFLECTION

God wants to bring his people to the land that "flows with milk and honey" (v. 27; 14:8). But most of the spies calculate their chances on their own terms instead of trusting God: "We are not able to go up against the people; for they are stronger than we" (v. 31). In response, the Lord asks, "How long will this people despise me? And how long will they not believe in me, in spite of all the signs which I have wrought among them?" (14:11). Jesus echoes this question in Mark 9:19 when his disciples fail to cast out a demon, apparently due to their failure to rely on God through "prayer and fasting" (Mk 9:29). The father of the afflicted child fares better with his moving plea, "I believe; help my unbelief!" (v. 24). He recognizes his limitations, but unlike the Israelites in the wilderness, he doesn't shrink God down to his own size. He becomes childlike in his dependence on God (see 10:13–16). The ultimate pattern of this divine childhood is Jesus himself, who is gloriously revealed as the Father's "beloved Son" (9:7). Psalm 57 provides a beautiful song of childlike trust that leads to praise of God's mercy and faithfulness. "How long" will we focus on our weakness rather than trusting in God's strength?

March 6

NUMBERS 15

The Lord said to Moses, [2]"Say to the sons of Israel, When you come into the land you are to inhabit, which I give you, [3]and you offer to the Lord from the herd or from the flock an offering by fire or a burnt offering or a sacrifice, to fulfil a vow or as a freewill offering or at your appointed feasts, to make a pleasing odor to the Lord, [4]then he who brings his offering shall offer to the Lord a cereal offering of a tenth of an ephah of fine flour, mixed with a fourth of a hin of oil; [5]and wine for the drink offering, a fourth of a hin, you shall prepare with the burnt offering, or for the sacrifice, for each lamb. [6]Or for a ram, you shall prepare for a cereal offering two tenths of an ephah of fine flour mixed with a third of a hin of oil; [7]and for the drink offering you shall offer a third of a hin of wine, a pleasing odor to the LORD. [8]And when you prepare a bull for a burnt offering, or for a sacrifice, to fulfil a vow, or for peace offerings to the LORD, [9]then you shall offer with the bull a cereal offering of three tenths of an ephah of fine flour, mixed with half a hin of oil, [10]and you shall offer for the drink offering half a hin of wine, as an offering by fire, a pleasing odor to the LORD.

[11]"Thus it shall be done for each bull or ram, or for each of the male lambs or the kids. [12]According to the number that you prepare, so shall you do with every one according to their number. [13]All who are native shall do these things in this way, in offering an offering by fire, a pleasing odor to the LORD. [14]And if a stranger is sojourning with you, or any one is among you throughout your generations, and he wishes to offer an offering by fire, a pleasing odor to the LORD, he shall do as you do. [15]For the assembly, there shall be one statute for you and for the stranger who sojourns with you, a perpetual statute throughout your generations; as you are, so shall the sojourner be before the LORD. [16]One law and one ordinance shall be for you and for the stranger who sojourns with you."

[17]The LORD said to Moses, [18]"Say to the sons of Israel, When you come into the land to which I bring you [19]and when you eat of the food of the land, you shall present an offering to the LORD. [20]Of the first of your coarse meal you shall present a cake as an offering; as an offering from the threshing floor, so shall you present it. [21]Of the first of your coarse meal you shall give to the Lord an offering throughout your generations.

[22]"But if you err, and do not observe all these commandments which the LORD has spoken to Moses, [23]all that the LORD has commanded you by Moses, from the day that the LORD gave commandment, and onward throughout your generations, [24]then if it was done unwittingly without the knowledge of the congregation, all the congregation shall offer one young bull for a burnt offering, a pleasing odor to the LORD, with its cereal offering and its drink offering, according to the ordinance, and one male goat for a sin offering. [25]And the priest shall make atonement for all the congregation of the sons of Israel, and they shall be forgiven; because it was an error, and they have brought their offering, an offering by fire to the LORD, and their sin offering before the LORD, for their error. [26]And all the congregation of the sons of Israel shall be forgiven, and the stranger who sojourns among them, because the whole population was involved in the error.

[27]"If one person sins unwittingly, he shall offer a female goat a year old for a sin offering. [28]And the priest shall make atonement before the LORD for the person who commits an error, when he sins unwittingly, to make atonement for him; and he shall be forgiven. [29]You shall have one law for him who does anything unwittingly, for him who is native among the sons of Israel, and for the stranger who sojourns among them. [30]But the person who does anything with a high hand, whether he is native or a sojourner, reviles the LORD, and that person shall be cut off from among his people. [31]Because he has despised the word of the LORD, and has broken his commandment, that person shall be utterly cut off; his iniquity shall be upon him."

[32]While the sons of Israel were in the wilderness, they found a man gathering sticks on the sabbath day. [33]And those who found him gathering sticks brought him to Moses and Aaron, and to all the congregation. [34]They put him in custody, because it had not been made plain what should be done to him. [35]And the LORD said to Moses, "The man shall be put to death; all the congregation shall stone him with stones outside the camp." [36]And all the congregation brought him outside the

camp, and stoned him to death with stones, as the LORD commanded Moses.

37The LORD said to Moses, 38“Speak to the sons of Israel, and bid them to make tassels on the corners of their garments throughout their generations, and to put upon the tassel of each corner a cord of blue; 39and it shall be to you a tassel to look upon and remember all the commandments of the LORD, to do them, not to follow after your own heart and your own eyes, which you are inclined to go after wantonly. 40So you shall remember and do all my commandments, and be holy to your God. 41I am the LORD your God, who brought you out of the land of Egypt, to be your God: I am the LORD your God.”

16 Now Ko′rah the son of Iz′har, son of Ko′hath, son of Levi, and Da′than and Abi′ram the sons of Eli′ab, and On the son of Pe′leth, sons of Reuben, 2took men; and they rose up before Moses, with a number of the sons of Israel, two hundred and fifty leaders of the congregation, chosen from the assembly, well-known men; 3and they assembled themselves together against Moses and against Aaron, and said to them, “You have gone too far! For all the congregation are holy, every one of them, and the LORD is among them; why then do you exalt yourselves above the assembly of the LORD?” 4When Moses heard it, he fell on his face; 5and he said to Ko′rah and all his company, “In the morning the LORD will show who is his, and who is holy, and will cause him to come near to him; him whom he will choose he will cause to come near to him. 6Do this: take censers, Ko′rah and all his company; 7put fire in them and put incense upon them before the LORD tomorrow, and the man whom the LORD chooses shall be the holy one. You have gone too far, sons of Levi!” 8And Moses said to Ko′rah, “Hear now, you sons of Levi: 9is it too small a thing for you that the God of Israel has separated you from the congregation of Israel, to bring you near to himself, to do service in the tabernacle of the LORD, and to stand before the congregation to minister to them; 10and that he has brought you near him, and all your brethren the sons of Levi with you? And would you seek the priesthood also? 11Therefore it is against the LORD that you and all your company have gathered together; what is Aaron that you murmur against him?”

12And Moses sent to call Da′than and Abi′ram the sons of Eli′ab; and they said, “We will not come up. 13Is it a small thing that you have brought us up out of a land flowing with milk and honey, to kill us in the wilderness, that you must also make yourself a prince over us? 14Moreover you have not brought us into a land flowing with milk and honey, nor given us inheritance of fields and vineyards. Will you put out the eyes of these men? We will not come up.”

15And Moses was very angry, and said to the LORD, “Do not respect their offering. I have not taken one donkey from them, and I have not harmed one of them.” 16And Moses said to Ko′rah, “Be present, you and all your company, before the LORD, you and they, and Aaron, tomorrow; 17and let every one of you take his censer, and put incense upon it, and every one of you bring before the LORD his censer, two hundred and fifty censers; you also, and Aaron, each his censer.” 18So every man took his censer, and they put fire in them and laid incense upon them, and they stood at the entrance of the tent of meeting with Moses and Aaron. 19Then Ko′rah assembled all the congregation against them at the entrance of the tent of meeting. And the glory of the LORD appeared to all the congregation.

To the choirmaster: according to Do Not Destroy.
A Miktam of David.

PSALM 58 [57]

Do you indeed decree what is right,
you gods?
Do you judge the sons of men uprightly?
2No, in your hearts you devise wrongs;
your hands deal out violence on earth.

3The wicked go astray from the womb,
they err from their birth, speaking lies.

[4]They have venom like the venom of
a serpent,
like the deaf adder that stops its ear,
[5]so that it does not hear the voice of charmers
or of the cunning enchanter.
[6]O God, break the teeth in their mouths;
tear out the fangs of the young lions,
O LORD!
[7]Let them vanish like water that runs away;
like grass let them be trodden down
and wither.
[8]Let them be like the snail which dissolves
into slime,
like the untimely birth that never sees
the sun.
[9]Sooner than your pots can feel the heat
of thorns,
whether green or ablaze, may he sweep
them away!

[10]The righteous will rejoice when he sees
the vengeance;
he will bathe his feet in the blood of
the wicked.
[11]Men will say, "Surely there is a reward for
the righteous;
surely there is a God who judges on earth."

MARK 9

[30]They went on from there and passed through Galilee. And he would not have any one know it; [31]for he was teaching his disciples, saying to them, "The Son of man will be delivered into the hands of men, and they will kill him; and when he is killed, after three days he will rise." [32]But they did not understand the saying, and they were afraid to ask him.

[33]And they came to Caper'na-um; and when he was in the house he asked them, "What were you discussing on the way?"
[34]But they were silent; for on the way they had discussed with one another who was the greatest. [35]And he sat down and called the Twelve and he said to them, "If any one would be first, he must be last of all and servant of all." [36]And he took a child, and put him in the midst of them; and taking him in his arms, he said to them, [37]"Whoever receives one such child in my name receives me; and whoever receives me, receives not me but him who sent me."

[38]John said to him, "Teacher, we saw a man casting out demons in your name, and we forbade him, because he was not following us." [39]But Jesus said, "Do not forbid him; for no one who does a mighty work in my name will be able soon after to speak evil of me.
[40]For he that is not against us is for us. [41]For truly, I say to you, whoever gives you a cup of water to drink because you bear the name of Christ, will by no means lose his reward.

[42]"Whoever causes one of these little ones who believe in me to sin, it would be better for him if a great millstone were hung round his neck and he were thrown into the sea. [43]And if your hand causes you to sin, cut it off; it is better for you to enter life maimed than with two hands to go to hell, to the unquenchable fire. [45]And if your foot causes you to sin, cut it off; it is better for you to enter life lame than with two feet to be thrown into hell. [47]And if your eye causes you to sin, pluck it out; it is better for you to enter the kingdom of God with one eye than with two eyes to be thrown into hell, [48]where their worm does not die, and the fire is not quenched. [49]For every one will be salted with fire. [50]Salt is good; but if the salt has lost its saltiness, how will you season it? Have salt in yourselves, and be at peace with one another."

REFLECTION

How many times have you been told to "follow your heart"? Today in Numbers, the Israelites are told to put tassels on the corners of their garments to remind them *not* "to follow after [their] own heart and [their] own eyes," but rather to remember God's commandments (Nm 15:38–39). Unfortunately, our hearts are all too prone to "go astray from the womb" (Ps 58:3), chasing after our often disordered desires and refusing to listen to truth, "like the deaf adder that stops its ear" (Ps 58:4).

What an image! The end of this road is death. The capital punishment we see in Numbers 15:35–36 seems harsh, to be sure. But Jesus is equally serious about sin in today's Gospel, warning about something far worse: spiritual death (see Mk 9:43–48). It's true that he's being hyperbolic; we aren't literally to self-amputate. But Jesus uses shocking language to communicate an important point, and we shouldn't let that point get dulled. Spiritual health is more important than bodily health. Sin is worse for us than the most grievous bodily injury, for sin weakens or, if it's mortal, destroys the communion with God that we were made for. Are there sins we just shrug off? What steps can you take today to "remember and do" God's Word, to be set apart for him (Nm 15:40)?

March 7

NUMBERS 16

20 And the Lord said to Moses
and to Aaron, 21 "Separate your-
selves from among this congregation,
that I may consume them in a moment."
22 And they fell on their faces, and said,
"O God, the God of the spirits of all flesh, shall
one man sin, and will you be angry with all
the congregation?" 23 And the Lord said to
Moses, 24 "Say to the congregation, Get away
from about the dwelling of Ko′rah, Da′than,
and Abi′ram."

25 Then Moses rose and went to Da′than
and Abi′ram; and the elders of Israel
followed him. 26 And he said to the
congregation, "Depart, I beg you, from
the tents of these wicked men, and touch
nothing of theirs, lest you be swept
away with all their sins." 27 So they got
away from about the dwelling of Ko′rah,
Da′than, and Abi′ram; and Dathan and
Abiram came out and stood at the door
of their tents, together with their wives,
their sons, and their little ones. 28 And
Moses said, "Hereby you shall know that
the Lord has sent me to do all these
works, and that it has not been of my own
accord. 29 If these men die the common
death of all men, or if they are visited by
the fate of all men, then the Lord has
not sent me. 30 But if the Lord creates
something new, and the ground opens its
mouth, and swallows them up, with all
that belongs to them, and they go down
alive into Sheol, then you shall know that
these men have despised the Lord."

31 And as he finished speaking all
these words, the ground under them
split asunder; 32 and the earth opened its
mouth and swallowed them up, with their
households and all the men that belonged
to Ko′rah and all their goods. 33 So they
and all that belonged to them went down
alive into Sheol; and the earth closed over
them, and they perished from the midst
of the assembly. 34 And all Israel that were
round about them fled at their cry; for
they said, "Lest the earth swallow us up!"
35 And fire came forth from the Lord, and
consumed the two hundred and fifty men
offering the incense.

36 Then the Lord said to Moses, 37 "Tell
El-ea′zar the son of Aaron the priest to
take up the censers out of the blaze; then
scatter the fire far and wide. For they are
holy, 38 the censers of these men who have
sinned at the cost of their lives; so let
them be made into hammered plates as
a covering for the altar, for they offered
them before the Lord; therefore they are
holy. Thus they shall be a sign to the sons
of Israel." 39 So Elea′zar the priest took
the bronze censers, which those who
were burned had offered; and they were
hammered out as a covering for the altar,
40 to be a reminder to the sons of Israel,
so that no one who is not a priest, who is
not of the descendants of Aaron, should
draw near to burn incense before the
Lord, lest he become as Ko′rah and as his
company—as the Lord said to Elea′zar
through Moses.

41But the next day all the congregation
of the sons of Israel murmured against
Moses and against Aaron, saying, "You
have killed the people of the LORD." 42And
when the congregation had assembled
against Moses and against Aaron, they
turned toward the tent of meeting;
and behold, the cloud covered it, and
the glory of the LORD appeared. 43And
Moses and Aaron came to the front of
the tent of meeting, 44and the LORD said
to Moses, 45"Get away from the midst of
this congregation, that I may consume
them in a moment." And they fell on their
faces. 46And Moses said to Aaron, "Take
your censer, and put fire therein from
off the altar, and lay incense on it, and
carry it quickly to the congregation, and
make atonement for them; for wrath has
gone forth from the LORD, the plague has
begun." 47So Aaron took it as Moses said,
and ran into the midst of the assembly;
and behold, the plague had already
begun among the people; and he put on
the incense, and made atonement for
the people. 48And he stood between the
dead and the living; and the plague was
stopped. 49Now those who died by the
plague were fourteen thousand seven
hundred, besides those who died in the
affair of Ko′rah. 50And Aaron returned
to Moses at the entrance of the tent of
meeting, when the plague was stopped.

17 The LORD said to Moses, 2"Speak to
the sons of Israel, and get from them
rods, one for each fathers' house, from all
their leaders according to their fathers'
houses, twelve rods. Write each man's
name upon his rod, 3and write Aaron's
name upon the rod of Levi. For there shall
be one rod for the head of each fathers'
house. 4Then you shall deposit them in the
tent of meeting before the covenant, where
I meet with you. 5And the rod of the man
whom I choose shall sprout; thus I will
make to cease from me the murmurings
of the sons of Israel, which they murmur
against you." 6Moses spoke to the sons of
Israel; and all their leaders gave him rods,
one for each leader, according to their
fathers' houses, twelve rods; and the rod of
Aaron was among their rods. 7And Moses
deposited the rods before the LORD in the
tent of the covenant.

8And the next day Moses went into the
tent of the covenant; and behold, the rod of
Aaron for the house of Levi had sprouted
and put forth buds, and produced blossoms,
and it bore ripe almonds. 9Then Moses
brought out all the rods from before the
LORD to all the sons of Israel; and they
looked, and each man took his rod. 10And
the LORD said to Moses, "Put back the rod
of Aaron before the covenant, to be kept as
a sign for the rebels, that you may make an
end of their murmurings against me, lest
they die." 11Thus did Moses; as the LORD
commanded him, so he did.

12And the sons of Israel said to Moses,
"Behold, we perish, we are undone, we are
all undone. 13Every one who comes near,
who comes near to the tabernacle of the
LORD, shall die. Are we all to perish?"

18 So the LORD said to Aaron, "You and
your sons and your fathers' house
with you shall bear iniquity in connection
with the sanctuary; and you and your sons
with you shall bear iniquity in connection
with your priesthood. 2And with you bring
your brethren also, the tribe of Levi, the
tribe of your father, that they may join you,
and minister to you while you and your
sons with you are before the tent of the
covenant. 3They shall attend you and attend
to all duties of the tent; but shall not come
near to the vessels of the sanctuary or to
the altar, lest they, and you, die. 4They shall
join you, and attend to the tent of meeting,
for all the service of the tent; and no one
else shall come near you. 5And you shall
attend to the duties of the sanctuary and the
duties of the altar, that there be wrath no
more upon the sons of Israel. 6And behold,
I have taken your brethren the Levites from
among the sons of Israel; they are a gift to
you, given to the LORD, to do the service of
the tent of meeting. 7And you and your sons
with you shall attend to your priesthood for
all that concerns the altar and that is within
the veil; and you shall serve. I give your

priesthood as a gift, and any one else who comes near shall be put to death."

To the choirmaster: according to Do Not Destroy.

A Miktam of David, when Saul sent men to watch his house in order to kill him.

PSALM 59 [58]

Deliver me from my enemies, O my God,
protect me from those who rise up against me,
2deliver me from those who work evil,
and save me from bloodthirsty men.

3For behold, they lie in wait for my life;
fierce men band themselves against me.
For no transgression or sin of mine, O LORD,
4 for no fault of mine, they run and make ready.
Rouse yourself, come to my help, and see!
5 You, LORD God of hosts, are God of Israel.
Awake to punish all the nations;
spare none of those who treacherously plot evil. *Selah*

6Each evening they come back,
howling like dogs
and prowling about the city.
7There they are, bellowing with their mouths,
and snarling with their lips—
for "Who," they think, "will hear us?"

8But you, O LORD, laugh at them;
you hold all the nations in derision.
9O my Strength, I will sing praises to you;
for you, O God, are my fortress.
10My God in his mercy will meet me;
my God will let me look in triumph on my enemies.

11Slay them not, lest my people forget;
make them totter by your power, and bring them down,
O Lord, our shield!
12For the sin of their mouths, the words of their lips,
let them be trapped in their pride.
For the cursing and lies which they utter,
13 consume them in wrath,
consume them till they are no more,
that men may know that God rules over Jacob
to the ends of the earth. *Selah*

14Each evening they come back,
howling like dogs
and prowling about the city.
15They roam about for food,
and growl if they do not get their fill.

16But I will sing of your might;
I will sing aloud of your mercy in the morning.
For you have been to me a fortress
and a refuge in the day of my distress.
17O my Strength, I will sing praises to you,
for you, O God, are my fortress,
the God who shows me mercy.

MARK 10

And he left there and went to the region of Judea and beyond the Jordan, and crowds gathered to him again; and again, as his custom was, he taught them.

2And Pharisees came up and in order to test
him asked, "Is it lawful for a man to divorce
his wife?" 3He answered them, "What did
Moses command you?" 4They said, "Moses
allowed a man to write a certificate of divorce, and to put her away." 5But Jesus said
to them, "For your hardness of heart he
wrote you this commandment. 6But from
the beginning of creation, 'God made them
male and female.' 7'For this reason a man
shall leave his father and mother and be
joined to his wife, 8and the two shall become
one flesh.' So they are no longer two but
one flesh. 9What therefore God has joined
together, let not man put asunder."
10And in the house the disciples asked
him again about this matter. 11And he said
to them, "Whoever divorces his wife and
marries another, commits adultery against

her; 12and if she divorces her husband and
marries another, she commits adultery."
13And they were bringing children to him,
that he might touch them; and the disciples
rebuked them. 14But when Jesus saw it he was
indignant, and said to them, "Let the children
come to me, do not hinder them; for to such
belongs the kingdom of God. 15Truly, I say to
you, whoever does not receive the kingdom
of God like a child shall not enter it." 16And
he took them in his arms and blessed them,
laying his hands upon them.
17And as he was setting out on his journey, a
man ran up and knelt before him, and asked
him, "Good Teacher, what must I do to inherit
eternal life?" 18And Jesus said to him, "Why
do you call me good? No one is good but
God alone. 19You know the commandments:
'Do not kill, Do not commit adultery, Do
not steal, Do not bear false witness, Do not
defraud, Honor your father and mother.'"
20And he said to him, "Teacher, all these I
have observed from my youth." 21And Jesus
looking upon him loved him, and said to
him, "You lack one thing; go, sell what you
have, and give to the poor, and you will have
treasure in heaven; and come, follow me." 22At
that saying his countenance fell, and he went
away sorrowful; for he had great possessions.
23And Jesus looked around and said to his
disciples, "How hard it will be for those who
have riches to enter the kingdom of God!"
24And the disciples were amazed at his words.
But Jesus said to them again, "Children, how
hard it is for those who trust in riches to
enter the kingdom of God! 25It is easier for a
camel to go through the eye of a needle than
for a rich man to enter the kingdom of God."
26And they were exceedingly astonished,
and said to him, "Then who can be saved?"
27Jesus looked at them and said, "With men it
is impossible, but not with God; for all things
are possible with God." 28Peter began to say
to him, "Behold, we have left everything
and followed you." 29Jesus said, "Truly, I say
to you, there is no one who has left house
or brothers or sisters or mother or father or
children or lands, for my sake and for the
gospel, 30who will not receive a hundredfold
now in this time, houses and brothers and
sisters and mothers and children and lands,
with persecutions, and in the age to come
eternal life. 31But many that are first will be
last, and the last first."

REFLECTION

Yesterday we read, "All the congregation are holy, every one of them, and the LORD is among them; why then do you exalt yourselves above the assembly of the LORD?" (Nm 16:3). Surely many of us can sympathize with this egalitarian protest of the 250 led by Korah, Dathan, and Abiram. There's certainly truth to it! Just a little earlier, all Israelites were exhorted to "be holy to your God" (15:40). The Fathers of Vatican II reminded us that "all the faithful of Christ of whatever rank or status, are called to the fullness of the Christian life" (*Lumen Gentium*, 40). In Christ, we enjoy fundamental equality as children of God. If we mistakenly equate hierarchy with self-interest and power, like Korah, we will rebel. Today we read of the tragic consequences. Note, however, that Moses and Aaron do not use force to assert their rights as divinely appointed leaders; they trust God to vindicate them. Even though it was written much later, we might imagine them praying, "O my God, protect me from those who rise up against me" (Ps 59:1). Even hierarchical leaders must "receive the kingdom of God like a child" (Mk 10:15) and be willing, in childlike faith, to give up everything for Jesus. Are there possessions you cling to that might cause you to "[go] away sorrowful" (v. 22)?

March 8

NUMBERS 18

**8Then the LORD said to Aaron,
"And behold, I have given you
whatever is kept of the offerings
made to me, all the consecrated things
of the sons of Israel; I have given them
to you as a portion, and to your sons as**

a perpetual debt. 9 This shall be yours of the most holy things, reserved from the fire; every offering of theirs, every cereal offering of theirs and every sin offering of theirs and every guilt offering of theirs, which they render to me, shall be most holy to you and to your sons. 10 In a most holy place shall you eat of it; every male may eat of it; it is holy to you. 11 This also is yours, the offering of their gift, all the wave offerings of the sons of Israel; I have given them to you, and to your sons and daughters with you, as a perpetual debt; every one who is clean in your house may eat of it. 12 All the best of the oil, and all the best of the wine and of the grain, the first fruits of what they give to the LORD, I give to you. 13 The first ripe fruits of all that is in their land, which they bring to the LORD, shall be yours; every one who is clean in your house may eat of it. 14 Every devoted thing in Israel shall be yours. 15 Everything that opens the womb of all flesh, whether man or beast, which they offer to the LORD, shall be yours; nevertheless the first-born of man you shall redeem, and the firstling of unclean beasts you shall redeem. 16 And their redemption price (at a month old you shall redeem them) you shall fix at five shekels in silver, according to the shekel of the sanctuary, which is twenty gerahs. 17 But the firstling of a cow, or the firstling of a sheep, or the firstling of a goat, you shall not redeem; they are holy. You shall sprinkle their blood upon the altar, and shall burn their fat as an offering by fire, a pleasing odor to the LORD; 18 but their flesh shall be yours, as the breast that is waved and as the right thigh are yours. 19 All the holy offerings which the sons of Israel present to the LORD I give to you, and to your sons and daughters with you, as a perpetual debt; it is a covenant of salt for ever before the LORD for you and for your offspring with you." 20 And the LORD said to Aaron, "You shall have no inheritance in their land, neither shall you have any portion among them; I am your portion and your inheritance among the sons of Israel.

21 "To the Levites I have given every tithe in Israel for an inheritance, in return for their service which they serve, their service in the tent of meeting. 22 And henceforth the sons of Israel shall not come near the tent of meeting, lest they bear sin and die. 23 But the Levites shall do the service of the tent of meeting, and they shall bear their iniquity; it shall be a perpetual statute throughout your generations; and among the sons of Israel they shall have no inheritance. 24 For the tithe of the sons of Israel, which they present as an offering to the LORD, I have given to the Levites for an inheritance; therefore I have said of them that they shall have no inheritance among the sons of Israel."

25 And the LORD said to Moses, 26 "Moreover you shall say to the Levites, 'When you take from the sons of Israel the tithe which I have given you from them for your inheritance, then you shall present an offering from it to the LORD, a tithe of the tithe. 27 And your offering shall be reckoned to you as though it were the grain of the threshing floor, and as the fulness of the wine press. 28 So shall you also present an offering to the LORD from all your tithes, which you receive from the sons of Israel; and from it you shall give the LORD's offering to Aaron the priest. 29 Out of all the gifts to you, you shall present every offering due to the LORD, from all the best of them, giving the hallowed part from them.' 30 Therefore you shall say to them, 'When you have offered from it the best of it, then the rest shall be reckoned to the Levites as produce of the threshing floor, and as produce of the wine press; 31 and you may eat it in any place, you and your households; for it is your reward in return for your service in the tent of meeting. 32 And you shall bear no sin by reason of it, when you have offered the best of it. And you shall not profane the holy things of the sons of Israel, lest you die.' "

19 Now the LORD said to Moses and to Aaron, 2 "This is the statute of the law which the LORD has commanded: Tell the sons of Israel to bring you a red heifer without defect, in which there is no blemish, and upon which a yoke has never come. 3 And you shall give her to Elea′zar the priest, and she shall be taken outside the camp and slaughtered before him; 4 and Elea′zar the

priest shall take some of her blood with
his finger, and sprinkle some of her blood
toward the front of the tent of meeting seven
times. 5 And the heifer shall be burned in his
sight; her skin, her flesh, and her blood,
with all her dung, shall be burned; 6 and the
priest shall take cedarwood and hyssop and
scarlet stuff, and cast them into the midst of
the burning of the heifer. 7 Then the priest
shall wash his clothes and bathe his body in
water, and afterwards he shall come into the
camp; and the priest shall be unclean until
evening. 8 He who burns the heifer shall
wash his clothes in water and bathe his body
in water, and shall be unclean until evening.
9 And a man who is clean shall gather up the
ashes of the heifer, and deposit them outside
the camp in a clean place; and they shall be
kept for the congregation of the sons of Israel
for the water for impurity, for the removal of
sin. 10 And he who gathers the ashes of the
heifer shall wash his clothes, and be unclean
until evening. And this shall be to the sons
of Israel, and to the stranger who sojourns
among them, a perpetual statute.

11 "He who touches the dead body of any
person shall be unclean seven days; 12 he
shall cleanse himself with the water on the
third day and on the seventh day, and so
be clean; but if he does not cleanse himself
on the third day and on the seventh day, he
will not become clean. 13 Whoever touches a
dead person, the body of any man who has
died, and does not cleanse himself, defiles
the tabernacle of the LORD, and that person
shall be cut off from Israel; because the
water for impurity was not thrown upon
him, he shall be unclean; his uncleanness is
still on him.

14 "This is the law when a man dies in a
tent: every one who comes into the tent, and
every one who is in the tent, shall be unclean
seven days. 15 And every open vessel, which
has no cover fastened upon it, is unclean.
16 Whoever in the open field touches one
who is slain with a sword, or a dead body, or
a bone of a man, or a grave, shall be unclean
seven days. 17 For the unclean they shall take
some ashes of the burnt sin offering, and
running water shall be added in a vessel;
18 then a clean person shall take hyssop, and
dip it in the water, and sprinkle it upon the
tent, and upon all the furnishings, and upon
the persons who were there, and upon him
who touched the bone, or the slain, or the
dead, or the grave; 19 and the clean person
shall sprinkle upon the unclean on the third
day and on the seventh day; thus on the
seventh day he shall cleanse him, and he
shall wash his clothes and bathe himself in
water, and at evening he shall be clean.

20 "But the man who is unclean and does
not cleanse himself, that person shall be cut
off from the midst of the assembly, since
he has defiled the sanctuary of the LORD;
because the water for impurity has not been
thrown upon him, he is unclean. 21 And it
shall be a perpetual statute for them. He
who sprinkles the water for impurity shall
wash his clothes; and he who touches the
water for impurity shall be unclean until
evening. 22 And whatever the unclean person
touches shall be unclean; and any one who
touches it shall be unclean until evening."

20 And the sons of Israel, the whole
congregation, came into the wilderness of Zin in the first month, and the
people stayed in Ka'desh; and Miriam died
there, and was buried there.

2 Now there was no water for the congregation; and they assembled themselves
together against Moses and against Aaron.
3 And the people contended with Moses, and
said, "Would that we had died when our
brethren died before the LORD! 4 Why have
you brought the assembly of the LORD into
this wilderness, that we should die here,
both we and our cattle? 5 And why have you
made us come up out of Egypt, to bring us
to this evil place? It is no place for grain, or
figs, or vines, or pomegranates; and there is
no water to drink." 6 Then Moses and Aaron
went from the presence of the assembly to the
door of the tent of meeting, and fell on their
faces. And the glory of the LORD appeared to
them, 7 and the LORD said to Moses, 8 "Take
the rod, and assemble the congregation, you
and Aaron your brother, and tell the rock
before their eyes to yield its water; so you
shall bring water out of the rock for them; so

you shall give drink to the congregation and
their cattle." 9And Moses took the rod from
before the LORD, as he commanded him.
10And Moses and Aaron gathered the
assembly together before the rock, and he
said to them, "Hear now, you rebels; shall we
bring forth water for you out of this rock?"
11And Moses lifted up his hand and struck the
rock with his rod twice; and water came forth
abundantly, and the congregation drank, and
their cattle. 12And the LORD said to Moses and
Aaron, "Because you did not believe in me, to
sanctify me in the eyes of the sons of Israel,
therefore you shall not bring this assembly
into the land which I have given them."
13These are the waters of Mer′ibah, where
the sons of Israel contended with the LORD,
and he showed himself holy among them.

To the choirmaster: according to Shushan Eduth. A Miktam of David; for instruction; when he strove with Aram-naharaim and with Aram-zobah, and when Joab on his return killed twelve thousand of Edom in the Valley of Salt.

PSALM 60 [59]

O God, you have rejected us, broken
our defenses;
you have been angry; oh, restore us.
2You have made the land to quake, you have
torn it open;
repair its breaches, for it totters.
3You have made your people suffer
hard things;
you have given us wine to drink that
made us reel.

4You have set up a banner for those who
fear you,
to rally to it from the bow. *Selah*
5That your beloved may be delivered,
give victory by your right hand and
answer us!

6God has spoken in his sanctuary:
"With exultation I will divide up Shechem
and portion out the Vale of Succoth.
7Gilead is mine; Manas′seh is mine;
E′phraim is my helmet;
Judah is my scepter.
8Moab is my washbasin;
upon Edom I cast my shoe;
over Philistia I shout in triumph."
9Who will bring me to the fortified city?
Who will lead me to Edom?
10Have you not rejected us, O God?
You do not go forth, O God, with
our armies.
11O grant us help against the foe,
for vain is the help of man!
12With God we shall do valiantly;
it is he who will tread down our foes.

MARK 10

**32And they were on the road, go-
ing up to Jerusalem, and Jesus
was walking ahead of them; and they
were amazed, and those who followed**
were afraid. And taking the Twelve again, he
began to tell them what was to happen to
him, 33saying, "Behold, we are going up to
Jerusalem; and the Son of man will be delivered to the chief priests and the scribes,
and they will condemn him to death, and
deliver him to the Gentiles; 34and they will
mock him, and spit upon him, and scourge
him, and kill him; and after three days he
will rise."
35And James and John, the sons of Zeb′e-
dee, came forward to him, and said to him,
"Teacher, we want you to do for us whatever
we ask of you." 36And he said to them, "What
do you want me to do for you?" 37And they
said to him, "Grant us to sit, one at your right
hand and one at your left, in your glory."
38But Jesus said to them, "You do not know
what you are asking. Are you able to drink
the chalice that I drink, or to be baptized
with the baptism with which I am baptized?"
39And they said to him, "We are able." And
Jesus said to them, "The chalice that I drink
you will drink; and with the baptism with
which I am baptized, you will be baptized;

[40]but to sit at my right hand or at my left is not mine to grant, but it is for those for whom it has been prepared." [41]And when the ten heard it, they began to be indignant at James and John. [42]And Jesus called them to him and said to them, "You know that those who are supposed to rule over the Gentiles lord it over them, and their great men exercise authority over them. [43]But it shall not be so among you; but whoever would be great among you must be your servant, [44]and whoever would be first among you must be slave of all. [45]For the Son of man also came not to be served but to serve, and to give his life as a ransom for many."

[46]And they came to Jericho; and as he was leaving Jericho with his disciples and a great multitude, Bartimae′us, a blind beggar, the son of Timae′us, was sitting by the roadside. [47]And when he heard that it was Jesus of Nazareth, he began to cry out and say, "Jesus, Son of David, have mercy on me!" [48]And many rebuked him, telling him to be silent; but he cried out all the more, "Son of David, have mercy on me!" [49]And Jesus stopped and said, "Call him." And they called the blind man, saying to him, "Take heart; rise, he is calling you." [50]And throwing off his cloak he sprang up and came to Jesus. [51]And Jesus said to him, "What do you want me to do for you?" And the blind man said to him, "Master, let me receive my sight." [52]And Jesus said to him, "Go your way; your faith has made you well." And immediately he received his sight and followed him on the way.

REFLECTION

When we're confronted with profound suffering, it's a mistake to hide behind pious platitudes. God doesn't need us to put on a happy face. It's okay to be honest with him, for that's where deep faith can really take hold. Psalm 60 reads almost like an argument with itself. The psalmist feels frustrated and abandoned by God: "You have made your people suffer hard things. . . . Have you not rejected us, O God?" (Ps 60:3, 10). Yet God remains the object of faith and hope (see vv. 4–8, 11–12). This is an important example, for if we follow the way of our Master, we should expect to share in his experience of rejection and suffering (see Mk 10:32–34). In Numbers 20:12, we hear the sad news that Moses and Aaron will not enter the Promised Land. Why? "Because you did not believe in me, to sanctify me in the eyes of the sons of Israel." It's difficult to pin down exactly where Moses and Aaron went wrong, but the key seems to be found in Numbers 20:10. Exasperated with the complaints of the Israelite "rebels," Moses asks, "Shall *we* bring forth water for you out of this rock?" (emphasis added). In Moses's frustration, his self-denying focus on God falters. What problems or hurts do you need to entrust to God today?

March 9

NUMBERS 20

[14]Moses sent messengers from Ka′desh to the king of E′dom, "Thus says your brother Israel: You know all the adversity that has befallen us: [15]how our fathers went down to Egypt, and we dwelt in Egypt a long time; and the Egyptians dealt harshly with us and our fathers; [16]and when we cried to the LORD, he heard our voice, and sent an angel and brought us forth out of Egypt; and here we are in Ka′desh, a city on the edge of your territory. [17]Now let us pass through your land. We will not pass through field or vineyard, neither will we drink water from a well; we will go along the King's Highway, we will not turn aside to the right hand or to the left, until we have passed through your territory." [18]But E′dom said to him, "You shall not pass through, lest I come out with the sword against you." [19]And the sons of Israel said to him, "We will go up by the

highway; and if we drink of your water, I and
my cattle, then I will pay for it; let me only
pass through on foot, nothing more." 20But
he said, "You shall not pass through." And
E´dom came out against them with many
men, and with a strong force. 21Thus E´dom
refused to give Israel passage through his
territory; so Israel turned away from him.

22And they journeyed from Ka´desh, and
the sons of Israel, the whole congregation,
came to Mount Hor. 23And the LORD said
to Moses and Aaron at Mount Hor, on the
border of the land of E´dom, 24"Aaron shall
be gathered to his people; for he shall not
enter the land which I have given to the
sons of Israel, because you rebelled against
my command at the waters of Mer´ibah.
25Take Aaron and Elea´zar his son, and
bring them up to Mount Hor; 26and strip
Aaron of his garments, and put them
upon Elea´zar his son; and Aaron shall be
gathered to his people, and shall die there."
27Moses did as the LORD commanded; and
they went up Mount Hor in the sight of
the congregation. 28And Moses stripped
Aaron of his garments, and put them upon
Elea´zar his son; and Aaron died there on
the top of the mountain. Then Moses and
Eleazar came down from the mountain.
29And when all the congregation saw that
Aaron was dead, all the house of Israel
wept for Aaron thirty days.

21 When the Canaanite, the king of
Ar´ad, who dwelt in the Neg´eb,
heard that Israel was coming by the way of
Ath´arim, he fought against Israel, and took
some of them captive. 2And Israel vowed
a vow to the LORD, and said, "If you will
indeed give this people into my hand, then
I will utterly destroy their cities." 3And the
LORD listened to the voice of Israel, and
gave over the Canaanites; and they utterly
destroyed them and their cities; so the name
of the place was called Hormah.

4From Mount Hor they set out by the way
to the Red Sea, to go around the land of
E´dom; and the people became impatient
on the way. 5And the people spoke against
God and against Moses, "Why have you
brought us up out of Egypt to die in the
wilderness? For there is no food and no
water, and we loathe this worthless food."
6Then the LORD sent fiery serpents among
the people, and they bit the people, so that
many sons of Israel died. 7And the people
came to Moses, and said, "We have sinned,
for we have spoken against the LORD and
against you; pray to the LORD, that he
take away the serpents from us." So Moses
prayed for the people. 8And the LORD said
to Moses, "Make a fiery serpent, and set it
up as a sign; and every one who is bitten,
when he sees it, shall live." 9So Moses made
a bronze serpent, and set it up as a sign;
and if a serpent bit any man, he would look
at the bronze serpent and live.

10And the sons of Israel set out, and
encamped in O´both. 11And they set
out from O´both, and encamped at
I´ye-ab´arim, in the wilderness which
is opposite Moab, toward the sunrise.
12From there they set out, and encamped
in the Valley of Ze´red. 13From there they
set out, and encamped on the other side
of the Arnon, which is in the wilderness
that extends from the boundary of the
Am´orites; for the Arnon is the boundary
of Moab, between Moab and the Amorites.
14Wherefore it is said in the Book of the
Wars of the LORD,

"Wa´heb in Su´phah,
and the valleys of the Arnon,
15and the slope of the valleys
that extends to the seat of Ar,
and leans to the border of Moab."

16And from there they continued to Be´er;
that is the well of which the LORD said to
Moses, "Gather the people together, and I
will give them water." 17Then Israel sang this
song:

"Spring up, O well!—Sing to it!—
18the well which the princes dug,
which the nobles of the people delved,
with the scepter and with their staves."

And from the wilderness they went on
to Mat´tanah, 19and from Mat´tanah to
Nahal´iel, and from Nahaliel to Ba´moth,
20and from Ba´moth to the valley lying in
the region of Moab by the top of Pisgah
which looks down upon the desert.

21Then Israel sent messengers to Si′hon king of the Am′orites, saying, 22"Let me pass through your land; we will not turn aside into field or vineyard; we will not drink the water of a well; we will go by the King's Highway, until we have passed through your territory." 23But Si′hon would not allow Israel to pass through his territory. He gathered all his men together, and went out against Israel to the wilderness, and came to Ja′haz, and fought against Israel. 24And Israel slew him with the edge of the sword, and took possession of his land from the Arnon to the Jabbok, as far as to the Am′monites; for Ja′zer was the boundary of the Ammonites. 25And Israel took all these cities, and Israel settled in all the cities of the Am′orites, in Heshbon, and in all its villages. 26For Heshbon was the city of Si′hon the king of the Am′orites, who had fought against the former king of Moab and taken all his land out of his hand, as far as the Arnon. 27Therefore the ballad singers say,

"Come to Heshbon, let it be built,
  let the city of Si′hon be established.
28For fire went forth from Heshbon,
  flame from the city of Si′hon.
It devoured Ar of Moab,
  the lords of the heights of the Arnon.
29Woe to you, O Moab!
  You are undone, O people of Che′mosh!
He has made his sons fugitives, and
  his daughters captives, to an Am′orite
  king, Si′hon.
30So their posterity perished from Heshbon,
  as far as Di′bon,
and we laid waste until fire spread to
  Med′eba."

31Thus Israel dwelt in the land of the Am′orites. 32And Moses sent to spy out Ja′zer; and they took its villages, and dispossessed the Am′orites that were there. 33Then they turned and went up by the way to Bashan; and Og the king of Bashan came out against them, he and all his people, to battle at Ed′re-i. 34But the LORD said to Moses, "Do not fear him; for I have given him into your hand, and all his people, and his land; and you shall do to him as you did to Si′hon king of the Am′orites, who dwelt at Heshbon." 35So they slew him, and his sons, and all his people, until there was not one survivor left to him; and they possessed his land.

22 Then the sons of Israel set out, and encamped in the plains of Moab beyond the Jordan at Jericho. 2And Balak the son of Zippor saw all that Israel had done to the Am′orites. 3And Moab was in great dread of the people, because they were many; Moab was overcome with fear of the sons of Israel. 4And Moab said to the elders of Mid′ian, "This horde will now lick up all that is round about us, as the ox licks up the grass of the field." So Balak the son of Zippor, who was king of Moab at that time, 5sent messengers to Balaam the son of Beor at Pe′thor, which is near the River, in the land of Am′aw to call him, saying, "Behold, a people has come out of Egypt; they cover the face of the earth, and they are dwelling opposite me. 6Come now, curse this people for me, since they are too mighty for me; perhaps I shall be able to defeat them and drive them from the land; for I know that he whom you bless is blessed, and he whom you curse is cursed."

7So the elders of Moab and the elders of Mid′ian departed with the fees for divination in their hand; and they came to Balaam, and gave him Balak's message. 8And he said to them, "Lodge here this night, and I will bring back word to you, as the LORD speaks to me"; so the princes of Moab stayed with Balaam. 9And God came to Balaam and said, "Who are these men with you?" 10And Balaam said to God, "Balak the son of Zippor, king of Moab, has sent to me, saying, 11'Behold, a people has come out of Egypt, and it covers the face of the earth; now come, curse them for me; perhaps I shall be able to fight against them and drive them out.'" 12God said to Balaam, "You shall not go with them; you shall not curse the people, for they are blessed." 13So Balaam rose in the morning, and said to the princes of Balak, "Go to your own land; for the LORD has refused to let me go with you." 14So the princes of Moab rose and went to Balak, and said, "Balaam refuses to come with us."

15Once again Balak sent princes, more in
number and more honorable than they. 16And
they came to Balaam and said to him, "Thus
says Balak the son of Zippor: 'Let nothing
hinder you from coming to me; 17for I will
surely do you great honor, and whatever you
say to me I will do; come, curse this people for
me.'" 18But Balaam answered and said to the
servants of Balak, "Though Balak were to give
me his house full of silver and gold, I could not
go beyond the command of the LORD my God,
to do less or more. 19Please, now, tarry here
this night also, that I may know what more
the LORD will say to me." 20And God came to
Balaam at night and said to him, "If the men
have come to call you, rise, go with them; but
only what I bid you, that shall you do."

To the choirmaster: with stringed instruments.
A Psalm of David.

PSALM 61 [60]

Hear my cry, O God,
listen to my prayer;
2from the end of the earth I call to you,
when my heart is faint.

Lead me
to the rock that is higher than I;
3for you are my refuge,
a strong tower against the enemy.

4Let me dwell in your tent for ever!
Oh, to be safe under the shelter of
your wings! *Selah*
5For you, O God, have heard my vows,
you have given me the heritage of those
who fear your name.

6Prolong the life of the king;
may his years endure to all generations!
7May he be enthroned for ever before God;
bid steadfast love and faithfulness watch
over him!
8So will I ever sing praises to your name,
as I pay my vows day after day.

MARK 11

**And when they drew near to
Jerusalem, to Beth′phage and
Beth′any, at the Mount of Olives,
he sent two of his disciples, 2and said
to them, "Go into the village opposite
you, and immediately as you enter it**
you will find a colt tied, on which no one
has ever sat; untie it and bring it. 3If any one
says to you, 'Why are you doing this?' say,
'The Lord has need of it and will send it back
here immediately.'" 4And they went away,
and found a colt tied at the door out in the
open street; and they untied it. 5And those
who stood there said to them, "What are
you doing, untying the colt?" 6And they told
them what Jesus had said; and they let them
go. 7And they brought the colt to Jesus, and
threw their garments on it; and he sat upon
it. 8And many spread their garments on the
road, and others spread leafy branches which
they had cut from the fields. 9And those who
went before and those who followed cried
out, "Hosanna! Blessed is he who comes
in the name of the Lord! 10Blessed is the
kingdom of our father David that is coming!
Hosanna in the highest!"

11And he entered Jerusalem, and went into
the temple; and when he had looked round
at everything, as it was already late, he went
out to Beth′any with the Twelve.

12On the following day, when they came
from Beth′any, he was hungry. 13And seeing
in the distance a fig tree in leaf, he went to
see if he could find anything on it. When he
came to it, he found nothing but leaves, for
it was not the season for figs. 14And he said
to it, "May no one ever eat fruit from you
again." And his disciples heard it.

15And they came to Jerusalem. And he
entered the temple and began to drive out
those who sold and those who bought in the
temple, and he overturned the tables of the
money-changers and the seats of those who
sold pigeons; 16and he would not allow any one
to carry anything through the temple. 17And
he taught, and said to them, "Is it not written,
'My house shall be called a house of prayer for

all the nations'? But you have made it a den of
robbers." 18And the chief priests and the scribes
heard it and sought a way to destroy him; for
they feared him, because all the multitude was
astonished at his teaching. 19And when evening
came they went out of the city.

REFLECTION

Psalm 61 beautifully encapsulates Israel's faith, centered on the great gifts of the Temple and the Davidic king. The "rock" (Ps 61:2) and the Lord's "tent" (v. 4) evoke the Temple, the place of praise, sacrifice, and communion with God. The king, when he responds to God's "steadfast love and faithfulness" (v. 7), makes God's reign concrete. Israelites can pray to God "from the end of the earth," when their "heart is faint" (v. 2), and they will find him a "refuge" and "a strong tower" (v. 3). Unfortunately, the king and the Temple's leadership did not always faithfully mediate God's mercy. Jesus comes to fulfill both Kingdom and Temple. He condemns abuses of the Temple just after entering Jerusalem as the returning Davidic king. But for this restoration to be definitive, Jesus needs to deal with the root of the Temple and kingdom's corruption. That is, he will be rejected and die for our sin. Israel's sin is handled in a surprising way in Numbers 21:5–9, but Jesus himself compares his Crucifixion to this event (see Jn 3:14–15). On the Cross, Jesus takes on the likeness of our sin, like the serpent, and thus deals with it once and for all, healing our relationship with God. How often do you thank him for this?

March 10

NUMBERS 22

21So Balaam rose in the morn-
ing, and saddled his donkey, and
went with the princes of Moab. 22But
God's anger was kindled because he
went; and the angel of the LORD took
his stand in the way as his adversary. Now
he was riding on the donkey, and his two
servants were with him. 23And the donkey
saw the angel of the LORD standing in the
road, with a drawn sword in his hand; and
the donkey turned aside out of the road,
and went into the field; and Balaam struck
the donkey, to turn her into the road.
24Then the angel of the LORD stood in a
narrow path between the vineyards, with a
wall on either side. 25And when the donkey saw the angel of the LORD, she pushed
against the wall, and pressed Balaam's foot
against the wall; so he struck her again.
26Then the angel of the LORD went ahead,
and stood in a narrow place, where there
was no way to turn either to the right or to
the left. 27When the donkey saw the angel
of the LORD, she lay down under Balaam;
and Balaam's anger was kindled, and he
struck the donkey with his staff. 28Then
the LORD opened the mouth of the donkey,
and she said to Balaam, "What have I done
to you, that you have struck me these three
times?" 29And Balaam said to the donkey,
"Because you have made sport of me. I
wish I had a sword in my hand, for then
I would kill you." 30And the donkey said
to Balaam, "Am I not your donkey, upon
which you have ridden all your life long to
this day? Was I ever accustomed to do so to
you?" And he said, "No."
31Then the LORD opened the eyes of
Balaam, and he saw the angel of the LORD
standing in the way, with his drawn sword
in his hand; and he bowed his head, and fell
on his face. 32And the angel of the LORD said
to him, "Why have you struck your donkey
these three times? Behold, I have come
forth to withstand you, because your way is
perverse before me; 33and the donkey saw
me, and turned aside before me these three
times. If she had not turned aside from me,
surely just now I would have slain you and let
her live." 34Then Balaam said to the angel of
the LORD, "I have sinned, for I did not know
that you stood in the road against me. Now
therefore, if it is evil in your sight, I will go
back again." 35And the angel of the LORD said
to Balaam, "Go with the men; but only the

word which I bid you, that shall you speak."
So Balaam went on with the princes of Balak.
36When Balak heard that Balaam had come,
he went out to meet him at the city of Moab,
on the boundary formed by the Arnon, at the
extremity of the boundary. 37And Balak said
to Balaam, "Did I not send to you to call you?
Why did you not come to me? Am I not able to
honor you?" 38Balaam said to Balak, "Behold, I
have come to you! Have I now any power at all
to speak anything? The word that God puts in
my mouth, that must I speak." 39Then Balaam
went with Balak, and they came to Kir′iath-
hu′zoth. 40And Balak sacrificed oxen and
sheep, and sent to Balaam and to the princes
who were with him.
41And the next day Balak took Balaam and
brought him up to Ba′moth-ba′al; and from
there he saw the nearest of the people.

23

1And Balaam said to Balak, "Build
for me here seven altars, and provide for me
here seven bulls and seven rams." 2Balak did
as Balaam had said; and Balak and Balaam
offered on each altar a bull and a ram. 3And
Balaam said to Balak, "Stand beside your burnt
offering, and I will go; perhaps the LORD will
come to meet me; and whatever he shows me
I will tell you." And he went to a bare height.
4And God met Balaam; and Balaam said to
him, "I have prepared the seven altars, and I
have offered upon each altar a bull and a ram."
5And the LORD put a word in Balaam's mouth,
and said, "Return to Balak, and thus you shall
speak." 6And he returned to him, and behold,
he and all the princes of Moab were standing
beside his burnt offering. 7And Balaam took
up his discourse, and said,

"From Ar′am Balak has brought me,
the king of Moab from the eastern
mountains:
'Come, curse Jacob for me,
and come, denounce Israel!'
8How can I curse whom God has not cursed?
How can I denounce whom the LORD
has not denounced?
9For from the top of the mountains I see him,
from the hills I behold him;
behold, a people dwelling alone,
and not reckoning itself among
the nations!
10Who can count the dust of Jacob,
or number the fourth part of Israel?
Let me die the death of the righteous,
and let my end be like his!"

11And Balak said to Balaam, "What have
you done to me? I took you to curse my
enemies, and behold, you have done nothing
but bless them." 12And he answered, "Must I
not take heed to speak what the LORD puts
in my mouth?"
13And Balak said to him, "Come with me to
another place, from which you may see them;
you shall see only the nearest of them, and
shall not see them all; then curse them for me
from there." 14And he took him to the field of
Zophim, to the top of Pisgah, and built seven
altars, and offered a bull and a ram on each
altar. 15Balaam said to Balak, "Stand here
beside your burnt offering, while I meet the
LORD yonder." 16And the LORD met Balaam,
and put a word in his mouth, and said,
"Return to Balak, and thus shall you speak."
17And he came to him, and, behold, he was
standing beside his burnt offering, and the
princes of Moab with him. And Balak said
to him, "What has the LORD spoken?" 18And
Balaam took up his discourse, and said,

"Rise, Balak, and hear;
hearken to me, O son of Zippor:
19God is not man, that he should lie,
or a son of man, that he should repent.
Has he said, and will he not do it?
Or has he spoken, and will he not fulfil it?
20Behold, I received a command to bless:
he has blessed, and I cannot revoke it.
21He has not beheld misfortune in Jacob;
nor has he seen trouble in Israel.
The LORD their God is with them,
and the shout of a king is among them.
22God brings them out of Egypt;
they have as it were the horns of the
wild ox.
23For there is no enchantment against Jacob,
no divination against Israel;
now it shall be said of Jacob and Israel,
'What has God wrought!'
24Behold, a people! As a lioness it rises up
and as a lion it lifts itself;
it does not lie down till it devours the prey,
and drinks the blood of the slain."

25 And Balak said to Balaam, "Neither
curse them at all, nor bless them at all." 26 But
Balaam answered Balak, "Did I not tell you,
'All that the LORD says, that I must do'?"
27 And Balak said to Balaam, "Come now,
I will take you to another place; perhaps it
will please God that you may curse them
for me from there." 28 So Balak took Balaam
to the top of Peor, that overlooks the desert.
29 And Balaam said to Balak, "Build for me
here seven altars, and provide for me here
seven bulls and seven rams." 30 And Balak
did as Balaam had said, and offered a bull
and a ram on each altar.

24 When Balaam saw that it pleased the
LORD to bless Israel, he did not go,
as at other times, to look for omens, but set
his face toward the wilderness. 2 And Balaam
lifted up his eyes, and saw Israel encamping
tribe by tribe. And the Spirit of God came
upon him, 3 and he took up his discourse,
and said,

"The oracle of Balaam the son of Beor,
the oracle of the man whose
eye is opened,
4 the oracle of him who hears the words
of God,
who sees the vision of the Almighty,
falling down, but having his
eyes uncovered:
5 How fair are your tents, O Jacob,
your encampments, O Israel!
6 Like valleys that stretch afar,
like gardens beside a river,
like aloes that the LORD has planted,
like cedar trees beside the waters.
7 Water shall flow from his buckets,
and his seed shall be in many waters,
his king shall be higher than Agag,
and his kingdom shall be exalted.
8 God brings him out of Egypt;
he has as it were the horns of the wild ox,
he shall eat up the nations his adversaries,
and shall break their bones in pieces,
and pierce them through with
his arrows.
9 He lurked, he lay down like a lion,
and like a lioness; who will rouse him up?
Blessed be every one who blesses you,
and cursed be every one who curses you."

10 And Balak's anger was kindled against
Balaam, and he struck his hands together;
and Balak said to Balaam, "I called you to
curse my enemies, and behold, you have
blessed them these three times. 11 Therefore
now flee to your place; I said, 'I will certainly
honor you,' but the LORD has held you back
from honor." 12 And Balaam said to Balak,
"Did I not tell your messengers whom you
sent to me, 13 'If Balak should give me his
house full of silver and gold, I would not be
able to go beyond the word of the LORD, to
do either good or bad of my own will; what
the LORD speaks, that will I speak'? 14 And
now, behold, I am going to my people; come,
I will let you know what this people will do
to your people in the latter days." 15 And he
took up his discourse, and said,

"The oracle of Balaam the son of Beor,
the oracle of the man whose eye
is opened,
16 the oracle of him who hears the
words of God,
and knows the knowledge of the
Most High,
who sees the vision of the Almighty,
falling down, but having his eyes uncovered:
17 I see him, but not now;
I behold him, but not near:
a star shall come forth out of Jacob,
and a scepter shall rise out of Israel;
it shall crush the forehead of Moab,
and break down all the sons of Sheth.
18 E´dom shall be dispossessed,
Se´ir also, his enemies, shall
be dispossessed,
while Israel does valiantly.
19 By Jacob shall dominion be exercised,
and the survivors of cities be destroyed!"

20 Then he looked on Am´alek, and took up
his discourse, and said,

"Amalek was the first of the nations,
but in the end he shall come to destruction."

21 And he looked on the Kenite, and took
up his discourse, and said,

"Enduring is your dwelling place,
and your nest is set in the rock;
22 nevertheless Kain shall be wasted.
How long shall Asshur take you
away captive?"

23And he took up his discourse, and said,
"Alas, who shall live when God does this?
24 But ships shall come from Kittim
and shall afflict Asshur and E'ber;
and he also shall come to destruction."
25Then Balaam rose, and went back to his
place; and Balak also went his way.

To the choirmaster: according to Jeduthun.
A Psalm of David.

PSALM 62 [61]

For God alone my soul waits in silence;
from him comes my salvation.
2He only is my rock and my salvation,
my fortress; I shall not be greatly moved.

3How long will you set upon a man
to shatter him, all of you,
like a leaning wall, a tottering fence?
4They only plan to thrust him down from
his eminence.
They take pleasure in falsehood.
They bless with their mouths,
but inwardly they curse. *Selah*

5For God alone my soul waits in silence,
for my hope is from him.
6He only is my rock and my salvation,
my fortress; I shall not be shaken.
7On God rests my deliverance and my honor;
my mighty rock, my refuge is God.

8Trust in him at all times, O people;
pour out your heart before him;
God is a refuge for us. *Selah*

9Men of low estate are but a breath,
men of high estate are a delusion;
in the balances they go up;
they are together lighter than a breath.
10Put no confidence in extortion,
set no vain hopes on robbery;
if riches increase, set not your heart
on them.

11Once God has spoken;
twice have I heard this:
that power belongs to God;
12 and that to you, O Lord, belongs
steadfast love.
For you repay a man
according to his work.

MARK 11

20As they passed by in the morn-
ing, they saw the fig tree with-
ered away to its roots. 21And Peter
remembered and said to him, "Master,
look! The fig tree which you cursed has
withered." 22And Jesus answered them,
"Have faith in God. 23Truly, I say to you,
whoever says to this mountain, 'Be taken up
and cast into the sea,' and does not doubt
in his heart, but believes that what he says
will come to pass, it will be done for him.
24Therefore I tell you, whatever you ask in
prayer, believe that you receive it, and you
will. 25And whenever you stand praying,
forgive, if you have anything against any
one; so that your Father also who is in heav-
en may forgive you your trespasses."
27And they came again to Jerusalem. And as
he was walking in the temple, the chief priests
and the scribes and the elders came to him,
28and they said to him, "By what authority are
you doing these things, or who gave you this
authority to do them?" 29Jesus said to them, "I
will ask you a question; answer me, and I will
tell you by what authority I do these things.
30Was the baptism of John from heaven or from
men? Answer me." 31And they argued with one
another, "If we say, 'From heaven,' he will say,
'Why then did you not believe him?' 32But
shall we say, 'From men'?"—they were afraid
of the people, for all held that John was a real
prophet. 33So they answered Jesus, "We do not
know." And Jesus said to them, "Neither will I
tell you by what authority I do these things."

REFLECTION

The story of Balaam is lengthy and complicated. Sometimes it's humorous. Balaam's talking donkey comes to mind, along with Balaam's apparent lack of surprise as he engages the donkey in conversation! So does Balak's increasing frustration with Balaam, who repeatedly blesses Israel instead of cursing them. Sometimes it's puzzling. Balaam's own motivations, as we'll see later in Numbers, may not always be what they seem. One thing that is crystal clear in this story is that God cannot be manipulated or his purposes thwarted. God has blessed Israel, and there's nothing Balak can do about that. We should keep this in mind when considering Jesus's teaching on the power of prayer. This power is not about manipulation, bending God's will to our own. Rather, it depends on a faith (see Mk 11:22) that leads us to imitate our forgiving Father (see v. 25). That is, it bends *our* will to God's, something Jesus will soon definitively model for us. When we seek God's will rather than our own, we can depend on his strength (see Ps 62:2, 5–7, 11–12) rather than counting on self-promoting gossip (see vv. 3–4) or financial exploits (see vv. 9–10). What steps can you take today to seek God's will in prayer?

March 11

NUMBERS 25

While Israel dwelt in Shittim the people began to play the harlot with the daughters of Moab. 2 These invited the people to the sacrifices of their gods, and the people ate, and bowed down to their gods. 3 So Israel yoked himself to Ba′al of Peor. And the anger of the LORD was kindled against Israel; 4 and the LORD said to Moses, "Take all the chiefs of the people, and hang them in the sun before the LORD, that the fierce anger of the LORD may turn away from Israel." 5 And Moses said to the judges of Israel, "Every one of you slay his men who have yoked themselves to Ba′al of Peor."

6 And behold, one of the sons of Israel came and brought a Mid′ianite woman to his family, in the sight of Moses and in the sight of the whole congregation of the sons of Israel, while they were weeping at the door of the tent of meeting. 7 When Phin′ehas the son of Elea′zar, son of Aaron the priest, saw it, he rose and left the congregation, and took a spear in his hand 8 and went after the man of Israel into the inner room, and pierced both of them, the man of Israel and the woman, through her body. Thus the plague was stayed from the sons of Israel. 9 Nevertheless those that died by the plague were twenty-four thousand.

10 And the LORD said to Moses, 11 "Phin′ehas the son of Elea′zar, son of Aaron the priest, has turned back my wrath from the sons of Israel, in that he was jealous with my jealousy among them, so that I did not consume the sons of Israel in my jealousy. 12 Therefore say, 'Behold, I give to him my covenant of peace; 13 and it shall be to him, and to his descendants after him, the covenant of a perpetual priesthood, because he was jealous for his God, and made atonement for the sons of Israel.'"

14 The name of the slain man of Israel, who was slain with the Mid′ianite woman, was Zimri the son of Sa′lu, head of a fathers' house belonging to the Simeonites. 15 And the name of the Mid′ianite woman who was slain was Cozbi the daughter of Zur, who was the head of the people of a fathers' house in Mid′ian.

16 And the LORD said to Moses, 17 "Harass the Mid′ianites, and strike them; 18 for they have harassed you with their wiles, with which they beguiled you in the matter of Peor, and in the matter of Cozbi, the daughter of the prince of Mid′ian, their sister, who was slain on the day of the plague on account of Peor."

26 After the plague the LORD said to Moses and to Elea′zar the son of Aaron, the priest, 2 "Take a census of all the congregation of the sons of Israel, from twenty years old and upward, by their fathers' houses, all in Israel who are able to go forth to war." 3 And Moses and Elea′zar the priest spoke with them in the plains of Moab by the Jordan at Jericho, saying, 4“Take a census of the people, from twenty years old and upward,” as the LORD commanded Moses. The sons of Israel, who came forth out of the land of Egypt, were:

5Reuben, the first-born of Israel; the sons of Reuben: of Ha′noch, the family of the Ha′nochites; of Pallu, the family of the Pal′luites; 6of Hezron, the family of the Hez′ronites; of Carmi, the family of the Carmites. 7These are the families of the Reubenites; and their number was forty-three thousand seven hundred and thirty. 8And the sons of Pallu: Eli′ab. 9The sons of Eli′ab: Nem′u-el, Da′than, and Abi′ram. These are the Dathan and Abiram, chosen from the congregation, who contended against Moses and Aaron in the company of Ko′rah, when they contended against the LORD, 10and the earth opened its mouth and swallowed them up together with Ko′rah, when that company died, when the fire devoured two hundred and fifty men; and they became a warning. 11Notwithstanding, the sons of Ko′rah did not die.

12The sons of Simeon according to their families: of Nem′u-el, the family of the Nem′u-elites; of Ja′min, the family of the Ja′minites; of Ja′chin, the family of the Ja′chinites; 13of Ze′rah, the family of the Ze′rahites; of Sha′ul, the family of the Sha′ulites. 14These are the families of the Simeonites, twenty-two thousand two hundred.

15The sons of Gad according to their families: of Ze′phon, the family of the Ze′phonites; of Hag′gi, the family of the Haggites; of Shu′ni, the family of the Shu′nites; 16of Ozni, the family of the Oznites; of E′ri, the family of the E′rites; 17of Ar′od, the family of the Ar′odites; of Are′li, the family of the Are′lites. 18These are the families of the sons of Gad according to their number, forty thousand five hundred.

19The sons of Judah were Er and O′nan; and Er and Onan died in the land of Canaan. 20And the sons of Judah according to their families were: of She′lah, the family of the She′lanites; of Per′ez, the family of the Per′ezites; of Ze′rah, the family of the Ze′rahites. 21And the sons of Per′ez were: of Hezron, the family of the Hez′ronites; of Ha′mul, the family of the Ha′mulites. 22These are the families of Judah according to their number, seventy-six thousand five hundred.

23The sons of Is′sachar according to their families: of To′la, the family of the To′laites; of Pu′vah, the family of the Pu′nites; 24of Jash′ub, the family of the Jash′ubites; of Shimron, the family of the Shim′ronites. 25These are the families of Is′sachar according to their number, sixty-four thousand three hundred.

26The sons of Zeb′ulun, according to their families: of Se′red, the family of the Se′redites; of E′lon, the family of the E′lonites; of Jah′leel, the family of the Jah′leelites. 27These are the families of the Zeb′ulunites according to their number, sixty thousand five hundred.

28The sons of Joseph according to their families: Manas′seh and E′phraim. 29The sons of Manas′seh: of Ma′chir, the family of the Ma′chirites; and Machir was the father of Gilead; of Gilead, the family of the Gileadites. 30These are the sons of Gilead: of Iez′er, the family of the Iez′erites; of He′lek, the family of the He′lekites; 31and of As′riel, the family of the As′rielites; and of She′chem, the family of the She′chemites; 32and of Shemi′da, the family of the Shemi′daites; and of He′pher, the family of the He′pherites. 33Now Zeloph′ehad the son of He′pher had no sons, but daughters: and the names of the daughters of Zelophehad were Mahlah, Noah, Hoglah, Milcah, and Tirzah. 34These are the families of Manas′seh; and their number was fifty-two thousand seven hundred.

35These are the sons of E′phraim according to their families: of Shu′thelah, the family of the Shu″thela′hites; of Be′cher, the family of the Be′cherites; of Ta′han, the family of the Ta′hanites. 36And these are the sons of Shu′thelah: of E′ran, the family of the E′ranites. 37These are the families of the sons of E′phraim according to their number, thirty-two thousand five hundred. These are the sons of Joseph according to their families.

38The sons of Benjamin according to their families: of Be′la, the family of the Be′laites; of Ash′bel, the family of the Ash′belites; of Ahi′ram, the family of the Ahi′ramites;

39of Shephu′pham, the family of the Shephu′phamites; of Hu′pham, the family of the Hu′phamites. 40And the sons of Be′la were Ard and Na′aman: of Ard, the family of the Ardites; of Naaman, the family of the Na′amites. 41These are the sons of Benjamin according to their families; and their number was forty-five thousand six hundred.

42These are the sons of Dan according to their families: of Shu′ham, the family of the Shu′hamites. These are the families of Dan according to their families. 43All the families of the Shu′hamites, according to their number, were sixty-four thousand four hundred.

44The sons of Asher according to their families: of Imnah, the family of the Imnites; of Ishvi, the family of the Ishvites; of Beri′ah, the family of the Beri′ites. 45Of the sons of Beri′ah: of He′ber, the family of the He′berites; of Mal′chi-el, the family of the Mal′chi-elites. 46And the name of the daughter of Asher was Se′rah. 47These are the families of the sons of Asher according to their number, fifty-three thousand four hundred.

48The sons of Naph′tali according to their families: of Jah′zeel, the family of the Jah′zeelites; of Gu′ni, the family of the Gu′nites; 49of Je′zer, the family of the Je′zerites; of Shillem, the family of the Shil′lemites. 50These are the families of Naph′tali according to their families; and their number was forty-five thousand four hundred.

51This was the number of the sons of Israel, six hundred and one thousand seven hundred and thirty.

52The LORD said to Moses: 53"To these the land shall be divided for inheritance according to the number of names. 54To a large tribe you shall give a large inheritance, and to a small tribe you shall give a small inheritance; every tribe shall be given its inheritance according to its numbers. 55But the land shall be divided by lot; according to the names of the tribes of their fathers they shall inherit. 56Their inheritance shall be divided according to lot between the larger and the smaller."

57These are the Levites as numbered according to their families: of Gershon, the family of the Ger′shonites; of Ko′hath, the family of the Ko′hathites; of Merar′i, the family of the Merar′ites. 58These are the families of Levi: the family of the Libnites, the family of the He′bronites, the family of the Mahlites, the family of the Mu′shites, the family of the Ko′rahites. And Ko′hath was the father of Amram. 59The name of Amram's wife was Joch′ebed the daughter of Levi, who was born to Levi in Egypt; and she bore to Amram Aaron and Moses and Miriam their sister. 60And to Aaron were born Na′dab, Abi′hu, Elea′zar and Ith′amar. 61But Na′dab and Abi′hu died when they offered unholy fire before the LORD. 62And those numbered of them were twenty-three thousand, every male from a month old and upward; for they were not numbered among the sons of Israel, because there was no inheritance given to them among the sons of Israel.

63These were those numbered by Moses and Elea′zar the priest, who numbered the sons of Israel in the plains of Moab by the Jordan at Jericho. 64But among these there was not a man of those numbered by Moses and Aaron the priest, who had numbered the sons of Israel in the wilderness of Sinai. 65For the LORD had said of them, "They shall die in the wilderness." There was not left a man of them, except Caleb the son of Jephun′neh and Joshua the son of Nun.

27 Then drew near the daughters of Zeloph′ehad the son of He′pher, son of Gilead, son of Ma′chir, son of Manas′seh, from the families of Manasseh the son of Joseph. The names of his daughters were: Mahlah, Noah, Hoglah, Milcah, and Tirzah. 2And they stood before Moses, and before Elea′zar the priest, and before the leaders and all the congregation, at the door of the tent of meeting, saying, 3"Our father died in the wilderness; he was not among the company of those who gathered themselves together against the LORD in the company of Ko′rah, but died for his own sin; and he had no sons. 4Why should the name of our father be taken away from his family, because he had no son? Give to us a possession among our father's brethren."

5 Moses brought their case before the
Lord. 6 And the Lord said to Moses,
7 "The daughters of Zeloph′ehad are right;
you shall give them possession of an
inheritance among their father's brethren
and cause the inheritance of their father to
pass to them. 8 And you shall say to the sons
of Israel, 'If a man dies, and has no son,
then you shall cause his inheritance to pass
to his daughter. 9 And if he has no daughter,
then you shall give his inheritance to his
brothers. 10 And if he has no brothers, then
you shall give his inheritance to his father's
brothers. 11 And if his father has no brothers,
then you shall give his inheritance to his
kinsman that is next to him of his family,
and he shall possess it. And it shall be to
the sons of Israel a statute and ordinance,
as the Lord commanded Moses.'"

A Psalm of David, when he was in
the Wilderness of Judah.

PSALM 63 [62]

O God, you are my God, I seek you,
  my soul thirsts for you;
my flesh faints for you,
  as in a dry and weary land where no
    water is.
2 So I have looked upon you in the sanctuary,
  beholding your power and glory.
3 Because your merciful love is better than life,
  my lips will praise you.
4 So I will bless you as long as I live;
  I will lift up my hands and call on
    your name.

5 My soul is feasted as with marrow and fat,
  and my mouth praises you with joyful lips,
6 when I think of you upon my bed,
  and meditate on you in the watches of
    the night;
7 for you have been my help,
  and in the shadow of your wings I sing
    for joy.
8 My soul clings to you;
  your right hand upholds me.

9 But those who seek to destroy my life
  shall go down into the depths of
    the earth;
10 they shall be given over to the power of
    the sword,
  they shall be prey for jackals.
11 But the king shall rejoice in God;
  all who swear by him shall glory;
  for the mouths of liars will be stopped.

MARK 12

**And he began to speak to them in
parables. "A man planted a vineyard, and set a hedge around it,
and dug a pit for the wine press, and
built a tower, and leased it to tenants,
and went into another country. 2 When**
the time came, he sent a servant to the
tenants, to get from them some of the
fruit of the vineyard. 3 And they took him
and beat him, and sent him away empty-
handed. 4 Again he sent to them another
servant, and they wounded him in the
head, and treated him shamefully. 5 And
he sent another, and him they killed; and
so with many others, some they beat and
some they killed. 6 He had still one other,
a beloved son; finally he sent him to
them, saying, 'They will respect my son.'
7 But those tenants said to one another,
'This is the heir; come, let us kill him,
and the inheritance will be ours.' 8 And
they took him and killed him, and cast
him out of the vineyard. 9 What will the
owner of the vineyard do? He will come
and destroy the tenants, and give the
vineyard to others. 10 Have you not read
this Scripture:
  'The very stone which the builders
    rejected
  has become the cornerstone;
11 this was the Lord's doing,
  and it is marvelous in our eyes'?"
12 And they tried to arrest him, but feared
the multitude, for they perceived that he
had told the parable against them; so they
left him and went away.

13And they sent to him some of the
Pharisees and some of the Hero′dians, to
entrap him in his talk. 14And they came
and said to him, "Teacher, we know that
you are true, and care for no man; for you
do not regard the position of men, but
truly teach the way of God. Is it lawful to
pay taxes to Caesar, or not? 15Should we
pay them, or should we not?" But knowing
their hypocrisy, he said to them, "Why
put me to the test? Bring me a coin, and
let me look at it." 16And they brought one.
And he said to them, "Whose likeness
and inscription is this?" They said to him,
"Caesar's." 17Jesus said to them, "Render to
Caesar the things that are Caesar's, and to
God the things that are God's." And they
were amazed at him.

REFLECTION

The Book of Numbers began with a census of Israel. Now we read of a second one. Why? This is a new generation. The Israelites counted earlier have died, the sad consequence of their refusal to trust God to bring them into Canaan. We also learn that part of the reason for the census is in preparation for the division of the Promised Land that will take place in Joshua 14–19. The exodus is almost over, and the Promised Land is near. But there's a catch. Remember Balaam, who was hired to curse Israel but couldn't? It turns out he was behind the fornication and idolatry we read about in Numbers 25 (see Nm 31:16; Rev 2:14). Balaam couldn't curse Israel, but they could turn their backs on their own blessing through sin. In today's Gospel, the vineyard in Jesus's parable represents the people of Israel in the Promised Land, and the tenants represent certain leaders of the people. Their behavior reminds us that simply being in the earthly Promised Land doesn't solve the problem of sin. Our true home, the heavenly Promised Land, is found in restful communion with God, whose "merciful love is better than life" (Ps 63:3), whose presence quenches our thirst from "a dry and weary land" (v. 1). How deeply do you thirst for God?

March 12

NUMBERS 27

**12The LORD said to Moses,
"Go up into this mountain of
Ab′arim, and see the land which
I have given to the sons of Israel. 13And
when you have seen it, you also shall be
gathered to your people, as your brother**
Aaron was gathered, 14because you rebelled against my word in the wilderness
of Zin during the strife of the congregation,
to sanctify me at the waters before their
eyes." (These are the waters of Mer′ibah of
Ka′desh in the wilderness of Zin.) 15Moses
said to the LORD, 16"Let the LORD, the God
of the spirits of all flesh, appoint a man over
the congregation, 17who shall go out before
them and come in before them, who shall
lead them out and bring them in; that the
congregation of the LORD may not be as
sheep which have no shepherd." 18And the
LORD said to Moses, "Take Joshua the son
of Nun, a man in whom is the spirit, and lay
your hand upon him; 19cause him to stand
before Elea′zar the priest and all the congregation, and you shall commission him
in their sight. 20You shall invest him with
some of your authority, that all the congregation of the sons of Israel may obey. 21And
he shall stand before Elea′zar the priest,
who shall inquire for him by the judgment
of the U′rim before the LORD; at his word
they shall go out, and at his word they shall
come in, both he and all the sons of Israel
with him, the whole congregation." 22And
Moses did as the LORD commanded him; he
took Joshua and caused him to stand before
Elea′zar the priest and the whole congregation, 23and he laid his hands upon him, and
commissioned him as the LORD directed
through Moses.

28 The LORD said to Moses, 2"Command
the sons of Israel, and say to them, 'My
offering, my food for my offerings by fire, my
pleasing odor, you shall take heed to offer to

me in its due season.' 3And you shall say to
them, This is the offering by fire which you
shall offer to the LORD: two male lambs a
year old without blemish, day by day, as a
continual offering. 4The one lamb you shall
offer in the morning, and the other lamb
you shall offer in the evening; 5also a tenth
of an ephah of fine flour for a cereal offering, mixed with a fourth of a hin of beaten
oil. 6It is a continual burnt offering, which
was ordained at Mount Sinai for a pleasing
odor, an offering by fire to the LORD. 7Its
drink offering shall be a fourth of a hin for
each lamb; in the holy place you shall pour
out a drink offering of strong drink to the
LORD. 8The other lamb you shall offer in
the evening; like the cereal offering of the
morning, and like its drink offering, you
shall offer it as an offering by fire, a pleasing odor to the LORD.

9"On the sabbath day two male lambs a
year old without blemish, and two tenths of
an ephah of fine flour for a cereal offering,
mixed with oil, and its drink offering:
10this is the burnt offering of every sabbath,
besides the continual burnt offering and its
drink offering.

11"At the beginnings of your months you
shall offer a burnt offering to the LORD:
two young bulls, one ram, seven male
lambs a year old without blemish; 12also
three tenths of an ephah of fine flour
for a cereal offering, mixed with oil, for
each bull; and two tenths of fine flour for
a cereal offering, mixed with oil, for the
one ram; 13and a tenth of fine flour mixed
with oil as a cereal offering for every lamb;
for a burnt offering of pleasing odor, an
offering by fire to the LORD. 14Their drink
offerings shall be half a hin of wine for
a bull, a third of a hin for a ram, and
a fourth of a hin for a lamb; this is the
burnt offering of each month throughout
the months of the year. 15Also one male
goat for a sin offering to the LORD; it shall
be offered besides the continual burnt
offering and its drink offering.

16"On the fourteenth day of the first
month is the LORD's Passover. 17And on the
fifteenth day of this month is a feast; seven
days shall unleavened bread be eaten.
18On the first day there shall be a holy
convocation: you shall do no laborious
work, 19but offer an offering by fire, a burnt
offering to the LORD: two young bulls, one
ram, and seven male lambs a year old; see
that they are without blemish; 20also their
cereal offering of fine flour mixed with
oil; three tenths of an ephah shall you
offer for a bull, and two tenths for a ram;
21a tenth shall you offer for each of the
seven lambs; 22also one male goat for a sin
offering, to make atonement for you. 23You
shall offer these besides the burnt offering
of the morning, which is for a continual
burnt offering. 24In the same way you
shall offer daily, for seven days, the food
of an offering by fire, a pleasing odor to
the LORD; it shall be offered besides the
continual burnt offering and its drink
offering. 25And on the seventh day you
shall have a holy convocation; you shall do
no laborious work.

26"On the day of the first fruits, when
you offer a cereal offering of new grain
to the LORD at your feast of weeks, you
shall have a holy convocation; you shall
do no laborious work, 27but offer a burnt
offering, a pleasing odor to the LORD: two
young bulls, one ram, seven male lambs
a year old; 28also their cereal offering of
fine flour mixed with oil, three tenths of
an ephah for each bull, two tenths for one
ram, 29a tenth for each of the seven lambs;
30with one male goat, to make atonement
for you. 31Besides the continual burnt
offering and its cereal offering, you shall
offer them and their drink offering. See
that they are without blemish.

29 "On the first day of the seventh month
you shall have a holy convocation;
you shall do no laborious work. It is a day
for you to blow the trumpets, 2and you
shall offer a burnt offering, a pleasing
odor to the LORD: one young bull, one
ram, seven male lambs a year old without
blemish; 3also their cereal offering of fine
flour mixed with oil, three tenths of an
ephah for the bull, two tenths for the ram,
4and one tenth for each of the seven lambs;

[5]with one male goat for a sin offering, to
make atonement for you; [6]besides the
burnt offering of the new moon, and its
cereal offering, and the continual burnt
offering and its cereal offering, and their
drink offering, according to the ordinance
for them, a pleasing odor, an offering by
fire to the LORD.
[7]"On the tenth day of this seventh month
you shall have a holy convocation, and
afflict yourselves; you shall do no work,
[8]but you shall offer a burnt offering to the
LORD, a pleasing odor: one young bull, one
ram, seven male lambs a year old; they
shall be to you without blemish; [9]and their
cereal offering of fine flour mixed with oil,
three tenths of an ephah for the bull, two
tenths for the one ram, [10]a tenth for each
of the seven lambs: [11]also one male goat
for a sin offering, besides the sin offering
of atonement, and the continual burnt
offering and its cereal offering, and their
drink offerings.
[12]"On the fifteenth day of the seventh
month you shall have a holy convocation;
you shall do no laborious work, and you
shall keep a feast to the LORD seven days;
[13]and you shall offer a burnt offering, an
offering by fire, a pleasing odor to the
LORD, thirteen young bulls, two rams,
fourteen male lambs a year old; they shall be
without blemish; [14]and their cereal offering
of fine flour mixed with oil, three tenths
of an ephah for each of the thirteen bulls,
two tenths for each of the two rams, [15]and a
tenth for each of the fourteen lambs; [16]also
one male goat for a sin offering, besides the
continual burnt offering, its cereal offering
and its drink offering.
[17]"On the second day twelve young bulls,
two rams, fourteen male lambs a year old
without blemish, [18]with the cereal offering
and the drink offerings for the bulls, for
the rams, and for the lambs, by number,
according to the ordinance; [19]also one male
goat for a sin offering, besides the continual
burnt offering and its cereal offering, and
their drink offerings.
[20]"On the third day eleven bulls, two rams,
fourteen male lambs a year old without
blemish, [21]with the cereal offering and the
drink offerings for the bulls, for the rams,
and for the lambs, by number, according to
the ordinance; [22]also one male goat for a sin
offering, besides the continual burnt offering
and its cereal offering and its drink offering.
[23]"On the fourth day ten bulls, two rams,
fourteen male lambs a year old without
blemish, [24]with the cereal offering and the
drink offerings for the bulls, for the rams,
and for the lambs, by number, according
to the ordinance; [25]also one male goat for
a sin offering, besides the continual burnt
offering, its cereal offering and its drink
offering.
[26]"On the fifth day nine bulls, two rams,
fourteen male lambs a year old without
blemish, [27]with the cereal offering and the
drink offerings for the bulls, for the rams,
and for the lambs, by number, according
to the ordinance; [28]also one male goat for
a sin offering; besides the continual burnt
offering and its cereal offering and its
drink offering.
[29]"On the sixth day eight bulls, two rams,
fourteen male lambs a year old without
blemish, [30]with the cereal offering and the
drink offerings for the bulls, for the rams,
and for the lambs, by number, according to
the ordinance; [31]also one male goat for a sin
offering; besides the continual burnt offering,
its cereal offering, and its drink offerings.
[32]"On the seventh day seven bulls, two
rams, fourteen male lambs a year old
without blemish, [33]with the cereal offering
and the drink offerings for the bulls, for
the rams, and for the lambs, by number,
according to the ordinance; [34]also one male
goat for a sin offering; besides the continual
burnt offering, its cereal offering, and its
drink offering.
[35]"On the eighth day you shall have a
solemn assembly: you shall do no laborious work, [36]but you shall offer a burnt offering, an offering by fire, a pleasing odor
to the LORD: one bull, one ram, seven
male lambs a year old without blemish,
[37]and the cereal offering and the drink offerings for the bull, for the ram, and for
the lambs, by number, according to the

ordinance; [38]also one male goat for a sin
offering; besides the continual burnt offering and its cereal offering and its drink
offering.
[39]"These you shall offer to the LORD at
your appointed feasts, in addition to your
votive offerings and your freewill offerings,
for your burnt offerings, and for your cereal
offerings, and for your drink offerings, and
for your peace offerings."
[40]And Moses told the sons of Israel everything just as the LORD had commanded
Moses.

To the choirmaster.
A Psalm of David.

PSALM 64 [63]

Hear my voice, O God, in my complaint;
preserve my life from dread of the enemy,
[2]hide me from the secret plots of the wicked,
from the scheming of evildoers,
[3]who whet their tongues like swords,
who aim bitter words like arrows,
[4]shooting from ambush at the blameless,
shooting at him suddenly and
without fear.
[5]They hold fast to their evil purpose;
they talk of laying snares secretly,
thinking, "Who can see us?
[6] Who can search out our crimes?
We have thought out a cunningly
conceived plot."
For the inward mind and heart of a man
are deep!

[7]But God will shoot his arrow at them;
they will be wounded suddenly.
[8]Because of their tongue he will bring
them to ruin;
all who see them will wag their heads.
[9]Then all men will fear;
they will tell what God has wrought,
and ponder what he has done.

[10]Let the righteous rejoice in the LORD,
and take refuge in him!
Let all the upright in heart glory!

MARK 12

**[18]And Sad′ducees came to him,
who say that there is no resurrection; and they asked him
a question, saying, [19]"Teacher, Moses
wrote for us that if a man's brother dies
and leaves a wife, but leaves no child,**
the man must take the wife, and raise
up children for his brother. [20]There were
seven brothers; the first took a wife, and
when he died left no children; [21]and the
second took her, and died, leaving no
children; and the third likewise; [22]and
the seven left no children. Last of all the
woman also died. [23]In the resurrection
whose wife will she be? For the seven had
her as wife."
[24]Jesus said to them, "Is not this why
you are wrong, that you know neither the
Scriptures nor the power of God? [25]For
when they rise from the dead, they neither
marry nor are given in marriage, but are
like angels in heaven. [26]And as for the dead
being raised, have you not read in the book
of Moses, in the passage about the bush, how
God said to him, 'I am the God of Abraham,
and the God of Isaac, and the God of Jacob'?
[27]He is not God of the dead, but of the living;
you are quite wrong."
[28]And one of the scribes came up and
heard them disputing with one another,
and seeing that he answered them well,
asked him, "Which commandment is the
first of all?" [29]Jesus answered, "The first
is, 'Hear, O Israel: The Lord our God, the
Lord is one; [30]and you shall love the Lord
your God with all your heart, and with
all your soul, and with all your mind, and
with all your strength.' [31]The second is this,
'You shall love your neighbor as yourself.'
There is no other commandment greater
than these." [32]And the scribe said to him,
"You are right, Teacher; you have truly
said that he is one, and there is no other
but he; [33]and to love him with all the heart,
and with all the understanding, and with
all the strength, and to love one's neighbor
as oneself, is much more than all whole

burnt offerings and sacrifices." 34And when
Jesus saw that he answered wisely, he said
to him, "You are not far from the kingdom
of God." And after that no one dared to ask
him any question.
35And as Jesus taught in the temple, he
said, "How can the scribes say that the
Christ is the son of David? 36David himself,
inspired by the Holy Spirit, declared,

'The Lord said to my Lord,
Sit at my right hand,
till I put your enemies under your feet.'

37David himself calls him Lord; so how is he
his son?" And the great throng heard him
gladly.
38And in his teaching he said, "Beware of
the scribes, who like to go about in long
robes, and to have salutations in the market
places 39and the best seats in the synagogues
and the places of honor at feasts, 40who
devour widows' houses and for a pretense
make long prayers. They will receive the
greater condemnation."
41And he sat down opposite the treasury,
and watched the multitude putting money
into the treasury. Many rich people put in
large sums. 42And a poor widow came, and
put in two copper coins, which make a penny.
43And he called his disciples to him, and
said to them, "Truly, I say to you, this poor
widow has put in more than all those who
are contributing to the treasury. 44For they
all contributed out of their abundance; but
she out of her poverty has put in everything
she had, her whole living."

REFLECTION

The psalmist complains of those who "whet their tongues like swords, who aim bitter words like arrows" (Ps 64:3). Their verbal attack is an "ambush," a trap (v. 4). In the Gospel, Jesus faces a series of such traps. In yesterday's reading, Jesus responds to the "ambush" of the Pharisees and Herodians, who try to paint him as either an idolater or a threat to the Roman government. Today, Jesus answers the challenges of the Sadducees and a scribe. One by one, Jesus bests his attackers. Jesus's verbal victories strikingly match the promise of God's defeat of slanderers in Psalm 64:7–9. This shouldn't surprise us, for Jesus is the divine Son of God as well as the Messiah, the Son of David, which is why David himself calls the Christ "Lord" (Mk 12:37). Turning back to our reading from Numbers, we see Israel continuing preparations to settle in the Promised Land. Moses appoints Joshua to succeed him as leader, and the liturgical feasts that govern the rhythm of Israel's worship are described. But even good and important things like a strong leader or regular worship will only bear fruit if the final goal is remembered: love of God and neighbor (see Mk 12:29–33). Are all of your thoughts, words, and deeds directed to love of God and others? How can you grow in this love today?

March 13

NUMBERS 30

Moses said to the heads of the tribes of the sons of Israel, "This is what the Lord has commanded.
2When a man vows a vow to the Lord, or
swears an oath to bind himself by a pledge,
he shall not break his word; he shall do
according to all that proceeds out of his
mouth. 3Or when a woman vows a vow to
the Lord, and binds herself by a pledge,
while within her father's house, in her
youth, 4and her father hears of her vow
and of her pledge by which she has bound
herself, and says nothing to her; then
all her vows shall stand, and her every
pledge by which she has bound herself
shall stand. 5But if her father expresses
disapproval to her on the day that he
hears of it, no vow of hers, no pledge by
which she has bound herself, shall stand;
and the Lord will forgive her, because her
father opposed her. 6And if she is married

to a husband, while under her vows or any
thoughtless utterance of her lips by which
she has bound herself, 7and her husband
hears of it, and says nothing to her on
the day that he hears; then her vows shall
stand, and her pledges by which she has
bound herself shall stand. 8But if, on
the day that her husband comes to hear
of it, he expresses disapproval, then he
shall make void her vow which was on
her, and the thoughtless utterance of her
lips, by which she bound herself; and the
LORD will forgive her. 9But any vow of a
widow or of a divorced woman, anything
by which she has bound herself, shall
stand against her. 10And if she vowed in
her husband's house, or bound herself by
a pledge with an oath, 11and her husband
heard of it, and said nothing to her, and
did not oppose her; then all her vows
shall stand, and every pledge by which
she bound herself shall stand. 12But if her
husband makes them null and void on
the day that he hears them, then whatever
proceeds out of her lips concerning her
vows, or concerning her pledge of herself,
shall not stand: her husband has made
them void, and the LORD will forgive her.
13Any vow and any binding oath to afflict
herself, her husband may establish, or
her husband may make void. 14But if her
husband says nothing to her from day to
day, then he establishes all her vows, or
all her pledges, that are upon her; he has
established them, because he said nothing
to her on the day that he heard of them.
15But if he makes them null and void after
he has heard of them, then he shall bear
her iniquity."
16These are the statutes which the LORD
commanded Moses, as between a man
and his wife, and between a father and his
daughter, while in her youth, within her
father's house.

31 The LORD said to Moses, 2"Avenge
the sons of Israel on the Mid'ianites;
afterward you shall be gathered to your
people." 3And Moses said to the people,
"Arm men from among you for the war,
that they may go against Mid'ian, to
execute the LORD's vengeance on Midian.
4You shall send a thousand from each of
the tribes of Israel to the war." 5So there
were provided, out of the thousands of
Israel, a thousand from each tribe, twelve
thousand armed for war. 6And Moses
sent them to the war, a thousand from
each tribe, together with Phin'ehas the
son of Elea'zar the priest, with the vessels
of the sanctuary and the trumpets for the
alarm in his hand. 7They warred against
Mid'ian, as the LORD commanded Moses,
and slew every male. 8They slew the kings
of Mid'ian with the rest of their slain,
E'vi, Re'kem, Zur, Hur, and Reba, the
five kings of Midian; and they also slew
Balaam the son of Beor with the sword.
9And the sons of Israel took captive the
women of Mid'ian and their little ones;
and they took as booty all their cattle,
their flocks, and all their goods. 10All their
cities in the places where they dwelt, and
all their encampments, they burned with
fire, 11and took all the spoil and all the
booty, both of man and of beast. 12Then
they brought the captives and the booty
and the spoil to Moses, and to Elea'zar
the priest, and to the congregation of the
sons of Israel, at the camp on the plains of
Moab by the Jordan at Jericho.
13Moses, and Elea'zar the priest, and all
the leaders of the congregation, went forth
to meet them outside the camp. 14And
Moses was angry with the officers of the
army, the commanders of thousands and
the commanders of hundreds, who had
come from service in the war. 15Moses
said to them, "Have you let all the women
live? 16Behold, these caused the sons of
Israel, by the counsel of Balaam, to act
treacherously against the LORD in the
matter of Peor, and so the plague came
among the congregation of the LORD.
17Now therefore, kill every male among
the little ones, and kill every woman who
has known man by lying with him. 18But
all the young girls who have not known
man by lying with him, keep alive for
yourselves. 19Encamp outside the camp
seven days; whoever of you has killed any

person, and whoever has touched any slain, purify yourselves and your captives on the third day and on the seventh day. 20You shall purify every garment, every article of skin, all work of goats' hair, and every article of wood."

21And Elea'zar the priest said to the men of war who had gone to battle: "This is the statute of the law which the LORD has commanded Moses: 22only the gold, the silver, the bronze, the iron, the tin, and the lead, 23everything that can stand the fire, you shall pass through the fire, and it shall be clean. Nevertheless it shall also be purified with the water of impurity; and whatever cannot stand the fire, you shall pass through the water. 24You must wash your clothes on the seventh day, and you shall be clean; and afterward you shall come into the camp."

25The LORD said to Moses, 26"Take the count of the booty that was taken, both of man and of beast, you and Elea'zar the priest and the heads of the fathers' houses of the congregation; 27and divide the booty into two parts, between the warriors who went out to battle and all the congregation. 28And levy for the LORD a tribute from the men of war who went out to battle, one out of five hundred, of the persons and of the oxen and of the donkeys and of the flocks; 29take it from their half, and give it to Elea'zar the priest as an offering to the LORD. 30And from the sons of Israel's half you shall take one drawn out of every fifty, of the persons, of the oxen, of the donkeys, and of the flocks, of all the cattle, and give them to the Levites who have charge of the tabernacle of the LORD." 31And Moses and Elea'zar the priest did as the LORD commanded Moses.

32Now the booty remaining of the spoil that the men of war took was: six hundred and seventy-five thousand sheep, 33seventy-two thousand cattle, 34sixty-one thousand donkeys, 35and thirty-two thousand persons in all, women who had not known man by lying with him. 36And the half, the portion of those who had gone out to war, was in number three hundred and thirty-seven thousand five hundred sheep, 37and the LORD's tribute of sheep was six hundred and seventy-five. 38The cattle were thirty-six thousand, of which the LORD's tribute was seventy-two. 39The donkeys were thirty thousand five hundred, of which the LORD's tribute was sixty-one. 40The persons were sixteen thousand, of which the LORD's tribute was thirty-two persons. 41And Moses gave the tribute, which was the offering for the LORD, to Elea'zar the priest, as the LORD commanded Moses.

42From the sons of Israel's half, which Moses separated from that of the men who had gone to war—43now the congregation's half was three hundred and thirty-seven thousand five hundred sheep, 44thirty-six thousand cattle, 45and thirty thousand five hundred donkeys, 46and sixteen thousand persons—47from the sons of Israel's half Moses took one of every fifty, both of persons and of beasts, and gave them to the Levites who had charge of the tabernacle of the LORD; as the LORD commanded Moses.

48Then the officers who were over the thousands of the army, the captains of thousands and the captains of hundreds, came near to Moses, 49and said to Moses, "Your servants have counted the men of war who are under our command, and there is not a man missing from us. 50And we have brought the LORD's offering, what each man found, articles of gold, armlets and bracelets, signet rings, earrings, and beads, to make atonement for ourselves before the LORD." 51And Moses and Elea'zar the priest received from them the gold, all wrought articles. 52And all the gold of the offering that they offered to the LORD, from the commanders of thousands and the commanders of hundreds, was sixteen thousand seven hundred and fifty shekels. 53(The men of war had taken booty, every man for himself.) 54And Moses and Elea'zar the priest received the gold from the commanders of thousands and of hundreds, and brought it into the tent of meeting, as a memorial for the sons of Israel before the LORD.

To the choirmaster. A Psalm of David. A Song.

PSALM 65 [64]

Praise is due to you,
O God, in Zion;
and to you shall vows be performed
in Jerusalem,
2 O you who hear prayer!
To you shall all flesh come
3 on account of sins.
When our transgressions prevail over us,
you forgive them.
4 Blessed is he whom you choose and
bring near,
to dwell in your courts!
We shall be satisfied with the goodness of
your house,
your holy temple!

5 By dread deeds you answer us
with deliverance,
O God of our salvation,
who are the hope of all the ends of the earth,
and of the farthest seas;
6 who by your strength have established
the mountains,
being girded with might;
7 who still the roaring of the seas,
the roaring of their waves,
the tumult of the peoples;
8 so that those who dwell at earth's
farthest bounds
are afraid at your signs;
you make the outgoings of the morning
and the evening
to shout for joy.

9 You visit the earth and water it,
you greatly enrich it;
the river of God is full of water;
you provide their grain,
for so you have prepared it.
10 You water its furrows abundantly,
settling its ridges,
softening it with showers,
and blessing its growth.
11 You crown the year with your bounty;
the tracks of your chariot overflow
with richness.
12 The pastures of the wilderness drip,
the hills gird themselves with joy,
13 the meadows clothe themselves
with flocks,
the valleys deck themselves with grain,
they shout and sing together for joy.

MARK 13

And as he came out of the temple, one of his disciples said to him, "Look, Teacher, what wonderful stones and what wonderful buildings!"
2 And Jesus said to him, "Do you see these
great buildings? There will not be left here
one stone upon another, that will not be
thrown down."
3 And as he sat on the Mount of Olives
opposite the temple, Peter and James and
John and Andrew asked him privately,
4 "Tell us, when will this be, and what will
be the sign when these things are all to be
accomplished?" 5 And Jesus began to say
to them, "Take heed that no one leads you
astray. 6 Many will come in my name, saying,
'I am he!' and they will lead many astray.
7 And when you hear of wars and rumors
of wars, do not be alarmed; this must take
place, but the end is not yet. 8 For nation will
rise against nation, and kingdom against
kingdom; there will be earthquakes in
various places, there will be famines; this is
but the beginning of the sufferings.
9 "But take heed to yourselves; for they
will deliver you up to councils; and you
will be beaten in synagogues; and you
will stand before governors and kings for
my sake, to bear testimony before them.
10 And the gospel must first be preached to
all nations. 11 And when they bring you to
trial and deliver you up, do not be anxious
beforehand about what you are to say; but
say whatever is given you in that hour, for
it is not you who speak, but the Holy Spirit.
12 And brother will deliver up brother to
death, and the father his child, and children
will rise against parents and have them put
to death; 13 and you will be hated by all for

my name's sake. But he who endures to the
end will be saved.
[14]"But when you see the desolating sacrilege set up where it ought not to be (let the
reader understand), then let those who are
in Judea flee to the mountains; [15]let him who
is on the housetop not go down, nor enter
his house, to take anything away; [16]and let
him who is in the field not turn back to get a
coat. [17]And alas for those who are with child
and for those who are nursing in those days!
[18]Pray that it may not happen in winter. [19]For
in those days there will be such tribulation
as has not been from the beginning of the
creation which God created until now, and
never will be. [20]And if the Lord had not
shortened the days, no human being would
be saved; but for the sake of the elect, whom
he chose, he shortened the days. [21]And then
if any one says to you, 'Look, here is the
Christ!' or 'Look, there he is!' do not believe
it. [22]False Christs and false prophets will
arise and show signs and wonders, to lead
astray, if possible, the elect. [23]But take heed;
I have told you all things beforehand."

REFLECTION

Today's readings from Numbers and Mark are both difficult and even disturbing. Fortunately, Psalm 65 provides a helpful way of approaching them. The psalm begins with an emphasis on the Temple in Jerusalem (see Ps 65:1–4), transitions to God's saving power in all the earth (see vv. 5–8), and ends with his provision of creation (see vv. 9–13). The very last verse comes full circle, for when the meadows and valleys "shout and sing together for joy," they echo the "praise" that is due to God at the Temple (v. 1). In Hebrew thought, the Temple is a microcosm of all creation. Conversely, creation should ideally be one giant Temple filled with God's glory. This can help us understand why Jesus's speech in Mark 13, which is primarily about the Temple's impending destruction, is also about the end of the world. Theologically, the two events are intimately linked. Furthermore, the Temple is the heart of the Promised Land, which was meant to be a partial reclaiming of creation corrupted by sin. This might help us comprehend the war of vengeance against Midian (see Nm 31:1–3). Midian had been an occasion of sin for Israel, and sin compromises the very purpose of Israel's election. How committed are you to avoiding occasions of sin so that you can be more fully dedicated to God's praise?

March 14

NUMBERS 32

Now the sons of Reuben and the sons of Gad had a very great multitude of cattle; and they saw the land of Ja′zer and the land of Gilead, and behold, the place was a place for
cattle. [2]So the sons of Gad and the sons
of Reuben came and said to Moses and
to Elea′zar the priest and to the leaders of
the congregation, [3]"At′aroth, Di′bon, Ja′zer,
Nimrah, Heshbon, E′lea′leh, Sebam, Nebo,
and Beon, [4]the land which the LORD struck
before the congregation of Israel, is a land
for cattle; and your servants have cattle."
[5]And they said, "If we have found favor in
your sight, let this land be given to your
servants for a possession; do not take us
across the Jordan."
[6]But Moses said to the sons of Gad and to
the sons of Reuben, "Shall your brethren go
to the war while you sit here? [7]Why will you
discourage the heart of the sons of Israel from
going over into the land which the LORD has
given them? [8]Thus did your fathers, when I
sent them from Ka′desh-bar′nea to see the
land. [9]For when they went up to the Valley of
Eshcol, and saw the land, they discouraged the
heart of the sons of Israel from going into the
land which the LORD had given them. [10]And
the LORD's anger was kindled on that day,
and he swore, saying, [11]'Surely none of the

men who came up out of Egypt, from twenty
years old and upward, shall see the land which
I swore to give to Abraham, to Isaac, and to
Jacob, because they have not wholly followed
me; 12none except Caleb the son of Jephun′neh
the Ken′izzite and Joshua the son of Nun, for
they have wholly followed the LORD.' 13And the
LORD's anger was kindled against Israel, and
he made them wander in the wilderness forty
years, until all the generation that had done evil
in the sight of the LORD was consumed. 14And
behold, you have risen in your fathers' stead, a
brood of sinful men, to increase still more the
fierce anger of the LORD against Israel! 15For
if you turn away from following him, he will
again abandon them in the wilderness; and
you will destroy all this people."

16Then they came near to him, and said,
"We will build sheepfolds here for our flocks,
and cities for our little ones, 17but we will take
up arms, ready to go before the sons of Israel,
until we have brought them to their place; and
our little ones shall live in the fortified cities
because of the inhabitants of the land. 18We
will not return to our homes until the sons of
Israel have inherited each his inheritance. 19For
we will not inherit with them on the other
side of the Jordan and beyond; because our
inheritance has come to us on this side of the
Jordan to the east." 20So Moses said to them, "If
you will do this, if you will take up arms to go
before the LORD for the war, 21and every armed
man of you will pass over the Jordan before the
LORD, until he has driven out his enemies from
before him 22and the land is subdued before the
LORD; then after that you shall return and be
free of obligation to the LORD and to Israel; and
this land shall be your possession before the
LORD. 23But if you will not do so, behold, you
have sinned against the LORD; and be sure your
sin will find you out. 24Build cities for your little
ones, and folds for your sheep; and do what you
have promised." 25And the sons of Gad and the
sons of Reuben said to Moses, "Your servants
will do as my lord commands. 26Our little
ones, our wives, our flocks, and all our cattle,
shall remain there in the cities of Gilead; 27but
your servants will pass over, every man who is
armed for war, before the LORD to battle, as my
lord orders."

28So Moses gave command concerning them
to Elea′zar the priest, and to Joshua the son of
Nun, and to the heads of the fathers' houses
of the tribes of the sons of Israel. 29And Moses
said to them, "If the sons of Gad and the sons
of Reuben, every man who is armed to battle
before the LORD, will pass with you over the
Jordan and the land shall be subdued before
you, then you shall give them the land of Gilead
for a possession; 30but if they will not pass over
with you armed, they shall have possessions
among you in the land of Canaan." 31And the
sons of Gad and the sons of Reuben answered,
"As the LORD has said to your servants, so
we will do. 32We will pass over armed before
the LORD into the land of Canaan, and the
possession of our inheritance shall remain
with us beyond the Jordan."

33And Moses gave to them, to the sons of
Gad and to the sons of Reuben and to the half-
tribe of Manas′seh the son of Joseph, the kingdom of Si′hon king of the Am′orites and the
kingdom of Og king of Bashan, the land and
its cities with their territories, the cities of the
land throughout the country. 34And the sons
of Gad built Di′bon, At′aroth, Aro′er, 35At′roth-
sho′phan, Ja′zer, Jog′behah, 36Beth-nim′rah
and Beth-har′an, fortified cities, and folds for
sheep. 37And the sons of Reuben built Heshbon, E′lea′leh, Kir″iatha′im, 38Nebo, and Ba′al-
me′on (their names to be changed), and Sibmah; and they gave other names to the cities
which they built. 39And the sons of Ma′chir the
son of Manas′seh went to Gilead and took it,
and dispossessed the Am′orites who were in it.
40And Moses gave Gilead to Ma′chir the son of
Manas′seh, and he settled in it. 41And Ja′ir the
son of Manas′seh went and took their villages,
and called them Hav′voth-ja′ir. 42And No′bah
went and took Ke′nath and its villages, and
called it Nobah, after his own name.

33 These are the stages of the sons of
Israel, when they went forth out of
the land of Egypt by their hosts under the
leadership of Moses and Aaron. 2Moses wrote
down their starting places, stage by stage, by
command of the LORD; and these are their
stages according to their starting places. 3They
set out from Ram′eses in the first month, on
the fifteenth day of the first month; on the day

after the Passover the sons of Israel went out
triumphantly in the sight of all the Egyptians,
4while the Egyptians were burying all their
first-born, whom the LORD had struck down
among them; upon their gods also the LORD
executed judgments.

5So the sons of Israel set out from Ram´eses,
and encamped at Succoth. 6And they set out
from Succoth, and encamped at E´tham,
which is on the edge of the wilderness. 7And
they set out from E´tham, and turned back to
Pi-hahi´roth, which is east of Ba´al-ze´phon;
and they encamped before Migdol. 8And
they set out from before Hahi´roth, and
passed through the midst of the sea into the
wilderness, and they went a three days' journey
in the wilderness of E´tham, and encamped
at Marah. 9And they set out from Marah,
and came to E´lim; at Elim there were twelve
springs of water and seventy palm trees, and
they encamped there. 10And they set out from
E´lim, and encamped by the Red Sea. 11And
they set out from the Red Sea, and encamped
in the wilderness of Sin. 12And they set out
from the wilderness of Sin, and encamped at
Dophkah. 13And they set out from Dophkah,
and encamped at A´lush. 14And they set out
from A´lush, and encamped at Reph´idim,
where there was no water for the people to
drink. 15And they set out from Reph´idim, and
encamped in the wilderness of Sinai. 16And
they set out from the wilderness of Sinai, and
encamped at Kib´roth-hatta´avah. 17And
they set out from Kib´roth-hatta´avah, and
encamped at Haze´roth. 18And they set out
from Haze´roth, and encamped at Rithmah.
19And they set out from Rithmah, and
encamped at Rim´mon-per´ez. 20And they
set out from Rim´mon-per´ez, and encamped
at Libnah. 21And they set out from Libnah,
and encamped at Rissah. 22And they set out
from Rissah, and encamped at Kehela´thah.
23And they set out from Kehela´thah, and
encamped at Mount She´pher. 24And they set
out from Mount She´pher, and encamped at
Hara´dah. 25And they set out from Hara´dah,
and encamped at Makhe´loth. 26And they
set out from Makhe´loth, and encamped at
Ta´hath. 27And they set out from Ta´hath, and
encamped at Te´rah. 28And they set out from
Te´rah, and encamped at Mithkah. 29And
they set out from Mithkah, and encamped
at Hashmo´nah. 30And they set out from
Hashmo´nah, and encamped at Mose´roth.
31And they set out from Mose´roth, and
encamped at Be´ne-ja´akan. 32And they set
out from Be´ne-ja´akan, and encamped at
Hor-haggid´gad. 33And they set out from
Hor-haggid´gad, and encamped at Jot´bathah.
34And they set out from Jot´bathah, and
encamped at Abro´nah. 35And they set out
from Abro´nah, and encamped at E´zion-
ge´ber. 36And they set out from E´zion-ge´ber,
and encamped in the wilderness of Zin (that
is, Ka´desh). 37And they set out from Ka´desh,
and encamped at Mount Hor, on the edge of
the land of E´dom.

38And Aaron the priest went up Mount
Hor at the command of the LORD, and died
there, in the fortieth year after the sons of
Israel had come out of the land of Egypt, on
the first day of the fifth month. 39And Aaron
was a hundred and twenty-three years old
when he died on Mount Hor.

40And the Canaanite, the king of Ar´ad, who
dwelt in the Neg´eb in the land of Canaan,
heard of the coming of the sons of Israel.

41And they set out from Mount Hor, and
encamped at Zalmo´nah. 42And they set out
from Zalmo´nah, and encamped at Pu´non.
43And they set out from Pu´non, and encamped
at O´both. 44And they set out from O´both,
and encamped at I´ye-ab´arim, in the territory
of Moab. 45And they set out from I´yim, and
encamped at Di´bon-gad. 46And they set out
from Di´bon-gad, and encamped at Al´mon-
diblatha´im. 47And they set out from Al´mon-
diblatha´im, and encamped in the mountains
of Ab´arim, before Nebo. 48And they set
out from the mountains of Ab´arim, and
encamped in the plains of Moab by the Jordan
at Jericho; 49they encamped by the Jordan from
Beth-jesh´imoth as far as A´bel-shit´tim in the
plains of Moab.

50And the LORD said to Moses in the
plains of Moab by the Jordan at Jericho,
51"Say to the sons of Israel, When you pass
over the Jordan into the land of Canaan,
52then you shall drive out all the inhabitants
of the land from before you, and destroy all

their figured stones, and destroy all their
molten images, and demolish all their high
places; 53and you shall take possession of
the land and settle in it, for I have given
the land to you to possess it. 54You shall
inherit the land by lot according to your
families; to a large tribe you shall give a
large inheritance, and to a small tribe you
shall give a small inheritance; wherever
the lot falls to any man, that shall be his;
according to the tribes of your fathers you
shall inherit. 55But if you do not drive out
the inhabitants of the land from before you,
then those of them whom you let remain
shall be as pricks in your eyes and thorns
in your sides, and they shall trouble you in
the land where you dwell. 56And I will do to
you as I thought to do to them."

To the choirmaster. A Song. A Psalm.

PSALM 66 [65]

Make a joyful noise to God, all the earth;
2 sing the glory of his name;
give to him glorious praise!
3Say to God, "How awesome are your deeds!
So great is your power that your enemies
cringe before you.
4All the earth worships you;
they sing praises to you,
sing praises to your name." *Selah*

5Come and see what God has done:
he is awesome in his deeds among men.
6He turned the sea into dry land;
men passed through the river on foot.
There did we rejoice in him,
7 who rules by his might for ever,
whose eyes keep watch on the nations—
let not the rebellious exalt
themselves. *Selah*

8Bless our God, O peoples,
let the sound of his praise be heard,
9who has kept us among the living,
and has not let our feet slip.
10For you, O God, have tested us;
you have tried us as silver is tried.
11You brought us into the net;
you laid affliction on our backs;
12you let men ride over our heads;
we went through fire and through water;
yet you have brought us forth to a
spacious place.

13I will come into your house with
burnt offerings;
I will pay you my vows,
14that which my lips uttered
and my mouth promised when
I was in trouble.
15I will offer to you burnt offerings of fatlings,
with the smoke of the sacrifice of rams;
I will make an offering of bulls
and goats. *Selah*

16Come and hear, all you who fear God,
and I will tell what he has done for me.
17I cried aloud to him,
and he was extolled with my tongue.
18If I had cherished iniquity in my heart,
the Lord would not have listened.
19But truly God has listened;
he has given heed to the voice of
my prayer.

20Blessed be God,
because he has not rejected my prayer
or removed his merciful love from me!

MARK 13

**24"But in those days, after that
tribulation, the sun will be
darkened, and the moon will
not give its light, 25and the stars will be
falling from heaven, and the powers
in the heavens will be shaken.** 26And
then they will see the Son of man coming
in clouds with great power and glory. 27And
then he will send out the angels, and gather
his elect from the four winds, from the ends
of the earth to the ends of heaven.
28"From the fig tree learn its lesson: as soon
as its branch becomes tender and puts forth

its leaves, you know that summer is near. 29So also, when you see these things taking place, you know that he is near, at the very gates. 30Truly, I say to you, this generation will not pass away before all these things take place. 31Heaven and earth will pass away, but my words will not pass away.

32"But of that day or that hour no one knows, not even the angels in heaven, nor the Son, but only the Father. 33Take heed, watch and pray; for you do not know when the time will come. 34It is like a man going on a journey, when he leaves home and puts his servants in charge, each with his work, and commands the doorkeeper to be on the watch. 35Watch therefore—for you do not know when the master of the house will come, in the evening, or at midnight, or at cockcrow, or in the morning—36lest he come suddenly and find you asleep. 37And what I say to you I say to all: Watch."

REFLECTION

Yesterday we noted that to understand Jesus's words in Mark 13, we need to keep in mind both the destruction of the Temple in the year AD 70 and the Second Coming of Christ. There are actually two more layers of meaning to note. First, Jesus himself is the new Temple, so his Passion is a sort of preview of the Temple's destruction. Jesus takes that judgment, in a sense, on himself (consider Mk 15:37–38). As the Body of Christ, believers are also the "temple." So it's no surprise that Jesus speaks of the disciples' suffering, too (see 13:9–13). This is why it's so important for believers, as Jesus repeats over and over, to *watch*, to pay close attention to God's Word, and to be vigilant in prayer. When we are tested, we must persevere, for God remains faithful. Psalm 66 is a beautiful prayer of praise after a time of perseverance through testing. And even when we have moments of rest in this life, we should remain aware of our struggling brothers and sisters, a lesson we might draw from Numbers 32. The Israelites who settle east of the Jordan are still members of the whole people, and Israel's battle is their battle. How can you increase your attentiveness to God's Word throughout the day? How can you encourage those around you?

March 15

NUMBERS 34

The Lord said to Moses, 2"Command the sons of Israel, and say to them, When you enter the land of Canaan (this is the land that shall fall to you for an inheritance, the land of Canaan in its full extent), 3your south side shall be from the wilderness of Zin along the side of E′dom, and your southern boundary shall be from the end of the Salt Sea on the east; 4and your boundary shall turn south of the ascent of Akrab′bim, and cross to Zin, and its end shall be south of Ka′desh-bar′nea; then it shall go on to Ha′zar-ad′dar, and pass along to Azmon; 5and the boundary shall turn from Azmon to the Brook of Egypt, and its termination shall be at the sea.

6"For the western boundary, you shall have the Great Sea and its coast; this shall be your western boundary.

7"This shall be your northern boundary: from the Great Sea you shall mark out your line to Mount Hor; 8from Mount Hor you shall mark it out to the entrance of Ha′math, and the end of the boundary shall be at Ze′dad; 9then the boundary shall extend to Ziphron, and its end shall be at Ha′zar-e′nan; this shall be your northern boundary.

10"You shall mark out your eastern boundary from Ha′zar-e′nan to She′pham; 11and the boundary shall go down from She′pham to Riblah on the east side of A′in; and the boundary shall go down, and reach to the shoulder of the sea of Chin′nereth on the east; 12and the boundary shall go down to the Jordan, and its end shall be at the Salt Sea. This shall be your land with its boundaries all round."

13Moses commanded the sons of Israel, saying, "This is the land which you shall inherit by lot, which the LORD has commanded to give to the nine tribes and to the half-tribe; 14for the tribe of the sons of

Reuben by fathers' houses and the tribe of
the sons of Gad by their fathers' houses have
received their inheritance, and also the half-
tribe of Manas'seh; 15the two tribes and the
half-tribe have received their inheritance
beyond the Jordan at Jericho eastward,
toward the sunrise."
16The LORD said to Moses, 17"These are the
names of the men who shall divide the land
to you for inheritance: Elea'zar the priest
and Joshua the son of Nun. 18You shall take
one leader of every tribe, to divide the land
for inheritance. 19These are the names of the
men: Of the tribe of Judah, Caleb the son
of Jephun'neh. 20Of the tribe of the sons of
Simeon, Shemu'el the son of Ammi'hud.
21Of the tribe of Benjamin, Eli'dad the son of
Chis'lon. 22Of the tribe of the sons of Dan a
leader, Bukki the son of Jogli. 23Of the sons of
Joseph: of the tribe of the sons of Manas'seh
a leader, Han'niel the son of E'phod. 24And
of the tribe of the sons of E'phraim a leader,
Ke'muel the son of Shiph'tan. 25Of the tribe
of the sons of Zeb'ulun a leader, Eliza'phan
the son of Parnach. 26Of the tribe of the
sons of Is'sachar a leader, Pal'ti-el the son of
Azzan. 27And of the tribe of the sons of Asher
a leader, Ahi'hud the son of Shelo'mi. 28Of
the tribe of the sons of Naph'tali a leader,
Pedah'el the son of Ammi'hud. 29These are
the men whom the LORD commanded to
divide the inheritance for the sons of Israel
in the land of Canaan."

35 The LORD said to Moses in the plains
of Moab by the Jordan at Jericho,
2"Command the sons of Israel, that they
give to the Levites, from the inheritance of
their possession, cities to dwell in; and you
shall give to the Levites pasture lands round
about the cities. 3The cities shall be theirs to
dwell in, and their pasture lands shall be for
their cattle and for their livestock and for
all their beasts. 4The pasture lands of the
cities, which you shall give to the Levites,
shall reach from the wall of the city outward
a thousand cubits all round. 5And you shall
measure, outside the city, for the east side
two thousand cubits, and for the south side
two thousand cubits, and for the west side
two thousand cubits, and for the north
side two thousand cubits, the city being
in the middle; this shall belong to them
as pasture land for their cities. 6The cities
which you give to the Levites shall be the
six cities of refuge, where you shall permit
the manslayer to flee, and in addition to
them you shall give forty-two cities. 7All the
cities which you give to the Levites shall be
forty-eight, with their pasture lands. 8And
as for the cities which you shall give from
the possession of the sons of Israel, from the
larger tribes you shall take many, and from
the smaller tribes you shall take few; each,
in proportion to the inheritance which it
inherits, shall give of its cities to the Levites."
9And the LORD said to Moses, 10"Say to the
sons of Israel, When you cross the Jordan
into the land of Canaan, 11then you shall
select cities to be cities of refuge for you, that
the manslayer who kills any person without
intent may flee there. 12The cities shall be
for you a refuge from the avenger, that the
manslayer may not die until he stands before
the congregation for judgment. 13And the
cities which you give shall be your six cities
of refuge. 14You shall give three cities beyond
the Jordan, and three cities in the land of
Canaan, to be cities of refuge. 15These six
cities shall be for refuge for the sons of Israel,
and for the stranger and for the sojourner
among them, that any one who kills any
person without intent may flee there.
16"But if he struck him down with an
instrument of iron, so that he died, he is
a murderer; the murderer shall be put to
death. 17And if he struck him down with a
stone in the hand, by which a man may die,
and he died, he is a murderer; the murderer
shall be put to death. 18Or if he struck him
down with a weapon of wood in the hand,
by which a man may die, and he died, he
is a murderer; the murderer shall be put to
death. 19The avenger of blood shall himself
put the murderer to death; when he meets
him, he shall put him to death. 20And if he
stabbed him from hatred, or hurled at him,
lying in wait, so that he died, 21or in enmity
struck him down with his hand, so that he
died, then he who struck the blow shall be
put to death; he is a murderer; the avenger

of blood shall put the murderer to death, when he meets him.

[22]“But if he stabbed him suddenly without enmity, or hurled anything on him without lying in wait, [23]or used a stone, by which a man may die, and without seeing him cast it upon him, so that he died, though he was not his enemy, and did not seek his harm; [24]then the congregation shall judge between the manslayer and the avenger of blood, in accordance with these ordinances; [25]and the congregation shall rescue the manslayer from the hand of the avenger of blood, and the congregation shall restore him to his city of refuge, to which he had fled, and he shall live in it until the death of the high priest who was anointed with the holy oil. [26]But if the manslayer shall at any time go beyond the bounds of his city of refuge to which he fled, [27]and the avenger of blood finds him outside the bounds of his city of refuge, and the avenger of blood slays the manslayer, he shall not be guilty of blood. [28]For the man must remain in his city of refuge until the death of the high priest; but after the death of the high priest the manslayer may return to the land of his possession.

[29]“And these things shall be for a statute and ordinance to you throughout your generations in all your dwellings. [30]If any one kills a person, the murderer shall be put to death on the evidence of witnesses; but no person shall be put to death on the testimony of one witness. [31]Moreover you shall accept no ransom for the life of a murderer, who is guilty of death; but he shall be put to death. [32]And you shall accept no ransom for him who has fled to his city of refuge, that he may return to dwell in the land before the death of the high priest. [33]You shall not thus pollute the land in which you live; for blood pollutes the land, and no expiation can be made for the land, for the blood that is shed in it, except by the blood of him who shed it. [34]You shall not defile the land in which you live, in the midst of which I dwell; for I the LORD dwell in the midst of the sons of Israel.”

36 The heads of the fathers’ houses of the families of the sons of Gilead the son of Ma′chir, son of Manas′seh, of the fathers’ houses of the sons of Joseph, came near and spoke before Moses and before the leaders, the heads of the fathers’ houses of the sons of Israel; [2]they said, “The LORD commanded my lord to give the land for inheritance by lot to the sons of Israel; and my lord was commanded by the LORD to give the inheritance of Zeloph′ehad our brother to his daughters. [3]But if they are married to any of the sons of the other tribes of the sons of Israel then their inheritance will be taken from the inheritance of our fathers, and added to the inheritance of the tribe to which they belong; so it will be taken away from the lot of our inheritance. [4]And when the jubilee of the sons of Israel comes, then their inheritance will be added to the inheritance of the tribe to which they belong; and their inheritance will be taken from the inheritance of the tribe of our fathers.”

[5]And Moses commanded the sons of Israel according to the word of the LORD, saying, “The tribe of the sons of Joseph is right. [6]This is what the LORD commands concerning the daughters of Zeloph′ehad, ‘Let them marry whom they think best; only, they shall marry within the family of the tribe of their father. [7]The inheritance of the sons of Israel shall not be transferred from one tribe to another; for every one of the sons of Israel shall cling to the inheritance of the tribe of his fathers. [8]And every daughter who possesses an inheritance in any tribe of the sons of Israel shall be wife to one of the family of the tribe of her father, so that every one of the sons of Israel may possess the inheritance of his fathers. [9]So no inheritance shall be transferred from one tribe to another; for each of the tribes of the sons of Israel shall cling to its own inheritance.’ ”

[10]The daughters of Zeloph′ehad did as the LORD commanded Moses; [11]for Mahlah, Tirzah, Hoglah, Milcah, and Noah, the daughters of Zeloph′ehad, were married to sons of their father’s brothers. [12]They were married into the families of the sons of Manas′seh the son of Joseph, and their inheritance remained in the tribe of the family of their father.

13These are the commandments and the ordinances which the LORD commanded by Moses to the sons of Israel in the plains of Moab by the Jordan at Jericho.

To the choirmaster: with stringed instruments.
A Psalm. A Song.

PSALM 67 [66]

May God be gracious to us and bless us
and make his face to shine upon us, *Selah*
2that your way may be known upon earth,
your saving power among all nations.
3Let the peoples praise you, O God;
let all the peoples praise you!

4Let the nations be glad and sing for joy,
for you judge the peoples with equity
and guide the nations upon earth. *Selah*
5Let the peoples praise you, O God;
let all the peoples praise you!

6The earth has yielded its increase;
God, our God, has blessed us.
7God has blessed us;
let all the ends of the earth fear him!

MARK 14

It was now two days before the Passover and the feast of Unleavened Bread. And the chief priests and the scribes were seeking how to arrest him by stealth, and kill him; 2for they said, "Not during the feast, lest there be a tumult of the people."

3And while he was at Beth′any in the house of Simon the leper, as he sat at table, a woman came with an alabaster jar of ointment of pure nard, very costly, and she broke the jar and poured it over his head. 4But there were some who said to themselves indignantly, "Why was the ointment thus wasted? 5For this ointment might have been sold for more than three hundred denarii, and given to the poor." And they reproached her. 6But Jesus said, "Let her alone; why do you trouble her? She has done a beautiful thing to me. 7For you always have the poor with you, and whenever you will, you can do good to them; but you will not always have me. 8She has done what she could; she has anointed my body beforehand for burying. 9And truly, I say to you, wherever the gospel is preached in the whole world, what she has done will be told in memory of her."

10Then Judas Iscariot, who was one of the Twelve, went to the chief priests in order to betray him to them. 11And when they heard it they were glad, and promised to give him money. And he sought an opportunity to betray him.

12And on the first day of Unleavened Bread, when they sacrificed the Passover lamb, his disciples said to him, "Where will you have us go and prepare for you to eat the Passover?" 13And he sent two of his disciples, and said to them, "Go into the city, and a man carrying a jar of water will meet you; follow him, 14and wherever he enters, say to the householder, 'The Teacher says, Where is my guest room, where I am to eat the Passover with my disciples?' 15And he will show you a large upper room furnished and ready; there prepare for us." 16And the disciples set out and went to the city, and found it as he had told them; and they prepared the Passover.

17And when it was evening he came with the Twelve. 18And as they were at table eating, Jesus said, "Truly, I say to you, one of you will betray me, one who is eating with me." 19They began to be sorrowful, and to say to him one after another, "Is it I?" 20He said to them, "It is one of the Twelve, one who is dipping bread in the same dish with me. 21For the Son of man goes as it is written of him, but woe to that man by whom the Son of man is betrayed! It would have been better for that man if he had not been born."

22And as they were eating, he took bread, and blessed, and broke it, and gave it to them, and said, "Take; this is my body." 23And he took a chalice, and when he had given thanks he gave it to them, and they all drank of it. 24And he said to them, "This is my blood of

the covenant, which is poured out for many.
[25]Truly, I say to you, I shall not drink again
of the fruit of the vine until that day when I
drink it new in the kingdom of God."

REFLECTION

As the Book of Numbers ends, we poignantly review the long years of wandering (see Nm 33, read yesterday). Israel then receives a few more instructions for stable organization in the Promised Land. Its boundaries are determined, as are the leaders who will divide it (see Nm 34:1–29), cities are designated for Levites (see 35:1–8), steps are taken to prevent blood-feuds from spiraling out of control (see vv. 9–34), and rules are established to enable smooth processes of inheritance. As Israel is poised to enter the Promised Land, it's good to recall with Psalm 67 the ultimate purpose of God's blessing of Israel: that his "saving power" might be known "among all nations" (Ps 67:2), and that "all the peoples" might praise him (v. 3). How fitting then, especially for those of us who are believers from "among all nations," to turn to St. Mark's account of the Last Supper. Earlier in Mark we see Jesus take, bless, break, and give bread to feed the hungry in the wilderness (see Mk 6:41; 8:6). Now he reveals his own Body and Blood, not only as nourishment for our "exodus," our way to the Promised Land, but as a sacrificial banquet that even now gives us a foretaste of our heavenly Homeland. Can you take a few minutes today to praise God for his amazing gift of the Eucharist?

March 16

DEUTERONOMY 1

**These are the words that Moses
spoke to all Israel beyond the
Jordan in the wilderness, in the
Ar′abah over against Suph, between
Par′an and To′phel, La′ban, Haze′roth,
and Di′zahab. [2]It is eleven days' journey**
from Horeb by the way of Mount Se′ir to
Ka′desh-bar′nea. [3]And in the fortieth year,
on the first day of the eleventh month,
Moses spoke to the sons of Israel according
to all that the LORD had given him in
commandment to them, [4]after he had
defeated Si′hon the king of the Am′orites,
who lived in Heshbon, and Og the king
of Bashan, who lived in Ash′taroth and in
Ed′re-i. [5]Beyond the Jordan, in the land of
Moab, Moses undertook to explain this law,
saying, [6]"The LORD our God said to us in
Horeb, 'You have stayed long enough at
this mountain; [7]turn and take your journey,
and go to the hill country of the Am′orites,
and to all their neighbors in the Ar′abah, in
the hill country and in the lowland, and in
the Neg′eb, and by the seacoast, the land of
the Canaanites, and Lebanon, as far as the
great river, the river Euphrates. [8]Behold,
I have set the land before you; go in and
take possession of the land which the LORD
swore to your fathers, to Abraham, to Isaac,
and to Jacob, to give to them and to their
descendants after them.'

[9]"At that time I said to you, 'I am not able
alone to bear you; [10]the LORD your God has
multiplied you, and behold, you are this
day as the stars of heaven for multitude.
[11]May the LORD, the God of your fathers,
make you a thousand times as many as
you are, and bless you, as he has promised
you! [12]How can I bear alone the weight and
burden of you and your strife? [13]Choose
wise, understanding, and experienced men,
according to your tribes, and I will appoint
them as your heads.' [14]And you answered
me, 'The thing that you have spoken is
good for us to do.' [15]So I took the heads of
your tribes, wise and experienced men, and
set them as heads over you, commanders
of thousands, commanders of hundreds,
commanders of fifties, commanders of tens,
and officers, throughout your tribes. [16]And
I charged your judges at that time, 'Hear
the cases between your brethren, and judge
righteously between a man and his brother
or the alien that is with him. [17]You shall not
be partial in judgment; you shall hear the
small and the great alike; you shall not be

afraid of the face of man, for the judgment is God's; and the case that is too hard for you, you shall bring to me, and I will hear it.' [18]And I commanded you at that time all the things that you should do.

[19]"And we set out from Horeb, and went through all that great and terrible wilderness which you saw, on the way to the hill country of the Am′orites, as the LORD our God commanded us; and we came to Ka′desh-bar′nea. [20]And I said to you, 'You have come to the hill country of the Am′orites, which the LORD our God gives us. [21]Behold, the LORD your God has set the land before you; go up, take possession, as the LORD, the God of your fathers, has told you; do not fear or be dismayed.' [22]Then all of you came near me, and said, 'Let us send men before us, that they may explore the land for us, and bring us word again of the way by which we must go up and the cities into which we shall come.' [23]The thing seemed good to me, and I took twelve men of you, one man for each tribe; [24]and they turned and went up into the hill country, and came to the Valley of Eshcol and spied it out. [25]And they took in their hands some of the fruit of the land and brought it down to us, and brought us word again, and said, 'It is a good land which the LORD our God gives us.'

[26]"Yet you would not go up, but rebelled against the command of the LORD your God; [27]and you murmured in your tents, and said, 'Because the LORD hated us he has brought us forth out of the land of Egypt, to give us into the hand of the Am′orites, to destroy us. [28]Where are we going up? Our brethren have made our hearts melt, saying, "The people are greater and taller than we; the cities are great and fortified up to heaven; and moreover we have seen the sons of the An′akim there."' [29]Then I said to you, 'Do not be in dread or afraid of them. [30]The LORD your God who goes before you will himself fight for you, just as he did for you in Egypt before your eyes, [31]and in the wilderness, where you have seen how the LORD your God bore you, as a man bears his son, in all the way that you went until you came to this place.' [32]Yet in spite of this word you did not believe the LORD your God, [33]who went before you in the way to seek you out a place to pitch your tents, in fire by night, to show you by what way you should go, and in the cloud by day.

[34]"And the LORD heard your words, and was angered, and he swore, [35]'Not one of these men of this evil generation shall see the good land which I swore to give to your fathers, [36]except Caleb the son of Jephun′neh; he shall see it, and to him and to his children I will give the land upon which he has trodden, because he has wholly followed the LORD!' [37]The LORD was angry with me also on your account, and said, 'You also shall not go in there; [38]Joshua the son of Nun, who stands before you, he shall enter; encourage him, for he shall cause Israel to inherit it. [39]Moreover your little ones, who you said would become a prey, and your children, who this day have no knowledge of good or evil, shall go in there, and to them I will give it, and they shall possess it. [40]But as for you, turn, and journey into the wilderness in the direction of the Red Sea.'

[41]"Then you answered me, 'We have sinned against the LORD; we will go up and fight, just as the LORD our God commanded us.' And every man of you belted on his weapons of war, and thought it easy to go up into the hill country. [42]And the LORD said to me, 'Say to them, Do not go up or fight, for I am not in the midst of you; lest you be defeated before your enemies.' [43]So I spoke to you, and you would not listen; but you rebelled against the command of the LORD, and were presumptuous and went up into the hill country. [44]Then the Am′orites who lived in that hill country came out against you and chased you as bees do and beat you down in Se′ir as far as Hormah. [45]And you returned and wept before the LORD; but the LORD did not listen to your voice or give ear to you. [46]So you remained at Ka′desh many days, the days that you remained there.

2 "Then we turned, and journeyed into the wilderness in the direction of the Red Sea, as the LORD told me; and for many days we went about Mount Se′ir. [2]Then the LORD said to me, [3]'You have been going

about this mountain country long enough;
turn northward. 4And command the people,
You are about to pass through the territory
of your brethren the sons of Esau, who live
in Se′ir; and they will be afraid of you. So
take good heed; 5do not contend with them;
for I will not give you any of their land, no,
not so much as for the sole of the foot to
tread on, because I have given Mount Se′ir
to Esau as a possession. 6You shall purchase
food from them for money, that you may
eat; and you shall also buy water of them for
money, that you may drink. 7For the LORD
your God has blessed you in all the work of
your hands; he knows your going through
this great wilderness; these forty years the
LORD your God has been with you; you
have lacked nothing.’ 8So we went on, away
from our brethren the sons of Esau who live
in Se′ir, away from the Ar′abah road from
E′lath and E′zion-ge′ber.

“And we turned and went in the direction
of the wilderness of Moab. 9And the LORD
said to me, ‘Do not harass Moab or contend
with them in battle, for I will not give you
any of their land for a possession, because
I have given Ar to the sons of Lot for a
possession.’ 10(The E′mim formerly lived
there, a people great and many, and tall as
the An′akim; 11like the An′akim they are
also known as Reph′aim, but the Moabites
call them E′mim. 12The Horites also lived
in Se′ir formerly, but the sons of Esau
dispossessed them, and destroyed them
from before them, and settled in their stead;
as Israel did to the land of their possession,
which the LORD gave to them.) 13‘Now rise
up, and go over the brook Ze′red.’ So we
went over the brook Zered. 14And the time
from our leaving Ka′desh-bar′nea until we
crossed the brook Ze′red was thirty-eight
years, until the entire generation, that is, the
men of war, had perished from the camp, as
the LORD had sworn to them. 15For indeed
the hand of the LORD was against them,
to destroy them from the camp, until they
had perished.

16“So when all the men of war had perished
and were dead from among the people, 17the
LORD said to me, 18‘This day you are to pass
over the boundary of Moab at Ar; 19and
when you approach the frontier of the sons
of Ammon, do not harass them or contend
with them, for I will not give you any of the
land of the sons of Ammon as a possession,
because I have given it to the sons of Lot for
a possession.’ 20(That also is known as a land
of Reph′aim; Rephaim formerly lived there,
but the Am′monites call them Zamzum′mim,
21a people great and many, and tall as the
An′akim; but the LORD destroyed them
before them; and they dispossessed them, and
settled in their stead; 22as he did for the sons of
Esau, who live in Se′ir, when he destroyed the
Horites before them, and they dispossessed
them, and settled in their stead even to this
day. 23As for the Avvim, who lived in villages
as far as Gaza, the Caphtorim, who came from
Caphtor, destroyed them and settled in their
stead.) 24‘Rise up, take your journey, and go
over the valley of the Arnon; behold, I have
given into your hand Si′hon the Am′orite,
king of Heshbon, and his land; begin to take
possession, and contend with him in battle.
25This day I will begin to put the dread and
fear of you upon the peoples that are under
the whole heaven, who shall hear the report
of you and shall tremble and be in anguish
because of you.’”

To the choirmaster.
A Psalm of David.
A Song.

PSALM 68 [67]

Let God arise, let his enemies be scattered;
let those who hate him flee before him!
2As smoke is driven away, so drive them away;
as wax melts before fire,
let the wicked perish before God!
3But let the righteous be joyful;
let them exult before God;
let them be jubilant with joy!

4Sing to God, sing praises to his name;
lift up a song to him who rides upon
the clouds;
his name is the LORD, exult before him!

5 Father of the fatherless and protector
of widows
is God in his holy habitation.
6 God gives the desolate a home to dwell in;
he leads out the prisoners to prosperity;
but the rebellious dwell in a parched land.

7 O God, when you went forth before
your people,
when you marched through the
wilderness, *Selah*
8 the earth quaked, the heavens poured
down rain,
at the presence of God;
yon Sinai quaked at the presence of God,
the God of Israel.

9 Rain in abundance, O God, you
showered abroad;
you restored your heritage as
it languished;
10 your flock found a dwelling in it;
in your goodness, O God, you provided
for the needy.

11 The Lord gives the command;
great is the host of those who bore
the tidings:
12 "The kings of the armies, they flee,
they flee!"
The women at home divide the spoil,
13 though they stay among the sheepfolds—
the wings of a dove covered with silver,
its pinions with green gold.
14 When the Almighty scattered kings there,
snow fell on Zalmon.

15 O mighty mountain, mountain of Bashan;
O many-peaked mountain, mountain
of Bashan!
16 Why do you look with envy, O many-
peaked mountain,
at the mount which God desired for
his abode,
yes, where the LORD will dwell for ever?

17 With mighty chariotry, twice ten thousand,
thousands upon thousands,
the Lord came from Sinai into the
holy place.
18 You ascended the high mount,
leading captives in your train,
and receiving gifts among men,
even among the rebellious, that the LORD
God may dwell there.

MARK 14

26 And when they had sung a hymn, they went out to the Mount of Olives. 27 And Jesus said to them, "You will all fall away; for it is written, 'I will strike the shep-
herd, and the sheep will be scattered.' 28 But
after I am raised up, I will go before you to
Galilee." 29 Peter said to him, "Even though
they all fall away, I will not." 30 And Jesus said
to him, "Truly, I say to you, this very night,
before the cock crows twice, you will deny
me three times." 31 But he said vehemently,
"If I must die with you, I will not deny you."
And they all said the same.
32 And they went to a place which was
called Gethsem′ane; and he said to his
disciples, "Sit here, while I pray." 33 And he
took with him Peter and James and John,
and began to be greatly distressed and
troubled. 34 And he said to them, "My soul is
very sorrowful, even to death; remain here,
and watch." 35 And going a little farther, he
fell on the ground and prayed that, if it were
possible, the hour might pass from him.
36 And he said, "Abba, Father, all things are
possible to you; remove this chalice from
me; yet not what I will, but what you will."
37 And he came and found them sleeping,
and he said to Peter, "Simon, are you asleep?
Could you not watch one hour? 38 Watch and
pray that you may not enter into temptation;
the spirit indeed is willing, but the flesh is
weak." 39 And again he went away and prayed,
saying the same words. 40 And again he came
and found them sleeping, for their eyes were
very heavy; and they did not know what to
answer him. 41 And he came the third time,
and said to them, "Are you still sleeping and
taking your rest? It is enough; the hour has
come; the Son of man is betrayed into the

hands of sinners. 42Rise, let us be going; see,
my betrayer is at hand."

REFLECTION

The Book of Deuteronomy has been called the "heartbeat" of the Old Testament. This is not merely a catchy phrase. It's hard to find a page in Deuteronomy where the Hebrew term "heart" (*levav*) does not appear. Although some see it as simply a book of legal code, the reality is very different. Deuteronomy is all about God winning back the hearts of a new generation. At this point in the biblical story, the Exodus generation is largely gone, and their children need to be prepared to finally enter the land that God had promised. Now, God desires to entreat his people and give them the tools to be a light to the world. Moses does this by reminding them of their story. It has been said that those who do not know history are doomed to repeat it. This is a profoundly apt description of the biblical story—and our story. Do you keep your story, the story of the Catholic Church, close to your mind and heart?

March 17

DEUTERONOMY 2

**26"So I sent messengers from
the wilderness of Ked′emoth to
Si′hon the king of Heshbon, with words
of peace, saying, 27'Let me pass through**
your land; I will go only by the road, I will
turn aside neither to the right nor to the left.
28You shall sell me food for money, that I
may eat, and give me water for money, that I
may drink; only let me pass through on foot,
29as the sons of Esau who live in Se′ir and the
Moabites who live in Ar did for me, until I
go over the Jordan into the land which the
LORD our God gives to us.' 30But Si′hon the
king of Heshbon would not let us pass by
him; for the LORD your God hardened his
spirit and made his heart obstinate, that he
might give him into your hand, as at this
day. 31And the LORD said to me, 'Behold,
I have begun to give Si′hon and his land
over to you; begin to take possession, that
you may occupy his land.' 32Then Si′hon
came out against us, he and all his people,
to battle at Ja′haz. 33And the LORD our
God gave him over to us; and we defeated
him and his sons and all his people. 34And
we captured all his cities at that time and
utterly destroyed every city, men, women,
and children; we left none remaining; 35only
the cattle we took as spoil for ourselves, with
the booty of the cities which we captured.
36From Aro′er, which is on the edge of the
valley of the Arnon, and from the city that is
in the valley, as far as Gilead, there was not a
city too high for us; the LORD our God gave
all into our hands. 37Only to the land of the
sons of Ammon you did not draw near, that
is, to all the banks of the river Jabbok and
the cities of the hill country, and wherever
the LORD our God forbade us.

3 "Then we turned and went up the way
to Bashan; and Og the king of Bashan
came out against us, he and all his people,
to battle at Ed′re-i. 2But the LORD said to
me, 'Do not fear him; for I have given him
and all his people and his land into your
hand; and you shall do to him as you did to
Si′hon the king of the Am′orites, who dwelt
at Heshbon.' 3So the LORD our God gave into
our hand Og also, the king of Bashan, and
all his people; and we struck him until no
survivor was left to him. 4And we took all his
cities at that time—there was not a city which
we did not take from them—sixty cities, the
whole region of Argob, the kingdom of Og
in Bashan. 5All these were cities fortified
with high walls, gates, and bars, besides very
many unwalled villages. 6And we utterly
destroyed them, as we did to Si′hon the king
of Heshbon, destroying every city, men,
women, and children. 7But all the cattle and
the spoil of the cities we took as our booty. 8So
we took the land at that time out of the hand
of the two kings of the Am′orites who were
beyond the Jordan, from the valley of the
Arnon to Mount Hermon 9(the Sido′nians

call Hermon Sir′ion, while the Am′orites call it Se′nir), [10]all the cities of the tableland and all Gilead and all Bashan, as far as Sal′ecah and Ed′re-i, cities of the kingdom of Og in Bashan. [11](For only Og the king of Bashan was left of the remnant of the Reph′aim; behold, his bedstead was a bedstead of iron; is it not in Rabbah of the Am′monites? Nine cubits was its length, and four cubits its breadth, according to the common cubit.)

[12]"When we took possession of this land at that time, I gave to the Reubenites and the Gadites the territory beginning at Aro′er, which is on the edge of the valley of the Arnon, and half the hill country of Gilead with its cities; [13]the rest of Gilead, and all Bashan, the kingdom of Og, that is, all the region of Argob, I gave to the half-tribe of Manas′seh. (The whole of that Bashan is called the land of Reph′aim. [14]Ja′ir the Manas′site took all the region of Argob, that is, Bashan, as far as the border of the Gesh′urites and the Ma-ac′athites, and called the villages after his own name, Hav′voth-ja′ir, as it is to this day.) [15]To Ma′chir I gave Gilead, [16]and to the Reubenites and the Gadites I gave the territory from Gilead as far as the valley of the Arnon, with the middle of the valley as a boundary, as far over as the river Jabbok, the boundary of the Am′monites; [17]the Ar′abah also, with the Jordan as the boundary, from Chin′nereth as far as the sea of the Arabah, the Salt Sea, under the slopes of Pisgah on the east.

[18]"And I commanded you at that time, saying, 'The LORD your God has given you this land to possess; all your men of valor shall pass over armed before your brethren the sons of Israel. [19]But your wives, your little ones, and your cattle (I know that you have many cattle) shall remain in the cities which I have given you, [20]until the LORD gives rest to your brethren, as to you, and they also occupy the land which the LORD your God gives them beyond the Jordan; then you shall return every man to his possession which I have given you.' [21]And I commanded Joshua at that time, 'Your eyes have seen all that the LORD your God has done to these two kings; so will the LORD do to all the kingdoms into which you are going over. [22]You shall not fear them; for it is the LORD your God who fights for you.'

[23]"And I begged the LORD at that time, saying, [24]'O Lord GOD, you have only begun to show your servant your greatness and your mighty hand; for what god is there in heaven or on earth who can do such works and mighty acts as yours? [25]Let me go over, I pray, and see the good land beyond the Jordan, that excellent hill country, and Lebanon.' [26]But the LORD was angry with me on your account, and would not listen to me; and the LORD said to me, 'Let it satisfy you; speak no more to me of this matter. [27]Go up to the top of Pisgah, and lift up your eyes westward and northward and southward and eastward, and behold it with your eyes; for you shall not go over this Jordan. [28]But charge Joshua, and encourage and strengthen him; for he shall go over at the head of this people, and he shall put them in possession of the land which you shall see.' [29]So we remained in the valley opposite Beth-pe′or.

4 "And now, O Israel, give heed to the statutes and the ordinances which I teach you, and do them; that you may live, and go in and take possession of the land which the LORD, the God of your fathers, gives you. [2]You shall not add to the word which I command you, nor take from it; that you may keep the commandments of the LORD your God which I command you. [3]Your eyes have seen what the LORD did at Ba′al-pe′or; for the LORD your God destroyed from among you all the men who followed the Ba′al of Peor; [4]but you who held fast to the LORD your God are all alive this day. [5]Behold, I have taught you statutes and ordinances, as the LORD my God commanded me, that you should do them in the land which you are entering to take possession of it. [6]Keep them and do them; for that will be your wisdom and your understanding in the sight of the peoples, who, when they hear all these statutes, will say, 'Surely this great nation is a wise and understanding people.' [7]For what great nation is there that has a god so near to it

as the LORD our God is to us, whenever we
call upon him? 8And what great nation is
there, that has statutes and ordinances so
righteous as all this law which I set before
you this day?
9"Only take heed, and keep your soul
diligently, lest you forget the things which
your eyes have seen, and lest they depart
from your heart all the days of your life;
make them known to your children and
your children's children—10how on the day
that you stood before the LORD your God
at Horeb, the LORD said to me, 'Gather the
people to me, that I may let them hear my
words, so that they may learn to fear me
all the days that they live upon the earth,
and that they may teach their children so.'
11And you came near and stood at the foot
of the mountain, while the mountain burned
with fire to the heart of heaven, wrapped in
darkness, cloud, and gloom. 12Then the LORD
spoke to you out of the midst of the fire; you
heard the sound of words, but saw no form;
there was only a voice. 13And he declared to
you his covenant, which he commanded you
to perform, that is, the ten commandments;
and he wrote them upon two tables of stone.
14And the LORD commanded me at that time
to teach you statutes and ordinances, that
you might do them in the land which you
are going over to possess.
15"Therefore take good heed to yourselves.
Since you saw no form on the day that the
LORD spoke to you at Horeb out of the midst
of the fire, 16beware lest you act corruptly by
making a graven image for yourselves, in the
form of any figure, the likeness of male or
female, 17the likeness of any beast that is on
the earth, the likeness of any winged bird that
flies in the air, 18the likeness of anything that
creeps on the ground, the likeness of any fish
that is in the water under the earth. 19And
beware lest you lift up your eyes to heaven,
and when you see the sun and the moon and
the stars, all the host of heaven, you be drawn
away and worship them and serve them,
things which the LORD your God has allotted
to all the peoples under the whole heaven.
20But the LORD has taken you, and brought
you forth out of the iron furnace, out of
Egypt, to be a people of his own possession,
as at this day. 21Furthermore the LORD was
angry with me on your account, and he swore
that I should not cross the Jordan, and that
I should not enter the good land which the
LORD your God gives you for an inheritance.
22For I must die in this land, I must not go
over the Jordan; but you shall go over and
take possession of that good land."

To the choirmaster.
A Psalm of David.
A Song.

PSALM 68 [67]

19Blessed be the Lord,
who daily bears us up;
God is our salvation. *Selah*
20Our God is a God of salvation;
and to GOD, the Lord, belongs escape
from death.

21But God will shatter the heads of
his enemies,
the hairy crown of him who walks
in his guilty ways.
22The Lord said,
"I will bring them back from Bashan,
I will bring them back from the depths
of the sea,
23that you may bathe your feet in blood,
that the tongues of your dogs may have
their portion from the foe."

24Your solemn processions are seen, O God,
the processions of my God, my King, into
the sanctuary—
25the singers in front, the minstrels last,
between them maidens playing timbrels:
26"Bless God in the great congregation,
the LORD, O you who are of Israel's
fountain!"
27There is Benjamin, the least of them,
in the lead,
the princes of Judah in their throng,
the princes of Zeb′ulun, the princes
of Naph′tali.

28Summon your might, O God;
show your strength, O God, you who
have wrought for us.
29Because of your temple at Jerusalem
kings bear gifts to you.
30Rebuke the beasts that dwell among
the reeds,
the herd of bulls with the calves of
the peoples.
Trample under foot those who lust
after tribute;
scatter the peoples who delight in war.
31Let bronze be brought from Egypt;
let Ethiopia hasten to stretch out her
hands to God.

32Sing to God, O kingdoms of the earth;
sing praises to the Lord, *Selah*
33to him who rides in the heavens, the
ancient heavens;
behold, he sends forth his voice, his
mighty voice.
34Ascribe power to God,
whose majesty is over Israel,
and his power is in the skies.
35Awesome is God in his sanctuary,
the God of Israel,
he gives power and strength to his people.

Blessed be God!

MARK 14

43**And immediately, while he was still speaking, Judas came, one of the Twelve, and with him a crowd with swords and clubs, from the chief priests and the scribes and the elders.** 44**Now the betrayer had given**
them a sign, saying, "The one I shall kiss is the man; seize him and lead him away safely." 45And
when he came, he went up to him at once, and said, "Master!" And he kissed him. 46And they
laid hands on him and seized him. 47But one of
those who stood by drew his sword, and struck the slave of the high priest and cut off his ear.
48And Jesus said to them, "Have you come out as against a robber, with swords and clubs to capture me? 49Day after day I was with you in the temple teaching, and you did not seize me. But let the Scriptures be fulfilled." 50And they
all deserted him and fled.
51And a young man followed him, with nothing but a linen cloth about his body; and they seized him, 52but he left the linen
cloth and ran away naked.

REFLECTION

Dying words in the Bible are always important. The Book of Deuteronomy can be seen as Moses's last will and testament. It's the last message of one of the most important figures in the Bible to a new generation of Israelites who are preparing to enter the Promised Land. As Moses tells this new generation the story of salvation history, one of the main things he wants to convey is that God will always fight for his children. If God is not fighting our battles, then we will surely lose. This is an important point for understanding what Jesus will do and teach in the Gospels. Jesus will fight the ultimate battle on our behalf, defeating sin and death itself. In the reading from the Gospel of Mark, St. Peter struggles to understand this concept. As Judas leads the soldiers to arrest Jesus, Peter takes matters into his own hands—as we are often prone to do. Jesus's response, however, is startling. After Peter cuts off the ear of one of the soldiers, Jesus actually heals it. He is not afraid. He is in complete control, even in the midst of his arrest. He's trying to show Peter, and us, that if we put our trust in him to fight our battles, we have nothing to fear. How can you put more trust in Jesus to take care of the difficulties that arise in your own life?

March 18

DEUTERONOMY 4

23**"Take heed to yourselves, lest you forget the covenant of the LORD your God, which he made with you, and make a graven image in the** form of anything which the LORD your God has forbidden you. 24 For the LORD your God is a devouring fire, a jealous God.

25 "When you beget children and children's children, and have grown old in the land, if you act corruptly by making a graven image in the form of anything, and by doing what is evil in the sight of the LORD your God, so as to provoke him to anger, 26 I call heaven and earth to witness against you this day, that you will soon utterly perish from the land which you are going over the Jordan to possess; you will not live long upon it, but will be utterly destroyed. 27 And the LORD will scatter you among the peoples, and you will be left few in number among the nations where the LORD will drive you. 28 And there you will serve gods of wood and stone, the work of men's hands, that neither see, nor hear, nor eat, nor smell. 29 But from there you will seek the LORD your God, and you will find him, if you search after him with all your heart and with all your soul. 30 When you are in tribulation, and all these things come upon you in the latter days, you will return to the LORD your God and obey his voice, 31 for the LORD your God is a merciful God; he will not fail you or destroy you or forget the covenant with your fathers which he swore to them.

32 "For ask now of the days that are past, which were before you, since the day that God created man upon the earth, and ask from one end of heaven to the other, whether such a great thing as this has ever happened or was ever heard of. 33 Did any people ever hear the voice of God speaking out of the midst of the fire, as you have heard, and still live? 34 Or has God ever attempted to go and take a nation for himself from the midst of another nation, by trials, by signs, by wonders, and by war, by a mighty hand and an outstretched arm, and by great terrors, according to all that the LORD your God did for you in Egypt before your eyes? 35 To you it was shown, that you might know that the LORD is God; there is no other besides him. 36 Out of heaven he let you hear his voice, that he might discipline you; and on earth he let you see his great fire, and you heard his words out of the midst of the fire. 37 And because he loved your fathers and chose their descendants after them, and brought you out of Egypt with his own presence, by his great power, 38 driving out before you nations greater and mightier than yourselves, to bring you in, to give you their land for an inheritance, as at this day; 39 know therefore this day, and lay it to your heart, that the LORD is God in heaven above and on the earth beneath; there is no other. 40 Therefore you shall keep his statutes and his commandments, which I command you this day, that it may go well with you, and with your children after you, and that you may prolong your days in the land which the LORD your God gives you for ever."

41 Then Moses set apart three cities in the east beyond the Jordan, 42 that the manslayer might flee there, who kills his neighbor unintentionally, without being at enmity with him in time past, and that by fleeing to one of these cities he might save his life: 43 Bezer in the wilderness on the tableland for the Reubenites, and Ramoth in Gilead for the Gadites, and Golan in Bashan for the Manas′sites.

44 This is the law which Moses set before the children of Israel; 45 these are the decrees, the statutes, and the ordinances, which Moses spoke to the children of Israel when they came out of Egypt, 46 beyond the Jordan in the valley opposite Beth-pe′or, in the land of Si′hon the king of the Am′orites, who lived at Heshbon, whom Moses and the children of Israel defeated when they came out of Egypt. 47 And they took possession of his land and the land of Og the king of Bashan, the two kings of the Am′orites, who lived to the east beyond the Jordan; 48 from Aro′er, which is on the edge of the valley of the Arnon, as far as Mount Sir′ion (that is, Hermon), 49 together with all the Ar′abah on the east side of the Jordan as far as the Sea of the Arabah, under the slopes of Pisgah.

5 And Moses summoned all Israel, and said to them, "Hear, O Israel, the statutes and the ordinances which I speak in your hearing this day, and you shall learn them and be careful to do them. 2 The LORD our

God made a covenant with us in Horeb. [3]Not with our fathers did the LORD make this covenant, but with us, who are all of us here alive this day. [4]The LORD spoke with you face to face at the mountain, out of the midst of the fire, [5]while I stood between the LORD and you at that time, to declare to you the word of the LORD; for you were afraid because of the fire, and you did not go up into the mountain. He said:

[6]“ ‘I am the LORD your God, who brought you out of the land of Egypt, out of the house of bondage.

[7]“ ‘You shall have no other gods before me.

[8]“ ‘You shall not make for yourself a graven image, or any likeness of anything that is in heaven above, or that is on the earth beneath, or that is in the water under the earth; [9]you shall not bow down to them or serve them; for I the LORD your God am a jealous God, visiting the iniquity of the fathers upon the children to the third and fourth generation of those who hate me, [10]but showing merciful love to thousands of those who love me and keep my commandments.

[11]“ ‘You shall not take the name of the LORD your God in vain: for the LORD will not hold him guiltless who takes his name in vain.

[12]“ ‘Observe the sabbath day, to keep it holy, as the LORD your God commanded you. [13]Six days you shall labor, and do all your work; [14]but the seventh day is a sabbath to the LORD your God; in it you shall not do any work, you, or your son, or your daughter, or your manservant, or your maidservant, or your ox, or your donkey, or any of your cattle, or the sojourner who is within your gates, that your manservant and your maidservant may rest as well as you. [15]You shall remember that you were a servant in the land of Egypt, and the LORD your God brought you out from there with a mighty hand and an outstretched arm; therefore the LORD your God commanded you to keep the sabbath day.

[16]“ ‘Honor your father and your mother, as the LORD your God commanded you; that your days may be prolonged, and that it may go well with you, in the land which the LORD your God gives you.

[17]“ ‘You shall not kill.

[18]“ ‘Neither shall you commit adultery.

[19]“ ‘Neither shall you steal.

[20]“ ‘Neither shall you bear false witness against your neighbor.

[21]“ ‘Neither shall you covet your neighbor’s wife; and you shall not desire your neighbor’s house, his field, or his manservant, or his maidservant, his ox, or his donkey, or anything that is your neighbor’s.’

[22]“These words the LORD spoke to all your assembly at the mountain out of the midst of the fire, the cloud, and the thick darkness, with a loud voice; and he added no more. And he wrote them upon two tables of stone, and gave them to me. [23]And when you heard the voice out of the midst of the darkness, while the mountain was burning with fire, you came near to me, all the heads of your tribes, and your elders; [24]and you said, ‘Behold, the LORD our God has shown us his glory and greatness, and we have heard his voice out of the midst of the fire; we have this day seen God speak with man and man still live. [25]Now therefore why should we die? For this great fire will consume us; if we hear the voice of the LORD our God any more, we shall die. [26]For who is there of all flesh, that has heard the voice of the living God speaking out of the midst of fire, as we have, and has still lived? [27]Go near, and hear all that the LORD our God will say; and speak to us all that the LORD our God will speak to you; and we will hear and do it.’

[28]“And the LORD heard your words, when you spoke to me; and the LORD said to me, ‘I have heard the words of this people, which they have spoken to you; they have rightly said all that they have spoken. [29]Oh that they had such a mind as this always, to fear me and to keep all my commandments, that it might go well with them and with their children for ever! [30]Go and say to them, “Return to your tents.” [31]But you, stand here by me, and I will tell you all the commandment and the statutes and the ordinances

which you shall teach them, that they may do them in the land which I give them to possess.' [32]You shall be careful to do therefore as the LORD your God has commanded you; you shall not turn aside to the right hand or to the left. [33]You shall walk in all the way which the LORD your God has commanded you, that you may live, and that it may go well with you, and that you may live long in the land which you shall possess."

To the choirmaster: according to Lilies.
A Psalm of David.

PSALM 69 [68]

Save me, O God!
For the waters have come up to my neck.
2 I sink in deep mire,
where there is no foothold;
I have come into deep waters,
and the flood sweeps over me.
3 I am weary with my crying;
my throat is parched.
My eyes grow dim
with waiting for my God.

4 More in number than the hairs of my head
are those who hate me without cause;
mighty are those who would destroy me,
those who attack me with lies.
What I did not steal
must I now restore?
5 O God, you know my folly;
the wrongs I have done are not hidden
from you.

6 Let not those who hope in you be put to
shame through me,
O Lord GOD of hosts;
let not those who seek you be brought to
dishonor through me,
O God of Israel.
7 For it is for your sake that I have
borne reproach,
that shame has covered my face.
8 I have become a stranger to my brethren,
an alien to my mother's sons.
9 For zeal for your house has consumed me,
and the insults of those who insult you
have fallen on me.
10 When I humbled my soul with fasting,
it became my reproach.
11 When I made sackcloth my clothing,
I became a byword to them.
12 I am the talk of those who sit in the gate,
and the drunkards make songs about me.

13 But as for me, my prayer is to you, O LORD.
At an acceptable time, O God,
in the abundance of your mercy answer me.
With your faithful help [14]rescue me
from sinking in the mire;
let me be delivered from my enemies
and from the deep waters.
15 Let not the flood sweep over me,
or the deep swallow me up,
or the pit close its mouth over me.

16 Answer me, O LORD, for your merciful
love is good;
according to your abundant compassion,
turn to me.
17 Hide not your face from your servant;
for I am in distress, make haste to
answer me.
18 Draw near to me, redeem me,
set me free because of my enemies!

MARK 14

[53]**And they led Jesus to the high priest; and all the chief priests and the elders and the scribes were assembled. [54]And Peter had followed him at a distance, right into the** courtyard of the high priest; and he was sitting with the guards, and warming himself at the fire. [55]Now the chief priests and the whole council sought testimony against Jesus to put him to death; but they found none. [56]For many bore false witness against him, and their witness did not agree. [57]And some stood up and bore false witness against him, saying, [58]"We heard him say, 'I will destroy this temple that is made with

hands, and in three days I will build another, not made with hands.' " 59Yet not even so
did their testimony agree. 60And the high
priest stood up in their midst, and asked
Jesus, "Have you no answer to make? What
is it that these men testify against you?"
61But he was silent and made no answer.
Again the high priest asked him, "Are you
the Christ, the Son of the Blessed?" 62And
Jesus said, "I am; and you will see the Son
of man sitting at the right hand of Power,
and coming with the clouds of heaven."
63And the high priest tore his clothes, and
said, "Why do we still need witnesses?
64You have heard his blasphemy. What is
your decision?" And they all condemned
him as deserving death. 65And some began
to spit on him, and to cover his face, and to
strike him, saying to him, "Prophesy!" And
the guards received him with blows.
66And as Peter was below in the courtyard,
one of the maids of the high priest came;
67and seeing Peter warming himself, she
looked at him, and said, "You also were
with the Nazarene, Jesus." 68But he denied
it, saying, "I neither know nor understand
what you mean." And he went out into the
gateway. 69And the maid saw him, and began
again to say to the bystanders, "This man is
one of them." 70But again he denied it. And
after a little while again the bystanders said
to Peter, "Certainly you are one of them; for
you are a Galilean." 71But he began to invoke
a curse on himself and to swear, "I do not
know this man of whom you speak." 72And
immediately the cock crowed a second time.
And Peter remembered how Jesus had said
to him, "Before the cock crows twice, you
will deny me three times." And he broke
down and wept.

REFLECTION

In chapters 1–3, Moses walked a new generation of Israelites through the story of salvation history—from Mt. Sinai, to the wilderness, through the military victories in the Book of Numbers, he recounted their family story. Now, in chapters 4 and 5, Moses gives a homiletical commentary on that story. What he stresses more than anything else is that the people of God are not to forget what the Lord had done for them. Ultimately, the story of the previous generation—those who fell to the sin of worshipping the golden calf—was that they forgot both who God is and what he had done for them. In Moses's message, however, remembering the past is not enough. Moses wants the people of God to use the events of the past as a lens for their present for the sake of their future. What are God's expectations for them now? Throughout Moses's speech, we see phrases like "today" or "this day" as a kind of reminder that God is not simply a god of the past, but he is a God of our here and now. How can you make God more present in your everyday life?

March 19

DEUTERONOMY 6

**"Now this is the command-
ment, the statutes and the ordinances which the LORD your
God commanded me to teach you,
that you may do them in the land to**
which you are going over, to possess it;
2that you may fear the LORD your God, you
and your son and your son's son, by keeping all his statutes and his commandments,
which I command you, all the days of your
life; and that your days may be prolonged.
3Hear therefore, O Israel, and be careful to
do them; that it may go well with you, and
that you may multiply greatly, as the LORD,
the God of your fathers, has promised you,
in a land flowing with milk and honey.
4"Hear, O Israel: The LORD our God is one
LORD; 5and you shall love the LORD your
God with all your heart, and with all your
soul, and with all your might. 6And these
words which I command you this day shall

be upon your heart; 7and you shall teach
them diligently to your children, and shall
talk of them when you sit in your house, and
when you walk by the way, and when you
lie down, and when you rise. 8And you shall
bind them as a sign upon your hand, and
they shall be as frontlets between your eyes.
9And you shall write them on the doorposts
of your house and on your gates.
10"And when the LORD your God brings
you into the land which he swore to your
fathers, to Abraham, to Isaac, and to Jacob,
to give you, with great and excellent cities,
which you did not build, 11and houses full of
all good things, which you did not fill, and
cisterns hewn out, which you did not hew,
and vineyards and olive trees, which you
did not plant, and when you eat and are full,
12then take heed lest you forget the LORD,
who brought you out of the land of Egypt,
out of the house of bondage. 13You shall fear
the LORD your God; you shall serve him,
and swear by his name. 14You shall not go
after other gods, of the gods of the peoples
who are round about you; 15for the LORD
your God in the midst of you is a jealous
God; lest the anger of the LORD your God
be kindled against you, and he destroy you
from off the face of the earth.
16"You shall not put the LORD your God to
the test, as you tested him at Massah. 17You
shall diligently keep the commandments of
the LORD your God, and his decrees, and
his statutes, which he has commanded you.
18And you shall do what is right and good
in the sight of the LORD, that it may go well
with you, and that you may go in and take
possession of the good land which the LORD
swore to give to your fathers 19by thrusting
out all your enemies from before you, as the
LORD has promised.
20"When your son asks you in time to
come, 'What is the meaning of the decrees
and the statutes and the ordinances which
the LORD our God has commanded you?'
21then you shall say to your son, 'We were
Pharaoh's slaves in Egypt; and the LORD
brought us out of Egypt with a mighty
hand; 22and the LORD showed signs and
wonders, great and grievous, against Egypt
and against Pharaoh and all his household,
before our eyes; 23and he brought us out
from there, that he might bring us in and
give us the land which he swore to give to
our fathers. 24And the LORD commanded
us to do all these statutes, to fear the LORD
our God, for our good always, that he might
preserve us alive, as at this day. 25And it will
be righteousness for us, if we are careful to
do all this commandment before the LORD
our God, as he has commanded us.'
7 "When the LORD your God brings you
into the land which you are entering
to take possession of it, and clears away
many nations before you, the Hittites, the
Gir′gashites, the Am′orites, the Canaanites,
the Per′izzites, the Hi′vites, and the Jeb′usites,
seven nations greater and mightier than
yourselves, 2and when the LORD your God
gives them over to you, and you defeat
them; then you must utterly destroy them;
you shall make no covenant with them, and
show no mercy to them. 3You shall not make
marriages with them, giving your daughters
to their sons or taking their daughters for
your sons. 4For they would turn away your
sons from following me, to serve other
gods; then the anger of the LORD would be
kindled against you, and he would destroy
you quickly. 5But thus shall you deal with
them: you shall break down their altars,
and dash in pieces their pillars, and hew
down their Ashe′rim, and burn their graven
images with fire.
6"For you are a people holy to the LORD your
God; the LORD your God has chosen you to
be a people for his own possession, out of all
the peoples that are on the face of the earth.
7It was not because you were more in number
than any other people that the LORD set his
love upon you and chose you, for you were
the fewest of all peoples; 8but it is because
the LORD loves you, and is keeping the oath
which he swore to your fathers, that the LORD
has brought you out with a mighty hand, and
redeemed you from the house of bondage,
from the hand of Pharaoh king of Egypt.
9Know therefore that the LORD your God is
God, the faithful God who keeps covenant
and merciful love with those who love him

and keep his commandments, to a thousand
generations, 10and repays to their face those
who hate him, by destroying them; he will not
be slack with him who hates him, he will repay
him to his face. 11You shall therefore be careful
to do the commandment, and the statutes,
and the ordinances, which I command you
this day.

12"And because you listen to these ordinances, and keep and do them, the LORD
your God will keep with you the covenant
and the merciful love which he swore to
your fathers to keep; 13he will love you,
bless you, and multiply you; he will also
bless the fruit of your body and the fruit
of your ground, your grain and your wine
and your oil, the increase of your cattle and
the young of your flock, in the land which
he swore to your fathers to give you. 14You
shall be blessed above all peoples; there shall
not be male or female barren among you, or
among your cattle. 15And the LORD will take
away from you all sickness; and none of the
evil diseases of Egypt, which you knew, will
he inflict upon you, but he will lay them
upon all who hate you. 16And you shall
destroy all the peoples that the LORD your
God will give over to you, your eye shall not
pity them; neither shall you serve their gods,
for that would be a snare to you.

17"If you say in your heart, 'These nations
are greater than I; how can I dispossess
them?' 18you shall not be afraid of them,
but you shall remember what the LORD
your God did to Pharaoh and to all Egypt,
19the great trials which your eyes saw, the
signs, the wonders, the mighty hand, and
the outstretched arm, by which the LORD
your God brought you out; so will the LORD
your God do to all the peoples of whom you
are afraid. 20Moreover the LORD your God
will send hornets among them, until those
who are left and hide themselves from you
are destroyed. 21You shall not be in dread of
them; for the LORD your God is in the midst
of you, a great and terrible God. 22The LORD
your God will clear away these nations
before you little by little; you may not make
an end of them at once, lest the wild beasts
grow too numerous for you. 23But the LORD
your God will give them over to you, and
throw them into great confusion, until they
are destroyed. 24And he will give their kings
into your hand, and you shall make their
name perish from under heaven; not a man
shall be able to stand against you, until you
have destroyed them. 25The graven images
of their gods you shall burn with fire; you
shall not covet the silver or the gold that is
on them, or take it for yourselves, lest you
be ensnared by it; for it is an abomination
to the LORD your God. 26And you shall
not bring an abominable thing into your
house, and become accursed like it; you
shall utterly detest and abhor it; for it is an
accursed thing."

To the choirmaster: according to Lilies.
A Psalm of David.

PSALM 69 [68]

19You know my reproach,
  and my shame and my dishonor;
  my foes are all known to you.
20Insults have broken my heart,
  so that I am in despair.
 I looked for pity, but there was none;
  and for comforters, but I found none.
21They gave me gall for food,
  and for my thirst they gave me vinegar
    to drink.

22Let their own table before them become a
    snare;
  let their sacrificial feasts be a trap.
23Let their eyes be darkened, so that they
    cannot see;
  and make their loins tremble continually.
24Pour out your indignation upon them,
  and let your burning anger overtake them.
25May their camp be a desolation,
  let no one dwell in their tents.
26For they persecute him whom you have
    struck down,
  and him whom you have wounded, they
    afflict still more.
27Add to them punishment upon punishment;
  may they have no acquittal from you.

[28]Let them be blotted out of the book
of the living;
let them not be enrolled among
the righteous.

[29]But I am afflicted and in pain;
let your salvation, O God, set me on high!

[30]I will praise the name of God with a song;
I will magnify him with thanksgiving.
[31]This will please the LORD more than an ox
or a bull with horns and hoofs.
[32]Let the humble see it and be glad;
you who seek God, let your hearts revive.
[33]For the LORD hears the needy,
and does not despise his own that
are in bonds.

[34]Let heaven and earth praise him,
the seas and everything that moves therein.
[35]For God will save Zion
and rebuild the cities of Judah;
and his servants shall dwell there and
possess it;
[36] the children of his servants shall
inherit it,
and those who love his name shall
dwell in it.

MARK 15

And as soon as it was morning the chief priests, with the elders and scribes, and the whole council held a consultation; and they bound Jesus and led him away and delivered him to Pilate.
[2]And Pilate asked him, "Are you the King
of the Jews?" And he answered him, "You
have said so." [3]And the chief priests accused
him of many things. [4]And Pilate again asked
him, "Have you no answer to make? See
how many charges they bring against you."
[5]But Jesus made no further answer, so that
Pilate wondered.

[6]Now at the feast he used to release for
them one prisoner for whom they asked.
[7]And among the rebels in prison, who had
committed murder in the insurrection,
there was a man called Barab'bas. [8]And the
crowd came up and began to ask Pilate to do
as he always did for them. [9]And he answered
them, "Do you want me to release for you
the King of the Jews?" [10]For he perceived
that it was out of envy that the chief priests
had delivered him up. [11]But the chief priests
stirred up the crowd to have him release for
them Barab'bas instead. [12]And Pilate again
said to them, "Then what shall I do with the
man whom you call the King of the Jews?"
[13]And they cried out again, "Crucify him."
[14]And Pilate said to them, "Why, what evil
has he done?" But they shouted all the more,
"Crucify him." [15]So Pilate, wishing to satisfy
the crowd, released for them Barab'bas; and
having scourged Jesus, he delivered him to
be crucified.

[16]And the soldiers led him away inside
the palace (that is, the praetorium); and
they called together the whole battalion.
[17]And they clothed him in a purple cloak,
and plaiting a crown of thorns they put it on
him. [18]And they began to salute him, "Hail,
King of the Jews!" [19]And they struck his
head with a reed, and spat upon him, and
they knelt down in homage to him. [20]And
when they had mocked him, they stripped
him of the purple cloak, and put his own
clothes on him. And they led him out to
crucify him.

REFLECTION

In Deuteronomy chapter 6, we read one of the most important passages of the Hebrew Scriptures, which is called the *Shema* prayer. In Hebrew, the word *shema* can mean both "listen" and "obey." This was understood by the ancients: the way we let God know we're listening is by obeying him. In this prayer we find the heart and soul of Judaism. In the time of Deuteronomy, there were no other nations or religions that believed in only one God. This belief set Judaism apart. In the Gospel of Mark, we get a rather shocking revelation of who this one God really is. St. Mark shows us a God on trial, scourged and abused by Roman soldiers, jeered at by his fellow countrymen, and ultimately led to his Crucifixion and

Death. The God spoken of and revealed in the Book of Deuteronomy, as Jesus shows us, is not just a God who is all powerful and deserving of our obedience, but, rather, he is also a God who is willing to pour himself out in a total and complete gift of love for the sake of his people. Do you sometimes fail to listen to and obey God?

March 20

DEUTERONOMY 8

"All the commandment which I command you this day you shall be careful to do, that you may live and multiply, and go in and possess the land which the Lord swore
to give to your fathers. [2]And you shall
remember all the way which the LORD
your God has led you these forty years
in the wilderness, that he might humble
you, testing you to know what was in
your heart, whether you would keep his
commandments, or not. [3]And he humbled
you and let you hunger and fed you with
manna, which you did not know, nor did
your fathers know; that he might make
you know that man does not live by bread
alone, but that man lives by everything that
proceeds out of the mouth of the LORD.
[4]Your clothing did not wear out upon you,
and your foot did not swell, these forty
years. [5]Know then in your heart that, as a
man disciplines his son, the LORD your
God disciplines you. [6]So you shall keep the
commandments of the LORD your God, by
walking in his ways and by fearing him.
[7]For the LORD your God is bringing you
into a good land, a land of brooks of water,
of fountains and springs, flowing forth in
valleys and hills, [8]a land of wheat and barley,
of vines and fig trees and pomegranates,
a land of olive trees and honey, [9]a land in
which you will eat bread without scarcity, in
which you will lack nothing, a land whose
stones are iron, and out of whose hills you
can dig copper. [10]And you shall eat and be
full, and you shall bless the LORD your God
for the good land he has given you.
[11]"Take heed lest you forget the LORD your
God, by not keeping his commandments
and his ordinances and his statutes, which I
command you this day: [12]lest, when you have
eaten and are full, and have built excellent
houses and live in them, [13]and when your
herds and flocks multiply, and your silver
and gold is multiplied, and all that you have
is multiplied, [14]then your heart be lifted
up, and you forget the LORD your God,
who brought you out of the land of Egypt,
out of the house of bondage, [15]who led you
through the great and terrible wilderness,
with its fiery serpents and scorpions and
thirsty ground where there was no water,
who brought you water out of the flinty
rock, [16]who fed you in the wilderness with
manna which your fathers did not know,
that he might humble you and test you, to do
you good in the end. [17]Beware lest you say in
your heart, 'My power and the might of my
hand have gotten me this wealth.' [18]You shall
remember the LORD your God, for it is he
who gives you power to get wealth; that he
may confirm his covenant which he swore
to your fathers, as at this day. [19]And if you
forget the LORD your God and go after other
gods and serve them and worship them, I
solemnly warn you this day that you shall
surely perish. [20]Like the nations that the
LORD makes to perish before you, so shall
you perish, because you would not obey the
voice of the LORD your God.

9 "Hear, O Israel; you are to pass over the
Jordan this day, to go in to dispossess
nations greater and mightier than yourselves, cities great and fortified up to heaven,
[2]a people great and tall, the sons of the
An′akim, whom you know, and of whom you
have heard it said, 'Who can stand before the
sons of A′nak?' [3]Know therefore this day that
he who goes over before you as a devouring
fire is the LORD your God; he will destroy
them and subdue them before you; so you

shall drive them out, and make them perish
quickly, as the LORD has promised you.
4“Do not say in your heart, after the LORD
your God has thrust them out before you,
‘It is because of my righteousness that
the LORD has brought me in to possess
this land’; whereas it is because of the
wickedness of these nations that the LORD is
driving them out before you. 5Not because
of your righteousness or the uprightness
of your heart are you going in to possess
their land; but because of the wickedness of
these nations the LORD your God is driving
them out from before you, and that he may
confirm the word which the LORD swore
to your fathers, to Abraham, to Isaac, and
to Jacob.
6“Know therefore, that the LORD your
God is not giving you this good land to
possess because of your righteousness; for
you are a stubborn people. 7Remember
and do not forget how you provoked the
LORD your God to wrath in the wilderness;
from the day you came out of the land of
Egypt, until you came to this place, you
have been rebellious against the LORD.
8Even at Horeb you provoked the LORD to
wrath, and the LORD was so angry with you
that he was ready to destroy you. 9When I
went up the mountain to receive the tables
of stone, the tables of the covenant which
the LORD made with you, I remained on
the mountain forty days and forty nights;
I neither ate bread nor drank water. 10And
the LORD gave me the two tables of stone
written with the finger of God; and on them
were all the words which the LORD had
spoken with you on the mountain out of the
midst of the fire on the day of the assembly.
11And at the end of forty days and forty
nights the LORD gave me the two tables of
stone, the tables of the covenant. 12Then the
LORD said to me, ‘Arise, go down quickly
from here; for your people whom you have
brought from Egypt have acted corruptly;
they have turned aside quickly out of the
way which I commanded them; they have
made themselves a molten image.’
13“Furthermore the LORD said to me, ‘I
have seen this people, and behold, it is a
stubborn people; 14let me alone, that I may
destroy them and blot out their name from
under heaven; and I will make of you a
nation mightier and greater than they.’ 15So I
turned and came down from the mountain,
and the mountain was burning with fire;
and the two tables of the covenant were in
my two hands. 16And I looked, and behold,
you had sinned against the LORD your God;
you had made yourselves a molten calf;
you had turned aside quickly from the way
which the LORD had commanded you. 17So
I took hold of the two tables, and cast them
out of my two hands, and broke them before
your eyes. 18Then I lay prostrate before the
LORD as before, forty days and forty nights;
I neither ate bread nor drank water, because
of all the sin which you had committed, in
doing what was evil in the sight of the LORD,
to provoke him to anger. 19For I was afraid
of the anger and hot displeasure which the
LORD bore against you, so that he was ready
to destroy you. But the LORD listened to me
that time also. 20And the LORD was so angry
with Aaron that he was ready to destroy
him; and I prayed for Aaron also at the same
time. 21Then I took the sinful thing, the calf
which you had made, and burned it with
fire and crushed it, grinding it very small,
until it was as fine as dust; and I threw the
dust of it into the brook that descended out
of the mountain.
22“At Tab′erah also, and at Massah, and
at Kib′roth-hatta′avah, you provoked the
LORD to wrath. 23And when the LORD sent
you from Ka′desh-bar′nea, saying, ‘Go up
and take possession of the land which I have
given you,’ then you rebelled against the
commandment of the LORD your God, and
did not believe him or obey his voice. 24You
have been rebellious against the LORD from
the day that I knew you.
25“So I lay prostrate before the LORD for
these forty days and forty nights, because
the LORD had said he would destroy you.
26And I prayed to the LORD, ‘O Lord GOD,
do not destroy your people and your
heritage, whom you have redeemed through
your greatness, whom you have brought out
of Egypt with a mighty hand. 27Remember

your servants, Abraham, Isaac, and Jacob;
do not regard the stubbornness of this
people, or their wickedness, or their sin,
[28]lest the land from which you brought us
say, "Because the LORD was not able to bring
them into the land which he promised them,
and because he hated them, he has brought
them out to slay them in the wilderness."
[29]For they are your people and your heritage,
whom you brought out by your great power
and by your outstretched arm.'

10 "At that time the LORD said to me,
'Hew two tables of stone like the first,
and come up to me on the mountain, and
make an ark of wood. [2]And I will write on the
tables the words that were on the first tables
which you broke, and you shall put them in
the ark.' [3]So I made an ark of acacia wood,
and hewed two tables of stone like the first,
and went up the mountain with the two tables
in my hand. [4]And he wrote on the tables, as
at the first writing, the ten commandments
which the LORD had spoken to you on the
mountain out of the midst of the fire on the
day of the assembly; and the LORD gave them
to me. [5]Then I turned and came down from
the mountain, and put the tables in the ark
which I had made; and there they are, as the
LORD commanded me.

[6]"(The sons of Israel journeyed from Be-
er'oth Be'ne-ja'akan to Mose'rah. There Aaron
died, and there he was buried; and his son
Elea'zar ministered as priest in his stead. [7]From
there they journeyed to Gud'godah, and from
Gudgodah to Jot'bathah, a land with brooks
of water. [8]At that time the LORD set apart the
tribe of Levi to carry the ark of the covenant of
the LORD, to stand before the LORD to minister
to him and to bless in his name, to this day.
[9]Therefore Levi has no portion or inheritance
with his brothers; the LORD is his inheritance,
as the LORD your God said to him.)

[10]"I stayed on the mountain, as at the
first time, forty days and forty nights, and
the LORD listened to me that time also; the
LORD was unwilling to destroy you. [11]And
the LORD said to me, 'Arise, go on your
journey at the head of the people, that they
may go in and possess the land, which I
swore to their fathers to give them.'"

To the choirmaster.
A Psalm of David, for the memorial offering.

PSALM 70 [69]

Be pleased, O God, to deliver me!
O LORD, make haste to help me!
[2]Let them be put to shame and confusion
who seek my life!
Let them be turned back and brought
to dishonor
who desire my harm!
[3]Let them be appalled because of
their shame
who say, "Aha, Aha!"

[4]May all who seek you
rejoice and be glad in you!
May those who love your salvation
say evermore, "God is great!"
[5]But I am poor and needy;
hasten to me, O God!
You are my help and my deliverer;
O LORD, do not delay!

MARK 15

[21]**And they compelled a passer-
by, Simon of Cyre'ne, who was
coming in from the country,
the father of Alexander and Rufus, to carry his cross. [22]And they brought him to the
place called Gol'gotha (which means the**
place of a skull). [23]And they offered him wine
mingled with myrrh; but he did not take
it. [24]And they crucified him, and divided his
garments among them, casting lots for them,
to decide what each should take. [25]And it was
the third hour, when they crucified him. [26]And
the inscription of the charge against him read,
"The King of the Jews." [27]And with him they
crucified two robbers, one on his right and one
on his left.* [29]And those who passed by derided him, shaking their heads, and saying, "Aha!
You who would destroy the temple and build it

* Other ancient authorities insert verse 28, *And the scripture was fulfilled which says, "He was reckoned with the transgressors."*

in three days, 30save yourself, and come down from the cross!" 31So also the chief priests mocked him to one another with the scribes, saying, "He saved others; he cannot save himself. 32Let the Christ, the King of Israel, come down now from the cross, that we may see and believe." Those who were crucified with him also reviled him.

33And when the sixth hour had come, there was darkness over the whole land until the ninth hour. 34And at the ninth hour Jesus cried with a loud voice, "E'lo-i, Elo-i, la'ma sabach-tha'ni?" which means, "My God, my God, why have you forsaken me?" 35And some of the bystanders hearing it said, "Behold, he is calling Eli'jah." 36And one ran and, filling a sponge full of vinegar, put it on a reed and gave it to him to drink, saying, "Wait, let us see whether Eli'jah will come to take him down." 37And Jesus uttered a loud cry, and breathed his last. 38And the curtain of the temple was torn in two, from top to bottom. 39And when the centurion, who stood facing him, saw that he thus breathed his last, he said, "Truly this man was the Son of God!"

40There were also women looking on from afar, among whom were Mary Mag'dalene, and Mary the mother of James the younger and of Joses, and Salo'me, 41who, when he was in Galilee, followed him, and ministered to him; and also many other women who came up with him to Jerusalem.

42And when evening had come, since it was the day of Preparation, that is, the day before the sabbath, 43Joseph of Arimathe'a, a respected member of the council, who was also himself looking for the kingdom of God, took courage and went to Pilate, and asked for the body of Jesus. 44And Pilate wondered if he were already dead; and summoning the centurion, he asked him whether he was already dead. 45And when he learned from the centurion that he was dead, he granted the body to Joseph. 46And he bought a linen shroud, and taking him down, wrapped him in the linen shroud, and laid him in a tomb which had been hewn out of the rock; and he rolled a stone against the door of the tomb. 47Mary Mag'dalene and Mary the mother of Joses saw where he was laid.

REFLECTION

Throughout the Book of Deuteronomy, God demonstrates that he desires Israel's heart—just as he does ours. In chapter 8, however, we are warned of dangers that seek to turn hearts away from God. Moses foretells that once the people enter the Promised Land, they will discover a land filled with bounty and blessing. The danger is that we can become self-sufficient and forget about our need for God. We can be lulled into thinking that we don't need to rely on him anymore. Moses says in chapter 9 that Israel will defeat great and powerful enemies in the land. This will also be a danger to their faith because they will begin to put their faith in their own greatness. What God wants Israel to know is that he didn't choose them because they were the strongest nation. Rather, he chose them because he loved them. Wrestling with God's love for us is one of life's greatest mysteries. God's utter greatness should leave us in awe, knowing that he's chosen to love, to care for, and even to die for us, despite our failures, frailties, and weaknesses. In what ways might you be self-satisfied with material comfort or success and fail to rely solely on God?

March 21

DEUTERONOMY 10

12"And now, Israel, what does the Lord your God require of you, but to fear the Lord your God, to walk in all his ways, to love him, to serve the Lord your God with all your heart and with all your soul, 13and to keep the commandments and statutes of the LORD, which I command you this day for your good? 14Behold, to the LORD your God belong heaven and the heaven of heavens, the earth with all that is in it; 15yet the LORD set his heart in love upon your fathers and chose their descendants after them, you above all peoples, as at this day. 16Circumcise therefore the foreskin of your heart, and be no longer stubborn. 17For the LORD your God is God of gods and Lord of lords, the great, the mighty, and the terrible God, who is not partial and takes no bribe. 18He executes justice for the fatherless and the widow, and loves the sojourner, giving him food and clothing. 19Love the sojourner therefore; for you were sojourners in the land of Egypt. 20You shall fear the LORD your God; you shall serve him and cling to him, and by his name you shall swear. 21He is your praise; he is your God, who has done for you these great and terrible things which your eyes have seen. 22Your fathers went down to Egypt seventy persons; and now the LORD your God has made you as the stars of heaven for multitude.

11 "You shall therefore love the LORD your God, and keep his charge, his statutes, his ordinances, and his commandments always. 2And consider this day (since I am not speaking to your children who have not known or seen it), consider the discipline of the LORD your God, his greatness, his mighty hand and his outstretched arm, 3his signs and his deeds which he did in Egypt to Pharaoh the king of Egypt and to all his land; 4and what he did to the army of Egypt, to their horses and to their chariots; how he made the water of the Red Sea overflow them as they pursued after you, and how the LORD has destroyed them to this day; 5and what he did to you in the wilderness, until you came to this place; 6and what he did to Da′than and Abi′ram the sons of Eli′ab, son of Reuben; how the earth opened its mouth and swallowed them up, with their households, their tents, and every living thing that followed them, in the midst of all Israel; 7for your eyes have seen all the great work of the LORD which he did.

8"You shall therefore keep all the commandment which I command you this day, that you may be strong, and go in and take possession of the land which you are going over to possess, 9and that you may live long in the land which the LORD swore to your fathers to give to them and to their descendants, a land flowing with milk and honey. 10For the land which you are entering to take possession of it is not like the land of Egypt, from which you have come, where you sowed your seed and watered it with your feet, like a garden of vegetables; 11but the land which you are going over to possess is a land of hills and valleys, which drinks water by the rain from heaven, 12a land which the LORD your God cares for; the eyes of the LORD your God are always upon it, from the beginning of the year to the end of the year.

13"And if you will obey my commandments which I command you this day, to love the LORD your God, and to serve him with all your heart and with all your soul, 14he will give the rain for your land in its season, the early rain and the later rain, that you may gather in your grain and your wine and your oil. 15And he will give grass in your fields for your cattle, and you shall eat and be full. 16Take heed lest your heart be deceived, and you turn aside and serve other gods and worship them, 17and the anger of the LORD be kindled against you, and he shut up the heavens, so that there be no rain, and the land yield no fruit, and you perish quickly off the good land which the LORD gives you.

18"You shall therefore lay up these words of mine in your heart and in your soul; and you shall bind them as a sign upon your hand, and they shall be as frontlets between your eyes. 19And you shall teach them to your children, talking of them when you are sitting in your house, and when you are walking by the way, and when you lie down, and when you rise. 20And you shall write them upon the doorposts of your house and upon your gates, 21that your days and the days of your children may be multiplied in the land which the LORD swore to your fathers to give them, as long as the heavens are above the earth. 22For if you will be careful to do all this commandment which I command you to do, loving the LORD your God, walking in all his ways, and clinging to him, 23then the LORD will drive out all these nations before you, and you will dispossess nations greater and mightier than yourselves. 24Every place on which the sole of your foot treads shall be yours; your territory shall be from the wilderness and Lebanon and from the River, the river Euphrates, to the western sea. 25No man shall be able to stand against you; the LORD your God will lay the fear of you and the dread of you upon all the land that you shall tread, as he promised you.

26"Behold, I set before you this day a blessing and a curse: 27the blessing, if you obey the commandments of the LORD your God, which I command you this day, 28and the curse, if you do not obey the commandments of the LORD your God, but turn aside from the way which I command you this day, to go after other gods which you have not known. 29And when the LORD your God brings you into the land which you are entering to take possession of it, you shall set the blessing on Mount Ger′izim and the curse on Mount E′bal. 30Are they not beyond the Jordan, west of the road, toward the going down of the sun, in the land of the Canaanites who live in the Ar′abah, over against Gilgal, beside the Oak of Mo′reh? 31For you are to pass over the Jordan to go in to take possession of the land which the LORD your God gives you; and when you possess it and live in it, 32you shall be careful to do all the statutes and the ordinances which I set before you this day.

12 "These are the statutes and ordinances which you shall be careful to do in the land which the LORD, the God of your fathers, has given you to possess, all the days that you live upon the earth. 2You shall surely destroy all the places where the nations whom you shall dispossess served their gods, upon the high mountains and upon the hills and under every green tree; 3you shall tear down their altars, and dash in pieces their pillars, and burn their Ashe′rim with fire; you shall hew down the graven images of their gods, and destroy their name out of that place. 4You shall not do so to the LORD your God. 5But you shall seek the place which the LORD your God will choose out of all your tribes to put his name and make his habitation there; there you shall go, 6and there you shall bring your burnt offerings and your sacrifices, your tithes and the offering that you present, your votive offerings, your freewill offerings, and the firstlings of your herd and of your flock; 7and there you shall eat before the LORD your God, and you shall rejoice, you and your households, in all that you undertake, in which the LORD your God has blessed you. 8You shall not do according to all that we are doing here this day, every man doing whatever is right in his own eyes; 9for you have not as yet come to the rest and to the inheritance which the LORD your God gives you. 10But when you go over the Jordan, and live in the land which the LORD your God gives you to inherit, and when he gives you rest from all your enemies round about, so that you live in safety, 11then to the place which the LORD your God will choose, to make his name dwell there, there you shall bring all that I command you: your burnt offerings and your sacrifices, your tithes and the offering that you present, and all your votive offerings which you vow to the LORD. 12And you shall rejoice before the LORD your God, you and your sons and your daughters, your menservants and your maidservants, and the Levite that is within your towns, since he has no portion or inheritance with you. 13Take heed that you do not offer your burnt offerings at every place that you see; 14but at the place which the LORD will choose in one of your tribes, there you shall offer your burnt offerings, and there you shall do all that I am commanding you."

PSALM 71 [70]

In you, O LORD, I take refuge;
let me never be put to shame!
2In your righteousness deliver me and rescue me;
incline your ear to me, and save me!
3Be to me a rock of refuge,
a strong fortress, to save me,
for you are my rock and my fortress.

4Rescue me, O my God, from the hand of the wicked,
from the grasp of the unjust and cruel man.

[5]For you, O Lord, are my hope,
my trust, O LORD, from my youth.
[6]Upon you I have leaned from my birth;
from my mother's womb, you have been
my strength.
My praise is continually of you.

[7]I have been as a portent to many;
but you are my strong refuge.
[8]My mouth is filled with your praise,
and with your glory all the day.
[9]Do not cast me off in the time of old age;
forsake me not when my strength
is spent.
[10]For my enemies speak concerning me,
those who watch for my life consult
together,
[11]and say, "God has forsaken him;
pursue and seize him,
for there is none to deliver him."

[12]O God, be not far from me;
O my God, make haste to help me!
[13]May my accusers be put to shame
and consumed;
with scorn and disgrace may they
be covered
who seek my harm.
[14]But I will hope continually,
and will praise you yet more and more.
[15]My mouth will tell of your righteous acts,
of your deeds of salvation all the day,
for their number is past my knowledge.
[16]With the mighty deeds of the Lord GOD
I will come,
I will praise your righteousness,
yours alone.

[17]O God, from my youth you have taught me,
and I still proclaim your wondrous deeds.
[18]So even to old age and gray hairs,
O God, do not forsake me,
till I proclaim your might
to all the generations to come.
Your power [19]and your righteousness,
O God,
reach the high heavens.

You who have done great things,
O God, who is like you?
[20]You who have made me see many
sore troubles
will revive me again;
from the depths of the earth
you will bring me up again.
[21]You will increase my honor,
and comfort me again.

[22]I will also praise you with the harp
for your faithfulness, O my God;
I will sing praises to you with the lyre,
O Holy One of Israel.
[23]My lips will shout for joy,
when I sing praises to you;
my soul also, which you have rescued.
[24]And my tongue will talk of your
righteous help
all the day long,
for they have been put to shame
and disgraced
who sought to do me harm.

MARK 16

And when the sabbath was past, Mary Mag′dalene, and Mary the mother of James, and Salo′me, bought spices, so that they might go and anoint
him. [2]And very early on the first day of
the week they went to the tomb when
the sun had risen. [3]And they were saying
to one another, "Who will roll away the
stone for us from the door of the tomb?"
[4]And looking up, they saw that the stone
was rolled back; for it was very large. [5]And
entering the tomb, they saw a young man
sitting on the right side, dressed in a white
robe; and they were amazed. [6]And he said
to them, "Do not be amazed; you seek Jesus
of Nazareth, who was crucified. He has
risen, he is not here; see the place where
they laid him. [7]But go, tell his disciples
and Peter that he is going before you to
Galilee; there you will see him, as he told
you." [8]And they went out and fled from the
tomb; for trembling and astonishment had
come upon them; and they said nothing to
any one, for they were afraid.

[9]Now when he rose early on the first
day of the week, he appeared first to Mary
Magdalene, from whom he had cast out
seven demons. [10]She went and told those
who had been with him, as they mourned
and wept. [11]But when they heard that he was
alive and had been seen by her, they would
not believe it.

[12]After this he appeared in another form
to two of them, as they were walking into
the country. [13]And they went back and told
the rest, but they did not believe them.

[14]Afterward he appeared to the Eleven
themselves as they sat at table; and he
upbraided them for their unbelief and
hardness of heart, because they had not
believed those who saw him after he had
risen. [15]And he said to them, "Go into all the
world and preach the gospel to the whole
creation. [16]He who believes and is baptized
will be saved; but he who does not believe
will be condemned. [17]And these signs will
accompany those who believe: in my name
they will cast out demons; they will speak
in new tongues; [18]they will pick up serpents,
and if they drink any deadly thing, it will
not hurt them; they will lay their hands on
the sick, and they will recover."

[19]So then the Lord Jesus, after he had
spoken to them, was taken up into heaven,
and sat down at the right hand of God. [20]And
they went forth and preached everywhere,
while the Lord worked with them and
confirmed the message by the signs that
attended it. Amen.

REFLECTION

Having recounted the story of salvation, Moses urges the people to fix, or literally "bind," the Commandments of God and the story of salvation onto their hearts (see Dt 11:18). God desires these things to be embedded deep within his people. In the Gospel, on the other hand, we read the story of Jesus's Resurrection from the dead, his appearance to Mary Magdalene, and his Ascension into Heaven. One gets the sense, in reading the story, that Mary Magdalene has the kind of heart that God desires. She has embedded the words of Jesus in her heart and, as a result, recognizes the truth of his Resurrection even before the Apostles. St. Mark reminds us of her story—that Jesus had cast seven demons out of her. In a very real way, Mary Magdalene has experienced her own exodus, moving from slavery to freedom through Jesus. By remembering this and embedding Jesus in her heart, she is able to recognize with the eyes of faith what no one else can. How can you embed God's Commandments and the story of salvation more deeply in your own heart?

March 22

DEUTERONOMY 12

[15]**"However, you may slaughter
and eat flesh within any of your
towns, as much as you desire,
according to the blessing of the LORD
your God which he has given you; the
unclean and the clean may eat of it, as**
of the gazelle and as of the deer. [16]Only you
shall not eat the blood; you shall pour it out
upon the earth like water. [17]You may not eat
within your towns the tithe of your grain or
of your wine or of your oil, or the firstlings
of your herd or of your flock, or any of your
votive offerings which you vow, or your
freewill offerings, or the offering that you
present; [18]but you shall eat them before the
LORD your God in the place which the LORD
your God will choose, you and your son and
your daughter, your manservant and your
maidservant, and the Levite who is within
your towns; and you shall rejoice before the
LORD your God in all that you undertake.
[19]Take heed that you do not forsake the
Levite as long as you live in your land.

[20]"When the LORD your God enlarges
your territory, as he has promised you, and
you say, 'I will eat flesh,' because you crave

flesh, you may eat as much flesh as you
desire. 21If the place which the LORD your
God will choose to put his name there is too
far from you, then you may kill any of your
herd or your flock, which the LORD has
given you, as I have commanded you; and
you may eat within your towns as much as
you desire. 22Just as the gazelle or the deer
is eaten, so you may eat of it; the unclean
and the clean alike may eat of it. 23Only be
sure that you do not eat the blood; for the
blood is the life, and you shall not eat the
life with the flesh. 24You shall not eat it; you
shall pour it out upon the earth like water.
25You shall not eat it; that all may go well
with you and with your children after you,
when you do what is right in the sight of
the LORD. 26But the holy things which are
due from you, and your votive offerings,
you shall take, and you shall go to the
place which the LORD will choose, 27and
offer your burnt offerings, the flesh and
the blood, on the altar of the LORD your
God; the blood of your sacrifices shall be
poured out on the altar of the LORD your
God, but the flesh you may eat. 28Be careful
to heed all these words which I command
you, that it may go well with you and with
your children after you for ever, when you
do what is good and right in the sight of the
LORD your God.

29"When the LORD your God cuts off
before you the nations whom you go in to
dispossess, and you dispossess them and
dwell in their land, 30take heed that you be
not ensnared to follow them, after they have
been destroyed before you, and that you do
not inquire about their gods, saying, 'How
did these nations serve their gods?—that I
also may do likewise.' 31You shall not do so
to the LORD your God; for every abominable
thing which the LORD hates they have done
for their gods; for they even burn their sons
and their daughters in the fire to their gods.

32"Everything that I command you you
shall be careful to do; you shall not add to it
or take from it.

13 "If a prophet arises among you, or a
dreamer of dreams, and gives you a
sign or a wonder, 2and the sign or wonder
which he tells you comes to pass, and if he
says, 'Let us go after other gods,' which you
have not known, 'and let us serve them,'
3you shall not listen to the words of that
prophet or to that dreamer of dreams; for
the LORD your God is testing you, to know
whether you love the LORD your God with
all your heart and with all your soul. 4You
shall walk after the LORD your God and fear
him, and keep his commandments and obey
his voice, and you shall serve him and cling
to him. 5But that prophet or that dreamer
of dreams shall be put to death, because he
has taught rebellion against the LORD your
God, who brought you out of the land of
Egypt and redeemed you out of the house
of bondage, to make you leave the way in
which the LORD your God commanded you
to walk. So you shall purge the evil from the
midst of you.

6"If your brother, the son of your mother,
or your son, or your daughter, or the wife of
your bosom, or your friend who is as your
own soul, entices you secretly, saying, 'Let
us go and serve other gods,' which neither
you nor your fathers have known, 7some
of the gods of the peoples that are round
about you, whether near you or far off from
you, from the one end of the earth to the
other, 8you shall not yield to him or listen
to him, nor shall your eye pity him, nor
shall you spare him, nor shall you conceal
him; 9but you shall kill him; your hand shall
be first against him to put him to death,
and afterwards the hand of all the people.
10You shall stone him to death with stones,
because he sought to draw you away from
the LORD your God, who brought you out
of the land of Egypt, out of the house of
bondage. 11And all Israel shall hear, and fear,
and never again do any such wickedness as
this among you.

12"If you hear in one of your cities, which
the LORD your God gives you to dwell
there, 13that certain base fellows have gone
out among you and have drawn away the
inhabitants of the city, saying, 'Let us go
and serve other gods,' which you have not
known, 14then you shall inquire and make
search and ask diligently; and behold, if it

be true and certain that such an abominable thing has been done among you, 15you shall surely put the inhabitants of that city to the sword, destroying it utterly, all who are in it and its cattle, with the edge of the sword. 16You shall gather all its spoil into the midst of its open square, and burn the city and all its spoil with fire, as a whole burnt offering to the LORD your God; it shall be a heap for ever, it shall not be built again. 17None of the devoted things shall cling to your hand; that the LORD may turn from the fierceness of his anger, and show you mercy, and have compassion on you, and multiply you, as he swore to your fathers, 18if you obey the voice of the LORD your God, keeping all his commandments which I command you this day, and doing what is right in the sight of the LORD your God.

14 "You are the sons of the LORD your God; you shall not cut yourselves or make any baldness on your foreheads for the dead. 2For you are a people holy to the LORD your God, and the LORD has chosen you to be a people for his own possession, out of all the peoples that are on the face of the earth.

3"You shall not eat any abominable thing. 4These are the animals you may eat: the ox, the sheep, the goat, 5the deer, the gazelle, the roebuck, the wild goat, the ibex, the antelope, and the mountain-sheep. 6Every animal that parts the hoof and has the hoof cloven in two, and chews the cud, among the animals, you may eat. 7Yet of those that chew the cud or have the hoof cloven you shall not eat these: The camel, the hare, and the rock badger, because they chew the cud but do not part the hoof, are unclean for you. 8And the swine, because it parts the hoof but does not chew the cud, is unclean for you. Their flesh you shall not eat, and their carcasses you shall not touch.

9"Of all that are in the waters you may eat these: Whatever has fins and scales you may eat. 10And whatever does not have fins and scales you shall not eat; it is unclean for you.

11"You may eat all clean birds. 12But these are the ones which you shall not eat: the eagle, the vulture, the osprey, 13the buzzard, the kite, after their kinds; 14every raven after its kind; 15the ostrich, the nighthawk, the sea gull, the hawk, after their kinds; 16the little owl and the great owl, the water hen 17and the pelican, the carrion vulture and the cormorant, 18the stork, the heron, after their kinds; the hoopoe and the bat. 19And all winged insects are unclean for you; they shall not be eaten. 20All clean winged things you may eat.

21"You shall not eat anything that dies of itself; you may give it to the alien who is within your towns, that he may eat it, or you may sell it to a foreigner; for you are a people holy to the LORD your God.

"You shall not boil a kid in its mother's milk."

A Psalm of Solomon.

PSALM 72 [71]

Give the king your justice, O God,
and your righteousness to the royal son!
2May he judge your people with
righteousness,
and your poor with justice!
3Let the mountains bear prosperity for
the people,
and the hills, in righteousness!
4May he defend the cause of the poor of
the people,
give deliverance to the needy,
and crush the oppressor!

5May he live while the sun endures,
and as long as the moon, throughout
all generations!
6May he be like rain that falls on the
mown grass,
like showers that water the earth!
7In his days may righteousness flourish,
and peace abound, till the moon be
no more!

8May he have dominion from sea to sea,
and from the River to the ends of
the earth!

[9]May his foes bow down before him,
and his enemies lick the dust!
[10]May the kings of Tarshish and of the isles
render him tribute,
may the kings of Sheba and Seba bring gifts!
[11]May all kings fall down before him,
all nations serve him!

[12]For he delivers the needy when he calls,
the poor and him who has no helper.
[13]He has pity on the weak and the needy,
and saves the lives of the needy.
[14]From oppression and violence he redeems
their souls;
and precious is their blood in his sight.

[15]Long may he live,
may gold of Sheba be given to him!
May prayer be made for him continually,
and blessings invoked for him all the day!
[16]May there be abundance of grain in
the land;
on the tops of the mountains may it wave;
may its fruit be like Lebanon;
and may men blossom forth from
the cities
like the grass of the field!
[17]May his name endure for ever,
his fame continue as long as the sun!
May men bless themselves by him,
all nations call him blessed!

[18]Blessed be the LORD, the God of Israel,
who alone does wondrous things.
[19]Blessed be his glorious name for ever;
may his glory fill the whole earth! Amen
and Amen!

[20]The prayers of David, the son of Jesse,
are ended.

LUKE 1

Inasmuch as many have undertaken to compile a narrative of the things which have been accomplished among us, [2]just as they were delivered to us by those who from the beginning were eyewitnesses and ministers of the word, [3]it seemed good to me also, having followed all things closely for some time past, to write an orderly account for you, most excellent Theophʹilus, [4]that you may know the truth concerning the things of which you have been informed.

[5]In the days of Herod, king of Judea, there was a priest named Zechariʹah, of the division of Abiʹjah; and he had a wife of the daughters of Aaron, and her name was Elizabeth. [6]And they were both righteous before God, walking in all the commandments and ordinances of the Lord blamelessly. [7]But they had no child, because Elizabeth was barren, and both were advanced in years.

[8]Now while he was serving as priest before God when his division was on duty,
[9]according to the custom of the priesthood, it fell to him by lot to enter the temple of the Lord and burn incense. [10]And the whole multitude of the people were praying outside at the hour of incense. [11]And there appeared to him an angel of the Lord standing on the right side of the altar of incense. [12]And Zechariʹah was troubled when he saw him, and fear fell upon him. [13]But the angel said to him, "Do not be afraid, Zechariʹah, for your prayer is heard, and your wife Elizabeth will bear you a son, and you shall call his name John.
[14]And you will have joy and gladness,
and many will rejoice at his birth;
[15]for he will be great before the Lord,
and he shall drink no wine nor
strong drink,
and he will be filled with the Holy Spirit,
even from his mother's womb.
[16]And he will turn many of the sons of Israel
to the Lord their God,
[17]and he will go before him in the spirit and
power of Eliʹjah,
to turn the hearts of the fathers to
the children,
and the disobedient to the wisdom of
the just,
to make ready for the Lord a
people prepared."

[18]And Zechari′ah said to the angel, "How
shall I know this? For I am an old man,
and my wife is advanced in years." [19]And
the angel answered him, "I am Gabriel,
who stand in the presence of God; and I
was sent to speak to you, and to bring you
this good news. [20]And behold, you will be
silent and unable to speak until the day
that these things come to pass, because
you did not believe my words, which
will be fulfilled in their time." [21]And the
people were waiting for Zechari′ah, and
they wondered at his delay in the temple.
[22]And when he came out, he could not
speak to them, and they perceived that he
had seen a vision in the temple; and he
made signs to them and remained mute.
[23]And when his time of service was ended,
he went to his home.
[24]After these days his wife Elizabeth conceived, and for five months she hid herself,
saying, [25]"Thus the Lord has done to me
in the days when he looked on me, to take
away my reproach among men."

REFLECTION

Many readers are confused by the Book of Deuteronomy. It contains many puzzling details about places of worship, liturgical furnishings, animal sacrifice, foods to be eaten and foods to be avoided, and various religious practices. Indeed, it's easy to get lost in all the details. But to do so is to miss the bigger picture of Deuteronomy. At this point in the story of salvation, God has freed Israel from slavery in Egypt and sought to win her over as his beloved. The Ten Commandments and the laws of the Old Testament can be seen within this love story as wedding vows. Viewed in this light, details about houses of worship, furnishings, food, etc., should be seen not merely as a detailed legal code but rather as a beloved family setting up their first home together. Reading Deuteronomy this way helps to bring the book to life. How do you view the Ten Commandments and precepts of the Church—as simply a legal code to follow, or as wedding vows directed toward building a better relationship with God?

March 23

DEUTERONOMY 14

[22]**"You shall tithe all the yield of
your seed, which comes forth
from the field year by year. [23]And before
the LORD your God, in the place which**
he will choose, to make his name dwell
there, you shall eat the tithe of your grain, of
your wine, and of your oil, and the firstlings
of your herd and flock; that you may learn
to fear the LORD your God always. [24]And if
the way is too long for you, so that you are
not able to bring the tithe, when the LORD
your God blesses you, because the place
is too far from you, which the LORD your
God chooses, to set his name there, [25]then
you shall turn it into money, and bind up
the money in your hand, and go to the
place which the LORD your God chooses,
[26]and spend the money for whatever you
desire, oxen, or sheep, or wine or strong
drink, whatever your appetite craves; and
you shall eat there before the LORD your
God and rejoice, you and your household.
[27]And you shall not forsake the Levite who
is within your towns, for he has no portion
or inheritance with you.
[28]"At the end of every three years you shall
bring forth all the tithe of your produce
in the same year, and lay it up within your
towns; [29]and the Levite, because he has no
portion or inheritance with you, and the
sojourner, the fatherless, and the widow,
who are within your towns, shall come and
eat and be filled; that the LORD your God
may bless you in all the work of your hands
that you do.
15 "At the end of every seven years you
shall grant a release. [2]And this is the
manner of the release: every creditor shall
release what he has lent to his neighbor;
he shall not exact it of his neighbor, his
brother, because the LORD's release has
been proclaimed. [3]Of a foreigner you may
exact it; but whatever of yours is with your

brother your hand shall release. [4]But there will be no poor among you (for the LORD will bless you in the land which the LORD your God gives you for an inheritance to possess), [5]if only you will obey the voice of the LORD your God, being careful to do all this commandment which I command you this day. [6]For the LORD your God will bless you, as he promised you, and you shall lend to many nations, but you shall not borrow; and you shall rule over many nations, but they shall not rule over you.

[7]"If there is among you a poor man, one of your brethren, in any of your towns within your land which the LORD your God gives you, you shall not harden your heart or shut your hand against your poor brother, [8]but you shall open your hand to him, and lend him sufficient for his need, whatever it may be. [9]Take heed lest there be a base thought in your heart, and you say, 'The seventh year, the year of release is near,' and your eye be hostile to your poor brother, and you give him nothing, and he cry to the LORD against you, and it be sin in you. [10]You shall give to him freely, and your heart shall not be grudging when you give to him; because for this the LORD your God will bless you in all your work and in all that you undertake. [11]For the poor will never cease out of the land; therefore I command you, You shall open wide your hand to your brother, to the needy and to the poor, in the land.

[12]"If your brother, a Hebrew man, or a Hebrew woman, is sold to you, he shall serve you six years, and in the seventh year you shall let him go free from you.[13]And when you let him go free from you, you shall not let him go empty-handed; [14]you shall furnish him liberally out of your flock, out of your threshing floor, and out of your wine press; as the LORD your God has blessed you, you shall give to him. [15]You shall remember that you were a slave in the land of Egypt, and the LORD your God redeemed you; therefore I command you this today. [16]But if he says to you, 'I will not go out from you,' because he loves you and your household, since he fares well with you, [17]then you shall take an awl, and thrust it through his ear into the door, and he shall be your bondman for ever. And to your bondwoman you shall do likewise. [18]It shall not seem hard to you, when you let him go free from you; for at half the cost of a hired servant he has served you six years. So the LORD your God will bless you in all that you do.

[19]"All the firstling males that are born of your herd and flock you shall consecrate to the LORD your God; you shall do no work with the firstling of your herd, nor shear the firstling of your flock. [20]You shall eat it, you and your household, before the LORD your God year by year at the place which the LORD will choose. [21]But if it has any blemish, if it is lame or blind, or has any serious blemish whatever, you shall not sacrifice it to the LORD your God. [22]You shall eat it within your towns; the unclean and the clean alike may eat it, as though it were a gazelle or a deer. [23]Only you shall not eat its blood; you shall pour it out on the ground like water.

16 "Observe the month of A'bib, and keep the Passover to the LORD your God; for in the month of Abib the LORD your God brought you out of Egypt by night. [2]And you shall offer the Passover sacrifice to the LORD your God, from the flock or the herd, at the place which the LORD will choose, to make his name dwell there. [3]You shall eat no leavened bread with it; seven days you shall eat it with unleavened bread, the bread of affliction—for you came out of the land of Egypt in hurried flight—that all the days of your life you may remember the day when you came out of the land of Egypt. [4]No leaven shall be seen with you in all your territory for seven days; nor shall any of the flesh which you sacrifice on the evening of the first day remain all night until morning. [5]You may not offer the Passover sacrifice within any of your towns which the LORD your God gives you; [6]but at the place which the LORD your God will choose, to make his name dwell in it, there you shall offer the Passover sacrifice, in the evening at the going down of the sun, at the time you came out of Egypt. [7]And you shall boil it and eat it at the place which the LORD your God will choose; and in the morning you shall turn and go to your tents. [8]For six days you shall eat unleavened bread; and on the seventh day

there shall be a solemn assembly to the LORD
your God; you shall do no work on it.
9“You shall count seven weeks; begin to
count the seven weeks from the time you
first put the sickle to the standing grain.
10Then you shall keep the feast of weeks
to the LORD your God with the tribute
of a freewill offering from your hand,
which you shall give as the LORD your
God blesses you; 11and you shall rejoice
before the LORD your God, you and your
son and your daughter, your manservant
and your maidservant, the Levite who
is within your towns, the sojourner, the
fatherless, and the widow who are among
you, at the place which the LORD your
God will choose, to make his name dwell
there. 12You shall remember that you were
a slave in Egypt; and you shall be careful
to observe these statutes.

13“You shall keep the feast of booths seven
days, when you make your ingathering from
your threshing floor and your wine press;
14you shall rejoice in your feast, you and your
son and your daughter, your manservant and
your maidservant, the Levite, the sojourner,
the fatherless, and the widow who are within
your towns. 15For seven days you shall keep
the feast to the LORD your God at the place
which the LORD will choose; because the
LORD your God will bless you in all your
produce and in all the work of your hands, so
that you will be altogether joyful.

16“Three times a year all your males shall
appear before the LORD your God at the
place which he will choose: at the feast of
unleavened bread, at the feast of weeks, and
at the feast of booths. They shall not appear
before the LORD empty-handed; 17every
man shall give as he is able, according to the
blessing of the LORD your God which he has
given you.

18“You shall appoint judges and officers in
all your towns which the LORD your God
gives you, according to your tribes; and
they shall judge the people with righteous
judgment. 19You shall not pervert justice; you
shall not show partiality; and you shall not
take a bribe, for a bribe blinds the eyes of the
wise and subverts the cause of the righteous.
20Justice, and only justice, you shall follow,
that you may live and inherit the land which
the LORD your God gives you.

21“You shall not plant any tree as an Ashe′rah
beside the altar of the LORD your God which
you shall make. 22And you shall not set up a
pillar, which the LORD your God hates.

17 “You shall not sacrifice to the LORD
your God an ox or a sheep in which
is a blemish, any defect whatever; for that is
an abomination to the LORD your God.

2“If there is found among you, within any
of your towns which the LORD your God
gives you, a man or woman who does what
is evil in the sight of the LORD your God, in
transgressing his covenant, 3and has gone
and served other gods and worshiped them,
or the sun or the moon or any of the host
of heaven, which I have forbidden, 4and
it is told you and you hear of it; then you
shall inquire diligently, and if it is true and
certain that such an abominable thing has
been done in Israel, 5then you shall bring
forth to your gates that man or woman who
has done this evil thing, and you shall stone
that man or woman to death with stones.
6On the evidence of two witnesses or of
three witnesses he that is to die shall be put
to death; a person shall not be put to death
on the evidence of one witness. 7The hand
of the witnesses shall be first against him to
put him to death, and afterward the hand
of all the people. So you shall purge the evil
from the midst of you.”

A Psalm of Asaph.

PSALM 73 [72]

Truly God is good to the upright,
to those who are pure in heart.
2But as for me, my feet had
almost stumbled,
my steps had well nigh slipped.
3For I was envious of the arrogant,
when I saw the prosperity of the wicked.
4For they have no pangs;
their bodies are sound and sleek.

[5]They are not in trouble as other men are;
they are not stricken like other men.
[6]Therefore pride is their necklace;
violence covers them as a garment.
[7]Their eyes swell out with fatness,
their hearts overflow with follies.
[8]They scoff and speak with malice;
loftily they threaten oppression.
[9]They set their mouths against the heavens,
and their tongue struts through the earth.

[10]Therefore the people turn and praise them;
and find no fault in them.
[11]And they say, "How can God know?
Is there knowledge in the Most High?"
[12]Behold, these are the wicked;
always at ease, they increase in riches.
[13]All in vain have I kept my heart clean
and washed my hands in innocence.
[14]For all the day long I have been stricken,
and chastened every morning.

[15]If I had said, "I will speak thus,"
I would have been untrue to the
generation of your children.
[16]But when I thought how to
understand this,
it seemed to me a wearisome task,
[17]until I went into the sanctuary of God;
then I perceived their end.
[18]Truly you set them in slippery places;
you make them fall to ruin.
[19]How they are destroyed in a moment,
swept away utterly by terrors!
[20]They are like a dream when one awakes,
on awaking you despise their phantoms.

LUKE 1

[26]In the sixth month the angel Gabriel was sent from God to a city of Galilee named Nazareth, [27]to a virgin betrothed to a man whose name was Joseph, of the house of David; and the virgin's name was Mary.
[28]And he came to her and said, "Hail, full of grace, the Lord is with you!"
[29]But she was greatly troubled at the saying, and considered in her mind what sort of greeting this might be.
[30]And the angel said to her, "Do not be afraid, Mary, for you have found favor with God.
[31]And behold, you will conceive in your womb and bear a son, and you shall call his name Jesus.
[32]He will be great, and will be called the Son
of the Most High;
and the Lord God will give to him the
throne of his father David,
[33]and he will reign over the house of Jacob
for ever;
and of his kingdom there will be no end."
[34]And Mary said to the angel, "How can this be, since I do not know man?"
[35]And the angel said to her,
"The Holy Spirit will come upon you,
and the power of the Most High will
overshadow you;
therefore the child to be born will be
called holy,
the Son of God.
[36]And behold, your kinswoman Elizabeth in her old age has also conceived a son; and this is the sixth month with her who was called barren.
[37]For with God nothing will be impossible."
[38]And Mary said, "Behold, I am the handmaid of the Lord; let it be to me according to your word." And the angel departed from her.

REFLECTION

In many ways, the Gospel of Luke is a story of reversals. The Annunciation to Mary by the Angel Gabriel demonstrates that God will often choose the most unlikely of candidates to do his greatest work. Mary was a young girl from a small and unimportant village. And yet, God chose Mary, in this place and time, to change the course of human history. One of the first things that Gabriel says to Mary in the Annunciation is "do not be afraid" (Lk 1:30), a phrase which some think paints Mary in a negative light. Did she not trust God? Did she not have enough faith? Understanding the biblical tradition, however, allows us to recognize the profundity of this statement. Indeed, right before the angel tells Mary not to be afraid, he says, "The Lord is with you" (v. 28). Everywhere this phrase occurs in the Old Testament, the person to whom it is spoken is about to be asked to do something profound. For example, these words were spoken to Moses at the burning bush before he was sent to challenge Pharaoh (see Ex 3:12). And Joshua was told this before he led God's people into the Promised Land (see Jos 1:5–7). Here, Mary's righteous fear demonstrates that she knows biblical tradition. She understands that, on her own, she doesn't have the capacity to perform the mission that will be given her. Her response shows that she needs God to assist her. Her trust is not in herself; it is in God alone. Are there times when you fail to trust in God?

March 24

DEUTERONOMY 17

8"If any case arises requiring decision between one kind of homicide and another, one kind of legal right and another, or one kind of assault and another, any case within your towns which is too difficult for you, then you shall arise and go up to the place which the LORD your God will choose, 9and coming to the Levitical priests, and to the judge who is in office in those days, you shall consult them, and they shall declare to you the decision. 10Then you shall do according to what they declare to you from that place which the LORD will choose; and you shall be careful to do according to all that they direct you; 11according to the instructions which they give you, and according to the decision which they pronounce to you, you shall do; you shall not turn aside from the verdict which they declare to you, either to the right hand or to the left. 12The man who acts presumptuously, by not obeying the priest who stands to minister there before the LORD your God, or the judge, that man shall die; so you shall purge the evil from Israel. 13And all the people shall hear, and fear, and not act presumptuously again.

14"When you come to the land which the LORD your God gives you, and you possess it and dwell in it, and then say, 'I will set a king over me, like all the nations that are round about me'; 15you may indeed set as king over you him whom the LORD your God will choose. One from among your brethren you shall set as king over you; you may not put a foreigner over you, who is not your brother. 16Only he must not multiply horses for himself, or cause the people to return to Egypt in order to multiply horses, since the LORD has said to you, 'You shall never return that way again.' 17And he shall not multiply wives for himself, lest his heart turn away; nor shall he greatly multiply for himself silver and gold.

18"And when he sits on the throne of his kingdom, he shall write for himself in a book a copy of this law, from that which is in the charge of the Levitical priests; 19and it shall be with him, and he shall read in it all the days of his life, that he may learn to fear the LORD his God, by keeping all the words of this law and these statutes, and doing them; 20that his heart may not be lifted up above his brethren, and that he may not turn aside from the commandment, either to the right hand or to the left; so that he may continue long in his kingdom, he and his children, in Israel.

18 "The Levitical priests, that is, all the tribe of Levi, shall have no portion or inheritance with Israel; they shall eat the offerings by fire to the LORD, and his rightful dues. 2They shall have no inheritance among their brethren; the LORD is their inheritance, as he promised them. 3And this shall be the priests' due from the people, from those offering a sacrifice, whether it be ox or sheep: they shall give to the priest the shoulder and the two cheeks and the stomach. 4The first fruits of your grain, of your wine and of your oil, and the first of the fleece of your sheep, you shall give him. 5For the LORD your God has chosen him out of all your tribes, to stand and minister in the name of the LORD, him and his sons for ever.

[6]"And if a Levite comes from any of your towns out of all Israel, where he lives—and he may come when he desires—to the place which the LORD will choose, [7]then he may minister in the name of the LORD his God, like all his fellow Levites who stand to minister there before the LORD. [8]They shall have equal portions to eat, besides what he receives from the sale of his patrimony.

[9]"When you come into the land which the LORD your God gives you, you shall not learn to follow the abominable practices of those nations. [10]There shall not be found among you any one who burns his son or his daughter as an offering, any one who practices divination, a soothsayer, or an augur, or a sorcerer, [11]or a charmer, or a medium, or a wizard, or a necromancer. [12]For whoever does these things is an abomination to the LORD; and because of these abominable practices the LORD your God is driving them out before you. [13]You shall be blameless before the LORD your God. [14]For these nations, which you are about to dispossess, give heed to soothsayers and to diviners; but as for you, the LORD your God has not allowed you so to do.

[15]"The LORD your God will raise up for you a prophet like me from among you, from your brethren—him you shall heed—[16]just as you desired of the LORD your God at Horeb on the day of the assembly, when you said, 'Let me not hear again the voice of the LORD my God, or see this great fire any more, lest I die.' [17]And the LORD said to me, 'They have rightly said all that they have spoken. [18]I will raise up for them a prophet like you from among their brethren; and I will put my words in his mouth, and he shall speak to them all that I command him. [19]And whoever will not give heed to my words which he shall speak in my name, I myself will require it of him. [20]But the prophet who presumes to speak a word in my name which I have not commanded him to speak, or who speaks in the name of other gods, that same prophet shall die.' [21]And if you say in your heart, 'How may we know the word which the LORD has not spoken?'—[22]when a prophet speaks in the name of the LORD, if the word does not come to pass or come true, that is a word which the LORD has not spoken; the prophet has spoken it presumptuously, you need not be afraid of him.

19 "When the LORD your God cuts off the nations whose land the LORD your God gives you, and you dispossess them and dwell in their cities and in their houses, [2]you shall set apart three cities for you in the land which the LORD your God gives you to possess. [3]You shall prepare the roads, and divide into three parts the area of the land which the LORD your God gives you as a possession, so that any manslayer can flee to them.

[4]"This is the provision for the manslayer, who by fleeing there may save his life. If any one kills his neighbor unintentionally without having been at enmity with him in time past—[5]as when a man goes into the forest with his neighbor to cut wood, and his hand swings the axe to cut down a tree, and the head slips from the handle and strikes his neighbor so that he dies—he may flee to one of these cities and save his life; [6]lest the avenger of blood in hot anger pursue the manslayer and overtake him, because the way is long, and wound him mortally, though the man did not deserve to die, since he was not at enmity with his neighbor in time past. [7]Therefore I command you, You shall set apart three cities. [8]And if the LORD your God enlarges your border, as he has sworn to your fathers, and gives you all the land which he promised to give to your fathers—[9]provided you are careful to keep all this commandment, which I command you this day, by loving the LORD your God and by walking ever in his ways—then you shall add three other cities to these three, [10]lest innocent blood be shed in your land which the LORD your God gives you for an inheritance, and so the guilt of bloodshed be upon you.

[11]"But if any man hates his neighbor, and lies in wait for him, and attacks him, and wounds him mortally so that he dies, and the man flees into one of these cities, [12]then the elders of his city shall send and fetch

him from there, and hand him over to the avenger of blood, so that he may die. [13]Your eye shall not pity him, but you shall purge the guilt of innocent blood from Israel, so that it may be well with you.

[14]“In the inheritance which you will hold in the land that the LORD your God gives you to possess, you shall not remove your neighbor’s landmark, which the men of old have set.

[15]“A single witness shall not prevail against a man for any crime or for any wrong in connection with any offense that he has committed; only on the evidence of two witnesses, or of three witnesses, shall a charge be sustained. [16]If a malicious witness rises against any man to accuse him of wrongdoing, [17]then both parties to the dispute shall appear before the LORD, before the priests and the judges who are in office in those days; [18]the judges shall inquire diligently, and if the witness is a false witness and has accused his brother falsely, [19]then you shall do to him as he had meant to do to his brother; so you shall purge the evil from the midst of you. [20]And the rest shall hear, and fear, and shall never again commit any such evil among you. [21]Your eye shall not pity; it shall be life for life, eye for eye, tooth for tooth, hand for hand, foot for foot.

20 “When you go forth to war against your enemies, and see horses and chariots and an army larger than your own, you shall not be afraid of them; for the LORD your God is with you, who brought you up out of the land of Egypt. [2]And when you draw near to the battle, the priest shall come forward and speak to the people, [3]and shall say to them, ‘Hear, O Israel, you draw near this day to battle against your enemies: let not your heart faint; do not fear, or tremble, or be in dread of them; [4]for the LORD your God is he that goes with you, to fight for you against your enemies, to give you the victory.’ [5]Then the officers shall speak to the people, saying, ‘What man is there that has built a new house and has not dedicated it? Let him go back to his house, lest he die in the battle and another man dedicate it. [6]And what man is there that has planted a vineyard and has not enjoyed its fruit? Let him go back to his house, lest he die in the battle and another man enjoy its fruit. [7]And what man is there that has betrothed a wife and has not taken her? Let him go back to his house, lest he die in the battle and another man take her.’ [8]And the officers shall speak further to the people, and say, ‘What man is there that is fearful and fainthearted? Let him go back to his house, lest the heart of his fellows melt as his heart.’ [9]And when the officers have made an end of speaking to the people, then commanders shall be appointed at the head of the people.

[10]“When you draw near to a city to fight against it, offer terms of peace to it. [11]And if its answer to you is peace and it opens to you, then all the people who are found in it shall do forced labor for you and shall serve you. [12]But if it makes no peace with you, but makes war against you, then you shall besiege it; [13]and when the LORD your God gives it into your hand you shall put all its males to the sword, [14]but the women and the little ones, the cattle, and everything else in the city, all its spoil, you shall take as booty for yourselves; and you shall enjoy the spoil of your enemies, which the LORD your God has given you. [15]Thus you shall do to all the cities which are very far from you, which are not cities of the nations here. [16]But in the cities of these peoples that the LORD your God gives you for an inheritance, you shall save alive nothing that breathes, [17]but you shall utterly destroy them, the Hittites and the Am′orites, the Canaanites and the Per′izzites, the Hi′vites and the Jeb′usites, as the LORD your God has commanded; [18]that they may not teach you to do according to all their abominable practices which they have done in the service of their gods, and so to sin against the LORD your God.

[19]“When you besiege a city for a long time, making war against it in order to take it, you shall not destroy its trees by wielding an axe against them; for you may eat of them, but you shall not cut them down. Are the trees in the field men that they should be besieged by you? [20]Only the trees which you know are not trees for food you may destroy and cut

down that you may build siegeworks against the city that makes war with you, until it falls."

A Psalm of Asaph.

PSALM 73 [72]

21When my soul was embittered,
when I was pricked in heart,
22I was stupid and ignorant,
I was like a beast toward you.
23Nevertheless I am continually with you;
you hold my right hand.
24You guide me with your counsel,
and afterward you will receive me
to glory.
25Whom have I in heaven but you?
And there is nothing upon earth that I
desire besides you.
26My flesh and my heart may fail,
but God is the strength of my heart and
my portion for ever.

27For behold, those who are far from you
shall perish;
you put an end to those who are false
to you.
28But for me it is good to be near God;
I have made the Lord GOD my refuge,
that I may tell of all your works.

LUKE 1

39In those days Mary arose and went with haste into the hill country, to a city of Judah, 40and she entered the house of Zechari′ah and greeted Elizabeth. 41And when Elizabeth heard the greeting of Mary, the child leaped in her womb; and Elizabeth was filled with the Holy Spirit 42and she exclaimed with a loud cry, "Blessed are you among women, and blessed is the fruit of your womb! 43And why is this granted me, that the mother of my Lord should come to me? 44For behold, when the voice of your greeting came to my ears, the child in my womb leaped for joy.
45And blessed is she who believed that there would be a fulfilment of what was spoken to her from the Lord." 46And Mary said,
"My soul magnifies the Lord,
47and my spirit rejoices in God my Savior,
48for he has regarded the low estate of his
handmaiden.
For behold, henceforth all generations will
call me blessed;
49for he who is mighty has done great things
for me,
and holy is his name.
50And his mercy is on those who fear him
from generation to generation.
51He has shown strength with his arm,
he has scattered the proud in the
imagination of their hearts,
52he has put down the mighty from
their thrones,
and exalted those of low degree;
53he has filled the hungry with good things,
and the rich he has sent empty away.
54He has helped his servant Israel,
in remembrance of his mercy,
55as he spoke to our fathers,
to Abraham and to his posterity for ever."
56And Mary remained with her about three
months, and returned to her home.

REFLECTION

As God continues to prepare his people for a new life in the Promised Land, he gives an interesting but chilling warning about their future kings. In chapter 17, Deuteronomy describes three things that the future kings of Israel should never to do. Simply put, they are never to acquire too much wealth, too many wives, or too much weaponry—one could call it "the three W's." Later on, so that they would not forget what God demanded of them, the kings were to handwrite the entire Book of Deuteronomy and keep it next to their throne. However, looking back on Israel's history, we see just how quickly the kings failed to follow these three things. One of the major themes of Deuteronomy is that of remembering. Unfortunately too many of Israel's leaders failed to remember and

> heed the Lord's words. Indeed, if the story of the Old Testament is rightly understood, it should make readers long for a king who transcends all of these shortcomings. It is designed to make Israel long for Christ. What are some ways that you "fail to remember" those things that God is asking of you?

March 25

DEUTERONOMY 21

"If in the land which the LORD your God gives you to possess, any one is found slain, lying in the open country, and it is not known who killed him, 2then your elders and your judges shall come forth, and they shall measure the distance to the cities which are around him that is slain; 3and the elders of the city which is nearest to the slain man shall take a heifer which has never been worked and which has not pulled in the yoke. 4And the elders of that city shall bring the heifer down to a valley with running water, which is neither plowed nor sown, and shall break the heifer's neck there in the valley. 5And the priests the sons of Levi shall come forward, for the LORD your God has chosen them to minister to him and to bless in the name of the LORD, and by their word every dispute and every assault shall be settled. 6And all the elders of that city nearest to the slain man shall wash their hands over the heifer whose neck was broken in the valley; 7and they shall testify, 'Our hands did not shed this blood, neither did our eyes see it shed. 8Forgive, O LORD, your people Israel, whom you have redeemed, and set not the guilt of innocent blood in the midst of your people Israel; but let the guilt of blood be forgiven them.' 9So you shall purge the guilt of innocent blood from your midst, when you do what is right in the sight of the LORD.

10"When you go forth to war against your enemies, and the LORD your God gives them into your hands, and you take them captive, 11and see among the captives a beautiful woman, and you have desire for her and would take her for yourself as wife, 12then you shall bring her home to your house, and she shall shave her head and pare her nails. 13And she shall put off her captive's garb, and shall remain in your house and bewail her father and her mother a full month; after that you may go in to her, and be her husband, and she shall be your wife. 14Then, if you have no delight in her, you shall let her go where she will; but you shall not sell her for money, you shall not treat her as a slave, since you have humiliated her.

15"If a man has two wives, the one loved and the other disliked, and they have borne him children, both the loved and the disliked, and if the first-born son is hers that is disliked, 16then on the day when he assigns his possessions as an inheritance to his sons, he may not treat the son of the loved as the first-born in preference to the son of the disliked, who is the first-born, 17but he shall acknowledge the first-born, the son of the disliked, by giving him a double portion of all that he has, for he is the first issue of his strength; the right of the first-born is his.

18"If a man has a stubborn and rebellious son, who will not obey the voice of his father or the voice of his mother, and, though they chastise him, will not give heed to them, 19then his father and his mother shall take hold of him and bring him out to the elders of his city at the gate of the place where he lives, 20and they shall say to the elders of his city, 'This our son is stubborn and rebellious, he will not obey our voice; he is a glutton and a drunkard.' 21Then all the men of the city shall stone him to death with stones; so you shall purge the evil from your midst; and all Israel shall hear, and fear.

22“And if a man has committed a crime punishable by death and he is put to death, and you hang him on a tree, 23his body shall not remain all night upon the tree, but you shall bury him the same day, for a hanged man is accursed by God; you shall not defile your land which the LORD your God gives you for an inheritance.

22 “You shall not see your brother’s ox or his sheep go astray, and withhold your help from them; you shall take them back to your brother. 2And if he is not near you, or if you do not know him, you shall bring it home to your house, and it shall be with you until your brother seeks it; then you shall restore it to him. 3And so you shall do with his donkey; so you shall do with his garment; so you shall do with any lost thing of your brother’s, which he loses and you find; you may not withhold your help. 4You shall not see your brother’s donkey or his ox fallen down by the way, and withhold your help from them; you shall help him to lift them up again.

5“A woman shall not wear anything that pertains to a man, nor shall a man put on a woman’s garment; for whoever does these things is an abomination to the LORD your God.

6“If you chance to come upon a bird’s nest, in any tree or on the ground, with young ones or eggs and the mother sitting upon the young or upon the eggs, you shall not take the mother with the young; 7you shall let the mother go, but the young you may take to yourself; that it may go well with you, and that you may live long.

8“When you build a new house, you shall make a parapet for your roof, that you may not bring the guilt of blood upon your house, if any one fall from it.

9“You shall not sow your vineyard with two kinds of seed, lest the whole yield be forfeited to the sanctuary, the crop which you have sown and the yield of the vineyard. 10You shall not plow with an ox and a donkey together. 11You shall not wear a mingled stuff, wool and linen together.

12“You shall make yourself tassels on the four corners of your cloak with which you cover yourself.

13“If any man takes a wife, and goes in to her, and then spurns her, 14and charges her with shameful conduct, and brings an evil name upon her, saying, ‘I took this woman, and when I came near her, I did not find in her the tokens of virginity,’ 15then the father of the young woman and her mother shall take and bring out the tokens of her virginity to the elders of the city in the gate; 16and the father of the young woman shall say to the elders, ‘I gave my daughter to this man to wife, and he spurns her; 17and behold, he has made shameful charges against her, saying, “I did not find in your daughter the tokens of virginity.” And yet these are the tokens of my daughter’s virginity.’ And they shall spread the garment before the elders of the city. 18Then the elders of that city shall take the man and whip him; 19and they shall fine him a hundred shekels of silver, and give them to the father of the young woman, because he has brought an evil name upon a virgin of Israel; and she shall be his wife; he may not put her away all his days. 20But if the thing is true, that the tokens of virginity were not found in the young woman, 21then they shall bring out the young woman to the door of her father’s house, and the men of her city shall stone her to death with stones, because she has wrought folly in Israel by playing the harlot in her father’s house; so you shall purge the evil from the midst of you.

22“If a man is found lying with the wife of another man, both of them shall die, the man who lay with the woman, and the woman; so you shall purge the evil from Israel.

23“If there is a betrothed virgin, and a man meets her in the city and lies with her, 24then you shall bring them both out to the gate of that city, and you shall stone them to death with stones, the young woman because she did not cry for help though she was in the city, and the man because he violated his neighbor’s wife; so you shall purge the evil from the midst of you.

[25]"But if in the open country a man meets a young woman who is betrothed, and the man seizes her and lies with her, then only the man who lay with her shall die. [26]But to the young woman you shall do nothing; in the young woman there is no offense punishable by death, for this case is like that of a man attacking and murdering his neighbor; [27]because he came upon her in the open country, and though the betrothed young woman cried for help there was no one to rescue her.

[28]"If a man meets a virgin who is not betrothed, and seizes her and lies with her, and they are found, [29]then the man who lay with her shall give to the father of the young woman fifty shekels of silver, and she shall be his wife, because he has violated her; he may not put her away all his days.

[30]"A man shall not take his father's wife, nor shall he uncover her who is his father's."

A Maskil of Asaph.

PSALM 74 [73]

O God, why do you cast us off for ever?
Why does your anger smoke against the sheep of your pasture?
[2]Remember your congregation, which you have gotten of old,
which you have redeemed to be the tribe of your heritage!
Remember Mount Zion, where you have dwelt.
[3]Direct your steps to the perpetual ruins;
the enemy has destroyed everything in the sanctuary!

[4]Your foes have roared in the midst of your holy place;
they set up their own signs for signs.
[5]At the upper entrance they hacked
the wooden trellis with axes.
[6]And then all its carved wood
they broke down with hatchets and hammers.
[7]They set your sanctuary on fire;
to the ground they desecrated the dwelling place of your name.
[8]They said to themselves, "We will utterly subdue them";
they burned all the meeting places of God in the land.

[9]We do not see our signs;
there is no longer any prophet,
and there is none among us who knows how long.
[10]How long, O God, is the foe to scoff?
Is the enemy to revile your name for ever?
[11]Why do you hold back your hand,
why do you keep your right hand in your bosom?

[12]Yet God my King is from of old,
working salvation in the midst of the earth.
[13]You divided the sea by your might;
you broke the heads of the dragons on the waters.
[14]You crushed the heads of Leviathan,
you gave him as food for the creatures of the wilderness.
[15]You cut open springs and brooks;
you dried up ever-flowing streams.
[16]Yours is the day, yours also the night;
you have established the luminaries and the sun.
[17]You have fixed all the bounds of the earth;
you have made summer and winter.

[18]Remember this, O LORD, how the enemy scoffs,
and an impious people reviles your name.
[19]Do not deliver the soul of your dove to the wild beasts;
do not forget the souls of your poor for ever.

[20]Have regard for your covenant;
for the dark places of the land are full of the habitations of violence.
[21]Let not the humble be put to shame;
let the poor and needy praise your name.

22 Arise, O God, plead your cause;
remember how the impious scoff at you
all the day!
23 Do not forget the clamor of your foes,
the uproar of your adversaries which
goes up continually!

LUKE 1

57 Now the time came for Eliz-
abeth to be delivered, and she
gave birth to a son. 58 And her
neighbors and kinsfolk heard that the
Lord had shown great mercy to her, and
they rejoiced with her. 59 And on the
eighth day they came to circumcise the
child; and they would have named him
Zechari´ah after his father, 60 but his mother said, "Not so; he shall be called John."
61 And they said to her, "None of your kindred is called by this name." 62 And they
made signs to his father, inquiring what
he would have him called. 63 And he asked
for a writing tablet, and wrote, "His name
is John." And they all marveled. 64 And
immediately his mouth was opened and
his tongue loosed, and he spoke, blessing
God. 65 And fear came on all their neighbors. And all these things were talked
about through all the hill country of Judea; 66 and all who heard them laid them
up in their hearts, saying, "What then will
this child be?" For the hand of the Lord
was with him.

67 And his father Zechari´ah was filled with
the Holy Spirit, and prophesied, saying,
68 "Blessed be the Lord God of Israel,
for he has visited and redeemed his people,
69 and has raised up a horn of salvation for us
in the house of his servant David,
70 as he spoke by the mouth of his holy
prophets from of old,
71 that we should be saved from our enemies,
and from the hand of all who hate us;
72 to perform the mercy promised to our
fathers,
and to remember his holy covenant,
73 the oath which he swore to our father
Abraham, 74 to grant us
that we, being delivered from the hand of
our enemies,
might serve him without fear,
75 in holiness and righteousness before him
all the days of our life.
76 And you, child, will be called the prophet
of the Most High;
for you will go before the Lord to prepare
his ways,
77 to give knowledge of salvation to his people
in the forgiveness of their sins,
78 through the tender mercy of our God,
when the day shall dawn upon us from
on high
79 to give light to those who sit in darkness
and in the shadow of death,
to guide our feet into the way of peace."
80 And the child grew and became strong in
spirit, and he was in the wilderness till the
day of his manifestation to Israel.

REFLECTION

Much of today's reading from Deuteronomy is based on the idea of anticipation. As God's people prepare to enter the Promised Land, they're given many stipulations for different social and legal circumstances that may arise. Many of these instructions are meant to deal with the problem of sin. They are not, however, definitive solutions. Jesus even says in the Gospels that at times Moses allowed concessions because of the hardness of Israel's heart, but in the beginning it was not so. Jesus wants to return humanity to a state of purity. He desires to lift his people from the burden of sin and the laws of Deuteronomy, which in many ways acted merely as a stopgap measure against sin. Once again, we see Deuteronomy anticipating the need for a Savior. Similarly, in the Gospel of Luke, we read the story of the birth of John the Baptist—the herald of the King—whose birth anticipates the Lord's salvation. Zechariah, John's father, sings his famous *Benedictus* hymn (see Lk 1:68–79), which is a commentary on how the long-awaited reign of sin and darkness is, at long last, coming to a close. Do you truly relish the freedom from sin and darkness won for us by Christ?

March 26

DEUTERONOMY 23

**"He whose testicles are crushed
or whose male member is cut
off shall not enter the assembly of the
LORD.**
2"No bastard shall enter the assembly of
the LORD; even to the tenth generation none
of his descendants shall enter the assembly
of the LORD.
3"No Am'monite or Moabite shall enter
the assembly of the LORD; even to the
tenth generation none belonging to them
shall enter the assembly of the LORD for
ever; 4because they did not meet you with
bread and with water on the way, when you
came forth out of Egypt, and because they
hired against you Balaam the son of Beor
from Pe'thor of Mesopota'mia, to curse
you. 5Nevertheless the LORD your God
would not listen to Balaam; but the LORD
your God turned the curse into a blessing
for you, because the LORD your God loved
you. 6You shall not seek their peace or their
prosperity all your days for ever.
7"You shall not abhor an E'domite, for
he is your brother; you shall not abhor an
Egyptian, because you were a sojourner
in his land. 8The children of the third
generation that are born to them may enter
the assembly of the LORD.
9"When you go forth against your enemies
and are in camp, then you shall keep yourself
from every evil thing.
10"If there is among you any man who is
not clean by reason of a nocturnal emission,
then he shall go outside the camp, he shall
not come within the camp; 11but when
evening comes on, he shall bathe himself in
water, and when the sun is down, he may
come within the camp.
12"You shall have a place outside the
camp and you shall go out to it; 13and you
shall have a stick with your weapons; and
when you relieve yourself outside, you
shall dig a hole with it, and turn back
and cover up your excrement. 14Because
the LORD your God walks in the midst
of your camp, to save you and to give up
your enemies before you, therefore your
camp must be holy, that he may not see
anything indecent among you, and turn
away from you.
15"You shall not give up to his master a
slave who has escaped from his master to
you; 16he shall dwell with you, in your midst,
in the place which he shall choose within
one of your towns, where it pleases him
best; you shall not oppress him.
17"There shall be no cult prostitute of the
daughters of Israel, neither shall there be a
cult prostitute of the sons of Israel. 18You shall
not bring the hire of a harlot, or the wages of
a dog, into the house of the LORD your God
in payment for any vow; for both of these are
an abomination to the LORD your God.
19"You shall not lend upon interest to
your brother, interest on money, interest
on victuals, interest on anything that is lent
for interest. 20To a foreigner you may lend
upon interest, but to your brother you shall
not lend upon interest; that the LORD your
God may bless you in all that you undertake
in the land which you are entering to take
possession of it.
21"When you make a vow to the LORD
your God, you shall not be slack to pay it;
for the LORD your God will surely require
it of you, and it would be sin in you. 22But
if you refrain from vowing, it shall be no
sin in you. 23You shall be careful to perform
what has passed your lips, for you have
voluntarily vowed to the LORD your God
what you have promised with your mouth.
24"When you go into your neighbor's vineyard, you may eat your fill of grapes, as many
as you wish, but you shall not put any in your
vessel. 25When you go into your neighbor's
standing grain, you may pluck the ears with
your hand, but you shall not put a sickle to
your neighbor's standing grain.

24 "When a man takes a wife and marries her, if then she finds no favor
in his eyes because he has found some
indecency in her, and he writes her a

bill of divorce and puts it in her hand and sends her out of his house, and she departs out of his house, 2and if she goes and becomes another man's wife, 3and the latter husband dislikes her and writes her a bill of divorce and puts it in her hand and sends her out of his house, or if the latter husband dies, who took her to be his wife, 4then her former husband, who sent her away, may not take her again to be his wife, after she has been defiled; for that is an abomination before the LORD, and you shall not bring guilt upon the land which the LORD your God gives you for an inheritance.

5"When a man is newly married, he shall not go out with the army or be charged with any business; he shall be free at home one year, to be happy with his wife whom he has taken.

6"No man shall take a mill or an upper millstone in pledge; for he would be taking a life in pledge.

7"If a man is found stealing one of his brethren, the sons of Israel, and if he treats him as a slave or sells him, then that thief shall die; so you shall purge the evil from the midst of you.

8"Take heed, in an attack of leprosy, to be very careful to do according to all that the Levitical priests shall direct you; as I commanded them, so you shall be careful to do. 9Remember what the LORD your God did to Miriam on the way as you came forth out of Egypt.

10"When you make your neighbor a loan of any sort, you shall not go into his house to fetch his pledge. 11You shall stand outside, and the man to whom you make the loan shall bring the pledge out to you. 12And if he is a poor man, you shall not sleep in his pledge; 13when the sun goes down, you shall restore to him the pledge that he may sleep in his cloak and bless you; and it shall be righteousness to you before the LORD your God.

14"You shall not oppress a hired servant who is poor and needy, whether he is one of your brethren or one of the sojourners who are in your land within your towns; 15you shall give him his hire on the day he earns it, before the sun goes down (for he is poor, and sets his heart upon it); lest he cry against you to the LORD, and it be sin in you.

16"The fathers shall not be put to death for the children, nor shall the children be put to death for the fathers; every man shall be put to death for his own sin.

17"You shall not pervert the justice due to the sojourner or to the fatherless, or take a widow's garment in pledge; 18but you shall remember that you were a slave in Egypt and the LORD your God redeemed you from there; therefore I command you to do this.

19"When you reap your harvest in your field, and have forgotten a sheaf in the field, you shall not go back to get it; it shall be for the sojourner, the fatherless, and the widow; that the LORD your God may bless you in all the work of your hands. 20When you beat your olive trees, you shall not go over the boughs again; it shall be for the sojourner, the fatherless, and the widow. 21When you gather the grapes of your vineyard, you shall not glean it afterward; it shall be for the sojourner, the fatherless, and the widow. 22You shall remember that you were a slave in the land of Egypt; therefore I command you to do this.

25 "If there is a dispute between men, and they come into court, and the judges decide between them, acquitting the innocent and condemning the guilty, 2then if the guilty man deserves to be beaten, the judge shall cause him to lie down and be beaten in his presence with a number of stripes in proportion to his offense. 3Forty stripes may be given him, but not more; lest, if one should go on to beat him with more stripes than these, your brother be degraded in your sight.

4"You shall not muzzle an ox when it treads out the grain.

5"If brothers dwell together, and one of them dies and has no son, the wife of the dead shall not be married outside the family to a stranger; her husband's brother shall go in to her, and take her

as his wife, and perform the duty of a
husband's brother to her. 6And the first
son whom she bears shall succeed to
the name of his brother who is dead,
that his name may not be blotted out of
Israel. 7And if the man does not wish to
take his brother's wife, then his brother's
wife shall go up to the gate to the elders,
and say, 'My husband's brother refuses to
perpetuate his brother's name in Israel; he
will not perform the duty of a husband's
brother to me.' 8Then the elders of his city
shall call him, and speak to him: and if he
persists, saying, 'I do not wish to take her,'
9then his brother's wife shall go up to him
in the presence of the elders, and pull his
sandal off his foot, and spit in his face;
and she shall answer and say, 'So shall it
be done to the man who does not build up
his brother's house.' 10And the name of his
house shall be called in Israel, The house
of him that had his sandal pulled off.

11"When men fight with one another, and
the wife of the one draws near to rescue her
husband from the hand of him who is beating
him, and puts out her hand and seizes him by
the private parts, 12then you shall cut off her
hand; your eye shall have no pity.

13"You shall not have in your bag two kinds
of weights, a large and a small. 14You shall not
have in your house two kinds of measures,
a large and a small. 15A full and just weight
you shall have, a full and just measure you
shall have; that your days may be prolonged
in the land which the LORD your God gives
you. 16For all who do such things, all who
act dishonestly, are an abomination to the
LORD your God.

17"Remember what Am'alek did to you
on the way as you came out of Egypt,
18how he attacked you on the way, when
you were faint and weary, and cut off at
your rear all who lagged behind you; and
he did not fear God. 19Therefore when the
LORD your God has given you rest from
all your enemies round about, in the land
which the LORD your God gives you for
an inheritance to possess, you shall blot
out the remembrance of Am'alek from
under heaven; you shall not forget."

To the choirmaster: according to Do Not Destroy.
A Psalm of Asaph. A song.

PSALM 75 [74]

We give thanks to you, O God; we give thanks;
we call on your name and recount your
wondrous deeds.

2At the set time which I appoint
I will judge with equity.
3When the earth totters, and all
its inhabitants,
it is I who keep steady its pillars. *Selah*
4I say to the boastful, "Do not boast,"
and to the wicked, "Do not lift up
your horn;
5do not lift up your horn on high,
or speak with insolent neck."

6For not from the east or from the west
and not from the wilderness comes
lifting up;
7but it is God who executes judgment,
putting down one and lifting up another.
8For in the hand of the LORD there is a cup,
with foaming wine, well mixed;
and he will pour a draught from it,
and all the wicked of the earth
shall drain it down to the dregs.

9But I will rejoice for ever,
I will sing praises to the God of Jacob.
10All the horns of the wicked he will cut off,
but the horns of the righteous shall
be exalted.

LUKE 2

**In those days a decree went out
from Caesar Augustus that all
the world should be enrolled.
2This was the first enrollment, when
Quirin'ius was governor of Syria. 3And
all went to be enrolled, each to his own**
city. 4And Joseph also went up from Galilee,
from the city of Nazareth, to Judea, to the
city of David, which is called Bethlehem,

because he was of the house and lineage of David, [5]to be enrolled with Mary his betrothed, who was with child. [6]And while they were there, the time came for her to be delivered. [7]And she gave birth to her first-born son and wrapped him in swaddling cloths, and laid him in a manger, because there was no place for them in the inn.

[8]And in that region there were shepherds out in the field, keeping watch over their flock by night. [9]And an angel of the Lord appeared to them, and the glory of the Lord shone around them, and they were filled with fear. [10]And the angel said to them, "Be not afraid; for behold, I bring you good news of a great joy which will come to all the people; [11]for to you is born this day in the city of David a Savior, who is Christ the Lord. [12]And this will be a sign for you: you will find a baby wrapped in swaddling cloths and lying in a manger." [13]And suddenly there was with the angel a multitude of the heavenly host praising God and saying,

[14]"Glory to God in the highest,
and on earth peace among men with whom
he is pleased!"

[15]When the angels went away from them into heaven, the shepherds said to one another, "Let us go over to Bethlehem and see this thing that has happened, which the Lord has made known to us." [16]And they went with haste, and found Mary and Joseph, and the baby lying in a manger. [17]And when they saw it they made known the saying which had been told them concerning this child; [18]and all who heard it wondered at what the shepherds told them. [19]But Mary kept all these things, pondering them in her heart. [20]And the shepherds returned, glorifying and praising God for all they had heard and seen, as it had been told them.

REFLECTION

The Bible loves to confound expectations. The story of the birth of Jesus is no exception. Indeed, Luke's Gospel begins with two births—the birth of John the Baptist and then the birth of Jesus. Both of these births are announced by an angel. Both are an answer to prayers. One of these birth announcements is given to a priest ministering in the Temple in Jerusalem. The other announcement is given to a poor young girl in a small village. One would expect the more important announcement to come to the priest, in the Temple, in the capital city. But of course, that expectation would be wrong. God loves to surprise. He loves to enter the hidden places to confound expectations. The birth of Jesus should remind us that the world is not always as it seems, that the poor are often kings and queens, and that his love for us will always transcend our self-imposed limitations. What are some ways in which God has confounded your own expectations?

March 27

DEUTERONOMY 26

"When you come into the land which the LORD your God gives you for an inheritance, and have taken possession of it, and live in it, [2]you shall take some of the first of all the fruit of the ground, which you harvest from your land that the LORD your God gives you, and you shall put it in a basket, and you shall go to the place which the LORD your God will choose, to make his name to dwell there. [3]And you shall go to the priest who is in office at that time, and say to him, 'I declare this day to the LORD your God that I have come into the land which the LORD swore to our fathers to give us.' [4]Then the priest shall take the basket from your hand, and set it down before the altar of the LORD your God.

[5]"And you shall make response before the LORD your God, 'A wandering Arame′an was my father; and he went down into Egypt and sojourned there, few in number; and there he became a nation, great, mighty,

and populous. [6]And the Egyptians treated
us harshly, and afflicted us, and laid upon us
hard bondage. [7]Then we cried to the LORD
the God of our fathers, and the LORD heard
our voice, and saw our affliction, our toil,
and our oppression; [8]and the LORD brought
us out of Egypt with a mighty hand and an
outstretched arm, with great terror, with
signs and wonders; [9]and he brought us
into this place and gave us this land, a land
flowing with milk and honey. [10]And behold,
now I bring the first of the fruit of the
ground, which you, O LORD, have given me.'
And you shall set it down before the LORD
your God, and worship before the LORD
your God; [11]and you shall rejoice in all the
good which the LORD your God has given to
you and to your house, you, and the Levite,
and the sojourner who is among you.

[12]"When you have finished paying all
the tithe of your produce in the third year,
which is the year of tithing, giving it to the
Levite, the sojourner, the fatherless, and the
widow, that they may eat within your towns
and be filled, [13]then you shall say before the
LORD your God, 'I have removed the sacred
portion out of my house, and moreover I
have given it to the Levite, the sojourner,
the fatherless, and the widow, according
to all your commandment which you have
commanded me; I have not transgressed
any of your commandments, neither have
I forgotten them; [14]I have not eaten of the
tithe while I was mourning, or removed any
of it while I was unclean, or offered any of it
to the dead; I have obeyed the voice of the
LORD my God, I have done according to all
that you have commanded me. [15]Look down
from your holy habitation, from heaven,
and bless your people Israel and the ground
which you have given us, as you swore to our
fathers, a land flowing with milk and honey.'

[16]"'This day the LORD your God commands
you to do these statutes and ordinances; you
shall therefore be careful to do them with
all your heart and with all your soul. [17]You
have declared this day concerning the LORD
that he is your God, and that you will walk
in his ways, and keep his statutes and his
commandments and his ordinances, and
will obey his voice; [18]and the LORD has
declared this day concerning you that you
are a people for his own possession, as he
has promised you, and that you are to keep
all his commandments, [19]that he will set you
high above all nations that he has made, in
praise and in fame and in honor, and that
you shall be a people holy to the LORD your
God, as he has spoken."

27 Now Moses and the elders of Israel
commanded the people, saying, "Keep
all the commandment which I command
you this day. [2]And on the day you pass over
the Jordan to the land which the LORD your
God gives you, you shall set up large stones,
and plaster them with plaster; [3]and you shall
write upon them all the words of this law,
when you pass over to enter the land which
the LORD your God gives you, a land flowing
with milk and honey, as the LORD, the God
of your fathers, has promised you. [4]And
when you have passed over the Jordan, you
shall set up these stones, concerning which I
command you this day, on Mount E'bal, and
you shall plaster them with plaster. [5]And
there you shall build an altar to the LORD
your God, an altar of stones; you shall lift
up no iron tool upon them. [6]You shall build
an altar to the LORD your God of unhewn
stones; and you shall offer burnt offerings
on it to the LORD your God; [7]and you shall
sacrifice peace offerings, and shall eat there;
and you shall rejoice before the LORD your
God. [8]And you shall write upon the stones
all the words of this law very plainly."

[9]And Moses and the Levitical priests said
to all Israel, "Keep silence and hear, O Israel:
this day you have become the people of the
LORD your God. [10]You shall therefore obey
the voice of the LORD your God, keeping his
commandments and his statutes, which I
command you this day."

[11]And Moses charged the people the same
day, saying, [12]"When you have passed over
the Jordan, these shall stand upon Mount
Ger'izim to bless the people: Simeon, Levi,
Judah, Is'sachar, Joseph, and Benjamin.
[13]And these shall stand upon Mount E'bal for
the curse: Reuben, Gad, Asher, Zeb'ulun,
Dan, and Naph'tali. [14]And the Levites shall

declare to all the men of Israel with a loud
voice:
15“ ‘Cursed be the man who makes a
graven or molten image, an abomination to
the LORD, a thing made by the hands of a
craftsman, and sets it up in secret.’ And all
the people shall answer and say, ‘Amen.’
16“ ‘Cursed be he who dishonors his father
or his mother.’ And all the people shall say,
‘Amen.’
17“ ‘Cursed be he who removes his neighbor’s landmark.’ And all the people shall say,
‘Amen.’
18“ ‘Cursed be he who misleads a blind
man on the road.’ And all the people shall
say, ‘Amen.’
19“ ‘Cursed be he who perverts the justice
due to the sojourner, the fatherless, and the
widow.’ And all the people shall say, ‘Amen.’
20“ ‘Cursed be he who lies with his father’s
wife, because he has uncovered her who
is his father’s.’ And all the people shall say,
‘Amen.’
21“ ‘Cursed be he who lies with any kind of
beast.’ And all the people shall say, ‘Amen.’
22“ ‘Cursed be he who lies with his sister,
whether the daughter of his father or the
daughter of his mother.’ And all the people
shall say, ‘Amen.’
23“ ‘Cursed be he who lies with his mother-
in-law.’ And all the people shall say, ‘Amen.’
24“ ‘Cursed be he who slays his neighbor in
secret.’ And all the people shall say, ‘Amen.’
25“ ‘Cursed be he who takes a bribe to slay
an innocent person.’ And all the people shall
say, ‘Amen.’
26“ ‘Cursed be he who does not confirm
the words of this law by doing them.’ And
all the people shall say, ‘Amen.’
28 “And if you obey the voice of the
LORD your God, being careful to do
all his commandments which I command
you this day, the LORD your God will set
you high above all the nations of the earth.
2And all these blessings shall come upon
you and overtake you, if you obey the voice
of the LORD your God. 3Blessed shall you be
in the city, and blessed shall you be in the
field. 4Blessed shall be the fruit of your body,
and the fruit of your ground, and the fruit
of your beasts, the increase of your cattle,
and the young of your flock. 5Blessed shall
be your basket and your kneading-trough.
6Blessed shall you be when you come in, and
blessed shall you be when you go out.
7“The LORD will cause your enemies who
rise against you to be defeated before you;
they shall come out against you one way, and
flee before you seven ways. 8The LORD will
command the blessing upon you in your
barns, and in all that you undertake; and he
will bless you in the land which the LORD your
God gives you. 9The LORD will establish you
as a people holy to himself, as he has sworn
to you, if you keep the commandments of the
LORD your God, and walk in his ways. 10And
all the peoples of the earth shall see that you are
called by the name of the LORD; and they shall
be afraid of you. 11And the LORD will make you
abound in prosperity, in the fruit of your body,
and in the fruit of your cattle, and in the fruit of
your ground, within the land which the LORD
swore to your fathers to give you. 12The LORD
will open to you his good treasury the heavens,
to give the rain of your land in its season and
to bless all the work of your hands; and you
shall lend to many nations, but you shall not
borrow. 13And the LORD will make you the
head, and not the tail; and you shall tend
upward only, and not downward; if you obey
the commandments of the LORD your God,
which I command you this day, being careful
to do them, 14and if you do not turn aside from
any of the words which I command you this
day, to the right hand or to the left, to go after
other gods to serve them.”

To the choirmaster: with stringed instruments.
A Psalm of Asaph. A Song.

PSALM 76 [75]

In Judah God is known,
his name is great in Israel.
2His abode has been established in Salem,
his dwelling place in Zion.
3There he broke the flashing arrows,
the shield, the sword, and the weapons
of war. *Selah*

4Glorious are you, more majestic
than the everlasting mountains.
5The stouthearted were stripped of their spoil;
they sank into sleep;
all the men of war
were unable to use their hands.
6At your rebuke, O God of Jacob,
both rider and horse lay stunned.

7But you, you are awesome!
Who can stand before you
when once your anger is roused?
8From the heavens you pronounced
judgment;
the earth feared and was still,
9when God arose to establish judgment
to save all the oppressed of
the earth. *Selah*

10Surely the wrath of men shall praise you;
the residue of wrath you will bind around
you.
11Make your vows to the LORD your God,
and perform them;
let all around him bring gifts
to him who is to be feared,
12who cuts off the spirit of princes,
who is awesome to the kings of the earth.

LUKE 2

21And at the end of eight days, when he was circumcised, he was called Jesus, the name given by the angel before he was conceived in the womb.

22And when the time came for their purification according to the law of Moses, they
brought him up to Jerusalem to present him
to the Lord 23(as it is written in the law of
the Lord, "Every male that opens the womb
shall be called holy to the Lord") 24and to
offer a sacrifice according to what is said in
the law of the Lord, "a pair of turtledoves, or
two young pigeons." 25Now there was a man
in Jerusalem, whose name was Simeon, and
this man was righteous and devout, looking
for the consolation of Israel, and the Holy
Spirit was upon him. 26And it had been
revealed to him by the Holy Spirit that he
should not see death before he had seen the
Lord's Christ. 27And inspired by the Spirit
he came into the temple; and when the
parents brought in the child Jesus, to do for
him according to the custom of the law, 28he
took him up in his arms and blessed God
and said,
29"Lord, now let your servant depart
in peace,
according to your word;
30for my eyes have seen your salvation
31which you have prepared in the presence
of all peoples,
32a light for revelation to the Gentiles,
and for glory to your people Israel."
33And his father and his mother marveled
at what was said about him; 34and Simeon
blessed them and said to Mary his mother,
"Behold, this child is set for the fall and
rising of many in Israel,
and for a sign that is spoken against
35(and a sword will pierce through your own
soul also),
that thoughts out of many hearts may
be revealed."
36And there was a prophetess, Anna, the
daughter of Phan′uel, of the tribe of Asher;
she was of a great age, having lived with
her husband seven years from her virginity,
37and as a widow till she was eighty-four. She
did not depart from the temple, worshiping
with fasting and prayer night and day. 38And
coming up at that very hour she gave thanks
to God, and spoke of him to all who were
looking for the redemption of Jerusalem.

REFLECTION

Jesus's Presentation in the Temple is a mystery that is often misunderstood. This event, however, is so important that it was chosen as one of the Joyful Mysteries of the Rosary. But what is the Presentation really about? The practice of presenting the firstborn son in the Temple goes back to the time of Deuteronomy. In God's original plan, the first-born son of every family was to be a priest to that family. However, after Israel's sin of the golden calf, the firstborn sons lost this privilege of priesthood, which became confined to the Tribe of Levi (the only Tribe of Israel that appeared to condemn the idolatry of the golden calf). From this point on, every firstborn son was to be presented to the Levitical priests, along with an offering, essentially thanking them for performing the priestly duties that they could no longer do. In this light, it's fascinating to see Mary and Joseph doing this as well. The humility of this event is striking. Jesus would be perfectly faithful to what God had asked of his people but was simultaneously pointing ahead to a time when the priesthood of the Old Testament would become obsolete and Jesus himself would become the once-and-for-all, eternal high priest. Are you faithful to what God has asked of you?

March 28

DEUTERONOMY 28

15"But if you will not obey the voice of the LORD your God or be careful to do all his commandments and his statutes which I command you this day, then all these curses shall come upon you and over-take you. 16Cursed shall you be in the city, and cursed shall you be in the field. 17Cursed shall be your basket and your kneading-trough. 18Cursed shall be the fruit of your body, and the fruit of your ground, the increase of your cattle, and the young of your flock. 19Cursed shall you be when you come in, and cursed shall you be when you go out.

20"The LORD will send upon you curses, confusion, and frustration, in all that you undertake to do, until you are destroyed and perish quickly, on account of the evil of your doings, because you have forsaken me. 21The LORD will make the pestilence cling to you until he has consumed you off the land which you are entering to take possession of it. 22The LORD will strike you with consumption, and with fever, inflammation, and fiery heat, and with drought, and with blasting, and with mildew; they shall pursue you until you perish. 23And the heavens over your head shall be brass, and the earth under you shall be iron. 24The LORD will make the rain of your land powder and dust; from heaven it shall come down upon you until you are destroyed.

25"The LORD will cause you to be defeated before your enemies; you shall go out one way against them, and flee seven ways before them; and you shall be a horror to all the kingdoms of the earth. 26And your dead body shall be food for all birds of the air, and for the beasts of the earth; and there shall be no one to frighten them away. 27The LORD will strike you with the boils of Egypt, and with the ulcers and the scurvy and the itch, of which you cannot be healed. 28The LORD will strike you with madness and blindness and confusion of mind; 29and you shall grope at noonday, as the blind grope in darkness, and you shall not prosper in your ways; and you shall be only oppressed and robbed continually, and there shall be no one to help you. 30You shall betroth a wife, and another man shall lie with her; you shall build a house, and you shall not dwell in it; you shall plant a vineyard, and you shall not use the fruit of it. 31Your ox shall be slain before your eyes, and you shall not eat of it; your donkey shall be violently taken away before your face, and shall not be restored to you; your sheep shall be given to your enemies, and there shall be no one to help you. 32Your sons and your daughters shall be given to another people, while your eyes look on and fail with longing for them all the day; and it shall not be in the power of your hand to prevent it. 33A nation which you have not known shall eat up the fruit of your ground and of all your labors; and you shall be only oppressed and crushed continually; 34so that you shall be driven mad by the sight which your eyes shall see. 35The LORD will strike you on the knees and on the legs with grievous boils of which you cannot be healed, from the sole of your foot to the crown of your head.

36“The LORD will bring you, and your king whom you set over you, to a nation that neither you nor your fathers have known; and there you shall serve other gods, of wood and stone. 37And you shall become a horror, a proverb, and a byword, among all the peoples where the LORD will lead you away. 38You shall carry much seed into the field, and shall gather little in; for the locust shall consume it. 39You shall plant vineyards and dress them, but you shall neither drink of the wine nor gather the grapes; for the worm shall eat them. 40You shall have olive trees throughout all your territory, but you shall not anoint yourself with the oil; for your olives shall drop off. 41You shall beget sons and daughters, but they shall not be yours; for they shall go into captivity. 42All your trees and the fruit of your ground the locust shall possess. 43The sojourner who is among you shall mount above you higher and higher; and you shall come down lower and lower. 44He shall lend to you, and you shall not lend to him; he shall be the head, and you shall be the tail. 45All these curses shall come upon you and pursue you and overtake you, till you are destroyed, because you did not obey the voice of the LORD your God, to keep his commandments and his statutes which he commanded you. 46They shall be upon you as a sign and a wonder, and upon your descendants for ever.

47“Because you did not serve the LORD your God with joyfulness and gladness of heart, by reason of the abundance of all things, 48therefore you shall serve your enemies whom the LORD will send against you, in hunger and thirst, in nakedness, and in want of all things; and he will put a yoke of iron upon your neck, until he has destroyed you. 49The LORD will bring a nation against you from afar, from the end of the earth, as swift as the eagle flies, a nation whose language you do not understand, 50a nation of stern countenance, who shall not regard the person of the old or show favor to the young, 51and shall eat the offspring of your cattle and the fruit of your ground, until you are destroyed; who also shall not leave you grain, wine, or oil, the increase of your cattle or the young of your flock, until they have caused you to perish. 52They shall besiege you in all your towns, until your high and fortified walls, in which you trusted, come down throughout all your land; and they shall besiege you in all your towns throughout all your land, which the LORD your God has given you. 53And you shall eat the offspring of your own body, the flesh of your sons and daughters, whom the LORD your God has given you, in the siege and in the distress with which your enemies shall distress you. 54The man who is the most tender and delicately bred among you will grudge food to his brother, to the wife of his bosom, and to the last of the children who remain to him; 55so that he will not give to any of them any of the flesh of his children whom he is eating, because he has nothing left him, in the siege and in the distress with which your enemy shall distress you in all your towns. 56The most tender and delicately bred woman among you, who would not venture to set the sole of her foot upon the ground because she is so delicate and tender, will grudge to the husband of her bosom, to her son and to her daughter, 57her afterbirth that comes out from between her feet and her children whom she bears, because she will eat them secretly, for want of all things, in the siege and in the distress with which your enemy shall distress you in your towns.

58“If you are not careful to do all the words of this law which are written in this book, that you may fear this glorious and awesome name, the LORD your God, 59then the LORD will bring on you and your offspring extraordinary afflictions, afflictions severe and lasting, and sicknesses grievous and lasting. 60And he will bring upon you again all the diseases of Egypt, which you were afraid of; and they shall cling to you. 61Every sickness also, and every affliction which is not recorded in the book of this law, the LORD will bring upon you, until you are destroyed. 62Whereas you were as the stars of heaven for multitude, you shall be left few in number; because you did not obey the voice of the LORD your God. 63And as the LORD took delight in doing you good and multiplying you, so the LORD will take delight

in bringing ruin upon you and destroying you;
and you shall be plucked off the land which
you are entering to take possession of it. 64And
the LORD will scatter you among all peoples,
from one end of the earth to the other; and
there you shall serve other gods, of wood and
stone, which neither you nor your fathers have
known. 65And among these nations you shall
find no ease, and there shall be no rest for the
sole of your foot; but the LORD will give you
there a trembling heart, and failing eyes, and
a languishing soul; 66your life shall hang in
doubt before you; night and day you shall be
in dread, and have no assurance of your life.
67In the morning you shall say, 'Would it were
evening!' and at evening you shall say, 'Would
it were morning!' because of the dread which
your heart shall fear, and the sights which
your eyes shall see. 68And the LORD will bring
you back in ships to Egypt, a journey which I
promised that you should never make again;
and there you shall offer yourselves for sale to
your enemies as male and female slaves, but no
man will buy you."

To the choirmaster: according to Jeduthun.
A Psalm of Asaph.

PSALM 77 [76]

I cry aloud to God,
aloud to God, that he may hear me.
2In the day of my trouble I seek the Lord;
in the night my hand is stretched out
without wearying;
my soul refuses to be comforted.

3I think of God, and I moan;
I meditate, and my spirit faints. *Selah*
4You keep my eyelids from closing;
I am so troubled that I cannot speak.
5I consider the days of old,
I remember the years long ago.
6I commune with my heart in the night;
I meditate and search my spirit:
7"Will the Lord spurn for ever,
and never again be favorable?
8Has his steadfast love for ever ceased?
Are his promises at an end for all time?
9Has God forgotten to be gracious?
Has he in anger shut up his compassion?"
Selah
10And I say, "It is my grief
that the right hand of the Most High
has changed."

11I will call to mind the deeds of the LORD;
yes, I will remember your wonders of old.
12I will meditate on all your work,
and muse on your mighty deeds.
13Your way, O God, is holy.
What god is great like our God?
14You are the God who works wonders,
who have manifested your might among
the peoples.
15With your arm you redeemed your people,
the sons of Jacob and Joseph. *Selah*

16When the waters saw you, O God,
when the waters saw you, they were afraid,
yes, the deep trembled.
17The clouds poured out water;
the skies gave forth thunder;
your arrows flashed on every side.
18The crash of your thunder was in the
whirlwind;
your lightnings lighted up the world;
the earth trembled and shook.
19Your way was through the sea,
your path through the great waters;
yet your footprints were unseen.
20You led your people like a flock
by the hand of Moses and Aaron.

LUKE 2

**39And when they had performed
everything according to the law
of the Lord, they returned into Galilee,
to their own city, Nazareth. 40And the**
child grew and became strong, filled with
wisdom; and the favor of God was upon him.
41Now his parents went to Jerusalem every
year at the feast of the Passover. 42And when he
was twelve years old, they went up according
to custom; 43and when the feast was ended,
as they were returning, the boy Jesus stayed

behind in Jerusalem. His parents did not know
it, 44but supposing him to be in the company
they went a day's journey, and they sought him
among their kinsfolk and acquaintances; 45and
when they did not find him, they returned
to Jerusalem, seeking him. 46After three days
they found him in the temple, sitting among
the teachers, listening to them and asking
them questions; 47and all who heard him were
amazed at his understanding and his answers.
48And when they saw him they were astonished;
and his mother said to him, "Son, why have
you treated us so? Behold, your father and I
have been looking for you anxiously." 49And he
said to them, "How is it that you sought me?
Did you not know that I must be in my Father's
house?" 50And they did not understand the
saying which he spoke to them. 51And he went
down with them and came to Nazareth, and
was obedient to them; and his mother kept all
these things in her heart.
52And Jesus increased in wisdom and in
stature, and in favor with God and man.

REFLECTION

Many parents know the horrible feeling of losing track of their children for a moment. Maybe in a crowded supermarket, or mall, or amusement park. "I thought *you* had him!" "No, I thought *you* did!" Imagine the sinking feeling that Mary and Joseph must have felt when they realized that Jesus was not with them on their long journey back from Jerusalem. In a large family setting, it would have been easy to think that the young, twelve-year-old Jesus was with an aunt, or uncle, or playing with cousins. Even after they realized that he was missing, it was still three more days until they finally found him in the Temple, "sitting among the teachers, listening to them and asking them questions" (Lk 2:46). What was happening in the hearts of Mary and Joseph? Were they angry? Hurt? Confused? Was there a sense within them that God was doing something bigger than they realized? They already knew the miraculous circumstances surrounding Jesus's Birth. How would you have responded to this situation? How do you respond to confusion within your own life? Does it throw you off course, or do you have the discernment that God might be doing more than you could imagine?

March 29

DEUTERONOMY 29

These are the words of the covenant which the LORD commanded Moses to make with the sons of Israel in the land of Moab, besides the covenant which he had made with them at Horeb.
2And Moses summoned all Israel and said
to them: "You have seen all that the LORD
did before your eyes in the land of Egypt, to
Pharaoh and to all his servants and to all his
land, 3the great trials which your eyes saw,
the signs, and those great wonders; 4but to
this day the LORD has not given you a mind
to understand, or eyes to see, or ears to hear.
5I have led you forty years in the wilderness;
your clothes have not worn out upon you, and
your sandals have not worn off your feet; 6you
have not eaten bread, and you have not drunk
wine or strong drink; that you may know
that I am the LORD your God. 7And when
you came to this place, Si′hon the king of
Heshbon and Og the king of Bashan came out
against us to battle, but we defeated them; 8we
took their land, and gave it for an inheritance
to the Reubenites, the Gadites, and the half-
tribe of the Manas′sites. 9Therefore be careful
to do the words of this covenant, that you may
prosper in all that you do.
10"You stand this day all of you before the
LORD your God; the heads of your tribes,
your elders, and your officers, all the men of
Israel, 11your little ones, your wives, and the
sojourner who is in your camp, both he who
hews your wood and he who draws your
water, 12that you may enter into the sworn
covenant of the LORD your God, which the
LORD your God makes with you this day;
13that he may establish you this day as his
people, and that he may be your God, as
he promised you, and as he swore to your
fathers, to Abraham, to Isaac, and to Jacob.
14Nor is it with you only that I make this
sworn covenant, 15but with him who is not

here with us this day as well as with him
who stands here with us this day before the
LORD our God.
16“You know how we dwelt in the land of
Egypt, and how we came through the midst of
the nations through which you passed; 17and
you have seen their detestable things, their
idols of wood and stone, of silver and gold,
which were among them. 18Beware lest there
be among you a man or woman or family or
tribe, whose heart turns away this day from
the LORD our God to go and serve the gods
of those nations; lest there be among you a
root bearing poisonous and bitter fruit, 19one
who, when he hears the words of this sworn
covenant, blesses himself in his heart, saying, ‘I
shall be safe, though I walk in the stubbornness
of my heart.’ This would lead to the sweeping
away of moist and dry alike. 20The LORD would
not pardon him, but rather the anger of the
LORD and his jealousy would smoke against
that man, and the curses written in this book
would settle upon him, and the LORD would
blot out his name from under heaven. 21And
the LORD would single him out from all the
tribes of Israel for calamity, in accordance
with all the curses of the covenant written in
this book of the law. 22And the generation to
come, your children who rise up after you,
and the foreigner who comes from a far land,
would say, when they see the afflictions of that
land and the sicknesses with which the LORD
has made it sick—23the whole land brimstone
and salt, and a burnt-out waste, unsown,
and growing nothing, where no grass can
sprout, an overthrow like that of Sodom and
Gomor′rah, Admah and Zeboi′im, which the
LORD overthrew in his anger and wrath—24yes,
all the nations would say, ‘Why has the LORD
done thus to this land? What means the heat
of this great anger?’ 25Then men would say,
‘It is because they forsook the covenant of the
LORD, the God of their fathers, which he made
with them when he brought them out of the
land of Egypt, 26and went and served other
gods and worshiped them, gods whom they
had not known and whom he had not allotted
to them; 27therefore the anger of the LORD
was kindled against this land, bringing upon
it all the curses written in this book; 28and the
LORD uprooted them from their land in anger
and fury and great wrath, and cast them into
another land, as at this day.’
29“The secret things belong to the LORD
our God; but the things that are revealed
belong to us and to our children for ever,
that we may do all the words of this law.

30 “And when all these things come
upon you, the blessing and the
curse, which I have set before you, and you
call them to mind among all the nations
where the LORD your God has driven you,
2and return to the LORD your God, you and
your children, and obey his voice in all that
I command you this day, with all your heart
and with all your soul; 3then the LORD your
God will restore your fortunes, and have
compassion upon you, and he will gather
you again from all the peoples where the
LORD your God has scattered you. 4If your
outcasts are in the uttermost parts of heaven,
from there the LORD your God will gather
you, and from there he will fetch you; 5and
the LORD your God will bring you into the
land which your fathers possessed, that you
may possess it; and he will make you more
prosperous and numerous than your fathers.
6And the LORD your God will circumcise
your heart and the heart of your offspring,
so that you will love the LORD your God
with all your heart and with all your soul,
that you may live. 7And the LORD your God
will put all these curses upon your foes and
enemies who persecuted you. 8And you shall
again obey the voice of the LORD, and keep
all his commandments which I command
you this day. 9The LORD your God will make
you abundantly prosperous in all the work of
your hand, in the fruit of your body, and in
the fruit of your cattle, and in the fruit of your
ground; for the LORD will again take delight
in prospering you, as he took delight in your
fathers, 10if you obey the voice of the LORD
your God, to keep his commandments and
his statutes which are written in this book of
the law, if you turn to the Lord your God with
all your heart and with all your soul.
11“For this commandment which I command you this day is not too hard for you,
neither is it far off. 12It is not in heaven, that

you should say, 'Who will go up for us to
heaven, and bring it to us, that we may hear
it and do it?' 13Neither is it beyond the sea,
that you should say, 'Who will go over the
sea for us, and bring it to us, that we may
hear it and do it?' 14But the word is very near
you; it is in your mouth and in your heart,
so that you can do it.

15"See, I have set before you this day life
and good, death and evil. 16If you obey
the commandments of the Lord your God
which I command you this day, by loving
the Lord your God, by walking in his ways,
and by keeping his commandments and
his statutes and his ordinances, then you
shall live and multiply, and the Lord your
God will bless you in the land which you
are entering to take possession of it. 17But
if your heart turns away, and you will not
hear, but are drawn away to worship other
gods and serve them, 18I declare to you this
day, that you shall perish; you shall not live
long in the land which you are going over
the Jordan to enter and possess. 19I call
heaven and earth to witness against you
this day, that I have set before you life and
death, blessing and curse; therefore choose
life, that you and your descendants may live,
20loving the LORD your God, obeying his
voice, and clinging to him; for that means
life to you and length of days, that you may
dwell in the land which the Lord swore to
your fathers, to Abraham, to Isaac, and to
Jacob, to give them."

31 So Moses continued to speak these
words to all Israel. 2And he said to
them, "I am a hundred and twenty years old
this day; I am no longer able to go out and
come in. The LORD has said to me, 'You shall
not go over this Jordan.' 3The LORD your
God himself will go over before you; he will
destroy these nations before you, so that you
shall dispossess them; and Joshua will go
over at your head, as the Lord has spoken.
4And the LORD will do to them as he did to
Si´hon and Og, the kings of the Am´orites,
and to their land, when he destroyed them.
5And the LORD will give them over to you,
and you shall do to them according to all the
commandment which I have commanded
you. 6Be strong and of good courage, do not
fear or be in dread of them: for it is the LORD
your God who goes with you; he will not fail
you or forsake you."

7Then Moses summoned Joshua, and said
to him in the sight of all Israel, "Be strong
and of good courage; for you shall go with
this people into the land which the LORD
has sworn to their fathers to give them; and
you shall put them in possession of it. 8It is
the LORD who goes before you; he will be
with you, he will not fail you or forsake you;
do not fear or be dismayed."

A Maskil of Asaph.

PSALM 78 [77]

Give ear, O my people, to my teaching;
incline your ears to the words of
my mouth!
2I will open my mouth in a parable;
I will utter dark sayings from of old,
3things that we have heard and known,
that our fathers have told us.
4We will not hide them from their children,
but tell to the coming generation
the glorious deeds of the LORD, and
his might,
and the wonders which he has wrought.

5He established a testimony in Jacob,
and appointed a law in Israel,
which he commanded our fathers
to teach to their children;
6that the next generation might know them,
the children yet unborn,
and arise and tell them to their children,
7 so that they should set their hope in God,
and not forget the works of God,
but keep his commandments;
8and that they should not be like
their fathers,
a stubborn and rebellious generation,
a generation whose heart was not steadfast,
whose spirit was not faithful to God.

9The E´phraimites, armed with the bow,
turned back on the day of battle.

10 They did not keep God's covenant,
but refused to walk according to his law.
11 They forgot what he had done,
and the miracles that he had shown them.
12 In the sight of their fathers he wrought
marvels
in the land of Egypt, in the fields of Zo′an.
13 He divided the sea and let them pass
through it,
and made the waters stand like a heap.
14 In the daytime he led them with a cloud,
and all the night with a fiery light.
15 He cleft rocks in the wilderness,
and gave them drink abundantly as from
the deep.
16 He made streams come out of the rock,
and caused waters to flow down like rivers.

LUKE 3

In the fifteenth year of the reign
of Tibe′rius Caesar, Pontius
Pilate being governor of Judea,
and Herod being tetrarch of Galilee,
and his brother Philip tetrarch of the re-
gion of Iturae′a and Trachoni′tis, and
Lysa′nias tetrarch of Abi-le′ne, 2 in the
high-priesthood of Annas and Cai′aphas,
the word of God came to John the son of
Zechari′ah in the wilderness; 3 and he went
into all the region about the Jordan, preaching
a baptism of repentance for the forgiveness of
sins. 4 As it is written in the book of the words
of Isaiah the prophet,

"The voice of one crying in the wilderness:
Prepare the way of the Lord,
make his paths straight.
5 Every valley shall be filled,
and every mountain and hill shall be
brought low,
and the crooked shall be made straight,
and the rough ways shall be made smooth;
6 and all flesh shall see the salvation of God."

7 He said therefore to the multitudes that came
out to be baptized by him, "You brood of vipers!
Who warned you to flee from the wrath to
come? 8 Bear fruits that befit repentance, and
do not begin to say to yourselves, 'We have
Abraham as our father'; for I tell you, God is
able from these stones to raise up children to
Abraham. 9 Even now the axe is laid to the root
of the trees; every tree therefore that does not
bear good fruit is cut down and thrown into
the fire."

10 And the multitudes asked him, "What then
shall we do?" 11 And he answered them, "He
who has two coats, let him share with him
who has none; and he who has food, let
him do likewise." 12 Tax collectors also came
to be baptized, and said to him, "Teacher,
what shall we do?" 13 And he said to them,
"Collect no more than is appointed you."
14 Soldiers also asked him, "And we, what
shall we do?" And he said to them, "Rob no
one by violence or by false accusation, and
be content with your wages."

15 As the people were in expectation, and all
men questioned in their hearts concerning
John, whether perhaps he were the Christ,
16 John answered them all, "I baptize you with
water; but he who is mightier than I is coming,
the thong of whose sandals I am not worthy to
untie; he will baptize you with the Holy Spirit
and with fire. 17 His winnowing fork is in his
hand, to clear his threshing floor, and to gather
the wheat into his granary, but the chaff he will
burn with unquenchable fire."

18 So, with many other exhortations, he
preached good news to the people. 19 But
Herod the tetrarch, who had been reproved by
him for Hero′di-as, his brother's wife, and for
all the evil things that Herod had done, 20 added
this to them all, that he shut up John in prison.

21 Now when all the people were baptized,
and when Jesus also had been baptized and
was praying, the heaven was opened, 22 and
the Holy Spirit descended upon him in bodily
form, as a dove, and a voice came from heaven,
"You are my beloved Son; with you I am well
pleased."

REFLECTION

Although most of Deuteronomy comes from the words of Moses, it is here, toward the end of the book, that Moses becomes his most passionate. In these passages, the text centers on the themes of *liturgy* and *torah*, in other words, how we worship and how we respond to God's Word. It is in this section that the Israelites will reach what is called the "Valley of Decision." As they prepare to enter the Promised Land, Moses asks them to choose between life (faithfulness to God and his Word) and death (unfaithfulness to God and his Word). It is here that they will be asked to once again swear themselves to the covenant that their parents broke and to decide what kind of a people they will be. In the midst of this, however, fully aware of the frailty of his own people, God promises his own faithfulness. More than anything else, these verses are meant to remind us that God alone is faithful and is always willing to fill in the gaps of our lives. Have you been faithful to your baptismal promises? In what ways have you failed? Do you trust in the faithfulness of God?

March 30

DEUTERONOMY 31

**[9]And Moses wrote this law, and
gave it to the priests the sons
of Levi, who carried the ark of the covenant of the LORD, and to all the elders**
of Israel. [10]And Moses commanded them, "At
the end of every seven years, at the set time of
the year of release, at the feast of booths, [11]when
all Israel comes to appear before the LORD your
God at the place which he will choose, you shall
read this law before all Israel in their hearing.
[12]Assemble the people, men, women, and little
ones, and the sojourner within your towns,
that they may hear and learn to fear the LORD
your God, and be careful to do all the words of
this law, [13]and that their children, who have not
known it, may hear and learn to fear the LORD
your God, as long as you live in the land which
you are going over the Jordan to possess."
[14]And the LORD said to Moses, "Behold, the
days approach when you must die; call Joshua,
and present yourselves in the tent of meeting,
that I may commission him." And Moses and
Joshua went and presented themselves in the
tent of meeting. [15]And the LORD appeared in
the tent in a pillar of cloud; and the pillar of
cloud stood by the door of the tent.
[16]And the LORD said to Moses, "Behold,
you are about to sleep with your fathers; then
this people will rise and play the harlot after
the strange gods of the land, where they go
to be among them, and they will forsake me
and break my covenant which I have made
with them. [17]Then my anger will be kindled
against them in that day, and I will forsake
them and hide my face from them, and they
will be devoured; and many evils and troubles
will come upon them, so that they will say in
that day, 'Have not these evils come upon us
because our God is not among us?' [18]And I will
surely hide my face in that day on account of
all the evil which they have done, because they
have turned to other gods. [19]Now therefore
write this song, and teach it to the sons of
Israel; put it in their mouths, that this song may
be a witness for me against the sons of Israel.
[20]For when I have brought them into the land
flowing with milk and honey, which I swore to
give to their fathers, and they have eaten and are
full and grown fat, they will turn to other gods
and serve them, and despise me and break my
covenant. [21]And when many evils and troubles
have come upon them, this song shall confront
them as a witness (for it will live unforgotten in
the mouths of their descendants); for I know
the purposes which they are already forming,
before I have brought them into the land that I
swore to give." [22]So Moses wrote this song the
same day, and taught it to the sons of Israel.
[23]And the LORD commissioned Joshua the
son of Nun and said, "Be strong and of good
courage; for you shall bring the children of
Israel into the land which I swore to give them:
I will be with you."
[24]When Moses had finished writing the
words of this law in a book, to the very end,
[25]Moses commanded the Levites who carried
the ark of the covenant of the LORD, [26]"Take
this book of the law, and put it by the side of the
ark of the covenant of the LORD your God, that
it may be there for a witness against you. [27]For

I know how rebellious and stubborn you are;
behold, while I am yet alive with you, today
you have been rebellious against the LORD;
how much more after my death! 28 Assemble
to me all the elders of your tribes, and your
officers, that I may speak these words in their
ears and call heaven and earth to witness
against them. 29 For I know that after my
death you will surely act corruptly, and turn
aside from the way which I have commanded
you; and in the days to come evil will befall
you, because you will do what is evil in the
sight of the LORD, provoking him to anger
through the work of your hands."

30 Then Moses spoke the words of this song
until they were finished, in the ears of all the
assembly of Israel:

32 "Give ear, O heavens, and I will speak;
and let the earth hear the words of
my mouth.
2 May my teaching drop as the rain,
my speech distil as the dew,
as the gentle rain upon the tender grass,
and as the showers upon the herb.
3 For I will proclaim the name of the LORD.
Ascribe greatness to our God!

4 "The Rock, his work is perfect;
for all his ways are justice.
A God of faithfulness and without iniquity,
just and right is he.
5 They have dealt corruptly with him,
they are no longer his children because
of their blemish;
they are a perverse and crooked
generation.
6 Do you thus repay the LORD,
you foolish and senseless people?
Is not he your father, who created you,
who made you and established you?
7 Remember the days of old,
consider the years of many generations;
ask your father, and he will show you;
your elders, and they will tell you.
8 When the Most High gave to the nations
their inheritance,
when he separated the sons of men,
he fixed the bounds of the peoples
according to the number of the sons
of Israel.
9 For the LORD's portion is his people,
Jacob his allotted heritage.

10 "He found him in a desert land,
and in the howling waste of
the wilderness;
he encircled him, he cared for him,
he kept him as the apple of his eye.
11 Like an eagle that stirs up its nest,
that flutters over its young,
spreading out its wings, catching them,
bearing them on its pinions,
12 the LORD alone did lead him,
and there was no foreign god with him.
13 He made him ride on the high places of
the earth,
and he ate the produce of the field;
and he made him suck honey out
of the rock,
and oil out of the flinty rock.
14 Curds from the herd, and milk from
the flock,
with fat of lambs and rams,
herds of Bashan and goats,
with the finest of the wheat—
and of the blood of the grape you
drank wine.

15 "But Jesh´urun waxed fat, and kicked;
you waxed fat, you grew thick, you
became sleek;
then he forsook God who made him,
and scoffed at the Rock of his salvation.
16 They stirred him to jealousy with
strange gods;
with abominable practices they provoked
him to anger.
17 They sacrificed to demons which were
no gods,
to gods they had never known,
to new gods that had come in of late,
whom your fathers had never dreaded.
18 You were unmindful of the Rock that
begot you,
and you forgot the God who gave
you birth.

19 "The LORD saw it, and spurned them,
because of the provocation of his sons
and his daughters.

20 And he said, 'I will hide my face from them,
I will see what their end will be,
for they are a perverse generation,
children in whom is no faithfulness.
21 They have stirred me to jealousy with what
is no god;
they have provoked me with their idols.
So I will stir them to jealousy with those
who are no people;
I will provoke them with a foolish nation.
22 For a fire is kindled by my anger,
and it burns to the depths of Sheol,
devours the earth and its increase,
and sets on fire the foundations of the
mountains.

23 " 'And I will heap evils upon them;
I will spend my arrows upon them;
24 they shall be wasted with hunger,
and devoured with burning heat
and poisonous pestilence;
and I will send the teeth of beasts
against them,
with venom of crawling things of the dust.
25 In the open the sword shall bereave,
and in the chambers shall be terror,
destroying both young man and virgin,
the sucking child with the man of
gray hairs.
26 I would have said, "I will scatter them afar,
I will make the remembrance of them
cease from among men,"
27 had I not feared provocation by the enemy,
lest their adversaries should judge amiss,
lest they should say, "Our hand is
triumphant,
the Lord has not wrought all this." '

28 "For they are a nation void of counsel,
and there is no understanding in them.
29 If they were wise, they would understand
this,
they would discern their latter end!
30 How should one chase a thousand,
and two put ten thousand to flight,
unless their Rock had sold them,
and the Lord had given them up?
31 For their rock is not as our Rock,
even our enemies themselves
being judges.
32 For their vine comes from the vine
of Sodom,
and from the fields of Gomor′rah;
their grapes are grapes of poison,
their clusters are bitter;
33 their wine is the poison of serpents,
and the cruel venom of asps.

34 "Is not this laid up in store with me,
sealed up in my treasuries?
35 Vengeance is mine, and recompense,
for the time when their foot shall slip;
for the day of their calamity is at hand,
and their doom comes swiftly.
36 For the Lord will vindicate his people
and have compassion on his servants,
when he sees that their power is gone,
and there is none remaining, bond
or free.
37 Then he will say, 'Where are their gods,
the rock in which they took refuge,
38 who ate the fat of their sacrifices,
and drank the wine of their drink
offering?
Let them rise up and help you,
let them be your protection!

39 " 'See now that I, even I, am he,
and there is no god beside me;
I kill and I make alive;
I wound and I heal;
and there is none that can deliver
out of my hand.
40 For I lift up my hand to heaven,
and swear, As I live for ever,
41 if I sharpen my glittering sword,
and my hand takes hold on judgment,
I will take vengeance on my adversaries,
and will repay those who hate me.
42 I will make my arrows drunk with blood,
and my sword shall devour flesh—
with the blood of the slain and the captives,
from the long-haired heads of
the enemy.'

43 "Praise his people, O you nations;
for he avenges the blood of his servants,
and takes vengeance on his adversaries,
and makes expiation for the land of
his people."

44 Moses came and recited all the words
of this song in the hearing of the people,
he and Joshua the son of Nun. 45 And
when Moses had finished speaking all
these words to all Israel, 46 he said to
them, "Lay to heart all the words which
I enjoin upon you this day, that you may
command them to your children, that
they may be careful to do all the words
of this law. 47 For it is no trifle for you, but
it is your life, and thereby you shall live
long in the land which you are going over
the Jordan to possess."

A Maskil of Asaph.

PSALM 78 [77]

17 Yet they sinned still more against him,
rebelling against the Most High in
the desert.
18 They tested God in their heart
by demanding the food they craved.
19 They spoke against God, saying,
"Can God spread a table in
the wilderness?
20 He struck the rock so that water
gushed out
and streams overflowed.
Can he also give bread,
or provide meat for his people?"

21 Therefore, when the LORD heard, he was
full of wrath;
a fire was kindled against Jacob,
his anger mounted against Israel;
22 because they had no faith in God,
and did not trust his saving power.
23 Yet he commanded the skies above,
and opened the doors of heaven;
24 and he rained down upon them manna
to eat,
and gave them the bread of heaven.
25 Man ate of the bread of the angels;
he sent them food in abundance.
26 He caused the east wind to blow in
the heavens,
and by his power he led out the
south wind;
27 he rained flesh upon them like dust,
winged birds like the sand of the seas;
28 he let them fall in the midst of their camp,
all around their habitations.
29 And they ate and were well filled,
for he gave them what they craved.
30 But before they had sated their craving,
while the food was still in their mouths,
31 the anger of God rose against them
and he slew the strongest of them,
and laid low the picked men of Israel.

32 In spite of all this they still sinned;
despite his wonders they did not believe.

LUKE 3

23 Jesus, when he began his min-
istry, was about thirty years of
age, being the son (as was sup-
posed) of Joseph, the son of He'li, 24 the
son of Matthat, the son of Levi, the son
of Melchi, the son of Jan'na-i, the son of
Joseph, 25 the son of Mattathi'as, the son of
Amos, the son of Na'hum, the son of Es'li,
the son of Nag'ga-i, 26 the son of Ma'ath,
the son of Mattathi'as, the son of Sem'e-
in, the son of Jo'sech, the son of Jo'da,
27 the son of Jo-an'an, the son of Rhesa,
the son of Zerub'babel, the son of She-al'-
ti-el, the son of Ne'ri, 28 the son of Melchi,
the son of Addi, the son of Co'sam, the
son of Elma'dam, the son of Er, 29 the son
of Joshua, the son of Elie'zer, the son of
Jo'rim, the son of Matthat, the son of Levi,
30 the son of Simeon, the son of Judah, the
son of Joseph, the son of Jo'nam, the son
of Eli'akim, 31 the son of Me'le-a, the son
of Menna, the son of Mat'tatha, the son
of Nathan, the son of David, 32 the son of
Jesse, the son of O'bed, the son of Boaz,
the son of Sa'la, the son of Nahshon, 33 the
son of Ammin'adab, the son of Admin,
the son of Arni, the son of Hezron, the
son of Per'ez, the son of Judah, 34 the son
of Jacob, the son of Isaac, the son of Abraham, the son of Te'rah, the son of Na'hor,

35 the son of Se´rug, the son of Re´u, the son of Pe´leg, the son of E´ber, the son of She´lah, 36 the son of Ca-i´nan, the son of Arpha´xad, the son of Shem, the son of Noah, the son of La´mech, 37 the son of Methu´selah, the son of E´noch, the son of Jar´ed, the son of Ma-ha´lale´´el, the son of Ca-i´nan, 38 the son of E´nos, the son of Seth, the son of Adam, the son of God.

REFLECTION

At the beginning of this reading from Deuteronomy, Moses gives the people of Israel the tablets of the Law to carry with them into the Promised Land. God's law is so important that the tablets will be placed in the Ark of the Covenant, which is kept in the Holy of Holies. We see then how important God's Word is for Israel! At this point, although Moses will not be able to lead the people into the Promised Land, he has given them three great gifts: Joshua as their new leader, God's Word as a reminder of who they are meant to be, and the Levitical priests to offer sacrifice and teach them. Then, in chapter 32, the people are given one last thing—a song. This chapter has been called the national anthem of Israel. Notice, though, that this hymn is not merely meant to inspire. Rather it is meant to *remind* and *convict*. It is perhaps in this remarkable song that Moses rises to his highest prophetic stature. As great as Moses was, however, his most important act was in pointing forward to God's ultimate act of faithfulness—the sending of his Son to be our Savior and Redeemer. Do you carry the Word of God in your heart?

March 31

DEUTERONOMY 32

48 And the LORD said to Moses that very day, 49 "Ascend this mountain of the Ab´arim, Mount Nebo, which is in the land of Moab, opposite Jericho; and view the land of Canaan, which I give to the sons of Israel for a possession; 50 and die on the mountain which you ascend, and be gathered to your people, as Aaron your brother died in Mount Hor and was gathered to his people; 51 because you broke faith with me in the midst of the sons of Israel at the waters of Mer´ibath-ka´desh, in the wilderness of Zin; because you did not revere me as holy in the midst of the sons of Israel. 52 For you shall see the land before you; but you shall not go there, into the land which I give to the sons of Israel."

33 This is the blessing with which Moses the man of God blessed the children of Israel before his death. 2 He said,

"The LORD came from Sinai,
and dawned from Se´ir upon us;
he shone forth from Mount Par´an,
he came from the ten thousands of
holy ones,
with flaming fire at his right hand.
3 Yes, he loved his people;
all those consecrated to him were
in his hand;
so they followed in your steps,
receiving direction from you,
4 when Moses commanded us a law,
as a possession for the assembly of Jacob.
5 Thus the LORD became king in Jesh´urun,
when the heads of the people
were gathered,
all the tribes of Israel together.

6 "Let Reuben live, and not die,
nor let his men be few."

7 And this he said of Judah:
"Hear, O LORD, the voice of Judah,
and bring him in to his people.
With your hands contend for him,
and be a help against his adversaries."

8 And of Levi he said,
"Give to Levi your Thummim,
and your U´rim to your godly one,
whom you tested at Massah,
with whom you strove at the waters
of Mer´ibah;

9who said of his father and mother,
'I regard them not';
he disowned his brothers,
and ignored his children.
For they observed your word,
and kept your covenant.
10They shall teach Jacob your ordinances,
and Israel your law;
they shall put incense before you,
and whole burnt offering upon
your altar.
11Bless, O LORD, his substance,
and accept the work of his hands;
crush the loins of his adversaries,
of those that hate him, that they
rise not again."

12Of Benjamin he said,
"The beloved of the LORD,
he dwells in safety by him;
he encompasses him all the day long,
and makes his dwelling between
his shoulders."

13And of Joseph he said,
"Blessed by the LORD be his land,
with the choicest gifts of heaven above,
and of the deep that lies beneath,
14with the choicest fruits of the sun,
and the rich yield of the months,
15with the finest produce of the ancient
mountains,
and the abundance of the
everlasting hills,
16with the best gifts of the earth and
its fulness,
and the favor of him that dwelt in the bush.
Let these come upon the head of Joseph,
and upon the crown of the head of him
that is prince among his brothers.
17His firstling bull has majesty,
and his horns are the horns of a wild ox;
with them he shall push the peoples,
all of them, to the ends of the earth;
such are the ten thousands of E′phraim,
and such are the thousands of Manas′seh."

18And of Zeb′ulun he said,
"Rejoice, Zebulun, in your going out;
and Is′sachar, in your tents.
19They shall call peoples to their mountain;
there they offer right sacrifices;
for they suck the affluence of the seas
and the hidden treasures of the sand."
20And of Gad he said,
"Blessed be he who enlarges Gad!
Gad lurks like a lion,
he tears the arm, and the crown of the head.
21He chose the best of the land for himself,
for there a commander's portion
was reserved;
and he came to the heads of the people,
with Israel he executed the commands
and just decrees of the LORD."

22And of Dan he said,
"Dan is a lion's whelp,
that leaps forth from Bashan."

23And of Naph′tali he said,
"O Naphtali, satisfied with favor,
and full of the blessing of the LORD,
possess the lake and the south."

24And of Asher he said,
"Blessed above sons be Asher;
let him be the favorite of his brothers,
and let him dip his foot in oil.
25Your bars shall be iron and bronze;
and as your days, so shall your strength be.

26"There is none like God, O Jesh′urun,
who rides through the heavens to
your help,
and in his majesty through the skies.
27The eternal God is your dwelling place,
and underneath are the everlasting arms.
And he thrust out the enemy before you,
and said, Destroy.
28So Israel dwelt in safety,
the fountain of Jacob alone,
in a land of grain and wine;
yes, his heavens drop down dew.
29Happy are you, O Israel! Who is like you,
a people saved by the LORD,
the shield of your help,
and the sword of your triumph!
Your enemies shall come fawning to you;
and you shall tread upon their high places."

34 And Moses went up from the plains
of Moab to Mount Nebo, to the
top of Pisgah, which is opposite Jericho.
And the LORD showed him all the land,
Gilead as far as Dan, [2]all Naph′tali, the
land of E′phraim and Manas′seh, all the
land of Judah as far as the western sea, [3]the
Neg′eb, and the Plain, that is, the valley
of Jericho the city of palm trees, as far as
Zoar. [4]And the LORD said to him, "This is
the land of which I swore to Abraham, to
Isaac, and to Jacob, 'I will give it to your
descendants.' I have let you see it with your
eyes, but you shall not go over there." [5]So
Moses the servant of the LORD died there
in the land of Moab, according to the word
of the LORD, [6]and he buried him in the
valley in the land of Moab opposite Beth-
pe′or; but no man knows the place of his
burial to this day. [7]Moses was a hundred
and twenty years old when he died; his eye
was not dim, nor his natural force abated.
[8]And the sons of Israel wept for Moses in
the plains of Moab thirty days; then the
days of weeping and mourning for Moses
were ended.
[9]And Joshua the son of Nun was full
of the spirit of wisdom, for Moses had
laid his hands upon him; so the sons of
Israel obeyed him, and did as the LORD
had commanded Moses. [10]And there has
not arisen a prophet since in Israel like
Moses, whom the LORD knew face to face,
[11]none like him for all the signs and the
wonders which the LORD sent him to do
in the land of Egypt, to Pharaoh and to
all his servants and to all his land, [12]and
for all the mighty power and all the great
and terrible deeds which Moses wrought
in the sight of all Israel.

A Maskil of Asaph.

PSALM 78 [77]

[33]So he made their days vanish like a breath,
and their years in terror.
[34]When he slew them, they sought for him;
they repented and sought God earnestly.
[35]They remembered that God was their rock,
the Most High God their redeemer.
[36]But they flattered him with their mouths;
they lied to him with their tongues.
[37]Their heart was not steadfast toward him;
they were not true to his covenant.
[38]Yet he, being compassionate,
forgave their iniquity,
and did not destroy them;
he restrained his anger often,
and did not stir up all his wrath.
[39]He remembered that they were but flesh,
a wind that passes and comes not again.
[40]How often they rebelled against him in
the wilderness
and grieved him in the desert!
[41]They tested him again and again,
and provoked the Holy One of Israel.
[42]They did not keep in mind his power,
or the day when he redeemed them
from the foe;
[43]when he wrought his signs in Egypt,
and his miracles in the fields of Zo′an.
[44]He turned their rivers to blood,
so that they could not drink of
their streams.
[45]He sent among them swarms of flies,
which devoured them,
and frogs, which destroyed them.
[46]He gave their crops to the caterpillar,
and the fruit of their labor to the locust.
[47]He destroyed their vines with hail,
and their sycamores with frost.
[48]He gave over their cattle to the hail,
and their flocks to thunderbolts.
[49]He let loose on them his fierce anger,
wrath, indignation, and distress,
a company of destroying angels.
[50]He made a path for his anger;
he did not spare them from death,
but gave their lives over to the plague.
[51]He struck all the first-born in Egypt,
the first issue of their strength in the
tents of Ham.
[52]Then he led forth his people like sheep,
and guided them in the wilderness
like a flock.
[53]He led them in safety, so that they were
not afraid;
but the sea overwhelmed their enemies.

54 And he brought them to his holy land,
to the mountain which his right hand
had won.
55 He drove out nations before them;
he apportioned them for a possession
and settled the tribes of Israel in
their tents.

LUKE 4

**And Jesus, full of the Holy Spirit,
returned from the Jordan, and
was led by the Spirit 2 for forty days
in the wilderness, tempted by the**
devil. And he ate nothing in those days;
and when they were ended, he was hungry. 3 The devil said to him, "If you are
the Son of God, command this stone to
become bread." 4 And Jesus answered him,
"It is written, 'Man shall not live by bread
alone.'" 5 And the devil took him up,
and showed him all the kingdoms of the
world in a moment of time, 6 and said to
him, "To you I will give all this authority and their glory; for it has been delivered to me, and I give it to whom I will.
7 If you, then, will worship me, it shall all
be yours." 8 And Jesus answered him, "It
is written,

'You shall worship the Lord your God,
and him only shall you serve.'"

9 And he took him to Jerusalem, and set
him on the pinnacle of the temple, and said
to him, "If you are the Son of God, throw
yourself down from here; 10 for it is written,

'He will give his angels charge of you, to
guard you,'

11 and

'On their hands they will bear you up,
lest you strike your foot against a stone.'"

12 And Jesus answered him, "It is said,
'You shall not tempt the Lord your God.'"
13 And when the devil had ended every
temptation, he departed from him until an
opportune time.

14 And Jesus returned in the power
of the Spirit into Galilee, and a report
concerning him went out through all the
surrounding country. 15 And he taught in
their synagogues, being glorified by all.

16 And he came to Nazareth, where he
had been brought up; and he went to the
synagogue, as was his custom, on the sabbath
day. And he stood up to read; 17 and there was
given to him the book of the prophet Isaiah.
He opened the book and found the place
where it was written,

18 "The Spirit of the Lord is upon me,
because he has anointed me to preach good
news to the poor.
He has sent me to proclaim release to the
captives
and recovering of sight to the blind,
to set at liberty those who are oppressed,
19 to proclaim the acceptable year of the
Lord."

20 And he closed the book, and gave it
back to the attendant, and sat down; and
the eyes of all in the synagogue were fixed
on him. 21 And he began to say to them,
"Today this Scripture has been fulfilled in
your hearing." 22 And all spoke well of him,
and wondered at the gracious words which
proceeded out of his mouth; and they said,
"Is not this Joseph's son?" 23 And he said to
them, "Doubtless you will quote to me this
proverb, 'Physician, heal yourself; what we
have heard you did at Caper'na-um, do here
also in your own country.'" 24 And he said,
"Truly, I say to you, no prophet is acceptable
in his own country. 25 But in truth, I tell
you, there were many widows in Israel in
the days of Eli'jah, when the heaven was
shut up three years and six months, when
there came a great famine over all the land;
26 and Eli'jah was sent to none of them but
only to Zar'ephath, in the land of Si'don,
to a woman who was a widow. 27 And there
were many lepers in Israel in the time of
the prophet Eli'sha; and none of them was
cleansed, but only Na'aman the Syrian."
28 When they heard this, all in the synagogue
were filled with wrath. 29 And they rose up
and put him out of the city, and led him
to the brow of the hill on which their city
was built, that they might throw him down
headlong. 30 But passing through the midst
of them he went away.

REFLECTION

In the final chapters of Deuteronomy, we see a recounting of Moses's death. This part of the book is almost exclusively focused on Israel's future. The theme is *What are God's plans, dreams, desires for you?* The last words of Moses are also his most passionate. They're focused on the hope for the future that God has promised to his people. This is a very difficult moment for Israel because their future won't include Moses—the man who had been their leader and father figure since the Exodus. It is a moment of endings and new beginnings. In the Gospel, Jesus experiences his own temptation in the wilderness, in which he begins to close the door on Satan's power and his domination of humanity, embodied in many ways by the exodus generation. Now it is Jesus who will lead the people of God into a new Promised Land—the likes of which Moses could never have dreamed. What are God's plans, dreams, and desires for your own life?

April 1

JOSHUA 1

After the death of Moses the servant of the LORD, the LORD said to Joshua the son of Nun, Moses' minister, [2]"Moses my servant is dead; now therefore arise, go over this Jordan, you and all this people, into the land which I am giving to them, to the sons of Israel. [3]Every place that the sole of your foot will tread upon I have given to you, as I promised to Moses. [4]From the wilderness and this Lebanon as far as the great river, the river Euphrates, all the land of the Hittites to the Great Sea toward the going down of the sun shall be your territory. [5]No man shall be able to stand before you all the days of your life; as I was with Moses, so I will be with you; I will not fail you or forsake you. [6]Be strong and of good courage; for you shall cause this people to inherit the land which I swore to their fathers to give them. [7]Only be strong and very courageous, being careful to do according to all the law which Moses my servant commanded you; turn not from it to the right hand or to the left, that you may have good success wherever you go. [8]This book of the law shall not depart out of your mouth, but you shall meditate on it day and night, that you may be careful to do according to all that is written in it; for then you shall make your way prosperous, and then you shall have good success. [9]Have I not commanded you? Be strong and of good courage; be not frightened, neither be dismayed; for the LORD your God is with you wherever you go."

[10]Then Joshua commanded the officers of the people, [11]"Pass through the camp, and command the people, 'Prepare your provisions; for within three days you are to pass over this Jordan, to go in to take possession of the land which the LORD your God gives you to possess.'"

[12]And to the Reubenites, the Gadites, and the half-tribe of Manas'seh Joshua said, [13]"Remember the word which Moses the servant of the LORD commanded you, saying, 'The LORD your God is providing you a place of rest, and will give you this land.' [14]Your wives, your little ones, and your cattle shall remain in the land which Moses gave you beyond the Jordan; but all the men of valor among you shall pass over armed before your brethren and shall help them, [15]until the LORD gives rest to your brethren as well as to you, and they also take possession of the land which the LORD your God is giving them; then you shall return to the land of your possession, and shall possess it, the land which Moses the servant of the LORD gave you beyond the Jordan toward the sunrise." [16]And they answered Joshua, "All that you have commanded us we will do, and wherever you send us we will go. [17]Just as we obeyed Moses in all things, so we will obey you; only may the LORD your God be with you, as he was with Moses! [18]Whoever rebels against your commandment and disobeys your words, whatever you command him, shall be put to death. Only be strong and of good courage."

2 And Joshua the son of Nun sent two men secretly from Shittim as spies, saying, "Go, view the land, especially Jericho." And they went, and came into the house of a harlot whose name was Ra'hab, and lodged there. [2]And it was told the king of Jericho, "Behold, certain men of Israel have come here tonight to search out the land." [3]Then the king of Jericho sent to Ra'hab, saying, "Bring forth the men that have come to you, who entered your house; for they have come to search out all the land." [4]But the woman had taken the two men and hidden them; and she said, "True, men came to me, but I did not know where they came from; [5]and when the gate was to be closed, at dark, the men went out; where the men went I do not know; pursue them quickly, for you will overtake them." [6]But she had brought them up to the roof, and hid them with the stalks of flax which she had laid in order on the roof. [7]So the men pursued after them on the way to the Jordan as far as the fords; and as soon as the pursuers had gone out, the gate was shut.

8 Before they lay down, she came up to them on the roof, 9 and said to the men, "I know that the LORD has given you the land, and that the fear of you has fallen upon us, and that all the inhabitants of the land melt away before you. 10 For we have heard how the LORD dried up the water of the Red Sea before you when you came out of Egypt, and what you did to the two kings of the Am′orites that were beyond the Jordan, to Si′hon and Og, whom you utterly destroyed. 11 And as soon as we heard it, our hearts melted, and there was no courage left in any man, because of you; for the LORD your God is he who is God in heaven above and on earth beneath. 12 Now then, swear to me by the LORD that as I have dealt kindly with you, you also will deal kindly with my father's house, and give me a sure sign, 13 and save alive my father and mother, my brothers and sisters, and all who belong to them, and deliver our lives from death." 14 And the men said to her, "Our life for yours! If you do not tell this business of ours, then we will deal kindly and faithfully with you when the LORD gives us the land."

15 Then she let them down by a rope through the window, for her house was built into the city wall, so that she dwelt in the wall. 16 And she said to them, "Go into the hills, lest the pursuers meet you; and hide yourselves there three days, until the pursuers have returned; then afterward you may go your way." 17 The men said to her, "We will be guiltless with respect to this oath of yours which you have made us swear. 18 Behold, when we come into the land, you shall bind this scarlet cord in the window through which you let us down; and you shall gather into your house your father and mother, your brothers, and all your father's household. 19 If any one goes out of the doors of your house into the street, his blood shall be upon his head, and we shall be guiltless; but if a hand is laid upon any one who is with you in the house, his blood shall be on our head. 20 But if you tell this business of ours, then we shall be guiltless with respect to your oath which you have made us swear." 21 And she said, "According to your words, so be it." Then she sent them away, and they departed; and she bound the scarlet cord in the window.

22 They departed, and went into the hills, and remained there three days, until the pursuers returned; for the pursuers had made search all along the way and found nothing. 23 Then the two men came down again from the hills, and passed over and came to Joshua the son of Nun; and they told him all that had befallen them. 24 And they said to Joshua, "Truly the LORD has given all the land into our hands; and moreover all the inhabitants of the land are fainthearted because of us."

3 Early in the morning Joshua rose and set out from Shittim, with all the sons of Israel; and they came to the Jordan, and lodged there before they passed over. 2 At the end of three days the officers went through the camp 3 and commanded the people, "When you see the ark of the covenant of the LORD your God being carried by the Levitical priests, then you shall set out from your place and follow it, 4 that you may know the way you shall go, for you have not passed this way before. Yet there shall be a space between you and it, a distance of about two thousand cubits; do not come near it." 5 And Joshua said to the people, "Sanctify yourselves; for tomorrow the LORD will do wonders among you." 6 And Joshua said to the priests, "Take up the ark of the covenant, and pass on before the people." And they took up the ark of the covenant, and went before the people.

7 And the LORD said to Joshua, "This day I will begin to exalt you in the sight of all Israel, that they may know that, as I was with Moses, so I will be with you. 8 And you shall command the priests who bear the ark of the covenant, 'When you come to the brink of the waters of the Jordan, you shall stand still in the Jordan.'" 9 And Joshua said to the sons of Israel, "Come here, and hear the words of the LORD your God." 10 And Joshua said, "Hereby you shall know that

the living God is among you, and that he
will without fail drive out from before you
the Canaanites, the Hittites, the Hi′vites, the
Per′izzites, the Gir′gashites, the Am′orites,
and the Jeb′usites. 11 Behold, the ark of the
covenant of the Lord of all the earth is to
pass over before you into the Jordan. 12 Now
therefore take twelve men from the tribes of
Israel, from each tribe a man. 13 And when
the soles of the feet of the priests who bear
the ark of the LORD, the Lord of all the earth,
shall rest in the waters of the Jordan, the
waters of the Jordan shall be stopped from
flowing, and the waters coming down from
above shall stand in one heap."

14 So, when the people set out from their
tents, to pass over the Jordan with the priests
bearing the ark of the covenant before the
people, 15 and when those who bore the ark
had come to the Jordan, and the feet of the
priests bearing the ark were dipped in the
brink of the water (the Jordan overflows all
its banks throughout the time of harvest),
16 the waters coming down from above stood
and rose up in a heap far off, at Adam, the city
that is beside Zar′ethan, and those flowing
down toward the sea of the Ar′abah, the
Salt Sea, were wholly cut off; and the people
passed over opposite Jericho. 17 And while all
Israel were passing over on dry ground, the
priests who bore the ark of the covenant of
the LORD stood on dry ground in the midst
of the Jordan, until all the nation finished
passing over the Jordan.

A Maskil of Asaph.

PSALM 78 [77]

56 Yet they tested and rebelled against the
Most High God,
and did not observe his decrees,
57 but turned away and acted treacherously
like their fathers;
they twisted like a deceitful bow.
58 For they provoked him to anger with their
high places;
they moved him to jealousy with their
graven images.
59 When God heard, he was full of wrath,
and he utterly rejected Israel.
60 He forsook his dwelling at Shiloh,
the tent where he dwelt among men,
61 and delivered his power to captivity,
his glory to the hand of the foe.
62 He gave his people over to the sword,
and vented his wrath on his heritage.
63 Fire devoured their young men,
and their maidens had no marriage song.
64 Their priests fell by the sword,
and their widows made no lamentation.
65 Then the Lord awoke as from sleep,
like a strong man shouting because
of wine.
66 And he put his adversaries to rout;
he put them to everlasting shame.

67 He rejected the tent of Joseph,
he did not choose the tribe of E′phraim;
68 but he chose the tribe of Judah,
Mount Zion, which he loves.
69 He built his sanctuary like the high
heavens,
like the earth, which he has founded
for ever.
70 He chose David his servant,
and took him from the sheepfolds;
71 from tending the ewes that had young he
brought him
to be the shepherd of Jacob his people,
of Israel his inheritance.
72 With upright heart he tended them,
and guided them with skilful hand.

LUKE 4

**31 And he went down to Caper′-
na-um, a city of Galilee. And
he was teaching them on the
sabbath; 32 and they were astonished
at his teaching, for his word was with**
authority. 33 And in the synagogue there was
a man who had the spirit of an unclean demon; and he cried out with a loud voice,
34 "Ah! What have you to do with us, Jesus
of Nazareth? Have you come to destroy us?
I know who you are, the Holy One of God."

35But Jesus rebuked him, saying, "Be silent,
and come out of him!" And when the demon had thrown him down in their midst,
he came out of him, having done him no
harm. 36And they were all amazed and said
to one another, "What is this word? For with
authority and power he commands the unclean spirits, and they come out." 37And reports of him went out into every place in the
surrounding region.

38And he arose and left the synagogue, and
entered Simon's house. Now Simon's mother-
in-law was ill with a high fever, and they
asked him about her. 39And he stood over
her and rebuked the fever, and it left her; and
immediately she rose and served them.

40Now when the sun was setting, all those
who had any that were sick with various
diseases brought them to him; and he laid
his hands on every one of them and healed
them. 41And demons also came out of many,
crying, "You are the Son of God!" But he
rebuked them, and would not allow them
to speak, because they knew that he was
the Christ.

42And when it was day he departed and
went into a lonely place. And the people
sought him and came to him, and would
have kept him from leaving them; 43but
he said to them, "I must preach the good
news of the kingdom of God to the other
cities also; for I was sent for this purpose."
44And he was preaching in the synagogues
of Judea."

REFLECTION

Often we feel as though our lives are in someone else's hands, or that our future is at the mercy of circumstances beyond our control. But God is in control and his order and intention bring clarity and direction. After Moses's death, the Lord establishes continuity in leadership by appointing Joshua as Moses's successor. Joshua recalls God's promise of land (see Jos 1:13) and understands it as the basis for the drama about to unfold—the conquest of Canaan. In Psalm 78, we see God's plan for his people opposed by disobedience, but not thwarted.

The Lord "chose the tribe of Judah," and "he chose David" (Ps 78:68, 70). His choice, not the winds of chance, provides a new leader for his people and their future. Even in the Gospel, we see Jesus rebuking the demons that try to name him (see Lk 4:34, 41), not because they are lying but because they are trying to control the situation. Jesus's mastery over them demonstrates that he is in control. How does God's order give direction to your life?

April 2

JOSHUA 4

**When all the nation had fin-
ished passing over the Jordan,
the LORD said to Joshua, 2"Take twelve
men from the people, from each tribe**
a man, 3and command them, 'Take twelve
stones from here out of the midst of the Jordan, from the very place where the priests'
feet stood, and carry them over with you,
and lay them down in the place where you
lodge tonight.'" 4Then Joshua called the
twelve men from the sons of Israel, whom
he had appointed, a man from each tribe;
5and Joshua said to them, "Pass on before
the ark of the LORD your God into the midst
of the Jordan, and take up each of you a
stone upon his shoulder, according to the
number of the tribes of the sons of Israel,
6that this may be a sign among you, when
your children ask in time to come, 'What do
those stones mean to you?' 7Then you shall
tell them that the waters of the Jordan were
cut off before the ark of the covenant of the
LORD; when it passed over the Jordan, the
waters of the Jordan were cut off. So these
stones shall be to the sons of Israel a memorial for ever."

8And the men of Israel did as Joshua
commanded, and took up twelve stones out

of the midst of the Jordan, according to the number of the tribes of the sons of Israel, as the LORD told Joshua; and they carried them over with them to the place where they lodged, and laid them down there. 9And Joshua set up twelve stones in the midst of the Jordan, in the place where the feet of the priests bearing the ark of the covenant had stood; and they are there to this day. 10For the priests who bore the ark stood in the midst of the Jordan, until everything was finished that the LORD commanded Joshua to tell the people, according to all that Moses had commanded Joshua.

The people passed over in haste; 11and when all the people had finished passing over, the ark of the LORD and the priests passed over before the people. 12The sons of Reuben and the sons of Gad and the half-tribe of Manas′seh passed over armed before the sons of Israel, as Moses had bidden them; 13about forty thousand ready armed for war passed over before the LORD for battle, to the plains of Jericho. 14On that day the LORD exalted Joshua in the sight of all Israel; and they stood in awe of him, as they had stood in awe of Moses, all the days of his life.

15And the LORD said to Joshua, 16"Command the priests who bear the ark of the covenant to come up out of the Jordan." 17Joshua therefore commanded the priests, "Come up out of the Jordan." 18And when the priests bearing the ark of the covenant of the LORD came up from the midst of the Jordan, and the soles of the priests' feet were lifted up on dry ground, the waters of the Jordan returned to their place and overflowed all its banks, as before.

19The people came up out of the Jordan on the tenth day of the first month, and they encamped in Gilgal on the east border of Jericho. 20And those twelve stones, which they took out of the Jordan, Joshua set up in Gilgal. 21And he said to the sons of Israel, "When your children ask their fathers in time to come, 'What do these stones mean?' 22then you shall let your children know, 'Israel passed over this Jordan on dry ground.' 23For the LORD your God dried up the waters of the Jordan for you until you passed over, as the LORD your God did to the Red Sea, which he dried up for us until we passed over, 24so that all the peoples of the earth may know that the hand of the LORD is mighty; that you may fear the LORD your God for ever."

5 When all the kings of the Am′orites that were beyond the Jordan to the west, and all the kings of the Canaanites that were by the sea, heard that the LORD had dried up the waters of the Jordan for the sons of Israel until they had crossed over, their heart melted, and there was no longer any spirit in them, because of the sons of Israel.

2At that time the LORD said to Joshua, "Make flint knives and circumcise the sons of Israel again the second time." 3So Joshua made flint knives, and circumcised the sons of Israel at Gib′eath-haar′aloth. 4And this is the reason why Joshua circumcised them: all the males of the people who came out of Egypt, all the men of war, had died on the way in the wilderness after they had come out of Egypt. 5Though all the people who came out had been circumcised, yet all the people that were born on the way in the wilderness after they had come out of Egypt had not been circumcised. 6For the sons of Israel walked forty years in the wilderness, till all the nation, the men of war that came forth out of Egypt, perished, because they did not listen to the voice of the LORD; to them the LORD swore that he would not let them see the land which the LORD had sworn to their fathers to give us, a land flowing with milk and honey. 7So it was their children, whom he raised up in their stead, that Joshua circumcised; for they were uncircumcised, because they had not been circumcised on the way.

8When the circumcising of all the nation was done, they remained in their places in the camp till they were healed. 9And the LORD said to Joshua, "This day I have rolled away the reproach of Egypt from you." And so the name of that place is called Gilgal to this day.

10While the sons of Israel were encamped in Gilgal they kept the Passover on the fourteenth day of the month at evening in the plains of Jericho. [11]And on the next day after the Passover, on that very day, they ate of the produce of the land, unleavened cakes and parched grain. [12]And the manna ceased on the next day, when they ate of the produce of the land; and the sons of Israel had manna no more, but ate of the fruit of the land of Canaan that year.

[13]When Joshua was by Jericho, he lifted up his eyes and looked, and behold, a man stood before him with his drawn sword in his hand; and Joshua went to him and said to him, "Are you for us, or for our adversaries?" [14]And he said, "No; but as commander of the army of the LORD I have now come." And Joshua fell on his face to the earth, and worshiped, and said to him, "What does my lord bid his servant?" [15]And the commander of the LORD's army said to Joshua, "Put off your shoes from your feet; for the place where you stand is holy." And Joshua did so.

6 Now Jericho was shut up from within and from without because of the sons of Israel; none went out, and none came in. [2]And the LORD said to Joshua, "See, I have given into your hand Jericho, with its king and mighty men of valor. [3]You shall march around the city, all the men of war going around the city once. Thus shall you do for six days. [4]And seven priests shall bear seven trumpets of rams' horns before the ark; and on the seventh day you shall march around the city seven times, the priests blowing the trumpets. [5]And when they make a long blast with the ram's horn, as soon as you hear the sound of the trumpet, then all the people shall shout with a great shout; and the wall of the city will fall down flat, and the people shall go up every man straight before him." [6]So Joshua the son of Nun called the priests and said to them, "Take up the ark of the covenant, and let seven priests bear seven trumpets of rams' horns before the ark of the LORD." [7]And he said to the people, "Go forward; march around the city, and let the armed men pass on before the ark of the LORD."

[8]And as Joshua had commanded the people, the seven priests bearing the seven trumpets of rams' horns before the LORD went forward, blowing the trumpets, with the ark of the covenant of the LORD following them. [9]And the armed men went before the priests who blew the trumpets, and the rear guard came after the ark, while the trumpets blew continually. [10]But Joshua commanded the people, "You shall not shout or let your voice be heard, neither shall any word go out of your mouth, until the day I bid you shout; then you shall shout." [11]So he caused the ark of the LORD to compass the city, going about it once; and they came into the camp, and spent the night in the camp.

[12]Then Joshua rose early in the morning, and the priests took up the ark of the LORD. [13]And the seven priests bearing the seven trumpets of rams' horns before the ark of the LORD passed on, blowing the trumpets continually; and the armed men went before them, and the rear guard came after the ark of the LORD, while the trumpets blew continually. [14]And the second day they marched around the city once, and returned into the camp. So they did for six days.

[15]On the seventh day they rose early at the dawn of day, and marched around the city in the same manner seven times: it was only on that day that they marched around the city seven times. [16]And at the seventh time, when the priests had blown the trumpets, Joshua said to the people, "Shout; for the LORD has given you the city. [17]And the city and all that is within it shall be devoted to the LORD for destruction; only Ra'hab the harlot and all who are with her in her house shall live, because she hid the messengers that we sent. [18]But you, keep yourselves from the things devoted to destruction, lest when you have devoted them you take any of the devoted things and make the camp of Israel a thing for destruction, and bring trouble upon it. [19]But all silver and gold, and vessels of bronze and iron, are sacred to the LORD; they shall go into the treasury of the LORD." [20]So the people

shouted, and the trumpets were blown.
As soon as the people heard the sound
of the trumpet, the people raised a great
shout, and the wall fell down flat, so that
the people went up into the city, every
man straight before him, and they took
the city. 21Then they utterly destroyed all
in the city, both men and women, young
and old, oxen, sheep, and donkeys, with
the edge of the sword.
22And Joshua said to the two men who
had spied out the land, "Go into the
harlot's house, and bring out from it the
woman, and all who belong to her, as you
swore to her." 23So the young men who
had been spies went in, and brought out
Ra'hab, and her father and mother and
brothers and all who belonged to her;
and they brought all her kindred, and set
them outside the camp of Israel. 24And
they burned the city with fire, and all
within it; only the silver and gold, and
the vessels of bronze and of iron, they
put into the treasury of the house of the
LORD. 25But Ra'hab the harlot, and her
father's household, and all who belonged
to her, Joshua saved alive; and she dwelt
in Israel to this day, because she hid the
messengers whom Joshua sent to spy
out Jericho.
26Joshua laid an oath upon them at that
time, saying, "Cursed before the LORD be
the man that rises up and rebuilds this
city, Jericho.
At the cost of his first-born shall he lay its
foundation,
and at the cost of his youngest son shall
he set up its gates."
27So the LORD was with Joshua; and his
fame was in all the land.

A Psalm of Asaph.

PSALM 79 [78]

O God, the heathen have come into
your inheritance;
they have defiled your holy temple;
they have laid Jerusalem in ruins.
2They have given the bodies of your servants
to the birds of the air for food,
the flesh of your saints to the beasts of
the earth.
3They have poured out their blood like water
round about Jerusalem,
and there was none to bury them.
4We have become a taunt to our neighbors,
mocked and derided by those round
about us.

5How long, O LORD? Will you be angry
for ever?
Will your jealous wrath burn like fire?
6Pour out your anger on the nations that do
not know you,
and on the kingdoms
that do not call on your name!
7For they have devoured Jacob,
and laid waste his habitation.

8Do not remember against us the iniquities
of our forefathers;
let your compassion come speedily to
meet us,
for we are brought very low.
9Help us, O God of our salvation,
for the glory of your name;
deliver us, and forgive our sins,
for your name's sake!
10Why should the nations say,
"Where is their God?"
Let the avenging of the outpoured blood of
your servants
be known among the nations before
our eyes!

11Let the groans of the prisoners come
before you;
according to your great power preserve
those doomed to die!
12Return sevenfold into the bosom of our
neighbors
the taunts with which they have taunted
you, O Lord!
13Then we your people, the flock of your
pasture,
will give thanks to you for ever;
from generation to generation we will
recount your praise.

LUKE 5

While the people pressed upon him to hear the word of God, he was standing by the lake of Gennes′aret. [2]And he saw two boats by the lake; but the fishermen had gone out of them and were washing their nets.
[3]Getting into one of the boats, which was Simon's, he asked him to put out a little from the land. And he sat down and taught the people from the boat. [4]And when he had ceased speaking, he said to Simon, "Put out into the deep and let down your nets for a catch." [5]And Simon answered, "Master, we toiled all night and took nothing! But at your word I will let down the nets." [6]And when they had done this, they enclosed a great shoal of fish; and as their nets were breaking, [7]they beckoned to their partners in the other boat to come and help them. And they came and filled both the boats, so that they began to sink. [8]But when Simon Peter saw it, he fell down at Jesus' knees, saying, "Depart from me, for I am a sinful man, O Lord." [9]For he was astonished, and all that were with him, at the catch of fish which they had taken; [10]and so also were James and John, sons of Zeb′edee, who were partners with Simon. And Jesus said to Simon, "Do not be afraid; henceforth you will be catching men." [11]And when they had brought their boats to land, they left everything and followed him.

[12]While he was in one of the cities, there came a man full of leprosy; and when he saw Jesus, he fell on his face and begged him, "Lord, if you will, you can make me clean." [13]And he stretched out his hand, and touched him, saying, "I will; be clean." And immediately the leprosy left him. [14]And he charged him to tell no one; but "go and show yourself to the priest, and make an offering for your cleansing, as Moses commanded, for a proof to the people." [15]But so much the more the report went abroad concerning him; and great multitudes gathered to hear and to be healed of their infirmities. [16]But he withdrew to the wilderness and prayed.

REFLECTION

We miss out on the miraculous because we are not willing to risk asking God for the extraordinary. Yet taking a risk to trust him and act on his word is part of prayer, part of faith. Joshua risks looking foolish by telling his whole army to shout instead of fight at Jericho. The Lord rewards his act of obedient faith and tears down Jericho's walls. Similarly, the first disciples could have kept their nets clean and dry, but they respond to Jesus's invitation to "put out into the deep" (Lk 5:4) with a generous faith. They too are rewarded for trusting in, and acting on, God's word. Likewise, the psalmist, against incredible odds, prays for God's deliverance. The Temple has been destroyed, and the enemies of Israel are triumphant, yet the psalmist has the audacity to pray for forgiveness and even divine judgment. Faith requires us to be audacious at times, trusting God, even daring him to act. Furthermore, acting on faith means that we risk looking foolish to others. It challenges our pride to yell at a stone wall, expecting it to fall. Are you willing to take risks for God and step out in faith?

April 3

JOSHUA 7

But the sons of Israel broke faith in regard to the devoted things; for A′chan the son of Carmi, son of Zabdi, son of Ze′rah, of the tribe of Judah, took some of the devoted things; and the anger of the LORD burned against the sons of Israel.

[2]Joshua sent men from Jericho to Ai, which is near Beth-a′ven, east of Bethel, and said to them, "Go up and spy out the land." And the men went up and spied out Ai. [3]And they returned to Joshua, and said to him, "Let not all the people go up, but let about two or

three thousand men go up and attack Ai; do not make the whole people toil up there, for they are but few." [4]So about three thousand went up there from the people; and they fled before the men of Ai, [5]and the men of Ai killed about thirty-six men of them, and chased them before the gate as far as Sheb′arim, and slew them at the descent. And the hearts of the people melted, and became as water.

[6]Then Joshua tore his clothes, and fell to the earth upon his face before the ark of the LORD until the evening, he and the elders of Israel; and they put dust upon their heads. [7]And Joshua said, "Alas, O Lord GOD, why have you brought this people over the Jordan at all, to give us into the hands of the Am′orites, to destroy us? Would that we had been content to dwell beyond the Jordan! [8]O Lord, what can I say, when Israel has turned their backs before their enemies! [9]For the Canaanites and all the inhabitants of the land will hear of it, and will surround us, and cut off our name from the earth; and what will you do for your great name?"

[10]The LORD said to Joshua, "Arise, why have you thus fallen upon your face? [11]Israel has sinned; they have transgressed my covenant which I commanded them; they have taken some of the devoted things; they have stolen, and lied, and put them among their own stuff. [12]Therefore the sons of Israel cannot stand before their enemies; they turn their backs before their enemies, because they have become a thing for destruction. I will be with you no more, unless you destroy the devoted things from among you. [13]Up, sanctify the people, and say, 'Sanctify yourselves for tomorrow; for thus says the LORD, God of Israel, "There are devoted things in the midst of you, O Israel; you cannot stand before your enemies, until you take away the devoted things from among you." [14]In the morning therefore you shall be brought near by your tribes; and the tribe which the LORD takes shall come near by families; and the family which the LORD takes shall come near by households; and the household which the LORD takes shall come near man by man. [15]And he who is taken with the devoted things shall be burned with fire, he and all that he has, because he has transgressed the covenant of the LORD, and because he has done a shameful thing in Israel.'"

[16]So Joshua rose early in the morning, and brought Israel near tribe by tribe, and the tribe of Judah was taken; [17]and he brought near the families of Judah, and the family of the Ze′rahites was taken; and he brought near the family of the Zerahites man by man, and Zabdi was taken; [18]and he brought near his household man by man, and A′chan the son of Carmi, son of Zabdi, son of Ze′rah of the tribe of Judah, was taken. [19]Then Joshua said to A′chan, "My son, give glory to the LORD God of Israel, and render praise to him; and tell me now what you have done; do not hide it from me." [20]And A′chan answered Joshua, "Of a truth I have sinned against the LORD God of Israel, and this is what I did: [21]when I saw among the spoil a beautiful mantle from Shi′nar, and two hundred shekels of silver, and a bar of gold weighing fifty shekels, then I coveted them, and took them; and behold, they are hidden in the earth inside my tent, with the silver underneath."

[22]So Joshua sent messengers, and they ran to the tent; and behold, it was hidden in his tent with the silver underneath. [23]And they took them out of the tent and brought them to Joshua and all the sons of Israel; and they laid them down before the LORD. [24]And Joshua and all Israel with him took A′chan the son of Ze′rah, and the silver and the mantle and the bar of gold, and his sons and daughters, and his oxen and donkeys and sheep, and his tent, and all that he had; and they brought them up to the Valley of A′chor. [25]And Joshua said, "Why did you bring trouble on us? The LORD brings trouble on you today." And all Israel stoned him with stones; they burned them with fire, and stoned them with stones. [26]And they raised over him a great heap of stones that remains to this day; then the LORD turned from his burning anger. Therefore to this day the name of that place is called the Valley of A′chor.

8 And the LORD said to Joshua, "Do not fear or be dismayed; take all the fighting

men with you, and arise, go up to Ai; see, I
have given into your hand the king of Ai,
and his people, his city, and his land; 2and
you shall do to Ai and its king as you did
to Jericho and its king; only its spoil and its
cattle you shall take as booty for yourselves;
lay an ambush against the city, behind it."

3So Joshua arose, and all the fighting men,
to go up to Ai; and Joshua chose thirty thousand mighty men of valor, and sent them
forth by night. 4And he commanded them,
"Behold, you shall lie in ambush against the
city, behind it; do not go very far from the
city, but hold yourselves all in readiness;
5and I, and all the people who are with me,
will approach the city. And when they come
out against us, as before, we shall flee before
them; 6and they will come out after us, till
we have drawn them away from the city; for
they will say, 'They are fleeing from us, as
before.' So we will flee from them; 7then you
shall rise up from the ambush, and seize the
city; for the LORD your God will give it into
your hand. 8And when you have taken the
city, you shall set the city on fire, doing as the
LORD has bidden; see, I have commanded
you." 9So Joshua sent them forth; and they
went to the place of ambush, and lay between
Bethel and Ai, to the west of Ai; but Joshua
spent that night among the people.

10And Joshua arose early in the morning
and mustered the people, and went up,
with the elders of Israel, before the people
to Ai. 11And all the fighting men who were
with him went up, and drew near before the
city, and encamped on the north side of Ai,
with a ravine between them and Ai. 12And
he took about five thousand men, and set
them in ambush between Bethel and Ai,
to the west of the city. 13So they stationed
the forces, the main encampment which
was north of the city and its rear guard
west of the city. But Joshua spent that
night in the valley. 14And when the king of
Ai saw this he and all his people, the men
of the city, made haste and went out early
to the descent toward the Arabah to meet
Israel in battle; but he did not know that
there was an ambush against him behind
the city. 15And Joshua and all Israel made
a pretense of being beaten before them,
and fled in the direction of the wilderness.
16So all the people who were in the city
were called together to pursue them, and
as they pursued Joshua they were drawn
away from the city. 17There was not a man
left in Ai or Bethel, who did not go out
after Israel; they left the city open, and
pursued Israel.

18Then the LORD said to Joshua, "Stretch
out the javelin that is in your hand toward
Ai; for I will give it into your hand." And
Joshua stretched out the javelin that was
in his hand toward the city. 19And the
ambush rose quickly out of their place, and
as soon as he had stretched out his hand,
they ran and entered the city and took
it; and they made haste to set the city on
fire. 20So when the men of Ai looked back,
behold, the smoke of the city went up to
heaven; and they had no power to flee this
way or that, for the people that fled to the
wilderness turned back upon the pursuers.
21And when Joshua and all Israel saw that
the ambush had taken the city, and that the
smoke of the city went up, then they turned
back and struck the men of Ai. 22And the
others came forth from the city against
them; so they were in the midst of Israel,
some on this side, and some on that side;
and Israel struck them, until there was left
none that survived or escaped. 23But the
king of Ai they took alive, and brought him
to Joshua.

24When Israel had finished slaughtering
all the inhabitants of Ai in the open wilderness where they pursued them, and
all of them to the very last had fallen by
the edge of the sword, all Israel returned
to Ai, and struck it with the edge of the
sword. 25And all who fell that day, both
men and women, were twelve thousand,
all the people of Ai. 26For Joshua did
not draw back his hand, with which he
stretched out the javelin, until he had
utterly destroyed all the inhabitants of Ai.
27Only the cattle and the spoil of that city
Israel took as their booty, according to the
word of the LORD which he commanded
Joshua. 28So Joshua burned Ai, and made

it for ever a heap of ruins, as it is to this
day. 29And he hanged the king of Ai on a
tree until evening; and at the going down
of the sun Joshua commanded, and they
took his body down from the tree, and
cast it at the entrance of the gate of the
city, and raised over it a great heap of
stones, which stands there to this day.

To the choirmaster: according to Lilies.
A testimony of Asaph.
A Psalm.

PSALM 80 [79]

Give ear, O Shepherd of Israel,
you who lead Joseph like a flock!
You who are enthroned upon the cherubim,
shine forth
2 before Ephraim and Benjamin and
Manas′seh!
Stir up your might,
and come to save us!

3Restore us, O God;
let your face shine, that we may be saved!

4O LORD God of hosts,
how long will you be angry with your
people's prayers?
5You have fed them with the bread of tears,
and given them tears to drink in full
measure.
6You make us the scorn of our neighbors;
and our enemies laugh among
themselves.
7Restore us, O God of hosts;
let your face shine, that we may be saved!

8You brought a vine out of Egypt;
you drove out the nations and planted it.
9You cleared the ground for it;
it took deep root and filled the land.
10The mountains were covered with its
shade,
the mighty cedars with its branches;
11it sent out its branches to the sea,
and its shoots to the River.
12Why then have you broken down its walls,
so that all who pass along the way pluck
its fruit?
13The boar from the forest ravages it,
and all that move in the field feed on it.

14Turn again, O God of hosts!
Look down from heaven, and see;
have regard for this vine,
15 the stock which your right hand planted.
16They have burned it with fire, they have
cut it down;
may they perish at the rebuke of your
countenance!
17But let your hand be upon the man of your
right hand,
the son of man whom you have made
strong for yourself!
18Then we will never turn back from you;
give us life, and we will call on your
name!

19Restore us, O LORD God of hosts!
let your face shine, that we may be saved!

LUKE 5

**17On one of those days, as he
was teaching, there were Pharisees and teachers of the law
sitting by, who had come from every
village of Galilee and Judea and from**
Jerusalem; and the power of the Lord was
with him to heal. 18And behold, men
were bringing on a bed a man who was
paralyzed, and they sought to bring him
in and lay him before Jesus; 19but finding no way to bring him in, because of
the crowd, they went up on the roof and
let him down with his bed through the
tiles into their midst before Jesus. 20And
when he saw their faith he said, "Man,
your sins are forgiven you." 21And the
scribes and the Pharisees began to question, saying, "Who is this that speaks
blasphemies? Who can forgive sins but
God only?" 22When Jesus perceived
their questionings, he answered them,

"Why do you question in your hearts?
23Which is easier, to say, 'Your sins are
forgiven you,' or to say, 'Rise and walk'?
24But that you may know that the Son of
man has authority on earth to forgive
sins"—he said to the man who was paralyzed—"I say to you, rise, take up your
bed and go home." 25And immediately
he rose before them, and took up that on
which he lay, and went home, glorifying
God. 26And amazement seized them all,
and they glorified God and were filled
with awe, saying, "We have seen strange
things today."
27After this he went out, and saw a tax
collector, named Levi, sitting at the tax
office; and he said to him, "Follow me."
28And he left everything, and rose and
followed him.
29And Levi made him a great feast in his
house; and there was a large company of
tax collectors and others sitting at table
with them. 30And the Pharisees and their
scribes murmured against his disciples,
saying, "Why do you eat and drink with
tax collectors and sinners?" 31And Jesus
answered them, "Those who are well have
no need of a physician, but those who are
sick; 32I have not come to call the righteous,
but sinners to repentance."
33And they said to him, "The disciples of
John fast often and offer prayers, and so do
the disciples of the Pharisees, but yours eat
and drink." 34And Jesus said to them, "Can
you make wedding guests fast while the
bridegroom is with them? 35The days will
come, when the bridegroom is taken away
from them, and then they will fast in those
days." 36He told them a parable also: "No
one tears a piece from a new garment and
puts it upon an old garment; if he does, he
will tear the new, and the piece from the
new will not match the old. 37And no one
puts new wine into old wineskins; if he
does, the new wine will burst the skins
and it will be spilled, and the skins will
be destroyed. 38But new wine must be put
into fresh wineskins. 39And no one after
drinking old wine desires new; for he says,
'The old is good.'"

REFLECTION

Sin is deceptive because its initial consequences often appear trivial or even nonexistent. Although Achan's covetousness and thievery go unnoticed amongst his neighbors, it does not go unnoticed by God, and it brings a terrible punishment upon both Achan and his household. In the gospel reading, when Jesus first meets the paralytic, he chooses to forgive the paralytic's sins before healing him. Not only does Jesus understand the seriousness of sin, but he also has the authority to do something about it. The Jews present are shocked by his outrageous claim to be able to forgive sins, and so Jesus heals the paralytic to prove his authority. The point is that forgiveness of sins is a far greater miracle than fixing a broken human body. Psalm 80 gives us the right prayer for forgiveness: "Restore us, O God of hosts; let your face shine, that we may be saved!" (Ps 80:7). Do you take sin seriously enough to seek God's forgiveness when you fall?

April 4

JOSHUA 8

**30Then Joshua built an altar
on Mount E′bal to the LORD,
the God of Israel, 31as Moses
the servant of the LORD had commanded the sons of Israel, as it is written in**
the book of the law of Moses, "an altar of
unhewn stones, upon which no man has
lifted an iron tool"; and they offered on it
burnt offerings to the LORD, and sacrificed
peace offerings. 32And there, in the presence
of the sons of Israel, he wrote upon the
stones a copy of the law of Moses, which
he had written. 33And all Israel, sojourner
as well as homeborn, with their elders and
officers and their judges, stood on opposite
sides of the ark before the Levitical priests

who carried the ark of the covenant of
the LORD, half of them in front of Mount
Ger′izim and half of them in front of Mount
E′bal, as Moses the servant of the LORD had
commanded at the first, that they should
bless the sons of Israel. [34]And afterward he
read all the words of the law, the blessing
and the curse, according to all that is written
in the book of the law. [35]There was not a
word of all that Moses commanded which
Joshua did not read before all the assembly
of Israel, and the women, and the little ones,
and the sojourners who lived among them.

9 When all the kings who were beyond
the Jordan in the hill country and in the
lowland all along the coast of the Great Sea
toward Lebanon, the Hittites, the Am′orites,
the Canaanites, the Per′izzites, the Hi′vites,
and the Jeb′usites, heard of this, [2]they
gathered together with one accord to fight
Joshua and Israel.

[3]But when the inhabitants of Gib′eon
heard what Joshua had done to Jericho
and to Ai, [4]they on their part acted with
cunning, and went and made ready
provisions, and took worn-out sacks upon
their donkeys, and wineskins, worn-out
and torn and mended, [5]with worn-out,
patched sandals on their feet, and worn-out
clothes; and all their provisions were dry
and moldy. [6]And they went to Joshua in the
camp at Gilgal, and said to him and to the
men of Israel, "We have come from a far
country; so now make a covenant with us."
[7]But the men of Israel said to the Hi′vites,
"Perhaps you live among us; then how can
we make a covenant with you?" [8]They said
to Joshua, "We are your servants." And
Joshua said to them, "Who are you? And
where do you come from?" [9]They said to
him, "From a very far country your servants have come, because of the name of
the LORD your God; for we have heard a
report of him, and all that he did in Egypt,
[10]and all that he did to the two kings of the
Am′orites who were beyond the Jordan,
Si′hon the king of Heshbon, and Og king
of Bashan, who dwelt in Ash′taroth. [11]And
our elders and all the inhabitants of our
country said to us, 'Take provisions in your
hand for the journey, and go to meet them,
and say to them, "We are your servants;
come now, make a covenant with us."'
[12]Here is our bread; it was still warm when
we took it from our houses as our food
for the journey, on the day we set forth to
come to you, but now, behold, it is dry and
moldy; [13]these wineskins were new when
we filled them, and behold, they are burst;
and these garments and shoes of ours are
worn out from the very long journey." [14]So
the men partook of their provisions, and
did not ask direction from the LORD. [15]And
Joshua made peace with them, and made
a covenant with them, to let them live;
and the leaders of the congregation swore
to them.

[16]At the end of three days after they had
made a covenant with them, they heard
that they were their neighbors, and that
they dwelt among them. [17]And the sons of
Israel set out and reached their cities on the
third day. Now their cities were Gib′eon,
Chephi′rah, Be-er′oth, and Kir′iath-je′arim.
[18]But the sons of Israel did not kill them,
because the leaders of the congregation
had sworn to them by the LORD, the God of
Israel. Then all the congregation murmured
against the leaders. [19]But all the leaders said
to all the congregation, "We have sworn to
them by the LORD, the God of Israel, and
now we may not touch them. [20]This we will
do to them, and let them live, lest wrath
be upon us, because of the oath which we
swore to them." [21]And the leaders said to
them, "Let them live." So they became
hewers of wood and drawers of water for
all the congregation, as the leaders had said
of them.

[22]Joshua summoned them, and he said
to them, "Why did you deceive us, saying,
'We are very far from you,' when you dwell
among us? [23]Now therefore you are cursed,
and some of you shall always be slaves,
hewers of wood and drawers of water for
the house of my God." [24]They answered
Joshua, "Because it was told to your servants for a certainty that the LORD your
God had commanded his servant Moses
to give you all the land, and to destroy all

the inhabitants of the land from before you; so we feared greatly for our lives because of you, and did this thing. 25And now, behold, we are in your hand: do as it seems good and right in your sight to do to us." 26So he did to them, and delivered them out of the hand of the sons of Israel; and they did not kill them. 27But Joshua made them that day hewers of wood and drawers of water for the congregation and for the altar of the LORD, to continue to this day, in the place which he should choose.

10 When Ado′ni-ze′dek king of Jerusalem heard how Joshua had taken Ai, and had utterly destroyed it, doing to Ai and its king as he had done to Jericho and its king, and how the inhabitants of Gib′eon had made peace with Israel and were among them, 2he feared greatly, because Gib′eon was a great city, like one of the royal cities, and because it was greater than Ai, and all its men were mighty. 3So Ado′ni-ze′dek king of Jerusalem sent to Hoham king of He′bron, to Piram king of Jarmuth, to Japhi′a king of La′chish, and to De′bir king of Eg′lon, saying, 4"Come up to me, and help me, and let us strike Gib′eon; for it has made peace with Joshua and with the sons of Israel." 5Then the five kings of the Am′orites, the king of Jerusalem, the king of He′bron, the king of Jarmuth, the king of La′chish, and the king of Eg′lon, gathered their forces, and went up with all their armies and encamped against Gib′eon, and made war against it.

6And the men of Gib′eon sent to Joshua at the camp in Gilgal, saying, "Do not relax your hand from your servants; come up to us quickly, and save us, and help us; for all the kings of the Am′orites that dwell in the hill country are gathered against us." 7So Joshua went up from Gilgal, he and all the people of war with him, and all the mighty men of valor. 8And the LORD said to Joshua, "Do not fear them, for I have given them into your hands; there shall not a man of them stand before you." 9So Joshua came upon them suddenly, having marched up all night from Gilgal. 10And the LORD threw them into a panic before Israel, who slew them with a great slaughter at Gib′eon, and chased them by the way of the ascent of Beth-ho′ron, and struck them as far as Aze′kah and Makke′dah. 11And as they fled before Israel, while they were going down the ascent of Beth-ho′ron, the LORD threw down great stones from heaven upon them as far as Aze′kah, and they died; there were more who died because of the hailstones than the men of Israel killed with the sword.

12Then spoke Joshua to the LORD in the day when the LORD gave the Am′orites over to the men of Israel; and he said in the sight of Israel,

"Sun, stand still at Gib′eon,
and you Moon in the valley of Ai′jalon."
13And the sun stood still, and the moon stayed,
until the nation took vengeance on their enemies.

Is this not written in the Book of Jash′ar? The sun stayed in the midst of heaven, and did not hasten to go down for about a whole day. 14There has been no day like it before or since, when the LORD listened to the voice of a man; for the LORD fought for Israel.

15Then Joshua returned, and all Israel with him, to the camp at Gilgal.

To the choirmaster: according to The Gittith.
A testimony of Asaph.

PSALM 81 [80]

Sing aloud to God our strength;
shout for joy to the God of Jacob!
2Raise a song, sound the timbrel,
the sweet lyre with the harp.
3Blow the trumpet at the new moon,
at the full moon, on our feast day.
4For it is a statute for Israel,
an ordinance of the God of Jacob.
5He made it a decree in Joseph,
when he went out over the land of Egypt.

I hear a voice I had not known:
6"I relieved your shoulder of the burden;
your hands were freed from the basket.

[7]In distress you called, and I delivered you;
I answered you in the secret place of
thunder;
I tested you at the waters of Mer′ibah.
Selah
[8]Hear, O my people, while I admonish you!
O Israel, if you would but listen to me!
[9]There shall be no strange god among you;
you shall not bow down to a foreign god.
[10]I am the LORD your God,
who brought you up out of the land
of Egypt.
Open your mouth wide, and I will fill it.

[11]"But my people did not listen to
my voice;
Israel would have none of me.
[12]So I gave them over to their stubborn
hearts,
to follow their own counsels.
[13]O that my people would listen to me,
that Israel would walk in my ways!
[14]I would soon subdue their enemies,
and turn my hand against their foes.
[15]Those who hate the LORD would cringe
toward him,
and their fate would last for ever.
[16]I would feed you with the finest of
the wheat,
and with honey from the rock I would
satisfy you."

LUKE 6

On a sabbath, while he was going through the grainfields, his disciples plucked and ate some heads of grain, rubbing them in their
hands. [2]But some of the Pharisees said, "Why
are you doing what is not lawful to do on the
sabbath?" [3]And Jesus answered, "Have you
not read what David did when he was hungry, he and those who were with him: [4]how
he entered the house of God, and took and ate
the showbread, which it is not lawful for any
but the priests to eat, and also gave it to those
with him?" [5]And he said to them, "The Son of
man is lord of the sabbath."

[6]On another sabbath, when he entered
the synagogue and taught, a man was there
whose right hand was withered. [7]And the
scribes and the Pharisees watched him, to
see whether he would heal on the sabbath,
so that they might find an accusation against
him. [8]But he knew their thoughts, and he
said to the man who had the withered hand,
"Come and stand here." And he rose and
stood there. [9]And Jesus said to them, "I ask
you, is it lawful on the sabbath to do good
or to do harm, to save life or to destroy it?"
[10]And he looked around on them all, and
said to him, "Stretch out your hand." And he
did so, and his hand was restored. [11]But they
were filled with fury and discussed with one
another what they might do to Jesus.

[12]In these days he went out to the hills to
pray; and all night he continued in prayer
to God. [13]And when it was day, he called
his disciples, and chose from them twelve,
whom he named apostles; [14]Simon, whom
he named Peter, and Andrew his brother,
and James and John, and Philip, and
Bartholomew, [15]and Matthew, and Thomas,
and James the son of Alphae′us, and Simon
who was called the Zealot, [16]and Judas
the son of James, and Judas Iscariot, who
became a traitor.

[17]And he came down with them and stood
on a level place, with a great crowd of his
disciples and a great multitude of people
from all Judea and Jerusalem and the
seacoast of Tyre and Si′don, who came to
hear him and to be healed of their diseases;
[18]and those who were troubled with unclean
spirits were cured. [19]And all the crowd
sought to touch him, for power came forth
from him and healed them all.

[20]And he lifted up his eyes on his disciples,
and said:

"Blessed are you poor, for yours is the
kingdom of God.

[21]"Blessed are you that hunger now, for
you shall be satisfied.

"Blessed are you that weep now, for you
shall laugh.

[22]"Blessed are you when men hate you,
and when they exclude you and revile you,
and cast out your name as evil, on account

of the Son of man! 23Rejoice in that day, and leap for joy, for behold, your reward is great in heaven; for so their fathers did to the prophets.

24"But woe to you that are rich, for you have received your consolation.

25"Woe to you that are full now, for you shall hunger.

"Woe to you that laugh now, for you shall mourn and weep.

26"Woe to you, when all men speak well of you, for so their fathers did to the false prophets.

27"But I say to you that hear, Love your enemies, do good to those who hate you, 28bless those who curse you, pray for those who abuse you. 29To him who strikes you on the cheek, offer the other also; and from him who takes away your cloak do not withhold your coat as well. 30Give to every one who begs from you; and of him who takes away your goods do not ask them again. 31And as you wish that men would do to you, do so to them.

32"If you love those who love you, what credit is that to you? For even sinners love those who love them. 33And if you do good to those who do good to you, what credit is that to you? For even sinners do the same. 34And if you lend to those from whom you hope to receive, what credit is that to you? Even sinners lend to sinners, to receive as much again. 35But love your enemies, and do good, and lend, expecting nothing in return; and your reward will be great, and you will be sons of the Most High; for he is kind to the ungrateful and the selfish. 36Be merciful, even as your Father is merciful."

REFLECTION

Joshua reaps the consequences of making a forbidden covenant (see Dt 7:2) with the deceptive Gibeonites when, soon afterward, his army is called upon to honor their newfound friendship by embarking on a military alliance against the five kings of the Amorites (see Jos 10:6). Joshua fulfills his covenant promises and aids the Gibeonites. The Lord even honors the ill-conceived pact with two miracles: lethal hailstones and a standstill sun. While Joshua fulfills the obligations of friendship, Jesus calls us to do the impossible. Consistently loving our friends is hard—especially if it means going to war on their behalf—but Jesus calls us to something much more difficult: to be like God, who is "kind to the ungrateful and the selfish" (Lk 6:35), and love our enemies. This kind of love is not natural to us; it is supernatural and is only made possible by grace. Jesus challenges any thinking that we might get points for loving our family and friends. He says, "If you love those who love you, what credit is that to you?" (v. 32). He gives us a higher call, to love those who don't love us. Which "enemy" in your life is Jesus challenging you to love? Begin today by praying for that person.

April 5

JOSHUA 10

16These five kings fled, and hid themselves in the cave at Makke′dah. 17And it was told Joshua, "The five kings have been found, hidden in the cave at Makke′dah." 18And Joshua said, "Roll great stones against the mouth of the cave, and set men by it to guard them; 19but do not stay there yourselves, pursue your enemies, fall upon their rear, do not let them enter their cities; for the LORD your God has given them into your hand." 20When Joshua and the men of Israel had finished slaying them with a very great slaughter, until they were wiped out, and when the remnant which remained of them had entered into the fortified cities, 21all the people returned safe to Joshua in the camp at Makke′dah; not a man moved his tongue against any of the sons of Israel.

[22]Then Joshua said, "Open the mouth of the cave, and bring those five kings out to me from the cave." [23]And they did so, and brought those five kings out to him from the cave, the king of Jerusalem, the king of He′bron, the king of Jarmuth, the king of La′chish, and the king of Eg′lon. [24]And when they brought those kings out to Joshua, Joshua summoned all the men of Israel, and said to the chiefs of the men of war who had gone with him, "Come near, put your feet upon the necks of these kings." Then they came near, and put their feet on their necks. [25]And Joshua said to them, "Do not be afraid or dismayed; be strong and of good courage; for thus the LORD will do to all your enemies against whom you fight." [26]And afterward Joshua struck them and put them to death, and he hung them on five trees. And they hung upon the trees until evening; [27]but at the time of the going down of the sun, Joshua commanded, and they took them down from the trees, and threw them into the cave where they had hidden themselves, and they set great stones against the mouth of the cave, which remain to this very day.

[28]And Joshua took Makke′dah on that day, and struck it and its king with the edge of the sword; he utterly destroyed every person in it, he left none remaining; and he did to the king of Makkedah as he had done to the king of Jericho.

[29]Then Joshua passed on from Makke′dah, and all Israel with him, to Libnah, and fought against Libnah; [30]and the LORD gave it also and its king into the hand of Israel; and he struck it with the edge of the sword, and every person in it; he left none remaining in it; and he did to its king as he had done to the king of Jericho.

[31]And Joshua passed on from Libnah, and all Israel with him, to La′chish, and laid siege to it, and assaulted it: [32]and the LORD gave La′chish into the hand of Israel, and he took it on the second day, and struck it with the edge of the sword, and every person in it, as he had done to Libnah.

[33]Then Horam king of Gezer came up to help La′chish; and Joshua struck him and his people, until he left none remaining.

[34]And Joshua passed on with all Israel from La′chish to Eg′lon; and they laid siege to it, and assaulted it; [35]and they took it on that day, and struck it with the edge of the sword; and every person in it he utterly destroyed that day, as he had done to La′chish.

[36]Then Joshua went up with all Israel from Eg′lon to He′bron; and they assaulted it, [37]and took it, and struck it with the edge of the sword, and its king and its towns, and every person in it; he left none remaining, as he had done to Eg′lon, and utterly destroyed it with every person in it.

[38]Then Joshua, with all Israel, turned back to De′bir and assaulted it,[39]and he took it with its king and all its towns; and they struck them with the edge of the sword, and utterly destroyed every person in it; he left none remaining; as he had done to Heb′ron and to Libnah and its king, so he did to De′bir and to its king.

[40]So Joshua defeated the whole land, the hill country and the Neg′eb and the lowland and the slopes, and all their kings; he left none remaining, but utterly destroyed all that breathed, as the LORD God of Israel commanded. [41]And Joshua defeated them from Ka′desh-bar′nea to Gaza, and all the country of Go′shen, as far as Gib′eon. [42]And Joshua took all these kings and their land at one time, because the LORD God of Israel fought for Israel. [43]Then Joshua returned, and all Israel with him, to the camp at Gilgal.

11 When Jabin king of Ha′zor heard of this, he sent to Jo′bab king of Madon, and to the king of Shimron, and to the king of Ach′shaph, [2]and to the kings who were in the northern hill country, and in the Ar′abah south of Chin′neroth, and in the lowland, and in Na′photh-dor on the west, [3]to the Canaanites in the east and the west, the Am′orites, the Hittites, the Per′izzites, and the Jeb′usites in the hill country, and the Hi′vites under Hermon in the land of Mizpah. [4]And they came out, with all their troops, a great host, in number like the sand that is upon the seashore, with very many horses and chariots. [5]And all these kings

joined their forces, and came and encamped together at the waters of Me′rom, to fight with Israel.

[6]And the LORD said to Joshua, "Do not be afraid of them, for tomorrow at this time I will give over all of them, slain, to Israel; you shall hamstring their horses, and burn their chariots with fire." [7]So Joshua came suddenly upon them with all his people of war, by the waters of Me′rom, and fell upon them. [8]And the LORD gave them into the hand of Israel, who struck them and chased them as far as Great Sidon and Mis′rephoth-ma′im, and eastward as far as the valley of Mizpeh; and they struck them, until they left none remaining. [9]And Joshua did to them as the LORD bade him; he hamstrung their horses, and burned their chariots with fire.

[10]And Joshua turned back at that time, and took Ha′zor, and struck its king with the sword; for Hazor formerly was the head of all those kingdoms. [11]And they put to the sword all who were in it, utterly destroying them; there was none left that breathed, and he burned Ha′zor with fire. [12]And all the cities of those kings, and all their kings, Joshua took, and struck them with the edge of the sword, utterly destroying them, as Moses the servant of the LORD had commanded. [13]But none of the cities that stood on mounds did Israel burn, except Ha′zor only; that Joshua burned. [14]And all the spoil of these cities and the cattle, the sons of Israel took for their booty; but every man they struck with the edge of the sword, until they had destroyed them, and they did not leave any that breathed. [15]As the LORD had commanded Moses his servant, so Moses commanded Joshua, and so Joshua did; he left nothing undone of all that the LORD had commanded Moses.

[16]So Joshua took all that land, the hill country and all the Neg′eb and all the land of Go′shen and the lowland and the Ar′abah and the hill country of Israel and its lowland [17]from Mount Ha′lak, that rises toward Se′ir, as far as Ba′al-gad in the valley of Lebanon below Mount Hermon. And he took all their kings, and struck them, and put them to death. [18]Joshua made war a long time with all those kings. [19]There was not a city that made peace with the sons of Israel, except the Hi′vites, the inhabitants of Gib′eon; they took all in battle. [20]For it was the LORD's doing to harden their hearts that they should come against Israel in battle, in order that they should be utterly destroyed, and should receive no mercy but be exterminated, as the LORD commanded Moses.

[21]And Joshua came at that time, and wiped out the An′akim from the hill country, from Heb′ron, from De′bir, from A′nab, and from all the hill country of Judah, and from all the hill country of Israel; Joshua utterly destroyed them with their cities. [22]There was none of the An′akim left in the land of the sons of Israel; only in Gaza, in Gath, and in Ashdod, did some remain. [23]So Joshua took the whole land, according to all that the LORD had spoken to Moses; and Joshua gave it for an inheritance to Israel according to their tribal allotments. And the land had rest from war.

12 Now these are the kings of the land, whom the sons of Israel defeated, and took possession of their land beyond the Jordan toward the sunrising, from the valley of the Arnon to Mount Hermon, with all the Ar′abah eastward: [2]Si′hon king of the Am′orites who dwelt at Heshbon, and ruled from Aro′er, which is on the edge of the valley of the Arnon, and from the middle of the valley as far as the river Jabbok, the boundary of the Am′monites, that is, half of Gilead, [3]and the Ar′abah to the Sea of Chin′neroth eastward, and in the direction of Beth-jesh′imoth, to the sea of the Arabah, the Salt Sea, southward to the foot of the slopes of Pisgah; [4]and Og king of Bashan, one of the remnant of the Reph′aim, who dwelt at Ash′taroth and at Ed′re-i [5]and ruled over Mount Hermon and Sal′ecah and all Bashan to the boundary of the Gesh′urites and the Ma-ac′athites, and over half of Gilead to the boundary of Si′hon king of Heshbon. [6]Moses, the servant of the LORD, and the sons of Israel defeated them; and Moses

the servant of the LORD gave their land
for a possession to the Reubenites and the
Gadites and the half-tribe of Manas′seh.
7And these are the kings of the land
whom Joshua and the sons of Israel
defeated on the west side of the Jordan,
from Ba′al-gad in the valley of Lebanon
to Mount Ha′lak, that rises toward Se′ir
(and Joshua gave their land to the tribes
of Israel as a possession according to
their allotments, 8in the hill country, in
the lowland, in the Ar′abah, in the slopes,
in the wilderness, and in the Neg′eb, the
land of the Hittites, the Am′orites, the
Canaanites, the Per′izzites, the Hi′vites,
and the Jeb′usites): 9the king of Jericho,
one; the king of Ai, which is beside Bethel,
one; 10the king of Jerusalem, one; the king
of He′bron, one; 11the king of Jarmuth,
one; the king of La′chish, one; 12the king
of Eg′lon, one; the king of Gezer, one; 13the
king of De′bir, one; the king of Geder,
one; 14the king of Hormah, one; the king
of Ar′ad, one; 15the king of Libnah, one;
the king of Adul′lam, one; 16the king of
Makke′dah, one; the king of Bethel, one;
17the king of Tap′pu-ah, one; the king of
He′pher, one; 18the king of A′phek, one;
the king of Lashar′on, one; 19the king of
Madon, one; the king of Ha′zor, one; 20the
king of Shim′ron-me′ron, one; the king
of Ach′shaph, one; 21the king of Ta′anach,
one; the king of Megid′do, one; 22the
king of Ke′desh, one; the king of Jok′ne-
am in Carmel, one; 23the king of Dor in
Na′phath-dor, one; the king of Goi′im in
Galilee, one; 24the king of Tirzah, one: in
all, thirty-one kings.

A Psalm of Asaph.

PSALM 82 [81]

God has taken his place in the
divine council;
in the midst of the angels he
holds judgment:
2"How long will you judge unjustly
and show partiality to the wicked? *Selah*
3Give justice to the weak and the fatherless;
maintain the right of the afflicted and
the destitute.
4Rescue the weak and the needy;
deliver them from the hand of
the wicked."

5They have neither knowledge nor
understanding,
they walk about in darkness;
all the foundations of the earth
are shaken.

6I say, "You are gods,
sons of the Most High, all of you;
7nevertheless, you shall die like men,
and fall like any prince."

8Arise, O God, judge the earth;
for to you belong all the nations!

LUKE 6

**37"Judge not, and you will not
be judged; condemn not, and
you will not be condemned; forgive,
and you will be forgiven; 38give, and it**
will be given to you; good measure, pressed
down, shaken together, running over, will
be put into your lap. For the measure you
give will be the measure you get back."
39He also told them a parable: "Can a blind
man lead a blind man? Will they not both
fall into a pit? 40A disciple is not above his
teacher, but every one when he is fully
taught will be like his teacher. 41Why do you
see the speck that is in your brother's eye,
but do not notice the log that is in your own
eye? 42Or how can you say to your brother,
'Brother, let me take out the speck that is in
your eye,' when you yourself do not see the
log that is in your own eye? You hypocrite,
first take the log out of your own eye, and
then you will see clearly to take out the
speck that is in your brother's eye.
43"For no good tree bears bad fruit, nor
again does a bad tree bear good fruit; 44for
each tree is known by its own fruit. For

figs are not gathered from thorns, nor
are grapes picked from a bramble bush.
[45]The good man out of the good treasure
of his heart produces good, and the evil
man out of his evil treasure produces evil;
for out of the abundance of the heart his
mouth speaks.
[46]"Why do you call me 'Lord, Lord,' and
not do what I tell you? [47]Every one who
comes to me and hears my words and does
them, I will show you what he is like: [48]he
is like a man building a house, who dug
deep, and laid the foundation upon rock;
and when a flood arose, the stream broke
against that house, and could not shake it,
because it had been well built. [49]But he who
hears and does not do them is like a man
who built a house on the ground without a
foundation; against which the stream broke,
and immediately it fell, and the ruin of that
house was great."

REFLECTION

It is important to find time to "take stock" of our lives, to assess our accomplishments and our failures, and to measure ourselves against the goals we have set. At the end of Joshua 12, we see a counting up, a stock-taking of the Israelites' conquest of Canaan. Amazingly, Joshua and his army defeat thirty-one kings—they bear good fruit. Jesus teaches that a "tree is known by its own fruit" (Lk 6:44). This saying is directed against hypocrisy, which is an outward show of righteousness not accompanied by interior virtue. Jesus explains that authentic virtue flows from the inside out. The truly faithful are not speck-finding, judgmental grudge-holders, but generous, forgiving, and obedient to God. Their lives are built upon a rock foundation. Joshua demonstrates obedience to God in leading the conquest of Canaan, and his efforts meet with success. Our own seeking to fulfill the Lord's command will only come to fruition if we truly allow his grace to transform our hearts so that his righteousness flows out of us. Pause and take stock: are you living your life as both a hearer and a doer of the Word?

April 6

JOSHUA 13

Now Joshua was old and ad-
vanced in years; and the LORD
said to him, "You are old and
advanced in years, and there remains
yet very much land to be possessed.
[2]This is the land that yet remains: all
the regions of the Philis′tines, and all those of
the Gesh′urites [3](from the Shi′hor, which is
east of Egypt, northward to the boundary of
Ek′ron, it is reckoned as Canaanite; there are
five rulers of the Philis′tines, those of Gaza,
Ash′dod, Ash′kelon, Gath, and Ek′ron), and
those of the Avvim, [4]in the south, all the
land of the Canaanites, and Me-ar′ah which
belongs to the Sido′nians, to A′phek, to the
boundary of the Am′orites, [5]and the land
of the Geb′alites, and all Lebanon, toward
the sunrising, from Ba′al-gad below Mount
Hermon to the entrance of Ha′math, [6]all
the inhabitants of the hill country from
Lebanon to Mis′rephoth-ma′im, even all
the Sido′nians. I will myself drive them out
from before the sons of Israel; only allot the
land to Israel for an inheritance, as I have
commanded you. [7]Now therefore divide this
land for an inheritance to the nine tribes
and half the tribe of Manas′seh."
[8]With the other half of the tribe of
Manas′seh the Reubenites and the Gadites
received their inheritance, which Moses
gave them, beyond the Jordan eastward, as
Moses the servant of the LORD gave them:
[9]from Aro′er, which is on the edge of the
valley of the Arnon, and the city that is
in the middle of the valley, and all the
tableland of Med′eba as far as Di′bon; [10]and
all the cities of Si′hon king of the Am′orites,
who reigned in Heshbon, as far as the
boundary of the Am′monites; [11]and Gilead,
and the region of the Gesh′urites and Ma-
ac′athites, and all Mount Hermon, and all
Bashan to Sal′ecah; [12]all the kingdom of Og
in Bashan, who reigned in Ash′taroth and

in Ed′re-i (he alone was left of the remnant of the Reph′aim); these Moses had defeated and driven out. 13Yet the sons of Israel did not drive out the Gesh′urites or the Ma-ac′athites; but Ge′shur and Ma′acath dwell in the midst of Israel to this day.

14To the tribe of Levi alone Moses gave no inheritance; the offerings by fire to the LORD God of Israel are their inheritance, as he said to him.

15And Moses gave an inheritance to the tribe of the Reubenites according to their families. 16So their territory was from Aro′er, which is on the edge of the valley of the Arnon, and the city that is in the middle of the valley, and all the tableland by Med′eba; 17with Heshbon, and all its cities that are in the tableland; Di′bon, and Ba′moth-ba′al, and Beth-ba′al-me′on, 18and Ja′haz, and Ked′e-moth, and Meph′a-ath, 19and Kir″iatha′im, and Sibmah, and Ze′reth-sha′har on the hill of the valley, 20and Beth-pe′or, and the slopes of Pisgah, and Beth-jesh′imoth, 21that is, all the cities of the tableland, and all the kingdom of Si′hon king of the Am′orites, who reigned in Heshbon, whom Moses defeated with the leaders of Mid′ian, E′vi and Re′kem and Zur and Hur and Reba, the princes of Si′hon, who dwelt in the land. 22Balaam also, the son of Beor, the soothsayer, the sons of Israel killed with the sword among the rest of their slain. 23And the border of the people of Reuben was the Jordan as a boundary. This was the inheritance of the Reubenites, according to their families with their cities and villages.

24And Moses gave an inheritance also to the tribe of the Gadites, according to their families. 25Their territory was Ja′zer, and all the cities of Gilead, and half the land of the Am′monites, to Aro′er, which is east of Rabbah, 26and from Heshbon to Ra′math-miz′peh and Bet′onim, and from Ma″hana′im to the territory of De′bir, 27and in the valley Beth-ha′ram, Beth-nim′rah, Succoth, and Za′phon, the rest of the kingdom of Si′hon king of Heshbon, having the Jordan as a boundary, to the lower end of the Sea of Chin′nereth, eastward beyond the Jordan. 28This is the inheritance of the Gadites according to their families, with their cities and villages.

29And Moses gave an inheritance to the half-tribe of Manas′seh; it was allotted to the half-tribe of the Manas′sites according to their families. 30Their region extended from Ma″hana′im, through all Bashan, the whole kingdom of Og king of Bashan, and all the towns of Ja′ir, which are in Bashan, sixty cities, 31and half Gilead, and Ash′taroth, and Ed′re-i, the cities of the kingdom of Og in Bashan; these were allotted to the people of Ma′chir the son of Manas′seh for the half of the Ma′chirites according to their families.

32These are the inheritances which Moses distributed in the plains of Moab, beyond the Jordan east of Jericho. 33But to the tribe of Levi Moses gave no inheritance; the LORD God of Israel is their inheritance, as he said to them.

14 And these are the inheritances which the sons of Israel received in the land of Canaan, which Elea′zar the priest, and Joshua the son of Nun, and the heads of the fathers′ houses of the tribes of the sons of Israel distributed to them. 2Their inheritance was by lot, as the LORD had commanded Moses for the nine and one-half tribes. 3For Moses had given an inheritance to the two and one-half tribes beyond the Jordan; but to the Levites he gave no inheritance among them. 4For the people of Joseph were two tribes, Manas′seh and E′phraim; and no portion was given to the Levites in the land, but only cities to dwell in, with their pasture lands for their cattle and their substance. 5The sons of Israel did as the LORD commanded Moses; they allotted the land.

6Then the people of Judah came to Joshua at Gilgal; and Caleb the son of Jephun′neh the Ken′izzite said to him, “You know what the LORD said to Moses the man of God in Ka′desh-bar′nea concerning you and me. 7I was forty years old when Moses the servant of the LORD sent me from Ka′desh-bar′nea to spy out the land; and I brought him word again as it was in my heart. 8But my brethren who went up with me made the heart of the people melt; yet I wholly followed the LORD my God. 9And Moses swore on that day,

saying, 'Surely the land on which your foot
has trodden shall be an inheritance for you
and your children for ever, because you have
wholly followed the LORD my God.' 10And
now, behold, the LORD has kept me alive, as
he said, these forty-five years since the time
that the LORD spoke this word to Moses,
while Israel walked in the wilderness; and
now, behold, I am this day eighty-five years
old. 11I am still as strong to this day as I was
in the day that Moses sent me; my strength
now is as my strength was then, for war,
and for going and coming. 12So now give
me this hill country of which the LORD
spoke on that day; for you heard on that
day how the An′akim were there, with great
fortified cities: it may be that the LORD will
be with me, and I shall drive them out as the
LORD said."

13Then Joshua blessed him; and he gave
He′bron to Caleb the son of Jephun′neh for
an inheritance. 14So He′bron became the
inheritance of Caleb the son of Jephun′neh
the Ken′izzite to this day, because he wholly
followed the LORD, the God of Israel. 15Now
the name of He′bron formerly was Kir′iath-ar′ba;
this Arba was the greatest man
among the An′akim. And the land had rest
from war.

A Song.
A Psalm of Asaph.

PSALM 83 [82]

O God, do not keep silence;
do not hold your peace or be still, O God!
2For behold, your enemies are in tumult;
those who hate you have raised their
heads.
3They lay crafty plans against your people;
they consult together against your
protected ones.
4They say, "Come, let us wipe them out as
a nation;
let the name of Israel be remembered
no more!"
5Yes, they conspire with one accord;
against you they make a covenant—
6the tents of Edom and the Ish′maelites,
Moab and the Hagrites,
7Gebal and Ammon and Am′alek,
Philistia with the inhabitants of Tyre;
8Assyria also has joined them;
they are the strong arm of the children
of Lot. *Selah*

9Do to them as you did to Mid′ian,
as to Sis′era and Jabin at the river Kishon,
10who were destroyed at En-dor,
who became dung for the ground.
11Make their nobles like Oreb and Zeeb,
all their princes like Zebah and
Zalmun′na,
12who said, "Let us take possession
for ourselves
of the pastures of God."

13O my God, make them like whirling dust,
like chaff before the wind.
14As fire consumes the forest,
as the flame sets the mountains ablaze,
15so you pursue them with your tempest
and terrify them with your hurricane!
16Fill their faces with shame,
that they may seek your name, O LORD.
17Let them be put to shame and dismayed
for ever;
let them perish in disgrace.
18Let them know that you alone,
whose name is the LORD,
are the Most High over all the earth.

LUKE 7

**After he had ended all his sayings in the hearing of the people
he entered Caper′na-um. 2Now
a centurion had a slave who was dear
to him, who was sick and at the point
of death. 3When he heard of Jesus, he**
sent to him elders of the Jews, asking him
to come and heal his slave. 4And when they
came to Jesus, they begged him earnestly,
saying, "He is worthy to have you do this
for him, 5for he loves our nation, and he
built us our synagogue." 6And Jesus went

with them. When he was not far from the house, the centurion sent friends to him, saying to him, "Lord, do not trouble yourself, for I am not worthy to have you come under my roof; [7]therefore I did not presume to come to you. But say the word, and let my servant be healed. [8]For I am a man set under authority, with soldiers under me: and I say to one, 'Go,' and he goes; and to another, 'Come,' and he comes; and to my slave, 'Do this,' and he does it." [9]When Jesus heard this he marveled at him, and turned and said to the multitude that followed him, "I tell you, not even in Israel have I found such faith." [10]And when those who had been sent returned to the house, they found the slave well.

[11]Soon afterward he went to a city called Na′in, and his disciples and a great crowd went with him. [12]As he drew near to the gate of the city, behold, a man who had died was being carried out, the only son of his mother, and she was a widow; and a large crowd from the city was with her. [13]And when the Lord saw her, he had compassion on her and said to her, "Do not weep." [14]And he came and touched the bier, and the bearers stood still. And he said, "Young man, I say to you, arise." [15]And the dead man sat up, and began to speak. And he gave him to his mother. [16]Fear seized them all; and they glorified God, saying, "A great prophet has arisen among us!" and "God has visited his people!" [17]And this report concerning him spread through the whole of Judea and all the surrounding country.

[18]The disciples of John told him of all these things. [19]And John, calling to him two of his disciples, sent them to the Lord, saying, "Are you he who is to come, or shall we look for another?" [20]And when the men had come to him, they said, "John the Baptist has sent us to you, saying, 'Are you he who is to come, or shall we look for another?'" [21]In that hour he cured many of diseases and plagues and evil spirits, and on many that were blind he bestowed sight. [22]And he answered them, "Go and tell John what you have seen and heard: the blind receive their sight, the lame walk, lepers are cleansed, and the deaf hear, the dead are raised up, the poor have good news preached to them. [23]And blessed is he who takes no offense at me."

[24]When the messengers of John had gone, he began to speak to the crowds concerning John: "What did you go out into the wilderness to behold? A reed shaken by the wind? [25]What then did you go out to see? A man clothed in soft raiment? Behold, those who are gorgeously appareled and live in luxury are in kings' courts. [26]What then did you go out to see? A prophet? Yes, I tell you, and more than a prophet. [27]This is he of whom it is written,

'Behold, I send my messenger before your face,
who shall prepare your way before you.'

[28]I tell you, among those born of women none is greater than John; yet he who is least in the kingdom of God is greater than he." [29](When they heard this all the people and the tax collectors justified God, having been baptized with the baptism of John; [30]but the Pharisees and the lawyers rejected the purpose of God for themselves, not having been baptized by him.)

[31]"To what then shall I compare the men of this generation, and what are they like? [32]They are like children sitting in the market place and calling to one another,

'We piped to you, and you did not dance;
we wailed, and you did not weep.'

[33]For John the Baptist has come eating no bread and drinking no wine; and you say, 'He has a demon.' [34]The Son of man has come eating and drinking; and you say, 'Behold, a glutton and a drunkard, a friend of tax collectors and sinners!' [35]Yet wisdom is justified by all her children."

REFLECTION

We often rely on the judgment of others. That is why publishers provide endorsements on books, employers ask for references or letters of recommendation, and character witnesses appear in court. But while our judgment of others is always limited and subjective, God's judgment is true. For this reason, when God enthusiastically endorses two men, Caleb and St. John the Baptist, we want to take note. Caleb is one of the original twelve spies sent into Canaan by Moses. He and Joshua are the only spies who recommend, against all odds, that God's people invade Canaan because they trust that God will provide for their success. The text says three times that Caleb "wholly followed the LORD" (Jos 14:8, 9, 14). Similarly, Jesus says that "among those born of women none is greater than John [the Baptist]" (Lk 7:28). These two men stand out for their fidelity to God, for their boldness in believing in his promises even in the midst of great difficulty. Caleb and John the Baptist exemplify what it means to follow the Lord. What would it take for you to "wholly follow the LORD" today?

April 7

JOSHUA 15

**The lot for the tribe of the peo-
ple of Judah according to their
families reached southward to
the boundary of E′dom, to the wilderness of Zin at the farthest south. [2]And**
their south boundary ran from the end of the
Salt Sea, from the bay that faces southward;
[3]it goes out southward of the ascent of Ak-
rab′bim, passes along to Zin, and goes up
south of Ka′desh-bar′nea, along by Hezron,
up to Addar, turns about to Karka, [4]passes
along to Azmon, goes out by the Brook of
Egypt, and comes to its end at the sea. This
shall be your south boundary. [5]And the east
boundary is the Salt Sea, to the mouth of the
Jordan. And the boundary on the north side
runs from the bay of the sea at the mouth
of the Jordan; [6]and the boundary goes up
to Beth-hog′lah, and passes along north of
Beth-ar′abah; and the boundary goes up to
the stone of Bohan the son of Reuben; [7]and
the boundary goes up to De′bir from the
Valley of A′chor, and so northward, turning
toward Gilgal, which is opposite the ascent
of Adum′mim, which is on the south side of
the valley; and the boundary passes along to
the waters of En-she′mesh, and ends at En-
ro′gel; [8]then the boundary goes up by the
valley of the son of Hinnom at the southern
shoulder of the Jeb′usite (that is, Jerusalem);
and the boundary goes up to the top of the
mountain that lies over against the valley of
Hinnom, on the west, at the northern end of
the valley of Reph′aim; [9]then the boundary
extends from the top of the mountain to the
spring of the Waters of Nephto′ah, and from
there to the cities of Mount E′phron; then the
boundary bends round to Ba′alah (that is,
Kir′iath-je′arim); [10]and the boundary circles
west of Ba′alah to Mount Se′ir, passes along
to the northern shoulder of Mount Je′arim
(that is, Ches′alon), and goes down to Beth-
she′mesh, and passes along by Timnah;
[11]the boundary goes out to the shoulder of
the hill north of Ek′ron, then the boundary
bends round to Shik′keron, and passes along
to Mount Ba′alah, and goes out to Jab′neel;
then the boundary comes to an end at the
sea. [12]And the west boundary was the Great
Sea with its coast-line. This is the boundary
round about the people of Judah according to
their families.

[13]According to the commandment of the
LORD to Joshua, he gave to Caleb the son
of Jephun′neh a portion among the people
of Judah, Kir′iath-ar′ba, that is, He′bron
(Arba was the father of A′nak). [14]And Caleb drove out from there the three sons of
A′nak, She′shai and Ahi′man and Talmai,
the descendants of Anak. [15]And he went
up from there against the inhabitants of
De′bir; now the name of Debir formerly was Kir′iath-se′pher. [16]And Caleb said,
"Whoever strikes Kir′iath-se′pher, and
takes it, to him will I give Ach′sah my
daughter as wife." [17]And Oth′ni-el the son
of Ke′naz, the brother of Caleb, took it;
and he gave him Ach′sah his daughter as
wife. [18]When she came to him, she urged
him to ask her father for a field; and she

alighted from her donkey, and Caleb said
to her, "What do you wish?" 19She said to
him, "Give me a present; since you have set
me in the land of the Neg′eb, give me also
springs of water." And Caleb gave her the
upper springs and the lower springs.
20This is the inheritance of the tribe of
the people of Judah according to their
families. 21The cities belonging to the tribe
of the people of Judah in the extreme
South, toward the boundary of E′dom, were
Kab′zeel, E′der, Jagur, 22Kinah, Dimo′nah,
Ada′dah, 23Ke′desh, Ha′zor, Ithnan, 24Ziph,
Telem, Be-a′loth, 25Ha′zor-hadat′tah, Ker′i-
oth-hez′ron (that is, Ha′zor), 26A′mam, Shema,
Mo′ladah, 27Ha′zar-gad′dah, Heshmon, Beth-
pel′et, 28Ha′zar-shu′al, Be′er-she′ba, Biziothi′ah,
29Ba′alah, I′im, E′zem, 30Elto′lad, Che′sil, Hormah, 31Zik′lag, Madman′nah, Sansan′nah,
32Leba′oth, Shilhim, A′in, and Rimmon: in all,
twenty-nine cities, with their villages.
33And in the lowland, Esh′ta-ol, Zorah,
Ashnah, 34Zano′ah, En-gan′nim, Tap′pu-
ah, E′nam, 35Jarmuth, Adul′lam, Socoh,
Aze′kah, 36Sha″ara′im, Aditha′im, Gede′rah,
Gede′rotha″im: fourteen cities with their
villages.
37Ze′nan, Hadash′ah, Mig′dal-gad, 38Di′lean,
Mizpeh, Jok′the-el, 39La′chish, Bozkath, Eg′lon,
40Cabbon, Lahmam, Chitlish, 41Gede′roth,
Beth-da′gon, Na′amah, and Makke′dah: sixteen cities with their villages.
42Libnah, E′ther, A′shan, 43Iphtah, Ash′nah,
Nezib, 44Kei′lah, Ach′zib, and Mare′shah:
nine cities with their villages.
45Ek′ron, with its towns and its villages;
46from Ek′ron to the sea, all that were by the
side of Ash′dod, with their villages.
47Ash′dod, its towns and its villages; Gaza,
its towns and its villages; to the Brook of
Egypt, and the Great Sea with its coast-line.
48And in the hill country, Sha′mir, Jat′tir,
Socoh, 49Dannah, Kir′iath-san′nah (that
is, De′bir), 50A′nab, Esh′temoh, A′nim,
51Goshen, Holon, and Giloh: eleven cities
with their villages.
52A′rab, Du′mah, E′shan, 53Ja′nim, Beth-
tap′pu-ah, Aphe′kah, 54Humtah, Kir′iath-
ar′ba (that is, He′bron), and Zior: nine cities
with their villages.
55Maon, Carmel, Ziph, Juttah, 56Jezre′el,
Jok′de-am, Zano′ah, 57Kain, Gib′e-ah, and
Timnah: ten cities with their villages.
58Halhul, Beth-zur, Gedor, 59Ma′arath,
Beth-a′noth, and El′tekon: six cities with
their villages.
60Kir′iath-ba′al (that is, Kir′iath-je′arim),
and Rabbah: two cities with their villages.
61In the wilderness, Beth-ar′abah, Middin,
Seca′cah, 62Nibshan, the City of Salt, and
En-ge′di: six cities with their villages.
63But the Jeb′usites, the inhabitants of
Jerusalem, the people of Judah could not
drive out; so the Jebusites dwell with the
people of Judah at Jerusalem to this day.

16 The allotment of the descendants
of Joseph went from the Jordan by
Jericho, east of the waters of Jericho, into
the wilderness, going up from Jericho into
the hill country to Bethel; 2then going from
Bethel to Luz, it passes along to At′aroth, the
territory of the Ar′chites; 3then it goes down
westward to the territory of the Japh′letites,
as far as the territory of Lower Beth-ho′ron,
then to Gezer, and it ends at the sea.
4The people of Joseph, Manas′seh and
E′phraim, received their inheritance.
5The territory of the E′phraimites by their
families was as follows: the boundary of
their inheritance on the east was At′aroth-
ad′dar as far as Upper Beth-ho′ron, 6and
the boundary goes thence to the sea; on the
north is Michme′thath; then on the east the
boundary turns round toward Ta′anath-
shi′loh, and passes along beyond it on the
east to Jano′ah, 7then it goes down from
Jano′ah to At′aroth and to Na′arah, and
touches Jericho, ending at the Jordan. 8From
Tap′pu-ah the boundary goes westward
to the brook Kanah, and ends at the sea.
Such is the inheritance of the tribe of the
E′phraimites by their families, 9together
with the towns which were set apart for
the E′phraimites within the inheritance of
the Manas′sites, all those towns with their
villages. 10However they did not drive out
the Canaanites that dwelt in Gezer: so
the Canaanites have dwelt in the midst of
E′phraim to this day but have become slaves
to do forced labor.

17 Then allotment was made to the
tribe of Manas´seh, for he was the
first-born of Joseph. To Ma´chir the first-
born of Manasseh, the father of Gilead,
were allotted Gilead and Bashan, because
he was a man of war. 2And allotments were
made to the rest of the tribe of Manas´seh,
by their families, Abi-e´zer, He´lek, As´ri-
el, She´chem, He´pher, and Shemi´da; these
were the male descendants of Manasseh the
son of Joseph, by their families.
3Now Zeloph´ehad the son of He´pher, son
of Gilead, son of Ma´chir, son of Manas´seh,
had no sons, but only daughters; and these are
the names of his daughters: Mahlah, Noah,
Hoglah, Milcah, and Tirzah. 4They came
before Elea´zar the priest and Joshua the son
of Nun and the leaders, and said, "The LORD
commanded Moses to give us an inheritance
along with our brethren." So according to the
commandment of the LORD he gave them an
inheritance among the brethren of their father.
5Thus there fell to Manas´seh ten portions,
besides the land of Gilead and Bashan, which
is on the other side of the Jordan; 6because the
daughters of Manas´seh received an inheritance
along with his sons. The land of Gilead was
allotted to the rest of the Manas´sites.
7The territory of Manas´seh reached from
Asher to Michme´thath, which is east of
She´chem; then the boundary goes along
southward to the inhabitants of En-tap´pu-ah.
8The land of Tap´pu-ah belonged to Manas´seh,
but the town of Tappu-ah on the boundary of
Manasseh belonged to the sons of E´phraim.
9Then the boundary went down to the brook
Kanah. The cities here, to the south of the
brook, among the cities of Manas´seh, belong
to E´phraim. Then the boundary of Manasseh
goes on the north side of the brook and ends at
the sea; 10the land to the south being E´phraim's
and that to the north being Manas´seh's, with
the sea forming its boundary; on the north
Asher is reached, and on the east Is´sachar.
11Also in Is´sachar and in Asher Manas´seh had
Beth-she´an and its villages, and Ib´leam and
its villages, and the inhabitants of Dor and its
villages, and the inhabitants of En-dor and its
villages, and the inhabitants of Ta´anach and
its villages, and the inhabitants of Megid´do
and its villages; the third is Na´phath. 12Yet the
sons of Manas´seh could not take possession
of those cities; but the Canaanites persisted in
dwelling in that land. 13But when the sons of
Israel grew strong, they put the Canaanites to
forced labor, and did not utterly drive them
out.
14And the tribe of Joseph spoke to Joshua,
saying, "Why have you given me but one lot
and one portion as an inheritance, although
I am a numerous people, since hitherto the
LORD has blessed me?" 15And Joshua said
to them, "If you are a numerous people,
go up to the forest, and there clear ground
for yourselves in the land of the Per´izzites
and the Reph´aim, since the hill country of
E´phraim is too narrow for you." 16The tribe of
Joseph said, "The hill country is not enough
for us; yet all the Canaanites who dwell in
the plain have chariots of iron, both those in
Beth-she´an and its villages and those in the
Valley of Jezre´el." 17Then Joshua said to the
house of Joseph, to E´phraim and Manas´seh,
"You are a numerous people, and have great
power; you shall not have one lot only, 18but
the hill country shall be yours, for though it
is a forest, you shall clear it and possess it to
its farthest borders; for you shall drive out
the Canaanites, though they have chariots of
iron, and though they are strong."

To the choirmaster: according to The Gittith.
A Psalm of the Sons of Korah.

PSALM 84 [83]

How lovely is your dwelling place,
O LORD of hosts!
2My soul longs, yes, faints
for the courts of the LORD;
my heart and flesh sing for joy
to the living God.

3Even the sparrow finds a home,
and the swallow a nest for herself,
where she may lay her young,
at your altars, O LORD of hosts,
my King and my God.

4Blessed are those who dwell in your house,
ever singing your praise! *Selah*
5Blessed are the men whose strength is
in you,
in whose heart are the highways to Zion.
6As they go through the valley of Baca
they make it a place of springs;
the early rain also covers it with pools.
7They go from strength to strength;
the God of gods will be seen in Zion.

8O Lord God of hosts, hear my prayer;
give ear, O God of Jacob! *Selah*
9Behold our shield, O God;
look upon the face of your anointed!

10For a day in your courts is better
than a thousand elsewhere.
I would rather be a doorkeeper in the
house of my God
than dwell in the tents of wickedness.
11For the Lord God is a sun and shield;
he bestows favor and honor.
No good thing does the Lord withhold
from those who walk uprightly.
12O Lord of hosts,
blessed is the man who trusts in you!

LUKE 7

36One of the Pharisees asked
him to eat with him, and he
went into the Pharisee's house, and sat
at table. 37And behold, a woman of the
city, who was a sinner, when she learned that
he was sitting at table in the Pharisee's house,
brought an alabaster flask of ointment, 38and
standing behind him at his feet, weeping,
she began to wet his feet with her tears, and
wiped them with the hair of her head, and
kissed his feet, and anointed them with the
ointment. 39Now when the Pharisee who had
invited him saw it, he said to himself, "If this
man were a prophet, he would have known
who and what sort of woman this is who
is touching him, for she is a sinner." 40And
Jesus answering said to him, "Simon, I have
something to say to you." And he answered,
"What is it, Teacher?" 41"A certain creditor had
two debtors; one owed five hundred denarii,
and the other fifty. 42When they could not pay,
he forgave them both. Now which of them will
love him more?" 43Simon answered, "The one,
I suppose, to whom he forgave more." And he
said to him, "You have judged rightly." 44Then
turning toward the woman he said to Simon,
"Do you see this woman? I entered your house,
you gave me no water for my feet, but she has
wet my feet with her tears and wiped them
with her hair. 45You gave me no kiss, but from
the time I came in she has not ceased to kiss
my feet. 46You did not anoint my head with oil,
but she has anointed my feet with ointment.
47Therefore I tell you, her sins, which are many,
are forgiven, for she loved much; but he who
is forgiven little, loves little." 48And he said to
her, "Your sins are forgiven." 49Then those who
were at table with him began to say among
themselves, "Who is this, who even forgives
sins?" 50And he said to the woman, "Your faith
has saved you; go in peace."

8 Soon afterward he went on through
cities and villages, preaching and bringing
the good news of the kingdom of God. And
the Twelve were with him, 2and also some
women who had been healed of evil spirits
and infirmities: Mary, called Mag′dalene,
from whom seven demons had gone out,
3and Jo-an′na, the wife of Chuza, Herod's
steward, and Susanna, and many others, who
provided for them out of their means.

REFLECTION

One of our hearts' deepest longings is for safety, security, and rest, for a place we can truly call home. The inventory of geographic locations here in Joshua gives the specific pieces of land that the different Israelite tribes and families will inherit. It is, in effect, the detailed specification of the land that the Lord promised to Abraham. These lands are given to each family in perpetuity, never to be taken away by creditors or enemies. This idea of having a true homeland, an inheritance in the land, is picked up in Psalm 84, which refers to the center of the Promised Land, the Temple. It is "your dwelling place," "a home," "a nest," "your house" (Ps 84:1, 3, 4). Later, when we find Jesus dining at the home of a Pharisee, a sinful woman steals the show by anointing his feet, and he sends her off forgiven and "in peace." The Pharisee does not understand Jesus's actions and even distances himself from the situation in his own home. The sinful woman finds her "home" in Jesus himself and receives the security we all long for in his words: "Go in peace" (Lk 7:50). When have you experienced that sense of peace and "home" most strongly in your life?

April 8

JOSHUA 18

Then the whole congregation of the sons of Israel assembled at Shiloh, and set up the tent of meeting there; the land lay subdued before them.

2There remained among the sons of Israel seven tribes whose inheritance had not yet been apportioned. 3So Joshua said to the sons of Israel, "How long will you be slack to go in and take possession of the land, which the LORD, the God of your fathers, has given you? 4Provide three men from each tribe, and I will send them out that they may set out and go up and down the land, writing a description of it with a view to their inheritances, and then come to me. 5They shall divide it into seven portions, Judah continuing in his territory on the south, and the house of Joseph in their territory on the north. 6And you shall describe the land in seven divisions and bring the description here to me; and I will cast lots for you here before the LORD our God. 7The Levites have no portion among you, for the priesthood of the LORD is their heritage; and Gad and Reuben and half the tribe of Manas′seh have received their inheritance beyond the Jordan eastward, which Moses the servant of the LORD gave them."

8So the men started on their way; and Joshua charged those who went to write the description of the land, saying, "Go up and down and write a description of the land, and come again to me; and I will cast lots for you here before the LORD in Shiloh." 9So the men went and passed up and down in the land and set down in a book a description of it by towns in seven divisions; then they came to Joshua in the camp at Shiloh, 10and Joshua cast lots for them in Shiloh before the LORD; and there Joshua apportioned the land to the sons of Israel, to each his portion.

11The lot of the tribe of Benjamin according to its families came up, and the territory allotted to it fell between the tribe of Judah and the tribe of Joseph. 12On the north side their boundary began at the Jordan; then the boundary goes up to the shoulder north of Jericho, then up through the hill country westward; and it ends at the wilderness of Beth-a′ven. 13From there the boundary passes along southward in the direction of Luz, to the shoulder of Luz (the same is Bethel), then the boundary goes down to At′aroth-ad′dar, upon the mountain that lies south of Lower Beth-ho′ron. 14Then the boundary goes in another direction, turning on the western side southward from the mountain that lies to the south, opposite Beth-ho′ron, and it ends at Kir′iath-ba′al (that is, Kir′iath-je′arim), a city belonging to the tribe of Judah. This forms the western side. 15And the southern side begins at the outskirts of Kir′iath-je′arim; and the boundary goes from there to E′phron, to the spring of the Waters of Nephto′ah; 16then the boundary goes down to the border of the mountain that overlooks the valley of the son of Hinnom, which is at the north end of the valley of Reph′aim; and it then goes down the valley of Hinnom, south of the shoulder of the Jeb′usites, and downward to En-ro′gel; 17then it bends in a northerly direction going on to En-she′mesh, and thence goes to Geli′loth, which is opposite the ascent of Adum′mim; then it goes down to the stone of Bohan the son of Reuben;

[18]and passing on to the north of the shoulder
of Beth-ar′abah it goes down to the Ar′abah;
[19]then the boundary passes on to the north
of the shoulder of Beth-hog′lah; and the
boundary ends at the northern bay of the
Salt Sea, at the south end of the Jordan: this
is the southern border. [20]The Jordan forms
its boundary on the eastern side. This is
the inheritance of the tribe of Benjamin,
according to its families, boundary by
boundary round about.

[21]Now the cities of the tribe of Benjamin
according to their families were Jericho,
Beth-hog′lah, E′mek-ke′ziz, [22]Beth-ar′abah,
Zemara′im, Bethel, [23]Avvim, Par′ah, Oph′rah,
[24]Che′phar-am′moni, Ophni, Ge′ba—twelve
cities with their villages: [25]Gib′eon, Ra′mah,
Be-er′oth, [26]Mizpeh, Chephi′rah, Mozah,
[27]Re′kem, Ir′peel, Tar′alah, [28]Ze′la, Ha-e′leph,
Je′bus (that is, Jerusalem), Gib′e-ah and
Kir′iath-je′arim—fourteen cities with their
villages. This is the inheritance of the tribe of
Benjamin according to its families.

19 The second lot came out for Simeon,
for the tribe of Simeon, according
to its families; and its inheritance was in
the midst of the inheritance of the tribe of
Judah. [2]And it had for its inheritance Be′er-
she′ba, Sheba, Mo′ladah, [3]Ha′zar-shu′al,
Balah, E′zem, [4]Elto′lad, Be′thul, Hormah,
[5]Zik′lag, Beth-mar′caboth, Ha′zar-su′sah,
[6]Beth-leba′oth, and Sharu′hen—thirteen
cities with their villages; [7]En-rim′mon,
E′ther, and A′shan—four cities with their
villages; [8]together with all the villages
round about these cities as far as Ba′alath-
be′er, Ra′mah of the Neg′eb. This was the
inheritance of the tribe of Simeon according
to its families. [9]The inheritance of the tribe
of Simeon formed part of the territory of
Judah; because the portion of the tribe
of Judah was too large for them, the tribe
of Simeon obtained an inheritance in the
midst of their inheritance.

[10]The third lot came up for the tribe of
Zeb′ulun, according to its families. And
the territory of its inheritance reached as
far as Sa′rid; [11]then its boundary goes up
westward, and on to Mar′eal, and touches
Dab′besheth, then the brook which is
east of Jok′ne-am; [12]from Sa′rid it goes
in the other direction eastward toward
the sunrise to the boundary of Chis′loth-
ta′bor; thence it goes to Dab′erath, then
up to Japhi′a; [13]from there it passes along
on the east toward the sunrise to Gath-
he′pher, to Eth-ka′zin, and going on to
Rimmon it bends toward Ne′ah; [14]then
on the north the boundary turns about to
Hanna′thon, and it ends at the valley of
Iph′tahel; [15]and Kattath, Nahal′al, Shimron,
I′dalah, and Bethlehem—twelve cities with
their villages. [16]This is the inheritance
of the tribe of Zeb′ulun, according to its
families—these cities with their villages.

[17]The fourth lot came out for Is′sachar, for
the tribe of Issachar, according to its families.
[18]Its territory included Jezre′el, Chesul′loth,
Shunem, [19]Haph′ara-im, Shi′on, Ana′harath,
[20]Rabbith, Kish′ion, E′bez, [21]Re′meth, En-
gan′nim, En-had′dah, Beth-paz′zez; [22]the
boundary also touches Tabor, Shahazu′mah,
and Beth-she′mesh, and its boundary ends
at the Jordan—sixteen cities with their villages. [23]This is the inheritance of the tribe
of Is′sachar, according to its families—the
cities with their villages.

[24]The fifth lot came out for the tribe
of Asher according to its families. [25]Its
territory included Helkath, Ha′li, Be′ten,
Ach′shaph, [26]Allam′melech, A′mad, and
Mi′shal; on the west it touches Carmel and
Shihorlib′nath, [27]then it turns eastward,
it goes to Beth-da′gon, and touches
Zeb′ulun and the valley of Iph′tahel
northward to Beth-e′mek and Nei′el;
then it continues in the north to Ca′bul,
[28]E′bron, Re′hob, Hammon, Kanah, as far
as Sidon the Great; [29]then the boundary
turns to Ra′mah, reaching to the fortified
city of Tyre; then the boundary turns to
Ho′sah, and it ends at the sea; Maha′lab,
Ach′zib, [30]Ummah, A′phek and Re′hob—
twenty-two cities with their villages.
[31]This is the inheritance of the tribe of
Asher according to its families—these
cities with their villages.

[32]The sixth lot came out for the tribe
of Naph′tali, for the tribe of Naphtali,
according to its families. [33]And its

boundary ran from He´leph, from the oak
in Za-anan´nim, and Ad´ami-nek´eb, and
Jab´neel, as far as Lakkum; and it ended
at the Jordan; 34then the boundary turns
westward to Az´noth-ta´bor, and goes from
there to Hukkok, touching Zeb´ulun at the
south, and Asher on the west, and Judah
on the east at the Jordan. 35The fortified
cities are Ziddim, Zer, Hammath, Rakkath,
Chin´nereth, 36Ad´amah, Ra´mah, Ha´zor,
37Ke´desh, Ed´re-i, En-ha´zor, 38Yi´ron,
Mig´dal-el, Horem, Beth-a´nath, and
Beth-she´mesh—nineteen cities with their
villages. 39This is the inheritance of the tribe
of Naph´tali according to its families—the
cities with their villages.

40The seventh lot came out for the tribe
of Dan, according to its families. 41And
the territory of its inheritance included
Zorah, Esh´ta-ol, Irshe´mesh, 42Sha-al-
ab´bin, Ai´jalon, Ithlah, 43E´lon, Timnah,
Ek´ron, 44El´tekeh, Gib´bethon, Ba´alath,
45Je´hud, Ben´e-be´rak, Gath-rim´mon,
46and Me-jar´kon and Rakkon with the
territory over against Joppa. 47When the
territory of the Da´nites was lost to them,
the Danites went up and fought against
Le´shem, and after capturing it and putting it to the sword they took possession
of it and settled in it, calling Leshem,
Dan, after the name of Dan their ancestor. 48This is the inheritance of the tribe
of Dan, according to their families—these
cities with their villages.

49When they had finished distribut-
ing the several territories of the land as
inheritances, the sons of Israel gave an
inheritance among them to Joshua the
son of Nun. 50By command of the LORD
they gave him the city which he asked,
Tim´nath-se´rah in the hill country of
E´phraim; and he rebuilt the city, and settled in it.

51These are the inheritances which
Elea´zar the priest and Joshua the son of
Nun and the heads of the fathers' houses
of the tribes of the sons of Israel distributed by lot at Shiloh before the LORD, at
the door of the tent of meeting. So they
finished dividing the land.

To the choirmaster.
A Psalm of the Sons of Korah.

PSALM 85 [84]

LORD, you were favorable to your land;
you brought back the captives of Jacob.
2You forgave the iniquity of your people;
you pardoned all their sin. *Selah*
3You withdrew all your wrath;
you turned from your hot anger.

4Restore us again, O God of our salvation,
and put away your indignation toward us!
5Will you be angry with us for ever?
Will you prolong your anger to
all generations?
6Will you not revive us again,
that your people may rejoice in you?
7Show us your merciful love, O LORD,
and grant us your salvation.

8Let me hear what God the LORD will speak,
for he will speak peace to his people,
to his saints, to those who turn to him in
their hearts.
9Surely his salvation is at hand for those who
fear him,
that glory may dwell in our land.

10Mercy and faithfulness will meet;
righteousness and peace will kiss
each other.
11Faithfulness will spring up from
the ground,
and righteousness will look down
from heaven.
12Yes, the LORD will give what is good,
and our land will yield its increase.
13Righteousness will go before him,
and make his footsteps a way.

LUKE 8

**4And when a great crowd came
together and people from town
after town came to him, he said in a
parable: 5"A sower went out to sow**

his seed; and as he sowed, some fell along the path, and was trodden under foot, and the birds of the air devoured it. [6]And some fell on the rock; and as it grew up, it withered away, because it had no moisture. [7]And some fell among thorns; and the thorns grew with it and choked it. [8]And some fell into good soil and grew, and yielded a hundredfold." As he said this, he called out, "He who has ears to hear, let him hear."

[9]And when his disciples asked him what this parable meant, [10]he said, "To you it has been given to know the secrets of the kingdom of God; but for others they are in parables, so that seeing they may not see, and hearing they may not understand. [11]Now the parable is this: The seed is the word of God. [12]The ones along the path are those who have heard; then the devil comes and takes away the word from their hearts, that they may not believe and be saved. [13]And the ones on the rock are those who, when they hear the word, receive it with joy; but these have no root, they believe for a while and in time of temptation fall away. [14]And as for what fell among the thorns, they are those who hear, but as they go on their way they are choked by the cares and riches and pleasures of life, and their fruit does not mature. [15]And as for that in the good soil, they are those who, hearing the word, hold it fast in an honest and good heart, and bring forth fruit with patience.

[16]"No one after lighting a lamp covers it with a vessel, or puts it under a bed, but puts it on a stand, that those who enter may see the light. [17]For nothing is hidden that shall not be made manifest, nor anything secret that shall not be known and come to light. [18]Take heed then how you hear; for to him who has will more be given, and from him who has not, even what he thinks that he has will be taken away."

[19]Then his mother and his brethren came to him, but they could not reach him for the crowd. [20]And he was told, "Your mother and your brethren are standing outside, desiring to see you." [21]But he said to them, "My mother and my brethren are those who hear the word of God and do it."

[22]One day he got into a boat with his disciples, and he said to them, "Let us go across to the other side of the lake." So they set out, [23]and as they sailed he fell asleep. And a storm of wind came down on the lake, and they were filling with water, and were in danger. [24]And they went and woke him, saying, "Master, Master, we are perishing!" And he awoke and rebuked the wind and the raging waves; and they ceased, and there was a calm. [25]He said to them, "Where is your faith?" And they were afraid, and they marveled, saying to one another, "Who then is this, that he commands even wind and water, and they obey him?"

[26]Then they arrived at the country of the Ger′asenes, which is opposite Galilee. [27]And as he stepped out on land, there met him a man from the city who had demons; for a long time he had worn no clothes, and he lived not in a house but among the tombs. [28]When he saw Jesus, he cried out and fell down before him, and said with a loud voice, "What have you to do with me, Jesus, Son of the Most High God? I beg you, do not torment me." [29]For he had commanded the unclean spirit to come out of the man. (For many a time it had seized him; he was kept under guard, and bound with chains and shackles, but he broke the bonds and was driven by the demon into the desert.) [30]Jesus then asked him, "What is your name?" And he said, "Legion"; for many demons had entered him. [31]And they begged him not to command them to depart into the abyss. [32]Now a large herd of swine was feeding there on the hillside; and they begged him to let them enter these. So he gave them leave. [33]Then the demons came out of the man and entered the swine, and the herd rushed down the steep bank into the lake and were drowned.

[34]When the herdsmen saw what had happened, they fled, and told it in the city and in the country. [35]Then people went out to see what had happened, and

they came to Jesus, and found the man from whom the demons had gone, sitting at the feet of Jesus, clothed and in his right mind; and they were afraid. 36And those who had seen it told them how he who had been possessed with demons was healed. 37Then all the people of the surrounding country of the Ger′asenes asked him to depart from them; for they were seized with great fear; so he got into the boat and returned. 38The man from whom the demons had gone begged that he might be with him; but he sent him away, saying, 39"Return to your home, and declare how much God has done for you." And he went away, proclaiming throughout the whole city how much Jesus had done for him.

REFLECTION

Nothing is more frustrating for a gardener than trying to grow a garden in bad soil. Even if your plants get plenty of sun, water, and fertilizer, contaminated or imbalanced soil will lead to a failed crop and wasted effort. In Jesus's famous parable of the sower, Jesus is the gardener and the seed he generously scatters is "the word of God," that is, Jesus's message of repentance and faith. Sadly, the soil upon which he sows is not all good soil. In some places the seed cannot take root; in other places the shallow soil allows for only short-term growth. We are the soil in which Jesus desires to plant his Word. The question is "What kind of soil are you?" Are you shallow soil such that "cares and riches and pleasures" (Lk 8:14) distract you from faith? Are you rocky ground in which God's Word can take no root, like the Gerasenes who kicked Jesus out after he performed a miracle (see v. 37)? Or are you the good soil; do you hear the Word and then "hold it fast in an honest and good heart" (v. 15)? Those of good soil are the ones in whom "faithfulness will spring up from the ground" (Ps 85:11). Jesus spreads the seed and invites us to follow him. Do you see it as your job to be good soil that can bear much fruit?

April 9

JOSHUA 20

Then the LORD said to Joshua, 2"Say to the sons of Israel, 'Appoint the cities of refuge, of which I spoke to you through Moses, 3that the manslayer who kills any person without intent or unwittingly may flee there; they shall be for you a refuge from the avenger of blood. 4He shall flee to one of these cities and shall stand at the entrance of the gate of the city, and explain his case to the elders of that city; then they shall take him into the city, and give him a place, and he shall remain with them. 5And if the avenger of blood pursues him, they shall not give up the slayer into his hand; because he killed his neighbor unwittingly, having had no enmity against him in times past. 6And he shall remain in that city until he has stood before the congregation for judgment, until the death of him who is high priest at the time: then the slayer may go again to his own town and his own home, to the town from which he fled.'"

7So they set apart Ke′desh in Galilee in the hill country of Naph′tali, and She′chem in the hill country of E′phraim, and Kir′iath-ar′ba (that is, He′bron) in the hill country of Judah. 8And beyond the Jordan east of Jericho, they appointed Be′zer in the wilderness on the tableland, from the tribe of Reuben, and Ra′moth in Gilead, from the tribe of Gad, and Golan in Bashan, from the tribe of Manas′seh. 9These were the cities designated for all the sons of Israel, and for the stranger sojourning among them, that any one who killed a person without intent could flee there, so that he might not die by the hand of the avenger of blood, till he stood before the congregation.

21 Then the heads of the fathers' houses of the Levites came to Elea′zar the priest and to Joshua the son of Nun and to the heads of the fathers' houses of the tribes of the sons of Israel; 2and they said to them at Shiloh in the land of Canaan, "The LORD commanded through Moses that we be given cities to dwell in, along with their pasture lands for our cattle." [3]So by command of the LORD the sons of Israel gave to the Levites the following cities and pasture lands out of their inheritance.

[4]The lot came out for the families of the Ko′hathites. So those Levites who were descendants of Aaron the priest received by lot from the tribes of Judah, Simeon, and Benjamin, thirteen cities.

[5]And the rest of the Ko′hathites received by lot from the families of the tribe of E′phraim, from the tribe of Dan and the half-tribe of Manas′seh, ten cities.

[6]The Ger′shonites received by lot from the families of the tribe of Is′sachar, from the tribe of Asher, from the tribe of Naph′tali, and from the half-tribe of Manas′seh in Bashan, thirteen cities.

[7]The Merar′ites according to their families received from the tribe of Reuben, the tribe of Gad, and the tribe of Zeb′ulun, twelve cities.

[8]These cities and their pasture lands the sons of Israel gave by lot to the Levites, as the LORD had commanded through Moses.

[9]Out of the tribe of Judah and the tribe of Simeon they gave the following cities mentioned by name, [10]which went to the descendants of Aaron, one of the families of the Ko′hathites who belonged to the Levites; since the lot fell to them first. [11]They gave them Kir′iath-ar′ba (Arba being the father of A′nak), that is He′bron, in the hill country of Judah, along with the pasture lands round about it. [12]But the fields of the city and its villages had been given to Caleb the son of Jephun′neh as his possession.

[13]And to the descendants of Aaron the priest they gave He′bron, the city of refuge for the slayer, with its pasture lands, Libnah with its pasture lands, [14]Jat′tir with its pasture lands, Eshtemo′a with its pasture lands, [15]Ho′lon with its pasture lands, De′bir with its pasture lands, [16]A′in with its pasture lands, Juttah with its pasture lands, Beth-she′mesh with its pasture lands—nine cities out of these two tribes; [17]then out of the tribe of Benjamin, Gib′eon with its pasture lands, Ge′ba with its pasture lands, [18]An′athoth with its pasture lands, and Al′mon with its pasture lands—four cities. [19]The cities of the descendants of Aaron, the priests, were in all thirteen cities with their pasture lands.

[20]As to the rest of the Ko′hathites belonging to the Kohathite families of the Levites, the cities allotted to them were out of the tribe of E′phraim. [21]To them were given She′chem, the city of refuge for the slayer, with its pasture lands in the hill country of E′phraim, Gezer with its pasture lands, [22]Kib′za-im with its pasture lands, Beth-ho′ron with its pasture lands—four cities; [23]and out of the tribe of Dan, El′teke with its pasture lands, Gib′bethon with its pasture lands, [24]Ai′jalon with its pasture lands, Gath-rim′mon with its pasture lands—four cities; [25]and out of the half-tribe of Manas′seh, Ta′anach with its pasture lands, and Gath-rim′mon with its pasture lands—two cities. [26]The cities of the families of the rest of the Ko′hathites were ten in all with their pasture lands.

[27]And to the Ger′shonites, one of the families of the Levites, were given out of the half-tribe of Manas′seh, Golan in Bashan with its pasture lands, the city of refuge for the slayer, and Be-eshte′rah with its pasture lands—two cities; [28]and out of the tribe of Is′sachar, Kish′ion with its pasture lands, Dab′erath with its pasture lands, [29]Jarmuth with its pasture lands, En-gan′nim with its pasture lands—four cities; [30]and out of the tribe of Asher, Mishal with its pasture lands, Abdon with its pasture lands, [31]Helkath with its pasture lands, and Re′hob with its pasture lands—four cities; [32]and out of the tribe of Naph′tali, Ke′desh in Galilee with its pasture lands, the city of refuge for the slayer, Ham′moth-dor with its pasture lands, and Kartan with its pasture lands—three cities. [33]The cities of the several families of the Ger′shonites were in all thirteen cities with their pasture lands.

[34]And to the rest of the Levites, the Merar′ite families, were given out of the tribe of Zeb′ulun, Jok′ne-am with its pasture lands, Kartah with its pasture lands,

[35]Dimnah with its pasture lands, Nahal′al with its pasture lands—four cities; [36]and out of the tribe of Reuben, Be′zer with its pasture lands, Ja′haz with its pasture lands, [37]Ked′emoth with its pasture lands, and Meph′a-ath with its pasture lands—four cities; [38]and out of the tribe of Gad, Ra′moth in Gilead with its pasture lands, the city of refuge for the slayer, Ma″hana′im with its pasture lands, [39]Heshbon with its pasture lands, Ja′zer with its pasture lands—four cities in all. [40]As for the cities of the several Merar′ite families, that is, the remainder of the families of the Levites, those allotted to them were in all twelve cities.

[41]The cities of the Levites in the midst of the possession of the sons of Israel were in all forty-eight cities with their pasture lands. [42]These cities had each its pasture lands round about it; so it was with all these cities.

[43]Thus the LORD gave to Israel all the land which he swore to give to their fathers; and having taken possession of it, they settled there. [44]And the LORD gave them rest on every side just as he had sworn to their fathers; not one of all their enemies had withstood them, for the LORD had given all their enemies into their hands. [45]Not one of all the good promises which the LORD had made to the house of Israel had failed; all came to pass.

22 Then Joshua summoned the Reubenites, and the Gadites, and the half-tribe of Manas′seh, [2]and said to them, "You have kept all that Moses the servant of the LORD commanded you, and have obeyed my voice in all that I have commanded you; [3]you have not forsaken your brethren these many days, down to this day, but have been careful to keep the charge of the LORD your God. [4]And now the LORD your God has given rest to your brethren, as he promised them; therefore turn and go to your home in the land where your possession lies, which Moses the servant of the LORD gave you on the other side of the Jordan. [5]Take good care to observe the commandment and the law which Moses the servant of the LORD commanded you, to love the LORD your God, and to walk in all his ways, and to keep his commandments, and to cling to him, and to serve him with all your heart and with all your soul." [6]So Joshua blessed them, and sent them away; and they went to their homes.

[7]Now to the one half of the tribe of Manas′seh Moses had given a possession in Bashan; but to the other half Joshua had given a possession beside their brethren in the land west of the Jordan. And when Joshua sent them away to their homes and blessed them, [8]he said to them, "Go back to your homes with much wealth, and with very many cattle, with silver, gold, bronze, and iron, and with much clothing; divide the spoil of your enemies with your brethren." [9]So the Reubenites and the Gadites and the half-tribe of Manas′seh returned home, parting from the sons of Israel at Shiloh, which is in the land of Canaan, to go to the land of Gilead, their own land of which they had possessed themselves by command of the LORD through Moses.

[10]And when they came to the region about the Jordan, that lies in the land of Canaan, the Reubenites and the Gadites and the half-tribe of Manas′seh built there an altar by the Jordan, an altar of great size. [11]And the sons of Israel heard say, "Behold, the Reubenites and the Gadites and the half-tribe of Manas′seh have built an altar at the frontier of the land of Canaan, in the region about the Jordan, on the side that belongs to the sons of Israel." [12]And when the sons of Israel heard of it, the whole assembly of the sons of Israel gathered at Shiloh, to make war against them.

[13]Then the sons of Israel sent to the Reubenites and the Gadites and the half-tribe of Manas′seh, in the land of Gilead, Phin′ehas the son of Elea′zar the priest, [14]and with him ten chiefs, one from each of the tribal families of Israel, every one of them the head of a family among the clans of Israel. [15]And they came to the Reubenites, the Gadites, and the half-tribe of Manas′seh, in the land of Gilead, and they said to them, [16]"Thus says the whole congregation of the LORD, 'What is this treachery which you have committed against the God of Israel

in turning away this day from following the LORD, by building yourselves an altar this day in rebellion against the LORD? [17]Have we not had enough of the sin at Peor from which even yet we have not cleansed ourselves, and for which there came a plague upon the congregation of the LORD, [18]that you must turn away this day from following the LORD? And if you rebel against the LORD today he will be angry with the whole congregation of Israel tomorrow. [19]But now, if your land is unclean, pass over into the LORD's land where the LORD's tabernacle stands, and take for yourselves a possession among us; only do not rebel against the LORD, or make us as rebels by building yourselves an altar other than the altar of the LORD our God. [20]Did not A'chan the son of Ze'rah break faith in the matter of the devoted things, and wrath fell upon all the congregation of Israel? And he did not perish alone for his iniquity.'

A Prayer of David.

PSALM 86 [85]

Incline your ear, O LORD, and answer me,
for I am poor and needy.
[2]Preserve my life, for I am godly;
save your servant who trusts in you.
You are my God; [3]have mercy on me, O Lord,
for to you do I cry all the day.
[4]Gladden the soul of your servant,
for to you, O Lord, do I lift up my soul.
[5]For you, O Lord, are good and forgiving,
abounding in mercy to all who call on you.
[6]Give ear, O LORD, to my prayer;
listen to my cry of supplication.
[7]In the day of my trouble I call on you,
for you do answer me.

[8]There is none like you among the gods, O Lord,
nor are there any works like yours.
[9]All the nations you have made shall come
and bow down before you, O Lord,
and shall glorify your name.
[10]For you are great and do wondrous things,
you alone are God.
[11]Teach me your way, O LORD,
that I may walk in your truth;
unite my heart to fear your name.
[12]I give thanks to you, O Lord my God, with my whole heart,
and I will glorify your name for ever.
[13]For great is your merciful love toward me;
you have delivered my soul from the depths of Sheol.

[14]O God, insolent men have risen up against me;
a band of ruthless men seek my life,
and they do not set you before them.
[15]But you, O Lord, are a God merciful and gracious,
slow to anger and abounding in mercy and faithfulness.
[16]Turn to me and take pity on me;
give your strength to your servant,
and save the son of your handmaid.
[17]Show me a sign of your favor,
that those who hate me may see and be put to shame
because you, LORD, have helped me and comforted me.

LUKE 8

**[40]Now when Jesus returned,
the crowd welcomed him, for
they were all waiting for him.
[41]And there came a man named Ja'irus,
who was a ruler of the synagogue; and**
falling at Jesus' feet he begged him to come
to his house, [42]for he had an only daughter,
about twelve years of age, and she was dying.
As he went, the people pressed round him.
[43]And a woman who had had a flow of blood
for twelve years and had spent all her living
upon physicians and could not be healed by
any one, [44]came up behind him, and touched
the fringe of his garment; and immediately
her flow of blood ceased. [45]And Jesus said,
"Who was it that touched me?" When all
denied it, Peter said, "Master, the multitudes

surround you and press upon you!" 46But
Jesus said, "Some one touched me; for I
perceive that power has gone forth from me."
47And when the woman saw that she was
not hidden, she came trembling, and falling
down before him declared in the presence
of all the people why she had touched him,
and how she had been immediately healed.
48And he said to her, "Daughter, your faith
has made you well; go in peace."
49While he was still speaking, a man from
the ruler's house came and said, "Your
daughter is dead; do not trouble the Teacher
any more." 50But Jesus on hearing this answered him, "Do not fear; only believe, and
she shall be well." 51And when he came to
the house, he permitted no one to enter with
him, except Peter and John and James, and
the father and mother of the child. 52And
all were weeping and bewailing her; but he
said, "Do not weep; for she is not dead but
sleeping." 53And they laughed at him, knowing that she was dead. 54But taking her by
the hand he called, saying, "Child, arise."
55And her spirit returned, and she got up at
once; and he directed that something should
be given her to eat. 56And her parents were
amazed; but he charged them to tell no one
what had happened.

REFLECTION

"I am poor and needy" (Ps 86:1). This is always our stance before God. We have nothing to offer the Almighty. No matter our accomplishments, we are mere creatures, wholly dependent on him for our next breath. Yet sometimes we forget just how helpless we are without him. In the reading from Luke's Gospel for today, we find two intertwined stories in which individuals come face to face with their own dependence. On the one hand, a father comes to Jesus on behalf of his gravely ill daughter; on the other, a woman with a chronic hemorrhage, which makes her ritually impure and therefore excludes her from Temple worship, reaches out to touch Jesus. Both of these people are humble enough to acknowledge their need and yet bold enough to ask Jesus for help. That combination—humility and courage—gives us insight into the seemingly imbalanced prayer of the psalmist. First he describes his plight with what sounds like despair, but then he suddenly shifts into expressing his overwhelming confidence in the Lord: "There is none like you among the gods, O Lord" (v. 8). Are you humble enough to admit your helplessness and yet bold enough to ask Jesus for help?

April 10

JOSHUA 22

21Then the Reubenites, the Ga-
dites, and the half-tribe of Ma-
nas'seh said in answer to the
heads of the families of Israel, 22"The
Mighty One, God, the LORD! The
Mighty One, God, the LORD! He knows; and
let Israel itself know! If it was in rebellion
or in breach of faith toward the LORD,
spare us not today 23for building an altar to
turn away from following the LORD; or if
we did so to offer burnt offerings or cereal
offerings or peace offerings on it, may the
LORD himself take vengeance. 24No, but we
did it from fear that in time to come your
children might say to our children, 'What
have you to do with the LORD, the God of
Israel? 25For the LORD has made the Jordan
a boundary between us and you, you Reubenites and Gadites; you have no portion
in the LORD.' So your children might make
our children cease to worship the LORD.
26Therefore we said, 'Let us now build an
altar, not for burnt offering, nor for sacrifice, 27but to be a witness between us and
you, and between the generations after
us, that we do perform the service of the
LORD in his presence with our burnt offerings and sacrifices and peace offerings; lest
your children say to our children in time to

come, "You have no portion in the LORD." '
[28]And we thought, If this should be said to
us or to our descendants in time to come,
we should say, 'Behold the copy of the altar
of the LORD, which our fathers made, not
for burnt offerings, nor for sacrifice, but to
be a witness between us and you.' [29]Far be
it from us that we should rebel against the
LORD, and turn away this day from following the LORD by building an altar for burnt
offering, cereal offering, or sacrifice, other than the altar of the LORD our God that
stands before his tabernacle!"

[30]When Phin′ehas the priest and the chiefs
of the congregation, the heads of the families
of Israel who were with him, heard the
words that the Reubenites and the Gadites
and the Manas′sites spoke, it pleased them
well. [31]And Phin′ehas the son of Elea′zar the
priest said to the Reubenites and the Gadites
and the Manas′sites, "Today we know that
the LORD is in the midst of us, because you
have not committed this treachery against
the LORD; now you have saved the sons of
Israel from the hand of the LORD."

[32]Then Phin′ehas the son of Elea′zar the
priest, and the chiefs, returned from the
Reubenites and the Gadites in the land of
Gilead to the land of Canaan, to the sons
of Israel, and brought back word to them.
[33]And the report pleased the sons of Israel;
and the sons of Israel blessed God and spoke
no more of making war against them, to
destroy the land where the Reubenites and
the Gadites were settled. [34]The Reubenites
and the Gadites called the altar Witness;
"For," said they, "it is a witness between us
that the LORD is God."

23 A long time afterward, when the
LORD had given rest to Israel from
all their enemies round about, and Joshua
was old and well advanced in years, [2]Joshua
summoned all Israel, their elders and heads,
their judges and officers, and said to them,
"I am now old and well advanced in years;
[3]and you have seen all that the LORD your
God has done to all these nations for your
sake, for it is the LORD your God who has
fought for you. [4]Behold, I have allotted to
you as an inheritance for your tribes those
nations that remain, along with all the
nations that I have already cut off, from the
Jordan to the Great Sea in the west. [5]The
LORD your God will push them back before
you, and drive them out of your sight; and
you shall possess their land, as the LORD
your God promised you. [6]Therefore be very
steadfast to keep and do all that is written
in the book of the law of Moses, turning
aside from it neither to the right hand nor
to the left, [7]that you may not be mixed with
these nations left here among you, or make
mention of the names of their gods, or
swear by them, or serve them, or bow down
yourselves to them, [8]but cling to the LORD
your God as you have done to this day. [9]For
the LORD has driven out before you great
and strong nations; and as for you, no man
has been able to withstand you to this day.
[10]One man of you puts to flight a thousand,
since it is the LORD your God who fights
for you, as he promised you. [11]Take good
heed to yourselves, therefore, to love the
LORD your God. [12]For if you turn back, and
join the remnant of these nations left here
among you, and make marriages with them,
so that you marry their women and they
yours, [13]know assuredly that the LORD your
God will not continue to drive out these
nations before you; but they shall be a snare
and a trap for you, a scourge on your sides,
and thorns in your eyes, till you perish from
off this good land which the LORD your God
has given you.

[14]"And now I am about to go the way of all
the earth, and you know in your hearts and
souls, all of you, that not one thing has failed
of all the good things which the LORD your
God promised concerning you; all have come
to pass for you, not one of them has failed.
[15]But just as all the good things which the
LORD your God promised concerning you
have been fulfilled for you, so the LORD will
bring upon you all the evil things, until he
has destroyed you from off this good land
which the LORD your God has given you,
[16]if you transgress the covenant of the LORD
your God, which he commanded you, and go
and serve other gods and bow down to them.
Then the anger of the LORD will be kindled

against you, and you shall perish quickly from
off the good land which he has given to you."
24 Then Joshua gathered all the tribes of
Israel to She'chem, and summoned
the elders, the heads, the judges, and the
officers of Israel; and they presented themselves before God. 2And Joshua said to all
the people, "Thus says the LORD, the God of
Israel, 'Your fathers lived of old beyond the
Euphrates, Te'rah, the father of Abraham
and of Na'hor; and they served other gods.
3Then I took your father Abraham from
beyond the River and led him through all
the land of Canaan, and made his offspring
many. I gave him Isaac; 4and to Isaac I gave
Jacob and Esau. And I gave Esau the hill
country of Se'ir to possess, but Jacob and
his children went down to Egypt. 5And
I sent Moses and Aaron, and I plagued
Egypt with what I did in the midst of it;
and afterwards I brought you out. 6Then I
brought your fathers out of Egypt, and you
came to the sea; and the Egyptians pursued
your fathers with chariots and horsemen
to the Red Sea. 7And when they cried to
the LORD, he put darkness between you
and the Egyptians, and made the sea come
upon them and cover them; and your eyes
saw what I did to Egypt; and you lived in
the wilderness a long time. 8Then I brought
you to the land of the Am'orites, who lived
on the other side of the Jordan; they fought
with you, and I gave them into your hand,
and you took possession of their land, and
I destroyed them before you. 9Then Balak
the son of Zippor, king of Moab, arose
and fought against Israel; and he sent and
invited Balaam the son of Beor to curse
you, 10but I would not listen to Balaam;
therefore he blessed you; so I delivered you
out of his hand. 11And you went over the
Jordan and came to Jericho, and the men
of Jericho fought against you, and also the
Am'orites, the Per'izzites, the Canaanites,
the Hittites, the Gir'gashites, the Hi'vites,
and the Jeb'usites; and I gave them into
your hand. 12And I sent the hornet before
you, which drove them out before you, the
two kings of the Am'orites; it was not by
your sword or by your bow. 13I gave you a
land on which you had not labored, and
cities which you had not built, and you
dwell therein; you eat the fruit of vineyards
and oliveyards which you did not plant.'

14"Now therefore fear the LORD, and serve
him in sincerity and in faithfulness; put
away the gods which your fathers served
beyond the River, and in Egypt, and serve
the LORD. 15And if you be unwilling to serve
the LORD, choose this day whom you will
serve, whether the gods your fathers served
in the region beyond the River, or the gods
of the Am'orites in whose land you dwell;
but as for me and my house, we will serve
the LORD."

16Then the people answered, "Far be it
from us that we should forsake the LORD, to
serve other gods; 17for it is the LORD our God
who brought us and our fathers up from the
land of Egypt, out of the house of bondage,
and who did those great signs in our sight,
and preserved us in all the way that we went,
and among all the peoples through whom
we passed; 18and the LORD drove out before
us all the peoples, the Am'orites who lived
in the land; therefore we also will serve the
LORD, for he is our God."

19But Joshua said to the people, "You
cannot serve the LORD; for he is a holy
God; he is a jealous God; he will not
forgive your transgressions or your sins.
20If you forsake the LORD and serve
foreign gods, then he will turn and do
you harm, and consume you, after having
done you good." 21And the people said to
Joshua, "No; but we will serve the LORD."
22Then Joshua said to the people, "You
are witnesses against yourselves that you
have chosen the LORD, to serve him." And
they said, "We are witnesses." 23He said,
"Then put away the foreign gods which
are among you, and incline your heart to
the LORD, the God of Israel." 24And the
people said to Joshua, "The LORD our
God we will serve, and his voice we will
obey." 25So Joshua made a covenant with
the people that day, and made statutes and
ordinances for them at She'chem. 26And
Joshua wrote these words in the book of
the law of God; and he took a great stone,

and set it up there under the oak in the
sanctuary of the LORD. [27]And Joshua said
to all the people, "Behold, this stone shall
be a witness against us; for it has heard all
the words of the LORD which he spoke to
us; therefore it shall be a witness against
you, lest you deal falsely with your God."
[28]So Joshua sent the people away, every
man to his inheritance.

[29]After these things Joshua the son of
Nun, the servant of the LORD, died, being
a hundred and ten years old. [30]And they
buried him in his own inheritance at
Tim′nath-se′rah, which is in the hill country
of E′phraim, north of the mountain of
Ga′ash.

[31]And Israel served the LORD all the days
of Joshua, and all the days of the elders who
outlived Joshua and had known all the work
which the LORD did for Israel.

[32]The bones of Joseph which the sons of
Israel brought up from Egypt were buried at
She′chem, in the portion of ground which
Jacob bought from the sons of Ha′mor the
father of She′chem for a hundred pieces
of money; it became an inheritance of the
descendants of Joseph.

[33]And Elea′zar the son of Aaron died; and
they buried him at Gib′e-ah, the town of
Phin′ehas his son, which had been given
him in the hill country of E′phraim.

A Psalm of the Sons of Korah.
A Song.

PSALM 87 [86]

On the holy mount stands the city
he founded;
2 the LORD loves the gates of Zion
more than all the dwelling places of Jacob.
[3]Glorious things are spoken of you,
O city of God. *Selah*

[4]Among those who know me I mention
Rahab and Babylon;
behold, Philis′tia and Tyre, with
Ethiopia—
"This one was born there," they say.
[5]And of Zion it shall be said,
"This one and that one were born in her";
for the Most High himself will
establish her.
[6]The LORD records as he registers the peoples,
"This one was born there." *Selah*

[7]Singers and dancers alike say,
"All my springs are in you."

LUKE 9

**And he called the Twelve to-
gether and gave them power
and authority over all demons
and to cure diseases, [2]and he sent them
out to preach the kingdom of God and
to heal. [3]And he said to them, "Take**
nothing for your journey, no staff, nor
bag, nor bread, nor money; and do not
have two tunics. [4]And whatever house you
enter, stay there, and from there depart.
[5]And wherever they do not receive you,
when you leave that town shake off the
dust from your feet as a testimony against
them." [6]And they departed and went
through the villages, preaching the gospel
and healing everywhere.

[7]Now Herod the tetrarch heard of all that
was done, and he was perplexed, because
it was said by some that John had been
raised from the dead, [8]by some that Eli′jah
had appeared, and by others that one of
the old prophets had risen. [9]Herod said,
"John I beheaded; but who is this about
whom I hear such things?" And he sought
to see him.

[10]On their return the apostles told him
what they had done. And he took them
and withdrew apart to a city called Beth-
sa′ida. [11]When the crowds learned it,
they followed him; and he welcomed
them and spoke to them of the kingdom
of God, and cured those who had need
of healing. [12]Now the day began to wear
away; and the Twelve came and said to
him, "Send the crowd away, to go into

the villages and country round about, to lodge and get provisions; for we are here in a lonely place." 13But he said to them, "You give them something to eat." They said, "We have no more than five loaves and two fish—unless we are to go and buy food for all these people." 14For there were about five thousand men. And he said to his disciples, "Make them sit down in companies, about fifty each." 15And they did so, and made them all sit down. 16And taking the five loaves and the two fish he looked up to heaven, and blessed and broke them, and gave them to the disciples to set before the crowd. 17And all ate and were satisfied. And they took up what was left over, twelve baskets of broken pieces.

REFLECTION

Once Joshua dismisses the Transjordan tribes—Gad, Reuben, and Manasseh—they build an altar that nearly provokes a civil war (see Jos 22:10–12). The other Israelites are concerned that these tribes are going on their own to start their own religion, and that they are no longer coming together with the other tribes for worship. But the Transjordan tribes explain that their altar is not an active sacrificial site, but a "witness" of the unity of all Israel. This spiritual unity is later signified by the city of Jerusalem, Zion, which Psalm 87 celebrates as the spiritual birthplace of all nations. "This one was born there" (Ps 87:4) is describing that even the Gentiles will come to know the Most High God. When Jesus sends out the Twelve, he gives them "power and authority" and "[sends] them out to preach the kingdom of God and to heal" (Lk 9:1–2). After Jesus's Crucifixion and Resurrection, the disciples will once again be sent out to preach, this time baptizing all the nations into the New Covenant. But the unity of the New Covenant people will shift from a geographic place to a person, from Jerusalem to Jesus himself, who is the fulfillment of all God's promises: "Not one of all the good promises which the LORD had made to the house of Israel had failed; all came to pass" (Jos 21:45). What promises has God fulfilled in your life?

April 11

JUDGES 1

After the death of Joshua the sons of Israel inquired of the LORD, "Who shall go up first for us against the Canaanites, to fight against them?" 2The LORD said, "Judah shall go up; behold, I have given the land into his hand." 3And Judah said to Simeon his brother, "Come up with me into the territory allotted to me, that we may fight against the Canaanites; and I likewise will go with you into the territory allotted to you." So Simeon went with him. 4Then Judah went up and the LORD gave the Canaanites and the Per′izzites into their hand; and they defeated ten thousand of them at Be′zek. 5They came upon Ado′ni-be′zek at Be′zek, and fought against him, and defeated the Canaanites and the Per′izzites. 6Ado′ni-be′zek fled; but they pursued him, and caught him, and cut off his thumbs and his great toes. 7And Ado′ni-be′zek said, "Seventy kings with their thumbs and their great toes cut off used to pick up scraps under my table; as I have done, so God has repaid me." And they brought him to Jerusalem, and he died there.

8And the men of Judah fought against Jerusalem, and took it, and struck it with the edge of the sword, and set the city on fire. 9And afterward the men of Judah went down to fight against the Canaanites who dwelt in the hill country, in the Neg′eb, and in the lowland. 10And Judah went against the Canaanites who dwelt in He′bron (now the name of Hebron was formerly Kir′iath-ar′ba); and they defeated Sheshai and Ahi′man and Talmai.

11From there they went against the inhabitants of De′bir. The name of Debir was formerly Kir′iath-se′pher. 12And Caleb said, "He who attacks Kir′iath-se′pher and takes it, I will give him Ach′sah my daughter as wife." 13And Oth′ni-el the son of Ke′naz,

Caleb's younger brother, took it; and he gave him Ach′sah his daughter as wife. [14]When she came to him, she urged him to ask her father for a field; and she alighted from her donkey, and Caleb said to her, "What do you wish?" [15]She said to him, "Give me a present; since you have set me in the land of the Neg′eb, give me also springs of water." And Caleb gave her the upper springs and the lower springs.

[16]And the descendants of the Ken′ite, Moses' father-in-law, went up with the people of Judah from the city of palms into the wilderness of Judah, which lies in the Negeb near Ar′ad; and they went and settled with the people. [17]And Judah went with Simeon his brother, and they defeated the Canaanites who inhabited Ze′phath, and utterly destroyed it. So the name of the city was called Hormah. [18]Judah also took Gaza with its territory, and Ash′kelon with its territory, and Ek′ron with its territory. [19]And the LORD was with Judah, and he took possession of the hill country, but he could not drive out the inhabitants of the plain, because they had chariots of iron. [20]And He′bron was given to Caleb, as Moses had said; and he drove out from it the three sons of A′nak. [21]But the people of Benjamin did not drive out the Jeb′usites who dwelt in Jerusalem; so the Jebusites have dwelt with the people of Benjamin in Jerusalem to this day.

[22]The house of Joseph also went up against Bethel; and the LORD was with them. [23]And the house of Joseph sent to spy out Bethel. (Now the name of the city was formerly Luz.) [24]And the spies saw a man coming out of the city, and they said to him, "Please, show us the way into the city, and we will deal kindly with you." [25]And he showed them the way into the city; and they struck the city with the edge of the sword, but they let the man and all his family go. [26]And the man went to the land of the Hittites and built a city, and called its name Luz; that is its name to this day.

[27]Manas′seh did not drive out the inhabitants of Beth-she′an and its villages, or Ta′anach and its villages, or the inhabitants of Dor and its villages, or the inhabitants of Ib′leam and its villages, or the inhabitants of Megid′do and its villages, but the Canaanites persisted in dwelling in that land. [28]When Israel grew strong, they put the Canaanites to forced labor, but did not utterly drive them out.

[29]And E′phraim did not drive out the Canaanites who dwelt in Gezer; but the Canaanites dwelt in Gezer among them.

[30]Zeb′ulun did not drive out the inhabitants of Kitron, or the inhabitants of Nahal′ol; but the Canaanites dwelt among them, and became subject to forced labor.

[31]Asher did not drive out the inhabitants of Ac′co, or the inhabitants of Si′don, or of Ahlab, or of Ach′zib, or of Helbah, or of A′phik, or of Re′hob; [32]but the Ash′erites dwelt among the Canaanites, the inhabitants of the land; for they did not drive them out.

[33]Naph′tali did not drive out the inhabitants of Beth-she′mesh, or the inhabitants of Beth-a′nath, but dwelt among the Canaanites, the inhabitants of the land; nevertheless the inhabitants of Beth-shemesh and of Beth-anath became subject to forced labor for them.

[34]The Am′orites pressed the Da′nites back into the hill country, for they did not allow them to come down to the plain; [35]the Am′orites persisted in dwelling in Har-he′res, in Ai′jalon, and in Sha-al′bim, but the hand of the house of Joseph rested heavily upon them, and they became subject to forced labor. [36]And the border of the Am′orites ran from the ascent of Akrab′bim, from Se′la and upward.

2 Now the angel of the LORD went up from Gilgal to Bochim. And he said, "I brought you up from Egypt, and brought you into the land which I swore to give to your fathers. I said, 'I will never break my covenant with you, [2]and you shall make no covenant with the inhabitants of this land; you shall break down their altars.' But you have not obeyed my command. What is this you have done? [3]So now I say, I will not drive them out before you; but they shall become adversaries to you, and their gods shall be a snare to you." [4]When the angel of

the LORD spoke these words to all the sons
of Israel, the people lifted up their voices
and wept. 5And they called the name of that
place Bochim; and they sacrificed there to
the LORD.

6When Joshua dismissed the people, the
sons of Israel went each to his inheritance to
take possession of the land. 7And the people
served the LORD all the days of Joshua, and
all the days of the elders who outlived Joshua,
who had seen all the great work which the
LORD had done for Israel. 8And Joshua the
son of Nun, the servant of the LORD, died at
the age of one hundred and ten years. 9And
they buried him within the bounds of his
inheritance in Tim′nath-he′res, in the hill
country of E′phraim, north of the mountain
of Ga′ash. 10And all that generation also were
gathered to their fathers; and there arose
another generation after them, who did not
know the LORD or the work which he had
done for Israel.

11And the sons of Israel did what was evil
in the sight of the LORD and served the
Ba′als; 12and they forsook the LORD, the God
of their fathers, who had brought them out
of the land of Egypt; they went after other
gods, from among the gods of the peoples
who were round about them, and bowed
down to them; and they provoked the LORD
to anger. 13They forsook the LORD, and
served the Ba′als and the Ash′taroth. 14So
the anger of the LORD was kindled against
Israel, and he gave them over to plunderers,
who plundered them; and he sold them into
the power of their enemies round about, so
that they could no longer withstand their
enemies. 15Whenever they marched out,
the hand of the LORD was against them for
evil, as the LORD had warned, and as the
LORD had sworn to them; and they were in
great distress.

16Then the LORD raised up judges, who
saved them out of the power of those who
plundered them. 17And yet they did not
listen to their judges; for they played the
harlot after other gods and bowed down
to them; they soon turned aside from the
way in which their fathers had walked,
who had obeyed the commandments of the
LORD, and they did not do so. 18Whenever
the LORD raised up judges for them, the
LORD was with the judge, and he saved
them from the hand of their enemies all the
days of the judge; for the LORD was moved
to pity by their groaning because of those
who afflicted and oppressed them. 19But
whenever the judge died, they turned back
and behaved worse than their fathers, going
after other gods, serving them and bowing
down to them; they did not drop any of
their practices or their stubborn ways. 20So
the anger of the LORD was kindled against
Israel; and he said, "Because this people
have transgressed my covenant which I
commanded their fathers, and have not
obeyed my voice, 21from now on I will not
drive out before them any of the nations
that Joshua left when he died, 22that by
them I may test Israel, whether they will
take care to walk in the way of the LORD as
their fathers did, or not." 23So the LORD left
those nations, not driving them out at once,
and he did not give them into the power
of Joshua.

A Song. A Psalm of the Sons of Korah.
To the choirmaster: according to Mahalath Leannoth.
A Maskhil of Heman the Ezrahite.

PSALM 88 [87]

O LORD, my God, I call for help by day;
  I cry out in the night before you.
2Let my prayer come before you,
  incline your ear to my cry!

3For my soul is full of troubles,
  and my life draws near to Sheol.
4I am reckoned among those who go down
  to the Pit;
  I am a man who has no strength,
5like one forsaken among the dead,
  like the slain that lie in the grave,
like those whom you remember no more,
  for they are cut off from your hand.
6You have put me in the depths of the Pit,
  in the regions dark and deep.

7 Your wrath lies heavy upon me,
and you overwhelm me with all your
waves. *Selah*
8 You have caused my companions to
shun me;
you have made me a thing of horror
to them.
I am shut in so that I cannot escape;
9 my eye grows dim through sorrow.
Every day I call upon you, O LORD;
I spread out my hands to you.
10 Do you work wonders for the dead?
Do the shades rise up to praise you?
Selah
11 Is your mercy declared in the grave,
or your faithfulness in Abad′don?
12 Are your wonders known in the darkness,
or your saving help in the land of
forgetfulness?

13 But I, O LORD, cry to you;
in the morning my prayer comes
before you.
14 O LORD, why do you cast me off?
Why do you hide your face from me?
15 Afflicted and close to death from my
youth,
I suffer your terrors; I am helpless.
16 Your wrath has swept over me;
your dread assaults destroy me.
17 They surround me like a flood all
day long;
they close in upon me together.
18 You have caused loved one and friend to
shun me;
my companions are in darkness.

LUKE 9

18 Now it happened that as he
was praying alone the disciples
were with him; and he asked them,
"Who do the people say that I am?"
19 And they answered, "John the Baptist; but
others say, Eli′jah; and others, that one of
the old prophets has risen." 20 And he said
to them, "But who do you say that I am?"
And Peter answered, "The Christ of God."
21 But he charged and commanded them to
tell this to no one, 22 saying, "The Son of man
must suffer many things, and be rejected by
the elders and chief priests and scribes, and
be killed, and on the third day be raised."
23 And he said to all, "If any man would
come after me, let him deny himself and
take up his cross daily and follow me.
24 For whoever would save his life will lose
it; and whoever loses his life for my sake,
he will save it. 25 For what does it profit
a man if he gains the whole world and
loses or forfeits himself? 26 For whoever is
ashamed of me and of my words, of him
will the Son of man be ashamed when he
comes in his glory and the glory of the
Father and of the holy angels. 27 But I tell
you truly, there are some standing here
who will not taste death before they see
the kingdom of God."
28 Now about eight days after these
sayings he took with him Peter and John
and James, and went up on the mountain
to pray. 29 And as he was praying, the
appearance of his countenance was
altered, and his clothing became dazzling
white. 30 And behold, two men talked with
him, Moses and Eli′jah, 31 who appeared
in glory and spoke of his exodus, which
he was to accomplish at Jerusalem. 32 Now
Peter and those who were with him were
heavy with sleep but kept awake, and they
saw his glory and the two men who stood
with him. 33 And as the men were parting
from him, Peter said to Jesus, "Master, it
is well that we are here; let us make three
booths, one for you and one for Moses
and one for Eli′jah"—not knowing what
he said. 34 As he said this, a cloud came
and overshadowed them; and they were
afraid as they entered the cloud. 35 And a
voice came out of the cloud, saying, "This
is my Son, my Chosen; listen to him!"
36 And when the voice had spoken, Jesus
was found alone. And they kept silence
and told no one in those days anything of
what they had seen.
37 On the next day, when they had come
down from the mountain, a great crowd
met him. 38 And behold, a man from the

crowd cried, "Teacher, I beg you to look
upon my son, for he is my only child;
[39]and behold, a spirit seizes him, and
he suddenly cries out; it convulses him
till he foams, and shatters him, and will
hardly leave him. [40]And I begged your
disciples to cast it out, but they could
not." [41]Jesus answered, "O faithless and
perverse generation, how long am I to
be with you and bear with you? Bring
your son here." [42]While he was coming,
the demon tore him and convulsed him.
But Jesus rebuked the unclean spirit, and
healed the boy, and gave him back to his
father. [43]And all were astonished at the
majesty of God.

But while they were all marveling at
everything he did, he said to his disciples,
[44]"Let these words sink into your ears;
for the Son of man is to be delivered
into the hands of men." [45]But they did
not understand this saying, and it was
concealed from them, that they should not
perceive it; and they were afraid to ask him
about this saying.

REFLECTION

An abstract God, who is hands-off with his creation and who demands nothing from us, is easy to believe in. But this is not the God we find in the Scriptures. Here we find a God who acts and interacts; who demands a response. Joshua, at the end of his life, recalls how the Lord delivered his people from Egypt, provided for them in their desert wandering, and fought for them in their conquest of the Promised Land. Here voiced by Joshua, the Lord asks his people for a response to his action in their lives: "Choose this day whom you will serve . . . but as for me and my house, we will serve the LORD" (Jos 24:15). Later, Jesus too requires a response from his disciples: "But who do you say that I am?" (Lk 9:20). Jesus challenges us further by saying that if anyone wants to follow him, "let him deny himself and take up his cross daily and follow me" (v. 23). We cannot stay on the fence about Jesus. We must either deny him, or deny ourselves and follow him. Which will it be for you?

April 12

JUDGES 3

**Now these are the nations which
the LORD left, to test Israel by
them, that is, all in Israel who had
no experience of any war in Canaan;
[2]it was only that the generations of the
sons of Israel might know war, that he**
might teach war to such at least as had not
known it before. [3]These are the nations:
the five lords of the Philis′tines, and all the
Canaanites, and the Sido′nians, and the
Hi′vites who dwelt on Mount Lebanon, from
Mount Ba′al-her′mon as far as the entrance
of Ha′math. [4]They were for the testing of
Israel, to know whether Israel would obey
the commandments of the LORD, which he
commanded their fathers by Moses. [5]So the
sons of Israel dwelt among the Canaanites,
the Hittites, the Am′orites, the Per′izzites,
the Hi′vites, and the Jeb′usites; [6]and they
took their daughters to themselves for
wives, and their own daughters they gave to
their sons; and they served their gods.

[7]And the sons of Israel did what was evil
in the sight of the LORD, forgetting the LORD
their God, and serving the Ba′als and the
Ashe′roth. [8]Therefore the anger of the LORD
was kindled against Israel, and he sold them
into the hand of Cu′shan-rishatha′im king
of Mesopota′mia; and the sons of Israel
served Cushan-rishathaim eight years. [9]But
when the sons of Israel cried to the LORD,
the LORD raised up a deliverer for the sons
of Israel, who delivered them, Oth′ni-el
the son of Ke′naz, Caleb's younger brother.
[10]The Spirit of the LORD came upon him,
and he judged Israel; he went out to war, and
the LORD gave Cu′shan-rishatha′im king of
Mesopota′mia into his hand; and his hand
prevailed over Cushan-rishathaim. [11]So the
land had rest forty years. Then Oth′ni-el the
son of Ke′naz died.

[12]And the sons of Israel again did what
was evil in the sight of the LORD; and the

LORD strengthened Eg´lon the king of Moab
against Israel, because they had done what
was evil in the sight of the LORD. 13He
gathered to himself the Am´monites and the
Amal´ekites, and went and defeated Israel;
and they took possession of the city of
palms. 14And the sons of Israel served Eg´lon
the king of Moab eighteen years.
15But when the sons of Israel cried to
the LORD, the LORD raised up for them
a deliverer, E´hud, the son of Gera, the
Benjaminite, a left-handed man. The sons
of Israel sent tribute by him to Eg´lon
the king of Moab. 16And E´hud made for
himself a sword with two edges, a cubit in
length; and he girded it on his right thigh
under his clothes. 17And he presented
the tribute to Eg´lon king of Moab. Now
Eglon was a very fat man. 18And when
E´hud had finished presenting the tribute,
he sent away the people that carried the
tribute. 19But he himself turned back at the
sculptured stones near Gilgal, and said,
"I have a secret message for you, O king."
And he commanded, "Silence." And all
his attendants went out from his presence.
20And E´hud came to him, as he was sitting
alone in his cool roof chamber. And Ehud
said, "I have a message from God for you."
And he arose from his seat. 21And E´hud
reached with his left hand, took the sword
from his right thigh, and thrust it into his
belly; 22and the hilt also went in after the
blade, and the fat closed over the blade,
for he did not draw the sword out of his
belly; and the dirt came out. 23Then E´hud
went out into the vestibule, and closed the
doors of the roof chamber upon him, and
locked them.
24When he had gone, the servants came;
and when they saw that the doors of the
roof chamber were locked, they thought,
"He is only relieving himself in the closet
of the cool chamber." 25And they waited till
they were utterly at a loss; but when he still
did not open the doors of the roof chamber,
they took the key and opened them; and
there lay their lord dead on the floor.
26E´hud escaped while they delayed, and
passed beyond the sculptured stones, and
escaped to Se-i´rah. 27When he arrived, he
sounded the trumpet in the hill country of
E´phraim; and the sons of Israel went down
with him from the hill country, having
him at their head. 28And he said to them,
"Follow after me; for the LORD has given
your enemies the Moabites into your hand."
So they went down after him, and seized the
fords of the Jordan against the Moabites,
and allowed no man to pass over. 29And they
killed at that time about ten thousand of the
Moabites, all strong, able-bodied men; not a
man escaped. 30So Moab was subdued that
day under the hand of Israel. And the land
had rest for eighty years.
31After him was Shamgar the son of A´nath,
who killed six hundred of the Philis´tines
with an oxgoad; and he too delivered Israel.
4 And the sons of Israel again did what
was evil in the sight of the LORD, after
E´hud died. 2And the LORD sold them into
the hand of Ja´bin king of Canaan, who
reigned in Ha´zor; the commander of his
army was Sis´era, who dwelt in Haro´sheth-
ha-goi´im. 3Then the sons of Israel cried to
the LORD for help; for he had nine hundred
chariots of iron, and oppressed the sons of
Israel cruelly for twenty years.
4Now Deborah, a prophetess, the wife of
Lap´pidoth, was judging Israel at that time.
5She used to sit under the palm of Deborah
between Ra´mah and Bethel in the hill
country of E´phraim; and the sons of Israel
came up to her for judgment. 6She sent and
summoned Barak the son of Abin´o-am
from Ke´desh in Naph´tali, and said to him,
"The LORD, the God of Israel, commands
you, 'Go, gather your men at Mount Ta´bor,
taking ten thousand from the tribe of
Naphtali and the tribe of Zeb´ulun. 7And I
will draw out Sis´era, the general of Ja´bin's
army, to meet you by the river Ki´shon with
his chariots and his troops; and I will give
him into your hand.' " 8Barak said to her, "If
you will go with me, I will go; but if you will
not go with me, I will not go." 9And she said,
"I will surely go with you; nevertheless, the
road on which you are going will not lead to
your glory, for the LORD will sell Sis´era into
the hand of a woman." Then Deborah arose,

and went with Barak to Ke´desh. 10And
Barak summoned Zeb´ulun and Naph´tali
to Ke´desh; and ten thousand men went
up at his heels; and Deborah went up with
him.

11Now He´ber the Kenite had separated
from the Kenites, the descendants of
Ho´bab the father-in-law of Moses, and had
pitched his tent as far away as the oak in Za-
anan´nim, which is near Ke´desh.

12When Sis´era was told that Barak the son
of Abin´o-am had gone up to Mount Ta´bor,
13Sis´era called out all his chariots, nine
hundred chariots of iron, and all the men
who were with him, from Haro´sheth-ha-
goi´im to the river Ki´shon. 14And Deborah
said to Barak, "Up! For this is the day in
which the LORD has given Sis´era into your
hand. Does not the LORD go out before
you?" So Barak went down from Mount
Ta´bor with ten thousand men following
him. 15And the LORD routed Sis´era and all
his chariots and all his army before Barak at
the edge of the sword; and Sisera alighted
from his chariot and fled away on foot.
16And Barak pursued the chariots and the
army to Haro´sheth-ha-goi´im, and all the
army of Sis´era fell by the edge of the sword;
not a man was left.

17But Sis´era fled away on foot to the tent
of Ja´el, the wife of He´ber the Kenite; for
there was peace between Ja´bin the king of
Ha´zor and the house of Heber the Kenite.
18And Ja´el came out to meet Sis´era, and
said to him, "Turn aside, my lord, turn aside
to me; have no fear." So he turned aside to
her into the tent, and she covered him with
a rug. 19And he said to her, "Please, give me
a little water to drink; for I am thirsty." So
she opened a skin of milk and gave him a
drink and covered him. 20And he said to her,
"Stand at the door of the tent, and if any man
comes and asks you, 'Is any one here?' say,
No." 21But Ja´el the wife of He´ber took a tent
peg, and took a hammer in her hand, and
went softly to him and drove the peg into
his temple, till it went down into the ground,
as he was lying fast asleep from weariness.
So he died. 22And behold, as Barak pursued
Sis´era, Ja´el went out to meet him, and said
to him, "Come, and I will show you the man
whom you are seeking." So he went in to her
tent; and there lay Sisera dead, with the tent
peg in his temple.

23So on that day God subdued Ja´bin the
king of Canaan before the sons of Israel.
24And the hand of the sons of Israel bore
harder and harder on Ja´bin the king of
Canaan, until they destroyed Jabin king
of Canaan.

A Maskil of Ethan the Ezrahite.

PSALM 89 [88]

I will sing of your mercies,
O LORD, for ever;
with my mouth I will proclaim your
faithfulness to all generations.
2For your merciful love was established
for ever,
your faithfulness is firm as the heavens.
3You have said, "I have made a covenant
with my chosen one,
I have sworn to David my servant:
4'I will establish your descendants for ever,
and build your throne for all
generations.'" *Selah*

5Let the heavens praise your wonders,
O LORD,
your faithfulness in the assembly of the
holy ones!
6For who in the skies can be compared to
the LORD?
Who among the heavenly beings is like
the LORD,
7a God feared in the council of the holy ones,
great and awesome above all that are
round about him?
8O LORD God of hosts,
who is mighty as you are, O LORD,
with your faithfulness round about you?
9You rule the raging of the sea;
when its waves rise, you still them.
10You crushed Rahab like a carcass,
you scattered your enemies with your
mighty arm.

11 The heavens are yours, the earth also
is yours;
the world and all that is in it, you have
founded them.
12 The north and the south, you have
created them;
Tabor and Hermon joyously praise
your name.
13 You have a mighty arm;
strong is your hand, high your
right hand.
14 Righteousness and justice are the
foundation of your throne;
steadfast love and faithfulness go
before you.
15 Blessed are the people who know the
festal shout,
who walk, O LORD, in the light of
your countenance,
16 who exult in your name all the day,
and extol your righteousness.
17 For you are the glory of their strength;
by your favor our horn is exalted.
18 For our shield belongs to the LORD,
our king to the Holy One of Israel.

LUKE 9

**46 And an argument arose a-
mong them as to which of them
was the greatest. 47 But when Jesus perceived the thought of their hearts, he**
took a child and put him by his side, 48 and
said to them, "Whoever receives this child in
my name receives me, and whoever receives
me receives him who sent me; for he who is
least among you all is the one who is great."
49 John answered, "Master, we saw a man
casting out demons in your name, and we
forbade him, because he does not follow
with us." 50 But Jesus said to him, "Do not
forbid him; for he that is not against you
is for you."
51 When the days drew near for him to
be received up, he set his face to go to Jerusalem. 52 And he sent messengers ahead
of him, who went and entered a village of
the Samaritans, to make ready for him;
53 but the people would not receive him,
because his face was set toward Jerusalem. 54 And when his disciples James and
John saw it, they said, "Lord, do you want
us to bid fire come down from heaven
and consume them?" 55 But he turned and
rebuked them. 56 And they went on to another village.
57 As they were going along the road,
a man said to him, "I will follow you
wherever you go." 58 And Jesus said to
him, "Foxes have holes, and birds of the
air have nests; but the Son of man has
nowhere to lay his head." 59 To another he
said, "Follow me." But he said, "Lord, let
me first go and bury my father." 60 But he
said to him, "Leave the dead to bury their
own dead; but as for you, go and proclaim the kingdom of God." 61 Another
said, "I will follow you, Lord; but let me
first say farewell to those at my home."
62 Jesus said to him, "No one who puts his
hand to the plow and looks back is fit for
the kingdom of God."

REFLECTION

The Book of Joshua gave us the good news about Israel's success in fulfilling God's command, but Judges opens with the bad news. Despite all the victories under Joshua, Israel failed to complete the conquest. Judges 3 lists the nations that the Israelites failed to conquer: "the five lords of the Philistines, and all the Canaanites, and the Sido'nians, and the Hivites who dwelt on Mount Lebanon" (Jgs 3:3). The people disobeyed the Lord and thus received the consequences. Beyond that, they fall into pagan worship, going after false gods. This sin sets up a cycle of disobedience repeated throughout the whole Book of Judges, wherein the Israelites engage in idolatry, the Lord makes use of their enemies to punish them, they cry out to God, he sends a judge to deliver them, and they return to serving the Lord. This cycle shows the Israelites to be fair-weather friends of the Lord, much like those who want to follow Jesus but are not ready for the sacrifice involved: "No one who puts his hand to the plow and looks back is fit for the kingdom of God" (Lk 9:62). The Lord's commitment to us is eternal, and he calls us to reciprocate with whole-hearted love and devotion. Jesus wants all that we have to give because he has given everything to us. Are you ready to give everything to him?

April 13

JUDGES 5

Then sang Deborah and Barak the son of Abin′o-am on that day:
2"**That the leaders took the lead in Israel,**
that the people offered themselves willingly,
bless the LORD!

3"Hear, O kings; give ear, O princes;
to the LORD I will sing,
I will make melody to the LORD, the God of Israel.
4"LORD, when you went forth from Se′ir,
when you marched from the region of E′dom,
the earth trembled,
and the heavens dropped,
yes, the clouds dropped water.
5The mountains quaked before the LORD,
the One of Sinai, before the LORD, the God of Israel.

6"In the days of Shamgar, son of A′nath,
in the days of Ja′el, caravans ceased
and travelers kept to the byways.
7The peasantry ceased in Israel, they ceased
until you arose, Deborah,
arose as a mother in Israel.
8When new gods were chosen,
then war was in the gates.
Was shield or spear to be seen
among forty thousand in Israel?
9My heart goes out to the commanders of Israel
who offered themselves willingly among the people.
Bless the LORD.

10"Tell of it, you who ride on tawny donkeys,
you who sit on rich carpets
and you who walk by the way.
11To the sound of musicians at the watering places,
there they repeat the triumphs of the LORD,
the triumphs of his peasantry in Israel.

"Then down to the gates marched
the people of the LORD.
12"Awake, awake, Deborah!
Awake, awake, utter a song!
Arise, Barak, lead away your captives,
O son of Abin′o-am.
13Then down marched the remnant of the noble;
the people of the LORD marched down for him against the mighty.
14From E′phraim they set out there into the valley,
following you, Benjamin, with your kinsmen;
from Ma′chir marched down the commanders,
and from Zeb′ulun those who bear the marshal's staff;
15the princes of Is′sachar came with Deborah,
and Issachar faithful to Barak;
into the valley they rushed forth at his heels.
Among the clans of Reuben
there were great searchings of heart.
16Why did you tarry among the sheepfolds,
to hear the piping for the flocks?
Among the clans of Reuben
there were great searchings of heart.
17Gilead stayed beyond the Jordan;
and Dan, why did he abide with the ships?
Asher sat still at the coast of the sea,
settling down by his landings.

[18]Zeb′ulun is a people that jeoparded their
lives to the death;
Naph′tali too, on the heights of the field.

[19]"The kings came, they fought;
then fought the kings of Canaan,
at Ta′anach, by the waters of Megid′do;
they got no spoils of silver.
[20]From heaven fought the stars,
from their courses they fought
against Sis′era.
[21]The torrent Ki′shon swept them away,
the onrushing torrent, the torrent Kishon.
March on, my soul, with might!

[22]"Then loud beat the horses' hoofs
with the galloping, galloping of
his steeds.

[23]"Curse Me′roz, says the angel of the LORD,
curse bitterly its inhabitants,
because they came not to the help of
the LORD,
to the help of the LORD against
the mighty.

[24]"Most blessed of women be Ja′el,
the wife of He′ber the Kenite,
of tent-dwelling women most blessed.
[25]He asked for water and she gave him milk,
she brought him curds in a lordly bowl.
[26]She put her hand to the tent peg
and her right hand to the
workmen's mallet;
she struck Sis′era a blow,
she crushed his head,
she shattered and pierced his temple.
[27]He sank, he fell,
he lay still at her feet;
at her feet he sank, he fell;
where he sank, there he fell dead.

[28]"Out of the window she peered,
the mother of Sis′era gazed through
the lattice:
'Why is his chariot so long in coming?
Why do the hoofbeats of his chariots
tarry?'
[29]Her wisest ladies make answer,
no, she gives answer to herself,
[30]'Are they not finding and dividing
the spoil?—
A maiden or two for every man;
spoil of dyed stuffs for Sis′era,
spoil of dyed stuffs embroidered,
two pieces of dyed work embroidered
for my neck as spoil?'

[31]"So perish all your enemies, O LORD!
But your friends be like the sun as he
rises in his might."

And the land had rest for forty years.

6 The sons of Israel did what was evil in
the sight of the LORD; and the LORD
gave them into the hand of Mid′ian seven
years. [2]And the hand of Mid′ian prevailed
over Israel; and because of Midian the
sons of Israel made for themselves the
dens which are in the mountains, and the
caves and the strongholds. [3]For whenever
the Israelites put in seed the Mid′ianites
and the Amal′ekites and the people of
the East would come up and attack them;
[4]they would encamp against them and
destroy the produce of the land, as far as
the neighborhood of Gaza, and leave no
sustenance in Israel, and no sheep or ox
or donkey. [5]For they would come up with
their cattle and their tents, coming like
locusts for number; both they and their
camels could not be counted; so that they
wasted the land as they came in. [6]And
Israel was brought very low because of
Mid′ian; and the sons of Israel cried for
help to the LORD.
[7]When the sons of Israel cried to the LORD
on account of the Mid′ianites, [8]the LORD
sent a prophet to the sons of Israel; and
he said to them, "Thus says the LORD, the
God of Israel: I led you up from Egypt, and
brought you out of the house of bondage;
[9]and I delivered you from the hand of the
Egyptians, and from the hand of all who
oppressed you, and drove them out before
you, and gave you their land; [10]and I said to
you, 'I am the LORD your God; you shall not
pay reverence to the gods of the Am′orites,
in whose land you dwell.' But you have not
given heed to my voice."

11 Now the angel of the LORD came and sat
under the oak at Oph′rah, which belonged
to Jo′ash the Abiez′rite, as his son Gideon
was beating out wheat in the wine press,
to hide it from the Mid′ianites. 12 And the
angel of the LORD appeared to him and
said to him, "The LORD is with you, you
mighty man of valor." 13 And Gideon said to
him, "Please, sir, if the LORD is with us, why
then has all this befallen us? And where are
all his wonderful deeds which our fathers
recounted to us, saying, 'Did not the LORD
bring us up from Egypt?' But now the LORD
has cast us off, and given us into the hand of
Mid′ian." 14 And the LORD turned to him and
said, "Go in this might of yours and deliver
Israel from the hand of Mid′ian; do not I
send you?" 15 And he said to him, "Please,
Lord, how can I deliver Israel? Behold, my
clan is the weakest in Manas′seh, and I am
the least in my family." 16 And the LORD said
to him, "But I will be with you, and you shall
strike the Mid′ianites as one man." 17 And he
said to him, "If now I have found favor with
you, then show me a sign that it is you who
speak with me. 18 Do not depart from here, I
beg you, until I come to you, and bring out
my present, and set it before you." And he
said, "I will stay till you return."
19 So Gideon went into his house and prepared a kid, and unleavened cakes from an
ephah of flour; the meat he put in a basket,
and the broth he put in a pot, and brought
them to him under the oak and presented
them. 20 And the angel of God said to him,
"Take the meat and the unleavened cakes,
and put them on this rock, and pour the
broth over them." And he did so. 21 Then the
angel of the LORD reached out the tip of the
staff that was in his hand, and touched the
meat and the unleavened cakes; and there
sprang up fire from the rock and consumed
the flesh and the unleavened cakes; and the
angel of the LORD vanished from his sight.
22 Then Gideon perceived that he was the
angel of the LORD; and Gideon said, "Alas, O
Lord GOD! For now I have seen the angel of
the LORD face to face." 23 But the LORD said
to him, "Peace be to you; do not fear, you
shall not die." 24 Then Gideon built an altar
there to the LORD, and called it, The LORD is
peace. To this day it still stands at Oph′rah,
which belongs to the Abiez′rites.
25 That night the LORD said to him, "Take
your father's bull, the second bull seven
years old, and pull down the altar of Ba′al
which your father has, and cut down the
Ashe′rah that is beside it; 26 and build an
altar to the LORD your God on the top of
the stronghold here, with stones laid in due
order; then take the second bull, and offer
it as a burnt offering with the wood of the
Ashe′rah which you shall cut down." 27 So
Gideon took ten men of his servants, and
did as the LORD had told him; but because
he was too afraid of his family and the men
of the town to do it by day, he did it by night.

A Maskil of Ethan the Ezrahite.

PSALM 89 [88]

19 Of old you spoke in a vision
to your faithful one, and said:
"I have set the crown upon one who
is mighty,
I have exalted one chosen from the people.
20 I have found David, my servant;
with my holy oil I have anointed him;
21 so that my hand shall ever abide with him,
my arm also shall strengthen him.
22 The enemy shall not outwit him,
the wicked shall not humble him.
23 I will crush his foes before him
and strike down those who hate him.
24 My faithfulness and my mercy shall be
with him,
and in my name shall his horn be exalted.
25 I will set his hand on the sea
and his right hand on the rivers.
26 He shall cry to me, 'You are my Father,
my God, and the Rock of my salvation.'
27 And I will make him the first-born,
the highest of the kings of the earth.
28 My merciful love I will keep for him for ever,
and my covenant will stand firm for him.
29 I will establish his line for ever
and his throne as the days of the heavens.

30If his children forsake my law
and do not walk according to
my ordinances,
31if they violate my statutes
and do not keep my commandments,
32then I will punish their transgression
with the rod
and their iniquity with scourges;
33but I will not remove from him my
merciful love,
or be false to my faithfulness.
34I will not violate my covenant,
or alter the word that went forth from
my lips.
35Once for all I have sworn by my holiness;
I will not lie to David.
36His line shall endure for ever,
his throne as long as the sun before me.
37Like the moon it shall be established
for ever;
it shall stand firm while the skies endure."
Selah

LUKE 10

**After this the Lord appointed
seventy others, and sent them
on ahead of him, two by two,
into every town and place where he
himself was about to come. 2And he**
said to them, "The harvest is plentiful, but the
laborers are few; pray therefore the Lord
of the harvest to send out laborers into
his harvest. 3Go your way; behold, I send
you out as lambs in the midst of wolves.
4Carry no purse, no bag, no sandals; and
salute no one on the road. 5Whatever
house you enter, first say, 'Peace be to this
house!' 6And if a son of peace is there,
your peace shall rest upon him; but if not,
it shall return to you. 7And remain in the
same house, eating and drinking what
they provide, for the laborer deserves his
wages; do not go from house to house.
8Whenever you enter a town and they
receive you, eat what is set before you;
9heal the sick in it and say to them, 'The
kingdom of God has come near to you.'
10But whenever you enter a town and they
do not receive you, go into its streets and
say, 11'Even the dust of your town that
clings to our feet, we wipe off against you;
nevertheless know this, that the kingdom
of God has come near.' 12I tell you, it shall
be more tolerable on that day for Sodom
than for that town.

13"Woe to you, Chora′zin! woe to you,
Beth-sa′ida! for if the mighty works done
in you had been done in Tyre and Si′don,
they would have repented long ago, sitting
in sackcloth and ashes. 14But it shall be
more tolerable in the judgment for Tyre and
Si′don than for you. 15And you, Caper′na-
um, will you be exalted to heaven? You shall
be brought down to Hades.

16"He who hears you hears me, and he who
rejects you rejects me, and he who rejects
me rejects him who sent me."

17The seventy returned with joy, saying,
"Lord, even the demons are subject
to us in your name!" 18And he said to
them, "I saw Satan fall like lightning
from heaven. 19Behold, I have given
you authority to tread upon serpents
and scorpions, and over all the power
of the enemy; and nothing shall hurt
you. 20Nevertheless do not rejoice in
this, that the spirits are subject to you;
but rejoice that your names are written
in heaven."

21In that same hour he rejoiced in the
Holy Spirit and said, "I thank you, Father,
Lord of heaven and earth, that you have
hidden these things from the wise and
understanding and revealed them to
infants; yes, Father, for such was your
gracious will. 22All things have been
delivered to me by my Father; and no one
knows who the Son is except the Father,
or who the Father is except the Son and
any one to whom the Son chooses to
reveal him."

23Then turning to the disciples he said
privately, "Blessed are the eyes which see
what you see! 24For I tell you that many
prophets and kings desired to see what you
see, and did not see it, and to hear what you
hear, and did not hear it."

REFLECTION

The cyclical sin-punishment-repentance-deliverance-faithfulness pattern in the Book of Judges does a great job depicting the temporary nature of earthly rest. Just as soon as we have fixed one problem, another one springs up. As soon as we have conquered one bad habit, another one overtakes us. The ebb and flow of Israel's obedience in Judges should give us pause, but more than that it ought to enkindle a desire for a greater destiny, a better, more permanent future. Psalm 89 points to this greater future when it goes on at length lauding "your faithful one . . . David, my servant" (Ps 89:19–20). David and his royal descendants are pictured as superheroes who defeat all their enemies, conquer the whole world, and enjoy divine favor. David points forward to a future permanent solution to the problems we face. Jesus himself is the "Davidic solution" to the impermanent conquest over evil that God's people experienced. He points his own disciples away from temporary victory and toward eternal triumph: "Do not rejoice in this, that the spirits are subject to you; but rejoice that your names are written in heaven" (Lk 10:20). How is God inviting your heart to rest in the permanent victory of Christ in the midst of the storms of earthly life?

April 14

JUDGES 6

**28When the men of the town
rose early in the morning, behold, the altar of Ba′al was broken down,
and the Ashe′rah beside it was cut down,**
and the second bull was offered upon the
altar which had been built. 29And they
said to one another, "Who has done this
thing?" And after they had made search
and inquired, they said, "Gideon the son
of Jo′ash has done this thing." 30Then the
men of the town said to Jo′ash, "Bring
out your son, that he may die, for he has
pulled down the altar of Ba′al and cut
down the Ashe′rah beside it." 31But Jo′ash
said to all who were arrayed against him,
"Will you contend for Ba′al? Or will you
defend his cause? Whoever contends for
him shall be put to death by morning.
If he is a god, let him contend for himself, because his altar has been pulled
down." 32Therefore on that day he was
called Jerubba′al, that is to say, "Let Ba′al
contend against him," because he pulled
down his altar.
33Then all the Mid′ianites and the Amal′e-
kites and the people of the East came
together, and crossing the Jordan they
encamped in the Valley of Jezre′el. 34But
the Spirit of the LORD took possession of
Gideon; and he sounded the trumpet, and
the Abiez′rites were called out to follow
him. 35And he sent messengers throughout
all Manas′seh; and they too were called out
to follow him. And he sent messengers to
Asher, Zeb′ulun, and Naph′tali; and they
went up to meet them.
36Then Gideon said to God, "If you will
deliver Israel by my hand, as you have said,
37behold, I am laying a fleece of wool on the
threshing floor; if there is dew on the fleece
alone, and it is dry on all the ground, then I
shall know that you will deliver Israel by my
hand, as you have said." 38And it was so. When
he rose early next morning and squeezed the
fleece, he wrung enough dew from the fleece
to fill a bowl with water. 39Then Gideon said
to God, "Let not your anger burn against
me, let me speak but this once; please, let
me make trial only this once with the fleece;
please, let it be dry only on the fleece, and on
all the ground let there be dew." 40And God
did so that night; for it was dry on the fleece
only, and on all the ground there was dew.

7 Then Jerubba′al (that is, Gideon) and all
the people who were with him rose early
and encamped beside the spring of Harod;
and the camp of Mid′ian was north of them,
by the hill of Mo′reh, in the valley.
2The LORD said to Gideon, "The people
with you are too many for me to give the

Mid′ianites into their hand, lest Israel vaunt themselves against me, saying, 'My own hand has delivered me.' [3]Now therefore proclaim in the ears of the people, saying, 'Whoever is fearful and trembling, let him return home.' " And Gideon tested them; twenty-two thousand returned, and ten thousand remained.

[4]And the LORD said to Gideon, "The people are still too many; take them down to the water and I will test them for you there; and he of whom I say to you, 'This man shall go with you,' shall go with you; and any of whom I say to you, 'This man shall not go with you,' shall not go." [5]So he brought the people down to the water; and the LORD said to Gideon, "Every one that laps the water with his tongue, as a dog laps, you shall set by himself; likewise every one that kneels down to drink." [6]And the number of those that lapped, putting their hands to their mouths, was three hundred men; but all the rest of the people knelt down to drink water. [7]And the LORD said to Gideon, "With the three hundred men that lapped I will deliver you and give the Mid′ianites into your hand; and let all the others go every man to his home." [8]So he took the jars of the people from their hands, and their trumpets; and he sent all the rest of Israel every man to his tent, but retained the three hundred men; and the camp of Mid′ian was below him in the valley.

[9]That same night the LORD said to him, "Arise, go down against the camp; for I have given it into your hand. [10]But if you fear to go down, go down to the camp with Pu′rah your servant; [11]and you shall hear what they say, and afterward your hands shall be strengthened to go down against the camp." Then he went down with Pu′rah his servant to the outposts of the armed men that were in the camp. [12]And the Mid′ianites and the Amal′ekites and all the people of the East lay along the valley like locusts for multitude; and their camels were without number, as the sand which is upon the seashore for multitude. [13]When Gideon came, behold, a man was telling a dream to his comrade; and he said, "Behold, I dreamed a dream; and a cake of barley bread tumbled into the camp of Mid′ian, and came to the tent, and struck it so that it fell, and turned it upside down, so that the tent lay flat." [14]And his comrade answered, "This is no other than the sword of Gideon the son of Jo′ash, a man of Israel; into his hand God has given Mid′ian and all the host."

[15]When Gideon heard the telling of the dream and its interpretation, he worshiped; and he returned to the camp of Israel, and said, "Arise; for the LORD has given the host of Mid′ian into your hand." [16]And he divided the three hundred men into three companies, and put trumpets into the hands of all of them and empty jars, with torches inside the jars. [17]And he said to them, "Look at me, and do likewise; when I come to the outskirts of the camp, do as I do. [18]When I blow the trumpet, I and all who are with me, then blow the trumpets also on every side of all the camp, and shout, 'For the LORD and for Gideon.' "

[19]So Gideon and the hundred men who were with him came to the outskirts of the camp at the beginning of the middle watch, when they had just set the watch; and they blew the trumpets and smashed the jars that were in their hands. [20]And the three companies blew the trumpets and broke the jars, holding in their left hands the torches, and in their right hands the trumpets to blow; and they cried, "A sword for the LORD and for Gideon!" [21]They stood every man in his place round about the camp, and all the army ran; they cried out and fled. [22]When they blew the three hundred trumpets, the LORD set every man's sword against his fellow and against all the army; and the army fled as far as Beth-shit′tah toward Zer′erah, as far as the border of Abel-meho′lah, by Tabbath. [23]And the men of Israel were called out from Naph′tali and from Asher and from all Manas′seh, and they pursued after Mid′ian.

[24]And Gideon sent messengers throughout all the hill country of E′phraim, saying, "Come down against the Mid′ianites and seize the waters against them, as far as Beth-bar′ah, and also the Jordan." So all the men of Ephraim were called out, and they seized the waters as far as Beth-barah, and also the

Jordan. [25]And they took the two princes of Mid′ian, Or′eb and Ze′eb; they killed Oreb at the rock of Oreb, and Zeeb they killed at the wine press of Zeeb, as they pursued Midian; and they brought the heads of Oreb and Zeeb to Gideon beyond the Jordan.

A Maskil of Ethan the Ezrahite.

PSALM 89 [88]

[38]But now you have cast off and rejected,
you are full of wrath against your
anointed.
[39]You have renounced the covenant with
your servant;
you have defiled his crown in the dust.
[40]You have breached all his walls;
you have laid his strongholds in ruins.
[41]All that pass by despoil him;
he has become the scorn of his neighbors.
[42]You have exalted the right hand of
his foes;
you have made all his enemies rejoice.
[43]Yes, you have turned back the edge of
his sword,
and you have not made him stand
in battle.
[44]You have removed the scepter from
his hand,
and cast his throne to the ground.
[45]You have cut short the days of his youth;
you have covered him with shame. *Selah*

[46]How long, O LORD? Will you hide
yourself for ever?
How long will your wrath burn like fire?
[47]Remember, O Lord, what the measure of
life is,
for what vanity you have created all the
sons of men!
[48]What man can live and never see death?
Who can deliver his soul from the power
of Sheol? *Selah*

[49]Lord, where is your steadfast love of old,
which by your faithfulness you swore
to David?
[50]Remember, O Lord, how your servant
is scorned;
how I bear in my bosom the insults of
the peoples,
[51]with which your enemies taunt, O LORD,
with which they mock the footsteps of
your anointed.

[52]Blessed be the LORD for ever! Amen and
Amen.

LUKE 10

**[25]And behold, a lawyer stood up
to put him to the test, saying,
"Teacher, what shall I do to inherit eternal life?" [26]He said to him, "What is written in the law? What do you read there?"**
[27]And he answered, "You shall love the Lord
your God with all your heart, and with all
your soul, and with all your strength, and
with all your mind; and your neighbor as
yourself." [28]And he said to him, "You have
answered right; do this, and you will live."
[29]But he, desiring to justify himself, said
to Jesus, "And who is my neighbor?" [30]Jesus
replied, "A man was going down from
Jerusalem to Jericho, and he fell among
robbers, who stripped him and beat him, and
departed, leaving him half dead. [31]Now by
chance a priest was going down that road; and
when he saw him he passed by on the other
side. [32]So likewise a Levite, when he came
to the place and saw him, passed by on the
other side. [33]But a Samaritan, as he journeyed,
came to where he was; and when he saw him,
he had compassion, [34]and went to him and
bound up his wounds, pouring on oil and
wine; then he set him on his own beast and
brought him to an inn, and took care of him.
[35]And the next day he took out two denarii
and gave them to the innkeeper, saying, 'Take
care of him; and whatever more you spend, I
will repay you when I come back.' [36]Which of
these three, do you think, proved neighbor to
the man who fell among the robbers?" [37]He
said, "The one who showed mercy on him."
And Jesus said to him, "Go and do likewise."

38Now as they went on their way, he entered a village; and a woman named Martha received him into her house. 39And she had a sister called Mary, who sat at the Lord's feet and listened to his teaching. 40But Martha was distracted with much serving; and she went to him and said, "Lord, do you not care that my sister has left me to serve alone? Tell her then to help me." 41But the Lord answered her, "Martha, Martha, you are anxious and troubled about many things; 42one thing is needful. Mary has chosen the good portion, which shall not be taken away from her."

11 He was praying in a certain place, and when he ceased, one of his disciples said to him, "Lord, teach us to pray, as John taught his disciples." 2And he said to them, "When you pray, say:

"Father, hallowed be your name. Your kingdom come. 3Give us each day our daily bread; 4and forgive us our sins, for we ourselves forgive every one who is indebted to us; and lead us not into temptation."

5And he said to them, "Which of you who has a friend will go to him at midnight and say to him, 'Friend, lend me three loaves; 6for a friend of mine has arrived on a journey, and I have nothing to set before him'; 7and he will answer from within, 'Do not bother me; the door is now shut, and my children are with me in bed; I cannot get up and give you anything'? 8I tell you, though he will not get up and give him anything because he is his friend, yet because of his importunity he will rise and give him whatever he needs. 9And I tell you, Ask, and it will be given you; seek, and you will find; knock, and it will be opened to you. 10For every one who asks receives, and he who seeks finds, and to him who knocks it will be opened. 11What father among you, if his son asks for a fish, will instead of a fish give him a serpent; 12or if he asks for an egg, will give him a scorpion? 13If you then, who are evil, know how to give good gifts to your children, how much more will the heavenly Father give the Holy Spirit to those who ask him!"

REFLECTION

When we see how great the needs of the world are, it often makes each one of us feel small. In such situations it is tempting to fall into Gideon's way of thinking: "Lord, how can I deliver Israel? Behold, my clan is the weakest in Manasseh, and I am the least in my family" (Jgs 6:15). Despite his social unimportance, Gideon was called by the Lord to accomplish great things. Often, the "great things" God calls us to do are so small, so seemingly unimportant, that it would be easy to miss them all together. When an argumentative lawyer confronts Jesus, the Lord tells him a story about a man who helped someone on the side of the road. When Martha complains about her workload, Jesus points out that "one thing is needful," that is, to sit at his feet (Lk 10:42). Fidelity often consists in doing simple things like helping a person in need, listening to Jesus, or asking God for gifts. God calls us to do great things, simple things, hidden things. How can you rise to the challenge?

April 15

JUDGES 8

And the men of E′phraim said to him, "What is this that you have done to us, not to call us when you went to fight with Mid′ian?" And they upbraided him violently. 2And he said to them, "What have I done now in comparison with you? Is not the gleaning of the grapes of E′phraim better than the vintage of Abie′zer? 3God has given into your hands the princes of Mid′ian, Or′eb and Ze′eb; what have I been able to do in comparison with you?" Then their anger against him was abated, when he had said this.

[4]And Gideon came to the Jordan and passed over, he and the three hundred men who were with him, faint yet pursuing. [5]So he said to the men of Succoth, "Please, give loaves of bread to the people who follow me; for they are faint, and I am pursuing after Zebah and Zalmun′na, the kings of Mid′ian." [6]And the officials of Succoth said, "Are Zebah and Zalmun′na already in your hand, that we should give bread to your army?" [7]And Gideon said, "Well then, when the LORD has given Zebah and Zalmun′na into my hand, I will flail your flesh with the thorns of the wilderness and with briers." [8]And from there he went up to Penu′el, and spoke to them in the same way; and the men of Penuel answered him as the men of Succoth had answered. [9]And he said to the men of Penu′el, "When I come again in peace, I will break down this tower."

[10]Now Zebah and Zalmun′na were in Karkor with their army, about fifteen thousand men, all who were left of all the army of the people of the East; for there had fallen a hundred and twenty thousand men who drew the sword. [11]And Gideon went up by the caravan route east of No′bah and Jog′behah, and attacked the army; for the army was off its guard. [12]And Zebah and Zalmun′na fled; and he pursued them and took the two kings of Mid′ian, Zebah and Zalmunna, and he threw all the army into a panic.

[13]Then Gideon the son of Jo′ash returned from the battle by the ascent of He′res. [14]And he caught a young man of Succoth, and questioned him; and he wrote down for him the officials and elders of Succoth, seventy-seven men. [15]And he came to the men of Succoth, and said, "Behold Zebah and Zalmun′na, about whom you taunted me, saying, 'Are Zebah and Zalmunna already in your hand, that we should give bread to your men who are faint?' " [16]And he took the elders of the city and he took thorns of the wilderness and briers and with them taught the men of Succoth. [17]And he broke down the tower of Penu′el, and slew the men of the city.

[18]Then he said to Zebah and Zalmun′na, "Where are the men whom you slew at Ta′bor?" They answered, "As you are, so were they, every one of them; they resembled the sons of a king." [19]And he said, "They were my brothers, the sons of my mother; as the LORD lives, if you had saved them alive, I would not slay you." [20]And he said to Je′ther his first-born, "Rise, and slay them." But the youth did not draw his sword; for he was afraid, because he was still a youth. [21]Then Zebah and Zalmun′na said, "Rise yourself, and fall upon us; for as the man is, so is his strength." And Gideon arose and slew Zebah and Zalmunna; and he took the crescents that were on the necks of their camels.

[22]Then the men of Israel said to Gideon, "Rule over us, you and your son and your grandson also; for you have delivered us out of the hand of Mid′ian." [23]Gideon said to them, "I will not rule over you, and my son will not rule over you; the LORD will rule over you." [24]And Gideon said to them, "Let me make a request of you; give me every man of you the earrings of his spoil." (For they had golden earrings, because they were Ish′maelites.) [25]And they answered, "We will willingly give them." And they spread a garment, and every man cast in it the earrings of his spoil. [26]And the weight of the golden earrings that he requested was one thousand seven hundred shekels of gold; besides the crescents and the pendants and the purple garments worn by the kings of Mid′ian, and besides the collars that were about the necks of their camels. [27]And Gideon made an ephod of it and put it in his city, in Oph′rah; and all Israel played the harlot after it there, and it became a snare to Gideon and to his family. [28]So Mid′ian was subdued before the sons of Israel, and they lifted up their heads no more. And the land had rest forty years in the days of Gideon.

[29]Jerubba′al the son of Jo′ash went and dwelt in his own house. [30]Now Gideon had seventy sons, his own offspring, for he had many wives. [31]And his concubine who was in She′chem also bore him a son, and he called his name Abim′elech. [32]And Gideon the son of Jo′ash died in a good old age, and was buried in the tomb of Jo′ash his father, at Oph′rah of the Abiez′rites.

[33]As soon as Gideon died, the sons of Israel turned again and played the harlot after the Ba′als, and made Ba′al-be′rith their god. [34]And the sons of Israel did not remember

the LORD their God, who had rescued them
from the hand of all their enemies on every
side; [35]and they did not show kindness to
the family of Jerubba′al (that is, Gideon)
in return for all the good that he had done
to Israel.

9 Now Abim′elech the son of Jerubba′al
went to She′chem to his mother's kinsmen and said to them and to the whole clan
of his mother's family, [2]"Say in the ears of all
the citizens of She′chem, 'Which is better for
you, that all seventy of the sons of Jerubba′al
rule over you, or that one rule over you?'
Remember also that I am your bone and your
flesh." [3]And his mother's kinsmen spoke all
these words on his behalf in the ears of all the
men of She′chem; and their hearts inclined to
follow Abim′elech, for they said, "He is our
brother." [4]And they gave him seventy pieces
of silver out of the house of Ba′al-be′rith
with which Abim′elech hired worthless and
reckless fellows, who followed him. [5]And
he went to his father's house at Oph′rah,
and slew his brothers the sons of Jerubba′al,
seventy men, upon one stone; but Jo′tham
the youngest son of Jerubbaal was left, for he
hid himself. [6]And all the citizens of She′chem
came together, and all Beth-mil′lo, and they
went and made Abim′elech king, by the oak
of the pillar at Shechem.

[7]When it was told to Jo′tham, he went and
stood on the top of Mount Ger′izim, and cried
aloud and said to them, "Listen to me, you men
of She′chem, that God may listen to you. [8]The
trees once went forth to anoint a king over
them; and they said to the olive tree, 'Reign
over us.' [9]But the olive tree said to them, 'Shall
I leave my fatness, by which gods and men are
honored, and go to sway over the trees?' [10]And
the trees said to the fig tree, 'Come you, and
reign over us.' [11]But the fig tree said to them,
'Shall I leave my sweetness and my good fruit,
and go to sway over the trees?' [12]And the trees
said to the vine, 'Come you, and reign over us.'
[13]But the vine said to them, 'Shall I leave my
wine which cheers gods and men, and go to
sway over the trees?' [14]Then all the trees said
to the bramble, 'Come you, and reign over us.'
[15]And the bramble said to the trees, 'If in good
faith you are anointing me king over you, then
come and take refuge in my shade; but if not,
let fire come out of the bramble and devour the
cedars of Lebanon.'

[16]"Now therefore, if you acted in good faith
and honor when you made Abim′elech king,
and if you have dealt well with Jerubba′al and
his house, and have done to him as his deeds
deserved—[17]for my father fought for you, and
risked his life, and rescued you from the hand
of Mid′ian; [18]and you have risen up against
my father's house this day, and have slain his
sons, seventy men on one stone, and have
made Abim′elech, the son of his maidservant,
king over the citizens of She′chem, because he
is your kinsman—[19]if you then have acted in
good faith and honor with Jerubba′al and with
his house this day, then rejoice in Abim′elech,
and let him also rejoice in you; [20]but if not, let
fire come out from Abim′elech, and devour the
citizens of She′chem, and Beth-mil′lo; and let
fire come out from the citizens of Shechem,
and from Beth-millo, and devour Abimelech."
[21]And Jo′tham ran away and fled, and went to
Be′er and dwelt there, for fear of Abim′elech
his brother.

A Prayer of Moses, the man of God.

PSALM 90 [89]

LORD, you have been our dwelling place
in all generations.
[2]Before the mountains were brought forth,
or ever you had formed the earth and
the world,
from everlasting to everlasting you
are God.

[3]You turn man back to the dust,
and say, "Turn back, O children of men!"
[4]For a thousand years in your sight
are but as yesterday when it is past,
or as a watch in the night.

[5]You sweep men away; they are like
a dream,
like grass which is renewed in
the morning:

[6]in the morning it flourishes and is renewed;
in the evening it fades and withers.
[7]For we are consumed by your anger;
by your wrath we are overwhelmed.
[8]You have set our iniquities before you,
our secret sins in the light of your
countenance.

[9]For all our days pass away under
your wrath,
our years come to an end like a sigh.
[10]The years of our life are threescore and ten,
or even by reason of strength fourscore;
yet their span is but toil and trouble;
they are soon gone, and we fly away.

[11]Who considers the power of your anger,
and your wrath according to the fear of you?
[12]So teach us to number our days
that we may get a heart of wisdom.

[13]Return, O LORD! How long?
Have pity on your servants!
[14]Satisfy us in the morning with your mercy,
that we may rejoice and be glad all
our days.
[15]Make us glad as many days as you have
afflicted us,
and as many years as we have seen evil.
[16]Let your work be manifest to your servants,
and your glorious power to their children.
[17]Let the favor of the Lord our God be
upon us,
and establish the work of our hands
upon us,
yes, establish the work of our hands.

LUKE 11

**[14]Now he was casting out a
demon that was mute; when
the demon had gone out, the mute
man spoke, and the people marveled.**
[15]But some of them said, "He casts out
demons by Be-el′zebul, the prince of demons"; [16]while others, to test him, sought from
him a sign from heaven. [17]But he, knowing
their thoughts, said to them, "Every kingdom
divided against itself is laid waste, and house
falls upon house. [18]And if Satan also is divided
against himself, how will his kingdom stand?
For you say that I cast out demons by Be-el′-
zebul. [19]And if I cast out demons by Be-el′-
zebul, by whom do your sons cast them out?
Therefore they shall be your judges. [20]But if it
is by the finger of God that I cast out demons,
then the kingdom of God has come upon you.
[21]When a strong man, fully armed, guards his
own palace, his goods are in peace; [22]but when
one stronger than he assails him and overcomes him, he takes away his armor in which
he trusted, and divides his spoil. [23]He who is
not with me is against me, and he who does not
gather with me scatters.
[24]"When the unclean spirit has gone out
of a man, he passes through waterless places
seeking rest; and finding none he says, 'I
will return to my house from which I came.'
[25]And when he comes he finds it swept and
put in order. [26]Then he goes and brings
seven other spirits more evil than himself,
and they enter and dwell there; and the
last state of that man becomes worse than
the first."
[27]As he said this, a woman in the crowd
raised her voice and said to him, "Blessed is
the womb that bore you, and the breasts that
you sucked!" [28]But he said, "Blessed rather are
those who hear the word of God and keep it!"
[29]When the crowds were increasing, he began
to say, "This generation is an evil generation;
it seeks a sign, but no sign shall be given to it
except the sign of Jonah. [30]For as Jonah became
a sign to the men of Nin′eveh, so will the Son
of man be to this generation. [31]The queen of
the South will arise at the judgment with the
men of this generation and condemn them; for
she came from the ends of the earth to hear the
wisdom of Solomon, and behold, something
greater than Solomon is here. [32]The men of
Nin′eveh will arise at the judgment with this
generation and condemn it; for they repented
at the preaching of Jonah, and behold,
something greater than Jonah is here.
[33]"No one after lighting a lamp puts it in a
cellar or under a bushel, but on a stand, that
those who enter may see the light. [34]Your eye
is the lamp of your body; when your eye is

sound, your whole body is full of light; but
when it is not sound, your body is full of
darkness. 35Therefore be careful lest the light
in you be darkness. 36If then your whole body
is full of light, having no part dark, it will be
wholly bright, as when a lamp with its rays
gives you light."

> **REFLECTION**
>
> Fear is a great motivator. In fact, the whole insurance industry is driven by fear—fear of fire, fear of car crashes, even fear of death. While it can be a powerful motivator, fear can often get in the way. In Judges 7, we saw how the Lord dismissed the fearful from Gideon's army. Gideon is left with a pitiable army of 300 water-lapping, nearly faint men, yet shockingly defeats Midian with only torches and trumpets. In Judges 8, Gideon's ragtag band continues to pursue their foes, winning battle after battle. With these miraculous victories, the Lord reminds Israel (and us) that there is nothing to fear when we trust in him. Fear of God is a good start—the beginning of wisdom—but it must give way to something greater, to a relationship of friendship and love. Psalm 90 meditates on the wrath of God and the fleeting nature of human life, but points beyond: "Satisfy us in the morning with your mercy, that we may rejoice and be glad all our days" (Ps 90:14). The Lord longs to be our "dwelling place in all generations" (v. 1), where we can dwell secure, free from fear. Are you driven by fear or by fear-dispelling faith?

April 16

JUDGES 9

**22Abim'elech ruled over Israel
three years. 23And God sent an
evil spirit between Abim'elech and
the men of She'chem; and the men of**
Shechem dealt treacherously with Abim'elech; 24that the violence done to the seventy
sons of Jerubba'al might come and their
blood be laid upon Abim'elech their brother, who slew them, and upon the men of
She'chem, who strengthened his hands
to slay his brothers. 25And the men of
She'chem put men in ambush against him
on the mountain tops, and they robbed all
who passed by them along that way; and it
was told Abim'elech.
26And Ga'al the son of E'bed moved into
She'chem with his kinsmen; and the men of
Shechem put confidence in him. 27And they
went out into the field, and gathered the
grapes from their vineyards and trod them,
and held festival, and went into the house
of their god, and ate and drank and reviled
Abim'elech. 28And Ga'al the son of E'bed
said, "Who is Abim'elech, and who are we
of She'chem, that we should serve him?
Did not the son of Jerubba'al and Ze'bul his
officer serve the men of Ha'mor the father
of Shechem? Why then should we serve
him? 29Would that this people were under
my hand! then I would remove Abim'elech.
I would say to Abimelech, 'Increase your
army, and come out.'"
30When Ze'bul the ruler of the city heard
the words of Ga'al the son of E'bed, his anger
was kindled. 31And he sent messengers to
Abim'elech at Aru'mah, saying, "Behold,
Ga'al the son of E'bed and his kinsmen have
come to She'chem, and they are stirring up
the city against you. 32Now therefore, go by
night, you and the men that are with you,
and lie in wait in the fields. 33Then in the
morning, as soon as the sun is up, rise early
and rush upon the city; and when he and
the men that are with him come out against
you, you may do to them as occasion offers."
34And Abim'elech and all the men that
were with him rose up by night, and laid
wait against She'chem in four companies.
35And Ga'al the son of E'bed went out and
stood in the entrance of the gate of the city;
and Abim'elech and the men that were with
him rose from the ambush. 36And when
Ga'al saw the men, he said to Ze'bul, "Look,
men are coming down from the mountain
tops!" And Zebul said to him, "You see the
shadow of the mountains as if they were

men." 37Ga´al spoke again and said, "Look, men are coming down from the center of the land, and one company is coming from the direction of the Diviners' Oak." 38Then Ze´bul said to him, "Where is your mouth now, you who said, 'Who is Abim´elech, that we should serve him?' Are not these the men whom you despised? Go out now and fight with them." 39And Ga´al went out at the head of the men of She´chem, and fought with Abim´elech. 40And Abim´elech chased him, and he fled before him; and many fell wounded, up to the entrance of the gate. 41And Abim´elech dwelt at Aru´mah; and Ze´bul drove out Ga´al and his kinsmen, so that they could not live on at She´chem.

42On the following day the men went out into the fields. And Abim´elech was told. 43He took his men and divided them into three companies, and laid wait in the fields; and he looked and saw the men coming out of the city, and he rose against them and slew them. 44Abim´elech and the company that was with him rushed forward and stood at the entrance of the gate of the city, while the two companies rushed upon all who were in the fields and slew them. 45And Abim´elech fought against the city all that day; he took the city, and killed the people that were in it; and he razed the city and sowed it with salt.

46When all the people of the Tower of She´chem heard of it, they entered the stronghold of the house of El-be´rith. 47Abim´elech was told that all the people of the Tower of She´chem were gathered together. 48And Abim´elech went up to Mount Zalmon, he and all the men that were with him; and Abimelech took an axe in his hand, and cut down a bundle of brushwood, and took it up and laid it on his shoulder. And he said to the men that were with him, "What you have seen me do, make haste to do, as I have done." 49So every one of the people cut down his bundle and following Abim´elech put it against the stronghold, and they set the stronghold on fire over them, so that all the people of the Tower of She´chem also died, about a thousand men and women.

50Then Abim´elech went to The´bez, and encamped against Thebez, and took it. 51But there was a strong tower within the city, and all the people of the city fled to it, all the men and women, and shut themselves in; and they went to the roof of the tower. 52And Abim´elech came to the tower, and fought against it, and drew near to the door of the tower to burn it with fire. 53And a certain woman threw an upper millstone upon Abim´elech's head, and crushed his skull. 54Then he called hastily to the young man his armor-bearer, and said to him, "Draw your sword and kill me, lest men say of me, 'A woman killed him.'" And his young man thrust him through, and he died. 55And when the men of Israel saw that Abim´elech was dead, they departed every man to his home. 56Thus God repaid the crime of Abim´elech, which he committed against his father in killing his seventy brothers; 57and God also made all the wickedness of the men of She´chem fall back upon their heads, and upon them came the curse of Jo´tham the son of Jerubba´al.

10 After Abim´elech there arose to deliver Israel Tola the son of Puah, son of Dodo, a man of Is´sachar; and he lived at Sha´mir in the hill country of E´phraim. 2And he judged Israel twenty-three years. Then he died, and was buried at Sha´mir.

3After him arose Ja´ir the Gileadite, who judged Israel twenty-two years. 4And he had thirty sons who rode on thirty donkeys; and they had thirty cities, called Hav´voth-ja´ir to this day, which are in the land of Gilead. 5And Ja´ir died, and was buried in Kamon.

6And the sons of Israel again did what was evil in the sight of the LORD, and served the Ba´als and the Ash´taroth, the gods of Syria, the gods of Sidon, the gods of Moab, the gods of the Am´monites, and the gods of the Philis´tines; and they forsook the LORD, and did not serve him. 7And the anger of the LORD was kindled against Israel, and he sold them into the hand of the Philis´tines and into the hand of the Am´monites, 8and they crushed and oppressed the children of Israel that year. For eighteen years they oppressed all the sons of Israel that were beyond the Jordan in the land of the Am′orites, which is in Gilead. 9And the Am′monites crossed the Jordan to fight also against Judah and against Benjamin and against the house of E′phraim; so that Israel was sorely distressed.

10And the sons of Israel cried to the LORD, saying, "We have sinned against you, because we have forsaken our God and have served the Ba′als." 11And the LORD said to the sons of Israel, "Did I not deliver you from the Egyptians and from the Am′orites, from the Am′monites and from the Philis′tines? 12The Sido′nians also, and the Amal′ekites, and the Ma′onites, oppressed you; and you cried to me, and I delivered you out of their hand. 13Yet you have forsaken me and served other gods; therefore I will deliver you no more. 14Go and cry to the gods whom you have chosen; let them deliver you in the time of your distress." 15And the sons of Israel said to the LORD, "We have sinned; do to us whatever seems good to you; only deliver us, we beg you, this day." 16So they put away the foreign gods from among them and served the LORD; and he became indignant over the misery of Israel.

17Then the Am′monites were called to arms, and they encamped in Gilead; and the sons of Israel came together, and they encamped at Mizpah. 18And the people, the leaders of Gilead, said one to another, "Who is the man that will begin to fight against the Am′monites? He shall be head over all the inhabitants of Gilead."

11 Now Jephthah the Gileadite was a mighty warrior, but he was the son of a harlot. Gilead was the father of Jephthah. 2And Gilead's wife also bore him sons; and when his wife's sons grew up, they thrust Jephthah out, and said to him, "You shall not inherit in our father's house; for you are the son of another woman." 3Then Jephthah fled from his brothers, and dwelt in the land of Tob; and worthless fellows collected round Jephthah, and went raiding with him.

4After a time the Am′monites made war against Israel. 5And when the Am′monites made war against Israel, the elders of Gilead went to bring Jephthah from the land of Tob; 6and they said to Jephthah, "Come and be our leader, that we may fight with the Am′monites." 7But Jephthah said to the elders of Gilead, "Did you not hate me, and drive me out of my father's house? Why have you come to me now when you are in trouble?" 8And the elders of Gilead said to Jephthah, "That is why we have turned to you now, that you may go with us and fight with the Am′monites, and be our head over all the inhabitants of Gilead." 9Jephthah said to the elders of Gilead, "If you bring me home again to fight with the Am′monites, and the LORD gives them over to me, I will be your head." 10And the elders of Gilead said to Jephthah, "The LORD will be witness between us; we will surely do as you say." 11So Jephthah went with the elders of Gilead, and the people made him head and leader over them; and Jephthah spoke all his words before the LORD at Mizpah.

PSALM 91 [90]

He who dwells in the shelter of the
Most High,
who abides in the shadow of the Almighty,
2will say to the LORD, "My refuge and
my fortress;
my God, in whom I trust."
3For he will deliver you from the snare of
the fowler
and from the deadly pestilence;
4he will cover you with his pinions,
and under his wings you will find refuge;
his faithfulness is a shield and buckler.
5You will not fear the terror of the night,
nor the arrow that flies by day,
6nor the pestilence that stalks in darkness,
nor the destruction that wastes at
noonday.

7A thousand may fall at your side,
ten thousand at your right hand;
but it will not come near you.
8You will only look with your eyes
and see the recompense of the wicked.

9 Because you have made the LORD
your refuge,
the Most High your habitation,
10 no evil shall befall you,
no scourge come near your tent.

11 For he will give his angels charge of you
to guard you in all your ways.
12 On their hands they will bear you up,
lest you dash your foot against a stone.
13 You will tread on the lion and the adder,
the young lion and the serpent you will
trample under foot.

14 Because he clings to me in love, I will
deliver him;
I will protect him, because he knows
my name.
15 When he calls to me, I will answer him;
I will be with him in trouble,
I will rescue him and honor him.
16 With long life I will satisfy him,
and show him my salvation.

LUKE 11

37 While he was speaking, a Phar-
isee asked him to dine with him;
so he went in and sat at table. 38 The
Pharisee was astonished to see that
he did not first wash before dinner. 39 And
the Lord said to him, "Now you Pharisees
cleanse the outside of the cup and of the
dish, but inside you are full of extortion and
wickedness. 40 You fools! Did not he who
made the outside make the inside also? 41 But
give for alms those things which are within;
and behold, everything is clean for you.
42 "But woe to you Pharisees! for you tithe
mint and rue and every herb, and neglect
justice and the love of God; these you ought
to have done, without neglecting the others.
43 Woe to you Pharisees! for you love the best
seat in the synagogues and salutations in the
market places. 44 Woe to you! for you are like
graves which are not seen, and men walk
over them without knowing it."
45 One of the lawyers answered him, "Teacher, in saying this you reproach us also." 46 And
he said, "Woe to you lawyers also! for you
load men with burdens hard to bear, and
you yourselves do not touch the burdens
with one of your fingers. 47 Woe to you! for
you build the tombs of the prophets whom
your fathers killed. 48 So you are witnesses
and consent to the deeds of your fathers; for
they killed them, and you build their tombs.
49 Therefore also the Wisdom of God said, 'I
will send them prophets and apostles, some
of whom they will kill and persecute,' 50 that
the blood of all the prophets, shed from the
foundation of the world, may be required of
this generation, 51 from the blood of Abel to the
blood of Zechari′ah, who perished between
the altar and the sanctuary. Yes, I tell you, it
shall be required of this generation. 52 Woe to
you lawyers! for you have taken away the key
of knowledge; you did not enter yourselves,
and you hindered those who were entering."
53 As he went away from there, the scribes
and the Pharisees began to press him hard,
and to provoke him to speak of many
things, 54 lying in wait for him, to catch him
in something he might say.

REFLECTION

It is always a challenge to keep our interior motivations aligned with our exterior actions. The Israelites demonstrate this problem when they turn to the gods of foreign nations. "The sons of Israel again did what was evil in the sight of the LORD . . . and did not serve him" (Jgs 10:6). The results of their sin are played out in their oppression by the nations of the very gods they had worshipped. Israel's duplicity is mirrored by the Pharisees and lawyers who fail in this area as well. They are obsessed with religious rules, procedures, and practices, but have lost sight of the goal: "justice and the love of God" (Lk 11:42). Jesus uncovers their hidden guilt and charges them to align their inner motivations with their exterior actions. External works without faith lose their meaning, and interior faith without external action is dead (see Jas 2:14–22). We must struggle daily to bring our internal dispositions and our external actions into alignment. What can you do to align your faith and actions?

April 17

JUDGES 11

12Then Jephthah sent messengers to the king of the Am′monites and said, "What have you against me, that you have come to me to fight against my land?" 13And the king of the Am′monites answered the messengers of Jephthah, "Because Israel on coming from Egypt took away my land, from the Arnon to the Jabbok and to the Jordan; now therefore restore it peaceably." 14And Jephthah sent messengers again to the king of the Am′monites 15and said to him, "Thus says Jephthah: Israel did not take away the land of Moab or the land of the Am′monites, 16but when they came up from Egypt, Israel went through the wilderness to the Red Sea and came to Ka′desh. 17Israel then sent messengers to the king of E′dom, saying, 'Let us pass, we beg, through your land'; but the king of Edom would not listen. And they sent also to the king of Moab, but he would not consent. So Israel remained at Ka′desh. 18Then they journeyed through the wilderness, and went around the land of E′dom and the land of Moab, and arrived on the east side of the land of Moab, and camped on the other side of the Arnon; but they did not enter the territory of Moab, for the Arnon was the boundary of Moab. 19Israel then sent messengers to Si′hon king of the Am′orites, king of Heshbon; and Israel said to him, 'Let us pass, we beg, through your land to our country.' 20But Si′hon did not trust Israel to pass through his territory; so Sihon gathered all his people together, and encamped at Ja′haz, and fought with Israel. 21And the LORD, the God of Israel, gave Si′hon and all his people into the hand of Israel, and they defeated them; so Israel took possession of all the land of the Am′orites, who inhabited that country. 22And they took possession of all the territory of the Am′orites from the Arnon to the Jabbok and from the wilderness to the Jordan. 23So then the LORD, the God of Israel, dispossessed the Am′orites from before his people Israel; and are you to take possession of them? 24Will you not possess what Che′mosh your god gives you to possess? And all that the LORD our God has dispossessed before us, we will possess. 25Now are you any better than Balak the son of Zippor, king of Moab? Did he ever strive against Israel, or did he ever go to war with them? 26While Israel dwelt in Heshbon and its villages, and in Aro′er and its villages, and in all the cities that are on the banks of the Arnon, three hundred years, why did you not recover them within that time? 27I therefore have not sinned against you, and you do me wrong by making war on me; the LORD, the Judge, decide this day between the sons of Israel and the people of Ammon." 28But the king of the Am′monites did not heed the message of Jephthah which he sent to him.

29Then the Spirit of the LORD came upon Jephthah, and he passed through Gilead and Manas′seh, and passed on to Mizpah of Gilead, and from Mizpah of Gilead he passed on to the Am′monites. 30And Jephthah made a vow to the LORD, and said, "If you will give the Am′monites into my hand, 31then whoever comes forth from the doors of my house to meet me, when I return victorious from the Am′monites, shall be the LORD's, and I will offer him up for a burnt offering." 32So Jephthah crossed over to the Am′monites to fight against them; and the LORD gave them into his hand. 33And he struck them from Aro′er to the neighborhood of Minnith, twenty cities, and as far as A′bel-ker′amim, with a very great slaughter. So the Am′monites were subdued before the sons of Israel.

34Then Jephthah came to his home at Mizpah; and behold, his daughter came out to meet him with timbrels and with dances; she was his only child; beside her he had neither son nor daughter. 35And when he saw her, he tore his clothes, and said, "Alas, my daughter! you have brought me very low, and you have become the cause of great trouble to me; for I have opened my mouth to the LORD, and I cannot take back my vow." 36 And she said to him, "My father, if you have opened your mouth to the LORD, do to me according to what has gone forth from your mouth, now that the LORD has avenged you on your enemies, on the Am′monites." 37 And she said to her father, "Let this thing be done for me; let me alone two months, that I may go and wander on the mountains, and bewail my virginity, I and my companions." 38 And he said, "Go." And he sent her away for two months; and she departed, she and her companions, and bewailed her virginity upon the mountains. 39 And at the end of two months, she returned to her father, who did with her according to his vow which he had made. She had never known a man. And it became a custom in Israel 40 that the daughters of Israel went year by year to lament the daughter of Jephthah the Gileadite four days in the year.

12 The men of E′phraim were called to arms, and they crossed to Za′phon and said to Jephthah, "Why did you cross over to fight against the Am′monites, and did not call us to go with you? We will burn your house over you with fire." 2 And Jephthah said to them, "I and my people had a great feud with the Am′monites; and when I called you, you did not deliver me from their hand. 3 And when I saw that you would not deliver me, I took my life in my hand, and crossed over against the Am′monites, and the LORD gave them into my hand; why then have you come up to me this day, to fight against me?" 4 Then Jephthah gathered all the men of Gilead and fought with E′phraim; and the men of Gilead struck Ephraim, because they said, "You are fugitives of Ephraim, you Gileadites, in the midst of Ephraim and Manas′seh." 5 And the Gileadites took the fords of the Jordan against the E′phraimites. And when any of the fugitives of E′phraim said, "Let me go over," the men of Gilead said to him, "Are you an Ephraimite?" When he said, "No," 6 they said to him, "Then say Shib′boleth," and he said, "Sib′boleth," for he could not pronounce it right; then they seized him and slew him at the fords of the Jordan. And there fell at that time forty-two thousand of the E′phraimites.

7 Jephthah judged Israel six years. Then Jephthah the Gileadite died, and was buried in his city in Gilead.

8 After him Ibzan of Bethlehem judged Israel. 9 He had thirty sons; and thirty daughters he gave in marriage outside his clan, and thirty daughters he brought in from outside for his sons. And he judged Israel seven years. 10 Then Ibzan died, and was buried at Bethlehem.

11 After him E′lon the Zeb′ulunite judged Israel; and he judged Israel ten years. 12 Then E′lon the Zeb′ulunite died, and was buried at Ai′jalon in the land of Zeb′ulun.

13 After him Abdon the son of Hillel the Pir′athonite judged Israel. 14 He had forty sons and thirty grandsons, who rode on seventy donkeys; and he judged Israel eight years. 15 Then Abdon the son of Hillel the Pir′athonite died, and was buried at Pir′athon in the land of E′phraim, in the hill country of the Amal′ekites.

13 And the sons of Israel again did what was evil in the sight of the LORD; and the LORD gave them into the hand of the Philis′tines for forty years.

2 And there was a certain man of Zorah, of the tribe of the Da′nites, whose name was Mano′ah; and his wife was barren and had no children. 3 And the angel of the LORD appeared to the woman and said to her, "Behold, you are barren and have no children; but you shall conceive and bear a son. 4 Therefore beware, and drink no wine or strong drink, and eat nothing unclean, 5 for behold, you shall conceive and bear a son. No razor shall come upon his head, for the boy shall be a Naz′irite to God from birth; and he shall begin to deliver Israel from the hand of the Philis′tines." 6 Then the woman came and told her husband, "A man of God came to me, and his countenance was like the countenance of the angel of God, very terrible; I did not ask him where he was from, and he did not tell me his name; 7 but he said to me, 'Behold, you shall conceive and bear a son; so then drink no wine or strong drink, and eat nothing unclean, for the boy shall be a Naz′irite to God from birth to the day of his death.'"

8 Then Mano′ah entreated the LORD, and
said, "O, LORD, I beg you, let the man of
God whom you sent come again to us, and
teach us what we are to do with the boy that
will be born." 9 And God listened to the voice
of Mano′ah, and the angel of God came
again to the woman as she sat in the field;
but Manoah her husband was not with her.
10 And the woman ran in haste and told her
husband, "Behold, the man who came to me
the other day has appeared to me." 11 And
Mano′ah arose and went after his wife,
and came to the man and said to him, "Are
you the man who spoke to this woman?"
And he said, "I am." 12 And Mano′ah said,
"Now when your words come true, what
is to be the boy's manner of life, and what
is he to do?" 13 And the angel of the LORD
said to Mano′ah, "Of all that I said to the
woman let her beware. 14 She may not eat of
anything that comes from the vine, neither
let her drink wine or strong drink, or eat any
unclean thing; all that I commanded her let
her observe."

15 Mano′ah said to the angel of the LORD,
"Please, let us detain you, and prepare a
kid for you." 16 And the angel of the LORD
said to Mano′ah, "If you detain me, I will
not eat of your food; but if you make
ready a burnt offering, then offer it to
the LORD." (For Manoah did not know
that he was the angel of the LORD.) 17 And
Mano′ah said to the angel of the LORD,
"What is your name, so that, when your
words come true, we may honor you?"
18 And the angel of the LORD said to him,
"Why do you ask my name, seeing it is
wonderful?" 19 So Mano′ah took the kid
with the cereal offering, and offered it
upon the rock to the LORD, to him who
works wonders. 20 And when the flame
went up toward heaven from the altar, the
angel of the LORD ascended in the flame
of the altar while Mano′ah and his wife
looked on; and they fell on their faces to
the ground.

21 The angel of the LORD appeared no more
to Mano′ah and to his wife. Then Manoah
knew that he was the angel of the LORD.
22 And Mano′ah said to his wife, "We shall
surely die, for we have seen God." 23 But his
wife said to him, "If the LORD had meant
to kill us, he would not have accepted a
burnt offering and a cereal offering at our
hands, or shown us all these things, or now
announced to us such things as these."
24 And the woman bore a son, and called his
name Samson; and the boy grew, and the
LORD blessed him. 25 And the Spirit of the
LORD began to stir him in Ma′haneh-dan,
between Zorah and Esh′ta-ol.

A Psalm.
A Song for the Sabbath.

PSALM 92 [91]

It is good to give thanks to the LORD,
to sing praises to your name, O
Most High;
2 to declare your merciful love in
the morning,
and your faithfulness by night,
3 to the music of the lute and the harp,
to the melody of the lyre.
4 For you, O LORD, have made me glad by
your work;
at the works of your hands I sing for joy.

5 How great are your works, O LORD!
Your thoughts are very deep!
6 The dull man cannot know,
the stupid cannot understand this:
7 that, though the wicked sprout like grass
and all evildoers flourish,
they are doomed to destruction for ever,
8 but you, O LORD, are on high for ever.
9 For, behold, your enemies, O LORD,
for, behold, your enemies shall perish;
all evildoers shall be scattered.

10 But you have exalted my horn like that of
the wild ox;
you have poured over me fresh oil.
11 My eyes have seen the downfall of
my enemies,
my ears have heard the doom of my
evil assailants.

12The righteous flourish like the palm tree,
and grow like a cedar in Lebanon.
13They are planted in the house of
the LORD,
they flourish in the courts of our God.
14They still bring forth fruit in old age,
they are ever full of sap and green,
15to show that the LORD is upright;
he is my rock, and there is no
unrighteousness in him.

LUKE 12

In the meantime, when so many
thousands of the multitude had
gathered together that they trod upon
one another, he began to say to his
disciples first, "Beware of the leaven of the
Pharisees, which is hypocrisy. 2Nothing
is covered up that will not be revealed, or
hidden that will not be known. 3Whatever
you have said in the dark shall be heard in
the light, and what you have whispered in
private rooms shall be proclaimed upon
the housetops.
4"I tell you, my friends, do not fear those
who kill the body, and after that have no
more that they can do. 5But I will warn you
whom to fear: fear him who, after he has
killed, has power to cast into hell; yes, I tell
you, fear him! 6Are not five sparrows sold
for two pennies? And not one of them is
forgotten before God. 7Why, even the hairs
of your head are all numbered. Fear not; you
are of more value than many sparrows.
8"And I tell you, every one who acknowledges me before men, the Son of man also will
acknowledge before the angels of God; 9but
he who denies me before men will be denied
before the angels of God. 10And every one who
speaks a word against the Son of man will be
forgiven; but he who blasphemes against the
Holy Spirit will not be forgiven. 11And when
they bring you before the synagogues and the
rulers and the authorities, do not be anxious
about how or what you are to answer or what
you are to say; 12for the Holy Spirit will teach
you in that very hour what you ought to say."
13One of the multitude said to him,
"Teacher, bid my brother divide the
inheritance with me." 14But he said to him,
"Man, who made me a judge or divider
over you?" 15And he said to them, "Take
heed, and beware of all covetousness;
for a man's life does not consist in the
abundance of his possessions." 16And he
told them a parable, saying, "The land
of a rich man brought forth plentifully;
17and he thought to himself, 'What shall
I do, for I have nowhere to store my
crops?' 18And he said, 'I will do this: I
will pull down my barns, and build larger
ones; and there I will store all my grain
and my goods. 19And I will say to my
soul, Soul, you have ample goods laid
up for many years; take your ease, eat,
drink, be merry.' 20But God said to him,
'Fool! This night your soul is required of
you; and the things you have prepared,
whose will they be?' 21So is he who lays
up treasure for himself, and is not rich
toward God."

REFLECTION

In the passage from Judges, Jephthah makes a foolish vow in order to manipulate God to award him a victory in battle (see Jgs 11:30–31). Yet the Lord, out of loyalty to his people, would have granted the victory anyway. After winning the battle, Jephthah comes home to find not a farm animal, but his very own daughter emerging from his house to greet him. He does not have the moral vision to see the misguided error of his vow and that his vow is null and void if it leads to sin, especially the grave sin of human sacrifice, and so he apparently offers his daughter as a sacrifice to the Lord—a repugnant act in God's sight (see Lv 20:2–5; Dt 12:31). Jephthath should have honored God's assistance by following the psalmist, "[giving] thanks to the LORD" and "[singing] praises to your name, O Most High" (Ps 92:1). What should you be giving thanks to the Lord for in your life? You may not try to manipulate God like Jepthath does, but do you expend your efforts trying to bend God to your will more than submitting your will to his?

April 18

JUDGES 14

Samson went down to Timnah, and at Timnah he saw one of the daughters of the Philis′tines. 2Then he came up, and told his father and mother, "I saw one of the daughters of the Philis′tines at Timnah; now get her for me as my wife." 3But his father and mother said to him, "Is there not a woman among the daughters of your kinsmen, or among all our people, that you must go to take a wife from the uncircumcised Philis′tines?" But Samson said to his father, "Get her for me; for she pleases me well."

4His father and mother did not know that it was from the LORD; for he was seeking an occasion against the Philis′tines. At that time the Philistines had dominion over Israel.

5Then Samson went down with his father and mother to Timnah, and he came to the vineyards of Timnah. And behold, a young lion roared against him; 6and the Spirit of the LORD came mightily upon him, and he tore the lion asunder as one tears a kid; and he had nothing in his hand. But he did not tell his father or his mother what he had done. 7Then he went down and talked with the woman; and she pleased Samson well. 8And after a while he returned to take her; and he turned aside to see the carcass of the lion, and behold, there was a swarm of bees in the body of the lion, and honey. 9He scraped it out into his hands, and went on, eating as he went; and he came to his father and mother, and gave some to them, and they ate. But he did not tell them that he had taken the honey from the carcass of the lion.

10And his father went down to the woman, and Samson made a feast there; for so the young men used to do. 11And when the people saw him, they brought thirty companions to be with him. 12And Samson said to them, "Let me now put a riddle to you; if you can tell me what it is, within the seven days of the feast, and find it out, then I will give you thirty linen garments and thirty festal garments; 13but if you cannot tell me what it is, then you shall give me thirty linen garments and thirty festal garments." And they said to him, "Put your riddle, that we may hear it." 14And he said to them,

"Out of the eater came something to eat.
Out of the strong came something sweet."

And they could not in three days tell what the riddle was.

15On the fourth day they said to Samson's wife, "Entice your husband to tell us what the riddle is, lest we burn you and your father's house with fire. Have you invited us here to impoverish us?" 16And Samson's wife wept before him, and said, "You only hate me, you do not love me; you have put a riddle to my countrymen, and you have not told me what it is." And he said to her, "Behold, I have not told my father nor my mother, and shall I tell you?" 17She wept before him the seven days that their feast lasted; and on the seventh day he told her, because she pressed him hard. Then she told the riddle to her countrymen. 18And the men of the city said to him on the seventh day before the sun went down,

"What is sweeter than honey?
What is stronger than a lion?"

And he said to them,

"If you had not plowed with my heifer,
you would not have found out my riddle."

19And the Spirit of the LORD came mightily upon him, and he went down to Ash′kelon and killed thirty men of the town, and took their spoil and gave the festal garments to those who had told the riddle. In hot anger he went back to his father's house. 20And Samson's wife was given to his companion, who had been his best man.

15 After a while, at the time of wheat harvest, Samson went to visit his wife with a kid; and he said, "I will go in to my wife in the chamber." But her father would not allow him to go in. 2And her father said, "I really thought that you utterly hated her; so I gave her to your companion. Is not her younger sister fairer than she? Please take her instead."

[3]And Samson said to them, "This time I shall
be blameless in regard to the Philis′tines, when
I do them mischief." [4]So Samson went and
caught three hundred foxes, and took torches;
and he turned them tail to tail, and put a torch
between each pair of tails. [5]And when he had
set fire to the torches, he let the foxes go into the
standing grain of the Philis′tines, and burned
up the shocks and the standing grain, as well as
the olive orchards. [6]Then the Philis′tines said,
"Who has done this?" And they said, "Samson,
the son-in-law of the Timnite, because he has
taken his wife and given her to his companion."
And the Philistines came up, and burned her
and her father with fire. [7]And Samson said to
them, "If this is what you do, I swear I will be
avenged upon you, and after that I will quit."
[8]And he struck them hip and thigh with great
slaughter; and he went down and stayed in the
cleft of the rock of E′tam.

[9]Then the Philis′tines came up and encamped in Judah, and made a raid on Lehi.
[10]And the men of Judah said, "Why have you
come up against us?" They said, "We have
come up to bind Samson, to do to him as
he did to us." [11]Then three thousand men
of Judah went down to the cleft of the rock
of E′tam, and said to Samson, "Do you not
know that the Philis′tines are rulers over
us? What then is this that you have done
to us?" And he said to them, "As they did
to me, so have I done to them." [12]And they
said to him, "We have come down to bind
you, that we may give you into the hands of
the Philis′tines." And Samson said to them,
"Swear to me that you will not fall upon me
yourselves." [13]They said to him, "No; we will
only bind you and give you into their hands;
we will not kill you." So they bound him with
two new ropes, and brought him up from
the rock.

[14]When he came to Lehi, the Philis′tines
came shouting to meet him; and the Spirit
of the LORD came mightily upon him, and
the ropes which were on his arms became
as flax that has caught fire, and his bonds
melted off his hands. [15]And he found a fresh
jawbone of a donkey, and put out his hand
and seized it, and with it he slew a thousand
men. [16]And Samson said,

"With the jawbone of a donkey,
heaps upon heaps,
with the jawbone of a donkey
have I slain a thousand men."

[17]When he had finished speaking, he threw
away the jawbone out of his hand; and that
place was called Ra′math-le′hi.

[18]And he was very thirsty, and he called on
the LORD and said, "You have granted this
great deliverance by the hand of your servant;
and shall I now die of thirst, and fall into the
hands of the uncircumcised?" [19]And God split
open the hollow place that is at Lehi, and there
came water from it; and when he drank, his
spirit returned, and he revived. Therefore the
name of it was called En-hakkor′e; it is at Lehi
to this day. [20]And he judged Israel in the days
of the Philis′tines twenty years.

PSALM 93 [92]

The LORD reigns; he is robed in majesty;
the LORD is robed, he is girded with
strength.
Yes, the world is established; it shall never
be moved;
[2] your throne is established from of old;
you are from everlasting.

[3]The floods have lifted up, O LORD,
the floods have lifted up their voice,
the floods lift up their roaring.
[4]Mightier than the thunders of many waters,
mightier than the waves of the sea,
the LORD on high is mighty!

[5]Your decrees are very sure;
holiness befits your house,
O LORD, for evermore.

LUKE 12

[22]And he said to his disciples, "Therefore I tell you, do not be anxious about your life, what you shall eat, nor about your body, what you shall put on. [23]For life is more

than food, and the body more than clothing.
24Consider the ravens: they neither sow nor
reap, they have neither storehouse nor barn,
and yet God feeds them. Of how much more
value are you than the birds! 25And which of
you by being anxious can add a cubit to his
span of life? 26If then you are not able to do
as small a thing as that, why are you anxious
about the rest? 27Consider the lilies, how they
grow; they neither toil nor spin; yet I tell you,
even Solomon in all his glory was not clothed
like one of these. 28But if God so clothes the
grass which is alive in the field today and
tomorrow is thrown into the oven, how
much more will he clothe you, O men of little
faith! 29And do not seek what you are to eat
and what you are to drink, nor be of anxious
mind. 30For all the nations of the world seek
these things; and your Father knows that you
need them. 31Instead, seek his kingdom, and
these things shall be yours as well.

32"Fear not, little flock, for it is your
Father's good pleasure to give you the
kingdom. 33Sell your possessions, and give
alms; provide yourselves with purses that do
not grow old, with a treasure in the heavens
that does not fail, where no thief approaches
and no moth destroys. 34For where your
treasure is, there will your heart be also.

35"Let your loins be girded and your lamps
burning, 36and be like men who are waiting
for their master to come home from the
marriage feast, so that they may open to
him at once when he comes and knocks.
37Blessed are those servants whom the
master finds awake when he comes; truly, I
say to you, he will put on his apron and have
them sit at table, and he will come and serve
them. 38If he comes in the second watch,
or in the third, and finds them so, blessed
are those servants! 39But know this, that if
the householder had known at what hour
the thief was coming, he would have been
awake and would not have left his house to
be broken into. 40You also must be ready; for
the Son of man is coming at an hour you do
not expect."

41Peter said, "Lord, are you telling this
parable for us or for all?" 42And the Lord
said, "Who then is the faithful and wise
steward, whom his master will set over his
household, to give them their portion of food
at the proper time? 43Blessed is that servant
whom his master when he comes will find so
doing. 44Truly I tell you, he will set him over
all his possessions. 45But if that servant says
to himself, 'My master is delayed in coming,'
and begins to beat the menservants and the
maidservants, and to eat and drink and get
drunk, 46the master of that servant will come
on a day when he does not expect him and at
an hour he does not know, and will punish
him, and put him with the unfaithful. 47And
that servant who knew his master's will, but
did not make ready or act according to his
will, shall receive a severe beating. 48But he
who did not know, and did what deserved
a beating, shall receive a light beating. Every
one to whom much is given, of him will
much be required; and of him to whom men
commit much they will demand the more.

49"I came to cast fire upon the earth; and
would that it were already kindled! 50I have
a baptism to be baptized with; and how I am
constrained until it is accomplished! 51Do
you think that I have come to give peace on
earth? No, I tell you, but rather division; 52for
henceforth in one house there will be five
divided, three against two and two against
three; 53they will be divided, father against
son and son against father, mother against
daughter and daughter against her mother,
mother-in-law against her daughter-in-law
and daughter-in-law against her mother-in-law."

REFLECTION

As we learn from a young age, every privilege brings with it a certain level of responsibility. The Lord grants a powerful anointing to Samson to be judge over Israel. Despite his Nazirite vow from birth (see Nm 6:1–21), Samson exhibits spiritual immaturity and an undisciplined life. It seems, in fact, that he is determined to act in direct contradiction to his calling. As soon as he grows up, he falls in love with a Philistine woman, a member of an enemy people. He eats unclean food in the form of honey from a lion's dead carcass. Beyond that, he abuses his God-given anointing to murder people. He abuses his privileges much like the irresponsible steward from Jesus's parable (see Lk 12:42–48), who beats the other servants and wastes his master's wealth on drunkenness. Jesus sums up the lesson powerfully: "Every one to whom much is given, of him will much be required" (v. 48). If we abuse the gifts and privileges we are given, spending them for our own good only and not for the good of others, we show that our treasure is not in the Lord: "For where your treasure is, there will your heart be also" (v. 34). Where is your treasure?

April 19

JUDGES 16

Samson went to Gaza, and there he saw a harlot, and he went in to her. [2]The Gazites were told, "Samson has come here," and they surrounded the place and lay in wait for him all night at the gate of the city. They kept quiet all night, saying, "Let us wait till the light of the morning; then we will kill him." [3]But Samson lay till midnight, and at midnight he arose and took hold of the doors of the gate of the city and the two posts, and pulled them up, bar and all, and put them on his shoulders and carried them to the top of the hill that is before He´bron.

[4]After this he loved a woman in the valley of Sorek, whose name was Deli´lah. [5]And the lords of the Philis´tines came to her and said to her, "Entice him, and see wherein his great strength lies, and by what means we may overpower him, that we may bind him to subdue him; and we will each give you eleven hundred pieces of silver." [6]And Deli´lah said to Samson, "Please tell me wherein your great strength lies, and how you might be bound, that one could subdue you." [7]And Samson said to her, "If they bind me with seven fresh bowstrings which have not been dried, then I shall become weak, and be like any other man." [8]Then the lords of the Philis´tines brought her seven fresh bowstrings which had not been dried, and she bound him with them. [9]Now she had men lying in wait in an inner chamber. And she said to him, "The Philis´tines are upon you, Samson!" But he snapped the bowstrings, as a tow line snaps when it touches the fire. So the secret of his strength was not known.

[10]And Deli´lah said to Samson, "Behold, you have mocked me, and told me lies; please tell me how you might be bound." [11]And he said to her, "If they bind me with new ropes that have not been used, then I shall become weak, and be like any other man." [12]So Deli´lah took new ropes and bound him with them, and said to him, "The Philis´tines are upon you, Samson!" And the men lying in wait were in an inner chamber. But he snapped the ropes off his arms like a thread.

[13]And Deli´lah said to Samson, "Until now you have mocked me, and told me lies; tell me how you might be bound." And he said to her, "If you weave the seven locks of my head with the web and make it tight with the pin, then I shall become weak, and be like any other man." [14]So while he slept, Deli´lah took the seven locks of his head and wove them into the web. And she made them tight with the pin, and said to him, "The Philis´tines are upon you, Samson!" But he awoke from his sleep, and pulled away the pin, the loom, and the web.

[15]And she said to him, "How can you say, 'I love you,' when your heart is not with me? You have mocked me these three times, and you have not told me wherein your great strength lies." [16]And when she pressed him hard with her words day after day, and urged him, his soul was vexed to death. [17]And he told her all his mind, and said to her, "A razor has never come upon my head; for I have been a Naz´irite to God from my mother's womb. If I be shaved, then my strength will leave me, and I shall become weak, and be like any other man."

[18]When Deli′lah saw that he had told her all
his mind, she sent and called the lords of the
Philis′tines, saying, "Come up this once, for
he has told me all his mind." Then the lords
of the Philistines came up to her, and brought
the money in their hands. [19]She made him
sleep upon her knees; and she called a man,
and had him shave off the seven locks of his
head. Then she began to torment him, and
his strength left him. [20]And she said, "The
Philis′tines are upon you, Samson!" And he
awoke from his sleep, and said, "I will go out
as at other times, and shake myself free." And
he did not know that the LORD had left him.
[21]And the Philis′tines seized him and gouged
out his eyes, and brought him down to Gaza,
and bound him with bronze fetters; and he
ground at the mill in the prison. [22]But the
hair of his head began to grow again after it
had been shaved.

[23]Now the lords of the Philis′tines gathered to offer a great sacrifice to Da′gon their
god, and to rejoice; for they said, "Our god
has given Samson our enemy into our hand."
[24]And when the people saw him, they praised
their god; for they said, "Our god has given
our enemy into our hand, the ravager of our
country, who has slain many of us." [25]And
when their hearts were merry, they said,
"Call Samson, that he may make sport for us."
So they called Samson out of the prison, and
he made sport before them. They made him
stand between the pillars; [26]and Samson said
to the lad who held him by the hand, "Let me
feel the pillars on which the house rests, that I
may lean against them." [27]Now the house was
full of men and women; all the lords of the
Philis′tines were there, and on the roof there
were about three thousand men and women,
who looked on while Samson made sport.

[28]Then Samson called to the LORD and
said, "O Lord GOD, remember me, I beg
you, and strengthen me, I beg you, only this
once, O God, that I may be avenged upon
the Philis′tines for one of my two eyes."
[29]And Samson grasped the two middle
pillars upon which the house rested, and
he leaned his weight upon them, his right
hand on the one and his left hand on the
other. [30]And Samson said, "Let me die with
the Philis′tines." Then he bowed with all his
might; and the house fell upon the lords and
upon all the people that were in it. So the
dead whom he slew at his death were more
than those whom he had slain during his
life. [31]Then his brothers and all his family
came down and took him and brought him
up and buried him between Zorah and
Esh′ta-ol in the tomb of Mano′ah his father.
He had judged Israel twenty years.

17 There was a man of the hill country
of E′phraim, whose name was Micah.
[2]And he said to his mother, "The eleven
hundred pieces of silver which were taken
from you, about which you uttered a curse,
and also spoke it in my ears, behold, the
silver is with me; I took it." And his mother
said, "Blessed be my son by the LORD." [3]And
he restored the eleven hundred pieces of
silver to his mother; and his mother said, "I
consecrate the silver to the LORD from my
hand for my son, to make a graven image
and a molten image; now therefore I will
restore it to you." [4]So when he restored
the money to his mother, his mother took
two hundred pieces of silver, and gave it to
the silversmith, who made it into a graven
image and a molten image; and it was in
the house of Micah. [5]And the man Micah
had a shrine, and he made an ephod and
teraphim, and installed one of his sons, who
became his priest. [6]In those days there was
no king in Israel; every man did what was
right in his own eyes.

[7]Now there was a young man of Bethlehem
in Judah, of the family of Judah, who was
a Levite; and he sojourned there. [8]And the
man departed from the town of Bethlehem
in Judah, to live where he could find a place;
and as he journeyed, he came to the hill
country of E′phraim to the house of Micah.
[9]And Micah said to him, "From where do
you come?" And he said to him, "I am a
Levite of Bethlehem in Judah, and I am
going to sojourn where I may find a place."
[10]And Micah said to him, "Stay with me, and
be to me a father and a priest, and I will give
you ten pieces of silver a year, and a suit of
apparel, and your living." [11]And the Levite
was content to dwell with the man; and the

young man became to him like one of his
sons. 12And Micah installed the Levite, and
the young man became his priest, and was
in the house of Micah. 13Then Micah said,
"Now I know that the LORD will prosper me,
because I have a Levite as priest."

18 In those days there was no king in
Israel. And in those days the tribe
of the Da′nites was seeking for itself an
inheritance to dwell in; for until then no
inheritance among the tribes of Israel had
fallen to them. 2So the Da′nites sent five able
men from the whole number of their tribe,
from Zorah and from Esh′ta-ol, to spy out
the land and to explore it; and they said to
them, "Go and explore the land." And they
came to the hill country of E′phraim, to the
house of Micah, and lodged there. 3When
they were by the house of Micah, they
recognized the voice of the young Levite;
and they turned aside and said to him, "Who
brought you here? What are you doing in this
place? What is your business here?" 4And he
said to them, "Thus and thus has Micah dealt
with me: he has hired me, and I have become
his priest." 5And they said to him, "Inquire of
God, we beg you, that we may know whether
the journey on which we are setting out will
succeed." 6And the priest said to them, "Go in
peace. The journey on which you go is under
the eye of the LORD."

PSALM 94 [93]

O LORD, you God of vengeance,
you God of vengeance, shine forth!
2Rise up, O judge of the earth;
render to the proud their deserts!
3O LORD, how long shall the wicked,
how long shall the wicked exult?

4They pour out their arrogant words,
they boast, all the evildoers.
5They crush your people, O LORD,
and afflict your heritage.
6They slay the widow and the sojourner,
and murder the fatherless;
7and they say, "The LORD does not see;
the God of Jacob does not perceive."
8Understand, O dullest of the people!
Fools, when will you be wise?
9He who planted the ear, does he not hear?
He who formed the eye, does he not see?
10He who chastens the nations, does he not
chastise?
He who teaches men knowledge,
11 the LORD, knows the thoughts of man,
that they are but a breath.

12Blessed is the man whom you chasten,
O LORD,
and whom you teach out of your law
13to give him respite from days of trouble,
until a pit is dug for the wicked.
14For the LORD will not forsake his people;
he will not abandon his heritage;
15for justice will return to the righteous,
and all the upright in heart will follow it.

16Who rises up for me against the wicked?
Who stands up for me against evildoers?
17If the LORD had not been my help,
my soul would soon have dwelt in the
land of silence.
18When I thought, "My foot slips,"
your mercy, O LORD, held me up.
19When the cares of my heart are many,
your consolations cheer my soul.
20Can wicked rulers be allied with you,
who frame mischief by statute?
21They band together against the life of the
righteous,
and condemn the innocent to death.
22But the LORD has become my stronghold,
and my God the rock of my refuge.
23He will bring back on them their iniquity
and wipe them out for their wickedness;
the LORD our God will wipe them out.

LUKE 12

**54He also said to the multitudes,
"When you see a cloud rising in
the west, you say at once, 'A shower is
coming'; and so it happens. 55And when**
you see the south wind blowing, you say,
'There will be scorching heat'; and it happens.

56You hypocrites! You know how to interpret
the appearance of earth and sky; but why do
you not know how to interpret the present
time?
57"And why do you not judge for yourselves
what is right? 58As you go with your accuser
before the magistrate, make an effort to
settle with him on the way, lest he drag you
to the judge, and the judge hand you over to
the officer, and the officer put you in prison.
59I tell you, you will never get out till you
have paid the very last copper."

13 There were some present at that very
time who told him of the Galileans
whose blood Pilate had mingled with
their sacrifices. 2And he answered them,
"Do you think that these Galileans were
worse sinners than all the other Galileans,
because they suffered thus? 3I tell you, No;
but unless you repent you will all likewise
perish. 4Or those eighteen upon whom the
tower in Silo′am fell and killed them, do you
think that they were worse offenders than
all the others who dwelt in Jerusalem? 5I tell
you, No; but unless you repent you will all
likewise perish."
6And he told this parable: "A man had a
fig tree planted in his vineyard; and he came
seeking fruit on it and found none. 7And
he said to the vinedresser, 'Behold, these
three years I have come seeking fruit on
this fig tree, and I find none. Cut it down;
why should it use up the ground?' 8And he
answered him, 'Let it alone, sir, this year
also, till I dig about it and put on manure.
9And if it bears fruit next year, well and
good; but if not, you can cut it down.' "

REFLECTION

In the Book of Judges we repeatedly hear that "every man did what was right in his own eyes" (Jgs 17:6). That is, instead of living according to God's standard of holiness, people fell into moral relativism. Samson is thus an emblem of his own era. Though he has a special anointing from God, he uses his strength to destroy property and kill people. While he sometimes attacks the enemies of God's people, the overall results of his judgeship are morally problematic. Jesus gives us the solution to such moral relativism: "Unless you repent . . . "(Lk 13:5). When we repent, we reject moral relativism and acknowledge the Lord's moral standard as supreme. Interior peace comes from recognizing Jesus's "lordship," his right to rule over our lives. "When the cares of my heart are many, your consolations cheer my soul" (Ps 94:19). The weight of guilt mires our souls, but our repentance and his forgiveness set us free. Are there areas where you have let moral relativism creep into your life? How can you begin to do what is right in God's eyes in those areas?

April 20

JUDGES 18

**7Then the five men departed, and
came to La′ish, and saw the people
who were there, how they dwelt in security, after the manner of the Sido′nians,**
quiet and unsuspecting, lacking nothing
that is in the earth, and possessing wealth,
and how they were far from the Sidonians
and had no dealings with any one. 8And
when they came to their brethren at Zorah
and Esh′ta-ol, their brethren said to them,
"What do you report?" 9They said, "Arise,
and let us go up against them; for we
have seen the land, and behold, it is very
fertile. And will you do nothing? Do not
be slow to go, and enter in and possess the
land. 10When you go, you will come to an
unsuspecting people. The land is broad; yes,
God has given it into your hands, a place
where there is no lack of anything that is in
the earth."
11And six hundred men of the tribe of Dan,
armed with weapons of war, set forth from
Zorah and Esh′ta-ol, 12and went up and
encamped at Kir′iath-je′arim in Judah. On
this account that place is called Ma′haneh-

dan to this day; behold, it is west of Kiriath-jearim. [13]And they passed on from there to the hill country of E′phraim, and came to the house of Micah.

[14]Then the five men who had gone to spy out the country of La′ish said to their brethren, “Do you know that in these houses there are an ephod, teraphim, a graven image, and a molten image? Now therefore consider what you will do.” [15]And they turned aside there, and came to the house of the young Levite, at the home of Micah, and asked him of his welfare. [16]Now the six hundred men of the Da′nites, armed with their weapons of war, stood by the entrance of the gate; [17]and the five men who had gone to spy out the land went up, and entered and took the graven image, the ephod, the teraphim, and the molten image, while the priest stood by the entrance of the gate with the six hundred men armed with weapons of war. [18]And when these went into Micah’s house and took the graven image, the ephod, the teraphim, and the molten image, the priest said to them, “What are you doing?” [19]And they said to him, “Keep quiet, put your hand upon your mouth, and come with us, and be to us a father and a priest. Is it better for you to be priest to the house of one man, or to be priest to a tribe and family in Israel?” [20]And the priest’s heart was glad; he took the ephod, and the teraphim, and the graven image, and went in the midst of the people.

[21]So they turned and departed, putting the little ones and the cattle and the goods in front of them. [22]When they were a good way from the home of Micah, the men who were in the houses near Micah’s house were called out, and they overtook the Da′nites. [23]And they shouted to the Da′nites, who turned round and said to Micah, “What ails you that you come with such a company?” [24]And he said, “You take my gods which I made, and the priest, and go away, and what have I left? How then do you ask me, ‘What ails you?’ ” [25]And the Da′nites said to him, “Do not let your voice be heard among us, lest angry fellows fall upon you, and you lose your life with the lives of your household.” [26]Then the Da′nites went their way; and when Micah saw that they were too strong for him, he turned and went back to his home.

[27]And taking what Micah had made, and the priest who belonged to him, the Da′nites came to La′ish, to a people quiet and unsuspecting, and struck them with the edge of the sword, and burned the city with fire. [28]And there was no deliverer because it was far from Si′don, and they had no dealings with any one. It was in the valley which belongs to Beth-re′hob. And they rebuilt the city, and dwelt in it. [29]And they named the city Dan, after the name of Dan their ancestor, who was born to Israel; but the name of the city was La′ish at the first. [30]And the Da′nites set up the graven image for themselves; and Jonathan the son of Gershom, son of Moses, and his sons were priests to the tribe of the Da′nites until the day of the captivity of the land. [31]So they set up Micah’s graven image which he made, as long as the house of God was at Shiloh.

19 In those days, when there was no king in Israel, a certain Levite was sojourning in the remote parts of the hill country of E′phraim, who took to himself a concubine from Bethlehem in Judah. [2]And his concubine became angry with him, and she went away from him to her father’s house at Bethlehem in Judah, and was there some four months. [3]Then her husband arose and went after her, to speak kindly to her and bring her back. He had with him his servant and a couple of donkeys. And he came to her father’s house; and when the girl’s father saw him, he came with joy to meet him. [4]And his father-in-law, the girl’s father, made him stay, and he remained with him three days; so they ate and drank, and lodged there. [5]And on the fourth day they arose early in the morning, and he prepared to go; but the girl’s father said to his son-in-law, “Strengthen your heart with a morsel of bread, and after that you may go.” [6]So the two men sat and ate and drank together; and the girl’s father said to the man, “Be pleased to spend the night, and let your heart be merry.” [7]And when the man

rose up to go, his father-in-law urged him,
till he lodged there again. 8And on the fifth
day he arose early in the morning to depart;
and the girl's father said, "Strengthen your
heart, and tarry until the day declines." So
they ate, both of them. 9And when the man
and his concubine and his servant rose
up to depart, his father-in-law, the girl's
father, said to him, "Behold, now the day
has waned toward evening; please tarry all
night. Behold, the day draws to its close;
lodge here and let your heart be merry;
and tomorrow you shall arise early in the
morning for your journey, and go home."

10But the man would not spend the night;
he rose up and departed, and arrived opposite Je′bus (that is, Jerusalem). He had
with him a couple of saddled donkeys, and
his concubine was with him. 11When they
were near Je′bus, the day was far spent, and
the servant said to his master, "Come now, let
us turn aside to this city of the Jeb′usites, and
spend the night in it." 12And his master said
to him, "We will not turn aside into the city
of foreigners, who do not belong to the sons
of Israel; but we will pass on to Gib′e-ah."
13And he said to his servant, "Come and let us
draw near to one of these places, and spend
the night at Gib′e-ah or at Ra′mah." 14So they
passed on and went their way; and the sun
went down on them near Gib′e-ah, which
belongs to Benjamin, 15and they turned aside
there, to go in and spend the night at Gib′e-
ah. And he went in and sat down in the open
square of the city; for no man took them into
his house to spend the night.

16And behold, an old man was coming
from his work in the field at evening; the
man was from the hill country of E′phraim,
and he was sojourning in Gib′e-ah; the men
of the place were Benjaminites. 17And he
lifted up his eyes, and saw the wayfarer in
the open square of the city; and the old man
said, "Where are you going? and from where
do you come?" 18And he said to him, "We
are passing from Bethlehem in Judah to the
remote parts of the hill country of E′phraim,
from which I come. I went to Bethlehem in
Judah; and I am going to my home; and
nobody takes me into his house. 19We have
straw and food for our donkeys, with bread
and wine for me and your maidservant and
the young man with your servants; there
is no lack of anything." 20And the old man
said, "Peace be to you; I will care for all your
wants; only, do not spend the night in the
square." 21So he brought him into his house,
and fed the donkeys; and they washed their
feet, and ate and drank.

22As they were making their hearts merry,
behold, the men of the city, base fellows,
surrounded the house, beating on the door;
and they said to the old man, the master of
the house, "Bring out the man who came
into your house, that we may know him."
23And the man, the master of the house,
went out to them and said to them, "No,
my brethren, do not act so wickedly; seeing
that this man has come into my house, do
not do this vile thing. 24Behold, here are
my virgin daughter and his concubine; let
me bring them out now. Ravish them and
do with them what seems good to you; but
against this man do not do so vile a thing."
25But the men would not listen to him. So
the man seized his concubine, and put her
out to them; and they knew her, and abused
her all night until the morning. And as the
dawn began to break, they let her go. 26And
as morning appeared, the woman came and
fell down at the door of the man's house
where her master was, till it was light.

27And her master rose up in the morning,
and when he opened the doors of the house
and went out to go on his way, behold, there
was his concubine lying at the door of the
house, with her hands on the threshold.
28He said to her, "Get up, let us be going."
But there was no answer. Then he put her
upon the donkey; and the man rose up
and went away to his home. 29And when
he entered his house, he took a knife, and
laying hold of his concubine he divided her,
limb by limb, into twelve pieces, and sent
her throughout all the territory of Israel.
30And all who saw it said, "Such a thing has
never happened or been seen from the day
that the sons of Israel came up out of the
land of Egypt until this day; consider it,
take counsel, and speak."

PSALM 95 [94]

O come, let us sing to the LORD;
let us make a joyful noise to the rock of our salvation!
2Let us come into his presence with thanksgiving;
let us make a joyful noise to him with songs of praise!
3For the LORD is a great God,
and a great King above all gods.
4In his hand are the depths of the earth;
the heights of the mountains are his also.
5The sea is his, for he made it;
for his hands formed the dry land.

6O come, let us worship and bow down,
let us kneel before the LORD, our Maker!
7For he is our God,
and we are the people of his pasture,
and the sheep of his hand.

O that today you would listen to his voice!
8 Harden not your hearts, as at Mer′ibah,
as on the day at Massah in the wilderness,
9when your fathers tested me,
and put me to the proof, though they had seen my work.
10For forty years I was wearied of that generation
and said, "They are a people who err in heart,
and they do not regard my ways."
11Therefore I swore in my anger
that they should not enter my rest.

LUKE 13

10Now he was teaching in one of
the synagogues on the sabbath.
11And there was a woman who had had a
spirit of infirmity for eighteen years; she
was bent over and could not fully straighten
herself. 12And when Jesus saw her, he called her
and said to her, "Woman, you are freed from
your infirmity." 13And he laid his hands upon
her, and immediately she was made straight,
and she praised God. 14But the ruler of the synagogue, indignant because Jesus had healed on
the sabbath, said to the people, "There are six
days on which work ought to be done; come
on those days and be healed, and not on the
sabbath day." 15Then the Lord answered him,
"You hypocrites! Does not each of you on the
sabbath untie his ox or his donkey from the
manger, and lead it away to water it? 16And
ought not this woman, a daughter of Abraham whom Satan bound for eighteen years,
be loosed from this bond on the sabbath day?"
17As he said this, all his adversaries were put to
shame; and all the people rejoiced at all the glorious things that were done by him.

18He said therefore, "What is the kingdom
of God like? And to what shall I compare
it? 19It is like a grain of mustard seed which
a man took and sowed in his garden; and it
grew and became a tree, and the birds of the
air made nests in its branches."
20And again he said, "To what shall I
compare the kingdom of God? 21It is like
leaven which a woman took and hid in three
measures of meal, till it was all leavened."
22He went on his way through towns and
villages, teaching, and journeying toward
Jerusalem. 23And some one said to him, "Lord,
will those who are saved be few?" And he said
to them, 24"Strive to enter by the narrow door;
for many, I tell you, will seek to enter and will
not be able. 25When once the householder has
risen up and shut the door, you will begin to
stand outside and to knock at the door, saying,
'Lord, open to us.' He will answer you, 'I do
not know where you come from.' 26Then you
will begin to say, 'We ate and drank in your
presence, and you taught in our streets.' 27But
he will say, 'I tell you, I do not know where you
come from; depart from me, all you workers of
iniquity!' 28There you will weep and gnash your
teeth, when you see Abraham and Isaac and
Jacob and all the prophets in the kingdom of
God and you yourselves thrust out. 29And men
will come from east and west, and from north
and south, and sit at table in the kingdom of
God. 30And behold, some are last who will be
first, and some are first who will be last."

31At that very hour some Pharisees came, and
said to him, "Get away from here, for Herod
wants to kill you." 32And he said to them, "Go
and tell that fox, 'Behold, I cast out demons

and perform cures today and tomorrow, and
the third day I finish my course. 33Nevertheless
I must go on my way today and tomorrow
and the day following; for it cannot be that a
prophet should perish away from Jerusalem.'
34O Jerusalem, Jerusalem, killing the prophets
and stoning those who are sent to you! How
often would I have gathered your children
together as a hen gathers her brood under
her wings, and you would not! 35Behold, your
house is forsaken. And I tell you, you will not
see me until you say, 'Blessed is he who comes
in the name of the Lord!'"

REFLECTION

In today's readings we are confronted with the terrible consequences of setting up our own gods in opposition to the Lord. Micah has set up his own idol-god with his own priest. It is stolen by the tribe of Dan, which builds its own rival sanctuary. The lack of fidelity to God leads to a situation of moral confusion and even terror. Judges 19 presents one of the darkest tales of the Bible, when the consequences of a sinful culture are put on full display. No actor in the story deals righteously. Everyone is treacherous. While most of us do not build literal idols to worship, the psalmist recalls for us the stubborn hearts of the wilderness generation—a type of idolatry a bit closer to home. Jesus confronts those who uphold the Sabbath itself as if it were an idol, so far as to deny a crippled woman Jesus's healing touch. The lesson is simple: if we set up our own gods, we will wander after anything and wind up in moral darkness. Yet, if we wish to respond to the God whose "hands formed the dry land" (Ps 95:5), then we must "strive to enter by the narrow door" (Lk 13:24). What are you striving for?

April 21

JUDGES 20

**Then all the sons of Israel came
out, from Dan to Be'er-she'ba,
including the land of Gilead, and the
congregation assembled as one man to**
the LORD at Mizpah. 2And the chiefs of all the
people, of all the tribes of Israel, presented
themselves in the assembly of the people of
God, four hundred thousand men on foot
that drew the sword. 3(Now the Benjaminites heard that the sons of Israel had gone
up to Mizpah.) And the sons of Israel said,
"Tell us, how was this wickedness brought
to pass?" 4And the Levite, the husband of
the woman who was murdered, answered
and said, "I came to Gib'e-ah that belongs
to Benjamin, I and my concubine, to spend
the night. 5And the men of Gib'e-ah rose
against me, and surrounded the house by
night; they meant to kill me, and they ravished my concubine, and she is dead. 6And
I took my concubine and cut her in pieces,
and sent her throughout all the country
of the inheritance of Israel; for they have
committed abomination and wantonness
in Israel. 7Behold, you sons of Israel, all of
you, give your advice and counsel here."
8And all the people arose as one man,
saying, "None of us will go to his tent, and
none of us will return to his house. 9But now
this is what we will do to Gib'e-ah: we will
go up against it by lot, 10and we will take ten
men of a hundred throughout all the tribes
of Israel, and a hundred of a thousand,
and a thousand of ten thousand, to bring
provisions for the people, that when they
come they may repay Gib'e-ah of Benjamin,
for all the wanton crime which they have
committed in Israel." 11So all the men of
Israel gathered against the city, united as
one man.
12And the tribes of Israel sent men through
all the tribe of Benjamin, saying, "What
wickedness is this that has taken place
among you? 13Now therefore give up the
men, the base fellows in Gib'e-ah, that we
may put them to death, and put away evil
from Israel." But the Benjaminites would
not listen to the voice of their brethren, the
sons of Israel. 14And the Benjaminites came
together out of the cities to Gib'e-ah, to go
out to battle against the sons of Israel. 15And
the Benjaminites mustered out of their cities
on that day twenty-six thousand men that
drew the sword, besides the inhabitants of

Gib′e-ah, who mustered seven hundred
picked men. 16Among all these were seven
hundred picked men who were left-handed;
every one could sling a stone at a hair, and
not miss. 17And the men of Israel, apart from
Benjamin, mustered four hundred thousand
men that drew sword; all these were men
of war.

18The sons of Israel arose and went up
to Bethel, and inquired of God, "Which
of us shall go up first to battle against the
Benjaminites?" And the LORD said, "Judah
shall go up first."

19Then the sons of Israel rose in the
morning, and encamped against Gib′e-ah.
20And the men of Israel went out to battle
against Benjamin; and the men of Israel drew
up the battle line against them at Gib′e-ah.
21The Benjaminites came out of Gib′e-ah,
and struck down on that day twenty-two
thousand men of the Israelites. 22But the
people, the men of Israel, took courage, and
again formed the battle line in the same
place where they had formed it on the first
day. 23And the sons of Israel went up and
wept before the LORD until the evening; and
they inquired of the LORD, "Shall we again
draw near to battle against our brethren the
Benjaminites?" And the LORD said, "Go up
against them."

24So the sons of Israel came near against
the Benjaminites the second day. 25And
Benjamin went against them out of Gib′e-ah
the second day, and struck down eighteen
thousand men of the sons of Israel; all these
were men who drew the sword. 26Then all
the sons of Israel, the whole army, went
up and came to Bethel and wept; they sat
there before the LORD, and fasted that day
until evening, and offered burnt offerings
and peace offerings before the LORD. 27And
the sons of Israel inquired of the LORD (for
the ark of the covenant of God was there
in those days, 28and Phin′ehas the son of
Elea′zar, son of Aaron, ministered before it
in those days), saying, "Shall we yet again
go out to battle against our brethren the
Benjaminites, or shall we cease?" And the
LORD said, "Go up; for tomorrow I will give
them into your hand."

29So Israel set men in ambush round about
Gib′e-ah. 30And the sons of Israel went
up against the Benjaminites on the third
day, and set themselves in array against
Gib′e-ah, as at other times. 31And the
Benjaminites went out against the people,
and were drawn away from the city; and as
at other times they began to strike and kill
some of the people, in the highways, one of
which goes up to Bethel and the other to
Gib′e-ah, and in the open country, about
thirty men of Israel. 32And the Benjaminites
said, "They are routed before us, as at the
first." But the men of Israel said, "Let us
flee, and draw them away from the city
to the highways." 33And all the men of
Israel rose up out of their place, and set
themselves in array at Ba′al-ta′mar; and the
men of Israel who were in ambush rushed
out of their place west of Ge′ba. 34And there
came against Gib′e-ah ten thousand picked
men out of all Israel, and the battle was
hard; but the Benjaminites did not know
that disaster was close upon them. 35And
the LORD defeated Benjamin before Israel;
and the men of Israel destroyed twenty-five
thousand one hundred men of Benjamin
that day; all these were men who drew the
sword. 36So the Benjaminites saw that they
were defeated.

The men of Israel gave ground to Benjamin, because they trusted to the men in
ambush whom they had set against Gib′e-
ah. 37And the men in ambush made haste
and rushed upon Gib′e-ah; the men in
ambush moved out and struck the whole
city with the edge of the sword. 38Now the
appointed signal between the men of Israel
and the men in ambush was that when
they made a great cloud of smoke rise up
out of the city 39the men of Israel should
turn in battle. Now Benjamin had begun to
strike and kill about thirty men of Israel;
they said, "Surely they are struck down
before us, as in the first battle." 40But when
the signal began to rise out of the city in a
column of smoke, the Benjaminites looked
behind them; and behold, the whole city
went up in smoke to heaven. 41Then the
men of Israel turned, and the men of

Benjamin were dismayed, for they saw that disaster was close upon them. [42]Therefore they turned their backs before the men of Israel in the direction of the wilderness; but the battle overtook them, and those who came out of the cities destroyed them in the midst of them. [43]Cutting down the Benjaminites, they pursued them and trod them down from Noʹhah as far as opposite Gibʹe-ah on the east. [44]Eighteen thousand men of Benjamin fell, all of them men of valor. [45]And they turned and fled toward the wilderness to the rock of Rimmon; five thousand men of them were cut down in the highways, and they were pursued hard to Giʹdom, and two thousand men of them were slain. [46]So all who fell that day of Benjamin were twenty-five thousand men that drew the sword, all of them men of valor. [47]But six hundred men turned and fled toward the wilderness to the rock of Rimmon, and abode at the rock of Rimmon four months. [48]And the men of Israel turned back against the Benjaminites, and struck them with the edge of the sword, men and beasts and all that they found. And all the towns which they found they set on fire.

21 Now the men of Israel had sworn at Mizpah, "No one of us shall give his daughter in marriage to Benjamin." [2]And the people came to Bethel, and sat there till evening before God, and they lifted up their voices and wept bitterly. [3]And they said, "O Lord, the God of Israel, why has this come to pass in Israel, that there should be today one tribe lacking in Israel?" [4]And the next day the people rose early, and built there an altar, and offered burnt offerings and peace offerings. [5]And the sons of Israel said, "Which of all the tribes of Israel did not come up in the assembly to the Lord?" For they had taken a great oath concerning him who did not come up to the Lord to Mizpah, saying, "He shall be put to death." [6]And the sons of Israel had compassion for Benjamin their brother, and said, "One tribe is cut off from Israel this day. [7]What shall we do for wives for those who are left, since we have sworn by the Lord that we will not give them any of our daughters for wives?"

[8]And they said, "What one is there of the tribes of Israel that did not come up to the Lord to Mizpah?" And behold, no one had come to the camp from Jaʹbesh-gilʹead, to the assembly. [9]For when the people were mustered, behold, not one of the inhabitants of Jaʹbesh-gilʹead was there. [10]So the congregation sent twelve thousand of their bravest men there, and commanded them, "Go and strike the inhabitants of Jaʹbesh-gilʹead with the edge of the sword; also the women and the little ones. [11]This is what you shall do; every male and every woman that has lain with a male you shall utterly destroy." [12]And they found among the inhabitants of Jaʹbesh-gilʹead four hundred young virgins who had not known man by lying with him; and they brought them to the camp at Shiloh, which is in the land of Canaan.

[13]Then the whole congregation sent word to the Benjaminites who were at the rock of Rimmon, and proclaimed peace to them. [14]And Benjamin returned at that time; and they gave them the women whom they had saved alive of the women of Jaʹbesh-gilʹead; but they did not suffice for them. [15]And the people had compassion on Benjamin because the Lord had made a breach in the tribes of Israel.

[16]Then the elders of the congregation said, "What shall we do for wives for those who are left, since the women are destroyed out of Benjamin?" [17]And they said, "There must be an inheritance for the survivors of Benjamin, that a tribe be not blotted out from Israel. [18]Yet we cannot give them wives of our daughters." For the sons of Israel had sworn, "Cursed be he who gives a wife to Benjamin." [19]So they said, "Behold, there is the yearly feast of the Lord at Shiloh, which is north of Bethel, on the east of the highway that goes up from Bethel to Sheʹchem, and south of Leboʹnah." [20]And they commanded the Benjaminites, saying, "Go and lie in wait in the vineyards, [21]and watch; if the daughters of Shiloh come

out to dance in the dances, then come
out of the vineyards and seize each man
his wife from the daughters of Shiloh,
and go to the land of Benjamin. 22And
when their fathers or their brothers come
to complain to us, we will say to them,
'Grant them graciously to us; because we
did not take for each man of them his
wife in battle, neither did you give them
to them, else you would now be guilty.' "
23And the Benjaminites did so, and took
their wives, according to their number,
from the dancers whom they carried
off; then they went and returned to
their inheritance, and rebuilt the towns,
and dwelt in them. 24And the sons of
Israel departed from there at that time,
every man to his tribe and family, and
they went out from there every man to
his inheritance.

25In those days there was no king in Israel;
every man did what was right in his own
eyes.

PSALM 96 [95]

O sing to the Lord a new song;
sing to the Lord, all the earth!
2Sing to the Lord, bless his name;
tell of his salvation from day to day.
3Declare his glory among the nations,
his marvelous works among all
the peoples!
4For great is the Lord, and greatly to
be praised;
he is to be feared above all gods.
5For all the gods of the peoples are idols;
but the Lord made the heavens.
6Honor and majesty are before him;
strength and beauty are in his sanctuary.

7Ascribe to the Lord, O families of
the peoples,
ascribe to the Lord glory and strength!
8Ascribe to the Lord the glory due his name;
bring an offering, and come into
his courts!
9Worship the Lord in holy attire;
tremble before him, all the earth!

10Say among the nations, "The Lord reigns!
Yes, the world is established, it shall never
be moved;
he will judge the peoples with equity."
11Let the heavens be glad, and let the
earth rejoice;
let the sea roar, and all that fills it;
12 let the field exult, and everything in it!
Then shall all the trees of the wood sing
for joy
13 before the Lord, for he comes,
for he comes to judge the earth.
He will judge the world with
righteousness,
and the peoples with his truth.

LUKE 14

One sabbath when he went to
dine at the house of a ruler who
belonged to the Pharisees, they were
watching him. 2And behold, there was a
man before him who had dropsy. 3And
Jesus spoke to the lawyers and Pharisees,
saying, "Is it lawful to heal on the sabbath,
or not?" 4But they were silent. Then he took
him and healed him, and let him go. 5And
he said to them, "Which of you, having a
son or an ox that has fallen into a well, will
not immediately pull him out on a sabbath
day?" 6And they could not reply to this.

7Now he told a parable to those who were
invited, when he marked how they chose the
places of honor, saying to them, 8"When you
are invited by any one to a marriage feast, do
not sit down in a place of honor, lest a more
eminent man than you be invited by him;
9and he who invited you both will come
and say to you, 'Give place to this man,' and
then you will begin with shame to take the
lowest place. 10But when you are invited,
go and sit in the lowest place, so that when
your host comes he may say to you, 'Friend,
go up higher'; then you will be honored in
the presence of all who sit at table with you.
11For every one who exalts himself will be
humbled, and he who humbles himself will
be exalted."

12He said also to the man who had invited him, "When you give a dinner or a banquet, do not invite your friends or your brothers or your kinsmen or rich neighbors, lest they also invite you in return, and you be repaid. 13But when you give a feast, invite the poor, the maimed, the lame, the blind, 14and you will be blessed, because they cannot repay you. You will be repaid at the resurrection of the just."

REFLECTION

After the outrageous violent crime of Judges 19, the whole nation of Israel is provoked to war against the tribe of Benjamin. Moreover, the other tribes of Israel swear not to give their daughters in marriage to any Benjaminites, which prompts a new bride-shortage crisis. They can only think of more violence and kidnapping to solve the new problem. Judges is the book of "what-not-to-do." The immorality and violence, which keep spiraling out of control, show the need for a national moral authority, a king. Indeed, it is the Lord's kingship over creation that holds the world together. Psalm 96:10 invites us to say, "The LORD reigns!" His kingly authority brings justice and truth to the world. Jesus invites us to participate in his magnanimous reign—the polar opposite of the chaotic anarchy of the judges' period—by inviting "the poor, the maimed, the lame, the blind" to our feasts (Lk 14:13–14). These lowly persons will not be able to reciprocate, so the Lord will repay on their behalf. When you have opportunity, will you fight or will you invite?

April 22

RUTH 1

In the days when the judges ruled there was a famine in the land, and a certain man of Bethlehem in Judah went to sojourn in the country of Moab, he and his wife and his two sons. 2The name of the man was Elim′elech and the name of his wife Na′omi, and the names of his two sons were Mahlon and Chil′ion; they were Eph′rathites from Bethlehem in Judah. They went into the country of Moab and remained there. 3But Elim′elech, the husband of Na′omi, died, and she was left with her two sons. 4These took Moabite wives; the name of the one was Orpah and the name of the other Ruth. They lived there about ten years; 5and both Mahlon and Chil′ion died, so that the woman was bereft of her two sons and her husband.

6Then she started with her daughters-in-law to return from the country of Moab, for she had heard in the country of Moab that the LORD had visited his people and given them food. 7So she set out from the place where she was, with her two daughters-in-law, and they went on the way to return to the land of Judah. 8But Na′omi said to her two daughters-in-law, "Go, return each of you to her mother's house. May the LORD deal kindly with you, as you have dealt with the dead and with me. 9The LORD grant that you may find a home, each of you in the house of her husband!" Then she kissed them, and they lifted up their voices and wept. 10And they said to her, "No, we will return with you to your people." 11But Na′omi said, "Turn back, my daughters, why will you go with me? Have I yet sons in my womb that they may become your husbands? 12Turn back, my daughters, go your way, for I am too old to have a husband. If I should say I have hope, even if I should have a husband this night and should bear sons, 13would you therefore wait till they were grown? Would you therefore refrain from marrying? No, my daughters, for it is exceedingly bitter to me for your sake that the hand of the LORD has gone forth against me." 14Then they lifted up their voices and wept again; and Orpah kissed her mother-in-law, but Ruth clung to her.

15And she said, "See, your sister-in-law has gone back to her people and to her gods; return after your sister-in-law." 16But Ruth said, "Entreat me not to leave you or to return from following you; for where you go I will go, and where you lodge I will lodge; your people shall be my people, and your God my God; 17where you die I will die, and there will I be buried. May the LORD do so to me and more also if even death parts me from you." 18And when Na´omi saw that she was determined to go with her, she said no more.

19So the two of them went on until they came to Bethlehem. And when they came to Bethlehem, the whole town was stirred because of them; and the women said, "Is this Na´omi?" 20She said to them, "Do not call me Na´omi, call me Mara, for the Almighty has dealt very bitterly with me. 21I went away full, and the LORD has brought me back empty. Why call me Na´omi, when the LORD has afflicted me and the Almighty has brought calamity upon me?"

22So Na´omi returned, and Ruth the Moabitess her daughter-in-law with her, who returned from the country of Moab. And they came to Bethlehem at the beginning of barley harvest.

2 Now Na´omi had a kinsman of her husband's, a man of wealth, of the family of Elim´elech, whose name was Boaz. 2And Ruth the Moabitess said to Na´omi, "Let me go to the field, and glean among the ears of grain after him in whose sight I shall find favor." And she said to her, "Go, my daughter." 3So she set forth and went and gleaned in the field after the reapers; and she happened to come to the part of the field belonging to Boaz, who was of the family of Elim´elech. 4And behold, Boaz came from Bethlehem; and he said to the reapers, "The LORD be with you!" And they answered, "The LORD bless you." 5Then Boaz said to his servant who was in charge of the reapers, "Whose maiden is this?" 6And the servant who was in charge of the reapers answered, "It is the Moabite maiden, who came back with Na´omi from the country of Moab. 7She said, 'Please, let me glean and gather among the sheaves after the reapers.' So she came, and she has continued from early morning until now, without resting even for a moment."

8Then Boaz said to Ruth, "Now, listen, my daughter, do not go to glean in another field or leave this one, but keep close to my maidens. 9Let your eyes be upon the field which they are reaping, and go after them. Have I not charged the young men not to molest you? And when you are thirsty, go to the vessels and drink what the young men have drawn." 10Then she fell on her face, bowing to the ground, and said to him, "Why have I found favor in your eyes, that you should take notice of me, when I am a foreigner?" 11But Boaz answered her, "All that you have done for your mother-in-law since the death of your husband has been fully told me, and how you left your father and mother and your native land and came to a people that you did not know before. 12The LORD recompense you for what you have done, and a full reward be given you by the LORD, the God of Israel, under whose wings you have come to take refuge!" 13Then she said, "You are most gracious to me, my lord, for you have comforted me and spoken kindly to your maidservant, though I am not one of your maidservants."

14And at mealtime Boaz said to her, "Come here, and eat some bread, and dip your morsel in the wine." So she sat beside the reapers, and he passed to her parched grain; and she ate until she was satisfied, and she had some left over. 15When she rose to glean, Boaz instructed his young men, saying, "Let her glean even among the sheaves, and do not reproach her. 16And also pull out some from the bundles for her, and leave it for her to glean, and do not rebuke her."

17So she gleaned in the field until evening; then she beat out what she had gleaned, and it was about an ephah of barley. 18And she took it up and went into the city; she showed her mother-in-law what she had gleaned, and she also brought out and gave her what food she had left over after being satisfied. 19And her mother-in-law said to her, "Where did you glean today? And where have you worked? Blessed be the man who took notice of you." So she told her mother-in-law with whom she had worked, and said, "The name of the man with whom I worked today is Boaz." 20And Na´omi said to her daughter-in-law, "Blessed be he by the LORD, whose kindness has not forsaken the living or the

dead!" Na'omi also said to her, "The man is a
relative of ours, one of our nearest kin." 21 And
Ruth the Moabitess said, "Besides, he said to
me, 'You shall keep close by my servants, till
they have finished all my harvest.'" 22 And
Na'omi said to Ruth, her daughter-in-law,
"It is well, my daughter, that you go out
with his maidens, lest in another field you be
molested." 23 So she kept close to the maidens
of Boaz, gleaning until the end of the barley
and wheat harvests; and she lived with her
mother-in-law.

PSALM 97 [96]

The LORD reigns; let the earth rejoice;
let the many islands be glad!
2 Clouds and thick darkness are round
about him;
righteousness and justice are the
foundation of his throne.
3 Fire goes before him,
and burns up his adversaries round about.
4 His lightnings lighten the world;
the earth sees and trembles.
5 The mountains melt like wax before
the LORD,
before the Lord of all the earth.

6 The heavens proclaim his righteousness;
and all the peoples behold his glory.
7 All worshipers of images are put to shame,
who make their boast in worthless idols;
let all his angels bow down before him.
8 Zion hears and is glad,
and the daughters of Judah rejoice,
because of your judgments, O God.
9 For you, O LORD, are most high over all
the earth;
you are exalted far above all gods.

10 The LORD loves those who hate evil;
he preserves the lives of his saints;
he delivers them from the hand of
the wicked.
11 Light dawns for the righteous,
and joy for the upright in heart.
12 Rejoice in the LORD, O you righteous,
and give thanks to his holy name!

LUKE 14

**15 When one of those who sat
at table with him heard this,
he said to him, "Blessed is he
who shall eat bread in the kingdom of
God!" 16 But he said to him, "A man
once gave a great banquet, and invited**
many; 17 and at the time for the banquet he
sent his servant to say to those who had
been invited, 'Come; for all is now ready.'
18 But they all alike began to make excuses.
The first said to him, 'I have bought a field,
and I must go out and see it; please, have me
excused.' 19 And another said, 'I have bought
five yoke of oxen, and I go to examine them;
please, have me excused.' 20 And another
said, 'I have married a wife, and therefore
I cannot come.' 21 So the servant came
and reported this to his master. Then the
householder in anger said to his servant,
'Go out quickly to the streets and lanes of
the city, and bring in the poor and maimed
and blind and lame.' 22 And the servant said,
'Sir, what you commanded has been done,
and still there is room.' 23 And the master
said to the servant, 'Go out to the highways
and hedges, and compel people to come in,
that my house may be filled. 24 For I tell you,
none of those men who were invited shall
taste my banquet.'"

25 Now great multitudes accompanied him;
and he turned and said to them, 26 "If any
one comes to me and does not hate his own
father and mother and wife and children and
brothers and sisters, yes, and even his own
life, he cannot be my disciple. 27 Whoever
does not bear his own cross and come after
me, cannot be my disciple. 28 For which
of you, desiring to build a tower, does not
first sit down and count the cost, whether
he has enough to complete it? 29 Otherwise,
when he has laid a foundation, and is not
able to finish, all who see it begin to mock
him, 30 saying, 'This man began to build, and
was not able to finish.' 31 Or what king, going
to encounter another king in war, will not
sit down first and take counsel whether he
is able with ten thousand to meet him who

comes against him with twenty thousand? 32 And if not, while the other is yet a great way off, he sends an embassy and asks terms of peace. 33 So therefore, whoever of you does not renounce all that he has cannot be my disciple.

34 "Salt is good; but if salt has lost its taste, how shall its saltiness be restored? 35 It is fit neither for the land nor for the dunghill; men throw it away. He who has ears to hear, let him hear."

15 Now the tax collectors and sinners were all drawing near to hear him. 2 And the Pharisees and the scribes murmured, saying, "This man receives sinners and eats with them."

3 So he told them this parable: 4 "What man of you, having a hundred sheep, if he has lost one of them, does not leave the ninety-nine in the wilderness, and go after the one which is lost, until he finds it? 5 And when he has found it, he lays it on his shoulders, rejoicing. 6 And when he comes home, he calls together his friends and his neighbors, saying to them, 'Rejoice with me, for I have found my sheep which was lost.' 7 Just so, I tell you, there will be more joy in heaven over one sinner who repents than over ninety-nine righteous persons who need no repentance.

8 "Or what woman, having ten silver coins, if she loses one coin, does not light a lamp and sweep the house and seek diligently until she finds it? 9 And when she has found it, she calls together her friends and neighbors, saying, 'Rejoice with me, for I have found the coin which I had lost.' 10 Just so, I tell you, there is joy before the angels of God over one sinner who repents."

REFLECTION

Many people think of God as issuing demands, but the Bible frequently depicts him as extending invitations instead. The Lord is the one hosting a "great banquet" (Lk 14:16), yet many who are invited make excuses and refuse to come. Here we see people preoccupied with worldly matters: marriage, property, oxen. They are so busy they do not have time for the banquet, so the master issues a new command: "Go out to the highways and hedges, and compel people to come in, that my house may be filled" (v. 23). The Lord is seeking those who will commit to him, not the complacent. Ruth is a great illustration of the kind of whole-hearted loyalty true discipleship requires. When Naomi tries to send her home, Ruth responds: "Where you will go I will go, and where you lodge I will lodge; your people shall be my people, and your God my God; where you die I will die, and there will I be buried" (Ru 1:16–17). Jesus seeks people like Ruth, those who are willing to "count the cost," "renounce all," and make a total life-commitment. Jesus invites you to follow him. Will you make excuses, or come after him with Ruth's dedication?

April 23

RUTH 3

Then Na′omi her mother-in-law said to her, "My daughter, should I not seek a home for you, that it may be well with you? 2 Now is not Boaz our kinsman, with whose maidens you were? See, he is winnowing barley tonight at the threshing floor. 3 Wash therefore and anoint yourself, and put on your best clothes and go down to the threshing floor; but do not make yourself known to the man until he has finished eating and drinking. 4 But when he lies down, observe the place where he lies; then, go and uncover his feet and lie down; and he will tell you what to do." 5 And she replied, "All that you say I will do."

6 So she went down to the threshing floor and did just as her mother-in-law had told her. 7 And when Boaz had eaten and drunk, and his heart was merry, he went to lie down

at the end of the heap of grain. Then she
came softly, and uncovered his feet, and lay
down. 8 At midnight the man was startled,
and turned over, and behold, a woman lay
at his feet! 9 He said, "Who are you?" And she
answered, "I am Ruth, your maidservant;
spread your garment over your maidservant,
for you are next of kin." 10 And he said, "May
you be blessed by the LORD, my daughter;
you have made this last kindness greater
than the first, in that you have not gone
after young men, whether poor or rich.
11 And now, my daughter, do not fear, I will
do for you all that you ask, for all my fellow
townsmen know that you are a woman of
worth. 12 And now it is true that I am a near
kinsman, yet there is a kinsman nearer than
I. 13 Remain this night, and in the morning, if
he will do the part of the next of kin for you,
well; let him do it; but if he is not willing to
do the part of the next of kin for you, then, as
the LORD lives, I will do the part of the next
of kin for you. Lie down until the morning."
14 So she lay at his feet until the morning, but
arose before one could recognize another; and
he said, "Let it not be known that the woman
came to the threshing floor." 15 And he said,
"Bring the mantle you are wearing and hold it
out." So she held it, and he measured out six
measures of barley, and laid it upon her; then
she went into the city. 16 And when she came
to her mother-in-law, she said, "How did you
fare, my daughter?" Then she told her all that
the man had done for her, 17 saying, "These
six measures of barley he gave to me, for he
said, 'You must not go back empty-handed to
your mother-in-law.'" 18 She replied, "Wait, my
daughter, until you learn how the matter turns
out, for the man will not rest, but will settle the
matter today."

4 And Boaz went up to the gate and sat
down there; and behold, the next of kin,
of whom Boaz had spoken, came by. So Boaz
said, "Turn aside, friend; sit down here"; and
he turned aside and sat down. 2 And he took
ten men of the elders of the city, and said, "Sit
down here"; so they sat down. 3 Then he said
to the next of kin, "Na'omi, who has come
back from the country of Moab, is selling
the parcel of land which belonged to our
kinsman Elim'elech. 4 So I thought I would
tell you of it, and say, Buy it in the presence
of those sitting here, and in the presence of
the elders of my people. If you will redeem it,
redeem it; but if you will not, tell me, that I
may know, for there is no one besides you to
redeem it, and I come after you." And he said,
"I will redeem it." 5 Then Boaz said, "The day
you buy the field from the hand of Na'omi,
you are also buying Ruth the Moabitess, the
widow of the dead, in order to restore the
name of the dead to his inheritance." 6 Then
the next of kin said, "I cannot redeem it for
myself, lest I impair my own inheritance.
Take my right of redemption yourself, for I
cannot redeem it."

7 Now this was the custom in former times in
Israel concerning redeeming and exchanging:
to confirm a transaction, the one drew off his
sandal and gave it to the other, and this was
the manner of attesting in Israel. 8 So when the
next of kin said to Boaz, "Buy it for yourself,"
he drew off his sandal. 9 Then Boaz said to the
elders and all the people, "You are witnesses
this day that I have bought from the hand of
Na'omi all that belonged to Elim'elech and all
that belonged to Chil'ion and to Mahlon. 10 Also
Ruth the Moabitess, the widow of Mahlon, I
have bought to be my wife, to perpetuate the
name of the dead in his inheritance, that the
name of the dead may not be cut off from
among his brethren and from the gate of his
native place; you are witnesses this day." 11 Then
all the people who were at the gate, and the
elders, said, "We are witnesses. May the LORD
make the woman, who is coming into your
house, like Rachel and Leah, who together
built up the house of Israel. May you prosper
in Eph'rathah and be renowned in Bethlehem;
12 and may your house be like the house of
Per'ez, whom Ta'mar bore to Judah, because of
the children that the LORD will give you by this
young woman."

13 So Boaz took Ruth and she became his
wife; and he went in to her, and the LORD gave
her conception, and she bore a son. 14 Then
the women said to Na'omi, "Blessed be the
LORD, who has not left you this day without
next of kin; and may his name be renowned
in Israel! 15 He shall be to you a restorer of

life and a nourisher of your old age; for
your daughter-in-law who loves you, who
is more to you than seven sons, has borne
him." [16]Then Na′omi took the child and laid
him in her bosom, and became his nurse.
[17]And the women of the neighborhood gave
him a name, saying, "A son has been born to
Na′omi." They named him O′bed; he was the
father of Jesse, the father of David.
[18]Now these are the descendants of Per′ez:
Perez was the father of Hezron, [19]Hezron of
Ram, Ram of Ammin′adab, [20]Ammin′adab
of Nahshon, Nahshon of Salmon, [21]Salmon
of Boaz, Boaz of O′bed, [22]O′bed of Jesse, and
Jesse of David.

A Psalm.

PSALM 98 [97]

O sing to the Lord a new song,
for he has done marvelous things!
His right hand and his holy arm
have gotten him victory.
[2]The Lord has made known his victory,
he has revealed his vindication in the
sight of the nations.
[3]He has remembered his mercy
and faithfulness
to the house of Israel.
All the ends of the earth have seen
the victory of our God.

[4]Make a joyful noise to the Lord, all
the earth;
break forth into joyous song and
sing praises!
[5]Sing praises to the Lord with the lyre,
with the lyre and the sound of melody!
[6]With trumpets and the sound of the horn
make a joyful noise before the King,
the Lord!

[7]Let the sea roar, and all that fills it;
the world and those who dwell in it!
[8]Let the floods clap their hands;
let the hills sing for joy together
[9]before the Lord, for he comes
to judge the earth.
He will judge the world with righteousness,
and the peoples with equity.

LUKE 15

**[11]And he said, "There was a
man who had two sons; [12]and
the younger of them said to
his father, 'Father, give me the share of
property that falls to me.' And he divided his living between them. [13]Not**
many days later, the younger son gathered
all he had and took his journey into a
far country, and there he squandered his
property in loose living. [14]And when he had
spent everything, a great famine arose in that
country, and he began to be in want. [15]So he
went and joined himself to one of the citizens
of that country, who sent him into his fields
to feed swine. [16]And he would gladly have
fed on the pods that the swine ate; and no
one gave him anything. [17]But when he came
to himself he said, 'How many of my father's
hired servants have bread enough and to
spare, but I perish here with hunger! [18]I will
arise and go to my father, and I will say to
him, "Father, I have sinned against heaven
and before you; [19]I am no longer worthy to
be called your son; treat me as one of your
hired servants."' [20]And he arose and came to
his father. But while he was yet at a distance,
his father saw him and had compassion,
and ran and embraced him and kissed him.
[21]And the son said to him, 'Father, I have
sinned against heaven and before you; I am
no longer worthy to be called your son.' [22]But
the father said to his servants, 'Bring quickly
the best robe, and put it on him; and put a
ring on his hand, and shoes on his feet; [23]and
bring the fatted calf and kill it, and let us eat
and make merry; [24]for this my son was dead,
and is alive again; he was lost, and is found.'
And they began to make merry.
[25]"Now his elder son was in the field; and
as he came and drew near to the house, he
heard music and dancing. [26]And he called
one of the servants and asked what this
meant. [27]And he said to him, 'Your brother

has come, and your father has killed the fatted calf, because he has received him safe and sound.' [28]But he was angry and refused to go in. His father came out and entreated him, [29]but he answered his father, 'Behold, these many years I have served you, and I never disobeyed your command; yet you never gave me a kid, that I might make merry with my friends. [30]But when this son of yours came, who has devoured your living with harlots, you killed for him the fatted calf!' [31]And he said to him, 'Son, you are always with me, and all that is mine is yours. [32]It was fitting to make merry and be glad, for this your brother was dead, and is alive; he was lost, and is found.' "

16 He also said to the disciples, "There was a rich man who had a steward, and charges were brought to him that this man was wasting his goods. [2]And he called him and said to him, 'What is this that I hear about you? Turn in the account of your stewardship, for you can no longer be steward.' [3]And the steward said to himself, 'What shall I do, since my master is taking the stewardship away from me? I am not strong enough to dig, and I am ashamed to beg. [4]I have decided what to do, so that people may receive me into their houses when I am put out of the stewardship.' [5]So, summoning his master's debtors one by one, he said to the first, 'How much do you owe my master?' [6]He said, 'A hundred measures of oil.' And he said to him, 'Take your bill, and sit down quickly and write fifty.' [7]Then he said to another, 'And how much do you owe?' He said, 'A hundred measures of wheat.' He said to him, 'Take your bill, and write eighty.' [8]The master commended the dishonest steward for his prudence; for the sons of this world are wiser in their own generation than the sons of light. [9]And I tell you, make friends for yourselves by means of unrighteous mammon, so that when it fails they may receive you into the eternal habitations.

[10]"He who is faithful in a very little is faithful also in much; and he who is dishonest in a very little is dishonest also in much. [11]If then you have not been faithful in the unrighteous mammon, who will entrust to you the true riches? [12]And if you have not been faithful in that which is another's, who will give you that which is your own? [13]No servant can serve two masters; for either he will hate the one and love the other, or he will be devoted to the one and despise the other. You cannot serve God and mammon."

[14]The Pharisees, who were lovers of money, heard all this, and they scoffed at him. [15]But he said to them, "You are those who justify yourselves before men, but God knows your hearts; for what is exalted among men is an abomination in the sight of God.

[16]"The law and the prophets were until John; since then the good news of the kingdom of God is preached, and every one enters it violently. [17]But it is easier for heaven and earth to pass away, than for one dot of the law to become void.

[18]"Every one who divorces his wife and marries another commits adultery, and he who marries a woman divorced from her husband commits adultery."

REFLECTION

Sometimes we find ourselves at a dead end, unable to find an escape or a way forward. The Lord, who wins "victory" with his "holy arm" (Ps 98:1), wants to deliver us from such stagnation. His salvation is about continuing the story, our story, rather than letting it come to an end. Ruth's story could have ended with no husband, no children, and no future, but instead she finds a faithful kinsman redeemer in Boaz, who provides for her material needs and also marries her. The prodigal son finds himself at a dead end in life: poor, desperate, and feeding pigs in a foreign land. His story could have ended there in despair, but he "came to himself" (Lk 15:17) and returned to his father in humble repentance. Sin is a dead end, a place from which we cannot extricate ourselves, a lonely territory away from God. When we turn to the Lord and repent, he is faithful to his promises, running to us like the prodigal's father, who "embraced him and kissed him" (v. 20). He welcomes us back, forgives our sins, and rejoices over us. When you come to a dead end, do you turn to the Lord?

April 24

1 SAMUEL 1

There was a certain man of Ra-matha′im-zo′phim of the hill country of E′phraim, whose name was Elka′nah the son of Jero′ham, son of Eli′hu, son of To′hu, son of Zuph, an E′ph-raimite. [2]He had two wives; the name of the one was Hannah, and the name of the other Penin′nah. And Peninnah had children, but Hannah had no children.

[3]Now this man used to go up year by year from his city to worship and to sacrifice to the LORD of hosts at Shiloh, where the two sons of Eli, Hoph′ni and Phin′ehas, were priests of the LORD. [4]On the day when Elka′nah sacrificed, he would give portions to Penin′nah his wife and to all her sons and daughters; [5]and, although he loved Hannah, he would give Hannah only one portion, because the LORD had closed her womb. [6]And her rival used to provoke her sorely, to irritate her, because the LORD had closed her womb. [7]So it went on year by year; as often as she went up to the house of the LORD, she used to provoke her. Therefore Hannah wept and would not eat. [8]And Elka′nah, her husband, said to her, "Hannah, why do you weep? And why do you not eat? And why is your heart sad? Am I not more to you than ten sons?"

[9]After they had eaten and drunk in Shiloh, Hannah rose. Now Eli the priest was sitting on the seat beside the doorpost of the temple of the LORD. [10]She was deeply distressed and prayed to the LORD, and wept bitterly. [11]And she vowed a vow and said, "O LORD of hosts, if you will indeed look on the affliction of your maidservant, and remember me, and not forget your maidservant, but will give to your maidservant a son, then I will give him to the LORD all the days of his life, and no razor shall touch his head."

[12]As she continued praying before the LORD, Eli observed her mouth. [13]Hannah was speaking in her heart; only her lips moved, and her voice was not heard; therefore Eli took her to be a drunken woman. [14]And Eli said to her, "How long will you be drunken? Put away your wine from you." [15]But Hannah answered, "No, my lord, I am a woman sorely troubled; I have drunk neither wine nor strong drink, but I have been pouring out my soul before the LORD. [16]Do not regard your maidservant as a base woman, for all along I have been speaking out of my great anxiety and vexation." [17]Then Eli answered, "Go in peace, and the God of Israel grant your petition which you have made to him." [18]And she said, "Let your maidservant find favor in your eyes." Then the woman went her way and ate, and her countenance was no longer sad.

[19]They rose early in the morning and worshiped before the LORD; then they went back to their house at Ra′mah. And Elka′nah knew Hannah his wife, and the LORD remembered her; [20]and in due time Hannah conceived and bore a son, and she called his name Samuel, for she said, "I have asked him of the LORD."

[21]And the man Elka′nah and all his house went up to offer to the LORD the yearly sacrifice, and to pay his vow. [22]But Hannah did not go up, for she said to her husband, "As soon as the child is weaned, I will bring him, that he may appear in the presence of the LORD, and abide there for ever." [23]Elka′nah her husband said to her, "Do what seems best to you, wait until you have weaned him; only, may the LORD establish his word." So the woman remained and nursed her son, until she weaned him. [24]And when she had weaned him, she took him up with her, along with a three-year-old bull, an ephah of flour, and a skin of wine; and she brought him to the house of the LORD at Shiloh; and the child was young. [25]Then they slew the bull, and they brought the child to Eli. [26]And she said, "Oh, my lord! As you live, my lord, I am the woman who was standing here in your presence, praying to the LORD. [27]For this child I prayed; and the LORD has granted me my petition which I made to him. [28]Therefore I have lent him to the LORD; as long as he lives, he is lent to the LORD."

And they worshiped the LORD there.

2 Hannah also prayed and said,
"My heart exults in the LORD;
my strength is exalted in the LORD.
My mouth derides my enemies,
because I rejoice in your salvation.

2 "There is none holy like the LORD,
there is none besides you;
there is no rock like our God.
3 Talk no more so very proudly,
let not arrogance come from your mouth;
for the LORD is a God of knowledge,
and by him actions are weighed.
4 The bows of the mighty are broken,
but the feeble gird on strength.
5 Those who were full have hired themselves
out for bread,
but those who were hungry have ceased
to hunger.
The barren has borne seven,
but she who has many children is forlorn.
6 The LORD kills and brings to life;
he brings down to Sheol and raises up.
7 The LORD makes poor and makes rich;
he brings low, he also exalts.
8 He raises up the poor from the dust;
he lifts the needy from the dung heap,
to make them sit with princes
and inherit a seat of honor.
For the pillars of the earth are the LORD's,
and on them he has set the world.

9 "He will guard the feet of his faithful ones;
but the wicked shall be cut off in
darkness;
for not by might shall a man prevail.
10 The adversaries of the LORD shall be
broken to pieces;
against them he will thunder in heaven.
The LORD will judge the ends of the earth;
he will give strength to his king,
and exalt the power of his anointed."

11 Then Elka′nah went home to Ra′mah.
And the boy ministered to the LORD, in the
presence of Eli the priest.
12 Now the sons of Eli were worthless men;
they had no regard for the LORD.
13 The cus-
tom of the priests with the people was that
when any man offered sacrifice, the priest's
servant would come, while the meat was
boiling, with a three-pronged fork in his
hand,
14 and he would thrust it into the pan,
or kettle, or caldron, or pot; all that the fork
brought up the priest would take for himself.
So they did at Shiloh to all the Israelites who
came there.
15 Moreover, before the fat was
burned, the priest's servant would come and
say to the man who was sacrificing, "Give
meat for the priest to roast; for he will not
accept boiled meat from you, but raw."
16 And
if the man said to him, "Let them burn the
fat first, and then take as much as you wish,"
he would say, "No, you must give it now; and
if not, I will take it by force."
17 Thus the sin of
the young men was very great in the sight of
the LORD; for the men treated the offering of
the LORD with contempt.

18 Samuel was ministering before the LORD,
a boy girded with a linen ephod.
19 And his
mother used to make for him a little robe
and take it to him each year, when she went
up with her husband to offer the yearly
sacrifice.
20 Then Eli would bless Elka′nah
and his wife, and say, "The LORD give you
children by this woman for the loan which
she lent to the LORD"; so then they would
return to their home.

21 And the LORD visited Hannah, and she
conceived and bore three sons and two
daughters. And the boy Samuel grew in the
presence of the LORD.

22 Now Eli was very old, and he heard all
that his sons were doing to all Israel, and how
they lay with the women who served at the
entrance to the tent of meeting.
23 And he said
to them, "Why do you do such things? For I
hear of your evil dealings from all the people.
24 No, my sons; it is no good report that I hear
the people of the LORD spreading abroad.
25 If
a man sins against a man, God will mediate
for him; but if a man sins against the LORD,
who can intercede for him?" But they would
not listen to the voice of their father; for it
was the will of the LORD to slay them.

26 Now the boy Samuel continued to grow
both in stature and in favor with the LORD
and with men.

27 And there came a man of God to Eli,
and said to him, "Thus the LORD has said, 'I
revealed myself to the house of your father

when they were in Egypt subject to the house of Pharaoh. [28]And I chose him out of all the tribes of Israel to be my priest, to go up to my altar, to burn incense, to wear an ephod before me; and I gave to the house of your father all my offerings by fire from the sons of Israel. [29]Why then look with greedy eye at my sacrifices and my offerings which I commanded, and honor your sons above me by fattening yourselves upon the choicest parts of every offering of my people Israel?' [30]Therefore the LORD the God of Israel declares: 'I promised that your house and the house of your father should go in and out before me for ever'; but now the LORD declares: 'Far be it from me; for those who honor me I will honor, and those who despise me shall be lightly esteemed. [31]Behold, the days are coming, when I will cut off your strength and the strength of your father's house, so that there will not be an old man in your house. [32]Then in distress you will look with envious eye on all the prosperity which shall be bestowed upon Israel; and there shall not be an old man in your house for ever. [33]The man of you whom I shall not cut off from my altar shall be spared to weep out his eyes and grieve his heart; and all the increase of your house shall die by the sword of men. [34]And this which shall befall your two sons, Hoph′ni and Phin′ehas, shall be the sign to you: both of them shall die on the same day. [35]And I will raise up for myself a faithful priest, who shall do according to what is in my heart and in my mind; and I will build him a sure house, and he shall go in and out before my anointed for ever. [36]And every one who is left in your house shall come to implore him for a piece of silver or a loaf of bread, and shall say, "Put me, I beg you, in one of the priest's places, that I may eat a morsel of bread."'"

PSALM 99 [98]

The LORD reigns; let the peoples tremble!
He sits enthroned upon the cherubim; let the earth quake!
[2]The LORD is great in Zion;
he is exalted over all the peoples.
[3]Let them praise your great and awesome name!
Holy is he!
[4]Mighty King, lover of justice,
you have established equity;
you have executed justice
and righteousness in Jacob.
[5]Extol the LORD our God;
worship at his footstool!
Holy is he!

[6]Moses and Aaron were among his priests,
Samuel also was among those who called on his name.
They cried to the LORD, and he answered them.
[7]He spoke to them in the pillar of cloud;
they kept his testimonies,
and the statutes that he gave them.

[8]O LORD our God, you answered them;
you were a forgiving God to them,
but an avenger of their wrongdoings.
[9]Extol the LORD our God,
and worship at his holy mountain;
for the LORD our God is holy!

LUKE 16

[19]"**There was a rich man, who was clothed in purple and fine linen and who feasted sumptuously every day. [20]And at his gate lay a poor** man named Laz′arus, full of sores, [21]who desired to be fed with what fell from the rich man's table; moreover the dogs came and licked his sores. [22]The poor man died and was carried by the angels to Abraham's bosom. The rich man also died and was buried; [23]and in Hades, being in torment, he lifted up his eyes, and saw Abraham far off and Laz′arus in his bosom. [24]And he called out, 'Father Abraham, have mercy upon me, and send Laz′arus to dip the end of his finger in water and cool my tongue; for I am in anguish in this flame.'

25But Abraham said, 'Son, remember that
you in your lifetime received your good
things, and Laz′arus in like manner evil
things; but now he is comforted here,
and you are in anguish. 26And besides all
this, between us and you a great chasm
has been fixed, in order that those who
would pass from here to you may not be
able, and none may cross from there to
us.' 27And he said, 'Then I beg you, father,
to send him to my father's house, 28for I
have five brothers, so that he may warn
them, lest they also come into this place
of torment.' 29But Abraham said, 'They
have Moses and the prophets; let them
hear them.' 30And he said, 'No, father
Abraham; but if some one goes to them
from the dead, they will repent.' 31He said
to him, 'If they do not hear Moses and the
prophets, neither will they be convinced
if some one should rise from the dead.' "

17 And he said to his disciples, "Temptations to sin are sure to come; but
woe to him by whom they come! 2It would
be better for him if a millstone were hung
round his neck and he were cast into the
sea, than that he should cause one of these
little ones to sin. 3Take heed to yourselves;
if your brother sins, rebuke him, and if he
repents, forgive him; 4and if he sins against
you seven times in the day, and turns to you
seven times, and says, 'I repent,' you must
forgive him."

5The apostles said to the Lord, "Increase
our faith!" 6And the Lord said, "If you had
faith as a grain of mustard seed, you could
say to this sycamine tree, 'Be rooted up, and
be planted in the sea,' and it would obey you.

7"Will any one of you, who has a servant
plowing or keeping sheep, say to him when
he has come in from the field, 'Come at once
and sit down at table'? 8Will he not rather
say to him, 'Prepare supper for me, and
put on your apron and serve me, till I eat
and drink; and afterward you shall eat and
drink'? 9Does he thank the servant because
he did what was commanded? 10So you also,
when you have done all that is commanded
you, say, 'We are unworthy servants; we
have only done what was our duty.' "

REFLECTION

"Hannah wept and would not eat" (1 Sm 1:7) because she is barren and her husband's other, more fertile wife mocks her. Hannah is powerless. Though her husband loves her, she cannot heal herself or change her situation. Instead, in her powerlessness, she cries out to God. In her prayer for a child, she vows to dedicate the baby as a Nazirite for the Lord. Indeed, the Lord hears her prayer, and she gives birth to the prophet Samuel, who is "among those who called on his name" (Ps 99:6). The poor man, Lazarus, in Jesus's parable is also powerless. But in his hunger and neediness, he relies on the Lord, who welcomes him to "Abraham's bosom" when he dies. In spite of all our resources, relationships, and accomplishments, before God we are all like Hannah and Lazarus—powerless. The rich man in the parable is also powerless, but he does not acknowledge the fact until it is too late. The lesson Hannah and Lazarus teach us is that we must recognize our helplessness before God and depend on him for deliverance. He is a "Mighty King" (v. 4), a powerful God who delights in saving us if we allow ourselves to depend on him. Do you recognize your own powerlessness before our powerful God?

April 25

1 SAMUEL 3

Now the boy Samuel was min-
istering to the LORD under Eli.
And the word of the LORD was rare in
those days; there was no frequent vision.
2At that time Eli, whose eyesight had
begun to grow dim, so that he could not
see, was lying down in his own place; 3the
lamp of God had not yet gone out, and
Samuel was lying down within the temple
of the LORD, where the ark of God was.
4Then the LORD called, "Samuel! Samuel!"

and he said, "Here I am!" 5and ran to Eli,
and said, "Here I am, for you called me."
But he said, "I did not call; lie down again."
So he went and lay down. 6And the LORD
called again, "Samuel!" And Samuel arose
and went to Eli, and said, "Here I am, for
you called me." But he said, "I did not call,
my son; lie down again." 7Now Samuel did
not yet know the LORD, and the word of
the LORD had not yet been revealed to
him. 8And the LORD called Samuel again
the third time. And he arose and went to
Eli, and said, "Here I am, for you called
me." Then Eli perceived that the LORD
was calling the boy. 9Therefore Eli said
to Samuel, "Go, lie down; and if he calls
you, you shall say, 'Speak, LORD, for your
servant hears.'" So Samuel went and lay
down in his place.

10And the LORD came and stood forth,
calling as at other times, "Samuel! Samuel!"
And Samuel said, "Speak, for your servant
hears." 11Then the LORD said to Samuel,
"Behold, I am about to do a thing in Israel,
at which the two ears of every one that
hears it will tingle. 12On that day I will
fulfil against Eli all that I have spoken
concerning his house, from beginning to
end. 13And I tell him that I am about to
punish his house for ever, for the iniquity
which he knew, because his sons were
blaspheming God, and he did not restrain
them. 14Therefore I swear to the house of
Eli that the iniquity of Eli's house shall
not be expiated by sacrifice or offering for
ever."

15Samuel lay until morning; then he opened the doors of the house of the LORD. And
Samuel was afraid to tell the vision to Eli.
16But Eli called Samuel and said, "Samuel,
my son." And he said, "Here I am." 17And
Eli said, "What was it that he told you? Do
not hide it from me. May God do so to you
and more also, if you hide anything from
me of all that he told you." 18So Samuel told
him everything and hid nothing from him.
And he said, "It is the LORD; let him do what
seems good to him."

19And Samuel grew, and the LORD was
with him and let none of his words fall to the
ground. 20And all Israel from Dan to Be′er-
she′ba knew that Samuel was established
as a prophet of the LORD. 21And the LORD
appeared again at Shiloh, for the LORD
revealed himself to Samuel at Shiloh by the
4 word of the LORD. 1And the word of
Samuel came to all Israel.

Now Israel went out to battle against the
Philis′tines; they encamped at Ebenezer,
and the Philistines encamped at A′phek.
2The Philis′tines drew up in line against
Israel, and when the battle spread, Israel
was defeated by the Philistines, who slew
about four thousand men on the field of
battle. 3And when the troops came to the
camp, the elders of Israel said, "Why has
the LORD put us to rout today before the
Philis′tines? Let us bring the ark of the
covenant of the LORD here from Shiloh,
that he may come among us and save
us from the power of our enemies." 4So
the people sent to Shiloh, and brought
from there the ark of the covenant of
the LORD of hosts, who is enthroned on
the cherubim; and the two sons of Eli,
Hoph′ni and Phin′ehas, were there with
the ark of the covenant of God.

5When the ark of the covenant of the LORD
came into the camp, all Israel gave a mighty
shout, so that the earth resounded. 6And
when the Philis′tines heard the noise of the
shouting, they said, "What does this great
shouting in the camp of the Hebrews mean?"
And when they learned that the ark of the
LORD had come to the camp, 7the Philis′tines
were afraid; for they said, "A god has come
into the camp." And they said, "Woe to us!
For nothing like this has happened before.
8Woe to us! Who can deliver us from the
power of these mighty gods? These are the
gods who struck the Egyptians with every
sort of plague in the wilderness. 9Take
courage, and acquit yourselves like men, O
Philis′tines, lest you become slaves to the
Hebrews as they have been to you; acquit
yourselves like men and fight."

10So the Philis′tines fought, and Israel was
defeated, and they fled, every man to his
home; and there was a very great slaughter,
for there fell of Israel thirty thousand foot

soldiers. [11]And the ark of God was captured;
and the two sons of Eli, Hoph′ni and
Phin′ehas, were slain.
[12]A man of Benjamin ran from the
battle line, and came to Shiloh the same
day, with his clothes torn and with earth
upon his head. [13]When he arrived, Eli was
sitting upon his seat by the road watching,
for his heart trembled for the ark of God.
And when the man came into the city
and told the news, all the city cried out.
[14]When Eli heard the sound of the outcry,
he said, "What is this uproar?" Then the
man hastened and came and told Eli.
[15]Now Eli was ninety-eight years old and
his eyes were set, so that he could not see.
[16]And the man said to Eli, "I am he who
has come from the battle; I fled from the
battle today." And he said, "How did it go,
my son?" [17]He who brought the tidings
answered and said, "Israel has fled before
the Philis′tines, and there has also been a
great slaughter among the people; your two
sons also, Hoph′ni and Phin′ehas, are dead,
and the ark of God has been captured."
[18]When he mentioned the ark of God, Eli
fell over backward from his seat by the side
of the gate; and his neck was broken and he
died, for he was an old man, and heavy. He
had judged Israel forty years.
[19]Now his daughter-in-law, the wife of
Phin′ehas, was with child, about to give
birth. And when she heard the tidings that
the ark of God was captured, and that her
father-in-law and her husband were dead,
she bowed and gave birth; for her pains
came upon her. [20]And about the time of
her death the women attending her said to
her, "Fear not, for you have borne a son."
But she did not answer or give heed. [21]And
she named the child Ich′abod, saying,
"The glory has departed from Israel!"
because the ark of God had been captured
and because of her father-in-law and her
husband. [22]And she said, "The glory has
departed from Israel, for the ark of God
has been captured."
5 When the Philis′tines captured the ark
of God, they carried it from Ebenezer
to Ash′dod; [2]then the Philis′tines took the
ark of God and brought it into the house
of Da′gon and set it up beside Dagon. [3]And
when the people of Ash′dod rose early the
next day, behold, Da′gon had fallen face
downward on the ground before the ark of
the LORD. So they took Dagon and put him
back in his place. [4]But when they rose early
on the next morning, behold, Da′gon had
fallen face downward on the ground before
the ark of the LORD, and the head of Dagon
and both his hands were lying cut off upon
the threshold; only the trunk of Dagon was
left to him. [5]This is why the priests of Da′gon
and all who enter the house of Dagon do not
tread on the threshold of Dagon in Ash′dod
to this day.
[6]The hand of the LORD was heavy upon
the people of Ash′dod, and he terrified
and afflicted them with tumors, both
Ashdod and its territory. [7]And when the
men of Ash′dod saw how things were,
they said, "The ark of the God of Israel
must not remain with us; for his hand
is heavy upon us and upon Da′gon our
god." [8]So they sent and gathered together
all the lords of the Philis′tines, and said,
"What shall we do with the ark of the God
of Israel?" They answered, "Let the ark
of the God of Israel be brought around
to Gath." So they brought the ark of the
God of Israel there. [9]But after they had
brought it around, the hand of the LORD
was against the city, causing a very great
panic, and he afflicted the men of the
city, both young and old, so that tumors
broke out upon them. [10]So they sent the
ark of God to Ek′ron. But when the ark of
God came to Ekron, the people of Ekron
cried out, "They have brought around to
us the ark of the God of Israel to slay us
and our people." [11]They sent therefore
and gathered together all the lords of the
Philis′tines, and said, "Send away the ark
of the God of Israel, and let it return to
its own place, that it may not slay us and
our people." For there was a deathly panic
throughout the whole city. The hand of
God was very heavy there; [12]the men who
did not die were stricken with tumors,
and the cry of the city went up to heaven.

A Psalm for the thank offering.

PSALM 100 [99]

Make a joyful noise to the LORD, all
the lands!
2 Serve the LORD with gladness!
Come into his presence with singing!

3 Know that the LORD is God!
It is he that made us, and we are his;
we are his people, and the sheep of
his pasture.

4 Enter his gates with thanksgiving,
and his courts with praise!
Give thanks to him, bless his name!

5 For the LORD is good;
his mercy endures for ever,
and his faithfulness to all generations.

LUKE 17

**[11]On the way to Jerusalem he was
passing along between Sama′ria
and Galilee. [12]And as he entered
a village, he was met by ten lepers, who
stood at a distance [13]and lifted up their
voices and said, "Jesus, Master, have**
mercy on us." [14]When he saw them he said to
them, "Go and show yourselves to the priests."
And as they went they were cleansed. [15]Then
one of them, when he saw that he was healed,
turned back, praising God with a loud voice;
[16]and he fell on his face at Jesus' feet, giving him
thanks. Now he was a Samaritan. [17]Then said
Jesus, "Were not ten cleansed? Where are the
nine? [18]Was no one found to return and give
praise to God except this foreigner?" [19]And he
said to him, "Rise and go your way; your faith
has made you well."

[20]Being asked by the Pharisees when the
kingdom of God was coming, he answered
them, "The kingdom of God is not coming
with signs to be observed; [21]nor will they say,
'Behold, here it is!' or 'There!' for behold,
the kingdom of God is in your midst."

[22]And he said to the disciples, "The days
are coming when you will desire to see
one of the days of the Son of man, and
you will not see it. [23]And they will say to
you, 'Behold, there!' or 'Behold, here!' Do
not go, do not follow them. [24]For as the
lightning flashes and lights up the sky
from one side to the other, so will the
Son of man be in his day. [25]But first he
must suffer many things and be rejected
by this generation. [26]As it was in the days
of Noah, so will it be in the days of the
Son of man. [27]They ate, they drank, they
married, they were given in marriage,
until the day when Noah entered the ark,
and the flood came and destroyed them
all. [28]Likewise as it was in the days of
Lot—they ate, they drank, they bought,
they sold, they planted, they built, [29]but
on the day when Lot went out from
Sodom, fire and brimstone rained from
heaven and destroyed them all—[30]so will
it be on the day when the Son of man is
revealed. [31]On that day, let him who is
on the housetop, with his goods in the
house, not come down to take them away;
and likewise let him who is in the field
not turn back. [32]Remember Lot's wife.
[33]Whoever seeks to gain his life will lose
it, but whoever loses his life will preserve
it. [34]I tell you, in that night there will be
two men in one bed; one will be taken
and the other left. [35]There will be two
women grinding together; one will be
taken and the other left." [37]And they said
to him, "Where, Lord?" He said to them,
"Where the body is, there the eagles will
be gathered together."

18 And he told them a parable, to the
effect that they ought always to pray
and not lose heart. [2]He said, "In a certain city
there was a judge who neither feared God
nor regarded man; [3]and there was a widow
in that city who kept coming to him and
saying, 'Vindicate me against my adversary.'
[4]For a while he refused; but afterward he
said to himself, 'Though I neither fear God
nor regard man, [5]yet because this widow
bothers me, I will vindicate her, or she will
wear me out by her continual coming.'" [6]And

the Lord said, "Hear what the unrighteous
judge says. 7And will not God vindicate his
elect, who cry to him day and night? Will
he delay long over them? 8I tell you, he will
vindicate them speedily. Nevertheless, when
the Son of man comes, will he find faith
on earth?"
9He also told this parable to some who
trusted in themselves that they were righteous and despised others: 10"Two men went
up into the temple to pray, one a Pharisee
and the other a tax collector. 11The Pharisee
stood and prayed thus with himself, 'God,
I thank you that I am not like other men,
extortioners, unjust, adulterers, or even
like this tax collector. 12I fast twice a week,
I give tithes of all that I get.' 13But the tax
collector, standing far off, would not even
lift up his eyes to heaven, but beat his breast,
saying, 'God, be merciful to me a sinner!' 14I
tell you, this man went down to his house
justified rather than the other; for every one
who exalts himself will be humbled, but he
who humbles himself will be exalted."

REFLECTION

The priestly sons of Eli were worthless men, who had no regard for the Lord and treated the sacrificial offerings with contempt. Their sinful pride, and their father's disregard, brings destruction on them all. Eli's sons epitomize the words of Jesus that those who seek their own gain, will lose their life. Eli and his sons were priestly ministers, but where we would expect to find them, instead we find the young Samuel, close to the ark where God's presence dwelt, ministering to the Lord. Jesus teaches, "Every one who exalts himself will be humbled, but he who humbles himself will be exalted" (Lk 18:14). Eli falls from his chair, he and his house brought low and cut off. But Samuel, humbly lying in the Temple, will be raised up to be the first prophet of Israel; he will hear and know the Lord, and thus be able to direct God's people. Samuel reminds us that humility is the foundation of prayer, it opens the door for us to see and to hear the Lord. Like Samuel, it is the one leper who humbly returns to Jesus who truly encounters the Lord. What can you do today to walk humbly with the Lord?

April 26

1 SAMUEL 6

**The ark of the LORD was in the
country of the Philis′tines sev-
en months. 2And the Philis′tines
called for the priests and the diviners
and said, "What shall we do with the ark
of the LORD? Tell us with what we shall**
send it to its place." 3They said, "If you send
away the ark of the God of Israel, do not
send it empty, but by all means return him a
guilt offering. Then you will be healed, and
it will be known to you why his hand does
not turn away from you." 4And they said,
"What is the guilt offering that we shall return to him?" They answered, "Five golden
tumors and five golden mice, according to
the number of the lords of the Philis′tines;
for the same plague was upon all of you and
upon your lords. 5So you must make images of your tumors and images of your mice
that ravage the land, and give glory to the
God of Israel; perhaps he will lighten his
hand from off you and your gods and your
land. 6Why should you harden your hearts
as the Egyptians and Pharaoh hardened
their hearts? After he had made sport of
them, did not they let the people go, and
they departed? 7Now then, take and prepare
a new cart and two milch cows upon which
there has never come a yoke, and yoke the
cows to the cart, but take their calves home,
away from them. 8And take the ark of the
LORD and place it on the cart, and put in
a box at its side the figures of gold, which
you are returning to him as a guilt offering.
Then send it off, and let it go its way. 9And
watch; if it goes up on the way to its own
land, to Beth-she′mesh, then it is he who
has done us this great harm; but if not, then
we shall know that it is not his hand that
struck us, it happened to us by chance."
10The men did so, and took two milch
cows and yoked them to the cart, and shut
up their calves at home. 11And they put the

ark of the LORD on the cart, and the box
with the golden mice and the images of
their tumors. [12]And the cows went straight
in the direction of Beth-she′mesh along one
highway, lowing as they went; they turned
neither to the right nor to the left, and the
lords of the Philis′tines went after them as
far as the border of Beth-shemesh. [13]Now
the people of Beth-she′mesh were reaping
their wheat harvest in the valley; and when
they lifted up their eyes and saw the ark,
they rejoiced to see it. [14]The cart came into
the field of Joshua of Beth-she′mesh, and
stopped there. A great stone was there;
and they split up the wood of the cart and
offered the cows as a burnt offering to the
LORD. [15]And the Levites took down the ark
of the LORD and the box that was beside it,
in which were the golden figures, and set
them upon the great stone; and the men of
Beth-she′mesh offered burnt offerings and
sacrificed sacrifices on that day to the LORD.
[16]And when the five lords of the Philis′tines
saw it, they returned that day to Ek′ron.

[17]These are the golden tumors, which the
Philis′tines returned as a guilt offering to
the LORD: one for Ash′dod, one for Gaza,
one for Ash′kelon, one for Gath, one for
Ek′ron; [18]also the golden mice, according to
the number of all the cities of the Philis′tines
belonging to the five lords, both fortified
cities and unwalled villages. The great stone,
beside which they set down the ark of the
LORD, is a witness to this day in the field of
Joshua of Beth-she′mesh.

[19]And he slew some of the men of Beth-
she′mesh, because they looked into the ark
of the LORD; he slew seventy men of them,
and the people mourned because the LORD
had made a great slaughter among the
people. [20]Then the men of Beth-she′mesh
said, "Who is able to stand before the LORD,
this holy God? And to whom shall he go up
away from us?" [21]So they sent messengers to
the inhabitants of Kir′iath-je′arim, saying,
"The Philis′tines have returned the ark of
the LORD. Come down and take it up to
7 you." [1]And the men of Kir′iath-je′arim
came and took up the ark of the LORD,
and brought it to the house of Abin′adab
on the hill; and they consecrated his son,
Elea′zar, to have charge of the ark of the
LORD. [2]From the day that the ark was lodged
at Kir′iath-je′arim, a long time passed, some
twenty years, and all the house of Israel
lamented after the LORD.

[3]Then Samuel said to all the house of
Israel, "If you are returning to the LORD with
all your heart, then put away the foreign
gods and the Ash′taroth from among you,
and direct your heart to the LORD, and serve
him only, and he will deliver you out of
the hand of the Philis′tines." [4]So Israel put
away the Ba′als and the Ash′taroth, and they
served the LORD only.

[5]Then Samuel said, "Gather all Israel at
Mizpah, and I will pray to the LORD for
you." [6]So they gathered at Mizpah, and drew
water and poured it out before the LORD,
and fasted on that day, and said there, "We
have sinned against the LORD." And Samuel
judged the sons of Israel at Mizpah. [7]Now
when the Philis′tines heard that the sons of
Israel had gathered at Mizpah, the lords of
the Philistines went up against Israel. And
when the sons of Israel heard of it they were
afraid of the Philistines. [8]And the sons of
Israel said to Samuel, "Do not cease to cry
to the LORD our God for us, that he may
save us from the hand of the Philis′tines."
[9]So Samuel took a suckling lamb and offered
it as a whole burnt offering to the LORD;
and Samuel cried to the LORD for Israel,
and the LORD answered him. [10]As Samuel
was offering up the burnt offering, the
Philis′tines drew near to attack Israel; but
the LORD thundered with a mighty voice
that day against the Philistines and threw
them into confusion; and they were routed
before Israel. [11]And the men of Israel went
out of Mizpah and pursued the Philis′tines,
and struck them, as far as below Beth-car.

[12]Then Samuel took a stone and set it up
between Mizpah and Jesha′nah, and called
its name Ebenezer; for he said, "Hitherto
the LORD has helped us." [13]So the Philis′tines
were subdued and did not again enter the
territory of Israel. And the hand of the LORD
was against the Philistines all the days of
Samuel. [14]The cities which the Philis′tines

had taken from Israel were restored to Israel, from Ek′ron to Gath; and Israel rescued their territory from the hand of the Philistines. There was peace also between Israel and the Am′orites.

15Samuel judged Israel all the days of his life. 16And he went on a circuit year by year to Bethel, Gilgal, and Mizpah; and he judged Israel in all these places. 17Then he would come back to Ra′mah, for his home was there, and there also he administered justice to Israel. And he built there an altar to the LORD.

8 When Samuel became old, he made his sons judges over Israel. 2The name of his first-born son was Joel, and the name of his second, Abi′jah; they were judges in Be′er-she′ba. 3Yet his sons did not walk in his ways, but turned aside after gain; they took bribes and perverted justice.

4Then all the elders of Israel gathered together and came to Samuel at Ra′mah, 5and said to him, "Behold, you are old and your sons do not walk in your ways; now appoint for us a king to govern us like all the nations." 6But the thing displeased Samuel when they said, "Give us a king to govern us." And Samuel prayed to the LORD. 7And the LORD said to Samuel, "Listen to the voice of the people in all that they say to you; for they have not rejected you, but they have rejected me from being king over them. 8According to all the deeds which they have done to me, from the day I brought them up out of Egypt even to this day, forsaking me and serving other gods, so they are also doing to you. 9Now then, listen to their voice; only, you shall solemnly warn them, and show them the ways of the king who shall reign over them."

10So Samuel told all the words of the LORD to the people who were asking a king from him. 11He said, "These will be the ways of the king who will reign over you: he will take your sons and appoint them to his chariots and to be his horsemen, and to run before his chariots; 12and he will appoint for himself commanders of thousands and commanders of fifties, and some to plow his ground and to reap his harvest, and to make his implements of war and the equipment of his chariots. 13He will take your daughters to be perfumers and cooks and bakers. 14He will take the best of your fields and vineyards and olive orchards and give them to his servants. 15He will take the tenth of your grain and of your vineyards and give it to his officers and to his servants. 16He will take your menservants and maidservants, and the best of your cattle and your donkeys, and put them to his work. 17He will take the tenth of your flocks, and you shall be his slaves. 18And in that day you will cry out because of your king, whom you have chosen for yourselves; but the LORD will not answer you in that day."

19But the people refused to listen to the voice of Samuel; and they said, "No! but we will have a king over us, 20that we also may be like all the nations, and that our king may govern us and go out before us and fight our battles." 21And when Samuel had heard all the words of the people, he repeated them in the ears of the LORD. 22And the LORD said to Samuel, "Listen to their voice, and make them a king." Samuel then said to the men of Israel, "Go every man to his city."

A Psalm of David.

PSALM 101 [100]

I will sing of mercy and of justice;
  to you, O LORD, I will sing.
2I will give heed to the way that is blameless.
  Oh, when will you come to me?

I will walk with integrity of heart
  within my house;
3I will not set before my eyes
  anything that is base.

I hate the work of those who fall away;
  it shall not cling to me.
4Perverseness of heart shall be far from me;
  I will know nothing of evil.

5Him who slanders his neighbor secretly
I will destroy.
The man of haughty looks and arrogant
heart
I will not endure.

6I will look with favor on the faithful in
the land,
that they may dwell with me;
he who walks in the way that is blameless
shall minister to me.

7No man who practices deceit
shall dwell in my house;
no man who utters lies
shall continue in my presence.

8Morning by morning I will destroy
all the wicked in the land,
cutting off all the evildoers
from the city of the LORD.

LUKE 18

15Now they were bringing even infants to him that he might touch them; and when the disciples saw it, they rebuked them. 16But Jesus
called them to him, saying, "Let the children
come to me, and do not hinder them; for to
such belongs the kingdom of God. 17Truly,
I say to you, whoever does not receive the
kingdom of God like a child shall not enter it."
18And a ruler asked him, "Good Teacher,
what shall I do to inherit eternal life?" 19And
Jesus said to him, "Why do you call me
good? No one is good but God alone. 20You
know the commandments: 'Do not commit
adultery, Do not kill, Do not steal, Do not
bear false witness, Honor your father and
mother.'" 21And he said, "All these I have
observed from my youth." 22And when Jesus
heard it, he said to him, "One thing you still
lack. Sell all that you have and distribute
to the poor, and you will have treasure in
heaven; and come, follow me." 23But when
he heard this he became sad, for he was
very rich. 24Jesus looking at him said, "How
hard it is for those who have riches to enter
the kingdom of God! 25For it is easier for a
camel to go through the eye of a needle than
for a rich man to enter the kingdom of God."
26Those who heard it said, "Then who can be
saved?" 27But he said, "What is impossible
with men is possible with God." 28And Peter
said, "Behold, we have left our homes and
followed you." 29And he said to them, "Truly, I
say to you, there is no man who has left house
or wife or brothers or parents or children, for
the sake of the kingdom of God, 30who will
not receive manifold more in this time, and
in the age to come eternal life."
31And taking the Twelve, he said to them,
"Behold, we are going up to Jerusalem, and
everything that is written of the Son of man
by the prophets will be accomplished. 32For
he will be delivered to the Gentiles, and will
be mocked and shamefully treated and spit
upon; 33they will scourge him and kill him,
and on the third day he will rise." 34But they
understood none of these things; this saying was hidden from them, and they did not
grasp what was said.
35As he drew near to Jericho, a blind man
was sitting by the roadside begging; 36and
hearing a multitude going by, he inquired
what this meant. 37They told him, "Jesus
of Nazareth is passing by." 38And he cried,
"Jesus, Son of David, have mercy on me!"
39And those who were in front rebuked him,
telling him to be silent; but he cried out all
the more, "Son of David, have mercy on me!"
40And Jesus stopped, and commanded him to
be brought to him; and when he came near,
he asked him, 41"What do you want me to
do for you?" He said, "Lord, let me receive
my sight." 42And Jesus said to him, "Receive
your sight; your faith has made you well."
43And immediately he received his sight and
followed him, glorifying God; and all the
people, when they saw it, gave praise to God.

REFLECTION

We see in these readings two ways in which power is exercised—two kinds of kingship. On the one hand, Samuel warns the Israelites that a human king will tax heavily, taking as much as he can from the people: "He will take your daughters to be perfumers and cooks and bakers. He will take the best of your fields and vineyards and olive orchards and give them to his servants" (1 Sm 8:13–14). The king will take, and take greedily, without giving in return. Jesus, on the other hand, is a king who gives. He gives mercy and justice (see Ps 101:1) and favor to the faithful (see v. 6). He restores the blind man's sight (see Lk 18:42) and even suffers physical torment for our sake (see vv. 32–33). No wonder, then, that he tells the rich young man to "sell all" (v. 22), lest he become like a greedy king, building his own empire without regard for others. To follow the true King, we need to be like him in generosity—to give, rather than take and hoard; to empty ourselves, rather than amass power and possessions. Do you pattern your life after the generous kingship of Jesus?

April 27

1 SAMUEL 9

There was a man of Benjamin
whose name was Kish, the son
of Abi′el, son of Ze′ror, son of
Beco′rath, son of Aphi′ah, a Benjamin-
ite, a man of wealth; 2and he had a son
whose name was Saul, a handsome
young man. There was not a man among the
sons of Israel more handsome than he; from
his shoulders upward he was taller than any
of the people.
3Now the donkeys of Kish, Saul's father,
were lost. So Kish said to Saul his son, "Take
one of the servants with you, and arise, go
and look for the donkeys." 4And they passed
through the hill country of E′phraim and
passed through the land of Shal′ishah, but
they did not find them. And they passed
through the land of Sha′alim, but they were
not there. Then they passed through the
land of Benjamin, but did not find them.
5When they came to the land of Zuph,
Saul said to his servant who was with him,
"Come, let us go back, lest my father cease to
care about the donkeys and become anxious
about us." 6But he said to him, "Behold,
there is a man of God in this city, and he is
a man that is held in honor; all that he says
comes true. Let us go there; perhaps he can
tell us about the journey on which we have
set out." 7Then Saul said to his servant, "But
if we go, what can we bring the man? For the
bread in our sacks is gone, and there is no
present to bring to the man of God. What
have we?" 8The servant answered Saul again,
"Here, I have with me the fourth part of a
shekel of silver, and I will give it to the man
of God, to tell us our way." 9(Formerly in
Israel, when a man went to inquire of God,
he said, "Come, let us go to the seer"; for he
who is now called a prophet was formerly
called a seer.) 10And Saul said to his servant,
"Well said; come, let us go." So they went to
the city where the man of God was.
11As they went up the hill to the city, they
met young maidens coming out to draw
water, and said to them, "Is the seer here?"
12They answered, "He is; behold, he is just
ahead of you. Make haste; he has come just
now to the city, because the people have a
sacrifice today on the high place. 13As soon
as you enter the city, you will find him,
before he goes up to the high place to eat; for
the people will not eat till he comes, since
he must bless the sacrifice; afterward those
eat who are invited. Now go up, for you will
meet him immediately." 14So they went up to
the city. As they were entering the city, they
saw Samuel coming out toward them on his
way up to the high place.
15Now the day before Saul came, the LORD
had revealed to Samuel: 16"Tomorrow about
this time I will send to you a man from the
land of Benjamin, and you shall anoint
him to be prince over my people Israel. He
shall save my people from the hand of the
Philis′tines; for I have seen the affliction of
my people, because their cry has come to
me." 17When Samuel saw Saul, the LORD

told him, "Here is the man of whom I spoke to you! He it is who shall rule over my people." 18Then Saul approached Samuel in the gate, and said, "Tell me where is the house of the seer?" 19Samuel answered Saul, "I am the seer; go up before me to the high place, for today you shall eat with me, and in the morning I will let you go and will tell you all that is on your mind. 20As for your donkeys that were lost three days ago, do not set your mind on them, for they have been found. And for whom is all that is desirable in Israel? Is it not for you and for all your father's house?" 21Saul answered, "Am I not a Benjaminite, from the least of the tribes of Israel? And is not my family the humblest of all the families of the tribe of Benjamin? Why then have you spoken to me in this way?"

22Then Samuel took Saul and his servant and brought them into the hall and gave them a place at the head of those who had been invited, who were about thirty persons. 23And Samuel said to the cook, "Bring the portion I gave you, of which I said to you, 'Put it aside.'" 24So the cook took up the leg and the upper portion and set them before Saul; and Samuel said, "See, what was kept is set before you. Eat; because it was kept for you until the hour appointed, that you might eat with the guests."

So Saul ate with Samuel that day. 25And when they came down from the high place into the city, a bed was spread for Saul upon the roof, and he lay down to sleep. 26Then at the break of dawn Samuel called to Saul upon the roof, "Up, that I may send you on your way." So Saul arose, and both he and Samuel went out into the street.

27As they were going down to the outskirts of the city, Samuel said to Saul, "Tell the servant to pass on before us, and when he has passed on stop here yourself for a while, that I may make known to you the word of God."

10 Then Samuel took a vial of oil and poured it on his head, and kissed him and said, "Has not the LORD anointed you to be prince over his people Israel? And you shall reign over the people of the LORD and you will save them from the hand of their enemies round about. And this shall be the sign to you that the LORD has anointed you to be prince over his heritage. 2When you depart from me today you will meet two men by Rachel's tomb in the territory of Benjamin at Zelzah, and they will say to you, 'The donkeys which you went to seek are found, and now your father has ceased to care about the donkeys and is anxious about you, saying, "What shall I do about my son?"' 3Then you shall go on from there further and come to the oak of Ta′bor; three men going up to God at Bethel will meet you there, one carrying three kids, another carrying three loaves of bread, and another carrying a skin of wine. 4And they will greet you and give you two loaves of bread, which you shall accept from their hand. 5After that you shall come to Gib′eath-elo′him, where there is a garrison of the Philis′tines; and there, as you come to the city, you will meet a band of prophets coming down from the high place with harp, tambourine, flute, and lyre before them, prophesying. 6Then the spirit of the LORD will come mightily upon you, and you shall prophesy with them and be turned into another man. 7Now when these signs meet you, do whatever your hand finds to do, for God is with you. 8And you shall go down before me to Gilgal; and behold, I am coming to you to offer burnt offerings and to sacrifice peace offerings. Seven days you shall wait, until I come to you and show you what you shall do."

9When he turned his back to leave Samuel, God gave him another heart; and all these signs came to pass that day. 10When they came to Gib′e-ah, behold, a band of prophets met him; and the spirit of God came mightily upon him, and he prophesied among them. 11And when all who knew him before saw how he prophesied with the prophets, the people said to one another, "What has come over the son of Kish? Is Saul also among the prophets?" 12And a man of the place answered, "And who is their father?" Therefore it became a proverb, "Is

Saul also among the prophets?" 13When he
had finished prophesying, he came to the
high place.
14Saul's uncle said to him and to his
servant, "Where did you go?" And he said,
"To seek the donkeys; and when we saw they
were not to be found, we went to Samuel."
15And Saul's uncle said, "Please, tell me what
Samuel said to you." 16And Saul said to his
uncle, "He told us plainly that the donkeys
had been found." But about the matter of the
kingdom, of which Samuel had spoken, he
did not tell him anything.
17Now Samuel called the people together to
the LORD at Mizpah; 18and he said to the sons
of Israel, "Thus says the LORD, the God of
Israel, 'I brought up Israel out of Egypt, and I
delivered you from the hand of the Egyptians
and from the hand of all the kingdoms that
were oppressing you.' 19But you have this day
rejected your God, who saves you from all
your calamities and your distresses; and you
have said, 'No! but set a king over us.' Now
therefore present yourselves before the LORD
by your tribes and by your thousands."
20Then Samuel brought all the tribes of
Israel near, and the tribe of Benjamin was
taken by lot. 21He brought the tribe of Benjamin near by its families, and the family
of the Ma'trites was taken by lot; finally he
brought the family of the Matrites near man
by man, and Saul the son of Kish was taken
by lot. But when they sought him, he could
not be found. 22So they inquired again of the
LORD, "Did the man come here?" and the
LORD said, "Behold, he has hidden himself
among the baggage." 23Then they ran and
fetched him from there; and when he stood
among the people, he was taller than any
of the people from his shoulders upward.
24And Samuel said to all the people, "Do you
see him whom the LORD has chosen? There
is none like him among all the people." And
all the people shouted, "Long live the king!"
25Then Samuel told the people the rights and
duties of the kingship; and he wrote them in
a book and laid it up before the LORD. Then
Samuel sent all the people away, each one to his
home. 26Saul also went to his home at Gib'e-ah,
and with him went men of valor whose hearts
God had touched. 27But some worthless fellows
said, "How can this man save us?" And they
despised him, and brought him no present. But
he held his peace.

A prayer of one afflicted, when he is faint and pours out his complaint before the LORD.

PSALM 102 [101]

Hear my prayer, O LORD;
let my cry come to you!
2Do not hide your face from me
in the day of my distress!
Incline your ear to me;
answer me speedily in the day when I call!

3For my days pass away like smoke,
and my bones burn like a furnace.
4My heart is struck down like grass,
and withered;
I forget to eat my bread.
5Because of my loud groaning
my bones cling to my flesh.
6I am like a vulture of the wilderness,
like an owl of the waste places;
7I lie awake,
I am like a lonely bird on the housetop.
8All the day my enemies taunt me,
those who deride me use my name for
a curse.
9For I eat ashes like bread,
and mingle tears with my drink,
10because of your indignation and anger;
for you have taken me up and thrown
me away.
11My days are like an evening shadow;
I wither away like grass.

12But you, O LORD, are enthroned for ever;
your name endures to all generations.
13You will arise and have pity on Zion;
it is the time to favor her;
the appointed time has come.
14For your servants hold her stones dear,
and have pity on her dust.
15The nations will fear the name of the LORD,
and all the kings of the earth your glory.

LUKE 19

He entered Jericho and was passing through. 2And there was a man named Zacchae´us; he was a chief tax collector, and rich. 3And he sought to see who Jesus was, but could not, on account of the crowd, because he was small of stature. 4So he ran on ahead and climbed up into a sycamore tree to see him, for he was to pass that way. 5And when Jesus came to the place, he looked up and said to him, "Zacchae´us, make haste and come down; for I must stay at your house today." 6So he made haste and came down, and received him joyfully. 7And when they saw it they all murmured, "He has gone in to be the guest of a man who is a sinner." 8And Zacchae´us stood and said to the Lord, "Behold, Lord, the half of my goods I give to the poor; and if I have defrauded any one of anything, I restore it fourfold." 9And Jesus said to him, "Today salvation has come to this house, since he also is a son of Abraham. 10For the Son of man came to seek and to save the lost."

11As they heard these things, he proceeded to tell a parable, because he was near to Jerusalem, and because they supposed that the kingdom of God was to appear immediately. 12He said therefore, "A nobleman went into a far country to receive kingly power and then return. 13Calling ten of his servants, he gave them ten pounds, and said to them, 'Trade with these till I come.' 14But his citizens hated him and sent an embassy after him, saying, 'We do not want this man to reign over us.' 15When he returned, having received the kingly power, he commanded these servants, to whom he had given the money, to be called to him, that he might know what they had gained by trading. 16The first came before him, saying, 'Lord, your pound has made ten pounds more.' 17And he said to him, 'Well done, good servant! Because you have been faithful in a very little, you shall have authority over ten cities.' 18And the second came, saying, 'Lord, your pound has made five pounds.' 19And he said to him, 'And you are to be over five cities.' 20Then another came, saying, 'Lord, here is your pound, which I kept laid away in a napkin; 21for I was afraid of you, because you are a severe man; you take up what you did not lay down, and reap what you did not sow.' 22He said to him, 'I will condemn you out of your own mouth, you wicked servant! You knew that I was a severe man, taking up what I did not lay down and reaping what I did not sow? 23Why then did you not put my money into the bank, and at my coming I should have collected it with interest?' 24And he said to those who stood by, 'Take the pound from him, and give it to him who has the ten pounds.' 25(And they said to him, 'Lord, he has ten pounds!') 26'I tell you, that to every one who has will more be given; but from him who has not, even what he has will be taken away. 27But as for these enemies of mine, who did not want me to reign over them, bring them here and slay them before me.'"

REFLECTION

After the people of Israel reject the Lord as their king, he grants them a human king—Saul. Samuel anoints Saul at the Lord's direction, and the spirit of prophecy descends on him. Yet it is clear that all is not well. This tall, handsome man lacks confidence. He complains about being from the smallest tribe and the least important family (see 1 Sm 9:21). Even worse, at the grand assembly of Israel where Saul is to be declared king, he exhibits cowardice, hiding himself among the baggage to dodge the responsibility. In the Gospel of Luke, we find in Zacchaeus—a rich, powerful tax collector so short in stature he has to climb a tree to see Jesus. In contrast to Saul's worries about what others think, Zacchaeus is willing to endure the likely derision of the crowd, many of whom he has probably cheated, and puts himself out on a limb in order to see Jesus. And when Jesus invites himself into Zacchaeus's home, he responds with joy, quickly takes responsibility for his past actions, promising to restore what he had stolen. Saul's fears keep him from trusting God to assist his kingship, but Zacchaeus has faith that God will provide all that he needs to be faithful.

April 28

1 SAMUEL 11

Then Na′hash the Am′monite went up and besieged Ja′besh-gil′ead; and all the men of Ja′besh said to Nahash, "Make a treaty with us, and we will serve you." 2But Na′hash the Am′monite said to them, "On this condition I will make a treaty with you, that I gouge out all your right eyes, and thus put disgrace upon all Israel." 3The elders of Ja′besh said to him, "Give us seven days respite that we may send messengers through all the territory of Israel. Then, if there is no one to save us, we will give ourselves up to you." 4When the messengers came to Gib′e-ah of Saul, they reported the matter in the hearing of the people; and all the people wept aloud.

5Now Saul was coming from the field behind the oxen; and Saul said, "What ails the people, that they are weeping?" So they told him the tidings of the men of Ja′besh. 6And the spirit of God came mightily upon Saul when he heard these words, and his anger was greatly kindled. 7He took a yoke of oxen, and cut them in pieces and sent them throughout all the territory of Israel by the hand of messengers, saying, "Whoever does not come out after Saul and Samuel, so shall it be done to his oxen!" Then the dread of the LORD fell upon the people, and they came out as one man. 8When he mustered them at Be′zek, the men of Israel were three hundred thousand, and the men of Judah thirty thousand. 9And they said to the messengers who had come, "Thus shall you say to the men of Ja′besh-gil′ead: 'Tomorrow, by the time the sun is hot, you shall have deliverance.'" When the messengers came and told the men of Ja′besh, they were glad. 10Therefore the men of Ja′besh said, "Tomorrow we will give ourselves up to you, and you may do to us whatever seems good to you." 11And the next day Saul put the people in three companies; and they came into the midst of the camp in the morning watch, and cut down the Am′monites until the heat of the day; and those who survived were scattered, so that no two of them were left together.

12Then the people said to Samuel, "Who is it that said, 'Shall Saul reign over us?' Bring the men, that we may put them to death." 13But Saul said, "Not a man shall be put to death this day, for today the LORD has wrought deliverance in Israel." 14Then Samuel said to the people, "Come, let us go to Gilgal and there renew the kingdom." 15So all the people went to Gilgal, and there they made Saul king before the LORD in Gilgal. There they sacrificed peace offerings before the LORD, and there Saul and all the men of Israel rejoiced greatly.

12 And Samuel said to all Israel, "Behold, I have listened to your voice in all that you have said to me, and have made a king over you. 2And now, behold, the king walks before you; and I am old and gray, and behold, my sons are with you; and I have walked before you from my youth until this day. 3Here I am; testify against me before the LORD and before his anointed. Whose ox have I taken? Or whose donkey have I taken? Or whom have I defrauded? Whom have I oppressed? Or from whose hand have I taken a bribe to blind my eyes with it? Testify against me and I will restore it to you." 4They said, "You have not defrauded us or oppressed us or taken anything from any man's hand." 5And he said to them, "The LORD is witness against you, and his anointed is witness this day, that you have not found anything in my hand." And they said, "He is witness."

6And Samuel said to the people, "The LORD is witness, who appointed Moses and

Aaron and brought your fathers up out of
the land of Egypt. 7Now therefore stand still,
that I may plead with you before the LORD
concerning all the saving deeds of the LORD
which he performed for you and for your
fathers. 8When Jacob went into Egypt and the
Egyptians oppressed them, then your fathers
cried to the LORD and the LORD sent Moses
and Aaron, who brought forth your fathers
out of Egypt, and made them dwell in this
place. 9But they forgot the LORD their God;
and he sold them into the hand of Sis′era,
commander of the army of Ja′bin king of
Ha′zor, and into the hand of the Philis′tines,
and into the hand of the king of Moab; and
they fought against them. 10And they cried to
the LORD, and said, 'We have sinned, because
we have forsaken the LORD, and have served
the Ba′als and the Ash′taroth; but now deliver
us out of the hand of our enemies, and we will
serve you.' 11And the LORD sent Jerubba′al
and Barak, and Jephthah, and Samuel, and
delivered you out of the hand of your enemies
on every side; and you dwelt in safety. 12And
when you saw that Na′hash the king of the
Am′monites came against you, you said to
me, 'No, but a king shall reign over us,' when
the LORD your God was your king. 13And
now behold the king whom you have chosen,
for whom you have asked; behold, the LORD
has set a king over you. 14If you will fear the
LORD and serve him and listen to his voice
and not rebel against the commandment of
the LORD, and if both you and the king who
reigns over you will follow the LORD your
God, it will be well; 15but if you will not listen
to the voice of the LORD, but rebel against the
commandment of the LORD, then the hand
of the LORD will be against you and your
king. 16Now therefore stand still and see this
great thing, which the LORD will do before
your eyes. 17Is it not wheat harvest today? I
will call upon the LORD, that he may send
thunder and rain; and you shall know and
see that your wickedness is great, which you
have done in the sight of the LORD, in asking
for yourselves a king." 18So Samuel called
upon the LORD, and the LORD sent thunder
and rain that day; and all the people greatly
feared the LORD and Samuel.

19And all the people said to Samuel, "Pray
for your servants to the LORD your God,
that we may not die; for we have added to all
our sins this evil, to ask for ourselves a king."
20And Samuel said to the people, "Fear not;
you have done all this evil, yet do not turn
aside from following the LORD, but serve the
LORD with all your heart; 21and do not turn
aside after vain things which cannot profit
or save, for they are vain. 22For the LORD will
not cast away his people, for his great name's
sake, because it has pleased the LORD to
make you a people for himself. 23Moreover
as for me, far be it from me that I should
sin against the LORD by ceasing to pray for
you; and I will instruct you in the good and
the right way. 24Only fear the LORD, and
serve him faithfully with all your heart; for
consider what great things he has done for
you. 25But if you still do wickedly, you shall
be swept away, both you and your king."

13 Saul was . . .* years old when he began
to reign; and he reigned . . . and two**
years over Israel.

2Saul chose three thousand men of Israel;
two thousand were with Saul in Mich′mash
and the hill country of Bethel, and a
thousand were with Jonathan in Gib′e-ah
of Benjamin; the rest of the people he sent
home, every man to his tent. 3Jonathan
defeated the garrison of the Philis′tines
which was at Ge′ba; and the Philistines
heard of it. And Saul blew the trumpet
throughout all the land, saying, "Let the
Hebrews hear." 4And all Israel heard it said
that Saul had defeated the garrison of the
Philis′tines, and also that Israel had become
odious to the Philistines. And the people
were called out to join Saul at Gilgal.

5And the Philis′tines mustered to fight
with Israel, thirty thousand chariots, and
six thousand horsemen, and troops like
the sand on the seashore in multitude; they
came up and encamped in Mich′mash,
to the east of Beth-a′ven. 6When the men
of Israel saw that they were in straits (for
the people were hard pressed), the people

* The number is lacking in Heb.
** *Two* is not the entire number. Something has dropped out.

hid themselves in caves and in holes and in rocks and in tombs and in cisterns, 7or crossed the fords of the Jordan to the land of Gad and Gilead. Saul was still at Gilgal, and all the people followed him trembling.

8He waited seven days, the time appointed by Samuel; but Samuel did not come to Gilgal, and the people were scattering from him. 9So Saul said, "Bring the burnt offering here to me, and the peace offerings." And he offered the burnt offering. 10As soon as he had finished offering the burnt offering, behold, Samuel came; and Saul went out to meet him and salute him. 11Samuel said, "What have you done?" And Saul said, "When I saw that the people were scattering from me, and that you did not come within the days appointed, and that the Philis′tines had mustered at Mich′mash, 12I said, 'Now the Philis′tines will come down upon me at Gilgal and I have not entreated the favor of the LORD'; so I forced myself, and offered the burnt offering." 13And Samuel said to Saul, "You have done foolishly; you have not kept the commandment of the LORD your God, which he commanded you; for now the LORD would have established your kingdom over Israel for ever. 14But now your kingdom shall not continue; the LORD has sought out a man after his own heart; and the LORD has appointed him to be prince over his people, because you have not kept what the LORD commanded you." 15And Samuel arose, and went up from Gilgal to Gib′e-ah of Benjamin.

And Saul numbered the people who were present with him, about six hundred men. 16And Saul, and Jonathan his son, and the people who were present with them, stayed in Ge′ba of Benjamin; but the Philis′tines encamped in Mich′mash. 17And raiders came out of the camp of the Philis′tines in three companies; one company turned toward Oph′rah, to the land of Shual, 18another company turned toward Beth-ho′ron, and another company turned toward the border that looks down upon the valley of Zebo′im toward the wilderness.

19Now there was no smith to be found throughout all the land of Israel; for the Philis′tines said, "Lest the Hebrews make themselves swords or spears"; 20but every one of the Israelites went down to the Philis′tines to sharpen his plowshare, his mattock, his axe, or his sickle; 21and the charge was a pim for the plowshares and for the mattocks, and a third of a shekel for sharpening the axes and for setting the goads. 22So on the day of the battle there was neither sword nor spear found in the hand of any of the people with Saul and Jonathan; but Saul and Jonathan his son had them. 23And the garrison of the Philis′tines went out to the pass of Mich′mash.

A prayer of one afflicted, when he is faint and pours out his complaint before the LORD.

PSALM 102 [101]

16For the LORD will build up Zion,
he will appear in his glory;
17he will regard the prayer of the destitute,
and will not despise their supplication.
18Let this be recorded for a generation
to come,
so that a people yet unborn may praise
the LORD:
19that he looked down from his holy height,
from heaven the LORD looked at
the earth,
20to hear the groans of the prisoners,
to set free those who were doomed to die;
21that men may declare in Zion the name
of the LORD,
and in Jerusalem his praise,
22when peoples gather together,
and kingdoms, to worship the LORD.

23He has broken my strength in mid-course;
he has shortened my days.
24"O my God," I say, "do not take me
from here
in the midst of my days,
you whose years endure
throughout all generations!"

25Of old you laid the foundation of the earth,
and the heavens are the work of your
hands.

26They will perish, but you endure;
they will all wear out like a garment.
You change them like clothing, and they
pass away;
27 but you are the same, and your years have
no end.
28The children of your servants shall dwell
secure;
their posterity shall be established
before you.

LUKE 19

**28And when he had said this,
he went on ahead, going up
to Jerusalem. 29When he drew
near to Beth′phage and Beth′any, at
the mount that is called Olivet, he sent
two of the disciples, 30saying, "Go into**
the village opposite, where on entering you
will find a colt tied, on which no one has
ever yet sat; untie it and bring it here. 31If
any one asks you, 'Why are you untying
it?' you shall say this, 'The Lord has need
of it.' " 32So those who were sent went away
and found it as he had told them. 33And
as they were untying the colt, its owners
said to them, "Why are you untying the
colt?" 34And they said, "The Lord has need
of it." 35And they brought it to Jesus, and
throwing their garments on the colt they set
Jesus upon it. 36And as he rode along, they
spread their garments on the road. 37As he
was now drawing near, at the descent of
the Mount of Olives, the whole multitude
of the disciples began to rejoice and praise
God with a loud voice for all the mighty
works that they had seen, 38saying, "Blessed
is the King who comes in the name of the
Lord! Peace in heaven and glory in the
highest!" 39And some of the Pharisees in
the multitude said to him, "Teacher, rebuke
your disciples." 40He answered, "I tell you,
if these were silent, the very stones would
cry out."
41And when he drew near and saw the
city he wept over it, 42saying, "Would that
even today you knew the things that make
for peace! But now they are hidden from
your eyes. 43For the days shall come upon
you, when your enemies will cast up a bank
about you and surround you, and hem you
in on every side, 44and dash you to the
ground, you and your children within you,
and they will not leave one stone upon
another in you; because you did not know
the time of your visitation."
45And he entered the temple and began to
drive out those who sold, 46saying to them,
"It is written, 'My house shall be a house
of prayer'; but you have made it a den of
robbers."
47And he was teaching daily in the temple.
The chief priests and the scribes and the
principal men of the people sought to
destroy him; 48but they did not find anything
they could do, for all the people hung upon
his words.

REFLECTION

If Samuel's generation of Israelites rejects the Lord as their king (see 1 Sm 12:12), then Jesus's generation gets a second chance—a chance to do it right. Near the end of his life, the prophet Samuel retells the story of salvation from Jacob to the present day (see vv. 8–11). Sadly, however, his speech ends with an indictment of the people who have rejected the Lord's kingship: "Your wickedness is great, which you have done in the sight of the LORD, in asking for yourselves a king" (v. 17). Centuries later, on Palm Sunday, Jesus rides into Jerusalem in triumph. The people even proclaim, "Blessed is the *King* who comes in the name of the LORD!" (Lk 19:38, emphasis added). Jerusalem could have undone the sin of its ancestors by recognizing Jesus as king, but, unfortunately, as Jesus tells the city through his tears, "You did not know the time of your visitation" (v. 44). Though the ancient Israelites and many of the Jews of Jesus's day missed their chance to make God their king, we have not. Every new day gives us the opportunity to let him reign in our hearts. How can the Lord more fully reign in your heart today?

April 29

1 SAMUEL 14

One day Jonathan the son of Saul said to the young man who bore his armor, "Come, let us go over to the Philis′tine garrison on yonder side." But he did not tell his father. [2]Saul was staying in the outskirts of Gib′e-ah under the pomegranate tree which is at Migron; the people who were with him were about six hundred men, [3]and Ahi′jah the son of Ahi′tub, Ich′abod's brother, son of Phin′ehas, son of Eli, the priest of the LORD in Shiloh, wearing an ephod. And the people did not know that Jonathan had gone. [4]In the pass, by which Jonathan sought to go over to the Philis′tine garrison, there was a rocky crag on the one side and a rocky crag on the other side; the name of the one was Bozez, and the name of the other Se′neh. [5]The one crag rose on the north in front of Mich′mash, and the other on the south in front of Ge′ba.

[6]And Jonathan said to the young man who bore his armor, "Come, let us go over to the garrison of these uncircumcised; it may be that the LORD will work for us; for nothing can hinder the LORD from saving by many or by few." [7]And his armor-bearer said to him, "Do all that your mind inclines to; behold, I am with you, as is your mind so is mine." [8]Then said Jonathan, "Behold, we will cross over to the men, and we will show ourselves to them. [9]If they say to us, 'Wait until we come to you,' then we will stand still in our place, and we will not go up to them. [10]But if they say, 'Come up to us,' then we will go up; for the LORD has given them into our hand. And this shall be the sign to us." [11]So both of them showed themselves to the garrison of the Philis′tines; and the Philistines said, "Look, Hebrews are coming out of the holes where they have hid themselves." [12]And the men of the garrison hailed Jonathan and his armor-bearer, and said, "Come up to us, and we will show you a thing." And Jonathan said to his armor-bearer, "Come up after me; for the LORD has given them into the hand of Israel." [13]Then Jonathan climbed up on his hands and feet, and his armor-bearer after him. And they fell before Jonathan, and his armor-bearer killed them after him; [14]and that first slaughter, which Jonathan and his armor-bearer made, was of about twenty men within as it were half a furrow's length in an acre of land. [15]And there was a panic in the camp, in the field, and among all the people; the garrison and even the raiders trembled; the earth quaked; and it became a very great panic.

[16]And the watchmen of Saul in Gib′e-ah of Benjamin looked; and behold, the multitude was surging here and there. [17]Then Saul said to the people who were with him, "Number and see who has gone from us." And when they had numbered, behold, Jonathan and his armor-bearer were not there. [18]And Saul said to Ahi′jah, "Bring the ark of God here." For the ark of God went at that time with the sons of Israel. [19]And while Saul was talking to the priest, the tumult in the camp of the Philis′tines increased more and more; and Saul said to the priest, "Withdraw your hand." [20]Then Saul and all the people who were with him rallied and went into the battle; and behold, every man's sword was against his fellow, and there was very great confusion. [21]Now the Hebrews who had been with the Philis′tines before that time and who had gone up with them into the camp, even they also turned to be with the Israelites who were with Saul and Jonathan. [22]Likewise, when all the men of Israel who had hid themselves in the hill country of E′phraim heard that the Philis′tines were fleeing, they too followed hard after them in the battle. [23]So the LORD delivered Israel that day; and the battle passed beyond Beth-a′ven.

[24]And the men of Israel were distressed that day; for Saul laid an oath on the people, saying, "Cursed be the man who eats food until it is evening and I am avenged on my enemies." So none of the people tasted food. [25]And all the people came into the forest; and there was honey on the ground. [26]And when the people entered the forest,

behold, the honey was dropping, but no man put his hand to his mouth; for the people feared the oath. 27But Jonathan had not heard his father charge the people with the oath; so he put forth the tip of the staff that was in his hand, and dipped it in the honeycomb, and put his hand to his mouth; and his eyes became bright. 28Then one of the people said, "Your father strictly charged the people with an oath, saying, 'Cursed be the man who eats food this day.'" And the people were faint. 29Then Jonathan said, "My father has troubled the land; see how my eyes have become bright, because I tasted a little of this honey. 30How much better if the people had eaten freely today of the spoil of their enemies which they found; for now the slaughter among the Philis′tines has not been great."

31They struck down the Philis′tines that day from Mich′mash to Ai′jalon. And the people were very faint; 32the people flew upon the spoil, and took sheep and oxen and calves, and slew them on the ground; and the people ate them with the blood. 33Then they told Saul, "Behold, the people are sinning against the LORD, by eating with the blood." And he said, "You have dealt treacherously; roll a great stone to me here." 34And Saul said, "Disperse yourselves among the people, and say to them, 'Let every man bring his ox or his sheep, and slay them here, and eat; and do not sin against the LORD by eating with the blood.'" So every one of the people brought his ox with him that night, and slew them there. 35And Saul built an altar to the LORD; it was the first altar that he built to the LORD.

36Then Saul said, "Let us go down after the Philis′tines by night and despoil them until the morning light; let us not leave a man of them." And they said, "Do whatever seems good to you." But the priest said, "Let us draw near here to God." 37And Saul inquired of God, "Shall I go down after the Philis′tines? Will you give them into the hand of Israel?" But he did not answer him that day. 38And Saul said, "Come here, all you leaders of the people; and know and see how this sin has arisen today. 39For as the LORD lives who saves Israel, though it be in Jonathan my son, he shall surely die." But there was not a man among all the people that answered him. 40Then he said to all Israel, "You shall be on one side, and I and Jonathan my son will be on the other side." And the people said to Saul, "Do what seems good to you." 41Therefore Saul said, "O LORD God of Israel, why have you not answered your servant this day? If this guilt is in me or in Jonathan my son, O LORD, God of Israel, give U′rim; but if this guilt is in your people Israel, give Thummim." And Jonathan and Saul were taken, but the people escaped. 42Then Saul said, "Cast the lot between me and my son Jonathan." And Jonathan was taken.

43Then Saul said to Jonathan, "Tell me what you have done." And Jonathan told him, "I tasted a little honey with the tip of the staff that was in my hand; here I am, I will die." 44And Saul said, "God do so to me and more also; you shall surely die, Jonathan." 45Then the people said to Saul, "Shall Jonathan die, who has wrought this great victory in Israel? Far from it! As the LORD lives, there shall not one hair of his head fall to the ground; for he has wrought with God this day." So the people ransomed Jonathan, that he did not die. 46Then Saul went up from pursuing the Philis′tines; and the Philistines went to their own place.

47When Saul had taken the kingship over Israel, he fought against all his enemies on every side, against Moab, against the Am′monites, against E′dom, against the kings of Zobah, and against the Philis′tines; wherever he turned he put them to the worse. 48And he did valiantly, and struck the Amal′ekites, and delivered Israel out of the hands of those who plundered them.

49Now the sons of Saul were Jonathan, Ishvi, and Mal″chishu′a; and the names of his two daughters were these: the name of the first-born was Merab, and the name of the younger Michal; 50and the name of Saul's wife was Ahin′o-am the daughter of Ahim′a-az. And the name of the commander of his army was Abner the son of Ner, Saul's uncle;

[51]Kish was the father of Saul, and Ner the father of Abner was the son of Abi′el.

[52]There was hard fighting against the Philis′tines all the days of Saul; and when Saul saw any strong man, or any valiant man, he attached him to himself.

A Psalm of David.

PSALM 103 [102]

Bless the LORD, O my soul;
and all that is within me, bless his holy name!
[2]Bless the LORD, O my soul,
and forget not all his benefits,
[3]who forgives all your iniquity,
who heals all your diseases,
[4]who redeems your life from the Pit,
who crowns you with mercy and compassion,
[5]who satisfies you with good as long as you live
so that your youth is renewed like the eagle's.

[6]The LORD works vindication
and justice for all who are oppressed.
[7]He made known his ways to Moses,
his acts to the people of Israel.
[8]The LORD is merciful and gracious,
slow to anger and abounding in mercy.
[9]He will not always chide,
nor will he keep his anger for ever.
[10]He does not deal with us according to our sins,
nor repay us according to our iniquities.
[11]For as the heavens are high above the earth,
so great is his mercy toward those who fear him;
[12]as far as the east is from the west,
so far does he remove our transgressions from us.
[13]As a father pities his children,
so the LORD pities those who fear him.
[14]For he knows our frame;
he remembers that we are dust.
[15]As for man, his days are like grass;
he flourishes like a flower of the field;
[16]for the wind passes over it, and it is gone,
and its place knows it no more.
[17]But the mercy of the LORD is from everlasting to everlasting
upon those who fear him,
and his righteousness to children's children,
[18]to those who keep his covenant
and remember to do his commandments.

[19]The LORD has established his throne in the heavens,
and his kingdom rules over all.
[20]Bless the LORD, O you his angels,
you mighty ones who do his word,
hearkening to the voice of his word!
[21]Bless the LORD, all his hosts,
his ministers that do his will!
[22]Bless the LORD, all his works,
in all places of his dominion.
Bless the LORD, O my soul!

LUKE 20

One day, as he was teaching the people in the temple and preaching the gospel, the chief priests and the scribes with the elders came up [2]and said to him, "Tell us by what authority you do these things, or
who it is that gave you this authority."
[3]He answered them, "I also will ask you a
question; now tell me, [4]Was the baptism of
John from heaven or from men?" [5]And they
discussed it with one another, saying, "If
we say, 'From heaven,' he will say, 'Why did
you not believe him?' [6]But if we say, 'From
men,' all the people will stone us; for they
are convinced that John was a prophet."
[7]So they answered that they did not know
where it was from. [8]And Jesus said to them,
"Neither will I tell you by what authority I
do these things."
[9]And he began to tell the people this
parable: "A man planted a vineyard, and
leased it to tenants, and went into another

country for a long while. 10When the time came, he sent a servant to the tenants, that they should give him some of the fruit of the vineyard; but the tenants beat him, and sent him away empty-handed. 11And he sent another servant; him also they beat and treated shamefully, and sent him away empty-handed. 12And he sent yet a third; this one they wounded and cast out. 13Then the owner of the vineyard said, 'What shall I do? I will send my beloved son; it may be they will respect him.' 14But when the tenants saw him, they said to themselves, 'This is the heir; let us kill him, that the inheritance may be ours.' 15And they cast him out of the vineyard and killed him. What then will the owner of the vineyard do to them? 16He will come and destroy those tenants, and give the vineyard to others." When they heard this, they said, "God forbid!" 17But he looked at them and said, "What then is this that is written:

'The very stone which the builders rejected
has become the cornerstone'?

18Every one who falls on that stone will be broken to pieces; but when it falls on any one it will crush him."

19The scribes and the chief priests tried to lay hands on him at that very hour, but they feared the people; for they perceived that he had told this parable against them. 20So they watched him, and sent spies, who pretended to be sincere, that they might take hold of what he said, so as to deliver him up to the authority and jurisdiction of the governor. 21They asked him, "Teacher, we know that you speak and teach rightly, and show no partiality, but truly teach the way of God. 22Is it lawful for us to give tribute to Caesar, or not?" 23But he perceived their craftiness, and said to them, 24"Show me a coin. Whose likeness and inscription has it?" They said, "Caesar's." 25He said to them, "Then render to Caesar the things that are Caesar's, and to God the things that are God's." 26And they were not able in the presence of the people to catch him by what he said; but marveling at his answer they were silent.

REFLECTION

Amid the busy-ness of daily life, we can forget some of the most important things. Yet living a life faithful to God requires a continual practice of remembering. Psalm 103 encourages us to "forget not all his benefits" (Ps 103:2). Here we see the Old Testament's covenant language: to be faithful to the covenant is to "remember," but to be unfaithful is to "forget." In God's goodness to us, he remembers "that we are dust" (v. 14). We are called to keep his covenant and remember his commandments (see v. 18). Remembering unleashes his bountiful blessings: he forgives, heals, redeems, crowns, and satisfies us (see vv. 3–5). King Saul, on the other hand, forgets his responsibilities and makes rash vows that imperil the life of his own son. The wicked tenants in Jesus's parable forget their duty to the owner of the vineyard, choosing violence and murder and bringing their own destruction. The question is, do you often "forget all his benefits"? What can you do today to begin a habit of "remembering" the Lord, his covenant, and all the gifts he has given you?

April 30

1 SAMUEL 15

And Samuel said to Saul, "The LORD sent me to anoint you king over his people Israel; now therefore listen to the words of the LORD. 2Thus says the LORD of hosts, 'I will punish what Am′alek did to Israel in opposing them on the way, when they came up out of Egypt. 3Now go and strike Am′alek, and utterly destroy all that they have; do not spare them, but kill both man and woman, infant and suckling, ox and sheep, camel and donkey.'"

4So Saul summoned the people, and numbered them in Tela′im, two hundred thousand men on foot, and ten thousand men of Judah. 5And Saul came to the city of Am′alek, and lay in wait in the valley. 6And Saul said to the Kenites, "Go, depart, go down from among the Amal′ekites, lest I destroy you with them; for you showed kindness to all the people of Israel when they came up out of Egypt." So the Kenites departed from among the Amalekites. 7And Saul defeated the Amal′ekites, from Hav′ilah as far as Shur, which is east of Egypt. 8And he took A′gag the king of the Amal′ekites alive, and utterly destroyed all the people with the edge of the sword. 9But Saul and the people spared A′gag, and the best of the sheep and of the oxen and of the fatlings, and the lambs, and all that was good, and would not utterly destroy them; all that was despised and worthless they utterly destroyed.

10The word of the LORD came to Samuel: 11"I repent that I have made Saul king; for he has turned back from following me, and has not performed my commandments." And Samuel was angry; and he cried to the LORD all night. 12And Samuel rose early to meet Saul in the morning; and it was told Samuel, "Saul came to Carmel, and behold, he set up a monument for himself and turned, and passed on, and went down to Gilgal." 13And Samuel came to Saul, and Saul said to him, "Blessed be you to the LORD; I have performed the commandment of the LORD." 14And Samuel said, "What then is this bleating of the sheep in my ears, and the lowing of the oxen which I hear?" 15Saul said, "They have brought them from the Amal′ekites; for the people spared the best of the sheep and of the oxen, to sacrifice to the LORD your God; and the rest we have utterly destroyed." 16Then Samuel said to Saul, "Stop! I will tell you what the LORD said to me this night." And he said to him, "Say on."

17And Samuel said, "Though you are little in your own eyes, are you not the head of the tribes of Israel? The LORD anointed you king over Israel. 18And the LORD sent you on a mission, and said, 'Go, utterly destroy the sinners, the Amal′ekites, and fight against them until they are consumed.' 19Why then did you not obey the voice of the LORD? Why did you swoop on the spoil, and do what was evil in the sight of the LORD?" 20And Saul said to Samuel, "I have obeyed the voice of the LORD, I have gone on the mission on which the LORD sent me, I have brought A′gag the king of Am′alek, and I have utterly destroyed the Amal′ekites. 21But the people took of the spoil, sheep and oxen, the best of the things devoted to destruction, to sacrifice to the LORD your God in Gilgal." 22And Samuel said,

"Has the LORD as great delight in burnt
offerings and sacrifices,
as in obeying the voice of
the LORD?
Behold, to obey is better than sacrifice,
and to listen than the fat of rams.
23For rebellion is as the sin of divination,
and stubbornness is as iniquity
and idolatry.
Because you have rejected the word of
the LORD,
he has also rejected you from being king."

24And Saul said to Samuel, "I have sinned; for I have transgressed the commandment of the LORD and your words, because I feared the people and obeyed their voice. 25Now therefore, I beg, pardon my sin, and return with me, that I may worship the LORD." 26And Samuel said to Saul, "I will not return with you; for you have rejected the word of the LORD, and the LORD has rejected you from being king over Israel." 27As Samuel turned to go away, Saul laid hold upon the skirt of his robe, and it tore. 28And Samuel said to him, "The LORD has torn the kingdom of Israel from you this day, and has given it to a neighbor of yours, who is better than you. 29And also the Glory of Israel will not lie or repent; for he is not a man, that he should repent." 30Then he said, "I have sinned; yet honor me now before the elders of my people and before Israel, and return with me, that I may worship the LORD your God." 31So Samuel turned back after Saul; and Saul worshiped the LORD.

32 Then Samuel said, "Bring here to me
A′gag the king of the Amal′ekites." And Agag
came to him cheerfully. Agag said, "Surely
the bitterness of death is past." 33 And Samuel
said, "As your sword has made women
childless, so shall your mother be childless
among women." And Samuel hewed A′gag in
pieces before the LORD in Gilgal.

34 Then Samuel went to Ra′mah; and Saul
went up to his house in Gib′e-ah of Saul.
35 And Samuel did not see Saul again until
the day of his death, but Samuel grieved
over Saul. And the LORD repented that he
had made Saul king over Israel.

16 The LORD said to Samuel, "How long
will you grieve over Saul, seeing I
have rejected him from being king over
Israel? Fill your horn with oil, and go; I
will send you to Jesse the Bethlehemite, for
I have provided for myself a king among
his sons." 2 And Samuel said, "How can I
go? If Saul hears it, he will kill me." And
the LORD said, "Take a heifer with you, and
say, 'I have come to sacrifice to the LORD.'
3 And invite Jesse to the sacrifice, and I will
show you what you shall do; and you shall
anoint for me him whom I name to you."
4 Samuel did what the LORD commanded,
and came to Bethlehem. The elders of
the city came to meet him trembling, and
said, "Do you come peaceably?" 5 And he
said, "Peaceably; I have come to sacrifice
to the LORD; consecrate yourselves, and
come with me to the sacrifice." And he
consecrated Jesse and his sons, and invited
them to the sacrifice.

6 When they came, he looked on Eli′ab
and thought, "Surely the LORD's anointed is before him." 7 But the LORD said to
Samuel, "Do not look on his appearance
or on the height of his stature, because I
have rejected him; for the LORD sees not
as man sees; man looks on the outward
appearance, but the LORD looks on the
heart." 8 Then Jesse called Abin′adab, and
made him pass before Samuel. And he
said, "Neither has the LORD chosen this
one." 9 Then Jesse made Shammah pass by.
And he said, "Neither has the LORD chosen this one." 10 And Jesse made seven of
his sons pass before Samuel. And Samuel
said to Jesse, "The LORD has not chosen
these." 11 And Samuel said to Jesse, "Are
all your sons here?" And he said, "There
remains yet the youngest, but behold, he
is keeping the sheep." And Samuel said
to Jesse, "Send and fetch him; for we will
not sit down till he comes here." 12 And
he sent, and brought him in. Now he was
ruddy, and had beautiful eyes, and was
handsome. And the LORD said, "Arise,
anoint him; for this is he." 13 Then Samuel
took the horn of oil, and anointed him in
the midst of his brothers; and the Spirit
of the LORD came mightily upon David
from that day forward. And Samuel rose
up, and went to Ra′mah.

14 Now the Spirit of the LORD departed
from Saul, and an evil spirit from the LORD
tormented him. 15 And Saul's servants said
to him, "Behold now, an evil spirit from
God is tormenting you. 16 Let our lord now
command your servants, who are before
you, to seek out a man who is skilful in
playing the lyre; and when the evil spirit
from God is upon you, he will play it,
and you will be well." 17 So Saul said to his
servants, "Provide for me a man who can
play well, and bring him to me." 18 One
of the young men answered, "Behold, I
have seen a son of Jesse the Bethlehemite,
who is skilful in playing, a man of valor, a
man of war, prudent in speech, and a man
of good presence; and the LORD is with
him." 19 Therefore Saul sent messengers
to Jesse, and said, "Send me David your
son, who is with the sheep." 20 And Jesse
took a donkey laden with bread, and a
skin of wine and a kid, and sent them by
David his son to Saul. 21 And David came
to Saul, and entered his service. And Saul
loved him greatly, and he became his
armor-bearer. 22 And Saul sent to Jesse,
saying, "Let David remain in my service,
for he has found favor in my sight." 23 And
whenever the evil spirit from God was
upon Saul, David took the lyre and played
it with his hand; so Saul was refreshed,
and was well, and the evil spirit departed
from him.

PSALM 104 [103]

Bless the LORD, O my soul!
O LORD my God, you are very great!
You are clothed with honor and majesty,
2 who cover yourself with light as with a garment,
who have stretched out the heavens like a tent,
3 who have laid the beams of your chambers on the waters,
who make the clouds your chariot,
who ride on the wings of the wind,
4 who make the winds your messengers,
fire and flame your ministers.

5 You set the earth on its foundations,
so that it should never be shaken.
6 You covered it with the deep as with a garment;
the waters stood above the mountains.
7 At your rebuke they fled;
at the sound of your thunder they took to flight.
8 The mountains rose, the valleys sank down
to the place which you appointed for them.
9 You set a bound which they should not pass,
so that they might not again cover the earth.

10 You make springs gush forth in the valleys;
they flow between the hills,
11 they give drink to every beast of the field;
the wild donkeys quench their thirst.
12 By them the birds of the air have their habitation;
they sing among the branches.
13 From your lofty abode you water the mountains;
the earth is satisfied with the fruit of your work.

LUKE 20

27 There came to him some Sad′ducees, those who say that here is no resurrection, 28 and they asked him a question, saying, "Teacher, Moses
wrote for us that if a man's brother dies, hav-
ing a wife but no children, the man must
take the wife and raise up children for his
brother. 29 Now there were seven brothers;
the first took a wife, and died without children; 30 and the second 31 and the third took
her, and likewise all seven left no children
and died. 32 Afterward the woman also died.
33 In the resurrection, therefore, whose wife
will the woman be? For the seven had her
as wife."
34 And Jesus said to them, "The sons of
this age marry and are given in marriage;
35 but those who are accounted worthy
to attain to that age and to the resurrection from the dead neither marry nor are
given in marriage, 36 for they cannot die
any more, because they are equal to angels and are sons of God, being sons of
the resurrection. 37 But that the dead are
raised, even Moses showed, in the passage about the bush, where he calls the
Lord the God of Abraham and the God
of Isaac and the God of Jacob. 38 Now he is
not God of the dead, but of the living; for
all live to him." 39 And some of the scribes
answered, "Teacher, you have spoken
well." 40 For they no longer dared to ask
him any question.
41 But he said to them, "How can they say
that the Christ is David's son? 42 For David
himself says in the Book of Psalms,
'The Lord said to my Lord,
Sit at my right hand,
43 till I make your enemies a stool for your feet.'
44 David thus calls him Lord; so how is he his
son?"
45 And in the hearing of all the people
he said to his disciples, 46 "Beware of the
scribes, who like to go about in long robes,
and love salutations in the market places
and the best seats in the synagogues and
the places of honor at feasts, 47 who devour
widows' houses and for a pretense make
long prayers. They will receive the greater
condemnation."

21 He looked up and saw the rich putting their gifts into the treasury;
2 and he saw a poor widow put in two

copper coins. 3And he said, "Truly I tell you, this poor widow has put in more than all of them; 4for they all contributed out of their abundance, but she out of her poverty put in all the living that she had."

REFLECTION

Some times our eyes play tricks on us. When Israel desires a king to rule over them, they are thrilled to place Saul on the throne. Tall and handsome (see 1 Sm 9:2), on the exterior he looks to be just the man for the job. But soon enough it becomes clear that he lacks the necessary confidence and virtue, disobeying the Lord grievously and failing to fulfill the mission God has given him. Thankfully God has 20/20 vision: "the LORD sees not as man sees; man looks on the outward appearance, but the LORD looks on the heart" (16:7). We tend to judge people based on the exterior— their clothing, material possessions, or external accomplishments—but the Lord has a "heart perspective." Similarly, when Jesus watches people placing their contributions in the Temple treasury, he is not impressed by the lavish gifts given by the wealthy for all to see. Rather, he praises the poor widow who gives her last two coins, honoring the woman's whole-hearted sacrifice and trust in God. How is your vision? Who do you need to take a second look at with God's perspective?

May 1

1 SAMUEL 17

**Now the Philis′tines gathered
their armies for battle; and they
were gathered at Socoh, which
belongs to Judah, and encamped between
Socoh and Aze′kah, in E′phes-dam′mim.**
[2]And Saul and the men of Israel were
gathered, and encamped in the valley of
E′lah, and drew up in line of battle against
the Philis′tines. [3]And the Philis′tines stood
on the mountain on the one side, and
Israel stood on the mountain on the other
side, with a valley between them. [4]And there
came out from the camp of the Philis′tines
a champion named Goliath, of Gath, whose
height was six cubits and a span. [5]He had a
helmet of bronze on his head, and he was
armed with a coat of mail, and the weight
of the coat was five thousand shekels of
bronze. [6]And he had greaves of bronze
upon his legs, and a javelin of bronze slung
between his shoulders. [7]And the shaft of
his spear was like a weaver's beam, and his
spear's head weighed six hundred shekels
of iron; and his shield-bearer went before
him. [8]He stood and shouted to the ranks
of Israel, "Why have you come out to draw
up for battle? Am I not a Philis′tine, and are
you not servants of Saul? Choose a man for
yourselves, and let him come down to me.
[9]If he is able to fight with me and kill me,
then we will be your servants; but if I prevail
against him and kill him, then you shall
be our servants and serve us." [10]And the
Philis′tine said, "I defy the ranks of Israel
this day; give me a man, that we may fight
together." [11]When Saul and all Israel heard
these words of the Philis′tine, they were
dismayed and greatly afraid.

[12]Now David was the son of an Eph′rathite
of Bethlehem in Judah, named Jesse, who
had eight sons. In the days of Saul the man
was already old and advanced in years. [13]The
three eldest sons of Jesse had followed Saul
to the battle; and the names of his three sons
who went to the battle were Eli′ab the first-
born, and next to him Abin′adab, and the
third Shammah. [14]David was the youngest;
the three eldest followed Saul, [15]but David
went back and forth from Saul to feed his
father's sheep at Bethlehem. [16]For forty days
the Philis′tine came forward and took his
stand, morning and evening.

[17]And Jesse said to David his son, "Take
for your brothers an ephah of this parched
grain, and these ten loaves, and carry them
quickly to the camp to your brothers; [18]also
take these ten cheeses to the commander of
their thousand. See how your brothers fare,
and bring some token from them."

[19]Now Saul, and they, and all the men of
Israel, were in the valley of E′lah, fighting
with the Philis′tines. [20]And David rose
early in the morning, and left the sheep
with a keeper, and took the provisions, and
went, as Jesse had commanded him; and he
came to the encampment as the host was
going forth to the battle line, shouting the
war cry. [21]And Israel and the Philis′tines
drew up for battle, army against army.
[22]And David left the things in charge of the
keeper of the baggage, and ran to the ranks,
and went and greeted his brothers. [23]As he
talked with them, behold, the champion, the
Philis′tine of Gath, Goliath by name, came
up out of the ranks of the Philistines, and
spoke the same words as before. And David
heard him.

[24]All the men of Israel, when they saw the
man, fled from him, and were much afraid.
[25]And the men of Israel said, "Have you seen
this man who has come up? Surely he has
come up to defy Israel; and the man who
kills him, the king will enrich with great
riches, and will give him his daughter, and
make his father's house free in Israel." [26]And
David said to the men who stood by him,
"What shall be done for the man who kills
this Philis′tine, and takes away the reproach
from Israel? For who is this uncircumcised
Philistine, that he should defy the armies of
the living God?" [27]And the people answered
him in the same way, "So shall it be done to
the man who kills him."

28Now Eli′ab his eldest brother heard when
he spoke to the men; and Eli′ab's anger was
kindled against David, and he said, "Why
have you come down? And with whom have
you left those few sheep in the wilderness?
I know your presumption, and the evil of
your heart; for you have come down to see
the battle." 29And David said, "What have I
done now? Was it not but a word?" 30And
he turned away from him toward another,
and spoke in the same way; and the people
answered him again as before.

31When the words which David spoke were
heard, they repeated them before Saul; and
he sent for him. 32And David said to Saul,
"Let no man's heart fail because of him; your
servant will go and fight with this Philis′tine."
33And Saul said to David, "You are not able to
go against this Philis′tine to fight with him;
for you are but a youth, and he has been a
man of war from his youth." 34But David said
to Saul, "Your servant used to keep sheep for
his father; and when there came a lion, or
a bear, and took a lamb from the flock, 35I
went after him and struck him and delivered
it out of his mouth; and if he arose against
me, I caught him by his beard, and struck
him and killed him. 36Your servant has killed
both lions and bears; and this uncircumcised
Philis′tine shall be like one of them, seeing
he has defied the armies of the living God."
37And David said, "The LORD who delivered
me from the paw of the lion and from the
paw of the bear, will deliver me from the
hand of this Philis′tine." And Saul said to
David, "Go, and the LORD be with you!"
38Then Saul clothed David with his armor;
he put a helmet of bronze on his head, and
clothed him with a coat of mail. 39And David
belted on his sword over his armor, and he
tried in vain to go, for he was not used to
them. Then David said to Saul, "I cannot
go with these; for I am not used to them."
And David put them off. 40Then he took
his staff in his hand, and chose five smooth
stones from the brook, and put them in his
shepherd's bag or wallet; his sling was in his
hand, and he drew near to the Philis′tine.

41And the Philis′tine came on and drew
near to David, with his shield-bearer in
front of him. 42And when the Philis′tine
looked, and saw David, he disdained him;
for he was but a youth, ruddy and comely
in appearance. 43And the Philis′tine said to
David, "Am I a dog, that you come to me with
sticks?" And the Philistine cursed David by
his gods. 44The Philis′tine said to David,
"Come to me, and I will give your flesh to
the birds of the air and to the beasts of the
field." 45Then David said to the Philis′tine,
"You come to me with a sword and with a
spear and with a javelin; but I come to you
in the name of the LORD of hosts, the God of
the armies of Israel, whom you have defied.
46This day the LORD will deliver you into
my hand, and I will strike you down, and
cut off your head; and I will give the dead
bodies of the host of the Philis′tines this day
to the birds of the air and to the wild beasts
of the earth; that all the earth may know that
there is a God in Israel, 47and that all this
assembly may know that the LORD saves not
with sword and spear; for the battle is the
LORD's and he will give you into our hand."

48When the Philis′tine arose and came and
drew near to meet David, David ran quickly
toward the battle line to meet the Philistine.
49And David put his hand in his bag and
took out a stone, and slung it, and struck the
Philis′tine on his forehead; the stone sank
into his forehead, and he fell on his face to
the ground.

50So David prevailed over the Philis′tine
with a sling and with a stone, and struck
the Philistine, and killed him; there was no
sword in the hand of David. 51Then David
ran and stood over the Philis′tine, and took
his sword and drew it out of its sheath, and
killed him, and cut off his head with it. When
the Philistines saw that their champion was
dead, they fled. 52And the men of Israel and
Judah rose with a shout and pursued the
Philis′tines as far as Gath and the gates of
Ek′ron, so that the wounded Philistines fell
on the way from Sha-ara′im as far as Gath
and Ekron. 53And the Israelites came back
from chasing the Philis′tines, and they
plundered their camp. 54And David took
the head of the Philis′tine and brought it to
Jerusalem; but he put his armor in his tent.

[55]When Saul saw David go forth against the Philis′tine, he said to Abner, the commander of the army, "Abner, whose son is this youth?" And Abner said, "As your soul lives, O king, I cannot tell." [56]And the king said, "Inquire whose son the stripling is." [57]And as David returned from the slaughter of the Philis′tine, Abner took him, and brought him before Saul with the head of the Philistine in his hand. [58]And Saul said to him, "Whose son are you, young man?" And David answered, "I am the son of your servant Jesse the Bethlehemite."

PSALM 104 [103]

[14]You cause the grass to grow for the cattle,
and plants for man to cultivate,
that he may bring forth food from
the earth,
[15] and wine to gladden the heart of man,
oil to make his face shine,
and bread to strengthen man's heart.
[16]The trees of the LORD are watered
abundantly,
the cedars of Lebanon which he planted.
[17]In them the birds build their nests;
the stork has her home in the fir trees.
[18]The high mountains are for the wild goats;
the rocks are a refuge for the badgers.
[19]You have made the moon to mark
the seasons;
the sun knows its time for setting.
[20]You make darkness, and it is night,
when all the beasts of the forest
creep forth.
[21]The young lions roar for their prey,
seeking their food from God.
[22]When the sun rises, they get them away
and lie down in their dens.
[23]Man goes forth to his work
and to his labor until the evening.

[24]O LORD, how manifold are your works!
In wisdom you have made them all;
the earth is full of your creatures.
[25]Yonder is the sea, great and wide,
which teems with things innumerable,
living things both small and great.
[26]There go the ships,
and Leviathan which you formed to sport
in it.
[27]These all look to you,
to give them their food in due season.
[28]When you give to them, they gather it up;
when you open your hand, they are filled
with good things.
[29]When you hide your face, they
are dismayed;
when you take away their spirit, they die
and return to their dust.
[30]When you send forth your Spirit, they
are created;
and you renew the face of the earth.

[31]May the glory of the LORD endure for ever,
may the LORD rejoice in his works,
[32]who looks on the earth and it trembles,
who touches the mountains and
they smoke!
[33]I will sing to the LORD as long as I live;
I will sing praise to my God while I
have being.
[34]May my meditation be pleasing to him,
for I rejoice in the LORD.
[35]Let sinners be consumed from the earth,
and let the wicked be no more!
Bless the LORD, O my soul!
Praise the LORD!

LUKE 21

[5]And as some spoke of the temple, how it was adorned with noble stones and offerings, he said, [6]"As for these things which you
see, the days will come when there shall not
be left here one stone upon another that will
not be thrown down." [7]And they asked him,
"Teacher, when will this be, and what will be
the sign when this is about to take place?"
[8]And he said, "Take heed that you are not
led astray; for many will come in my name,
saying, 'I am he!' and, 'The time is at hand!'
Do not go after them. [9]And when you hear
of wars and tumults, do not be terrified; for

this must first take place, but the end will not be at once."

[10]Then he said to them, "Nation will rise against nation, and kingdom against kingdom; [11]there will be great earthquakes, and in various places famines and pestilences; and there will be terrors and great signs from heaven. [12]But before all this they will lay their hands on you and persecute you, delivering you up to the synagogues and prisons, and you will be brought before kings and governors for my name's sake. [13]This will be a time for you to bear testimony. [14]Settle it therefore in your minds, not to meditate beforehand how to answer; [15]for I will give you a mouth and wisdom, which none of your adversaries will be able to withstand or contradict. [16]You will be delivered up even by parents and brothers and kinsmen and friends, and some of you they will put to death; [17]you will be hated by all for my name's sake. [18]But not a hair of your head will perish. [19]By your endurance you will gain your lives.

[20]"But when you see Jerusalem surrounded by armies, then know that its desolation has come near. [21]Then let those who are in Judea flee to the mountains, and let those who are inside the city depart, and let not those who are out in the country enter it; [22]for these are days of vengeance, to fulfil all that is written. [23]Alas for those who are with child and for those who are nursing in those days! For great distress shall be upon the earth and wrath upon this people; [24]they will fall by the edge of the sword, and be led captive among all nations; and Jerusalem will be trodden down by the Gentiles, until the times of the Gentiles are fulfilled.

[25]"And there will be signs in sun and moon and stars, and upon the earth distress of nations in perplexity at the roaring of the sea and the waves, [26]men fainting with fear and with foreboding of what is coming on the world; for the powers of the heavens will be shaken. [27]And then they will see the Son of man coming in a cloud with power and great glory. [28]Now when these things begin to take place, look up and raise your heads, because your redemption is drawing near."

REFLECTION

The Israelites look upon the giant Goliath with great fear; his stature, six cubits, and his armor, such as his spearhead weighing six hundred shekels of iron, send them running. The repetition of the number six in Goliath's description hearkens back to the sixth day of creation, when God creates the beasts, as well as man and woman. We are created on the sixth day with the animals, but called into the seventh day and the covenant relationship with God. David shows us how to live that covenant relationship; he trusts in the living God to deliver him. David is indignant at Goliath's insults, replying, "I come to you in the name of the Lord of hosts . . . that all the earth may know that there is a God in Israel" (1 Sm 17:45–46). And David is triumphant, bringing just five smooth stones (recalling the five books of the Torah) to the battle. Jesus warns us about the days of persecution to come, but encourages us not to be afraid. Like David before the giant Goliath, if we live in the covenant relationship with God, we can overcome terrifying realities and not be dismayed. How can you imitate David and trust God in the midst of the fearful situations in your own life?

May 2

1 SAMUEL 18

When he had finished speaking to Saul, the soul of Jonathan was knit to the soul of David, and Jonathan loved him as his own soul. [2]**And**
Saul took him that day, and would not let
him return to his father's house. [3]Then Jonathan made a covenant with David, because
he loved him as his own soul. [4]And Jonathan
stripped himself of the robe that was upon
him, and gave it to David, and his armor,
and even his sword and his bow and his
belt. [5]And David went out and was successful wherever Saul sent him; so that Saul set

him over the men of war. And this was good
in the sight of all the people and also in the
sight of Saul's servants.
6As they were coming home, when David
returned from slaying the Philis'tine, the
women came out of all the cities of Israel,
singing and dancing, to meet King Saul,
with timbrels, with songs of joy, and with
instruments of music. 7And the women
sang to one another as they made merry,
"Saul has slain his thousands,
and David his ten thousands."
8And Saul was very angry, and this saying
displeased him; he said, "They have ascribed
to David ten thousands, and to me they
have ascribed thousands; and what more
can he have but the kingdom?" 9And Saul
eyed David from that day on.
10And the next day an evil spirit from God
rushed upon Saul, and he raved within his
house, while David was playing the lyre,
as he did day by day. Saul had his spear in
his hand; 11and Saul cast the spear, for he
thought, "I will pin David to the wall." But
David evaded him twice.
12Saul was afraid of David, because the
LORD was with him but had departed from
Saul. 13So Saul removed him from his
presence, and made him a commander of
a thousand; and he went out and came in
before the people. 14And David had success
in all his undertakings; for the LORD was
with him. 15And when Saul saw that he had
great success, he stood in awe of him. 16But
all Israel and Judah loved David; for he went
out and came in before them.
17Then Saul said to David, "Here is my
elder daughter Merab; I will give her to
you for a wife; only be valiant for me and
fight the LORD's battles." For Saul thought,
"Let not my hand be upon him, but let the
hand of the Philis'tines be upon him." 18And
David said to Saul, "Who am I, and who are
my kinsfolk, my father's family in Israel, that
I should be son-in-law to the king?" 19But
at the time when Merab, Saul's daughter,
should have been given to David, she was
given to A'dri-el the Meho'lathite for a wife.
20Now Saul's daughter Michal loved David;
and they told Saul, and the thing pleased
him. 21Saul thought, "Let me give her to him,
that she may be a snare for him, and that the
hand of the Philis'tines may be against him."
Therefore Saul said to David a second time,
"You shall now be my son-in-law." 22And Saul
commanded his servants, "Speak to David in
private and say, 'Behold, the king has delight
in you, and all his servants love you; now
then become the king's son-in-law.'" 23And
Saul's servants spoke those words in the ears
of David. And David said, "Does it seem to
you a little thing to become the king's son-
in-law, seeing that I am a poor man and of
no repute?" 24And the servants of Saul told
him, "Thus and so did David speak." 25Then
Saul said, "Thus shall you say to David, 'The
king desires no marriage present except a
hundred foreskins of the Philis'tines, that he
may be avenged of the king's enemies.'" Now
Saul thought to make David fall by the hand
of the Philistines. 26And when his servants
told David these words, it pleased David
well to be the king's son-in-law. Before the
time had expired, 27David arose and went,
along with his men, and killed two hundred
of the Philis'tines; and David brought their
foreskins, which were given in full number
to the king, that he might become the king's
son-in-law. And Saul gave him his daughter
Michal for a wife. 28But when Saul saw and
knew that the LORD was with David, and
that all Israel loved him, 29Saul was still
more afraid of David. So Saul was David's
enemy continually.
30Then the princes of the Philis'tines came
out to battle, and as often as they came
out David had more success than all the
servants of Saul; so that his name was highly
esteemed.

19 And Saul spoke to Jonathan his son
and to all his servants, that they
should kill David. But Jonathan, Saul's son,
delighted much in David. 2And Jonathan
told David, "Saul my father seeks to kill
you; therefore take heed to yourself in the
morning, stay in a secret place and hide
yourself; 3and I will go out and stand beside
my father in the field where you are, and I
will speak to my father about you; and if I
learn anything I will tell you." 4And Jonathan

spoke well of David to Saul his father, and said to him, "Let not the king sin against his servant David; because he has not sinned against you, and because his deeds have been of good service to you; [5]for he took his life in his hand and he slew the Philis′tine, and the LORD wrought a great victory for all Israel. You saw it, and rejoiced; why then will you sin against innocent blood by killing David without cause?" [6]And Saul listened to the voice of Jonathan; Saul swore, "As the LORD lives, he shall not be put to death." [7]And Jonathan called David, and Jonathan showed him all these things. And Jonathan brought David to Saul, and he was in his presence as before.

[8]And there was war again; and David went out and fought with the Philis′tines, and made a great slaughter among them, so that they fled before him. [9]Then an evil spirit from the LORD came upon Saul, as he sat in his house with his spear in his hand; and David was playing the lyre. [10]And Saul sought to pin David to the wall with the spear; but he eluded Saul, so that he struck the spear into the wall. And David fled, and escaped.

[11]That night Saul sent messengers to David's house to watch him, that he might kill him in the morning. But Michal, David's wife, told him, "If you do not save your life tonight, tomorrow you will be killed." [12]So Michal let David down through the window; and he fled away and escaped. [13]Michal took an image and laid it on the bed and put a pillow of goats' hair at its head, and covered it with the clothes. [14]And when Saul sent messengers to take David, she said, "He is sick." [15]Then Saul sent the messengers to see David, saying, "Bring him up to me in the bed, that I may kill him." [16]And when the messengers came in, behold, the image was in the bed, with the pillow of goats' hair at its head. [17]Saul said to Michal, "Why have you deceived me thus, and let my enemy go, so that he has escaped?" And Michal answered Saul, "He said to me, 'Let me go; why should I kill you?'"

[18]Now David fled and escaped, and he came to Samuel at Ra′mah, and told him all that Saul had done to him. And he and Samuel went and dwelt at Naioth. [19]And it was told Saul, "Behold, David is at Naioth in Ra′mah." [20]Then Saul sent messengers to take David; and when they saw the company of the prophets prophesying, and Samuel standing as head over them, the Spirit of God came upon the messengers of Saul, and they also prophesied. [21]When it was told Saul, he sent other messengers, and they also prophesied. And Saul sent messengers again the third time, and they also prophesied. [22]Then he himself went to Ra′mah, and came to the great well that is in Secu; and he asked, "Where are Samuel and David?" And one said, "Behold, they are at Naioth in Ra′mah." [23]And he went from there to Naioth in Ra′mah; and the Spirit of God came upon him also, and as he went he prophesied, until he came to Naioth in Ramah. [24]And he too stripped off his clothes, and he too prophesied before Samuel, and lay naked all that day and all that night. Hence it is said, "Is Saul also among the prophets?"

PSALM 105 [104]

O give thanks to the LORD, call on his name,
make known his deeds among
the peoples!
[2]Sing to him, sing praises to him,
tell of all his wonderful works!
[3]Glory in his holy name;
let the hearts of those who seek
the LORD rejoice!
[4]Seek the LORD and his strength,
seek his presence continually!
[5]Remember the wonderful works that he
has done,
his miracles, and the judgments
he uttered,
[6]O offspring of Abraham his servant,
sons of Jacob, his chosen ones!

[7]He is the LORD our God;
his judgments are in all the earth.
[8]He is mindful of his covenant for ever,
of the word that he commanded, for a
thousand generations,
[9]the covenant which he made with Abraham,
his sworn promise to Isaac,

[10]which he confirmed to Jacob as a statute,
to Israel as an everlasting covenant,
[11]saying, "To you I will give the land of Canaan
as your portion for an inheritance."

[12]When they were few in number,
of little account, and sojourners in it,
[13]wandering from nation to nation,
from one kingdom to another people,
[14]he allowed no one to oppress them;
he rebuked kings on their account,
[15]saying, "Touch not my anointed ones,
do my prophets no harm!"

LUKE 21

[29]**And he told them a parable: "Look at the fig tree, and all the trees; [30]as soon as they come out in leaf, you see for yourselves and know**
that the summer is already near. [31]So also,
when you see these things taking place,
you know that the kingdom of God is near.
[32]Truly, I say to you, this generation will not
pass away till all has taken place. [33]Heaven
and earth will pass away, but my words will
not pass away.
[34]"But take heed to yourselves lest your
hearts be weighed down with dissipation and
drunkenness and cares of this life, and that
day come upon you suddenly like a snare;
[35]for it will come upon all who dwell upon
the face of the whole earth. [36]But watch at all
times, praying that you may have strength to
escape all these things that will take place,
and to stand before the Son of man."
[37]And every day he was teaching in the
temple, but at night he went out and lodged
on the mount called Olivet. [38]And early in
the morning all the people came to him in
the temple to hear him.

22 Now the feast of Unleavened Bread
drew near, which is called the Passover. [2]And the chief priests and the scribes
were seeking how to put him to death; for
they feared the people.
[3]Then Satan entered into Judas called
Iscariot, who was of the number of the
Twelve; [4]he went away and conferred with
the chief priests and captains how he might
betray him to them. [5]And they were glad,
and engaged to give him money. [6]So he
agreed, and sought an opportunity to betray
him to them in the absence of the multitude.
[7]Then came the day of Unleavened Bread,
on which the Passover lamb had to be
sacrificed. [8]So Jesus sent Peter and John,
saying, "Go and prepare the Passover for
us, that we may eat it." [9]They said to him,
"Where will you have us prepare it?" [10]He
said to them, "Behold, when you have
entered the city, a man carrying a jar of water
will meet you; follow him into the house
which he enters, [11]and tell the householder,
'The Teacher says to you, Where is the guest
room, where I am to eat the Passover with
my disciples?' [12]And he will show you a large
upper room furnished; there make ready."
[13]And they went, and found it as he had told
them; and they prepared the Passover.

REFLECTION

"Jonathan loved [David] as his own soul" (1 Sm 18:1). True friends seek the good of the other even more than themselves. They rejoice at the accomplishments and blessings of their friends and are saddened by their sorrows, as if the blessings and sorrows were their very own. Jonathan's friendship compels him to take off his own armor and clothing and give them to David. He protects David and helps him escape, not out of self-interest but out of love. Jonathan himself, as the son of the king, could have hoped to follow in his father's royal footsteps, but instead he supports David and even David's claim to the throne. Immediately after David's triumph over Goliath, Saul becomes jealous. Jealousy and envy undermine the heart of friendship; one who is jealous sees the good of another and wishes to have it for oneself, and one who is envious seeks to destroy the good in the other. Indeed, Saul's jealousy of David's popularity and success drives him to a dark envy, an envy that spurs Saul to seek David's life. To whom can you be a better friend and promoter of the good? Of whom are you envious; and what first step can you make to change this relationship?

May 3

1 SAMUEL 20

**Then David fled from Naioth
in Raʹmah, and came and said
before Jonathan, "What have I
done? What is my guilt? And what
is my sin before your father, that he
seeks my life?" 2And he said to him,**
"Far from it! You shall not die. Behold, my
father does nothing either great or small
without disclosing it to me; and why should
my father hide this from me? It is not so."
3But David replied, "Your father knows well
that I have found favor in your eyes; and he
thinks, 'Let not Jonathan know this, lest he
be grieved.' But truly, as the LORD lives and
as your soul lives, there is but a step between
me and death." 4Then said Jonathan to David,
"Whatever you say, I will do for you." 5David
said to Jonathan, "Behold, tomorrow is the
new moon, and I should not fail to sit at
table with the king; but let me go, that I
may hide myself in the field till the third
day at evening. 6If your father misses me at
all, then say, 'David earnestly asked leave of
me to run to Bethlehem his city; for there
is a yearly sacrifice there for all the family.'
7If he says, 'Good!' it will be well with your
servant; but if he is angry, then know that
evil is determined by him. 8Therefore deal
kindly with your servant, for you have
brought your servant into a sacred covenant
with you. But if there is guilt in me, slay me
yourself; for why should you bring me to
your father?" 9And Jonathan said, "Far be it
from you! If I knew that it was determined
by my father that evil should come upon
you, would I not tell you?" 10Then said David
to Jonathan, "Who will tell me if your father
answers you roughly?" 11And Jonathan said
to David, "Come, let us go out into the field."
So they both went out into the field.

12And Jonathan said to David, "The
LORD, the God of Israel, be witness! When
I have sounded my father, about this time
tomorrow, or the third day, behold, if he is
well disposed toward David, shall I not then
send and disclose it to you? 13But should it
please my father to do you harm, the LORD
do so to Jonathan, and more also, if I do
not disclose it to you, and send you away,
that you may go in safety. May the LORD
be with you, as he has been with my father.
14If I am still alive, show me the loyal love
of the LORD, that I may not die; 15and do
not cut off your loyalty from my house for
ever. When the LORD cuts off every one of
the enemies of David from the face of the
earth, 16let not the name of Jonathan be cut
off from the house of David. And may the
LORD take vengeance on David's enemies."
17And Jonathan made David swear again
by his love for him; for he loved him as he
loved his own soul.

18Then Jonathan said to him, "Tomorrow
is the new moon; and you will be missed,
because your seat will be empty. 19And on
the third day you will be greatly missed; then
go to the place where you hid yourself when
the matter was in hand, and remain beside
yonder stone heap. 20And I will shoot three
arrows to the side of it, as though I shot at
a mark. 21And behold, I will send the lad,
saying, 'Go, find the arrows.' If I say to the
lad, 'Look, the arrows are on this side of you,
take them,' then you are to come, for, as the
LORD lives, it is safe for you and there is no
danger. 22But if I say to the youth, 'Look, the
arrows are beyond you,' then go; for the LORD
has sent you away. 23And as for the matter of
which you and I have spoken, behold, the
LORD is between you and me for ever."

24So David hid himself in the field; and
when the new moon came, the king sat
down to eat food. 25The king sat upon his
seat, as at other times, upon the seat by the
wall; Jonathan sat opposite, and Abner sat
by Saul's side, but David's place was empty.

26Yet Saul did not say anything that day;
for he thought, "Something has befallen
him; he is not clean, surely he is not clean."
27But on the second day, the next day after
the new moon, David's place was empty.
And Saul said to Jonathan his son, "Why has
not the son of Jesse come to the meal, either

yesterday or today?" 28Jonathan answered Saul, "David earnestly asked leave of me to go to Bethlehem; 29he said, 'Let me go; for our family holds a sacrifice in the city, and my brother has commanded me to be there. So now, if I have found favor in your eyes, let me get away, and see my brothers.' For this reason he has not come to the king's table."

30Then Saul's anger was kindled against Jonathan, and he said to him, "You son of a perverse, rebellious woman, do I not know that you have chosen the son of Jesse to your own shame, and to the shame of your mother's nakedness? 31For as long as the son of Jesse lives upon the earth, neither you nor your kingdom shall be established. Therefore send and fetch him to me, for he shall surely die." 32Then Jonathan answered Saul his father, "Why should he be put to death? What has he done?" 33But Saul cast his spear at him to strike him; so Jonathan knew that his father was determined to put David to death. 34And Jonathan rose from the table in fierce anger and ate no food the second day of the month, for he was grieved for David, because his father had disgraced him.

35In the morning Jonathan went out into the field to the appointment with David, and with him a little lad. 36And he said to his lad, "Run and find the arrows which I shoot." As the lad ran, he shot an arrow beyond him. 37And when the lad came to the place of the arrow which Jonathan had shot, Jonathan called after the lad and said, "Is not the arrow beyond you?" 38And Jonathan called after the lad, "Hurry, make haste, stay not." So Jonathan's lad gathered up the arrows, and came to his master. 39But the lad knew nothing; only Jonathan and David knew the matter. 40And Jonathan gave his weapons to his lad, and said to him, "Go and carry them to the city." 41And as soon as the lad had gone, David rose from beside the stone heap and fell on his face to the ground, and bowed three times; and they kissed one another, and wept with one another, until David recovered himself. 42Then Jonathan said to David, "Go in peace, forasmuch as we have sworn both of us in the name of the LORD, saying, 'The LORD shall be between me and you, and between my descendants and your descendants, for ever.' " And he rose and departed; and Jonathan went into the city.

21 Then came David to Nob to Ahim′elech the priest; and Ahimelech came to meet David trembling, and said to him, "Why are you alone, and no one with you?" 2And David said to Ahim′elech the priest, "The king has charged me with a matter, and said to me, 'Let no one know anything of the matter about which I send you, and with which I have charged you.' I have made an appointment with the young men for such and such a place. 3Now then, what have you at hand? Give me five loaves of bread, or whatever is here." 4And the priest answered David, "I have no common bread at hand, but there is holy bread; if only the young men have kept themselves from women." 5And David answered the priest, "Of a truth women have been kept from us as always when I go on an expedition; the vessels of the young men are holy, even when it is a common journey; how much more today will their vessels be holy?" 6So the priest gave him the holy bread; for there was no bread there but the bread of the Presence, which is removed from before the LORD, to be replaced by hot bread on the day it is taken away.

7Now a certain man of the servants of Saul was there that day, detained before the LORD; his name was Do′eg the E′domite, the chief of Saul's herdsmen.

8And David said to Ahim′elech, "And have you not here a spear or a sword at hand? For I have brought neither my sword nor my weapons with me, because the king's business required haste." 9And the priest said, "The sword of Goliath the Philis′tine, whom you killed in the valley of E′lah, behold, it is here wrapped in a cloth behind the ephod; if you will take that, take it, for there is none but that here." And David said, "There is none like that; give it to me."

10And David rose and fled that day from Saul, and went to A′chish the king of Gath. 11And the servants of A′chish said to him, "Is not this David the king of the land? Did they not sing to one another of him in dances,

'Saul has slain his thousands,
and David his ten thousands'?"
12And David took these words to heart, and
was much afraid of A′chish the king of Gath.
13So he changed his behavior before them, and
feigned himself mad in their hands, and made
marks on the doors of the gate, and let his
spittle run down his beard. 14Then said A′chish
to his servants, "Behold, you see the man is
mad; why then have you brought him to me?
15Do I lack madmen, that you have brought
this fellow to play the madman in my presence?
Shall this fellow come into my house?"

PSALM 105 [104]

16When he summoned a famine on the land,
and broke every staff of bread,
17he had sent a man ahead of them,
Joseph, who was sold as a slave.
18His feet were hurt with shackles,
his neck was put in a collar of iron;
19until what he had said came to pass
the word of the LORD tested him.
20The king sent and released him,
the ruler of the peoples set him free;
21he made him lord of his house,
and ruler of all his possessions,
22to instruct his princes at his pleasure,
and to teach his elders wisdom.

23Then Israel came to Egypt;
Jacob sojourned in the land of Ham.
24And the LORD made his people very
fruitful,
and made them stronger than their foes.
25He turned their hearts to hate his people,
to deal craftily with his servants.

LUKE 22

**14And when the hour came, he
sat at table, and the apostles
with him. 15And he said to them,
"I have earnestly desired to eat this**
Passover with you before I suffer; 16for I tell
you I shall not eat it until it is fulfilled in the
kingdom of God." 17And he took a chalice,
and when he had given thanks he said, "Take
this, and divide it among yourselves; 18for I
tell you that from now on I shall not drink
of the fruit of the vine until the kingdom of
God comes." 19And he took bread, and when
he had given thanks he broke it and gave it
to them, saying, "This is my body which is
given for you. Do this in remembrance of
me." 20And likewise the chalice after supper,
saying, "This chalice which is poured out
for you is the new covenant in my blood."
21But behold the hand of him who betrays
me is with me on the table. 22For the Son
of man goes as it has been determined; but
woe to that man by whom he is betrayed!"
23And they began to question one another,
which of them it was that would do this.

24A dispute also arose among them, which of
them was to be regarded as the greatest. 25And
he said to them, "The kings of the Gentiles
exercise lordship over them; and those in
authority over them are called benefactors.
26But not so with you; rather let the greatest
among you become as the youngest, and
the leader as one who serves. 27For which is
the greater, one who sits at table, or one who
serves? Is it not the one who sits at table? But I
am among you as one who serves.

28"You are those who have continued with
me in my trials; 29as my Father appointed
a kingdom for me, so do I appoint for you
30that you may eat and drink at my table in
my kingdom, and sit on thrones judging the
twelve tribes of Israel.

31"Simon, Simon, behold, Satan demanded
to have you, that he might sift you like
wheat, 32but I have prayed for you that your
faith may not fail; and when you have turned
again, strengthen your brethren." 33And he
said to him, "Lord, I am ready to go with you
to prison and to death." 34He said, "I tell you,
Peter, the cock will not crow this day, until
you three times deny that you know me."

35And he said to them, "When I sent you
out with no purse or bag or sandals, did you
lack anything?" They said, "Nothing." 36He
said to them, "But now, let him who has a
purse take it, and likewise a bag. And let
him who has no sword sell his cloak and buy

one. 37For I tell you that this Scripture must
be fulfilled in me, 'And he was reckoned with
transgressors'; for what is written about me
has its fulfilment." 38And they said, "Look,
Lord, here are two swords." And he said to
them, "It is enough."
39And he came out, and went, as was his
custom, to the Mount of Olives; and the
disciples followed him. 40And when he came
to the place he said to them, "Pray that you
may not enter into temptation." 41And he
withdrew from them about a stone's throw,
and knelt down and prayed, 42"Father, if
you are willing, remove this chalice from
me; nevertheless not my will, but yours, be
done." 43And there appeared to him an angel
from heaven, strengthening him. 44And
being in an agony he prayed more earnestly;
and his sweat became like great drops
of blood falling down upon the ground.
45And when he rose from prayer, he came
to the disciples and found them sleeping for
sorrow, 46and he said to them, "Why do you
sleep? Rise and pray that you may not enter
into temptation."

REFLECTION

Jonathan stands in stark contrast to the disciples of Jesus. David calls on Jonathan to be true to the "sacred covenant" that they had made with one another (1 Sm 20:8), and Jonathan comes through by warning him of danger. Jesus, similarly, tells the disciples to pray for strength to resist temptation (see Lk 22:40), but instead he finds them sleeping (see v. 45)—or worse, betraying and denying him. As he flees from Saul, David goes to the sanctuary of the Lord and eats the sacred Bread of the Presence that was reserved in the Holy Place. Jesus, as the new David, but also as the new High Priest, offers his body in sacrifice as the new Bread of the Presence at the Last Supper when he says, "This is my body which is given for you" (v. 19). Jesus and Jonathan show us what true friendship is like: it extends all the way to giving your own life in sacrificial covenant for another. Jonathan, willingly, is cursed by his father in order to save his friend (see 1 Sm 20:30). Jesus, also willingly, becomes "a curse for us" that we might be saved (Gal 3:13). What sacrifices do you make for your friends?

May 4

1 SAMUEL 22

**David departed from there and
escaped to the cave of Adul'lam;
and when his brothers and
all his father's house heard it, they
went down there to him. 2And every
one who was in distress, and every**
one who was in debt, and every one who
was discontented, gathered to him; and he
became captain over them. And there were
with him about four hundred men.
3And David went from there to Mizpeh
of Moab; and he said to the king of Moab,
"Please let my father and my mother stay
with you, till I know what God will do for
me." 4And he left them with the king of
Moab, and they stayed with him all the time
that David was in the stronghold. 5Then the
prophet Gad said to David, "Do not remain
in the stronghold; depart, and go into the
land of Judah." So David departed, and went
into the forest of He'reth.
6Now Saul heard that David was discovered, and the men who were with
him. Saul was sitting at Gib'e-ah, under
the tamarisk tree on the height, with his
spear in his hand, and all his servants were
standing about him. 7And Saul said to his
servants who stood about him, "Hear now,
you Benjaminites; will the son of Jesse give
every one of you fields and vineyards, will
he make you all commanders of thousands
and commanders of hundreds, 8that all of
you have conspired against me? No one
discloses to me when my son makes a
league with the son of Jesse, none of you
is sorry for me or discloses to me that
my son has stirred up my servant against
me, to lie in wait, as at this day." 9Then
answered Do'eg the E'domite, who stood
by the servants of Saul, "I saw the son of
Jesse coming to Nob, to Ahim'elech the
son of Ahi'tub, 10and he inquired of the
LORD for him, and gave him provisions,

and gave him the sword of Goliath the Philis′tine."

[11]Then the king sent to summon Ahim′elech the priest, the son of Ahi′tub, and all his father's house, the priests who were at Nob; and all of them came to the king. [12]And Saul said, "Hear now, son of Ahi′tub." And he answered, "Here I am, my lord." [13]And Saul said to him, "Why have you conspired against me, you and the son of Jesse, in that you have given him bread and a sword, and have inquired of God for him, so that he has risen against me, to lie in wait, as at this day?" [14]Then Ahim′elech answered the king, "And who among all your servants is so faithful as David, who is the king's son-in-law, and captain over your bodyguard, and honored in your house? [15]Is today the first time that I have inquired of God for him? No! Let not the king impute anything to his servant or to all the house of my father; for your servant has known nothing of all this, much or little." [16]And the king said, "You shall surely die, Ahim′elech, you and all your father's house." [17]And the king said to the guard who stood about him, "Turn and kill the priests of the LORD; because their hand also is with David, and they knew that he fled, and did not disclose it to me." But the servants of the king would not put forth their hand to fall upon the priests of the LORD. [18]Then the king said to Do′eg, "You turn and fall upon the priests." And Doeg the E′domite turned and fell upon the priests, and he killed on that day eighty-five persons who wore the linen ephod. [19]And Nob, the city of the priests, he put to the sword; both men and women, children and sucklings, oxen, donkeys and sheep, he put to the sword.

[20]But one of the sons of Ahim′elech the son of Ahi′tub, named Abi′athar, escaped and fled after David. [21]And Abi′athar told David that Saul had killed the priests of the LORD. [22]And David said to Abi′athar, "I knew on that day, when Do′eg the E′domite was there, that he would surely tell Saul. I have occasioned the death of all the persons of your father's house. [23]Stay with me, fear not; for he that seeks my life seeks your life; with me you shall be in safekeeping."

23 Now they told David, "Behold, the Philis′tines are fighting against Kei′lah, and are robbing the threshing floors." [2]Therefore David inquired of the LORD, "Shall I go and attack these Philis′tines?" And the LORD said to David, "Go and attack the Philistines and save Kei′lah." [3]But David's men said to him, "Behold, we are afraid here in Judah; how much more then if we go to Kei′lah against the armies of the Philis′tines?" [4]Then David inquired of the LORD again. And the LORD answered him, "Arise, go down to Kei′lah; for I will give the Philis′tines into your hand." [5]And David and his men went to Kei′lah, and fought with the Philis′tines, and brought away their cattle, and made a great slaughter among them. So David delivered the inhabitants of Keilah.

[6]When Abi′athar the son of Ahim′elech fled to David to Kei′lah, he came down with an ephod in his hand. [7]Now it was told Saul that David had come to Kei′lah. And Saul said, "God has given him into my hand; for he has shut himself in by entering a town that has gates and bars." [8]And Saul summoned all the people to war, to go down to Kei′lah, to besiege David and his men. [9]David knew that Saul was plotting evil against him; and he said to Abi′athar the priest, "Bring the ephod here." [10]Then said David, "O LORD, the God of Israel, your servant has surely heard that Saul seeks to come to Kei′lah, to destroy the city on my account. [11]Will the men of Kei′lah surrender me into his hand? Will Saul come down, as your servant has heard? O LORD, the God of Israel, I beg you, tell your servant." And the LORD said, "He will come down." [12]Then said David, "Will the men of Kei′lah surrender me and my men into the hand of Saul?" And the LORD said, "They will surrender you." [13]Then David and his men, who were about six hundred, arose and departed from Kei′lah, and they went wherever they could go. When Saul was told that David had escaped from Keilah, he gave up the expedition. [14]And David remained in the strongholds in the wilderness, in the hill country of the wilderness of Ziph. And Saul

sought him every day, but God did not give
him into his hand.
15And David was afraid because Saul
had come out to seek his life. David was
in the wilderness of Ziph at Horesh. 16And
Jonathan, Saul's son, rose, and went to
David at Horesh, and strengthened his
hand in God. 17And he said to him, "Fear
not; for the hand of Saul my father shall not
find you; you shall be king over Israel, and
I shall be next to you; Saul my father also
knows this." 18And the two of them made a
covenant before the LORD; David remained
at Horesh, and Jonathan went home.
19Then the Ziphites went up to Saul at
Gib'e-ah, saying, "Does not David hide
among us in the strongholds at Horesh,
on the hill of Hachi'lah, which is south of
Jeshi'mon? 20Now come down, O king, according to all your heart's desire to come
down; and our part shall be to surrender
him into the king's hand." 21And Saul
said, "May you be blessed by the LORD;
for you have had compassion on me.
22Go, make yet more sure; know and see
the place where his haunt is, and who
has seen him there; for it is told me that
he is very cunning. 23See therefore, and
take note of all the lurking places where
he hides, and come back to me with sure
information. Then I will go with you; and
if he is in the land, I will search him
out among all the thousands of Judah."
24And they arose, and went to Ziph ahead
of Saul.

Now David and his men were in the
wilderness of Maon, in the Ar'abah to the
south of Jeshi'mon. 25And Saul and his men
went to seek him. And David was told;
therefore he went down to the rock which
is in the wilderness of Maon. And when
Saul heard that, he pursued after David in
the wilderness of Maon. 26Saul went on one
side of the mountain, and David and his
men on the other side of the mountain; and
David was making haste to get away from
Saul, as Saul and his men were closing in
upon David and his men to capture them,
27when a messenger came to Saul, saying,
"Make haste and come; for the Philis'tines
have made a raid upon the land." 28So Saul
returned from pursuing after David, and
went against the Philis'tines; therefore that
place was called the Rock of Escape. 29And
David went up from there, and dwelt in the
strongholds of En-ge'di.

PSALM 105 [104]

26He sent Moses his servant,
  and Aaron whom he had chosen.
27They wrought his signs among them,
  and miracles in the land of Ham.
28He sent darkness, and made the land dark;
  they rebelled against his words.
29He turned their waters into blood,
  and caused their fish to die.
30Their land swarmed with frogs,
  even in the chambers of their kings.
31He spoke, and there came swarms of flies,
  and gnats throughout their country.
32He gave them hail for rain,
  and lightning that flashed through
    their land.
33He struck their vines and fig trees,
  and shattered the trees of their country.
34He spoke, and the locusts came,
  and young locusts without number;
35which devoured all the vegetation in
    their land,
  and ate up the fruit of their ground.
36He struck all the first-born in their land,
  the first issue of all their strength.

37Then he led forth Israel with silver and gold,
  and there was none among his tribes who
    stumbled.
38Egypt was glad when they departed,
  for dread of them had fallen upon it.
39He spread a cloud for a covering,
  and fire to give light by night.
40They asked, and he brought quails,
  and gave them bread from heaven
    in abundance.
41He opened the rock, and water
    gushed forth;
  it flowed through the desert like a river.
42For he remembered his holy promise,
  and Abraham his servant.

43So he led forth his people with joy,
his chosen ones with singing.
44And he gave them the lands of the nations;
and they took possession of the fruit of
the peoples' toil,
45to the end that they should keep
his statutes,
and observe his laws.
Praise the LORD!

LUKE 22

47While he was still speaking, there came a crowd, and the man called Judas, one of the Twelve, was leading them. He drew near to Jesus to kiss him; 48but Jesus said to him, "Judas, would you betray the Son of man with a kiss?" 49And when those who were about him saw what would follow, they said, "Lord, shall we strike with the sword?" 50And one of them struck the slave of the high priest and cut off his right ear.
51But Jesus said, "No more of this!" And he touched his ear and healed him. 52Then Jesus said to the chief priests and captains of the temple and elders, who had come out against him, "Have you come out as against a robber, with swords and clubs? 53When I was with you day after day in the temple, you did not lay hands on me. But this is your hour, and the power of darkness."
54Then they seized him and led him away, bringing him into the high priest's house. Peter followed at a distance; 55and when they had kindled a fire in the middle of the courtyard and sat down together, Peter sat among them. 56Then a maid, seeing him as he sat in the light and gazing at him, said, "This man also was with him." 57But he denied it, saying, "Woman, I do not know him." 58And a little later some one else saw him and said, "You also are one of them." But Peter said, "Man, I am not." 59And after an interval of about an hour still another insisted, saying, "Certainly this man also was with him; for he is a Galilean." 60But Peter said, "Man, I do not know what you are saying." And immediately, while he was still speaking, the cock crowed. 61And the Lord turned and looked at Peter. And Peter remembered the word of the Lord, how he had said to him, "Before the cock crows today, you will deny me three times." 62And he went out and wept bitterly.
63Now the men who were holding Jesus mocked him and beat him; 64they also blindfolded him and asked him, "Prophesy! Who is it that struck you?" 65And they spoke many other words against him, reviling him.
66When day came, the assembly of the elders of the people gathered together, both chief priests and scribes; and they led him away to their council, and they said, 67"If you are the Christ, tell us." But he said to them, "If I tell you, you will not believe; 68and if I ask you, you will not answer. 69But from now on the Son of man shall be seated at the right hand of the power of God." 70And they all said, "Are you the Son of God, then?" And he said to them, "You say that I am." 71And they said, "What further testimony do we need? We have heard it ourselves from his own lips."

REFLECTION

We know to run from some dangers, such as a burning building or a terrorist attack. Even if we will eventually mount a response, often we first need to seek safety in order to regroup, catch our breath, and gather our resources. Life has a way of assaulting us with many pressures and dangers: temptations, financial problems, difficulties in our relationships, and even persecution for our faith. At times, then, we can feel harried and harassed like Abiathar—the lone survivor from King Saul's massacre of the high priestly family (see 1 Sm 22:18–20). In his terror, he runs to David, the Lord's anointed. David speaks reassuring words to him: "Stay with me, fear not; for he that seeks my life seeks your life; with me you shall be in safekeeping" (v. 23). These words, spoken by a king who foreshadows Christ, give us hope when we feel harassed, tempted, or attacked. With Jesus is safety. If we stay closely to him, we will not go wrong. The disciples failed to stay close to Jesus in the hour of trial. How closely are you following Jesus?

May 5

1 SAMUEL 24

When Saul returned from following the Philis′tines, he was told, "Behold, David is in the wilderness of En-ge′di." 2Then Saul took three thousand chosen men out of all Israel, and went to seek David and his men in front of the Wildgoats' Rocks. 3And he came to the sheepfolds by the way, where there was a cave; and Saul went in to relieve himself. Now David and his men were sitting in the innermost parts of the cave. 4And the men of David said to him, "Here is the day of which the LORD said to you, 'Behold, I will give your enemy into your hand, and you shall do to him as it shall seem good to you.'" Then David arose and stealthily cut off the skirt of Saul's robe. 5And afterward David's heart struck him, because he had cut off Saul's skirt. 6He said to his men, "The LORD forbid that I should do this thing to my lord, the LORD's anointed, to put forth my hand against him, seeing he is the LORD's anointed." 7So David persuaded his men with these words, and did not permit them to attack Saul. And Saul rose up and left the cave, and went upon his way.

8Afterward David also arose, and went out of the cave, and called after Saul, "My lord the king!" And when Saul looked behind him, David bowed with his face to the earth, and did obeisance. 9And David said to Saul, "Why do you listen to the words of men who say, 'Behold, David seeks your hurt'? 10Behold, this day your eyes have seen how the LORD gave you today into my hand in the cave; and some bade me kill you, but I spared you. I said, 'I will not put forth my hand against my lord; for he is the LORD's anointed.' 11See, my father, see the skirt of your robe in my hand; for by the fact that I cut off the skirt of your robe, and did not kill you, you may know and see that there is no wrong or treason in my hands. I have not sinned against you, though you hunt my life to take it. 12May the LORD judge between me and you, may the LORD avenge me upon you; but my hand shall not be against you. 13As the proverb of the ancients says, 'Out of the wicked comes forth wickedness'; but my hand shall not be against you. 14After whom has the king of Israel come out? After whom do you pursue? After a dead dog! After a flea! 15May the LORD therefore be judge, and give sentence between me and you, and see to it, and plead my cause, and deliver me from your hand."

16When David had finished speaking these words to Saul, Saul said, "Is this your voice, my son David?" And Saul lifted up his voice and wept. 17He said to David, "You are more righteous than I; for you have repaid me good, whereas I have repaid you evil. 18And you have declared this day how you have dealt well with me, in that you did not kill me when the LORD put me into your hands. 19For if a man finds his enemy, will he let him go away safe? So may the LORD reward you with good for what you have done to me this day. 20And now, behold, I know that you shall surely be king, and that the kingdom of Israel shall be established in your hand. 21Swear to me therefore by the LORD that you will not cut off my descendants after me, and that you will not destroy my name out of my father's house." 22And David swore this to Saul. Then Saul went home; but David and his men went up to the stronghold.

25 Now Samuel died; and all Israel assembled and mourned for him, and they buried him in his house at Ra′mah.

Then David rose and went down to the wilderness of Par′an. 2And there was a man in Maon, whose business was in Carmel. The man was very rich; he had three thousand sheep and a thousand goats. He was shearing his sheep in Carmel. 3Now the name of the man was Nabal, and the name of his wife Ab′igail. The woman was of good understanding and beautiful, but the man was churlish and ill-behaved; he was a Ca′lebite. 4David heard in the wilderness that Nabal was shearing his sheep. 5So David sent ten young men; and David said

to the young men, "Go up to Carmel, and go
to Nabal, and greet him in my name. 6And
thus you shall salute him: 'Peace be to you,
and peace be to your house, and peace be
to all that you have. 7I hear that you have
shearers; now your shepherds have been
with us, and we did them no harm, and they
missed nothing, all the time they were in
Carmel. 8Ask your young men, and they will
tell you. Therefore let my young men find
favor in your eyes; for we come on a feast
day. Please, give whatever you have at hand
to your servants and to your son David.' "

9When David's young men came, they
said all this to Nabal in the name of
David; and then they waited. 10And Nabal
answered David's servants, "Who is David?
Who is the son of Jesse? There are many
servants nowadays who are breaking away
from their masters. 11Shall I take my bread
and my water and my meat that I have
killed for my shearers, and give it to men
who come from I do not know where?" 12So
David's young men turned away, and came
back and told him all this. 13And David
said to his men, "Every man belt on his
sword!" And every man of them belted on
his sword; David also belted on his sword;
and about four hundred men went up after
David, while two hundred remained with
the baggage.

14But one of the young men told Ab′igail,
Nabal's wife, "Behold, David sent messengers
out of the wilderness to salute our master;
and he railed at them. 15Yet the men were
very good to us, and we suffered no harm,
and we did not miss anything when we were
in the fields, as long as we went with them;
16they were a wall to us both by night and
by day, all the while we were with them
keeping the sheep. 17Now therefore know
this and consider what you should do; for
evil is determined against our master and
against all his house, and he is so ill-natured
that one cannot speak to him."

18Then Ab′igail made haste, and took two
hundred loaves, and two skins of wine, and
five sheep ready dressed, and five measures
of parched grain, and a hundred clusters of
raisins, and two hundred cakes of figs, and
laid them on donkeys. 19And she said to
her young men, "Go on before me; behold,
I come after you." But she did not tell her
husband Nabal. 20And as she rode on the
donkey, and came down under cover of
the mountain, behold, David and his men
came down toward her; and she met them.
21Now David had said, "Surely in vain have
I guarded all that this fellow has in the
wilderness, so that nothing was missed of all
that belonged to him; and he has returned
me evil for good. 22God do so to David and
more also, if by morning I leave so much as
one male of all who belong to him."

23When Ab′igail saw David, she made
haste, and alighted from the donkey, and fell
before David on her face, and bowed to the
ground. 24She fell at his feet and said, "Upon
me alone, my lord, be the guilt; please let
your handmaid speak in your hearing, and
hear the words of your handmaid. 25Let
not my lord regard this ill-natured fellow,
Nabal; for as his name is, so is he; Nabal is
his name, and folly is with him; but I your
handmaid did not see the young men of my
lord, whom you sent. 26Now then, my lord,
as the LORD lives, and as your soul lives,
seeing the LORD has restrained you from
bloodguilt, and from taking vengeance with
your own hand, now then let your enemies
and those who seek to do evil to my lord
be as Nabal. 27And now let this present
which your servant has brought to my lord
be given to the young men who follow my
lord. 28Please forgive the trespass of your
handmaid; for the LORD will certainly make
my lord a sure house, because my lord is
fighting the battles of the LORD; and evil
shall not be found in you so long as you live.
29If men rise up to pursue you and to seek
your life, the life of my lord shall be bound
in the bundle of the living in the care of
the LORD your God; and the lives of your
enemies he shall sling out as from the hollow
of a sling. 30And when the LORD has done to
my lord according to all the good that he has
spoken concerning you, and has appointed
you prince over Israel, 31my lord shall have
no cause of grief, or pangs of conscience, for
having shed blood without cause or for my

lord taking vengeance himself. And when
the LORD has dealt well with my lord, then
remember your handmaid."
[32]And David said to Ab′igail, "Blessed be
the LORD, the God of Israel, who sent you this
day to meet me! [33]Blessed be your discretion,
and blessed be you, who have kept me this
day from bloodguilt and from avenging
myself with my own hand! [34]For as surely
as the LORD the God of Israel lives, who has
restrained me from hurting you, unless you
had made haste and come to meet me, truly
by morning there had not been left to Nabal
so much as one male." [35]Then David received
from her hand what she had brought him;
and he said to her, "Go up in peace to your
house; see, I have listened to your voice, and
I have granted your petition."
[36]And Ab′igail came to Nabal; and behold,
he was holding a feast in his house, like the
feast of a king. And Nabal's heart was merry
within him, for he was very drunk; so she
told him nothing at all until the morning
light. [37]And in the morning, when the wine
had gone out of Nabal, his wife told him these
things, and his heart died within him, and he
became as a stone. [38]And about ten days later
the LORD struck Nabal; and he died.
[39]When David heard that Nabal was dead,
he said, "Blessed be the LORD who has
avenged the insult I received at the hand of
Nabal, and has kept back his servant from
evil; the LORD has returned the evil-doing of
Nabal upon his own head." Then David sent
and wooed Ab′igail, to make her his wife.
[40]And when the servants of David came to
Ab′igail at Carmel, they said to her, "David
has sent us to you to take you to him as his
wife." [41]And she rose and bowed with her
face to the ground, and said, "Behold, your
handmaid is a servant to wash the feet of the
servants of my lord." [42]And Ab′igail made
haste and rose and mounted on a donkey,
and her five maidens attended her; she went
after the messengers of David, and became
his wife.
[43]David also took Ahin′o-am of Jezre′el;
and both of them became his wives. [44]Saul
had given Michal his daughter, David's wife,
to Palti the son of La′ish, who was of Gallim.

PSALM 106 [105]

Praise the LORD!
O give thanks to the LORD, for he is good;
for his mercy endures for ever!
[2]Who can utter the mighty doings of
the LORD,
or show forth all his praise?
[3]Blessed are they who observe justice,
who do righteousness at all times!

[4]Remember me, O LORD, when you show
favor to your people;
help me when you deliver them;
[5]that I may see the prosperity of your
chosen ones,
that I may rejoice in the gladness of
your nation,
that I may glory with your heritage.

[6]Both we and our fathers have sinned;
we have committed iniquity, we have
done wickedly.
[7]Our fathers, when they were in Egypt,
did not consider your wonderful works;
they did not remember the abundance of
your mercy,
but rebelled against the Most High at
the Red Sea.
[8]Yet he saved them for his name's sake,
that he might make known his
mighty power.
[9]He rebuked the Red Sea, and it became dry;
and he led them through the deep as
through a desert.
[10]So he saved them from the hand of the foe,
and delivered them from the power of
the enemy.
[11]And the waters covered their adversaries;
not one of them was left.
[12]Then they believed his words;
they sang his praise.

[13]But they soon forgot his works;
they did not wait for his counsel.
[14]But they had a wanton craving in
the wilderness,
and put God to the test in the desert;
[15]he gave them what they asked,
but sent a wasting disease among them.

LUKE 23

Then the whole company of them arose, and brought him before Pilate. 2And they began to accuse him, saying, "We found this man perverting our nation, and forbidding us to give tribute to Caesar, and saying that he himself is Christ a king." 3And Pilate asked him, "Are you the King of the Jews?" And he answered him, "You have said so." 4And Pilate said to the chief priests and the multitudes, "I find no crime in this man." 5But they were urgent, saying, "He stirs up the people, teaching throughout all Judea, from Galilee even to this place."

6When Pilate heard this, he asked whether the man was a Galilean. 7And when he learned that he belonged to Herod's jurisdiction, he sent him over to Herod, who was himself in Jerusalem at that time. 8When Herod saw Jesus, he was very glad, for he had long desired to see him, because he had heard about him, and he was hoping to see some sign done by him. 9So he questioned him at some length; but he made no answer. 10The chief priests and the scribes stood by, vehemently accusing him. 11And Herod with his soldiers treated him with contempt and mocked him; then, clothing him in gorgeous apparel, he sent him back to Pilate. 12And Herod and Pilate became friends with each other that very day, for before this they had been at enmity with each other.

REFLECTION

God is always faithful to us, even when we prove unfaithful. This is a consolation, but also a challenge. Today, David shows us what it means to be faithful to someone even when that person is unfaithful. David served Saul with great loyalty and honor, but Saul, realizing that his kingdom is coming to an end, seeks to kill David. In this scene, David has a chance to murder the king when Saul is vulnerable and unaware, but David resists the temptation and the prodding of his men. He pledges, "I will not put forth my hand against my lord; for he is the LORD's anointed" (1 Sm 24:10). Saul acknowledges David's guiltlessness, saying, "You have repaid me good, whereas I have repaid you evil" (v. 17). In the next chapter, Nabal is faithless, not honoring David for protecting his flocks, nor taking care to guard his family from David's vengeance. His wife, Abigail, however, shows true fidelity to her husband by making a gift to David and his men. The Lord was faithful to his people, saving and redeeming them (see Ps 106:8–10), but his people "soon forgot his works" (v. 13). How can you better imitate David and Abigail, living up to your commitments to others even when they do not fulfill their commitments to you?

May 6

1 SAMUEL 26

Then the Ziphites came to Saul at Gib′eah, saying, "Is not David hiding himself on the hill of Hachi′lah, which is on the east of Jeshi′mon?" 2So Saul arose and went down to the wilderness of Ziph, with three thousand chosen men of Israel, to seek David in the wilderness of Ziph. 3And Saul encamped on the hill of Hachi′lah, which is beside the road on the east of Jeshi′mon. But David remained in the wilderness; and when he saw that Saul came after him into the wilderness, 4David sent out spies, and learned of a certainty that Saul had come. 5Then David rose and came to the place where Saul had encamped; and David saw the place where Saul lay, with Abner the son of Ner, the commander of his army; Saul was lying within the encampment, while the army was encamped around him.

6Then David said to Ahim′elech the Hittite, and to Jo′ab's brother Abi′shai the son of Zeru′iah, "Who will go down with me into the camp to Saul?" And Abishai said, "I will go down with you." 7So David and Abi′shai went to the army by night; and there lay Saul sleeping within the encampment, with his

spear stuck in the ground at his head; and
Abner and the army lay around him. [8]Then
said Abi′shai to David, "God has given
your enemy into your hand this day; now
therefore let me pin him to the earth with
one stroke of the spear, and I will not strike
him twice." [9]But David said to Abi′shai, "Do
not destroy him; for who can put forth his
hand against the LORD's anointed, and be
guiltless?" [10]And David said, "As the LORD
lives, the LORD will strike him; or his day
shall come to die; or he shall go down into
battle and perish. [11]The LORD forbid that
I should put forth my hand against the
LORD's anointed; but take now the spear
that is at his head, and the jar of water, and
let us go." [12]So David took the spear and the
jar of water from Saul's head; and they went
away. No man saw it, or knew it, nor did
any awake; for they were all asleep, because
a deep sleep from the LORD had fallen
upon them.

[13]Then David went over to the other
side, and stood afar off on the top of the
mountain, with a great space between them;
[14]and David called to the army, and to Abner
the son of Ner, saying, "Will you not answer,
Abner?" Then Abner answered, "Who are
you that calls to the king?" [15]And David said
to Abner, "Are you not a man? Who is like
you in Israel? Why then have you not kept
watch over your lord the king? For one of
the people came in to destroy the king your
lord. [16]This thing that you have done is not
good. As the LORD lives, you deserve to die,
because you have not kept watch over your
lord, the LORD's anointed. And now see
where the king's spear is, and the jar of water
that was at his head."

[17]Saul recognized David's voice, and said,
"Is this your voice, my son David?" And
David said, "It is my voice, my lord, O king."
[18]And he said, "Why does my lord pursue
after his servant? For what have I done?
What guilt is on my hands? [19]Now therefore
let my lord the king hear the words of his
servant. If it is the LORD who has stirred you
up against me, may he accept an offering; but
if it is men, may they be cursed before the
LORD, for they have driven me out this day
that I should have no share in the heritage
of the LORD, saying, 'Go, serve other gods.'
[20]Now therefore, let not my blood fall to the
earth away from the presence of the LORD;
for the king of Israel has come out to seek
my life, like one who hunts a partridge in
the mountains."

[21]Then Saul said, "I have done wrong;
return, my son David, for I will no more
do you harm, because my life was precious
in your eyes this day; behold, I have played
the fool, and have erred exceedingly." [22]And
David made answer, "Here is the spear, O
king! Let one of the young men come over
and fetch it. [23]The LORD rewards every man
for his righteousness and his faithfulness;
for the LORD gave you into my hand today,
and I would not put forth my hand against
the LORD's anointed. [24]Behold, as your
life was precious this day in my sight, so
may my life be precious in the sight of
the LORD, and may he deliver me out of
all tribulation." [25]Then Saul said to David,
"Blessed be you, my son David! You will do
many things and will succeed in them." So
David went his way, and Saul returned to
his place.

27 And David said in his heart, "I shall
now perish one day by the hand
of Saul; there is nothing better for me
than that I should escape to the land of
the Philis′tines; then Saul will despair of
seeking me any longer within the borders
of Israel, and I shall escape out of his
hand." [2]So David arose and went over, he
and the six hundred men who were with
him, to A′chish the son of Ma′och, king
of Gath. [3]And David dwelt with A′chish at
Gath, he and his men, every man with his
household, and David with his two wives,
Ahin′o-am of Jezre′el, and Ab′igail of
Carmel, Nabal's widow. [4]And when it was
told Saul that David had fled to Gath, he
sought for him no more.

[5]Then David said to A′chish, "If I have
found favor in your eyes, let a place be
given me in one of the country towns, that
I may dwell there; for why should your
servant dwell in the royal city with you?"
[6]So that day A′chish gave him Zik′lag;

therefore Zik′lag has belonged to the kings of Judah to this day. 7 And the number of the days that David dwelt in the country of the Philis′tines was a year and four months.

8 Now David and his men went up, and made raids upon the Gesh′urites, the Girzites, and the Amal′ekites; for these were the inhabitants of the land from of old, as far as Shur, to the land of Egypt. 9 And David struck the land, and left neither man nor woman alive, but took away the sheep, the oxen, the donkeys, the camels, and the garments, and came back to A′chish. 10 When A′chish asked, "Against whom have you made a raid today?" David would say, "Against the Neg′eb of Judah," or "Against the Negeb of the Jerah′meelites," or, "Against the Negeb of the Kenites." 11 And David saved neither man nor woman alive, to bring tidings to Gath, thinking, "Lest they should tell about us, and say, 'So David has done.'" Such was his custom all the while he dwelt in the country of the Philis′tines. 12 And A′chish trusted David, thinking, "He has made himself utterly abhorred by his people Israel; therefore he shall be my servant always."

28 In those days the Philis′tines gathered their forces for war, to fight against Israel. And A′chish said to David, "Understand that you and your men are to go out with me in the army." 2 David said to A′chish, "Very well, you shall know what your servant can do." And Achish said to David, "Very well, I will make you my bodyguard for life."

3 Now Samuel had died, and all Israel had mourned for him and buried him in Ra′mah, his own city. And Saul had put the mediums and the wizards out of the land. 4 The Philis′tines assembled, and came and encamped at Shu′nem; and Saul gathered all Israel, and they encamped at Gilbo′a. 5 When Saul saw the army of the Philis′tines, he was afraid, and his heart trembled greatly. 6 And when Saul inquired of the LORD, the LORD did not answer him, either by dreams, or by U′rim, or by prophets. 7 Then Saul said to his servants, "Seek out for me a woman who is a medium, that I may go to her and inquire of her." And his servants said to him, "Behold, there is a medium at En-dor."

8 So Saul disguised himself and put on other garments, and went, he and two men with him; and they came to the woman by night. And he said, "Divine for me by a spirit, and bring up for me whomever I shall name to you." 9 The woman said to him, "Surely you know what Saul has done, how he has cut off the mediums and the wizards from the land. Why then are you laying a snare for my life to bring about my death?" 10 But Saul swore to her by the LORD, "As the LORD lives, no punishment shall come upon you for this thing." 11 Then the woman said, "Whom shall I bring up for you?" He said, "Bring up Samuel for me." 12 When the woman saw Samuel, she cried out with a loud voice; and the woman said to Saul, "Why have you deceived me? You are Saul." 13 The king said to her, "Have no fear; what do you see?" And the woman said to Saul, "I see a god coming up out of the earth." 14 He said to her, "What is his appearance?" And she said, "An old man is coming up; and he is wrapped in a robe." And Saul knew that it was Samuel, and he bowed with his face to the ground, and did obeisance.

15 Then Samuel said to Saul, "Why have you disturbed me by bringing me up?" Saul answered, "I am in great distress; for the Philis′tines are warring against me, and God has turned away from me and answers me no more, either by prophets or by dreams; therefore I have summoned you to tell me what I shall do." 16 And Samuel said, "Why then do you ask me, since the LORD has turned from you and become your enemy? 17 The LORD has done to you as he spoke by me; for the LORD has torn the kingdom out of your hand, and given it to your neighbor, David. 18 Because you did not obey the voice of the LORD, and did not carry out his fierce wrath against Am′alek, therefore the LORD has done this thing to you this day. 19 Moreover the LORD will give Israel also with you into the hand of the Philis′tines; and tomorrow you and your sons shall be with me; the LORD will

give the army of Israel also into the hand of the Philistines."

[20]Then Saul fell at once full length upon the ground, filled with fear because of the words of Samuel; and there was no strength in him, for he had eaten nothing all day and all night. [21]And the woman came to Saul, and when she saw that he was terrified, she said to him, "Behold, your handmaid has listened to you; I have taken my life in my hand, and have listened to what you have said to me. [22]Now therefore, you also listen to your handmaid; let me set a morsel of bread before you; and eat, that you may have strength when you go on your way." [23]He refused, and said, "I will not eat." But his servants, together with the woman, urged him; and he listened to their words. So he arose from the earth, and sat upon the bed. [24]Now the woman had a fatted calf in the house, and she quickly killed it, and she took flour, and kneaded it and baked unleavened bread of it, [25]and she put it before Saul and his servants; and they ate. Then they rose and went away that night.

PSALM 106 [105]

[16]When men in the camp were jealous
of Moses
and Aaron, the holy one of the LORD,
[17]the earth opened and swallowed up Dathan,
and covered the company of Abi′ram.
[18]Fire also broke out in their company;
the flame burned up the wicked.

[19]They made a calf in Horeb
and worshiped a molten image.
[20]They exchanged the glory of God
for the image of an ox that eats grass.
[21]They forgot God, their Savior,
who had done great things in Egypt,
[22]wondrous works in the land of Ham,
and awesome things by the Red Sea.
[23]Therefore he said he would destroy them—
had not Moses, his chosen one,
stood in the breach before him,
to turn away his wrath from
destroying them.

[24]Then they despised the pleasant land,
having no faith in his promise.
[25]They murmured in their tents,
and did not obey the voice of the LORD.
[26]Therefore he raised his hand and swore
to them
that he would make them fall in
the wilderness,
[27]and would disperse their descendants
among the nations,
scattering them over the lands.

[28]Then they attached themselves to the Ba′al
of Peor,
and ate sacrifices offered to the dead;
[29]they provoked the LORD to anger with
their doings,
and a plague broke out among them.
[30]Then Phin′ehas stood up and interposed,
and the plague was stayed.
[31]And that has been reckoned to him
as righteousness
from generation to generation for ever.

LUKE 23

[13]Pilate then called together
the chief priests and the rulers
and the people, [14]and said to
them, "You brought me this man as
one who was perverting the people;
and after examining him before you, behold,
I did not find this man guilty of any of your
charges against him; [15]neither did Herod,
for he sent him back to us. Behold, nothing
deserving death has been done by him; [16]I
will therefore chastise him and release him."*

[18]But they all cried out together, "Away with
this man, and release to us Barab′bas"—[19]a
man who had been thrown into prison for
an insurrection started in the city, and for
murder. [20]Pilate addressed them once more,
desiring to release Jesus; [21]but they shouted
out, "Crucify, crucify him!" [22]A third time he
said to them, "Why, what evil has he done? I

* Here, or after verse 19, other ancient authorities add verse 17, *Now he was obliged to release one man to them at the festival.*

have found in him no crime deserving death; I will therefore chastise him and release him."
23But they were urgent, demanding with loud cries that he should be crucified. And their voices prevailed.
24So Pilate gave sentence that their demand should be granted.
25He released the man who had been thrown into prison for insurrection and murder, whom they asked for; but Jesus he delivered up to their will.

REFLECTION

Sadly, people are not always truthful—they lie. Lying breaks down the fundamental bonds of trust that unite us. Lying is opposed to truth; and it is an offense against justice, since we owe others the truth. Saul lies in order to deceive David when he responds to David's protestations of innocence with an apparent confession: "I have done wrong; return, my son David, for I will no more do you harm" (1 Sm 26:21). Saul has proven himself false repeatedly, and as a result his promises of peaceful welcome cannot be trusted. Indeed, we find Saul giving David's wife to another man (see 25:44). In the trial of Jesus, Pilate pronounces the verdict three times: not guilty (see Lk 23:14, 15, 22). Jesus is innocent, and Pilate knows this to be true. Yet the Roman governor does not have the will to back up his truthful words with right action in the face of Jesus's accusers. Despite the "not guilty" verdict, Pilate sentences Jesus to death. The punishment does not fit the "crime," nor even the judge's own verdict! Proverbs reminds us, "Lying lips are an abomination to the LORD, but those who act faithfully are his delight" (Prv 12:22). What can you do to grow in the virtue of honesty—in word and deed?

May 7

1 SAMUEL 29

Now the Philis′tines gathered all their forces at A′phek; and the Israelites were encamped by the fountain which is in Jezre′el.
2As the
lords of the Philis′tines were passing on by hundreds and by thousands, and David and his men were passing on in the rear with A′chish,
3the commanders of the Philis′tines said, "What are these Hebrews doing here?" And A′chish said to the commanders of the Philistines, "Is not this David, the servant of Saul, king of Israel, who has been with me now for days and years, and since he deserted to me I have found no fault in him to this day."
4But the commanders of the Philis′tines were angry with him; and the commanders of the Philistines said to him, "Send the man back, that he may return to the place to which you have assigned him; he shall not go down with us to battle, lest in the battle he become an adversary to us. For how could this fellow reconcile himself to his lord? Would it not be with the heads of the men here?
5Is not this David, of whom they sing to one another in dances,

'Saul has slain his thousands,
and David his ten thousands'?"

6Then A′chish called David and said to him, "As the LORD lives, you have been honest, and to me it seems right that you should march out and in with me in the campaign; for I have found nothing wrong in you from the day of your coming to me to this day. Nevertheless the lords do not approve of you.
7So go back now; and go peaceably, that you may not displease the lords of the Philis′tines."
8And David said to A′chish, "But what have I done? What have you found in your servant from the day I entered your service until now, that I may not go and fight against the enemies of my lord the king?"
9And A′chish made answer to David, "I know that you are as blameless in my sight as an angel of God; nevertheless the commanders of the Philis′tines have said, 'He shall not go up with us to the battle.'
10Now then rise early in the morning with the servants of your lord who came with you; and start early in the morning, and depart as soon as you have light."
11So David set out with his men early in the morning, to return to the land of the Philis′tines. But the Philistines went up to Jezre′el.

30 Now when David and his men
came to Zik´lag on the third day,
the Amal´ekites had made a raid upon
the Neg´eb and upon Ziklag. They had
overcome Ziklag, and burned it with fire,
2and taken captive the women and all who
were in it, both small and great; they killed
no one, but carried them off, and went their
way. 3And when David and his men came to
the city, they found it burned with fire, and
their wives and sons and daughters taken
captive. 4Then David and the people who
were with him raised their voices and wept,
until they had no more strength to weep.
5David's two wives also had been taken
captive, Ahin´o-am of Jezre´el, and Ab´igail
the widow of Nabal of Carmel. 6And David
was greatly distressed; for the people spoke
of stoning him, because all the people
were bitter in soul, each for his sons and
daughters. But David strengthened himself
in the LORD his God.

7And David said to Abi´athar the priest, the
son of Ahim´elech, "Bring me the ephod." So
Abiathar brought the ephod to David. 8And
David inquired of the LORD, "Shall I pursue
after this band? Shall I overtake them?" He
answered him, "Pursue; for you shall surely
overtake and shall surely rescue." 9So David
set out, and the six hundred men who were
with him, and they came to the brook Be´sor,
where those stayed who were left behind.
10But David went on with the pursuit, he
and four hundred men; two hundred stayed
behind, who were too exhausted to cross the
brook Be´sor.

11They found an Egyptian in the open
country, and brought him to David; and they
gave him bread and he ate, they gave him
water to drink, 12and they gave him a piece
of a cake of figs and two clusters of raisins.
And when he had eaten, his spirit revived;
for he had not eaten bread or drunk water
for three days and three nights. 13And David
said to him, "To whom do you belong? And
where are you from?" He said, "I am a young
man of Egypt, servant to an Amal´ekite; and
my master left me behind because I fell sick
three days ago. 14We had made a raid upon
the Neg´eb of the Cher´ethites and upon that
which belongs to Judah and upon the Negeb
of Caleb; and we burned Zik´lag with fire."
15And David said to him, "Will you take me
down to this band?" And he said, "Swear
to me by God, that you will not kill me, or
deliver me into the hands of my master, and
I will take you down to this band."

16And when he had taken him down,
behold, they were spread abroad over all
the land, eating and drinking and dancing,
because of all the great spoil they had taken
from the land of the Philis´tines and from the
land of Judah. 17And David struck them from
twilight until the evening of the next day;
and not a man of them escaped, except four
hundred young men, who mounted camels
and fled. 18David recovered all that the
Amal´ekites had taken; and David rescued his
two wives. 19Nothing was missing, whether
small or great, sons or daughters, spoil or
anything that had been taken; David brought
back all. 20David also captured all the flocks
and herds; and the people drove those cattle
before him, and said, "This is David's spoil."

21Then David came to the two hundred
men, who had been too exhausted to follow
David, and who had been left at the brook
Be´sor; and they went out to meet David
and to meet the people who were with him;
and when David drew near to the people he
saluted them. 22Then all the wicked and base
fellows among the men who had gone with
David said, "Because they did not go with
us, we will not give them any of the spoil
which we have recovered, except that each
man may lead away his wife and children,
and depart." 23But David said, "You shall
not do so, my brothers, with what the LORD
has given us; he has preserved us and given
into our hand the band that came against us.
24Who would listen to you in this matter?
For as his share is who goes down into the
battle, so shall his share be who stays by the
baggage; they shall share alike." 25And from
that day forward he made it a statute and an
ordinance for Israel to this day.

26When David came to Zik´lag, he sent
part of the spoil to his friends, the elders
of Judah, saying, "Here is a present for you
from the spoil of the enemies of the LORD";

27it was for those in Bethel, in Ra′moth of the Neg′eb, in Jat′tir, 28in Aro′er, in Siphmoth, in Eshtemo′a, 29in Racal, in the cities of the Jerah′meelites, in the cities of the Kenites, 30in Hormah, in Borash′an, in A′thach, 31in He′bron, for all the places where David and his men had roamed.

31 Now the Philis′tines fought against Israel; and the men of Israel fled before the Philistines, and fell slain on Mount Gilbo′a. 2And the Philis′tines overtook Saul and his sons; and the Philistines slew Jonathan and Abin′adab and Mal″chishu′a, the sons of Saul. 3The battle pressed hard upon Saul, and the archers found him; and he was badly wounded by the archers. 4Then Saul said to his armor-bearer, "Draw your sword, and thrust me through with it, lest these uncircumcised come and thrust me through, and make sport of me." But his armor-bearer would not; for he feared greatly. Therefore Saul took his own sword, and fell upon it. 5And when his armor-bearer saw that Saul was dead, he also fell upon his sword, and died with him. 6Thus Saul died, and his three sons, and his armor-bearer, and all his men, on the same day together. 7And when the men of Israel who were on the other side of the valley and those beyond the Jordan saw that the men of Israel had fled and that Saul and his sons were dead, they forsook their cities and fled; and the Philis′tines came and dwelt in them.

8On the next day, when the Philis′tines came to strip the slain, they found Saul and his three sons fallen on Mount Gilbo′a. 9And they cut off his head, and stripped off his armor, and sent messengers throughout the land of the Philis′tines, to carry the good news to their idols and to the people. 10They put his armor in the temple of Ash′taroth; and they fastened his body to the wall of Beth-shan. 11But when the inhabitants of Ja′besh-gil′ead heard what the Philis′tines had done to Saul, 12all the valiant men arose, and went all night, and took the body of Saul and the bodies of his sons from the wall of Beth-shan; and they came to Ja′besh and burnt them there. 13And they took their bones and buried them under the tamarisk tree in Ja′besh, and fasted seven days.

PSALM 106 [105]

32They angered him at the waters
of Mer′ibah,
and it went ill with Moses on their account;
33for they made his spirit bitter,
and he spoke words that were rash.

34They did not destroy the peoples,
as the LORD commanded them,
35but they mingled with the nations
and learned to do as they did.
36They served their idols,
which became a snare to them.
37They sacrificed their sons
and their daughters to the demons;
38they poured out innocent blood,
the blood of their sons and daughters,
whom they sacrificed to the idols
of Canaan;
and the land was polluted with blood.
39Thus they became unclean by their acts,
and played the harlot in their doings.

40Then the anger of the LORD was kindled
against his people,
and he abhorred his heritage;
41he gave them into the hand of the nations,
so that those who hated them ruled
over them.
42Their enemies oppressed them,
and they were brought into subjection
under their power.
43Many times he delivered them,
but they were rebellious in their purposes,
and were brought low through
their iniquity.
44Nevertheless he regarded their distress,
when he heard their cry.
45He remembered for their sake
his covenant,
and relented according to the abundance
of his mercy.

46 He caused them to be pitied
by all those who held them captive.

47 Save us, O LORD our God,
and gather us from among the nations,
that we may give thanks to your holy name
and glory in your praise.

48 Blessed be the LORD, the God of Israel,
from everlasting to everlasting!
And let all the people say, "Amen!"
Praise the LORD!

LUKE 23

26 And as they led him away, they
seized one Simon of Cyre′ne,
who was coming in from the
country, and laid on him the cross, to
carry it behind Jesus. 27 And there fol-
lowed him a great multitude of the
people, and of women who bewailed and
lamented him. 28 But Jesus turning to them
said, "Daughters of Jerusalem, do not weep
for me, but weep for yourselves and for your
children. 29 For behold, the days are coming
when they will say, 'Blessed are the barren,
and the wombs that never bore, and the
breasts that never nursed!' 30 Then they will
begin to say to the mountains, 'Fall on us';
and to the hills, 'Cover us.' 31 For if they do
this when the wood is green, what will happen when it is dry?"

32 Two others also, who were criminals,
were led away to be put to death with him.
33 And when they came to the place which is
called The Skull, there they crucified him, and
the criminals, one on the right and one on the
left. 34 And Jesus said, "Father, forgive them; for
they know not what they do." And they cast
lots to divide his garments. 35 And the people
stood by, watching; but the rulers scoffed at
him, saying, "He saved others; let him save
himself, if he is the Christ of God, his Chosen
One!" 36 The soldiers also mocked him, coming
up and offering him vinegar, 37 and saying, "If
you are the King of the Jews, save yourself!"
38 There was also an inscription over him, "This
is the King of the Jews."

39 One of the criminals who were hanged
railed at him, saying, "Are you not the
Christ? Save yourself and us!" 40 But the
other rebuked him, saying, "Do you not fear
God, since you are under the same sentence
of condemnation? 41 And we indeed justly;
for we are receiving the due reward of
our deeds; but this man has done nothing
wrong." 42 And he said, "Jesus, remember
me when you come in your kingly power."
43 And he said to him, "Truly, I say to you,
today you will be with me in Paradise."

44 It was now about the sixth hour,
and there was darkness over the whole
land until the ninth hour, 45 while the
sun's light failed; and the curtain of the
temple was torn in two. 46 Then Jesus,
crying with a loud voice, said, "Father,
into your hands I commit my spirit!"
And having said this he breathed his
last. 47 Now when the centurion saw what
had taken place, he praised God, and
said, "Certainly this man was innocent!"
48 And all the multitudes who assembled
to see the sight, when they saw what had
taken place, returned home beating their
breasts. 49 And all his acquaintances and
the women who had followed him from
Galilee stood at a distance and saw these
things.

50 Now there was a man named Joseph
from the Jewish town of Arimathe′a. He
was a member of the council, a good and
righteous man, 51 who had not consented to
their purpose and deed, and he was looking
for the kingdom of God. 52 This man went
to Pilate and asked for the body of Jesus.
53 Then he took it down and wrapped it in a
linen shroud, and laid him in a rock-hewn
tomb, where no one had ever yet been laid.
54 It was the day of Preparation, and the
sabbath was beginning. 55 The women who
had come with him from Galilee followed,
and saw the tomb, and how his body was
laid; 56 then they returned, and prepared
spices and ointments.

On the sabbath they rested according to
the commandment.

REFLECTION

Today, we read about two violent deaths, both tragic; but while one is self-serving, the other is self-sacrificial. First, we read about King Saul, chosen by God to be Israel's first king but who refuses to obey the Lord. Saul finds himself overtaken by the Philistines in battle. He watches his sons die in combat, realizing that even if his life is preserved, his line will fail. Fearing the mockery of the Philistines if he is captured, Saul falls on his own sword, a tragic end to a life that began with so much promise but ended with growing disobedience. Then we witness the Crucifixion and Death of Jesus, the King of kings. Even in the midst of his suffering, Jesus looks not to himself, but to the needs of others—he prays, "Father, forgive them" (Lk 23:34) and tells the repentant thief, "Today you will be with me in Paradise" (v. 43). Obedient to the last, Jesus endures the mockery of the soldiers and willingly lays down his life for others, for us. While his Death is surely tragic, it is not a tragedy. The Father in Heaven—Jesus's Father, and ours—will raise his Son from the dead and offer us a share in this new life if we imitate his Son. If we hope to be obedient to the last like Jesus, we need to begin today with obedience in small things.

May 8

2 SAMUEL 1

After the death of Saul, when David had returned from the slaughter of the Amal′ekites, David remained two days in Zik′lag; 2and on the third day, behold, a man came from
Saul's camp, with his clothes torn and earth
upon his head. And when he came to David,
he fell to the ground and did obeisance.
3David said to him, "Where do you come
from?" And he said to him, "I have escaped
from the camp of Israel." 4And David said
to him, "How did it go? Tell me." And he
answered, "The people have fled from the
battle, and many of the people also have
fallen and are dead; and Saul and his son
Jonathan are also dead." 5Then David said
to the young man who told him, "How do
you know that Saul and his son Jonathan are
dead?" 6And the young man who told him
said, "By chance I happened to be on Mount
Gilbo′a; and there was Saul leaning upon
his spear; and behold, the chariots and the
horsemen were close upon him. 7And when
he looked behind him, he saw me, and called
to me. And I answered, 'Here I am.' 8And he
said to me, 'Who are you?' I answered him, 'I
am an Amal′ekite.' 9And he said to me, 'Stand
beside me and slay me; for anguish has seized
me, and yet my life still lingers.' 10So I stood
beside him, and slew him, because I was sure
that he could not live after he had fallen; and
I took the crown which was on his head and
the armlet which was on his arm, and I have
brought them here to my lord."

11Then David took hold of his clothes, and
tore them; and so did all the men who were
with him; 12and they mourned and wept and
fasted until evening for Saul and for Jonathan
his son and for the people of the LORD and
for the house of Israel, because they had
fallen by the sword. 13And David said to the
young man who told him, "Where do you
come from?" And he answered, "I am the
son of a sojourner, an Amal′ekite." 14David
said to him, "How is it you were not afraid
to put forth your hand to destroy the LORD's
anointed?" 15Then David called one of the
young men and said, "Go, fall upon him."
And he struck him so that he died. 16And
David said to him, "Your blood be upon
your head; for your own mouth has testified
against you, saying, 'I have slain the LORD's
anointed.'"

17And David lamented with this lamentation over Saul and Jonathan his son, 18and
he said it should be taught to the people of
Judah; behold, it is written in the Book of
Jashar. He said:

19"Your glory, O Israel, is slain upon your
high places!
How are the mighty fallen!
20Tell it not in Gath,
publish it not in the streets of Ash′kelon;

lest the daughters of the Philis′tines rejoice,
lest the daughters of the uncircumcised
exult.

21"You mountains of Gilbo′a,
let there be no dew or rain upon you,
nor upsurging of the deep!
For there the shield of the mighty
was defiled,
the shield of Saul, not anointed with oil.

22"From the blood of the slain,
from the fat of the mighty,
the bow of Jonathan turned not back,
and the sword of Saul returned
not empty.

23"Saul and Jonathan, beloved and lovely!
In life and in death they were not divided;
they were swifter than eagles,
they were stronger than lions.

24"You daughters of Israel, weep over Saul,
who clothed you daintily in scarlet,
who put ornaments of gold upon
your apparel.

25"How are the mighty fallen
in the midst of the battle!

"Jonathan lies slain upon your high places.
26 I am distressed for you, my brother
Jonathan;
very pleasant have you been to me;
your love to me was wonderful,
passing the love of women.

27"How are the mighty fallen,
and the weapons of war perished!"

2 After this David inquired of the LORD,
"Shall I go up into any of the cities of
Judah?" And the LORD said to him, "Go
up." David said, "To which shall I go up?"
And he said, "To He′bron." 2So David went
up there, and his two wives also, Ahin′o-am
of Jezre′el, and Ab′igail the widow of Nabal
of Carmel. 3And David brought up his men
who were with him, every one with his
household; and they dwelt in the towns of
He′bron. 4And the men of Judah came, and
there they anointed David king over the
house of Judah.
When they told David, "It was the men of
Ja′besh-gil′ead who buried Saul," 5David sent
messengers to the men of Ja′besh-gil′ead,
and said to them, "May you be blessed by
the LORD, because you showed this loyalty
to Saul your lord, and buried him! 6Now
may the LORD show mercy and faithfulness
to you! And I will do good to you because
you have done this thing. 7Now therefore let
your hands be strong, and be valiant; for Saul
your lord is dead, and the house of Judah has
anointed me king over them."
8Now Abner the son of Ner, commander
of Saul's army, had taken Ish-bo′sheth
the son of Saul, and brought him over to
Ma′′hana′im; 9and he made him king over
Gilead and the Ash′urites and Jezre′el and
E′phraim and Benjamin and all Israel. 10Ish-
bo′sheth, Saul's son, was forty years old
when he began to reign over Israel, and he
reigned two years. But the house of Judah
followed David. 11And the time that David
was king in He′bron over the house of Judah
was seven years and six months.
12Abner the son of Ner, and the servants of
Ish-bo′sheth the son of Saul, went out from
Ma′′hana′im to Gib′eon. 13And Jo′ab the son
of Zeru′iah, and the servants of David, went
out and met them at the pool of Gib′eon;
and they sat down, the one on the one side
of the pool, and the other on the other side
of the pool. 14And Abner said to Jo′ab, "Let
the young men arise and play before us."*
And Joab said, "Let them arise." 15Then they
arose and passed over by number, twelve for
Benjamin and Ish-bo′sheth the son of Saul,
and twelve of the servants of David. 16And
each caught his opponent by the head, and
thrust his sword in his opponent's side;
so they fell down together. Therefore that
place was called Hel′kath-hazzu′rim, which
is at Gib′eon. 17And the battle was very
fierce that day; and Abner and the men
of Israel were beaten before the servants
of David.

* *play*: he meant "do battle." The idea was to settle the matter by a fight between two select groups of soldiers.

18 And the three sons of Zeru′iah were
there, Jo′ab, Abi′shai, and As′ahel. Now
Asahel was as swift of foot as a wild gazelle;
19 and As′ahel pursued Abner, and as he went
he turned neither to the right hand nor to
the left from following Abner. 20 Then Abner
looked behind him and said, “Is it you,
As′ahel?” And he answered, “It is I.” 21 Abner
said to him, “Turn aside to your right hand
or to your left, and seize one of the young
men, and take his spoil.” But As′ahel would
not turn aside from following him. 22 And
Abner said again to As′ahel, “Turn aside
from following me; why should I strike you
to the ground? How then could I lift up my
face to your brother Jo′ab?” 23 But he refused
to turn aside; therefore Abner struck him in
the belly with the butt of his spear, so that
the spear came out at his back; and he fell
there, and died where he was. And all who
came to the place where As′ahel had fallen
and died, stood still.
24 But Jo′ab and Abi′shai pursued Abner;
and as the sun was going down they came to
the hill of Ammah, which lies before Giah
on the way to the wilderness of Gib′eon.
25 And the Benjaminites gathered themselves
together behind Abner, and became one
band, and took their stand on the top of a
hill. 26 Then Abner called to Jo′ab, “Shall the
sword devour for ever? Do you not know
that the end will be bitter? How long will it
be before you bid your people turn from the
pursuit of their brethren?” 27 And Jo′ab said,
“As God lives, if you had not spoken, surely
the men would have given up the pursuit of
their brethren in the morning.” 28 So Jo′ab
blew the trumpet; and all the men stopped,
and pursued Israel no more, nor did they
fight any more.
29 And Abner and his men went all that
night through the Ar′abah; they crossed the
Jordan, and marching the whole forenoon
they came to Ma′hana′im. 30 Jo′ab returned
from the pursuit of Abner; and when he had
gathered all the people together, there were
missing of David’s servants nineteen men
besides As′ahel. 31 But the servants of David
had slain of Benjamin three hundred and
sixty of Abner’s men. 32 And they took up
As′ahel, and buried him in the tomb of his
father, which was at Bethlehem. And Jo′ab
and his men marched all night, and the day
broke upon them at He′bron.

PSALM 107 [106]

O give thanks to the LORD, for he is good;
for his mercy endures for ever!
2 Let the redeemed of the LORD say so,
whom he has redeemed from trouble
3 and gathered in from the lands,
from the east and from the west,
from the north and from the south.

4 Some wandered in desert wastes,
finding no way to a city to dwell in;
5 hungry and thirsty,
their soul fainted within them.
6 Then they cried to the LORD in
their trouble,
and he delivered them from their distress;
7 he led them by a straight way,
till they reached a city to dwell in.
8 Let them thank the LORD for his
merciful love,
for his wonderful works to the sons
of men!
9 For he satisfies him who is thirsty,
and the hungry he fills with good things.

10 Some sat in darkness and in gloom,
prisoners in affliction and in irons,
11 for they had rebelled against the words
of God,
and spurned the counsel of the Most High.
12 Their hearts were bowed down with
hard labor;
they fell down, with none to help.
13 Then they cried to the LORD in
their trouble,
and he delivered them from their distress;
14 he brought them out of darkness
and gloom,
and broke their bonds asunder.
15 Let them thank the LORD for his
steadfast love,
for his wonderful works to the sons
of men!

16 For he shatters the doors of bronze,
and cuts in two the bars of iron.

17 Some were sick through their sinful ways,
and because of their iniquities suffered
affliction;
18 they loathed any kind of food,
and they drew near to the gates of death.
19 Then they cried to the LORD in their
trouble,
and he delivered them from their distress;
20 he sent forth his word, and healed them,
and delivered them from destruction.
21 Let them thank the LORD for his steadfast
love,
for his wonderful works to the sons
of men!
22 And let them offer sacrifices of
thanksgiving,
and tell of his deeds in songs of joy!

LUKE 24

**But on the first day of the week,
at early dawn, they went to the
tomb, taking the spices which
they had prepared. 2 And they found
the stone rolled away from the tomb,**
3 but when they went in they did not find the
body. 4 While they were perplexed about this,
behold, two men stood by them in dazzling
apparel; 5 and as they were frightened and
bowed their faces to the ground, the men
said to them, "Why do you seek the living
among the dead? He is not here, but has
risen. 6 Remember how he told you, while
he was still in Galilee, 7 that the Son of man
must be delivered into the hands of sinful
men, and be crucified, and on the third day
rise." 8 And they remembered his words, 9 and
returning from the tomb they told all this to
the Eleven and to all the rest. 10 Now it was
Mary Mag′dalene and Jo-an′na and Mary
the mother of James and the other women
with them who told this to the apostles;
11 but these words seemed to them an idle
tale, and they did not believe them. 12 But
Peter rose and ran to the tomb; stooping
and looking in, he saw the linen cloths by
themselves; and he went home wondering at
what had happened.
13 That very day two of them were going
to a village named Emma′us, about seven
miles from Jerusalem, 14 and talking with
each other about all these things that had
happened. 15 While they were talking and
discussing together, Jesus himself drew near
and went with them. 16 But their eyes were
kept from recognizing him. 17 And he said to
them, "What is this conversation which you
are holding with each other as you walk?"
And they stood still, looking sad. 18 Then
one of them, named Cle′opas, answered
him, "Are you the only visitor to Jerusalem
who does not know the things that have
happened there in these days?" 19 And he
said to them, "What things?" And they said
to him, "Concerning Jesus of Nazareth, who
was a prophet mighty in deed and word
before God and all the people, 20 and how
our chief priests and rulers delivered him
up to be condemned to death, and crucified
him. 21 But we had hoped that he was the one
to redeem Israel. Yes, and besides all this, it
is now the third day since this happened.
22 Moreover, some women of our company
amazed us. They were at the tomb early in
the morning 23 and did not find his body;
and they came back saying that they had
even seen a vision of angels, who said that
he was alive. 24 Some of those who were with
us went to the tomb, and found it just as the
women had said; but him they did not see."

REFLECTION

So often we take God's blessings for granted or we don't even recognize what he has accomplished for us. Psalm 107 exhorts those who have been delivered by the Lord to acknowledge the fact and to praise him: "Let the redeemed of the LORD say so" (Ps 107:2). It recounts the plight of the exiles, who had been trapped in a foreign land, imprisoned and sick because of sin. But "they cried to the Lord in their trouble, and he delivered them from their distress" (vv. 6, 13, 19). Such deliverance should result in an abundance of thanksgiving. When the disciples first hear about the Resurrection of Jesus, they are incredulous—judging the testimony of the women as an "idle tale" (Lk 24:11). Cleopas, in speaking with the risen Jesus whose identity is shrouded, repeats the women's story, yet ironically, while looking at Jesus himself, says, "But him they did not see" (v. 24). Like the disciples we often don't recognize God's presence in our lives, or like the exiles we forget to give thanks. We too have been delivered from sin in Baptism, and the Lord is with us at all times; therefore we too have reason to give thanks. In what ways has God redeemed and blessed you this week? How can you offer him thanksgiving?

May 9

2 SAMUEL 3

**There was a long war between
the house of Saul and the house
of David; and David grew stronger
and stronger, while the house of Saul
became weaker and weaker.**
[2]And sons were born to David at He´bron:
his first-born was Amnon, of Ahin´o-am
of Jezre´el; [3]and his second, Chil´e-ab, of
Ab´igail the widow of Nabal of Carmel; and
the third, Ab´salom the son of Ma´acah the
daughter of Talmai king of Ge´shur; [4]and the
fourth, Adoni´jah the son of Haggith; and
the fifth, Shephati´ah the son of Abi´tal; [5]and
the sixth, Ith´re-am of Eglah, David's wife.
These were born to David in He´bron.
[6]While there was war between the house
of Saul and the house of David, Abner was
making himself strong in the house of Saul.
[7]Now Saul had a concubine, whose name
was Rizpah, the daughter of Ai´ah; and
Ish-bo´sheth said to Abner, "Why have you
gone in to my father's concubine?" [8]Then
Abner was very angry over the words of
Ish-bo´sheth, and said, "Am I a dog's head
of Judah? This day I keep showing loyalty
to the house of Saul your father, to his
brothers, and to his friends, and have not
given you into the hand of David; and yet
you charge me today with a fault concerning
a woman. [9]God do so to Abner and more
also, if I do not accomplish for David what
the LORD has sworn to him, [10]to transfer the
kingdom from the house of Saul, and set
up the throne of David over Israel and over
Judah, from Dan to Be´er-she´ba." [11]And Ish-
bo´sheth could not answer Abner another
word, because he feared him.
[12]And Abner sent messengers to David at
He´bron, saying, "To whom does the land
belong? Make your covenant with me, and
behold, my hand shall be with you to bring
over all Israel to you." [13]And he said, "Good;
I will make a covenant with you; but one
thing I require of you; that is, you shall not
see my face, unless you first bring Michal,
Saul's daughter, when you come to see my
face." [14]Then David sent messengers to Ish-
bo´sheth Saul's son, saying, "Give me my
wife Michal, whom I betrothed at the price
of a hundred foreskins of the Philis´tines."
[15]And Ish-bo´sheth sent, and took her from
her husband Pal´ti-el the son of La´ish. [16]But
her husband went with her, weeping after
her all the way to Bahu´rim. Then Abner
said to him, "Go, return"; and he returned.
[17]And Abner conferred with the elders
of Israel, saying, "For some time past you
have been seeking David as king over you.
[18]Now then bring it about; for the LORD has
promised David, saying, 'By the hand of my
servant David I will save my people Israel
from the hand of the Philis´tines, and from
the hand of all their enemies.'" [19]Abner also
spoke to Benjamin; and then Abner went to
tell David at He´bron all that Israel and the
whole house of Benjamin thought good to do.
[20]When Abner came with twenty men to
David at He´bron, David made a feast for
Abner and the men who were with him.
[21]And Abner said to David, "I will arise and
go, and will gather all Israel to my lord the
king, that they may make a covenant with
you, and that you may reign over all that
your heart desires." So David sent Abner
away; and he went in peace.

[22]Just then the servants of David arrived
with Jo′ab from a raid, bringing much spoil
with them. But Abner was not with David at
He′bron, for he had sent him away, and he
had gone in peace. [23]When Jo′ab and all the
army that was with him came, it was told Joab,
"Abner the son of Ner came to the king, and
he has let him go, and he has gone in peace."
[24]Then Jo′ab went to the king and said, "What
have you done? Behold, Abner came to you;
why is it that you have sent him away, so that
he is gone? [25]You know that Abner the son of
Ner came to deceive you, and to know your
going out and your coming in, and to know
all that you are doing."

[26]When Jo′ab came out from David's presence, he sent messengers after Abner, and
they brought him back from the cistern
of Sirah; but David did not know about it.
[27]And when Abner returned to He′bron,
Jo′ab took him aside into the midst of the
gate to speak with him privately, and there
he struck him in the belly, so that he died, for
the blood of As′ahel his brother. [28]Afterward,
when David heard of it, he said, "I and my
kingdom are for ever guiltless before the
LORD for the blood of Abner the son of
Ner. [29]May it fall upon the head of Jo′ab,
and upon all his father's house; and may the
house of Joab never be without one who has
a discharge, or who is leprous, or who holds
a spindle, or who is slain by the sword, or
who lacks bread!" [30]So Jo′ab and Abi′shai his
brother slew Abner, because he had killed
their brother As′ahel in the battle at Gib′eon.

[31]Then David said to Jo′ab and to all the
people who were with him, "Tear your
clothes, and put on sackcloth, and mourn
before Abner." And King David followed
the bier. [32]They buried Abner at He′bron;
and the king lifted up his voice and wept at
the grave of Abner; and all the people wept.
[33]And the king lamented for Abner, saying,

"Should Abner die as a fool dies?
[34]Your hands were not bound,
your feet were not fettered;
as one falls before the wicked
you have fallen."

And all the people wept again over him.
[35]Then all the people came to persuade David
to eat bread while it was yet day; but David
swore, saying, "God do so to me and more
also, if I taste bread or anything else till the
sun goes down!" [36]And all the people took
notice of it, and it pleased them; as everything
that the king did pleased all the people. [37]So
all the people and all Israel understood that
day that it had not been the king's will to slay
Abner the son of Ner. [38]And the king said to
his servants, "Do you not know that a prince
and a great man has fallen this day in Israel?
[39]And I am this day weak, though anointed
king; these men the sons of Zeru′iah are too
hard for me. The LORD repay the evildoer
according to his wickedness!"

PSALM 107 [106]

[23]Some went down to the sea in ships,
doing business on the great waters;
[24]they saw the deeds of the LORD,
his wondrous works in the deep.
[25]For he commanded, and raised the
stormy wind,
which lifted up the waves of the sea.
[26]They mounted up to heaven, they went
down to the depths;
their courage melted away in their
evil plight;
[27]they reeled and staggered like
drunken men,
and were at their wits' end.
[28]Then they cried to the LORD in
their trouble,
and he delivered them from their distress;
[29]he made the storm be still,
and the waves of the sea were hushed.
[30]Then they were glad because they
had quiet,
and he brought them to their
desired haven.
[31]Let them thank the LORD for his
merciful love,
for his wonderful works to the sons
of men!
[32]Let them extol him in the congregation of
the people,
and praise him in the assembly
of the elders.

33 He turns rivers into a desert,
springs of water into thirsty ground,
34 a fruitful land into a salty waste,
because of the wickedness of
its inhabitants.
35 He turns a desert into pools of water,
a parched land into springs of water.
36 And there he lets the hungry dwell,
and they establish a city to live in;
37 they sow fields, and plant vineyards,
and get a fruitful yield.
38 By his blessing they multiply greatly;
and he does not let their cattle decrease.
39 When they are diminished and brought low
through oppression, trouble, and sorrow,
40 he pours contempt upon princes
and makes them wander in
trackless wastes;
41 but he raises up the needy out of affliction,
and makes their families like flocks.
42 The upright see it and are glad;
and all wickedness stops its mouth.
43 Whoever is wise, let him give heed to
these things;
let men consider the steadfast love of the
of the LORD.

LUKE 24

**25 And he said to them, "O foolish
men, and slow of heart to believe
all that the prophets have spoken! 26 Was it
not necessary that the Christ should suffer
these things and enter into his glory?"**
27 And beginning with Moses and all the
prophets, he interpreted to them in all the
Scriptures the things concerning himself.

28 So they drew near to the village to which
they were going. He appeared to be going
further, 29 but they constrained him, saying,
"Stay with us, for it is toward evening and
the day is now far spent." So he went in
to stay with them. 30 When he was at table
with them, he took the bread and blessed
and broke it, and gave it to them. 31 And
their eyes were opened and they recognized
him; and he vanished out of their sight.
32 They said to each other, "Did not our
hearts burn within us while he talked to
us on the road, while he opened to us the
Scriptures?" 33 And they rose that same hour
and returned to Jerusalem; and they found
the Eleven gathered together and those who
were with them, 34 who said, "The Lord has
risen indeed, and has appeared to Simon!"
35 Then they told what had happened on the
road, and how he was known to them in the
breaking of the bread.

36 As they were saying this, Jesus himself
stood among them, and said to them,
"Peace to you." 37 But they were startled and
frightened, and supposed that they saw a
spirit. 38 And he said to them, "Why are you
troubled, and why do questionings rise in
your hearts? 39 See my hands and my feet,
that it is I myself; handle me, and see; for
a spirit has not flesh and bones as you see
that I have." 40 And when he had said this
he showed them his hands and his feet.
41 And while they still disbelieved for joy,
and wondered, he said to them, "Have you
anything here to eat?" 42 They gave him a
piece of broiled fish, 43 and he took it and ate
before them.

44 Then he said to them, "These are my
words which I spoke to you, while I was still
with you, that everything written about me
in the law of Moses and the prophets and the
psalms must be fulfilled." 45 Then he opened
their minds to understand the Scriptures,
46 and said to them, "Thus it is written, that
the Christ should suffer and on the third day
rise from the dead, 47 and that repentance
and forgiveness of sins should be preached
in his name to all nations, beginning from
Jerusalem. 48 You are witnesses of these
things. 49 And behold, I send the promise of
my Father upon you; but stay in the city, until
you are clothed with power from on high."

50 Then he led them out as far as Beth′any,
and lifting up his hands he blessed them.
51 While he blessed them, he parted from
them, and was carried up into heaven.*
52 And they worshiped him, and returned

* Other ancient authorities omit *and said to them "Peace be with you."*

to Jerusalem with great joy, [53]and were continually in the temple blessing God.

REFLECTION

Our sinful desires breed every type of conflict and division. Adam and Eve's sin not only brings their expulsion from the Garden of Eden, but it is also shortly followed by Cain's murder of his brother and division at the Tower of Babel. In the aftermath of Saul's death, sin and conflict continue as the Israelites are divided between David and Saul's son, Ish-bosheth. When Abner tries to reconcile the factions, his attempt is foiled, and Joab, desiring revenge for the death of his brother Asahel, murders Abner. Sin spirals into sin in this cycle of conflict, division, and death. The Resurrection of Jesus overcomes this pattern of conflict. As they walked to Emmaus, Jesus "interpreted to them in all the Scriptures" (Lk 24:27) and showed himself to be the promised messiah. He speaks consoling words: "Peace to you" (v. 36) and then gives the means by which this peace is to be obtained: "That repentance and forgiveness of sins should be preached" (v. 47) and you shall be "clothed with power from on high" (v. 49). Jesus has conquered the death-spiral of sin and initiates a new era of peace, both in our relationship with God and with one another. How can the peace of Christ help you today to overcome conflict in your relationships?

May 10

2 SAMUEL 4

When Ish-bo´sheth, Saul's son, heard that Abner had died at He´bron, his courage failed, and all Israel was dismayed. [2]Now Saul's son had two men who were captains of raiding bands; the name of the one was Ba´anah, and the name of the other Re´chab, sons of Rimmon a man of Benjamin from Be-er´oth (for Be-eroth also is reckoned to Benjamin; [3]the Be-er´othites fled to Gitta´im, and have been sojourners there to this day).

[4]Jonathan, the son of Saul, had a son who was crippled in his feet. He was five years old when the news about Saul and Jonathan came from Jezre´el; and his nurse took him up, and fled; and, as she fled in her haste, he fell, and became lame. And his name was Mephib´osheth.

[5]Now the sons of Rimmon the Be-er´othite, Re´chab and Ba´anah, set out, and about the heat of the day they came to the house of Ish-bo´sheth, as he was taking his noonday rest. [6]And behold, the doorkeeper of the house had been cleaning wheat, but she grew drowsy and slept; so Re´chab and Ba´anah his brother slipped in. [7]When they came into the house, as he lay on his bed in his bedchamber, they struck him, and slew him, and beheaded him. They took his head, and went by the way of the Ar´abah all night, [8]and brought the head of Ish-bo´sheth to David at He´bron. And they said to the king, "Here is the head of Ish-bosheth, the son of Saul, your enemy, who sought your life; the LORD has avenged my lord the king this day on Saul and on his offspring." [9]But David answered Re´chab and Ba´anah his brother, the sons of Rimmon the Be-er´othite, "As the LORD lives, who has redeemed my life out of every adversity, [10]when one told me, 'Behold, Saul is dead,' and thought he was bringing good news, I seized him and slew him at Zik´lag, which was the reward I gave him for his news. [11]How much more, when wicked men have slain a righteous man in his own house upon his bed, shall I not now require his blood at your hand, and destroy you from the earth?" [12]And David commanded his young men, and they killed them, and cut off their hands and feet, and hanged them beside the pool at He´bron. But they took the head of Ish-bo´sheth, and buried it in the tomb of Abner at Hebron.

5 Then all the tribes of Israel came to David at He´bron, and said, "Behold, we are your bone and flesh. [2]In times past, when Saul was king over us, it was you that led out and brought in Israel; and the LORD

said to you, 'You shall be shepherd of my people Israel, and you shall be prince over Israel.'" 3So all the elders of Israel came to the king at He′bron; and King David made a covenant with them at Hebron before the LORD, and they anointed David king over Israel. 4David was thirty years old when he began to reign, and he reigned forty years. 5At He′bron he reigned over Judah seven years and six months; and at Jerusalem he reigned over all Israel and Judah thirty-three years.

6And the king and his men went to Jerusalem against the Jeb′usites, the inhabitants of the land, who said to David, "You will not come in here, but the blind and the lame will ward you off"—thinking, "David cannot come in here." 7Nevertheless David took the stronghold of Zion, that is, the city of David. 8And David said on that day, "Whoever would strike the Jeb′usites, let him get up the water shaft to attack the lame and the blind, who are hated by David's soul." Therefore it is said, "The blind and the lame shall not come into the house." 9And David dwelt in the stronghold, and called it the city of David. And David built the city round about from the Millo inward. 10And David became greater and greater, for the LORD, the God of hosts, was with him.

11And Hiram king of Tyre sent messengers to David, and cedar trees, also carpenters and masons who built David a house. 12And David perceived that the LORD had established him king over Israel, and that he had exalted his kingdom for the sake of his people Israel.

13And David took more concubines and wives from Jerusalem, after he came from He′bron; and more sons and daughters were born to David. 14And these are the names of those who were born to him in Jerusalem: Sham′mu-a, Shobab, Nathan, Solomon, 15Ib′har, Eli′shu-a, Ne′pheg, Japhi′a, 16Elish′ama, Eli′ada, and Eliph′elet.

17When the Philis′tines heard that David had been anointed king over Israel, all the Philistines went up in search of David; but David heard of it and went down to the stronghold. 18Now the Philis′tines had come and spread out in the valley of Reph′aim. 19And David inquired of the LORD, "Shall I go up against the Philis′tines? Will you give them into my hand?" And the LORD said to David, "Go up; for I will certainly give the Philistines into your hand." 20And David came to Ba′al-pera′zim, and David defeated them there; and he said, "The LORD has broken through my enemies before me, like a bursting flood." Therefore the name of that place is called Ba′al-pera′zim. 21And the Philis′tines left their idols there, and David and his men carried them away.

22And the Philis′tines came up yet again, and spread out in the valley of Reph′aim. 23And when David inquired of the LORD, he said, "You shall not go up; go around to their rear, and come upon them opposite the balsam trees. 24And when you hear the sound of marching in the tops of the balsam trees, then bestir yourself; for then the LORD has gone out before you to strike the army of the Philis′tines." 25And David did as the LORD commanded him, and struck the Philis′tines from Ge′ba to Gezer.

6 David again gathered all the chosen men of Israel, thirty thousand. 2And David arose and went with all the people who were with him from Ba′ale-ju′dah, to bring up from there the ark of God, which is called by the name of the LORD of hosts who sits enthroned on the cherubim. 3And they carried the ark of God upon a new cart, and brought it out of the house of Abin′adab which was on the hill; and Uzzah and Ahi′o, the sons of Abinadab, were driving the new cart 4with the ark of God; and Ahi′o went before the ark. 5And David and all the house of Israel were making merry before the LORD with all their might, with songs and lyres and harps and tambourines and castanets and cymbals.

6And when they came to the threshing floor of Nacon, Uzzah put out his hand to the ark of God and took hold of it, for the oxen stumbled. 7And the anger of the LORD was kindled against Uzzah; and God struck him there because he put forth his hand to the ark; and he died there beside the ark of God. 8And David

was angry because the LORD had broken
forth upon Uzzah; and that place is called
Per′ez-uz′zah, to this day. 9And David was
afraid of the LORD that day; and he said,
"How can the ark of the LORD come to
me?" 10So David was not willing to take
the ark of the LORD into the city of David;
but David took it aside to the house of
O′bed-e′dom the Gittite. 11And the ark
of the LORD remained in the house of
O′bed-e′dom the Gittite three months;
and the LORD blessed Obed-edom and all
his household.

12And it was told King David, "The LORD
has blessed the household of O′bed-e′dom
and all that belongs to him, because of the
ark of God." So David went and brought
up the ark of God from the house of Obed-
edom to the city of David with rejoicing;
13and when those who bore the ark of the
LORD had gone six paces, he sacrificed an
ox and a fatling. 14And David danced before
the LORD with all his might; and David was
belted with a linen ephod. 15So David and all
the house of Israel brought up the ark of the
LORD with shouting, and with the sound of
the horn.

16As the ark of the LORD came into the
city of David, Michal the daughter of Saul
looked out of the window, and saw King
David leaping and dancing before the
LORD; and she despised him in her heart.
17And they brought in the ark of the LORD,
and set it in its place, inside the tent which
David had pitched for it; and David offered
burnt offerings and peace offerings before
the LORD. 18And when David had finished
offering the burnt offerings and the peace
offerings, he blessed the people in the name
of the LORD of hosts, 19and distributed
among all the people, the whole multitude
of Israel, both men and women, to each a
cake of bread, a portion of meat, and a cake
of raisins. Then all the people departed,
each to his house.

20And David returned to bless his
household. But Michal the daughter of
Saul came out to meet David, and said,
"How the king of Israel honored himself
today, uncovering himself today before
the eyes of his servants' maids, as one of
the vulgar fellows shamelessly uncovers
himself!" 21And David said to Michal,
"It was before the LORD, who chose me
above your father, and above all his house,
to appoint me as prince over Israel, the
people of the LORD—and I will make
merry before the LORD. 22I will make
myself yet more contemptible than this,
and I will be abased in your eyes; but
by the maids of whom you have spoken,
by them I shall be held in honor." 23And
Michal the daughter of Saul had no child
to the day of her death.

A Song.
A Psalm of David.

PSALM 108 [107]

My heart is steadfast, O God, my heart
is steadfast!
I will sing and make melody!
Awake, my soul!
2Awake, O harp and lyre!
I will awake the dawn!
3I will give thanks to you, O LORD, among
the peoples,
I will sing praises to you among
the nations.
4For your steadfast love is great above
the heavens,
your faithfulness reaches to the clouds.

5Be exalted, O God, above the heavens!
Let your glory be over all the earth!
6That your beloved may be delivered,
give help by your right hand,
and answer me!

7God has promised in his sanctuary:
"With exultation I will divide up
She′chem,
and portion out the Vale of Succoth.
8Gilead is mine; Manas′seh is mine;
E′phraim is my helmet;
Judah my scepter.
9Moab is my washbasin;
upon E′dom I cast my shoe;
over Philistia I shout in triumph."

10Who will bring me to the fortified city?
Who will lead me to E′dom?
11Have you not rejected us, O God?
You do not go forth, O God, with
our armies.
12O grant us help against the foe,
for vain is the help of man!
13With God we shall do valiantly;
it is he who will tread down our foes.

JOHN 1

**In the beginning was the Word,
and the Word was with God,
and the Word was God. 2He
was in the beginning with God; 3all
things were made through him, and
without him was not anything made**
that was made. 4In him was life, and the life was
the light of men. 5The light shines in the darkness, and the darkness has not overcome it.

6There was a man sent from God, whose
name was John. 7He came for testimony,
to bear witness to the light, that all might
believe through him. 8He was not the light,
but came to bear witness to the light.

9The true light that enlightens every
man was coming into the world. 10He was
in the world, and the world was made
through him, yet the world knew him
not. 11He came to his own home, and his
own people received him not. 12But to all
who received him, who believed in his
name, he gave power to become children
of God; 13who were born, not of blood
nor of the will of the flesh nor of the will
of man, but of God.

14And the Word became flesh and dwelt
among us, full of grace and truth; we have
beheld his glory, glory as of the only-begotten
Son from the Father. 15(John bore witness to
him, and cried, "This was he of whom I said,
'He who comes after me ranks before me, for
he was before me.'") 16And from his fulness
have we all received, grace upon grace. 17For
the law was given through Moses; grace and
truth came through Jesus Christ. 18No one
has ever seen God; the only-begotten Son,
who is in the bosom of the Father, he has
made him known.

REFLECTION

Our cares, circumstances, troubles, and worries can cloud our vision of God. We forget the wonder, amazement, and awe that our God and his self-revelation should inspire. David here sets the example for enthusiastic wonder and worship: "David and all the house of Israel were making merry before the LORD with all their might, with songs and lyres and harps and tambourines and castanets and cymbals" (2 Sm 6:5). He brings the ark of God to Jerusalem "inside the tent which David had pitched for it" (v. 17). In fact, he dances before the Lord with such enthusiasm that his wife is embarrassed, but rather than yield to her concerns for social standing, he insists, "I will make myself yet more contemptible than this" (v. 22). While our worship takes a different form than David's, his whole-hearted praise should inspire us. For we do not have a tent merely pitched by humans, but "the Word [who] became flesh and dwelt among us" (Jn 1:14). The underlying Greek word for "dwelt" means to "spread a tent." David pitched a tent for the Lord, but now Jesus has come and pitched his own tent in our midst by becoming one of us. How can you follow David's example and worship the Lord with greater wonder and awe?

May 11

---

2 SAMUEL 7

**Now when the king dwelt in his
house, and the LORD had given
him rest from all his enemies
round about, 2the king said to Nathan
the prophet, "See now, I dwell in a house
of cedar, but the ark of God dwells in a**
tent." 3And Nathan said to the king, "Go,
do all that is in your heart; for the LORD
is with you."

4But that same night the word of the
LORD came to Nathan, 5"Go and tell my
servant David, 'Thus says the LORD:
Would you build me a house to dwell in?
6I have not dwelt in a house since the day I
brought up the sons of Israel from Egypt to
this day, but I have been moving about in
a tent for my dwelling. 7In all places where
I have moved with all the sons of Israel,
did I speak a word with any of the judges
of Israel, whom I commanded to shepherd
my people Israel, saying, "Why have you
not built me a house of cedar?"' 8Now
therefore thus you shall say to my servant
David, 'Thus says the LORD of hosts, I
took you from the pasture, from following
the sheep, that you should be prince over
my people Israel; 9and I have been with
you wherever you went, and have cut off
all your enemies from before you; and I
will make for you a great name, like the
name of the great ones of the earth. 10And
I will appoint a place for my people Israel,
and will plant them, that they may dwell
in their own place, and be disturbed no
more; and violent men shall afflict them
no more, as formerly, 11from the time that
I appointed judges over my people Israel;
and I will give you rest from all your
enemies. Moreover the LORD declares to
you that the LORD will make you a house.
12When your days are fulfilled and you
lie down with your fathers, I will raise up
your offspring after you, who shall come
forth from your body, and I will establish
his kingdom. 13He shall build a house for
my name, and I will establish the throne
of his kingdom for ever. 14I will be his
father, and he shall be my son. When
he commits iniquity, I will chasten him
with the rod of men, with the stripes of
the sons of men; 15but I will not take my
merciful love from him, as I took it from
Saul, whom I put away from before you.
16And your house and your kingdom shall
be made sure for ever before me; your
throne shall be established for ever.'" 17In
accordance with all these words, and in
accordance with all this vision, Nathan
spoke to David.

18Then King David went in and sat before
the LORD, and said, "Who am I, O Lord
GOD, and what is my house, that you have
brought me thus far? 19And yet this was a
small thing in your eyes, O Lord GOD; you
have spoken also of your servant's house
for a great while to come, and have shown
me future generations, O Lord GOD!
20And what more can David say to you?
For you know your servant, O Lord GOD!
21Because of your promise, and according
to your own heart, you have wrought all
this greatness, to make your servant know
it. 22Therefore you are great, O LORD
God; for there is none like you, and there
is no God besides you, according to all
that we have heard with our ears. 23What
other nation on earth is like your people
Israel, whom God went to redeem to be
his people, making himself a name, and
doing for them great and terrible things,
by driving out before his people a nation
and its gods? 24And you established for
yourself your people Israel to be your
people for ever; and you, O LORD, became
their God. 25And now, O LORD God,
confirm for ever the word which you
have spoken concerning your servant and
concerning his house, and do as you have
spoken; 26and your name will be magnified
for ever, saying, 'The LORD of hosts is God
over Israel,' and the house of your servant
David will be established before you. 27For
you, O LORD of hosts, the God of Israel,
have made this revelation to your servant,
saying, 'I will build you a house'; therefore
your servant has found courage to pray
this prayer to you. 28And now, O Lord GOD,
you are God, and your words are true, and
you have promised this good thing to your
servant; 29now therefore may it please you
to bless the house of your servant, that it
may continue for ever before you; for you,
O Lord GOD, have spoken, and with your
blessing shall the house of your servant be
blessed for ever."

8 After this David defeated the Philis′tines
and subdued them, and David took
Meth′eg-am′mah out of the hand of the
Philistines.

2And he defeated Moab, and measured
them with a line, making them lie down on
the ground; two lines he measured to be put
to death, and one full line to be spared. And
the Moabites became servants to David and
brought tribute.

3David also defeated Hadade´zer the son of
Re´hob, king of Zobah, as he went to restore
his power at the river Euphrates. 4And
David took from him a thousand and seven
hundred horsemen, and twenty thousand
foot soldiers; and David hamstrung all
the chariot horses, but left enough for a
hundred chariots. 5And when the Syrians
of Damascus came to help Hadade´zer king
of Zobah, David slew twenty-two thousand men of the Syrians. 6Then David put
garrisons in Ar´am of Damascus; and the
Syrians became servants to David and
brought tribute. And the LORD gave victory
to David wherever he went. 7And David
took the shields of gold which were carried
by the servants of Hadade´zer, and brought
them to Jerusalem. 8And from Betah and
from Bero´thai, cities of Hadade´zer, King
David took very much bronze.

9When To´i king of Ha´math heard that
David had defeated the whole army of
Hadade´zer, 10To´i sent his son Jo´ram to King
David, to greet him, and to congratulate him
because he had fought against Hadade´zer
and defeated him; for Hadadezer had often
been at war with Toi. And Joram brought with
him articles of silver, of gold, and of bronze;
11these also King David dedicated to the LORD,
together with the silver and gold which he
dedicated from all the nations he subdued,
12from E´dom, Moab, the Am´monites, the
Philis´tines, Am´alek, and from the spoil of
Hadade´zer the son of Re´hob, king of Zobah.

13And David won a name for himself. When
he returned, he slew eighteen thousand
E´domites in the Valley of Salt. 14And he put
garrisons in E´dom; throughout all Edom he
put garrisons, and all the E´domites became
David's servants. And the LORD gave victory
to David wherever he went.

15So David reigned over all Israel; and
David administered justice and equity to all
his people. 16And Jo´ab the son of Zeru´iah
was over the army; and Jehosh´aphat the
son of Ahi´lud was recorder; 17and Zad´ok
the son of Ahi´tub and Ahim´elech the
son of Abi´athar were priests; and Serai´ah
was secretary; 18and Bena´iah the son of
Jehoi´ada was over the Cher´ethites and the
Pel´ethites; and David's sons were priests.

9 And David said, "Is there still any one
left of the house of Saul, that I may show
him kindness for Jonathan's sake?" 2Now
there was a servant of the house of Saul
whose name was Zi´ba, and they called him
to David; and the king said to him, "Are you
Ziba?" And he said, "Your servant is he."
3And the king said, "Is there not still some
one of the house of Saul, that I may show
the kindness of God to him?" Zi´ba said to
the king, "There is still a son of Jonathan;
he is crippled in his feet." 4The king said to
him, "Where is he?" And Zi´ba said to the
king, "He is in the house of Ma´chir the
son of Am´miel, at Lo-de´bar." 5Then King
David sent and brought him from the house
of Ma´chir the son of Am´miel, at Lo-de´bar.
6And Mephib´osheth the son of Jonathan,
son of Saul, came to David, and fell on
his face and did obeisance. And David
said, "Mephibosheth!" And he answered,
"Behold, your servant." 7And David said
to him, "Do not fear; for I will show
you kindness for the sake of your father
Jonathan, and I will restore to you all the
land of Saul your father; and you shall eat
at my table always." 8And he did obeisance,
and said, "What is your servant, that you
should look upon a dead dog such as I?"

9Then the king called Zi´ba, Saul's servant,
and said to him, "All that belonged to Saul
and to all his house I have given to your
master's son. 10And you and your sons and
your servants shall till the land for him,
and shall bring in the produce, that your
master's son may have bread to eat; but
Mephib´osheth your master's son shall
always eat at my table." Now Zi´ba had fifteen
sons and twenty servants. 11Then Zi´ba said
to the king, "According to all that my lord
the king commands his servant, so will your
servant do." So Mephib´osheth ate at David's
table, like one of the king's sons. 12And

Mephib′osheth had a young son, whose name was Mica. And all who dwelt in Zi′ba's house became Mephib′osheth's servants. 13So Mephib′osheth dwelt in Jerusalem; for he ate always at the king's table. Now he was lame in both his feet.

To the choirmaster.
A Psalm of David.

PSALM 109 [108]

Be not silent, O God of my praise!
2For wicked and deceitful mouths are opened against me,
speaking against me with lying tongues.
3They beset me with words of hate,
and attack me without cause.
4In return for my love they accuse me,
even as I make prayer for them.
5So they reward me evil for good,
and hatred for my love.

6Appoint a wicked man against him;
let an accuser bring him to trial.
7When he is tried, let him come forth guilty;
let his prayer be counted as sin!
8May his days be few;
may another seize his goods!
9May his children be fatherless,
and his wife a widow!
10May his children wander about and beg;
may they be driven out of the ruins they inhabit!
11May the creditor seize all that he has;
may strangers plunder the fruits of his toil!
12Let there be none to extend kindness to him,
nor any to pity his fatherless children!
13May his posterity be cut off;
may his name be blotted out in the second generation!
14May the iniquity of his fathers be remembered before the LORD,
and let not the sin of his mother be blotted out!
15Let them be before the LORD continually;
and may his memory be cut off from the earth!
16For he did not remember to show kindness,
but pursued the poor and needy
and the brokenhearted to their death.
17He loved to curse; let curses come on him!
He did not like blessing; may it be far from him!
18He clothed himself with cursing as his coat,
may it soak into his body like water,
like oil into his bones!
19May it be like a garment which he wraps round him,
like a belt with which he daily girds himself!

20May this be the reward of my accusers from the LORD,
of those who speak evil against my life!
21But you, O GOD my Lord,
deal on my behalf for your name's sake;
because your mercy is good, deliver me!

JOHN 1

19And this is the testimony of John, when the Jews sent priests and Levites from Jerusalem to ask him, "Who are you?" 20He confessed, he did
not deny, but confessed, "I am not the Christ."
21And they asked him, "What then? Are you Eli′jah?" He said, "I am not." "Are you the prophet?" And he answered, "No." 22They said to him then, "Who are you? Let us have an answer for those who sent us. What do you say about yourself?" 23He said, "I am the voice of one crying in the wilderness, 'Make straight the way of the Lord,' as the prophet Isaiah said."
24Now they had been sent from the Pharisees. 25They asked him, "Then why are you baptizing, if you are neither the Christ, nor Eli′jah, nor the prophet?" 26John answered them, "I baptize with water; but among you stands one whom you do not know, 27even he who comes after me, the thong of whose sandal I am not worthy to untie." 28This took place in Beth′any beyond the Jordan, where John was baptizing.
29The next day he saw Jesus coming toward him, and said, "Behold, the Lamb of God,

who takes away the sin of the world! [30]This is he of whom I said, 'After me comes a man who ranks before me, for he was before me.' [31]I myself did not know him; but for this I came baptizing with water, that he might be revealed to Israel." [32]And John bore witness, "I saw the Spirit descend as a dove from heaven and remain on him. [33]I myself did not know him; but he who sent me to baptize with water said to me, 'He on whom you see the Spirit descend and remain, this is he who baptizes with the Holy Spirit.' [34]And I have seen and have borne witness that this is the Son of God."

REFLECTION

The Lord will not be outdone in generosity. After all his successes, David has "rest" from all his enemies and his mind turns toward building projects. He has a royal palace, but the Lord is still "dwelling" in a tent—the Tabernacle. David decides to begin construction on the Temple as a gift to the Lord, but the Lord responds with an even greater gift to David—a dynasty. The Lord here promises David, "Your house and your kingdom shall be made sure for ever before me; your throne shall be established for ever (2 Sm 7:16). He pledges to give him "a great name" (v. 9), that is, a lasting kingship in his family line. This great promise sets the stage for the rest of the story of the kings of Israel and Judah, and for the rest of the Bible. It is ultimately fulfilled when Jesus himself takes up the scepter of the House of David and reigns eternally as King—an astounding fulfillment of a seemingly simple political promise. David responds to the Lord with appropriate humility: "Who am I, O Lord God?" (v. 18), yet he gratefully asks God to confirm and do what he has promised. How has God displayed his generosity in your life?

May 12

2 SAMUEL 10

After this the king of the Am′monites died, and Ha′nun his son reigned in his stead. [2]And David said, "I will deal loyally with Ha′nun the son
of Na′hash, as his father dealt loyally with me." So David sent by his servants to console him concerning his father. And David's servants came into the land of the Am′monites. [3]But the princes of the Am′monites said to Ha′nun their lord, "Do you think, because David has sent comforters to you, that he is honoring your father? Has not David sent his servants to you to search the city, and to spy it out, and to overthrow it?" [4]So Ha′nun took David's servants, and shaved off half the beard of each, and cut off their garments in the middle, at their hips, and sent them away. [5]When it was told David, he sent to meet them, for the men were greatly ashamed. And the king said, "Remain at Jericho until your beards have grown, and then return."

[6]When the Am′monites saw that they had become odious to David, the Ammonites sent and hired the Syrians of Beth-re′hob, and the Syrians of Zobah, twenty thousand foot soldiers, and the king of Ma′acah with a thousand men, and the men of Tob, twelve thousand men. [7]And when David heard of it, he sent Jo′ab and all the host of the mighty men. [8]And the Am′monites came out and drew up in battle array at the entrance of the gate; and the Syrians of Zobah and of Re′hob, and the men of Tob and Ma′acah, were by themselves in the open country.

[9]When Jo′ab saw that the battle was set against him both in front and in the rear, he chose some of the picked men of Israel, and arrayed them against the Syrians; [10]the rest of his men he put in the charge of Abi′shai his brother, and he arrayed them against the Am′monites. [11]And he said, "If the Syrians are too strong for me, then you shall help me; but if the Am′monites are too strong for you, then I will come and help you. [12]Be of good courage, and let us play the man for our people, and for the cities of our God; and may the Lord do what seems good to him." [13]So Jo′ab and the people who were with him drew near to battle against the Syrians; and they fled before him. [14]And when the Am′monites saw that the Syrians fled, they likewise fled before Abi′shai, and entered the city. Then Jo′ab returned from

fighting against the Ammonites, and came
to Jerusalem.

[15]But when the Syrians saw that they
had been defeated by Israel, they gathered
themselves together. [16]And Hadade´zer sent,
and brought out the Syrians who were
beyond the Euphra´tes; and they came to
He´lam, with Shobach the commander of
the army of Hadadezer at their head. [17]And
when it was told David, he gathered all Israel
together, and crossed the Jordan, and came to
He´lam. And the Syrians arrayed themselves
against David, and fought with him. [18]And
the Syrians fled before Israel; and David slew
of the Syrians the men of seven hundred
chariots, and forty thousand horsemen, and
wounded Shobach the commander of their
army, so that he died there. [19]And when all
the kings who were servants of Hadade´zer
saw that they had been defeated by Israel,
they made peace with Israel, and became
subject to them. So the Syrians feared to help
the Am´monites any more.

11 In the spring of the year, the time
when kings go forth to battle, David
sent Jo´ab, and his servants with him, and
all Israel; and they ravaged the Am´monites,
and besieged Rabbah. But David remained
at Jerusalem.

[2]It happened, late one afternoon, when
David arose from his couch and was walking
upon the roof of the king's house, that he
saw from the roof a woman bathing; and the
woman was very beautiful. [3]And David sent
and inquired about the woman. And one
said, "Is not this Bathshe´ba, the daughter
of Eli´am, the wife of Uri´ah the Hittite?"
[4]So David sent messengers, and took her;
and she came to him, and he lay with her.
(Now she was purifying herself from her
uncleanness.) Then she returned to her
house. [5]And the woman conceived; and she
sent and told David, "I am with child."

[6]So David sent word to Jo´ab, "Send me
Uri´ah the Hittite." And Joab sent Uriah to
David. [7]When Uri´ah came to him, David
asked how Jo´ab was doing, and how the
people fared, and how the war prospered.
[8]Then David said to Uri´ah, "Go down
to your house, and wash your feet." And
Uriah went out of the king's house, and
there followed him a present from the king.
[9]But Uri´ah slept at the door of the king's
house with all the servants of his lord, and
did not go down to his house. [10]When they
told David, "Uri´ah did not go down to his
house," David said to Uriah, "Have you
not come from a journey? Why did you
not go down to your house?" [11]Uri´ah said
to David, "The ark and Israel and Judah
dwell in booths; and my lord Jo´ab and the
servants of my lord are camping in the open
field; shall I then go to my house, to eat and
to drink, and to lie with my wife? As you
live, and as your soul lives, I will not do this
thing." [12]Then David said to Uri´ah, "Remain
here today also, and tomorrow I will let you
depart." So Uriah remained in Jerusalem
that day, and the next. [13]And David invited
him, and he ate in his presence and drank,
so that he made him drunk; and in the
evening he went out to lie on his couch with
the servants of his lord, but he did not go
down to his house.

[14]In the morning David wrote a letter to
Jo´ab, and sent it by the hand of Uri´ah.
[15]In the letter he wrote, "Set Uri´ah in the
forefront of the hardest fighting, and then
draw back from him, that he may be struck
down, and die." [16]And as Jo´ab was besieging
the city, he assigned Uri´ah to the place
where he knew there were valiant men.
[17]And the men of the city came out and
fought with Jo´ab; and some of the servants
of David among the people fell. Uri´ah the
Hittite was slain also. [18]Then Jo´ab sent and
told David all the news about the fighting;
[19]and he instructed the messenger, "When
you have finished telling all the news about
the fighting to the king, [20]then, if the king's
anger rises, and if he says to you, 'Why
did you go so near the city to fight? Did
you not know that they would shoot from
the wall? [21]Who killed Abim´elech the son
of Jerub´besheth? Did not a woman cast
an upper millstone upon him from the
wall, so that he died at The´bez? Why did
you go so near the wall?' then you shall
say, 'Your servant Uri´ah the Hittite is
dead also.' "

22So the messenger went, and came and told
David all that Jo′ab had sent him to tell. 23The
messenger said to David, "The men gained
an advantage over us, and came out against
us in the field; but we drove them back to the
entrance of the gate. 24Then the archers shot
at your servants from the wall; some of the
king's servants are dead; and your servant
Uri′ah the Hittite is dead also." 25David said to
the messenger, "Thus shall you say to Jo′ab,
'Do not let this matter trouble you, for the
sword devours now one and now another;
strengthen your attack upon the city, and
overthrow it.' And encourage him."
26When the wife of Uri′ah heard that
Uriah her husband was dead, she made
lamentation for her husband. 27And when
the mourning was over, David sent and
brought her to his house, and she became
his wife, and bore him a son. But the thing
that David had done displeased the LORD.

To the choirmaster.
A Psalm of David.

PSALM 109 [108]

22For I am poor and needy,
and my heart is stricken within me.
23I am gone, like a shadow at evening;
I am shaken off like a locust.
24My knees are weak through fasting;
my body has become gaunt.
25I am an object of scorn to my accusers;
when they see me, they wag their heads.

26Help me, O LORD my God!
Save me according to your merciful love!
27Let them know that this is your hand;
you, O LORD, have done it!
28Let them curse, but do bless!
Let my assailants be put to shame; may
your servant be glad!
29May my accusers be clothed with dishonor;
may they be wrapped in their own shame
as in a mantle!

30With my mouth I will give great thanks to
the LORD;
I will praise him in the midst of
the throng.
31For he stands at the right hand of
the needy,
to save him from those who condemn
him to death.

JOHN 1

35The next day again John was
standing with two of his dis-
ciples; 36and he looked at Jesus as he
walked, and said, "Behold, the Lamb
of God!" 37The two disciples heard
him say this, and they followed Jesus.
38Jesus turned, and saw them following,
and said to them, "What do you seek?"
And they said to him, "Rabbi" (which
means Teacher), "where are you staying?"
39He said to them, "Come and see." They
came and saw where he was staying; and
they stayed with him that day, for it was
about the tenth hour. 40One of the two
who heard John speak, and followed him,
was Andrew, Simon Peter's brother. 41He
first found his brother Simon, and said to
him, "We have found the Messiah" (which
means Christ). 42He brought him to Jesus.
Jesus looked at him, and said, "So you
are Simon the son of John? You shall be
called Ce′phas" (which means Peter).
43The next day Jesus decided to go to
Galilee. And he found Philip and said to him,
"Follow me." 44Now Philip was from Beth-
sa′ida, the city of Andrew and Peter. 45Philip
found Nathan′a-el, and said to him, "We have
found him of whom Moses in the law and
also the prophets wrote, Jesus of Nazareth,
the son of Joseph." 46Nathan′a-el said to him,
"Can anything good come out of Nazareth?"
Philip said to him, "Come and see." 47Jesus
saw Nathan′a-el coming to him, and said of
him, "Behold, an Israelite indeed, in whom is
no guile!" 48Nathan′a-el said to him, "How do
you know me?" Jesus answered him, "Before
Philip called you, when you were under the
fig tree, I saw you." 49Nathan′a-el answered
him, "Rabbi, you are the Son of God! You

are the King of Israel!" 50 Jesus answered him, "Because I said to you, I saw you under the fig tree, do you believe? You shall see greater things than these." 51 And he said to him, "Truly, truly, I say to you, you will see heaven opened, and the angels of God ascending and descending upon the Son of man."

2 On the third day there was a marriage at Cana in Galilee, and the mother of Jesus was there; 2 Jesus also was invited to the marriage, with his disciples. 3 When the wine failed, the mother of Jesus said to him, "They have no wine." 4 And Jesus said to her, "O woman, what have you to do with me? My hour has not yet come." 5 His mother said to the servants, "Do whatever he tells you." 6 Now six stone jars were standing there, for the Jewish rites of purification, each holding twenty or thirty gallons. 7 Jesus said to them, "Fill the jars with water." And they filled them up to the brim. 8 He said to them, "Now draw some out, and take it to the steward of the feast." So they took it. 9 When the steward of the feast tasted the water now become wine, and did not know where it came from (though the servants who had drawn the water knew), the steward of the feast called the bridegroom 10 and said to him, "Every man serves the good wine first; and when men have drunk freely, then the poor wine; but you have kept the good wine until now." 11 This, the first of his signs, Jesus did at Cana in Galilee, and manifested his glory; and his disciples believed in him.

12 After this he went down to Caper′naum, with his mother and his brethren and his disciples; and there they stayed for a few days.

13 The Passover of the Jews was at hand, and Jesus went up to Jerusalem. 14 In the temple he found those who were selling oxen and sheep and pigeons, and the money-changers at their business. 15 And making a whip of cords, he drove them all, with the sheep and oxen, out of the temple; and he poured out the coins of the money-changers and overturned their tables. 16 And he told those who sold the pigeons, "Take these things away; you shall not make my Father's house a house of trade." 17 His disciples remembered that it was written, "Zeal for your house will consume me." 18 The Jews then said to him, "What sign have you to show us for doing this?" 19 Jesus answered them, "Destroy this temple, and in three days I will raise it up." 20 The Jews then said, "It has taken forty-six years to build this temple, and will you raise it up in three days?" 21 But he spoke of the temple of his body. 22 When therefore he was raised from the dead, his disciples remembered that he had said this; and they believed the Scripture and the word which Jesus had spoken.

23 Now when he was in Jerusalem at the Passover feast, many believed in his name when they saw the signs which he did; 24 but Jesus did not trust himself to them, 25 because he knew all men and needed no one to bear witness of man; for he himself knew what was in man.

REFLECTION

Today's readings quite candidly describe the grave sins that result from David's disobedience to God's commands: "David sent messengers, and took her; and she came to him, and he lay with her" (2 Sm 11:4). Then David heaps sin upon sin by giving orders that will assure Bathsheba's husband is killed in battle. David sinned, plain and simple. Thankfully, the remedy to sin is also very straightforward. Jesus sums up the whole Christian life when he says, "Follow me" (Jn 1:43). That's it, plain and simple. If we obey that one command, or rather, if we respond to that one invitation, then everything else starts to fall into place. Mary, Jesus's mother, puts a very similar charge to the servants at Cana: "Do whatever he tells you" (2:5). Yes, the spiritual life will require discernment and struggle, and there will be questions and doubts, but in the end it's quite straightforward: Follow Jesus and do whatever he tells you. The first disciples responded to Jesus's call, giving up everything and following Jesus wholeheartedly. Because they followed Jesus closely, they saw great miracles and even tasted "the good wine" (v. 10). Even in the midst of your struggles and failings, Jesus is calling you to follow him. How is Jesus calling you to follow him more closely today?

May 13

2 SAMUEL 12

And the LORD sent Nathan to David. He came to him, and said to him, "There were two men in a certain city, the one rich and the other poor. [2]The rich man had very many flocks and herds; [3]but the poor man had nothing but one little ewe lamb, which he had bought. And he brought it up, and it grew up with him and with his children; it used to eat of his morsel, and drink from his cup, and lie in his bosom, and it was like a daughter to him. [4]Now there came a traveler to the rich man, and he was unwilling to take one of his own flock or herd to prepare for the wayfarer who had come to him, but he took the poor man's lamb, and prepared it for the man who had come to him." [5]Then David's anger was greatly kindled against the man; and he said to Nathan, "As the LORD lives, the man who has done this deserves to die; [6]and he shall restore the lamb fourfold, because he did this thing, and because he had no pity."

[7]Nathan said to David, "You are the man. Thus says the LORD, the God of Israel, 'I anointed you king over Israel, and I delivered you out of the hand of Saul; [8]and I gave you your master's house, and your master's wives into your bosom, and gave you the house of Israel and of Judah; and if this were too little, I would add to you as much more. [9]Why have you despised the word of the LORD, to do what is evil in his sight? You have struck down Uri′ah the Hittite with the sword, and have taken his wife to be your wife, and have slain him with the sword of the Am′monites. [10]Now therefore the sword shall never depart from your house, because you have despised me, and have taken the wife of Uri′ah the Hittite to be your wife.' [11]Thus says the LORD, 'Behold, I will raise up evil against you out of your own house; and I will take your wives before your eyes, and give them to your neighbor, and he shall lie with your wives in the sight of this sun. [12]For you did it secretly; but I will do this thing before all Israel, and before the sun.'" [13]David said to Nathan, "I have sinned against the LORD." And Nathan said to David, "The LORD also has put away your sin; you shall not die. [14]Nevertheless, because by this deed you have utterly scorned the LORD, the child that is born to you shall die." [15]Then Nathan went to his house.

And the LORD struck the child that Uri′ah's wife bore to David, and it became sick. [16]David therefore besought God for the child; and David fasted, and went in and lay all night upon the ground. [17]And the elders of his house stood beside him, to raise him from the ground; but he would not, nor did he eat food with them. [18]On the seventh day the child died. And the servants of David feared to tell him that the child was dead; for they said, "Behold, while the child was yet alive, we spoke to him, and he did not listen to us; how then can we say to him the child is dead? He may do himself some harm." [19]But when David saw that his servants were whispering together, David perceived that the child was dead; and David said to his servants, "Is the child dead?" They said, "He is dead." [20]Then David arose from the earth, and washed, and anointed himself, and changed his clothes; and he went into the house of the LORD, and worshiped; he then went to his own house; and when he asked, they set food before him, and he ate. [21]Then his servants said to him, "What is this thing that you have done? You fasted and wept for the child while it was alive; but when the child died, you arose and ate food." [22]He said, "While the child was still alive, I fasted and wept; for I said, 'Who knows whether the LORD will be gracious to me, that the child may live?' [23]But now he is dead; why should I fast? Can I bring him back again? I shall go to him, but he will not return to me."

[24]Then David comforted his wife, Bath-she′ba, and went in to her, and lay with her; and she bore a son, and he called his name Solomon. And the LORD loved him, [25]and sent

a message by Nathan the prophet; so he called his name Jedidi´ah, because of the LORD.

26Now Jo´ab fought against Rabbah of the Am´monites, and took the royal city. 27And Jo´ab sent messengers to David, and said, "I have fought against Rabbah; moreover, I have taken the city of waters. 28Now, then, gather the rest of the people together, and encamp against the city, and take it; lest I take the city, and it be called by my name." 29So David gathered all the people together and went to Rabbah, and fought against it and took it. 30And he took the crown of their king from his head; the weight of it was a talent of gold, and in it was a precious stone; and it was placed on David's head. And he brought forth the spoil of the city, a very great amount. 31And he brought forth the people who were in it, and set them to labor with saws and iron picks and iron axes, and made them toil at the brick-kilns; and thus he did to all the cities of the Am´monites. Then David and all the people returned to Jerusalem.

13 Now Ab´salom, David's son, had a beautiful sister, whose name was Ta´mar; and after a time Amnon, David's son, loved her. 2And Amnon was so tormented that he made himself ill because of his sister Ta´mar; for she was a virgin, and it seemed impossible to Amnon to do anything to her. 3But Amnon had a friend, whose name was Jon´adab, the son of Shim´e-ah, David's brother; and Jonadab was a very crafty man. 4And he said to him, "O son of the king, why are you so haggard morning after morning? Will you not tell me?" Amnon said to him, "I love Ta´mar, my brother Ab´salom's sister." 5Jon´adab said to him, "Lie down on your bed, and pretend to be ill; and when your father comes to see you, say to him, 'Let my sister Ta´mar come and give me bread to eat, and prepare the food in my sight, that I may see it, and eat it from her hand.'" 6So Amnon lay down, and pretended to be ill; and when the king came to see him, Amnon said to the king, "Please let my sister Ta´mar come and make a couple of cakes in my sight, that I may eat from her hand."

7Then David sent home to Ta´mar, saying, "Go to your brother Amnon's house, and prepare food for him." 8So Ta´mar went to her brother Amnon's house, where he was lying down. And she took dough, and kneaded it, and made cakes in his sight, and baked the cakes. 9And she took the pan and emptied it out before him, but he refused to eat. And Amnon said, "Send out every one from me." So every one went out from him. 10Then Amnon said to Ta´mar, "Bring the food into the chamber, that I may eat from your hand." And Tamar took the cakes she had made, and brought them into the chamber to Amnon her brother. 11But when she brought them near him to eat, he took hold of her, and said to her, "Come, lie with me, my sister." 12She answered him, "No, my brother, do not force me; for such a thing is not done in Israel; do not do this wanton folly. 13As for me, where could I carry my shame? And as for you, you would be as one of the wanton fools in Israel. Now therefore, I beg you, speak to the king; for he will not withhold me from you." 14But he would not listen to her; and being stronger than she, he forced her, and lay with her.

15Then Amnon hated her with very great hatred; so that the hatred with which he hated her was greater than the love with which he had loved her. And Amnon said to her, "Arise, be gone." 16But she said to him, "No, my brother; for this wrong in sending me away is greater than the other which you did to me." But he would not listen to her. 17He called the young man who served him and said, "Put this woman out of my presence, and bolt the door after her." 18Now she was wearing a long robe with sleeves; for thus were the virgin daughters of the king clad of old. So his servant put her out, and bolted the door after her. 19And Ta´mar put ashes on her head, and tore the long robe which she wore; and she laid her hand on her head, and went away, crying aloud as she went.

20And her brother Ab´salom said to her, "Has Amnon your brother been with you? Now hold your peace, my sister; he is your brother; do not take this to heart." So Ta´mar dwelt, a desolate woman, in her brother Ab´salom's house. 21When King David heard of all these things, he was very angry. 22But

Ab′salom spoke to Amnon neither good nor
bad; for Absalom hated Amnon, because he
had forced his sister Ta′mar.
23After two full years Ab′salom had
sheepshearers at Ba′al-ha′zor, which is near
E′phraim, and Absalom invited all the king's
sons. 24And Ab′salom came to the king, and
said, "Behold, your servant has sheepshearers;
please let the king and his servants go with
your servant." 25But the king said to Ab′salom,
"No, my son, let us not all go, lest we be
burdensome to you." He pressed him, but
he would not go but gave him his blessing.
26Then Ab′salom said, "If not, please let my
brother Amnon go with us." And the king said
to him, "Why should he go with you?" 27But
Ab′salom pressed him until he let Amnon
and all the king's sons go with him. 28Then
Ab′salom commanded his servants, "Mark
when Amnon's heart is merry with wine, and
when I say to you, 'Strike Amnon,' then kill
him. Fear not; have I not commanded you? Be
courageous and be valiant." 29So the servants
of Ab′salom did to Amnon as Absalom had
commanded. Then all the king's sons arose,
and each mounted his mule and fled.
30While they were on the way, tidings came
to David, "Ab′salom has slain all the king's sons,
and not one of them is left." 31Then the king
arose, and tore his garments, and lay on the
earth; and all his servants who were standing
by tore their garments. 32But Jon′adab the son
of Shim′e-ah, David's brother, said, "Let not
my lord suppose that they have killed all the
young men the king's sons, for Amnon alone is
dead, for by the command of Ab′salom this has
been determined from the day he forced his
sister Ta′mar. 33Now therefore let not my lord
the king so take it to heart as to suppose that
all the king's sons are dead; for Amnon alone
is dead."
34But Ab′salom fled. And the young man
who kept the watch lifted up his eyes, and
looked, and behold, many people were
coming from the Horona′im road by the
side of the mountain. 35And Jon′adab said
to the king, "Behold, the king's sons have
come; as your servant said, so it has come
about." 36And as soon as he had finished
speaking, behold, the king's sons came, and
lifted up their voice and wept; and the king
also and all his servants wept very bitterly.
37But Ab′salom fled, and went to Talmai
the son of Ammi′hud, king of Ge′shur. And
David mourned for his son day after day. 38So
Ab′salom fled, and went to Ge′shur, and was
there three years. 39And the spirit of the king
longed to go forth to Ab′salom; for he was
comforted about Amnon, seeing he was dead.

A Psalm of David.

PSALM 110 [109]

The LORD says to my lord:
"Sit at my right hand,
till I make your enemies your footstool."

2The LORD sends forth from Zion
your mighty scepter.
Rule in the midst of your foes!
3Yours is dominion
on the day you lead your host
in holy splendor.
From the womb of the morning
I begot you.
4The LORD has sworn
and will not change his mind,
"You are a priest for ever
according to the order of Melchiz′edek."

5The Lord is at your right hand;
he will shatter kings on the day of
his wrath.
6He will execute judgment among the nations,
filling them with corpses;
he will shatter chiefs
over the wide earth.
7He will drink from the brook by the way;
therefore he will lift up his head.

JOHN 3

**Now there was a man of the
Pharisees, named Nicode′mus,
a ruler of the Jews. 2This man came to
Jesus by night and said to him, "Rabbi,
we know that you are a teacher come**

from God; for no one can do these signs that you do, unless God is with him." 3Jesus answered him, "Truly, truly, I say to you, unless one is born anew, he cannot see the kingdom of God." 4Nicode′mus said to him, "How can a man be born when he is old? Can he enter a second time into his mother's womb and be born?" 5Jesus answered, "Truly, truly, I say to you, unless one is born of water and the Spirit, he cannot enter the kingdom of God. 6That which is born of the flesh is flesh, and that which is born of the Spirit is spirit. 7Do not marvel that I said to you, 'You must be born anew.' 8The wind blows where it wills, and you hear the sound of it, but you do not know where it comes from or where it goes; so it is with every one who is born of the Spirit." 9Nicode′mus said to him, "How can this be?" 10Jesus answered him, "Are you a teacher of Israel, and yet you do not understand this? 11Truly, truly, I say to you, we speak of what we know, and bear witness to what we have seen; but you do not receive our testimony. 12If I have told you earthly things and you do not believe, how can you believe if I tell you heavenly things? 13No one has ascended into heaven but he who descended from heaven, the Son of man. 14And as Moses lifted up the serpent in the wilderness, so must the Son of man be lifted up, 15that whoever believes in him may have eternal life."

16For God so loved the world that he gave his only-begotten Son, that whoever believes in him should not perish but have eternal life. 17For God sent the Son into the world, not to condemn the world, but that the world might be saved through him. 18He who believes in him is not condemned; he who does not believe is condemned already, because he has not believed in the name of the only-begotten Son of God. 19And this is the judgment, that the light has come into the world, and men loved darkness rather than light, because their deeds were evil. 20For every one who does evil hates the light, and does not come to the light, lest his deeds should be exposed. 21But he who does what is true comes to the light, that it may be clearly seen that his deeds have been wrought in God.

REFLECTION

Our actions have consequences, for good or for ill. David's sins, which he tried to cover up, are brought into the light by the prophet Nathan. He does not shrink from accusing even his own king: "You are the man" (2 Sm 12:7). Soon after being promised an everlasting throne, David falls into grave sin. With those sins, he throws away the Lord's blessing and is told: "Now therefore the sword shall never depart from your house" (v. 10). This ominous prophecy not only points to the series of tragedies that follow—the death of David's child, the rape of Tamar, and the murder of Amnon—but also to the story of the kings who will succeed David. Bloodshed indeed follows the house of David. We see here the ramifications of one man's sin. But Jesus shows us how one holy act, his sacrifice, will have eternal benefit, opening salvation to all who will believe. Jesus emphasizes the primacy of our faith response to him: "Whoever believes in him may have eternal life" (Jn 3:15). While sinners, like David, conceal sin to hide from the light, those who believe come to the light and are transformed by it (see vv. 20–21). Can you think of times when one sin led to another, or conversely, how one good deed you did created momentum toward greater virtue and a deeper relationship with God?

May 14

2 SAMUEL 14

Now Jo′ab the son of Zeru′iah perceived that the king's heart went out to Ab′salom. 2And Jo′ab sent to Teko′a, and fetched from there a wise woman, and said to her, "Pretend to be a mourner, and put on mourning garments; do not anoint yourself with oil, but behave like a woman who has been mourning many days for the dead; 3and go to the king, and speak thus to him." So Jo′ab put the words in her mouth.

4When the woman of Teko′a came to the king, she fell on her face to the ground, and did obeisance, and said, "Help, O king." 5And the king said to her, "What is your trouble?" She answered, "Alas, I am a widow; my husband is dead. [6]And your handmaid had two sons, and they quarreled with one another in the field; there was no one to part them, and one struck the other and killed him. [7]And now the whole family has risen against your handmaid, and they say, 'Give up the man who struck his brother, that we may kill him for the life of his brother whom he slew'; and so they would destroy the heir also. Thus they would quench my coal which is left, and leave to my husband neither name nor remnant upon the face of the earth."

[8]Then the king said to the woman, "Go to your house, and I will give orders concerning you." [9]And the woman of Teko′a said to the king, "On me be the guilt, my lord the king, and on my father's house; let the king and his throne be guiltless." [10]The king said, "If any one says anything to you, bring him to me, and he shall never touch you again." [11]Then she said, "Please let the king invoke the LORD your God, that the avenger of blood slay no more, and my son be not destroyed." He said, "As the LORD lives, not one hair of your son shall fall to the ground."

[12]Then the woman said, "Please let your handmaid speak a word to my lord the king." He said, "Speak." [13]And the woman said, "Why then have you planned such a thing against the people of God? For in giving this decision the king convicts himself, inasmuch as the king does not bring his banished one home again. [14]We must all die, we are like water spilt on the ground, which cannot be gathered up again; but God will not take away the life of him who devises means not to keep his banished one an outcast. [15]Now I have come to say this to my lord the king because the people have made me afraid; and your handmaid thought, 'I will speak to the king; it may be that the king will perform the request of his servant. [16]For the king will hear, and deliver his servant from the hand of the man who would destroy me and my son together from the heritage of God.' [17]And your handmaid thought, 'The word of my lord the king will set me at rest'; for my lord the king is like the angel of God to discern good and evil. The LORD your God be with you!"

[18]Then the king answered the woman, "Do not hide from me anything I ask you." And the woman said, "Let my lord the king speak." [19]The king said, "Is the hand of Jo′ab with you in all this?" The woman answered and said, "As surely as you live, my lord the king, one cannot turn to the right hand or to the left from anything that my lord the king has said. It was your servant Joab who bade me; it was he who put all these words in the mouth of your handmaid. [20]In order to change the course of affairs your servant Jo′ab did this. But my lord has wisdom like the wisdom of the angel of God to know all things that are on the earth."

[21]Then the king said to Jo′ab, "Behold now, I grant this; go, bring back the young man Ab′salom." [22]And Jo′ab fell on his face to the ground, and did obeisance, and blessed the king; and Joab said, "Today your servant knows that I have found favor in your sight, my lord the king, in that the king has granted the request of his servant." [23]So Jo′ab arose and went to Ge′shur, and brought Ab′salom to Jerusalem. [24]And the king said, "Let him dwell apart in his own house; he is not to come into my presence." So Ab′salom dwelt apart in his own house, and did not come into the king's presence.

[25]Now in all Israel there was no one so much to be praised for his beauty as Ab′salom; from the sole of his foot to the crown of his head there was no blemish in him. [26]And when he cut the hair of his head (for at the end of every year he used to cut it; when it was heavy on him, he cut it), he weighed the hair of his head, two hundred shekels by the king's weight. [27]There were born to Ab′salom three sons, and one daughter whose name was Ta′mar; she was a beautiful woman.

[28]So Ab′salom dwelt two full years in Jerusalem, without coming into the king's presence. [29]Then Ab′salom sent for Jo′ab, to send him to the king; but Joab would not come to him. And he sent a second time, but

Joab would not come. [30]Then he said to his servants, "See, Jo´ab's field is next to mine, and he has barley there; go and set it on fire." So Ab´salom's servants set the field on fire. [31]Then Jo´ab arose and went to Ab´salom at his house, and said to him, "Why have your servants set my field on fire?" [32]Ab´salom answered Jo´ab, "Behold, I sent word to you, 'Come here, that I may send you to the king, to ask, "Why have I come from Ge´shur? It would be better for me to be there still." Now therefore let me go into the presence of the king; and if there is guilt in me, let him kill me.'" [33]Then Jo´ab went to the king, and told him; and he summoned Ab´salom. So he came to the king, and bowed himself on his face to the ground before the king; and the king kissed Absalom.

15 After this Ab´salom got himself a chariot and horses, and fifty men to run before him. [2]And Ab´salom used to rise early and stand beside the way of the gate; and when any man had a suit to come before the king for judgment, Absalom would call to him, and say, "From what city are you?" And when he said, "Your servant is of such and such a tribe in Israel," [3]Ab´salom would say to him, "See, your claims are good and right; but there is no man deputed by the king to hear you." [4]Ab´salom said moreover, "Oh that I were judge in the land! Then every man with a suit or cause might come to me, and I would give him justice." [5]And whenever a man came near to do obeisance to him, he would put out his hand, and take hold of him, and kiss him. [6]Thus Ab´salom did to all of Israel who came to the king for judgment; so Absalom stole the hearts of the men of Israel.

[7]And at the end of four years Ab´salom said to the king, "Please let me go and pay my vow, which I have vowed to the LORD, in He´bron. [8]For your servant vowed a vow while I dwelt at Ge´shur in Ar´am, saying, 'If the LORD will indeed bring me back to Jerusalem, then I will offer worship to the LORD.'" [9]The king said to him, "Go in peace." So he arose, and went to He´bron. [10]But Ab´salom sent secret messengers throughout all the tribes of Israel, saying, "As soon as you hear the sound of the trumpet, then say, 'Ab´salom is king at He´bron!'" [11]With Ab´salom went two hundred men from Jerusalem who were invited guests, and they went in their simplicity, and knew nothing. [12]And while Ab´salom was offering the sacrifices, he sent for Ahith´ophel the Gi´lonite, David's counselor, from his city Gi´loh. And the conspiracy grew strong, and the people with Absalom kept increasing.

[13]And a messenger came to David, saying, "The hearts of the men of Israel have gone after Ab´salom." [14]Then David said to all his servants who were with him at Jerusalem, "Arise, and let us flee; or else there will be no escape for us from Ab´salom; go in haste, lest he overtake us quickly, and bring down evil upon us, and strike the city with the edge of the sword." [15]And the king's servants said to the king, "Behold, your servants are ready to do whatever my lord the king decides." [16]So the king went forth, and all his household after him. And the king left ten concubines to keep the house. [17]And the king went forth, and all the people after him; and they halted at the last house. [18]And all his servants passed by him; and all the Cher´ethites, and all the Pel´ethites, and all the six hundred Gittites who had followed him from Gath, passed on before the king.

[19]Then the king said to Ittai the Gittite, "Why do you also go with us? Go back, and stay with the king; for you are a foreigner, and also an exile from your home. [20]You came only yesterday, and shall I today make you wander about with us, seeing I go I know not where? Go back, and take your brethren with you; and may the LORD show mercy and faithfulness to you." [21]But Ittai answered the king, "As the LORD lives, and as my lord the king lives, wherever my lord the king shall be, whether for death or for life, there also will your servant be." [22]And David said to Ittai, "Go then, pass on." So Ittai the Gittite passed on, with all his men and all the little ones who were with him. [23]And all the country wept aloud as all the people passed by, and the king crossed the

brook Kidron, and all the people passed on toward the wilderness.

[24]And Abi′athar came up, and behold, Za′dok came also, with all the Levites, bearing the ark of the covenant of God; and they set down the ark of God, until the people had all passed out of the city. [25]Then the king said to Za′dok, "Carry the ark of God back into the city. If I find favor in the eyes of the LORD, he will bring me back and let me see both it and his habitation; [26]but if he says, 'I have no pleasure in you,' behold, here I am, let him do to me what seems good to him." [27]The king also said to Za′dok the priest, "Look, go back to the city in peace, you and Abi′athar, with your two sons, Ahim′a-az your son, and Jonathan the son of Abiathar. [28]See, I will wait at the fords of the wilderness, until word comes from you to inform me." [29]So Za′dok and Abi′athar carried the ark of God back to Jerusalem; and they remained there.

[30]But David went up the ascent of the Mount of Olives, weeping as he went, barefoot and with his head covered; and all the people who were with him covered their heads, and they went up, weeping as they went. [31]And it was told David, "Ahith′ophel is among the conspirators with Ab′salom." And David said, "O LORD, I pray you, turn the counsel of Ahithophel into foolishness."

[32]When David came to the summit, where God was worshiped, behold, Hu′shai the Ar′chite came to meet him with his coat torn and earth upon his head. [33]David said to him, "If you go on with me, you will be a burden to me. [34]But if you return to the city, and say to Ab′salom, 'I will be your servant, O king; as I have been your father's servant in time past, so now I will be your servant,' then you will defeat for me the counsel of Ahith′ophel. [35]Are not Za′dok and Abi′athar the priests with you there? So whatever you hear from the king's house, tell it to Zadok and Abiathar the priests. [36]Behold, their two sons are with them there, Ahim′a-az, Za′dok's son, and Jonathan, Abi′athar's son; and by them you shall send to me everything you hear." [37]So Hu′shai, David's friend, came into the city, just as Ab′salom was entering Jerusalem.

PSALM 111 [110]

Praise the LORD!
I will give thanks to the LORD with my
whole heart,
in the company of the upright, in
the congregation.
[2]Great are the works of the LORD,
studied by all who have pleasure in them.
[3]Full of honor and majesty is his work,
and his righteousness endures for ever.
[4]He has caused his wonderful works to
be remembered;
the LORD is gracious and merciful.
[5]He provides food for those who fear him;
he is ever mindful of his covenant.
[6]He has shown his people the power of
his works,
in giving them the heritage of the nations.
[7]The works of his hands are faithful and just;
all his precepts are trustworthy,
[8]they are established for ever and ever,
to be performed with faithfulness
and uprightness.
[9]He sent redemption to his people;
he has commanded his covenant for ever.
Holy and awesome is his name!
[10]The fear of the LORD is the beginning
of wisdom;
a good understanding have all those who
practice it.
His praise endures for ever!

JOHN 3

[22]After this Jesus and his disciples went into the land of Judea; there he remained with them and baptized. [23]John also was baptizing at Ae′non near Sa′lim, because there was much water there; and people came and were baptized. [24]For John had not yet been put in prison.

[25]Now a discussion arose between John's disciples and a Jew over purifying. [26]And they came to John, and said to him, "Rabbi, he who was with you beyond the Jordan, to whom you bore witness, here he is, baptizing, and all are going to him." [27]John

answered, "No one can receive anything except what is given him from heaven. [28]You yourselves bear me witness, that I said, I am not the Christ, but I have been sent before him. [29]He who has the bride is the bridegroom; the friend of the bridegroom, who stands and hears him, rejoices greatly at the bridegroom's voice; therefore this joy of mine is now full. [30]He must increase, but I must decrease."

[31]He who comes from above is above all; he who is of the earth belongs to the earth, and of the earth he speaks; he who comes from heaven is above all. [32]He bears witness to what he has seen and heard, yet no one receives his testimony; [33]he who receives his testimony sets his seal to this, that God is true. [34]For he whom God has sent utters the words of God, for it is not by measure that he gives the Spirit; [35]the Father loves the Son, and has given all things into his hand. [36]He who believes in the Son has eternal life; he who does not obey the Son shall not see life, but the wrath of God rests upon him.

REFLECTION

Sometimes it takes a lot to grab our attention. The routine of life can hypnotize and lull us into a state of spiritual complacency, from which we need a wake-up call. In today's readings, Absalom's actions provide us a vivid image of just such a wake-up call. Absalom twice sends the commander Joab a message, but Joab ignores him. So Absalom takes drastic measures to get Joab's attention. He tells his servants to look at Joab's barley field; then he says, "Go and set it on fire" (2 Sm 14:30). That gets Joab's attention in a hurry, and he comes immediately. While Absalom is a negative character—who murders his brother and tries to wrest the kingdom from his own father—his dramatic communication style parallels what God occasionally has to do to get through to us. When we ignore him and allow ourselves to become spiritually deaf, he can break through our shell by "setting our field on fire," as when Jesus performs miracles or drives out the money-changers from the Temple. In your life right now, are you listening to God with a wide open heart, or does he need to "set [your] field on fire" to get your attention?

May 15

2 SAMUEL 16

When David had passed a little beyond the summit, Zi′ba the servant of Mephib′osheth met him, with a couple of donkeys saddled, bearing two hundred loaves of bread, a hundred bunches of raisins, a hundred of summer fruits, and a skin of wine. [2]And the king said to Zi′ba, "Why have you brought these?" Ziba answered, "The donkeys are for the king's household to ride on, the bread and summer fruit for the young men to eat, and the wine for those who faint in the wilderness to drink." [3]And the king said, "And where is your master's son?" Zi′ba said to the king, "Behold, he remains in Jerusalem; for he said, 'Today the house of Israel will give me back the kingdom of my father.'" [4]Then the king said to Zi′ba, "Behold, all that belonged to Mephib′osheth is now yours." And Ziba said, "I do obeisance; let me ever find favor in your sight, my lord the king."

[5]When King David came to Bahu′rim, there came out a man of the family of the house of Saul, whose name was Shim′e-i, the son of Gera; and as he came he cursed continually. [6]And he threw stones at David, and at all the servants of King David; and all the people and all the mighty men were on his right hand and on his left. [7]And Shim′e-i said as he cursed, "Begone, begone, you man of blood, you worthless fellow! [8]The LORD has avenged upon you all the blood of the house of Saul, in whose place you have reigned; and the LORD has given the kingdom into the hand of your son Ab′salom. See, your ruin is on you; for you are a man of blood."

[9]Then Abi′shai the son of Zeru′iah said to the king, "Why should this dead dog curse my lord the king? Let me go over and take off his head." [10]But the king said, "What have I to do with you, you sons of Zeru′iah?

If he is cursing because the LORD has said
to him, 'Curse David,' who then shall say,
'Why have you done so?' " 11And David said
to Abi′shai and to all his servants, "Behold,
my own son seeks my life; how much more
now may this Benjaminite! Let him alone,
and let him curse; for the LORD has bidden
him. 12It may be that the LORD will look
upon my affliction, and that the LORD will
repay me with good for this cursing of me
today." 13So David and his men went on
the road, while Shim′e-i went along on
the hillside opposite him and cursed as he
went, and threw stones at him and flung
dust. 14And the king, and all the people who
were with him, arrived weary at the Jordan;
and there he refreshed himself.

15Now Ab′salom and all the people, the
men of Israel, came to Jerusalem, and
Ahith′ophel with him. 16And when Hu′shai
the Ar′chite, David's friend, came to
Ab′salom, Hushai said to Absalom, "Long
live the king! Long live the king!" 17And
Ab′salom said to Hu′shai, "Is this your
loyalty to your friend? Why did you not
go with your friend?" 18And Hu′shai said
to Ab′salom, "No; for whom the LORD and
this people and all the men of Israel have
chosen, his I will be, and with him I will
remain. 19And again, whom should I serve?
Should it not be his son? As I have served
your father, so I will serve you."

20Then Ab′salom said to Ahith′ophel,
"Give your counsel; what shall we do?"
21Ahith′ophel said to Ab′salom, "Go in to
your father's concubines, whom he has
left to keep the house; and all Israel will
hear that you have made yourself odious
to your father, and the hands of all who
are with you will be strengthened." 22So
they pitched a tent for Ab′salom upon the
roof; and Absalom went in to his father's
concubines in the sight of all Israel.
23Now in those days the counsel which
Ahith′ophel gave was as if one consulted
the oracle of God; so was all the counsel
of Ahithophel esteemed, both by David
and by Ab′salom.

17 Moreover Ahith′ophel said to Ab′salom,
"Let me choose twelve thousand men,
and I will set out and pursue David tonight.
2I will come upon him while he is weary and
discouraged, and throw him into a panic;
and all the people who are with him will
flee. I will strike down the king only, 3and
I will bring all the people back to you as a
bride comes home to her husband. You seek
the life of only one man, and all the people
will be at peace." 4And the advice pleased
Ab′salom and all the elders of Israel.

5Then Ab′salom said, "Call Hu′shai the
Ar′chite also, and let us hear what he
has to say." 6And when Hu′shai came to
Ab′salom, Absalom said to him, "Thus
has Ahith′ophel spoken; shall we do as he
advises? If not, you speak." 7Then Hu′shai
said to Ab′salom, "This time the counsel
which Ahith′ophel has given is not good."
8Hu′shai said moreover, "You know that
your father and his men are mighty men,
and that they are enraged, like a bear
robbed of her cubs in the field. Besides,
your father is expert in war; he will not
spend the night with the people. 9Behold,
even now he has hidden himself in one
of the pits, or in some other place. And
when some of the people fall at the first
attack, whoever hears it will say, 'There
has been a slaughter among the people
who follow Ab′salom.' 10Then even the
valiant man, whose heart is like the heart
of a lion, will utterly melt with fear; for all
Israel knows that your father is a mighty
man, and that those who are with him are
valiant men. 11But my counsel is that all
Israel be gathered to you, from Dan to
Be′er-she′ba, as the sand by the sea for
multitude, and that you go to battle in
person. 12So we shall come upon him in
some place where he is to be found, and
we shall light upon him as the dew falls
on the ground; and of him and all the
men with him not one will be left. 13If he
withdraws into a city, then all Israel will
bring ropes to that city, and we shall drag
it into the valley, until not even a pebble
is to be found there." 14And Ab′salom and
all the men of Israel said, "The counsel
of Hu′shai the Ar′chite is better than the
counsel of Ahith′ophel." For the LORD

had ordained to defeat the good counsel
of Ahithophel, so that the LORD might
bring evil upon Ab′salom.
15 Then Hu′shai said to Za′dok and
Abi′athar the priests, "Thus and so did
Ahith′ophel counsel Ab′salom and the
elders of Israel; and thus and so have I
counseled. 16 Now therefore send quickly
and tell David, 'Do not lodge tonight at
the fords of the wilderness, but by all
means pass over; lest the king and all the
people who are with him be swallowed
up.'" 17 Now Jonathan and Ahim′a-az were
waiting at En-ro′gel; a maidservant used to
go and tell them, and they would go and
tell King David; for they must not be seen
entering the city. 18 But a lad saw them, and
told Ab′salom; so both of them went away
quickly, and came to the house of a man at
Bahu′rim, who had a well in his courtyard;
and they went down into it. 19 And the
woman took and spread a covering over
the well's mouth, and scattered grain upon
it; and nothing was known of it. 20 When
Ab′salom's servants came to the woman at
the house, they said, "Where are Ahim′a-
az and Jonathan?" And the woman said
to them, "They have gone over the brook
of water." And when they had sought
and could not find them, they returned
to Jerusalem.
21 After they had gone, the men came up
out of the well, and went and told King
David. They said to David, "Arise, and go
quickly over the water; for thus and so has
Ahith′ophel counseled against you." 22 Then
David arose, and all the people who were
with him, and they crossed the Jordan; by
daybreak not one was left who had not
crossed the Jordan.
23 When Ahith′ophel saw that his counsel
was not followed, he saddled his donkey,
and went off home to his own city. And he
set his house in order, and hanged himself;
and he died, and was buried in the tomb of
his father.
24 Then David came to Ma′hana′im. And
Ab′salom crossed the Jordan with all the men
of Israel. 25 Now Ab′salom had set Ama′sa
over the army instead of Jo′ab. Amasa was
the son of a man named Ithra the Ish′maelite,
who had married Ab′igail the daughter of
Na′hash, sister of Zeru′iah, Jo′ab's mother.
26 And Israel and Ab′salom encamped in the
land of Gilead.
27 When David came to Ma′hana′im, Shobi
the son of Na′hash from Rabbah of the
Am′monites, and Ma′chir the son of
Am′mi-el from Lo-de′bar, and Barzil′lai
the Gileadite from Ro′gelim, 28 brought
beds, basins, and earthen vessels, wheat,
barley, meal, parched grain, beans and
lentils, 29 honey and curds and sheep and
cheese from the herd, for David and the
people with him to eat; for they said, "The
people are hungry and weary and thirsty in
the wilderness."

PSALM 112 [111]

Praise the LORD!
Blessed is the man who fears the LORD,
who greatly delights in
his commandments!
2 His descendants will be mighty in the land;
the generation of the upright will
be blessed.
3 Wealth and riches are in his house;
and his righteousness endures for ever.
4 Light rises in the darkness for the upright;
the LORD is gracious, merciful,
and righteous.
5 It is well with the man who deals generously
and lends,
who conducts his affairs with justice.
6 For the righteous will never be moved;
he will be remembered for ever.
7 He is not afraid of evil tidings;
his heart is firm, trusting in the LORD.
8 His heart is steady, he will not be afraid,
until he sees his desire on his adversaries.
9 He has distributed freely, he has given to
the poor;
his righteousness endures for ever;
his horn is exalted in honor.
10 The wicked man sees it and is angry;
he gnashes his teeth and melts away;
the desire of the wicked man comes
to nought.

JOHN 4

Now when the Lord knew that the Pharisees had heard that Jesus was making and baptizing more disciples than John 2(although Jesus himself did not baptize, but only his disciples), 3he left Judea and departed again to Galilee. 4He had to pass through Samar′ia. 5So he came to a city of Samar′ia, called Sy′char, near the field that Jacob gave to his son Joseph. 6Jacob's well was there, and so Jesus, wearied as he was with his journey, sat down beside the well. It was about the sixth hour.

7There came a woman of Samar′ia to draw water. Jesus said to her, "Give me a drink." 8For his disciples had gone away into the city to buy food. 9The Samaritan woman said to him, "How is it that you, a Jew, ask a drink of me, a woman of Samar′ia?" For Jews have no dealings with Samaritans. 10Jesus answered her, "If you knew the gift of God, and who it is that is saying to you, 'Give me a drink,' you would have asked him and he would have given you living water." 11The woman said to him, "Sir, you have nothing to draw with, and the well is deep; where do you get that living water? 12Are you greater than our father Jacob, who gave us the well, and drank from it himself, and his sons, and his cattle?" 13Jesus said to her, "Every one who drinks of this water will thirst again, 14but whoever drinks of the water that I shall give him will never thirst; the water that I shall give him will become in him a spring of water welling up to eternal life." 15The woman said to him, "Sir, give me this water, that I may not thirst, nor come here to draw."

16Jesus said to her, "Go, call your husband, and come here." 17The woman answered him, "I have no husband." Jesus said to her, "You are right in saying, 'I have no husband'; 18for you have had five husbands, and he whom you now have is not your husband; this you said truly." 19The woman said to him, "Sir, I perceive that you are a prophet. 20Our fathers worshiped on this mountain; and you say that in Jerusalem is the place where men ought to worship." 21Jesus said to her, "Woman, believe me, the hour is coming when neither on this mountain nor in Jerusalem will you worship the Father. 22You worship what you do not know; we worship what we know, for salvation is from the Jews. 23But the hour is coming, and now is, when the true worshipers will worship the Father in spirit and truth, for such the Father seeks to worship him. 24God is spirit, and those who worship him must worship in spirit and truth." 25The woman said to him, "I know that Messiah is coming (he who is called Christ); when he comes, he will show us all things." 26Jesus said to her, "I who speak to you am he."

27Just then his disciples came. They marveled that he was talking with a woman, but none said, "What do you wish?" or, "Why are you talking with her?" 28So the woman left her water jar, and went away into the city, and said to the people, 29"Come, see a man who told me all that I ever did. Can this be the Christ?" 30They went out of the city and were coming to him.

REFLECTION

When everything falls apart, it can be hard to keep trusting in the Lord. Yet Psalm 112 tells us about the righteous man: "He is not afraid of evil tidings; his heart is firm, trusting in the LORD" (Ps 112:7). David, at this point in the story, has seemingly lost his kingdom to his rebellious son, Absalom. The evil sequence of events started with David's lust after Bathsheba and led to the rape of Tamar and the death of Amnon. Now Absalom, in seeking to steal the throne, sleeps with David's concubines on the palace roof—the very place where David was viewing Bathsheba bathing. Yet David remains steadfast even in his downfall, allowing himself to be publicly cursed (see 2 Sm 16:10). The Lord protects David and causes the advice of his spy, Hushai, to influence Absalom (see 17:14). David's fearlessness exhibits a trust in the Lord mirrored by the Samaritan woman. Though she may have been dismayed at

Jesus's recounting of the struggles, sins, and failures in her personal life, she does not shy away from the encounter with the Lord. And as a result, she recognizes the truth of Jesus's self-revelation as the Messiah and invites all her neighbors to come and meet him (see Jn 4:29). Is your trust in the Lord shaken by bad news? Or do you pray for strength and trust the Lord in spite of the difficulty?

May 16

2 SAMUEL 18

Then David mustered the men who were with him, and set over them commanders of thousands and commanders of hundreds. 2And David sent forth the army, one third under the command of Jo′ab, one third
under the command of Abi′shai the son of Zeru′iah, Jo′ab's brother, and one third under the command of Ittai the Gittite. And the king said to the men, "I myself will also go out with you." 3But the men said, "You shall not go out. For if we flee, they will not care about us. If half of us die, they will not care about us. But you are worth ten thousand of us; therefore it is better that you send us help from the city." 4The king said to them, "Whatever seems best to you I will do." So the king stood at the side of the gate, while all the army marched out by hundreds and by thousands. 5And the king ordered Jo′ab and Abi′shai and Ittai, "Deal gently for my sake with the young man Ab′salom." And all the people heard when the king gave orders to all the commanders about Absalom.

6So the army went out into the field against Israel; and the battle was fought in the forest of E′phraim. 7And the men of Israel were defeated there by the servants of David, and the slaughter there was great on that day, twenty thousand men. 8The battle spread over the face of all the country; and the forest devoured more people that day than the sword.

9And Ab′salom chanced to meet the servants of David. Absalom was riding upon his mule, and the mule went under the thick branches of a great oak, and his head caught fast in the oak, and he was left hanging between heaven and earth, while the mule that was under him went on. 10And a certain man saw it, and told Jo′ab, "Behold, I saw Ab′salom hanging in an oak." 11Jo′ab said to the man who told him, "What, you saw him! Why then did you not strike him there to the ground? I would have been glad to give you ten pieces of silver and a belt." 12But the man said to Jo′ab, "Even if I felt in my hand the weight of a thousand pieces of silver, I would not put forth my hand against the king's son; for in our hearing the king commanded you and Abi′shai and Ittai, 'For my sake protect the young man Ab′salom.' 13On the other hand, if I had dealt treacherously against his life (and there is nothing hidden from the king), then you yourself would have stood aloof." 14Jo′ab said, "I will not waste time like this with you." And he took three darts in his hand, and thrust them into the heart of Ab′salom, while he was still alive in the oak. 15And ten young men, Jo′ab's armor-bearers, surrounded Ab′salom and struck him, and killed him.

16Then Jo′ab blew the trumpet, and the troops came back from pursuing Israel; for Joab restrained them. 17And they took Ab′salom, and threw him into a great pit in the forest, and raised over him a very great heap of stones; and all Israel fled every one to his own home. 18Now Ab′salom in his lifetime had taken and set up for himself the pillar which is in the King's Valley, for he said, "I have no son to keep my name in remembrance"; he called the pillar after his own name, and it is called Absalom's monument to this day.

19Then said Ahim′a-az the son of Za′dok, "Let me run, and carry tidings to the king that the LORD has delivered him from the power of his enemies." 20And Jo′ab said to him, "You are not to carry tidings today;

you may carry tidings another day, but
today you shall carry no tidings, because
the king's son is dead." 21Then Jo'ab said to
the Cushite, "Go, tell the king what you have
seen." The Cushite bowed before Jo'ab, and
ran. 22Then Ahim'a-az the son of Za'dok said
again to Jo'ab, "Come what may, let me also
run after the Cushite." And Jo'ab said, "Why
will you run, my son, seeing that you will
have no reward for the tidings?" 23"Come
what may," he said, "I will run." So he said to
him, "Run." Then Ahim'a-az ran by the way
of the plain, and outran the Cushite.

24Now David was sitting between the two
gates; and the watchman went up to the
roof of the gate by the wall, and when he
lifted up his eyes and looked, he saw a man
running alone. 25And the watchman called
out and told the king. And the king said, "If
he is alone, there are tidings in his mouth."
And he came apace, and drew near. 26And
the watchman saw another man running;
and the watchman called to the gate and
said, "See, another man running alone!"
The king said, "He also brings tidings."
27And the watchman said, "I think the
running of the foremost is like the running
of Ahim'a-az the son of Za'dok." And the
king said, "He is a good man, and comes
with good tidings."

28Then Ahim'a-az cried out to the king,
"All is well." And he bowed before the king
with his face to the earth, and said, "Blessed
be the LORD your God, who has delivered up
the men who raised their hand against my
lord the king." 29And the king said, "Is it well
with the young man Ab'salom?" Ahim'a-az
answered, "When Jo'ab sent your servant, I
saw a great tumult, but I do not know what
it was." 30And the king said, "Turn aside, and
stand here." So he turned aside, and stood
still.

31And behold, the Cushite came; and the
Cushite said, "Good tidings for my lord the
king! For the LORD has delivered you this day
from the power of all who rose up against
you." 32The king said to the Cushite, "Is it
well with the young man Ab'salom?" And
the Cushite answered, "May the enemies of
my lord the king, and all who rise up against
you for evil, be like that young man." 33And
the king was deeply moved, and went up to
the chamber over the gate, and wept; and as
he went, he said, "O my son Ab'salom, my
son, my son Absalom! Would I had died
instead of you, O Absalom, my son, my son!"

PSALM 113 [112]

Praise the LORD!
Praise, O servants of the LORD,
praise the name of the LORD!

2Blessed be the name of the LORD
from this time forth and for evermore!
3From the rising of the sun to its setting
the name of the LORD is to be praised!
4The LORD is high above all nations,
and his glory above the heavens!

5Who is like the LORD our God,
who is seated on high,
6who looks far down
upon the heavens and the earth?
7He raises the poor from the dust,
and lifts the needy from the ash heap,
8to make them sit with princes,
with the princes of his people.
9He gives the barren woman a home,
making her the joyous mother
of children.
Praise the LORD!

JOHN 4

31Meanwhile the disciples begged
him, saying, "Rabbi, eat." 32But he
said to them, "I have food to eat
of which you do not know." 33So the dis-
ciples said to one another, "Has any
one brought him food?" 34Jesus said to
them, "My food is to do the will of him who
sent me, and to accomplish his work. 35Do
you not say, 'There are yet four months, then
comes the harvest'? I tell you, lift up your
eyes, and see how the fields are already white
for harvest. 36He who reaps receives wages,

and gathers fruit for eternal life, so that sower and reaper may rejoice together. 37For here the saying holds true, 'One sows and another reaps.' 38I sent you to reap that for which you did not labor; others have labored, and you have entered into their labor."

39Many Samaritans from that city believed in him because of the woman's testimony, "He told me all that I ever did." 40So when the Samaritans came to him, they asked him to stay with them; and he stayed there two days. 41And many more believed because of his word. 42They said to the woman, "It is no longer because of your words that we believe, for we have heard for ourselves, and we know that this is indeed the Savior of the world."

43After the two days he departed to Galilee. 44For Jesus himself testified that a prophet has no honor in his own country. 45So when he came to Galilee, the Galileans welcomed him, having seen all that he had done in Jerusalem at the feast, for they too had gone to the feast.

46So he came again to Cana in Galilee, where he had made the water wine. And at Caper′na-um there was an official whose son was ill. 47When he heard that Jesus had come from Judea to Galilee, he went and begged him to come down and heal his son, for he was at the point of death. 48Jesus therefore said to him, "Unless you see signs and wonders you will not believe." 49The official said to him, "Sir, come down before my child dies." 50Jesus said to him, "Go; your son will live." The man believed the word that Jesus spoke to him and went his way. 51As he was going down, his servants met him and told him that his son was living. 52So he asked them the hour when he began to mend, and they said to him, "Yesterday at the seventh hour the fever left him." 53The father knew that was the hour when Jesus had said to him, "Your son will live"; and he himself believed, and all his household. 54This was now the second sign that Jesus did when he had come from Judea to Galilee.

5 After this there was a feast of the Jews, and Jesus went up to Jerusalem.

2Now there is in Jerusalem by the Sheep Gate a pool, in Hebrew called Beth-za′tha, which has five porticoes. 3In these lay a multitude of invalids, blind, lame, paralyzed.* 5One man was there, who had been ill for thirty-eight years. 6When Jesus saw him and knew that he had been lying there a long time, he said to him, "Do you want to be healed?" 7The sick man answered him, "Sir, I have no man to put me into the pool when the water is troubled, and while I am going another steps down before me." 8Jesus said to him, "Rise, take up your pallet, and walk." 9And at once the man was healed, and he took up his pallet and walked.

Now that day was the sabbath. 10So the Jews said to the man who was cured, "It is the sabbath, it is not lawful for you to carry your pallet." 11But he answered them, "The man who healed me said to me, 'Take up your pallet, and walk.'" 12They asked him, "Who is the man who said to you, 'Take up your pallet, and walk'?" 13Now the man who had been healed did not know who it was, for Jesus had withdrawn, as there was a crowd in the place. 14Afterward, Jesus found him in the temple, and said to him, "See, you are well! Sin no more, that nothing worse befall you." 15The man went away and told the Jews that it was Jesus who had healed him. 16And this was why the Jews persecuted Jesus, because he did this on the sabbath. 17But Jesus answered them, "My Father is working still, and I am working." 18This was why the Jews sought all the more to kill him, because he not only broke the sabbath but also called God his Father, making himself equal with God.

19Jesus said to them, "Truly, truly, I say to you, the Son can do nothing of his own accord, but only what he sees the Father doing; for whatever he does, that the Son does likewise. 20For the Father loves the Son, and shows him all that he himself is doing; and greater works than these will he show him, that you may marvel. 21For as the

* Other ancient authorities insert, wholly or in part, *waiting for the moving of the water; 4for an angel of the Lord went down at certain seasons into the pool, and troubled the water; whoever stepped in first after the troubling of the water was healed of whatever disease he had.*

Father raises the dead and gives them life,
so also the Son gives life to whom he will.
[22]The Father judges no one, but has given all
judgment to the Son, [23]that all may honor
the Son, even as they honor the Father. He
who does not honor the Son does not honor
the Father who sent him. [24]Truly, truly, I say
to you, he who hears my word and believes
him who sent me, has eternal life; he does
not come into judgment, but has passed
from death to life.
[25]"Truly, truly, I say to you, the hour is
coming, and now is, when the dead will
hear the voice of the Son of God, and those
who hear will live. [26]For as the Father has
life in himself, so he has granted the Son
also to have life in himself, [27]and has given
him authority to execute judgment, because
he is the Son of man. [28]Do not marvel at
this; for the hour is coming when all who
are in the tombs will hear his voice [29]and
come forth, those who have done good, to
the resurrection of life, and those who have
done evil, to the resurrection of judgment.

REFLECTION

The Lord is a God who reverses fortunes, who lifts up the lowly and brings down the mighty. "He raises the poor from the dust, and lifts the needy from the ash heap; to make them sit with princes" (Ps 113:7–8). In today's readings, we find two fathers worried over their sons. Though he is at war with Absalom, David is troubled over his son. When he finally hears that Absalom is dead, David blurts out, "O my son Absalom, my son, my son Absalom! Would I had died instead of you, O Absalom, my son!" (2 Sm 18:33). David's beautiful and moving mourning for his son shows the sincerity of his love even in the face of his son's rebellion. David the mighty had been brought low by Absalom's rebellion, but now Absalom the usurper lies dead. In the reading from John, we find an official who humbles himself and begs Jesus, "Sir, come down before my child dies" (Jn 4:49). Jesus reverses the man's fortunes: "Go; your son will live" (v. 50). Indeed, we should rely on the Lord who reverses fortunes and can raise us up. Are you confident in the Lord's power to turn your world right-side up?

May 17

2 SAMUEL 19

**It was told Jo′ab, "Behold, the
king is weeping and mourning
for Ab′salom." [2]So the victory that day
was turned into mourning for all the
people; for the people heard that day,**
"The king is grieving for his son." [3]And the
people stole into the city that day as people
steal in who are ashamed when they flee in
battle. [4]The king covered his face, and the
king cried with a loud voice, "O my son
Ab′salom, O Absalom, my son, my son!"
[5]Then Jo′ab came into the house to the king,
and said, "You have today covered with
shame the faces of all your servants, who
have this day saved your life, and the lives
of your sons and your daughters, and the
lives of your wives and your concubines,
[6]because you love those who hate you and
hate those who love you. For you have made
it clear today that commanders and servants
are nothing to you; for today I perceive that
if Ab′salom were alive and all of us were
dead today, then you would be pleased.
[7]Now therefore arise, go out and speak
kindly to your servants; for I swear by the
LORD, if you do not go, not a man will stay
with you this night; and this will be worse
for you than all the evil that has come upon
you from your youth until now." [8]Then the
king arose, and took his seat in the gate.
And the people were all told, "Behold, the
king is sitting in the gate"; and all the people
came before the king.
Now Israel had fled every man to his own
home. [9]And all the people were at strife
throughout all the tribes of Israel, saying,
"The king delivered us from the hand of our
enemies, and saved us from the hand of the
Philis′tines; and now he has fled out of the
land from Ab′salom. [10]But Ab′salom, whom
we anointed over us, is dead in battle. Now
therefore why do you say nothing about
bringing the king back?"

[11]And King David sent this message to Za′dok and Abi′athar the priests, "Say to the elders of Judah, 'Why should you be the last to bring the king back to his house, when the word of all Israel has come to the king? [12]You are my kinsmen, you are my bone and my flesh; why then should you be the last to bring back the king?' [13]And say to Ama′sa, 'Are you not my bone and my flesh? God do so to me, and more also, if you are not commander of my army henceforth in place of Jo′ab.'" [14]And he swayed the heart of all the men of Judah as one man; so that they sent word to the king, "Return, both you and all your servants." [15]So the king came back to the Jordan; and Judah came to Gilgal to meet the king and to bring the king over the Jordan.

[16]And Shim′e-i the son of Gera, the Benjaminite, from Bahu′rim, made haste to come down with the men of Judah to meet King David; [17]and with him were a thousand men from Benjamin. And Zi′ba the servant of the house of Saul, with his fifteen sons and his twenty servants, rushed down to the Jordan before the king, [18]and they crossed the ford to bring over the king's household, and to do his pleasure. And Shim′e-i the son of Gera fell down before the king, as he was about to cross the Jordan, [19]and said to the king, "Let not my lord hold me guilty or remember how your servant did wrong on the day my lord the king left Jerusalem; let not the king bear it in mind. [20]For your servant knows that I have sinned; therefore, behold, I have come this day, the first of all the house of Joseph to come down to meet my lord the king." [21]Abi′shai the son of Zeru′iah answered, "Shall not Shim′e-i be put to death for this, because he cursed the LORD's anointed?" [22]But David said, "What have I to do with you, you sons of Zeru′iah, that you should this day be as an adversary to me? Shall any one be put to death in Israel this day? For do I not know that I am this day king over Israel?" [23]And the king said to Shim′e-i, "You shall not die." And the king gave him his oath.

[24]And Mephib′osheth the son of Saul came down to meet the king; he had neither dressed his feet, nor trimmed his beard, nor washed his clothes, from the day the king departed until the day he came back in safety. [25]And when he came from Jerusalem to meet the king, the king said to him, "Why did you not go with me, Mephib′osheth?" [26]He answered, "My lord, O king, my servant deceived me; for your servant said to him, 'Saddle a donkey for me, that I may ride upon it and go with the king.' For your servant is lame. [27]He has slandered your servant to my lord the king. But my lord the king is like the angel of God; do therefore what seems good to you. [28]For all my father's house were but men doomed to death before my lord the king; but you set your servant among those who eat at your table. What further right have I, then, to cry to the king?" [29]And the king said to him, "Why speak any more of your affairs? I have decided: you and Zi′ba shall divide the land." [30]And Mephib′osheth said to the king, "Oh, let him take it all, since my lord the king has come safely home."

[31]Now Barzil′lai the Gileadite had come down from Ro′gelim; and he went on with the king to the Jordan, to escort him over the Jordan. [32]Barzil′lai was a very aged man, eighty years old; and he had provided the king with food while he stayed at Ma′′hana′im; for he was a very wealthy man. [33]And the king said to Barzil′lai, "Come over with me, and I will provide for you with me in Jerusalem." [34]But Barzil′lai said to the king, "How many years have I still to live, that I should go up with the king to Jerusalem? [35]I am this day eighty years old; can I discern what is pleasant and what is not? Can your servant taste what he eats or what he drinks? Can I still listen to the voice of singing men and singing women? Why then should your servant be an added burden to my lord the king? [36]Your servant will go a little way over the Jordan with the king. Why should the king recompense me with such a reward? [37]Please let your servant return, that I may die in my own city, near the grave of my father and my mother. But here is your servant Chimham; let him go over with my lord the king; and do for him whatever seems good to you." [38]And the king answered, "Chimham shall go over

with me, and I will do for him whatever
seems good to you; and all that you desire
of me I will do for you." 39Then all the
people went over the Jordan, and the king
went over; and the king kissed Barzil'lai
and blessed him, and he returned to his
own home. 40The king went on to Gilgal,
and Chimham went on with him; all the
people of Judah, and also half the sons of
Israel, brought the king on his way.
41Then all the men of Israel came to the
king, and said to the king, "Why have our
brethren the men of Judah stolen you away,
and brought the king and his household over
the Jordan, and all David's men with him?"
42All the men of Judah answered the men of
Israel, "Because the king is near of kin to us.
Why then are you angry over this matter?
Have we eaten at all at the king's expense?
Or has he given us any gift?" 43And the men
of Israel answered the men of Judah, "We
have ten shares in the king, and in David
also we have more than you. Why then did
you despise us? Were we not the first to
speak of bringing back our king?" But the
words of the men of Judah were fiercer than
the words of the men of Israel.

PSALM 114 [113]

When Israel went forth from Egypt,
the house of Jacob from a people of
strange language,
2Judah became his sanctuary,
Israel his dominion.

3The sea looked and fled,
Jordan turned back.
4The mountains skipped like rams,
the hills like lambs.

5What ails you, O sea, that you flee?
O Jordan, that you turn back?
6O mountains, that you skip like rams?
O hills, like lambs?

7Tremble, O earth, at the presence of
the LORD,
at the presence of the God of Jacob,
8who turns the rock into a pool of water,
the flint into a spring of water.

JOHN 5

30**"I can do nothing on my own
authority; as I hear, I judge; and
my judgment is just, because I seek
not my own will but the will of him**
who sent me. 31If I bear witness to myself,
my testimony is not true; 32there is another
who bears witness to me, and I know that
the testimony which he bears to me is true.
33You sent to John, and he has borne witness
to the truth. 34Not that the testimony which
I receive is from man; but I say this that
you may be saved. 35He was a burning and
shining lamp, and you were willing to rejoice
for a while in his light. 36But the testimony
which I have is greater than that of John; for
the works which the Father has granted me
to accomplish, these very works which I am
doing, bear me witness that the Father has
sent me. 37And the Father who sent me has
himself borne witness to me. His voice you
have never heard, his form you have never
seen; 38and you do not have his word abiding
in you, for you do not believe him whom he
has sent. 39You search the Scriptures, because
you think that in them you have eternal life;
and it is they that bear witness to me; 40yet
you refuse to come to me that you may have
life. 41I do not receive glory from men. 42But
I know that you have not the love of God
within you. 43I have come in my Father's
name, and you do not receive me; if another
comes in his own name, him you will receive.
44How can you believe, who receive glory
from one another and do not seek the glory
that comes from the only God? 45Do not
think that I shall accuse you to the Father;
it is Moses who accuses you, on whom you
set your hope. 46If you believed Moses, you
would believe me, for he wrote of me. 47But if
you do not believe his writings, how will you
believe my words?"

6 After this Jesus went to the other side
of the Sea of Galilee, which is the Sea

of Tibe´ri-as. 2And a multitude followed
him, because they saw the signs which he
did on those who were diseased. 3Jesus
went up into the hills, and there sat down
with his disciples. 4Now the Passover, the
feast of the Jews, was at hand. 5Lifting up
his eyes, then, and seeing that a multitude
was coming to him, Jesus said to Philip,
"How are we to buy bread, so that these
people may eat?" 6This he said to test
him, for he himself knew what he would
do. 7Philip answered him, "Two hundred
denarii would not buy enough bread for
each of them to get a little." 8One of his
disciples, Andrew, Simon Peter's brother,
said to him, 9"There is a lad here who has
five barley loaves and two fish; but what
are they among so many?" 10Jesus said,
"Make the people sit down." Now there
was much grass in the place; so the men
sat down, in number about five thousand.
11Jesus then took the loaves, and when he
had given thanks, he distributed them to
those who were seated; so also the fish,
as much as they wanted. 12And when they
had eaten their fill, he told his disciples,
"Gather up the fragments left over, that
nothing may be lost." 13So they gathered
them up and filled twelve baskets with
fragments from the five barley loaves,
left by those who had eaten. 14When the
people saw the sign which he had done,
they said, "This is indeed the prophet
who is to come into the world!"

15Perceiving then that they were about to
come and take him by force to make him
king, Jesus withdrew again to the hills by
himself.

16When evening came, his disciples went
down to the sea, 17got into a boat, and started
across the sea to Caper´na-um. It was now
dark, and Jesus had not yet come to them.
18The sea rose because a strong wind was
blowing. 19When they had rowed about three
or four miles, they saw Jesus walking on the
sea and drawing near to the boat. They were
frightened, 20but he said to them, "It is I; do
not be afraid." 21Then they were glad to take
him into the boat, and immediately the boat
was at the land to which they were going.

REFLECTION

David's prolonged mourning over Absalom's death brings a rebuke from his army commander, Joab: "You love those who hate you and hate those who love you" (2 Sm 19:6). From Joab's perspective, David is disloyal to those who fought on his behalf, but loyal to those who rebelled against him. Too often we show such divided loyalty in our relationship with God, loving him and seeking his will one day, then rebelling and seeking only our own desires the next. When David returns to Jerusalem, he receives the repentant rebels back, forgiving them and healing the relationship, just as God desires to do for us when we have turned away from him. Jesus tells us, "Do not be afraid" (Jn 6:20) and calls us to follow his example: "I seek not my will but the will of him who sent me" (5:30). Jesus shows us that happiness is to be found in surrender to the will of his Father, who is our Father, too. Today, how can you better conform your will to that of your Father in Heaven who loves you?

May 18

2 SAMUEL 20

Now there happened to be there a worthless fellow, whose name was Sheba, the son of Bichri, a Benjaminite; and he blew the trumpet, and said,

"We have no portion in David,
and we have no inheritance in the son
of Jesse;
every man to his tents, O Israel!"

2So all the men of Israel withdrew from
David, and followed Sheba the son of Bichri;
but the men of Judah followed their king
steadfastly from the Jordan to Jerusalem.

3And David came to his house at Jerusalem;
and the king took the ten concubines whom
he had left to care for the house, and put
them in a house under guard, and provided

for them, but did not go in to them. So they
were shut up until the day of their death,
living as if in widowhood.
4Then the king said to Ama´sa, "Call the
men of Judah together to me within three
days, and be here yourself." 5So Ama´sa went
to summon Judah; but he delayed beyond
the set time which had been appointed him.
6And David said to Abi´shai, "Now Sheba
the son of Bichri will do us more harm
than Ab´salom; take your lord's servants
and pursue him, lest he get himself fortified
cities, and cause us trouble." 7And there went
out after Abi´shai, Jo´ab and the Cher´ethites
and the Pel´ethites, and all the mighty men;
they went out from Jerusalem to pursue
Sheba the son of Bichri. 8When they were at
the great stone which is in Gib´eon, Ama´sa
came to meet them. Now Jo´ab was wearing
a soldier's garment, and over it was a belt
with a sword in its sheath fastened upon
his loins, and as he went forward it fell out.
9And Jo´ab said to Ama´sa, "Is it well with
you, my brother?" And Joab took Amasa by
the beard with his right hand to kiss him.
10But Ama´sa did not observe the sword
which was in Jo´ab's hand; so Joab struck
him with it in the body, and shed his bowels
to the ground, without striking a second
blow; and he died.

Then Joab and Abi´shai his brother
pursued Sheba the son of Bichri. 11And one
of Jo´ab's men took his stand by Ama´sa,
and said, "Whoever favors Joab, and whoever is for David, let him follow Joab."
12And Ama´sa lay wallowing in his blood
in the highway. And any one who came by,
seeing him, stopped; and when the man
saw that all the people stopped, he carried
Amasa out of the highway into the field,
and threw a garment over him. 13When he
was taken out of the highway, all the people
went on after Jo´ab to pursue Sheba the son
of Bichri.
14And Sheba passed through all the tribes
of Israel to Abel of Beth-ma´acah; and all
the Bichrites assembled, and followed him
in. 15And all the men who were with Jo´ab
came and besieged him in Abel of Beth-
ma´acah; they cast up a mound against
the city, and it stood against the rampart;
and they were battering the wall, to throw
it down. 16Then a wise woman called from
the city, "Hear! Hear! Tell Jo´ab, 'Come
here, that I may speak to you.'" 17And he
came near her; and the woman said, "Are
you Jo´ab?" He answered, "I am." Then she
said to him, "Listen to the words of your
maidservant." And he answered, "I am
listening." 18Then she said, "They were wont
to say in old time, 'Let them but ask counsel
at Abel'; and so they settled a matter. 19I am
one of those who are peaceable and faithful
in Israel; you seek to destroy a city which is
a mother in Israel; why will you swallow up
the heritage of the LORD?" 20Jo´ab answered,
"Far be it from me, far be it, that I should
swallow up or destroy! 21That is not true.
But a man of the hill country of E´phraim,
called Sheba the son of Bichri, has lifted up
his hand against King David; give up him
alone, and I will withdraw from the city."
And the woman said to Jo´ab, "Behold, his
head shall be thrown to you over the wall."
22Then the woman went to all the people in
her wisdom. And they cut off the head of
Sheba the son of Bichri, and threw it out
to Jo´ab. So he blew the trumpet, and they
dispersed from the city, every man to his
home. And Joab returned to Jerusalem to
the king.
23Now Jo´ab was in command of all the army
of Israel; and Bena´iah the son of Jehoi´ada
was in command of the Cher´ethites and the
Pel´ethites; 24and Ador´am was in charge of
the forced labor; and Jehosh´aphat the son
of Ahi´lud was the recorder; 25and Sheva was
secretary; and Za´dok and Abi´athar were
priests; 26and Ira the Ja´irite was also David's
priest.

21 Now there was a famine in the days
of David for three years, year after year;
and David sought the face of the LORD. And
the LORD said, "There is bloodguilt on Saul and
on his house, because he put the Gib´eonites
to death." 2So the king called the Gib´eonites.
Now the Gibeonites were not of the sons of
Israel, but of the remnant of the Am´orites;
although the sons of Israel had sworn to spare
them, Saul had sought to slay them in his zeal

for the sons of Israel and Judah. 3And David
said to the Gib′eonites, "What shall I do for
you? And how shall I make expiation, that
you may bless the heritage of the LORD?" 4The
Gib′eonites said to him, "It is not a matter of
silver or gold between us and Saul or his house;
neither is it for us to put any man to death in
Israel." And he said, "What do you say that
I shall do for you?" 5They said to the king,
"The man who consumed us and planned to
destroy us, so that we should have no place in
all the territory of Israel, 6let seven of his sons
be given to us, so that we may hang them up
before the LORD at Gib′eon on the mountain
of the LORD." And the king said, "I will
give them."

7But the king spared Mephib′osheth, the
son of Saul's son Jonathan, because of the
oath of the LORD which was between them,
between David and Jonathan the son of Saul.
8The king took the two sons of Rizpah the
daughter of Ai′ah, whom she bore to Saul,
Armo′ni and Mephib′osheth; and the five
sons of Merab the daughter of Saul, whom
she bore to A′dri-el the son of Barzil′lai the
Meho′lathite; 9and he gave them into the
hands of the Gib′eonites, and they hanged
them on the mountain before the LORD, and
the seven of them perished together. They
were put to death in the first days of harvest,
at the beginning of barley harvest.

10Then Rizpah the daughter of Ai′ah took
sackcloth, and spread it for herself on the
rock, from the beginning of harvest until
rain fell upon them from the heavens;
and she did not allow the birds of the air
to come upon them by day, or the beasts
of the field by night. 11When David was
told what Rizpah the daughter of Ai′ah,
the concubine of Saul, had done, 12David
went and took the bones of Saul and the
bones of his son Jonathan from the men of
Ja′besh-gil′ead, who had stolen them from
the public square of Beth-shan, where
the Philis′tines had hanged them, on the
day the Philistines killed Saul on Gilbo′a;
13and he brought up from there the bones
of Saul and the bones of his son Jonathan;
and they gathered the bones of those who
were hanged. 14And they buried the bones
of Saul and his son Jonathan in the land
of Benjamin in Ze′la, in the tomb of Kish
his father; and they did all that the king
commanded. And after that God heeded
supplications for the land.

15The Philis′tines had war again with Israel,
and David went down together with his servants, and they fought against the Philistines;
and David grew weary. 16And Ish′bi-be′nob,
one of the descendants of the giants, whose
spear weighed three hundred shekels of
bronze, and who was armed with a new sword,
thought to kill David. 17But Abi′shai the son
of Zeru′iah came to his aid, and attacked the
Philis′tine and killed him. Then David's men
adjured him, "You shall no more go out with
us to battle, lest you quench the lamp of Israel."

18After this there was again war with
the Philis′tines at Gob; then Sib′becai the
Hu′shathite slew Saph, who was one of
the descendants of the giants. 19And there
was again war with the Philis′tines at Gob;
and Elha′nan the son of Ja′are-or′egim, the
Bethlehemite, slew Goliath the Gittite, the
shaft of whose spear was like a weaver's
beam. 20And there was again war at Gath,
where there was a man of great stature, who
had six fingers on each hand, and six toes on
each foot, twenty-four in number; and he
also was descended from the giants. 21And
when he taunted Israel, Jonathan the son of
Shim′e-i, David's brother, slew him. 22These
four were descended from the giants in
Gath; and they fell by the hand of David and
by the hand of his servants.

PSALM 115

Not to us, O LORD, not to us,
but to your name give glory,
for the sake of your mercy and
your faithfulness!
2Why should the nations say,
"Where is their God?"

3Our God is in the heavens;
he does whatever he pleases.
4Their idols are silver and gold,
the work of men's hands.

5 They have mouths, but do not speak;
eyes, but do not see.
6 They have ears, but do not hear;
noses, but do not smell.
7 They have hands, but do not feel;
feet, but do not walk;
and they do not make a sound in
their throat.
8 Those who make them are like them;
so are all who trust in them.

9 O Israel, trust in the LORD!
He is their help and their shield.
10 O house of Aaron, put your trust in the LORD!
He is their help and their shield.
11 You who fear the LORD, trust in the LORD!
He is their help and their shield.

12 The LORD has been mindful of us; he will
bless us;
he will bless the house of Israel;
he will bless the house of Aaron;
13 he will bless those who fear the LORD,
both small and great.

14 May the LORD give you increase,
you and your children!
15 May you be blessed by the LORD,
who made heaven and earth!

16 The heavens are the LORD's heavens,
but the earth he has given to the sons
of men.
17 The dead do not praise the LORD,
nor do any that go down into silence.
18 But we will bless the LORD
from this time forth and for evermore.
Praise the LORD!

JOHN 6

22 On the next day the people who
remained on the other side of
the sea saw that there had been
only one boat there, and that Jesus had
not entered the boat with his disciples,
but that his disciples had gone away alone.
23 However, boats from Tibe′ri-as came
near the place where they ate the bread
after the Lord had given thanks. 24 So
when the people saw that Jesus was not
there, nor his disciples, they themselves
got into the boats and went to Caper′na-
um, seeking Jesus.
25 When they found him on the other
side of the sea, they said to him, "Rabbi,
when did you come here?" 26 Jesus
answered them, "Truly, truly, I say to
you, you seek me, not because you saw
signs, but because you ate your fill of the
loaves. 27 Do not labor for the food which
perishes, but for the food which endures
to eternal life, which the Son of man
will give to you; for on him has God the
Father set his seal." 28 Then they said to
him, "What must we do, to be doing the
works of God?" 29 Jesus answered them,
"This is the work of God, that you believe
in him whom he has sent." 30 So they said
to him, "Then what sign do you do, that
we may see, and believe you? What work
do you perform? 31 Our fathers ate the
manna in the wilderness; as it is written,
'He gave them bread from heaven to eat.'"
32 Jesus then said to them, "Truly, truly, I
say to you, it was not Moses who gave you
the bread from heaven; my Father gives
you the true bread from heaven. 33 For the
bread of God is that which comes down
from heaven, and gives life to the world."
34 They said to him, "Lord, give us this
bread always."
35 Jesus said to them, "I am the bread of
life; he who comes to me shall not hunger,
and he who believes in me shall never
thirst. 36 But I said to you that you have seen
me and yet do not believe. 37 All that the
Father gives me will come to me; and him
who comes to me I will not cast out. 38 For
I have come down from heaven, not to do
my own will, but the will of him who sent
me; 39 and this is the will of him who sent
me, that I should lose nothing of all that
he has given me, but raise it up at the last
day. 40 For this is the will of my Father, that
every one who sees the Son and believes
in him should have eternal life; and I will
raise him up at the last day."

REFLECTION

So many things in life clamor for our attention that it can be hard to keep our priorities straight and to spend our time doing the right things. It would be easy to keep focused on ourselves and try to accumulate as much money, fame, or power as possible. Yet, Scripture points in a different direction: "Not to us, O LORD, not to us, but to your name give glory" (Ps 115:1). The world is filled with glory-seekers, but God wants us to be glory-givers, those who give glory to him. Jesus points out that many of his followers are seeking him for the wrong reasons: "You seek me, not because you saw signs, but because you ate your fill of the loaves" (Jn 6:26). Jesus charges many in the crowd with coming after him just to fill their bellies with the bread he provides—a base, self-seeking motive. He redirects them, and us, in the right way: "This is the work of God, that you believe in him whom he has sent" (v. 29). What can you do today that will take the focus off of you, and give greater glory to God?

May 19

2 SAMUEL 22

And David spoke to the LORD the words of this song on the day when the LORD delivered him from the hand of all his enemies, and from the hand of Saul. [2]**He said,**

"The LORD is my rock, and my fortress,
and my deliverer,
[3] my God, my rock, in whom I
take refuge,
my shield and the horn of my salvation,
my stronghold and my refuge,
my savior; you save me from violence.
[4]I call upon the LORD, who is worthy to
be praised,
and I am saved from my enemies.

[5]"For the waves of death encompassed me,
the torrents of perdition assailed me;
[6]the cords of Sheol entangled me,
the snares of death confronted me.

[7]"In my distress I called upon the LORD;
to my God I called.
From his temple he heard my voice,
and my cry came to his ears.

[8]"Then the earth reeled and rocked;
the foundations of the heavens trembled
and quaked, because he was angry.
[9]Smoke went up from his nostrils,
and devouring fire from his mouth;
glowing coals flamed forth from him.
[10]He bowed the heavens, and came down;
thick darkness was under his feet.
[11]He rode on a cherub, and flew;
he was seen upon the wings
of the wind.
[12]He made darkness around him
his canopy, thick clouds, a gathering
of water.
[13]Out of the brightness before him
coals of fire flamed forth.
[14]The LORD thundered from heaven,
and the Most High uttered his voice.
[15]And he sent out arrows, and scattered them;
lightning, and routed them.
[16]Then the channels of the sea were seen,
the foundations of the world were
laid bare,
at the rebuke of the LORD,
at the blast of the breath of his nostrils.

[17]"He reached from on high, he took me,
he drew me out of many waters.
[18]He delivered me from my strong enemy,
from those who hated me;
for they were too mighty for me.
[19]They came upon me in the day of
my calamity;
but the LORD was my stay.
[20]He brought me forth into a broad place;
he delivered me, because he delighted
in me.

[21]"The LORD rewarded me according to my
righteousness;
according to the cleanness of my hands
he recompensed me.

22For I have kept the ways of the LORD,
and have not wickedly departed from
my God.
23For all his ordinances were before me,
and from his statutes I did not turn aside.
24I was blameless before him,
and I kept myself from guilt.
25Therefore the LORD has recompensed me
according to my righteousness,
according to my cleanness in his sight.

26"With the loyal you show yourself loyal;
with the blameless man you show
yourself blameless;
27with the pure you show yourself pure,
and with the crooked you show
yourself perverse.
28You deliver a humble people,
but your eyes are upon the haughty to
bring them down.
29Yes, you are my lamp, O LORD,
and my God lightens my darkness.
30Yes, by you I can crush a troop,
and by my God I can leap over a wall.
31This God—his way is perfect;
the promise of the LORD proves true;
he is a shield for all those who take
refuge in him.

32"For who is God, but the LORD?
And who is a rock, except our God?
33This God is my strong refuge,
and has made my way safe.
34He made my feet like deer's feet,
and set me secure on the heights.
35He trains my hands for war,
so that my arms can bend a bow of bronze.
36You have given me the shield of
your salvation,
and your help made me great.
37You gave a wide place for my steps under me,
and my feet did not slip;
38I pursued my enemies and destroyed them,
and did not turn back until they
were consumed.
39I consumed them; I thrust them through,
so that they did not rise;
they fell under my feet.
40For you girded me with strength for the battle;
you made my assailants sink under me.
41You made my enemies turn their backs
to me,
those who hated me, and I
destroyed them.
42They looked, but there was none to save;
they cried to the LORD, but he did not
answer them.
43I beat them fine as the dust of the earth,
I crushed them and stamped them
down like the mire of the streets.

44"You delivered me from strife with
the peoples;
you kept me as the head of the nations;
people whom I had not known served me.
45Foreigners came cringing to me;
as soon as they heard of me, they
obeyed me.
46Foreigners lost heart,
and came trembling out of
their fastnesses.

47"The LORD lives; and blessed be my rock,
and exalted be my God, the rock of
my salvation,
48the God who gave me vengeance
and brought down peoples under me,
49who brought me out from my enemies;
you exalted me above my adversaries,
you delivered me from men
of violence.

50"For this I will extol you, O LORD, among
the nations,
and sing praises to your name.
51Great triumphs he gives to his king,
and shows mercy to his anointed,
to David, and his descendants for ever."

PSALM 116 [114]

I love the LORD, because he has heard
my voice and my supplications.
2Because he inclined his ear to me,
therefore I will call on him as long as
I live.
3The snares of death encompassed me;
the pangs of Sheol laid hold on me;
I suffered distress and anguish.

[4]Then I called on the name of the LORD:
  "O LORD, I beg you, save my life!"

[5]Gracious is the LORD, and righteous;
  our God is merciful.
[6]The LORD preserves the simple;
  when I was brought low, he saved me.
[7]Return, O my soul, to your rest;
  for the LORD has dealt bountifully
    with you.

[8]For you have delivered my soul from death,
  my eyes from tears,
  my feet from stumbling;
[9]I walk before the LORD
  in the land of the living.
[115] [10]I kept my faith, even when I said,
  "I am greatly afflicted";
[11]I said in my consternation,
  "Men are all a vain hope."

[12]What shall I render to the LORD
  for all his bounty to me?
[13]I will lift up the chalice of salvation
  and call on the name of the LORD,
[14]I will pay my vows to the LORD
  in the presence of all his people.
[15]Precious in the sight of the LORD
  is the death of his saints.
[16]O LORD, I am your servant;
  I am your servant, the son of
    your handmaid.
  You have loosed my bonds.
[17]I will offer to you the sacrifice
    of thanksgiving
  and call on the name of the LORD.
[18]I will pay my vows to the LORD
  in the presence of all his people,
[19]in the courts of the house of the LORD,
  in your midst, O Jerusalem.
Praise the LORD!

JOHN 6

[41]The Jews then murmured at
him, because he said, "I am the
bread which came down from heaven."
[42]They said, "Is not this Jesus, the son of
Joseph, whose father and mother we know?
How does he now say, 'I have come down
from heaven'?" [43]Jesus answered them,
"Do not murmur among yourselves. [44]No
one can come to me unless the Father
who sent me draws him; and I will raise
him up at the last day. [45]It is written in
the prophets, 'And they shall all be taught
by God.' Every one who has heard and
learned from the Father comes to me.
[46]Not that any one has seen the Father
except him who is from God; he has seen
the Father. [47]Truly, truly, I say to you, he
who believes has eternal life. [48]I am the
bread of life. [49]Your fathers ate the manna
in the wilderness, and they died. [50]This
is the bread which comes down from
heaven, that a man may eat of it and not
die. [51]I am the living bread which came
down from heaven; if any one eats of this
bread, he will live for ever; and the bread
which I shall give for the life of the world
is my flesh."

[52]The Jews then disputed among themselves, saying, "How can this man give us
his flesh to eat?" [53]So Jesus said to them,
"Truly, truly, I say to you, unless you eat
the flesh of the Son of man and drink his
blood, you have no life in you; [54]he who
eats my flesh and drinks my blood has
eternal life, and I will raise him up at the
last day. [55]For my flesh is food indeed,
and my blood is drink indeed. [56]He who
eats my flesh and drinks my blood abides
in me, and I in him. [57]As the living Father
sent me, and I live because of the Father,
so he who eats me will live because of
me. [58]This is the bread which came down
from heaven, not such as the fathers ate
and died; he who eats this bread will live
for ever." [59]This he said in the synagogue,
as he taught at Caper′na-um.

[60]Many of his disciples, when they heard
it, said, "This is a hard saying; who can
listen to it?" [61]But Jesus, knowing in
himself that his disciples murmured at it,
said to them, "Do you take offense at this?
[62]Then what if you were to see the Son of
man ascending where he was before? [63]It
is the Spirit that gives life, the flesh is of

no avail; the words that I have spoken to you are Spirit and life. 64But there are some of you that do not believe." For Jesus knew from the first who those were that did not believe, and who it was that would betray him. 65And he said, "This is why I told you that no one can come to me unless it is granted him by the Father."

66After this many of his disciples drew back and no longer walked with him. 67Jesus said to the Twelve, "Will you also go away?" 68Simon Peter answered him, "Lord, to whom shall we go? You have the words of eternal life; 69and we have believed, and have come to know, that you are the Holy One of God." 70Jesus answered them, "Did I not choose you, the Twelve, and one of you is a devil?" 71He spoke of Judas the son of Simon Iscariot, for he, one of the Twelve, was to betray him.

REFLECTION

Life is good. That's a biblical message that our often glum world could use. David's song, which also appears in Psalm 18, celebrates the Lord's help in battle and his preservation of David's life. God is a "rock" and a "refuge" who keeps his servant safe and gives him strength. "The Lord lives; and blessed be my rock" (2 Sm 22:47). Life is not primarily about me; it is about sharing in the life of the Lord. The same message comes to us in Psalm 116. The psalmist says, "I love the LORD, because he has heard my voice" (Ps 116:1). But what is he asking the Lord? "O LORD, I beg you, save *my life*" (v. 4, emphasis added). The Lord saves life, preserves life, protects life, and even "deliver[s] my soul from death" (v. 8). When Jesus tells us he is the "bread of life" and that if we believe in him we gain "eternal life" and that if we eat his flesh we will "live for ever" (Jn 6:48, 54, 58), he is reaffirming the good life to which we are called. He gives us his Body to eat in the Eucharist, not for an interesting religious symbol, but so that we might participate in the divine life, the blessed life of God himself. How has God been a "rock" and a "refuge" for you?

May 20

2 SAMUEL 23

Now these are the last words of David:
The oracle of David, the son of Jesse,
the oracle of the man who was raised on high,
the anointed of the God of Jacob,
the sweet psalmist of Israel:

2"The Spirit of the LORD speaks by me,
his word is upon my tongue.
3The God of Israel has spoken,
the Rock of Israel has said to me:
When one rules justly over men,
ruling in the fear of God,
4he dawns on them like the morning light,
like the sun shining forth upon a cloudless morning,
like rain that makes grass to sprout from the earth.
5Yes, does not my house stand so with God?
For he has made with me an everlasting covenant,
ordered in all things and secure.
For will he not cause to prosper
all my help and my desire?
6But godless men are all like thorns that are thrown away;
for they cannot be taken with the hand;
7but the man who touches them
arms himself with iron and the shaft of a spear,
and they are utterly consumed with fire."

8These are the names of the mighty men whom David had: Jo'sheb-basshe'beth a Tah-che'monite; he was chief of the three; he wielded his spear against eight hundred whom he slew at one time.

9And next to him among the three mighty men was Elea'zar the son of Dodo, son of Aho'hi. He was with David when they defied the Philis'tines who were gathered there for battle, and the men of Israel withdrew. 10He
rose and struck down the Philis'tines until

his hand was weary, and his hand clung to
the sword; and the LORD wrought a great
victory that day; and the men returned after
him only to strip the slain.
11 And next to him was Shammah, the
son of Agee the Har′arite. The Philis′tines
gathered together at Lehi, where there was
a plot of ground full of lentils; and the men
fled from the Philistines. 12 But he took his
stand in the midst of the plot, and defended
it, and slew the Philis′tines; and the LORD
wrought a great victory.
13 And three of the thirty chief men went
down, and came about harvest time to
David at the cave of Adul′lam, when a
band of Philis′tines was encamped in the
valley of Reph′aim. 14 David was then in
the stronghold; and the garrison of the
Philis′tines was then at Bethlehem. 15 And
David said longingly, "O that some one
would give me water to drink from the well
of Bethlehem which is by the gate!" 16 Then
the three mighty men broke through the
camp of the Philis′tines, and drew water
out of the well of Bethlehem which was by
the gate, and took and brought it to David.
But he would not drink of it; he poured it
out to the LORD, 17 and said, "Far be it from
me, O LORD, that I should do this. Shall I
drink the blood of the men who went at
the risk of their lives?" Therefore he would
not drink it. These things did the three
mighty men.
18 Now Abi′shai, the brother of Jo′ab, the
son of Zeru′iah, was chief of the thirty. And
he wielded his spear against three hundred
men and slew them, and won a name beside
the three. 19 He was the most renowned of
the thirty, and became their commander;
but he did not attain to the three.
20 And Bena′iah the son of Jehoi′ada was
a valiant man of Kab′zeel, a doer of great
deeds; he struck two Ariels of Moab. He
also went down and slew a lion in a pit on a
day when snow had fallen. 21 And he slew an
Egyptian, a handsome man. The Egyptian
had a spear in his hand; but Bena′iah went
down to him with a staff, and snatched the
spear out of the Egyptian's hand, and slew
him with his own spear. 22 These things did
Bena′iah the son of Jehoi′ada, and won a
name beside the three mighty men. 23 He
was renowned among the thirty, but he did
not attain to the three. And David set him
over his bodyguard.
24 As′ahel the brother of Jo′ab was one
of the thirty; Elha′nan the son of Dodo
of Bethlehem, 25 Shammah of Harod,
Eli′ka of Harod, 26 He′lez the Paltite, Ira
the son of Ikkesh of Teko′a, 27 Abie′zer, of
An′athoth, Mebun′nai the Hu′shathite,
28 Zalmon the Aho′hite, Ma′harai of
Netoph′ah, 29 He′leb the son of Ba′anah of
Netoph′ah, Ittai the son of Ribai of Gib′e-
ah of the Benjaminites, 30 Bena′iah of
Pir′athon, Hiddai of the brooks of Ga′ash,
31 A′bi-al′bon the Ar′bathite, Az′maveth
of Bahu′rim, 32 Eli′ahba of Sha-al′bon, the
sons of Jashen, Jonathan, 33 Shammah the
Har′arite, Ahi′am the son of Sharar the
Hararite, 34 Eliph′elet the son of Ahas′bai
of Ma′acah, Eli′am the son of Ahith′ophel
of Gilo, 35 Hezro of Carmel, Pa′arai the
Arbite, 36 I′gal the son of Nathan of Zobah,
Ba′ni the Gadite, 37 Zelek the Am′monite,
Na′harai of Be-er′oth, the armor-bearer
of Jo′ab the son of Zeru′iah, 38 Ira the
Ithrite, Ga′reb the Ithrite, 39 Uri′ah the
Hittite: thirty-seven in all.

24 Again the anger of the LORD was
kindled against Israel, and he incited
David against them, saying, "Go, number
Israel and Judah." 2 So the king said to
Jo′ab and the commanders of the army,
who were with him, "Go through all the
tribes of Israel, from Dan to Be′er-she′ba,
and number the people, that I may know
the number of the people." 3 But Jo′ab said
to the king, "May the LORD your God add
to the people a hundred times as many
as they are, while the eyes of my lord the
king still see it; but why does my lord
the king delight in this thing?" 4 But the
king's word prevailed against Jo′ab and
the commanders of the army. So Joab and
the commanders of the army went out
from the presence of the king to number
the people of Israel. 5 They crossed the
Jordan, and began from Aro′er, and from
the city that is in the middle of the valley,

toward Gad and on to Ja´zer. [6]Then they came to Gilead, and to Ka´desh in the land of the Hittites; and they came to Dan, and from Dan they went around to Si´don, [7]and came to the fortress of Tyre and to all the cities of the Hi´vites and Canaanites; and they went out to the Neg´eb of Judah at Be´er-she´ba. [8]So when they had gone through all the land, they came to Jerusalem at the end of nine months and twenty days. [9]And Jo´ab gave the sum of the numbering of the people to the king: in Israel there were eight hundred thousand valiant men who drew the sword, and the men of Judah were five hundred thousand.

[10]But David's heart struck him after he had numbered the people. And David said to the LORD, "I have sinned greatly in what I have done. But now, O LORD, I pray you, take away the iniquity of your servant; for I have done very foolishly." [11]And when David arose in the morning, the word of the LORD came to the prophet Gad, David's seer, saying, [12]"Go and say to David, 'Thus says the LORD, Three things I offer you; choose one of them, that I may do it to you.'" [13]So Gad came to David and told him, and said to him, "Shall three years of famine come to you in your land? Or will you flee three months before your foes while they pursue you? Or shall there be three days' pestilence in your land? Now consider, and decide what answer I shall return to him who sent me." [14]Then David said to Gad, "I am in great distress; let us fall into the hand of the LORD, for his mercy is great; but let me not fall into the hand of man."

[15]So the LORD sent a pestilence upon Israel from the morning until the appointed time; and there died of the people from Dan to Be´er-she´ba seventy thousand men. [16]And when the angel stretched forth his hand toward Jerusalem to destroy it, the LORD repented of the evil, and said to the angel who was working destruction among the people, "It is enough; now stay your hand." And the angel of the LORD was by the threshing floor of Arau´nah the Jeb´usite. [17]Then David spoke to the LORD when he saw the angel who was striking down the people, and said, "Behold, I have sinned, and I have done wickedly; but these sheep, what have they done? Let your hand, I pray you, be against me and against my father's house."

[18]And Gad came that day to David, and said to him, "Go up, rear an altar to the LORD on the threshing floor of Arau´nah the Jeb´usite." [19]So David went up at Gad's word, as the LORD commanded. [20]And when Arau´nah looked down, he saw the king and his servants coming on toward him; and Araunah went forth, and did obeisance to the king with his face to the ground. [21]And Arau´nah said, "Why has my lord the king come to his servant?" David said, "To buy the threshing floor of you, in order to build an altar to the LORD, that the plague may be averted from the people." [22]Then Arau´nah said to David, "Let my lord the king take and offer up what seems good to him; here are the oxen for the burnt offering, and the threshing sledges and the yokes of the oxen for the wood. [23]All this, O king, Arau´nah gives to the king." And Araunah said to the king, "The LORD your God accept you." [24]But the king said to Arau´nah, "No, but I will buy it of you for a price; I will not offer burnt offerings to the LORD my God which cost me nothing." So David bought the threshing floor and the oxen for fifty shekels of silver. [25]And David built there an altar to the LORD, and offered burnt offerings and peace offerings. So the LORD heeded supplications for the land, and the plague was averted from Israel.

PSALM 117 [116]

Praise the LORD, all nations!
  Extol him, all peoples!
[2]For great is his mercy toward us;
  and the faithfulness of the LORD endures
    for ever.
Praise the LORD!

JOHN 7

After this Jesus went about in Galilee; he would not go about in Judea, because the Jews sought to kill him. [2]Now the Jews' feast of Tabernacles was at hand. [3]So his brethren said to him, "Leave here and go to Judea, that your disciples may see the works you are doing. [4]For no man works in secret if he seeks to be known openly. If you do these things, show yourself to the world." [5]For even his brethren did not believe in him. [6]Jesus said to them, "My time has not yet come, but your time is always here. [7]The world cannot hate you, but it hates me because I testify of it that its works are evil. [8]Go to the feast yourselves; I am not going up to this feast, for my time has not yet fully come." [9]So saying, he remained in Galilee.

[10]But after his brethren had gone up to the feast, then he also went up, not publicly but in private. [11]The Jews were looking for him at the feast, and saying, "Where is he?" [12]And there was much muttering about him among the people. While some said, "He is a good man," others said, "No, he is leading the people astray." [13]Yet for fear of the Jews no one spoke openly of him.

[14]About the middle of the feast Jesus went up into the temple and taught. [15]The Jews marveled at it, saying, "How is it that this man has learning, when he has never studied?" [16]So Jesus answered them, "My teaching is not mine, but his who sent me; [17]if any man's will is to do his will, he shall know whether the teaching is from God or whether I am speaking on my own authority. [18]He who speaks on his own authority seeks his own glory; but he who seeks the glory of him who sent him is true, and in him there is no falsehood. [19]Did not Moses give you the law? Yet none of you keeps the law. Why do you seek to kill me?" [20]The people answered, "You have a demon! Who is seeking to kill you?" [21]Jesus answered them, "I did one deed, and you all marvel at it. [22]Moses gave you circumcision (not that it is from Moses, but from the fathers), and you circumcise a man upon the sabbath. [23]If on the sabbath a man receives circumcision, so that the law of Moses may not be broken, are you angry with me because on the sabbath I made a man's whole body well? [24]Do not judge by appearances, but judge with right judgment."

REFLECTION

Our spiritual life is largely about trust—will I trust in myself or in God? Toward the end of his life, David shows that he is trusting in himself and his human resources rather than in the Lord. How? He takes a census. Though not forbidden by God's law, David uses the census to tally the number of soldiers he can muster to exhibit the great power he possesses. With such military might, who needs to rely on the Lord for help? Soon David is seized with guilt: "David's heart struck him" (2 Sm 24:10). How easy it is to return to trusting in ourselves rather than the Lord! If our heart is not fully converted, we will put too much stock in the visible world and its allure of money, security, and power, and not nearly enough in the power of the Lord, who reigns supreme over all other powers. Jesus warns his opponents against such false thinking: "Do not judge by appearances, but judge with right judgment" (Jn 7:24). Trusting in God, in his knowledge and in his wisdom, sometimes takes all the courage and faith we can muster. If you took a census of what you put your trust in, what, or who, would come out on top?

May 21

1 KINGS 1

Now King David was old and advanced in years; and although they covered him with clothes, he could not get warm. [2]Therefore his servants said to him, "Let a young maiden be sought for my lord the king, and let her wait upon the king, and be his

nurse; let her lie in your bosom, that my
lord the king may be warm." 3So they sought
for a beautiful maiden throughout all the
territory of Israel, and found Ab′ishag the
Shu′nammite, and brought her to the king.
4The maiden was very beautiful; and she
became the king's nurse and ministered to
him; but the king knew her not.

5Now Adoni′jah the son of Haggith exalted himself, saying, "I will be king"; and he
prepared for himself chariots and horsemen,
and fifty men to run before him. 6His father
had never at any time displeased him by
asking, "Why have you done thus and so?" He
was also a very handsome man; and he was
born next after Ab′salom. 7He conferred with
Jo′ab the son of Zeru′iah and with Abi′athar
the priest; and they followed Adoni′jah and
helped him. 8But Za′dok the priest, and
Bena′iah the son of Jehoi′ada, and Nathan the
prophet, and Shim′e-i, and Re′i, and David's
mighty men were not with Adoni′jah.

9Adoni′jah sacrificed sheep, oxen, and
fatlings by the Serpent's Stone, which is
beside En-ro′gel, and he invited all his
brothers, the king's sons, and all the royal
officials of Judah, 10but he did not invite
Nathan the prophet or Bena′iah or the
mighty men or Solomon his brother.

11Then Nathan said to Bathshe′ba the
mother of Solomon, "Have you not heard
that Adoni′jah the son of Haggith has
become king and David our lord does not
know it? 12Now therefore come, let me give
you counsel, that you may save your own
life and the life of your son Solomon. 13Go in
at once to King David, and say to him, 'Did
you not, my lord the king, swear to your
maidservant, saying, "Solomon your son
shall reign after me, and he shall sit upon
my throne"? Why then is Adoni′jah king?'
14Then while you are still speaking with
the king, I also will come in after you and
confirm your words."

15So Bathshe′ba went to the king into
his chamber (now the king was very
old, and Ab′ishag the Shu′nammite was
ministering to the king). 16Bathshe′ba
bowed and did obeisance to the king,
and the king said, "What do you desire?"
17She said to him, "My lord, you swore
to your maidservant by the LORD your
God, saying, 'Solomon your son shall
reign after me, and he shall sit upon my
throne.' 18And now, behold, Adoni′jah
is king, although you, my lord the king,
do not know it. 19He has sacrificed oxen,
fatlings, and sheep in abundance, and has
invited all the sons of the king, Abi′athar
the priest, and Jo′ab the commander of
the army; but Solomon your servant he
has not invited. 20And now, my lord the
king, the eyes of all Israel are upon you,
to tell them who shall sit on the throne of
my lord the king after him. 21Otherwise it
will come to pass, when my lord the king
sleeps with his fathers, that I and my son
Solomon will be counted offenders."

22While she was still speaking with the
king, Nathan the prophet came in. 23And
they told the king, "Here is Nathan the
prophet." And when he came in before the
king, he bowed before the king, with his
face to the ground. 24And Nathan said, "My
lord the king, have you said, 'Adoni′jah shall
reign after me, and he shall sit upon my
throne'? 25For he has gone down this day,
and has sacrificed oxen, fatlings, and sheep
in abundance, and has invited all the king's
sons, Jo′ab the commander of the army,
and Abi′athar the priest; and behold, they
are eating and drinking before him, and
saying, 'Long live King Adoni′jah!' 26But
me, your servant, and Za′dok the priest,
and Bena′iah the son of Jehoi′ada, and your
servant Solomon, he has not invited. 27Has
this thing been brought about by my lord
the king and you have not told your servants
who should sit on the throne of my lord the
king after him?"

28Then King David answered, "Call Bathshe′ba
to me." So she came into the king's presence,
and stood before the king. 29And the king
swore, saying, "As the LORD lives, who has
redeemed my soul out of every adversity,
30as I swore to you by the LORD, the God of
Israel, saying, 'Solomon your son shall reign
after me, and he shall sit upon my throne
in my stead'; even so will I do this day."
31Then Bathshe′ba bowed with her face to the

ground, and did obeisance to the king, and said, "May my lord King David live for ever!"

32King David said, "Call to me Za′dok the priest, Nathan the prophet, and Bena′iah the son of Jehoi′ada." So they came before the king. 33And the king said to them, "Take with you the servants of your lord, and cause Solomon my son to ride on my own mule, and bring him down to Gi′hon; 34and let Za′dok the priest and Nathan the prophet there anoint him king over Israel; then blow the trumpet, and say, 'Long live King Solomon!' 35You shall then come up after him, and he shall come and sit upon my throne; for he shall be king in my stead; and I have appointed him to be ruler over Israel and over Judah." 36And Bena′iah the son of Jehoi′ada answered the king, "Amen! May the LORD, the God of my lord the king, say so. 37As the LORD has been with my lord the king, even so may he be with Solomon, and make his throne greater than the throne of my lord King David."

38So Za′dok the priest, Nathan the prophet, and Bena′iah the son of Jehoi′ada, and the Cher′ethites and the Pel′ethites, went down and caused Solomon to ride on King David's mule, and brought him to Gi′hon. 39There Za′dok the priest took the horn of oil from the tent, and anointed Solomon. Then they blew the trumpet; and all the people said, "Long live King Solomon!" 40And all the people went up after him, playing on pipes, and rejoicing with great joy, so that the earth was split by their noise.

41Adoni′jah and all the guests who were with him heard it as they finished feasting. And when Jo′ab heard the sound of the trumpet, he said, "What does this uproar in the city mean?" 42While he was still speaking, behold, Jonathan the son of Abi′athar the priest came; and Adoni′jah said, "Come in, for you are a worthy man and bring good news." 43Jonathan answered Adoni′jah, "No, for our lord King David has made Solomon king; 44and the king has sent with him Za′dok the priest, Nathan the prophet, and Bena′iah the son of Jehoi′ada, and the Cher′ethites and the Pel′ethites; and they have caused him to ride on the king's mule; 45and Za′dok the priest and Nathan the prophet have anointed him king at Gi′hon; and they have gone up from there rejoicing, so that the city is in an uproar. This is the noise that you have heard. 46Solomon sits upon the royal throne. 47Moreover the king's servants came to congratulate our lord King David, saying, 'Your God make the name of Solomon more famous than yours, and make his throne greater than your throne.' And the king bowed himself upon the bed. 48And the king also said, 'Blessed be the LORD, the God of Israel, who has granted one of my offspring to sit on my throne this day, my own eyes seeing it.' "

49Then all the guests of Adoni′jah trembled, and rose, and each went his own way. 50And Adoni′jah feared Solomon; and he arose, and went, and caught hold of the horns of the altar. 51And it was told Solomon, "Behold, Adoni′jah fears King Solomon; for behold, he has laid hold of the horns of the altar, saying, 'Let King Solomon swear to me first that he will not slay his servant with the sword.' " 52And Solomon said, "If he prove to be a worthy man, not one of his hairs shall fall to the earth; but if wickedness is found in him, he shall die." 53So King Solomon sent, and they brought him down from the altar. And he came and did obeisance to King Solomon; and Solomon said to him, "Go to your house."

PSALM 118 [117]

O give thanks to the LORD, for he is good;
his mercy endures for ever!

2Let Israel say,
"His mercy endures for ever."
3Let the house of Aaron say,
"His mercy endures for ever."
4Let those who fear the LORD say,
"His mercy endures for ever."

5Out of my distress I called on the LORD;
the LORD answered me and set me free.
6With the LORD on my side I do not fear.
What can man do to me?

7The LORD is on my side to help me;
I shall look in triumph on those who
hate me.
8It is better to take refuge in the LORD
than to put confidence in man.
9It is better to take refuge in the LORD
than to put confidence in princes.

10All nations surrounded me;
in the name of the LORD I cut them off!
11They surrounded me, surrounded me on
every side;
in the name of the LORD I cut them off!
12They surrounded me like bees,
they blazed like a fire of thorns;
in the name of the LORD I cut them off!
13I was pushed hard, so that I was falling,
but the LORD helped me.
14The LORD is my strength and my song;
he has become my salvation.

JOHN 7

**25Some of the people of Jerusa-
lem therefore said, "Is not this
the man whom they seek to kill?
26And here he is, speaking openly, and
they say nothing to him! Can it be that
the authorities really know that this**
is the Christ? 27Yet we know where this
man comes from; and when the Christ
appears, no one will know where he
comes from." 28So Jesus proclaimed, as he
taught in the temple, "You know me, and
you know where I come from? But I have
not come of my own accord; he who sent
me is true, and him you do not know. 29I
know him, for I come from him, and he
sent me." 30So they sought to arrest him;
but no one laid hands on him, because his
hour had not yet come. 31Yet many of the
people believed in him; they said, "When
the Christ appears, will he do more signs
than this man has done?"
32The Pharisees heard the crowd thus
muttering about him, and the chief
priests and Pharisees sent officers to
arrest him. 33Jesus then said, "I shall be
with you a little longer, and then I go
to him who sent me; 34you will seek me
and you will not find me; where I am
you cannot come." 35The Jews said to one
another, "Where does this man intend to
go that we shall not find him? Does he
intend to go to the Dispersion among
the Greeks and teach the Greeks? 36What
does he mean by saying, 'You will seek me
and you will not find me,' and, 'Where I
am you cannot come'?"
37On the last day of the feast, the great
day, Jesus stood up and proclaimed, "If
any one thirst, let him come to me and
drink. 38He who believes in me, as the
Scripture has said, 'Out of his heart shall
flow rivers of living water.'" 39Now this
he said about the Spirit, which those who
believed in him were to receive; for as yet
the Spirit had not been given, because
Jesus was not yet glorified.
40When they heard these words, some of
the people said, "This is really the prophet."
41Others said, "This is the Christ." But some
said, "Is the Christ to come from Galilee?
42Has not the Scripture said that the Christ
is descended from David, and comes from
Bethlehem, the village where David was?"
43So there was a division among the people
over him. 44Some of them wanted to arrest
him, but no one laid hands on him.
45The officers then went back to the
chief priests and Pharisees, who said to
them, "Why did you not bring him?" 46The
officers answered, "No man ever spoke like
this man!" 47The Pharisees answered them,
"Are you led astray, you also? 48Have any of
the authorities or of the Pharisees believed
in him? 49But this crowd, who do not know
the law, are accursed." 50Nicode´mus, who
had gone to him before, and who was
one of them, said to them, 51"Does our
law judge a man without first giving him
a hearing and learning what he does?"
52They replied, "Are you from Galilee too?
Search and you will see that no prophet is
to rise from Galilee."
8 53They went each to his own house, 1but
Jesus went to the Mount of Olives.

REFLECTION

Loving God entails committing to a life-and-death struggle. Our decision to love brings not only unity and joy, but also division and separation. Choosing to marry one person is a rejection of all others. Choosing to follow Jesus is a rejection of all other gods. In the first chapter of 1 Kings, Adonijah seeks to steal the kingdom for himself, but David, true to his promises, grants succession to his other son, Solomon. The followers of Adonijah flee in shame, while Solomon magnanimously pardons his brother for his rebellion. David's faithfulness to his promise to make Solomon king is patterned after the Lord's fidelity to us: "His mercy (*hesed*) endures forever" (Ps 118:1). *Hesed* is the Hebrew word for covenant loyalty or fidelity, which is often translated "steadfast love." Jesus's identity prompts crisis and division in John 7. Is he the Messiah? Where is he from? What do his signs mean? When he comes on the scene, by the sheer power of his presence, Jesus forces people to make a decision for or against him. His presence ignites more questions than answers. In choosing Jesus, what have you been willing to separate yourself from, or give up for the Lord?

May 22

1 KINGS 2

When David's time to die drew
near, he charged Solomon his
son, saying, 2"I am about to go
the way of all the earth. Be strong, and
show yourself a man, 3and keep the
charge of the LORD your God, walking
in his ways and keeping his statutes, his
commandments, his ordinances, and his
testimonies, as it is written in the law of
Moses, that you may prosper in all that you
do and wherever you turn; 4that the LORD
may establish his word which he spoke
concerning me, saying, 'If your sons take
heed to their way, to walk before me in
faithfulness with all their heart and with all
their soul, there shall not fail you a man on
the throne of Israel.'
5"Moreover you know also what Jo′ab the
son of Zeru′iah did to me, how he dealt with
the two commanders of the armies of Israel,
Abner the son of Ner, and Ama′sa the son
of Je′ther, whom he murdered, avenging in
time of peace blood which had been shed in
war, and putting innocent blood upon the
belt about my loins, and upon the sandals
on my feet. 6Act therefore according to
your wisdom, but do not let his gray head
go down to Sheol in peace. 7But deal loyally
with the sons of Barzil′lai the Gileadite, and
let them be among those who eat at your
table; for with such loyalty they met me
when I fled from Ab′salom your brother.
8And there is also with you Shim′e-i the son
of Gera, the Benjaminite from Bahu′rim,
who cursed me with a grievous curse on the
day when I went to Ma″hana′im; but when
he came down to meet me at the Jordan, I
swore to him by the LORD, saying, 'I will
not put you to death with the sword.' 9Now
therefore hold him not guiltless, for you are
a wise man; you will know what you ought
to do to him, and you shall bring his gray
head down with blood to Sheol."
10Then David slept with his fathers, and
was buried in the city of David. 11And the
time that David reigned over Israel was forty
years; he reigned seven years in He′bron, and
thirty-three years in Jerusalem. 12So Solomon
sat upon the throne of David his father; and
his kingdom was firmly established.
13Then Adoni′jah the son of Haggith came
to Bathshe′ba the mother of Solomon. And
she said, "Do you come peaceably?" He
said, "Peaceably." 14Then he said, "I have
something to say to you." She said, "Say on."
15He said, "You know that the kingdom was
mine, and that all Israel fully expected me
to reign; however the kingdom has turned
about and become my brother's, for it
was his from the LORD. 16And now I have
one request to make of you; do not refuse

me." She said to him, "Say on." 17And he said, "Please ask King Solomon—he will not refuse you—to give me Ab′ishag the Shu′nammite as my wife." 18Bathshe′ba said, "Very well; I will speak for you to the king."

19So Bathshe′ba went to King Solomon, to speak to him on behalf of Adoni′jah. And the king rose to meet her, and bowed down to her; then he sat on his throne, and had a seat brought for the king's mother; and she sat on his right. 20Then she said, "I have one small request to make of you; do not refuse me." And the king said to her, "Make your request, my mother; for I will not refuse you." 21She said, "Let Ab′ishag the Shu′nammite be given to Adoni′jah your brother as his wife." 22King Solomon answered his mother, "And why do you ask Ab′ishag the Shu′nammite for Adoni′jah? Ask for him the kingdom also; for he is my elder brother, and on his side are Abi′athar the priest and Jo′ab the son of Zeru′iah." 23Then King Solomon swore by the LORD, saying, "God do so to me and more also if this word does not cost Adoni′jah his life! 24Now therefore as the LORD lives, who has established me, and placed me on the throne of David my father, and who has made me a house, as he promised, Adoni′jah shall be put to death this day." 25So King Solomon sent Bena′iah the son of Jehoi′ada; and he struck him down, and he died.

26And to Abi′athar the priest the king said, "Go to An′athoth, to your estate; for you deserve death. But I will not at this time put you to death, because you bore the ark of the Lord GOD before David my father, and because you shared in all the affliction of my father." 27So Solomon expelled Abi′athar from being priest to the LORD, thus fulfilling the word of the LORD which he had spoken concerning the house of Eli in Shi′loh.

28When the news came to Jo′ab—for Joab had supported Adoni′jah although he had not supported Ab′salom—Joab fled to the tent of the LORD and caught hold of the horns of the altar. 29And when it was told King Solomon, "Jo′ab has fled to the tent of the LORD, and behold, he is beside the altar," Solomon sent Bena′iah the son of Jehoi′ada, saying, "Go, strike him down." 30So Bena′iah came to the tent of the LORD, and said to him, "The king commands, 'Come forth.'" But he said, "No, I will die here." Then Benaiah brought the king word again, saying, "Thus said Jo′ab, and thus he answered me." 31The king replied to him, "Do as he has said, strike him down and bury him; and thus take away from me and from my father's house the guilt for the blood which Jo′ab shed without cause. 32The LORD will bring back his bloody deeds upon his own head, because, without the knowledge of my father David, he attacked and slew with the sword two men more righteous and better than himself, Abner the son of Ner, commander of the army of Israel, and Ama′sa the son of Je′ther, commander of the army of Judah. 33So shall their blood come back upon the head of Jo′ab and upon the head of his descendants for ever; but to David, and to his descendants, and to his house, and to his throne, there shall be peace from the LORD for evermore." 34Then Bena′iah the son of Jehoi′ada went up, and struck him down and killed him; and he was buried in his own house in the wilderness. 35The king put Bena′iah the son of Jehoi′ada over the army in place of Jo′ab, and the king put Za′dok the priest in the place of Abi′athar.

36Then the king sent and summoned Shim′e-i, and said to him, "Build yourself a house in Jerusalem, and dwell there, and do not go forth from there to any place whatever. 37For on the day you go forth, and cross the brook Kidron, know for certain that you shall die; your blood shall be upon your own head." 38And Shim′e-i said to the king, "What you say is good; as my lord the king has said, so will your servant do." So Shime-i dwelt in Jerusalem many days.

39But it happened at the end of three years that two of Shim′e-i's slaves ran away to A′chish, son of Ma′acah, king of Gath. And when it was told Shime-i, "Behold, your slaves are in Gath," 40Shim′e-i arose and saddled a donkey, and went to Gath to A′chish, to seek his slaves; Shime-i went and brought his slaves from Gath. 41And when Solomon was told that Shim′e-i had

gone from Jerusalem to Gath and returned,
42the king sent and summoned Shim′e-i,
and said to him, "Did I not make you swear
by the LORD, and solemnly admonish you,
saying, 'Know for certain that on the day
you go forth and go to any place whatever,
you shall die'? And you said to me, 'What
you say is good; I obey.' 43Why then have
you not kept your oath to the LORD and
the commandment with which I charged
you?" 44The king also said to Shim′e-i, "You
know in your own heart all the evil that you
did to David my father; so the LORD will
bring back your evil upon your own head.
45But King Solomon shall be blessed, and
the throne of David shall be established
before the LORD for ever." 46Then the king
commanded Bena′iah the son of Jehoi′ada;
and he went out and struck him down, and
he died.

So the kingdom was established in the hand of Solomon.

PSALM 118 [117]

15Listen, glad songs of victory
in the tents of the righteous:
"The right hand of the LORD does valiantly!
16 The right hand of the LORD is exalted;
the right hand of the LORD
does valiantly!"
17I shall not die, but I shall live,
and recount the deeds of the LORD.
18The LORD has chastened me sorely,
but he has not given me over to death.

19Open to me the gates of righteousness,
that I may enter through them
and give thanks to the LORD.

20This is the gate of the LORD;
the righteous shall enter through it.

21I thank you that you have answered me
and have become my salvation.
22The stone which the builders rejected
has become the cornerstone.
23This is the LORD's doing;
it is marvelous in our eyes.
24This is the day which the LORD has made;
let us rejoice and be glad in it.
25Save us, we beg you, O LORD!
O LORD, we beg you, give us success!
26Blessed be he who enters in the name of
the LORD!
We bless you from the house of the LORD.
27The LORD is God,
and he has given us light.
Bind the festal procession with branches,
up to the horns of the altar!
28You are my God, and I will give thanks
to you;
you are my God, I will extol you.
29O give thanks to the LORD, for he is good;
for his mercy endures for ever!

JOHN 8

2Early in the morning he came again to the temple; all the people came to him, and he sat down and taught them. 3The scribes and the Pharisees brought a woman who had
been caught in adultery, and placing her
in their midst 4they said to him, "Teacher,
this woman has been caught in the act of
adultery. 5Now in the law Moses commanded us to stone such. What do you
say about her?" 6This they said to test
him, that they might have some charge
to bring against him. Jesus bent down
and wrote with his finger on the ground.
7And as they continued to ask him, he
stood up and said to them, "Let him who
is without sin among you be the first to
throw a stone at her." 8And once more he
bent down and wrote with his finger on
the ground. 9But when they heard it, they
went away, one by one, beginning with
the eldest, and Jesus was left alone with
the woman standing before him. 10Jesus
looked up and said to her, "Woman,
where are they? Has no one condemned
you?" 11She said, "No one, Lord." And

Jesus said, “Neither do I condemn you; go, and do not sin again.”

12Again Jesus spoke to them, saying, “I am the light of the world; he who follows me will not walk in darkness, but will have the light of life.” 13The Pharisees then said to him, “You are bearing witness to yourself; your testimony is not true.” 14Jesus answered, “Even if I do bear witness to myself, my testimony is true, for I know where I have come from and where I am going, but you do not know where I come from or where I am going. 15You judge according to the flesh, I judge no one. 16Yet even if I do judge, my judgment is true, for it is not I alone that judge, but I and he who sent me. 17In your law it is written that the testimony of two men is true; 18I bear witness to myself, and the Father who sent me bears witness to me.” 19They said to him therefore, “Where is your Father?” Jesus answered, “You know neither me nor my Father; if you knew me, you would know my Father also.” 20These words he spoke in the treasury, as he taught in the temple; but no one arrested him, because his hour had not yet come.

21Again he said to them, “I go away, and you will seek me and die in your sin; where I am going, you cannot come.” 22Then said the Jews, “Will he kill himself, since he says, ‘Where I am going, you cannot come’?” 23He said to them, “You are from below, I am from above; you are of this world, I am not of this world. 24I told you that you would die in your sins, for you will die in your sins unless you believe that I am he.” 25They said to him, “Who are you?” Jesus said to them, “Even what I have told you from the beginning. 26I have much to say about you and much to judge; but he who sent me is true, and I declare to the world what I have heard from him.” 27They did not understand that he spoke to them of the Father. 28So Jesus said, “When you have lifted up the Son of man, then you will know that I am he, and that I do nothing on my own authority but speak thus as the Father taught me. 29And he who sent me is with me; he has not left me alone, for I always do what is pleasing to him.” 30As he spoke thus, many believed in him.

REFLECTION

Old Testament command-and-control kingship contrasts sharply with the New Testament kingship of Jesus. Here the dying David commissions Solomon, not just to follow the Law of Moses, but to execute David’s enemies, particularly Joab and Shime-i. Solomon follows through, killing not only Joab and Shime-i but also his brother, Adonijah, who makes a foolishly treasonous request for David’s former concubine. In classic Machiavellian style, Solomon’s rule is only cemented with a blood-letting: “So the kingdom was established in the hand of Solomon” (1 Kgs 2:46). In contrast, Jesus’s reign is marked by mercy. Some of his opponents drag a poor woman caught in adultery before Jesus for summary judgment. They want to see if he will execute the Law of Moses and spurn Roman authority by having her stoned. Yet he demurs, telling her, “Neither do I condemn you; go, and do not sin again” (Jn 8:11). Rather than killing his enemies like Solomon did, Jesus will actually die for their sins. He is a just judge: “Even if I do judge, my judgment is true, for it is not I alone that judge, but I and he who sent me” (v. 16). But he is also a merciful, self-sacrificial Savior. How can you imitate Jesus’s merciful kingship?

May 23

1 KINGS 3

Solomon made a marriage alliance with Pharaoh king of Egypt; he took Pharaoh’s daughter, and brought her into the city of David, until he had finished building his own house and the house of the Lord and the wall around Jerusalem. 2The people were

sacrificing at the high places, however,
because no house had yet been built for
the name of the LORD.
3 Solomon loved the LORD, walking in
the statutes of David his father; only, he
sacrificed and burnt incense at the high
places. 4 And the king went to Gib′eon to
sacrifice there, for that was the great high
place; Solomon used to offer a thousand
burnt offerings upon that altar. 5 At Gib′eon
the LORD appeared to Solomon in a dream
by night; and God said, “Ask what I shall give
you.” 6 And Solomon said, “You have shown
great and merciful love to your servant
David my father, because he walked before
you in faithfulness, in righteousness, and in
uprightness of heart toward you; and you
have kept for him this great and merciful
love, and have given him a son to sit on his
throne this day. 7 And now, O LORD my God,
you have made your servant king in place
of David my father, although I am but a
little child; I do not know how to go out or
come in. 8 And your servant is in the midst
of your people whom you have chosen, a
great people, that cannot be numbered or
counted for multitude. 9 Give your servant
therefore an understanding mind to govern
your people, that I may discern between
good and evil; for who is able to govern this
great people of yours?”
10 It pleased the LORD that Solomon had
asked this. 11 And God said to him, “Because
you have asked this, and have not asked
for yourself long life or riches or the life of
your enemies, but have asked for yourself
understanding to discern what is right,
12 behold, I now do according to your word.
Behold, I give you a wise and discerning
mind, so that none like you has been before
you and none like you shall arise after you. 13 I
give you also what you have not asked, both
riches and honor, so that no other king shall
compare with you, all your days. 14 And if you
will walk in my ways, keeping my statutes and
my commandments, as your father David
walked, then I will lengthen your days.”
15 And Solomon awoke, and behold, it was
a dream. Then he came to Jerusalem, and
stood before the ark of the covenant of the
LORD, and offered up burnt offerings and
peace offerings, and made a feast for all his
servants.
16 Then two harlots came to the king, and
stood before him. 17 The one woman said,
“Oh, my lord, this woman and I dwell in the
same house; and I gave birth to a child while
she was in the house. 18 Then on the third
day after I was delivered, this woman also
gave birth; and we were alone; there was
no one else with us in the house, only we
two were in the house. 19 And this woman’s
son died in the night, because she lay on it.
20 And she arose at midnight, and took my
son from beside me, while your maidservant
slept, and laid it in her bosom, and laid her
dead son in my bosom. 21 When I rose in the
morning to nurse my child, behold, it was
dead; but when I looked at it closely in the
morning, behold, it was not the child that
I had borne.” 22 But the other woman said,
“No, the living child is mine, and the dead
child is yours.” The first said, “No, the dead
child is yours, and the living child is mine.”
Thus they spoke before the king.
23 Then the king said, “The one says, ‘This
is my son that is alive, and your son is dead’;
and the other says, ‘No; but your son is dead,
and my son is the living one.’ ” 24 And the
king said, “Bring me a sword.” So a sword
was brought before the king. 25 And the king
said, “Divide the living child in two, and give
half to the one, and half to the other.” 26 Then
the woman whose son was alive said to the
king, because her heart yearned for her son,
“Oh, my lord, give her the living child, and
by no means slay it.” But the other said, “It
shall be neither mine nor yours; divide it.”
27 Then the king answered and said, “Give
the living child to the first woman, and by
no means slay it; she is its mother.” 28 And
all Israel heard of the judgment which the
king had rendered; and they stood in awe
of the king, because they perceived that the
wisdom of God was in him, to render justice.
4 King Solomon was king over all Israel,
2 and these were his high officials:
Azari′ah the son of Za′dok was the priest;
3 Elihor′eph and Ahi′jah the sons of Shi′sha
were secretaries; Jehosh′aphat the son of

Ahi′lud was recorder; 4Bena′iah the son of
Jehoi′ada was in command of the army;
Za′dok and Abi′athar were priests; 5Azari′ah
the son of Nathan was over the officers;
Zabud the son of Nathan was priest and
king's friend; 6Ahi′shar was in charge of the
palace; and Adoni′ram the son of Abda was
in charge of the forced labor.

7Solomon had twelve officers over all
Israel, who provided food for the king
and his household; each man had to make
provision for one month in the year. 8These
were their names: Ben-hur, in the hill
country of E′phraim; 9Ben-de′ker, in Makaz,
Sha-al′bim, Beth-she′mesh, and E′lonbeth-
ha′nan; 10Ben-he′sed, in Arub′both (to him
belonged Socoh and all the land of He′pher);
11Ben-abin′adab, in all Na′phath-dor (he
had Ta′phath the daughter of Solomon as
his wife); 12Ba′ana the son of Ahi′lud, in
Ta′anach, Megid′do, and all Beth-she′an
which is beside Zar′ethan below Jezre′el, and
from Beth-shean to A′bel-meho′lah, as far as
the other side of Jok′meam; 13Ben-ge′ber, in
Ra′moth-gil′ead (he had the villages of Ja′ir
the son of Manas′seh, which are in Gilead,
and he had the region of Argob, which is
in Bashan, sixty great cities with walls and
bronze bars); 14Ahin′adab the son of Iddo,
in Ma′hana′im; 15Ahi′ma-az, in Naph′tali
(he had taken Bas′emath the daughter of
Solomon as his wife); 16Ba′ana the son of
Hu′shai, in Asher and Bea′loth; 17Jehosh′aphat
the son of Paru′ah, in Is′sachar; 18Shim′e-i
the son of E′la, in Benjamin; 19Geber the son
of U′ri, in the land of Gilead, the country of
Si′hon king of the Am′orites and of Og king
of Bashan. And there was one officer in the
land of Judah.

20Judah and Israel were as many as the
sand by the sea; they ate and drank and
were happy. 21Solomon ruled over all the
kingdoms from the Euphrates to the land of
the Philis′tines and to the border of Egypt;
they brought tribute and served Solomon all
the days of his life.

22Solomon's provision for one day was
thirty cors of fine flour, and sixty cors of
meal, 23ten fat oxen, and twenty pasture-
fed cattle, a hundred sheep, besides deer,
gazelles, roebucks, and fatted fowl. 24For he
had dominion over all the region west of the
Euphra′tes from Tiphsah to Gaza, over all the
kings west of the Euphrates; and he had peace
on all sides round about him. 25And Judah
and Israel dwelt in safety, from Dan even to
Be′er-she′ba, every man under his vine and
under his fig tree, all the days of Solomon.
26Solomon also had forty thousand stalls of
horses for his chariots, and twelve thousand
horsemen. 27And those officers supplied
provisions for King Solomon, and for all who
came to King Solomon's table, each one in his
month; they let nothing be lacking. 28Barley
also and straw for the horses and swift
steeds they brought to the place where it was
required, each according to his charge.

PSALM 119 [118]

Blessed are those whose way is blameless,
who walk in the law of the LORD!
2Blessed are those who keep his testimonies,
who seek him with their whole heart,
3who also do no wrong,
but walk in his ways!
4You have commanded your precepts
to be kept diligently.
5O that my ways may be steadfast
in keeping your statutes!
6Then I shall not be put to shame,
having my eyes fixed on all your
commandments.
7I will praise you with an upright heart,
when I learn your righteous ordinances.
8I will observe your statutes;
O forsake me not utterly!

9How can a young man keep his way pure?
By guarding it according to your word.
10With my whole heart I seek you;
let me not wander from your
commandments!
11I have laid up your word in my heart,
that I might not sin against you.
12Blessed are you, O LORD;
teach me your statutes!
13With my lips I declare
all the ordinances of your mouth.

[14]In the way of your testimonies I delight
as much as in all riches.
[15]I will meditate on your precepts,
and fix my eyes on your ways.
[16]I will delight in your statutes;
I will not forget your word.

JOHN 8

**[31]Jesus then said to the Jews
who had believed in him, "If
you continue in my word, you are truly
my disciples, [32]and you will know the
truth, and the truth will make you free."**
[33]They answered him, "We are descendants
of Abraham, and have never been in
bondage to any one. How is it that you say,
'You will be made free'?"
[34]Jesus answered them, "Truly, truly, I say
to you, every one who commits sin is a slave
to sin. [35]The slave does not continue in the
house for ever; the son continues for ever.
[36]So if the Son makes you free, you will be free
indeed. [37]I know that you are descendants of
Abraham; yet you seek to kill me, because my
word finds no place in you. [38]I speak of what
I have seen with my Father, and you do what
you have heard from your father."
[39]They answered him, "Abraham is our
father." Jesus said to them, "If you were
Abraham's children, you would do what
Abraham did, [40]but now you seek to kill me,
a man who has told you the truth which I
heard from God; this is not what Abraham
did. [41]You do the works of your father."
They said to him, "We were not born of
fornication; we have one Father, even God."
[42]Jesus said to them, "If God were your
Father, you would love me, for I proceeded
and came forth from God; I came not of
my own accord, but he sent me. [43]Why do
you not understand what I say? It is because
you cannot bear to hear my word. [44]You are
of your father the devil, and your will is to
do your father's desires. He was a murderer
from the beginning, and has nothing to do
with the truth, because there is no truth in
him. When he lies, he speaks according to
his own nature, for he is a liar and the father
of lies. [45]But, because I tell the truth, you
do not believe me. [46]Which of you convicts
me of sin? If I tell the truth, why do you not
believe me? [47]He who is of God hears the
words of God; the reason why you do not
hear them is that you are not of God."
[48]The Jews answered him, "Are we not
right in saying that you are a Samaritan and
have a demon?" [49]Jesus answered, "I have
not a demon; but I honor my Father, and
you dishonor me. [50]Yet I do not seek my own
glory; there is One who seeks it and he will
be the judge. [51]Truly, truly, I say to you, if any
one keeps my word, he will never see death."
[52]The Jews said to him, "Now we know that
you have a demon. Abraham died, as did
the prophets; and you say, 'If any one keeps
my word, he will never taste death.' [53]Are
you greater than our father Abraham, who
died? And the prophets died! Who do you
claim to be?" [54]Jesus answered, "If I glorify
myself, my glory is nothing; it is my Father
who glorifies me, of whom you say that he
is your God. [55]But you have not known him;
I know him. If I said, I do not know him, I
should be a liar like you; but I do know him
and I keep his word. [56]Your father Abraham
rejoiced that he was to see my day; he saw it
and was glad." [57]The Jews then said to him,
"You are not yet fifty years old, and have
you seen Abraham?" [58]Jesus said to them,
"Truly, truly, I say to you, before Abraham
was, I am." [59]So they took up stones to throw
at him; but Jesus hid himself, and went out
of the temple.

REFLECTION

It is so easy for us to look for wisdom and the meaning of life in all the wrong places. In today's readings Solomon gives us a great example to follow. At the beginning of his reign, Solomon prays for the right thing: wisdom. In humility before God, he admits his own inadequacy: "I am but a little child; I do not know how to go out or come in" (1 Kgs 3:7). He needs the Lord's wisdom in order to govern. His prayer is so apt, so humble, so on-target that God is delighted. Instead of asking for his own health, wealth, and security, Solomon asks for wisdom for the good of others, so that he can lead God's people well. Because of Solomon's prayer, God blesses him, and Israel prospers in his reign with peace, productivity, expansion of territory, and even foreign tribute. His reign is the high watermark of Israel's kingship. It exemplifies Jesus's saying that "the truth will make you free" (Jn 8:31). In our humanity, we tend to look at worldly goods as providing us with freedom—freedom to buy things, freedom from fear, freedom from death—but in fact, these good things are very limited. Only the truth truly frees us. When you pray, what do you ask from the Lord?

May 24

1 KINGS 4

29And God gave Solomon wisdom and understanding beyond measure, and largeness of mind like the sand on the seashore, 30so that Solomon's wisdom surpassed the wisdom of all the people of the east, and all the wisdom of Egypt. 31For he was wiser than all other men, wiser than Ethan the Ez′rahite, and He′man, Calcol, and Darda, the sons of Mahol; and his fame was in all the nations round about. 32He also uttered three thousand proverbs; and his songs were a thousand and five. 33He spoke of trees, from the cedar that is in Lebanon to the hyssop that grows out of the wall; he spoke also of beasts, and of birds, and of reptiles, and of fish. 34And men came from all peoples to hear the wisdom of Solomon, and from all the kings of the earth, who had heard of his wisdom.

5 Now Hiram king of Tyre sent his servants to Solomon, when he heard that they had anointed him king in place of his father; for Hiram always loved David. 2And Solomon sent word to Hiram, 3"You know that David my father could not build a house for the name of the LORD his God because of the warfare with which his enemies surrounded him, until the LORD put them under the soles of his feet. 4But now the LORD my God has given me rest on every side; there is neither adversary nor misfortune. 5And so I purpose to build a house for the name of the LORD my God, as the LORD said to David my father, 'Your son, whom I will set upon your throne in your place, shall build the house for my name.' 6Now therefore command that cedars of Lebanon be cut for me; and my servants will join your servants, and I will pay you for your servants such wages as you set; for you know that there is no one among us who knows how to cut timber like the Sido′nians."

7When Hiram heard the words of Solomon, he rejoiced greatly, and said, "Blessed be the LORD this day, who has given to David a wise son to be over this great people." 8And Hiram sent to Solomon, saying, "I have heard the message which you have sent to me; I am ready to do all you desire in the matter of cedar and cypress timber. 9My servants shall bring it down to the sea from Lebanon; and I will make it into rafts to go by sea to the place you direct, and I will have them broken up there, and you shall receive it; and you shall meet my wishes by providing food for my household." 10So Hiram supplied Solomon with all the timber of cedar and cypress that he desired, 11while Solomon gave Hiram twenty thousand cors of wheat as food for his household, and twenty thousand cors of beaten oil. Solomon gave this to Hiram year by year. 12And the LORD gave Solomon wisdom, as he promised him; and there was peace between Hiram and Solomon; and the two of them made a treaty.

13King Solomon raised a levy of forced labor out of all Israel; and the levy numbered thirty thousand men. 14And he sent them to Lebanon, ten thousand a month in relays; they would be a month in Lebanon and two months at home; Adoni′ram was in charge of the levy. 15Solomon also had seventy thousand burden-bearers and eighty thousand hewers of stone in the hill country, 16besides Solomon's three thousand three hundred chief officers who were over the work, who had charge of the people who carried on the work. 17At the king's command, they quarried out great, costly stones in order to lay the foundation of the house with dressed stones. 18So Solomon's builders and Hiram's builders and the men of Ge'bal did the hewing and prepared the timber and the stone to build the house.

6 In the four hundred and eightieth year after the sons of Israel came out of the land of Egypt, in the fourth year of Solomon's reign over Israel, in the month of Ziv, which is the second month, he began to build the house of the LORD. 2The house which King Solomon built for the LORD was sixty cubits long, twenty cubits wide, and thirty cubits high. 3The vestibule in front of the nave of the house was twenty cubits long, equal to the width of the house, and ten cubits deep in front of the house. 4And he made for the house windows with recessed frames. 5He also built a structure against the wall of the house, running round the walls of the house, both the nave and the inner sanctuary; and he made side chambers all around. 6The lowest story was five cubits broad, the middle one was six cubits broad, and the third was seven cubits broad; for around the outside of the house he made offsets on the wall in order that the supporting beams should not be inserted into the walls of the house.

7When the house was built, it was with stone prepared at the quarry; so that neither hammer nor axe nor any tool of iron was heard in the temple, while it was being built.

8The entrance for the lowest story was on the south side of the house; and one went up by stairs to the middle story, and from the middle story to the third. 9So he built the house, and finished it; and he made the ceiling of the house of beams and planks of cedar. 10He built the structure against the whole house, each story five cubits high, and it was joined to the house with timbers of cedar.

11Now the word of the LORD came to Solomon, 12"Concerning this house which you are building, if you will walk in my statutes and obey my ordinances and keep all my commandments and walk in them, then I will establish my word with you, which I spoke to David your father. 13And I will dwell among the children of Israel, and will not forsake my people Israel."

14So Solomon built the house, and finished it. 15He lined the walls of the house on the inside with boards of cedar; from the floor of the house to the rafters of the ceiling, he covered them on the inside with wood; and he covered the floor of the house with boards of cypress. 16He built twenty cubits of the rear of the house with boards of cedar from the floor to the rafters, and he built this within as an inner sanctuary, as the most holy place. 17The house, that is, the nave in front of the inner sanctuary, was forty cubits long. 18The cedar within the house was carved in the form of gourds and open flowers; all was cedar, no stone was seen. 19The inner sanctuary he prepared in the innermost part of the house, to set there the ark of the covenant of the LORD. 20The inner sanctuary was twenty cubits long, twenty cubits wide, and twenty cubits high; and he overlaid it with pure gold. He also made an altar of cedar. 21And Solomon overlaid the inside of the house with pure gold, and he drew chains of gold across, in front of the inner sanctuary, and overlaid it with gold. 22And he overlaid the whole house with gold, until all the house was finished. Also the whole altar that belonged to the inner sanctuary he overlaid with gold.

23In the inner sanctuary he made two cherubim of olivewood, each ten cubits high. 24Five cubits was the length of one wing of the cherub, and five cubits the length of the other wing of the cherub; it was ten cubits from the tip of one wing to the tip of the other. 25The other cherub also measured ten cubits; both cherubim had the same measure and the same form.

26The height of one cherub was ten cubits,
and so was that of the other cherub.
27He put the cherubim in the innermost
part of the house; and the wings of the
cherubim were spread out so that a wing
of one touched the one wall, and a wing of
the other cherub touched the other wall;
their other wings touched each other in
the middle of the house. 28And he overlaid
the cherubim with gold.

29He carved all the walls of the house
round about with carved figures of
cherubim and palm trees and open flowers,
in the inner and outer rooms. 30The floor of
the house he overlaid with gold in the inner
and outer rooms.

31For the entrance to the inner sanctuary
he made doors of olivewood; the lintel and
the doorposts formed a pentagon. 32He
covered the two doors of olivewood with
carvings of cherubim, palm trees, and open
flowers; he overlaid them with gold, and
spread gold upon the cherubim and upon
the palm trees.

33So also he made for the entrance to the
nave doorposts of olivewood, in the form
of a square, 34and two doors of cypress
wood; the two leaves of the one door were
folding, and the two leaves of the other
door were folding. 35On them he carved
cherubim and palm trees and open
flowers; and he overlaid them with gold
evenly applied upon the carved work.
36He built the inner court with three
courses of hewn stone and one course of
cedar beams.

37In the fourth year the foundation of the
house of the LORD was laid, in the month of
Ziv. 38And in the eleventh year, in the month
of Bul, which is the eighth month, the house
was finished in all its parts, and according
to all its specifications. He was seven years
in building it.

PSALM 119 [118]

17Deal bountifully with your servant,
that I may live and observe your word.
18Open my eyes, that I may behold
wondrous things out of your law.
19I am a sojourner on earth;
hide not your commandments from me!
20My soul is consumed with longing
for your ordinances at all times.
21You rebuke the insolent, accursed ones,
who wander from your commandments;
22take away from me their scorn
and contempt,
for I have kept your testimonies.
23Even though princes sit plotting against me,
your servant will meditate on
your statutes.
24Your testimonies are my delight,
they are my counselors.

25My soul clings to the dust;
revive me according to your word!
26When I told of my ways, you answered me;
teach me your statutes!
27Make me understand the way of
your precepts,
and I will meditate on your
wondrous works.
28My soul melts away for sorrow;
strengthen me according to your word!
29Put false ways far from me;
and graciously teach me your law!
30I have chosen the way of faithfulness,
I set your ordinances before me.
31I cling to your testimonies, O LORD;
let me not be put to shame!
32I will run in the way of your commandments
when you enlarge my understanding!

JOHN 9

**As he passed by, he saw a man
blind from his birth. 2And his
disciples asked him, "Rabbi, who sinned,
this man or his parents, that he was born**
blind?" 3Jesus answered, "It was not that
this man sinned, or his parents, but that
the works of God might be made manifest
in him. 4We must work the works of him
who sent me, while it is day; night comes,
when no one can work. 5As long as I am

in the world, I am the light of the world."
6As he said this, he spat on the ground and
made clay of the spittle and anointed the
man's eyes with the clay, 7saying to him,
"Go, wash in the pool of Silo′am" (which
means Sent). So he went and washed
and came back seeing. 8The neighbors
and those who had seen him before as
a beggar, said, "Is not this the man who
used to sit and beg?" 9Some said, "It is he";
others said, "No, but he is like him." He
said, "I am the man." 10They said to him,
"Then how were your eyes opened?" 11He
answered, "The man called Jesus made
clay and anointed my eyes and said to me,
'Go to Silo′am and wash'; so I went and
washed and received my sight." 12They
said to him, "Where is he?" He said, "I do
not know."

REFLECTION

The Old Testament frames love for God in terms of obedience to the Law, while the New Testament describes it in terms of faith in Christ. For example, as Solomon begins to construct the Temple, the Lord speaks to him: "If you will walk in my statutes and obey my ordinances and keep all my commandments and walk in them, then I will establish my word with you" (1 Kgs 6:12). Psalm 119 similarly is a multifaceted celebration of the laws, commandments, statutes, and testimonies of the Lord. It uses many synonyms to describe the same reality: the word God spoke to man. St. Paul beautifully sums up the connection between Old and New Testament when he says, "Christ is the end (*telos*) of the law" (Rom 10:4). He is the Word that God spoke to man: "the light of the world" (Jn 9:5). When the ancient Israelites loved the Law and obeyed the commandments, they were loving and obeying Christ. Similarly, when we believe in him, when we love and follow him, we are fulfilling the law (see Rom 13:10). We can thus reread all the Old Testament celebration of rules, commandments, and ordinances in terms of Christ. Why do you think that Jesus is interchangeable with the Law?

May 25

1 KINGS 7

Solomon was building his own house thirteen years, and he finished his entire house.
2He built the House of the Forest of
Lebanon; its length was a hundred cubits,
and its breadth fifty cubits, and its height
thirty cubits, and it was built upon three rows
of cedar pillars, with cedar beams upon the
pillars. 3And it was covered with cedar above
the chambers that were upon the forty-five
pillars, fifteen in each row. 4There were window frames in three rows, and window opposite window in three tiers. 5All the doorways
and windows had square frames, and window
was opposite window in three tiers.
6And he made the Hall of Pillars; its length
was fifty cubits, and its breadth thirty cubits;
there was a porch in front with pillars, and a
canopy before them.
7And he made the Hall of the Throne
where he was to pronounce judgment, even
the Hall of Judgment; it was finished with
cedar from floor to rafters.
8His own house where he was to dwell, in
the other court back of the hall, was of like
workmanship. Solomon also made a house
like this hall for Pharaoh's daughter whom
he had taken in marriage.
9All these were made of costly stones,
hewn according to measure, sawed with
saws, back and front, even from the foundation to the coping, and from the court of
the house of the LORD to the great court.
10The foundation was of costly stones, huge
stones, stones of eight and ten cubits. 11And
above were costly stones, hewn according to
measurement, and cedar. 12The great court
had three courses of hewn stone round
about, and a course of cedar beams; so had
the inner court of the house of the LORD,
and the vestibule of the house.
13And King Solomon sent and brought
Hiram from Tyre. 14He was the son of a

widow of the tribe of Naph′tali, and his father was a man of Tyre, a worker in bronze; and he was full of wisdom, understanding, and skill, for making any work in bronze. He came to King Solomon, and did all his work.

[15]He cast two pillars of bronze. Eighteen cubits was the height of one pillar, and a line of twelve cubits measured its circumference; it was hollow, and its thickness was four fingers; the second pillar was the same. [16]He also made two capitals of molten bronze, to set upon the tops of the pillars; the height of the one capital was five cubits, and the height of the other capital was five cubits. [17]Then he made two nets of checker work with wreaths of chain work for the capitals upon the tops of the pillars; a net for the one capital, and a net for the other capital. [18]Likewise he made pomegranates; in two rows round about upon the one network, to cover the capital that was upon the top of the pillar; and he did the same with the other capital. [19]Now the capitals that were upon the tops of the pillars in the vestibule were of lily-work, four cubits. [20]The capitals were upon the two pillars and also above the rounded projection which was beside the network; there were two hundred pomegranates, in two rows round about; and so with the other capital. [21]He set up the pillars at the vestibule of the temple; he set up the pillar on the south and called its name Ja′chin; and he set up the pillar on the north and called its name Boaz. [22]And upon the tops of the pillars was lily-work. Thus the work of the pillars was finished.

[23]Then he made the molten sea; it was round, ten cubits from brim to brim, and five cubits high, and a line of thirty cubits measured its circumference. [24]Under its brim were gourds, for thirty cubits, compassing the sea round about; the gourds were in two rows, cast with it when it was cast. [25]It stood upon twelve oxen, three facing north, three facing west, three facing south, and three facing east; the sea was set upon them, and all their posterior parts were inward. [26]Its thickness was a handbreadth; and its brim was made like the brim of a cup, like the flower of a lily; it held two thousand baths.

[27]He also made the ten stands of bronze; each stand was four cubits long, four cubits wide, and three cubits high. [28]This was the construction of the stands: they had panels, and the panels were set in the frames [29]and on the panels that were set in the frames were lions, oxen, and cherubim. Upon the frames, both above and below the lions and oxen, there were wreaths of beveled work. [30]Moreover each stand had four bronze wheels and axles of bronze; and at the four corners were supports for a laver. The supports were cast, with wreaths at the side of each. [31]Its opening was within a crown which projected upward one cubit; its opening was round, as a pedestal is made, a cubit and a half deep. At its opening there were carvings; and its panels were square, not round. [32]And the four wheels were underneath the panels; the axles of the wheels were of one piece with the stands; and the height of a wheel was a cubit and a half. [33]The wheels were made like a chariot wheel; their axles, their rims, their spokes, and their hubs, were all cast. [34]There were four supports at the four corners of each stand; the supports were of one piece with the stands. [35]And on the top of the stand there was a round band half a cubit high; and on the top of the stand its stays and its panels were of one piece with it. [36]And on the surfaces of its stays and on its panels, he carved cherubim, lions, and palm trees, according to the space of each, with wreaths round about. [37]After this manner he made the ten stands; all of them were cast alike, of the same measure and the same form.

[38]And he made ten lavers of bronze; each laver held forty baths, each laver measured four cubits, and there was a laver for each of the ten stands. [39]And he set the stands, five on the south side of the house, and five on the north side of the house; and he set the sea at the southeast corner of the house.

[40]Hiram also made the pots, the shovels, and the basins. So Hiram finished all the work that he did for King Solomon on the house of the LORD: [41]the two pillars, the two bowls of the capitals that were on the tops of the pillars, and the two networks to cover the two bowls of the capitals that were on

the tops of the pillars; [42]and the four hundred pomegranates for the two networks, two rows of pomegranates for each network, to cover the two bowls of the capitals that were upon the pillars; [43]the ten stands, and the ten lavers upon the stands; [44]and the one sea, and the twelve oxen underneath the sea.

[45]Now the pots, the shovels, and the basins, all these vessels in the house of the LORD, which Hiram made for King Solomon, were of burnished bronze. [46]In the plain of the Jordan the king cast them, in the clay ground between Succoth and Zar′ethan. [47]And Solomon left all the vessels unweighed, because there were so many of them; the weight of the bronze was not found out.

[48]So Solomon made all the vessels that were in the house of the LORD: the golden altar, the golden table for the bread of the Presence, [49]the lampstands of pure gold, five on the south side and five on the north, before the inner sanctuary; the flowers, the lamps, and the tongs, of gold; [50]the cups, snuffers, basins, dishes for incense, and firepans, of pure gold; and the sockets of gold, for the doors of the innermost part of the house, the most holy place, and for the doors of the nave of the temple.

[51]Thus all the work that King Solomon did on the house of the LORD was finished. And Solomon brought in the things which David his father had dedicated, the silver, the gold, and the vessels, and stored them in the treasuries of the house of the LORD.

PSALM 119 [118]

[33]Teach me, O LORD, the way of
your statutes;
and I will keep it to the end.
[34]Give me understanding, that I may keep
your law
and observe it with my whole heart.
[35]Lead me in the path of your
commandments,
for I delight in it.
[36]Incline my heart to your testimonies,
and not to gain!
[37]Turn my eyes from looking at vanities;
and give me life in your ways.
[38]Confirm to your servant your promise,
which is for those who fear you.
[39]Turn away the reproach which I dread;
for your ordinances are good.
[40]Behold, I long for your precepts;
in your righteousness give me life!

[41]Let your mercy come to me, O LORD,
your salvation according to your promise;
[42]then shall I have an answer for those who
taunt me,
for I trust in your word.
[43]And take not the word of truth utterly out
of my mouth,
for my hope is in your ordinances.
[44]I will keep your law continually,
for ever and ever;
[45]and I shall walk at liberty,
for I have sought your precepts.
[46]I will also speak of your testimonies
before kings,
and shall not be put to shame;
[47]for I find my delight in your commandments,
which I love.
[48]I revere your commandments, which I love,
and I will meditate on your statutes.

JOHN 9

[13]They brought to the Pharisees the man who had formerly been blind. [14]Now it was a sabbath day when Jesus made the clay and opened his eyes.
[15]The Pharisees again asked him how he had received his sight. And he said to them, "He put clay on my eyes, and I washed, and I see." [16]Some of the Pharisees said, "This man is not from God, for he does not keep the sabbath." But others said, "How can a man who is a sinner do such signs?" There was a division among them. [17]So they again said to the blind man, "What do you say about him, since he has opened your eyes?" He said, "He is a prophet."

[18]The Jews did not believe that he had been blind and had received his sight, until

they called the parents of the man who had received his sight, 19and asked them, "Is this your son, who you say was born blind? How then does he now see?" 20His parents answered, "We know that this is our son, and that he was born blind; 21but how he now sees we do not know, nor do we know who opened his eyes. Ask him; he is of age, he will speak for himself." 22His parents said this because they feared the Jews, for the Jews had already agreed that if any one should confess him to be Christ, he was to be put out of the synagogue. 23Therefore his parents said, "He is of age, ask him."

24So for the second time they called the man who had been blind, and said to him, "Give God the praise; we know that this man is a sinner." 25He answered, "Whether he is a sinner, I do not know; one thing I know, that though I was blind, now I see." 26They said to him, "What did he do to you? How did he open your eyes?" 27He answered them, "I have told you already, and you would not listen. Why do you want to hear it again? Do you too want to become his disciples?" 28And they reviled him, saying, "You are his disciple, but we are disciples of Moses. 29We know that God has spoken to Moses, but as for this man, we do not know where he comes from." 30The man answered, "Why, this is a marvel! You do not know where he comes from, and yet he opened my eyes. 31We know that God does not listen to sinners, but if any one is a worshiper of God and does his will, God listens to him. 32Never since the world began has it been heard that any one opened the eyes of a man born blind. 33If this man were not from God, he could do nothing." 34They answered him, "You were born in utter sin, and would you teach us?" And they cast him out.

35Jesus heard that they had cast him out, and having found him he said, "Do you believe in the Son of man?" 36He answered, "And who is he, sir, that I may believe in him?" 37Jesus said to him, "You have seen him, and it is he who speaks to you." 38He said, "Lord, I believe"; and he worshiped him. 39Jesus said, "For judgment I came into this world, that those who do not see may see, and that those who see may become blind." 40Some of the Pharisees near him heard this, and they said to him, "Are we also blind?" 41Jesus said to them, "If you were blind, you would have no guilt; but now that you say, 'We see,' your guilt remains."

REFLECTION

The Book of Kings narrates in elaborate detail the building of Solomon's palace, as well as the Temple and its many instruments for worship. As a dark hint of things to come, the narrator mentions that it took Solomon seven years to build the Temple but thirteen to build his own house. The priests used the sacred objects described in today's reading for worship in the Temple—for stoking the fire on the altar, for ritual washings, for blood rituals, and for animal sacrifices. The Temple worship of God was meant to go hand in hand with obedience to the Law, and lead to a spiritual life free from fear: "I shall walk in liberty, for I have sought your precepts" (Ps 119:45). Jesus demonstrates that his opponents are spiritually blind to the true meaning of God's Law, revelation, and the Temple worship. The blind man has greater sight than the Pharisees: "One thing I know, that though I was blind, now I see" (Jn 9:25). The blind man professes faith in Jesus, but the others reject Jesus and are judged. "For judgment I came into this world, that those who do not see may see, and that those who see may become blind" (v. 39). Are you attentive to the small details in your life and how they can serve God, or are there blind-spots that need healing?

May 26

1 KINGS 8

Then Solomon assembled the elders of Israel and all the heads of the tribes, the leaders of the fathers' houses of the sons of Israel, before King Solomon in Jerusalem, to bring up the

ark of the covenant of the LORD out of the
city of David, which is Zion. 2And all the
men of Israel assembled to King Solomon at
the feast in the month Eth´anim, which is the
seventh month. 3And all the elders of Israel
came, and the priests took up the ark. 4And
they brought up the ark of the LORD, the
tent of meeting, and all the holy vessels that
were in the tent; the priests and the Levites
brought them up. 5And King Solomon
and all the congregation of Israel, who
had assembled before him, were with him
before the ark, sacrificing so many sheep
and oxen that they could not be counted or
numbered. 6Then the priests brought the
ark of the covenant of the LORD to its place,
in the inner sanctuary of the house, in the
most holy place, underneath the wings of
the cherubim. 7For the cherubim spread out
their wings over the place of the ark, so that
the cherubim made a covering above the ark
and its poles. 8And the poles were so long
that the ends of the poles were seen from
the holy place before the inner sanctuary;
but they could not be seen from outside;
and they are there to this day. 9There was
nothing in the ark except the two tables
of stone which Moses put there at Horeb,
where the LORD made a covenant with
the sons of Israel, when they came out of
the land of Egypt. 10And when the priests
came out of the holy place, a cloud filled
the house of the LORD, 11so that the priests
could not stand to minister because of the
cloud; for the glory of the LORD filled the
house of the LORD.

12Then Solomon said,

"The LORD has set the sun in the heavens,
but has said that he would dwell in thick
darkness.
13I have built you an exalted house,
a place for you to dwell in for ever."

14Then the king faced about, and blessed all
the assembly of Israel, while all the assembly
of Israel stood. 15And he said, "Blessed be
the LORD, the God of Israel, who with his
hand has fulfilled what he promised with his
mouth to David my father, saying, 16'Since
the day that I brought my people Israel out
of Egypt, I chose no city in all the tribes of
Israel in which to build a house, that my
name might be there; but I chose David to
be over my people Israel.' 17Now it was in the
heart of David my father to build a house for
the name of the LORD, the God of Israel. 18But
the LORD said to David my father, 'Whereas
it was in your heart to build a house for my
name, you did well that it was in your heart;
19nevertheless you shall not build the house,
but your son who shall be born to you shall
build the house for my name.' 20Now the
LORD has fulfilled his promise which he
made; for I have risen in the place of David
my father, and sit on the throne of Israel,
as the LORD promised, and I have built the
house for the name of the LORD, the God of
Israel. 21And there I have provided a place
for the ark, in which is the covenant of the
LORD which he made with our fathers, when
he brought them out of the land of Egypt."

22Then Solomon stood before the altar of
the LORD in the presence of all the assembly
of Israel, and spread forth his hands toward
heaven; 23and said, "O LORD, God of Israel,
there is no God like you, in heaven above
or on earth beneath, keeping covenant and
showing mercy to your servants who walk
before you with all their heart; 24who have
kept with your servant David my father
what you declared to him; yes, you spoke
with your mouth, and with your hand have
fulfilled it this day. 25Now therefore, O
LORD, God of Israel, keep with your servant
David my father what you have promised
him, saying, 'There shall never fail you a
man before me to sit upon the throne of
Israel, if only your sons take heed to their
way, to walk before me as you have walked
before me.' 26Now therefore, O God of Israel,
let your word be confirmed, which you have
spoken to your servant David my father.

27"But will God indeed dwell on the earth?
Behold, heaven and the highest heaven
cannot contain you; how much less this
house which I have built! 28Yet have regard
to the prayer of your servant and to his
supplication, O LORD my God, listening to
the cry and to the prayer which your servant
prays before you this day; 29that your eyes
may be open night and day toward this

house, the place of which you have said, 'My
name shall be there,' that you may listen to
the prayer which your servant offers toward
this place. 30And hear the supplication of
your servant and of your people Israel,
when they pray toward this place; yes, hear
in heaven your dwelling place; and when
you hear, forgive.

31"If a man sins against his neighbor and
is made to take an oath, and comes and
swears his oath before your altar in this
house, 32then hear in heaven, and act, and
judge your servants, condemning the guilty
by bringing his conduct upon his own head,
and vindicating the righteous by rewarding
him according to his righteousness.

33"When your people Israel are defeated
before the enemy because they have sinned
against you, if they turn again to you, and
acknowledge your name, and pray and
make supplication to you in this house;
34then hear in heaven, and forgive the sin of
your people Israel, and bring them again to
the land which you gave to their fathers.

35"When heaven is shut up and there is no
rain because they have sinned against you, if
they pray toward this place, and acknowledge
your name, and turn from their sin, when
you afflict them, 36then hear in heaven, and
forgive the sin of your servants, your people
Israel, when you teach them the good way in
which they should walk; and grant rain upon
your land, which you have given to your
people as an inheritance.

37"If there is famine in the land, if there is
pestilence or blight or mildew or locust or
caterpillar; if their enemy besieges them in
any of their cities; whatever plague, whatever sickness there is; 38whatever prayer,
whatever supplication is made by any man
or by all your people Israel, each knowing
the affliction of his own heart and stretching
out his hands toward this house; 39then hear
in heaven your dwelling place, and forgive,
and act, and render to each whose heart you
know, according to all his ways (for you, you
only, know the hearts of all the children of
men); 40that they may fear you all the days
that they live in the land which you gave to
our fathers.

41"Likewise when a foreigner, who is not of
your people Israel, comes from a far country
for your name's sake 42(for they shall hear of
your great name, and your mighty hand,
and of your outstretched arm), when he
comes and prays toward this house, 43hear
in heaven your dwelling place, and do
according to all for which the foreigner calls
to you; in order that all the peoples of the
earth may know your name and fear you,
as do your people Israel, and that they may
know that this house which I have built is
called by your name.

44"If your people go out to battle against
their enemy, by whatever way you shall send
them, and they pray to the LORD toward
the city which you have chosen and the
house which I have built for your name,
45then hear in heaven their prayer and their
supplication, and maintain their cause.

46"If they sin against you—for there is no
man who does not sin—and you are angry
with them, and give them to an enemy, so
that they are carried away captive to the
land of the enemy, far off or near; 47yet
if they lay it to heart in the land to which
they have been carried captive, and repent,
and make supplication to you in the land
of their captors, saying, 'We have sinned,
and have acted perversely and wickedly';
48if they repent with all their mind and with
all their heart in the land of their enemies,
who carried them captive, and pray to you
toward their land, which you gave to their
fathers, the city which you have chosen,
and the house which I have built for your
name; 49then hear in heaven your dwelling
place their prayer and their supplication,
and maintain their cause 50and forgive
your people who have sinned against you,
and all their transgressions which they
have committed against you; and grant
them compassion in the sight of those
who carried them captive, that they may
have compassion on them 51(for they are
your people, and your heritage, which you
brought out of Egypt, from the midst of the
iron furnace). 52Let your eyes be open to
the supplication of your servant, and to the
supplication of your people Israel, giving

ear to them whenever they call to you. 53For you separated them from among all the peoples of the earth, to be your heritage, as you declared through Moses, your servant, when you brought our fathers out of Egypt, O Lord GOD."

PSALM 119 [118]

49Remember your word to your servant,
in which you have made me hope.
50This is my comfort in my affliction
that your promise gives me life.
51Godless men utterly deride me,
but I do not turn away from your law.
52When I think of your ordinances from
of old,
I take comfort, O LORD.
53Hot indignation seizes me because of
the wicked,
who forsake your law.
54Your statutes have been my songs
in the house of my pilgrimage.
55I remember your name in the night, O LORD,
and keep your law.
56This blessing has fallen to me,
that I have kept your precepts.
57The LORD is my portion;
I promise to keep your words.
58I entreat your favor with all my heart;
be gracious to me according to
your promise.
59When I think of your ways,
I turn my feet to your testimonies;
60I hasten and do not delay
to keep your commandments.
61Though the cords of the wicked ensnare me,
I do not forget your law.
62At midnight I rise to praise you,
because of your righteous ordinances.
63I am a companion of all who fear you,
of those who keep your precepts.
64The earth, O LORD, is full of your
steadfast love;
teach me your statutes!

65You have dealt well with your servant,
O LORD, according to your word.
66Teach me good judgment and knowledge,
for I believe in your commandments.
67Before I was afflicted I went astray;
but now I keep your word.
68You are good and do good;
teach me your statutes.
69The godless besmear me with lies,
but with my whole heart I keep
your precepts;
70their heart is gross like fat,
but I delight in your law.
71It is good for me that I was afflicted,
that I might learn your statutes.
72The law of your mouth is better to me
than thousands of gold and silver pieces.

JOHN 10

"Truly, truly, I say to you, he who does not enter the sheepfold by the door but climbs in by another way, that man is a thief and a robber; 2but
he who enters by the door is the shepherd
of the sheep. 3To him the gatekeeper opens;
the sheep hear his voice, and he calls his own
sheep by name and leads them out. 4When he
has brought out all his own, he goes before
them, and the sheep follow him, for they
know his voice. 5A stranger they will not
follow, but they will flee from him, for they
do not know the voice of strangers." 6This
figure Jesus used with them, but they did not
understand what he was saying to them.
7So Jesus again said to them, "Truly, truly,
I say to you, I am the door of the sheep.
8All who came before me are thieves and
robbers; but the sheep did not heed them.
9I am the door; if any one enters by me, he
will be saved, and will go in and out and
find pasture. 10The thief comes only to steal
and kill and destroy; I came that they may
have life, and have it abundantly. 11I am the
good shepherd. The good shepherd lays
down his life for the sheep. 12He who is a
hireling and not a shepherd, whose own
the sheep are not, sees the wolf coming
and leaves the sheep and flees; and the wolf
snatches them and scatters them. 13He flees

because he is a hireling and cares nothing for the sheep. [14]I am the good shepherd; I know my own and my own know me, [15]as the Father knows me and I know the Father; and I lay down my life for the sheep. [16]And I have other sheep, that are not of this fold; I must bring them also, and they will heed my voice. So there shall be one flock, one shepherd. [17]For this reason the Father loves me, because I lay down my life, that I may take it again. [18]No one takes it from me, but I lay it down of my own accord. I have power to lay it down, and I have power to take it again; this charge I have received from my Father."

[19]There was again a division among the Jews because of these words. [20]Many of them said, "He has a demon, and he is mad; why listen to him?" [21]Others said, "These are not the sayings of one who has a demon. Can a demon open the eyes of the blind?"

REFLECTION

God wants to bless us. His whole design for the universe aims at one goal: that we might share in his blessed life. When Solomon dedicates the new Temple, he blesses the people and recalls the Lord's promises to them, which culminate in this climactic moment when the Ark of the Covenant is installed in the Holy of Holies so that God might dwell amongst his people. If the Holy Land represents the blessed rest that the Lord wants to share with his people, then the Temple is the center of that land, the most holy of all places, the location that represents the rest of God in its most intense form. During the Temple's dedication, Solomon turns to the Lord in prayer. He acknowledges the Lord's covenant faithfulness and then pleads with him eight times to "hear in heaven" the cries of his people, to forgive their sins, and to act on their behalf. God's people will need forgiveness and mercy if God is to dwell in their midst. What God's presence in the Temple foreshadowed comes to fulfillment with Jesus: "I came that they may have life, and have it abundantly" (Jn 10:10). His love for us is about life, about flourishing in his presence, and about enjoying the rest granted by the Good Shepherd.

May 27

1 KINGS 8

[54]Now as Solomon finished offering all this prayer and supplication to the LORD, he arose from before the altar of the LORD, where he had knelt with hands outstretched toward heaven; [55]and he stood, and blessed all the assembly of Israel with a loud voice, saying, [56]"Blessed be the LORD who has given rest to his people Israel, according to all that he promised; not one word has failed of all his good promise, which he uttered by Moses his servant. [57]The LORD our God be with us, as he was with our fathers; may he not leave us or forsake us; [58]that he may incline our hearts to him, to walk in all his ways, and to keep his commandments, his statutes, and his ordinances, which he commanded our fathers. [59]Let these words of mine, wherewith I have made supplication before the LORD, be near to the LORD our God day and night, and may he maintain the cause of his servant, and the cause of his people Israel, as each day requires; [60]that all the peoples of the earth may know that the LORD is God; there is no other. [61]Let your heart therefore be wholly true to the LORD our God, walking in his statutes and keeping his commandments, as at this day."

[62]Then the king, and all Israel with him, offered sacrifice before the LORD. [63]Solomon offered as peace offerings to the LORD twenty-two thousand oxen and a hundred and twenty thousand sheep. So the king and all the sons of Israel dedicated the house of the LORD. [64]The same day the king consecrated the middle of the court that was before the house of the LORD; for there he offered the burnt offering and the cereal offering and the fat pieces of the peace offerings, because the bronze altar that was before the LORD was too small to receive the burnt offering and the cereal offering and the fat pieces of the peace offerings.

65So Solomon held the feast at that time, and all Israel with him, a great assembly, from the entrance of Ha´math to the Brook of Egypt, before the LORD our God, seven days. 66On the eighth day he sent the people away; and they blessed the king, and went to their homes joyful and glad of heart for all the goodness that the LORD had shown to David his servant and to Israel his people.

9 When Solomon had finished building the house of the LORD and the king's house and all that Solomon desired to build, 2the LORD appeared to Solomon a second time, as he had appeared to him at Gib´eon. 3And the LORD said to him, "I have heard your prayer and your supplication, which you have made before me; I have consecrated this house which you have built, and put my name there for ever; my eyes and my heart will be there for all time. 4And as for you, if you will walk before me, as David your father walked, with integrity of heart and uprightness, doing according to all that I have commanded you, and keeping my statutes and my ordinances, 5then I will establish your royal throne over Israel for ever, as I promised David your father, saying, 'There shall not fail you a man upon the throne of Israel.' 6But if you turn aside from following me, you or your children, and do not keep my commandments and my statutes which I have set before you, but go and serve other gods and worship them, 7then I will cut off Israel from the land which I have given them; and the house which I have consecrated for my name I will cast out of my sight; and Israel will become a proverb and a byword among all peoples. 8And this house will become a heap of ruins; every one passing by it will be astonished, and will hiss; and they will say, 'Why has the LORD done thus to this land and to this house?' 9Then they will say, 'Because they forsook the LORD their God who brought their fathers out of the land of Egypt, and laid hold on other gods, and worshiped them and served them; therefore the LORD has brought all this evil upon them.' "

10At the end of twenty years, in which Solomon had built the two houses, the house of the LORD and the king's house, 11and Hiram king of Tyre had supplied Solomon with cedar and cypress timber and gold, as much as he desired, King Solomon gave to Hiram twenty cities in the land of Galilee. 12But when Hiram came from Tyre to see the cities which Solomon had given him, they did not please him. 13Therefore he said, "What kind of cities are these which you have given me, my brother?" So they are called the land of Ca´bul to this day. 14Hiram had sent to the king one hundred and twenty talents of gold.

15And this is the account of the forced labor which King Solomon levied to build the house of the LORD and his own house and the Millo and the wall of Jerusalem and Ha´zor and Megid´do and Gezer 16(Pharaoh king of Egypt had gone up and captured Gezer and burnt it with fire, and had slain the Canaanites who dwelt in the city, and had given it as dowry to his daughter, Solomon's wife; 17so Solomon rebuilt Gezer) and Lower Beth-ho´ron 18and Ba´alath and Ta´mar in the wilderness, in the land of Judah, 19and all the store-cities that Solomon had, and the cities for his chariots, and the cities for his horsemen, and whatever Solomon desired to build in Jerusalem, in Lebanon, and in all the land of his dominion. 20All the people who were left of the Am´orites, the Hittites, the Per´izzites, the Hi´vites, and the Jeb´usites, who were not of the sons of Israel—21their descendants who were left after them in the land, whom the sons of Israel were unable to destroy utterly—these Solomon made a forced levy of slaves, and so they are to this day. 22But of the sons of Israel Solomon made no slaves; they were the soldiers, they were his officials, his commanders, his captains, his chariot commanders and his horsemen.

23These were the chief officers who were over Solomon's work: five hundred and fifty, who had charge of the people who carried on the work.

24But Pharaoh's daughter went up from the city of David to her own house which Solomon had built for her; then he built the Millo.

25Three times a year Solomon used to offer
up burnt offerings and peace offerings upon
the altar which he built to the LORD, burning
incense before the LORD. So he finished the
house.
26King Solomon built a fleet of ships at
E′zion-ge′ber, which is near E′loth on the
shore of the Red Sea, in the land of E′dom.
27And Hiram sent with the fleet his servants,
seamen who were familiar with the sea,
together with the servants of Solomon;
28and they went to O′phir, and brought from
there gold, to the amount of four hundred
and twenty talents; and they brought it to
King Solomon.
10 Now when the queen of Sheba heard
of the fame of Solomon concerning
the name of the LORD, she came to test
him with hard questions. 2She came to
Jerusalem with a very great retinue, with
camels bearing spices, and very much
gold, and precious stones; and when she
came to Solomon, she told him all that was
on her mind. 3And Solomon answered all
her questions; there was nothing hidden
from the king which he could not explain
to her. 4And when the queen of Sheba
had seen all the wisdom of Solomon, the
house that he had built, 5the food of his
table, the seating of his officials, and the
attendance of his servants, their clothing,
his cupbearers, and his burnt offerings
which he offered at the house of the
LORD, there was no more spirit in her.
6And she said to the king, "The report
was true which I heard in my own land
of your affairs and of your wisdom, 7but
I did not believe the reports until I came
and my own eyes had seen it; and behold,
the half was not told me; your wisdom
and prosperity surpass the report which
I heard. 8Happy are your wives! Happy
are these your servants, who continually
stand before you and hear your wisdom!
9Blessed be the LORD your God, who has
delighted in you and set you on the throne
of Israel! Because the LORD loved Israel
for ever, he has made you king, that you
may execute justice and righteousness."
10Then she gave the king a hundred and
twenty talents of gold, and a very great
quantity of spices, and precious stones;
never again came such an abundance of
spices as these which the queen of Sheba
gave to King Solomon.
11Moreover the fleet of Hiram, which
brought gold from O′phir, brought from
Ophir a very great amount of almug wood
and precious stones. 12And the king made
of the almug wood supports for the house
of the LORD, and for the king's house,
lyres also and harps for the singers; no
such almug wood has come or been seen,
to this day.
13And King Solomon gave to the queen of
Sheba all that she desired, whatever she asked
besides what was given her by the bounty of
King Solomon. So she turned and went back
to her own land, with her servants.

PSALM 119 [118]

73Your hands have made and fashioned me;
give me understanding that I may learn
your commandments.
74Those who fear you shall see me
and rejoice,
because I have hoped in your word.
75I know, O LORD, that your judgments
are right,
and that in faithfulness you have
afflicted me.
76Let your mercy be ready to comfort me
according to your promise to
your servant.
77Let your compassion come to me, that I
may live;
for your law is my delight.
78Let the godless be put to shame,
because they have subverted me
with guile;
as for me, I will meditate on your precepts.
79Let those who fear you turn to me,
that they may know your testimonies.
80May my heart be blameless in your statutes,
that I may not be put to shame!

81My soul languishes for your salvation;
I hope in your word.

82My eyes fail with watching for
your promise;
I ask, "When will you comfort me?"
83For I have become like a wineskin in
the smoke,
yet I have not forgotten your statutes.
84How long must your servant endure?
When will you judge those who
persecute me?
85Godless men have dug pitfalls for me,
men who do not conform to your law.
86All your commandments are sure;
they persecute me with falsehood; help me!
87They have almost made an end of me
on earth;
but I have not forsaken your precepts.
88In your mercy spare my life,
that I may keep the testimonies of
your mouth.

JOHN 10

22It was the feast of the Dedication at Jerusalem; 23it was winter, and Jesus was walking in the temple, in the portico of Solomon. 24So the Jews gathered round him and said to him, "How long will you keep us in suspense? If you are the Christ, tell us
plainly." 25Jesus answered them, "I told you,
and you do not believe. The works that I do in my Father's name, they bear witness to
me; 26but you do not believe, because you do
not belong to my sheep. 27My sheep hear my voice, and I know them, and they follow me;
28and I give them eternal life, and they shall never perish, and no one shall snatch them out of my hand. 29My Father, who has given them to me, is greater than all, and no one is able to snatch them out of the Father's hand.
30I and the Father are one."
31The Jews took up stones again to stone
him. 32Jesus answered them, "I have shown you many good works from the Father; for which of these do you stone me?" 33The
Jews answered him, "We stone you for no good work but for blasphemy; because you, being a man, make yourself God." 34Jesus answered them, "Is it not written in your law, 'I said, you are gods'? 35If he called them
gods to whom the word of God came (and Scripture cannot be nullified), 36do you say
of him whom the Father consecrated and sent into the world, 'You are blaspheming,' because I said, 'I am the Son of God'? 37If I
am not doing the works of my Father, then do not believe me; 38but if I do them, even
though you do not believe me, believe the works, that you may know and understand that the Father is in me and I am in the
Father." 39Again they tried to arrest him, but
he escaped from their hands.
40He went away again across the Jordan to the place where John at first baptized, and there he remained. 41And many came
to him; and they said, "John did no sign, but everything that John said about this man was true." 42And many believed in
him there.

REFLECTION

Doing something half-heartedly never works. Half-hearted soldiers don't win battles. Half-hearted athletes don't win games. Likewise, half-hearted devotion to God crumbles before the pressures of the world. Because of this, Solomon encourages the people, "Let your heart therefore be wholly true to the LORD our God" (1 Kgs 8:61). Whole-hearted devotion is linked with God's blessing, which leads to our happiness. When the Queen of Sheba visits Solomon, she recognizes the hand of God blessing the Israelites: "Happy are your wives! Happy are these your servants, who continually stand before you and hear your wisdom!" (10:8). When our hearts align with the Lord's purposes for our lives and we experience his blessing, happiness is the predictable result. Happiness is found in Jesus's promises: "I give them eternal life, and they shall never perish, and no one shall snatch them out of my hand" (Jn 10:28). It is a happiness based on hope, rather than on possession. Giving ourselves away in whole-hearted love like Jesus—seeking to give, not to gain—makes for happiness. Are you half-hearted in your love for the Lord, or are you "wholly true" to him?

May 28

1 KINGS 10

14Now the weight of gold that came to Solomon in one year was six hundred and sixty-six talents of gold, 15besides that which came from the traders and from the traffic of the merchants, and from all the kings of Arabia and from the governors of the land. 16King Solomon made two hundred large shields of beaten gold; six hundred shekels of gold went into each shield. 17And he made three hundred shields of beaten gold; three minas of gold went into each shield; and the king put them in the House of the Forest of Lebanon. 18The king also made a great ivory throne, and overlaid it with the finest gold. 19The throne had six steps, and at the back of the throne was a calf's head, and on each side of the seat were arm rests and two lions standing beside the arm rests, 20while twelve lions stood there, one on each end of a step on the six steps. The like of it was never made in any kingdom. 21All King Solomon's drinking vessels were of gold, and all the vessels of the House of the Forest of Lebanon were of pure gold; none were of silver, it was not considered as anything in the days of Solomon. 22For the king had a fleet of ships of Tar′shish at sea with the fleet of Hiram. Once every three years the fleet of ships of Tarshish used to come bringing gold, silver, ivory, apes, and peacocks.

23Thus King Solomon excelled all the kings of the earth in riches and in wisdom. 24And the whole earth sought the presence of Solomon to hear his wisdom, which God had put into his mind. 25Every one of them brought his present, articles of silver and gold, garments, myrrh, spices, horses, and mules, so much year by year.

26And Solomon gathered together chariots and horsemen; he had fourteen hundred chariots and twelve thousand horsemen, whom he stationed in the chariot cities and with the king in Jerusalem. 27And the king made silver as common in Jerusalem as stone, and he made cedar as plentiful as the sycamore of the Shephe′lah. 28And Solomon's import of horses was from Egypt and Ku′e, and the king's traders received them from Kue at a price. 29A chariot could be imported from Egypt for six hundred shekels of silver, and a horse for a hundred and fifty; and so through the king's traders they were exported to all the kings of the Hittites and the kings of Syria.

11 Now King Solomon loved many foreign women: the daughter of Pharaoh, and Moabite, Am′monite, E′domite, Sido′nian, and Hittite women, 2from the nations concerning which the LORD had said to the sons of Israel, "You shall not enter into marriage with them, neither shall they with you, for surely they will turn away your heart after their gods"; Solomon clung to these in love. 3He had seven hundred wives, princesses, and three hundred concubines; and his wives turned away his heart. 4For when Solomon was old his wives turned away his heart after other gods; and his heart was not wholly true to the LORD his God, as was the heart of David his father. 5For Solomon went after Ash′toreth the goddess of the Sido′nians, and after Milcom the abomination of the Am′monites. 6So Solomon did what was evil in the sight of the LORD, and did not wholly follow the LORD, as David his father had done. 7Then Solomon built a high place for Che′mosh the abomination of Moab, and for Mo′lech the abomination of the Am′monites, on the mountain east of Jerusalem. 8And so he did for all his foreign wives, who burned incense and sacrificed to their gods.

9And the LORD was angry with Solomon, because his heart had turned away from the LORD, the God of Israel, who had appeared to him twice, 10and had commanded him concerning this thing, that he should not go after other gods; but he did not keep what the LORD commanded. 11Therefore the LORD said to Solomon, "Since this has been your mind and you have not kept my covenant

and my statutes which I have commanded
you, I will surely tear the kingdom from you
and will give it to your servant. [12]Yet for the
sake of David your father I will not do it in
your days, but I will tear it out of the hand
of your son. [13]However I will not tear away
all the kingdom; but I will give one tribe to
your son, for the sake of David my servant
and for the sake of Jerusalem which I have
chosen."

[14]And the LORD raised up an adversary
against Solomon, Ha′dad the E′domite; he
was of the royal house in E′dom. [15]For when
David was in E′dom, and Jo′ab the commander of the army went up to bury the
slain, he slew every male in Edom [16](for Jo′ab
and all Israel remained there six months,
until he had cut off every male in E′dom);
[17]but Ha′dad fled to Egypt, together with
certain E′domites of his father's servants,
Hadad being yet a little child. [18]They set out
from Mid′ian and came to Par′an, and took
men with them from Paran and came to
Egypt, to Pharaoh king of Egypt, who gave
him a house, and assigned him an allowance
of food, and gave him land. [19]And Ha′dad
found great favor in the sight of Pharaoh,
so that he gave him in marriage the sister
of his own wife, the sister of Tah′penes the
queen. [20]And the sister of Tah′penes bore
him Genu′bath his son, whom Tahpenes
weaned in Pharaoh's house; and Genubath
was in Pharaoh's house among the sons of
Pharaoh. [21]But when Ha′dad heard in Egypt
that David slept with his fathers and that
Jo′ab the commander of the army was dead,
Hadad said to Pharaoh, "Let me depart, that
I may go to my own country." [22]But Pharaoh
said to him, "What have you lacked with me
that you are now seeking to go to your own
country?" And he said to him, "Only let
me go."

[23]God also raised up as an adversary to
him, Re′zon the son of Eli′ada, who had fled
from his master Ha′dad-e′zer king of Zobah.
[24]And he gathered men about him and
became leader of a marauding band, after
the slaughter by David; and they went to
Damascus, and dwelt there, and made him
king in Damascus. [25]He was an adversary
of Israel all the days of Solomon, doing
mischief as Ha′dad did; and he abhorred
Israel, and reigned over Syria.

[26]Jerobo′am the son of Ne′bat, an E′ph-
raimite of Zer′edah, a servant of Solomon,
whose mother's name was Zeru′ah, a widow,
also lifted up his hand against the king.
[27]And this was the reason why he lifted up
his hand against the king. Solomon built the
Millo, and closed up the breach of the city
of David his father. [28]The man Jerobo′am
was very able, and when Solomon saw
that the young man was industrious he
gave him charge over all the forced labor
of the house of Joseph. [29]And at that time,
when Jerobo′am went out of Jerusalem, the
prophet Ahi′jah the Shi′lonite found him on
the road. Now Ahijah had clad himself with
a new garment; and the two of them were
alone in the open country. [30]Then Ahi′jah
laid hold of the new garment that was on
him, and tore it into twelve pieces. [31]And
he said to Jerobo′am, "Take for yourself
ten pieces; for thus says the LORD, the God
of Israel, 'Behold, I am about to tear the
kingdom from the hand of Solomon, and
will give you ten tribes [32](but he shall have
one tribe, for the sake of my servant David
and for the sake of Jerusalem, the city which
I have chosen out of all the tribes of Israel),
[33]because he has forsaken me, and worshiped
Ash′toreth the goddess of the Sido′nians,
Che′mosh the god of Moab, and Milcom the
god of the Am′monites, and has not walked
in my ways, doing what is right in my sight
and keeping my statutes and my ordinances,
as David his father did. [34]Nevertheless I will
not take the whole kingdom out of his hand;
but I will make him ruler all the days of his
life, for the sake of David my servant whom
I chose, who kept my commandments and
my statutes; [35]but I will take the kingdom
out of his son's hand, and will give it to you,
ten tribes. [36]Yet to his son I will give one
tribe, that David my servant may always
have a lamp before me in Jerusalem, the city
where I have chosen to put my name. [37]And
I will take you, and you shall reign over all
that your soul desires, and you shall be king
over Israel. [38]And if you will listen to all that

I command you, and will walk in my ways,
and do what is right in my eyes by keeping
my statutes and my commandments, as
David my servant did, I will be with you,
and will build you a sure house, as I built for
David, and I will give Israel to you. 39And
I will for this afflict the descendants of
David, but not for ever.' " 40Solomon sought
therefore to kill Jerobo'am; but Jeroboam
arose, and fled into Egypt, to Shi'shak king
of Egypt, and was in Egypt until the death of
Solomon.
41Now the rest of the acts of Solomon,
and all that he did, and his wisdom, are
they not written in the book of the acts of
Solomon? 42And the time that Solomon
reigned in Jerusalem over all Israel was
forty years. 43And Solomon slept with his
fathers, and was buried in the city of David
his father; and Rehobo'am his son reigned
in his stead.

PSALM 119 [118]

89For ever, O LORD, your word
is firmly fixed in the heavens.
90Your faithfulness endures to all
generations;
you have established the earth, and it
stands fast.
91By your appointment they stand this day;
for all things are your servants.
92If your law had not been my delight,
I should have perished in my affliction.
93I will never forget your precepts;
for by them you have given me life.
94I am yours, save me;
for I have sought your precepts.
95The wicked lie in wait to destroy me;
but I consider your testimonies.
96I have seen a limit to all perfection,
but your commandment is
exceedingly broad.

97Oh, how I love your law!
It is my meditation all the day.
98Your commandment makes me wiser than
my enemies,
for it is ever with me.
99I have more understanding than all
my teachers,
for your testimonies are my meditation.
100I understand more than the aged,
for I keep your precepts.
101I hold back my feet from every evil way,
in order to keep your word.
102I do not turn aside from your ordinances,
for you have taught me.
103How sweet are your words to my taste,
sweeter than honey to my mouth!
104Through your precepts I get
understanding;
therefore I hate every false way.

JOHN 11

**Now a certain man was ill, Laz'a-
rus of Beth'any, the village of
Mary and her sister Martha. 2It
was Mary who anointed the Lord with
ointment and wiped his feet with her
hair, whose brother Laz'arus was ill.**
3So the sisters sent to him, saying, "Lord, he
whom you love is ill." 4But when Jesus heard
it he said, "This illness is not unto death; it is
for the glory of God, so that the Son of God
may be glorified by means of it."
5Now Jesus loved Martha and her sister and
Laz'arus. 6So when he heard that he was ill, he
stayed two days longer in the place where he
was. 7Then after this he said to the disciples,
"Let us go into Judea again." 8The disciples
said to him, "Rabbi, the Jews were but now
seeking to stone you, and are you going
there again?" 9Jesus answered, "Are there not
twelve hours in the day? If any one walks in
the day, he does not stumble, because he sees
the light of this world. 10But if any one walks
in the night, he stumbles, because the light
is not in him." 11Thus he spoke, and then he
said to them, "Our friend Laz'arus has fallen
asleep, but I go to awake him out of sleep."
12The disciples said to him, "Lord, if he has
fallen asleep, he will recover." 13Now Jesus had
spoken of his death, but they thought that he
meant taking rest in sleep. 14Then Jesus told
them plainly, "Laz'arus is dead; 15and for your

sake I am glad that I was not there, so that you may believe. But let us go to him."
16Thomas, called the Twin, said to his fellow disciples, "Let us also go, that we may die with him."

REFLECTION

With his prayer for wisdom and his building of the Temple, Solomon's reign begins well; but now things begin to unravel. He starts to do the exact things that Moses had warned against in Deuteronomy 17:16–17: he acquires many horses (military power), many wives (diplomatic power), and great wealth (through heavily taxing God's people). Inevitably, he begins to worship the gods of his foreign wives "and his heart was not wholly true to the LORD his God" (1 Kgs 11:4). It is a sad story of moral compromise. What began as an attempt to secure peace for God's people through diplomatic intermarriage and military might leads to a betrayal of the Lord. Solomon shows himself unfaithful to the covenant and so the Lord brings down judgment against him. New enemies arise, but most remarkably, the Lord sends the prophet Ahijah to spur Jeroboam to action. He grants Jeroboam ten of the tribes and transfers some of the blessings of David to him, if only he will keep faith (see v. 38). Two warnings stand out for us: first, that we guard against the slippery slope of compromise; second, that if we disobey the Lord, we will forsake his blessings. What temptations to compromise do you face?

May 29

1 KINGS 12

Rehobo'am went to She'chem, for all Israel had come to Shechem to make him king.
2And when Jerobo'am the son of Ne'bat heard of it (for he was
still in Egypt, whither he had fled from King Solomon), then Jeroboam returned from Egypt.
3And they sent and called him; and Jerobo'am and all the assembly of Israel came and said to Rehobo'am,
4"Your father made our yoke heavy. Now therefore lighten the hard service of your father and his heavy yoke upon us, and we will serve you."
5He said to them, "Depart for three days, then come again to me." So the people went away.
6Then King Rehobo'am took counsel with the old men, who had stood before Solomon his father while he was yet alive, saying, "How do you advise me to answer this people?"
7And they said to him, "If you will be a servant to this people today and serve them, and speak good words to them when you answer them, then they will be your servants for ever."
8But he forsook the counsel which the old men gave him, and took counsel with the young men who had grown up with him and stood before him.
9And he said to them, "What do you advise that we answer this people who have said to me, 'Lighten the yoke that your father put upon us'?"
10And the young men who had grown up with him said to him, "Thus shall you speak to this people who said to you, 'Your father made our yoke heavy, but please lighten it for us'; thus shall you say to them, 'My little finger is thicker than my father's loins.
11And now, whereas my father laid upon you a heavy yoke, I will add to your yoke. My father chastised you with whips, but I will chastise you with scorpions.'"
12So Jerobo'am and all the people came to Rehobo'am the third day, as the king said, "Come to me again the third day."
13And the king answered the people harshly, and forsaking the counsel which the old men had given him,
14he spoke to them according to the counsel of the young men, saying, "My father made your yoke heavy, but I will add to your yoke; my father chastised you with whips, but I will chastise you with scorpions."
15So the king did not listen to the people; for it was a turn of affairs brought about by the LORD that he might fulfil his word, which the LORD spoke by Ahi'jah the Shi'lonite to Jerobo'am the son of Ne'bat.

16And when all Israel saw that the king did
not listen to them, the people answered the
king,

"What portion have we in David?
We have no inheritance in the son of
Jesse.
To your tents, O Israel!
Look now to your own house, David."

So Israel departed to their tents. 17But Rehobo'am reigned over the sons of Israel who
dwelt in the cities of Judah. 18Then King Rehobo'am sent Ador'am, who was taskmaster
over the forced labor, and all Israel stoned
him to death with stones. And King Rehoboam made haste to mount his chariot, to
flee to Jerusalem. 19So Israel has been in rebellion against the house of David to this day.
20And when all Israel heard that Jerobo'am
had returned, they sent and called him to the
assembly and made him king over all Israel.
There was none that followed the house of
David, but the tribe of Judah only.

21When Rehobo'am came to Jerusalem,
he assembled all the house of Judah, and
the tribe of Benjamin, a hundred and eighty
thousand chosen warriors, to fight against
the house of Israel, to restore the kingdom
to Rehoboam the son of Solomon. 22But the
word of God came to Shemai'ah the man
of God: 23"Say to Rehobo'am the son of
Solomon, king of Judah, and to all the house
of Judah and Benjamin, and to the rest of the
people, 24'Thus says the LORD, You shall not
go up or fight against your kinsmen the sons
of Israel. Return every man to his home, for
this thing is from me.'" So they listened to
the word of the LORD, and went home again,
according to the word of the LORD.

25Then Jerobo'am built She'chem in the hill
country of E'phraim, and dwelt there; and
he went out from there and built Penu'el.
26And Jerobo'am said in his heart, "Now
the kingdom will turn back to the house of
David; 27if this people go up to offer sacrifices
in the house of the LORD at Jerusalem, then
the heart of this people will turn again to their
lord, to Rehobo'am king of Judah, and they
will kill me and return to Rehoboam king of
Judah." 28So the king took counsel, and made
two calves of gold. And he said to the people,
"You have gone up to Jerusalem long enough.
Behold your gods, O Israel, who brought you
up out of the land of Egypt." 29And he set one
in Bethel, and the other he put in Dan. 30And
this thing became a sin, for the people went
to the one at Bethel and to the other as far as
Dan. 31He also made houses on high places,
and appointed priests from among all the
people, who were not of the Levites. 32And
Jerobo'am appointed a feast on the fifteenth
day of the eighth month like the feast that
was in Judah, and he offered sacrifices upon
the altar; so he did in Bethel, sacrificing to
the calves that he had made. And he placed
in Bethel the priests of the high places that
he had made. 33He went up to the altar which
he had made in Bethel on the fifteenth day in
the eighth month, in the month which he had
devised of his own heart; and he ordained a
feast for the sons of Israel, and went up to the
altar to burn incense.

PSALM 119 [118]

105Your word is a lamp to my feet
and a light to my path.
106I have sworn an oath and confirmed it,
to observe your righteous ordinances.
107I am sorely afflicted;
give me life, O LORD, according to
your word!
108Accept my offerings of praise, O LORD,
and teach me your ordinances.
109I hold my life in my hand continually,
but I do not forget your law.
110The wicked have laid a snare for me,
but I do not stray from your precepts.
111Your testimonies are my heritage for ever;
yes, they are the joy of my heart.
112I incline my heart to perform your statutes
for ever, to the end.

113I hate double-minded men,
but I love your law.
114You are my hiding place and my shield;
I hope in your word.
115Depart from me, you evildoers,
that I may keep the commandments of
my God.

116 Uphold me according to your promise,
that I may live,
and let me not be put to shame in
my hope!
117 Hold me up, that I may be safe
and have regard for your statutes
continually!
118 You spurn all who go astray from
your statutes;
yes, their cunning is in vain.
119 All the wicked of the earth you count
as dross;
therefore I love your testimonies.
120 My flesh trembles for fear of you,
and I am afraid of your judgments.

121 I have done what is just and right;
do not leave me to my oppressors.
122 Be surety for your servant for good;
let not the godless oppress me.
123 My eyes fail with watching for
your salvation,
and for the fulfilment of your
righteous promise.
124 Deal with your servant according to your
steadfast love,
and teach me your statutes.
125 I am your servant; give me understanding,
that I may know your testimonies!
126 It is time for the LORD to act,
for your law has been broken.
127 Therefore I love your commandments
above gold, above fine gold.
128 Therefore I direct my steps by all
your precepts;
I hate every false way.

JOHN 11

**17 Now when Jesus came, he found
that Laz′arus had already been
in the tomb four days. 18 Beth′any
was near Jerusalem, about two miles
off, 19 and many of the Jews had come
to Martha and Mary to console them**
concerning their brother. 20 When Martha
heard that Jesus was coming, she went
and met him, while Mary sat in the house.
21 Martha said to Jesus, "Lord, if you had
been here, my brother would not have died.
22 And even now I know that whatever you
ask from God, God will give you." 23 Jesus
said to her, "Your brother will rise again."
24 Martha said to him, "I know that he will
rise again in the resurrection at the last day."
25 Jesus said to her, "I am the resurrection
and the life; he who believes in me, though
he die, yet shall he live, 26 and whoever lives
and believes in me shall never die. Do you
believe this?" 27 She said to him, "Yes, Lord;
I believe that you are the Christ, the Son of
God, he who is coming into the world."

28 When she had said this, she went and called
her sister Mary, saying quietly, "The Teacher is
here and is calling for you." 29 And when she
heard it, she rose quickly and went to him.
30 Now Jesus had not yet come to the village,
but was still in the place where Martha had met
him. 31 When the Jews who were with her in the
house, consoling her, saw Mary rise quickly and
go out, they followed her, supposing that she
was going to the tomb to weep there. 32 Then
Mary, when she came where Jesus was and
saw him, fell at his feet, saying to him, "Lord, if
you had been here, my brother would not have
died." 33 When Jesus saw her weeping, and the
Jews who came with her also weeping, he was
deeply moved in spirit and troubled; 34 and he
said, "Where have you laid him?" They said to
him, "Lord, come and see." 35 Jesus wept. 36 So
the Jews said, "See how he loved him!" 37 But
some of them said, "Could not he who opened
the eyes of the blind man have kept this man
from dying?"

38 Then Jesus, deeply moved again, came
to the tomb; it was a cave, and a stone lay
upon it. 39 Jesus said, "Take away the stone."
Martha, the sister of the dead man, said to
him, "Lord, by this time there will be an
odor, for he has been dead four days." 40 Jesus
said to her, "Did I not tell you that if you
would believe you would see the glory of
God?" 41 So they took away the stone. And
Jesus lifted up his eyes and said, "Father, I
thank you that you have heard me. 42 I knew
that you always hear me, but I have said
this on account of the people standing by,
that they may believe that you sent me."

[43]When he had said this, he cried with a
loud voice, "Laz′arus, come out." [44]The dead
man came out, his hands and feet bound
with bandages, and his face wrapped with a
cloth. Jesus said to them, "Unbind him, and
let him go."

REFLECTION

In today's Old Testament reading, we see the sad consequences of sin. The peaceful kingdom of Solomon is torn asunder by his son, Rehoboam, and by the challenger, Jeroboam. From this time on, there will be two kingdoms instead of one. Rehoboam errs by oppressing his subjects in a foolish show of force, which results in the ten northern tribes breaking away under Jeroboam. Jeroboam rejects the blessing of the Lord by setting up idolatrous golden calves so that his subjects will not travel to the Temple in Jerusalem and leave his political boundaries for their worship. Thus already at its outset the northern kingdom's demise is set. The sins of Rehoboam and Jeroboam bring division and idolatry to God's people. In contrast, Jesus, the true King, comes to unite all people in the worship of the one true God. Jesus raises Lazarus to glorify God and to exhibit the significance of his messianic identity: "I am the resurrection and the life; he who believes in me, though he die, yet shall he live" (Jn 11:25). Jesus grants Lazarus what the psalmist prays for: "Give me life, O LORD, according to your word" (Ps 119:107). Jesus gives life to Lazarus and thus foreshadows his own Resurrection in which death will finally be defeated. Can you think of examples of sin leading to deep divisions among friends?

May 30

1 KINGS 13

**And behold, a man of God came
out of Judah by the word of the
Lord to Bethel. Jerobo′am was standing
by the altar to burn incense. [2]And the**
man cried against the altar by the word of the
LORD, and said, "O altar, altar, thus says the
LORD: 'Behold, a son shall be born to the
house of David, Josi′ah by name; and he
shall sacrifice upon you the priests of the
high places who burn incense upon you,
and men's bones shall be burned upon you.'"
[3]And he gave a sign the same day, saying,
"This is the sign that the LORD has spoken:
'Behold, the altar shall be torn down, and
the ashes that are upon it shall be poured
out.'" [4]And when the king heard the saying
of the man of God, which he cried against
the altar at Bethel, Jerobo′am stretched out
his hand from the altar, saying, "Lay hold
of him." And his hand, which he stretched
out against him, dried up, so that he could
not draw it back to himself. [5]The altar also
was torn down, and the ashes poured out
from the altar, according to the sign which
the man of God had given by the word of
the LORD. [6]And the king said to the man of
God, "Entreat now the favor of the LORD
your God, and pray for me, that my hand
may be restored to me." And the man of
God entreated the LORD; and the king's
hand was restored to him, and became as it
was before. [7]And the king said to the man
of God, "Come home with me, and refresh
yourself, and I will give you a reward." [8]And
the man of God said to the king, "If you give
me half your house, I will not go in with
you. And I will not eat bread or drink water
in this place; [9]for so was it commanded
me by the word of the LORD, saying, 'You
shall neither eat bread, nor drink water, nor
return by the way that you came.'" [10]So he
went another way, and did not return by the
way that he came to Bethel.

[11]Now there dwelt an old prophet in Bethel.
And his sons came and told him all that the
man of God had done that day in Bethel; the
words also which he had spoken to the king,
they told to their father. [12]And their father said
to them, "Which way did he go?" And his sons
showed him the way which the man of God
who came from Judah had gone. [13]And he said
to his sons, "Saddle the donkey for me." So they
saddled the donkey for him and he mounted
it. [14]And he went after the man of God, and

found him sitting under an oak; and he said to
him, "Are you the man of God who came from
Judah?" And he said, "I am." [15]Then he said
to him, "Come home with me and eat bread."
[16]And he said, "I may not return with you, or go
in with you; neither will I eat bread nor drink
water with you in this place; [17]for it was said to
me by the word of the LORD, 'You shall neither
eat bread nor drink water there, nor return by
the way that you came.'" [18]And he said to him,
"I also am a prophet as you are, and an angel
spoke to me by the word of the LORD, saying,
'Bring him back with you into your house that
he may eat bread and drink water.'" But he lied
to him. [19]So he went back with him, and ate
bread in his house, and drank water.

[20]And as they sat at the table, the word of the
LORD came to the prophet who had brought
him back; [21]and he cried to the man of God
who came from Judah, "Thus says the LORD,
'Because you have disobeyed the word of the
LORD, and have not kept the commandment
which the LORD your God commanded you,
[22]but have come back, and have eaten bread
and drunk water in the place of which he said
to you, "Eat no bread, and drink no water";
your body shall not come to the tomb of your
fathers.'" [23]And after he had eaten bread and
drunk, he saddled the donkey for the prophet
whom he had brought back. [24]And as he went
away a lion met him on the road and killed
him. And his body was thrown in the road,
and the donkey stood beside it; the lion also
stood beside the body. [25]And behold, men
passed by, and saw the body thrown in the
road, and the lion standing by the body. And
they came and told it in the city where the old
prophet dwelt.

[26]And when the prophet who had
brought him back from the way heard
of it, he said, "It is the man of God, who
disobeyed the word of the LORD; therefore
the LORD has given him to the lion, which
has torn him and slain him, according to
the word which the LORD spoke to him."
[27]And he said to his sons, "Saddle the
donkey for me." And they saddled it. [28]And
he went and found his body thrown in the
road, and the donkey and the lion standing
beside the body. The lion had not eaten the
body or torn the donkey. [29]And the prophet
took up the body of the man of God and
laid it upon the donkey, and brought it
back to the city, to mourn and to bury him.
[30]And he laid the body in his own grave;
and they mourned over him, saying, "Alas,
my brother!" [31]And after he had buried
him, he said to his sons, "When I die, bury
me in the grave in which the man of God
is buried; lay my bones beside his bones.
[32]For the saying which he cried by the word
of the LORD against the altar in Bethel, and
against all the houses of the high places
which are in the cities of Samar′ia, shall
surely come to pass."

[33]After this incident Jerobo′am did not
turn from his evil way, but made priests
for the high places again from among all
the people; any who would, he consecrated
to be priests of the high places. [34]And this
thing became sin to the house of Jerobo′am,
so as to cut it off and to destroy it from the
face of the earth.

14 At that time Abi′jah the son of Jero-
bo′am fell sick. [2]And Jerobo′am said
to his wife, "Arise, and disguise yourself,
that it be not known that you are the wife of
Jeroboam, and go to Shiloh; behold, Ahi′jah
the prophet is there, who said of me that I
should be king over this people. [3]Take with
you ten loaves, some cakes, and a jar of
honey, and go to him; he will tell you what
shall happen to the child."

[4]Jerobo′am's wife did so; she arose, and
went to Shiloh, and came to the house of
Ahi′jah. Now Ahijah could not see, for his
eyes were dim because of his age. [5]And the
LORD said to Ahi′jah, "Behold, the wife
of Jerobo′am is coming to inquire of you
concerning her son; for he is sick. Thus and
thus shall you say to her."

When she came, she pretended to be
another woman. [6]But when Ahi′jah heard
the sound of her feet, as she came in at the
door, he said, "Come in, wife of Jerobo′am;
why do you pretend to be another? For I
am charged with heavy tidings for you.
[7]Go, tell Jerobo′am, 'Thus says the LORD,
the God of Israel: "Because I exalted you
from among the people, and made you

leader over my people Israel, [8]and tore the
kingdom away from the house of David
and gave it to you; and yet you have not
been like my servant David, who kept my
commandments, and followed me with all
his heart, doing only that which was right
in my eyes, [9]but you have done evil above
all that were before you and have gone and
made for yourself other gods, and molten
images, provoking me to anger, and have
cast me behind your back; [10]therefore
behold, I will bring evil upon the house of
Jerobo′am, and will cut off from Jeroboam
every male, both bond and free in Israel,
and will utterly consume the house of
Jeroboam, as a man burns up dung until
it is all gone. [11]Any one belonging to
Jerobo′am who dies in the city the dogs
shall eat; and any one who dies in the open
country the birds of the air shall eat; for
the LORD has spoken it."' [12]Arise therefore,
go to your house. When your feet enter
the city, the child shall die. [13]And all Israel
shall mourn for him, and bury him; for he
only of Jerobo′am shall come to the grave,
because in him there is found something
pleasing to the LORD, the God of Israel,
in the house of Jeroboam. [14]Moreover
the LORD will raise up for himself a king
over Israel, who shall cut off the house
of Jerobo′am today. And henceforth [15]the
LORD will strike Israel, as a reed is shaken
in the water, and root up Israel out of this
good land which he gave to their fathers,
and scatter them beyond the Euphrates,
because they have made their Ashe′rim,
provoking the LORD to anger. [16]And he
will give Israel up because of the sins of
Jerobo′am, which he sinned and which he
made Israel to sin."

PSALM 119 [118]

[129]Your testimonies are wonderful;
therefore my soul keeps them.
[130]The unfolding of your words gives light;
it imparts understanding to the simple.
[131]With open mouth I pant,
because I long for your commandments.
[132]Turn to me and be gracious to me,
as you always do toward those who love your name.
[133]Keep steady my steps according to your promise,
and let no iniquity get dominion over me.
[134]Redeem me from man's oppression,
that I may keep your precepts.
[135]Make your face shine upon your servant,
and teach me your statutes.
[136]My eyes shed streams of tears,
because men do not keep your law.

[137]You are righteous, O LORD,
and right are your judgments.
[138]You have appointed your testimonies in righteousness
and in all faithfulness.
[139]My zeal consumes me,
because my foes forget your words.
[140]Your promise is well tried,
and your servant loves it.
[141]I am small and despised,
yet I do not forget your precepts.
[142]Your righteousness is righteous for ever,
and your law is true.
[143]Trouble and anguish have come upon me,
but your commandments are my delight.
[144]Your testimonies are righteous for ever;
give me understanding that I may live.

[145]With my whole heart I cry; answer me, O LORD!
I will keep your statutes.
[146]I cry to you; save me,
that I may observe your testimonies.
[147]I rise before dawn and cry for help;
I hope in your words.
[148]My eyes are awake before the watches of the night,
that I may meditate upon your promise.
[149]Hear my voice in your steadfast love;
O LORD, in your justice preserve my life.
[150]They draw near who persecute me with evil purpose;
they are far from your law.
[151]But you are near, O LORD,
and all your commandments are true.
[152]Long have I known from your testimonies
that you have founded them for ever.

JOHN 11

**45Many of the Jews therefore,
who had come with Mary and
had seen what he did, believed in him;
46but some of them went to the Pharisees**
and told them what Jesus had done. 47So the
chief priests and the Pharisees gathered the
council, and said, "What are we to do? For
this man performs many signs. 48If we let
him go on like this, every one will believe
in him, and the Romans will come and
destroy both our holy place and our nation."
49But one of them, Cai′aphas, who was high
priest that year, said to them, "You know
nothing at all; 50you do not understand that
it is expedient for you that one man should
die for the people, and that the whole nation
should not perish." 51He did not say this of his
own accord, but being high priest that year
he prophesied that Jesus should die for the
nation, 52and not for the nation only, but to
gather into one the children of God who are
scattered abroad. 53So from that day on they
took counsel about how to put him to death.
54Jesus therefore no longer went about
openly among the Jews, but went from there
to the country near the wilderness, to a town
called E′phraim; and there he stayed with the
disciples.
55Now the Passover of the Jews was at
hand, and many went up from the country
to Jerusalem before the Passover, to purify
themselves. 56They were looking for Jesus
and saying to one another as they stood in
the temple, "What do you think? That he
will not come to the feast?" 57Now the chief
priests and the Pharisees had given orders
that if any one knew where he was, he should
let them know, so that they might arrest him.
12 Six days before the Passover, Jesus
came to Beth′any, where Laz′arus was,
whom Jesus had raised from the dead. 2There
they made him a supper; Martha served, and
Laz′arus was one of those at table with him.
3Mary took a pound of costly ointment of pure
nard and anointed the feet of Jesus and wiped
his feet with her hair; and the house was filled
with the fragrance of the ointment. 4But Judas
Iscariot, one of his disciples (he who was to
betray him), said, 5"Why was this ointment not
sold for three hundred denarii and given to the
poor?" 6This he said, not that he cared for the
poor but because he was a thief, and as he had
the money box he used to take what was put
into it. 7Jesus said, "Let her alone, let her keep it
for the day of my burial. 8The poor you always
have with you, but you do not always have me."

REFLECTION

Today we see a great contrast between exacting judgment and extravagant devotion. Jeroboam has led the people of Israel into false worship and so a "man of God" is sent to condemn his actions. In one of the most dramatic and miraculous prophecies of the Old Testament, he curses the altar of Jeroboam at Bethel, predicts the coming of King Josiah by name hundreds of years in advance, and causes Jeroboam's hand to wither and then be healed. To cap it all off, the man of God disobeys the Lord and is then killed by a lion. This unnamed prophet displays God's heart for his people, as described by the psalmist: "My eyes shed streams of tears, because men do not keep your law" (Ps 119:136). In the New Testament, the sad story of disobedience to God will continue as men seek to put Jesus to death. In contrast, Mary of Bethany puts on the most extravagant display of devotion in the Bible: "Mary took a pound of costly ointment of pure nard and anointed the feet of Jesus and wiped his feet with her hair" (Jn 12:3). Mary shows what true devotion to the Lord looks like as she prepares his body for burial. What extravagance are you willing to give in your worship of God?

May 31

1 KINGS 14

**17Then Jerobo′am's wife arose,
and departed, and came to Tirzah. And as she came to the threshold of
the house, the child died. 18And all Israel buried him and mourned for him,**

according to the word of the LORD, which
he spoke by his servant Ahi′jah the prophet.
[19]Now the rest of the acts of Jerobo′am, how
he warred and how he reigned, behold, they
are written in the Book of the Chronicles of
the Kings of Israel. [20]And the time that Je-
robo′am reigned was twenty-two years; and
he slept with his fathers, and Na′dab his son
reigned in his stead.

[21]Now Rehobo′am the son of Solomon
reigned in Judah. Rehoboam was forty-
one years old when he began to reign, and
he reigned seventeen years in Jerusalem,
the city which the LORD had chosen out
of all the tribes of Israel, to put his name
there. His mother's name was Na′amah
the Am′monitess. [22]And Judah did what
was evil in the sight of the LORD, and they
provoked him to jealousy with their sins
which they committed, more than all that
their fathers had done. [23]For they also built
for themselves high places, and pillars, and
Ashe′rim on every high hill and under
every green tree; [24]and there were also
male cult prostitutes in the land. They did
according to all the abominations of the
nations which the LORD drove out before
the sons of Israel.

[25]In the fifth year of King Rehobo′am,
Shi′shak king of Egypt came up against
Jerusalem; [26]he took away the treasures of the
house of the LORD and the treasures of the
king's house; he took away everything. He
also took away all the shields of gold which
Solomon had made; [27]and King Rehobo′am
made in their stead shields of bronze, and
committed them to the hands of the officers
of the guard, who kept the door of the king's
house. [28]And as often as the king went into
the house of the LORD, the guard bore them
and brought them back to the guardroom.

[29]Now the rest of the acts of Rehobo′am,
and all that he did, are they not written in the
Book of the Chronicles of the Kings of Judah?
[30]And there was war between Rehobo′am and
Jerobo′am continually. [31]And Rehobo′am
slept with his fathers and was buried with
his fathers in the city of David. His mother's
name was Na′amah the Am′monitess. And
Abi′jam his son reigned in his stead.

15 Now in the eighteenth year of King
Jerobo′am the son of Ne′bat, Abi′jam
began to reign over Judah. [2]He reigned for
three years in Jerusalem. His mother's name
was Ma′acah the daughter of Abish′alom. [3]And
he walked in all the sins which his father did
before him; and his heart was not wholly true
to the LORD his God, as the heart of David
his father. [4]Nevertheless for David's sake the
LORD his God gave him a lamp in Jerusalem,
setting up his son after him, and establishing
Jerusalem; [5]because David did what was right
in the eyes of the LORD, and did not turn aside
from anything that he commanded him all the
days of his life, except in the matter of Uri′ah
the Hittite. [6]Now there was war between
Rehobo′am and Jerobo′am all the days of his
life. [7]The rest of the acts of Abi′jam, and all
that he did, are they not written in the Book
of the Chronicles of the Kings of Judah? And
there was war between Abijam and Jerobo′am.
[8]And Abi′jam slept with his fathers; and they
buried him in the city of David. And Asa his
son reigned in his stead.

[9]In the twentieth year of Jerobo′am king of
Israel Asa began to reign over Judah, [10]and
he reigned forty-one years in Jerusalem. His
mother's name was Ma′acah the daughter of
Abish′alom. [11]And Asa did what was right in
the eyes of the LORD, as David his father had
done. [12]He put away the male cult prostitutes
out of the land, and removed all the idols
that his fathers had made. [13]He also removed
Ma′acah his mother from being queen mother
because she had an abominable image made
for Ashe′rah; and Asa cut down her image and
burned it at the brook Kidron. [14]But the high
places were not taken away. Nevertheless the
heart of Asa was wholly true to the LORD all his
days. [15]And he brought into the house of the
LORD the votive gifts of his father and his own
votive gifts, silver, and gold, and vessels.

[16]And there was war between Asa and
Ba′asha king of Israel all their days. [17]Ba′asha
king of Israel went up against Judah, and built
Ra′mah, that he might permit no one to go
out or come in to Asa king of Judah. [18]Then
Asa took all the silver and the gold that were
left in the treasures of the house of the LORD
and the treasures of the king's house, and

gave them into the hands of his servants; and
King Asa sent them to Ben-ha´dad the son
of Tabrim´mon, the son of He´zi-on, king of
Syria, who dwelt in Damascus, saying, 19“Let
there be a league between me and you, as
between my father and your father: behold, I
am sending to you a present of silver and gold;
go, break your league with Ba´asha king of
Israel, that he may withdraw from me.” 20And
Ben-ha´dad listened to King Asa, and sent the
commanders of his armies against the cities of
Israel, and conquered I´jon, Dan, A´bel-beth-
ma´acah, and all Chin´neroth, with all the land
of Naph´tali. 21And when Ba´asha heard of it,
he stopped building Ra´mah, and he dwelt in
Tirzah. 22Then King Asa made a proclamation
to all Judah, none was exempt, and they carried
away the stones of Ra´mah and its timber, with
which Ba´asha had been building; and with
them King Asa built Ge´ba of Benjamin and
Mizpah. 23Now the rest of all the acts of Asa,
all his might, and all that he did, and the cities
which he built, are they not written in the Book
of the Chronicles of the Kings of Judah? But in
his old age he was diseased in his feet. 24And
Asa slept with his fathers, and was buried with
his fathers in the city of David his father; and
Jehosh´aphat his son reigned in his stead.

25Nadab the son of Jerobo´am began to
reign over Israel in the second year of Asa
king of Judah; and he reigned over Israel two
years. 26He did what was evil in the sight of
the LORD, and walked in the way of his father,
and in his sin which he made Israel to sin.

27Ba´asha the son of Ahi´jah, of the house of
Is´sachar, conspired against him; and Baasha
struck him down at Gib´bethon, which
belonged to the Philis´tines; for Na´dab and
all Israel were laying siege to Gibbethon. 28So
Ba´asha killed him in the third year of Asa
king of Judah, and reigned in his stead. 29And
as soon as he was king, he killed all the house
of Jerobo´am; he left to the house of Jeroboam
not one that breathed, until he had destroyed
it, according to the word of the LORD which
he spoke by his servant Ahi´jah the Shi´lonite;
30it was for the sins of Jerobo´am which he
sinned and which he made Israel to sin, and
because of the anger to which he provoked
the LORD, the God of Israel.

31Now the rest of the acts of Na´dab, and
all that he did, are they not written in the
Book of the Chronicles of the Kings of
Israel? 32And there was war between Asa
and Ba´asha king of Israel all their days.

33In the third year of Asa king of Judah,
Ba´asha the son of Ahi´jah began to reign over
all Israel at Tirzah, and reigned twenty-four
years. 34He did what was evil in the sight of the
LORD, and walked in the way of Jerobo´am and
in his sin which he made Israel to sin.

PSALM 119 [118]

153Look on my affliction and deliver me,
for I do not forget your law.
154Plead my cause and redeem me;
give me life according to your promise!
155Salvation is far from the wicked,
for they do not seek your statutes.
156Great is your mercy, O LORD;
give me life according to your justice.
157Many are my persecutors and
my adversaries,
but I do not swerve from your testimonies.
158I look at the faithless with disgust,
because they do not keep
your commands.
159Consider how I love your precepts!
Preserve my life according to your
steadfast love.
160The sum of your word is truth;
and every one of your righteous
ordinances endures for ever.

161Princes persecute me without cause,
but my heart stands in awe of your words.
162I rejoice at your word
like one who finds great spoil.
163I hate and abhor falsehood,
but I love your law.
164Seven times a day I praise you
for your righteous ordinances.
165Great peace have those who love your law;
nothing can make them stumble.
166I hope for your salvation, O LORD,
and I do your commandments.
167My soul keeps your testimonies;
I love them exceedingly.

168I keep your precepts and testimonies,
for all my ways are before you.
169Let my cry come before you, O LORD;
give me understanding according to your word!
170Let my supplication come before you;
deliver me according to your word.
171My lips will pour forth praise
that you teach me your statutes.
172My tongue will sing of your word,
for all your commandments are right.
173Let your hand be ready to help me,
for I have chosen your precepts.
174I long for your salvation, O LORD,
and your law is my delight.
175Let my soul live, that I may praise you,
and let your ordinances help me.
176I have gone astray like a lost sheep; seek your servant,
for I do not forget your commandments.

JOHN 12

9When the great crowd of the Jews learned that he was there, they came, not only on account of Jesus but also to see Laz′arus, whom he had
raised from the dead. 10So the chief priests planned to put Laz′arus also to death, 11because on account of him many of the Jews were going away and believing in Jesus.
12The next day a great crowd who had come to the feast heard that Jesus was coming to Jerusalem. 13So they took branches of palm trees and went out to meet him, crying, "Hosanna! Blessed is he who comes in the name of the Lord, even the King of Israel!"
14And Jesus found a young donkey and sat upon it; as it is written,
15"Fear not, daughter of Zion;
behold, your king is coming,
sitting on a donkey's colt!"
16His disciples did not understand this at first; but when Jesus was glorified, then they remembered that this had been written of him and had been done to him.
17The crowd that had been with him when he called Laz′arus out of the tomb and raised him from the dead bore witness.
18The reason why the crowd went to meet him was that they heard he had done this sign.
19The Pharisees then said to one another, "You see that you can do nothing; look, the world has gone after him."
20Now among those who went up to worship at the feast were some Greeks.
21So these came to Philip, who was from Beth-sa′ida in Galilee, and said to him, "Sir, we wish to see Jesus."
22Philip went and told Andrew; Andrew went with Philip and they told Jesus.
23And Jesus answered them, "The hour has come for the Son of man to be glorified.
24Truly, truly, I say to you, unless a grain of wheat falls into the earth and dies, it remains alone; but if it dies, it bears much fruit.
25He who loves his life loses it, and he who hates his life in this world will keep it for eternal life.
26If any one serves me, he must follow me; and where I am, there shall my servant be also; if any one serves me, the Father will honor him."

REFLECTION

With the death of Jeroboam, 1 Kings begins to narrate the reigns of the kings of Judah and Israel at a blistering pace. If a king "walked in the ways of his father David," then he proved righteous before God; but if he "walked in the ways of Jeroboam," then he promoted false worship and apostasy. Israel (which now refers to the northern kingdom that broke away under Jeroboam), as a whole, is well characterized by the last line of Psalm 119: "I have gone astray like a lost sheep; seek your servant" (Ps 119:176). Israel was lost and needed the Lord to come after the nation and bring it back. Likewise, each of us is akin to a lost sheep. We cannot seek God all by ourselves, but in fact, we need him to come looking for us. Jesus indeed comes looking for us, his people, and exemplifies sacrificial love: "Unless a grain of wheat falls into the earth and dies, it remains alone; but if it dies, it bears much fruit" (Jn 12:24). Jesus, of course, is talking about himself and his sacrifice for us, which bears great spiritual fruit in the salvation of the world. Yet he also invites us to "die" with him and to participate in his suffering. How has the Lord sought you out?

June 1

1 KINGS 16

And the word of the Lord came to Je´hu the son of Hana´ni against Ba´asha, saying, [2]"Since I exalted you out of the dust and made you leader over my people Israel, and you have walked in the way of Jerobo´am, and have made my people Israel to sin, provoking me to anger with their sins, [3]behold, I will utterly sweep away Ba´asha and his house, and I will make your house like the house of Jerobo´am the son of Ne´bat. [4]Any one belonging to Ba´asha who dies in the city the dogs shall eat; and any one of his who dies in the field the birds of the air shall eat."

[5]Now the rest of the acts of Ba´asha, and what he did, and his might, are they not written in the Book of the Chronicles of the Kings of Israel? [6]And Ba´asha slept with his fathers, and was buried at Tirzah; and E´lah his son reigned in his stead. [7]Moreover the word of the Lord came by the prophet Je´hu the son of Hana´ni against Ba´asha and his house, both because of all the evil that he did in the sight of the Lord, provoking him to anger with the work of his hands, in being like the house of Jerobo´am, and also because he destroyed it.

[8]In the twenty-sixth year of Asa king of Judah, E´lah the son of Ba´asha began to reign over Israel in Tirzah, and he reigned two years. [9]But his servant Zimri, commander of half his chariots, conspired against him. When he was at Tirzah, drinking himself drunk in the house of Arza, who was over the household in Tirzah, [10]Zimri came in and struck him down and killed him, in the twenty-seventh year of Asa king of Judah, and reigned in his stead.

[11]When he began to reign, as soon as he had seated himself on his throne, he killed all the house of Ba´asha; he did not leave him a single male of his kinsmen or his friends. [12]Thus Zimri destroyed all the house of Ba´asha, according to the word of the Lord, which he spoke against Baasha by Je´hu the prophet, [13]for all the sins of Ba´asha and the sins of E´lah his son which they sinned, and which they made Israel to sin, provoking the Lord God of Israel to anger with their idols. [14]Now the rest of the acts of E´lah, and all that he did, are they not written in the Book of the Chronicles of the Kings of Israel?

[15]In the twenty-seventh year of Asa king of Judah, Zimri reigned seven days in Tirzah. Now the troops were encamped against Gib´bethon, which belonged to the Philis´tines, [16]and the troops who were encamped heard it said, "Zimri has conspired, and he has killed the king"; therefore all Israel made Omri, the commander of the army, king over Israel that day in the camp. [17]So Omri went up from Gib´bethon, and all Israel with him, and they besieged Tirzah. [18]And when Zimri saw that the city was taken, he went into the citadel of the king's house, and burned the king's house over him with fire, and died, [19]because of his sins which he committed, doing evil in the sight of the Lord, walking in the way of Jerobo´am, and for his sin which he committed, making Israel to sin. [20]Now the rest of the acts of Zimri, and the conspiracy which he made, are they not written in the Book of the Chronicles of the Kings of Israel?

[21]Then the sons of Israel were divided into two parts; half of the people followed Tibni the son of Ginath, to make him king, and half followed Omri. [22]But the people who followed Omri overcame the people who followed Tibni the son of Ginath; so Tibni died, and Omri became king. [23]In the thirty-first year of Asa king of Judah, Omri began to reign over Israel, and reigned for twelve years; six years he reigned in Tirzah. [24]He bought the hill of Samar´ia from She´mer for two talents of silver; and he fortified the hill, and called the name of the city which he built, Samaria, after the name of Shemer, the owner of the hill.

[25]Omri did what was evil in the sight of the Lord, and did more evil than all who were before him. [26]For he walked in all the way of Jerobo´am the son of Ne´bat, and in the

sins which he made Israel to sin, provoking
the LORD, the God of Israel, to anger by
their idols. [27]Now the rest of the acts of
Omri which he did, and the might that he
showed, are they not written in the Book of
the Chronicles of the Kings of Israel? [28]And
Omri slept with his fathers, and was buried
in Samar′ia; and A′hab his son reigned in
his stead.

[29]In the thirty-eighth year of Asa king
of Judah, A′hab the son of Omri began to
reign over Israel, and Ahab the son of Omri
reigned over Israel in Samar′ia twenty-two
years. [30]And A′hab the son of Omri did evil
in the sight of the LORD more than all that
were before him. [31]And as if it had been a
light thing for him to walk in the sins of
Jerobo′am the son of Ne′bat, he took for
his wife Jez′ebel the daughter of Ethba′al
king of the Sido′nians, and went and served
Ba′al, and worshiped him. [32]He erected an
altar for Ba′al in the house of Baal, which
he built in Samar′ia. [33]And A′hab made an
Ashe′rah. Ahab did more to provoke the
LORD, the God of Israel, to anger than all the
kings of Israel who were before him. [34]In his
days Hiel of Bethel built Jericho; he laid its
foundation at the cost of Abi′ram his first-
born, and set up its gates at the cost of his
youngest son Segub, according to the word
of the LORD, which he spoke by Joshua the
son of Nun.

17 Now Eli′jah the Tishbite, of Tishbe
in Gilead, said to A′hab, "As the LORD
the God of Israel lives, before whom I stand,
there shall be neither dew nor rain these
years, except by my word." [2]And the word of
the LORD came to him, [3]"Depart from here
and turn eastward, and hide yourself by the
brook Cherith, that is east of the Jordan.
[4]You shall drink from the brook, and I have
commanded the ravens to feed you there."
[5]So he went and did according to the word
of the LORD; he went and dwelt by the brook
Cherith that is east of the Jordan. [6]And
the ravens brought him bread and meat in
the morning, and bread and meat in the
evening; and he drank from the brook. [7]And
after a while the brook dried up, because
there was no rain in the land.

[8]Then the word of the LORD came to him.
[9]"Arise, go to Zar′ephath, which belongs
to Si′don, and dwell there. Behold, I have
commanded a widow there to feed you."
[10]So he arose and went to Zar′ephath; and
when he came to the gate of the city, behold,
a widow was there gathering sticks; and he
called to her and said, "Bring me a little
water in a vessel, that I may drink." [11]And
as she was going to bring it, he called to
her and said, "Bring me a morsel of bread
in your hand." [12]And she said, "As the LORD
your God lives, I have nothing baked, only
a handful of meal in a jar, and a little oil in
a pitcher; and now, I am gathering a couple
of sticks, that I may go in and prepare it for
myself and my son, that we may eat it, and
die." [13]And Eli′jah said to her, "Fear not;
go and do as you have said; but first make
me a little cake of it and bring it to me, and
afterward make for yourself and your son.
[14]For thus says the LORD the God of Israel,
'The jar of meal shall not be spent, and the
pitcher of oil shall not fail, until the day that
the LORD sends rain upon the earth.'" [15]And
she went and did as Eli′jah said; and she, and
he, and her household ate for many days.
[16]The jar of meal was not spent, neither did
the pitcher of oil fail, according to the word
of the LORD which he spoke by Eli′jah.

[17]After this the son of the woman, the
mistress of the house, became ill; and his
illness was so severe that there was no
breath left in him. [18]And she said to Eli′jah,
"What have you against me, O man of God?
You have come to me to bring my sin to
remembrance, and to cause the death of my
son!" [19]And he said to her, "Give me your
son." And he took him from her bosom,
and carried him up into the upper chamber,
where he lodged, and laid him upon his own
bed. [20]And he cried to the LORD, "O LORD my
God, have you brought calamity even upon
the widow with whom I sojourn, by slaying
her son?" [21]Then he stretched himself upon
the child three times, and cried to the LORD,
"O LORD my God, let this child's soul come
into him again." [22]And the LORD listened
to the voice of Eli′jah; and the soul of the
child came into him again, and he revived.

23 And Eli′jah took the child, and brought
him down from the upper chamber into the
house, and delivered him to his mother; and
Elijah said, "See, your son lives." 24 And the
woman said to Eli′jah, "Now I know that
you are a man of God, and that the word of
the LORD in your mouth is truth."

A Song of Ascents.

PSALM 120 [119]

In my distress I cry to the LORD,
  that he may answer me:
2 "Deliver me, O LORD,
  from lying lips,
  from a deceitful tongue."

3 What shall be given to you?
  And what more shall be done to you,
  you deceitful tongue?
4 A warrior's sharp arrows,
  with glowing coals of the broom tree!

5 Woe is me, that I sojourn in Meshech,
  that I dwell among the tents
    of Kedar!
6 Too long have I had my dwelling
  among those who hate peace.
7 I am for peace;
  but when I speak,
  they are for war!

JOHN 12

27 "Now is my soul troubled. And
what shall I say? 'Father, save me
from this hour'? No, for this purpose I
have come to this hour. 28 Father, glorify
your name." Then a voice came from
heaven, "I have glorified it, and I will glorify
it again." 29 The crowd standing by heard it
and said that it had thundered. Others said,
"An angel has spoken to him." 30 Jesus answered, "This voice has come for your sake,
not for mine. 31 Now is the judgment of this
world, now shall the ruler of this world be
cast out; 32 and I, when I am lifted up from
the earth, will draw all men to myself." 33 He
said this to show by what death he was to
die. 34 The crowd answered him, "We have
heard from the law that the Christ remains
for ever. How can you say that the Son of
man must be lifted up? Who is this Son of
man?" 35 Jesus said to them, "The light is
with you for a little longer. Walk while you
have the light, lest the darkness overtake
you; he who walks in the darkness does
not know where he goes. 36 While you have
the light, believe in the light, that you may
become sons of light."

When Jesus had said this, he departed
and hid himself from them. 37 Though he
had done so many signs before them, yet
they did not believe in him; 38 it was that the
word spoken by the prophet Isaiah might be
fulfilled:

"Lord, who has believed our report,
and to whom has the arm of the Lord been
  revealed?"

39 Therefore they could not believe. For
Isaiah again said,

40 "He has blinded their eyes and hardened
  their heart,
lest they should see with their eyes and
  perceive with their heart,
and turn for me to heal them."

41 Isaiah said this because he saw his glory
and spoke of him. 42 Nevertheless many even
of the authorities believed in him, but for
fear of the Pharisees they did not confess it,
lest they should be put out of the synagogue:
43 for they loved the praise of men more than
the praise of God.

44 And Jesus cried out and said, "He who
believes in me, believes not in me but in him
who sent me. 45 And he who sees me sees
him who sent me. 46 I have come as light into
the world, that whoever believes in me may
not remain in darkness. 47 If any one hears
my sayings and does not keep them, I do
not judge him; for I did not come to judge
the world but to save the world. 48 He who
rejects me and does not receive my sayings
has a judge; the word that I have spoken
will be his judge on the last day. 49 For I
have not spoken on my own authority; the

Father who sent me has himself given me commandment what to say and what to speak. 50 And I know that his commandment is eternal life. What I say, therefore, I say as the Father has bidden me."

REFLECTION

Good leadership can make all the difference. The ongoing history of the kings of Israel and Judah reads like a litany of evils almost without interruption. Repeatedly we hear that the king "did evil in the sight of the LORD" (1 Kgs 16:30), some even more than the kings that were before them (see vv. 16:25, 30); and often these evil kings made God's people, Israel, to sin (see vv. 16:2, 13, 19). All aspirations that a king might reverse the cycle of sin seen during the time of the judges are quickly dashed. But God intervenes. A prophet comes on the scene—Elijah—whose holy life and fidelity to God will redirect God's people. Elijah's story interrupts the list of evil kings with miraculous marvels. He prophesies a drought. He is fed by ravens. He provides food for the widow at Zarephath and raises her son from the dead. Just as Israel follows Elijah because of his mighty signs, so too many will follow Jesus. But Jesus will heal not just bodies, but souls, giving his grace so that they will sin no more. The evil kings led others astray by their lives. Elijah led others back to God. What example and direction will your life give to others today?

June 2

1 KINGS 18

After many days the word of the LORD came to Eli′jah, in the third year, saying, "Go, show yourself to A′hab; and I will send rain upon the earth." 2 So Eli′jah went to show himself to A′hab. Now the famine was severe in Samar′ia. 3 And A′hab called Obadi′ah, who was over the household. (Now Obadiah revered the LORD greatly; 4 and when Jez′ebel cut off the prophets of the LORD, Obadi′ah took a hundred prophets and hid them by fifties in a cave, and fed them with bread and water.) 5 And A′hab said to Obadi′ah, "Go through the land to all the springs of water and to all the valleys; perhaps we may find grass and save the horses and mules alive, and not lose some of the animals." 6 So they divided the land between them to pass through it; A′hab went in one direction by himself, and Obadi′ah went in another direction by himself.

7 And as Obadi′ah was on the way, behold, Eli′jah met him; and Obadiah recognized him, and fell on his face, and said, "Is it you, my lord Elijah?" 8 And he answered him, "It is I. Go, tell your lord, 'Behold, Eli′jah is here.'" 9 And he said, "Wherein have I sinned, that you would give your servant into the hand of A′hab, to kill me? 10 As the LORD your God lives, there is no nation or kingdom whither my lord has not sent to seek you; and when they would say, 'He is not here,' he would take an oath of the kingdom or nation, that they had not found you. 11 And now you say, 'Go, tell your lord, "Behold, Eli′jah is here."' 12 And as soon as I have gone from you, the Spirit of the LORD will carry you I know not where; and so, when I come and tell A′hab and he cannot find you, he will kill me, although I your servant have revered the LORD from my youth. 13 Has it not been told my lord what I did when Jez′ebel killed the prophets of the LORD, how I hid a hundred men of the LORD's prophets by fifties in a cave, and fed them with bread and water? 14 And now you say, 'Go, tell your lord, "Behold, Eli′jah is here"'; and he will kill me." 15 And Eli′jah said, "As the LORD of hosts lives, before whom I stand, I will surely show myself to him today." 16 So Obadi′ah went to meet A′hab, and told him; and Ahab went to meet Eli′jah.

17 When A′hab saw Eli′jah, Ahab said to him, "Is it you, you troubler of Israel?" 18 And he answered, "I have not troubled Israel; but you have, and your father's house, because you have forsaken the commandments of

the LORD and followed the Ba′als. [19]Now therefore send and gather all Israel to me at Mount Carmel, and the four hundred and fifty prophets of Ba′al and the four hundred prophets of Ashe′rah, who eat at Jez′ebel's table."

[20]So A′hab sent to all the sons of Israel, and gathered the prophets together at Mount Carmel. [21]And Eli′jah came near to all the people, and said, "How long will you go limping with two different opinions? If the LORD is God, follow him; but if Ba′al, then follow him." And the people did not answer him a word. [22]Then Eli′jah said to the people, "I, even I only, am left a prophet of the LORD; but Ba′al's prophets are four hundred and fifty men. [23]Let two bulls be given to us; and let them choose one bull for themselves, and cut it in pieces and lay it on the wood, but put no fire to it; and I will prepare the other bull and lay it on the wood, and put no fire to it. [24]And you call on the name of your god and I will call on the name of the LORD; and the God who answers by fire, he is God." And all the people answered, "It is well spoken." [25]Then Eli′jah said to the prophets of Ba′al, "Choose for yourselves one bull and prepare it first, for you are many; and call on the name of your god, but put no fire to it." [26]And they took the bull which was given them, and they prepared it, and called on the name of Ba′al from morning until noon, saying, "O Baal, answer us!" But there was no voice, and no one answered. And they limped about the altar which they had made. [27]And at noon Eli′jah mocked them, saying, "Cry aloud, for he is a god; either he is musing, or he has gone aside, or he is on a journey, or perhaps he is asleep and must be awakened." [28]And they cried aloud, and cut themselves after their custom with swords and lances, until the blood gushed out upon them. [29]And as midday passed, they raved on until the time of the offering of the oblation, but there was no voice; no one answered, no one heeded.

[30]Then Eli′jah said to all the people, "Come near to me"; and all the people came near to him. And he repaired the altar of the LORD that had been thrown down; [31]Eli′jah took twelve stones, according to the number of the tribes of the sons of Jacob, to whom the word of the LORD came, saying, "Israel shall be your name"; [32]and with the stones he built an altar in the name of the LORD. And he made a trench about the altar, as great as would contain two measures of seed. [33]And he put the wood in order, and cut the bull in pieces and laid it on the wood. And he said, "Fill four jars with water, and pour it on the burnt offering, and on the wood." [34]And he said, "Do it a second time"; and they did it a second time. And he said, "Do it a third time"; and they did it a third time. [35]And the water ran round about the altar, and filled the trench also with water.

[36]And at the time of the offering of the oblation, Eli′jah the prophet came near and said, "O LORD, God of Abraham, Isaac, and Israel, let it be known this day that you are God in Israel, and that I am your servant, and that I have done all these things at your word. [37]Answer me, O LORD, answer me, that this people may know that you, O LORD, are God, and that you have turned their hearts back." [38]Then the fire of the LORD fell, and consumed the burnt offering, and the wood, and the stones, and the dust, and licked up the water that was in the trench. [39]And when all the people saw it, they fell on their faces; and they said, "The LORD, he is God; the LORD, he is God." [40]And Eli′jah said to them, "Seize the prophets of Ba′al; let not one of them escape." And they seized them; and Elijah brought them down to the brook Ki′shon, and killed them there.

[41]And Eli′jah said to A′hab, "Go up, eat and drink; for there is a sound of the rushing of rain." [42]So A′hab went up to eat and to drink. And Eli′jah went up to the top of Carmel; and he bowed himself down upon the earth, and put his face between his knees. [43]And he said to his servant, "Go up now, look toward the sea." And he went up and looked, and said, "There is nothing." And he said, "Go again seven times." [44]And at the seventh time he said, "Behold, a little cloud like a man's hand is rising out of the sea." And he said, "Go up, say to A′hab, 'Prepare your chariot and go down, lest the rain stop you.'" [45]And

in a little while the heavens grew black with
clouds and wind, and there was a great rain.
And A′hab rode and went to Jezre′el. [46]And
the hand of the LORD was on Eli′jah; and he
girded up his loins and ran before A′hab to
the entrance of Jezre′el.

19 A′hab told Jez′ebel all that Eli′jah
had done, and how he had slain all
the prophets with the sword. [2]Then Jez′ebel
sent a messenger to Eli′jah, saying, "So may
the gods do to me, and more also, if I do not
make your life as the life of one of them by
this time tomorrow." [3]Then he was afraid,
and he arose and went for his life, and came
to Be′er-she′ba, which belongs to Judah, and
left his servant there.

[4]But he himself went a day's journey into
the wilderness, and came and sat down
under a broom tree; and he asked that he
might die, saying, "It is enough; now, O
LORD, take away my life; for I am no better
than my fathers." [5]And he lay down and
slept under a broom tree; and behold, an
angel touched him, and said to him, "Arise
and eat." [6]And he looked, and behold, there
was at his head a cake baked on hot stones
and a jar of water. And he ate and drank, and
lay down again. [7]And the angel of the LORD
came again a second time, and touched him,
and said, "Arise and eat, else the journey will
be too great for you." [8]And he arose, and
ate and drank, and walked in the strength
of that food forty days and forty nights to
Horeb the mount of God.

[9]And there he came to a cave, and lodged
there; and behold, the word of the LORD came
to him, and he said to him, "What are you
doing here, Eli′jah?" [10]He said, "I have been
very jealous for the LORD, the God of hosts; for
the sons of Israel have forsaken your covenant,
thrown down your altars, and slain your
prophets with the sword; and I, even I only,
am left; and they seek my life, to take it away."
[11]And he said, "Go forth, and stand upon the
mount before the LORD." And behold, the
LORD passed by, and a great and strong wind
tore the mountains, and broke in pieces the
rocks before the LORD, but the LORD was not
in the wind; and after the wind an earthquake,
but the LORD was not in the earthquake; [12]and
after the earthquake a fire, but the LORD was
not in the fire; and after the fire a still small
voice. [13]And when Eli′jah heard it, he wrapped
his face in his mantle and went out and stood
at the entrance of the cave. And behold, there
came a voice to him, and said, "What are you
doing here, Eli′jah?" [14]He said, "I have been
very jealous for the LORD, the God of hosts; for
the sons of Israel have forsaken your covenant,
thrown down your altars, and slain your
prophets with the sword; and I, even I only,
am left; and they seek my life, to take it away."
[15]And the LORD said to him, "Go, return on
your way to the wilderness of Damascus; and
when you arrive, you shall anoint Haz′ael to be
king over Syria; [16]and Je′hu the son of Nimshi
you shall anoint to be king over Israel; and
Eli′sha the son of Sha′phat of A′bel-meho′lah
you shall anoint to be prophet in your place.
[17]And him who escapes from the sword of
Haz′ael shall Je′hu slay; and him who escapes
from the sword of Jehu shall Eli′sha slay. [18]Yet I
will leave seven thousand in Israel, all the knees
that have not bowed to Ba′al, and every mouth
that has not kissed him."

[19]So he departed from there, and found
Eli′sha the son of Sha′phat, who was plowing,
with twelve yoke of oxen before him, and he
was with the twelfth. Eli′jah passed by him
and cast his mantle upon him. [20]And he left
the oxen, and ran after Eli′jah, and said, "Let
me kiss my father and my mother, and then
I will follow you." And he said to him, "Go
back again; for what have I done to you?"
[21]And he returned from following him,
and took the yoke of oxen, and slew them,
and boiled their flesh with the yokes of the
oxen, and gave it to the people, and they ate.
Then he arose and went after Eli′jah, and
ministered to him.

A Song of Ascents.

PSALM 121 [120]

I lift up my eyes to the hills.
From where does my help come?
[2]My help comes from the LORD,
who made heaven and earth.

[3]He will not let your foot be moved,
he who keeps you will not slumber.
[4]Behold, he who keeps Israel
will neither slumber nor sleep.

[5]The LORD is your keeper;
the LORD is your shade
on your right hand.
[6]The sun shall not strike you by day,
nor the moon by night.

[7]The LORD will keep you from all evil;
he will keep your life.
[8]The LORD will keep
your going out and your coming in
from this time forth and for evermore.

JOHN 13

Now before the feast of the Passover, when Jesus knew that his hour had come to depart out of this world to the Father, having loved his own who were in the world, he loved them to the end. [2]And during
supper, when the devil had already put it into the heart of Judas Iscariot, Simon's son, to betray him, [3]Jesus, knowing that the Father had given all things into his hands, and that he had come from God and was going to God, [4]rose from supper, laid aside his garments, and tied a towel around himself. [5]Then he poured water into a basin, and began to wash the disciples' feet, and to wipe them with the towel that was tied around him. [6]He came to Simon Peter; and Peter said to him, "Lord, do you wash my feet?" [7]Jesus answered him, "What I am doing you do not know now, but afterward you will understand." [8]Peter said to him, "You shall never wash my feet." Jesus answered him, "If I do not wash you, you have no part in me." [9]Simon Peter said to him, "Lord, not my feet only but also my hands and my head!" [10]Jesus said to him, "He who has bathed does not need to wash, except for his feet, but he is clean all over; and you are clean, but not all of you." [11]For he knew who was to betray him; that was why he said, "You are not all clean."

[12]When he had washed their feet, and taken his garments, and resumed his place, he said to them, "Do you know what I have done to you? [13]You call me Teacher and Lord; and you are right, for so I am. [14]If I then, your Lord and Teacher, have washed your feet, you also ought to wash one another's feet. [15]For I have given you an example, that you also should do as I have done to you. [16]Truly, truly, I say to you, a servant is not greater than his master; nor is he who is sent greater than he who sent him. [17]If you know these things, blessed are you if you do them. [18]I am not speaking of you all; I know whom I have chosen; it is that the Scripture may be fulfilled, 'He who ate my bread has lifted his heel against me.' [19]I tell you this now, before it takes place, that when it does take place you may believe that I am he. [20]Truly, truly, I say to you, he who receives any one whom I send receives me; and he who receives me receives him who sent me."

REFLECTION

Elijah's famous contest with the prophets of Baal is one of the premier mountain-top experiences of God in the Bible. After challenging the false prophets to a showdown of divinities, and after watching them fail to summon fire from Baal, Elijah calls down fire from Heaven on his water-logged altar. "Then the fire of the LORD fell, and consumed the burnt offering, and the wood, and the stones, and the dust, and licked up the water that was in the trench" (1 Kgs 18:38). As if this mighty show was not enough, Elijah concludes the contest by ending the three-year drought. Fleeing persecution, Elijah is directed to a second mountain-top encounter. Despite the drama of wind, earthquake, and fire, the Lord's presence arrives in a "still small voice" (19:12). Though our Lord is the Creator of the cosmos and the King of all kings, he longs for us to come to him in the quiet intimacy of faith. Are you regularly listening for the still small voice of the Lord?

June 3

1 KINGS 20

Ben-ha′dad the king of Syria gathered all his army together; thirty-two kings were with him, and horses and chariots; and he went up and besieged Samar′ia, and fought against it. [2]And he sent messengers into the city to A′hab king of Israel, and said to him, "Thus says Ben-ha′dad: [3]'Your silver and your gold are mine; your fairest wives and children also are mine.'" [4]And the king of Israel answered, "As you say, my lord, O king, I am yours, and all that I have." [5]The messengers came again, and said, "Thus says Ben-ha′dad: 'I sent to you, saying, "Deliver to me your silver and your gold, your wives and your children"; [6]nevertheless I will send my servants to you tomorrow about this time, and they shall search your house and the houses of your servants, and lay hands on whatever pleases them, and take it away.'"

[7]Then the king of Israel called all the elders of the land, and said, "Mark, now, and see how this man is seeking trouble; for he sent to me for my wives and my children, and for my silver and my gold, and I did not refuse him." [8]And all the elders and all the people said to him, "Do not heed or consent." [9]So he said to the messengers of Ben-ha′dad, "Tell my lord the king, 'All that you first demanded of your servant I will do; but this thing I cannot do.'" And the messengers departed and brought him word again. [10]Ben-ha′dad sent to him and said, "The gods do so to me, and more also, if the dust of Samar′ia shall suffice for handfuls for all the people who follow me." [11]And the king of Israel answered, "Tell him, 'Let not him that belts on his armor boast himself as he that puts it off.'" [12]When Ben-ha′dad heard this message as he was drinking with the kings in the booths, he said to his men, "Take your positions." And they took their positions against the city.

[13]And behold, a prophet came near to A′hab king of Israel and said, "Thus says the LORD, Have you seen all this great multitude? Behold, I will give it into your hand this day; and you shall know that I am the LORD." [14]And A′hab said, "By whom?" He said, "Thus says the LORD, By the servants of the governors of the districts." Then he said, "Who shall begin the battle?" He answered, "You." [15]Then he mustered the servants of the governors of the districts, and they were two hundred and thirty-two; and after them he mustered all the sons of Israel, seven thousand.

[16]And they went out at noon, while Ben-ha′dad was drinking himself drunk in the booths, he and the thirty-two kings who helped him. [17]The servants of the governors of the districts went out first. And Ben-ha′dad sent out scouts, and they reported to him, "Men are coming out from Samar′ia." [18]He said, "If they have come out for peace, take them alive; or if they have come out for war, take them alive."

[19]So these went out of the city, the servants of the governors of the districts, and the army which followed them. [20]And each killed his man; the Syrians fled and Israel pursued them, but Ben-ha′dad king of Syria escaped on a horse with horsemen. [21]And the king of Israel went out, and captured the horses and chariots, and killed the Syrians with a great slaughter.

[22]Then the prophet came near to the king of Israel, and said to him, "Come, strengthen yourself, and consider well what you have to do; for in the spring the king of Syria will come up against you."

[23]And the servants of the king of Syria said to him, "Their gods are gods of the hills, and so they were stronger than we; but let us fight against them in the plain, and surely we shall be stronger than they. [24]And do this: remove the kings, each from his post, and put commanders in their places; [25]and muster an army like the army that you have lost, horse for horse, and chariot for chariot; then we will fight against them in the plain, and surely we shall be stronger than they." And he listened to their voice, and did so.

[26]In the spring Ben-ha′dad mustered the Syrians, and went up to A′phek, to fight against Israel. [27]And the sons of Israel were mustered, and were provisioned, and went against them; the sons of Israel encamped before them like two little flocks of goats, but the Syrians filled the country. [28]And a man of God came near and said to the king of Israel, "Thus says the LORD, 'Because the Syrians have said, "The LORD is a god of the hills but he is not a god of the valleys," therefore I will give all this great multitude into your hand, and you shall know that I am the LORD.'" [29]And they encamped opposite one another seven days. Then on the seventh day the battle was joined; and the sons of Israel struck a hundred thousand Syrian foot soldiers in one day. [30]And the rest fled into the city of A′phek; and the wall fell upon twenty-seven thousand men that were left.

Ben-ha′dad also fled, and entered an inner chamber in the city. [31]And his servants said to him, "Behold now, we have heard that the kings of the house of Israel are merciful kings; let us put sackcloth on our loins and ropes upon our heads, and go out to the king of Israel; perhaps he will spare your life." [32]So they belted sackcloth on their loins, and put ropes on their heads, and went to the king of Israel and said, "Your servant Ben-ha′dad says, 'Please, let me live.'" And he said, "Does he still live? He is my brother." [33]Now the men were watching for an omen, and they quickly took it up from him and said, "Yes, your brother Ben-ha′dad." Then he said, "Go and bring him." Then Ben-hadad came forth to him; and he caused him to come up into the chariot. [34]And Ben-ha′dad said to him, "The cities which my father took from your father I will restore; and you may establish bazaars for yourself in Damascus, as my father did in Samar′ia." And A′hab said, "I will let you go on these terms." So he made a covenant with him and let him go.

[35]And a certain man of the sons of the prophets said to his fellow at the command of the LORD, "Strike me, I beg you." But the man refused to strike him. [36]Then he said to him, "Because you have not obeyed the voice of the LORD, behold, as soon as you have gone from me, a lion shall kill you." And as soon as he had departed from him, a lion met him and killed him. [37]Then he found another man, and said, "Strike me, I beg you." And the man struck him, hitting and wounding him. [38]So the prophet departed, and waited for the king by the way, disguising himself with a bandage over his eyes. [39]And as the king passed, he cried to the king and said, "Your servant went out into the midst of the battle; and behold, a soldier turned and brought a man to me, and said, 'Keep this man; if by any means he be missing, your life shall be for his life, or else you shall pay a talent of silver.' [40]And as your servant was busy here and there, he was gone." The king of Israel said to him, "So shall your judgment be; you yourself have decided it." [41]Then he made haste to take the bandage away from his eyes; and the king of Israel recognized him as one of the prophets. [42]And he said to him, "Thus says the LORD, 'Because you have let go out of your hand the man whom I had devoted to destruction, therefore your life shall go for his life, and your people for his people.'" [43]And the king of Israel went to his house resentful and sullen, and came to Samar′ia.

21 Now Naboth the Jezre′elite had a vineyard in Jezre′el, beside the palace of A′hab king of Samar′ia. [2]And after this A′hab said to Naboth, "Give me your vineyard, that I may have it for a vegetable garden, because it is near my house; and I will give you a better vineyard for it; or, if it seems good to you, I will give you its value in money." [3]But Naboth said to A′hab, "The LORD forbid that I should give you the inheritance of my fathers." [4]And A′hab went into his house vexed and sullen because of what Naboth the Jezre′elite had said to him; for he had said, "I will not give you the inheritance of my fathers." And he lay down on his bed, and turned away his face, and would eat no food.

[5]But Jez′ebel his wife came to him, and said to him, "Why is your spirit so vexed that you eat no food?" [6]And he said to her, "Because I spoke to Naboth the Jezre′elite,

and said to him, 'Give me your vineyard
for money; or else, if it please you, I will
give you another vineyard for it'; and he
answered, 'I will not give you my vineyard.'"
7And Jez′ebel his wife said to him, "Do you
now govern Israel? Arise, and eat bread, and
let your heart be cheerful; I will give you the
vineyard of Naboth the Jezre′elite."
8So she wrote letters in A′hab's name and
sealed them with his seal, and she sent the
letters to the elders and the nobles who dwelt
with Naboth in his city. 9And she wrote in
the letters, "Proclaim a fast, and set Naboth
on high among the people; 10and set two base
fellows opposite him, and let them bring a
charge against him, saying, 'You have cursed
God and the king.' Then take him out, and
stone him to death." 11And the men of his city,
the elders and the nobles who dwelt in his city,
did as Jez′ebel had sent word to them. As it
was written in the letters which she had sent to
them, 12they proclaimed a fast, and set Naboth
on high among the people. 13And the two base
fellows came in and sat opposite him; and the
base fellows brought a charge against Naboth,
in the presence of the people, saying, "Naboth
cursed God and the king." So they took him
outside the city, and stoned him to death with
stones. 14Then they sent to Jez′ebel, saying,
"Naboth has been stoned; he is dead."
15As soon as Jez′ebel heard that Naboth
had been stoned and was dead, Jezebel
said to A′hab, "Arise, take possession of the
vineyard of Naboth the Jezre′elite, which he
refused to give you for money; for Naboth is
not alive, but dead." 16And as soon as A′hab
heard that Naboth was dead, Ahab arose
to go down to the vineyard of Naboth the
Jezre′elite, to take possession of it.

A Song of Ascents.
Of David.

PSALM 122 [121]

I was glad when they said to me,
"Let us go to the house of the LORD!"
2Our feet have been standing
within your gates, O Jerusalem!

3Jerusalem, built as a city
which is bound firmly together,
4to which the tribes go up,
the tribes of the LORD,
as was decreed for Israel,
to give thanks to the name of the LORD.
5There thrones for judgment were set,
the thrones of the house of David.

6Pray for the peace of Jerusalem!
"May they prosper who love you!
7Peace be within your walls,
and security within your towers!"
8For my brethren and companions' sake
I will say, "Peace be within you!"
9For the sake of the house of the LORD
our God,
I will seek your good.

A Song of Ascents.

123 [122] To you I lift up my eyes,
O you who are enthroned in the heavens!
2Behold, as the eyes of servants
look to the hand of their master,
as the eyes of a maid
to the hand of her mistress,
so our eyes look to the LORD our God,
till he have mercy upon us.

3Have mercy upon us, O LORD, have mercy
upon us,
for we have had more than enough of
contempt.
4Too long our soul has been sated
with the scorn of those who are at ease,
the contempt of the proud.

JOHN 13

21When Jesus had thus spoken,
he was troubled in spirit, and
testified, "Truly, truly, I say to you, one
of you will betray me." 22The disciples
looked at one another, uncertain of whom he
spoke. 23One of his disciples, whom Jesus
loved, was lying close to the breast of Jesus;
24so Simon Peter beckoned to him and said,

"Tell us who it is of whom he speaks." 25 So
lying thus, close to the breast of Jesus, he
said to him, "Lord, who is it?" 26 Jesus answered, "It is he to whom I shall give this
morsel when I have dipped it." So when he
had dipped the morsel, he gave it to Judas,
the son of Simon Iscariot. 27 Then after the
morsel, Satan entered into him. Jesus said to
him, "What you are going to do, do quickly."
28 Now no one at the table knew why he said
this to him. 29 Some thought that, because
Judas had the money box, Jesus was telling
him, "Buy what we need for the feast"; or,
that he should give something to the poor.
30 So, after receiving the morsel, he immediately went out; and it was night.
31 When he had gone out, Jesus said, "Now
is the Son of man glorified, and in him God
is glorified; 32 if God is glorified in him,
God will also glorify him in himself, and
glorify him at once. 33 Little children, yet a
little while I am with you. You will seek me;
and as I said to the Jews so now I say to you,
'Where I am going you cannot come.' 34 A
new commandment I give to you, that you
love one another; even as I have loved you,
that you also love one another. 35 By this all
men will know that you are my disciples, if
you have love for one another."
36 Simon Peter said to him, "Lord, where are
you going?" Jesus answered, "Where I am
going you cannot follow me now; but you
shall follow afterward." 37 Peter said to him,
"Lord, why can I not follow you now? I will
lay down my life for you." 38 Jesus answered,
"Will you lay down your life for me? Truly,
truly, I say to you, the cock will not crow, till
you have denied me three times."

REFLECTION

Today, our readings show two opposing philosophies of life—one of acquisitiveness, the other of generous service. King Ahab acts the part of a typical politician—going to war and then seeking the best economic concessions he can get once he wins the battle. He does not finish off the enemy king, but spares him for political reasons against the command of the Lord (see 1 Kgs 20:42). In addition, Ahab stays up late at night scheming how to get his hands on a certain piece of real estate. The owner refuses to sell for theological reasons: he does not want to abandon the "inheritance of his fathers." But Ahab's Gentile wife, Jezebel, has the owner murdered so his property can be stolen. The psalm and the Gospel go in the opposite direction, where our eyes look to the hand of the Lord for mercy like a servant's eyes look upon his master's hand. In addition, Jesus gives the new commandment: "Love one another" (Jn 13:34). Sadly, Judas adopts Ahab's philosophy and betrays Jesus for money even as Jesus gives him a morsel of food. Each of us has a choice, too: Will you live out a philosophy of "getting" or of "giving"? Will you seek to acquire more things or to give generously of yourself?

June 4

1 KINGS 21

**17 Then the word of the LORD
came to Eli′jah the Tishbite,
saying, 18 "Arise, go down to meet A′hab
king of Israel, who is in Samar′ia; behold,**
he is in the vineyard of Naboth, where he
has gone to take possession. 19 And you shall
say to him, 'Thus says the LORD, "Have you
killed, and also taken possession?"' And you
shall say to him, 'Thus says the LORD: "In
the place where dogs licked up the blood of
Naboth shall dogs lick your own blood."'"
20 A′hab said to Eli′jah, "Have you found
me, O my enemy?" He answered, "I have
found you, because you have sold yourself
to do what is evil in the sight of the LORD.
21 Behold, I will bring evil upon you; I will
utterly sweep you away, and will cut off
from A′hab every male, bond or free, in
Israel; 22 and I will make your house like the
house of Jerobo′am the son of Ne′bat, and
like the house of Ba′asha the son of Ahi′jah,

for the anger to which you have provoked me, and because you have made Israel to sin. 23And of Jez′ebel the LORD also said, 'The dogs shall eat Jezebel within the bounds of Jezre′el.' 24Any one belonging to A′hab who dies in the city the dogs shall eat; and any one of his who dies in the open country the birds of the air shall eat."

25(There was none who sold himself to do what was evil in the sight of the LORD like A′hab, whom Jez′ebel his wife incited. 26He did very abominably in going after idols, as the Am′orites had done, whom the LORD cast out before the sons of Israel.)

27And when A′hab heard those words, he tore his clothes, and put sackcloth upon his flesh, and fasted and lay in sackcloth, and went about dejectedly. 28And the word of the LORD came to Eli′jah the Tishbite, saying, 29"Have you seen how Ahab has humbled himself before me? Because he has humbled himself before me, I will not bring the evil in his days; but in his son's days I will bring the evil upon his house."

22 For three years Syria and Israel continued without war. 2But in the third year Jehosh′aphat the king of Judah came down to the king of Israel. 3And the king of Israel said to his servants, "Do you know that Ra′moth-gil′ead belongs to us, and we keep quiet and do not take it out of the hand of the king of Syria?" 4And he said to Jehosh′aphat, "Will you go with me to battle at Ra′moth-gil′ead?" And Jehoshaphat said to the king of Israel, "I am as you are, my people as your people, my horses as your horses."

5And Jehosh′aphat said to the king of Israel, "Inquire first for the word of the LORD." 6Then the king of Israel gathered the prophets together, about four hundred men, and said to them, "Shall I go to battle against Ra′moth-gil′ead, or shall I forbear?" And they said, "Go up; for the Lord will give it into the hand of the king." 7But Jehosh′aphat said, "Is there not here another prophet of the LORD of whom we may inquire?" 8And the king of Israel said to Jehosh′aphat, "There is yet one man by whom we may inquire of the LORD, Micai′ah the son of Imlah; but I hate him, for he never prophesies good concerning me, but evil." And Jehosh′aphat said, "Let not the king say so." 9Then the king of Israel summoned an officer and said, "Bring quickly Micai′ah the son of Imlah." 10Now the king of Israel and Jehosh′aphat the king of Judah were sitting on their thrones, wearing their robes, at the threshing floor at the entrance of the gate of Samar′ia; and all the prophets were prophesying before them. 11And Zedeki′ah the son of Chena′anah made for himself horns of iron, and said, "Thus says the LORD, 'With these you shall push the Syrians until they are destroyed.'" 12And all the prophets prophesied so, and said, "Go up to Ra′moth-gil′ead and triumph; the LORD will give it into the hand of the king."

13And the messenger who went to summon Micai′ah said to him, "Behold, the words of the prophets with one accord are favorable to the king; let your word be like the word of one of them, and speak favorably." 14But Micai′ah said, "As the LORD lives, what the LORD says to me, that I will speak." 15And when he had come to the king, the king said to him, "Micai′ah, shall we go to Ra′moth-gil′ead to battle, or shall we forbear?" And he answered him, "Go up and triumph; the LORD will give it into the hand of the king." 16But the king said to him, "How many times shall I adjure you that you speak to me nothing but the truth in the name of the LORD?" 17And he said, "I saw all Israel scattered upon the mountains, as sheep that have no shepherd; and the LORD said, 'These have no master; let each return to his home in peace.'" 18And the king of Israel said to Jehosh′aphat, "Did I not tell you that he would not prophesy good concerning me, but evil?" 19And Micai′ah said, "Therefore hear the word of the LORD: I saw the LORD sitting on his throne, and all the host of heaven standing beside him on his right hand and on his left; 20and the LORD said, 'Who will entice A′hab, that he may go up and fall at Ra′moth-gil′ead?' And one said one thing, and another said another. 21Then a spirit came forward and stood before the LORD, saying, 'I will entice him.' 22And the LORD said to him, 'By what means?' And he said, 'I will go forth, and will be a lying spirit in the mouth of all his prophets.' And he said, 'You are to entice him, and you shall succeed; go forth and do so.' [23]Now therefore behold, the LORD has put a lying spirit in the mouth of all these your prophets; the LORD has spoken evil concerning you."

[24]Then Zedeki'ah the son of Chena'anah came near and struck Micai'ah on the cheek, and said, "How did the Spirit of the LORD go from me to speak to you?" [25]And Micai'ah said, "Behold, you shall see on that day when you go into an inner chamber to hide yourself." [26]And the king of Israel said, "Seize Micai'ah, and take him back to A'mon the governor of the city and to Jo'ash the king's son; [27]and say, 'Thus says the king, "Put this fellow in prison, and feed him with scant fare of bread and water, until I come in peace."'" [28]And Micai'ah said, "If you return in peace, the LORD has not spoken by me." And he said, "Hear, all you peoples!"

[29]So the king of Israel and Jehosh'aphat the king of Judah went up to Ra'moth-gil'ead. [30]And the king of Israel said to Jehosh'aphat, "I will disguise myself and go into battle, but you wear your robes." And the king of Israel disguised himself and went into battle. [31]Now the king of Syria had commanded the thirty-two captains of his chariots, "Fight with neither small nor great, but only with the king of Israel." [32]And when the captains of the chariots saw Jehosh'aphat, they said, "It is surely the king of Israel." So they turned to fight against him; and Jehoshaphat cried out. [33]And when the captains of the chariots saw that it was not the king of Israel, they turned back from pursuing him. [34]But a certain man drew his bow by chance, and struck the king of Israel between the scale armor and the breastplate; therefore he said to the driver of his chariot, "Turn about, and carry me out of the battle, for I am wounded." [35]And the battle grew hot that day, and the king was propped up in his chariot facing the Syrians, until at evening he died; and the blood of the wound flowed into the bottom of the chariot. [36]And about sunset a cry went through the army, "Every man to his city, and every man to his country!"

[37]So the king died, and was brought to Samar'ia; and they buried the king in Samaria. [38]And they washed the chariot by the pool of Samar'ia, and the dogs licked up his blood, and the harlots washed themselves in it, according to the word of the LORD which he had spoken. [39]Now the rest of the acts of A'hab, and all that he did, and the ivory house which he built, and all the cities that he built, are they not written in the Book of the Chronicles of the Kings of Israel? [40]So A'hab slept with his fathers; and Ahazi'ah his son reigned in his stead.

[41]Jehosh'aphat the son of Asa began to reign over Judah in the fourth year of A'hab king of Israel. [42]Jehosh'aphat was thirty-five years old when he began to reign, and he reigned twenty-five years in Jerusalem. His mother's name was Azu'bah the daughter of Shilhi. [43]He walked in all the way of Asa his father; he did not turn aside from it, doing what was right in the sight of the LORD; yet the high places were not taken away, and the people still sacrificed and burned incense on the high places. [44]Jehosh'aphat also made peace with the king of Israel.

[45]Now the rest of the acts of Jehosh'aphat, and his might that he showed, and how he warred, are they not written in the Book of the Chronicles of the Kings of Judah? [46]And the remnant of the male cult prostitutes who remained in the days of his father Asa, he exterminated from the land.

[47]There was no king in E'dom; a deputy was king. [48]Jehosh'aphat made ships of Tar'shish to go to O'phir for gold; but they did not go, for the ships were wrecked at E'zion-ge'ber. [49]Then Ahazi'ah the son of A'hab said to Jehosh'aphat, "Let my servants go with your servants in the ships," but Jehoshaphat was not willing. [50]And Jehosh'aphat slept with his fathers, and was buried with his fathers in the city of David his father; and Jeho'ram his son reigned in his stead.

[51]Ahazi'ah the son of A'hab began to reign over Israel in Samar'ia in the seventeenth year of Jehosh'aphat king of Judah,

and he reigned two years over Israel. [52]He
did what was evil in the sight of the LORD,
and walked in the way of his father, and
in the way of his mother, and in the way
of Jerobo´am the son of Ne´bat, who made
Israel to sin. [53]He served Ba´al and worshiped him, and provoked the LORD, the
God of Israel, to anger in every way that
his father had done.

A Song of Ascents.
Of David.

PSALM 124 [123]

If it had not been the LORD who was on
our side,
let Israel now say—
[2]if it had not been the LORD who was on
our side,
when men rose up against us,
[3]then they would have swallowed us
up alive,
when their anger was kindled against us;
[4]then the flood would have swept us away,
the torrent would have gone over us;
[5]then over us would have gone
the raging waters.

[6]Blessed be the LORD,
who has not given us
as prey to their teeth!
[7]We have escaped as a bird
from the snare of the fowlers;
the snare is broken,
and we have escaped!

[8]Our help is in the name of the LORD,
who made heaven and earth.

A Song of Ascents.

125 [124] Those who trust in the LORD are
like Mount Zion,
which cannot be moved, but abides for ever.
[2]As the mountains are round about
Jerusalem,
so the LORD is round about his people,
from this time forth and for evermore.
[3]For the scepter of wickedness shall not rest
upon the land allotted to the righteous,
lest the righteous put forth
their hands to do wrong.
[4]Do good, O LORD, to those who are good,
and to those who are upright in their
hearts!
[5]But those who turn aside upon their
crooked ways
the LORD will lead away with evildoers!
Peace be in Israel!

JOHN 14

**"Let not your hearts be troubled;
believe in God, believe also in
me. [2]In my Father's house are
many rooms; if it were not so, would
I have told you that I go to prepare
a place for you? [3]And when I go and**
prepare a place for you, I will come again
and will take you to myself, that where I
am you may be also. [4]And you know the
way where I am going." [5]Thomas said to
him, "Lord, we do not know where you are
going; how can we know the way?" [6]Jesus
said to him, "I am the way, and the truth,
and the life; no one comes to the Father, but
by me. [7]If you had known me, you would
have known my Father also; henceforth you
know him and have seen him."
[8]Philip said to him, "Lord, show us the
Father, and we shall be satisfied." [9]Jesus said
to him, "Have I been with you so long, and
yet you do not know me, Philip? He who
has seen me has seen the Father; how can
you say, 'Show us the Father'? [10]Do you
not believe that I am in the Father and the
Father is in me? The words that I say to you
I do not speak on my own authority; but the
Father who dwells in me does his works.
[11]Believe me that I am in the Father and the
Father is in me; or else believe me for the
sake of the works themselves.
[12]"Truly, truly, I say to you, he who believes
in me will also do the works that I do; and
greater works than these will he do, because

I go to the Father. 13Whatever you ask in my
name, I will do it, that the Father may be
glorified in the Son; 14if you ask anything in
my name, I will do it."

REFLECTION

King Ahab of Israel responds to the Lord inconsistently. After Elijah rebukes him for his serious sins, Ahab surprisingly humbles himself before God in repentance, which prompts the Lord to delay his judgment. But the next time a prophet tells him things he does not want to hear, he throws the prophet into prison on scant rations. The Lord wants us to rely on him consistently—in the midst of flood, torrent, and the raging waters of the world (see Ps 124:4–5). He desires our confidence: "Let not your hearts be troubled; believe in God, believe also in me" (Jn 14:1). Worry, fear, pain, and the challenges of life always threaten to overwhelm us. Yet in the midst of the storm, the Lord wants us to cling to him for security. A consistent response of faith is full of confidence—not prideful confidence in oneself, but hopeful confidence in God, in his power to save us. It is his mission after all: "I will come again and will take you to myself, that where I am you may be also" (Jn 14:3). Do you consistently believe that Jesus will do what he said he would do?

June 5

2 KINGS 1

After the death of A′hab, Moab rebelled against Israel.

2Now Ahazi′ah fell through the lattice
in his upper chamber in Samar′ia, and
lay sick; so he sent messengers, telling them,
"Go, inquire of Ba′al-ze′bub, the god of
Ek′ron, whether I shall recover from this
sickness." 3But the angel of the LORD said
to Eli′jah the Tishbite, "Arise, go up to meet
the messengers of the king of Samar′ia, and
say to them, 'Is it because there is no God in
Israel that you are going to inquire of Ba′al-
ze′bub, the god of Ek′ron?' 4Now therefore
thus says the LORD, 'You shall not come
down from the bed to which you have gone,
but you shall surely die.'" So Eli′jah went.
5The messengers returned to the king, and
he said to them, "Why have you returned?"
6And they said to him, "There came a man
to meet us, and said to us, 'Go back to the
king who sent you, and say to him, Thus
says the LORD, Is it because there is no God
in Israel that you are sending to inquire of
Ba′al-ze′bub, the god of Ek′ron? Therefore
you shall not come down from the bed to
which you have gone, but shall surely die.'"
7He said to them, "What kind of man was he
who came to meet you and told you these
things?" 8They answered him, "He wore a
garment of haircloth, with a belt of leather
about his loins." And he said, "It is Eli′jah
the Tishbite."
9Then the king sent to him a captain of
fifty men with his fifty. He went up to Eli′jah,
who was sitting on the top of a hill, and
said to him, "O man of God, the king says,
'Come down.'" 10But Eli′jah answered the
captain of fifty, "If I am a man of God, let fire
come down from heaven and consume you
and your fifty." Then fire came down from
heaven, and consumed him and his fifty.
11Again the king sent to him another
captain of fifty men with his fifty. And he
went up and said to him, "O man of God, this
is the king's order, 'Come down quickly!'"
12But Eli′jah answered them, "If I am a man
of God, let fire come down from heaven and
consume you and your fifty." Then the fire of
God came down from heaven and consumed
him and his fifty.
13Again the king sent the captain of a third
fifty with his fifty. And the third captain of
fifty went up, and came and fell on his knees
before Eli′jah, and entreated him, "O man
of God, I beg you, let my life, and the life of
these fifty servants of yours, be precious in
your sight. 14Behold, fire came down from
heaven, and consumed the two former
captains of fifty men with their fifties; but

now let my life be precious in your sight." [15]Then the angel of the LORD said to Eli′jah, "Go down with him; do not be afraid of him." So he arose and went down with him to the king, [16]and said to him, "Thus says the LORD, 'Because you have sent messengers to inquire of Ba′al-ze′bub, the god of Ek′ron—is it because there is no God in Israel to inquire of his word?—therefore you shall not come down from the bed to which you have gone, but you shall surely die.'"

[17]So he died according to the word of the LORD which Eli′jah had spoken. Jeho′ram, his brother, became king in his stead in the second year of Jehoram the son of Jehosh′aphat, king of Judah, because Ahazi′ah had no son. [18]Now the rest of the acts of Ahazi′ah which he did, are they not written in the Book of the Chronicles of the Kings of Israel?

2 Now when the LORD was about to take Eli′jah up to heaven by a whirlwind, Elijah and Eli′sha were on their way from Gilgal. [2]And Eli′jah said to Eli′sha, "Tarry here, I beg you; for the LORD has sent me as far as Bethel." But Elisha said, "As the LORD lives, and as you yourself live, I will not leave you." So they went down to Bethel. [3]And the sons of the prophets who were in Bethel came out to Eli′sha, and said to him, "Do you know that today the LORD will take away your master from over you?" And he said, "Yes, I know it; hold your peace."

[4]Eli′jah said to him, "Eli′sha, tarry here, I beg you; for the LORD has sent me to Jericho." But he said, "As the LORD lives, and as you yourself live, I will not leave you." So they came to Jericho. [5]The sons of the prophets who were at Jericho drew near to Eli′sha, and said to him, "Do you know that today the LORD will take away your master from over you?" And he answered, "Yes, I know it; hold your peace."

[6]Then Eli′jah said to him, "Tarry here, I beg you; for the LORD has sent me to the Jordan." But he said, "As the LORD lives, and as you yourself live, I will not leave you." So the two of them went on. [7]Fifty men of the sons of the prophets also went, and stood at some distance from them, as they both were standing by the Jordan. [8]Then Eli′jah took his coat, and rolled it up, and struck the water, and the water was parted to the one side and to the other, till the two of them could go over on dry ground.

[9]When they had crossed, Eli′jah said to Eli′sha, "Ask what I shall do for you, before I am taken from you." And Elisha said, "I beg you, let me inherit a double share of your spirit." [10]And he said, "You have asked a hard thing; yet, if you see me as I am being taken from you, it shall be so for you; but if you do not see me, it shall not be so." [11]And as they still went on and talked, behold, a chariot of fire and horses of fire separated the two of them. And Eli′jah went up by a whirlwind into heaven. [12]And Eli′sha saw it and he cried, "My father, my father! the chariots of Israel and its horsemen!" And he saw him no more.

Then he took hold of his own clothes and tore them in two pieces. [13]And he took up the coat of Eli′jah that had fallen from him, and went back and stood on the bank of the Jordan. [14]Then he took the coat of Eli′jah that had fallen from him, and struck the water, saying, "Where is the LORD, the God of Elijah?" And when he had struck the water, the water was parted to the one side and to the other; and Eli′sha went over.

[15]Now when the sons of the prophets who were at Jericho saw him over against them, they said, "The spirit of Eli′jah rests on Eli′sha." And they came to meet him, and bowed to the ground before him. [16]And they said to him, "Behold now, there are with your servants fifty strong men; please, let them go, and seek your master; it may be that the Spirit of the LORD has caught him up and cast him upon some mountain or into some valley." And he said, "You shall not send." [17]But when they urged him till he was ashamed, he said, "Send." They sent therefore fifty men; and for three days they sought him but did not find him. [18]And they came back to him, while he tarried at Jericho, and he said to them, "Did I not say to you, Do not go?"

19Now the men of the city said to Eli′sha, "Behold, the situation of this city is pleasant, as my lord sees; but the water is bad, and the land is unfruitful." 20He said, "Bring me a new bowl, and put salt in it." So they brought it to him. 21Then he went to the spring of water and threw salt in it, and said, "Thus says the LORD, I have made this water wholesome; henceforth neither death nor miscarriage shall come from it." 22So the water has been wholesome to this day, according to the word which Eli′sha spoke.

23He went up from there to Bethel; and while he was going up on the way, some small boys came out of the city and jeered at him, saying, "Go up, you baldhead! Go up, you baldhead!" 24And he turned around, and when he saw them, he cursed them in the name of the LORD. And two she-bears came out of the woods and tore forty-two of the boys. 25From there he went on to Mount Carmel, and thence he returned to Samar′ia.

A Song of Ascents.

PSALM 126 [125]

When the LORD restored the fortunes
of Zion,
we were like those who dream.
2Then our mouth was filled with laughter,
and our tongue with shouts of joy;
then they said among the nations,
"The LORD has done great things
for them."
3The LORD has done great things for us;
we are glad.

4Restore our fortunes, O LORD,
like the watercourses in the Neg′eb!
5May those who sow in tears
reap with shouts of joy!
6He that goes forth weeping,
bearing the seed for sowing,
shall come home with shouts of joy,
bringing his sheaves with him.

JOHN 14

15"If you love me, you will keep my commandments. 16And I will ask the Father, and he will give you another Counselor, to be with you for
ever, 17even the Spirit of truth, whom the world cannot receive, because it neither sees him nor knows him; you know him, for he dwells with you, and will be in you.

18"I will not leave you desolate; I will come to you. 19Yet a little while, and the world will see me no more, but you will see me; because I live, you will live also. 20In that day you will know that I am in my Father, and you in me, and I in you. 21He who has my commandments and keeps them, he it is who loves me; and he who loves me will be loved by my Father, and I will love him and manifest myself to him." 22Judas (not Iscariot) said to him, "Lord, how is it that you will manifest yourself to us, and not to the world?" 23Jesus answered him, "If a man loves me, he will keep my word, and my Father will love him, and we will come to him and make our home with him. 24He who does not love me does not keep my words; and the word which you hear is not mine but the Father's who sent me.

25"These things I have spoken to you, while I am still with you. 26But the Counselor, the Holy Spirit, whom the Father will send in my name, he will teach you all things, and bring to your remembrance all that I have said to you. 27Peace I leave with you; my peace I give to you; not as the world gives do I give to you. Let not your hearts be troubled, neither let them be afraid. 28You heard me say to you, 'I go away, and I will come to you.' If you loved me, you would have rejoiced, because I go to the Father; for the Father is greater than I. 29And now I have told you before it takes place, so that when it does take place, you may believe. 30I will no longer talk much with you, for the ruler of this world is coming. He has no power over me; 31but I do as the Father has commanded me, so that the world may know that I love the Father. Rise, let us go from here.

15 "I am the true vine, and my Father is the vinedresser. 2Every branch of mine that bears no fruit, he takes away, and every branch that does bear fruit he prunes, that it may bear more fruit. 3You are already made clean by the word which I have spoken to you. 4Abide in me, and I in you. As the branch cannot bear fruit by itself, unless it abides in the vine, neither can you, unless you abide in me. 5I am the vine, you are the branches. He who abides in me, and I in him, he it is that bears much fruit, for apart from me you can do nothing. 6If a man does not abide in me, he is cast forth as a branch and withers; and the branches are gathered, thrown into the fire and burned. 7If you abide in me, and my words abide in you, ask whatever you will, and it shall be done for you. 8By this my Father is glorified, that you bear much fruit, and so prove to be my disciples. 9As the Father has loved me, so have I loved you; abide in my love. 10If you keep my commandments, you will abide in my love, just as I have kept my Father's commandments and abide in his love. 11These things I have spoken to you, that my joy may be in you, and that your joy may be full.

12"This is my commandment, that you love one another as I have loved you. 13Greater love has no man than this, that a man lay down his life for his friends. 14You are my friends if you do what I command you. 15No longer do I call you servants, for the servant does not know what his master is doing; but I have called you friends, for all that I have heard from my Father I have made known to you. 16You did not choose me, but I chose you and appointed you that you should go and bear fruit and that your fruit should abide; so that whatever you ask the Father in my name, he may give it to you. 17This I command you, to love one another."

REFLECTION

Elisha asks his master, Elijah, for a "double share of [his] spirit" (2 Kgs 2:9). It is a bold request, but Elisha receives what he asks for and puts it to good use working even more miracles than Elijah. Jesus, our Master, promises to give us his Spirit, the "Spirit of truth" to dwell with us and be in us (Jn 14:17). The Holy Spirit enables us to do what Jesus commands: "If you love me, you will keep my commandments" (Jn 15:5). The Holy Spirit empowers us to love Jesus and put his teaching into action. Our moral action and our evangelistic mission flow from our relationship with Jesus. When we seek him in prayer, our work will be fruitful like Elijah's and Elisha's. If we cut off our relationship with him, then our efforts fall flat, "for apart from [him] you can do nothing" (v. 5). Jesus wants us to rely on his Spirit and his love, not just on our own human efforts. What good work today do you need to boldly begin with prayer?

June 6

2 KINGS 3

In the eighteenth year of Je-hosh′a-phat king of Judah, Je-ho′ram the son of A′hab became king over Israel in Samar′ia, and he reigned twelve years. 2He did what was evil in the sight of the LORD, though not like his father and mother, for he put away the pillar of Ba′al which his father had made. 3Nevertheless he clung to the sin of Jerobo′am the son of Ne′bat, which he made Israel to sin; he did not depart from it.

4Now Me′sha king of Moab was a sheep breeder; and he had to deliver annually to the king of Israel a hundred thousand lambs, and the wool of a hundred thousand rams. 5But when A′hab died, the king of Moab rebelled against the king of Israel. 6So King Jeho′ram marched out of Samar′ia at that time and mustered all Israel. 7And he went and sent word to Jehosh′aphat king of Judah, "The king of Moab has rebelled against me; will you go with me to battle against Moab?" And he said, "I will go; I am as you are, my

people as your people, my horses as your
horses." 8Then he said, "By which way shall
we march?" Jeho′ram answered, "By the way
of the wilderness of E′dom."
9So the king of Israel went with the king
of Judah and the king of E′dom. And when
they had made a circuitous march of seven
days, there was no water for the army or
for the beasts which followed them. 10Then
the king of Israel said, "Alas! The LORD has
called these three kings to give them into the
hand of Moab." 11And Jehosh′aphat said, "Is
there no prophet of the LORD here, through
whom we may inquire of the LORD?" Then
one of the king of Israel's servants answered,
"Eli′sha the son of Sha′phat is here, who
poured water on the hands of Eli′jah."
12And Jehosh′aphat said, "The word of the
LORD is with him." So the king of Israel and
Jehoshaphat and the king of E′dom went
down to him.
13And Eli′sha said to the king of Israel,
"What have I to do with you? Go to the
prophets of your father and the prophets
of your mother." But the king of Israel said
to him, "No; it is the LORD who has called
these three kings to give them into the hand
of Moab." 14And Eli′sha said, "As the LORD
of hosts lives, whom I serve, were it not that
I have regard for Jehosh′aphat the king of
Judah, I would neither look at you, nor see
you. 15But now bring me a minstrel." And
when the minstrel played, the power of
the LORD came upon him. 16And he said,
"Thus says the LORD, 'I will make this dry
stream-bed full of pools.' 17For thus says the
LORD, 'You shall not see wind or rain, but
that stream-bed shall be filled with water,
so that you shall drink, you, your cattle,
and your beasts.' 18This is a light thing in
the sight of the LORD; he will also give the
Moabites into your hand, 19and you shall
conquer every fortified city, and every
choice city, and shall fell every good tree,
and stop up all springs of water, and ruin
every good piece of land with stones." 20The
next morning, about the time of offering
the sacrifice, behold, water came from the
direction of E′dom, till the country was
filled with water.
21When all the Moabites heard that the
kings had come up to fight against them,
all who were able to put on armor, from the
youngest to the oldest, were called out, and
were drawn up at the frontier. 22And when
they rose early in the morning, and the sun
shone upon the water, the Moabites saw
the water opposite them as red as blood.
23And they said, "This is blood; the kings
have surely fought together, and slain one
another. Now then, Moab, to the spoil!"
24But when they came to the camp of Israel,
the Israelites rose and attacked the Moabites,
till they fled before them; and they went
forward, slaughtering the Moabites as they
went. 25And they overthrew the cities, and
on every good piece of land every man
threw a stone, until it was covered; they
stopped every spring of water, and felled all
the good trees; till only its stones were left in
Kir-har′-eseth, and the slingers surrounded
and conquered it. 26When the king of Moab
saw that the battle was going against him, he
took with him seven hundred swordsmen
to break through, opposite the king of
E′dom; but they could not. 27Then he took
his eldest son who was to reign in his stead,
and offered him for a burnt offering upon
the wall. And there came great wrath upon
Israel; and they withdrew from him and
returned to their own land.
4 Now the wife of one of the sons of the
prophets cried to Eli′sha, "Your servant
my husband is dead; and you know that your
servant feared the LORD, but the creditor
has come to take my two children to be his
slaves." 2And Eli′sha said to her, "What shall
I do for you? Tell me; what have you in the
house?" And she said, "Your maidservant
has nothing in the house, except a jar of oil."
3Then he said, "Go outside, borrow vessels
of all your neighbors, empty vessels and
not too few. 4Then go in, and shut the door
upon yourself and your sons, and pour into
all these vessels; and when one is full, set
it aside." 5So she went from him and shut
the door upon herself and her sons; and as
she poured they brought the vessels to her.
6When the vessels were full, she said to her
son, "Bring me another vessel." And he said

to her, "There is not another." Then the oil stopped flowing. 7She came and told the man of God, and he said, "Go, sell the oil and pay your debts, and you and your sons can live on the rest."

8One day Eli′sha went on to Shu′nem, where a wealthy woman lived, who urged him to eat some food. So whenever he passed that way, he would turn in there to eat food. 9And she said to her husband, "Behold now, I perceive that this is a holy man of God, who is continually passing our way. 10Let us make a small roof chamber with walls, and put there for him a bed, a table, a chair, and a lamp, so that whenever he comes to us, he can go in there."

11One day he came there, and he turned into the chamber and rested there. 12And he said to Geha′zi his servant, "Call this Shu′nammite." When he had called her, she stood before him. 13And he said to him, "Say now to her, See, you have taken all this trouble for us; what is to be done for you? Would you have a word spoken on your behalf to the king or to the commander of the army?" She answered, "I dwell among my own people." 14And he said, "What then is to be done for her?" Geha′zi answered, "Well, she has no son, and her husband is old." 15He said, "Call her." And when he had called her, she stood in the doorway. 16And he said, "At this season, when the time comes round, you shall embrace a son." And she said, "No, my lord, O man of God; do not lie to your maidservant." 17But the woman conceived, and she bore a son about that time the following spring, as Eli′sha had said to her.

18When the child had grown, he went out one day to his father among the reapers. 19And he said to his father, "Oh, my head, my head!" The father said to his servant, "Carry him to his mother." 20And when he had lifted him, and brought him to his mother, the child sat on her lap till noon, and then he died. 21And she went up and laid him on the bed of the man of God, and shut the door upon him, and went out. 22Then she called to her husband, and said, "Send me one of the servants and one of the donkeys, that I may quickly go to the man of God, and come back again." 23And he said, "Why will you go to him today? It is neither new moon nor sabbath." She said, "It will be well." 24Then she saddled the donkey, and she said to her servant, "Urge the beast on; do not slacken the pace for me unless I tell you." 25So she set out, and came to the man of God at Mount Carmel.

When the man of God saw her coming, he said to Geha′zi his servant, "Look, yonder is the Shu′nammite; 26run at once to meet her, and say to her, Is it well with you? Is it well with your husband? Is it well with the child?" And she answered, "It is well." 27And when she came to the mountain to the man of God, she caught hold of his feet. And Geha′zi came to thrust her away. But the man of God said, "Let her alone, for she is in bitter distress; and the LORD has hidden it from me, and has not told me." 28Then she said, "Did I ask my lord for a son? Did I not say, Do not deceive me?" 29He said to Geha′zi, "Gird up your loins, and take my staff in your hand, and go. If you meet any one, do not salute him; and if any one salutes you, do not reply; and lay my staff upon the face of the child." 30Then the mother of the child said, "As the LORD lives, and as you yourself live, I will not leave you." So he arose and followed her. 31Geha′zi went on ahead and laid the staff upon the face of the child, but there was no sound or sign of life. Therefore he returned to meet him, and told him, "The child has not awaked."

32When Eli′sha came into the house, he saw the child lying dead on his bed. 33So he went in and shut the door upon the two of them, and prayed to the LORD. 34Then he went up and lay upon the child, putting his mouth upon his mouth, his eyes upon his eyes, and his hands upon his hands; and as he stretched himself upon him, the flesh of the child became warm. 35Then he got up again, and walked once back and forth in the house, and went up, and stretched himself upon him; the child sneezed seven times, and the child opened his eyes. 36Then he summoned Geha′zi and said, "Call this Shu′nammite." So he called her. And when she came to him, he said, "Take up your son." 37She came and fell at his feet, bowing to the ground; then she took up her son and went out.

38And Eli´sha came again to Gilgal when
there was a famine in the land. And as the
sons of the prophets were sitting before
him, he said to his servant, "Put on the
great pot, and boil pottage for the sons of
the prophets." 39One of them went out into
the field to gather herbs, and found a wild
vine and gathered from it his lap full of wild
gourds, and came and cut them up into the
pot of pottage, not knowing what they were.
40And they poured out for the men to eat.
But while they were eating of the pottage,
they cried out, "O man of God, there is
death in the pot!" And they could not eat it.
41He said, "Then bring meal." And he threw
it into the pot, and said, "Pour out for the
men, that they may eat." And there was no
harm in the pot.
42A man came from Ba´al-shal´ishah, bringing the man of God bread of the first fruits,
twenty loaves of barley, and fresh ears of
grain in his sack. And Eli´sha said, "Give to the
men, that they may eat." 43But his servant said,
"How am I to set this before a hundred men?"
So he repeated, "Give them to the men, that
they may eat, for thus says the LORD, 'They
shall eat and have some left.'" 44So he set it
before them. And they ate, and had some left,
according to the word of the LORD.

A Song of Ascents.
Of Solomon.

PSALM 127 [126]

Unless the LORD builds the house,
those who build it labor in vain.
Unless the LORD watches over the city,
the watchman stays awake in vain.
2It is in vain that you rise up early
and go late to rest,
eating the bread of anxious toil;
for he gives to his beloved sleep.

3Behold, sons are a heritage from the LORD,
the fruit of the womb a reward.
4Like arrows in the hand of a warrior
are the sons of one's youth.
5Happy is the man who has
his quiver full of them!
He shall not be put to shame
when he speaks with his enemies in
the gate.

A Song of Ascents.

128 [127] Blessed is every one who fears
the LORD,
who walks in his ways!
2You shall eat the fruit of the labor of
your hands;
you shall be happy, and it shall be
well with you.

3Your wife will be like a fruitful vine
within your house;
your children will be like olive shoots
around your table.
4Behold, thus shall the man be blessed
who fears the LORD.

5The LORD bless you from Zion!
May you see the prosperity of Jerusalem
all the days of your life!
6May you see your children's children!
Peace be upon Israel!

JOHN 15

**18"If the world hates you, know
that it has hated me before it
hated you. 19If you were of the
world, the world would love its own; but
because you are not of the world, but**
I chose you out of the world, therefore the
world hates you. 20Remember the word that
I said to you, 'A servant is not greater than
his master.' If they persecuted me, they will
persecute you; if they kept my word, they will
keep yours also. 21But all this they will do to you
on my account, because they do not know him
who sent me. 22If I had not come and spoken to
them, they would not have sin; but now they
have no excuse for their sin. 23He who hates me
hates my Father also. 24If I had not done among
them the works which no one else did, they

would not have sin; but now they have seen
and hated both me and my Father. 25 It is to
fulfil the word that is written in their law, 'They
hated me without a cause.' 26 But when the
Counselor comes, whom I shall send to you
from the Father, even the Spirit of truth, who
proceeds from the Father, he will bear witness
to me; 27 and you also are witnesses, because
you have been with me from the beginning."

REFLECTION

At first, the ordinary God-given blessings of human life are in tension with the sufferings we can expect as Christians. On the one hand, if you fear the Lord, the Bible promises, "You shall eat the fruit of the labor of your hands; you shall be happy, and it shall be well with you" (Ps 128:2). On the other hand, Jesus teaches, as we know from the Psalms as well, "the world hates you" (Jn 15:19). We would relish it if our lives were constantly filled to overflowing with miraculously multiplied oil and bread, miracle babies, and our family members being raised from the dead. While we may see some miracles in our lives, these works of God are meant to point beyond themselves. They point to Jesus, in whom is our hope. "Unless the Lord builds the house, those who build it labor in vain" (Ps 127:1). Our hope is bigger than merely enjoying the temporal pleasures of life. If we encounter Jesus, then his words speak to us: "You also are witnesses" (Jn 15:27). We will experience God's blessings and at the same time experience the scorn of the world, yet the Lord builds our house. Are you looking for blessing without suffering, or are you willing to accept suffering along with blessing?

June 7

2 KINGS 5

**Na'aman, commander of the
army of the king of Syria, was
a great man with his master and in
high favor, because by him the LORD**
had given victory to Syria. He was a mighty
man of valor, but he was a leper. 2 Now the
Syrians on one of their raids had carried off
a little maid from the land of Israel, and she
waited on Na'aman's wife. 3 She said to her
mistress, "Would that my lord were with
the prophet who is in Samar'ia! He would
cure him of his leprosy." 4 So Na'aman went
in and told his lord, "Thus and so spoke the
maiden from the land of Israel." 5 And the
king of Syria said, "Go now, and I will send
a letter to the king of Israel."

So he went, taking with him ten talents of
silver, six thousand shekels of gold, and ten
festal garments. 6 And he brought the letter
to the king of Israel, which read, "When this
letter reaches you, know that I have sent to
you Na'aman my servant, that you may cure
him of his leprosy." 7 And when the king of
Israel read the letter, he tore his clothes and
said, "Am I God, to kill and to make alive,
that this man sends word to me to cure a
man of his leprosy? Only consider, and see
how he is seeking a quarrel with me."

8 But when Eli'sha the man of God heard
that the king of Israel had torn his clothes,
he sent to the king, saying, "Why have
you torn your clothes? Let him come now
to me, that he may know that there is a
prophet in Israel." 9 So Na'aman came with
his horses and chariots, and halted at the
door of Eli'sha's house. 10 And Eli'sha sent
a messenger to him, saying, "Go and wash
in the Jordan seven times, and your flesh
shall be restored, and you shall be clean."
11 But Na'aman was angry, and went away,
saying, "Behold, I thought that he would
surely come out to me, and stand, and call
on the name of the LORD his God, and wave
his hand over the place, and cure the leper.
12 Are not Aba'na and Pharpar, the rivers
of Damascus, better than all the waters of
Israel? Could I not wash in them, and be
clean?" So he turned and went away in
a rage. 13 But his servants came near and
said to him, "My father, if the prophet had
commanded you to do some great thing,
would you not have done it? How much
rather, then, when he says to you, 'Wash,
and be clean'?" 14 So he went down and

dipped himself seven times in the Jordan,
according to the word of the man of God;
and his flesh was restored like the flesh of a
little child, and he was clean.
[15]Then he returned to the man of God, he
and all his company, and he came and stood
before him; and he said, "Behold, I know
that there is no God in all the earth but in
Israel; so accept now a present from your
servant." [16]But he said, "As the LORD lives,
whom I serve, I will receive none." And he
urged him to take it, but he refused. [17]Then
Na′aman said, "If not, I beg you, let there be
given to your servant two mules' burden of
earth; for henceforth your servant will not
offer burnt offering or sacrifice to any god
but the LORD. [18]In this matter may the LORD
pardon your servant: when my master goes
into the house of Rimmon to worship there,
leaning on my arm, and I bow myself in the
house of Rimmon, when I bow myself in the
house of Rimmon, the LORD pardon your
servant in this matter." [19]He said to him, "Go
in peace."
But when Na′aman had gone from him
a short distance, [20]Geha′zi, the servant of
Eli′sha the man of God, said, "See, my master
has spared this Na′aman the Syrian, in not
accepting from his hand what he brought.
As the LORD lives, I will run after him,
and get something from him." [21]So Geha′zi
followed Na′aman. And when Naaman saw
some one running after him, he alighted
from the chariot to meet him, and said,
"Is all well?" [22]And he said, "All is well. My
master has sent me to say, 'There have just
now come to me from the hill country of
E′phraim two young men of the sons of the
prophets; please, give them a talent of silver
and two festal garments.'" [23]And Na′aman
said, "Be pleased to accept two talents." And
he urged him, and tied up two talents of
silver in two bags, with two festal garments,
and laid them upon two of his servants; and
they carried them before Geha′zi. [24]And
when he came to the hill, he took them from
their hand, and put them in the house; and
he sent the men away, and they departed.
[25]He went in, and stood before his master,
and Eli′sha said to him, "Where have you
been, Geha′zi?" And he said, "Your servant
went nowhere." [26]But he said to him, "Did
I not go with you in spirit when the man
turned from his chariot to meet you? Was it
a time to accept money and garments, olive
orchards and vineyards, sheep and oxen,
menservants and maidservants? [27]Therefore
the leprosy of Na′aman shall cling to you,
and to your descendants for ever." So he
went out from his presence a leper, as white
as snow.

6 Now the sons of the prophets said to
Eli′sha, "See, the place where we dwell
under your charge is too small for us. [2]Let
us go to the Jordan and each of us get there
a log, and let us make a place for us to dwell
there." And he answered, "Go." [3]Then one
of them said, "Be pleased to go with your
servants." And he answered, "I will go." [4]So
he went with them. And when they came to
the Jordan, they cut down trees. [5]But as one
was felling a log, his axe head fell into the
water; and he cried out, "Alas, my master! It
was borrowed." [6]Then the man of God said,
"Where did it fall?" When he showed him
the place, he cut off a stick, and threw it in
there, and made the iron float. [7]And he said,
"Take it up." So he reached out his hand and
took it.
[8]Once when the king of Syria was warring
against Israel, he took counsel with his
servants, saying, "At such and such a place
shall be my camp." [9]But the man of God sent
word to the king of Israel, "Beware that you
do not pass this place, for the Syrians are
going down there." [10]And the king of Israel
sent to the place of which the man of God
told him. Thus he used to warn him, so
that he saved himself there more than once
or twice.
[11]And the mind of the king of Syria was
greatly troubled because of this incident;
and he called his servants and said to them,
"Will you not show me who of us is for the
king of Israel?" [12]And one of his servants
said, "None, my lord, O king; but Eli′sha,
the prophet who is in Israel, tells the king
of Israel the words that you speak in your
bedchamber." [13]And he said, "Go and see
where he is, that I may send and seize him."

It was told him, "Behold, he is in Do´than." [14]So he sent there horses and chariots and a great army; and they came by night, and surrounded the city.

[15]When the servant of the man of God rose early in the morning and went out, behold, an army with horses and chariots was round about the city. And the servant said, "Alas, my master! What shall we do?" [16]He said, "Fear not, for those who are with us are more than those who are with them." [17]Then Eli´sha prayed, and said, "O LORD, I beg you, open his eyes that he may see." So the LORD opened the eyes of the young man, and he saw; and behold, the mountain was full of horses and chariots of fire round about Eli´sha. [18]And when the Syrians came down against him, Eli´sha prayed to the LORD, and said, "Strike this people, I pray you, with blindness." So he struck them with blindness in accordance with the prayer of Elisha. [19]And Eli´sha said to them, "This is not the way, and this is not the city; follow me, and I will bring you to the man whom you seek." And he led them to Samar´ia.

[20]As soon as they entered Samar´ia, Eli´sha said, "O LORD, open the eyes of these men, that they may see." So the LORD opened their eyes, and they saw; and behold, they were in the midst of Samaria. [21]When the king of Israel saw them he said to Eli´sha, "My father, shall I slay them? Shall I slay them?" [22]He answered, "You shall not slay them. Would you slay those whom you have taken captive with your sword and with your bow? Set bread and water before them, that they may eat and drink and go to their master." [23]So he prepared for them a great feast; and when they had eaten and drunk, he sent them away, and they went to their master. And the Syrians came no more on raids into the land of Israel.

[24]Afterward Ben-ha´dad king of Syria mustered his entire army, and went up, and besieged Samar´ia. [25]And there was a great famine in Samar´ia, as they besieged it, until a donkey's head was sold for eighty shekels of silver, and the fourth part of a kab of dove's dung for five shekels of silver. [26]Now as the king of Israel was passing by upon the wall, a woman cried out to him, saying, "Help, my lord, O king!" [27]And he said, "If the LORD will not help you, how shall I help you? From the threshing floor, or from the wine press?" [28]And the king asked her, "What is your trouble?" She answered, "This woman said to me, 'Give your son, that we may eat him today, and we will eat my son tomorrow.' [29]So we boiled my son, and ate him. And on the next day I said to her, 'Give your son, that we may eat him'; but she has hidden her son." [30]When the king heard the words of the woman he tore his clothes—now he was passing by upon the wall—and the people looked, and behold, he had sackcloth beneath upon his body—[31]and he said, "May God do so to me, and more also, if the head of Eli´sha the son of Sha´phat remains on his shoulders today."

[32]Eli´sha was sitting in his house, and the elders were sitting with him. Now the king had dispatched a man from his presence; but before the messenger arrived Elisha said to the elders, "Do you see how this murderer has sent to take off my head? Look, when the messenger comes, shut the door, and hold the door fast against him. Is not the sound of his master's feet behind him?" [33]And while he was still speaking with them, the king came down to him and said, "This trouble is from the LORD! Why should I wait for the LORD any longer?"

A Song of Ascents.

PSALM 129 [128]

"Sorely have they afflicted me from
 my youth,"
 let Israel now say—
[2]"Sorely have they afflicted me from
 my youth,
 yet they have not prevailed against me.
[3]The plowers plowed upon my back;
 they made long their furrows."
[4]The LORD is righteous;
 he has cut the cords of the wicked.
[5]May all who hate Zion
 be put to shame and turned backward!

6Let them be like the grass on
the housetops,
which withers before it grows up,
7with which the reaper does not fill
his hand
or the binder of sheaves his arms,
8while those who pass by do not say,
"The blessing of the LORD be upon you!
We bless you in the name of the LORD!"

JOHN 16

"I have said all this to you to keep
you from falling away. 2They
will put you out of the synagogues;
indeed, the hour is coming when who-
ever kills you will think he is offering service
to God. 3And they will do this because they
have not known the Father, nor me. 4But
I have said these things to you, that when
their hour comes you may remember that I
told you of them.
"I did not say these things to you from
the beginning, because I was with you.
5But now I am going to him who sent
me; yet none of you asks me, 'Where are
you going?' 6But because I have said these
things to you, sorrow has filled your hearts.
7Nevertheless I tell you the truth: it is to
your advantage that I go away, for if I do
not go away, the Counselor will not come
to you; but if I go, I will send him to you.
8And when he comes, he will convince
the world of sin and of righteousness and
of judgment: 9of sin, because they do not
believe in me; 10of righteousness, because
I go to the Father, and you will see me no
more; 11of judgment, because the ruler of
this world is judged.
12"I have yet many things to say to you,
but you cannot bear them now. 13When the
Spirit of truth comes, he will guide you into
all the truth; for he will not speak on his
own authority, but whatever he hears he
will speak, and he will declare to you the
things that are to come. 14He will glorify
me, for he will take what is mine and
declare it to you. 15All that the Father has is
mine; therefore I said that he will take what
is mine and declare it to you."

REFLECTION

We have much to learn from Naaman the Syrian. Though he is a powerful army commander, in his desperation for a cure from his leprosy, he listens to the testimony of a little servant girl and makes a long journey bringing rich gifts, seeking healing from the Lord. And though he is offended by the prophet's standoffish attitude, he humbles himself to follow his instructions. So often we seek personal gain, enrichment, and advancement that we forget to become like little children as Jesus requires and to approach God in all humility. In order to remain firm in childlike faith, we need manly courage, since "the hour is coming when whoever kills you will think he is offering service to God" (Jn 16:2). Persecuted Christians can also join the voice of the psalmist: "Sorely have they afflicted me from my youth, yet they have not prevailed against me" (Ps 129:2). And such is our spirituality: a humble, childlike trust that is so strong it can withstand the onslaught of persecution and opposition from the world. Are you willing to humble yourself like Naaman to receive healing from the Lord?

June 8

2 KINGS 7

But Eli′sha said, "Hear the word
of the LORD: thus says the LORD,
Tomorrow about this time a measure
of fine meal shall be sold for a shekel,
and two measures of barley for a shekel, at
the gate of Samar′ia." 2Then the captain on
whose hand the king leaned said to the man
of God, "If the LORD himself should make
windows in heaven, could this thing be?"

But he said, "You shall see it with your own eyes, but you shall not eat of it."

3Now there were four men who were lepers at the entrance to the gate; and they said to one another, "Why do we sit here till we die? 4If we say, 'Let us enter the city,' the famine is in the city, and we shall die there; and if we sit here, we die also. So now come, let us go over to the camp of the Syrians; if they spare our lives we shall live, and if they kill us we shall but die." 5So they arose at twilight to go to the camp of the Syrians; but when they came to the edge of the camp of the Syrians, behold, there was no one there. 6For the LORD had made the army of the Syrians hear the sound of chariots, and of horses, the sound of a great army, so that they said to one another, "Behold, the king of Israel has hired against us the kings of the Hittites and the kings of Egypt to come upon us." 7So they fled away in the twilight and forsook their tents, their horses, and their donkeys, leaving the camp as it was, and fled for their lives. 8And when these lepers came to the edge of the camp, they went into a tent, and ate and drank, and they carried off silver and gold and clothing, and went and hid them; then they came back, and entered another tent, and carried off things from it, and went and hid them.

9Then they said to one another, "We are not doing right. This day is a day of good news; if we are silent and wait until the morning light, punishment will overtake us; now therefore come, let us go and tell the king's household." 10So they came and called to the gatekeepers of the city, and told them, "We came to the camp of the Syrians, and behold, there was no one to be seen or heard there, nothing but the horses tied, and the donkeys tied, and the tents as they were." 11Then the gatekeepers called out, and it was told within the king's household. 12And the king rose in the night, and said to his servants, "I will tell you what the Syrians have prepared against us. They know that we are hungry; therefore they have gone out of the camp to hide themselves in the open country, thinking, 'When they come out of the city, we shall take them alive and get into the city.'" 13And one of his servants said, "Let some men take five of the remaining horses, seeing that those who are left here will fare like the whole multitude of Israel that have already perished; let us send and see." 14So they took two mounted men, and the king sent them after the army of the Syrians, saying, "Go and see." 15So they went after them as far as the Jordan; and, behold, all the way was littered with garments and equipment which the Syrians had thrown away in their haste. And the messengers returned, and told the king.

16Then the people went out, and plundered the camp of the Syrians. So a measure of fine meal was sold for a shekel, and two measures of barley for a shekel, according to the word of the LORD. 17Now the king had appointed the captain on whose hand he leaned to have charge of the gate; and the people trod upon him in the gate, so that he died, as the man of God had said when the king came down to him. 18For when the man of God had said to the king, "Two measures of barley shall be sold for a shekel, and a measure of fine meal for a shekel, about this time tomorrow in the gate of Samar′ia," 19the captain had answered the man of God, "If the LORD himself should make windows in heaven, could such a thing be?" And he had said, "You shall see it with your own eyes, but you shall not eat of it." 20And so it happened to him, for the people trod upon him in the gate and he died.

8 Now Eli′sha had said to the woman whose son he had restored to life, "Arise, and depart with your household, and sojourn wherever you can; for the LORD has called for a famine, and it will come upon the land for seven years." 2So the woman arose, and did according to the word of the man of God; she went with her household and sojourned in the land of the Philis′tines seven years. 3And at the end of the seven years, when the woman returned from the land of the Philis′tines, she went forth to appeal to the king for her house and her land. 4Now the king was talking with Geha′zi the servant of the man of God, saying, "Tell me all the great things that

Eli´sha has done." [5]And while he was telling
the king how Eli´sha had restored the dead
to life, behold, the woman whose son he
had restored to life appealed to the king for
her house and her land. And Geha´zi said,
"My lord, O king, here is the woman, and
here is her son whom Elisha restored to
life." [6]And when the king asked the woman,
she told him. So the king appointed an
official for her, saying, "Restore all that was
hers, together with all the produce of the
fields from the day that she left the land
until now."

[7]Now Eli´sha came to Damascus. Ben-
ha´dad the king of Syria was sick; and
when it was told him, "The man of God
has come here," [8]the king said to Haz´ael,
"Take a present with you and go to meet
the man of God, and inquire of the LORD
through him, saying, 'Shall I recover from
this sickness?'" [9]So Haz´ael went to meet
him, and took a present with him, all kinds
of goods of Damascus, forty camel loads.
When he came and stood before him, he
said, "Your son Ben-ha´dad king of Syria
has sent me to you, saying, 'Shall I recover
from this sickness?'" [10]And Eli´sha said to
him, "Go, say to him, 'You shall certainly
recover'; but the LORD has shown me
that he shall certainly die." [11]And he fixed
his gaze and stared at him, until he was
ashamed. And the man of God wept. [12]And
Haz´ael said, "Why does my lord weep?"
He answered, "Because I know the evil that
you will do to the sons of Israel; you will
set on fire their fortresses, and you will
slay their young men with the sword, and
dash in pieces their little ones, and rip up
their women with child." [13]And Haz´ael
said, "What is your servant, who is but a
dog, that he should do this great thing?"
Eli´sha answered, "The LORD has shown me
that you are to be king over Syria." [14]Then
he departed from Eli´sha, and came to his
master, who said to him, "What did Elisha
say to you?" And he answered, "He told me
that you would certainly recover." [15]But the
next day he took the coverlet and dipped it
in water and spread it over his face, till he
died. And Haz´ael became king in his stead.

[16]In the fifth year of Jo´ram the son of
A´hab, king of Israel, Jeho´ram the son of
Jehosh´aphat, king of Judah, began to reign.
[17]He was thirty-two years old when he
became king, and he reigned eight years in
Jerusalem. [18]And he walked in the way of
the kings of Israel, as the house of A´hab had
done, for the daughter of Ahab was his wife.
And he did what was evil in the sight of the
LORD. [19]Yet the LORD would not destroy
Judah, for the sake of David his servant,
since he promised to give a lamp to him and
to his sons for ever.

[20]In his days E´dom revolted from the
rule of Judah, and set up a king of their
own. [21]Then Jo´ram passed over to Za´ir
with all his chariots, and rose by night, and
he and his chariot commanders struck the
E´domites who had surrounded him; but his
army fled home. [22]So E´dom revolted from
the rule of Judah to this day. Then Libnah
revolted at the same time. [23]Now the rest of
the acts of Jo´ram, and all that he did, are they
not written in the Book of the Chronicles of
the Kings of Judah? [24]So Jo´ram slept with
his fathers, and was buried with his fathers
in the city of David; and Ahazi´ah his son
reigned in his stead.

[25]In the twelfth year of Jo´ram the son of
A´hab, king of Israel, Ahazi´ah the son of
Jeho´ram, king of Judah, began to reign.
[26]Ahazi´ah was twenty-two years old when
he began to reign, and he reigned one
year in Jerusalem. His mother's name was
Athali´ah; she was a granddaughter of Omri
king of Israel. [27]He also walked in the way
of the house of A´hab, and did what was
evil in the sight of the LORD, as the house of
Ahab had done, for he was son-in-law to the
house of Ahab.

[28]He went with Jo´ram the son of A´hab to
make war against Haz´ael king of Syria at
Ra´moth-gil´ead, where the Syrians wounded Joram. [29]And King Jo´ram returned to be
healed in Jezre´el of the wounds which the
Syrians had given him at Ra´mah, when he
fought against Haz´ael king of Syria. And
Ahazi´ah the son of Jeho´ram king of Judah
went down to see Joram the son of A´hab in
Jezre´el, because he was sick.

A Song of Ascents.

PSALM 130 [129]

Out of the depths I cry to you, O LORD!
[2] Lord, hear my voice!
Let your ears be attentive
to the voice of my supplications!

[3]If you, O LORD, should mark iniquities,
Lord, who could stand?
[4]But there is forgiveness with you,
that you may be feared.

[5]I wait for the LORD, my soul waits,
and in his word I hope;
[6]my soul waits for the LORD
more than watchmen for the morning,
more than watchmen for the morning.

[7]O Israel, hope in the LORD!
For with the LORD there is mercy,
and with him is plenteous redemption.
[8]And he will redeem Israel
from all his iniquities.

A Song of Ascents.
Of David.

131 [130] O LORD, my heart is not lifted up,
my eyes are not raised too high;
I do not occupy myself with things
too great and too marvelous for me.
[2]But I have calmed and quieted my soul,
like a child quieted at its mother's breast;
like a child that is quieted is my soul.

[3]O Israel, hope in the LORD
from this time forth and for evermore.

JOHN 16

[16]"A little while, and you will see
me no more; again a little while,
and you will see me." [17]Some of
his disciples said to one another, "What
is this that he says to us, 'A little while,
and you will not see me, and again a little
while, and you will see me'; and, 'because I
go to the Father'?" [18]They said, "What does
he mean by 'a little while'? We do not know
what he means." [19]Jesus knew that they
wanted to ask him; so he said to them, "Is
this what you are asking yourselves, what
I meant by saying, 'A little while, and you
will not see me, and again a little while,
and you will see me'? [20]Truly, truly, I say
to you, you will weep and lament, but the
world will rejoice; you will be sorrowful,
but your sorrow will turn into joy.
[21]When a woman is in labor, she has pain,
because her hour has come; but when she
is delivered of the child, she no longer
remembers the anguish, for joy that a
child is born into the world. [22]So you have
sorrow now, but I will see you again and
your hearts will rejoice, and no one will
take your joy from you. [23]In that day you
will ask nothing of me. Truly, truly, I say to
you, if you ask anything of the Father, he
will give it to you in my name. [24]Until now
you have asked nothing in my name; ask,
and you will receive, that your joy may
be full.

[25]"I have said this to you in figures; the
hour is coming when I shall no longer speak
to you in figures but tell you plainly of the
Father. [26]In that day you will ask in my
name; and I do not say to you that I shall ask
the Father for you; [27]for the Father himself
loves you, because you have loved me and
have believed that I came from the Father.
[28]I came from the Father and have come into
the world; again, I am leaving the world and
going to the Father."

[29]His disciples said, "Ah, now you are
speaking plainly, not in any figure! [30]Now
we know that you know all things, and need
none to question you; by this we believe
that you came from God." [31]Jesus answered
them, "Do you now believe? [32]The hour is
coming, indeed it has come, when you will
be scattered, every man to his home, and
will leave me alone; yet I am not alone, for
the Father is with me. [33]I have said this to
you, that in me you may have peace. In the
world you have tribulation; but be of good
cheer, I have overcome the world."

REFLECTION

Too often we trust in ourselves rather than in the Lord, but he is the one who delivers victory. In Elisha's time, the Syrian army laid siege to Samaria. When the besieged Israelites were on the brink of starvation, "the Lord made the army of the Syrians hear the sound of chariots, and of horses, the sound of a great army" (2 Kgs 7:6). The Syrians fled and God gave Israel victory. Referring to his Death and Resurrection, Jesus warns his worrisome disciples, "You will be sorrowful, but your sorrow will turn into joy" (Jn 16:20). While we have to endure times of sorrow and suffering, the joy of Jesus's victory over sin trumps our troubles. Our job, in the midst of troubles, is to be like the psalmist: "I have calmed and quieted my soul, like a child quieted at its mother's breast" (Ps 131:2). If we trust in ourselves to fix everything, we will be plagued by worry and doubt; but if we trust in Jesus's victory over sin, death, and the world, then our souls can rest in him. How can you calm and quiet your soul in the Lord?

June 9

2 KINGS 9

Then Eli´sha the prophet called
one of the sons of the prophets
and said to him, "Gird up your
loins, and take this flask of oil in your
hand, and go to Ra´moth-gil´ead. 2And
when you arrive, look there for Je´hu
the son of Jehosh´aphat, son of Nimshi;
and go in and bid him rise from among his
fellows, and lead him to an inner chamber.
3Then take the flask of oil, and pour it on his
head, and say, 'Thus says the LORD, I anoint
you king over Israel.' Then open the door
and flee; do not tarry."
4So the young man, the prophet, went
to Ra´moth-gil´ead. 5And when he came,
behold, the commanders of the army were
in council; and he said, "I have an errand
to you, O commander." And Je´hu said, "To
which of us all?" And he said, "To you, O
commander." 6So he arose, and went into
the house; and the young man poured the
oil on his head, saying to him, "Thus says
the LORD the God of Israel, I anoint you
king over the people of the LORD, over
Israel. 7And you shall strike down the house
of A´hab your master, that I may avenge
on Jez´ebel the blood of my servants the
prophets, and the blood of all the servants
of the LORD. 8For the whole house of A´hab
shall perish; and I will cut off from Ahab
every male, bond or free, in Israel. 9And I
will make the house of A´hab like the house
of Jerobo´am the son of Ne´bat, and like the
house of Ba´asha the son of Ahi´jah. 10And
the dogs shall eat Jez´ebel in the territory of
Jezre´el, and none shall bury her." Then he
opened the door, and fled.
11When Je´hu came out to the servants of
his master, they said to him, "Is all well?
Why did this mad fellow come to you?" And
he said to them, "You know the fellow and
his talk." 12And they said, "That is not true;
tell us now." And he said, "Thus and so he
spoke to me, saying, 'Thus says the LORD, I
anoint you king over Israel.'" 13Then in haste
every man of them took his garment, and
put it under him on the bare steps, and they
blew the trumpet, and proclaimed, "Je´hu
is king."
14Thus Je´hu the son of Jehosh´aphat the
son of Nimshi conspired against Jo´ram.
(Now Joram with all Israel had been on
guard at Ra´moth-gil´ead against Haz´ael
king of Syria; 15but King Jo´ram had returned
to be healed in Jezre´el of the wounds which
the Syrians had given him, when he fought
with Haz´ael king of Syria.) So Je´hu said, "If
this is your mind, then let no one slip out of
the city to go and tell the news in Jezreel."
16Then Je´hu mounted his chariot, and
went to Jezre´el, for Jo´ram lay there. And
Ahazi´ah king of Judah had come down to
visit Joram.

17 Now the watchman was standing on the tower in Jezre´el, and he spied the company of Je´hu as he came, and said, "I see a company." And Jo´ram said, "Take a horseman, and send to meet them, and let him say, 'Is it peace?'" 18 So a man on horseback went to meet him, and said, "Thus says the king, 'Is it peace?'" And Je´hu said, "What have you to do with peace? Turn round and ride behind me." And the watchman reported, saying, "The messenger reached them, but he is not coming back." 19 Then he sent out a second horseman, who came to them, and said, "Thus the king has said, 'Is it peace?'" And Je´hu answered, "What have you to do with peace? Turn round and ride behind me." 20 Again the watchman reported, "He reached them, but he is not coming back. And the driving is like the driving of Je´hu the son of Nimshi; for he drives furiously."

21 Jo´ram said, "Make ready." And they made ready his chariot. Then Joram king of Israel and Ahazi´ah king of Judah set out, each in his chariot, and went to meet Je´hu, and met him at the property of Naboth the Jezre´elite. 22 And when Jo´ram saw Je´hu, he said, "Is it peace, Jehu?" He answered, "What peace can there be, so long as the harlotries and the sorceries of your mother Jez´ebel are so many?" 23 Then Jo´ram reined about and fled, saying to Ahazi´ah, "Treachery, O Ahaziah!" 24 And Je´hu drew his bow with his full strength, and shot Jo´ram between the shoulders, so that the arrow pierced his heart, and he sank in his chariot. 25 Je´hu said to Bidkar his aide, "Take him up, and cast him on the plot of ground belonging to Naboth the Jezre´elite; for remember, when you and I rode side by side behind A´hab his father, how the LORD uttered this oracle against him: 26 'As surely as I saw yesterday the blood of Naboth and the blood of his sons—says the LORD—I will repay you on this plot of ground.' Now therefore take him up and cast him on the plot of ground, in accordance with the word of the LORD."

27 When Ahazi´ah the king of Judah saw this, he fled in the direction of Beth-hag´gan. And Je´hu pursued him, and said, "Shoot him also"; and they shot him in the chariot at the ascent of Gur, which is by Ib´leam. And he fled to Megid´do, and died there. 28 His servants carried him in a chariot to Jerusalem, and buried him in his tomb with his fathers in the city of David.

29 In the eleventh year of Jo´ram the son of A´hab, Ahazi´ah began to reign over Judah.

30 When Je´hu came to Jezre´el, Jez´ebel heard of it; and she painted her eyes, and adorned her head, and looked out of the window. 31 And as Je´hu entered the gate, she said, "Is it peace, you Zimri, murderer of your master?" 32 And he lifted up his face to the window, and said, "Who is on my side? Who?" Two or three eunuchs looked out at him. 33 He said, "Throw her down." So they threw her down; and some of her blood spattered on the wall and on the horses, and they trampled on her. 34 Then he went in and ate and drank; and he said, "See now to this cursed woman, and bury her; for she is a king's daughter." 35 But when they went to bury her, they found no more of her than the skull and the feet and the palms of her hands. 36 When they came back and told him, he said, "This is the word of the LORD, which he spoke by his servant Eli´jah the Tishbite, 'In the territory of Jezre´el the dogs shall eat the flesh of Jez´ebel; 37 and the corpse of Jez´ebel shall be as dung upon the face of the field in the territory of Jezre´el, so that no one can say, This is Jezebel.'"

10 Now A´hab had seventy sons in Samar´ia. So Je´hu wrote letters, and sent them to Samar´ia, to the rulers of the city, to the elders, and to the guardians of the sons of Ahab, saying, 2 "Now then, as soon as this letter comes to you, seeing your master's sons are with you, and there are with you chariots and horses, fortified cities also, and weapons, 3 select the best and fittest of your master's sons and set him on his father's throne, and fight for your master's house." 4 But they were exceedingly afraid, and said, "Behold, the two kings could not stand before him; how then can we stand?" 5 So he who was over the palace, and he who was over the city, together with the elders and the guardians, sent to Je´hu, saying, "We are your servants, and we will

do all that you bid us. We will not make
any one king; do whatever is good in your
eyes." 6Then he wrote to them a second
letter, saying, "If you are on my side, and
if you are ready to obey me, take the heads
of your master's sons, and come to me at
Jezre'el tomorrow at this time." Now the
king's sons, seventy persons, were with the
great men of the city, who were bringing
them up. 7And when the letter came to
them, they took the king's sons, and slew
them, seventy persons, and put their heads
in baskets, and sent them to him at Jezre'el.
8When the messenger came and told him,
"They have brought the heads of the king's
sons," he said, "Lay them in two heaps at
the entrance of the gate until the morning."
9Then in the morning, when he went out,
he stood, and said to all the people, "You
are innocent. It was I who conspired against
my master, and slew him; but who struck
down all these? 10Know then that there shall
fall to the earth nothing of the word of the
LORD, which the LORD spoke concerning
the house of A'hab; for the LORD has done
what he said by his servant Eli'jah." 11So
Je'hu slew all that remained of the house of
A'hab in Jezre'el, all his great men, and his
familiar friends, and his priests, until he left
him none remaining.

12Then he set out and went to Samar'ia.
On the way, when he was at Beth-ek'ed of
the Shepherds, 13Je'hu met the kinsmen of
Ahazi'ah king of Judah, and he said, "Who
are you?" And they answered, "We are the
kinsmen of Ahazi'ah, and we came down
to visit the royal princes and the sons of the
queen mother." 14He said, "Take them alive."
And they took them alive, and slew them at
the pit of Beth-ek'ed, forty-two persons, and
he spared none of them.

15And when he departed from there, he
met Jehon'adab the son of Re'chab coming
to meet him; and he greeted him, and said to
him, "Is your heart true to my heart as mine
is to yours?" And Jehonadab answered, "It
is." Je'hu said, "If it is, give me your hand."
So he gave him his hand. And Jehu took
him up with him into the chariot. 16And he
said, "Come with me, and see my zeal for
the LORD." So he had him ride in his chariot.
17And when he came to Samar'ia, he slew all
that remained to A'hab in Samaria, till he
had wiped them out, according to the word
of the LORD which he spoke to Eli'jah.

A Song of Ascents.

PSALM 132 [131]

Remember, O LORD, in David's favor,
his humility;
2how he swore to the LORD
and vowed to the Mighty One of Jacob,
3"I will not enter my house
or get into my bed;
4I will not give sleep to my eyes
or slumber to my eyelids,
5until I find a place for the LORD,
a dwelling place for the Mighty One
of Jacob."

6Behold, we heard of it in Eph'rathah,
we found it in the fields of Ja'ar.
7"Let us go to his dwelling place;
let us worship at his footstool!"

8Arise, O LORD, and go to your resting place,
you and the ark of your might.
9Let your priests be clothed with righteousness,
and let your saints shout for joy.
10For your servant David's sake
do not turn away the face of your
anointed one.

11The LORD swore to David a sure oath
from which he will not turn back:
"One of the sons of your body
I will set on your throne.
12If your sons keep my covenant
and my testimonies which I shall
teach them,
their sons also for ever
shall sit upon your throne."

13For the LORD has chosen Zion;
he has desired it for his habitation:
14"This is my resting place for ever;
here I will dwell, for I have desired it.

[15]I will abundantly bless her provisions;
I will satisfy her poor with bread.
[16]Her priests I will clothe with salvation,
and her saints will shout for joy.
[17]There I will make a horn to sprout
for David;
I have prepared a lamp for my anointed.
[18]His enemies I will clothe with shame,
but upon himself his crown will shed
its luster."

JOHN 17

When Jesus had spoken these words, he lifted up his eyes to heaven and said, "Father, the hour has come; glorify your Son that the Son
may glorify you, [2]since you have given
him power over all flesh, to give eternal
life to all whom you have given him. [3]And
this is eternal life, that they know you the
only true God, and Jesus Christ whom you
have sent. [4]I glorified you on earth, having
accomplished the work which you gave me
to do; [5]and now, Father, glorify me in your
own presence with the glory which I had
with you before the world was made.
[6]"I have manifested your name to the men
whom you gave me out of the world; they
were yours, and you gave them to me, and
they have kept your word. [7]Now they know
that everything that you have given me is
from you; [8]for I have given them the words
which you gave me, and they have received
them and know in truth that I came from
you; and they have believed that you sent me.
[9]I am praying for them; I am not praying for
the world but for those whom you have given
me, for they are yours; [10]all mine are yours,
and yours are mine, and I am glorified in
them. [11]And now I am no more in the world,
but they are in the world, and I am coming to
you. Holy Father, keep them in your name,
which you have given me, that they may be
one, even as we are one. [12]While I was with
them, I kept them in your name, which you
have given me; I have guarded them, and none
of them is lost but the son of perdition, that
the Scripture might be fulfilled. [13]But now I
am coming to you; and these things I speak in
the world, that they may have my joy fulfilled
in themselves."

REFLECTION

Ahab and Jezebel now reap what they sowed by their idolatrous and murderous ways. The ferocity of divine judgment in the downfall of Ahab's house, the death of his descendants, and the desecration of Jezebel's body are matched only by how this wicked king and queen brought about the downfall of God's people by leading them astray to worship false gods, or Jezebel's obsession to cut off the prophets of the Lord. In the gospel reading we see the Lord's judgment on Judas the betrayer, who "is lost" (Jn 17:12). Of course, the Lord would rather bless his followers than curse his enemies. He promises to be with his people: "This is my resting place for ever; here I will dwell, for I have desired it" (Ps 132:14). Indeed, Jesus defines eternal life as knowing God and being known by him "that they know you the only true God, and Jesus Christ whom you have sent" (Jn 17:3). Jesus prays for the unity of his followers in love "that they may be one, even as we are one" (v. 11). Sin brings about division, violence, and death. Obedience to the Lord leads to unity with God and with one another.

June 10

---

2 KINGS 10

[18]Then Je'hu assembled all the people, and said to them, "A'hab served Ba'al a little; but Jehu will serve him much. [19]Now therefore call to me all the prophets of Ba'al, all his worshipers and all his priests; let
none be missing, for I have a great sacrifice
to offer to Baal; whoever is missing shall
not live." But Je'hu did it with cunning in

order to destroy the worshipers of Ba′al. 20And Je′hu ordered, "Sanctify a solemn assembly for Ba′al." So they proclaimed it. 21And Je′hu sent throughout all Israel; and all the worshipers of Ba′al came, so that there was not a man left who did not come. And they entered the house of Baal, and the house of Baal was filled from one end to the other. 22He said to him who was in charge of the wardrobe, "Bring out the vestments for all the worshipers of Ba′al." So he brought out the vestments for them. 23Then Je′hu went into the house of Ba′al with Jehon′adab the son of Re′chab; and he said to the worshipers of Baal, "Search, and see that there is no servant of the LORD here among you, but only the worshipers of Baal." 24Then he went in to offer sacrifices and burnt offerings.

Now Je′hu had stationed eighty men outside, and said, "The man who allows any of those whom I give into your hands to escape shall forfeit his life." 25So as soon as he had made an end of offering the burnt offering, Je′hu said to the guard and to the officers, "Go in and slay them; let not a man escape." So when they put them to the sword, the guard and the officers cast them out and went into the inner room of the house of Ba′al 26and they brought out the pillar that was in the house of Ba′al, and burned it. 27And they demolished the pillar of Ba′al, and demolished the house of Baal, and made it a latrine to this day.

28Thus Je′hu wiped out Ba′al from Israel. 29But Je′hu did not turn aside from the sins of Jerobo′am the son of Ne′bat, which he made Israel to sin, the golden calves that were in Bethel, and in Dan. 30And the LORD said to Je′hu, "Because you have done well in carrying out what is right in my eyes, and have done to the house of A′hab according to all that was in my heart, your sons of the fourth generation shall sit on the throne of Israel." 31But Je′hu was not careful to walk in the law of the LORD the God of Israel with all his heart; he did not turn from the sins of Jerobo′am, which he made Israel to sin.

32In those days the LORD began to cut off parts of Israel. Haz′ael defeated them throughout the territory of Israel: 33from the Jordan eastward, all the land of Gilead, the Gadites, and the Reubenites, and the Manas′sites, from Aro′er, which is by the valley of the Arnon, that is, Gilead and Bashan. 34Now the rest of the acts of Je′hu, and all that he did, and all his might, are they not written in the Book of the Chronicles of the Kings of Israel? 35So Je′hu slept with his fathers, and they buried him in Samar′ia. And Jeho′ahaz his son reigned in his stead. 36The time that Je′hu reigned over Israel in Samar′ia was twenty-eight years.

11 Now when Athali′ah the mother of Ahazi′ah saw that her son was dead, she arose and destroyed all the royal family. 2But Jehosh′eba, the daughter of King Jo′ram, sister of Ahazi′ah, took Jo′ash the son of Ahaziah, and stole him away from among the king's sons who were about to be slain, and she put him and his nurse in a bedchamber. Thus she hid him from Athali′ah, so that he was not slain; 3and he remained with her six years, hid in the house of the LORD, while Athali′ah reigned over the land.

4But in the seventh year Jehoi′ada sent and brought the captains of the Cari′tes and of the guards, and had them come to him in the house of the LORD; and he made a covenant with them and put them under oath in the house of the LORD, and he showed them the king's son. 5And he commanded them, "This is the thing that you shall do: one third of you, those who come off duty on the sabbath and guard the king's house 6(another third being at the gate Sur and a third at the gate behind the guards), shall guard the palace; 7and the two divisions of you, which come on duty in force on the sabbath and guard the house of the LORD, 8shall surround the king, each with his weapons in his hand; and whoever approaches the ranks is to be slain. Be with the king when he goes out and when he comes in."

9The captains did according to all that Jehoi′ada the priest commanded, and each brought his men who were to go off duty on the sabbath, with those who were to come on duty on the sabbath, and came to Jehoiada

the priest. [10]And the priest delivered to
the captains the spears and shields that
had been King David's, which were in the
house of the LORD; [11]and the guards stood,
every man with his weapons in his hand,
from the south side of the house to the
north side of the house, around the altar
and the house. [12]Then he brought out the
king's son, and put the crown upon him,
and gave him the covenant; and they
proclaimed him king, and anointed him;
and they clapped their hands, and said,
"Long live the king!"
[13]When Athali'ah heard the noise of the
guard and of the people, she went into the
house of the LORD to the people; [14]and when
she looked, there was the king standing by
the pillar, according to the custom, and
the captains and the trumpeters beside the
king, and all the people of the land rejoicing
and blowing trumpets. And Athali'ah tore
her clothes, and cried, "Treason! Treason!"
[15]Then Jehoi'ada the priest commanded
the captains who were set over the army,
"Bring her out between the ranks; and slay
with the sword any one who follows her."
For the priest said, "Let her not be slain in
the house of the LORD." [16]So they laid hands
on her; and she went through the horses'
entrance to the king's house, and there she
was slain.
[17]And Jehoi'ada made a covenant between
the LORD and the king and people, that
they should be the LORD's people; and also
between the king and the people. [18]Then
all the people of the land went to the house
of Ba'al, and tore it down; his altars and
his images they broke in pieces, and they
slew Mattan the priest of Baal before the
altars. And the priest posted watchmen
over the house of the LORD. [19]And he took
the captains, the Cari'tes, the guards, and
all the people of the land; and they brought
the king down from the house of the LORD,
marching through the gate of the guards to
the king's house. And he took his seat on the
throne of the kings. [20]So all the people of the
land rejoiced; and the city was quiet after
Athali'ah had been slain with the sword at
the king's house.

[21]Jeho'ash was seven years old when he
began to reign.

12 In the seventh year of Je'hu Jeho'ash
began to reign, and he reigned forty
years in Jerusalem. His mother's name was
Zib'iah of Be'er-she'ba. [2]And Jeho'ash did
what was right in the eyes of the LORD all his
days, because Jehoi'ada the priest instructed
him. [3]Nevertheless the high places were not
taken away; the people continued to sacrifice and burn incense on the high places.
[4]Jeho'ash said to the priests, "All the money
of the holy things which is brought into the
house of the LORD, the money for which
each man is assessed—the money from
the assessment of persons—and the money
which a man's heart prompts him to bring
into the house of the LORD, [5]let the priests
take, each from his acquaintance; and let
them repair the house wherever any need
of repairs is discovered." [6]But by the twenty-
third year of King Jeho'ash the priests had
made no repairs on the house. [7]Therefore
King Jeho'ash summoned Jehoi'ada the
priest and the other priests and said to them,
"Why are you not repairing the house? Now
therefore take no more money from your
acquaintances, but hand it over for the
repair of the house." [8]So the priests agreed
that they should take no more money from
the people, and that they should not repair
the house.
[9]Then Jehoi'ada the priest took a chest,
and bored a hole in the lid of it, and set
it beside the altar on the right side as one
entered the house of the LORD; and the
priests who guarded the threshold put in
it all the money that was brought into the
house of the LORD. [10]And whenever they
saw that there was much money in the chest,
the king's secretary and the high priest came
up and they counted and tied up in bags the
money that was found in the house of the
LORD. [11]Then they would give the money
that was weighed out into the hands of
the workmen who had the oversight of the
house of the LORD; and they paid it out to
the carpenters and the builders who worked
upon the house of the LORD, [12]and to the
masons and the stonecutters, as well as to

buy timber and quarried stone for making
repairs on the house of the LORD, and for
any outlay upon the repairs of the house.
13But there were not made for the house of
the LORD basins of silver, snuffers, bowls,
trumpets, or any vessels of gold, or of silver,
from the money that was brought into the
house of the LORD, 14for that was given to
the workmen who were repairing the house
of the LORD with it. 15And they did not ask
an accounting from the men into whose
hand they delivered the money to pay out
to the workmen, for they dealt honestly.
16The money from the guilt offerings and
the money from the sin offerings was not
brought into the house of the LORD; it
belonged to the priests.

17At that time Haz′ael king of Syria went
up and fought against Gath, and took it. But
when Hazael set his face to go up against
Jerusalem, 18Jeho′ash king of Judah took
all the votive gifts that Jehosh′aphat and
Jeho′ram and Ahazi′ah, his fathers, the kings
of Judah, had dedicated, and his own votive
gifts, and all the gold that was found in the
treasuries of the house of the LORD and of
the king's house, and sent these to Haz′ael
king of Syria. Then Hazael went away from
Jerusalem.

19Now the rest of the acts of Jo′ash, and all
that he did, are they not written in the Book
of the Chronicles of the Kings of Judah?
20His servants arose and made a conspiracy,
and slew Jo′ash in the house of Millo, on the
way that goes down to Silla. 21It was Jo′zacar
the son of Shim′eath and Jeho′zabad the son
of Shomer, his servants, who struck him
down, so that he died. And they buried him
with his fathers in the city of David, and
Amazi′ah his son reigned in his stead.

A Song of Ascents.

PSALM 133 [132]

Behold, how good and pleasant it is
when brothers dwell in unity!
2It is like the precious oil upon the head,
running down upon the beard,
upon the beard of Aaron,
running down on the collar of his robes!
3It is like the dew of Hermon,
which falls on the mountains of Zion!
For there the LORD has commanded
the blessing,
life for evermore.

A Song of Ascents.

PSALM 134 [133]

Come, bless the LORD,
all you servants of the LORD,
who stand by night in the house of
the LORD!
2Lift up your hands to the holy place,
and bless the LORD!

3May the LORD bless you from Zion,
he who made heaven and earth!

JOHN 17

**14"I have given them your word;
and the world has hated them
because they are not of the world, even
as I am not of the world. 15I do not pray**
that you should take them out of the world,
but that you should keep them from the evil
one. 16They are not of the world, even as I am
not of the world. 17Sanctify them in the truth;
your word is truth. 18As you sent me into the
world, so I have sent them into the world.
19And for their sake I consecrate myself, that
they also may be consecrated in truth.

20"I do not pray for these only, but also for
those who believe in me through their word,
21that they may all be one; even as you, Father,
are in me, and I in you, that they also may be in
us, so that the world may believe that you have
sent me. 22The glory which you have given me I
have given to them, that they may be one even
as we are one, 23I in them and you in me, that
they may become perfectly one, so that the
world may know that you have sent me and
have loved them even as you have loved me.
24Father, I desire that they also, whom you

have given me, may be with me where I am, to behold my glory which you have given me in your love for me before the foundation of the world. 25O righteous Father, the world has not known you, but I have known you; and these know that you have sent me. 26I made known to them your name, and I will make it known, that the love with which you have loved me may be in them, and I in them."

REFLECTION

Many of us are tempted to embrace "bus-stop Christianity," where we simply wait around until Jesus comes to pick us up so we can finally get to Heaven and rest. If that idea were right, we would almost expect Jesus to take us out of the world as soon as we come to faith. Yet he does not. In fact, he says to the Father, "I do not pray that you should take them out of the world" (Jn 17:15). We are supposed to be here. Beyond that, he sees us as participating in his mission: "As you sent me into the world, so I have sent them into the world" (v. 18). We are not just waiting around for death or the Apocalypse. Rather, our role as Christians is to participate in the mission of Christ to the world by spreading the Gospel and living lives conformed to his. We are meant to "dwell in unity" (Ps 133:1) with one another and even to "stand by night in the house of the LORD," seeking him in prayer (Ps 134:1). We are not "of the world," but we are most definitely "in the world," called to bring Christ with us wherever we go. How can you participate in Christ's mission to the world?

June 11

2 KINGS 13

In the twenty-third year of Jo'ash the son of Ahazi'ah, king of Judah, Jeho'ahaz the son of Je'hu began to reign over Israel in Samar'ia, and he reigned seventeen years. 2He did what was evil in the sight of the LORD, and followed the sins of Jerobo'am the son of Ne'bat, which he made Israel to sin; he did not depart from them. 3And the anger of the LORD was kindled against Israel, and he gave them continually into the hand of Haz'ael king of Syria and into the hand of Ben-ha'dad the son of Hazael. 4Then Jeho'ahaz besought the LORD, and the LORD listened to him; for he saw the oppression of Israel, how the king of Syria oppressed them. 5(Therefore the LORD gave Israel a savior, so that they escaped from the hand of the Syrians; and the sons of Israel dwelt in their homes as formerly. 6Nevertheless they did not depart from the sins of the house of Jerobo'am, which he made Israel to sin, but walked in them; and the Ashe'rah also remained in Samar'ia.) 7For there was not left to Jeho'ahaz an army of more than fifty horsemen and ten chariots and ten thousand footmen; for the king of Syria had destroyed them and made them like the dust at threshing. 8Now the rest of the acts of Jeho'ahaz and all that he did, and his might, are they not written in the Book of the Chronicles of the Kings of Israel? 9So Jeho'ahaz slept with his fathers, and they buried him in Samar'ia; and Jo'ash his son reigned in his stead.

10In the thirty-seventh year of Jo'ash king of Judah Jeho'ash the son of Jeho'ahaz began to reign over Israel in Samar'ia, and he reigned sixteen years. 11He also did what was evil in the sight of the LORD; he did not depart from all the sins of Jerobo'am the son of Ne'bat, which he made Israel to sin, but he walked in them. 12Now the rest of the acts of Jo'ash, and all that he did, and the might with which he fought against Amazi'ah king of Judah, are they not written in the Book of the Chronicles of the Kings of Israel? 13So Jo'ash slept with his fathers, and Jerobo'am sat upon his throne; and Joash was buried in Samar'ia with the kings of Israel.

14Now when Eli'sha had fallen sick with the illness of which he was to die, Jo'ash king of Israel went down to him, and wept before him, crying, "My father, my father! The chariots of Israel and its horsemen!" 15And Eli'sha said to him, "Take a bow and arrows"; so he took a bow and arrows.

16Then he said to the king of Israel, "Draw
the bow"; and he drew it. And Eli′sha laid
his hands upon the king's hands. 17And he
said, "Open the window eastward"; and he
opened it. Then Eli′sha said, "Shoot"; and
he shot. And he said, "The LORD's arrow of
victory, the arrow of victory over Syria! For
you shall fight the Syrians in A′phek until
you have made an end of them." 18And he
said, "Take the arrows"; and he took them.
And he said to the king of Israel, "Strike
the ground with them"; and he struck three
times, and stopped. 19Then the man of God
was angry with him, and said, "You should
have struck five or six times; then you would
have struck down Syria until you had made
an end of it, but now you will strike down
Syria only three times."

20So Eli′sha died, and they buried him.
Now bands of Moabites used to invade the
land in the spring of the year. 21And as a
man was being buried, behold, a marauding
band was seen and the man was cast into
the grave of Eli′sha; and as soon as the man
touched the bones of Elisha, he revived, and
stood on his feet.

22Now Haz′ael king of Syria oppressed Israel
all the days of Jeho′ahaz. 23But the LORD was
gracious to them and had compassion on
them, and he turned toward them, because of
his covenant with Abraham, Isaac, and Jacob,
and would not destroy them; nor has he cast
them from his presence until now.

24When Haz′ael king of Syria died, Ben-
ha′dad his son became king in his stead.
25Then Jeho′ash the son of Jeho′ahaz took
again from Ben-ha′dad the son of Haz′ael
the cities which he had taken from Jehoahaz
his father in war. Three times Jo′ash defeated
him and recovered the cities of Israel.

14 In the second year of Jo′ash the son
of Jo′ahaz, king of Israel, Amazi′ah
the son of Joash, king of Judah, began to
reign. 2He was twenty-five years old when
he began to reign, and he reigned twenty-
nine years in Jerusalem. His mother's name
was Je′ho-ad′din of Jerusalem. 3And he did
what was right in the eyes of the LORD, yet
not like David his father; he did in all things
as Jo′ash his father had done. 4But the high
places were not removed; the people still
sacrificed and burned incense on the high
places. 5And as soon as the royal power was
firmly in his hand he killed his servants who
had slain the king his father. 6But he did not
put to death the children of the murderers;
according to what is written in the book
of the law of Moses, where the LORD commanded, "The fathers shall not be put to
death for the children, or the children be
put to death for the fathers; but every man
shall die for his own sin."

7He killed ten thousand E′domites in
the Valley of Salt and took Se′la by storm,
and called it Jok′the-el, which is its name
to this day.

8Then Amazi′ah sent messengers to
Jeho′ash the son of Jeho′ahaz, son of Je′hu,
king of Israel, saying, "Come, let us look one
another in the face." 9And Jeho′ash king of
Israel sent word to Amazi′ah king of Judah,
"A thistle in Lebanon sent to a cedar in
Lebanon, saying, 'Give your daughter to my
son for a wife'; and a wild beast of Lebanon
passed by and trampled down the thistle.
10You have indeed struck down E′dom, and
your heart has lifted you up. Be content with
your glory, and stay at home; for why should
you provoke trouble so that you fall, you
and Judah with you?"

11But Amazi′ah would not listen. So Jeho′ash
king of Israel went up, and he and Amaziah
king of Judah faced one another in battle
at Beth-she′mesh, which belongs to Judah.
12And Judah was defeated by Israel, and every
man fled to his home. 13And Jeho′ash king of
Israel captured Amazi′ah king of Judah, the
son of Jehoash, son of Ahazi′ah, at Beth-
she′mesh, and came to Jerusalem, and broke
down the wall of Jerusalem for four hundred
cubits, from the E′phraim Gate to the Corner
Gate. 14And he seized all the gold and silver,
and all the vessels that were found in the
house of the LORD and in the treasuries of the
king's house, also hostages, and he returned
to Samar′ia.

15Now the rest of the acts of Jeho′ash which
he did, and his might, and how he fought
with Amazi′ah king of Judah, are they not
written in the Book of the Chronicles of the

Kings of Israel? 16And Jeho′ash slept with
his fathers, and was buried in Samar′ia with
the kings of Israel; and Jerobo′am his son
reigned in his stead.
17Amazi′ah the son of Jo′ash, king of
Judah, lived fifteen years after the death
of Jeho′ash son of Jeho′ahaz, king of Israel.
18Now the rest of the deeds of Amazi′ah,
are they not written in the Book of the
Chronicles of the Kings of Judah? 19And
they made a conspiracy against him in
Jerusalem, and he fled to La′chish. But
they sent after him to Lachish, and slew
him there. 20And they brought him upon
horses; and he was buried in Jerusalem
with his fathers in the city of David. 21And
all the people of Judah took Azari′ah, who
was sixteen years old, and made him king
instead of his father Amazi′ah. 22He built
E′lath and restored it to Judah, after the
king slept with his fathers.
23In the fifteenth year of Amazi′ah the son
of Jo′ash, king of Judah, Jerobo′am the son
of Joash, king of Israel, began to reign in
Samar′ia, and he reigned forty-one years.
24And he did what was evil in the sight of
the LORD; he did not depart from all the sins
of Jerobo′am the son of Ne′bat, which he
made Israel to sin. 25He restored the border
of Israel from the entrance of Ha′math as
far as the Sea of the Ar′abah, according to
the word of the LORD, the God of Israel,
which he spoke by his servant Jonah the
son of Amit′tai, the prophet, who was from
Gath-he′pher. 26For the LORD saw that the
affliction of Israel was very bitter, for there
was none left, bond or free, and there was
none to help Israel. 27But the LORD had not
said that he would blot out the name of
Israel from under heaven, so he saved them
by the hand of Jerobo′am the son of Jo′ash.
28Now the rest of the acts of Jerobo′am,
and all that he did, and his might, how
he fought, and how he recovered for
Israel Damascus and Ha′math, which had
belonged to Judah, are they not written in
the Book of the Chronicles of the Kings
of Israel? 29And Jerobo′am slept with his
fathers, the kings of Israel, and Zechari′ah
his son reigned in his stead.

PSALM 135 [134]

Praise the LORD!
Praise the name of the LORD,
give praise, O servants of the LORD,
2you that stand in the house of the LORD,
in the courts of the house of our God!
3Praise the LORD, for the LORD is good;
sing to his name, for he is gracious!
4For the LORD has chosen Jacob for himself,
Israel as his own possession.

5For I know that the LORD is great,
and that our Lord is above all gods.
6Whatever the LORD pleases he does,
in heaven and on earth,
in the seas and all deeps.
7He it is who makes the clouds rise at the
end of the earth,
who makes lightnings for the rain
and brings forth the wind from his
storehouses.

8He it was who struck the first-born
of Egypt,
both of man and of beast;
9who in your midst, O Egypt,
sent signs and wonders
against Pharaoh and all his servants;
10who struck many nations
and slew mighty kings,
11Sihon, king of the Amorites,
and Og, king of Bashan,
and all the kingdoms of Canaan,
12and gave their land as a heritage,
a heritage to his people Israel.

13Your name, O LORD, endures for ever,
your renown, O LORD, throughout
all ages.

JOHN 18

When Jesus had spoken these words, he went forth with his disciples across the Kidron valley, where there was a garden, which he and his disciples entered. 2Now Judas, who

betrayed him, also knew the place; for Jesus often met there with his disciples.
3So Judas, procuring a band of soldiers and some officers from the chief priests and the Pharisees, went there with lanterns and torches and weapons.
4Then Jesus, knowing all that was to befall him, came forward and said to them, "Whom do you seek?"
5They answered him, "Jesus of Nazareth." Jesus said to them, "I am he." Judas, who betrayed him, was standing with them.
6When he said to them, "I am he," they drew back and fell to the ground.
7Again he asked them, "Whom do you seek?" And they said, "Jesus of Nazareth."
8Jesus answered, "I told you that I am he; so, if you seek me, let these men go."
9This was to fulfil the word which he had spoken, "Of those whom you gave me I lost not one."
10Then Simon Peter, having a sword, drew it and struck the high priest's slave and cut off his right ear. The slave's name was Malchus.
11Jesus said to Peter, "Put your sword into its sheath; shall I not drink the chalice which the Father has given me?"

12So the band of soldiers and their captain and the officers of the Jews seized Jesus and bound him.
13First they led him to Annas; for he was the father-in-law of Cai′aphas, who was high priest that year.
14It was Cai′aphas who had given counsel to the Jews that it was expedient that one man should die for the people.

15Simon Peter followed Jesus, and so did another disciple. As this disciple was known to the high priest, he entered the court of the high priest along with Jesus,
16while Peter stood outside at the door. So the other disciple, who was known to the high priest, went out and spoke to the maid who kept the door, and brought Peter in.
17The maid who kept the door said to Peter, "Are not you also one of this man's disciples?" He said, "I am not."
18Now the servants and officers had made a charcoal fire, because it was cold, and they were standing and warming themselves; Peter also was with them, standing and warming himself.

REFLECTION

It is all too easy to content ourselves with the regular stuff of life. Two tales from today's reading take aim at our spiritual complacency. The prophet Elisha tells the king to perform prophetic actions of victory: to shoot a bow and to strike the ground with a fistful of arrows. While the king obeys, he exhibits complacency, a lack of interest in the prophet's spiritual antics, and he only strikes the ground three times with the arrows. If the king will give only half-heartedly to God, then he will receive only half of a victory. When Jesus pronounces his divine and messianic identity with the words *ego eimi*, "I am" (Jn 18:5), the bevy of soldiers and officials who have come to arrest him fall to the ground involuntarily. The soldiers proceed with the arrest, seemingly oblivious of who is before them and the miraculous sign they have witnessed. When Jesus knocks us down with his words, we should probably pause and reconsider what we're doing. What complacency is God trying to shake you out of?

June 12

2 KINGS 15

In the twenty-seventh year of Jerobo′am king of Israel Azari′ah the son of Amazi′ah, king of Judah, began to reign.
2He was sixteen years old when he began to reign, and he reigned fifty-two years in Jerusalem. His mother's name was Jecoli′ah of Jerusalem.
3And he did what was right in the eyes of the LORD, according to all that his father Amazi′ah had done.
4Nevertheless the high places were not taken away; the people still sacrificed and burned incense on the high places.
5And the LORD struck the king, so that he was a leper to the day of his death, and he dwelt in a separate house.

And Jo´tham the king's son was over the
household, governing the people of the
land. 6Now the rest of the acts of Azari´ah,
and all that he did, are they not written in
the Book of the Chronicles of the Kings of
Judah? 7And Azari´ah slept with his fathers,
and they buried him with his fathers in the
city of David, and Jo´tham his son reigned
in his stead.

8In the thirty-eighth year of Azari´ah king
of Judah Zechari´ah the son of Jerobo´am
reigned over Israel in Samar´ia six months.
9And he did what was evil in the sight of
the LORD, as his fathers had done. He did
not depart from the sins of Jerobo´am the
son of Ne´bat, which he made Israel to
sin. 10Shallum the son of Ja´besh conspired
against him, and struck him down at Ib´leam,
and killed him, and reigned in his stead.
11Now the rest of the deeds of Zechari´ah,
behold, they are written in the Book of the
Chronicles of the Kings of Israel. 12(This was
the promise of the LORD which he gave to
Je´hu, "Your sons shall sit upon the throne
of Israel to the fourth generation." And so it
came to pass.)

13Shallum the son of Ja´besh began to
reign in the thirty-ninth year of Uzzi´ah
king of Judah, and he reigned one month
in Samar´ia. 14Then Men´ahem the son of
Gadi came up from Tirzah and came to
Samar´ia, and he struck down Shallum the
son of Ja´besh in Samaria and slew him,
and reigned in his stead. 15Now the rest of
the deeds of Shallum, and the conspiracy
which he made, behold, they are written
in the Book of the Chronicles of the Kings
of Israel. 16At that time Men´ahem sacked
Tap´pu-ah and all who were in it and its
territory from Tirzah on; because they did
not open it to him, therefore he sacked it,
and he ripped up all the women in it who
were with child.

17In the thirty-ninth year of Azari´ah
king of Judah Men´ahem the son of Gadi
began to reign over Israel, and he reigned
ten years in Samar´ia. 18And he did what
was evil in the sight of the LORD; he did
not depart all his days from all the sins of
Jerobo´am the son of Ne´bat, which he made
Israel to sin. 19Pul the king of Assyria came
against the land; and Men´ahem gave Pul
a thousand talents of silver, that he might
help him to confirm his hold of the royal
power. 20Men´ahem exacted the money
from Israel, that is, from all the wealthy
men, fifty shekels of silver from every man,
to give to the king of Assyria. So the king of
Assyria turned back, and did not stay there
in the land. 21Now the rest of the deeds of
Men´ahem, and all that he did, are they not
written in the Book of the Chronicles of the
Kings of Israel? 22And Men´ahem slept with
his fathers, and Pekahi´ah his son reigned in
his stead.

23In the fiftieth year of Azari´ah king
of Judah Pekahi´ah the son of Men´ahem
began to reign over Israel in Samar´ia, and
he reigned two years. 24And he did what was
evil in the sight of the LORD; he did not turn
away from the sins of Jerobo´am the son of
Ne´bat, which he made Israel to sin. 25And
Pe´kah the son of Remali´ah, his captain,
conspired against him with fifty men of
the Gileadites, and slew him in Samar´ia, in
the citadel of the king's house; he slew him,
and reigned in his stead. 26Now the rest of
the deeds of Pekahi´ah, and all that he did,
behold, they are written in the Book of the
Chronicles of the Kings of Israel.

27In the fifty-second year of Azari´ah
king of Judah Pe´kah the son of Remali´ah
began to reign over Israel in Samar´ia, and
he reigned twenty years. 28And he did what
was evil in the sight of the LORD; he did not
depart from the sins of Jerobo´am the son of
Ne´bat, which he made Israel to sin.

29In the days of Pe´kah king of Israel Tig´lath-
pile´ser king of Assyria came and captured
I´jon, A´bel-beth-ma´acah, Jano´ah, Ke´desh,
Ha´zor, Gilead, and Galilee, all the land of
Naph´tali; and he carried the people captive
to Assyria. 30Then Hoshe´a the son of E´lah
made a conspiracy against Pe´kah the son of
Remali´ah, and struck him down, and slew
him, and reigned in his stead, in the twentieth
year of Jo´tham the son of Uzzi´ah. 31Now the
rest of the acts of Pe´kah, and all that he did,
behold, they are written in the Book of the
Chronicles of the Kings of Israel.

32 In the second year of Pe′kah the son of Remali′ah, king of Israel, Jo′tham the son of Uzzi′ah, king of Judah, began to reign. 33 He was twenty-five years old when he began to reign, and he reigned sixteen years in Jerusalem. His mother's name was Jeru′sha the daughter of Za′dok. 34 And he did what was right in the eyes of the LORD, according to all that his father Uzzi′ah had done. 35 Nevertheless the high places were not removed; the people still sacrificed and burned incense on the high places. He built the upper gate of the house of the LORD. 36 Now the rest of the acts of Jotham, and all that he did, are they not written in the Book of the Chronicles of the Kings of Judah? 37 In those days the LORD began to send Re′zin the king of Syria and Pe′kah the son of Remali′ah against Judah. 38 Jo′tham slept with his fathers, and was buried with his fathers in the city of David his father; and A′haz his son reigned in his stead.

16 In the seventeenth year of Pe′kah the son of Remali′ah, A′haz the son of Jo′tham, king of Judah, began to reign. 2 Ahaz was twenty years old when he began to reign, and he reigned sixteen years in Jerusalem. And he did not do what was right in the eyes of the LORD his God, as his father David had done, 3 but he walked in the way of the kings of Israel. He even burned his son as an offering, according to the abominable practices of the nations whom the LORD drove out before the people of Israel. 4 And he sacrificed and burned incense on the high places, and on the hills, and under every green tree.

5 Then Re′zin king of Syria and Pe′kah the son of Remali′ah, king of Israel, came up to wage war on Jerusalem, and they besieged A′haz but could not conquer him. 6 At that time the king of E′dom recovered E′lath for Edom, and drove the men of Judah from Elath; and the E′domites came to Elath, where they dwell to this day. 7 So A′haz sent messengers to Tig′lath-pile′ser king of Assyria, saying, "I am your servant and your son. Come up, and rescue me from the hand of the king of Syria and from the hand of the king of Israel, who are attacking me." 8 A′haz also took the silver and gold that was found in the house of the LORD and in the treasures of the king's house, and sent a present to the king of Assyria. 9 And the king of Assyria listened to him; the king of Assyria marched up against Damascus, and took it, carrying its people captive to Kir, and he killed Re′zin.

10 When King A′haz went to Damascus to meet Tig′lath-pile′ser king of Assyria, he saw the altar that was at Damascus. And King Ahaz sent to Uri′ah the priest a model of the altar, and its pattern, exact in all its details. 11 And Uri′ah the priest built the altar; in accordance with all that King A′haz had sent from Damascus, so Uriah the priest made it, before King Ahaz arrived from Damascus. 12 And when the king came from Damascus, the king viewed the altar. Then the king drew near to the altar, and went up on it, 13 and burned his burnt offering and his cereal offering, and poured his drink offering, and threw the blood of his peace offerings upon the altar. 14 And the bronze altar which was before the LORD he removed from the front of the house, from the place between his altar and the house of the LORD, and put it on the north side of his altar. 15 And King A′haz commanded Uri′ah the priest, saying, "Upon the great altar burn the morning burnt offering, and the evening cereal offering, and the king's burnt offering, and his cereal offering, with the burnt offering of all the people of the land, and their cereal offering, and their drink offering; and throw upon it all the blood of the burnt offering, and all the blood of the sacrifice; but the bronze altar shall be for me to inquire by." 16 Uri′ah the priest did all this, as King A′haz commanded.

17 And King A′haz cut off the frames of the stands, and removed the laver from them, and he took down the sea from off the bronze oxen that were under it, and put it upon a pediment of stone. 18 And the covered way for the sabbath which had been built inside the palace, and the outer entrance for the king he removed from the house of the LORD, because of the king of Assyria. 19 Now the rest of the acts of A′haz which

he did, are they not written in the Book of the Chronicles of the Kings of Judah? 20And A′haz slept with his fathers, and was buried with his fathers in the city of David; and Hezeki′ah his son reigned in his stead.

PSALM 135 [134]

14For the LORD will vindicate his people,
and have compassion on his servants.

15The idols of the nations are silver and gold,
the work of men's hands.
16They have mouths, but they speak not,
they have eyes, but they see not,
17they have ears, but they hear not,
nor is there any breath in their mouths.
18Like them be those who make them!—
yes, every one who trusts in them!

19O house of Israel, bless the LORD!
O house of Aaron, bless the LORD!
20O house of Levi, bless the LORD!
You that fear the LORD, bless the LORD!
21Blessed be the LORD from Zion,
he who dwells in Jerusalem!
Praise the LORD!

JOHN 18

19The high priest then questioned Jesus about his disciples and his teaching. 20Jesus answered him, "I have spoken openly to the world; I have always taught in synagogues and in the temple, where all Jews come together; I have said nothing secretly. 21Why do you ask me? Ask those who have heard me, what I said to them; they know what I said." 22When he had said this, one of the officers standing by struck Jesus with his hand, saying, "Is that how you answer the high priest?" 23Jesus answered him, "If I have spoken wrongly, bear witness to the wrong; but if I have spoken rightly, why do you strike me?" 24Annas then sent him bound to Cai′aphas the high priest.

25Now Simon Peter was standing and warming himself. They said to him, "Are not you also one of his disciples?" He denied it and said, "I am not." 26One of the servants of the high priest, a kinsman of the man whose ear Peter had cut off, asked, "Did I not see you in the garden with him?" 27Peter again denied it; and at once the cock crowed.

28Then they led Jesus from the house of Cai′aphas to the praetorium. It was early. They themselves did not enter the praetorium, so that they might not be defiled, but might eat the Passover. 29So Pilate went out to them and said, "What accusation do you bring against this man?" 30They answered him, "If this man were not an evildoer, we would not have handed him over." 31Pilate said to them, "Take him yourselves and judge him by your own law." The Jews said to him, "It is not lawful for us to put any man to death." 32This was to fulfil the word which Jesus had spoken to show by what death he was to die.

33Pilate entered the praetorium again and called Jesus, and said to him, "Are you the King of the Jews?" 34Jesus answered, "Do you say this of your own accord, or did others say it to you about me?" 35Pilate answered, "Am I a Jew? Your own nation and the chief priests have handed you over to me; what have you done?" 36Jesus answered, "My kingship is not of this world; if my kingship were of this world, my servants would fight, that I might not be handed over to the Jews; but my kingship is not from the world." 37Pilate said to him, "So you are a king?" Jesus answered, "You say that I am a king. For this I was born, and for this I have come into the world, to bear witness to the truth. Every one who is of the truth hears my voice." 38Pilate said to him, "What is truth?"

After he had said this, he went out to the Jews again, and told them, "I find no crime in him. 39But you have a custom that I should release one man for you at the Passover; will you have me release for you the King of the Jews?" 40They cried out again, "Not this man, but Barab′bas!" Now Barab′bas was a robber.

REFLECTION

King Ahaz is seduced by the world. Not only does he give himself over to "the abominable practices of the nations" (2 Kgs 16:3) and pay tribute to a foreign power (see v. 8), he also tries to import foreign religious customs into the Temple itself. He has a new, Syrian-style altar installed in the Temple, and he himself officiates at the sacrifices as if he were a priest. Clearly, Ahaz is a king who acts as though he is God. In the Gospel we see God refusing to act as the kings of the world, for Jesus's kingship is of a much higher order. Rather than asserting royal authority to get his way, Jesus holds back the exercise of his royal rights in order to do his Father's will. Who acts as the true king, Ahaz or Jesus? In what ways can you say true power and self-possession is exercised more by what Jesus does not do or say? Why does Jesus refuse to act like a king, and in what way is that a critique of how the world wields power and authority? The Jerusalem authorities who seek to kill Jesus likewise are capitulating to the world and its system. They are trying to use the Roman legal apparatus to murder Jesus, since they cannot put anyone to death under their own legal authority (see Jn 18:31).

June 13

2 KINGS 17

In the twelfth year of A′haz king of Judah Hoshe′a the son of E′lah began to reign in Samar′ia over Israel, and he reigned nine years. 2And he did what was evil in the sight of the LORD, yet not as the kings of Israel who were before him. 3Against him came up Shalmane′ser king of Assyria; and Hoshe′a became his vassal, and paid him tribute. 4But the king of Assyria found treachery in Hoshe′a; for he had sent messengers to So, king of Egypt, and offered no tribute to the king of Assyria, as he had done year by year; therefore the king of Assyria shut him up, and bound him in prison. 5Then the king of Assyria invaded all the land and came to Samar′ia, and for three years he besieged it. 6In the ninth year of Hoshe′a the king of Assyria captured Samar′ia, and he carried the Israelites away to Assyria, and placed them in Ha′lah, and on the Ha′bor, the river of Gozan, and in the cities of the Medes.

7And this was so, because the sons of Israel had sinned against the LORD their God, who had brought them up out of the land of Egypt from under the hand of Pharaoh king of Egypt, and had feared other gods 8and walked in the customs of the nations whom the LORD drove out before the sons of Israel, and in the customs which the kings of Israel had introduced. 9And the sons of Israel did secretly against the LORD their God things that were not right. They built for themselves high places at all their towns, from watchtower to fortified city; 10they set up for themselves pillars and Ashe′rim on every high hill and under every green tree; 11and there they burned incense on all the high places, as the nations did whom the LORD carried away before them. And they did wicked things, provoking the LORD to anger, 12and they served idols, of which the LORD had said to them, "You shall not do this." 13Yet the LORD warned Israel and Judah by every prophet and every seer, saying, "Turn from your evil ways and keep my commandments and my statutes, in accordance with all the law which I commanded your fathers, and which I sent to you by my servants the prophets." 14But they would not listen, but were stubborn, as their fathers had been, who did not believe in the LORD their God. 15They despised his statutes, and his covenant that he made with their fathers, and the warnings which he gave them. They went after false idols, and became false, and they followed the nations that were round about them, concerning whom the LORD had commanded them that they should not do like them. 16And they forsook all the commandments of the LORD their God, and made for themselves molten images of two calves; and they made

an Ashe´rah, and worshiped all the host
of heaven, and served Ba´al. [17]And they
burned their sons and their daughters as
offerings, and used divination and sorcery,
and sold themselves to do evil in the sight
of the LORD, provoking him to anger.
[18]Therefore the LORD was very angry with
Israel, and removed them out of his sight;
none was left but the tribe of Judah only.

[19]Judah also did not keep the commandments of the LORD their God, but walked
in the customs which Israel had introduced.
[20]And the LORD rejected all the descendants
of Israel, and afflicted them, and gave them
into the hand of spoilers, until he had cast
them out of his sight.

[21]When he had torn Israel from the house
of David they made Jerobo´am the son of
Ne´bat king. And Jeroboam drove Israel from
following the LORD and made them commit
great sin. [22]The sons of Israel walked in all
the sins which Jerobo´am did; they did not
depart from them, [23]until the LORD removed
Israel out of his sight, as he had spoken by
all his servants the prophets. So Israel was
exiled from their own land to Assyria until
this day.

[24]And the king of Assyria brought people
from Babylon, Cu´thah, Avva, Ha´math, and
Sepharva´im, and placed them in the cities
of Samar´ia instead of the sons of Israel; and
they took possession of Samaria, and dwelt
in its cities. [25]And at the beginning of their
dwelling there, they did not fear the LORD;
therefore the LORD sent lions among them,
which killed some of them. [26]So the king of
Assyria was told, "The nations which you
have carried away and placed in the cities of
Samar´ia do not know the law of the god of
the land; therefore he has sent lions among
them, and behold, they are killing them,
because they do not know the law of the
god of the land." [27]Then the king of Assyria
commanded, "Send there one of the priests
whom you carried away from there; and let
him go and dwell there, and teach them the
law of the god of the land." [28]So one of the
priests whom they had carried away from
Samar´ia came and dwelt in Bethel, and
taught them how they should fear the LORD.

[29]But every nation still made gods of its
own, and put them in the shrines of the high
places which the Samar´itans had made,
every nation in the cities in which they
dwelt; [30]the men of Babylon made Suc´coth-
be´noth, the men of Cuth made Ner´gal, the
men of Ha´math made Ashi´ma, [31]and the
Avvites made Nibhaz and Tartak; and the
Sephar´vites burned their children in the
fire to Adram´melech and Anam´melech,
the gods of Sepharva´im. [32]They also feared
the LORD, and appointed from among
themselves all sorts of people as priests of
the high places, who sacrificed for them
in the shrines of the high places. [33]So they
feared the LORD but also served their own
gods, after the manner of the nations from
among whom they had been carried away.
[34]To this day they do according to the
former manner.

They do not fear the LORD, and they do
not follow the statutes or the ordinances or
the law or the commandment which the
LORD commanded the children of Jacob,
whom he named Israel. [35]The LORD made
a covenant with them, and commanded
them, "You shall not fear other gods or
bow yourselves to them or serve them or
sacrifice to them; [36]but you shall fear the
LORD, who brought you out of the land
of Egypt with great power and with an
outstretched arm; you shall bow yourselves
to him, and to him you shall sacrifice.
[37]And the statutes and the ordinances and
the law and the commandment which he
wrote for you, you shall always be careful
to do. You shall not fear other gods, [38]and
you shall not forget the covenant that I
have made with you. You shall not fear
other gods, [39]but you shall fear the LORD
your God, and he will deliver you out of the
hand of all your enemies." [40]However they
would not listen, but they did according to
their former manner.

[41]So these nations feared the LORD, and also
served their graven images; their children
likewise, and their children's children—as
their fathers did, so they do to this day.

18 In the third year of Hoshe´a son of
E´lah, king of Israel, Hezeki´ah the

son of A´haz, king of Judah, began to reign.
2He was twenty-five years old when he
began to reign, and he reigned twenty-
nine years in Jerusalem. His mother's
name was Abi the daughter of Zechari´ah.
3And he did what was right in the eyes
of the LORD, according to all that David
his father had done. 4He removed the
high places, and broke the pillars, and cut
down the Ashe´rah. And he broke in pieces
the bronze serpent that Moses had made,
for until those days the sons of Israel
had burned incense to it; it was called
Nehush´tan. 5He trusted in the LORD the
God of Israel; so that there was none like
him among all the kings of Judah after
him, nor among those who were before
him. 6For he held fast to the LORD; he
did not depart from following him, but
kept the commandments which the LORD
commanded Moses. 7And the LORD was
with him; wherever he went forth, he
prospered. He rebelled against the king
of Assyria, and would not serve him. 8He
struck the Philis´tines as far as Gaza and
its territory, from watchtower to fortified
city.
9In the fourth year of King Hezeki´ah,
which was the seventh year of Hoshe´a
son of E´lah, king of Israel, Shalmane´ser
king of Assyria came up against Samar´ia
and besieged it 10and at the end of three
years he took it. In the sixth year of
Hezeki´ah, which was the ninth year of
Hoshe´a king of Israel, Samar´ia was taken.
11The king of Assyria carried the Israelites
away to Assyria, and put them in Ha´lah,
and on the Ha´bor, the river of Gozan, and
in the cities of the Medes, 12because they did
not obey the voice of the LORD their God
but transgressed his covenant, even all that
Moses the servant of the LORD commanded;
they neither listened nor obeyed.

PSALM 136 [135]

O give thanks to the LORD, for he is good,
for his mercy endures for ever.
2O give thanks to the God of gods,
for his mercy endures for ever.
3O give thanks to the Lord of lords,
for his mercy endures for ever;

4to him who alone does great wonders,
for his mercy endures for ever;
5to him who by understanding made
the heavens,
for his mercy endures for ever;
6to him who spread out the earth upon
the waters,
for his mercy endures for ever;
7to him who made the great lights,
for his mercy endures for ever;
8the sun to rule over the day,
for his mercy endures for ever;
9the moon and stars to rule over the night,
for his mercy endures for ever;

10to him who struck the first-born of Egypt,
for his mercy endures for ever;
11and brought Israel out from among them,
for his mercy endures for ever;
12with a strong hand and an
outstretched arm,
for his mercy endures for ever;
13to him who divided the Red Sea in two,
for his mercy endures for ever;
14and made Israel pass through the midst
of it,
for his mercy endures for ever;
15but overthrew Pharaoh and his host in the
Red Sea,
for his mercy endures for ever;
16to him who led his people through
the wilderness,
for his mercy endures for ever;
17to him who struck great kings,
for his mercy endures for ever;
18and slew famous kings,
for his mercy endures for ever;
19Sihon, king of the Amorites,
for his mercy endures for ever;
20and Og, king of Bashan,
for his mercy endures for ever;
21and gave their land as a heritage,
for his mercy endures for ever;
22a heritage to Israel his servant,
for his mercy endures for ever.

23It is he who remembered us in our
low estate,
for his mercy endures for ever;
24and rescued us from our foes,
for his mercy endures for ever;
25he who gives food to all flesh,
for his mercy endures for ever.

26O give thanks to the God of heaven,
for his mercy endures for ever.

JOHN 19

**Then Pilate took Jesus and
scourged him. 2And the soldiers
plaited a crown of thorns, and put it on
his head, and clothed him in a purple**
robe; 3they came up to him, saying, "Hail,
King of the Jews!" and struck him with their
hands. 4Pilate went out again, and said to them,
"Behold, I am bringing him out to you, that
you may know that I find no crime in him." 5So
Jesus came out, wearing the crown of thorns
and the purple robe. Pilate said to them, "Here
is the man!" 6When the chief priests and the
officers saw him, they cried out, "Crucify him,
crucify him!" Pilate said to them, "Take him
yourselves and crucify him, for I find no crime
in him." 7The Jews answered him, "We have a
law, and by that law he ought to die, because
he has made himself the Son of God." 8When
Pilate heard these words, he was even more
afraid; 9he entered the praetorium again and
said to Jesus, "Where are you from?" But Jesus
gave no answer. 10Pilate therefore said to him,
"You will not speak to me? Do you not know
that I have power to release you, and power
to crucify you?" 11Jesus answered him, "You
would have no power over me unless it had
been given you from above; therefore he who
delivered me to you has the greater sin."
12Upon this Pilate sought to release him, but
the Jews cried out, "If you release this man, you
are not Caesar's friend; every one who makes
himself a king sets himself against Caesar."
13When Pilate heard these words, he brought
Jesus out and sat down on the judgment seat
at a place called The Pavement, and in Hebrew,
Gab′batha. 14Now it was the day of Preparation
of the Passover; it was about the sixth hour. He
said to the Jews, "Here is your King!" 15They
cried out, "Away with him, away with him,
crucify him!" Pilate said to them, "Shall I crucify
your King?" The chief priests answered, "We
have no king but Caesar." 16Then he handed
him over to them to be crucified.

REFLECTION

Hezekiah demonstrates how conversion works. He cleans out the old sins—tearing down pagan shrines—and renews the nation's commitment to the Lord. Simply, "he trusted in the LORD the God of Israel" (2 Kgs 18:5). Psalm 136 recounts the Lord's trustworthiness by telling the Exodus story again: "For his mercy [*hesed*] endures forever." *Hesed* is the Lord's covenant loyalty, his steadfast love, which is on full display on Good Friday. Jesus stands before the crowd, crowned, robed, and bleeding while they shout, "Crucify him!" Little do they know that he truly is their king and by his suffering that day, their sins will be blotted out. Jesus's accusers say, "We have no king but Caesar" (Jn 19:15), showing how much they have gone along with the world. Hezekiah rejects Judah's foreign overlord by refusing to pay tribute to Assyria (see 2 Kgs 18:7). He prefers trusting God to friendship with the world. We are tested every day in this regard—whether our trust and our *hesed* is invested in the world or in God. Will you be like Hezekiah and raze the old sins to the ground, inspired by the face of mercy marred by the scourging and the beatings? Do not Jesus's sufferings move us to deeper conversion and love?

June 14

---

2 KINGS 18

**13In the fourteenth year of King
Hezeki′ah Sennach′erib king of
Assyria came up against all the fortified cities of Judah and took them.**

[14]And Hezeki′ah king of Judah sent to the
king of Assyria at La′chish, saying, "I have
done wrong; withdraw from me; whatever
you impose on me I will bear." And the
king of Assyria required of Hezekiah
king of Judah three hundred talents of
silver and thirty talents of gold. [15]And
Hezeki′ah gave him all the silver that was
found in the house of the LORD, and in
the treasuries of the king's house. [16]At
that time Hezeki′ah stripped the gold
from the doors of the temple of the LORD,
and from the doorposts which Hezekiah
king of Judah had overlaid and gave it
to the king of Assyria. [17]And the king of
Assyria sent the Tartan, the Rab′saris, and
the Rab′shakeh with a great army from
La′chish to King Hezeki′ah at Jerusalem.
And they went up and came to Jerusalem.
When they arrived, they came and stood
by the conduit of the upper pool, which
is on the highway to the Fuller's Field.
[18]And when they called for the king,
there came out to them Eli′akim the son
of Hilki′ah, who was over the household,
and Shebnah the secretary, and Jo′ah the
son of A′saph, the recorder.

[19]And the Rab′shakeh said to them, "Say
to Hezeki′ah, 'Thus says the great king, the
king of Assyria: On what do you rest this
confidence of yours? [20]Do you think that
mere words are strategy and power for war?
On whom do you now rely, that you have
rebelled against me? [21]Behold, you are
relying now on Egypt, that broken reed
of a staff, which will pierce the hand of
any man who leans on it. Such is Pharaoh
king of Egypt to all who rely on him. [22]But
if you say to me, "We rely on the LORD
our God," is it not he whose high places
and altars Hezeki′ah has removed, saying
to Judah and to Jerusalem, "You shall
worship before this altar in Jerusalem"?
[23]Come now, make a wager with my master
the king of Assyria: I will give you two
thousand horses, if you are able on your
part to set riders upon them. [24]How then
can you repulse a single captain among the
least of my master's servants, when you rely
on Egypt for chariots and for horsemen?
[25]Moreover, is it without the LORD that I
have come up against this place to destroy
it? The LORD said to me, Go up against this
land, and destroy it.'"

[26]Then Eli′akim the son of Hilki′ah, and
Shebnah, and Jo′ah, said to the Rab′shakeh,
"Please, speak to your servants in the
Arama′ic language, for we understand it;
do not speak to us in the language of Judah
within the hearing of the people who are
on the wall." [27]But the Rab′shakeh said to
them, "Has my master sent me to speak
these words to your master and to you, and
not to the men sitting on the wall, who are
doomed with you to eat their own dung and
to drink their own urine?"

[28]Then the Rab′shakeh stood and called
out in a loud voice in the language of Judah:
"Hear the word of the great king, the king
of Assyria! [29]Thus says the king: 'Do not let
Hezeki′ah deceive you, for he will not be able
to deliver you out of my hand. [30]Do not let
Hezeki′ah make you to rely on the LORD by
saying, The LORD will surely deliver us, and
this city will not be given into the hand of the
king of Assyria.' [31]Do not listen to Hezeki′ah;
for thus says the king of Assyria: 'Make your
peace with me and come out to me; then
every one of you will eat of his own vine,
and every one of his own fig tree, and every
one of you will drink the water of his own
cistern; [32]until I come and take you away to a
land like your own land, a land of grain and
wine, a land of bread and vineyards, a land
of olive trees and honey, that you may live,
and not die. And do not listen to Hezeki′ah
when he misleads you by saying, The LORD
will deliver us. [33]Has any of the gods of the
nations ever delivered his land out of the
hand of the king of Assyria? [34]Where are
the gods of Ha′math and Arpad? Where are
the gods of Sepharva′im, He′na, and Ivvah?
Have they delivered Samar′ia out of my
hand? [35]Who among all the gods of the
countries have delivered their countries
out of my hand, that the LORD should
deliver Jerusalem out of my hand?'"

[36]But the people were silent and answered him not a word, for the king's
command was, "Do not answer him." [37]Then

Eli´akim the son of Hilki´ah, who was over
the household, and Shebna the secretary,
and Jo´ah the son of A´saph, the recorder,
came to Hezeki´ah with their clothes torn,
and told him the words of the Rab´shakeh.

19 When King Hezeki´ah heard it, he
tore his clothes, and covered
himself with sackcloth, and went into
the house of the Lord. 2And he sent
Eli´akim, who was over the household,
and Shebna the secretary, and the senior
priests, covered with sackcloth, to the
prophet Isai´ah the son of A´moz. 3They
said to him, "Thus says Hezeki´ah, This
day is a day of distress, of rebuke, and of
disgrace; children have come to the birth,
and there is no strength to bring them
forth. 4It may be that the Lord your God
heard all the words of the Rab´shakeh,
whom his master the king of Assyria has
sent to mock the living God, and will
rebuke the words which the Lord your
God has heard; therefore lift up your
prayer for the remnant that is left." 5When
the servants of King Hezeki´ah came to
Isai´ah, 6Isai´ah said to them, "Say to your
master, 'Thus says the Lord: Do not be
afraid because of the words that you have
heard, with which the servants of the king
of Assyria have reviled me. 7Behold, I will
put a spirit in him, so that he shall hear a
rumor and return to his own land; and I
will cause him to fall by the sword in his
own land.' "

8The Rab´shakeh returned, and found the
king of Assyria fighting against Libnah; for
he heard that the king had left La´chish.
9And when the king heard concerning
Tirha´kah king of Ethiopia, "Behold, he
has set out to fight against you," he sent
messengers again to Hezeki´ah, saying,
10"Thus shall you speak to Hezeki´ah king
of Judah: 'Do not let your God on whom
you rely deceive you by promising that
Jerusalem will not be given into the hand
of the king of Assyria. 11Behold, you have
heard what the kings of Assyria have done
to all lands, destroying them utterly. And
shall you be delivered? 12Have the gods of
the nations delivered them, the nations
which my fathers destroyed, Gozan,
Haran, Rezeph, and the people of Eden
who were in Tel-as´sar? 13Where is the king
of Ha´math, the king of Arpad, the king of
the city of Sepharva´im, the king of He´na,
or the king of Ivvah?' "

14Hezeki´ah received the letter from
the hand of the messengers, and read
it; and Hezekiah went up to the house
of the Lord, and spread it before the
Lord. 15And Hezeki´ah prayed before
the Lord, and said: "O Lord the God
of Israel, who are enthroned above the
cherubim, you are the God, you alone, of
all the kingdoms of the earth; you have
made heaven and earth. 16Incline your
ear, O Lord, and hear; open your eyes,
O Lord, and see; and hear the words of
Sennach´erib, which he has sent to mock
the living God. 17Of a truth, O Lord,
the kings of Assyria have laid waste the
nations and their lands, 18and have cast
their gods into the fire; for they were no
gods, but the work of men's hands, wood
and stone; therefore they were destroyed.
19So now, O Lord our God, save us, I beg
you, from his hand, that all the kingdoms
of the earth may know that you, O Lord,
are God alone."

20Then Isai´ah the son of A´moz sent to
Hezeki´ah, saying, "Thus says the Lord,
the God of Israel: Your prayer to me about
Sennach´erib king of Assyria I have heard.
21This is the word that the Lord has spoken
concerning him:

"She despises you, she scorns you—
the virgin daughter of Zion;
she wags her head behind you—
the daughter of Jerusalem.

22"Whom have you mocked and reviled?
Against whom have you raised your voice
and haughtily lifted your eyes?
Against the Holy One of Israel!
23By your messengers you have mocked
the Lord,
and you have said, 'With my
many chariots
I have gone up the heights of the mountains,
to the far recesses of Lebanon;

I felled its tallest cedars,
its choicest cypresses;
I entered its farthest retreat,
its densest forest.
24I dug wells
and drank foreign waters,
and I dried up with the sole of my foot
all the streams of Egypt.'

25"Have you not heard
that I determined it long ago?
I planned from days of old
what now I bring to pass,
that you should turn fortified cities
into heaps of ruins,
26while their inhabitants, shorn of strength,
are dismayed and confounded,
and have become like plants of the field,
and like tender grass,
like grass on the housetops;
blighted before it is grown?

27"But I know your sitting down
and your going out and coming in,
and your raging against me.
28Because you have raged against me
and your arrogance has come into
my ears,
I will put my hook in your nose
and my bit in your mouth,
and I will turn you back on the way
by which you came.

29"And this shall be the sign for you: this
year you shall eat what grows of itself,
and in the second year what springs
of the same; then in the third year sow,
and reap, and plant vineyards, and eat
their fruit. 30And the surviving remnant
of the house of Judah shall again take
root downward, and bear fruit upward;
31for out of Jerusalem shall go forth a
remnant, and out of Mount Zion a band
of survivors. The zeal of the LORD will do
this.
32"Therefore thus says the LORD concerning the king of Assyria, He shall not
come into this city or shoot an arrow there,
or come before it with a shield or cast up a
siege mound against it. 33By the way that
he came, by the same he shall return, and
he shall not come into this city, says the
LORD. 34For I will defend this city to save
it, for my own sake and for the sake of my
servant David."
35And that night the angel of the LORD
went forth, and slew a hundred and
eighty-five thousand in the camp of the
Assyrians; and when men arose early in
the morning, behold, these were all dead
bodies. 36Then Sennach′erib king of Assyria departed, and went home, and dwelt
at Nin′eveh. 37And as he was worshiping in
the house of Nisroch his god, Adram′mel-
ech and Share′zer, his sons, slew him with
the sword, and escaped into the land of
Ar′arat. And Esarhad′don his son reigned
in his stead.

PSALM 137 [136]

By the waters of Babylon, there we sat down
and wept,
when we remembered Zion.
2On the willows there
we hung up our lyres.
3For there our captors
required of us songs,
and our tormentors, mirth, saying,
"Sing us one of the songs of Zion!"

4How shall we sing the LORD's song
in a foreign land?
5If I forget you, O Jerusalem,
let my right hand wither!
6Let my tongue cleave to the roof of my mouth,
if I do not remember you,
if I do not set Jerusalem
above my highest joy!

7Remember, O LORD, against the E′domites
the day of Jerusalem,
how they said, "Raze it, raze it!
Down to its foundations!"

8O daughter of Babylon, you devastator!
Happy shall he be who repays you
with what you have done to us!
9Happy shall he be who takes your little ones
and dashes them against the rock!

JOHN 19

**17So they took Jesus, and he went
out, bearing his own cross, to the
place called the place of a skull,
which is called in Hebrew Gol′gotha.
18There they crucified him, and with**
him two others, one on either side, and Jesus
between them. 19Pilate also wrote a title and
put it on the cross; it read, "Jesus of Nazareth,
the King of the Jews." 20Many of the Jews
read this title, for the place where Jesus was
crucified was near the city; and it was written
in Hebrew, in Latin, and in Greek. 21The chief
priests of the Jews then said to Pilate, "Do not
write, 'The King of the Jews,' but, 'This man
said, I am King of the Jews.'" 22Pilate answered,
"What I have written I have written."

23When the soldiers had crucified Jesus they
took his garments and made four parts, one
for each soldier; also his tunic. But the tunic
was without seam, woven from top to bottom;
24so they said to one another, "Let us not tear
it, but cast lots for it to see whose it shall be."
This was to fulfil the Scripture,

"They parted my garments among them,
and for my clothing they cast lots."

25So the soldiers did this. But standing by the
cross of Jesus were his mother, and his mother's
sister, Mary the wife of Clopas, and Mary
Mag′dalene. 26When Jesus saw his mother,
and the disciple whom he loved standing near,
he said to his mother, "Woman, behold, your
son!" 27Then he said to the disciple, "Behold,
your mother!" And from that hour the disciple
took her to his own home.

28After this Jesus, knowing that all was now
finished, said (to fulfil the Scripture), "I thirst."
29A bowl full of vinegar stood there; so they put
a sponge full of the vinegar on hyssop and held
it to his mouth. 30When Jesus had received the
vinegar, he said, "It is finished"; and he bowed
his head and gave up his spirit.

REFLECTION

Assyria overran Israel. Now Sennacherib's army has conquered all of Judah except for the capital, Jerusalem. The chief representatives of Assyria offer terms, mocking the bravery of the little army of Judah holding out in Jerusalem. Yet the king still trusts the Lord and asks for a word from Isaiah, which comes back, "Do not be afraid" (2 Kgs 19:6). Indeed, Hezekiah prays, "O LORD our God, save us, I beg you, from his hand, that all the kingdoms of the earth may know that you, O LORD, are God alone" (v. 19). Rather than surrender to the superior military force, Hezekiah surrenders to the Lord and even prays for the renown of the Lord's name. His faithfulness is rewarded when the Lord strikes down the Assyrian army (see v. 35). Jesus's courage, however, trumps Hezekiah's. Jesus is not delivered from suffering but rather delivers us through his Passion. At the Cross, he does not forget us, but gives us his mother, the Virgin Mary, to be our spiritual mother. He accomplishes our salvation through his Death: "It is finished" (Jn 19:30). May we have the fearless courage of Hezekiah to face down enemies and the heroic virtue to suffer like Jesus in conformity to his Cross. Most of the disciples fled from the Cross; does St. John stay because of his connection to Mary? Do you ask Mary to give you strength in times of trial?

June 15

2 KINGS 20

**In those days Hezeki′ah became
sick and was at the point of
death. And Isai′ah the prophet the
son of A′moz came to him, and said to**
him, "Thus says the LORD, 'Set your house
in order; for you shall die, you shall not
recover.'" 2Then Hezeki′ah turned his face
to the wall, and prayed to the LORD, saying,
3"Remember now, O LORD, I beg you, how
I have walked before you in faithfulness and
with a whole heart, and have done what is
good in your sight." And Hezeki′ah wept
bitterly. 4And before Isai′ah had gone out of
the middle court, the word of the LORD came

to him: 5“Turn back, and say to Hezeki′ah the
prince of my people, Thus says the LORD, the
God of David your father: I have heard your
prayer, I have seen your tears; behold, I will
heal you; on the third day you shall go up to
the house of the LORD. 6And I will add fifteen
years to your life. I will deliver you and this
city out of the hand of the king of Assyria,
and I will defend this city for my own sake
and for my servant David’s sake.” 7And Isai′ah
said, “Bring a cake of figs. And let them take
and lay it on the boil, that he may recover.”

8And Hezeki′ah said to Isai′ah, “What shall
be the sign that the LORD will heal me, and
that I shall go up to the house of the LORD
on the third day?” 9And Isai′ah said, “This is
the sign to you from the LORD, that the LORD
will do the thing that he has promised: shall
the shadow go forward ten steps, or go back
ten steps?” 10And Hezeki′ah answered, “It
is an easy thing for the shadow to lengthen
ten steps; rather let the shadow go back ten
steps.” 11And Isai′ah the prophet cried to the
LORD; and he brought the shadow back ten
steps, by which the sun had declined on the
dial of A′haz.

12At that time Mer′odach-bal′adan the son
of Bal′adan, king of Babylon, sent envoys
with letters and a present to Hezeki′ah; for
he heard that Hezekiah had been sick. 13And
Hezeki′ah welcomed them, and he showed
them all his treasure house, the silver, the
gold, the spices, the precious oil, his armory,
all that was found in his storehouses; there
was nothing in his house or in all his realm
that Hezekiah did not show them. 14Then
Isai′ah the prophet came to King Hezeki′ah,
and said to him, “What did these men say?
And from where did they come to you?”
And Hezekiah said, “They have come from
a far country, from Babylon.” 15He said,
“What have they seen in your house?” And
Hezeki′ah answered, “They have seen all
that is in my house; there is nothing in my
storehouses that I did not show them.”

16Then Isai′ah said to Hezeki′ah, “Hear the
word of the LORD: 17Behold, the days are
coming, when all that is in your house, and
that which your fathers have stored up till
this day, shall be carried to Babylon; nothing
shall be left, says the LORD. 18And some of
your own sons, who are born to you, shall
be taken away; and they shall be eunuchs in
the palace of the king of Babylon.” 19Then
said Hezeki′ah to Isai′ah, “The word of the
LORD which you have spoken is good.” For
he thought, “Why not, if there will be peace
and security in my days?”

20The rest of the deeds of Hezeki′ah, and
all his might, and how he made the pool
and the conduit and brought water into
the city, are they not written in the Book
of the Chronicles of the Kings of Judah?
21And Hezeki′ah slept with his fathers; and
Manas′seh his son reigned in his stead.

21 Manas′seh was twelve years old when
he began to reign, and he reigned
fifty-five years in Jerusalem. His mother’s
name was Heph′zibah. 2And he did what
was evil in the sight of the LORD, according
to the abominable practices of the nations
whom the LORD drove out before the
people of Israel. 3For he rebuilt the high
places which Hezeki′ah his father had
destroyed; and he erected altars for Ba′al,
and made an Ashe′rah, as A′hab king of
Israel had done, and worshiped all the host
of heaven, and served them. 4And he built
altars in the house of the LORD, of which the
LORD had said, “In Jerusalem will I put my
name.” 5And he built altars for all the host
of heaven in the two courts of the house
of the LORD. 6And he burned his son as an
offering, and practiced soothsaying and
augury, and dealt with mediums and with
wizards. He did much evil in the sight of
the LORD, provoking him to anger. 7And
the graven image of Ashe′rah that he had
made he set in the house of which the LORD
said to David and to Solomon his son, “In
this house, and in Jerusalem, which I have
chosen out of all the tribes of Israel, I will
put my name for ever; 8and I will not cause
the feet of Israel to wander any more out
of the land which I gave to their fathers, if
only they will be careful to do according
to all that I have commanded them, and
according to all the law that my servant
Moses commanded them.” 9But they did not
listen, and Manas′seh seduced them to do

more evil than the nations had done whom
the LORD destroyed before the sons of Israel.
[10]And the LORD said by his servants the
prophets, [11]"Because Manas′seh king of
Judah has committed these abominations,
and has done things more wicked than all
that the Am′orites did, who were before
him, and has made Judah also to sin with
his idols; [12]therefore thus says the LORD,
the God of Israel, Behold, I am bringing
upon Jerusalem and Judah such evil that
the ears of every one who hears of it will
tingle. [13]And I will stretch over Jerusalem
the measuring line of Samar′ia, and the
plummet of the house of A′hab; and I
will wipe Jerusalem as one wipes a dish,
wiping it and turning it upside down.
[14]And I will cast off the remnant of my
heritage, and give them into the hand
of their enemies, and they shall become
a prey and a spoil to all their enemies,
[15]because they have done what is evil in
my sight and have provoked me to anger,
since the day their fathers came out of
Egypt, even to this day."
[16]Moreover Manas′seh shed very much
innocent blood, till he had filled Jerusalem
from one end to another, besides the sin
which he made Judah to sin so that they did
what was evil in the sight of the LORD.
[17]Now the rest of the acts of Manas′seh,
and all that he did, and the sin that he
committed, are they not written in the Book
of the Chronicles of the Kings of Judah?
[18]And Manas′seh slept with his fathers, and
was buried in the garden of his house, in the
garden of Uzza; and A′mon his son reigned
in his stead.
[19]A′mon was twenty-two years old when
he began to reign, and he reigned two years
in Jerusalem. His mother's name was Me-
shul′lemeth the daughter of Haruz of Jot-
bah. [20]And he did what was evil in the sight
of the LORD, as Manas′seh his father had
done. [21]He walked in all the way in which
his father walked, and served the idols that
his father served, and worshiped them;
[22]he forsook the LORD, the God of his fathers, and did not walk in the way of the
LORD. [23]And the servants of A′mon conspired against him, and killed the king in
his house. [24]But the people of the land slew
all those who had conspired against King
A′mon, and the people of the land made
Josi′ah his son king in his stead. [25]Now the
rest of the acts of A′mon which he did, are
they not written in the Book of the Chronicles of the Kings of Judah? [26]And he was
buried in his tomb in the garden of Uzza;
and Josi′ah his son reigned in his stead.

22 Josi′ah was eight years old when
he began to reign, and he reigned
thirty-one years in Jerusalem. His mother's
name was Jedi′dah the daughter of Adai′ah
of Bozkath. [2]And he did what was right in
the eyes of the LORD, and walked in all the
way of David his father, and he did not turn
aside to the right hand or to the left.
[3]In the eighteenth year of King Josi′ah, the
king sent Sha′phan the son of Azali′ah, son
of Meshul′lam, the secretary, to the house
of the LORD, saying, [4]"Go up to Hilki′ah the
high priest, that he may reckon the amount
of the money which has been brought into
the house of the LORD, which the keepers
of the threshold have collected from the
people; [5]and let it be given into the hand of
the workmen who have the oversight of the
house of the LORD; and let them give it to
the workmen who are at the house of the
LORD, repairing the house, [6]that is, to the
carpenters, and to the builders, and to the
masons, as well as for buying timber and
quarried stone to repair the house. [7]But no
accounting shall be asked from them for the
money which is delivered into their hand,
for they deal honestly."
[8]And Hilki′ah the high priest said to
Sha′phan the secretary, "I have found the
book of the law in the house of the LORD."
And Hilkiah gave the book to Shaphan, and
he read it. [9]And Sha′phan the secretary came
to the king, and reported to the king, "Your
servants have emptied out the money that
was found in the house, and have delivered
it into the hand of the workmen who have
the oversight of the house of the LORD."
[10]Then Sha′phan the secretary told the king,
"Hilki′ah the priest has given me a book."
And Shaphan read it before the king.

A Psalm of David.

PSALM 138 [137]

I give you thanks, O LORD, with my
whole heart;
before the angels I sing your praise;
2I bow down toward your holy temple
and give thanks to your name for your
mercy and your faithfulness;
for you have exalted above everything
your name and your word.
3On the day I called, you answered me,
my strength of soul you increased.

4All the kings of the earth shall praise you,
O LORD,
for they have heard the words of your
mouth;
5and they shall sing of the ways of the LORD,
for great is the glory of the LORD.
6For though the LORD is high, he regards
the lowly;
but the haughty he knows from afar.

7Though I walk in the midst of trouble,
you preserve my life;
you stretch out your hand against the wrath
of my enemies,
and your right hand delivers me.
8The LORD will fulfil his purpose for me;
your mercy, O LORD, endures for ever.
Do not forsake the work of your hands.

JOHN 19

31Since it was the day of Preparation, in order to prevent the bodies from remaining on the cross on the sabbath (for that sabbath was a high day), the Jews asked Pilate that their legs might be broken, and
that they might be taken away. 32So the
soldiers came and broke the legs of the first,
and of the other who had been crucified with
him; 33but when they came to Jesus and saw
that he was already dead, they did not break
his legs. 34But one of the soldiers pierced his
side with a spear, and at once there came out
blood and water. 35He who saw it has borne
witness—his testimony is true, and he knows
that he tells the truth—that you also may
believe. 36For these things took place that the
Scripture might be fulfilled, "Not a bone of
him shall be broken." 37And again another
Scripture says, "They shall look on him
whom they have pierced."

38After this Joseph of Arimathe′a, who
was a disciple of Jesus, but secretly, for fear
of the Jews, asked Pilate that he might take
away the body of Jesus, and Pilate gave him
leave. So he came and took away his body.
39Nicode′mus also, who had at first come to
him by night, came bringing a mixture of
myrrh and aloes, about a hundred pounds'
weight. 40They took the body of Jesus, and
bound it in linen cloths with the spices, as
is the burial custom of the Jews. 41Now in
the place where he was crucified there was a
garden, and in the garden a new tomb where
no one had ever been laid. 42So because of the
Jewish day of Preparation, as the tomb was
close at hand, they laid Jesus there.

REFLECTION

Late in his reign, Hezekiah shows off his wealth to the Babylonian ambassadors: "He showed them all his treasure house, the silver, the gold, the spices, the precious oil, his armory, all that was found in his storehouses" (2 Kgs 20:13). Showing off wealth is a typical way to boost one's prestige, but in the ancient world it was even more so. Hezekiah is trying to impress a foreign power, to show that his kingdom might be a helpful ally or a formidable foe, to give them a sense of how much power he possesses. Hezekiah's sin here is very similar to David's error in initiating a census to measure his military might. Hezekiah uses his wealth to gain worldly renown. Nicodemus and Joseph of Arimathea use their wealth in a different way, "bringing a mixture of myrrh and aloes, about a hundred pounds' weight" to anoint the body of Jesus (Jn 19:39). They use their wealth to express their devotion to the Lord, not to play power politics on the international stage. Money has a purpose, but often we use it for the wrong things. In the ways you manage your money, who is glorified more, you or the Lord?

June 16

2 KINGS 22

11And when the king heard the
words of the book of the law, he
tore his clothes. 12And the king
commanded Hilki′ah the priest, and
Ahi′kam the son of Sha′phan, and Achbor
the son of Micai′ah, and Shaphan the
secretary, and Asai′ah the king's servant,
saying, 13"Go, inquire of the LORD for me, and
for the people, and for all Judah, concerning
the words of this book that has been found; for
great is the wrath of the LORD that is kindled
against us, because our fathers have not obeyed
the words of this book, to do according to all
that is written concerning us."

14So Hilki′ah the priest, and Ahi′kam, and
Achbor, and Sha′phan, and Asai′ah went to
Huldah the prophetess, the wife of Shallum
the son of Tikvah, son of Harhas, keeper of
the wardrobe (now she dwelt in Jerusalem in
the Second Quarter); and they talked with her.
15And she said to them, "Thus says the LORD,
the God of Israel: 'Tell the man who sent you to
me, 16Thus says the LORD, Behold, I will bring
evil upon this place and upon its inhabitants,
all the words of the book which the king of
Judah has read. 17Because they have forsaken
me and have burned incense to other gods,
that they might provoke me to anger with all
the work of their hands, therefore my wrath
will be kindled against this place, and it will
not be quenched. 18But as to the king of Judah,
who sent you to inquire of the LORD, thus shall
you say to him, Thus says the LORD, the God
of Israel: Regarding the words which you have
heard, 19because your heart was penitent, and
you humbled yourself before the LORD, when
you heard how I spoke against this place, and
against its inhabitants, that they should become
a desolation and a curse, and you have torn
your clothes and wept before me, I also have
heard you, says the LORD. 20Therefore, behold, I
will gather you to your fathers, and you shall be
gathered to your grave in peace, and your eyes
shall not see all the evil which I will bring upon
this place.'" And they brought back word to
the king.

23 Then the king sent, and all the elders
of Judah and Jerusalem were gathered
to him. 2And the king went up to the house of
the LORD, and with him all the men of Judah
and all the inhabitants of Jerusalem, and the
priests and the prophets, all the people, both
small and great; and he read in their hearing all
the words of the book of the covenant which
had been found in the house of the LORD.
3And the king stood by the pillar and made
a covenant before the LORD, to walk after the
LORD and to keep his commandments and his
covenants and his statutes, with all his heart
and all his soul, to perform the words of this
covenant that were written in this book; and all
the people joined in the covenant.

4And the king commanded Hilki′ah, the
high priest, and the priests of the second order,
and the keepers of the threshold, to bring out
of the temple of the LORD all the vessels made
for Ba′al, for Ashe′rah, and for all the host of
heaven; he burned them outside Jerusalem in
the fields of the Kidron, and carried their ashes
to Bethel. 5And he deposed the idolatrous
priests whom the kings of Judah had ordained
to burn incense in the high places at the cities
of Judah and round about Jerusalem; those
also who burned incense to Ba′al, to the sun,
and the moon, and the constellations, and all
the host of the heavens. 6And he brought out
the Ashe′rah from the house of the LORD,
outside Jerusalem, to the brook Kidron, and
burned it at the brook Kidron, and beat it to
dust and cast the dust of it upon the graves of
the common people. 7And he broke down the
houses of the male cult prostitutes which were
in the house of the LORD, where the women
wove hangings for the Ashe′rah. 8And he
brought all the priests out of the cities of Judah,
and defiled the high places where the priests
had burned incense, from Ge′ba to Be′er-
she′ba; and he broke down the high places of
the gates that were at the entrance of the gate of
Joshua the governor of the city, which were on
one's left at the gate of the city. 9However, the
priests of the high places did not come up to
the altar of the LORD in Jerusalem, but they ate

unleavened bread among their brethren. [10]And
he defiled To´pheth, which is in the valley of the
sons of Hin´nom, that no one might burn his
son or his daughter as an offering to Mo´lech.
[11]And he removed the horses that the kings of
Judah had dedicated to the sun, at the entrance
to the house of the LORD, by the chamber of
Na´than-me´lech the chamberlain, which was
in the precincts; and he burned the chariots
of the sun with fire. [12]And the altars on the
roof of the upper chamber of A´haz, which the
kings of Judah had made, and the altars which
Manas´seh had made in the two courts of the
house of the LORD, he pulled down and broke
in pieces, and cast the dust of them into the
brook Kidron. [13]And the king defiled the high
places that were east of Jerusalem, to the south
of the mount of corruption, which Solomon
the king of Israel had built for Ash´toreth
the abomination of the Sido´nians, and for
Che´mosh the abomination of Moab, and for
Milcom the abomination of the Am´monites.
[14]And he broke in pieces the pillars, and cut
down the Ashe´rim, and filled their places with
the bones of men.

[15]Moreover the altar at Bethel, the high place
erected by Jerobo´am the son of Ne´bat, who
made Israel to sin, that altar with the high
place he pulled down and he broke in pieces its
stones, crushing them to dust; also he burned
the Ashe´rah. [16]And as Josi´ah turned, he saw
the tombs there on the mount; and he sent and
took the bones out of the tombs, and burned
them upon the altar, and defiled it, according
to the word of the LORD which the man of God
proclaimed, who had predicted these things.
[17]Then he said, "What is yonder monument
that I see?" And the men of the city told him,
"It is the tomb of the man of God who came
from Judah and predicted these things which
you have done against the altar at Bethel."
[18]And he said, "Let him be; let no man move
his bones." So they let his bones alone, with the
bones of the prophet who came out of Samar´ia.
[19]And all the shrines also of the high places that
were in the cities of Samar´ia, which kings of
Israel had made, provoking the LORD to anger,
Josi´ah removed; he did to them according to
all that he had done at Bethel. [20]And he slew all
the priests of the high places who were there,
upon the altars, and burned the bones of men
upon them. Then he returned to Jerusalem.

[21]And the king commanded all the people,
"Keep the Passover to the LORD your God,
as it is written in this book of the covenant."
[22]For no such Passover had been kept since
the days of the judges who judged Israel, or
during all the days of the kings of Israel or
of the kings of Judah; [23]but in the eighteenth
year of King Josi´ah this Passover was kept to
the LORD in Jerusalem.

[24]Moreover Josi´ah put away the mediums
and the wizards and the teraphim and the idols
and all the abominations that were seen in the
land of Judah and in Jerusalem, that he might
establish the words of the law which were
written in the book that Hilki´ah the priest
found in the house of the LORD. [25]Before him
there was no king like him, who turned to the
LORD with all his heart and with all his soul
and with all his might, according to all the law
of Moses; nor did any like him arise after him.

[26]Still the LORD did not turn from the
fierceness of his great wrath, by which his
anger was kindled against Judah, because of
all the provocations with which Manas´seh
had provoked him. [27]And the LORD said, "I
will remove Judah also out of my sight, as I
have removed Israel, and I will cast off this city
which I have chosen, Jerusalem, and the house
of which I said, My name shall be there."

To the choirmaster.
A Psalm of David.

PSALM 139 [138]

O LORD, you have searched me and
known me!
[2]You know when I sit down and when I rise up;
you discern my thoughts from afar.
[3]You search out my path and my lying down,
and are acquainted with all my ways.
[4]Even before a word is on my tongue,
behold, O LORD, you know it altogether.
[5]You beset me behind and before,
and lay your hand upon me.
[6]Such knowledge is too wonderful for me;
it is high, I cannot attain it.

7 Where shall I go from your Spirit?
Or where shall I flee from your presence?
8 If I ascend to heaven, you are there!
If I make my bed in Sheol, you are there!
9 If I take the wings of the morning
and dwell in the uttermost parts of the sea,
10 even there your hand shall lead me,
and your right hand shall hold me.
11 If I say, "Let only darkness cover me,
and the light about me be night,"
12 even the darkness is not dark to you,
the night is bright as the day;
for darkness is as light with you.

13 For you formed my inward parts,
you knitted me together in my mother's
womb.
14 I praise you, for I am wondrously made.
Wonderful are your works!
You know me right well;
15 my frame was not hidden from you,
when I was being made in secret,
intricately wrought in the depths of
the earth.
16 Your eyes beheld my unformed substance;
in your book were written, every one
of them,
the days that were formed for me,
when as yet there was none of them.
17 How precious to me are your thoughts,
O God!
How vast is the sum of them!
18 If I would count them, they are more than
the sand.
When I awake, I am still with you.

19 O that you would slay the wicked, O God,
and that men of blood would depart
from me,
20 men who maliciously defy you,
who lift themselves up against you for evil!
21 Do I not hate them that hate you, O LORD?
And do I not loathe them that rise up
against you?
22 I hate them with perfect hatred;
I count them my enemies.
23 Search me, O God, and know my heart!
Try me and know my thoughts!
24 And see if there be any wicked way in me,
and lead me in the way everlasting!

JOHN 20

Now on the first day of the week, Mary Mag'dalene came to the tomb early, while it was still dark, and saw that the stone had been taken away from the tomb.
2 So she ran, and went to Simon Peter and the other
disciple, the one whom Jesus loved, and said
to them, "They have taken the Lord out of the
tomb, and we do not know where they have
laid him."
3 Peter then came out with the other
disciple, and they went toward the tomb.
4 They
both ran, but the other disciple outran Peter
and reached the tomb first;
5 and stooping to
look in, he saw the linen cloths lying there,
but he did not go in.
6 Then Simon Peter came,
following him, and went into the tomb; he saw
the linen cloths lying,
7 and the napkin, which
had been on his head, not lying with the linen
cloths but rolled up in a place by itself.
8 Then
the other disciple, who reached the tomb first,
also went in, and he saw and believed;
9 for as
yet they did not know the Scripture, that he
must rise from the dead.
10 Then the disciples
went back to their homes.
11 But Mary stood weeping outside the
tomb, and as she wept she stooped to look
into the tomb;
12 and she saw two angels in
white, sitting where the body of Jesus had
lain, one at the head and one at the feet.
13 They said to her, "Woman, why are you
weeping?" She said to them, "Because they
have taken away my Lord, and I do not know
where they have laid him."
14 Saying this, she
turned round and saw Jesus standing, but
she did not know that it was Jesus.
15 Jesus
said to her, "Woman, why are you weeping?
Whom do you seek?" Supposing him to be
the gardener, she said to him, "Sir, if you have
carried him away, tell me where you have
laid him, and I will take him away."
16 Jesus
said to her, "Mary." She turned and said to
him in Hebrew, "Rab-bo'ni!" (which means
Teacher).
17 Jesus said to her, "Do not hold
me, for I have not yet ascended to the Father;
but go to my brethren and say to them, I am
ascending to my Father and your Father, to
my God and your God."
18 Mary Mag'dalene

went and said to the disciples, "I have seen the Lord"; and she told them that he had said these things to her.

REFLECTION

Josiah shows us what it means to be faithful. He "turned to the LORD with all his heart and with all his soul and with all his might" (2 Kgs 23:25). After so many evil kings and so many duplicitous worshippers, Josiah finally destroys all the pagan sanctuaries, north and south. He puts an end to false worship and fulfills the prophecy of the "man of God" (1 Kgs 13:1). Despite Josiah's ironclad fidelity, the fate of the nation is sealed. Judgment is coming. Josiah's whole-hearted devotion to the Lord is paralleled by Mary Magdalene on Easter Sunday. She arrives at the empty tomb first, weeping genuine tears. Jesus rewards her devotion by appearing to her and then sends her back to bring the Good News to the Apostles so that the Church calls her "The Apostle to the Apostles." Faithfulness to the Lord is rooted in a close relationship with him, where we appreciate his powerful love for us. Psalm 139 explores his all-encompassing knowledge of us and his mysterious omnipresence: "Where shall I go from your Spirit? Or where shall I flee from your presence?" (139:7). Josiah and Mary Magdalene knew the power of the Lord's presence, and they surrendered to him. Will you do the same?

June 17

2 KINGS 23

[28]Now the rest of the acts of Josi´ah, and all that he did, are they not written in the Book of the Chronicles of the Kings of Judah? [29]In his days Pharaoh Neco king of Egypt went up to the king of Assyria to the river Euphra´tes. King Josi´ah went to meet him; and Pharaoh Neco slew him at Megid´do, when he saw him. [30]And his servants carried him dead in a chariot from Megid´do, and brought him to Jerusalem, and buried him in his own tomb. And the people of the land took Jeho´ahaz the son of Josi´ah, and anointed him, and made him king in his father's stead.

[31]Jeho´ahaz was twenty-three years old when he began to reign, and he reigned three months in Jerusalem. His mother's name was Hamu´tal the daughter of Jeremi´ah of Libnah. [32]And he did what was evil in the sight of the LORD, according to all that his fathers had done. [33]And Pharaoh Neco put him in bonds at Riblah in the land of Ha´math, that he might not reign in Jerusalem, and laid upon the land a tribute of a hundred talents of silver and a talent of gold. [34]And Pharaoh Ne´co made Eli´akim the son of Josi´ah king in the place of Josiah his father, and changed his name to Jehoi´akim. But he took Jeho´ahaz away; and he came to Egypt, and died there. [35]And Jehoi´akim gave the silver and the gold to Pharaoh, but he taxed the land to give the money according to the command of Pharaoh. He exacted the silver and the gold of the people of the land, from every one according to his assessment, to give it to Pharaoh Neco.

[36]Jehoi´akim was twenty-five years old when he began to reign, and he reigned eleven years in Jerusalem. His mother's name was Zebi´dah the daughter of Pedai´ah of Ru´mah. [37]And he did what was evil in the sight of the LORD, according to all that his fathers had done.

24 In his days Nebuchadnez´zar king of Babylon came up, and Jehoi´akim became his servant three years; then he turned and rebelled against him. [2]And the LORD sent against him bands of the Chalde´ans, and bands of the Syrians, and bands of the Moabites, and bands of the Am´monites, and sent them against Judah to destroy it, according to the word of the LORD which he spoke by his servants the prophets. [3]Surely this came upon Judah at the command of the LORD, to remove them out of his sight, for the sins of Manas´seh, according to all that he had done, 4and also for the innocent blood that he had shed; for he filled Jerusalem with innocent blood, and the LORD would not pardon. 5Now the rest of the deeds of Jehoi′akim, and all that he did, are they not written in the Book of the Chronicles of the Kings of Judah? 6So Jehoi′akim slept with his fathers, and Jehoi′achin his son reigned in his stead. 7And the king of Egypt did not come again out of his land, for the king of Babylon had taken all that belonged to the king of Egypt from the Brook of Egypt to the river Euphrates.

8Jehoi′achin was eighteen years old when he became king, and he reigned three months in Jerusalem. His mother's name was Nehush′ta the daughter of Elna′than of Jerusalem. 9And he did what was evil in the sight of the LORD, according to all that his father had done.

10At that time the servants of Nebuchadnez′zar king of Babylon came up to Jerusalem, and the city was besieged. 11And Nebuchadnez′zar king of Babylon came to the city, while his servants were besieging it; 12and Jehoi′achin the king of Judah gave himself up to the king of Babylon, himself, and his mother, and his servants, and his princes, and his palace officials. The king of Babylon took him prisoner in the eighth year of his reign, 13and carried off all the treasures of the house of the LORD, and the treasures of the king's house, and cut in pieces all the vessels of gold in the temple of the LORD, which Solomon king of Israel had made, as the LORD had foretold. 14He carried away all Jerusalem, and all the princes, and all the mighty men of valor, ten thousand captives, and all the craftsmen and the smiths; none remained, except the poorest people of the land. 15And he carried away Jehoi′achin to Babylon; the king's mother, the king's wives, his officials, and the chief men of the land, he took into captivity from Jerusalem to Babylon. 16And the king of Babylon brought captive to Babylon all the men of valor, seven thousand, and the craftsmen and the smiths, one thousand, all of them strong and fit for war. 17And the king of Babylon made Mattani′ah, Jehoi′achin's uncle, king in his stead, and changed his name to Zedeki′ah.

18Zedeki′ah was twenty-one years old when he became king, and he reigned eleven years in Jerusalem. His mother's name was Hamu′tal the daughter of Jeremi′ah of Libnah. 19And he did what was evil in the sight of the LORD, according to all that Jehoi′akim had done. 20For because of the anger of the LORD it came to the point in Jerusalem and Judah that he cast them out from his presence.

And Zedeki′ah rebelled against the king of Babylon.

25 And in the ninth year of his reign, in the tenth month, on the tenth day of the month, Nebuchadnez′zar king of Babylon came with all his army against Jerusalem, and laid siege to it; and they built siegeworks against it round about. 2So the city was besieged till the eleventh year of King Zedeki′ah. 3On the ninth day of the fourth month the famine was so severe in the city that there was no food for the people of the land. 4Then a breach was made in the city; the king with all the men of war fled by night by the way of the gate between the two walls, by the king's garden, though the Chalde′ans were around the city. And they went in the direction of the Ar′abah. 5But the army of the Chalde′ans pursued the king, and overtook him in the plains of Jericho; and all his army was scattered from him. 6Then they captured the king, and brought him up to the king of Babylon at Rib′lah, who passed sentence upon him. 7They slew the sons of Zedeki′ah before his eyes, and put out the eyes of Zedekiah, and bound him in fetters, and took him to Babylon.

8In the fifth month, on the seventh day of the month—which was the nineteenth year of King Nebuchadnez′zar, king of Babylon—Nebu″zarad′an, the captain of the bodyguard, a servant of the king of Babylon, came to Jerusalem. 9And he burned the house of the LORD, and the king's house and all the houses of Jerusalem; every great house he burned down. 10And all the army of the Chalde′ans, who were with the captain of the guard, broke down the walls around Jerusalem. 11And the rest of the people who were left in the city and the deserters who had deserted to the king of Babylon, together with the rest of the multitude, Nebu″zarad′an the captain of the guard carried into exile. 12 But the captain of the guard left some of the poorest of the land to be vinedressers and plowmen.

13 And the pillars of bronze that were in the house of the LORD, and the stands and the bronze sea that were in the house of the LORD, the Chalde′ans broke in pieces, and carried the bronze to Babylon. 14 And they took away the pots, and the shovels, and the snuffers, and the dishes for incense and all the vessels of bronze used in the temple service, 15 the firepans also, and the bowls. What was of gold the captain of the guard took away as gold, and what was of silver, as silver. 16 As for the two pillars, the one sea, and the stands, which Solomon had made for the house of the LORD, the bronze of all these vessels was beyond weight. 17 The height of the one pillar was eighteen cubits, and upon it was a capital of bronze; the height of the capital was three cubits; a network and pomegranates, all of bronze, were upon the capital round about. And the second pillar had the like, with the network.

18 And the captain of the guard took Serai′ah the chief priest, and Zephani′ah the second priest, and the three keepers of the threshold; 19 and from the city he took an officer who had been in command of the men of war, and five men of the king's council who were found in the city; and the secretary of the commander of the army who mustered the people of the land; and sixty men of the people of the land who were found in the city. 20 And Nebu″zarad′an the captain of the guard took them, and brought them to the king of Babylon at Riblah. 21 And the king of Babylon struck them, and put them to death at Riblah in the land of Ha′math. So Judah was taken into exile out of its land.

22 And over the people who remained in the land of Judah, whom Nebuchadnez′zar king of Babylon had left, he appointed Gedali′ah the son of Ahi′kam, son of Sha′phan, governor. 23 Now when all the captains of the forces in the open country and their men heard that the king of Babylon had appointed Gedali′ah governor, they came with their men to Gedaliah at Mizpah, namely, Ish′mael the son of Nethani′ah, and Joha′nan the son of Kare′ah, and Serai′ah the son of Ta′humeth the Netoph′athite, and Ja-azani′ah the son of the Ma-ac′athite. 24 And Gedali′ah swore to them and their men, saying, "Do not be afraid because of the Chalde′an officials; dwell in the land, and serve the king of Babylon, and it shall be well with you." 25 But in the seventh month, Ish′mael the son of Nethani′ah, son of Elish′ama, of the royal family, came with ten men, and attacked and killed Gedali′ah and the Jews and the Chalde′ans who were with him at Mizpah. 26 Then all the people, both small and great, and the captains of the forces arose, and went to Egypt; for they were afraid of the Chalde′ans.

27 And in the thirty-seventh year of the exile of Jehoi′achin king of Judah, in the twelfth month, on the twenty-seventh day of the month, E′vil-mer′odach king of Babylon, in the year that he began to reign, graciously freed Jehoi′achin king of Judah from prison; 28 and he spoke kindly to him, and gave him a seat above the seats of the kings who were with him in Babylon. 29 So Jehoi′achin put off his prison garments. And every day of his life he dined regularly at the king's table; 30 and for his allowance, a regular allowance was given him by the king, every day a portion, as long as he lived.

To the choirmaster.
A Psalm of David.

PSALM 140 [139]

Deliver me, O LORD, from evil men;
preserve me from violent men,
2 who plan evil things in their heart,
and stir up wars continually.
3 They make their tongue sharp as a serpent's,
and under their lips is the poison
of vipers. *Selah*
4 Guard me, O LORD, from the hands of
the wicked;
preserve me from violent men,
who have planned to trip up my feet.

5Arrogant men have hidden a trap for me,
and with cords they have spread a net,
by the wayside they have set snares
for me. *Selah*

6I say to the LORD, You are my God;
give ear to the voice of my supplications,
O LORD!
7O LORD, my Lord, my strong deliverer,
you have covered my head in the day
of battle.
8Grant not, O LORD, the desires of the wicked;
do not further his evil plot! *Selah*

9Those who surround me lift up their head,
let the mischief of their lips overwhelm
them!
10Let burning coals fall upon them!
Let them be cast into pits, no more to rise!
11Let not the slanderer be established in
the land;
let evil hunt down the violent
man speedily!

12I know that the LORD maintains the cause
of the afflicted,
and executes justice for the needy.
13Surely the righteous shall give thanks to
your name;
the upright shall dwell in your presence.

JOHN 20

19On the evening of that day,
the first day of the week, the
doors being shut where the dis-
ciples were, for fear of the Jews, Jesus
came and stood among them and said
to them, "Peace be with you." 20When he had
said this, he showed them his hands and his
side. Then the disciples were glad when they
saw the Lord. 21Jesus said to them again,
"Peace be with you. As the Father has sent
me, even so I send you." 22And when he had
said this, he breathed on them, and said to
them, "Receive the Holy Spirit. 23If you forgive the sins of any, they are forgiven; if you
retain the sins of any, they are retained."
24Now Thomas, one of the Twelve, called the
Twin, was not with them when Jesus came.
25So the other disciples told him, "We have
seen the Lord." But he said to them, "Unless I
see in his hands the print of the nails, and place
my finger in the mark of the nails, and place
my hand in his side, I will not believe."
26Eight days later, his disciples were again in
the house, and Thomas was with them. The
doors were shut, but Jesus came and stood
among them, and said, "Peace be with you."
27Then he said to Thomas, "Put your finger
here, and see my hands; and put out your hand,
and place it in my side; do not be faithless, but
believing." 28Thomas answered him, "My Lord
and my God!" 29Jesus said to him, "You have
believed because you have seen me. Blessed are
those who have not seen and yet believe."
30Now Jesus did many other signs in the
presence of the disciples, which are not
written in this book; 31but these are written
that you may believe that Jesus is the Christ,
the Son of God, and that believing you may
have life in his name.

REFLECTION

Today we read about victory and defeat. After hundreds of years of repeated failure to follow the Lord, the kingdom of Judah is finally conquered. Nebuchadnezzar brings the armies of Babylon to first subjugate Jerusalem and then finally to destroy it. He burns the Temple, takes all its treasure, and sends the people into exile. The Promised Land is reduced to smoldering rubble, and even the people left in the land flee back to Egypt—"that place of slavery." All that the Lord accomplished through Moses, Joshua, and David now is lost. Yet this Old Covenant failure set the stage for the coming of a new David with a new kind of victory. He does not deliver people from literal exile in a foreign country or from literal slavery in Egypt. Rather, he delivers us from the exile and slavery of sin: "If you forgive the sins of any, they are forgiven" (Jn 20:23). Jesus delivers true peace. "Blessed are those who have not seen and yet believe" (v. 29). The Lord is able to bring glorious victory out of apparent defeat. In what ways has he brought victory out of defeat in your life?

June 18

1 CHRONICLES 1

Adam, Seth, E´nosh; 2Ke´nan, Ma-hal´alel, Jar´ed; 3E´noch, Me-thu´selah, La´mech; 4Noah, Shem, Ham, and Ja´pheth.

5The sons of Ja´pheth: Gomer, Ma´gog, Ma´dai, Ja´van, Tu´bal, Me´shech, and Ti´ras. 6The sons of Gomer: Ash´kenaz, Di´phath, and Togar´mah. 7The sons of Ja´van: Eli´shah, Tar´shish, Kittim, and Ro´danim.

8The sons of Ham: Cush, Egypt, Put, and Canaan. 9The sons of Cush: Seba, Hav´ilah, Sabta, Ra´ama, and Sab´teca. The sons of Ra´amah: Sheba and De´dan. 10Cush was the father of Nimrod; he began to be a mighty one in the earth.

11Egypt was the father of Lu´dim, An´amim, Leha´bim, Naph´tuhim, 12Pathru´sim, Caslu´him (from whom came the Philis´tines), and Caph´torim.

13Canaan was the father of Si´don his first-born, and Heth, 14and the Jeb´usites, the Am´orites, the Gir´gashites, 15the Hi´vites, the Arkites, the Si´nites, 16the Ar´vadites, the Zem´arites, and the Ha´mathites.

17The sons of Shem: E´lam, Asshur, Arpach´shad, Lud, Ar´am, Uz, Hul, Ge´ther, and Me´shech. 18Arpach´shad was the father of She´lah; and Shelah was the father of E´ber. 19To E´ber were born two sons: the name of the one was Pe´leg (for in his days the earth was divided), and the name of his brother Joktan. 20Joktan was the father of Almo´dad, She´leph, Ha´´zarma´veth, Je´rah, 21Hador´am, U´zal, Diklah, 22E´bal, Abim´a-el, Sheba, 23O´phir, Hav´ilah, and Jo´bab; all these were the sons of Joktan.

24Shem, Arpach´shad, She´lah; 25E´ber, Pe´leg, Re´u; 26Se´rug, Na´hor, Te´rah; 27Abram, that is, Abraham.

28The sons of Abraham: Isaac and Ish´-mael. 29These are their genealogies: the first-born of Ish´mael, Neba´ioth; and Ke´-dar, Ad´beel, Mibsam, 30Mishma, Du´mah, Massa, Ha´dad, Te´ma, 31Je´tur, Naphish, and Ked´emah. These are the sons of Ish´-mael. 32The sons of Ketu´rah, Abraham's concubine: she bore Zimran, Jok´shan, Me´dan, Mid´ian, Ishbak, and Shuah. The sons of Jokshan: Sheba and De´dan. 33The sons of Mid´ian: E´phah, E´pher, Ha´noch, Abi´da, and Elda´ah. All these were the de-scendants of Ketu´rah.

34Abraham was the father of Isaac. The sons of Isaac: Esau and Israel. 35The sons of Esau: Eli´phaz, Reu´el, Je´ush, Ja´lam, and Ko´rah. 36The sons of Eli´phaz: Te´man, Omar, Zephi, Ga´tam, Ke´naz, Timna, and Am´alek. 37The sons of Reu´el: Na´hath, Ze´rah, Shammah, and Mizzah.

38The sons of Se´ir: Lo´tan, Sho´bal, Zib´eon, An´ah, Di´shon, E´zer, and Di´shan. 39The sons of Lo´tan: Ho´ri and Homam; and Lotan's sister was Timna. 40The sons of Sho´bal: Al´ian, Man´ahath, E´bal, She´phi, and O´nam. The sons of Zib´eon: Ai´ah and An´ah. 41The sons of An´ah: Di´shon. The sons of Dishon: Hamran, Eshban, Ithran, and Che´ran. 42The sons of E´zer: Bilhan, Za´avan, and Ja´akan. The sons of Di´shan: Uz and A´ran.

43These are the kings who reigned in the land of E´dom before any king reigned over the Israelites: Be´la the son of Beor, the name of whose city was Din´habah. 44When Be´la died, Jobab the son of Ze´rah of Bozrah reigned in his stead. 45When Jobab died, Hu´sham of the land of the Te´manites reigned in his stead. 46When Hu´sham died, Ha´dad the son of Be´dad, who defeated Mid´ian in the country of Moab, reigned in his stead; and the name of his city was A´vith. 47When Ha´dad died, Samlah of Masre´kah reigned in his stead. 48When Samlah died, Sha´ul of Reho´both on the Euphra´tes reigned in his stead. 49When Sha´ul died, Ba´al-ha´nan, the son of Achbor, reigned in his stead. 50When Ba´al-ha´nan died, Ha´dad reigned in his stead; and the name of his city was Pa´i, and his wife's name Mehet´abel the daughter of Ma´tred, the daughter of Me´zahab. 51And Ha´dad died.

The chiefs of E´dom were: chiefs Timna, Al´iah, Je´theth, 52Oholiba´mah, E´lah, Pi´non,

53Ke´naz, Te´man, Mibzar, 54Mag´di-el, and I´ram; these are the chiefs of E´dom.

2 These are the sons of Israel: Reuben, Simeon, Levi, Judah, Is´sachar, Zeb´ulun, 2Dan, Joseph, Benjamin, Naph´tali, Gad, and Ash´er. 3The sons of Judah: Er, O´nan, and She´lah; these three Bath-shu´a the Canaanitess bore to him. Now Er, Judah's first-born, was wicked in the sight of the LORD, and he slew him. 4His daughter-in-law Ta´mar also bore him Per´ez and Ze´rah. Judah had five sons in all.

5The sons of Per´ez: Hezron and Ha´mul. 6The sons of Ze´rah: Zimri, Ethan, He´man, Calcol, and Dara, five in all. 7The sons of Carmi: A´char, the troubler of Israel, who transgressed in the matter of the devoted thing; 8and Ethan's son was Azari´ah.

9The sons of Hezron, that were born to him: Jerah´meel, Ram, and Chelu´bai. 10Ram was the father of Ammin´adab, and Amminadab was the father of Nahshon, prince of the sons of Judah. 11Nahshon was the father of Salma, Salma of Boaz, 12Boaz of O´bed, Obed of Jesse. 13Jesse was the father of Eli´ab his first-born, Abin´adab the second, Shim´e-a the third, 14Nethan´el the fourth, Raddai the fifth, 15Ozem the sixth, David the seventh; 16and their sisters were Zeru´iah and Ab´igail. The sons of Zeruiah: Abi´shai, Jo´ab, and As´ahel, three. 17Ab´igail bore Ama´sa, and the father of Amasa was Je´ther the Ish´maelite.

18Caleb the son of Hezron had children by his wife Azu´bah, and by Jer´ioth; and these were her sons: Jesher, Shobab, and Ardon. 19When Azu´bah died, Caleb married Eph´rath, who bore him Hur. 20Hur was the father of U´ri, and Uri was the father of Bez´alel.

21Afterward Hezron went in to the daughter of Ma´chir the father of Gilead, whom he married when he was sixty years old; and she bore him Segub; 22and Segub was the father of Ja´ir, who had twenty-three cities in the land of Gilead. 23But Ge´shur and Ar´am took from them Hav´voth-ja´ir, Ke´nath and its villages, sixty towns. All these were descendants of Ma´chir, the father of Gilead. 24After the death of Hezron, Caleb went in to Eph´rathah, the wife of Hezron his father, and she bore him Ash´hur, the father of Teko´a.

25The sons of Jerah´meel, the first-born of Hezron: Ram, his first-born, Bunah, Oren, Ozem, and Ahi´jah. 26Jerah´meel also had another wife, whose name was At´arah; she was the mother of O´nam. 27The sons of Ram, the first-born of Jerah´meel: Ma´az, Ja´min, and E´ker. 28The sons of O´nam: Shammai and Jada. The sons of Shammai: Na´dab and Abi´shur. 29The name of Abi´shur's wife was Ab´ihail, and she bore him Ahban and Molid. 30The sons of Na´dab: Se´led and Ap´pa-im; and Seled died childless. 31The sons of Ap´pa-im: Ishi. The sons of Ishi: Sheshan. The sons of Sheshan: Ahlai. 32The sons of Jada, Shammai's brother: Je´ther and Jonathan; and Jether died childless. 33The sons of Jonathan: Pe´leth and Zaza. These were the descendants of Jerah´meel. 34Now Sheshan had no sons, only daughters; but Sheshan had an Egyptian slave, whose name was Jarha. 35So Sheshan gave his daughter in marriage to Jarha his slave; and she bore him Attai. 36Attai was the father of Nathan, and Nathan of Zabad. 37Zabad was the father of Ephlal, and Ephlal of O´bed. 38O´bed was the father of Je´hu, and Jehu of Azari´ah. 39Azari´ah was the father of He´lez, and Helez of E´le-a´sah. 40E´le-a´sah was the father of Sismai, and Sismai of Shallum. 41Shallum was the father of Jekami´ah, and Jekamiah of Elish´ama.

42The sons of Caleb the brother of Jerah´meel: Mare´shah his first-born, who was the father of Ziph. The sons of Mareshah: He´bron. 43The sons of He´bron: Ko´rah, Tap´pu-ah, Re´kem, and Shema. 44Shema was the father of Raham, the father of Jor´ke-am; and Re´kem was the father of Shammai. 45The son of Shammai: Maon; and Maon was the father of Beth-zur. 46E´phah also, Caleb's concubine, bore Haran, Moza, and Gazez; and Haran was the father of Gazez. 47The sons of Jahdai: Re´gem, Jo´tham, Geshan, Pe´let, E´phah, and Sha´aph. 48Ma´acah, Caleb's concubine, bore Sheber and Tir´hanah. 49She also bore Sha´aph the father of Madman´nah, Sheva the father of Machbe´nah and the father of Gib´e-a; and the daughter of Caleb was Achsah. 50These were the descendants of Caleb.

The sons of Hur the first-born of Eph′ra-
thah: Sho′bal the father of Kir′iath-je′arim,
51Salma, the father of Bethlehem, and Hareph
the father of Beth-ga′der. 52Sho′bal the father
of Kir′iath-je′arim had other sons: Haro′eh,
half of the Menu′hoth. 53And the families of
Kir′iath-je′arim: the Ithrites, the Puthites, the
Shu′mathites, and the Mish′raites; from these
came the Zorathites and the Esh′taolites. 54The
sons of Salma: Bethlehem, the Netoph′athites,
At′roth-beth-jo′ab, and half of the Man″a-
ha′thites, the Zorites. 55The families also of the
scribes that dwelt at Ja′bez: the Ti′rathites, the
Shim′e-athites, and the Su′cathites. These are
the Kenites who came from Hammath, the father of the house of Re′chab.

A Psalm of David.

PSALM 141 [140]

I call upon you, O Lord; make haste to me!
Give ear to my voice, when I call to you!
2Let my prayer be counted as incense before you,
and the lifting up of my hands as an evening sacrifice!

3Set a guard over my mouth, O Lord,
keep watch over the door of my lips!
4Incline not my heart to any evil,
to busy myself with wicked deeds
in company with men who work iniquity;
and let me not eat of their dainties!

5Let a good man strike or rebuke me in kindness,
but let the oil of the wicked never anoint my head;
for my prayer is continually against their wicked deeds.
6When they are given over to those who shall condemn them,
then they shall learn that the word of the Lord is true.
7As a rock which one cleaves and shatters on the land,
so shall their bones be strewn at the mouth of Sheol.
8But my eyes are toward you, O Lord God;
in you I seek refuge; leave me not defenseless!
9Keep me from the trap which they have laid for me,
and from the snares of evildoers!
10Let the wicked together fall into their own nets,
while I escape.

JOHN 21

**After this Jesus revealed him-
self again to the disciples by the
Sea of Tibe′ri-as; and he revealed himself in this way. 2Simon Peter, Thomas**
called the Twin, Nathan′a-el of Cana in Galilee, the sons of Zeb′edee, and two others
of his disciples were together. 3Simon Peter
said to them, "I am going fishing." They said
to him, "We will go with you." They went
out and got into the boat; but that night they
caught nothing.

4Just as day was breaking, Jesus stood on
the beach; yet the disciples did not know that
it was Jesus. 5Jesus said to them, "Children,
have you any fish?" They answered him,
"No." 6He said to them, "Cast the net on
the right side of the boat, and you will find
some." So they cast it, and now they were
not able to haul it in, for the quantity of
fish. 7That disciple whom Jesus loved said
to Peter, "It is the Lord!" When Simon Peter
heard that it was the Lord, he put on his
clothes, for he was stripped for work, and
sprang into the sea. 8But the other disciples
came in the boat, dragging the net full of
fish, for they were not far from the land, but
about a hundred yards off.

9When they got out on land, they saw a
charcoal fire there, with fish lying on it,
and bread. 10Jesus said to them, "Bring
some of the fish that you have just caught."
11So Simon Peter went aboard and hauled
the net ashore, full of large fish, a hundred
and fifty-three of them; and although there
were so many, the net was not torn. 12Jesus
said to them, "Come and have breakfast."

Now none of the disciples dared ask him, "Who are you?" They knew it was the Lord.
13Jesus came and took the bread and gave it to them, and so with the fish.
14This was now the third time that Jesus was revealed to the disciples after he was raised from the dead.
15When they had finished breakfast, Jesus said to Simon Peter, "Simon, son of John, do you love me more than these?" He said to him, "Yes, Lord; you know that I love you." He said to him, "Feed my lambs."
16A second time he said to him, "Simon, son of John, do you love me?" He said to him, "Yes, Lord; you know that I love you." He said to him, "Tend my sheep."
17He said to him the third time, "Simon, son of John, do you love me?" Peter was grieved because he said to him the third time, "Do you love me?" And he said to him, "Lord, you know everything; you know that I love you." Jesus said to him, "Feed my sheep.
18Truly, truly, I say to you, when you were young, you fastened your own belt and walked where you would; but when you are old, you will stretch out your hands, and another will fasten your belt for you and carry you where you do not wish to go."
19(This he said to show by what death he was to glorify God.) And after this he said to him, "Follow me."
20Peter turned and saw following them the disciple whom Jesus loved, who had lain close to his breast at the supper and had said, "Lord, who is it that is going to betray you?"
21When Peter saw him, he said to Jesus, "Lord, what about this man?"
22Jesus said to him, "If it is my will that he remain until I come, what is that to you? Follow me!"
23The saying spread abroad among the brethren that this disciple was not to die; yet Jesus did not say to him that he was not to die, but, "If it is my will that he remain until I come, what is that to you?"
24This is the disciple who is bearing witness to these things, and who has written these things; and we know that his testimony is true.
25But there are also many other things which Jesus did; were every one of them to be written, I suppose that the world itself could not contain the books that would be written.

REFLECTION

Reading through the first few chapters of 1 Chronicles is like flipping through a family photo album. The story of Genesis is recapitulated with the genealogies of Adam, Abraham, and Jacob. Almost every name contains a mysterious meaning: Shem meaning "name"; Isaac, "he laughs"; David, "beloved." Each line in the genealogy is merely the beginning of a story—whether the story of Israel or the story of the nations near Israel: Ammon, Edom, or Egypt. Every Israelite could find his place in history, the point at which his own story dovetailed with the Bible's story, by locating his own family in the genealogy. Far from being alienating, the genealogies would be highly personalizing, bringing the story of salvation close to home. We truly need a personal encounter with the Lord and a personal appropriation of the Word in order for it to impact our lives. St. Peter shows how a soul who has come to know the Word personally can respond in faith. When he sees the risen Jesus on the shore, he "sprang into the sea" to swim to him (Jn 21:7). He is soon confronted with his own sins and invited to join Jesus afresh by declaring his love for him. In what ways have you made the story of salvation your own?

June 19

1 CHRONICLES 3

These are the sons of David that were born to him in He′bron: the first-born Amnon, by Ahin′o-am the Jezre′elitess; the second Daniel, by
Ab′igail the Car′melitess, 2the third Ab′sa-
lom, whose mother was Ma′acah, the daughter of Talmai, king of Ge′shur; the fourth
Adoni′jah, whose mother was Haggith; 3the
fifth Shephati′ah, by Abi′tal; the sixth Ith′re-
am, by his wife Eglah; 4six were born to him
in He′bron, where he reigned for seven years

and six months. And he reigned thirty-three
years in Jerusalem. 5These were born to him
in Jerusalem: Shim′e-a, Sho′bab, Nathan, and
Solomon, four by Bath-shu′a, the daughter of
Am′mi-el; 6then Ibhar, Elish′ama, Eliph′elet,
7No′gah, Ne′pheg, Japhi′a, 8Elish′ama, Eli′ada,
and Eliph′elet, nine. 9All these were David's
sons, besides the sons of the concubines; and
Ta′mar was their sister.
10The descendants of Solomon: Rehobo′am,
Abi′jah his son, Asa his son, Jehosh′aphat his
son, 11Jo′ram his son, Ahazi′ah his son, Jo′ash
his son, 12Amazi′ah his son, Azari′ah his son,
Jo′tham his son, 13A′haz his son, Hezeki′ah
his son, Manas′seh his son, 14A′mon his son,
Josi′ah his son. 15The sons of Josi′ah: Joha′nan
the first-born, the second Jehoi′akim, the
third Zedeki′ah, the fourth Shallum. 16The
descendants of Jehoi′akim: Jeconi′ah his son,
Zedeki′ah his son; 17and the sons of Jeconi′ah,
the captive: She-al′ti-el his son, 18Malchi′ram,
Pedai′ah, Shenaz′zar, Jekami′ah, Hosh′ama,
and Nedabi′ah; 19and the sons of Pedai′ah:
Zerub′babel and Shim′e-i; and the sons of
Zerubbabel: Meshul′lam and Hanani′ah, and
Shelo′mith was their sister; 20and Hashu′bah,
O′hel, Berechi′ah, Hasadi′ah, and Ju′shab-
he′sed, five. 21The sons of Hanani′ah: Pelati′ah
and Jesha′iah, his son Rephai′ah, his son
Arnan, his son Obadi′ah, his son Shecani′ah.
22The sons of Shecani′ah: Shemai′ah. And
the sons of Shemaiah: Hattush, I′gal, Bari′ah,
Neari′ah, and Sha′phat, six. 23The sons of
Neari′ah: El′i-o-e′nai, Hizki′aj, and Azri′kam,
three. 24The sons of El′i-o-e′nai: Hod″avi′ah,
Eli′ashib, Pelai′ah, Akkub, Joha′nan, Delai′ah,
and Ana′ni, seven.

4 The sons of Judah: Per′ez, Hezron, Carmi,
Hur, and Sho′bal. 2Re-ai′ah the son
of Sho′bal was the father of Jahath, and Jahath was the father of Ahu′mai and Lahad.
These were the families of the Zo′rathites.
3These were the sons of E′tam: Jezre′el, Ish-
ma, and Idbash; and the name of their sister was Hazzelelpo′ni, 4and Penu′el was
the father of Gedor, and E′zer the father of
Hu′shah. These were the sons of Hur, the
first-born of Eph′rathah, the father of Bethlehem. 5Ash′hur, the father of Teko′a, had
two wives, He′lah and Na′arah; 6Na′arah
bore him Ahuz′zam, He′pher, Te′meni,
and Ha-a-hash′tari. These were the sons of
Naarah. 7The sons of He′lah: Ze′reth, Izhar,
and Ethnan. 8Koz was the father of A′nub,
Zobe′bah, and the families of Ahar′hel the
son of Harum. 9Ja′bez was more honorable
than his brothers; and his mother called
his name Jabez, saying, "Because I bore
him in pain." 10Ja′bez called on the God
of Israel, saying, "Oh that you would bless
me and enlarge my border, and that your
hand might be with me, and that you would
keep me from harm so that it might not
hurt me!" And God granted what he asked.
11Che′lub, the brother of Shu′hah, was the
father of Me′hir, who was the father of Esh-
ton. 12Eshton was the father of Bethra′pha,
Pase′ah, and Tehin′nah the father of Ir-
na′hash. These are the men of Re′cah. 13The
sons of Ke′naz: Oth′ni-el and Serai′ah;
and the sons of Othni-el: Ha′thath and
Meo′nothai. 14Meo′nothai was the father
of Oph′rah; and Serai′ah was the father of
Jo′ab the father of Ge-har′ashim, so-called
because they were craftsmen. 15The sons of
Caleb the son of Jephun′neh: Iru, E′lah, and
Na′am; and the sons of Elah: Ke′naz. 16The
sons of Jehal′lelel: Ziph, Ziphah, Tir′i-a, and
As′arel. 17The sons of Ezrah: Je′ther, Me′red,
E′pher, and Ja′lon. These are the sons of
Bith′i-ah, the daughter of Pharaoh, whom
Mered married; and she conceived and
bore Miriam, Sham′mai, and Ish′bah, the
father of Eshtemo′a. 18And his Jewish wife
bore Je′red the father of Gedor, He′ber the
father of Soco, and Jeku′thiel the father of
Zano′ah. 19The sons of the wife of Hodi′ah,
the sister of Na′ham, were the fathers of
Kei′lah the Garmite and Eshtemo′a the Ma-
ac′athite. 20The sons of Shimon: Amnon,
Rinnah, Ben-ha′nan, and Ti′lon. The sons
of Ishi: Zoheth and Ben-zo′heth. 21The sons
of She′lah the son of Judah: Er the father
of Lecah, La′adah the father of Mare′shah,
and the families of the house of linen workers at Beth-ashbe′a; 22and Jokim, and the
men of Coze′ba, and Jo′ash, and Saraph,
who ruled in Moab and returned to Lehem
(now the records are ancient). 23These were
the potters and inhabitants of Neta′im and

Gede´rah; they dwelt there with the king for his work.

24The sons of Simeon: Nem´u-el, Ja´min, Ja´rib, Ze´rah, Sha´ul; 25Shallum was his son, Mib´sam his son, Mishma his son. 26The sons of Mishma: Ham´mu-el his son, Zaccur his son, Shim´e-i his son. 27Shim´e-i had sixteen sons and six daughters; but his brothers had not many children, nor did all their family multiply like the men of Judah. 28They dwelt in Be´er-she´ba, Mo´ladah, Ha´zar-shu´al, 29Bilhah, E´zem, To´lad, 30Bethu´el, Hormah, Zik´lag, 31Beth-mar´caboth, Ha´zar-su´sim, Beth-bir´i, and Sha-ara´im. These were their cities until David reigned. 32And their villages were E´tam, A´in, Rimmon, Tochen, and A´shan, five cities, 33along with all their villages which were round about these cities as far as Ba´al. These were their settlements, and they kept a genealogical record.

34Mesho´bab, Jamlech, Joshah the son of Amazi´ah, 35Joel, Je´hu the son of Joshibi´ah, son of Serai´ah, son of As´i-el, 36Eli-o-e´nai, Ja″ako´bah, Jeshohai´ah, Asai´ah, Ad´i-el, Jesim´i-el, Bena´iah, 37Ziza the son of Shi´phi, son of Allon, son of Jedai´ah, son of Shimri, son of Shemai´ah—38these mentioned by name were princes in their families, and their fathers' houses increased greatly. 39They journeyed to the entrance of Gedor, to the east side of the valley, to seek pasture for their flocks, 40where they found rich, good pasture, and the land was very broad, quiet, and peaceful; for the former inhabitants there belonged to Ham. 41These, registered by name, came in the days of Hezeki´ah, king of Judah, and destroyed their tents and the Me-u´nim who were found there, and exterminated them to this day, and settled in their place, because there was pasture there for their flocks. 42And some of them, five hundred men of the Simeonites, went to Mount Se´ir, having as their leaders Pelati´ah, Ne-ari´ah, Rephai´ah, and Uz´ziel, the sons of Ishi; 43and they destroyed the remnant of the Amal´ekites that had escaped, and they have dwelt there to this day.

5 The sons of Reuben the first-born of Israel (for he was the first-born; but because he polluted his father's couch, his birthright was given to the sons of Joseph the son of Israel, so that he is not enrolled in the genealogy according to the birthright; 2though Judah became strong among his brothers and a prince was from him, yet the birthright belonged to Joseph), 3the sons of Reuben, the first-born of Israel: Ha´noch, Pallu, Hezron, and Carmi. 4The sons of Joel: Shemai´ah his son, Gog his son, Shim´e-i his son, 5Micah his son, Re-ai´ah his son, Ba´al his son, 6Beer´ah his son, whom Til´gath-pilne´ser king of Assyria carried away into exile; he was a chieftain of the Reubenites. 7And his kinsmen by their families, when the genealogy of their generations was reckoned: the chief, Je-i´el, and Zechari´ah, 8and Be´la the son of A´zaz, son of She´ma, son of Joel, who dwelt in Aro´er, as far as Nebo and Ba´al-me´on. 9He also dwelt to the east as far as the entrance of the desert this side of the Euphrates, because their cattle had multiplied in the land of Gilead. 10And in the days of Saul they made war on the Hag´rites, who fell by their hand; and they dwelt in their tents throughout all the region east of Gilead.

11The sons of Gad dwelt over against them in the land of Bashan as far as Sal´ecah: 12Joel the chief, Sha´pham the second, Ja´nai, and Sha´phat in Bashan. 13And their kinsmen according to their fathers' houses: Michael, Meshul´lam, Sheba, Jo´rai, Ja´can, Zia, and E´ber, seven. 14These were the sons of Ab´ihail the son of Huri, son of Jaro´ah, son of Gilead, son of Michael, son of Jeshish´ai, son of Jahdo, son of Buz; 15A´hi the son of Ab´di-el, son of Gu´ni, was chief in their fathers' houses; 16and they dwelt in Gilead, in Bashan and in its towns, and in all the pasture lands of Sharon to their limits. 17All of these were enrolled by genealogies in the days of Jo´tham king of Judah, and in the days of Jerobo´am king of Israel.

18The Reubenites, the Gadites, and the half-tribe of Manas´seh had valiant men, who carried shield and sword, and drew the bow, expert in war, forty-four thousand seven hundred and sixty, ready for service. 19They made war upon the Hag´rites, Je´tur, Na´phish, and No´dab; 20and when they received help against them, the Hag´rites and all who were with them were given into their hands, for they cried to God in the battle, and he granted their

entreaty because they trusted in him. [21]They
carried off their livestock: fifty thousand of
their camels, two hundred and fifty thousand
sheep, two thousand donkeys, and a hundred
thousand men alive. [22]For many fell slain,
because the war was of God. And they dwelt in
their place until the exile.
[23]The members of the half-tribe of Manas′seh
dwelt in the land; they were very numerous
from Ba′shan to Ba′al-her′mon, Se′nir, and
Mount Hermon. [24]These were the heads of
their fathers' houses: E′pher, Ishi, Eli′el, Az′ri-
el, Jeremi′ah, Hod″avi′ah, and Jah′di-el, mighty
warriors, famous men, heads of their fathers'
houses. [25]But they transgressed against the God
of their fathers, and played the harlot after the
gods of the peoples of the land, whom God had
destroyed before them. [26]So the God of Israel
stirred up the spirit of Pul king of Assyria, the
spirit of Til′gath-pilne′ser king of Assyria, and
he carried them away, namely, the Reubenites,
the Gadites, and the half-tribe of Manas′seh,
and brought them to Ha′lah, Ha′bor, Hara, and
the river Gozan, to this day.

A Maskil of David, when he was in the cave.

A Prayer.

PSALM 142 [141]

I cry with my voice to the LORD,
with my voice I make supplication to
the LORD,
[2]I pour out my complaint before him,
I tell my trouble before him.
[3]When my spirit is faint,
you know my way!

In the path where I walk
they have hidden a trap for me.
[4]I look to the right and watch,
but there is none who takes notice of me;
no refuge remains to me,
no man cares for me.

[5]I cry to you, O LORD;
I say, You are my refuge,
my portion in the land of the living.
[6]Give heed to my cry;
for I am brought very low!

Deliver me from my persecutors;
for they are too strong for me!
[7]Bring me out of prison,
that I may give thanks to your name!
The righteous will surround me;
for you will deal bountifully with me.

A Psalm of David.

PSALM 143 [142]

Hear my prayer, O LORD; give ear
to my supplications!
In your faithfulness answer me, in your
righteousness!
[2]Enter not into judgment with your servant;
for no man living is righteous before you.

[3]For the enemy has pursued me;
he has crushed my life to the ground;
he has made me sit in darkness like those
long dead.
[4]Therefore my spirit faints within me;
my heart within me is appalled.

[5]I remember the days of old,
I meditate on all that you have done;
I muse on what your hands have wrought.
[6]I stretch out my hands to you;
my soul thirsts for you like a parched land.
Selah

[7]Make haste to answer me, O LORD!
My spirit fails!
Hide not your face from me,
lest I be like those who go down to the Pit.
[8]Let me hear in the morning of your
merciful love,
for in you I put my trust.
Teach me the way I should go,
for to you I lift up my soul.

[9]Deliver me, O LORD, from my enemies!
I have fled to you for refuge!
[10]Teach me to do your will,
for you are my God!
Let your good spirit lead me
on a level path!

11For your name's sake, O LORD, preserve
my life!
In your righteousness bring me out
of trouble!
12And in your steadfast love cut off
my enemies,
and destroy all my adversaries,
for I am your servant.

ACTS 1

In the first book, O Theoph′ilus,
I have dealt with all that Jesus
began to do and teach, 2until the
day when he was taken up, after he had
given commandment through the Holy
Spirit to the apostles whom he had
chosen. 3To them he presented himself alive
after his passion by many proofs, appearing
to them during forty days, and speaking of
the kingdom of God. 4And while staying
with them he charged them not to depart
from Jerusalem, but to wait for the promise
of the Father, which, he said, "you heard
from me, 5for John baptized with water,
but before many days you shall be baptized
with the Holy Spirit."
6So when they had come together, they
asked him, "Lord, will you at this time
restore the kingdom to Israel?" 7He said
to them, "It is not for you to know times
or seasons which the Father has fixed by
his own authority. 8But you shall receive
power when the Holy Spirit has come
upon you; and you shall be my witnesses
in Jerusalem and in all Judea and Samar′ia
and to the end of the earth." 9And when
he had said this, as they were looking on,
he was lifted up, and a cloud took him
out of their sight. 10And while they were
gazing into heaven as he went, behold,
two men stood by them in white robes,
11and said, "Men of Galilee, why do you
stand looking into heaven? This Jesus,
who was taken up from you into heaven,
will come in the same way as you saw him
go into heaven."

REFLECTION

Part of prayer is acknowledging our powerlessness and putting our trust in God's power instead. Psalms 142 and 143 show us a complaining supplicant, telling his troubles to God: "I am brought very low!" (Ps 142:6); "he has crushed my life to the ground" (Ps 143:3). The psalmist entrusts himself to God's power with his petitions: "You are my refuge" (Ps 142:5). The urgency of his cry for divine help is undiminished as he begs the Lord to hurry and not hide, to hear and to deliver. The famous prayer of Jabez likewise exhibits reliance on the Lord for help and blessing (see 1 Chr 4:10). Moreover, Jesus's last instruction to the Apostles shows how they need God's power, not human cleverness, to accomplish the mission: "You shall receive power when the Holy Spirit has come upon you" (Acts 1:8). When we powerless people petition the powerful God, these passages remind us to recall his mighty deeds. Acts of remembrance figure prominently in the psalmist's plea (see Ps 143:5). Recalling the Lord's record of faithfulness inspires our confidence in prayer. We cannot fix all of our own problems but need to depend on the one who is mightier than us. How can you more fully entrust yourself to the Lord's powerful help?

June 20

---

1 CHRONICLES 6

The sons of Levi: Gershom,
Ko′hath, and Merar′i. 2The sons
of Ko′hath: Amram, Izhar, Heb′ron,
and Uz′ziel. 3The children of Amram:
Aaron, Moses, and Miriam. The sons of
Aaron: Na′dab, Abi′hu, Elea′zar, and Ith′amar.
4Elea′zar was the father of Phin′ehas,
Phinehas of Abishu′a, 5Abishu′a of Bukki,
Bukki of Uzzi, 6Uzzi of Zerahi′ah, Zerahiah of
Mera′ioth, 7Mera′ioth of Amari′ah, Amariah
of Ahi′tub, 8Ahi′tub of Za′dok, Zadok of

Ahim′a-az, [9]Ahim′a-az of Azari′ah, Azariah of Joha′nan, [10]and Joha′nan of Azari′ah (it was he who served as priest in the house that Solomon built in Jerusalem). [11]Azari′ah was the father of Amari′ah, Amariah of Ahi′tub, [12]Ahi′tub of Za′dok, Zadok of Shallum, [13]Shallum of Hilki′ah, Hilkiah of Azari′ah, [14]Azari′ah of Serai′ah, Seraiah of Jehoz′adak; [15]and Jehoz′adak went into exile when the LORD sent Judah and Jerusalem into exile by the hand of Nebuchadnez′zar.

[16]The sons of Levi: Gershom, Ko′hath, and Merar′i. [17]And these are the names of the sons of Gershom: Libni and Shim′e-i. [18]The sons of Ko′hath: Amram, Izhar, He′bron, and Uz′ziel. [19]The sons of Merar′i: Mah′li and Mu′shi. These are the families of the Levites according to their fathers. [20]Of Gershom: Libni his son, Jahath his son, Zimmah his son, [21]Jo′ah his son, Iddo his son, Ze′rah his son, Je-ath′erai his son. [22]The sons of Ko′hath: Ammin′adab his son, Ko′rah his son, Assir his son, [23]Elka′nah his son, Ebi′asaph his son, Assir his son, [24]Ta′hath his son, Uri′el his son, Uzzi′ah his son, and Sha′ul his son. [25]The sons of Elka′nah: Ama′sai and Ahi′moth, [26]Elka′nah his son, Zo′phai his son, Na′hath his son, [27]Eli′ab his son, Jero′ham his son, Elka′nah his son. [28]The sons of Samuel: Joel his first-born, the second Abi′jah. [29]The sons of Merar′i: Mah′li, Libni his son, Shim′e-i his son, Uzzah his son, [30]Shim′e-a his son, Haggi′ah his son, and Asai′ah his son.

[31]These are the men whom David put in charge of the service of song in the house of the LORD, after the ark rested there. [32]They ministered with song before the tabernacle of the tent of meeting, until Solomon had built the house of the LORD in Jerusalem; and they performed their service in due order. [33]These are the men who served and their sons. Of the sons of the Ko′hathites: He′man the singer the son of Joel, son of Samuel, [34]son of Elka′nah, son of Jero′ham, son of Eli′el, son of To′ah, [35]son of Zuph, son of Elka′nah, son of Mahath, son of Ama′sai, [36]son of Elka′nah, son of Joel, son of Azari′ah, son of Zephani′ah, [37]son of Ta′hath, son of Assir, son of Ebi′asaph, son of Ko′rah, [38]son of Izhar, son of Ko′hath, son of Levi, son of Israel; [39]and his brother A′saph, who stood on his right hand, namely, Asaph the son of Berechi′ah, son of Shim′e-a, [40]son of Michael, son of Ba-ase′iah, son of Malchi′jah, [41]son of Ethni, son of Ze′rah, son of Adai′ah, [42]son of Ethan, son of Zimmah, son of Shim′e-i, [43]son of Jahath, son of Gershom, son of Levi. [44]On the left hand were their brethren the sons of Merar′i: Ethan the son of Kishi, son of Abdi, son of Mal′luch, [45]son of Hashabi′ah, son of Amazi′ah, son of Hilki′ah, [46]son of Amzi, son of Ba′ni, son of She′mer, [47]son of Mah′li, son of Mu′shi, son of Merar′i, son of Levi; [48]and their brethren the Levites were appointed for all the service of the tabernacle of the house of God.

[49]But Aaron and his sons made offerings upon the altar of burnt offering and upon the altar of incense for all the work of the most holy place, and to make atonement for Israel, according to all that Moses the servant of God had commanded. [50]These are the sons of Aaron: Elea′zar his son, Phin′ehas his son, Abishu′a his son, [51]Bukki his son, Uzzi his son, Zerahi′ah his son, [52]Mera′ioth his son, Amari′ah his son, Ahi′tub his son, [53]Za′dok his son, Ahim′a-az his son.

[54]These are their dwelling places according to their settlements within their borders: to the sons of Aaron of the families of Ko′hathites, for theirs was the lot, [55]to them they gave He′bron in the land of Judah and its surrounding pasture lands, [56]but the fields of the city and its villages they gave to Caleb the son of Jephun′neh. [57]To the sons of Aaron they gave the cities of refuge: He′bron, Libnah with its pasture lands, Jat′tir, Eshtemo′a with its pasture lands, [58]Hilen with its pasture lands, De′bir with its pasture lands, [59]A′shan with its pasture lands, and Beth-she′mesh with its pasture lands; [60]and from the tribe of Benjamin, Ge′ba with its pasture lands, Al′emeth with its pasture lands, and An′athoth with its pasture lands. All their cities throughout their families were thirteen.

[61]To the rest of the Ko′hathites were given by lot out of the family of the tribe, out of the

half-tribe, the half of Manas′seh, ten cities.
62To the Ger′shomites according to their
families were allotted thirteen cities out of
the tribes of Is′sachar, Asher, Naph′tali, and
Manas′seh in Bashan. 63To the Merar′ites
according to their families were allotted
twelve cities out of the tribes of Reuben,
Gad, and Zeb′ulun. 64So the sons of Israel
gave the Levites the cities with their pasture
lands. 65They also gave them by lot out of
the tribes of Judah, Simeon, and Benjamin
these cities which are mentioned by name.
66And some of the families of the sons of
Ko′hath had cities of their territory out of
the tribe of E′phraim. 67They were given the
cities of refuge: She′chem with its pasture
lands in the hill country of E′phraim, Gezer
with its pasture lands, 68Jok′me-am with its
pasture lands, Beth-ho′ron with its pasture
lands, 69Ai′jalon with its pasture lands,
Gath-rim′mon with its pasture lands, 70and
out of the half-tribe of Manas′seh, A′ner
with its pasture lands, and Bil′e-am with its
pasture lands, for the rest of the families of
the Ko′hathites.
71To the Ger′shomites were given out of
the half-tribe of Manas′seh: Golan in Bashan
with its pasture lands and Ash′taroth with
its pasture lands; 72and out of the tribe of
Is′sachar: Ke′desh with its pasture lands,
Dab′erath with its pasture lands, 73Ra′moth
with its pasture lands, and A′nem with its
pasture lands; 74out of the tribe of Asher:
Mashal with its pasture lands, Abdon with
its pasture lands, 75Hukok with its pasture
lands, and Re′hob with its pasture lands;
76and out of the tribe of Naph′tali: Ke′desh
in Galilee with its pasture lands, Ham′mon
with its pasture lands, and Kir″iatha′im
with its pasture lands. 77To the rest of the
Merar′ites were allotted out of the tribe of
Zeb′ulun: Rim′mono with its pasture lands,
Ta′bor with its pasture lands, 78and beyond
the Jordan at Jericho, on the east side of
the Jordan, out of the tribe of Reuben:
Bezer in the steppe with its pasture lands,
Jah′zah with its pasture lands, 79Ked′emoth
with its pasture lands, and Meph′a-ath with
its pasture lands; 80and out of the tribe of
Gad: Ra′moth in Gilead with its pasture
lands, Ma″hana′im with its pasture lands,
81Hesh′bon with its pasture lands, and Ja′zer
with its pasture lands.

A Psalm of David.

PSALM 144 [143]

Blessed be the Lord, my rock,
who trains my hands for war,
and my fingers for battle;
2my mercy and my fortress,
my stronghold and my deliverer,
my shield and he in whom I take refuge,
who subdues my people under me.

3O Lord, what is man that you regard him,
or the son of man that you think of him?
4Man is like a breath,
his days are like a passing shadow.

5Bow your heavens, O Lord, and
come down!
Touch the mountains that they smoke!
6Flash forth the lightning and scatter them,
send out your arrows and rout them!
7Stretch forth your hand from on high,
rescue me and deliver me from the
many waters,
from the hand of aliens,
8whose mouths speak lies,
and whose right hand is a right hand
of falsehood.

9I will sing a new song to you, O God;
upon a ten-stringed harp I will play to you,
10who give victory to kings,
who rescue David your servant from the
cruel sword.
11Rescue me from the cruel sword,
and deliver me from the hand of aliens,
whose mouths speak lies,
and whose right hand is a right hand
of falsehood.

12May our sons in their youth
be like plants full grown,
our daughters like corner pillars
cut for the structure of a palace;

[13]may our garners be full,
providing all manner of store;
may our sheep bring forth thousands
and ten thousands in our fields;
[14]may our cattle be heavy with young,
suffering no mischance or failure
in bearing;
may there be no cry of distress in our streets!
[15]Happy the people to whom such
blessings fall!
Happy the people whose God is the LORD!

ACTS 1

[12]Then they returned to Jeru-
salem from the mount called
Olivet, which is near Jerusalem, a sabbath
day's journey away; [13]and when they had
entered, they went up to the upper room,
where they were staying, Peter and John
and James and Andrew, Philip and Thomas,
Bartholomew and Matthew, James the son
of Alphae´us and Simon the Zealot and
Judas the son of James. [14]All these with
one accord devoted themselves to prayer,
together with the women and Mary the
mother of Jesus, and with his brethren.
[15]In those days Peter stood up among the
brethren (the company of persons was in
all about a hundred and twenty), and said,
[16]"Brethren, the Scripture had to be fulfilled,
which the Holy Spirit spoke beforehand
by the mouth of David, concerning Judas
who was guide to those who arrested Jesus.
[17]For he was numbered among us, and was
allotted his share in this ministry. [18](Now
this man bought a field with the reward
of his wickedness; and falling headlong he
burst open in the middle and all his bowels
gushed out. [19]And it became known to all
the inhabitants of Jerusalem, so that the field
was called in their language Akel´dama, that
is, Field of Blood.) [20]For it is written in the
book of Psalms,
'Let his habitation become desolate,
and let there be no one to live in it';
and
'His office let another take.'
[21]So one of the men who have accompanied us during all the time that the
Lord Jesus went in and out among us,
[22]beginning from the baptism of John until
the day when he was taken up from us—
one of these men must become with us
a witness to his resurrection." [23]And
they put forward two, Joseph called
Barsab´bas, who was surnamed Justus,
and Matthi´as. [24]And they prayed and
said, "Lord, you know the hearts of all
men, show which one of these two you
have chosen [25]to take the place in this
ministry and apostleship from which
Judas turned aside, to go to his own
place." [26]And they cast lots for them,
and the lot fell on Matthi´as; and he was
enrolled with the eleven apostles.

2 When the day of Pentecost had come,
they were all together in one place.
[2]And suddenly a sound came from heaven
like the rush of a mighty wind, and it filled
all the house where they were sitting.
[3]And there appeared to them tongues as
of fire, distributed and resting on each
one of them. [4]And they were all filled with
the Holy Spirit and began to speak in other
tongues, as the Spirit gave them utterance.
[5]Now there were dwelling in Jerusalem
Jews, devout men from every nation
under heaven. [6]And at this sound the
multitude came together, and they were
bewildered, because each one heard them
speaking in his own language. [7]And they
were amazed and wondered, saying,
"Are not all these who are speaking
Galileans? [8]And how is it that we hear,
each of us in his own native language?
[9]Par´thians and Medes and E´la-mites and
residents of Mesopota´mia, Judea and
Cappado´cia, Pontus and Asia, [10]Phryg´ia
and Pamphyl´ia, Egypt and the parts of
Libya belonging to Cyre´ne, and visitors
from Rome, both Jews and proselytes,
[11]Cretans and Arabians, we hear them
telling in our own tongues the mighty
works of God." [12]And all were amazed and
perplexed, saying to one another, "What
does this mean?" [13]But others mocking
said, "They are filled with new wine."

REFLECTION

Whereas 1 Chronicles 3 presented the kings of Judah, here we have the genealogy of Levites, priests, and high priests. The text also lists the ancestral lands given to the Levites, recording their legal right to possess certain cities and pastures. Land was destiny for the ancients. To have an ancestral claim on land was to have not only a past but a future with the Lord in the land. Land was not just an economic necessity but a tangible connection to God's promises. Psalm 144 builds on this idea, asking for the Lord's peace and for his blessing on children, farms, and animals: "May our sons in their youth be like plants full grown" (v. 12); "may our sheep bring forth thousands" (v. 13). The corporeal blessings that the psalmist longs for give way to spiritual blessings in the New Testament. The Apostles appear to be "filled with new wine," but, in fact, they are not drunk on any agricultural abundance but on the power of the promised Holy Spirit. The possession of the Promised Land and all its benefits has been translated to its awesome meaning: possessing access to the inner life of God, the "rest" of salvation that he gives. What will your future with the Lord be like?

June 21

1 CHRONICLES 7

The sons of Is′sachar: To′la, Puah, Jash′ub, and Shim′ron, four. 2The sons of To′la: Uzzi, Rephai′ah, Je′ri-el, Jahmai, Ibsam, and Shemu′el, heads of their fathers' houses, namely of Tola, mighty warriors of their generations, their number in the days of David being twenty-two thousand six hundred. 3The sons of Uzzi: Izrahi′ah. And the sons of Izrahiah: Michael, Obad′iah, Joel, and Isshi′ah, five, all of them chief men; 4and along with them, by their generations, according to their fathers' houses, were units of the army for war, thirty-six thousand, for they had many wives and sons. 5Their kinsmen belonging to all the families of Is′sachar were in all eighty-seven thousand mighty warriors, enrolled by genealogy.

6The sons of Benjamin: Be′la, Be′cher, and Jedi′a-el, three. 7The sons of Be′la: Ezbon, Uzzi, Uz′ziel, Jer′imoth, and Iri, five, heads of fathers' houses, mighty warriors; and their enrollment by genealogies was twenty-two thousand and thirty-four. 8The sons of Be′cher: Zemi′rah, Jo′ash, Elie′zer, El′i-o-e′nai, Omri, Jer′emoth, Abi′jah, An′athoth, and Al′emeth. All these were the sons of Becher; 9and their enrollment by genealogies, according to their generations, as heads of their fathers' houses, mighty warriors, was twenty thousand two hundred. 10The sons of Jedi′a-el: Bilhan. And the sons of Bilhan: Je′ush, Benjamin, E′hud, Chena′anah, Zethan, Tar′shish, and Ahish′ahar. 11All these were the sons of Jedi′a-el according to the heads of their fathers' houses, mighty warriors, seventeen thousand and two hundred, ready for service in war. 12And Shuppim and Huppim were the sons of Ir, Hu′shim the sons of A′her.

13The sons of Naph′tali: Jah′zi-el, Gu′ni, Je′zer, and Shallum, the offspring of Bilhah.

14The sons of Manas′seh: As′ri-el, whom his Arame′an concubine bore; she bore Ma′chir the father of Gilead. 15And Ma′chir took a wife for Huppim and for Shuppim. The name of his sister was Ma′acah. And the name of the second was Zeloph′ehad; and Zelophehad had daughters. 16And Ma′acah the wife of Ma′chir bore a son, and she called his name Peresh; and the name of his brother was Sheresh; and his sons were Ulam and Rakem. 17The sons of Ulam: Be′dan. These were the sons of Gilead the son of Ma′chir, son of Manas′seh. 18And his sister Hammo′lecheth bore Ish′hod, Abie′zer, and Mahlah. 19The sons of Shemi′da were Ahi′an, She′chem, Likhi, and Ani′am.

20The sons of E′phraim: Shuthe′lah, and Be′red his son, Ta′hath his son, Ele-a′dah his son, Tahath his son, 21Zabad his son, Shuthe′lah his son, and E′zer and E′le-ad, whom the men of Gath who were born in the land slew, because they came down to raid their cattle. 22And E′phraim their father mourned many

days, and his brothers came to comfort him.
23And E'phraim went in to his wife, and she
conceived and bore a son; and he called his
name Beri'ah, because evil had befallen his
house. 24His daughter was She'erah, who
built both Lower and Upper Beth-ho'ron,
and Uz'zen-she'erah. 25Rephah was his son,
Resheph his son, Te'lah his son, Ta'han his son,
26Ladan his son, Ammi'hud his son, Elish'ama
his son, 27Nun his son, Joshua his son. 28Their
possessions and settlements were Bethel and
its towns, and eastward Na'aran, and westward
Gezer and its towns, She'chem and its towns,
and Ayyah and its towns; 29also along the
borders of the Manas'sites, Beth-she'an and its
towns, Ta'anach and its towns, Megid'do and
its towns, Dor and its towns. In these dwelt the
sons of Joseph the son of Israel.

30The sons of Asher: Imnah, Ishvah, Ishvi,
Beri'ah, and their sister Se'rah. 31The sons of
Beri'ah: He'ber and Mal'chi-el, who was the
father of Bir'zaith. 32He'ber was the father of
Japhlet, Shomer, Ho'tham, and their sister
Shua. 33The sons of Japhlet: Pasach, Bimhal,
and Ashvath. These are the sons of Japhlet.
34The sons of She'mer his brother: Rohgah,
Jehub'bah, and Ar'am. 35The sons of He'lem
his brother: Zo'phah, Imna, Shelesh, and
A'mal. 36The sons of Zo'phah: Su'ah, Har'n-
epher, Shual, Beri, Imrah, 37Bezer, Hod,
Shamma, Shilshah, Ithran, and Be-e'ra. 38The
sons of Je'ther: Jephun'neh, Pispa, and Ar'a.
39The sons of Ulla: A'rah, Han'niel, and Rizi'a.
40All of these were men of Asher, heads of
fathers' houses, approved, mighty warriors,
chief of the princes. Their number enrolled by
genealogies, for service in war, was twenty-six
thousand men.

8 Benjamin was the father of Be'la his
first-born, Ash'bel the second, A'harah
the third, 2No'hah the fourth, and Ra'pha
the fifth. 3And Be'la had sons: Addar, Gera,
Abi'hud, 4Abishu'a, Na'aman, Aho'ah, 5Gera,
Shephu'phan, and Hu'ram. 6These are the
sons of E'hud (they were heads of fathers'
houses of the inhabitants of Ge'ba, and
they were carried into exile to Mana'hath):
7Na'aman, Ahi'jah, and Gera, that is, Heglam,
who was the father of Uzza and Ahi'hud.
8And Sha'hara'im had sons in the country
of Moab after he had sent away Hu'shim and
Ba'ara his wives. 9He had sons by Hodesh
his wife: Jo'bab, Zib'ia, Me'sha, Malcam,
10Je'uz, Sachi'a, and Mirmah. These were
his sons, heads of fathers' houses. 11He also
had sons by Hu'shim: Abi'tub and Elpa'al.
12The sons of Elpa'al: E'ber, Misham, and
She'med, who built Ono and Lod with its
towns, 13and Beri'ah and She'ma (they were
heads of fathers' houses of the inhabitants of
Ai'jalon, who put to flight the inhabitants of
Gath); 14and Ahi'o, Shashak, and Jer'emoth.
15Zebadi'ah, Ar'ad, E'der, 16Michael, Ishpah,
and Joha were sons of Beri'ah. 17Zebadi'ah,
Meshul'lam, Hizki, He'ber, 18Ish'merai, Izli'ah,
and Jo'bab were the sons of Elpa'al. 19Ja'kim,
Zich'ri, Zabdi, 20E'li-e'nai, Zil'le-thai, Eli'el,
21Adai'ah, Bera'iah, and Shimrath were
the sons of Shim'e-i. 22Ishpan, E'ber, Eli'el,
23Abdon, Zich'ri, Ha'nan, 24Hanani'ah,
E'lam, Anthothi'jah, 25Iphde'iah, and Penu'el
were the sons of Shashak. 26Sham'sherai,
Shehari'ah, Athali'ah, 27Ja-areshi'ah, Eli'jah,
and Zich'ri were the sons of Jero'ham.
28These were the heads of fathers' houses,
according to their generations, chief men.
These dwelt in Jerusalem.

29Je-i'el the father of Gib'eon dwelt in
Gibeon, and the name of his wife was
Ma'acah. 30His first-born son: Abdon, then
Zur, Kish, Ba'al, Na'dab, 31Gedor, Ahi'o,
Zecher, 32and Mikloth (he was the father of
Shim'e-ah). Now these also dwelt opposite
their kinsmen in Jerusalem, with their
kinsmen. 33Ner was the father of Kish, Kish
of Saul, Saul of Jonathan, Mal"chishu'a,
Abin'adab, and Eshba'al; 34and the son of
Jonathan was Mer'ib-ba'al; and Merib-baal
was the father of Micah. 35The sons of Micah:
Pithon, Melech, Tare'a, and A'haz. 36A'haz
was the father of Jeho'addah; and Jehoaddah
was the father of Al'emeth, Az'maveth, and
Zimri; Zimri was the father of Moza. 37Moza
was the father of Bin'e-a; Ra'phah was his son,
El-e-a'sah his son, A'zel his son. 38A'zel had
six sons, and these are their names: Azri'kam,
Bo'cheru, Ish'mael, Sheari'ah, Obadi'ah,
and Ha'nan. All these were the sons of Azel.
39The sons of E'shek his brother: Ulam his
first-born, Je'ush the second, and Eliph'elet

the third. 40 The sons of Ulam were men who
were mighty warriors, bowmen, having
many sons and grandsons, one hundred and
fifty. All these were Benjaminites.

9 So all Israel was enrolled by genealogies;
and these are written in the Book of the
Kings of Israel. And Judah was taken into exile
in Babylon because of their unfaithfulness.
2 Now the first to dwell again in their possessions
in their cities were Israel, the priests, the
Levites, and the temple servants. 3 And some of
the people of Judah, Benjamin, E´phraim, and
Manas´seh dwelt in Jerusalem: 4 Uthai the son
of Ammi´hud, son of Omri, son of Imri, son of
Ba´ni, from the sons of Per´ez the son of Judah.
5 And of the Shi´lonites: Asai´ah the first-born,
and his sons. 6 Of the sons of Ze´rah: Jeu´el and
their kinsmen, six hundred and ninety. 7 Of the
Benjaminites: Sallu the son of Meshul´lam, son
of Hod″avi´ah, son of Hassenu´ah, 8 Ibne´iah
the son of Jero´ham, E´lah the son of Uzzi,
son of Michri, and Meshul´lam the son of
Shephati´ah, son of Reu´el, son of Ibni´jah; 9 and
their kinsmen according to their generations,
nine hundred and fifty-six. All these were
heads of fathers' houses according to their
fathers' houses.

A Psalm of Praise.
Of David.

PSALM 145 [144]

I will extol you, my God and King,
and bless your name for ever and ever.
2 Every day I will bless you,
and praise your name for ever and ever.
3 Great is the LORD, and greatly to be praised,
and his greatness is unsearchable.

4 One generation shall laud your works
to another,
and shall declare your mighty acts.
5 On the glorious splendor of your majesty,
and on your wondrous works, I
will meditate.
6 Men shall proclaim the might of your
awesome acts,
and I will declare your greatness.
7 They shall pour forth the fame of your
abundant goodness,
and shall sing aloud of your righteousness.

8 The LORD is gracious and merciful,
slow to anger and abounding in mercy.
9 The LORD is good to all,
and his compassion is over all that he
has made.

10 All your works shall give thanks to you,
O LORD,
and all your saints shall bless you!
11 They shall speak of the glory of your kingdom,
and tell of your power,
12 to make known to the sons of men your
mighty deeds,
and the glorious splendor of your kingdom.
13 Your kingdom is an everlasting kingdom,
and your dominion endures throughout
all generations.

The LORD is faithful in all his words,
and gracious in all his deeds.
14 The LORD upholds all who are falling,
and raises up all who are bowed down.
15 The eyes of all look to you,
and you give them their food in due season.
16 You open your hand,
you satisfy the desire of every living thing.
17 The LORD is just in all his ways,
and kind in all his doings.
18 The LORD is near to all who call upon him,
to all who call upon him in truth.
19 He fulfils the desire of all who fear him,
he also hears their cry, and saves them.
20 The LORD preserves all who love him;
but all the wicked he will destroy.

21 My mouth will speak the praise of the LORD,
and let all flesh bless his holy name for
ever and ever.

ACTS 2

14 But Peter, standing with the Eleven, lifted up his voice and addressed them, "Men of Judea and all who dwell in Jerusalem, let this be

known to you, and give ear to my words. 15For
these men are not drunk, as you suppose,
since it is only the third hour of the day; 16but
this is what was spoken by the prophet Joel:
17'And in the last days it shall be, God
declares,
that I will pour out my Spirit upon all flesh,
and your sons and your daughters shall
prophesy,
and your young men shall see visions,
and your old men shall dream dreams;
18yes, and on my menservants and my
maidservants in those days
I will pour out my Spirit; and they
shall prophesy.
19And I will show wonders in the
heaven above
and signs on the earth beneath,
blood, and fire, and vapor of smoke;
20the sun shall be turned into darkness
and the moon into blood,
before the day of the Lord comes,
the great and manifest day.
21And it shall be that whoever calls on the
name of the Lord shall be saved.'
22"Men of Israel, hear these words: Jesus of
Nazareth, a man attested to you by God with
mighty works and wonders and signs which
God did through him in your midst, as you
yourselves know—23this Jesus, delivered up
according to the definite plan and foreknowledge of God, you crucified and killed by the
hands of lawless men. 24But God raised him
up, having loosed the pangs of death, because
it was not possible for him to be held by it. 25For
David says concerning him,
'I saw the Lord always before me,
for he is at my right hand that I may not
be shaken;
26therefore my heart was glad, and my
tongue rejoiced;
moreover my flesh will dwell in hope.
27For you will not abandon my soul to Hades,
nor let your Holy One see corruption.
28You have made known to me the ways
of life;
you will make me full of gladness with
your presence.'
29"Brethren, I may say to you confidently
of the patriarch David that he both died
and was buried, and his tomb is with us to
this day. 30Being therefore a prophet, and
knowing that God had sworn with an oath to
him that he would set one of his descendants
upon his throne, 31he foresaw and spoke of
the resurrection of the Christ, that he was
not abandoned to Hades, nor did his flesh see
corruption. 32This Jesus God raised up, and
of that we all are witnesses. 33Being therefore
exalted at the right hand of God, and having
received from the Father the promise of the
Holy Spirit, he has poured out this which you
see and hear. 34For David did not ascend into
the heavens; but he himself says,
'The Lord said to my Lord, Sit at my
right hand,
35till I make your enemies a stool for
your feet.'
36Let all the house of Israel therefore know
assuredly that God has made him both Lord
and Christ, this Jesus whom you crucified."

REFLECTION

Prayer is daily. "Every day I will bless you" (Ps 145:2). Though we might fail sometimes to pray, prayer by its nature is a daily activity, a daily recognition of our Creator's greatness and our own weakness. Prayer is intergenerational. "One generation shall laud your works to another" (v. 4). Parents teach their children to praise God for his magnificent deeds, and so a life of prayer and praise is handed down from one generation to the next. Prayer is creation-wide. "All your works shall give thanks to you, O LORD" (v. 10). The prophecy of Joel, which St. Peter quotes on Pentecost morning, depicts the sun, the moon, and the earth all participating in God's revelation, displaying his wonders. Prayer is part of God's plan for us. Just as he intended all Israel to enjoy intergenerational blessing in their "possessions" in the Promised Land, so now he intends for us to hand on the blessings of a life with God from generation to generation that we might enjoy the "Sabbath rest" of redemption in Christ. Though our sins "crucified and killed" Jesus (Acts 2:23), the grave could not hold him. "God raised him up" from death (v. 24), that by the power of his indestructible life, we might gain salvation. How can you prioritize prayer in your life?

June 22

1 CHRONICLES 9

10Of the priests: Jedai′ah, Je-
hoi′a-rib, Ja′chin, 11and Azari′ah
the son of Hilki′ah, son of Me-
shul′lam, son of Za′dok, son of Mer-
a′ioth, son of Ahi′tub, the chief officer
of the house of God; 12and Adai′ah
the son of Jero′ham, son of Pashhur, son of
Malchi′jah, and Ma′asai the son of Ad′i-el,
son of Jah′zerah, son of Meshul′lam, son of
Meshil′lemith, son of Immer; 13besides their
kinsmen, heads of their fathers' houses, one
thousand seven hundred and sixty, very able
men for the work of the service of the house
of God.

14Of the Levites: Shemai′ah the son of
Hasshub, son of Azri′kam, son of Hashabi′ah,
of the sons of Merar′i; 15and Bakbak′kar,
He′resh, Ga′lal, and Mattani′ah the son of
Mica, son of Zich′ri, son of A′saph; 16and
Obadi′ah the son of Shemai′ah, son of Galal,
son of Jedu′thun, and Berechi′ah the son
of Asa, son of Elka′nah, who dwelt in the
villages of the Netoph′athites.

17The gatekeepers were: Shallum, Akkub,
Talmon, Ahi′man, and their kinsmen (Shallum being the chief), 18stationed hitherto
in the king's gate on the east side. These
were the gatekeepers of the camp of the
Levites. 19Shallum the son of Ko′re, son of
Ebi′asaph, son of Ko′rah, and his kinsmen
of his fathers' house, the Ko′rahites, were in
charge of the work of the service, keepers
of the thresholds of the tent, as their
fathers had been in charge of the camp of
the LORD, keepers of the entrance. 20And
Phin′ehas the son of Elea′zar was the ruler
over them in time past; the LORD was with
him. 21Zechari′ah the son of Meshelemi′ah
was gatekeeper at the entrance of the tent
of meeting. 22All these, who were chosen
as gatekeepers at the thresholds, were two
hundred and twelve. They were enrolled
by genealogies in their villages. David and
Samuel the seer established them in their
office of trust. 23So they and their sons
were in charge of the gates of the house of
the LORD, that is, the house of the tent, as
guards. 24The gatekeepers were on the four
sides, east, west, north, and south; 25and their
kinsmen who were in their villages were
obliged to come in every seven days, from
time to time, to be with these; 26for the four
chief gatekeepers, who were Levites, were in
charge of the chambers and the treasures of
the house of God. 27And they lodged round
about the house of God; for upon them lay
the duty of watching, and they had charge of
opening it every morning.

28Some of them had charge of the utensils
of service, for they were required to count
them when they were brought in and taken
out. 29Others of them were appointed over
the furniture, and over all the holy utensils,
also over the fine flour, the wine, the oil, the
incense, and the spices. 30Others, of the sons
of the priests, prepared the mixing of the
spices, 31and Mattithi′ah, one of the Levites,
the first-born of Shallum the Ko′rahite, was
in charge of making the flat cakes. 32Also
some of their kinsmen of the Ko′hathites
had charge of the showbread, to prepare it
every sabbath.

33Now these are the singers, the heads of
fathers' houses of the Levites, dwelling in
the chambers of the temple free from other
service, for they were on duty day and night.
34These were heads of fathers' houses of the
Levites, according to their generations,
leaders, who lived in Jerusalem.

35In Gib′eon dwelt the father of Gibeon, Je-
i′el, and the name of his wife was Ma′acah,
36and his first-born son Abdon, then Zur,
Kish, Ba′al, Ner, Na′dab, 37Gedor, Ahi′o,
Zechari′ah, and Mikloth; 38and Mikloth was
the father of Shim′e-am; and these also dwelt
opposite their kinsmen in Jerusalem, with
their kinsmen. 39Ner was the father of Kish,
Kish of Saul, Saul of Jonathan, Mal″chishu′a,
Abin′adab, and Eshba′al; 40and the son of
Jonathan was Mer′ib-ba′al; and Merib-
baal was the father of Micah. 41The sons of
Micah: Pithon, Melech, Tah′re-a, and A′haz;
42and A′haz was the father of Jarah, and

Jarah of Al´emeth, Az´maveth, and Zimri;
and Zimri was the father of Moza. 43Moza
was the father of Bin´e-a; and Rephai´ah
was his son, Ele-a´sah his son, A´zel his
son. 44A´zel had six sons and these are
their names: Azri´kam, Bo´cheru, Ish´mael,
Sheari´ah, Obadi´ah, and Ha´nan; these were
the sons of Azel.

10 Now the Philis´tines fought against
Israel; and the men of Israel fled
before the Philis´tines, and fell slain on
Mount Gilbo´a. 2And the Philis´tines overtook
Saul and his sons; and the Philistines slew
Jonathan and Abin´adab and Mal″chishu´a,
the sons of Saul. 3The battle pressed hard
upon Saul, and the archers found him;
and he was wounded by the archers. 4Then
Saul said to his armor-bearer, "Draw your
sword, and thrust me through with it, lest
these uncircumcised come and make sport
of me." But his armor-bearer would not; for
he feared greatly. Therefore Saul took his
own sword, and fell upon it. 5And when his
armor-bearer saw that Saul was dead, he
also fell upon his sword, and died. 6Thus
Saul died; he and his three sons and all his
house died together. 7And when all the men
of Israel who were in the valley saw that the
army had fled and that Saul and his sons
were dead, they forsook their cities and fled;
and the Philis´tines came and dwelt in them.

8The next day, when the Philis´tines came
to strip the slain, they found Saul and his
sons fallen on Mount Gilbo´a. 9And they
stripped him and took his head and his
armor, and sent messengers throughout the
land of the Philis´tines, to carry the good
news to their idols and to the people. 10And
they put his armor in the temple of their
gods, and fastened his head in the temple of
Da´gon. 11But when all Ja´besh-gil´ead heard
all that the Philis´tines had done to Saul, 12all
the valiant men arose, and took away the
body of Saul and the bodies of his sons, and
brought them to Ja´besh. And they buried
their bones under the oak in Jabesh, and
fasted seven days.

13So Saul died for his unfaithfulness; he
was unfaithful to the LORD in that he did
not keep the command of the LORD, and
also consulted a medium, seeking guidance,
14and did not seek guidance from the LORD.
Therefore the LORD slew him, and turned
the kingdom over to David the son of Jesse.

11 Then all Israel gathered together to
David at He´bron, and said, "Behold,
we are your bone and flesh. 2In times
past, even when Saul was king, it was you
that led out and brought in Israel; and the
LORD your God said to you, 'You shall be
shepherd of my people Israel, and you shall
be prince over my people Israel.'" 3So all the
elders of Israel came to the king at He´bron;
and David made a covenant with them at
Hebron before the LORD, and they anointed
David king over Israel, according to the
word of the LORD by Samuel.

4And David and all Israel went to Jerusalem,
that is Je´bus, where the Jeb´usites were, the
inhabitants of the land. 5The inhabitants of
Je´bus said to David, "You will not come in
here." Nevertheless David took the stronghold
of Zion, that is, the city of David. 6David said,
"Whoever shall strike the Jeb´usites first shall
be chief and commander." And Jo´ab the son
of Zeru´iah went up first, so he became chief.
7And David dwelt in the stronghold; therefore
it was called the city of David. 8And he built the
city round about from the Millo in complete
circuit; and Jo´ab repaired the rest of the city.
9And David became greater and greater, for the
LORD of hosts was with him.

PSALM 146 [145]

Praise the LORD!
  Praise the LORD, O my soul!
2I will praise the LORD as long as I live;
  I will sing praises to my God while I
    have being.

3Put not your trust in princes,
  in a son of man, in whom there is no help.
4When his breath departs he returns to
    his earth;
  on that very day his plans perish.

5Happy is he whose help is the God of Jacob,
  whose hope is in the LORD his God,

6 who made heaven and earth,
the sea, and all that is in them;
who keeps faith for ever;
7 who executes justice for the oppressed;
who gives food to the hungry.

The LORD sets the prisoners free;
8 the LORD opens the eyes of the blind.
The LORD lifts up those who are
bowed down;
the LORD loves the righteous.
9 The LORD watches over the sojourners,
he upholds the widow and the fatherless;
but the way of the wicked he brings to ruin.

10 The LORD will reign for ever,
your God, O Zion, to all generations.
Praise the LORD!

ACTS 2

**37 Now when they heard this they
were cut to the heart, and said
to Peter and the rest of the apostles, "Brethren, what shall we do?" 38 And
Peter said to them, "Repent, and be bap-**
tized every one of you in the name of Jesus
Christ for the forgiveness of your sins; and
you shall receive the gift of the Holy Spirit. 39 For the promise is to you and to your
children and to all that are far off, every
one whom the Lord our God calls to him."
40 And he testified with many other words
and exhorted them, saying, "Save yourselves
from this crooked generation." 41 So those
who received his word were baptized, and
there were added that day about three thousand souls. 42 And they held steadfastly to
the apostles' teaching and fellowship, to the
breaking of the bread and to the prayers.

43 And fear came upon every soul; and
many wonders and signs were done through
the apostles. 44 And all who believed were
together and had all things in common;
45 and they sold their possessions and goods
and distributed them to all, as any had need.
46 And day by day, attending the temple
together and breaking bread in their homes,
they partook of food with glad and generous
hearts, 47 praising God and having favor
with all the people. And the Lord added to
their number day by day those who were
being saved.

3 Now Peter and John were going up to the
temple at the hour of prayer, the ninth
hour. 2 And a man lame from birth was
being carried, whom they laid daily at that
gate of the temple which is called Beautiful
to ask alms of those who entered the temple.
3 Seeing Peter and John about to go into
the temple, he asked for alms. 4 And Peter
directed his gaze at him, with John, and said,
"Look at us." 5 And he fixed his attention
upon them, expecting to receive something
from them. 6 But Peter said, "I have no silver
and gold, but I give you what I have; in the
name of Jesus Christ of Nazareth, rise and
walk." 7 And he took him by the right hand
and raised him up; and immediately his feet
and ankles were made strong. 8 And leaping
up he stood and walked and entered the
temple with them, walking and leaping and
praising God. 9 And all the people saw him
walking and praising God, 10 and recognized
him as the one who sat for alms at the
Beautiful Gate of the temple; and they were
filled with wonder and amazement at what
had happened to him.

11 While he clung to Peter and John, all the
people ran together to them in the portico
called Solomon's, astounded. 12 And when
Peter saw it he addressed the people, "Men
of Israel, why do you wonder at this, or why
do you stare at us, as though by our own
power or piety we had made him walk? 13 The
God of Abraham and of Isaac and of Jacob,
the God of our fathers, glorified his servant
Jesus, whom you delivered up and denied in
the presence of Pilate, when he had decided
to release him. 14 But you denied the Holy and
Righteous One, and asked for a murderer to
be granted to you, 15 and killed the Author of
life, whom God raised from the dead. To this
we are witnesses. 16 And his name, by faith in
his name, has made this man strong whom
you see and know; and the faith which is
through Jesus has given the man this perfect
health in the presence of you all.

17“And now, brethren, I know that you
acted in ignorance, as did also your rulers.
18But what God foretold by the mouth of all
the prophets, that his Christ should suffer,
he thus fulfilled. 19Repent therefore, and
turn again, that your sins may be blotted
out, that times of refreshing may come
from the presence of the Lord, 20and that
he may send the Christ appointed for you,
Jesus, 21whom heaven must receive until
the time for establishing all that God spoke
by the mouth of his holy prophets from of
old. 22Moses said, ‘The Lord God will raise
up for you a prophet from your brethren
as he raised me up. You shall listen to him
in whatever he tells you. 23And it shall
be that every soul that does not listen to
that prophet shall be destroyed from the
people.’ 24And all the prophets who have
spoken, from Samuel and those who came
afterwards, also proclaimed these days.
25You are the sons of the prophets and of the
covenant which God gave to your fathers,
saying to Abraham, ‘And in your posterity
shall all the families of the earth be blessed.’
26God, having raised up his servant, sent
him to you first, to bless you in turning
every one of you from your wickedness.”

REFLECTION

Sin is a spiral that ends in death, as we see in King Saul’s self-destructive suicide (see 1 Chr 10:4). Without God, there is no escape from sin’s inexorable pattern of ruin. But with God, things change. St. Peter preaches to the people in Jerusalem, saying that they “killed the Author of life, whom God raised from the dead” (Acts 3:15). Despite our failure, God succeeds. Peter shows us how to escape the death-spiral of sin: “Repent therefore, and turn again, that your sins may be blotted out” (v. 19). Jesus came to free us from the dire consequences of our own actions, our own sins. Peter explains how Jesus fulfills two central Old Testament predictions. First, he is the prophet whom Moses prophesied (see v. 22). Second, he brings about the global blessing that God promised through Abraham (see v. 25). Jesus does not come to destroy us but to save us and to bless us (see v. 26). He “sets prisoners free” and “opens the eyes of the blind” (Ps 146:7–8). His work of salvation brings us true happiness: “Happy is he whose help is the God of Jacob” (v. 5). How can you more fully live a life of repentance and more fully enjoy the blessings that Jesus purchased for you by his Death?

June 23

1 CHRONICLES 11

**10Now these are the chiefs of
David’s mighty men, who gave
him strong support in his kingdom, together with all Israel, to make
him king, according to the word of the
Lord concerning Israel. 11This is an**
account of David’s mighty men: Jashoʹbe-
am, a Hachʹmonite, was chief of the three;
he wielded his spear against three hundred
whom he slew at one time.
12And next to him among the three
mighty men was Eleaʹzar the son of Dodo,
the Ahoʹhite. 13He was with David at Pas-
damʹmim when the Philisʹtines were gathered there for battle. There was a plot of
ground full of barley, and the men fled from
the Philistines. 14But he took his stand in the
midst of the plot, and defended it, and slew
the Philisʹtines; and the Lord saved them by
a great victory.
15Three of the thirty chief men went down
to the rock to David at the cave of Adulʹlam,
when the army of Philisʹtines was encamped
in the valley of Rephʹaim. 16David was then
in the stronghold; and the garrison of the
Philisʹtines was then at Bethlehem. 17And
David said longingly, “O that some one
would give me water to drink from the well
of Bethlehem which is by the gate!” 18Then
the three mighty men broke through the

camp of the Philis´tines, and drew water out
of the well of Bethlehem which was by the
gate, and took and brought it to David. But
David would not drink of it; he poured it out
to the LORD, [19]and said, "Far be it from me
before my God that I should do this. Shall I
drink the lifeblood of these men? For at the
risk of their lives they brought it." Therefore
he would not drink it. These things did the
three mighty men.
[20]Now Abi´shai, the brother of Jo´ab, was
chief of the thirty. And he wielded his spear
against three hundred men and slew them,
and won a name beside the three. [21]He was
the most renowned of the thirty, and became
their commander; but he did not attain to
the three.
[22]And Bena´iah the son of Jehoi´ada was
a valiant man of Kab´zeel, a doer of great
deeds; he struck two Ariels of Moab. He
also went down and slew a lion in a pit on
a day when snow had fallen. [23]And he slew
an Egyptian, a man of great stature, five
cubits tall. The Egyptian had in his hand
a spear like a weaver's beam; but Bena´iah
went down to him with a staff, and snatched
the spear out of the Egyptian's hand, and
slew him with his own spear. [24]These things
did Bena´iah the son of Jehoi´ada, and won
a name beside the three mighty men. [25]He
was renowned among the thirty, but he did
not attain to the three. And David set him
over his bodyguard.
[26]The mighty men of the armies were
As´ahel the brother of Jo´ab, Elha´nan the
son of Dodo of Bethlehem, [27]Shammoth
of Harod, He´lez the Pel´onite, [28]Ira the son
of Ikkesh of Teko´a, Abie´zer of An´athoth,
[29]Sib´becai the Hu´shathite, Ilai the Aho´hite,
[30]Ma´harai of Netoph´ah, He´led the son of
Ba´anah of Netophah, [31]Ithai the son of Ri´bai
of Gib´e-ah of the Benjaminites, Bena´iah
of Pir´athon, [32]Hurai of the brooks of
Ga´ash, Abi´el the Ar´bathite, [33]Az´maveth of
Baha´rum, Eli´ahba of Sha-al´bon, [34]Hashem
the Gi´zonite, Jonathan the son of Sha´gee
the Har´arite, [35]Ahi´am the son of Sachar the
Har´arite, Eli´phal the son of Ur, [36]He´pher
the Meche´rathite, Ahi´jah the Pel´onite,
[37]Hezro of Carmel, Na´arai the son of Ezbai,
[38]Joel the brother of Nathan, Mibhar the son
of Hagri, [39]Zelek the Am´monite, Na´harai
of Be-er´oth, the armor-bearer of Jo´ab the
son of Zeru´iah, [40]Ira the Ithrite, Ga´reb
the Ithrite, [41]Uri´ah the Hittite, Zabad the
son of Ahlai, [42]Ad´ina the son of Shiza the
Reubenite, a leader of the Reubenites, and
thirty with him, [43]Ha´nan the son of Ma´acah,
and Josh´aphat the Mithnite, [44]Uzzi´a the
Ash´terathite, Shama and Je-i´el the sons
of Ho´tham the Aro´erite, [45]Jedi´a-el the
son of Shimri, and Joha his brother, the
Ti´zite, [46]Eli´el the Ma´havite, and Jer´ibai,
and Joshavi´ah, the sons of El´na-am, and
Ithmah the Moabite, [47]Eli´el, and O´bed, and
Ja-asi´el the Mezo´baite.

12 Now these are the men who came to
David at Zik´lag, while he could not
move about freely because of Saul the son
of Kish; and they were among the mighty
men who helped him in war. [2]They were
bowmen, and could shoot arrows and sling
stones with either the right or the left hand;
they were Benjaminites, Saul's kinsmen.
[3]The chief was Ahie´zer, then Jo´ash, both
sons of Shema´ah of Gib´e-ah; also Je´zi-el
and Pe´let the sons of Az´maveth; Ber´acah,
Je´hu of An´athoth, [4]Ishma´iah of Gib´eon,
a mighty man among the thirty and a
leader over the thirty; Jeremi´ah, Jaha´ziel,
Joha´nan, Joz´abad of Gede´rah, [5]Elu´zai,
Jer´imoth, Beali´ah, Shemari´ah, Shephati´ah
the Har´uphite; [6]Elka´nah, Isshi´ah, Az´arel,
Jo-e´zer, and Jasho´be-am, the Ko´rahites;
[7]and Jo-e´lah and Zebadi´ah, the sons of
Jero´ham of Gedor.
[8]From the Gadites there went over to
David at the stronghold in the wilderness
mighty and experienced warriors, expert
with shield and spear, whose faces were
like the faces of lions, and who were swift
as gazelles upon the mountains: [9]E´zer
the chief, Obadi´ah second, Eli´ab third,
[10]Mishman´nah fourth, Jeremi´ah fifth,
[11]Attai sixth, Eli´el seventh, [12]Joha´nan
eighth, Elza´bad ninth, [13]Jeremi´ah tenth,
Mach´bannai eleventh. [14]These Gadites
were officers of the army, the lesser over a
hundred and the greater over a thousand.
[15]These are the men who crossed the Jordan

in the first month, when it was overflowing all its banks, and put to flight all those in the valleys, to the east and to the west.

16And some of the men of Benjamin and Judah came to the stronghold to David. 17David went out to meet them and said to them, "If you have come to me in friendship to help me, my heart will be knit to you; but if to betray me to my adversaries, although there is no wrong in my hands, then may the God of our fathers see and rebuke you." 18Then the Spirit came upon Ama′sai, chief of the thirty, and he said,

"We are yours, O David;
 and with you, O son of Jesse!
Peace, peace to you,
 and peace to your helpers!
For your God helps you."

Then David received them, and made them officers of his troops.

19Some of the men of Manas′seh deserted to David when he came with the Philis′tines for the battle against Saul. (Yet he did not help them, for the rulers of the Philistines took counsel and sent him away, saying, "At peril to our heads he will desert to his master Saul.") 20As he went to Zik′lag these men of Manas′seh deserted to him: Adnah, Joz′abad, Jedi′a-el, Michael, Jozabad, Eli′hu, and Zil′lethai, chiefs of thousands in Manasseh. 21They helped David against the band of raiders; for they were all mighty men of valor, and were commanders in the army. 22For from day to day men kept coming to David to help him, until there was a great army, like an army of God.

23These are the numbers of the divisions of the armed troops, who came to David in He′bron, to turn the kingdom of Saul over to him, according to the word of the LORD. 24The men of Judah bearing shield and spear were six thousand eight hundred armed troops. 25Of the Simeonites, mighty men of valor for war, seven thousand one hundred. 26Of the Levites four thousand six hundred. 27The prince Jehoi′ada, of the house of Aaron, and with him three thousand seven hundred. 28Za′dok, a young man mighty in valor, and twenty-two commanders from his own father's house. 29Of the Benjaminites, the kinsmen of Saul, three thousand, of whom the majority had hitherto kept their allegiance to the house of Saul. 30Of the E′phraimites twenty thousand eight hundred, mighty men of valor, famous men in their fathers' houses. 31Of the half-tribe of Manas′seh eighteen thousand, who were expressly named to come and make David king. 32Of Is′sachar men who had understanding of the times, to know what Israel ought to do, two hundred chiefs, and all their kinsmen under their command. 33Of Zeb′ulun fifty thousand seasoned troops, equipped for battle with all the weapons of war, to help David with singleness of purpose. 34Of Naph′tali a thousand commanders with whom were thirty-seven thousand men armed with shield and spear. 35Of the Danites twenty-eight thousand six hundred men equipped for battle. 36Of Asher forty thousand seasoned troops ready for battle. 37Of the Reubenites and Gadites and the half-tribe of Manas′seh from beyond the Jordan, one hundred and twenty thousand men armed with all the weapons of war.

38All these, men of war, arrayed in battle order, came to He′bron with full intent to make David king over all Israel; likewise all the rest of Israel were of a single mind to make David king. 39And they were there with David for three days, eating and drinking, for their brethren had made preparation for them. 40And also their neighbors, from as far as Is′sachar and Zeb′ulun and Naph′tali, came bringing food on donkeys and on camels and on mules and on oxen, abundant provisions of meal, cakes of figs, clusters of raisins, and wine and oil, oxen and sheep, for there was joy in Israel.

PSALM 147 [146]

Praise the LORD!
For it is good to sing praises to our God;
 for he is gracious, and a song of praise
  is seemly.
2The LORD builds up Jerusalem;
 he gathers the outcasts of Israel.
3He heals the brokenhearted,
 and binds up their wounds.

[4]He determines the number of the stars,
he gives to all of them their names.
[5]Great is our LORD, and abundant in power;
his understanding is beyond measure.
[6]The LORD lifts up the downtrodden,
he casts the wicked to the ground.

[7]Sing to the LORD with thanksgiving;
make melody to our God upon the lyre!
[8]He covers the heavens with clouds,
he prepares rain for the earth,
he makes grass grow upon the hills.
[9]He gives to the beasts their food,
and to the young ravens which cry.
[10]His delight is not in the strength of the horse,
nor his pleasure in the legs of a man;
[11]but the LORD takes pleasure in those who fear him,
in those who hope in his steadfast love.

[147] [12]Praise the LORD, O Jerusalem!
Praise your God, O Zion!
[13]For he strengthens the bars of your gates;
he blesses your sons within you.
[14]He makes peace in your borders;
he fills you with the finest of the wheat.
[15]He sends forth his command to the earth;
his word runs swiftly.
[16]He gives snow like wool;
he scatters hoarfrost like ashes.
[17]He casts forth his ice like morsels;
who can stand before his cold?
[18]He sends forth his word, and melts them;
he makes his wind blow, and the waters flow.
[19]He declares his word to Jacob,
his statutes and ordinances to Israel.
[20]He has not dealt thus with any other nation;
they do not know his ordinances.
Praise the LORD!

ACTS 4

And as they were speaking to the people, the priests and the captain of the temple and the Sad′ducees came upon them, [2]annoyed because they were teaching the people and proclaiming in Jesus the resurrection from the dead. [3]And they
arrested them and put them in custody until the next day, for it was already evening. [4]But
many of those who heard the word believed; and the number of the men came to about five thousand.

[5]On the next day their rulers and elders and scribes were gathered together in Jerusalem,
[6]with Annas the high priest and Cai′aphas and John and Alexander, and all who were of the high-priestly family. [7]And when they had set them in their midst, they inquired, "By what power or by what name did you do this?"
[8]Then Peter, filled with the Holy Spirit, said to them, "Rulers of the people and elders, [9]if we
are being examined today concerning a good deed done to a cripple, by what means this man has been healed, [10]be it known to you all, and
to all the people of Israel, that by the name of Jesus Christ of Nazareth, whom you crucified, whom God raised from the dead, by him this man is standing before you well. [11]This is the
stone which was rejected by you builders, but which has become the cornerstone. [12]And
there is salvation in no one else, for there is no other name under heaven given among men by which we must be saved."

[13]Now when they saw the boldness of Peter and John, and perceived that they were uneducated, common men, they wondered; and they recognized that they had been with Jesus. [14]But seeing the man that had
been healed standing beside them, they had nothing to say in opposition. [15]But when they
had commanded them to go aside out of the council, they conferred with one another,
[16]saying, "What shall we do with these men?
For that a notable sign has been performed through them is manifest to all the inhabitants of Jerusalem, and we cannot deny it. [17]But in
order that it may spread no further among the people, let us warn them to speak no more to any one in this name." [18]So they called them and
charged them not to speak or teach at all in the name of Jesus. [19]But Peter and John answered
them, "Whether it is right in the sight of God to listen to you rather than to God, you must judge; [20]for we cannot but speak of what we
have seen and heard." [21]And when they had

further threatened them, they let them go,
finding no way to punish them, because of
the people; for all men praised God for what
had happened. 22For the man on whom this
sign of healing was performed was more
than forty years old.

REFLECTION

Finding reliable friends is one of the great quests of life. When a group of soldiers approach David in his wilderness hideout, he tests them: "If you have come to me in friendship to help me, my heart will be knit to you" (1 Chr 12:17). David shows himself to be a true friend to those who are faithful to him and beautifully expresses that deep connection, that sharing of souls, which true friends find. The band's representative prophesies in response, "We are yours, O David; and with you, O son of Jesse!" (v. 18). Not only do friends share their hearts, they "possess" one another in a certain sense. David "owns" his friends and they own him. Psalm 147 explores the friendship of God and man, stating that "the LORD takes pleasure in those who fear him" (v. 11). Our praise is a continual giving back to the God who gives to us, which the psalmist explains through a series of verbs describing God's actions: he builds up, gathers, heals, binds up, determines, gives, lifts up, strengthens, and makes peace. Sts. Peter and John give back to God by determining to obey him rather than men (see Acts 4:19–20) and so risk their lives. How can you cultivate your friendship with God?

June 24

1 CHRONICLES 13

**David consulted with the commanders of thousands and of
hundreds, with every leader. 2And David
said to all the assembly of Israel, "If it
seems good to you, and if it is the will**
of the LORD our God, let us send abroad to
our brethren who remain in all the land of
Israel, and with them to the priests and
Levites in the cities that have pasture
lands, that they may come together to us.
3Then let us bring again the ark of our
God to us; for we neglected it in the days
of Saul." 4All the assembly agreed to do
so, for the thing was right in the eyes of
all the people.

5So David assembled all Israel from the
Shihor of Egypt to the entrance of Ha′math,
to bring the ark of God from Kir′iath-je′arim.
6And David and all Israel went up to Ba′alah,
that is, to Kir′iath-je′arim which belongs to
Judah, to bring up from there the ark of God,
which is called by the name of the LORD
who sits enthroned above the cherubim.
7And they carried the ark of God upon a
new cart, from the house of Abin′adab, and
Uzzah and Ahi′o were driving the cart. 8And
David and all Israel were making merry
before God with all their might, with song
and lyres and harps and tambourines and
cymbals and trumpets.

9And when they came to the threshing
floor of Chidon, Uzzah put out his hand to
hold the ark, for the oxen stumbled. 10And
the anger of the LORD was kindled against
Uzzah; and he struck him because he put
forth his hand to the ark; and he died there
before God. 11And David was angry because
the LORD had broken forth upon Uzzah; and
that place is called Pe′rez-uzza to this day.
12And David was afraid of God that day; and
he said, "How can I bring the ark of God
home to me?" 13So David did not take the
ark home into the city of David, but took it
aside to the house of O′bed-e′dom the Gittite.
14And the ark of God remained with the
household of O′bed-e′dom in his house three
months; and the LORD blessed the household
of Obed-edom and all that he had.

14 And Hiram king of Tyre sent messengers to David, and cedar trees,
also masons and carpenters to build a house
for him. 2And David perceived that the
LORD had established him king over Israel,
and that his kingdom was highly exalted for
the sake of his people Israel.

3And David took more wives in Jerusalem, and David begot more sons and daughters. 4These are the names of the children whom he had in Jerusalem: Sham′mu-a, Sho′bab, Nathan, Solomon, 5Ibhar, Eli′shu-a, El′pelet, 6No′gah, Ne′pheg, Japhi′a, 7Elish′ama, Beeli′ada, and Eliph′elet.

8When the Philis′tines heard that David had been anointed king over all Israel, all the Philistines went up in search of David; and David heard of it and went out against them. 9Now the Philis′tines had come and made a raid in the valley of Reph′aim. 10And David inquired of God, "Shall I go up against the Philis′tines? Will you give them into my hand?" And the LORD said to him, "Go up, and I will give them into your hand." 11And he went up to Ba′al-pera′zim, and David defeated them there; and David said, "God has broken through my enemies by my hand, like a bursting flood." Therefore the name of that place is called Baal-perazim. 12And they left their gods there, and David gave command, and they were burned.

13And the Philis′tines yet again made a raid in the valley. 14And when David again inquired of God, God said to him, "You shall not go up after them; go around and come upon them opposite the balsam trees. 15And when you hear the sound of marching in the tops of the balsam trees, then go out to battle; for God has gone out before you to strike the army of the Philis′tines." 16And David did as God commanded him, and they struck the Philis′tine army from Gib′eon to Gezer. 17And the fame of David went out into all lands, and the LORD brought the fear of him upon all nations.

15 David built houses for himself in the city of David; and he prepared a place for the ark of God, and pitched a tent for it. 2Then David said, "No one but the Levites may carry the ark of God, for the LORD chose them to carry the ark of the LORD and to minister to him for ever." 3And David assembled all Israel at Jerusalem, to bring up the ark of the LORD to its place, which he had prepared for it. 4And David gathered together the sons of Aaron and the Levites: 5of the sons of Ko′hath, Uri′el the chief, with a hundred and twenty of his brethren; 6of the sons of Merar′i, Asai′ah the chief, with two hundred and twenty of his brethren; 7of the sons of Gershom, Joel the chief, with a hundred and thirty of his brethren; 8of the sons of Eliza′phan, Shemai′ah the chief, with two hundred of his brethren; 9of the sons of He′bron, Eli′el the chief, with eighty of his brethren; 10of the sons of Uz′ziel, Ammin′adab the chief, with a hundred and twelve of his brethren. 11Then David summoned the priests Za′dok and Abi′athar, and the Levites Uri′el, Asai′ah, Joel, Shemai′ah, Eli′el, and Ammin′adab, 12and said to them, "You are the heads of the fathers' houses of the Levites; sanctify yourselves, you and your brethren, so that you may bring up the ark of the LORD, the God of Israel, to the place that I have prepared for it. 13Because you did not carry it the first time, the LORD our God broke forth upon us, because we did not care for it in the way that is ordained." 14So the priests and the Levites sanctified themselves to bring up the ark of the LORD, the God of Israel. 15And the Levites carried the ark of God upon their shoulders with the poles, as Moses had commanded according to the word of the LORD.

16David also commanded the chiefs of the Levites to appoint their brethren as the singers who should play loudly on musical instruments, on harps and lyres and cymbals, to raise sounds of joy. 17So the Levites appointed He′man the son of Joel; and of his brethren A′saph the son of Berechi′ah; and of the sons of Merar′i, their brethren, Ethan the son of Kusha′iah; 18and with them their brethren of the second order, Zechari′ah, Ja-a′ziel, Shemir′amoth, Jehi′el, Unni, Eli′ab, Bena′iah, Ma″asei′ah, Mattithi′ah, Eliph′elehu, and Mikne′iah, and the gatekeepers O′bed-e′dom and Je-i′el. 19The singers, He′man, A′saph, and Ethan, were to sound bronze cymbals; 20Zechari′ah, A′zi-el, Shemir′amoth, Jehi′el, Unni, Eli′ab, Ma″asei′ah, and Bena′iah were to play harps according to Al′amoth; 21but Mattithi′ah, Eliph′elehu, Mikne′iah, O′bed-e′dom, Je-i′el, and Azazi′ah were to lead with lyres

according to the Shem′inith. 22Chenani′ah,
leader of the Levites in music, should direct
the music, for he understood it. 23Berechi′ah
and Elka′nah were to be gatekeepers for
the ark. 24Shebani′ah, Josh′aphat, Nethan′el,
Ama′sai, Zechari′ah, Bena′iah, and Elie′zer,
the priests, should blow the trumpets before
the ark of God. O′bed-e′dom and Jehi′ah
also were to be gatekeepers for the ark.
25So David and the elders of Israel, and the
commanders of thousands, went to bring
up the ark of the covenant of the LORD from
the house of O′bed-e′dom with rejoicing.
26And because God helped the Levites who
were carrying the ark of the covenant of the
LORD, they sacrificed seven bulls and seven
rams. 27David was clothed with a robe of
fine linen, as also were all the Levites who
were carrying the ark, and the singers, and
Chenani′ah the leader of the music of the
singers; and David wore a linen ephod. 28So
all Israel brought up the ark of the covenant
of the LORD with shouting, to the sound of
the horn, trumpets, and cymbals, and made
loud music on harps and lyres.
29And as the ark of the covenant of the
LORD came to the city of David, Michal the
daughter of Saul looked out of the window,
and saw King David dancing and making
merry; and she despised him in her heart.

PSALM 148

Praise the LORD!
Praise the LORD from the heavens,
praise him in the heights!
2Praise him, all his angels,
praise him, all his host!

3Praise him, sun and moon,
praise him, all you shining stars!
4Praise him, you highest heavens,
and you waters above the heavens!

5Let them praise the name of the LORD!
For he commanded and they were created.
6And he established them for ever and ever;
he fixed their bounds which cannot
be passed.

7Praise the LORD from the earth,
you sea monsters and all deeps,
8fire and hail, snow and frost,
stormy wind fulfilling his command!

9Mountains and all hills,
fruit trees and all cedars!
10Beasts and all cattle,
creeping things and flying birds!

11Kings of the earth and all peoples,
princes and all rulers of the earth!
12Young men and maidens together,
old men and children!

13Let them praise the name of the LORD,
for his name alone is exalted;
his glory is above earth and heaven.
14He has raised up a horn for his people,
praise for all his saints,
for the people of Israel who are near to him.
Praise the LORD!

ACTS 4

23When they were released they
went to their friends and reported
what the chief priests and the elders had
said to them. 24And when they heard it,
they lifted their voices together to God and
said, "Sovereign Lord, who made the heaven
and the earth and the sea and everything
in them, 25who by the mouth of our father
David, your servant, said by the Holy Spirit,
'Why did the Gentiles rage,
and the peoples imagine vain things?
26The kings of the earth set themselves
in array,
and the rulers were gathered together,
against the Lord and against his Anointed'—
27for truly in this city there were gathered
together against your holy servant Jesus,
whom you anointed, both Herod and
Pontius Pilate, with the Gentiles and the
peoples of Israel, 28to do whatever your
hand and your plan had predestined to take
place. 29And now, Lord, look upon their
threats, and grant to your servants to speak

your word with all boldness, 30while you stretch out your hand to heal, and signs and wonders are performed through the name of your holy servant Jesus." 31And when they had prayed, the place in which they were gathered together was shaken; and they were all filled with the Holy Spirit and spoke the word of God with boldness.

32Now the company of those who believed were of one heart and soul, and no one said that any of the things which he possessed was his own, but they had everything in common. 33And with great power the apostles gave their testimony to the resurrection of the Lord Jesus, and great grace was upon them all. 34There was not any one needy among them, for as many as were possessors of lands or houses sold them, and brought the proceeds of what was sold 35and laid it at the apostles' feet; and distribution was made to each as any had need. 36Thus Joseph who was surnamed by the apostles Barnabas (which means, Son of encouragement), a Levite, a native of Cyprus, 37sold a field which belonged to him, and brought the money and laid it at the apostles' feet.

5 But a man named Anani′as with his wife Sapphi′ra sold a piece of property, 2and with his wife's knowledge he kept back some of the proceeds, and brought only a part and laid it at the apostles' feet. 3But Peter said, "Anani′as, why has Satan filled your heart to lie to the Holy Spirit and to keep back part of the proceeds of the land? 4While it remained unsold, did it not remain your own? And after it was sold, was it not at your disposal? How is it that you have contrived this deed in your heart? You have not lied to men but to God." 5When Anani′as heard these words, he fell down and died. And great fear came upon all who heard of it. 6The young men rose and wrapped him up and carried him out and buried him.

7After an interval of about three hours his wife came in, not knowing what had happened. 8And Peter said to her, "Tell me whether you sold the land for so much." And she said, "Yes, for so much." 9But Peter said to her, "How is it that you have agreed together to tempt the Spirit of the Lord? Listen, the feet of those that have buried your husband are at the door, and they will carry you out." 10Immediately she fell down at his feet and died. When the young men came in they found her dead, and they carried her out and buried her beside her husband. 11And great fear came upon the whole Church, and upon all who heard of these things.

12Now many signs and wonders were done among the people by the hands of the apostles. And they were all together in Solomon's Portico. 13None of the rest dared join them, but the people held them in high honor. 14And more than ever believers were added to the Lord, multitudes both of men and women, 15so that they even carried out the sick into the streets, and laid them on beds and pallets, that as Peter came by at least his shadow might fall on some of them. 16The people also gathered from the towns around Jerusalem, bringing the sick and those afflicted with unclean spirits, and they were all healed.

REFLECTION

The presence of God is holy—so holy in fact that we cannot approach him without trepidation. Uzzah, who reaches out and touches the Ark to save it from toppling, is struck dead by the powerful, holy presence of God. Similarly, Ananias and Sapphira die before God when they lie to him by pretending to make an offering of the whole proceeds of a land sale, when, in fact, they held back some of the money: "You have not lied to men but to God" (Acts 5:4). These moments reveal God's holiness and power—like the lightning on Mt. Sinai or the fire Elijah calls down from Heaven. He is not a god to be trifled with, but fierce, holy, and set apart. While his wrath "broke out" against Uzzah, he also causes David's army to "break out" against the Philistines, thus securing the title *baal-perazim,* meaning "Lord of breakthrough" (see 1 Chr 14:11). While the Lord holds us accountable for violating his holiness, he also enriches us with many blessings. The early Christians in Jerusalem share their possessions with one another (see Acts 4:32), showing the kind of self-sacrificial generosity and shared blessing possible in Christ. How do you honor the holiness of the Lord and share in his blessings?

June 25

1 CHRONICLES 16

**And they brought in the ark of
God, and set it inside the tent
which David had pitched for it;
and they offered burnt offerings and
peace offerings before God. [2]And when
David had finished offering the burnt**
offerings and the peace offerings, he blessed
the people in the name of the LORD, [3]and
distributed to all Israel, both men and wom-
en, to each a loaf of bread, a portion of meat,
and a cake of raisins.
[4]Moreover he appointed certain of the
Levites as ministers before the ark of the
LORD, to invoke, to thank, and to praise the
LORD, the God of Israel. [5]A′saph was the
chief, and second to him were Zechari′ah,
Je-i′el, Shemir′amoth, Jehi′el, Mattithi′ah,
Eli′ab, Bena′iah, O′bed-e′dom, and Je-iel,
who were to play harps and lyres; Asaph was
to sound the cymbals, [6]and Bena′iah and
Jaha′ziel the priests were to blow trumpets
continually, before the ark of the covenant
of God.
[7]Then on that day David first appointed
that thanksgiving be sung to the LORD by
A′saph and his brethren.

[8]O give thanks to the LORD, call on his name,
make known his deeds among
the peoples!
[9]Sing to him, sing praises to him,
tell of all his wonderful works!
[10]Glory in his holy name;
let the hearts of those who seek the
LORD rejoice!
[11]Seek the LORD and his strength,
seek his presence continually!
[12]Remember the wonderful works that he
has done,
the wonders he wrought, the judgments
he uttered,
[13]O offspring of Abraham his servant,
sons of Jacob, his chosen ones!
[14]He is the LORD our God;
his judgments are in all the earth.
[15]He is mindful of his covenant for ever,
of the word that he commanded, for a
thousand generations,
[16]the covenant which he made with Abraham,
his sworn promise to Isaac,
[17]which he confirmed as a statute to Jacob,
as an everlasting covenant to Israel,
[18]saying, "To you I will give the land
of Canaan,
as your portion for an inheritance."
[19]When they were few in number,
and of little account, and sojourners in it,
[20]wandering from nation to nation,
from one kingdom to another people,
[21]he allowed no one to oppress them;
he rebuked kings on their account,
[22]saying, "Touch not my anointed ones,
do my prophets no harm!"
[23]Sing to the LORD, all the earth!
Tell of his salvation from day to day.
[24]Declare his glory among the nations,
his marvelous works among all
the peoples!
[25]For great is the LORD, and greatly to
be praised,
and he is to be held in awe above all gods.
[26]For all the gods of the peoples are idols;
but the LORD made the heavens.
[27]Honor and majesty are before him;
strength and joy are in his place.
[28]Ascribe to the LORD, O families of the
peoples,
ascribe to the LORD glory and strength!
[29]Ascribe to the LORD the glory due his name;
bring an offering, and come before him!
Worship the LORD in holy attire;
[30]tremble before him, all the earth;
yes, the world stands firm, never to
be moved.
[31]Let the heavens be glad, and let the
earth rejoice,
and let them say among the nations,
"The LORD reigns!"
[32]Let the sea roar, and all that fills it,
let the field exult, and everything in it!

33Then shall the trees of the wood sing for joy
before the LORD, for he comes to judge
the earth.
34O give thanks to the LORD, for he is good;
for his mercy endures for ever!

35Say also:
"Deliver us, O God of our salvation,
and gather and save us from among
the nations,
that we may give thanks to your holy name,
and glory in your praise.
36Blessed be the LORD, the God of Israel,
from everlasting to everlasting!"
Then all the people said "Amen!" and
praised the LORD.

37So David left A′saph and his brethren
there before the ark of the covenant of the
LORD to minister continually before the ark
as each day required, 38and also O′bed-e′dom
and his sixty-eight brethren; while Obed-
edom, the son of Jedu′thun, and Hosah were
to be gatekeepers. 39And he left Za′dok the
priest and his brethren the priests before the
tabernacle of the LORD in the high place that
was at Gib′eon, 40to offer burnt offerings to
the LORD upon the altar of burnt offering
continually morning and evening, according
to all that is written in the law of the LORD
which he commanded Israel. 41With them
were He′man and Jedu′thun, and the rest of
those chosen and expressly named to give
thanks to the LORD, for his mercy endures for
ever. 42He′man and Jedu′thun had trumpets
and cymbals for the music and instruments
for sacred song. The sons of Jeduthun were
appointed to the gate.

43Then all the people departed each to his
house, and David went home to bless his
household.

17 Now when David dwelt in his house,
David said to Nathan the prophet,
"Behold, I dwell in a house of cedar, but the
ark of the covenant of the LORD is under a
tent." 2And Nathan said to David, "Do all
that is in your heart, for God is with you."

3But that same night the word of the LORD
came to Nathan, 4"Go and tell my servant
David, 'Thus says the LORD: You shall not
build me a house to dwell in. 5For I have
not dwelt in a house since the day I led up
Israel to this day, but I have gone from tent
to tent and from dwelling to dwelling. 6In all
places where I have moved with all Israel,
did I speak a word with any of the judges of
Israel, whom I commanded to shepherd my
people, saying, "Why have you not built me
a house of cedar?"' 7Now therefore thus shall
you say to my servant David, 'Thus says the
LORD of hosts, I took you from the pasture,
from following the sheep, that you should
be prince over my people Israel; 8and I have
been with you wherever you went, and have
cut off all your enemies from before you; and
I will make for you a name, like the name
of the great ones of the earth. 9And I will
appoint a place for my people Israel, and will
plant them, that they may dwell in their own
place, and be disturbed no more; and violent
men shall waste them no more, as formerly,
10from the time that I appointed judges over
my people Israel; and I will subdue all your
enemies. Moreover I declare to you that the
LORD will build you a house. 11When your
days are fulfilled to go to be with your fathers,
I will raise up your offspring after you, one
of your own sons, and I will establish his
kingdom. 12He shall build a house for me,
and I will establish his throne for ever. 13I
will be his father, and he shall be my son;
I will not take my merciful love from him,
as I took it from him who was before you,
14but I will confirm him in my house and in
my kingdom for ever and his throne shall be
established for ever.'" 15In accordance with
all these words, and in accordance with all
this vision, Nathan spoke to David.

16Then King David went in and sat before
the LORD, and said, "Who am I, O LORD
God, and what is my house, that you have
brought me thus far? 17And this was a small
thing in your eyes, O God; you have also
spoken of your servant's house for a great
while to come, and have shown me future
generations, O LORD God! 18And what more
can David say to you for honoring your
servant? For you know your servant. 19For
your servant's sake, O LORD, and according
to your own heart, you have wrought all this
greatness, in making known all these great

things. [20]There is none like you, O LORD,
and there is no God besides you, according
to all that we have heard with our ears.
[21]What other nation on earth is like your
people Israel, whom God went to redeem to
be his people, making for yourself a name
for great and terrible things, in driving
out nations before your people whom you
redeemed from Egypt? [22]And you made
your people Israel to be your people for
ever; and you, O LORD, became their God.
[23]And now, O LORD, let the word which
you have spoken concerning your servant
and concerning his house be established for
ever, and do as you have spoken; [24]and your
name will be established and magnified for
ever, saying, 'The LORD of hosts, the God of
Israel, is Israel's God,' and the house of your
servant David will be established before you.
[25]For you, my God, have revealed to your
servant that you will build a house for him;
therefore your servant has found courage
to pray before you. [26]And now, O LORD,
you are God, and you have promised this
good thing to your servant; [27]now therefore
may it please you to bless the house of your
servant, that it may continue for ever before
you; for what you, O LORD, have blessed is
blessed for ever."

PSALM 149

Praise the LORD!
Sing to the LORD a new song,
his praise in the assembly of the faithful!
[2]Let Israel be glad in his Maker,
let the sons of Zion rejoice in their King!
[3]Let them praise his name with dancing,
making melody to him with timbrel
and lyre!
[4]For the LORD takes pleasure in his people;
he adorns the humble with victory.
[5]Let the faithful exult in glory;
let them sing for joy on their couches.
[6]Let the high praises of God be in
their throats
and two-edged swords in their hands,
[7]to wreak vengeance on the nations
and chastisement on the peoples,
[8]to bind their kings with chains
and their nobles with fetters of iron,
[9]to execute on them the judgment written!
This is glory for all his faithful ones.
Praise the LORD!

PSALM 150

Praise the LORD!
Praise God in his sanctuary;
praise him in his mighty firmament!
[2]Praise him for his mighty deeds;
praise him according to his
exceeding greatness!
[3]Praise him with trumpet sound;
praise him with lute and harp!
[4]Praise him with timbrel and dance;
praise him with strings and pipe!
[5]Praise him with sounding cymbals;
praise him with loud clashing cymbals!
[6]Let everything that breathes praise the LORD!
Praise the LORD!

ACTS 5

[17]But the high priest rose up and
all who were with him, that is, the
party of the Sad´ducees, and filled with
jealousy [18]they arrested the apostles and
put them in the common prison. [19]But at
night an angel of the Lord opened the prison
doors and brought them out and said, [20]"Go
and stand in the temple and speak to the
people all the words of this Life." [21]And when
they heard this, they entered the temple at
daybreak and taught.
Now the high priest came and those who
were with him and called together the council
and all the senate of Israel, and sent to the
prison to have them brought. [22]But when
the officers came, they did not find them in
the prison, and they returned and reported,
[23]"We found the prison securely locked and
the sentries standing at the doors, but when
we opened it we found no one inside." [24]Now
when the captain of the temple and the chief
priests heard these words, they were much

perplexed about them, wondering what this
would come to. 25 And some one came and
told them, "The men whom you put in prison
are standing in the temple and teaching
the people." 26 Then the captain with the
officers went and brought them, but without
violence, for they were afraid of being stoned
by the people.
27 And when they had brought them,
they set them before the council. And the
high priest questioned them, 28 saying, "We
strictly charged you not to teach in this
name, yet here you have filled Jerusalem
with your teaching and you intend to bring
this man's blood upon us." 29 But Peter and
the apostles answered, "We must obey God
rather than men. 30 The God of our fathers
raised Jesus whom you killed by hanging
him on a tree. 31 God exalted him at his
right hand as Leader and Savior, to give
repentance to Israel and forgiveness of sins.
32 And we are witnesses to these things, and
so is the Holy Spirit whom God has given to
those who obey him."
33 When they heard this they were enraged
and wanted to kill them. 34 But a Pharisee in
the council named Gama'li-el, a teacher of
the law, held in honor by all the people, stood
up and ordered the men to be put outside for
a while. 35 And he said to them, "Men of Israel,
take care what you do with these men. 36 For
before these days Theu'das arose, claiming to
be somebody, and a number of men, about
four hundred, joined him; but he was slain
and all who followed him were dispersed
and came to nothing. 37 After him Judas the
Galilean arose in the days of the census and
drew away some of the people after him;
he also perished, and all who followed him
were scattered. 38 So in the present case I tell
you, keep away from these men and let them
alone; for if this plan or this undertaking is of
men, it will fail; 39 but if it is of God, you will
not be able to overthrow them. You might
even be found opposing God!"
40 So they took his advice, and when they
had called in the apostles, they beat them
and charged them not to speak in the name
of Jesus, and let them go. 41 Then they left the
presence of the council, rejoicing that they
were counted worthy to suffer dishonor for
the name. 42 And every day in the temple and
at home they did not cease teaching and
preaching Jesus as the Christ.

REFLECTION

When the Ark of the Covenant is brought to the tent of the Lord in Jerusalem, David rejoices heartily. Not only does he worship the Lord with sacrifices, but he generously bestows gifts on the people: "To each a loaf of bread, a portion of meat, and a cake of raisins" (1 Chr 16:3). Beyond that, he establishes regular offerings and a round-the-clock worship team of Levites to sing to the Lord. Rejoicing characterizes his response to the Lord. When David generously wants to build a Temple, the Lord tells him: "You shall not build me a house to dwell in. . . . I declare to you that the LORD will build you a house" (1 Chr 17:4, 10). And indeed, the Lord blesses him with an everlasting throne. The Apostles, too, are characterized by rejoicing. Even when the Sanhedrin beats them for preaching Jesus, they walk away "rejoicing that they were counted worthy to suffer dishonor for the name" (Acts 5:41). In addition, they disobey the Sanhedrin's commands and keep preaching about Jesus to anyone who will listen. David's attitude of grateful rejoicing before the Lord and the Apostles' courage in the face of persecution should inspire us. Suffering for Christ should not lead us to despair but to joy. Is your life characterized by rejoicing in the Lord?

June 26

1 CHRONICLES 18

After this David defeated the Philis'tines and subdued them, and he took Gath and its villages out of the hand of the Philistines.

2And he defeated Moab, and the Moabites
became servants to David and brought
tribute.
3David also defeated Hadade′zer king
of Zobah, toward Ha′math, as he went to
set up his monument at the river Euphrates. 4And David took from him a thousand
chariots, seven thousand horsemen, and
twenty thousand foot soldiers; and David
hamstrung all the chariot horses, but left
enough for a hundred chariots. 5And when
the Syrians of Damascus came to help Ha-
dade′zer king of Zobah, David slew twenty-
two thousand men of the Syrians. 6Then David put garrisons in Syria of Damascus; and
the Syrians became servants to David, and
brought tribute. And the LORD gave victory to David wherever he went. 7And David
took the shields of gold which were carried
by the servants of Hadade′zer, and brought
them to Jerusalem. 8And from Tibhath and
from Cun, cities of Hadade′zer, David took
very much bronze; with it Solomon made
the bronze sea and the pillars and the vessels of bronze.
9When To′u king of Ha′math heard that
David had defeated the whole army of Ha-
dade′zer, king of Zobah, 10he sent his son
Hador′am to King David, to greet him, and
to congratulate him because he had fought
against Hadade′zer and defeated him; for
Hadadezer had often been at war with To′u.
And he sent all sorts of articles of gold, of
silver, and of bronze; 11these also King David dedicated to the LORD, together with
the silver and gold which he had carried off
from all the nations, from E′dom, Moab, the
Am′monites, the Philis′tines, and Am′alek.
12And Abi′shai, the son of Zeru′iah, slew
eighteen thousand E′domites in the Valley
of Salt. 13And he put garrisons in E′dom;
and all the E′domites became David's
servants. And the LORD gave victory to
David wherever he went.
14So David reigned over all Israel; and he
administered justice and equity to all his
people. 15And Jo′ab the son of Zeru′iah was
over the army; and Jehosh′aphat the son of
Ahi′lud was recorder; 16and Za′dok the son of
Ahi′tub and Ahim′elech the son of Abi′athar
were priests; and Shavsha was secretary; 17and
Bena′iah the son of Jehoi′ada was over the
Cher′ethites and the Pel′ethites; and David's
sons were the chief officials in the service of
the king.

19 Now after this Na′hash the king of
the Am′monites died, and his son
reigned in his stead. 2And David said, "I
will deal loyally with Ha′nun the son of
Na′hash, for his father dealt loyally with
me." So David sent messengers to console
him concerning his father. And David's
servants came to Ha′nun in the land of
the Am′monites, to console him. 3But the
princes of the Am′monites said to Ha′nun,
"Do you think, because David has sent
comforters to you, that he is honoring your
father? Have not his servants come to you to
search and to overthrow and to spy out the
land?" 4So Ha′nun took David's servants,
and shaved them, and cut off their garments
in the middle, at their hips, and sent them
away; 5and they departed. When David was
told concerning the men, he sent to meet
them, for the men were greatly ashamed.
And the king said, "Remain at Jericho until
your beards have grown, and then return."
6When the Am′monites saw that they had
made themselves odious to David, Ha′nun
and the Ammonites sent a thousand talents
of silver to hire chariots and horsemen
from Mesopota′mia, from Ar′am-ma′acah,
and from Zobah. 7They hired thirty-two
thousand chariots and the king of Ma′acah
with his army, who came and encamped
before Med′eba. And the Am′monites were
mustered from their cities and came to
battle. 8When David heard of it, he sent Jo′ab
and all the army of the mighty men. 9And
the Am′monites came out and drew up in
battle array at the entrance of the city, and
the kings who had come were by themselves
in the open country.
10When Jo′ab saw that the battle was set
against him both in front and in the rear,
he chose some of the picked men of Israel,
and arrayed them against the Syrians; 11the
rest of his men he put in the charge of
Abi′shai his brother, and they were arrayed
against the Am′monites. 12And he said, "If

the Syrians are too strong for me, then you shall help me; but if the Am′monites are too strong for you, then I will help you. [13]Be of good courage, and let us play the man for our people, and for the cities of our God; and may the LORD do what seems good to him." [14]So Jo′ab and the people who were with him drew near before the Syrians for battle; and they fled before him. [15]And when the Am′monites saw that the Syrians fled, they likewise fled before Abi′shai, Jo′ab's brother, and entered the city. Then Joab came to Jerusalem.

[16]But when the Syrians saw that they had been defeated by Israel, they sent messengers and brought out the Syrians who were beyond the Euphra′tes, with Shophach the commander of the army of Hadade′zer at their head. [17]And when it was told David, he gathered all Israel together, and crossed the Jordan, and came to them, and drew up his forces against them. And when David set the battle in array against the Syrians, they fought with him. [18]And the Syrians fled before Israel; and David slew of the Syrians the men of seven thousand chariots, and forty thousand foot soldiers, and killed also Shophach the commander of their army. [19]And when the servants of Hadade′zer saw that they had been defeated by Israel, they made peace with David, and became subject to him. So the Syrians were not willing to help the Am′monites any more.

20 In the spring of the year, the time when kings go forth to battle, Jo′ab led out the army, and ravaged the country of the Am′monites, and came and besieged Rabbah. But David remained at Jerusalem. And Jo′ab struck Rabbah, and overthrew it. [2]And David took the crown of their king from his head; he found that it weighed a talent of gold, and in it was a precious stone; and it was placed on David's head. And he brought forth the spoil of the city, a very great amount. [3]And he brought forth the people who were in it, and set them to labor with saws and iron picks and axes; and thus David did to all the cities of the Am′monites. Then David and all the people returned to Jerusalem.

[4]And after this there arose war with the Philis′tines at Gezer; then Sib′becai the Hu′shathite slew Sippai, who was one of the descendants of the giants; and the Philistines were subdued. [5]And there was again war with the Philis′tines; and Elha′nan the son of Ja′ir slew Lahmi the brother of Goliath the Gittite, the shaft of whose spear was like a weaver's beam. [6]And there was again war at Gath, where there was a man of great stature, who had six fingers on each hand, and six toes on each foot, twenty-four in number; and he also was descended from the giants. [7]And when he taunted Israel, Jonathan the son of Shim′e-a, David's brother, slew him. [8]These were descended from the giants in Gath; and they fell by the hand of David and by the hand of his servants.

PROVERBS 1

The proverbs of Solomon, son of David, king of Israel:

[2]That men may know wisdom
and instruction,
understand words of insight,
[3]receive instruction in wise dealing,
righteousness, justice, and equity;
[4]that prudence may be given to the simple,
knowledge and discretion to the youth—
[5]the wise man also may hear and increase
in learning,
and the man of understanding
acquire skill,
[6]to understand a proverb and a figure,
the words of the wise and their riddles.

[7]The fear of the LORD is the beginning
of knowledge;
fools despise wisdom and instruction.

[8]Hear, my son, your father's instruction,
and reject not your mother's teaching;
[9]for they are a fair garland for your head,
and pendants for your neck.
[10]My son, if sinners entice you,
do not consent.

[11]If they say, "Come with us, let us lie in wait
for blood,
let us wantonly ambush the innocent;
[12]like Sheol let us swallow them alive
and whole, like those who go down to
the Pit;
[13]we shall find all precious goods,
we shall fill our houses with spoil;
[14]throw in your lot among us,
we will all have one purse"—
[15]my son, do not walk in the way with them,
hold back your foot from their paths;
[16]for their feet run to evil,
and they make haste to shed blood.
[17]For in vain is a net spread
in the sight of any bird;
[18]but these men lie in wait for their
own blood,
they set an ambush for their own lives.
[19]Such are the ways of all who get gain
by violence;
it takes away the life of its possessors.

ACTS 6

Now in these days when the disciples were increasing in number, the Hellenists murmured against the Hebrews because their widows were
neglected in the daily distribution. [2]And the
Twelve summoned the body of the disciples
and said, "It is not right that we should give
up preaching the word of God to serve
tables. [3]Therefore, brethren, pick out from
among you seven men of good repute, full
of the Spirit and of wisdom, whom we may
appoint to this duty. [4]But we will devote
ourselves to prayer and to the ministry of
the word." [5]And what they said pleased the
whole multitude, and they chose Stephen, a
man full of faith and of the Holy Spirit, and
Philip, and Proch′orus, and Nica′nor, and
Ti′mon, and Par′menas, and Nicola′us, a
proselyte of Antioch. [6]These they set before
the apostles, and they prayed and laid their
hands upon them.
[7]And the word of God increased; and the
number of the disciples multiplied greatly in
Jerusalem, and a great many of the priests were
obedient to the faith.
[8]And Stephen, full of grace and power, did
great wonders and signs among the people.
[9]Then some of those who belonged to the
synagogue of the Freedmen (as it was called),
and of the Cyre′nians, and of the Alexandrians,
and of those from Cili′cia and Asia, arose and
disputed with Stephen. [10]But they could not
withstand the wisdom and the Spirit with
which he spoke. [11]Then they secretly instigated
men, who said, "We have heard him speak
blasphemous words against Moses and God."
[12]And they stirred up the people and the elders
and the scribes, and they came upon him
and seized him and brought him before the
council, [13]and set up false witnesses who said,
"This man never ceases to speak words against
this holy place and the law; [14]for we have heard
him say that this Jesus of Nazareth will destroy
this place, and will change the customs which
Moses delivered to us." [15]And gazing at him, all
who sat in the council saw that his face was like
the face of an angel.

REFLECTION

The Book of Proverbs starts off with an invitation to wisdom rather than a series of maxims. Amidst many synonyms for wisdom, it gives us the key to the whole book: "The fear of the LORD is the beginning of knowledge" (Prv 1:7). Seeking wisdom is thus always oriented toward God. When one truly seeks wisdom, its God-given blessings are ubiquitous: "And the LORD gave victory to David wherever he went" (1 Chr 18:13). While the foolish "get gain by violence," it backfires on them (Prv 1:19). They end up worse for the wear, but the wise man is different. In seeking after wisdom, he gains blessing in every arena. St. Stephen is a great example of a wisdom-seeker. He is described as a man "full of the Spirit and of wisdom . . . full of faith and of the Holy Spirit . . . full of grace and power . . . the wisdom and the Spirit" (Acts 6:3–10). He is falsely accused but "his face was like the face of an angel" (v. 15). God blessed him and filled him with wisdom in spite of others' hatred. Wisdom is a mysterious gift from God that orients our whole lives in the right direction. Are you daily seeking wisdom?

June 27

1 CHRONICLES 21

**Satan stood up against Israel,
and incited David to number
Israel. 2So David said to Jo′ab
and the commanders of the army, "Go,
number Israel, from Be′er-she′ba to
Dan, and bring me a report, that I may**
know their number." 3But Jo′ab said, "May
the LORD add to his people a hundred times
as many as they are! Are they not, my lord
the king, all of them my lord's servants?
Why then should my lord require this?
Why should he bring guilt upon Israel?"
4But the king's word prevailed against Jo′ab.
So Joab departed and went throughout all
Israel, and came back to Jerusalem. 5And
Jo′ab gave the sum of the numbering of the
people to David. In all Israel there were one
million one hundred thousand men who
drew the sword, and in Judah four hundred
and seventy thousand who drew the sword.
6But he did not include Levi and Benjamin
in the numbering, for the king's command
was abhorrent to Jo′ab.

7But God was displeased with this thing,
and he struck Israel. 8And David said to
God, "I have sinned greatly in that I have
done this thing. But now, I pray you, take
away the iniquity of your servant; for I have
done very foolishly." 9And the LORD spoke
to Gad, David's seer, saying, 10"Go and say to
David, 'Thus says the LORD, Three things I
offer you; choose one of them, that I may do
it to you.' " 11So Gad came to David and said
to him, "Thus says the LORD, 'Take which
you will: 12either three years of famine; or
three months of devastation by your foes,
while the sword of your enemies overtakes
you; or else three days of the sword of the
LORD, pestilence upon the land, and the
angel of the LORD destroying throughout
all the territory of Israel.' Now decide what
answer I shall return to him who sent me."
13Then David said to Gad, "I am in great
distress; let me fall into the hand of the
LORD, for his mercy is very great; but let me
not fall into the hand of man."

14So the LORD sent a pestilence upon
Israel; and there fell seventy thousand
men of Israel. 15And God sent the angel
to Jerusalem to destroy it; but when he
was about to destroy it, the LORD saw, and
he repented of the evil; and he said to the
destroying angel, "It is enough; now stay
your hand." And the angel of the LORD was
standing by the threshing floor of Ornan
the Jeb′usite. 16And David lifted his eyes and
saw the angel of the LORD standing between
earth and heaven, and in his hand a drawn
sword stretched out over Jerusalem. Then
David and the elders, clothed in sackcloth,
fell upon their faces. 17And David said to
God, "Was it not I who gave command to
number the people? It is I who have sinned
and done very wickedly. But these sheep,
what have they done? Let your hand, I pray
you, O LORD my God, be against me and
against my father's house; but let not the
plague be upon your people."

18Then the angel of the LORD commanded
Gad to say to David that David should go
up and raise an altar to the LORD on the
threshing floor of Ornan the Jeb′usite. 19So
David went up at Gad's word, which he had
spoken in the name of the LORD. 20Now
Ornan was threshing wheat; he turned and
saw the angel, and his four sons who were
with him hid themselves. 21As David came
to Ornan, Ornan looked and saw David and
went forth from the threshing floor, and
did obeisance to David with his face to the
ground. 22And David said to Ornan, "Give
me the site of the threshing floor that I may
build on it an altar to the LORD—give it to
me at its full price—that the plague may be
averted from the people." 23Then Ornan said
to David, "Take it; and let my lord the king
do what seems good to him; see, I give the
oxen for burnt offerings, and the threshing
sledges for the wood, and the wheat for a
cereal offering. I give it all." 24But King David
said to Ornan, "No, but I will buy it for the
full price; I will not take for the LORD what
is yours, nor offer burnt offerings which

cost me nothing." [25]So David paid Ornan six hundred shekels of gold by weight for the site. [26]And David built there an altar to the LORD and presented burnt offerings and peace offerings, and called upon the LORD, and he answered him with fire from heaven upon the altar of burnt offering. [27]Then the LORD commanded the angel; and he put his sword back into its sheath.

[28]At that time, when David saw that the LORD had answered him at the threshing floor of Ornan the Jeb´usite, he made his sacrifices there. [29]For the tabernacle of the LORD, which Moses had made in the wilderness, and the altar of burnt offering were at that time in the high place at Gib´eon; [30]but David could not go before it to inquire of God, for he was afraid of the sword of the angel of the LORD.

22 Then David said, "Here shall be the house of the LORD God and here the altar of burnt offering for Israel."

[2]David commanded to gather together the aliens who were in the land of Israel, and he set stonecutters to prepare dressed stones for building the house of God. [3]David also provided great stores of iron for nails for the doors of the gates and for clamps, as well as bronze in quantities beyond weighing, [4]and cedar timbers without number; for the Sido´nians and Ty´rians brought great quantities of cedar to David. [5]For David said, "Solomon my son is young and inexperienced, and the house that is to be built for the LORD must be exceedingly magnificent, of fame and glory throughout all lands; I will therefore make preparation for it." So David provided materials in great quantity before his death.

[6]Then he called for Solomon his son, and charged him to build a house for the LORD, the God of Israel. [7]David said to Solomon, "My son, I had it in my heart to build a house to the name of the LORD my God. [8]But the word of the LORD came to me, saying, 'You have shed much blood and have waged great wars; you shall not build a house to my name, because you have shed so much blood before me upon the earth. [9]Behold, a son shall be born to you; he shall be a man of peace. I will give him peace from all his enemies round about; for his name shall be Solomon, and I will give peace and quiet to Israel in his days. [10]He shall build a house for my name. He shall be my son, and I will be his father, and I will establish his royal throne in Israel for ever.' [11]Now, my son, the LORD be with you, so that you may succeed in building the house of the LORD your God, as he has spoken concerning you. [12]Only, may the LORD grant you discretion and understanding, that when he gives you charge over Israel you may keep the law of the LORD your God. [13]Then you will prosper if you are careful to observe the statutes and the ordinances which the LORD commanded Moses for Israel. Be strong, and of good courage. Fear not; be not dismayed. [14]With great pains I have provided for the house of the LORD a hundred thousand talents of gold, a million talents of silver, and bronze and iron beyond weighing, for there is so much of it; timber and stone too I have provided. To these you must add. [15]You have an abundance of workmen: stonecutters, masons, carpenters, and all kinds of craftsmen without number, skilled in working [16]gold, silver, bronze, and iron. Arise and be doing! The LORD be with you!"

[17]David also commanded all the leaders of Israel to help Solomon his son, saying, [18]"Is not the LORD your God with you? And has he not given you peace on every side? For he has delivered the inhabitants of the land into my hand; and the land is subdued before the LORD and his people. [19]Now set your mind and heart to seek the LORD your God. Arise and build the sanctuary of the LORD God, so that the ark of the covenant of the LORD and the holy vessels of God may be brought into a house built for the name of the LORD."

PROVERBS 1

[20]Wisdom cries aloud in the street;
in the markets she raises her voice;
[21]on the top of the walls she cries out;
at the entrance of the city gates she speaks:

22“How long, O simple ones, will you love
being simple?
How long will scoffers delight in their
scoffing
and fools hate knowledge?
23Give heed to my reproof;
behold, I will pour out my thoughts to you;
I will make my words known to you.
24Because I have called and you refused
to listen,
have stretched out my hand and no one
has heeded,
25and you have ignored all my counsel
and would have none of my reproof,
26I also will laugh at your calamity;
I will mock when panic strikes you,
27when panic strikes you like a storm,
and your calamity comes like a whirlwind,
when distress and anguish come upon you.
28Then they will call upon me, but I will
not answer;
they will seek me diligently but will not
find me.
29Because they hated knowledge
and did not choose the fear of the LORD,
30would have none of my counsel,
and despised all my reproof,
31therefore they shall eat the fruit of their way
and be sated with their own devices.
32For the simple are killed by their
turning away,
and the complacence of fools
destroys them;
33but he who listens to me will dwell secure
and will be at ease, without dread of evil.”

ACTS 7

And the high priest said, “Is this so?” 2And Stephen said:
**“Brethren and fathers, hear me. The
God of glory appeared to our father**
Abraham, when he was in Mesopota′mia,
before he lived in Haran, 3and said to him,
‘Depart from your land and from your
kindred and go into the land which I will
show you.’ 4Then he departed from the land
of the Chalde′ans, and lived in Haran. And
after his father died, God removed him from
there into this land in which you are now
living; 5yet he gave him no inheritance in it,
not even a foot’s length, but promised to give
it to him in possession and to his posterity
after him, though he had no child. 6And God
spoke to this effect, that his posterity would
be aliens in a land belonging to others, who
would enslave them and ill-treat them four
hundred years. 7‘But I will judge the nation
which they serve,’ said God, ‘and after that
they shall come out and worship me in this
place.’ 8And he gave him the covenant of
circumcision. And so Abraham became the
father of Isaac, and circumcised him on the
eighth day; and Isaac became the father of
Jacob, and Jacob of the twelve patriarchs.

9“And the patriarchs, jealous of Joseph, sold
him into Egypt; but God was with him, 10and
rescued him out of all his afflictions, and
gave him favor and wisdom before Pharaoh,
king of Egypt, who made him governor over
Egypt and over all his household. 11Now
there came a famine throughout all Egypt
and Canaan, and great affliction, and our
fathers could find no food. 12But when Jacob
heard that there was grain in Egypt, he sent
forth our fathers the first time. 13And at the
second visit Joseph made himself known
to his brothers, and Joseph’s family became
known to Pharaoh. 14And Joseph sent and
called to him Jacob his father and all his
kindred, seventy-five souls; 15and Jacob went
down into Egypt. And he died, himself and
our fathers, 16and they were carried back to
She′chem and laid in the tomb that Abraham
had bought for a sum of silver from the sons
of Hamor in Shechem.

17“But as the time of the promise drew
near, which God had granted to Abraham,
the people grew and multiplied in Egypt
18till there arose over Egypt another king
who had not known Joseph. 19He dealt
craftily with our race and forced our fathers
to expose their infants, that they might not
be kept alive. 20At this time Moses was born,
and was beautiful before God. And he was
brought up for three months in his father’s
house; 21and when he was exposed, Pharaoh’s
daughter adopted him and brought him up

as her own son. 22And Moses was instructed in all the wisdom of the Egyptians, and he was mighty in his words and deeds.

23"When he was forty years old, it came into his heart to visit his brethren, the sons of Israel. 24And seeing one of them being wronged, he defended the oppressed man and avenged him by striking the Egyptian. 25He supposed that his brethren understood that God was giving them deliverance by his hand, but they did not understand. 26And on the following day he appeared to them as they were quarreling and would have reconciled them, saying, 'Men, you are brethren, why do you wrong each other?' 27But the man who was wronging his neighbor thrust him aside, saying, 'Who made you a ruler and a judge over us? 28Do you want to kill me as you killed the Egyptian yesterday?' 29At this retort Moses fled, and became an exile in the land of Mid′ian, where he became the father of two sons."

REFLECTION

So many of our faults lie in not doing, rather than doing. It is easy to focus on the problems our actions bring about, but so many problems arise because of our inaction. David, like a good father, warns his son against such procrastination and heartily encourages him to do what God wants: build the Temple. David declares, "Be strong, and of good courage. Fear not; be not dismayed" (1 Chr 22:13). He essentially commissions Solomon to accomplish the project in his heart. He provides workmen and materials, giving his son everything necessary. To conclude his charge, David issues a powerful command, "Arise and be doing! The LORD be with you" (v. 16). Upon David's death, Solomon could have ignored his father's advice and simply enjoyed the privileges of being king, yet he follows through and actually builds the Temple. The Lord can accomplish great things through us, but we must be willing to stand up and act when the time comes. We must follow Wisdom when she calls in order that we might "dwell secure" (Prv 1:33). Indeed, we might be called upon to witness before powerful men like St. Stephen was (see Acts 7). In what ways should you "arise and be doing"?

June 28

1 CHRONICLES 23

When David was old and full of days, he made Solomon his son king over Israel.

2David assembled all the leaders of Israel and the priests and the Levites. 3The Levites, thirty years old and upward, were numbered, and the total was thirty-eight thousand men. 4"Twenty-four thousand of these," David said, "shall have charge of the work in the house of the LORD, six thousand shall be officers and judges, 5four thousand gatekeepers, and four thousand shall offer praises to the LORD with the instruments which I have made for praise." 6And David organized them in divisions corresponding to the sons of Levi: Gershom, Ko′hath, and Merar′i.

7The sons of Gershom were Ladan and Shim′e-i. 8The sons of Ladan: Jehi′el the chief, and Zetham, and Joel, three. 9The sons of Shim′e-i: Shelo′moth, Ha′zi-el, and Haran, three. These were the heads of the fathers' houses of Ladan. 10And the sons of Shim′e-i: Jahath, Zina, and Je′ush, and Beri′ah. These four were the sons of Shim′e-i. 11Jahath was the chief, and Zizah the second; but Je′ush and Beri′ah had not many sons, therefore they became a father's house in one reckoning.

12The sons of Ko′hath: Amram, Izhar, He′bron, and Uz′ziel, four. 13The sons of Amram: Aaron and Moses. Aaron was set apart to consecrate the most holy things, that he and his sons for ever should burn incense before the LORD, and minister to him and pronounce blessings in his name for ever. 14But the sons of Moses the man of God were named among the tribe of Levi. 15The sons of Moses: Gershom and Elie′zer. 16The sons of Gershom: Shebu′el the chief. 17The sons of Elie′zer: Rehabi′ah the chief; Eliezer had no other sons, but the sons of Rehabiah were very many. 18The sons of Izhar: Shelo′mith the chief. 19The sons of

He′bron: Jeri′ah the chief, Amari′ah the second, Jaha′ziel the third, and Jekame′am the fourth. [20]The sons of Uz′ziel: Micah the chief and Isshi′ah the second.

[21]The sons of Merar′i: Mah′li and Mu′shi. The sons of Mahli: Elea′zar and Kish. [22]Elea′zar died having no sons, but only daughters; their kinsmen, the sons of Kish, married them. [23]The sons of Mu′shi: Mah′li, E′der, and Jer′emoth, three.

[24]These were the sons of Levi by their fathers' houses, the heads of fathers' houses as they were registered according to the number of the names of the individuals from twenty years old and upward who were to do the work for the service of the house of the LORD. [25]For David said, "The LORD, the God of Israel, has given peace to his people; and he dwells in Jerusalem for ever. [26]And so the Levites no longer need to carry the tabernacle or any of the things for its service"—[27]for by the last words of David these were the number of the Levites from twenty years old and upward—[28]"but their duty shall be to assist the sons of Aaron for the service of the house of the LORD, having the care of the courts and the chambers, the cleansing of all that is holy, and any work for the service of the house of God; [29]to assist also with the showbread, the flour for the cereal offering, the wafers of unleavened bread, the baked offering, the offering mixed with oil, and all measures of quantity or size. [30]And they shall stand every morning, thanking and praising the LORD, and likewise at evening, [31]and whenever burnt offerings are offered to the LORD on sabbaths, new moons, and feast days, according to the number required of them, continually before the LORD. [32]Thus they shall keep charge of the tent of meeting and the sanctuary, and shall attend the sons of Aaron, their brethren, for the service of the house of the LORD."

24 The divisions of the sons of Aaron were these. The sons of Aaron: Na′dab, Abi′hu, Elea′zar, and Ith′amar. [2]But Na′dab and Abi′hu died before their father, and had no children, so Elea′zar and Ith′amar became the priests. [3]With the help of Za′dok of the sons of Elea′zar, and Ahim′elech of the sons of Ith′amar, David organized them according to the appointed duties in their service. [4]Since more chief men were found among the sons of Elea′zar than among the sons of Ith′amar, they organized them under sixteen heads of fathers' houses of the sons of Eleazar, and eight of the sons of Ithamar. [5]They organized them by lot, all alike, for there were officers of the sanctuary and officers of God among both the sons of Elea′zar and the sons of Ith′amar. [6]And the scribe Shemai′ah the son of Nethan′el, a Levite, recorded them in the presence of the king, and the princes, and Za′dok the priest, and Ahim′elech the son of Abi′athar, and the heads of the fathers' houses of the priests and of the Levites; one father's house being chosen for Elea′zar and one chosen for Ith′amar.

[7]The first lot fell to Jehoi′arib, the second to Jedai′ah, [8]the third to Harim, the fourth to Seo′rim, [9]the fifth to Malchi′jah, the sixth to Mi′jamin, [10]the seventh to Hakkoz, the eighth to Abi′jah, [11]the ninth to Jesh′ua, the tenth to Shecani′ah, [12]the eleventh to Eli′ashib, the twelfth to Ja′kim, [13]the thirteenth to Huppah, the fourteenth to Jesheb′e-ab, [14]the fifteenth to Bilgah, the sixteenth to Immer, [15]the seventeenth to He′zir, the eighteenth to Hap′pizzez, [16]the nineteenth to Pethahi′ah, the twentieth to Jehez′kel, [17]the twenty-first to Ja′chin, the twenty-second to Gamul, [18]the twenty-third to Delai′ah, the twenty-fourth to Ma-azi′ah. [19]These had as their appointed duty in their service to come into the house of the LORD according to the procedure established for them by Aaron their father, as the LORD God of Israel had commanded him.

[20]And of the rest of the sons of Levi: of the sons of Amram, Shu′ba-el; of the sons of Shuba-el, Jehde′iah. [21]Of Rehabi′ah: of the sons of Rehabiah, Isshi′ah the chief. [22]Of the Iz′harites, Shelo′moth; of the sons of Shelomoth, Jahath. [23]The sons of He′bron: Jeri′ah the chief, Amari′ah the second, Jahazi′el the third, Jekame′am the fourth. [24]The sons of Uz′ziel, Micah; of the sons of Micah, Sha′mir. [25]The brother of Micah, Isshi′ah; of the sons of Isshiah, Zechari′ah.

26The sons of Merar´i: Mah´li and Mu´shi. The sons of Ja-azi´ah: Beno. 27The sons of Merar´i: of Ja-azi´ah, Beno, Shoham, Zaccur, and Ibri. 28Of Mah´li: Elea´zar, who had no sons. 29Of Kish, the sons of Kish: Jerah´meel. 30The sons of Mu´shi: Mah´li, E´der, and Jer´imoth. These were the sons of the Levites according to their fathers' houses. 31These also, the head of each father's house and his younger brother alike, cast lots, just as their brethren the sons of Aaron, in the presence of King David, Za´dok, Ahim´elech, and the heads of fathers' houses of the priests and of the Levites.

25 David and the chiefs of the service also set apart for the service certain of the sons of A´saph, and of He´man, and of Jedu´thun, who should prophesy with lyres, with harps, and with cymbals. The list of those who did the work and of their duties was: 2Of the sons of A´saph: Zaccur, Joseph, Nethani´ah, and Ashare´lah, sons of Asaph, under the direction of Asaph, who prophesied under the direction of the king. 3Of Jedu´thun, the sons of Jeduthun: Gedali´ah, Zeri, Jeshai´ah, Shim´e-i, Hashabi´ah, and Mattithi´ah, six, under the direction of their father Jeduthun, who prophesied with the lyre in thanksgiving and praise to the LORD. 4Of He´man, the sons of Heman: Bukki´ah, Mattani´ah, Uz´ziel, Shebu´el, and Jer´imoth, Hanani´ah, Hana´ni, Eli´athah, Giddal´ti, and Romam´ti-e´zer, Joshbekash´ah, Mallo´thi, Hothir, Maha´zi-oth. 5All these were the sons of He´man the king's seer, according to the promise of God to exalt him; for God had given Heman fourteen sons and three daughters. 6They were all under the direction of their father in the music in the house of the LORD with cymbals, harps, and lyres for the service of the house of God. A´saph, Jedu´thun, and He´man were under the order of the king. 7The number of them along with their brethren, who were trained in singing to the LORD, all who were skilful, was two hundred and eighty-eight. 8And they cast lots for their duties, small and great, teacher and pupil alike.

9The first lot fell for A´saph to Joseph; the second to Gedali´ah, to him and his brethren and his sons, twelve; 10the third to Zaccur, his sons and his brethren, twelve; 11the fourth to Izri, his sons and his brethren, twelve; 12the fifth to Nethani´ah, his sons and his brethren, twelve; 13the sixth to Bukki´ah, his sons and his brethren, twelve; 14the seventh to Jeshare´lah, his sons and his brethren, twelve; 15the eighth to Jesha´iah, his sons and his brethren, twelve; 16the ninth to Mattani´ah, his sons and his brethren, twelve; 17the tenth to Shim´e-i, his sons and his brethren, twelve; 18the eleventh to Az´arel, his sons and his brethren, twelve; 19the twelfth to Hashabi´ah, his sons and his brethren, twelve; 20to the thirteenth, Shu´ba-el, his sons and his brethren, twelve; 21to the fourteenth, Mattithi´ah, his sons and his brethren, twelve; 22to the fifteenth, to Jer´emoth, his sons and his brethren, twelve; 23to the sixteenth, to Hanani´ah, his sons and his brethren, twelve; 24to the seventeenth, to Joshbekash´ah, his sons and his brethren, twelve; 25to the eighteenth, to Hana´ni, his sons and his brethren, twelve; 26to the nineteenth, to Mallo´thi, his sons and his brethren, twelve; 27to the twentieth, to Eli´athah, his sons and his brethren, twelve; 28to the twenty-first, to Hothir, his sons and his brethren, twelve; 29to the twenty-second, to Giddal´ti, his sons and his brethren, twelve; 30to the twenty-third, to Maha´zi-oth, his sons and his brethren, twelve; 31to the twenty-fourth, to Romam´ti-e´zer, his sons and his brethren, twelve.

PROVERBS 2

My son, if you receive my words
and treasure up my commandments
with you,
2making your ear attentive to wisdom
and inclining your heart to understanding;
3yes, if you cry out for insight
and raise your voice for understanding,
4if you seek it like silver
and search for it as for hidden treasures;
5then you will understand the fear of the LORD
and find the knowledge of God.
6For the LORD gives wisdom;
from his mouth come knowledge and
understanding;

7 he stores up sound wisdom for the upright;
he is a shield to those who walk in integrity,
8 guarding the paths of justice
and preserving the way of his saints.
9 Then you will understand righteousness
and justice
and equity, every good path;
10 for wisdom will come into your heart,
and knowledge will be pleasant to
your soul;
11 discretion will watch over you;
understanding will guard you;
12 delivering you from the way of evil,
from men of perverted speech,
13 who forsake the paths of uprightness
to walk in the ways of darkness,
14 who rejoice in doing evil
and delight in the perverseness of evil;
15 men whose paths are crooked,
and who are devious in their ways.

16 You will be saved from the loose woman,
from the adventuress with her smooth
words,
17 who forsakes the companion of her youth
and forgets the covenant of her God;
18 for her house sinks down to death,
and her paths to the shades;
19 none who go to her come back
nor do they regain the paths of life.

20 So you will walk in the way of good men
and keep to the paths of the righteous.
21 For the upright will inhabit the land,
and men of integrity will remain in it;
22 but the wicked will be cut off from the land,
and the treacherous will be rooted out of it.

ACTS 7

30 "Now when forty years had
passed, an angel appeared to
him in the wilderness of Mount Sinai,
in a flame of fire in a bush. 31 When
Moses saw it he wondered at the sight;
and as he drew near to look, the voice of the
Lord came, 32 'I am the God of your fathers,
the God of Abraham and of Isaac and of
Jacob.' And Moses trembled and did not dare
to look. 33 And the Lord said to him, 'Take off
the shoes from your feet, for the place where
you are standing is holy ground. 34 I have
surely seen the ill-treatment of my people
that are in Egypt and heard their groaning,
and I have come down to deliver them. And
now come, I will send you to Egypt.'
35 "This Moses whom they refused, saying,
'Who made you a ruler and a judge?' God sent
as both ruler and deliverer by the hand of the
angel that appeared to him in the bush. 36 He
led them out, having performed wonders and
signs in Egypt and at the Red Sea, and in the
wilderness for forty years. 37 This is the Moses
who said to the Israelites, 'God will raise up
for you a prophet from your brethren as he
raised me up.' 38 This is he who was in the
congregation in the wilderness with the angel
who spoke to him at Mount Sinai, and with
our fathers; and he received living oracles to
give to us. 39 Our fathers refused to obey him,
but thrust him aside, and in their hearts they
turned to Egypt, 40 saying to Aaron, 'Make
for us gods to go before us; as for this Moses
who led us out from the land of Egypt, we
do not know what has become of him.' 41 And
they made a calf in those days, and offered a
sacrifice to the idol and rejoiced in the works
of their hands. 42 But God turned and gave
them over to worship the host of heaven, as
it is written in the book of the prophets:
'Did you offer to me slain beasts
and sacrifices,
forty years in the wilderness, O house
of Israel?
43 And you took up the tent of Mo´loch,
and the star of the god Re´phan,
the figures which you made to worship;
and I will remove you beyond Babylon.'
44 "Our fathers had the tent of witness in
the wilderness, even as he who spoke to
Moses directed him to make it, according to
the pattern that he had seen. 45 Our fathers
in turn brought it in with Joshua when they
dispossessed the nations which God thrust
out before our fathers. So it was until the days
of David, 46 who found favor in the sight of
God and asked leave to find a habitation for
the God of Jacob. 47 But it was Solomon who

built a house for him. [48]Yet the Most High
does not dwell in houses made with hands;
as the prophet says,
[49]'Heaven is my throne,
and earth my footstool.
What house will you build for me, says
the Lord,
or what is the place of my rest?
[50] Did not my hand make all these things?'"

REFLECTION

Solomon is both the wisest of men and the builder of the Temple. His example shows us what it means to seek after wisdom, how seeking after the Lord himself is actually at the heart of the search for wisdom. Proverbs encourages us to seek wisdom, to "treasure up my commandments with you" (2:1) and to "seek it like silver and search for it as for hidden treasures" (v. 4). Yet it also insists that wisdom is a gift: "The LORD gives wisdom" (v. 6). David makes Solomon king to build the Temple, yet he also organizes the priests and Levites to supply the liturgy that will take place in that Temple. What begins as a search for wisdom becomes a building project and then a liturgical life of worship. However, St. Stephen reminds us that, though Solomon was the great temple-builder, "the Most High does not dwell in houses made with hands" (Acts 7:48). No matter how great a building we make for him, it cannot contain his presence since he is the creator of all. Seeking the treasure of wisdom leads us into action. Yet action, like Solomon's building, leads us to worship, to seek the Lord himself. How are you living out the search for wisdom?

June 29

1 CHRONICLES 26

As for the divisions of the gatekeepers: of the Ko′rahites, Meshelemi′ah the son of Ko′re, of the sons of A′saph. [2]And Meshelemi′ah had sons:
Zechari′ah the first-born, Jedi′ael the second,
Zebadi′ah the third, Jath′ni-el the fourth,
[3]E′lam the fifth, Je′ho-ha′nan the sixth, El′ie-
ho-e′nai the seventh. [4]And O′bed-e′dom had
sons: Shemai′ah the first-born, Jeho′zabad
the second, Jo′ah the third, Sachar the
fourth, Nethan′el the fifth, [5]Am′mi-el the
sixth, Is′sachar the seventh, Pe-ul′lethai the
eighth; for God blessed him. [6]Also to his
son Shemai′ah were sons born who were
rulers in their fathers' houses, for they were
men of great ability. [7]The sons of Shemai′ah:
Othni, Reph′a-el, O′bed, and Elza′bad,
whose brethren were able men, Eli′hu and
Semachi′ah. [8]All these were of the sons of
O′bed-e′dom with their sons and brethren,
able men qualified for the service; sixty-
two of Obed-edom. [9]And Meshelemi′ah
had sons and brethren, able men, eighteen.
[10]And Ho′sah, of the sons of Merar′i, had
sons: Shimri the chief (for though he was
not the first-born, his father made him
chief), [11]Hilki′ah the second, Tebali′ah the
third, Zechari′ah the fourth: all the sons and
brethren of Ho′sah were thirteen.

[12]These divisions of the gatekeepers, corresponding to their chief men, had duties,
just as their brethren did, ministering in
the house of the LORD; [13]and they cast lots
by fathers' houses, small and great alike,
for their gates. [14]The lot for the east fell to
Shelemi′ah. They cast lots also for his son
Zechari′ah, a shrewd counselor, and his lot
came out for the north. [15]O′bed-e′dom's
came out for the south, and to his sons was
allotted the storehouse. [16]For Shuppim and
Ho′sah it came out for the west, at the gate
of Shal′lecheth on the road that goes up.
Watch corresponded to watch. [17]On the east
there were six each day, on the north four
each day, on the south four each day, as well
as two and two at the storehouse; [18]and for
the parbar on the west there were four at
the road and two at the parbar. [19]These were
the divisions of the gatekeepers among the
Ko′rahites and the sons of Merar′i.

[20]And of the Levites, Ahi′jah had charge
of the treasuries of the house of God and
the treasuries of the dedicated gifts. [21]The
sons of Ladan, the sons of the Ger′shonites

belonging to Ladan, the heads of the fathers' houses belonging to Ladan the Gershonite: Jehi′eli.

[22]The sons of Jehi′eli, Zetham and Joel his brother, were in charge of the treasuries of the house of the LORD. [23]Of the Am′ramites, the Iz′harites, the He′bronites, and the Uz′zielites—[24]and Shebu′el the son of Gershom, son of Moses, was chief officer in charge of the treasuries. [25]His brethren: from Elie′zer were his son Rehabi′ah, and his son Jeshai′ah, and his son Jo′ram, and his son Zich′ri, and his son Shelo′moth. [26]This Shelo′moth and his brethren were in charge of all the treasuries of the dedicated gifts which David the king, and the heads of the fathers' houses, and the officers of the thousands and the hundreds, and the commanders of the army, had dedicated. [27]From spoil won in battles they dedicated gifts for the maintenance of the house of the LORD. [28]Also all that Samuel the seer, and Saul the son of Kish, and Abner the son of Ner, and Jo′ab the son of Zeru′iah had dedicated—all dedicated gifts were in the care of Shelo′moth and his brethren.

[29]Of the Iz′harites, Chenani′ah and his sons were appointed to outside duties for Israel, as officers and judges. [30]Of the He′bronites, Hashabi′ah and his brethren, one thousand seven hundred men of ability, had the oversight of Israel westward of the Jordan for all the work of the LORD and for the service of the king. [31]Of the He′bronites, Jeri′jah was chief of the Hebronites of whatever genealogy or fathers' houses. (In the fortieth year of David's reign search was made and men of great ability among them were found at Ja′zer in Gilead.) [32]King David appointed him and his brethren, two thousand seven hundred men of ability, heads of fathers' houses, to have the oversight of the Reubenites, the Gadites, and the half-tribe of the Manas′sites for everything pertaining to God and for the affairs of the king.

27 This is the list of the people of Israel, the heads of fathers' houses, the commanders of thousands and hundreds, and their officers who served the king in all matters concerning the divisions that came and went, month after month throughout the year, each division numbering twenty-four thousand:

[2]Jasho′beam the son of Zab′diel was in charge of the first division in the first month; in his division were twenty-four thousand. [3]He was a descendant of Per′ez, and was chief of all the commanders of the army for the first month. [4]Dodai the Aho′hite was in charge of the division of the second month; in his division were twenty-four thousand. [5]The third commander, for the third month, was Bena′iah, the son of Jehoi′ada the priest, as chief; in his division were twenty-four thousand. [6]This is the Bena′iah who was a mighty man of the thirty and in command of the thirty; Ammiz′abad his son was in charge of his division. [7]As′ahel the brother of Jo′ab was fourth, for the fourth month, and his son Zebadi′ah after him; in his division were twenty-four thousand. [8]The fifth commander, for the fifth month, was Shamhuth, the Iz′rahite; in his division were twenty-four thousand. [9]Sixth, for the sixth month, was Ira, the son of Ikkesh the Teko′ite; in his division were twenty-four thousand. [10]Seventh, for the seventh month, was He′lez the Pel′onite, of the sons of E′phraim; in his division were twenty-four thousand. [11]Eighth, for the eighth month, was Sib′becai the Hu′shathite, of the Ze′rahites; in his division were twenty-four thousand. [12]Ninth, for the ninth month, was Abie′zer of An′athoth, a Benjaminite; in his division were twenty-four thousand. [13]Tenth, for the tenth month, was Ma′harai of Netoph′ah, of the Ze′rahites; in his division were twenty-four thousand. [14]Eleventh, for the eleventh month, was Bena′iah of Pir′athon, of the sons of E′phraim; in his division were twenty-four thousand. [15]Twelfth, for the twelfth month, was Heldai the Netoph′athite, of Oth′ni-el; in his division were twenty-four thousand.

[16]Over the tribes of Israel, for the Reubenites Elie′zer the son of Zich′ri was chief officer; for the Simeonites, Shephati′ah the son of Ma′acah; [17]for Levi, Hashabi′ah the son of Kemu′el; for Aaron, Za′dok; [18]for Judah, Eli′hu, one of David's brothers; for Is′sachar, Omri the son of Michael; [19]for Zeb′ulun,

Ishma´iah the son of Obadi´ah; for Naph´ta-
li, Jer´emoth the son of Az´ri-el; [20]for the
E´phraimites, Hoshe´a the son of Azazi´ah; for
the half-tribe of Manas´seh, Joel the son of Pe-
dai´ah; [21]for the half-tribe of Manas´seh in Gilead, Iddo the son of Zechari´ah; for Benjamin,
Ja-asi´el the son of Abner; [22]for Dan, Az´arel the
son of Jero´ham. These were the leaders of the
tribes of Israel. [23]David did not number those
below twenty years of age, for the LORD had
promised to make Israel as many as the stars
of heaven. [24]Jo´ab the son of Zeru´iah began
to number, but did not finish; yet wrath came
upon Israel for this, and the number was not
entered in the chronicles of King David.

[25]Over the king's treasuries was Az´maveth
the son of Ad´i-el; and over the treasuries in the
country, in the cities, in the villages and in the
towers, was Jonathan the son of Uzzi´ah; [26]and
over those who did the work of the field for
tilling the soil was Ezri the son of Che´lub; [27]and
over the vineyards was Shim´e-i the Ra´mathite;
and over the produce of the vineyards for the
wine cellars was Zabdi the Shiphmite. [28]Over
the olive and sycamore trees in the Shephe´lah
was Ba´al-ha´nan the Gede´rite; and over the
stores of oil was Jo´ash. [29]Over the herds that
pastured in Sharon was Shitrai the Sharonite;
over the herds in the valleys was Sha´phat the
son of Ad´lai. [30]Over the camels was Obil the
Ish´maelite; and over the she-donkeys was
Jehde´iah the Meron´othite. Over the flocks
was Jaziz the Hag´rite. [31]All these were stewards
of King David's property.

[32]Jonathan, David's uncle, was a counselor,
being a man of understanding and a scribe;
he and Jehi´el the son of Hach´moni attended
the king's sons. [33]Ahith´ophel was the king's
counselor, and Hu´shai the Ar´chite was the
king's friend. [34]Ahith´ophel was succeeded by
Jehoi´ada the son of Bena´iah, and Abi´athar.
Jo´ab was commander of the king's army.

PROVERBS 3

My son, do not forget my teaching,
but let your heart keep my commandments;
[2]for length of days and years of life
and abundant welfare will they give you.
[3]Let not loyalty and faithfulness forsake you;
bind them about your neck,
write them on the tablet of your heart.
[4]So you will find favor and good repute
in the sight of God and man.

[5]Trust in the LORD with all your heart,
and do not rely on your own insight.
[6]In all your ways acknowledge him,
and he will make straight your paths.
[7]Be not wise in your own eyes;
fear the LORD, and turn away from evil.
[8]It will be healing to your flesh
and refreshment to your bones.

[9]Honor the LORD with your substance
and with the first fruits of all your produce;
[10]then your barns will be filled with plenty,
and your vats will be bursting with wine.

[11]My son, do not despise the LORD's discipline
or be weary of his reproof,
[12]for the LORD reproves him whom he loves,
as a father the son in whom he delights.

[13]Happy is the man who finds wisdom,
and the man who gets understanding,
[14]for the gain from it is better than gain
from silver
and its profit better than gold.
[15]She is more precious than jewels,
and nothing you desire can compare with her.
[16]Long life is in her right hand;
in her left hand are riches and honor.
[17]Her ways are ways of pleasantness,
and all her paths are peace.
[18]She is a tree of life to those who lay hold of her;
those who hold her fast are called happy.

ACTS 7

[51]"**You stiff-necked people, uncircumcised in heart and ears, you always resist the Holy Spirit. As your fathers did, so do you.** [52]**Which of**
the prophets did not your fathers persecute?
And they killed those who announced beforehand the coming of the Righteous One,

whom you have now betrayed and murdered, [53]you who received the law as delivered by angels and did not keep it."

[54]Now when they heard these things they were enraged, and they ground their teeth against him. [55]But he, full of the Holy Spirit, gazed into heaven and saw the glory of God, and Jesus standing at the right hand of God; [56]and he said, "Behold, I see the heavens opened, and the Son of man standing at the right hand of God." [57]But they cried out with a loud voice and stopped their ears and rushed together upon him. [58]Then they cast him out of the city and stoned him; and the witnesses laid down their garments at the feet of a young man named Saul. [59]And as they were stoning Stephen, he prayed, "Lord Jesus, receive my spirit." [60]And he knelt down and cried with a loud voice, "Lord, do not hold this sin against them." And when he had said this, he fell asleep. 8 [1]And Saul was consenting to his death.

And on that day a great persecution arose against the Church in Jerusalem; and they were all scattered throughout the region of Judea and Sama′ria, except the apostles. [2]Devout men buried Stephen, and made great lamentation over him. [3]But Saul laid waste the Church, and entering house after house, he dragged off men and women and committed them to prison.

[4]Now those who were scattered went about preaching the word. [5]Philip went down to a city of Samar′ia, and proclaimed to them the Christ. [6]And the multitudes with one accord gave heed to what was said by Philip, when they heard him and saw the signs which he did. [7]For unclean spirits came out of many who were possessed, crying with a loud voice; and many who were paralyzed or lame were healed. [8]So there was much joy in that city.

REFLECTION

St. Stephen is an example of the wise man. Proverbs promises "length of days and years of life" (3:2) to the man who seeks wisdom, yet Stephen dies by public stoning. Stephen testifies before the Sanhedrin about Jesus and calls them to account for their refusal to follow him. His violent fate, however, is not a tragedy in the strictest sense. Rather, the Church celebrates Stephen as the "proto-martyr." His death is not the end but instead an entry into eternal life. At the moment of death, he says, "Lord Jesus, receive my spirit" (Acts 7:59), showing his death to be patterned after the Lord's. Here he truly epitomizes what Proverbs teaches: "Trust in the LORD with all your heart, and do not rely on your own insight" (v. 3:5). While wisdom promises long life, riches, honor, pleasantness, peace, and happiness (see vv. 16–18), these rewards may not come on earth but in Heaven. Proverbs promises the "tree of life to those who lay hold of her; those who hold her fast are called happy" (v. 18). Stephen, whose Greek name means *crown*, wins by his fidelity the glorious crown of martyrdom. Adopting an eternal perspective will help us to stay true to him in times of testing and look for our happiness not merely in earthly realities but in the life to come. What are you hoping for in this life and the next?

June 30

1 CHRONICLES 28

David assembled at Jerusalem all the officials of Israel, the officials of the tribes, the officers of the divisions that served the king, the commanders of thousands, the commanders of hundreds, the stewards of all the property and cattle of the king and his sons, together with the palace officials, the mighty men, and all the seasoned warriors. [2]Then King David rose to his feet and said: "Hear me, my brethren and my people. I had it in my heart to build a house of rest for the ark of the covenant of the LORD, and for the footstool of our God; and I made preparations for building. [3]But God said

to me, ‘You may not build a house for my
name, for you are a warrior and have shed
blood.’ 4Yet the LORD God of Israel chose
me from all my father’s house to be king
over Israel for ever; for he chose Judah as
leader, and in the house of Judah my father’s
house, and among my father’s sons he took
pleasure in me to make me king over all
Israel. 5And of all my sons (for the LORD
has given me many sons) he has chosen
Solomon my son to sit upon the throne of
the kingdom of the LORD over Israel. 6He
said to me, ‘It is Solomon your son who
shall build my house and my courts, for I
have chosen him to be my son, and I will be
his father. 7I will establish his kingdom for
ever if he continues resolute in keeping my
commandments and my ordinances, as he
is today.’ 8Now therefore in the sight of all
Israel, the assembly of the LORD, and in the
hearing of our God, observe and seek out all
the commandments of the LORD your God;
that you may possess this good land, and
leave it for an inheritance to your children
after you for ever.

9“And you, Solomon my son, know the
God of your father, and serve him with a
whole heart and with a willing mind; for the
LORD searches all hearts, and understands
every plan and thought. If you seek him, he
will be found by you; but if you forsake him,
he will cast you off for ever. 10Take heed now,
for the LORD has chosen you to build a house
for the sanctuary; be strong, and do it.”

11Then David gave Solomon his son the
plan of the vestibule of the temple, and of
its houses, its treasuries, its upper rooms,
and its inner chambers, and of the room for
the mercy seat; 12and the plan of all that he
had in mind for the courts of the house of
the LORD, all the surrounding chambers,
the treasuries of the house of God, and
the treasuries for dedicated gifts; 13for the
divisions of the priests and of the Levites,
and all the work of the service in the house
of the LORD; for all the vessels for the service
in the house of the LORD, 14the weight of
gold for all golden vessels for each service,
the weight of silver vessels for each service,
15the weight of the golden lampstands and
their lamps, the weight of gold for each
lampstand and its lamps, the weight of silver
for a lampstand and its lamps, according to
the use of each lampstand in the service,
16the weight of gold for each table for the
showbread, the silver for the silver tables,
17and pure gold for the forks, the basins,
and the cups; for the golden bowls and the
weight of each; for the silver bowls and the
weight of each; 18for the altar of incense
made of refined gold, and its weight; also his
plan for the golden chariot of the cherubim
that spread their wings and covered the ark
of the covenant of the LORD. 19All this he
made clear by the writing from the hand of
the LORD concerning it, all the work to be
done according to the plan.

20Then David said to Solomon his son, “Be
strong and of good courage, and do it. Fear
not, be not dismayed; for the LORD God,
even my God, is with you. He will not fail
you or forsake you, until all the work for the
service of the house of the LORD is finished.
21And behold the divisions of the priests and
the Levites for all the service of the house
of God; and with you in all the work will
be every willing man who has skill for any
kind of service; also the officers and all the
people will be wholly at your command.”

29 And David the king said to all the
assembly, “Solomon my son, whom
alone God has chosen, is young and
inexperienced, and the work is great; for the
palace will not be for man but for the LORD
God. 2So I have provided for the house of
my God, so far as I was able, the gold for
the things of gold, the silver for the things
of silver, and the bronze for the things of
bronze, the iron for the things of iron,
and wood for the things of wood, besides
great quantities of onyx and stones for
setting, antimony, colored stones, all sorts
of precious stones, and marble. 3Moreover,
in addition to all that I have provided for
the holy house, I have a treasure of my
own of gold and silver, and because of my
devotion to the house of my God I give it
to the house of my God: 4three thousand
talents of gold, of the gold of Ophir, and
seven thousand talents of refined silver,

for overlaying the walls of the house, [5]and for all the work to be done by craftsmen, gold for the things of gold and silver for the things of silver. Who then will offer willingly, consecrating himself today to the LORD?"

[6]Then the heads of fathers' houses made their freewill offerings, as did also the leaders of the tribes, the commanders of thousands and of hundreds, and the officers over the king's work. [7]They gave for the service of the house of God five thousand talents and ten thousand darics of gold, ten thousand talents of silver, eighteen thousand talents of bronze, and a hundred thousand talents of iron. [8]And whoever had precious stones gave them to the treasury of the house of the LORD, in the care of Jehi′el the Ger′shonite. [9]Then the people rejoiced because these had given willingly, for with a whole heart they had offered freely to the LORD; David the king also rejoiced greatly.

[10]Therefore David blessed the LORD in the presence of all the assembly; and David said: "Blessed are you, O LORD, the God of Israel our father, for ever and ever. [11]Yours, O LORD, is the greatness, and the power, and the glory, and the victory, and the majesty; for all that is in the heavens and in the earth is yours; yours is the kingdom, O LORD, and you are exalted as head above all. [12]Both riches and honor come from you, and you rule over all. In your hand are power and might; and in your hand it is to make great and to give strength to all. [13]And now we thank you, our God, and praise your glorious name.

[14]"But who am I, and what is my people, that we should be able thus to offer willingly? For all things come from you, and of your own have we given you. [15]For we are strangers before you, and sojourners, as all our fathers were; our days on the earth are like a shadow, and there is no abiding. [16]O LORD our God, all this abundance that we have provided for building you a house for your holy name comes from your hand and is all your own. [17]I know, my God, that you try the heart, and have pleasure in uprightness; in the uprightness of my heart I have freely offered all these things, and now I have seen your people, who are present here, offering freely and joyously to you. [18]O LORD, the God of Abraham, Isaac, and Israel, our fathers, keep for ever such purposes and thoughts in the hearts of your people, and direct their hearts toward you. [19]Grant to Solomon my son that with a whole heart he may keep your commandments, your covenants, and your statutes, performing all, and that he may build the palace for which I have made provision."

[20]Then David said to all the assembly, "Bless the LORD your God." And all the assembly blessed the LORD, the God of their fathers, and bowed their heads, and worshiped the LORD, and did obeisance to the king. [21]And they performed sacrifices to the LORD, and on the next day offered burnt offerings to the LORD, a thousand bulls, a thousand rams, and a thousand lambs, with their drink offerings, and sacrifices in abundance for all Israel; [22]and they ate and drank before the LORD on that day with great gladness.

And they made Solomon the son of David king the second time, and they anointed him as prince for the LORD, and Za′dok as priest. [23]Then Solomon sat on the throne of the LORD as king instead of David his father; and he prospered, and all Israel obeyed him. [24]All the leaders and the mighty men, and also all the sons of King David, pledged their allegiance to King Solomon. [25]And the LORD gave Solomon great repute in the sight of all Israel, and bestowed upon him such royal majesty as had not been on any king before him in Israel.

[26]Thus David the son of Jesse reigned over all Israel. [27]The time that he reigned over Israel was forty years; he reigned seven years in He′bron, and thirty-three years in Jerusalem. [28]Then he died in a good old age, full of days, riches, and honor; and Solomon his son reigned in his stead. [29]Now the acts of King David, from first to last, are written in the Chronicles of Samuel the seer, and in the Chronicles of Nathan the prophet, and in the Chronicles of Gad the seer, [30]with accounts of all his rule and his might and of the circumstances that came upon him and

upon Israel, and upon all the kingdoms of the countries.

35The wise will inherit honor,
but fools get disgrace.

PROVERBS 3

19The LORD by wisdom founded the earth;
by understanding he established the heavens;
20by his knowledge the deeps broke forth,
and the clouds drop down the dew.

21My son, keep sound wisdom
and discretion;
let them not escape from your sight,
22and they will be life for your soul
and adornment for your neck.
23Then you will walk on your way securely
and your foot will not stumble.
24If you sit down, you will not be afraid;
when you lie down, your sleep will be sweet.
25Do not be afraid of sudden panic,
or of the ruin of the wicked, when it comes;
26for the LORD will be your confidence
and will keep your foot from being caught.
27Do not withhold good from those to whom it is due,
when it is in your power to do it.

28Do not say to your neighbor, "Go, and come again,
tomorrow I will give it"—when you have it with you.
29Do not plan evil against your neighbor
who dwells trustingly beside you.
30Do not contend with a man for no reason,
when he has done you no harm.
31Do not envy a man of violence
and do not choose any of his ways;
32for the perverse man is an abomination to the LORD,
but the upright are in his confidence.
33The LORD's curse is on the house of the wicked,
but he blesses the abode of the righteous.
34Toward the scorners he is scornful,
but to the humble he shows favor.

ACTS 8

**9But there was a man named Si-
mon who had previously practiced magic in the city and
amazed the nation of Samar'ia, saying
that he himself was somebody great.**
10They all listened to him, from the least to
the greatest, saying, "This man is that power
of God which is called Great." 11And they listened to him, because for a long time he had
amazed them with his magic. 12But when
they believed Philip as he preached good
news about the kingdom of God and the
name of Jesus Christ, they were baptized,
both men and women. 13Even Simon himself believed, and after being baptized he
continued with Philip. And seeing signs and
great miracles performed, he was amazed.
14Now when the apostles at Jerusalem heard
that Samar'ia had received the word of God,
they sent to them Peter and John, 15who came
down and prayed for them that they might
receive the Holy Spirit; 16for the Spirit had not
yet fallen on any of them, but they had only
been baptized in the name of the Lord Jesus.
17Then they laid their hands on them and
they received the Holy Spirit. 18Now when
Simon saw that the Spirit was given through
the laying on of the apostles' hands, he offered
them money, 19saying, "Give me also this
power, that any one on whom I lay my hands
may receive the Holy Spirit." 20But Peter said
to him, "Your silver perish with you, because
you thought you could obtain the gift of
God with money! 21You have neither part
nor lot in this matter, for your heart is not
right before God. 22Repent therefore of this
wickedness of yours, and pray to the Lord
that, if possible, the intent of your heart may
be forgiven you. 23For I see that you are in the
gall of bitterness and in the bond of iniquity."
24And Simon answered, "Pray for me to the
Lord, that nothing of what you have said may
come upon me."

25Now when they had testified and spoken the word of the Lord, they returned to Jerusalem, preaching the gospel to many villages of the Samaritans.

REFLECTION

Sometimes we just need to acknowledge our smallness and God's greatness. David sets a great example for us when he prays, "Yours, O LORD, is the greatness, and the power, and the glory, and the victory, and the majesty" (1 Chr 29:11). David shows us that God alone possesses all the things that human kings seek after. Likewise, he acknowledges God's ownership of everything: "All that is in the heavens and in the earth is yours" (v. 11). But David goes further, pointing out that all the sacrifices he and the people of Israel make to the Lord have their origin in him: "For all things come from you, and of your own have we given you. . . . All this abundance that we have provided for building you a house for your holy name comes from your hand and is all your own" (vv. 14, 16). Essentially, he is saying that no matter what we give to God, it was originally from God in the first place. We cannot "obtain the gift of God with money" as Simon Magus tries to do (Acts 8:20). We can only receive his Spirit as a gift and then give the gifts he gives us back to him. In what ways do you receive from God and give back to him?

July 1

2 CHRONICLES 1

**Solomon the son of David estab-
lished himself in his kingdom,
and the LORD his God was with him
and made him exceedingly great.**
[2]Solomon spoke to all Israel, to the commanders of thousands and of hundreds, to
the judges, and to all the leaders in all Israel,
the heads of fathers' houses. [3]And Solomon,
and all the assembly with him, went to the
high place that was at Gib′eon; for the tent
of meeting of God, which Moses the servant
of the LORD had made in the wilderness,
was there. [4](But David had brought up the
ark of God from Kir′iath-je′arim to the
place that David had prepared for it, for
he had pitched a tent for it in Jerusalem.)
[5]Moreover the bronze altar that Bez′alel
the son of U′ri, son of Hur, had made, was
there before the tabernacle of the LORD.
And Solomon and the assembly sought the
LORD. [6]And Solomon went up there to the
bronze altar before the LORD, which was at
the tent of meeting, and offered a thousand
burnt offerings upon it.
[7]In that night God appeared to Solomon,
and said to him, "Ask what I shall give you."
[8]And Solomon said to God, "You have
shown great and merciful love to David my
father, and have made me king in his stead.
[9]O LORD God, let your promise to David my
father be now fulfilled, for you have made
me king over a people as many as the dust
of the earth. [10]Give me now wisdom and
knowledge to go out and come in before this
people, for who can rule this your people,
that is so great?" [11]God answered Solomon,
"Because this was in your heart, and you
have not asked possessions, wealth, honor,
or the life of those who hate you, and have
not even asked long life, but have asked
wisdom and knowledge for yourself that
you may rule my people over whom I have
made you king, [12]wisdom and knowledge
are granted to you. I will also give you riches,
possessions, and honor, such as none of the
kings had who were before you, and none
after you shall have the like." [13]So Solomon
came from the high place at Gib′eon, from
before the tent of meeting, to Jerusalem.
And he reigned over Israel.
[14]Solomon gathered together chariots and
horsemen; he had fourteen hundred chariots
and twelve thousand horsemen, whom he
stationed in the chariot cities and with the
king in Jerusalem. [15]And the king made
silver and gold as common in Jerusalem
as stone, and he made cedar as plentiful
as the sycamore of the Shephe′lah. [16]And
Solomon's import of horses was from Egypt
and Ku′e, and the king's traders received
them from Kue for a price. [17]They imported
a chariot from Egypt for six hundred shekels
of silver, and a horse for a hundred and fifty;
likewise through them these were exported
to all the kings of the Hittites and the kings
of Syria.

2 Now Solomon purposed to build a
temple for the name of the LORD, and
a royal palace for himself. [2]And Solomon
assigned seventy thousand men to bear
burdens and eighty thousand to quarry
in the hill country, and three thousand six
hundred to oversee them. [3]And Solomon
sent word to Hu′ram the king of Tyre: "As
you dealt with David my father and sent him
cedar to build himself a house to dwell in, so
deal with me. [4]Behold, I am about to build
a house for the name of the LORD my God
and dedicate it to him for the burning of
incense of sweet spices before him, and for
the continual offering of the showbread, and
for burnt offerings morning and evening,
on the sabbaths and the new moons and
the appointed feasts of the LORD our God,
as ordained for ever for Israel. [5]The house
which I am to build will be great, for our
God is greater than all gods. [6]But who is able
to build him a house, since heaven, even
highest heaven, cannot contain him? Who
am I to build a house for him, except as a
place to burn incense before him? [7]So now
send me a man skilled to work in gold, silver,
bronze, and iron, and in purple, crimson,

and blue fabrics, trained also in engraving, to be with the skilled workers who are with me in Judah and Jerusalem, whom David my father provided. [8]Send me also cedar, cypress, and algum timber from Lebanon, for I know that your servants know how to cut timber in Lebanon. And my servants will be with your servants, [9]to prepare timber for me in abundance, for the house I am to build will be great and wonderful. [10]I will give for your servants, the hewers who cut timber, twenty thousand cors of crushed wheat, twenty thousand cors of barley, twenty thousand baths of wine, and twenty thousand baths of oil."

[11]Then Hu′ram the king of Tyre answered in a letter which he sent to Solomon, "Because the LORD loves his people he has made you king over them." [12]Hu′ram also said, "Blessed be the LORD God of Israel, who made heaven and earth, who has given King David a wise son, endued with discretion and understanding, who will build a temple for the LORD, and a royal palace for himself.

[13]"Now I have sent a skilled man, endued with understanding, Hu′ram-a′bi, [14]the son of a woman of the daughters of Dan, and his father was a man of Tyre. He is trained to work in gold, silver, bronze, iron, stone, and wood, and in purple, blue, and crimson fabrics and fine linen, and to do all sorts of engraving and execute any design that may be assigned him, with your craftsmen, the craftsmen of my lord, David your father. [15]Now therefore the wheat and barley, oil and wine, of which my lord has spoken, let him send to his servants; [16]and we will cut whatever timber you need from Lebanon, and bring it to you in rafts by sea to Joppa, so that you may take it up to Jerusalem."

[17]Then Solomon took a census of all the aliens who were in the land of Israel, after the census of them which David his father had taken; and there were found a hundred and fifty-three thousand six hundred. [18]Seventy thousand of them he assigned to bear burdens, eighty thousand to quarry in the hill country, and three thousand six hundred as overseers to make the people work.

3 Then Solomon began to build the house of the LORD in Jerusalem on Mount Mori′ah, where the LORD had appeared to David his father, at the place that David had appointed, on the threshing floor of Ornan the Jeb′usite. [2]He began to build in the second month of the fourth year of his reign. [3]These are Solomon's measurements for building the house of God: the length, in cubits of the old standard, was sixty cubits, and the breadth twenty cubits. [4]The vestibule in front of the nave of the house was twenty cubits long, equal to the width of the house; and its height was a hundred and twenty cubits. He overlaid it on the inside with pure gold. [5]The nave he lined with cypress, and covered it with fine gold, and made palms and chains on it. [6]He adorned the house with settings of precious stones. The gold was gold of Parva′im. [7]So he lined the house with gold—its beams, its thresholds, its walls, and its doors; and he carved cherubim on the walls.

[8]And he made the most holy place; its length, corresponding to the breadth of the house, was twenty cubits, and its breadth was twenty cubits; he overlaid it with six hundred talents of fine gold. [9]The weight of the nails was one shekel to fifty shekels of gold. And he overlaid the upper chambers with gold.

[10]In the most holy place he made two cherubim of wood and overlaid them with gold. [11]The wings of the cherubim together extended twenty cubits: one wing of the one, of five cubits, touched the wall of the house, and its other wing, of five cubits, touched the wing of the other cherub; [12]and of this cherub, one wing, of five cubits, touched the wall of the house, and the other wing, also of five cubits, was joined to the wing of the first cherub. [13]The wings of these cherubim extended twenty cubits; the cherubim stood on their feet, facing the nave. [14]And he made the veil of blue and purple and crimson fabrics and fine linen, and worked cherubim on it.

[15]In front of the house he made two pillars thirty-five cubits high, with a capital of five cubits on the top of each. [16]He made chains like a necklace and put them on the

tops of the pillars; and he made a hundred pomegranates, and put them on the chains. 17He set up the pillars in front of the temple, one on the south, the other on the north; that on the south he called Ja´chin, and that on the north Boaz.

PROVERBS 4

Hear, O sons, a father's instruction,
and be attentive, that you may gain insight;
2for I give you good precepts:
do not forsake my teaching.
3When I was a son with my father,
tender, the only one in the sight of
my mother,
4he taught me, and said to me,
"Let your heart hold fast my words;
keep my commandments, and live;
5do not forget, and do not turn away from
the words of my mouth.
Get wisdom; get insight.
6Do not forsake her, and she will keep you;
love her, and she will guard you.
7The beginning of wisdom is this: Get wisdom,
and whatever you get, get insight.
8Prize her highly, and she will exalt you;
she will honor you if you embrace her.
9She will place on your head a fair garland;
she will bestow on you a beautiful crown."

10Hear, my son, and accept my words,
that the years of your life may be many.
11I have taught you the way of wisdom;
I have led you in the paths of uprightness.
12When you walk, your step will not
be hampered;
and if you run, you will not stumble.
13Keep hold of instruction, do not let go;
guard her, for she is your life.

ACTS 8

26But an angel of the Lord said to Philip, "Rise and go toward the south to the road that goes down from Jerusalem to Gaza." This is a desert
road. 27And he rose and went. And behold,
an Ethiopian, a eunuch, a minister of Can-
da´ce the queen of the Ethiopians, in charge
of all her treasure, had come to Jerusalem to
worship 28and was returning; seated in his
chariot, he was reading the prophet Isaiah.
29And the Spirit said to Philip, "Go up and
join this chariot." 30So Philip ran to him, and
heard him reading Isaiah the prophet, and
asked, "Do you understand what you are
reading?" 31And he said, "How can I, unless
some one guides me?" And he invited Philip
to come up and sit with him. 32Now the passage of the Scripture which he was reading
was this:

"As a sheep led to the slaughter
or a lamb before its shearer is silent,
so he opens not his mouth.
33In his humiliation justice was denied him.
Who can describe his generation?
For his life is taken up from the earth."

34And the eunuch said to Philip, "Please,
about whom does the prophet say this, about
himself or about some one else?" 35Then
Philip opened his mouth, and beginning
with this Scripture he told him the good news
of Jesus. 36And as they went along the road
they came to some water, and the eunuch
said, "See, here is water! What is to prevent
my being baptized?" 38And he commanded
the chariot to stop, and they both went down
into the water, Philip and the eunuch, and
he baptized him. 39And when they came up
out of the water, the Spirit of the Lord caught
up Philip; and the eunuch saw him no more,
and went on his way rejoicing. 40But Philip
was found at Azo´tus, and passing on he
preached the gospel to all the towns till he
came to Caesare´a.

REFLECTION

Whether we admit it or not, we all need guidance. It could come from a parent, a coach, a teacher, a priest, a spiritual director, or a friend, but none of us can make our way through life well without wise direction. Solomon, in his humility, recognizes this need, praying, "Give me now wisdom and knowledge" (2 Chr 1:10). He thus shows what it means to "get wisdom; get insight" (Prv 4:5). This part of Proverbs is framed as a "father's instruction" (v. 1), and Solomon thus puts himself in the role of the son, receiving wisdom and guidance from God. Proverbs promises that wisdom will "keep you . . . guard you . . . exalt you . . . honor you" (vv. 6–8). And indeed, Solomon receives "riches, possessions, and honor" (2 Chr 1:12) from the Lord for his request. The Ethiopian eunuch manifests a similar spiritual humility when reading the prophecy of Isaiah, admitting his lack of understanding: "How can I, unless some one guides me?" (Acts 8:31). Fortunately, the Holy Spirit brings Philip onto the scene to interpret the Scripture and preach the Gospel to him. In an age of self-reliance, it takes serious humility to admit your need for a guide. Who has God put in your life to help speak wisdom to you? Take time to pray for this person(s).

July 2

2 CHRONICLES 4

He made an altar of bronze, twenty cubits long, and twenty cubits wide, and ten cubits high. 2Then he made the molten sea; it was round,
ten cubits from brim to brim, and five cubits high, and a line of thirty cubits measured
its circumference. 3Under it were figures of gourds, for thirty cubits, compassing the sea round about; the gourds were in two rows,
cast with it when it was cast. 4It stood upon twelve oxen, three facing north, three facing west, three facing south, and three facing east; the sea was set upon them, and all their
posterior parts were inward. 5Its thickness was a handbreadth; and its brim was made like the brim of a cup, like the flower of a lily; it held over three thousand baths. 6He
also made ten lavers in which to wash, and set five on the south side, and five on the north side. In these they were to rinse off what was used for the burnt offering, and the sea was for the priests to wash in.
7And he made ten golden lampstands as prescribed, and set them in the temple, five
on the south side and five on the north. 8He also made ten tables, and placed them in the temple, five on the south side and five on the north. And he made a hundred basins of
gold. 9He made the court of the priests, and the great court, and doors for the court, and
overlaid their doors with bronze; 10and he set the sea at the southeast corner of the house.
11Hu′ram also made the pots, the shovels, and the basins. So Huram finished the work that he did for King Solomon on the
house of God: 12the two pillars, the bowls, and the two capitals on the top of the pillars; and the two networks to cover the two bowls of the capitals that were on the
top of the pillars; 13and the four hundred pomegranates for the two networks, two rows of pomegranates for each network, to cover the two bowls of the capitals that were
upon the pillars. 14He made the stands also,
and the lavers upon the stands, 15and the one sea, and the twelve oxen underneath
it. 16The pots, the shovels, the forks, and all the equipment for these Hu′ram-a′bi made of burnished bronze for King Solomon for
the house of the LORD. 17In the plain of the Jordan the king cast them, in the clay ground between Succoth and Zer′edah.
18Solomon made all these things in great quantities, so that the weight of the bronze was not ascertained.
19So Solomon made all the things that were in the house of God: the golden altar, the tables for the bread of the Presence,
20the lampstands and their lamps of pure gold to burn before the inner sanctuary,
as prescribed; 21the flowers, the lamps, and
the tongs, of purest gold; 22the snuffers, basins, dishes for incense, and firepans, of pure gold; and the sockets of the temple, for the inner doors to the most holy place and for the doors of the nave of the temple were of gold.

5 Thus all the work that Solomon did for the house of the LORD was finished.

And Solomon brought in the things which
David his father had dedicated, and stored
the silver, the gold, and all the vessels in the
treasuries of the house of God.
2 Then Solomon assembled the elders of
Israel and all the heads of the tribes, the
leaders of the fathers' houses of the sons
of Israel, in Jerusalem, to bring up the ark
of the covenant of the LORD out of the city
of David, which is Zion. 3 And all the men
of Israel assembled before the king at the
feast which is in the seventh month. 4 And
all the elders of Israel came, and the Levites
took up the ark. 5 And they brought up the
ark, the tent of meeting, and all the holy
vessels that were in the tent; the priests and
the Levites brought them up. 6 And King
Solomon and all the congregation of Israel,
who had assembled before him, were
before the ark, sacrificing so many sheep
and oxen that they could not be counted
or numbered. 7 So the priests brought the
ark of the covenant of the LORD to its place,
in the inner sanctuary of the house, in the
most holy place, underneath the wings of
the cherubim. 8 For the cherubim spread
out their wings over the place of the ark, so
that the cherubim made a covering above
the ark and its poles. 9 And the poles were
so long that the ends of the poles were
seen from the holy place before the inner
sanctuary; but they could not be seen from
outside; and they are there to this day.
10 There was nothing in the ark except the
two tables which Moses put there at Horeb,
where the LORD made a covenant with
the sons of Israel, when they came out of
Egypt. 11 Now when the priests came out
of the holy place (for all the priests who
were present had sanctified themselves,
without regard to their divisions; 12 and all
the Levitical singers, A′saph, He′man, and
Jedu′thun, their sons and kinsmen, arrayed
in fine linen, with cymbals, harps, and
lyres, stood east of the altar with a hundred
and twenty priests who were trumpeters;
13 and it was the duty of the trumpeters
and singers to make themselves heard in
unison in praise and thanksgiving to the
LORD), and when the song was raised, with
trumpets and cymbals and other musical
instruments, in praise to the LORD,

"For he is good,
for his mercy endures for ever,"

the house, the house of the LORD, was filled
with a cloud, 14 so that the priests could not
stand to minister because of the cloud; for
the glory of the LORD filled the house of God.

6 Then Solomon said,
"The LORD has said that he would dwell
in thick darkness.
2 I have built you an exalted house,
a place for you to dwell in for ever."

3 Then the king faced about, and blessed all
the assembly of Israel, while all the assembly
of Israel stood. 4 And he said, "Blessed be
the LORD, the God of Israel, who with his
hand has fulfilled what he promised with
his mouth to David my father, saying, 5 'Since
the day that I brought my people out of the
land of Egypt, I chose no city in all the tribes
of Israel in which to build a house, that my
name might be there, and I chose no man
as prince over my people Israel; 6 but I have
chosen Jerusalem that my name may be there
and I have chosen David to be over my people
Israel.' 7 Now it was in the heart of David my
father to build a house for the name of the
LORD, the God of Israel. 8 But the LORD said
to David my father, 'Whereas it was in your
heart to build a house for my name, you did
well that it was in your heart; 9 nevertheless
you shall not build the house, but your son
who shall be born to you shall build the house
for my name.' 10 Now the LORD has fulfilled
his promise which he made; for I have risen
in the place of David my father, and sit on
the throne of Israel, as the LORD promised,
and I have built the house for the name of the
LORD, the God of Israel. 11 And there I have
set the ark, in which is the covenant of the
LORD which he made with the sons of Israel."

PROVERBS 4

14 Do not enter the path of the wicked,
and do not walk in the way of evil men.
15 Avoid it; do not go on it;
turn away from it and pass on.

[16]For they cannot sleep unless they have
done wrong;
they are robbed of sleep unless they have
made someone stumble.
[17]For they eat the bread of wickedness
and drink the wine of violence.
[18]But the path of the righteous is like the
light of dawn,
which shines brighter and brighter until
full day.
[19]The way of the wicked is like deep darkness;
they do not know over what they stumble.

[20]My son, be attentive to my words;
incline your ear to my sayings.
[21]Let them not escape from your sight;
keep them within your heart.
[22]For they are life to him who finds them,
and healing to all his flesh.
[23]Keep your heart with all vigilance;
for from it flow the springs of life.
[24]Put away from you crooked speech,
and put devious talk far from you.
[25]Let your eyes look directly forward,
and your gaze be straight before you.
[26]Take heed to the path of your feet,
then all your ways will be sure.
[27]Do not swerve to the right or to the left;
turn your foot away from evil.

ACTS 9

**But Saul, still breathing threats
and murder against the disci-
ples of the Lord, went to the high priest
[2]and asked him for letters to the syna-**
gogues at Damascus, so that if he found any
belonging to the Way, men or women, he
might bring them bound to Jerusalem. [3]Now
as he journeyed he approached Damascus,
and suddenly a light from heaven flashed
about him. [4]And he fell to the ground and
heard a voice saying to him, "Saul, Saul, why
do you persecute me?" [5]And he said, "Who
are you, Lord?" And he said, "I am Jesus,
whom you are persecuting; [6]but rise and
enter the city, and you will be told what you
are to do." [7]The men who were traveling with
him stood speechless, hearing the voice but
seeing no one. [8]Saul arose from the ground;
and when his eyes were opened, he could see
nothing; so they led him by the hand and
brought him into Damascus. [9]And for three
days he was without sight, and neither ate
nor drank.

[10]Now there was a disciple at Damascus
named Anani'as. The Lord said to him in a
vision, "Ananias." And he said, "Here I am,
Lord." [11]And the Lord said to him, "Rise and
go to the street called Straight, and inquire in
the house of Judas for a man of Tarsus named
Saul; for behold, he is praying, [12]and he has
seen a man named Anani'as come in and lay
his hands on him so that he might regain
his sight." [13]But Anani'as answered, "Lord,
I have heard from many about this man,
how much evil he has done to your saints at
Jerusalem; [14]and here he has authority from
the chief priests to bind all who call upon
your name." [15]But the Lord said to him,
"Go, for he is a chosen instrument of mine
to carry my name before the Gentiles and
kings and the sons of Israel; [16]for I will show
him how much he must suffer for the sake
of my name." [17]So Anani'as departed and
entered the house. And laying his hands on
him he said, "Brother Saul, the Lord Jesus
who appeared to you on the road by which
you came, has sent me that you may regain
your sight and be filled with the Holy Spirit."
[18]And immediately something like scales
fell from his eyes and he regained his sight.
Then he rose and was baptized, [19]and took
food and was strengthened.

For several days he was with the disciples
at Damascus. [20]And in the synagogues immediately he proclaimed Jesus, saying, "He
is the Son of God." [21]And all who heard
him were amazed, and said, "Is not this the
man who made havoc in Jerusalem of those
who called on this name? And he has come
here for this purpose, to bring them bound
before the chief priests." [22]But Saul increased
all the more in strength, and confounded
the Jews who lived in Damascus by proving
that Jesus was the Christ.

[23]When many days had passed, the Jews
plotted to kill him, [24]but their plot became

known to Saul. They were watching the gates day and night, to kill him; [25]but his disciples took him by night and let him down over the wall, lowering him in a basket.

[26]And when he had come to Jerusalem he attempted to join the disciples; and they were all afraid of him, for they did not believe that he was a disciple. [27]But Barnabas took him, and brought him to the apostles, and declared to them how on the road he had seen the Lord, who spoke to him, and how at Damascus he had preached boldly in the name of Jesus. [28]So he went in and out among them at Jerusalem, [29]preaching boldly in the name of the Lord. And he spoke and disputed against the Hellenists; but they were seeking to kill him. [30]And when the brethren knew it, they brought him down to Caesare′a, and sent him off to Tarsus.

[31]So the Church throughout all Judea and Galilee and Samar′ia had peace and was built up; and walking in the fear of the Lord and in the comfort of the Holy Spirit it was multiplied.

REFLECTION

Observing the news on any given day, one is tempted to believe that the history of humanity is moved forward by the decisions of powerful men, the crimes of the evil, and the projects of the creative. Yet the Bible insists that history is driven by the choosing of the Lord. Solomon cites the Lord's words to David that though he had chosen no city for a Temple in Israel, now he has chosen Jerusalem; and though he had chosen no man to be a leader, now he has chosen David (see 2 Chr 6:5–6). Similarly, when Ananias balks at going to Saul, the former persecutor, the Lord tells him, "Go, for he is a chosen instrument of mine to carry my name before the Gentiles" (Acts 9:15). In each case, we see God's choice intervening in human history to move the story forward. The cares and trials of this world distract us from listening for the deeper undertones of God's hand in history. Proverbs encourages us to stay focused: "Let your eyes look directly forward, and your gaze be straight before you" (Prv 4:25). How can you see God's hand at work in your own life and keep your eyes looking "directly forward"?

July 3

2 CHRONICLES 6

[12]Then Solomon stood before the altar of the LORD in the presence of all the assembly of Israel, and spread forth his hands. [13]Solomon had made a bronze platform five cubits long, five cubits wide, and three cubits high, and had set it in the court; and he stood upon it. Then he knelt upon his knees in the presence of all the assembly of Israel, and spread forth his hands toward heaven; [14]and said, "O LORD, God of Israel, there is no God like you, in heaven or on earth, keeping covenant and showing mercy to your servants who walk before you with all their heart; [15]who have kept with your servant David my father what you declared to him; yes, you spoke with your mouth, and with your hand have fulfilled it this day. [16]Now therefore, O LORD, God of Israel, keep with your servant David my father what you have promised him, saying, 'There shall never fail you a man before me to sit upon the throne of Israel, if only your sons take heed to their way, to walk in my law as you have walked before me.' [17]Now therefore, O LORD, God of Israel, let your word be confirmed, which you have spoken to your servant David.

[18]"But will God dwell indeed with man on the earth? Behold, heaven and the highest heaven cannot contain you; how much less this house which I have built! [19]Yet have regard to the prayer of your servant and to his supplication, O LORD my God, listening to the cry and to the prayer which your servant prays before you; [20]that your eyes may be open day and night toward this house, the place where you have promised to set your name, that you may listen to the prayer which your servant offers toward this place. [21]And listen to the supplications of your servant and of your people Israel, when they pray toward this place; yes, hear

from heaven your dwelling place; and when
you hear, forgive.
22“If a man sins against his neighbor and is
made to take an oath, and comes and swears
his oath before your altar in this house, 23then
hear from heaven, and act, and judge your
servants, repaying the guilty by bringing his
conduct upon his own head, and vindicating
the righteous by rewarding him according to
his righteousness.
24“If your people Israel are defeated before
the enemy because they have sinned against
you, when they turn again and acknowledge
your name, and pray and make supplication to
you in this house, 25then hear from heaven, and
forgive the sin of your people Israel, and bring
them again to the land which you gave to them
and to their fathers.
26“When heaven is shut up and there is no
rain because they have sinned against you, if
they pray toward this place, and acknowledge
your name, and turn from their sin, when you
afflict them, 27then hear in heaven, and forgive
the sin of your servants, your people Israel,
when you teach them the good way in which
they should walk; and grant rain upon your
land, which you have given to your people as
an inheritance.
28“If there is famine in the land, if there is
pestilence or blight or mildew or locust or
caterpillar; if their enemies besiege them in
any of their cities; whatever plague, whatever
sickness there is; 29whatever prayer, whatever
supplication is made by any man or by all
your people Israel, each knowing his own
affliction, and his own sorrow and stretching
out his hands toward this house; 30then hear
from heaven your dwelling place, and forgive,
and render to each whose heart you know,
according to all his ways (for you, you only,
know the hearts of the children of men); 31that
they may fear you and walk in your ways all the
days that they live in the land which you gave
to our fathers.
32“Likewise when a foreigner, who is not of
your people Israel, comes from a far country
for the sake of your great name, and your
mighty hand, and your outstretched arm,
when he comes and prays toward this house,
33hear from heaven your dwelling place, and
do according to all for which the foreigner
calls to you; in order that all the peoples of the
earth may know your name and fear you, as
do your people Israel, and that they may know
that this house which I have built is called by
your name.
34“If your people go out to battle against their
enemies, by whatever way you shall send them,
and they pray to you toward this city which you
have chosen and the house which I have built
for your name, 35then hear from heaven their
prayer and their supplication, and maintain
their cause.
36“If they sin against you—for there is no man
who does not sin—and you are angry with
them, and give them to an enemy, so that they
are carried away captive to a land far or near;
37yet if they lay it to heart in the land to which
they have been carried captive, and repent, and
make supplication to you in the land of their
captivity, saying, ‘We have sinned, and have
acted perversely and wickedly’; 38if they repent
with all their mind and with all their heart in
the land of their captivity, to which they were
carried captive, and pray toward their land,
which you gave to their fathers, the city which
you have chosen, and the house which I have
built for your name, 39then hear from heaven
your dwelling place their prayer and their
supplications, and maintain their cause and
forgive your people who have sinned against
you. 40Now, O my God, let your eyes be open
and your ears attentive to a prayer of this place.

41“And now arise, O Lord God, and go to
your resting place,
you and the ark of your might.
Let your priests, O Lord God, be clothed
with salvation,
and let your saints rejoice in your
goodness.
42O Lord God, do not turn away the face of
your anointed one!
Remember your merciful love for David
your servant.”

7 When Solomon had ended his prayer, fire
came down from heaven and consumed
the burnt offering and the sacrifices, and the
glory of the Lord filled the temple. 2And
the priests could not enter the house of the
Lord, because the glory of the Lord filled

the LORD's house. 3When all the children of Israel saw the fire come down and the glory of the LORD upon the temple, they bowed down with their faces to the earth on the pavement, and worshiped and gave thanks to the LORD, saying,

"For he is good,
for his mercy endures for ever."

4Then the king and all the people offered sacrifice before the LORD. 5King Solomon offered as a sacrifice twenty-two thousand oxen and a hundred and twenty thousand sheep. So the king and all the people dedicated the house of God. 6The priests stood at their posts; the Levites also, with the instruments for music to the LORD which King David had made for giving thanks to the LORD—for his mercy endures for ever—whenever David offered praises by their ministry; opposite them the priests sounded trumpets; and all Israel stood.

7And Solomon consecrated the middle of the court that was before the house of the LORD; for there he offered the burnt offering and the fat of the peace offerings, because the bronze altar Solomon had made could not hold the burnt offering and the cereal offering and the fat.

8At that time Solomon held the feast for seven days, and all Israel with him, a very great congregation, from the entrance of Ha′math to the Brook of Egypt. 9And on the eighth day they held a solemn assembly; for they had kept the dedication of the altar seven days and the feast seven days. 10On the twenty-third day of the seventh month he sent the people away to their homes, joyful and glad of heart for the goodness that the LORD had shown to David and to Solomon and to Israel his people.

11Thus Solomon finished the house of the LORD and the king's house; all that Solomon had planned to do in the house of the LORD and in his own house he successfully accomplished. 12Then the LORD appeared to Solomon in the night and said to him: "I have heard your prayer, and have chosen this place for myself as a house of sacrifice. 13When I shut up the heavens so that there is no rain, or command the locust to devour the land, or send pestilence among my people, 14if my people who are called by my name humble themselves, and pray and seek my face, and turn from their wicked ways, then I will hear from heaven, and will forgive their sin and heal their land. 15Now my eyes will be open and my ears attentive to the prayer that is made in this place. 16For now I have chosen and consecrated this house that my name may be there for ever; my eyes and my heart will be there for all time. 17And as for you, if you walk before me, as David your father walked, doing according to all that I have commanded you and keeping my statutes and my ordinances, 18then I will establish your royal throne, as I covenanted with David your father, saying, 'There shall not fail you a man to rule Israel.'

19"But if you turn aside and forsake my statutes and my commandments which I have set before you, and go and serve other gods and worship them, 20then I will pluck you up from the land which I have given you; and this house, which I have consecrated for my name, I will cast out of my sight, and will make it a proverb and a byword among all peoples. 21And at this house, which is exalted, every one passing by will be astonished, and say, 'Why has the LORD done thus to this land and to this house?' 22Then they will say, 'Because they forsook the LORD the God of their fathers who brought them out of the land of Egypt, and laid hold on other gods, and worshiped them and served them; therefore he has brought all this evil upon them.'"

PROVERBS 5

My son, be attentive to my wisdom,
incline your ear to my understanding;
2that you may keep discretion,
and your lips may guard knowledge.
3For the lips of a loose woman drip honey,
and her speech is smoother than oil;
4but in the end she is bitter as wormwood,
sharp as a two-edged sword.
5Her feet go down to death;
her steps follow the path to Sheol;
6she does not take heed to the path of life;
her ways wander, and she does not know it.

[7]And now, O sons, listen to me,
and do not depart from the words of
my mouth.
[8]Keep your way far from her,
and do not go near the door of her house;
[9]lest you give your honor to others
and your years to the merciless;
[10]lest strangers take their fill of your strength,
and your labors go to the house of an alien;
[11]and at the end of your life you groan,
when your flesh and body are consumed,
[12]and you say, "How I hated discipline,
and my heart despised reproof!
[13]I did not listen to the voice of my teachers
or incline my ear to my instructors.
[14]I was at the point of utter ruin
in the assembled congregation."

[15]Drink water from your own cistern,
flowing water from your own well.
[16]Should your springs be scattered abroad,
streams of water in the streets?
[17]Let them be for yourself alone,
and not for strangers with you.
[18]Let your fountain be blessed,
and rejoice in the wife of your youth,
[19] a lovely deer, a graceful doe.
Let her affection fill you at all times
with delight,
be infatuated always with her love.
[20]Why should you be infatuated, my son,
with a loose woman
and embrace the bosom of an adventuress?
[21]For a man's ways are before the eyes of
the LORD,
and he watches all his paths.
[22]The iniquities of the wicked ensnare him,
and he is caught in the toils of his sin.
[23]He dies for lack of discipline,
and because of his great folly he is lost.

ACTS 9

**[32]Now as Peter went here and
there among them all, he came
down also to the saints that lived
at Lydda. [33]There he found a man named
Aene′as, who had been bedridden for**
eight years and was paralyzed. [34]And Peter
said to him, "Aene′as, Jesus Christ heals
you; rise and make your bed." And immediately he rose. [35]And all the residents
of Lydda and Sharon saw him, and they
turned to the Lord.
[36]Now there was at Joppa a disciple named
Tabitha, which means Dorcas or Gazelle.
She was full of good works and acts of
charity. [37]In those days she fell sick and died;
and when they had washed her, they laid her
in an upper room. [38]Since Lydda was near
Joppa, the disciples, hearing that Peter was
there, sent two men to him entreating him,
"Please come to us without delay." [39]So Peter
rose and went with them. And when he had
come, they took him to the upper room.
All the widows stood beside him weeping,
and showing coats and garments which
Dorcas made while she was with them.
[40]But Peter put them all outside and knelt
down and prayed; then turning to the body
he said, "Tabitha, rise." And she opened her
eyes, and when she saw Peter she sat up.
[41]And he gave her his hand and lifted her
up. Then calling the saints and widows he
presented her alive. [42]And it became known
throughout all Joppa, and many believed in
the Lord. [43]And he stayed in Joppa for many
days with one Simon, a tanner.

REFLECTION

The Lord keeps his promises to us. Solomon's beautiful prayer of dedication reminds the Lord of his promises to David and asks him to be faithful to the covenant he has made and to honor the newly built Temple with his presence. Solomon repeatedly asks the Lord to "hear from heaven" (2 Chr 6:21) the petitions of those who worship at the Temple and to forgive those who repent. The Lord responds by sending down fire from Heaven to ignite the sacrifices and by filling the Temple with his glory and, thus, his presence. His fidelity to us should motivate us to be faithful to him. Proverbs warns us against the temptations of the loose woman who represents folly, the opposite of wisdom. Her enticements lead to bitter disappointment, death, and Sheol. Instead of falling for the temptations of folly, we are called to be faithful to wisdom, "the wife of your youth" (Prv 5:18). St. Peter's example shows the rewards of being faithful to God, as he heals a paralyzed man and raises a woman from the dead, just like Jesus did in his earthly ministry. Infidelity to the Lord is tempting, but keeping covenant with him is far more rewarding. What can you do today to remain in God's presence and walk on the "path of life"?

July 4

2 CHRONICLES 8

**At the end of twenty years, in
which Solomon had built the
house of the LORD and his own
house, [2]Solomon rebuilt the cities which
Hu′ram had given to him, and settled
the sons of Israel in them.**
[3]And Solomon went to Ha′math-zo′bah,
and took it. [4]He built Tadmor in the
wilderness and all the store-cities which
he built in Ha′math. [5]He also built Upper
Beth-ho′ron and Lower Beth-horon, fortified cities with walls, gates, and bars,
[6]and Ba′alath, and all the store-cities that
Solomon had, and all the cities for his
chariots, and the cities for his horsemen,
and whatever Solomon desired to build in
Jerusalem, in Lebanon, and in all the land of
his dominion. [7]All the people who were left
of the Hittites, the Am′orites, the Per′izzites,
the Hi′vites, and the Jeb′usites, who were not
of Israel, [8]from their descendants who were
left after them in the land, whom the sons
of Israel had not destroyed—these Solomon
made a forced levy and so they are to this
day. [9]But of the sons of Israel Solomon made
no slaves for his work; they were soldiers,
and his officers, the commanders of his
chariots, and his horsemen. [10]And these
were the chief officers of King Solomon, two
hundred and fifty, who exercised authority
over the people.
[11]Solomon brought Pharaoh's daughter up
from the city of David to the house which he
had built for her, for he said, "My wife shall
not live in the house of David king of Israel,
for the places to which the ark of the LORD
has come are holy."
[12]Then Solomon offered up burnt offerings
to the LORD upon the altar of the LORD
which he had built before the vestibule,
[13]as the duty of each day required, offering
according to the commandment of Moses
for the sabbaths, the new moons, and the
three annual feasts—the feast of unleavened
bread, the feast of weeks, and the feast of
tabernacles. [14]According to the ordinance of
David his father, he appointed the divisions
of the priests for their service, and the Levites
for their offices of praise and ministry before
the priests as the duty of each day required,
and the gatekeepers in their divisions for the
several gates; for so David the man of God
had commanded. [15]And they did not turn
aside from what the king had commanded
the priests and Levites concerning any
matter and concerning the treasuries.
[16]Thus was accomplished all the work
of Solomon from the day the foundation
of the house of the LORD was laid until it
was finished. So the house of the LORD was
completed.
[17]Then Solomon went to E′zion-ge′ber and
E′loth on the shore of the sea, in the land
of E′dom. [18]And Hu′ram sent him by his
servants ships and servants familiar with
the sea, and they went to O′phir together
with the servants of Solomon, and fetched
from there four hundred and fifty talents of
gold and brought it to King Solomon.
9 Now when the queen of Sheba heard
of the fame of Solomon she came to
Jerusalem to test him with hard questions,
having a very great retinue and camels
bearing spices and very much gold and
precious stones. When she came to Solomon, she told him all that was on her mind.
[2]And Solomon answered all her questions;

there was nothing hidden from Solomon
which he could not explain to her. [3]And
when the queen of Sheba had seen the
wisdom of Solomon, the house that he had
built, [4]the food of his table, the seating of his
officials, and the attendance of his servants,
and their clothing, his cupbearers, and their
clothing, and his burnt offerings which he
offered at the house of the LORD, there was
no more spirit in her.

[5]And she said to the king, "The report
was true which I heard in my own land of
your affairs and of your wisdom, [6]but I did
not believe the reports until I came and
my own eyes had seen it; and behold, half
the greatness of your wisdom was not told
me; you surpass the report which I heard.
[7]Happy are your wives! Happy are these
your servants, who continually stand before
you and hear your wisdom! [8]Blessed be the
LORD your God, who has delighted in you
and set you on his throne as king for the
LORD your God! Because your God loved
Israel and would establish them for ever, he
has made you king over them, that you may
execute justice and righteousness." [9]Then
she gave the king a hundred and twenty
talents of gold, and a very great quantity
of spices, and precious stones: there were
no spices such as those which the queen of
Sheba gave to King Solomon.

[10]Moreover the servants of Hu′ram and
the servants of Solomon, who brought gold
from O′phir, brought algum wood and
precious stones. [11]And the king made of the
algum wood steps for the house of the LORD
and for the king's house, lyres also and harps
for the singers; there never was seen the like
of them before in the land of Judah.

[12]And King Solomon gave to the queen
of Sheba all that she desired, whatever she
asked besides what she had brought to the
king. So she turned and went back to her
own land, with her servants.

[13]Now the weight of gold that came to
Solomon in one year was six hundred and
sixty-six talents of gold, [14]besides that which
the traders and merchants brought; and all
the kings of Arabia and the governors of the
land brought gold and silver to Solomon.
[15]King Solomon made two hundred large
shields of beaten gold; six hundred shekels
of beaten gold went into each shield. [16]And
he made three hundred shields of beaten
gold; three hundred shekels of gold went
into each shield; and the king put them in
the House of the Forest of Lebanon. [17]The
king also made a great ivory throne, and
overlaid it with pure gold. [18]The throne
had six steps and a footstool of gold, which
were attached to the throne, and on each
side of the seat were arm rests and two
lions standing beside the arm rests, [19]while
twelve lions stood there, one on each end
of a step on the six steps. The like of it was
never made in any kingdom. [20]All King
Solomon's drinking vessels were of gold,
and all the vessels of the House of the
Forest of Lebanon were of pure gold; silver
was not considered as anything in the days
of Solomon. [21]For the king's ships went to
Tar′shish with the servants of Hu′ram; once
every three years the ships of Tarshish used
to come bringing gold, silver, ivory, apes,
and peacocks.

[22]Thus King Solomon excelled all the
kings of the earth in riches and in wisdom.
[23]And all the kings of the earth sought the
presence of Solomon to hear his wisdom,
which God had put into his mind. [24]Every
one of them brought his present, articles of
silver and of gold, garments, myrrh, spices,
horses, and mules, so much year by year.
[25]And Solomon had four thousand stalls for
horses and chariots, and twelve thousand
horsemen, whom he stationed in the chariot
cities and with the king in Jerusalem.
[26]And he ruled over all the kings from the
Euphrates to the land of the Philis′tines, and
to the border of Egypt. [27]And the king made
silver as common in Jerusalem as stone, and
cedar as plentiful as the sycamore of the
Shephe′lah. [28]And horses were imported for
Solomon from Egypt and from all lands.

[29]Now the rest of the acts of Solomon,
from first to last, are they not written in
the history of Nathan the prophet, and in
the prophecy of Ahi′jah the Shi′lonite, and
in the visions of Iddo the seer concerning
Jerobo′am the son of Ne′bat? [30]Solomon

reigned in Jerusalem over all Israel forty years. [31]And Solomon slept with his fathers, and was buried in the city of David his father; and Rehobo′am his son reigned in his stead.

PROVERBS 6

My son, if you have become surety for
your neighbor,
have given your pledge for a stranger;
[2]if you are snared in the utterance of your lips,
caught in the words of your mouth;
[3]then do this, my son, and save yourself,
for you have come into your
neighbor's power:
go, hasten, and importune your neighbor.
[4]Give your eyes no sleep
and your eyelids no slumber;
[5]save yourself like a gazelle from the hunter,
like a bird from the hand of the fowler.

[6]Go to the ant, O sluggard;
consider her ways, and be wise.
[7]Without having any chief,
officer or ruler,
[8]she prepares her food in summer,
and gathers her sustenance in harvest.
[9]How long will you lie there, O sluggard?
When will you arise from your sleep?
[10]A little sleep, a little slumber,
a little folding of the hands to rest,
[11]and poverty will come upon you
like a vagabond,
and want like an armed man.

[12]A worthless person, a wicked man,
goes about with crooked speech,
[13]winks with his eyes, scrapes with his feet,
points with his finger,
[14]with perverted heart devises evil,
continually sowing discord;
[15]therefore calamity will come upon
him suddenly;
in a moment he will be broken
beyond healing.

[16]There are six things which the LORD hates,
seven which are an abomination to him:
[17]haughty eyes, a lying tongue,
and hands that shed innocent blood,
[18]a heart that devises wicked plans,
feet that make haste to run to evil,
[19]a false witness who breathes out lies,
and a man who sows discord
among brothers.

ACTS 10

At Caesare′a there was a man named Cornelius, a centurion of what was known as the Italian Cohort,
[2]a devout man who feared God with all
his household, gave alms liberally to the people, and prayed constantly to God.
[3]About the ninth hour of the day he saw clearly in a vision an angel of God coming in and saying to him, "Cornelius." [4]And he stared at him in terror, and said, "What is it, Lord?" And he said to him, "Your prayers and your alms have ascended as a memorial before God. [5]And now send men to Joppa, and bring one Simon who is called Peter;
[6]he is lodging with Simon, a tanner, whose house is by the seaside." [7]When the angel who spoke to him had departed, he called two of his servants and a devout soldier from among those that waited on him, [8]and having related everything to them, he sent them to Joppa.

[9]The next day, as they were on their journey and coming near the city, Peter went up on the housetop to pray, about the sixth hour. [10]And he became hungry and desired something to eat; but while they were preparing it, he fell into a trance [11]and saw the heaven opened, and something descending, like a great sheet, let down by four corners upon the earth. [12]In it were all kinds of animals and reptiles and birds of the air. [13]And there came a voice to him, "Rise, Peter; kill and eat." [14]But Peter said, "No, Lord; for I have never eaten anything that is common or unclean." [15]And the voice came to him again a second time, "What God has cleansed, you must not call common." [16]This happened three times,

and the thing was taken up at once to
heaven.
[17]Now while Peter was inwardly perplexed
as to what the vision which he had seen
might mean, behold, the men that were
sent by Cornelius, having made inquiry for
Simon's house, stood before the gate [18]and
called out to ask whether Simon who was
called Peter was lodging there. [19]And while
Peter was pondering the vision, the Spirit
said to him, "Behold, three men are looking
for you. [20]Rise and go down, and accompany
them without hesitation; for I have sent
them." [21]And Peter went down to the men
and said, "I am the one you are looking
for; what is the reason for your coming?"
[22]And they said, "Cornelius, a centurion, an
upright and God-fearing man, who is well
spoken of by the whole Jewish nation, was
directed by a holy angel to send for you to
come to his house, and to hear what you
have to say." [23]So he called them in to be
his guests.
The next day he rose and went off with
them, and some of the brethren from Joppa
accompanied him.

REFLECTION

Much of earthly life centers on work. Proverbs gives us encouragement in the ordinary virtues of hard work, avoiding debt, and staying out of poverty: "go to the ant" and "consider her ways" (Prv 6:6). It is no small thing to wake up early, work hard all day, and persevere in this over the years of our lives. We need to learn the wisdom of persevering in our work and also making it a prayer to God. As Solomon's life comes to an end, we see the success of his hard work; his kingdom is overflowing with silver, gold, cedar, horses, ivory, spices, and other riches. But we also see that this wise king has turned away from the wisdom of God. He has amassed an army (note the number of horses, chariots, and horsemen), a harem of wives and concubines (see 1 Kgs 11:3) and much gold—all things the Lord specifically directed Israel's king not to do. Solomon accomplishes the work of building the house of the Lord, but he lets his heart turn away from God. In contrast, we see Cornelius dedicated to his work, a centurion in a premier cohort of the Roman military, but also "a devout man who feared God," who "gave alms liberally" and "prayed constantly" (Acts 10:2). How can you work well and pray well?

July 5

2 CHRONICLES 10

**Rehobo´am went to She´chem, for
all Israel had come to Shechem
to make him king. [2]And when
Jerobo´am the son of Ne´bat heard of it
(for he was in Egypt, whither he had fled
from King Solomon), then Jeroboam**
returned from Egypt. [3]And they sent and
called him; and Jerobo´am and all Israel
came and said to Rehobo´am, [4]"Your father
made our yoke heavy. Now therefore lighten
the hard service of your father and his heavy
yoke upon us, and we will serve you." [5]He
said to them, "Come to me again in three
days." So the people went away.
[6]Then King Rehobo´am took counsel
with the old men, who had stood before
Solomon his father while he was yet alive,
saying, "How do you advise me to answer
this people?" [7]And they said to him, "If
you will be kind to this people and please
them, and speak good words to them, then
they will be your servants for ever." [8]But
he forsook the counsel which the old men
gave him, and took counsel with the young
men who had grown up with him and stood
before him. [9]And he said to them, "What do
you advise that we answer this people who
have said to me, 'Lighten the yoke that your
father put upon us'?" [10]And the young men
who had grown up with him said to him,
"Thus shall you speak to the people who
said to you, 'Your father made our yoke

heavy, but please lighten it for us'; thus shall
you say to them, 'My little finger is thicker
than my father's loins. [11]And now, whereas
my father laid upon you a heavy yoke, I
will add to your yoke. My father chastised
you with whips, but I will chastise you with
scorpions.'"

[12]So Jerobo'am and all the people came
to Rehobo'am the third day, as the king
said, "Come to me again the third day."
[13]And the king answered them harshly, and
forsaking the counsel of the old men, [14]King
Rehobo'am spoke to them according to
the counsel of the young men, saying, "My
father made your yoke heavy, but I will add
to it; my father chastised you with whips, but
I will chastise you with scorpions." [15]So the
king did not listen to the people; for it was
a turn of affairs brought about by God that
the LORD might fulfil his word, which he
spoke by Ahi'jah the Shi'lonite to Jerobo'am
the son of Ne'bat.

[16]And when all Israel saw that the king did
not listen to them, the people answered the
king,

"What portion have we in David?
We have no inheritance in the son
of Jesse.
Each of you to your tents, O Israel!
Look now to your own house, David."

So all Israel departed to their tents. [17]But
Rehobo'am reigned over the sons of Israel
who dwelt in the cities of Judah. [18]Then
King Rehobo'am sent Hador'am, who was
taskmaster over the forced labor, and the
sons of Israel stoned him to death with
stones. And King Rehoboam made haste
to mount his chariot, to flee to Jerusalem.
[19]So Israel has been in rebellion against the
house of David to this day.

11 When Rehobo'am came to Jerusalem,
he assembled the house of Judah, and
Benjamin, a hundred and eighty thousand
chosen warriors, to fight against Israel, to
restore the kingdom to Rehoboam. [2]But the
word of the LORD came to Shemai'ah the
man of God: [3]"Say to Rehobo'am the son of
Solomon king of Judah, and to all Israel in
Judah and Benjamin, [4]'Thus says the LORD,
You shall not go up or fight against your
brethren. Return every man to his home,
for this thing is from me.'" So they listened
to the word of the LORD, and returned and
did not go against Jerobo'am.

[5]Rehobo'am dwelt in Jerusalem, and he
built cities for defense in Judah. [6]He built
Bethlehem, E'tam, Teko'a, [7]Beth-zur, Soco,
Adul'lam, [8]Gath, Mare'shah, Ziph, [9]Adora'im,
La'chish, Aze'kah, [10]Zorah, Ai'jalon, and
He'bron, fortified cities which are in Judah and
in Benjamin. [11]He made the fortresses strong,
and put commanders in them, and stores of
food, oil, and wine. [12]And he put shields and
spears in all the cities, and made them very
strong. So he held Judah and Benjamin.

[13]And the priests and the Levites that were
in all Israel presented themselves to him
from all places where they lived. [14]For the
Levites left their common lands and their
holdings and came to Judah and Jerusalem,
because Jerobo'am and his sons cast them
out from serving as priests of the LORD,
[15]and he appointed his own priests for the
high places, and for the satyrs, and for the
calves which he had made. [16]And those
who had set their hearts to seek the LORD
God of Israel came after them from all the
tribes of Israel to Jerusalem to sacrifice to
the LORD, the God of their fathers. [17]They
strengthened the kingdom of Judah, and for
three years they made Rehobo'am the son of
Solomon secure, for they walked for three
years in the way of David and Solomon.

[18]Rehobo'am took as wife Ma'halath the
daughter of Jer'imoth the son of David, and
of Ab'ihail the daughter of Eli'ab the son
of Jesse; [19]and she bore him sons, Je'ush,
Shemari'ah, and Zaham. [20]After her he
took Ma'acah the daughter of Ab'salom,
who bore him Abi'jah, Attai, Ziza, and
Shelo'mith. [21]Rehobo'am loved Ma'acah the
daughter of Ab'salom above all his wives
and concubines (he took eighteen wives
and sixty concubines, and had twenty-eight
sons and sixty daughters); [22]and Rehobo'am
appointed Abi'jah the son of Ma'acah as chief
prince among his brothers, for he intended
to make him king. [23]And he dealt wisely, and
distributed some of his sons through all the
districts of Judah and Benjamin, in all the

fortified cities; and he gave them abundant provisions, and procured wives for them.

12 When the rule of Rehobo′am was established and was strong, he forsook the law of the LORD, and all Israel with him. [2]In the fifth year of King Rehobo′am, because they had been unfaithful to the LORD, Shishak king of Egypt came up against Jerusalem [3]with twelve hundred chariots and sixty thousand horsemen. And the people were without number who came with him from Egypt—Libyans, Suk′kiim, and Ethiopians. [4]And he took the fortified cities of Judah and came as far as Jerusalem. [5]Then Shemai′ah the prophet came to Rehobo′am and to the princes of Judah, who had gathered at Jerusalem because of Shishak, and said to them, "Thus says the LORD, 'You abandoned me, so I have abandoned you to the hand of Shishak.'" [6]Then the princes of Israel and the king humbled themselves and said, "The LORD is righteous." [7]When the LORD saw that they humbled themselves, the word of the LORD came to Shemai′ah: "They have humbled themselves; I will not destroy them, but I will grant them some deliverance, and my wrath shall not be poured out upon Jerusalem by the hand of Shishak. [8]Nevertheless they shall be servants to him, that they may know my service and the service of the kingdoms of the countries."

[9]So Shishak king of Egypt came up against Jerusalem; he took away the treasures of the house of the LORD and the treasures of the king's house; he took away everything. He also took away the shields of gold which Solomon had made; [10]and King Rehobo′am made in their stead shields of bronze, and committed them to the hands of the officers of the guard, who kept the door of the king's house. [11]And as often as the king went into the house of the LORD, the guard came and bore them, and brought them back to the guardroom. [12]And when he humbled himself the wrath of the LORD turned from him, so as not to make a complete destruction; moreover, conditions were good in Judah.

[13]So King Rehobo′am established himself in Jerusalem and reigned. Rehoboam was forty-one years old when he began to reign, and he reigned seventeen years in Jerusalem, the city which the LORD had chosen out of all the tribes of Israel to put his name there. His mother's name was Na′amah the Am′monitess. [14]And he did evil, for he did not set his heart to seek the LORD.

[15]Now the acts of Rehobo′am, from first to last, are they not written in the chronicles of Shemai′ah the prophet and of Iddo the seer? There were continual wars between Rehobo′am and Jerobo′am. [16]And Rehobo′am slept with his fathers, and was buried in the city of David; and Abi′jah his son reigned in his stead.

PROVERBS 6

[20]My son, keep your father's commandment,
and forsake not your mother's teaching.
[21]Bind them upon your heart always;
tie them about your neck.
[22]When you walk, they will lead you;
when you lie down, they will watch over you;
and when you awake, they will talk with you.
[23]For the commandment is a lamp and the teaching a light,
and the reproofs of discipline are the way of life,
[24]to preserve you from the evil woman,
from the smooth tongue of the adventuress.
[25]Do not desire her beauty in your heart,
and do not let her capture you with her eyelashes;
[26]for a harlot may be hired for a loaf of bread,
but an adulteress stalks a man's very life.
[27]Can a man carry fire in his bosom
and his clothes not be burned?
[28]Or can one walk upon hot coals
and his feet not be scorched?
[29]So is he who goes in to his neighbor's wife;
none who touches her will go unpunished.
[30]Men do not despise a thief if he steals
to satisfy his appetite when he is hungry.
[31]And if he is caught, he will pay sevenfold;
he will give all the goods of his house.

32He who commits adultery has no sense;
he who does it destroys himself.
33Wounds and dishonor will he get,
and his disgrace will not be wiped away.
34For jealousy makes a man furious,
and he will not spare when he
takes revenge.
35He will accept no compensation,
nor be appeased though you multiply gifts.

ACTS 10

24And on the following day they entered Caesare′a. Cornelius was expecting them and had called together his kinsmen and close friends. 25When Peter entered, Cornelius met him and fell down at his feet and worshiped him. 26But Peter lifted him up, saying, "Stand up; I too am a man." 27And as he talked with him, he went in and found many persons gathered; 28and he said to them, "You yourselves know how unlawful it is for a Jew to associate with or to visit any one of another nation; but God has shown me that I should not call any man common or unclean. 29So when I was sent for, I came without objection. I ask then why you sent for me."

30And Cornelius said, "Four days ago, about this hour, I was keeping the ninth hour of prayer in my house; and behold, a man stood before me in bright apparel, 31saying, 'Cornelius, your prayer has been heard and your alms have been remembered before God. 32Send therefore to Joppa and ask for Simon who is called Peter; he is lodging in the house of Simon, a tanner, by the seaside.' 33So I sent to you at once, and you have been kind enough to come. Now therefore we are all here present in the sight of God, to hear all that you have been commanded by the Lord."

34And Peter opened his mouth and said: "Truly I perceive that God shows no partiality, 35but in every nation any one who fears him and does what is right is acceptable to him. 36You know the word which he sent to the sons of Israel, preaching good news of peace by Jesus Christ (he is Lord of all), 37the word which was proclaimed throughout all Judea, beginning from Galilee after the baptism which John preached: 38how God anointed Jesus of Nazareth with the Holy Spirit and with power; how he went about doing good and healing all that were oppressed by the devil, for God was with him. 39And we are witnesses to all that he did both in the country of the Jews and in Jerusalem. They put him to death by hanging him on a tree; 40but God raised him on the third day and made him manifest; 41not to all the people but to us who were chosen by God as witnesses, who ate and drank with him after he rose from the dead. 42And he commanded us to preach to the people, and to testify that he is the one ordained by God to be judge of the living and the dead. 43To him all the prophets bear witness that every one who believes in him receives forgiveness of sins through his name."

REFLECTION

Rehoboam, King Solomon's son, "forsook the counsel which the old men gave him" (2 Chr 10:8). Rehoboam foolishly rejects the sage advice of the elders and embraces the opinions of his friends, setting in motion a rebellion that splits the kingdom. While he had inherited a glorious, unified, and wealthy kingdom, now he squanders his inheritance for an intransigent power play. His self-assertion is misguided and disastrous. Cornelius, a man of stature in the Roman military, doesn't lord his position over the simple fisherman who enters his house. Instead he receives St. Peter graciously, as a messenger from God. Cornelius exemplifies receptivity to God's wisdom: "The commandment is a lamp and the teaching a light, and the reproofs of discipline are the way of life" (Prv 6:23). By his docility to the wisdom of God, Cornelius prepares himself to receive the Gospel and eternal life. How can you be more docile to the wisdom of God?

July 6

2 CHRONICLES 13

In the eighteenth year of King Jerobo′am Abi′jah began to reign over Judah. 2He reigned for three years in Jerusalem. His mother's name was Micai′ah the daughter of U′riel of Gib′e-ah.

Now there was war between Abi′jah and Jerobo′am. 3Abi′jah went out to battle having an army of valiant men of war, four hundred thousand picked men; and Jerobo′am drew up his line of battle against him with eight hundred thousand picked mighty warriors. 4Then Abi′jah stood up on Mount Zemara′im which is in the hill country of E′phraim, and said, "Hear me, O Jerobo′am and all Israel! 5Ought you not to know that the LORD God of Israel gave the kingship over Israel for ever to David and his sons by a covenant of salt? 6Yet Jerobo′am the son of Ne′bat, a servant of Solomon the son of David, rose up and rebelled against his lord; 7and certain worthless scoundrels gathered about him and defied Rehobo′am the son of Solomon, when Rehoboam was young and irresolute and could not withstand them.

8"And now you think to withstand the kingdom of the LORD in the hand of the sons of David, because you are a great multitude and have with you the golden calves which Jerobo′am made you for gods. 9Have you not driven out the priests of the LORD, the sons of Aaron, and the Levites, and made priests for yourselves like the peoples of other lands? Whoever comes to consecrate himself with a young bull or seven rams becomes a priest of what are no gods. 10But as for us, the LORD is our God, and we have not forsaken him. We have priests ministering to the LORD who are sons of Aaron, and Levites for their service. 11They offer to the LORD every morning and every evening burnt offerings and incense of sweet spices, set out the showbread on the table of pure gold, and care for the golden lampstand that its lamps may burn every evening; for we keep the charge of the LORD our God, but you have forsaken him. 12Behold, God is with us at our head, and his priests with their battle trumpets to sound the call to battle against you. O sons of Israel, do not fight against the LORD, the God of your fathers; for you cannot succeed."

13Jerobo′am had sent an ambush around to come on them from behind; thus his troops were in front of Judah, and the ambush was behind them. 14And when Judah looked, behold, the battle was before and behind them; and they cried to the LORD, and the priests blew the trumpets. 15Then the men of Judah raised the battle shout. And when the men of Judah shouted, God defeated Jerobo′am and all Israel before Abi′jah and Judah. 16The men of Israel fled before Judah, and God gave them into their hand. 17Abi′jah and his people slew them with a great slaughter; so there fell slain of Israel five hundred thousand picked men. 18Thus the men of Israel were subdued at that time, and the men of Judah prevailed, because they relied upon the LORD, the God of their fathers. 19And Abi′jah pursued Jerobo′am, and took cities from him, Bethel with its villages and Jesha′nah with its villages and E′phron with its villages. 20Jerobo′am did not recover his power in the days of Abi′jah; and the LORD struck him, and he died. 21But Abi′jah grew mighty. And he took fourteen wives, and had twenty-two sons and sixteen daughters. 22The rest of the acts of Abi′jah, his ways and his sayings, are written in the story of the prophet Iddo.

14
So Abi′jah slept with his fathers, and they buried him in the city of David; and Asa his son reigned in his stead. In his days the land had rest for ten years. 2And Asa did what was good and right in the eyes of the LORD his God. 3He took away the foreign altars and the high places, and broke down the pillars and hewed down the Ashe′rim, 4and commanded Judah to seek the LORD, the God of their fathers, and to keep the law and the commandment. 5He also took out of all the cities of Judah the high places and

the incense altars. And the kingdom had rest
under him. 6He built fortified cities in Judah,
for the land had rest. He had no war in those
years, for the LORD gave him peace. 7And
he said to Judah, "Let us build these cities,
and surround them with walls and towers,
gates and bars; the land is still ours, because
we have sought the LORD our God; we have
sought him, and he has given us peace on
every side." So they built and prospered. 8And
Asa had an army of three hundred thousand
from Judah, armed with bucklers and spears,
and two hundred and eighty thousand men
from Benjamin, that carried shields and drew
bows; all these were mighty men of valor.
9Ze′rah the Ethiopian came out against
them with an army of a million men and
three hundred chariots, and came as far
as Mare′shah. 10And Asa went out to meet
him, and they drew up their lines of battle
in the valley of Zeph′athah at Mare′shah.
11And Asa cried to the LORD his God,
"O LORD, there is none like you to help,
between the mighty and the weak. Help
us, O LORD our God, for we rely on you,
and in your name we have come against
this multitude. O LORD, you are our God;
let man not prevail against you." 12So the
LORD defeated the Ethiopians before Asa
and before Judah, and the Ethiopians fled.
13Asa and the people that were with him
pursued them as far as Ge′rar, and the
Ethiopians fell until none remained alive;
for they were broken before the LORD and
his army. The men of Judah carried away
very much booty. 14And they struck all the
cities round about Ge′rar, for the fear of the
LORD was upon them. They plundered all
the cities, for there was much plunder in
them. 15And they struck the tents of those
who had cattle, and carried away sheep in
abundance and camels. Then they returned
to Jerusalem.

15 The Spirit of God came upon Az-
ari′ah the son of O′ded, 2and he went
out to meet Asa, and said to him, "Hear
me, Asa, and all Judah and Benjamin: The
LORD is with you, while you are with him.
If you seek him, he will be found by you,
but if you forsake him, he will forsake you.
3For a long time Israel was without the
true God, and without a teaching priest,
and without law; 4but when in their distress they turned to the LORD, the God of
Israel, and sought him, he was found by
them. 5In those times there was no peace
to him who went out or to him who came
in, for great disturbances afflicted all the
inhabitants of the lands. 6They were broken in pieces, nation against nation and
city against city, for God troubled them
with every sort of distress. 7But you, take
courage! Do not let your hands be weak,
for your work shall be rewarded."
8When Asa heard these words, the prophecy of Azari′ah the son of O′ded, he took
courage, and put away the abominable
idols from all the land of Judah and
Benjamin and from the cities which he
had taken in the hill country of E′phraim,
and he repaired the altar of the LORD that
was in front of the vestibule of the house
of the LORD. 9And he gathered all Judah
and Benjamin, and those from E′phraim,
Manas′seh, and Simeon who were
sojourning with them, for great numbers
had deserted to him from Israel when they
saw that the LORD his God was with him.
10They were gathered at Jerusalem in the
third month of the fifteenth year of the
reign of Asa. 11They sacrificed to the LORD
on that day, from the spoil which they had
brought, seven hundred oxen and seven
thousand sheep. 12And they entered into
a covenant to seek the LORD, the God of
their fathers, with all their heart and with
all their soul; 13and that whoever would not
seek the LORD, the God of Israel, should be
put to death, whether young or old, man
or woman. 14They took oath to the LORD
with a loud voice, and with shouting, and
with trumpets, and with horns. 15And all
Judah rejoiced over the oath; for they had
sworn with all their heart, and had sought
him with their whole desire, and he was
found by them, and the LORD gave them
rest round about.
16Even Ma′acah, his mother, King Asa
removed from being queen mother because she had made an abominable image

for Ashe´rah. Asa cut down her image,
crushed it, and burned it at the brook
Kidron. 17But the high places were not tak-
en out of Israel. Nevertheless the heart of
Asa was blameless all his days. 18And he
brought into the house of God the votive
gifts of his father and his own votive gifts,
silver, and gold, and vessels. 19And there
was no more war until the thirty-fifth year
of the reign of Asa.

PROVERBS 7

My son, keep my words
  and treasure up my commandments
    with you;
2keep my commandments and live,
  keep my teachings as the apple of your eye;
3bind them on your fingers,
  write them on the tablet of your heart.
4Say to wisdom, "You are my sister,"
  and call insight your intimate friend;
5to preserve you from the loose woman,
  from the adventuress with her
    smooth words.

6For at the window of my house
  I have looked out through my lattice,
7and I have seen among the simple,
  I have perceived among the youths,
  a young man without sense,
8passing along the street near her corner,
  taking the road to her house
9in the twilight, in the evening,
  at the time of night and darkness.

ACTS 10

**44While Peter was still saying
this, the Holy Spirit fell on all
who heard the word. 45And the believers
from among the circumcised who came**
with Peter were amazed, because the gift of
the Holy Spirit had been poured out even on
the Gentiles. 46For they heard them speaking in tongues and extolling God. Then Peter declared, 47"Can any one forbid water for
baptizing these people who have received
the Holy Spirit just as we have?" 48And he
commanded them to be baptized in the
name of Jesus Christ. Then they asked him
to remain for some days.

11 Now the apostles and the brethren
who were in Judea heard that the
Gentiles also had received the word of
God. 2So when Peter went up to Jerusalem, the circumcision party criticized him,
3saying, "Why did you go to uncircumcised
men and eat with them?" 4But Peter began
and explained to them in order: 5"I was in
the city of Joppa praying; and in a trance I
saw a vision, something descending, like a
great sheet, let down from heaven by four
corners; and it came down to me. 6Looking
at it closely I observed animals and beasts
of prey and reptiles and birds of the air.
7And I heard a voice saying to me, 'Rise,
Peter; kill and eat.' 8But I said, 'No, Lord;
for nothing common or unclean has ever
entered my mouth.' 9But the voice answered
a second time from heaven, 'What God
has cleansed you must not call common.'
10This happened three times, and all was
drawn up again into heaven. 11At that very
moment three men arrived at the house in
which we were, sent to me from Caesare´a.
12And the Spirit told me to go with them,
making no distinction. These six brethren
also accompanied me, and we entered the
man's house. 13And he told us how he had
seen the angel standing in his house and
saying, 'Send to Joppa and bring Simon
called Peter; 14he will declare to you a message by which you will be saved, you and
all your household.' 15As I began to speak,
the Holy Spirit fell on them just as on us
at the beginning. 16And I remembered the
word of the Lord, how he said, 'John baptized with water, but you shall be baptized
with the Holy Spirit.' 17If then God gave the
same gift to them as he gave to us when
we believed in the Lord Jesus Christ, who
was I that I could withstand God?" 18When
they heard this they were silenced. And
they glorified God, saying, "Then to the
Gentiles also God has granted repentance
unto life."

REFLECTION

Life presents us with challenges, problems, tragedies, sorrows, and surprises. The torrent can be overwhelming at times, and in those moments we need to seek solace in a God who is far bigger than our troubles. When Azariah prophesies to King Asa, he recounts Israel's former difficulties in being apart from God, his priests, and his law: "When in their distress they turned to the LORD, the God of Israel, and sought him, he was found by them" (2 Chr 15:4). Sometimes God seems unfindable, beyond our reach, far away, and silent. It is precisely at these times that we must "seek" him, which can be as simple as quiet prayer, Bible reading, or receiving the sacraments. He comes to us and helps us, even if we don't experience lightning bolts or goosebumps. At times we find him in unexpected situations, like when St. Peter preaches to the Gentiles and the Holy Spirit falls upon them in power (see Acts 11:15). Peter interprets the Gentiles' receiving of the Holy Spirit as evidence of their eligibility for Baptism: "Who was I that I could withstand God?" (v. 17). In our struggles, we need to seek after the Lord, and, when he comes unexpectedly, we must not stand in his way. What are some ways that you can seek the Lord?

July 7

2 CHRONICLES 16

**In the thirty-sixth year of the
reign of Asa, Ba′asha king of
Israel went up against Judah, and built
Ra′mah, that he might permit no one**
to go out or come in to Asa king of Judah.
[2]Then Asa took silver and gold from the
treasures of the house of the LORD and the
king's house, and sent them to Ben-ha′dad
king of Syria, who dwelt in Damascus,
saying, [3]"Let there be a league between
me and you, as between my father and
your father; behold, I am sending to you
silver and gold; go, break your league with
Ba′asha king of Israel, that he may withdraw
from me." [4]And Ben-ha′dad listened to
King Asa, and sent the commanders of his
armies against the cities of Israel, and they
conquered I′jon, Dan, A′bel-ma′im, and
all the store-cities of Naph′tali. [5]And when
Ba′asha heard of it, he stopped building
Ra′mah, and let his work cease. [6]Then King
Asa took all Judah, and they carried away
the stones of Ra′mah and its timber, with
which Ba′asha had been building, and with
them he built Ge′ba and Mizpah.
[7]At that time Hana′ni the seer came to Asa
king of Judah, and said to him, "Because
you relied on the king of Syria, and did not
rely on the LORD your God, the army of the
king of Syria has escaped you. [8]Were not the
Ethiopians and the Libyans a huge army with
exceedingly many chariots and horsemen?
Yet because you relied on the LORD, he gave
them into your hand. [9]For the eyes of the
LORD move back and forth throughout the
whole earth, to show his might in behalf
of those whose heart is blameless toward
him. You have done foolishly in this; for
from now on you will have wars." [10]Then
Asa was angry with the seer, and put him
in the stocks, in prison, for he was in a rage
with him because of this. And Asa inflicted
cruelties upon some of the people at the
same time.
[11]The acts of Asa, from first to last, are
written in the Book of the Kings of Judah
and Israel. [12]In the thirty-ninth year of
his reign Asa was diseased in his feet, and
his disease became severe; yet even in his
disease he did not seek the LORD, but sought
help from physicians. [13]And Asa slept with
his fathers, dying in the forty-first year of
his reign. [14]They buried him in the tomb
which he had hewn out for himself in the
city of David. They laid him on a bier which
had been filled with various kinds of spices
prepared by the perfumer's art; and they
made a very great fire in his honor.

17 Jehosh′aphat his son reigned in his
stead, and strengthened himself against

Israel. 2He placed forces in all the fortified
cities of Judah, and set garrisons in the land
of Judah, and in the cities of E′phraim which
Asa his father had taken. 3The LORD was with
Jehosh′aphat, because he walked in the earlier
ways of his father; he did not seek the Ba′als,
4but sought the God of his father and walked
in his commandments, and not according
to the ways of Israel. 5Therefore the LORD
established the kingdom in his hand; and all
Judah brought tribute to Jehosh′aphat; and
he had great riches and honor. 6His heart
was courageous in the ways of the LORD; and
furthermore he took the high places and the
Ashe′rim out of Judah.

7In the third year of his reign he sent his
princes, Ben-ha′il, Obadi′ah, Zechari′ah,
Nethan′el, and Micai′ah, to teach in the
cities of Judah; 8and with them the Levites,
Shemai′ah, Nethani′ah, Zebadi′ah, As′ahel,
Shemi′ramoth, Jehon′athan, Adoni′jah,
Tobi′jah, and Tobadoni′jah; and with these
Levites, the priests Elish′ama and Jeho′ram.
9And they taught in Judah, having the book
of the law of the LORD with them; they went
about through all the cities of Judah and
taught among the people.

10And the fear of the LORD fell upon all
the kingdoms of the lands that were round
about Judah, and they made no war against
Jehosh′aphat. 11Some of the Philis′tines
brought Jehosh′aphat presents, and silver
for tribute; and the Arabs also brought him
seven thousand seven hundred rams and
seven thousand seven hundred he-goats.
12And Jehosh′aphat grew steadily greater.
He built in Judah fortresses and store-
cities, 13and he had great stores in the cities
of Judah. He had soldiers, mighty men of
valor, in Jerusalem. 14This was the muster
of them by fathers' houses: Of Judah, the
commanders of thousands: Adnah the
commander, with three hundred thousand
mighty men of valor, 15and next to him
Je′ho-ha′nan the commander, with two
hundred and eighty thousand, 16and next
to him Amasi′ah the son of Zich′ri, a
volunteer for the service of the LORD, with
two hundred thousand mighty men of
valor. 17Of Benjamin: Eli′ada, a mighty man
of valor, with two hundred thousand men
armed with bow and shield, 18and next to
him Jeho′zabad with a hundred and eighty
thousand armed for war. 19These were in
the service of the king, besides those whom
the king had placed in the fortified cities
throughout all Judah.

18 Now Jehosh′aphat had great riches
and honor; and he made a marriage alliance with A′hab. 2After some
years he went down to A′hab in Samar′ia.
And Ahab killed an abundance of sheep
and oxen for him and for the people who
were with him, and induced him to go
up against Ra′moth-gil′ead. 3A′hab king
of Israel said to Jehosh′aphat king of Judah, "Will you go with me to Ra′moth-
gil′ead?" He answered him, "I am as you
are, my people as your people. We will be
with you in the war."

4And Jehosh′aphat said to the king of
Israel, "Inquire first for the word of the
LORD." 5Then the king of Israel gathered
the prophets together, four hundred men,
and said to them, "Shall we go to battle
against Ra′moth-gil′ead, or shall I forbear?" And they said, "Go up; for God will
give it into the hand of the king." 6But Je-
hosh′aphat said, "Is there not here another prophet of the LORD of whom we may
inquire?" 7And the king of Israel said to
Jehosh′aphat, "There is yet one man by
whom we may inquire of the LORD, Mic-
ai′ah the son of Imlah; but I hate him, for
he never prophesies good concerning me,
but always evil." And Jehoshaphat said, "Let
not the king say so." 8Then the king of Israel summoned an officer and said, "Bring
quickly Micai′ah the son of Imlah." 9Now
the king of Israel and Jehosh′aphat the king
of Judah were sitting on their thrones, at-
tired in their robes; and they were sitting
at the threshing floor at the entrance of the
gate of Samar′ia; and all the prophets were
prophesying before them. 10And Zedeki′ah
the son of Chena′anah made for himself
horns of iron, and said, "Thus says the
LORD, 'With these you shall push the Syrians until they are destroyed.'" 11And all the
prophets prophesied so, and said, "Go up

to Ra´moth-gil´ead and triumph; the LORD
will give it into the hand of the king."
12And the messenger who went to summon
Micai´ah said to him, "Behold, the words of
the prophets with one accord are favorable
to the king; let your word be like the word
of one of them, and speak favorably." 13But
Micai´ah said, "As the LORD lives, what my
God says, that I will speak." 14And when he
had come to the king, the king said to him,
"Mica´ah, shall we go to Ra´moth-gil´ead to
battle, or shall I forbear?" And he answered,
"Go up and triumph; they will be given into
your hand." 15But the king said to him, "How
many times shall I adjure you that you speak
to me nothing but the truth in the name of
the LORD?" 16And he said, "I saw all Israel scattered upon the mountains, as sheep
that have no shepherd; and the LORD said,
'These have no master; let each return to
his home in peace.' " 17And the king of Israel
said to Jehosh´aphat, "Did I not tell you that
he would not prophesy good concerning
me, but evil?" 18And Micai´ah said, "Therefore hear the word of the LORD: I saw the
LORD sitting on his throne, and all the host
of heaven standing on his right hand and
on his left; 19and the LORD said, 'Who will
entice A´hab the king of Israel, that he may
go up and fall at Ra´moth-gil´ead?' And
one said one thing, and another said another. 20Then a spirit came forward and
stood before the LORD, saying, 'I will entice
him.' And the LORD said to him, 'By what
means?' 21And he said, 'I will go forth, and
will be a lying spirit in the mouth of all his
prophets.' And he said, 'You are to entice
him, and you shall succeed; go forth and
do so.' 22Now therefore behold, the LORD
has put a lying spirit in the mouth of these
your prophets; the LORD has spoken evil
concerning you."
23Then Zedeki´ah the son of Chena´anah
came near and struck Micai´ah on the cheek,
and said, "Which way did the Spirit of the
LORD go from me to speak to you?" 24And
Micai´ah said, "Behold, you shall see on that
day when you go into an inner chamber
to hide yourself." 25And the king of Israel
said, "Seize Micai´ah, and take him back to
A´mon the governor of the city and to Jo´ash
the king's son; 26and say, 'Thus says the king,
Put this fellow in prison, and feed him with
scant fare of bread and water, until I return
in peace.' " 27And Micai´ah said, "If you return
in peace, the LORD has not spoken by me."
And he said, "Hear, all you peoples!"
28So the king of Israel and Jehosh´aphat
the king of Judah went up to Ra´moth-
gil´ead. 29And the king of Israel said to
Jehosh´aphat, "I will disguise myself and
go into battle, but you wear your robes."
And the king of Israel disguised himself;
and they went into battle. 30Now the king
of Syria had commanded the captains of
his chariots, "Fight with neither small nor
great, but only with the king of Israel."
31And when the captains of the chariots saw
Jehosh´aphat, they said, "It is the king of
Israel." So they turned to fight against him;
and Jehoshaphat cried out, and the LORD
helped him. God drew them away from
him, 32for when the captains of the chariots
saw that it was not the king of Israel, they
turned back from pursuing him. 33But a
certain man drew his bow and unknowingly
struck the king of Israel between the scale
armor and the breastplate; therefore he said
to the driver of his chariot, "Turn about,
and carry me out of the battle, for I am
wounded." 34And the battle grew hot that
day, and the king of Israel propped himself
up in his chariot facing the Syrians until
evening; then at sunset he died.

PROVERBS 7

10And behold, a woman meets him,
dressed as a harlot, wily of heart.
11She is loud and wayward,
her feet do not stay at home;
12now in the street, now in the market,
and at every corner she lies in wait.
13She seizes him and kisses him,
and with impudent face she says to him:
14"I had to offer sacrifices,
and today I have paid my vows;
15so now I have come out to meet you,
to seek you eagerly, and I have found you.

[16]I have decked my couch with coverings,
colored spreads of Egyptian linen;
[17]I have perfumed my bed with myrrh,
aloes, and cinnamon.
[18]Come, let us take our fill of love
till morning;
let us delight ourselves with love.
[19]For my husband is not at home;
he has gone on a long journey;
[20]he took a bag of money with him;
at full moon he will come home."

[21]With much seductive speech she
persuades him;
with her smooth talk she compels him.
[22]All at once he follows her,
as an ox goes to the slaughter,
or as a stag is caught fast
[23] till an arrow pierces its entrails;
as a bird rushes into a snare;
he does not know that it will cost him
his life.

[24]And now, O sons, listen to me,
and be attentive to the words of my mouth.
[25]Let not your heart turn aside to her ways,
do not stray into her paths;
[26]for many a victim has she laid low;
yes, all her slain are a mighty host.
[27]Her house is the way to Sheol,
going down to the chambers of death.

ACTS 11

[19]Now those who were scattered because of the persecution that arose over Stephen traveled as far as Phoeni′cia and Cyprus and Antioch,
speaking the word to none except Jews.
[20]But there were some of them, men of
Cyprus and Cyre′ne, who on coming to
Antioch spoke to the Greeks also, preaching
the Lord Jesus. [21]And the hand of the Lord
was with them, and a great number that
believed turned to the Lord. [22]News of this
came to the ears of the Church in Jerusalem,
and they sent Barnabas to Antioch. [23]When
he came and saw the grace of God, he was
glad; and he exhorted them all to remain
faithful to the Lord with steadfast purpose;
[24]for he was a good man, full of the Holy
Spirit and of faith. And a large company was
added to the Lord. [25]So Barnabas went to
Tarsus to look for Saul; [26]and when he had
found him, he brought him to Antioch. For
a whole year they met with the Church, and
taught a large company of people; and in
Antioch the disciples were for the first time
called Christians.
[27]Now in these days prophets came down
from Jerusalem to Antioch. [28]And one of
them named Ag′abus stood up and foretold
by the Spirit that there would be a great
famine over all the world; and this took place
in the days of Claudius. [29]And the disciples
determined, every one according to his
ability, to send relief to the brethren who
lived in Judea; [30]and they did so, sending it to
the elders by the hand of Barnabas and Saul.

REFLECTION

Taking a stand for the truth is always tougher than telling people what they want to hear. The prophet Micaiah faces a tough situation when two powerful kings plan to go to battle against the Syrians. They have already consulted multiple prophets who have supported their plans with prophecies from a "lying spirit" (2 Chr 18:21). Finally, Micaiah is summoned before the kings. Initially, he lies, telling the kings what they want to hear: "Go up and triumph; they will be given into your hand" (v. 18:14). One can imagine him delivering this line with a perfunctory tone of voice, showing his unwilling compliance with the sentiments of the kings. But King Ahab presses him for a true prophecy, at which point Micaiah delivers up a negative prophecy and advises against attacking Syria, explaining the "lying spirit" of the other prophets. Foolishly, the kings reject his words and go to battle anyway, whereupon Ahab is killed by a random arrow. The kings are like the "young man without sense" (Prv 7:7), who is seduced by Lady Folly "as an ox goes to the slaughter" (v. 22). We must take care not to be silent when the truth is called for, nor to ignore the truth when it is spoken to us. Are you courageous enough to speak the truth?

July 8

2 CHRONICLES 19

**Jehosh′aphat the king of Judah
returned in safety to his house
in Jerusalem. [2]But Je′hu the son
of Hana′ni the seer went out to meet
him, and said to King Jehosh′aphat,
"Should you help the wicked and love**
those who hate the LORD? Because of this,
wrath has gone out against you from the
LORD. [3]Nevertheless some good is found
in you, for you destroyed the Ashe′rahs
out of the land, and have set your heart
to seek God."
[4]Jehosh′aphat dwelt at Jerusalem; and he
went out again among the people, from
Be′er-she′ba to the hill country of E′phraim,
and brought them back to the LORD, the
God of their fathers. [5]He appointed judges
in the land in all the fortified cities of
Judah, city by city, [6]and said to the judges,
"Consider what you do, for you judge not
for man but for the LORD; he is with you
in giving judgment. [7]Now then, let the fear
of the LORD be upon you; take heed what
you do, for there is no perversion of justice
with the LORD our God, or partiality, or
taking bribes."
[8]Moreover in Jerusalem Jehosh′aphat
appointed certain Levites and priests and
heads of families of Israel, to give judgment for the LORD and to decide disputed
cases. They had their seat at Jerusalem.
[9]And he charged them: "Thus you shall
do in the fear of the LORD, in faithfulness,
and with your whole heart: [10]whenever
a case comes to you from your brethren
who live in their cities, concerning bloodshed, law or commandment, statutes or
ordinances, then you shall instruct them,
that they may not incur guilt before the
LORD and wrath may not come upon you
and your brethren. Thus you shall do, and
you will not incur guilt. [11]And behold,
Amari′ah the chief priest is over you in
all matters of the LORD; and Zebadi′ah
the son of Ish′mael, the governor of the
house of Judah, in all the king's matters;
and the Levites will serve you as officers.
Deal courageously, and may the LORD be
with the upright!"

20 After this the Moabites and Am′mon-
ites, and with them some of the Me-
u′nites, came against Jehosh′aphat for battle.
[2]Some men came and told Jehosh′aphat, "A
great multitude is coming against you from
E′dom, from beyond the sea; and, behold,
they are in Haz′azon-ta′mar" (that is, En-
ge′di). [3]Then Jehosh′aphat feared, and set
himself to seek the LORD, and proclaimed
a fast throughout all Judah. [4]And Judah
assembled to seek help from the LORD;
from all the cities of Judah they came to
seek the LORD.
[5]And Jehosh′aphat stood in the assembly of Judah and Jerusalem, in the house
of the LORD, before the new court, [6]and
said, "O LORD, God of our fathers, are you
not God in heaven? Do you not rule over
all the kingdoms of the nations? In your
hand are power and might, so that none
is able to withstand you. [7]Did you not, O
our God, drive out the inhabitants of this
land before your people Israel, and give it
for ever to the descendants of Abraham
your friend? [8]And they have dwelt in it,
and have built you in it a sanctuary for
your name, saying, [9]'If evil comes upon
us, the sword, judgment, or pestilence, or
famine, we will stand before this house,
and before you, for your name is in this
house, and cry to you in our affliction,
and you will hear and save.' [10]And now
behold, the men of Ammon and Moab
and Mount Se′ir, whom you would not let
Israel invade when they came from the
land of Egypt, and whom they avoided
and did not destroy—[11]behold, they reward us by coming to drive us out of your
possession, which you have given us to
inherit. [12]O our God, will you not execute
judgment upon them? For we are powerless against this great multitude that is
coming against us. We do not know what
to do, but our eyes are upon you."

13Meanwhile all the men of Judah stood
before the LORD, with their little ones,
their wives, and their children. 14And the
Spirit of the LORD came upon Jahazi′el
the son of Zechari′ah, son of Bena′iah,
son of Je-i′el, son of Mattani′ah, a Levite
of the sons of A′saph, in the midst of the
assembly. 15And he said, "Listen, all Judah
and inhabitants of Jerusalem, and King
Jehosh′aphat: Thus says the LORD to you,
'Fear not, and be not dismayed at this
great multitude; for the battle is not yours
but God's. 16Tomorrow go down against
them; behold, they will come up by the
ascent of Ziz; you will find them at the
end of the valley, east of the wilderness
of Jeru′el. 17You will not need to fight in
this battle; take your position, stand still,
and see the victory of the LORD on your
behalf, O Judah and Jerusalem.' Fear not,
and be not dismayed; tomorrow go out
against them, and the LORD will be with
you."

18Then Jehosh′aphat bowed his head with
his face to the ground, and all Judah and
the inhabitants of Jerusalem fell down
before the LORD, worshiping the LORD.
19And the Levites, of the Ko′hathites and
the Ko′rahites, stood up to praise the LORD,
the God of Israel, with a very loud voice.

20And they rose early in the morning and
went out into the wilderness of Teko′a;
and as they went out, Jehosh′aphat stood
and said, "Hear me, Judah and inhabitants
of Jerusalem! Believe in the LORD your
God, and you will be established; believe
his prophets, and you will succeed." 21And
when he had taken counsel with the
people, he appointed those who were to
sing to the LORD and praise him in holy
splendor, as they went before the army,
and say,

"Give thanks to the LORD,
for his mercy endures for ever."

22And when they began to sing and praise,
the LORD set an ambush against the men
of Ammon, Moab, and Mount Se′ir, who
had come against Judah, so that they were
routed. 23For the men of Ammon and Moab
rose against the inhabitants of Mount Se′ir,
destroying them utterly, and when they had
made an end of the inhabitants of Seir, they
all helped to destroy one another.

24When Judah came to the watchtower
of the wilderness, they looked toward the
multitude; and behold, they were dead bodies lying on the ground; none had escaped.
25When Jehosh′aphat and his people came
to take the spoil from them, they found cattle in great numbers, goods, clothing, and
precious things, which they took for themselves until they could carry no more. They
were three days in taking the spoil, it was
so much. 26On the fourth day they assembled in the Valley of Bera′cah, for there they
blessed the LORD; therefore the name of that
place has been called the Valley of Beracah
to this day. 27Then they returned, every man
of Judah and Jerusalem, and Jehosh′aphat at
their head, returning to Jerusalem with joy,
for the LORD had made them rejoice over
their enemies. 28They came to Jerusalem,
with harps and lyres and trumpets, to the
house of the LORD. 29And the fear of God
came on all the kingdoms of the countries
when they heard that the LORD had fought
against the enemies of Israel. 30So the realm
of Jehosh′aphat was quiet, for his God gave
him rest round about.

31Thus Jehosh′aphat reigned over Judah.
He was thirty-five years old when he began to reign, and he reigned twenty-five
years in Jerusalem. His mother's name
was Azu′bah the daughter of Shilhi. 32He
walked in the way of Asa his father and
did not turn aside from it; he did what
was right in the sight of the LORD. 33The
high places, however, were not taken
away; the people had not yet set their
hearts upon the God of their fathers.

34Now the rest of the acts of Jehosh′aphat,
from first to last, are written in the chronicles
of Je′hu the son of Hana′ni, which are recorded in the Book of the Kings of Israel.

35After this Jehosh′aphat king of Judah
joined with Ahazi′ah king of Israel, who
did wickedly. 36He joined him in building
ships to go to Tar′shish, and they built the
ships in E′zion-ge′ber. 37Then Elie′zer the
son of Dodav′ahu of Mare′shah prophesied

against Jehosh′aphat, saying, "Because you have joined with Ahazi′ah, the LORD will destroy what you have made." And the ships were wrecked and were not able to go to Tar′shish.

PROVERBS 8

Does not wisdom call,
does not understanding raise her voice?
2On the heights beside the way,
in the paths she takes her stand;
3beside the gates in front of the town,
at the entrance of the portals she
cries aloud:
4"To you, O men, I call,
and my cry is to the sons of men.
5O simple ones, learn prudence;
O foolish men, pay attention.
6Hear, for I will speak noble things,
and from my lips will come what is right;
7for my mouth will utter truth;
wickedness is an abomination to my lips.
8All the words of my mouth are righteous;
there is nothing twisted or crooked
in them.
9They are all straight to him
who understands
and right to those who find knowledge.
10Take my instruction instead of silver,
and knowledge rather than choice gold;
11for wisdom is better than jewels,
and all that you may desire cannot
compare with her.
12I, wisdom, dwell in prudence,
and I find knowledge and discretion.
13The fear of the LORD is hatred of evil.
Pride and arrogance and the way of evil
and perverted speech I hate.
14I have counsel and sound wisdom,
I have insight, I have strength.
15By me kings reign,
and rulers decree what is just;
16by me princes rule,
and nobles govern the earth.
17I love those who love me,
and those who seek me diligently find me.
18Riches and honor are with me,
enduring wealth and prosperity.
19My fruit is better than gold, even fine gold,
and my yield than choice silver.
20I walk in the way of righteousness,
in the paths of justice,
21endowing with wealth those who love me,
and filling their treasuries.

ACTS 12

About that time Herod the king laid violent hands upon some who belonged to the Church. 2He killed James the brother of John with the
sword; 3and when he saw that it pleased the
Jews, he proceeded to arrest Peter also. This
was during the days of Unleavened Bread.
4And when he had seized him, he put him
in prison, and delivered him to four squads
of soldiers to guard him, intending after the
Passover to bring him out to the people. 5So
Peter was kept in prison; but earnest prayer for
him was made to God by the Church.

6The very night when Herod was about to
bring him out, Peter was sleeping between two
soldiers, bound with two chains, and sentries
before the door were guarding the prison;
7and behold, an angel of the Lord appeared,
and a light shone in the cell; and he struck
Peter on the side and woke him, saying, "Get
up quickly." And the chains fell off his hands.
8And the angel said to him, "Dress yourself
and put on your sandals." And he did so. And
he said to him, "Wrap your cloak around you
and follow me." 9And he went out and followed
him; he did not know that what was done by
the angel was real, but thought he was seeing
a vision. 10When they had passed the first and
the second guard, they came to the iron gate
leading into the city. It opened to them of its
own accord, and they went out and passed on
through one street; and immediately the angel
left him. 11And Peter came to himself, and said,
"Now I am sure that the Lord has sent his angel
and rescued me from the hand of Herod and
from all that the Jewish people were expecting."

12When he realized this, he went to the house
of Mary, the mother of John whose other name
was Mark, where many were gathered together

and were praying.[13]And when he knocked at
the door of the gateway, a maid named Rhoda
came to answer. [14]Recognizing Peter's voice, in
her joy she did not open the gate but ran in and
told that Peter was standing at the gate. [15]They
said to her, "You are mad." But she insisted
that it was so. They said, "It is his angel!"
[16]But Peter continued knocking; and when
they opened, they saw him and were amazed.
[17]But motioning to them with his hand to be
silent, he described to them how the Lord had
brought him out of the prison. And he said,
"Tell this to James and to the brethren." Then
he departed and went to another place.
[18]Now when day came, there was no small
stir among the soldiers over what had become
of Peter. [19]And when Herod had sought for
him and could not find him, he examined the
sentries and ordered that they should be put
to death. Then he went down from Judea to
Caesare′a, and remained there.

REFLECTION

Following the Lord's way in this world invites opposition. King Jehoshaphat appoints judges throughout his kingdom and instructs them: "You judge not for man but for the LORD" (2 Chr 19:6). Yet soon after he initiates his project of justice, multiple enemy nations form an alliance and plan an attack. When Jehoshaphat finds out, he seeks the Lord and "proclaim[s] a fast throughout all Judah" (20:3). Rather than relying on his own strategic cleverness, he relies on the Lord. As battle approaches, he again prays to the Lord, "O our God, will you not execute judgment upon them? For we are powerless against this great multitude that is coming against us. We do not know what to do, but our eyes are upon you" (v. 12). This is a prayer of abandonment to God's will in desperate times. Jehoshaphat models for us how to rely on the Lord in the midst of the storms of life. Similarly, when he is imprisoned for the Gospel, St. Peter relies on the Lord, who sends an angel to rescue him. Both of them show the reality of what Lady Wisdom promises: "I love those who love me, and those who seek me diligently find me" (Prv 8:17). How can you seek God diligently today?

July 9

2 CHRONICLES 21

Jehosh′aphat slept with his fathers, and was buried with his fathers in the city of David; and Jeho′ram his son reigned in his stead.
[2]He had brothers, the sons of Jehosh′aphat:
Azari′ah, Jehi′el, Zechari′ah, Azariah, Michael, and Shephati′ah; all these were the sons
of Jehoshaphat king of Judah. [3]Their father
gave them great gifts, of silver, gold, and valuable possessions, together with fortified cities
in Judah; but he gave the kingdom to Jeho′ram,
because he was the first-born. [4]When Jeho′ram
had ascended the throne of his father and was
established, he slew all his brothers with the
sword, and also some of the princes of Israel.
[5]Jeho′ram was thirty-two years old when he
became king, and he reigned eight years in
Jerusalem. [6]And he walked in the way of the
kings of Israel, as the house of A′hab had done;
for the daughter of Ahab was his wife. And
he did what was evil in the sight of the LORD.
[7]Yet the LORD would not destroy the house of
David, because of the covenant which he had
made with David, and since he had promised
to give a lamp to him and to his sons for ever.
[8]In his days E′dom revolted from the rule of
Judah, and set up a king of their own. [9]Then
Jeho′ram passed over with his commanders
and all his chariots, and he rose by night and
struck the E′domites who had surrounded
him and his chariot commanders. [10]So E′dom
revolted from the rule of Judah to this day. At
that time Libnah also revolted from his rule,
because he had forsaken the LORD, the God of
his fathers.
[11]Moreover he made high places in the hill
country of Judah, and led the inhabitants
of Jerusalem into unfaithfulness, and made
Judah go astray. [12]And a letter came to him
from Eli′jah the prophet, saying, "Thus says the
LORD, the God of David your father, 'Because
you have not walked in the ways of Jehosh′aphat
your father, or in the ways of Asa king of Judah,

13but have walked in the way of the kings of
Israel, and have led Judah and the inhabitants
of Jerusalem into unfaithfulness, as the house
of A'hab led Israel into unfaithfulness, and
also you have killed your brothers, of your
father's house, who were better than yourself;
14behold, the LORD will bring a great plague on
your people, your children, your wives, and all
your possessions, 15and you yourself will have
a severe sickness with a disease of your bowels,
until your bowels come out because of the
disease, day by day.'"
16And the LORD stirred up against Jeho'ram
the anger of the Philis'tines and of the Arabs
who are near the Ethiopians; 17and they came
up against Judah, and invaded it, and carried
away all the possessions they found that
belonged to the king's house, and also his sons
and his wives, so that no son was left to him
except Jeho'ahaz, his youngest son.
18And after all this the LORD struck him
in his bowels with an incurable disease. 19In
course of time, at the end of two years, his
bowels came out because of the disease, and
he died in great agony. His people made no
fire in his honor, like the fires made for his
fathers. 20He was thirty-two years old when
he began to reign, and he reigned eight years
in Jerusalem; and he departed with no one's
regret. They buried him in the city of David,
but not in the tombs of the kings.
22 And the inhabitants of Jerusalem
made Ahazi'ah his youngest son king
in his stead; for the band of men that came with
the Arabs to the camp had slain all the older
sons. So Ahaziah the son of Jeho'ram king of
Judah reigned. 2Ahazi'ah was forty-two years
old when he began to reign, and he reigned
one year in Jerusalem. His mother's name was
Athali'ah, the granddaughter of Omri. 3He also
walked in the ways of the house of A'hab, for
his mother was his counselor in doing wickedly. 4He did what was evil in the sight of the
LORD, as the house of A'hab had done; for after
the death of his father they were his counselors,
to his undoing. 5He even followed their counsel, and went with Jeho'ram the son of A'hab
king of Israel to make war against Haz'ael
king of Syria at Ra'moth-gil'ead. And the Syrians wounded Jo'ram, 6and he returned to be
healed in Jezre'el of the wounds which he had
received at Ra'mah, when he fought against
Haz'ael king of Syria. And Ahazi'ah the son
of Jeho'ram king of Judah went down to see
Jo'ram the son of A'hab in Jezreel, because he
was sick.
7But it was ordained by God that the downfall of Ahazi'ah should come about through his
going to visit Jo'ram. For when he came there
he went out with Jeho'ram to meet Je'hu the
son of Nimshi, whom the LORD had anointed to destroy the house of A'hab. 8And when
Je'hu was executing judgment upon the house
of A'hab, he met the princes of Judah and
the sons of Ahazi'ah's brothers, who attended
Ahaziah, and he killed them. 9He searched for
Ahazi'ah, and he was captured while hiding in
Samar'ia, and he was brought to Je'hu and put
to death. They buried him, for they said, "He
is the grandson of Jehosh'aphat, who sought
the LORD with all his heart." And the house of
Ahaziah had no one able to rule the kingdom.
10Now when Athali'ah the mother of Ahazi'ah
saw that her son was dead, she arose and
destroyed all the royal family of the house of
Judah. 11But Je'ho-shab'e-ath, the daughter of
the king, took Jo'ash the son of Ahazi'ah, and
stole him away from among the king's sons
who were about to be slain, and she put him
and his nurse in a bedchamber. Thus Jeho-
shabe-ath, the daughter of King Jeho'ram and
wife of Jehoi'ada the priest, because she was a
sister of Ahaziah, hid him from Athali'ah, so
that she did not slay him; 12and he remained
with them six years, hid in the house of God,
while Athali'ah reigned over the land.

PROVERBS 8

22The LORD created me at the beginning of
his work,
the first of his acts of old.
23Ages ago I was set up,
at the first, before the beginning
of the earth.
24When there were no depths I was
brought forth,
when there were no springs abounding
with water.

[25]Before the mountains had been shaped,
before the hills, I was brought forth;
[26]before he had made the earth with
its fields,
or the first of the dust of the world.
[27]When he established the heavens,
I was there,
when he drew a circle on the face
of the deep,
[28]when he made firm the skies above,
when he established the fountains
of the deep,
[29]when he assigned to the sea its limit,
so that the waters might not transgress
his command,
when he marked out the foundations
of the earth,
[30] then I was beside him, like a
master workman;
and I was daily his delight,
rejoicing before him always,
[31]rejoicing in his inhabited world
and delighting in the sons of men.

[32]And now, my sons, listen to me:
happy are those who keep my ways.
[33]Hear instruction and be wise,
and do not neglect it.
[34]Happy is the man who listens to me,
watching daily at my gates,
waiting beside my doors.
[35]For he who finds me finds life
and obtains favor from the LORD;
[36]but he who misses me injures himself;
all who hate me love death."

ACTS 12

[20]Now Herod was angry with
the people of Tyre and Si′don;
and they came to him in a body, and
having persuaded Blastus, the king's
chamberlain, they asked for peace, because
their country depended on the king's
country for food. [21]On an appointed day
Herod put on his royal robes, took his
seat upon the throne, and made an ora-
tion to them. [22]And the people shouted,
"The voice of a god, and not of man!"
[23]Immediately an angel of the Lord struck
him, because he did not give God the glory; and he was eaten by worms and died.
[24]But the word of God grew and multiplied.
[25]And Barnabas and Saul returned from
Jerusalem when they had fulfilled their
mission, bringing with them John whose
other name was Mark.

13 Now in the Church at Antioch there
were prophets and teachers, Barnabas, Symeon who was called Ni′ger, Lucius
of Cyre′ne, Man′a-en a member of the court
of Herod the tetrarch, and Saul. [2]While they
were worshiping the Lord and fasting, the
Holy Spirit said, "Set apart for me Barnabas
and Saul for the work to which I have called
them." [3]Then after fasting and praying they
laid their hands on them and sent them off.
[4]So, being sent out by the Holy Spirit, they
went down to Seleu′cia; and from there
they sailed to Cyprus. [5]When they arrived
at Sal′amis, they proclaimed the word of
God in the synagogues of the Jews. And
they had John to assist them. [6]When they
had gone through the whole island as
far as Pa′phos, they came upon a certain
magician, a Jewish false prophet, named
Bar-Jesus. [7]He was with the proconsul,
Sergius Paulus, a man of intelligence, who
summoned Barnabas and Saul and sought
to hear the word of God. [8]But El′ymas the
magician (for that is the meaning of his
name) withstood them, seeking to turn
away the proconsul from the faith. [9]But
Saul, who is also called Paul, filled with
the Holy Spirit, looked intently at him
[10]and said, "You son of the devil, you enemy of all righteousness, full of all deceit
and villainy, will you not stop making
crooked the straight paths of the Lord?
[11]And now, behold, the hand of the Lord
is upon you, and you shall be blind and
unable to see the sun for a time." Immediately mist and darkness fell upon him and
he went about seeking people to lead him
by the hand. [12]Then the proconsul believed, when he saw what had occurred,
for he was astonished at the teaching of
the Lord.

13Now Paul and his company set sail from
Pa′phos, and came to Perga in Pamphyl′ia.
And John left them and returned to Jerusalem;
14but they passed on from Perga and came to
Antioch of Pisid′ia. And on the sabbath day
they went into the synagogue and sat down.
15After the reading of the law and the prophets,
the rulers of the synagogue sent to them, saying, "Brethren, if you have any word of exhortation for the people, say it." 16So Paul stood up,
and motioning with his hand said:
"Men of Israel, and you that fear God, listen.
17The God of this people Israel chose our fathers and made the people great during their
stay in the land of Egypt, and with uplifted
arm he led them out of it. 18And for about forty years he bore with them in the wilderness.
19And when he had destroyed seven nations
in the land of Canaan, he gave them their land
as an inheritance, for about four hundred and
fifty years. 20And after that he gave them judges until Samuel the prophet. 21Then they asked
for a king; and God gave them Saul the son of
Kish, a man of the tribe of Benjamin, for forty years. 22And when he had removed him, he
raised up David to be their king; of whom he
testified and said, 'I have found in David, the
son of Jesse, a man after my heart, who will do
all my will.' 23Of this man's posterity God has
brought to Israel a Savior, Jesus, as he promised. 24Before his coming John had preached a
baptism of repentance to all the people of Israel. 25And as John was finishing his course, he
said, 'What do you suppose that I am? I am not
he. No, but after me one is coming, the sandals
of whose feet I am not worthy to untie.'"

REFLECTION

Today's readings contain two dramatic examples of divine judgment. First, for his crimes of murdering his brothers and leading Judah astray, Jehoram is struck by God "with a disease of [his] bowels" (2 Chr 21:15) as Elijah prophesies. Second, after allowing himself to be worshipped as a god, Herod Agrippa is struck down by an angel and "was eaten by worms and died" (Acts 12:23). These sad examples demonstrate the gravity of sin for us. Men in power, having an opportunity to do great good, end up sinning against the Lord and suffer the dire consequences of their actions. Similarly, the magician named Bar-Jesus is struck with blindness after he tries to prevent the spread of the Gospel (see 13:8–11). Sin brings death as its natural consequence. However, if we turn to wisdom, she tells us, "He who finds me finds life" (Prv 8:35). Wisdom is wrapped up in the mystery of creation, the origin of life. She says that at the beginning "I was beside him [God], like a master workman; and I was daily his delight" (v. 30). If we take delight in God and his wisdom, we find life eternal. Memorize one of the verses from Proverbs, and take delight in God's wisdom by repeating it often today.

July 10

2 CHRONICLES 23

**But in the seventh year Jehoi′ada
took courage, and entered into a
compact with the commanders
of hundreds, Azari′ah the son of Jero′ham,
Ish′mael the son of Je′ho-ha′nan, Azariah
the son of O′bed, Ma-asei′ah the son of**
Adai′ah, and Elisha′phat the son of Zich′ri.
2And they went about through Judah and
gathered the Levites from all the cities of
Judah, and the heads of fathers' houses of
Israel, and they came to Jerusalem. 3And
all the assembly made a covenant with the
king in the house of God. And Jehoi′ada
said to them, "Behold, the king's son! Let
him reign, as the LORD spoke concerning
the sons of David. 4This is the thing that
you shall do: of you priests and Levites
who come off duty on the sabbath, one
third shall be gatekeepers, 5and one third
shall be at the king's house and one third
at the Gate of the Foundation; and all
the people shall be in the courts of the

house of the LORD. [6]Let no one enter the house of the LORD except the priests and ministering Levites; they may enter, for they are holy, but all the people shall keep the charge of the LORD. [7]The Levites shall surround the king, each with his weapons in his hand; and whoever enters the house shall be slain. Be with the king when he comes in, and when he goes out."

[8]The Levites and all Judah did according to all that Jehoi′ada the priest commanded. They each brought his men, who were to go off duty on the sabbath, with those who were to come on duty on the sabbath; for Jehoiada the priest did not dismiss the divisions. [9]And Jehoi′ada the priest delivered to the captains the spears and the large and small shields that had been King David's, which were in the house of God; [10]and he set all the people as a guard for the king, every man with his weapon in his hand, from the south side of the house to the north side of the house, around the altar and the house. [11]Then he brought out the king's son, and put the crown upon him, and gave him the covenant; and they proclaimed him king, and Jehoi′ada and his sons anointed him, and they said, "Long live the king."

[12]When Athali′ah heard the noise of the people running and praising the king, she went into the house of the LORD to the people; [13]and when she looked, there was the king standing by his pillar at the entrance, and the captains and the trumpeters beside the king, and all the people of the land rejoicing and blowing trumpets, and the singers with their musical instruments leading in the celebration. And Athali′ah tore her clothes, and cried, "Treason! Treason!" [14]Then Jehoi′ada the priest brought out the captains who were set over the army, saying to them, "Bring her out between the ranks; any one who follows her is to be slain with the sword." For the priest said, "Do not slay her in the house of the LORD." [15]So they laid hands on her; and she went into the entrance of the horse gate of the king's house, and they slew her there.

[16]And Jehoi′ada made a covenant between himself and all the people and the king that they should be the LORD's people. [17]Then all the people went to the house of Ba′al, and tore it down; his altars and his images they broke in pieces, and they slew Mattan the priest of Baal before the altars. [18]And Jehoi′ada posted watchmen for the house of the LORD under the direction of the Levitical priests and the Levites whom David had organized to be in charge of the house of the LORD, to offer burnt offerings to the LORD, as it is written in the law of Moses, with rejoicing and with singing, according to the order of David. [19]He stationed the gatekeepers at the gates of the house of the LORD so that no one should enter who was in any way unclean. [20]And he took the captains, the nobles, the governors of the people, and all the people of the land; and they brought the king down from the house of the LORD, marching through the upper gate to the king's house. And they set the king upon the royal throne. [21]So all the people of the land rejoiced; and the city was quiet, after Athali′ah had been slain with the sword.

24 Jo′ash was seven years old when he began to reign, and he reigned forty years in Jerusalem; his mother's name was Zib′iah of Be′er-she′ba. [2]And Jo′ash did what was right in the eyes of the LORD all the days of Jehoi′ada the priest. [3]Jehoi′ada got for him two wives, and he had sons and daughters.

[4]After this Jo′ash decided to restore the house of the LORD. [5]And he gathered the priests and the Levites, and said to them, "Go out to the cities of Judah, and gather from all Israel money to repair the house of your God from year to year; and see that you hasten the matter." But the Levites did not hasten it. [6]So the king summoned Jehoi′ada the chief, and said to him, "Why have you not required the Levites to bring in from Judah and Jerusalem the tax levied by Moses, the servant of the LORD, on the congregation of Israel for the tent of covenant?" [7]For the sons of Athali′ah, that wicked woman, had broken into the house of God; and had also used all the dedicated things of the house of the LORD for the Ba′als.

[8]So the king commanded, and they made a chest, and set it outside the gate of the house

of the LORD. [9]And proclamation was made
throughout Judah and Jerusalem, to bring in
for the LORD the tax that Moses the servant of
God laid upon Israel in the wilderness. [10]And
all the princes and all the people rejoiced and
brought their tax and dropped it into the chest
until they had finished. [11]And whenever the
chest was brought to the king's officers by the
Levites, when they saw that there was much
money in it, the king's secretary and the officer
of the chief priest would come and empty the
chest and take it and return it to its place. Thus
they did day after day, and collected money
in abundance. [12]And the king and Jehoi'ada
gave it to those who had charge of the work
of the house of the LORD, and they hired
masons and carpenters to restore the house
of the LORD, and also workers in iron and
bronze to repair the house of the LORD. [13]So
those who were engaged in the work labored,
and the repairing went forward in their
hands, and they restored the house of God
to its proper condition and strengthened it.
[14]And when they had finished, they brought
the rest of the money before the king and
Jehoi'ada, and with it were made utensils for
the house of the LORD, both for the service
and for the burnt offerings, and dishes for
incense, and vessels of gold and silver. And
they offered burnt offerings in the house of
the LORD continually all the days of Jehoiada.
[15]But Jehoi'ada grew old and full of days,
and died; he was a hundred and thirty
years old at his death. [16]And they buried
him in the city of David among the kings,
because he had done good in Israel, and
toward God and his house.

PROVERBS 9

Wisdom has built her house,
she has set up her seven pillars.
[2]She has slaughtered her beasts, she has
mixed her wine,
she has also set her table.
[3]She has sent out her maids to call
from the highest places in the town,
[4]"Whoever is simple, let him turn in here!"
To him who is without sense she says,
[5]"Come, eat of my bread
and drink of the wine I have mixed.
[6]Leave simpleness, and live,
and walk in the way of insight."

[7]He who corrects a scoffer gets himself abuse,
and he who reproves a wicked man
incurs injury.
[8]Do not reprove a scoffer, or he will hate you;
reprove a wise man, and he will love you.
[9]Give instruction to a wise man, and he will
be still wiser;
teach a righteous man and he will
increase in learning.
[10]The fear of the LORD is the beginning
of wisdom,
and the knowledge of the Holy One
is insight.
[11]For by me your days will be multiplied,
and years will be added to your life.
[12]If you are wise, you are wise for yourself;
if you scoff, you alone will bear it.

[13]A foolish woman is noisy;
she is wanton and knows no shame.
[14]She sits at the door of her house,
she takes a seat on the high places
of the town,
[15]calling to those who pass by,
who are going straight on their way,
[16]"Whoever is simple, let him turn in here!"
And to him who is without sense
she says,
[17]"Stolen water is sweet,
and bread eaten in secret is pleasant."
[18]But he does not know that the dead are there,
that her guests are in the depths of Sheol.

ACTS 13

[26]"Brethren, sons of the family of Abraham, and those among you that fear God, to us has been sent the message of this salvation. [27]For those who live in Jerusalem and their rulers, because they did not recognize him nor understand the utterances of the prophets which are read every

sabbath, fulfilled these by condemning him.
28Though they could charge him with nothing deserving death, yet they asked Pilate to
have him killed. 29And when they had fulfilled all that was written of him, they took
him down from the tree, and laid him in a
tomb. 30But God raised him from the dead;
31and for many days he appeared to those
who came up with him from Galilee to Jerusalem, who are now his witnesses to the
people. 32And we bring you the good news
that what God promised to the fathers, 33this
he has fulfilled to us their children by raising Jesus; as also it is written in the second
psalm,

'You are my Son,
today I have begotten you.'

34And as for the fact that he raised him from
the dead, no more to return to corruption,
he spoke in this way,

'I will give you the holy and sure blessings
of David.'

35Therefore he says also in another psalm,

'You will not let your Holy One see
corruption.'

36For David, after he had served the
counsel of God in his own generation,
fell asleep, and was laid with his fathers,
and saw corruption; 37but he whom God
raised up saw no corruption. 38Let it be
known to you therefore, brethren, that
through this man forgiveness of sins is
proclaimed to you, 39and by him every
one that believes is freed from everything
from which you could not be freed by the
law of Moses. 40Beware, therefore, lest
there come upon you what is said in the
prophets:

41'Behold, you scoffers, and wonder,
and perish;
for I do a deed in your days,
a deed you will never believe,
if one declares it to you.'"

42As they went out, the people begged that
these things might be told them the next
sabbath. 43And when the meeting of the
synagogue broke up, many Jews and devout
converts to Judaism followed Paul and
Barnabas, who spoke to them and urged
them to continue in the grace of God.

44The next sabbath almost the whole city
gathered together to hear the word of God.
45But when the Jews saw the multitudes, they
were filled with jealousy, and contradicted
what was spoken by Paul, and reviled him.
46And Paul and Barnabas spoke out boldly,
saying, "It was necessary that the word of
God should be spoken first to you. Since
you thrust it from you, and judge yourselves
unworthy of eternal life, behold, we turn
to the Gentiles. 47For so the Lord has commanded us, saying,

'I have set you to be a light for the Gentiles,
that you may bring salvation to the
uttermost parts of the earth.'"

48And when the Gentiles heard this, they
were glad and glorified the word of God;
and as many as were ordained to eternal life
believed. 49And the word of the Lord spread
throughout all the region. 50But the Jews
incited the devout women of high standing
and the leading men of the city, and stirred
up persecution against Paul and Barnabas,
and drove them out of their district. 51But
they shook off the dust from their feet
against them, and went to Ico′nium. 52And
the disciples were filled with joy and with
the Holy Spirit.

REFLECTION

Oftentimes our true motivations are hidden, which is why we need to examine our consciences daily to check ourselves—our words, deeds, and intentions. When St. Paul proclaims the Gospel of Jesus to the Jews in Antioch, initially they are enthusiastic. He and Barnabas recruit a multitude of followers, but, by the next weekend, most of these converts abandon the Gospel. Why? They are jealous of the large crowds of Gentiles that Paul and Barnabas are able to draw with their preaching. Paul does his best to explain not just the life of Jesus, but how his life fulfilled the Old Testament prophecies, such as Psalm 2, Isaiah 55, Psalm 16, and Habbakuk 1. Yet these listeners allow their jealousy to extinguish their zeal for the true fulfillment of Scripture. Sadly, they exemplify the warning in Proverbs: "Do not reprove a scoffer, or he will hate you" (Prv 9:8). True wisdom-seeking requires humility: "Reprove a wise man, and he will love you" (v. 8). No one enjoys being corrected, as correction wounds the ego. Yet if we are truly humble, we should welcome reproof gladly, since such correction given in love is for our good, keeping us on the narrow way of Christ. Take time today to make an examination of conscience and offer a prayer of contrition for your sins.

July 11

2 CHRONICLES 24

17 **Now after the death of Jehoi′ada
the princes of Judah came and
did obeisance to the king; then the king
listened to them.** 18 **And they forsook the**
house of the LORD, the God of their fathers,
and served the Ashe′rim and the idols. And
wrath came upon Judah and Jerusalem for this
their guilt. 19 Yet he sent prophets among them
to bring them back to the LORD; these testified
against them, but they would not give heed.
20 Then the Spirit of God took possession
of Zechari′ah the son of Jehoi′ada the priest;
and he stood above the people, and said to
them, "Thus says God, 'Why do you transgress the commandments of the LORD, so
that you cannot prosper? Because you have
forsaken the LORD, he has forsaken you.'"
21 But they conspired against him, and by
command of the king they stoned him with
stones in the court of the house of the LORD.
22 Thus Jo′ash the king did not remember
the kindness which Jehoi′ada, Zechari′ah's
father, had shown him, but killed his son.
And when he was dying, he said, "May the
LORD see and avenge!"
23 At the end of the year the army of the
Syrians came up against Jo′ash. They came to
Judah and Jerusalem, and destroyed all the
princes of the people from among the people,
and sent all their spoil to the king of Damascus.
24 Though the army of the Syrians had come
with few men, the LORD delivered into their
hand a very great army, because they had
forsaken the LORD, the God of their fathers.
Thus they executed judgment on Jo′ash.
25 When they had departed from him, leaving
him severely wounded, his servants conspired
against him because of the blood of the son of
Jehoi′ada the priest, and slew him on his bed.
So he died; and they buried him in the city
of David, but they did not bury him in the
tombs of the kings. 26 Those who conspired
against him were Zabad the son of Shim′e-ath
the Am′monitess, and Jeho′zabad the son of
Shimrith the Moabitess. 27 Accounts of his sons,
and of the many oracles against him, and of the
rebuilding of the house of God are written in
the Commentary on the Book of the Kings.
And Amazi′ah his son reigned in his stead.

25 Amazi′ah was twenty-five years old
when he began to reign, and he reigned
twenty-nine years in Jerusalem. His mother's
name was Je′ho-ad′dan of Jerusalem. 2 And he
did what was right in the eyes of the LORD, yet
not with a blameless heart. 3 And as soon as the
royal power was firmly in his hand he killed
his servants who had slain the king his father.
4 But he did not put their children to death,
according to what is written in the law, in the
book of Moses, where the LORD commanded,
"The fathers shall not be put to death for the
children, or the children be put to death for the
fathers; but every man shall die for his own sin."
5 Then Amazi′ah assembled the men of
Judah, and set them by fathers' houses under
commanders of thousands and of hundreds
for all Judah and Benjamin. He mustered those
twenty years old and upward, and found that
they were three hundred thousand picked
men, fit for war, able to handle spear and shield.
6 He hired also a hundred thousand mighty
men of valor from Israel for a hundred talents
of silver. 7 But a man of God came to him and
said, "O king, do not let the army of Israel go
with you, for the LORD is not with Israel, with
all these E′phraimites. 8 But if you suppose that
in this way you will be strong for war, God will
cast you down before the enemy; for God has
power to help or to cast down." 9 And Amazi′ah
said to the man of God, "But what shall we

do about the hundred talents which I have given to the army of Israel?" The man of God answered, "The LORD is able to give you much more than this." 10Then Amazi′ah discharged the army that had come to him from E′phraim, to go home again. And they became very angry with Judah, and returned home in fierce anger. 11But Amazi′ah took courage, and led out his people, and went to the Valley of Salt and struck ten thousand men of Se′ir. 12The men of Judah captured another ten thousand alive, and took them to the top of a rock and threw them down from the top of the rock; and they were all dashed to pieces. 13But the men of the army whom Amazi′ah sent back, not letting them go with him to battle, fell upon the cities of Judah, from Samar′ia to Beth-ho′ron, and killed three thousand people in them, and took much spoil.

14After Amazi′ah came from the slaughter of the E′domites, he brought the gods of the men of Se′ir, and set them up as his gods, and worshiped them, making offerings to them. 15Therefore the LORD was angry with Amazi′ah and sent to him a prophet, who said to him, "Why have you resorted to the gods of a people, which did not deliver their own people from your hand?" 16But as he was speaking the king said to him, "Have we made you a royal counselor? Stop! Why should you be put to death?" So the prophet stopped, but said, "I know that God has determined to destroy you, because you have done this and have not listened to my counsel."

17Then Amazi′ah king of Judah took counsel and sent to Jo′ash the son of Jeho′ahaz, son of Je′hu, king of Israel, saying, "Come, let us look one another in the face." 18And Jo′ash the king of Israel sent word to Amazi′ah king of Judah, "A thistle on Lebanon sent to a cedar on Lebanon, saying, 'Give your daughter to my son for a wife'; and a wild beast of Lebanon passed by and trampled down the thistle. 19You say, 'See, I have struck Edom,' and your heart has lifted you up in boastfulness. But now stay at home; why should you provoke trouble so that you fall, you and Judah with you?"

20But Amazi′ah would not listen; for it was of God, in order that he might give them into the hand of their enemies, because they had sought the gods of E′dom. 21So Jo′ash king of Israel went up; and he and Amazi′ah king of Judah faced one another in battle at Beth-she′mesh, which belongs to Judah. 22And Judah was defeated by Israel, and every man fled to his home. 23And Jo′ash king of Israel captured Amazi′ah king of Judah, the son of Joash, son of Ahazi′ah, at Beth-she′mesh, and brought him to Jerusalem, and broke down the wall of Jerusalem for four hundred cubits, from the E′phraim Gate to the Corner Gate. 24And he seized all the gold and silver, and all the vessels that were found in the house of God, and O′bed-e′dom with them; he seized also the treasuries of the king's house, and hostages, and he returned to Samar′ia.

25Amazi′ah the son of Jo′ash king of Judah lived fifteen years after the death of Joash the son of Jeho′ahaz, king of Israel. 26Now the rest of the deeds of Amazi′ah, from first to last, are they not written in the Book of the Kings of Judah and Israel? 27From the time when he turned away from the LORD they made a conspiracy against him in Jerusalem, and he fled to La′chish. But they sent after him to Lachish, and slew him there. 28And they brought him upon horses; and he was buried with his fathers in the city of David.

PROVERBS 10

A wise son makes a glad father,
  but a foolish son is a sorrow to his mother.
2Treasures gained by wickedness
    do not profit,
  but righteousness delivers from death.
3The LORD does not let the righteous
    go hungry,
  but he thwarts the craving of the wicked.
4A slack hand causes poverty,
  but the hand of the diligent makes rich.
5A son who gathers in summer is prudent,
  but a son who sleeps in harvest
    brings shame.
6Blessings are on the head of the righteous,
  but the mouth of the wicked
    conceals violence.
7The memory of the righteous is a blessing,
  but the name of the wicked will rot.

8 The wise of heart will heed commandments,
but a prating fool will come to ruin.
9 He who walks in integrity walks securely,
but he who perverts his ways will be
found out.
10 He who winks the eye causes trouble,
but he who boldly reproves makes peace.
11 The mouth of the righteous is a fountain
of life,
but the mouth of the wicked
conceals violence.
12 Hatred stirs up strife,
but love covers all offenses.
13 On the lips of him who has understanding
wisdom is found,
but a rod is for the back of him who
lacks sense.
14 Wise men lay up knowledge,
but the babbling of a fool brings ruin near.
15 A rich man's wealth is his strong city;
the poverty of the poor is their ruin.
16 The wage of the righteous leads to life,
the gain of the wicked to sin.
17 He who heeds instruction is on the path
to life,
but he who rejects reproof goes astray.
18 He who conceals hatred has lying lips,
and he who utters slander is a fool.
19 When words are many, transgression is
not lacking,
but he who restrains his lips is prudent.
20 The tongue of the righteous is choice silver;
the mind of the wicked is of little worth.
21 The lips of the righteous feed many,
but fools die for lack of sense.

ACTS 14

**Now at Ico′nium they entered
together into the Jewish synagogue, and so spoke that a great company believed, both of Jews and of**
Greeks. 2 But the unbelieving Jews stirred up
the Gentiles and poisoned their minds against
the brethren. 3 So they remained for a long
time, speaking boldly for the Lord, who bore
witness to the word of his grace, granting signs
and wonders to be done by their hands. 4 But
the people of the city were divided; some sided with the Jews, and some with the apostles.
5 When an attempt was made by both Gentiles
and Jews, with their rulers, to molest them
and to stone them, 6 they learned of it and fled
to Lystra and Der′be, cities of Lycao′nia, and
to the surrounding country; 7 and there they
preached the gospel.

8 Now at Lystra there was a man sitting, who
could not use his feet; he was a cripple from
birth, who had never walked. 9 He listened to
Paul speaking; and Paul, looking intently at
him and seeing that he had faith to be made
well, 10 said in a loud voice, "Stand upright
on your feet." And he sprang up and walked.
11 And when the crowds saw what Paul had
done, they lifted up their voices, saying in
Lycao′nian, "The gods have come down to
us in the likeness of men!" 12 Barnabas they
called Zeus, and Paul, because he was the chief
speaker, they called Hermes. 13 And the priest
of Zeus, whose temple was in front of the city,
brought oxen and garlands to the gates and
wanted to offer sacrifice with the people. 14 But
when the apostles Barnabas and Paul heard
of it, they tore their garments and rushed out
among the multitude, crying, 15 "Men, why are
you doing this? We also are men, of like nature
with you, and bring you good news, that you
should turn from these vain things to a living
God who made the heaven and the earth and
the sea and all that is in them. 16 In past generations he allowed all the nations to walk in
their own ways; 17 yet he did not leave himself
without witness, for he did good and gave you
from heaven rains and fruitful seasons, satisfy-
ing your hearts with food and gladness." 18 With
these words they scarcely restrained the people
from offering sacrifice to them.

19 But Jews came there from Antioch and
Ico′nium; and having persuaded the people,
they stoned Paul and dragged him out of the
city, supposing that he was dead. 20 But when the
disciples gathered about him, he rose up and
entered the city; and on the next day he went
on with Barnabas to Derbe. 21 When they had
preached the gospel to that city and had made
many disciples, they returned to Lystra and
to Ico′nium and to Antioch, 22 strengthening
the souls of the disciples, exhorting them to

continue in the faith, and saying that through many tribulations we must enter the kingdom of God. [23]And when they had appointed elders for them in every church, with prayer and fasting, they committed them to the Lord in whom they believed.

REFLECTION

Many sins involve talking: "When words are many, transgression is not lacking, but he who restrains his lips is prudent" (Prv 10:19). The prudent man holds back unkind words, gossip, and negative opinions. In the same place, Proverbs commends the speaking of the wise man: "The tongue of the righteous is choice silver . . . . the lips of the righteous feed many" (vv. 20–21). Restraint in our words is commendable but is to be combined with appropriate speech. The adventures of Paul and Barnabas on their mission journey show us how these principles work in practice. On the one hand, they speak "boldly for the Lord" (Acts 14:3), "[preach] the gospel" (v. 21); and declare "[we] bring you good news" (v. 15). In doing so, they fulfill the words of Proverbs: "The mouth of the righteous is a fountain of life" (Prv 10:11) and, "On the lips of him who has understanding wisdom is found" (v. 13). They are preaching the life-giving message of the Gospel, which is the truest wisdom. Their opponents, however, commit sins of the tongue: They "poisoned their minds" (Acts 14:2) and "persuaded the people" to stone Paul (v. 19). They epitomize the saying: "The mouth of the wicked conceals violence" (Prv 10:6). Do your words harm others or do they bring life?

July 12

2 CHRONICLES 26

And all the people of Judah took Uzzi′ah, who was sixteen years old, and made him king instead of his father Amazi′ah. [2]He built E′loth and restored it to Judah, after the king slept
with his fathers. [3]Uzzi′ah was sixteen years
old when he began to reign, and he reigned
fifty-two years in Jerusalem. His mother's
name was Jecoli′ah of Jerusalem. [4]And he
did what was right in the eyes of the LORD,
according to all that his father Amazi′ah
had done. [5]He set himself to seek God in the
days of Zechari′ah, who instructed him in
the fear of God; and as long as he sought the
LORD, God made him prosper.

[6]He went out and made war against the
Philis′tines, and broke down the wall of
Gath and the wall of Jabneh and the wall of
Ash′dod; and he built cities in the territory
of Ashdod and elsewhere among the Philistines. [7]God helped him against the Phil-
is′tines, and against the Arabs that dwelt in
Gurba′al, and against the Me-u′nites. [8]The
Am′monites paid tribute to Uzzi′ah, and his
fame spread even to the border of Egypt, for
he became very strong. [9]Moreover Uzzi′ah
built towers in Jerusalem at the Corner Gate
and at the Valley Gate and at the Angle, and
fortified them. [10]And he built towers in the
wilderness, and hewed out many cisterns, for
he had large herds, both in the Shephe′lah
and in the plain, and he had farmers and
vinedressers in the hills and in the fertile
lands, for he loved the soil. [11]Moreover
Uzzi′ah had an army of soldiers, fit for war,
in divisions according to the numbers in
the muster made by Je-i′el the secretary and
Ma-asei′ah the officer, under the direction
of Hanani′ah, one of the king's commanders.
[12]The whole number of the heads of
fathers' houses of mighty men of valor was
two thousand six hundred. [13]Under their
command was an army of three hundred
and seven thousand five hundred, who
could make war with mighty power, to help
the king against the enemy. [14]And Uzzi′ah
prepared for all the army shields, spears,
helmets, coats of mail, bows, and stones for
slinging. [15]In Jerusalem he made engines,
invented by skilful men, to be on the towers
and the corners, to shoot arrows and great
stones. And his fame spread far, for he was
marvelously helped, till he was strong.

[16]But when he was strong he grew proud, to
his destruction. For he was false to the LORD

his God, and entered the temple of the LORD to burn incense on the altar of incense. 17But Azari´ah the priest went in after him, with eighty priests of the LORD who were men of valor; 18and they withstood King Uzzi´ah, and said to him, "It is not for you, Uzziah, to burn incense to the LORD, but for the priests the sons of Aaron, who are consecrated to burn incense. Go out of the sanctuary; for you have done wrong, and it will bring you no honor from the LORD God." 19Then Uzzi´ah was angry. Now he had a censer in his hand to burn incense, and when he became angry with the priests leprosy broke out on his forehead, in the presence of the priests in the house of the LORD, by the altar of incense. 20And Azari´ah the chief priest, and all the priests, looked at him, and behold, he was leprous in his forehead! And they thrust him out quickly, and he himself hastened to go out, because the LORD had struck him down. 21And King Uzzi´ah was a leper to the day of his death, and being a leper dwelt in a separate house, for he was excluded from the house of the LORD. And Jo´tham his son was over the king's household, governing the people of the land.

22Now the rest of the acts of Uzzi´ah, from first to last, Isai´ah the prophet the son of A´moz wrote. 23And Uzzi´ah slept with his fathers, and they buried him with his fathers in the burial field which belonged to the kings, for they said, "He is a leper." And Jo´tham his son reigned in his stead.

27 Jo´tham was twenty-five years old when he began to reign, and he reigned sixteen years in Jerusalem. His mother's name was Jeru´shah the daughter of Za´dok. 2And he did what was right in the eyes of the LORD according to all that his father Uzzi´ah had done—only he did not invade the temple of the LORD. But the people still followed corrupt practices. 3He built the upper gate of the house of the LORD, and did much building on the wall of O´phel. 4Moreover he built cities in the hill country of Judah, and forts and towers on the wooded hills. 5He fought with the king of the Am´monites and prevailed against them. And the Ammonites gave him that year a hundred talents of silver, and ten thousand cors of wheat and ten thousand of barley. The Ammonites paid him the same amount in the second and the third years. 6So Jo´tham became mighty, because he ordered his ways before the LORD his God. 7Now the rest of the acts of Jo´tham, and all his wars, and his ways, behold, they are written in the Book of the Kings of Israel and Judah. 8He was twenty-five years old when he began to reign, and he reigned sixteen years in Jerusalem. 9And Jo´tham slept with his fathers, and they buried him in the city of David; and A´haz his son reigned in his stead.

28 A´haz was twenty years old when he began to reign, and he reigned sixteen years in Jerusalem. And he did not do what was right in the eyes of the LORD, like his father David, 2but walked in the ways of the kings of Israel. He even made molten images for the Ba´als; 3and he burned incense in the valley of the son of Hinnom, and burned his sons as an offering, according to the abominable practices of the nations whom the LORD drove out before the sons of Israel. 4And he sacrificed and burned incense on the high places, and on the hills, and under every green tree.

5Therefore the LORD his God gave him into the hand of the king of Syria, who defeated him and took captive a great number of his people and brought them to Damascus. He was also given into the hand of the king of Israel, who defeated him with great slaughter. 6For Pe´kah the son of Remali´ah slew a hundred and twenty thousand in Judah in one day, all of them men of valor, because they had forsaken the LORD, the God of their fathers. 7And Zich´ri, a mighty man of E´phraim, slew Ma-asei´ah the king's son and Azri´kam the commander of the palace and Elka´nah the next in authority to the king.

8The men of Israel took captive two hundred thousand of their kinsfolk, women, sons, and daughters; they also took much spoil from them and brought the spoil to Samar´ia. 9But a prophet of the LORD was there, whose name was O´ded; and he went out to meet the army that came

to Samar′ia, and said to them, "Behold,
because the LORD, the God of your fathers,
was angry with Judah, he gave them into
your hand, but you have slain them in
a rage which has reached up to heaven.
10And now you intend to subjugate the
people of Judah and Jerusalem, male and
female, as your slaves. Have you not sins
of your own against the LORD your God?
11Now hear me, and send back the captives
from your kinsfolk whom you have taken,
for the fierce wrath of the LORD is upon
you." 12Certain chiefs also of the men of
E′phraim, Azari′ah the son of Joha′nan,
Berechi′ah the son of Meshil′lemoth,
Jehizki′ah the son of Shallum, and Ama′sa
the son of Hadlai, stood up against those
who were coming from the war, 13and said
to them, "You shall not bring the captives
in here, for you propose to bring upon
us guilt against the LORD in addition to
our present sins and guilt. For our guilt
is already great, and there is fierce wrath
against Israel." 14So the armed men left the
captives and the spoil before the princes
and all the assembly. 15And the men who
have been mentioned by name rose and
took the captives, and with the spoil they
clothed all that were naked among them;
they clothed them, gave them sandals,
provided them with food and drink, and
anointed them; and carrying all the feeble
among them on donkeys, they brought
them to their kinsfolk at Jericho, the city of
palm trees. Then they returned to Samar′ia.
16At that time King A′haz sent to the
king of Assyria for help. 17For the E′domites
had again invaded and defeated Judah, and
carried away captives. 18And the Philis′tines
had made raids on the cities in the
Shephe′lah and the Neg′eb of Judah, and had
taken Beth-she′mesh, Ai′jalon, Gede′roth,
Soco with its villages, Timnah with its
villages, and Gimzo with its villages; and
they settled there. 19For the LORD brought
Judah low because of A′haz king of Israel,
for he had dealt wantonly in Judah and had
been faithless to the LORD. 20So Til′gath-
pilne′ser king of Assyria came against him,
and afflicted him instead of strengthening
him. 21For A′haz took from the house of
the LORD and the house of the king and of
the princes, and gave tribute to the king of
Assyria; but it did not help him.
22In the time of his distress he became yet
more faithless to the LORD—this same
King A′haz. 23For he sacrificed to the
gods of Damascus which had defeated
him, and said, "Because the gods of
the kings of Syria helped them, I will
sacrifice to them that they may help me."
But they were the ruin of him, and of
all Israel. 24And A′haz gathered together
the vessels of the house of God and cut
in pieces the vessels of the house of God,
and he shut up the doors of the house of
the LORD; and he made himself altars in
every corner of Jerusalem. 25In every city
of Judah he made high places to burn
incense to other gods, provoking to anger
the LORD, the God of his fathers. 26Now
the rest of his acts and all his ways, from
first to last, behold, they are written in
the Book of the Kings of Judah and Israel.
27And A′haz slept with his fathers, and
they buried him in the city, in Jerusalem,
for they did not bring him into the tombs
of the kings of Israel. And Hezeki′ah his
son reigned in his stead.

PROVERBS 10

22The blessing of the LORD makes rich,
and he adds no sorrow with it.
23It is like sport to a fool to do wrong,
but wise conduct is pleasure to a man
of understanding.
24What the wicked dreads will come
upon him,
but the desire of the righteous will
be granted.
25When the tempest passes, the wicked is
no more,
but the righteous is established for ever.
26Like vinegar to the teeth, and smoke
to the eyes,
so is the sluggard to those who send him.
27The fear of the LORD prolongs life,
but the years of the wicked will be short.

28 The hope of the righteous ends in gladness,
but the expectation of the wicked comes
to nothing.
29 The LORD is a stronghold to him whose
way is upright,
but destruction to evildoers.
30 The righteous will never be removed,
but the wicked will not dwell in the land.
31 The mouth of the righteous brings forth
wisdom,
but the perverse tongue will be cut off.
32 The lips of the righteous know what
is acceptable,
but the mouth of the wicked, what
is perverse.

ACTS 14

24 Then they passed through Pis-
id'ia, and came to Pamphyl'ia.
25 And when they had spoken the
word in Perga, they went down to Attali'a;
26 and from there they sailed to Antioch,
where they had been commended to the
grace of God for the work which they had
fulfilled. 27 And when they arrived, they
gathered the Church together and declared
all that God had done with them, and
how he had opened a door of faith to the
Gentiles. 28 And they remained no little time
with the disciples.
15 But some men came down from
Judea and were teaching the brethren,
"Unless you are circumcised according
to the custom of Moses, you cannot be
saved." 2 And when Paul and Barnabas had
no small dissension and debate with them,
Paul and Barnabas and some of the others
were appointed to go up to Jerusalem to the
apostles and the elders about this question.
3 So, being sent on their way by the Church,
they passed through both Phoeni'cia and
Samar'ia, reporting the conversion of the
Gentiles, and they gave great joy to all the
brethren. 4 When they came to Jerusalem,
they were welcomed by the Church and
the apostles and the elders, and they
declared all that God had done with them.
5 But some believers who belonged to the
party of the Pharisees rose up, and said,
"It is necessary to circumcise them, and
to charge them to keep the law of Moses."
6 The apostles and the elders were gathered together to consider this matter.
7 And after there had been much debate,
Peter rose and said to them, "Brethren,
you know that in the early days God made
choice among you, that by my mouth the
Gentiles should hear the word of the
gospel and believe. 8 And God who knows
the heart bore witness to them, giving
them the Holy Spirit just as he did to us;
9 and he made no distinction between us
and them, but cleansed their hearts by
faith. 10 Now therefore why do you make
trial of God by putting a yoke upon the
neck of the disciples which neither our
fathers nor we have been able to bear?
11 But we believe that we shall be saved
through the grace of the Lord Jesus, just
as they will."

REFLECTION

In today's reading, we find the long-reigning King Uzziah making a grave error. He personally enters the sanctuary of the Temple to offer incense before the Lord—a holy task reserved to the priests alone. When the priests tell him to leave, he becomes annoyed with them and immediately is struck with leprosy. Leprosy was not only a devastating skin disease, but it made any person who contracted it ritually impure and therefore ineligible to even enter the Temple, let alone perform official liturgical functions. Uzziah embodies the proverb: "It is like sport to a fool to do wrong" (Prv 10:23). He does not take God's holy presence seriously enough, and presumptuously profanes the Temple. On the opposite end of the spectrum, some of the early Christians cannot believe that God is actually admitting the Gentiles into the plan of salvation, and insist that they must become Jewish first before they can become followers of Jesus. Their strictness is actually constraining God's plan. Are you overly scrupulous in following God's commands?

July 13

2 CHRONICLES 29

**Hezeki'ah began to reign when
he was twenty-five years old,
and he reigned twenty-nine years in Jerusalem. His mother's name was Abi'jah the**
daughter of Zechari'ah. 2And he did what
was right in the eyes of the LORD, according
to all that David his father had done.
3In the first year of his reign, in the first
month, he opened the doors of the house of
the LORD, and repaired them. 4He brought
in the priests and the Levites, and assembled
them in the square on the east, 5and said
to them, "Hear me, Levites! Now sanctify
yourselves, and sanctify the house of the
LORD, the God of your fathers, and carry
out the filth from the holy place. 6For our
fathers have been unfaithful and have done
what was evil in the sight of the LORD our
God; they have forsaken him, and have
turned away their faces from the habitation
of the LORD, and turned their backs. 7They
also shut the doors of the vestibule and put
out the lamps, and have not burned incense
or offered burnt offerings in the holy place
to the God of Israel. 8Therefore the wrath
of the LORD came on Judah and Jerusalem,
and he has made them an object of horror,
of astonishment, and of hissing, as you see
with your own eyes. 9For behold, our fathers
have fallen by the sword and our sons and
our daughters and our wives are in captivity
for this. 10Now it is in my heart to make a
covenant with the LORD, the God of Israel,
that his fierce anger may turn away from
us. 11My sons, do not now be negligent, for
the LORD has chosen you to stand in his
presence, to minister to him, and to be his
ministers and burn incense to him."
12Then the Levites arose, Mahath the son
of Ama'sai, and Joel the son of Azari'ah,
of the sons of the Ko'hathites; and of the
sons of Merar'i, Kish the son of Abdi, and
Azariah the son of Jehal'lelel; and of the
Ger'shonites, Jo'ah the son of Zimmah, and
Eden the son of Joah; 13and of the sons of
Eliza'phan, Shimri and Jeu'el; and of the
sons of A'saph, Zechari'ah and Mattani'ah;
14and of the sons of He'man, Jehu'el and
Shim'e-i; and of the sons of Jedu'thun,
Shemai'ah and Uz'ziel. 15They gathered their
brethren, and sanctified themselves, and
went in as the king had commanded, by the
words of the LORD, to cleanse the house of
the LORD. 16The priests went into the inner
part of the house of the LORD to cleanse it,
and they brought out all the uncleanness
that they found in the temple of the LORD
into the court of the house of the LORD; and
the Levites took it and carried it out to the
brook Kidron. 17They began to sanctify on
the first day of the first month, and on the
eighth day of the month they came to the
vestibule of the LORD; then for eight days
they sanctified the house of the LORD, and
on the sixteenth day of the first month they
finished. 18Then they went in to Hezeki'ah
the king and said, "We have cleansed all
the house of the LORD, the altar of burnt
offering and all its utensils, and the table for
the showbread and all its utensils. 19All the
utensils which King A'haz discarded in his
reign when he was faithless, we have made
ready and sanctified; and behold, they are
before the altar of the LORD."
20Then Hezeki'ah the king rose early and
gathered the officials of the city, and went
up to the house of the LORD. 21And they
brought seven bulls, seven rams, seven
lambs, and seven he-goats for a sin offering
for the kingdom and for the sanctuary and
for Judah. And he commanded the priests
the sons of Aaron to offer them on the altar
of the LORD. 22So they killed the bulls, and
the priests received the blood and threw it
against the altar; and they killed the rams
and their blood was thrown against the altar;
and they killed the lambs and their blood was
thrown against the altar. 23Then the he-goats
for the sin offering were brought to the king
and the assembly, and they laid their hands
upon them, 24and the priests killed them and
made a sin offering with their blood on the
altar, to make atonement for all Israel. For the

king commanded that the burnt offering and
the sin offering should be made for all Israel.
25And he stationed the Levites in the house
of the LORD with cymbals, harps, and lyres,
according to the commandment of David
and of Gad the king's seer and of Nathan the
prophet; for the commandment was from
the LORD through his prophets. 26The Levites
stood with the instruments of David, and the
priests with the trumpets. 27Then Hezeki′ah
commanded that the burnt offering be
offered on the altar. And when the burnt
offering began, the song to the LORD began
also, and the trumpets, accompanied by
the instruments of David king of Israel.
28The whole assembly worshiped, and the
singers sang, and the trumpeters sounded;
all this continued until the burnt offering
was finished. 29When the offering was
finished, the king and all who were present
with him bowed themselves and worshiped.
30And Hezeki′ah the king and the princes
commanded the Levites to sing praises to the
LORD with the words of David and of A′saph
the seer. And they sang praises with gladness,
and they bowed down and worshiped.
31Then Hezeki′ah said, "You have now
consecrated yourselves to the LORD; come
near, bring sacrifices and thank offerings to
the house of the LORD." And the assembly
brought sacrifices and thank offerings; and
all who were of a willing heart brought
burnt offerings. 32The number of the burnt
offerings which the assembly brought was
seventy bulls, a hundred rams, and two
hundred lambs; all these were for a burnt
offering to the LORD. 33And the consecrated
offerings were six hundred bulls and three
thousand sheep. 34But the priests were too
few and could not flay all the burnt offerings,
so until other priests had sanctified themselves their brethren the Levites helped
them, until the work was finished—for the
Levites were more upright in heart than the
priests in sanctifying themselves. 35Besides
the great number of burnt offerings there
was the fat of the peace offerings, and there
were the libations for the burnt offerings.
Thus the service of the house of the LORD
was restored. 36And Hezeki′ah and all the
people rejoiced because of what God had
done for the people; for the thing came
about suddenly.

30 Hezeki′ah sent to all Israel and Judah,
and wrote letters also to E′phraim
and Manas′seh, that they should come to
the house of the LORD at Jerusalem, to
keep the Passover to the LORD the God of
Israel. 2For the king and his princes and
all the assembly in Jerusalem had taken
counsel to keep the Passover in the second
month—3for they could not keep it in its
time because the priests had not sanctified
themselves in sufficient number, nor had
the people assembled in Jerusalem—4and
the plan seemed right to the king and all
the assembly. 5So they decreed to make a
proclamation throughout all Israel, from
Be′er-she′ba to Dan, that the people should
come and keep the Passover to the LORD
the God of Israel, at Jerusalem; for they had
not kept it in great numbers as prescribed.
6So couriers went throughout all Israel and
Judah with letters from the king and his
princes, as the king had commanded, saying,
"O people of Israel, return to the LORD, the
God of Abraham, Isaac, and Israel, that he
may turn again to the remnant of you who
have escaped from the hand of the kings of
Assyria. 7Do not be like your fathers and
your brethren, who were faithless to the
LORD God of their fathers, so that he made
them a desolation, as you see. 8Do not now
be stiff-necked as your fathers were, but
yield yourselves to the LORD, and come to
his sanctuary, which he has sanctified for
ever, and serve the LORD your God, that his
fierce anger may turn away from you. 9For if
you return to the LORD, your brethren and
your children will find compassion with
their captors, and return to this land. For the
LORD your God is gracious and merciful,
and will not turn away his face from you, if
you return to him."
10So the couriers went from city to city
through the country of E′phraim and
Manas′seh, and as far as Zeb′ulun; but they
laughed them to scorn, and mocked them.
11Only a few men of Asher, of Manas′seh,
and of Zeb′ulun humbled themselves and

came to Jerusalem. 12The hand of God was
also upon Judah to give them one heart to do
what the king and the princes commanded
by the word of the LORD.
13And many people came together in Jerusalem to keep the feast of unleavened bread
in the second month, a very great assembly.
14They set to work and removed the altars
that were in Jerusalem, and all the altars
for burning incense they took away and
threw into the Kidron valley. 15And they
killed the Passover lamb on the fourteenth
day of the second month. And the priests
and the Levites were put to shame, so that
they sanctified themselves, and brought
burnt offerings into the house of the LORD.
16They took their accustomed posts according to the law of Moses the man of God; the
priests sprinkled the blood which they received from the hand of the Levites. 17For
there were many in the assembly who had
not sanctified themselves; therefore the
Levites had to kill the Passover lamb for every one who was not clean, to make it holy
to the LORD. 18For a multitude of the people,
many of them from E′phraim, Manas′seh,
Is′sachar, and Zeb′ulun, had not cleansed
themselves, yet they ate the Passover otherwise than as prescribed. For Hezeki′ah had
prayed for them, saying, "The good LORD
pardon every one 19who sets his heart to
seek God, the LORD the God of his fathers,
even though not according to the sanctuary's rules of cleanness." 20And the LORD
heard Hezeki′ah, and healed the people.
21And the sons of Israel that were present
at Jerusalem kept the feast of unleavened
bread seven days with great gladness; and
the Levites and the priests praised the LORD
day by day, singing with all their might to
the LORD. 22And Hezeki′ah spoke encouragingly to all the Levites who showed good
skill in the service of the LORD. So the people ate the food of the festival for seven days,
sacrificing peace offerings and giving thanks
to the LORD the God of their fathers.
23Then the whole assembly agreed together to keep the feast for another seven
days; so they kept it for another seven days
with gladness. 24For Hezeki′ah king of Judah
gave the assembly a thousand bulls and seven
thousand sheep for offerings, and the princes
gave the assembly a thousand bulls and ten
thousand sheep. And the priests sanctified
themselves in great numbers. 25The whole
assembly of Judah, and the priests and the
Levites, and the whole assembly that came
out of Israel, and the sojourners who came
out of the land of Israel, and the sojourners
who dwelt in Judah, rejoiced. 26So there
was great joy in Jerusalem, for since the
time of Solomon the son of David king of
Israel there had been nothing like this in
Jerusalem. 27Then the priests and the Levites
arose and blessed the people, and their voice
was heard, and their prayer came to his holy
habitation in heaven.

PROVERBS 11

A false balance is an abomination to the LORD,
  but a just weight is his delight.
2When pride comes, then comes disgrace;
  but with the humble is wisdom.
3The integrity of the upright guides them,
  but the crookedness of the treacherous
    destroys them.
4Riches do not profit in the day of wrath,
  but righteousness delivers from death.
5The righteousness of the blameless keeps
    his way straight,
  but the wicked falls by his own wickedness.
6The righteousness of the upright
    delivers them,
  but the treacherous are taken captive by
    their lust.
7When the wicked dies, his hope perishes,
  and the expectation of the godless comes
    to nothing.
8The righteous is delivered from trouble,
  and the wicked gets into it instead.
9With his mouth the godless man would
    destroy his neighbor,
  but by knowledge the righteous
    are delivered.
10When it goes well with the righteous, the
    city rejoices;
  and when the wicked perish there are
    shouts of gladness.

[11]By the blessing of the upright a city
is exalted,
but it is overthrown by the mouth
of the wicked.

ACTS 15

**[12]And all the assembly kept si-
lence; and they listened to Barnabas and Paul as they related
what signs and wonders God had done
through them among the Gentiles.** [13]Af-
ter they finished speaking, James replied,
"Brethren, listen to me. [14]Symeon has related how God first visited the Gentiles, to take
out of them a people for his name. [15]And
with this the words of the prophets agree,
as it is written,
[16]'After this I will return,
and I will rebuild the dwelling of David,
which has fallen;
I will rebuild its ruins,
and I will set it up,
[17]that the rest of men may seek the Lord,
and all the Gentiles who are called by
my name,
[18]says the Lord, who has made these things
known from of old.'
[19]Therefore my judgment is that we should
not trouble those of the Gentiles who turn
to God, [20]but should write to them to abstain
from the pollutions of idols and from
unchastity and from what is strangled and
from blood. [21]For from early generations
Moses has had in every city those who
preach him, for he is read every sabbath in
the synagogues."

REFLECTION

Proverbs insists that "righteousness delivers from death" (Prv 11:4). As Christians, we see how this statement is true in an eternal way. Jesus's righteous act of redemption delivers us from death. King Hezekiah understands how grave the consequences of sin really are, and so he determines to set the nation on a new course: "Now it is in my heart to make a covenant with the LORD, the God of Israel, that his fierce anger may turn away from us" (2 Chr 29:10). He leverages all of his political capital to restore Temple worship, to re-sanctify the priests and Levites, to cleanse the altar, to re-organize the Temple musicians, and to bring the whole nation to observe the Passover. Hezekiah's efforts bring greater joy to Jerusalem than since the days of Solomon (see 30:26). His work demonstrates the proverb that "when it goes well with the righteous, the city rejoices" (Prv 11:10). His wholehearted commitment to the Lord sets a great example for us to follow. What good work, what righteous act, can you do today to bring life to another?

July 14

2 CHRONICLES 31

**Now when all this was finished,
all Israel who were present went
out to the cities of Judah and
broke in pieces the pillars and hewed
down the Ashe'rim and broke down
the high places and the altars through-**
out all Judah and Benjamin, and in E'phraim
and Manas'seh, until they had destroyed
them all. Then all the sons of Israel returned
to their cities, every man to his possession.
[2]And Hezeki'ah appointed the divisions
of the priests and of the Levites, division by
division, each according to his service, the
priests and the Levites, for burnt offerings
and peace offerings, to minister in the gates
of the camp of the LORD and to give thanks
and praise. [3]The contribution of the king
from his own possessions was for the burnt
offerings: the burnt offerings of morning
and evening, and the burnt offerings for the
sabbaths, the new moons, and the appointed
feasts, as it is written in the law of the LORD.
[4]And he commanded the people who lived

in Jerusalem to give the portion due to the priests and the Levites, that they might give themselves to the law of the LORD. [5]As soon as the command was spread abroad, the sons of Israel gave in abundance the first fruits of grain, wine, oil, honey, and of all the produce of the field; and they brought in abundantly the tithe of everything. [6]And the sons of Israel and Judah who lived in the cities of Judah also brought in the tithe of cattle and sheep, and the dedicated things which had been consecrated to the LORD their God, and laid them in heaps. [7]In the third month they began to pile up the heaps, and finished them in the seventh month. [8]When Hezeki′ah and the princes came and saw the heaps, they blessed the LORD and his people Israel. [9]And Hezeki′ah questioned the priests and the Levites about the heaps. [10]Azari′ah the chief priest, who was of the house of Za′dok, answered him, "Since they began to bring the contributions into the house of the LORD we have eaten and had enough and have plenty left; for the LORD has blessed his people, so that we have this great store left."

[11]Then Hezeki′ah commanded them to prepare chambers in the house of the LORD; and they prepared them. [12]And they faithfully brought in the contributions, the tithes and the dedicated things. The chief officer in charge of them was Conani′ah the Levite, with Shim′e-i his brother as second; [13]while Jehi′el, Azazi′ah, Na′hath, As′ahel, Jer′imoth, Joz′abad, Eli′el, Ismachi′ah, Mahath, and Bena′iah were overseers assisting Conani′ah and Shim′e-i his brother, by the appointment of Hezeki′ah the king and Azari′ah the chief officer of the house of God. [14]And Ko′re the son of Imnah the Levite, keeper of the east gate, was over the freewill offerings to God, to apportion the contribution reserved for the LORD and the most holy offerings. [15]Eden, Mini′amin, Jesh′ua, Shemai′ah, Amari′ah, and Shecani′ah were faithfully assisting him in the cities of the priests, to distribute the portions to their brethren, old and young alike, by divisions, [16]except those enrolled by genealogy, males from three years old and upwards, all who entered the house of the LORD as the duty of each day required, for their service according to their offices, by their divisions. [17]The enrollment of the priests was according to their fathers' houses; that of the Levites from twenty years old and upwards was according to their offices, by their divisions. [18]The priests were enrolled with all their little children, their wives, their sons, and their daughters, the whole multitude; for they were faithful in keeping themselves holy. [19]And for the sons of Aaron, the priests, who were in the fields of common land belonging to their cities, there were men in the several cities who were designated by name to distribute portions to every male among the priests and to every one among the Levites who was enrolled.

[20]Thus Hezeki′ah did throughout all Judah; and he did what was good and right and faithful before the LORD his God. [21]And every work that he undertook in the service of the house of God and in accordance with the law and the commandments, seeking his God, he did with all his heart, and prospered.

32 After these things and these acts of faithfulness Sennach′erib king of Assyria came and invaded Judah and encamped against the fortified cities, thinking to win them for himself. [2]And when Hezeki′ah saw that Sennach′erib had come and intended to fight against Jerusalem, [3]he planned with his officers and his mighty men to stop the water of the springs that were outside the city; and they helped him. [4]A great many people were gathered, and they stopped all the springs and the brook that flowed through the land, saying, "Why should the kings of Assyria come and find much water?" [5]He set to work resolutely and built up all the wall that was broken down, and raised towers upon it, and outside it he built another wall; and he strengthened the Millo in the city of David. He also made weapons and shields in abundance. [6]And he set combat commanders over the people, and gathered them together to him in the square at the gate of the city and spoke encouragingly to them, saying, [7]"Be strong

and of good courage. Do not be afraid or
dismayed before the king of Assyria and all
the horde that is with him; for there is one
greater with us than with him. 8 With him is
an arm of flesh; but with us is the LORD our
God, to help us and to fight our battles."
And the people took confidence from the
words of Hezeki′ah king of Judah.

9 After this Sennach′erib king of Assyria,
who was besieging La′chish with all his
forces, sent his servants to Jerusalem to
Hezeki′ah king of Judah and to all the
people of Judah that were in Jerusalem,
saying, 10 "Thus says Sennach′erib king of
Assyria, 'On what are you relying, that you
stand siege in Jerusalem? 11 Is not Hezeki′ah
misleading you, that he may give you over
to die by famine and by thirst, when he
tells you, "The LORD our God will deliver
us from the hand of the king of Assyria"?
12 Has not this same Hezeki′ah taken
away his high places and his altars and
commanded Judah and Jerusalem, "Before
one altar you shall worship, and upon it
you shall burn your sacrifices"? 13 Do you
not know what I and my fathers have done
to all the peoples of other lands? Were the
gods of the nations of those lands at all
able to deliver their lands out of my hand?
14 Who among all the gods of those nations
which my fathers utterly destroyed was
able to deliver his people from my hand,
that your God should be able to deliver
you from my hand? 15 Now therefore do
not let Hezeki′ah deceive you or mislead
you in this fashion, and do not believe
him, for no god of any nation or kingdom
has been able to deliver his people from
my hand or from the hand of my fathers.
How much less will your God deliver you
out of my hand!' "

16 And his servants said still more against
the Lord GOD and against his servant
Hezeki′ah. 17 And he wrote letters to cast
contempt on the LORD the God of Israel
and to speak against him, saying, "Like the
gods of the nations of the lands who have
not delivered their people from my hands,
so the God of Hezeki′ah will not deliver his
people from my hand." 18 And they shouted
it with a loud voice in the language of
Judah to the people of Jerusalem who were
upon the wall, to frighten and terrify them,
in order that they might take the city. 19 And
they spoke of the God of Jerusalem as they
spoke of the gods of the peoples of the
earth, which are the work of men's hands.

20 Then Hezeki′ah the king and Isai′ah the
prophet, the son of A′moz, prayed because
of this and cried to heaven. 21 And the LORD
sent an angel, who cut off all the mighty
warriors and commanders and officers
in the camp of the king of Assyria. So he
returned with shame of face to his own
land. And when he came into the house of
his god, some of his own sons struck him
down there with the sword. 22 So the LORD
saved Hezeki′ah and the inhabitants of
Jerusalem from the hand of Sennach′erib
king of Assyria and from the hand of all
his enemies; and he gave them rest on
every side. 23 And many brought gifts to
the LORD to Jerusalem and precious things
to Hezeki′ah king of Judah, so that he was
exalted in the sight of all nations from that
time onward.

PROVERBS 11

12 He who belittles his neighbor lacks sense,
but a man of understanding
remains silent.
13 He who goes about as a talebearer
reveals secrets,
but he who is trustworthy in spirit keeps
a thing hidden.
14 Where there is no guidance, a people falls;
but in an abundance of counselors there
is safety.
15 He who gives surety for a stranger will
smart for it,
but he who hates suretyship is secure.
16 A gracious woman gets honor,
and violent men get riches.
17 A man who is kind benefits himself,
but a cruel man hurts himself.
18 A wicked man earns deceptive wages,
but one who sows righteousness gets a
sure reward.

19 He who is steadfast in righteousness
will live,
but he who pursues evil will die.
20 Men of perverse mind are an abomination
to the LORD,
but those of blameless ways are his delight.
21 Be assured, an evil man will not
go unpunished,
but those who are righteous will
be delivered.
22 Like a gold ring in a swine's snout
is a beautiful woman without discretion.
23 The desire of the righteous ends only
in good;
the expectation of the wicked in wrath.
24 One man gives freely, yet grows all
the richer;
another withholds what he should give,
and only suffers want.
25 A liberal man will be enriched,
and one who waters will himself be watered.
26 The people curse him who holds
back grain,
but a blessing is on the head of him who
sells it.
27 He who diligently seeks good seeks favor,
but evil comes to him who searches for it.
28 He who trusts in his riches will wither,
but the righteous will flourish like a
green leaf.
29 He who troubles his household will
inherit wind,
and the fool will be servant to the wise.
30 The fruit of the righteous is a tree of life,
but lawlessness takes away lives.
31 If the righteous is repaid on earth,
how much more the wicked and the sinner!

ACTS 15

22 Then it seemed good to the
apostles and the elders, with the
whole Church, to choose men from
among them and send them to Antioch
with Paul and Barnabas. They sent Judas
called Barsab′bas, and Silas, leading men
among the brethren, 23 with the following letter: "The brethren, both the apostles and the
elders, to the brethren who are of the Gentiles in Antioch and Syria and Cili′cia, greeting. 24 Since we have heard that some persons
from us have troubled you with words, unsettling your minds, although we gave them
no instructions, 25 it has seemed good to us
in assembly to choose men and send them
to you with our beloved Barnabas and Paul,
26 men who have risked their lives for the sake
of our Lord Jesus Christ. 27 We have therefore
sent Judas and Silas, who themselves will tell
you the same things by word of mouth. 28 For
it has seemed good to the Holy Spirit and to
us to lay upon you no greater burden than
these necessary things: 29 that you abstain
from what has been sacrificed to idols and
from blood and from what is strangled and
from unchastity. If you keep yourselves from
these, you will do well. Farewell."

30 So when they were sent off, they went
down to Antioch; and having gathered
the congregation together, they delivered
the letter. 31 And when they read it, they
rejoiced at the exhortation. 32 And Judas
and Silas, who were themselves prophets,
exhorted the brethren with many words
and strengthened them.* 33 And after they
had spent some time, they were sent off in
peace by the brethren to those who had sent
them. 35 But Paul and Barnabas remained in
Antioch, teaching and preaching the word
of the Lord, with many others also.

36 And after some days Paul said to Barnabas,
"Come, let us return and visit the brethren
in every city where we proclaimed the word
of the Lord, and see how they are." 37 And
Barnabas wanted to take with them John called
Mark. 38 But Paul thought best not to take with
them one who had withdrawn from them in
Pamphyl′ia, and had not gone with them to the
work. 39 And there arose a sharp contention, so
that they separated from each other; Barnabas
took Mark with him and sailed away to
Cyprus, 40 but Paul chose Silas and departed,
being commended by the brethren to the grace
of the Lord. 41 And he went through Syria and
Cili′cia, strengthening the churches.

* Other ancient authorities insert verse 34, *But it seemed good to Silas to remain there.*

REFLECTION

The world lies to us. It tries to convince us that we can fix all our problems with things that can be bought. It tries to take away our confidence in God by mocking our faith. When the Assyrian army invades Judah, the king of Assyria sends out propaganda messengers who shout to the defenders of Jerusalem: "No god of any nation or kingdom has been able to deliver his people from my hand or from the hand of my fathers. How much less will your God deliver you out of my hand!" (2 Chr 32:15). Yet the soldiers and people of Jerusalem keep King Hezekiah's words in their hearts: "Do not be afraid or dismayed before the king of Assyria and all the horde that is with him; for there is one greater with us than with him" (v. 7). Indeed, the angel of the Lord comes to strike down the army of Assyria, and Sennacherib himself is assassinated by his own sons. When we are insulted for our faith or when the pressures and temptations of the world surround us, we need to remember Hezekiah's encouragement that "there is one greater with us" than with our enemies. How do you find confidence in the Lord in times of conflict?

July 15

2 CHRONICLES 32

[24]In those days Hezeki'ah became sick and was at the point of death, and he prayed to the LORD; and he answered him and gave him a sign. [25]But Hezeki'ah did not make return according to the benefit done to him, for his heart was proud. Therefore wrath came upon him and Judah and Jerusalem. [26]But Hezeki'ah humbled himself for the pride of his heart, both he and the inhabitants of Jerusalem, so that the wrath of the LORD did not come upon them in the days of Hezekiah.

[27]And Hezeki'ah had very great riches and honor; and he made for himself treasuries for silver, for gold, for precious stones, for spices, for shields, and for all kinds of costly vessels; [28]storehouses also for the yield of grain, wine, and oil; and stalls for all kinds of cattle, and sheepfolds. [29]He likewise provided cities for himself, and flocks and herds in abundance; for God had given him very great possessions. [30]This same Hezeki'ah closed the upper outlet of the waters of Gi'hon and directed them down to the west side of the city of David. And Hezekiah prospered in all his works. [31]And so in the matter of the envoys of the princes of Babylon, who had been sent to him to inquire about the sign that had been done in the land, God left him to himself, in order to try him and to know all that was in his heart.

[32]Now the rest of the acts of Hezeki'ah, and his good deeds, behold, they are written in the vision of Isaiah the prophet the son of A'moz, in the Book of the Kings of Judah and Israel. [33]And Hezeki'ah slept with his fathers, and they buried him in the ascent of the tombs of the sons of David; and all Judah and the inhabitants of Jerusalem did him honor at his death. And Manas'seh his son reigned in his stead.

33 Manas'seh was twelve years old when he began to reign, and he reigned fifty-five years in Jerusalem. [2]He did what was evil in the sight of the LORD, according to the abominable practices of the nations whom the LORD drove out before the sons of Israel. [3]For he rebuilt the high places which his father Hezeki'ah had broken down, and erected altars to the Ba'als, and made Ashe'rahs, and worshiped all the host of heaven, and served them. [4]And he built altars in the house of the LORD, of which the LORD had said, "In Jerusalem shall my name be for ever." [5]And he built altars for all the host of heaven in the two courts of the house of the LORD. [6]And he burned his sons as an offering in the valley of the son of Hinnom, and practiced soothsaying and augury and sorcery, and dealt with mediums and with wizards. He did much evil in the sight of the LORD, provoking him

to anger. 7And the image of the idol which
he had made he set in the house of God, of
which God said to David and to Solomon
his son, "In this house, and in Jerusalem,
which I have chosen out of all the tribes of
Israel, I will put my name for ever; 8and I
will no more remove the foot of Israel from
the land which I appointed for your fathers,
if only they will be careful to do all that I
have commanded them, all the law, the
statutes, and the ordinances given through
Moses." 9Manas′seh seduced Judah and the
inhabitants of Jerusalem, so that they did
more evil than the nations whom the LORD
destroyed before the sons of Israel.
10The LORD spoke to Manas′seh and to his
people, but they gave no heed. 11Therefore the
LORD brought upon them the commanders
of the army of the king of Assyria, who
took Manas′seh with hooks and bound
him with fetters of bronze and brought
him to Babylon. 12And when he was in
distress he entreated the favor of the LORD
his God and humbled himself greatly
before the God of his fathers. 13He prayed
to him, and God received his entreaty and
heard his supplication and brought him
again to Jerusalem into his kingdom. Then
Manas′seh knew that the LORD was God.
14Afterwards he built an outer wall for the
city of David west of Gi′hon, in the valley,
and for the entrance into the Fish Gate, and
carried it round O′phel, and raised it to a
very great height; he also put commanders
of the army in all the fortified cities in Judah.
15And he took away the foreign gods and the
idol from the house of the LORD, and all the
altars that he had built on the mountain of
the house of the LORD and in Jerusalem,
and he threw them outside of the city. 16He
also restored the altar of the LORD and
offered upon it sacrifices of peace offerings
and of thanksgiving; and he commanded
Judah to serve the LORD the God of Israel.
17Nevertheless the people still sacrificed
at the high places, but only to the LORD
their God.
18Now the rest of the acts of Manas′seh,
and his prayer to his God, and the words
of the seers who spoke to him in the name
of the LORD the God of Israel, behold, they
are in the Chronicles of the Kings of Israel.
19And his prayer, and how God received his
entreaty, and all his sin and his faithlessness,
and the sites on which he built high places
and set up the Ashe′rim and the images,
before he humbled himself, behold, they are
written in the Chronicles of the Seers. 20So
Manas′seh slept with his fathers, and they
buried him in his house; and A′mon his son
reigned in his stead.
21A′mon was twenty-two years old when
he began to reign, and he reigned two
years in Jerusalem. 22He did what was evil
in the sight of the LORD, as Manas′seh his
father had done. A′mon sacrificed to all the
images that Manasseh his father had made,
and served them. 23And he did not humble
himself before the LORD, as Manas′seh his
father had humbled himself, but this A′mon
incurred guilt more and more. 24And his
servants conspired against him and killed
him in his house. 25But the people of the
land slew all those who had conspired
against King A′mon; and the people of the
land made Josi′ah his son king in his stead.

34 Josi′ah was eight years old when he
began to reign, and he reigned thirty-
one years in Jerusalem. 2He did what was
right in the eyes of the LORD, and walked in
the ways of David his father; and he did not
turn aside to the right or to the left. 3For in
the eighth year of his reign, while he was yet
a boy, he began to seek the God of David his
father; and in the twelfth year he began to
purge Judah and Jerusalem of the high places,
the Ashe′rim, and the graven and the molten
images. 4And they broke down the altars
of the Ba′als in his presence; and he hewed
down the incense altars which stood above
them; and he broke in pieces the Ashe′rim
and the graven and the molten images, and
he made dust of them and strewed it over the
graves of those who had sacrificed to them.
5He also burned the bones of the priests on
their altars, and purged Judah and Jerusalem.
6And in the cities of Manas′seh, E′phraim,
and Simeon, and as far as Naph′tali, in their
ruins round about, 7he broke down the altars,
and beat the Ashe′rim and the images into

powder, and hewed down all the incense altars throughout all the land of Israel. Then he returned to Jerusalem.

PROVERBS 12

Whoever loves discipline loves knowledge,
but he who hates reproof is stupid.
2A good man obtains favor from the LORD,
but a man of evil devices he condemns.
3A man is not established by wickedness,
but the root of the righteous will never be moved.
4A good wife is the crown of her husband,
but she who brings shame is like rottenness in his bones.
5The thoughts of the righteous are just;
the counsels of the wicked are treacherous.
6The words of the wicked lie in wait for blood,
but the mouth of the upright delivers men.
7The wicked are overthrown and are no more,
but the house of the righteous will stand.
8A man is commended according to his good sense,
but one of perverse mind is despised.
9Better is a man of humble standing who works for himself
than one who plays the great man but lacks bread.
10A righteous man has regard for the life of his beast,
but the mercy of the wicked is cruel.
11He who tills his land will have plenty of bread,
but he who follows worthless pursuits has no sense.
12The strong tower of the wicked comes to ruin,
but the root of the righteous stands firm.
13An evil man is ensnared by the transgression of his lips,
but the righteous escapes from trouble.
14From the fruit of his words a man is satisfied with good,
and the work of a man's hand comes back to him.
15The way of a fool is right in his own eyes,
but a wise man listens to advice.
16The vexation of a fool is known at once,
but the prudent man ignores an insult.
17He who speaks the truth gives honest evidence,
but a false witness utters deceit.
18There is one whose rash words are like sword thrusts,
but the tongue of the wise brings healing.
19Truthful lips endure for ever,
but a lying tongue is but for a moment.
20Deceit is in the heart of those who devise evil,
but those who plan good have joy.
21No ill befalls the righteous,
but the wicked are filled with trouble.
22Lying lips are an abomination to the LORD,
but those who act faithfully are his delight.
23A prudent man conceals his knowledge,
but fools proclaim their folly.
24The hand of the diligent will rule,
while the slothful will be put to forced labor.
25Anxiety in a man's heart weighs him down,
but a good word makes him glad.
26A righteous man turns away from evil,
but the way of the wicked leads them astray.
27A slothful man will not catch his prey,
but the diligent man will get precious wealth.
28In the path of righteousness is life,
but the way of error leads to death.

ACTS 16

And he came also to Derbe and to Lystra. A disciple was there, named Timothy, the son of a Jewish woman who was a believer; but his
father was a Greek. 2He was well spoken of
by the brethren at Lystra and Ico´nium. 3Paul
wanted Timothy to accompany him; and he
took him and circumcised him because of
the Jews that were in those places, for they
all knew that his father was a Greek. 4As
they went on their way through the cities,
they delivered to them for observance the
decisions which had been reached by the
apostles and elders who were at Jerusalem.

5So the churches were strengthened in the
faith, and they increased in numbers daily.
6And they went through the region
of Phry′gia and Galatia, having been
forbidden by the Holy Spirit to speak the
word in Asia. 7And when they had come
opposite My′sia, they attempted to go
into Bithyn′ia, but the Spirit of Jesus did
not allow them; 8so, passing by My′sia,
they went down to Troas. 9And a vision
appeared to Paul in the night: a man of
Macedonia was standing pleading with
him and saying, "Come over to Macedonia
and help us." 10And when he had seen
the vision, immediately we sought to
go on into Macedonia, concluding that
God had called us to preach the gospel
to them.
11Setting sail therefore from Troas, we
made a direct voyage to Sam′othrace, and
the following day to Ne-ap′olis, 12and from
there to Philip′pi, which is the leading city
of the district of Macedonia, and a Roman
colony. We remained in this city some
days; 13and on the sabbath day we went
outside the gate to the riverside, where we
supposed there was a place of prayer; and
we sat down and spoke to the women who
had come together. 14One who heard us
was a woman named Lydia, from the city
of Thyati′ra, a seller of purple goods, who
was a worshiper of God. The Lord opened
her heart to listen to what was said by
Paul. 15And when she was baptized, with
her household, she begged us, saying, "If
you have judged me to be faithful to the
Lord, come to my house and stay." And
she prevailed upon us.

REFLECTION

Our love for God begins in the heart. "Deceit is in the heart of those who devise evil, but those who plan good have joy" (Prv 12:20). King Manasseh, the son of righteous Hezekiah, sadly misleads the nation of Judah. He brings back all the baals (the pagan gods), idols, and altars, even sacrificing his own son to a false god. His heart of "deceit" builds evil systems of blasphemy and perversion. Truly, "Manasseh seduced Judah and the inhabitants of Jerusalem" (2 Chr 33:9). Leaders and authorities, when their hearts are in the wrong place, can lead whole peoples into sin and away from God. Sadly, Manasseh did not learn the way of his father King Hezekiah, who when he realized that he had sinned "humbled himself for the pride of his heart . . . so that the wrath of the LORD did not come upon them" (32:26). His sincere and heartfelt repentance is honored by God and leads to many blessings: "Hezekiah prospered in all his works" (v. 30). Lydia, too, "opened her heart to listen" to the Gospel (Acts 16:14). If we close our hearts to God and resist his Word, we end up far away from him; yet if we repent and open our hearts to him, he can give us the joy for which we long. How can you open your heart to the Lord?

July 16

2 CHRONICLES 34

**8Now in the eighteenth year of
his reign, when he had purged
the land and the house, he sent Sha′phan
the son of Azali′ah, and Maasei′ah the**
governor of the city, and Jo′ah the son of
Jo′ahaz, the recorder, to repair the house of
the LORD his God. 9They came to Hilki′ah
the high priest and delivered the money
that had been brought into the house of
God, which the Levites, the keepers of the
threshold, had collected from Manas′seh
and E′phraim and from all the remnant
of Israel and from all Judah and Benjamin
and from the inhabitants of Jerusalem.
10They delivered it to the workmen who
had the oversight of the house of the LORD;
and the workmen who were working in
the house of the LORD gave it for repairing and restoring the house. 11They gave it
to the carpenters and the builders to buy

quarried stone, and timber for binders and
beams for the buildings which the kings of
Judah had let go to ruin. [12]And the men did
the work faithfully. Over them were set Jahath and Obadi´ah the Levites, of the sons
of Merar´i, and Zechari´ah and Meshul´lam,
of the sons of the Ko´hathites, to have oversight. The Levites, all who were skilful
with instruments of music, [13]were over the
burden-bearers and directed all who did
work in every kind of service; and some of
the Levites were scribes, and officials, and
gatekeepers.

[14]While they were bringing out the money
that had been brought into the house of the
LORD, Hilki´ah the priest found the book of
the law of the LORD given through Moses.
[15]Then Hilki´ah said to Sha´phan the
secretary, "I have found the book of the law
in the house of the LORD"; and Hilkiah gave
the book to Shaphan. [16]Sha´phan brought
the book to the king, and further reported
to the king, "All that was committed to
your servants they are doing. [17]They have
emptied out the money that was found in
the house of the LORD and have delivered
it into the hand of the overseers and the
workmen." [18]Then Sha´phan the secretary
told the king, "Hilki´ah the priest has given
me a book." And Shaphan read it before
the king.

[19]When the king heard the words of the
law he tore his clothes. [20]And the king
commanded Hilki´ah, Ahi´kam the son
of Sha´phan, Abdon the son of Micah,
Shaphan the secretary, and Asai´ah the
king's servant, saying, [21]"Go, inquire of the
LORD for me and for those who are left in
Israel and in Judah, concerning the words
of the book that has been found; for great is
the wrath of the LORD that is poured out on
us, because our fathers have not kept the
word of the LORD, to do according to all
that is written in this book."

[22]So Hilki´ah and those whom the king
had sent went to Huldah the prophetess,
the wife of Shallum the son of Tokhath, son
of Hasrah, keeper of the wardrobe (now she
dwelt in Jerusalem in the Second Quarter)
and spoke to her to that effect. [23]And she
said to them, "Thus says the LORD, the
God of Israel: 'Tell the man who sent you
to me, [24]Thus says the LORD, Behold, I will
bring evil upon this place and upon its
inhabitants, all the curses that are written
in the book which was read before the king
of Judah. [25]Because they have forsaken me
and have burned incense to other gods,
that they might provoke me to anger with
all the works of their hands, therefore my
wrath will be poured out upon this place
and will not be quenched. [26]But to the king
of Judah, who sent you to inquire of the
LORD, thus shall you say to him, Thus says
the LORD, the God of Israel: Regarding the
words which you have heard, [27]because
your heart was penitent and you humbled
yourself before God when you heard his
words against this place and its inhabitants,
and you have humbled yourself before me,
and have torn your clothes and wept before
me, I also have heard you, says the LORD.
[28]Behold, I will gather you to your fathers,
and you shall be gathered to your grave in
peace, and your eyes shall not see all the
evil which I will bring upon this place and
its inhabitants.'" And they brought back
word to the king.

[29]Then the king sent and gathered
together all the elders of Judah and
Jerusalem. [30]And the king went up to the
house of the LORD, with all the men of
Judah and the inhabitants of Jerusalem and
the priests and the Levites, all the people
both great and small; and he read in their
hearing all the words of the book of the
covenant which had been found in the
house of the LORD. [31]And the king stood in
his place and made a covenant before the
LORD, to walk after the LORD and to keep
his commandments and his covenants and
his statutes, with all his heart and all his
soul, to perform the words of the covenant
that were written in this book. [32]Then he
made all who were present in Jerusalem
and in Benjamin stand to it. And the
inhabitants of Jerusalem did according
to the covenant of God, the God of their
fathers. [33]And Josi´ah took away all the
abominations from all the territory that

belonged to the sons of Israel, and made
all who were in Israel serve the LORD
their God. All his days they did not turn
away from following the LORD the God of
their fathers.

35 Josi´ah kept a Passover to the LORD
in Jerusalem; and they killed the
Passover lamb on the fourteenth day of the
first month. 2He appointed the priests to
their offices and encouraged them in the
service of the house of the LORD. 3And he
said to the Levites who taught all Israel and
who were holy to the LORD, "Put the holy
ark in the house which Solomon the son
of David, king of Israel, built; you need no
longer carry it upon your shoulders. Now
serve the LORD your God and his people
Israel. 4Prepare yourselves according to
your fathers' houses by your divisions,
following the directions of David king of
Israel and the directions of Solomon his
son. 5And stand in the holy place according
to the groupings of the fathers' houses of
your brethren the lay people, and let there
be for each a part of a father's house of the
Levites. 6And kill the Passover lamb, and
sanctify yourselves, and prepare for your
brethren, to do according to the word of the
LORD by Moses."

7Then Josi´ah contributed to the lay people, as Passover offerings for all that were
present, lambs and kids from the flock to
the number of thirty thousand, and three
thousand bulls; these were from the king's
possessions. 8And his princes contributed
willingly to the people, to the priests, and to
the Levites. Hilki´ah, Zechari´ah, and Jehi´el,
the chief officers of the house of God, gave
to the priests for the Passover offerings two
thousand six hundred lambs and kids and
three hundred bulls. 9Conani´ah also, and
Shemai´ah and Nethan´el his brothers, and
Hashabi´ah and Je-i´el and Joz´abad, the
chiefs of the Levites, gave to the Levites for
the Passover offerings five thousand lambs
and kids and five hundred bulls.

10When the service had been prepared
for, the priests stood in their place, and
the Levites in their divisions according to
the king's command. 11And they killed the
Passover lamb, and the priests sprinkled
the blood which they received from them
while the Levites flayed the victims. 12And
they set aside the burnt offerings that they
might distribute them according to the
groupings of the fathers' houses of the lay
people, to offer to the LORD, as it is written
in the book of Moses. And so they did with
the bulls. 13And they roasted the Passover
lamb with fire according to the ordinance;
and they boiled the holy offerings in pots,
in caldrons, and in pans, and carried them
quickly to all the lay people. 14And afterward
they prepared for themselves and for the
priests, because the priests the sons of Aaron
were busied in offering the burnt offerings
and the fat parts until night; so the Levites
prepared for themselves and for the priests
the sons of Aaron. 15The singers, the sons
of A´saph, were in their place according to
the command of David, and Asaph, and
He´man, and Jedu´thun the king's seer; and
the gatekeepers were at each gate; they did
not need to depart from their service, for
their brethren the Levites prepared for them.

16So all the service of the LORD was prepared that day, to keep the Passover and to
offer burnt offerings on the altar of the LORD,
according to the command of King Josi´ah.
17And the sons of Israel who were present
kept the Passover at that time, and the feast of
unleavened bread seven days. 18No Passover
like it had been kept in Israel since the days
of Samuel the prophet; none of the kings of
Israel had kept such a Passover as was kept
by Josi´ah, and the priests and the Levites,
and all Judah and Israel who were present,
and the inhabitants of Jerusalem. 19In the
eighteenth year of the reign of Josi´ah this
Passover was kept.

PROVERBS 13

A wise son hears his father's instruction,
but a scoffer does not listen to rebuke.
2From the fruit of his mouth a good man
eats good,
but the desire of the treacherous is
for violence.

3 He who guards his mouth preserves his life;
he who opens wide his lips comes to ruin.
4 The soul of the sluggard craves, and
gets nothing,
while the soul of the diligent is
richly supplied.
5 A righteous man hates falsehood,
but a wicked man acts shamefully and
disgracefully.
6 Righteousness guards him whose way
is upright,
but sin overthrows the wicked.
7 One man pretends to be rich, yet has nothing;
another pretends to be poor, yet has
great wealth.
8 The ransom of a man's life is his wealth,
but a poor man has no means
of redemption.
9 The light of the righteous rejoices,
but the lamp of the wicked will be put out.
10 By insolence the heedless make strife,
but with those who take advice is wisdom.

ACTS 16

16 **As we were going to the place
of prayer, we were met by a
slave girl who had a spirit of divination
and brought her owners much gain by**
soothsaying. 17 She followed Paul and us,
crying, "These men are servants of the Most
High God, who proclaim to you the way of
salvation." 18 And this she did for many days.
But Paul was annoyed, and turned and said to
the spirit, "I charge you in the name of Jesus
Christ to come out of her." And it came out
that very hour.
19 But when her owners saw that their hope of
gain was gone, they seized Paul and Silas and
dragged them into the market place before
the rulers; 20 and when they had brought them
to the magistrates they said, "These men are
Jews and they are disturbing our city. 21 They
advocate customs which it is not lawful for us
Romans to accept or practice." 22 The crowd
joined in attacking them; and the magistrates
tore the garments off them and gave orders
to beat them with rods. 23 And when they had
inflicted many blows upon them, they threw
them into prison, charging the jailer to keep
them safely. 24 Having received this charge, he
put them into the inner prison and fastened
their feet in the stocks.
25 But about midnight Paul and Silas were
praying and singing hymns to God, and the
prisoners were listening to them, 26 and suddenly there was a great earthquake, so that
the foundations of the prison were shaken;
and immediately all the doors were opened
and every one's chains were unfastened.
27 When the jailer woke and saw that the
prison doors were open, he drew his sword
and was about to kill himself, supposing
that the prisoners had escaped. 28 But Paul
cried with a loud voice, "Do not harm yourself, for we are all here." 29 And he called for
lights and rushed in, and trembling with
fear he fell down before Paul and Silas, 30 and
brought them out and said, "Men, what
must I do to be saved?" 31 And they said,
"Believe in the Lord Jesus, and you will be
saved, you and your household." 32 And they
spoke the word of the Lord to him and to all
that were in his house. 33 And he took them
the same hour of the night, and washed
their wounds, and he was baptized at once,
with all his family. 34 Then he brought them
up into his house, and set food before them;
and he rejoiced with all his household that
he had believed in God.
35 But when it was day, the magistrates sent
the police, saying, "Let those men go." 36 And
the jailer reported the words to Paul, saying,
"The magistrates have sent to let you go; now
therefore come out and go in peace." 37 But Paul
said to them, "They have beaten us publicly,
uncondemned, men who are Roman citizens,
and have thrown us into prison; and do they
now cast us out secretly? No! let them come
themselves and take us out." 38 The police
reported these words to the magistrates, and
they were afraid when they heard that they
were Roman citizens; 39 so they came and
apologized to them. And they took them out
and asked them to leave the city. 40 So they went
out of the prison, and visited Lydia; and when
they had seen the brethren, they exhorted
them and departed.

REFLECTION

The normal human response to bad news and bad circumstances is sadness. When we experience setbacks, we tend to become disheartened. Yet, in today's readings, we find believers responding to adverse situations in an entirely different manner. King Josiah, after his robe-tearing repentance, hears a dreadful prophecy from Huldah: "Behold, I will bring evil upon this place and upon its inhabitants, all the curses that are written in the book" (2 Chr 34:24). Though this message of judgment is a tragic blow to the righteous king, he does not lose heart. Instead, he renews the covenant with the Lord and lavishly celebrates the Passover. In a moment that seems ripe for discouragement, Josiah chooses to worship the Lord with all his heart. Similarly, when Sts. Paul and Silas find themselves in prison for preaching the Gospel, they begin "praying and singing hymns to God" (Acts 16:25). Their paradoxical response of praise during suffering leads to their miraculous deliverance by earthquake. These examples show us that when we confront the world and our problems in faith, our total reliance on God leads us to the logical response of giving praise and worship to the only one who can help us. Problems and hindrances need to lead us into praise rather than discouragement. What discouragement in your life needs to be turned to God in praise?

July 17

2 CHRONICLES 35

[20]**After all this, when Josi′ah**
had prepared the temple, Neco
king of Egypt went up to fight
at Car′chemish on the Euphrates and
Josiah went out against him. [21]**But he**
sent envoys to him, saying, "What have
we to do with each other, king of Judah?
I am not coming against you this day, but
against the house with which I am at war;
and God has commanded me to make haste.
Cease opposing God, who is with me, lest he
destroy you." [22]Nevertheless Josi′ah would
not turn away from him, but disguised
himself in order to fight with him. He did
not listen to the words of Neco from the
mouth of God, but joined battle in the plain
of Megid′do. [23]And the archers shot King
Josi′ah; and the king said to his servants,
"Take me away, for I am badly wounded."
[24]So his servants took him out of the chariot
and carried him in his second chariot and
brought him to Jerusalem. And he died, and
was buried in the tombs of his fathers. All
Judah and Jerusalem mourned for Josi′ah.
[25]Jeremi′ah also uttered a lament for Josi′ah;
and all the singing men and singing women
have spoken of Josiah in their laments to this
day. They made these an ordinance in Israel;
behold, they are written in the Laments.
[26]Now the rest of the acts of Josi′ah, and his
good deeds according to what is written in
the law of the LORD, [27]and his acts, first and
last, behold, they are written in the Book of
the Kings of Israel and Judah.

36 The people of the land took Jeho′ahaz
the son of Josi′ah and made him king
in his father's stead in Jerusalem. [2]Jeho′ahaz
was twenty-three years old when he began
to reign; and he reigned three months in
Jerusalem. [3]Then the king of Egypt deposed
him in Jerusalem and laid upon the land a
tribute of a hundred talents of silver and
a talent of gold. [4]And the king of Egypt
made Eli′akim his brother king over Judah
and Jerusalem, and changed his name to
Jehoi′akim; but Neco took Jeho′ahaz his
brother and carried him to Egypt.

[5]Jehoi′akim was twenty-five years old
when he began to reign, and he reigned
eleven years in Jerusalem. He did what
was evil in the sight of the LORD his God.
[6]Against him came up Nebuchadnez′zar
king of Babylon, and bound him in fetters
to take him to Babylon. [7]Nebuchadnez′zar
also carried part of the vessels of the house
of the LORD to Babylon and put them in his
palace in Babylon. [8]Now the rest of the acts
of Jehoi′akim, and the abominations which

he did, and what was found against him,
behold, they are written in the Book of the
Kings of Israel and Judah; and Jehoi´achin
his son reigned in his stead.
9Jehoi´achin was eight years old when he
began to reign, and he reigned three months
and ten days in Jerusalem. He did what was
evil in the sight of the LORD. 10In the spring
of the year King Nebuchadnez´zar sent and
brought him to Babylon, with the precious
vessels of the house of the LORD, and made
his brother Zedeki´ah king over Judah and
Jerusalem.
11Zedeki´ah was twenty-one years old
when he began to reign, and he reigned
eleven years in Jerusalem. 12He did what
was evil in the sight of the LORD his God.
He did not humble himself before Jeremi´ah
the prophet, who spoke from the mouth of
the LORD. 13He also rebelled against King
Nebuchadnez´zar, who had made him swear
by God; he stiffened his neck and hardened
his heart against turning to the LORD,
the God of Israel. 14All the leading priests
and the people likewise were exceedingly
unfaithful, following all the abominations
of the nations; and they polluted the house
of the LORD which he had hallowed in
Jerusalem.
15The LORD, the God of their fathers, sent
persistently to them by his messengers,
because he had compassion on his people
and on his dwelling place; 16but they kept
mocking the messengers of God, despising
his words, and scoffing at his prophets,
till the wrath of the LORD rose against his
people, till there was no remedy.
17Therefore he brought up against them
the king of the Chalde´ans, who slew their
young men with the sword in the house of
their sanctuary, and had no compassion
on young man or virgin, old man or aged;
he gave them all into his hand. 18And all
the vessels of the house of God, great and
small, and the treasures of the house of
the LORD, and the treasures of the king
and of his princes, all these he brought to
Babylon. 19And they burned the house of
God, and broke down the wall of Jerusalem,
and burned all its palaces with fire, and
destroyed all its precious vessels. 20He took
into exile in Babylon those who had escaped
from the sword, and they became servants to
him and to his sons until the establishment
of the kingdom of Persia, 21to fulfil the word
of the LORD by the mouth of Jeremi´ah, until
the land had enjoyed its sabbaths. All the
days that it lay desolate it kept sabbath, to
fulfil seventy years.
22Now in the first year of Cyrus king of
Persia, that the word of the LORD by the
mouth of Jeremi´ah might be accomplished,
the LORD stirred up the spirit of Cyrus king
of Persia so that he made a proclamation
throughout all his kingdom and also put
it in writing: 23"Thus says Cyrus king of
Persia, 'The LORD, the God of heaven, has
given me all the kingdoms of the earth, and
he has charged me to build him a house at
Jerusalem, which is in Judah. Whoever is
among you of all his people, may the LORD
his God be with him. Let him go up.'"

PROVERBS 13

11Wealth hastily gotten will dwindle,
but he who gathers little by little will
increase it.
12Hope deferred makes the heart sick,
but a desire fulfilled is a tree of life.
13He who despises the word brings
destruction on himself,
but he who respects the commandment
will be rewarded.
14The teaching of the wise is a fountain of life,
that one may avoid the snares of death.
15Good sense wins favor,
but the way of the faithless is their ruin.
16In everything a prudent man acts with
knowledge,
but a fool flaunts his folly.
17A bad messenger plunges men into trouble,
but a faithful envoy brings healing.
18Poverty and disgrace come to him who
ignores instruction,
but he who heeds reproof is honored.
19A desire fulfilled is sweet to the soul;
but to turn away from evil is an
abomination to fools.

20He who walks with wise men becomes wise,
but the companion of fools will
suffer harm.
21Misfortune pursues sinners,
but prosperity rewards the righteous.
22A good man leaves an inheritance to his
children's children,
but the sinner's wealth is laid up for
the righteous.
23The fallow ground of the poor yields
much food,
but it is swept away through injustice.
24He who spares the rod hates his son,
but he who loves him is diligent to
discipline him.
25The righteous has enough to satisfy
his appetite,
but the belly of the wicked suffers want.

ACTS 17

Now when they had passed through Amphip´olis and Apollo´nia, they came to Thessaloni´ca, where there was a synagogue of the Jews. 2And Paul went in, as was his custom, and for three weeks he argued with them from the Scriptures, 3explaining and proving that it was necessary for the Christ to suffer and to rise from the dead, and saying, "This Jesus, whom I proclaim to you, is the Christ." 4And some of them were persuaded, and joined Paul and Silas; as did a great many of the devout Greeks and not a few of the leading women. 5But the Jews were jealous, and taking some wicked fellows of the rabble, they gathered a crowd, set the city in an uproar, and attacked the house of Jason, seeking to bring them out to the people. 6And when they could not find them, they dragged Jason and some of the brethren before the city authorities, crying, "These men who have turned the world upside down have come here also, 7and Jason has received them; and they are all acting against the decrees of Caesar, saying that there is another king, Jesus." 8And the people and the city authorities were disturbed when they heard this. 9And when they had taken security from Jason and the rest, they let them go.

10The brethren immediately sent Paul and Silas away by night to Beroe´a; and when they arrived they went into the Jewish synagogue. 11Now these Jews were more noble than those in Thessaloni´ca, for they received the word with all eagerness, examining the Scriptures daily to see if these things were so. 12Many of them therefore believed, with not a few Greek women of high standing as well as men. 13But when the Jews of Thessaloni´ca learned that the word of God was proclaimed by Paul at Beroe´a also, they came there too, stirring up and inciting the crowds. 14Then the brethren immediately sent Paul off on his way to the sea, but Silas and Timothy remained there. 15Those who conducted Paul brought him as far as Athens; and receiving a command for Silas and Timothy to come to him as soon as possible, they departed.

16Now while Paul was waiting for them at Athens, his spirit was provoked within him as he saw that the city was full of idols. 17So he argued in the synagogue with the Jews and the devout persons, and in the market place every day with those who chanced to be there. 18Some also of the Epicurean and Stoic philosophers met him. And some said, "What would this babbler say?" Others said, "He seems to be a preacher of foreign divinities"—because he preached Jesus and the resurrection. 19And they took hold of him and brought him to the Are-op´agus, saying, "May we know what this new teaching is which you present? 20For you bring some strange things to our ears; we wish to know therefore what these things mean." 21Now all the Athenians and the foreigners who lived there spent their time in nothing except telling or hearing something new.

22So Paul, standing in the middle of the Are-op´agus, said: "Men of Athens, I perceive that in every way you are very religious. 23For as I passed along, and observed the objects of your worship, I found also an altar with this inscription, 'To an unknown god.' What therefore you worship as unknown, this I proclaim to you. 24The God who made the world and everything in it, being Lord of heaven and earth, does not live in shrines made by man, 25nor is he served by human hands, as though he needed anything, since he himself gives to all men life and breath and everything. 26And he made from one every nation of men to live on all the face of the earth, having determined allotted periods and the boundaries of their habitation, 27that they should seek God, in the hope that they might feel after him and find him. Yet he is not far from each one of us, 28for

'In him we live and move and have
our being';

as even some of your poets have said,

'For we are indeed his offspring.'

29Being then God's offspring, we ought not to think that the Deity is like gold, or silver, or stone, a representation by the art and imagination of man. 30The times of ignorance God overlooked, but now he commands all men everywhere to repent, 31because he has fixed a day on which he will judge the world in righteousness by a man whom he has appointed, and of this he has given assurance to all men by raising him from the dead."

32Now when they heard of the resurrection of the dead, some mocked; but others said, "We will hear you again about this." 33So Paul went out from among them. 34But some men joined him and believed, among them Dionys'ius the Are-op'agite and a woman named Dam'aris and others with them.

18 After this he left Athens and went to Corinth. 2And he found a Jew named Aqui'la, a native of Pontus, lately come from Italy with his wife Priscilla, because Claudius had commanded all the Jews to leave Rome. And he went to see them; 3and because he was of the same trade he stayed with them, and they worked, for by trade they were tentmakers. 4And he argued in the synagogue every sabbath, and persuaded Jews and Greeks.

5When Silas and Timothy arrived from Macedonia, Paul was occupied with preaching, testifying to the Jews that the Christ was Jesus. 6And when they opposed and reviled him, he shook out his garments and said to them, "Your blood be upon your heads! I am innocent. From now on I will go to the Gentiles." 7And he left there and went to the house of a man named Titius Justus, a worshiper of God; his house was next door to the synagogue. 8Crispus, the ruler of the synagogue, believed in the Lord, together with all his household; and many of the Corinthians hearing Paul believed and were baptized. 9And the Lord said to Paul one night in a vision, "Do not be afraid, but speak and do not be silent; 10for I am with you, and no man shall attack you to harm you; for I have many people in this city." 11And he stayed a year and six months, teaching the word of God among them.

REFLECTION

Proverbs continually compares wise living to foolish living, helping us contemplate all of the repercussions of sin and righteousness. For example, "He who walks with wise men becomes wise, but the companion of fools will suffer harm" (Prv 13:20). Sadly, at the end of his life, Josiah, this good reformer king, made a foolhardy decision when "he did not listen to the words of Neco from the mouth of God" (2 Chr 35:22). He should have heeded Pharaoh's dismissal, but instead confronts him in battle and loses his life. St. Paul confronts the foolishness of pagan worship with the wisdom of the Gospel in his famous speech at the Areopagus in Athens. Upon seeing the false gods of the Greeks, "his spirit was provoked within him" (Acts 17:16). When given an invitation to speak before the Greeks, Paul wisely finds common ground (the crowd's pious, although pagan, practice of religion), from which he introduces them to the one true God. Paul rejects the foolishness of idol-worship and preaches the Gospel with wisdom. When you share your faith with unbelievers, do you speak in such an inviting way?

July 18

EZRA 1

In the first year of Cyrus king of Persia, that the word of the LORD by the mouth of Jeremi′ah might be accomplished, the LORD stirred up the spirit of Cyrus king of Persia so that he made a proclamation throughout all his kingdom and also put it in writing:

[2]"Thus says Cyrus king of Persia: The LORD, the God of heaven, has given me all the kingdoms of the earth, and he has charged me to build him a house at Jerusalem, which is in Judah. [3]Whoever is among you of all his people, may his God be with him, and let him go up to Jerusalem, which is in Judah, and rebuild the house of the LORD, the God of Israel—he is the God who is in Jerusalem; [4]and let each survivor, in whatever place he sojourns, be assisted by the men of his place with silver and gold, with goods and with beasts, besides freewill offerings for the house of God which is in Jerusalem."

[5]Then rose up the heads of the fathers' houses of Judah and Benjamin, and the priests and the Levites, every one whose spirit God had stirred to go up to rebuild the house of the LORD which is in Jerusalem; [6]and all who were about them aided them with vessels of silver, with gold, with goods, with beasts, and with costly wares, besides all that was freely offered. [7]Cyrus the king also brought out the vessels of the house of the LORD which Nebuchadnez′zar had carried away from Jerusalem and placed in the house of his gods. [8]Cyrus king of Persia brought these out in charge of Mith′redath the treasurer, who counted them out to Shesh-baz′zar the prince of Judah. [9]And this was the number of them: a thousand basins of gold, a thousand basins of silver, twenty-nine censers, [10]thirty bowls of gold, two thousand four hundred and ten bowls of silver, and a thousand other vessels; [11]all the vessels of gold and of silver were five thousand four hundred and sixty-nine. All these did Shesh-baz′zar bring up, when the exiles were brought up from Babylonia to Jerusalem.

2 Now these were the people of the province who came up out of the captivity of those exiles whom Nebuchadnez′zar the king of Babylon had carried captive to Babylonia; they returned to Jerusalem and Judah, each to his own town. [2]They came with Zerub′babel, Jesh′ua, Nehemi′ah, Serai′ah, Re-elai′ah, Mor′decai, Bilshan, Mispar, Bigvai, Re′hum, and Ba′anah.

The number of the men of the sons of Israel: [3]the sons of Parosh, two thousand one hundred and seventy-two. [4]The sons of Shephati′ah, three hundred and seventy-two. [5]The sons of A′rah, seven hundred and seventy-five. [6]The sons of Pa′hath-mo′ab, namely the sons of Jesh′ua and Jo′ab, two thousand eight hundred and twelve. [7]The sons of E′lam, one thousand two hundred and fifty-four. [8]The sons of Zattu, nine hundred and forty-five. [9]The sons of Zaccai, seven hundred and sixty. [10]The sons of Ba′ni, six hundred and forty-two. [11]The sons of Bebai, six hundred and twenty-three. [12]The sons of Azgad, one thousand two hundred and twenty-two. [13]The sons of Adoni′kam, six hundred and sixty-six. [14]The sons of Bigvai, two thousand and fifty-six. [15]The sons of A′din, four hundred and fifty-four. [16]The sons of A′ter, namely of Hezeki′ah, ninety-eight. [17]The sons of Bezai, three hundred and twenty-three. [18]The sons of Jo′rah, one hundred and twelve. [19]The sons of Hashum, two hundred and twenty-three. [20]The sons of Gibbar, ninety-five. [21]The sons of Bethlehem, one hundred and twenty-three. [22]The men of Netoph′ah, fifty-six. [23]The men of An′athoth, one hundred and twenty-eight. [24]The sons of Az′maveth, forty-two. [25]The sons of Kir″iathar′im, Chephi′rah, and Be-er′oth, seven hundred and forty-three. [26]The sons of Ra′mah and Ge′ba, six hundred and twenty-one. [27]The men of Michmas, one hundred and twenty-two. [28]The men of Bethel and Ai, two hundred and twenty-three. [29]The sons of Nebo, fifty-two. [30]The sons of Magbish, one

hundred and fifty-six. 31 The sons of the other
E´lam, one thousand two hundred and fifty-
four. 32 The sons of Harim, three hundred and
twenty. 33 The sons of Lod, Ha´did, and Ono,
seven hundred and twenty-five. 34 The sons of
Jericho, three hundred and forty-five. 35 The
sons of Sena´ah, three thousand six hundred
and thirty.

36 The priests: the sons of Jedai´ah, of the
house of Jesh´ua, nine hundred and seventy-
three. 37 The sons of Immer, one thousand and
fifty-two. 38 The sons of Pashhur, one thousand
two hundred and forty-seven. 39 The sons of
Harim, one thousand and seventeen.

40 The Levites: the sons of Jesh´ua and
Kad´mi-el, of the sons of Hod´´avi´ah, seventy-
four. 41 The singers: the sons of A´saph, one
hundred and twenty-eight. 42 The sons of the
gatekeepers: the sons of Shallum, the sons of
A´ter, the sons of Talmon, the sons of Akkub,
the sons of Hati´ta, and the sons of Shobai, in
all one hundred and thirty-nine.

43 The temple servants: the sons of Ziha, the
sons of Hasu´pha, the sons of Tabba´oth, 44 the
sons of Keros, the sons of Si´aha, the sons of
Padon, 45 the sons of Leba´nah, the sons of
Hag´abah, the sons of Akkub, 46 the sons of
Hagab, the sons of Shamlai, the sons of Ha´nan,
47 the sons of Giddel, the sons of Gahar, the
sons of Re-ai´ah, 48 the sons of Re´zin, the sons
of Neko´da, the sons of Gazzam, 49 the sons of
Uzza, the sons of Pase´ah, the sons of Besai,
50 the sons of Asnah, the sons of Me-u´nim,
the sons of Nephi´sim, 51 the sons of Bakbuk,
the sons of Haku´pha, the sons of Harhur,
52 the sons of Bazluth, the sons of Mehi´da, the
sons of Harsha, 53 the sons of Barkos, the sons
of Sis´era, the sons of Te´mah, 54 the sons of
Nezi´ah, and the sons of Hati´pha.

55 The sons of Solomon's servants: the sons
of Sotai, the sons of Hasso´phereth, the sons
of Peru´da, 56 the sons of Ja´alah, the sons of
Darkon, the sons of Giddel, 57 the sons of
Shephati´ah, the sons of Hattil, the sons of
Po´chereth-hazzeba´im, and the sons of A´mi.

58 All the temple servants and the sons of
Solomon's servants were three hundred and
ninety-two.

59 The following were those who came up
from Tel-me´lah, Tel-har´sha, Cherub, Addan,
and Immer, though they could not prove
their fathers' houses or their descent, whether
they belonged to Israel: 60 the sons of Delai´ah,
the sons of Tobi´ah, and the sons of Neko´da,
six hundred and fifty-two. 61 Also, of the sons
of the priests: the sons of Habai´ah, the sons
of Hakkoz, and the sons of Barzil´lai (who had
taken a wife from the daughters of Barzillai
the Gileadite, and was called by their name).
62 These sought their registration among those
enrolled in the genealogies, but they were not
found there, and so they were excluded from
the priesthood as unclean; 63 the governor
told them that they were not to partake of the
most holy food, until there should be a priest
to consult U´rim and Thummim.

64 The whole assembly together was
forty-two thousand three hundred and
sixty, 65 besides their menservants and
maidservants, of whom there were seven
thousand three hundred and thirty-seven;
and they had two hundred male and
female singers. 66 Their horses were seven
hundred and thirty-six, their mules were
two hundred and forty-five, 67 their camels
were four hundred and thirty-five, and
their donkeys were six thousand seven
hundred and twenty.

68 Some of the heads of families, when
they came to the house of the LORD which
is in Jerusalem, made freewill offerings
for the house of God, to erect it on its site;
69 according to their ability they gave to the
treasury of the work sixty-one thousand
darics of gold, five thousand minas of silver,
and one hundred priests' garments.

70 The priests, the Levites, and some of the
people lived in Jerusalem and its vicinity;
and the singers, the gatekeepers, and the
temple servants lived in their towns, and all
Israel in their towns.

PROVERBS 14

Wisdom builds her house,
but folly with her own hands tears it down.
2 He who walks in uprightness fears the LORD,
but he who is devious in his ways
despises him.

[3]The talk of a fool is a rod for his back,
but the lips of the wise will preserve them.
[4]Where there are no oxen, there is no grain;
but abundant crops come by the strength
of the ox.
[5]A faithful witness does not lie,
but a false witness breathes out lies.
[6]A scoffer seeks wisdom in vain,
but knowledge is easy for a man
of understanding.
[7]Leave the presence of a fool,
for there you do not meet words
of knowledge.
[8]The wisdom of a prudent man is to discern
his way,
but the folly of fools is deceiving.
[9]God scorns the wicked,
but the upright enjoy his favor.
[10]The heart knows its own bitterness,
and no stranger shares its joy.
[11]The house of the wicked will be destroyed,
but the tent of the upright will flourish.
[12]There is a way which seems right to a man,
but its end is the way to death.
[13]Even in laughter the heart is sad,
and the end of joy is grief.
[14]A perverse man will be filled with the fruit
of his ways,
and a good man with the fruit
of his deeds.
[15]The simple believes everything,
but the prudent looks where he is going.
[16]A wise man is cautious and turns away
from evil,
but a fool throws off restraint
and is careless.
[17]A man of quick temper acts foolishly,
but a man of discretion is patient.

ACTS 18

[12]But when Gallio was proconsul of Acha'ia, the Jews made a united attack upon Paul and brought him before the tribunal, [13]saying, "This
man is persuading men to worship God
contrary to the law." [14]But when Paul was
about to open his mouth, Gallio said to the
Jews, "If it were a matter of wrongdoing or
vicious crime, I should have reason to bear
with you, O Jews; [15]but since it is a matter of
questions about words and names and your
own law, see to it yourselves; I refuse to be a
judge of these things." [16]And he drove them
from the tribunal. [17]And they all seized
Sos'thenes, the ruler of the synagogue, and
beat him in front of the tribunal. But Gallio
paid no attention to this.

[18]After this Paul stayed many days longer,
and then took leave of the brethren and
sailed for Syria, and with him Priscilla and
Aqui'la. At Cen'chre-ae he cut his hair, for
he had a vow. [19]And they came to Ephesus,
and he left them there; but he himself
went into the synagogue and argued with
the Jews. [20]When they asked him to stay
for a longer period, he declined; [21]but on
taking leave of them he said, "I will return
to you if God wills," and he set sail from
Ephesus.

[22]When he had landed at Caesare'a, he
went up and greeted the Church, and then
went down to Antioch. [23]After spending
some time there he departed and went
from place to place through the region
of Galatia and Phryg'ia, strengthening all
the disciples.

[24]Now a Jew named Apol'los, a native of
Alexandria, came to Ephesus. He was an
eloquent man, well versed in the Scriptures.
[25]He had been instructed in the way of the
Lord; and being fervent in spirit, he spoke
and taught accurately the things concerning
Jesus, though he knew only the baptism
of John. [26]He began to speak boldly in the
synagogue; but when Priscilla and Aqui'la
heard him, they took him and expounded to
him the way of God more accurately. [27]And
when he wished to cross to Acha'ia, the
brethren encouraged him, and wrote to the
disciples to receive him. When he arrived,
he greatly helped those who through grace
had believed, [28]for he powerfully confuted
the Jews in public, showing by the Scriptures
that the Christ was Jesus.

19 While Apol'los was at Corinth, Paul
passed through the upper country
and came to Ephesus. There he found some

disciples. [2]And he said to them, "Did you
receive the Holy Spirit when you believed?"
And they said, "No, we have never even
heard that there is a Holy Spirit." [3]And he
said, "Into what then were you baptized?"
They said, "Into John's baptism." [4]And Paul
said, "John baptized with the baptism of
repentance, telling the people to believe in
the one who was to come after him, that is,
Jesus." [5]On hearing this, they were baptized
in the name of the Lord Jesus. [6]And when
Paul had laid his hands upon them, the Holy
Spirit came on them; and they spoke with
tongues and prophesied. [7]There were about
twelve of them in all.
[8]And he entered the synagogue and for
three months spoke boldly, arguing and
pleading about the kingdom of God; [9]but
when some were stubborn and disbelieved,
speaking evil of the Way before the congregation, he withdrew from them, taking the
disciples with him, and argued daily in the
hall of Tyran′nus. [10]This continued for two
years, so that all the residents of Asia heard
the word of the Lord, both Jews and Greeks.

REFLECTION

The Bible's recounting of Israel's history skips from the end of 2 Chronicles, which narrates the downfall of Jerusalem, to the beginning of Ezra, which sets forth the return of the exiled Jews. In between these two events, the Babylonians exile the leading Jews to Babylon. Then the Persian king, Cyrus, conquers the Babylonian empire and incorporates it into his own kingdom. While the Babylonians had a repressive policy of conquest, capture, and exile, the Persians take a more peaceful approach and allow the Jews to return to their homeland to worship their own God. Cyrus even partially finances the reconstruction of the Temple and returns Temple items that had been stolen by the Babylonians. His humility exemplifies the proverb that "wisdom builds her house" (Prv 14:1). In a similar vein, the early evangelist Apollos exhibits profound humility when, after preaching publicly about Jesus, he allows his theology to be corrected by the more knowledgeable Christians, Priscilla and Aquila. Some of the believers who he evangelized had only received John's baptism, and they are corrected by Paul. After this, they receive full Christian Baptism and the power of the Spirit. Are you humble enough to receive correction when it is given?

July 19

EZRA 3

**When the seventh month came,
and the sons of Israel were in
the towns, the people gathered
as one man to Jerusalem. [2]Then arose
Jesh′ua the son of Jo′zadak, with his
fellow priests, and Zerub′babel the son**
of She-al′ti-el with his kinsmen, and they
built the altar of the God of Israel, to offer
burnt offerings upon it, as it is written in
the law of Moses the man of God. [3]They set
the altar in its place, for fear was upon them
because of the peoples of the lands, and they
offered burnt offerings upon it to the LORD,
burnt offerings morning and evening. [4]And
they kept the feast of booths, as it is written,
and offered the daily burnt offerings by
number according to the ordinance, as each
day required, [5]and after that the continual
burnt offerings, the offerings at the new
moon and at all the appointed feasts of the
LORD, and the offerings of every one who
made a freewill offering to the LORD. [6]From
the first day of the seventh month they began
to offer burnt offerings to the LORD. But
the foundation of the temple of the LORD
was not yet laid. [7]So they gave money to the
masons and the carpenters, and food, drink,
and oil to the Sido′nians and the Tyr′ians to
bring cedar trees from Lebanon to the sea, to

Joppa, according to the grant which they had from Cyrus king of Persia.

8Now in the second year of their coming to the house of God at Jerusalem, in the second month, Zerub´babel the son of She-al´ti-el and Jesh´ua the son of Jo´zadak made a beginning, together with the rest of their brethren, the priests and the Levites and all who had come to Jerusalem from the captivity. They appointed the Levites, from twenty years old and upward, to have the oversight of the work of the house of the LORD. 9And Jesh´ua with his sons and his kinsmen, and Kad´mi-el and his sons, the sons of Judah, together took the oversight of the workmen in the house of God, along with the sons of Hen´adad and the Levites, their sons and kinsmen.

10And when the builders laid the foundation of the temple of the LORD, the priests in their vestments came forward with trumpets, and the Levites, the sons of A´saph, with cymbals, to praise the LORD, according to the directions of David king of Israel; 11and they sang responsively, praising and giving thanks to the LORD,

"For he is good,
for his mercy endures for ever toward Israel."

And all the people shouted with a great shout, when they praised the LORD, because the foundation of the house of the LORD was laid. 12But many of the priests and Levites and heads of fathers' houses, old men who had seen the first house, wept with a loud voice when they saw the foundation of this house being laid, though many shouted aloud for joy; 13so that the people could not distinguish the sound of the joyful shout from the sound of the people's weeping, for the people shouted with a great shout, and the sound was heard afar.

4 Now when the adversaries of Judah and Benjamin heard that the returned exiles were building a temple to the LORD, the God of Israel, 2they approached Zerub´babel and the heads of fathers' houses and said to them, "Let us build with you; for we worship your God as you do, and we have been sacrificing to him ever since the days of E´sar-had´don king of Assyria who brought us here." 3But Zerub´babel, Jesh´ua, and the rest of the heads of fathers' houses in Israel said to them, "You have nothing to do with us in building a house to our God; but we alone will build to the LORD, the God of Israel, as King Cyrus the king of Persia has commanded us."

4Then the people of the land discouraged the people of Judah, and made them afraid to build, 5and hired counselors against them to frustrate their purpose, all the days of Cyrus king of Persia, even until the reign of Dari´us king of Persia.

6And in the reign of Ahas´u-e´rus, in the beginning of his reign, they wrote an accusation against the inhabitants of Judah and Jerusalem.

7And in the days of Ar-ta-xerx´es, Bishlam and Mith´redath and Ta´be-el and the rest of their associates wrote to Ar-ta-xerxes king of Persia; the letter was written in Arama´ic and translated. 8Re´hum the commander and Shimshai the scribe wrote a letter against Jerusalem to Ar-ta-xerx´es the king as follows—9then wrote Re´hum the commander, Shimshai the scribe, and the rest of their associates, the judges, the governors, the officials, the Persians, the men of E´rech, the Babylonians, the men of Susa, that is, the E´lamites, 10and the rest of the nations whom the great and noble Osnap´par deported and settled in the cities of Samar´ia and in the rest of the province Beyond the River, and now 11this is a copy of the letter that they sent—"To Ar-ta-xerx´es the king: Your servants, the men of the province Beyond the River, send greeting. And now 12be it known to the king that the Jews who came up from you to us have gone to Jerusalem. They are rebuilding that rebellious and wicked city; they are finishing the walls and repairing the foundations. 13Now be it known to the king that, if this city is rebuilt and the walls finished, they will not pay tribute, custom, or toll, and the royal revenue will be impaired. 14Now because we eat the salt of the palace and it is not fitting for us to witness the king's dishonor, therefore we send and inform the king, 15in order that search may be made in the book of the records of your fathers. You will find in the book of the records and learn

that this city is a rebellious city, hurtful to kings
and provinces, and that sedition was stirred up
in it from of old. That was why this city was
laid waste. 16 We make known to the king that,
if this city is rebuilt and its walls finished, you
will then have no possession in the province
Beyond the River."
17 The king sent an answer: "To Re'hum the
commander and Shimshai the scribe and the
rest of their associates who live in Samar'ia
and in the rest of the province Beyond the
River, greeting. And now 18 the letter which
you sent to us has been plainly read before
me. 19 And I made a decree, and search has
been made, and it has been found that this
city from of old has risen against kings,
and that rebellion and sedition have been
made in it. 20 And mighty kings have been
over Jerusalem, who ruled over the whole
province Beyond the River, to whom tribute,
custom, and toll were paid. 21 Therefore make
a decree that these men be made to cease,
and that this city be not rebuilt, until a decree
is made by me. 22 And take care not to be slack
in this matter; why should damage grow to
the hurt of the king?"
23 Then, when the copy of King Ar-ta-xerx'es'
letter was read before Re'hum and Shimshai
the scribe and their associates, they went in
haste to the Jews at Jerusalem and by force
and power made them cease. 24 Then the work
on the house of God which is in Jerusalem
stopped; and it ceased until the second year of
the reign of Dari'us king of Persia.

PROVERBS 14

18 The simple acquire folly,
but the prudent are crowned
with knowledge.
19 The evil bow down before the good,
the wicked at the gates of the righteous.
20 The poor is disliked even by his neighbor,
but the rich has many friends.
21 He who despises his neighbor is a sinner,
but happy is he who is kind to the poor.
22 Do they not err that devise evil?
Those who devise good meet loyalty
and faithfulness.
23 In all toil there is profit,
but mere talk tends only to want.
24 The crown of the wise is their wisdom,
but folly is the garland of fools.
25 A truthful witness saves lives,
but one who utters lies is a betrayer.
26 In the fear of the LORD one has
strong confidence,
and his children will have a refuge.
27 The fear of the LORD is a fountain of life,
that one may avoid the snares of death.
28 In a multitude of people is the glory of a king,
but without people a prince is ruined.
29 He who is slow to anger has
great understanding,
but he who has a hasty temper exalts folly.
30 A tranquil mind gives life to the flesh,
but passion makes the bones rot.
31 He who oppresses a poor man insults
his Maker,
but he who is kind to the needy honors him.
32 The wicked is overthrown through his
evil-doing,
but the righteous finds refuge through
his integrity.
33 Wisdom abides in the mind of a man
of understanding,
but it is not known in the heart of fools.
34 Righteousness exalts a nation,
but sin is a reproach to any people.
35 A servant who deals wisely has the
king's favor,
but his wrath falls on one who
acts shamefully.

ACTS 19

**11 And God did extraordinary
miracles by the hands of Paul,**
**12 so that handkerchiefs or aprons were
carried away from his body to the sick,**
and diseases left them and the evil spirits
came out of them. 13 Then some of the
itinerant Jewish exorcists undertook to
pronounce the name of the Lord Jesus
over those who had evil spirits, saying,
"I adjure you by the Jesus whom Paul
preaches." 14 Seven sons of a Jewish high

priest named Sceva were doing this. 15But the evil spirit answered them, "Jesus I know, and Paul I know; but who are you?" 16And the man in whom the evil spirit was leaped on them, mastered all of them, and overpowered them, so that they fled out of that house naked and wounded. 17And this became known to all residents of Ephesus, both Jews and Greeks; and fear fell upon them all; and the name of the Lord Jesus was extolled. 18Many also of those who were now believers came, confessing and divulging their practices. 19And a number of those who practiced magic arts brought their books together and burned them in the sight of all; and they counted the value of them and found it came to fifty thousand pieces of silver. 20So the word of the Lord grew and prevailed mightily.

21Now after these events Paul resolved in the Spirit to pass through Macedonia and Acha′ia and go to Jerusalem, saying, "After I have been there, I must also see Rome." 22And having sent into Macedonia two of his helpers, Timothy and Eras′tus, he himself stayed in Asia for a while.

23About that time there arose no little stir concerning the Way. 24For a man named Deme′trius, a silversmith, who made silver shrines of Ar′temis, brought no little business to the craftsmen. 25These he gathered together, with the workmen of like occupation, and said, "Men, you know that from this business we have our wealth. 26And you see and hear that not only at Ephesus but almost throughout all Asia this Paul has persuaded and turned away a considerable company of people, saying that gods made with hands are not gods. 27And there is danger not only that this trade of ours may come into disrepute but also that the temple of the great goddess Ar′temis may count for nothing, and that she may even be deposed from her magnificence, she whom all Asia and the world worship."

28When they heard this they were enraged, and cried out, "Great is Ar′temis of the Ephesians!" 29So the city was filled with the confusion; and they rushed together into the theater, dragging with them Ga′ius and Aristar′chus, Macedonians who were Paul's companions in travel. 30Paul wished to go in among the crowd, but the disciples would not let him; 31some of the A′si-archs also, who were friends of his, sent to him and begged him not to venture into the theater. 32Now some cried one thing, some another; for the assembly was in confusion, and most of them did not know why they had come together. 33Some of the crowd prompted Alexander, whom the Jews had put forward. And Alexander motioned with his hand, wishing to make a defense to the people. 34But when they recognized that he was a Jew, for about two hours they all with one voice cried out, "Great is Ar′temis of the Ephesians!" 35And when the town clerk had quieted the crowd, he said, "Men of Ephesus, what man is there who does not know that the city of the Ephesians is temple keeper of the great Ar′temis, and of the sacred stone that fell from the sky? 36Seeing then that these things cannot be contradicted, you ought to be quiet and do nothing rash. 37For you have brought these men here who are neither sacrilegious nor blasphemers of our goddess. 38If therefore Deme′trius and the craftsmen with him have a complaint against any one, the courts are open, and there are proconsuls; let them bring charges against one another. 39But if you seek anything further, it shall be settled in the regular assembly. 40For we are in danger of being charged with rioting today, there being no cause that we can give to justify this commotion." 41And when he had said this, he dismissed the assembly.

REFLECTION

Protecting our self-interest is important, but we must be careful not to end up opposing God. In today's readings, we find plenty of people worried about money, their personal profits, and how they might be impacted by people's devotion to God. Once the Jews begin rebuilding the Temple after the exile, the surrounding nations write a warning letter to the Persian king that the Jews "will not pay tribute, custom, or toll, and the royal revenue will be impaired" (Ezr 4:13). They appeal to the king's greed, and he halts the

Temple construction project. In Ephesus, St. Paul's evangelistic efforts are so successful that the silversmiths who make souvenir copies of the idol of Artemis in their city throw a riot to protect their profits: "Men, you know that from this business we have our wealth" (Acts 19:25). Making money is an important part of life: "In all toil there is profit, but mere talk tends only to want" (Prv 14:23). Yet we need to make sure we have our priorities straight and that our money-making activities are honest and not put ahead of the Lord and his will for our lives. Sometimes we might even have to forego a profitable opportunity in order to remain faithful to the Lord. Are your work, business, and investments in harmony with the Gospel?

July 20

EZRA 5

Now the prophets, Hag′gai and Zechari′ah the son of Iddo, prophesied to the Jews who were in Judah and Jerusalem, in the name of the God of Israel who was over them. 2Then Zerub′babel the son of She-al′ti-el and Jesh′ua the son of Jo′za-dak arose and began to rebuild the house of God which is in Jerusalem; and with them were the prophets of God, helping them.

3At the same time Tat′tenai the governor of the province Beyond the River and She′thar-boz′enai and their associates came to them and spoke to them thus, "Who gave you a decree to build this house and to finish this structure?" 4They also asked them this, "What are the names of the men who are building this building?" 5But the eye of their God was upon the elders of the Jews, and they did not stop them till a report should reach Dari′us and then answer be returned by letter concerning it.

6The copy of the letter which Tat′tenai the governor of the province Beyond the River and She′thar-boz′enai and his associates the governors who were in the province Beyond the River sent to Dari′us the king; 7they sent him a report, in which was written as follows: "To Dari′us the king, all peace. 8Be it known to the king that we went to the province of Judah, to the house of the great God. It is being built with huge stones, and timber is laid in the walls; this work goes on diligently and prospers in their hands. 9Then we asked those elders and spoke to them thus, 'Who gave you a decree to build this house and to finish this structure?' 10We also asked them their names, for your information, that we might write down the names of the men at their head. 11And this was their reply to us: 'We are the servants of the God of heaven and earth, and we are rebuilding the house that was built many years ago, which a great king of Israel built and finished. 12But because our fathers had angered the God of heaven, he gave them into the hand of Nebuchadnez′zar king of Babylon, the Chalde′an, who destroyed this house and carried away the people to Babylonia. 13However in the first year of Cyrus king of Babylon, Cyrus the king made a decree that this house of God should be rebuilt. 14And the gold and silver vessels of the house of God, which Nebuchadnez′zar had taken out of the temple that was in Jerusalem and brought into the temple of Babylon, these Cyrus the king took out of the temple of Babylon, and they were delivered to one whose name was Shesh-baz′zar, whom he had made governor; 15and he said to him, "Take these vessels, go and put them in the temple which is in Jerusalem, and let the house of God be rebuilt on its site." 16Then this Shesh-baz′zar came and laid the foundations of the house of God which is in Jerusalem; and from that time until now it has been in building, and it is not yet finished.' 17Therefore, if it seem good to the king, let search be made in the royal archives there in Babylon, to see whether a decree was issued by Cyrus the king for

the rebuilding of this house of God in
Jerusalem. And let the king send us his
pleasure in this matter."

6 Then Dari´us the king made a decree,
and search was made in Babylonia,
in the house of the archives where the
documents were stored. 2And in Ecbat´ana,
the capital which is in the province of
Med´ia, a scroll was found on which this
was written: "A record. 3In the first year
of Cyrus the king, Cyrus the king issued
a decree: Concerning the house of God
at Jerusalem, let the house be rebuilt, the
place where sacrifices are offered and
burnt offerings are brought; its height shall
be sixty cubits and its breadth sixty cubits,
4with three courses of great stones and one
course of timber; let the cost be paid from
the royal treasury. 5And also let the gold
and silver vessels of the house of God,
which Nebuchadnez´zar took out of the
temple that is in Jerusalem and brought to
Babylon, be restored and brought back to
the temple which is in Jerusalem, each to
its place; you shall put them in the house
of God.

6"Now therefore, Tat´tenai, governor
of the province Beyond the River,
She´thar-boz´enai, and your associates the
governors who are in the province Beyond
the River, keep away; 7let the work on this
house of God alone; let the governor of
the Jews and the elders of the Jews rebuild
this house of God on its site. 8Moreover
I make a decree regarding what you shall
do for these elders of the Jews for the
rebuilding of this house of God; the cost is
to be paid to these men in full and without
delay from the royal revenue, the tribute
of the province from Beyond the River.
9And whatever is needed—young bulls,
rams, or sheep for burnt offerings to the
God of heaven, wheat, salt, wine, or oil, as
the priests at Jerusalem require—let that
be given to them day by day without fail,
10that they may offer pleasing sacrifices to
the God of heaven, and pray for the life
of the king and his sons. 11Also I make a
decree that if any one alters this edict, a
beam shall be pulled out of his house, and
he shall be impaled upon it, and his house
shall be made a dunghill. 12May the God
who has caused his name to dwell there
overthrow any king or people that shall
put forth a hand to alter this, or to destroy
this house of God which is in Jerusalem. I
Dari´us make a decree; let it be done with
all diligence."

13Then, according to the word sent by
Dari´us the king, Tat´tenai, the governor
of the province Beyond the River,
She´thar-boz´enai, and their associates
did with all diligence what Darius the
king had ordered. 14And the elders of the
Jews built and prospered, through the
prophesying of Hag´gai the prophet and
Zechari´ah the son of Iddo. They finished
their building by command of the God of
Israel and by decree of Cyrus and Dari´us
and Ar-ta-xerx´es king of Persia; 15and
this house was finished on the third day
of the month of Adar´, in the sixth year of
the reign of Dari´us the king.

16And the sons of Israel, the priests and
the Levites, and the rest of the returned
exiles, celebrated the dedication of this
house of God with joy. 17They offered at
the dedication of this house of God one
hundred bulls, two hundred rams, four
hundred lambs, and as a sin offering for
all Israel twelve he-goats, according to the
number of the tribes of Israel. 18And they
set the priests in their divisions and the
Levites in their courses, for the service of
God at Jerusalem, as it is written in the
book of Moses.

19On the fourteenth day of the first
month the returned exiles kept the
Passover. 20For the priests and the Levites
had purified themselves together; all
of them were clean. So they killed the
Passover lamb for all the returned
exiles, for their fellow priests, and for
themselves; 21it was eaten by the sons of
Israel who had returned from exile, and
also by every one who had joined them
and separated himself from the pollutions
of the peoples of the land to worship the
LORD, the God of Israel. 22And they kept
the feast of unleavened bread seven days

with joy; for the LORD had made them joyful, and had turned the heart of the king of Assyria to them, so that he aided them in the work of the house of God, the God of Israel.

PROVERBS 15

A soft answer turns away wrath,
but a harsh word stirs up anger.
2The tongue of the wise dispenses knowledge,
but the mouths of fools pour out folly.
3The eyes of the LORD are in every place,
keeping watch on the evil and the good.
4A gentle tongue is a tree of life,
but perverseness in it breaks the spirit.
5A fool despises his father's instruction,
but he who heeds admonition is prudent.
6In the house of the righteous there is
much treasure,
but trouble befalls the income of the wicked.
7The lips of the wise spread knowledge;
not so the minds of fools.
8The sacrifice of the wicked is an
abomination to the LORD,
but the prayer of the upright is his delight.
9The way of the wicked is an abomination
to the LORD,
but he loves him who pursues
righteousness.
10There is severe discipline for him who
forsakes the way;
he who hates reproof will die.
11Sheol and Abad′don lie open before
the LORD,
how much more the hearts of men!
12A scoffer does not like to be reproved;
he will not go to the wise.
13A glad heart makes a cheerful countenance,
but by sorrow of heart the spirit is broken.
14The mind of him who has understanding
seeks knowledge,
but the mouths of fools feed on folly.
15All the days of the afflicted are evil,
but a cheerful heart has a continual feast.
16Better is a little with the fear of the LORD
than great treasure and trouble with it.
17Better is a dinner of herbs where love is
than a fatted ox and hatred with it.
18A hot-tempered man stirs up strife,
but he who is slow to anger
quiets contention.
19The way of a sluggard is overgrown
with thorns,
but the path of the upright is
a level highway.
20A wise son makes a glad father,
but a foolish man despises his mother.
21Folly is a joy to him who has no sense,
but a man of understanding walks aright.

ACTS 20

After the uproar ceased, Paul sent for the disciples and having exhorted them took leave of them and departed for Macedonia. 2When he had
gone through these parts and had given
them much encouragement, he came to
Greece. 3There he spent three months,
and when a plot was made against him by the Jews as he was about to set sail for Syria, he determined to return through
Macedonia. 4Sop′ater of Beroe′a, the son of Pyrrhus, accompanied him; and of the Thessalo′nians, Aristar′chus and Secun′dus; and Ga′ius of Derbe, and Timothy; and the
Asians, Tych′icus and Troph′imus. 5These
went on and were waiting for us at Troas,
6but we sailed away from Philip′pi after the days of Unleavened Bread, and in five days we came to them at Troas, where we stayed for seven days.
7On the first day of the week, when we
were gathered together to break bread, Paul talked with them, intending to depart on the next day; and he prolonged
his speech until midnight. 8There were
many lights in the upper chamber
where we were gathered. 9And a young
man named Eu′tychus was sitting in the window. He sank into a deep sleep as Paul talked still longer; and being overcome by sleep, he fell down from the third story
and was taken up dead. 10But Paul went
down and bent over him, and embracing him said, "Do not be alarmed, for his life

is in him." [11]And when Paul had gone
up and had broken bread and eaten, he
conversed with them a long while, until
daybreak, and so departed. [12]And they
took the lad away alive, and were not a
little comforted.
[13]But going ahead to the ship, we set sail
for Assos, intending to take Paul aboard
there; for so he had arranged, intending
himself to go by land. [14]And when he met us
at Assos, we took him on board and came
to Mityle′ne. [15]And sailing from there we
came the following day opposite Chi′os; the
next day we touched at Sa′mos; and the day
after that we came to Mile′tus. [16]For Paul
had decided to sail past Ephesus, so that
he might not have to spend time in Asia;
for he was hastening to be at Jerusalem, if
possible, on the day of Pentecost.

REFLECTION

Faith takes courage. The sad exiles who had finally returned to Jerusalem and then had their Temple-building project stopped by the authorities must have been discouraged. The project had been halted for about ten years, but the Lord stirs his people into action through the prophecies of Haggai and Zechariah. The Jews finally begin to work again on the Temple and yet are opposed by a local governor. With great bravery they respond, "We are the servants of the God of heaven and earth" (Ezr 5:11). We could use that sort of courage in faith whenever we take a risk for the Lord. Every time we confront temptation, we should keep these words in mind. Like Haggai and Zechariah, St. Paul encourages the believers with his preaching. Yet he speaks so long and so late into the night that one of his listeners falls out of a window to his death! Even so, Paul undauntedly prays for the man and keeps on preaching till daybreak, when the dead man rises to life (see Acts 20:9–12). Whether we think of Paul's bold faith to pray for a resurrection or the Jews' bravery in rebuilding the Temple, we should call these examples to mind when our faith needs encouragement. Is your faith timid or courageous?

July 21

EZRA 7

**Now after this, in the reign of
Ar-ta-xerx′es king of Persia,
Ezra the son of Serai′ah, son of
Azari′ah, son of Hilki′ah, [2]son of Shallum, son of Za′dok, son of Ahi′tub,
[3]son of Amari′ah, son of Azari′ah,**
son of Mera′ioth, [4]son of Zerahi′ah, son of
Uzzi, son of Bukki, [5]son of Abishu′a, son
of Phin′ehas, son of Elea′zar, son of Aaron
the chief priest—[6]this Ezra went up from
Babylonia. He was a scribe skilled in the
law of Moses which the LORD the God of
Israel had given; and the king granted him
all that he asked, for the hand of the LORD
his God was upon him.
[7]And there went up also to Jerusalem, in the
seventh year of Ar-ta-xerx′es the king, some
of the sons of Israel, and some of the priests
and Levites, the singers and gatekeepers,
and the temple servants. [8]And he came to
Jerusalem in the fifth month, which was
in the seventh year of the king; [9]for on the
first day of the first month he began to go
up from Babylonia, and on the first day of
the fifth month he came to Jerusalem, for the
good hand of his God was upon him. [10]For
Ezra had set his heart to study the law of the
LORD, and to do it, and to teach his statutes
and ordinances in Israel.
[11]This is a copy of the letter which King Ar-
ta-xerx′es gave to Ezra the priest, the scribe,
learned in matters of the commandments of
the LORD and his statutes for Israel: [12]"Ar-
ta-xerx′es, king of kings, to Ezra the priest,
the scribe of the law of the God of heaven.
And now [13]I make a decree that any one of
the sons of Israel or their priests or Levites
in my kingdom, who freely offers to go to
Jerusalem, may go with you. [14]For you are
sent by the king and his seven counselors to
make inquiries about Judah and Jerusalem
according to the law of your God, which is
in your hand, [15]and also to convey the silver

and gold which the king and his counselors
have freely offered to the God of Israel,
whose dwelling is in Jerusalem, 16with all
the silver and gold which you shall find in
the whole province of Babylonia, and with
the freewill offerings of the people and the
priests, vowed willingly for the house of
their God which is in Jerusalem. 17With this
money, then, you shall with all diligence
buy bulls, rams, and lambs, with their cereal
offerings and their drink offerings, and
you shall offer them upon the altar of the
house of your God which is in Jerusalem.
18Whatever seems good to you and your
brethren to do with the rest of the silver and
gold, you may do, according to the will of
your God. 19The vessels that have been given
you for the service of the house of your
God, you shall deliver before the God of
Jerusalem. 20And whatever else is required
for the house of your God, which you have
occasion to provide, you may provide it out
of the king's treasury.

21"And I, Ar-ta-xerx′es the king, make a
decree to all the treasurers in the province
Beyond the River: Whatever Ezra the
priest, the scribe of the law of the God of
heaven, requires of you, be it done with all
diligence, 22up to a hundred talents of silver,
a hundred cors of wheat, a hundred baths
of wine, a hundred baths of oil, and salt
without prescribing how much. 23Whatever
is commanded by the God of heaven, let it
be done in full for the house of the God of
heaven, lest his wrath be against the realm of
the king and his sons. 24We also notify you
that it shall not be lawful to impose tribute,
custom, or toll upon any one of the priests,
the Levites, the singers, the doorkeepers, the
temple servants, or other servants of this
house of God.

25"And you, Ezra, according to the wisdom
of your God which is in your hand, appoint
magistrates and judges who may judge all
the people in the province Beyond the River,
all such as know the laws of your God; and
those who do not know them, you shall teach.
26Whoever will not obey the law of your
God and the law of the king, let judgment
be strictly executed upon him, whether for
death or for banishment or for confiscation
of his goods or for imprisonment."

27Blessed be the LORD, the God of our
fathers, who put such a thing as this into the
heart of the king, to beautify the house of
the LORD which is in Jerusalem, 28and who
extended to me his merciful love before the
king and his counselors, and before all the
king's mighty officers. I took courage, for
the hand of the LORD my God was upon me,
and I gathered leading men from Israel to
go up with me.

8 These are the heads of their fathers'
houses, and this is the genealogy of those
who went up with me from Babylonia, in the
reign of Ar-ta-xerx′es the king: 2Of the sons of
Phin′ehas, Gershom. Of the sons of Ith′amar,
Daniel. Of the sons of David, Hattush, 3of the
sons of Shecani′ah. Of the sons of Pa′rosh,
Zechari′ah, with whom were registered one
hundred and fifty men. 4Of the sons of Pa′hath-
mo′ab, El′ie-ho-e′nai the son of Zerahi′ah, and
with him two hundred men. 5Of the sons of
Zattu, Shecani′ah the son of Jaha′ziel, and with
him three hundred men. 6Of the sons of A′din,
E′bed the son of Jonathan, and with him fifty
men. 7Of the sons of E′lam, Jeshai′ah the son
of Athali′ah, and with him seventy men. 8Of
the sons of Shephati′ah, Zebadi′ah the son of
Michael, and with him eighty men. 9Of the
sons of Jo′ab, Obadi′ah the son of Jehi′el, and
with him two hundred and eighteen men.
10Of the sons of Ba′ni, Shelo′mith the son of
Josiphi′ah, and with him a hundred and sixty
men. 11Of the sons of Bebai, Zechari′ah, the
son of Bebai, and with him twenty-eight men.
12Of the sons of Azgad, Joha′nan the son of
Hak′katan, and with him a hundred and ten
men. 13Of the sons of Adoni′kam, those who
came later, their names being Eliph′elet, Jeu′el,
and Shemai′ah, and with them sixty men. 14Of
the sons of Bigvai, Uthai and Zaccur, and with
them seventy men.

15I gathered them to the river that runs to
Aha′va, and there we encamped three days.
As I reviewed the people and the priests, I
found there none of the sons of Levi. 16Then I
sent for Elie′zer, Ar′iel, Shemai′ah, Elna′than,
Jarib, Elnathan, Nathan, Zechari′ah, and
Meshul′lam, leading men, and for Joi′arib and

Elnathan, who were men of insight, 17and sent
them to Iddo, the leading man at the place
Casiphi′a, telling them what to say to Iddo
and his brethren the temple servants at the
place Casiphia, namely, to send us ministers
for the house of our God. 18And by the good
hand of our God upon us, they brought us a
man of discretion, of the sons of Mah′li the
son of Levi, son of Israel, namely, Sherebi′ah
with his sons and kinsmen, eighteen; 19also
Hashabi′ah and with him Jeshai′ah of the
sons of Merar′i, with his kinsmen and their
sons, twenty; 20besides two hundred and
twenty of the temple servants, whom David
and his officials had set apart to attend the
Levites. These were all mentioned by name.

21Then I proclaimed a fast there, at the river
Aha′va, that we might humble ourselves
before our God, to seek from him a straight
way for ourselves, our children, and all our
goods. 22For I was ashamed to ask the king for
a band of soldiers and horsemen to protect
us against the enemy on our way; since we
had told the king, "The hand of our God
is for good upon all that seek him, and the
power of his wrath is against all that forsake
him." 23So we fasted and besought our God
for this, and he listened to our entreaty.

24Then I set apart twelve of the leading
priests: Sherebi′ah, Hashabi′ah, and ten of
their kinsmen with them. 25And I weighed out
to them the silver and the gold and the vessels,
the offering for the house of our God which
the king and his counselors and his lords
and all Israel there present had offered; 26I
weighed out into their hand six hundred and
fifty talents of silver, and silver vessels worth
a hundred talents, and a hundred talents of
gold, 27twenty bowls of gold worth a thousand
darics, and two vessels of fine bright bronze
as precious as gold. 28And I said to them,
"You are holy to the LORD, and the vessels are
holy; and the silver and the gold are a freewill
offering to the LORD, the God of your fathers.
29Guard them and keep them until you weigh
them before the chief priests and the Levites
and the heads of fathers' houses in Israel at
Jerusalem, within the chambers of the house
of the LORD." 30So the priests and the Levites
took over the weight of the silver and the gold
and the vessels, to bring them to Jerusalem, to
the house of our God.

31Then we departed from the river Aha′va
on the twelfth day of the first month, to go
to Jerusalem; the hand of our God was upon
us, and he delivered us from the hand of the
enemy and from ambushes by the way. 32We
came to Jerusalem, and there we remained
three days. 33On the fourth day, within the
house of our God, the silver and the gold and
the vessels were weighed into the hands of
Mer′emoth the priest, son of Uri′ah, and with
him was Elea′zar the son of Phin′ehas, and
with them were the Levites, Joz′abad the son
of Jesh′ua and No-adi′ah the son of Bin′nui.
34The whole was counted and weighed, and
the weight of everything was recorded.

35At that time those who had come from
captivity, the returned exiles, offered burnt
offerings to the God of Israel, twelve bulls
for all Israel, ninety-six rams, seventy-seven
lambs, and as a sin offering twelve he-goats;
all this was a burnt offering to the LORD.
36They also delivered the king's commissions
to the king's satraps and to the governors of
the province Beyond the River; and they
aided the people and the house of God.

PROVERBS 15

22Without counsel plans go wrong,
but with many advisers they succeed.
23To make an apt answer is a joy to a man,
and a word in season, how good it is!
24The wise man's path leads upward to life,
that he may avoid Sheol beneath.
25The LORD tears down the house
of the proud,
but maintains the widow's boundaries.
26The thoughts of the wicked are an
abomination to the LORD,
the words of the pure are pleasing to him.
27He who is greedy for unjust gain makes
trouble for his household,
but he who hates bribes will live.
28The mind of the righteous ponders how
to answer,
but the mouth of the wicked pours out
evil things.

29The LORD is far from the wicked,
but he hears the prayer of the righteous.
30The light of the eyes rejoices the heart,
and good news refreshes the bones.
31He whose ear heeds wholesome admonition
will abide among the wise.
32He who ignores instruction
despises himself,
but he who heeds admonition
gains understanding.
33The fear of the LORD is instruction
in wisdom,
and humility goes before honor.

ACTS 20

17And from Mile´tus he sent to Ephesus and called to him the elders of the Church. 18And when they came to him, he said to them:
"You yourselves know how I lived among
you all the time from the first day that I
set foot in Asia, 19serving the Lord with
all humility and with tears and with trials
which befell me through the plots of the
Jews; 20how I did not shrink from declaring
to you anything that was profitable, and
teaching you in public and from house
to house, 21testifying both to Jews and to
Greeks of repentance to God and of faith in
our Lord Jesus Christ. 22And now, behold,
I am going to Jerusalem, bound in the
Spirit, not knowing what shall befall me
there; 23except that the Holy Spirit testifies
to me in every city that imprisonment and
afflictions await me. 24But I do not account
my life of any value nor as precious to
myself, if only I may accomplish my course
and the ministry which I received from the
Lord Jesus, to testify to the gospel of the
grace of God. 25And now, behold, I know
that all you among whom I have gone about
preaching the kingdom will see my face no
more. 26Therefore I testify to you this day
that I am innocent of the blood of all of
you, 27for I did not shrink from declaring to
you the whole counsel of God. 28Take heed
to yourselves and to all the flock, in which
the Holy Spirit has made you guardians,
to feed the Church of the Lord which he
obtained with his own blood. 29I know that
after my departure fierce wolves will come
in among you, not sparing the flock; 30and
from among your own selves will arise men
speaking perverse things, to draw away the
disciples after them. 31Therefore be alert,
remembering that for three years I did not
cease night or day to admonish every one
with tears. 32And now I commend you to
God and to the word of his grace, which
is able to build you up and to give you
the inheritance among all those who are
sanctified. 33I coveted no one's silver or gold
or apparel. 34You yourselves know that these
hands ministered to my necessities, and to
those who were with me. 35In all things I
have shown you that by so toiling one must
help the weak, remembering the words
of the Lord Jesus, how he said, 'It is more
blessed to give than to receive.' "
36And when he had spoken thus, he knelt
down and prayed with them all. 37And they
all wept and embraced Paul and kissed him,
38sorrowing most of all because of the word
he had spoken, that they should see his face
no more. And they brought him to the ship.

REFLECTION

Today's readings give us the testimonies of two great men of God: Ezra and Paul. Both embody the proverb that "the fear of the LORD is instruction in wisdom, and humility goes before honor" (Prv 15:33). Ezra is born in exile to a priestly family, and he "had set his heart to study the law of the LORD, and to do it, and to teach his statutes and ordinances in Israel" (Ezr 7:10). Now he leads a group of exiles back to Jerusalem about fifty years after the reconstruction of the Temple. His life of prayerful study leads him to zealous action for the Lord, recruiting priests, proclaiming a fast, and organizing the renewal of Temple worship. St. Paul, here, gives his last major speech to Christian elders. In this speech, he does little teaching but mainly testifies about God's work in his apostolic ministry and how he surrendered himself to the Lord's plan: "But I do not account my life of any value nor as precious to myself, if only I may accomplish my course and the ministry" (Acts 20:24). Both Ezra and Paul give us an example of Christlike self-sacrifice for the sake of the kingdom, and their lives call us to do as they have done. How can you give your life for the Kingdom of God today?

July 22

EZRA 9

After these things had been done, the officials approached me and said, "The sons of Israel and the priests and the Levites have not separated themselves from the peoples of the lands with their abominations, from the Canaanites, the Hittites, the Per′izzites, the Jeb′usites, the Am′monites, the Moabites, the Egyptians, and the
Am′orites. 2For they have taken some of
their daughters to be wives for themselves and for their sons; so that the holy race has mixed itself with the peoples of the lands. And in this faithlessness the hand of the officials and chief men has been foremost."
3When I heard this, I tore my garments and
my mantle, and pulled hair from my head
and beard, and sat appalled. 4Then all who
trembled at the words of the God of Israel, because of the faithlessness of the returned exiles, gathered round me while I sat appalled until the evening sacrifice. 5And at
the evening sacrifice I rose from my fasting, with my garments and my mantle torn, and fell upon my knees and spread out my hands
to the LORD my God, 6saying:

"O my God, I am ashamed and blush to lift my face to you, my God, for our iniquities have risen higher than our heads, and our
guilt has mounted up to the heavens. 7From
the days of our fathers to this day we have been in great guilt; and for our iniquities we, our kings, and our priests have been given into the hand of the kings of the lands, to the sword, to captivity, to plundering, and
to utter shame, as at this day. 8But now for
a brief moment favor has been shown by the LORD our God, to leave us a remnant, and to give us a secure hold within his holy place, that our God may brighten our eyes and grant us a little reviving in our bondage.
9For we are bondmen; yet our God has
not forsaken us in our bondage, but has extended to us his mercy before the kings of Persia, to grant us some reviving to set up the house of our God, to repair its ruins, and to give us protection in Judea and Jerusalem.
10"And now, O our God, what shall we
say after this? For we have forsaken your
commandments, 11which you commanded
by your servants the prophets, saying, 'The land which you are entering, to take possession of it, is a land unclean with the pollutions of the peoples of the lands, with their abominations which have filled it from end to end with their uncleanness.
12Therefore give not your daughters to
their sons, neither take their daughters for your sons, and never seek their peace or prosperity, that you may be strong, and eat the good of the land, and leave it for an inheritance to your children for ever.'
13And after all that has come upon us for
our evil deeds and for our great guilt, seeing that you, our God, have punished us less than our iniquities deserved and
have given us such a remnant as this, 14shall
we break your commandments again and intermarry with the peoples who practice these abominations? Would you not be angry with us till you would consume us, so that there should be no remnant, nor any
to escape? 15O LORD the God of Israel, you
are just, for we are left a remnant that has escaped, as at this day. Behold, we are before you in our guilt, for none can stand before you because of this."

10 While Ezra prayed and made confession, weeping and casting himself
down before the house of God, a very great

assembly of men, women, and children, gathered to him out of Israel; for the people wept bitterly. [2]And Shecani´ah the son of Jehi´el, of the sons of E´lam, addressed Ezra: "We have broken faith with our God and have married foreign women from the peoples of the land, but even now there is hope for Israel in spite of this. [3]Therefore let us make a covenant with our God to put away all these wives and their children, according to the counsel of my lord and of those who tremble at the commandment of our God; and let it be done according to the law. [4]Arise, for it is your task, and we are with you; be strong and do it." [5]Then Ezra arose and made the leading priests and Levites and all Israel take oath that they would do as had been said. So they took the oath.

[6]Then Ezra withdrew from before the house of God, and went to the chamber of Je´ho-ha´nan the son of Eli´ashib, where he spent the night, neither eating bread nor drinking water; for he was mourning over the faithlessness of the exiles. [7]And a proclamation was made throughout Judah and Jerusalem to all the returned exiles that they should assemble at Jerusalem, [8]and that if any one did not come within three days, by order of the officials and the elders all his property should be forfeited, and he himself banned from the congregation of the exiles.

[9]Then all the men of Judah and Benjamin assembled at Jerusalem within the three days; it was the ninth month, on the twentieth day of the month. And all the people sat in the open square before the house of God, trembling because of this matter and because of the heavy rain. [10]And Ezra the priest stood up and said to them, "You have trespassed and married foreign women, and so increased the guilt of Israel. [11]Now then make confession to the LORD the God of your fathers, and do his will; separate yourselves from the peoples of the land and from the foreign wives." [12]Then all the assembly answered with a loud voice, "It is so; we must do as you have said. [13]But the people are many, and it is a time of heavy rain; we cannot stand in the open. Nor is this a work for one day or for two; for we have greatly transgressed in this matter. [14]Let our officials stand for the whole assembly; let all in our cities who have taken foreign wives come at appointed times, and with them the elders and judges of every city, till the fierce wrath of our God over this matter be averted from us." [15]Only Jonathan the son of As´ahel and Jahzei´ah the son of Tikvah opposed this, and Meshul´lum and Shab´bethai the Levite supported them.

[16]Then the returned exiles did so. Ezra the priest selected men, heads of fathers' houses, according to their fathers' houses, each of them designated by name. On the first day of the tenth month they sat down to examine the matter; [17]and by the first day of the first month they had come to the end of all the men who had married foreign women.

[18]Of the sons of the priests who had married foreign women were found Ma-asei´ah, Elie´zer, Ja´rib, and Gedali´ah, of the sons of Jesh´ua the son of Jo´zadak and his brethren. [19]They pledged themselves to put away their wives, and their guilt offering was a ram of the flock for their guilt. [20]Of the sons of Immer: Hana´ni and Zebadi´ah. [21]Of the sons of Harim: Ma-asei´ah, Eli´jah, Shemai´ah, Jehi´el, and Uzzi´ah. [22]Of the sons of Pashhur: El´i-o-e´nai, Ma-asei´ah, Ish´mael, Nethan´el, Joz´abad, and Ela´sah.

[23]Of the Levites: Joz´abad, Shim´e-i, Kelai´ah (that is, Keli´ta), Peth´a-hi´ah, Judah, and Elie´zer. [24]Of the singers: Eli´ashib. Of the gatekeepers: Shallum, Telem, and U´ri.

[25]And of Israel: of the sons of Pa´rosh: Rami´ah, Izzi´ah, Malchi´jah, Mi´jamin, El-ea´zar, Hashabi´ah, and Bena´iah. [26]Of the sons of E´lam: Mattani´ah, Zechari´ah, Jehi´el, Abdi, Jer´emoth, and Eli´jah. [27]Of the sons of Zattu: El´i-o-e´nai, Eli´ashib, Mattani´ah, Jer´emoth, Zabad, and Azi´za. [28]Of the sons of Bebai were Je´ho-ha´nan, Hanani´ah, Zabbai, and Athlai. [29]Of the sons of Ba´ni were Meshul´lam, Malluch, Adai´ah, Jash´ub, She´al, and Jer´emoth. [30]Of the sons of Pa´hath-mo´ab: Adna, Chelal, Bena´iah, Ma-asei´ah, Mattani´ah, Bez´alel, Bin´nui, and Manas´seh. [31]Of the sons of Harim: Elie´zer, Isshi´jah, Malchi´jah, Shemai´ah, Shim´e-on, [32]Benjamin, Malluch, and Shemari´ah. [33]Of

the sons of Hashum: Matte´nai, Mattat´tah,
Zabad, Eliph´elet, Jer´emai, Manas´seh, and
Shim´e-i. 34Of the sons of Ba´ni: Ma-ada´i,
Amram, U´el, 35Bena´iah, Bedei´ah, Chel´uhi,
36Vani´ah, Mer´emoth, Eli´ashib, 37Mat-
tani´ah, Matte´nai, Jaa´su. 38Of the sons of
Bin´nui: Shim´e-i, 39Shelemi´ah, Nathan,
Adai´ah, 40Machnad´ebai, Shashai, Sharai,
41Az´arel, Shelemi´ah, Shemari´ah, 42Shallum,
Amari´ah, and Joseph. 43Of the sons of
Nebo: Je-i´el, Mattithi´ah, Zabad, Zebi´na,
Jaddai, Joel, and Bena´iah. 44All these had
married foreign women, and they put them
away with their children.

PROVERBS 16

The plans of the mind belong to man,
but the answer of the tongue is from the LORD.
2All the ways of a man are pure in his own eyes,
but the LORD weighs the spirit.
3Commit your work to the LORD,
and your plans will be established.
4The LORD has made everything for its purpose,
even the wicked for the day of trouble.
5Every one who is arrogant is an abomination to the LORD;
be assured, he will not go unpunished.
6By loyalty and faithfulness iniquity is atoned for,
and by the fear of the LORD a man avoids evil.
7When a man's ways please the LORD,
he makes even his enemies to be at peace with him.
8Better is a little with righteousness
than great revenues with injustice.
9A man's mind plans his way,
but the LORD directs his steps.
10Inspired decisions are on the lips of a king;
his mouth does not sin in judgment.
11A just balance and scales are the LORD's;
all the weights in the bag are his work.
12It is an abomination to kings to do evil,
for the throne is established by righteousness.
13Righteous lips are the delight of a king,
and he loves him who speaks what is right.
14A king's wrath is a messenger of death,
and a wise man will appease it.
15In the light of a king's face there is life,
and his favor is like the clouds that bring the spring rain.
16To get wisdom is better than gold;
to get understanding is to be chosen rather than silver.

ACTS 21

And when we had parted from
them and set sail, we came by
a straight course to Cos, and the
next day to Rhodes, and from there to
Pat´ara. 2And having found a ship crossing
to Phoeni´cia, we went aboard, and set sail.
3When we had come in sight of Cyprus,
leaving it on the left we sailed to Syria,
and landed at Tyre; for there the ship was
to unload its cargo. 4And having sought
out the disciples, we stayed there for seven
days. Through the Spirit they told Paul not
to go on to Jerusalem. 5And when our days
there were ended, we departed and went
on our journey; and they all, with wives
and children, brought us on our way till we
were outside the city; and kneeling down on
the beach we prayed and bade one another
farewell. 6Then we went on board the ship,
and they returned home.

7When we had finished the voyage from
Tyre, we arrived at Ptolema´is; and we
greeted the brethren and stayed with them
for one day. 8The next day we departed and
came to Caesare´a; and we entered the house
of Philip the evangelist, who was one of the
seven, and stayed with him. 9And he had
four unmarried daughters, who prophesied.
10While we were staying for some days, a
prophet named Ag´abus came down from
Judea. 11And coming to us he took Paul's
belt and bound his own feet and hands, and
said, "Thus says the Holy Spirit, 'So shall the
Jews at Jerusalem bind the man who owns

this belt and deliver him into the hands of the Gentiles.'" 12When we heard this, we and the people there begged him not to go up to Jerusalem. 13Then Paul answered, "What are you doing, weeping and breaking my heart? For I am ready not only to be imprisoned but even to die at Jerusalem for the name of the Lord Jesus." 14And when he would not be persuaded, we ceased and said, "The will of the Lord be done."

15After these days we made ready and went up to Jerusalem. 16And some of the disciples from Caesare′a went with us, bringing us to the house of Mnason of Cyprus, an early disciple, with whom we should lodge.

17When we had come to Jerusalem, the brethren received us gladly. 18On the following day Paul went in with us to James; and all the elders were present. 19After greeting them, he related one by one the things that God had done among the Gentiles through his ministry. 20And when they heard it, they glorified God. And they said to him, "You see, brother, how many thousands there are among the Jews of those who have believed; they are all zealous for the law, 21and they have been told about you that you teach all the Jews who are among the Gentiles to forsake Moses, telling them not to circumcise their children or observe the customs. 22What then is to be done? They will certainly hear that you have come. 23Do therefore what we tell you. We have four men who are under a vow; 24take these men and purify yourself along with them and pay their expenses, so that they may shave their heads. Thus all will know that there is nothing in what they have been told about you but that you yourself live in observance of the law. 25But as for the Gentiles who have believed, we have sent a letter with our judgment that they should abstain from what has been sacrificed to idols and from blood and from what is strangled and from unchastity." 26Then Paul took the men, and the next day he purified himself with them and went into the temple, to give notice when the days of purification would be fulfilled and the offering presented for every one of them.

27When the seven days were almost completed, the Jews from Asia, who had seen him in the temple, stirred up all the crowd, and laid hands on him, 28crying out, "Men of Israel, help! This is the man who is teaching men everywhere against the people and the law and this place; moreover he also brought Greeks into the temple, and he has defiled this holy place." 29For they had previously seen Troph′imus the Ephesian with him in the city, and they supposed that Paul had brought him into the temple. 30Then all the city was aroused, and the people ran together; they seized Paul and dragged him out of the temple, and at once the gates were shut. 31And as they were trying to kill him, word came to the tribune of the cohort that all Jerusalem was in confusion. 32He at once took soldiers and centurions, and ran down to them; and when they saw the tribune and the soldiers, they stopped beating Paul. 33Then the tribune came up and arrested him, and ordered him to be bound with two chains. He inquired who he was and what he had done. 34Some in the crowd shouted one thing, some another; and as he could not learn the facts because of the uproar, he ordered him to be brought into the barracks. 35And when he came to the steps, he was actually carried by the soldiers because of the violence of the crowd; 36for the mob of the people followed, crying, "Away with him!"

REFLECTION

Sometimes, being faithful to the Lord requires great sacrifice and even suffering. When Ezra learns that many of Jews, even Levites and priests, have intermarried with the pagan peoples against God's command, he strongly reacts: "I tore my garments and my mantle, and pulled hair from my head and beard, and sat appalled" (Ezr 9:3). These Jews have broken the Law and apparently are even entering into the "abominations" (v. 1) of pagan worship. Ezra sees their action as a betrayal of the whole purpose of their return to the land, and the only remedy is separation. Repentance, change, and renewal are required here: "By loyalty and faithfulness iniquity is atoned for" (Prv 16:6). St. Paul feels a strong calling by God to return to Jerusalem, though he is warned by prophecies that he will be targeted. Indeed, when he goes to worship at the Temple, the Jews throw a riot and the mob delivers him over to the Romans under arrest. Yet he is not scared: "I am ready not only to be imprisoned but even to die at Jerusalem for the name of the Lord Jesus" (Acts 21:13). Most likely our sacrifices for the Lord will be less extreme, but we are called to make an offering of our lives nonetheless. What small sacrifice can you make today out of love for the Lord?

July 23

NEHEMIAH 1

**The words of Nehemi′ah the
son of Hacali′ah. Now it happened in the month of Chis′lev, in the
twentieth year, as I was in Susa the cap-**
ital, 2that Hana′ni, one of my brethren,
came with certain men out of Judah; and
I asked them concerning the Jews that
survived, who had escaped exile, and
concerning Jerusalem. 3And they said to
me, "The survivors there in the province
who escaped exile are in great trouble and
shame; the wall of Jerusalem is broken
down, and its gates are destroyed by fire."
4When I heard these words I sat down
and wept, and mourned for days; and I
continued fasting and praying before the
God of heaven. 5And I said, "O LORD
God of heaven, the great and terrible
God who keeps covenant and merciful
love with those who love him and keep
his commandments; 6let your ear be
attentive, and your eyes open, to hear the
prayer of your servant which I now pray
before you day and night for the sons
of Israel your servants, confessing the
sins of the sons of Israel, which we have
sinned against you. Yes, I and my father's
house have sinned. 7We have acted very
corruptly against you, and have not kept
the commandments, the statutes, and
the ordinances which you commanded
your servant Moses. 8Remember the word
which you commanded your servant
Moses, saying, 'If you are unfaithful, I will
scatter you among the peoples; 9but if you
return to me and keep my commandments
and do them, though your dispersed be
under the farthest skies, I will gather them
from there and bring them to the place
which I have chosen, to make my name
dwell there.' 10They are your servants and
your people, whom you have redeemed
by your great power and by your strong
hand. 11O Lord, let your ear be attentive
to the prayer of your servant, and to the
prayer of your servants who delight to
fear your name; and give success to your
servant today, and grant him mercy in the
sight of this man."
Now I was cupbearer to the king.

2 In the month of Ni′san, in the twentieth
year of King Ar-ta-xerx′es, when wine
was before him, I took up the wine and
gave it to the king. Now I had not been
sad in his presence. 2And the king said
to me, "Why is your face sad, seeing you
are not sick? This is nothing else but
sadness of the heart." Then I was very
much afraid. 3I said to the king, "Let the
king live for ever! Why should not my
face be sad, when the city, the place of
my fathers' sepulchres, lies waste, and
its gates have been destroyed by fire?"
4Then the king said to me, "For what do
you make request?" So I prayed to the
God of heaven. 5And I said to the king,
"If it pleases the king, and if your servant
has found favor in your sight, that you
send me to Judah, to the city of my fathers'
sepulchres, that I may rebuild it." 6And the
king said to me (the queen sitting beside
him), "How long will you be gone, and
when will you return?" So it pleased the
king to send me; and I set him a time. 7And

I said to the king, "If it pleases the king, let
letters be given me to the governors of the
province Beyond the River, that they may
let me pass through until I come to Judah;
[8]and a letter to A′saph, the keeper of the
king's forest, that he may give me timber to
make beams for the gates of the fortress of
the temple, and for the wall of the city, and
for the house which I shall occupy." And
the king granted me what I asked, for the
good hand of my God was upon me.
[9]Then I came to the governors of the
province Beyond the River, and gave them
the king's letters. Now the king had sent with
me officers of the army and horsemen. [10]But
when Sanbal′lat the Hor′onite and Tobi′ah
the servant, the Am′monite, heard this, it
displeased them greatly that some one had
come to seek the welfare of the children
of Israel.
[11]So I came to Jerusalem and was there
three days. [12]Then I arose in the night, I
and a few men with me; and I told no one
what my God had put into my heart to
do for Jerusalem. There was no beast with
me but the beast on which I rode. [13]I went
out by night by the Valley Gate to the
Jackal's Well and to the Dung Gate, and
I inspected the walls of Jerusalem which
were broken down and its gates which
had been destroyed by fire. [14]Then I went
on to the Fountain Gate and to the King's
Pool; but there was no place for the beast
that was under me to pass. [15]Then I went
up in the night by the valley and inspected
the wall; and I turned back and entered by
the Valley Gate, and so returned. [16]And
the officials did not know where I had
gone or what I was doing; and I had not
yet told the Jews, the priests, the nobles,
the officials, and the rest that were to do
the work.
[17]Then I said to them, "You see the
trouble we are in, how Jerusalem lies in
ruins with its gates burned. Come, let
us build the wall of Jerusalem, that we
may no longer suffer disgrace." [18]And I
told them of the hand of my God which
had been upon me for good, and also of
the words which the king had spoken to
me. And they said, "Let us rise up and
build." So they strengthened their hands
for the good work. [19]But when Sanbal′lat
the Hor′onite and Tobi′ah the servant,
the Am′monite, and Geshem the Arab
heard of it, they derided us and despised
us and said, "What is this thing that you
are doing? Are you rebelling against the
king?" [20]Then I replied to them, "The
God of heaven will make us prosper, and
we his servants will arise and build; but
you have no portion or right or memorial
in Jerusalem."

PROVERBS 16

[17]The highway of the upright turns aside
from evil;
he who guards his way preserves his life.
[18]Pride goes before destruction,
and a haughty spirit before a fall.
[19]It is better to be of a lowly spirit with
the poor
than to divide the spoil with the proud.
[20]He who gives heed to the word will prosper,
and happy is he who trusts in the LORD.
[21]The wise of heart is called a man
of discernment,
and pleasant speech increases
persuasiveness.
[22]Wisdom is a fountain of life to him who
has it,
but folly is the chastisement of fools.
[23]The mind of the wise makes his
speech judicious,
and adds persuasiveness to his lips.
[24]Pleasant words are like a honeycomb,
sweetness to the soul and health
to the body.
[25]There is a way which seems right to a man,
but its end is the way to death.
[26]A worker's appetite works for him;
his mouth urges him on.
[27]A worthless man plots evil,
and his speech is like a scorching fire.
[28]A perverse man spreads strife,
and a whisperer separates close friends.
[29]A man of violence entices his neighbor
and leads him in a way that is not good.

30He who winks his eyes plans
perverse things,
he who compresses his lips brings evil
to pass.
31A hoary head is a crown of glory;
it is gained in a righteous life.
32He who is slow to anger is better than
the mighty,
and he who rules his spirit than he who
takes a city.
33The lot is cast into the lap,
but the decision is wholly from the LORD.

ACTS 21

37As Paul was about to be brought
into the barracks, he said to the
tribune, "May I say something to
you?" And he said, "Do you know Greek?
38Are you not the Egyptian, then, who
recently stirred up a revolt and led the
four thousand men of the Assassins out into
the wilderness?" 39Paul replied, "I am a Jew,
from Tarsus in Cili′cia, a citizen of no mean
city; I beg you, let me speak to the people."
40And when he had given him leave, Paul,
standing on the steps, motioned with his
hand to the people; and when there was a
great hush, he spoke to them in the Hebrew
language, saying:

22 "Brethren and fathers, hear the defense which I now make before you."
2And when they heard that he addressed
them in the Hebrew language, they were the
more quiet. And he said:
3"I am a Jew, born at Tarsus in Cili′cia, but
brought up in this city at the feet of Gama′li-
el, educated according to the strict
manner of the law of our fathers, being
zealous for God as you all are this day. 4I
persecuted this Way to the death, binding
and delivering to prison both men and
women, 5as the high priest and the whole
council of elders bear me witness. From
them I received letters to the brethren,
and I journeyed to Damascus to take
those also who were there and bring them
in bonds to Jerusalem to be punished.
6"As I made my journey and drew near
to Damascus, about noon a great light
from heaven suddenly shone about me.
7And I fell to the ground and heard a
voice saying to me, 'Saul, Saul, why do you
persecute me?' 8And I answered, 'Who are
you, Lord?' And he said to me, 'I am Jesus
of Nazareth whom you are persecuting.'
9Now those who were with me saw the
light but did not hear the voice of the one
who was speaking to me. 10And I said,
'What shall I do, Lord?' And the Lord said
to me, 'Rise, and go into Damascus, and
there you will be told all that is appointed
for you to do.' 11And when I could not see
because of the brightness of that light, I
was led by the hand by those who were
with me, and came into Damascus.
12"And one Anani′as, a devout man according to the law, well spoken of by all
the Jews who lived there, 13came to me,
and standing by me said to me, 'Brother
Saul, receive your sight.' And in that very
hour I received my sight and saw him.
14And he said, 'The God of our fathers
appointed you to know his will, to see
the Just One and to hear a voice from
his mouth; 15for you will be a witness for
him to all men of what you have seen and
heard. 16And now why do you wait? Rise
and be baptized, and wash away your
sins, calling on his name.'
17"When I had returned to Jerusalem and
was praying in the temple, I fell into a trance
18and saw him saying to me, 'Make haste and
get quickly out of Jerusalem, because they
will not accept your testimony about me.'
19And I said, 'Lord, they themselves know
that in every synagogue I imprisoned and
beat those who believed in you. 20And when
the blood of Stephen your witness was shed,
I also was standing by and approving, and
keeping the garments of those who killed
him.' 21And he said to me, 'Depart; for I will
send you far away to the Gentiles.'"
22Up to this word they listened to him;
then they lifted up their voices and said,
"Away with such a fellow from the earth!
For he ought not to live." 23And as they cried
out and waved their garments and threw

dust into the air, [24]the tribune commanded
him to be brought into the barracks, and
ordered him to be examined by scourging,
to find out why they shouted thus against
him. [25]But when they had tied him up
with the thongs, Paul said to the centurion
who was standing by, "Is it lawful for you
to scourge a man who is a Roman citizen,
and uncondemned?" [26]When the centurion
heard that, he went to the tribune and said
to him, "What are you about to do? For this
man is a Roman citizen." [27]So the tribune
came and said to him, "Tell me, are you a
Roman citizen?" And he said, "Yes." [28]The
tribune answered, "I bought this citizenship
for a large sum." Paul said, "But I was born
a citizen." [29]So those who were about to
examine him withdrew from him instantly;
and the tribune also was afraid, for he
realized that Paul was a Roman citizen and
that he had bound him.

REFLECTION

It is so easy to get comfortable with the daily routine of our lives. Yet the life of faith calls for action. Today's readings present two men who take action: Nehemiah and Paul. Nehemiah, who is roughly contemporaneous with Ezra, hears of the sorry state of the city of Jerusalem, which essentially lies in ruins despite the rebuilding of the Temple. He is moved to tears by the state of the city and decides to do something about it. He prays and then bravely approaches the Persian king for help. Having procured an official assignment, he sets out to do the work. St. Paul, too, decides to take a stand in a risky moment. As the Roman soldiers are taking him away from an angry mob, he courageously offers to give a speech, wherein he testifies to Jesus, tells his conversion story, and explains his calling as the Apostle to the Gentiles. He could have gone away silently but instead jumps at the chance to preach. Our lives might usually feel boring or repetitive rather than adventuresome, yet it could be that we are not building opportunities or seizing the ones that arise. Are you just letting life go by, or are you taking action for good?

July 24

NEHEMIAH 3

**Then Eli′ashib the high priest
rose up with his brethren the
priests and they built the Sheep Gate.
They consecrated it and set its doors;**
they consecrated it as far as the Tower of the
Hundred, as far as the Tower of Hanan′el.
[2]And next to him the men of Jericho built.
And next to them Zaccur the son of Imri
built.
[3]And the sons of Hassena′ah built the
Fish Gate; they laid its beams and set its
doors, its bolts, and its bars. [4]And next to
them Mer′emoth the son of Uri′ah, son
of Hakkoz repaired. And next to them
Meshul′lam the son of Berechi′ah, son of
Meshez′abel repaired. And next to them
Za′dok the son of Ba′ana repaired. [5]And
next to them the Teko′ites repaired; but
their nobles did not put their necks to the
work of their Lord.
[6]And Joi′ada the son of Pase′ah and
Meshul′lam the son of Besodei′ah
repaired the Old Gate; they laid its
beams and set its doors, its bolts, and
its bars. [7]And next to them repaired
Melati′ah the Gib′eonite and Ja′don the
Meron′othite, the men of Gib′eon and of
Mizpah, who were under the jurisdiction
of the governor of the province Beyond
the River. [8]Next to them Uzziel the son
of Harhai′ah, goldsmiths, repaired. Next
to him Hanani′ah, one of the perfumers,
repaired; and they restored Jerusalem as far
as the Broad Wall. [9]Next to them Rephai′ah
the son of Hur, ruler of half the district of
Jerusalem, repaired. [10]Next to them Jedai′a
the son of Haru′maph repaired opposite
his house; and next to him Hattush the
son of Hashabnei′ah repaired. [11]Malchi′jah
the son of Harim and Hasshub the son of
Pa′hath-mo′ab repaired another section
and the Tower of the Ovens. [12]Next to him
Shallum the son of Hallo′hesh, ruler of

half the district of Jerusalem, repaired, he
and his daughters.
13Ha′nun and the inhabitants of Zano′ah
repaired the Valley Gate; they rebuilt it
and set its doors, its bolts, and its bars,
and repaired a thousand cubits of the
wall, as far as the Dung Gate.
14Malchi′jah the son of Re′chab, ruler of
the district of Beth-hacche′rem, repaired
the Dung Gate; he rebuilt it and set its
doors, its bolts, and its bars.
15And Shallum the son of Colho′zeh,
ruler of the district of Mizpah, repaired
the Fountain Gate; he rebuilt it and
covered it and set its doors, its bolts, and
its bars; and he built the wall of the Pool
of She′lah of the king's garden, as far as
the stairs that go down from the City of
David. 16After him Nehemi′ah the son
of Azbuk, ruler of half the district of
Beth-zur, repaired to a point opposite
the sepulchres of David, to the artificial
pool, and to the house of the mighty
men. 17After him the Levites repaired:
Re′hum the son of Ba′ni; next to him
Hashabi′ah, ruler of half the district of
Kei′lah, repaired for his district. 18After
him their brethren repaired: Bavvai the
son of Hen′adad, ruler of half the district
of Kei′lah; 19next to him E′zer the son of
Jeshu′a, ruler of Mizpah, repaired another
section opposite the ascent to the armory
at the Angle. 20After him Baruch the son of
Zabbai repaired another section from the
Angle to the door of the house of Eli′ashib
the high priest. 21After him Mer′emoth
the son of Uri′ah, son of Hakkoz repaired
another section from the door of the
house of Eli′ashib to the end of the house
of Eliashib. 22After him the priests, the
men of the Plain, repaired. 23After them
Benjamin and Hasshub repaired opposite
their house. After them Azari′ah the son
of Ma-asei′ah, son of Anani′ah repaired
beside his own house. 24After him Bin′nui
the son of Hen′adad repaired another
section, from the house of Azari′ah to the
Angle 25and to the corner. Pa′lal the son of
U′zai repaired opposite the Angle and the
tower projecting from the upper house of
the king at the court of the guard. After
him Pedai′ah the son of Pa′rosh 26and the
temple servants living on O′phel repaired
to a point opposite the Water Gate on the
east and the projecting tower. 27After him
the Teko′ites repaired another section
opposite the great projecting tower as far
as the wall of O′phel.
28Above the Horse Gate the priests
repaired, each one opposite his own house.
29After them Za′dok the son of Immer
repaired opposite his own house. After
him Shemai′ah the son of Shecani′ah, the
keeper of the East Gate, repaired. 30After
him Hanani′ah the son of Shelemi′ah and
Ha′nun the sixth son of Za′laph repaired
another section. After him Meshul′lam
the son of Berechi′ah repaired opposite
his chamber. 31After him Malchi′jah, one
of the goldsmiths, repaired as far as the
house of the temple servants and of the
merchants, opposite the Muster Gate, and
to the upper chamber of the corner. 32And
between the upper chamber of the corner
and the Sheep Gate the goldsmiths and
the merchants repaired.

4 Now when Sanbal′lat heard that we were
building the wall, he was angry and
greatly enraged, and he ridiculed the
Jews. 2And he said in the presence of his
brethren and of the army of Samar′ia,
"What are these feeble Jews doing? Will
they restore things? Will they sacrifice?
Will they finish up in a day? Will they
revive the stones out of the heaps of
rubbish, and burned ones at that?"
3Tobi′ah the Am′monite was by him, and
he said, "Yes, what they are building—if
a fox goes up on it he will break down
their stone wall!" 4Hear, O our God, for
we are despised; turn back their taunt
upon their own heads, and give them up
to be plundered in a land where they are
captives. 5Do not cover their guilt, and
let not their sin be blotted out from your
sight; for they have provoked you to anger
before the builders.
6So we built the wall; and all the wall was
joined together to half its height. For the
people had a mind to work.

[7]But when Sanbal′lat and Tobi′ah and
the Arabs and the Am′monites and the
Ash′dodites heard that the repairing of
the walls of Jerusalem was going forward
and that the breaches were beginning to
be closed, they were very angry; [8]and they
all plotted together to come and fight
against Jerusalem and to cause confusion
in it. [9]And we prayed to our God, and set
a guard as a protection against them day
and night.
[10]But Judah said, "The strength of the
burden-bearers is failing, and there is
much rubbish; we are not able to work on
the wall." [11]And our enemies said, "They
will not know or see till we come into the
midst of them and kill them and stop the
work." [12]When the Jews who lived by them
came they said to us ten times, "From all
the places where they live they will come
up against us." [13]So in the lowest parts of
the space behind the wall, in open places,
I stationed the people according to their
families, with their swords, their spears,
and their bows. [14]And I looked, and arose,
and said to the nobles and to the officials
and to the rest of the people, "Do not be
afraid of them. Remember the Lord, who
is great and terrible, and fight for your
brethren, your sons, your daughters, your
wives, and your homes."
[15]When our enemies heard that it was
known to us and that God had frustrated
their plan, we all returned to the wall,
each to his work. [16]From that day on, half
of my servants worked on construction,
and half held the spears, shields, bows,
and coats of mail; and the leaders stood
behind all the house of Judah, [17]who were
building on the wall. Those who carried
burdens were laden in such a way that each
with one hand labored on the work and with
the other held his weapon. [18]And each of
the builders had his sword belted at his side
while he built. The man who sounded the
trumpet was beside me. [19]And I said to the
nobles and to the officials and to the rest of the
people, "The work is great and widely spread,
and we are separated on the wall, far from one
another. [20]In the place where you hear the
sound of the trumpet, rally to us there. Our
God will fight for us."
[21]So we labored at the work, and half of
them held the spears from the break of dawn
till the stars came out. [22]I also said to the
people at that time, "Let every man and his
servant pass the night within Jerusalem, that
they may be a guard for us by night and may
labor by day." [23]So neither I nor my brethren
nor my servants nor the men of the guard
who followed me, none of us took off our
clothes; each kept his weapon in his hand.

PROVERBS 17

Better is a dry morsel with quiet
than a house full of feasting with strife.
[2]A slave who deals wisely will rule over a son who acts shamefully,
and will share the inheritance as one of the brothers.
[3]The crucible is for silver, and the furnace is for gold,
and the LORD tries hearts.
[4]An evildoer listens to wicked lips;
and a liar gives heed to a mischievous tongue.
[5]He who mocks the poor insults his Maker;
he who is glad at calamity will not go unpunished.
[6]Grandchildren are the crown of the aged,
and the glory of sons is their fathers.
[7]Fine speech is not becoming to a fool;
still less is false speech to a prince.
[8]A bribe is like a magic stone in the eyes of him who gives it;
wherever he turns he prospers.
[9]He who forgives an offense seeks love,
but he who repeats a matter alienates a friend.
[10]A rebuke goes deeper into a man of understanding
than a hundred blows into a fool.
[11]An evil man seeks only rebellion,
and a cruel messenger will be sent against him.
[12]Let a man meet a she-bear robbed of her cubs,
rather than a fool in his folly.

13 If a man returns evil for good,
evil will not depart from his house.
14 The beginning of strife is like letting
out water;
so quit before the quarrel breaks out.

ACTS 22

**30 But the next day, desiring to
know the real reason why the
Jews accused him, he unbound him, and
commanded the chief priests and all the**
council to meet, and he brought Paul down
and set him before them.

23 And Paul, looking intently at the
council, said, "Brethren, I have
lived before God in all good conscience up
to this day." 2 And the high priest Anani'as
commanded those who stood by him to
strike him on the mouth. 3 Then Paul said to
him, "God shall strike you, you whitewashed
wall! Are you sitting to judge me according
to the law, and yet contrary to the law you
order me to be struck?" 4 Those who stood
by said, "Would you revile God's high
priest?" 5 And Paul said, "I did not know,
brethren, that he was the high priest; for it
is written, 'You shall not speak evil of a ruler
of your people.' "

6 But when Paul perceived that one part
were Sad'ducees and the other Pharisees,
he cried out in the council, "Brethren, I
am a Pharisee, a son of Pharisees; with
respect to the hope and the resurrection
of the dead I am on trial." 7 And when he
had said this, a dissension arose between
the Pharisees and the Sad'ducees; and the
assembly was divided. 8 For the Sad'ducees
say that there is no resurrection, nor angel,
nor spirit; but the Pharisees acknowledge
them all. 9 Then a great clamor arose; and
some of the scribes of the Pharisees' party
stood up and contended, "We find nothing
wrong in this man. What if a spirit or an
angel spoke to him?" 10 And when the
dissension became violent, the tribune,
afraid that Paul would be torn in pieces
by them, commanded the soldiers to go
down and take him by force from among
them and bring him into the barracks.

11 The following night the Lord stood by
him and said, "Take courage, for as you
have testified about me at Jerusalem, so
you must bear witness also at Rome."

12 When it was day, the Jews made a plot
and bound themselves by an oath neither
to eat nor drink till they had killed Paul.
13 There were more than forty who made
this conspiracy. 14 And they went to the
chief priests and elders, and said, "We
have strictly bound ourselves by an oath
to taste no food till we have killed Paul.
15 You therefore, along with the council,
give notice now to the tribune to bring
him down to you, as though you were
going to determine his case more exactly.
And we are ready to kill him before he
comes near."

16 Now the son of Paul's sister heard of
their ambush; so he went and entered the
barracks and told Paul. 17 And Paul called
one of the centurions and said, "Take
this young man to the tribune; for he has
something to tell him." 18 So he took him
and brought him to the tribune and said,
"Paul the prisoner called me and asked
me to bring this young man to you, as
he has something to say to you." 19 The
tribune took him by the hand, and going
aside asked him privately, "What is it that
you have to tell me?" 20 And he said, "The
Jews have agreed to ask you to bring Paul
down to the council tomorrow, as though
they were going to inquire somewhat
more closely about him. 21 But do not
yield to them; for more than forty of their
men lie in ambush for him, having bound
themselves by an oath neither to eat nor
drink till they have killed him; and now
they are ready, waiting for the promise
from you." 22 So the tribune dismissed the
young man, charging him, "Tell no one
that you have informed me of this."

23 Then he called two of the centurions
and said, "At the third hour of the night
get ready two hundred soldiers with
seventy horsemen and two hundred
spearmen to go as far as Caesare'a. 24 Also

provide mounts for Paul to ride, and bring him safely to Felix the governor." [25]And he wrote a letter to this effect:

[26]"Claudius Lys'ias to his Excellency the governor Felix, greeting. [27]This man was seized by the Jews, and was about to be killed by them, when I came upon them with the soldiers and rescued him, having learned that he was a Roman citizen. [28]And desiring to know the charge on which they accused him, I brought him down to their council. [29]I found that he was accused about questions of their law, but charged with nothing deserving death or imprisonment. [30]And when it was disclosed to me that there would be a plot against the man, I sent him to you at once, ordering his accusers also to state before you what they have against him."

[31]So the soldiers, according to their instructions, took Paul and brought him by night to Antip'atris. [32]And the next day they returned to the barracks, leaving the horsemen to go on with him. [33]When they came to Caesare'a and delivered the letter to the governor, they presented Paul also before him. [34]On reading the letter, he asked to what province he belonged. When he learned that he was from Cili'cia [35]he said, "I will hear you when your accusers arrive." And he commanded him to be guarded in Herod's praetorium.

REFLECTION

When we seek to follow the Lord, we will be greeted with opposition from the world, the flesh, and the devil. That is, the people we know might try to thwart us, our own temptations will assail us, and evil spirits will plot against us. Nehemiah and the Jews face violent persecution for trying to rebuild Jerusalem's walls. The walls are not merely a security system but a true fortification. Once a city had walls, it could declare political independence and defend itself from attack—an unwelcome change for the Jews' opponents. St. Paul shows himself dangerous as an evangelist. Even on trial before the Sanhedrin, he is clever enough to cause a division in his opponents by declaring that his trial is about the resurrection of the dead, a Pharisee doctrine. That declaration gets the Pharisees on his side, but provokes some of the Jews to swear an oath to kill him so that he must be taken out of the city at night with almost five hundred soldiers as guards. When the world, the flesh, and the devil attack us, we might have to be like Nehemiah, spending half our time fighting them off and the other half building the city of God. How do you respond when your faith runs into hostility?

July 25

NEHEMIAH 5

Now there arose a great outcry of the people and of their wives against their Jewish brethren. [2]For there were those who said, "With our sons and our daughters, we are many; let us get grain, that we may eat and keep alive." [3]There were also those who said, "We are mortgaging our fields, our vineyards, and our houses to get grain because of the famine." [4]And there were those who said, "We have borrowed money for the king's tax upon our fields and our vineyards. [5]Now our flesh is as the flesh of our brethren, our children are as their children; yet we are forcing our sons and our daughters to be slaves, and some of our daughters have already been enslaved; but it is not in our power to help it, for other men have our fields and our vineyards."

[6]I was very angry when I heard their outcry and these words. [7]I took counsel with myself, and I brought charges against the nobles and the officials. I said to them, "You are exacting interest, each from his brother." And I held a great assembly against them, [8]and said to them, "We, as far as we are able, have bought back our Jewish brethren who have been sold to the nations; but you even sell your brethren that they may be sold to us!" They were silent,

and could not find a word to say. [9]So I said, "The thing that you are doing is not good. Ought you not to walk in the fear of our God to prevent the taunts of the nations our enemies? [10]Moreover I and my brethren and my servants are lending them money and grain. Let us leave off this interest. [11]Return to them this very day their fields, their vineyards, their olive orchards, and their houses, and the hundredth of money, grain, wine, and oil which you have been exacting of them." [12]Then they said, "We will restore these and require nothing from them. We will do as you say." And I called the priests, and took an oath of them to do as they had promised. [13]I also shook out my garment and said, "So may God shake out every man from his house and from his labor who does not perform this promise. So may he be shaken out and emptied." And all the assembly said "Amen" and praised the LORD. And the people did as they had promised.

[14]Moreover from the time that I was appointed to be their governor in the land of Judah, from the twentieth year to the thirty-second year of Ar-ta-xerx′es the king, twelve years, neither I nor my brethren ate the food allowance of the governor. [15]The former governors who were before me laid heavy burdens upon the people, and took from them food and wine, besides forty shekels of silver. Even their servants lorded it over the people. But I did not do so, because of the fear of God. [16]I also held to the work on this wall, and acquired no land; and all my servants were gathered there for the work. [17]Moreover there were at my table a hundred and fifty men, Jews and officials, besides those who came to us from the nations which were about us. [18]Now that which was prepared for one day was one ox and six choice sheep; fowls likewise were prepared for me, and every ten days skins of wine in abundance; yet with all this I did not demand the food allowance of the governor, because the servitude was heavy upon this people. [19]Remember for my good, O my God, all that I have done for this people.

6 Now when it was reported to Sanbal′lat and Tobi′ah and to Geshem the Arab and to the rest of our enemies that I had built the wall and that there was no breach left in it (although up to that time I had not set up the doors in the gates), [2]Sanbal′lat and Geshem sent to me, saying, "Come and let us meet together in one of the villages in the plain of Ono." But they intended to do me harm. [3]And I sent messengers to them, saying, "I am doing a great work and I cannot come down. Why should the work stop while I leave it and come down to you?" [4]And they sent to me four times in this way and I answered them in the same manner. [5]In the same way Sanbal′lat for the fifth time sent his servant to me with an open letter in his hand. [6]In it was written, "It is reported among the nations, and Geshem also says it, that you and the Jews intend to rebel; that is why you are building the wall; and you wish to become their king, according to this report. [7]And you have also set up prophets to proclaim concerning you in Jerusalem, 'There is a king in Judah.' And now it will be reported to the king according to these words. So now come, and let us take counsel together." [8]Then I sent to him, saying, "No such things as you say have been done, for you are inventing them out of your own mind." [9]For they all wanted to frighten us, thinking, "Their hands will drop from the work, and it will not be done." But now, O God, strengthen my hands.

[10]Now when I went into the house of Shemai′ah the son of Delai′ah, son of Mehet′abel, who was shut up, he said, "Let us meet together in the house of God, within the temple, and let us close the doors of the temple; for they are coming to kill you, at night they are coming to kill you." [11]But I said, "Should such a man as I flee? And what man such as I could go into the temple and live? I will not go in." [12]And I understood, and saw that God had not sent him, but he had pronounced the prophecy against me because Tobi′ah and Sanbal′lat had hired him. [13]For this purpose he was hired, that I should be afraid and act in this way and sin, and so they could give me an evil name, in order to taunt me. [14]Remember Tobi′ah and Sanbal′lat, O my God, according to these things that they did, and also the prophetess No-adi′ah and the rest of the prophets who wanted to make me afraid.

[15]So the wall was finished on the twenty-fifth
day of the month E'lul, in fifty-two days. [16]And
when all our enemies heard of it, all the nations
round about us were afraid and fell greatly in
their own esteem; for they perceived that this
work had been accomplished with the help of
our God. [17]Moreover in those days the nobles of
Judah sent many letters to Tobi'ah, and Tobiah's
letters came to them. [18]For many in Judah were
bound by oath to him, because he was the son-
in-law of Shecani'ah the son of A'rah: and his
son Je'ho-ha'nan had taken the daughter
of Meshul'lam the son of Berechi'ah as his
wife. [19]Also they spoke of his good deeds
in my presence, and reported my words to
him. And Tobi'ah sent letters to make me
afraid.

7 Now when the wall had been built and I
had set up the doors, and the gatekeepers,
the singers, and the Levites had been
appointed, [2]I gave my brother Hana'ni and
Hanani'ah the governor of the castle charge
over Jerusalem, for he was a more faithful
and God-fearing man than many. [3]And I said
to them, "Let not the gates of Jerusalem be
opened until the sun is hot; and while they
are still standing guard let them shut and bar
the doors. Appoint guards from among the
inhabitants of Jerusalem, each to his station
and each opposite his own house." [4]The city
was wide and large, but the people within it
were few and no houses had been built.

PROVERBS 17

[15]He who justifies the wicked and he who
condemns the righteous
are both alike an abomination to the LORD.
[16]Why should a fool have a price in his hand
to buy wisdom,
when he has no mind?
[17]A friend loves at all times,
and a brother is born for adversity.
[18]A man without sense gives a pledge,
and becomes surety in the presence
of his neighbor.
[19]He who loves transgression loves strife;
he who makes his door high
seeks destruction.
[20]A man of crooked mind does not prosper,
and one with a perverse tongue falls
into calamity.
[21]A stupid son is a grief to a father;
and the father of a fool has no joy.
[22]A cheerful heart is a good medicine,
but a downcast spirit dries up the bones.
[23]A wicked man accepts a bribe from
the bosom
to pervert the ways of justice.
[24]A man of understanding sets his face
toward wisdom,
but the eyes of a fool are on the ends of
the earth.
[25]A foolish son is a grief to his father
and bitterness to her who bore him.
[26]To impose a fine on a righteous man is
not good;
to flog noble men is wrong.
[27]He who restrains his words has knowledge,
and he who has a cool spirit is a man
of understanding.
[28]Even a fool who keeps silent is
considered wise;
when he closes his lips, he is deemed
intelligent.

ACTS 24

And after five days the high priest
Anani'as came down with some
elders and a spokesman, one Ter-
tul'lus. They laid before the governor their
case against Paul; [2]and when he was called,
Tertul'lus began to accuse him, saying:
"Since through you we enjoy much
peace, and since by your provision, most
excellent Felix, reforms are introduced
on behalf of this nation, [3]in every way
and everywhere we accept this with all
gratitude. [4]But, to detain you no further, I
beg you in your kindness to hear us briefly.
[5]For we have found this man a pestilent
fellow, an agitator among all the Jews
throughout the world, and a ringleader of
the sect of the Nazarenes. [6]He even tried to
profane the temple, but we seized him. [8]By
examining him yourself you will be able to

learn from him about everything of which we accuse him."
9The Jews also joined in the charge, affirming that all this was so.
10And when the governor had motioned to him to speak, Paul replied:
"Realizing that for many years you have been judge over this nation, I cheerfully make my defense. 11As you may ascertain, it is not more than twelve days since I went up to worship at Jerusalem; 12and they did not find me disputing with any one or stirring up a crowd, either in the temple or in the synagogues, or in the city. 13Neither can they prove to you what they now bring up against me. 14But this I admit to you, that according to the Way, which they call a sect, I worship the God of our fathers, believing everything laid down by the law or written in the prophets, 15having a hope in God which these themselves accept, that there will be a resurrection of both the just and the unjust. 16So I always take pains to have a clear conscience toward God and toward men. 17Now after some years I came to bring to my nation alms and offerings. 18As I was doing this, they found me purified in the temple, without any crowd or tumult. But some Jews from Asia—19they ought to be here before you and to make an accusation, if they have anything against me. 20Or else let these men themselves say what wrongdoing they found when I stood before the council, 21except this one thing which I cried out while standing among them, 'With respect to the resurrection of the dead I am on trial before you this day.'"
22But Felix, having a rather accurate knowledge of the Way, put them off, saying, "When Lys′ias the tribune comes down, I will decide your case." 23Then he gave orders to the centurion that he should be kept in custody but should have some liberty, and that none of his friends should be prevented from attending to his needs.
24After some days Felix came with his wife Drusil′la, who was Jewish; and he sent for Paul and heard him speak upon faith in Christ Jesus. 25And as he argued about justice and self-control and future judgment, Felix was alarmed and said, "Go away for the present; when I have an opportunity I will summon you." 26At the same time he hoped that money would be given him by Paul. So he sent for him often and conversed with him. 27But when two years had elapsed, Felix was succeeded by Por′cius Festus; and desiring to do the Jews a favor, Felix left Paul in prison.

REFLECTION

Proverbs reminds us that "a cheerful heart is a good medicine, but a downcast spirit dries up the bones" (Prv 17:22). Nehemiah exhibits a cheerful generosity to the poor Jews who have returned to Judah. He chastises those charging usurious interest on loans that push the people into poverty, and then grants the poor an abundance of food from his own table. In addition, he does not collect all the tax due from the people to himself (see Neh 5:18). In his vigorous joy, Nehemiah determinedly finishes the wall of Jerusalem to bring peace to his people. Despite being under arrest and accused, which could lead anyone into a downcast state, St. Paul says, "I cheerfully make my defense" (Acts 24:10). Faith in God brings with it a redoubtable joyfulness that imbues every saint's heart. It comes from a deep trust in what God says and a concrete reliance on the truth of his word. The truth, when fully grasped, that God is in control, makes way for a vigorously cheerful disposition. Do you bring a cheerful heart to everyone you meet?

July 26

NEHEMIAH 7

5Then God put it into my mind to assemble the nobles and the officials and the people to be enrolled by genealogy. And I found the book of the genealogy of those who came up at the first, and I found written in it:

6These were the people of the province who came up out of the captivity of those exiles whom Nebuchadnez′zar the king of Babylon had carried into exile; they returned to Jerusalem and Judah, each to his town. 7They came with Zerub′babel, Jesh′ua, Nehemi′ah, Azari′ah, Raami′ah, Naham′ani, Mor′decai, Bilshan, Mis′pereth, Bigvai, Nehum, Ba′anah.

The number of the men of the sons of Israel: 8the sons of Pa′rosh, two thousand a hundred and seventy-two. 9The sons of Shephati′ah, three hundred and seventy-two. 10The sons of A′rah, six hundred and fifty-two. 11The sons of Pa′hath-mo′ab, namely the sons of Jesh′ua and Jo′ab, two thousand eight hundred and eighteen. 12The sons of E′lam, a thousand two hundred and fifty-four. 13The sons of Zattu, eight hundred and forty-five. 14The sons of Zaccai, seven hundred and sixty. 15The sons of Bin′nui, six hundred and forty-eight. 16The sons of Bebai, six hundred and twenty-eight. 17The sons of Azgad, two thousand three hundred and twenty-two. 18The sons of Adoni′kam, six hundred and sixty-seven. 19The sons of Bigvai, two thousand and sixty-seven. 20The sons of A′din, six hundred and fifty-five. 21The sons of A′ter, namely of Hezeki′ah, ninety-eight. 22The sons of Hashum, three hundred and twenty-eight. 23The sons of Bezai, three hundred and twenty-four. 24The sons of Hariph, a hundred and twelve. 25The sons of Gib′eon, ninety-five. 26The men of Bethlehem and Netoph′ah, a hundred and eighty-eight. 27The men of An′athoth, a hundred and twenty-eight. 28The men of Beth-az′maveth, forty-two. 29The men of Kir′iath-je′arim, Chephi′rah, and Beer′oth, seven hundred and forty-three. 30The men of Ra′mah and Ge′ba, six hundred and twenty-one. 31The men of Michmas, a hundred and twenty-two. 32The men of Bethel and Ai, a hundred and twenty-three. 33The men of the other Nebo, fifty-two. 34The sons of the other E′lam, a thousand two hundred and fifty-four. 35The sons of Harim, three hundred and twenty. 36The sons of Jericho, three hundred and forty-five. 37The sons of Lod, Hadid, and Ono, seven hundred and twenty-one. 38The sons of Sena′ah, three thousand nine hundred and thirty.

39The priests: the sons of Jedai′ah, namely the house of Jesh′ua, nine hundred and seventy-three. 40The sons of Immer, a thousand and fifty-two. 41The sons of Pashhur, a thousand two hundred and forty-seven. 42The sons of Harim, a thousand and seventeen.

43The Levites: the sons of Jesh′ua, namely of Kad′mi-el of the sons of Ho′devah, seventy-four. 44The singers: the sons of A′saph, a hundred and forty-eight. 45The gatekeepers: the sons of Shallum, the sons of A′ter, the sons of Talmon, the sons of Akkub, the sons of Hati′ta, the sons of Shobai, a hundred and thirty-eight.

46The temple servants: the sons of Ziha, the sons of Hasu′pha, the sons of Tabba′oth, 47the sons of Keros, the sons of Sia, the sons of Pa′don, 48the sons of Leba′na, the sons of Hag′aba, the sons of Shalmai, 49the sons of Ha′nan, the sons of Giddel, the sons of Ga′har, 50the sons of Re-ai′ah, the sons of Re′zin, the sons of Neko′da, 51the sons of Gazzam, the sons of Uzza, the sons of Pase′ah, 52the sons of Besai, the sons of Me-u′nim, the sons of Nephush′esim, 53the sons of Bakbuk, the sons of Haku′pha, the sons of Harhur, 54the sons of Bazlith, the sons of Mehi′da, the sons of Harsha, 55the sons of Barkos, the sons of Sis′era, the sons of Te′mah, 56the sons of Nezi′ah, the sons of Hati′pha.

57The sons of Solomon's servants: the sons of Sotai, the sons of So′phereth, the sons of Peri′da, 58the sons of Ja′ala, the sons of Darkon, the sons of Giddel, 59the sons of Shephati′ah, the sons of Hattil, the sons of Po′chereth-hazzeba′im, the sons of A′mon.

60All the temple servants and the sons of Solomon's servants were three hundred and ninety-two.

61The following were those who came up from Tel-me′lah, Tel-har′sha, Cherub, Addon, and Immer, but they could not prove their fathers' houses nor their descent, whether they belonged to Israel: [62]the sons of Delai′ah, the sons of Tobi′ah, the sons of Neko′da, six hundred and forty-two. [63]Also, of the priests: the sons of Hobai′ah, the sons of Hakkoz, the sons of Barzil′lai (who had taken a wife of the daughters of Barzillai the Gileadite and was called by their name). [64]These sought their registration among those enrolled in the genealogies, but it was not found there, so they were excluded from the priesthood as unclean; [65]the governor told them that they were not to partake of the most holy food, until a priest with U′rim and Thummim should arise.

[66]The whole assembly together was forty-two thousand three hundred and sixty, [67]besides their menservants and maid-servants, of whom there were seven thousand three hundred and thirty-seven; and they had two hundred and forty-five singers, male and female. [68]Their horses were seven hundred and thirty-six, their mules two hundred and forty-five, [69]their camels four hundred and thirty-five, and their donkeys six thousand seven hundred and twenty.

[70]Now some of the heads of fathers' houses gave to the work. The governor gave to the treasury a thousand darics of gold, fifty basins, five hundred and thirty priests' garments. [71]And some of the heads of fathers' houses gave into the treasury of the work twenty thousand darics of gold and two thousand two hundred minas of silver. [72]And what the rest of the people gave was twenty thousand darics of gold, two thousand minas of silver, and sixty-seven priests' garments.

[73]So the priests, the Levites, the gatekeepers, the singers, some of the people, the temple servants, and all Israel, lived in their towns.

8 And when the seventh month had come, the children of Israel were in their towns. [1]And all the people gathered as one man into the square before the Water Gate; and they told Ezra the scribe to bring the book of the law of Moses which the LORD had given to Israel. [2]And Ezra the priest brought the law before the assembly, both men and women and all who could hear with understanding, on the first day of the seventh month. [3]And he read from it facing the square before the Water Gate from early morning until midday, in the presence of the men and the women and those who could understand; and the ears of all the people were attentive to the book of the law. [4]And Ezra the scribe stood on a wooden pulpit which they had made for the purpose; and beside him stood Mattithi′ah, Shema, Anai′ah, Uri′ah, Hilki′ah, and Ma-asei′ah on his right hand; and Pedai′ah, Mish′a-el, Malchi′jah, Hashum, Hash-bad′danah, Zechari′ah, and Meshul′lam on his left hand. [5]And Ezra opened the book in the sight of all the people, for he was above all the people; and when he opened it all the people stood. [6]And Ezra blessed the LORD, the great God; and all the people answered, "Amen, Amen," lifting up their hands; and they bowed their heads and worshiped the LORD with their faces to the ground. [7]Also Jesh′ua, Ba′ni, Sherebi′ah, Ja′min, Akkub, Shab′bethai, Hodi′ah, Ma-asei′ah, Keli′ta, Azari′ah, Jo′za-bad, Ha′nan, Pelai′ah, the Levites, helped the people to understand the law, while the people remained in their places. [8]And they read from the book, from the law of God, clearly; and they gave the sense, so that the people understood the reading.

[9]And Nehemi′ah, who was the governor, and Ezra the priest and scribe, and the Levites who taught the people said to all the people, "This day is holy to the LORD your God; do not mourn or weep." For all the people wept when they heard the words of the law. [10]Then he said to them, "Go your way, eat the fat and drink sweet wine and send portions to him for whom nothing is prepared; for this day is holy to our Lord; and do not be grieved, for the joy of the LORD is your strength." [11]So the Levites stilled all the people, saying, "Be quiet, for this day is holy; do not be grieved." [12]And all the people went their

way to eat and drink and to send portions and to make great rejoicing, because they had understood the words that were declared to them.

PROVERBS 18

He who is estranged seeks pretexts
to break out against all sound judgment.
2 A fool takes no pleasure in understanding,
but only in expressing his opinion.
3 When wickedness comes, contempt
comes also;
and with dishonor comes disgrace.
4 The words of a man's mouth are deep waters;
the fountain of wisdom is a
gushing stream.
5 It is not good to be partial to a wicked man,
or to deprive a righteous man of justice.
6 A fool's lips bring strife,
and his mouth invites a flogging.
7 A fool's mouth is his ruin,
and his lips are a snare to himself.
8 The words of a whisperer are like
delicious morsels;
they go down into the inner parts
of the body.
9 He who is slack in his work
is a brother to him who destroys.
10 The name of the LORD is a strong tower;
the righteous man runs into it and is safe.
11 A rich man's wealth is his strong city,
and like a high wall protecting him.
12 Before destruction a man's heart is haughty,
but humility goes before honor.
13 If one gives answer before he hears,
it is his folly and shame.
14 A man's spirit will endure sickness;
but a broken spirit who can bear?
15 An intelligent mind acquires knowledge,
and the ear of the wise seeks knowledge.
16 A man's gift makes room for him
and brings him before great men.
17 He who states his case first seems right,
until the other comes and examines him.
18 The lot puts an end to disputes
and decides between powerful contenders.
19 A brother helped is like a strong city,
but quarreling is like the bars of a castle.
20 From the fruit of his mouth a man
is satisfied;
he is satisfied by the yield of his lips.
21 Death and life are in the power
of the tongue,
and those who love it will eat its fruits.
22 He who finds a wife finds a good thing,
and obtains favor from the LORD.
23 The poor use entreaties,
but the rich answer roughly.
24 There are friends who pretend
to be friends,
but there is a friend who sticks closer
than a brother.

ACTS 25

Now when Festus had come into his province, after three days he went up to Jerusalem from Caesare′a.
2 And the chief priests and the principal
men of the Jews informed him against
Paul; and they urged him, 3 asking as a
favor to have the man sent to Jerusalem,
planning an ambush to kill him on the way.
4 Festus replied that Paul was being kept at
Caesare′a, and that he himself intended to go
there shortly. 5 "So," said he, "let the men of
authority among you go down with me, and
if there is anything wrong about the man, let
them accuse him."
6 When he had stayed among them not
more than eight or ten days, he went down to
Caesare′a; and the next day he took his seat on
the tribunal and ordered Paul to be brought.
7 And when he had come, the Jews who had
gone down from Jerusalem stood about him,
bringing against him many serious charges
which they could not prove. 8 Paul said in his
defense, "Neither against the law of the Jews,
nor against the temple, nor against Caesar
have I offended at all." 9 But Festus, wishing
to do the Jews a favor, said to Paul, "Do you
wish to go up to Jerusalem, and there be tried
on these charges before me?" 10 But Paul said,
"I am standing before Caesar's tribunal, where
I ought to be tried; to the Jews I have done no
wrong, as you know very well. 11 If then I am a

wrongdoer, and have committed anything for which I deserve to die, I do not seek to escape death; but if there is nothing in their charges against me, no one can give me up to them. I appeal to Caesar." [12]Then Festus, when he had conferred with his council, answered, "You have appealed to Caesar; to Caesar you shall go."

[13]Now when some days had passed, Agrippa the king and Bernice arrived at Caesare'a to welcome Festus. [14]And as they stayed there many days, Festus laid Paul's case before the king, saying, "There is a man left prisoner by Felix; [15]and when I was at Jerusalem, the chief priests and the elders of the Jews gave information about him, asking for sentence against him. [16]I answered them that it was not the custom of the Romans to give up any one before the accused met the accusers face to face, and had opportunity to make his defense concerning the charge laid against him. [17]When therefore they came together here, I made no delay, but on the next day took my seat on the tribunal and ordered the man to be brought in. [18]When the accusers stood up, they brought no charge in his case of such evils as I supposed; [19]but they had certain points of dispute with him about their own superstition and about one Jesus, who was dead, but whom Paul asserted to be alive. [20]Being at a loss how to investigate these questions, I asked whether he wished to go to Jerusalem and be tried there regarding them. [21]But when Paul had appealed to be kept in custody for the decision of the emperor, I commanded him to be held until I could send him to Caesar." [22]And Agrippa said to Festus, "I should like to hear the man myself." "Tomorrow," said he, "you shall hear him."

[23]So the next day Agrippa and Bernice came with great pomp, and they entered the audience hall with the military tribunes and the prominent men of the city. Then by command of Festus Paul was brought in. [24]And Festus said, "King Agrippa and all who are present with us, you see this man about whom the whole Jewish people petitioned me, both at Jerusalem and here, shouting that he ought not to live any longer. [25]But I found that he had done nothing deserving death; and as he himself appealed to the emperor, I decided to send him. [26]But I have nothing definite to write to my lord about him. Therefore I have brought him before you, and, especially before you, King Agrippa, that, after we have examined him, I may have something to write. [27]For it seems to me unreasonable, in sending a prisoner, not to indicate the charges against him."

REFLECTION

The Jews who return to the land of Judah serve as a great example for us in their approach to the Word of God. They come out in large numbers to hear Ezra the priest read the book of the Law aloud. Here the people exemplify the proverb that "an intelligent mind acquires knowledge, and the ear of the wise seeks knowledge" (Prv 18:15). While they are practicing their religion, it appears that few of them have ever heard large portions of the Law before, so this moment becomes a powerful and revelatory experience for them. When they hear the Word, they say, "Amen, Amen," and then "they [bow] their heads and [worship] the LORD with their faces to the ground" (Neh 8:6). Indeed the Word makes them weep (see v. 9), similar to the impact it had on Josiah long before (see 2 Chr 34:19). Rather than weep, Nehemiah and Ezra encourage them to rejoice, to feast, and to celebrate the holy day. God's people rejoice in the truth proclaimed to them in God's Word. What in the Word of God have you read today brings joy to your heart?

July 27

NEHEMIAH 8

[13]On the second day the heads of fathers' houses of all the people, with the priests and the Levites, came together to Ezra the scribe in order to study the words of the law. [14]And they

found it written in the law that the LORD had
commanded by Moses that the sons of Israel
should dwell in booths during the feast of
the seventh month, 15and that they should
publish and proclaim in all their towns and
in Jerusalem, "Go out to the hills and bring
branches of olive, wild olive, myrtle, palm,
and other leafy trees to make booths, as it is
written." 16So the people went out and brought
them and made booths for themselves, each on
his roof, and in their courts and in the courts
of the house of God, and in the square at the
Water Gate and in the square at the Gate of
E′phraim. 17And all the assembly of those who
had returned from the captivity made booths
and dwelt in the booths; for from the days of
Jesh′ua the son of Nun to that day the sons of
Israel had not done so. And there was very
great rejoicing. 18And day by day, from the
first day to the last day, he read from the book
of the law of God. They kept the feast seven
days; and on the eighth day there was a solemn
assembly, according to the ordinance.

9 Now on the twenty-fourth day of this
month the sons of Israel were assembled
with fasting and in sackcloth, and with earth
upon their heads. 2And the Israelites separated
themselves from all foreigners, and stood and
confessed their sins and the iniquities of their
fathers. 3And they stood up in their place and
read from the book of the law of the LORD their
God for a fourth of the day; for another fourth
of it they made confession and worshiped the
LORD their God. 4Upon the stairs of the Levites
stood Jesh′ua, Ba′ni, Kad′mi-el, Shebani′ah,
Bunni, Sherebi′ah, Bani, and Chena′ni; and
they cried with a loud voice to the LORD their
God. 5Then the Levites, Jesh′ua, Kad′mi-el,
Ba′ni, Hashabnei′ah, Sherebi′ah, Hodi′ah,
Shebani′ah, and Pethahi′ah, said, "Stand up
and bless the LORD your God from everlasting
to everlasting. Blessed be your glorious name
which is exalted above all blessing and praise."

6And Ezra said: "You are the LORD, you
alone; you have made heaven, the heaven of
heavens, with all their host, the earth and all
that is on it, the seas and all that is in them;
and you preserve all of them; and the host of
heaven worships you. 7You are the LORD, the
God who chose Abram and brought him forth
out of Ur of the Chalde′ans and gave him the
name Abraham; 8and you found his heart
faithful before you, and made with him the
covenant to give to his descendants the land
of the Canaanite, the Hittite, the Am′orite, the
Per′izzite, the Jeb′usite, and the Gir′gashite; and
you have fulfilled your promise, for you are
righteous.

9"And you saw the affliction of our fathers in
Egypt and heard their cry at the Red Sea, 10and
performed signs and wonders against Pharaoh
and all his servants and all the people of his
land, for you knew that they acted insolently
against our fathers; and you got yourself a
name, as it is to this day. 11And you divided the
sea before them, so that they went through the
midst of the sea on dry land; and you cast their
pursuers into the depths, as a stone into mighty
waters. 12By a pillar of cloud you led them in
the day, and by a pillar of fire in the night to
light for them the way in which they should
go. 13You came down upon Mount Sinai, and
spoke with them from heaven and gave them
right ordinances and true laws, good statutes
and commandments, 14and you made known
to them your holy sabbath and commanded
them commandments and statutes and a law
by Moses your servant. 15You gave them bread
from heaven for their hunger and brought
forth water for them from the rock for their
thirst, and you told them to go in to possess the
land which you had sworn to give them.

16"But they and our fathers acted presumptuously and stiffened their neck and did
not obey your commandments; 17they refused
to obey, and were not mindful of the wonders
which you performed among them; but they
stiffened their neck and appointed a leader to
return to their bondage in Egypt. But you are
a God ready to forgive, gracious and merciful,
slow to anger and abounding in mercy, and did
not forsake them. 18Even when they had made
for themselves a molten calf and said, 'This is
your God who brought you up out of Egypt,'
and had committed great blasphemies, 19you in
your great mercies did not forsake them in the
wilderness; the pillar of cloud which led them
in the way did not depart from them by day,
nor the pillar of fire by night which lighted for
them the way by which they should go. 20You

gave your good Spirit to instruct them, and did
not withhold your manna from their mouth,
and gave them water for their thirst. 21 Forty
years you sustained them in the wilderness,
and they lacked nothing; their clothes did not
wear out and their feet did not swell. 22 And you
gave them kingdoms and peoples, and allotted
to them every corner; so they took possession
of the land of Si'hon king of Heshbon and the
land of Og king of Bashan. 23 You multiplied
their descendants as the stars of heaven, and
you brought them into the land which you had
told their fathers to enter and possess. 24 So the
descendants went in and possessed the land,
and you subdued before them the inhabitants
of the land, the Canaanites, and gave them into
their hands, with their kings and the peoples of
the land, that they might do with them as they
would. 25 And they captured fortified cities and
a rich land, and took possession of houses full
of all good things, cisterns hewn out, vineyards,
olive orchards and fruit trees in abundance; so
they ate, and were filled and became fat, and
delighted themselves in your great goodness.

26 "Nevertheless they were disobedient and
rebelled against you and cast your law behind
their back and killed your prophets, who had
warned them in order to turn them back to
you, and they committed great blasphemies.
27 Therefore you gave them into the hand of
their enemies, who made them suffer; and
in the time of their suffering they cried to
you and you heard them from heaven; and
according to your great mercies you gave them
saviors who saved them from the hand of their
enemies. 28 But after they had rest they did evil
again before you, and you abandoned them
to the hand of their enemies, so that they had
dominion over them; yet when they turned
and cried to you, you heard from heaven, and
many times you delivered them according
to your mercies. 29 And you warned them in
order to turn them back to your law. Yet they
acted presumptuously and did not obey your
commandments, but sinned against your
ordinances, by the observance of which a man
shall live, and turned a stubborn shoulder
and stiffened their neck and would not obey.
30 Many years you bore with them, and warned
them by your Spirit through your prophets; yet
they would not give ear. Therefore you gave
them into the hand of the peoples of the lands.
31 Nevertheless in your great mercies you did
not make an end of them or forsake them; for
you are a gracious and merciful God.

32 "Now therefore, our God, the great and
mighty and awesome God, who keep covenant
and mercy, let not all the hardship seem little
to you that has come upon us, upon our kings,
our princes, our priests, our prophets, our
fathers, and all your people, since the time
of the kings of Assyria until this day. 33 Yet
you have been just in all that has come upon
us, for you have dealt faithfully and we have
acted wickedly; 34 our kings, our princes, our
priests, and our fathers have not kept your
law or heeded your commandments and your
warnings which you gave them. 35 They did not
serve you in their kingdom, and in your great
goodness which you gave them, and in the
large and rich land which you set before them;
and they did not turn from their wicked works.
36 Behold, we are slaves this day; in the land that
you gave to our fathers to enjoy its fruit and
its good gifts, behold, we are slaves. 37 And its
rich yield goes to the kings whom you have set
over us because of our sins; they have power
also over our bodies and over our cattle at their
pleasure, and we are in great distress."

PROVERBS 19

Better is a poor man who walks in
his integrity
than a man who is perverse in speech,
and is a fool.
2 It is not good for a man to be
without knowledge,
and he who makes haste with his feet
misses his way.
3 When a man's folly brings his way to ruin,
his heart rages against the LORD.
4 Wealth brings many new friends,
but a poor man is deserted by his friend.
5 A false witness will not go unpunished,
and he who utters lies will not escape.
6 Many seek the favor of a generous man,
and every one is a friend to a man who
gives gifts.

7 All a poor man's brothers hate him;
how much more do his friends go far
from him!
He pursues them with words, but does not
have them.
8 He who gets wisdom loves himself;
he who keeps understanding will prosper.
9 A false witness will not go unpunished,
and he who utters lies will perish.
10 It is not fitting for a fool to live in luxury,
much less for a slave to rule over princes.
11 Good sense makes a man slow to anger,
and it is his glory to overlook an offense.
12 A king's wrath is like the growling of a lion,
but his favor is like dew upon the grass.
13 A foolish son is ruin to his father,
and a wife's quarreling is a continual
dripping of rain.
14 House and wealth are inherited from fathers,
but a prudent wife is from the LORD.

ACTS 26

Agrippa said to Paul, "You have permission to speak for yourself."
Then Paul stretched out his hand and made his defense:
2 "I think myself fortunate that it is before
you, King Agrippa, I am to make my defense
today against all the accusations of the Jews,
3 because you are especially familiar with
all customs and controversies of the Jews;
therefore I beg you to listen to me patiently.
4 "My manner of life from my youth, spent
from the beginning among my own nation
and at Jerusalem, is known by all the Jews.
5 They have known for a long time, if they
are willing to testify, that according to the
strictest party of our religion I have lived as
a Pharisee. 6 And now I stand here on trial
for hope in the promise made by God to our
fathers, 7 to which our twelve tribes hope to
attain, as they earnestly worship night and
day. And for this hope I am accused by
Jews, O king! 8 Why is it thought incredible
by any of you that God raises the dead?
9 "I myself was convinced that I ought
to do many things in opposing the name
of Jesus of Nazareth. 10 And I did so in
Jerusalem; I not only shut up many of the
saints in prison, by authority from the chief
priests, but when they were put to death I
cast my vote against them. 11 And I punished
them often in all the synagogues and tried
to make them blaspheme; and in raging
fury against them, I persecuted them even
to foreign cities.
12 "Thus I journeyed to Damascus with
the authority and commission of the chief
priests. 13 At midday, O king, I saw on the
way a light from heaven, brighter than
the sun, shining round me and those who
journeyed with me. 14 And when we had all
fallen to the ground, I heard a voice saying
to me in the Hebrew language, 'Saul, Saul,
why do you persecute me? It hurts you
to kick against the goads.' 15 And I said,
'Who are you, Lord?' And the Lord said,
'I am Jesus whom you are persecuting.
16 But rise and stand upon your feet; for
I have appeared to you for this purpose,
to appoint you to serve and bear witness
to the things in which you have seen me
and to those in which I will appear to you,
17 delivering you from the people and from
the Gentiles—to whom I send you 18 to
open their eyes, that they may turn from
darkness to light and from the power
of Satan to God, that they may receive
forgiveness of sins and a place among
those who are sanctified by faith in me.'
19 "Wherefore, O King Agrippa, I was not
disobedient to the heavenly vision, 20 but
declared first to those at Damascus, then at
Jerusalem and throughout all the country
of Judea, and also to the Gentiles, that
they should repent and turn to God and
perform deeds worthy of their repentance.
21 For this reason the Jews seized me in the
temple and tried to kill me. 22 To this day
I have had the help that comes from God,
and so I stand here testifying both to small
and great, saying nothing but what the
prophets and Moses said would come to
pass: 23 that the Christ must suffer, and that,
by being the first to rise from the dead, he
would proclaim light both to the people
and to the Gentiles."

REFLECTION

It is hard for us to fathom how the God of the universe can be both a righteous and just judge who hates sin, and at the same time the God of loving kindness who bestows abundant mercy on his repentant children. Ezra's prayer on the people's behalf does an amazing job of comparing the continual mercy of God and the repeated failures of his people. Ezra recounts, "Our fathers acted presumptuously and stiffened their neck and did not obey your commandments" (Neh 9:16), but God blesses them with his presence, with manna from Heaven, and with the Promised Land. When they finally enter into the land, however, they "cast [God's] law behind their back" (v. 26). In sum, "[God has] dealt faithfully and [the people] have acted wickedly" (v. 33). St. Paul deals with a similar dichotomy in his own testimony, since he had been a zealous Jewish persecutor of the early Christians and then does an about-face when he has a vision of Jesus. Once we know how broken and sinful we are, we realize how great God's mercy must be that he is willing to reach out and save us. How does God's perfect mercy resolve your imperfection?

July 28

NEHEMIAH 9

[38]Because of all this we make
a firm covenant and write it,
and our princes, our Levites, and our
priests set their seal to it.

10 Those who set their seal are Nehe-
mi′ah the governor, the son of
Hacali′ah, Zedeki′ah, [2]Serai′ah, Azari′ah,
Jeremi′ah, [3]Pashhur, Amari′ah, Malchi′jah,
[4]Hattush, Shebani′ah, Malluch, [5]Harim,
Mer′emoth, Obadi′ah, [6]Daniel, Gin′nethon,
Baruch, [7]Meshul′lam, Abi′jah, Mi′jamin, [8]Ma-
azi′ah, Bilgai, Shemai′ah; these are the priests.
[9]And the Levites: Jesh′ua the son of Azani′ah,
Bin′nui of the sons of Hen′adad, Kad′mi-el; [10]and
their brethren, Shebani′ah, Hodi′ah, Keli′ta,
Pelai′ah, Hanan, [11]Mica, Re′hob, Hashabi′ah,
[12]Zaccur, Sherebi′ah, Shebani′ah, [13]Hodi′ah,
Ba′ni, Beni′nu. [14]The chiefs of the people:
Pa′rosh, Pa′hath-mo′ab, E′lam, Zattu, Ba′ni,
[15]Bunni, Azgad, Bebai, [16]Adoni′jah, Bigvai,
A′din, [17]A′ter, Hezeki′ah, Azzur, [18]Hodi′ah,
Hashum, Bezai, [19]Hariph, An′athoth, Nebai,
[20]Mag′piash, Meshul′lam, He′zir, [21]Meshez′abel,
Za′dok, Jad′du-a, [22]Pelati′ah, Hanan, Anai′ah,
[23]Hoshe′a, Hanani′ah, Hasshub, [24]Hallo′hesh,
Pilha, Shobek, [25]Re′hum, Hashab′nah, Ma-
asei′ah, [26]Ahi′ah, Ha′nan, A′nan, [27]Malluch,
Harim, Ba′anah.

[28]The rest of the people, the priests, the
Levites, the gatekeepers, the singers, the
temple servants, and all who have separated
themselves from the peoples of the lands to
the law of God, their wives, their sons, their
daughters, all who have knowledge and
understanding, [29]join with their brethren,
their nobles, and enter into a curse and
an oath to walk in God's law which was
given by Moses the servant of God, and to
observe and do all the commandments of
the LORD our Lord and his ordinances and
his statutes. [30]We will not give our daughters
to the peoples of the land or take their
daughters for our sons; [31]and if the peoples
of the land bring in wares or any grain on
the sabbath day to sell, we will not buy from
them on the sabbath or on a holy day; and
we will forego the crops of the seventh year
and the exaction of every debt.

[32]We also lay upon ourselves the obligation
to charge ourselves yearly with the third part
of a shekel for the service of the house of
our God: [33]for the showbread, the continual
cereal offering, the continual burnt offering,
the sabbaths, the new moons, the appointed
feasts, the holy things, and the sin offerings
to make atonement for Israel, and for all the
work of the house of our God. [34]We have
likewise cast lots, the priests, the Levites,
and the people, for the wood offering, to
bring it into the house of our God, according
to our fathers' houses, at times appointed,
year by year, to burn upon the altar of the
LORD our God, as it is written in the law.
[35]We obligate ourselves to bring the first

fruits of our ground and the first fruits of all
fruit of every tree, year by year, to the house
of the LORD; 36also to bring to the house
of our God, to the priests who minister
in the house of our God, the first-born of
our sons and of our cattle, as it is written
in the law, and the firstlings of our herds
and of our flocks; 37and to bring the first
of our coarse meal, and our contributions,
the fruit of every tree, the wine and the oil,
to the priests, to the chambers of the house
of our God; and to bring to the Levites the
tithes from our ground, for it is the Levites
who collect the tithes in all our rural towns.
38And the priest, the son of Aaron, shall be
with the Levites when the Levites receive
the tithes; and the Levites shall bring up the
tithe of the tithes to the house of our God,
to the chambers, to the storehouse. 39For
the sons of Israel and the sons of Levi shall
bring the contribution of grain, wine, and
oil to the chambers, where are the vessels of
the sanctuary, and the priests that minister,
and the gatekeepers and the singers. We will
not neglect the house of our God.

11 Now the leaders of the people lived
in Jerusalem; and the rest of the
people cast lots to bring one out of ten to
live in Jerusalem the holy city, while nine
tenths remained in the other towns. 2And
the people blessed all the men who willingly
offered to live in Jerusalem.

3These are the chiefs of the province who
lived in Jerusalem; but in the towns of
Judah every one lived on his property in
their towns: Israel, the priests, the Levites,
the temple servants, and the descendants of
Solomon's servants. 4And in Jerusalem lived
certain of the sons of Judah and of the sons
of Benjamin. Of the sons of Judah: Athai′ah
the son of Uzzi′ah, son of Zechari′ah, son of
Amari′ah, son of Shephati′ah, son of Ma-
hal′alel, of the sons of Per′ez; 5and Ma-asei′ah
the son of Baruch, son of Col-ho′zeh, son of
Hazai′ah, son of Adai′ah, son of Joi′arib, son
of Zechari′ah, son of the Shilon′ite. 6All the
sons of Per′ez who lived in Jerusalem were
four hundred and sixty-eight valiant men.

7And these are the sons of Benjamin:
Sallu the son of Meshul′lam, son of Jo′ed,
son of Pedai′ah, son of Kolai′ah, son of Ma-
asei′ah, son of I′thi-el, son of Jeshai′ah. 8And
after him Gabba′i, Sallai, nine hundred
and twenty-eight. 9Joel the son of Zich′ri
was their overseer; and Judah the son of
Hassenu′ah was second over the city.

10Of the priests: Jedai′ah the son of Joi′arib,
Ja′chin, 11Serai′ah the son of Hilki′ah, son of
Meshul′lam, son of Za′dok, son of Mera′ioth,
son of Ahi′tub, ruler of the house of God, 12and
their brethren who did the work of the house,
eight hundred and twenty-two; and Adai′ah
the son of Jero′ham, son of Pelali′ah, son of
Amzi, son of Zechari′ah, son of Pashhur, son
of Malchi′jah, 13and his brethren, heads of
fathers' houses, two hundred and forty-two;
and Amash′sai, the son of Az′arel, son of
Ahzai, son of Meshil′lemoth, son of Immer,
14and their brethren, mighty men of valor,
a hundred and twenty-eight; their overseer
was Zab′diel the son of Haggedo′lim.

15And of the Levites: Shemai′ah the son of
Hasshub, son of Azri′kam, son of Hashabi′ah,
son of Bunni; 16and Shab′bethai and Jo′zabad,
of the chiefs of the Levites, who were over
the outside work of the house of God; 17and
Mattani′ah the son of Mica, son of Zabdi,
son of A′saph, who was the leader to begin
the thanksgiving in prayer, and Bakbuki′ah,
the second among his brethren; and Abda
the son of Sham′mu-a, son of Galal, son of
Jedu′thun. 18All the Levites in the holy city
were two hundred and eighty-four.

19The gatekeepers, Akkub, Talmon and
their brethren, who kept watch at the gates,
were a hundred and seventy-two. 20And
the rest of Israel, and of the priests and the
Levites, were in all the towns of Judah, every
one in his inheritance. 21But the temple
servants lived on O′phel; and Ziha and
Gishpa were over the temple servants.

22The overseer of the Levites in Jerusalem
was Uzzi the son of Ba′ni, son of Hashabi′ah,
son of Mattani′ah, son of Mica, of the sons
of A′saph, the singers, over the work of the
house of God. 23For there was a command
from the king concerning them, and a
settled provision for the singers, as every
day required. 24And Pethahi′ah the son of
Meshez′abel, of the sons of Ze′rah the son of

Judah, was at the king's hand in all matters concerning the people.

25And as for the villages, with their fields, some of the people of Judah lived in Kir′iath-ar′ba and its villages, and in Di′bon and its villages, and in Jekab′zeel and its villages, 26and in Jesh′ua and in Mo′ladah and Beth-pel′et, 27in Ha′zar-shu′al, in Be′er-she′ba and its villages, 28in Zik′lag, in Meco′nah and its villages, 29in En-rim′mon, in Zo′rah, in Jarmuth, 30Zano′ah, Adul′lam, and their villages, La′chish and its fields, and Aze′kah and its villages. So they encamped from Be′er-she′ba to the valley of Hinnom. 31The people of Benjamin also lived from Ge′ba onward, at Michmash, Aija, Bethel and its villages, 32An′athoth, Nob, Anani′ah, 33Ha′zor, Ra′mah, Git′taim, 34Hadid, Zebo′im, Nebal′lat, 35Lod, and Ono, the valley of craftsmen. 36And certain divisions of the Levites in Judah were joined to Benjamin.

12 These are the priests and the Levites who came up with Zerub′babel the son of She-al′tiel, and Jesh′ua: Serai′ah, Jeremi′ah, Ezra, 2Amari′ah, Malluch, Hattush, 3Shecani′ah, Re′hum, Mer′emoth, 4Iddo, Gin′nethoi, Abi′jah, 5Mi′jamin, Ma-adi′ah, Bilgah, 6Shemai′ah, Joi′arib, Jedai′ah, 7Sallu, A′mok, Hilki′ah, Jedai′ah. These were the chiefs of the priests and of their brethren in the days of Jesh′ua.

8And the Levites: Jesh′ua, Bin′nui, Kad′mi-el, Sherebi′ah, Judah, and Mattani′ah, who with his brethren was in charge of the songs of thanksgiving. 9And Bakbuki′ah and Unno their brethren stood opposite them in the service. 10And Jesh′ua was the father of Joi′akim, Joiakim the father of Eli′ashib, Eliashib the father of Joi′ada, 11Joi′ada the father of Jonathan, and Jonathan the father of Jad′du-a.

12And in the days of Joi′akim were priests, heads of fathers' houses: of Serai′ah, Merai′ah; of Jeremi′ah, Hanani′ah; 13of Ezra, Meshul′lam; of Amari′ah, Jeho-ha′nan; 14of Mal′luchi, Jonathan; of Shebani′ah, Joseph; 15of Harim, Adna; of Mera′ioth, Helkai; 16of Iddo, Zechari′ah; of Gin′nethon, Meshul′lam; 17of Abi′jah, Zich′ri; of Mini′amin, of Moadi′ah, Piltai; 18of Bilgah, Sham′mu-a; of Shemai′ah, Jehon′athan; 19of Joi′arib, Matte′nai; of Jedai′ah, Uzzi; 20of Sallai, Kallai; of A′mok, E′ber; 21of Hilki′ah, Hashabi′ah; of Jedai′ah, Nethan′el.

22As for the Levites, in the days of Eli′ashib, Joi′ada, Joha′nan, and Jad′du-a, there were recorded the heads of fathers' houses; also the priests until the reign of Dari′us the Persian. 23The sons of Levi, heads of fathers' houses, were written in the Book of the Chronicles until the days of Joha′nan the son of Eli′ashib. 24And the chiefs of the Levites: Hashabi′ah, Sherebi′ah, and Jesh′ua the son of Kad′mi-el, with their brethren over against them, to praise and to give thanks, according to the commandment of David the man of God, watch corresponding to watch. 25Mattani′ah, Bakbuki′ah, Obadi′ah, Meshul′lam, Talmon, and Akkub were gatekeepers standing guard at the storehouses of the gates. 26These were in the days of Joi′akim the son of Jesh′ua son of Jo′zadak, and in the days of Nehemi′ah the governor and of Ezra the priest the scribe.

PROVERBS 19

15Slothfulness casts into a deep sleep,
and an idle person will suffer hunger.
16He who keeps the commandment keeps
his life;
he who despises the word will die.
17He who is kind to the poor lends to
the LORD,
and he will repay him for his deed.
18Discipline your son while there is hope;
do not set your heart on his destruction.
19A man of great wrath will pay the penalty;
for if you deliver him, you will only have
to do it again.
20Listen to advice and accept instruction,
that you may gain wisdom for the future.
21Many are the plans in the mind of a man,
but it is the purpose of the LORD that will
be established.
22What is desired in a man is loyalty,
and a poor man is better than a liar.
23The fear of the LORD leads to life;
and he who has it rests satisfied;
he will not be visited by harm.

[24]The sluggard buries his hand in the dish,
and will not even bring it back to
his mouth.
[25]Strike a scoffer, and the simple will
learn prudence;
reprove a man of understanding, and he
will gain knowledge.
[26]He who does violence to his father and
chases away his mother
is a son who causes shame and
brings reproach.
[27]Cease, my son, to hear instruction
only to stray from the words of knowledge.
[28]A worthless witness mocks at justice,
and the mouth of the wicked
devours iniquity.
[29]Condemnation is ready for scoffers,
and flogging for the backs of fools.

ACTS 26

**[24]And as he thus made his de-
fense, Festus said with a loud
voice, "Paul, you are mad; your great
learning is turning you mad." [25]But Paul**
said, "I am not mad, most excellent Festus,
but I am speaking the sober truth. [26]For the
king knows about these things, and to him I
speak freely; for I am persuaded that none of
these things has escaped his notice, for this
was not done in a corner. [27]King Agrippa,
do you believe the prophets? I know that
you believe." [28]And Agrippa said to Paul,
"In a short time you think to make me a
Christian!" [29]And Paul said, "Whether short
or long, I would to God that not only you but
also all who hear me this day might become
such as I am—except for these chains."
[30]Then the king rose, and the governor and
Bernice and those who were sitting with them;
[31]and when they had withdrawn, they said
to one another, "This man is doing nothing
to deserve death or imprisonment." [32]And
Agrippa said to Festus, "This man could have
been set free if he had not appealed to Caesar."

27 And when it was decided that we
should sail for Italy, they delivered
Paul and some other prisoners to a centurion
of the Augustan Cohort, named Julius. [2]And
embarking in a ship of Adramyt´tium, which
was about to sail to the ports along the coast
of Asia, we put to sea, accompanied by Aris-
tar´chus, a Macedonian from Thessaloni´ca.
[3]The next day we put in at Si´don; and Julius treated Paul kindly, and gave him leave
to go to his friends and be cared for. [4]And
putting to sea from there we sailed under
the lee of Cyprus, because the winds were
against us. [5]And when we had sailed across
the sea which is off Cili´cia and Pamphyl´ia,
we came to Myra in Ly´cia. [6]There the centurion found a ship of Alexandria sailing for
Italy, and put us on board. [7]We sailed slowly
for a number of days, and arrived with difficulty off Cni´dus, and as the wind did not
allow us to go on, we sailed under the lee of
Crete off Salmo´ne. [8]Coasting along it with
difficulty, we came to a place called Fair Ha-
vens, near which was the city of Lase´a.
[9]As much time had been lost, and the
voyage was already dangerous because the
fast had already gone by, Paul advised them,
[10]saying, "Sirs, I perceive that the voyage will
be with injury and much loss, not only of
the cargo and the ship, but also of our lives."
[11]But the centurion paid more attention to
the captain and to the owner of the ship
than to what Paul said. [12]And because the
harbor was not suitable to winter in, the
majority advised to put to sea from there,
on the chance that somehow they could
reach Phoenix, a harbor of Crete, looking
northeast and southeast, and winter there.

REFLECTION

Most people, except maybe for lawyers, forget about the contracts they sign. Detailed stipulations are often only informally observed until a problem arises and the courts get involved. Nehemiah wants to make sure that the Jews he governs do not forget the details of their covenant with God, so he initiates a covenant renewal ceremony, including a signed document. Here the people recommit to the Lord and to obey his Law—a reminder that our vows to him need constant renewal. For "many are the plans in the mind of a man, but it is the purpose of the LORD that will be established" (Prv 19:21). No matter how many ideas we come up with, we need to look to the Lord's will and trust in his providence and his plan. We see this principle in St. Paul's life, when he prophesies to the sailing crew ferrying him to Rome that shipwreck will come and advises them to wait. Yet the majority overrule him and soon embrace their unlucky fate. God knows what is going to happen and even sends his messenger to prevent it. When we are up against difficult situations, let's hope that we are patient enough to listen to what the Lord is saying to us. Do you regularly recommit to the Lord and entrust yourself to his plan?

July 29

NEHEMIAH 12

27 And at the dedication of the wall of Jerusalem they sought the Levites in all their places, to bring them to Jerusalem to celebrate the dedication with gladness, with thanksgivings and with singing, with cymbals, harps, and lyres. 28 And the sons of the singers gathered together from the circuit round Jerusalem and from the villages of the Netoph´athites; 29 also from Beth-gil´gal and from the region of Ge´ba and Az´maveth; for the singers had built for themselves villages around Jerusalem. 30 And the priests and the Levites purified themselves; and they purified the people and the gates and the wall.

31 Then I brought up the princes of Judah upon the wall, and appointed two great companies which gave thanks and went in procession. One went to the right upon the wall to the Dung Gate; 32 and after them went Hoshai´ah and half of the princes of Judah, 33 and Azari´ah, Ezra, Meshul´lam, 34 Judah, Benjamin, Shemai´ah, and Jeremi´ah, 35 and certain of the priests' sons with trumpets: Zechari´ah the son of Jonathan, son of Shemai´ah, son of Mattani´ah, son of Micai´ah, son of Zaccur, son of A´saph; 36 and his kinsmen, Shemai´ah, Az´arel, Mil´alai, Gil´alai, Ma´ai, Nethan´el, Judah, and Hana´ni, with the musical instruments of David the man of God; and Ezra the scribe went before them. 37 At the Fountain Gate they went up straight before them by the stairs of the city of David, at the ascent of the wall, above the house of David, to the Water Gate on the east.

38 The other company of those who gave thanks went to the left, and I followed them with half of the people, upon the wall, above the Tower of the Ovens, to the Broad Wall, 39 and above the Gate of E´phraim, and by the Old Gate, and by the Fish Gate and the Tower of Hanan´el and the Tower of the Hundred, to the Sheep Gate; and they came to a halt at the Gate of the Guard. 40 So both companies of those who gave thanks stood in the house of God, and I and half of the officials with me; 41 and the priests Eli´akim, Ma-asei´ah, Mini´amin, Micai´ah, El´i-o-e´nai, Zechari´ah, and Hanani´ah, with trumpets; 42 and Ma-asei´ah, Shemai´ah, Elea´zar, Uzzi, Je´ho-ha´nan, Malchi´jah, E´lam, and E´zer. And the singers sang with Jezrahi´ah as their leader. 43 And they offered great sacrifices that day and rejoiced, for God had made them rejoice with great joy; the women and children also rejoiced. And the joy of Jerusalem was heard afar off.

44 On that day men were appointed over the chambers for the stores, the contributions, the first fruits, and the tithes, to gather into them the portions required by the law for the priests and for the Levites according to the fields of the towns; for Judah rejoiced over the priests and the Levites who ministered. 45 And they performed the service of their God and the service of purification, as did the singers and the gatekeepers, according to the command of David and his son Solomon. 46 For in the days of David and A´saph of old there was a chief of the singers, and there were songs of praise and thanksgiving to God. 47 And all Israel in the days of Zerub´babel and in the

days of Nehemi′ah gave the daily portions for the singers and the gatekeepers; and they set apart that which was for the Levites; and the Levites set apart that which was for the sons of Aaron.

13 On that day they read from the book of Moses in the hearing of the people; and in it was found written that no Am′monite or Moabite should ever enter the assembly of God; [2]for they did not meet the children of Israel with bread and water, but hired Balaam against them to curse them—yet our God turned the curse into a blessing. [3]When the people heard the law, they separated from Israel all those of foreign descent.

[4]Now before this, Eli′ashib the priest, who was appointed over the chambers of the house of our God, and who was connected with Tobi′ah, [5]prepared for Tobi′ah a large chamber where they had previously put the cereal offering, the frankincense, the vessels, and the tithes of grain, wine, and oil, which were given by commandment to the Levites, singers, and gatekeepers, and the contributions for the priests. [6]While this was taking place I was not in Jerusalem, for in the thirty-second year of Ar-ta-xerx′es king of Babylon I went to the king. And after some time I asked leave of the king [7]and came to Jerusalem, and I then discovered the evil that Eli′ashib had done for Tobi′ah, preparing for him a chamber in the courts of the house of God. [8]And I was very angry, and I threw all the household furniture of Tobi′ah out of the chamber. [9]Then I gave orders and they cleansed the chambers; and I brought back there the vessels of the house of God, with the cereal offering and the frankincense.

[10]I also found out that the portions of the Levites had not been given to them; so that the Levites and the singers, who did the work, had fled each to his field. [11]So I remonstrated with the officials and said, "Why is the house of God forsaken?" And I gathered them together and set them in their stations. [12]Then all Judah brought the tithe of the grain, wine, and oil into the storehouses. [13]And I appointed as treasurers over the storehouses Shelemi′ah the priest, Za′dok the scribe, and Pedai′ah of the Levites, and as their assistant Ha′nan the son of Zaccur, son of Mattani′ah, for they were counted faithful; and their duty was to distribute to their brethren. [14]Remember me, O my God, concerning this, and wipe not out my good deeds that I have done for the house of my God and for his service.

[15]In those days I saw in Judah men treading wine presses on the sabbath, and bringing in heaps of grain and loading them on donkeys; and also wine, grapes, figs, and all kinds of burdens, which they brought into Jerusalem on the sabbath day; and I warned them on the day when they sold food. [16]Men of Tyre also, who lived in the city, brought in fish and all kinds of wares and sold them on the sabbath to the people of Judah, and in Jerusalem. [17]Then I remonstrated with the nobles of Judah and said to them, "What is this evil thing which you are doing, profaning the sabbath day? [18]Did not your fathers act in this way, and did not our God bring all this evil on us and on this city? Yet you bring more wrath upon Israel by profaning the sabbath."

[19]When it began to be dark at the gates of Jerusalem before the sabbath, I commanded that the doors should be shut and gave orders that they should not be opened until after the sabbath. And I set some of my servants over the gates, that no burden might be brought in on the sabbath day. [20]Then the merchants and sellers of all kinds of wares lodged outside Jerusalem once or twice. [21]But I warned them and said to them, "Why do you lodge before the wall? If you do so again I will lay hands on you." From that time on they did not come on the sabbath. [22]And I commanded the Levites that they should purify themselves and come and guard the gates, to keep the sabbath day holy. Remember this also in my favor, O my God, and spare me according to the greatness of your mercy.

[23]In those days also I saw the Jews who had married women of Ash′dod, Ammon, and Moab; [24]and half of their children spoke the language of Ash′dod, and they

could not speak the language of Judah, but
the language of each people. 25And I contended with them and cursed them and beat
some of them and pulled out their hair; and
I made them take oath in the name of God,
saying, "You shall not give your daughters to
their sons, or take their daughters for your
sons or for yourselves. 26Did not Solomon
king of Israel sin on account of such women?
Among the many nations there was no king
like him, and he was beloved by his God, and
God made him king over all Israel; nevertheless foreign women made even him to sin.
27Shall we then listen to you and do all this
great evil and act treacherously against our
God by marrying foreign women?"
28And one of the sons of Jehoi′ada, the son
of Eli′ashib the high priest, was the son-in-
law of Sanbal′lat the Hor′onite; therefore I
chased him from me. 29Remember them,
O my God, because they have defiled the
priesthood and the covenant of the priesthood and the Levites.
30Thus I cleansed them from everything
foreign, and I established the duties of
the priests and Levites, each in his work;
31and I provided for the wood offering, at
appointed times, and for the first fruits.
Remember me, O my God, for good.

PROVERBS 20

Wine is a mocker, strong drink a brawler;
and whoever is led astray by it is not wise.
2The dread wrath of a king is like the
growling of a lion;
he who provokes him to anger forfeits
his life.
3It is an honor for a man to keep aloof
from strife;
but every fool will be quarreling.
4The sluggard does not plow in the autumn;
he will seek at harvest and have nothing.
5The purpose in a man's mind is like
deep water,
but a man of understanding will
draw it out.
6Many a man proclaims his own loyalty,
but a faithful man who can find?
7A righteous man who walks in his
integrity—
blessed are his sons after him!
8A king who sits on the throne of judgment
winnows all evil with his eyes.
9Who can say, "I have made my heart clean;
I am pure from my sin"?
10Diverse weights and diverse measures
are both alike an abomination to
the LORD.
11Even a child makes himself known by
his acts,
whether what he does is pure and right.
12The hearing ear and the seeing eye,
the LORD has made them both.
13Love not sleep, lest you come to poverty;
open your eyes, and you will have plenty
of bread.
14"It is bad, it is bad," says the buyer;
but when he goes away, then he boasts.
15There is gold, and abundance of costly
stones;
but the lips of knowledge are a
precious jewel.

ACTS 27

13And when the south wind blew
gently, supposing that they had
obtained their purpose, they
weighed anchor and sailed along Crete,
close inshore. 14But soon a tempestuous
wind, called the northeaster, struck down
from the land; 15and when the ship was
caught and could not face the wind, we
gave way to it and were driven. 16And
running under the lee of a small island
called Cau′da, we managed with difficulty
to secure the boat; 17after hoisting it up,
they took measures to undergird the ship;
then, fearing that they should run on the
Syr′tis, they lowered the gear, and so were
driven. 18As we were violently storm-
tossed, they began next day to throw the
cargo overboard; 19and the third day they
cast out with their own hands the tackle of
the ship. 20And when neither sun nor stars
appeared for many a day, and no small

tempest lay on us, all hope of our being saved was at last abandoned.

21As they had been long without food, Paul then came forward among them and said, "Men, you should have listened to me, and should not have set sail from Crete and incurred this injury and loss. 22I now bid you take heart; for there will be no loss of life among you, but only of the ship. 23For this very night there stood by me an angel of the God to whom I belong and whom I worship, 24and he said, 'Do not be afraid, Paul; you must stand before Caesar; and behold, God has granted you all those who sail with you.' 25So take heart, men, for I have faith in God that it will be exactly as I have been told. 26But we shall have to run on some island."

27When the fourteenth night had come, as we were drifting across the sea of A´dria, about midnight the sailors suspected that they were nearing land. 28So they sounded and found twenty fathoms; a little farther on they sounded again and found fifteen fathoms. 29And fearing that we might run on the rocks, they let out four anchors from the stern, and prayed for day to come. 30And as the sailors were seeking to escape from the ship, and had lowered the boat into the sea, under pretense of laying out anchors from the bow, 31Paul said to the centurion and the soldiers, "Unless these men stay in the ship, you cannot be saved." 32Then the soldiers cut away the ropes of the boat, and let it go.

33As day was about to dawn, Paul urged them all to take some food, saying, "Today is the fourteenth day that you have continued in suspense and without food, having taken nothing. 34Therefore I urge you to take some food; it will give you strength, since not a hair is to perish from the head of any of you." 35And when he had said this, he took bread, and giving thanks to God in the presence of all, he broke it and began to eat. 36Then they all were encouraged and ate some food themselves. 37(We were in all two hundred and seventy-six persons in the ship.) 38And when they had eaten enough, they lightened the ship, throwing out the wheat into the sea.

39Now when it was day, they did not recognize the land, but they noticed a bay with a beach, on which they planned if possible to bring the ship ashore. 40So they cast off the anchors and left them in the sea, at the same time loosening the ropes that tied the rudders; then hoisting the foresail to the wind they made for the beach. 41But striking a shoal they ran the vessel aground; the bow stuck and remained immovable, and the stern was broken up by the surf. 42The soldiers' plan was to kill the prisoners, lest any should swim away and escape; 43but the centurion, wishing to save Paul, kept them from carrying out their purpose. He ordered those who could swim to throw themselves overboard first and make for the land, 44and the rest on planks or on pieces of the ship. And so it was that all escaped to land.

REFLECTION

One of the worst feelings in the world comes from feeling trapped and in danger. Being on a sailing ship in the middle of a days-long storm in rough seas, constantly on the verge of shipwreck and drowning, is a quick way to get that feeling. St. Paul, though, in the midst of that exact circumstance, stays steady in faith. He even receives a message from an angel pledging his safety and the safety of all aboard. While he reminds the sailors, "You should have listened to me," he does not dwell on it, but encourages them to "take heart" (Acts 27:21–22). St. Paul's presence brings divine protection and guidance. If we adopt a worldly perspective when storms hit our lives, we can fall into panic. The Lord does not abandon us in our need, but wants to guide us and be near to us in the midst of life's trials. Nehemiah's generation, in their zeal to re-establish Jerusalem, must have deep trust in the Lord, which they symbolically enact by gathering together in "gladness, with thanksgivings" (Neh 12:27) with musical instruments and singing to "rejoice with great joy" (v. 43). Do you rely on the joy of the Lord when times are tough?

July 30

TOBIT 1

The book of the acts of Tobit the
son of Tobi′el, son of Anan′iel,
son of Adu′el, son of Gab′ael, of the
descendants of As′i-el and the tribe of
Naph′tali, 2who in the days of Shalmane′ser,
king of the Assyrians, was taken into
captivity from Thisbe, which is to the south
of Ke′desh Naph′tali in Galilee above Asher.
3I, Tobit, walked in the ways of truth
and righteousness all the days of my life,
and I performed many acts of charity to
my brethren and countrymen who went
with me into the land of the Assyrians,
to Nin′eveh. 4Now when I was in my
own country, in the land of Israel, while I
was still a young man, the whole tribe of
Naph′tali my forefather deserted the house
of Jerusalem. This was the place which had
been chosen from among all the tribes of
Israel, where all the tribes should sacrifice
and where the temple of the dwelling of the
Most High was consecrated and established
for all generations for ever.
5All the tribes that joined in apostasy
used to sacrifice to the calf Ba′al, and so
did the house of Naph′tali my forefather.
6But I alone went often to Jerusalem for
the feasts, as it is ordained for all Israel
by an everlasting decree. Taking the first
fruits and the tithes of my produce and the
first shearings, I would give these to the
priests, the sons of Aaron, at the altar. 7Of
all my produce I would give a tenth to the
sons of Levi who ministered at Jerusalem;
a second tenth I would sell, and I would
go and spend the proceeds each year at
Jerusalem; 8the third tenth I would give to
those to whom it was my duty, as Deborah
my father's mother had commanded me,
for I was left an orphan by my father.
9When I became a man I married Anna, a
member of our family, and by her I became
the father of Tobi′as.
10Now when I was carried away captive to
Nin′eveh, all my brethren and my relatives
ate the food of the Gentiles; 11but I kept
myself from eating it, 12because I remembered
God with all my heart. 13Then the Most High
gave me favor and good appearance in the
sight of Shalmane′ser, and I was his buyer
of provisions. 14So I used to go into Med′ia,
and once at Ra′ges in Med′ia I left ten talents
of silver in trust with Gab′ael, the brother
of Ga′brias. 15But when Shalmane′ser died,
Sennach′erib his son reigned in his place; and
under him the highways were unsafe, so that I
could no longer go into Med′ia.
16In the days of Shalmane′ser I performed
many acts of charity to my brethren. 17I
would give my bread to the hungry and my
clothing to the naked; and if I saw any one of
my people dead and thrown out behind the
wall of Nin′eveh, I would bury him. 18And
if Sennach′erib the king put to death any
who came fleeing from Judea, I buried them
secretly. For in his anger he put many to death.
When the bodies were sought by the king,
they were not found. 19Then one of the men
of Nin′eveh went and informed the king about
me, that I was burying them; so I hid myself.
When I learned that I was being searched for,
to be put to death, I left home in fear. 20Then
all my property was confiscated and nothing
was left to me except my wife Anna and my
son Tobi′as.
21But not fifty days passed before two of
Sennach′erib's sons killed him, and they fled to
the mountains of Ar′arat. Then E′sar-had′don,
his son, reigned in his place; and he appointed
Ahi′kar, the son of my brother An′ael, over
all the accounts of his kingdom and over the
entire administration. 22Ahi′kar interceded for
me, and I returned to Nin′eveh. Now Ahikar
was cupbearer, keeper of the signet, and in
charge of administration of the accounts,
for E′sar-had′don had appointed him
second to himself. He was my nephew.

2 When I arrived home and my wife Anna
and my son Tobi′as were restored to
me, at the feast of Pentecost, which is the
sacred festival of the seven weeks, a good
dinner was prepared for me and I sat down
to eat. 2Upon seeing the abundance of food I

said to my son, "Go and bring whatever poor
man of our brethren you may find among
the exiles in Nineveh, who is mindful of the
Lord, and he shall eat together with me. I will
wait for you until you come back." 3So Tobias
went out to look for some poor person of our
people. When he came back, he said, "Father!"
And I replied, "Here I am, my child." And
he went on to say, "Look, Father, one of our
own people has been murdered and thrown
into the market place, and now he lies there
strangled." 4So before I tasted anything I sprang
up and removed the body to a place of shelter
until sunset when I might bury it. 5And when
I returned I washed myself and ate my food in
sorrow. 6Then I remembered the prophecy of
Amos, how he said against Bethel,

"Your feasts shall be turned into mourning,
and all your songs into lamentation."

And I wept.

7When the sun had set I went and dug a
grave and buried the body. 8And my neighbors
laughed at me and said, "He is still not afraid;
he has already been hunted down to be put to
death for doing this, and he ran away, yet here
he is burying the dead again!" 9On the same
night after I, Tobit, returned from burying
the dead, I went into my courtyard and slept
by the wall of the courtyard, and my face was
uncovered because of the heat. 10I did not
know that there were sparrows on the wall
and their fresh droppings fell into my open
eyes and white films formed on my eyes. I
went to physicians to be healed, but the more
they treated me with ointments, the more my
vision was obscured by the white films, until
I became completely blind. For four years I
remained unable to see. All my kindred were
sorry for me, and Ahi′kar took care of me for
two years until he went to El″yma′is.

11Then my wife Anna earned money at
women's work. 12She used to send the product
to the owners, and they paid her wages. One
day, the seventh of Dystrus, when she cut off
a piece she had woven and sent it to the
owners, they paid her full wages and they
also gave her a kid. 13When she returned
to me it began to bleat. So I called her and
said to her, "Where did you get the kid? It
is not stolen, is it? Return it to the owners;
for it is not right to eat what is stolen."
14And she said, "It was given to me as a
gift in addition to my wages." But I did
not believe her, and told her to return it
to the owners; and I blushed for her. Then
she replied to me, "Where are your charities
and your righteous deeds? You seem to
know everything!"

3 Then in my grief I wept, and I prayed in
anguish, saying, 2"Righteous are you, O
Lord; all your deeds are just and all your
ways are mercy and truth, and you render true
and righteous judgment for ever. 3And now, O
Lord, remember me and look favorably upon
me; do not punish me for my sins and for my
unwitting offenses and those which my fathers
committed before you. 4For we disobeyed
your commandments, and you gave us over
to plunder, captivity, and death; you made us
the talk, the byword, and an object of reproach
in all the nations among which you have
dispersed us. 5And now your many judgments
are true in exacting penalty from me for my
sins and those of my fathers, because we did
not keep your commandments. For we did not
walk in truth before you. 6And now deal with
me according to your pleasure; command my
spirit to be taken up, that I may be released
from the face of the earth and become dust. For
it is better for me to die than to live, because I
have heard false reproaches, and great is the
sorrow within me. Command that I now be
released from my distress; release me to go to
the eternal abode; and do not, O Lord, turn
your face away from me. For it is better for me
to die than to see so much distress in my life
and listen to such insults."

7On the same day, at Ecbat′ana in Med′ia,
it also happened that Sarah, the daughter
of Rag′uel, was reproached by her father's
maids, 8because she had been given to seven
husbands, and the evil demon As″mode′us
had slain each of them before he had been
with her as his wife. So the maids said to her,
"You are the one who kills your husbands!
See, you already have had seven and have had
no benefit from any of them. 9Why do you
beat us? Because your husbands are dead?
Go with them! May we never see a son or
daughter of yours!"

[10]On that day she was deeply grieved in spirit
and wept. When she had gone up to her father's
upper room, she intended to hang herself.
But she thought it over and said, "Never
shall they reproach my father, saying to him,
'You only had one beloved daughter but she
hanged herself because of her distress.' And
I shall bring his old age down in sorrow
to the grave. It is better for me not to hang
myself, but to pray the Lord that I may die
and not listen to these reproaches any more."
[11]At that same time, with hands outstretched
toward the window, she prayed and said,
"Blessed are you, O Lord, merciful God, and
blessed is your holy and honored name for
ever. May all your works praise you for ever.
[12]And now, O Lord, I have turned my eyes
and my face toward you. [13]Command that
I be released from the earth and that I hear
reproach no more. [14]You know, O Lord, that
I am innocent of any sin with man, [15]and that
I did not stain my name or the name of my
father in the land of my captivity. I am my
father's only child, and he has no child to be
his heir, no near kinsman or kinsman's son for
whom I should keep myself as wife. Already
seven husbands of mine are dead. Why should
I live? But if it be not pleasing to you to take
my life, command that respect be shown to
me and pity be taken upon me, and that I hear
reproach no more."
[16]At that very moment the prayer of both was
heard in the presence of the glory of the great
God. [17]And Ra′phael was sent to heal the two
of them: to scale away the white films of Tobit's
eyes; to give Sarah the daughter of Rag′uel in
marriage to Tobi′as the son of Tobit, and to
bind As″mode′us the evil demon, because
Tobias was entitled to possess her. At that very
moment Tobit returned and entered his house
and Sarah the daughter of Raguel came down
from her upper room.

PROVERBS 20

[16]Take a man's garment when he has given
surety for a stranger,
and hold him in pledge when he gives
surety for foreigners.
[17]Bread gained by deceit is sweet to a man,
but afterward his mouth will be full
of gravel.
[18]Plans are established by counsel;
by wise guidance wage war.
[19]He who goes about gossiping
reveals secrets;
therefore do not associate with one who
speaks foolishly.
[20]If one curses his father or his mother,
his lamp will be put out in utter darkness.
[21]An inheritance gotten hastily in
the beginning
will in the end not be blessed.
[22]Do not say, "I will repay evil";
wait for the LORD, and he will help you.
[23]Diverse weights are an abomination to
the LORD,
and false scales are not good.
[24]A man's steps are ordered by the LORD;
how then can man understand his way?
[25]It is a snare for a man to say rashly, "It
is holy,"
and to reflect only after making his vows.
[26]A wise king winnows the wicked,
and drives the wheel over them.
[27]The spirit of man is the lamp of the LORD,
searching all his innermost parts.
[28]Loyalty and faithfulness preserve the king
and his throne is upheld by righteousness.
[29]The glory of young men is their strength,
but the beauty of old men is their gray hair.
[30]Blows that wound cleanse away evil;
strokes make clean the innermost parts.

ACTS 28

**After we had escaped, we then
learned that the island was
called Malta. [2]And the natives showed
us unusual kindness, for they kindled**
a fire and welcomed us all, because it had
begun to rain and was cold. [3]Paul had
gathered a bundle of sticks and put them
on the fire, when a viper came out because
of the heat and fastened on his hand. [4]When
the natives saw the creature hanging from
his hand, they said to one another, "No

doubt this man is a murderer. Though he has
escaped from the sea, justice has not allowed
him to live." 5He, however, shook off the
creature into the fire and suffered no harm.
6They waited, expecting him to swell up or
suddenly fall down dead; but when they had
waited a long time and saw no misfortune
come to him, they changed their minds and
said that he was a god.
7Now in the neighborhood of that place
were lands belonging to the chief man of
the island, named Pub′lius, who received
us and entertained us hospitably for three
days. 8It happened that the father of Pub′lius
lay sick with fever and dysentery; and Paul
visited him and prayed, and putting his
hands on him healed him. 9And when this
had taken place, the rest of the people on the
island who had diseases also came and were
cured. 10They presented many gifts to us; and
when we sailed, they put on board whatever
we needed.
11After three months we set sail in a ship
which had wintered in the island, a ship
of Alexandria, with the Twin Brothers as
figurehead. 12Putting in at Syracuse, we
stayed there for three days. 13And from there
we made a circuit and arrived at Rhe′gium;
and after one day a south wind sprang up,
and on the second day we came to Pute′oli.
14There we found brethren, and were invited
to stay with them for seven days. And so we
came to Rome. 15And the brethren there,
when they heard of us, came as far as the
Forum of Ap′pius and Three Taverns to meet
us. On seeing them Paul thanked God and
took courage. 16And when we came into
Rome, Paul was allowed to stay by himself,
with the soldier that guarded him.

REFLECTION

God answers our prayers, but not always in the way we would expect. "A man's steps are ordered by the LORD" (Prv 20:24). Both Tobit and his future daughter-in-law, Sarah, are deeply depressed and pray to the Lord for death at the exact same time. God decides to answer their prayers, but not in the way that they expect. Rather, he sends the Archangel Raphael to accomplish the mission. The only solutions they can see are darkness and dead-ends, but God wants to bring life to them: a happy marriage, restored sight, children, and grandchildren. Similarly, when St. Paul is bitten by a poisonous snake, the observers think he has been divinely condemned for his sins, but, in fact, God miraculously preserves Paul from the viper's venom. Not only does he avoid death, but he actually brings the Lord's healing to the local ruler and many other sick people. These stories show us the power of God's providence. When we cannot see a way forward and feel like our road has come to nothing, he knows the path forward. In fact, he directs our steps—we only need to trust in him. And where we see death alone as a solution, he longs to fill us with his abundant life. How has God directed your steps?

July 31

TOBIT 4

**On that day Tobit remembered
the money which he had left
in trust with Gab′ael at Ra′ges in
Med′ia, and he said to himself: 2"I have
asked for death. Why do I not call my son
Tobi′as so that I may explain to him about**
the money before I die?" 3So he called him
and said, "My son, when I die, bury me, and
do not neglect your mother. Honor her all
the days of your life; do what is pleasing to
her, and do not grieve her. 4Remember, my
son, that she faced many dangers for you
while you were yet unborn. When she dies,
bury her beside me in the same grave.
5"Remember the Lord our God all your
days, my son, and refuse to sin or to transgress
his commandments. Live uprightly all the
days of your life, and do not walk in the
ways of wrongdoing. 6For if you do what is
true, your ways will prosper through your

deeds. 7Give alms from your possessions to
all who live uprightly, and do not let your
eye begrudge the gift when you make it.
Do not turn your face away from any
poor man, and the face of God will not be
turned away from you. 8If you have many
possessions, make your gift from them
in proportion; if few, do not be afraid to
give according to the little you have. 9So
you will be laying up a good treasure for
yourself against the day of necessity. 10For
charity delivers from death and keeps
you from entering the darkness; 11and for
all who practice it charity is an excellent
offering in the presence of the Most High.
12"Beware, my son, of all immorality.
First of all take a wife from among the
descendants of your fathers and do not
marry a foreign woman, who is not of
your father's tribe; for we are the sons of
the prophets. Remember, my son, that
Noah, Abraham, Isaac, and Jacob, our
fathers of old, all took wives from among
their brethren. They were blessed in their
children, and their posterity will inherit
the land. 13So now, my son, love your
brethren, and in your heart do not disdain
your brethren and the sons and daughters
of your people by refusing to take a wife
for yourself from among them. For in
pride there is ruin and great confusion;
and in shiftlessness there is loss and great
want, because shiftlessness is the mother
of famine. 14Do not hold over till the next
day the wages of any man who works for
you, but pay him at once; and if you serve
God you will receive payment.
"Watch yourself, my son, in everything
you do, and be disciplined in all your
conduct. 15And what you hate, do not do
to any one. Do not drink wine to excess
or let drunkenness go with you on your
way. 16Give of your bread to the hungry,
and of your clothing to the naked. Give
all your surplus to charity, and do not
let your eye begrudge the gift when you
make it. 17Place your bread on the grave
of the righteous, but give none to sinners.
18Seek advice from every wise man, and
do not despise any useful counsel. 19Bless
the Lord God on every occasion; ask him
that your ways may be made straight
and that all your paths and plans may
prosper. For none of the nations has
understanding; but the Lord himself gives
all good things, and according to his will
he humbles whomever he wishes.
"So, my son, remember my commands,
and do not let them be blotted out of your
mind. 20And now let me explain to you
about the ten talents of silver which I left
in trust with Gab'ael the son of Ga'brias
at Ra'ges in Med'ia. 21Do not be afraid,
my son, because we have become poor.
You have great wealth if you fear God
and refrain from every sin and do what is
pleasing in his sight."
5 Then Tobi'as answered him, "Father,
I will do everything that you have commanded me; 2but how can I obtain the
money when I do not know the man?"
3Then Tobit gave him the receipt, and said
to him, "Find a man to go with you and I
will pay him wages as long as I live; and
go and get the money." 4So he went to look
for a man; and he found Ra'phael, who
was an angel, 5but Tobi'as did not know it.
Tobias said to him, "Can you go with me
to Ra'ges in Med'ia? Are you acquainted
with that region?" 6The angel replied, "I
will go with you; I am familiar with the
way, and I have stayed with our brother
Gab'ael." 7Then Tobi'as said to him, "Wait
for me, and I shall tell my father." 8And
he said to him, "Go, and do not delay." So
he went in and said to his father, "I have
found some one to go with me." He said,
"Call him to me, so that I may learn to
what tribe he belongs, and whether he is
a reliable man to go with you."
9So Tobi'as invited him in; he entered
and they greeted each other. 10Then Tobit
said to him, "My brother, to what tribe and
family do you belong? Tell me." 11But he
answered, "Are you looking for a tribe and
a family or for a man whom you will pay to
go with your son?" And Tobit said to him,
"I should like to know, my brother, your
people and your name." 12He replied, "I am
Azari'as the son of the great Anani'as, one

of your relatives." [13]Then Tobit said to him, "You are welcome, my brother. Do not be angry with me because I tried to learn your tribe and family. You are a relative of mine, of a good and noble lineage. For I used to know Anani′as and Ja′than, the sons of the great Shemai′ah, when we went together to Jerusalem to worship and offered the first-born of our flocks and the tithes of our produce. They did not go astray in the error of our brethren. My brother, you come of good stock. [14]But tell me, what wages am I to pay you—a drachma a day, and expenses for yourself as for my son? [15]And besides, I will add to your wages if you both return safe and sound." So they agreed to these terms.

[16]Then he said to Tobi′as, "Get ready for the journey, and good success to you both." So his son made the preparations for the journey. And his father said to him, "Go with this man; God who dwells in heaven will prosper your way, and may his angel attend you." So they both went out and departed, and the young man's dog was with them.

[17]But Anna, his mother, began to weep, and said to Tobit, "Why have you sent our child away? Is he not the staff of our hands as he goes in and out before us? [18]Do not add money to money, but consider it rubbish as compared to our child. [19]For the life that is given to us by the Lord is enough for us." [20]And Tobit said to her, "Do not worry, my sister; he will return safe and sound, and your eyes will see him. [21]For a good angel will go with him; his journey will be successful, and he will come back safe and sound." [22]So she stopped weeping.

6 Now as they proceeded on their way they came at evening to the Tigris river and camped there. [2]Then the young man went down to wash himself. A fish leaped up from the river and would have swallowed the young man; [3]and the angel said to him, "Catch the fish." So the young man seized the fish and threw it up on the land. [4]Then the angel said to him, "Cut open the fish and take the heart and liver and gall and put them away safely." [5]So the young man did as the angel told him; and they roasted and ate the fish.

And they both continued on their way until they came near to Ecbat′ana. [6]Then the young man said to the angel, "Brother Azari′as, of what use is the liver and heart and gall of the fish?" [7]He replied, "As for the heart and liver, if a demon or evil spirit gives trouble to any one, you make a smoke from these before the man or woman, and that person will never be troubled again. [8]And as for the gall, anoint with it a man who has white films in his eyes, and he will be cured."

[9]When he entered Med′ia and was already approaching Ecbat′ana, [10]Ra′phael said to the young man, "Brother Tobi′as!" "Here I am," he answered. Then Raphael said to him, "We must stay this night in the home of Ra′guel. He is your relative, and he has a daughter named Sarah. He has no male heir and no daughter except Sarah only, and you, as next of kin to her, have before all other men a hereditary claim on her. [11]Also, it is right for you to inherit her father's possessions. [12]Moreover, the girl is sensible, brave, and very beautiful, and her father is a good man."

[13]Then the young man said to the angel, "Brother Azari′as, I have heard that the girl has been given to seven husbands and that each died in the bridal chamber. [14]Now I am the only son my father has, and I am afraid that if I go in I will die as those before me did, for a demon is in love with her, and he harms no one except those who approach her. So now I fear that I may die and bring the lives of my father and mother to the grave in sorrow on my account. And they have no other son to bury them."

[15]But the angel said to him, "Do you not remember the words with which your father commanded you to take a wife from among your own people? Now listen to me, brother, for she will become your wife; and do not worry about the demon, for this very night she will be given to you in marriage. [16]When you enter the bridal chamber, you shall take live ashes of incense and lay upon them some of

the heart and liver of the fish so as to make a
smoke. 17Then the demon will smell it and flee
away, and will never again return. And when
you approach her, rise up, both of you, and cry
out to the merciful God, and he will save you
and have mercy on you. Do not be afraid, for
she was destined for you from eternity. You
will save her, and she will go with you, and I
suppose that you will have children by her."
When Tobi′as heard these things, he fell in love
with her and yearned deeply for her.

PROVERBS 21

The king's heart is a stream of water in the
hand of the Lord;
he turns it wherever he will.
2Every way of a man is right in his own eyes,
but the Lord weighs the heart.
3To do righteousness and justice
is more acceptable to the Lord
than sacrifice.
4Haughty eyes and a proud heart,
the lamp of the wicked, are sin.
5The plans of the diligent lead surely
to abundance,
but every one who is hasty comes only
to want.
6The getting of treasures by a lying tongue
is a fleeting vapor and a snare of death.
7The violence of the wicked will sweep
them away,
because they refuse to do what is just.
8The way of the guilty is crooked,
but the conduct of the pure is right.
9It is better to live in a corner of the housetop
than in a house shared with a
contentious woman.
10The soul of the wicked desires evil;
his neighbor finds no mercy in his eyes.
11When a scoffer is punished, the simple
becomes wise;
when a wise man is instructed, he gains
knowledge.
12The righteous observes the house
of the wicked;
the wicked are cast down to ruin.
13He who closes his ear to the cry of the poor
will himself cry out and not be heard.
14A gift in secret averts anger;
and a bribe in the bosom, strong wrath.
15When justice is done, it is a joy
to the righteous,
but dismay to evildoers.

ACTS 28

17After three days he called to-
gether the local leaders of the
Jews; and when they had gathered, he
said to them, "Brethren, though I had
done nothing against the people or the
customs of our fathers, yet I was delivered
prisoner from Jerusalem into the hands of the
Romans. 18When they had examined me, they
wished to set me at liberty, because there was
no reason for the death penalty in my case.
19But when the Jews objected, I was compelled
to appeal to Caesar—though I had no charge
to bring against my nation. 20For this reason
therefore I have asked to see you and speak
with you, since it is because of the hope of Israel
that I am bound with this chain." 21And they
said to him, "We have received no letters from
Judea about you, and none of the brethren
coming here has reported or spoken any evil
about you. 22But we desire to hear from you
what your views are; for with regard to this sect
we know that everywhere it is spoken against."
23When they had appointed a day for him,
they came to him at his lodging in great
numbers. And he expounded the matter to
them from morning till evening, testifying to
the kingdom of God and trying to convince
them about Jesus both from the law of Moses
and from the prophets. 24And some were
convinced by what he said, while others
disbelieved. 25So, as they disagreed among
themselves, they departed, after Paul had
made one statement: "The Holy Spirit was
right in saying to your fathers through Isaiah
the prophet:
26'Go to this people, and say,
You shall indeed hear but
never understand,
and you shall indeed see but
never perceive.

[27]For this people's heart has grown dull,
and their ears are heavy of hearing,
and their eyes they have closed;
lest they should perceive with
their eyes,
and hear with their ears,
and understand with their heart,
and turn for me to heal them.'

[28]Let it be known to you then that this salvation of God has been sent to the Gentiles; they will listen."

[30]And he lived there two whole years at his own expense, and welcomed all who came to him, [31]preaching the kingdom of God and teaching about the Lord Jesus Christ quite openly and unhindered.

REFLECTION

Sometimes we have to confront our fears. Tobias gets his chance to look fear in the face when the disguised angel Raphael suggests, even insists, that he marry Sarah. She had already married seven men, all of whom were killed by a demon, and Tobias has no intention of becoming the eighth victim. Though she is "sensible, brave, and very beautiful" (Tb 6:12), he is afraid. Raphael presses him, "Do not be afraid, for she was destined for you from eternity" (v. 17). Heartened by Raphael's words, Tobias decides to trust God's plan, and falls in love with Sarah. He yields to the Lord's way like Proverbs teaches: "The king's heart is a stream of water in the hand of the LORD; he turns it wherever he will" (Prv 21:1). Tobias allows himself to be swayed by the voice of an angel. St. Paul, too, though arrested, in chains and under guard, keeps preaching the Gospel to anyone who will listen. He garners an audience of Jews in Rome and witnesses to them about Jesus and the plan of salvation extending to Gentiles. He preaches without fear, in the midst of suffering, trusting completely in the Lord. Is your heart like a stream of water in the hand of the Lord?

August 1

TOBIT 7

Now when they reached Ecbat´ana, Tobi´as said to him, "Brother Azari´ah, take me straight to our brother Rag´uel." So he took him to the house of Raguel, and they found Raguel sitting beside the courtyard door. They greeted him first, and he replied, "Joyous greetings, brothers; welcome and good health!" Then he brought them into his house. 2Then Rag´uel said to his wife Edna, "How much the young man resembles my cousin Tobit!" 3And Rag´uel asked them, "Where are you from, brethren?" They answered him, "We belong to the sons of Naph´tali, who are captives in Nin´eveh." 4So he said to them, "Do you know our brother Tobit?" And they said, "Yes, we do." And he asked them, "Is he in good health?" 5They replied, "He is alive and in good health." And Tobi´as said, "He is my father." 6Then Rag´uel sprang up and kissed him and wept. 7And he blessed him and exclaimed, "Son of that good and noble man!" When he heard that Tobit had lost his sight, he was stricken with grief and wept. 8And his wife Edna and his daughter Sarah wept.

9Then Rag´uel killed a ram from the flock and received them very warmly. When they had bathed and washed themselves and had reclined to dine, Tobi´as said to Ra´phael, "Brother Azari´as, ask Raguel to give me my kinswoman Sarah." 10But Rag´uel overheard it and said to Tobi´as, "Eat, drink, and be merry; for no one except you, brother, has the right to marry my daughter Sarah. Likewise, I am not at liberty to give her to any other man than yourself, because you are my nearest relative. 11But let me explain the true situation to you. I have given my daughter to seven men of our kinsmen, and when each came to her he died in the night. But for the present, my child, eat and drink, and the Lord will act on behalf of you both." But Tobi´as said, "I will eat nothing here unless you make a binding agreement with me." 12So Rag´uel said, "I will do so. She is given to you in accordance with the decree in the book of Moses, and it has been decreed from heaven that she be given to you. Take your kinswoman; from now on you are her brother and she is your sister. She is given to you from today and for ever. May the Lord of heaven, my child, guide and prosper you both this night and grant you mercy and peace." 13Then he called his daughter Sarah, and taking her by the hand he gave her to Tobi´as to be his wife, saying, "Here she is; take her to be your wife in accordance with the law and the decree written in the book of Moses. Take her and bring her safely to your father. And may the God of heaven prosper your journey with his peace." 14Then he called her mother and told her to bring writing material; and he wrote out a copy of the marriage contract, to the effect that he gave her to him as wife according to the law of Moses. 15Then they began to eat and drink.

16And Rag´uel called his wife Edna and said to her, "Sister, make up the other room, and take her into it." 17So she did as he said, and took her there; and the girl began to weep. But the mother comforted her daughter in her tears, and said to her, 18"Be brave, my child; the Lord of heaven and earth grant you joy in place of this sorrow of yours. Be brave, my daughter."

8 When they had finished eating and drinking, they wanted to retire; so they took the young man and brought him into the bedroom. 2As he went he remembered the words of Ra´phael, and he took the live ashes of incense and put the heart and liver of the fish upon them and made a smoke. 3And when the demon smelled the odor he fled to the remotest parts of Egypt, and the angel bound him. 4When the door was shut and the two were alone, Tobi´as got up from the bed and said, "Sister, get up, and let us pray and implore our Lord that he grant us mercy and safety." 5And they began to say,

"Blessed are you, O God of our fathers,
and blessed be your holy and glorious
name for ever.
Let the heavens and all your creatures
bless you.
6You made Adam and gave him Eve his wife
as a helper and support.
From them the race of mankind
has sprung.
You said, 'It is not good that the man
should be alone;
let us make a helper for him like himself.'
7And now, O Lord, I am not taking this
sister of mine because of lust, but with
sincerity. Grant that I may find mercy and
may grow old together with her." 8And they
both said, "Amen, amen." 9Then they both
went to sleep for the night.

But Rag'uel arose and went and dug a
grave, 10with the thought, "Perhaps he too
will die." 11Then Rag'uel went into his house
12and said to his wife Edna, "Send one of
the maids to see whether he is alive; and if
he is not, let us bury him without any one
knowing about it." 13So the maid opened
the door and went in, and found them both
asleep. 14And she came out and told them
that he was alive. 15Then Rag'uel blessed
God and said,

"Blessed are you, O God, with every pure
and holy blessing.
Let your saints and all your creatures
bless you;
let all your angels and your chosen
people bless you for ever.
16Blessed are you, because you have made
me glad.
It has not happened to me as I expected;
but you have treated us according to
your great mercy.
17Blessed are you, because you have had
compassion on two only children.
Show them mercy, O Lord;
and bring their lives to fulfilment in
health and happiness and mercy."

18Then he ordered his servants to fill in the
grave.

19After this he gave a wedding feast for
them which lasted fourteen days. 20And before the days of the feast were over, Rag'uel
declared by oath to Tobi'as that he should
not leave until the fourteen days of the wedding feast were ended, 21that then he should
take half of Rag'uel's property and return in
safety to his father, and that the rest would
be his "when my wife and I die."

9 Then Tobi'as called Ra'phael and said to
him, 2"Brother Azari'as, take a servant
and two camels with you and go to Gab'ael
at Ra'ges in Med'ia and get the money for
me; and bring him to the wedding feast.
3For Rag'uel has sworn that I should not
leave; 4but my father is counting the days,
and if I delay long he will be greatly distressed." 5So Ra'phael made the journey
and stayed overnight with Gab'ael. He
gave him the receipt, and Gabael brought
out the money bags with their seals intact
and gave them to him. 6In the morning
they both got up early and came to the
wedding feast. And Gab'ael blessed Tobi'as
and his wife.

10 Now his father Tobit was counting
each day, and when the days for the
journey had expired and they did not arrive, 2he said, "Is it possible that he has been
detained? Or is it possible that Gab'ael has
died and there is no one to give him the
money?" 3And he was greatly distressed.
4And his wife said to him, "The lad has perished; his long delay proves it." Then she
began to mourn for him, and said, 5"Am I
not distressed, my child, that I let you go,
you who are the light of my eyes?" 6But Tobit said to her, "Be still and stop worrying;
he is well." 7And she answered him, "Be still
and stop deceiving me; my child has perished." And she went out every day to the
road by which they had left; she ate nothing in the daytime, and throughout the
nights she never stopped mourning for her
son Tobi'as, until the fourteen days of the
wedding feast had expired which Rag'uel
had sworn that he should spend there.

At that time Tobias said to Raguel, "Send
me back, for my father and mother have
given up hope of ever seeing me again."
8But his father-in-law said to him, "Stay
with me, and I will send messengers to
your father, and they will inform him how

things are with you." 9Tobi′as replied, "No,
send me back to my father." 10So Rag′uel
arose and gave him his wife Sarah and half
of his property in slaves, cattle, and money.
11And when he had blessed them he sent
them away, saying, "The God of heaven
will prosper you, my children, before I die."
12He said also to his daughter, "Honor your
father-in-law and your mother-in-law; they
are now your parents. Let me hear a good
report of you." And he kissed her. And Edna
said to Tobi′as, "The Lord of heaven bring
you back safely, dear brother, and grant me
to see your children by my daughter Sarah,
that I may rejoice before the Lord. See, I am
entrusting my daughter to you; do nothing
to grieve her."

PROVERBS 21

16A man who wanders from the way
of understanding
will rest in the assembly of the dead.
17He who loves pleasure will be a poor man;
he who loves wine and oil will not be rich.
18The wicked is a ransom for the righteous,
and the faithless for the upright.
19It is better to live in a desert land
than with a contentious and
fretful woman.
20Precious treasure remains in a
wise man's dwelling,
but a foolish man devours it.
21He who pursues righteousness
and kindness
will find life and honor.
22A wise man scales the city of the mighty
and brings down the stronghold in which
they trust.
23He who keeps his mouth and his tongue
keeps himself out of trouble.
24"Scoffer" is the name of the proud,
haughty man
who acts with arrogant pride.
25The desire of the sluggard kills him
for his hands refuse to labor.
26All day long the wicked covets,
but the righteous gives and does not
hold back.
27The sacrifice of the wicked is
an abomination;
how much more when he brings it with
evil intent.
28A false witness will perish,
but the word of a man who hears
will endure.
29A wicked man puts on a bold face,
but an upright man considers his ways.
30No wisdom, no understanding, no counsel,
can avail against the LORD.
31The horse is made ready for the day
of battle,
but the victory belongs to the LORD.

ROMANS 1

Paul, a servant of Jesus Christ,
called to be an apostle, set apart
for the gospel of God 2which
he promised beforehand through his
prophets in the holy Scriptures, 3the
gospel concerning his Son, who was descended from David according to the
flesh 4and designated Son of God in power according to the Spirit of holiness by
his resurrection from the dead, Jesus
Christ our Lord, 5through whom we have
received grace and apostleship to bring
about the obedience of faith for the sake
of his name among all the nations, 6in-
cluding yourselves who are called to belong to Jesus Christ;

7To all God's beloved in Rome, who are
called to be saints:

Grace to you and peace from God our
Father and the Lord Jesus Christ.

8First, I thank my God through Jesus
Christ for all of you, because your faith
is proclaimed in all the world. 9For God
is my witness, whom I serve with my
spirit in the gospel of his Son, that without ceasing I mention you always in my
prayers, 10asking that somehow by God's
will I may now at last succeed in coming to you. 11For I long to see you, that
I may impart to you some spiritual gift
to strengthen you, 12that is, that we may

be mutually encouraged by each other's faith, both yours and mine. 13I want you to know, brethren, that I have often intended to come to you (but thus far have been prevented), in order that I may reap some harvest among you as well as among the rest of the Gentiles. 14I am under obligation both to Greeks and to barbarians, both to the wise and to the foolish: 15so I am eager to preach the gospel to you also who are in Rome.

16For I am not ashamed of the gospel: it is the power of God for salvation to every one who has faith, to the Jew first and also to the Greek. 17For in it the righteousness of God is revealed through faith for faith; as it is written, "He who through faith is righteous shall live."

REFLECTION

The way we use our words matters. It is too easy to let our words come out without thinking—to use our words to hurt other people, to tarnish reputations, to complain, or to discourage. Yet "he who keeps his mouth and his tongue keeps himself out of trouble" (Prv 21:23). When we watch our words carefully and think before we speak, we can use our words for building up instead of tearing down. In today's readings, Tobias and Raguel use their words to pray and commit themselves to one another, while Tobit's wife, Anna, uses her words to despair and grumble. St. Paul uses words not only to offer holy greetings to the Christians at Rome, but more importantly to give thanks to God on their behalf. He hopes to visit and speak encouraging words to the Romans and to be encouraged by them (see Rom 1:11–12). While most of us shrink from evangelistic encounters for fear of social awkwardness, Paul leaps at the opportunity: "I am eager to preach the gospel to you also who are in Rome" (v. 15). Watching biblical characters speak out of differing motivations helps us learn the right way to talk. We can honor God, lift our brothers and sisters up, and preach the Gospel with what we say. How do you use your words?

August 2

TOBIT 11

After this Tobi′as went on his way, praising God because he had made his journey a success. And he blessed Rag′uel and his wife Edna. So he continued on his way until they came near to Nin′eveh. 2Then Ra′phael said to Tobi′as, "Are you not aware, brother, of how you left your father? 3Let us run ahead of your wife and prepare the house. 4And take the gall of the fish with you." So they went their way, and the dog went along behind them.

5Now Anna sat looking intently down the road for her son. 6And she caught sight of him coming, and said to his father, "Behold, your son is coming, and so is the man who went with him!"

7Ra′phael said to Tobi′as, before they approached his father, "I know that his eyes will be opened. 8Smear the gall of the fish on his eyes, and the medicine will cause the white films to fall away. And your father will regain his sight and see the light."

9Then Anna ran to meet them, and embraced her son, and said to him, "I have seen you, my child; now I am ready to die." And she wept. 10Tobit got up, and came stumbling out through the courtyard door. But his son ran to him 11with the gall of the fish in his hand, and holding him firmly, he blew into his eyes, saying, "Take courage, Father." 12With this he applied the medicine on his eyes. 13Next, with both his hands, he peeled off the white films from the corners of his eyes. 14Then he saw his son and embraced him, and he wept and said, "Here I see my son, the light of my eyes!" Then he said, "Blessed be God, and blessed be his great name, and blessed be all his holy angels. May his holy name be blessed throughout all the ages. 15Though he afflicted me, he has had mercy on me. Now I see my son Tobi′as!"

16 And his son went in rejoicing, and he
reported to his father the great things that
had happened to him in Med′ia. Then
Tobit went out to meet his daughter-in-
law at the gate of Nin′eveh, rejoicing and
praising God. Those who saw him as he
went were amazed because he could see.
17 And Tobit gave thanks before them that
God had been merciful to him. When Tobit
came near to Sarah his daughter-in-law, he
blessed her, saying, "Welcome, daughter!
Blessed is God who has brought you to
us, and blessed are your father and your
mother." So there was rejoicing among all
his brethren in Nin′eveh. 18 Ahi′kar and
his nephew Na′dab came, 19 and Tobi′as'
marriage was celebrated for seven days
with great festivity.

12 Tobit then called his son Tobi′as
and said to him, "My son, see to the
wages of the man who went with you; and
he must also be given more." 2 He replied,
"Father, it would do me no harm to give
him half of what I have brought back. 3 For
he has led me back to you safely, he cured
my wife, he obtained the money for me, and
he also healed you." 4 The old man said, "He
deserves it." 5 So he called the angel and said
to him, "Take for your wages half of all that
you two have brought back, and farewell."
6 Then the angel called the two of them
privately and said to them: "Praise God
and give thanks to him; exalt him and give
thanks to him in the presence of all the
living for what he has done for you. It is
good to praise God and to exalt his name,
worthily declaring the works of God, and
with fitting honor to acknowledge him.
Do not be slow to give him thanks. 7 It is
good to guard the secret of a king, but
gloriously to reveal the works of God,
and with fitting honor to acknowledge
him. Do good, and evil will not overtake
you. 8 Prayer is good when accompanied
by fasting, almsgiving, and righteousness.
A little with righteousness is better than
much with wrongdoing. It is better to
give alms than to treasure up gold. 9 For
almsgiving delivers from death, and it will
purge away every sin. Those who perform
deeds of charity and of righteousness
will have fulness of life; 10 but those who
commit sin are the enemies of their own
lives.
11 "I will now declare the whole truth to
you and I will not conceal anything from
you. I have said, 'It is good to guard the
secret of a king, but gloriously to reveal
the works of God.' 12 And so, when you
and your daughter-in-law Sarah prayed, I
brought a reminder of your prayer before
the Holy One; and when you buried the
dead, I was likewise present with you.
13 When you did not hesitate to rise and
leave your dinner in order to go and lay
out the dead, I was sent to test you. 14 So
now God sent me to heal you and your
daughter-in-law Sarah. 15 I am Ra′phael,
one of the seven holy angels who present
the prayers of the saints and enter into
the presence of the glory of the Lord."
16 They were both alarmed; and they fell
upon their faces, for they were afraid. 17 But
he said to them, "Do not be afraid; you will
be safe. But praise God for ever. 18 For I did
not come as a favor on my part, but by the
will of our God. Therefore praise him for
ever. 19 All these days I merely appeared to
you and did not eat or drink, but you were
seeing a vision. 20 And now bless the Lord
upon the earth and give thanks to God, for
I am ascending to him who sent me. Write
in a book everything that has happened
to you." 21 Then they stood up; but they
saw him no more. 22 So they confessed the
great and wonderful works of God, and
acknowledged that the angel of the Lord
had appeared to them.

PROVERBS 22

A good name is to be chosen rather than
great riches,
and favor is better than silver or gold.
2 The rich and the poor meet together;
the LORD is the maker of them all.
3 A prudent man sees danger and
hides himself;
but the simple go on, and suffer for it.

4 The reward for humility and fear of
the LORD
is riches and honor and life.
5 Thorns and snares are in the way
of the perverse;
he who guards himself will keep far
from them.
6 Train up a child in the way he should go,
and when he is old he will not depart
from it.
7 The rich rules over the poor,
and the borrower is the slave of the lender.
8 He who sows injustice will reap calamity,
and the rod of his fury will fail.
9 He who has a bountiful eye will be blessed,
for he shares his bread with the poor.
10 Drive out a scoffer, and strife will go out,
and quarreling and abuse will cease.
11 He who loves purity of heart,
and whose speech is gracious, will have
the king as his friend.
12 The eyes of the LORD keep watch
over knowledge,
but he overthrows the words
of the faithless.
13 The sluggard says, "There is a lion outside!
I shall be slain in the streets!"
14 The mouth of a loose woman is a deep pit;
he with whom the LORD is angry will fall
into it.
15 Folly is bound up in the heart of a child,
but the rod of discipline drives it far
from him.
16 He who oppresses the poor to increase his
own wealth,
or gives to the rich, will only come to want.

ROMANS 1

18 For the wrath of God is re-
vealed from heaven against all
ungodliness and wickedness of men
who by their wickedness suppress the
truth. 19 For what can be known about God
is plain to them, because God has shown
it to them. 20 Ever since the creation of the
world his invisible nature, namely, his
eternal power and deity, has been clearly
perceived in the things that have been
made. So they are without excuse; 21 for
although they knew God they did not
honor him as God or give thanks to him,
but they became futile in their thinking
and their senseless minds were darkened.
22 Claiming to be wise, they became fools,
23 and exchanged the glory of the immortal God for images resembling mortal
man or birds or animals or reptiles.
24 Therefore God gave them up in the lusts
of their hearts to impurity, to the dishonoring
of their bodies among themselves, 25 because
they exchanged the truth about God for a
lie and worshiped and served the creature
rather than the Creator, who is blessed for
ever! Amen.
26 For this reason God gave them up
to dishonorable passions. Their women
exchanged natural relations for unnatural,
27 and the men likewise gave up natural
relations with women and were consumed
with passion for one another, men committing shameless acts with men and receiving
in their own persons the due penalty for
their error.
28 And since they did not see fit to acknowledge God, God gave them up to
a base mind and to improper conduct.
29 They were filled with all manner of wickedness, evil, covetousness, malice. Full of
envy, murder, strife, deceit, malignity, they
are gossips, 30 slanderers, haters of God, insolent, haughty, boastful, inventors of evil,
disobedient to parents, 31 foolish, faithless,
heartless, ruthless. 32 Though they know
God's decree that those who do such things
deserve to die, they not only do them but
approve those who practice them.
2 Therefore you have no excuse, O man,
whoever you are, when you judge
another; for in passing judgment upon
him you condemn yourself, because
you, the judge, are doing the very same
things. 2 We know that the judgment
of God rightly falls upon those who do
such things. 3 Do you suppose, O man,
that when you judge those who do such
things and yet do them yourself, you will
escape the judgment of God? 4 Or do you

presume upon the riches of his kindness
and forbearance and patience? Do you
not know that God's kindness is meant
to lead you to repentance? 5But by your
hard and impenitent heart you are storing up wrath for yourself on the day of
wrath when God's righteous judgment
will be revealed. 6For he will render to
every man according to his works: 7to
those who by patience in well-doing seek
for glory and honor and immortality, he
will give eternal life; 8but for those who
are factious and do not obey the truth,
but obey wickedness, there will be wrath
and fury. 9There will be tribulation and
distress for every human being who does
evil, the Jew first and also the Greek, 10but
glory and honor and peace for every one
who does good, the Jew first and also the
Greek. 11For God shows no partiality.
12All who have sinned without the law
will also perish without the law, and all who
have sinned under the law will be judged
by the law. 13For it is not the hearers of
the law who are righteous before God, but
the doers of the law who will be justified.
14When Gentiles who have not the law do
by nature what the law requires, they are a
law to themselves, even though they do not
have the law. 15They show that what the law
requires is written on their hearts, while
their conscience also bears witness and
their conflicting thoughts accuse or perhaps
excuse them 16on that day when, according
to my gospel, God judges the secrets of men
by Christ Jesus.

REFLECTION

God's generosity is hard to outdo, but that doesn't mean that we shouldn't try. When Tobit's sorrows are turned to joy with his restored sight, his son's return, and his new daughter-in-law, he does not turn inward in self-satisfaction. Rather, he turns outward to the Lord, pouring out praise and thanksgiving, and acknowledging God as the source of his happiness. Beyond that, his praise overflows in generosity, giving half of the money he had saved to Tobias's mysterious companion. The angel Raphael then reveals his true identity and praises Tobit's quickness to do good: "You did not hesitate to rise and leave your dinner" (Tb 12:13) and advises him that "almsgiving delivers from death" (v. 9). Proverbs similarly teaches that God blesses the one who "shares his bread with the poor" (Prv 22:9). And St. Paul insists that "it is not the hearers of the law who are righteous before God, but the doers of the law who will be justified" (Rom 2:13). Actions speak louder than words, and the Lord wants us to mirror his generosity by being generous with others, particularly the poor. When we respond to his work in gratitude like Tobit, our hearts will overflow with praise to God and openhandedness to others. How can you share your bread with the poor?

August 3

TOBIT 13

Then Tobit wrote a prayer of rejoicing, and said:

"Blessed is God who lives for ever,
and blessed is his kingdom.
2For he afflicts, and he shows mercy;
he leads down to Hades, and brings
up again,
and there is no one who can escape
his hand.
3Acknowledge him before the nations,
O sons of Israel;
for he has scattered us among them.
4Make his greatness known there,
and exalt him in the presence of all
the living;
because he is our Lord and God,
he is our Father for ever.
5He will afflict us for our iniquities;
and again he will show mercy,
and will gather us from all the nations
among whom you have been scattered.

6 If you turn to him with all your heart and
with all your soul,
to do what is true before him,
then he will turn to you
and will not hide his face from you.
But see what he will do with you;
give thanks to him with your full voice.
Praise the Lord of righteousness,
and exalt the King of the ages.
I give him thanks in the land of my captivity,
and I show his power and majesty to a
nation of sinners.
Turn back, you sinners, and do right
before him;
who knows if he will accept you and
have mercy on you?
7 I exalt my God;
my soul exalts the King of heaven,
and will rejoice in his majesty.
8 Bless the Lord, all you his chosen ones,
all of you, praise his glory.
Celebrate days of joy, and give thanks to him.
9 O Jerusalem, the holy city,
he will afflict you for the deeds
of your sons,
but again he will show mercy to the
sons of the righteous.
10 Give thanks worthily to the Lord,
and praise the King of the ages,
that his tent may be raised for you again
with joy.
May he cheer those within you who
are captives,
and love those within you who
are distressed,
to all generations for ever.
11 Many nations will come from afar to the
name of the Lord God,
bearing gifts in their hands, gifts for the
King of heaven.
Generations of generations will give you
joyful praise.
12 Cursed are all who hate you;
blessed for ever will be all who love you.
13 Rejoice and be glad for the sons
of the righteous;
for they will be gathered together,
and will praise the Lord of the righteous.
14 How blessed are those who love you!
They will rejoice in your peace.
Blessed are those who grieved over all
your afflictions;
for they will rejoice for you upon seeing
all your glory,
and they will be made glad for ever.
15 Let my soul praise God the great King.
16 For Jerusalem will be built with sapphires
and emeralds,
her walls with precious stones,
and her towers and battlements with
pure gold.
17 The streets of Jerusalem will be paved with
beryl and ruby and stones of O′phir;
18 all her lanes will cry 'Hallelujah!' and
will give praise,
saying, 'Blessed is God, who has exalted
you for ever.'"

14 Here Tobit ended his words of praise.
2 He was fifty-eight years old when
he lost his sight, and after eight years he
regained it. He gave alms, and he continued to fear the Lord God and to praise
him. 3 When he had grown very old he
called his son and grandsons, and said to
him, "My son, take your sons; behold, I
have grown old and am about to depart
this life. 4 Go to Med′ia, my son, for I fully
believe what Jonah the prophet said about
Nin′eveh, that it will be overthrown. But
in Media there will be peace for a time.
Our brethren will be scattered over the
earth from the good land, and Jerusalem
will be desolate. The house of God in it
will be burned down and will be in ruins for a time. 5 But God will again have
mercy on them, and bring them back
into their land; and they will rebuild the
house of God, though it will not be like
the former one until the times of the age
are completed. After this they will return
from the places of their captivity, and will
rebuild Jerusalem in splendor. And the
house of God will be rebuilt there with a
glorious building for all generations for
ever, just as the prophets said of it. 6 Then
all the Gentiles will turn to fear the Lord
God in truth, and will bury their idols.
7 All the Gentiles will praise the Lord, and
his people will give thanks to God, and
the Lord will exalt his people. And all

who love the Lord God in truth and righteousness will rejoice, showing mercy to our brethren.

8“So now, my son, leave Nin′eveh, because what the prophet Jonah said will surely happen. 9But keep the law and the commandments, and be merciful and just, so that it may be well with you. 10Bury me properly, and your mother with me. And do not live in Nin′eveh any longer. See, my son, what Na′dab did to Ahi′kar who had reared him, how he brought him from light into darkness, and with what he repaid him. But Ahikar was saved, and the other received repayment as he himself went down into the darkness. Ahikar gave alms and escaped the deathtrap which Nadab had set for him; but Nadab fell into the trap and perished. 11So now, my children, consider what almsgiving accomplishes and how righteousness delivers.” As he said this he died in his bed. He was a hundred and fifty-eight years old; and Tobi′as gave him a magnificent funeral. 12And when Anna died he buried her with his father.

Then Tobi′as returned with his wife and his sons to Ecbat′ana, to Rag′uel his father-in-law. 13He grew old with honor, and he gave his father-in-law and mother-in-law magnificent funerals. He inherited their property and that of his father Tobit. 14He died in Ecbat′ana of Med′ia at the age of a hundred and twenty-seven years. 15But before he died he heard of the destruction of Nin′eveh, which Nebuchadnez′zar and Ahas′u-erus had captured. Before his death he rejoiced over Nineveh.

PROVERBS 22

17Incline your ear, and hear the words
of the wise,
and apply your mind to my knowledge;
18for it will be pleasant if you keep them
within you,
if all of them are ready on your lips.
19That your trust may be in the LORD,
I have made them known to you today,
even to you.
20Have I not written for you thirty sayings
of admonition and knowledge,
21to show you what is right and true,
that you may give a true answer to those
who sent you?

22Do not rob the poor, because he is poor,
or crush the afflicted at the gate;
23for the LORD will plead their cause
and despoil of life those who
despoil them.
24Make no friendship with a man given
to anger,
nor go with a wrathful man,
25lest you learn his ways
and entangle yourself in a snare.
26Be not one of those who give pledges,
who become surety for debts.
27If you have nothing with which to pay,
why should your bed be taken from
under you?
28Remove not the ancient landmark
which your fathers have set.
29Do you see a man skilful in his work?
he will stand before kings;
he will not stand before obscure men.

ROMANS 2

17But if you call yourself a Jew and rely upon the law and boast of your relation to God 18and know his will and approve what is excellent, because you are instructed in the law, 19and if you are sure that you are a guide to the blind, a light to those who are in darkness, 20a corrector of the foolish, a teacher of children, having in the law the embodiment of knowledge and truth—21you then who teach others, will you not teach yourself? While you preach against stealing, do you steal? 22You who say that one must not commit adultery, do you commit adultery? You who abhor idols, do you rob temples? 23You who boast in the law, do you dishonor God by breaking the law? 24For, as it is written, “The name of God is blasphemed among the Gentiles because of you.”

25 Circumcision indeed is of value if you obey the law; but if you break the law, your circumcision becomes uncircumcision. 26 So, if a man who is uncircumcised keeps the precepts of the law, will not his uncircumcision be regarded as circumcision? 27 Then those who are physically uncircumcised but keep the law will condemn you who have the written code and circumcision but break the law. 28 For he is not a real Jew who is one outwardly, nor is true circumcision something external and physical. 29 He is a Jew who is one inwardly, and real circumcision is a matter of the heart, spiritual and not literal. His praise is not from men but from God.

3 Then what advantage has the Jew? Or what is the value of circumcision?
2 Much in every way. To begin with, the Jews are entrusted with the oracles of God.
3 What if some were unfaithful? Does their faithlessness nullify the faithfulness of God?
4 By no means! Let God be true though every man be false, as it is written,

"That you may be justified in your words,
and prevail when you are judged."

5 But if our wickedness serves to show the justice of God, what shall we say? That God is unjust to inflict wrath on us? (I speak in a human way.)
6 By no means! For then how could God judge the world?
7 But if through my falsehood God's truthfulness abounds to his glory, why am I still being condemned as a sinner?
8 And why not do evil that good may come?—as some people slanderously charge us with saying. Their condemnation is just.
9 What then? Are we Jews any better off? No, not at all; for I have already charged that all men, both Jews and Greeks, are under the power of sin,
10 as it is written:

"None is righteous, no, not one;
11 no one understands, no one seeks for God.
12 All have turned aside, together they have gone wrong;
no one does good, not even one."
13 "Their throat is an open grave,
they use their tongues to deceive."
"The venom of asps is under their lips."
14 "Their mouth is full of curses and bitterness."
15 "Their feet are swift to shed blood,
16 in their paths are ruin and misery,
17 and the way of peace they do not know."
18 "There is no fear of God before their eyes."

19 Now we know that whatever the law says it speaks to those who are under the law, so that every mouth may be stopped, and the whole world may be held accountable to God.
20 For no human being will be justified in his sight by works of the law, since through the law comes knowledge of sin.

REFLECTION

Tobit's beautiful song meditates on the mystery of Divine Providence: "For he afflicts, and he shows mercy" (Tb 13:2). Tobit interprets the "afflictions" or wrath of God as a healing medicine, a warning of discipline. When the Lord punishes, he calls to us, "Turn back, you sinners, and do right before him" (v. 6). After we turn, he can heal us in his mercy. While Tobit sees these patterns of providence in the destruction and rebuilding of Jerusalem and in the judgment of Nineveh, they are truly personal patterns. We can learn from our mistakes when we face the consequences of our actions. It is easy to think of God's wrath and mercy as opposites, but Tobit sees them together, with God's wrath opening opportunities for his mercy to be received. St. Paul also sees a pattern of divine punishment and mercy, a true accountability before God. Outward practices are empty without inward devotion: "Real circumcision is a matter of the heart" (Rom 2:29). How can you see God's "afflictions" and mercy at work in your own life?

August 4

JUDITH 1

In the twelfth year of the reign of Nebuchadnez′zar, who ruled over the Assyrians in the great city of Nin′eveh, in the days of Arpha′xad, who ruled over the Medes in

Ecbat′ana—2he is the king who built walls
about Ecbat′ana with hewn stones three cubits thick and six cubits long; he made the
walls seventy cubits high and fifty cubits
wide; 3at the gates he built towers a hundred
cubits high and sixty cubits wide at the foundations; 4and he made its gates, which were
seventy cubits high and forty cubits wide,
so that his armies could march out in force
and his infantry form their ranks—5it was
in those days that King Nebuchadnez′zar
made war against King Arpha′xad in the
great plain which is on the borders of Ragae.
6He was joined by all the people of the hill
country and all those who lived along the
Euphrates and the Tigris and the Hydas′pes
and in the plain where Ar′ioch ruled the
El″ymae′ans. Many nations joined the forces
of the Chalde′ans.

7Then Nebuchadnez′zar king of the
Assyrians sent to all who lived in Persia and
to all who lived in the west, those who lived
in Cili′cia and Damascus and Lebanon and
An″ti-leb′anon and all who lived along the
seacoast, 8and those among the nations of
Carmel and Gilead, and Upper Galilee and
the great Plain of Esdrae′lon, 9and all who
were in Samar′ia and its surrounding towns,
and beyond the Jordan as far as Jerusalem
and Beth′any and Chelous and Ka′desh
and the river of Egypt, and Tah′panhes and
Ra-am′ses and the whole land of Go′shen,
10even beyond Tanis and Memphis, and all
who lived in Egypt as far as the borders
of Ethiopia. 11But all who lived in the
whole region disregarded the orders of
Nebuchadnez′zar king of the Assyrians,
and refused to join him in the war; for they
were not afraid of him, but looked upon
him as only one man, and they sent back his
messengers empty-handed and shamefaced.
12Then Nebuchadnez′zar was very angry
with this whole region, and swore by his
throne and kingdom that he would surely
take revenge on the whole territory of
Cili′cia and Damascus and Syria, that he
would kill by the sword all the inhabitants
of the land of Moab, and the people of
Ammon, and all Jude′a, and every one in
Egypt, as far as the coasts of the two seas. 13In
the seventeenth year he led his forces against
King Arpha′xad, and defeated him in battle,
and overthrew the whole army of Arphaxad,
and all his cavalry and all his chariots. 14Thus
he took possession of his cities, and came to
Ecbat′ana, captured its towers, plundered its
markets, and turned its beauty into shame.
15He captured Arpha′xad in the mountains
of Ragae and struck him down with hunting
spears; and he utterly destroyed him, to
this day. 16Then he returned with them to
Nin′eveh, he and all his combined forces,
a vast body of troops; and there he and his
forces rested and feasted for one hundred
and twenty days.

2 In the eighteenth year, on the twenty-
second day of the first month, there
was talk in the palace of Nebuchadnez′zar
king of the Assyrians about carrying out
his revenge on the whole region, just as
he said. 2He called together all his officers
and all his nobles and set forth to them his
secret plan and recounted fully, with his own
lips, all the wickedness of the region; 3and
it was decided that every one who had not
obeyed his command should be destroyed.
4When he had finished setting forth his plan,
Nebuchadnez′zar king of the Assyrians called
Hol″ofer′nes, the chief general of his army,
second only to himself, and said to him,

5"Thus says the Great King, the lord of the
whole earth: When you leave my presence,
take with you men confident in their
strength, to the number of one hundred
and twenty thousand foot soldiers and
twelve thousand cavalry. 6Go and attack the
whole west country, because they disobeyed
my orders. 7Tell them to prepare earth and
water, for I am coming against them in my
anger, and will cover the whole face of the
earth with the feet of my armies, and will
hand them over to be plundered by my
troops, 8till their wounded shall fill their
valleys, and every brook and river shall
be filled with their dead, and overflow;
9and I will lead them away captive to the
ends of the whole earth. 10You shall go and
seize all their territory for me in advance.
They will yield themselves to you, and you
shall hold them for me till the day of their

punishment. 11But if they refuse, your eye shall not spare and you shall hand them over to slaughter and plunder throughout your whole region. 12For as I live, and by the power of my kingdom, what I have spoken my hand will execute. 13And you—take care not to transgress any of your sovereign's commands, but be sure to carry them out just as I have ordered you; and do not delay about it."

14So Hol″ofer′nes left the presence of his master, and called together all the commanders, generals, and officers of the Assyrian army, 15and mustered the picked troops by divisions as his lord had ordered him to do, one hundred and twenty thousand of them, together with twelve thousand archers on horseback, 16and he organized them as a great army is marshaled for a campaign. 17He collected a vast number of camels and donkeys and mules for transport, and innumerable sheep and oxen and goats for provision; 18also plenty of food for every man, and a huge amount of gold and silver from the royal palace. 19So he set out with his whole army, to go ahead of King Nebuchadnez′zar and to cover the whole face of the earth to the west with their chariots and horsemen and picked troops of infantry. 20Along with them went a mixed crowd like a swarm of locusts, like the dust of the earth—a multitude that could not be counted.

21They marched for three days from Nin′eveh to the plain of Bec′tileth, and camped opposite Bectileth near the mountain which is to the north of Upper Cili′cia. 22From there Hol″ofer′nes took his whole army, his infantry, cavalry, and chariots, and went up into the hill country 23and ravaged Put and Lud, and plundered all the people of Rassis and the Ish′maelites who lived along the desert, south of the country of the Chel′leans. 24Then he followed the Euphrates and passed through Mesopota′mia and destroyed all the hilltop cities along the brook Abron, as far as the sea. 25He also seized the territory of Cili′cia, and killed every one who resisted him, and came to the southern borders of Ja′pheth, fronting toward Arabia. 26He surrounded all the Mid′ianites, and burned their tents and plundered their sheepfolds. 27Then he went down into the plain of Damascus during the wheat harvest, and burned all their fields and destroyed their flocks and herds and sacked their cities and ravaged their lands and put to death all their young men with the edge of the sword.

28So fear and terror of him fell upon all the people who lived along the seacoast, at Si′don and Tyre, and those who lived in Sur and Oci′na and all who lived in Jam′nia. Those who lived in Azo′tus and Asca′lon feared him exceedingly.

3 So they sent messengers to sue for peace, and said, 2"Behold, we the servants of Nebuchadnez′zar, the Great King, lie prostrate before you. Do with us whatever you will. 3Behold, our buildings, and all our land, and all our wheat fields, and our flocks and herds, and all our sheepfolds with their tents, lie before you; do with them whatever you please. 4Our cities also and their inhabitants are your slaves; come and deal with them in any way that seems good to you."

5The men came to Hol″ofer′nes and told him all this. 6Then he went down to the seacoast with his army and stationed garrisons in the hilltop cities and took picked men from them as his allies. 7And these people and all in the country round about welcomed him with garlands and dances and tambourines. 8And he demolished all their shrines and cut down their sacred groves; for it had been given to him to destroy all the gods of the land, so that all nations should worship Nebuchadnez′zar only, and all their tongues and tribes should call upon him as god.

9Then he came to the edge of Esdrae′lon, near Do′than, fronting the great ridge of Jude′a; 10here he camped between Ge′ba and Scythop′olis, and remained for a whole month in order to assemble all the supplies for his army.

4 By this time the people of Israel living in Judea heard of everything that Hol″ofer′nes, the general of Nebuchad-nez′zar the king of the Assyrians, had done to the nations, and how he had plundered and destroyed all their temples;

2they were therefore very greatly terrified at
his approach, and were alarmed both for Jerusalem and for the temple of the Lord their
God. 3For they had only recently returned
from the captivity, and all the people of Jude′a
were newly gathered together, and the sacred
vessels and the altar and the temple had been
consecrated after their profanation. 4So they
sent to every district of Samar′ia, and to Kona
and Beth-ho′ron and Bel′main and Jericho
and to Choba and Aeso′ra and the valley of
Salem, 5and immediately seized all the high
hilltops and fortified the villages on them
and stored up food in preparation for war—
since their fields had recently been harvested.
6And Jo′akim, the high priest, who was in Jerusalem at that time, wrote to the people of
Beth″uli′a and Bet″omestha′im, which faces
Esdrae′lon opposite the plain near Do′than,
7ordering them to seize the passes up into the
hills, since by them Jude′a could be invaded,
and it was easy to stop any who tried to enter, for the approach was narrow, only wide
enough for two men at the most.

PROVERBS 23

When you sit down to eat with a ruler,
observe carefully what is before you;
2and put a knife to your throat
if you are a man given to appetite.
3Do not desire his delicacies,
for they are deceptive food.
4Do not toil to acquire wealth;
be wise enough to desist.
5When your eyes light upon it, it is gone;
for suddenly it takes to itself wings,
flying like an eagle toward heaven.
6Do not eat the bread of a man who is stingy;
do not desire his delicacies;
7for he is like one who is inwardly reckoning.
"Eat and drink!" he says to you;
but his heart is not with you.
8You will vomit up the morsels which you
have eaten,
and waste your pleasant words.
9Do not speak in the hearing of a fool,
for he will despise the wisdom
of your words.
10Do not remove an ancient landmark
or enter the fields of the fatherless;
11for their Redeemer is strong;
he will plead their cause against you.
12Apply your mind to instruction
and your ear to words of knowledge.
13Do not withhold discipline from a child;
if you beat him with a rod, he will not die.
14If you beat him with the rod
you will save his life from Sheol.
15My son, if your heart is wise,
my heart too will be glad.
16My soul will rejoice
when your lips speak what is right.
17Let not your heart envy sinners,
but continue in the fear of the LORD all
the day.
18Surely there is a future,
and your hope will not be cut off.

ROMANS 3

**21But now the righteousness of
God has been manifested apart
from law, although the law and the
prophets bear witness to it, 22the righ-**
teousness of God through faith in Jesus
Christ for all who believe. For there is no
distinction; 23since all have sinned and fall
short of the glory of God, 24they are justified by his grace as a gift, through the redemption which is in Christ Jesus, 25whom
God put forward as an expiation by his
blood, to be received by faith. This was
to show God's righteousness, because in
his divine forbearance he had passed over
former sins; 26it was to prove at the present
time that he himself is righteous and that
he justifies him who has faith in Jesus.
27Then what becomes of our boasting?
It is excluded. On what principle? On the
principle of works? No, but on the principle
of faith. 28For we hold that a man is justified
by faith apart from works of law. 29Or is
God the God of Jews only? Is he not the
God of Gentiles also? Yes, of Gentiles also,
30since God is one; and he will justify the
circumcised on the ground of their faith and

the uncircumcised through their faith. 31Do we then overthrow the law by this faith? By no means! On the contrary, we uphold the law.

REFLECTION

When we are in distress, it is then that we most need to turn to the Lord. The Israelites in the narrative of Judith are up against a wall. The enemy general, Holofernes, is wreaking havoc through many cities and lands and is on his way to attack them. They prepare for war by fortifying hilltops and storing food, but also, as we will see tomorrow, by pleading before the Lord: "And all the men and women of Israel, and their children, living at Jerusalem, prostrated themselves before the temple and put ashes on their heads and spread out their sackcloth before the Lord" (Jdt 4:11). They come to the Lord in their hour of need, in desperation and fasting, and he hears their prayer. We too are desperate, for "all have sinned and fall short of the glory of God" (Rom 3:23). Our need, then, is great indeed. In Christ, we "are justified by his grace as a gift" (v. 24). We receive our salvation as a gift; we do not earn our way to Heaven. We cannot boast except in the Lord. Take a few moments today to give thanks for your savior Jesus Christ, who saved you at the cost of his own blood.

August 5

JUDITH 4

8So the Israelites did as Jo′akim the high priest and the senate of the whole people of Israel, in session at Jerusalem, had given order. 9And
every man of Israel cried out to God with great fervor, and they humbled themselves with much fasting. 10They and their wives and their children and their cattle and every resident alien and hired laborer and purchased slave—they all clothed themselves with sackcloth. 11And all the men and women of Israel, and their children, living at Jerusalem, prostrated themselves before the temple and put ashes on their heads and spread out their sackcloth before the Lord. 12They even surrounded the altar with sackcloth and cried out in unison, praying earnestly to the God of Israel not to give up their infants as prey and their wives as booty, and the cities they had inherited to be destroyed, and the sanctuary to be profaned and desecrated to the malicious joy of the Gentiles. 13So the Lord heard their prayers and looked upon their affliction; for the people fasted many days throughout Jude′a and in Jerusalem before the sanctuary of the Lord Almighty. 14And Jo′akim the high priest and all the priests who stood before the Lord and ministered to the Lord, with their loins clothed with sackcloth, offered the continual burnt offerings and the vows and freewill offerings of the people. 15With ashes upon their turbans, they cried out to the Lord with all their might to look with favor upon the whole house of Israel.

5 When Hol″ofer′nes, the general of the Assyrian army, heard that the people of Israel had prepared for war and had closed the passes in the hills and had fortified all the high hilltops and set up barricades in the plains, 2he was very angry. So he called together all the princes of Moab and the commanders of Ammon and all the governors of the coastland, 3and said to them, "Tell me, you Canaanites, what people is this that lives in the hill country? What cities do they inhabit? How large is their army, and in what does their power or strength consist? Who rules over them as king, leading their army? 4And why have they alone, of all who live in the west, refused to come out and meet me?"

5Then A′chior, the leader of all the Am′monites, said to him, "Let my lord now hear a word from the mouth of your servant, and I will tell you the truth about this people that dwells in the nearby mountain district. No falsehood shall come from your servant's mouth. 6This people is descended from the Chalde′ans. [7]At one time they lived in Mesopota′mia, because they would not follow the gods of their fathers who were in Chaldea. [8]For they had left the ways of their ancestors, and they worshiped the God of heaven, the God they had come to know; hence they drove them out from the presence of their gods; and they fled to Mesopota′mia, and lived there for a long time. [9]Then their God commanded them to leave the place where they were living and go to the land of Canaan. There they settled, and prospered, with much gold and silver and very many cattle. [10]When a famine spread over Canaan they went down to Egypt and lived there as long as they had food; and there they became a great multitude—so great that they could not be counted. [11]So the king of Egypt became hostile to them; he took advantage of them and set them to making bricks, and humbled them and made slaves of them. [12]Then they cried out to their God, and he afflicted the whole land of Egypt with incurable plagues; and so the Egyptians drove them out of their sight. [13]Then God dried up the Red Sea before them, [14]and he led them by the way of Sinai and Ka′desh-bar′nea, and drove out all the people of the wilderness. [15]So they lived in the land of the Am′orites, and by their might destroyed all the inhabitants of Heshbon; and crossing over the Jordan they took possession of all the hill country. [16]And they drove out before them the Canaanites and the Per′izzites and the Jeb′usites and the She′chemites and all the Ger′gesites, and lived there a long time. [17]As long as they did not sin against their God they prospered, for the God who hates iniquity is with them. [18]But when they departed from the way which he had appointed for them, they were utterly defeated in many battles and were led away captive to a foreign country; the temple of their God was razed to the ground, and their cities were captured by their enemies. [19]But now they have returned to their God, and have come back from the places to which they were scattered, and have occupied Jerusalem, where their sanctuary is, and have settled in the hill country, because it was uninhabited. [20]Now therefore, my master and lord, if there is any unwitting error in this people and they sin against their God and we find out their offense, then we will go up and defeat them. [21]But if there is no transgression in their nation, then let my lord pass them by; for their Lord will defend them, and their God will protect them, and we shall be put to shame before the whole world."

[22]When A′chior had finished saying this, all the men standing around the tent began to complain; Hol″ofer′nes' officers and all the men from the seacoast and from Moab insisted that he must be put to death. [23]"For," they said, "we will not be afraid of the Israelites; they are a people with no strength or power for making war. [24]Therefore let us go up, Lord Hol″ofer′nes, and they will be devoured by your vast army."

6 When the disturbance made by the men outside the council died down, Hol″ofer′nes, the commander of the Assyrian army, said to A′chior and all the Moabites in the presence of all the foreign contingents:

[2]"And who are you, A′chior, and you hirelings of E′phraim, to prophesy among us as you have done today and tell us not to make war against the people of Israel because their God will defend them? Who is God except Nebuchadnez′zar? [3]He will send his forces and will destroy them from the face of the earth, and their God will not deliver them—we the king's servants will destroy them as one man. They cannot resist the might of our cavalry. [4]We will burn them up, and their mountains will be drunk with their blood, and their fields will be full of their dead. They cannot withstand us, but will utterly perish. So says King Nebuchadnez′zar, the lord of the whole earth. For he has spoken; none of his words shall be in vain.

[5]"But you, A′chior, you Am′monite hireling, who have said these words on the day of your iniquity, you shall not see my face

again from this day until I take revenge
on this race that came out of Egypt. [6]Then
the sword of my army and the spear of my
servants shall pierce your sides, and you
shall fall among their wounded, when I
return. [7]Now my slaves are going to take
you back into the hill country and put you
in one of the cities beside the passes, [8]and
you will not die until you perish along with
them. [9]If you really hope in your heart
that they will not be taken, do not look
downcast! I have spoken and none of my
words shall fail."

[10]Then Hol″ofer′nes ordered his slaves,
who waited on him in his tent, to seize
A′chior and take him to Beth″uli′a and
hand him over to the men of Israel. [11]So the
slaves took him and led him out of the camp
into the plain, and from the plain they went
up into the hill country and came to the
springs below Beth″uli′a. [12]When the men
of the city saw them, they caught up their
weapons and ran out of the city to the top
of the hill, and all the slingers kept them
from coming up by casting stones at them.
[13]However, they got under the shelter of the
hill and they bound A′chior and left him
lying at the foot of the hill, and returned to
their master.

[14]Then the men of Israel came down
from their city and found him; and
they untied him and brought him into
Beth″uli′a and placed him before the
magistrates of their city, [15]who in those
days were Uzzi′ah the son of Micah, of
the tribe of Simeon, and Chabris the son
of Gotho′niel, and Charmis the son of
Melchi′el. [16]They called together all the
elders of the city, and all their young men
and their women ran to the assembly; and
they set A′chior in the midst of all their
people, and Uzzi′ah asked him what had
happened. [17]He answered and told them
what had taken place at the council of
Hol″ofer′nes, and all that he had said in
the presence of the Assyrian leaders, and
all that Holofernes had said so boastfully
against the house of Israel. [18]Then the
people fell down and worshiped God, and
cried out to him, and said,

[19]"O Lord God of heaven, behold their
arrogance, and have pity on the humiliation
of our people, and look this day upon the
faces of those who are consecrated to you."

[20]Then they consoled A′chior, and praised
him greatly. [21]And Uzzi′ah took him from
the assembly to his own house and gave a
banquet for the elders; and all that night
they called on the God of Israel for help.

PROVERBS 23

[19]Hear, my son, and be wise,
and direct your mind in the way.
[20]Be not among winebibbers,
or among gluttonous eaters of meat;
[21]for the drunkard and the glutton will come
to poverty,
and drowsiness will clothe a man
with rags.

[22]Listen to your father who begot you,
and do not despise your mother when
she is old.
[23]Buy truth, and do not sell it;
buy wisdom, instruction, and
understanding.
[24]The father of the righteous will
greatly rejoice;
he who begets a wise son will be glad in him.
[25]Let your father and mother be glad,
let her who bore you rejoice.

[26]My son, give me your heart,
and let your eyes observe my ways.
[27]For a harlot is a deep pit;
an adventuress is a narrow well.
[28]She lies in wait like a robber
and increases the faithless among men.

[29]Who has woe? Who has sorrow?
Who has strife? Who has complaining?
Who has wounds without cause? Who has
redness of eyes?
[30]Those who tarry long over wine,
those who go to try mixed wine.
[31]Do not look at wine when it is red,
when it sparkles in the cup
and goes down smoothly.

32 At the last it bites like a serpent,
and stings like an adder.
33 Your eyes will see strange things,
and your mind utter perverse things.
34 You will be like one who lies down in the
midst of the sea,
like one who lies on the top of a mast.
35 "They struck me," you will say, "but I was
not hurt;
they beat me, but I did not feel it.
When shall I awake?
I will seek another drink."

ROMANS 4

What then shall we say about Abraham, our forefather according to the flesh? 2For if Abraham was justified by works, he has something to boast about, but not
before God. 3For what does the Scripture
say? "Abraham believed God, and it was
reckoned to him as righteousness." 4Now
to one who works, his wages are not reckoned as a gift but as his due. 5And to one
who does not work but trusts him who justifies the ungodly, his faith is reckoned as
righteousness. 6So also David pronounces a
blessing upon the man to whom God reckons righteousness apart from works:
7 "Blessed are those whose iniquities are
forgiven, and whose sins are covered;
8 blessed is the man against whom the Lord
will not reckon his sin."
9 Is this blessing pronounced only upon
the circumcised, or also upon the uncircumcised? We say that faith was reckoned
to Abraham as righteousness. 10How then
was it reckoned to him? Was it before or
after he had been circumcised? It was not
after, but before he was circumcised. 11He
received circumcision as a sign or seal of the
righteousness which he had by faith while
he was still uncircumcised. The purpose was
to make him the father of all who believe
without being circumcised and who thus
have righteousness reckoned to them, 12and
likewise the father of the circumcised who
are not merely circumcised but also follow
the example of the faith which our father
Abraham had before he was circumcised.

REFLECTION

We are taught that salvation history demonstrates that God is always worthy of trust. That principle shapes the advice that Achior the Ammonite gives to the general Holofernes in regard to the Israelites. Simply, he explains that if the Israelites have sinned, Holofernes will win in battle, but if they have not, then "their Lord will defend them" (Jdt 5:21). Rather than taking this advice under consideration, Holofernes has Achior tossed out. In contrast to Holofernes's self-trust, Abraham models trust in the Lord. St. Paul explains that Abraham believed God and was justified (see Gen 15) and then later was circumcised (see Gen 17). Thus, Abraham was justified apart from the Law regarding circumcision, and so he became the father not only of the Jews (who are circumcised) but also of the Gentiles (who are uncircumcised). Circumcision is not necessary for salvation, but what is necessary is faith. The one thing necessary for us to please God and draw close to him is our faith, which is trust in who he is and what he has done for us—rather than in who we are and what we do. The difference between Holofernes and Abraham is who they put their trust in. Who do you trust?

August 6

JUDITH 7

The next day Hol″ofer′nes ordered his whole army, and all the allies who had joined him, to break camp and move against Beth″uli′a, and
to seize the passes up into the hill country
and make war on the Israelites. 2So all their
warriors moved their camp that day; their
force of men of war was one hundred and

seventy thousand infantry and twelve thousand cavalry, together with the baggage and the foot soldiers handling it, a very great multitude. 3They encamped in the valley near Beth″uli′a, beside the spring, and they spread out in breadth over Do′than as far as Balba′im and in length from Bethulia to Cy′amon, which faces Esdrae′lon.

4When the Israelites saw their vast numbers they were greatly terrified, and every one said to his neighbor, "These men will now lick up the face of the whole land; neither the high mountains nor the valleys nor the hills will bear their weight." 5Then each man took up his weapons, and when they had kindled fires on their towers they remained on guard all that night.

6On the second day Hol″ofer′nes led out all his cavalry in full view of the Israelites in Beth″uli′a, 7and examined the approaches to the city, and visited the springs that supplied their water, and seized them and set guards of soldiers over them, and then returned to his army.

8Then all the chieftains of the people of Esau and all the leaders of the Moabites and the commanders of the coastland came to him and said, 9"Let our lord hear a word, lest his army be defeated. 10For these people, the Israelites, do not rely on their spears but on the height of the mountains where they live, for it is not easy to reach the tops of their mountains. 11Therefore, my lord, do not fight against them in battle array, and not a man of your army will fall. 12Remain in your camp, and keep all the men in your forces with you; only let your servants take possession of the spring of water that flows from the foot of the mountain—13for this is where all the people of Beth″uli′a get their water. So thirst will destroy them, and they will give up their city. We and our people will go up to the tops of the nearby mountains and camp there to keep watch that not a man gets out of the city. 14They and their wives and children will waste away with famine, and before the sword reaches them they will be strewn about in the streets where they live. 15So you will pay them back with evil, because they rebelled and did not receive you peaceably."

16These words pleased Hol″ofer′nes and all his servants, and he gave orders to do as they had said. 17So the army of the Am′monites moved forward, together with five thousand Assyrians, and they encamped in the valley and seized the water supply and the springs of the Israelites. 18And the sons of Esau and the sons of Ammon went up and encamped in the hill country opposite Do′than; and they sent some of their men toward the south and the east, toward Ac′raba, which is near Chu′si beside the brook Moch′mur. The rest of the Assyrian army encamped in the plain, and covered the whole face of the land, and their tents and supply trains spread out in great number, and they formed a vast multitude.

19The people of Israel cried out to the Lord their God, for their courage failed, because all their enemies had surrounded them and there was no way of escape from them. 20The whole Assyrian army, their infantry, chariots, and cavalry, surrounded them for thirty-four days, until all the vessels of water belonging to every inhabitant of Beth″uli′a were empty; 21their cisterns were going dry, and they did not have enough water to drink their fill for a single day, because it was measured out to them to drink. 22Their children lost heart, and the women and young men fainted from thirst and fell down in the streets of the city and in the passages through the gates; there was no strength left in them any longer.

23Then all the people, the young men, the women, and the children, gathered about Uzzi′ah and the rulers of the city and cried out with a loud voice, and said before all the elders, 24"God be judge between you and us! For you have done us a great injury in not making peace with the Assyrians. 25For now we have no one to help us; God has sold us into their hands, to strew us on the ground before them with thirst and utter destruction. 26Now call them in and surrender the whole city to the army of Hol″ofer′nes and to all his forces, to be plundered. 27For it would be better for us to be captured by them; for we will be slaves, but our lives will be spared, and we shall not witness the death of our infants before our eyes, or see our wives and children draw their last breath. 28We call to

witness against you heaven and earth and our
God, the Lord of our fathers, who punishes
us according to our sins and the sins of our
fathers. Let him not do this day the things
which we have described!"
29Then great and general lamentation arose
throughout the assembly, and they cried out
to the Lord God with a loud voice. 30And
Uzzi′ah said to them, "Have courage, my
brothers! Let us hold out for five more days;
by that time the Lord our God will restore
to us his mercy, for he will not forsake us
utterly. 31But if these days pass by, and no
help comes for us, I will do what you say."
32Then he dismissed the people to their
various posts, and they went up on the
walls and towers of their city. The women
and children he sent home. And they were
greatly depressed in the city.
8 At that time Judith heard about these
things: she was the daughter of Merar′i
the son of Ox, son of Joseph, son of O′ziel,
son of Elki′ah, son of Anani′as, son of
Gideon, son of Raph′aim, son of Ahi′tub,
son of Eli′jah, son of Hilki′ah, son of Eliab,
son of Nathan′a-el, son of Sala′miel, son
of Sara′sadai, son of Israel. 2Her husband
Manas′seh, who belonged to her tribe and
family, had died during the barley harvest.
3For as he stood overseeing the men who were
binding sheaves in the field, he was overcome
by the burning heat, and took to his bed and
died in Beth″uli′a his city. So they buried him
with his fathers in the field between Do′than
and Bal′amon. 4Judith had lived at home as a
widow for three years and four months. 5She
set up a tent for herself on the roof of her
house, and belted sackcloth about her loins
and wore the garments of her widowhood.
6She fasted all the days of her widowhood,
except the day before the sabbath and the
sabbath itself, the day before the new moon
and the day of the new moon, and the feasts
and days of rejoicing of the house of Israel.
7She was beautiful in appearance, and had
a very lovely face; she was prudent of heart,
discerning in judgment, and quite virtuous.
Her husband Manas′seh, the son of Joseph,
the son of Ahi′tub, the son of Melchis, the
son of E′liab, the son of Nathan′a-el, the son
of Sara′sadai, the son of Simeon, had left her
gold and silver, and men and women slaves,
and cattle, and fields; and she maintained this
estate. 8No one spoke ill of her, for she feared
God with great devotion.
9When Judith heard the wicked words
spoken by the people against the ruler,
because they were faint for lack of water,
and when she heard all that Uzziah said to
them, and how he promised them under
oath to surrender the city to the Assyrians
after five days, 10she sent her maid, who was
in charge of all she possessed, to summon
Chabris and Charmis, the elders of her city.
11They came to her, and she said to them,
"Listen to me, rulers of the people of
Beth″uli′a! What you have said to the people
today is not right; you have even sworn and
pronounced this oath between God and
you, promising to surrender the city to our
enemies unless the Lord turns and helps us
within so many days. 12Who are you, that
have put God to the test this day, and are
setting yourselves up in the place of God
among the sons of men? 13You are putting
the Lord Almighty to the test—but you
will never know anything! 14You cannot
plumb the depths of the human heart, nor
find out what a man is thinking; how do
you expect to search out God, who made
all these things, and find out his mind or
comprehend his thought? No, my brethren,
do not provoke the Lord our God to anger.
15For if he does not choose to help us within
these five days, he has power to protect
us within any time he pleases, or even to
destroy us in the presence of our enemies.
16Do not try to bind the purposes of the
Lord our God; for God is not like man, to
be threatened, nor like a human being, to be
won over by pleading. 17Therefore, while we
wait for his deliverance, let us call upon him
to help us, and he will hear our voice, if it
pleases him.
18"For never in our generation, nor in
these present days, has there been any tribe
or family or people or city of ours which
worshiped gods made with hands, as was
done in days gone by—19and that was why
our fathers were handed over to the sword,

and to be plundered, and so they suffered
a great catastrophe before our enemies.
20But we know no other god but him, and
therefore we hope that he will not disdain
us or any of our nation. 21For if we are
captured all Jude´a will be captured and our
sanctuary will be plundered; and he will
exact of us the penalty for its desecration.
22And the slaughter of our brethren and the
captivity of the land and the desolation of
our inheritance—all this he will bring upon
our heads among the Gentiles, wherever we
serve as slaves; and we shall be an offense
and a reproach in the eyes of those who
acquire us. 23For our slavery will not bring
us into favor, but the Lord our God will turn
it to dishonor.

24"Now therefore, brethren, let us set an
example to our brethren, for their lives
depend upon us, and the sanctuary and the
temple and the altar rest upon us. 25In spite
of everything let us give thanks to the Lord
our God, who is putting us to the test as he
did our forefathers. 26Remember what he did
with Abraham, and how he tested Isaac, and
what happened to Jacob in Mesopota´mia
in Syria, while he was keeping the sheep of
La´ban, his mother's brother. 27For he has not
tried us with fire, as he did them, to search
their hearts, nor has he taken revenge upon
us; but the Lord scourges those who draw
near to him, in order to admonish them."

28Then Uzzi´ah said to her, "All that you have
said has been spoken out of a true heart, and
there is no one who can deny your words.
29Today is not the first time your wisdom
has been shown, but from the beginning of
your life all the people have recognized your
understanding, for your heart's disposition
is right. 30But the people were very thirsty,
and they compelled us to do for them what
we have promised, and made us take an oath
which we cannot break. 31So pray for us,
since you are a devout woman, and the Lord
will send us rain to fill our cisterns and we
will no longer be faint."

32Judith said to them, "Listen to me. I am
about to do a thing which will go down
through all generations of our descendants.
33Stand at the city gate tonight, and I will go
out with my maid; and within the days after
which you have promised to surrender the
city to our enemies, the Lord will deliver
Israel by my hand. 34Only, do not try to find
out what I plan; for I will not tell you until I
have finished what I am about to do."

35Uzzi´ah and the rulers said to her, "Go
in peace, and may the Lord God go before
you, to take revenge upon our enemies."
36So they returned from the tent and went
to their posts.

PROVERBS 24

Be not envious of evil men,
  nor desire to be with them;
2for their minds devise violence,
  and their lips talk of mischief.

3By wisdom a house is built,
  and by understanding it is established;
4by knowledge the rooms are filled
  with all precious and pleasant riches.
5A wise man is mightier than a strong man,
  and a man of knowledge than he who
    has strength;
6for by wise guidance you can wage your war,
  and in abundance of counselors there
    is victory.
7Wisdom is too high for a fool;
  in the gate he does not open his mouth.
8He who plans to do evil
  will be called a mischief-maker.
9The devising of folly is sin,
  and the scoffer is an abomination to men.

10If you faint in the day of adversity,
  your strength is small.
11Rescue those who are being taken away
    to death;
  hold back those who are stumbling
    to the slaughter.
12If you say, "Behold, we did not know this,"
  does not he who weighs the heart
    perceive it?
Does not he who keeps watch over your
    soul know it,
  and will he not repay man according to
    his work?

ROMANS 4

**13 The promise to Abraham and
his descendants, that they
should inherit the world, did not come
through the law but through the right-**
eousness of faith. 14 If it is the adherents of
the law who are to be the heirs, faith is null
and the promise is void. 15 For the law brings
wrath, but where there is no law there is no
transgression.
16 That is why it depends on faith, in order
that the promise may rest on grace and be
guaranteed to all his descendants—not only
to the adherents of the law but also to those
who share the faith of Abraham, for he is
the father of us all, 17 as it is written, "I have
made you the father of many nations"—
in the presence of the God in whom he
believed, who gives life to the dead and calls
into existence the things that do not exist.
18 In hope he believed against hope, that he
should become the father of many nations; as
he had been told, "So shall your descendants
be." 19 He did not weaken in faith when he
considered his own body, which was as good
as dead because he was about a hundred years
old, or when he considered the barrenness of
Sarah's womb. 20 No distrust made him waver
concerning the promise of God, but he grew
strong in his faith as he gave glory to God,
21 fully convinced that God was able to do
what he had promised. 22 That is why his faith
was "reckoned to him as righteousness." 23 But
the words, "it was reckoned to him," were
written not for his sake alone, 24 but for ours
also. It will be reckoned to us who believe in
him that raised from the dead Jesus our Lord,
25 who was put to death for our trespasses and
raised for our justification.

REFLECTION

Regarding Abraham, St. Paul writes, "In hope he believed against hope" (Rom 4:18). That is exactly what we need—a faith that contradicts the hopelessness around us. Judith had a powerful faith. At a moment when the people of her city run out of water and they lack courage (see Jdt 7:19–28), she steps forward to remind them of God's providence and chides them for putting him to the test. She understands that the Lord disciplines his followers "in order to admonish them" (8:27), not to destroy them. Despite the city's presumption in issuing a time limit to God, she professes a rock-solid faith: "The Lord will deliver Israel by my hand" (v. 33). Faith brings victory to Judith and justification to Abraham. For us, Proverbs advises, "By wisdom a house is built" (Prv 24:3), shedding light on the constructive nature of faith and wisdom. A confident faith confronts the threats around us with a belief stronger than fear. Faith in God fills us with courage to live a holy life, to surrender our fears to him, and to break the hold that fear often has over us. Does your faith have the strength to stand up to anxiety and fear like Judith and Abraham?

August 7

JUDITH 9

**Then Judith fell upon her face,
and put ashes on her head, and
uncovered the sackcloth she was wearing;
and at the very time when that evening's**
incense was being offered in the house of
God in Jerusalem, Judith cried out to the
Lord with a loud voice, and said,
2 "O Lord God of my father Simeon, to
whom you gave a sword to take revenge on
the strangers who had loosed the girdle of a
virgin to defile her, and uncovered her thigh
to put her to shame, and polluted her womb
to disgrace her; for you have said, 'It shall not
be done'—yet they did it. 3 So you gave up their
rulers to be slain, and their bed, which was
ashamed of the deceit they had practiced, to
be stained with blood, and you struck down
slaves along with princes, and princes on their
thrones; 4 and you gave their wives for a prey
and their daughters to captivity, and all their
booty to be divided among your beloved sons,

who were zealous for you, and abhorred the pollution of their blood, and called on you for help—O God, my God, hear me also, a widow.

5“For you have done these things and those that went before and those that followed; you have designed the things that are now, and those that are to come. Yes, the things you intended came to pass, 6and the things you willed presented themselves and said, ‘Behold, we are here’; for all your ways are prepared in advance, and your judgment is with foreknowledge.

7“Behold now, the Assyrians are increased in their might; they are exalted, with their horses and riders; they glory in the strength of their foot soldiers; they trust in shield and spear, in bow and sling, and know not that you are the Lord who crushes wars; the Lord is your name. 8Break their strength by your might, and bring down their power in your anger; for they intend to defile your sanctuary, and to pollute the tabernacle where your glorious name rests, and to cast down the horn of your altar with the sword. 9Behold their pride, and send your wrath upon their heads; give to me, a widow, the strength to do what I plan. 10By the deceit of my lips strike down the slave with the prince and the prince with his servant; crush their arrogance by the hand of a woman.

11“For your power depends not upon numbers, nor your might upon men of strength; for you are God of the lowly, helper of the oppressed, upholder of the weak, protector of the forlorn, savior of those without hope. 12Hear, O hear me, God of my father, God of the inheritance of Israel, Lord of heaven and earth, Creator of the waters, King of all your creation, hear my prayer! 13Make my deceitful words to be their wound and stripe, for they have planned cruel things against your covenant, and against your consecrated house, and against the top of Zion, and against the house possessed by your children. 14And cause your whole nation and every tribe to know and understand that you are God, the God of all power and might, and that there is no other who protects the people of Israel but you alone!”

10 When Judith had ceased crying out to the God of Israel, and had ended all these words, 2she rose from where she lay prostrate and called her maid and went down into the house where she lived on sabbaths and on her feast days; 3and she removed the sackcloth which she had been wearing, and took off her widow’s garments, and bathed her body with water, and anointed herself with precious ointment, and combed her hair and put on a tiara, and arrayed herself in her most festive apparel, which she used to wear while her husband Manas′seh was living. 4And she put sandals on her feet, and put on her anklets and bracelets and rings, and her earrings and all her ornaments, and made herself very beautiful, to entice the eyes of all men who might see her. 5And she gave her maid a bottle of wine and a flask of oil, and filled a bag with parched grain and a cake of dried fruit and fine bread; and she wrapped up all her vessels and gave them to her to carry.

6Then they went out to the city gate of Beth″uli′a, and found Uzzi′ah standing there with the elders of the city, Chabris and Charmis. 7When they saw her, and noted how her face was altered and her clothing changed, they greatly admired her beauty, and said to her, 8“May the God of our fathers grant you favor and fulfil your plans, that the people of Israel may glory and Jerusalem may be exalted.” And she worshiped God.

9Then she said to them, “Order the gate of the city to be opened for me, and I will go out and accomplish the things about which you spoke with me.” So they ordered the young men to open the gate for her, as she had said. 10When they had done this, Judith went out, she and her maid with her; and the men of the city watched her until she had gone down the mountain and passed through the valley and they could no longer see her.

11The women went straight on through the valley; and an Assyrian patrol met her 12and took her into custody, and asked her, “To what people do you belong, and where are you coming from, and where are you going?” She replied, “I am a daughter of the Hebrews, but I am fleeing from them, for they are about to be handed over to you

to be devoured. [13]I am on my way to the
presence of Hol″ofer′nes the commander of
your army, to give him a true report; and I
will show him a way by which he can go and
capture all the hill country without losing
one of his men, captured or slain."
[14]When the men heard her words, and
observed her face—she was in their eyes
marvelously beautiful—they said to her,
[15]"You have saved your life by hurrying
down to the presence of our lord. Go at
once to his tent; some of us will escort you
and hand you over to him. [16]And when you
stand before him, do not be afraid in your
heart, but tell him just what you have said,
and he will treat you well."
[17]They chose from their number a
hundred men to accompany her and
her maid, and they brought them to the
tent of Hol″ofer′nes. [18]There was great
excitement in the whole camp, for her
arrival was reported from tent to tent, and
they came and stood around her as she
waited outside the tent of Hol″ofer′nes
while they told him about her. [19]And
they marveled at her beauty, and admired
the Israelites, judging them by her, and
every one said to his neighbor, "Who can
despise these people, who have women
like this among them? Surely not a man
of them had better be left alive, for if we
let them go they will be able to ensnare
the whole world!"

PROVERBS 24

[13]My son, eat honey, for it is good,
and the drippings of the honeycomb are
sweet to your taste.
[14]Know that wisdom is such to your soul;
if you find it, there will be a future,
and your hope will not be cut off.

[15]Lie not in wait as a wicked man against
the dwelling of the righteous;
do not violence to his home;
[16]for a righteous man falls seven times, and
rises again;
but the wicked are overthrown by calamity.

[17]Do not rejoice when your enemy falls,
and let not your heart be glad when
he stumbles;
[18]lest the LORD see it, and be displeased,
and turn away his anger from him.

[19]Fret not yourself because of evildoers,
and be not envious of the wicked;
[20]for the evil man has no future;
the lamp of the wicked will be put out.

[21]My son, fear the LORD and the king,
and do not disobey either of them;
[22]for disaster from them will rise suddenly,
and who knows the ruin that will come
from them both?

[23] These also are sayings of the wise.

Partiality in judging is not good.
[24]He who says to the wicked, "You
are innocent,"
will be cursed by peoples, abhorred
by nations;
[25]but those who rebuke the wicked will
have delight,
and a good blessing will be upon them.
[26]He who gives a right answer
kisses the lips.

[27]Prepare your work outside,
get everything ready for you in the field;
and after that build your house.

[28]Be not a witness against your neighbor
without cause,
and do not deceive with your lips.
[29]Do not say, "I will do to him as he has done
to me;
I will pay the man back for what he
has done."

[30]I passed by the field of a sluggard,
by the vineyard of a man without sense;
[31]and behold, it was all overgrown
with thorns;
the ground was covered with nettles,
and its stone wall was broken down.
[32]Then I saw and considered it;
I looked and received instruction.

33 A little sleep, a little slumber,
a little folding of the hands to rest,
34 and poverty will come upon you like
a robber,
and want like an armed man.

ROMANS 5

**Therefore, since we are justified
by faith, we have peace with God
through our Lord Jesus Christ.
2 Through him we have obtained access
to this grace in which we stand, and
we rejoice in our hope of sharing the**
glory of God. 3 More than that, we rejoice in
our sufferings, knowing that suffering produces endurance, 4 and endurance produces
character, and character produces hope, 5 and
hope does not disappoint us, because God's
love has been poured into our hearts through
the Holy Spirit who has been given to us.

6 While we were yet helpless, at the right
time Christ died for the ungodly. 7 Why, one
will hardly die for a righteous man—though
perhaps for a good man one will dare even
to die. 8 But God shows his love for us in that
while we were yet sinners Christ died for us.
9 Since, therefore, we are now justified by his
blood, much more shall we be saved by him
from the wrath of God. 10 For if while we were
enemies we were reconciled to God by the
death of his Son, much more, now that we are
reconciled, shall we be saved by his life. 11 Not
only so, but we also rejoice in God through
our Lord Jesus Christ, through whom we
have now received our reconciliation.

12 Therefore as sin came into the world
through one man and death through sin, and
so death spread to all men because all men
sinned—13 sin indeed was in the world before
the law was given, but sin is not counted where
there is no law. 14 Yet death reigned from Adam
to Moses, even over those whose sins were not
like the transgression of Adam, who was a type
of the one who was to come.

15 But the free gift is not like the trespass.
For if many died through one man's trespass,
much more have the grace of God and the
free gift in the grace of that one man Jesus
Christ abounded for many. 16 And the free gift
is not like the effect of that one man's sin. For
the judgment following one trespass brought
condemnation, but the free gift following
many trespasses brings justification. 17 If,
because of one man's trespass, death reigned
through that one man, much more will those
who receive the abundance of grace and the
free gift of righteousness reign in life through
the one man Jesus Christ.

18 Then as one man's trespass led to
condemnation for all men, so one man's act
of righteousness leads to acquittal and life for
all men. 19 For as by one man's disobedience
many were made sinners, so by one man's
obedience many will be made righteous.
20 Law came in, to increase the trespass; but
where sin increased, grace abounded all the
more, 21 so that, as sin reigned in death, grace
also might reign through righteousness to
eternal life through Jesus Christ our Lord.

REFLECTION

Judith models a deep trust in the providence of God. At a moment of crisis, when her city is about to be overwhelmed by powerful enemies, she places herself in the Lord's hands: "For you have done these things and those that went before and those that followed; you have designed the things that are now, and those that are to come" (Jdt 9:5). Prayer is founded on God's lordship over, and care for, all his creation. Nothing escapes his notice, and when we pray in faith, we recognize that the whole universe is under his control. Faith like that allows us to "rejoice in our sufferings" (Rom 5:3), a paradox to the world. Yet our confidence in God means that "hope does not disappoint us" (v. 5). Rather, the Lord has overcome even our worst enemy, death, which came to have power over us through the Original Sin of Adam. Now, he has given us the "free gift" (v. 15) of justification through Christ. Rather than cowering under the reign of death, we now "reign in life" (v. 17). Jesus's conquest over sin empowers us to be like the righteous man who "falls seven times, and rises again" (Prv 24:16). Do you trust, like Judith, that the future unfolds according to God's master plan?

August 8

JUDITH 10

[20]Then Hol″ofer′nes’ companions and all his servants came out and led her into the tent. [21]Hol″ofer′nes was resting on his bed, under a canopy which was woven with purple and gold and emeralds and precious stones. [22]When they told him of her he came forward to the front of the tent, with silver lamps carried before him. [23]And when Judith came into the presence of Hol″ofer′nes and his servants, they all marveled at the beauty of her face; and she prostrated herself and made obeisance to him, and his slaves raised her up.

11 Then Hol″ofer′nes said to her, “Take courage, woman, and do not be afraid in your heart, for I have never hurt any one who chose to serve Nebuchadnez′zar, the king of all the earth. [2]And even now, if your people who live in the hill country had not slighted me, I would never have lifted my spear against them; but they have brought all this on themselves. [3]And now tell me why you have fled from them and have come over to us—since you have come to safety. [4]Have courage; you will live, tonight and from now on. No one will hurt you, but all will treat you well, as they do the servants of my lord King Nebuchadnez′zar.”

[5]Judith replied to him, “Accept the words of your servant, and let your maidservant speak in your presence, and I will tell nothing false to my lord this night. [6]And if you follow out the words of your maidservant, God will accomplish something through you, and my lord will not fail to achieve his purposes. [7]Nebuchadnez′zar the king of the whole earth lives, and as his power endures, who had sent you to direct every living soul, not only do men serve him because of you, but also the beasts of the field and the cattle and the birds of the air will live by your power under Nebuchadnezzar and all his house. [8]For we have heard of your wisdom and skill, and it is reported throughout the whole world that you are the one good man in the whole kingdom, thoroughly informed and marvelous in military strategy.

[9]“Now as for the things A′chior said in your council, we have heard his words, for the men of Beth″uli′a spared him and he told them all he had said to you. [10]Therefore, my lord and master, do not disregard what he said, but keep it in your mind, for it is true: our nation cannot be punished, nor can the sword prevail against them, unless they sin against their God.

[11]“And now, in order that my lord may not be defeated and his purpose frustrated, death will fall upon them, for a sin has overtaken them by which they are about to provoke their God to anger when they do what is wrong. [12]Since their food supply is exhausted and their water has almost given out, they have planned to kill their cattle and have determined to use all that God by his laws has forbidden them to eat. [13]They have decided to consume the first fruits of the grain and the tithes of the wine and oil, which they had consecrated and set aside for the priests who minister in the presence of our God at Jerusalem—although it is not lawful for any of the people so much as to touch these things with their hands. [14]They have sent men to Jerusalem, because even the people living there have been doing this, to bring back to them permission from the senate. [15]When the word reaches them and they proceed to do this, on that day they will be handed over to you to be destroyed.

[16]“Therefore, when I, your servant, learned all this, I fled from them; and God has sent me to accomplish with you things that will astonish the whole world, as many as shall hear about them. [17]For your servant is religious, and serves the God of heaven day and night; therefore, my lord, I will remain with you, and every night your servant will go out into the valley, and I will pray to God and he will tell me when they have committed their sins. [18]And I will come and tell you, and then you shall go out with your whole army, and not one of them will withstand you. [19]Then I will lead you through the middle of Jude′a, till you come to Jerusalem; and

I will set your throne in the midst of it; and you will lead them like sheep that have no shepherd, and not a dog will so much as open its mouth to growl at you. For this has been told me, by my foreknowledge; it was announced to me, and I was sent to tell you."

[20]Her words pleased Hol′ofer′nes and all his servants, and they marveled at her wisdom and said, [21]"There is not such a woman from one end of the earth to the other, either for beauty of face or wisdom of speech!" [22]And Hol′ofer′nes said to her, "God has done well to send you before the people, to lend strength to our hands and to bring destruction upon those who have slighted my lord. [23]You are not only beautiful in appearance, but wise in speech; and if you do as you have said, your God shall be my God, and you shall live in the house of King Nebuchadnez′zar and be renowned throughout the whole world."

12 Then he commanded them to bring her in where his silver dishes were kept, and ordered them to set a table for her with some of his own food and to serve her with his own wine. [2]But Judith said, "I cannot eat it, lest it be an offense; but I will be provided from the things I have brought with me." [3]Hol′ofer′nes said to her, "If your supply runs out, where can we get more like it for you? For none of your people is here with us." [4]Judith replied, "As your soul lives, my lord, your servant will not use up the things I have with me before the Lord carries out by my hand what he has determined to do."

[5]Then the servants of Hol′ofer′nes brought her into the tent, and she slept until midnight. Along toward the morning watch she arose [6]and sent to Hol′ofer′nes and said, "Let my lord now command that your servant be permitted to go out and pray." [7]So Hol′ofer′nes commanded his guards not to hinder her. And she remained in the camp for three days, and went out each night to the valley of Beth′uli′a, and bathed at the spring in the camp. [8]When she came up from the spring she prayed the Lord God of Israel to direct her way for the raising up of her people. [9]So she returned clean and stayed in the tent until she ate her food toward evening.

[10]On the fourth day Hol′ofer′nes held a banquet for his slaves only, and did not invite any of his officers. [11]And he said to Bago′as, the eunuch who had charge of all his personal affairs, "Go now and persuade the Hebrew woman who is in your care to join us and eat and drink with us. [12]For it will be a disgrace if we let such a woman go without enjoying her company, for if we do not embrace her she will laugh at us." [13]So Bago′as went out from the presence of Hol′ofer′nes, and approached her and said, "This beautiful maidservant will please come to my lord and be honored in his presence, and drink wine and be merry with us, and become today like one of the daughters of the Assyrians who serve in the house of Nebuchadnez′zar." [14]And Judith said, "Who am I, to refuse my lord? Surely whatever pleases him I will do at once, and it will be a joy to me until the day of my death!" [15]So she got up and arrayed herself in all her woman's finery, and her maid went and spread on the ground for her before Hol′ofer′nes the soft fleeces which she had received from Bago′as for her daily use, so that she might recline on them when she ate.

[16]Then Judith came in and lay down, and Hol′ofer′nes' heart was ravished with her and he was moved with great desire to possess her; for he had been waiting for an opportunity to deceive her, ever since the day he first saw her. [17]So Hol′ofer′nes said to her, "Drink now, and be merry with us!" [18]Judith said, "I will drink now, my lord, because my life means more to me today than in all the days since I was born." [19]Then she took and ate and drank before him what her maid had prepared. [20]And Hol′ofer′nes was greatly pleased with her, and drank a great quantity of wine, much more than he had ever drunk in any one day since he was born.

PROVERBS 25

These also are proverbs of Solomon which the men of Hezeki′ah king of Judah copied.

[2]It is the glory of God to conceal things,
but the glory of kings is to search
things out.

[3]As the heavens for height, and the earth
for depth,
so the mind of kings is unsearchable.
[4]Take away the dross from the silver,
and the smith has material for a vessel;
[5]take away the wicked from the presence of
the king,
and his throne will be established
in righteousness.
[6]Do not put yourself forward in the
king's presence
or stand in the place of the great;
[7]for it is better to be told, "Come up here,"
than to be put lower in the presence of
the prince.

What your eyes have seen
8 do not hastily bring into court;
for what will you do in the end,
when your neighbor puts you to shame?
[9]Argue your case with your
neighbor himself,
and do not disclose another's secret;
[10]lest he who hears you bring shame upon you,
and your ill repute have no end.

[11]A word fitly spoken
is like apples of gold in a setting of silver.
[12]Like a gold ring or an ornament of gold
is a wise reprover to a listening ear.
[13]Like the cold of snow in the time of harvest
is a faithful messenger to those who
send him,
he refreshes the spirit of his masters.
[14]Like clouds and wind without rain
is a man who boasts of a gift he does
not give.

ROMANS 6

What shall we say then? Are
we to continue in sin that grace
may abound? [2]By no means! How can
we who died to sin still live in it? [3]Do
you not know that all of us who have been
baptized into Christ Jesus were baptized
into his death? [4]We were buried therefore
with him by baptism into death, so that
as Christ was raised from the dead by the
glory of the Father, we too might walk in
newness of life.
[5]For if we have been united with him in a
death like his, we shall certainly be united
with him in a resurrection like his. [6]We
know that our former man was crucified
with him so that the sinful body might
be destroyed, and we might no longer be
enslaved to sin. [7]For he who has died is
freed from sin. [8]But if we have died with
Christ, we believe that we shall also live
with him. [9]For we know that Christ being
raised from the dead will never die again;
death no longer has dominion over him.
[10]The death he died he died to sin, once for
all, but the life he lives he lives to God. [11]So
you also must consider yourselves dead to
sin and alive to God in Christ Jesus.
[12]Let not sin therefore reign in your mortal
bodies, to make you obey their passions. [13]Do
not yield your members to sin as instruments
of wickedness, but yield yourselves to
God as men who have been brought from
death to life, and your members to God as
instruments of righteousness. [14]For sin will
have no dominion over you, since you are
not under law but under grace.
[15]What then? Are we to sin because we
are not under law but under grace? By no
means! [16]Do you not know that if you yield
yourselves to any one as obedient slaves,
you are slaves of the one whom you obey,
either of sin, which leads to death, or of
obedience, which leads to righteousness?
[17]But thanks be to God, that you who
were once slaves of sin have become
obedient from the heart to the standard
of teaching to which you were committed,
[18]and, having been set free from sin, have
become slaves of righteousness. [19]I am
speaking in human terms, because of
your natural limitations. For just as you
once yielded your members to impurity
and to greater and greater iniquity, so
now yield your members to righteousness
for sanctification.
[20]When you were slaves of sin, you were
free in regard to righteousness. [21]But then
what return did you get from the things

of which you are now ashamed? The end of those things is death. [22]But now that you have been set free from sin and have become slaves of God, the return you get is sanctification and its end, eternal life. [23]For the wages of sin is death, but the free gift of God is eternal life in Christ Jesus our Lord.

7 Do you not know, brethren—for I am speaking to those who know the law—that the law is binding on a person only during his life? [2]Thus a married woman is bound by law to her husband as long as he lives; but if her husband dies she is discharged from the law concerning the husband. [3]Accordingly, she will be called an adulteress if she lives with another man while her husband is alive. But if her husband dies she is free from that law, and if she marries another man she is not an adulteress.

[4]Likewise, my brethren, you have died to the law through the body of Christ, so that you may belong to another, to him who has been raised from the dead in order that we may bear fruit for God. [5]While we were living in the flesh, our sinful passions, aroused by the law, were at work in our members to bear fruit for death. [6]But now we are discharged from the law, dead to that which held us captive, so that we serve not under the old written code but in the new life of the Spirit.

[7]What then shall we say? That the law is sin? By no means! Yet, if it had not been for the law, I should not have known sin. I should not have known what it is to covet if the law had not said, "You shall not covet." [8]But sin, finding opportunity in the commandment, wrought in me all kinds of covetousness. Apart from the law sin lies dead. [9]I was once alive apart from the law, but when the commandment came, sin revived and I died; [10]the very commandment which promised life proved to be death to me. [11]For sin, finding opportunity in the commandment, deceived me and by it killed me. [12]So the law is holy, and the commandment is holy and just and good.

REFLECTION

St. Paul calls us, challenges us, to "walk in newness of life" (Rom 6:4). What is impossible for the unbeliever, and those under the Old Covenant, is now possible for us who have been "baptized into Christ Jesus" (v. 3). Holofernes's lust of Judith is a reminder of the many sins that we are now set free from by the Death and Resurrection of Jesus Christ. But since our fallen nature can easily tend toward sin because of concupiscence, this gift of freedom which was won for us on the Cross demands our cooperation with God's grace. Thus St. Paul urges us, "Do not yield" (v. 12) to sin, do not return to being slaves to sin, but, rather, be "obedient from the heart" (v. 17) and yield to righteous. The good news is that because of our baptism we now "belong to another" (7:4), to our Lord, and he will provide all we need in our struggle. Just as Judith will overcome the wicked Holofernes, we can overcome the allurements of sin and walk in newness of life in Christ. What can you do today to be more "obedient from the heart"?

August 9

JUDITH 13

When evening came, his slaves quickly withdrew, and Bago′as closed the tent from outside and shut out the attendants from his master's presence; and they went to bed, for they all were weary because the banquet had lasted long. [2]So Judith was left alone in the tent, with Hol″ofer′nes stretched out on his bed, for he was overcome with wine.

[3]Now Judith had told her maid to stand outside the bedchamber and to wait for her to come out, as she did every day; for she said she would be going out for her prayers. And she had said the same thing to Bago′as. [4]So every one went out, and no one, either small or great, was left in the bedchamber.

Then Judith, standing beside his bed, said in
her heart, "O Lord God of all might, look in
this hour upon the work of my hands for the
exaltation of Jerusalem. 5For now is the time
to help your inheritance, and to carry out my
undertaking for the destruction of the enemies who have risen up against us."
6She went up to the post at the end of the
bed, above Hol″ofer′nes' head, and took
down his sword that hung there. 7She came
close to his bed and took hold of the hair of
his head, and said, "Give me strength this
day, O Lord God of Israel!" 8And she struck
his neck twice with all her might, and severed
his head from his body. 9Then she tumbled
his body off the bed and pulled down the
canopy from the posts; after a moment she
went out, and gave Hol″ofer′nes' head to her
maid, 10who placed it in her food bag.
Then the two of them went out together, as
they were accustomed to go for prayer; and
they passed through the camp and circled
around the valley and went up the mountain
to Beth″uli′a and came to its gates. 11Judith
called out from afar to the watchmen at the
gates, "Open, open the gate! God, our God,
is still with us, to show his power in Israel,
and his strength against our enemies, even
as he has done this day!"
12When the men of her city heard her
voice, they hurried down to the city gate and
called together the elders of the city. 13They
all ran together, both small and great, for it
was unbelievable that she had returned; they
opened the gate and admitted them, and
they kindled a fire for light, and gathered
around them. 14Then she said to them with a
loud voice, "Praise God, O praise him! Praise
God, who has not withdrawn his mercy
from the house of Israel, but has destroyed
our enemies by my hand this very night!"
15Then she took the head out of the bag
and showed it to them, and said, "See, here
is the head of Hol″ofer′nes, the commander
of the Assyrian army, and here is the canopy
beneath which he lay in his drunken stupor.
The Lord has struck him down by the hand
of a woman. 16As the Lord lives, who has
protected me in the way I went, it was my
face that tricked him to his destruction, and
yet he committed no act of sin with me, to
defile and shame me."
17All the people were greatly astonished,
and bowed down and worshiped God, and
said with one accord, "Blessed are you, our
God, who have brought into contempt this
day the enemies of your people."
18And Uzzi′ah said to her, "O daughter, you
are blessed by the Most High God above all
women on earth; and blessed be the Lord
God, who created the heavens and the earth,
who has guided you to strike the head of
the leader of our enemies. 19Your hope will
never depart from the hearts of men, as they
remember the power of God. 20May God
grant this to be a perpetual honor to you, and
may he visit you with blessings, because you
did not spare your own life when our nation
was brought low, but have avenged our ruin,
walking in the straight path before our God."
And all the people said, "So be it, so be it!"

14 Then Judith said to them, "Listen to
me, my brethren, and take this head
and hang it upon the parapet of your wall. 2And
as soon as morning comes and the sun rises,
let every valiant man take his weapons and go
out of the city, and set a captain over them, as
if you were going down to the plain against the
Assyrian outpost; only do not go down. 3Then
they will seize their arms and go into the camp
and rouse the officers of the Assyrian army;
and they will rush into the tent of Hol″ofer′nes,
and will not find him. Then fear will come over
them, and they will flee before you, 4and you
and all who live within the borders of Israel
shall pursue them and cut them down as they
flee. 5But before you do all this, bring A′chior
the Am′monite to me, and let him see and
recognize the man who despised the house of
Israel and sent him to us as if to his death."
6So they summoned A′chior from the house
of Uzzi′ah. And when he came and saw the
head of Hol″ofer′nes in the hand of one of the
men at the gathering of the people, he fell down
on his face and his spirit failed him. 7And when
they raised him up he fell at Judith's feet, and
knelt before her, and said, "Blessed are you in
every tent of Judah! In every nation those who
hear your name will be alarmed. 8Now tell me
what you have done during these days."

Then Judith described to him in the presence
of the people all that she had done, from the
day she left until the moment of her speaking to
them. 9And when she had finished, the people
raised a great shout and made a joyful noise
in their city. 10And when A′chior saw all that
the God of Israel had done, he believed firmly
in God, and was circumcised, and joined the
house of Israel, remaining so to this day.
11As soon as it was dawn they hung the head
of Hol″ofer′nes on the wall, and every man took
his weapons, and they went out in companies
to the passes in the mountains. 12And when
the Assyrians saw them they sent word to their
commanders, and they went to the generals
and the captains and to all their officers. 13So
they came to Hol″ofer′nes' tent and said to the
steward in charge of all his personal affairs,
"Wake up our lord, for the slaves have been so
bold as to come down against us to give battle
in order to be destroyed completely."
14So Bago′as went in and knocked at the
door of the tent, for he supposed that he
was sleeping with Judith. 15But when no one
answered, he opened it and went into the
bedchamber and found him thrown down
on the platform dead, with his head cut off
and missing. 16And he cried out with a loud
voice and wept and groaned and shouted,
and tore his garments. 17Then he went to the
tent where Judith had stayed, and when he
did not find her he rushed out to the people
and shouted, 18"The slaves have tricked us!
One Hebrew woman has brought disgrace
upon the house of King Nebuchadnez′zar!
For look, here is Hol″ofer′nes lying on the
ground, and his head is not on him!"
19When the leaders of the Assyrian army
heard this, they tore their tunics and were
greatly dismayed, and their loud cries and
shouts arose in the midst of the camp.

PROVERBS 25

15With patience a ruler may be persuaded,
and a soft tongue will break a bone.
16If you have found honey, eat only enough
for you,
lest you be sated with it and vomit it.
17Let your foot be seldom in your
neighbor's house,
lest he become weary of you and hate you.
18A man who bears false witness against
his neighbor
is like a war club, or a sword, or
a sharp arrow.
19Trust in a faithless man in time of trouble
is like a bad tooth or a foot that slips.
20He who sings songs to a heavy heart
is like one who takes off a garment on a
cold day,
and like vinegar on a wound.
21If your enemy is hungry, give him bread
to eat;
and if he is thirsty, give him water to drink;
22for you will heap coals of fire on his head,
and the LORD will reward you.
23The north wind brings forth rain;
and a backbiting tongue, angry looks.
24It is better to live in a corner of the housetop
than in a house shared with a
contentious woman.
25Like cold water to a thirsty soul,
so is good news from a far country.
26Like a muddied spring or a polluted
fountain
is a righteous man who gives way before
the wicked.
27It is not good to eat much honey,
so be sparing of complimentary words.
28A man without self-control
is like a city broken into and left
without walls.

ROMANS 7

13Did that which is good, then,
bring death to me? By no means!
It was sin, working death in me through
what is good, in order that sin might be
shown to be sin, and through the commandment might become sinful beyond measure.
14We know that the law is spiritual; but I am
carnal, sold under sin. 15I do not understand
my own actions. For I do not do what I want,
but I do the very thing I hate. 16Now if I do
what I do not want, I agree that the law is

good. [17]So then it is no longer I that do it, but
sin which dwells within me. [18]For I know that
nothing good dwells within me, that is, in my
flesh. I can will what is right, but I cannot do it.
[19]For I do not do the good I want, but the evil
I do not want is what I do. [20]Now if I do what I
do not want, it is no longer I that do it, but sin
which dwells within me.
[21]So I find it to be a law that when I want
to do right, evil lies close at hand. [22]For I
delight in the law of God, in my inmost
self, [23]but I see in my members another law
at war with the law of my mind and making
me captive to the law of sin which dwells
in my members. [24]Wretched man that I
am! Who will deliver me from this body of
death? [25]Thanks be to God through Jesus
Christ our Lord! So then, I of myself serve
the law of God with my mind, but with my
flesh I serve the law of sin.

8 There is therefore now no condemnation
for those who are in Christ Jesus. [2]For
the law of the Spirit of life in Christ Jesus has
set me free from the law of sin and death.
[3]For God has done what the law, weakened
by the flesh, could not do: sending his own
Son in the likeness of sinful flesh and for
sin, he condemned sin in the flesh, [4]in order
that the just requirement of the law might
be fulfilled in us, who walk not according
to the flesh but according to the Spirit. [5]For
those who live according to the flesh set
their minds on the things of the flesh, but
those who live according to the Spirit set
their minds on the things of the Spirit. [6]To
set the mind on the flesh is death, but to set
the mind on the Spirit is life and peace. [7]For
the mind that is set on the flesh is hostile to
God; it does not submit to God's law, indeed
it cannot; [8]and those who are in the flesh
cannot please God.
[9]But you are not in the flesh, you are
in the Spirit, if the Spirit of God really
dwells in you. Any one who does not
have the Spirit of Christ does not belong
to him. [10]But if Christ is in you, although
your bodies are dead because of sin, your
spirits are alive because of righteousness.
[11]If the Spirit of him who raised Jesus from
the dead dwells in you, he who raised
Christ Jesus from the dead will give life
to your mortal bodies also through his
Spirit who dwells in you.
[12]So then, brethren, we are debtors, not
to the flesh, to live according to the flesh
[13]for if you live according to the flesh you
will die, but if by the Spirit you put to
death the deeds of the body you will live.
[14]For all who are led by the Spirit of God
are sons of God. [15]For you did not receive
the spirit of slavery to fall back into
fear, but you have received the spirit of
sonship. When we cry, "Abba! Father!" [16]it
is the Spirit himself bearing witness with
our spirit that we are children of God,
[17]and if children, then heirs, heirs of God
and fellow heirs with Christ, provided we
suffer with him in order that we may also
be glorified with him.

REFLECTION

Judith's bravery saves her people. It would have been easy to cower in fear of the enemy's powerful army, to run away, or even to become a traitor, but Judith stays true to the Lord. When she gets a chance to be alone with Holofernes, she fearlessly takes his sword and cuts off his head. She could have been discovered at any moment and killed, but Judith risks her life to save her people. When she returns to the city, Judith is told, "You are blessed by the Most High God above all women on earth" (Jdt 13:18). Judith crushes the head of the enemy of Israel and so is called blessed among women, a prophetic title that will be given to Mary by Elizabeth at the Visitation (see Lk 1:42). The news of Judith's victory must have been "like cold water to a thirsty soul" (Prv 25:25). Jesus likewise won a victory, but over a much greater foe. He delivered us from the power of sin and death so that we might have life in his Spirit. We are thus able to "walk not according to the flesh but according to the Spirit" (Rom 8:4). By the power of the Holy Spirit we can live in victory over sin and temptation, just as Judith was victorious over Holofernes. Like Judith, Mary is called "blessed among women" (Lk 1:42). Why do you think Mary is given this title?

August 10

JUDITH 15

When the men in the tents heard it, they were amazed at what had happened. 2Fear and trembling came over them, so that they did not wait for one another, but with one impulse all rushed out and fled by every path across the plain and through the hill country. 3Those who had camped in the hills around Beth″uli′a also took to flight. Then the men of Israel, every one that was a soldier, rushed out upon them. 4And Uzz′iah sent men to Bet″o-mastha′im and Bebai and Choba and Ko′-la, and to all the frontiers of Israel, to tell what had taken place and to urge all to rush out upon their enemies to destroy them. 5And when the Israelites heard it, with one accord they fell upon the enemy, and cut them down as far as Cho′ba. Those in Jerusalem and all the hill country also came, for they were told what had happened in the camp of the enemy; and those in Gilead and in Galilee outflanked them with great slaughter, even beyond Damascus and its borders. 6The rest of the people of Beth″uli′a fell upon the Assyrian camp and plundered it, and were greatly enriched. 7And the Israelites, when they returned from the slaughter, took possession of what remained, and the villages and towns in the hill country and in the plain got a great amount of booty, for there was a vast quantity of it.

8Then Jo′akim the high priest, and the senate of the people of Israel who lived at Jerusalem, came to witness the good things which the Lord had done for Israel, and to see Judith and to greet her. 9And when they met her they all blessed her with one accord and said to her, "You are the exaltation of Jerusalem, you are the great glory of Israel, you are the great pride of our nation! 10You have done all this singlehanded; you have done great good to Israel, and God is well pleased with it. May the Almighty Lord bless you for ever!" And all the people said, "So be it!"

11So all the people plundered the camp for thirty days. They gave Judith the tent of Hol″ofer′nes and all his silver dishes and his beds and his bowls and all his furniture; and she took them and loaded her mule and hitched up her carts and piled the things on them.

12Then all the women of Israel gathered to see her, and blessed her, and some of them performed a dance for her; and she took branches in her hands and gave them to the women who were with her; 13and they crowned themselves with olive wreaths, she and those who were with her; and she went before all the people in the dance, leading all the women, while all the men of Israel followed, bearing their arms and wearing garlands and with songs on their lips.

16 Then Judith began this thanksgiving before all Israel, and all the people loudly sang this song of praise. 2And Judith said,

Begin a song to my God with tambourines,
sing to my Lord with cymbals.
Raise to him a new psalm;
exalt him, and call upon his name.
3For God is the Lord who crushes wars;
for he has delivered me out of the hands
of my pursuers,
and brought me to his camp, in the
midst of the people.

4The Assyrian came down from the
mountains of the north;
he came with myriads of his warriors;
their multitude blocked up the valleys,
their cavalry covered the hills.
5He boasted that he would burn up
my territory,
and kill my young men with the sword,
and dash my infants to the ground
and seize my children as prey,
and take my virgins as booty.

6But the Lord Almighty has foiled them
by the hand of a woman.

7For their mighty one did not fall by the
hands of the young men,
nor did the sons of the Titans strike him,
nor did tall giants set upon him;
but Judith the daughter of Merar′i
undid him
with the beauty of her countenance.

8For she took off her widow's mourning
to exalt the oppressed in Israel.
She anointed her face with ointment
and fastened her hair with a tiara
and put on a linen gown to deceive him.
9Her sandal ravished his eyes,
her beauty captivated his mind,
and the sword severed his neck.
10The Persians trembled at her boldness,
the Medes were daunted at her daring.

11Then my oppressed people shouted for joy;
my weak people shouted and the
enemy trembled;
they lifted up their voices, and the
enemy were turned back.
12The sons of maidservants have pierced
them through;
they were wounded like the children
of fugitives,
they perished before the army of my Lord.

13I will sing to my God a new song:
O Lord, you are great and glorious,
wonderful in strength, invincible.
14Let all your creatures serve you,
for you spoke, and they were made.
You sent forth your Spirit, and it
formed them;
there is none that can resist your voice.
15For the mountains shall be shaken to their
foundations with the waters;
at your presence the rocks shall melt
like wax,
but to those who fear you
you will continue to show mercy.
16For every sacrifice as a fragrant offering is
a small thing,
and all fat for burnt offerings to you is a
very little thing,
but he who fears the Lord shall be great
for ever.

17Woe to the nations that rise up against
my people!
The Lord Almighty will take vengeance
on them in the day of judgment;
fire and worms he will give to their flesh;
they shall weep in pain for ever.

18When they arrived at Jerusalem they
worshiped God. As soon as the people were
purified, they offered their burnt offerings,
their freewill offerings, and their gifts.
19Judith also dedicated to God all the vessels
of Hol″ofer′nes, which the people had given
her; and the canopy which she took for
herself from his bedchamber she gave as a
votive offering to the Lord. 20So the people
continued feasting in Jerusalem before the
sanctuary for three months, and Judith
remained with them.

21After this every one returned home to
his own inheritance, and Judith went to
Beth″uli′a, and remained on her estate, and
was honored in her time throughout the
whole country. 22Many desired to marry her,
but she remained a widow all the days of her
life after Manas′seh her husband died and
was gathered to his people. 23She became
more and more famous, and grew old in her
husband's house, until she was one hundred
and five years old. She set her maid free. She
died in Beth″uli′a, and they buried her in
the cave of her husband Manas′seh, 24and
the house of Israel mourned for her seven
days. Before she died she distributed her
property to all those who were next of kin
to her husband Manas′seh, and to her own
nearest kindred. 25And no one ever again
spread terror among the people of Israel in
the days of Judith, or for a long time after
her death.

PROVERBS 26

Like snow in summer or rain in harvest,
so honor is not fitting for a fool.
2Like a sparrow in its flitting, like a swallow
in its flying,
a curse that is causeless does not alight.
3A whip for the horse, a bridle for the donkey,
and a rod for the back of fools.

4 Answer not a fool according to his folly,
lest you be like him yourself.
5 Answer a fool according to his folly,
lest he be wise in his own eyes.
6 He who sends a message by the hand of
a fool
cuts off his own feet and drinks violence.
7 Like a lame man's legs, which hang useless,
is a proverb in the mouth of fools.
8 Like one who binds the stone in the sling
is he who gives honor to a fool.
9 Like a thorn that goes up into the hand of
a drunkard
is a proverb in the mouth of fools.
10 Like an archer who wounds everybody
is he who hires a passing fool or drunkard.
11 Like a dog that returns to his vomit
is a fool who repeats his folly.
12 Do you see a man who is wise in his
own eyes?
There is more hope for a fool than for him.
13 The sluggard says, "There is a lion
in the road!
There is a lion in the streets!"
14 As a door turns on its hinges,
so does a sluggard on his bed.
15 The sluggard buries his hand in the dish;
it wears him out to bring it back
to his mouth.
16 The sluggard is wiser in his own eyes
than seven men who can
answer discreetly.

ROMANS 8

18 I consider that the sufferings of
this present time are not worth
comparing with the glory that is to be
revealed to us. 19 For the creation waits
with eager longing for the revealing of the
sons of God; 20 for the creation was subjected
to futility, not of its own will but by the will
of him who subjected it in hope; 21 because
the creation itself will be set free from its
bondage to decay and obtain the glorious
liberty of the children of God. 22 We know
that the whole creation has been groaning
with labor pains together until now; 23 and
not only the creation, but we ourselves,
who have the first fruits of the Spirit, groan
inwardly as we wait for adoption as sons, the
redemption of our bodies. 24 For in this hope
we were saved. Now hope that is seen is not
hope. For who hopes for what he sees? 25 But
if we hope for what we do not see, we wait
for it with patience.

26 Likewise the Spirit helps us in our
weakness; for we do not know how to pray
as we ought, but the Spirit himself intercedes
for us with sighs too deep for words. 27 And
he who searches the hearts of men knows
what is the mind of the Spirit, because the
Spirit intercedes for the saints according to
the will of God.

28 We know that in everything God works
for good with those who love him, who are
called according to his purpose. 29 For those
whom he foreknew he also predestined to be
conformed to the image of his Son, in order
that he might be the first-born among many
brethren. 30 And those whom he predestined
he also called; and those whom he called he
also justified; and those whom he justified
he also glorified.

31 What then shall we say to this? If God is
for us, who is against us? 32 He who did not
spare his own Son but gave him up for us all,
will he not also give us all things with him?
33 Who shall bring any charge against God's
elect? It is God who justifies; 34 who is to
condemn? Is it Christ Jesus, who died, yes,
who was raised from the dead, who is at the
right hand of God, who indeed intercedes
for us? 35 Who shall separate us from the
love of Christ? Shall tribulation, or distress,
or persecution, or famine, or nakedness, or
peril, or sword? 36 As it is written,

"For your sake we are being killed all the
day long;
we are regarded as sheep to be slaughtered."

37 No, in all these things we are more than
conquerors through him who loved us.
38 For I am sure that neither death, nor life,
nor angels, nor principalities, nor things
present, nor things to come, nor powers,
39 nor height, nor depth, nor anything else in
all creation, will be able to separate us from
the love of God in Christ Jesus our Lord.

REFLECTION

Our fear betrays our lack of trust in God. Ironically, all the soldiers of Bethulia cringed in hiding while a woman sallied forth alone against the enemy. Judith's confidence in God triumphs over the enemy: "Her beauty captivated his mind, and the sword severed his neck" (Jdt 16:9). She shows why we undermine the power of our own faith in a God who is "wonderful in strength, invincible" when we hide in fear (v. 13). While Judith's victory culminates in wealth and feasting, our victory in Christ leads to the eternal banqueting hall of Heaven. St. Paul speaks of our destiny when he says, "I consider that the sufferings of this present time are not worth comparing with the glory that is to be revealed to us" (Rom 8:18). He argued earlier that we should rejoice in our sufferings and view ourselves as co-crucified with Christ. Now he fills out the picture. No matter how great our suffering on earth, our glorious destiny in Heaven far outweighs it. While it seems like the terrors of the world—distress, persecution, famine, sword—will cut us off from God, in fact, "we are more than conquerors" (v. 37), and nothing "will be able to separate us from the love of God" (v. 39). In the midst of trials do you find consolation in the future hope of glory to come?

August 11

ESTHER 11

2In the second year of the reign of
Artaxerxes the Great, on the first
day of Nisan, Mordecai the son of Jair,
son of Shimei, son of Kish, of the tribe of
Benjamin, had a dream. 3He was a Jew,
dwelling in the city of Susa, a great man, serv-
ing in the court of the king. 4He was one of the
captives whom Nebuchadnezzar king of Baby-
lon had brought from Jerusalem with Jeconiah
king of Judea. And this was his dream:
5Behold, noise and confusion, thunders and
earthquake, tumult upon the earth! 6And
behold, two great dragons came forward,
both ready to fight, and they roared terribly.
7And at their roaring every nation prepared
for war, to fight against the nation of the
righteous. 8And behold, a day of darkness and
gloom, tribulation and distress, affliction and
great tumult upon the earth! 9And the whole
righteous nation was troubled; they feared
the evils that threatened them, and were
ready to perish. 10Then they cried to God; and
from their cry, as though from a tiny spring,
there came a great river, with abundant
water; 11light came, and the sun rose, and the
lowly were exalted and consumed those held
in honor.
12Mordecai saw in this dream what God
had determined to do, and after he awoke
he had it on his mind and sought all day to
understand it in every detail.

12 *Now Mordecai took his rest in the*
courtyard with Gabatha and Tharra,
the two eunuchs of the king who kept
watch in the courtyard. 2He overheard
their conversation and inquired into their
purposes, and learned that they were
preparing to lay hands upon Artaxerxes the
king; and he informed the king concerning
them. 3Then the king examined the two
eunuchs, and when they confessed they were
led to execution. 4The king made a permanent
record of these things, and Mordecai wrote
an account of them. 5And the king ordered
Mordecai to serve in the court and rewarded
him for these things. 6But Haman, the son
of Hammedatha, a Bougaean, was in great
honor with the king, and he sought to injure
Mordecai and his people because of the two
eunuchs of the king.

1 In the days of Ahas′u-e′rus, the Ahasuerus who reigned from India to
Ethiopia over one hundred and twenty-
seven provinces, 2in those days when King
Ahas′u-e′rus sat on his royal throne in Susa
the capital, 3in the third year of his reign
he gave a banquet for all his princes and

* The disarrangement of the chapter and verse order is due to the insertion of the deuterocanonical portions in their logical place in the story of Esther, as narrated in the Greek version from which they are taken. They are printed in italics to enable the reader to recognize them at once.

servants, the army chiefs of Persia and Med′ia and the nobles and governors of the provinces being before him, 4while he showed the riches of his royal glory and the splendor and pomp of his majesty for many days, a hundred and eighty days. 5And when these days were completed, the king gave for all the people present in Susa the capital, both great and small, a banquet lasting for seven days, in the court of the garden of the king's palace. 6There were white cotton curtains and blue hangings caught up with cords of fine linen and purple to silver rings and marble pillars, and also couches of gold and silver on a mosaic pavement of porphyry, marble, mother-of-pearl and precious stones. 7Drinks were served in golden goblets, goblets of different kinds, and the royal wine was lavished according to the bounty of the king. 8And drinking was according to the law, no one was compelled; for the king had given orders to all the officials of his palace to do as every man desired. 9Queen Vashti also gave a banquet for the women in the palace which belonged to King Ahas′u-e′rus.

10On the seventh day, when the heart of the king was merry with wine, he commanded Mehu′man, Biztha, Harbo′na, Bigtha and Abagtha, Ze′thar and Car′kas, the seven eunuchs who served King Ahas′u-e′rus as chamberlains, 11to bring Queen Vashti before the king with her royal crown, in order to show the peoples and the princes her beauty; for she was fair to behold. 12But Queen Vashti refused to come at the king's command conveyed by the eunuchs. At this the king was enraged, and his anger burned within him.

13Then the king said to the wise men who knew the times—for this was the king's procedure toward all who were versed in law and judgment, 14the men next to him being Carshe′na, She′thar, Adma′tha, Tar′shish, Me′res, Marse′na, and Memu′can, the seven princes of Persia and Med′ia, who saw the king's face, and sat first in the kingdom—: 15"According to the law, what is to be done to Queen Vashti, because she has not performed the command of King Ahas′u-e′rus conveyed by the eunuchs?" 16Then Memu′can said in presence of the king and the princes, "Not only to the king has Queen Vashti done wrong, but also to all the princes and all the peoples who are in all the provinces of King Ahas′u-e′rus. 17For this deed of the queen will be made known to all women, causing them to look with contempt upon their husbands, since they will say, 'King Ahas′u-e′rus commanded Queen Vashti to be brought before him, and she did not come.' 18This very day the ladies of Persia and Med′ia who have heard of the queen's behavior will be telling it to all the king's princes, and there will be contempt and wrath in plenty. 19If it please the king, let a royal order go forth from him, and let it be written among the laws of the Persians and the Medes so that it may not be altered, that Vashti is to come no more before King Ahas′u-e′rus; and let the king give her royal position to another who is better than she. 20So when the decree made by the king is proclaimed throughout all his kingdom, vast as it is, all women will give honor to their husbands, high and low." 21This advice pleased the king and the princes, and the king did as Memu′can proposed; 22he sent letters to all the royal provinces, to every province in its own script and to every people in its own language, that every man be lord in his own house and speak according to the language of his people.

2 After these things, when the anger of King Ahas′u-e′rus had abated, he remembered Vashti and what she had done and what had been decreed against her. 2Then the king's servants who attended him said, "Let beautiful young virgins be sought out for the king. 3And let the king appoint officers in all the provinces of his kingdom to gather all the beautiful young virgins to the harem in Susa the capital, under custody of Hegai the king's eunuch who is in charge of the women; let their ointments be given them. 4And let the maiden who pleases the king be queen instead of Vashti." This pleased the king, and he did so.

[5]Now there was a Jew in Susa the capital
whose name was Mor′decai, the son
of Ja′ir, son of Shim′e-i, son of Kish, a
Benjaminite, [6]who had been carried away
from Jerusalem among the captives carried
away with Jeconi′ah king of Judah, whom
Nebuchadnez′zar king of Babylon had
carried away. [7]He had brought up Hadas′sah,
that is Esther, the daughter of his uncle,
for she had neither father nor mother; the
maiden was beautiful and lovely, and when
her father and her mother died, Mor′decai
adopted her as his own daughter. [8]So when the
king's order and his edict were proclaimed,
and when many maidens were gathered in
Susa the capital in custody of Hegai, Esther
also was taken into the king's palace and put
in custody of Hegai who had charge of the
women. [9]And the maiden pleased him and
won his favor; and he quickly provided her
with her ointments and her portion of food,
and with seven chosen maids from the king's
palace, and advanced her and her maids to
the best place in the harem. [10]Esther had
not made known her people or kindred, for
Mor′decai had charged her not to make it
known. [11]And every day Mor′decai walked
in front of the court of the harem, to learn
how Esther was and how she fared.

[12]Now when the turn came for each
maiden to go in to King Ahas′u-e′rus, after
being twelve months under the regulations
for the women, since this was the regular
period of their beautifying, six months with
oil of myrrh and six months with spices and
ointments for women—[13]when the maiden
went in to the king in this way she was
given whatever she desired to take with her
from the harem to the king's palace. [14]In the
evening she went, and in the morning she
came back to the second harem in custody
of Shaash′gaz the king's eunuch who was in
charge of the concubines; she did not go in
to the king again, unless the king delighted
in her and she was summoned by name.

[15]When the turn came for Esther the
daughter of Ab′ihail the uncle of Mor′decai,
who had adopted her as his own daughter,
to go in to the king, she asked for nothing
except what Hegai the king's eunuch, who
had charge of the women, advised. Now
Esther found favor in the eyes of all who saw
her. [16]And when Esther was taken to King
Ahas′u-e′rus into his royal palace in the
tenth month, which is the month of Te′beth,
in the seventh year of his reign, [17]the king
loved Esther more than all the women, and
she found grace and favor in his sight more
than all the virgins, so that he set the royal
crown on her head and made her queen
instead of Vashti. [18]Then the king gave a
great banquet to all his princes and servants;
it was Esther's banquet. He also granted
a remission of taxes to the provinces, and
gave gifts with royal liberality.

PROVERBS 26

[17]He who meddles in a quarrel not his own
is like one who takes a passing dog
by the ears.
[18]Like a madman who throws firebrands,
arrows, and death,
[19]is the man who deceives his neighbor
and says, "I am only joking!"
[20]For lack of wood the fire goes out;
and where there is no whisperer,
quarreling ceases.
[21]As charcoal to hot embers and wood to fire,
so is a quarrelsome man for kindling strife.
[22]The words of a whisperer are like
delicious morsels;
they go down into the inner parts
of the body.
[23]Like the glaze covering an earthen vessel
are smooth lips with an evil heart.
[24]He who hates, dissembles with his lips
and harbors deceit in his heart;
[25]when he speaks graciously, believe him not,
for there are seven abominations
in his heart;
[26]though his hatred be covered with guile,
his wickedness will be exposed
in the assembly.
[27]He who digs a pit will fall into it,
and a stone will come back upon him
who starts it rolling.
[28]A lying tongue hates its victims,
and a flattering mouth works ruin.

ROMANS 9

**I am speaking the truth in
Christ, I am not lying; my conscience bears me witness in
the Holy Spirit, 2that I have great
sorrow and unceasing anguish in my
heart. 3For I could wish that I myself**
were accursed and cut off from Christ for
the sake of my brethren, my kinsmen according to the flesh. 4They are Israelites,
and to them belong the sonship, the glory, the covenants, the giving of the law,
the worship, and the promises; 5to them
belong the patriarchs, and of their race,
according to the flesh, is the Christ, who
is God over all, blessed for ever. Amen.

6But it is not as though the word of God
had failed. For not all who are descended
from Israel belong to Israel, 7and not all are
children of Abraham because they are his
descendants; but "Through Isaac shall your
descendants be named." 8This means that it
is not the children of the flesh who are the
children of God, but the children of the
promise are reckoned as descendants. 9For
this is what the promise said, "About this
time I will return and Sarah shall have a son."
10And not only so, but also when Rebecca
had conceived children by one man, our
forefather Isaac, 11though they were not yet
born and had done nothing either good or
bad, in order that God's purpose of election
might continue, not because of works but
because of his call, 12she was told, "The elder
will serve the younger." 13As it is written,
"Jacob I loved, but Esau I hated."

14What shall we say then? Is there injustice
on God's part? By no means! 15For he says to
Moses, "I will have mercy on whom I have
mercy, and I will have compassion on whom
I have compassion." 16So it depends not upon
man's will or exertion, but upon God's mercy.
17For the Scripture says to Pharaoh, "I have
raised you up for the very purpose of showing
my power in you, so that my name may be
proclaimed in all the earth." 18So then he
has mercy upon whomever he wills, and he
hardens the heart of whomever he wills.

19You will say to me then, "Why does he still
find fault? For who can resist his will?" 20But
who are you, a man, to answer back to God?
Will what is molded say to its molder, "Why
have you made me thus?" 21Has the potter no
right over the clay, to make out of the same
lump one vessel for beauty and another for
menial use? 22What if God, desiring to show
his wrath and to make known his power, has
endured with much patience the vessels of
wrath made for destruction, 23in order to
make known the riches of his glory for the
vessels of mercy, which he has prepared
beforehand for glory, 24even us whom he has
called, not from the Jews only but also from
the Gentiles?
25As indeed he says in Hose′a,
"Those who were not my people
I will call 'my people,'
and her who was not beloved
I will call 'my beloved.'"
26"And in the very place where it was said to
them, 'You are not my people,'
they will be called 'sons of the living God.'"
27And Isaiah cries out concerning Israel:
"Though the number of the sons of Israel
be as the sand of the sea, only a remnant of
them will be saved; 28for the Lord will execute
his sentence upon the earth with rigor and
dispatch." 29And as Isaiah predicted,
"If the Lord of hosts had not left us children,
we would have fared like Sodom and been
made like Gomor′rah."

REFLECTION

Today's readings continue to call us to strive for holiness, all the while trusting in God's grace for our success. On the one hand, Proverbs and the example of Esther encourage us to work hard to attain what is good. Proverbs condemns the fool, the sluggard, the meddlesome, and the quarrelsome. Esther shows herself wise as she wins the favor of Hegai, and then, in turn, wins the exuberant favor of the king, Ahasuerus, himself: "The king loved Esther more than all the women, and she found grace and favor in his sight more than all the virgins, so that he set the royal crown on her head and made her queen instead of Vashti" (Est 2:17). Esther's grace in dealing with others wins her great favor and sets her up to be in a position of great influence. On the other hand, St. Paul teaches us about God's "purpose of election" (Rom 9:11), which is the driving force behind salvation history: "So it depends not upon man's will or exertion, but upon God's mercy" (v. 16). It is God's gracious mercy and love that brings about our salvation, but our loving God calls us as his sons and daughters to love him with all our strength. How can you personally work hard for good and also depend on God's purpose?

August 12

ESTHER 2

19 When the virgins were gathered together the second time, Mor´decai was sitting at the king's gate. 20 Now Esther had not made known her kindred or her people, as Mor´decai had charged her; for Esther obeyed Mordecai just as when she was brought up by him. 21 And in those days, as Mor´decai was sitting at the king's gate, Bigthan and Te´resh, two of the king's eunuchs, who guarded the threshold, became angry and sought to lay hands on King Ahas´u-e´rus. 22 And this came to the knowledge of Mor´decai, and he told it to Queen Esther, and Esther told the king in the name of Mordecai. 23 When the affair was investigated and found to be so, the men were both hanged on the gallows. And it was recorded in the Book of the Chronicles in the presence of the king.

3 After these things King Ahas´u-e´rus promoted Ha´man the Ag´agite, the son of Hammeda´tha, and advanced him and set his seat above all the princes who were with him. 2 And all the king's servants who were at the king's gate bowed down and did obeisance to Ha´man; for the king had so commanded concerning him. But Mor´decai did not bow down or do obeisance. 3 Then the king's servants who were at the king's gate said to Mor´decai, "Why do you transgress the king's command?" 4 And when they spoke to him day after day and he would not listen to them, they told Ha´man, in order to see whether Mor´decai's words would avail; for he had told them that he was a Jew. 5 And when Ha´man saw that Mor´decai did not bow down or do obeisance to him, Ha´man was filled with fury. 6 But he disdained to lay hands on Mor´decai alone. So, as they had made known to him the people of Mordecai, Ha´man sought to destroy all the Jews, the people of Mordecai, throughout the whole kingdom of Ahas´u-e´rus.

7 In the first month, which is the month of Ni´san, in the twelfth year of King Ahas´u-e´rus, they cast Pur, that is the lot, before Ha´man day after day; and they cast it month after month till the twelfth month, which is the month of Adar´. 8 Then Ha´man said to King Ahas´u-e´rus, "There is a certain people scattered abroad and dispersed among the peoples in all the provinces of your kingdom; their laws are different from those of every other people, and they do not keep the king's laws, so that it is not for the king's profit to tolerate them. 9 If it please the king, let it be decreed that they be destroyed, and I will pay ten thousand talents of silver into the hands of those who have charge of the king's business, that they may put it into the king's treasuries." 10 So the king took his signet ring from his hand and gave it to Ha´man the Ag´agite, the son of Hammeda´tha, the enemy of the Jews. 11 And the king said to Ha´man, "The money is given to you, the people also, to do with them as it seems good to you."

12 Then the king's secretaries were summoned on the thirteenth day of the first month, and an edict, according to all that Ha´man commanded, was written to the king's satraps and to the governors over all the provinces and to the princes of all the peoples, to every province in its own script and every people in its own language; it was

written in the name of King Ahas′u-e′rus
and sealed with the king's ring. 13Letters were
sent by couriers to all the king's provinces,
to destroy, to slay, and to annihilate all Jews,
young and old, women and children, in one
day, the thirteenth day of the twelfth month,
which is the month of Adar′, and to plunder
their goods.

13 *This is a copy of the letter: "The Great*
King, Artaxerxes, to the rulers of the
hundred and twenty-seven provinces from
India to Ethiopia and to the governors under
them, writes thus:
2*"Having become ruler of many nations*
and master of the whole world, not elated
with presumption of authority but always
acting reasonably and with kindness, I have
determined to settle the lives of my subjects
in lasting tranquillity and, in order to make
my kingdom peaceable and open to travel
throughout all its extent, to re-establish the
peace which all men desire.
3*"When I asked my counselors how this might*
be accomplished, Haman, who excels among
us in sound judgment, and is distinguished for
his unchanging good will and steadfast fidelity,
and has attained the second place in the
kingdom, 4*pointed out to us that among all the*
nations in the world there is scattered a certain
hostile people, who have laws contrary to those
of every nation and continually disregard the
ordinances of the kings, so that the unifying
of the kingdom which we honorably intend
cannot be brought about. 5*We understand that*
this people, and it alone, stands constantly in
opposition to all men, perversely following
a strange manner of life and laws, and is ill-
disposed to our government, doing all the
harm they can so that our kingdom may not
attain stability.
6*"Therefore we have decreed that those*
indicated to you in the letters of Haman,
who is in charge of affairs and is our
second father, shall all, with their wives and
children, be utterly destroyed by the sword
of their enemies, without pity or mercy, on
the fourteenth day of the twelfth month,
Adar, of this present year, 7*so that those who*
have long been and are now hostile may in
one day go down in violence to Hades, and
leave our government completely secure and
untroubled hereafter."
14A copy of the document was to be issued as
a decree in every province by proclamation
to all the peoples to be ready for that day.
15The couriers went in haste by order of the
king, and the decree was issued in Susa the
capital. And the king and Ha′man sat down
to drink; but the city of Susa was perplexed.

4 When Mor′decai learned all that had
been done, Mordecai tore his clothes
and put on sackcloth and ashes, and went
out into the midst of the city, wailing with
a loud and bitter cry; 2he went up to the
entrance of the king's gate, for no one might
enter the king's gate clothed with sackcloth.
3And in every province, wherever the king's
command and his decree came, there was
great mourning among the Jews, with
fasting and weeping and lamenting, and
most of them lay in sackcloth and ashes.
4When Esther's maids and her eunuchs
came and told her, the queen was deeply
distressed; she sent garments to clothe
Mor′decai, so that he might take off his
sackcloth, but he would not accept them.
5Then Esther called for Ha′thach, one of the
king's eunuchs, who had been appointed
to attend her, and ordered him to go to
Mor′decai to learn what this was and why
it was. 6Ha′thach went out to Mor′decai in
the open square of the city in front of the
king's gate, 7and Mor′decai told him all
that had happened to him, and the exact
sum of money that Ha′man had promised
to pay into the king's treasuries for the
destruction of the Jews. 8Mor′decai also
gave him a copy of the written decree
issued in Susa for their destruction, that
he might show it to Esther and explain it
to her and charge her to go to the king to
make supplication to him and entreat him
for her people, *"Remembering the days of*
your lowliness, when you were cared for by
me, because Haman, who is next to the king,
spoke against us for our destruction. Beseech
the Lord and speak to the king concerning us
and deliver us from death." 9And Ha′thach
went and told Esther what Mor′decai had
said. 10Then Esther spoke to Ha′thach and

gave him a message for Mor′decai, saying,
11“All the king's servants and the people of
the king's provinces know that if any man
or woman goes to the king inside the inner
court without being called, there is but one
law; all alike are to be put to death, except
the one to whom the king holds out the
golden scepter that he may live. And I have
not been called to come in to the king these
thirty days.” 12And they told Mor′decai what
Esther had said. 13Then Mor′decai told them
to return answer to Esther, “Think not that
in the king's palace you will escape any
more than all the other Jews. 14For if you
keep silence at such a time as this, relief
and deliverance will rise for the Jews from
another quarter, but you and your father's
house will perish. And who knows whether
you have not come to the kingdom for such
a time as this?” 15Then Esther told them to
reply to Mor′decai, 16“Go, gather all the Jews
to be found in Susa, and hold a fast on my
behalf, and neither eat nor drink for three
days, night or day. I and my maids will also
fast as you do. Then I will go to the king,
though it is against the law; and if I perish, I
perish.” 17Mor′decai then went away and did
everything as Esther had ordered him.

[13] 8*Then Mordecai prayed to the Lord,
and said: “O God of Abraham, God of Isaac,
God of Jacob, blessed are you:*

9*“O Lord, Lord, King who rule over all
things, for the universe is in your power and
there is no one who can oppose you if it is
your will to save Israel.* 10*For you have made
heaven and earth and every wonderful thing
under heaven,* 11*and you are Lord of all, and
there is no one who can resist you.* 12*You
know all things;* 13*you know, O Lord, that I
would have been willing to kiss the soles of
Haman's feet to save Israel!* 14*But I did not
do this, lest I set the glory of man above the
glory of God; I will not bow down to any
one but you, O Lord, my God.* 15*And now,
O Lord God and King, God of Abraham,
God of Isaac, and God of Jacob, spare your
people; for the eyes of our foes are upon us
to annihilate us, and they desire to destroy
your inheritance.* 16*Do not neglect your
portion, which you redeemed for yourself
out of the land of Egypt.* 17*Hear my prayer,
and have mercy upon your inheritance; turn
our mourning into feasting, that we may live
and sing praise to your name, O Lord; do
not destroy the mouth of those who praise
you.”*

18*And all Israel cried out mightily, for their
death was before their eyes.*

PROVERBS 27

Do not boast about tomorrow,
  for you do not know what a day may
    bring forth.
2Let another praise you, and not your
    own mouth;
  a stranger, and not your own lips.
3A stone is heavy, and sand is weighty,
  but a fool's provocation is heavier
    than both.
4Wrath is cruel, anger is overwhelming;
  but who can stand before jealousy?
5Better is open rebuke
  than hidden love.
6Faithful are the wounds of a friend;
  profuse are the kisses of an enemy.
7He who is sated loathes honey,
  but to one who is hungry everything
    bitter is sweet.
8Like a bird that strays from its nest,
  is a man who strays from his home.
9Oil and perfume make the heart glad,
  but the soul is torn by trouble.
10Your friend, and your father's friend, do
    not forsake;
  and do not go to your brother's house in
    the day of your calamity.
Better is a neighbor who is near
  than a brother who is far away.
11Be wise, my son, and make my heart glad,
  that I may answer him who
    reproaches me.
12A prudent man sees danger and
    hides himself;
  but the simple go on, and suffer for it.
13Take a man's garment when he has given
    surety for a stranger,
  and hold him in pledge when he gives
    surety for foreigners.

ROMANS 9

**[30]What shall we say, then? That
Gentiles who did not pursue
righteousness have attained it,
that is, righteousness through faith; [31]but
that Israel who pursued the righteousness which is based on law did not suc-**
ceed in fulfilling that law. [32]Why? Because
they did not pursue it through faith, but as if
it were based on works. They have stumbled
over the stumbling stone, [33]as it is written,

"Behold, I am laying in Zion a stone that
will make men stumble,
a rock that will make them fall;
and he who believes in him will not be put
to shame."

10 Brethren, my heart's desire and prayer
to God for them is that they may be
saved. [2]I bear them witness that they have
a zeal for God, but it is not enlightened.
[3]For, being ignorant of the righteousness
that comes from God, and seeking to
establish their own, they did not submit to
God's righteousness. [4]For Christ is the end
of the law, that every one who has faith
may be justified.
[5]Moses writes that the man who practices
the righteousness which is based on the law
shall live by it. [6]But the righteousness based
on faith says, Do not say in your heart, "Who
will ascend into heaven?" (that is, to bring
Christ down) [7]or "Who will descend into
the abyss?" (that is, to bring Christ up from
the dead). [8]But what does it say? The word
is near you, on your lips and in your heart
(that is, the word of faith which we preach);
[9]because, if you confess with your lips that
Jesus is Lord and believe in your heart that
God raised him from the dead, you will
be saved. [10]For man believes with his heart
and so is justified, and he confesses with his
lips and so is saved. [11]The Scripture says,
"No one who believes in him will be put to
shame." [12]For there is no distinction between
Jew and Greek; the same Lord is Lord of all
and bestows his riches upon all who call
upon him. [13]For, "every one who calls upon
the name of the Lord will be saved."
[14]But how are men to call upon him in
whom they have not believed? And how are
they to believe in him of whom they have
never heard? And how are they to hear
without a preacher? [15]And how can men
preach unless they are sent? As it is written,
"How beautiful are the feet of those who
preach good news!" [16]But they have not all
heeded the gospel; for Isaiah says, "Lord,
who has believed what he has heard from
us?" [17]So faith comes from what is heard,
and what is heard comes by the preaching
of Christ.
[18]But I ask, have they not heard? Indeed
they have; for

"Their voice has gone out to all the earth,
and their words to the ends of the world."

[19]Again I ask, did Israel not understand?
First Moses says,

"I will make you jealous of those who are
not a nation;
with a foolish nation I will make you angry."

[20]Then Isaiah is so bold as to say,

"I have been found by those who did not
seek me;
I have shown myself to those who did not
ask for me."

[21]But of Israel he says, "All day long I have
held out my hands to a disobedient and
contrary people."

REFLECTION

Mordecai takes a stand against the pagan culture of his day: He "did not bow down or do obeisance" to the Persian official, Haman (Est 3:2). When the king's servants press him to comply, he refuses, "for he had told them that he was a Jew" (v. 4). His bold act of fidelity to the Lord, by which he refuses to worship a man as if he were a god, draws Haman's ire. Haman sets his heart on genocide, the central plot of the Book of Esther. While Mordecai's action may seem overly bold and risky, he sets a pattern for our own courageous profession of faith. St. Paul teaches, "If you confess with your lips that Jesus is Lord and believe in your heart that God raised him from the dead, you will be saved" (Rom 10:9). We too might be called upon to take courageous steps in our witness for Jesus Christ and the Gospel. Though we might feel secure today, "Do not boast about tomorrow, for you do not know what a day may bring forth" (Prv 27:1). Mordecai risked his life to honor the Lord. We too should be willing to joyfully suffer ridicule or exclusion for our faith. In what ways are you tempted to "do obeisance" to the world?

August 13

ESTHER 14

And Esther the queen, seized with deathly anxiety, fled to the Lord; 2she took off her splendid apparel and put on the garments of distress and *mourning, and instead of costly perfumes she covered her head with ashes and dung, and she utterly humbled her body, and every part that she loved to adorn she covered with her tangled hair. 3And she lay on the earth together with all her maidservants, from morning until evening, and said: "God of Abraham, God of Isaac, and God of Jacob, blessed are you; help me, who am alone and have no helper but you, 4for my danger is in my hand. 5Ever since I was born I have heard in the tribe of my family that you, O Lord, took Israel out of all the nations, and our fathers from among all their ancestors, for an everlasting inheritance, and that you did for them all that you promised. 6And now we have sinned before you, and you have given us into the hands of our enemies, 7because we glorified their gods. You are righteous, O Lord! 8And now they are not satisfied that we are in bitter slavery, but they have covenanted with their idols 9to abolish what your mouth has ordained and to destroy your inheritance, to stop the mouths of those who praise you and to quench your altar and the glory of your house, 10to open the mouths of the nations for the praise of vain idols, and to magnify for ever a mortal king. 11O Lord, do not surrender your scepter to what has no being; and do not let them mock at our downfall; but turn their plan against themselves, and make an example of the man who began this against us. I have heard from the books of my ancestors that you liberate all those who are pleasing to you, O Lord, until the very end. And now, assist me, who am all alone, and have no one but you, O Lord, my God. Come to my aid, for I am an orphan. 12Remember, O Lord; make yourself known in this time of our affliction, and give me courage, O King of the gods and Master of all dominion! 13Put eloquent speech in my mouth before the lion, and turn his heart to hate the man who is fighting against us, so that there may be an end of him and those who agree with him. 14But save us from the hand of our enemies; turn our mourning into gladness and our affliction into well-being. 15You have knowledge of all things; and you know that I hate the splendor of the wicked and abhor the bed of the uncircumcised and of any alien. 16You know my necessity—that I abhor the sign of my proud position, which is upon my head on the days when I appear in public. I abhor it like a menstruous rag, and I do not wear it on the days when I am at leisure. 17And your servant has not eaten at Haman's table, and I have not honored the king's feast or drunk the wine of the libations. 18Your servant has had no joy since the day that I was brought here until now, except in you, O Lord God of Abraham. 19O God, whose might is over all, hear the voice of the despairing, and save us from the hands of evildoers. And save me from my fear!"*

15 *On the third day, when she ended her prayer, she took off the garments in which she had worshiped, and clothed herself in splendid attire. 2Then, majestically adorned, after invoking the aid of the all-seeing God and Savior, she took her two maids with her, 3leaning daintily on one, 4while the other followed carrying her train. 5She was radiant with perfect beauty, and she looked happy, as if beloved, but her heart was frozen with fear. 6When she had gone through all the doors, she stood before the king. He was*

seated on his royal throne, clothed in the full
array of his majesty, all covered with gold and
precious stones. And he was most terrifying.
7Lifting his face, flushed with splendor, he
looked at her in fierce anger. And the queen
faltered, and turned pale and faint, and
collapsed upon the head of the maid who
went before her. 8Then God changed the
spirit of the king to gentleness, and in alarm
he sprang from his throne and took her in
his arms until she came to herself. And he
comforted her with soothing words, and said
to her, 9"What is it, Esther? I am your brother.
Take courage; 10you shall not die, for our law
applies only to the people. Come near."
11Then he raised the golden scepter and
touched it to her neck; 12and he embraced
her, and said, "Speak to me." 13And she said
to him, "I saw you, my lord, like an angel of
God, and my heart was shaken with fear at
your glory. 14For you are wonderful, my lord,
and your countenance is full of grace." 15But
as she was speaking, she fell fainting. 16And
the king was agitated, and all his servants
sought to comfort her.
[5] 3And the king said to her, "What is it,
Queen Esther? What is your request? It shall
be given you, even to the half of my kingdom."
4And Esther said, "If it please the king, let the
king and Ha´man come this day to a dinner
that I have prepared for the king." 5Then said
the king, "Bring Ha´man quickly, that we may
do as Esther desires." So the king and Ha´man
came to the dinner that Esther had prepared.
6And as they were drinking wine, the king
said to Esther, "What is your petition? It shall
be granted you. And what is your request?
Even to the half of my kingdom, it shall be
fulfilled." 7But Esther said, "My petition and
my request is: 8If I have found favor in the
sight of the king, and if it please the king to
grant my petition and fulfil my request, let
the king and Ha´man come tomorrow to the
dinner which I will prepare for them, and
tomorrow I will do as the king has said."
9And Ha´man went out that day joyful
and glad of heart. But when Haman saw
Mor´decai in the king's gate, that he neither
rose nor trembled before him, he was filled
with wrath against Mordecai. 10Nevertheless
Ha´man restrained himself, and went home;
and he sent and fetched his friends and his
wife Ze´resh. 11And Ha´man recounted to
them the splendor of his riches, the number
of his sons, all the promotions with which
the king had honored him, and how he had
advanced him above the princes and the
servants of the king. 12And Ha´man added,
"Even Queen Esther let no one come with
the king to the banquet she prepared but
myself. And tomorrow also I am invited by
her together with the king. 13Yet all this does
me no good, so long as I see Mor´decai the
Jew sitting at the king's gate." 14Then his wife
Ze´resh and all his friends said to him, "Let
a gallows fifty cubits high be made, and in
the morning tell the king to have Mor´decai
hanged upon it; then go merrily with the
king to the dinner." This counsel pleased
Ha´man, and he had the gallows made.

PROVERBS 27

14He who blesses his neighbor with
a loud voice,
rising early in the morning,
will be counted as cursing.
15A continual dripping on a rainy day
and a contentious woman are alike;
16to restrain her is to restrain the wind
or to grasp oil in one's right hand.
17Iron sharpens iron,
and one man sharpens another.
18He who tends a fig tree will eat its fruit,
and he who guards his master will
be honored.
19As in water face answers to face,
so the mind of man reflects the man.
20Sheol and Abad´don are never satisfied,
and never satisfied are the eyes of man.
21The crucible is for silver, and the furnace
is for gold,
and a man is judged by his praise.
22Crush a fool in a mortar with a pestle
along with crushed grain,
yet his folly will not depart from him.

23Know well the condition of your flocks,
and give attention to your herds;

[24]for riches do not last for ever;
and does a crown endure to
all generations?
[25]When the grass is gone, and the new
growth appears,
and the herbage of the mountains
is gathered,
[26]the lambs will provide your clothing,
and the goats the price of a field;
[27]there will be enough goats' milk for your food,
for the food of your household
and maintenance for your maidens.

ROMANS 11

I ask, then, has God rejected his people? By no means! I myself am an Israelite, a descendant of Abraham, a member of the tribe of Benjamin. [2]God has not rejected his people whom he foreknew. Do you not know what the Scripture says of Eli′jah, how he pleads with God against Israel? [3]"Lord, they have killed your prophets, they have demolished your altars, and I alone am left, and they seek my life." [4]But what is God's reply to him? "I have kept for myself seven thousand men who have not bowed the knee to Ba′al." [5]So too at the present time there is a remnant, chosen by grace. [6]But if it is by grace, it is no longer on the basis of works; otherwise grace would no longer be grace.

[7]What then? Israel failed to obtain what it sought. The elect obtained it, but the rest were hardened, [8]as it is written,

"God gave them a spirit of stupor,
eyes that should not see and ears that
should not hear,
down to this very day."

[9]And David says,

"Let their feast become a snare and a trap,
a pitfall and a retribution for them;
[10]let their eyes be darkened so that they
cannot see,
and bend their backs for ever."

[11]So I ask, have they stumbled so as to fall? By no means! But through their trespass salvation has come to the Gentiles, so as to make Israel jealous. [12]Now if their trespass means riches for the world, and if their failure means riches for the Gentiles, how much more will their full inclusion mean!

[13]Now I am speaking to you Gentiles. Inasmuch then as I am an apostle to the Gentiles, I magnify my ministry [14]in order to make my fellow Jews jealous, and thus save some of them. [15]For if their rejection means the reconciliation of the world, what will their acceptance mean but life from the dead? [16]If the dough offered as first fruits is holy, so is the whole batch; and if the root is holy, so are the branches.

[17]But if some of the branches were broken off, and you, a wild olive shoot, were grafted in their place to share the richness of the olive tree, [18]do not boast over the branches. If you do boast, remember it is not you that support the root, but the root that supports you. [19]You will say, "Branches were broken off so that I might be grafted in." [20]That is true. They were broken off because of their unbelief, but you stand fast only through faith. So do not become proud, but stand in awe. [21]For if God did not spare the natural branches, neither will he spare you. [22]Note then the kindness and the severity of God: severity toward those who have fallen, but God's kindness to you, provided you continue in his kindness; otherwise you too will be cut off. [23]And even the others, if they do not persist in their unbelief, will be grafted in, for God has the power to graft them in again. [24]For if you have been cut from what is by nature a wild olive tree, and grafted, contrary to nature, into a cultivated olive tree, how much more will these natural branches be grafted back into their own olive tree.

[25]Lest you be wise in your own conceits, I want you to understand this mystery, brethren: a hardening has come upon part of Israel, until the full number of the Gentiles come in, [26]and so all Israel will be saved; as it is written,

"The Deliverer will come from Zion,
he will banish ungodliness from Jacob";
[27]"and this will be my covenant with them
when I take away their sins."

28 As regards the gospel they are enemies of God, for your sake; but as regards election they are beloved for the sake of their forefathers. 29 For the gifts and the call of God are irrevocable. 30 Just as you were once disobedient to God but now have received mercy because of their disobedience, 31 so they have now been disobedient in order that by the mercy shown to you they also may receive mercy. 32 For God has consigned all men to disobedience, that he may have mercy upon all.

33 O the depth of the riches and wisdom and knowledge of God! How unsearchable are his judgments and how inscrutable his ways!

34 "For who has known the mind of the Lord,
or who has been his counselor?"
35 "Or who has given a gift to him
that he might be repaid?"
36 For from him and through him and to him are all things. To him be glory for ever. Amen.

REFLECTION

Esther, like Judith, humbles herself in prayer. Though she is a beautiful queen, she fasts and covers herself with "the garments of distress and mourning," even putting "ashes and dung" on her head (Est 14:2). These actions symbolize her lowliness before the Lord. At the heart of her prayer, she gives voice to something we at times might also feel: "And now, assist me, who am all alone, and have no one but you, O Lord, my God. Come to my aid, for I am an orphan" (v. 11). She comes to the Lord in her loneliness, asking for his help and deliverance. Courageously she goes forth to meet her fate: "She was radiant with perfect beauty, and she looked happy, as if beloved, but her heart was frozen with fear" (15:5). The contrast between her outward appearance and her inward experience could not be greater, yet with complete reliance on the Lord she enters the king's presence on behalf of her people. Her success will show that "God has not rejected his people whom he foreknew" (Rom 11:2) and that "all Israel will be saved" (v. 26). Esther exhibits great bravery in faith, which brings salvation for the Jews. What can you imitate from her prayer and boldness?

August 14

ESTHER 6

On that night the king could not sleep; and he gave orders to bring the book of memorable deeds, the chronicles, and they were read before the king. 2 And it was found written how Mor′decai had told about Big′thana and Te′resh, two of the king's eunuchs, who guarded the threshold, and who had sought to lay hands upon King Ahas′u-e′rus. 3 And the king said, "What honor or dignity has been bestowed on Mor′decai for this?" The king's servants who attended him said, "Nothing has been done for him." 4 And the king said, "Who is in the court?" Now Ha′man had just entered the outer court of the king's palace to speak to the king about having Mor′decai hanged on the gallows that he had prepared for him. 5 So the king's servants told him, "Ha′man is there, standing in the court." And the king said, "Let him come in." 6 So Ha′man came in, and the king said to him, "What shall be done to the man whom the king delights to honor?" And Haman said to himself, "Whom would the king delight to honor more than me?" 7 And Ha′man said to the king, "For the man whom the king delights to honor, 8 let royal robes be brought, which the king has worn, and the horse which the king has ridden, and on whose head a royal crown is set; 9 and let the robes and the horse be handed over to one of the king's most noble princes; let him clothe the man whom the king delights to honor, and let him conduct the man on horseback through the open square of the city, proclaiming before him: 'Thus shall it be done to the man whom the king delights to honor.'" 10 Then the king said to Ha′man, "Make haste, take the robes and the horse, as you have said, and do so to Mor′decai the Jew who sits at the king's gate. Leave out nothing that you have mentioned." 11 So Ha′man took the robes and the horse, and he clothed Mor′decai and made him ride through the open square of the city, proclaiming, “Thus shall it be done to the man whom the king delights to honor.”

[12]Then Mor′decai returned to the king’s gate. But Ha′man hurried to his house, mourning and with his head covered. [13]And Ha′man told his wife Ze′resh and all his friends everything that had befallen him. Then his wise men and his wife Zeresh said to him, “If Mor′decai, before whom you have begun to fall, is of the Jewish people, you will not prevail against him but will surely fall before him.”

[14]While they were yet talking with him, the king’s eunuchs arrived and brought Ha′man in haste to the banquet that Esther had prepared.

7 So the king and Ha′man went in to feast with Queen Esther. [2]And on the second day, as they were drinking wine, the king again said to Esther, “What is your petition, Queen Esther? It shall be granted you. And what is your request? Even to the half of my kingdom, it shall be fulfilled.” [3]Then Queen Esther answered, “If I have found favor in your sight, O king, and if it please the king, let my life be given me at my petition, and my people at my request. [4]For we are sold, I and my people, to be destroyed, to be slain, and to be annihilated. If we had been sold merely as slaves, men and women, I would have held my peace; for our affliction is not to be compared with the loss to the king.” [5]Then King Ahas′u-e′rus said to Queen Esther, “Who is he, and where is he, that would presume to do this?” [6]And Esther said, “A foe and enemy! This wicked Ha′man!” Then Ha′man was in terror before the king and the queen. [7]And the king rose from the feast in wrath and went into the palace garden; but Ha′man stayed to beg his life from Queen Esther, for he saw that evil was determined against him by the king. [8]And the king returned from the palace garden to the place where they were drinking wine, as Ha′man was falling on the couch where Esther was; and the king said, “Will he even assault the queen in my presence, in my own house?” As the words left the mouth of the king, they covered Haman’s face. [9]Then said Harbo′na, one of the eunuchs in attendance on the king, “Moreover, the gallows which Ha′man has prepared for Mor′decai, whose word saved the king, is standing in Haman’s house, fifty cubits high.” [10]And the king said, “Hang him on that.” So they hanged Ha′man on the gallows which he had prepared for Mor′decai. Then the anger of the king abated.

8 On that day King Ahas′u-e′rus gave to Queen Esther the house of Ha′man, the enemy of the Jews. And Mor′decai came before the king, for Esther had told what he was to her; [2]and the king took off his signet ring, which he had taken from Ha′man, and gave it to Mor′decai. And Esther set Mordecai over the house of Haman.

[3]Then Esther spoke again to the king; she fell at his feet and besought him with tears to avert the evil design of Ha′man the Ag′agite and the plot which he had devised against the Jews. [4]And the king held out the golden scepter to Esther, [5]and Esther rose and stood before the king. And she said, “If it please the king, and if I have found favor in his sight, and if the thing seem right before the king, and I be pleasing in his eyes, let an order be written to revoke the letters devised by Ha′man the Ag′agite, the son of Hammeda′tha, which he wrote to destroy the Jews who are in all the provinces of the king. [6]For how can I endure to see the calamity that is coming to my people? Or how can I endure to see the destruction of my kindred?” [7]Then King Ahas′u-e′rus said to Queen Esther and to Mor′decai the Jew, “Behold, I have given Esther the house of Ha′man, and they have hanged him on the gallows, because he would lay hands on the Jews. [8]And you may write as you please with regard to the Jews, in the name of the king, and seal it with the king’s ring; for an edict written in the name of the king and sealed with the king’s ring cannot be revoked.”

[9]The king’s secretaries were summoned at that time, in the third month, which is the month of Si′van, on the twenty-third day; and an edict was written according to all that Mor′decai commanded concerning the Jews to the satraps and the governors and the princes of the provinces from India to Ethiopia, a hundred and twenty-seven provinces, to every

province in its own script and to every people in its own language, and also to the Jews in their script and their language. 10The writing was in the name of King Ahas′u-e′rus and sealed with the king's ring, and letters were sent by mounted couriers riding on swift horses that were used in the king's service, bred from the royal stud. 11By these the king allowed the Jews who were in every city to gather and defend their lives, to destroy, to slay, and to annihilate any armed force of any people or province that might attack them, with their children and women, and to plunder their goods, 12upon one day throughout all the provinces of King Ahas′u-e′rus, on the thirteenth day of the twelfth month, which is the month of Adar′.

16 *The following is a copy of this letter: "The Great King, Artaxerxes, to the rulers of the provinces from India to Ethiopia, one hundred and twenty-seven satrapies, and to those who are loyal to our government, greeting.*

2*"The more often they are honored by the too great kindness of their benefactors, the more proud do many men become.* 3*They not only seek to injure our subjects, but in their inability to stand prosperity they even undertake to scheme against their own benefactors.* 4*They not only take away thankfulness from among men, but, carried away by the boasts of those who know nothing of goodness, they suppose that they will escape the evil-hating justice of God, who always sees everything.* 5*And often many of those who are set in places of authority have been made in part responsible for the shedding of innocent blood, and have been involved in irremediable calamities, by the persuasion of friends who have been entrusted with the administration of public affairs,* 6*when these men by the false trickery of their evil natures beguile the sincere good will of their sovereigns.*

7*"What has been wickedly accomplished through the pestilent behavior of those who exercise authority unworthily, can be seen not so much from the more ancient records which we hand on as from investigation of matters close at hand.* 8*For the future we will take care to render our kingdom quiet and peaceable for all men,* 9*by changing our methods and always judging what comes before our eyes with more equitable consideration.* 10*For Haman, the son of Hammedatha, a Macedonian (really an alien to the Persian blood, and quite devoid of our kindliness), having become our guest,* 11*so far enjoyed the good will that we have for every nation that he was called our father and was continually bowed down to by all as the person second to the royal throne.* 12*But, unable to restrain his arrogance, he undertook to deprive us of our kingdom and our life,* 13*and with intricate craft and deceit asked for the destruction of Mordecai, our savior and perpetual benefactor, and of Esther, the blameless partner of our kingdom, together with their whole nation.* 14*He thought that in this way he would find us undefended and would transfer the kingdom of the Persians to the Macedonians.*

15*"But we find that the Jews, who were consigned to annihilation by this thrice accursed man, are not evildoers but are governed by most righteous laws* 16*and are sons of the Most High, the most mighty living God, who has directed the kingdom both for us and for our fathers in the most excellent order.*

17*"You will therefore do well not to put in execution the letters sent by Haman the son of Hammedatha,* 18*because the man himself who did these things has been hanged at the gate of Susa, with all his household. For God, who rules over all things, has speedily inflicted on him the punishment he deserved.*

19*"Therefore post a copy of this letter publicly in every place, and permit the Jews to live under their own laws.* 20*And give them reinforcements, so that on the thirteenth day of the twelfth month, Adar, on that very day they may defend themselves against those who attack them at the time of their affliction.* 21*For God, who rules over all things, has made this day to be a joy to his chosen people instead of a day of destruction for them.*

22*"Therefore you shall observe this with all good cheer as a notable day among your commemorative festivals,* 23*so that both now and hereafter it may mean salvation for us and the loyal Persians, but that for those who plot against us it may be a reminder of destruction.*

24*"Every city and country, without exception, which does not act accordingly, shall* *be destroyed in wrath with spear and fire. It shall be made not only impassable for men, but also most hateful for all time to beasts and birds."*

PROVERBS 28

The wicked flee when no one pursues,
but the righteous are bold as a lion.
2When a land transgresses
it has many rulers;
but with men of understanding
and knowledge
its stability will long continue.
3A poor man who oppresses the poor
is a beating rain that leaves no food.
4Those who forsake the law praise the wicked,
but those who keep the law strive
against them.
5Evil men do not understand justice,
but those who seek the LORD understand
it completely.
6Better is a poor man who walks in
his integrity
than a rich man who is perverse in
his ways.
7He who keeps the law is a wise son,
but a companion of gluttons shames
his father.
8He who augments his wealth by interest
and increase
gathers it for him who is kind to the poor.
9If one turns away his ear from hearing the law,
even his prayer is an abomination.
10He who misleads the upright into an evil way
will fall into his own pit;
but the blameless will have an
excellent inheritance.
11A rich man is wise in his own eyes,
but a poor man who has understanding
will find him out.
12When the righteous triumph, there is
great glory;
but when the wicked rise, men
hide themselves.
13He who conceals his transgressions will
not prosper,
but he who confesses and forsakes them
will obtain mercy.

ROMANS 12

**I appeal to you therefore, breth-
ren, by the mercies of God, to
present your bodies as a living sacrifice,
holy and acceptable to God, which is**
your spiritual worship. 2Do not be conformed to this world but be transformed
by the renewal of your mind, that you may
prove what is the will of God, what is good
and acceptable and perfect.
3For by the grace given to me I bid every
one among you not to think of himself more
highly than he ought to think, but to think
with sober judgment, each according to the
measure of faith which God has assigned
him. 4For as in one body we have many
members, and all the members do not have
the same function, 5so we, though many,
are one body in Christ, and individually
members one of another. 6Having gifts that
differ according to the grace given to us, let
us use them: if prophecy, in proportion to
our faith; 7if service, in our serving; he who
teaches, in his teaching; 8he who exhorts,
in his exhortation; he who contributes, in
liberality; he who gives aid, with zeal; he
who does acts of mercy, with cheerfulness.
9Let love be genuine; hate what is evil, hold
fast to what is good; 10love one another with
brotherly affection; outdo one another in
showing honor. 11Never flag in zeal, be aglow
with the Spirit, serve the Lord. 12Rejoice
in your hope, be patient in tribulation, be
constant in prayer. 13Contribute to the needs
of the saints, practice hospitality.
14Bless those who persecute you; bless and
do not curse them. 15Rejoice with those who
rejoice, weep with those who weep. 16Live
in harmony with one another; do not be
haughty, but associate with the lowly; never
be conceited. 17Repay no one evil for evil,
but take thought for what is noble in the
sight of all. 18If possible, so far as it depends
upon you, live peaceably with all. 19Beloved,
never avenge yourselves, but leave it to the
wrath of God; for it is written, "Vengeance
is mine, I will repay, says the Lord." 20No,
"if your enemy is hungry, feed him; if he is
thirsty, give him drink; for by so doing you

will heap burning coals upon his head." 21Do
not be overcome by evil, but overcome evil
with good.

REFLECTION

When Haman's genocidal plan against the Jews reaches fever pitch, Esther presents her petition before the king: "Let my life be given me at my petition, and my people at my request" (Est 7:3). As she accuses Haman, the king immediately changes his mind. He has Haman executed and countermands his order, allowing the Jews to defend themselves against attack. Esther and Mordecai's example reminds us of St. Paul's words: "Do not be overcome by evil, but overcome evil with good" (Rom 12:21). They did not launch a war, but sought help from God, who aids them through the decisions of the king. The king's new decree cites "the evil-hating justice of God" (Est 16:4), which matches with the attitude St. Paul promotes: "Hate what is evil, hold fast to what is good" (Rom 12:9). In our tumultuous world, it is easy to lose our understanding of the truth and allow ourselves to be seduced by the errors that surround us. Paul warns us strongly to take a firm stand against evil, and so reflect the justice of God. Are you willing and ready to take a strong stand against evil and injustice?

August 15

ESTHER 8

13A copy of what was written
was to be issued as a decree in
every province, and by proc-
lamation to all peoples, and the Jews
were to be ready on that day to avenge
themselves upon their enemies. 14So the
couriers, mounted on their swift horses that
were used in the king's service, rode out in
haste, urged by the king's command; and the
decree was issued in Susa the capital.
15Then Mor′decai went out from the
presence of the king in royal robes of blue
and white, with a great golden crown and a
mantle of fine linen and purple, while the city
of Susa shouted and rejoiced. 16The Jews had
light and gladness and joy and honor. 17And
in every province and in every city, wherever
the king's command and his edict came, there
was gladness and joy among the Jews, a feast
and a holiday. And many from the peoples of
the country declared themselves Jews, for the
fear of the Jews had fallen upon them.

9 Now in the twelfth month, which is the
month of Adar′, on the thirteenth day of
the same, when the king's command and edict
were about to be executed, on the very day
when the enemies of the Jews hoped to get
the mastery over them, but which had been
changed to a day when the Jews should get
the mastery over their foes, 2the Jews gathered
in their cities throughout all the provinces of
King Ahas′u-e′rus to lay hands on such as
sought their hurt. And no one could make a
stand against them, for the fear of them had
fallen upon all peoples. 3All the princes of the
provinces and the satraps and the governors
and the royal officials also helped the Jews,
for the fear of Mor′decai had fallen upon
them. 4For Mor′decai was great in the king's
house, and his fame spread throughout all the
provinces; for the man Mordecai grew more
and more powerful. 5So the Jews struck all
their enemies with the sword, slaughtering,
and destroying them, and did as they pleased
to those who hated them. 6In Susa the
capital itself the Jews slew and destroyed five
hundred men, 7and also slew Par-shan-da′tha
and Dalphon and Aspa′tha 8and Pora′tha and
Ada′lia and Arida′tha 9and Parmash′ta and
Ar′isai and Ar′idai and Vaiza′tha, 10the ten
sons of Ha′man the son of Hammeda′tha, the
enemy of the Jews; but they laid no hand on
the plunder.
11That very day the number of those slain
in Susa the capital was reported to the king.
12And the king said to Queen Esther, "In Susa
the capital the Jews have slain five hundred

men and also the ten sons of Ha′man. What then have they done in the rest of the king's provinces! Now what is your petition? It shall be granted you. And what further is your request? It shall be fulfilled." [13]And Esther said, "If it please the king, let the Jews who are in Susa be allowed tomorrow also to do according to this day's edict. And let the ten sons of Ha′man be hanged on the gallows." [14]So the king commanded this to be done; a decree was issued in Susa, and the ten sons of Ha′man were hanged. [15]The Jews who were in Susa gathered also on the fourteenth day of the month of Adar′ and they slew three hundred men in Susa; but they laid no hands on the plunder.

[16]Now the other Jews who were in the king's provinces also gathered to defend their lives, and got relief from their enemies, and slew seventy-five thousand of those who hated them; but they laid no hands on the plunder. [17]This was on the thirteenth day of the month of Adar′, and on the fourteenth day they rested and made that a day of feasting and gladness. [18]But the Jews who were in Susa gathered on the thirteenth day and on the fourteenth, and rested on the fifteenth day, making that a day of feasting and gladness. [19]Therefore the Jews of the villages, who live in the open towns, hold the fourteenth day of the month of Adar′ as a day for gladness and feasting and holiday-making, and a day on which they send choice portions to one another.

[20]And Mor′decai recorded these things, and sent letters to all the Jews who were in all the provinces of King Ahas′u-e′rus, both near and far, [21]enjoining them that they should keep the fourteenth day of the month Adar′ and also the fifteenth day of the same, year by year, [22]as the days on which the Jews got relief from their enemies, and as the month that had been turned for them from sorrow into gladness and from mourning into a holiday; that they should make them days of feasting and gladness, days for sending choice portions to one another and gifts to the poor.

[23]So the Jews undertook to do as they had begun, and as Mor′decai had written to them. [24]For Ha′man the Ag′agite, the son of Hammeda′tha, the enemy of all the Jews, had plotted against the Jews to destroy them, and had cast Pur, that is the lot, to crush and destroy them; [25]but when Esther came before the king, he gave orders in writing that his wicked plot which he had devised against the Jews should come upon his own head, and that he and his sons should be hanged on the gallows. [26]Therefore they called these days Purim, after the term Pur. And therefore, because of all that was written in this letter, and of what they had faced in this matter, and of what had befallen them, [27]the Jews ordained and took it upon themselves and their descendants and all who joined them, that without fail they would keep these two days according to what was written and at the time appointed every year, [28]that these days should be remembered and kept throughout every generation, in every family, province, and city, and that these days of Purim should never fall into disuse among the Jews, nor should the commemoration of these days cease among their descendants.

[29]Then Queen Esther, the daughter of Ab′ihail, and Mor′decai the Jew gave full written authority, confirming this second letter about Purim. [30]Letters were sent to all the Jews, to the hundred and twenty-seven provinces of the kingdom of Ahas′u-e′rus, in words of peace and truth, [31]that these days of Purim should be observed at their appointed seasons, as Mor′decai the Jew and Queen Esther enjoined upon the Jews, and as they had laid down for themselves and for their descendants, with regard to their fasts and their lamenting. [32]The command of Queen Esther fixed these practices of Purim, and it was recorded in writing.

10 King Ahas′u-e′rus laid tribute on the land and on the coastlands of the sea. [2]And all the acts of his power and might, and the full account of the high honor of Mor′decai, to which the king advanced him, are they not written in the Book of the Chronicles of the kings of Med′ia and Persia? [3]For Mor′decai the Jew was next in rank to King Ahas′u-e′rus, and he was great among the Jews and popular with the multitude of his brethren, for he sought the

welfare of his people and spoke peace to all
his people.

10 [4]*And Mordecai said, "These things*
have come from God. [5]*For I remem-*
ber the dream that I had concerning these
matters, and none of them has failed to be
fulfilled. [6]*The tiny spring which became a river,*
and there was light and the sun and abundant
water—the river is Esther, whom the king
married and made queen. [7]*The two dragons*
are Haman and myself. [8]*The nations are those*
that gathered to destroy the name of the Jews.
[9]*And my nation, this is Israel, who cried out to*
God and were saved. The Lord has saved his
people; the Lord has delivered us from all these
evils; God has done great signs and wonders,
which have not occurred among the nations.
[10]*For this purpose he made two lots, one for*
the people of God and one for all the nations.
[11]*And these two lots came to the hour and*
moment and day of decision before God and
among all the nations. [12]*And God remembered*
his people and vindicated his inheritance. [13]*So*
they will observe these days in the month of
Adar, on the fourteenth and fifteenth of that
month, with an assembly and joy and gladness
before God, from generation to generation for
ever among his people Israel."

11 [1]*In the fourth year of the reign of*
Ptolemy and Cleopatra, Dositheus,
who said that he was a priest and a Levite,
and Ptolemy his son brought to Egypt the
preceeding Letter of Purim, which they said
was genuine and had been translated by
Lysimachus the son of Ptolemy, one of the
residents of Jerusalem.

PROVERBS 28

[14]Blessed is the man who fears
the LORD always;
but he who hardens his heart will fall
into calamity.
[15]Like a roaring lion or a charging bear
is a wicked ruler over a poor people.
[16]A ruler who lacks understanding is a
cruel oppressor;
but he who hates unjust gain will prolong
his days.
[17]If a man is burdened with the blood
of another,
let him be a fugitive until death;
let no one help him.
[18]He who walks in integrity will be delivered,
but he who is perverse in his ways will
fall into a pit.
[19]He who tills his land will have plenty
of bread,
but he who follows worthless pursuits
will have plenty of poverty.
[20]A faithful man will abound with blessings,
but he who hastens to be rich will not
go unpunished.
[21]To show partiality is not good;
but for a piece of bread a man will
do wrong.
[22]A miserly man hastens after wealth,
and does not know that want will come
upon him.
[23]He who rebukes a man will afterward find
more favor
than he who flatters with his tongue.
[24]He who robs his father or his mother
and says, "That is no transgression,"
is the companion of a man who destroys.
[25]A greedy man stirs up strife,
but he who trusts in the LORD will
be enriched.
[26]He who trusts in his own mind is a fool;
but he who walks in wisdom will
be delivered.
[27]He who gives to the poor will not want,
but he who hides his eyes will get many
a curse.
[28]When the wicked rise, men hide themselves,
but when they perish, the righteous
increase.

ROMANS 13

Let every person be subject to
the governing authorities. For
there is no authority except from God,
and those that exist have been instituted
by God. [2]Therefore he who resists the authorities resists what God has appointed, and
those who resist will incur judgment. [3]For

rulers are not a terror to good conduct, but to bad. Would you have no fear of him who is in authority? Then do what is good, and you will receive his approval, 4for he is God's servant for your good. But if you do wrong, be afraid, for he does not bear the sword in vain; he is the servant of God to execute his wrath on the wrongdoer. 5Therefore one must be subject, not only to avoid God's wrath but also for the sake of conscience. 6For the same reason you also pay taxes, for the authorities are ministers of God, attending to this very thing. 7Pay all of them their dues, taxes to whom taxes are due, revenue to whom revenue is due, respect to whom respect is due, honor to whom honor is due.

8Owe no one anything, except to love one another; for he who loves his neighbor has fulfilled the law. 9The commandments, "You shall not commit adultery, You shall not kill, You shall not steal, You shall not covet," and any other commandment, are summed up in this sentence, "You shall love your neighbor as yourself." 10Love does no wrong to a neighbor; therefore love is the fulfilling of the law.

11Besides this you know what hour it is, how it is full time now for you to wake from sleep. For salvation is nearer to us now than when we first believed; 12the night is far gone, the day is at hand. Let us then cast off the works of darkness and put on the armor of light; 13let us conduct ourselves becomingly as in the day, not in reveling and drunkenness, not in debauchery and licentiousness, not in quarreling and jealousy. 14But put on the Lord Jesus Christ, and make no provision for the flesh, to gratify its desires.

14 As for the man who is weak in faith, welcome him, but not for disputes over opinions. 2One believes he may eat anything, while the weak man eats only vegetables. 3Let not him who eats despise him who abstains, and let not him who abstains pass judgment on him who eats; for God has welcomed him. 4Who are you to pass judgment on the servant of another? It is before his own master that he stands or falls. And he will be upheld, for the Master is able to make him stand.

5One man esteems one day as better than another, while another man esteems all days alike. Let every one be fully convinced in his own mind. 6He who observes the day, observes it in honor of the Lord. He also who eats, eats in honor of the Lord, since he gives thanks to God; while he who abstains, abstains in honor of the Lord and gives thanks to God. 7None of us lives to himself, and none of us dies to himself. 8If we live, we live to the Lord, and if we die, we die to the Lord; so then, whether we live or whether we die, we are the Lord's. 9For to this end Christ died and lived again, that he might be Lord both of the dead and of the living.

10Why do you pass judgment on your brother? Or you, why do you despise your brother? For we shall all stand before the judgment seat of God; 11for it is written,

"As I live, says the Lord, every knee shall
bow to me,
and every tongue shall give praise to God."

12So each of us shall give account of himself to God.

REFLECTION

Once the king issues his countermanding edict, the Jews arm themselves and organize a defense. On the appointed day of violence, they successfully defend themselves from attack, thus achieving the deliverance engineered by Mordecai and Queen Esther. Esther is described in Mordecai's vision as a "tiny spring which became a river, and there was light and the sun and abundant water" (Est 10:6). Her decision to intercede on the Jews' behalf begins as a small, seemingly insignificant thing, but it grows until it saves the lives of thousands of people. In celebration, the holiday of Purim is established, and the Jews celebrate it to this day. St. Paul encourages us to love one another and teaches us that "love is the fulfilling of the law" (Rom 13:10). Esther's life is a great reminder that our fidelity to God, expressed in love for others, can begin in such a small, quiet way, by simply winning favor and friends. What starts as a hidden expression of love for Christ in the other can increase to the point of being truly heroic. What are the small and hidden ways in which Jesus is inviting you to love him more?

August 16

JOB 1

There was a man in the land of Uz, whose name was Job; and that man was blameless and upright, one who feared God, and turned away from evil. 2There were born to him seven sons and three daughters. 3He had seven thousand sheep, three thousand camels, five hundred yoke of oxen, and five hundred she-donkeys, and very many servants; so that this man was the greatest of all the people of the east. 4His sons used to go and hold a feast in the house of each on his day; and they would send and invite their three sisters to eat and drink with them. 5And when the days of the feast had run their course, Job would send and sanctify them, and he would rise early in the morning and offer burnt offerings according to the number of them all; for Job said, "It may be that my sons have sinned, and cursed God in their hearts." Thus Job did continually.

6Now there was a day when the sons of God came to present themselves before the LORD, and Satan also came among them. 7The LORD said to Satan, "From where have you come?" Satan answered the LORD, "From going back and forth on the earth, and from walking up and down on it." 8And the LORD said to Satan, "Have you considered my servant Job, that there is none like him on the earth, a blameless and upright man, who fears God and turns away from evil?" 9Then Satan answered the LORD, "Does Job fear God for nothing? 10Have you not put a hedge about him and his house and all that he has, on every side? You have blessed the work of his hands, and his possessions have increased in the land. 11But put forth your hand now, and touch all that he has, and he will curse you to your face." 12And the LORD said to Satan, "Behold, all that he has is in your power; only upon himself do not put forth your hand." So Satan went forth from the presence of the LORD.

13Now there was a day when his sons and daughters were eating and drinking wine in their eldest brother's house; 14and there came a messenger to Job, and said, "The oxen were plowing and the donkeys feeding beside them; 15and the Sabe′ans fell upon them and took them, and slew the servants with the edge of the sword; and I alone have escaped to tell you." 16While he was yet speaking, there came another, and said, "The fire of God fell from heaven and burned up the sheep and the servants, and consumed them; and I alone have escaped to tell you." 17While he was yet speaking, there came another, and said, "The Chalde′ans formed three companies, and made a raid upon the camels and took them, and slew the servants with the edge of the sword; and I alone have escaped to tell you." 18While he was yet speaking, there came another, and said, "Your sons and daughters were eating and drinking wine in their eldest brother's house; 19and behold, a great wind came across the wilderness, and struck the four corners of the house, and it fell upon the young people, and they are dead; and I alone have escaped to tell you."

20Then Job arose, and tore his robe, and shaved his head, and fell upon the ground, and worshiped. 21And he said, "Naked I came from my mother's womb, and naked shall I return; the LORD gave, and the LORD has taken away; blessed be the name of the LORD."

22In all this Job did not sin or charge God with wrong.

2 Again there was a day when the sons of God came to present themselves before the LORD, and Satan also came among them to present himself before the LORD. 2And the LORD said to Satan, "From where have you come?" Satan answered the LORD, "From going back and forth on the earth, and from walking up and down on it." 3And the LORD said to Satan, "Have you considered my servant Job, that there is none like him on the earth, a blameless and upright man, who fears God and turns away from evil? He still holds fast his integrity, although you moved me against him, to destroy him without cause." 4Then Satan answered the

LORD, "Skin for skin! All that a man has he
will give for his life. 5But put forth your hand
now, and touch his bone and his flesh, and he
will curse you to your face." 6And the LORD
said to Satan, "Behold, he is in your power;
only spare his life."

7So Satan went forth from the presence of
the LORD, and afflicted Job with loathsome
sores from the sole of his foot to the crown of
his head. 8And he took a potsherd with which
to scrape himself, and sat among the ashes.

9Then his wife said to him, "Do you still
hold fast your integrity? Curse God, and
die." 10But he said to her, "You speak as one
of the foolish women would speak. Shall we
receive good at the hand of God, and shall
we not receive evil?" In all this Job did not
sin with his lips.

11Now when Job's three friends heard of
all this evil that had come upon him, they
came each from his own place, Eli′phaz
the Te′manite, Bildad the Shuhite, and
Zo′phar the Na′amathite. They made an
appointment together to come to condole
with him and comfort him. 12And when
they saw him from afar, they did not
recognize him; and they raised their voices
and wept; and they tore their robes and
sprinkled dust upon their heads toward
heaven. 13And they sat with him on the
ground seven days and seven nights, and
no one spoke a word to him, for they saw
that his suffering was very great.

3 After this Job opened his mouth and cursed the day of his birth.

2And Job said:

3"Let the day perish wherein I was born,
and the night which said,
'A man-child is conceived.'
4Let that day be darkness!
May God above not seek it,
nor light shine upon it.
5Let gloom and deep darkness claim it.
Let clouds dwell upon it;
let the blackness of the day terrify it.
6That night—let thick darkness seize it!
let it not rejoice among the days
of the year,
let it not come into the number
of the months.
7Yes, let that night be barren;
let no joyful cry be heard in it.
8Let those curse it who curse the day,
who are skilled to rouse up Levi′athan.
9Let the stars of its dawn be dark;
let it hope for light, but have none,
nor see the eyelids of the morning;
10because it did not shut the doors of my
mother's womb,
nor hide trouble from my eyes.

11"Why did I not die at birth,
come forth from the womb and expire?
12Why did the knees receive me?
Or why the breasts, that I should suck?
13For then I should have lain down and
been quiet;
I should have slept; then I should have
been at rest,
14with kings and counselors of the earth
who rebuilt ruins for themselves,
15or with princes who had gold,
who filled their houses with silver.
16Or why was I not as a hidden
untimely birth,
as infants that never see the light?
17There the wicked cease from troubling,
and there the weary are at rest.
18There the prisoners are at ease together;
they hear not the voice of the taskmaster.
19The small and the great are there,
and the slave is free from his master.

20"Why is light given to him who is in misery,
and life to the bitter in soul,
21who long for death, but it comes not,
and dig for it more than for
hidden treasures;
22who rejoice exceedingly,
and are glad, when they find the grave?
23Why is light given to a man whose way
is hidden,
whom God has hedged in?
24For my sighing comes as my bread,
and my groanings are poured out
like water.
25For the thing that I fear comes upon me,
and what I dread befalls me.
26I am not at ease, nor am I quiet;
I have no rest; but trouble comes."

PROVERBS 29

He who is often reproved, yet stiffens his neck,
will suddenly be broken beyond healing.
2When the righteous are in authority, the
people rejoice;
but when the wicked rule,
the people groan.
3He who loves wisdom makes his father glad,
but one who keeps company with harlots
squanders his substance.
4By justice a king gives stability to the land,
but one who exacts gifts ruins it.
5A man who flatters his neighbor
spreads a net for his feet.
6An evil man is ensnared in his transgression,
but a righteous man sings and rejoices.
7A righteous man knows the rights
of the poor;
a wicked man does not understand
such knowledge.
8Scoffers set a city aflame,
but wise men turn away wrath.
9If a wise man has an argument with a fool,
the fool only rages and laughs, and there
is no quiet.
10Bloodthirsty men hate one who
is blameless,
and the wicked seek his life.
11A fool gives full vent to his anger,
but a wise man quietly holds it back.
12If a ruler listens to falsehood,
all his officials will be wicked.
13The poor man and the oppressor
meet together;
the LORD gives light to the eyes of both.
14If a king judges the poor with equity
his throne will be established for ever.

ROMANS 14

**13Then let us no more pass judg-
ment on one another, but rather
decide never to put a stumbling block or
hindrance in the way of a brother. 14I know**
and am persuaded in the Lord Jesus that nothing is unclean in itself; but it is unclean for any
one who thinks it unclean. 15If your brother is
being injured by what you eat, you are no longer
walking in love. Do not let what you eat cause
the ruin of one for whom Christ died. 16So do
not let what is good to you be spoken of as evil.
17For the kingdom of God does not mean food
and drink but righteousness and peace and joy
in the Holy Spirit; 18he who thus serves Christ
is acceptable to God and approved by men.
19Let us then pursue what makes for peace and
for mutual upbuilding. 20Do not, for the sake
of food, destroy the work of God. Everything
is indeed clean, but it is wrong for any one to
make others fall by what he eats; 21it is right
not to eat meat or drink wine or do anything
that makes your brother stumble. 22The faith
that you have, keep between yourself and God;
happy is he who has no reason to judge himself
for what he approves. 23But he who has doubts
is condemned, if he eats, because he does not
act from faith; for whatever does not proceed
from faith is sin.

15 We who are strong ought to bear
with the failings of the weak, and not
to please ourselves; 2let each of us please his
neighbor for his good, to edify him. 3For Christ
did not please himself; but, as it is written, "The
reproaches of those who reproached you fell
on me." 4For whatever was written in former
days was written for our instruction, that by
steadfastness and by the encouragement of the
Scriptures we might have hope. 5May the God
of steadfastness and encouragement grant you
to live in such harmony with one another, in
accord with Christ Jesus, 6that together you
may with one voice glorify the God and Father
of our Lord Jesus Christ.

7Welcome one another, therefore, as Christ
has welcomed you, for the glory of God. 8For
I tell you that Christ became a servant to the
circumcised to show God's truthfulness, in
order to confirm the promises given to the
patriarchs, 9and in order that the Gentiles might
glorify God for his mercy. As it is written,

"Therefore I will praise you among
the Gentiles,
and sing to your name";

10and again it is said,

"Rejoice, O Gentiles, with his people";

11and again,

"Praise the Lord, all Gentiles,
and let all the peoples praise him";

[12]and further Isaiah says,
"The root of Jesse shall come,
he who rises to rule the Gentiles;
in him shall the Gentiles hope."
[13]May the God of hope fill you with all joy
and peace in believing, so that by the power
of the Holy Spirit you may abound in hope.

REFLECTION

The suffering in our lives can seem more than we're able to bear. We are wearied by the trials we are given and, at times, nearly broken by tragedy. We struggle to find meaning in these moments, desperately seeking to know God's grander purpose. However, the answer to our prayers is often silence. Think of the righteous Job. In the midst of disaster and heartbreak, this godly man's lament (see Jb 3) goes unanswered. We see that fidelity to God prevents neither pain nor struggle. Yet Job refuses to curse God, choosing instead to acknowledge his own frailty and to depend upon his Creator: "Naked I came from my mother's womb, and naked shall I return; the LORD gave, and the LORD has taken away; blessed be the name of the LORD" (1:21). In this passage, Job is a model for all the faithful who suffer. But we, as part of the believing community in Christ, need not struggle alone. St. Paul shows us the importance of encouraging our brethren, especially when they stumble and fall. We cannot scorn each other's weaknesses. Do you encourage and edify your family and friends during their times of struggle, or do you hinder them by your actions?

August 17

JOB 4

Then Eli´phaz the Te´manite answered:
[2]"If one ventures a word with you, will you be offended?
Yet who can keep from speaking?
[3]Behold, you have instructed many,
and you have strengthened the weak hands.
[4]Your words have upheld him who was stumbling,
and you have made firm the feeble knees.
[5]But now it has come to you, and you are impatient;
it touches you, and you are dismayed.
[6]Is not your fear of God your confidence,
and the integrity of your ways your hope?

[7]"Think now, who that was innocent ever perished?
Or where were the upright cut off?
[8]As I have seen, those who plow iniquity
and sow trouble reap the same.
[9]By the breath of God they perish,
and by the blast of his anger they are consumed.
[10]The roar of the lion, the voice of the fierce lion,
the teeth of the young lions, are broken.
[11]The strong lion perishes for lack of prey,
and the whelps of the lioness are scattered.

[12]"Now a word was brought to me stealthily,
my ear received the whisper of it.
[13]Amid thoughts from visions of the night,
when deep sleep falls on men,
[14]dread came upon me, and trembling,
which made all my bones shake.
[15]A spirit glided past my face;
the hair of my flesh stood up.
[16]It stood still,
but I could not discern its appearance.
A form was before my eyes;
there was silence, then I heard a voice:
[17]'Can mortal man be righteous before God?
Can a man be pure before his Maker?
[18]Even in his servants he puts no trust,
and his angels he charges with error;
[19]how much more those who dwell in houses of clay,
whose foundation is in the dust,
who are crushed before the moth.
[20]Between morning and evening they are destroyed;
they perish for ever without any regarding it.

21 If their tent-cord is plucked up within them,
do they not die, and that without wisdom?'

5 "Call now; is there any one who will answer you?
To which of the holy ones will you turn?
2 Surely vexation kills the fool,
and jealousy slays the simple.
3 I have seen the fool taking root,
but suddenly I cursed his dwelling.
4 His sons are far from safety,
they are crushed in the gate,
and there is no one to deliver them.
5 His harvest the hungry eat,
and he takes it even out of thorns;
and the thirsty pant after his wealth.
6 For affliction does not come from the dust,
nor does trouble sprout from the ground;
7 but man is born to trouble
as the sparks fly upward.

8 "As for me, I would seek God,
and to God would I commit my cause;
9 who does great things and unsearchable,
marvelous things without number:
10 he gives rain upon the earth
and sends waters upon the fields;
11 he sets on high those who are lowly,
and those who mourn are lifted to safety.
12 He frustrates the devices of the crafty,
so that their hands achieve no success.
13 He takes the wise in their own craftiness;
and the schemes of the wily are brought to a quick end.
14 They meet with darkness in the daytime,
and grope at noonday as in the night.
15 But he saves the fatherless from their mouth,
the needy from the hand of the mighty.
16 So the poor have hope,
and injustice shuts her mouth.

17 "Behold, happy is the man whom God reproves;
therefore despise not the chastening of the Almighty.
18 For he wounds, but he binds up;
he strikes, but his hands heal.
19 He will deliver you from six troubles;
in seven there shall no evil touch you.
20 In famine he will redeem you from death,
and in war from the power of the sword.
21 You shall be hidden from the scourge of the tongue,
and shall not fear destruction when it comes.
22 At destruction and famine you shall laugh,
and shall not fear the beasts of the earth.
23 For you shall be in league with the stones of the field,
and the beasts of the field shall be at peace with you.
24 You shall know that your tent is safe,
and you shall inspect your fold and miss nothing.
25 You shall know also that your descendants shall be many,
and your offspring as the grass of the earth.
26 You shall come to your grave in ripe old age,
as a shock of grain comes up to the threshing floor in its season.
27 Behold, this we have searched out; it is true.
Hear, and know it for your good."

6 Then Job answered:
2 "O that my vexation were weighed,
and all my calamity laid in the balances!
3 For then it would be heavier than the sand of the sea;
therefore my words have been rash.
4 For the arrows of the Almighty are in me;
my spirit drinks their poison;
the terrors of God are arrayed against me.
5 Does the wild donkey bray when he has grass,
or the ox low over his fodder?
6 Can that which is tasteless be eaten without salt,
or is there any taste in the slime of the purslane?
7 My appetite refuses to touch them;
they are as food that is loathsome to me.

8 "O that I might have my request,
and that God would grant my desire;
9 that it would please God to crush me,
that he would let loose his hand and cut me off!
10 This would be my consolation;
I would even exult in pain unsparing;
for I have not denied the words of the Holy One.

11What is my strength, that I should wait?
And what is my end, that I should
be patient?
12Is my strength the strength of stones,
or is my flesh bronze?
13In truth I have no help in me,
and any resource is driven from me.

14"He who withholds kindness from a friend
forsakes the fear of the Almighty.
15My brethren are treacherous as a torrent-bed,
as freshets that pass away,
16which are dark with ice,
and where the snow hides itself.
17In time of heat they disappear;
when it is hot, they vanish from
their place.
18The caravans turn aside from
their course;
they go up into the waste, and perish.
19The caravans of Te′ma look,
the travelers of Sheba hope.
20They are disappointed because they
were confident;
they come there and are confounded.
21Such you have now become to me;
you see my calamity, and are afraid.
22Have I said, 'Make me a gift'?
Or, 'From your wealth offer a bribe
for me'?
23Or, 'Deliver me from the adversary's hand'?
Or, 'Ransom me from the hand of
oppressors'?

24"Teach me, and I will be silent;
make me understand how I have erred.
25How forceful are honest words!
But what does reproof from you reprove?
26Do you think that you can reprove words,
when the speech of a despairing man
is wind?
27You would even cast lots over the fatherless,
and bargain over your friend.

28"But now, be pleased to look at me;
for I will not lie to your face.
29Turn, I beg, let no wrong be done.
Turn now, my vindication is at stake.
30Is there any wrong on my tongue?
Cannot my taste discern calamity?

7 "Has not man a hard service upon earth,
and are not his days like the days
of a hireling?
2Like a slave who longs for the shadow,
and like a hireling who looks
for his wages,
3so I am allotted months of emptiness,
and nights of misery are apportioned
to me.
4When I lie down I say, 'When shall I arise?'
But the night is long,
and I am full of tossing till the dawn.
5My flesh is clothed with worms and dirt;
my skin hardens, then breaks out afresh.
6My days are swifter than a weaver's shuttle,
and come to their end without hope.

7"Remember that my life is a breath;
my eye will never again see good.
8The eye of him who sees me will behold me
no more;
while your eyes are upon me, I shall be gone.
9As the cloud fades and vanishes,
so he who goes down to Sheol does not
come up;
10he returns no more to his house,
nor does his place know him any more.

11"Therefore I will not restrain my mouth;
I will speak in the anguish of my spirit;
I will complain in the bitterness
of my soul.
12Am I the sea, or a sea monster,
that you set a guard over me?
13When I say, 'My bed will comfort me,
my couch will ease my complaint,'
14then you scare me with dreams
and terrify me with visions,
15so that I would choose strangling
and death rather than my bones.
16I loathe my life; I would not live for ever.
Let me alone, for my days are a breath.
17What is man, that you make so much
of him,
and that you set your mind upon him,
18visit him every morning,
and test him every moment?
19How long will you not look away
from me,
nor let me alone till I swallow my spittle?

20 If I sin, what do I do to you, you watcher
of men?
Why have you made me your mark?
Why have I become a burden to you?
21 Why do you not pardon my transgression
and take away my iniquity?
For now I shall lie in the earth;
you will seek me, but I shall not be."

PROVERBS 29

15 The rod and reproof give wisdom,
but a child left to himself brings shame to
his mother.
16 When the wicked are in authority,
transgression increases;
but the righteous will look upon
their downfall.
17 Discipline your son, and he will give
you rest;
he will give delight to your heart.
18 Where there is no prophecy the people
cast off restraint,
but blessed is he who keeps the law.
19 By mere words a servant is not disciplined,
for though he understands, he will not
give heed.
20 Do you see a man who is hasty in his words?
There is more hope for a fool than
for him.
21 He who pampers his servant
from childhood,
will in the end find him his heir.
22 A man of wrath stirs up strife,
and a man given to anger causes much
transgression.
23 A man's pride will bring him low,
but he who is lowly in spirit will
obtain honor.
24 The partner of a thief hates his own life;
he hears the curse, but discloses nothing.
25 The fear of man lays a snare,
but he who trusts in the LORD is safe.
26 Many seek the favor of a ruler,
but from the LORD a man gets justice.
27 An unjust man is an abomination
to the righteous,
but he whose way is straight is an
abomination to the wicked.

ROMANS 15

**14 I myself am satisfied about
you, my brethren, that you yourselves are full of goodness, filled with all
knowledge, and able to instruct one an-**
other. 15 But on some points I have written to
you very boldly by way of reminder, because
of the grace given me by God 16 to be a minister
of Christ Jesus to the Gentiles in the priestly
service of the gospel of God, so that the offering of the Gentiles may be acceptable, sanctified by the Holy Spirit. 17 In Christ Jesus, then,
I have reason to be proud of my work for God.
18 For I will not venture to speak of anything except what Christ has wrought through me to
win obedience from the Gentiles, by word and
deed, 19 by the power of signs and wonders, by
the power of the Holy Spirit, so that from Jerusalem and as far round as Illyr′icum I have fully
preached the gospel of Christ, 20 thus making it
my ambition to preach the gospel, not where
Christ has already been named, lest I build on
another man's foundation, 21 but as it is written,
"They shall see who have never been told
of him,
and they shall understand who have never
heard of him."
22 This is the reason why I have so often been
hindered from coming to you. 23 But now,
since I no longer have any room for work
in these regions, and since I have longed for
many years to come to you, 24 I hope to see
you in passing as I go to Spain, and to be
sped on my journey there by you, once I
have enjoyed your company for a little. 25 At
present, however, I am going to Jerusalem
with aid for the saints. 26 For Macedonia and
Acha′ia have been pleased to make some
contribution for the poor among the saints
at Jerusalem; 27 they were pleased to do it, and
indeed they are in debt to them, for if the
Gentiles have come to share in their spiritual
blessings, they ought also to be of service to
them in material blessings. 28 When therefore
I have completed this, and have delivered to
them what has been raised, I shall go on by
way of you to Spain; 29 and I know that when I
come to you I shall come in the fulness of the
blessing of Christ.

[30]I appeal to you, brethren, by our Lord Jesus Christ and by the love of the Spirit, to strive together with me in your prayers to God on my behalf, [31]that I may be delivered from the unbelievers in Judea, and that my service for Jerusalem may be acceptable to the saints, [32]so that by God's will I may come to you with joy and be refreshed in your company. [33]The God of peace be with you all. Amen.

REFLECTION

St. Paul is pleased with the Christian community in Rome. They possess "goodness" and "knowledge," and they "instruct one another" (Rom 15:14). But Paul also reminds his audience that he has written to them "very boldly by way of reminder" (v. 15). We must not grow complacent in our faith. We should be ready to accept instruction, and even reproof, from our brethren. Similarly, it is one of the responsibilities of Church leaders to encourage us, guide us, and correct our failings, and we should not resist this correction. Even our life's trials, when borne with faith and reliance on God, are opportunities to grow in holiness. For God, who does not will our suffering but allows it, seeks always to conform us more perfectly to himself, even though at times this may be painful and unpleasant. Today's readings from both Job and Proverbs show us that our response to trials and strife can strengthen us. Humility and trust in God is the proper response. Do you resent your daily sufferings, or do you accept them as opportunities to grow in holiness?

August 18

JOB 8

Then Bildad the Shuhite answered:
[2]"How long will you say these things,
and the words of your mouth be a great wind?
[3]Does God pervert justice?
Or does the Almighty pervert the right?
[4]If your children have sinned against him,
he has delivered them into the power of their transgression.
[5]If you will seek God
and make supplication to the Almighty,
[6]if you are pure and upright,
surely then he will rouse himself for you
and reward you with a rightful habitation.
[7]And though your beginning was small,
your latter days will be very great.

[8]"For inquire, I beg you, of bygone ages,
and consider what the fathers have found;
[9]for we are but of yesterday, and know nothing,
for our days on earth are a shadow.
[10]Will they not teach you, and tell you,
and utter words out of their understanding?

[11]"Can papyrus grow where there is no marsh?
Can reeds flourish where there is no water?
[12]While yet in flower and not cut down,
they wither before any other plant.
[13]Such are the paths of all who forget God;
the hope of the godless man shall perish.
[14]His confidence breaks in sunder,
and his trust is a spider's web.
[15]He leans against his house, but it does not stand;
he lays hold of it, but it does not endure.
[16]He thrives before the sun,
and his shoots spread over his garden.
[17]His roots twine about the stone-heap;
he lives among the rocks.
[18]If he is destroyed from his place,
then it will deny him, saying, 'I have never seen you.'
[19]Behold, this is the joy of his way;
and out of the earth others will spring.

[20]"Behold, God will not reject a blameless man,
nor take the hand of evildoers.
[21]He will yet fill your mouth with laughter,
and your lips with shouting.
[22]Those who hate you will be clothed with shame,
and the tent of the wicked will be no more."

9 Then Job answered:
[2]"Truly I know that it is so:
But how can a man be just before God?
[3]If one wished to contend with him,
one could not answer him once in a
thousand times.
[4]He is wise in heart, and mighty in strength
—who has hardened himself against
him, and succeeded?—
[5]he who removes mountains, and they know
it not,
when he overturns them in his anger;
[6]who shakes the earth out of its place,
and its pillars tremble;
[7]who commands the sun, and it does
not rise;
who seals up the stars;
[8]who alone stretched out the heavens,
and trampled the waves of the sea;
[9]who made the Bear and Ori′on,
the Plei′ades and the chambers
of the south;
[10]who does great things beyond
understanding,
and marvelous things without number.
[11]Behold, he passes by me, and I see him not;
he moves on, but I do not perceive him.
[12]Behold, he snatches away; who can
hinder him?
Who will say to him, 'What are
you doing?'

[13]"God will not turn back his anger;
beneath him bowed the helpers of Ra′hab.
[14]How then can I answer him,
choosing my words with him?
[15]Though I am innocent, I cannot
answer him;
I must appeal for mercy to my accuser.
[16]If I summoned him and he answered me,
I would not believe that he was listening
to my voice.
[17]For he crushes me with a tempest,
and multiplies my wounds
without cause;
[18]he will not let me get my breath,
but fills me with bitterness.
[19]If it is a contest of strength, behold him!
If it is a matter of justice, who can
summon him?
[20]Though I am innocent, my own mouth
would condemn me;
though I am blameless, he would prove
me perverse.
[21]I am blameless; I regard not myself;
I loathe my life.
[22]It is all one; therefore I say,
he destroys both the blameless
and the wicked.
[23]When disaster brings sudden death,
he mocks at the calamity of the innocent.
[24]The earth is given into the hand of the wicked;
he covers the faces of its judges—
if it is not he, who then is it?

[25]"My days are swifter than a runner;
they flee away, they see no good.
[26]They go by like skiffs of reed,
like an eagle swooping on the prey.
[27]If I say, 'I will forget my complaint,
I will put off my sad countenance, and
be of good cheer,'
[28]I become afraid of all my suffering,
for I know you will not hold me innocent.
[29]I shall be condemned;
why then do I labor in vain?
[30]If I wash myself with snow,
and cleanse my hands with lye,
[31]yet you will plunge me into a pit,
and my own clothes will abhor me.
[32]For he is not a man, as I am, that I might
answer him,
that we should come to trial together.
[33]There is no umpire between us,
who might lay his hand upon us both.
[34]Let him take his rod away from me,
and let not dread of him terrify me.
[35]Then I would speak without fear of him,
for I am not so in myself.

10 "I loathe my life;
I will give free utterance to my
complaint;
I will speak in the bitterness of my soul.
[2]I will say to God, Do not condemn me;
let me know why you contend against me.
[3]Does it seem good to you to oppress,
to despise the work of your hands
and favor the designs of the wicked?
[4]Do you have eyes of flesh?
Do you see as man sees?

5Are your days as the days of man,
or your years as man's years,
6that you seek out my iniquity
and search for my sin,
7although you know that I am
not guilty,
and there is none to deliver out
of your hand?
8Your hands fashioned and made me;
and now you turn about
and destroy me.
9Remember that you have made me
of clay;
and will you turn me to dust again?
10Did you not pour me out like milk
and curdle me like cheese?
11You clothed me with skin and flesh,
and knit me together with bones
and sinews.
12You have granted me life and mercy;
and your care has preserved
my spirit.
13Yet these things you hid in your heart;
I know that this was your purpose.
14If I sin, you mark me,
and do not acquit me of my iniquity.
15If I am wicked, woe to me!
If I am righteous, I cannot lift up
my head,
for I am filled with disgrace
and look upon my affliction.
16And if I lift myself up, you hunt me like
a lion,
and again work wonders against me;
17you renew your witnesses against me,
and increase your vexation
toward me;
you bring fresh hosts against me.

18"Why did you bring me forth from
the womb?
Would that I had died before any eye
had seen me,
19and were as though I had not been,
carried from the womb to the grave.
20Are not the days of my life few?
Let me alone, that I may find a
little comfort
21before I go from where I shall not return,
to the land of gloom and deep darkness,
22the land of gloom and chaos,
where light is as darkness."

11 Then Zo′phar the Na′amathite answered:

2"Should a multitude of words go unanswered,
and a man full of talk be vindicated?
3Should your babble silence men,
and when you mock, shall no one
shame you?
4For you say, 'My doctrine is pure,
and I am clean in God's eyes.'
5But oh, that God would speak,
and open his lips to you,
6and that he would tell you the secrets
of wisdom!
For he is manifold in understanding.
Know then that God exacts of you less than
your guilt deserves.

7"Can you find out the deep things of God?
Can you find out the limit
of the Almighty?
8It is higher than heaven—what can you do?
Deeper than Sheol—what can you know?
9Its measure is longer than the earth,
and broader than the sea.
10If he passes through, and imprisons,
and calls to judgment, who can
hinder him?
11For he knows worthless men;
when he sees iniquity, will he not
consider it?
12But a stupid man will get understanding,
when a wild donkey's colt is born a man.

13"If you set your heart aright,
you will stretch out your hands
toward him.
14If iniquity is in your hand, put it far away,
and let not wickedness dwell in
your tents.
15Surely then you will lift up your face
without blemish;
you will be secure, and will not fear.
16You will forget your misery;
you will remember it as waters that have
passed away.
17And your life will be brighter than
the noonday;
its darkness will be like the morning.

[18]And you will have confidence, because
there is hope;
you will be protected and take your rest
in safety.
[19]You will lie down, and none will make
you afraid;
many will entreat your favor.
[20]But the eyes of the wicked will fail;
all way of escape will be lost to them,
and their hope is to breathe their last."

PROVERBS 30

The words of Agur son of Ja′keh of Mas′sa.

The man says to Ith′iel,
to Ithiel and U′cal:
[2]Surely I am too stupid to be a man.
I have not the understanding of a man.
[3]I have not learned wisdom,
nor have I knowledge of the Holy One.
[4]Who has ascended to heaven and
come down?
Who has gathered the wind in his fists?
Who has wrapped up the waters in
a garment?
Who has established all the ends of
the earth?
What is his name, and what is his
son's name?
Surely you know!

[5]Every word of God proves true;
he is a shield to those who take refuge
in him.
[6]Do not add to his words,
lest he rebuke you, and you be found a liar.

[7]Two things I ask of you;
deny them not to me before I die:
[8]Remove far from me falsehood
and lying;
give me neither poverty nor riches;
feed me with the food that is needful
for me,
[9]lest I be full, and deny you,
and say, "Who is the LORD?"
or lest I be poor, and steal,
and profane the name of my God.

[10]Do not slander a servant to his master,
lest he curse you, and you be held guilty.

[11]There are those who curse their fathers
and do not bless their mothers.
[12]There are those who are pure in their
own eyes
but are not cleansed of their filth.
[13]There are those—how lofty are
their eyes,
how high their eyelids lift!
[14]There are those whose teeth are swords,
whose teeth are knives,
to devour the poor from off the earth,
the needy from among men.

[15]The leech has two daughters;
"Give, give," they cry.
Three things are never satisfied;
four never say, "Enough":
[16]Sheol, the barren womb,
the earth ever thirsty for water,
and the fire which never says, "Enough."

[17]The eye that mocks a father
and scorns to obey a mother
will be picked out by the ravens of the valley
and eaten by the vultures.

ROMANS 16

I commend to you our sister Phoebe, a deaconess of the Church at Cen′chre-ae, [2]that you may receive her in the Lord as befits the saints, and help her in whatever she may require from you, for she has been a helper of many and of myself as well.
[3]Greet Prisca and Aqui′la, my fellow workers
in Christ Jesus, [4]who risked their necks for
my life, to whom not only I but also all the
churches of the Gentiles give thanks; [5]greet also
the church in their house. Greet my beloved
Epae′netus, who was the first convert in Asia
for Christ. [6]Greet Mary, who has worked hard
among you. [7]Greet Andron′icus and Ju′nias,
my kinsmen and my fellow prisoners; they

are men of note among the apostles, and they
were in Christ before me. 8Greet Amplia´tus,
my beloved in the Lord. 9Greet Urba´nus,
our fellow worker in Christ, and my beloved
Stachys. 10Greet Apel´les, who is approved in
Christ. Greet those who belong to the family of
Aristob´ulus. 11Greet my kinsman Hero´dion.
Greet those in the Lord who belong to the
family of Narcis´sus. 12Greet those workers in
the Lord, Tryphae´na and Trypho´sa. Greet
the beloved Persis, who has worked hard in
the Lord. 13Greet Rufus, eminent in the Lord,
also his mother and mine. 14Greet Asyn´critus,
Phlegon, Hermes, Patro´bas, Hermas, and
the brethren who are with them. 15Greet
Philol´ogus, Julia, Nereus and his sister, and
Olympas, and all the saints who are with them.
16Greet one another with a holy kiss. All the
churches of Christ greet you.

REFLECTION

In the midst of Job's experience, questions arise as to the reason behind his immense suffering. Is he being punished for his sinfulness? But if the righteous Job deserves such wrath, how can anyone be blameless before God? Sometimes we can fall into the trap of thinking "I'm not good or holy enough for God, so why bother?" Or perhaps we feel that if even the righteous suffer, what good does it do to strive for holiness? However, there is a difference between being humble and feeling worthless, and suffering is not an excuse for a complacent faith life. An important question is put to Job: "Can you find out the deep things of God? Can you find out the limit of the Almighty?" (Jb 11:7). When things happen that don't make sense to us, we are called to trust in a Creator whose plans transcend our ability to understand. It is humbling to know and acknowledge that the fullness of wisdom is beyond our human grasp. Yet, we are invited to continually pursue wisdom, which is God himself. When things seem senseless to you, do you give up, saying, "Nothing I do matters so why bother?" Or do you surrender yourself to God's plan even when you don't understand his grander purpose for your welfare?

August 19

JOB 12

Then Job answered:
2"No doubt you are the people,
and wisdom will die with you.
3But I have understanding as well as you;
I am not inferior to you.
Who does not know such things as these?
4I am a laughingstock to my friends;
I, who called upon God and he answered me,
a just and blameless man, am a laughingstock.
5In the thought of one who is at ease there is contempt for misfortune;
it is ready for those whose feet slip.
6The tents of robbers are at peace,
and those who provoke God are secure,
who bring their god in their hand.

7"But ask the beasts, and they will teach you;
the birds of the air, and they will tell you;
8or the plants of the earth, and they will teach you;
and the fish of the sea will declare to you.
9Who among all these does not know
that the hand of the LORD has done this?
10In his hand is the life of every living thing
and the breath of all mankind.
11Does not the ear try words
as the palate tastes food?
12Wisdom is with the aged,
and understanding in length of days.

13"With God are wisdom and might;
he has counsel and understanding.
14If he tears down, none can rebuild;
if he shuts a man in, none can open.
15If he withholds the waters, they dry up;
if he sends them out, they overwhelm the land.
16With him are strength and wisdom;
the deceived and the deceiver are his.

17He leads counselors away stripped,
and judges he makes fools.
18He looses the bonds of kings,
and binds a waistcloth on their loins.
19He leads priests away stripped,
and overthrows the mighty.
20He deprives of speech those who are trusted,
and takes away the discernment of the elders.
21He pours contempt on princes,
and looses the belt of the strong.
22He uncovers the deeps out of darkness,
and brings deep darkness to light.
23He makes nations great, and he destroys them:
he enlarges nations, and leads them away.
24He takes away understanding from the chiefs of the people of the earth,
and makes them wander in a pathless waste.
25They grope in the dark without light;
and he makes them stagger like a drunken man.

13 "Behold, my eye has seen all this,
my ear has heard and understood it.
2What you know, I also know;
I am not inferior to you.
3But I would speak to the Almighty,
and I desire to argue my case with God.
4As for you, you whitewash with lies;
worthless physicians are you all.
5Oh, that you would keep silent,
and it would be your wisdom!
6Hear now my reasoning,
and listen to the pleadings of my lips.
7Will you speak falsely for God,
and speak deceitfully for him?
8Will you show partiality toward him,
will you plead the case for God?
9Will it be well with you when he searches you out?
Or can you deceive him, as one deceives a man?
10He will surely rebuke you
if in secret you show partiality.
11Will not his majesty terrify you,
and the dread of him fall upon you?
12Your maxims are proverbs of ashes,
your defenses are defenses of clay.
13"Let me have silence, and I will speak,
and let come on me what may.
14I will take my flesh in my teeth,
and put my life in my hand.
15Behold, he will slay me; I have no hope;
yet I will defend my ways to his face.
16This will be my salvation,
that a godless man shall not come before him.
17Listen carefully to my words,
and let my declaration be in your ears.
18Behold, I have prepared my case;
I know that I shall be vindicated.
19Who is there that will contend with me?
For then I would be silent and die.
20Only grant two things to me,
then I will not hide myself from your face:
21withdraw your hand far from me,
and let not dread of you terrify me.
22Then call, and I will answer;
or let me speak, and do reply to me.
23How many are my iniquities and my sins?
Make me know my transgression and my sin.
24Why do you hide your face,
and count me as your enemy?
25Will you frighten a driven leaf
and pursue dry chaff?
26For you write bitter things against me,
and make me inherit the iniquities of my youth.
27You put my feet in the stocks,
and watch all my paths;
you set a bound to the soles of my feet.
28Man wastes away like a rotten thing,
like a garment that is moth-eaten.

14 "Man that is born of a woman is of few days, and full of trouble.
2He comes forth like a flower, and withers;
he flees like a shadow, and continues not.
3And do you open your eyes upon such a one
and bring him into judgment with you?
4Who can bring a clean thing out of an unclean?
There is not one.
5Since his days are determined,
and the number of his months is with you,
and you have appointed his bounds that he cannot pass,

[6]look away from him, and desist,
that he may enjoy, like a hireling, his day.

[7]"For there is hope for a tree,
if it be cut down, that it will
sprout again,
and that its shoots will not cease.
[8]Though its root grow old in the earth,
and its stump die in the ground,
[9]yet at the scent of water it will bud
and put forth branches like a
young plant.
[10]But man dies, and is laid low;
man breathes his last, and where is he?
[11]As waters fail from a lake,
and a river wastes away and dries up,
[12]so man lies down and rises not again;
till the heavens are no more he will
not awake,
or be roused out of his sleep.
[13]Oh, that you would hide me in Sheol,
that you would conceal me until your
wrath be past,
that you would appoint me a set time,
and remember me!
[14]If a man die, shall he live again?
All the days of my service I would wait,
till my release should come.
[15]You would call, and I would answer you;
you would long for the work of
your hands.
[16]For then you would number my steps,
you would not keep watch over my sin;
[17]my transgression would be sealed up in
a bag,
and you would cover over my iniquity.

[18]"But the mountain falls and crumbles away,
and the rock is removed from its place;
[19]the waters wear away the stones;
the torrents wash away the soil of
the earth;
so you destroy the hope of man.
[20]You prevail for ever against him, and
he passes;
you change his countenance, and send
him away.
[21]His sons come to honor, and he does not
know it;
they are brought low, and he perceives it not.
[22]He feels only the pain of his own body,
and he mourns only for himself."

15 Then Eli′phaz the Te′manite answered:
[2]"Should a wise man answer with
windy knowledge,
and fill himself with the east wind?
[3]Should he argue in unprofitable talk,
or in words with which he can do
no good?
[4]But you are doing away with the fear
of God,
and hindering meditation before God.
[5]For your iniquity teaches your mouth,
and you choose the tongue of the crafty.
[6]Your own mouth condemns you, and not I;
your own lips testify against you.

[7]"Are you the first man that was born?
Or were you brought forth before
the hills?
[8]Have you listened in the council of God?
And do you limit wisdom to yourself?
[9]What do you know that we do not know?
What do you understand that is not
clear to us?
[10]Both the gray-haired and the aged are
among us,
older than your father.
[11]Are the consolations of God too small
for you,
or the word that deals gently with you?
[12]Why does your heart carry you away,
and why do your eyes flash,
[13]that you turn your spirit against God,
and let such words go out of your mouth?
[14]What is man, that he can be clean?
Or he who is born of a woman, that he
can be righteous?
[15]Behold, God puts no trust in his holy ones,
and the heavens are not clean in his sight;
[16]how much less one who is abominable
and corrupt,
a man who drinks iniquity like water!

[17]"I will show you, hear me;
and what I have seen I will declare
[18](what wise men have told,
and their fathers have not hidden,
[19]to whom alone the land was given,
and no stranger passed among them).

[20]The wicked man writhes in pain all
his days,
through all the years that are laid up for
the ruthless.
[21]Terrifying sounds are in his ears;
in prosperity the destroyer will come
upon him.
[22]He does not believe that he will return out
of darkness,
and he is destined for the sword.
[23]He wanders abroad for bread, saying,
'Where is it?'
He knows that a day of darkness is
ready at his hand;
[24]distress and anguish terrify him;
they prevail against him, like a king
prepared for battle.
[25]Because he has stretched forth his hand
against God,
and bids defiance to the Almighty,
[26]running stubbornly against him
with a thick-bossed shield;
[27]because he has covered his face with
his fat,
and gathered fat upon his loins,
[28]and has lived in desolate cities,
in houses which no man should inhabit,
which were destined to become heaps
of ruins;
[29]he will not be rich, and his wealth will not
endure,
nor will he strike root in the earth;
[30]he will not escape from darkness;
the flame will dry up his shoots,
and his blossom will be swept away by
the wind.
[31]Let him not trust in emptiness,
deceiving himself;
for emptiness will be his recompense.
[32]It will be paid in full before his time,
and his branch will not be green.
[33]He will shake off his unripe grape,
like the vine,
and cast off his blossom, like the
olive tree.
[34]For the company of the godless is barren,
and fire consumes the tents of bribery.
[35]They conceive mischief and bring
forth evil
and their heart prepares deceit."

PROVERBS 30

[18]Three things are too wonderful
for me;
four I do not understand:
[19]the way of an eagle in the sky,
the way of a serpent on a rock,
the way of a ship on the high seas,
and the way of a man with a maiden.
[20]This is the way of an adulteress:
she eats, and wipes her mouth,
and says, "I have done no wrong."

[21]Under three things the earth trembles;
under four it cannot bear up:
[22]a slave when he becomes king,
and a fool when he is filled with food;
[23]an unloved woman when she gets
a husband,
and a maid when she succeeds
her mistress.

[24]Four things on earth are small,
but they are exceedingly wise:
[25]the ants are a people not strong,
yet they provide their food in
the summer;
[26]the badgers are a people not mighty,
yet they make their homes in
the rocks;
[27]the locusts have no king,
yet all of them march in rank;
[28]the lizard you can take in your hands,
yet it is in kings' palaces.

[29]Three things are stately in their tread;
four are stately in their stride:
[30]the lion, which is mightiest among beasts
and does not turn back before any;
[31]the strutting cock, the he-goat,
and a king striding before his people.

[32]If you have been foolish, exalting
yourself,
or if you have been devising evil,
put your hand on your mouth.
[33]For pressing milk produces curds,
pressing the nose produces blood,
and pressing anger produces strife.

ROMANS 16

[17]I appeal to you, brethren, to take note of those who create dissensions and difficulties, in opposition to the doctrine which you have been taught; avoid them. [18]For such persons do not serve our Lord Christ, but their own appetites, and by fair and flattering words they deceive the hearts of the simple-minded.
[19]For while your obedience is known to all, so that I rejoice over you, I would have you wise as to what is good and guileless as to what is evil; [20]then the God of peace will soon crush Satan under your feet. The grace of our Lord Jesus Christ be with you.

[21]Timothy, my fellow worker, greets you; so do Lucius and Jason and Sosip′ater, my kinsmen.

[22]I Tertius, the writer of this letter, greet you in the Lord.

[23]Ga′ius, who is host to me and to the whole Church, greets you. Eras′tus, the city treasurer, and our brother Quartus, greet you.

[25] Now to him who is able to strengthen you according to my gospel and the preaching of Jesus Christ, according to the revelation of the mystery which was kept secret for long ages [26]but is now disclosed and through the prophetic writings is made known to all nations, according to the command of the eternal God, to bring about the obedience of faith—[27]to the only wise God be glory for evermore through Jesus Christ! Amen.

REFLECTION

God is a great gathering force. Throughout the Scriptures he is continually drawing people of disparate backgrounds to himself. God desires all humanity to be one people, one believing community, living in covenant with him. Thus, unity is often viewed as a mark of God's presence and blessing. Conversely, disunity is often a result of opposition to God and his divine will. So, what should the believing Christian do when he or she encounters disunity or outright hostility? St. Paul advises the Roman community: "Take note of those who create dissensions and difficulties, in opposition to the doctrine which you have been taught; avoid them" (Rom 16:17). Often God places people in our lives in order to bring about spiritual growth—both ours and theirs. For instance, if we encounter someone who has a mistaken view about God or his Church, we must by word and example testify to the truth. However, we are not to go out on God's behalf looking for an argument. If confrontation finds us, we are called to respond with truth in love. Otherwise, it is good to avoid the dissenters, lest in our zeal we sow more disunity. Do you seek to evangelize by word and example for the glory of God and his living community, or do you seek out dissenters so that you may win debates and elevate your own standing?

August 20

JOB 16

Then Job answered:
[2]"I have heard many such things;
miserable comforters are you all.
[3]Shall windy words have an end?
Or what provokes you that you answer?
[4]I also could speak as you do,
if you were in my place;
I could join words together against you,
and shake my head at you.
[5]I could strengthen you with my mouth,
and the solace of my lips would assuage your pain.

[6]"If I speak, my pain is not assuaged,
and if I forbear, how much of it leaves me?
[7]Surely now God has worn me out;
he has made desolate all my company.

8And he has shriveled me up,
which is a witness against me;
and my leanness has risen up against me,
it testifies to my face.
9He has torn me in his wrath, and hated me;
he has gnashed his teeth at me;
my adversary sharpens his eyes
against me.
10Men have gaped at me with their mouth,
they have struck me insolently upon
the cheek,
they mass themselves together against me.
11God gives me up to the ungodly,
and casts me into the hands of the wicked.
12I was at ease, and he broke me asunder;
he seized me by the neck and dashed
me to pieces;
he set me up as his target,
13 his archers surround me.
He slashes open my kidneys, and does
not spare;
he pours out my gall on the ground.
14He breaks me with breach upon breach;
he runs upon me like a warrior.
15I have sewn sackcloth upon my skin,
and have laid my strength in the dust.
16My face is red with weeping,
and on my eyelids is deep darkness;
17although there is no violence in my hands,
and my prayer is pure.

18"O earth, cover not my blood,
and let my cry find no resting place.
19Even now, behold, my witness is in heaven,
and he that vouches for me is on high.
20My friends scorn me;
my eye pours out tears to God,
21that he would maintain the right of a man
with God,
like that of a man with his neighbor.
22For when a few years have come
I shall go the way from where I shall
not return.

17 My spirit is broken, my days are extinct,
the grave is ready for me.
2Surely there are mockers about me,
and my eye dwells on their provocation.

3"Lay down a pledge for me with yourself;
who is there that will give surety for me?
4Since you have closed their minds to
understanding,
therefore you will not let them triumph.
5He who informs against his friends to get a
share of their property,
the eyes of his children will fail.

6"He has made me a byword of the peoples,
and I am one before whom men spit.
7My eye has grown dim from grief,
and all my members are like a shadow.
8Upright men are appalled at this,
and the innocent stirs himself up
against the godless.
9Yet the righteous holds to his way,
and he that has clean hands grows
stronger and stronger.
10But you, come on again, all of you,
and I shall not find a wise man among you.
11My days are past, my plans are broken off,
the desires of my heart.
12They make night into day;
'The light,' they say, 'is near to
the darkness.'
13If I look for Sheol as my house,
if I spread my couch in darkness,
14if I say to the pit, 'You are my father,'
and to the worm, 'My mother,' or
'My sister,'
15where then is my hope?
Who will see my hope?
16Will it go down to the bars of Sheol?
Shall we descend together into the dust?"

18 Then Bildad the Shuhite answered:
2"How long will you hunt for words?
Consider, and then we will speak.
3Why are we counted as cattle?
Why are we stupid in your sight?
4You who tear yourself in your anger,
shall the earth be forsaken for you,
or the rock be removed out of its place?

5"Yes, the light of the wicked is put out,
and the flame of his fire does not shine.
6The light is dark in his tent,
and his lamp above him is put out.
7His strong steps are shortened
and his own schemes throw him down.
8For he is cast into a net by his own feet,
and he walks on a pitfall.

[9]A trap seizes him by the heel,
a snare lays hold of him.
[10]A rope is hid for him in the ground,
a trap for him in the path.
[11]Terrors frighten him on every side,
and chase him at his heels.
[12]His strength is hunger-bitten,
and calamity is ready for his stumbling.
[13]By disease his skin is consumed,
the first-born of death consumes
his limbs.
[14]He is torn from the tent in which he trusted,
and is brought to the king of terrors.
[15]In his tent dwells that which is none of his;
brimstone is scattered upon his habitation.
[16]His roots dry up beneath,
and his branches wither above.
[17]His memory perishes from the earth,
and he has no name in the street.
[18]He is thrust from light into darkness,
and driven out of the world.
[19]He has no offspring or descendant among
his people,
and no survivor where he used to live.
[20]They of the west are appalled at his day,
and horror seizes them of the east.
[21]Surely such are the dwellings of the ungodly,
such is the place of him who knows
not God."

19 Then Job answered:
[2]"How long will you torment me,
and break me in pieces with words?
[3]These ten times you have cast reproach
upon me;
are you not ashamed to wrong me?
[4]And even if it be true that I have erred,
my error remains with myself.
[5]If indeed you magnify yourselves against me,
and make my humiliation an argument
against me,
[6]know then that God has put me in
the wrong,
and closed his net about me.
[7]Behold, I cry out, 'Violence!' but I am not
answered;
I call aloud, but there is no justice.
[8]He has walled up my way, so that I
cannot pass,
and he has set darkness upon
my paths.
[9]He has stripped from me my glory,
and taken the crown from my head.
[10]He breaks me down on every side, and I
am gone,
and my hope has he pulled up like a tree.
[11]He has kindled his wrath against me,
and counts me as his adversary.
[12]His troops come on together;
they have cast up siegeworks against me,
and encamp round about my tent.

[13]"He has put my brethren far from me,
and my acquaintances are wholly
estranged from me.
[14]My kinsfolk and my close friends have
failed me;
[15] the guests in my house have forgotten me;
my maidservants count me as a stranger;
I have become an alien in their eyes.
[16]I call to my servant, but he gives me
no answer;
I must beseech him with my mouth.
[17]I am repulsive to my wife,
loathsome to the sons of my own mother.
[18]Even young children despise me;
when I rise they talk against me.
[19]All my intimate friends abhor me,
and those whom I loved have turned
against me.
[20]My bones cling to my skin and to my flesh,
and I have escaped by the skin of my teeth.
[21]Have pity on me, have pity on me, O you
my friends,
for the hand of God has touched me!
[22]Why do you, like God, pursue me?
Why are you not satisfied with my flesh?

[23]"Oh, that my words were written!
Oh, that they were inscribed in a book!
[24]Oh, that with an iron pen and lead
they were graven in the rock for ever!
[25]For I know that my Redeemer lives,
and at last he will stand upon the earth;
[26]and after my skin has been thus destroyed,
then from my flesh I shall see God,
[27]whom I shall see on my side,
and my eyes shall behold, and not another.
My heart faints within me!
[28]If you say, 'How we will pursue him!'
and, 'The root of the matter is found in him';

[29]be afraid of the sword,
for wrath brings the punishment
of the sword,
that you may know there is a judgment."

PROVERBS 31

The words of Lem′uel, king of Massa, which his mother taught him:

[2]What, my son? What, son of my womb?
What, son of my vows?
[3]Give not your strength to women,
your ways to those who destroy kings.
[4]It is not for kings, O Lem′uel,
it is not for kings to drink wine,
or for rulers to desire strong drink;
[5]lest they drink and forget what has
been decreed,
and pervert the rights of all the afflicted.
[6]Give strong drink to him who is perishing,
and wine to those in bitter distress;
[7]let them drink and forget their poverty,
and remember their misery no more.
[8]Open your mouth for the mute,
for the rights of all who are left desolate.
[9]Open your mouth, judge righteously,
maintain the rights of the poor and needy.

---

1 CORINTHIANS 1

Paul, called by the will of God to be an apostle of Christ Jesus, and our brother Sos′thenes,

[2]To the Church of God which is at Corinth, to those sanctified in Christ Jesus, called to be saints together with all those who in every place call on the name of our Lord Jesus Christ, both their Lord and ours:

[3]Grace to you and peace from God our Father and the Lord Jesus Christ.

[4]I give thanks to God always for you
because of the grace of God which was given
you in Christ Jesus, [5]that in every way you
were enriched in him with all speech and all
knowledge—[6]even as the testimony to Christ
was confirmed among you—[7]so that you are
not lacking in any spiritual gift, as you wait for
the revealing of our Lord Jesus Christ; [8]who
will sustain you to the end, guiltless in the day
of our Lord Jesus Christ. [9]God is faithful, by
whom you were called into the fellowship of
his Son, Jesus Christ our Lord.

[10]I appeal to you, brethren, by the name of
our Lord Jesus Christ, that all of you agree and
that there be no dissensions among you, but
that you be united in the same mind and the
same judgment. [11]For it has been reported to
me by Chlo′e's people that there is quarreling
among you, my brethren. [12]What I mean is that
each one of you says, "I belong to Paul," or "I
belong to Apol′los," or "I belong to Ce′phas," or
"I belong to Christ." [13]Is Christ divided? Was
Paul crucified for you? Or were you baptized
in the name of Paul? [14]I am thankful that I
baptized none of you except Crispus and
Ga′ius; [15]lest any one should say that you were
baptized in my name. [16](I did baptize also the
household of Steph′anas. Beyond that, I do not
know whether I baptized any one else.) [17]For
Christ did not send me to baptize but to preach
the gospel, and not with eloquent wisdom, lest
the cross of Christ be emptied of its power.

[18]For the word of the cross is folly to those
who are perishing, but to us who are being
saved it is the power of God. [19]For it is written,
"I will destroy the wisdom of the wise,
and the cleverness of the clever I will thwart."
[20]Where is the wise man? Where is the scribe?
Where is the debater of this age? Has not God
made foolish the wisdom of the world? [21]For
since, in the wisdom of God, the world did not
know God through wisdom, it pleased God
through the folly of what we preach to save
those who believe. [22]For Jews demand signs
and Greeks seek wisdom, [23]but we preach
Christ crucified, a stumbling block to Jews and
folly to Gentiles, [24]but to those who are called,
both Jews and Greeks, Christ the power of God
and the wisdom of God. [25]For the foolishness
of God is wiser than men, and the weakness of
God is stronger than men.

[26]For consider your call, brethren; not many
of you were wise according to the flesh, not
many were powerful, not many were of noble
birth; [27]but God chose what is foolish in the

world to shame the wise, God chose what is weak in the world to shame the strong, [28]God chose what is low and despised in the world, even things that are not, to bring to nothing things that are, [29]so that no flesh might boast in the presence of God. [30]He is the source of your life in Christ Jesus, whom God made our wisdom, our righteousness and sanctification and redemption; [31]therefore, as it is written, "Let him who boasts, boast of the Lord."

REFLECTION

"Is Christ divided? Was Paul crucified for you? Or were you baptized in the name of Paul?" (1 Cor 1:13). In St. Paul's opening message to the Corinthians he urges his audience to shift their focus back to God. A disordered focus on the ministers of God, like Peter, Paul, and Apollos had led to quarreling and divisions. Perhaps one minister is more eloquent than another, or cares for his flock in a preferred way, etc., and as a result cliques begin to form. For Paul, to turn one's focus away from Jesus leads to the loss of unity. Thus, the Apostle summons the Corinthians to remember that they were baptized into Jesus Christ, all of them, regardless of who ministered to and baptized them, they were washed in Christ. Eloquent rhetoric, preaching, music, or programs are not the substance of the Gospel. These are accidental; the Cross is essential. At Calvary there is only naked love giving of self, and that is the heart of God, and thus Christian unity. Are we tempted today to evaluate the Church based on worldly wisdom and criteria, or by the Cross?

August 21

JOB 20

Then Zoʹphar the Naʹamathite answered:

[2]"Therefore my thoughts answer me,
because of my haste within me.
[3]I hear censure which insults me,
and out of my understanding a spirit answers me.
[4]Do you not know this from of old,
since man was placed upon earth,
[5]that the exulting of the wicked is short,
and the joy of the godless but for a moment?
[6]Though his height mount up to the heavens,
and his head reach to the clouds,
[7]he will perish for ever like his own dung;
those who have seen him will say, 'Where is he?'
[8]He will fly away like a dream, and not be found;
he will be chased away like a vision of the night.
[9]The eye which saw him will see him no more,
nor will his place any more behold him.
[10]His children will seek the favor of the poor,
and his hands will give back his wealth.
[11]His bones are full of youthful vigor,
but it will lie down with him in the dust.

[12]"Though wickedness is sweet in his mouth,
though he hides it under his tongue,
[13]though he is loath to let it go,
and holds it in his mouth,
[14]yet his food is turned in his stomach;
it is the gall of asps within him.
[15]He swallows down riches and vomits them up again;
God casts them out of his belly.
[16]He will suck the poison of asps;
the tongue of a viper will kill him.
[17]He will not look upon the rivers,
the streams flowing with honey and curds.
[18]He will give back the fruit of his toil,
and will not swallow it down;
from the profit of his trading
he will get no enjoyment.
[19]For he has crushed and abandoned the poor,
he has seized a house which he did not build.

[20]"Because his greed knew no rest,
he will not save anything in which he delights.
[21]There was nothing left after he had eaten;
therefore his prosperity will not endure.

22 In the fulness of his sufficiency he will be
in straits;
all the force of misery will come upon him.
23 To fill his belly to the full
God will send his fierce anger into him,
and rain it upon him as his food.
24 He will flee from an iron weapon;
a bronze arrow will strike him through.
25 It is drawn forth and comes out of his body,
the glittering point comes out of his gall;
terrors come upon him.
26 Utter darkness is laid up for his treasures;
a fire not blown upon will devour him;
what is left in his tent will be consumed.
27 The heavens will reveal his iniquity,
and the earth will rise up against him.
28 The possessions of his house will be
carried away,
dragged off in the day of God's wrath.
29 This is the wicked man's portion from God,
the heritage decreed for him by God."

21 Then Job answered:
2 "Listen carefully to my words,
and let this be your consolation.
3 Bear with me, and I will speak,
and after I have spoken, mock on.
4 As for me, is my complaint against man?
Why should I not be impatient?
5 Look at me, and be appalled,
and lay your hand upon your mouth.
6 When I think of it I am dismayed,
and shuddering seizes my flesh.
7 Why do the wicked live,
reach old age, and grow mighty in power?
8 Their children are established in
their presence,
and their offspring before their eyes.
9 Their houses are safe from fear,
and no rod of God is upon them.
10 Their bull breeds without fail;
their cow calves, and does not cast her calf.
11 They send forth their little ones like a flock,
and their children dance.
12 They sing to the tambourine and the lyre,
and rejoice to the sound of the pipe.
13 They spend their days in prosperity,
and in peace they go down to Sheol.
14 They say to God, 'Depart from us!
We do not desire the knowledge of
your ways.
15 What is the Almighty, that we should
serve him?
And what profit do we get if we pray
to him?'
16 Behold, is not their prosperity in their hand?
The counsel of the wicked is far from me.

17 "How often is it that the lamp of the wicked
is put out?
That their calamity comes upon them?
That God distributes pains in his anger?
18 That they are like straw before the wind,
and like chaff that the storm carries away?
19 You say, 'God stores up their iniquity for
their sons.'
Let him recompense it to themselves,
that they may know it.
20 Let their own eyes see their destruction,
and let them drink of the wrath of
the Almighty.
21 For what do they care for their houses
after them,
when the number of their months is
cut off?
22 Will any teach God knowledge,
seeing that he judges those that are
on high?
23 One dies in full prosperity,
being wholly at ease and secure,
24 his body full of fat
and the marrow of his bones moist.
25 Another dies in bitterness of soul,
never having tasted of good.
26 They lie down alike in the dust,
and the worms cover them.

27 "Behold, I know your thoughts,
and your schemes to wrong me.
28 For you say, 'Where is the house of
the prince?
Where is the tent in which the
wicked dwelt?'
29 Have you not asked those who travel
the roads,
and do you not accept their testimony
30 that the wicked man is spared in the day
of calamity,
that he is rescued in the day of wrath?
31 Who declares his way to his face,
and who repays him for what he has done?

32 When he is borne to the grave,
watch is kept over his tomb.
33 The clods of the valley are sweet to him;
all men follow after him,
and those who go before him
are innumerable.
34 How then will you comfort me with
empty nothings?
There is nothing left of your answers
but falsehood."

22 Then Eli′phaz the Te′manite answered:
2 "Can a man be profitable to God?
Surely he who is wise is profitable
to himself.
3 Is it any pleasure to the Almighty if you
are righteous,
or is it gain to him if you make your
ways blameless?
4 Is it for your fear of him that he reproves you,
and enters into judgment with you?
5 Is not your wickedness great?
There is no end to your iniquities.
6 For you have exacted pledges of your
brothers for nothing,
and stripped the naked of their clothing.
7 You have given no water to the weary
to drink,
and you have withheld bread from
the hungry.
8 The man with power possessed the land,
and the favored man dwelt in it.
9 You have sent widows away empty,
and the arms of the fatherless
were crushed.
10 Therefore snares are round about you,
and sudden terror overwhelms you;
11 your light is darkened, so that you cannot see,
and a flood of water covers you.

12 "Is not God high in the heavens?
See the highest stars, how lofty they are!
13 Therefore you say, 'What does God know?
Can he judge through the deep darkness?
14 Thick clouds enwrap him, so that he does
not see,
and he walks on the vault of heaven.'
15 Will you keep to the old way
which wicked men have trod?
16 They were snatched away before their time;
their foundation was washed away.
17 They said to God, 'Depart from us,'
and 'What can the Almighty do to us?'
18 Yet he filled their houses with
good things—
but the counsel of the wicked is far
from me.
19 The righteous see it and are glad;
the innocent laugh them to scorn,
20 saying, 'Surely our adversaries are cut off,
and what they left the fire has consumed.'

21 "Agree with God, and be at peace;
thereby good will come to you.
22 Receive instruction from his mouth,
and lay up his words in your heart.
23 If you return to the Almighty and
humble yourself,
if you remove unrighteousness far from
your tents,
24 if you lay gold in the dust,
and gold of O′phir among the stones of
the torrent bed,
25 and if the Almighty is your gold,
and your precious silver;
26 then you will delight yourself in
the Almighty,
and lift up your face to God.
27 You will make your prayer to him, and he
will hear you;
and you will pay your vows.
28 You will decide on a matter, and it will be
established for you,
and light will shine on your ways.
29 For God abases the proud,
but he saves the lowly.
30 He delivers the innocent man;
you will be delivered through the
cleanness of your hands."

23 Then Job answered:
2 "Today also my complaint is bitter,
his hand is heavy in spite of my groaning.
3 Oh, that I knew where I might find him,
that I might come even to his seat!
4 I would lay my case before him
and fill my mouth with arguments.
5 I would learn what he would answer me,
and understand what he would say to me.
6 Would he contend with me in the greatness
of his power?
No; he would give heed to me.

7There an upright man could reason with him,
and I should be acquitted for ever by
my judge.

8"Behold, I go forward, but he is not there;
and backward, but I cannot perceive him;
9on the left hand I seek him, but I cannot
behold him;
I turn to the right hand, but I cannot
see him.
10But he knows the way that I take;
when he has tried me, I shall come forth
as gold.
11My foot has held fast to his steps;
I have kept his way and have not
turned aside.
12I have not departed from the commandment
of his lips;
I have treasured in my bosom the words
of his mouth.
13But he is unchangeable and who can
turn him?
What he desires, that he does.
14For he will complete what he appoints
for me;
and many such things are in his mind.
15Therefore I am terrified at his presence;
when I consider, I am in dread of him.
16God has made my heart faint;
the Almighty has terrified me;
17for I am hemmed in by darkness,
and thick darkness covers my face."

PROVERBS 31

10Who can find a good wife?
She is far more precious than jewels.
11The heart of her husband trusts in her,
and he will have no lack of gain.
12She does him good, and not harm,
all the days of her life.
13She seeks wool and flax,
and works with willing hands.
14She is like the ships of the merchant,
she brings her food from afar.
15She rises while it is yet night
and provides food for her household
and tasks for her maidens.
16She considers a field and buys it;
with the fruit of her hands she plants
a vineyard.
17She clothes her loins with strength
and makes her arms strong.
18She perceives that her merchandise
is profitable.
Her lamp does not go out at night.
19She puts her hands to the distaff,
and her hands hold the spindle.
20She opens her hand to the poor,
and reaches out her hands to the needy.
21She is not afraid of snow for her household,
for all her household are clothed
in scarlet.
22She makes herself coverings;
her clothing is fine linen and purple.
23Her husband is known in the gates,
when he sits among the elders of the land.
24She makes linen garments and sells them;
she delivers sashes to the merchant.
25Strength and dignity are her clothing,
and she laughs at the time to come.
26She opens her mouth with wisdom,
and the teaching of kindness is on
her tongue.
27She looks well to the ways of her household,
and does not eat the bread of idleness.
28Her children rise up and call her blessed;
her husband also, and he praises her:
29"Many women have done excellently,
but you surpass them all."
30Charm is deceitful, and beauty is vain,
but a woman who fears the LORD is to
be praised.
31Give her of the fruit of her hands,
and let her works praise her in the gates.

---

1 CORINTHIANS 2

**When I came to you, brethren,
I did not come proclaiming to
you the testimony of God in lofty words
or wisdom. 2For I decided to know nothing among you except Jesus Christ and**
him crucified. 3And I was with you in weakness and in much fear and trembling;
4and my speech and my message were
not in plausible words of wisdom, but in

demonstration of the Spirit and of power,
5that your faith might not rest in the wisdom of men but in the power of God.

6Yet among the mature we do impart wisdom, although it is not a wisdom of this age or of the rulers of this age, who are doomed to pass away.
7But we impart a secret and hidden wisdom of God, which God decreed before the ages for our glorification.
8None of the rulers of this age understood this; for if they had, they would not have crucified the Lord of glory.
9But, as it is written,

"What no eye has seen, nor ear heard,
nor the heart of man conceived,
what God has prepared for those who
love him,"

10God has revealed to us through the Spirit. For the Spirit searches everything, even the depths of God.
11For what person knows a man's thoughts except the spirit of the man which is in him? So also no one comprehends the thoughts of God except the Spirit of God.
12Now we have received not the spirit of the world, but the Spirit which is from God, that we might understand the gifts bestowed on us by God.
13And we impart this in words not taught by human wisdom but taught by the Spirit, interpreting spiritual truths to those who possess the Spirit.

14The unspiritual man does not receive the gifts of the Spirit of God, for they are folly to him, and he is not able to understand them because they are spiritually discerned.
15The spiritual man judges all things, but is himself to be judged by no one.
16"For who has known the mind of the Lord so as to instruct him?" But we have the mind of Christ.

REFLECTION

In Proverbs 31, the mother of Lemuel describes for her son the character of the godly wife. This chapter, according to Jewish tradition, was the advice of the queen mother Bathsheba for her son King Solomon. In verse 10 the term "good wife" literally means valiant, or strong, for indeed she is in this account. She is of tremendous value, and what is first noted is the depth of her relationship with her husband, marked by deep trust. Second, she is not only industrious, she is entrepreneurial. Her work and house management lead to abundance for her family, but even beyond her family to care for the poor (Prv 31:20). She can give generously because she does not fear the future; because she is prudent she is without anxiety. The root of her fearlessness stems from what she gives her children: "wisdom" and "the teaching of kindness," which literally means the Torah, that is the Word of God. She is the teacher of faith, and thus she provides something of better value than prosperity and security, and so her children and husband will praise her, for "a woman who fears the Lord is to be praised" (v. 30). Scripture lauds the valiant woman. Who is a woman you know with these qualities?

August 22

JOB 24

"Why are not times of judgment kept by the Almighty,
and why do those who know him
never see his days?
2Men remove landmarks;
they seize flocks and pasture them.
3They drive away the donkey of
the fatherless;
they take the widow's ox for a pledge.
4They thrust the poor off the road;
the poor of the earth all hide themselves.
5Behold, like wild donkeys in the desert
they go forth to their toil,
seeking prey in the wilderness
as food for their children.
6They gather their fodder in the field
and they glean the vineyard of the
wicked man.
7They lie all night naked, without clothing,
and have no covering in the cold.
8They are wet with the rain of the mountains,
and cling to the rock for want of shelter.

9(There are those who snatch the fatherless
child from the breast,
and take in pledge the infant of the poor.)
10They go about naked, without clothing;
hungry, they carry the sheaves;
11among the olive rows of the wicked they
make oil;
they tread the wine presses, but
suffer thirst.
12From out of the city the dying groan,
and the soul of the wounded cries
for help;
yet God pays no attention to their prayer.

13"There are those who rebel against the light,
who are not acquainted with its ways,
and do not stay in its paths.
14The murderer rises in the dark,
that he may kill the poor and needy;
and in the night he is as a thief.
15The eye of the adulterer also waits for
the twilight,
saying, 'No eye will see me';
and he disguises his face.
16In the dark they dig through houses;
by day they shut themselves up;
they do not know the light.
17For deep darkness is morning to all of them;
for they are friends with the terrors of
deep darkness.

18"You say, 'They are swiftly carried away
upon the face of the waters;
their portion is cursed in the land;
no treader turns toward their vineyards.
19Drought and heat snatch away the
snow waters;
so does Sheol those who have sinned.
20The squares of the town forget them;
their name is no longer remembered;
so wickedness is broken like a tree.'

21"They feed on the barren childless woman,
and do no good to the widow.
22Yet God prolongs the life of the mighty by
his power;
they rise up when they despair of life.
23He gives them security, and they
are supported;
and his eyes are upon their ways.
24They are exalted a little while, and then
are gone;
they wither and fade like the mallow;
they are cut off like the heads of grain.
25If it is not so, who will prove me a liar,
and show that there is nothing in what
I say?"

25 Then Bildad the Shuhite answered:
2"Dominion and fear are with God;
he makes peace in his high heaven.
3Is there any number to his armies?
Upon whom does his light not arise?
4How then can man be righteous before God?
How can he who is born of woman
be clean?
5Behold, even the moon is not bright
and the stars are not clean in his sight;
6how much less man, who is a maggot,
and the son of man, who is a worm!"

26 Then Job answered:
2"How you have helped him who has
no power!
How you have saved the arm that has
no strength!
3How you have counseled him who has
no wisdom,
and plentifully declared sound
knowledge!
4With whose help have you uttered words,
and whose spirit has come forth from you?
5The shades below tremble,
the waters and their inhabitants.
6Sheol is naked before God,
and Abad′don has no covering.
7He stretches out the north over the void,
and hangs the earth upon nothing.
8He binds up the waters in his thick clouds,
and the cloud is not torn under them.
9He covers the face of the moon,
and spreads over it his cloud.
10He has described a circle upon the face of
the waters
at the boundary between light
and darkness.
11The pillars of heaven tremble,
and are astounded at his rebuke.
12By his power he stilled the sea;
by his understanding he struck Ra′hab.
13By his wind the heavens were made fair;
his hand pierced the fleeing serpent.

14Behold, these are but the outskirts of his ways;
and how small a whisper do we hear of him!
But the thunder of his power who can
understand?"

27 And Job again took up his discourse,
and said:
2"As God lives, who has taken away my right,
and the Almighty, who has made my
soul bitter;
3as long as my breath is in me,
and the spirit of God is in my nostrils;
4my lips will not speak falsehood,
and my tongue will not utter deceit.
5Far be it from me to say that you are right;
till I die I will not put away my integrity
from me.
6I hold fast my righteousness, and will not
let it go;
my heart does not reproach me for any
of my days.

7"Let my enemy be as the wicked,
and let him that rises up against me be
as the unrighteous.
8For what is the hope of the godless when
God cuts him off,
when God takes away his life?
9Will God hear his cry,
when trouble comes upon him?
10Will he take delight in the Almighty?
Will he call upon God at all times?
11I will teach you concerning the hand of God;
what is with the Almighty I will
not conceal.
12Behold, all of you have seen it yourselves;
why then have you become
altogether vain?

13"This is the portion of a wicked man
with God,
and the heritage which oppressors
receive from the Almighty:
14If his children are multiplied, it is for
the sword;
and his offspring have not enough to eat.
15Those who survive him the
pestilence buries,
and their widows make no lamentation.
16Though he heap up silver like dust,
and pile up clothing like clay;
17he may pile it up, but the just will wear it,
and the innocent will divide the silver.
18The house which he builds is like a
spider's web,
like a booth which a watchman makes.
19He goes to bed rich, but will do so
no more;
he opens his eyes, and his wealth is gone.
20Terrors overtake him like a flood;
in the night a whirlwind carries him off.
21The east wind lifts him up and he is gone;
it sweeps him out of his place.
22It hurls at him without pity;
he flees from its power in
headlong flight.
23It claps its hands at him,
and hisses at him from its place.

28 "Surely there is a mine for silver,
and a place for gold which they refine.
2Iron is taken out of the earth,
and copper is smelted from the ore.
3Men put an end to darkness,
and search out to the farthest bound
the ore in gloom and deep darkness.
4They open shafts in a valley away from
where men live;
they are forgotten by travelers,
they hang afar from men, they swing
back and forth.
5As for the earth, out of it comes bread;
but underneath it is turned up as by fire.
6Its stones are the place of sapphires,
and it has dust of gold.

7"That path no bird of prey knows,
and the falcon's eye has not seen it.
8The proud beasts have not trodden it;
the lion has not passed over it.

9"Man puts his hand to the flinty rock,
and overturns mountains by the roots.
10He cuts out channels in the rocks,
and his eye sees every precious thing.
11He binds up the streams so that they do
not trickle,
and the thing that is hidden he brings
forth to light.

12"But where shall wisdom be found?
And where is the place of understanding?

13 Man does not know the way to it,
and it is not found in the land of
the living.
14 The deep says, 'It is not in me,'
and the sea says, 'It is not with me.'
15 It cannot be gotten for gold,
and silver cannot be weighed as
its price.
16 It cannot be valued in the gold of O′phir,
in precious onyx or sapphire.
17 Gold and glass cannot equal it,
nor can it be exchanged for jewels of
fine gold.
18 No mention shall be made of coral or
of crystal;
the price of wisdom is above pearls.
19 The topaz of Ethiopia cannot compare
with it,
nor can it be valued in pure gold.

20 "From where does wisdom come?
And where is the place of understanding?
21 It is hidden from the eyes of all living,
and concealed from the birds of the air.
22 Abad′don and Death say,
'We have heard a rumor of it with
our ears.'

23 "God understands the way to it,
and he knows its place.
24 For he looks to the ends of the earth,
and sees everything under the heavens.
25 When he gave to the wind its weight,
and meted out the waters by measure;
26 when he made a decree for the rain,
and a way for the lightning of
the thunder;
27 then he saw it and declared it;
he established it, and searched it out.
28 And he said to man,
'Behold, the fear of the Lord, that is wisdom;
and to depart from evil is understanding.'"

ECCLESIASTES 1

The words of the Preacher, the son of David,
king in Jerusalem.
2 Vanity of vanities, says the Preacher,
vanity of vanities! All is vanity.
3 What does man gain by all the toil
at which he toils under the sun?
4 A generation goes, and a generation comes,
but the earth remains for ever.
5 The sun rises and the sun goes down,
and hastens to the place where it rises.
6 The wind blows to the south,
and goes round to the north;
round and round goes the wind,
and on its circuits the wind returns.
7 All streams run to the sea,
but the sea is not full;
to the place where the streams flow,
there they flow again.
8 All things are full of weariness;
a man cannot utter it;
the eye is not satisfied with seeing,
nor the ear filled with hearing.
9 What has been is what will be,
and what has been done is what will
be done;
and there is nothing new under the sun.
10 Is there a thing of which it is said,
"See, this is new"?
It has been already,
in the ages before us.
11 There is no remembrance of former things,
nor will there be any remembrance
of later things yet to happen
among those who come after.
12 I the Preacher have been king over Israel
in Jerusalem. 13 And I applied my mind to
seek and to search out by wisdom all that is
done under heaven; it is an unhappy business
that God has given to the sons of men to be
busy with. 14 I have seen everything that is
done under the sun; and behold, all is vanity
and a striving after wind.
15 What is crooked cannot be made straight,
and what is lacking cannot be numbered.
16 I said to myself, "I have acquired great
wisdom, surpassing all who were over
Jerusalem before me; and my mind has had
great experience of wisdom and knowledge."
17 And I applied my mind to know wisdom
and to know madness and folly. I perceived
that this also is but a striving after wind.
18 For in much wisdom is much vexation,
and he who increases knowledge
increases sorrow.

1 CORINTHIANS 3

But I, brethren, could not address you as spiritual men, but as men of the flesh, as infants in Christ. 2I fed you with milk, not solid food; for you were not ready for it; and even yet you are not ready, 3for you are still of the flesh. For while there is jealousy and strife among you, are you not of the flesh, and behaving like ordinary men? 4For when one says, "I belong to Paul," and another, "I belong to Apol′los," are you not merely men?

5What then is Apol′los? What is Paul? Servants through whom you believed, as the Lord assigned to each. 6I planted, Apol′los watered, but God gave the growth. 7So neither he who plants nor he who waters is anything, but only God who gives the growth. 8He who plants and he who waters are equal, and each shall receive his wages according to his labor. 9For we are God's fellow workers; you are God's field, God's building.

10According to the commission of God given to me, like a skilled master builder I laid a foundation, and another man is building upon it. Let each man take care how he builds upon it. 11For no other foundation can any one lay than that which is laid, which is Jesus Christ. 12Now if any one builds on the foundation with gold, silver, precious stones, wood, hay, straw—13each man's work will become manifest; for the Day will disclose it, because it will be revealed with fire, and the fire will test what sort of work each one has done. 14If the work which any man has built on the foundation survives, he will receive a reward. 15If any man's work is burned up, he will suffer loss, though he himself will be saved, but only as through fire.

16Do you not know that you are God's temple and that God's Spirit dwells in you? 17If any one destroys God's temple, God will destroy him. For God's temple is holy, and that temple you are.

18Let no one deceive himself. If any one among you thinks that he is wise in this age, let him become a fool that he may become wise. 19For the wisdom of this world is folly with God. For it is written, "He catches the wise in their craftiness," 20and again, "The Lord knows that the thoughts of the wise are futile." 21So let no one boast of men. For all things are yours, 22whether Paul or Apol′los or Ce′phas or the world or life or death or the present or the future, all are yours; 23and you are Christ's; and Christ is God's.

REFLECTION

"But where shall wisdom be found? And where is the place of understanding? Man does not know the way to it, and it is not found in the land of the living" (Jb 28:12–13). True wisdom is not something that can be mined, traded, or purchased, yet it is something every human heart naturally yearns to attain. Ecclesiastes reminds us that all creation is temporary and finite, and the things of this world can never satisfy us. The poet has seen "everything that is done under the sun; and behold, all is vanity" (Eccl 1:14). However, the divine transcends the created order, and in God we find our true fulfillment. For St. Paul, when the wisdom of the world is compared with the ways of God, it is mere folly. This is his message to the Corinthians, who are preoccupied with petty matters of prestige rather than the spiritual significance of the Gospel. Often, we all need to be reminded that Jesus is our only true and lasting foundation. It is incumbent upon us, as God's temples in which the Holy Spirit dwells, to forsake earthly vanities in the pursuit of spiritual wisdom. Only this will lead to spiritual fulfillment. Do you seek fulfillment from spiritual things, or from things of this world?

August 23

JOB 29

And Job again took up his discourse, and said:

2"Oh, that I were as in the months of old,
as in the days when God watched over me;

[3]when his lamp shone upon my head,
and by his light I walked through darkness;
[4]as I was in my autumn days,
when the friendship of God was upon
my tent;
[5]when the Almighty was yet with me,
when my children were about me;
[6]when my steps were washed with milk,
and the rock poured out for me streams
of oil!
[7]When I went out to the gate of the city,
when I prepared my seat in the square,
[8]the young men saw me and withdrew,
and the aged rose and stood;
[9]the princes refrained from talking,
and laid their hand on their mouth;
[10]the voice of the nobles was hushed,
and their tongue cleaved to the roof of
their mouth.
[11]When the ear heard, it called me blessed,
and when the eye saw, it approved;
[12]because I delivered the poor who cried,
and the fatherless who had none to
help him.
[13]The blessing of him who was about to
perish came upon me,
and I caused the widow's heart to sing
for joy.
[14]I put on righteousness, and it clothed me;
my justice was like a robe and a turban.
[15]I was eyes to the blind,
and feet to the lame.
[16]I was a father to the poor,
and I searched out the cause of him
whom I did not know.
[17]I broke the fangs of the unrighteous,
and made him drop his prey from
his teeth.
[18]Then I thought, 'I shall die in my nest,
and I shall multiply my days as
the sand,
[19]my roots spread out to the waters,
with the dew all night on my branches,
[20]my glory fresh with me,
and my bow ever new in my hand.'

[21]"Men listened to me, and waited,
and kept silence for my counsel.
[22]After I spoke they did not speak again,
and my word dropped upon them.
[23]They waited for me as for the rain;
and they opened their mouths as for the
spring rain.
[24]I smiled on them when they had
no confidence;
and the light of my countenance they did
not cast down.
[25]I chose their way, and sat as chief,
and I dwelt like a king among
his troops,
like one who comforts mourners.

30 "But now they make sport of me,
men who are younger than I,
whose fathers I would have disdained
to set with the dogs of my flock.
[2]What could I gain from the strength of
their hands,
men whose vigor is gone?
[3]Through want and hard hunger
they gnaw the dry and desolate ground;
[4]they pick mallow and the leaves of bushes,
and to warm themselves the roots of
the broom.
[5]They are driven out from among men;
they shout after them as after a thief.
[6]In the gullies of the torrents they
must dwell,
in holes of the earth and of the rocks.
[7]Among the bushes they bray;
under the nettles they huddle together.
[8]A senseless, a disreputable brood,
they have been whipped out of the land.
[9]"And now I have become their song,
I am a byword to them.
[10]They abhor me, they keep aloof from me;
they do not hesitate to spit at the sight
of me.
[11]Because God has loosed my cord and
humbled me,
they have cast off restraint in my presence.
[12]On my right hand the rabble rise,
they drive me forth,
they cast up against me their ways
of destruction.
[13]They break up my path,
they promote my calamity;
no one restrains them.
[14]As through a wide breach they come;
amid the crash they roll on.

15Terrors are turned upon me;
my honor is pursued as by the wind,
and my prosperity has passed away like
a cloud.

16"And now my soul is poured out
within me;
days of affliction have taken hold of me.
17The night racks my bones,
and the pain that gnaws me takes no rest.
18With violence it seizes my garment;
it binds me about like the collar of
my tunic.
19God has cast me into the mire,
and I have become like dust and ashes.
20I cry to you and you do not answer me;
I stand, and you do not heed me.
21You have turned cruel to me;
with the might of your hand you
persecute me.
22You lift me up on the wind, you make me
ride on it,
and you toss me about in the roar of
the storm.
23Yes, I know that you will bring me to death,
and to the house appointed for all living.
24"Yet does not one in a heap of ruins stretch
out his hand,
and in his disaster cry for help?
25Did not I weep for him whose day was hard?
Was not my soul grieved for the poor?
26But when I looked for good, evil came;
and when I waited for light,
darkness came.
27My heart is in turmoil, and is never still;
days of affliction come to meet me.
28I go about blackened, but not by the sun;
I stand up in the assembly, and cry
for help.
29I am a brother of jackals,
and a companion of ostriches.
30My skin turns black and falls from me,
and my bones burn with heat.
31My lyre is turned to mourning,
and my pipe to the voice of those
who weep.

31 "I have made a covenant with my
eyes;
how then could I look upon a virgin?
2What would be my portion from God above,
and my heritage from the Almighty on
high?
3Does not calamity befall the unrighteous,
and disaster the workers of iniquity?
4Does not he see my ways,
and number all my steps?

5"If I have walked with falsehood,
and my foot has hastened to deceit;
6(Let me be weighed in a just balance,
and let God know my integrity!)
7if my step has turned aside from the way,
and my heart has gone after my eyes,
and if any spot has clung to my hands;
8then let me sow, and another eat;
and let what grows for me be rooted out.

9"If my heart has been enticed to a woman,
and I have lain in wait at my
neighbor's door;
10then let my wife grind for another,
and let others bow down upon her.
11For that would be a heinous crime;
that would be an iniquity to be punished
by the judges;
12for that would be a fire which consumes
unto Abad´don,
and it would burn to the root all
my increase.

13"If I have rejected the cause of my
manservant or my maidservant,
when they brought a complaint
against me;
14what then shall I do when God rises up?
When he makes inquiry, what shall I
answer him?
15Did not he who made me in the womb
make him?
And did not one fashion us in the womb?

16"If I have withheld anything that the
poor desired,
or have caused the eyes of the widow to fail,
17or have eaten my morsel alone,
and the fatherless has not eaten of it
18(for from his youth I reared him as a father,
and from his mother's womb I
guided him);

19 if I have seen any one perish for lack
of clothing,
or a poor man without covering;
20 if his loins have not blessed me,
and if he was not warmed with the fleece
of my sheep;
21 if I have raised my hand against the
fatherless,
because I saw help in the gate;
22 then let my shoulder blade fall from
my shoulder,
and let my arm be broken from its socket.
23 For I was in terror of calamity from God,
and I could not have faced his majesty.

24 "If I have made gold my trust,
or called fine gold my confidence;
25 if I have rejoiced because my wealth was great,
or because my hand had gotten much;
26 if I have looked at the sun when it shone,
or the moon moving in splendor,
27 and my heart has been secretly enticed,
and my mouth has kissed my hand;
28 this also would be an iniquity to be
punished by the judges,
for I should have been false to God above.

29 "If I have rejoiced at the ruin of him that
hated me,
or exulted when evil overtook him
30 (I have not let my mouth sin
by asking for his life with a curse);
31 if the men of my tent have not said,
'Who is there that has not been filled
with his meat?'
32 (the sojourner has not lodged in the street;
I have opened my doors to the wayfarer);
33 if I have concealed my transgressions
from men,
by hiding my iniquity in my bosom,
34 because I stood in great fear of
the multitude,
and the contempt of families terrified me,
so that I kept silence, and did not go out
of doors—
35 Oh, that I had one to hear me!
(Here is my signature! let the Almighty
answer me!)
Oh, that I had the indictment written by
my adversary!
36 Surely I would carry it on my shoulder;
I would bind it on me as a crown;
37 I would give him an account of all my steps;
like a prince I would approach him.

38 "If my land has cried out against me,
and its furrows have wept together;
39 if I have eaten its yield without payment,
and caused the death of its owners;
40 let thorns grow instead of wheat,
and foul weeds instead of barley."

The words of Job are ended.

ECCLESIASTES 2

I said to myself, "Come now, I will make a test of
pleasure; enjoy yourself." But behold, this also
was vanity. 2 I said of laughter, "It is mad," and of
pleasure, "What use is it?" 3 I searched with my
mind how to cheer my body with wine—my
mind still guiding me with wisdom—and how
to lay hold on folly, till I might see what was
good for the sons of men to do under heaven
during the few days of their life. 4 I made great
works; I built houses and planted vineyards
for myself; 5 I made myself gardens and parks,
and planted in them all kinds of fruit trees. 6 I
made myself pools from which to water the
forest of growing trees. 7 I bought male and
female slaves, and had slaves who were born
in my house; I had also great possessions of
herds and flocks, more than any who had been
before me in Jerusalem. 8 I also gathered for
myself silver and gold and the treasure of kings
and provinces; I got singers, both men and
women, and many concubines, man's delight.

9 So I became great and surpassed all who
were before me in Jerusalem; also my wisdom
remained with me. 10 And whatever my eyes
desired I did not keep from them; I kept my
heart from no pleasure, for my heart found
pleasure in all my toil, and this was my reward
for all my toil. 11 Then I considered all that
my hands had done and the toil I had spent
in doing it, and behold, all was vanity and a
striving after wind, and there was nothing to
be gained under the sun.

1 CORINTHIANS 4

This is how one should regard us, as servants of Christ and stewards of the mysteries of God. [2]Moreover it is required of stewards that they be found trustworthy. [3]But with me it is a very small thing that I should be judged by you or by any human court. I do not even judge myself. [4]I am not aware of anything against myself, but I am not thereby acquitted. It is the Lord who judges me. [5]Therefore do not pronounce judgment before the time, before the Lord comes, who will bring to light the things now hidden in darkness and will disclose the purposes of the heart. Then every man will receive his commendation from God.

[6]I have applied all this to myself and Apol′los for your benefit, brethren, that you may learn by us not to go beyond what is written, that none of you may be puffed up in favor of one against another. [7]For who sees anything different in you? What have you that you did not receive? If then you received it, why do you boast as if it were not a gift?

[8]Already you are filled! Already you have become rich! Without us you have become kings! And would that you did reign, so that we might share the rule with you! [9]For I think that God has exhibited us apostles as last of all, like men sentenced to death; because we have become a spectacle to the world, to angels and to men. [10]We are fools for Christ's sake, but you are wise in Christ. We are weak, but you are strong. You are held in honor, but we in disrepute. [11]To the present hour we hunger and thirst, we are poorly clothed and buffeted and homeless, [12]and we labor, working with our own hands. When reviled, we bless; when persecuted, we endure; [13]when slandered, we try to conciliate; we have become, and are now, as the refuse of the world, the dregs of all things.

[14]I do not write this to make you ashamed, but to admonish you as my beloved children. [15]For though you have countless guides in Christ, you do not have many fathers. For I became your father in Christ Jesus through the gospel. [16]I urge you, then, be imitators of me. [17]Therefore I sent to you Timothy, my beloved and faithful child in the Lord, to remind you of my ways in Christ, as I teach them everywhere in every church. [18]Some are arrogant, as though I were not coming to you. [19]But I will come to you soon, if the Lord wills, and I will find out not the talk of these arrogant people but their power. [20]For the kingdom of God does not consist in talk but in power. [21]What do you wish? Shall I come to you with a rod, or with love in a spirit of gentleness?

REFLECTION

St. Paul warns us against our propensity to judge others. Of course, some judgment is necessary. Any civilized culture and society must have laws to help govern its citizens. These laws are especially important when they protect the powerless and disenfranchised. It is the duty of a society to "judge" when a law has been broken and to deliver a fitting punishment to the offender. This is not the type of judgment Paul is prohibiting. He is warning the Corinthians against judging the righteousness of another person. That task is reserved for God alone. "It is the Lord who judges me. Therefore do not pronounce judgment before the time, before the Lord comes, who will bring to light the things now hidden in darkness and will disclose the purposes of the heart. Then every man will receive his commendation from God" (1 Cor 4:4–5). While it is proper for a society to judge certain actions of another person, only God can discern a person's heart. Moreover, not only are we incapable of assessing another's righteousness, but casually judging others leads to our thinking we are superior in our holiness. This is the sin of pride, which can block us from charity. Do you not find it true that when you judge someone, it is very hard to treat them, or think of them, with charity? Why is that?

August 24

JOB 32

So these three men ceased to answer Job, because he was righteous in his own eyes. [2]Then Eli'hu the son of Bar'achel the Buzite, of the family of Ram, became angry. He
was angry at Job because he justified him-
self rather than God; [3]he was angry also at
Job's three friends because they had found
no answer, although they had declared Job
to be in the wrong. [4]Now Eli'hu had waited
to speak to Job because they were older than
he. [5]And when Eli'hu saw that there was no
answer in the mouths of these three men, he
became angry.

[6]And Eli'hu the son of Bar'achel the Buzite answered:

"I am young in years,
and you are aged;
therefore I was timid and afraid
to declare my opinion to you.
[7]I said, 'Let days speak,
and many years teach wisdom.'
[8]But it is the spirit in a man,
the breath of the Almighty, that makes him understand.
[9]It is not the old that are wise,
nor the aged that understand what is right.
[10]Therefore I say, 'Listen to me;
let me also declare my opinion.'

[11]"Behold, I waited for your words,
I listened for your wise sayings,
while you searched out what to say.
[12]I gave you my attention,
and, behold, there was none that confuted Job,
or that answered his words, among you.
[13]Beware lest you say, 'We have found wisdom;
God may vanquish him, not man.'
[14]He has not directed his words against me,
and I will not answer him with your speeches.

[15]"They are discomfited, they answer no more;
they have not a word to say.
[16]And shall I wait, because they do not speak,
because they stand there, and answer no more?
[17]I also will give my answer;
I also will declare my opinion.
[18]For I am full of words,
the spirit within me constrains me.
[19]Behold, my heart is like wine that has no vent;
like new wineskins, it is ready to burst.
[20]I must speak, that I may find relief;
I must open my lips and answer.
[21]I will not show partiality to any person
or use flattery toward any man.
[22]For I do not know how to flatter,
else would my Maker soon put an end to me.

33 "But now, hear my speech, O Job,
and listen to all my words.
[2]Behold, I open my mouth;
the tongue in my mouth speaks.
[3]My words declare the uprightness of my heart,
and what my lips know they speak sincerely.
[4]The spirit of God has made me,
and the breath of the Almighty gives me life.
[5]Answer me, if you can;
set your words in order before me; take your stand.
[6]Behold, I am toward God as you are;
I too was formed from a piece of clay.
[7]Behold, no fear of me need terrify you;
my pressure will not be heavy upon you.

[8]"Surely, you have spoken in my hearing,
and I have heard the sound of your words.
[9]You say, 'I am clean, without transgression;
I am pure, and there is no iniquity in me.
[10]Behold, he finds occasions against me,
he counts me as his enemy;
[11]he puts my feet in the stocks,
and watches all my paths.'

[12]"Behold, in this you are not right. I will answer you.
God is greater than man.

[13]Why do you contend against him,
saying, 'He will answer none of my words'?
[14]For God speaks in one way,
and in two, though man does not
perceive it.
[15]In a dream, in a vision of the night,
when deep sleep falls upon men,
while they slumber on their beds,
[16]then he opens the ears of men,
and terrifies them with warnings,
[17]that he may turn man aside from his deed,
and cut off pride from man;
[18]he keeps back his soul from the Pit,
his life from perishing by the sword.

[19]"Man is also chastened with pain upon
his bed,
and with continual strife in his bones;
[20]so that his life loathes bread,
and his appetite dainty food.
[21]His flesh is so wasted away that it cannot
be seen;
and his bones which were not seen
stick out.
[22]His soul draws near the Pit,
and his life to those who bring death.
[23]If there be for him an angel,
a mediator, one of the thousand,
to declare to man what is right for him;
[24]and he is gracious to him, and says,
'Deliver him from going down into
the Pit,
I have found a ransom;
[25]let his flesh become fresh with youth;
let him return to the days of his
youthful vigor';
[26]then man prays to God, and he accepts him,
he comes into his presence with joy.
He recounts to men his salvation,
[27] and he sings before men, and says:
'I sinned and perverted what was right,
and it was not repaid to me.
[28]He has redeemed my soul from going
down into the Pit,
and my life shall see the light.'

[29]"Behold, God does all these things,
twice, three times, with a man,
[30]to bring back his soul from the Pit,
that he may see the light of life.
[31]Give heed, O Job, listen to me;
be silent, and I will speak.
[32]If you have anything to say, answer me;
speak, for I desire to justify you.
[33]If not, listen to me;
be silent, and I will teach you wisdom."

34 Then Eli'hu said:
[2]"Hear my words, you wise men,
and give ear to me, you who know;
[3]for the ear tests words
as the palate tastes food.
[4]Let us choose what is right;
let us determine among ourselves what
is good.
[5]For Job has said, 'I am innocent,
and God has taken away my right;
[6]in spite of my right I am counted a liar;
my wound is incurable, though I am
without transgression.'
[7]What man is like Job,
who drinks up scoffing like water,
[8]who goes in company with evildoers
and walks with wicked men?
[9]For he has said, 'It profits a man nothing
that he should take delight in God.'

[10]"Therefore, hear me, you men
of understanding,
far be it from God that he should do
wickedness,
and from the Almighty that he should
do wrong.
[11]For according to the work of a man he will
repay him,
and according to his ways he will make it
befall him.
[12]Of a truth, God will not do wickedly,
and the Almighty will not pervert justice.
[13]Who gave him charge over the earth
and who laid on him the whole world?
[14]If he should take back his spirit to himself,
and gather to himself his breath,
[15]all flesh would perish together,
and man would return to dust.

[16]"If you have understanding, hear this;
listen to what I say.
[17]Shall one who hates justice govern?
Will you condemn him who is righteous
and mighty,

18who says to a king, 'Worthless one,'
and to nobles, 'Wicked man';
19who shows no partiality to princes,
nor regards the rich more than the poor,
for they are all the work of his hands?
20In a moment they die;
at midnight the people are shaken and
pass away,
and the mighty are taken away by no
human hand.

21"For his eyes are upon the ways of a man,
and he sees all his steps.
22There is no gloom or deep darkness
where evildoers may hide themselves.
23For he has not appointed a time for any man
to go before God in judgment.
24He shatters the mighty without investigation,
and sets others in their place.
25Thus, knowing their works,
he overturns them in the night, and they
are crushed.
26He strikes them for their wickedness
in the sight of men,
27because they turned aside from
following him,
and had no regard for any of his ways,
28so that they caused the cry of the poor to
come to him,
and he heard the cry of the afflicted—
29When he is quiet, who can condemn?
When he hides his face, who can
behold him,
whether it be a nation or a man?—
30that a godless man should not reign,
that he should not ensnare the people.

31"For has any one said to God,
'I have borne chastisement; I will not
offend any more;
32teach me what I do not see;
if I have done iniquity, I will do it no more'?
33Will he then make repayment to suit you,
because you reject it?
For you must choose, and not I;
therefore declare what you know.
34Men of understanding will say to me,
and the wise man who hears me will say:
35'Job speaks without knowledge,
his words are without insight.'
36Would that Job were judged to the end,
because he answers like wicked men.
37For he adds rebellion to his sin;
he claps his hands among us,
and multiplies his words against God."

35 And Eli'hu said:
2"Do you think this to be just?
Do you say, 'It is my right before God,'
3that you ask, 'What advantage have I?
How am I better off than if I had
sinned?'
4I will answer you
and your friends with you.
5Look at the heavens, and see;
and behold the clouds, which are higher
than you.
6If you have sinned, what do you accomplish
against him?
And if your transgressions are multiplied,
what do you do to him?
7If you are righteous, what do you give to him;
or what does he receive from
your hand?
8Your wickedness concerns a man
like yourself,
and your righteousness a son of man.

9"Because of the multitude of oppressions
people cry out;
they call for help because of the arm of
the mighty.
10But none says, 'Where is God my Maker,
who gives songs in the night,
11who teaches us more than the beasts of
the earth,
and makes us wiser than the birds of
the air?'
12There they cry out, but he does not answer,
because of the pride of evil men.
13Surely God does not hear an empty cry,
nor does the Almighty regard it.
14How much less when you say that you do
not see him,
that the case is before him, and you are
waiting for him!
15And now, because his anger does not punish,
and he does not greatly heed
transgression,
16Job opens his mouth in empty talk,
he multiplies words without knowledge."

ECCLESIASTES 2

12So I turned to consider wisdom and
madness and folly; for what can the
man do who comes after the king? Only
what he has already done. 13Then I saw
that wisdom excels folly as light excels
darkness. 14The wise man has his eyes in
his head, but the fool walks in darkness;
and yet I perceived that one fate comes to
all of them. 15Then I said to myself, "What
befalls the fool will befall me also; why
then have I been so very wise?" And I said
to myself that this also is vanity. 16For of
the wise man as of the fool there is no
enduring remembrance, seeing that in
the days to come all will have been long
forgotten. How the wise man dies just like
the fool! 17So I hated life, because what is
done under the sun was grievous to me;
for all is vanity and a striving after wind.

18I hated all my toil in which I had toiled
under the sun, seeing that I must leave it
to the man who will come after me; 19and
who knows whether he will be a wise man
or a fool? Yet he will be master of all for
which I toiled and used my wisdom under
the sun. This also is vanity. 20So I turned
about and gave my heart up to despair
over all the toil of my labors under the sun,
21because sometimes a man who has toiled
with wisdom and knowledge and skill must
leave all to be enjoyed by a man who did
not toil for it. This also is vanity and a great
evil. 22What has a man from all the toil and
strain with which he toils beneath the sun?
23For all his days are full of pain, and his
work is a vexation; even in the night his
mind does not rest. This also is vanity.

24There is nothing better for a man
than that he should eat and drink and
find enjoyment in his toil. This also, I
saw, is from the hand of God; 25for apart
from him who can eat or who can have
enjoyment? 26For to the man who pleases
him God gives wisdom and knowledge
and joy; but to the sinner he gives the
work of gathering and heaping, only to
give to one who pleases God. This also is
vanity and a striving after wind.

1 CORINTHIANS 5

**It is actually reported that there
is immorality among you, and
of a kind that is not found even among
pagans; for a man is living with his**
father's wife. 2And you are arrogant! Ought
you not rather to mourn? Let him who has
done this be removed from among you.

3For though absent in body I am present
in spirit, and as if present, I have already
pronounced judgment 4in the name of the
Lord Jesus on the man who has done such
a thing. When you are assembled, and my
spirit is present, with the power of our Lord
Jesus, 5you are to deliver this man to Satan
for the destruction of the flesh, that his spirit
may be saved in the day of the Lord Jesus.

6Your boasting is not good. Do you not
know that a little leaven leavens all the
dough? 7Cleanse out the old leaven that
you may be new dough, as you really are
unleavened. For Christ, our Paschal Lamb,
has been sacrificed. 8Let us, therefore,
celebrate the festival, not with the old leaven,
the leaven of malice and evil, but with the
unleavened bread of sincerity and truth.

9I wrote to you in my letter not to associate
with immoral men; 10not at all meaning the
immoral of this world, or the greedy and
robbers, or idolaters, since then you would
need to go out of the world. 11But rather I
wrote to you not to associate with any one
who bears the name of brother if he is guilty
of immorality or greed, or is an idolater,
reviler, drunkard, or robber—not even to
eat with such a one. 12For what have I to do
with judging outsiders? Is it not those inside
the Church whom you are to judge? 13God
judges those outside. "Drive out the wicked
person from among you."

REFLECTION

Although it is important to avoid judging another's righteousness before God in our day-to-day lives, this doesn't mean we should tolerate immorality. On the contrary, we should reject any attempt to normalize immoral behavior among our Christian brethren. Sometimes it is easier to look the other way and not speak up when we are confronted with behavior that we know is contrary to Catholic teaching. Indeed, only God knows what is in another person's heart, and none of us leads a sinless life. But this does not mean we should sacrifice truth for the sake of tolerance. In today's reading from 1 Corinthians, St. Paul reminds us that, in certain situations, we are duty-bound to fraternally correct our fellow Christians. To speak out against immoral living and sinful behavior is not to pass judgment on the state of another's soul, but rather to defend the holy way of life God desires for us all. Paul explains the proper motivation for this type of judgment: "That his spirit may be saved in the day of the Lord Jesus" (1 Cor 5:5). When you speak out against immorality, do you do so out of love? Do you reject immorality while reserving the judgment of another's soul for God alone?

August 25

JOB 36

And Eli′hu continued, and said:
2"Bear with me a little, and I
will show you,
for I have yet something to say on
God's behalf.
3I will fetch my knowledge from afar,
and ascribe righteousness to my Maker.
4For truly my words are not false;
one who is perfect in knowledge is with you.

5"Behold, God is mighty, and does not
despise any;
he is mighty in strength of understanding.
6He does not keep the wicked alive,
but gives the afflicted their right.
7He does not withdraw his eyes from
the righteous,
but with kings upon the throne
he sets them for ever, and they are exalted.
8And if they are bound in fetters
and caught in the cords of affliction,
9then he declares to them their work
and their transgressions, that they are
behaving arrogantly.
10He opens their ears to instruction,
and commands that they return
from iniquity.
11If they listen and serve him,
they complete their days in prosperity,
and their years in pleasantness.
12But if they do not listen, they perish by
the sword,
and die without knowledge.

13"The godless in heart cherish anger;
they do not cry for help when he
binds them.
14They die in youth,
and their life ends in shame.
15He delivers the afflicted by their affliction,
and opens their ear by adversity.
16He also allured you out of distress
into a broad place where there was
no cramping,
and what was set on your table was full of
rich food.

17"But you are full of the judgment on
the wicked;
judgment and justice seize you.
18Beware lest wrath entice you into scoffing;
and let not the greatness of the ransom
turn you aside.
19Will your cry avail to keep you from distress,
or all the force of your strength?
20Do not long for the night,
when peoples are cut off in their place.
21Take heed, do not turn to iniquity,
for this you have chosen rather
than affliction.
22Behold, God is exalted in his power;
who is a teacher like him?
23Who has prescribed for him his way,
or who can say, 'You have done wrong'?
24"Remember to extol his work,
of which men have sung.
25All men have looked on it;
man beholds it from afar.

26 Behold, God is great, and we know him not;
the number of his years is unsearchable.
27 For he draws up the drops of water,
he distils his mist in rain
28 which the skies pour down,
and drop upon man abundantly.
29 Can any one understand the spreading of
the clouds,
the thunderings of his pavilion?
30 Behold, he scatters his lightning about him,
and covers the roots of the sea.
31 For by these he judges peoples;
he gives food in abundance.
32 He covers his hands with the lightning,
and commands it to strike the mark.
33 Its crashing declares concerning him,
who is jealous with anger against iniquity.

37 "At this also my heart trembles,
and leaps out of its place.
2 Listen to the thunder of his voice
and the rumbling that comes from
his mouth.
3 Under the whole heaven he lets it go,
and his lightning to the corners of
the earth.
4 After it his voice roars;
he thunders with his majestic voice
and he does not restrain the bolts of
lightning when his voice is heard.
5 God thunders wondrously with his voice;
he does great things which we
cannot comprehend.
6 For to the snow he says, 'Fall on the earth';
and to the shower and the rain, 'Be strong.'
7 He seals up the hand of every man,
that all men may know his work.
8 Then the beasts go into their lairs,
and remain in their dens.
9 From its chamber comes the whirlwind,
and cold from the scattering winds.
10 By the breath of God ice is given,
and the broad waters are frozen fast.
11 He loads the thick cloud with moisture;
the clouds scatter his lightning.
12 They turn round and round by
his guidance,
to accomplish all that he command them
on the face of the habitable world.
13 Whether for correction, or for his land,
or for love, he causes it to happen.

14 "Hear this, O Job;
stop and consider the wondrous works
of God.
15 Do you know how God lays his command
upon them,
and causes the lightning of his cloud
to shine?
16 Do you know the balancings of the clouds,
the wondrous works of him who is
perfect in knowledge,
17 you whose garments are hot
when the earth is still because of the
south wind?
18 Can you, like him, spread out the skies,
hard as a molten mirror?
19 Teach us what we shall say to him;
we cannot draw up our case because of
darkness.
20 Shall it be told him that I would speak?
Did a man ever wish that he would be
swallowed up?

21 "And now men cannot look on the light
when it is bright in the skies,
when the wind has passed and
cleared them.
22 Out of the north comes golden splendor;
God is clothed with awesome
majesty.
23 The Almighty—we cannot find him;
he is great in power and justice,
and abundant righteousness he will
not violate.
24 Therefore men fear him;
he does not regard any who are wise in
their own conceit."

38 Then the LORD answered Job out of
the whirlwind:
2 "Who is this that darkens counsel by words
without knowledge?
3 Gird up your loins like a man,
I will question you, and you shall declare
to me.

4 "Where were you when I laid the foundation
of the earth?
Tell me, if you have understanding.
5 Who determined its measurements—
surely you know!
Or who stretched the line upon it?

6On what were its bases sunk,
or who laid its cornerstone,
7when the morning stars sang together,
and all the sons of God shouted for joy?

8"Or who shut in the sea with doors,
when it burst forth from the womb;
9when I made clouds its garment,
and thick darkness its swaddling band;
10and prescribed bounds for it,
and set bars and doors,
11and said, 'Thus far shall you come, and no farther,
and here shall your proud waves be stayed'?

12"Have you commanded the morning since your days began,
and caused the dawn to know its place,
13that it might take hold of the skirts of the earth,
and the wicked be shaken out of it?
14It is changed like clay under the seal,
and it is dyed like a garment.
15From the wicked their light is withheld,
and their uplifted arm is broken.

16"Have you entered into the springs of the sea,
or walked in the recesses of the deep?
17Have the gates of death been revealed to you,
or have you seen the gates of deep darkness?
18Have you comprehended the expanse of the earth?
Declare, if you know all this.

19"Where is the way to the dwelling of light,
and where is the place of darkness,
20that you may take it to its territory
and that you may discern the paths to its home?
21You know, for you were born then,
and the number of your days is great!

22"Have you entered the storehouses of the snow,
or have you seen the storehouses of the hail,
23which I have reserved for the time of trouble,
for the day of battle and war?
24What is the way to the place where the light is distributed,
or where the east wind is scattered upon the earth?

25"Who has cleft a channel for the torrents of rain,
and a way for the thunderbolt,
26to bring rain on a land where no man is,
on the desert in which there is no man;
27to satisfy the waste and desolate land,
and to make the ground put forth grass?

28"Has the rain a father,
or who has begotten the drops of dew?
29From whose womb did the ice come forth,
and who has given birth to the hoarfrost of heaven?
30The waters become hard like stone,
and the face of the deep is frozen.

31"Can you bind the chains of the Plei′ades,
or loose the cords of Ori′on?
32Can you lead forth the Maz′zaroth in their season,
or can you guide the Bear with its children?
33Do you know the ordinances of the heavens?
Can you establish their rule on the earth?

34"Can you lift up your voice to the clouds,
that a flood of waters may cover you?
35Can you send forth bolts of lightning, that they may go
and say to you, 'Here we are'?
36Who has put wisdom in the clouds,
or given understanding to the mists?
37Who can number the clouds by wisdom?
Or who can tilt the waterskins of the heavens,
38when the dust runs into a mass
and the clods cling tightly together?

39"Can you hunt the prey for the lion,
or satisfy the appetite of the young lions,
40when they crouch in their dens,
or lie in wait in their hiding places?
41Who provides for the raven its prey,
when its young ones cry to God,
and wander about for lack of food?"

ECCLESIASTES 3

For everything there is a season, and a time for every matter under heaven:
2a time to be born, and a time to die;
a time to plant, and a time to pluck up what is planted;
3a time to kill, and a time to heal;
a time to break down, and a time to build up;
4a time to weep, and a time to laugh;
a time to mourn, and a time to dance;
5a time to cast away stones, and a time to gather stones together;
a time to embrace, and a time to refrain from embracing;
6a time to seek, and a time to lose;
a time to keep, and a time to cast away;
7a time to tear, and a time to sew;
a time to keep silence, and a time to speak;
8a time to love, and a time to hate;
a time for war, and a time for peace.
9What gain has the worker from his toil?

10I have seen the business that God has
given to the sons of men to be busy with.
11He has made everything beautiful in its
time; also he has put eternity into man's
mind, yet so that he cannot find out what
God has done from the beginning to the
end. 12I know that there is nothing better for
them than to be happy and enjoy themselves
as long as they live; 13also that it is God's gift
to man that every one should eat and drink
and take pleasure in all his toil. 14I know
that whatever God does endures for ever;
nothing can be added to it, nor anything
taken from it; God has made it so, in order
that men should fear before him. 15That
which is, already has been; that which is to
be, already has been; and God seeks what
has been driven away.

---

1 CORINTHIANS 6

When one of you has a grievance against a brother, does he dare go to law before the unrighteous instead of the saints? 2Do you not know
that the saints will judge the world? And if
the world is to be judged by you, are you
incompetent to try trivial cases? 3Do you
not know that we are to judge angels? How
much more, matters pertaining to this life!
4If then you have such cases, why do you lay
them before those who are least esteemed
by the Church? 5I say this to your shame.
Can it be that there is no man among you
wise enough to decide between members of
the brotherhood, 6but brother goes to law
against brother, and that before unbelievers?

7To have lawsuits at all with one another
is defeat for you. Why not rather suffer
wrong? Why not rather be defrauded? 8But
you yourselves wrong and defraud, and that
even your own brethren.

9Do you not know that the unrighteous will
not inherit the kingdom of God? Do not be
deceived; neither the immoral, nor idolaters,
nor adulterers, nor homosexuals, 10nor
thieves, nor the greedy, nor drunkards, nor
revilers, nor robbers will inherit the kingdom
of God. 11And such were some of you. But
you were washed, you were sanctified, you
were justified in the name of the Lord Jesus
Christ and in the Spirit of our God.

12"All things are lawful for me," but not all
things are helpful. "All things are lawful for
me," but I will not be enslaved by anything.
13"Food is meant for the stomach and the
stomach for food"—and God will destroy
both one and the other. The body is not
meant for immorality, but for the Lord, and
the Lord for the body. 14And God raised the
Lord and will also raise us up by his power.
15Do you not know that your bodies are
members of Christ? Shall I therefore take
the members of Christ and make them
members of a prostitute? Never! 16Do you
not know that he who joins himself to a
prostitute becomes one body with her? For,
as it is written, "The two shall become one."
17But he who is united to the Lord becomes
one spirit with him. 18Shun immorality.
Every other sin which a man commits is
outside the body; but the immoral man sins
against his own body. 19Do you not know
that your body is a temple of the Holy Spirit
within you, which you have from God? You

are not your own; [20]you were bought with a price. So glorify God in your body.

REFLECTION

Job has been searching for meaning to his suffering. Trials and tragedy often seem senseless, and they leave us pleading with God to reveal his greater purpose. At the very least, we would like God to give us a reason for our struggle. In today's readings Job finally gets a reply from God, but it is not exactly the satisfactory response for which he was hoping. "Where were you when I laid the foundation of the earth? . . . Have you entered into the springs of the sea, or walked in the recesses of the deep? Have the gates of death been revealed to you, or have you seen the gates of deep darkness?" (Jb 38:4, 16–17). As this passage reminds us, our finite minds are never truly prepared to grasp the eternal ways of God. But, as Ecclesiastes underscores, all things, all the patterns and rhythms of life, are ordained by God, who ultimately desires our welfare. Many things will remain a mystery to us. Are you willing to trust in God and participate in his plan for you, even when it doesn't make sense or brings hardship? As you encounter the inevitable ups and downs of daily life, do you remember that even unpleasantness and suffering can make you holy if you surrender to God's control?

August 26

JOB 39

"Do you know when the
mountain goats bring forth?
Do you observe the deer bringing
forth their young?
[2]Can you number the months that they fulfil,
and do you know the time when they
bring forth,
[3]when they crouch, bring forth their offspring,
and are delivered of their young?
[4]Their young ones become strong, they
grow up in the open;
they go forth, and do not return to them.

[5]"Who has let the wild donkey go free?
Who has loosed the bonds of the
swift donkey,
[6]to whom I have given the steppe for
his home,
and the salt land for his dwelling place?
[7]He scorns the tumult of the city;
he hears not the shouts of the driver.
[8]He ranges the mountains as his pasture,
and he searches after every green thing.

[9]"Is the wild ox willing to serve you?
Will he spend the night at your crib?
[10]Can you bind him in the furrow with ropes,
or will he harrow the valleys after you?
[11]Will you depend on him because his
strength is great,
and will you leave to him your labor?
[12]Do you have faith in him that he will return,
and bring your grain to your
threshing floor?

[13]"The wings of the ostrich wave proudly;
but are they the pinions and plumage
of love?
[14]For she leaves her eggs to the earth,
and lets them be warmed on the ground,
[15]forgetting that a foot may crush them,
and that the wild beast may
trample them.
[16]She deals cruelly with her young, as if they
were not hers;
though her labor be in vain, yet she has
no fear;
[17]because God has made her forget wisdom,
and given her no share in understanding.
[18]When she rouses herself to flee,
she laughs at the horse and his rider.

[19]"Do you give the horse his might?
Do you clothe his neck with strength?
[20]Do you make him leap like the locust?
His majestic snorting is terrible.
[21]He paws in the valley, and exults in
his strength;
he goes out to meet the weapons.

22He laughs at fear, and is not dismayed;
he does not turn back from the sword.
23Upon him rattle the quiver,
the flashing spear and the javelin.
24With fierceness and rage he swallows
the ground;
he cannot stand still at the sound of
the trumpet.
25When the trumpet sounds, he says 'Aha!'
He smells the battle from afar,
the thunder of the captains, and
the shouting.

26"Is it by your wisdom that the hawk soars,
and spreads his wings toward the south?
27Is it at your command that the eagle
mounts up
and makes his nest on high?
28On the rock he dwells and makes
his home
in the fastness of the rocky crag.
29From there he spies out the prey;
his eyes behold it afar off.
30His young ones suck up blood;
and where the slain are, there is he."

40 And the LORD said to Job:
2"Shall a faultfinder contend with the
Almighty?
He who argues with God, let him
answer it."

3Then Job answered the LORD:
4"Behold, I am of small account; what shall
I answer you?
I lay my hand on my mouth.
5I have spoken once, and I will not answer;
twice, but I will proceed no further."

6Then the LORD answered Job out of
the whirlwind:
7"Gird up your loins like a man;
I will question you, and you declare to me.
8Will you even put me in the wrong?
Will you condemn me that you may
be justified?
9Have you an arm like God,
and can you thunder with a voice like his?
10"Deck yourself with majesty and dignity;
clothe yourself with glory and splendor.
11Pour forth the overflowings of your anger,
and look on every one that is proud, and
abase him.
12Look on every one that is proud, and bring
him low;
and tread down the wicked where
they stand.
13Hide them all in the dust together;
bind their faces in the world below.
14Then will I also acknowledge to you,
that your own right hand can give
you victory.

15"Behold, Be'hemoth,
which I made as I made you;
he eats grass like an ox.
16Behold, his strength in his loins,
and his power in the muscles of his belly.
17He makes his tail stiff like a cedar;
the sinews of his thighs are knit together.
18His bones are tubes of bronze,
his limbs like bars of iron.

19"He is the first of the works of God;
let him who made him bring near his sword!
20For the mountains yield food for him
where all the wild beasts play.
21Under the lotus plants he lies,
in the hiding place of the reeds and in
the marsh.
22For his shade the lotus trees cover him;
the willows of the brook surround him.
23Behold, if the river is turbulent he is
not frightened;
he is confident though Jordan rushes
against his mouth.
24Can one take him with hooks,
or pierce his nose with a snare?

41 "Can you draw out Levi'athan with a
fishhook,
or press down his tongue with a cord?
2Can you put a rope in his nose,
or pierce his jaw with a hook?
3Will he make many supplications to you?
Will he speak to you soft words?
4Will he make a covenant with you
to take him for your servant for ever?
5Will you play with him as with a bird,
or will you put him on leash for
your maidens?

6Will traders bargain over him?
Will they divide him up among the merchants?
7Can you fill his skin with harpoons,
or his head with fishing spears?
8Lay hands on him;
think of the battle; you will not do it again!
9Behold, the hope of a man is disappointed;
he is laid low even at the sight of him.
10No one is so fierce that he dares to stir him up.
Who then is he that can stand before me?
11Who has given to me, that I should repay him?
Whatever is under the whole heaven is mine.

12"I will not keep silence concerning his limbs,
or his mighty strength, or his large frame.
13Who can strip off his outer garment?
Who can penetrate his double coat of mail?
14Who can open the doors of his face?
Round about his teeth is terror.
15His back is made of rows of shields,
shut up closely as with a seal.
16One is so near to another
that no air can come between them.
17They are joined one to another;
they clasp each other and cannot be separated.
18His sneezings flash forth light,
and his eyes are like the eyelids of the dawn.
19Out of his mouth go flaming torches;
sparks of fire leap forth.
20Out of his nostrils comes forth smoke,
as from a boiling pot and burning rushes.
21His breath kindles coals,
and a flame comes forth from his mouth.
22In his neck abides strength,
and terror dances before him.
23The folds of his flesh cling together,
firmly cast upon him and immovable.
24His heart is hard as a stone,
hard as the nether millstone.
25When he raises himself up the mighty are afraid;
at the crashing they are beside themselves.
26Though the sword reaches him, it does not avail;
nor the spear, the dart, or the javelin.
27He counts iron as straw,
and bronze as rotten wood.
28The arrow cannot make him flee;
for him slingstones are turned to stubble.
29Clubs are counted as stubble;
he laughs at the rattle of javelins.
30His underparts are like sharp potsherds;
he spreads himself like a threshing sledge on the mire.
31He makes the deep boil like a pot;
he makes the sea like a pot of ointment.
32Behind him he leaves a shining wake;
one would think the deep to be hoary.
33Upon earth there is not his like,
a creature without fear.
34He beholds everything that is high;
he is king over all the sons of pride."

42 Then Job answered the LORD:
2"I know that you can do all things,
and that no purpose of yours can be thwarted.
3'Who is this that hides counsel without knowledge?'
Therefore I have uttered what I did not understand,
things too wonderful for me, which I did not know.
4'Hear, and I will speak;
I will question you, and you declare to me.'
5I had heard of you by the hearing of the ear,
but now my eye sees you;
6therefore I despise myself,
and repent in dust and ashes."

7After the LORD had spoken these words
to Job, the LORD said to Eli′phaz the
Te′manite: "My wrath is kindled against
you and against your two friends; for you
have not spoken of me what is right, as my
servant Job has. 8Now therefore take seven
bulls and seven rams, and go to my servant
Job, and offer up for yourselves a burnt
offering; and my servant Job shall pray for
you, for I will accept his prayer not to deal
with you according to your folly; for you
have not spoken of me what is right, as my
servant Job has." 9So Eli′phaz the Te′manite

and Bildad the Shuhite and Zo′phar the Na′amathite went and did what the LORD had told them; and the LORD accepted Job's prayer.

[10]And the LORD restored the fortunes of Job, when he had prayed for his friends; and the LORD gave Job twice as much as he had before. [11]Then came to him all his brothers and sisters and all who had known him before, and ate bread with him in his house; and they showed him sympathy and comforted him for all the evil that the LORD had brought upon him; and each of them gave him a piece of money and a ring of gold. [12]And the LORD blessed the latter days of Job more than his beginning; and he had fourteen thousand sheep, six thousand camels, a thousand yoke of oxen, and a thousand she-donkeys. [13]He had also seven sons and three daughters. [14]And he called the name of the first Jemi′mah; and the name of the second Kezi′ah; and the name of the third Ker′en-hap′puch. [15]And in all the land there were no women so fair as Job's daughters; and their father gave them inheritance among their brothers. [16]And after this Job lived a hundred and forty years, and saw his sons, and his sons' sons, four generations. [17]And Job died, an old man, and full of days.

ECCLESIASTES 3

[16]Moreover I saw under the sun that in the place of justice, even there was wickedness, and in the place of righteousness, even there was wickedness. [17]I said in my heart, God will judge the righteous and the wicked, for he has appointed a time for every matter, and for every work. [18]I said in my heart with regard to the sons of men that God is testing them to show them that they are but beasts. [19]For the fate of the sons of men and the fate of beasts is the same; as one dies, so dies the other. They all have the same breath, and man has no advantage over the beasts; for all is vanity. [20]All go to one place; all are from the dust, and all turn to dust again. [21]Who knows whether the spirit of man goes upward and the spirit of the beast goes down to the earth? [22]So I saw that there is nothing better than that a man should enjoy his work, for that is his lot; who can bring him to see what will be after him?

4 Again I saw all the oppressions that are practiced under the sun. And behold, the tears of the oppressed, and they had no one to comfort them! On the side of their oppressors there was power, and there was no one to comfort them. [2]And I thought the dead who are already dead more fortunate than the living who are still alive; [3]but better than both is he who has not yet been, and has not seen the evil deeds that are done under the sun.

[4]Then I saw that all toil and all skill in work come from a man's envy of his neighbor. This also is vanity and a striving after wind.

[5]The fool folds his hands, and eats his own flesh.

[6]Better is a handful of quietness than two hands full of toil and a striving after wind.

[7]Again, I saw vanity under the sun: [8]a person who has no one, either son or brother, yet there is no end to all his toil, and his eyes are never satisfied with riches, so that he never asks, "For whom am I toiling and depriving myself of pleasure?" This also is vanity and an unhappy business.

---

1 CORINTHIANS 7

Now concerning the matters about which you wrote. It is well for a man not to touch a woman. [2]But because of the temptation to immorality, each man should have his own wife and each woman her own husband. [3]The husband should give to his wife her conjugal rights, and likewise the wife to her husband. [4]For the wife does not rule over her own body, but the husband does; likewise the husband does not

rule over his own body, but the wife does.
[5]Do not refuse one another except perhaps by agreement for a season, that you
may devote yourselves to prayer; but then
come together again, lest Satan tempt you
through lack of self-control. [6]I say this by
way of concession, not of command. [7]I
wish that all were as I myself am. But each
has his own special gift from God, one of
one kind and one of another.
[8]To the unmarried and the widows I say
that it is well for them to remain single as I
do. [9]But if they cannot exercise self-control,
they should marry. For it is better to marry
than to be aflame with passion.
[10]To the married I give charge, not I but
the Lord, that the wife should not separate
from her husband [11](but if she does, let her
remain single or else be reconciled to her
husband)—and that the husband should
not divorce his wife.
[12]To the rest I say, not the Lord, that if any
brother has a wife who is an unbeliever, and
she consents to live with him, he should not
divorce her. [13]If any woman has a husband
who is an unbeliever, and he consents to live
with her, she should not divorce him. [14]For
the unbelieving husband is consecrated
through his wife, and the unbelieving
wife is consecrated through her husband.
Otherwise, your children would be unclean,
but as it is they are holy. [15]But if the unbelieving partner desires to separate, let it
be so; in such a case the brother or sister is
not bound. For God has called us to peace.
[16]Wife, how do you know whether you will
save your husband? Husband, how do you
know whether you will save your wife?

REFLECTION

"I said in my heart, God will judge the righteous and the wicked, for he has appointed a time for every matter, and for every work" (Eccl 3:17). God is in control of everything, and all creation is under his dominion. In order to participate fruitfully in God's plan for our salvation, the entire structure of our lives and each choice we make should be ordered to him. In today's passage from 1 Corinthians, St. Paul stresses that our state in life should be determined by how we can best attain holiness and serve God. Contrary to some interpretations, Paul is not against marriage. Rather, marriage can be an excellent opportunity to structure one's life and priorities properly. Alternatively, it can also be a blessing to remain single and thereby order oneself fully to God. In either case—married or single—we are each called to live beyond ourselves as a path to sanctification. Indeed, everything in our lives, from the seemingly insignificant daily choices we make to discerning our vocation, should be approached in full recognition of, and in total surrender to, God's economy of salvation. Given your state in life, how does God want you to serve him?

August 27

ISAIAH 1

The vision of Isai′ah the son of A′moz, which he saw concerning Judah and Jerusalem in the days of Uzzi′ah, Jo′tham, A′haz, and Hezeki′ah, kings of Judah.

[2]Hear, O heavens, and give ear, O earth;
  for the LORD has spoken:
"Sons have I reared and brought up,
  but they have rebelled against me.
[3]The ox knows its owner,
  and the donkey its master's crib;
but Israel does not know,
  my people does not understand."

[4]Ah, sinful nation,
  a people laden with iniquity,
offspring of evildoers,
  sons who deal corruptly!
They have forsaken the LORD,
  they have despised the Holy One of Israel,
  they are utterly estranged.

5Why will you still be struck down,
that you continue to rebel?
The whole head is sick,
and the whole heart faint.
6From the sole of the foot even to
the head,
there is no soundness in it,
but bruises and sores
and bleeding wounds;
they are not pressed out, or bound up,
or softened with oil.

7Your country lies desolate,
your cities are burned with fire;
in your very presence
strangers devour your land;
it is desolate, as overthrown
by strangers.
8And the daughter of Zion is left
like a booth in a vineyard,
like a lodge in a cucumber field,
like a besieged city.

9If the LORD of hosts
had not left us a few survivors,
we should have been like Sodom,
and become like Gomor′rah.

10Hear the word of the LORD,
you rulers of Sodom!
Give ear to the teaching of our God,
you people of Gomor′rah!
11"What to me is the multitude of
your sacrifices?
says the LORD;
I have had enough of burnt offerings
of rams
and the fat of fed beasts;
I do not delight in the blood of bulls,
or of lambs, or of he-goats.

12"When you come to appear before me,
who requires of you
this trampling of my courts?
13Bring no more vain offerings;
incense is an abomination to me.
New moon and sabbath and the calling of
assemblies—
I cannot endure iniquity and solemn
assembly.
14Your new moons and your appointed feasts
my soul hates;
they have become a burden to me,
I am weary of bearing them.
15When you spread forth your hands,
I will hide my eyes from you;
even though you make many prayers,
I will not listen;
your hands are full of blood.
16Wash yourselves; make yourselves clean;
remove the evil of your doings
from before my eyes;
cease to do evil,
17 learn to do good;
seek justice,
correct oppression;
defend the fatherless,
plead for the widow.

18"Come now, let us reason together,
says the LORD:
though your sins are like scarlet,
they shall be as white as snow;
though they are red like crimson,
they shall become like wool.
19If you are willing and obedient,
you shall eat the good of the land;
20but if you refuse and rebel,
you shall be devoured by the sword;
for the mouth of the LORD has spoken."
21How the faithful city
has become a harlot,
she that was full of justice!
Righteousness lodged in her,
but now murderers.
22Your silver has become dross,
your wine mixed with water.
23Your princes are rebels
and companions of thieves.
Every one loves a bribe
and runs after gifts.
They do not defend the fatherless,
and the widow's cause does not come to
them.

24Therefore the Lord says,
the LORD of hosts,
the Mighty One of Israel:
"Ah, I will vent my wrath on my enemies,
and avenge myself on my foes.

[25]I will turn my hand against you
and will smelt away your dross as
with lye
and remove all your alloy.
[26]And I will restore your judges as at the first,
and your counselors as at the beginning.
Afterward you shall be called the city of
righteousness,
the faithful city."

[27]Zion shall be redeemed by justice,
and those in her who repent,
by righteousness.
[28]But rebels and sinners shall be destroyed
together,
and those who forsake the LORD shall
be consumed.
[29]For you shall be ashamed of the oaks
in which you delighted;
and you shall blush for the gardens
which you have chosen.
[30]For you shall be like an oak
whose leaf withers,
and like a garden without water.
[31]And the strong shall become tow,
and his work a spark,
and both of them shall burn together,
with none to quench them.

2 The word which Isai′ah the son of A′moz
saw concerning Judah and Jerusalem.
[2]It shall come to pass in the latter days
that the mountain of the house of the LORD
shall be established as the highest of the
mountains,
and shall be raised above the hills;
and all the nations shall flow to it,
[3] and many peoples shall come, and say:
"Come, let us go up to the mountain of
the LORD,
to the house of the God of Jacob;
that he may teach us his ways
and that we may walk in his paths."
For out of Zion shall go forth the law,
and the word of the LORD from Jerusalem.
[4]He shall judge between the nations,
and shall decide for many peoples;
and they shall beat their swords into
plowshares,
and their spears into
pruning hooks;
nation shall not lift up sword against nation,
neither shall they learn war any more.

[5]O house of Jacob,
come, let us walk
in the light of the LORD.

[6]For you have rejected your people,
the house of Jacob,
because they are full of diviners from the east
and of soothsayers like the Philis′tines,
and they strike hands with foreigners.
[7]Their land is filled with silver and gold,
and there is no end to their treasures;
their land is filled with horses,
and there is no end to their chariots.
[8]Their land is filled with idols;
they bow down to the work of their hands,
to what their own fingers have made.
[9]So man is humbled,
and men are brought low—
forgive them not!
[10]Enter into the rock,
and hide in the dust
from before the terror of the LORD,
and from the glory of his majesty.
[11]The haughty looks of man shall be
brought low,
and the pride of men shall be humbled;
and the LORD alone will be exalted in
that day.

[12]For the LORD of hosts has a day
against all that is proud and lofty,
against all that is lifted up and high;
[13]against all the cedars of Lebanon,
lofty and lifted up;
and against all the oaks of Bashan;
[14]against all the high mountains,
and against all the lofty hills;
[15]against every high tower,
and against every fortified wall;
[16]against all the ships of Tar′shish,
and against all the beautiful craft.
[17]And the haughtiness of man shall
be humbled,
and the pride of men shall be brought low;
and the LORD alone will be exalted in
that day.
[18]And the idols shall utterly pass away.

[19]And men shall enter the caves of the rocks
and the holes of the ground,
from before the terror of the LORD,
and from the glory of his majesty,
when he rises to terrify the earth.

[20]In that day men will cast forth
their idols of silver and their idols of gold,
which they made for themselves
to worship,
to the moles and to the bats,
[21]to enter the caverns of the rocks and the
clefts of the cliffs,
from before the terror of the LORD,
and from the glory of his majesty,
when he rises to terrify the earth.
[22]Turn away from man
in whose nostrils is breath,
for of what account is he?

ECCLESIASTES 4

[9]Two are better than one, because they have
a good reward for their toil. [10]For if they fall,
one will lift up his fellow; but woe to him who
is alone when he falls and has not another to
lift him up. [11]Again, if two lie together, they are
warm; but how can one be warm alone? [12]And
though a man might prevail against one who
is alone, two will withstand him. A threefold
cord is not quickly broken.
[13]Better is a poor and wise youth than an
old and foolish king, who will no longer take
advice, [14]even though he had gone from prison
to the throne or in his own kingdom had been
born poor. [15]I saw all the living who move
about under the sun, as well as that youth, who
was to stand in his place; [16]there was no end of
all the people; he was over all of them. Yet those
who come later will not rejoice in him. Surely
this also is vanity and a striving after wind.
5 Guard your steps when you go to the
house of God; to draw near to listen is
better than to offer the sacrifice of fools; for
they do not know that they are doing evil.
[2]Be not rash with your mouth, nor let your
heart be hasty to utter a word before God,
for God is in heaven, and you upon earth;
therefore let your words be few.
[3]For a dream comes with much business,
and a fool's voice with many words.
[4]When you vow a vow to God, do not delay
paying it; for he has no pleasure in fools. Pay
what you vow. [5]It is better that you should not
vow than that you should vow and not pay.
[6]Let not your mouth lead you into sin, and
do not say before the messenger that it was
a mistake; why should God be angry at your
voice, and destroy the work of your hands?
[7]For when dreams increase, empty words
grow many: but you must fear God.
[8]If you see in a province the poor oppressed and justice and right violently taken
away, do not be amazed at the matter; for
the high official is watched by a higher, and
there are yet higher ones over them. [9]But
in all, a king is an advantage to a land with
cultivated fields.
[10]He who loves money will not be satisfied
with money; nor he who loves wealth, with
gain: this also is vanity.
[11]When goods increase, they increase who
eat them; and what gain has their owner but
to see them with his eyes?
[12]Sweet is the sleep of a laborer, whether he
eats little or much; but the surfeit of the rich
will not let him sleep.

1 CORINTHIANS 7

**[17]Only, let every one lead the life
which the Lord has assigned to
him, and in which God has called him.
This is my rule in all the churches. [18]Was**
any one at the time of his call already circumcised? Let him not seek to remove the marks
of circumcision. Was any one at the time of his
call uncircumcised? Let him not seek circumcision. [19]For neither circumcision counts for
anything nor uncircumcision, but keeping the
commandments of God. [20]Every one should
remain in the state in which he was called.
[21]Were you a slave when called? Never mind.
But if you can gain your freedom, avail yourself
of the opportunity. [22]For he who was called in
the Lord as a slave is a freedman of the Lord.
Likewise he who was free when called is a slave

of Christ. [23]You were bought with a price; do
not become slaves of men. [24]So, brethren, in
whatever state each was called, there let him
remain with God.
[25]Now concerning the unmarried, I have no
command of the Lord, but I give my opinion as
one who by the Lord's mercy is trustworthy. [26]I
think that in view of the impending distress it
is well for a person to remain as he is. [27]Are you
bound to a wife? Do not seek to be free. Are you
free from a wife? Do not seek marriage. [28]But if
you marry, you do not sin, and if a girl marries
she does not sin. Yet those who marry will have
worldly troubles, and I would spare you that. [29]I
mean, brethren, the appointed time has grown
very short; from now on, let those who have
wives live as though they had none, [30]and those
who mourn as though they were not mourning,
and those who rejoice as though they were not
rejoicing, and those who buy as though they
had no goods, [31]and those who deal with the
world as though they had no dealings with it.
For the form of this world is passing away.
[32]I want you to be free from anxieties. The
unmarried man is anxious about the affairs
of the Lord, how to please the Lord; [33]but the
married man is anxious about worldly affairs,
how to please his wife, [34]and his interests
are divided. And the unmarried woman
or virgin is anxious about the affairs of the
Lord, how to be holy in body and spirit; but
the married woman is anxious about worldly
affairs, how to please her husband. [35]I say this
for your own benefit, not to lay any restraint
upon you, but to promote good order and to
secure your undivided devotion to the Lord.
[36]If any one thinks that he is not behaving
properly toward his betrothed, if his passions
are strong, and it has to be, let him do as he
wishes: let them marry—it is no sin. [37]But
whoever is firmly established in his heart,
being under no necessity but having his desire
under control, and has determined this in his
heart, to keep her as his betrothed, he will do
well. [38]So that he who marries his betrothed
does well; and he who refrains from marriage
will do better.
[39]A wife is bound to her husband as long
as he lives. If the husband dies, she is free to
be married to whom she wishes, only in the
Lord. [40]But in my judgment she is happier if
she remains as she is. And I think that I have
the Spirit of God.

REFLECTION

The opening of the Book of Isaiah describes the vision of a horrible situation. Israel is conquered by the Babylonians, and the people are sent into exile. What is the reason given for this calamity? Isaiah does not speak about military failure but about moral failure. The suffering of Israel has resulted from its sin, especially from its neglect of the lowly—the widow, the orphan, and the poor. In a similar vein, Ecclesiastes describes proper human relationships as a source of strength and St. Paul, in 1 Corinthians, lays out guidelines for different kinds of people to live together as Christians. We are therefore challenged to extend the love of God to all people, especially those who are difficult to love. If someone is different from us in class or status, in age or ability, in race or culture, will we regard them as our brother or sister? Will we see such people as God sees them, or as the world does? When we seek to understand our neighbor in light of God's Word and to love them as ourselves, we cultivate in our hearts a longing for eternal peace, a true desire to beat our "swords into plowshares" (Is 2:4), and to regard no one as an enemy. How do you treat others, especially those described by Isaiah?

August 28

ISAIAH 3

For behold, the Lord, the LORD
of hosts,
is taking away from Jerusalem and
from Judah
stay and staff,
the whole stay of bread,
and the whole stay of water;

[2]the mighty man and the soldier,
the judge and the prophet,
the diviner and the elder,
[3]the captain of fifty
and the man of rank,
the counselor and the skilful magician
and the expert in charms.
[4]And I will make boys their princes,
and infants shall rule over them.
[5]And the people will oppress one another,
every man his fellow
and every man his neighbor;
the youth will be insolent to the elder,
and the base fellow to the honorable.

[6]When a man takes hold of his brother
in the house of his father, saying:
"You have a mantle;
you shall be our leader,
and this heap of ruins
shall be under your rule";
[7]in that day he will speak out, saying:
"I will not be a healer;
in my house there is neither bread
nor mantle;
you shall not make me
leader of the people."
[8]For Jerusalem has stumbled,
and Judah has fallen;
because their speech and their deeds are
against the LORD,
defying his glorious presence.

[9]Their partiality witnesses against them;
they proclaim their sin like Sodom,
they do not hide it.
Woe to them!
For they have brought evil upon
themselves.
[10]Tell the righteous that it shall be well
with them,
for they shall eat the fruit of their deeds.
[11]Woe to the wicked! It shall be ill
with him,
for what his hands have done shall be
done to him.
[12]My people—children are their oppressors,
and women rule over them.
O my people, your leaders mislead you,
and confuse the course of your paths.

[13]The LORD has taken his place to contend,
he stands to judge his people.
[14]The LORD enters into judgment
with the elders and princes of his people:
"It is you who have devoured the vineyard,
the spoil of the poor is in your houses.
[15]What do you mean by crushing my people,
by grinding the face of the poor?" says
the Lord GOD of hosts.

[16]The LORD said:
Because the daughters of Zion are haughty
and walk with outstretched necks,
glancing wantonly with their eyes,
mincing along as they go,
tinkling with their feet;
[17]the Lord will strike with a scab
the heads of the daughters of Zion,
and the LORD will lay bare their secret parts.
[18]In that day the Lord will take away the
finery of the anklets, the headbands, and the
crescents; [19]the pendants, the bracelets, and the
scarfs; [20]the headdresses, the armlets, the sashes, the perfume boxes, and the amulets; [21]the
signet rings and nose rings; [22]the festal robes,
the mantles, the cloaks, and the handbags; [23]the
garments of gauze, the linen garments, the turbans, and the veils.
[24]Instead of perfume there will be rottenness;
and instead of a belt, a rope;
and instead of well-set hair, baldness;
and instead of a rich robe, a putting on
of sackcloth;
instead of beauty, shame.
[25]Your men shall fall by the sword
and your mighty men in battle.
[26]And her gates shall lament and mourn;
ravaged, she shall sit upon the ground.

4 And seven women shall take hold of one
man in that day, saying, "We will eat our own
bread and wear our own clothes, only let us be
called by your name; take away our reproach."

[2]In that day the branch of the LORD shall be
beautiful and glorious, and the fruit of the land
shall be the pride and glory of the survivors of
Israel. [3]And he who is left in Zion and remains
in Jerusalem will be called holy, every one
who has been recorded for life in Jerusalem,
[4]when the Lord shall have washed away the

filth of the daughters of Zion and cleansed the
bloodstains of Jerusalem from its midst by a
spirit of judgment and by a spirit of burning.
5 Then the LORD will create over the whole site
of Mount Zion and over her assemblies a cloud
by day, and smoke and the shining of a flaming
fire by night; for over all the glory there will be
a canopy and a pavilion. 6 It will be for a shade
by day from the heat, and for a refuge and a
shelter from the storm and rain.

5 Let me sing for my beloved
a love song concerning his vineyard:
My beloved had a vineyard
on a very fertile hill.
2 He dug it and cleared it of stones,
and planted it with choice vines;
he built a watchtower in the midst of it,
and hewed out a wine vat in it;
and he looked for it to yield grapes,
but it yielded wild grapes.

3 And now, O inhabitants of Jerusalem
and men of Judah,
judge, I beg you, between me
and my vineyard.
4 What more was there to do for my vineyard,
that I have not done in it?
When I looked for it to yield grapes,
why did it yield wild grapes?

5 And now I will tell you
what I will do to my vineyard.
I will remove its hedge,
and it shall be devoured;
I will break down its wall,
and it shall be trampled down.
6 I will make it a waste;
it shall not be pruned or hoed,
and briers and thorns shall grow up;
I will also command the clouds
that they rain no rain upon it.

7 For the vineyard of the LORD of hosts
is the house of Israel,
and the men of Judah
are his pleasant planting;
and he looked for justice,
but behold, bloodshed;
for righteousness,
but behold, a cry!

8 Woe to those who join house to house,
who add field to field,
until there is no more room,
and you are made to dwell alone
in the midst of the land.
9 The LORD of hosts has sworn in my hearing:
"Surely many houses shall be desolate,
large and beautiful houses, without
inhabitant.
10 For ten acres of vineyard shall yield but
one bath,
and a homer of seed shall yield but an ephah."

11 Woe to those who rise early in the morning,
that they may run after strong drink,
who linger late into the evening
till wine inflames them!
12 They have lyre and harp,
timbrel and flute and wine at their feasts;
but they do not regard the deeds of the LORD,
or see the work of his hands.

13 Therefore my people go into exile for want
of knowledge;
their honored men are dying of hunger,
and their multitude is parched with thirst.
14 Therefore Sheol has enlarged its appetite
and opened its mouth beyond measure,
and the nobility of Jerusalem and her
multitude go down,
her throng and he who exults in her.
15 Man is bowed down, and men are
brought low,
and the eyes of the haughty are humbled.
16 But the LORD of hosts is exalted in justice,
and the Holy God shows himself holy in
righteousness.
17 Then shall the lambs graze as in their
pasture,
fatlings and kids shall feed among the ruins.

18 Woe to those who draw iniquity with
cords of falsehood,
who draw sin as with cart ropes,
19 who say: "Let him make haste,
let him speed his work
that we may see it;
let the purpose of the Holy One of Israel
draw near,
and let it come, that we may know it!"

20Woe to those who call evil good and
good evil,
who put darkness for light
and light for darkness,
who put bitter for sweet
and sweet for bitter!
21Woe to those who are wise in their
own eyes,
and shrewd in their own sight!
22Woe to those who are heroes at
drinking wine,
and valiant men in mixing strong drink,
23who acquit the guilty for a bribe,
and deprive the innocent of his right!

24Therefore, as the tongue of fire devours
the stubble,
and as dry grass sinks down in the flame,
so their root will be as rottenness,
and their blossom go up like dust;
for they have rejected the law of the LORD
of hosts,
and have despised the word of the Holy
One of Israel.
25Therefore the anger of the LORD was
kindled against his people,
and he stretched out his hand against
them and struck them,
and the mountains quaked;
and their corpses were as refuse
in the midst of the streets.
For all this his anger is not turned away
and his hand is stretched out still.

26He will raise a signal for a nation afar off,
and whistle for it from the ends of the
earth;
and behold, swiftly, speedily it comes!
27None is weary, none stumbles,
none slumbers or sleeps,
not a waistcloth is loose,
not a sandal-thong broken;
28their arrows are sharp,
all their bows bent,
their horses' hoofs seem like flint,
and their wheels like the whirlwind.
29Their roaring is like a lion,
like young lions they roar;
they growl and seize their prey,
they carry it off, and none can rescue.
30They will growl over it on that day,
like the roaring of the sea.
And if one look to the land,
behold, darkness and distress;
and the light is darkened by its clouds.

ECCLESIASTES 5

13There is a grievous evil which I have seen
under the sun: riches were kept by their owner
to his hurt, 14and those riches were lost in a
bad venture; and he is father of a son, but he
has nothing in his hand. 15As he came from his
mother's womb he shall go again, naked as he
came, and shall take nothing for his toil, which
he may carry away in his hand. 16This also is
a grievous evil: just as he came, so shall he go;
and what gain has he that he toiled for the wind,
17and spent all his days in darkness and grief, in
much vexation and sickness and resentment?
18Behold, what I have seen to be good
and to be fitting is to eat and drink and find
enjoyment in all the toil with which one toils
under the sun the few days of his life which
God has given him, for this is his lot. 19Every
man also to whom God has given wealth and
possessions and power to enjoy them, and to
accept his lot and find enjoyment in his toil—
this is the gift of God. 20For he will not much
remember the days of his life because God
keeps him occupied with joy in his heart.
6 There is an evil which I have seen
under the sun, and it lies heavy upon men:
2a man to whom God gives wealth, possessions,
and honor, so that he lacks nothing of all that
he desires, yet God does not give him power
to enjoy them, but a stranger enjoys them; this
is vanity; it is a sore affliction. 3If a man begets
a hundred children, and lives many years, so
that the days of his years are many, but he does
not enjoy life's good things, and also has no
burial, I say that an untimely birth is better off
than he. 4For it comes into vanity and goes into
darkness, and in darkness its name is covered;
5moreover it has not seen the sun or known
anything; yet it finds rest rather than he. 6Even
though he should live a thousand years twice
told, yet enjoy no good—do not all go to the
one place?

[7]All the toil of man is for his mouth, yet his appetite is not satisfied. [8]For what advantage has the wise man over the fool? And what does the poor man have who knows how to conduct himself before the living? [9]Better is the sight of the eyes than the wandering of desire; this also is vanity and a striving after wind.

[10]Whatever has come to be has already been named, and it is known what man is, and that he is not able to dispute with one stronger than he. [11]The more words, the more vanity, and what is man the better? [12]For who knows what is good for man while he lives the few days of his vain life, which he passes like a shadow? For who can tell man what will be after him under the sun?

---

1 CORINTHIANS 8

Now concerning food offered to idols: we know that "all of us possess knowledge." "Knowledge" puffs up, but love builds up. [2]If any one imagines that he knows something, he does not yet know as he ought to know. [3]But if one loves God, one is known by him.

[4]Hence, as to the eating of food offered to idols, we know that "an idol has no real existence," and that "there is no God but one." [5]For although there may be so-called gods in heaven or on earth—as indeed there are many "gods" and many "lords"—[6]yet for us there is one God, the Father, from whom are all things and for whom we exist, and one Lord, Jesus Christ, through whom are all things and through whom we exist.

[7]However, not all possess this knowledge. But some, through being until now accustomed to idols, eat food as really offered to an idol; and their conscience, being weak, is defiled. [8]Food will not commend us to God. We are no worse off if we do not eat, and no better off if we do. [9]Only take care lest this liberty of yours somehow become a stumbling block to the weak. [10]For if any one sees you, a man of knowledge, at table in an idol's temple, might he not be encouraged, if his conscience is weak, to eat food offered to idols? [11]And so by your knowledge this weak man is destroyed, the brother for whom Christ died. [12]Thus, sinning against your brethren and wounding their conscience when it is weak, you sin against Christ. [13]Therefore, if food is a cause of my brother's falling, I will never eat meat, lest I cause my brother to fall.

REFLECTION

It is regarded as a platitude that money cannot buy happiness, but do we really live as if this is true? How often are our decisions based on material considerations? How often do we delay service to God, family, or neighbor for the sake of our careers or our financial benefit? In Isaiah, the prophet speaks of Israel's punishment: the people will be stripped of their wealthy trappings, of their land, and of their livelihood. These severe losses will remind the people that all things are a gift from God. Although material possessions can be good and are necessary for our everyday life, we can easily allow them to take precedence over God. Ecclesiastes makes the point even more starkly. If we horde possessions, it is to our own detriment. When we die we take nothing with us. Too often we forget that the good things we have are not the ultimate good. We must resist the temptation to let our talents and treasures puff us up, as St. Paul says. When we have good and beautiful things, we should praise God and not ourselves. Consider the true tests of whether you love material possessions more than God: How do you react when you lose them? And for whom do you use your material possessions? Do you sometimes put material possessions before God and others?

August 29

ISAIAH 6

In the year that King Uzzi′ah died I saw the Lord sitting upon a throne, high and lifted up; and his train filled the temple. [2]Above him stood the

seraphim; each had six wings: with two he
covered his face, and with two he covered
his feet, and with two he flew. 3And one
called to another and said:
"Holy, holy, holy is the LORD of hosts;
the whole earth is full of his glory."
4And the foundations of the thresholds
shook at the voice of him who called, and
the house was filled with smoke. 5And I
said: "Woe is me! For I am lost; for I am a
man of unclean lips, and I dwell in the midst
of a people of unclean lips; for my eyes have
seen the King, the LORD of hosts!"
6Then flew one of the seraphim to me,
having in his hand a burning coal which he
had taken with tongs from the altar. 7And he
touched my mouth, and said: "Behold, this
has touched your lips; your guilt is taken
away, and your sin forgiven." 8And I heard
the voice of the Lord saying, "Whom shall I
send, and who will go for us?" Then I said,
"Here am I! Send me." 9And he said, "Go,
and say to this people:
'Hear and hear, but do not understand;
see and see, but do not perceive.'
10Make the heart of this people fat,
and their ears heavy,
and shut their eyes;
lest they see with their eyes,
and hear with their ears,
and understand with their hearts,
and turn and be healed."
11Then I said, "How long, O Lord?"
And he said:
"Until cities lie waste
without inhabitant,
and houses without men,
and the land is utterly desolate,
12and the LORD removes men far away,
and the forsaken places are many in the
midst of the land.
13And though a tenth remain in it,
it will be burned again,
like a terebinth or an oak,
whose stump remains standing
when it is felled."
The holy seed is its stump.

7 In the days of A'haz the son of Jo'tham,
son of Uzzi'ah, king of Judah, Re'zin
the king of Syria and Pe'kah the son of
Remali'ah the king of Israel came up to
Jerusalem to wage war against it, but they
could not conquer it. 2When the house of
David was told, "Syria is in league with
E'phraim," his heart and the heart of his
people shook as the trees of the forest shake
before the wind.
3And the LORD said to Isai'ah, "Go forth
to meet A'haz, you and She'arjash''ub
your son, at the end of the conduit of the
upper pool on the highway to the Fuller's
Field, 4and say to him, 'Take heed, be quiet,
do not fear, and do not let your heart be
faint because of these two smoldering
stumps of firebrands, at the fierce anger of
Re'zin and Syria and the son of Remali'ah.
5Because Syria, with E'phraim and the son
of Remali'ah, has devised evil against you,
saying, 6"Let us go up against Judah and
terrify it, and let us conquer it for ourselves,
and set up the son of Ta'be-el as king in the
midst of it," 7thus says the Lord GOD:
It shall not stand,
and it shall not come to pass.
8For the head of Syria is Damascus,
and the head of Damascus is Re'zin.
(Within sixty-five years E'phraim will be
broken to pieces so that it will no longer be
a people.)
9And the head of E'phraim is Samar'ia,
and the head of Samaria is the son
of Remali'ah.
If you will not believe,
surely you shall not be established.'"
10Again the LORD spoke to A'haz, 11"Ask
a sign of the LORD your God; let it be deep
as Sheol or high as heaven." 12But A'haz
said, "I will not ask, and I will not put the
LORD to the test." 13And he said, "Hear
then, O house of David! Is it too little
for you to weary men, that you weary my
God also? 14Therefore the Lord himself
will give you a sign. Behold, a virgin
shall conceive and bear a son, and shall
call his name Imman'u-el. 15He shall eat
curds and honey when he knows how to
refuse the evil and choose the good. 16For
before the child knows how to refuse the
evil and choose the good, the land before
whose two kings you are in dread will

be deserted. 17The LORD will bring upon
you and upon your people and upon your
father's house such days as have not come
since the day that E′phraim departed
from Judah—the king of Assyria."
18In that day the LORD will whistle for the
fly which is at the sources of the streams of
Egypt, and for the bee which is in the land
of Assyria. 19And they will all come and
settle in the steep ravines, and in the clefts
of the rocks, and on all the thornbushes,
and on all the pastures.
20In that day the Lord will shave with a razor
which is hired beyond the River—with the
king of Assyria—the head and the hair of the
feet, and it will sweep away the beard also.
21In that day a man will keep alive a young
cow and two sheep; 22and because of the
abundance of milk which they give, he will
eat curds; for every one that is left in the
land will eat curds and honey.
23In that day every place where there used
to be a thousand vines, worth a thousand
shekels of silver, will become briers and
thorns. 24With bow and arrows men will
come there, for all the land will be briers
and thorns; 25and as for all the hills which
used to be hoed with a hoe, you will not
come there for fear of briers and thorns;
but they will become a place where cattle
are let loose and where sheep tread.

8 Then the LORD said to me, "Take a large
tablet and write upon it in common
characters, 'Belonging to Ma′her-shal′al-
hash″-baz.'" 2And I got reliable witnesses,
Uri′ah the priest and Zechari′ah the son of
Jeberechi′ah, to attest for me. 3And I went to
the prophetess, and she conceived and bore
a son. Then the LORD said to me, "Call his
name Ma′her-shal′al-hash″-baz; 4for before
the child knows how to cry 'My father' or
'My mother,' the wealth of Damascus and
the spoil of Samar′ia will be carried away
before the king of Assyria."
5The LORD spoke to me again: 6"Because
this people have refused the waters of
Shilo′ah that flow gently, and melt in fear
before Re′zin and the son of Remali′ah;
7therefore, behold, the Lord is bringing
up against them the waters of the River,
mighty and many, the king of Assyria and
all his glory; and it will rise over all its
channels and go over all its banks; 8and it
will sweep on into Judah, it will overflow
and pass on, reaching even to the neck; and
its outspread wings will fill the breadth of
your land, O Imman′u-el."

9Be broken, you peoples, and be dismayed;
give ear, all you far countries;
gird yourselves and be dismayed;
gird yourselves and be dismayed.
10Take counsel together, but it will come to
nought;
speak a word, but it will not stand,
for God is with us.

11For the LORD spoke thus to me with his
strong hand upon me, and warned me not to
walk in the way of this people, saying: 12"Do
not call conspiracy all that this people call
conspiracy, and do not fear what they fear, nor
be in dread. 13But the LORD of hosts, him you
shall regard as holy; let him be your fear, and
let him be your dread. 14And he will become a
sanctuary, and a stone of offense, and a rock of
stumbling to both houses of Israel, a trap and
a snare to the inhabitants of Jerusalem. 15And
many shall stumble thereon; they shall fall and
be broken; they shall be snared and taken."
16Bind up the testimony, seal the teaching among my disciples. 17I will wait for
the LORD, who is hiding his face from the
house of Jacob, and I will hope in him. 18Be-
hold, I and the children whom the LORD
has given me are signs and portents in Israel from the LORD of hosts, who dwells on
Mount Zion. 19And when they say to you,
"Consult the mediums and the wizards
who chirp and mutter," should not a people
consult their God? Should they consult the
dead on behalf of the living? 20To the teaching and to the testimony! Surely for this
word which they speak there is no dawn.
21They will pass through the land, greatly distressed and hungry; and when they
are hungry, they will be enraged and will
curse their king and their God, and turn
their faces upward; 22and they will look to
the earth, but behold, distress and darkness, the gloom of anguish; and they will
be thrust into thick darkness.

ECCLESIASTES 7

A good name is better than precious
ointment;
and the day of death, than the day
of birth.
2 It is better to go to the house of mourning
than to go to the house of feasting;
for this is the end of all men,
and the living will lay it to heart.
3 Sorrow is better than laughter,
for by sadness of countenance the heart is
made glad.
4 The heart of the wise is in the house
of mourning;
but the heart of fools is in the house
of mirth.
5 It is better for a man to hear the rebuke of
the wise
than to hear the song of fools.
6 For as the crackling of thorns under a pot,
so is the laughter of the fools;
this also is vanity.
7 Surely oppression makes the wise
man foolish,
and a bribe corrupts the mind.
8 Better is the end of a thing than its beginning;
and the patient in spirit is better than the
proud in spirit.
9 Be not quick to anger,
for anger lodges in the bosom of fools.
10 Say not, "Why were the former days better
than these?"
For it is not from wisdom that you
ask this.
11 Wisdom is good with an inheritance,
an advantage to those who see the sun.
12 For the protection of wisdom is like the
protection of money;
and the advantage of knowledge is that
wisdom preserves the life of him who
has it.
13 Consider the work of God;
who can make straight what he has
made crooked?

14 In the day of prosperity be joyful, and
in the day of adversity consider; God has
made the one as well as the other, so that
man may not find out anything that will
be after him.

1 CORINTHIANS 9

Am I not free? Am I not an
apostle? Have I not seen Jesus
our Lord? Are you not my workman-
ship in the Lord? 2 If to others I am not
an apostle, at least I am to you;for you are
the seal of my apostleship in the Lord.
3 This is my defense to those who would
examine me. 4 Do we not have the right to
our food and drink? 5 Do we not have the
right to be accompanied by a wife, as the
other apostles and the brethren of the Lord
and Cephas? 6 Or is it only Barnabas and I
who have no right to refrain from working
for a living? 7 Who serves as a soldier at
his own expense? Who plants a vineyard
without eating any of its fruit? Who tends a
flock without getting some of the milk?
8 Do I say this on human authority? Does
not the law say the same? 9 For it is written
in the law of Moses, "You shall not muzzle
an ox when it is treading out the grain." Is
it for oxen that God is concerned? 10 Does
he not speak entirely for our sake? It was
written for our sake, because the plowman
should plow in hope and the thresher thresh
in hope of a share in the crop. 11 If we have
sown spiritual good among you, is it too
much if we reap your material benefits? 12 If
others share this rightful claim upon you,
do not we still more?

Nevertheless, we have not made use of this
right, but we endure anything rather than
put an obstacle in the way of the gospel of
Christ. 13 Do you not know that those who
are employed in the temple service get their
food from the temple, and those who serve
at the altar share in the sacrificial offerings?
14 In the same way, the Lord commanded
that those who proclaim the gospel should
get their living by the gospel.
15 But I have made no use of any of these
rights, nor am I writing this to secure any
such provision. For I would rather die than
have any one deprive me of my ground
for boasting. 16 For if I preach the gospel,
that gives me no ground for boasting. For
necessity is laid upon me. Woe to me if I do
not preach the gospel! 17 For if I do this of my

own will, I have a reward; but if not of my own will, I am entrusted with a commission.
18What then is my reward? Just this: that in my preaching I may make the gospel free of charge, not making full use of my right in the gospel.

REFLECTION

In chapter 6 of Isaiah, the prophet sees a heavenly vision and hears the angels singing "holy, holy, holy" (Is 6:3). This angelic refrain is part of the *Sanctus* sung at Mass. But when does Isaiah hear this glorious song? He hears it just as he is being called to preach a difficult message, and as he learns about the great suffering Israel must endure. Likewise in Ecclesiastes, the author tells us that sorrow is better than laughter, and mourning better than feasting. In these passages we glimpse a mystery that lies at the heart of the Gospel. Somehow, it is in our suffering and in our mortal toil that God's glory should be especially evident to us. This is also the mystery of the Cross—that God chose to enter fully into human suffering. When we sing the *Sanctus* at Mass, we truly join the angelic hosts that Isaiah saw praising God in Heaven. If we find ourselves suffering, in difficult situations, or sad when we are about to sing this heavenly refrain, we should join in even more fully, seeing it as an opportunity to offer a sacrifice of praise. Do you remember to praise God in times of suffering or sadness?

August 30

ISAIAH 9

But there will be no gloom for her that was in anguish. In the former time he brought into contempt the land of Zeb′ulun and the land of Naph′tali, but in the latter time he will make glorious the way of the sea, the land beyond the Jordan, Galilee of the nations.

2The people who walked in darkness
have seen a great light;
those who dwelt in a land of deep darkness,
on them has light shined.
3You have multiplied the nation,
you have increased its joy;
they rejoice before you
as with joy at the harvest,
as men rejoice when they divide the spoil.
4For the yoke of his burden,
and the staff for his shoulder,
the rod of his oppressor,
you have broken as on the day of Mid′ian.
5For every boot of the tramping warrior in battle tumult
and every garment rolled in blood
will be burned as fuel for the fire.
6For to us a child is born,
to us a son is given;
and the government will be upon his shoulder,
and his name will be called
"Wonderful Counselor, Mighty God,
Everlasting Father, Prince of Peace."
7Of the increase of his government and of peace
there will be no end,
upon the throne of David, and over his kingdom,
to establish it, and to uphold it
with justice and with righteousness
from this time forth and for evermore.
The zeal of the LORD of hosts will do this.

8The Lord has sent a word against Jacob,
and it will light upon Israel;
9and all the people will know,
E′phraim and the inhabitants of Samar′ia,
who say in pride and in arrogance of heart:
10"The bricks have fallen,
but we will build with dressed stones;
the sycamores have been cut down,
but we will put cedars in their place."
11So the LORD raises adversaries against them,
and stirs up their enemies.
12The Syrians on the east and the Philis′tines on the west
devour Israel with open mouth.
For all this his anger is not turned away
and his hand is stretched out still.

13The people did not turn to him who
struck them,
nor seek the LORD of hosts.
14So the LORD cut off from Israel head
and tail,
palm branch and reed in one day—
15the elder and honored man is the head,
and the prophet who teaches lies is the tail;
16for those who lead this people lead
them astray,
and those who are led by them are
swallowed up.
17Therefore the Lord does not rejoice over
their young men,
and has no compassion on their fatherless
and widows;
for every one is godless and an evildoer,
and every mouth speaks folly.
For all this his anger is not turned away
and his hand is stretched out still.

18For wickedness burns like a fire,
it consumes briers and thorns;
it kindles the thickets of the forest,
and they roll upward in a column of smoke.
19Through the wrath of the LORD of hosts
the land is burned,
and the people are like fuel for the fire;
no man spares his brother.
20They snatch on the right, but are still hungry,
and they devour on the left, but are
not satisfied;
each devours his neighbor's flesh,
21Manas′seh E′phraim, and Ephraim
Manasseh,
and together they are against Judah.
For all this his anger is not turned away
and his hand is stretched out still.

10 Woe to those who decree iniquitous
decrees,
and the writers who keep writing
oppression,
2to turn aside the needy from justice
and to rob the poor of my people of
their right,
that widows may be their spoil,
and that they may make the fatherless
their prey!
3What will you do on the day of punishment,
in the storm which will come from afar?
To whom will you flee for help,
and where will you leave your wealth?
4Nothing remains but to crouch among
the prisoners
or fall among the slain.
For all this his anger is not turned away
and his hand is stretched out still.

5Ah, Assyria, the rod of my anger,
the staff of my fury!
6Against a godless nation I send him,
and against the people of my wrath I
command him,
to take spoil and seize plunder,
and to tread them down like the mire of
the streets.
7But he does not so intend,
and his mind does not so think;
but it is in his mind to destroy,
and to cut off nations not a few;
8for he says:
"Are not my commanders all kings?
9Is not Calno like Car′chemish?
Is not Ha′math like Arpad?
Is not Samar′ia like Damascus?
10As my hand has reached to the kingdoms
of the idols
whose graven images were greater than
those of Jerusalem and Samar′ia,
11shall I not do to Jerusalem and her idols
as I have done to Samar′ia and her images?"

12When the Lord has finished all his work
on Mount Zion and on Jerusalem he will
punish the arrogant boasting of the king of
Assyria and his haughty pride. 13For he says:
"By the strength of my hand I have done it,
and by my wisdom, for I have
understanding;
I have removed the boundaries of peoples,
and have plundered their treasures;
like a bull I have brought down those
who sat on thrones.
14My hand has found like a nest
the wealth of the peoples;
and as men gather eggs that have
been forsaken
so I have gathered all the earth;
and there was none that moved a wing,
or opened the mouth, or chirped."

[15]Shall the axe vaunt itself over him who
hews with it,
or the saw magnify itself against him who
wields it?
As if a rod should wield him who lifts it,
or as if a staff should lift him who is
not wood!
[16]Therefore the Lord, the LORD of hosts,
will send wasting sickness among his
stout warriors,
and under his glory a burning will
be kindled,
like the burning of fire.
[17]The light of Israel will become a fire,
and his Holy One a flame;
and it will burn and devour
his thorns and briers in one day.
[18]The glory of his forest and of his
fruitful land
the LORD will destroy, both soul and body,
and it will be as when a sick man
wastes away.
[19]The remnant of the trees of his forest will
be so few
that a child can write them down.
[20]In that day the remnant of Israel and
the survivors of the house of Jacob will no
more lean upon him that struck them, but
will lean upon the LORD, the Holy One of
Israel, in truth. [21]A remnant will return, the
remnant of Jacob, to the mighty God. [22]For
though your people Israel be as the sand of
the sea, only a remnant of them will return.
Destruction is decreed, overflowing with
righteousness. [23]For the Lord, the LORD of
hosts, will make a full end, as decreed, in the
midst of all the earth.
[24]Therefore thus says the Lord, the LORD
of hosts: "O my people, who dwell in
Zion, be not afraid of the Assyrians when
they strike with the rod and lift up their
staff against you as the Egyptians did.
[25]For in a very little while my indignation
will come to an end, and my anger will be
directed to their destruction. [26]And the
LORD of hosts will wield against them a
scourge, as when he struck Mid′ian at the
rock of Or′eb; and his rod will be over the
sea, and he will lift it as he did in Egypt.
[27]And in that day his burden will depart
from your shoulder, and his yoke will be
destroyed from your neck."

He has gone up from Rimmon,
[28] he has come to Ai′ath;
he has passed through Migron,
at Mich′mash he stores his baggage;
[29]they have crossed over the pass,
at Ge′ba they lodge for the night;
Ra′mah trembles,
Gib′eah of Saul has fled.
[30]Cry aloud, O daughter of Gallim!
Listen, O La′ishah!
Answer her, O An′athoth!
[31]Madme′nah is in flight,
the inhabitants of Gebim flee for safety.
[32]This very day he will halt at Nob,
he will shake his fist
at the mount of the daughter of Zion,
the hill of Jerusalem.

[33]Behold, the Lord, the LORD of hosts
will lop the boughs with terrifying power;
the great in height will be hewn down,
and the lofty will be brought low.
[34]He will cut down the thickets of the forest
with an axe,
and Lebanon with its majestic trees will fall.

11 There shall come forth a shoot from
the stump of Jesse,
and a branch shall grow out of his roots.
[2]And the Spirit of the LORD shall rest upon
him,
the spirit of wisdom and understanding,
the spirit of counsel and might,
the spirit of knowledge and the fear
of the LORD.
[3]And his delight shall be in the fear of
the LORD.

He shall not judge by what his eyes see,
or decide by what his ears hear;
[4]but with righteousness he shall judge
the poor,
and decide with equity for the meek of
the earth;
and he shall strike the earth with the rod of
his mouth,
and with the breath of his lips he shall
slay the wicked.

5Righteousness shall be the belt of his waist,
and faithfulness the belt of his loins.
6The wolf shall dwell with the lamb,
and the leopard shall lie down with the kid,
and the calf and the lion and the fatling
together,
and a little child shall lead them.
7The cow and the bear shall feed;
their young shall lie down together;
and the lion shall eat straw like the ox.
8The sucking child shall play over the hole
of the asp,
and the weaned child shall put his hand
on the adder's den.
9They shall not hurt or destroy
in all my holy mountain;
for the earth shall be full of the knowledge
of the LORD
as the waters cover the sea.

10In that day the root of Jesse shall stand as
an ensign to the peoples; him shall the nations
seek, and his dwellings shall be glorious.
11In that day the Lord will extend his hand
yet a second time to recover the remnant
which is left of his people, from Assyria,
from Egypt, from Path′ros, from Ethiopia,
from E′lam, from Shi′nar, from Ha′math,
and from the islands of the sea.
12He will raise an ensign for the nations,
and will assemble the outcasts of Israel,
and gather the dispersed of Judah
from the four corners of the earth.
13The jealousy of E′phraim shall depart,
and those who harass Judah shall be
cut off;
Ephraim shall not be jealous of Judah,
and Judah shall not harass Ephraim.
14But they shall swoop down upon the
shoulder of the Philis′tines in the west,
and together they shall plunder the
people of the east.
They shall put forth their hand against
E′dom and Moab,
and the Am′monites shall obey them.
15And the LORD will utterly destroy
the tongue of the sea of Egypt;
and will wave his hand over the River
with his scorching wind,
and strike it into seven channels
that men may cross dryshod.
16And there will be a highway from Assyria
for the remnant which is left of
his people,
as there was for Israel
when they came up from the land
of Egypt.

12 You will say in that day:
"I will give thanks to you, O LORD,
for though you were angry with me,
your anger turned away,
and you did comfort me.

2"Behold, God is my salvation;
I will trust, and will not be afraid;
for the LORD GOD is my strength and
my song,
and he has become my salvation."

3With joy you will draw water from the wells
of salvation. 4And you will say in that day:
"Give thanks to the LORD,
call upon his name;
make known his deeds among the nations,
proclaim that his name is exalted.

5"Sing praises to the LORD, for he has done
gloriously;
let this be known in all the earth.
6Shout, and sing for joy, O inhabitant of Zion,
for great in your midst is the Holy One
of Israel."

ECCLESIASTES 7

15In my vain life I have seen everything;
there is a righteous man who perishes in his
righteousness, and there is a wicked man
who prolongs his life in his evil-doing. 16Be
not righteous overmuch, and do not make
yourself overwise; why should you destroy
yourself? 17Be not wicked overmuch, neither be a fool; why should you die before
your time? 18It is good that you should take
hold of this, and from that withhold not
your hand; for he who fears God shall come
forth from them all.

19Wisdom gives strength to the wise man
more than ten rulers that are in a city.
20Surely there is not a righteous man on
earth who does good and never sins.
21Do not give heed to all the things that
men say, lest you hear your servant cursing
you; 22your heart knows that many times
you have yourself cursed others.
23All this I have tested by wisdom; I said, "I
will be wise"; but it was far from me. 24That
which is, is far off, and deep, very deep; who
can find it out? 25I turned my mind to know and
to search out and to seek wisdom and the sum
of things, and to know the wickedness of folly
and the foolishness which is madness. 26And I
found more bitter than death the woman whose
heart is snares and nets, and whose hands are
fetters; he who pleases God escapes her, but the
sinner is taken by her. 27Behold, this is what I
found, says the Preacher, adding one thing to
another to find the sum, 28which my mind has
sought repeatedly, but I have not found. One
man among a thousand I found, but a woman
among all these I have not found. 29Behold, this
alone I found, that God made man upright, but
they have sought out many devices.

1 CORINTHIANS 9

**19For though I am free from
all men, I have made myself a
slave to all, that I might win the more.
20To the Jews I became as a Jew, in order**
to win Jews; to those under the law I became as
one under the law—though not being myself
under the law—that I might win those under
the law. 21To those outside the law I became as
one outside the law—not being without law
toward God but under the law of Christ—that I
might win those outside the law. 22To the weak
I became weak, that I might win the weak. I
have become all things to all men, that I might
by all means save some. 23I do it all for the sake
of the gospel, that I may share in its blessings.
24Do you not know that in a race all the
runners compete, but only one receives the
prize? So run that you may obtain it. 25Every
athlete exercises self-control in all things. They
do it to receive a perishable wreath, but we an
imperishable. 26Well, I do not run aimlessly, I do
not box as one beating the air; 27but I pommel
my body and subdue it, lest after preaching to
others I myself should be disqualified.

REFLECTION

Ecclesiastes poses the problem of life's unfairness in stark terms: "There is a righteous man who perishes in his righteousness, and there is a wicked man who prolongs his life in his evil-doing" (Eccl 7:15). The heart wonders why God, in his justice, would allow such upside-down circumstances to persist. Yet his answer does not come in the form of revised judicial procedures, but in the person of his Son. Isaiah eloquently proclaims the coming of the Messiah: "The people who walked in darkness have seen a great light" (Is 9:2). The darkness of injustice is wiped away by his arrival. This "child" will be "Wonderful Counselor, Mighty God, Everlasting Father, Prince of Peace" (v. 6). The Messiah will not be an outsider, but a son of David from the "stump of Jesse," David's father (11:1). Through him, "a remnant will return, the remnant of Jacob, to the mighty God" (10:21). Jesus, as the fulfillment of these prophecies, ushers in an era of salvation, of light, of return to the Lord. While we might still experience unfairness or injustice in our earthly lives, we can rest with confidence in his eternal justice, knowing that one day he will "judge the world in righteousness" (Acts 17:31). How can you rest in the justice of God in the midst of life's unfairness?

August 31

ISAIAH 13

**The oracle concerning Babylon
which Isai′ah the son of A′moz
saw.
2On a bare hill raise a signal,
cry aloud to them;**
wave the hand for them to enter
the gates of the nobles.

3 I myself have commanded my
consecrated ones,
have summoned my mighty men to
execute my anger,
my proudly exulting ones.

4 Listen, a tumult on the mountains
as of a great multitude!
Listen, an uproar of kingdoms,
of nations gathering together!
The LORD of hosts is mustering
a host for battle.
5 They come from a distant land,
from the end of the heavens,
the LORD and the weapons of his indignation,
to destroy the whole earth.

6 Wail, for the day of the LORD is near;
as destruction from the Almighty
it will come!
7 Therefore all hands will be feeble,
and every man's heart will melt,
8 and they will be dismayed.
Pangs and agony will seize them;
they will be in anguish like a woman with
labor pains.
They will look aghast at one another;
their faces will be aflame.

9 Behold, the day of the LORD comes,
cruel, with wrath and fierce anger,
to make the earth a desolation
and to destroy its sinners from it.
10 For the stars of the heavens and their
constellations
will not give their light;
the sun will be dark at its rising
and the moon will not shed its light.
11 I will punish the world for its evil,
and the wicked for their iniquity;
I will put an end to the pride of the arrogant,
and lay low the haughtiness of
the ruthless.
12 I will make men more rare than fine gold,
and mankind than the gold of O´phir.
13 Therefore I will make the heavens tremble,
and the earth will be shaken out of
its place,
at the wrath of the LORD of hosts
in the day of his fierce anger.
14 And like a hunted gazelle,
or like sheep with none to gather them,
every man will turn to his own people,
and every man will flee to his own land.
15 Whoever is found will be thrust through,
and whoever is caught will fall by
the sword.
16 Their infants will be dashed in pieces
before their eyes;
their houses will be plundered
and their wives ravished.

17 Behold, I am stirring up the Medes
against them,
who have no regard for silver
and do not delight in gold.
18 Their bows will slaughter the young men;
they will have no mercy on the fruit of
the womb;
their eyes will not pity children.
19 And Babylon, the glory of kingdoms,
the splendor and pride of the Chalde´ans,
will be like Sodom and Gomor´rah
when God overthrew them.
20 It will never be inhabited
or dwelt in for all generations;
no Arab will pitch his tent there,
no shepherds will make their flocks lie
down there.
21 But wild beasts will lie down there,
and its houses will be full of howling
creatures;
there ostriches will dwell,
and there satyrs will dance.
22 Hyenas will cry in its towers,
and jackals in the pleasant palaces;
its time is close at hand
and its days will not be prolonged.

14 The LORD will have compassion on
Jacob and will again choose Israel,
and will set them in their own land, and
strangers will join them and will cling to the
house of Jacob. 2 And the peoples will take
them and bring them to their place, and the
house of Israel will possess them in the LORD's
land as male and female slaves; they will take
captive those who were their captors, and rule
over those who oppressed them.
3 When the LORD has given you rest from
your pain and turmoil and the hard service

with which you were made to serve, 4you
will take up this taunt against the king of
Babylon:

"How the oppressor has ceased,
 the insolent fury ceased!
5The LORD has broken the staff of the wicked,
 the scepter of rulers,
6that struck the peoples in wrath
 with unceasing blows,
that ruled the nations in anger
 with unrelenting persecution.
7The whole earth is at rest and quiet;
 they break forth into singing.
8The cypresses rejoice at you,
 the cedars of Lebanon, saying,
'Since you were laid low,
 no hewer comes up against us.'
9Sheol beneath is stirred up
 to meet you when you come,
it rouses the shades to greet you,
 all who were leaders of the earth;
it raises from their thrones
 all who were kings of the nations.
10All of them will speak
 and say to you:
'You too have become as weak as we!
 You have become like us!'
11Your pomp is brought down to Sheol,
 the sound of your harps;
maggots are the bed beneath you,
 and worms are your covering.

12"How you are fallen from heaven,
 O Day Star, son of Dawn!
How you are cut down to the ground,
 you who laid the nations low!
13You said in your heart,
 'I will ascend to heaven;
above the stars of God
 I will set my throne on high;
I will sit on the mount of assembly
 in the far north;
14I will ascend above the heights of the clouds,
 I will make myself like the Most High.'
15But you are brought down to Sheol,
 to the depths of the Pit.
16Those who see you will stare at you,
 and ponder over you:
'Is this the man who made the earth tremble,
 who shook kingdoms,
17who made the world like a desert
 and overthrew its cities,
 who did not let his prisoners go home?'
18All the kings of the nations lie in glory,
 each in his own tomb;
19but you are cast out, away from
 your sepulchre,
 like a loathed untimely birth,
clothed with the slain, those pierced
 by the sword,
 who go down to the stones of the Pit,
 like a dead body trodden under foot.
20You will not be joined with them
 in burial,
 because you have destroyed your land,
 you have slain your people.

"May the descendants of evildoers
 nevermore be named!
21Prepare slaughter for his sons
 because of the guilt of their fathers,
lest they rise and possess the earth,
 and fill the face of the world with cities."

22"I will rise up against them," says the
LORD of hosts, "and will cut off from Babylon name and remnant, offspring and
posterity, says the LORD. 23And I will make
it a possession of the hedgehog, and pools of
water, and I will sweep it with the broom of
destruction, says the LORD of hosts."

24The LORD of hosts has sworn:
"As I have planned,
 so shall it be,
and as I have purposed,
 so shall it stand,
25that I will break the Assyrian in my land,
 and upon my mountains trample him
 under foot;
and his yoke shall depart from them,
 and his burden from their shoulder."
26This is the purpose that is purposed
 concerning the whole earth;
and this is the hand that is stretched out
 over all the nations.
27For the LORD of hosts has purposed,
 and who will annul it?
His hand is stretched out,
 and who will turn it back?

[28]In the year that King Aʹhaz died came
this oracle:
[29]"Rejoice not, O Philisʹtia, all of you,
that the rod which struck you is broken,
for from the serpent's root will come forth
an adder,
and its fruit will be a flying serpent.
[30]And the first-born of the poor will feed,
and the needy lie down in safety;
but I will kill your root with famine,
and your remnant I will slay.
[31]Wail, O gate; cry, O city;
melt in fear, O Philisʹtia, all of you!
For smoke comes out of the north,
and there is no straggler in his ranks."

[32]What will one answer the messengers of
the nation?
"The LORD has founded Zion,
and in her the afflicted of his people
find refuge."

ECCLESIASTES 8

Who is like the wise man?
And who knows the interpretation of
a thing?
A man's wisdom makes his face shine,
and the hardness of his countenance
is changed.

[2]Keep the king's command, and because
of your sacred oath be not dismayed; [3]go
from his presence, do not delay when
the matter is unpleasant, for he does
whatever he pleases. [4]For the word of the
king is supreme, and who may say to him,
"What are you doing?" [5]He who obeys
a command will meet no harm, and the
mind of a wise man will know the time
and way. [6]For every matter has its time
and way, although man's trouble lies
heavy upon him. [7]For he does not know
what is to be, for who can tell him how it
will be? [8]No man has power to retain the
spirit, or authority over the day of death;
there is no discharge from war, nor will
wickedness deliver those who are given to
it. [9]All this I observed while applying my
mind to all that is done under the sun,
while man lords it over man to his hurt.
[10]Then I saw the wicked buried; they
used to go in and out of the holy place,
and were praised in the city where they
had done such things. This also is vanity.
[11]Because sentence against an evil deed
is not executed speedily, the heart of
the sons of men is fully set to do evil.
[12]Though a sinner does evil a hundred
times and prolongs his life, yet I know
that it will be well with those who fear
God, because they fear before him; [13]but
it will not be well with the wicked, neither
will he prolong his days like a shadow,
because he does not fear before God.
[14]There is a vanity which takes place
on earth, that there are righteous men
to whom it happens according to the
deeds of the wicked, and there are wicked
men to whom it happens according to
the deeds of the righteous. I said that
this also is vanity. [15]And I commend
enjoyment, for man has no good thing
under the sun but to eat and drink and
enjoy himself, for this will go with him
in his toil through the days of life which
God gives him under the sun.
[16]When I applied my mind to know wisdom, and to see the business that is done
on earth, how neither day nor night one's
eyes see sleep; [17]then I saw all the work of
God, that man cannot find out the work
that is done under the sun. However much
man may toil in seeking, he will not find
it out; even though a wise man claims to
know, he cannot find it out.

1 CORINTHIANS 10

**I want you to know, brethren,
that our fathers were all under
the cloud, and all passed through the
sea, [2]and all were baptized into Moses**
in the cloud and in the sea, [3]and all ate
the same supernatural food [4]and all drank
the same supernatural drink. For they

drank from the supernatural Rock which
followed them, and the Rock was Christ.
[5]Nevertheless with most of them God was
not pleased; for they were overthrown in
the wilderness.

[6]Now these things are warnings for us,
not to desire evil as they did. [7]Do not be
idolaters as some of them were; as it is
written, "The people sat down to eat and
drink and rose up to dance." [8]We must
not indulge in immorality as some of
them did, and twenty-three thousand fell
in a single day. [9]We must not put the Lord
to the test, as some of them did and were
destroyed by serpents; [10]nor grumble, as
some of them did and were destroyed
by the Destroyer. [11]Now these things
happened to them as a warning, but they
were written down for our instruction,
upon whom the end of the ages has come.
[12]Therefore let any one who thinks that
he stands take heed lest he fall. [13]No
temptation has overtaken you that is not
common to man. God is faithful, and he
will not let you be tempted beyond your
strength, but with the temptation will
also provide the way of escape, that you
may be able to endure it.

[14]Therefore, my beloved, shun the
worship of idols. [15]I speak as to sensible
men; judge for yourselves what I say.
[16]The cup of blessing which we bless,
is it not a participation in the blood of
Christ? The bread which we break, is it
not a participation in the body of Christ?
[17]Because there is one bread, we who are
many are one body, for we all partake of
the one bread. [18]Consider the people of
Israel; are not those who eat the sacrifices
partners in the altar? [19]What do I imply
then? That food offered to idols is anything,
or that an idol is anything? [20]No, I imply
that what pagans sacrifice they offer to
demons and not to God. I do not want you
to be partners with demons. [21]You cannot
drink the cup of the Lord and the cup of
demons. You cannot partake of the table of
the Lord and the table of demons. [22]Shall
we provoke the Lord to jealousy? Are we
stronger than he?

REFLECTION

We need to admit our powerlessness before God. While we can organize our lives to avoid trouble, poverty, or confusion, "no man has power to retain the spirit, or authority over the day of death" (Eccl 8:8). Our lives are in God's hands, and we do not know the day of our departure from this earth. This powerlessness can make us impatient with God, wishing that he would hurry up and help us, yet "we must not put the LORD to the test as some of them did and were destroyed by serpents" (1 Cor 10:9). St. Paul is pointing back to the wilderness generation that complained against Moses in the desert (see Nm 21:4–9). We must be patient with the Lord's redemptive justice—sometimes it is delayed until eternity. Appropriately, the Lord is also patient with us. He gives his people a second chance: "The LORD will have compassion on Jacob and will again choose Israel, and will set them in their own land" (Is 14:1). After all their disobedience and covenant-breaking, the Lord will remake and re-establish his people. In response to his merciful patience, we should acknowledge our helplessness and dependence on him despite the timeline of his justice. In what way can you surrender your impatience with God and simply trust in his power?

September 1

ISAIAH 15

An oracle concerning Moab.
Because Ar is laid waste in a night
Moab is undone;
because Kir is laid waste in a night
Moab is undone.
2The daughter of Di'bon has gone up
to the high places to weep;
over Nebo and over Med'eba
Moab wails.
On every head is baldness,
every beard is shorn;
3in the streets they put on sackcloth;
on the housetops and in the squares
every one wails and melts in tears.
4Heshbon and E'lea'leh cry out,
their voice is heard as far as Ja'haz;
therefore the armed men of Moab
cry aloud;
his soul trembles.
5My heart cries out for Moab;
his fugitives flee to Zoar,
to Eg'lath-shelish'iyah.
For at the ascent of Lu'hith
they go up weeping;
on the road to Horona'im
they raise a cry of destruction;
6the waters of Nimrim
are a desolation;
the grass is withered, the new growth fails,
the verdure is no more.
7Therefore the abundance they have gained
and what they have laid up
they carry away
over the Brook of the Willows.
8For a cry has gone
round the land of Moab;
the wailing reaches to Egla'im,
the wailing reaches to Be'er-e'lim.
9For the waters of Di'bon are full of blood;
yet I will bring upon Dibon even more,
a lion for those of Moab who escape,
for the remnant of the land.

16 They have sent lambs
to the ruler of the land,
from Se'la, by way of the desert,
to the mount of the daughter of Zion.
2Like fluttering birds,
like scattered nestlings,
so are the daughters of Moab
at the fords of the Arnon.
3"Give counsel,
grant justice;
make your shade like night
at the height of noon;
hide the outcasts,
betray not the fugitive;
4let the outcasts of Moab
sojourn among you;
be a refuge to them
from the destroyer.
When the oppressor is no more,
and destruction has ceased,
and he who tramples under foot
has vanished from the land,
5then a throne will be established in
steadfast love
and on it will sit in faithfulness
in the tent of David
one who judges and seeks justice
and is swift to do righteousness."

6We have heard of the pride of Moab,
how proud he was;
of his arrogance, his pride, and his
insolence—
his boasts are false.
7Therefore let Moab wail,
let every one wail for Moab.
Mourn, utterly stricken,
for the raisin-cakes of Kir'-har'eseth.

8For the fields of Heshbon languish,
and the vine of Sibmah;
the lords of the nations
have struck down its branches,
which reached to Ja'zer
and strayed to the desert;
its shoots spread abroad
and passed over the sea.
9Therefore I weep with the weeping
of Ja'zer
for the vine of Sibmah;

I drench you with my tears,
O Heshbon and E′lea′leh;
for upon your fruit and your harvest
the battle shout has fallen.
10 And joy and gladness are taken away
from the fruitful field;
and in the vineyards no songs are sung,
no shouts are raised;
no treader treads out wine in the presses;
the vintage shout is hushed.
11 Therefore my soul moans like a lyre
for Moab,
and my heart for Kirhe′res.

12 And when Moab presents himself, when
he wearies himself upon the high place,
when he comes to his sanctuary to pray, he
will not prevail.

13 This is the word which the LORD spoke
concerning Moab in the past. 14 But now
the LORD says, "In three years, like the
years of a hireling, the glory of Moab will
be brought into contempt, in spite of all his
great multitude, and those who survive will
be very few and feeble."

17 An oracle concerning Damascus.
Behold, Damascus will cease to be a
city,
and will become a heap of ruins.
2 Her cities will be deserted for ever;
they will be for flocks,
which will lie down, and none will make
them afraid.
3 The fortress will disappear from E′phraim,
and the kingdom from Damascus;
and the remnant of Syria will be
like the glory of the children of Israel,
says the LORD of hosts.

4 And in that day
the glory of Jacob will be brought low,
and the fat of his flesh will grow lean.
5 And it shall be as when the reaper gathers
standing grain
and his arm harvests the ears,
and as when one gleans the ears of grain
in the Valley of Reph′aim.
6 Gleanings will be left in it,
as when an olive tree is beaten—
two or three berries
in the top of the highest bough,
four or five
on the branches of a fruit tree,
says the LORD God of Israel.

7 In that day men will regard their Maker,
and their eyes will look to the Holy One of
Israel; 8 they will not have regard for the altars,
the work of their hands, and they will not
look to what their own fingers have made,
either the Ashe′rim or the altars of incense.

9 In that day their strong cities will be like
the deserted places of the Hi′vites and the
Am′orites, which they deserted because
of the children of Israel, and there will be
desolation.

10 For you have forgotten the God of
your salvation,
and have not remembered the Rock
of your refuge;
therefore, though you plant pleasant plants
and set out slips of an alien god,
11 though you make them grow on the day
that you plant them,
and make them blossom in the morning
that you sow;
yet the harvest will flee away
in a day of grief and incurable pain.

12 Ah, the thunder of many peoples,
they thunder like the thundering of the sea!
Ah, the roar of nations,
they roar like the roaring of mighty waters!
13 The nations roar like the roaring of many
waters,
but he will rebuke them, and they will
flee far away,
chased like chaff on the mountains before
the wind
and whirling dust before the storm.
14 At evening time, behold, terror!
Before morning, they are no more!
This is the portion of those who despoil us,
and the lot of those who plunder us.

18 Ah, land of whirring wings
which is beyond the rivers of
Ethiopia;
2 which sends ambassadors by the Nile,
in vessels of papyrus upon the waters!

Go, you swift messengers,
to a nation, tall and smooth,
to a people feared near and far,
a nation mighty and conquering,
whose land the rivers divide.

3 All you inhabitants of the world,
you who dwell on the earth,
when a signal is raised on the
mountains, look!
When a trumpet is blown, hear!
4 For thus the LORD said to me:
"I will quietly look from my dwelling
like clear heat in sunshine,
like a cloud of dew in the heat of harvest."
5 For before the harvest, when the blossom
is over,
and the flower becomes a ripening grape,
he will cut off the shoots with pruning hooks,
and the spreading branches he will
hew away.
6 They shall all of them be left
to the birds of prey of the mountains
and to the beasts of the earth.
And the birds of prey will summer
upon them,
and all the beasts of the earth will winter
upon them.

7 At that time gifts will be brought to the
LORD of hosts
from a people tall and smooth,
from a people feared near and far,
a nation mighty and conquering,
whose land the rivers divide,
to Mount Zion, the place of the name of the
LORD of hosts.

19 An oracle concerning Egypt.
Behold, the LORD is riding on a
swift cloud
and comes to Egypt;
and the idols of Egypt will tremble at his
presence,
and the heart of the Egyptians will melt
within them.
2 And I will stir up Egyptians against Egyptians,
and they will fight, every man against
his brother
and every man against his neighbor,
city against city, kingdom against kingdom;
3 and the spirit of the Egyptians within them
will be emptied out,
and I will confound their plans;
and they will consult the idols and
the sorcerers,
and the mediums and the wizards;
4 and I will give over the Egyptians
into the hand of a hard master;
and a fierce king will rule over them,
says the Lord, the LORD of hosts.
5 And the waters of the Nile will be
dried up,
and the river will be parched and dry;
6 and its canals will become foul,
and the branches of Egypt's Nile will
diminish and dry up,
reeds and rushes will rot away.
7 There will be bare places by the Nile,
on the brink of the Nile,
and all that is sown by the Nile will dry up,
be driven away, and be no more.
8 The fishermen will mourn and lament,
all who cast hook in the Nile;
and they will languish
who spread nets upon the water.
9 The workers in combed flax will be
in despair,
and the weavers of white cotton.
10 Those who are the pillars of the land will
be crushed,
and all who work for hire will
be grieved.

11 The princes of Zoan are utterly foolish;
the wise counselors of Pharaoh give
stupid counsel.
How can you say to Pharaoh,
"I am a son of the wise,
a son of ancient kings"?
12 Where then are your wise men?
Let them tell you and make known
what the LORD of hosts has purposed
against Egypt.
13 The princes of Zoan have become fools,
and the princes of Memphis are
deluded;
those who are the cornerstones of
her tribes
have led Egypt astray.

14The LORD has mingled within her a spirit
of confusion;
and they have made Egypt stagger in all
her doings
as a drunken man staggers in his vomit.
15And there will be nothing for Egypt
which head or tail, palm branch or reed,
may do.

16In that day the Egyptians will be like
women, and tremble with fear before the
hand which the LORD of hosts shakes over
them. 17And the land of Judah will become
a terror to the Egyptians; every one to
whom it is mentioned will fear because of
the purpose which the LORD of hosts has
purposed against them.
18In that day there will be five cities in the
land of Egypt which speak the language of
Canaan and swear allegiance to the LORD of
hosts. One of these will be called the City of
the Sun.
19In that day there will be an altar to the
LORD in the midst of the land of Egypt,
and a pillar to the LORD at its border. 20It
will be a sign and a witness to the LORD
of hosts in the land of Egypt; when they
cry to the LORD because of oppressors he
will send them a savior, and will defend
and deliver them. 21And the LORD will
make himself known to the Egyptians;
and the Egyptians will know the LORD in
that day and worship with sacrifice and
burnt offering, and they will make vows
to the LORD and perform them. 22And
the LORD will strike Egypt, striking and
healing, and they will return to the LORD,
and he will heed their supplications and
heal them.
23In that day there will be a highway from
Egypt to Assyria, and the Assyrian will come
into Egypt, and the Egyptian into Assyria,
and the Egyptians will worship with the
Assyrians.
24In that day Israel will be the third with
Egypt and Assyria, a blessing in the midst
of the earth, 25whom the LORD of hosts
has blessed, saying, "Blessed be Egypt my
people, and Assyria the work of my hands,
and Israel my heritage."

ECCLESIASTES 9

But all this I laid to heart, examining it all,
how the righteous and the wise and their
deeds are in the hand of God; whether it is
love or hate man does not know. Everything
before them is vanity, 2since one fate comes
to all, to the righteous and the wicked, to
the good and the evil, to the clean and the
unclean, to him who sacrifices and him who
does not sacrifice. As is the good man, so is
the sinner; and he who swears is as he who
shuns an oath. 3This is an evil in all that is
done under the sun, that one fate comes to
all; also the hearts of men are full of evil, and
madness is in their hearts while they live,
and after that they go to the dead. 4But he
who is joined with all the living has hope,
for a living dog is better than a dead lion.
5For the living know that they will die, but
the dead know nothing, and they have no
more reward; but the memory of them is
lost. 6Their love and their hate and their
envy have already perished, and they have
no more for ever any share in all that is done
under the sun.
7Go, eat your bread with enjoyment, and
drink your wine with a merry heart; for God
has already approved what you do.
8Let your garments be always white; let
not oil be lacking on your head.
9Enjoy life with the wife whom you love,
all the days of your vain life which he has
given you under the sun, because that
is your portion in life and in your toil at
which you toil under the sun. 10Whatever
your hand finds to do, do it with your
might; for there is no work or thought or
knowledge or wisdom in Sheol, to which
you are going.
11Again I saw that under the sun the race is
not to the swift, nor the battle to the strong,
nor bread to the wise, nor riches to the intelligent, nor favor to the men of skill; but time
and chance happen to them all. 12For man
does not know his time. Like fish which are
taken in an evil net, and like birds which
are caught in a snare, so the sons of men are
snared at an evil time, when it suddenly falls
upon them.

[13]I have also seen this example of wisdom under the sun, and it seemed great to me. [14]There was a little city with few men in it; and a great king came against it and besieged it, building great siegeworks against it. [15]But there was found in it a poor wise man, and he by his wisdom delivered the city. Yet no one remembered that poor man. [16]But I say that wisdom is better than might, though the poor man's wisdom is despised, and his words are not heeded.

[17]The words of the wise heard in quiet are better than the shouting of a ruler among fools. [18]Wisdom is better than weapons of war, but one sinner destroys much good.

1 CORINTHIANS 10

[23]"All things are lawful," but not all things are helpful. "All things are lawful," but not all things build up. [24]Let no one seek his own good, but the good of his neighbor. [25]Eat whatever is sold in the meat market without raising any question on the ground of conscience. [26]For "the earth is the Lord's, and everything in it." [27]If one of the unbelievers invites you to dinner and you are disposed to go, eat whatever is set before you without raising any question on the ground of conscience. [28](But if some one says to you, "This has been offered in sacrifice," then out of consideration for the man who informed you, and for conscience' sake—[29]I mean his conscience, not yours—do not eat it.) For why should my liberty be determined by another man's scruples? [30]If I partake with thankfulness, why am I denounced because of that for which I give thanks?

[31]So, whether you eat or drink, or whatever you do, do all to the glory of God. [32]Give no offense to Jews or to Greeks or to the Church of God, [33]just as I try to please all men in everything I do, not seeking my own advantage, but that of many, that they may be saved.

REFLECTION

"In that day men will regard their Maker, and their eyes will look to the Holy One of Israel" (Is 17:7). Isaiah describes that, when the restoration of Israel comes, the redeemed remnant will look to the Lord instead of the false gods their ancestors worshipped (see v. 8). Isaiah extends this restoration by predicting that not only will Israel return to the Lord, but even the traditional enemies of God's people, such as Egypt and Assyria, will likewise be converted. Through the Lord's "striking and healing," these nations "will return to the LORD, and he will heed their supplications and heal them" (19:22). These prophecies find a beautiful fulfillment in the Corinthians, who turn away from "mute idols" (1 Cor 12:2) to look to the Lord. Some of the newer Christian Corinthians were being scandalized by the consumption of meat sold from the pagan temples. St. Paul wants to make sure that these new Christians continue to look to the one true God and not return to the worship of idols. While St. Paul insists that it is acceptable in principle for Christians to eat meat that has been offered to Greek idols, he warns Christians to defer to others' more sensitive consciences. In either case, he says, "Whether you eat or drink . . . do all to the glory of God" (10:31). How can you give glory to God today by encouraging someone else who is growing in the faith?

September 2

ISAIAH 20

In the year that the commander in chief, who was sent by Sargon the king of Assyria, came to Ash′dod and fought against it and took it,—[2]at that time the LORD had spoken by Isai′ah the son of A′moz, saying, "Go, and loose the sackcloth from your loins and take off your shoes from your feet," and he had done so, walking naked and barefoot—[3]the LORD said, "As my servant

Isai′ah has walked naked and barefoot for three
years as a sign and a portent against Egypt and
Ethiopia, 4 so shall the king of Assyria lead away
the Egyptians captives and the Ethiopians exiles, both the young and old, naked and barefoot, with buttocks uncovered, to the shame
of Egypt. 5 Then they shall be dismayed and
confounded because of Ethiopia their hope
and of Egypt their boast. 6 And the inhabitants
of this coastland will say in that day, 'Behold,
this is what has happened to those in whom
we hoped and to whom we fled for help to be
delivered from the king of Assyria! And we,
how shall we escape?'"

21 The oracle concerning the wilderness of the sea.

As whirlwinds in the Neg′eb sweep on,
it comes from the desert,
from a terrible land.
2 A stern vision is told to me;
the plunderer plunders,
and the destroyer destroys.
Go up, O E′lam,
lay siege, O Med′ia;
all the sighing she has caused
I bring to an end.
3 Therefore my loins are filled with anguish;
pangs have seized me,
like the pangs of a woman with labor pains;
I am bowed down so that I cannot hear,
I am dismayed so that I cannot see.
4 My mind reels, horror has appalled me;
the twilight I longed for
has been turned for me into trembling.
5 They prepare the table,
they spread the rugs,
they eat, they drink.
Arise, O princes,
oil the shield!
6 For thus the Lord said to me:
"Go, set a watchman,
let him announce what he sees.
7 When he sees riders, horsemen in pairs,
riders on donkeys, riders on camels,
let him listen diligently,
very diligently."
8 Then he who saw cried:
"Upon a watchtower I stand, O LORD,
continually by day,
and at my post I am stationed whole nights.
9 And, behold, here come riders,
horsemen in pairs!"
And he answered,
"Fallen, fallen is Babylon;
and all the images of her gods
he has shattered to the ground."
10 O my threshed and winnowed one,
what I have heard from the LORD of hosts,
the God of Israel, I announce to you.

11 The oracle concerning Du′mah.
One is calling to me from Se′ir,
"Watchman, what of the night?
Watchman, what of the night?"
12 The watchman says:
"Morning comes, and also the night.
If you will inquire, inquire;
come back again."

13 The oracle concerning Arabia.
In the thickets in Arabia you will lodge,
O caravans of De′danites.
14 To the thirsty bring water,
meet the fugitive with bread,
O inhabitants of the land of Te′ma.
15 For they have fled from the swords,
from the drawn sword,
from the bent bow,
and from the press of battle.

16 For thus the Lord said to me, "Within a
year, according to the years of a hireling, all
the glory of Ke′dar will come to an end; 17 and
the remainder of the archers of the mighty
men of the sons of Ke′dar will be few; for the
LORD, the God of Israel, has spoken."

22 The oracle concerning the valley of vision.

What do you mean that you have gone up,
all of you, to the housetops,
2 you who are full of shoutings,
tumultuous city, exultant town?
Your slain are not slain with the sword
or dead in battle.
3 All your rulers have fled together,
without the bow they were captured.
All of you who were found were captured,
though they had fled far away.
4 Therefore I said:
"Look away from me,
let me weep bitter tears;

do not labor to comfort me
for the destruction of the daughter of
my people."
[5]For the Lord GOD of hosts has a day
of tumult and trampling and confusion
in the valley of vision,
a battering down of walls
and a shouting to the mountains.
[6]And E'lam bore the quiver
with chariots and horsemen,
and Kir uncovered the shield.
[7]Your choicest valleys were full of chariots,
and the horsemen took their stand at
the gates.
[8]He has taken away the covering of Judah.

In that day you looked to the weapons
of the House of the Forest, [9]and you saw
that the breaches of the city of David were
many, and you collected the waters of the
lower pool, [10]and you counted the houses of
Jerusalem, and you broke down the houses
to fortify the wall. [11]You made a reservoir
between the two walls for the water of the
old pool. But you did not look to him who
did it, or have regard for him who planned
it long ago.

[12]In that day the Lord GOD of hosts
called to weeping and mourning,
to baldness and putting on of sackcloth;
[13]and behold, joy and gladness,
slaying oxen and killing sheep,
eating flesh and drinking wine.
"Let us eat and drink,
for tomorrow we die."
[14]The LORD of hosts has revealed himself
in my ears:
"Surely this iniquity will not be
forgiven you
till you die,"
says the Lord GOD of hosts.

[15]Thus says the Lord GOD of hosts,
"Come, go to this steward, to Shebna, who
is over the household, and say to him:
[16]What have you to do here and whom
have you here, that you have hewn here
a tomb for yourself, you who hew a tomb
on the height, and carve a habitation for
yourself in the rock? [17]Behold, the LORD
will hurl you away violently, O you strong
man. He will seize firm hold on you, [18]and
whirl you round and round, and throw
you like a ball into a wide land; there you
shall die, and there shall be your splendid chariots, you shame of your master's
house. [19]I will thrust you from your office, and you will be cast down from your
station. [20]In that day I will call my servant
Eli'akim the son of Hilki'ah, [21]and I will
clothe him with your robe, and will bind
your belt on him, and will commit your
authority to his hand; and he shall be a
father to the inhabitants of Jerusalem and
to the house of Judah. [22]And I will place
on his shoulder the key of the house of
David; he shall open, and none shall shut;
and he shall shut, and none shall open.
[23]And I will fasten him like a peg in a
sure place, and he will become a throne
of honor to his father's house. [24]And they
will hang on him the whole weight of his
father's house, the offspring and issue,
every small vessel, from the cups to all
the flagons. [25]In that day, says the LORD
of hosts, the peg that was fastened in a
sure place will give way; and it will be cut
down and fall, and the burden that was
upon it will be cut off, for the LORD has
spoken."

23 The oracle concerning Tyre.
Wail, O ships of Tar'shish,
for Tyre is laid waste, without house
or haven!
From the land of Cyprus
it is revealed to them.
[2]Be still, O inhabitants of the coast,
O merchants of Si'don;
your messengers passed over the sea
[3] and were on many waters;
your revenue was the grain of Shihor,
the harvest of the Nile;
you were the merchant of the nations.
[4]Be ashamed, O Si'don, for the sea has spoken,
the stronghold of the sea, saying:
"I have neither endured labor pains nor
given birth,
I have neither reared young men nor
brought up virgins."

[5]When the report comes to Egypt,
they will be in anguish over the report
about Tyre.
[6]Pass over to Tar′shish,
wail, O inhabitants of the coast!
[7]Is this your exultant city
whose origin is from days of old,
whose feet carried her
to settle afar?
[8]Who has purposed this
against Tyre, the bestower of crowns,
whose merchants were princes,
whose traders were the honored of
the earth?
[9]The LORD of hosts has purposed it,
to defile the pride of all glory,
to dishonor all the honored of the earth.
[10]Overflow your land like the Nile,
O daughter of Tar′shish;
there is no restraint any more.
[11]He has stretched out his hand over the sea,
he has shaken the kingdoms;
the LORD has given command concerning
Canaan
to destroy its strongholds.
[12]And he said:
"You will no more exult,
O oppressed virgin daughter of Si′don;
arise, pass over to Cyprus,
even there you will have no rest."

[13]Behold the land of the Chalde′ans! This
is the people; it was not Assyria. They destined Tyre for wild beasts. They erected
their siege towers, they razed her palaces,
they made her a ruin.
[14]Wail, O ships of Tar′shish,
for your stronghold is laid waste.
[15]In that day Tyre will be forgotten for
seventy years, like the days of one king. At
the end of seventy years, it will happen to
Tyre as in the song of the harlot:
[16]"Take a harp,
go about the city,
O forgotten harlot!
Make sweet melody,
sing many songs,
that you may be remembered."
[17]At the end of seventy years, the LORD
will visit Tyre, and she will return to her
hire, and will play the harlot with all the
kingdoms of the world upon the face of
the earth. [18]Her merchandise and her hire
will be dedicated to the LORD; it will not
be stored or hoarded, but her merchandise
will supply abundant food and fine clothing
for those who dwell before the LORD.

ECCLESIASTES 10

Dead flies make the perfumer's ointment
give off an evil odor;
so a little folly outweighs wisdom
and honor.
[2]A wise man's heart inclines him toward
the right,
but a fool's heart toward the left.
[3]Even when the fool walks on the road, he
lacks sense,
and he says to every one that he is
a fool.
[4]If the anger of the ruler rises against you,
do not leave your place,
for deference will make amends for
great offenses.
[5]There is an evil which I have seen under
the sun, as it were an error proceeding from
the ruler: [6]folly is set in many high places,
and the rich sit in a low place. [7]I have seen
slaves on horses, and princes walking on
foot like slaves.
[8]He who digs a pit will fall into it;
and a serpent will bite him who breaks
through a wall.
[9]He who quarries stones is hurt by them;
and he who splits logs is endangered
by them.
[10]If the iron is blunt, and one does not whet
the edge,
he must put forth more strength;
but wisdom helps one to succeed.
[11]If the serpent bites before it is charmed,
there is no advantage in a
charmer.
[12]The words of a wise man's mouth win
him favor,
but the lips of a fool consume him.

[13]The beginning of the words of his mouth
is foolishness,
and the end of his talk is wicked madness.
[14]A fool multiplies words,
though no man knows what is to be,
and who can tell him what will be after him?
[15]The toil of a fool wearies him,
so that he does not know the way to
the city.

[16]Woe to you, O land, when your king is
a child,
and your princes feast in the morning!
[17]Happy are you, O land, when your king is
the son of free men,
and your princes feast at the
proper time,
for strength, and not for drunkenness!
[18]Through sloth the roof sinks in,
and through indolence the house leaks.
[19]Bread is made for laughter,
and wine gladdens life,
and money answers everything.
[20]Even in your thought, do not curse
the king,
nor in your bedchamber curse the rich;
for a bird of the air will carry your voice,
or some winged creature tell the matter.

---

1 CORINTHIANS 11

Be imitators of me, as I am of Christ.

**[2]I commend you because you remem-
ber me in everything and maintain the
traditions even as I have delivered**
them to you. [3]But I want you to understand
that the head of every man is Christ, the
head of a woman is her husband, and the
head of Christ is God. [4]Any man who prays
or prophesies with his head covered dishonors his head, [5]but any woman who prays or
prophesies with her head unveiled dishonors her head—it is the same as if her head
were shaven. [6]For if a woman will not veil
herself, then she should cut off her hair; but
if it is disgraceful for a woman to be shorn
or shaven, let her wear a veil. [7]For a man
ought not to cover his head, since he is the
image and glory of God; but woman is the
glory of man. [8](For man was not made from
woman, but woman from man. [9]Neither
was man created for woman, but woman
for man.) [10]That is why a woman ought to
have a veil on her head, because of the angels. [11](Nevertheless, in the Lord woman is
not independent of man nor man of woman; [12]for as woman was made from man, so
man is now born of woman. And all things
are from God.) [13]Judge for yourselves; is it
proper for a woman to pray to God with her
head uncovered? [14]Does not nature itself
teach you that for a man to wear long hair is
degrading to him, [15]but if a woman has long
hair, it is her pride? For her hair is given to
her for a covering. [16]If any one is disposed to
be contentious, we recognize no other practice, nor do the churches of God.

REFLECTION

In one of the most unexpected prophetic displays in the Bible, Isaiah walks around naked for three years (see Is 20:2–4). His radical obedience to the Lord is held up for our imitation. While Isaiah praises the people for preparing water resources for a siege, he criticizes them for trusting in their own efforts rather than in the Lord (see 22:8–11). He also condemns the self-serving government official, Shebna, who has been building himself an elaborate tomb rather than serving the people (see vv. 15–18). Similarly, Ecclesiastes warns us against childish rulers who allow their princes to "feast in the morning," the normal time for work (Eccl 10:16). On the other hand, he tells us, "Happy are you, O land, when your king is the son of free men, and your princes feast at the proper time, for strength, and not for drunkenness!" (v. 17). While lazy, selfish rulers are a burden on the people, hard-working public servants can be a blessing. If we respond to St. Paul's urging and become "imitators of me, as I am of Christ" (1 Cor 11:1), we will be good servants of all around us. Who in your life offers a Christlike example for you to imitate?

September 3

ISAIAH 24

Behold, the LORD will lay waste the earth and make it desolate,
and he will twist its surface and scatter its inhabitants.
2And it shall be, as with the people, so with the priest;
as with the slave, so with his master;
as with the maid, so with her mistress;
as with the buyer, so with the seller;
as with the lender, so with the borrower;
as with the creditor, so with the debtor.
3The earth shall be utterly laid waste and utterly despoiled;
for the LORD has spoken this word.
4The earth mourns and withers,
the world languishes and withers;
the heavens languish together with the earth.
5The earth lies polluted
under its inhabitants;
for they have transgressed the laws,
violated the statutes,
broken the everlasting covenant.
6Therefore a curse devours the earth,
and its inhabitants suffer for their guilt;
therefore the inhabitants of the earth are scorched,
and few men are left.
7The wine mourns,
the vine languishes,
all the merry-hearted sigh.
8The mirth of the timbrels is stilled,
the noise of the jubilant has ceased,
the mirth of the lyre is stilled.
9No more do they drink wine with singing;
strong drink is bitter to those who drink it.
10The city of chaos is broken down,
every house is shut up so that none can enter.
11There is an outcry in the streets for lack of wine;
all joy has reached its eventide;
the gladness of the earth is banished.
12Desolation is left in the city,
the gates are battered into ruins.
13For thus it shall be in the midst of the earth among the nations,
as when an olive tree is beaten,
as at the gleaning when the vintage is done.

14They lift up their voices, they sing for joy;
over the majesty of the LORD they shout from the west.
15Therefore in the east give glory to the LORD;
in the islands of the sea, to the name of the LORD, the God of Israel.
16From the ends of the earth we hear songs of praise,
of glory to the Righteous One.
But I say, "I pine away,
I pine away. Woe is me!
For the treacherous deal treacherously,
the treacherous deal very treacherously."
17Terror, and the pit, and the snare are upon you, O inhabitant of the earth!
18He who flees at the sound of the terror
shall fall into the pit;
and he who climbs out of the pit shall be caught in the snare.
For the windows of heaven are opened,
and the foundations of the earth tremble.
19The earth is utterly broken,
the earth is torn apart,
the earth is violently shaken.
20The earth staggers like a drunken man,
it sways like a hut;
its transgression lies heavy upon it,
and it falls, and will not rise again.

21On that day the LORD will punish
the host of heaven, in heaven,
and the kings of the earth, on the earth.
22They will be gathered together
as prisoners in a pit;
they will be shut up in a prison,
and after many days they will be punished.
23Then the moon will be confounded,
and the sun ashamed;
for the LORD of hosts will reign
on Mount Zion and in Jerusalem
and before his elders he will manifest his glory.

25 O LORD, you are my God;
I will exalt you, I will praise your name;
for you have done wonderful things,
plans formed of old, faithful and sure.
[2]For you have made the city a heap,
the fortified city a ruin;
the palace of strangers is a city no more,
it will never be rebuilt.
[3]Therefore strong peoples will glorify you;
cities of ruthless nations will fear you.
[4]For you have been a stronghold to the poor,
a stronghold to the needy in his distress,
a shelter from the storm and a shade from the heat;
for the blast of the ruthless is like a storm against a wall,
[5] like heat in a dry place.
You subdue the noise of the strangers;
as heat by the shade of a cloud,
so the song of the ruthless is stilled.

[6]On this mountain the LORD of hosts will
make for all peoples a feast of fat things,
a feast of choice wines—of fat things full
of marrow, of choice wines well refined.
[7]And he will destroy on this mountain the
covering that is cast over all peoples, the
veil that is spread over all nations. [8]He will
swallow up death for ever, and the Lord
GOD will wipe away tears from all faces,
and the reproach of his people he will take
away from all the earth, for the LORD has
spoken.
[9]It will be said on that day, "Behold, this
is our God; we have waited for him, that he
might save us. This is the LORD; we have
waited for him; let us be glad and rejoice in
his salvation."
[10]For the hand of the LORD will rest
on this mountain, and Moab shall be
trodden down in his place, as straw is
trodden down in a dung-pit. [11]And he
will spread out his hands in the midst of
it as a swimmer spreads his hands out to
swim; but the LORD will lay low his pride
together with the skill of his hands. [12]And
the high fortifications of his walls he
will bring down, lay low, and cast to the
ground, even to the dust.

26 In that day this song will be sung in the land of Judah:
"We have a strong city;
he sets up salvation
as walls and bulwarks.
[2]Open the gates,
that the righteous nation which keeps faith
may enter in.
[3]You keep him in perfect peace,
whose mind is stayed on you,
because he trusts in you.
[4]Trust in the LORD for ever,
for the LORD GOD
is an everlasting rock.
[5]For he has brought low
the inhabitants of the height,
the lofty city.
He lays it low, lays it low to the ground,
casts it to the dust.
[6]The foot tramples it,
the feet of the poor,
the steps of the needy."

[7]The way of the righteous is level;
you make smooth the path of the righteous.
[8]In the path of your judgments,
O LORD, we wait for you;
your memorial name
is the desire of our soul.
[9]My soul yearns for you in the night,
my spirit within me earnestly seeks you.
For when your judgments are in the earth,
the inhabitants of the world learn righteousness.
[10]If favor is shown to the wicked,
he does not learn righteousness;
in the land of uprightness he deals perversely
and does not see the majesty of the LORD.
[11]O LORD, your hand is lifted up,
but they see it not.
Let them see your zeal for your people,
and be ashamed.
Let the fire for your adversaries
consume them.

12O Lord, you will ordain peace for us,
you have wrought for us all our works.
13O Lord our God,
other lords besides you have ruled over us,
but your name alone we acknowledge.
14They are dead, they will not live;
they are shades, they will not arise;
to that end you have visited them with destruction
and wiped out all remembrance of them.
15But you have increased the nation, O Lord,
you have increased the nation; you are glorified;
you have enlarged all the borders of the land.

16O Lord, in distress they sought you,
they poured out a prayer
when your chastening was upon them.
17Like a woman with child,
who writhes and cries out in her pangs,
when she is near her time,
so were we because of you, O Lord;
18 we were with child, we writhed,
but we gave birth only to wind.
We have wrought no deliverance in the earth,
and the inhabitants of the world have not fallen.
19Your dead shall live, their bodies shall rise.
O dwellers in the dust, awake and sing for joy!
For your dew is a dew of light,
and on the land of the shades you will let it fall.

20Come, my people, enter your chambers,
and shut your doors behind you;
hide yourselves for a little while
until the wrath is past.
21For behold, the Lord is coming forth out of his place
to punish the inhabitants of the earth for their iniquity,
and the earth will disclose the blood shed upon her,
and will no more cover her slain.

27 In that day the Lord with his hard and great and strong sword will punish Levi′athan the fleeing serpent, Leviathan the twisting serpent, and he will slay the dragon that is in the sea.

2In that day:
"A pleasant vineyard, sing of it!
3 I, the Lord, am its keeper;
every moment I water it.
Lest any one harm it,
I guard it night and day;
4 I have no wrath.
Would that I had thorns and briers to battle!
I would set out against them,
I would burn them up together.
5Or let them lay hold of my protection,
let them make peace with me,
let them make peace with me."

6In days to come Jacob shall take root,
Israel shall blossom and put forth shoots,
and fill the whole world with fruit.

7Has he struck them down as he struck those who struck them?
Or have they been slain as their slayers were slain?
8Measure by measure, by exile you contended with them;
he removed them with his fierce blast in the day of the east wind.
9Therefore by this the guilt of Jacob will be expiated,
and this will be the full fruit of the removal of his sin:
when he makes all the stones of the altars
like chalkstones crushed to pieces,
no Ashe′rim or incense altars will remain standing.
10For the fortified city is solitary,
a habitation deserted and forsaken, like the wilderness;
there the calf grazes,
there he lies down, and strips its branches.
11When its boughs are dry, they are broken;
women come and make a fire of them.
For this is a people without discernment;
therefore he who made them will not have compassion on them,
he that formed them will show them no favor.

[12]In that day from the river Euphra´tes to
the Brook of Egypt the LORD will thresh out
the grain, and you will be gathered one by
one, O people of Israel. [13]And in that day a
great trumpet will be blown, and those who
were lost in the land of Assyria and those
who were driven out to the land of Egypt
will come and worship the LORD on the
holy mountain at Jerusalem.

ECCLESIASTES 11

Cast your bread upon the waters,
for you will find it after many days.
[2]Give a portion to seven, or even to eight,
for you know not what evil may happen
on earth.
[3]If the clouds are full of rain,
they empty themselves on the earth;
and if a tree falls to the south or to
the north,
in the place where the tree falls, there it
will lie.
[4]He who observes the wind will not sow;
and he who regards the clouds will
not reap.

[5]As you do not know how the spirit comes
to the bones in the womb of a woman with
child, so you do not know the work of God
who makes everything.

[6]In the morning sow your seed, and at
evening withhold not your hand; for you do
not know which will prosper, this or that, or
whether both alike will be good.

[7]Light is sweet, and it is pleasant for the
eyes to behold the sun.

[8]For if a man lives many years, let him
rejoice in them all; but let him remember
that the days of darkness will be many. All
that comes is vanity.

[9]Rejoice, O young man, in your youth,
and let your heart cheer you in the days of
your youth; walk in the ways of your heart
and the sight of your eyes. But know that
for all these things God will bring you into
judgment.

[10]Remove vexation from your mind, and
put away pain from your body; for youth
and the dawn of life are vanity.

1 CORINTHIANS 11

**[17]But in the following instruc-
tions I do not commend you,
because when you come together it is
not for the better but for the worse.
[18]For, in the first place, when you assemble**
as a Church, I hear that there are divisions
among you; and I partly believe it, [19]for there
must be factions among you in order that
those who are genuine among you may be recognized. [20]When you meet together, it is not
the Lord's supper that you eat. [21]For in eating,
each one goes ahead with his own meal, and
one is hungry and another is drunk. [22]What!
Do you not have houses to eat and drink in?
Or do you despise the Church of God and hu-
miliate those who have nothing? What shall I
say to you? Shall I commend you in this? No,
I will not.

[23]For I received from the Lord what I also
delivered to you, that the Lord Jesus on the
night when he was betrayed took bread,
[24]and when he had given thanks, he broke
it, and said, "This is my body which is for
you. Do this in remembrance of me." [25]In
the same way also the chalice, after supper,
saying, "This chalice is the new covenant
in my blood. Do this, as often as you drink
it, in remembrance of me." [26]For as often as
you eat this bread and drink the chalice, you
proclaim the Lord's death until he comes.

[27]Whoever, therefore, eats the bread or
drinks the cup of the Lord in an unworthy
manner will be guilty of profaning the body
and blood of the Lord. [28]Let a man examine
himself, and so eat of the bread and drink of
the cup. [29]For any one who eats and drinks
without discerning the body eats and drinks
judgment upon himself. [30]That is why many
of you are weak and ill, and some have died.
[31]But if we judged ourselves truly, we should
not be judged. [32]But when we are judged by
the Lord, we are chastened so that we may
not be condemned along with the world.

[33]So then, my brethren, when you come
together to eat, wait for one another—[34]if any
one is hungry, let him eat at home—lest you
come together to be condemned. About the
other things I will give directions when I come.

REFLECTION

In the midst of trying times and challenging circumstances, we need to look forward to the mysterious consummation of history. Isaiah gives us a glimpse past the history of this world, past the time of judgment, to a glorious future with God. He says, "On this mountain the LORD of hosts will make for all peoples a feast of fat things, a feast of choice wines—of fat things full of marrow, of choice wines well refined" (Is 25:6). This eschatological meal represents the Lord's restoration of his people, and the salvation and communion he offers us. At this meal, "he will swallow up death forever" (v. 8), a powerful foreshadowing of Jesus's victory on the Cross and its Eucharistic commemoration. The Eucharist is meant to draw us into union with God and with his Church, rather than divide us into "factions" (1 Cor 11:19). It is a mysterious means the Lord employs to draw us to himself: "As you do not know how the spirit comes to the bones in the womb of a woman with child, so you do not know the work of God who makes everything" (Eccl 11:5). How will you enter more fully into the mysterious work of God in the Eucharist?

September 4

ISAIAH 28

Woe to the proud crown of the
drunkards of E′phraim,
and to the fading flower of its
glorious beauty,
which is on the head of the rich valley of
those overcome with wine!
2Behold, the Lord has one who is mighty
and strong;
like a storm of hail, a destroying tempest,
like a storm of mighty, overflowing waters,
he will cast down to the earth with
violence.
3The proud crown of the drunkards
of E′phraim
will be trodden under foot;
4and the fading flower of its glorious beauty,
which is on the head of the rich valley,
will be like a first-ripe fig before the summer:
when a man sees it, he eats it up
as soon as it is in his hand.

5In that day the LORD of hosts will be a
crown of glory,
and a diadem of beauty, to the remnant of
his people;
6and a spirit of justice to him who sits in
judgment,
and strength to those who turn back the
battle at the gate.

7These also reel with wine
and stagger with strong drink;
the priest and the prophet reel with
strong drink,
they are confused with wine,
they stagger with strong drink;
they err in vision,
they stumble in giving judgment.
8For all tables are full of vomit,
no place is without filthiness.

9"Whom will he teach knowledge,
and to whom will he explain
the message?
Those who are weaned from the milk,
those taken from the breast?
10For it is precept upon precept, precept
upon precept,
line upon line, line upon line,
here a little, there a little."

11No, but by men of strange lips
and with an alien tongue
the LORD will speak to this people,
12 to whom he has said,
"This is rest;
give rest to the weary;
and this is repose";
yet they would not hear.
13Therefore the word of the LORD will be
to them
precept upon precept, precept upon
precept,
line upon line, line upon line,
here a little, there a little;

that they may go, and fall backward,
and be broken, and snared, and taken.

14 Therefore hear the word of the LORD,
you scoffers,
who rule this people in Jerusalem!
15 Because you have said, "We have made a covenant with death,
and with Sheol we have an agreement;
when the overwhelming scourge passes through
it will not come to us;
for we have made lies our refuge,
and in falsehood we have taken shelter";
16 therefore thus says the Lord GOD,
"Behold, I am laying in Zion for a foundation
a stone, a tested stone,
a precious cornerstone, of a sure foundation:
'He who believes will not be in haste.'
17 And I will make justice the line,
and righteousness the plummet;
and hail will sweep away the refuge of lies,
and waters will overwhelm the shelter."
18 Then your covenant with death will be annulled,
and your agreement with Sheol will not stand;
when the overwhelming scourge passes through
you will be beaten down by it.
19 As often as it passes through it will take you;
for morning by morning it will pass through,
by day and by night;
and it will be sheer terror to understand the message.
20 For the bed is too short to stretch oneself on it,
and the covering too narrow to wrap oneself in it.
21 For the LORD will rise up as on Mount Pera′zim,
he will rage as in the valley of Gib′eon;
to do his deed—strange is his deed!
and to work his work—alien is his work!
22 Now therefore do not scoff,
lest your bonds be made strong;
for I have heard a decree of destruction
from the Lord GOD of hosts upon the whole land.

23 Give ear, and hear my voice;
listen, and hear my speech.
24 Does he who plows for sowing plow continually?
does he continually open and harrow his ground?
25 When he has leveled its surface,
does he not scatter dill, sow cummin,
and put in wheat in rows
and barley in its proper place,
and spelt as the border?
26 For he is instructed rightly;
his God teaches him.

27 Dill is not threshed with a threshing sledge,
nor is a cart wheel rolled over cummin;
but dill is beaten out with a stick,
and cummin with a rod.
28 Does one crush bread grain?
No, he does not thresh it for ever;
when he drives his cart wheel over it
with his horses, he does not crush it.
29 This also comes from the LORD of hosts;
he is wonderful in counsel,
and excellent in wisdom.

29 Ho Ar′iel, Ariel,
the city where David encamped!
Add year to year;
let the feasts run their round.
2 Yet I will distress Ar′iel,
and there shall be moaning and lamentation,
and she shall be to me like an Ariel.
3 And I will encamp against you round about,
and will besiege you with towers
and I will raise siegeworks against you.
4 Then deep from the earth you shall speak,
from low in the dust your words shall come;
your voice shall come from the ground
like the voice of a ghost,
and your speech shall whisper out of the dust.

5But the multitude of your foes shall be like
small dust,
and the multitude of the ruthless like
passing chaff.
And in an instant, suddenly,
6 you will be visited by the LORD of hosts
with thunder and with earthquake and
great noise,
with whirlwind and tempest, and the
flame of a devouring fire.
7And the multitude of all the nations that
fight against Ar′iel,
all that fight against her and her
stronghold and distress her,
shall be like a dream, a vision of the night.
8As when a hungry man dreams he is eating
and awakes with his hunger not satisfied,
or as when a thirsty man dreams he is
drinking
and awakes faint, with his thirst not
quenched,
so shall the multitude of all the nations be
that fight against Mount Zion.

9Stupefy yourselves and be in a stupor,
blind yourselves and be blind!
Be drunk, but not with wine;
stagger, but not with strong drink!
10For the LORD has poured out upon you
a spirit of deep sleep,
and has closed your eyes, the prophets,
and covered your heads, the seers.
11And the vision of all this has become to
you like the words of a book that is sealed.
When men give it to one who can read,
saying, "Read this," he says, "I cannot, for it
is sealed." 12And when they give the book to
one who cannot read, saying, "Read this," he
says, "I cannot read."

13And the Lord said:
"Because this people draw near with
their mouth
and honor me with their lips,
while their hearts are far from me,
and their fear of me is a commandment of
men learned by rote;
14therefore, behold, I will again
do marvelous things with this people,
wonderful and marvelous;
and the wisdom of their wise men shall
perish,
and the discernment of their discerning
men shall be hidden."

15Woe to those who hide deep from the
LORD their counsel,
whose deeds are in the dark,
and who say, "Who sees us? Who
knows us?"
16You turn things upside down!
Shall the potter be regarded as the clay;
that the thing made should say of its maker,
"He did not make me";
or the thing formed say of him who
formed it,
"He has no understanding"?

17Is it not yet a very little while
until Lebanon shall be turned into a
fruitful field,
and the fruitful field shall be regarded as
a forest?
18In that day the deaf shall hear the words
of a book,
and out of their gloom and darkness
the eyes of the blind shall see.
19The meek shall obtain fresh joy in the LORD,
and the poor among men shall exult in
the Holy One of Israel.
20For the ruthless shall come to nothing and
the scoffer cease,
and all who watch to do evil shall be
cut off,
21who by a word make a man out to be
an offender,
and lay a snare for him who reproves in
the gate,
and with an empty plea turn aside him
who is in the right.
22Therefore thus says the LORD, who
redeemed Abraham, concerning the house
of Jacob:
"Jacob shall no more be ashamed,
no more shall his face grow pale.
23For when he sees his children,
the work of my hands, in his midst,
they will sanctify my name;
they will sanctify the Holy One of Jacob,
and will stand in awe of the God of Israel.

24And those who err in spirit will come to
understanding,
and those who murmur will accept
instruction."

ECCLESIASTES 12

Remember also your Creator in the days of
your youth, before the evil days come, and
the years draw nigh, when you will say, "I
have no pleasure in them"; 2before the sun
and the light and the moon and the stars
are darkened and the clouds return after
the rain; 3in the day when the keepers of the
house tremble, and the strong men are bent,
and the grinders cease because they are few,
and those that look through the windows
are dimmed, 4and the doors on the street
are shut; when the sound of the grinding is
low, and one rises up at the voice of a bird,
and all the daughters of song are brought
low; 5they are afraid also of what is high,
and terrors are in the way; the almond tree
blossoms, the grasshopper drags itself along
and desire fails; because man goes to his
eternal home, and the mourners go about
the streets; 6before the silver cord is snapped,
or the golden bowl is broken, or the pitcher
is broken at the fountain, or the wheel
broken at the cistern, 7and the dust returns
to the earth as it was, and the spirit returns
to God who gave it. 8Vanity of vanities, says
the Preacher; all is vanity.

9Besides being wise, the Preacher also
taught the people knowledge, weighing and
studying and arranging proverbs with great
care. 10The Preacher sought to find pleasing
words, and uprightly he wrote words of truth.

11The sayings of the wise are like goads,
and like nails firmly fixed are the collected
sayings which are given by one Shepherd.
12My son, beware of anything beyond these.
Of making many books there is no end, and
much study is a weariness of the flesh.

13The end of the matter; all has been heard.
Fear God, and keep his commandments; for
this is the whole duty of man. 14For God will
bring every deed into judgment, with every
secret thing, whether good or evil.

1 CORINTHIANS 12

**Now concerning spiritual gifts,
brethren, I do not want you to
be uninformed. 2You know that when
you were heathen, you were led astray**
to mute idols, however you may have been
moved. 3Therefore I want you to understand that no one speaking by the Spirit
of God ever says "Jesus be cursed!" and no
one can say "Jesus is Lord" except by the
Holy Spirit.

4Now there are varieties of gifts, but
the same Spirit; 5and there are varieties of
service, but the same Lord; 6and there are
varieties of working, but it is the same God
who inspires them all in every one. 7To
each is given the manifestation of the Spirit
for the common good. 8To one is given
through the Spirit the utterance of wisdom,
and to another the utterance of knowledge
according to the same Spirit, 9to another
faith by the same Spirit, to another gifts of
healing by the one Spirit, 10to another the
working of miracles, to another prophecy,
to another the ability to distinguish between
spirits, to another various kinds of tongues,
to another the interpretation of tongues.
11All these are inspired by one and the
same Spirit, who apportions to each one
individually as he wills.

12For just as the body is one and has
many members, and all the members of
the body, though many, are one body, so it
is with Christ. 13For by one Spirit we were
all baptized into one body—Jews or Greeks,
slaves or free—and all were made to drink
of one Spirit.

14For the body does not consist of one
member but of many. 15If the foot should say,
"Because I am not a hand, I do not belong to
the body," that would not make it any less a
part of the body. 16And if the ear should say,
"Because I am not an eye, I do not belong to
the body," that would not make it any less a
part of the body. 17If the whole body were
an eye, where would be the hearing? If the
whole body were an ear, where would be the
sense of smell? 18But as it is, God arranged
the organs in the body, each one of them, as

he chose. 19If all were a single organ, where would the body be? 20As it is, there are many parts, yet one body. 21The eye cannot say to the hand, "I have no need of you," nor again the head to the feet, "I have no need of you." 22On the contrary, the parts of the body which seem to be weaker are indispensable, 23and those parts of the body which we think less honorable we invest with the greater honor, and our unpresentable parts are treated with greater modesty, 24which our more presentable parts do not require. But God has so composed the body, giving the greater honor to the inferior part, 25that there may be no discord in the body, but that the members may have the same care for one another. 26If one member suffers, all suffer together; if one member is honored, all rejoice together.

27Now you are the body of Christ and individually members of it. 28And God has appointed in the Church first apostles, second prophets, third teachers, then workers of miracles, then healers, helpers, administrators, speakers in various kinds of tongues. 29Are all apostles? Are all prophets? Are all teachers? Do all work miracles? 30Do all possess gifts of healing? Do all speak with tongues? Do all interpret?

REFLECTION

As Isaiah enumerates God's judgments against the rebellious, he highlights how our relationship with God can break down. It gets to the point where the people cannot understand the Lord's law; his message is merely "precept upon precept, precept upon precept, line upon line, line upon line, here a little, there a little" (Is 28:10). Rather than trusting in the Lord, they have made "a covenant with death" (v. 15), drawing near to the Lord only with their mouths and lips, "while their hearts are far from [him]" (29:13). God anticipates this possible breakdown in the New Covenant, giving us "the manifestation of the Spirit for the common good" (1 Cor 12:7). That is, the Lord gives us the Spirit, which empowers us to live the Christian life, as well as spiritual gifts, which help us live together as a community. As he enumerates the different kinds of Spirit-given gifts, St. Paul emphasizes that all the diverse gifts contribute to the unity and upbuilding of the whole "body of Christ" (v. 27). To ward off a collapse of our relationship with God, we would do well to take the parting advice of Ecclesiastes: "Fear God, and keep his commandments; for this is the whole duty of man" (Eccl 12:13). What spiritual gifts has the Lord given you, and how are you employing them?

September 5

ISAIAH 30

"Woe to the rebellious
children," says the LORD,
"who carry out a plan, but not mine;
and who make a league, but not of my
spirit,
that they may add sin to sin;
2who set out to go down to Egypt,
without asking for my counsel,
to take refuge in the protection of Pharaoh,
and to seek shelter in the shadow of Egypt!
3Therefore the protection of Pharaoh shall
turn to your shame,
and the shelter in the shadow of Egypt to
your humiliation.
4For though his officials are at Zoan
and his envoys reach Han′es,
5every one comes to shame
through a people that cannot profit them,
that brings neither help nor profit,
but shame and disgrace."

6An oracle on the beasts of the Neg′eb.
Through a land of trouble and anguish,
from where come the lioness and the lion,
the viper and the flying serpent,
they carry their riches on the backs
of donkeys,
and their treasures on the humps of camels,
to a people that cannot profit them.
7For Egypt's help is worthless and empty,
therefore I have called her
"Ra′hab who sits still."

8 And now, go, write it before them on
a tablet,
and inscribe it in a book,
that it may be for the time to come as a
witness for ever.
9 For they are a rebellious people,
lying sons,
sons who will not hear
the instruction of the LORD;
10 who say to the seers, "See not";
and to the prophets, "Prophesy not to us
what is right;
speak to us smooth things,
prophesy illusions,
11 leave the way, turn aside from the path,
let us hear no more of the Holy One
of Israel."
12 Therefore thus says the Holy One
of Israel,
"Because you despise this word,
and trust in oppression and
perverseness,
and rely on them;
13 therefore this iniquity shall be to you
like a break in a high wall, bulging out,
and about to collapse,
whose crash comes suddenly, in an instant;
14 and its breaking is like that of a potter's
vessel
which is smashed so ruthlessly
that among its fragments not a shard
is found
with which to take fire from the hearth,
or to dip up water out of the cistern."

15 For thus said the Lord GOD, the Holy One
of Israel,
"In returning and rest you shall be saved;
in quietness and in trust shall be your
strength."
And you would not, 16 but you said,
"No! We will speed upon horses,"
therefore you shall speed away;
and, "We will ride upon swift steeds,"
therefore your pursuers shall be swift.
17 A thousand shall flee at the threat of one,
at the threat of five you shall flee,
till you are left
like a flagstaff on the top of a mountain,
like a signal on a hill.

18 Therefore the LORD waits to be gracious
to you;
therefore he exalts himself to show
mercy to you.
For the LORD is a God of justice;
blessed are all those who wait for him.

19 Yes, O people in Zion who dwell at
Jerusalem; you shall weep no more. He will
surely be gracious to you at the sound of your
cry; when he hears it, he will answer you.
20 And though the Lord give you the bread of
adversity and the water of affliction, yet your
Teacher will not hide himself any more, but
your eyes shall see your Teacher. 21 And your
ears shall hear a word behind you, saying,
"This is the way, walk in it," when you turn
to the right or when you turn to the left.
22 Then you will defile your silver-covered
graven images and your gold-plated molten
images. You will scatter them as unclean
things; you will say to them, "Begone!"

23 And he will give rain for the seed with
which you sow the ground, and grain, the
produce of the ground, which will be rich and
plenteous. In that day your flock will be given
pasture, and the lamb will graze in open fields;
24 and the oxen and the donkeys that till the
ground will eat salted food, which has been
winnowed with shovel and fork. 25 And upon
every lofty mountain and every high hill there
will be brooks running with water, in the day
of the great slaughter, when the towers fall.
26 Moreover the light of the moon will be as the
light of the sun, and the light of the sun will be
sevenfold, as the light of seven days, in the day
when the LORD binds up the hurt of his people,
and heals the wounds inflicted by his blow.

27 Behold, the name of the LORD comes
from far,
burning with his anger, and in thick
rising smoke;
his lips are full of indignation,
and his tongue is like a devouring fire;
28 his breath is like an overflowing stream
that reaches up to the neck;
to sift the nations with the sieve of
destruction,
and to place on the jaws of the peoples a
bridle that leads astray.

29 You shall have a song as in the night when
a holy feast is kept; and gladness of heart, as
when one sets out to the sound of the flute
to go to the mountain of the LORD, to the
Rock of Israel. 30 And the LORD will cause his
majestic voice to be heard and the descending
blow of his arm to be seen, in furious
anger and a flame of devouring fire, with a
cloudburst and tempest and hailstones. 31 The
Assyrians will be terror-stricken at the voice
of the LORD, when he strikes with his rod.
32 And every stroke of the staff of punishment
which the LORD lays upon them will be to
the sound of timbrels and lyres; battling with
brandished arm he will fight with them. 33 For
a burning place has long been prepared;
yes, for the king it is made ready, its pyre
made deep and wide, with fire and wood in
abundance; the breath of the LORD, like a
stream of brimstone, kindles it.

31 Woe to those who go down to Egypt
for help
and rely on horses,
who trust in chariots because they are many
and in horsemen because they are very
strong,
but do not look to the Holy One of Israel
or consult the LORD!
2 And yet he is wise and brings disaster,
he does not call back his words,
but will arise against the house of
the evildoers,
and against the helpers of those who
work iniquity.
3 The Egyptians are men, and not God;
and their horses are flesh, and not spirit.
When the LORD stretches out his hand,
the helper will stumble, and he who is
helped will fall,
and they will all perish together.

4 For thus the LORD said to me,
As a lion or a young lion growls over his prey,
and when a band of shepherds is called
forth against him
is not terrified by their shouting
or daunted at their noise,
so the LORD of hosts will come down
to fight upon Mount Zion and upon
its hill.
5 Like birds hovering, so the LORD of hosts
will protect Jerusalem;
he will protect and deliver it,
he will spare and rescue it.

6 Turn to him from whom you have deeply
revolted, O people of Israel. 7 For in that day
every one shall cast away his idols of silver
and his idols of gold, which your hands have
sinfully made for you.
8 "And the Assyrian shall fall by a sword, not
of man;
and a sword, not of man, shall devour him;
and he shall flee from the sword,
and his young men shall be put to
forced labor.
9 His rock shall pass away in terror,
and his officers desert the standard
in panic,"
says the LORD, whose fire is in Zion,
and whose furnace is in Jerusalem.

32 Behold, a king will reign in
righteousness,
and princes will rule in justice.
2 Each will be like a hiding place from
the wind,
a covert from the tempest,
like streams of water in a dry place,
like the shade of a great rock in a
weary land.
3 Then the eyes of those who see will
not be closed,
and the ears of those who hear will listen.
4 The mind of the rash will have good
judgment,
and the tongue of the stammerers will
speak readily and distinctly.
5 The fool will no more be called noble,
nor the knave said to be honorable.
6 For the fool speaks folly,
and his mind plots iniquity:
to practice ungodliness,
to utter error concerning the LORD,
to leave the craving of the hungry
unsatisfied,
and to deprive the thirsty of drink.
7 The knaveries of the knave are evil;
he devises wicked devices
to ruin the poor with lying words,
even when the plea of the needy is right.

8But he who is noble devises noble things,
and by noble things he stands.
9Rise up, you women who are at ease, hear my voice;
you complacent daughters, give ear to my speech.
10In little more than a year
you will shudder, you complacent women;
for the vintage will fail,
the fruit harvest will not come.
11Tremble, you women who are at ease,
shudder, you complacent ones;
strip, and make yourselves bare,
and put sackcloth upon your loins.
12Beat upon your breasts for the pleasant fields,
for the fruitful vine,
13for the soil of my people
growing up in thorns and briers;
yes, for all the joyous houses
in the joyful city.
14For the palace will be forsaken,
the populous city deserted;
the hill and the watchtower
will become dens for ever,
a joy of wild donkeys,
a pasture of flocks;
15until the Spirit is poured upon us
from on high,
and the wilderness becomes a fruitful field,
and the fruitful field is deemed a forest.
16Then justice will dwell in the wilderness,
and righteousness abide in the fruitful field.
17And the effect of righteousness will be peace,
and the result of righteousness, quietness and trust for ever.
18My people will abide in a peaceful habitation,
in secure dwellings, and in quiet resting places.
19And the forest will utterly go down,
and the city will be utterly laid low.
20Happy are you who sow beside all waters,
who let the feet of the ox and the donkey range free.

WISDOM 1

Love righteousness, you rulers of the earth,
think of the Lord with uprightness,
and seek him with sincerity of heart;
2because he is found by those who do not put him to the test,
and manifests himself to those who do not distrust him.
3For perverse thoughts separate men from God,
and when his power is tested, it convicts the foolish;
4because wisdom will not enter a deceitful soul,
nor dwell in a body enslaved to sin.
5For a holy and disciplined spirit will flee from deceit,
and will rise and depart from foolish thoughts,
and will be ashamed at the approach of unrighteousness.

6For wisdom is a kindly spirit
and will not free a blasphemer from the guilt of his words;
because God is witness of his inmost feelings,
and a true observer of his heart, and a hearer of his tongue.
7Because the Spirit of the Lord has filled the world,
and that which holds all things together knows what is said;
8therefore no one who utters unrighteous things will escape notice,
and justice, when it punishes, will not pass him by.
9For inquiry will be made into the counsels of an ungodly man,
and a report of his words will come to the Lord,
to convict him of his lawless deeds;
10because a jealous ear hears all things,
and the sound of murmurings does not go unheard.
11Beware then of useless murmuring,
and keep your tongue from slander;
because no secret word is without result,
and a lying mouth destroys the soul.

[12]Do not invite death by the error of your life,
nor bring on destruction by the works of
your hands;
[13]because God did not make death, and
he does not delight in the death of the living.
[14]For he created all things that they might exist,
and the creatures of the world are wholesome,
and there is no destructive poison in them;
and the dominion of Hades is not on earth.
[15]For righteousness is immortal.

[16]But ungodly men by their words and deeds
summoned death;
considering him a friend, they pined away,
and they made a covenant with him,
because they are fit to belong to his party.

1 CORINTHIANS 12

[31]But earnestly desire the higher gifts.

And I will show you a still more excellent way.

13 If I speak in the tongues of men and
of angels, but have not love, I am a
noisy gong or a clanging cymbal. [2]And if I
have prophetic powers, and understand all
mysteries and all knowledge, and if I have
all faith, so as to remove mountains, but
have not love, I am nothing. [3]If I give away
all I have, and if I deliver my body to be
burned, but have not love, I gain nothing.
[4]Love is patient and kind; love is not
jealous or boastful; [5]it is not arrogant or
rude. Love does not insist on its own way;
it is not irritable or resentful; [6]it does not
rejoice at wrong, but rejoices in the right.
[7]Love bears all things, believes all things,
hopes all things, endures all things.
[8]Love never ends; as for prophecies, they
will pass away; as for tongues, they will cease;
as for knowledge, it will pass away. [9]For our
knowledge is imperfect and our prophecy is
imperfect; [10]but when the perfect comes, the
imperfect will pass away. [11]When I was a child,
I spoke like a child, I thought like a child, I
reasoned like a child; when I became a man,
I gave up childish ways. [12]For now we see in
a mirror dimly, but then face to face. Now I
know in part; then I shall understand fully,
even as I have been fully understood. [13]So
faith, hope, love abide, these three; but the
greatest of these is love.

REFLECTION

Sin has a way of snowballing—a bad act becomes a bad habit, and bad habits enslave us. Isaiah laments the tendency of the people who have become like stubborn children, "who carry out a plan, but not mine; and who make a league, but not of my spirit, that they may add sin to sin" (Is 30:1). They prevent God from rescuing them by refusing his wisdom, since "wisdom will not enter a deceitful soul" (Wis 1:4). When we sin, we actually "invite death" (v. 12), bringing it upon ourselves. "God did not make death" (v. 13), but instead invites us to love as he loves. St. Paul explains the "more excellent way" (1 Cor 12:31) of love, or in Greek, *agape*. Agape is not mere enjoyment or happiness in another person, it is a love that gives itself away for the other. It is a love that God pours into our hearts (see Rom 5:5), and we, in turn, should pass it on in loving service to others. "Love bears all things, believes all things, hopes all things, endures all things" (1 Cor 13:7). It will endure forever as the most powerful force in all creation. How can you exercise patience, kindness, and generous Christlike love to others today?

September 6

ISAIAH 33

Woe to you, destroyer,
who yourself have not been
destroyed;
you treacherous one,
with whom none has dealt
treacherously!
When you have ceased to destroy,
you will be destroyed;
and when you have made an end of dealing
treacherously,
you will be dealt with treacherously.

2O Lord, be gracious to us; we wait for you.
Be our arm every morning,
our salvation in the time of trouble.
3At the thunderous noise peoples flee,
at the lifting up of yourself nations
are scattered;
4and spoil is gathered as the caterpillar
gathers;
as locusts leap, men leap upon it.

5The Lord is exalted, for he dwells on high;
he will fill Zion with justice and
righteousness;
6and he will be the stability of your times,
abundance of salvation, wisdom, and
knowledge;
the fear of the Lord is his treasure.

7Behold, the valiant ones cry without;
the envoys of peace weep bitterly.
8The highways lie waste,
the wayfaring man ceases.
Covenants are broken,
witnesses are despised,
there is no regard for man.
9The land mourns and languishes;
Lebanon is confounded and withers away;
Sharon is like a desert;
and Bashan and Carmel shake off their
leaves.

10"Now I will arise," says the Lord,
"now I will lift myself up;
now I will be exalted.
11You conceive chaff, you bring forth stubble;
your breath is a fire that will consume
you.
12And the peoples will be as if burned to lime,
like thorns cut down, that are burned in
the fire."

13Hear, you who are far off, what I have done;
and you who are near, acknowledge my
might.
14The sinners in Zion are afraid;
trembling has seized the godless:
"Who among us can dwell with the
devouring fire?
Who among us can dwell with
everlasting burnings?"
15He who walks righteously and
speaks uprightly,
who despises the gain of oppressions,
who shakes his hands, lest they hold
a bribe,
who stops his ears from hearing of
bloodshed
and shuts his eyes from looking
upon evil,
16he will dwell on the heights;
his place of defense will be the fortresses
of rocks;
his bread will be given him, his water will
be sure.

17Your eyes will see the king in his beauty;
they will behold a land that stretches afar.
18Your mind will muse on the terror:
"Where is he who counted, where is he
who weighed the tribute?
Where is he who counted the towers?"
19You will see no more the insolent people,
the people of an obscure speech which
you cannot comprehend,
stammering in a tongue which you
cannot understand.
20Look upon Zion, the city of our
appointed feasts!
Your eyes will see Jerusalem,
a quiet habitation, an immovable tent,
whose stakes will never be plucked up,
nor will any of its cords be broken.
21But there the Lord in majesty will be for us
a place of broad rivers and streams,
where no galley with oars can go,
nor stately ship can pass.
22For the Lord is our judge, the Lord is
our ruler,
the Lord is our king; he will save us.

23Your tackle hangs loose;
it cannot hold the mast firm in its place,
or keep the sail spread out.

Then prey and spoil in abundance will be
divided;
even the lame will take the prey.
24And no inhabitant will say, "I am sick";
the people who dwell there will be
forgiven their iniquity.

34 Draw near, O nations, to hear,
and listen, O peoples!
Let the earth listen, and all that fills it;
the world, and all that comes from it.
2For the LORD is enraged against all
the nations,
and furious against all their host,
he has doomed them, has given them
over for slaughter.
3Their slain shall be cast out,
and the stench of their corpses shall rise;
the mountains shall flow with their blood.
4All the host of heaven shall rot away,
and the skies roll up like a scroll.
All their host shall fall,
as leaves fall from the vine,
like leaves falling from the fig tree.

5For my sword has drunk its fill in
the heavens;
behold, it descends for judgment
upon E′dom,
upon the people I have doomed.
6The LORD has a sword; it is sated
with blood,
it is gorged with fat,
with the blood of lambs and goats,
with the fat of the kidneys of rams.
For the LORD has a sacrifice in Bozrah,
a great slaughter in the land of E′dom.
7Wild oxen shall fall with them,
and young steers with the mighty bulls.
Their land shall be soaked with blood,
and their soil made rich with fat.

8For the LORD has a day of vengeance,
a year of recompense for the cause of Zion.
9And the streams of E′dom shall be turned
into pitch,
and her soil into brimstone;
her land shall become burning pitch.
10Night and day it shall not be quenched;
its smoke shall go up for ever.
From generation to generation it shall
lie waste;
none shall pass through it for ever
and ever.
11But the hawk and the porcupine shall
possess it,
the owl and the raven shall dwell in it.
He shall stretch the line of confusion over it,
and the plummet of chaos over its nobles.
12They shall name it No Kingdom There,
and all its princes shall be nothing.

13Thorns shall grow over its strongholds,
nettles and thistles in its fortresses.
It shall be the haunt of jackals,
an abode for ostriches.
14And wild beasts shall meet with hyenas,
the satyr shall cry to his fellow;
yes, there shall the night creature alight,
and find for herself a resting place.

15There shall the owl nest and lay
and hatch and gather her young in her
shadow;
yes, there shall the kites be gathered,
each one with her mate.
16Seek and read from the book of
the LORD:
Not one of these shall be missing;
none shall be without her mate.
For the mouth of the LORD has
commanded,
and his Spirit has gathered them.
17He has cast the lot for them,
his hand has portioned it out to them
with the line;
they shall possess it for ever,
from generation to generation they shall
dwell in it.

35 The wilderness and the dry land
shall be glad,
the desert shall rejoice and blossom;
like the lily 2it shall blossom abundantly,
and rejoice with joy and singing.
The glory of Lebanon shall be given to it,
the majesty of Car′mel and Sharon.
They shall see the glory of the LORD,
the majesty of our God.

3Strengthen the weak hands,
and make firm the feeble knees.
4Say to those who are of a fearful heart,
"Be strong, fear not!
Behold, your God
will come with vengeance,
with the recompense of God.
He will come and save you."

5 Then the eyes of the blind shall be opened,
  and the ears of the deaf unstopped;
6 then shall the lame man leap like a deer,
  and the tongue of the mute sing for joy.
For waters shall break forth in the
    wilderness,
  and streams in the desert;
7 the burning sand shall become a pool,
  and the thirsty ground springs of water;
the haunt of jackals shall become a swamp,
  the grass shall become reeds and rushes.

8 And a highway shall be there,
  and it shall be called the Holy Way;
the unclean shall not pass over it,
  and fools shall not err therein.
9 No lion shall be there,
  nor shall any ravenous beast come
    up on it;
they shall not be found there,
  but the redeemed shall walk there.
10 And the ransomed of the LORD
    shall return,
  and come to Zion with singing;
everlasting joy shall be upon their heads;
  they shall obtain joy and gladness,
  and sorrow and sighing shall flee away.

36 In the fourteenth year of King Heze-
ki′ah, Sennach′erib king of Assyria
came up against all the fortified cities of
Judah and took them. 2 And the king of
Assyria sent the Rab′shakeh from La′chish
to King Hezeki′ah at Jerusalem, with a great
army. And he stood by the conduit of the
upper pool on the highway to the Fuller's
Field. 3 And there came out to him Eli′akim
the son of Hilki′ah, who was over the
household, and Shebna the secretary, and
Jo′ah the son of A′saph, the recorder.
4 And the Rab′shakeh said to them, "Say
to Hezeki′ah, 'Thus says the great king, the
king of Assyria: On what do you rest this
confidence of yours? 5 Do you think that
mere words are strategy and power for war?
On whom do you now rely, that you have
rebelled against me? 6 Behold, you are relying
on Egypt, that broken reed of a staff, which
will pierce the hand of any man who leans on
it. Such is Pharaoh king of Egypt to all who
rely on him. 7 But if you say to me, "We rely on
the LORD our God," is it not he whose high
places and altars Hezeki′ah has removed,
saying to Judah and to Jerusalem, "You shall
worship before this altar"? 8 Come now, make
a wager with my master the king of Assyria: I
will give you two thousand horses, if you are
able on your part to set riders upon them.
9 How then can you repulse a single captain
among the least of my master's servants,
when you rely on Egypt for chariots and
for horsemen? 10 Moreover, is it without the
LORD that I have come up against this land
to destroy it? The LORD said to me, Go up
against this land, and destroy it.'"
11 Then Eli′akim, Shebna, and Jo′ah said
to the Rab′shakeh, "Please, speak to your
servants in Arama′ic, for we understand it;
do not speak to us in the language of Judah
within the hearing of the people who are on
the wall." 12 But the Rab′shakeh said, "Has my
master sent me to speak these words to your
master and to you, and not to the men sitting
on the wall, who are doomed with you to eat
their own dung and drink their own urine?"
13 Then the Rab′shakeh stood and called
out in a loud voice in the language of Judah:
"Hear the words of the great king, the king
of Assyria! 14 Thus says the king: 'Do not let
Hezeki′ah deceive you, for he will not be able
to deliver you. 15 Do not let Hezeki′ah make
you rely on the LORD by saying, "The LORD
will surely deliver us; this city will not be
given into the hand of the king of Assyria."
16 Do not listen to Hezeki′ah; for thus says
the king of Assyria: Make your peace with
me and come out to me; then every one of
you will eat of his own vine, and every one
of his own fig tree, and every one of you will
drink the water of his own cistern; 17 until
I come and take you away to a land like
your own land, a land of grain and wine, a
land of bread and vineyards. 18 Beware lest
Hezeki′ah mislead you by saying, "The LORD
will deliver us." Has any of the gods of the
nations delivered his land out of the hand of
the king of Assyria? 19 Where are the gods of
Ha′math and Arpad? Where are the gods of
Sepharva′im? Have they delivered Samar′ia
out of my hand? 20 Who among all the gods
of these countries have delivered their

countries out of my hand, that the LORD should deliver Jerusalem out of my hand?'"
21But they were silent and answered him not a word, for the king's command was, "Do not answer him." 22Then Eli′akim the son of Hilki′ah, who was over the household, and Sheb′na the secretary, and Jo′ah the son of A′saph, the recorder, came to Hezeki′ah with their clothes torn, and told him the words of the Rab′shakeh.

WISDOM 2

For they reasoned unsoundly, saying
to themselves,
"Short and sorrowful is our life,
and there is no remedy when a man comes
to his end,
and no one has been known to return
from Hades.
2Because we were born by mere chance,
and hereafter we shall be as though we had
never been;
because the breath in our nostrils is smoke,
and reason is a spark kindled by the beating
of our hearts.
3When it is extinguished, the body will turn
to ashes,
and the spirit will dissolve like empty air.
4Our name will be forgotten in time,
and no one will remember our works;
our life will pass away like the traces
of a cloud,
and be scattered like mist
that is chased by the rays of the sun
and overcome by its heat.
5For our allotted time is the passing
of a shadow,
and there is no return from our death,
because it is sealed up and no one
turns back.

6"Come, therefore, let us enjoy the good
things that exist,
and make use of the creation to the full as
in youth.
7Let us take our fill of costly wine and
perfumes,
and let no flower of spring pass by us.
8Let us crown ourselves with rosebuds
before they wither.
9Let none of us fail to share in our revelry,
everywhere let us leave signs of enjoyment,
because this is our portion, and this our lot.
10Let us oppress the righteous poor man;
let us not spare the widow
nor regard the gray hairs of the aged.
11But let our might be our law of right,
for what is weak proves itself to be useless.

1 CORINTHIANS 14

Make love your aim, and earnestly desire the spiritual gifts,
especially that you may prophesy. 2For
one who speaks in a tongue speaks not
to men but to God; for no one understands
him, but he utters mysteries in the Spirit.
3On the other hand, he who prophesies
speaks to men for their upbuilding and
encouragement and consolation. 4He who
speaks in a tongue edifies himself, but he
who prophesies edifies the Church. 5Now I
want you all to speak in tongues, but even
more to prophesy. He who prophesies is
greater than he who speaks in tongues,
unless some one interprets, so that the
Church may be edified.
6Now, brethren, if I come to you speaking
in tongues, how shall I benefit you unless
I bring you some revelation or knowledge
or prophecy or teaching? 7If even lifeless
instruments, such as the flute or the harp,
do not give distinct notes, how will any one
know what is played? 8And if the bugle gives
an indistinct sound, who will get ready for
battle? 9So with yourselves; if you in a tongue
utter speech that is not intelligible, how will
any one know what is said? For you will be
speaking into the air. 10There are doubtless
many different languages in the world, and
none is without meaning; 11but if I do not
know the meaning of the language, I shall be
a foreigner to the speaker and the speaker a
foreigner to me. 12So with yourselves; since
you are eager for manifestations of the Spirit,
strive to excel in building up the Church.

REFLECTION

The book of Wisdom lets us peer into the minds of the ungodly, who see life as "short and sorrowful," thinking "we were born by mere chance" (Wis 2:1–2). They do not believe in the existence of an eternal soul, thinking instead that "hereafter we shall be as though we had never been" (v. 2) and "the spirit will dissolve like empty air" (v. 3). Nothing could be further from the truth. Christianity understands that the human person is created with both a body and a soul. Not only do we understand that the soul is immortal and will live forever we also profess, as a central Tenant of our Faith, the Resurrection of Jesus Christ, who will raise us up, body and soul, to new life. There is a "return from our death"! For this reason, we who believe and have been baptized into Christ Jesus do not live only for this temporal, passing life, we also look forward to the life to come, and this changes (or should change) how we live. St. Paul exhorts us, "Make love your aim" (1 Cor 14:1). If we love with the love of Christ, we will see the glory of the Lord (see Is 35:2), and we will bring others with us. How can you make love your aim today?

September 7

ISAIAH 37

When King Hezeki′ah heard it, he tore his clothes, and covered himself with sackcloth, and went into the house of the LORD.
2And he sent Eli′akim, who was over the household, and Shebna the secre-tary, and the senior priests, clothed with
sackcloth, to the prophet Isai′ah the son
of A′moz. 3They said to him, "Thus says
Hezeki′ah, 'This day is a day of distress,
of rebuke, and of disgrace; children have
come to the birth, and there is no strength
to bring them forth. 4It may be that the
LORD your God heard the words of the Rab′shakeh, whom his master the king of Assyria has sent to mock the living God, and will rebuke the words which the LORD your God has heard; therefore lift up your prayer for the remnant that is left.' "
5When the servants of King Hezeki′ah
came to Isai′ah, 6Isai′ah said to them, "Say to your master, 'Thus says the LORD: Do not be afraid because of the words that you have heard, with which the servants of the king of
Assyria have reviled me. 7Behold, I will put a spirit in him, so that he shall hear a rumor, and return to his own land; and I will make him fall by the sword in his own land.' "
8The Rab′shakeh returned, and found the king of Assyria fighting against Libnah; for he had heard that the king had left
La′chish. 9Now the king heard concerning Tirha′kah king of Ethiopia, "He has set out to fight against you." And when he heard it, he sent messengers to Hezeki′ah, saying,
10"Thus shall you speak to Hezeki′ah king of Judah: 'Do not let your God on whom you rely deceive you by promising that Jerusalem will not be given into the hand
of the king of Assyria. 11Behold, you have heard what the kings of Assyria have done to all lands, destroying them utterly. And
shall you be delivered? 12Have the gods of the nations delivered them, the nations which my fathers destroyed, Gozan, Haran, Rezeph, and the people of Eden
who were in Telas′sar? 13Where is the king of Ha′math, the king of Arpad, the king of the city of Sepharva′im, the king of He′na, or the king of Ivvah?' "
14Hezeki′ah received the letter from the hand of the messengers, and read it; and Hezekiah went up to the house of the LORD, and spread it before the LORD.
15And Hezeki′ah prayed to the LORD: 16"O
LORD of hosts, God of Israel, who are enthroned above the cherubim, you are the God, you alone, of all the kingdoms of the earth; you have made heaven and earth.
17Incline your ear, O LORD, and hear; open your eyes, O LORD, and see; and hear all the words of Sennach′erib, which
he has sent to mock the living God. 18Of a

truth, O LORD, the kings of Assyria have
laid waste all the nations and their lands,
[19]and have cast their gods into the fire; for
they were no gods, but the work of men's
hands, wood and stone; therefore they
were destroyed. [20]So now, O LORD our
God, save us from his hand, that all the
kingdoms of the earth may know that you
alone are the LORD."

[21]Then Isai′ah the son of A′moz sent to
Hezeki′ah, saying, "Thus says the LORD,
the God of Israel: Because you have prayed
to me concerning Sennach′erib king of
Assyria, [22]this is the word that the LORD has
spoken concerning him:

'She despises you, she scorns you—
the virgin daughter of Zion;
she wags her head behind you—
the daughter of Jerusalem.

[23]'Whom have you mocked and reviled?
Against whom have you raised your voice
and haughtily lifted your eyes?
Against the Holy One of Israel!
[24]By your servants you have mocked
the Lord,
and you have said, With my many chariots
I have gone up the heights of the mountains,
to the far recesses of Lebanon;
I felled its tallest cedars,
its choicest cypresses;
I came to its remotest height,
its densest forest.
[25]I dug wells
and drank waters,
and I dried up with the sole of my foot
all the streams of Egypt.

[26]'Have you not heard
that I determined it long ago?
I planned from days of old
what now I bring to pass,
that you should make fortified cities
crash into heaps of ruins,
[27]while their inhabitants, shorn of strength,
are dismayed and confounded,
and have become like plants of the field
and like tender grass,
like grass on the housetops,
blighted before it is grown.

[28]'I know your sitting down
and your going out and coming in,
and your raging against me.
[29]Because you have raged against me
and your arrogance has come to my ears,
I will put my hook in your nose
and my bit in your mouth,
and I will turn you back on the way
by which you came.'

[30]"And this shall be the sign for you: this
year eat what grows of itself, and in the
second year what springs of the same; then
in the third year sow and reap, and plant
vineyards, and eat their fruit. [31]And the
surviving remnant of the house of Judah
shall again take root downward, and bear
fruit upward; [32]for out of Jerusalem shall go
forth a remnant, and out of Mount Zion a
band of survivors. The zeal of the LORD of
hosts will accomplish this.

[33]"Therefore thus says the LORD concerning the king of Assyria: He shall not come
into this city, or shoot an arrow there, or
come before it with a shield, or cast up a siege
mound against it. [34]By the way that he came,
by the same he shall return, and he shall not
come into this city, says the LORD. [35]For I will
defend this city to save it, for my own sake
and for the sake of my servant David."

[36]And the angel of the LORD went forth,
and slew a hundred and eighty-five thousand in the camp of the Assyrians; and
when men arose early in the morning,
behold, these were all dead bodies. [37]Then
Sennach′erib king of Assyria departed,
and went home and dwelt at Nin′eveh.
[38]And as he was worshiping in the house
of Nis′roch his god, Adram′melech
and Share′zer, his sons, slew him with
the sword, and escaped into the land
of Ar′arat. And E′sar-had′don his son
reigned in his stead.

38 In those days Hezeki′ah became sick
and was at the point of death. And
Isai′ah the prophet the son of A′moz came
to him, and said to him, "Thus says the
LORD: Set your house in order; for you
shall die, you shall not recover." [2]Then
Hezeki′ah turned his face to the wall, and

prayed to the LORD, 3and said, "Remember
now, O LORD, I beseech you, how I have
walked before you in faithfulness and
with a whole heart, and have done what is
good in your sight." And Hezeki´ah wept
bitterly. 4Then the word of the LORD came
to Isai´ah: 5"Go and say to Hezeki´ah,
Thus says the LORD, the God of David
your father: I have heard your prayer, I
have seen your tears; behold, I will add
fifteen years to your life. 6I will deliver
you and this city out of the hand of the
king of Assyria, and defend this city.
7"This is the sign to you from the LORD,
that the LORD will do this thing that he
has promised: 8Behold, I will make the
shadow cast by the declining sun on the
dial of A´haz turn back ten steps." So the
sun turned back on the dial the ten steps by
which it had declined.

9A writing of Hezeki´ah king of Judah,
after he had been sick and had recovered
from his sickness:

10I said, In the noontide of my days
I must depart;
I am consigned to the gates of Sheol
for the rest of my years.
11I said, I shall not see the LORD
in the land of the living;
I shall look upon man no more
among the inhabitants of the world.
12My dwelling is plucked up and removed
from me
like a shepherd's tent;
like a weaver I have rolled up my life;
he cuts me off from the loom;
from day to night you bring me to an end;
13 I cry for help until morning;
like a lion he breaks all my bones;
from day to night you bring me to an end.

14Like a swallow or a crane I clamor,
I moan like a dove.
My eyes are weary with looking upward.
O Lord, I am oppressed; be my security!
15But what can I say? For he has spoken to me,
and he himself has done it.
All my sleep has fled
because of the bitterness of my soul.

16O Lord, by these things men live,
and in all these is the life of my spirit.
Oh, restore me to health and make me live!
17Behold, it was for my welfare
that I had great bitterness;
but you have held back my life
from the pit of destruction,
for you have cast all my sins behind
your back.
18For Sheol cannot thank you,
death cannot praise you;
those who go down to the pit cannot hope
for your faithfulness.
19The living, the living, he thanks you,
as I do this day;
the father makes known to the children
your faithfulness.

20The LORD will save me,
and we will sing to stringed instruments
all the days of our life,
at the house of the LORD.

21Now Isai´ah had said, "Let them take a
cake of figs, and apply it to the boil, that
he may recover." 22Hezeki´ah also had said,
"What is the sign that I shall go up to the
house of the LORD?"

39 At that time Mer´odach-bal´adan the
son of Bal´adan, king of Babylon, sent
envoys with letters and a present to Hezeki´ah,
for he heard that he had been sick and had
recovered. 2And Hezeki´ah welcomed them;
and he showed them his treasure house, the
silver, the gold, the spices, the precious oil,
his whole armory, all that was found in his
storehouses. There was nothing in his house
or in all his realm that Hezekiah did not show
them. 3Then Isai´ah the prophet came to King
Hezeki´ah, and said to him, "What did these
men say? And from where did they come to
you?" Hezeki´ah said, "They have come to
me from a far country, from Babylon." 4He
said, "What have they seen in your house?"
Hezeki´ah answered, "They have seen all
that is in my house; there is nothing in my
storehouses that I did not show them."

5Then Isai´ah said to Hezeki´ah, "Hear the
word of the LORD of hosts: 6Behold, the days
are coming, when all that is in your house,

and that which your fathers have stored up till
this day, shall be carried to Babylon; nothing
shall be left, says the LORD. 7And some of your
own sons, who are born to you, shall be taken
away; and they shall be eunuchs in the palace
of the king of Babylon." 8Then said Hezeki′ah
to Isai′ah, "The word of the LORD which you
have spoken is good." For he thought, "There
will be peace and security in my days."

WISDOM 2

12"Let us lie in wait for the righteous man,
because he is inconvenient to us and
opposes our actions;
he reproaches us for sins against the law,
and accuses us of sins against our training.
13He professes to have knowledge of God,
and calls himself a child of the Lord.
14He became to us a reproof of our thoughts;
15the very sight of him is a burden to us,
because his manner of life is unlike that
of others,
and his ways are strange.
16We are considered by him as
something base,
and he avoids our ways as unclean;
he calls the last end of the righteous happy,
and boasts that God is his father.
17Let us see if his words are true,
and let us test what will happen at the end
of his life;
18for if the righteous man is God's son, he
will help him,
and will deliver him from the hand of
his adversaries.
19Let us test him with insult and torture,
that we may find out how gentle he is,
and make trial of his forbearance.
20Let us condemn him to a shameful death,
for, according to what he says, he will
be protected."

21Thus they reasoned, but they were led astray,
for their wickedness blinded them,
22and they did not know the secret purposes
of God,
nor hope for the wages of holiness,
nor discern the prize for blameless souls;
23for God created man for
incorruption,
and made him in the image of his
own eternity,
24but through the devil's envy death
entered the world,
and those who belong to his party
experience it.

1 CORINTHIANS 14

**13Therefore, he who speaks in
a tongue should pray for the
power to interpret. 14For if I pray in a
tongue, my spirit prays but my mind is**
unfruitful. 15What am I to do? I will
pray with the spirit and I will pray with
the mind also; I will sing with the spirit
and I will sing with the mind also. 16Oth-
erwise, if you bless with the spirit, how can
any one in the position of an outsider say
the "Amen" to your thanksgiving when he
does not know what you are saying? 17For
you may give thanks well enough, but the
other man is not edified. 18I thank God that
I speak in tongues more than you all; 19nev-
ertheless, in church I would rather speak
five words with my mind, in order to instruct others, than ten thousand words in
a tongue.

20Brethren, do not be children in your
thinking; be infants in evil, but in thinking be
mature. 21In the law it is written, "By men of
strange tongues and by the lips of foreigners
will I speak to this people, and even then
they will not listen to me, says the Lord."
22Thus, tongues are a sign not for believers
but for unbelievers, while prophecy is not for
unbelievers but for believers. 23If, therefore,
the whole Church assembles and all speak in
tongues, and outsiders or unbelievers enter,
will they not say that you are mad? 24But if
all prophesy, and an unbeliever or outsider
enters, he is convicted by all, he is called to
account by all, 25the secrets of his heart are
disclosed; and so, falling on his face, he will
worship God and declare that God is really
among you.

REFLECTION

In this historical interlude in Isaiah, we see the Assyrian army laying siege to Jerusalem. Even in the face of such a threat, Isaiah tells King Hezekiah, "Do not be afraid" (Is 37:6). Hezekiah obeys and prays to the Lord for deliverance. The Lord responds by striking down the army of the Assyrians (see v. 36). Hezekiah thus exemplifies Wisdom's saying: "If the righteous man is God's son, he will help him, and will deliver him from the hand of his adversaries" (Wis 2:18). Though he cements his reputation as a faithful king, at the end of his life he errs by displaying the wealth of his kingdom to envoys of another foreign power, Babylon (see Is 39:2). It is the first step in a long, sad road that leads to the exile of God's people in Babylon. St. Paul encourages us to "be infants in evil, but in thinking be mature" (1 Cor 14:20) as he instructs the Corinthians about the appropriate use of spiritual gifts or *charisms*. This advice would have served Hezekiah well, possibly preventing his vain, prideful display before the Babylonian entourage. Do you realize that you are God's son or daughter and that you can go to him when you need help?

September 8

ISAIAH 40

Comfort, comfort my people,
says your God.
2Speak tenderly to Jerusalem,
and cry to her
that her warfare is ended,
that her iniquity is pardoned,
that she has received from the LORD's hand
double for all her sins.

3A voice cries:
"In the wilderness prepare the way of the LORD,
make straight in the desert a highway for
our God.
4Every valley shall be lifted up,
and every mountain and hill be made low;
the uneven ground shall become level,
and the rough places a plain.
5And the glory of the LORD shall be revealed,
and all flesh shall see it together,
for the mouth of the LORD has spoken."

6A voice says, "Cry!"
And I said, "What shall I cry?"
All flesh is grass,
and all its beauty is like the flower
of the field.
7The grass withers, the flower fades,
when the breath of the LORD blows
upon it;
surely the people is grass.
8The grass withers, the flower fades;
but the word of our God will stand
for ever.
9Get you up to a high mountain,
O Zion, herald of good tidings;
lift up your voice with strength,
O Jerusalem, herald of good tidings,
lift it up, fear not;
say to the cities of Judah,
"Behold your God!"
10Behold, the Lord GOD comes with might,
and his arm rules for him;
behold, his reward is with him,
and his recompense before him.
11He will feed his flock like a shepherd,
he will gather the lambs in his arms,
he will carry them in his bosom,
and gently lead those that are with young.

12Who has measured the waters in the
hollow of his hand
and marked off the heavens with a span,
enclosed the dust of the earth in a measure
and weighed the mountains in scales
and the hills in a balance?
13Who has directed the Spirit of the LORD,
or as his counselor has instructed him?
14Whom did he consult for his
enlightenment,
and who taught him the path of justice,
and taught him knowledge,
and showed him the way of
understanding?

[15]Behold, the nations are like a drop
from a bucket,
and are accounted as the dust on
the scales;
behold, he takes up the isles like fine dust.
[16]Lebanon would not suffice for fuel,
nor are its beasts enough for a burnt
offering.
[17]All the nations are as nothing before him,
they are accounted by him as less than
nothing and emptiness.

[18]To whom then will you liken God,
or what likeness compare with him?
[19]The idol! a workman casts it,
and a goldsmith overlays it with gold,
and casts for it silver chains.
[20]He who is impoverished chooses
for an offering
wood that will not rot;
he seeks out a skilful craftsman
to set up an image that will not move.

[21]Have you not known? Have you not heard?
Has it not been told you from the
beginning?
Have you not understood from the
foundations of the earth?
[22]It is he who sits above the circle of the earth,
and its inhabitants are like grasshoppers;
who stretches out the heavens like a curtain,
and spreads them like a tent to dwell in;
[23]who brings princes to nought,
and makes the rulers of the earth
as nothing.

[24]Scarcely are they planted, scarcely sown,
scarcely has their stem taken root in
the earth,
when he blows upon them, and they wither,
and the tempest carries them off like
stubble.

[25]To whom then will you compare me,
that I should be like him?
says the Holy One.
[26]Lift up your eyes on high and see:
who created these?
He who brings out their host by number,
calling them all by name;
by the greatness of his might,
and because he is strong in power
not one is missing.

[27]Why do you say, O Jacob,
and speak, O Israel,
"My way is hidden from the LORD,
and my right is disregarded by my God"?
[28]Have you not known? Have you not heard?
The LORD is the everlasting God,
the Creator of the ends of the earth.
He does not faint or grow weary,
his understanding is unsearchable.
[29]He gives power to the faint,
and to him who has no might he increases
strength.
[30]Even youths shall faint and be weary,
and young men shall fall exhausted;
[31]but they who wait for the LORD shall renew
their strength,
they shall mount up with wings
like eagles,
they shall run and not be weary,
they shall walk and not faint.

41 Listen to me in silence, O islands;
let the peoples renew their strength;
let them approach, then let them speak;
let us together draw near for judgment.

[2]Who stirred up one from the east
whom victory meets at every step?
He gives up nations before him,
so that he tramples kings under foot;
he makes them like dust with his sword,
like driven stubble with his bow.
[3]He pursues them and passes on safely,
by paths his feet have not trod.
[4]Who has performed and done this,
calling the generations from the
beginning?
I, the LORD, the first,
and with the last; I am He.
[5]The islands have seen and are afraid,
the ends of the earth tremble;
they have drawn near and come.
[6]Every one helps his neighbor,
and says to his brother, "Take courage!"
[7]The craftsman encourages the goldsmith,
and he who smooths with the hammer
him who strikes the anvil,

saying of the soldering, "It is good";
and they fasten it with nails so that it
cannot be moved.

8But you, Israel, my servant,
Jacob, whom I have chosen,
the offspring of Abraham, my friend;
9you whom I took from the ends of
the earth,
and called from its farthest corners,
saying to you, "You are my servant,
I have chosen you and not cast you off";
10fear not, for I am with you,
be not dismayed, for I am your God;
I will strengthen you, I will help you,
I will uphold you with my victorious
right hand.

11Behold, all who are incensed against you
shall be put to shame and confounded;
those who strive against you
shall be as nothing and shall perish.
12You shall seek those who contend with you,
but you shall not find them;
those who war against you
shall be as nothing at all.
13For I, the LORD your God,
hold your right hand;
it is I who say to you, "Fear not,
I will help you."

14Fear not, you worm Jacob,
you men of Israel!
I will help you, says the LORD;
your Redeemer is the Holy One of Israel.
15Behold, I will make of you a threshing
sledge,
new, sharp, and having teeth;
you shall thresh the mountains and
crush them,
and you shall make the hills like chaff;
16you shall winnow them and the wind shall
carry them away,
and the tempest shall scatter them.
And you shall rejoice in the LORD;
in the Holy One of Israel you shall glory.

17When the poor and needy seek water,
and there is none,
and their tongue is parched with thirst,
I the LORD will answer them,
I the God of Israel will not forsake them.
18I will open rivers on the bare heights,
and fountains in the midst of the valleys;
I will make the wilderness a pool of water,
and the dry land springs of water.
19I will put in the wilderness the cedar,
the acacia, the myrtle, and the olive;
I will set in the desert the cypress,
the plane and the pine together;
20that men may see and know,
may consider and understand together,
that the hand of the LORD has done this,
the Holy One of Israel has created it.

21Set forth your case, says the LORD;
bring your proofs, says the King of Jacob.
22Let them bring them, and tell us
what is to happen.
Tell us the former things, what they are,
that we may consider them,
that we may know their outcome;
or declare to us the things to come.
23Tell us what is to come hereafter,
that we may know that you are gods;
do good, or do harm,
that we may be dismayed and terrified.
24Behold, you are nothing,
and your work is nought;
an abomination is he who chooses you.

25I stirred up one from the north, and he
has come,
from the rising of the sun, and he shall
call on my name;
he shall trample on rulers as on mortar,
as the potter treads clay.
26Who declared it from the beginning, that
we might know,
and beforetime, that we might say,
"He is right"?
There was none who declared it, none
who proclaimed,
none who heard your words.
27I first have declared it to Zion,
and I give to Jerusalem a herald of
good tidings.
28But when I look there is no one;
among these there is no counselor
who, when I ask, gives an answer.

29Behold, they are all a delusion;
their works are nothing;
their molten images are empty wind.

WISDOM 3

But the souls of the righteous are in the hand of God,
and no torment will ever touch them.
2In the eyes of the foolish they seemed to have died,
and their departure was thought to be an affliction,
3and their going from us to be their destruction;
but they are at peace.
4For though in the sight of men they were punished,
their hope is full of immortality.
5Having been disciplined a little, they will receive great good,
because God tested them and found them worthy of himself;
6like gold in the furnace he tried them,
and like a sacrificial burnt offering he accepted them.
7In the time of their visitation they will shine forth,
and will run like sparks through the stubble.
8They will govern nations and rule over peoples,
and the Lord will reign over them for ever.
9Those who trust in him will understand truth,
and the faithful will abide with him in love,
because grace and mercy are upon his elect,
and he watches over his holy ones.
10But the ungodly will be punished as their reasoning deserves,
who disregarded the righteous man and rebelled against the Lord;
11for whoever despises wisdom and instruction is miserable.
Their hope is vain, their labors are unprofitable,
and their works are useless.
12Their wives are foolish, and their children evil;
13their offspring are accursed.
For blessed is the barren woman who is undefiled,
who has not entered into a sinful union;
she will have fruit when God examines souls.
14Blessed also is the eunuch whose hands have done no lawless deed,
and who has not devised wicked things against the Lord;
for special favor will be shown him for his faithfulness,
and a place of great delight in the temple of the Lord.
15For the fruit of good labors is renowned,
and the root of understanding does not fail.
16But children of adulterers will not come to maturity,
and the offspring of an unlawful union will perish.
17Even if they live long they will be held of no account,
and finally their old age will be without honor.
18If they die young, they will have no hope
and no consolation in the day of decision.
19For the end of an unrighteous generation is grievous.

1 CORINTHIANS 14

26What then, brethren? When you come together, each one has a hymn, a lesson, a revelation, a tongue, or an interpretation. Let all things be done for edification. 27If any speak in a tongue, let there be only two or at most three, and each in turn; and let one interpret. 28But if there is no one to interpret, let each of them keep silence in church and speak to himself and to God.
29Let two or three prophets speak, and let the others weigh what is said. 30If a revelation is made to another sitting by, let the

first be silent. [31]For you can all prophesy
one by one, so that all may learn and all
be encouraged; [32]and the spirits of prophets are subject to prophets. [33]For God is
not a God of confusion but of peace.
As in all the churches of the saints,
[34]the women should keep silence in the
churches. For they are not permitted to
speak, but should be subordinate, as even
the law says. [35]If there is anything they
desire to know, let them ask their husbands
at home. For it is shameful for a woman to
speak in church. [36]What! Did the word of
God originate with you, or are you the only
ones it has reached?
[37]If any one thinks that he is a prophet, or
spiritual, he should acknowledge that what
I am writing to you is a command of the
Lord. [38]If any one does not recognize this,
he is not recognized. [39]So, my brethren, earnestly desire to prophesy, and do not forbid
speaking in tongues; [40]but all things should
be done decently and in order.

15 Now I would remind you, brethren,
in what terms I preached to you
the gospel, which you received, in which
you stand, [2]by which you are saved, if you
hold it fast—unless you believed in vain.
[3]For I delivered to you as of first importance what I also received, that Christ
died for our sins in accordance with the
Scriptures, [4]that he was buried, that he
was raised on the third day in accordance with the Scriptures, [5]and that he
appeared to Ce′phas, then to the Twelve.
[6]Then he appeared to more than five hundred brethren at one time, most of whom
are still alive, though some have fallen
asleep. [7]Then he appeared to James, then
to all the apostles. [8]Last of all, as to one
untimely born, he appeared also to me.
[9]For I am the least of the apostles, unfit to
be called an apostle, because I persecuted
the Church of God. [10]But by the grace of
God I am what I am, and his grace toward
me was not in vain. On the contrary, I
worked harder than any of them, though
it was not I, but the grace of God which is
with me. [11]Whether then it was I or they,
so we preach and so you believed.

REFLECTION

The major turn in the Book of Isaiah comes with the opening verses of chapter 40: "Comfort, comfort my people, says your God" (Is 40:1). Isaiah switches from primarily foretelling the Lord's judgment on the disobedient, to describing his merciful restoration. He sees the Lord coming as a gentle shepherd (see v. 11) and making his people fly like eagles (see v. 31). After judgment comes repentance, and after repentance comes the glorious restoration of God's people. Isaiah's prophecies show that "the souls of the righteous are in the hand of God" (Wis 3:1). He interprets Israel's history differently than unbelievers, a contrast Wisdom brings out: "Though in the sight of men they were punished, their hope is full of immortality" (v. 4). The Lord's discipline is not meant to lead to despair, but to conversion and healing. In the community of the redeemed, St. Paul envisions a harmonious and dynamic interplay: "When you come together, each one has a hymn, a lesson, a revelation, a tongue, or an interpretation" (1 Cor 14:26). He sees the Christian community worshipping in peace, not confusion, "decently and in order" (v. 40). When you are confronted by discouraging circumstances, do you look back to the story of Scripture, which moves from plight to praise?

September 9

ISAIAH 42

Behold my servant, whom I uphold,
my chosen, in whom my soul delights;
I have put my Spirit upon him,
he will bring forth justice to the nations.
[2]He will not cry or lift up his voice,
or make it heard in the street;

3a bruised reed he will not break,
and a dimly burning wick he will
not quench;
he will faithfully bring forth justice.
4He will not fail or be discouraged
till he has established justice in
the earth;
and the islands wait for his law.

5Thus says God, the LORD,
who created the heavens and stretched
them out,
who spread forth the earth and what
comes from it,
who gives breath to the people upon it
and spirit to those who walk in it:
6"I am the LORD, I have called you in
righteousness,
I have taken you by the hand and
kept you;
I have given you as a covenant to the people,
a light to the nations,
7 to open the eyes that are blind,
to bring out the prisoners from the dungeon,
from the prison those who sit in
darkness.
8I am the LORD, that is my name;
my glory I give to no other,
nor my praise to graven images.
9Behold, the former things have come to pass,
and new things I now declare;
before they spring forth
I tell you of them."

10Sing to the LORD a new song,
his praise from the end of the earth!
Let the sea roar and all that fills it,
the islands and their inhabitants.
11Let the desert and its cities lift up
their voice,
the villages that Ke´dar inhabits;
let the inhabitants of Se´la sing for joy,
let them shout from the top of the
mountains.
12Let them give glory to the LORD,
and declare his praise in the islands.
13The LORD goes forth like a mighty man,
like a man of war he stirs up his fury;
he cries out, he shouts aloud,
he shows himself mighty against his foes.
14For a long time I have held my peace,
I have kept still and restrained myself;
now I will cry out like a woman with
labor pains,
I will gasp and pant.
15I will lay waste mountains and hills,
and dry up all their herbage;
I will turn the rivers into islands,
and dry up the pools.
16And I will lead the blind
in a way that they know not,
in paths that they have not known
I will guide them.
I will turn the darkness before them
into light,
the rough places into level ground.
These are the things I will do,
and I will not forsake them.
17They shall be turned back and utterly
put to shame,
who trust in graven images,
who say to molten images,
"You are our gods."

18Hear, you deaf;
and look, you blind, that you may see!
19Who is blind but my servant,
or deaf as my messenger whom I send?
Who is blind as my dedicated one,
or blind as the servant of the LORD?
20He sees many things, but does not
observe them;
his ears are open, but he does not hear.
21The LORD was pleased, for his
righteousness' sake,
to magnify his law and make it glorious.
22But this is a people robbed and plundered,
they are all of them trapped in holes
and hidden in prisons;
they have become a prey with none
to rescue,
a spoil with none to say, "Restore!"
23Who among you will give ear to this,
will attend and listen for the time to come?
24Who gave up Jacob to the spoiler,
and Israel to the robbers?
Was it not the LORD, against whom we
have sinned,
in whose ways they would not walk,
and whose law they would not obey?

25 So he poured upon him the heat of
his anger
and the might of battle;
it set him on fire round about, but he
did not understand;
it burned him, but he did not take it to
heart.

43 But now thus says the LORD, he who
created you, O Jacob,
he who formed you, O Israel:
"Fear not, for I have redeemed you;
I have called you by name, you
are mine.
2 When you pass through the waters I will be
with you;
and through the rivers, they shall not
overwhelm you;
when you walk through fire you shall not
be burned,
and the flame shall not consume you.
3 For I am the LORD your God,
the Holy One of Israel, your Savior.
I give Egypt as your ransom,
Ethiopia and Seba in exchange for you.
4 Because you are precious in my eyes,
and honored, and I love you,
I give men in return for you,
peoples in exchange for your life.
5 Fear not, for I am with you;
I will bring your offspring from
the east,
and from the west I will gather you;
6 I will say to the north, Give up,
and to the south, Do not withhold;
bring my sons from afar
and my daughters from the end of
the earth,
7 every one who is called by my name,
whom I created for my glory,
whom I formed and made."

8 Bring forth the people who are blind, yet
have eyes,
who are deaf, yet have ears!
9 Let all the nations gather together,
and let the peoples assemble.
Who among them can declare this,
and show us the former things?
Let them bring their witnesses to justify them,
and let them hear and say, It is true.
10 "You are my witnesses," says the LORD,
"and my servant whom I have chosen,
that you may know and believe me
and understand that I am He.
Before me no god was formed,
nor shall there be any after me.
11 I, I am the LORD,
and besides me there is no savior.
12 I declared and saved and proclaimed,
when there was no strange god
among you;
and you are my witnesses," says the LORD.
13 "I am God, and also henceforth I am He;
there is none who can deliver from
my hand;
I work and who can hinder it?"

14 Thus says the LORD,
your Redeemer, the Holy One of Israel:
"For your sake I will send to Babylon
and break down all the bars,
and the shouting of the Chalde´ans will
be turned to lamentations.
15 I am the LORD, your Holy One,
the Creator of Israel, your King."
16 Thus says the LORD,
who makes a way in the sea,
a path in the mighty waters,
17 who brings forth chariot and horse,
army and warrior;
they lie down, they cannot rise,
they are extinguished, quenched like
a wick:
18 "Remember not the former things,
nor consider the things of old.
19 Behold, I am doing a new thing;
now it springs forth, do you not
perceive it?
I will make a way in the wilderness and
rivers in the desert.
20 The wild beasts will honor me,
the jackals and the ostriches;
for I give water in the wilderness,
rivers in the desert,
to give drink to my chosen people,
21 the people whom I formed for myself
that they might declare my praise.

22 "Yet you did not call upon me, O Jacob;
but you have been weary of me, O Israel!

[23]You have not brought me your sheep for
burnt offerings,
or honored me with your sacrifices.
I have not burdened you with offerings,
or wearied you with frankincense.
[24]You have not bought me sweet cane
with money,
or satisfied me with the fat of your sacrifices.
But you have burdened me with your sins,
you have wearied me with your
iniquities.

[25]"I, I am He
who blots out your transgressions for my
own sake,
and I will not remember your sins.
[26]Put me in remembrance, let us argue
together;
set forth your case, that you may be
proved right.
[27]Your first father sinned,
and your mediators transgressed
against me.
[28]Therefore I profaned the princes of
the sanctuary,
I delivered Jacob to utter
destruction and Israel to reviling."

WISDOM 4

Better than this is childlessness with virtue,
for in the memory of virtue is immortality,
because it is known both by God and by men.
[2]When it is present, men imitate it,
and they long for it when it has gone;
and throughout all time it marches crowned
in triumph,
victor in the contest for prizes that are
undefiled.
[3]But the prolific brood of the ungodly will
be of no use,
and none of their illegitimate seedlings will
strike a deep root
or take a firm hold.
[4]For even if they put forth boughs for a while,
standing insecurely they will be shaken by
the wind,
and by the violence of the winds they will
be uprooted.
[5]The branches will be broken off before they
come to maturity,
and their fruit will be useless,
not ripe enough to eat, and good for nothing.
[6]For children born of unlawful unions
are witnesses of evil against their parents
when God examines them.

[7]But the righteous man, though he die early,
will be at rest.
[8]For old age is not honored for length of time,
nor measured by number of years;
[9]but understanding is gray hair for men,
and a blameless life is ripe old age.

[10]There was one who pleased God and was
loved by him,
and while living among sinners he was
taken up.
[11]He was caught up lest evil change his
understanding
or guile deceive his soul.
[12]For the fascination of wickedness obscures
what is good,
and roving desire perverts the innocent
mind.
[13]Being perfected in a short time, he fulfilled
long years;
[14]for his soul was pleasing to the Lord,
therefore he took him quickly from the
midst of wickedness.
[15]Yet the peoples saw and did not
understand,
nor take such a thing to heart,
that God's grace and mercy are with
his elect,
and he watches over his holy ones.

[16]The righteous man who has died will
condemn the ungodly who are living,
and youth that is quickly perfected will
condemn the prolonged old age of the
unrighteous man.
[17]For they will see the end of the wise man,
and will not understand what the Lord
purposed for him,
and for what he kept him safe.
[18]They will see, and will have contempt
for him,
but the Lord will laugh them to scorn.

After this they will become dishonored
corpses,
and an outrage among the dead for ever;
[19]because he will dash them speechless to
the ground,
and shake them from the foundations;
they will be left utterly dry and barren,
and they will suffer anguish,
and the memory of them will perish.

[20]They will come with dread when their sins
are reckoned up,
and their lawless deeds will convict them
to their face.

---

1 CORINTHIANS 15

**[12]Now if Christ is preached as
raised from the dead, how can
some of you say that there is no
resurrection of the dead? [13]But if there is
no resurrection of the dead, then Christ
has not been raised; [14]if Christ has not**
been raised, then our preaching is in vain
and your faith is in vain. [15]We are even found
to be misrepresenting God, because we testified of God that he raised Christ, whom he
did not raise if it is true that the dead are not
raised. [16]For if the dead are not raised, then
Christ has not been raised. [17]If Christ has not
been raised, your faith is futile and you are
still in your sins. [18]Then those also who have
fallen asleep in Christ have perished. [19]If for
this life only we have hoped in Christ, we are
of all men most to be pitied.
[20]But in fact Christ has been raised from the
dead, the first fruits of those who have fallen
asleep. [21]For as by a man came death, by a man
has come also the resurrection of the dead. [22]For
as in Adam all die, so also in Christ shall all be
made alive. [23]But each in his own order: Christ
the first fruits, then at his coming those who
belong to Christ. [24]Then comes the end, when
he delivers the kingdom to God the Father
after destroying every rule and every authority
and power. [25]For he must reign until he has
put all his enemies under his feet. [26]The last
enemy to be destroyed is death. [27]"For God has
put all things in subjection under his feet." But
when it says, "All things are put in subjection
under him," it is plain that he is excepted who
put all things under him. [28]When all things are
subjected to him, then the Son himself will also
be subjected to him who put all things under
him, that God may be everything to every one.
[29]Otherwise, what do people mean by being
baptized on behalf of the dead? If the dead are
not raised at all, why are people baptized on
their behalf? [30]Why am I in peril every hour?
[31]I protest, brethren, by my pride in you which
I have in Christ Jesus our Lord, I die every
day! [32]What do I gain if, humanly speaking, I
fought with beasts at Ephesus? If the dead are
not raised, "Let us eat and drink, for tomorrow we die." [33]Do not be deceived: "Bad company ruins good morals." [34]Come to your right
mind, and sin no more. For some have no
knowledge of God. I say this to your shame.
[35]But some one will ask, "How are the
dead raised? With what kind of body do
they come?" [36]You foolish man! What you
sow does not come to life unless it dies.
[37]And what you sow is not the body which
is to be, but a bare kernel, perhaps of wheat
or of some other grain. [38]But God gives it
a body as he has chosen, and to each kind
of seed its own body. [39]For not all flesh is
alike, but there is one kind for men, another
for animals, another for birds, and another
for fish. [40]There are celestial bodies and
there are terrestrial bodies; but the glory
of the celestial is one, and the glory of the
terrestrial is another. [41]There is one glory of
the sun, and another glory of the moon, and
another glory of the stars; for star differs
from star in glory.
[42]So is it with the resurrection of the dead.
What is sown is perishable, what is raised
is imperishable. [43]It is sown in dishonor, it
is raised in glory. It is sown in weakness,
it is raised in power. [44]It is sown a physical
body, it is raised a spiritual body. If there
is a physical body, there is also a spiritual
body. [45]Thus it is written, "The first man
Adam became a living soul"; the last Adam
became a life-giving spirit. [46]But it is not
the spiritual which is first but the physical,
and then the spiritual.

REFLECTION

Isaiah offers us his first song about the suffering servant (see Is 42:1–9), a man appointed by God, anointed with his Spirit, who will be a "covenant to the people, a light to the nations" (v. 6), freeing prisoners and giving sight to the blind (see v. 7). Jesus fulfills these predictions, anointed by the Spirit at his baptism in the Jordan, freeing us from the prison of sin, and leading us out of darkness toward his marvelous light. Isaiah helps us see how intimately personal our calling from God is: "Fear not, for I have redeemed you; I have called you by name, you are mine" (43:1). God calls each one of us in a particular and personal manner. He calls us to be made alive in Christ. St. Paul points us toward the final destiny of this call in his reflection on the resurrection: "What is sown is perishable, what is raised is imperishable" (1 Cor 15:42). Our bodies may die, but they will be raised and made glorious. How do you sense the Lord's call as truly personal to you?

September 10

ISAIAH 44

"But now hear, O Jacob my servant,
Israel whom I have chosen!
2Thus says the LORD who made you,
who formed you from the womb
and will help you:
Fear not, O Jacob my servant,
Jesh′urun whom I have chosen.
3For I will pour water on the thirsty land,
and streams on the dry ground;
I will pour my Spirit upon your descendants,
and my blessing on your offspring.
4They shall spring up like grass amid waters,
like willows by flowing streams.
5This one will say, 'I am the LORD's,'
another will call himself by the name
of Jacob,
and another will write on his hand,
'The LORD's,'
and surname himself by the name
of Israel."

6Thus says the LORD, the King of Israel
and his Redeemer, the LORD of hosts:
"I am the first and I am the last;
besides me there is no god.
7Who is like me? Let him proclaim it,
let him declare and set it forth before me.
Who has announced from of old the things
to come?
Let them tell us what is yet to be.
8Fear not, nor be afraid;
have I not told you from of old and
declared it?
And you are my witnesses!
Is there a God besides me?
There is no Rock; I know not any."

9All who make idols are nothing, and the
things they delight in do not profit; their
witnesses neither see nor know, that they
may be put to shame. 10Who fashions a
god or casts an image, that is profitable for
nothing? 11Behold, all his fellows shall be
put to shame, and the craftsmen are but
men; let them all assemble, let them stand
forth, they shall be terrified, they shall be
put to shame together.

12The ironsmith fashions it and works it
over the coals; he shapes it with hammers,
and forges it with his strong arm; he becomes hungry and his strength fails, he
drinks no water and is faint. 13The carpenter stretches a line, he marks it out with
a pencil; he fashions it with planes, and
marks it with a compass; he shapes it into
the figure of a man, with the beauty of a
man, to dwell in a house. 14He cuts down
cedars; or he chooses a holm tree or an oak
and lets it grow strong among the trees of
the forest; he plants a cedar and the rain
nourishes it. 15Then it becomes fuel for a
man; he takes a part of it and warms himself, he kindles a fire and bakes bread; also
he makes a god and worships it, he makes
it a graven image and falls down before it.
16Half of it he burns in the fire; over the half
he eats flesh, he roasts meat and is satisfied;

also he warms himself and says, "Aha, I am
warm, I have seen the fire!" 17And the rest
of it he makes into a god, his idol; and falls
down to it and worships it; he prays to it
and says, "Deliver me, for you are my god!"
18They know not, nor do they discern;
for he has shut their eyes, so that they
cannot see, and their minds, so that they
cannot understand. 19No one considers,
nor is there knowledge or discernment to
say, "Half of it I burned in the fire, I also
baked bread on its coals, I roasted flesh and
have eaten; and shall I make the residue of
it an abomination? Shall I fall down before
a block of wood?" 20He feeds on ashes; a
deluded mind has led him astray, and he
cannot deliver himself or say, "Is there not
a lie in my right hand?"

21Remember these things, O Jacob,
and Israel, for you are my servant;
I formed you, you are my servant;
O Israel, you will not be forgotten by me.
22I have swept away your transgressions like a cloud,
and your sins like mist;
return to me, for I have redeemed you.

23Sing, O heavens, for the LORD has done it;
shout, O depths of the earth;
break forth into singing, O mountains,
O forest, and every tree in it!
For the LORD has redeemed Jacob,
and will be glorified in Israel.

24Thus says the LORD, your Redeemer,
who formed you from the womb:
"I am the LORD, who made all things,
who stretched out the heavens alone,
who spread out the earth—Who was with me?—
25who frustrates the omens of liars,
and makes fools of diviners;
who turns wise men back,
and makes their knowledge foolish;
26who confirms the word of his servant,
and performs the counsel of his messengers;
who says of Jerusalem, 'She shall be inhabited,'
and of the cities of Judah, 'They shall be built,
and I will raise up their ruins';
27who says to the deep, 'Be dry,
I will dry up your rivers';
28who says of Cyrus, 'He is my shepherd,
and he shall fulfil all my purpose';
saying of Jerusalem, 'She shall be built,'
and of the temple, 'Your foundation shall be laid.'"

45 Thus says the LORD to his anointed, to Cyrus,
whose right hand I have grasped,
to subdue nations before him
and uncover the loins of kings,
to open doors before him
that gates may not be closed:
2"I will go before you
and level the mountains,
I will break in pieces the doors of bronze
and cut asunder the bars of iron,
3I will give you the treasures of darkness
and the hoards in secret places,
that you may know that it is I, the LORD,
the God of Israel, who call you by your name.
4For the sake of my servant Jacob,
and Israel my chosen,
I call you by your name,
I surname you, though you do not know me.
5I am the LORD, and there is no other,
besides me there is no God;
I clothe you, though you do not know me,
6that men may know, from the rising of the sun
and from the west, that there is none besides me;
I am the LORD, and there is no other.
7I form light and create darkness,
I make well-being and create woe,
I am the LORD, who do all these things.

8"Shower, O heavens, from above,
and let the skies rain down righteousness;
let the earth open, that salvation may sprout forth,
and let it cause righteousness to spring up also;
I the LORD have created it.

9"Woe to him who strives with his Maker,
an earthen vessel with the potter!
Does the clay say to him who fashions it,
'What are you making?'
or 'Your work has no handles'?
10Woe to him who says to a father, 'What are
you begetting?'
or to a woman, 'With what are you
suffering labor pains?'"
11Thus says the LORD,
the Holy One of Israel, and his Maker:
"Will you question me about my
children,
or command me concerning the work
of my hands?
12I made the earth,
and created man upon it;
it was my hands that stretched out
the heavens,
and I commanded all their host.
13I have aroused him in righteousness,
and I will make straight all his ways;
he shall build my city
and set my exiles free,
not for price or reward,"
says the LORD of hosts.

14Thus says the LORD:
"The wealth of Egypt and the merchandise
of Ethiopia,
and the Sabe'ans, men of stature,
shall come over to you and be yours,
they shall follow you;
they shall come over in chains and bow
down to you.
They will make supplication to you,
saying:
'God is with you only, and there is
no other,
no god besides him.'"
15Truly, you are a God who hide yourself,
O God of Israel, the Savior.
16All of them are put to shame
and confounded,
the makers of idols go in confusion
together.
17But Israel is saved by the LORD
with everlasting salvation;
you shall not be put to shame or confounded
to all eternity.

18For thus says the LORD,
who created the heavens
(he is God!),
who formed the earth and made it
(he established it;
he did not create it a chaos,
he formed it to be inhabited!):
"I am the LORD, and there is no other.
19I did not speak in secret,
in a land of darkness;
I did not say to the offspring of Jacob,
'Seek me in chaos.'
I the LORD speak the truth,
I declare what is right.

20"Assemble yourselves and come,
draw near together,
you survivors of the nations!
They have no knowledge
who carry about their wooden idols,
and keep on praying to a god
that cannot save.
21Declare and present your case;
let them take counsel together!
Who told this long ago?
Who declared it of old?
Was it not I, the LORD?
And there is no other god
besides me,
a righteous God and a Savior;
there is none besides me.

22"Turn to me and be saved,
all the ends of the earth!
For I am God, and there is no other.
23By myself I have sworn,
from my mouth has gone forth
in righteousness
a word that shall not return:
'To me every knee shall bow,
every tongue shall swear.'

24"Only in the LORD, it shall be said of me,
are righteousness and strength;
to him shall come and be ashamed,
all who were incensed against him.
25In the LORD all the offspring of Israel
shall triumph and glory."

46 Bel bows down, Nebo stoops,
their idols are on beasts and cattle;

these things you carry are loaded
as burdens on weary beasts.
2They stoop, they bow down together,
they cannot save the burden,
but themselves go into captivity.

3"Listen to me, O house of Jacob,
all the remnant of the house of Israel,
who have been borne by me from
your birth,
carried from the womb;
4even to your old age I am He,
and to gray hairs I will carry you.
I have made, and I will bear;
I will carry and will save.

5"To whom will you liken me and make
me equal,
and compare me, that we may be alike?
6Those who lavish gold from the purse,
and weigh out silver in the scales,
hire a goldsmith, and he makes it into a god;
then they fall down and worship!
7They lift it upon their shoulders, they
carry it,
they set it in its place, and it stands there;
it cannot move from its place.
If one cries to it, it does not answer
or save him from his trouble.

8"Remember this and consider,
recall it to mind, you transgressors,
9 remember the former things of old;
for I am God, and there is no other;
I am God, and there is none like me,
10declaring the end from the beginning
and from ancient times things not yet done,
saying, 'My counsel shall stand,
and I will accomplish all my purpose,'
11calling a bird of prey from the east,
the man of my counsel from a far country.
I have spoken, and I will bring it to pass;
I have planned, and I will do it.

12"Listen to me, you stubborn of heart,
you who are far from deliverance:
13I bring near my deliverance, it is not far off,
and my salvation will not tarry;
I will put salvation in Zion,
for Israel my glory."

WISDOM 5

Then the righteous man will stand
with great confidence
in the presence of those who have
afflicted him,
and those who make light of his labors.
2When they see him, they will be shaken
with dreadful fear,
and they will be amazed at his unexpected
salvation.
3They will speak to one another in
repentance,
and in anguish of spirit they will groan,
and say,
4"This is the man whom we once held
in derision
and made a byword of reproach—we fools!
We thought that his life was madness
and that his end was without honor.
5Why has he been numbered among the
sons of God?
And why is his lot among the saints?
6So it was we who strayed from the way
of truth,
and the light of righteousness did not
shine on us,
and the sun did not rise upon us.
7We took our fill of the paths of lawlessness
and destruction,
and we journeyed through trackless deserts,
but the way of the Lord we have not known.
8What has our arrogance profited us?
And what good has our boasted wealth
brought us?
9"All those things have vanished like
a shadow,
and like a rumor that passes by;
10like a ship that sails through the
billowy water,
and when it has passed no trace
can be found,
nor track of its keel in the waves;
11or as, when a bird flies through the air,
no evidence of its passage is found;
the light air, lashed by the beat of its pinions
and pierced by the force of its rushing flight,
is traversed by the movement of its wings,
and afterward no sign of its coming is
found there;

[12]or as, when an arrow is shot at a target,
the air, thus divided, comes together at once,
so that no one knows its pathway.
[13]So we also, as soon as we were born,
ceased to be,
and we had no sign of virtue to show,
but were consumed in our wickedness."
[14]Because the hope of the ungodly man is
like chaff carried by the wind,
and like a light hoarfrost driven away by
a storm;
it is dispersed like smoke before the wind,
and it passes like the remembrance of a
guest who stays but a day.

[15]But the righteous live for ever,
and their reward is with the Lord;
the Most High takes care of them.
[16]Therefore they will receive a glorious crown
and a beautiful diadem from the hand of
the Lord,
because with his right hand he will
cover them,
and with his arm he will shield them.
[17]The Lord will take his zeal as his
whole armor,
and will arm all creation to repel
his enemies;
[18]he will put on righteousness as a
breastplate,
and wear impartial justice as a helmet;
[19]he will take holiness as an invincible
shield,
[20]and sharpen stern wrath for a sword,
and creation will join with him to fight
against the madmen.
[21]Shafts of lightning will fly with true aim,
and will leap to the target as from a
well-drawn bow of clouds,
[22]and hailstones full of wrath will be hurled
as from a catapult;
the water of the sea will rage against them,
and rivers will relentlessly overwhelm
them;
[23]a mighty wind will rise against them,
and like a tempest it will winnow
them away.
Lawlessness will lay waste the whole earth,
and evil-doing
will overturn the thrones of rulers.

1 CORINTHIANS 15

**[47]The first man was from the
earth, a man of dust; the second
man is from heaven. [48]As was
the man of dust, so are those who are of
the dust; and as is the man of heaven,
so are those who are of heaven. [49]Just**
as we have borne the image of the man of
dust, we shall also bear the image of the
man of heaven. [50]I tell you this, brethren:
flesh and blood cannot inherit the
kingdom of God, nor does the perishable
inherit the imperishable.
[51]Behold! I tell you a mystery. We shall not
all sleep, but we shall all be changed, [52]in a
moment, in the twinkling of an eye, at the
last trumpet. For the trumpet will sound,
and the dead will be raised imperishable,
and we shall be changed. [53]For this perishable nature must put on the imperishable,
and this mortal nature must put on immortality. [54]When the perishable puts on
the imperishable, and the mortal puts on
immortality, then shall come to pass the
saying that is written:
"Death is swallowed up in victory."
[55]"O death, where is your victory?
O death, where is your sting?"
[56]The sting of death is sin, and the power
of sin is the law. [57]But thanks be to God, who
gives us the victory through our Lord Jesus
Christ.
[58]Therefore, my beloved brethren, be steadfast, immovable, always abounding in the
work of the Lord, knowing that in the Lord
your labor is not in vain.

REFLECTION

Sometimes our vision can become so crowded with distractions—screens, advertisements, financial struggles, health problems—that we can lose sight of the end, the goal, the purpose of our lives. Our final destiny can seem so far off as to be unimportant. Isaiah, with his poetic descriptions of our salvation, tries to draw our vision back to God: the Lord will pour out water on dry ground (see Is 44:3), call us "my servant" (v. 21), and proclaim, "Return to me, for I have redeemed you" (v. 22). For the exiled Jews at the time of the prophecy, he sends the Persian king, Cyrus, to save them from their plight (see 44:28; 45:1). But the ultimate savior of the people will not be Cyrus, but rather the Lord Jesus Christ. Our destiny is to be rescued, saved from death, and brought into communion with the God who has the power to deliver. In the end, "the righteous live forever, and their reward is with the Lord" (Wis 5:15). Sin and death will not win, but in Christ we will be victorious over them (see 1 Cor 15:54–55). When you get distracted, how can the habit of prayer draw you back to first things, that is, to God?

September 11

ISAIAH 47

Come down and sit in the dust,
O virgin daughter of Babylon;
sit on the ground without a throne,
O daughter of the Chalde′ans!
For you shall no more be called
tender and delicate.
2Take the millstones and grind meal,
put off your veil,
strip off your robe, uncover your legs,
pass through the rivers.
3Your nakedness shall be uncovered,
and your shame shall be seen.
I will take vengeance,
and I will spare no man.
4Our Redeemer—the LORD of hosts is
his name—
is the Holy One of Israel.

5Sit in silence, and go into darkness,
O daughter of the Chalde′ans;
for you shall no more be called
the mistress of kingdoms.
6I was angry with my people,
I profaned my heritage;
I gave them into your hand,
you showed them no mercy;
on the aged you made your yoke
exceedingly heavy.
7You said, "I shall be mistress for ever,"
so that you did not lay these things
to heart
or remember their end.

8Now therefore hear this, you lover
of pleasures,
who sit securely,
who say in your heart,
"I am, and there is no one besides me;
I shall not sit as a widow
or know the loss of children":
9These two things shall come to you
in a moment, in one day;
the loss of children and widowhood
shall come upon you in full measure,
in spite of your many sorceries
and the great power of your enchantments.

10You felt secure in your wickedness,
you said, "No one sees me";
your wisdom and your knowledge
led you astray,
and you said in your heart,
"I am, and there is no one besides me."
11But evil shall come upon you,
for which you cannot atone;
disaster shall fall upon you,
which you will not be able to expiate;
and ruin shall come on you suddenly,
of which you know nothing.

12Stand fast in your enchantments
and your many sorceries,
with which you have labored from
your youth;
perhaps you may be able to succeed,
perhaps you may inspire terror.
13You are wearied with your many counsels;
let them stand forth and save you,
those who divide the heavens,
who gaze at the stars,
who at the new moons predict
what shall befall you.

14Behold, they are like stubble,
the fire consumes them;
they cannot deliver themselves
from the power of the flame.
No coal for warming oneself is this,
no fire to sit before!
15Such to you are those with whom you
have labored,
who have trafficked with you from
your youth;
they wander about each in his own
direction;
there is no one to save you.

48 Hear this, O house of Jacob,
who are called by the name of Israel,
and who came forth from the loins of
Judah;
who swear by the name of the LORD,
and confess the God of Israel,
but not in truth or right.
2For they call themselves after the holy city,
and stay themselves on the God of Israel;
the LORD of hosts is his name.

3"The former things I declared of old,
they went forth from my mouth and
I made them known;
then suddenly I did them and they
came to pass.
4Because I know that you are obstinate,
and your neck is an iron sinew
and your forehead brass,
5I declared them to you from of old,
before they came to pass I announced
them to you,
lest you should say, 'My idol did them,
my graven image and my molten image
commanded them.'

6"You have heard; now see all this;
and will you not declare it?
From this time forth I make you hear
new things,
hidden things which you have not known.
7They are created now, not long ago;
before today you have never heard of them,
lest you should say, 'Behold, I knew them.'
8You have never heard, you have never
known,
from of old your ear has not been opened.
For I knew that you would deal very
treacherously,
and that from birth you were called
a rebel.

9"For my name's sake I defer my anger,
for the sake of my praise I restrain it
for you,
that I may not cut you off.
10Behold, I have refined you, but not
like silver;
I have tried you in the furnace of
affliction.
11For my own sake, for my own sake, I do it,
for how should my name be profaned?
My glory I will not give to another.

12"Listen to me, O Jacob,
and Israel, whom I called!
I am He, I am the first,
and I am the last.
13My hand laid the foundation of the earth,
and my right hand spread out the heavens;
when I call to them,
they stand forth together.

14"Assemble, all of you, and hear!
Who among them has declared
these things?
The LORD loves him;
he shall perform his purpose on Babylon,
and his arm shall be against the Chalde'ans.
15I, even I, have spoken and called him,
I have brought him, and he will prosper
in his way.
16Draw near to me, hear this:
from the beginning I have not spoken
in secret,
from the time it came to be I have
been there."
And now the Lord GOD has sent me and
his Spirit.

17Thus says the LORD,
your Redeemer, the Holy One of Israel:
"I am the LORD your God, who teaches
you to profit,
who leads you in the way you should go.
18O that you had listened to my
commandments!

Then your peace would have been like
a river,
and your righteousness like the waves of
the sea;
19 your offspring would have been like the sand,
and your descendants like its grains;
their name would never be cut off
or destroyed from before me."
20 Go forth from Babylon, flee from Chalde′a,
declare this with a shout of joy, proclaim it,
send it forth to the end of the earth;
say, "The LORD has redeemed his
servant Jacob!"
21 They thirsted not when he led them
through the deserts;
he made water flow for them from the rock;
he cleft the rock and the water gushed out.
22 "There is no peace," says the LORD, "for the
wicked."

49 Listen to me, O islands,
and pay attention, you peoples
from afar.
The LORD called me from the womb,
from the body of my mother he named
my name.
2 He made my mouth like a sharp sword,
in the shadow of his hand he hid me;
he made me a polished arrow,
in his quiver he hid me away.
3 And he said to me, "You are my servant,
Israel, in whom I will be glorified."
4 But I said, "I have labored in vain,
I have spent my strength for nothing
and vanity;
yet surely my right is with the LORD,
and my recompense with my God."

5 And now the LORD says,
who formed me from the womb to be
his servant,
to bring Jacob back to him,
and that Israel might be gathered to him,
for I am honored in the eyes of the LORD,
and my God has become my strength—
6 he says:
"It is too light a thing that you should be
my servant
to raise up the tribes of Jacob
and to restore the preserved of Israel;
I will give you as a light to the nations,
that my salvation may reach to the end of
the earth."

7 Thus says the LORD,
the Redeemer of Israel and his Holy One,
to one deeply despised, abhorred by the nations,
the servant of rulers:
"Kings shall see and arise;
princes, and they shall prostrate
themselves;
because of the LORD, who is faithful,
the Holy One of Israel, who has
chosen you."
8 Thus says the LORD:
"In a time of favor I have answered you,
in a day of salvation I have helped you;
I have kept you and given you
as a covenant to the people,
to establish the land,
to apportion the desolate heritages;
9 saying to the prisoners, 'Come forth,'
to those who are in darkness, 'Appear.'
They shall feed along the ways,
on all bare heights shall be their pasture;
10 they shall not hunger or thirst,
neither scorching wind nor sun shall
strike them,
for he who has pity on them will lead them,
and by springs of water will guide them.
11 And I will make all my mountains a way,
and my highways shall be raised up.
12 Behold, these shall come from afar,
and behold, these from the north and
from the west,
and these from the land of Sye′ne."
13 Sing for joy, O heavens, and exult,
O earth;
break forth, O mountains, into singing!
For the LORD has comforted his people,
and will have compassion on
his afflicted.

WISDOM 6

Listen therefore, O kings, and understand;
learn, O judges of the ends of the earth.

2 Give ear, you that rule over multitudes,
and boast of many nations.
3 For your dominion was given you from
the Lord,
and your sovereignty from the Most High,
who will search out your works and inquire
into your plans.
4 Because as servants of his kingdom you did
not rule rightly,
nor keep the law,
nor walk according to the purpose of God,
5 he will come upon you terribly and swiftly,
because severe judgment falls on those in
high places.
6 For the lowliest man may be pardoned
in mercy,
but mighty men will be mightily tested.
7 For the Lord of all will not stand in awe
of any one,
nor show deference to greatness;
because he himself made both small
and great,
and he takes thought for all alike.
8 But a strict inquiry is in store for the
mighty.
9 To you then, O monarchs, my words
are directed,
that you may learn wisdom and not
transgress.
10 For they will be made holy who observe
holy things in holiness,
and those who have been taught them will
find a defense.
11 Therefore set your desire on my words;
long for them, and you will be instructed.

---

1 CORINTHIANS 16

Now concerning the contribu-
tion for the saints: as I directed
the churches of Galatia, so you also are
to do. 2 On the first day of every week,
each of you is to put something aside and
store it up, as he may prosper, so that
contributions need not be made when
I come. 3 And when I arrive, I will send
those whom you accredit by letter to
carry your gift to Jerusalem. 4 If it seems
advisable that I should go also, they will
accompany me.
5 I will visit you after passing through
Macedonia, for I intend to pass through
Macedonia, 6 and perhaps I will stay with
you or even spend the winter, so that you
may speed me on my journey, wherever I
go. 7 For I do not want to see you now just
in passing; I hope to spend some time with
you, if the Lord permits. 8 But I will stay in
Ephesus until Pentecost, 9 for a wide door for
effective work has opened to me, and there
are many adversaries.
10 When Timothy comes, see that you put
him at ease among you, for he is doing the
work of the Lord, as I am. 11 So let no one
despise him. Speed him on his way in peace,
that he may return to me; for I am expecting
him with the brethren.
12 As for our brother Apol′los, I strongly urged him to visit you with the other
brethren, but it was not at all his will to
come now. He will come when he has opportunity.
13 Be watchful, stand firm in your faith,
be courageous, be strong. 14 Let all that
you do be done in love.
15 Now, brethren, you know that the
household of Steph′anas were the first
converts in Acha′ia, and they have devoted
themselves to the service of the saints; 16 I
urge you to be subject to such men and
to every fellow worker and laborer. 17 I
rejoice at the coming of Steph′anas and
Fortuna′tus and Acha′icus, because they
have made up for your absence; 18 for they
refreshed my spirit as well as yours. Give
recognition to such men.
19 The churches of Asia send greetings.
Aqui′la and Prisca, together with the
church in their house, send you hearty
greetings in the Lord. 20 All the brethren
send greetings. Greet one another with a
holy kiss.
21 I, Paul, write this greeting with my
own hand. 22 If any one has no love for
the Lord, let him be accursed. Our Lord,
come! 23 The grace of the Lord Jesus be
with you. 24 My love be with you all in
Christ Jesus. Amen.

REFLECTION

Evildoers seem to get away with a lot. The sinful sometimes prosper because of their sin. Yet the Bible assures us that divine judgment awaits the wicked. In prophesying against the sins of "daughter Babylon," Isaiah exclaims, "You felt secure in your wickedness . . . but evil shall come upon you" (Is 47:10–11). Similarly, he prophesies, "'There is no peace,' says the LORD, 'for the wicked'" (48:22). Sins like stealing and dishonesty might bring temporal wealth, but we are assured that "a strict inquiry is in store for the mighty" (Wis 6:8). The antidote to sin and the source of freedom from divine judgment comes from the Suffering Servant, who is called by God "from the womb" to bring Israel back to the land, and to be "a light to the nations" (Is 49:1, 6). Jesus upends the world, casting down the mighty from their thrones and lifting up the lowly (see Lk 1:52). He reverses society's unethical logic of cutthroat competition. Instead, St. Paul teaches, "Let all that you do be done in love" (1 Cor 16:14). Who do you know who best embodies the virtues of the suffering servant?

September 12

ISAIAH 49

14But Zion said, "The LORD has
forsaken me,
my Lord has forgotten me."
15"Can a woman forget her sucking child,
that she should have no compassion
on the son of her womb?
Even these may forget,
yet I will not forget you.
16Behold, I have graven you on the palms of
my hands;
your walls are continually before me.
17Your builders outstrip your destroyers,
and those who laid you waste go forth
from you.
18Lift up your eyes round about and see;
they all gather, they come to you.
As I live, says the LORD,
you shall put them all on as an ornament,
you shall bind them on as a bride does.

19"Surely your waste and your desolate places
and your devastated land—
surely now you will be too narrow for
your inhabitants,
and those who swallowed you up will
be far away.
20The children born in the time of your
bereavement
will yet say in your ears:
'The place is too narrow for me;
make room for me to dwell in.'
21Then you will say in your heart:
'Who has borne me these?
I was bereaved and barren,
exiled and put away,
but who has brought up these?
Behold, I was left alone;
from where then have these come?'"

22Thus says the Lord GOD:
"Behold, I will lift up my hand to
the nations,
and raise my signal to the peoples;
and they shall bring your sons in
their bosom,
and your daughters shall be carried on
their shoulders.
23Kings shall be your foster fathers,
and their queens your nursing
mothers.
With their faces to the ground they shall
bow down to you, and lick the dust
of your feet.
Then you will know that I am the LORD;
those who wait for me shall not be put
to shame."

24Can the prey be taken from the mighty,
or the captives of a tyrant be rescued?
25Surely, thus says the LORD:
"Even the captives of the mighty shall
be taken,
and the prey of the tyrant be rescued,
for I will contend with those who contend
with you,
and I will save your children.

[26]I will make your oppressors eat their
own flesh,
and they shall be drunk with their own
blood as with wine.
Then all flesh shall know
that I am the LORD your Savior,
and your Redeemer, the Mighty One
of Jacob."

50 Thus says the LORD:
"Where is your mother's bill of divorce,
with which I put her away?
Or which of my creditors is it
to whom I have sold you?
Behold, for your iniquities you were sold,
and for your transgressions your mother
was put away.
[2]Why, when I came, was there no man?
When I called, was there no one to answer?
Is my hand shortened, that it cannot redeem?
Or have I no power to deliver?
Behold, by my rebuke I dry up the sea,
I make the rivers a desert;
their fish stink for lack of water,
and die of thirst.
[3]I clothe the heavens with blackness,
and make sackcloth their covering."

[4]The Lord GOD has given me
the tongue of those who are taught,
that I may know how to sustain with
a word
him that is weary.
Morning by morning he wakens,
he wakens my ear
to hear as those who are taught.
[5]The Lord GOD has opened my ear,
and I was not rebellious,
I turned not backward.
[6]I gave my back to those who struck me,
and my cheeks to those who pulled out
the beard;
I hid not my face
from shame and spitting.

[7]For the Lord GOD helps me;
therefore I have not been confounded;
therefore I have set my face like a flint,
and I know that I shall not be put
to shame;
[8] he who vindicates me is near.
Who will contend with me?
Let us stand up together.
Who is my adversary?
Let him come near to me.
[9]Behold, the Lord GOD helps me;
who will declare me guilty?
Behold, all of them will wear out
like a garment;
the moth will eat them up.

[10]Who among you fears the LORD
and obeys the voice of his servant,
who walks in darkness
and has no light,
yet trusts in the name of the LORD
and relies upon his God?
[11]Behold, all you who kindle a fire,
who set brands alight.
Walk by the light of your fire,
and by the brands which you have kindled!
This shall you have from my hand:
you shall lie down in torment.

51 "Listen to me, you who pursue
deliverance,
you who seek the LORD;
look to the rock from which you were hewn,
and to the quarry from which you were
dug.
[2]Look to Abraham your father
and to Sarah who bore you;
for when he was but one I called him,
and I blessed him and made him many.
[3]For the LORD will comfort Zion:
he will comfort all her waste places,
and will make her wilderness like Eden,
her desert like the garden of the LORD;
joy and gladness will be found in her,
thanksgiving and the voice of song.

[4]"Listen to me, my people,
and give ear to me, my nation;
for a law will go forth from me,
and my justice for a light to the peoples.
[5]My deliverance draws near speedily,
my salvation has gone forth,
and my arms will rule the peoples;
the islands wait for me,
and for my arm they hope.
[6]Lift up your eyes to the heavens,
and look at the earth beneath;

for the heavens will vanish like smoke,
the earth will wear out like a garment,
and they who dwell in it will die
like gnats;
but my salvation will be for ever,
and my deliverance will never be ended.

7 "Listen to me, you who know righteousness,
the people in whose heart is my law;
fear not the reproach of men,
and be not dismayed at their revilings.
8 For the moth will eat them up like
a garment,
and the worm will eat them like wool;
but my deliverance will be for ever,
and my salvation to all generations."

9 Awake, awake, put on strength,
O arm of the LORD;
awake, as in days of old,
the generations of long ago.
Was it not you who cut Ra′hab in pieces,
who pierced the dragon?
10 Was it not you who dried up the sea,
the waters of the great deep;
who made the depths of the sea a way
for the redeemed to pass over?
11 And the ransomed of the LORD
shall return,
and come to Zion with singing;
everlasting joy shall be upon their heads;
they shall obtain joy and gladness,
and sorrow and sighing shall flee away.

12 "I, I am he who comforts you;
who are you that you are afraid of man
who dies,
of the son of man who is made like grass,
13 and have forgotten the LORD,
your Maker,
who stretched out the heavens
and laid the foundations of the earth,
and fear continually all the day
because of the fury of the oppressor,
when he sets himself to destroy?
And where is the fury of the oppressor?
14 He who is bowed down shall speedily
be released;
he shall not die and go down to the Pit,
neither shall his bread fail.
15 For I am the LORD your God,
who stirs up the sea so that its
waves roar—
the LORD of hosts is his name.
16 And I have put my words in
your mouth,
and hid you in the shadow of my hand,
stretching out the heavens
and laying the foundations
of the earth,
and saying to Zion, 'You are my people.'"

17 Rouse yourself, rouse yourself,
stand up, O Jerusalem,
you who have drunk at the hand of
the LORD
the cup of his wrath,
who have drunk to the dregs
the bowl of staggering.
18 There is none to guide her
among all the sons she has borne;
there is none to take her by the hand
among all the sons she has
brought up.
19 These two things have befallen you—
who will condole with you?—
devastation and destruction, famine
and sword;
who will comfort you?
20 Your sons have fainted,
they lie at the head of every street
like an antelope in a net;
they are full of the wrath of the LORD,
the rebuke of your God.

21 Therefore hear this, you who are afflicted,
who are drunk, but not with wine:
22 Thus says your Lord, the LORD,
your God who pleads the cause of
his people:
"Behold, I have taken from your hand
the cup of staggering;
the bowl of my wrath
you shall drink no more;
23 and I will put it into the hand of
your tormentors,
who have said to you,
'Bow down, that we may pass over';
and you have made your back like the ground
and like the street for them to pass over."

WISDOM 6

[12]Wisdom is radiant and unfading,
and she is easily discerned by those who love her,
and is found by those who seek her.
[13]She hastens to make herself known to those who desire her.
[14]He who rises early to seek her will have no difficulty,
for he will find her sitting at his gates.
[15]To fix one's thought on her is perfect understanding,
and he who is vigilant on her account will soon be free from care,
[16]because she goes about seeking those worthy of her,
and she graciously appears to them in their paths,
and meets them in every thought.

[17]The beginning of wisdom is the most sincere desire for instruction,
and concern for instruction is love of her,
[18]and love of her is the keeping of her laws,
and giving heed to her laws is assurance of immortality,
[19]and immortality brings one near to God;
[20]so the desire for wisdom leads to a kingdom.

[21]Therefore if you delight in thrones and scepters, O monarchs over the peoples,
honor wisdom, that you may reign forever.
[22]I will tell you what wisdom is and how she came to be,
and I will hide no secrets from you,
but I will trace her course from the beginning of creation,
and make knowledge of her clear,
and I will not pass by the truth;
[23]neither will I travel in the company of sickly envy,
for envy does not associate with wisdom.
[24]A multitude of wise men is the salvation of the world,
and a sensible king is the stability of his people.
[25]Therefore be instructed by my words,
and you will profit.

2 CORINTHIANS 1

Paul, an apostle of Christ Jesus by the will of God, and Timothy our brother.

To the Church of God which is at Corinth, with all the saints who are in the whole of Acha'ia:

[2]Grace to you and peace from God our
Father and the Lord Jesus Christ.
[3]Blessed be the God and Father of our
Lord Jesus Christ, the Father of mercies
and God of all comfort, [4]who comforts us
in all our affliction, so that we may be able
to comfort those who are in any affliction,
with the comfort with which we ourselves
are comforted by God. [5]For as we share
abundantly in Christ's sufferings, so through
Christ we share abundantly in comfort too.
[6]If we are afflicted, it is for your comfort and
salvation; and if we are comforted, it is for
your comfort, which you experience when
you patiently endure the same sufferings that
we suffer. [7]Our hope for you is unshaken; for
we know that as you share in our sufferings,
you will also share in our comfort.

[8]For we do not want you to be ignorant,
brethren, of the affliction we experienced
in Asia; for we were so utterly, unbearably
crushed that we despaired of life itself. [9]Why,
we felt that we had received the sentence of
death; but that was to make us rely not on
ourselves but on God who raises the dead;
[10]he delivered us from so deadly a peril, and
he will deliver us; on him we have set our
hope that he will deliver us again. [11]You also
must help us by prayer, so that many will
give thanks on our behalf for the blessing
granted us in answer to many prayers.

[12]For our boast is this, the testimony of
our conscience that we have behaved in
the world, and still more toward you, with
holiness and godly sincerity, not by earthly
wisdom but by the grace of God. [13]For we
write you nothing but what you can read
and understand; I hope you will understand
fully, [14]as you have understood in part, that
you can be proud of us as we can be of you,
on the day of the Lord Jesus.

15Because I was sure of this, I wanted to
come to you first, so that you might have a
double pleasure; 16I wanted to visit you on
my way to Macedonia, and to come back
to you from Macedonia and have you send
me on my way to Judea. 17Was I vacillating
when I wanted to do this? Do I make my
plans like a worldly man, ready to say
Yes and No at once? 18As surely as God is
faithful, our word to you has not been Yes
and No. 19For the Son of God, Jesus Christ,
whom we preached among you, Silva′nus
and Timothy and I, was not Yes and No; but
in him it is always Yes. 20For all the promises
of God find their Yes in him. That is why we
utter the Amen through him, to the glory
of God. 21But it is God who establishes us
with you in Christ, and has commissioned
us; 22he has put his seal upon us and given
us his Spirit in our hearts as a guarantee.

23But I call God to witness against me—
it was to spare you that I refrained from
coming to Corinth. 24Not that we lord it over
your faith; we work with you for your joy,
for you stand firm in your faith.

REFLECTION

Being human, we often feel small, just a number among billions of people, an insignificant point in a vast universe. That sense of insignificance can turn into a false humility: "Why would God care about me?" But the Lord confronts our feelings with a promise, saying that even if a nursing mother forgets her child, "yet I will not forget you" (Is 49:15). He declares his identity, "I am the LORD your Savior" (v. 26), as he pledges to bring the sons and daughters of Israel back to the Promised Land. Isaiah assures us of the permanence of God's fidelity by contrasting it to the dissolution of the most permanent-seeming things: the heavens and the earth. Even though they will pass away, he promises, "my salvation will be for ever" (51:6). To respond to the Lord's awesome salvation, we need to rise above our self-pity and seek after wisdom by loving and desiring it, rising early, being vigilant, and seeking instruction (see Wis 6:12–17). Indeed, St. Paul instructs that we can respond to the promises of God by saying "yes" with Christ: "In him it is always Yes. For all the promises of God find their Yes in him" (2 Cor 1:19–20). Why is it easier to think God is loving, and yet so hard to believe he loves you?

September 13

ISAIAH 52

Awake, awake,
put on your strength, O Zion;
put on your beautiful garments,
O Jerusalem, the holy city;
for there shall no more come into you
the uncircumcised and the unclean.
2Shake yourself from the dust, arise,
O captive Jerusalem;
loose the bonds from your neck,
O captive daughter of Zion.

3For thus says the LORD: "You were sold for
nothing, and you shall be redeemed without
money. 4For thus says the Lord GOD: My
people went down at the first into Egypt to
sojourn there, and the Assyrian oppressed
them for nothing. 5Now therefore what have
I here, says the LORD, seeing that my people
are taken away for nothing? Their rulers wail,
says the LORD, and continually all the day my
name is despised. 6Therefore my people shall
know my name; therefore in that day they
shall know that it is I who speak; here am I."

7How beautiful upon the mountains
are the feet of him who brings
good tidings,
who publishes peace, who brings good
tidings of good,
who publishes salvation,
who says to Zion, "Your God reigns."
8Listen, your watchmen lift up their voice,
together they sing for joy;
for eye to eye they see
the return of the LORD to Zion.

9Break forth together into singing,
you waste places of Jerusalem;
for the LORD has comforted his people,
he has redeemed Jerusalem.
10The LORD has bared his holy arm
before the eyes of all the nations;
and all the ends of the earth shall see
the salvation of our God.

11Depart, depart, go out from there,
touch no unclean thing;
go out from the midst of her, purify
yourselves,
you who bear the vessels of
the LORD.
12For you shall not go out in haste,
and you shall not go in flight,
for the LORD will go before you,
and the God of Israel will be your
rear guard.

13Behold, my servant shall prosper,
he shall be exalted and lifted up,
and shall be very high.
14As many were astonished at him—
his appearance was so marred, beyond
human semblance,
and his form beyond that of the sons
of men—
15so shall he startle many nations;
kings shall shut their mouths because
of him;
for that which has not been told them
they shall see,
and that which they have not heard
they shall understand.

53 Who has believed what we have heard?
And to whom has the arm of the LORD
been revealed?
2For he grew up before him like a
young plant,
and like a root out of dry ground;
he had no form or comeliness that we
should look at him,
and no beauty that we should
desire him.
3He was despised and rejected by men;
a man of sorrows, and acquainted
with grief;
and as one from whom men hide their faces
he was despised, and we esteemed him not.

4Surely he has borne our griefs
and carried our sorrows;
yet we esteemed him stricken,
struck down by God, and afflicted.
5But he was wounded for our
transgressions,
he was bruised for our iniquities;
upon him was the chastisement that
made us whole,
and with his stripes we are healed.
6All we like sheep have gone astray;
we have turned every one to his own way;
and the LORD has laid on him
the iniquity of us all.

7He was oppressed, and he was afflicted,
yet he opened not his mouth;
like a lamb that is led to the slaughter,
and like a sheep that before its shearers
is silent,
so he opened not his mouth.
8By oppression and judgment he was
taken away;
and as for his generation, who considered
that he was cut off out of the land of
the living,
stricken for the transgression of
my people?
9And they made his grave with the wicked
and with a rich man in his death,
although he had done no violence,
and there was no deceit in his mouth.

10Yet it was the will of the LORD to
bruise him;
he has put him to grief;
when he makes himself an offering for sin,
he shall see his offspring, he shall prolong
his days;
the will of the LORD shall prosper in
his hand;
11 he shall see the fruit of the travail of
his soul and be satisfied;
by his knowledge shall the righteous one,
my servant,
make many to be accounted righteous;
and he shall bear their iniquities.

12Therefore I will divide him a portion with
the great,
and he shall divide the spoil with the strong;
because he poured out his soul to death,
and was numbered with the transgressors;
yet he bore the sin of many,
and made intercession for the
transgressors.

54 "Sing, O barren one, who did not
bear;
break forth into singing and cry aloud,
you who have not had labor pains!
For the children of the desolate one will
be more
than the children of her that is married,
says the LORD.
2Enlarge the place of your tent,
and let the curtains of your habitations be
stretched out;
hold not back, lengthen your cords
and strengthen your stakes.
3For you will spread abroad to the right and
to the left,
and your descendants will possess
the nations
and will people the desolate cities.

4"Fear not, for you will not be ashamed;
be not confounded, for you will not be
put to shame;
for you will forget the shame of your youth,
and the reproach of your widowhood
you will remember no more.
5For your Maker is your husband,
the LORD of hosts is his name;
and the Holy One of Israel is your
Redeemer,
the God of the whole earth he is called.
6For the LORD has called you
like a wife forsaken and grieved in spirit,
like a wife of youth when she is cast off,
says your God.
7For a brief moment I forsook you,
but with great compassion I will
gather you.
8In overflowing wrath for a moment
I hid my face from you,
but with everlasting mercy I will have
compassion on you,
says the LORD, your Redeemer.

9"For this is like the days of Noah to me:
as I swore that the waters of Noah
should no more go over the earth,
so I have sworn that I will not be angry
with you
and will not rebuke you.
10For the mountains may depart
and the hills be removed,
but my mercy shall not depart from you,
and my covenant of peace shall not
be removed,
says the LORD, who has compassion
on you.

11"O afflicted one, storm-tossed, and not
comforted,
behold, I will set your stones in antimony,
and lay your foundations with sapphires.
12I will make your pinnacles of agate,
your gates of carbuncles,
and all your wall of precious stones.
13All your sons shall be taught by the LORD,
and great shall be the prosperity of
your sons.
14In righteousness you shall be established;
you shall be far from oppression, for you
shall not fear;
and from terror, for it shall not come
near you.
15If any one stirs up strife,
it is not from me;
whoever stirs up strife with you
shall fall because of you.
16Behold, I have created the smith
who blows the fire of coals,
and produces a weapon for its purpose.
I have also created the ravager to
destroy;
17 no weapon that is fashioned against you
shall prosper,
and you shall confute every tongue that
rises against you in judgment.
This is the heritage of the servants of
the LORD
and their vindication from me, says
the LORD."

55 "Ho, every one who thirsts,
come to the waters;
and he who has no money,
come, buy and eat!

Come, buy wine and milk
without money and without price.
2Why do you spend your money for that which is not bread,
and your labor for that which does not satisfy?
Listen diligently to me, and eat what is good,
and delight yourselves in rich food.
3Incline your ear, and come to me;
hear, that your soul may live;
and I will make with you an everlasting covenant,
my steadfast, merciful love for David.
4Behold, I made him a witness to the peoples,
a leader and commander for the peoples.
5Behold, you shall call nations that you know not,
and nations that knew you not shall run to you,
because of the LORD your God, and of the Holy One of Israel,
for he has glorified you.

6"Seek the LORD while he may be found,
call upon him while he is near;
7let the wicked forsake his way,
and the unrighteous man his thoughts;
let him return to the LORD, that he may have mercy on him,
and to our God, for he will abundantly pardon.
8For my thoughts are not your thoughts,
neither are your ways my ways, says the LORD.
9For as the heavens are higher than the earth,
so are my ways higher than your ways
and my thoughts than your thoughts.

10"For as the rain and the snow come down from heaven,
and do not return there but water the earth,
making it bring forth and sprout,
giving seed to the sower and bread to the eater,
11so shall my word be that goes forth from my mouth;
it shall not return to me empty,
but it shall accomplish that which I intend,
and prosper in the thing for which I sent it.
12"For you shall go out in joy,
and be led forth in peace;
the mountains and the hills before you
shall break forth into singing,
and all the trees of the field shall clap their hands.
13Instead of the thorn shall come up the cypress;
instead of the brier shall come up the myrtle;
and it shall be to the LORD for a memorial,
for an everlasting sign which shall not be cut off."

WISDOM 7

I also am mortal, like all men,
a descendant of the first-formed child of earth;
and in the womb of a mother I was molded into flesh,
2within the period of ten months, compacted with blood,
from the seed of a man and the pleasure of marriage.
3And when I was born, I began to breathe the common air,
and fell upon the kindred earth,
and my first sound was a cry, like that of all.
4I was nursed with care in swaddling cloths.
5For no king has had a different beginning of existence;
6there is for all mankind one entrance into life, and a common departure.

7Therefore I prayed, and understanding was given me;
I called upon God, and the spirit of wisdom came to me.
8I preferred her to scepters and thrones,
and I accounted wealth as nothing in comparison with her.
9Neither did I liken to her any priceless gem,
because all gold is but a little sand in her sight,
and silver will be accounted as clay before her.
10I loved her more than health and beauty,

and I chose to have her rather than light,
because her radiance never ceases.
11All good things came to me along with her,
and in her hands uncounted wealth.
12I rejoiced in them all, because wisdom
leads them;
but I did not know that she was their
mother.
13I learned without guile and I impart
without grudging;
I do not hide her wealth,
14for it is an unfailing treasure for men;
those who get it obtain friendship
with God,
commended for the gifts that come from
instruction.
15May God grant that I speak with judgment
and have thoughts worthy of what I have
received,
for he is the guide even of wisdom
and the corrector of the wise.
16For both we and our words are in his hand,
as are all understanding and skill in crafts.
17For it is he who gave me unerring
knowledge of what exists,
to know the structure of the world and the
activity of the elements;
18the beginning and end and middle of times,
the alternations of the solstices and the
changes of the seasons,
19the cycles of the year and the constellations
of the stars,
20the natures of animals and the tempers of
wild beasts,
the powers of spirits and the reasonings
of men,
the varieties of plants and the virtues
of roots.

2 CORINTHIANS 2

For I made up my mind not to make you another painful visit.
2For if I cause you pain, who is there to make me glad but the one whom I have pained?
3And I wrote as I did, so that when I came I might not suffer pain from those who should have made me rejoice, for I felt sure of all of you, that my joy would be the joy of you all.
4For I wrote you out of much affliction and anguish of heart and with many tears, not to cause you pain but to let you know the abundant love that I have for you.
5But if any one has caused pain, he has caused it not to me, but in some measure—not to put it too severely—to you all.
6For such a one this punishment by the majority is enough;
7so you should rather turn to forgive and comfort him, or he may be overwhelmed by excessive sorrow.
8So I beg you to reaffirm your love for him.
9For this is why I wrote, that I might test you and know whether you are obedient in everything.
10Any one whom you forgive, I also forgive. What I have forgiven, if I have forgiven anything, has been for your sake in the presence of Christ,
11to keep Satan from gaining the advantage over us; for we are not ignorant of his designs.
12When I came to Troas to preach the gospel of Christ, a door was opened for me in the Lord;
13but my mind could not rest because I did not find my brother Titus there. So I took leave of them and went on to Macedonia.
14But thanks be to God, who in Christ always leads us in triumph, and through us spreads the fragrance of the knowledge of him everywhere.
15For we are the aroma of Christ to God among those who are being saved and among those who are perishing,
16to one a fragrance from death to death, to the other a fragrance from life to life. Who is sufficient for these things?
17For we are not, like so many, peddlers of God's word; but as men of sincerity, as commissioned by God, in the sight of God we speak in Christ.

REFLECTION

It can be tempting to think that certain people have innate talent, inherited money, or special circumstances that explain their success. We sometimes hate to admit that a skilled person has worked hard or suffered for their achievements because this can make us feel sinfully lazy. Yet Wisdom emphasizes, "For no king has had a different beginning of existence; there is for all mankind one entrance into life, and a common departure" (Wis 7:5–6). Every one of us is born and dies, the same as anyone else. Solomon prays for wisdom and receives it as a gift from God. Jesus, as Wisdom incarnate, eschews the glamour of the world and instead seeks the lowest place of most grievous suffering: marred, wounded, without beauty, without majesty, despised by all. Isaiah says, "But he was wounded for our transgressions, he was bruised for our iniquities; upon him was the chastisement that made us whole, and with his stripes we are healed" (Is 53:5). Jesus does not save us the easy way, but undertakes great suffering, hard work, in order to redeem us. Similarly, we cannot take the easy path of becoming "peddlers of God's word" (2 Cor 2:17), but like St. Paul we must deal with pain and affliction in the midst of carrying out the Lord's work. Is there anyone you know whose success makes you feel envy? Why?

September 14

ISAIAH 56

Thus says the LORD:
"Keep justice, and do
righteousness,
for soon my salvation will come,
and my deliverance be revealed.
2**Blessed is the man who does this,**
and the son of man who holds it fast,
who keeps the sabbath, not profaning it,
and keeps his hand from doing any evil."

3Let not the foreigner who has joined
himself to the LORD say,
"The LORD will surely separate me from
his people";
and let not the eunuch say,
"Behold, I am a dry tree."
4For thus says the LORD:
"To the eunuchs who keep my sabbaths,
who choose the things that please me
and hold fast my covenant,
5I will give in my house and within
my walls
a monument and a name
better than sons and daughters;
I will give them an everlasting name
which shall not be cut off.

6"And the foreigners who join themselves to
the LORD,
to minister to him, to love the name
of the LORD,
and to be his servants,
every one who keeps the sabbath, and does
not profane it,
and holds fast my covenant—
7these I will bring to my holy mountain,
and make them joyful in my house
of prayer;
their burnt offerings and their sacrifices
will be accepted on my altar;
for my house shall be called a house
of prayer
for all peoples.
8Thus says the Lord GOD,
who gathers the outcasts of Israel,
I will gather yet others to him
besides those already gathered."

9All you beasts of the field, come to devour—
all you beasts in the forest.
10His watchmen are blind,
they are all without knowledge;
they are all mute dogs,
they cannot bark;
dreaming, lying down,
loving to slumber.
11The dogs have a mighty appetite;
they never have enough.
The shepherds also have no
understanding;
they have all turned to their own way,
each to his own gain, one and all.
12"Come," they say, "let us get wine,
let us fill ourselves with strong drink;
and tomorrow will be like this day,
great beyond measure."

57 The righteous man perishes,
and no one lays it to heart;
devout men are taken away,
while no one understands.
For the righteous man is taken away
from calamity,
2 he enters into peace;
they rest in their beds
who walk in their uprightness.
3 But you, draw near to here,
sons of the sorceress,
offspring of the adulterer and the harlot.
4 Of whom are you making sport?
Against whom do you open your
mouth wide
and put out your tongue?
Are you not children of transgression,
the offspring of deceit,
5 you who burn with lust among the oaks,
under every green tree;
who slay your children in the valleys,
under the clefts of the rocks?
6 Among the smooth stones of the valley is
your portion;
they, they, are your lot;
to them you have poured out a
drink offering,
you have brought a cereal offering.
Shall I be appeased for these things?
7 Upon a high and lofty mountain
you have set your bed,
and from there you went up to
offer sacrifice.
8 Behind the door and the doorpost
you have set up your symbol;
for, deserting me, you have uncovered
your bed,
you have gone up to it,
you have made it wide;
and you have made a bargain for yourself
with them,
you have loved their bed,
you have looked on nakedness.
9 You journeyed to Mo'lech with oil
and multiplied your perfumes;
you sent your envoys far off,
and sent down even to Sheol.
10 You were wearied with the length of
your way,
but you did not say, "It is hopeless";
you found new life for your strength,
and so you were not faint.
11 Whom did you dread and fear,
so that you lied,
and did not remember me,
did not give me a thought?
Have I not held my peace, even for a
long time,
and so you do not fear me?
12 I will tell of your righteousness and
your doings,
but they will not help you.
13 When you cry out, let your collection of
idols deliver you!
The wind will carry them off,
a breath will take them away.
But he who takes refuge in me shall possess
the land,
and shall inherit my holy mountain.

14 And it shall be said,
"Build up, build up, prepare the way,
remove every obstruction from my
people's way."
15 For thus says the high and lofty One
who inhabits eternity, whose name
is Holy:
"I dwell in the high and holy place,
and also with him who is of a contrite
and humble spirit,
to revive the spirit of the humble,
and to revive the heart of the contrite.
16 For I will not contend for ever,
nor will I always be angry;
for from me proceeds the spirit,
and I have made the breath of life.
17 Because of the iniquity of his covetousness
I was angry,
I struck him, I hid my face and
was angry;
but he went on backsliding in the way of
his own heart.
18 I have seen his ways, but I will heal him;
I will lead him and repay him with comfort,
creating for his mourners the fruit of
the lips.
19 Peace, peace, to the far and to the near,
says the LORD;
and I will heal him.

[20]But the wicked are like the tossing sea;
for it cannot rest,
and its waters toss up mire and dirt.
[21]There is no peace, says my God, for the
wicked."

58 "Cry aloud, spare not,
lift up your voice like a trumpet;
declare to my people their transgression,
to the house of Jacob their sins.
[2]Yet they seek me daily,
and delight to know my ways,
as if they were a nation that did righteousness
and did not forsake the ordinance of
their God;
they ask of me righteous judgments,
they delight to draw near to God.
[3]'Why have we fasted, and you see it not?
Why have we humbled ourselves, and
you take no knowledge of it?'
Behold, in the day of your fast you seek
your own pleasure,
and oppress all your workers.
[4]Behold, you fast only to quarrel and to fight
and to hit with wicked fist.
Fasting like yours this day
will not make your voice to be heard
on high.
[5]Is such the fast that I choose,
a day for a man to humble himself?
Is it to bow down his head like a rush,
and to spread sackcloth and ashes
under him?
Will you call this a fast,
and a day acceptable to the LORD?

[6]"Is not this the fast that I choose:
to loose the bonds of wickedness,
to undo the thongs of the yoke,
to let the oppressed go free,
and to break every yoke?
[7]Is it not to share your bread with the hungry,
and bring the homeless poor into your
house;
when you see the naked, to cover him,
and not to hide yourself from your
own flesh?
[8]Then shall your light break forth like
the dawn,
and your healing shall spring up speedily;
your righteousness shall go before you,
the glory of the LORD shall be your
rear guard.
[9]Then you shall call, and the LORD will answer;
you shall cry, and he will say, Here I am.

"If you take away from the midst of you
the yoke,
the pointing of the finger, and speaking
wickedness,
[10]if you pour yourself out for the hungry
and satisfy the desire of the afflicted,
then shall your light rise in the darkness
and your gloom be as the noonday.
[11]And the LORD will guide you continually,
and satisfy your desire with good things,
and make your bones strong;
and you shall be like a watered garden,
like a spring of water,
whose waters do not fail.
[12]And your ancient ruins shall be rebuilt;
you shall raise up the foundations of
many generations;
you shall be called the repairer of the breach,
the restorer of streets to dwell in.

[13]"If you turn back your foot from the sabbath,
from doing your pleasure on my holy day,
and call the sabbath a delight
and the holy day of the LORD
honorable;
if you honor it, not going your own ways,
or seeking your own pleasure, or talking
idly;
[14]then you shall take delight in the LORD,
and I will make you ride upon the heights
of the earth;
I will feed you with the heritage of Jacob
your father,
for the mouth of the LORD has spoken."

59 Behold, the LORD's hand is not
shortened, that it cannot save,
or his ear dull, that it cannot hear;
[2]but your iniquities have made a separation
between you and your God,
and your sins have hidden his face from you
so that he does not hear.
[3]For your hands are defiled with blood
and your fingers with iniquity;
your lips have spoken lies,
your tongue mutters wickedness.

4No one enters suit justly,
no one goes to law honestly;
they rely on empty pleas, they speak lies,
they conceive mischief and bring forth
iniquity.
5They hatch adders' eggs,
they weave the spider's web;
he who eats their eggs dies,
and from one which is crushed a viper
is hatched.
6Their webs will not serve as clothing;
men will not cover themselves with what
they make.
Their works are works of iniquity,
and deeds of violence are in
their hands.
7Their feet run to evil,
and they make haste to shed
innocent blood;
their thoughts are thoughts of iniquity,
desolation and destruction are in
their highways.
8The way of peace they know not,
and there is no justice in their paths;
they have made their roads crooked,
no one who goes in them knows peace.

9Therefore justice is far from us,
and righteousness does not overtake us;
we look for light, and behold, darkness,
and for brightness, but we walk in gloom.
10We grope for the wall like the blind,
we grope like those who have no eyes;
we stumble at noon as in the twilight,
among those in full vigor we are like
dead men.
11We all growl like bears,
we moan and moan like doves;
we look for justice, but there is none;
for salvation, but it is far from us.
12For our transgressions are multiplied
before you,
and our sins testify against us;
for our transgressions are with us,
and we know our iniquities:
13transgressing, and denying the LORD,
and turning away from following our God,
speaking oppression and revolt,
conceiving and uttering from the heart
lying words.
14Justice is turned back,
and righteousness stands afar off;
for truth has fallen in the public squares,
and uprightness cannot enter.
15Truth is lacking,
and he who departs from evil makes
himself a prey.

The LORD saw it, and it displeased him
that there was no justice.
16He saw that there was no man,
and wondered that there was no one
to intervene;
then his own arm brought him victory,
and his righteousness upheld him.
17He put on righteousness as a breastplate,
and a helmet of salvation upon his head;
he put on garments of vengeance for
clothing,
and wrapped himself in fury as a mantle.
18According to their deeds, so will he repay,
wrath to his adversaries, repayment to
his enemies;
to the islands he will render repayment.
19So they shall fear the name of the LORD
from the west,
and his glory from the rising of the sun;
for he will come like a rushing stream,
which the wind of the LORD drives.

20"And he will come to Zion as Redeemer,
to those in Jacob who turn from
transgression, says the LORD.

21"And as for me, this is my covenant with
them, says the LORD: my spirit which is upon
you, and my words which I have put in your
mouth, shall not depart out of your mouth,
or out of the mouth of your children, or out
of the mouth of your children's children,
says the LORD, from this time forth and for
evermore."

WISDOM 7

21I learned both what is secret and what
is manifest,
22for wisdom, the fashioner of all things,
taught me.

For in her there is a spirit that is
intelligent, holy,
unique, manifold, subtle,
mobile, clear, unpolluted,
distinct, invulnerable, loving the
good, keen,
irresistible, 23beneficent, humane,
steadfast, sure, free from anxiety,
all-powerful, overseeing all,
and penetrating through all spirits
that are intelligent and pure and most subtle.
24For wisdom is more mobile than
any motion;
because of her pureness she pervades and
penetrates all things.
25For she is a breath of the power of God,
and a pure emanation of the glory of
the Almighty;
therefore nothing defiled gains entrance
into her.
26For she is a reflection of eternal light,
a spotless mirror of the working of God,
and an image of his goodness.
27Though she is but one, she can do all things,
and while remaining in herself, she renews
all things;
in every generation she passes into
holy souls
and makes them friends of God, and
prophets;
28for God loves nothing so much as the man
who lives with wisdom.
29For she is more beautiful than the sun,
and excels every constellation of the stars.
Compared with the light she is found to
be superior,
30for it is succeeded by the night,
but against wisdom evil does not prevail.

---

2 CORINTHIANS 3

Are we beginning to commend ourselves again? Or do we need, as some do, letters of recommendation to you, or from you? 2You yourselves are our letter of recommendation, written on your hearts, to be known and read by all men; 3and you show that you are a letter from Christ delivered by us, written not with ink but with the Spirit of the living God, not on tablets of stone but on tablets of human hearts.

4Such is the confidence that we have through
Christ toward God. 5Not that we are sufficient
of ourselves to claim anything as coming from
us; our sufficiency is from God, 6who has
qualified us to be ministers of a new covenant,
not in a written code but in the Spirit; for the
written code kills, but the Spirit gives life.
7Now if the dispensation of death, carved
in letters on stone, came with such splendor
that the Israelites could not look at Moses'
face because of its brightness, fading as this
was, 8will not the dispensation of the Spirit be
attended with greater splendor? 9For if there
was splendor in the dispensation of condemnation, the dispensation of righteousness
must far exceed it in splendor. 10Indeed, in
this case, what once had splendor has come
to have no splendor at all, because of the
splendor that surpasses it. 11For if what faded
away came with splendor, what is permanent
must have much more splendor.
12Since we have such a hope, we are very
bold, 13not like Moses, who put a veil over
his face so that the Israelites might not see
the end of the fading splendor. 14But their
minds were hardened; for to this day, when
they read the old covenant, that same veil
remains unlifted, because only through
Christ is it taken away. 15Yes, to this day
whenever Moses is read a veil lies over their
minds; 16but when a man turns to the Lord
the veil is removed. 17Now the Lord is the
Spirit, and where the Spirit of the Lord is,
there is freedom. 18And we all, with unveiled
face, beholding the glory of the Lord, are
being changed into his likeness from one
degree of glory to another; for this comes
from the Lord who is the Spirit.

REFLECTION

Isaiah's vision of restoration redefines traditional boundaries. He foresees a time when ritual qualifications for membership in God's people will give way to welcome authentic worshippers who don't meet traditional external standards. Even the eunuchs and the Gentiles, technically unclean persons under Old Covenant Law, if they "hold fast [God's] covenant" (Is 56:4), will not be excluded from Temple worship. Similarly, those who perform religious fasts yet oppress their neighbors will be excluded, while those who "share [their] bread with the hungry and bring the homeless poor into [their] house" (58:7), will be honored as keeping the fast that God desires. These prophecies remind us that external religious practices alone do nothing for us. It is only when our hearts and our actions together align with God's purposes that our actions become meritorious. Then we can truly seek out wisdom, "a reflection of eternal light" (Wis 7:26). St. Paul envisions our pursuit of the light of wisdom: "And we all, with unveiled face, beholding the glory of the Lord, are being changed into his likeness from one degree of glory to another" (2 Cor 3:18). We will never be transformed into glory with Christ by merely going through the motions of devotion. Do you sincerely put your heart into your worship?

September 15

ISAIAH 60

Arise, shine; for your light
has come,
and the glory of the LORD
has risen upon you.
2For behold, darkness shall cover the earth,
and thick darkness the peoples;
but the LORD will arise upon you,
and his glory will be seen upon you.
3And nations shall walk by your light,
and kings in the brightness of your rising.

4Lift up your eyes round about, and see;
they all gather together, they come to you;
your sons shall come from far,
and your daughters shall be carried in
the arms.
5Then you shall see and be radiant,
your heart shall thrill and rejoice;
because the abundance of the sea shall be
turned to you,
the wealth of the nations shall come
to you.
6A multitude of camels shall cover you,
the young camels of Mid′ian and E′phah;
all those from Sheba shall come.
They shall bring gold and frankincense,
and shall proclaim the praise of the LORD.
7All the flocks of Ke′dar shall be gathered
to you,
the rams of Nebai′oth shall minister to you;
they shall come up with acceptance on
my altar,
and I will glorify my glorious house.

8Who are these that fly like a cloud,
and like doves to their windows?
9For the islands shall wait for me,
the ships of Tar′shish first,
to bring your sons from far,
their silver and gold with them,
for the name of the LORD your God,
and for the Holy One of Israel,
because he has glorified you.

10Foreigners shall build up your walls,
and their kings shall minister to you;
for in my wrath I struck you,
but in my favor I have had mercy on you.
11Your gates shall be open continually;
day and night they shall not be shut;
that men may bring to you the wealth of
the nations,
with their kings led in procession.
12For the nation and kingdom
that will not serve you shall perish;
those nations shall be utterly laid waste.
13The glory of Lebanon shall come to you,
the cypress, the plane, and the pine,
to beautify the place of my sanctuary;
and I will make the place of my feet glorious.
14The sons of those who oppressed you
shall come bending low to you;
and all who despised you
shall bow down at your feet;
they shall call you the City of the LORD,
the Zion of the Holy One of Israel.

15Whereas you have been forsaken and hated,
with no one passing through,
I will make you majestic for ever,
a joy from age to age.
16You shall suck the milk of nations,
you shall suck the breast of kings;
and you shall know that I, the LORD, am
your Savior
and your Redeemer, the Mighty One
of Jacob.

17Instead of bronze I will bring gold,
and instead of iron I will bring silver;
instead of wood, bronze,
instead of stones, iron.
I will make your overseers peace
and your taskmasters righteousness.
18Violence shall no more be heard in
your land,
devastation or destruction within
your borders;
you shall call your walls Salvation,
and your gates Praise.

19The sun shall no longer be
your light by day,
nor for brightness shall the moon
give light to you by night;
but the LORD will be your everlasting light,
and your God will be your glory.
20Your sun shall no more go down,
nor your moon withdraw itself;
for the LORD will be your everlasting light,
and your days of mourning shall be
ended.
21Your people shall all be righteous;
they shall possess the land for ever,
the shoot of my planting, the work of
my hands,
that I might be glorified.
22The least one shall become a clan,
and the smallest one a mighty nation;
I am the LORD;
in its time I will hasten it.

61 The Spirit of the Lord GOD is upon me,
because the LORD has anointed me
to bring good tidings to the afflicted;
he has sent me to bind up the
brokenhearted,
to proclaim liberty to the captives,
and the opening of the prison to those
who are bound;
2to proclaim the year of the LORD's favor,
and the day of vengeance of our God;
to comfort all who mourn;
3to grant to those who mourn in Zion—
to give them a garland instead of ashes,
the oil of gladness instead of mourning,
the mantle of praise instead of a faint
spirit;
that they may be called oaks of
righteousness,
the planting of the LORD, that he may
be glorified.
4They shall build up the ancient ruins,
they shall raise up the former
devastations;
they shall repair the ruined cities,
the devastations of many generations.

5Aliens shall stand and feed your flocks,
foreigners shall be your plowmen and
vinedressers;
6but you shall be called the priests of
the LORD,
men shall speak of you as the ministers of
our God;
you shall eat the wealth of the nations,
and in their riches you shall glory.
7Instead of your shame you shall have a
double portion,
instead of dishonor you shall rejoice in
your lot;
therefore in your land you shall possess a
double portion;
yours shall be everlasting joy.

8For I the LORD love justice,
I hate robbery and wrong;
I will faithfully give them their
recompense,
and I will make an everlasting covenant
with them.
9Their descendants shall be known among
the nations,
and their offspring in the midst of the
peoples;
all who see them shall acknowledge them,
that they are a people whom the LORD
has blessed.

10I will greatly rejoice in the LORD,
my soul shall exult in my God;
for he has clothed me with the garments of salvation,
he has covered me with the robe of righteousness,
as a bridegroom decks himself with a garland,
and as a bride adorns herself with her jewels.
11For as the earth brings forth its shoots,
and as a garden causes what is sown in it to spring up,
so the Lord GOD will cause righteousness and praise
to spring forth before all the nations.

62 For Zion's sake I will not keep silent,
and for Jerusalem's sake I will not rest,
until her vindication goes forth as brightness,
and her salvation as a burning torch.
2The nations shall see your vindication,
and all the kings your glory;
and you shall be called by a new name
which the mouth of the LORD will give.
3You shall be a crown of beauty in the hand of the LORD,
and a royal diadem in the hand of your God.
4You shall no more be termed Forsaken,
and your land shall no more be termed Desolate;
but you shall be called My delight is in her,
and your land Married;
for the LORD delights in you,
and your land shall be married.
5For as a young man marries a virgin,
so shall your sons marry you,
and as the bridegroom rejoices over the bride,
so shall your God rejoice over you.

6Upon your walls, O Jerusalem,
I have set watchmen;
all the day and all the night
they shall never be silent.
You who put the LORD in remembrance,
take no rest,
7and give him no rest
until he establishes Jerusalem
and makes it a praise in the earth.
8The LORD has sworn by his right hand
and by his mighty arm:
"I will not again give your grain
to be food for your enemies,
and foreigners shall not drink your wine
for which you have labored;
9but those who garner it shall eat it
and praise the LORD,
and those who gather it shall drink it
in the courts of my sanctuary."

10Go through, go through the gates,
prepare the way for the people;
build up, build up the highway,
clear it of stones,
lift up an ensign over the peoples.
11Behold, the LORD has proclaimed
to the end of the earth:
Say to the daughter of Zion,
"Behold, your salvation comes;
behold, his reward is with him,
and his recompense before him."
12And they shall be called The holy people,
The redeemed of the LORD;
and you shall be called Sought out,
a city not forsaken.

63 Who is this that comes from E´dom,
in crimsoned garments from Bozrah,
he that is glorious in his apparel,
marching in the greatness of his strength?

"It is I, announcing vindication,
mighty to save."

2Why is your apparel red,
and your garments like his who treads in the wine press?

3"I have trodden the wine press alone,
and from the peoples no one was with me;
I trod them in my anger
and trampled them in my wrath;
their lifeblood is sprinkled upon my garments,
and I have stained all my clothing.
4For the day of vengeance was in my heart,
and my year of redemption has come.

[5]I looked, but there was no one to help;
I was appalled, but there was no one
to uphold;
so my own arm brought me victory,
and my wrath upheld me.
[6]I trod down the peoples in my anger,
I made them drunk in my wrath,
and I poured out their lifeblood on
the earth."

[7]I will recount the merciful love of the LORD,
the praises of the LORD,
according to all that the LORD has granted us,
and the great goodness to the house
of Israel
which he has granted them according to
his mercy,
according to the abundance of his
steadfast love.
[8]For he said, Surely they are my people,
sons who will not deal falsely;
and he became their Savior.
[9]In all their affliction he was afflicted,
and the angel of his presence saved them;
in his love and in his pity he redeemed them;
he lifted them up and carried them all the
days of old.

[10]But they rebelled
and grieved his holy Spirit;
therefore he turned to be their enemy,
and himself fought against them.
[11]Then he remembered the days of old,
of Moses his servant.
Where is he who brought up out of the sea
the shepherds of his flock?
Where is he who put in the midst of them
his holy Spirit,
[12]who caused his glorious arm
to go at the right hand of Moses,
who divided the waters before them
to make for himself an everlasting
name,
[13] who led them through the depths?
Like a horse in the desert,
they did not stumble.
[14]Like cattle that go down into the valley,
the Spirit of the LORD gave them rest.
So you led your people,
to make for yourself a glorious name.

[15]Look down from heaven and see,
from your holy and glorious habitation.
Where are your zeal and your might?
The yearning of your heart and
your compassion
are withheld from me.
[16]For you are our Father,
though Abraham does not know us
and Israel does not acknowledge us;
you, O LORD, are our Father,
our Redeemer from of old is your name.
[17]O LORD, why do you make us err from
your ways
and harden our heart, so that we fear
you not?
Return for the sake of your servants,
the tribes of your heritage.
[18]Your holy people possessed your sanctuary
a little while;
our adversaries have trodden it down.
[19]We have become like those over whom
you have never ruled,
like those who are not called by
your name.

WISDOM 8

She reaches mightily from one end of the
earth to the other,
and she orders all things well.

[2]I loved her and sought her from my youth,
and I desired to take her for my bride,
and I became enamored of her beauty.
[3]She glorifies her noble birth by living
with God,
and the Lord of all loves her.
[4]For she is an initiate in the knowledge of God,
and an associate in his works.
[5]If riches are a desirable possession in life,
what is richer than wisdom who effects
all things?
[6]And if understanding is effective,
who more than she is fashioner of what exists?
[7]And if any one loves righteousness,
her labors are virtues;
for she teaches self-control and prudence,
justice and courage;

nothing in life is more profitable for men
than these.
8 And if any one longs for wide experience,
she knows the things of old, and infers the
things to come;
she understands turns of speech and the
solutions of riddles;
she has foreknowledge of signs and wonders
and of the outcome of seasons and times.
9 Therefore I determined to take her to live
with me,
knowing that she would give me good
counsel
and encouragement in cares and grief.
10 Because of her I shall have glory among
the multitudes
and honor in the presence of the elders,
though I am young.

2 CORINTHIANS 4

**Therefore, having this ministry
by the mercy of God, we do not
lose heart.**
**2 We have renounced disgrace-
ful, underhanded ways; we refuse to**
practice cunning or to tamper with God's
word, but by the open statement of the truth
we would commend ourselves to every man's
conscience in the sight of God.
3 And even if
our gospel is veiled, it is veiled only to those
who are perishing.
4 In their case the god of
this world has blinded the minds of the unbelievers, to keep them from seeing the light
of the gospel of the glory of Christ, who is
the likeness of God.
5 For what we preach is
not ourselves, but Jesus Christ as Lord, with
ourselves as your servants for Jesus' sake.
6 For
it is the God who said, "Let light shine out
of darkness," who has shone in our hearts to
give the light of the knowledge of the glory of
God in the face of Christ.

7 But we have this treasure in earthen vessels,
to show that the transcendent power belongs
to God and not to us.
8 We are afflicted in ev-
ery way, but not crushed; perplexed, but not
driven to despair;
9 persecuted, but not forsak-
en; struck down, but not destroyed;
10 always
carrying in the body the death of Jesus, so that
the life of Jesus may also be manifested in our
bodies.
11 For while we live we are always being
given up to death for Jesus' sake, so that the life
of Jesus may be manifested in our mortal flesh.
12 So death is at work in us, but life in you.

13 Since we have the same spirit of faith
as he had who wrote, "I believed, and so
I spoke," we too believe, and so we speak,
14 knowing that he who raised the Lord Jesus
will raise us also with Jesus and bring us with
you into his presence.
15 For it is all for your
sake, so that as grace extends to more and
more people it may increase thanksgiving,
to the glory of God.

16 So we do not lose heart. Though our
outer man is wasting away, our inner man
is being renewed every day.
17 For this slight
momentary affliction is preparing for us an
eternal weight of glory beyond all comparison,
18 because we look not to the things that are
seen but to the things that are unseen; for
the things that are seen are transient, but the
things that are unseen are eternal.

REFLECTION

The world measures us by our accomplishments, our appearance, and personality. But God sees the heart. When our hearts are given over to him, we shine with his light. Isaiah envisions our future glorification in the Lord: "Arise, shine; for your light has come, and the glory of the LORD has risen upon you" (Is 60:1). God promises to "make you majestic for ever, a joy from age to age" (v. 15). Indeed, the sun will be outshone by the light of the Lord, "your everlasting light" (v. 19). In this glorious future, the Lord shines on us, and we reflect his light back in an endless, happy exchange. "As the bridegroom rejoices over the bride, so shall your God rejoice over you" (62:5). St. Paul likewise announces a time when the light of God has shone in our hearts, where our "outer man" is afflicted, but our "inner man" is daily renewed (2 Cor 4:16). He says we are being prepared for "an eternal weight of glory beyond all comparison" (v. 17). Why do you think that those full of joy and life often seem to have eyes that light up? How does that relate to the image of light in these passages?

September 16

ISAIAH 64

O that you would tear the heavens and come down,
that the mountains might quake at your presence—
2 as when fire kindles brushwood
and the fire causes water to boil—
to make your name known to your adversaries,
and that the nations might tremble at your presence!
3 When you did terrible things which we looked not for,
you came down, the mountains quaked at your presence.
4 From of old no one has heard
or perceived by the ear,
no eye has seen a God besides you,
who works for those who wait for him.
5 You meet him that joyfully works righteousness,
those that remember you in your ways.
Behold, you were angry, and we sinned;
in our sins we have been a long time, and shall we be saved?
6 We have all become like one who is unclean,
and all our righteous deeds are like a polluted garment.
We all fade like a leaf,
and our iniquities, like the wind, take us away.
7 There is no one that calls upon your name,
that bestirs himself to take hold of you;
for you have hidden your face from us,
and have delivered us into the hand of our iniquities.

8 Yet, O LORD, you are our Father;
we are the clay, and you are our potter;
we are all the work of your hand.
9 Be not exceedingly angry, O LORD,
and remember not iniquity for ever.
Behold, consider, we are all your people.
10 Your holy cities have become a wilderness,
Zion has become a wilderness,
Jerusalem a desolation.
11 Our holy and beautiful house,
where our fathers praised you,
has been burned by fire,
and all our pleasant places have become ruins.
12 Will you restrain yourself at these things,
O LORD?
Will you keep silent, and afflict us sorely?

65 I was ready to be sought by those who did not ask for me;
I was ready to be found by those who did not seek me.
I said, "Here am I, here am I,"
to a nation that did not call on my name.
2 I spread out my hands all the day
to a rebellious people,
who walk in a way that is not good,
following their own devices;
3 a people who provoke me
to my face continually,
sacrificing in gardens
and burning incense upon bricks;
4 who sit in tombs,
and spend the night in secret places;
who eat swine's flesh,
and broth of abominable things is in their vessels;
5 who say, "Keep to yourself,
do not come near me, for I am set apart from you."
These are a smoke in my nostrils,
a fire that burns all the day.
6 Behold, it is written before me:
"I will not keep silent, but I will repay,
yes, I will repay into their bosom
7 their iniquities and their fathers' iniquities together,
says the LORD;
because they burned incense upon the mountains
and reviled me upon the hills,
I will measure into their bosom
payment for their former doings."

8 Thus says the LORD:
"As the wine is found in the cluster,
and they say, 'Do not destroy it,
for there is a blessing in it,'

so I will do for my servants' sake,
and not destroy them all.
9 I will bring forth descendants from Jacob,
and from Judah inheritors of my mountains;
my chosen shall inherit it,
and my servants shall dwell there.
10 Sharon shall become a pasture for flocks,
and the Valley of A′chor a place for herds to lie down,
for my people who have sought me.
11 But you who forsake the LORD,
who forget my holy mountain,
who set a table for Fortune
and fill cups of mixed wine for Destiny;
12 I will destine you to the sword,
and all of you shall bow down to the slaughter;
because, when I called, you did not answer,
when I spoke, you did not listen,
but you did what was evil in my eyes,
and chose what I did not delight in."

13 Therefore thus says the Lord GOD:
"Behold, my servants shall eat,
but you shall be hungry;
behold, my servants shall drink,
but you shall be thirsty;
behold, my servants shall rejoice,
but you shall be put to shame;
14 behold, my servants shall sing for gladness of heart,
but you shall cry out for pain of heart,
and shall wail for anguish of spirit.
15 You shall leave your name to my chosen for a curse,
and the Lord GOD will slay you;
but his servants he will call by a different name.
16 So that he who blesses himself in the land
shall bless himself by the God of truth,
and he who takes an oath in the land
shall swear by the God of truth;
because the former troubles are forgotten
and are hidden from my eyes.

17 "For behold, I create new heavens
and a new earth;
and the former things shall not be remembered
or come into mind.
18 But be glad and rejoice for ever
in that which I create;
for behold, I create Jerusalem a rejoicing,
and her people a joy.
19 I will rejoice in Jerusalem,
and be glad in my people;
no more shall be heard in it the sound of weeping
and the cry of distress.
20 No more shall there be in it
an infant that lives but a few days,
or an old man who does not fill out his days,
for the child shall die a hundred years old,
and the sinner a hundred years old shall be accursed.
21 They shall build houses and inhabit them;
they shall plant vineyards and eat their fruit.
22 They shall not build and another inhabit;
they shall not plant and another eat;
for like the days of a tree shall the days of my people be,
and my chosen shall long enjoy the work of their hands.
23 They shall not labor in vain,
or bear children for calamity;
for they shall be the offspring of the blessed of the LORD,
and their children with them.
24 Before they call I will answer,
while they are yet speaking I will hear.
25 The wolf and the lamb shall feed together,
the lion shall eat straw like the ox;
and dust shall be the serpent's food.
They shall not hurt or destroy
in all my holy mountain,
says the LORD."

66 Thus says the LORD:
Heaven is my throne
and the earth is my footstool;
what is the house which you would build for me,
and what is the place of my rest?
2 All these things my hand has made,
and so all these things are mine,
says the LORD.

But this is the man to whom I will look,
he that is humble and contrite in spirit,
and trembles at my word.

3"He who slaughters an ox is like him who kills a man;
he who sacrifices a lamb, like him who breaks a dog's neck;
he who presents a cereal offering, like him who offers swine's blood;
he who makes a memorial offering of frankincense, like him who blesses an idol.
These have chosen their own ways,
and their soul delights in their abominations;
4I also will choose affliction for them,
and bring their fears upon them;
because, when I called, no one answered,
when I spoke they did not listen;
but they did what was evil in my eyes,
and chose that in which I did not delight."
5Hear the word of the LORD,
you who tremble at his word:
"Your brethren who hate you
and cast you out for my name's sake
have said, 'Let the LORD be glorified,
that we may see your joy';
but it is they who shall be put to shame.

6"Listen, an uproar from the city!
A voice from the temple!
The voice of the LORD,
rendering recompense to his enemies!

7"Before she was in labor
she gave birth;
before her pain came upon her
she was delivered of a son.
8Who has heard such a thing?
Who has seen such things?
Shall a land be born in one day?
Shall a nation be brought forth in one moment?
For as soon as Zion was in labor
she brought forth her sons.
9Shall I bring to the birth and not cause to bring forth?
says the LORD;
shall I, who cause to bring forth, shut the womb?
says your God.

10"Rejoice with Jerusalem, and be glad for her,
all you who love her;
rejoice with her in joy,
all you who mourn over her;
11that you may suck and be satisfied
with her consoling breasts;
that you may drink deeply with delight
from the abundance of her glory."

12For thus says the LORD:
"Behold, I will extend prosperity to her like a river,
and the wealth of the nations like an overflowing stream;
and you shall suck, you shall be carried upon her hip,
and fondled upon her knees.
13As one whom his mother comforts,
so I will comfort you;
you shall be comforted in Jerusalem.
14You shall see, and your heart shall rejoice;
your bones shall flourish like the grass;
and it shall be known that the hand of the LORD is with his servants,
and his indignation is against his enemies.

15"For behold, the LORD will come in fire,
and his chariots like the stormwind,
to render his anger in fury,
and his rebuke with flames of fire.
16For by fire will the LORD execute judgment,
and by his sword, upon all flesh;
and those slain by the LORD shall be many.

17"Those who sanctify and purify themselves to go into the gardens, following one in the midst, eating swine's flesh and the abomination and mice, shall come to an end together, says the LORD.

18"For I know their works and their thoughts, and I am coming to gather all nations and tongues; and they shall come and shall
see my glory, 19and I will set a sign among

them. And from them I will send survivors
to the nations, to Tar′shish, Put, and Lud,
who draw the bow, to Tu′bal and Ja′van,
to the islands afar off, that have not heard
my fame or seen my glory; and they shall
declare my glory among the nations. 20And
they shall bring all your brethren from
all the nations as an offering to the LORD,
upon horses, and in chariots, and in litters,
and upon mules, and upon dromedaries,
to my holy mountain Jerusalem, says the
LORD, just as the sons of Israel bring their
cereal offering in a clean vessel to the house
of the LORD. 21And some of them also I
will take for priests and for Levites, says
the LORD.

22"For as the new heavens and the new earth
which I will make
shall remain before me, says the LORD;
so shall your descendants and your name
remain.
23From new moon to new moon,
and from sabbath to sabbath,
all flesh shall come to worship before me,
says the LORD.

24"And they shall go forth and look on the
dead bodies of the men that have rebelled
against me; for their worm shall not die,
their fire shall not be quenched, and they
shall be an abhorrence to all flesh."

WISDOM 8

11I shall be found keen in judgment,
and in the sight of rulers I shall be admired.
12When I am silent they will wait for me,
and when I speak they will give heed;
and when I speak at greater length
they will put their hands on their mouths.
13Because of her I shall have immortality,
and leave an everlasting remembrance to
those who come after me.
14I shall govern peoples,
and nations will be subject to me;
15dread monarchs will be afraid of me when
they hear of me;
among the people I shall show myself
capable, and courageous in war.
16When I enter my house, I shall find rest
with her,
for companionship with her has no
bitterness,
and life with her has no pain, but gladness
and joy.
17When I considered these things inwardly,
and thought upon them in my mind,
that in kinship with wisdom there is
immortality,
18and in friendship with her, pure delight,
and in the labors of her hands, unfailing
wealth,
and in the experience of her company,
understanding,
and renown in sharing her words,
I went about seeking how to get her
for myself.
19As a child I was by nature well endowed,
and a good soul fell to my lot;
20or rather, being good, I entered an
undefiled body.
21But I perceived that I would not possess
wisdom unless God gave her to me—
and it was a mark of insight to know whose
gift she was—
so I appealed to the Lord and implored him,
and with my whole heart I said:

2 CORINTHIANS 5

For we know that if the earthly tent we live in is destroyed, we have a building from God, a house not made with hands, eternal in the heavens.
2Here indeed we groan, and long to put on
our heavenly dwelling, 3so that by putting it
on we may not be found naked. 4For while
we are still in this tent, we sigh with anxiety;
not that we would be unclothed, but that
we would be further clothed, so that what is
mortal may be swallowed up by life. 5He who
has prepared us for this very thing is God,
who has given us the Spirit as a guarantee.

6So we are always of good courage; we
know that while we are at home in the body
we are away from the Lord, 7for we walk by
faith, not by sight. 8We are of good courage,

and we would rather be away from the body
and at home with the Lord. 9So whether we
are at home or away, we make it our aim to
please him. 10For we must all appear before
the judgment seat of Christ, so that each one
may receive good or evil, according to what
he has done in the body.
11Therefore, knowing the fear of the Lord,
we persuade men; but what we are is known
to God, and I hope it is known also to your
conscience. 12We are not commending ourselves to you again but giving you cause to
be proud of us, so that you may be able to
answer those who pride themselves on a
man's position and not on his heart. 13For
if we are beside ourselves, it is for God; if
we are in our right mind, it is for you. 14For
the love of Christ urges us on, because we
are convinced that one has died for all;
therefore all have died. 15And he died for all,
that those who live might live no longer for
themselves but for him who for their sake
died and was raised.
16From now on, therefore, we regard no
one according to the flesh; even though we
once regarded Christ according to the flesh,
we regard him thus no longer. 17Therefore,
if any one is in Christ, he is a new creation;
the old has passed away, behold, the new has
come. 18All this is from God, who through
Christ reconciled us to himself and gave us the
ministry of reconciliation; 19that is, in Christ
God was reconciling the world to himself, not
counting their trespasses against them, and
entrusting to us the message of reconciliation.
20So we are ambassadors for Christ, God
making his appeal through us. We beg you on
behalf of Christ, be reconciled to God. 21For
our sake he made him to be sin who knew
no sin, so that in him we might become the
righteousness of God.

REFLECTION

As the Lord draws us closer to himself, our hearts begin to yearn for the definitive revelation of his justice and mercy. Isaiah invites his judgment: "O that you would tear the heavens and come down" (Is 64:1). Yet quickly, he declares our sinfulness, but also our trust in the Lord: "We are the clay, and you are our potter" (v. 8). He depicts a time when "the wolf and the lamb shall feed together" (65:25) and the Lord will welcome those who are "humble and contrite in spirit" (66:2). When we truly believe in and depend upon the Lord, we welcome his presence and his judgment of the world, since it is through his judgment that we enter salvation. St. Paul expresses this same view by emphasizing the resurrection, when we will shed our "earthly tent," our mortal body (2 Cor 5:1). In its place, we will take on "a house not made with hands," a "heavenly dwelling," a glorified body (vv. 1–2). We have already become a "new creation" in Christ (v. 17). The Day of Judgment and the end of time often sound frightening, yet they usher in an eternal era of "prosperity . . . like a river" (Is 66:12). Do you look forward to the coming of the Lord?

September 17

JEREMIAH 1

**The words of Jeremi′ah, the son
of Hilki′ah, of the priests who
were in An′athoth in the land of
Benjamin, 2to whom the word of the
Lord came in the days of Josi′ah the
son of A′mon, king of Judah, in the**
thirteenth year of his reign. 3It came also in
the days of Jehoi′akim the son of Josi′ah, king
of Judah, and until the end of the eleventh
year of Zedeki′ah, the son of Josiah, king of
Judah, until the captivity of Jerusalem in the
fifth month.
4Now the word of the Lord came to me
saying,
5"Before I formed you in the womb I
knew you,
and before you were born I consecrated
you;
I appointed you a prophet to the nations."

6Then I said, "Ah, Lord GOD! Behold, I do
not know how to speak, for I am only a
youth." 7But the LORD said to me,
"Do not say, 'I am only a youth';
for to all to whom I send you you shall go,
and whatever I command you you
shall speak.
8Be not afraid of them,
for I am with you to deliver you,
says the LORD."
9Then the LORD put forth his hand and
touched my mouth; and the LORD said to me,
"Behold, I have put my words in
your mouth.
10See, I have set you this day over nations
and over kingdoms,
to pluck up and to break down,
to destroy and to overthrow,
to build and to plant."

11And the word of the LORD came to
me, saying, "Jeremi'ah, what do you see?"
And I said, "I see a rod of almond." 12Then
the LORD said to me, "You have seen well,
for I am watching over my word to perform it."

13The word of the LORD came to me a
second time, saying, "What do you see?" And
I said, "I see a boiling pot, facing away from
the north." 14Then the LORD said to me, "Out
of the north evil shall break forth upon all the
inhabitants of the land. 15For, behold, I am
calling all the tribes of the kingdoms of the
north, says the LORD; and they shall come and
every one shall set his throne at the entrance
of the gates of Jerusalem, against all its walls
round about, and against all the cities of
Judah. 16And I will utter my judgments against
them, for all their wickedness in forsaking
me; they have burned incense to other gods,
and worshiped the works of their own hands.
17But you, gird up your loins; arise, and say to
them everything that I command you. Do not
be dismayed by them, lest I dismay you before
them. 18And I, behold, I make you this day a
fortified city, an iron pillar, and bronze walls,
against the whole land, against the kings of
Judah, its princes, its priests, and the people
of the land. 19They will fight against you; but
they shall not prevail against you, for I am
with you, says the LORD, to deliver you."

2 The word of the LORD came to me,
saying, 2"Go and proclaim in the hearing
of Jerusalem, Thus says the LORD,
I remember the devotion of your youth,
your love as a bride,
how you followed me in the wilderness,
in a land not sown.
3Israel was holy to the LORD,
the first fruits of his harvest.
All who ate of it became guilty;
evil came upon them,
says the LORD."

4Hear the word of the LORD, O house of
Jacob, and all the families of the house of
Israel. 5Thus says the LORD:
"What wrong did your fathers find in me
that they went far from me,
and went after worthlessness, and
became worthless?
6They did not say, 'Where is the LORD
who brought us up from the land
of Egypt,
who led us in the wilderness,
in a land of deserts and pits,
in a land of drought and deep darkness,
in a land that none passes through,
where no man dwells?'
7And I brought you into a plentiful land
to enjoy its fruits and its good things.
But when you came in you defiled my land,
and made my heritage an abomination.
8The priests did not say, 'Where is the LORD?'
Those who handle the law did not
know me;
the rulers transgressed against me;
the prophets prophesied by Ba'al,
and went after things that do not profit.

9"Therefore I still contend with you,
says the LORD,
and with your children's children I will
contend.
10For cross to the coasts of Cyprus and see,
or send to Kedar and examine with care;
see if there has been such a thing.
11Has a nation changed its gods,
even though they are no gods?
But my people have changed their glory
for that which does not profit.

12Be appalled, O heavens, at this,
be shocked, be utterly desolate,
says the LORD,
13for my people have committed two evils:
they have forsaken me,
the fountain of living waters,
and hewed out cisterns for themselves,
broken cisterns,
that can hold no water.

14"Is Israel a slave? Is he a homeborn servant?
Why then has he become a prey?
15The lions have roared against him,
they have roared loudly.
They have made his land a waste;
his cities are in ruins, without inhabitant.
16Moreover, the men of Memphis and
Tah′panhes
have broken the crown of your head.
17Have you not brought this upon yourself
by forsaking the LORD your God,
when he led you in the way?
18And now what do you gain by going
to Egypt,
to drink the waters of the Nile?
Or what do you gain by going to Assyria,
to drink the waters of the Euphra′tes?
19Your wickedness will chasten you,
and your apostasy will reprove you.
Know and see that it is evil and bitter
for you to forsake the LORD your God;
the fear of me is not in you,
says the Lord GOD of hosts.

20"For long ago you broke your yoke
and burst your bonds;
and you said, 'I will not serve.'
Yes, upon every high hill
and under every green tree
you bowed down as a harlot.
21Yet I planted you a choice vine,
wholly of pure seed.
How then have you turned degenerate
and become a wild vine?
22Though you wash yourself with lye
and use much soap,
the stain of your guilt is still before me,
says the Lord GOD.
23How can you say, 'I am not defiled,
I have not gone after the Ba′als'?
Look at your way in the valley;
know what you have done—
a restive young camel interlacing her tracks,
24 a wild donkey used to the wilderness,
in her heat sniffing the wind!
Who can restrain her lust?
None who seek her need weary
themselves;
in her month they will find her.
25Keep your feet from going unshod
and your throat from thirst.
But you said, 'It is hopeless,
for I have loved strangers,
and after them I will go.'

26"As a thief is shamed when caught,
so the house of Israel shall be shamed:
they, their kings, their princes,
their priests, and their prophets,
27who say to a tree, 'You are my father,'
and to a stone, 'You gave me birth.'
For they have turned their back to me,
and not their face.
But in the time of their trouble they say,
'Arise and save us!'
28But where are your gods
that you made for yourself?
Let them arise, if they can save you,
in your time of trouble;
for as many as your cities
are your gods, O Judah.

29"Why do you complain against me?
You have all rebelled against me,
says the LORD.
30In vain have I struck down your children,
they took no correction;
your own sword devoured your prophets
like a ravening lion.
31And you, O generation, heed the word of
the LORD.
Have I been a wilderness to Israel,
or a land of thick darkness?
Why then do my people say, 'We are free,
we will come no more to you'?
32Can a maiden forget her ornaments,
or a bride her attire?
Yet my people have forgotten me
days without number.

33"How well you direct your course
to seek lovers!
So that even to wicked women
you have taught your ways.
34Also on your skirts is found
the lifeblood of guiltless poor;
you did not find them breaking in.
Yet in spite of all these things
35you say, 'I am innocent;
surely his anger has turned from me.'
Behold, I will bring you to judgment
for saying, 'I have not sinned.'
36How lightly you gad about,
changing your way!
You shall be put to shame by Egypt
as you were put to shame by Assyria.
37From it too you will come away
with your hands upon your head,
for the LORD has rejected those in whom
you trust,
and you will not prosper by them."

WISDOM 9

"O God of my fathers and Lord of mercy,
who have made all things by your word,
2and by your wisdom have formed man,
to have dominion over the creatures you
have made,
3and rule the world in holiness and
righteousness,
and pronounce judgment in uprightness
of soul,
4give me the wisdom that sits by your throne,
and do not reject me from among
your servants.
5For I am your slave and the son of your
maidservant,
a man who is weak and short-lived,
with little understanding of judgment
and laws;
6for even if one is perfect among the sons
of men,
yet without the wisdom that comes from
you he will be regarded as nothing.
7You have chosen me to be king of your people
and to be judge over your sons and daughters.
8You have given command to build a temple
on your holy mountain,
and an altar in the city of your habitation,
a copy of the holy tent which you prepared
from the beginning.
9With you is wisdom, who knows your works
and was present when you made the world,
and who understands what is pleasing in
your sight
and what is right according to your
commandments.
10Send her forth from the holy heavens,
and from the throne of your glory send her,
that she may be with me and toil,
and that I may learn what is pleasing to you.
11For she knows and understands all things,
and she will guide me wisely in my actions
and guard me with her glory.
12Then my works will be acceptable,
and I shall judge your people justly,
and shall be worthy of the throne of
my father.
13For what man can learn the counsel of God?
Or who can discern what the Lord wills?
14For the reasoning of mortals is worthless,
and our designs are likely to fail,
15for a perishable body weighs down
the soul,
and this earthy tent burdens the thoughtful
mind.
16We can hardly guess at what is on earth,
and what is at hand we find with labor;
but who has traced out what is in the heavens?
17Who has learned your counsel, unless you
have given wisdom
and sent your holy Spirit from on high?
18And thus the paths of those on earth were
set right,
and men were taught what pleases you,
and were saved by wisdom."

2 CORINTHIANS 6

Working together with him, then, we entreat you not to accept the grace of God in vain. 2For he says,
"At the acceptable time I have listened
to you,
and helped you on the day of salvation."

Behold, now is the acceptable time; behold, now is the day of salvation. 3We
put no obstacle in any one's way, so that
no fault may be found with our ministry, 4but as servants of God we commend
ourselves in every way: through great
endurance, in afflictions, hardships, calamities, 5beatings, imprisonments, tumults, labors, watching, hunger; 6by
purity, knowledge, forbearance, kindness,
the Holy Spirit, genuine love, 7truthful
speech, and the power of God; with the
weapons of righteousness for the right
hand and for the left; 8in honor and dishonor, in ill repute and good repute. We
are treated as impostors, and yet are true;
9as unknown, and yet well known; as
dying, and behold we live; as punished,
and yet not killed; 10as sorrowful, yet always rejoicing; as poor, yet making many
rich; as having nothing, and yet possessing everything.

11Our mouth is open to you, Corinthians;
our heart is wide. 12You are not restricted
by us, but you are restricted in your own
affections. 13In return—I speak as to
children—widen your hearts also.

14Do not be mismated with unbelievers.
For what partnership have righteousness
and iniquity? Or what fellowship has
light with darkness? 15What accord has
Christ with Be′lial? Or what has a believer
in common with an unbeliever? 16What
agreement has the temple of God with
idols? For we are the temple of the living
God; as God said,

"I will live in them and move among them,
and I will be their God,
and they shall be my people.
17Therefore come out from them,
and be separate from them, says the Lord,
and touch nothing unclean;
then I will welcome you,
18and I will be a father to you,
and you shall be my sons and daughters,
says the Lord Almighty."

7 Since we have these promises, beloved,
let us cleanse ourselves from every defilement of body and spirit, and make holiness
perfect in the fear of God.

REFLECTION

At the beginning of the Book of Jeremiah, the prophet worries that he is not worthy of his calling. Jeremiah shies away from God's command because of his youth, but God reassures him. Likewise, in the Book of Wisdom, the author recognizes his human limitations and yet also his great responsibilities. Both men are made capable by the Wisdom or Word of God. Christians do not understand this Wisdom or Word to be an abstract intellectual gift, but rather the "Word" is Christ, the second Person of the Blessed Trinity. The Book of Wisdom speaks of "Wisdom" precisely as a person, one who was present at the creation of the world. What does this mean for our daily Christian lives? It means we must not be afraid to answer God's call. Despite our failings, we can acquire the kinds of virtues that St. Paul describes (kindness, genuine love, perfect speech, etc). In short, no matter who we are, we can be holy. This may seem unrealistic. But holiness does not come from our own strength of will, since we are "weak and short-lived" (Wis 9:5), but rather from Christ. How often do you consider how Wisdom can help you grow in holiness?

September 18

JEREMIAH 3

"If a man divorces his wife
and she goes from him
and becomes another man's wife,
will he return to her?
Would not that land be greatly polluted?
You have played the harlot with many lovers;
and would you return to me?
says the LORD.
2Lift up your eyes to the bare heights, and see!
Where have you not been lain with?
By the waysides you have sat awaiting lovers
like an Arab in the wilderness.
You have polluted the land
with your vile harlotry.

3Therefore the showers have been withheld,
and the spring rain has not come;
yet you have a harlot's brow,
you refuse to be ashamed.
4Have you not just now called to me,
'My father, you are the friend of my youth—
5will he be angry for ever,
will he be indignant to the end?'
Behold, you have spoken,
but you have done all the evil that
you could."

6The LORD said to me in the days of King
Josi′ah: "Have you seen what she did, that
faithless one, Israel, how she went up on
every high hill and under every green tree,
and there played the harlot? 7And I thought,
'After she has done all this she will return
to me'; but she did not return, and her false
sister Judah saw it. 8She saw that for all the
adulteries of that faithless one, Israel, I had
sent her away with a decree of divorce; yet
her false sister Judah did not fear, but she
too went and played the harlot. 9Because
harlotry was so light to her, she polluted
the land, committing adultery with stone
and tree. 10Yet for all this her false sister
Judah did not return to me with her whole
heart, but in pretense, says the LORD."

11And the LORD said to me, "Faithless
Israel has shown herself less guilty than
false Judah. 12Go, and proclaim these words
toward the north, and say,
'Return, faithless Israel,
says the LORD.
I will not look on you in anger,
for I am merciful,
says the LORD;
I will not be angry for ever.
13Only acknowledge your guilt,
that you rebelled against the LORD your God
and scattered your favors among strangers
under every green tree,
and that you have not obeyed my voice,
says the LORD.
14Return, O faithless children,
says the LORD;
for I am your master;
I will take you, one from a city and two
from a family,
and I will bring you to Zion.

15" 'And I will give you shepherds after
my own heart, who will feed you with
knowledge and understanding. 16And
when you have multiplied and increased
in the land, in those days, says the LORD,
they shall no more say, "The ark of the
covenant of the LORD." It shall not come
to mind, or be remembered, or missed; it
shall not be made again. 17At that time Jerusalem shall be called the throne of the
LORD, and all nations shall gather to it,
to the presence of the LORD in Jerusalem,
and they shall no more stubbornly follow
their own evil heart. 18In those days the
house of Judah shall join the house of Israel, and together they shall come from
the land of the north to the land that I
gave your fathers for a heritage.
19" 'I thought
how I would set you among my sons,
and give you a pleasant land,
a heritage most beauteous of all nations.
And I thought you would call me, My Father,
and would not turn from following me.
20Surely, as a faithless wife leaves her husband,
so have you been faithless to me, O house
of Israel,
says the LORD.' "

21A voice on the bare heights is heard,
the weeping and pleading of Israel's
sons,
because they have perverted their way,
they have forgotten the LORD their God.
22"Return, O faithless sons,
I will heal your faithlessness."
"Behold, we come to you;
for you are the LORD our God.
23Truly the hills are a delusion,
the orgies on the mountains.
Truly in the LORD our God
is the salvation of Israel.

24"But from our youth the shameful thing
has devoured all for which our fathers labored,
their flocks and their herds, their sons and their
daughters. 25Let us lie down in our shame, and
let our dishonor cover us; for we have sinned
against the LORD our God, we and our fathers,
from our youth even to this day; and we have
not obeyed the voice of the LORD our God."

4 "If you return, O Israel,
says the LORD,
to me you should return.
If you remove your abominations from
my presence,
and do not waver,
2 and if you swear, 'As the LORD lives,'
in truth, in justice, and in uprightness,
then nations shall bless themselves in him,
and in him shall they glory."

3 For thus says the LORD to the men of
Judah and to the inhabitants of Jerusalem:
"Break up your fallow ground,
and sow not among thorns.
4 Circumcise yourselves to the LORD,
remove the foreskin of your hearts,
O men of Judah and inhabitants of
Jerusalem;
lest my wrath go forth like fire,
and burn with none to quench it,
because of the evil of your doings."

5 Declare in Judah, and proclaim in Jerusalem, and say,
"Blow the trumpet through the land;
cry aloud and say,
'Assemble, and let us go
into the fortified cities!'
6 Raise a standard toward Zion,
flee for safety, stay not,
for I bring evil from the north,
and great destruction.
7 A lion has gone up from his thicket,
a destroyer of nations has set out;
he has gone forth from his place
to make your land a waste;
your cities will be ruins
without inhabitant.
8 For this clothe yourself with sackcloth,
lament and wail;
for the fierce anger of the LORD
has not turned back from us."

9 "In that day, says the LORD, courage shall
fail both king and princes; the priests shall
be appalled and the prophets astounded."
10 Then I said, "Ah, Lord GOD, surely you
have utterly deceived this people and
Jerusalem, saying, 'It shall be well with
you'; whereas the sword has reached their
very life."

11 At that time it will be said to this people and to Jerusalem, "A hot wind from
the bare heights in the desert toward the
daughter of my people, not to winnow or
cleanse, 12 a wind too full for this comes
for me. Now it is I who speak in judgment
upon them."
13 Behold, he comes up like clouds,
his chariots like the whirlwind;
his horses are swifter than eagles—
woe to us, for we are ruined!
14 O Jerusalem, wash your heart from
wickedness,
that you may be saved.
How long shall your evil thoughts
lodge within you?
15 For a voice declares from Dan
and proclaims evil from Mount E′phraim.
16 Warn the nations that he is coming;
announce to Jerusalem,
"Besiegers come from a distant land;
they shout against the cities of Judah.
17 Like keepers of a field they are against her
round about,
because she has rebelled against me,
says the LORD.

18 Your ways and your doings
have brought this upon you.
This is your doom, and it is bitter;
it has reached your very heart."

19 My anguish, my anguish! I writhe in pain!
Oh, the walls of my heart!
My heart is beating wildly;
I cannot keep silent;
for I hear the sound of the trumpet,
the alarm of war.
20 Disaster follows hard on disaster,
the whole land is laid waste.
Suddenly my tents are destroyed,
my curtains in a moment.
21 How long must I see the standard,
and hear the sound of the trumpet?
22 "For my people are foolish,
they know me not;
they are stupid children,
they have no understanding.
They are skilled in doing evil,
but how to do good they know not."

23 I looked on the earth, and behold, it was
waste and void;
and to the heavens, and they had no light.
24 I looked on the mountains, and behold,
they were quaking,
and all the hills moved back and forth.
25 I looked, and behold, there was no man,
and all the birds of the air had fled.
26 I looked, and behold, the fruitful land was
a desert,
and all its cities were laid in ruins
before the LORD, before his fierce anger.
27 For thus says the LORD, "The whole land
shall be a desolation; yet I will not make a
full end.
28 For this the earth shall mourn,
and the heavens above be black,
for I have spoken, I have planned;
I have not relented nor will I turn back."

29 At the noise of horseman and archer
every city takes to flight;
they enter thickets; they climb
among rocks;
all the cities are forsaken,
and no man dwells in them.
30 And you, O desolate one,
what do you mean that you dress in scarlet,
that you deck yourself with ornaments
of gold,
that you enlarge your eyes with paint?
In vain you beautify yourself.
Your lovers despise you;
they seek your life.
31 For I heard a cry as of a woman with
labor pains,
anguish as of one bringing forth her
first child,
the cry of the daughter of Zion gasping
for breath,
stretching out her hands,
"Woe is me! I am fainting before murderers."

WISDOM 10

Wisdom protected the first-formed
father of the world,
when he alone had been created;
she delivered him from his transgression,
2 and gave him strength to rule all things.
3 But when an unrighteous man departed
from her in his anger,
he perished because in rage he slew his
brother.
4 When the earth was flooded because of
him, wisdom again saved it,
steering the righteous man by a paltry piece
of wood.

5 Wisdom also, when the nations in wicked
agreement had been confounded,
recognized the righteous man and
preserved him blameless before God,
and kept him strong in the face of his
compassion for his child.
6 Wisdom rescued a righteous man when the
ungodly were perishing;
he escaped the fire that descended on the
Five Cities.
7 Evidence of their wickedness still
remains:
a continually smoking wasteland,
plants bearing fruit that does not ripen,
and a pillar of salt standing as a monument
to an unbelieving soul.
8 For because they passed wisdom by,
they not only were hindered from
recognizing the good,
but also left for mankind a reminder of
their folly,
so that their failures could never go
unnoticed.

9 Wisdom rescued from troubles those who
served her.
10 When a righteous man fled from his
brother's wrath,
she guided him on straight paths;
she showed him the kingdom of God,
and gave him knowledge of angels;
she prospered him in his labors,
and increased the fruit of his toil.
11 When his oppressors were covetous,
she stood by him and made him rich.
12 She protected him from his enemies,
and kept him safe from those who lay in
wait for him;
in his arduous contest she gave him
the victory,

so that he might learn that godliness is
more powerful than anything.

13When a righteous man was sold, wisdom
did not desert him,
but delivered him from sin.
She descended with him into the dungeon,
14and when he was in prison she did not
leave him,
until she brought him the scepter of
a kingdom
and authority over his masters.
Those who accused him she showed
to be false,
and she gave him everlasting honor.

15A holy people and blameless race
wisdom delivered from a nation
of oppressors.
16She entered the soul of a servant of
the Lord,
and withstood dread kings with wonders
and signs.
17She gave to holy men the reward of their
labors;
she guided them along a marvelous way,
and became a shelter to them by day,
and a starry flame through the night.
18She brought them over the Red Sea,
and led them through deep waters;
19but she drowned their enemies,
and cast them up from the depth of the sea.
20Therefore the righteous plundered the
ungodly;
they sang hymns, O Lord, to your holy name,
and praised with one accord your defending
hand,
21because wisdom opened the mouth
of the mute,
and made the tongues of infants
speak clearly.

---

2 CORINTHIANS 7

**2Open your hearts to us; we
have wronged no one, we have
corrupted no one, we have taken advantage of no one. 3I do not say this to**
condemn you, for I said before that you
are in our hearts, to die together and to
live together. 4I have great confidence in
you; I have great pride in you; I am filled
with comfort. With all our affliction, I am
overjoyed.

5For even when we came into Macedonia,
our bodies had no rest but we were afflicted
at every turn—fighting without and
fear within. 6But God, who comforts the
downcast, comforted us by the coming of
Titus, 7and not only by his coming but also
by the comfort with which he was comforted
in you, as he told us of your longing, your
mourning, your zeal for me, so that I rejoiced
still more. 8For even if I made you sorry with
my letter, I do not regret it (though I did
regret it), for I see that that letter grieved
you, though only for a while. 9As it is, I
rejoice, not because you were grieved, but
because you were grieved into repenting; for
you felt a godly grief, so that you suffered no
loss through us. 10For godly grief produces a
repentance that leads to salvation and brings
no regret, but worldly grief produces death.
11For see what earnestness this godly grief
has produced in you, what eagerness to clear
yourselves, what indignation, what alarm,
what longing, what zeal, what punishment!
At every point you have proved yourselves
guiltless in the matter. 12So although I wrote
to you, it was not on account of the one
who did the wrong, nor on account of the
one who suffered the wrong, but in order
that your zeal for us might be revealed to
you in the sight of God. 13Therefore we are
comforted.

And besides our own comfort we
rejoiced still more at the joy of Titus,
because his mind has been set at rest
by you all. 14For if I have expressed to
him some pride in you, I was not put to
shame; but just as everything we said to
you was true, so our boasting before Titus
has proved true. 15And his heart goes out
all the more to you, as he remembers
the obedience of you all, and the fear
and trembling with which you received
him. 16I rejoice, because I have perfect
confidence in you.

REFLECTION

We may find the imagery used in Jeremiah striking, and even scandalous. Jeremiah describes the idolatry of the Israelites (that is, their worship of objects in nature and of other gods) as prostitution. Vividly, the prophet tells us that "upon every high hill and under every green tree" (Jer 2:20) the people committed adultery. The Bible often employs marital imagery when speaking about the relationship of God to his people or to his Church. Marriage is a rich and complex human analog for the intimacy of our relationship with God. Another image of intimacy appears in the Book of Wisdom, which describes God's intervention at every stage of salvation history as a personal interaction—with Adam, Abel, Moses, etc. Likewise, St. Paul in 2 Corinthians speaks to his fellow Christians as if to family members. These images do not completely capture our love of God and of the Church, but they transform our vision. How does it change our understanding of sin, for example, if we think of it as a betrayal or the damaging of a relationship, rather than simply failing to follow rules? What would the Sacrament of Penance mean to you if you saw it as an opportunity to reconcile with a loved one, rather than as an obligation?

September 19

JEREMIAH 5

Run back and forth through
the streets of Jerusalem,
look and take note!
Search her squares to see
if you can find a man,
one who does justice
and seeks truth;
that I may pardon her.
2Though they say, "As the LORD lives,"
yet they swear falsely.
3O LORD, do not your eyes look for truth?
You have struck them down,
but they felt no anguish;
you have consumed them,
but they refused to take correction.
They have made their faces harder than rock;
they have refused to repent.

4Then I said, "These are only the poor,
they have no sense;
for they do not know the way of the LORD,
the law of their God.
5I will go to the great,
and will speak to them;
for they know the way of the LORD,
the law of their God."
But they all alike had broken the yoke,
they had burst the bonds.

6Therefore a lion from the forest shall slay them,
a wolf from the desert shall
destroy them.
A leopard is watching against their cities,
every one who goes out of them shall be
torn in pieces;
because their transgressions are many,
their apostasies are great.
7"How can I pardon you?
Your children have forsaken me,
and have sworn by those who are no gods.
When I fed them to the full,
they committed adultery
and trooped to the houses of harlots.
8They were well-fed lusty stallions,
each neighing for his neighbor's wife.
9Shall I not punish them for these things?
says the LORD;
and shall I not avenge myself
on a nation such as this?

10"Go up through her vine-rows and destroy,
but make not a full end;
strip away her branches,
for they are not the LORD's.
11For the house of Israel and the house
of Judah
have been utterly faithless to me,
says the LORD.
12They have spoken falsely of the LORD,
and have said, 'He will do nothing;
no evil will come upon us,
nor shall we see sword or famine.

13The prophets will become wind;
the word is not in them.
Thus shall it be done to them!'"

14Therefore thus says the LORD, the God of hosts:
"Because they have spoken this word,
behold, I am making my words in your mouth a fire,
and this people wood, and the fire shall devour them.
15Behold, I am bringing upon you
a nation from afar, O house of Israel,
says the LORD.
It is an enduring nation,
it is an ancient nation,
a nation whose language you do not know,
nor can you understand what they say.
16Their quiver is like an open tomb,
they are all mighty men.
17They shall eat up your harvest and your food;
they shall eat up your sons and your daughters;
they shall eat up your flocks and your herds;
they shall eat up your vines and your fig trees;
your fortified cities in which you trust
they shall destroy with the sword."

18"But even in those days, says the LORD,
I will not make a full end of you. 19And
when your people say, 'Why has the LORD
our God done all these things to us?' you
shall say to them, 'As you have forsaken
me and served foreign gods in your land,
so you shall serve strangers in a land that
is not yours.'"

20Declare this in the house of Jacob,
proclaim it in Judah:
21"Hear this, O foolish and senseless people,
who have eyes, but see not,
who have ears, but hear not.
22Do you not fear me? says the LORD;
Do you not tremble before me?
I placed the sand as the bound for the sea,
a perpetual barrier which it cannot pass;
though the waves toss, they cannot prevail,
though they roar, they cannot pass over it.
23But this people has a stubborn and rebellious heart;
they have turned aside and gone away.
24They do not say in their hearts,
'Let us fear the LORD our God,
who gives the rain in its season,
the autumn rain and the spring rain,
and keeps for us
the weeks appointed for the harvest.'
25Your iniquities have turned these away,
and your sins have kept good from you.
26For wicked men are found among my people;
they lurk like fowlers lying in wait.
They set a trap;
they catch men.
27Like a basket full of birds,
their houses are full of treachery;
therefore they have become great and rich,
28 they have grown fat and sleek.
They know no bounds in deeds of wickedness;
they judge not with justice
the cause of the fatherless, to make it prosper,
and they do not defend the rights of the needy.
29Shall I not punish them for these things?
says the LORD,
and shall I not avenge myself
on a nation such as this?"

30An appalling and horrible thing
has happened in the land:
31the prophets prophesy falsely,
and the priests rule at their direction;
my people love to have it so,
but what will you do when the end comes?

6 Flee for safety, O people of Benjamin,
from the midst of Jerusalem!
Blow the trumpet in Teko′a,
and raise a signal on Beth″-hacche′rem;
for evil looms out of the north,
and great destruction.
2The comely and delicately bred I will destroy,
the daughter of Zion.
3Shepherds with their flocks shall come against her;
they shall pitch their tents around her,
they shall pasture, each in his place.

4"Prepare war against her;
up, and let us attack at noon!"
"Woe to us, for the day declines,
for the shadows of evening lengthen!"
5"Up, and let us attack by night,
and destroy her palaces!"

6For thus says the LORD of hosts:
"Hew down her trees;
cast up a siege mound against Jerusalem.
This is the city which must be punished;
there is nothing but oppression within her.
7As a well keeps its water fresh,
so she keeps fresh her wickedness;
violence and destruction are heard
within her;
sickness and wounds are ever before me.
8Be warned, O Jerusalem,
lest I be alienated from you;
lest I make you a desolation,
an uninhabited land."

9Thus says the LORD of hosts:
"Glean thoroughly as a vine
the remnant of Israel;
like a grape-gatherer pass your hand again
over its branches."
10To whom shall I speak and give warning,
that they may hear?
Behold, their ears are closed,
they cannot listen;
behold, the word of the LORD is to them an
object of scorn,
they take no pleasure in it.
11Therefore I am full of the wrath of the LORD;
I am weary of holding it in.
"Pour it out upon the children in the street,
and upon the gatherings of young men,
also;
both husband and wife shall be taken,
the old folk and the very aged.
12Their houses shall be turned over to others,
their fields and wives together;
for I will stretch out my hand
against the inhabitants of the land,"
says the LORD.
13"For from the least to the greatest of them,
every one is greedy for unjust gain;
and from prophet to priest,
every one deals falsely.
14They have healed the wound of my
people lightly,
saying, 'Peace, peace,'
when there is no peace.
15Were they ashamed when they committed
abomination?
No, they were not at all ashamed;
they did not know how to blush.
Therefore they shall fall among those
who fall;
at the time that I punish them, they shall
be overthrown,"
says the LORD.

16Thus says the LORD:
"Stand by the roads, and look,
and ask for the ancient paths,
where the good way is; and walk in it,
and find rest for your souls.
But they said, 'We will not walk in it.'
17I set watchmen over you, saying,
'Give heed to the sound of the trumpet!'
But they said, 'We will not give heed.'
18Therefore hear, O nations,
and know, O congregation, what will
happen to them.
19Hear, O earth; behold, I am bringing evil
upon this people,
the fruit of their devices,
because they have not given heed to my words;
and as for my law, they have rejected it.
20To what purpose does frankincense come
to me from Sheba,
or sweet cane from a distant land?
Your burnt offerings are not acceptable,
nor your sacrifices pleasing to me.
21Therefore thus says the LORD:
'Behold, I will lay before this people
stumbling blocks against which they
shall stumble;
fathers and sons together,
neighbor and friend shall perish.'"

22Thus says the LORD:
"Behold, a people is coming from the north
country,
a great nation is stirring from the farthest
parts of the earth.
23They lay hold on bow and spear,
they are cruel and have no mercy,

the sound of them is like the roaring sea;
they ride upon horses,
set in array as a man for battle,
against you, O daughter of Zion!"
24 We have heard the report of it,
our hands fall helpless;
anguish has taken hold of us,
pain as of a woman with labor pains.
25 Go not forth into the field,
nor walk on the road;
for the enemy has a sword,
terror is on every side.
26 O daughter of my people, put on sackcloth,
and roll in ashes;
make mourning as for an only son,
most bitter lamentation;
for suddenly the destroyer
will come upon us.
27 "I have made you an assayer and tester
among my people,
that you may know and assay their ways.
28 They are all stubbornly rebellious,
going about with slanders;
they are bronze and iron,
all of them act corruptly.
29 The bellows blow fiercely,
the lead is consumed by the fire;
in vain the refining goes on,
for the wicked are not removed.
30 Refuse silver they are called,
for the LORD has rejected them."

WISDOM 11

Wisdom prospered their works by the hand
of a holy prophet.
2 They journeyed through an uninhabited
wilderness,
and pitched their tents in untrodden places.
3 They withstood their enemies and fought
off their foes.
4 When they thirsted they called upon you,
and water was given them out of flinty rock,
and slaking of thirst from hard stone.
5 For through the very things by which their
enemies were punished,
they themselves received benefit in
their need.
6 Instead of the fountain of an ever-flowing
river,
stirred up and defiled with blood
7 in rebuke for the decree to slay the infants,
you gave them abundant water unexpectedly,
8 showing by their thirst at that time
how you punished their enemies.
9 For when they were tried, though they were
being disciplined in mercy,
they learned how the ungodly were
tormented when judged in wrath.
10 For you tested them as a father does
in warning,
but you examined the ungodly as a stern
king does in condemnation.
11 Whether absent or present, they were
equally distressed,
12 for a twofold grief possessed them,
and a groaning at the memory of what
had occurred.
13 For when they heard that through their
own punishments
the righteous had received benefit, they
perceived it was the Lord's doing.
14 For though they had mockingly rejected
him who long before had been cast
out and exposed,
at the end of the events they marveled
at him,
for their thirst was not like that of the
righteous.

2 CORINTHIANS 8

We want you to know, brethren, about the grace of God which has been shown in the churches of Macedonia, 2 for in a severe test of affliction, their abundance of joy and their extreme poverty have overflowed
in a wealth of liberality on their part. 3 For
they gave according to their means, as I
can testify, and beyond their means, of
their own free will, 4 begging us earnestly
for the favor of taking part in the relief of
the saints—5 and this, not as we expected,
but first they gave themselves to the Lord

and to us by the will of God. 6Accordingly
we have urged Titus that as he had already
made a beginning, he should also complete
among you this gracious work. 7Now as you
excel in everything—in faith, in utterance,
in knowledge, in all earnestness, and in
your love for us—see that you excel in this
gracious work also.

8I say this not as a command, but to prove
by the earnestness of others that your love
also is genuine. 9For you know the grace of
our Lord Jesus Christ, that though he was
rich, yet for your sake he became poor, so
that by his poverty you might become rich.
10And in this matter I give my advice: it is
best for you now to complete what a year
ago you began not only to do but to desire,
11so that your readiness in desiring it may be
matched by your completing it out of what
you have. 12For if the readiness is there, it
is acceptable according to what a man has,
not according to what he has not. 13I do not
mean that others should be eased and you
burdened, 14but that as a matter of equality
your abundance at the present time should
supply their want, so that their abundance
may supply your want, that there may be
equality. 15As it is written, "He who gathered
much had nothing over, and he who gathered little had no lack."

16But thanks be to God who puts the same
earnest care for you into the heart of Titus.
17For he not only accepted our appeal, but
being himself very earnest he is going to
you of his own accord. 18With him we are
sending the brother who is famous among
all the churches for his preaching of the
gospel; 19and not only that, but he has been
appointed by the churches to travel with us
in this gracious work which we are carrying
on, for the glory of the Lord and to show our
good will. 20We intend that no one should
blame us about this liberal gift which we
are administering, 21for we aim at what is
honorable not only in the Lord's sight but
also in the sight of men. 22And with them
we are sending our brother whom we have
often tested and found earnest in many
matters, but who is now more earnest
than ever because of his great confidence
in you. 23As for Titus, he is my partner
and fellow worker in your service; and as
for our brethren, they are messengers of
the churches, the glory of Christ. 24So give
proof, before the churches, of your love and
of our boasting about you to these men.

REFLECTION

It is easy to become overwhelmed by the evils in the world. We are tempted to despair. According to Jeremiah, the Israelites give way to this temptation and begin to doubt the presence of God and his justice. They say to themselves, "He will do nothing; no evil will come upon us" (Jer 5:12). The people decide that it is irrelevant whether they live a good life or a sinful one, since God does not seem to care. In the midst of our personal trials or tragic events in the world, we should remember that if we lose our fear of the Lord and our faith in God's justice, we ourselves can easily be led into sin. It often takes years of reflection, a new perspective, or even a prophetic voice for us to see how God's justice is working. In the Book of Wisdom, for example, it is in retrospect that the author has come to a deeper understanding of the exodus from Egypt. We, like the people at Corinth, need to be encouraged to persist in our works of love. Do you ever become discouraged and feel that God is indifferent? Will you have the patience to wait for God's justice to be revealed?

September 20

JEREMIAH 7

**The word that came to Jeremi′ah
from the LORD: 2"Stand in the
gate of the LORD's house, and
proclaim there this word, and say, Hear
the word of the LORD, all you men of
Judah who enter these gates to worship**
the LORD. 3Thus says the LORD of hosts, the
God of Israel, Amend your ways and your

doings, and I will let you dwell in this place.
4Do not trust in these deceptive words: 'This
is the temple of the LORD, the temple of the
LORD, the temple of the LORD.'

5"For if you truly amend your ways and
your doings, if you truly execute justice
one with another, 6if you do not oppress
the alien, the fatherless or the widow, or
shed innocent blood in this place, and if
you do not go after other gods to your own
hurt, 7then I will let you dwell in this place,
in the land that I gave of old to your fathers
for ever.

8"Behold, you trust in deceptive words
to no avail. 9Will you steal, murder,
commit adultery, swear falsely, burn
incense to Ba′al, and go after other gods
that you have not known, 10and then
come and stand before me in this house,
which is called by my name, and say, 'We
are delivered!'—only to go on doing all
these abominations? 11Has this house,
which is called by my name, become a
den of robbers in your eyes? Behold, I
myself have seen it, says the LORD. 12Go
now to my place that was in Shiloh, where
I made my name dwell at first, and see
what I did to it for the wickedness of my
people Israel. 13And now, because you
have done all these things, says the LORD,
and when I spoke to you persistently you
did not listen, and when I called you, you
did not answer, 14therefore I will do to the
house which is called by my name, and in
which you trust, and to the place which I
gave to you and to your fathers, as I did
to Shiloh. 15And I will cast you out of my
sight, as I cast out all your kinsmen, all
the offspring of E′phraim.

16"As for you, do not pray for this people,
or lift up cry or prayer for them, and do
not intercede with me, for I do not hear
you. 17Do you not see what they are doing
in the cities of Judah and in the streets of
Jerusalem? 18The children gather wood, the
fathers kindle fire, and the women knead
dough, to make cakes for the queen of
heaven; and they pour out drink offerings
to other gods, to provoke me to anger. 19Is
it I whom they provoke? says the LORD. Is
it not themselves, to their own confusion?
20Therefore thus says the Lord GOD: Behold,
my anger and my wrath will be poured out
on this place, upon man and beast, upon the
trees of the field and the fruit of the ground;
it will burn and not be quenched."

21Thus says the LORD of hosts, the God
of Israel: "Add your burnt offerings to your
sacrifices, and eat the flesh. 22For in the day
that I brought them out of the land of Egypt,
I did not speak to your fathers or command
them concerning burnt offerings and sacrifices. 23But this command I gave them,
'Obey my voice, and I will be your God,
and you shall be my people; and walk in all
the way that I command you, that it may be
well with you.' 24But they did not obey or
incline their ear, but walked in their own
counsels and the stubbornness of their
evil hearts, and went backward and not
forward. 25From the day that your fathers
came out of the land of Egypt to this day,
I have persistently sent all my servants the
prophets to them, day after day; 26yet they
did not listen to me, or incline their ear, but
stiffened their neck. They did worse than
their fathers.

27"So you shall speak all these words to
them, but they will not listen to you. You
shall call to them, but they will not answer
you. 28And you shall say to them, 'This is the
nation that did not obey the voice of the LORD
their God, and did not accept discipline;
truth has perished; it is cut off from their lips.
29Cut off your hair and cast it away;
  raise a lamentation on the bare heights,
for the LORD has rejected and forsaken
  the generation of his wrath.'

30"For the sons of Judah have done evil
in my sight, says the LORD; they have set
their abominations in the house which is
called by my name, to defile it. 31And they
have built the high place of To′pheth, which
is in the valley of the son of Hin′nom, to
burn their sons and their daughters in the
fire; which I did not command, nor did it
come into my mind. 32Therefore, behold,
the days are coming, says the LORD, when
it will no more be called To′pheth, or the
valley of the son of Hinnom, but the valley

of Slaughter: for they will bury in Topheth,
because there is no room elsewhere. 33And
the dead bodies of this people will be food
for the birds of the air, and for the beasts of
the earth; and none will frighten them away.
34And I will make to cease from the cities of
Judah and from the streets of Jerusalem the
voice of mirth and the voice of gladness, the
voice of the bridegroom and the voice of the
bride; for the land shall become a waste.

8 "At that time, says the LORD, the bones
of the kings of Judah, the bones of its
princes, the bones of the priests, the bones of
the prophets, and the bones of the inhabitants
of Jerusalem shall be brought out of their
tombs; 2and they shall be spread before the sun
and the moon and all the host of heaven, which
they have loved and served, which they have
gone after, and which they have sought and
worshiped; and they shall not be gathered or
buried; they shall be as dung on the surface of
the ground. 3Death shall be preferred to life by
all the remnant that remains of this evil family
in all the places where I have driven them, says
the LORD of hosts.

4"You shall say to them, Thus says the LORD:
When men fall, do they not rise again?
If one turns away, does he not return?
5Why then has this people turned away
in perpetual backsliding?
They hold fast to deceit,
they refuse to return.
6I have given heed and listened,
but they have not spoken rightly;
no man repents of his wickedness,
saying, 'What have I done?'
Every one turns to his own course,
like a horse plunging headlong into battle.
7Even the stork in the heavens
knows her times;
and the turtledove, swallow, and crane
keep the time of their coming;
but my people know not
the ordinance of the LORD.

8"How can you say, 'We are wise,
and the law of the LORD is with us'?
But, behold, the false pen of the scribes
has made it into a lie.
9The wise men shall be put to shame,
they shall be dismayed and taken;
behold, they have rejected the word of
the LORD,
and what wisdom is in them?
10Therefore I will give their wives
to others
and their fields to conquerors,
because from the least to the greatest
every one is greedy for unjust gain;
from prophet to priest
every one deals falsely.
11They have healed the wound of my
people lightly,
saying, 'Peace, peace,'
when there is no peace.
12Were they ashamed when they committed
abomination?
No, they were not at all ashamed;
they did not know how to blush.
Therefore they shall fall among the fallen;
when I punish them, they shall be
overthrown,
says the LORD.
13When I would gather them, says the LORD,
there are no grapes on the vine,
nor figs on the fig tree;
even the leaves are withered,
and what I gave them has passed away
from them."

14Why do we sit still?
Gather together, let us go into the
fortified cities
and perish there;
for the LORD our God has doomed
us to perish,
and has given us poisoned water to drink,
because we have sinned against the LORD.
15We looked for peace, but no good came,
for a time of healing, but behold, terror.

16"The snorting of their horses is heard
from Dan;
at the sound of the neighing of their
stallions
the whole land quakes.
They come and devour the land and
all that fills it,
the city and those who dwell in it.

[17]For behold, I am sending among
you serpents,
adders which cannot be charmed,
and they shall bite you,"
says the LORD.

[18]My grief is beyond healing,
my heart is sick within me.
[19]Listen, the cry of the daughter of my people
from the length and breadth of the
land:
"Is the LORD not in Zion?
Is her King not in her?"
"Why have they provoked me to anger with
their graven images,
and with their foreign idols?"
[20]"The harvest is past, the summer is ended,
and we are not saved."
[21]For the wound of the daughter of my
people my heart is wounded,
I mourn, and dismay has taken hold on me.

[22]Is there no balm in Gilead?
Is there no physician there?
Why then has the health of the daughter of
my people
not been restored?

WISDOM 11

[15]In return for their foolish and wicked
thoughts,
which led them astray to worship irrational
serpents and worthless animals,
you sent upon them a multitude of
irrational creatures to punish them,
[16]that they might learn that one is punished
by the very things by which he sins.
[17]For your all-powerful hand,
which created the world out of
formless matter,
did not lack the means to send upon them
a multitude of bears, or bold lions,
[18]or newly created unknown beasts full of rage,
or such as breathe out fiery breath,
or belch forth a thick pall of smoke,
or flash terrible sparks from their eyes;
[19]not only could their damage
exterminate men,
but the mere sight of them could kill
by fright.
[20]Even apart from these, men could fall at a
single breath
when pursued by justice
and scattered by the breath of your power.
But you have arranged all things by
measure and number and weight.

[21]For it is always in your power to show
great strength,
and who can withstand the might of your arm?
[22]Because the whole world before you is like
speck that tips the scales,
and like a drop of morning dew that falls
upon the ground.
[23]But you are merciful to all, for you can
do all things,
and you overlook men's sins, that they
may repent.
[24]For you love all things that exist,
and you loathe none of the things which
you have made,
for you would not have made anything if
you had hated it.
[25]How would anything have endured if you
had not willed it?
Or how would anything not called forth by
you have been preserved?
[26]You spare all things, for they are yours, O
Lord who love the living.

2 CORINTHIANS 9

Now it is superfluous for me to write to you about the offering for the saints, [2]for I know your readiness, of which I boast about you to the
people of Macedonia, saying that Acha'ia
has been ready since last year; and your
zeal has stirred up most of them. [3]But I am
sending the brethren so that our boasting
about you may not prove vain in this case,
so that you may be ready, as I said you
would be; [4]lest if some Macedonians come
with me and find that you are not ready, we
be humiliated—to say nothing of you—for
being so confident. [5]So I thought it necessary

to urge the brethren to go on to you before me, and arrange in advance for this gift you have promised, so that it may be ready not as an exaction but as a willing gift.

6The point is this: he who sows sparingly will also reap sparingly, and he who sows bountifully will also reap bountifully. 7Each one must do as he has made up his mind, not reluctantly or under compulsion, for God loves a cheerful giver. 8And God is able to provide you with every blessing in abundance, so that you may always have enough of everything and may provide in abundance for every good work. 9As it is written,

"He scatters abroad, he gives to the poor;
his righteousness endures for ever."

10He who supplies seed to the sower and bread for food will supply and multiply your resources and increase the harvest of your righteousness. 11You will be enriched in every way for great generosity, which through us will produce thanksgiving to God; 12for the rendering of this service not only supplies the wants of the saints but also overflows in many thanksgivings to God. 13Under the test of this service, you will glorify God by your obedience in acknowledging the gospel of Christ, and by the generosity of your contribution for them and for all others; 14while they long for you and pray for you, because of the surpassing grace of God in you. 15Thanks be to God for his inexpressible gift!

10 I, Paul, myself entreat you, by the meekness and gentleness of Christ—I who am humble when face to face with you, but bold to you when I am away!—2I beg of you that when I am present I may not have to show boldness with such confidence as I count on showing against some who suspect us of acting in worldly fashion. 3For though we live in the world we are not carrying on a worldly war, 4for the weapons of our warfare are not worldly but have divine power to destroy strongholds. 5We destroy arguments and every proud obstacle to the knowledge of God, and take every thought captive to obey Christ, 6being ready to punish every disobedience, when your obedience is complete.

REFLECTION

Throughout the Old Testament, idolatry is condemned; both Jeremiah and the Book of Wisdom denounce the worship of false gods in today's readings. We may think that this sin is irrelevant to the modern Christian, and even feel a sense of smugness when we read about how often the Israelites worshipped foreign gods. But idolatry is broader than what it might at first appear. Idolatry is, in a sense, the quintessential human sin because it is the worship of *anything* that is not God: money, accomplishment, or even family. The worst form of idolatry is pride, that is, the worship of oneself and the desire to make oneself the center of the universe. It is idolatry to define morality by our own standards and to attempt to be the final judge of what is meaningful in life. It is this kind of idolatry that might make us chafe at St. Paul's suggestion that we be completely obedient to God (see 2 Cor 10:5–6). Independence, persistence, and even rebelliousness are seen as virtues in our society, but certainly not obedience! True worship of God, however, entails obedience to him and is the only alternative to idolatry. Do you think of obedience to God or to the Church as a positive, active decision?

September 21

JEREMIAH 9

O that my head were waters,
and my eyes a fountain of tears,
that I might weep day and night
for the slain of the daughter of my people!
2O that I had in the desert
a wayfarers' lodging place,
that I might leave my people
and go away from them!
For they are all adulterers,
a company of treacherous men.

[3]They bend their tongue like a bow;
falsehood and not truth has grown strong in the land;
for they proceed from evil to evil,
and they do not know me, says the LORD.

[4]Let every one beware of his neighbor,
and put no trust in any brother;
for every brother is a supplanter,
and every neighbor goes about as a slanderer.
[5]Every one deceives his neighbor,
and no one speaks the truth;
they have taught their tongue to speak lies;
they commit iniquity and are too weary to repent.
[6]Heaping oppression upon oppression, and deceit upon deceit,
they refuse to know me, says the LORD.

[7]Therefore thus says the LORD of hosts:
"Behold, I will refine them and test them,
for what else can I do, because of my people?
[8]Their tongue is a deadly arrow;
it speaks deceitfully;
with his mouth each speaks peaceably to his neighbor,
but in his heart he plans an ambush for him.
[9]Shall I not punish them for these things? says the LORD;
and shall I not avenge myself
on a nation such as this?

[10]"Take up weeping and wailing for the mountains,
and a lamentation for the pastures of the wilderness,
because they are laid waste so that no one passes through,
and the lowing of cattle is not heard;
both the birds of the air and the beasts
have fled and are gone.
[11]I will make Jerusalem a heap of ruins,
a lair of jackals;
and I will make the cities of Judah a desolation,
without inhabitant."

[12]Who is the man so wise that he can
understand this? To whom has the mouth
of the LORD spoken, that he may declare it?
Why is the land ruined and laid waste like a
wilderness, so that no one passes through?
[13]And the LORD says: "Because they have
forsaken my law which I set before them,
and have not obeyed my voice, or walked
in accord with it, [14]but have stubbornly
followed their own hearts and have gone
after the Ba′als, as their fathers taught them.
[15]Therefore thus says the LORD of hosts, the
God of Israel: Behold, I will feed this people
with wormwood, and give them poisonous
water to drink. [16]I will scatter them among the
nations whom neither they nor their fathers
have known; and I will send the sword after
them, until I have consumed them."

[17]Thus says the LORD of hosts:
"Consider, and call for the mourning women to come;
send for the skilful women to come;
[18]let them make haste and raise a wailing over us,
that our eyes may run down with tears,
and our eyelids gush with water.
[19]For a sound of wailing is heard from Zion:
'How we are ruined!
We are utterly shamed,
because we have left the land,
because they have cast down our dwellings.' "

[20]Hear, O women, the word of the LORD,
and let your ear receive the word of his mouth;
teach to your daughters a lament,
and each to her neighbor a dirge.
[21]For death has come up into our windows,
it has entered our palaces,
cutting off the children from the streets
and the young men from the squares.
[22]Speak, "Thus says the LORD:
'The dead bodies of men shall fall
like dung upon the open field,
like sheaves after the reaper,
and none shall gather them.' "

23Thus says the LORD: "Let not the wise man
glory in his wisdom, let not the mighty man
glory in his might, let not the rich man glory
in his riches; 24but let him who glories glory
in this, that he understands and knows me,
that I am the LORD who practice steadfast
love, justice, and righteousness in the earth;
for in these things I delight, says the LORD."
25"Behold, the days are coming, says the
LORD, when I will punish all those who
are circumcised but yet uncircumcised—
26Egypt, Judah, E′dom, the sons of Ammon,
Moab, and all who dwell in the desert that
cut the corners of their hair; for all these
nations are uncircumcised, and all the
house of Israel is uncircumcised in heart."

10 Hear the word which the LORD speaks
to you, O house of Israel. 2Thus says
the LORD:

"Learn not the way of the nations,
nor be dismayed at the signs of the heavens
because the nations are dismayed at them,
3for the customs of the peoples are false.
A tree from the forest is cut down,
and worked with an axe by the hands of
a craftsman.
4Men deck it with silver and gold;
they fasten it with hammer and nails
so that it cannot move.
5Their idols are like scarecrows in a
cucumber field,
and they cannot speak;
they have to be carried,
for they cannot walk.
Be not afraid of them,
for they cannot do evil,
neither is it in them to do good."

6There is none like you, O LORD;
you are great, and your name is great
in might.
7Who would not fear you, O King of
the nations?
For this is your due;
for among all the wise ones of
the nations
and in all their kingdoms
there is none like you.
8They are both stupid and foolish;
the instruction of idols is but wood!
9Beaten silver is brought from Tar′shish,
and gold from U′phaz.
They are the work of the craftsman and of
the hands of the goldsmith;
their clothing is violet and purple;
they are all the work of skilled men.
10But the LORD is the true God;
he is the living God and the everlasting King.
At his wrath the earth quakes,
and the nations cannot endure
his indignation.

11Thus shall you say to them: "The gods
who did not make the heavens and the earth
shall perish from the earth and from under
the heavens."

12It is he who made the earth by his power,
who established the world by his wisdom,
and by his understanding stretched out
the heavens.
13When he utters his voice there is a tumult
of waters in the heavens,
and he makes the mist rise from the ends
of the earth.
He makes lightning for the rain,
and he brings forth the wind from
his storehouses.
14Every man is stupid and without
knowledge;
every goldsmith is put to shame by his idols;
for his images are false,
and there is no breath in them.
15They are worthless, a work of delusion;
at the time of their punishment they
shall perish.
16Not like these is he who is the portion
of Jacob,
for he is the one who formed all things,
and Israel is the tribe of his inheritance;
the LORD of hosts is his name.

17Gather up your bundle from the ground,
O you who dwell under siege!
18For thus says the LORD:
"Behold, I am slinging out the inhabitants
of the land
at this time,
and I will bring distress on them,
that they may feel it."

[19]Woe is me because of my hurt!
My wound is grievous.
But I said, "Truly this is an affliction,
and I must bear it."
[20]My tent is destroyed,
and all my cords are broken;
my children have gone from me,
and they are not;
there is no one to spread my tent again,
and to set up my curtains.
[21]For the shepherds are stupid,
and do not inquire of the LORD;
therefore they have not prospered,
and all their flock is scattered.

[22]Listen, a rumor! Behold, it comes!—
a great commotion out of the north
country
to make the cities of Judah a desolation,
a lair of jackals.

[23]I know, O LORD, that the way of man is not
in himself,
that it is not in man who walks to direct
his steps.
[24]Correct me, O LORD, but in just measure;
not in your anger, lest you bring me
to nothing.

[25]Pour out your wrath upon the nations that
know you not,
and upon the peoples that call not on
your name;
for they have devoured Jacob;
they have devoured him and
consumed him,
and have laid waste his habitation.

11 The word that came to Jeremi′ah
from the LORD: [2]"Hear the words
of this covenant, and speak to the men of
Judah and the inhabitants of Jerusalem.
[3]You shall say to them, Thus says the LORD,
the God of Israel: Cursed be the man who
does not heed the words of this covenant
[4]which I commanded your fathers when I
brought them out of the land of Egypt, from
the iron furnace, saying, Listen to my voice,
and do all that I command you. So shall
you be my people, and I will be your God,
[5]that I may perform the oath which I swore
to your fathers, to give them a land flowing
with milk and honey, as at this day." Then I
answered, "So be it, LORD."
[6]And the LORD said to me, "Proclaim all
these words in the cities of Judah, and in
the streets of Jerusalem: Hear the words of
this covenant and do them. [7]For I solemnly
warned your fathers when I brought them
up out of the land of Egypt, warning them
persistently, even to this day, saying, Obey my
voice. [8]Yet they did not obey or incline their
ear, but every one walked in the stubbornness
of his evil heart. Therefore I brought upon
them all the words of this covenant, which I
commanded them to do, but they did not."

WISDOM 12

For your immortal spirit is in all things.
[2]Therefore you correct little by little those
who trespass,
and remind and warn them of the things
wherein they sin,
that they may be freed from wickedness
and put their trust in you, O Lord.

[3]Those who dwelt of old in your holy land
[4]you hated for their detestable practices,
their works of sorcery and unholy rites,
[5]their merciless slaughter of children,
and their sacrificial feasting on human
flesh and blood.
These initiates from the midst of a
heathen cult,
[6]these parents who murder helpless lives,
you wanted to destroy by the hands of
our fathers,
[7]that the land most precious of all to you
might receive a worthy colony of the
servants of God.
[8]But even these you spared, since they were
but men,
and sent wasps as forerunners of your army,
to destroy them little by little,
[9]though you were not unable to give the
ungodly into the hands of the
righteous in battle,
or to destroy them at one blow by dread
wild beasts or your stern word.

10But judging them little by little you gave
them a chance to repent,
though you were not unaware that their
origin was evil
and their wickedness inborn,
and that their way of thinking would
never change.
11For they were an accursed race from
the beginning,
and it was not through fear of any one that
you left them unpunished for their sins.

12For who will say, "What have you done?"
Or who will resist your judgment?
Who will accuse you for the destruction of
nations which you made?
Or who will come before you to plead as an
advocate for unrighteous men?
13For neither is there any god besides you,
whose care is for all men,
to whom you should prove that you have
not judged unjustly;
14nor can any king or monarch confront you
about those whom you have punished.

---

2 CORINTHIANS 10

**7Look at what is before your
eyes. If any one is confident
that he is Christ's, let him remind himself that as he is Christ's, so are we. 8For**
even if I boast a little too much of our authority, which the Lord gave for building
you up and not for destroying you, I shall
not be put to shame. 9I would not seem to be
frightening you with letters. 10For they say,
"His letters are weighty and strong, but his
bodily presence is weak, and his speech of
no account." 11Let such people understand
that what we say by letter when absent, we
do when present. 12Not that we venture to
class or compare ourselves with some of
those who commend themselves. But when
they measure themselves by one another,
and compare themselves with one another,
they are without understanding.
13But we will not boast beyond limit, but
will keep to the limits God has apportioned
us, to reach even to you. 14For we are not
overextending ourselves, as though we did
not reach you; we were the first to come all the
way to you with the gospel of Christ. 15We do
not boast beyond limit, in other men's labors;
but our hope is that as your faith increases,
our field among you may be greatly enlarged,
16so that we may preach the gospel in lands
beyond you, without boasting of work already
done in another's field. 17"Let him who boasts,
boast of the Lord." 18For it is not the man who
commends himself that is accepted, but the
man whom the Lord commends.
11 I wish you would bear with me in a
little foolishness. Do bear with me! 2I
feel a divine jealousy for you, for I betrothed
you to Christ to present you as a pure bride
to her one husband. 3But I am afraid that
as the serpent deceived Eve by his cunning,
your thoughts will be led astray from a
sincere and pure devotion to Christ. 4For if
some one comes and preaches another Jesus
than the one we preached, or if you receive
a different spirit from the one you received,
or if you accept a different gospel from the
one you accepted, you submit to it readily
enough. 5I think that I am not in the least
inferior to these superlative apostles. 6Even
if I am unskilled in speaking, I am not in
knowledge; in every way we have made this
plain to you in all things.
7Did I commit a sin in abasing myself so
that you might be exalted, because I preached
God's gospel without cost to you? 8I robbed
other churches by accepting support from
them in order to serve you. 9And when I was
with you and was in want, I did not burden
any one, for my needs were supplied by the
brethren who came from Macedonia. So I
refrained and will refrain from burdening
you in any way. 10As the truth of Christ is in
me, this boast of mine shall not be silenced in
the regions of Acha′ia. 11And why? Because I
do not love you? God knows I do!
12And what I do I will continue to do, in
order to undermine the claim of those who
would like to claim that in their boasted
mission they work on the same terms as we
do. 13For such men are false apostles, deceitful
workmen, disguising themselves as apostles

of Christ. 14 And no wonder, for even Satan
disguises himself as an angel of light. 15 So
it is not strange if his servants also disguise
themselves as servants of righteousness.
Their end will correspond to their deeds.

REFLECTION

Both St. Paul and Jeremiah tell us in today's readings to boast in the Lord and not in our own wisdom, might, or riches. Jeremiah says that, instead, we ought to glory in the Lord who is just and righteous and who "practice[s] steadfast love" (Jer 9:24). What sort of a boast is this? These qualities would not look very good on a résumé or college application. Nevertheless, the God who is all-wise and almighty and who possesses everything tells us to boast in his love for us and our love for him. We are being asked, therefore, not only to put aside our own pride, but also to change the way we judge what is valuable. God's "steadfast love" is, by his own reckoning, his most glorious quality, and so it should be with us. We are even told what this steadfast love looks like in practice. For example, despite the Israelites' repeated failures, God will not abandon them but correct them (see v. 7). The Book of Wisdom also tells us about God's patience in guiding everyone "little by little" (Wis 12:2). How can you imitate God's patient love, especially when you are serving as a role model, teacher, or parent?

September 22

JEREMIAH 11

9 Again the LORD said to me,
"There is revolt among the men
of Judah and the inhabitants
of Jerusalem. 10 They have turned back
to the iniquities of their forefathers, who
refused to hear my words; they have gone
after other gods to serve them; the house of
Israel and the house of Judah have broken
my covenant which I made with their
fathers. 11 Therefore, thus says the LORD,
Behold, I am bringing evil upon them which
they cannot escape; though they cry to me,
I will not listen to them. 12 Then the cities of
Judah and the inhabitants of Jerusalem will
go and cry to the gods to whom they burn
incense, but they cannot save them in the
time of their trouble. 13 For your gods have
become as many as your cities, O Judah;
and as many as the streets of Jerusalem are
the altars you have set up to shame, altars to
burn incense to Ba′al.

14 "Therefore do not pray for this people,
or lift up a cry or prayer on their behalf, for
I will not listen when they call to me in the
time of their trouble. 15 What right has my
beloved in my house, when she has done vile
deeds? Can vows and sacrificial flesh avert
your doom? Can you then exult? 16 The LORD
once called you, 'A green olive tree, fair with
excellent fruit'; but with the roar of a great
tempest he will set fire to it, and its branches
will be consumed. 17 The LORD of hosts, who
planted you, has pronounced evil against you,
because of the evil which the house of Israel
and the house of Judah have done, provoking
me to anger by burning incense to Ba′al."

18 The LORD made it known to me and
    I knew;
  then you showed me their evil deeds.
19 But I was like a gentle lamb
  led to the slaughter.
I did not know it was against me
  they devised schemes, saying,
"Let us destroy the tree with its fruit,
  let us cut him off from the land of
    the living,
  that his name be remembered no more."
20 But, O LORD of hosts, who judge
    righteously,
  who test the heart and the mind,
let me see your vengeance upon them,
  for to you have I committed my cause.

21 Therefore thus says the LORD concerning
the men of An′athoth, who seek your life, and
say, "Do not prophesy in the name of the LORD,
or you will die by our hand"—22 therefore thus
says the LORD of hosts: "Behold, I will punish
them; the young men shall die by the sword;

their sons and their daughters shall die by famine; [23]and none of them shall be left. For I will bring evil upon the men of An′athoth, the year of their punishment."

12 Righteous are you, O LORD, when I
complain to you;
yet I would plead my case before you.
Why does the way of the wicked prosper?
Why do all who are treacherous thrive?
2 You plant them, and they take root;
they grow and bring forth fruit;
you are near in their mouth
and far from their heart.
3 But you, O LORD, know me;
you see me, and test my mind toward you.
Pull them out like sheep for the slaughter,
and set them apart for the day of slaughter.
4 How long will the land mourn,
and the grass of every field wither?
For the wickedness of those who dwell in it
the beasts and the birds are swept away,
because men said, "He will not see our
latter end."

5 "If you have raced with men on foot, and
they have wearied you,
how will you compete with horses?
And if in a safe land you fall down,
how will you do in the jungle of
the Jordan?
6 For even your brothers and the house of
your father,
even they have dealt treacherously
with you;
they are in full cry after you;
believe them not,
though they speak fair words to you."

7 "I have forsaken my house,
I have abandoned my heritage;
I have given the beloved of my soul
into the hands of her enemies.
8 My heritage has become to me
like a lion in the forest,
she has lifted up her voice against me;
therefore I hate her.
9 Is my heritage to me like a speckled
bird of prey?
Are the birds of prey against her
round about?
Go, assemble all the wild beasts;
bring them to devour.
10 Many shepherds have destroyed
my vineyard,
they have trampled down my portion,
they have made my pleasant portion
a desolate wilderness.
11 They have made it a desolation;
desolate, it mourns to me.
The whole land is made desolate,
but no man lays it to heart.
12 Upon all the bare heights in the desert
destroyers have come;
for the sword of the LORD devours
from one end of the land to the other;
no flesh has peace.
13 They have sown wheat and have reaped
thorns,
they have tired themselves out but
profit nothing.
They shall be ashamed of their harvests
because of the fierce anger of the LORD."

14 Thus says the LORD concerning all my
evil neighbors who touch the heritage
which I have given my people Israel to
inherit: "Behold, I will pluck them up from
their land, and I will pluck up the house
of Judah from among them. 15 And after I
have plucked them up, I will again have
compassion on them, and I will bring them
again each to his heritage and each to his
land. 16 And it shall come to pass, if they
will diligently learn the ways of my people,
to swear by my name, 'As the LORD lives,'
even as they taught my people to swear
by Ba′al, then they shall be built up in the
midst of my people. 17 But if any nation will
not listen, then I will utterly pluck it up and
destroy it, says the LORD."

13 Thus said the LORD to me, "Go and
buy a linen waistcloth, and put it on
your loins, and do not dip it in water." 2 So I
bought a waistcloth according to the word
of the LORD, and put it on my loins. 3 And
the word of the LORD came to me a second
time, 4 "Take the waistcloth which you have
bought, which is upon your loins, and arise,
go to the Euphra′tes, and hide it there in a
cleft of the rock." 5 So I went, and hid it by
the Euphra′tes, as the LORD commanded

me. 6And after many days the LORD said
to me, "Arise, go to the Euphra´tes, and
take from there the waistcloth which I
commanded you to hide there." 7Then I
went to the Euphra´tes, and dug, and I took
the waistcloth from the place where I had
hidden it. And behold, the waistcloth was
spoiled; it was good for nothing.

8Then the word of the LORD came to me:
9"Thus says the LORD: Even so will I spoil
the pride of Judah and the great pride of
Jerusalem. 10This evil people, who refuse
to hear my words, who stubbornly follow
their own heart and have gone after other
gods to serve them and worship them,
shall be like this waistcloth, which is good
for nothing. 11For as the waistcloth clings
to the loins of a man, so I made the whole
house of Israel and the whole house of
Judah cling to me, says the LORD, that they
might be for me a people, a name, a praise,
and a glory, but they would not listen.

12"You shall speak to them this word:
'Thus says the LORD, the God of Israel,
"Every jar shall be filled with wine."'
And they will say to you, 'Do we not
indeed know that every jar will be filled
with wine?' 13Then you shall say to them,
'Thus says the LORD: Behold, I will fill
with drunkenness all the inhabitants of
this land: the kings who sit on David's
throne, the priests, the prophets, and all
the inhabitants of Jerusalem. 14And I will
dash them one against another, fathers and
sons together, says the LORD. I will not pity
or spare or have compassion, that I should
not destroy them.'"

15Hear and give ear; be not proud,
for the LORD has spoken.
16Give glory to the LORD your God
before he brings darkness,
before your feet stumble
on the twilight mountains,
and while you look for light
he turns it into gloom
and makes it deep darkness.
17But if you will not listen,
my soul will weep in secret for
your pride;
my eyes will weep bitterly and run down
with tears,
because the LORD's flock has been
taken captive.

18Say to the king and the queen mother:
"Take a lowly seat,
for your beautiful crown
has come down from your head."
19The cities of the Neg´eb are shut up,
with none to open them;
all Judah is taken into exile,
wholly taken into exile.

20"Lift up your eyes and see
those who come from the north.
Where is the flock that was given you,
your beautiful flock?
21What will you say when they set as head
over you
those whom you yourself have taught
to be friends to you?
Will not pangs take hold of you,
like those of a woman with labor pains?
22And if you say in your heart,
'Why have these things come upon me?'
it is for the greatness of your iniquity
that your skirts are lifted up,
and you suffer violence.
23Can the Ethiopian change his skin
or the leopard his spots?
Then also you can do good
who are accustomed to do evil.
24I will scatter you like chaff
driven by the wind from the desert.
25This is your lot,
the portion I have measured out to you,
says the LORD,
because you have forgotten me
and trusted in lies.
26I myself will lift up your skirts over
your face,
and your shame will be seen.
27I have seen your abominations,
your adulteries and neighings, your
lewd harlotries,
on the hills in the field.
Woe to you, O Jerusalem!
How long will it be
before you are made clean?"

WISDOM 12

15You are righteous and rule all things righteously,
deeming it alien to your power
to condemn him who does not deserve to be punished.
16For your strength is the source of righteousness,
and your sovereignty over all causes you to spare all.
17For you show your strength when men doubt the completeness of your power,
and rebuke any insolence among those who know it.
18You who are sovereign in strength judge with mildness,
and with great forbearance you govern us;
for you have power to act whenever you choose.

19Through such works you have taught your people
that the righteous man must be kind,
and you have filled your sons with good hope,
because you give repentance for sins.
20For if you punished with such great care and indulgence
the enemies of your servants and those deserving of death,
granting them time and opportunity to give up their wickedness,
21with what strictness you have judged your sons,
to whose fathers you gave oaths and covenants full of good promises!
22So while chastening us you scourge our enemies ten thousand times more,
so that we may meditate upon your goodness when we judge,
and when we are judged we may expect mercy.

23Therefore those who in folly of life lived unrighteously
you tormented through their own abominations.
24For they went far astray on the paths of error,
accepting as gods those animals which even their enemies despised;
they were deceived like foolish infants.
25Therefore, as to thoughtless children,
you sent your judgment to mock them.
26But those who have not heeded the warning of light rebukes
will experience the deserved judgment of God.
27For when in their suffering they became incensed
at those creatures which they had thought to be gods, being punished by means of them,
they saw and recognized as the true God him whom they had before refused to know.
Therefore the utmost condemnation came upon them.

2 CORINTHIANS 11

16I repeat, let no one think me foolish; but even if you do, accept me as a fool, so that I too may boast a little. 17(What I am saying I say not with the Lord's authority but as a fool, in this boastful confidence;
18since many boast of worldly things, I too
will boast.) 19For you gladly bear with fools,
being wise yourselves! 20For you bear it if a
man makes slaves of you, or preys upon you,
or takes advantage of you, or puts on airs,
or strikes you in the face. 21To my shame, I
must say, we were too weak for that!

But whatever any one dares to boast of—I am speaking as a fool—I also dare to boast of
that. 22Are they Hebrews? So am I. Are they
Israelites? So am I. Are they descendants
of Abraham? So am I. 23Are they servants
of Christ? I am a better one—I am talking like a madman—with far greater labors, far more imprisonments, with countless
beatings, and often near death. 24Five times
I have received at the hands of the Jews the
forty lashes less one. 25Three times I have

been beaten with rods; once I was stoned. Three times I have been shipwrecked; a night and a day I have been adrift at sea;
[26]on frequent journeys, in danger from rivers, danger from robbers, danger from my own people, danger from Gentiles, danger in the city, danger in the wilderness, danger at sea, danger from false brethren;
[27]in toil and hardship, through many a sleepless night, in hunger and thirst, often without food, in cold and exposure.
[28]And, apart from other things, there is the daily pressure upon me of my anxiety for all the churches.
[29]Who is weak, and I am not weak? Who is made to fall, and I am not indignant?

[30]If I must boast, I will boast of the things that show my weakness.
[31]The God and Father of the Lord Jesus, he who is blessed for ever, knows that I do not lie.
[32]At Damascus, the governor under King Ar′etas guarded the city of Damascus in order to seize me,
[33]but I was let down in a basket through a window in the wall, and escaped his hands.

REFLECTION

At Jeremiah 11:18–20 there is a change in tone. Jeremiah turns from speaking about the trials and punishments of the people and speaks directly to God about his own suffering, specifically, a plot against his life. This passage may sound familiar because it is also understood to refer to Christ's suffering. This is the nature of biblical prophecy; by the Spirit, a text may have a meaning in its own time and place but also foreshadow future events or enrich our understanding of them. One of the links between Christ's suffering and Jeremiah's is each man's obscurity. Jeremiah's foes want to kill him and erase any memory of him (see Jer 11:19). Likewise, it seemed that Jesus, a poor prophet from Nazareth, would soon be forgotten after his Death. But despite their obscurity, both Jeremiah and Jesus are being remembered as we read these passages thousands of years later. St. Paul's so-called "boasting" is also a boasting about his obscurity and lowliness. He prides himself on having been shipwrecked and beaten (see 2 Cor 11:25). We should remind ourselves, therefore, that acts done in love will be remembered in eternity, even if not on earth. What seems obscure now is glorious in God's sight. Do you have the fortitude to do what is right, even if it goes unnoticed in this life?

September 23

JEREMIAH 14

The word of the Lord which came to Jeremi′ah concerning the drought:

[2]"Judah mourns
and her gates languish;
her people lament on the ground,
and the cry of Jerusalem goes up.
[3]Her nobles send their servants for water;
they come to the cisterns,
they find no water,
they return with their vessels empty;
they are ashamed and confounded
and cover their heads.
[4]Because of the ground which is dismayed,
since there is no rain on the land,
the farmers are ashamed,
they cover their heads.
[5]Even the deer in the field forsakes her newborn fawn
because there is no grass.
[6]The wild donkeys stand on the bare heights,
they pant for air like jackals;
their eyes fail
because there is no herbage.

[7]"Though our iniquities testify against us,
act, O Lord, for your name's sake;
for our backslidings are many,
we have sinned against you.
[8]O you hope of Israel,
its savior in time of trouble,
why should you be like a stranger in the land,
like a wayfarer who turns aside to linger for a night?

9Why should you be like a man confused,
like a mighty man who cannot save?
Yet you, O LORD, are in the midst of us,
and we are called by your name;
leave us not."

10Thus says the LORD concerning this people:
"They have loved to wander thus,
they have not restrained their feet;
therefore the LORD does not accept them,
now he will remember their iniquity
and punish their sins."

11The LORD said to me: "Do not pray for
the welfare of this people. 12Though they
fast, I will not hear their cry, and though
they offer burnt offering and cereal
offering, I will not accept them; but I will
consume them by the sword, by famine,
and by pestilence."

13Then I said: "Ah, Lord GOD, behold,
the prophets say to them, 'You shall not
see the sword, nor shall you have famine,
but I will give you assured peace in this
place.'" 14And the LORD said to me: "The
prophets are prophesying lies in my name;
I did not send them, nor did I command
them or speak to them. They are prophesying to you a lying vision, worthless
divination, and the deceit of their own
minds. 15Therefore thus says the LORD
concerning the prophets who prophesy in
my name although I did not send them,
and who say, 'Sword and famine shall not
come on this land': By sword and famine
those prophets shall be consumed. 16And
the people to whom they prophesy shall be
cast out in the streets of Jerusalem, victims
of famine and sword, with none to bury
them—them, their wives, their sons, and
their daughters. For I will pour out their
wickedness upon them.

17"You shall say to them this word:
'Let my eyes run down with tears night
and day,
and let them not cease,
for the virgin daughter of my people is
struck down with a great wound,
with a very grievous blow.
18If I go out into the field,
behold, those slain by the sword!
And if I enter the city,
behold, the diseases of famine!
For both prophet and priest ply their trade
through the land,
and have no knowledge.'"

19Have you utterly rejected Judah?
Does your soul loathe Zion?
Why have you struck us down
so that there is no healing for us?
We looked for peace, but no good came;
for a time of healing, but behold, terror.
20We acknowledge our wickedness, O LORD,
and the iniquity of our fathers,
for we have sinned against you.
21Do not spurn us, for your name's sake;
do not dishonor your glorious throne;
remember and do not break your
covenant with us.
22Are there any among the false gods of the
nations that can bring rain?
Or can the heavens give showers?
Are you not he, O LORD our God?
We set our hope on you,
for you do all these things.

15 Then the LORD said to me, "Though
Moses and Samuel stood before me,
yet my heart would not turn toward this
people. Send them out of my sight, and let
them go! 2And when they ask you, 'Where
shall we go?' you shall say to them, 'Thus
says the LORD:
"Those who are for pestilence,
to pestilence,
and those who are for the sword,
to the sword;
those who are for famine,
to famine,
and those who are for captivity,
to captivity."'

3"I will appoint over them four kinds of
destroyers, says the LORD: the sword to
slay, the dogs to tear, and the birds of the
air and the beasts of the earth to devour
and destroy. 4And I will make them a horror to all the kingdoms of the earth because
of what Manas'seh the son of Hezeki'ah,
king of Judah, did in Jerusalem.

[5]"Who will have pity on you, O Jerusalem,
or who will bemoan you?
Who will turn aside
to ask about your welfare?
[6]You have rejected me, says the LORD,
you keep going backward;
so I have stretched out my hand against you
and destroyed you;—
I am weary of relenting.
[7]I have winnowed them with a winnowing
fork
in the gates of the land;
I have bereaved them, I have destroyed
my people;
they did not turn from their ways.
[8]I have made their widows more in number
than the sand of the seas;
I have brought against the mothers of
young men
a destroyer at noonday;
I have made anguish and terror
fall upon them suddenly.
[9]She who bore seven has languished;
she has swooned away;
her sun went down while it was yet day;
she has been shamed and disgraced.
And the rest of them I will give to the sword
before their enemies,
says the LORD."

[10]Woe is me, my mother, that you bore
me, a man of strife and contention to the
whole land! I have not lent, nor have I
borrowed, yet all of them curse me. [11]So
let it be, O LORD, if I have not entreated
you for their good, if I have not pleaded
with you on behalf of the enemy in the
time of trouble and in the time of distress! [12]Can one break iron, iron from the
north, and bronze?

[13]"Your wealth and your treasures I will
give as spoil, without price, for all your sins,
throughout all your territory. [14]I will make
you serve your enemies in a land which
you do not know, for in my anger a fire is
kindled which shall burn for ever."

[15]O LORD, you know;
remember me and visit me,
and take vengeance for me on
my persecutors.
In your forbearance take me not away;
know that for your sake I bear reproach.
[16]Your words were found, and I ate them,
and your words became to me a joy
and the delight of my heart;
for I am called by your name,
O LORD, God of hosts.
[17]I did not sit in the company
of merrymakers,
nor did I rejoice;
I sat alone, because your hand was
upon me,
for you had filled me with indignation.
[18]Why is my pain unceasing,
my wound incurable,
refusing to be healed?
Will you be to me like a deceitful brook,
like waters that fail?

[19]Therefore thus says the LORD:
"If you return, I will restore you,
and you shall stand before me.
If you utter what is precious, and not what
is worthless,
you shall be as my mouth.
They shall turn to you,
but you shall not turn to them.
[20]And I will make you to this people
a fortified wall of bronze;
they will fight against you,
but they shall not prevail over you,
for I am with you
to save you and deliver you, says the LORD.
[21]I will deliver you out of the hand of the
wicked,
and redeem you from the grasp of the
ruthless."

16 The word of the LORD came to me:
[2]"You shall not take a wife, nor shall
you have sons or daughters in this place. [3]For
thus says the LORD concerning the sons and
daughters who are born in this place, and
concerning the mothers who bore them and
the fathers who begot them in this land: [4]They
shall die of deadly diseases. They shall not be
lamented, nor shall they be buried; they shall
be as dung on the surface of the ground. They
shall perish by the sword and by famine, and
their dead bodies shall be food for the birds of
the air and for the beasts of the earth.

5“For thus says the LORD: Do not enter
the house of mourning, or go to lament,
or bemoan them; for I have taken away
my peace from this people, says the LORD,
my steadfast love and mercy. 6Both great
and small shall die in this land; they shall
not be buried, and no one shall lament
for them or cut himself or make himself
bald for them. 7No one shall break bread
for the mourner, to comfort him for the
dead; nor shall any one give him the cup
of consolation to drink for his father or his
mother. 8You shall not go into the house of
feasting to sit with them, to eat and drink.
9For thus says the LORD of hosts, the God
of Israel: Behold, I will make to cease from
this place, before your eyes and in your
days, the voice of mirth and the voice of
gladness, the voice of the bridegroom and
the voice of the bride.

10“And when you tell this people all these
words, and they say to you, ‘Why has the
LORD pronounced all this great evil against
us? What is our iniquity? What is the sin
that we have committed against the LORD
our God?’ 11then you shall say to them:
‘Because your fathers have forsaken me,
says the LORD, and have gone after other
gods and have served and worshiped them,
and have forsaken me and have not kept
my law, 12and because you have done worse
than your fathers, for behold, every one of
you follows his stubborn evil will, refusing
to listen to me; 13therefore I will hurl you out
of this land into a land which neither you
nor your fathers have known, and there you
shall serve other gods day and night, for I
will show you no favor.’

14“Therefore, behold, the days are coming,
says the LORD, when it shall no longer be
said, ‘As the LORD lives who brought up the
sons of Israel out of the land of Egypt,’ 15but
‘As the LORD lives who brought up the sons
of Israel out of the north country and out of
all the countries where he had driven them.’
For I will bring them back to their own land
which I gave to their fathers.

16“Behold, I am sending for many fishers,
says the LORD, and they shall catch them;
and afterwards I will send for many hunters,
and they shall hunt them from every mountain and every hill, and out of the clefts of the
rocks. 17For my eyes are upon all their ways;
they are not hidden from me, nor is their
iniquity concealed from my eyes. 18And I
will doubly recompense their iniquity and
their sin, because they have polluted my
land with the carcasses of their detestable
idols, and have filled my inheritance with
their abominations.”

19O LORD, my strength and my stronghold,
my refuge in the day of trouble,
to you shall the nations come
from the ends of the earth and say:
“Our fathers have inherited nothing but lies,
worthless things in which there is
no profit.
20Can man make for himself gods?
Such are no gods!”

21“Therefore, behold, I will make them
know, this once I will make them know my
power and my might, and they shall know
that my name is the LORD.”

WISDOM 13

For all men who were ignorant of God were
foolish by nature;
and they were unable from the good things
that are seen to know him who exists,
nor did they recognize the craftsman while
paying heed to his works;
2but they supposed that either fire or wind
or swift air,
or the circle of the stars, or turbulent water,
or the luminaries of heaven were the gods
that rule the world.
3If through delight in the beauty of these
things men assumed them to be gods,
let them know how much better than these
is their Lord,
for the author of beauty created them.
4And if men were amazed at their power
and working,
let them perceive from them
how much more powerful is he who
formed them.

5For from the greatness and beauty of
created things
comes a corresponding perception of
their Creator.
6Yet these men are little to be blamed,
for perhaps they go astray
while seeking God and desiring to find him.
7For as they live among his works they keep
searching,
and they trust in what they see, because the
things that are seen are beautiful.
8Yet again, not even they are to be excused;
9for if they had the power to know so much
that they could investigate the world,
how did they fail to find sooner the Lord of
these things?

---

2 CORINTHIANS 12

**I must boast; there is nothing
to be gained by it, but I will go
on to visions and revelations of the Lord.
2I know a man in Christ who fourteen**
years ago was caught up to the third heaven—
whether in the body or out of the body I do
not know, God knows. 3And I know that this
man was caught up into Paradise—whether
in the body or out of the body I do not know,
God knows—4and he heard things that
cannot be told, which man may not utter.
5On behalf of this man I will boast, but on
my own behalf I will not boast, except of
my weaknesses. 6Though if I wish to boast,
I shall not be a fool, for I shall be speaking
the truth. But I refrain from it, so that no one
may think more of me than he sees in me or
hears from me. 7And to keep me from being
too elated by the abundance of revelations, a
thorn was given me in the flesh, a messenger
of Satan, to harass me, to keep me from
being too elated. 8Three times I begged the
Lord about this, that it should leave me;
9but he said to me, "My grace is sufficient
for you, for my power is made perfect in
weakness." I will all the more gladly boast
of my weaknesses, that the power of Christ
may rest upon me. 10For the sake of Christ,
then, I am content with weaknesses, insults,
hardships, persecutions, and calamities; for
when I am weak, then I am strong.
11I have been a fool! You forced me to it,
for I ought to have been commended by
you. For I am not at all inferior to these
superlative apostles, even though I am
nothing. 12The signs of a true apostle were
performed among you in all patience, with
signs and wonders and mighty works. 13For
in what were you less favored than the rest
of the churches, except that I myself did not
burden you? Forgive me this wrong!
14Here for the third time I am ready to come
to you. And I will not be a burden, for I seek
not what is yours but you; for children ought
not to lay up for their parents, but parents for
their children. 15I will most gladly spend and
be spent for your souls. If I love you the more,
am I to be loved the less? 16But granting that
I myself did not burden you, I was crafty, you
say, and got the better of you by guile. 17Did
I take advantage of you through any of those
whom I sent to you? 18I urged Titus to go,
and sent the brother with him. Did Titus take
advantage of you? Did we not act in the same
spirit? Did we not take the same steps?
19Have you been thinking all along that
we have been defending ourselves before
you? It is in the sight of God that we have
been speaking in Christ, and all for your
upbuilding, beloved. 20For I fear that perhaps
I may come and find you not what I wish, and
that you may find me not what you wish; that
perhaps there may be quarreling, jealousy,
anger, selfishness, slander, gossip, conceit,
and disorder. 21I fear that when I come again
my God may humble me before you, and
I may have to mourn over many of those
who sinned before and have not repented of
the impurity, immorality, and licentiousness
which they have practiced.

REFLECTION

In 2 Corinthians, St. Paul says that he repeatedly prayed to God to take away a thorn in his flesh (see 2 Cor 12:7–8). We do not know what this "thorn" refers to, but God answers Paul's prayer not by healing him but with the words "my grace is sufficient for you, for my power is made perfect in weakness" (v. 9). This command to rely on God's grace is not easy; not for Paul, and not for us. In Jeremiah, we can glimpse a world without grace. When the people are given over to their own wickedness, the results are dire (see Jer 14–15). Even reading about their suffering is difficult. The images in Jeremiah are suggestive, however, of what our own lives would be without the sacraments: we would have no water and thirst always (Baptism); the land would yield no food (the Eucharist); God would not listen to our cries for forgiveness (Penance); and we would have no solace in death (the Anointing of the Sick). Through these harsh images, we can begin to see that grace is not some added bonus to the Christian life. The Christian life, and all of life, is only possible in and by grace. Can the suffering of Israel help you to love the sacraments, which mediate God's grace, more deeply?

September 24

JEREMIAH 17

"The sin of Judah is written with a pen of iron; with a point of diamond it is engraved on the tablet of their heart, and on the horns of their altars,
2while their children remember their altars
and their Ashe′rim, beside every green tree,
and on the high hills, 3on the mountains in
the open country. Your wealth and all your
treasures I will give for spoil as the price of
your sin throughout all your territory. 4You
shall loosen your hand from your heritage
which I gave to you, and I will make you
serve your enemies in a land which you do
not know, for in my anger a fire is kindled
which shall burn for ever."

5Thus says the LORD:
"Cursed is the man who trusts in man
and makes flesh his arm,
whose heart turns away from the LORD.
6He is like a shrub in the desert,
and shall not see any good come.
He shall dwell in the parched places of
the wilderness,
in an uninhabited salt land.

7"Blessed is the man who trusts in the LORD,
whose trust is the LORD.
8He is like a tree planted by water,
that sends out its roots by the stream,
and does not fear when heat comes,
for its leaves remain green,
and is not anxious in the year of drought,
for it does not cease to bear fruit."

9The heart is deceitful above all things,
and desperately corrupt;
who can understand it?
10"I the LORD search the mind
and test the heart,
to give to every man according to his ways,
according to the fruit of his doings."

11Like the partridge that gathers a brood
which she did not hatch,
so is he who gets riches but not by right;
in the midst of his days they will leave him,
and at his end he will be a fool.

12A glorious throne set on high from
the beginning
is the place of our sanctuary.
13O LORD, the hope of Israel,
all who forsake you shall be put to shame;
those who turn away from you shall be
written in the earth,
for they have forsaken the LORD, the
fountain of living water.

14Heal me, O LORD, and I shall be healed;
save me, and I shall be saved;
for you are my praise.
15Behold, they say to me,
"Where is the word of the LORD?
Let it come!"
16I have not pressed you to send evil,
nor have I desired the day of disaster,
you know;
that which came out of my lips
was before your face.

17 Be not a terror to me;
you are my refuge in the day of evil.
18 Let those be put to shame who persecute me,
but let me not be put to shame;
let them be dismayed,
but let me not be dismayed;
bring upon them the day of evil;
destroy them with double destruction!

19 Thus said the LORD to me: "Go and
stand in the Benjamin Gate, by which the
kings of Judah enter and by which they
go out, and in all the gates of Jerusalem,
20 and say: 'Hear the word of the LORD,
you kings of Judah, and all Judah, and all
the inhabitants of Jerusalem, who enter
by these gates. 21 Thus says the LORD: Take
heed for the sake of your lives, and do not
bear a burden on the sabbath day or bring
it in by the gates of Jerusalem. 22 And do
not carry a burden out of your houses on
the sabbath or do any work, but keep the
sabbath day holy, as I commanded your
fathers. 23 Yet they did not listen or incline
their ear, but stiffened their neck, that they
might not hear and receive instruction.
24 " 'But if you listen to me, says the
LORD, and bring in no burden by the
gates of this city on the sabbath day, but
keep the sabbath day holy and do no work
on it, 25 then there shall enter by the gates
of this city kings who sit on the throne of
David, riding in chariots and on horses,
they and their princes, the men of Judah
and the inhabitants of Jerusalem; and
this city shall be inhabited for ever. 26 And
people shall come from the cities of Judah
and the places round about Jerusalem,
from the land of Benjamin, from the
Shephe′lah, from the hill country, and
from the Neg′eb, bringing burnt offerings and sacrifices, cereal offerings
and frankincense, and bringing thank
offerings to the house of the LORD. 27 But
if you do not listen to me, to keep the
sabbath day holy, and not to bear a burden
and enter by the gates of Jerusalem on the
sabbath day, then I will kindle a fire in its
gates, and it shall devour the palaces of
Jerusalem and shall not be quenched.' "

18 The word that came to Jeremi′ah
from the LORD: 2 "Arise, and go down
to the potter's house, and there I will let
you hear my words." 3 So I went down to the
potter's house, and there he was working at
his wheel. 4 And the vessel he was making of
clay was spoiled in the potter's hand, and he
reworked it into another vessel, as it seemed
good to the potter to do.
5 Then the word of the LORD came to me:
6 "O house of Israel, can I not do with you as
this potter has done? says the LORD. Behold,
like the clay in the potter's hand, so are you
in my hand, O house of Israel. 7 If at any time
I declare concerning a nation or a kingdom,
that I will pluck up and break down and
destroy it, 8 and if that nation, concerning
which I have spoken, turns from its evil, I
will repent of the evil that I intended to do
to it. 9 And if at any time I declare concerning
a nation or a kingdom that I will build and
plant it, 10 and if it does evil in my sight, not
listening to my voice, then I will repent of
the good which I had intended to do to it.
11 Now, therefore, say to the men of Judah
and the inhabitants of Jerusalem: 'Thus says
the LORD, Behold, I am shaping evil against
you and devising a plan against you. Return,
every one from his evil way, and amend
your ways and your doings.'
12 "But they say, 'That is in vain! We will
follow our own plans, and everyone will act
according to the stubbornness of his evil
heart.'

13 "Therefore thus says the LORD:
Ask among the nations,
who has heard the like of this?
The virgin Israel
has done a very horrible thing.
14 Does the snow of Lebanon leave
the crags of Sir′ion?
Do the mountain waters run dry,
the cold flowing streams?
15 But my people have forgotten me,
they burn incense to false gods;
they have stumbled in their ways,
in the ancient roads,
and have gone into bypaths,
not the highway,

16 making their land a horror,
a thing to be hissed at for ever.
Every one who passes by it is horrified
and shakes his head.
17 Like the east wind I will scatter them
before the enemy.
I will show them my back, not my face,
in the day of their calamity."

18 Then they said, "Come, let us make
plots against Jeremi′ah, for the law shall not
perish from the priest, nor counsel from the
wise, nor the word from the prophet. Come,
let us strike him with the tongue, and let us
not heed any of his words."

19 Give heed to me, O Lord,
and listen to my plea.
20 Is evil a recompense for good?
Yet they have dug a pit for my life.
Remember how I stood before you
to speak good for them,
to turn away your wrath from them.
21 Therefore deliver up their children
to famine;
give them over to the power of the sword,
let their wives become childless and
widowed.
May their men meet death by pestilence,
their youths be slain by the sword
in battle.
22 May a cry be heard from their houses,
when you bring the marauder suddenly
upon them!
For they have dug a pit to take me,
and laid snares for my feet.
23 Yet, you, O Lord, know
all their plotting to slay me.
Forgive not their iniquity,
nor blot out their sin from your sight.
Let them be overthrown before you;
deal with them in the time of your anger.

19 Thus said the Lord, "Go, buy a potter's earthen flask, and take some
of the elders of the people and some of the
senior priests, 2 and go out to the valley of the
son of Hinnom at the entry of the Potsherd
Gate, and proclaim there the words that I
tell you. 3 You shall say, 'Hear the word of the
Lord, O kings of Judah and inhabitants of
Jerusalem. Thus says the Lord of hosts, the
God of Israel, Behold, I am bringing such
evil upon this place that the ears of every
one who hears of it will tingle. 4 Because the
people have forsaken me, and have profaned
this place by burning incense in it to other
gods whom neither they nor their fathers nor
the kings of Judah have known; and because
they have filled this place with the blood of
innocents, 5 and have built the high places of
Ba′al to burn their sons in the fire as burnt
offerings to Baal, which I did not command
or decree, nor did it come into my mind;
6 therefore, behold, days are coming, says
the Lord, when this place shall no more be
called To′pheth, or the valley of the son of
Hinnom, but the valley of Slaughter. 7 And in
this place I will make void the plans of Judah
and Jerusalem, and will cause their people
to fall by the sword before their enemies,
and by the hand of those who seek their life.
I will give their dead bodies for food to the
birds of the air and to the beasts of the earth.
8 And I will make this city a horror, a thing
to be hissed at; every one who passes by it
will be horrified and will hiss because of all
its disasters. 9 And I will make them eat the
flesh of their sons and their daughters, and
every one shall eat the flesh of his neighbor
in the siege and in the distress, with which
their enemies and those who seek their life
afflict them.'

10 "Then you shall break the flask in the
sight of the men who go with you, 11 and shall
say to them, 'Thus says the Lord of hosts: So
will I break this people and this city, as one
breaks a potter's vessel, so that it can never
be mended. Men shall bury in To′pheth
because there will be no place else to bury.
12 Thus will I do to this place, says the Lord,
and to its inhabitants, making this city like
To′pheth. 13 The houses of Jerusalem and the
houses of the kings of Judah—all the houses
upon whose roofs incense has been burned
to all the host of heaven, and drink offerings
have been poured out to other gods—shall
be defiled like the place of To′pheth.'"

14 Then Jeremi′ah came from To′pheth,
where the Lord had sent him to prophesy,
and he stood in the court of the Lord's
house, and said to all the people: 15 "Thus says

the LORD of hosts, the God of Israel, Behold, I am bringing upon this city and upon all its towns all the evil that I have pronounced against it, because they have stiffened their neck, refusing to hear my words."

WISDOM 13

10But miserable, with their hopes set on
dead things, are the men
who give the name "gods" to the works of
men's hands,
gold and silver fashioned with skill,
and likenesses of animals,
or a useless stone, the work of an
ancient hand.
11A skilled woodcutter may saw down a tree
easy to handle
and skilfully strip off all its bark,
and then with pleasing workmanship
make a useful vessel that serves life's needs,
12and burn the castoff pieces of his work
to prepare his food, and eat his fill.
13But a castoff piece from among them,
useful for nothing,
a stick crooked and full of knots,
he takes and carves with care in his leisure,
and shapes it with skill gained in idleness;
he forms it like the image of a man,
14or makes it like some worthless animal,
giving it a coat of red paint and coloring its
surface red
and covering every blemish in it with paint;
15then he makes for it a niche that befits it,
and sets it in the wall, and fastens it there
with iron.
16So he takes thought for it, that it may
not fall,
because he knows that it cannot help itself,
for it is only an image and has need of help.
17When he prays about possessions and his
marriage and children,
he is not ashamed to address a lifeless thing.
18For health he appeals to a thing that is weak;
for life he prays to a thing that is dead;
for aid he entreats a thing that is utterly
inexperienced;
for a prosperous journey, a thing that
cannot take a step;
19for money-making and work and success
with his hands
he asks strength of a thing whose hands
have no strength.

14 Again, one preparing to sail and about
to voyage over raging waves
calls upon a piece of wood more fragile
than the ship which carries him.
2For it was desire for gain that planned
that vessel,
and wisdom was the craftsman who built it;
3but it is your providence, O Father, that
steers its course,
because you have given it a path in the sea,
and a safe way through the waves,
4showing that you can save from every
danger,
so that even if a man lacks skill, he may
put to sea.
5It is your will that works of your wisdom
should not be without effect;
therefore men trust their lives even to the
smallest piece of wood,
and passing through the billows on a raft
they come safely to land.
6For even in the beginning, when arrogant
giants were perishing,
the hope of the world took refuge on a raft,
and guided by your hand left to the world
the seed of a new generation.
7For blessed is the wood by which
righteousness comes.

2 CORINTHIANS 13

This is the third time I am coming to you. Any charge must be sustained by the evidence of two or three witnesses. 2I warned those who sinned
before and all the others, and I warn them
now while absent, as I did when present on
my second visit, that if I come again I will
not spare them—3since you desire proof
that Christ is speaking in me. He is not weak
in dealing with you, but is powerful in you.
4For he was crucified in weakness, but lives
by the power of God. For we are weak in

him, but in dealing with you we shall live with him by the power of God.

5 Examine yourselves, to see whether you are holding to your faith. Test yourselves. Do you not realize that Jesus Christ is in you?—unless indeed you fail to meet the test! 6 I hope you will find out that we have not failed. 7 But we beg God that you may not do wrong—not that we may appear to have met the test, but that you may do what is right, though we may seem to have failed. 8 For we cannot do anything against the truth, but only for the truth. 9 For we are glad when we are weak and you are strong. What we pray for is your improvement. 10 I write this while I am away from you, in order that when I come I may not have to be severe in my use of the authority which the Lord has given me for building up and not for tearing down.

11 Finally, brethren, rejoice. Mend your ways, heed my appeal, agree with one another, live in peace, and the God of love and peace will be with you. 12 Greet one another with a holy kiss. 13 All the saints greet you.

14 The grace of the Lord Jesus Christ and the love of God and the fellowship of the Holy Spirit be with you all.

REFLECTION

In order to teach Jeremiah, God commands the prophet to engage in some hands-on learning. Jeremiah is told to visit a potter at his wheel, where he can see a spoiled vessel being reshaped (see Jer 18:1–4). Then Jeremiah understands that God can either break down or renew Israel. Jeremiah is also told to smash some pottery on the ground in order to demonstrate the irreversible damage that will be done to Jerusalem by its enemies (see 19:10–13). The Book of Wisdom likewise uses analogies from human handiwork to explain why we should trust in God and not in our own skill. God does not disdain to speak to us in a language we can understand, using the elements of our own lives. The Bible communicates profound truths and uses many beautiful images in a relatable and human way. God is not concerned with mere appearance, and he is not speaking in order to acquire prestige. He does not mind visiting a potter's shed. And, in Christ, he shows that he is not ashamed to fully enter human life, even as the son of a carpenter. Do you look for God's truth in the mundane tasks of everyday life?

September 25

JEREMIAH 20

Now Pashhur the priest, the son of Im′mer, who was chief officer in the house of the LORD, heard Jeremi′ah prophesying these things. 2 Then Pashhur beat Jeremi′ah the prophet, and put him in the stocks that were in the upper Benjamin Gate of the house of the LORD. 3 On the next day, when Pashhur released Jeremi′ah from the stocks, Jeremi′ah said to him, "The LORD does not call your name Pashhur, but Terror on every side. 4 For thus says the LORD: Behold, I will make you a terror to yourself and to all your friends. They shall fall by the sword of their enemies while you look on. And I will give all Judah into the hand of the king of Babylon; he shall carry them captive to Babylon, and shall slay them with the sword. 5 Moreover, I will give all the wealth of the city, all its gains, all its prized belongings, and all the treasures of the kings of Judah into the hand of their enemies, who shall plunder them, and seize them, and carry them to Babylon. 6 And you, Pashhur, and all who dwell in your house, shall go into captivity; to Babylon you shall go; and there you shall die, and there you shall be buried, you and all your friends, to whom you have prophesied falsely."

[7]O LORD, you have deceived me,
and I was deceived;
you are stronger than I,
and you have prevailed.
I have become a laughingstock all the day;
every one mocks me.
[8]For whenever I speak, I cry out,
I shout, "Violence and destruction!"
For the word of the LORD has become
for me
a reproach and derision all day long.
[9]If I say, "I will not mention him,
or speak any more in his name,"
there is in my heart as it were a burning fire
shut up in my bones,
and I am weary with holding it in,
and I cannot.
[10]For I hear many whispering.
Terror is on every side!
"Denounce him! Let us denounce him!"
say all my familiar friends,
watching for my fall.
"Perhaps he will be deceived,
then we can overcome him,
and take our revenge on him."
[11]But the LORD is with me as a dread warrior;
therefore my persecutors will stumble,
they will not overcome me.
They will be greatly shamed,
for they will not succeed.
Their eternal dishonor
will never be forgotten.
[12]O LORD of hosts, who test the righteous,
who see the heart and the mind,
let me see your vengeance upon them,
for to you have I committed my cause.

[13]Sing to the LORD;
praise the LORD!
For he has delivered the life of the needy
from the hand of evildoers.

[14]Cursed be the day
on which I was born!
The day when my mother bore me,
let it not be blessed!
[15]Cursed be the man
who brought the news to my father,
"A son is born to you,"
making him very glad.
[16]Let that man be like the cities
which the LORD overthrew without pity;
let him hear a cry in the morning
and an alarm at noon,
[17]because he did not kill me in the womb;
so my mother would have been my grave,
and her womb for ever great.
[18]Why did I come forth from the womb
to see toil and sorrow,
and spend my days in shame?

21 This is the word which came to Jeremi'ah from the LORD, when King
Zedeki'ah sent to him Pashhur the son of
Malchi'ah and Zephani'ah the priest, the
son of Ma-asei'ah, saying, [2]"Inquire of the
LORD for us, for Nebuchadrez'zar king of
Babylon is making war against us; perhaps
the LORD will deal with us according to all
his wonderful deeds, and will make him
withdraw from us."
[3]Then Jeremi'ah said to them: [4]"Thus
you shall say to Zedeki'ah, 'Thus says
the LORD, the God of Israel: Behold, I
will turn back the weapons of war which
are in your hands and with which you
are fighting against the king of Babylon
and against the Chalde'ans who are
besieging you outside the walls; and I
will bring them together into the midst
of this city. [5]I myself will fight against you
with outstretched hand and strong arm,
in anger, and in fury, and in great wrath.
[6]And I will strike the inhabitants of this
city, both man and beast; they shall die
of a great pestilence. [7]Afterward, says the
LORD, I will give Zedeki'ah king of Judah,
and his servants, and the people in this city
who survive the pestilence, sword, and
famine, into the hand of Nebuchadrez'zar
king of Babylon and into the hand of their
enemies, into the hand of those who seek
their lives. He shall strike them with the
edge of the sword; he shall not pity them,
or spare them, or have compassion.'
[8]"And to this people you shall say: 'Thus
says the LORD: Behold, I set before you the
way of life and the way of death. [9]He who
stays in this city shall die by the sword, by
famine, and by pestilence; but he who goes
out and surrenders to the Chalde'ans who

are besieging you shall live and shall have his life as a prize of war. 10For I have set my face against this city for evil and not for good, says the LORD: it shall be given into the hand of the king of Babylon, and he shall burn it with fire.'

11"And to the house of the king of Judah say, 'Hear the word of the LORD, 12O house of David! Thus says the LORD:

"'Execute justice in the morning,
and deliver from the hand of the oppressor
him who has been robbed,
lest my wrath go forth like fire,
and burn with none to quench it,
because of your evil doings.'"

13"Behold, I am against you, O inhabitant of the valley,
O rock of the plain,
says the LORD;
you who say, 'Who shall come down against us,
or who shall enter our habitations?'
14I will punish you according to the fruit of your doings,
says the LORD;
I will kindle a fire in her forest,
and it shall devour all that is round about her."

22 Thus says the LORD: "Go down to the house of the king of Judah, and speak there this word, 2and say, 'Hear the word of the LORD, O King of Judah, who sit on the throne of David, you, and your servants, and your people who enter these gates. 3Thus says the LORD: Do justice and righteousness, and deliver from the hand of the oppressor him who has been robbed. And do no wrong or violence to the alien, the fatherless, and the widow, nor shed innocent blood in this place. 4For if you will indeed obey this word, then there shall enter the gates of this house kings who sit on the throne of David, riding in chariots and on horses, they, and their servants, and their people. 5But if you will not heed these words, I swear by myself, says the LORD, that this house shall become a desolation. 6For thus says the LORD concerning the house of the king of Judah:

"'You are as Gilead to me,
as the summit of Lebanon,
yet surely I will make you a desert,
an uninhabited city.
7I will prepare destroyers against you,
each with his weapons;
and they shall cut down your choicest cedars,
and cast them into the fire.

8"'And many nations will pass by this city, and every man will say to his neighbor, "Why has the LORD dealt thus with this great city?" 9And they will answer, "Because they forsook the covenant of the LORD their God, and worshiped other gods and served them."'"

10Weep not for him who is dead,
nor bemoan him;
but weep bitterly for him who goes away,
for he shall return no more
to see his native land.

11For thus says the LORD concerning Shallum the son of Josi'ah, king of Judah, who reigned instead of Josiah his father, and who went away from this place: "He shall return here no more, 12but in the place where they have carried him captive, there shall he die, and he shall never see this land again."

13"Woe to him who builds his house by unrighteousness,
and his upper rooms by injustice;
who makes his neighbor serve him for nothing,
and does not give him his wages;
14who says, 'I will build myself a great house
with spacious upper rooms,'
and cuts out windows for it,
paneling it with cedar,
and painting it with vermilion.
15Do you think you are a king
because you compete in cedar?
Did not your father eat and drink
and do justice and righteousness?
Then it was well with him.
16He judged the cause of the poor and needy;
then it was well.
Is not this to know me?
says the LORD.

[17]But you have eyes and heart
only for your dishonest gain,
for shedding innocent blood,
and for practicing oppression
and violence."
[18]Therefore thus says the LORD concerning
Jehoi′akim the son of Josi′ah, king
of Judah:
"They shall not lament for him, saying,
'Ah my brother!' or 'Ah sister!'
They shall not lament for him, saying,
'Ah lord!' or 'Ah his majesty!'
[19]With the burial of a donkey he shall
be buried,
dragged and cast forth beyond the gates
of Jerusalem."

[20]"Go up to Lebanon, and cry out,
and lift up your voice in Bashan;
cry from Ab′arim,
for all your lovers are destroyed.
[21]I spoke to you in your prosperity,
but you said, 'I will not listen.'
This has been your way from your youth,
that you have not obeyed my voice.
[22]The wind shall shepherd all your
shepherds,
and your lovers shall go into captivity;
then you will be ashamed and confounded
because of all your wickedness.
[23]O inhabitant of Lebanon,
nested among the cedars,
how you will groan when pangs come
upon you,
pain as of a woman with labor pains!"

[24]"As I live, says the LORD, though Coni′ah
the son of Jehoi′akim, king of Judah, were
the signet ring on my right hand, yet I would
tear you off [25]and give you into the hand of
those who seek your life, into the hand of
those of whom you are afraid, even into the
hand of Nebuchadrez′zar king of Babylon
and into the hand of the Chalde′ans. [26]I will
hurl you and the mother who bore you into
another country, where you were not born,
and there you shall die. [27]But to the land to
which they will long to return, there they
shall not return."
[28]Is this man Coni′ah a despised, broken pot,
a vessel no one cares for?
Why are he and his children hurled
and cast
into a land which they do not know?
[29]O land, land, land,
hear the word of the LORD!
[30]Thus says the LORD:
"Write this man down as childless,
a man who shall not succeed in his days;
for none of his offspring shall succeed
in sitting on the throne of David,
and ruling again in Judah."

WISDOM 14

[8]But the idol made with hands is
accursed,
and so is he who made it;
because he did the work, and the perishable
thing was named a god.
[9]For equally hateful to God are the ungodly
man and his ungodliness,
[10]for what was done will be punished
together with him who did it.
[11]Therefore there will be a visitation also
upon the heathen idols,
because, though part of what God created,
they became an abomination,
and became traps for the souls of men
and a snare to the feet of the foolish.

[12]For the idea of making idols was the
beginning of fornication,
and the invention of them was the
corruption of life,
[13]for neither have they existed from the
beginning
nor will they exist for ever.
[14]For through the vanity of men they entered
the world,
and therefore their speedy end has been
planned.
[15]For a father, consumed with grief at an
untimely bereavement,
made an image of his child, who had been
suddenly taken from him;
and he now honored as a god what was
once a dead human being,
and handed on to his dependents secret
rites and initiations.

[16]Then the ungodly custom, grown strong
with time, was kept as a law,
and at the command of monarchs graven
images were worshiped.

GALATIANS 1

Paul an apostle—not from men nor through man, but through Jesus Christ and God the Father, who raised him from the dead—[2]and all the brethren who are with me,

To the churches of Galatia:

[3]Grace to you and peace from God the Father and our Lord Jesus Christ, [4]who gave himself for our sins to deliver us from the present evil age, according to the will of our God and Father; [5]to whom be the glory for ever and ever. Amen.

[6]I am astonished that you are so quickly deserting him who called you in the grace of Christ and turning to a different gospel—[7]not that there is another gospel, but there are some who trouble you and want to pervert the gospel of Christ. [8]But even if we, or an angel from heaven, should preach to you a gospel contrary to that which we preached to you, let him be accursed. [9]As we have said before, so now I say again, If any one is preaching to you a gospel contrary to that which you received, let him be accursed.

[10]Am I now seeking the favor of men, or of God? Or am I trying to please men? If I were still pleasing men, I should not be a servant of Christ.

[11]Brethren, I would have you know that the gospel which was preached by me is not man's gospel. [12]For I did not receive it from man, nor was I taught it, but it came through a revelation of Jesus Christ. [13]For you have heard of my former life in Judaism, how I persecuted the Church of God violently and tried to destroy it; [14]and I advanced in Judaism beyond many of my own age among my people, so extremely zealous was I for the traditions of my fathers. [15]But when he who had set me apart before I was born, and had called me through his grace, [16]was pleased to reveal his Son to me, in order that I might preach him among the Gentiles, I did not confer with flesh and blood, [17]nor did I go up to Jerusalem to those who were apostles before me, but I went away into Arabia; and again I returned to Damascus.

[18]Then after three years I went up to Jerusalem to visit Ce´phas, and remained with him fifteen days. [19]But I saw none of the other apostles except James the Lord's brother. [20](In what I am writing to you, before God, I do not lie!) [21]Then I went into the regions of Syria and Cili´cia. [22]And I was still not known by sight to the churches of Christ in Judea; [23]they only heard it said, "He who once persecuted us is now preaching the faith he once tried to destroy." [24]And they glorified God because of me.

REFLECTION

St. Paul is writing to the church at Galatia to warn them against false teachers and to remind them of the true Gospel that he has preached to them. Jeremiah also struggles to be heard amidst false prophets. He suffers at the hands of the priest Pashhur, who rejects Jeremiah's prophecies about the destruction of Jerusalem. But how can we tell who is a true prophet? Surely most people who preach believe that they are speaking the truth. Even in matters of day-to-day importance, we are persuaded that we know best and might wish we could shout out, "Listen to me! I am right!" But St. Paul does more than merely state that his word is true; he vouches for his teaching with the evidence of his own life (see Gal 1:13–24). His life-changing conversion and his good works serve as proof of his authenticity. We should therefore remember that no one can be argued into faith. Persuasive arguments, theological sophistication, and careful reading of the Scriptures are essential to our own spiritual growth and to evangelization, but ultimately it is the witness of the Christian life that is the visible proof of God's love in the world. When you cannot convince those with whom you disagree, will you show them the truth by the way you live?

September 26

JEREMIAH 23

"Woe to the shepherds who destroy and scatter the sheep of my pasture!" says the LORD.
2Therefore thus says the LORD, the God of Israel, concerning the shepherds who care for my people: "You have scattered
my flock, and have driven them away, and you have not attended to them. Behold, I will attend to you for your evil doings, says the LORD.
3Then I will gather the remnant of my flock out of all the countries where I have driven them, and I will bring them back to their fold, and they shall be fruitful and multiply.
4I will set shepherds over them who will care for them, and they shall fear no more, nor be dismayed, neither shall any be missing, says the LORD.

5"Behold, the days are coming, says the LORD, when I will raise up for David a righteous Branch, and he shall reign as king and deal wisely, and shall execute justice and righteousness in the land.
6In his days Judah will be saved, and Israel will dwell securely. And this is the name by which he will be called: 'The LORD is our righteousness.'

7"Therefore, behold, the days are coming, says the LORD, when men shall no longer say, 'As the LORD lives who brought up the sons of Israel out of the land of Egypt,'
8but 'As the LORD lives who brought up and led the descendants of the house of Israel out of the north country and out of all the countries where he had driven them.' Then they shall dwell in their own land."

9Concerning the prophets:
My heart is broken within me,
all my bones shake;
I am like a drunken man,
like a man overcome by wine,
because of the LORD
and because of his holy words.
10For the land is full of adulterers;
because of the curse the land mourns,
and the pastures of the wilderness are dried up.
Their course is evil,
and their might is not right.
11"Both prophet and priest are ungodly;
even in my house I have found their wickedness,
says the LORD.
12Therefore their way shall be to them
like slippery paths in the darkness,
into which they shall be driven and fall;
for I will bring evil upon them
in the year of their punishment,
says the LORD.
13In the prophets of Samar′ia
I saw an unsavory thing:
they prophesied by Ba′al
and led my people Israel astray.
14But in the prophets of Jerusalem
I have seen a horrible thing:
they commit adultery and walk in lies;
they strengthen the hands of evildoers,
so that no one turns from his wickedness;
all of them have become like Sodom to me,
and its inhabitants like Gomor′rah."
15Therefore thus says the LORD of hosts
concerning the prophets:
"Behold, I will feed them with wormwood,
and give them poisoned water to drink;
for from the prophets of Jerusalem
ungodliness has gone forth into all the land."

16Thus says the LORD of hosts: "Do not listen to the words of the prophets who prophesy to you, filling you with vain hopes; they speak visions of their own minds, not from the mouth of the LORD.
17They say continually to those who despise the word of the LORD, 'It shall be well with you'; and to every one who stubbornly follows his own heart, they say, 'No evil shall come upon you.'"

18For who among them has stood in the council of the LORD
to perceive and to hear his word,
or who has given heed to his word
and listened?

[19]Behold, the storm of the Lord!
Wrath has gone forth,
a whirling tempest;
it will burst upon the head of
the wicked.
[20]The anger of the Lord will not turn back
until he has executed and accomplished
the intents of his mind.
In the latter days you will understand
it clearly.

[21]"I did not send the prophets,
yet they ran;
I did not speak to them,
yet they prophesied.
[22]But if they had stood in my council,
then they would have proclaimed my
words to my people,
and they would have turned them from
their evil way,
and from the evil of their doings.

[23]"Am I a God at hand, says the Lord,
and not a God afar off? [24]Can a man hide
himself in secret places so that I cannot see him? says the Lord. Do I not
fill heaven and earth? says the Lord. [25]I
have heard what the prophets have said
who prophesy lies in my name, saying,
'I have dreamed, I have dreamed!' [26]How
long shall there be lies in the heart of the
prophets who prophesy lies, and who
prophesy the deceit of their own heart,
[27]who think to make my people forget my
name by their dreams which they tell one
another, even as their fathers forgot my
name for Ba'al? [28]Let the prophet who has
a dream tell the dream, but let him who
has my word speak my word faithfully.
What has straw in common with wheat?
says the Lord. [29]Is not my word like fire,
says the Lord, and like a hammer which
breaks the rock in pieces? [30]Therefore,
behold, I am against the prophets, says
the Lord, who steal my words from one
another. [31]Behold, I am against the prophets, says the Lord, who use their tongues
and say, 'Says the Lord.' [32]Behold, I am
against those who prophesy lying dreams,
says the Lord, and who tell them and lead
my people astray by their lies and their
recklessness, when I did not send them
or charge them; so they do not profit this
people at all, says the Lord.

[33]"When one of this people, or a prophet,
or a priest asks you, 'What is the burden of
the Lord?' you shall say to them, 'You are
the burden, and I will cast you off, says the
Lord.' [34]And as for the prophet, priest, or
one of the people who says, 'The burden
of the Lord,' I will punish that man and
his household. [35]Thus shall you say, every
one to his neighbor and every one to his
brother, 'What has the Lord answered?'
or 'What has the Lord spoken?' [36]But 'the
burden of the Lord' you shall mention
no more, for the burden is every man's
own word, and you pervert the words
of the living God, the Lord of hosts, our
God. [37]Thus you shall say to the prophet,
'What has the Lord answered you?' or
'What has the Lord spoken?' [38]But if you
say, 'The burden of the Lord,' thus says
the Lord, 'Because you have said these
words, "The burden of the Lord," when I
sent to you, saying, "You shall not say, 'The
burden of the Lord,'" [39]therefore, behold,
I will surely lift you up and cast you away
from my presence, you and the city which
I gave to you and your fathers. [40]And I
will bring upon you everlasting reproach
and perpetual shame, which shall not be
forgotten.'"

24 After Nebuchadrez'zar king of Babylon had taken into exile from Jerusalem Jeconi'ah the son of Jehoi'akim,
king of Judah, together with the princes
of Judah, the craftsmen, and the smiths,
and had brought them to Babylon, the
Lord showed me this vision: Behold, two
baskets of figs placed before the temple of
the Lord. [2]One basket had very good figs,
like first-ripe figs, but the other basket had
very bad figs, so bad that they could not be
eaten. [3]And the Lord said to me, "What do
you see, Jeremi'ah?" I said, "Figs, the good
figs very good, and the bad figs very bad,
so bad that they cannot be eaten."

[4]Then the word of the Lord came to
me: [5]"Thus says the Lord, the God of Israel: Like these good figs, so I will regard

as good the exiles from Judah, whom I
have sent away from this place to the
land of the Chalde′ans. [6]I will set my eyes
upon them for good, and I will bring
them back to this land. I will build them
up, and not tear them down; I will plant
them, and not uproot them. [7]I will give
them a heart to know that I am the LORD;
and they shall be my people and I will
be their God, for they shall return to me
with their whole heart.
[8]"But thus says the LORD: Like the bad
figs which are so bad they cannot be eat-
en, so will I treat Zedeki′ah the king of
Judah, his princes, the remnant of Jerusalem who remain in this land, and those
who dwell in the land of Egypt. [9]I will
make them a horror to all the kingdoms
of the earth, to be a reproach, a byword, a
taunt, and a curse in all the places where I
shall drive them. [10]And I will send sword,
famine, and pestilence upon them, until they shall be utterly destroyed from
the land which I gave to them and their
fathers."

WISDOM 14

[17]When men could not honor monarchs in
their presence, since they lived at
a distance,
they imagined their appearance far away,
and made a visible image of the king
whom they honored,
so that by their zeal they might flatter the
absent one as though present.
[18]Then the ambition of the craftsman
impelled
even those who did not know the king to
intensify their worship.
[19]For he, perhaps wishing to please his ruler,
skilfully forced the likeness to take more
beautiful form,
[20]and the multitude, attracted by the charm
of his work,
now regarded as an object of worship the
one whom shortly before they had
honored as a man.
[21]And this became a hidden trap for
mankind,
because men, in bondage to misfortune or
to royal authority,
bestowed on objects of stone or wood the
name that ought not to be shared.

[22]Afterward it was not enough for them to
err about the knowledge of God,
but they live in great strife due to ignorance,
and they call such great evils peace.
[23]For whether they kill children in their
initiations, or celebrate secret
mysteries,
or hold frenzied revels with strange
customs,
[24]they no longer keep either their lives or
their marriages pure,
but they either treacherously kill one another
or grieve one another by adultery,
[25]and all is a raging riot of blood and murder,
theft and deceit, corruption,
faithlessness, tumult, perjury,
[26]confusion over what is good, forgetfulness
of favors,
pollution of souls, sex perversion,
disorder in marriage, adultery, and
debauchery.
[27]For the worship of idols not to be named
is the beginning and cause and end of
every evil.
[28]For their worshipers either rave in
exultation, or prophesy lies,
or live unrighteously, or readily
commit perjury;
[29]for because they trust in lifeless idols
they swear wicked oaths and expect to
suffer no harm.
[30]But just penalties will overtake them on
two counts:
because they thought wickedly of God in
devoting themselves to idols,
and because in deceit they swore
unrighteously through contempt
for holiness.
[31]For it is not the power of the things by
which men swear,
but the just penalty for those who sin,
that always pursues the transgression of
the unrighteous.

GALATIANS 2

Then after fourteen years I went up again to Jerusalem with Barnabas, taking Titus along with me. [2]I went up by revelation; and I laid before them (but privately before those who were of repute) the gospel which I preach among the Gentiles, lest somehow I should be running or had run in vain. [3]But even Titus, who was with me, was not compelled to be circumcised, though he was a Greek. [4]But because of false brethren secretly brought in, who slipped in to spy out our freedom which we have in Christ Jesus, that they might bring us into bondage—[5]to them we did not yield submission even for a moment, that the truth of the gospel might be preserved for you. [6]And from those who were reputed to be something (what they were makes no difference to me; God shows no partiality)—those, I say, who were of repute added nothing to me; [7]but on the contrary, when they saw that I had been entrusted with the gospel to the uncircumcised, just as Peter had been entrusted with the gospel to the circumcised [8](for he who worked through Peter for the mission to the circumcised worked through me also for the Gentiles), [9]and when they perceived the grace that was given to me, James and Ce′phas and John, who were reputed to be pillars, gave to me and Barnabas the right hand of fellowship, that we should go to the Gentiles and they to the circumcised; [10]only they would have us remember the poor, which very thing I was eager to do.

[11]But when Cephas came to Antioch I opposed him to his face, because he stood condemned. [12]For before certain men came from James, he ate with the Gentiles; but when they came he drew back and separated himself, fearing the circumcision party. [13]And with him the rest of the Jews acted insincerely, so that even Barnabas was carried away by their insincerity. [14]But when I saw that they were not straightforward about the truth of the gospel, I said to Cephas before them all, "If you, though a Jew, live like a Gentile and not like a Jew, how can you compel the Gentiles to live like Jews?" [15]We ourselves, who are Jews by birth and not Gentile sinners, [16]yet who know that a man is not justified by works of the law but through faith in Jesus Christ, even we have believed in Christ Jesus, in order to be justified by faith in Christ, and not by works of the law, because by works of the law shall no flesh be justified. [17]But if, in our endeavor to be justified in Christ, we ourselves were found to be sinners, is Christ then an agent of sin? Certainly not! [18]But if I build up again those things which I tore down, then I prove myself a transgressor. [19]For I through the law died to the law, that I might live to God. [20]I have been crucified with Christ; it is no longer I who live, but Christ who lives in me; and the life I now live in the flesh I live by faith in the Son of God, who loved me and gave himself for me. [21]I do not nullify the grace of God; for if justification were through the law, then Christ died to no purpose.

REFLECTION

The saying "the grass is always greener on the other side" means that things we see from a distance always look more attractive than what is near to us. The Book of Wisdom contemplates this same truth in describing a strange phenomenon: when people make a statue in honor of their king, the statue becomes more idealized and more beautiful when the people are further removed from that king (see Wis 14:17–21). This can also be true of unrequited love. When we are rejected by someone, or we feel we have missed a romantic opportunity, we sometimes imagine our would-be lover in a distorted way. We remember only their good qualities and exaggerate their virtues. Jeremiah tells us that God, our true King and true beloved, does not want us to have a false image of him. He is a God who is "at hand" and who fills the whole earth (Jer 23:23). God is near to us because he wants us to know him truly. You would surely feel honored if an earthly king wanted to make your acquaintance, but do you appreciate that the King of the universe desires to make himself known? And do you, in imitation of God, seek to remove all pretenses when you communicate with others?

September 27

JEREMIAH 25

The word that came to Jeremi′ah concerning all the people of Judah, in the fourth year of Jehoi′a-kim the son of Josi′ah, king of Judah (that was the first year of Nebu-chadrez′zar king of Babylon), [2]which Jeremi′ah the prophet spoke to all the people of Judah and all the inhabitants of Jerusalem: [3]"For twenty-three years, from the thirteenth year of Josi′ah the son of A′mon, king of Judah, to this day, the word of the LORD has come to me, and I have spoken persistently to you, but you have not listened. [4]You have neither listened nor inclined your ears to hear, although the LORD persistently sent to you all his servants the prophets, [5]saying, 'Turn now, every one of you, from his evil way and wrong doings, and dwell upon the land which the LORD has given to you and your fathers from of old and for ever; [6]do not go after other gods to serve and worship them, or provoke me to anger with the work of your hands. Then I will do you no harm.' [7]Yet you have not listened to me, says the LORD, that you might provoke me to anger with the work of your hands to your own harm.

[8]"Therefore thus says the LORD of hosts: Because you have not obeyed my words, [9]behold, I will send for all the tribes of the north, says the LORD, and for Nebuchadrez′zar the king of Babylon, my servant, and I will bring them against this land and its inhabitants, and against all these nations round about; I will utterly destroy them, and make them a horror, a hissing, and an everlasting reproach. [10]Moreover, I will banish from them the voice of mirth and the voice of gladness, the voice of the bridegroom and the voice of the bride, the grinding of the millstones and the light of the lamp. [11]This whole land shall become a ruin and a waste, and these nations shall serve the king of Babylon seventy years. [12]Then after seventy years are completed, I will punish the king of Babylon and that nation, the land of the Chalde′ans, for their iniquity, says the LORD, making the land an everlasting waste. [13]I will bring upon that land all the words which I have uttered against it, everything written in this book, which Jeremi′ah prophesied against all the nations. [14]For many nations and great kings shall make slaves even of them; and I will recompense them according to their deeds and the work of their hands."

[15]Thus the LORD, the God of Israel, said to me: "Take from my hand this cup of the wine of wrath, and make all the nations to whom I send you drink it. [16]They shall drink and stagger and be crazed because of the sword which I am sending among them."

[17]So I took the cup from the LORD's hand, and made all the nations to whom the Lord sent me drink it: [18]Jerusalem and the cities of Judah, its kings and princes, to make them a desolation and a waste, a hissing and a curse, as at this day; [19]Pharaoh king of Egypt, his servants, his princes, all his people, [20]and all the foreign folk among them; all the kings of the land of Uz and all the kings of the land of the Philis′tines (Ash′kelon, Gaza, Ek′ron, and the remnant of Ash′dod); [21]E′dom, Moab, and the sons of Ammon; [22]all the kings of Tyre, all the kings of Sidon, and the kings of the islands across the sea; [23]De′dan, Te′ma, Buz, and all who cut the corners of their hair; [24]all the kings of Arabia and all the kings of the mixed tribes that dwell in the desert; [25]all the kings of Zimri, all the kings of E′lam, and all the kings of Med′ia; [26]all the kings of the north, far and near, one after another, and all the kingdoms of the world which are on the face of the earth. And after them the king of Babylon shall drink.

[27]"Then you shall say to them, 'Thus says the LORD of hosts, the God of Israel: Drink, be drunk and vomit, fall and rise no more,

because of the sword which I am sending
among you.'
28"And if they refuse to accept the cup
from your hand to drink, then you shall say
to them, 'Thus says the LORD of hosts: You
must drink! 29For behold, I begin to work
evil at the city which is called by my name,
and shall you go unpunished? You shall
not go unpunished, for I am summoning
a sword against all the inhabitants of the
earth, says the LORD of hosts.'
30"You, therefore, shall prophesy against
them all these words, and say to them:
'The LORD will roar from on high,
and from his holy habitation utter
his voice;
he will roar mightily against his fold,
and shout, like those who tread grapes,
against all the inhabitants of the earth.
31The clamor will resound to the ends of
the earth,
for the LORD has an indictment against
the nations;
he is entering into judgment with all
flesh,
and the wicked he will put to the sword,
says the LORD.'

32"Thus says the LORD of hosts:
Behold, evil is going forth
from nation to nation,
and a great tempest is stirring
from the farthest parts of the earth!
33"And those slain by the LORD on that
day shall extend from one end of the earth
to the other. They shall not be lamented, or
gathered, or buried; they shall be dung on
the surface of the ground.
34"Wail, you shepherds, and cry,
and roll in ashes, you lords of the flock,
for the days of your slaughter and
dispersion have come,
and you shall fall like choice rams.
35No refuge will remain for the shepherds,
nor escape for the lords of the flock.
36Listen, the cry of the shepherds,
and the wail of the lords of the flock!
For the LORD is despoiling their pasture,
37and the peaceful folds are devastated,
because of the fierce anger of the LORD.
38Like a lion he has left his den,
for their land has become a waste
because of the sword of the oppressor,
and because of his fierce anger."

26 In the beginning of the reign of
Jehoi'akim the son of Josi'ah, king
of Judah, this word came from the LORD,
2"Thus says the LORD: Stand in the court
of the LORD's house, and speak to all the
cities of Judah which come to worship in
the house of the LORD all the words that I
command you to speak to them; do not hold
back a word. 3It may be they will listen, and
every one turn from his evil way, that I may
repent of the evil which I intend to do to
them because of their evil doings. 4You shall
say to them, 'Thus says the LORD: If you will
not listen to me, to walk in my law which I
have set before you, 5and to heed the words
of my servants the prophets whom I send to
you urgently, though you have not heeded,
6then I will make this house like Shiloh,
and I will make this city a curse for all the
nations of the earth.'"
7The priests and the prophets and all
the people heard Jeremi'ah speaking these
words in the house of the LORD. 8And when
Jeremi'ah had finished speaking all that the
LORD had commanded him to speak to all
the people, then the priests and the prophets
and all the people laid hold of him, saying,
"You shall die! 9Why have you prophesied in
the name of the LORD, saying, 'This house
shall be like Shiloh, and this city shall be
desolate, without inhabitant'?" And all the
people gathered about Jeremi'ah in the
house of the LORD.
10When the princes of Judah heard these
things, they came up from the king's house
to the house of the LORD and took their seat
in the entry of the New Gate of the house of
the LORD. 11Then the priests and the prophets
said to the princes and to all the people, "This
man deserves the sentence of death, because
he has prophesied against this city, as you
have heard with your own ears."
12Then Jeremi'ah spoke to all the princes
and all the people, saying, "The LORD sent
me to prophesy against this house and this
city all the words you have heard. 13Now

therefore amend your ways and your doings,
and obey the voice of the LORD your God,
and the LORD will repent of the evil which
he has pronounced against you. 14But as for
me, behold, I am in your hands. Do with me
as seems good and right to you. 15Only know
for certain that if you put me to death, you
will bring innocent blood upon yourselves
and upon this city and its inhabitants, for in
truth the LORD sent me to you to speak all
these words in your ears."

16Then the princes and all the people said
to the priests and the prophets, "This man
does not deserve the sentence of death, for
he has spoken to us in the name of the LORD
our God." 17And certain of the elders of the
land arose and spoke to all the assembled
people, saying, 18"Micah of Mo′resheth
prophesied in the days of Hezeki′ah king of
Judah, and said to all the people of Judah:
'Thus says the LORD of hosts,

Zion shall be plowed as a field;
Jerusalem shall become a heap of ruins,
and the mountain of the house a wooded
height.'

19Did Hezeki′ah king of Judah and all Judah
put him to death? Did he not fear the LORD
and entreat the favor of the LORD, and did
not the LORD repent of the evil which he
had pronounced against them? But we are
about to bring great evil upon ourselves."

20There was another man who prophesied
in the name of the LORD, Uri′ah the son
of Shemai′ah from Kir′iath-je′arim. He
prophesied against this city and against this
land in words like those of Jeremi′ah. 21And
when King Jehoi′akim, with all his warriors
and all the princes, heard his words, the
king sought to put him to death; but when
Uri′ah heard of it, he was afraid and fled and
escaped to Egypt. 22Then King Jehoi′akim
sent to Egypt certain men, Elna′than the son
of Achbor and others with him, 23and they
fetched Uri′ah from Egypt and brought him
to King Jehoi′akim, who slew him with the
sword and cast his dead body into the burial
place of the common people.

24But the hand of Ahi′kam the son of
Sha′phan was with Jeremi′ah so that he was
not given over to the people to be put to death.

WISDOM 15

But you, our God, are kind and true,
patient, and ruling all things in mercy.
2For even if we sin we are yours, knowing
your power;
but we will not sin, because we know that
we are considered yours.
3For to know you is complete
righteousness,
and to know your power is the root of
immortality.
4For neither has the evil intent of human art
misled us,
nor the fruitless toil of painters,
a figure stained with varied colors,
5whose appearance arouses yearning
in fools,
so that they desire the lifeless form of a
dead image.
6Lovers of evil things and fit for such objects
of hope
are those who either make or desire or
worship them.

7For when a potter kneads the soft earth
and laboriously molds each vessel for
our service,
he fashions out of the same clay
both the vessels that serve clean uses
and those for contrary uses, making all in
like manner;
but which shall be the use of each of these
the worker in clay decides.
8With misspent toil, he forms a futile god
from the same clay—
this man who was made of earth a short
time before
and after a little while goes to the earth
from which he was taken,
when he is required to return the soul that
was lent him.
9But he is not concerned that he is destined
to die
or that his life is brief,
but he competes with workers in gold
and silver,
and imitates workers in copper;
and he counts it his glory that he molds
counterfeit gods.

10His heart is ashes, his hope is cheaper
than dirt,
and his life is of less worth than clay,
11because he failed to know the one who
formed him
and inspired him with an active soul
and breathed into him a living spirit.
12But he considered our existence an
idle game,
and life a festival held for profit,
for he says one must get money however
one can, even by base means.
13For this man, more than all others, knows
that he sins
when he makes from earthy matter fragile
vessels and graven images.

GALATIANS 3

O foolish Galatians! Who has bewitched you, before whose eyes Jesus Christ was publicly portrayed as crucified?
2Let me ask you only this: Did you receive the Spirit by works of the law, or by hearing with
faith? 3Are you so foolish? Having begun with the Spirit, are you now ending with the flesh? 4Did you experience so many
things in vain?—if it really is in vain. 5Does
he who supplies the Spirit to you and works miracles among you do so by works of the law, or by hearing with faith?

6Thus Abraham "believed God, and it was reckoned to him as righteousness."
7So you see that it is men of faith who are the sons of Abraham.
8And the Scripture, foreseeing that God would justify the Gentiles by faith, preached the gospel beforehand to Abraham, saying, "In you shall all the nations be blessed."
9So then, those who are men of faith are blessed with Abraham who had faith.

10For all who rely on works of the law are under a curse; for it is written, "Cursed be every one who does not abide by all things written in the book of the law, and do them."
11Now it is evident that no man is justified before God by the law; for "He who through faith is righteous shall live";
12but the law does not rest on faith, for "He who does them shall live by them."
13Christ redeemed us from the curse of the law, having become a curse for us—for it is written, "Cursed be every one who hangs on a tree"—
14that in Christ Jesus the blessing of Abraham might come upon the Gentiles, that we might receive the promise of the Spirit through faith.

15To give a human example, brethren: no one annuls even a man's will, or adds to it, once it has been ratified.
16Now the promises were made to Abraham and to his offspring. It does not say, "And to offsprings," referring to many; but, referring to one, "And to your offspring," which is Christ.
17This is what I mean: the law, which came four hundred and thirty years afterward, does not annul a covenant previously ratified by God, so as to make the promise void.
18For if the inheritance is by the law, it is no longer by promise; but God gave it to Abraham by a promise.

REFLECTION

In Galatians 3, we find some common Pauline theological ideas. St. Paul explains that we receive the Spirit not by works of the Law, but by faith (see Gal 3:2), and yet the Law is a continuation of the covenant made with Abraham (see vv. 15–18), which in no way is annulled by Christ. So, what is the relationship between the Law and the Spirit? The Book of Wisdom raises a similar question. The author describes the potter's work as useless due to his mortality, and says that the labor of a craftsman who fashions idols is "misspent" (Wis 15:8). Does this mean that all works on earth, whether the works of the Law or the works of our hands, are meaningless? Of course not! But our works are futile if they are made an end unto themselves without reference to God. The craftsman, if he works to compete with others in making idols (see Wis 15:9) or merely to earn money (see Wis 15:12), has wasted his brief time on earth. Likewise, we waste our time on earth if we perform the works of the Law without understanding those works as a response to God's loving promise. Do you compartmentalize your work and your faith, or do you see everything you do as being oriented toward God?

September 28

JEREMIAH 27

**In the beginning of the reign
of Zedeki′ah the son of Josi′ah,
king of Judah, this word came to
Jeremi′ah from the LORD. 2Thus the LORD
said to me: "Make yourself thongs and
yoke-bars, and put them on your neck.**
3Send word to the king of E′dom, the king
of Moab, the king of the sons of Ammon,
the king of Tyre, and the king of Si′don by
the hand of the envoys who have come to
Jerusalem to Zedeki′ah king of Judah. 4Give
them this charge for their masters: 'Thus
says the LORD of hosts, the God of Israel:
This is what you shall say to your masters:
5"It is I who by my great power and my
outstretched arm have made the earth, with
the men and animals that are on the earth,
and I give it to whomever it seems right to
me. 6Now I have given all these lands into
the hand of Nebuchadnez′zar, the king of
Babylon, my servant, and I have given him
also the beasts of the field to serve him. 7All
the nations shall serve him and his son and
his grandson, until the time of his own land
comes; then many nations and great kings
shall make him their slave.

8" ' "But if any nation or kingdom will not
serve this Nebuchadnez′zar king of Babylon,
and put its neck under the yoke of the king
of Babylon, I will punish that nation with the
sword, with famine, and with pestilence, says
the LORD, until I have consumed it by his
hand. 9So do not listen to your prophets, your
diviners, your dreamers, your soothsayers, or
your sorcerers, who are saying to you, 'You
shall not serve the king of Babylon.' 10For it is
a lie which they are prophesying to you, with
the result that you will be removed far from
your land, and I will drive you out, and you
will perish. 11But any nation which will bring
its neck under the yoke of the king of Babylon
and serve him, I will leave on its own land, to
till it and dwell there, says the LORD." ' "

12To Zedeki′ah king of Judah I spoke in
like manner: "Bring your necks under the
yoke of the king of Babylon, and serve him
and his people, and live. 13Why will you and
your people die by the sword, by famine,
and by pestilence, as the LORD has spoken
concerning any nation which will not serve
the king of Babylon? 14Do not listen to the
words of the prophets who are saying to you,
'You shall not serve the king of Babylon,' for
it is a lie which they are prophesying to you.
15I have not sent them, says the LORD, but
they are prophesying falsely in my name,
with the result that I will drive you out and
you will perish, you and the prophets who
are prophesying to you."

16Then I spoke to the priests and to
all this people, saying, "Thus says the
LORD: Do not listen to the words of your
prophets who are prophesying to you,
saying, 'Behold, the vessels of the LORD's
house will now shortly be brought back
from Babylon,' for it is a lie which they
are prophesying to you. 17Do not listen to
them; serve the king of Babylon and live.
Why should this city become a desolation?
18If they are prophets, and if the word of the
LORD is with them, then let them intercede
with the LORD of hosts, that the vessels
which are left in the house of the LORD,
in the house of the king of Judah, and in
Jerusalem may not go to Babylon. 19For
thus says the LORD of hosts concerning
the pillars, the sea, the stands, and the rest
of the vessels which are left in this city,
20which Nebuchadnez′zar king of Babylon
did not take away, when he took into exile
from Jerusalem to Babylon Jeconi′ah the
son of Jehoi′akim, king of Judah, and all
the nobles of Judah and Jerusalem—21thus
says the LORD of hosts, the God of Israel,
concerning the vessels which are left in the
house of the LORD, in the house of the king
of Judah, and in Jerusalem: 22They shall be
carried to Babylon and remain there until
the day when I give attention to them, says
the LORD. Then I will bring them back and
restore them to this place."

28 In that same year, at the beginning
of the reign of Zedeki′ah king of

Judah, in the fifth month of the fourth year,
Hanani′ah the son of Azzur, the prophet
from Gib′eon, spoke to me in the house of
the LORD, in the presence of the priests and
all the people, saying, 2"Thus says the LORD
of hosts, the God of Israel: I have broken
the yoke of the king of Babylon. 3Within
two years I will bring back to this place
all the vessels of the LORD's house, which
Nebuchadnez′zar king of Babylon took away
from this place and carried to Babylon. 4I
will also bring back to this place Jeconi′ah
the son of Jehoi′akim, king of Judah, and all
the exiles from Judah who went to Babylon,
says the LORD, for I will break the yoke of
the king of Babylon."

5Then the prophet Jeremi′ah spoke to
Hanani′ah the prophet in the presence of
the priests and all the people who were
standing in the house of the LORD; 6and the
prophet Jeremi′ah said, "Amen! May the
LORD do so; may the LORD make the words
which you have prophesied come true, and
bring back to this place from Babylon the
vessels of the house of the LORD, and all
the exiles. 7Yet hear now this word which I
speak in your hearing and in the hearing of
all the people. 8The prophets who preceded
you and me from ancient times prophesied
war, famine, and pestilence against many
countries and great kingdoms. 9As for the
prophet who prophesies peace, when the
word of that prophet comes to pass, then it
will be known that the LORD has truly sent
the prophet."

10Then the prophet Hanani′ah took the
yoke-bars from the neck of Jeremi′ah the
prophet, and broke them. 11And Hanani′ah
spoke in the presence of all the people,
saying, "Thus says the LORD: Even so will
I break the yoke of Nebuchadnez′zar king
of Babylon from the neck of all the nations
within two years." But Jeremi′ah the prophet
went his way.

12Sometime after the prophet Hanani′ah
had broken the yoke-bars from off the
neck of Jeremi′ah the prophet, the word
of the LORD came to Jeremi′ah: 13"Go, tell
Hanani′ah, 'Thus says the LORD: You have
broken wooden bars, but I will make in
their place bars of iron. 14For thus says the
LORD of hosts, the God of Israel: I have put
upon the neck of all these nations an iron
yoke of servitude to Nebuchadnez′zar king
of Babylon, and they shall serve him, for
I have given to him even the beasts of the
field.'" 15And Jeremi′ah the prophet said to
the prophet Hanani′ah, "Listen, Hananiah,
the LORD has not sent you, and you have
made this people trust in a lie. 16Therefore
thus says the LORD: 'Behold, I will remove
you from the face of the earth. This very
year you shall die, because you have uttered
rebellion against the LORD.'"

17In that same year, in the seventh month,
the prophet Hanani′ah died.

29 These are the words of the letter
which Jeremi′ah the prophet sent
from Jerusalem to the elders of the exiles,
and to the priests, the prophets, and all the
people, whom Nebuchadnez′zar had taken
into exile from Jerusalem to Babylon. 2This
was after King Jeconi′ah, and the queen
mother, the eunuchs, the princes of Judah
and Jerusalem, the craftsmen, and the
smiths had departed from Jerusalem. 3The
letter was sent by the hand of Ela′sah the
son of Sha′phan and Gemari′ah the son of
Hilki′ah, whom Zedeki′ah king of Judah
sent to Babylon to Nebuchadnez′zar king
of Babylon. It said: 4"Thus says the LORD
of hosts, the God of Israel, to all the exiles
whom I have sent into exile from Jerusalem
to Babylon: 5Build houses and live in
them; plant gardens and eat their produce.
6Take wives and have sons and daughters;
take wives for your sons, and give your
daughters in marriage, that they may bear
sons and daughters; multiply there, and do
not decrease. 7But seek the welfare of the
city where I have sent you into exile, and
pray to the LORD on its behalf, for in its
welfare you will find your welfare. 8For thus
says the LORD of hosts, the God of Israel:
Do not let your prophets and your diviners
who are among you deceive you, and do
not listen to the dreams which they dream,
9for it is a lie which they are prophesying to
you in my name; I did not send them, says
the LORD.

10“For thus says the LORD: When seventy
years are completed for Babylon, I will visit
you, and I will fulfil to you my promise and
bring you back to this place. 11For I know
the plans I have for you, says the LORD,
plans for welfare and not for evil, to give
you a future and a hope. 12Then you will call
upon me and come and pray to me, and I
will hear you. 13You will seek me and find
me; when you seek me with all your heart,
14I will be found by you, says the LORD, and
I will restore your fortunes and gather you
from all the nations and all the places where
I have driven you, says the LORD, and I will
bring you back to the place from which I
sent you into exile.

15“Because you have said, ‘The LORD has
raised up prophets for us in Babylon,’—
16Thus says the LORD concerning the
king who sits on the throne of David, and
concerning all the people who dwell in
this city, your kinsmen who did not go out
with you into exile: 17‘Thus says the LORD
of hosts, Behold, I am sending on them
sword, famine, and pestilence, and I will
make them like vile figs which are so bad
they cannot be eaten. 18I will pursue them
with sword, famine, and pestilence, and will
make them a horror to all the kingdoms of
the earth, to be a curse, a terror, a hissing,
and a reproach among all the nations where
I have driven them, 19because they did not
heed my words, says the LORD, which I
persistently sent to you by my servants the
prophets, but you would not listen, says the
LORD.’—20Hear the word of the LORD, all
you exiles whom I sent away from Jerusalem
to Babylon: 21‘Thus says the LORD of hosts,
the God of Israel, concerning A′hab the son
of Kolai′ah and Zedeki′ah the son of Ma-
asei′ah, who are prophesying a lie to you
in my name: Behold, I will deliver them
into the hand of Nebuchadrez′zar king of
Babylon, and he shall slay them before your
eyes. 22Because of them this curse shall be
used by all the exiles from Judah in Babylon:
“The LORD make you like Zedeki′ah and
A′hab, whom the king of Babylon roasted
in the fire,” 23because they have committed
folly in Israel, they have committed adultery
with their neighbors’ wives, and they have
spoken in my name lying words which I
did not command them. I am the one who
knows, and I am witness, says the LORD.’ ”

WISDOM 15

14But most foolish, and more miserable than
an infant,
are all the enemies who oppressed your
people.
15For they thought that all their heathen
idols were gods,
though these have neither the use of their
eyes to see with,
nor nostrils with which to draw breath,
nor ears with which to hear,
nor fingers to feel with,
and their feet are of no use for walking.
16For a man made them,
and one whose spirit is borrowed
formed them;
for no man can form a god which is
like himself.
17He is mortal, and what he makes with
lawless hands is dead,
for he is better than the objects
he worships,
since he has life, but they never have.

18The enemies of your people worship even
the most hateful animals,
which are worse than all others, when
judged by their lack of intelligence;
19and even as animals they are not so
beautiful in appearance that one
would desire them,
but they have escaped both the praise of
God and his blessing.

16 Therefore those men were deservedly
punished through such creatures,
and were tormented by a multitude of
animals.
2Instead of this punishment you showed
kindness to your people,
and you prepared quails to eat,
a delicacy to satisfy the desire of appetite;
3in order that those men, when they
desired food,

might lose the least remnant of appetite
because of the odious creatures sent
to them,
while your people, after suffering want a
short time,
might partake of delicacies.
4For it was necessary that upon those
oppressors inexorable want
should come,
while to these it was merely shown how
their enemies were being tormented.

GALATIANS 3

19Why then the law? It was added because of transgressions, till the offspring should come to whom the promise had been made; and it was ordained by
angels through an intermediary. 20Now an
intermediary implies more than one; but
God is one.
21Is the law then against the promises
of God? Certainly not; for if a law had
been given which could make alive, then
righteousness would indeed be by the law.
22But the Scripture consigned all things to
sin, that what was promised to faith in Jesus
Christ might be given to those who believe.
23Now before faith came, we were confined
under the law, kept under restraint until faith
should be revealed. 24So that the law was our
custodian until Christ came, that we might be
justified by faith. 25But now that faith has come,
we are no longer under a custodian; 26for in
Christ Jesus you are all sons of God, through
faith. 27For as many of you as were baptized
into Christ have put on Christ. 28There is
neither Jew nor Greek, there is neither slave
nor free, there is neither male nor female; for
you are all one in Christ Jesus. 29And if you
are Christ's, then you are Abraham's offspring,
heirs according to promise.
4 I mean that the heir, as long as he is a
child, is no better than a slave, though
he is the owner of all the estate; 2but he is
under guardians and trustees until the date
set by the father. 3So with us; when we were
children, we were slaves to the elemental
spirits of the universe. 4But when the time
had fully come, God sent forth his Son, born
of woman, born under the law, 5to redeem
those who were under the law, so that
we might receive adoption as sons. 6And
because you are sons, God has sent the Spirit
of his Son into our hearts, crying, "Abba!
Father!" 7So through God you are no longer
a slave but a son, and if a son then an heir.

REFLECTION

Jeremiah 29:11 ("For I know the plans I have for you, says the LORD, plans for welfare and not for evil, to give you a future and a hope") is a very popular verse, printed on bookmarks and cited on social media. Why? Taken out of context, this verse might sound like something out of a spiritual self-help book, like a Christian version of positive thinking. But in context, this verse challenges us to trust in a God whose providence spans the entire universe and whose plan encompasses all of humankind. This verse follows Jeremiah's prophecy that the people will return to Israel after seventy years (see v. 10)—when most of the recipients of the prophecy would be dead! This prophecy stands in stark contrast with the false prophecy of Hananiah, who promised restoration after only two years (see 28:3–4). Likewise, St. Paul speaks about a plan of salvation that plays out over thousands of years and which is only fully revealed in Christ (see Gal 3:25–26). This plan of salvation does not promise personal prosperity, but rather the "you" refers to all of God's people together, i.e., the Church. Do you have faith in God's plan, even if your own small part does involve evil or suffering?

September 29

JEREMIAH 29

24To Shemai′ah of Nehel′am you shall say: 25"Thus says the LORD of hosts, the God of Israel: You have sent letters in your name to all the people

who are in Jerusalem, and to Zephani′ah
the son of Ma-asei′ah the priest, and to all
the priests, saying, 26“The LORD has made
you priest instead of Jehoi′ada the priest, to
have charge in the house of the LORD over
every madman who prophesies, to put him
in the stocks and collar. 27Now why have you
not rebuked Jeremi′ah of An′athoth who is
prophesying to you? 28For he has sent to us
in Babylon, saying, “Your exile will be long;
build houses and live in them, and plant
gardens and eat their produce.” ’ ”

29Zephani′ah the priest read this letter in the
hearing of Jeremi′ah the prophet. 30Then the
word of the LORD came to Jeremi′ah: 31“Send
to all the exiles, saying, ‘Thus says the LORD
concerning Shemai′ah of Nehel′am: Because
Shemaiah has prophesied to you when I did
not send him, and has made you trust in a
lie, 32therefore thus says the LORD: Behold,
I will punish Shemai′ah of Nehel′am and his
descendants; he shall not have any one living
among this people to see the good that I will
do to my people, says the LORD, for he has
talked rebellion against the LORD.’ ”

30 The word that came to Jeremi′ah
from the LORD: 2“Thus says the
LORD, the God of Israel: Write in a book all
the words that I have spoken to you. 3For
behold, days are coming, says the LORD,
when I will restore the fortunes of my people,
Israel and Judah, says the LORD, and I will
bring them back to the land which I gave to
their fathers, and they shall take possession
of it.”

4These are the words which the LORD
spoke concerning Israel and Judah:

5“Thus says the LORD:
We have heard a cry of panic,
of terror, and no peace.
6Ask now, and see,
can a man bear a child?
Why then do I see every man
with his hands on his loins like a woman
in labor?
Why has every face turned pale?
7Alas! that day is so great
there is none like it;
it is a time of distress for Jacob;
yet he shall be saved out of it.

8“And it shall come to pass in that day,
says the LORD of hosts, that I will break the
yoke from off their neck, and I will burst
their bonds, and strangers shall no more
make servants of them. 9But they shall serve
the LORD their God and David their king,
whom I will raise up for them.

10“Then fear not, O Jacob my servant, says
the LORD,
nor be dismayed, O Israel;
for behold, I will save you from afar,
and your offspring from the land of
their captivity.
Jacob shall return and have quiet and ease,
and none shall make him afraid.
11For I am with you to save you,
says the LORD;
I will make a full end of all the nations
among whom I scattered you,
but of you I will not make a full end.
I will chasten you in just measure,
and I will by no means leave you
unpunished.

12“For thus says the LORD:
Your hurt is incurable,
and your wound is grievous.
13There is none to uphold your cause,
no medicine for your wound,
no healing for you.
14All your lovers have forgotten you;
they care nothing for you;
for I have dealt you the blow of an enemy,
the punishment of a merciless foe,
because your guilt is great,
because your sins are flagrant.
15Why do you cry out over your hurt?
Your pain is incurable.
Because your guilt is great,
because your sins are flagrant,
I have done these things to you.
16Therefore all who devour you shall
be devoured,
and all your foes, every one of them, shall
go into captivity;
those who despoil you shall become
a spoil,
and all who prey on you I will make
a prey.

17For I will restore health to you,
and your wounds I will heal,
says the LORD,
because they have called you an outcast:
'It is Zion, for whom no one cares!'

18"Thus says the LORD:
Behold, I will restore the fortunes of the tents of Jacob,
and have compassion on his dwellings;
the city shall be rebuilt upon its mound,
and the palace shall stand where it used to be.
19Out of them shall come songs of thanksgiving,
and the voices of those who make merry.
I will multiply them, and they shall not be few;
I will make them honored, and they shall not be small.
20Their children shall be as they were of old,
and their congregation shall be established before me;
and I will punish all who oppress them.
21Their prince shall be one of themselves,
their ruler shall come forth from their midst;
I will make him draw near, and he shall approach me,
for who would dare of himself to approach me?
says the LORD.
22And you shall be my people,
and I will be your God."
23Behold the storm of the LORD!
Wrath has gone forth,
a whirling tempest;
it will burst upon the head of the wicked.
24The fierce anger of the LORD will not turn back
until he has executed and accomplished
the intents of his mind.
In the latter days you will understand this.

31 "At that time, says the LORD, I will be the God of all the families of Israel, and they shall be my people."
2Thus says the LORD:
"The people who survived the sword
found grace in the wilderness;
when Israel sought for rest,
3 the LORD appeared to him from afar.
I have loved you with an everlasting love;
therefore I have continued my faithfulness to you.
4Again I will build you, and you shall be built,
O virgin Israel!
Again you shall adorn yourself with timbrels,
and shall go forth in the dance of the merrymakers.
5Again you shall plant vineyards
upon the mountains of Samar′ia;
the planters shall plant,
and shall enjoy the fruit.
6For there shall be a day when watchmen will call
in the hill country of E′phraim:
'Arise, and let us go up to Zion,
to the LORD our God.'"

7For thus says the LORD:
"Sing aloud with gladness for Jacob,
and raise shouts for the chief of the nations;
proclaim, give praise, and say,
'The LORD has saved his people,
the remnant of Israel.'
8Behold, I will bring them from the north country,
and gather them from the farthest parts of the earth,
among them the blind and the lame,
the woman with child and her who has labor pains, together;
a great company, they shall return here.
9With weeping they shall come,
and with consolations I will lead them back,
I will make them walk by brooks of water,
in a straight path in which they shall not stumble;
for I am a father to Israel,
and E′phraim is my first-born.

10"Hear the word of the LORD, O nations,
and declare it in the islands afar off;
say, 'He who scattered Israel will gather him,
and will keep him as a shepherd keeps his flock.'
11For the LORD has ransomed Jacob,
and has redeemed him from hands too strong for him.

12They shall come and sing aloud on the
height of Zion,
and they shall be radiant over the
goodness of the LORD,
over the grain, the wine, and the oil,
and over the young of the flock and the
herd;
their life shall be like a watered garden,
and they shall languish no more.
13Then shall the maidens rejoice in the dance,
and the young men and the old shall
be merry.
I will turn their mourning into joy,
I will comfort them, and give them
gladness for sorrow.
14I will feast the soul of the priests with
abundance,
and my people shall be satisfied with
my goodness,
says the LORD."

15Thus says the LORD:
"A voice is heard in Ra′mah,
lamentation and bitter weeping.
Rachel is weeping for her children;
she refuses to be comforted for
her children,
because they are not."
16Thus says the LORD:
"Keep your voice from weeping,
and your eyes from tears;
for your work shall be rewarded, says
the LORD,
and they shall come back from the land
of the enemy.
17There is hope for your future,
says the LORD,
and your children shall come back to
their own country.
18I have heard E′phraim bemoaning,
'You have chastened me, and I was
chastened,
like an untrained calf;
bring me back that I may be restored,
for you are the LORD my God.
19For after I had turned away I repented;
and after I was instructed, I struck
my thigh;
I was ashamed, and I was confounded,
because I bore the disgrace of my youth.'
20Is E′phraim my dear son?
Is he my darling child?
For as often as I speak against
him,
I do remember him still.
Therefore my heart yearns for him;
I will surely have mercy on him,
says the LORD.

21"Set up waymarks for yourself,
make yourself guideposts;
consider well the highway,
the road by which you went.
Return, O virgin Israel,
return to these your cities.
22How long will you waver,
O faithless daughter?
For the LORD has created a new thing on
the earth:
a woman protects a man."

23Thus says the LORD of hosts, the God
of Israel: "Once more they shall use these
words in the land of Judah and in its cities,
when I restore their fortunes:
'The LORD bless you, O habitation of
righteousness,
O holy hill!'
24And Judah and all its cities shall dwell there
together, and the farmers and those who
wander with their flocks. 25For I will satisfy
the weary soul, and every languishing soul I
will replenish."
26Thereupon I awoke and looked, and my
sleep was pleasant to me.
27"Behold, the days are coming, says the
LORD, when I will sow the house of Israel
and the house of Judah with the seed
of man and the seed of beast. 28And it
shall come to pass that as I have watched
over them to pluck up and break down,
to overthrow, destroy, and bring evil, so
I will watch over them to build and to
plant, says the LORD. 29In those days they
shall no longer say:
'The fathers have eaten sour grapes,
and the children's teeth are set on edge.'
30But every one shall die for his own sin;
each man who eats sour grapes, his teeth
shall be set on edge."

WISDOM 16

5For when the terrible rage of wild beasts
came upon your people
and they were being destroyed by the bites
of writhing serpents,
your wrath did not continue to the end;
6they were troubled for a little while as
a warning,
and received a token of deliverance to
remind them of your law's command.
7For he who turned toward it was saved, not
by what he saw,
but by you, the Savior of all.
8And by this also you convinced our enemies
that it is you who deliver from every evil.
9For they were killed by the bites of locusts
and flies,
and no healing was found for them,
because they deserved to be punished by
such things;
10but your sons were not conquered even by
the teeth of venomous serpents,
for your mercy came to their help and
healed them.
11To remind them of your oracles they
were bitten,
and then were quickly delivered,
lest they should fall into deep forgetfulness
and become unresponsive to your
kindness.
12For neither herb nor poultice cured them,
but it was your word, O Lord, which heals
all men.
13For you have power over life and death;
you lead men down to the gates of Hades
and back again.
14A man in his wickedness kills another,
but he cannot bring back the departed spirit,
nor set free the imprisoned soul.
15To escape from your hand is impossible;
16for the ungodly, refusing to know you,
were scourged by the strength of your arm,
pursued by unusual rains and hail and
relentless storms,
and utterly consumed by fire.
17For—most incredible of all—in the water,
which quenches all things,
the fire had still greater effect,
for the universe defends the righteous.

GALATIANS 4

8Formerly, when you did not
know God, you were in bondage
to beings that by nature are no gods; 9but
now that you have come to know God,
or rather to be known by God, how can you
turn back again to the weak and beggarly
elemental spirits, whose slaves you want to be
once more? 10You observe days, and months,
and seasons, and years! 11I am afraid I have
labored over you in vain.

12Brethren, I beg you, become as I am, for I
also have become as you are. You did me no
wrong; 13you know it was because of a bodily
ailment that I preached the gospel to you at
first; 14and though my condition was a trial
to you, you did not scorn or despise me, but
received me as an angel of God, as Christ Jesus.
15What has become of the satisfaction you felt?
For I bear you witness that, if possible, you
would have plucked out your eyes and given
them to me. 16Have I then become your enemy
by telling you the truth? 17They make much
of you, but for no good purpose; they want
to shut you out, that you may make much of
them. 18For a good purpose it is always good
to be made much of, and not only when I am
present with you. 19My little children, with
whom I am again in travail until Christ be
formed in you! 20I could wish to be present
with you now and to change my tone, for I am
perplexed about you.

21Tell me, you who desire to be under law,
do you not hear the law? 22For it is written that
Abraham had two sons, one by a slave and
one by a free woman. 23But the son of the slave
was born according to the flesh, the son of the
free woman through promise. 24Now this is
an allegory: these women are two covenants.
One is from Mount Sinai, bearing children
for slavery; she is Hagar. 25Now Hagar is
Mount Sinai in Arabia; she corresponds to the
present Jerusalem, for she is in slavery with her
children. 26But the Jerusalem above is free, and
she is our mother. 27For it is written,
"Rejoice, O barren one who does
not bear;
break forth and shout, you who are not
with labor pains;

for the desolate has more children
than she who has a husband."
28Now we, brethren, like Isaac, are children of
promise. 29But as at that time he who was born
according to the flesh persecuted him who was
born according to the Spirit, so it is now. 30But
what does the Scripture say? "Cast out the slave
and her son; for the son of the slave shall not
inherit with the son of the free woman." 31So,
brethren, we are not children of the slave but of
the free woman.

REFLECTION

Today, Jeremiah and the Book of Wisdom both speak about receiving mercy from God after a period of punishment. Jeremiah, who has been prophesying Israel's condemnation, now preaches God's mercy and love. The people, who have been weeping tears of grief, will weep tears of joy (see Jer 31:13). Wisdom describes Israel's slavery in Egypt and wandering in the desert quite gently, saying, "They were troubled for a little while as a warning" (Wis 16:6). Both Wisdom and Jeremiah speak of the period of trial as an illness. Wisdom calls it the bite of a snake (see v. 11), and Jeremiah describes it as a deep wound and incurable hurt (see Jer 30:12). The medical imagery resonates with us as it did with ancient people, since we too are required to undergo painful treatments in order to achieve greater healing. Although it would be a grave mistake to interpret all human suffering as punishment or correction from God, it can help us persevere through hard times to recognize that God is the great healer. As in the Book of Wisdom, when we look back, our hard times may indeed seem brief. Will you allow God to use your suffering in order to heal you?

September 30

JEREMIAH 31

31"Behold, the days are coming,
says the LORD, when I will make
a new covenant with the house of Israel
and the house of Judah, 32not like the
covenant which I made with their fathers
when I took them by the hand to bring them
out of the land of Egypt, my covenant which
they broke, and I showed myself their Master,
says the LORD. 33But this is the covenant which
I will make with the house of Israel after those
days, says the LORD: I will put my law within
them, and I will write it upon their hearts;
and I will be their God, and they shall be my
people. 34And no longer shall each man teach
his neighbor and each his brother, saying,
'Know the LORD,' for they shall all know me,
from the least of them to the greatest, says the
LORD; for I will forgive their iniquity, and I
will remember their sin no more."

35Thus says the LORD,
who gives the sun for light by day
and the fixed order of the moon and the
stars for light by night,
who stirs up the sea so that its
waves roar—
the LORD of hosts is his name:
36"If this fixed order departs
from before me, says the LORD,
then shall the descendants of Israel cease
from being a nation before me for ever."
37Thus says the LORD:
"If the heavens above can be measured,
and the foundations of the earth below
can be explored,
then I will cast off all the descendants
of Israel
for all that they have done,
says the LORD."

38"Behold, the days are coming, says the
LORD, when the city shall be rebuilt for the
LORD from the tower of Hanan′el to the
Corner Gate. 39And the measuring line shall
go out farther, straight to the hill Ga′reb, and
shall then turn to Goah. 40The whole valley
of the dead bodies and the ashes, and all
the fields as far as the brook Kid′ron, to the
corner of the Horse Gate toward the east,
shall be sacred to the LORD. It shall not be
uprooted or overthrown any more for ever."

32 The word that came to Jeremi′ah
from the LORD in the tenth year

of Zedeki′ah king of Judah, which was the eighteenth year of Nebuchadrez′zar. 2At that time the army of the king of Babylon was besieging Jerusalem, and Jeremi′ah the prophet was shut up in the court of the guard which was in the palace of the king of Judah. 3For Zedeki′ah king of Judah had imprisoned him, saying, "Why do you prophesy and say, 'Thus says the LORD: Behold, I am giving this city into the hand of the king of Babylon, and he shall take it; 4Zedeki′ah king of Judah shall not escape out of the hand of the Chalde′ans, but shall surely be given into the hand of the king of Babylon, and shall speak with him face to face and see him eye to eye; 5and he shall take Zedeki′ah to Babylon, and there he shall remain until I visit him, says the LORD; though you fight against the Chalde′ans, you shall not succeed'?"

6Jeremi′ah said, "The word of the LORD came to me: 7Behold, Han′amel the son of Shallum your uncle will come to you and say, 'Buy my field which is at An′athoth, for the right of redemption by purchase is yours.' 8Then Han′amel my cousin came to me in the court of the guard, in accordance with the word of the LORD, and said to me, 'Buy my field which is at An′athoth in the land of Benjamin, for the right of possession and redemption is yours; buy it for yourself.' Then I knew that this was the word of the LORD.

9"And I bought the field at An′athoth from Han′amel my cousin, and weighed out the money to him, seventeen shekels of silver. 10I signed the deed, sealed it, got witnesses, and weighed the money on scales. 11Then I took the sealed deed of purchase, containing the terms and conditions, and the open copy; 12and I gave the deed of purchase to Baruch the son of Neri′ah son of Mah′seiah, in the presence of Han′amel my cousin, in the presence of the witnesses who signed the deed of purchase, and in the presence of all the Jews who were sitting in the court of the guard. 13I charged Baruch in their presence, saying, 14'Thus says the LORD of hosts, the God of Israel: Take these deeds, both this sealed deed of purchase and this open deed, and put them in an earthenware vessel, that they may last for a long time. 15For thus says the LORD of hosts, the God of Israel: Houses and fields and vineyards shall again be bought in this land.'

16"After I had given the deed of purchase to Baruch the son of Neri′ah, I prayed to the LORD, saying: 17'Ah Lord GOD! It is you who have made the heavens and the earth by your great power and by your outstretched arm! Nothing is too hard for you, 18who show mercy to thousands, but repay the guilt of fathers to their children after them, O great and mighty God whose name is the LORD of hosts, 19great in counsel and mighty in deed; whose eyes are open to all the ways of men, rewarding every man according to his ways and according to the fruit of his doings; 20who have shown signs and wonders in the land of Egypt, and to this day in Israel and among all mankind, and have made you a name, as at this day. 21You brought your people Israel out of the land of Egypt with signs and wonders, with a strong hand and outstretched arm, and with great terror; 22and you gave them this land, which you swore to their fathers to give them, a land flowing with milk and honey; 23and they entered and took possession of it. But they did not obey your voice or walk in your law; they did nothing of all you commanded them to do. Therefore you have made all this evil come upon them. 24Behold, the siege mounds have come up to the city to take it, and because of sword and famine and pestilence the city is given into the hands of the Chalde′ans who are fighting against it. What you spoke has come to pass, and behold, you see it. 25Yet you, O Lord GOD, have said to me, "Buy the field for money and get witnesses"—though the city is given into the hands of the Chalde′ans.' "

26The word of the LORD came to Jeremi′ah: 27"Behold, I am the LORD, the God of all flesh; is anything too hard for me? 28Therefore, thus says the LORD: Behold, I am giving this city into the hands of the Chalde′ans and into the hand of Nebuchadrez′zar king of Babylon, and he shall take it. 29The Chalde′ans who are fighting against this city shall come and

set this city on fire, and burn it, with the
houses on whose roofs incense has been
offered to Ba′al and drink offerings have
been poured out to other gods, to provoke
me to anger. 30For the sons of Israel and the
sons of Judah have done nothing but evil
in my sight from their youth; the sons of
Israel have done nothing but provoke me
to anger by the work of their hands, says
the LORD. 31This city has aroused my anger
and wrath, from the day it was built to this
day, so that I will remove it from my sight
32because of all the evil of the sons of Israel
and the sons of Judah which they did to
provoke me to anger—their kings and their
princes, their priests and their prophets,
the men of Judah and the inhabitants of
Jerusalem. 33They have turned to me their
back and not their face; and though I have
taught them persistently they have not
listened to receive instruction. 34They set
up their abominations in the house which
is called by my name, to defile it. 35They
built the high places of Ba′al in the valley
of the son of Hinnom, to offer up their
sons and daughters to Mo′lech, though I
did not command them, nor did it enter
into my mind, that they should do this
abomination, to cause Judah to sin.

36"Now therefore thus says the LORD, the
God of Israel, concerning this city of which
you say, 'It is given into the hand of the
king of Babylon by sword, by famine, and
by pestilence': 37Behold, I will gather them
from all the countries to which I drove
them in my anger and my wrath and in
great indignation; I will bring them back
to this place, and I will make them dwell in
safety. 38And they shall be my people, and
I will be their God. 39I will give them one
heart and one way, that they may fear me
for ever, for their own good and the good of
their children after them. 40I will make with
them an everlasting covenant, that I will not
turn away from doing good to them; and I
will put the fear of me in their hearts, that
they may not turn from me. 41I will rejoice
in doing them good, and I will plant them
in this land in faithfulness, with all my heart
and all my soul.

42"For thus says the LORD: Just as I have
brought all this great evil upon this people,
so I will bring upon them all the good that
I promise them. 43Fields shall be bought
in this land of which you are saying, It is a
desolation, without man or beast; it is given
into the hands of the Chalde′ans. 44Fields
shall be bought for money, and deeds shall
be signed and sealed and witnessed, in
the land of Benjamin, in the places about
Jerusalem, and in the cities of Judah, in the
cities of the hill country, in the cities of the
Shephe′lah, and in the cities of the Neg′eb;
for I will restore their fortunes, says the
LORD."

WISDOM 16

18At one time the flame was restrained,
so that it might not consume the creatures
sent against the ungodly,
but that seeing this they might know
that they were being pursued by the
judgment of God;
19and at another time even in the midst
of water it burned more intensely
than fire,
to destroy the crops of the unrighteous land.
20Instead of these things you gave your
people the food of angels,
and without their toil you supplied them
from heaven with bread ready to eat,
providing every pleasure and suited to
every taste.
21For your sustenance manifested your
sweetness toward your children;
and the bread, ministering to the desire of
the one who took it,
was changed to suit every one's liking.
22Snow and ice withstood fire without
melting,
so that they might know that the crops of
their enemies
were being destroyed by the fire that blazed
in the hail
and flashed in the showers of rain;
23whereas the fire, in order that the righteous
might be fed,
even forgot its native power.

24For creation, serving you who have made it,
exerts itself to punish the unrighteous,
and in kindness relaxes on behalf of those
who trust in you.
25Therefore at that time also, changed into
all forms,
it served your all-nourishing bounty,
according to the desire of those who
had need,
26so that your sons, whom you loved, O
Lord, might learn
that it is not the production of crops that
feeds man,
but that your word preserves those who
trust in you.
27For what was not destroyed by fire
was melted when simply warmed by a
fleeting ray of the sun,
28to make it known that one must rise before
the sun to give you thanks,
and must pray to you at the dawning of
the light;
29for the hope of an ungrateful man will melt
like wintry frost,
and flow away like waste water.

GALATIANS 5

For freedom Christ has set us free; stand fast therefore, and do not submit again to a yoke of slavery.
2Now I, Paul, say to you that if you re-
ceive circumcision, Christ will be of
no advantage to you. 3I testify again to
every man who receives circumcision
that he is bound to keep the whole law.
4You are severed from Christ, you who
would be justified by the law; you have
fallen away from grace. 5For through the
Spirit, by faith, we wait for the hope of
righteousness. 6For in Christ Jesus neither
circumcision nor uncircumcision is of any
avail, but faith working through love. 7You
were running well; who hindered you from
obeying the truth? 8This persuasion is not
from him who called you. 9A little leaven
leavens all the dough. 10I have confidence
in the Lord that you will take no other view
than mine; and he who is troubling you
will bear his judgment, whoever he is. 11But
if I, brethren, still preach circumcision,
why am I still persecuted? In that case
the stumbling block of the cross has been
removed. 12I wish those who unsettle you
would mutilate themselves!
13For you were called to freedom, brethren; only do not use your freedom as an
opportunity for the flesh, but through love
be servants of one another. 14For the whole
law is fulfilled in one word, "You shall love
your neighbor as yourself." 15But if you bite
and devour one another take heed that you
are not consumed by one another.

REFLECTION

If your stockbroker told you to buy shares in a company that would soon be bankrupt, how would you respond? God makes a similar demand of Jeremiah: to buy a field that would soon be taken by the Babylonians (see Jer 32:6–15). The request is an analogy for God's new covenant, which is described in Jeremiah 31. This covenant cannot be reduced to a piece of paper like a deed of ownership, but instead the New Covenant is one of the heart. Jeremiah does not trust in the land purchased, but in God's Word. St. Paul likewise insists on a transformation of the Law. Whereas literal circumcision (a requirement of the Law) now profits nothing, the law of Christ demands circumcision of the heart (see Rom 2:29). The Old Covenant, Jeremiah's covenant, and Christ's covenant are of a piece, and yet there is also transformation. These developments in the relationship of humankind with God do not lessen our obligations; after all, Jeremiah still has to spend his precious silver on the field. But, if our hearts are transformed, we can come to love God's will, rather than follow it as an external imposition. In short, we become grateful rather than resentful (see Wis 16:29). Have you ever found that after doing a good thing grudgingly, you come to love your good work?

October 1

JEREMIAH 33

The word of the LORD came to Jeremi′ah a second time, while he was still shut up in the court of the guard: 2“Thus says the LORD who made the earth, the LORD who formed it to establish it—the LORD is his name: 3Call to me and I will answer you, and will tell you great and hidden things which you have not known. 4For thus says the LORD, the God of Israel, concerning the houses of this city and the houses of the kings of Judah which were torn down to make a defense against the siege mounds and before the sword: 5The Chalde′ans are coming in to fight and to fill them with the dead bodies of men whom I shall strike in my anger and my wrath, for I have hidden my face from this city because of all their wickedness. 6Behold, I will bring to it health and healing, and I will heal them and reveal to them abundance of prosperity and security. 7I will restore the fortunes of Judah and the fortunes of Israel, and rebuild them as they were at first. 8I will cleanse them from all the guilt of their sin against me, and I will forgive all the guilt of their sin and rebellion against me. 9And this city shall be to me a name of joy, a praise and a glory before all the nations of the earth who shall hear of all the good that I do for them; they shall fear and tremble because of all the good and all the prosperity I provide for it.

10“Thus says the LORD: In this place of which you say, ‘It is a waste without man or beast,’ in the cities of Judah and the streets of Jerusalem that are desolate, without man or inhabitant or beast, there shall be heard again 11the voice of mirth and the voice of gladness, the voice of the bridegroom and the voice of the bride, the voices of those who sing, as they bring thank offerings to the house of the LORD:

‘Give thanks to the LORD of hosts,
for the LORD is good,
for his mercy endures for ever!’

For I will restore the fortunes of the land as at first, says the LORD.

12“Thus says the LORD of hosts: In this place which is waste, without man or beast, and in all of its cities, there shall again be habitations of shepherds resting their flocks. 13In the cities of the hill country, in the cities of the Shephe′lah, and in the cities of the Neg′eb, in the land of Benjamin, the places about Jerusalem, and in the cities of Judah, flocks shall again pass under the hands of the one who counts them, says the LORD.

14“Behold, the days are coming, says the LORD, when I will fulfil the promise I made to the house of Israel and the house of Judah. 15In those days and at that time I will cause a righteous Branch to spring forth for David; and he shall execute justice and righteousness in the land. 16In those days Judah will be saved and Jerusalem will dwell securely. And this is the name by which it will be called: ‘The LORD is our righteousness.’

17“For thus says the LORD: David shall never lack a man to sit on the throne of the house of Israel, 18and the Levitical priests shall never lack a man in my presence to offer burnt offerings, to burn cereal offerings, and to make sacrifices for ever.”

19The word of the LORD came to Jeremi′ah: 20“Thus says the LORD: If you can break my covenant with the day and my covenant with the night, so that day and night will not come at their appointed time, 21then also my covenant with David my servant may be broken, so that he shall not have a son to reign on his throne, and my covenant with the Levitical priests my ministers. 22As the host of heaven cannot be numbered and the sands of the sea cannot be measured, so I will multiply the descendants of David my servant, and the Levitical priests who minister to me.”

23The word of the LORD came to Jeremi′ah: 24“Have you not observed what these people

are saying, 'The LORD has rejected the two
families which he chose'? Thus they have
despised my people so that they are no
longer a nation in their sight. 25Thus says the
LORD: If I have not established my covenant
with day and night and the ordinances of
heaven and earth, 26then I will reject the
descendants of Jacob and David my servant
and will not choose one of his descendants
to rule over the seed of Abraham, Isaac, and
Jacob. For I will restore their fortunes, and
will have mercy upon them."

34 The word which came to Jeremi'ah
from the LORD, when Nebuchadrez'zar
king of Babylon and all his army and all the
kingdoms of the earth under his dominion
and all the peoples were fighting against
Jerusalem and all of its cities: 2"Thus says
the LORD, the God of Israel: Go and speak
to Zedeki'ah king of Judah and say to him,
'Thus says the LORD: Behold, I am giving
this city into the hand of the king of Babylon,
and he shall burn it with fire. 3You shall not
escape from his hand, but shall surely be
captured and delivered into his hand; you
shall see the king of Babylon eye to eye and
speak with him face to face; and you shall
go to Babylon.' 4Yet hear the word of the
LORD, O Zedeki'ah king of Judah! Thus says
the LORD concerning you: 'You shall not die
by the sword. 5You shall die in peace. And
as spices were burned for your fathers, the
former kings who were before you, so men
shall burn spices for you and lament for you,
saying, "Alas, lord!"' For I have spoken the
word, says the LORD."

6Then Jeremi'ah the prophet spoke all
these words to Zedeki'ah king of Judah, in
Jerusalem, 7when the army of the king of
Babylon was fighting against Jerusalem and
against all the cities of Judah that were left,
La'chish and Aze'kah; for these were the
only fortified cities of Judah that remained.

8The word which came to Jeremi'ah from
the LORD, after King Zedeki'ah had made a
covenant with all the people in Jerusalem
to make a proclamation of liberty to them,
9that every one should set free his Hebrew
slaves, male and female, so that no one
should enslave a Jew, his brother. 10And
they obeyed, all the princes and all the
people who had entered into the covenant
that every one would set free his slave,
male or female, so that they would not be
enslaved again; they obeyed and set them
free. 11But afterward they turned around
and took back the male and female slaves
they had set free, and brought them into
subjection as slaves. 12The word of the
LORD came to Jeremi'ah from the LORD:
13"Thus says the LORD, the God of Israel: I
made a covenant with your fathers when I
brought them out of the land of Egypt, out
of the house of bondage, saying, 14'At the
end of six years each of you must set free
the fellow Hebrew who has been sold to
you and has served you six years; you must
set him free from your service.' But your
fathers did not listen to me or incline their
ears to me. 15You recently repented and did
what was right in my eyes by proclaiming
liberty, each to his neighbor, and you made
a covenant before me in the house which is
called by my name; 16but then you turned
around and profaned my name when each
of you took back his male and female
slaves, whom you had set free according
to their desire, and you brought them into
subjection to be your slaves. 17Therefore,
thus says the LORD: You have not obeyed
me by proclaiming liberty, every one to
his brother and to his neighbor; behold,
I proclaim to you liberty to the sword,
to pestilence, and to famine, says the
LORD. I will make you a horror to all the
kingdoms of the earth. 18And the men who
transgressed my covenant and did not keep
the terms of the covenant which they made
before me, I will make like the calf which
they cut in two and passed between its
parts—19the princes of Judah, the princes of
Jerusalem, the eunuchs, the priests, and all
the people of the land who passed between
the parts of the calf; 20and I will give them
into the hand of their enemies and into the
hand of those who seek their lives. Their
dead bodies shall be food for the birds of
the air and the beasts of the earth. 21And
Zedeki'ah king of Judah, and his princes
I will give into the hand of their enemies

and into the hand of those who seek their
lives, into the hand of the army of the king
of Babylon which has withdrawn from you.
22 Behold, I will command, says the LORD,
and will bring them back to this city; and
they will fight against it, and take it, and
burn it with fire. I will make the cities of
Judah a desolation without inhabitant."

35 The word which came to Jeremi´ah
from the LORD in the days of Je-
hoi´akim the son of Josi´ah, king of Judah:
2 "Go to the house of the Re´chabites,
and speak with them, and bring them to
the house of the LORD, into one of the
chambers; then offer them wine to drink."
3 So I took Ja-azani´ah the son of Jeremi´ah,
son of Ha´bazzini´ah, and his brothers, and
all his sons, and the whole house of the
Re´chabites. 4 I brought them to the house of
the LORD into the chamber of the sons of
Ha´nan the son of Igdali´ah, the man of God,
which was near the chamber of the princes,
above the chamber of Ma-asei´ah the son of
Shallum, keeper of the threshold. 5 Then I set
before the Re´chabites pitchers full of wine,
and cups; and I said to them, "Drink wine."
6 But they answered, "We will drink no wine,
for Jon´adab the son of Re´chab, our father,
commanded us, 'You shall not drink wine,
neither you nor your sons for ever; 7 you
shall not build a house; you shall not sow
seed; you shall not plant or have a vineyard;
but you shall live in tents all your days, that
you may live many days in the land where
you sojourn.' 8 We have obeyed the voice
of Jon´adab the son of Re´chab, our father,
in all that he commanded us, to drink no
wine all our days, ourselves, our wives, our
sons, or our daughters, 9 and not to build
houses to dwell in. We have no vineyard or
field or seed; 10 but we have lived in tents,
and have obeyed and done all that Jon´adab
our father commanded us. 11 But when
Nebuchadrez´zar king of Babylon came up
against the land, we said, 'Come, and let us
go to Jerusalem for fear of the army of the
Chalde´ans and the army of the Syrians.' So
we are living in Jerusalem."

12 Then the word of the LORD came to
Jeremi´ah: 13 "Thus says the LORD of hosts,
the God of Israel: Go and say to the men of
Judah and the inhabitants of Jerusalem, Will
you not receive instruction and listen to my
words? says the LORD. 14 The command which
Jon´adab the son of Re´chab gave to his sons,
to drink no wine, has been kept; and they
drink none to this day, for they have obeyed
their father's command. I have spoken to
you persistently, but you have not listened to
me. 15 I have sent to you all my servants the
prophets, sending them persistently, saying,
'Turn now every one of you from his evil way,
and amend your doings, and do not go after
other gods to serve them, and then you shall
dwell in the land which I gave to you and
your fathers.' But you did not incline your
ear or listen to me. 16 The sons of Jon´adab
the son of Re´chab have kept the command
which their father gave them, but this people
has not obeyed me. 17 Therefore, thus says the
LORD, the God of hosts, the God of Israel:
Behold, I am bringing on Judah and all the
inhabitants of Jerusalem all the evil that I
have pronounced against them; because
I have spoken to them and they have not
listened, I have called to them and they have
not answered."

18 But to the house of the Re´chabites Je-
remi´ah said, "Thus says the LORD of hosts,
the God of Israel: Because you have obeyed
the command of Jon´adab your father, and
kept all his precepts, and done all that he
commanded you, 19 therefore thus says the
LORD of hosts, the God of Israel: Jon´adab
the son of Re´chab shall never lack a man to
stand before me."

WISDOM 17

Great are your judgments and hard
to describe;
therefore uninstructed souls have
gone astray.
2 For when lawless men supposed that they
held the holy nation in their power,
they themselves lay as captives of darkness
and prisoners of long night,
shut in under their roofs, exiles from
eternal providence.

[3]For thinking that in their secret sins they
were unobserved
behind a dark curtain of forgetfulness,
they were scattered, terribly alarmed,
and appalled by specters.
[4]For not even the inner chamber that held
them protected them from fear,
but terrifying sounds rang out around them,
and dismal phantoms with gloomy
faces appeared.
[5]And no power of fire was able to give light,
nor did the brilliant flames of the stars
avail to illumine that hateful night.
[6]Nothing was shining through to them
except a dreadful, self-kindled fire,
and in terror they deemed the things
which they saw
to be worse than that unseen appearance.
[7]The delusions of their magic art lay humbled,
and their boasted wisdom was
scornfully rebuked.
[8]For those who promised to drive off the
fears and disorders of a sick soul
were sick themselves with ridiculous fear.
[9]For even if nothing disturbing
frightened them,
yet, scared by the passing of beasts and the
hissing of serpents,
[10]they perished in trembling fear,
refusing to look even at the air, though it
nowhere could be avoided.
[11]For wickedness is a cowardly thing,
condemned by its own testimony;
distressed by conscience, it has always
exaggerated the difficulties.
[12]For fear is nothing but surrender of the
helps that come from reason;
[13]and the inner expectation of help,
being weak,
prefers ignorance of what causes
the torment.

GALATIANS 5

[16]But I say, walk by the Spirit,
and do not gratify the desires
of the flesh. [17]For the desires of the flesh
are against the Spirit, and the desires of
the Spirit are against the flesh; for these are
opposed to each other, to prevent you from
doing what you would. [18]But if you are led by
the Spirit you are not under the law. [19]Now
the works of the flesh are plain: immorality,
impurity, licentiousness, [20]idolatry, sorcery,
enmity, strife, jealousy, anger, selfishness,
dissension, party spirit, [21]envy, drunkenness,
carousing, and the like. I warn you, as I
warned you before, that those who do such
things shall not inherit the kingdom of God.
[22]But the fruit of the Spirit is love, joy, peace,
patience, kindness, goodness, faithfulness,
[23]gentleness, self-control; against such
there is no law. [24]And those who belong to
Christ Jesus have crucified the flesh with its
passions and desires.
[25]If we live by the Spirit, let us also walk
by the Spirit. [26]Let us have no self-conceit,
no provoking of one another, no envy of one
another.

REFLECTION

The Book of Wisdom tells us that when lawless people imagine themselves to be in complete control, they become "captives of darkness and prisoners of long night" (Wis 17:2). Their feigned power is proven to be a delusion, and their wisdom to be simply a boast (see v. 7). Likewise, when the Israelites seek to have mastery over other human beings, that is, by keeping slaves, they themselves became captives (see Jer 34:16–17). These reversals are not just some Christian version of cosmic revenge, whereby people get what they deserve. Rather, the Bible is warning us against pride, and against the idea that we can be master of everything—of other people and even of ourselves. Slavery is the most perverse form of this mastery, since we claim total ownership of another human being. Even if we would never dream of being a slaveholder, we often seek to gain the upper hand over someone else, to speak rather than to listen, and to have things go our way. The Bible warns us that the more we desire to control others, the more we lose control of ourselves. Is there someone you have tried to gain power over by either coercion or persuasion? How can you begin to set that relationship right?

October 2

JEREMIAH 36

In the fourth year of Jehoi′akim the son of Josi′ah, king of Judah, this word came to Jeremi′ah from the LORD: 2"Take a scroll and write on it all the words that I have spoken to you against Israel and Judah and all the nations, from the day I spoke to you, from the days of Josi′ah until today. 3It may be that the house of Judah will hear all the evil which I intend to do to them, so that every one may turn from his evil way, and that I may forgive their iniquity and their sin."

4Then Jeremi′ah called Baruch the son of Neri′ah, and Baruch wrote upon a scroll at the dictation of Jeremi′ah all the words of the LORD which he had spoken to him. 5And Jeremi′ah ordered Baruch, saying, "I am debarred from going to the house of the LORD; 6so you are to go, and on a fast day in the hearing of all the people in the LORD's house you shall read the words of the LORD from the scroll which you have written at my dictation. You shall read them also in the hearing of all the men of Judah who come out of their cities. 7It may be that their supplication will come before the LORD, and that every one will turn from his evil way, for great is the anger and wrath that the LORD has pronounced against this people." 8And Baruch the son of Neri′ah did all that Jeremi′ah the prophet ordered him about reading from the scroll the words of the LORD in the LORD's house.

9In the fifth year of Jehoi′akim the son of Josi′ah, king of Judah, in the ninth month, all the people in Jerusalem and all the people who came from the cities of Judah to Jerusalem proclaimed a fast before the LORD. 10Then, in the hearing of all the people, Baruch read the words of Jeremi′ah from the scroll, in the house of the LORD, in the chamber of Gemari′ah the son of Sha′phan the secretary, which was in the upper court, at the entry of the New Gate of the LORD's house.

11When Micai′ah the son of Gemari′ah, son of Sha′phan, heard all the words of the LORD from the scroll, 12he went down to the king's house, into the secretary's chamber; and all the princes were sitting there: Elish′ama the secretary, Delai′ah the son of Shemai′ah, Elna′than the son of Achbor, Gemari′ah the son of Sha′phan, Zedeki′ah the son of Hanani′ah, and all the princes. 13And Micai′ah told them all the words that he had heard, when Baruch read the scroll in the hearing of the people. 14Then all the princes sent Jehu′di the son of Nethani′ah, son of Shelemi′ah, son of Cu′shi, to say to Baruch, "Take in your hand the scroll that you read in the hearing of the people, and come." So Baruch the son of Neri′ah took the scroll in his hand and came to them. 15And they said to him, "Sit down and read it." So Baruch read it to them. 16When they heard all the words, they turned one to another in fear; and they said to Baruch, "We must report all these words to the king." 17Then they asked Baruch, "Tell us, how did you write all these words? Was it at his dictation?" 18Baruch answered them, "He dictated all these words to me, while I wrote them with ink on the scroll." 19Then the princes said to Baruch, "Go and hide, you and Jeremi′ah, and let no one know where you are."

20So they went into the court to the king, having put the scroll in the chamber of Elish′ama the secretary; and they reported all the words to the king. 21Then the king sent Jehu′di to get the scroll, and he took it from the chamber of Elish′ama the secretary; and Jehudi read it to the king and all the princes who stood beside the king. 22It was the ninth month, and the king was sitting in the winter house and there was a fire burning in the brazier before him. 23As Jehu′di read three or four columns, the king would cut them off with a penknife and throw them into the fire in the brazier, until the entire scroll was consumed in the fire that was in the brazier. 24Yet neither the king, nor any of his servants who heard all these words, was afraid, nor did they tear their garments. 25Even when Elna′than and Delai′ah and Gemari′ah urged the king not to burn the scroll, he would not listen to them. 26And the

king commanded Jerah´meel the king's son and
Serai´ah the son of Az´ri-el and Shelemi´ah the
son of Abde´el to seize Baruch the secretary and
Jeremi´ah the prophet, but the LORD hid them.
27Now, after the king had burned the scroll
with the words which Baruch wrote at
Jeremi´ah's dictation, the word of the LORD
came to Jeremi´ah: 28"Take another scroll and
write on it all the former words that were in the
first scroll, which Jehoi´akim the king of Judah
has burned. 29And concerning Jehoi´akim king
of Judah you shall say, 'Thus says the LORD,
You have burned this scroll, saying, "Why have
you written in it that the king of Babylon will
certainly come and destroy this land, and will
cut off from it man and beast?" 30Therefore
thus says the LORD concerning Jehoi´akim
king of Judah, He shall have none to sit upon
the throne of David, and his dead body shall
be cast out to the heat by day and the frost by
night. 31And I will punish him and his offspring
and his servants for their iniquity; I will bring
upon them, and upon the inhabitants of
Jerusalem, and upon the men of Judah, all the
evil that I have pronounced against them, but
they would not hear.'"
32Then Jeremi´ah took another scroll and
gave it to Baruch the scribe, the son of Ner-
i´ah, who wrote on it at the dictation of
Jeremi´ah all the words of the scroll which
Jehoi´akim king of Judah had burned in the
fire; and many similar words were added to
them.

37 Zedeki´ah the son of Josi´ah, whom
Nebuchadrez´zar king of Babylon made
king in the land of Judah, reigned instead of
Coni´ah the son of Jehoi´akim. 2But neither
he nor his servants nor the people of the land
listened to the words of the LORD which he
spoke through Jeremi´ah the prophet.
3King Zedeki´ah sent Jehu´cal the son of
Shelemi´ah, and Zephani´ah the priest, the son
of Ma-asei´ah, to Jeremi´ah the prophet, saying,
"Pray for us to the LORD our God." 4Now
Jeremi´ah was still going in and out among the
people, for he had not yet been put in prison.
5The army of Pharaoh had come out of Egypt;
and when the Chalde´ans who were besieging
Jerusalem heard news of them, they withdrew
from Jerusalem.
6Then the word of the LORD came to Jer-
emi´ah the prophet: 7"Thus says the LORD,
God of Israel: Thus shall you say to the king
of Judah who sent you to me to inquire of
me, 'Behold, Pharaoh's army which came
to help you is about to return to Egypt, to
its own land. 8And the Chalde´ans shall
come back and fight against this city; they
shall take it and burn it with fire. 9Thus says
the LORD, Do not deceive yourselves, saying, "The Chalde´ans will surely stay away
from us," for they will not stay away. 10For
even if you should defeat the whole army
of Chalde´ans who are fighting against you,
and there remained of them only wounded
men, every man in his tent, they would rise
up and burn this city with fire.'"
11Now when the Chalde´an army had
withdrawn from Jerusalem at the approach
of Pharaoh's army, 12Jeremi´ah set out from
Jerusalem to go to the land of Benjamin to
receive his portion there among the people.
13When he was at the Benjamin Gate, a sentry
there named Iri´jah the son of Shelemi´ah, son
of Hanani´ah, seized Jeremi´ah the prophet,
saying, "You are deserting to the Chalde´ans."
14And Jeremi´ah said, "It is false; I am not
deserting to the Chalde´ans." But Iri´jah would
not listen to him, and seized Jeremiah and
brought him to the princes. 15And the princes
were enraged at Jeremi´ah, and they beat him
and imprisoned him in the house of Jonathan
the secretary, for it had been made a prison.
16When Jeremi´ah had come to the dungeon
cells, and remained there many days, 17King
Zedeki´ah sent for him, and received him. The
king questioned him secretly in his house,
and said, "Is there any word from the LORD?"
Jeremi´ah said, "There is." Then he said, "You
shall be delivered into the hand of the king
of Babylon." 18Jeremi´ah also said to King
Zedeki´ah, "What wrong have I done to you
or your servants or this people, that you have
put me in prison? 19Where are your prophets
who prophesied to you, saying, 'The king of
Babylon will not come against you and against
this land'? 20Now hear, I beg you, O my lord
the king: let my humble plea come before
you, and do not send me back to the house
of Jonathan the secretary, lest I die there."

[21]So King Zedeki′ah gave orders, and they committed Jeremi′ah to the court of the guard; and a loaf of bread was given him daily from the bakers' street, until all the bread of the city was gone. So Jeremiah remained in the court of the guard.

WISDOM 17

[14]But throughout the night, which was
really powerless,
and which beset them from the recesses of
powerless Hades,
they all slept the same sleep,
[15]and now were driven by
monstrous specters,
and now were paralyzed by their
souls' surrender,
for sudden and unexpected fear
overwhelmed them.
[16]And whoever was there fell down,
and thus was kept shut up in a prison not
made of iron;
[17]for whether he was a farmer or a shepherd
or a workman who toiled in the wilderness,
he was seized, and endured the
inescapable fate;
for with one chain of darkness they all
were bound.
[18]Whether there came a whistling wind,
or a melodious sound of birds in
wide-spreading branches,
or the rhythm of violently rushing water,
[19]or the harsh crash of rocks hurled down,
or the unseen running of leaping animals,
or the sound of the most savage
roaring beasts,
or an echo thrown back from a hollow of
the mountains,
it paralyzed them with terror.
[20]For the whole world was illumined with
brilliant light,
and was engaged in unhindered work,
[21]while over those men alone heavy night
was spread,
an image of the darkness that was destined
to receive them;
but still heavier than darkness were they
to themselves.

18 But for your holy ones there was very
great light.
Their enemies heard their voices but did
not see their forms,
and counted them happy for not
having suffered,
[2]and were thankful that your holy ones,
though previously wronged, were
doing them no injury;
and they begged their pardon for having
been at variance with them.
[3]Therefore you provided a flaming pillar
of fire
as a guide for your people's unknown
journey,
and a harmless sun for their glorious
wandering.
[4]For their enemies deserved to be deprived
of light and imprisoned in darkness,
those who had kept your sons imprisoned,
through whom the imperishable light of the
law was to be given to the world.

[5]When they had resolved to kill the infants
of your holy ones,
and one child had been exposed
and rescued,
in punishment you took away a multitude
of their children;
and you destroyed them all together by a
mighty flood.
[6]That night was made known beforehand to
our fathers,
so that they might rejoice in sure knowledge
of the oaths in which they trusted.
[7]The deliverance of the righteous and the
destruction of their enemies
were expected by your people.
[8]For by the same means by which you
punished our enemies
you called us to yourself and glorified us.
[9]For in secret the holy children of good men
offered sacrifices,
and with one accord agreed to the
divine law,
that the saints would share alike the
same things,
both blessings and dangers;
and already they were singing the praises of
the fathers.

[10]But the discordant cry of their enemies
echoed back,
and their piteous lament for their children
was spread abroad.
[11]The slave was punished with the same
penalty as the master,
and the common man suffered the same
loss as the king;
[12]and they all together, by the one form
of death,
had corpses too many to count.
For the living were not sufficient even to
bury them,
since in one instant their most valued
children had been destroyed.
[13]For though they had disbelieved
everything because of their magic arts,
yet, when their first-born were destroyed,
they acknowledged your people to be
God's son.

GALATIANS 6

Brethren, if a man is overtaken in any trespass, you who are spiritual should restore him in a spirit of gentleness. Look to yourself, lest you too
be tempted. [2]Bear one another's burdens,
and so fulfil the law of Christ. [3]For if any
one thinks he is something, when he is
nothing, he deceives himself. [4]But let each
one test his own work, and then his reason
to boast will be in himself alone and not in
his neighbor. [5]For each man will have to
bear his own load.

[6]Let him who is taught the word share all
good things with him who teaches.

[7]Do not be deceived; God is not mocked,
for whatever a man sows, that he will also
reap. [8]For he who sows to his own flesh will
from the flesh reap corruption; but he who
sows to the Spirit will from the Spirit reap
eternal life. [9]And let us not grow weary in
well-doing, for in due season we shall reap,
if we do not lose heart. [10]So then, as we have
opportunity, let us do good to all men, and
especially to those who are of the household
of faith.

[11]See with what large letters I am writing to you with my own hand. [12]It is those
who want to make a good showing in the
flesh that would compel you to be circumcised, and only in order that they may
not be persecuted for the cross of Christ.
[13]For even those who receive circumcision do not themselves keep the law, but
they desire to have you circumcised that
they may glory in your flesh. [14]But far be
it from me to glory except in the cross of
our Lord Jesus Christ, by which the world
has been crucified to me, and I to the
world. [15]For neither circumcision counts
for anything, nor uncircumcision, but a
new creation. [16]Peace and mercy be upon
all who walk by this rule, upon the Israel
of God.

[17]Henceforth let no man trouble me; for I
bear on my body the marks of Jesus.

[18]The grace of our Lord Jesus Christ be
with your spirit, brethren. Amen.

REFLECTION

When Jeremiah preaches to King Zedekiah, the words go in one ear and out the other, as the saying goes. The image of the king sitting and listening to the scroll of Jeremiah's prophecies, but then casually slicing it up with a penknife and dropping it into the fire, is a memorable one (see Jer 36:21–23). Those in the king's court remain completely unmoved by the words. Although Zedekiah's actions show flagrant disregard for God's prophet, they are not so different from how we often behave today. When we hear a homily and do not put its teaching into practice, it is as if we had picked up God's Word only to throw it straight into a fire, where it does no good in our hearts or in our lives. Even an impressive preacher like St. Paul goes to great lengths to be heard, writing his letter in extra-large print to get the attention of his readers (see Gal 6:11). We should always try to make some small space in our hearts for the words of a preacher, even if they are not eloquent. How often do you make a point to recall the content or a key point of a homily even a week, or even an hour or a day, after you have heard it?

October 3

JEREMIAH 38

Now Shephati′ah the son of Mattan, Gedali′ah the son of Pashhur, Ju′cal the son of Shelemi′ah, and Pashhur the son of Malchi′ah heard the words that Jeremi′ah was saying to all the people, 2"Thus says the LORD, He who stays in this city shall die by the sword, by famine, and by pestilence; but he who goes out to the Chalde′ans shall live; he shall have his life as a prize of war, and live. 3Thus says the LORD, This city shall surely be given into the hand of the army of the king of Babylon and be taken." 4Then the princes said to the king, "Let this man be put to death, for he is weakening the hands of the soldiers who are left in this city, and the hands of all the people, by speaking such words to them. For this man is not seeking the welfare of this people, but their harm." 5King Zedeki′ah said, "Behold, he is in your hands; for the king can do nothing against you." 6So they took Jeremi′ah and cast him into the cistern of Malchi′ah, the king's son, which was in the court of the guard, letting Jeremiah down by ropes. And there was no water in the cistern, but only mire, and Jeremiah sank in the mire.

7When E′bed-mel′ech the Ethiopian, a eunuch, who was in the king's house, heard that they had put Jeremi′ah into the cistern—the king was sitting in the Benjamin Gate—8E′bed-mel′ech went from the king's house and said to the king, 9"My lord the king, these men have done evil in all that they did to Jeremi′ah the prophet by casting him into the cistern; and he will die there of hunger, for there is no bread left in the city." 10Then the king commanded E′bed-mel′ech, the Ethiopian, "Take three men with you from here, and lift Jeremi′ah the prophet out of the cistern before he dies." 11So E′bed-mel′ech took the men with him and went to the house of the king, to a wardrobe of the storehouse, and took from there old rags and worn-out clothes, which he let down to Jeremi′ah in the cistern by ropes. 12Then E′bed-mel′ech the Ethiopian said to Jeremi′ah, "Put the rags and clothes between your armpits and the ropes." Jeremiah did so. 13Then they drew Jeremi′ah up with ropes and lifted him out of the cistern. And Jeremiah remained in the court of the guard.

14King Zedeki′ah sent for Jeremi′ah the prophet and received him at the third entrance of the temple of the LORD. The king said to Jeremi′ah, "I will ask you a question; hide nothing from me." 15Jeremi′ah said to Zedeki′ah, "If I tell you, will you not be sure to put me to death? And if I give you counsel, you will not listen to me." 16Then King Zedeki′ah swore secretly to Jeremi′ah, "As the LORD lives, who made our souls, I will not put you to death or deliver you into the hand of these men who seek your life."

17Then Jeremi′ah said to Zedeki′ah, "Thus says the LORD, the God of hosts, the God of Israel, If you will surrender to the princes of the king of Babylon, then your life shall be spared, and this city shall not be burned with fire, and you and your house shall live. 18But if you do not surrender to the princes of the king of Babylon, then this city shall be given into the hand of the Chalde′ans, and they shall burn it with fire, and you shall not escape from their hand." 19King Zedeki′ah said to Jeremi′ah, "I am afraid of the Jews who have deserted to the Chalde′ans, lest I be handed over to them and they abuse me." 20Jeremi′ah said, "You shall not be given to them. Obey now the voice of the LORD in what I say to you, and it shall be well with you, and your life shall be spared. 21But if you refuse to surrender, this is the vision which the LORD has shown to me: 22Behold, all the women left in the house of the king of Judah were being led out to the princes of the king of Babylon and were saying,

'Your trusted friends have deceived you
and prevailed against you;
now that your feet are sunk in the mire,
they turn away from you.'

23All your wives and your sons shall be led out to the Chalde′ans, and you yourself shall not escape from their hand, but shall be seized by the king of Babylon; and this city shall be burned with fire."

[24]Then Zedeki´ah said to Jeremi´ah, "Let no one know of these words and you shall not die. [25]If the princes hear that I have spoken with you and come to you and say to you, 'Tell us what you said to the king and what the king said to you; hide nothing from us and we will not put you to death,' [26]then you shall say to them, 'I made a humble plea to the king that he would not send me back to the house of Jonathan to die there.'" [27]Then all the princes came to Jeremi´ah and asked him, and he answered them as the king had instructed him. So they left off speaking with him, for the conversation had not been overheard. [28]And Jeremi´ah remained in the court of the guard until the day that Jerusalem was taken.

39 In the ninth year of Zedeki´ah king of Judah, in the tenth month, Nebuchadrez´zar king of Babylon and all his army came against Jerusalem and besieged it; [2]in the eleventh year of Zedeki´ah, in the fourth month, on the ninth day of the month, a breach was made in the city. [3]When Jerusalem was taken, all the princes of the king of Babylon came and sat in the middle gate: Ner´gal-share´zer, Sam´gar-ne´bo, Sar´sechim the Rab´saris, Nergal-sharezer the Rabmag, with all the rest of the officers of the king of Babylon. [4]When Zedeki´ah king of Judah and all the soldiers saw them, they fled, going out of the city at night by way of the king's garden through the gate between the two walls; and they went toward the Ar´abah. [5]But the army of the Chalde´ans pursued them, and overtook Zedeki´ah in the plains of Jericho; and when they had taken him, they brought him up to Nebuchadrez´zar king of Babylon, at Riblah, in the land of Ha´math; and he passed sentence upon him. [6]The king of Babylon slew the sons of Zedeki´ah at Riblah before his eyes; and the king of Babylon slew all the nobles of Judah. [7]He put out the eyes of Zedeki´ah, and bound him in chains to take him to Babylon. [8]The Chalde´ans burned the king's house and the house of the people, and broke down the walls of Jerusalem. [9]Then Nebu´zarad´an, the captain of the guard, carried into exile to Babylon the rest of the people who were left in the city, those who had deserted to him, and the people who remained. [10]Nebu´zarad´an, the captain of the guard, left in the land of Judah some of the poor people who owned nothing, and gave them vineyards and fields at the same time.

[11]Nebuchadrez´zar king of Babylon gave command concerning Jeremi´ah through Nebu´zarad´an, the captain of the guard, saying, [12]"Take him, look after him well and do him no harm, but deal with him as he tells you." [13]So Nebu´zarad´an the captain of the guard, Nebushaz´ban the Rab´saris, Ner´gal-share´zer the Rabmag, and all the chief officers of the king of Babylon [14]sent and took Jeremi´ah from the court of the guard. They entrusted him to Gedali´ah the son of Ahi´kam, son of Sha´phan, that he should take him home. So he dwelt among the people.

[15]The word of the LORD came to Jeremi´ah while he was shut up in the court of the guard: [16]"Go, and say to E´bed-mel´ech the Ethiopian, 'Thus says the LORD of hosts, the God of Israel: Behold, I will fulfil my words against this city for evil and not for good, and they shall be accomplished before you on that day. [17]But I will deliver you on that day, says the LORD, and you shall not be given into the hand of the men of whom you are afraid. [18]For I will surely save you, and you shall not fall by the sword; but you shall have your life as a prize of war, because you have put your trust in me, says the LORD.'"

40 The word that came to Jeremi´ah from the LORD after Nebu´zarad´an the captain of the guard had let him go from Ra´mah, when he took him bound in chains along with all the captives of Jerusalem and Judah who were being exiled to Babylon. [2]The captain of the guard took Jeremi´ah and said to him, "The LORD your God pronounced this evil against this place; [3]the LORD has brought it about, and has done as he said. Because you sinned against the LORD, and did not obey his voice, this thing has come upon you. [4]Now, behold, I release you today from the chains on your hands,

If it seems good to you to come with me
to Babylon, come, and I will look after you
well; but if it seems wrong to you to come
with me to Babylon, do not come. See, the
whole land is before you; go wherever you
think it good and right to go. [5]If you remain,
then return to Gedali′ah the son of Ahi′kam,
son of Sha′phan, whom the king of Babylon
appointed governor of the cities of Judah,
and dwell with him among the people; or
go wherever you think it right to go." So the
captain of the guard gave him an allowance
of food and a present, and let him go. [6]Then
Jeremi′ah went to Gedali′ah the son of
Ahi′kam, at Mizpah, and dwelt with him
among the people who were left in the land.
[7]When all the captains of the forces in
the open country and their men heard
that the king of Babylon had appointed
Gedali′ah the son of Ahi′kam governor in
the land, and had committed to him men,
women, and children, those of the poorest
of the land who had not been taken into
exile to Babylon, [8]they went to Gedali′ah at
Mizpah—Ish′mael the son of Nethani′ah,
Joha′nan the son of Kare′ah, Serai′ah the
son of Tan′humeth, the sons of E′phai the
Netoph′athite, Jezani′ah the son of the Ma-
ac′athite, they and their men. [9]Gedali′ah
the son of Ahi′kam, son of Sha′phan, swore
to them and their men, saying, "Do not be
afraid to serve the Chalde′ans. Dwell in the
land, and serve the king of Babylon, and it
shall be well with you. [10]As for me, I will
dwell at Mizpah, to stand for you before
the Chalde′ans who will come to us; but
as for you, gather wine and summer fruits
and oil, and store them in your vessels, and
dwell in your cities that you have taken."
[11]Likewise, when all the Jews who were in
Moab and among the Am′monites and in
E′dom and in other lands heard that the
king of Babylon had left a remnant in Judah
and had appointed Gedali′ah the son of
Ahi′kam, son of Sha′phan, as governor over
them, [12]then all the Jews returned from all
the places to which they had been driven
and came to the land of Judah, to Gedali′ah
at Mizpah; and they gathered wine and
summer fruits in great abundance.
[13]Now Joha′nan the son of Kare′ah and all
the leaders of the forces in the open country
came to Gedali′ah at Mizpah [14]and said to
him, "Do you know that Ba′alis the king of
the Am′monites has sent Ish′mael the son of
Nethani′ah to take your life?" But Gedali′ah
the son of Ahi′kam would not believe them.
[15]Then Joha′nan the son of Kare′ah spoke
secretly to Gedali′ah at Mizpah, "Let me
go and slay Ish′mael the son of Nethani′ah,
and no one will know it. Why should he
take your life, so that all the Jews who are
gathered about you would be scattered,
and the remnant of Judah would perish?"
[16]But Gedali′ah the son of Ahi′kam said to
Joha′nan the son of Kare′ah, "You shall not
do this thing, for you are speaking falsely of
Ish′mael."

WISDOM 18

[14]For while gentle silence enveloped
all things,
and night in its swift course was now
half gone,
[15]your all-powerful word leaped from
heaven, from the royal throne,
into the midst of the land that was doomed,
a stern warrior [16]carrying the sharp sword
of your authentic command,
and stood and filled all things with death,
and touched heaven while standing on
the earth.
[17]Then at once apparitions in dreadful
reams greatly troubled them,
and unexpected fears assailed them;
[18]and one here and another there, hurled
down half dead,
made known why they were dying;
[19]for the dreams which disturbed them
forewarned them of this,
so that they might not perish without
knowing why they suffered.

[20]The experience of death touched also
the righteous,
and a plague came upon the multitude
in the desert,
but the wrath did not long continue.

[21]For a blameless man was quick to act
as their champion;
he brought forward the shield of
his ministry,
prayer and propitiation by incense;
he withstood the anger and put an end
to the disaster,
showing that he was your servant.
[22]He conquered the wrath not by strength
of body,
and not by force of arms,
but by his word he subdued the punisher,
appealing to the oaths and covenants given
to our fathers.
[23]For when the dead had already fallen on
one another in heaps,
he intervened and held back the wrath,
and cut off its way to the living.
[24]For upon his long robe the whole world
was depicted,
and the glories of the fathers were engraved
on the four rows of stones,
and your majesty on the diadem upon
his head.
[25]To these the destroyer yielded, these
he feared;
for merely to test the wrath was enough.

EPHESIANS 1

Paul, an apostle of Christ Jesus by the will of God,
To the saints who are also faithful in Christ Jesus:
[2]Grace to you and peace from God our Father and the Lord Jesus Christ.
[3]Blessed be the God and Father of our
Lord Jesus Christ, who has blessed us in
Christ with every spiritual blessing in the
heavenly places, [4]even as he chose us in
him before the foundation of the world,
that we should be holy and blameless
before him. [5]He destined us in love to be
his sons through Jesus Christ, according
to the purpose of his will, [6]to the praise
of his glorious grace which he freely
bestowed on us in the Beloved. [7]In him we
have redemption through his blood, the
forgiveness of our trespasses, according to
the riches of his grace [8]which he lavished
upon us. [9]For he has made known to us
in all wisdom and insight the mystery of
his will, according to his purpose which
he set forth in Christ [10]as a plan for the
fulness of time, to unite all things in him,
things in heaven and things on earth.
[11]In him, according to the purpose of
him who accomplishes all things according to the counsel of his will, [12]we who
first hoped in Christ have been destined
and appointed to live for the praise of his
glory. [13]In him you also, who have heard
the word of truth, the gospel of your salvation, and have believed in him, were
sealed with the promised Holy Spirit,
[14]who is the guarantee of our inheritance
until we acquire possession of it, to the
praise of his glory.

REFLECTION

At the beginning of Ephesians, St. Paul speaks frequently about God's plan. In the fullness of time, he explains, Christ came to unite all things in himself, to grant forgiveness, and to destine us "to live for the praise of his glory" (Eph 1:12). The providence of God, however, is not a cause for rejoicing in Jeremiah. Zedekiah, although he seems to believe Jeremiah's prophecy, does not delight in God's will and does not surrender to the Babylonians. Perhaps these two situations feel incongruent, as if the will of God is cruel in one moment and then forgiving in another. But the joy spoken of in the Letter to the Ephesians is the fruit of Christ's complete conformity to God's will. Unlike Zedekiah, Christ agrees to be handed over to his enemies, even unto death. When God's plan is hard and difficult, our course must still be "to live for the praise of his glory"—otherwise, we, like Zedekiah, will end up both miserable and blind. Jeremiah teaches us that it is better to be at the bottom of a cistern while trusting in God than to sit on a throne resisting him. Do you ever feel resentful of, or resistant to, the will of God, even after you know you have correctly discerned that will?

October 4

JEREMIAH 41

In the seventh month, Ish´mael the son of Nethani´ah, son of Elish´ama, of the royal family, one of the chief officers of the king, came with ten men to Gedali´ah the son of Ahi´kam, at Mizpah. As they ate bread together there at Mizpah, 2Ish´mael the son of Nethani´ah and the ten men with him rose up and struck down Gedali´ah the son of Ahi´kam, son of Sha´phan, with the sword, and killed him, whom the king of Babylon had appointed governor in the land. 3Ish´mael also slew all the Jews who were with Gedali´ah at Mizpah, and the Chalde´an soldiers who happened to be there.

4On the day after the murder of Gedali´ah, before any one knew of it, 5eighty men arrived from She´chem and Shiloh and Samar´ia, with their beards shaved and their clothes torn, and their bodies gashed, bringing cereal offerings and incense to present at the temple of the LORD. 6And Ish´mael the son of Nethani´ah came out from Mizpah to meet them, weeping as he came. As he met them, he said to them, "Come in to Gedali´ah the son of Ahi´kam." 7When they came into the city, Ish´mael the son of Nethani´ah and the men with him slew them, and cast them into a cistern. 8But there were ten men among them who said to Ish´mael, "Do not kill us, for we have stores of wheat, barley, oil, and honey hidden in the fields." So he refrained and did not kill them with their companions.

9Now the cistern into which Ish´mael cast all the bodies of the men whom he had slain was the large cistern which King Asa had made for defense against Ba´asha king of Israel; Ishmael the son of Nethani´ah filled it with the slain. 10Then Ish´mael took captive all the rest of the people who were in Mizpah, the king's daughters and all the people who were left at Mizpah whom Nebu´zarad´an, the captain of the guard, had committed to Gedali´ah the son of Ahi´kam. Ish´mael the son of Nethani´ah took them captive and set out to cross over to the Am´monites.

11But when Joha´nan the son of Kare´ah and all the leaders of the forces with him heard of all the evil which Ish´mael the son of Nethani´ah had done, 12they took all their men and went to fight against Ish´mael the son of Nethani´ah. They came upon him at the great pool which is in Gib´eon. 13And when all the people who were with Ish´mael saw Joha´nan the son of Kare´ah and all the leaders of the forces with him, they rejoiced. 14So all the people whom Ish´mael had carried away captive from Mizpah turned about and came back, and went to Joha´nan the son of Kare´ah. 15But Ish´mael the son of Nethani´ah escaped from Joha´nan with eight men, and went to the Am´monites. 16Then Joha´nan the son of Kare´ah and all the leaders of the forces with him took all the rest of the people whom Ish´mael the son of Nethani´ah had carried away captive from Mizpah after he had slain Gedali´ah the son of Ahi´kam—soldiers, women, children, and eunuchs, whom Johanan brought back from Gib´eon. 17And they went and stayed at Ge´ruth Chimham near Bethlehem, intending to go to Egypt 18because of the Chalde´ans; for they were afraid of them, because Ish´mael the son of Nethani´ah had slain Gedali´ah the son of Ahi´kam, whom the king of Babylon had made governor over the land.

42 Then all the commanders of the forces, and Joha´nan the son of Kare´ah and Azari´ah the son of Hoshai´ah, and all the people from the least to the greatest, came near 2and said to Jeremi´ah the prophet, "Let our supplication come before you, and pray to the LORD your God for us, for all this remnant (for we are left but a few of many, as your eyes see us), 3that the LORD your God may show us the way we should go, and the thing that we should do." 4Jeremi´ah the prophet said to them, "I have heard you; behold, I will pray to the LORD your God according to your request, and whatever the LORD answers you I will tell you; I will keep nothing back from you."

5 Then they said to Jeremi´ah, "May the LORD be a true and faithful witness against us if we do not act according to all the word with which the LORD your God sends you to us. 6 Whether it is good or evil, we will obey the voice of the LORD our God to whom we are sending you, that it may be well with us when we obey the voice of the LORD our God."

7 At the end of ten days the word of the LORD came to Jeremi´ah. 8 Then he summoned Joha´nan the son of Kare´ah and all the commanders of the forces who were with him, and all the people from the least to the greatest, 9 and said to them, "Thus says the LORD, the God of Israel, to whom you sent me to present your supplication before him: 10 If you will remain in this land, then I will build you up and not pull you down; I will plant you, and not pluck you up; for I repent of the evil which I did to you. 11 Do not fear the king of Babylon, of whom you are afraid; do not fear him, says the LORD, for I am with you, to save you and to deliver you from his hand. 12 I will grant you mercy, that he may have mercy on you and let you remain in your own land. 13 But if you say, 'We will not remain in this land,' disobeying the voice of the LORD your God 14 and saying, 'No, we will go to the land of Egypt, where we shall not see war, or hear the sound of the trumpet, or be hungry for bread, and we will dwell there,' 15 then hear the word of the LORD, O remnant of Judah. Thus says the LORD of hosts, the God of Israel: If you set your faces to enter Egypt and go to live there, 16 then the sword which you fear shall overtake you there in the land of Egypt; and the famine of which you are afraid shall follow hard after you to Egypt; and there you shall die. 17 All the men who set their faces to go to Egypt to live there shall die by the sword, by famine, and by pestilence; they shall have no remnant or survivor from the evil which I will bring upon them.

18 "For thus says the LORD of hosts, the God of Israel: As my anger and my wrath were poured out on the inhabitants of Jerusalem, so my wrath will be poured out on you when you go to Egypt. You shall become an execration, a horror, a curse, and a taunt. You shall see this place no more. 19 The LORD has said to you, O remnant of Judah, 'Do not go to Egypt.' Know for a certainty that I have warned you this day 20 that you have gone astray at the cost of your lives. For you sent me to the LORD your God, saying, 'Pray for us to the LORD our God, and whatever the LORD our God says declare to us and we will do it.' 21 And I have this day declared it to you, but you have not obeyed the voice of the LORD your God in anything that he sent me to tell you. 22 Now therefore know for a certainty that you shall die by the sword, by famine, and by pestilence in the place where you desire to go to live."

43 When Jeremi´ah finished speaking to all the people all these words of the LORD their God, with which the LORD their God had sent him to them, 2 Azari´ah the son of Hoshai´ah and Joha´nan the son of Kare´ah and all the insolent men said to Jeremi´ah, "You are telling a lie. The LORD our God did not send you to say, 'Do not go to Egypt to live there'; 3 but Baruch the son of Neri´ah has set you against us, to deliver us into the hand of the Chalde´ans, that they may kill us or take us into exile in Babylon." 4 So Joha´nan the son of Kare´ah and all the commanders of the forces and all the people did not obey the voice of the LORD, to remain in the land of Judah. 5 But Joha´nan the son of Kare´ah and all the commanders of the forces took all the remnant of Judah who had returned to live in the land of Judah from all the nations to which they had been driven— 6 the men, the women, the children, the princesses, and every person whom Nebu´zarad´an the captain of the guard had left with Gedali´ah the son of Ahi´kam, son of Sha´phan; also Jeremi´ah the prophet and Baruch the son of Neri´ah. 7 And they came into the land of Egypt, for they did not obey the voice of the LORD. And they arrived at Tah´panhes.

8 Then the word of the LORD came to Jeremi´ah in Tah´panhes: 9 "Take in your hands large stones, and hide them in the mortar in the pavement which is at the entrance to Pharaoh's palace in Tah´panhes, in the sight of the men of Judah, 10 and say to them, 'Thus says the LORD of hosts, the God of Israel: Behold, I will send and take Nebuchadrez´zar the king of Babylon, my servant, and he will

set his throne above these stones which I have
hid, and he will spread his royal canopy over
them. [11]He shall come and strike the land of
Egypt, giving to the pestilence those who are
doomed to the pestilence, to captivity those
who are doomed to captivity, and to the
sword those who are doomed to the sword.
[12]He shall kindle a fire in the temples of the
gods of Egypt; and he shall burn them and
carry them away captive; and he shall clean
the land of Egypt, as a shepherd cleans his
cloak of vermin; and he shall go away from
there in peace. [13]He shall break the obelisks
of He′liop′olis which is in the land of Egypt;
and the temples of the gods of Egypt he shall
burn with fire.'"

WISDOM 19

But the ungodly were assailed to the end
by pitiless anger,
for God knew in advance even their
future actions,
[2]that, though they themselves had permitted
your people to depart
and hastily sent them forth,
they would change their minds and
pursue them.
[3]For while they were still busy at mourning,
and were lamenting at the graves of
their dead,
they reached another foolish decision,
and pursued as fugitives those whom they
had begged and compelled to depart.
[4]For the fate they deserved drew them on to
this end,
and made them forget what had happened,
in order that they might fill up the
punishment which their torments
still lacked,
[5]and that your people might experience an
incredible journey,
but they themselves might meet a
strange death.

[6]For the whole creation in its nature was
fashioned anew,
complying with your commands,
that your children might be kept unharmed.
[7]The cloud was seen overshadowing the camp,
and dry land emerging where water had
stood before,
an unhindered way out of the Red Sea,
and a grassy plain out of the raging waves,
[8]where those protected by your hand passed
through as one nation,
after gazing on marvelous wonders.
[9]For they ranged like horses,
and leaped like lambs,
praising you, O Lord, who delivered them.
[10]For they still recalled the events of
their sojourn,
how instead of producing animals the
earth brought forth gnats,
and instead of fish the river spewed out
vast numbers of frogs.
[11]Afterward they saw also a new kind
of birds,
when desire led them to ask for
luxurious food;
[12]for, to give them relief, quails came up
from the sea.

[13]The punishments did not come upon
the sinners
without prior signs in the violence
of thunder,
for they justly suffered because of their
wicked acts;
for they practiced a more bitter hatred
of strangers.
[14]Others had refused to receive strangers
when they came to them,
but these made slaves of guests who were
their benefactors.
[15]And not only so, but punishment of some
sort will come upon the former
for their hostile reception of the strangers;
[16]but the latter, after receiving them with
festal celebrations,
afflicted with terrible sufferings
those who had already shared the
same rights.
[17]They were stricken also with loss of sight—
just as were those at the door of the
righteous man—
when, surrounded by yawning darkness,
each tried to find the way through his
own door.

18For the elements changed places with
one another,
as on a harp the notes vary the nature
of the rhythm,
while each note remains the same.
This may be clearly inferred from the
sight of what took place.
19For land animals were transformed
into water creatures,
and creatures that swim moved
over to the land.
20Fire even in water retained its
normal power,
and water forgot its fire-quenching nature.
21Flames, on the contrary, failed to consume
the flesh of perishable creatures that walked
among them,
nor did they melt the crystalline, easily
melted kind of heavenly food.

22For in everything, O Lord, you have
exalted and glorified your people;
and you have not neglected to help them at
all times and in all places.

EPHESIANS 1

15For this reason, because I have heard of your faith in the Lord Jesus and your love toward all the saints, 16I do not cease to give thanks for you, remembering you in my prayers, 17that the God of our Lord Jesus Christ, the Father of glory, may give you a spirit of wisdom and of revelation in the knowledge of him, 18having the eyes of your hearts enlightened, that you may know what is the hope to which he has called you, what are the riches of his glorious inheritance in the saints, 19and what is the immeasurable greatness of his power in us who believe, according to the working of his great might 20which he accomplished in Christ when he raised him from the dead and made him sit at his right hand in the heavenly places, 21far above all rule and authority and power and dominion, and above every name that is named, not only in this age but also in that which is to come; 22and he has put all things under his feet and has made him the head over all things for the Church, 23which is his body, the fulness of him who fills all in all.

2 And you he made alive, when you were dead through the trespasses and sins
2in which you once walked, following the course of this world, following the prince of the power of the air, the spirit that is now at work in the sons of disobedience.
3Among these we all once lived in the passions of our flesh, following the desires of body and mind, and so we were by nature children of wrath, like the rest of mankind.
4But God, who is rich in mercy, out of the great love with which he loved us,
5even when we were dead through our trespasses, made us alive together with Christ (by grace you have been saved),
6and raised us up with him, and made us sit with him in the heavenly places in Christ Jesus,
7that in the coming ages he might show the immeasurable riches of his grace in kindness toward us in Christ Jesus.
8For by grace you have been saved through faith; and this is not your own doing, it is the gift of God—
9not because of works, lest any man should boast.
10For we are his workmanship, created in Christ Jesus for good works, which God prepared beforehand, that we should walk in them.

REFLECTION

The people left to work the land find themselves in a stressful situation. The man appointed to govern the "remnant of Judah" (Jer 42:15) has been murdered, and they are uncertain whether to stay or to flee to Egypt. They come to Jeremiah to ask for his advice and request that he intercede with God on their behalf. After Jeremiah speaks his prophecy, the people promptly ignore him and call him a liar (see 43:2–3). Oftentimes God's Word calls us to things we find difficult. Our first response is to ignore what we have heard, even if we know its truth in our hearts. Openness to the Word of God cannot be obtained simply by our own strength. According to St. Paul, we need the grace of God to acquire the "spirit of wisdom and of revelation" (Eph 1:17). We must, therefore, not only read Scripture and listen to those who preach, but also pray for an openness to these words, for patience, and for obedience. Do you ever pray that you might be open to the wisdom of God found in the Scriptures, and in the words of other people, even people you do not like?

October 5

JEREMIAH 44

**The word that came to Jer-
emi′ah concerning all the Jews
that dwelt in the land of Egypt,
at Migdol, at Tah′panhes, at Memphis,
and in the land of Path′ros, 2"Thus says
the LORD of hosts, the God of Israel:**
You have seen all the evil that I brought
upon Jerusalem and upon all the cities of
Judah. Behold, this day they are a desolation, and no one dwells in them, 3because
of the wickedness which they committed,
provoking me to anger, in that they went to
burn incense and serve other gods that they
knew not, neither they, nor you, nor your
fathers. 4Yet I persistently sent to you all
my servants the prophets, saying, 'Oh, do
not do this abominable thing that I hate!'
5But they did not listen or incline their ear,
to turn from their wickedness and burn no
incense to other gods. 6Therefore my wrath
and my anger were poured forth and kindled in the cities of Judah and in the streets
of Jerusalem; and they became a waste and
a desolation, as at this day. 7And now thus
says the LORD God of hosts, the God of
Israel: Why do you commit this great evil
against yourselves, to cut off from you man
and woman, infant and child, from the
midst of Judah, leaving you no remnant?
8Why do you provoke me to anger with
the works of your hands, burning incense
to other gods in the land of Egypt where
you have come to live, that you may be cut
off and become a curse and a taunt among
all the nations of the earth? 9Have you
forgotten the wickedness of your fathers,
the wickedness of the kings of Judah, the
wickedness of their wives, your own wickedness, and the wickedness of your wives,
which they committed in the land of Judah
and in the streets of Jerusalem? 10They have
not humbled themselves even to this day,
nor have they feared, nor walked in my law
and my statutes which I set before you and
before your fathers.

11"Therefore thus says the LORD of hosts,
the God of Israel: Behold, I will set my face
against you for evil, to cut off all Judah. 12I
will take the remnant of Judah who have set
their faces to come to the land of Egypt to
live, and they shall all be consumed; in the
land of Egypt they shall fall; by the sword
and by famine they shall be consumed; from
the least to the greatest, they shall die by the
sword and by famine; and they shall become
an execration, a horror, a curse, and a taunt.
13I will punish those who dwell in the land
of Egypt, as I have punished Jerusalem, with
the sword, with famine, and with pestilence,
14so that none of the remnant of Judah who
have come to live in the land of Egypt shall
escape or survive or return to the land of
Judah, to which they desire to return to
dwell there; for they shall not return, except
some fugitives."

15Then all the men who knew that their
wives had offered incense to other gods,
and all the women who stood by, a great
assembly, all the people who dwelt in
Path′ros in the land of Egypt, answered
Jeremi′ah: 16"As for the word which you
have spoken to us in the name of the
LORD, we will not listen to you. 17But we
will do everything that we have vowed,
burn incense to the queen of heaven
and pour out libations to her, as we did,
both we and our fathers, our kings and
our princes, in the cities of Judah and in
the streets of Jerusalem; for then we had
plenty of food, and prospered, and saw no

evil. 18But since we left off burning incense
to the queen of heaven and pouring out
libations to her, we have lacked everything
and have been consumed by the sword
and by famine." 19And the women said,
"When we burned incense to the queen
of heaven and poured out libations to her,
was it without our husbands' approval
that we made cakes for her bearing her
image and poured out libations to her?"
20Then Jeremi′ah said to all the people, men
and women, all the people who had given
him this answer: 21"As for the incense that
you burned in the cities of Judah and in the
streets of Jerusalem, you and your fathers,
your kings and your princes, and the people
of the land, did not the LORD remember it?
Did it not come into his mind? 22The LORD
could no longer bear your evil doings and
the abominations which you committed;
therefore your land has become a desolation
and a waste and a curse, without inhabitant,
as it is this day. 23It is because you burned
incense, and because you sinned against
the LORD and did not obey the voice of the
LORD or walk in his law and in his statutes
and in his testimonies, that this evil has
befallen you, as at this day."
24Jeremi′ah said to all the people and all
the women, "Hear the word of the LORD,
all you of Judah who are in the land of
Egypt, 25Thus says the LORD of hosts, the
God of Israel: You and your wives have
declared with your mouths, and have
fulfilled it with your hands, saying, 'We
will surely perform our vows that we have
made, to burn incense to the queen of
heaven and to pour out libations to her.'
Then confirm your vows and perform
your vows! 26Therefore hear the word of
the LORD, all you of Judah who dwell in the
land of Egypt: Behold, I have sworn by my
great name, says the LORD, that my name
shall no more be invoked by the mouth of
any man of Judah in all the land of Egypt,
saying, 'As the Lord GOD lives.' 27Behold,
I am watching over them for evil and not
for good; all the men of Judah who are in
the land of Egypt shall be consumed by the
sword and by famine, until there is an end
of them. 28And those who escape the sword
shall return from the land of Egypt to the
land of Judah, few in number; and all the
remnant of Judah, who came to the land
of Egypt to live, shall know whose word
will stand, mine or theirs. 29This shall be
the sign to you, says the LORD, that I will
punish you in this place, in order that you
may know that my words will surely stand
against you for evil: 30Thus says the LORD,
Behold, I will give Pharaoh Hoph′ra king
of Egypt into the hand of his enemies and
into the hand of those who seek his life, as I
gave Zedeki′ah king of Judah into the hand
of Nebuchadrez′zar king of Babylon, who
was his enemy and sought his life."

45 The word that Jeremi′ah the prophet
spoke to Baruch the son of Neri′ah,
when he wrote these words in a book at the
dictation of Jeremiah, in the fourth year of
Jehoi′akim the son of Josi′ah, king of Judah:
2"Thus says the LORD, the God of Israel, to
you, O Baruch: 3You said, 'Woe is me! for
the LORD has added sorrow to my pain; I
am weary with my groaning, and I find no
rest.' 4Thus shall you say to him, Thus says
the LORD: Behold, what I have built I am
breaking down, and what I have planted I
am plucking up—that is, the whole land.
5And do you seek great things for yourself?
Seek them not; for behold, I am bringing
evil upon all flesh, says the LORD; but I will
give you your life as a prize of war in all
places to which you may go."

46 The word of the LORD which came
to Jeremi′ah the prophet concerning
the nations.
2About Egypt. Concerning the army of
Pharaoh Neco, king of Egypt, which was
by the river Euphra′tes at Car′chemish and
which Nebuchadrez′zar king of Babylon
defeated in the fourth year of Jehoi′akim the
son of Josi′ah, king of Judah:
3"Prepare buckler and shield,
and advance for battle!
4Harness the horses;
mount, O horsemen!
Take your stations with your helmets,
polish your spears,
put on your coats of mail!

[5]Why have I seen it?
They are dismayed
and have turned backward.
Their warriors are beaten down,
and have fled in haste;
they look not back—
terror on every side!
says the LORD.
[6]The swift cannot flee away,
nor the warrior escape;
in the north by the river Euphra´tes
they have stumbled and fallen.
[7]"Who is this, rising like the Nile,
like rivers whose waters surge?
[8]Egypt rises like the Nile,
like rivers whose waters surge.
He said, I will rise, I will cover the earth,
I will destroy cities and their inhabitants.
[9]Advance, O horses,
and rage, O chariots!
Let the warriors go forth:
men of Ethiopia and Put who handle
the shield,
men of Lud, skilled in handling the bow.
[10]That day is the day of the Lord GOD of hosts,
a day of vengeance,
to avenge himself on his foes.
The sword shall devour and be sated,
and drink its fill of their blood.
For the Lord GOD of hosts holds a sacrifice
in the north country by the river Euphra´tes.
[11]Go up to Gilead, and take balm,
O virgin daughter of Egypt!
In vain you have used many medicines;
there is no healing for you.
[12]The nations have heard of your shame,
and the earth is full of your cry;
for warrior has stumbled against warrior;
they have both fallen together."

[13]The word which the LORD spoke to
Jeremi´ah the prophet about the coming of
Nebuchadrez´zar king of Babylon to strike
the land of Egypt:
[14]"Declare in Egypt, and proclaim in Migdol;
proclaim in Memphis and Tah´panhes;
Say, 'Stand ready and be prepared,
for the sword shall devour round
about you.'
[15]Why has A´pis fled?
Why did not your bull stand?
Because the LORD thrust him down.
[16]Your multitude stumbled and fell,
and they said one to another,
'Arise, and let us go back to our own people
and to the land of our birth,
because of the sword of the oppressor.'
[17]Call the name of Pharaoh, king of Egypt,
'Noisy one who lets the hour go by.'
[18]"As I live, says the King,
whose name is the LORD of hosts,
like Ta´bor among the mountains,
and like Carmel by the sea, shall one come.
[19]Prepare yourselves baggage for exile,
O inhabitants of Egypt!
For Memphis shall become a waste,
a ruin, without inhabitant.
[20]"A beautiful heifer is Egypt,
but a gadfly from the north has come
upon her.
[21]Even her hired soldiers in her midst
are like fatted calves;
yes, they have turned and fled together,
they did not stand;
for the day of their calamity has come
upon them,
the time of their punishment.
[22]"She makes a sound like a serpent
gliding away;
for her enemies march in force,
and come against her with axes,
like those who fell trees.
[23]They shall cut down her forest,
says the LORD,
though it is impenetrable,
because they are more numerous
than locusts;
they are without number.
[24]The daughter of Egypt shall be put to shame,
she shall be delivered into the hand of a
people from the north."

[25]The LORD of hosts, the God of Israel,
said: "Behold, I am bringing punishment
upon A´mon of Thebes, and Pharaoh, and
Egypt and her gods and her kings, upon

Pharaoh and those who trust in him. 26I will deliver them into the hand of those who seek their life, into the hand of Nebuchadrez′zar king of Babylon and his officers. Afterward Egypt shall be inhabited as in the days of old, says the LORD.

27"But fear not, O Jacob my servant,
nor be dismayed, O Israel;
for behold, I will save you from afar,
and your offspring from the land of their captivity.
Jacob shall return and have quiet and ease,
and none shall make him afraid.
28Fear not, O Jacob my servant,
says the LORD,
for I am with you.
I will make a full end of all the nations
to which I have driven you,
but of you I will not make a full end.
I will chasten you in just measure,
and I will by no means leave you
unpunished."

SIRACH

Whereas many great teachings have been given to us through the law and the prophets and the others that followed them, on account of which we should praise Israel for instruction and wisdom; and since it is necessary not only that the readers themselves should acquire understanding but also that those who love learning should be able to help the outsiders by both speaking and writing, my grandfather Jesus, after devoting himself especially to the reading of the law and the prophets and the other books of our fathers, and after acquiring considerable proficiency in them, was himself also led to write something pertaining to instruction and wisdom, in order that, by becoming conversant with this also, those who love learning should make even greater progress in living according to the law.

You are urged therefore to read with good will and attention, and to be indulgent in cases where, despite our diligent labor in translating, we may seem to have rendered some phrases imperfectly. For what was originally expressed in Hebrew does not have exactly the same sense when translated into another language. Not only this work, but even the law itself, the prophecies, and the rest of the books differ not a little as originally expressed.

When I came to Egypt in the thirty-eighth year of the reign of Euer′getes and stayed for some time, I found opportunity for no little instruction. It seemed highly necessary that I should myself devote some pains and labor to the translation of the following book, using in that period of time great watchfulness and skill in order to complete and publish the book for those living abroad who wished to gain learning, being prepared in character to live according to the law.

EPHESIANS 2

11Therefore remember that at one time you Gentiles in the flesh, called the uncircumcision by what is called the circumcision, which is made
in the flesh by hands—12remember that you
were at that time separated from Christ,
alienated from the commonwealth of Israel,
and strangers to the covenants of promise,
having no hope and without God in the
world. 13But now in Christ Jesus you who
once were far off have been brought near in
the blood of Christ. 14For he is our peace, who
has made us both one, and has broken down
the dividing wall of hostility, 15by abolishing
in his flesh the law of commandments and
ordinances, that he might create in himself
one new man in place of the two, so making
peace, 16and might reconcile us both to God
in one body through the cross, thereby
bringing the hostility to an end. 17And he
came and preached peace to you who were
far off and peace to those who were near;
18for through him we both have access in
one Spirit to the Father. 19So then you are no
longer strangers and sojourners, but you are
fellow citizens with the saints and members
of the household of God, 20built upon the

foundation of the apostles and prophets, Christ Jesus himself being the cornerstone,
21in whom the whole structure is joined together and grows into a holy temple in the Lord;
22in whom you also are built into it for a dwelling place of God in the Spirit.

REFLECTION

The prologue to Sirach discusses the problem of translating the book from Hebrew into Greek. Translation is a laborious process, the author explains, and it can be difficult to express ideas originally written in another language. This problem of translation is not just an ancient one, nor one that pertains strictly to language. St. Paul speaks about a different kind of translation, where the Jewish covenant is "translated" (we might say) by Christ into a universal language that invites all people. Christians are always "translating" the Gospel into new languages, but also into new cultures and new situations. In Jeremiah, the Israelites have been physically translated (i.e., moved) into Egypt, but rather than taking their ancient faith into their new situation, they have abandoned it. When we bring the Gospel with us into the world, we should reflect on which words we can use to authentically express the truth to modern culture. It is an art to find the appropriate language to effectively preach the Gospel, without allowing the surrounding culture to dictate our forms of expression. Do you ever spend time thinking about how themes found in modern books, movies, or other media can help you explain the Faith, while also considering their limitations?

October 6

JEREMIAH 47

The word of the LORD that came to Jeremi′ah the prophet concerning the Philis′tines, before Pharaoh struck Gaza.

2"Thus says the LORD:
Behold, waters are rising out of the north,
and shall become an overflowing torrent;
they shall overflow the land and all that fills it,
the city and those who dwell in it.
Men shall cry out,
and every inhabitant of the land shall wail.
3At the noise of the stamping of the hoofs of his stallions,
at the rushing of his chariots, at the rumbling of their wheels,
the fathers look not back to their children,
so feeble are their hands,
4because of the day that is coming to destroy all the Philis′tines,
to cut off from Tyre and Si′don
every helper that remains.
For the LORD is destroying the Philistines,
the remnant of the coastland of Caphtor.
5Baldness has come upon Gaza,
Ash′kelon has perished.
O remnant of the An′akim,
how long will you gash yourselves?
6Ah, sword of the LORD!
How long till you are quiet?
Put yourself into your scabbard,
rest and be still!
7How can it be quiet,
when the LORD has given it a charge?
Against Ash′kelon and against the seashore
he has appointed it."

48 Concerning Moab.
Thus says the LORD of hosts, the God of Israel:
"Woe to Nebo, for it is laid waste!
Kir″iatha′im is put to shame, it is taken;
the fortress is put to shame and broken down;
2 the renown of Moab is no more.
In Heshbon they planned evil against her:
'Come, let us cut her off from being a nation!'
You also, O Madmen, shall be brought to silence;
the sword shall pursue you.
3"Listen! a cry from Horona′im,
'Desolation and great destruction!'

[4]Moab is destroyed;
a cry is heard as far as Zoar.
[5]For at the ascent of Lu′hith
they go up weeping;
for at the descent of Horona′im
they have heard the cry of destruction.
[6]Flee! Save yourselves!
Be like a wild donkey in the desert!
[7]For, because you trusted in your strongholds
and your treasures,
you also shall be taken;
and Che′mosh shall go forth into exile,
with his priests and his princes.
[8]The destroyer shall come upon every city,
and no city shall escape;
the valley shall perish,
and the plain shall be destroyed,
as the LORD has spoken.

[9]"Give wings to Moab,
for she would fly away;
her cities shall become a desolation,
with no inhabitant in them.

[10]"Cursed is he who does the work of the
LORD with slackness; and cursed is he who
keeps back his sword from bloodshed.

[11]"Moab has been at ease from his youth
and has settled on his dregs;
he has not been emptied from vessel
to vessel,
nor has he gone into exile;
so his taste remains in him,
and his scent is not changed.
[12]"Therefore, behold, the days are coming,
says the LORD, when I shall send to him tilters
who will tilt him, and empty his vessels, and
break his jars in pieces. [13]Then Moab shall be
ashamed of Che′mosh, as the house of Israel
was ashamed of Bethel, their confidence.

[14]"How do you say, 'We are heroes
and mighty men of war'?
[15]The destroyer of Moab and his cities has
come up,
and the choicest of his young men have
gone down to slaughter,
says the King, whose name is the LORD
of hosts.
[16]The calamity of Moab is near at hand
and his affliction hastens apace.
[17]Bemoan him, all you who are round
about him,
and all who know his name;
say, 'How the mighty scepter is broken,
the glorious staff.'

[18]"Come down from your glory,
and sit on the parched ground,
O inhabitant of Di′bon!
For the destroyer of Moab has come up
against you;
he has destroyed your strongholds.
[19]Stand by the way and watch,
O inhabitant of Aro′er!
Ask him who flees and her who escapes;
say, 'What has happened?'
[20]Moab is put to shame, for it is broken;
wail and cry!
Tell it by the Arnon,
that Moab is laid waste.

[21]"Judgment has come upon the tableland,
upon Ho′lon, and Jah′zah, and Meph′a-
ath, [22]and Di′bon, and Nebo, and Beth″-
diblatha′im, [23]and Kir″iatha′im, and Beth-
ga′mul, and Beth-me′on, [24]and Ker′ioth,
and Bozrah, and all the cities of the land of
Moab, far and near. [25]The horn of Moab is
cut off, and his arm is broken, says the LORD.
[26]"Make him drunk, because he magnified
himself against the LORD; so that Moab shall
wallow in his vomit, and he too shall be
held in derision. [27]Was not Israel a derision
to you? Was he found among thieves, that
whenever you spoke of him you wagged
your head?

[28]"Leave the cities, and dwell in the rock,
O inhabitants of Moab!
Be like the dove that nests
in the sides of the mouth of a gorge.
[29]We have heard of the pride of Moab—
he is very proud—
of his loftiness, his pride, and his arrogance,
and the haughtiness of his heart.
[30]I know his insolence, says the LORD;
his boasts are false,
his deeds are false.

[31]Therefore I wail for Moab;
I cry out for all Moab;
for the men of Kir-he′res I mourn.
[32]More than for Ja′zer I weep for you,
O vine of Sibmah!
Your branches passed over the sea,
reached as far as Jazer,
upon your summer fruits and your vintage
the destroyer has fallen.
[33]Gladness and joy have been taken away
from the fruitful land of Moab;
I have made the wine cease from the wine presses;
no one treads them with shouts of joy;
the shouting is not the shout of joy.

[34]"Heshbon and Ele-a′leh cry out; as far as
Ja′haz they utter their voice, from Zoar to
Horona′im and Eg′lath-shelish′iyah. For the
waters of Nimrim also have become desolate.
[35]And I will bring to an end in Moab, says the
LORD, him who offers sacrifice in the high place
and burns incense to his god. [36]Therefore my
heart moans for Moab like a flute, and my heart
moans like a flute for the men of Kir-he′res;
therefore the riches they gained have perished.
[37]"For every head is shaved and every beard
cut off; upon all the hands are gashes, and on
the loins is sackcloth. [38]On all the housetops
of Moab and in the squares there is nothing
but lamentation; for I have broken Moab like
a vessel for which no one cares, says the LORD.
[39]How it is broken! How they wail! How Moab
has turned his back in shame! So Moab has
become a derision and a horror to all that are
round about him."
[40]For thus says the LORD:
"Behold, one shall fly swiftly like an eagle,
and spread his wings against Moab;
[41]the cities shall be taken
and the strongholds seized.
The heart of the warriors of Moab shall be
in that day
like the heart of a woman with her labor pains;
[42]Moab shall be destroyed and be no longer
a people,
because he magnified himself against
the LORD.
[43]Terror, pit, and snare
are before you, O inhabitant of Moab!
says the LORD.
[44]He who flees from the terror
shall fall into the pit,
and he who climbs out of the pit
shall be caught in the snare.
For I will bring these things upon Moab
in the year of their punishment,
says the LORD.

[45]"In the shadow of Heshbon
fugitives stop without strength;
for a fire has gone forth from Heshbon,
a flame from the house of Si′hon;
it has destroyed the forehead of Moab,
the crown of the sons of tumult.
[46]Woe to you, O Moab!
The people of Che′mosh is undone;
for your sons have been taken captive,
and your daughters into captivity.
[47]Yet I will restore the fortunes
of Moab
in the latter days, says the LORD."
Thus far is the judgment on Moab.

SIRACH 1

All wisdom comes from the Lord
and is with him for ever.
[2]The sand of the sea, the drops of rain,
and the days of eternity—who can
count them?
[3]The height of heaven, the breadth of the earth,
the abyss, and wisdom—who can search
them out?
[4]Wisdom was created before all things,
and prudent understanding from eternity.
[5]The source of wisdom is God's word in the
highest heaven,
and her ways are the eternal
commandments.
[6]The root of wisdom—to whom has it been
revealed?
Her clever devices—who knows them?
[7]The knowledge of wisdom—to whom was
it manifested?
And her abundant experience—who has
understood it?
[8]There is One who is wise, the Creator of all,
the King greatly to be feared, sitting upon
his throne, and ruling as God.

9The Lord himself created wisdom in the
holy spirit;
he saw her and apportioned her,
he poured her out upon all his works.
10She dwells with all flesh according to
his gift,
and he supplied her to those who love him.

11The fear of the Lord is glory and exultation,
and gladness and a crown of rejoicing.
12The fear of the Lord delights the heart,
and gives gladness and joy and long life.
13With him who fears the Lord it will go well
at the end;
on the day of his death he will be blessed.

14To fear the Lord is the beginning of wisdom;
she is created with the faithful in the womb.
15She made among men an eternal foundation,
and among their descendants she will
be trusted.
16To fear the Lord is wisdom's full measure;
she satisfies men with her fruits;
17she fills their whole house with
desirable goods,
and their storehouses with her produce.
18The fear of the Lord is the crown of wisdom,
making peace and perfect health
to flourish.
19He saw her and apportioned her;
he rained down knowledge and
discerning comprehension,
and he exalted the glory of those who
held her fast.
20To fear the Lord is the root of wisdom,
and her branches are long life.

22Unrighteous anger cannot be justified,
for a man's anger tips the scale to his ruin.
23A patient man will endure until the
right moment,
and then joy will burst forth for him.
24He will hide his words until the
right moment,
and the lips of many will tell of his
good sense.
25In the treasuries of wisdom are
wise sayings,
but godliness is an abomination to
a sinner.
26If you desire wisdom, keep the
commandments,
and the Lord will supply it for you.
27For the fear of the Lord is wisdom and
instruction,
and he delights in fidelity and meekness.
28Do not disobey the fear of the Lord;
do not approach him with a divided mind.
29Be not a hypocrite in men's sight,
and keep watch over your lips.
30Do not exalt yourself lest you fall,
and thus bring dishonor upon yourself.
The Lord will reveal your secrets
and cast you down in the midst of the
congregation,
because you did not come in the fear of
the Lord,
and your heart was full of deceit.

EPHESIANS 3

For this reason I, Paul, a prisoner for Christ Jesus on behalf of you Gentiles—2assuming that you have heard of the stewardship of God's grace
that was given to me for you, 3how the mys-
tery was made known to me by revelation,
as I have written briefly. 4When you read this
you can perceive my insight into the mystery
of Christ, 5which was not made known to
the sons of men in other generations as it has
now been revealed to his holy apostles and
prophets by the Spirit; 6that is, how the Gentiles are fellow heirs, members of the same
body, and partakers of the promise in Christ
Jesus through the gospel.
7Of this gospel I was made a minister
according to the gift of God's grace which was
given me by the working of his power. 8To me,
though I am the very least of all the saints, this
grace was given, to preach to the Gentiles the
unsearchable riches of Christ, 9and to make all
men see what is the plan of the mystery hidden
for ages in God who created all things; 10that
through the Church the manifold wisdom
of God might now be made known to the
principalities and powers in the heavenly
places. 11This was according to the eternal

purpose which he has realized in Christ Jesus our Lord, [12]in whom we have boldness and confidence of access through our faith in him. [13]So I ask you not to lose heart over what I am suffering for you, which is your glory.

REFLECTION

Sirach praises the fear of God, calling it "the beginning of wisdom" (Sir 1:14) and "wisdom's full measure" (v. 16). To modern ears, this can sound like an absurdity. Fear of the Lord is seen by many as superstitious at best and oppressive at worst. The words of Jeremiah, who prophesies the devastating effects of wickedness, are sometimes seen as dreadful and even barbaric. But consider this oft-quoted line from Fyodor Dostoevsky's novel *The Brothers Karamazov*: "Without God and the future life . . . everything is permitted" (Part 4, Book 11, Chapter 4). This statement suggests that when we recognize God's existence and the presence of eternal truth in the universe, our moral compass and indeed the entire orientation of our lives is dramatically shifted. That is why Sirach calls the fear of the Lord the beginning of wisdom. To gain wisdom, we must recognize that its origin is not human, but lies in God, a God who is ultimately beyond our comprehension. Our initial reaction to this revelation should be fear, not strictly a servile fear of punishment, but the filial fear of a son or daughter who loves his or her father and desires to honor and obey him. When we lose this fear, we lose a necessary constraint. Have you ever felt this holy fear, perhaps expressed as reverence or awe?

October 7

JEREMIAH 49

Concerning the Am′monites.
Thus says the Lord:
"Has Israel no sons?
Has he no heir?

Why then has Milcom dispossessed Gad,
and his people settled in its cities?
[2]Therefore, behold, the days are coming,
says the Lord,
when I will cause the battle cry to be heard
against Rabbah of the Am′monites;
it shall become a desolate mound,
and its villages shall be burned with fire;
then Israel shall dispossess those who
dispossessed him,
says the Lord.
[3]"Wail, O Heshbon, for Ai is laid waste!
Cry, O daughters of Rabbah!
Clothe yourselves with sackcloth,
lament, and run to and fro among
the hedges!
For Milcom shall go into exile,
with his priests and his princes.
[4]Why do you boast of your valleys,
O faithless daughter,
who trusted in her treasures, saying,
'Who will come against me?'
[5]Behold, I will bring terror upon you,
says the Lord God of hosts,
from all who are round about you,
and you shall be driven out, every man
straight before him,
with none to gather the fugitives.
[6]But afterward I will restore the fortunes of
the Am′monites, says the Lord."
[7]Concerning E′dom.
Thus says the Lord of hosts:
"Is wisdom no more in Te′man?
Has counsel perished from the prudent?
Has their wisdom vanished?
[8]Flee, turn back, dwell in the depths,
O inhabitants of De′dan!
For I will bring the calamity of Esau
upon him,
the time when I punish him.
[9]If grape-gatherers came to you,
would they not leave gleanings?
If thieves came by night,
would they not destroy only enough
for themselves?
[10]But I have stripped Esau bare,
I have uncovered his hiding places,
and he is not able to conceal himself.
His children are destroyed, and
his brothers,
and his neighbors; and he is no more.

11 Leave your fatherless children, I will keep
them alive;
and let your widows trust in me."
12 For thus says the LORD: "If those who
did not deserve to drink the cup must drink
it, will you go unpunished? You shall not
go unpunished, but you must drink. 13 For I
have sworn by myself, says the LORD, that
Bozrah shall become a horror, a taunt, a
waste, and a curse; and all her cities shall be
perpetual wastes."
14 I have heard tidings from the LORD,
and a messenger has been sent among
the nations:
"Gather yourselves together and come
against her,
and rise up for battle!"
15 For behold, I will make you small among
the nations,
despised among men.
16 The horror you inspire has deceived you,
and the pride of your heart,
you who live in the clefts of the rock,
who hold the height of the hill.
Though you make your nest as high as
the eagle's,
I will bring you down from there,
says the LORD.
17 "E′dom shall become a horror; every
one who passes by it will be horrified and
will hiss because of all its disasters. 18 As
when Sodom and Gomor′rah and their
neighbor cities were overthrown, says the
LORD, no man shall dwell there, no man
shall sojourn in her. 19 Behold, like a lion
coming up from the jungle of the Jordan
against a strong sheepfold, I will suddenly make them run away from her; and I
will appoint over her whomever I choose.
For who is like me? Who will summon
me? What shepherd can stand before me?
20 Therefore hear the plan which the LORD
has made against E′dom and the purposes
which he has formed against the inhabitants of Te′man: Even the little ones of the
flock shall be dragged away; surely their
fold shall be appalled at their fate. 21 At the
sound of their fall the earth shall tremble;
the sound of their cry shall be heard at
the Red Sea. 22 Behold, one shall mount up
and fly swiftly like an eagle, and spread
his wings against Bozrah, and the heart of
the warriors of E′dom shall be in that day
like the heart of a woman with her labor
pains."
23 Concerning Damascus.
"Ha′math and Arpad are confounded,
for they have heard evil tidings;
they melt in fear, they are troubled like
the sea
which cannot be quiet.
24 Damascus has become feeble, she turned
to flee,
and panic seized her;
anguish and sorrows have taken hold of her,
as of a woman with labor pains.
25 How the famous city is forsaken,
the joyful city!
26 Therefore her young men shall fall in
her squares,
and all her soldiers shall be destroyed
in that day,
says the LORD of hosts.
27 And I will kindle a fire in the wall of
Damascus,
and it shall devour the strongholds of
Benha′dad."
28 Concerning Ke′dar and the kingdoms
of Ha′zor which Nebuchadrez′zar king of
Babylon struck.
Thus says the LORD:
"Rise up, advance against Kedar!
Destroy the people of the east!
29 Their tents and their flocks shall be taken,
their curtains and all their goods;
their camels shall be borne away from them,
and men shall cry to them: 'Terror on
every side!'
30 Flee, wander far away, dwell in the depths,
O inhabitants of Ha′zor!
says the LORD.
For Nebuchadrez′zar king of Babylon
has made a plan against you,
and formed a purpose against you.

31 "Rise up, advance against a nation at ease,
that dwells securely,
says the LORD,
that has no gates or bars,
that dwells alone.

32 Their camels shall become booty,
their herds of cattle a spoil.
I will scatter to every wind
those who cut the corners of their hair,
and I will bring their calamity
from every side of them,
says the LORD.
33 Ha′zor shall become a haunt of jackals,
an everlasting waste;
no man shall dwell there,
no man shall sojourn in her."

34 The word of the LORD that came to
Jeremi′ah the prophet concerning E′lam, in
the beginning of the reign of Zedeki′ah king
of Judah.
35 Thus says the LORD of hosts: "Behold, I
will break the bow of E′lam, the mainstay of
their might; 36 and I will bring upon E′lam
the four winds from the four quarters of
heaven; and I will scatter them to all those
winds, and there shall be no nation to which
those driven out of Elam shall not come. 37 I
will terrify E′lam before their enemies, and
before those who seek their life; I will bring
evil upon them, my fierce anger, says the
LORD. I will send the sword after them, until
I have consumed them; 38 and I will set my
throne in E′lam, and destroy their king and
princes, says the LORD.
39 "But in the latter days I will restore the
fortunes of E′lam, says the LORD."

50 The word which the LORD spoke concerning Babylon, concerning the land
of the Chalde′ans, by Jeremi′ah the prophet:
2 "Declare among the nations and proclaim,
set up a banner and proclaim,
conceal it not, and say:
'Babylon is taken,
Bel is put to shame,
Mer′odach is dismayed.
Her images are put to shame,
her idols are dismayed.'

3 "For out of the north a nation has come
up against her, which shall make her land a
desolation, and none shall dwell in it; both
man and beast shall flee away.

4 "In those days and in that time, says the
LORD, the people of Israel and the people
of Judah shall come together, weeping as
they come; and they shall seek the LORD
their God. 5 They shall ask the way to
Zion, with faces turned toward it, saying,
'Come, let us join ourselves to the LORD
in an everlasting covenant which will
never be forgotten.'

6 "My people have been lost sheep; their
shepherds have led them astray, turning
them away on the mountains; from
mountain to hill they have gone, they
have forgotten their fold. 7 All who found
them have devoured them, and their
enemies have said, 'We are not guilty, for
they have sinned against the LORD, their
true habitation, the LORD, the hope of
their fathers.'

8 "Flee from the midst of Babylon, and
go out of the land of the Chalde′ans,
and be as he-goats before the flock. 9 For
behold, I am stirring up and bringing
against Babylon a company of great nations, from the north country; and they
shall array themselves against her; from
there she shall be taken. Their arrows are
like a skilled warrior who does not return empty-handed. 10 Chalde′a shall be
plundered; all who plunder her shall be
sated, says the LORD.

11 "Though you rejoice, though you exult,
O plunderers of my heritage,
though you are wanton as a heifer at grass,
and neigh like stallions,
12 your mother shall be utterly shamed,
and she who bore you shall be disgraced.
Behold, she shall be the last of the nations,
a wilderness dry and desert.
13 Because of the wrath of the LORD she shall
not be inhabited,
but shall be an utter desolation;
every one who passes by Babylon shall
be appalled,
and hiss because of all her wounds.
14 Set yourselves in array against Babylon
round about,
all you that bend the bow;
shoot at her, spare no arrows,
for she has sinned against the LORD.

[15]Raise a shout against her round about,
she has surrendered;
her bulwarks have fallen,
her walls are thrown down.
For this is the vengeance of the LORD:
take vengeance on her,
do to her as she has done.
[16]Cut off from Babylon the sower,
and the one who handles the sickle in
time of harvest;
because of the sword of the oppressor,
every one shall turn to his own people,
and every one shall flee to his own land.

[17]"Israel is a hunted sheep driven away by
lions. First the king of Assyria devoured him,
and now at last Nebuchadrez′zar king of
Babylon has gnawed his bones. [18]Therefore,
thus says the LORD of hosts, the God of Israel:
Behold, I am bringing punishment on the king
of Babylon and his land, as I punished the king
of Assyria. [19]I will restore Israel to his pasture,
and he shall feed on Car′mel and in Ba′shan,
and his desire shall be satisfied on the hills of
E′phraim and in Gilead. [20]In those days and
in that time, says the LORD, iniquity shall be
sought in Israel, and there shall be none; and
sin in Judah, and none shall be found; for I will
pardon those whom I leave as a remnant.

[21]"Go up against the land of Meratha′im,
and against the inhabitants of Pe′kod.
Slay, and utterly destroy after them, says
the LORD,
and do all that I have commanded you.
[22]The noise of battle is in the land,
and great destruction!
[23]How the hammer of the whole earth
is cut down and broken!
How Babylon has become
a horror among the nations!
[24]I set a snare for you and you were taken,
O Babylon,
and you did not know it;
you were found and caught,
because you strove against the LORD.
[25]The LORD has opened his armory,
and brought out the weapons of his wrath,
for the Lord GOD of hosts has a work to do
in the land of the Chalde′ans.
[26]Come against her from every quarter;
open her granaries;
pile her up like heaps of grain, and destroy
her utterly;
let nothing be left of her.
[27]Slay all her bulls,
let them go down to the slaughter.
Woe to them, for their day has come,
the time of their punishment."

SIRACH 2

My son, if you come forward to serve
the Lord,
remain in justice and in fear,
and prepare yourself for temptation.
[2]Set your heart right and be steadfast,
incline your ear, and receive words
of understanding,
and do not be hasty in time of calamity.
[3]Await God's patience, cling to him and do
not depart,
that you may be wise in all your ways.
[4]Accept whatever is brought upon you,
and endure it in sorrow;
in changes that humble you be patient.
[5]For gold and silver are tested in the fire,
and acceptable men in the furnace of
humiliation.
[6]Trust in God, and he will help you;
hope in him, and he will make your
ways straight.
Stay in fear of him, and grow old in him.
[7]You who fear the Lord, wait for his mercy;
and turn not aside, lest you fall.
[8]You who fear the Lord, trust in him,
and your reward will not fail;
[9]you who fear the Lord, hope for good things,
for everlasting joy and mercy.
You who fear the Lord, love him,
and your hearts will be made radiant.
[10]Consider the ancient generations and see:
who ever trusted in the Lord and was put
to shame?
Or who ever persevered in his
commandments and was forsaken?
Or who ever called upon him and was
overlooked?

11 For the Lord is compassionate
and merciful;
he forgives sins and saves in time
of affliction,
and he is the shield of all who seek him
in truth.

EPHESIANS 3

14 For this reason I bow my knees
before the Father, 15 from whom
every family in heaven and on earth is
named, 16 that according to the riches of
his glory he may grant you to be strengthened
with might through his Spirit in the inner
man, 17 and that Christ may dwell in your
hearts through faith; that you, being rooted
and grounded in love, 18 may have power to
comprehend with all the saints what is the
breadth and length and height and depth,
19 and to know the love of Christ which
surpasses knowledge, that you may be filled
with all the fulness of God.
20 Now to him who by the power at work
within us is able to do far more abundantly
than all that we ask or think, 21 to him be
glory in the Church and in Christ Jesus to
all generations, for ever and ever. Amen.

4 I therefore, a prisoner for the Lord, beg
you to walk in a manner worthy of the
calling to which you have been called, 2 with
all lowliness and meekness, with patience,
forbearing one another in love, 3 eager to
maintain the unity of the Spirit in the bond
of peace. 4 There is one body and one Spirit,
just as you were called to the one hope that
belongs to your call, 5 one Lord, one faith,
one baptism, 6 one God and Father of us all,
who is above all and through all and in all.
7 But grace was given to each of us according
to the measure of Christ's gift. 8 Therefore it
is said,
"When he ascended on high he led a host
of captives,
and he gave gifts to men."
9 (In saying, "He ascended," what does it mean
but that he had also descended into the lower
parts of the earth? 10 He who descended is he
who also ascended far above all the heavens,
that he might fill all things.) 11 And his gifts
were that some should be apostles, some
prophets, some evangelists, some pastors
and teachers, 12 to equip the saints for the
work of ministry, for building up the body
of Christ, 13 until we all attain to the unity of
the faith and of the knowledge of the Son
of God, to mature manhood, to the measure
of the stature of the fulness of Christ; 14 so
that we may no longer be children, tossed
back and forth and carried about with every
wind of doctrine, by the cunning of men, by
their craftiness in deceitful wiles. 15 Rather,
speaking the truth in love, we are to grow up
in every way into him who is the head, into
Christ, 16 from whom the whole body, joined
and knit together by every joint with which
it is supplied, when each part is working
properly, makes bodily growth and upbuilds
itself in love.

REFLECTION

Today, the Book of Sirach tells us that "gold and silver are tested in the fire, and acceptable men in the furnace of humiliation" (Sir 2:5). St. Paul likewise attests that it is in "lowliness and meekness" that we become the Body of Christ (Eph 4:2). Humility—and even humiliation—is the way in which we are perfected both individually and collectively. In Jeremiah, the concept of collective humiliation is especially evident. Just as Babylon had conquered and subdued many nations (including Israel), Babylon would soon be brought low (see Jer 50:9–12). Taken together, these texts offer a twofold lesson. First, the way to perfection is in lowliness, in imitation of the God who humbled himself in Christ. Second, this call to humility applies not only to ourselves as individuals, but also to all human institutions. To boast of and trust in any nation or human power is to place your hope in that which will fail. It is only through incorporation into the heavenly Kingdom as the Body of Christ, the Church, that we have an eternal hope. Do you ever invest yourself too heavily in an earthly kingdom, either by boasting at its glory or despairing because of its failings?

October 8

JEREMIAH 50

28"Listen! they flee and escape from the land of Babylon, to declare in Zion the vengeance of the LORD our God, vengeance for his temple.

29"Summon archers against Babylon, all those who bend the bow. Encamp round about her; let no one escape. Repay her according to her deeds, do to her according to all that she has done; for she has proudly defied the LORD, the Holy One of Israel.
30Therefore her young men shall fall in her squares, and all her soldiers shall be destroyed on that day, says the LORD.

31"Behold, I am against you, O proud one,
says the Lord GOD of hosts;
for your day has come,
the time when I will punish you.
32The proud one shall stumble and fall,
with none to raise him up,
and I will kindle a fire in his cities,
and it will devour all that is round
about him.

33"Thus says the LORD of hosts: The people of Israel are oppressed, and the people of Judah with them; all who took them captive have held them fast, they refuse to let them go.
34Their Redeemer is strong; the LORD of hosts is his name. He will surely plead their cause, that he may give rest to the earth, but unrest to the inhabitants of Babylon.

35"A sword upon the Chalde′ans, says
the LORD,
and upon the inhabitants of Babylon,
and upon her princes and her wise men!
36A sword upon the diviners,
that they may become fools!
A sword upon her warriors,
that they may be destroyed!
37A sword upon her horses and upon
her chariots,
and upon all the foreign troops in
her midst,
that they may become women!
A sword upon all her treasures,
that they may be plundered!
38A drought upon her waters,
that they may be dried up!
For it is a land of images,
and they are mad over idols.

39"Therefore wild beasts shall dwell with hyenas in Babylon, and ostriches shall dwell in her; she shall be peopled no more for ever, nor inhabited for all generations.
40As when God overthrew Sodom and Gomor′rah and their neighbor cities, says the LORD, so no man shall dwell there, and no son of man shall sojourn in her.

41"Behold, a people comes from the north;
a mighty nation and many kings
are stirring from the farthest parts of
the earth.
42They lay hold of bow and spear;
they are cruel, and have no mercy.
The sound of them is like the roaring of
the sea;
they ride upon horses,
clothed as a man for battle
against you, O daughter of Babylon!

43"The king of Babylon heard the report
of them,
and his hands fell helpless;
anguish seized him,
pain as of a woman in labor.

44"Behold, like a lion coming up from the jungle of the Jordan against a strong sheepfold, I will suddenly make them run away from her; and I will appoint over her whomever I choose. For who is like me? Who will summon me? What shepherd can stand before me?
45Therefore hear the plan which the LORD has made against Babylon, and the purposes which he has formed against the land of the Chalde′ans: Surely the little ones of their flock shall be dragged away; surely their fold shall be appalled at their fate.
46At the sound of the

capture of Babylon the earth shall tremble,
and her cry shall be heard among the nations."

51 Thus says the LORD:
Behold, I will stir up the spirit of a
destroyer against Babylon,
against the inhabitants of Chalde′a;
2and I will send to Babylon winnowers,
and they shall winnow her,
and they shall empty her land,
when they come against her from
every side
on the day of trouble.
3Let not the archer bend his bow,
and let him not stand up in his coat
of mail.
Spare not her young men;
utterly destroy all her host.
4They shall fall down slain in the land
of the Chalde′ans,
and wounded in her streets.
5For Israel and Judah have not been forsaken
by their God, the LORD of hosts;
but the land of the Chalde′ans is full of guilt
against the Holy One of Israel.

6"Flee from the midst of Babylon,
let every man save his life!
Be not cut off in her punishment,
for this is the time of the LORD's vengeance,
the repayment he is rendering her.
7Babylon was a golden cup in the
LORD's hand,
making all the earth drunken;
the nations drank of her wine,
therefore the nations went mad.
8Suddenly Babylon has fallen and
been broken;
wail for her!
Take balm for her pain;
perhaps she may be healed.
9We would have healed Babylon,
but she was not healed.
Forsake her, and let us go
each to his own country;
for her judgment has reached up to heaven
and has been lifted up even to the skies.
10The LORD has brought forth
our vindication;
come, let us declare in Zion
the work of the LORD our God.

11"Sharpen the arrows!
Take up the shields!
The LORD has stirred up the spirit of the
kings of the Medes, because his purpose
concerning Babylon is to destroy it, for that
is the vengeance of the LORD, the vengeance
for his temple.
12Set up a standard against the walls
of Babylon;
make the watch strong;
set up watchmen;
prepare the ambushes;
for the LORD has both planned and done
what he spoke concerning the inhabitants
of Babylon.
13O you who dwell by many waters,
rich in treasures,
your end has come,
the thread of your life is cut.
14The LORD of hosts has sworn by himself:
Surely I will fill you with men, as many
as locusts,
and they shall raise the shout of victory
over you.

15"It is he who made the earth by his power,
who established the world by his wisdom,
and by his understanding
stretched out the heavens.
16When he utters his voice there is a tumult
of waters in the heavens,
and he makes the mist rise from the ends
of the earth.
He makes lightning for the rain,
and he brings forth the wind from
his storehouses.
17Every man is stupid and without
knowledge;
every goldsmith is put to shame by
his idols;
for his images are false,
and there is no breath in them.
18They are worthless, a work of delusion;
at the time of their punishment they
shall perish.
19Not like these is he who is the portion
of Jacob,
for he is the one who formed all things,
and Israel is the tribe of his inheritance;
the LORD of hosts is his name.

[20]"You are my hammer and weapon of war:
with you I break nations in pieces;
with you I destroy kingdoms;
[21]with you I break in pieces the horse and
his rider;
with you I break in pieces the chariot and
the charioteer;
[22]with you I break in pieces man and woman;
with you I break in pieces the old man
and the youth;
with you I break in pieces the young man
and the maiden;
[23] with you I break in pieces the shepherd
and his flock;
with you I break in pieces the farmer and
his team;
with you I break in pieces governors and
commanders.
[24]"I will repay Babylon and all the inhabitants
of Chalde'a before your very eyes for all the evil
that they have done in Zion, says the LORD.

[25]"Behold, I am against you, O destroying
mountain,
says the LORD,
which destroys the whole earth;
I will stretch out my hand against you,
and roll you down from the crags,
and make you a burnt mountain.
[26]No stone shall be taken from you for a corner
and no stone for a foundation,
but you shall be a perpetual waste,
says the LORD.

[27]"Set up a standard on the earth,
blow the trumpet among the nations;
prepare the nations for war against her,
summon against her the kingdoms,
Ar'arat, Minni, and Ash'kenaz;
appoint a marshal against her,
bring up horses like bristling locusts.
[28]Prepare the nations for war against her,
the kings of the Medes, with their
governors and deputies,
and every land under their dominion.
[29]The land trembles and writhes in pain,
for the LORD's purposes against
Babylon stand,
to make the land of Babylon a desolation,
without inhabitant.
[30]The warriors of Babylon have ceased fighting,
they remain in their strongholds;
their strength has failed,
they have become women;
her dwellings are on fire,
her bars are broken.
[31]One runner runs to meet another,
and one messenger to meet another,
to tell the king of Babylon
that his city is taken on every side;
[32]the fords have been seized,
the bulwarks are burned with fire,
and the soldiers are in panic.
[33]For thus says the LORD of hosts, the God
of Israel:
The daughter of Babylon is like a
threshing floor
at the time when it is trodden;
yet a little while
and the time of her harvest will come."
[34]"Nebuchadrez'zar the king of Babylon has
devoured me,
he has crushed me;
he has made me an empty vessel,
he has swallowed me like a monster;
he has filled his belly with my delicacies,
he has rinsed me out.
[35]The violence done to me and to my
kinsmen be upon Babylon,"
let the inhabitant of Zion say.
"My blood be upon the inhabitants of Chalde'a,"
let Jerusalem say.
[36]Therefore thus says the LORD:
"Behold, I will plead your cause
and take vengeance for you.
I will dry up her sea
and make her fountain dry;
[37]and Babylon shall become a heap of ruins,
the haunt of jackals,
a horror and a hissing,
without inhabitant.

[38]"They shall roar together like lions;
they shall growl like lions' whelps.
[39]While they are inflamed I will prepare
them a feast
and make them drunk, till they swoon away
and sleep a perpetual sleep
and not wake, says the LORD.

[40]I will bring them down like lambs to
the slaughter,
like rams and he-goats."

SIRACH 2

[12]Woe to timid hearts and to slack hands,
and to the sinner who walks along two ways!
[13]Woe to the faint heart, for it has no trust!
Therefore it will not be sheltered.
[14]Woe to you who have lost your endurance!
What will you do when the Lord
punishes you?
[15]Those who fear the Lord will not disobey
his words,
and those who love him will keep his ways.
[16]Those who fear the Lord will seek his
approval,
and those who love him will be filled
with the law.
[17]Those who fear the Lord will prepare
their hearts,
and will humble themselves before him.
[18]Let us fall into the hands of the Lord,
but not into the hands of men;
for as his majesty is,
so also is his mercy.

3 Listen to me your father, O children;
and act accordingly, that you may be
kept in safety.
[2]For the Lord honored the father above
the children,
and he confirmed the right of the mother
over her sons.
[3]Whoever honors his father atones for sins,
and preserves himself from them.
When he prays, he is heard;
[4] and whoever glorifies his mother is like
one who lays up treasure.
[5]Whoever honors his father will be
gladdened by his own children,
and when he prays he will be heard.
[6]Whoever glorifies his father will have long life,
and whoever obeys the Lord will refresh
his mother;
[7] he will serve his parents as his masters.
[8]Honor your father by word and deed,
that a blessing from him may come
upon you.
[9]For a father's blessing strengthens the
houses of the children,
but a mother's curse uproots their
foundations.
[10]Do not glorify yourself by dishonoring
your father,
for your father's dishonor is no glory
to you.
[11]For a man's glory comes from honoring
his father,
and it is a disgrace for children not to
respect their mother.
[12]O son, help your father in his old age,
and do not grieve him as long as he lives;
[13]even if he is lacking in understanding,
show forbearance;
and do not despise him all the days of
his life.
[14]For kindness to a father will not be
forgotten,
and against your sins it will be credited
to you
—a house raised in justice to you.
[15]in the day of your affliction it will be
remembered in your favor;
as frost in fair weather, your sins will
melt away.
[16]Whoever forsakes his father is like a
blasphemer,
and whoever angers his mother is cursed
by the Lord.

EPHESIANS 4

[17]Now this I affirm and testify in the Lord, that you must no longer walk as the Gentiles walk, in the futility of their minds; [18]they are darkened in their understanding, alienated from the life of God because of the ignorance that is in them, due to their hardness of heart; [19]they have become callous and have given themselves up to licentiousness, greedy to practice every kind of uncleanness. [20]You did not so learn Christ!—[21]assuming that you have heard about him and were taught in him, as the truth is in

Jesus. 22Put off the old man that belongs to
your former manner of life and is corrupt
through deceitful lusts, 23and be renewed
in the spirit of your minds, 24and put on the
new man, created after the likeness of God
in true righteousness and holiness.
25Therefore, putting away falsehood,
let every one speak the truth with his
neighbor, for we are members one of
another. 26Be angry but do not sin; do not
let the sun go down on your anger, 27and
give no opportunity to the devil. 28Let the
thief no longer steal, but rather let him
labor, doing honest work with his hands, so
that he may be able to give to those in need.
29Let no evil talk come out of your mouths,
but only such as is good for edifying, as fits
the occasion, that it may impart grace to
those who hear. 30And do not grieve the
Holy Spirit of God, in whom you were
sealed for the day of redemption. 31Let all
bitterness and wrath and anger and clamor
and slander be put away from you, with
all malice, 32and be kind to one another,
tenderhearted, forgiving one another, as
God in Christ forgave you.

5 Therefore be imitators of God, as beloved children. 2And walk in love, as
Christ loved us and gave himself up for us, a
fragrant offering and sacrifice to God.

REFLECTION

In Ephesians, St. Paul explains how we should behave in order to live righteously. He sums up his exhortation by telling us to "be imitators of God, as beloved children" (Eph 5:1). The Book of Sirach likewise speaks about the parent-child relationship, meditating on the meaning of the Fourth Commandment (to honor one's mother and father). The Book of Sirach can help illuminate Paul's letter by way of analogy. Especially as we get older, we begin to see our parents' strengths and virtues and long to imitate them. So much the greater should our desire be to imitate our heavenly Father as we come to know him more intimately. Although not all have had a good relationship with their parents or with their children, we may still have some sense of God's love for us by reflecting on the bond between parent and child. And, in light of that love, we can better understand Paul's call to moral action. We should not treat God worse than we treat our earthly parents. Or, to put ourselves in God's place, we should love God at least as well as we want our own children to love us. Can calling God your Father help you to envision your good works as acts of love and devotion?

October 9

JEREMIAH 51

41"How Babylon is taken,
the praise of the whole earth
seized!
How Babylon has become
a horror among the nations!
42The sea has come up on Babylon;
she is covered with its tumultuous
waves.
43Her cities have become a horror,
a land of drought and a desert,
a land in which no one dwells,
and through which no son of
man passes.
44And I will punish Bel in Babylon,
and take out of his mouth what he
has swallowed.
The nations shall no longer flow to him;
the wall of Babylon has fallen.

45"Go out of the midst of her, my people!
Let every man save his life
from the fierce anger of the LORD!
46Let not your heart faint, and be not fearful
at the report heard in the land,
when a report comes in one year
and afterward a report in another year,
and violence is in the land,
and ruler is against ruler.

[47]"Therefore, behold, the days are coming
when I will punish the images of Babylon;
her whole land shall be put to shame,
and all her slain shall fall in the midst
of her.
[48]Then the heavens and the earth,
and all that is in them,
shall sing for joy over Babylon;
for the destroyers shall come against
them out of the north,
says the LORD.
[49]Babylon must fall for the slain of Israel,
as for Babylon have fallen the slain of all
the earth.

[50]"You that have escaped from the sword,
go, stand not still!
Remember the LORD from afar,
and let Jerusalem come into your mind:
[51]'We are put to shame, for we have heard
reproach;
dishonor has covered our face,
for aliens have come
into the holy places of the LORD's house.'

[52]"Therefore, behold, the days are coming,
says the LORD,
when I will execute judgment upon
her images,
and through all her land
the wounded shall groan.
[53]Though Babylon should mount up to heaven,
and though she should fortify her strong
height,
yet destroyers would come from me upon her,
says the LORD.

[54]"Listen! a cry from Babylon!
The noise of great destruction from the
land of the Chalde'ans!
[55]For the LORD is laying Babylon waste,
and stilling her mighty voice.
Their waves roar like many waters,
the noise of their voice is raised;
[56]for a destroyer has come upon her,
upon Babylon;
her warriors are taken,
their bows are broken in pieces;
for the LORD is a God of recompense,
he will surely repay.
[57]I will make drunk her princes and her
wise men,
her governors, her commanders, and
her warriors;
they shall sleep a perpetual sleep and not wake,
says the King, whose name is the LORD
of hosts.

[58]"Thus says the LORD of hosts:
The broad wall of Babylon
shall be leveled to the ground
and her high gates
shall be burned with fire.
The peoples labor for nothing,
and the nations weary themselves
only for fire."

[59]The word which Jeremi'ah the prophet
commanded Serai'ah the son of Neri'ah, son
of Mahsei'ah, when he went with Zedeki'ah
king of Judah to Babylon, in the fourth year
of his reign. Seraiah was the quartermaster.
[60]Jeremi'ah wrote in a book all the evil that
should come upon Babylon, all these words
that are written concerning Babylon. [61]And
Jeremi'ah said to Serai'ah: "When you come
to Babylon, see that you read all these words,
[62]and say, 'O LORD, you have said concerning this place that you will cut it off, so
that nothing shall dwell in it, neither man
nor beast, and it shall be desolate for ever.'
[63]When you finish reading this book, bind a
stone to it, and cast it into the midst of the
Euphra'tes, [64]and say, 'Thus shall Babylon
sink, to rise no more, because of the evil that
I am bringing upon her.'"
Thus far are the words of Jeremi'ah.

52 Zedeki'ah was twenty-one years old
when he became king; and he reigned
eleven years in Jerusalem. His mother's
name was Hamu'tal the daughter of Jeremi'ah of Libnah. [2]And he did what was evil
in the sight of the LORD, according to all
that Jehoi'akim had done. [3]Surely because of
the anger of the LORD things came to such
a pass in Jerusalem and Judah that he cast
them out from his presence.
And Zedeki'ah rebelled against the king of
Babylon. [4]And in the ninth year of his reign,
in the tenth month, on the tenth day of the
month, Nebuchadrez'zar king of Babylon

came with all his army against Jerusalem,
and they laid siege to it and built siegeworks
against it round about. [5]So the city was
besieged till the eleventh year of King
Zedeki′ah. [6]On the ninth day of the fourth
month the famine was so severe in the city,
that there was no food for the people of the
land. [7]Then a breach was made in the city;
and all the men of war fled and went out
from the city by night by the way of a gate
between the two walls, by the king's garden,
while the Chalde′ans were round about the
city. And they went in the direction of the
Ar′abah. [8]But the army of the Chalde′ans
pursued the king, and overtook Zedeki′ah
in the plains of Jericho; and all his army was
scattered from him. [9]Then they captured
the king, and brought him up to the king of
Babylon at Riblah in the land of Ha′math,
and he passed sentence upon him. [10]The
king of Babylon slew the sons of Zedeki′ah
before his eyes, and also slew all the princes
of Judah at Riblah. [11]He put out the eyes of
Zedeki′ah, and bound him in chains, and the
king of Babylon took him to Babylon, and
put him in prison till the day of his death.

[12]In the fifth month, on the tenth day of
the month—which was the nineteenth year
of King Nebuchadrez′zar, king of Babylon—
Nebu′zarad′an the captain of the bodyguard
who served the king of Babylon, entered
Jerusalem. [13]And he burned the house of
the LORD, and the king's house and all the
houses of Jerusalem; every great house he
burned down. [14]And all the army of the
Chalde′ans, who were with the captain of
the guard, broke down all the walls round
about Jerusalem. [15]And Nebu′zarad′an the
captain of the guard carried away captive
some of the poorest of the people and the
rest of the people who were left in the city
and the deserters who had deserted to the
king of Babylon, together with the rest of
the artisans. [16]But Nebu′zarad′an the captain
of the guard left some of the poorest of the
land to be vinedressers and plowmen.

[17]And the pillars of bronze that were in
the house of the LORD, and the stands and
the bronze sea that were in the house of the
LORD, the Chalde′ans broke in pieces, and
carried all the bronze to Babylon. [18]And
they took away the pots, and the shovels,
and the snuffers, and the basins, and the
dishes for incense, and all the vessels of
bronze used in the temple service; [19]also
the small bowls, and the firepans, and the
basins, and the pots, and the lampstands,
and the dishes for incense, and the bowls
for libation. What was of gold the captain
of the guard took away as gold, and what
was of silver, as silver. [20]As for the two
pillars, the one sea, the twelve bronze
bulls which were under the sea, and the
stands, which Solomon the king had made
for the house of the LORD, the bronze of
all these things was beyond weight. [21]As
for the pillars, the height of the one pillar
was eighteen cubits, its circumference
was twelve cubits, and its thickness was
four fingers, and it was hollow. [22]Upon it
was a capital of bronze; the height of the
one capital was five cubits; a network and
pomegranates, all of bronze, were upon the
capital round about. And the second pillar
had the like, with pomegranates. [23]There
were ninety-six pomegranates on the sides;
all the pomegranates were a hundred upon
the network round about.

[24]And the captain of the guard took Se-
rai′ah the chief priest, and Zephani′ah the
second priest, and the three keepers of the
threshold; [25]and from the city he took an
officer who had been in command of the
men of war, and seven men of the king's
council, who were found in the city; and
the secretary of the commander of the
army who mustered the people of the
land; and sixty men of the people of the
land, who were found in the midst of the
city. [26]And Nebu′zarad′an the captain of
the guard took them, and brought them
to the king of Babylon at Riblah. [27]And
the king of Babylon struck them, and
put them to death at Riblah in the land
of Ha′math. So Judah was carried captive
out of its land.

[28]This is the number of the people whom
Nebuchadrez′zar carried away captive:
in the seventh year, three thousand and
twenty-three Jews; [29]in the eighteenth year

of Nebuchadrez′zar he carried away captive
from Jerusalem eight hundred and thirty-
two persons; 30in the twenty-third year of
Nebuchadrez′zar, Nebu′zarad′an the captain
of the guard carried away captive of the
Jews seven hundred and forty-five persons;
all the persons were four thousand and
six hundred.
31And in the thirty-seventh year of the
captivity of Jehoi′achin king of Judah, in
the twelfth month, on the twenty-fifth
day of the month, E′vil-mer′odach king of
Babylon, in the year that he became king,
lifted up the head of Jehoiachin king of
Judah and brought him out of prison; 32and
he spoke kindly to him, and gave him a seat
above the seats of the kings who were with
him in Babylon. 33So Jehoi′achin put off his
prison garments. And every day of his life
he dined regularly at the king's table; 34as for
his allowance, a regular allowance was given
him by the king according to his daily need,
until the day of his death as long as he lived.

SIRACH 3

17My son, perform your tasks in meekness;
then you will be loved more than a giver
of gifts.
18The greater you are, the more you must
humble yourself;
so you will find favor with God.
19There are many who are noble
and renowned,
but it is to the humble that he reveals
his mysteries.
20For great is the might of the Lord;
he is glorified by the humble.
21Seek not what is too difficult for you,
nor investigate what is beyond your power.
22Reflect upon what has been assigned to you,
and do not be curious about many of
his works,
for you do not need to see with your eyes
what is hidden.
23Do not meddle in what is beyond
your tasks,
for matters too great for human
understanding have been shown you.
24For their hasty judgment has led
many astray,
and wrong opinion has caused their
thoughts to slip.
26A stubborn mind will be afflicted at the end,
and whoever loves danger will perish by it.
27A stubborn mind will be burdened by
troubles,
and the sinner will heap sin upon sin.
28The affliction of the proud has no healing,
for a plant of wickedness has taken root
in them,
though it will not be perceived.
29The mind of the wise man will ponder the
words of the wise,
and an attentive ear is the wise
man's desire.
30Water extinguishes a blazing fire:
so almsgiving atones for sin.
31Whoever repays favors gives thought
to the future;
at the moment of his falling he will
find support.

EPHESIANS 5

**3But immorality and all impu-
rity or covetousness must not
even be named among you, as
is fitting among saints. 4Let there be
no filthiness, nor silly talk, nor levity,
which are not fitting; but instead let**
there be thanksgiving. 5Be sure of this, that
no immoral or impure man, or one who is
covetous (that is, an idolater), has any inheritance in the kingdom of Christ and of God.
6Let no one deceive you with empty words,
for it is because of these things that the
wrath of God comes upon the sons of disobedience. 7Therefore do not associate with
them, 8for once you were darkness, but now
you are light in the Lord; walk as children
of light 9(for the fruit of light is found in all
that is good and right and true), 10and try to
learn what is pleasing to the Lord. 11Take no
part in the unfruitful works of darkness, but
instead expose them. 12For it is a shame even

to speak of the things that they do in secret;
13but when anything is exposed by the light
it becomes visible, for anything that becomes visible is light. 14Therefore it is said,
"Awake, O sleeper, and arise from the dead,
and Christ shall give you light."
15Look carefully then how you walk, not
as unwise men but as wise, 16making the
most of the time, because the days are evil.
17Therefore do not be foolish, but understand what the will of the Lord is. 18And
do not get drunk with wine, for that is debauchery; but be filled with the Spirit, 19ad-
dressing one another in psalms and hymns
and spiritual songs, singing and making
melody to the Lord with all your heart, 20al-
ways and for everything giving thanks in
the name of our Lord Jesus Christ to God
the Father.

REFLECTION

In today's reading, Paul may seem too serious or too moralizing. He tells us to avoid all talk that is filthy, silly, and trivial (see Eph 5:4). St. Paul is not commanding us to avoid happiness, nor banning every form of joyful fellowship. We are, after all, not to avoid wine, but drunkenness (see v. 18). To reject silliness does not mean that we must be serious, but that we must be grateful (see v. 4). Gratefulness is the opposite of pride because it requires that we do not congratulate ourselves. Rather, those who are grateful seek for the one to whom they should be grateful, namely God—and so gratefulness is also the foundation of love. And, as Sirach tells us, the more we have, the more humble (and therefore more grateful) we must be (see Sir 3:17–20). Of course, the hard part is that when we find ourselves in a difficult situation, and when all our treasures have been carried off to Babylon (see Jer 52:17–23), even then we should give thanks. If we live a life of thanksgiving, we will see everything as grace, whether we have much or little, whether we can do much or little. What would your day look like if you lived it in an attitude of gratefulness? What small act of thanksgiving can you make today to begin living this way?

October 10

LAMENTATIONS 1

How lonely sits the city
that was full of people!
How like a widow has she become,
she that was great among the nations!
She that was a princess among the cities
has become a vassal.

2She weeps bitterly in the night,
tears on her cheeks;
among all her lovers
she has none to comfort her;
all her friends have dealt treacherously
with her,
they have become her enemies.

3Judah has gone into exile because
of affliction
and hard servitude;
she dwells now among the nations,
but finds no resting place;
her pursuers have all overtaken her
in the midst of her distress.

4The roads to Zion mourn,
for none come to the appointed feasts;
all her gates are desolate,
her priests groan;
her maidens have been dragged away,
and she herself suffers bitterly.

5Her foes have become the head,
her enemies prosper,
because the LORD has made her suffer
for the multitude of her transgressions;
her children have gone away,
captives before the foe.

6From the daughter of Zion has departed
all her majesty.
Her princes have become like deer
that find no pasture;
they fled without strength
before the pursuer.

7Jerusalem remembers
in the days of her affliction
and bitterness
all the precious things
that were hers from days of old.
When her people fell into the hand
of the foe,
and there was none to help her,
the foe gloated over her,
mocking at her downfall.

8Jerusalem sinned grievously,
therefore she became filthy;
all who honored her despise her,
for they have seen her nakedness;
yes, she herself groans,
and turns her face away.

9Her uncleanness was in her skirts;
she took no thought of her doom;
therefore her fall is terrible,
she has no comforter.
"O LORD, behold my affliction,
for the enemy has triumphed!"

10The enemy has stretched out his hands
over all her precious things;
yes, she has seen the nations
invade her sanctuary,
those whom you forbade
to enter your congregation.

11All her people groan
as they search for bread;
they trade their treasures for food
to revive their strength.
"Look, O LORD, and behold,
for I am despised."

12"Is it nothing to you, all you who pass by?
Look and see
if there is any sorrow like my sorrow
which was brought upon me,
which the LORD inflicted
on the day of his fierce anger.

13"From on high he sent fire;
into my bones he made it descend;
he spread a net for my feet;
he turned me back;
he has left me stunned,
faint all the day long.

14"My transgressions were bound into
a yoke;
by his hand they were fastened together;
they were set upon my neck;
he caused my strength to fail;
the Lord gave me into the hands
of those whom I cannot withstand.

15"The LORD flouted all my mighty men
in the midst of me;
he summoned an assembly against me
to crush my young men;
the Lord has trodden as in a wine press
the virgin daughter of Judah.

16"For these things I weep;
my eyes flow with tears;
for a comforter is far from me,
one to revive my courage;
my children are desolate,
for the enemy has prevailed."

17Zion stretches out her hands,
but there is none to comfort her;
the LORD has commanded against Jacob
that his neighbors should be his foes;
Jerusalem has become
a filthy thing among them.

18"The LORD is in the right,
for I have rebelled against his word;
but hear, all you peoples,
and behold my suffering;
my maidens and my young men
have gone into captivity.

19"I called to my lovers
but they deceived me;
my priests and elders
perished in the city,
while they sought food
to revive their strength.

20"Behold, O LORD, for I am in distress,
my soul is in tumult,
my heart is wrung within me,
because I have been very rebellious.

In the street the sword bereaves;
in the house it is like death.

21 "Hear how I groan;
there is none to comfort me.
All my enemies have heard of my trouble;
they are glad that you have done it.
Bring the day you have announced,
and let them be as I am.

22 "Let all their evil-doing come before you;
and deal with them
as you have dealt with me
because of all my transgressions;
for my groans are many
and my heart is faint."

2 How the Lord in his anger
has set the daughter of Zion
under a cloud!
He has cast down from heaven to earth
the splendor of Israel;
he has not remembered his footstool
in the day of his anger.

2 The Lord has destroyed without mercy
all the habitations of Jacob;
in his wrath he has broken down
the strongholds of the daughter of Judah;
he has brought down to the ground in
dishonor
the kingdom and its rulers.

3 He has cut down in fierce anger
all the might of Israel;
he has withdrawn from them his right
hand
in the face of the enemy;
he has burned like a flaming fire in Jacob,
consuming all around.

4 He has bent his bow like an enemy,
with his right hand set like a foe;
and he has slain all the pride of our eyes
in the tent of the daughter of Zion;
he has poured out his fury like fire.

5 The Lord has become like an enemy,
he has destroyed Israel;
he has destroyed all its palaces,
laid in ruins its strongholds;
and he has multiplied in the daughter
of Judah
mourning and lamentation.

6 He has broken down his booth like that of
a garden,
laid in ruins the place of his appointed
feasts;
the LORD has brought to an end in Zion
appointed feast and sabbath,
and in his fierce indignation has spurned
king and priest.

7 The Lord has scorned his altar,
disowned his sanctuary;
he has delivered into the hand of the enemy
the walls of her palaces;
a clamor was raised in the house of
the LORD
as on the day of an appointed feast.

8 The LORD determined to lay in ruins
the wall of the daughter of Zion;
he marked it off by the line;
he restrained not his hand from
destroying;
he caused rampart and wall to lament,
they languish together.

9 Her gates have sunk into the ground;
he has ruined and broken her bars;
her king and princes are among the nations;
the law is no more,
and her prophets obtain
no vision from the LORD.

10 The elders of the daughter of Zion
sit on the ground in silence;
they have cast dust on their heads
and put on sackcloth;
the maidens of Jerusalem
have bowed their heads to the ground.

11 My eyes are spent with weeping;
my soul is in tumult;
my heart is poured out in grief
because of the destruction of the daughter
of my people,
because infants and babies faint
in the streets of the city.

12 They cry to their mothers,
"Where is bread and wine?"
as they faint like wounded men
in the streets of the city,
as their life is poured out
on their mothers' bosom.

13 What can I say for you, to what compare you,
O daughter of Jerusalem?
What can I liken to you, that I may
comfort you,
O virgin daughter of Zion?
For vast as the sea is your ruin;
who can restore you?

14 Your prophets have seen for you
false and deceptive visions;
they have not exposed your iniquity
to restore your fortunes,
but have seen for you oracles
false and misleading.

15 All who pass along the way
clap their hands at you;
they hiss and wag their heads
at the daughter of Jerusalem;
"Is this the city which was called
the perfection of beauty,
the joy of all the earth?"

16 All your enemies
rail against you;
they hiss, they gnash their teeth,
they cry: "We have destroyed her!
Ah, this is the day we longed for;
now we have it; we see it!"

17 The LORD has done what he planned,
has carried out his threat;
as he ordained long ago,
he has demolished without pity;
he has made the enemy rejoice over you,
and exalted the might of your foes.

18 Cry aloud to the Lord!
O daughter of Zion!
Let tears stream down like a torrent
day and night!
Give yourself no rest,
your eyes no respite!

19 Arise, cry out in the night,
at the beginning of the watches!
Pour out your heart like water
before the presence of the Lord!
Lift your hands to him
for the lives of your children,
who faint for hunger
at the head of every street.

20 Look, O LORD, and see!
With whom have you dealt thus?
Should women eat their offspring,
the children of their tender care?
Should priest and prophet be slain
in the sanctuary of the Lord?

21 In the dust of the streets
lie the young and the old;
my maidens and my young men
have fallen by the sword;
in the day of your anger you have slain them,
slaughtering without mercy.

22 You invited as to the day of an
appointed feast
my terrors on every side;
and on the day of the anger of the LORD
none escaped or survived;
those whom I dandled and reared
my enemy destroyed.

SIRACH 4

My son, deprive not the poor of his living,
and do not keep needy eyes waiting.
2 Do not grieve the one who is hungry,
nor anger a man in want.
3 Do not add to the troubles of an angry mind,
nor delay your gift to a beggar.
4 Do not reject an afflicted suppliant,
nor turn your face away from the poor.
5 Do not avert your eye from the needy,
nor give a man occasion to curse you;
6 for if in bitterness of soul he calls down a
curse upon you,
his Creator will hear his prayer.
7 Make yourself beloved in the congregation;
bow your head low to a great man.

8 Incline your ear to the poor,
and answer him peaceably and gently.
9 Deliver him who is wronged from the hand
of the wrongdoer;
and do not be fainthearted in judging
a case.
10 Be like a father to orphans,
and instead of a husband to their mother;
you will then be like a son of the Most High,
and he will love you more than does
your mother.

11 Wisdom breathes life into her sons
and gives help to those who seek her.
12 Whoever loves her loves life,
and those who seek her early
will win the Lord's good favor.
13 Whoever holds her fast will obtain glory,
and the Lord will bless the place she enters.
14 Those who serve her will minister to the
Holy One;
the Lord loves those who love her.
15 He who obeys her will judge the nations,
and whoever gives heed to her will
dwell secure.
16 If he has faith in her he will obtain her;
and his descendants will remain in
possession of her.
17 For she will walk with him in disguise,
and at first she will put him to the test;
she will bring fear and cowardice upon him,
and will torment him by her discipline
until he holds her in his thoughts,
and she trusts him.
18 Then she will come straight back to him
and strengthen him,
she will gladden him and will reveal her
secrets to him,
and store up for him knowledge
and the discernment of what is right.
19 But if he goes astray she will forsake him,
and give him over into the hands of his foe.

EPHESIANS 5

**21 Be subject to one another out
of reverence for Christ. 22 Wives,
be subject to your husbands, as to the
Lord. 23 For the husband is the head of**
the wife as Christ is the head of the Church,
his body, and is himself its Savior. 24 As the
Church is subject to Christ, so let wives also
be subject in everything to their husbands.
25 Husbands, love your wives, as Christ loved
the Church and gave himself up for her,
26 that he might sanctify her, having cleansed
her by the washing of water with the word,
27 that he might present the Church to
himself in splendor, without spot or wrinkle
or any such thing, that she might be holy
and without blemish. 28 Even so husbands
should love their wives as their own bodies.
He who loves his wife loves himself. 29 For no
man ever hates his own flesh, but nourishes
and cherishes it, as Christ does the Church,
30 because we are members of his body. 31 "For
this reason a man shall leave his father and
mother and be joined to his wife, and the
two shall become one flesh." 32 This is a great
mystery, and I mean in reference to Christ
and the Church; 33 however, let each one of
you love his wife as himself, and let the wife
see that she respects her husband.

REFLECTION

As modern readers, when we hear the words "wives, be subject to your husbands" (Eph 5:22), we may become defensive or apologetic. We may even be tempted to think that St. Paul's words have no place in modern society. But Scripture is as relevant today as it was when it was written and will still be relevant long after we are gone. God's Word is eternal, and if the reader is open to receiving God's Word, it will bear much fruit. Paul is revealing a mystery and uses nuptial language to get to the heart of the matter. He begins by saying we should all "be subject to one another out of reverence for Christ" (v. 21). He then describes the mystery of the Church. The Church is the bride of Christ and we are called to be obedient to her, not out of some mistaken sense of duty, but out of love. Christ, the bridegroom, loves his spouse so much that he sanctified her and died for her so he could present her to the Father without spot or blemish. We should never doubt that God's Word contains many lessons on how to live in right relationship in this world so we can live with Christ in the next. Pray before reading Scripture and ask the Lord to open your heart to the truth of his Word. Do you sometimes resist God's call to obedience?

October 11

LAMENTATIONS 3

I am the man who has seen affliction
under the rod of his wrath;
2 he has driven and brought me
into darkness without any light;
3 surely against me he turns his hand
again and again the whole day long.

4 He has made my flesh and my skin
waste away,
and broken my bones;
5 he has besieged and enveloped me
with bitterness and tribulation;
6 he has made me dwell in darkness
like the dead of long ago.

7 He has walled me about so that I
cannot escape;
he has put heavy chains on me;
8 though I call and cry for help,
he shuts out my prayer;
9 he has blocked my ways with hewn stones,
he has made my paths crooked.

10 He is to me like a bear lying in wait,
like a lion in hiding;
11 he led me off my way and tore me
to pieces;
he has made me desolate;
12 he bent his bow and set me
as a mark for his arrow.

13 He drove into my heart
the arrows of his quiver;
14 I have become the laughingstock of
all peoples,
the burden of their songs all day long.
15 He has filled me with bitterness,
he has sated me with wormwood.

16 He has made my teeth grind on gravel,
and made me cower in ashes;
17 my soul is bereft of peace,
I have forgotten what happiness is;
18 so I say, "Gone is my glory,
and my expectation from the LORD."

19 Remember my affliction and my bitterness,
the wormwood and the gall!
20 My soul continually thinks of it
and is bowed down within me.
21 But this I call to mind,
and therefore I have hope:

22 The steadfast love of the LORD
never ceases,
his mercies never come to an end;
23 they are new every morning;
great is your faithfulness.
24 "The LORD is my portion," says my soul,
"therefore I will hope in him."

25 The LORD is good to those who wait
for him,
to the soul that seeks him.
26 It is good that one should wait quietly
for the salvation of the LORD.
27 It is good for a man that he bear
the yoke in his youth.

28 Let him sit alone in silence
when he has laid it on him;
29 let him put his mouth in the dust—
there may yet be hope;
30 let him give his cheek to the one who
strikes him,
and be filled with insults.

31 For the Lord will not
cast off for ever,
32 but, though he cause grief, he will
have compassion
according to the abundance of his
steadfast love;

33for he does not willingly afflict
or grieve the sons of men.

34To crush under foot
all the prisoners of the earth,
35to turn aside the right of a man
in the presence of the Most High,
36to subvert a man in his cause,
the Lord does not approve.

37Who has commanded and it came to pass,
unless the Lord has ordained it?
38Is it not from the mouth of the Most High
that good and evil come?
39Why should a living man complain,
a man, about the punishment of his sins?

40Let us test and examine our ways,
and return to the LORD!
41Let us lift up our hearts and hands
to God in heaven:
42"We have transgressed and rebelled,
and you have not forgiven.

43"You have wrapped yourself with anger
and pursued us,
slaying without pity;
44you have wrapped yourself with a cloud
so that no prayer can pass through.
45You have made us offscouring and refuse
among the peoples.

46"All our enemies
rail against us;
47panic and pitfall have come upon us,
devastation and destruction;
48my eyes flow with rivers of tears
because of the destruction of the daughter
of my people.

49"My eyes will flow without ceasing,
without respite,
50until the LORD from heaven
looks down and sees;
51my eyes cause me grief
at the fate of all the maidens of my city.

52"I have been hunted like a bird
by those who were my enemies
without cause;
53they flung me alive into the pit
and cast stones on me;
54water closed over my head;
I said, 'I am lost.'

55"I called on your name, O LORD,
from the depths of the pit;
56you heard my plea, 'Do not close
your ear to my cry for help!'
57You came near when I called on you;
you said, 'Do not fear!'

58"You have taken up my cause, O Lord,
you have redeemed my life.
59You have seen the wrong done to me,
O LORD;
do judge my cause.
60You have seen all their vengeance,
all their devices against me.

61"You have heard their taunts, O LORD,
all their devices against me.
62The lips and thoughts of my
assailants
are against me all the day long.
63Behold their sitting and their rising;
I am the burden of their songs.

64"You will repay them, O LORD,
according to the work of their hands.
65You will give them dullness of heart;
your curse will be on them.
66You will pursue them in anger and
destroy them
from under your heavens, O LORD."

4 How the gold has grown dim,
how the pure gold is changed!
The holy stones lie scattered
at the head of every street.

2The precious sons of Zion,
worth their weight in fine gold,
how they are reckoned as earthen pots,
the work of a potter's hands!

3Even the jackals give the breast
and suckle their young,
but the daughter of my people has
become cruel,
like the ostriches in the wilderness.

4The tongue of the infant clings
to the roof of its mouth for thirst;
the children beg for food,
but no one gives to them.

5Those who feasted on dainties
perish in the streets;
those who were brought up in purple
lie on ash heaps.

6For the chastisement of the daughter of my
people has been greater
than the punishment of Sodom,
which was overthrown in a moment,
no hand being laid on it.

7Her princes were purer than snow,
whiter than milk;
their bodies were more ruddy than coral,
the beauty of their form was
like sapphire.

8Now their visage is blacker than soot,
they are not recognized in the streets;
their skin has shriveled upon their bones,
it has become as dry as wood.

9Happier were the victims of the sword
than the victims of hunger,
who pined away, stricken
by want of the fruits of the field.

10The hands of compassionate women
have boiled their own children;
they became their food
in the destruction of the daughter
of my people.

11The LORD gave full vent to his wrath,
he poured out his hot anger;
and he kindled a fire in Zion,
which consumed its foundations.

12The kings of the earth did not believe,
or any of the inhabitants of the world,
that foe or enemy could enter
the gates of Jerusalem.

13This was for the sins of her prophets
and the iniquities of her priests,
who shed in the midst of her
the blood of the righteous.

14They wandered, blind, through
the streets,
so defiled with blood
that none could touch
their garments.

15"Away! Unclean!" men cried at them;
"Away! Away! Touch not!"

So they became fugitives and wanderers;
men said among the nations,
"They shall stay with us no longer."

16The LORD himself has scattered them,
he will regard them no more;
no honor was shown to the priests,
no favor to the elders.

17Our eyes failed, ever watching
vainly for help;
in our watching we watched
for a nation which could not save.

18Men dogged our steps
so that we could not walk in our streets;
our end drew near; our days were numbered;
for our end had come.

19Our pursuers were swifter
than the vultures in the heavens;
they chased us on the mountains,
they lay in wait for us in the wilderness.

20The breath of our nostrils, the LORD's anointed,
was taken in their pits,
he of whom we said, "Under his shadow
we shall live among the nations."

21Rejoice and be glad, O daughter of E′dom,
dweller in the land of Uz;
but to you also the cup shall pass;
you shall become drunk and strip
yourself bare.

22The punishment of your iniquity,
O daughter of Zion, is accomplished,
he will keep you in exile no longer;

but your iniquity, O daughter of E′dom, he
will punish,
he will uncover your sins.

5 Remember, O LORD, what has befallen us;
behold, and see our disgrace!
2Our inheritance has been turned over to
strangers,
our homes to aliens.
3We have become orphans, fatherless;
our mothers are like widows.

4We must pay for the water we drink,
the wood we get must be bought.
5With a yoke on our necks we are
hard driven;
we are weary, we are given no rest.
6We have given the hand to Egypt,
and to Assyria, to get bread enough.
7Our fathers sinned, and are no more;
and we bear their iniquities.
8Slaves rule over us;
there is none to deliver us from
their hand.
9We get our bread at the peril of our lives,
because of the sword in the wilderness.
10Our skin is hot as an oven
with the burning heat of famine.
11Women are ravished in Zion,
virgins in the towns of Judah.
12Princes are hung up by their hands;
no respect is shown to the elders.
13Young men are compelled to grind
at the mill;
and boys stagger under loads of wood.
14The old men have quit the city gate,
the young men their music.
15The joy of our hearts has ceased;
our dancing has been turned
to mourning.
16The crown has fallen from our head;
woe to us, for we have sinned!
17For this our heart has become sick,
for these things our eyes have grown dim,
18for Mount Zion which lies desolate;
jackals prowl over it.

19But you, O LORD, reign for ever;
your throne endures to all generations.
20Why do you forget us for ever,
why do you so long forsake us?
21Restore us to yourself, O LORD, that we
may be restored!
Renew our days as of old!
22Or have you utterly rejected us?
Are you exceedingly angry with us?

SIRACH 4

20Observe the right time, and beware
of evil;
and do not bring shame on yourself.
21For there is a shame which brings sin,
and there is a shame which is glory
and favor.
22Do not show partiality, to your own harm,
or deference, to your downfall.
23Do not refrain from speaking at the
crucial time,
and do not hide your wisdom.
24For wisdom is known through speech,
and education through the words
of the tongue.
25Never speak against the truth,
but be mindful of your ignorance.
26Do not be ashamed to confess your sins,
and do not try to stop the current
of a river.
27Do not subject yourself to a foolish fellow,
nor show partiality to a ruler.
28Strive even to death for the truth
and the Lord God will fight for you.

29Do not be reckless in your speech,
or sluggish and remiss in your deeds.
30Do not be like a lion in your home,
nor be a faultfinder with your servants.
31Let not your hand be extended to receive,
but withdrawn when it is time to repay.

EPHESIANS 6

Children, obey your parents in
the Lord, for this is right. 2"Honor
your father and mother" (this is the first
commandment with a promise), 3"that it
may be well with you and that you may live
long on the earth." 4Fathers, do not provoke

your children to anger, but bring them up in the discipline and instruction of the Lord.

[5]Slaves, be obedient to those who are your earthly masters, with fear and trembling, in singleness of heart, as to Christ; [6]not in the way of eye-service, as men-pleasers, but as servants of Christ, doing the will of God from the heart, [7]rendering service with a good will as to the Lord and not to men, [8]knowing that whatever good any one does, he will receive the same again from the Lord, whether he is a slave or free. [9]Masters, do the same to them, and forbear threatening, knowing that he who is both their Master and yours is in heaven, and that there is no partiality with him.

[10]Finally, be strong in the Lord and in the strength of his might. [11]Put on the whole armor of God, that you may be able to stand against the wiles of the devil. [12]For we are not contending against flesh and blood, but against the principalities, against the powers, against the world rulers of this present darkness, against the spiritual hosts of wickedness in the heavenly places. [13]Therefore take the whole armor of God, that you may be able to withstand in the evil day, and having done all, to stand. [14]Stand therefore, having fastened the belt of truth around your waist, and having put on the breastplate of righteousness, [15]and having shod your feet with the equipment of the gospel of peace; [16]besides all these, taking the shield of faith, with which you can quench all the flaming darts of the Evil One. [17]And take the helmet of salvation, and the sword of the Spirit, which is the word of God. [18]Pray at all times in the Spirit, with all prayer and supplication. To that end keep alert with all perseverance, making supplication for all the saints, [19]and also for me, that utterance may be given me in opening my mouth boldly to proclaim the mystery of the gospel, [20]for which I am an ambassador in chains; that I may declare it boldly, as I ought to speak.

[21]Now that you also may know how I am and what I am doing, Tych′icus the beloved brother and faithful minister in the Lord will tell you everything. [22]I have sent him to you for this very purpose, that you may know how we are, and that he may encourage your hearts.

[23]Peace be to the brethren, and love with faith, from God the Father and the Lord Jesus Christ. [24]Grace be with all who love our Lord Jesus Christ with love undying.

REFLECTION

Sacred Scripture gives us instructions on how to live rightly, yet we fail, over and over again. Sin damages us in such a way that we may even doubt that we are worthy of God's love and forgiveness. Satan wants us to despair, but there is always hope: "The steadfast love of the LORD never ceases, his mercies never come to an end" (Lam 3:22). We should never fall into despair! God asks us to turn to him: "Do not be ashamed to confess your sins" (Sir 4:26). The Lord understands the brokenness of our world and Satan's desire to turn us from him. That is why the Lord tells us who our true enemy is and equips us with the "armor of God" (Eph 6:11): the belt of truth, the breastplate of righteousness, the gospel of peace, the shield of faith, and the helmet of salvation. You may notice that these items are intended to help us defend ourselves against Satan, but God also gave us one weapon: the sword of the Holy Spirit, which is the Word of God. Prayer and the Word of God are two indispensable aids in our battle against this present darkness. We should never doubt God's love and mercy and always turn to him for strength. Do you trust in God and use the gifts that he gave you when faced with temptation?

October 12

BARUCH 1

These are the words of the book which Baruch the son of Nerai′ah, son of Mah′seiah, son of Zedeki′ah, son of Hasadi′ah, son of Hilki′ah, wrote in Babylon, [2]in the fifth year, on the seventh day of the month, at the time when the

Chalde′ans took Jerusalem and burned it
with fire. 3And Baruch read the words of
this book in the hearing of Jeconi′ah the
son of Jehoi′akim, king of Judah, and in the
hearing of all the people who came to hear
the book, 4and in the hearing of the mighty
men and the princes, and in the hearing
of the elders, and in the hearing of all the
people, small and great, all who dwelt in
Babylon by the river Sud.
5Then they wept, and fasted, and prayed
before the Lord; 6and they collected money,
each giving what he could; 7and they sent it
to Jerusalem to Jehoi′akim the high priest,
the son of Hilki′ah, son of Shallum, and
to the priests, and to all the people who
were present with him in Jerusalem. 8At
the same time, on the tenth day of Si′van,
Baruch took the vessels of the house of the
Lord, which had been carried away from
the temple, to return them to the land of
Judah—the silver vessels which Zedeki′ah
the son of Josi′ah, king of Judah, had made,
9after Nebuchadnez′zar king of Babylon
had carried away from Jerusalem Jeconi′ah
and the princes and the prisoners and the
mighty men and the people of the land, and
brought them to Babylon.
10And they said: "Herewith we send you
money; so buy with the money burnt offerings and sin offerings and incense, and
prepare a cereal offering, and offer them
upon the altar of the Lord our God; 11and
pray for the life of Nebuchadnez′zar king
of Babylon, and for the life of Belshaz′zar
his son, that their days on earth may be like
the days of heaven. 12And the Lord will give
us strength, and he will give light to our
eyes, and we shall live under the protection
of Nebuchadnez′zar king of Babylon, and
under the protection of Belshaz′zar his son,
and we shall serve them many days and find
favor in their sight. 13And pray for us to the
Lord our God, for we have sinned against
the Lord our God, and to this day the anger
of the Lord and his wrath have not turned
away from us. 14And you shall read this book
which we are sending you, to make your
confession in the house of the Lord on the
days of the feasts and at appointed seasons.

15"And you shall say: 'Righteousness belongs to the Lord our God, but confusion of
face, as at this day, to us, to the men of Judah,
to the inhabitants of Jerusalem, 16and to our
kings and our princes and our priests and our
prophets and our fathers, 17because we have
sinned before the Lord, 18and have disobeyed
him, and have not heeded the voice of the
Lord our God, to walk in the statutes of
the Lord which he set before us. 19From the
day when the Lord brought our fathers out
of the land of Egypt until today, we have
been disobedient to the Lord our God, and
we have been negligent, in not heeding his
voice. 20So to this day there have clung to us
the calamities and the curse which the Lord
declared through Moses his servant at the
time when he brought our fathers out of the
land of Egypt to give to us a land flowing with
milk and honey. 21We did not heed the voice
of the Lord our God in all the words of the
prophets whom he sent to us, but we each
followed the intent of his own wicked heart
by serving other gods and doing what is evil
in the sight of the Lord our God.
2 " 'So the Lord confirmed his word, which
he spoke against us, and against our
judges who judged Israel, and against our
kings and against our princes and against
the men of Israel and Judah. 2Under the
whole heaven there has not been done the
like of what he has done in Jerusalem, in
accordance with what is written in the law of
Moses, 3that we should eat, one the flesh of
his son and another the flesh of his daughter.
4And he gave them into subjection to all
the kingdoms around us, to be a reproach
and a desolation among all the surrounding
peoples, where the Lord has scattered them.
5They were brought low and not raised up,
because we sinned against the Lord our God,
in not heeding his voice.
6" 'Righteousness belongs to the Lord our
God, but confusion of face to us and our
fathers, as at this day. 7All those calamities
with which the Lord threatened us have
come upon us. 8Yet we have not entreated
the favor of the Lord by turning away, each
of us, from the thoughts of his wicked heart.
9And the Lord has kept the calamities ready,

and the Lord has brought them upon us, for
the Lord is righteous in all his works which
he has commanded us to do. 10Yet we have
not obeyed his voice, to walk in the statutes
of the Lord which he set before us.
11"'And now, O Lord God of Israel, who
brought your people out of the land of
Egypt with a mighty hand and with signs
and wonders and with great power and
outstretched arm, and have made you a
name, as at this day, 12we have sinned, we
have been ungodly, we have done wrong, O
Lord our God, against all your ordinances.
13Let your anger turn away from us, for we
are left, few in number, among the nations
where you have scattered us. 14Hear, O
Lord, our prayer and our supplication, and
for your own sake deliver us, and grant us
favor in the sight of those who have carried
us into exile; 15that all the earth may know
that you are the Lord our God, for Israel
and his descendants are called by your
name. 16O Lord, look down from your holy
habitation, and consider us. Incline your
ear, O Lord, and hear; 17open your eyes,
O Lord, and see; for the dead who are in
Hades, whose spirit has been taken from
their bodies, will not ascribe glory or justice
to the Lord, 18but the person that is greatly
distressed, that goes about bent over and
feeble, and the eyes that are failing, and the
person that hungers, will ascribe to you
glory and righteousness, O Lord. 19For it is
not because of any righteous deeds of our
fathers or our kings that we bring before
you our prayer for mercy, O Lord our God.
20For you have sent your anger and your
wrath upon us, as you declared by your
servants the prophets, saying: 21"Thus says
the Lord: Bend your shoulders and serve
the king of Babylon, and you will remain in
the land which I gave to your fathers. 22But
if you will not obey the voice of the Lord
and will not serve the king of Babylon, 23I
will make to cease from the cities of Judah
and from the region about Jerusalem the
voice of mirth and the voice of gladness,
the voice of the bridegroom and the voice
of the bride, and the whole land will be a
desolation without inhabitants."
24"'But we did not obey your voice, to
serve the king of Babylon; and you have
confirmed your words, which you spoke
by your servants the prophets, that the
bones of our kings and the bones of our
fathers would be brought out of their
graves; 25and behold, they have been cast
out to the heat of day and the frost of
night. They perished in great misery, by
famine and sword and pestilence. 26And
the house which is called by your name
you have made as it is today, because of
the wickedness of the house of Israel and
the house of Judah.'"

SIRACH 5

Do not set your heart on your wealth,
nor say, "I have enough."
2Do not follow your inclination and strength,
walking according to the desires of
your heart.
3Do not say, "Who will have power over me?"
or "Who will bring me down because of
my deeds?"
for God will surely punish you.

4Do not say, "I sinned, and what happened
to me?"
for the Most High is slow to anger.
5Do not be so confident of atonement
that you add sin to sin.
6Do not say, "His mercy is great,
he will forgive the multitude of my sins,"
for both mercy and wrath are with him,
and his anger rests on sinners.
7Do not delay to turn to the Lord,
nor postpone it from day to day;
for suddenly the wrath of the Lord
will go forth,
and at the time of punishment
you will perish.

8Do not depend on dishonest wealth,
for it will not benefit you in the
day of calamity.
9Do not winnow with every wind,
nor follow every path:
the double-tongued sinner does that.

[10]Be steadfast in your understanding,
and let your speech be consistent.
[11]Be quick to hear,
and be deliberate in answering.
[12]If you have understanding, answer
your neighbor;
but if not, put your hand on your mouth.
[13]Glory and dishonor come from speaking,
and a man's tongue is his downfall.

[14]Do not be called a slanderer,
and do not lie in ambush with your tongue;
for shame comes to the thief,
and severe condemnation to the
double-tongued.
[15]In great or small matters do not act amiss,
and do not become an enemy instead
of a friend.

PHILIPPIANS 1

Paul and Timothy, servants of Christ Jesus,

To all the saints in Christ Jesus who are at Philip´pi, with the bishops and deacons:

[2]Grace to you and peace from God our
Father and the Lord Jesus Christ.
[3]I thank my God in all my remembrance
of you, [4]always in every prayer of mine for
you all making my prayer with joy, [5]thankful
for your partnership in the gospel from the
first day until now. [6]And I am sure that he
who began a good work in you will bring
it to completion at the day of Jesus Christ.
[7]It is right for me to feel this way about you
all, because I hold you in my heart, for you
are all partakers with me of grace, both in
my imprisonment and in the defense and
confirmation of the gospel. [8]For God is
my witness, how I yearn for you all with
the affection of Christ Jesus. [9]And it is my
prayer that your love may abound more and
more, with knowledge and all discernment,
[10]so that you may approve what is excellent,
and may be pure and blameless for the
day of Christ, [11]filled with the fruits of
righteousness which come through Jesus
Christ, to the glory and praise of God.
[12]I want you to know, brethren, that
what has happened to me has really
served to advance the gospel, [13]so that it
has become known throughout the whole
praetorian guard and to all the rest that
my imprisonment is for Christ; [14]and
most of the brethren have been made
confident in the Lord because of my imprisonment, and are much more bold to
speak the word of God without fear.
[15]Some indeed preach Christ from envy
and rivalry, but others from good will. [16]The
latter do it out of love, knowing that I am
put here for the defense of the gospel; [17]the
former proclaim Christ out of partisanship,
not sincerely but thinking to afflict me in my
imprisonment. [18]What then? Only that in
every way, whether in pretense or in truth,
Christ is proclaimed; and in that I rejoice.

REFLECTION

God's love and mercy know no bounds, but we must be careful about being so confident in this that we think we can commit any sin and God will forgive us. Sirach tells us, "Do not be so confident of atonement that you add sin to sin" (Sir 5:5). Baruch describes how Israel falls into just this problem. They mistakenly believe that God's mercy means there will be no consequences for their sins. Israel's repeated sins of idolatry, among others, lead to God withdrawing his presence from the Temple and its eventual destruction. The people realize their mistake and beg God for forgiveness. They recognize that God is faithful to his warnings, and, in the midst of the single worst event in Israel's history, they praise him for his faithfulness. We see a similar attitude with St. Paul in his epistle to the Philippians. The theme of this letter is joy, yet Paul is in prison for preaching the Gospel. Despite his dire circumstances, Paul is joyful, saying, "My imprisonment is for Christ" (Phil 1:13). Living a Christ-centered life does not mean we are safe from suffering. Our hope should always be that one day we "may be pure and blameless for the day of Christ" (Phil 1:10). Are you joyful, even when faced with suffering or hardship?

October 13

BARUCH 2

27“ ‘Yet you have dealt with us,
O Lord our God, in all your
kindness and in all your great
compassion, 28as you spoke by your servant
Moses on the day when you commanded
him to write your law in the presence of the
people of Israel, saying, 29“If you will not
obey my voice, this very great multitude
will surely turn into a small number
among the nations, where I will scatter
them. 30For I know that they will not obey
me, for they are a stiff-necked people. But
in the land of their exile they will come
to themselves, 31and they will know that
I am the Lord their God. I will give them
a heart that obeys and ears that hear;
32and they will praise me in the land of
their exile, and will remember my name,
33and will turn from their stubbornness
and their wicked deeds; for they will
remember the ways of their fathers, who
sinned before the Lord. 34I will bring
them again into the land which I swore
to give to their fathers, to Abraham and
to Isaac and to Jacob, and they will rule
over it; and I will increase them, and they
will not be diminished. 35I will make an
everlasting covenant with them to be
their God and they shall be my people;
and I will never again remove my people
Israel from the land which I have given
them.”

3 “ ‘O Lord Almighty, God of Israel, the
soul in anguish and the wearied spirit
cry out to you. 2Hear, O Lord, and have
mercy, for we have sinned before you.
3For you are enthroned for ever, and we
are perishing for ever. 4O Lord Almighty,
God of Israel, hear now the prayer of the
dead of Israel and of the sons of those
who sinned before you, who did not heed
the voice of the Lord their God, so that
calamities have clung to us. 5Remember
not the iniquities of our fathers, but in
this crisis remember your power and
your name. 6For you are the Lord our
God, and you, O Lord, will we praise. 7For
you have put the fear of you in our hearts
in order that we should call upon your
name; and we will praise you in our exile,
for we have put away from our hearts all
the iniquity of our fathers who sinned
before you. 8Behold, we are today in our
exile where you have scattered us, to be
reproached and cursed and punished
for all the iniquities of our fathers who
forsook the Lord our God.’ ”

9Hear the commandments of life, O Israel;
give ear, and learn wisdom!
10Why is it, O Israel, why is it that you are in
the land of your enemies,
that you are growing old in a foreign
country,
that you are defiled with the dead,
11 that you are counted among those
in Hades?
12You have forsaken the fountain of wisdom.
13If you had walked in the way of God,
you would be dwelling in peace for ever.
14Learn where there is wisdom,
where there is strength,
where there is understanding,
that you may at the same time discern
where there is length of days, and life,
where there is light for the eyes, and peace.

15Who has found her place?
And who has entered her storehouses?
16Where are the princes of the nations,
and those who rule over the beasts
on the earth;
17those who have sport with the birds
of the air,
and who hoard up silver and gold,
in which men trust,
and there is no end to their getting;
18those who scheme to get silver, and are
anxious,
whose labors are beyond measure?
19They have vanished and gone down
to Hades,
and others have arisen in their place.

[20]Young men have seen the light of day,
and have dwelt upon the earth;
but they have not learned the way
to knowledge,
nor understood her paths,
nor laid hold of her.
[21]Their sons have strayed far from
her way.
[22]She has not been heard of in Canaan,
nor seen in Te′man;
[23]the sons of Hagar, who seek for
understanding on the earth,
the merchants of Merran and Te′man,
the story-tellers and the seekers
for understanding,
have not learned the way to wisdom,
nor given thought to her paths.

[24]O Israel, how great is the house of God!
And how vast the territory that
he possesses!
[25]It is great and has no bounds;
it is high and immeasurable.
[26]The giants were born there, who were
famous of old,
great in stature, expert in war.
[27]God did not choose them,
nor give them the way to knowledge;
[28]so they perished because they had
no wisdom,
they perished through their folly.
[29]Who has gone up into heaven, and
taken her,
and brought her down from the clouds?
[30]Who has gone over the sea, and found her,
and will buy her for pure gold?
[31]No one knows the way to her,
or is concerned about the path to her.
[32]But he who knows all things knows her,
he found her by his understanding.
He who prepared the earth for all time
filled it with four-footed creatures;
[33]he who sends forth the light, and it goes,
called it, and it obeyed him in fear;
[34]the stars shone in their watches, and
were glad;
he called them, and they said, "Here
we are!"
They shone with gladness for him who
made them.
[35]This is our God;
no other can be compared to him!
[36]He found the whole way to knowledge,
and gave her to Jacob his servant
and to Israel whom he loved.
[37]Afterward she appeared upon earth and
lived among men.

4 She is the book of the commandments
of God,
and the law that endures for ever.
All who hold her fast will live,
and those who forsake her will die.
[2]Turn, O Jacob, and take her;
walk toward the shining of her light.
[3]Do not give your glory to another,
or your advantages to an alien people.
[4]Happy are we, O Israel,
for we know what is pleasing to God.

[5]Take courage, my people,
O memorial of Israel!
[6]It was not for destruction
that you were sold to the nations,
but you were handed over to
your enemies
because you angered God.
[7]For you provoked him who made you,
by sacrificing to demons and not to God.
[8]You forgot the everlasting God, who
brought you up,
and you grieved Jerusalem, who
reared you.
[9]For she saw the wrath that came upon you
from God,
and she said:
"Listen, you neighbors of Zion,
God has brought great sorrow upon me;
[10]for I have seen the captivity of my sons and
daughters,
which the Everlasting brought
upon them.
[11]With joy I nurtured them,
but I sent them away with weeping
and sorrow.
[12]Let no one rejoice over me, a widow
and bereaved of many;
I was left desolate because of the sins
of my children,
because they turned away from the
law of God.

[13]They had no regard for his statutes;
they did not walk in the ways of
God's commandments,
nor tread the paths of discipline in
his righteousness.
[14]Let the neighbors of Zion come;
remember the capture of my sons
and daughters,
which the Everlasting brought upon them.
[15]For he brought against them a nation
from afar,
a shameless nation, of a strange language,
who had no respect for an old man,
and had no pity for a child.
[16]They led away the widow's beloved sons,
and bereaved the lonely woman of
her daughters.

SIRACH 6

For a bad name incurs shame and reproach:
so fares the double-tongued sinner.

[2]Do not exalt yourself through your
soul's counsel,
lest your soul be torn in pieces like a bull.
[3]You will devour your leaves and destroy
your fruit,
and will be left like a withered tree.
[4]An evil soul will destroy him who has it,
and make him the laughingstock of
his enemies.

[5]A pleasant voice multiplies friends and
softens enemies,
and a gracious tongue multiplies
courtesies.
[6]Let those that are at peace with you be many,
but let your advisers be one in a thousand.
[7]When you gain a friend, gain him through
testing,
and do not trust him hastily.
[8]For there is a friend who is such at his
own convenience,
but will not stand by you in your day
of trouble.
[9]And there is a friend who changes into
an enemy,
and will disclose a quarrel to your disgrace.
[10]And there is a friend who is a
table companion,
but will not stand by you in your
day of trouble.
[11]In prosperity he will make himself
your equal,
and be bold with your servants;
[12]but if you are brought low he will turn
against you,
and will hide himself from your presence.
[13]Keep yourself far from your enemies,
and be on guard toward your friends.

[14]A faithful friend is a sturdy shelter:
he that has found one has found
a treasure.
[15]There is nothing so precious as a
faithful friend,
and no scales can measure his excellence.
[16]A faithful friend is an elixir of life;
and those who fear the Lord will find him.
[17]Whoever fears the Lord directs his
friendship aright,
for as he is, so is his neighbor also.

PHILIPPIANS 1

[19]Yes, and I shall rejoice. For I know that through your prayers and the help of the Spirit of Jesus Christ this will turn out for my deliverance,
[20]as it is my eager expectation and hope
that I shall not be at all ashamed, but that
with full courage now as always Christ will
be honored in my body, whether by life
or by death. [21]For to me to live is Christ,
and to die is gain. [22]If it is to be life in the
flesh, that means fruitful labor for me. Yet
which I shall choose I cannot tell. [23]I am
hard pressed between the two. My desire is
to depart and be with Christ, for that is far
better. [24]But to remain in the flesh is more
necessary on your account. [25]Convinced of
this, I know that I shall remain and continue
with you all, for your progress and joy in the
faith, [26]so that in me you may have ample
cause to glory in Christ Jesus, because of my
coming to you again.

[27]Only let your manner of life be worthy of the gospel of Christ, so that whether I come and see you or am absent, I may hear of you that you stand firm in one spirit, with one mind striving side by side for the faith of the gospel, [28]and not frightened in anything by your opponents. This is a clear omen to them of their destruction, but of your salvation, and that from God. [29]For it has been granted to you that for the sake of Christ you should not only believe in him but also suffer for his sake, [30]engaged in the same conflict which you saw and now hear to be mine.

2 So if there is any encouragement in Christ, any incentive of love, any participation in the Spirit, any affection and sympathy, [2]complete my joy by being of the same mind, having the same love, being in full accord and of one mind. [3]Do nothing from selfishness or conceit, but in humility count others better than yourselves. [4]Let each of you look not only to his own interests, but also to the interests of others. [5]Have this mind among yourselves, which was in Christ Jesus, [6]who, though he was in the form of God, did not count equality with God a thing to be grasped, [7]but emptied himself, taking the form of a servant, being born in the likeness of men. [8]And being found in human form he humbled himself and became obedient unto death, even death on a cross. [9]Therefore God has highly exalted him and bestowed on him the name which is above every name, [10]that at the name of Jesus every knee should bow, in heaven and on earth and under the earth, [11]and every tongue confess that Jesus Christ is Lord, to the glory of God the Father.

[12]Therefore, my beloved, as you have always obeyed, so now, not only as in my presence but much more in my absence, work out your own salvation with fear and trembling; [13]for God is at work in you, both to will and to work for his good pleasure.

[14]Do all things without grumbling or questioning, [15]that you may be blameless and innocent, children of God without blemish in the midst of a crooked and perverse generation, among whom you shine as lights in the world, [16]holding fast the word of life, so that in the day of Christ I may be proud that I did not run in vain or labor in vain. [17]Even if I am to be poured as a libation upon the sacrificial offering of your faith, I am glad and rejoice with you all. [18]Likewise you also should be glad and rejoice with me.

REFLECTION

Sacred Scripture gives us the best advice on how to live a fruitful and holy life. Wisdom, however, is not just good advice or a nice concept; it is the very word of God that is offered to us. Baruch tells us, "She [wisdom] is the book of the commandments of God . . . all who hold her fast will live" (Bar 4:1). Sirach implores the reader to search for wisdom and, when she is found, to never let her go, for she brings rest and joy (see Sir 6:27–28). Despite Paul's hardships, he accepts the gift of wisdom and embraces his sufferings with joy, for his people and for Christ. He stresses the necessity of humility and being at the service of others. St. Paul uses Jesus's *kenosis*, or self-emptying, as an example of not only dying for others but living for them as well. Unfortunately, due to Original Sin, we all suffer. But uniting our sufferings to Christ and living a life of joy is a choice. Our actions follow our attitude. Living a life of humility in Christ and doing so with joy is a powerful witness to the Gospel. How can you spend more time in the wisdom of the Word of God?

October 14

BARUCH 4

[17]"But I, how can I help you?
[18]For he who brought these
calamities upon you
will deliver you from the hand of
your enemies.
[19]Go, my children, go;
for I have been left desolate.

[20]I have taken off the robe of peace
and put on the sackcloth of my
supplication;
I will cry to the Everlasting all my days.

[21]"Take courage, my children, cry to God,
and he will deliver you from the power
and hand of the enemy.
[22]For I have put my hope in the Everlasting
to save you,
and joy has come to me from the Holy One,
because of the mercy which soon will come
to you
from your everlasting Savior.
[23]For I sent you out with sorrow and weeping,
but God will give you back to me with joy
and gladness for ever.
[24]For as the neighbors of Zion have now
seen your capture,
so they soon will see your salvation by God,
which will come to you with great glory
and with the splendor of the Everlasting.
[25]My children, endure with patience the
wrath that has come upon you
from God.
Your enemy has overtaken you,
but you will soon see their destruction
and will tread upon their necks.
[26]My tender sons have traveled rough roads;
they were taken away like a flock carried
off by the enemy.

[27]"Take courage, my children, and cry to God,
for you will be remembered by him who
brought this upon you.
[28]For just as you planned to go astray
from God,
return with tenfold zeal to seek him.
[29]For he who brought these calamities upon you
will bring you everlasting joy with
your salvation."

[30]Take courage, O Jerusalem,
for he who named you will comfort you.
[31]Wretched will be those who afflicted you
and rejoiced at your fall.
[32]Wretched will be the cities which your
children served as slaves;
wretched will be the city which received
your sons.
[33]For just as she rejoiced at your fall
and was glad for your ruin,
so she will be grieved at her own desolation.
[34]And I will take away her pride in her
great population,
and her insolence will be turned to grief.
[35]For fire will come upon her from the
Everlasting for many days,
and for a long time she will be inhabited
by demons.

[36]Look toward the east, O Jerusalem,
and see the joy that is coming to you
from God!
[37]Behold, your sons are coming, whom you
sent away;
they are coming, gathered from east
and west,
at the word of the Holy One,
rejoicing in the glory of God.

5 Take off the garment of your sorrow and
affliction, O Jerusalem,
and put on for ever the beauty of the
glory from God.
[2]Put on the robe of the righteousness from God;
put on your head the diadem of the glory
of the Everlasting.
[3]For God will show your splendor
everywhere under heaven.
[4]For your name will for ever be called by God,
"Peace of righteousness and glory of
godliness."

[5]Arise, O Jerusalem, stand upon the height
and look toward the east,
and see your children gathered from west
and east,
at the word of the Holy One,
rejoicing that God has remembered them.
[6]For they went forth from you on foot,
led away by their enemies;
but God will bring them back to you,
carried in glory, as on a royal throne.
[7]For God has ordered that every high
mountain and the everlasting hills be
made low
and the valleys filled up, to make level
ground,
so that Israel may walk safely in the glory
of God.

8The woods and every fragrant tree
have shaded Israel at God's command.
9For God will lead Israel with joy,
in the light of his glory,
with the mercy and righteousness that
come from him.

6 A copy of a letter which Jeremi′ah sent
to those who were to be taken to Babylon
as captives by the king of the Babylonians,
to give them the message which God had
commanded him.

2Because of the sins which you have
committed before God, you will be taken
to Babylon as captives by Nebuchadnez′zar,
king of the Babylonians. 3Therefore when you
have come to Babylon you will remain there
for many years, for a long time, up to seven
generations; after that I will bring you away
from there in peace. 4Now in Babylon you will
see gods made of silver and gold and wood,
which are carried on men's shoulders and
inspire fear in the heathen. 5So take care not to
become at all like the foreigners or to let fear
for these gods possess you, when you see the
multitude before and behind them worshiping
them. 6But say in your heart, "It is you, O Lord,
whom we must worship." 7For my angel is with
you, and he is watching your lives.

8Their tongues are smoothed by the craftsman, and they themselves are overlaid with
gold and silver; but they are false and cannot
speak. 9People take gold and make crowns
for the heads of their gods, as they would for
a girl who loves ornaments; 10and sometimes
the priests secretly take gold and silver from
their gods and spend it upon themselves,
11and even give some of it to the harlots in
the brothel. They deck their gods out with
garments like men—these gods of silver
and gold and wood, 12which cannot save
themselves from rust and corrosion. When
they have been dressed in purple robes,
13their faces are wiped because of the dust
from the temple, which is thick upon them.
14Like a local ruler the god holds a scepter,
though unable to destroy any one who
offends it. 15It has a dagger in its right hand,
and has an axe; but it cannot save itself from
war and robbers. 16Therefore they evidently
are not gods; so do not fear them.

17For just as one's dish is useless when it
is broken, so are the gods of the heathen,
when they have been set up in the temples.
Their eyes are full of the dust raised by the
feet of those who enter. 18And just as the
gates are shut on every side upon a man
who has offended a king, as though he were
sentenced to death, so the priests make
their temples secure with doors and locks
and bars, in order that they may not be
plundered by robbers. 19They light lamps,
even more than they light for themselves,
though their gods can see none of them.
20They are just like a beam of the temple,
but men say their hearts have melted, when
worms from the earth devour them and
their robes. They do not notice 21when their
faces have been blackened by the smoke of
the temple. 22Bats, swallows, and birds light
on their bodies and heads; and so do cats.
23From this you will know that they are not
gods; so do not fear them.

SIRACH 6

18My son, from your youth up choose
instruction,
and until you are old you will keep
finding wisdom.
19Come to her like one who plows and sows,
and wait for her good harvest.
For in her service you will toil a little while,
and soon you will eat of her produce.
20She seems very harsh to the uninstructed;
a weakling will not remain with her.
21She will weigh him down like a heavy
testing stone,
and he will not be slow to cast her off.
22For wisdom is like her name,
and is not manifest to many.

23Listen, my son, and accept my judgment;
do not reject my counsel.
24Put your feet into her chains,
and your neck into her collar.
25Put your shoulder under her and carry her,
and do not fret under her bonds.
26Come to her with all your soul,
and keep her ways with all your might.

[27]Search out and seek, and she will become
known to you;
and when you get hold of her, do not let
her go.
[28]For at last you will find the rest she gives,
and she will be changed into joy for you.
[29]Then her chains will become for you a
strong protection,
and her collar a glorious robe.
[30]Her yoke is a golden ornament,
and her bonds are a cord of blue.
[31]You will wear her like a glorious robe,
and put her on like a crown of gladness.

[32]If you are willing, my son, you will
be taught,
and if you apply yourself you will
become clever.
[33]If you love to listen you will gain knowledge,
and if you incline your ear you will
become wise.
[34]Stand in the assembly of the elders.
Who is wise? Cling to him.
[35]Be ready to listen to every narrative,
and do not let wise proverbs escape you.
[36]If you see an intelligent man, visit
him early;
let your foot wear out his doorstep.
[37]Reflect on the statutes of the Lord,
and meditate at all times on his
commandments.
It is he who will give insight to your mind,
and your desire for wisdom will be
granted.

7 Do no evil, and evil will never befall you.
[2]Stay away from wrong, and it will turn
away from you.
[3]My son, do not sow the furrows of injustice,
and you will not reap a sevenfold crop.

[4]Do not seek from the Lord the
highest office,
nor the seat of honor from the king.
[5]Do not assert your righteousness before
the Lord,
nor display your wisdom before the king.
[6]Do not seek to become a judge,
lest you be unable to remove iniquity,
lest you be partial to a powerful man,
and thus put a blot on your integrity.
[7]Do not offend against the public,
and do not disgrace yourself among
the people.

PHILIPPIANS 2

[19]I hope in the Lord Jesus to
send Timothy to you soon, so
that I may be cheered by news of you.
[20]I have no one like him, who will be
genuinely anxious for your welfare. [21]They
all look after their own interests, not those
of Jesus Christ. [22]But Timothy's worth
you know, how as a son with a father he
has served with me in the gospel. [23]I hope
therefore to send him just as soon as I see
how it will go with me; [24]and I trust in the
Lord that shortly I myself shall come also.
[25]I have thought it necessary to send to you
Epaphrodi'tus my brother and fellow worker
and fellow soldier, and your messenger
and minister to my need, [26]for he has been
longing for you all, and has been distressed
because you heard that he was ill. [27]Indeed he
was ill, near to death. But God had mercy on
him, and not only on him but on me also, lest
I should have sorrow upon sorrow. [28]I am the
more eager to send him, therefore, that you
may rejoice at seeing him again, and that I
may be less anxious. [29]So receive him in the
Lord with all joy; and honor such men, [30]for
he nearly died for the work of Christ, risking
his life to complete your service to me.

3 Finally, my brethren, rejoice in the Lord.
To write the same things to you is not
irksome to me, and is safe for you.
[2]Look out for the dogs, look out for the evil-
workers, look out for those who mutilate the
flesh. [3]For we are the true circumcision, who
worship God in spirit, and glory in Christ
Jesus, and put no confidence in the flesh.
[4]Though I myself have reason for confidence
in the flesh also. If any other man thinks he has
reason for confidence in the flesh, I have more:
[5]circumcised on the eighth day, of the people of
Israel, of the tribe of Benjamin, a Hebrew born
of Hebrews; as to the law a Pharisee, [6]as to zeal
a persecutor of the Church, as to righteousness

under the law blameless. [7]But whatever gain
I had, I counted as loss for the sake of Christ.
[8]Indeed I count everything as loss because of
the surpassing worth of knowing Christ Jesus
my Lord. For his sake I have suffered the loss
of all things, and count them as refuse, in
order that I may gain Christ [9]and be found in
him, not having a righteousness of my own,
based on law, but that which is through faith
in Christ, the righteousness from God that
depends on faith; [10]that I may know him and
the power of his resurrection, and may share
his sufferings, becoming like him in his death,
[11]that if possible I may attain the resurrection
from the dead.
[12]Not that I have already obtained this or am
already perfect; but I press on to make it my
own, because Christ Jesus has made me his
own. [13]Brethren, I do not consider that I have
made it my own; but one thing I do, forgetting
what lies behind and straining forward to what
lies ahead, [14]I press on toward the goal for
the prize of the upward call of God in Christ
Jesus. [15]Let those of us who are mature be thus
minded; and if in anything you are otherwise
minded, God will reveal that also to you. [16]Only
let us hold true to what we have attained.
[17]Brethren, join in imitating me, and mark
those who so walk as you have an example
in us. [18]For many, of whom I have often told
you and now tell you even with tears, walk
as enemies of the cross of Christ. [19]Their
end is destruction, their god is the belly, and
they glory in their shame, with minds set
on earthly things. [20]But our commonwealth
is in heaven, and from it we await a Savior,
the Lord Jesus Christ, [21]who will change
our lowly body to be like his glorious body,
by the power which enables him even to
subject all things to himself.

REFLECTION

Suffering has been part of the human condition since the Fall, and, unfortunately, there is no way around it. Although it doesn't seem fair, it is in suffering that we often gain wisdom, patience, endurance, and perseverance. But God does not will us to suffer. Rather, he walks with us in the midst of it and gives us hope, just as he gave hope to Israel after the destruction of Jerusalem and the Temple: "Take courage, my children, cry to God, and he will deliver you from the power and hand of the enemy" (Bar 4:21). God promised to redeem all of creation and has done so through his Son, Jesus Christ. Though Jesus was completely sinless, he suffered and died for the sins of the world. St. Paul conveys the hope he has in Christ as he speaks of his own suffering and the suffering of his friend, explaining that suffering only makes sense in the light of Christ. It is by sharing in the sufferings of Christ that we have the hope of sharing in his Resurrection (see Phil 3:9). Although it is admittedly difficult to rejoice in your sufferings like St. Paul, do you ask God for hope in the midst of suffering?

October 15

BARUCH 6

**[24]As for the gold which they
wear for beauty—they will not
shine unless some one wipes off the rust;
for even when they were being cast, they**
had no feeling. [25]They are bought at any cost,
but there is no breath in them. [26]Having no
feet, they are carried on men's shoulders,
revealing to mankind their worthlessness.
[27]And those who serve them are ashamed
because through them these gods are made
to stand, lest they fall to the ground. If any
one sets one of them upright, it cannot move
of itself; and if it is tipped over, it cannot
straighten itself; but gifts are placed before
them just as before the dead. [28]The priests sell
the sacrifices that are offered to these gods
and use the money; and likewise their wives
preserve some with salt, but give none to the
poor or helpless. [29]Sacrifices to them may be
touched by women in menstruation or at
childbirth. Since you know by these things
that they are not gods, do not fear them.

30For why should they be called gods? Women serve meals for gods of silver and gold and wood; 31and in their temples the priests sit with their clothes torn, their heads and beards shaved, and their heads uncovered. 32They howl and shout before their gods as some do at a funeral feast for a man who has died. 33The priests take some of the clothing of their gods to clothe their wives and children. 34Whether one does evil to them or good, they will not be able to repay it. They cannot set up a king or depose one. 35Likewise they are not able to give either wealth or money; if one makes a vow to them and does not keep it, they will not require it. 36They cannot save a man from death or rescue the weak from the strong. 37They cannot restore sight to a blind man; they cannot rescue a man who is in distress. 38They cannot take pity on a widow or do good to an orphan. 39These things that are made of wood and overlaid with gold and silver are like stones from the mountain, and those who serve them will be put to shame. 40Why then must any one think that they are gods, or call them gods?

Besides, even the Chalde´ans themselves dishonor them; 41for when they see a mute man, who cannot speak, they bring him and pray Bel that the man may speak, as though Bel were able to understand. 42Yet they themselves cannot perceive this and abandon them, for they have no sense. 43And the women, with cords about them, sit along the passageways, burning bran for incense; and when one of them is led off by one of the passersby and is lain with, she derides the woman next to her, because she was not as attractive as herself and her cord was not broken. 44Whatever is done for them is false. Why then must any one think that they are gods, or call them gods?

45They are made by carpenters and goldsmiths; they can be nothing but what the craftsmen wish them to be. 46The men that make them will certainly not live very long themselves; how then can the things that are made by them be gods? 47They have left only lies and reproach for those who come after. 48For when war or calamity comes upon them, the priests consult together as to where they can hide themselves and their gods. 49How then can one fail to see that these are not gods, for they cannot save themselves from war or calamity? 50Since they are made of wood and overlaid with gold and silver, it will afterward be known that they are false. 51It will be manifest to all the nations and kings that they are not gods but the work of men's hands, and that there is no work of God in them. 52Who then can fail to know that they are not gods?

53For they cannot set up a king over a country or give rain to men. 54They cannot judge their own cause or deliver one who is wronged, for they have no power; they are like crows between heaven and earth. 55When fire breaks out in a temple of wooden gods overlaid with gold or silver, their priests will flee and escape, but the gods will be burned in two like beams. 56Besides, they can offer no resistance to a king or any enemies. Why then must any one admit or think that they are gods?

57Gods made of wood and overlaid with silver and gold are not able to save themselves from thieves and robbers. 58Strong men will strip them of their gold and silver and of the robes they wear, and go off with this booty, and they will not be able to help themselves. 59So it is better to be a king who shows his courage, or a household utensil that serves its owner's need, than to be these false gods; better even the door of a house that protects its contents, than these false gods; better also a wooden pillar in a palace, than these false gods.

60For sun and moon and stars, shining and sent forth for service, are obedient. 61So also the lightning, when it flashes, is widely seen; and the wind likewise blows in every land. 62When God commands the clouds to go over the whole world, they carry out his command. 63And the fire sent from above to consume mountains and woods does what it is ordered. But these idols are not to be compared with them in appearance or power. 64Therefore one must not think that they are gods nor call them gods, for they are not able either to decide a case or to do

good to men. 65Since you know then that they
are not gods, do not fear them.
66For they can neither curse nor bless kings;
67they cannot show signs in the heavens and
among the nations, or shine like the sun or
give light like the moon. 68The wild beasts
are better than they are, for they can flee
to cover and help themselves. 69So we have
no evidence whatever that they are gods;
therefore do not fear them.
70Like a scarecrow in a cucumber bed, that
guards nothing, so are their gods of wood,
overlaid with gold and silver. 71In the same
way, their gods of wood, overlaid with gold
and silver, are like a thorn bush in a garden, on
which every bird sits; or like a dead body cast
out in the darkness. 72By the purple and linen
that rot upon them you will know that they
are not gods; and they will finally themselves
be consumed, and be a reproach in the land.
73Better therefore is a just man who has no
idols, for he will be far from reproach.

SIRACH 7

8Do not commit a sin twice;
even for one you will not go unpunished.
9Do not say, "He will consider the multitude
of my gifts,
and when I make an offering to the Most
High God he will accept it."
10Do not be fainthearted in your prayer,
nor neglect to give alms.

11Do not ridicule a man who is bitter in soul,
for there is One who abases and exalts.
12Do not devise a lie against your brother,
nor do the like to a friend.
13Refuse to utter any lie,
for the habit of lying serves no good.
14Do not prattle in the assembly of the elders,
nor repeat yourself in your prayer.

15Do not hate toilsome labor,
or farm work, which were created by the
Most High.
16Do not count yourself among the crowd
of sinners;
remember that wrath does not delay.
17Humble yourself greatly,
for the punishment of the ungodly is fire
and worms.

18Do not exchange a friend for money,
or a real brother for the gold of Ophir.
19Do not deprive yourself of a wise and
good wife,
for her charm is worth more than gold.
20Do not abuse a servant who performs his
work faithfully,
or a hired laborer who devotes himself to you.
21Let your soul love an intelligent servant;
do not withhold from him his freedom.

22Do you have cattle? Look after them;
if they are profitable to you, keep them.
23Do you have children? Discipline them,
and make them obedient from their youth.
24Do you have daughters? Be concerned for
their chastity,
and do not show yourself too indulgent
with them.
25Give a daughter in marriage; you will have
finished a great task.
But give her to a man of understanding.
26If you have a wife who pleases you, do not
cast her out;
but do not trust yourself to one whom
you detest.
27With all your heart honor your father,
and do not forget the birth pangs of
your mother.
28Remember that through your parents you
were born;
and what can you give back to them that
equals their gift to you?

29With all your soul fear the Lord,
and honor his priests.
30With all your might love your Maker,
and do not forsake his ministers.
31Fear the Lord and honor the priest,
and give him his portion, as is
commanded you:
the first fruits, the guilt offering, the gift of
the shoulders,
the sacrifice of sanctification, and the
first fruits of the holy things.

32 Stretch forth your hand to the poor,
so that your blessing may be complete.
33 Give graciously to all the living,
and withhold not kindness from the dead.
34 Do not fail those who weep,
but mourn with those who mourn.
35 Do not shrink from visiting a sick man,
because for such deeds you will be loved.
36 In all you do, remember the end of your life,
and then you will never sin.

PHILIPPIANS 4

Therefore, my brethren, whom
I love and long for, my joy and
crown, stand firm in this way in the
Lord, my beloved.
2 I entreat Eu-o′dia and I entreat Syn′tyche
to agree in the Lord. 3 And I also ask you, who
are a true co-worker, help these women, for
they have labored side by side with me in
the gospel together with Clement and the
rest of my fellow workers, whose names are
in the book of life.
4 Rejoice in the Lord always; again I will
say, Rejoice. 5 Let all men know your forbearance. The Lord is at hand. 6 Have no
anxiety about anything, but in everything by
prayer and supplication with thanksgiving
let your requests be made known to God.
7 And the peace of God, which passes all
understanding, will keep your hearts and
your minds in Christ Jesus.
8 Finally, brethren, whatever is true, whatever is honorable, whatever is just, whatever
is pure, whatever is lovely, whatever is
gracious, if there is any excellence, if there
is anything worthy of praise, think about
these things. 9 What you have learned and
received and heard and seen in me, do; and
the God of peace will be with you.
10 I rejoice in the Lord greatly that now at
length you have revived your concern for
me; you were indeed concerned for me,
but you had no opportunity. 11 Not that
I complain of want; for I have learned,
in whatever state I am, to be content. 12 I
know how to be abased, and I know how
to abound; in any and all circumstances I
have learned the secret of facing plenty and
hunger, abundance and want. 13 I can do all
things in him who strengthens me.
14 Yet it was kind of you to share my
trouble. 15 And you Philippians yourselves
know that in the beginning of the gospel,
when I left Macedonia, no church entered
into partnership with me in giving and
receiving except you only; 16 for even in
Thessaloni′ca you sent me help once and
again. 17 Not that I seek the gift; but I seek
the fruit which increases to your credit. 18 I
have received full payment, and more; I am
filled, having received from Epaphrodi′tus
the gifts you sent, a fragrant offering, a
sacrifice acceptable and pleasing to God.
19 And my God will supply every need of
yours according to his riches in glory in
Christ Jesus. 20 To our God and Father be
glory for ever and ever. Amen.
21 Greet every saint in Christ Jesus. The
brethren who are with me greet you. 22 All
the saints greet you, especially those of
Caesar's household.
23 The grace of the Lord Jesus Christ be
with your spirit.

REFLECTION

As parents and caring adults, we try to preserve the innocence of our children as long as possible. In our role as protectors, we may forget that we too need protection from things that are, at best, of no benefit to the salvation of our souls and, at worst, deadly. Oftentimes, we either don't know or don't believe that we are always under attack and being tempted by Satan. That's why St. Paul reminds the Philippians, in his closing words to them, to stay focused on the things of God: "Whatever is true, whatever is honorable, whatever is just . . . think about these things" (Phil 4:8). It's an enormously difficult task in a culture that prides itself on instant access to almost anything. Satan longs to see the destruction of as many souls as possible and will use whatever means necessary to accomplish his task. We must remember that each one of us is a child of God, made in his image and likeness and a temple of the Holy Spirit. We need to be as diligent at guarding ourselves as we are of our children. If it seems an impossible task, remember St. Paul's words: "I can do all things in him who strengthens me" (v. 13). What is one way that you can practice custody of the senses today?

October 16

EZEKIEL 1

In the thirtieth year, in the fourth month, on the fifth day of the month, as I was among the exiles by the river Che′bar, the heavens were opened,
and I saw visions of God. [2]On the fifth day
of the month (it was the fifth year of the
exile of King Jehoi′achin), [3]the word of the
LORD came to Ezek′iel the priest, the son of
Buzi, in the land of the Chalde′ans by the
river Che′bar; and the hand of the LORD was
upon him there.

[4]As I looked, behold, a stormy wind
came out of the north, and a great cloud,
with brightness round about it, and fire
flashing forth continually, and in the midst
of the fire, as it were gleaming bronze. [5]And
from the midst of it came the likeness of
four living creatures. And this was their
appearance: they had the form of men, [6]but
each had four faces, and each of them had
four wings. [7]Their legs were straight, and
the soles of their feet were like the sole of a
calf's foot; and they sparkled like burnished
bronze. [8]Under their wings on their four
sides they had human hands. And the four
had their faces and their wings thus: [9]their
wings touched one another; they went every
one straight forward, without turning as
they went. [10]As for the likeness of their faces,
each had the face of a man in front; the four
had the face of a lion on the right side, the
four had the face of an ox on the left side,
and the four had the face of an eagle at the
back. [11]Such were their faces. And their
wings were spread out above; each creature
had two wings, each of which touched the
wing of another, while two covered their
bodies. [12]And each went straight forward;
wherever the spirit would go, they went,
without turning as they went. [13]In the midst
of the living creatures there was something
that looked like burning coals of fire, like
torches moving back and forth among the
living creatures; and the fire was bright, and
out of the fire went forth lightning. [14]And
the living creatures darted back and forth,
like a flash of lightning.

[15]Now as I looked at the living creatures, I
saw a wheel upon the earth beside the living
creatures, one for each of the four of them.
[16]As for the appearance of the wheels and
their construction: their appearance was like
the gleaming of a chrysolite; and the four had
the same likeness, their construction being
as it were a wheel within a wheel. [17]When
they went, they went in any of their four
directions without turning as they went.
[18]The four wheels had rims and they had
spokes; and their rims were full of eyes round
about. [19]And when the living creatures went,
the wheels went beside them; and when
the living creatures rose from the earth, the
wheels rose. [20]Wherever the spirit would go,
they went, and the wheels rose along with
them; for the spirit of the living creatures
was in the wheels. [21]When those went, these
went; and when those stood, these stood; and
when those rose from the earth, the wheels
rose along with them; for the spirit of the
living creatures was in the wheels.

[22]Over the heads of the living creatures
there was the likeness of a firmament,
shining like crystal, spread out above their
heads. [23]And under the firmament their
wings were stretched out straight, one
toward another; and each creature had two
wings covering its body. [24]And when they
went, I heard the sound of their wings like
the sound of many waters, like the thunder
of the Almighty, a sound of tumult like the
sound of a host; when they stood still, they
let down their wings. [25]And there came a

voice from above the firmament over their
heads; when they stood still, they let down
their wings.
26And above the firmament over their
heads there was the likeness of a throne, in
appearance like sapphire; and seated above
the likeness of a throne was a likeness as it
were of a human form. 27And upward from
what had the appearance of his loins I saw as
it were gleaming bronze, like the appearance
of fire enclosed round about; and downward
from what had the appearance of his loins
I saw as it were the appearance of fire, and
there was brightness round about him.
28Like the appearance of the bow that is
in the cloud on the day of rain, so was the
appearance of the brightness round about.

Such was the appearance of the likeness of
the glory of the LORD. And when I saw it, I
fell upon my face, and I heard the voice of
one speaking.

2 And he said to me, "Son of man, stand
upon your feet, and I will speak with
you." 2And when he spoke to me, the Spirit
entered into me and set me upon my feet;
and I heard him speaking to me. 3And he
said to me, "Son of man, I send you to the
sons of Israel, to a nation of rebels, who
have rebelled against me; they and their
fathers have transgressed against me to this
very day. 4The people also are impudent
and stubborn: I send you to them; and
you shall say to them, 'Thus says the Lord
GOD.' 5And whether they hear or refuse to
hear (for they are a rebellious house) they
will know that there has been a prophet
among them. 6And you, son of man, be not
afraid of them, nor be afraid of their words,
though briers and thorns are with you
and you sit upon scorpions; be not afraid
of their words, nor be dismayed at their
looks, for they are a rebellious house. 7And
you shall speak my words to them, whether
they hear or refuse to hear; for they are a
rebellious house.

8"But you, son of man, hear what I say to
you; be not rebellious like that rebellious
house; open your mouth, and eat what I give
you." 9And when I looked, behold, a hand was
stretched out to me, and behold, a written
scroll was in it; 10and he spread it before me;
and it had writing on the front and on the
back, and there were written on it words of
lamentation and mourning and woe.

SIRACH 8

Do not contend with a powerful man,
lest you fall into his hands.
2Do not quarrel with a rich man,
lest his resources outweigh yours;
for gold has ruined many,
and has perverted the minds of kings.
3Do not argue with a chatterer,
nor heap wood on his fire.

4Do not jest with an ill-bred person,
lest your ancestors be disgraced.
5Do not reproach a man who is turning
away from sin;
remember that we all deserve
punishment.
6Do not disdain a man when he is old,
for some of us are growing old.
7Do not rejoice over any one's death;
remember that we all must die.
8Do not slight the discourse of the sages,
but busy yourself with their maxims;
because from them you will gain instruction
and learn how to serve great men.
9Do not disregard the discourse of the aged,
for they themselves learned from their
fathers;
because from them you will gain
understanding
and learn how to give an answer in time
of need.

10Do not kindle the coals of a sinner,
lest you be burned in his flaming fire.
11Do not get up and leave an insolent fellow,
lest he lie in ambush against your words.
12Do not lend to a man who is stronger than
you;
but if you do lend anything, be as one
who has lost it.
13Do not give surety beyond your means,
but if you give surety, be concerned as
one who must pay.

14Do not go to law against a judge,
for the decision will favor him because of
his standing.
15Do not travel on the road with a
foolhardy fellow,
lest he be burdensome to you;
for he will act as he pleases,
and through his folly you will perish
with him.
16Do not fight with a wrathful man,
and do not cross the wilderness with him;
because blood is as nothing in his sight,
and where no help is at hand, he will
strike you down.
17Do not consult with a fool,
for he will not be able to keep a secret.
18In the presence of a stranger do nothing
that is to be kept secret,
for you do not know what he will divulge.
19Do not reveal your thoughts to every one,
lest you drive away your good luck.

9 Do not be jealous of the wife of your
bosom,
and do not teach her an evil lesson to
your own hurt.
2Do not give yourself to a woman
so that she gains mastery over
your strength.
3Do not go to meet a loose woman,
lest you fall into her snares.
4Do not associate with a woman singer,
lest you be caught in her intrigues.
5Do not look intently at a virgin,
lest you stumble and incur penalties
for her.
6Do not give yourself to harlots
lest you lose your inheritance.
7Do not look around in the streets of a city,
nor wander about in its deserted sections.
8Turn away your eyes from a shapely woman,
and do not look intently at beauty
belonging to another;
many have been misled by a
woman's beauty,
and by it passion is kindled like a fire.
9Never dine with another man's wife,
nor revel with her at wine;
lest your heart turn aside to her,
and in blood you be plunged
into destruction.
10Forsake not an old friend,
for a new one does not compare
with him.
A new friend is like new wine;
when it has aged you will drink it with
pleasure.

COLOSSIANS 1

Paul, an apostle of Christ Jesus by the will of God, and Timothy our brother,

**2To the saints and faithful brethren
in Christ at Colos´sae:**

Grace to you and peace from God our
Father.
3We always thank God, the Father of our
Lord Jesus Christ, when we pray for you,
4because we have heard of your faith in
Christ Jesus and of the love which you have
for all the saints, 5because of the hope laid
up for you in heaven. Of this you have heard
before in the word of the truth, the gospel
6which has come to you, as indeed in the
whole world it is bearing fruit and growing—
so among yourselves, from the day you heard
and understood the grace of God in truth, 7as
you learned it from Ep´aphras our beloved
fellow servant. He is a faithful minister of
Christ on our behalf 8and has made known
to us your love in the Spirit.
9And so, from the day we heard of it, we
have not ceased to pray for you, asking
that you may be filled with the knowledge
of his will in all spiritual wisdom and
understanding, 10to lead a life worthy of
the Lord, fully pleasing to him, bearing
fruit in every good work and increasing
in the knowledge of God. 11May you be
strengthened with all power, according
to his glorious might, for all endurance
and patience with joy, 12giving thanks to
the Father, who has qualified us to share
in the inheritance of the saints in light.
13He has delivered us from the dominion
of darkness and transferred us to the
kingdom of his beloved Son, 14in whom we
have redemption, the forgiveness of sins.

[15]He is the image of the invisible God, the
first-born of all creation; [16]for in him all
things were created, in heaven and on earth,
visible and invisible, whether thrones or
dominions or principalities or authorities—
all things were created through him and for
him. [17]He is before all things, and in him all
things hold together. [18]He is the head of the
body, the Church; he is the beginning, the
first-born from the dead, that in everything
he might be pre-eminent. [19]For in him all
the fulness of God was pleased to dwell,
[20]and through him to reconcile to himself
all things, whether on earth or in heaven,
making peace by the blood of his cross.
[21]And you, who once were estranged
and hostile in mind, doing evil deeds, [22]he
has now reconciled in his body of flesh
by his death, in order to present you holy
and blameless and irreproachable before
him, [23]provided that you continue in the
faith, stable and steadfast, not shifting
from the hope of the gospel which you
heard, which has been preached to every
creature under heaven, and of which I,
Paul, became a minister.

REFLECTION

In the first chapter of Ezekiel, the prophet receives one of the most intense visions of God found in all of Scripture. In the vision of the wheel chariot, covered in eyes, never turning direction, and yet always moving forward, we glimpse the omnipotent, omniscient God, who is nevertheless still beyond Ezekiel's sight—the prophet sees only "the likeness of the glory of the LORD" (Ez 1:28). The vision is said to reveal merely the likeness of God's glory because God is transcendent, beyond the physical world and all our imagining, which is why the figure representing God appears "above the firmament," i.e., in the dome of the sky (see v. 26). Truly this is the God of whom St. Paul speaks, the Creator of all, the one in whom all things hold together (see Col 1:16–17). But where is Ezekiel when he is given this message? Ezekiel is in exile in Babylon (see Ez 1:1). Although God's house (the Temple) has been destroyed, God has no trouble making his presence known. The vision is therefore a powerful reminder of the character of our God. He is a God who is both completely magnificent and transcendent, yet also mobile and present. Have you ever experienced God's presence as both beyond you and yet near you at the same time?

October 17

EZEKIEL 3

**And he said to me, "Son of man,
eat what is offered to you; eat
this scroll, and go, speak to the
house of Israel." [2]So I opened my mouth,
and he gave me the scroll to eat. [3]And he
said to me, "Son of man, eat this scroll**
that I give you and fill your stomach with
it." Then I ate it; and it was in my mouth as
sweet as honey.
[4]And he said to me, "Son of man, go, get you
to the house of Israel, and speak with my words
to them. [5]For you are not sent to a people of
foreign speech and a hard language, but to
the house of Israel—[6]not to many peoples of
foreign speech and a hard language, whose
words you cannot understand. Surely, if I sent
you to such, they would listen to you. [7]But the
house of Israel will not listen to you; for they
are not willing to listen to me; because all the
house of Israel are of a hard forehead and of
a stubborn heart. [8]Behold, I have made your
face hard against their faces, and your forehead
hard against their foreheads. [9]Like adamant
harder than flint have I made your forehead;
fear them not, nor be dismayed at their looks,
for they are a rebellious house." [10]Moreover he
said to me, "Son of man, all my words that I
shall speak to you receive in your heart, and
hear with your ears. [11]And go, get you to the
exiles, to your people, and say to them, 'Thus
says the Lord GOD'; whether they hear or
refuse to hear."

12 Then the Spirit lifted me up, and as the
glory of the LORD arose from its place, I heard
behind me the sound of a great earthquake;
13 it was the sound of the wings of the living
creatures as they touched one another, and
the sound of the wheels beside them, that
sounded like a great earthquake. 14 The Spirit
lifted me up and took me away, and I went in
bitterness in the heat of my spirit, the hand of
the LORD being strong upon me; 15 and I came
to the exiles at Tel-a'bib, who dwelt by the river
Che'bar. And I sat there overwhelmed among
them seven days.

16 And at the end of seven days, the word of
the LORD came to me: 17 "Son of man, I have
made you a watchman for the house of Israel;
whenever you hear a word from my mouth,
you shall give them warning from me. 18 If I
say to the wicked, 'You shall surely die,' and
you give him no warning, nor speak to warn
the wicked from his wicked way, in order to
save his life, that wicked man shall die in his
iniquity; but his blood I will require at your
hand. 19 But if you warn the wicked, and he
does not turn from his wickedness, or from his
wicked way, he shall die in his iniquity; but you
will have saved your life. 20 Again, if a righteous
man turns from his righteousness and
commits iniquity, and I lay a stumbling block
before him, he shall die; because you have not
warned him, he shall die for his sin, and his
righteous deeds which he has done shall not
be remembered; but his blood I will require
at your hand. 21 Nevertheless if you warn the
righteous man not to sin, and he does not sin,
he shall surely live, because he took warning;
and you will have saved your life."

22 And the hand of the LORD was there upon
me; and he said to me, "Arise, go forth into
the plain, and there I will speak with you."
23 So I arose and went forth into the plain; and
behold, the glory of the LORD stood there,
like the glory which I had seen by the river
Che'bar; and I fell on my face. 24 But the Spirit
entered into me, and set me upon my feet; and
he spoke with me and said to me, "Go, shut
yourself within your house. 25 And you, O son
of man, behold, cords will be placed upon you,
and you shall be bound with them, so that you
cannot go out among the people; 26 and I will
make your tongue cleave to the roof of your
mouth, so that you shall be mute and unable to
reprove them; for they are a rebellious house.
27 But when I speak with you, I will open your
mouth, and you shall say to them, 'Thus says
the Lord GOD'; he that will hear, let him hear;
and he that will refuse to hear, let him refuse;
for they are a rebellious house.

4 "And you, O son of man, take a brick
and lay it before you, and portray upon
it a city, even Jerusalem; 2 and put siegeworks
against it, and build a siege wall against it, and
cast up a mound against it; set camps also
against it, and plant battering rams against it
round about. 3 And take an iron plate, and place
it as an iron wall between you and the city; and
set your face toward it, and let it be in a state
of siege, and press the siege against it. This is a
sign for the house of Israel.

4 "Then lie upon your left side, and I will lay
the punishment of the house of Israel upon
you; for the number of the days that you lie
upon it, you shall bear their punishment.
5 For I assign to you a number of days, three
hundred and ninety days, equal to the
number of the years of their punishment;
so long shall you bear the punishment of
the house of Israel. 6 And when you have
completed these, you shall lie down a
second time, but on your right side, and
bear the punishment of the house of Judah;
forty days I assign you, a day for each year.
7 And you shall set your face toward the siege
of Jerusalem, with your arm bared; and you
shall prophesy against the city. 8 And behold,
I will put cords upon you, so that you cannot
turn from one side to the other, till you have
completed the days of your siege.

9 "And you, take wheat and barley, beans
and lentils, millet and spelt, and put them
into a single vessel, and make bread of them.
During the number of days that you lie
upon your side, three hundred and ninety
days, you shall eat it. 10 And the food which
you eat shall be by weight, twenty shekels a
day; once a day you shall eat it. 11 And water
you shall drink by measure, the sixth part
of a hin; once a day you shall drink. 12 And
you shall eat it as a barley cake, baking it
in their sight on human dung." 13 And the

LORD said, "Thus shall the people of Israel eat their bread unclean, among the nations where I will drive them." [14]Then I said, "Ah, Lord GOD! behold, I have never defiled myself; from my youth up till now I have never eaten what died of itself or was torn by beasts, nor has foul flesh come into my mouth." [15]Then he said to me, "See, I will let you have cow's dung instead of human dung, on which you may prepare your bread." [16]Moreover he said to me, "Son of man, behold, I will break the staff of bread in Jerusalem; they shall eat bread by weight and with fearfulness; and they shall drink water by measure and in dismay. [17]I will do this that they may lack bread and water, and look at one another in dismay, and waste away under their punishment."

SIRACH 9

[11]Do not envy the honors of a sinner,
for you do not know what his end will be.
[12]Do not delight in what pleases the ungodly;
remember that they will not be held
guiltless as long as they live.

[13]Keep far from a man who has the power
to kill,
and you will not be worried by the fear
of death.
But if you approach him, make no misstep,
lest he rob you of your life.
Know that you are walking in the midst
of snares,
and that you are going about on the
city battlements.

[14]As much as you can, aim to know
your neighbors,
and consult with the wise.
[15]Let your conversation be with men
of understanding,
and let all your discussion be about the
law of the Most High.
[16]Let righteous men be your
dinner companions,
and let your glorying be in the fear
of the Lord.

[17]A work will be praised for the skill
of the craftsmen;
so a people's leader is proved wise
by his words.
[18]A babbler is feared in his city,
and the man who is reckless in speech
will be hated.

10 A wise magistrate will educate
his people,
and the rule of an understanding man
will be well ordered.
[2]Like the magistrate of the people, so are
his officials;
and like the ruler of the city, so are all
its inhabitants.
[3]An undisciplined king will ruin his people,
but a city will grow through the
understanding of its rulers.
[4]The government of the earth is in the hands
of the Lord,
and over it he will raise up the right man
for the time.
[5]The success of a man is in the hands of
the Lord,
and he confers his honor upon the person
of the scribe.

[6]Do not be angry with your neighbor for
any injury,
and do not attempt anything by acts
of insolence.
[7]Arrogance is hateful before the Lord and
before men,
and injustice is outrageous to both.
[8]Sovereignty passes from nation to nation
on account of injustice and insolence
and wealth.
[9]How can he who is dust and ashes be proud?
for even in life his bowels decay.
[10]A long illness baffles the physician;
the king of today will die tomorrow.
[11]For when a man is dead,
he will inherit creeping things, and wild
beasts, and worms.
[12]The beginning of man's pride is to depart
from the Lord;
his heart has forsaken his Maker.
[13]For the beginning of pride is sin,
and the man who clings to it pours out
abominations.

Therefore the Lord brought upon them
extraordinary afflictions,
and destroyed them utterly.
14 The Lord has cast down the thrones
of rulers,
and has seated the lowly in their place.
15 The Lord has plucked up the roots
of the nations,
and has planted the humble in
their place.
16 The Lord has overthrown the lands
of the nations,
and has destroyed them to the
foundations of the earth.
17 He has removed some of them and
destroyed them,
and has extinguished the memory of
them from the earth.
18 Pride was not created for men,
nor fierce anger for those born of women.

COLOSSIANS 1

**24 Now I rejoice in my sufferings
for your sake, and in my flesh
I complete what is lacking in
Christ's afflictions for the sake of his
body, that is, the Church, 25 of which
I became a minister according to the**
divine office which was given to me for you,
to make the word of God fully known, 26 the
mystery hidden for ages and generations
but now made manifest to his saints. 27 To
them God chose to make known how great
among the Gentiles are the riches of the
glory of this mystery, which is Christ in
you, the hope of glory. 28 Him we proclaim,
warning every man and teaching every
man in all wisdom, that we may present
every man mature in Christ. 29 For this I
toil, striving with all the energy which he
mightily inspires within me.

2 For I want you to know how greatly I
strive for you, and for those at La-odice´a,
and for all who have not seen my face, 2 that
their hearts may be encouraged as they are
knit together in love, to have all the riches of
assured understanding and the knowledge
of God's mystery, of Christ, 3 in whom are
hidden all the treasures of wisdom and
knowledge. 4 I say this in order that no one
may delude you with beguiling speech. 5 For
though I am absent in body, yet I am with
you in spirit, rejoicing to see your good order
and the firmness of your faith in Christ.
6 As therefore you received Christ Jesus the
Lord, so live in him, 7 rooted and built up in
him and established in the faith, just as you
were taught, abounding in thanksgiving.
8 See to it that no one makes a prey of
you by philosophy and empty deceit,
according to human tradition, according
to the elemental spirits of the universe,
and not according to Christ. 9 For in
him the whole fulness of deity dwells
bodily, 10 and you have come to fulness
of life in him, who is the head of all rule
and authority. 11 In him also you were
circumcised with a circumcision made
without hands, by putting off the body of
flesh in the circumcision of Christ; 12 and
you were buried with him in baptism,
in which you were also raised with him
through faith in the working of God,
who raised him from the dead. 13 And
you, who were dead in trespasses and the
uncircumcision of your flesh, God made
alive together with him, having forgiven
us all our trespasses, 14 having canceled the
bond which stood against us with its legal
demands; this he set aside, nailing it to
the cross. 15 He disarmed the principalities
and powers and made a public example of
them, triumphing over them in him.
16 Therefore let no one pass judgment
on you in questions of food and drink or
with regard to a festival or a new moon
or a sabbath. 17 These are only a shadow
of what is to come; but the substance
belongs to Christ. 18 Let no one disqualify
you, insisting on self-abasement and
worship of angels, taking his stand on
visions, puffed up without reason by his
sensuous mind, 19 and not holding fast to
the Head, from whom the whole body,
nourished and knit together through its
joints and ligaments, grows with a growth
that is from God.

REFLECTION

The prophet Ezekiel is given a difficult commission: he is told to preach to the people of Israel, even though they will not listen. Although this task may seem futile, Ezekiel is told that if he fails to preach, the blame for the unrepentant hearts of the people will fall on him. We too are priests, prophets, and kings by our Baptism, and we must follow along Ezekiel's path. We must speak the Word of God, even to a tough audience, or we will be held accountable for our silence. Yet, when Ezekiel eats the scroll of lamentation and woe that God gives him, it tastes "as sweet as honey" (Ez 3:3). Our prophetic vocation, although difficult, is ultimately given its flavor, its sweetness, and its success by God. To speak the Word of God, we must therefore rely on him and not ourselves. Like Ezekiel, we must trust God even in failure. It can be daunting to think of ourselves as prophets, but Sirach offers some advice for beginners: "As much as you can, aim to know your neighbors" (Sir 9:14). As in the case of Ezekiel, we are most often called to preach to those near at hand. Do you have any friends who could benefit from spiritual conversation? Begin praying for a chance to share with them God's goodness.

October 18

EZEKIEL 5

"And you, O son of man, take a sharp sword; use it as a barber's razor and pass it over your head and your beard; then take balances for weighing, and divide the hair. 2A third part you shall burn in the fire in the midst of the city, when the days of the siege are completed; and a third part you shall take and strike with the sword round about the city; and a third part you shall scatter to the wind, and I will unsheathe the sword after them. 3And you shall take from these a small number, and bind them in the skirts of your robe. 4And of these again you shall take some, and cast them into the fire, and burn them in the fire; from there a fire will come forth into all the house of Israel. 5Thus says the Lord GOD: This is Jerusalem; I have set her in the center of the nations, with countries round about her. 6And she has wickedly rebelled against my ordinances more than the nations, and against my statutes more than the countries round about her, by rejecting my ordinances and not walking in my statutes. 7Therefore thus says the Lord GOD: Because you are more turbulent than the nations that are round about you, and have not walked in my statutes or kept my ordinances, but have acted according to the ordinances of the nations that are round about you; 8therefore thus says the Lord GOD: Behold, I, even I, am against you; and I will execute judgments in the midst of you in the sight of the nations. 9And because of all your abominations I will do with you what I have never yet done, and the like of which I will never do again. 10Therefore fathers shall eat their sons in the midst of you, and sons shall eat their fathers; and I will execute judgments on you, and any of you who survive I will scatter to all the winds. 11Wherefore, as I live, says the Lord GOD, surely, because you have defiled my sanctuary with all your detestable things and with all your abominations, therefore I will cut you down; my eye will not spare, and I will have no pity. 12A third part of you shall die of pestilence and be consumed with famine in the midst of you; a third part shall fall by the sword round about you; and a third part I will scatter to all the winds and will unsheathe the sword after them.

13"Thus shall my anger spend itself, and I will vent my fury upon them and satisfy myself; and they shall know that I, the LORD, have spoken in my jealousy, when I spend my fury upon them. 14Moreover I will make you a desolation and an object of reproach among the nations round about you and in the sight of all that pass by. 15You shall be a reproach and a taunt, a warning and a horror, to the nations round about you, when I execute judgments on

you in anger and fury, and with furious
chastisements—I, the LORD, have spoken—
[16]when I loose against you my deadly arrows
of famine, arrows for destruction, which I
will loose to destroy you, and when I bring
more and more famine upon you, and break
your staff of bread. [17]I will send famine and
wild beasts against you, and they will rob
you of your children; pestilence and blood
shall pass through you; and I will bring the
sword upon you. I, the LORD, have spoken."

6 The word of the LORD came to me:
[2]"Son of man, set your face toward the
mountains of Israel, and prophesy against
them, [3]and say, You mountains of Israel,
hear the word of the Lord GOD! Thus says
the Lord GOD to the mountains and the
hills, to the ravines and the valleys: Behold,
I, even I, will bring a sword upon you, and
I will destroy your high places. [4]Your altars
shall become desolate, and your incense
altars shall be broken; and I will cast down
your slain before your idols. [5]And I will
lay the dead bodies of the people of Israel
before their idols; and I will scatter your
bones round about your altars. [6]Wherever
you dwell your cities shall be waste and your
high places ruined, so that your altars will
be waste and ruined, your idols broken and
destroyed, your incense altars cut down,
and your works wiped out. [7]And the slain
shall fall in the midst of you, and you shall
know that I am the LORD.

[8]"Yet I will leave some of you alive. When
you have among the nations some who
escape the sword, and when you are scattered
through the countries, [9]then those of you
who escape will remember me among the
nations where they are carried captive, when
I have broken their wanton heart which has
departed from me, and blinded their eyes
which turn wantonly after their idols; and
they will be loathsome in their own sight for
the evils which they have committed, for all
their abominations. [10]And they shall know
that I am the LORD; I have not said in vain
that I would do this evil to them."

[11]Thus says the Lord GOD: "Clap your
hands, and stamp your foot, and say, Alas!
because of all the evil abominations of the
house of Israel; for they shall fall by the
sword, by famine, and by pestilence. [12]He
that is far off shall die of pestilence; and
he that is near shall fall by the sword; and
he that is left and is preserved shall die of
famine. Thus I will spend my fury upon
them. [13]And you shall know that I am the
LORD, when their slain lie among their
idols round about their altars, upon every
high hill, on all the mountain tops, under
every green tree, and under every leafy oak,
wherever they offered pleasing odor to all
their idols. [14]And I will stretch out my hand
against them, and make the land desolate
and waste, throughout all their habitations,
from the wilderness to Riblah. Then they
will know that I am the LORD."

7 The word of the LORD came to me:
[2]"And you, O son of man, thus says the
Lord GOD to the land of Israel: An end!
The end has come upon the four corners of
the land. [3]Now the end is upon you, and I
will let loose my anger upon you, and will
judge you according to your ways; and I will
punish you for all your abominations. [4]And
my eye will not spare you, nor will I have
pity; but I will punish you for your ways,
while your abominations are in your midst.
Then you will know that I am the LORD.

[5]"Thus says the Lord GOD: Disaster after
disaster! Behold, it comes. [6]An end has
come, the end has come; it has awakened
against you. Behold, it comes. [7]Your doom
has come to you, O inhabitant of the land;
the time has come, the day is near, a day
of tumult, and not of joyful shouting upon
the mountains. [8]Now I will soon pour out
my wrath upon you, and spend my anger
against you, and judge you according to
your ways; and I will punish you for all
your abominations. [9]And my eye will not
spare, nor will I have pity; I will punish
you according to your ways, while your
abominations are in your midst. Then you
will know that I am the LORD, who strike.

[10]"Behold, the day! Behold, it comes! Your
doom has come, injustice has blossomed,
pride has budded. [11]Violence has grown
up into a rod of wickedness; none of them
shall remain, nor their abundance, nor their

wealth; neither shall there be preeminence among them. [12]The time has come, the day draws near. Let not the buyer rejoice, nor the seller mourn, for wrath is upon all their multitude. [13]For the seller shall not return to what he has sold, while they live. For wrath is upon all their multitude; it shall not turn back; and because of his iniquity, none can maintain his life."

SIRACH 10

19What race is worthy of honor? The
human race.
What race is worthy of honor? Those
who fear the Lord.
What race is unworthy of honor? The
human race.
What race is unworthy of honor? Those
who transgress the commandments.
20Among brothers their leader is worthy
of honor,
and those who fear the Lord are worthy
of honor in his eyes.
22The rich, and the eminent, and the poor—
their glory is the fear of the Lord.
23It is not right to despise an intelligent
poor man,
nor is it proper to honor a sinful man.
24The nobleman, and the judge, and the
ruler will be honored,
but none of them is greater than the man
who fears the Lord.
25Free men will be at the service of a
wise servant,
and a man of understanding will
not grumble.
26Do not make a display of your wisdom
when you do your work,
nor glorify yourself at a time when you
are in want.
27Better is a man who works and has an
abundance of everything,
than one who goes about boasting, but
lacks bread.
28My son, glorify yourself with humility,
and ascribe to yourself honor according
to your worth.
29Who will justify the man that sins
against himself?
And who will honor the man that
dishonors his own life?
30A poor man is honored for his
knowledge,
while a rich man is honored for
his wealth.
31A man honored in poverty, how much
more in wealth!
And a man dishonored in wealth, how
much more in poverty!

11 The wisdom of a humble man will
lift up his head,
and will seat him among the great.

2Do not praise a man for his good looks,
nor loathe a man because of his
appearance.
3The bee is small among flying creatures,
but her product is the best of sweet
things.
4Do not boast about wearing fine clothes,
nor exalt yourself in the day that you
are honored;
for the works of the Lord are wonderful,
and his works are concealed from men.
5Many kings have had to sit on the ground,
but one who was never thought of has
worn a crown.
6Many rulers have been greatly disgraced,
and illustrious men have been handed
over to others.

7Do not find fault before you investigate;
first consider, and then reprove.
8Do not answer before you have heard,
nor interrupt a speaker in the midst
of his words.
9Do not argue about a matter which does
not concern you,
nor sit with sinners when they judge
a case.

10My son, do not busy yourself with
many matters;
if you multiply activities you will not
go unpunished,
and if you pursue you will not overtake,
and by fleeing you will not escape.

11There is a man who works, and toils, and
presses on,
but is so much the more in want.
12There is another who is slow and
needs help,
who lacks strength and abounds
in poverty;
but the eyes of the Lord look upon him for
his good;
he lifts him out of his low estate
13and raises up his head,
so that many are amazed at him.
14Good things and bad, life and death,
poverty and wealth, come from the Lord.

COLOSSIANS 2

**20If with Christ you died to the
elemental spirits of the universe, why do you live as if you
still belonged to the world? Why do you
submit to regulations, 21"Do not handle,
Do not taste, Do not touch" 22(referring**
to things which all perish as they are used),
according to human precepts and doctrines?
23These have indeed an appearance of
wisdom in promoting rigor of devotion and
self-abasement and severity to the body,
but they are of no value in checking the
indulgence of the flesh.

3 If then you have been raised with Christ,
seek the things that are above, where
Christ is, seated at the right hand of God.
2Set your minds on things that are above,
not on things that are on earth. 3For you
have died, and your life is hidden with
Christ in God. 4When Christ who is our life
appears, then you also will appear with him
in glory.

5Put to death therefore what is earthly
in you: immorality, impurity, passion, evil
desire, and covetousness, which is idolatry.
6On account of these the wrath of God is
coming. 7In these you once walked, when
you lived in them. 8But now put them all
away: anger, wrath, malice, slander, and
foul talk from your mouth. 9Do not lie to
one another, seeing that you have put off
the old man with his practices 10and have
put on the new man, who is being renewed
in knowledge after the image of his creator.
11Here there cannot be Greek and Jew,
circumcised and uncircumcised, barbarian,
Scyth′ian, slave, free man, but Christ is all,
and in all.

12Put on then, as God's chosen ones, holy
and beloved, compassion, kindness, lowliness, meekness, and patience, 13forbearing
one another and, if one has a complaint
against another, forgiving each other; as
the Lord has forgiven you, so you also must
forgive. 14And over all these put on love,
which binds everything together in perfect
harmony. 15And let the peace of Christ rule
in your hearts, to which indeed you were
called in the one body. And be thankful.
16Let the word of Christ dwell in you richly,
as you teach and admonish one another in all
wisdom, and as you sing psalms and hymns
and spiritual songs with thankfulness in
your hearts to God. 17And whatever you do,
in word or deed, do everything in the name
of the Lord Jesus, giving thanks to God the
Father through him.

REFLECTION

You may have heard the phrase "preaching to the choir," but you probably have never heard of anyone preaching to mountains (see Ez 6:1–3). The image of Ezekiel shouting at immovable rock is surely meant to remind us of the hard hearts of the Israelites, which the words of the prophet cannot penetrate (see 3:7–9). And yet, the condemnation of the mountains for their complicity in the idolatry of the Israelites by housing altars to false gods reminds us of our responsibility toward all of creation. We are meant to love and use the goods of the material world, but when we love them more than God, they become an occasion for sin. We, then, draw created things into our sin and turn them to an evil purpose. In short, it is we who bring condemnation on the mountains. St. Paul says that our lives are hidden in Christ (see Col 3:3), the one in whom all things were made, and so the good of creation is also hidden in him. Learning to love the earth properly means, therefore, learning to love Christ properly. Do you understand your love or care for natural things as springing from your love for Christ?

October 19

EZEKIEL 7

14"They have blown the trumpet and made all ready; but none goes to battle, for my wrath is upon all their multitude. 15The sword is without, pestilence and famine are within; he that is in the field dies by the
sword; and him that is in the city famine and
pestilence devour. 16And if any survivors
escape, they will be on the mountains, like
doves of the valleys, all of them moaning,
every one over his iniquity. 17All hands
are feeble, and all knees weak as water.
18They clothe themselves with sackcloth,
and horror covers them; shame is upon
all faces, and baldness on all their heads.
19They cast their silver into the streets, and
their gold is like an unclean thing; their
silver and gold are not able to deliver them
in the day of the wrath of the LORD; they
cannot satisfy their hunger or fill their
stomachs with it. For it was the stumbling
block of their iniquity. 20Their beautiful
ornament they used for vainglory, and
they made their abominable images and
their detestable things of it; therefore I will
make it an unclean thing to them. 21And I
will give it into the hands of foreigners for
a prey, and to the wicked of the earth for a
spoil; and they shall profane it. 22I will turn
my face from them, that they may profane
my precious place; robbers shall enter and
profane it, 23and make a desolation.

"Because the land is full of bloody crimes
and the city is full of violence, 24I will bring
the worst of the nations to take possession
of their houses; I will put an end to their
proud might, and their holy places shall
be profaned. 25When anguish comes, they
will seek peace, but there shall be none.
26Disaster comes upon disaster, rumor
follows rumor; they seek a vision from
the prophet, but the law perishes from the
priest, and counsel from the elders. 27The
king mourns, the prince is wrapped in
despair, and the hands of the people of the
land are palsied by terror. According to their
way I will do to them, and according to their
own judgments I will judge them; and they
shall know that I am the LORD."

8 In the sixth year, in the sixth month,
on the fifth day of the month, as I sat in
my house, with the elders of Judah sitting
before me, the hand of the Lord GOD fell
there upon me. 2Then I beheld a form that
had the appearance of a man; below what
appeared to be his loins it was fire, and
above his loins it was like the appearance
of brightness, like gleaming bronze. 3He
put forth the form of a hand, and took me
by a lock of my head; and the Spirit lifted
me up between earth and heaven, and
brought me in visions of God to Jerusalem,
to the entrance of the gateway of the inner
court that faces north, where was the seat
of the image of jealousy, which provokes to
jealousy. 4And behold, the glory of the God
of Israel was there, like the vision that I saw
in the plain.

5Then he said to me, "Son of man, lift up
your eyes now in the direction of the north."
So I lifted up my eyes toward the north,
and behold, north of the altar gate, in the
entrance, was this image of jealousy. 6And
he said to me, "Son of man, do you see what
they are doing, the great abominations that
the house of Israel are committing here, to
drive me far from my sanctuary? But you
will see still greater abominations."

7And he brought me to the door of the
court; and when I looked, behold, there was a
hole in the wall. 8Then said he to me, "Son of
man, dig in the wall"; and when I dug in the

wall, behold, there was a door. [9]And he said to me, "Go in, and see the vile abominations that they are committing here." [10]So I went in and saw; and there, portrayed upon the wall round about, were all kinds of creeping things, and loathsome beasts, and all the idols of the house of Israel. [11]And before them stood seventy men of the elders of the house of Israel, with Ja-azani′ah the son of Sha′phan standing among them. Each had his censer in his hand, and the smoke of the cloud of incense went up. [12]Then he said to me, "Son of man, have you seen what the elders of the house of Israel are doing in the dark, every man in his room of pictures? For they say, 'The LORD does not see us, the LORD has forsaken the land.'" [13]He said also to me, "You will see still greater abominations which they commit."

[14]Then he brought me to the entrance of the north gate of the house of the LORD; and behold, there sat women weeping for Tammuz. [15]Then he said to me, "Have you seen this, O son of man? You will see still greater abominations than these."

[16]And he brought me into the inner court of the house of the LORD; and behold, at the door of the temple of the LORD, between the porch and the altar, were about twenty-five men, with their backs to the temple of the LORD, and their faces toward the east, worshiping the sun toward the east. [17]Then he said to me, "Have you seen this, O son of man? Is it too slight a thing for the house of Judah to commit the abominations which they commit here, that they should fill the land with violence, and provoke me further to anger? Behold, they put the branch to their nose. [18]Therefore I will deal in wrath; my eye will not spare, nor will I have pity; and though they cry in my ears with a loud voice, I will not hear them."

9 Then he cried in my ears with a loud voice, saying, "Draw near, you executioners of the city, each with his destroying weapon in his hand." [2]And behold, six men came from the direction of the upper gate, which faces north, every man with his weapon for slaughter in his hand, and with them was a man clothed in linen, with a writing case at his side. And they went in and stood beside the bronze altar.

[3]Now the glory of the God of Israel had gone up from the cherubim on which it rested to the threshold of the house; and he called to the man clothed in linen, who had the writing case at his side. [4]And the LORD said to him, "Go through the city, through Jerusalem, and put a mark upon the foreheads of the men who sigh and groan over all the abominations that are committed in it." [5]And to the others he said in my hearing, "Pass through the city after him, and kill; your eye shall not spare, and you shall show no pity; [6]slay old men outright, young men and maidens, little children and women, but touch no one upon whom is the mark. And begin at my sanctuary." So they began with the elders who were before the house. [7]Then he said to them, "Defile the house, and fill the courts with the slain. Go forth." So they went forth, and killed in the city. [8]And while they were killing, and I was left alone, I fell upon my face, and cried, "Ah, Lord GOD! will you destroy all that remains of Israel in the outpouring of your wrath upon Jerusalem?"

[9]Then he said to me, "The guilt of the house of Israel and Judah is exceedingly great; the land is full of blood, and the city full of injustice; for they say, 'The LORD has forsaken the land, and the LORD does not see.' [10]As for me, my eye will not spare, nor will I have pity, but I will repay their deeds upon their heads."

[11]And behold, the man clothed in linen, with the writing case at his side, brought back word, saying, "I have done as you commanded me."

SIRACH 11

[17]The gift of the Lord endures for those who
are godly,
and what he approves will have lasting
success.
[18]There is a man who is rich through his
diligence and self-denial,
and this is the reward allotted to him:

[19]when he says, "I have found rest,
and now I shall enjoy my goods!"
he does not know how much time will pass
until he leaves them to others and dies.
[20]Stand by your covenant and attend to it,
and grow old in your work.

[21]Do not wonder at the works of a sinner,
but trust in the Lord and keep at
your toil;
for it is easy in the sight of the Lord
to enrich a poor man quickly and suddenly.
[22]The blessing of the Lord is the reward of
the godly,
and quickly God causes his blessing
to flourish.
[23]Do not say, "What do I need,
and what prosperity could be mine
in the future?"
[24]Do not say, "I have enough,
and what calamity could happen to me
in the future?"
[25]In the day of prosperity, adversity is forgotten,
and in the day of adversity, prosperity is
not remembered.
[26]For it is easy in the sight of the Lord
to reward a man on the day of death
according to his conduct.
[27]The misery of an hour makes one
forget luxury,
and at the close of a man's life his deeds
will be revealed.
[28]Call no one happy before his death;
a man will be known through his children.

[29]Do not bring every man into your home,
for many are the wiles of the crafty.
[30]Like a decoy partridge in a cage, so is the
mind of a proud man,
and like a spy he observes your weakness;
[31]for he lies in wait, turning good into evil,
and to worthy actions he will attach blame.
[32]From a spark of fire come many
burning coals,
and a sinner lies in wait to shed blood.
[33]Beware of a scoundrel, for he devises evil,
lest he give you a lasting blemish.
[34]Receive a stranger into your home and he
will upset you with commotion,
and will estrange you from your family.

COLOSSIANS 3

[18]Wives, be subject to your hus-
bands, as is fitting in the Lord.
[19]Husbands, love your wives, and do not
be harsh with them. [20]Children, obey
your parents in everything, for this pleases
the Lord. [21]Fathers, do not provoke your
children, lest they become discouraged.
[22]Slaves, obey in everything those who are
your earthly masters, not with eyeservice,
as men-pleasers, but in singleness of heart,
fearing the Lord. [23]Whatever your task,
work heartily, as serving the Lord and not
men, [24]knowing that from the Lord you
will receive the inheritance as your reward;
you are serving the Lord Christ. [25]For the
wrongdoer will be paid back for the wrong
he has done, and there is no partiality.

4 Masters, treat your slaves justly and
fairly, knowing that you also have a
Master in heaven.

[2]Continue steadfastly in prayer, being
watchful in it with thanksgiving; [3]and pray
for us also, that God may open to us a door
for the word, to declare the mystery of
Christ, on account of which I am in prison,
[4]that I may make it clear, as I ought to speak.

[5]Conduct yourselves wisely toward outsiders, making the most of the time. [6]Let
your speech always be gracious, seasoned
with salt, so that you may know how you
ought to answer every one.

[7]Tych′icus will tell you all about my affairs; he is a beloved brother and faithful
minister and fellow servant in the Lord. [8]I
have sent him to you for this very purpose,
that you may know how we are and that he
may encourage your hearts, [9]and with him
Ones′imus, the faithful and beloved brother,
who is one of yourselves. They will tell you
of everything that has taken place here.

[10]Aristar′chus my fellow prisoner greets
you, and Mark the cousin of Barnabas
(concerning whom you have received
instructions—if he comes to you, receive
him), [11]and Jesus who is called Justus.
These are the only men of the circumcision
among my fellow workers for the kingdom
of God, and they have been a comfort to

me. [12]Ep′aphras, who is one of yourselves,
a servant of Christ Jesus, greets you, always
remembering you earnestly in his prayers,
that you may stand mature and fully
assured in all the will of God. [13]For I bear
him witness that he has worked hard for
you and for those in La-odice′a and in Hi-
erap′olis. [14]Luke the beloved physician and
Demas greet you. [15]Give my greetings to
the brethren at La-odice′a, and to Nympha
and the church in her house. [16]And when
this letter has been read among you, have it
read also in the Church of the La-odice′ans;
and see that you read also the letter from
La-odice′a. [17]And say to Archip′pus, "See
that you fulfil the ministry which you have
received in the Lord."

[18]I, Paul, write this greeting with my own
hand. Remember my chains. Grace be with
you.

REFLECTION

We often think of prophecy as simply telling the future, but a prophet is someone who accurately describes the present. Since prophets, by the grace of God, come to see with clarity what is happening, they can also predict what *will* happen. The prophets' message, therefore, remains timeless because their observations about the world and human nature remain true, and remain prophetic in any time and place. For example, Ezekiel in today's reading speaks this oracle: "Their silver and gold are not able to deliver them in the day of the wrath of the LORD" (Ez 7:19). In what age is this prophecy not true? Prophetic texts are not cryptic messages about the future for us to decode, but challenges for us here and now. In this case, Ezekiel is warning us not to become so comfortable with our state in life that we think God is superfluous. Sirach gives a similar warning: "Call no one happy before his death" (Sir 11:28). This saying suggests that even if you have fortune and health now, you may not tomorrow. The happiness of your life can only fully be measured once it has reached its conclusion. Do you ever let your material possessions become the source of your happiness?

October 20

EZEKIEL 10

**Then I looked, and behold, on
the firmament that was over
the heads of the cherubim there
appeared above them something like a
sapphire, in form resembling a throne.**
[2]And he said to the man clothed in linen,
"Go in among the whirling wheels underneath the cherubim; fill your hands with
burning coals from between the cherubim,
and scatter them over the city."

And he went in before my eyes. [3]Now the
cherubim were standing on the south side
of the house, when the man went in; and a
cloud filled the inner court. [4]And the glory of
the LORD went up from the cherubim to the
threshold of the house; and the house was
filled with the cloud, and the court was full
of the brightness of the glory of the LORD.
[5]And the sound of the wings of the cherubim
was heard as far as the outer court, like the
voice of God Almighty when he speaks.

[6]And when he commanded the man
clothed in linen, "Take fire from between
the whirling wheels, from between the
cherubim," he went in and stood beside a
wheel. [7]And a cherub stretched forth his
hand from between the cherubim to the
fire that was between the cherubim, and
took some of it, and put it into the hands
of the man clothed in linen, who took it
and went out. [8]The cherubim appeared
to have the form of a human hand under
their wings.

[9]And I looked, and behold, there were
four wheels beside the cherubim, one
beside each cherub; and the appearance of
the wheels was like sparkling chrysolite.
[10]And as for their appearance, the four
had the same likeness, as if a wheel were
within a wheel. [11]When they went, they
went in any of their four directions without
turning as they went, but in whatever
direction the front wheel faced the others

followed without turning as they went.
[12]And their rims, and their spokes, and the
wheels were full of eyes round about—the
wheels that the four of them had. [13]As for
the wheels, they were called in my hearing
the whirling wheels. [14]And every one had
four faces: the first face was the face of the
cherub, and the second face was the face of
a man, and the third the face of a lion, and
the fourth the face of an eagle.

[15]And the cherubim mounted up. These
were the living creatures that I saw by the
river Che′bar. [16]And when the cherubim
went, the wheels went beside them; and
when the cherubim lifted up their wings to
mount up from the earth, the wheels did
not turn from beside them. [17]When they
stood still, these stood still, and when they
mounted up, these mounted up with them;
for the spirit of the living creatures was
in them.

[18]Then the glory of the LORD went forth
from the threshold of the house, and stood
over the cherubim. [19]And the cherubim
lifted up their wings and mounted up from
the earth in my sight as they went forth,
with the wheels beside them; and they stood
at the door of the east gate of the house of
the LORD; and the glory of the God of Israel
was over them.

[20]These were the living creatures that I
saw underneath the God of Israel by the
river Che′bar; and I knew that they were
cherubim. [21]Each had four faces, and each
four wings, and underneath their wings
the semblance of human hands. [22]And as
for the likeness of their faces, they were the
very faces whose appearance I had seen
by the river Che′bar. They went every one
straight forward.

11 The Spirit lifted me up, and brought
me to the east gate of the house of
the LORD, which faces east. And behold, at
the door of the gateway there were twenty-
five men; and I saw among them Ja-azani′ah
the son of Azzur, and Pelati′ah the son of
Bena′iah, princes of the people. [2]And he said
to me, "Son of man, these are the men who
devise iniquity and who give wicked counsel
in this city; [3]who say, 'The time is not near
to build houses; this city is the caldron, and
we are the flesh.' [4]Therefore prophesy against
them, prophesy, O son of man."

[5]And the Spirit of the LORD fell upon
me, and he said to me, "Say, Thus says the
LORD: So you think, O house of Israel; for I
know the things that come into your mind.
[6]You have multiplied your slain in this city,
and have filled its streets with the slain.
[7]Therefore thus says the Lord GOD: Your
slain whom you have laid in the midst of
it, they are the flesh, and this city is the
caldron; but you shall be brought forth
out of the midst of it. [8]You have feared the
sword; and I will bring the sword upon you,
says the Lord GOD. [9]And I will bring you
forth out of the midst of it, and give you
into the hands of foreigners, and execute
judgments upon you. [10]You shall fall by
the sword; I will judge you at the border
of Israel; and you shall know that I am the
LORD. [11]This city shall not be your caldron,
nor shall you be the flesh in the midst of
it; I will judge you at the border of Israel;
[12]and you shall know that I am the LORD;
for you have not walked in my statutes, nor
executed my ordinances, but have acted
according to the ordinances of the nations
that are round about you."

[13]And it came to pass, while I was prophesying, that Pelati′ah the son of Bena′iah
died. Then I fell down upon my face, and
cried with a loud voice, and said, "Ah,
Lord GOD! will you make a full end of the
remnant of Israel?"

[14]And the word of the LORD came to me:
[15]"Son of man, your brethren, even your
brethren, your fellow exiles, the whole
house of Israel, all of them, are those of
whom the inhabitants of Jerusalem have
said, 'They have gone far from the LORD;
to us this land is given for a possession.'
[16]Therefore say, 'Thus says the Lord GOD:
Though I removed them far off among the
nations, and though I scattered them among
the countries, yet I have been a sanctuary
to them for a while in the countries where
they have gone.' [17]Therefore say, 'Thus
says the Lord GOD: I will gather you from
the peoples, and assemble you out of the

countries where you have been scattered,
and I will give you the land of Israel.' [18]And
when they come there, they will remove
from it all its detestable things and all its
abominations. [19]And I will give them one
heart, and put a new spirit within them; I
will take the stony heart out of their flesh
and give them a heart of flesh, [20]that they
may walk in my statutes and keep my
ordinances and obey them; and they shall
be my people, and I will be their God. [21]But
as for those whose heart goes after their
detestable things and their abominations,
I will repay their deeds upon their own
heads, says the Lord GOD."

[22]Then the cherubim lifted up their
wings, with the wheels beside them; and
the glory of the God of Israel was over
them. [23]And the glory of the LORD went up
from the midst of the city, and stood upon
the mountain which is on the east side of
the city. [24]And the Spirit lifted me up and
brought me in the vision by the Spirit of
God into Chalde′a, to the exiles. Then the
vision that I had seen went up from me.
[25]And I told the exiles all the things that the
LORD had showed me.

SIRACH 12

If you do a kindness, know to whom
you do it,
and you will be thanked for your
good deeds.
[2]Do good to a godly man, and you
will be repaid—
if not by him, certainly by the Most High.
[3]No good will come to the man who persists
in evil
or to him who does not give alms.
[4]Give to the godly man, but do not help
the sinner.
[5] Do good to the humble, but do not give
to the ungodly;
hold back his bread, and do not give
it to him,
lest by means of it he subdue you;
for you will receive twice as much evil
for all the good which you do to him.
[6]For the Most High also hates sinners
and will inflict punishment on the ungodly.
[7]Give to the good man, but do not help
the sinner.

[8]A friend will not be known in prosperity,
nor will an enemy be hidden
in adversity.
[9]A man's enemies are grieved when
he prospers,
and in his adversity even his friend will
separate from him.
[10]Never trust your enemy,
for like the rusting of copper, so is
his wickedness.
[11]Even if he humbles himself and goes
about cringing,
watch yourself, and be on your guard
against him;
and you will be to him like one who has
polished a mirror,
and you will know that it was not
hopelessly tarnished.
[12]Do not put him next to you,
lest he overthrow you and take your place;
do not have him sit at your right,
lest he try to take your seat of honor,
and at last you will realize the truth of
my words,
and be stung by what I have said.

[13]Who will pity a snake charmer bitten
by a serpent,
or any who go near wild beasts?
[14]So no one will pity a man who associates
with a sinner
and becomes involved in his sins.
[15]He will stay with you for a time,
but if you falter, he will not stand by you.

[16]An enemy will speak sweetly with his lips,
but in his mind he will plan to throw you
into a pit;
an enemy will weep with his eyes,
but if he finds an opportunity his thirst
for blood will be insatiable.
[17]If calamity befalls you, you will find him
there ahead of you;
and while pretending to help you, he will
trip you by the heel;

18he will shake his head, and clap his hands,
and whisper much, and change his
expression.

---

1 THESSALONIANS 1

**Paul, Silva′nus, and Timothy,
To the Church of the Thessa-lo′nians in God the Father and the Lord Jesus Christ:**

Grace to you and peace.

2We give thanks to God always for you all, constantly mentioning you in our prayers, 3remembering before our God and Father your work of faith and labor of love and steadfastness of hope in our Lord Jesus Christ. 4For we know, brethren beloved by God, that he has chosen you; 5for our gospel came to you not only in word, but also in power and in the Holy Spirit and with full conviction. You know what kind of men we proved to be among you for your sake. 6And you became imitators of us and of the Lord, for you received the word in much affliction, with joy inspired by the Holy Spirit; 7so that you became an example to all the believers in Macedonia and in Acha′ia. 8For not only has the word of the Lord sounded forth from you in Macedonia and Acha′ia, but your faith in God has gone forth everywhere, so that we need not say anything. 9For they themselves report concerning us what a welcome we had among you, and how you turned to God from idols, to serve a living and true God, 10and to wait for his Son from heaven, whom he raised from the dead, Jesus who delivers us from the wrath to come.

2 For you yourselves know, brethren, that our visit to you was not in vain; 2but though we had already suffered and been shamefully treated at Philip′pi, as you know, we had courage in our God to declare to you the gospel of God in the face of great opposition. 3For our appeal does not spring from error or uncleanness, nor is it made with guile; 4but just as we have been approved by God to be entrusted with the gospel, so we speak, not to please men, but to please God who tests our hearts. 5For we never used either words of flattery, as you know, or a cloak for greed, as God is witness; 6nor did we seek glory from men, whether from you or from others, though we might have made demands as apostles of Christ. 7But we were gentle among you, like a nurse taking care of her children. 8So, being affectionately desirous of you, we were ready to share with you not only the gospel of God but also our own selves, because you had become very dear to us.

9For you remember our labor and toil, brethren; we worked night and day, that we might not burden any of you, while we preached to you the gospel of God. 10You are witnesses, and God also, how holy and righteous and blameless was our behavior to you believers; 11for you know how, like a father with his children, we exhorted each one of you and encouraged you and charged you 12to walk in a manner worthy of God, who calls you into his own kingdom and glory.

13And we also thank God constantly for this, that when you received the word of God which you heard from us, you accepted it not as the word of men but as what it really is, the word of God, which is at work in you believers. 14For you, brethren, became imitators of the churches of God in Christ Jesus which are in Judea; for you suffered the same things from your own countrymen as they did from the Jews, 15who killed both the Lord Jesus and the prophets, and drove us out, and displease God and oppose all men 16by hindering us from speaking to the Gentiles that they may be saved—so as always to fill up the measure of their sins. But God's wrath has come upon them at last!

REFLECTION

The Book of Sirach tells us to "give to the godly man, but do not help the sinner" (Sir 12:4) and to "never trust your enemy" (v. 10). These statements seem to contradict the command of Christ to give to anyone who asks and to love your enemies (see Mt 5:42–43).

Although Sirach does offer sage advice for the protection of material property, Christ expands the Law so that our concern with spiritual matters relativizes some of the conventional wisdom that Sirach preserves. These words of Scripture, however, are certainly not meant to be cast aside. Christ came to fulfill the Law, not to destroy it (see v. 17). Understood in light of Christ, therefore, these words can have a spiritual sense. We should, after all, never trust our true enemy (the devil), nor should we yield anything to him. St. Paul also tells us to put off the old man (Adam) and put on the new man (Christ), and, therefore, we should in this sense give only to the godly man (Christ) and deny the sinful man (Adam) (see Rm 6:5–7; Eph 4:22–24). Ezekiel needed visions to understand God's plan, and we need grace to understand the coherency of Scripture. Do you pray before reading Scripture and ask for help in understanding a difficult passage?

October 21

EZEKIEL 12

The word of the LORD came to
me: 2"Son of man, you dwell in
the midst of a rebellious house,
who have eyes to see, but see not, who
have ears to hear, but hear not; 3for
they are a rebellious house. Therefore,
son of man, prepare for yourself an exile's
baggage, and go into exile by day in their
sight; you shall go like an exile from your
place to another place in their sight. Perhaps
they will understand, though they are a
rebellious house. 4You shall bring out your
baggage by day in their sight, as baggage
for exile; and you shall go forth yourself
at evening in their sight, as men do who
must go into exile. 5Dig through the wall in
their sight, and go out through it. 6In their
sight you shall lift the baggage upon your
shoulder, and carry it out in the dark; you
shall cover your face, that you may not see
the land; for I have made you a sign for the
house of Israel."
7And I did as I was commanded. I brought
out my baggage by day, as baggage for exile,
and in the evening I dug through the wall
with my own hands; I went forth in the
dark, carrying my outfit upon my shoulder
in their sight.
8In the morning the word of the LORD
came to me: 9"Son of man, has not the house
of Israel, the rebellious house, said to you,
'What are you doing?' 10Say to them, 'Thus
says the Lord GOD: This oracle concerns
the prince in Jerusalem and all the house of
Israel who are in it.' 11Say, 'I am a sign for
you: as I have done, so shall it be done to
them; they shall go into exile, into captivity.'
12And the prince who is among them
shall lift his baggage upon his shoulder in
the dark, and shall go forth; he shall dig
through the wall and go out through it; he
shall cover his face, that he may not see the
land with his eyes. 13And I will spread my
net over him, and he shall be taken in my
snare; and I will bring him to Babylon in the
land of the Chalde´ans, yet he shall not see
it; and he shall die there. 14And I will scatter
toward every wind all who are round about
him, his helpers and all his troops; and I
will unsheathe the sword after them. 15And
they shall know that I am the LORD, when
I disperse them among the nations and
scatter them through the countries. 16But I
will let a few of them escape from the sword,
from famine and pestilence, that they may
confess all their abominations among the
nations where they go, and may know that
I am the LORD."
17Moreover the word of the LORD came
to me: 18"Son of man, eat your bread with
quaking, and drink water with trembling
and with fearfulness; 19and say of the people
of the land, Thus says the Lord GOD concerning the inhabitants of Jerusalem in the
land of Israel: They shall eat their bread
with fearfulness, and drink water in dismay,
because their land will be stripped of all it
contains, on account of the violence of all

those who dwell in it. 20And the inhabited
cities shall be laid waste, and the land shall
become a desolation; and you shall know
that I am the LORD."
21And the word of the LORD came to me:
22"Son of man, what is this proverb that you
have about the land of Israel, saying, 'The
days grow long, and every vision comes
to nothing'? 23Tell them therefore, 'Thus
says the Lord GOD: I will put an end to this
proverb, and they shall no more use it as a
proverb in Israel.' But say to them, The days
are at hand, and the fulfilment of every vision.
24For there shall be no more any false vision
or flattering divination within the house of
Israel. 25But I the LORD will speak the word
which I will speak, and it will be performed.
It will no longer be delayed, but in your days,
O rebellious house, I will speak the word and
perform it, says the Lord GOD."
26Again the word of the LORD came to me:
27"Son of man, behold, they of the house of
Israel say, 'The vision that he sees is for many
days hence, and he prophesies of times far
off.' 28Therefore say to them, Thus says the
Lord GOD: None of my words will be delayed
any longer, but the word which I speak will
be performed, says the Lord GOD."

13 The word of the LORD came to me:
2"Son of man, prophesy against the
prophets of Israel, prophesy and say to
those who prophesy out of their own minds:
'Hear the word of the LORD!' 3Thus says the
Lord GOD, Woe to the foolish prophets
who follow their own spirit, and have seen
nothing! 4Your prophets have been like
foxes among ruins, O Israel. 5You have not
gone up into the breaches, or built up a wall
for the house of Israel, that it might stand
in battle in the day of the LORD. 6They have
spoken falsehood and divined a lie; they say,
'Says the LORD,' when the LORD has not sent
them, and yet they expect him to fulfil their
word. 7Have you not seen a delusive vision,
and uttered a lying divination, whenever
you have said, 'Says the LORD,' although I
have not spoken?"
8Therefore thus says the Lord God: "Because you have uttered delusions and seen
lies, therefore behold, I am against you, says
the Lord GOD. 9My hand will be against the
prophets who see delusive visions and who
give lying divinations; they shall not be in
the council of my people, nor be enrolled in
the register of the house of Israel, nor shall
they enter the land of Israel; and you shall
know that I am the Lord GOD. 10Because,
yes, because they have misled my people,
saying, 'Peace,' when there is no peace; and
because, when the people build a wall, these
prophets daub it with whitewash; 11say to
those who daub it with whitewash that
it shall fall! There will be a deluge of rain,
great hailstones will fall, and a stormy wind
break out; 12and when the wall falls, will it
not be said to you, 'Where is the daubing
with which you daubed it?' 13Therefore thus
says the Lord GOD: I will make a stormy
wind break out in my wrath; and there shall
be a deluge of rain in my anger, and great
hailstones in wrath to destroy it. 14And I will
break down the wall that you have daubed
with whitewash, and bring it down to the
ground, so that its foundation will be laid
bare; when it falls, you shall perish in the
midst of it; and you shall know that I am the
LORD. 15Thus will I spend my wrath upon
the wall, and upon those who have daubed
it with whitewash; and I will say to you,
The wall is no more, nor those who daubed
it, 16the prophets of Israel who prophesied
concerning Jerusalem and saw visions of
peace for her, when there was no peace, says
the Lord GOD.
17"And you, son of man, set your face against
the daughters of your people, who prophesy
out of their own minds; prophesy against them
18and say, Thus says the Lord GOD: Woe to the
women who sew magic bands upon all wrists,
and make veils for the heads of persons of every
stature, in the hunt for souls! Will you hunt
down souls belonging to my people, and keep
other souls alive for your profit? 19You have
profaned me among my people for handfuls of
barley and for pieces of bread, putting to death
persons who should not die and keeping alive
persons who should not live, by your lies to my
people, who listen to lies.
20"Wherefore thus says the Lord GOD:
Behold, I am against your magic bands with

which you hunt the souls, and I will tear
them from your arms; and I will let the souls
that you hunt go free like birds. 21 Your veils
also I will tear off, and deliver my people
out of your hand, and they shall be no more
in your hand as prey; and you shall know
that I am the LORD. 22 Because you have
disheartened the righteous falsely, although
I have not disheartened him, and you have
encouraged the wicked, that he should not
turn from his wicked way to save his life;
23 therefore you shall no more see delusive
visions nor practice divination; I will deliver
my people out of your hand. Then you will
know that I am the LORD."

SIRACH 13

Whoever touches pitch will be defiled,
  and whoever associates with a proud man will become like him.
2 Do not lift a weight beyond your strength,
  nor associate with a man mightier and richer than you.
How can the clay pot associate with the iron kettle?
  The pot will strike against it, and will itself be broken.
3 A rich man does wrong, and he even adds reproaches;
  a poor man suffers wrong, and he must add apologies.
4 A rich man will exploit you if you can be of use to him,
  but if you are in need he will forsake you.
5 If you own something, he will live with you;
  he will drain your resources and he will not care.
6 When he needs you he will deceive you,
  he will smile at you and give you hope.
He will speak to you kindly and say, "What do you need?"
7 He will shame you with his foods,
  until he has drained you two or three times;
  and finally he will deride you.
Should he see you afterwards, he will forsake you,
  and shake his head at you.
8 Take care not to be led astray,
  and not to be humiliated in your feasting.
9 When a powerful man invites you, be reserved;
  and he will invite you the more often.
10 Do not push forward, lest you be repulsed;
  and do not remain at a distance, lest you be forgotten.
11 Do not try to treat him as an equal,
  nor trust his abundance of words;
for he will test you through much talk,
  and while he smiles he will be examining you.
12 Cruel is he who does not keep words to himself;
  he will not hesitate to injure or to imprison.
13 Keep words to yourself and be very watchful,
  for you are walking about with your own downfall.

15 Every creature loves its like,
  and every person his neighbor;
16 all living beings associate by species,
  and a man clings to one like himself.
17 What fellowship has a wolf with a lamb?
  No more has a sinner with a godly man.
18 What peace is there between a hyena and a dog?
  And what peace between a rich man and a poor man?
19 Wild donkeys in the wilderness are the prey of lions;
  likewise the poor are pastures for the rich.
20 Humility is an abomination to a proud man;
  likewise a poor man is an abomination to a rich one.

1 THESSALONIANS 2

17 But since we were deprived of
you, brethren, for a short time,
in person not in heart, we endeavored
the more eagerly and with great desire
to see you face to face; 18 because we wanted
to come to you—I, Paul, again and again—
but Satan hindered us. 19 For what is our
hope or joy or crown of boasting before our

Lord Jesus at his coming? Is it not you? 20For
you are our glory and joy.
3 Therefore when we could bear it no
longer, we were willing to be left behind
at Athens alone, 2and we sent Timothy, our
brother and God's servant in the gospel of
Christ, to establish you in your faith and to
exhort you, 3that no one be moved by these
afflictions. You yourselves know that this is
to be our lot. 4For when we were with you,
we told you beforehand that we were to
suffer affliction; just as it has come to pass,
and as you know. 5For this reason, when I
could bear it no longer, I sent that I might
know your faith, for fear that somehow the
tempter had tempted you and that our labor
would be in vain.
6But now that Timothy has come to us
from you, and has brought us the good news
of your faith and love and reported that you
always remember us kindly and long to see
us, as we long to see you—7for this reason,
brethren, in all our distress and affliction
we have been comforted about you through
your faith; 8for now we live, if you stand fast
in the Lord. 9For what thanksgiving can
we render to God for you, for all the joy
which we feel for your sake before our God,
10praying earnestly night and day that we
may see you face to face and supply what is
lacking in your faith?
11Now may our God and Father himself,
and our Lord Jesus, direct our way to you;
12and may the Lord make you increase
and abound in love to one another and to
all men, as we do to you, 13so that he may
establish your hearts unblamable in holiness
before our God and Father, at the coming of
our Lord Jesus with all his saints.

REFLECTION

Today the Book of Sirach uses a vivid image to warn us against throwing our lot in with the proud: "Whoever touches pitch will be defiled, and whoever associates with a proud man will become like him" (Sir 13:1). We have all had experiences of being around people who gossip and complain, and we can find ourselves drawn into their mindset, stuck in their pitch, and we soon complain and gossip along with them. Likewise, if we spend our time around those who prioritize wealth and power, we may find ourselves captivated by their lifestyle and influenced to order other things ahead of God and neighbor. If a proud man is like a tar that mires us, then perhaps a prophet could be described as a fire that purifies us. If we spent our time with Ezekiel, for example, we would be forced to pack our bags and climb through a hole in the wall, but he will also lead us to a place of greater trust in God, rather than a greater trust in earthly possessions. Do you trust and listen to the prophets in your life, or to the proud?

October 22

EZEKIEL 14

**Then came certain of the elders
of Israel to me; and sat before
me. 2And the word of the LORD
came to me: 3"Son of man, these men have
taken their idols into their hearts, and
set the stumbling block of their iniquity**
before their faces; should I let myself be
inquired of at all by them? 4Therefore speak
to them, and say to them, Thus says the
Lord GOD: Any man of the house of Israel
who takes his idols into his heart and sets
the stumbling block of his iniquity before
his face, and yet comes to the prophet, I the
LORD will answer him myself because of the
multitude of his idols, 5that I may lay hold of
the hearts of the house of Israel, who are all
estranged from me through their idols.
6"Therefore say to the house of Israel,
Thus says the Lord GOD: Repent and turn
away from your idols; and turn away your
faces from all your abominations. 7For any
one of the house of Israel, or of the strangers that sojourn in Israel, who separates

himself from me, taking his idols into his heart and putting the stumbling block of his iniquity before his face, and yet comes to a prophet to inquire for himself of me, I the LORD will answer him myself; [8]and I will set my face against that man, I will make him a sign and a byword and cut him off from the midst of my people; and you shall know that I am the LORD. [9]And if the prophet be deceived and speak a word, I, the LORD, have deceived that prophet, and I will stretch out my hand against him, and will destroy him from the midst of my people Israel. [10]And they shall bear their punishment—the punishment of the prophet and the punishment of the inquirer shall be alike—[11]that the house of Israel may go no more astray from me, nor defile themselves any more with all their transgressions, but that they may be my people and I may be their God, says the Lord GOD."

[12]And the word of the LORD came to me: [13]"Son of man, when a land sins against me by acting faithlessly, and I stretch out my hand against it, and break its staff of bread and send famine upon it, and cut off from it man and beast, [14]even if these three men, Noah, Daniel, and Job, were in it, they would deliver but their own lives by their righteousness, says the Lord GOD. [15]If I cause wild beasts to pass through the land, and they ravage it, and it be made desolate, so that no man may pass through because of the beasts; [16]even if these three men were in it, as I live, says the Lord GOD, they would deliver neither sons nor daughters; they alone would be delivered, but the land would be desolate. [17]Or if I bring a sword upon that land, and say, Let a sword go through the land; and I cut off from it man and beast; [18]though these three men were in it, as I live, says the Lord GOD, they would deliver neither sons nor daughters, but they alone would be delivered. [19]Or if I send a pestilence into that land, and pour out my wrath upon it with blood, to cut off from it man and beast; [20]even if Noah, Daniel, and Job were in it, as I live, says the Lord GOD, they would deliver neither son nor daughter; they would deliver but their own lives by their righteousness.

[21]"For thus says the Lord GOD: How much more when I send upon Jerusalem my four sore acts of judgment, sword, famine, evil beasts, and pestilence, to cut off from it man and beast! [22]Yet, if there should be left in it any survivors to lead out sons and daughters, when they come forth to you, and you see their ways and their doings, you will be consoled for the evil that I have brought upon Jerusalem, for all that I have brought upon it. [23]They will console you, when you see their ways and their doings; and you shall know that I have not done without cause all that I have done in it, says the Lord GOD."

15 And the word of the LORD came to me: [2]"Son of man, how does the wood of the vine surpass any wood, the vine branch which is among the trees of the forest? [3]Is wood taken from it to make anything? Do men take a peg from it to hang any vessel on? [4]Behold, it is given to the fire for fuel; when the fire has consumed both ends of it, and the middle of it is charred, is it useful for anything? [5]Behold, when it was whole, it was used for nothing; how much less, when the fire has consumed it and it is charred, can it ever be used for anything! [6]Therefore thus says the Lord GOD: Like the wood of the vine among the trees of the forest, which I have given to the fire for fuel, so will I give up the inhabitants of Jerusalem. [7]And I will set my face against them; though they escape from the fire, the fire shall yet consume them; and you will know that I am the LORD, when I set my face against them. [8]And I will make the land desolate, because they have acted faithlessly, says the Lord GOD."

SIRACH 13

[21]When a rich man totters, he is steadied
by friends,
but when a humble man falls, he is even
pushed away by friends.

[22]If a rich man slips, his helpers are many;
he speaks unseemly words, and they justify him.
If a humble man slips, they even reproach him;
he speaks sensibly, and receives no attention.
[23]When the rich man speaks all are silent,
and they extol to the clouds what he says.
When the poor man speaks they say, "Who is this fellow?"
And should he stumble, they even push him down.
[24]Riches are good if they are free from sin,
and poverty is evil in the opinion of the ungodly.
[25]A man's heart changes his countenance,
either for good or for evil.
[26]The mark of a happy heart is a cheerful face,
but to devise proverbs requires painful thinking.

14 Blessed is the man who does not blunder with his lips
and need not suffer grief for sin.
[2]Blessed is he whose heart does not condemn him,
and who has not given up his hope.

[3]Riches are not seemly for a stingy man;
and of what use is property to an envious man?
[4]Whoever accumulates by depriving himself, accumulates for others;
and others will live in luxury on his goods.
[5]If a man is mean to himself, to whom will he be generous?
He will not enjoy his own riches.
[6]No one is meaner than the man who is grudging to himself,
and this is the retribution for his baseness;
[7]even if he does good, he does it unintentionally,
and betrays his baseness in the end.
[8]Evil is the man with a grudging eye;
he averts his face and disregards people.
[9]A greedy man's eye is not satisfied with a portion,
and mean injustice withers the soul.
[10]A stingy man's eye begrudges bread,
and it is lacking at his table.

[11]My son, treat yourself well, according to your means,
and present worthy offerings to the Lord.
[12]Remember that death will not delay,
and the decree of Hades has not been shown to you.
[13]Do good to a friend before you die,
and reach out and give to him as much as you can.
[14]Do not deprive yourself of a happy day;
let not your share of desired good pass by you.
[15]Will you not leave the fruit of your labors to another,
and what you acquired by toil to be divided by lot?
[16]Give, and take, and beguile yourself,
because in Hades one cannot look for luxury.
[17]All living beings become old like a garment,
for the decree from of old is, "You must surely die!"
[18]Like flourishing leaves on a spreading tree
which sheds some and puts forth others,
so are the generations of flesh and blood:
one dies and another is born.
[19]Every product decays and ceases to exist,
and the man who made it will pass away with it.

1 THESSALONIANS 4

Finally, brethren, we beg and exhort you in the Lord Jesus, that as you learned from us how you ought to walk and to please God, just
as you are doing, you do so more and more.
[2]For you know what instructions we gave you
through the Lord Jesus. [3]For this is the will of
God, your sanctification: that you abstain from
immorality; [4]that each one of you know how
to control his own body in holiness and honor,
[5]not in the passion of lust like heathens who do
not know God; [6]that no man transgress, and
wrong his brother in this matter, because the

Lord is an avenger in all these things, as we solemnly forewarned you. 7For God has not called
us for uncleanness, but in holiness. 8Therefore
whoever disregards this, disregards not man
but God, who gives his Holy Spirit to you.
9But concerning love of the brethren you
have no need to have any one write to you,
for you yourselves have been taught by God
to love one another; 10and indeed you do
love all the brethren throughout Macedonia.
But we exhort you, brethren, to do so more
and more, 11to aspire to live quietly, to mind
your own affairs, and to work with your
hands, as we charged you; 12so that you may
command the respect of outsiders, and be
dependent on nobody.
13But we would not have you ignorant,
brethren, concerning those who are asleep,
that you may not grieve as others do who
have no hope. 14For since we believe that
Jesus died and rose again, even so, through
Jesus, God will bring with him those who
have fallen asleep. 15For this we declare to
you by the word of the Lord, that we who
are alive, who are left until the coming of the
Lord, shall not precede those who have fallen
asleep. 16For the Lord himself will descend
from heaven with a cry of command, with
the archangel's call, and with the sound of
the trumpet of God. And the dead in Christ
will rise first; 17then we who are alive, who are
left, shall be caught up together with them in
the clouds to meet the Lord in the air; and so
we shall always be with the Lord. 18Therefore
comfort one another with these words.
5 But as to the times and the seasons,
brethren, you have no need to have anything
written to you. 2For you yourselves know well
that the day of the Lord will come like a thief
in the night. 3When people say, "There is peace
and security," then sudden destruction will
come upon them as labor pains come upon a
woman with child, and there will be no escape.
4But you are not in darkness, brethren, for that
day to surprise you like a thief. 5For you are all
sons of light and sons of the day; we are not
of the night or of darkness. 6So then let us not
sleep, as others do, but let us keep awake and be
sober. 7For those who sleep sleep at night, and
those who get drunk are drunk at night. 8But,
since we belong to the day, let us be sober, and
put on the breastplate of faith and love, and
for a helmet the hope of salvation. 9For God
has not destined us for wrath, but to obtain
salvation through our Lord Jesus Christ, 10who
died for us so that whether we wake or sleep
we might live with him. 11Therefore encourage
one another and build one another up, just as
you are doing.

REFLECTION

We have all witnessed the strange phenomenon known as celebrity endorsement, that is, when a company hires someone famous to be its spokesperson. This person is almost never an expert in the type of product he or she is selling. What difference should it make to me if my favorite actor drives a certain kind of car or wears a certain perfume? We, at some level, know the answer, and the Book of Sirach explains it concisely: we will listen to a rich person and not a poor one (see Sir 13:23). We respect those who have worldly success and ignore those who do not, and we do this almost instinctively. It is for this reason that the prophets are ignored, and even righteous men like Daniel, Job, and Noah would not have been able to turn aside the judgment coming on Israel (see Ez 14:14). As Christians, we must therefore be vigilant, as St. Paul instructs, because "the day of the Lord will come like a thief in the night" (1 Thes 5:2). We must pursue truth and be on our guard against the endless vanities that surround us. How much time do you spend listening to those on television or social media? Do you ever ignore a person who seems unimportant or has no worldly prestige?

October 23

EZEKIEL 16

**Again the word of the LORD
came to me: 2"Son of man, make
known to Jerusalem her abominations,
3and say, Thus says the Lord GOD to**

Jerusalem: Your origin and your birth are
of the land of the Canaanites; your father
was an Am′orite, and your mother a Hittite.
4And as for your birth, on the day you were
born your navel string was not cut, nor were
you washed with water to cleanse you, nor
rubbed with salt, nor swathed with bands.
5No eye pitied you, to do any of these things
to you out of compassion for you; but you
were cast out on the open field, for you were
abhorred, on the day that you were born.
6"And when I passed by you, and saw you
weltering in your blood, I said to you in your
blood, 'Live, 7and grow up like a plant of the
field.' And you grew up and became tall and
arrived at full maidenhood; your breasts
were formed, and your hair had grown; yet
you were naked and bare.
8"When I passed by you again and looked
upon you, behold, you were at the age for love;
and I spread my skirt over you, and covered
your nakedness: yes, I pledged myself to you
and entered into a covenant with you, says
the Lord GOD, and you became mine. 9Then
I bathed you with water and washed off your
blood from you, and anointed you with
oil. 10I clothed you also with embroidered
cloth and shod you with leather, I wrapped
you in fine linen and covered you with silk.
11And I decked you with ornaments, and put
bracelets on your arms, and a chain on your
neck. 12And I put a ring on your nose, and
earrings in your ears, and a beautiful crown
upon your head. 13Thus you were decked
with gold and silver; and your clothing was
of fine linen, and silk, and embroidered
cloth; you ate fine flour and honey and oil.
You grew exceedingly beautiful, and came to
regal estate. 14And your renown went forth
among the nations because of your beauty,
for it was perfect through the splendor which
I had bestowed upon you, says the Lord GOD.
15"But you trusted in your beauty, and
played the harlot because of your renown,
and lavished your harlotries on any passer-
by. 16You took some of your garments, and
made for yourself gaily decked shrines, and
on them played the harlot; the like has never
been, nor ever shall be. 17You also took your
fair jewels of my gold and of my silver, which
I had given you, and made for yourself
images of men, and with them played the
harlot; 18and you took your embroidered
garments to cover them, and set my oil and
my incense before them. 19Also my bread
which I gave you—I fed you with fine flour
and oil and honey—you set before them for
a pleasing odor, says the Lord GOD. 20And
you took your sons and your daughters,
whom you had borne to me, and these you
sacrificed to them to be devoured. Were
your harlotries so small a matter 21that you
slaughtered my children and delivered them
up as an offering by fire to them? 22And in all
your abominations and your harlotries you
did not remember the days of your youth,
when you were naked and bare, weltering in
your blood.
23"And after all your wickedness (woe,
woe to you! says the Lord GOD), 24you
built yourself a vaulted chamber, and made
yourself a lofty place in every square; 25at
the head of every street you built your lofty
place and prostituted your beauty, offering
yourself to any passer-by, and multiplying
your harlotry. 26You also played the harlot
with the Egyptians, your lustful neighbors,
multiplying your harlotry, to provoke me
to anger. 27Behold, therefore, I stretched out
my hand against you, and diminished your
allotted portion, and delivered you to the
greed of your enemies, the daughters of the
Philis′tines, who were ashamed of your lewd
behavior. 28You played the harlot also with
the Assyrians, because you were insatiable;
yes, you played the harlot with them, and
still you were not satisfied. 29You multiplied
your harlotry also with the trading land
of Chalde′a; and even with this you were
not satisfied.
30"How lovesick is your heart, says the
Lord GOD, seeing you did all these things,
the deeds of a brazen harlot; 31building your
vaulted chamber at the head of every street,
and making your lofty place in every square.
Yet you were not like a harlot, because you
scorned hire. 32Adulterous wife, who receives
strangers instead of her husband! 33Men give
gifts to all harlots; but you gave your gifts to
all your lovers, bribing them to come to you

from every side for your harlotries. [34]So you
were different from other women in your
harlotries: none solicited you to play the
harlot; and you gave hire, while no hire was
given to you; therefore you were different.
[35]"Wherefore, O harlot, hear the word of
the LORD: [36]Thus says the Lord GOD, Because
your shame was laid bare and your nakedness
uncovered in your harlotries with your lovers,
and because of all your idols, and because of
the blood of your children that you gave to
them, [37]therefore, behold, I will gather all
your lovers, with whom you took pleasure, all
those you loved and all those you loathed; I
will gather them against you from every side,
and will uncover your nakedness to them,
that they may see all your nakedness. [38]And I
will judge you as women who break wedlock
and shed blood are judged, and bring upon
you the blood of wrath and jealousy. [39]And
I will give you into the hand of your lovers,
and they shall throw down your vaulted
chamber and break down your lofty places;
they shall strip you of your clothes and take
your fair jewels, and leave you naked and
bare. [40]They shall bring up a host against
you, and they shall stone you and cut you
to pieces with their swords. [41]And they shall
burn your houses and execute judgments
upon you in the sight of many women; I will
make you stop playing the harlot, and you
shall also give hire no more. [42]So will I satisfy
my fury on you, and my jealousy shall depart
from you; I will be calm, and will no more be
angry. [43]Because you have not remembered
the days of your youth, but have enraged me
with all these things; therefore, behold, I will
repay your deeds upon your head, says the
Lord GOD.

"Have you not committed lewdness in
addition to all your abominations? [44]Be-
hold, every one who uses proverbs will use
this proverb about you, 'Like mother, like
daughter.' [45]You are the daughter of your
mother, who loathed her husband and
her children; and you are the sister of your
sisters, who loathed their husbands and their
children. Your mother was a Hit′tite and your
father an Am′orite. [46]And your elder sister is
Samar′ia, who lived with her daughters to
the north of you; and your younger sister,
who lived to the south of you, is Sodom with
her daughters. [47]Yet you were not content to
walk in their ways, or do according to their
abominations; within a very little time you
were more corrupt than they in all your ways.
[48]As I live, says the Lord GOD, your sister
Sodom and her daughters have not done as
you and your daughters have done. [49]Behold,
this was the guilt of your sister Sodom: she
and her daughters had pride, surfeit of food,
and prosperous ease, but did not aid the
poor and needy. [50]They were haughty, and
did abominable things before me; therefore
I removed them, when I saw it. [51]Samar′ia
has not committed half your sins; you have
committed more abominations than they,
and have made your sisters appear righteous
by all the abominations which you have
committed. [52]Bear your disgrace, you also, for
you have made judgment favorable to your
sisters; because of your sins in which you
acted more abominably than they, they are
more in the right than you. So be ashamed,
you also, and bear your disgrace, for you have
made your sisters appear righteous.

[53]"I will restore their fortunes, both the
fortunes of Sodom and her daughters, and
the fortunes of Samar′ia and her daughters,
and I will restore your own fortunes in
the midst of them, [54]that you may bear
your disgrace and be ashamed of all that
you have done, becoming a consolation to
them. [55]As for your sisters, Sodom and her
daughters shall return to their former estate,
and Samar′ia and her daughters shall return
to their former estate; and you and your
daughters shall return to your former estate.
[56]Was not your sister Sodom a byword
in your mouth in the day of your pride,
[57]before your wickedness was uncovered?
Now you have become like her an object of
reproach for the daughters of E′dom and all
her neighbors, and for the daughters of the
Philis′tines, those round about who despise
you. [58]You bear the penalty of your lewdness
and your abominations, says the LORD.

[59]"Yes, thus says the Lord GOD: I will
deal with you as you have done, who have
despised the oath in breaking the covenant,

[60]yet I will remember my covenant with
you in the days of your youth, and I will
establish with you an everlasting covenant.
[61]Then you will remember your ways, and
be ashamed when I take your sisters, both
your elder and your younger, and give them
to you as daughters, but not on account of
the covenant with you. [62]I will establish my
covenant with you, and you shall know that
I am the LORD, [63]that you may remember
and be confounded, and never open your
mouth again because of your shame, when
I forgive you all that you have done, says the
Lord GOD."

SIRACH 14

[20]Blessed is the man who meditates
on wisdom
and who reasons intelligently.
[21]He who reflects in his mind on her ways
will also ponder her secrets.
[22]Pursue wisdom like a hunter,
and lie in wait on her paths.
[23]He who peers through her windows
will also listen at her doors;
[24]he who encamps near her house
will also fasten his tent peg to her walls;
[25]he will pitch his tent near her,
and will lodge in an excellent on
on place;
[26]he will place his children under her shelter,
and will camp under her boughs;
[27]he will be sheltered by her from
the heat,
and will dwell in the midst of her glory.

1 THESSALONIANS 5

[12]But we beg you, brethren,
to respect those who labor
among you and are over you in
the Lord and admonish you,
[13]and to esteem them very highly in
love because of their work. Be at peace
among yourselves. [14]And we exhort you,
brethren, admonish the idle, encourage
the fainthearted, help the weak, be patient
with them all. [15]See that none of you repays
evil for evil, but always seek to do good to
one another and to all. [16]Rejoice always,
[17]pray constantly, [18]give thanks in all
circumstances; for this is the will of God in
Christ Jesus for you. [19]Do not quench the
Spirit, [20]do not despise prophesying, [21]but
test everything; hold fast what is good,
[22]abstain from every form of evil.
[23]May the God of peace himself sanctify
you wholly; and may your spirit and soul
and body be kept sound and blameless at
the coming of our Lord Jesus Christ. [24]He
who calls you is faithful, and he will do it.
[25]Brethren, pray for us.
[26]Greet all the brethren with a holy kiss.
[27]I adjure you by the Lord that this letter
be read to all the brethren.
[28]The grace of our Lord Jesus Christ be
with you.

REFLECTION

In Ezekiel, Israel is compared to a woman who has been nurtured and loved by God, given the finest clothing and food, but who worships and abuses the fine things she has received rather than love God for them. The image is one of extreme ingratitude. Although St. Paul tells us not to repay evil with evil (see 1 Thes 5:15), Israel has done even worse, because they have repaid good with evil. Since the woman in Ezekiel's parable is so thankless, perhaps we think there is little comparison between her actions and ours; but we too are often the least grateful to those who have done the most for us: God, our spouse, our parents, or our dearest friends. We can come to take those closest to us for granted, and even to attribute to ourselves things that others have given to us. Therefore, if we lose patience with aging parents, a careless spouse, or even with God himself, let us keep this powerful image of the ungrateful woman from Ezekiel before us as a warning because we would not want to find ourselves likened to her. Is there someone in your life who could benefit from a show of your appreciation?

October 24

EZEKIEL 17

The word of the LORD came to
me: 2“Son of man, propound a
riddle, and speak an allegory
to the house of Israel; 3say, Thus says
the Lord GOD: A great eagle with
great wings and long pinions, rich in
plumage of many colors, came to Lebanon
and took the top of the cedar; 4he broke off
the topmost of its young twigs and carried
it to a land of trade, and set it in a city of
merchants. 5Then he took of the seed of the
land and planted it in fertile soil; he placed
it beside abundant waters. He set it like a
willow twig, 6and it sprouted and became a
low spreading vine, and its branches turned
toward him, and its roots remained where
it stood. So it became a vine, and brought
forth branches and put forth foliage.

7“But there was another great eagle with
great wings and much plumage; and behold,
this vine bent its roots toward him, and
shot forth its branches toward him that he
might water it. From the bed where it was
planted 8he transplanted it to good soil by
abundant waters, that it might bring forth
branches, and bear fruit, and become a
noble vine. 9Say, Thus says the Lord GOD:
Will it thrive? Will he not pull up its roots
and cut off its branches, so that all its fresh
sprouting leaves wither? It will not take a
strong arm or many people to pull it from
its roots. 10Behold, when it is transplanted,
will it thrive? Will it not utterly wither when
the east wind strikes it—wither away on the
bed where it grew?”

11Then the word of the LORD came to
me: 12“Say now to the rebellious house, Do
you not know what these things mean? Tell
them, Behold, the king of Babylon came to
Jerusalem, and took her king and her princes
and brought them to him to Babylon. 13And
he took one of the royal offspring and made a
covenant with him, putting him under oath.
(The chief men of the land he had taken
away, 14that the kingdom might be humble
and not lift itself up, and that by keeping his
covenant it might stand.) 15But he rebelled
against him by sending ambassadors to
Egypt, that they might give him horses and
a large army. Will he succeed? Can a man
escape who does such things? Can he break
the covenant and yet escape? 16As I live, says
the Lord GOD, surely in the place where the
king dwells who made him king, whose oath
he despised, and whose covenant with him
he broke, in Babylon he shall die. 17Pharaoh
with his mighty army and great company
will not help him in war, when mounds
are cast up and siege walls built to cut off
many lives. 18Because he despised the oath
and broke the covenant, because he gave his
hand and yet did all these things, he shall
not escape. 19Therefore thus says the Lord
GOD: As I live, surely my oath which he
despised, and my covenant which he broke,
I will repay upon his head. 20I will spread my
net over him, and he shall be taken in my
snare, and I will bring him to Babylon and
enter into judgment with him there for the
treason he has committed against me. 21And
all the pick of his troops shall fall by the
sword, and the survivors shall be scattered
to every wind; and you shall know that I, the
LORD, have spoken.”

22Thus says the Lord GOD: “I myself will
take a sprig from the lofty top of the cedar,
and will set it out; I will break off from the
topmost of its young twigs a tender one, and
I myself will plant it upon a high and lofty
mountain; 23on the mountain height of Israel
will I plant it, that it may bring forth boughs
and bear fruit, and become a noble cedar;
and under it will dwell all kinds of beasts; in
the shade of its branches birds of every sort
will nest. 24And all the trees of the field shall
know that I the LORD bring low the high
tree, and make high the low tree, dry up the
green tree, and make the dry tree flourish. I
the LORD have spoken, and I will do it.”

18 The word of the LORD came to me
again: 2“What do you mean by repeating this proverb concerning the land of
Israel, ‘The fathers have eaten sour grapes,

and the children's teeth are set on edge'? [3]As I live, says the Lord GOD, this proverb shall no more be used by you in Israel. [4]Behold, all souls are mine; the soul of the father as well as the soul of the son is mine: the soul that sins shall die.

[5]"If a man is righteous and does what is lawful and right—[6]if he does not eat upon the mountains or lift up his eyes to the idols of the house of Israel, does not defile his neighbor's wife or approach a woman in her time of impurity, [7]does not oppress any one, but restores to the debtor his pledge, commits no robbery, gives his bread to the hungry and covers the naked with a garment, [8]does not lend at interest or take any increase, withholds his hand from iniquity, executes true justice between man and man, [9]walks in my statutes, and is careful to observe my ordinances—he is righteous, he shall surely live, says the Lord GOD.

[10]"If he begets a son who is a robber, a shedder of blood, [11]who does none of these duties, but eats upon the mountains, defiles his neighbor's wife, [12]oppresses the poor and needy, commits robbery, does not restore the pledge, lifts up his eyes to the idols, commits abomination, [13]lends at interest, and takes increase; shall he then live? He shall not live. He has done all these abominable things; he shall surely die; his blood shall be upon himself.

[14]"But if this man begets a son who sees all the sins which his father has done, and fears, and does not do likewise, [15]who does not eat upon the mountains or lift up his eyes to the idols of the house of Israel, does not defile his neighbor's wife, [16]does not wrong any one, exacts no pledge, commits no robbery, but gives his bread to the hungry and covers the naked with a garment, [17]withholds his hand from iniquity, takes no interest or increase, observes my ordinances, and walks in my statutes; he shall not die for his father's iniquity; he shall surely live. [18]As for his father, because he practiced extortion, robbed his brother, and did what is not good among his people, behold, he shall die for his iniquity.

[19]"Yet you say, 'Why should not the son suffer for the iniquity of the father?' When the son has done what is lawful and right, and has been careful to observe all my statutes, he shall surely live. [20]The soul that sins shall die. The son shall not suffer for the iniquity of the father, nor the father suffer for the iniquity of the son; the righteousness of the righteous shall be upon himself, and the wickedness of the wicked shall be upon himself.

[21]"But if a wicked man turns away from all his sins which he has committed and keeps all my statutes and does what is lawful and right, he shall surely live; he shall not die. [22]None of the transgressions which he has committed shall be remembered against him; for the righteousness which he has done he shall live. [23]Have I any pleasure in the death of the wicked, says the Lord GOD, and not rather that he should turn from his way and live? [24]But when a righteous man turns away from his righteousness and commits iniquity and does the same abominable things that the wicked man does, shall he live? None of the righteous deeds which he has done shall be remembered; for the treachery of which he is guilty and the sin he has committed, he shall die.

[25]"Yet you say, 'The way of the Lord is not just.' Hear now, O house of Israel: Is my way not just? Is it not your ways that are not just? [26]When a righteous man turns away from his righteousness and commits iniquity, he shall die for it; for the iniquity which he has committed he shall die. [27]Again, when a wicked man turns away from the wickedness he has committed and does what is lawful and right, he shall save his life. [28]Because he considered and turned away from all the transgressions which he had committed, he shall surely live, he shall not die. [29]Yet the house of Israel says, 'The way of the Lord is not just.' O house of Israel, are my ways not just? Is it not your ways that are not just?

[30]"Therefore I will judge you, O house of Israel, every one according to his ways, says the Lord GOD. Repent and turn from all your transgressions, lest iniquity be your ruin. [31]Cast away from you all the transgressions

which you have committed against me, and
get yourselves a new heart and a new spirit!
Why will you die, O house of Israel? 32 For
I have no pleasure in the death of any one,
says the Lord GOD; so turn, and live."

SIRACH 15

The man who fears the Lord will do this,
and he who holds to the law will obtain
wisdom.
2 She will come to meet him like a mother,
and like the wife of his youth she will
welcome him.
3 She will feed him with the bread of
understanding,
and give him the water of wisdom to drink.
4 He will lean on her and will not fall,
and he will rely on her and will not be put
to shame.
5 She will exalt him above his neighbors,
and will open his mouth in the midst of
the assembly;
she will fill him with a spirit of wisdom
and understanding,
and clothe him with a robe of glory.
6 He will find gladness and a crown
of rejoicing,
and will acquire an everlasting name.
7 Foolish men will not obtain her,
and sinful men will not see her.
8 She is far from men of pride,
and liars will never think of her.
9 A hymn of praise is not fitting on the lips
of a sinner,
for it has not been sent from the Lord.
10 For a hymn of praise should be uttered
in wisdom,
and the Lord will prosper it.

11 Do not say, "Because of the Lord I left the
right way";
for he will not do what he hates.
12 Do not say, "It was he who led me astray";
for he has no need of a sinful man.
13 The Lord hates all abominations,
and they are not loved by those who
fear him.
14 It was he who created man in the
beginning,
and he left him in the power of his
own inclination.
15 If you will, you can keep the
commandments, they will save you;
if you trust in God, you too shall live.
16 He has placed before you fire and water:
stretch out your hand for whichever
you wish.
17 Before a man are life and death, good and evil,
and whichever he chooses will be given
to him.
18 For great is the wisdom of the Lord;
he is mighty in power and sees everything.
19 The eyes of the Lord are on those who
fear him,
and he knows every deed of man.
20 He has not commanded any one to be
ungodly,
and he has not given any one permission
to sin.

2 THESSALONIANS 1

**Paul, Silva´nus, and Timothy,
To the Church of the Thes-
salo´nians in God our Father and the
Lord Jesus Christ:**
2 Grace to you and peace from God the
Father and the Lord Jesus Christ.
3 We are bound to give thanks to God always
for you, brethren, as is fitting, because your
faith is growing abundantly, and the love of
every one of you for one another is increasing.
4 Therefore we ourselves boast of you in the
churches of God for your steadfastness and
faith in all your persecutions and in the
afflictions which you are enduring.
5 This is evidence of the righteous judgment of God, that you may be made worthy
of the kingdom of God, for which you are
suffering— 6 since indeed God deems it just
to repay with affliction those who afflict
you, 7 and to grant rest with us to you who
are afflicted, when the Lord Jesus is revealed
from heaven with his mighty angels in
flaming fire, 8 inflicting vengeance upon

those who do not know God and upon those
who do not obey the gospel of our Lord
Jesus. 9They shall suffer the punishment of
eternal destruction and exclusion from the
presence of the Lord and from the glory of
his might, 10when he comes on that day to
be glorified in his saints, and to be marveled
at in all who have believed, because our
testimony to you was believed. 11To this end
we always pray for you, that our God may
make you worthy of his call, and may fulfil
every good resolve and work of faith by his
power, 12so that the name of our Lord Jesus
may be glorified in you, and you in him,
according to the grace of our God and the
Lord Jesus Christ.

2 Now concerning the coming of our
Lord Jesus Christ and our assembling
to meet him, we beg you, brethren, 2not to
be quickly shaken in mind or excited, either
by spirit or by word, or by letter purporting
to be from us, to the effect that the day of
the Lord has come. 3Let no one deceive
you in any way; for that day will not come,
unless the rebellion comes first, and the
man of lawlessness is revealed, the son of
perdition, 4who opposes and exalts himself
against every so-called god or object of
worship, so that he takes his seat in the
temple of God, proclaiming himself to be
God. 5Do you not remember that when I
was still with you I told you this? 6And you
know what is restraining him now so that
he may be revealed in his time. 7For the
mystery of lawlessness is already at work;
only he who now restrains it will do so until
he is out of the way. 8And then the lawless
one will be revealed, and the Lord Jesus
will slay him with the breath of his mouth
and destroy him by his appearing and his
coming. 9The coming of the lawless one by
the activity of Satan will be with all power
and with pretended signs and wonders,
10and with all wicked deception for those
who are to perish, because they refused to
love the truth and so be saved. 11Therefore
God sends upon them a strong delusion, to
make them believe what is false, 12so that all
may be condemned who did not believe the
truth but had pleasure in unrighteousness.

REFLECTION

All three of the readings today speak about free will and the justice of God. In Ezekiel, God explains how he judges each of us for our own deeds and accuses Israel of failing to understand the nature of justice (see Ez 18:5–29). Likewise, Sirach tells us that we have life and death as well as good and evil before us, and whatever we choose will be given to us (see Sir 15:17). St. Paul in 2 Thessalonians says that those who oppose the Gospel will suffer "exclusion from the presence of the Lord" (2 Thes 1:9). Modern people tend to shy away from these verses and to have a vague notion that nice people go to Heaven. But what is Heaven, and what is Hell? St. Paul tells us that the ultimate punishment is being separated from God and his glory. This judgment, therefore, is not one imposed from the outside, but, as Sirach says, it is our own choice. If we do not wish to be with God, we will not be forced to be with him. If God were to compel us to love him, to force us to desire Heaven, it would not only be a violation of our free will but a grave injustice. Do you imagine Heaven as simply some perfect place, or as being in eternal communion with God? Are you actively pursuing that communion?

October 25

EZEKIEL 19

And you, take up a lamentation for the princes of Israel, 2and say:

What a lioness was your mother
among lions!
She lurked in the midst of young lions,
rearing her whelps.
3And she brought up one of her whelps;
he became a young lion,
and he learned to catch prey;
he devoured men.

4The nations sounded an alarm
against him;
he was taken in their pit;
and they brought him with hooks
to the land of Egypt.
5When she saw that she was baffled,
that her hope was lost,
she took another of her whelps
and made him a young lion.
6He prowled among the lions;
he became a young lion,
and he learned to catch prey;
he devoured men.
7And he ravaged their strongholds,
and laid waste their cities;
and the land was appalled and all
who were in it
at the sound of his roaring.
8Then the nations set against him
snares on every side;
they spread their net over him;
he was taken in their pit.
9With hooks they put him in a cage,
and brought him to the king of Babylon;
they brought him into custody,
that his voice should no more be heard
upon the mountains of Israel.

10Your mother was like a vine in a vineyard
transplanted by the water,
fruitful and full of branches
by reason of abundant water.
11Its strongest stem became
a ruler's scepter;
it towered aloft
among the thick boughs;
it was seen in its height
with the mass of its branches.
12But the vine was plucked up in fury,
cast down to the ground;
the east wind dried it up;
its fruit was stripped off,
its strong stem was withered;
the fire consumed it.
13Now it is transplanted in the wilderness,
in a dry and thirsty land.
14And fire has gone out from its stem,
has consumed its branches and fruit,
so that there remains in it no strong stem,
no scepter for a ruler.

This is a lamentation, and has become a
lamentation.

20 In the seventh year, in the fifth
month, on the tenth day of the
month, certain of the elders of Israel came
to inquire of the LORD, and sat before
me. 2And the word of the LORD came to
me: 3"Son of man, speak to the elders of
Israel, and say to them, Thus says the
Lord GOD, Is it to inquire of me that you
come? As I live, says the Lord GOD, I will
not be inquired of by you. 4Will you judge
them, son of man, will you judge them?
Then let them know the abominations of
their fathers, 5and say to them, Thus says
the Lord GOD: On the day when I chose
Israel, I swore to the seed of the house of
Jacob, making myself known to them in
the land of Egypt, I swore to them, saying,
I am the LORD your God. 6On that day I
swore to them that I would bring them
out of the land of Egypt into a land that I
had searched out for them, a land flowing
with milk and honey, the most glorious
of all lands. 7And I said to them, Cast
away the detestable things your eyes feast
on, every one of you, and do not defile
yourselves with the idols of Egypt; I am
the LORD your God. 8But they rebelled
against me and would not listen to me;
they did not every man cast away the
detestable things their eyes feasted on,
nor did they forsake the idols of Egypt.
"Then I thought I would pour out my
wrath upon them and spend my anger
against them in the midst of the land of
Egypt. 9But I acted for the sake of my name,
that it should not be profaned in the sight
of the nations among whom they dwelt, in
whose sight I made myself known to them
in bringing them out of the land of Egypt.
10So I led them out of the land of Egypt and
brought them into the wilderness. 11I gave
them my statutes and showed them my
ordinances, by whose observance man shall
live. 12Moreover I gave them my sabbaths,
as a sign between me and them, that they
might know that I the LORD sanctify them.
13But the house of Israel rebelled against
me in the wilderness; they did not walk in

my statutes but rejected my ordinances, by
whose observance man shall live; and my
sabbaths they greatly profaned.
"Then I thought I would pour out my
wrath upon them in the wilderness, to make
a full end of them. 14But I acted for the sake
of my name, that it should not be profaned
in the sight of the nations, in whose sight I
had brought them out. 15Moreover I swore
to them in the wilderness that I would not
bring them into the land which I had given
them, a land flowing with milk and honey,
the most glorious of all lands, 16because they
rejected my ordinances and did not walk
in my statutes, and profaned my sabbaths;
for their heart went after their idols.
17Nevertheless my eye spared them, and I
did not destroy them or make a full end of
them in the wilderness.
18"And I said to their children in the
wilderness, Do not walk in the statutes of
your fathers, nor observe their ordinances,
nor defile yourselves with their idols. 19I the
LORD am your God; walk in my statutes,
and be careful to observe my ordinances,
20and hallow my sabbaths that they may
be a sign between me and you, that you
may know that I the LORD am your God.
21But the children rebelled against me; they
did not walk in my statutes, and were not
careful to observe my ordinances, by whose
observance man shall live; they profaned
my sabbaths.
"Then I thought I would pour out my wrath
upon them and spend my anger against
them in the wilderness. 22But I withheld my
hand, and acted for the sake of my name,
that it should not be profaned in the sight
of the nations, in whose sight I had brought
them out. 23Moreover I swore to them in the
wilderness that I would scatter them among
the nations and disperse them through the
countries, 24because they had not executed
my ordinances, but had rejected my statutes
and profaned my sabbaths, and their eyes
were set on their fathers' idols. 25Moreover
I gave them statutes that were not good and
ordinances by which they could not have
life; 26and I defiled them through their very
gifts in making them offer by fire all their
first-born, that I might horrify them; I did it
that they might know that I am the LORD.
27"Therefore, son of man, speak to the
house of Israel and say to them, Thus says
the Lord GOD: In this again your fathers
blasphemed me, by dealing treacherously
with me. 28For when I had brought them
into the land which I swore to give them,
then wherever they saw any high hill or any
leafy tree, there they offered their sacrifices
and presented the provocation of their
offering; there they sent up their soothing
odors, and there they poured out their drink
offerings. 29(I said to them, What is the high
place to which you go? So its name is called
Ba′mah to this day.) 30Wherefore say to the
house of Israel, Thus says the Lord GOD:
Will you defile yourselves after the manner
of your fathers and go astray after their
detestable things? 31When you offer your
gifts and sacrifice your sons by fire, you
defile yourselves with all your idols to this
day. And shall I be inquired of by you, O
house of Israel? As I live, says the Lord GOD,
I will not be inquired of by you.
32"What is in your mind shall never
happen—the thought, 'Let us be like the
nations, like the tribes of the countries, and
worship wood and stone.'"

SIRACH 16

Do not desire a multitude of
useless children,
nor rejoice in ungodly sons.
2If they multiply, do not rejoice in them,
unless the fear of the Lord is in them.
3Do not trust in their survival,
and do not rely on their multitude;
for one is better than a thousand,
and to die childless is better than to have
ungodly children.
4For through one man of understanding a
city will be filled with people,
but through a tribe of lawless men it will
be made desolate.
5Many such things my eye has seen,
and my ear has heard things more
striking than these.

6In an assembly of sinners a fire will
be kindled,
and in a disobedient nation wrath
was kindled.
7He was not propitiated for the ancient giants
who revolted in their might.
8He did not spare the neighbors of Lot,
whom he loathed on account of
their insolence.
9He showed no pity for a nation devoted
to destruction,
for those destroyed in their sins;
10nor for the six hundred thousand men
on foot,
who rebelliously assembled in their
stubbornness.
11Even if there is only one stiffnecked
person,
it will be a wonder if he remains
unpunished.
For mercy and wrath are with the Lord;
he is mighty to forgive, and he pours
out wrath.
12As great as his mercy, so great is also
his reproof;
he judges a man according to his deeds.
13The sinner will not escape with his plunder,
and the patience of the godly will not
be frustrated.
14He will make room for every act of mercy;
every one will receive in accordance with
his deeds.

17Do not say, "I shall be hidden from
the Lord,
and who from on high will
remember me?
Among so many people I shall not
be known,
for what is my soul in the boundless
creation?
18Behold, heaven and the highest heaven,
the abyss and the earth, will tremble at
his visitation.
19The mountains also and the foundations
of the earth
shake with trembling when he looks
upon them.
20And no mind will reflect on this.
Who will ponder his ways?
21Like a tempest which no man can see,
so most of his works are concealed.
22Who will announce his acts of justice?
Or who will await them? For the covenant
is far off."
23This is what one devoid of understanding
thinks;
a senseless and misguided man
thinks foolishly.

2 THESSALONIANS 2

**13But we are bound to give
thanks to God always for you,
brethren beloved by the Lord, because
God chose you from the beginning to**
be saved through sanctification by the Spirit
and belief in the truth. 14To this he called
you through our gospel, so that you may
obtain the glory of our Lord Jesus Christ.
15So then, brethren, stand firm and hold to
the traditions which you were taught by us,
either by word of mouth or by letter.
16Now may our Lord Jesus Christ himself,
and God our Father, who loved us and gave
us eternal comfort and good hope through
grace, 17comfort your hearts and establish
them in every good work and word.

3 Finally, brethren, pray for us, that the
word of the Lord may speed on and
triumph, as it did among you, 2and that
we may be delivered from wicked and evil
men; for not all have faith. 3But the Lord is
faithful; he will strengthen you and guard
you from evil. 4And we have confidence
in the Lord about you, that you are doing
and will do the things which we command.
5May the Lord direct your hearts to the love
of God and to the steadfastness of Christ.
6Now we command you, brethren, in the
name of our Lord Jesus Christ, that you
keep away from any brother who is walking
in idleness and not in accord with the
tradition that you received from us. 7For you
yourselves know how you ought to imitate
us; we were not idle when we were with
you, 8we did not eat any one's bread without
paying, but with toil and labor we worked

night and day, that we might not burden
any of you. 9It was not because we have not
that right, but to give you in our conduct
an example to imitate. 10For even when we
were with you, we gave you this command:
If any one will not work, let him not eat.
11For we hear that some of you are walking
in idleness, mere busybodies, not doing any
work. 12Now such persons we command
and exhort in the Lord Jesus Christ to do
their work in quietness and to earn their
own living. 13Brethren, do not be weary in
well-doing.
14If any one refuses to obey what we say in
this letter, note that man, and have nothing
to do with him, that he may be ashamed.
15Do not look on him as an enemy, but warn
him as a brother.
16Now may the Lord of peace himself give
you peace at all times in all ways. The Lord
be with you all.

17I, Paul, write this greeting with my own
hand. This is the mark in every letter of
mine; it is the way I write. 18The grace of our
Lord Jesus Christ be with you all.

REFLECTION

Today, the Book of Sirach tells us that having a multitude of children should not be counted as a blessing if those children are without God (see Sir 16:1–2). This saying is hard, especially for those of us who have children or other relatives who have rejected God, despite the best efforts of their parents and family members. But God himself has experienced this bitterness fully—the children of Israel have forsaken him many times, as Ezekiel tells us, despite the fact that God has shown them the best way to live (see Ez 20:11–13) and given them everything they need (see v. 6). When we struggle to show others the love of God, we should be comforted knowing that God has entered into our struggle, even coming himself to be with his children, only to be rejected by them on the Cross. We must treasure the words of St. Paul, who tells us that although "not all have faith . . . the Lord is faithful" (2 Thes 3:2–3). We, like God, must be faithful and steadfast in our love even toward those who have rejected God and who may have even rejected us. Do you continue to love and pray for those close to you who have abandoned religion, even if they have hurt you personally?

October 26

EZEKIEL 20

33"As I live, says the Lord God,
surely with a mighty hand and
an outstretched arm, and with wrath
poured out, I will be king over you. 34I
will bring you out from the peoples and
gather you out of the countries where
you are scattered, with a mighty hand
and an outstretched arm, and with wrath
poured out; 35and I will bring you into
the wilderness of the peoples, and there
I will enter into judgment with you face
to face. 36As I entered into judgment with
your fathers in the wilderness of the land
of Egypt, so I will enter into judgment
with you, says the Lord God. 37I will make
you pass under the rod, and I will let you
go in by number. 38I will purge out the
rebels from among you, and those who
transgress against me; I will bring them
out of the land where they sojourn, but
they shall not enter the land of Israel.
Then you will know that I am the Lord.
39"As for you, O house of Israel, thus says
the Lord God: Go serve every one of you
his idols, now and hereafter, if you will not
listen to me; but my holy name you shall no
more profane with your gifts and your idols.
40"For on my holy mountain, the
mountain height of Israel, says the Lord
God, there all the house of Israel, all of
them, shall serve me in the land; there I
will accept them, and there I will require
your contributions and the choicest of your
gifts, with all your sacred offerings. 41As

a pleasing odor I will accept you, when I
bring you out from the peoples, and gather
you out of the countries where you have
been scattered; and I will manifest my
holiness among you in the sight of the
nations. [42]And you shall know that I am
the LORD, when I bring you into the land
of Israel, the country which I swore to
give to your fathers. [43]And there you shall
remember your ways and all the doings
with which you have polluted yourselves;
and you shall loathe yourselves for all the
evils that you have committed. [44]And you
shall know that I am the LORD, when I deal
with you for my name's sake, not according
to your evil ways, nor according to your
corrupt doings, O house of Israel, says the
Lord GOD."

[45]And the word of the LORD came to
me: [46]"Son of man, set your face toward
the south, preach against the south, and
prophesy against the forest land in the
Neg′eb; [47]say to the forest of the Neg′eb,
Hear the word of the LORD: Thus says the
Lord GOD, Behold, I will kindle a fire in you,
and it shall devour every green tree in you
and every dry tree; the blazing flame shall
not be quenched, and all faces from south
to north shall be scorched by it. [48]All flesh
shall see that I the LORD have kindled it; it
shall not be quenched." [49]Then I said, "Ah,
Lord GOD! they are saying of me, 'Is he not
a maker of allegories?' "

21 The word of the LORD came to me:
[2]"Son of man, set your face toward
Jerusalem and preach against the sanctuaries; prophesy against the land of Israel
[3]and say to the land of Israel, Thus says the
LORD: Behold, I am against you, and will
draw forth my sword out of its sheath, and
will cut off from you both righteous and
wicked. [4]Because I will cut off from you
both righteous and wicked, therefore my
sword shall go out of its sheath against all
flesh from south to north; [5]and all flesh shall
know that I the LORD have drawn my sword
out of its sheath; it shall not be sheathed
again. [6]Sigh therefore, son of man; sigh
with breaking heart and bitter grief before
their eyes. [7]And when they say to you, 'Why
do you sigh?' you shall say, 'Because of the
tidings. When it comes, every heart will
melt and all hands will be feeble, every spirit
will faint and all knees will be weak as water.
Behold, it comes and it will be fulfilled,' "
says the Lord GOD.

[8]And the word of the LORD came to me:
[9]"Son of man, prophesy and say, Thus says
the Lord, Say:

A sword, a sword is sharpened
 and also polished,
[10]sharpened for slaughter,
 polished to flash like lightning!

Or do we make mirth? You have despised
the rod, my son, with everything of wood.
[11]So the sword is given to be polished, that
it may be handled; it is sharpened and
polished to be given into the hand of the
slayer. [12]Cry and wail, son of man, for it
is against my people; it is against all the
princes of Israel; they are delivered over to
the sword with my people. Strike therefore
upon your thigh. [13]For it will not be a
testing—what could it do if you despise the
rod?" says the Lord GOD.

[14]"Prophesy therefore, son of man; clap
your hands and let the sword come down
twice, yes, thrice, the sword for those to be
slain; it is the sword for the great slaughter,
which encompasses them, [15]that their
hearts may melt, and many fall at all their
gates. I have given the glittering sword;
ah! it is made like lightning, it is polished
for slaughter. [16]Cut sharply to right and left
where your edge is directed. [17]I also will clap
my hands, and I will satisfy my fury; I the
LORD have spoken."

[18]The word of the LORD came to me again:
[19]"Son of man, mark two ways for the sword
of the king of Babylon to come; both of
them shall come forth from the same land.
And make a signpost, make it at the head of
the way to a city; [20]mark a way for the sword
to come to Rabbah of the Am′monites and
to Judah and to Jerusalem the fortified. [21]For
the king of Babylon stands at the parting of
the way, at the head of the two ways, to use
divination; he shakes the arrows, he consults
the teraphim, he looks at the liver. [22]Into his
right hand comes the lot for Jerusalem, to

open the mouth with a cry, to lift up the voice
with shouting, to set battering rams against
the gates, to cast up mounds, to build siege
towers. 23But to them it will seem like a false
divination; they have sworn solemn oaths;
but he brings their guilt to remembrance,
that they may be captured.

24"Therefore thus says the Lord GOD:
Because you have made your guilt to be
remembered, in that your transgressions are
uncovered, so that in all your doings your
sins appear—because you have come to
remembrance, you shall be taken in them.
25And you, O unhallowed wicked one,
prince of Israel, whose day has come, the
time of your final punishment, 26thus says
the Lord GOD: Remove the turban, and take
off the crown; things shall not remain as
they are; exalt that which is low, and abase
that which is high. 27A ruin, ruin, ruin I will
make it; there shall not be even a trace of it
until he comes whose right it is; and to him
I will give it.

28"And you, son of man, prophesy, and
say, Thus says the Lord GOD concerning
the Am'monites, and concerning their
reproach; say, A sword, a sword is drawn
for the slaughter, it is polished to glitter
and to flash like lightning—29while they
see for you false visions, while they make
up lies for you—to be laid on the necks of
the unhallowed wicked, whose day has
come, the time of their final punishment.
30Return it to its sheath. In the place where
you were created, in the land of your origin,
I will judge you. 31And I will pour out my
indignation upon you; I will blow upon you
with the fire of my wrath; and I will deliver
you into the hands of brutal men, skilful to
destroy. 32You shall be fuel for the fire; your
blood shall be in the midst of the land; you
shall be no more remembered; for I the
LORD have spoken."

SIRACH 16

24Listen to me, my son, and acquire
knowledge,
and pay close attention to my words.
25I will impart instruction by weight,
and declare knowledge accurately.
26The works of the Lord have existed from
the beginning by his creation,
and when he made them, he determined
their divisions.
27He arranged his works in an eternal order,
and their dominion for all generations;
they neither hunger nor grow weary,
and they do not cease from their labors.
28They do not crowd one another aside,
and they will never disobey his word.
29After this the Lord looked upon the earth,
and filled it with his good things;
30with all kinds of living beings he covered
its surface,
and to it they return.

17 The Lord created man out of earth,
and made him into his own image;
2he turned him back into earth again,
but clothed him in strength like his own.
3He gave to men few days, a limited time,
but granted them authority over the
things upon the earth.
4He placed the fear of them in all flesh,
and granted them dominion over beasts
and birds.
6He made for them discretion, with a tongue
and eyes and ears;
he gave them a mind for thinking,
and filled them with the discipline
of discernment.
7He created in them the knowledge
of the spirit;
he filled their hearts with understanding,
and showed them good and evil.
8He placed the fear of him into their hearts,
showing them the majesty of his works.
9He made them glory in his wondrous deeds,
10 that they might praise his holy name,
to proclaim the grandeur of his works.
11He bestowed knowledge upon them,
and allotted to them the law of life.
12He established with them an eternal
covenant,
and showed them his justice and
his judgments.
13Their eyes saw his glorious majesty,
and their ears heard the glory of his voice.

[14]And he said to them, "Beware of all unrighteousness."
And he gave commandment to each of them concerning his neighbor.

[15]Their ways are always before him,
they will not be hidden from his eyes.

---

1 TIMOTHY 1

Paul, an apostle of Christ Jesus by command of God our Savior and of Christ Jesus our hope,

[2]To Timothy, my true child in the faith:

Grace, mercy, and peace from God the Father and Christ Jesus our Lord.

[3]As I urged you when I was going to Macedonia, remain at Ephesus that you may charge certain persons not to teach any different doctrine, [4]nor to occupy themselves with myths and endless genealogies which promote speculations rather than the divine training that is in faith; [5]whereas the aim of our charge is love that issues from a pure heart and a good conscience and sincere faith. [6]Certain persons by swerving from these have wandered away into vain discussion, [7]desiring to be teachers of the law, without understanding either what they are saying or the things about which they make assertions.

[8]Now we know that the law is good, if any one uses it lawfully, [9]understanding this, that the law is not laid down for the just but for the lawless and disobedient, for the ungodly and sinners, for the unholy and profane, for murderers of fathers and murderers of mothers, for manslayers, [10]immoral persons, sodomites, kidnapers, liars, perjurers, and whatever else is contrary to sound doctrine, [11]in accordance with the glorious gospel of the blessed God with which I have been entrusted.

[12]I thank him who has given me strength for this, Christ Jesus our Lord, because he judged me faithful by appointing me to his service, [13]though I formerly blasphemed and persecuted and insulted him; but I received mercy because I had acted ignorantly in unbelief, [14]and the grace of our Lord overflowed for me with the faith and love that are in Christ Jesus. [15]The saying is sure and worthy of full acceptance, that Christ Jesus came into the world to save sinners. And I am the foremost of sinners; [16]but I received mercy for this reason, that in me, as the foremost, Jesus Christ might display his perfect patience for an example to those who were to believe in him for eternal life. [17]To the King of ages, immortal, invisible, the only God, be honor and glory for ever and ever. Amen.

[18]This charge I commit to you, Timothy, my son, in accordance with the prophetic utterances which pointed to you, that inspired by them you may wage the good warfare, [19]holding faith and a good conscience. By rejecting conscience, certain persons have made shipwreck of their faith, [20]among them Hymenae´us and Alexander, whom I have delivered to Satan that they may learn not to blaspheme.

REFLECTION

In praise of God's mercy, St. Paul says this short prayer: "King of ages, immortal, invisible, the only God, be honor and glory for ever and ever. Amen" (1 Tm 1:17). We often pray to God our Father or Lord, but what does it mean to call him king? In Ezekiel, God uses this title to remind his wayward people that they are not ruler over themselves: "As I live, says the Lord GOD . . . I will be king over you" (Ez 20:33). God also commands the prince of Israel to remove his crown (see 21:26). Calling God our king, therefore, is a statement about his power and authority, his dominion over all things great and small, and about the subordination of earthly powers to him. But we must not think of God's kingship as a version of earthly kingship, only amplified. Unlike earthly power, God's power is not based in corruption, wealth, coercion, violence, or deceit. The reason God invokes his kingship in Ezekiel is to remind us of his just judgments, and Paul uses the title to praise God's mercy. When we seek power in this life, let that power, therefore, be found in love and justice. When you love and act justly, do you see this as a kind of kingly act?

October 27

EZEKIEL 22

**Moreover the word of the LORD
came to me, saying, 2"And you,
son of man, will you judge, will
you judge the bloody city? Then declare
to her all her abominable deeds. 3You
shall say, Thus says the Lord GOD: A**
city that sheds blood in the midst of her, that
her time may come, and that makes idols to
defile herself! 4You have become guilty by
the blood which you have shed, and defiled
by the idols which you have made; and you
have brought your day near, the appointed
time of your years has come. Therefore I
have made you a reproach to the nations,
and a mocking to all the countries. 5Those
who are near and those who are far from
you will mock you, you infamous one, full
of tumult.

6"Behold, the princes of Israel in you,
every one according to his power, have been
bent on shedding blood. 7Father and mother
are treated with contempt in you; the
sojourner suffers extortion in your midst;
the fatherless and the widow are wronged
in you. 8You have despised my holy things,
and profaned my sabbaths. 9There are men
in you who slander to shed blood, and men
in you who eat upon the mountains; men
commit lewdness in your midst. 10In you
men uncover their fathers' nakedness; in
you they humble women who are unclean in
their impurity. 11One commits abomination
with his neighbor's wife; another lewdly
defiles his daughter-in-law; another in you
defiles his sister, his father's daughter. 12In
you men take bribes to shed blood; you
take interest and increase and make gain of
your neighbors by extortion; and you have
forgotten me, says the Lord GOD.

13"Behold, therefore, I strike my hands
together at the dishonest gain which you have
made, and at the blood which has been in the
midst of you. 14Can your courage endure, or
can your hands be strong, in the days that I
shall deal with you? I the LORD have spoken,
and I will do it. 15I will scatter you among
the nations and disperse you through the
countries, and I will consume your filthiness
out of you. 16And I shall be profaned through
you in the sight of the nations; and you shall
know that I am the LORD."

17And the word of the LORD came to
me: 18"Son of man, the house of Israel has
become dross to me; all of them, silver and
bronze and tin and iron and lead in the
furnace, have become dross. 19Therefore
thus says the Lord GOD: Because you have
all become dross, therefore, behold, I will
gather you into the midst of Jerusalem. 20As
men gather silver and bronze and iron and
lead and tin into a furnace, to blow the fire
upon it in order to melt it; so I will gather
you in my anger and in my wrath, and I
will put you in and melt you. 21I will gather
you and blow upon you with the fire of my
wrath, and you shall be melted in the midst
of it. 22As silver is melted in a furnace, so you
shall be melted in the midst of it; and you
shall know that I the LORD have poured out
my wrath upon you."

23And the word of the LORD came to me:
24"Son of man, say to her, You are a land that
is not cleansed, or rained upon in the day
of indignation. 25Her princes in the midst
of her are like a roaring lion tearing the
prey; they have devoured human lives; they
have taken treasure and precious things;
they have made many widows in the midst
of her. 26Her priests have done violence to
my law and have profaned my holy things;
they have made no distinction between the
holy and the common, neither have they
taught the difference between the unclean
and the clean, and they have disregarded
my sabbaths, so that I am profaned among
them. 27Her princes in the midst of her are
like wolves tearing the prey, shedding blood,
destroying lives to get dishonest gain. 28And
her prophets have daubed for them with
whitewash, seeing false visions and making
up lies for them, saying, 'Thus says the
Lord GOD,' when the LORD has not spoken.
29The people of the land have practiced

extortion and committed robbery; they have
oppressed the poor and needy, and have
extorted from the sojourner without redress.
30And I sought for a man among them who
should build up the wall and stand in the
breach before me for the land, that I should
not destroy it; but I found none. 31Therefore
I have poured out my indignation upon
them; I have consumed them with the fire of
my wrath; their way have I repaid upon their
heads, says the Lord GOD."

23 The word of the LORD came to me:
2"Son of man, there were two women,
the daughters of one mother; 3they played
the harlot in Egypt; they played the harlot in
their youth; there their breasts were pressed
and their virgin bosoms handled. 4Oho′lah
was the name of the elder and Ohol′ibah the
name of her sister. They became mine, and
they bore sons and daughters. As for their
names, Oholah is Samar′ia, and Oholibah is
Jerusalem.

5"Oho′lah played the harlot while she
was mine; and she doted on her lovers the
Assyrians, 6warriors clothed in purple,
governors and commanders, all of them
desirable young men, horsemen riding on
horses. 7She bestowed her harlotries upon
them, the choicest men of Assyria all of
them; and she defiled herself with all the
idols of every one on whom she doted. 8She
did not give up her harlotry which she had
practiced since her days in Egypt; for in her
youth men had lain with her and handled
her virgin bosom and poured out their lust
upon her. 9Therefore I delivered her into the
hands of her lovers, into the hands of the
Assyrians, upon whom she doted. 10These
uncovered her nakedness; they seized her
sons and her daughters; and her they slew
with the sword; and she became a byword
among women, when judgment had been
executed upon her.

11"Her sister Ohol′ibah saw this, yet she
was more corrupt than she in her doting
and in her harlotry, which was worse than
that of her sister. 12She doted upon the
Assyrians, governors and commanders,
warriors clothed in full armor, horsemen
riding on horses, all of them desirable young
men. 13And I saw that she was defiled; they
both took the same way. 14But she carried
her harlotry further; she saw men portrayed
upon the wall, the images of the Chalde′ans
portrayed in vermilion, 15with belts around
their waists, with flowing turbans on their
heads, all of them looking like officers, a
picture of Babylonians whose native land
was Chalde′a. 16When she saw them she
doted upon them, and sent messengers to
them in Chalde′a. 17And the Babylonians
came to her into the bed of love, and they
defiled her with their lust; and after she
was polluted by them, she turned from
them in disgust. 18When she carried on
her harlotry so openly and flaunted her
nakedness, I turned in disgust from her,
as I had turned from her sister. 19Yet she
increased her harlotry, remembering the
days of her youth, when she played the
harlot in the land of Egypt 20and doted upon
her paramours there, whose members were
like those of donkeys, and whose issue was
like that of horses. 21Thus you longed for the
lewdness of your youth, when the Egyptians
handled your bosom and pressed your
young breasts."

SIRACH 17

17He appointed a ruler for every nation,
but Israel is the Lord's own portion.
19All their works are as the sun before him,
and his eyes are continually upon
their ways.
20Their iniquities are not hidden from him,
and all their sins are before the Lord.
22A man's almsgiving is like a signet with
the Lord,
and he will keep a person's kindness like
the apple of his eye.
23Afterward he will arise and repay them,
and he will bring their recompense on
their heads.
24Yet to those who repent he grants a return,
and he encourages those whose
endurance is failing,
and he has appointed to them the lot
of truth.

25 Turn to the Lord and forsake your sins;
pray in his presence and lessen
your offenses.
26 Return to the Most High and turn away
from iniquity,
and hate abominations intensely.
Know the justice and the judgments
of God,
and stand firm the lot that is set
before you,
in prayer to God, the Almighty.
27 Who will sing praises to the Most High
in Hades,
as do those who are alive and give thanks?
Tarry not in the waywardness of
the ungodly,
and give thanks before death.
28 From the dead, as from one who does not
exist, thanksgiving has ceased;
he who is alive and well sings the
Lord's praises.
29 How great is the mercy of the Lord,
and his forgiveness for those who turn
to him!
30 For all things cannot be in men,
since a son of man is not immortal.
31 What is brighter than the sun? Yet its
light fails.
So flesh and blood devise evil.
32 He marshals the host of the height
of heaven;
but all men are dust and ashes.

---

1 TIMOTHY 2

**First of all, then, I urge that supplications, prayers, intercessions, and thanksgivings be made for all
men, 2 for kings and all who are in high
positions, that we may lead a quiet and
peaceable life, godly and respectful in**
every way. 3 This is good, and it is acceptable in the sight of God our Savior, 4 who
desires all men to be saved and to come to
the knowledge of the truth. 5 For there is one
God, and there is one mediator between God
and men, the man Christ Jesus, 6 who gave
himself as a ransom for all, the testimony to
which was given at the proper time. 7 For this
I was appointed a preacher and apostle (I am
telling the truth, I am not lying), a teacher of
the Gentiles in faith and truth.

8 I desire then that in every place the men
should pray, lifting holy hands without anger
or quarreling; 9 also that women should adorn
themselves modestly and sensibly in seemly
apparel, not with braided hair or gold or pearls
or costly attire 10 but by good deeds, as befits
women who profess religion. 11 Let a woman
learn in silence with all submissiveness. 12 I permit no woman to teach or to have authority
over men; she is to keep silent. 13 For Adam was
formed first, then Eve; 14 and Adam was not
deceived, but the woman was deceived and became a transgressor. 15 Yet woman will be saved
through bearing children, if she continues in
faith and love and holiness, with modesty.

3 The saying is sure: If any one aspires
to the office of bishop, he desires a
noble task. 2 Now a bishop must be above
reproach, the husband of one wife, temperate,
sensible, dignified, hospitable, an apt teacher,
3 no drunkard, not violent but gentle, not
quarrelsome, and no lover of money. 4 He must
manage his own household well, keeping his
children submissive and respectful in every
way; 5 for if a man does not know how to
manage his own household, how can he care
for God's Church? 6 He must not be a recent
convert, or he may be puffed up with conceit
and fall into the condemnation of the devil;
7 moreover he must be well thought of by
outsiders, or he may fall into reproach and the
snare of the devil.

8 Deacons likewise must be serious, not
double-tongued, not addicted to much wine,
not greedy for gain; 9 they must hold the
mystery of the faith with a clear conscience.
10 And let them also be tested first; then if they
prove themselves blameless let them serve
as deacons. 11 The women likewise must be
serious, no slanderers, but temperate, faithful
in all things. 12 Let deacons be the husband of
one wife, and let them manage their children
and their households well; 13 for those who
serve well as deacons gain a good standing for
themselves and also great confidence in the
faith which is in Christ Jesus.

REFLECTION

St. Paul's instructions to women in 1 Timothy might make us uneasy, but we must not think that we moderns are the first to struggle with their meaning. St. Augustine, for example, rejects that Paul's words, a "woman will be saved through bearing children" (1 Tm 2:15), imply that a woman without children is denied salvation (see *The Trinity* XII.11). Augustine also notes that, based on 1 Timothy 2:14, Adam's sin is actually worse than Eve's because he is not deceived, and he sins with his eyes open (see *City of God* XIV.11). Like Augustine, therefore, we can understand Scripture's use of gender or gendered imagery as an invitation to read more deeply. In Ezekiel, we find a similar invitation, since the two female figures (the faithless daughters) represent all the people (see Ez 23:1–21). Indeed, the Church is often imaged as a bride or a mother. If we identify with the women of whom Paul is speaking, the words can resonate with every person; for our salvation does consist in bearing fruit for the kingdom of God. And, like Paul's godly woman (and unlike the harlots of Ezekiel), we should take more care for our inward righteousness than for outward appearances. Understood in this way, can St. Paul's exhortation to take off fine jewelry remind us all not to worry about the way we look in other people's eyes?

October 28

EZEKIEL 23

[22]Therefore, O Ohol′ibah, thus
says the Lord God: "Behold, I
will rouse against you your lovers from
whom you turned in disgust, and I will
bring them against you from every side:
[23]the Babylonians and all the Chalde′ans,
Pe′kod and Shoa and Koa, and all the
Assyrians with them, desirable young men,
governors and commanders all of them,
officers and warriors, all of them riding on
horses. [24]And they shall come against you
from the north with chariots and wagons and
a host of peoples; they shall set themselves
against you on every side with buckler, shield,
and helmet, and I will commit the judgment
to them, and they shall judge you according
to their judgments. [25]And I will direct my
indignation against you, that they may deal
with you in fury. They shall cut off your nose
and your ears, and your survivors shall fall
by the sword. They shall seize your sons and
your daughters, and your survivors shall be
devoured by fire. [26]They shall also strip you of
your clothes and take away your fine jewels.
[27]Thus I will put an end to your lewdness and
your harlotry brought from the land of Egypt;
so that you shall not lift up your eyes to the
Egyptians or remember them any more. [28]For
thus says the Lord God: Behold, I will deliver
you into the hands of those whom you hate,
into the hands of those from whom you turned
in disgust; [29]and they shall deal with you in
hatred, and take away all the fruit of your
labor, and leave you naked and bare, and the
nakedness of your harlotry shall be uncovered.
Your lewdness and your harlotry [30]have
brought this upon you, because you played the
harlot with the nations, and polluted yourself
with their idols. [31]You have gone the way of
your sister; therefore I will give her cup into
your hand. [32]Thus says the Lord God:

"You shall drink your sister's cup
which is deep and large;
you shall be laughed at and held in derision,
for it contains much;
[33]you will be filled with drunkenness
and sorrow.
A cup of horror and desolation,
is the cup of your sister Samar′ia;
[34]you shall drink it and drain it out,
and pluck out your hair,
and tear your breasts;

for I have spoken, says the Lord God.
[35]Therefore thus says the Lord God: Because
you have forgotten me and cast me behind
your back, therefore bear the consequences
of your lewdness and harlotry."

[36]The Lord said to me: "Son of man, will you
judge Oho′lah and Ohol′ibah? Then declare to
them their abominable deeds. [37]For they have
committed adultery, and blood is upon their

hands; with their idols they have committed
adultery; and they have even offered up to
them for food the sons whom they had borne
to me. [38]Moreover this they have done to me:
they have defiled my sanctuary on the same
day and profaned my sabbaths. [39]For when
they had slaughtered their children in sacrifice
to their idols, on the same day they came into
my sanctuary to profane it. And behold, this
is what they did in my house. [40]They even
sent for men to come from far, to whom a
messenger was sent, and behold, they came.
For them you bathed yourself, painted your
eyes, and decked yourself with ornaments;
[41]you sat upon a stately couch, with a table
spread before it on which you had placed my
incense and my oil. [42]The sound of a carefree
multitude was with her; and with men of the
common sort drunkards were brought from
the wilderness; and they put bracelets upon
the hands of the women, and beautiful crowns
upon their heads.

[43]"Then I said, Do not men now commit
adultery when they practice harlotry with
her? [44]For they have gone in to her, as men go
in to a harlot. Thus they went in to Oho′lah
and to Ohol′ibah to commit lewdness. [45]But
righteous men shall pass judgment on them
with the sentence of adulteresses, and with
the sentence of women that shed blood;
because they are adulteresses, and blood is
upon their hands."

[46]For thus says the Lord God: "Bring up a
host against them, and make them an object
of terror and a spoil. [47]And the host shall stone
them and dispatch them with their swords;
they shall slay their sons and their daughters,
and burn up their houses. [48]Thus will I put an
end to lewdness in the land, that all women
may take warning and not commit lewdness
as you have done. [49]And your lewdness shall
be repaid upon you, and you shall bear the
penalty for your sinful idolatry; and you shall
know that I am the Lord God."

24 In the ninth year, in the tenth month,
on the tenth day of the month, the
word of the Lord came to me: [2]"Son of
man, write down the name of this day, this
very day. The king of Babylon has laid siege
to Jerusalem this very day. [3]And utter an
allegory to the rebellious house and say to
them, Thus says the Lord God:

Set on the pot, set it on,
  pour in water also;
[4]put in it the pieces of flesh,
  all the good pieces, the thigh and
    the shoulder;
  fill it with choice bones.
[5]Take the choicest one of the flock,
  pile the logs under it;
boil its pieces,
  seethe also its bones in it.

[6]"Therefore thus says the Lord God: Woe
to the bloody city, to the pot whose rust
is in it, and whose rust has not gone out of
it! Take out of it piece after piece, without
making any choice. [7]For the blood she has
shed is still in the midst of her; she put it
on the bare rock, she did not pour it upon
the ground to cover it with dust. [8]To rouse
my wrath, to take vengeance, I have set on
the bare rock the blood she has shed, that
it may not be covered. [9]Therefore thus says
the Lord God: Woe to the bloody city! I also
will make the pile great. [10]Heap on the logs,
kindle the fire, boil well the flesh, and empty
out the broth, and let the bones be burned
up. [11]Then set it empty upon the coals, that
it may become hot, and its copper may burn,
that its filthiness may be melted in it, its rust
consumed. [12]In vain I have wearied myself;
its thick rust does not go out of it by fire. [13]Its
rust is your filthy lewdness. Because I would
have cleansed you and you were not cleansed
from your filthiness, you shall not be cleansed
any more till I have satisfied my fury upon
you. [14]I the Lord have spoken; it shall come
to pass, I will do it; I will not go back, I will
not spare, I will not repent; according to your
ways and your doings I will judge you, says
the Lord God."

[15]Also the word of the Lord came to me:
[16]"Son of man, behold, I am about to take
the delight of your eyes away from you at
a stroke; yet you shall not mourn or weep
nor shall your tears run down. [17]Sigh, but
not aloud; make no mourning for the dead.
Bind on your turban, and put your shoes
on your feet; do not cover your lips, nor eat
the bread of mourners." [18]So I spoke to the

people in the morning, and at evening my wife died. And on the next morning I did as I was commanded.

19 And the people said to me, "Will you not tell us what these things mean for us, that you are acting thus?" 20 Then I said to them, "The word of the LORD came to me: 21 'Say to the house of Israel, Thus says the Lord GOD: Behold, I will profane my sanctuary, the pride of your power, the delight of your eyes, and the desire of your soul; and your sons and your daughters whom you left behind shall fall by the sword. 22 And you shall do as I have done; you shall not cover your lips, nor eat the bread of mourners. 23 Your turbans shall be on your heads and your shoes on your feet; you shall not mourn or weep, but you shall pine away in your iniquities and groan to one another. 24 Thus shall Ezek′iel be to you a sign; according to all that he has done you shall do. When this comes, then you will know that I am the Lord GOD.'

25 "And you, son of man, on the day when I take from them their stronghold, their joy and glory, the delight of their eyes and their heart's desire, and also their sons and daughters, 26 on that day a fugitive will come to you to report to you the news. 27 On that day your mouth will be opened to the fugitive, and you shall speak and be no longer mute. So you will be a sign to them; and they will know that I am the LORD."

25 The word of the LORD came to me: 2 "Son of man, set your face toward the Am′monites, and prophesy against them. 3 Say to the Am′monites, Hear the word of the Lord GOD: Thus says the Lord GOD, Because you said, 'Aha!' over my sanctuary when it was profaned, and over the land of Israel when it was made desolate, and over the house of Judah when it went into exile; 4 therefore I am handing you over to the people of the East for a possession, and they shall set their encampments among you and make their dwellings in your midst; they shall eat your fruit, and they shall drink your milk. 5 I will make Rabbah a pasture for camels and the cities of the Am′monites a fold for flocks. Then you will know that I am the LORD. 6 For thus says the Lord GOD: Because you have clapped your hands and stamped your feet and rejoiced with all the malice within you against the land of Israel, 7 therefore, behold, I have stretched out my hand against you, and will hand you over as spoil to the nations; and I will cut you off from the peoples and will make you perish out of the countries; I will destroy you. Then you will know that I am the LORD.

8 "Thus says the Lord GOD: Because Moab said, Behold, the house of Judah is like all the other nations, 9 therefore I will lay open the flank of Moab from the cities on its frontier, the glory of the country, Beth-jesh′imoth, Ba′al-me′on, and Kir″iatha′im. 10 I will give it along with the Am′monites to the people of the East as a possession, that it may be remembered no more among the nations, 11 and I will execute judgments upon Moab. Then they will know that I am the LORD."

SIRACH 18

He who lives for ever created the whole
    universe;
2 the Lord alone will be declared righteous.*
4 To none has he given power to proclaim
    his works;
  and who can search out his mighty
    deeds?
5 Who can measure his majestic power?
  And who can fully recount his mercies?
6 It is not possible to diminish or increase
    them,
  nor is it possible to trace the wonders
    of the Lord.
7 When a man has finished, he is just
    beginning,
  and when he stops, he will be at a loss.
8 What is man, and of what use is he?
  What is his good and what is his evil?
9 The number of a man's days is great if he
    reaches a hundred years.
10 Like a drop of water from the sea and a
    grain of sand
  so are a few years in the day of eternity.
11 Therefore the Lord is patient with them
  and pours out his mercy upon them.

* Other authorities add *and there is no other beside him; 3 he steers the world with the span of his hand, and all things obey his will; for he is king of all things, by his power separating among them the holy things from the profane.*

12He sees and recognizes that their end will
be evil;
therefore he grants them forgiveness in
abundance.
13The compassion of man is for his neighbor,
but the compassion of the Lord is for all
living beings.
He rebukes and trains and teaches them,
and turns them back, as a shepherd
his flock.
14He has compassion on those who accept
his discipline
and who are eager for his judgments.

---

1 TIMOTHY 3

14I hope to come to you soon, but
I am writing these instructions
to you so that, 15if I am delayed, you may
know how one ought to behave in the
household of God, which is the Church of
the living God, the pillar and bulwark of
the truth. 16Great indeed, we confess, is the
mystery of our religion:

He was manifested in the flesh,
vindicated in the Spirit,
seen by angels,
preached among the nations,
believed on in the world,
taken up in glory.

4 Now the Spirit expressly says that in
later times some will depart from the
faith by giving heed to deceitful spirits and
doctrines of demons, 2through the preten-
sions of liars whose consciences are seared,
3who forbid marriage and enjoin abstinence
from foods which God created to be received
with thanksgiving by those who believe and
know the truth. 4For everything created by
God is good, and nothing is to be rejected if
it is received with thanksgiving; 5for then it is
consecrated by the word of God and prayer.

6If you put these instructions before the
brethren, you will be a good minister of
Christ Jesus, nourished on the words of the
faith and of the good doctrine which you have
followed. 7Have nothing to do with godless
and silly myths. Train yourself in godliness;
8for while bodily training is of some value,
godliness is of value in every way, as it holds
promise for the present life and also for the
life to come. 9The saying is sure and worthy
of full acceptance. 10For to this end we toil
and strive, because we have our hope set on
the living God, who is the Savior of all men,
especially of those who believe.

11Command and teach these things. 12Let
no one despise your youth, but set the
believers an example in speech and conduct, in love, in faith, in purity. 13Till I come,
attend to the public reading of Scripture,
to preaching, to teaching. 14Do not neglect
the gift you have, which was given you by
prophetic utterance when the elders laid
their hands upon you. 15Practice these
duties, devote yourself to them, so that
all may see your progress. 16Take heed to
yourself and to your teaching; hold to that,
for by so doing you will save both yourself
and your hearers.

REFLECTION

In Ezekiel, God likens the judgment of Israel to the cooking of meat in a pot; everything will be boiled, even the choicest flesh (see Ez 24:3–14). This image is a gruesome one, and it parallels the bloodshed that has been committed in Israel, such as child sacrifice (see Ez 23:39). In other words, since Israel has treated human beings like meat, so they will be treated likewise. This analogy, however unsettling, can help us reflect on the tendency in our own world to reject anything spiritual and treat human beings as simply flesh and bones. If we reduce life to its material dimension alone, we can end up treating human beings as inconveniences or even commodities. Both Sirach and St. Paul, however, speak of material things in a different way—as created (see Sir 18:1; 1 Tm 4:4–5). St. Paul insists that "everything created by God is good, and nothing is to be rejected if it is received with thanksgiving" (v. 4). According to St. Paul, we love things in the world not because they are meat in the pot to feed our appetites (so to speak), but because they are created by God. Do you think of everything you use and everyone you see as having their worth in Christ?

October 29

EZEKIEL 25

12"Thus says the Lord God: Because E´dom acted revengefully against the house of Judah and has grievously offended in taking vengeance upon them, 13therefore thus says the Lord God, I will stretch out my hand against E´dom, and cut off from it man and beast; and I will make it desolate; from Te´man even to De´dan they shall fall by the sword. 14And I will lay my vengeance upon E´dom by the hand of my people Israel; and they shall do in Edom according to my anger and according to my wrath; and they shall know my vengeance, says the Lord God.

15"Thus says the Lord God: Because the Philis´tines acted revengefully and took vengeance with malice of heart to destroy in never-ending enmity; 16therefore thus says the Lord God, Behold, I will stretch out my hand against the Philis´tines, and I will cut off the Cher´ethites, and destroy the rest of the seacoast. 17I will execute great vengeance upon them with wrathful chastisements. Then they will know that I am the Lord, when I lay my vengeance upon them."

26 In the eleventh year, on the first day of the month, the word of the Lord came to me: 2"Son of man, because Tyre said concerning Jerusalem, 'Aha, the gate of the peoples is broken, it has swung open to me; I shall be replenished, now that she is laid waste,' 3therefore thus says the Lord God: Behold, I am against you, O Tyre, and will bring up many nations against you, as the sea brings up its waves. 4They shall destroy the walls of Tyre, and break down her towers; and I will scrape her soil from her, and make her a bare rock. 5She shall be in the midst of the sea a place for the spreading of nets; for I have spoken, says the Lord God; and she shall become a spoil to the nations; 6and her daughters on the mainland shall be slain by the sword. Then they will know that I am the Lord.

7"For thus says the Lord God: Behold, I will bring upon Tyre from the north Nebuchadrez´zar king of Babylon, king of kings, with horses and chariots, and with horsemen and a host of many soldiers. 8He will slay with the sword your daughters on the mainland; he will set up a siege wall against you, and throw up a mound against you, and raise a roof of shields against you. 9He will direct the shock of his battering rams against your walls, and with his axes he will break down your towers. 10His horses will be so many that their dust will cover you; your walls will shake at the noise of the horsemen and wagons and chariots, when he enters your gates as one enters a city which has been breached. 11With the hoofs of his horses he will trample all your streets; he will slay your people with the sword; and your mighty pillars will fall to the ground. 12They will make a spoil of your riches and a prey of your merchandise; they will break down your walls and destroy your pleasant houses; your stones and timber and soil they will cast into the midst of the waters. 13And I will stop the music of your songs, and the sound of your lyres shall be heard no more. 14I will make you a bare rock; you shall be a place for the spreading of nets; you shall never be rebuilt; for I the Lord have spoken, says the Lord God.

15"Thus says the Lord God to Tyre: Will not the islands shake at the sound of your fall, when the wounded groan, when slaughter is made in the midst of you? 16Then all the princes of the sea will step down from their thrones, and remove their robes, and strip off their embroidered garments; they will clothe themselves with trembling; they will sit upon the ground and tremble every moment, and be appalled at you. 17And they will raise a lamentation over you, and say to you,

'How you have vanished from the seas,
O city renowned,
that was mighty on the sea,
you and your inhabitants,
who imposed your terror
on all the mainland!
18Now the isles tremble
on the day of your fall;
yes, the isles that are in the sea
are dismayed at your passing.'

19"For thus says the Lord God: When I make
you a city laid waste, like the cities that are
not inhabited, when I bring up the deep over
you, and the great waters cover you, 20then I
will thrust you down with those who descend
into the Pit, to the people of old, and I will
make you to dwell in the nether world, among
primeval ruins, with those who go down to the
Pit, so that you will not be inhabited or have a
place in the land of the living. 21I will bring you
to a dreadful end, and you shall be no more;
though you be sought for, you will never be
found again, says the Lord God."

27 The word of the Lord came to me:
2"Now you, son of man, raise a lamentation over Tyre, 3and say to Tyre, who
dwells at the entrance to the sea, merchant
of the peoples on many islands, thus says the
Lord God:

"O Tyre, you have said,
'I am perfect in beauty.'
4Your borders are in the heart of the seas;
your builders made perfect your beauty.
5They made all your planks
of fir trees from Se′nir;
they took a cedar from Lebanon
to make a mast for you.
6Of oaks of Ba′shan
they made your oars;
they made your deck of pines
from the coasts of Cyprus,
inlaid with ivory.
7Of fine embroidered linen from Egypt
was your sail,
serving as your ensign;
blue and purple from the coasts of Eli′shah
was your awning.
8The inhabitants of Si′don and Arvad
were your rowers;
skilled men of Ze′mer were in you,
they were your pilots.
9The elders of Ge′bal and her skilled men
were in you,
caulking your seams;
all the ships of the sea with their mariners
were in you,
to barter for your wares.

10"Persia and Lud and Put were in your army
as your men of war; they hung the shield and
helmet in you; they gave you splendor. 11The
men of Arvad and He′lech were upon your walls
round about, and men of Ga′mad were in your
towers; they hung their shields upon your walls
round about; they made perfect your beauty.

12"Tar′shish trafficked with you because of
your great wealth of every kind; silver, iron,
tin, and lead they exchanged for your wares.
13Ja′van, Tu′bal, and Me′shech traded with
you; they exchanged the persons of men
and vessels of bronze for your merchandise.
14Beth″-togar′mah exchanged for your wares
horses, war horses, and mules. 15The men of
Rhodes traded with you; many islands were
your own special markets, they brought you
in payment ivory tusks and ebony. 16E′dom
trafficked with you because of your abundant
goods; they exchanged for your wares
emeralds, purple, embroidered work, fine
linen, coral, and agate. 17Judah and the land
of Israel traded with you; they exchanged for
your merchandise wheat, olives and early figs,
honey, oil, and balm. 18Damascus trafficked
with you for your abundant goods, because
of your great wealth of every kind; wine of
Helbon, and white wool, 19and wine from
U′zal they exchanged for your wares; wrought
iron, cassia, and calamus were bartered for
your merchandise. 20De′dan traded with you
in saddlecloths for riding. 21Arabia and all the
princes of Ke′dar were your favored dealers in
lambs, rams, and goats; in these they trafficked
with you. 22The traders of Sheba and Ra′amah
traded with you; they exchanged for your
wares the best of all kinds of spices, and all
precious stones, and gold. 23Haran, Canneh,
Eden, Asshur, and Chil′mad traded with you.
24These traded with you in choice garments,
in clothes of blue and embroidered work, and
in carpets of colored stuff, bound with cords
and made secure; in these they traded with
you. 25The ships of Tar′shish traveled for you
with your merchandise.

"So you were filled and heavily laden
in the heart of the seas.
26Your rowers have brought you out
into the high seas.
The east wind has wrecked you
in the heart of the seas.
27Your riches, your wares, your merchandise,
your mariners and your pilots,

your caulkers, your dealers in merchandise,
and all your men of war who are in you,
with all your company
that is in your midst,
sink into the heart of the seas
on the day of your ruin.
28At the sound of the cry of your pilots
the countryside shakes,
29and down from their ships
come all that handle the oar.
The mariners and all the pilots of the sea
stand on the shore
30and wail aloud over you,
and cry bitterly.
They cast dust on their heads
and wallow in ashes;
31they make themselves bald for you,
and put on sackcloth,
and they weep over you in bitterness
of soul,
with bitter mourning.
32In their wailing they raise a lamentation
for you,
and lament over you:
'Who was ever destroyed like Tyre
in the midst of the sea?
33When your wares came from the seas,
you satisfied many peoples;
with your abundant wealth and merchandise
you enriched the kings of the earth.
34Now you are wrecked by the seas,
in the depths of the waters;
your merchandise and all your crew
have sunk with you.
35All the inhabitants of the islands
are appalled at you;
and their kings are horribly afraid,
their faces are convulsed.
36The merchants among the peoples hiss
at you;
you have come to a dreadful end
and shall be no more for ever.'"

SIRACH 18

15My son, do not mix reproach with your
good deeds,
nor cause grief by your words when you
present a gift.
16Does not the dew assuage the scorching heat?
So a word is better than a gift.
17Indeed, does not a word surpass a
good gift?
Both are to be found in a gracious man.
18A fool is ungracious and abusive,
and the gift of a grudging man makes the
eyes dim.
19Before you speak, learn,
and before you fall ill, take care of
your health.
20Before judgment, examine yourself,
and in the hour of visitation you will
find forgiveness.
21Before falling ill, humble yourself,
and when you are on the point of sinning,
turn back.
22Let nothing hinder you from paying a
vow promptly,
and do not wait until death to be released
from it.
23Before making a vow, prepare yourself;
and do not be like a man who tempts
the Lord.
24Think of his wrath on the day of death,
and of the moment of vengeance when he
turns away his face.
25In the time of plenty think of the time
of hunger;
in the days of wealth think of poverty
and need.
26From morning to evening conditions change,
and all things move swiftly before the Lord.

1 TIMOTHY 5

Do not rebuke an older man but exhort him as you would a father; treat younger men like brothers,
2older women like mothers, younger women like sisters, in all purity.
3Honor widows who are real widows. 4If
a widow has children or grandchildren, let
them first learn their religious duty to their
own family and make some return to their
parents; for this is acceptable in the sight of
God. 5She who is a real widow, and is left all

alone, has set her hope on God and continues in supplications and prayers night and day; 6whereas she who is self-indulgent is dead even while she lives. 7Command this, so that they may be without reproach. 8If any one does not provide for his relatives, and especially for his own family, he has disowned the faith and is worse than an unbeliever.

9Let a widow be enrolled if she is not less than sixty years of age, having been the wife of one husband; 10and she must be well attested for her good deeds, as one who has brought up children, shown hospitality, washed the feet of the saints, relieved the afflicted, and devoted herself to doing good in every way. 11But refuse to enrol younger widows; for when they grow wanton against Christ they desire to marry, 12and so they incur condemnation for having violated their first pledge. 13Besides that, they learn to be idlers, gadding about from house to house, and not only idlers but gossips and busybodies, saying what they should not. 14So I would have younger widows marry, bear children, rule their households, and give the enemy no occasion to revile us. 15For some have already strayed after Satan. 16If any believing woman has relatives who are widows, let her assist them; let the Church not be burdened, so that it may assist those who are real widows.

17Let the elders who rule well be considered worthy of double honor, especially those who labor in preaching and teaching; 18for the Scripture says, "You shall not muzzle an ox when it is treading out the grain," and, "The laborer deserves his wages." 19Never admit any charge against an elder except on the evidence of two or three witnesses. 20As for those who persist in sin, rebuke them in the presence of all, so that the rest may stand in fear. 21In the presence of God and of Christ Jesus and of the elect angels I charge you to keep these rules without favor, doing nothing from partiality. 22Do not be hasty in the laying on of hands, nor participate in another man's sins; keep yourself pure.

23No longer drink only water, but use a little wine for the sake of your stomach and your frequent ailments.

24The sins of some men are conspicuous, pointing to judgment, but the sins of others appear later. 25So also good deeds are conspicuous; and even when they are not, they cannot remain hidden.

REFLECTION

The words of God regarding the Philistines—"I will execute great vengeance upon them with wrathful chastisements. Then they will know that I am the LORD, when I lay my vengeance upon them" (Ez 25:17)—are nothing short of terrifying. Why should God be made known in wrath and judgment? Why can't the Philistines come to know the Lord by his love, by the beauty of his creation, or by any other means? Perhaps we can gain some understanding of this verse by contemplating a human analogy. When a daughter has done something wrong, how will her father make her understand her wrongdoing? How will a mother make herself known as a mother to a disobedient son? Of course, parents love their children and take no pleasure in punishing them, but for a child to be loved truly, he or she must also be wisely corrected in accord with the wrongdoing. If God wants to lead us to perfection, he must sometimes make his name known with "wrathful chastisements." Sirach therefore wisely advises that we do not forget God's righteous anger (see Sir 18:24). When you see yourself as a child of God, do you also understand yourself to be entirely under God's care, even if it means being corrected?

October 30

EZEKIEL 28

The word of the LORD came to me: 2"Son of man, say to the prince of Tyre, Thus says the Lord GOD:
"Because your heart is proud,
and you have said, 'I am a god,
I sit in the seat of the gods,
in the heart of the seas,'
yet you are but a man, and no god,
though you consider yourself as wise
as a god—

[3]you are indeed wiser than Daniel;
no secret is hidden from you;
[4]by your wisdom and your understanding
you have gotten wealth for yourself,
and have gathered gold and silver
into your treasuries;
[5]by your great wisdom in trade
you have increased your wealth,
and your heart has become proud in
your wealth—
[6]therefore thus says the Lord GOD:
"Because you consider yourself
as wise as a god,
[7]therefore, behold, I will bring strangers
upon you,
the most terrible of the nations;
and they shall draw their swords
against the beauty of your wisdom
and defile your splendor.
[8]They shall thrust you down into the Pit,
and you shall die the death of the slain
in the heart of the seas.
[9]Will you still say, 'I am a god,'
in the presence of those who slay you,
though you are but a man, and no god,
in the hands of those who wound you?
[10]You shall die the death of the uncircumcised
by the hand of foreigners;
for I have spoken, says the Lord GOD."

[11]Moreover the word of the LORD came to
me: [12]"Son of man, raise a lamentation over
the king of Tyre, and say to him, Thus says
the Lord GOD:

"You were the signet of perfection,
full of wisdom
and perfect in beauty.
[13]You were in Eden, the garden of God;
every precious stone was your covering,
carnelian, topaz, and jasper,
chrysolite, beryl, and onyx,
sapphire, carbuncle, and emerald;
and wrought in gold were your settings
and your engravings.
On the day that you were created
they were prepared.
[14]With an anointed guardian cherub I
placed you;
you were on the holy mountain of God;
in the midst of the stones of fire
you walked.
[15]You were blameless in your ways
from the day you were created,
till iniquity was found in you.
[16]In the abundance of your trade
you were filled with violence, and
you sinned;
so I cast you as a profane thing from the
mountain of God,
and the guardian cherub drove you out
from the midst of the stones of fire.
[17]Your heart was proud because of
your beauty;
you corrupted your wisdom for the sake
of your splendor.
I cast you to the ground;
I exposed you before kings,
to feast their eyes on you.
[18]By the multitude of your iniquities,
in the unrighteousness of your trade
you profaned your sanctuaries;
so I brought forth fire from the midst
of you;
it consumed you,
and I turned you to ashes upon the earth
in the sight of all who saw you.
[19]All who know you among the peoples
are appalled at you;
you have come to a dreadful end
and shall be no more for ever."

[20]The word of the LORD came to me:
[21]"Son of man, set your face toward Si′don,
and prophesy against her [22]and say, Thus
says the Lord GOD:

"Behold, I am against you, O Si′don,
and I will manifest my glory in the midst
of you.
And they shall know that I am the LORD
when I execute judgments in her,
and manifest my holiness in her;
[23]for I will send pestilence into her,
and blood into her streets;
and the slain shall fall in the midst of her,
by the sword that is against her on
every side.
Then they will know that I am the LORD.

[24]"And for the house of Israel there shall be
no more a brier to prick or a thorn to hurt
them among all their neighbors who have
treated them with contempt. Then they will
know that I am the Lord GOD.

25“Thus says the Lord GOD: When I gather
the house of Israel from the peoples among
whom they are scattered, and manifest my
holiness in them in the sight of the nations,
then they shall dwell in their own land which
I gave to my servant Jacob. 26And they shall
dwell securely in it, and they shall build
houses and plant vineyards. They shall dwell
securely, when I execute judgments upon all
their neighbors who have treated them with
contempt. Then they will know that I am the
LORD their God.”

29 In the tenth year, in the tenth month,
on the twelfth day of the month,
the word of the LORD came to me: 2“Son
of man, set your face against Pharaoh king
of Egypt, and prophesy against him and
against all Egypt; 3speak, and say, Thus says
the Lord GOD:

“Behold, I am against you,
Pharaoh king of Egypt,
the great dragon that lies
in the midst of his streams,
that says, ‘My Nile is my own;
I made it.’
4I will put hooks in your jaws,
and make the fish of your streams stick to
your scales;
and I will draw you up out of the midst of
your streams,
with all the fish of your streams
which stick to your scales.
5And I will cast you forth into the wilderness,
you and all the fish of your streams;
you shall fall upon the open field,
and not be gathered and buried.
To the beasts of the earth and to the birds
of the air
I have given you as food.

6“Then all the inhabitants of Egypt shall
know that I am the LORD. Because you
have been a staff of reed to the house of
Israel; 7when they grasped you with the
hand, you broke, and tore all their shoulders; and when they leaned upon you, you
broke, and made all their loins to shake;
8therefore thus says the Lord GOD: Behold, I will bring a sword upon you, and
will cut off from you man and beast; 9and
the land of Egypt shall be a desolation
and a waste. Then they will know that I
am the LORD.

“Because you said, ‘The Nile is mine, and
I made it,’ 10therefore, behold, I am against
you, and against your streams, and I will
make the land of Egypt an utter waste and
desolation, from Migdol to Sye′ne, as far
as the border of Ethiopia. 11No foot of man
shall pass through it, and no foot of beast
shall pass through it; it shall be uninhabited
forty years. 12And I will make the land of
Egypt a desolation in the midst of desolated
countries; and her cities shall be a desolation
forty years among cities that are laid waste. I
will scatter the Egyptians among the nations,
and disperse them among the countries.

13“For thus says the Lord GOD: At the end
of forty years I will gather the Egyptians from
the peoples among whom they were scattered;
14and I will restore the fortunes of Egypt, and
bring them back to the land of Path′ros, the
land of their origin; and there they shall be
a lowly kingdom. 15It shall be the most lowly
of the kingdoms, and never again exalt itself
above the nations; and I will make them so
small that they will never again rule over
the nations. 16And it shall never again be the
reliance of the house of Israel, recalling their
iniquity, when they turn to them for aid. Then
they will know that I am the Lord GOD.”

17In the twenty-seventh year, in the first
month, on the first day of the month, the word
of the LORD came to me: 18“Son of man, Ne-
buchadrez′zar king of Babylon made his army
labor hard against Tyre; every head was made
bald and every shoulder was rubbed bare; yet
neither he nor his army got anything from Tyre
to pay for the labor that he had performed
against it. 19Therefore thus says the Lord GOD:
Behold, I will give the land of Egypt to Nebu-
chadrez′zar king of Babylon; and he shall carry
off its wealth and despoil it and plunder it; and
it shall be the wages for his army. 20I have given
him the land of Egypt as his recompense for
which he labored, because they worked for me,
says the Lord GOD.

21“On that day I will cause a horn to spring
forth to the house of Israel, and I will open
your lips among them. Then they will know
that I am the LORD.”

30 The word of the LORD came to me: [2]"Son of man, prophesy, and say, Thus says the Lord GOD:
"Wail, 'Alas for the day!'
3 For the day is near,
the day of the LORD is near;
it will be a day of clouds,
a time of doom for the nations.
4 A sword shall come upon Egypt,
and anguish shall be in Ethiopia,
when the slain fall in Egypt,
and her wealth is carried away,
and her foundations are torn down.
5 Ethiopia, and Put, and Lud, and all Arabia,
and Libya, and the people of the land that is
in league, shall fall with them by the sword.

6 "Thus says the LORD:
Those who support Egypt shall fall,
and her proud might shall come down;
from Migdol to Sye′ne
they shall fall within her by the sword,
says the Lord GOD.
7 And she shall be desolated in the midst of
desolated countries
and her cities shall be in the midst of
cities that are laid waste.
8 Then they will know that I am the LORD,
when I have set fire to Egypt,
and all her helpers are broken.
9 "On that day swift messengers shall go
forth from me to terrify the unsuspecting
Ethiopians; and anguish shall come upon
them on the day of Egypt's doom; for
behold, it comes!

10 "Thus says the Lord GOD:
I will put an end to the wealth of Egypt,
by the hand of Nebuchadrez′zar king
of Babylon.
11 He and his people with him, the most
terrible of the nations,
shall be brought in to destroy
the land;
and they shall draw their swords
against Egypt,
and fill the land with the slain.
12 And I will dry up the Nile,
and will sell the land into the hand of
evil men;
I will bring desolation upon the land and
everything in it,
by the hand of foreigners;
I, the LORD, have spoken.

13 "Thus says the Lord GOD:
I will destroy the idols,
and put an end to the images, in Memphis;
there shall no longer be a prince in the land
of Egypt;
so I will put fear in the land of Egypt.
14 I will make Path′ros a desolation,
and will set fire to Zoan,
and will execute acts of judgment
upon Thebes.
15 And I will pour my wrath upon Pelu′sium,
the stronghold of Egypt,
and cut off the multitude of Thebes.
16 And I will set fire to Egypt;
Pelu′sium shall be in great agony;
Thebes shall be breached,
and its walls broken down.
17 The young men of On and of Pibe′seth
shall fall by the sword;
and the women shall go into captivity.
18 At Tehaph′nehes the day shall be dark,
when I break there the dominion of Egypt,
and her proud might shall come to an end;
she shall be covered by a cloud,
and her daughters shall go into captivity.
19 Thus I will execute acts of judgment
upon Egypt.
Then they will know that I am
the LORD."

SIRACH 18

27 A wise man is cautious in everything,
and in days of sin he guards against
wrongdoing.
28 Every intelligent man knows wisdom,
and he praises the one who finds her.
29 Those who understand sayings become
skilled themselves,
and pour forth apt proverbs.

30 Do not follow your base desires,
but restrain your appetites.

[31]If you allow your soul to take pleasure in
base desire,
it will make you the laughingstock of
your enemies.
[32]Do not revel in great luxury,
lest you become impoverished by its
expense.
[33]Do not become a beggar by feasting with
borrowed money,
when you have nothing in your purse.

---

1 TIMOTHY 6

**Let all who are under the yoke
of slavery regard their masters
as worthy of all honor, so that the name
of God and the teaching may not be**
defamed. [2]Those who have believing masters
must not be disrespectful on the ground that
they are brethren; rather they must serve all
the better since those who benefit by their
service are believers and beloved.
Teach and urge these duties. [3]If any one
teaches otherwise and does not agree with the
sound words of our Lord Jesus Christ and the
teaching which accords with godliness, [4]he is
puffed up with conceit, he knows nothing; he
has a morbid craving for controversy and for
disputes about words, which produce envy,
dissension, slander, base suspicions, [5]and
wrangling among men who are depraved in
mind and bereft of the truth, imagining that
godliness is a means of gain. [6]There is great gain
in godliness with contentment; [7]for we brought
nothing into the world, and we cannot take
anything out of the world; [8]but if we have food
and clothing, with these we shall be content.
[9]But those who desire to be rich fall into
temptation, into a snare, into many senseless
and hurtful desires that plunge men into ruin
and destruction. [10]For the love of money is the
root of all evils; it is through this craving that
some have wandered away from the faith and
pierced their hearts with many pangs.
[11]But as for you, man of God, shun all this;
aim at righteousness, godliness, faith, love,
steadfastness, gentleness. [12]Fight the good
fight of the faith; take hold of the eternal life
to which you were called when you made
the good confession in the presence of many
witnesses. [13]In the presence of God who gives
life to all things, and of Christ Jesus who in
his testimony before Pontius Pilate made
the good confession, [14]I charge you to keep
the commandment unstained and free from
reproach until the appearing of our Lord
Jesus Christ; [15]and this will be made manifest
at the proper time by the blessed and only
Sovereign, the King of kings and Lord of lords,
[16]who alone has immortality and dwells in
unapproachable light, whom no man has ever
seen or can see. To him be honor and eternal
dominion. Amen.
[17]As for the rich in this world, charge
them not to be haughty, nor to set their
hopes on uncertain riches but on God who
richly furnishes us with everything to enjoy.
[18]They are to do good, to be rich in good
deeds, liberal and generous, [19]thus laying
up for themselves a good foundation for the
future, so that they may take hold of the life
which is life indeed.
[20]O Timothy, guard what has been
entrusted to you. Avoid the godless chatter
and contradictions of what is falsely called
knowledge, [21]for by professing it some have
missed the mark as regards the faith.
Grace be with you.

REFLECTION

Ezekiel's denunciation of Tyre and of Egypt is a denunciation of pride. Tyre calls itself a god, and Egypt claims "the Nile is mine, and I made it" (Ez 29:9). It seems unbelievable that a people could be so deluded as to think they literally created the river Nile, but perhaps they behave as if they had created it. This prophecy therefore can condemn our pride as well because we too can become incredibly possessive of our personal property, of the land to which we have a deed, and of our home country. We may well say in our hearts, "My property is mine; I made it" or "Our country belongs to us; we made it." Of course, properties and countries pass from one hand to another, as is evident in the case presented of Tyre and of Egypt. God alone, however, is Creator and master of the earth.

> As Sirach recommends, then, let us not feast on borrowed money (see Sir 18:33). Let us not live beyond our means, but also let us not exploit our borrowed earth, and let us not waste our borrowed time. As St. Paul reminds us, we came into the world with nothing and will leave it with nothing (see 1 Tm 6:7), and so what kind of ownership of land and country can we truly claim?

October 31

EZEKIEL 30

20 **In the eleventh year, in the**
first month, on the seventh day
of the month, the word of the Lord
came to me: 21 **"Son of man, I have broken**
the arm of Pharaoh king of Egypt; and
behold, it has not been bound up, to heal
it by binding it with a bandage, so that it
may become strong to wield the sword.
22 Therefore thus says the Lord God: Behold,
I am against Pharaoh king of Egypt, and
will break his arms, both the strong arm
and the one that was broken; and I will
make the sword fall from his hand. 23 I will
scatter the Egyptians among the nations,
and disperse them throughout the lands.
24 And I will strengthen the arms of the king
of Babylon, and put my sword in his hand;
but I will break the arms of Pharaoh, and he
will groan before him like a man mortally
wounded. 25 I will strengthen the arms of the
king of Babylon, but the arms of Pharaoh
shall fall; and they shall know that I am the
Lord. When I put my sword into the hand
of the king of Babylon, he shall stretch it
out against the land of Egypt; 26 and I will
scatter the Egyptians among the nations and
disperse them throughout the countries.
Then they will know that I am the Lord."

31 In the eleventh year, in the third
month, on the first day of the month,
the word of the Lord came to me: 2 "Son of
man, say to Pharaoh king of Egypt and to
his multitude:

"Whom are you like in your greatness?
3 Behold, I will liken you to a cedar
in Lebanon,
with fair branches and forest shade,
and of great height,
its top among the clouds.
4 The waters nourished it,
the deep made it grow tall,
making its rivers flow
round the place of its planting,
sending forth its streams
to all the trees of the forest.
5 So it towered high
above all the trees of the forest;
its boughs grew large
and its branches long,
from abundant water in its shoots.
6 All the birds of the air
made their nests in its boughs;
under its branches all the beasts
of the field
brought forth their young;
and under its shadow
dwelt all great nations.
7 It was beautiful in its greatness,
in the length of its branches;
for its roots went down
to abundant waters.
8 The cedars in the garden of God could not
rival it,
nor the fir trees equal its boughs;
the plane trees were as nothing
compared with its branches;
no tree in the garden of God
was like it in beauty.
9 I made it beautiful
in the mass of its branches,
and all the trees of Eden envied it,
that were in the garden of God.

10 "Therefore thus says the Lord God:
Because it towered high and set its top
among the clouds, and its heart was proud
of its height, 11 I will give it into the hand of
a mighty one of the nations; he shall surely
deal with it as its wickedness deserves.
I have cast it out. 12 Foreigners, the most
terrible of the nations, will cut it down and
leave it. On the mountains and in all the

valleys its branches will fall, and its boughs
will lie broken in all the watercourses of the
land; and all the peoples of the earth will
go from its shadow and leave it. [13]Upon its
ruin will dwell all the birds of the air, and
upon its branches will be all the beasts of
the field. [14]All this is in order that no trees
by the waters may grow to lofty height or
set their tops among the clouds, and that
no trees that drink water may reach up to
them in height; for they are all given over
to death, to the nether world among mortal
men, with those who go down to the Pit.
[15]"Thus says the Lord GOD: When it goes
down to Sheol I will make the deep mourn
for it, and restrain its rivers, and many waters
shall be stopped; I will clothe Lebanon in
gloom for it, and all the trees of the field shall
faint because of it. [16]I will make the nations
quake at the sound of its fall, when I cast it
down to Sheol with those who go down to
the Pit; and all the trees of Eden, the choice
and best of Lebanon, all that drink water, will
be comforted in the nether world. [17]They also
shall go down to Sheol with it, to those who
are slain by the sword; yes, those who dwelt
under its shadow among the nations shall
perish. [18]Whom are you thus like in glory
and in greatness among the trees of Eden?
You shall be brought down with the trees of
Eden to the nether world; you shall lie among
the uncircumcised, with those who are slain
by the sword.

"This is Pharaoh and all his multitude,
says the Lord GOD."

32 In the twelfth year, in the twelfth
month, on the first day of the month,
the word of the LORD came to me: [2]"Son of
man, raise a lamentation over Pharaoh king
of Egypt, and say to him:

"You consider yourself a lion among
the nations,
but you are like a dragon in the seas;
you burst forth in your rivers,
trouble the waters with your feet,
and foul their rivers.
[3]Thus says the Lord GOD:
I will throw my net over you
with a host of many peoples;
and I will haul you up in my dragnet.
[4]And I will cast you on the ground,
on the open field I will fling you,
and will cause all the birds of the air to
settle on you,
and I will gorge the beasts of the whole
earth with you.
[5]I will strew your flesh upon the mountains,
and fill the valleys with your carcass.
[6]I will drench the land even to
the mountains
with your flowing blood;
and the watercourses will be full of you.
[7]When I blot you out, I will cover the heavens,
and make their stars dark;
I will cover the sun with a cloud,
and the moon shall not give its light.
[8]All the bright lights of heaven
will I make dark over you,
and put darkness upon your land,
says the Lord GOD.

[9]"I will trouble the hearts of many peoples, when I carry you captive among the
nations, into the countries which you have
not known. [10]I will make many peoples appalled at you, and their kings shall shudder
because of you, when I brandish my sword
before them; they shall tremble every moment, every one for his own life, on the day
of your downfall. [11]For thus says the Lord
GOD: The sword of the king of Babylon
shall come upon you. [12]I will cause your
multitude to fall by the swords of mighty
ones, all of them most terrible among the
nations.

"They shall bring to nothing the pride
of Egypt,
and all its multitude shall perish.
[13]I will destroy all its beasts
from beside many waters;
and no foot of man shall trouble them
any more,
nor shall the hoofs of beasts trouble them.
[14]Then I will make their waters clear,
and cause their rivers to run like oil,
says the Lord GOD.
[15]When I make the land of Egypt desolate
and when the land is stripped of all that
fills it,
when I strike all who dwell in it,
then they will know that I am the LORD.

16 This is a lamentation which shall be chanted; the daughters of the nations shall chant it; over Egypt, and over all her multitude, shall they chant it, says the Lord GOD."

17 In the twelfth year, in the first month, on the fifteenth day of the month, the word of the LORD came to me: 18 "Son of man, wail over the multitude of Egypt, and send them down, her and the daughters of majestic nations, to the nether world, to those who have gone down to the Pit:

19 'Whom do you surpass in beauty?
Go down, and be laid with the
uncircumcised.'

20 They shall fall amid those who are slain by the sword, and with her shall lie all her multitudes. 21 The mighty chiefs shall speak of them, with their helpers, out of the midst of Sheol: 'They have come down, they lie still, the uncircumcised, slain by the sword.'

22 "Assyria is there, and all her company, their graves round about her, all of them slain, fallen by the sword; 23 whose graves are set in the uttermost parts of the Pit, and her company is round about her grave; all of them slain, fallen by the sword, who spread terror in the land of the living.

24 "E'lam is there, and all her multitude about her grave; all of them slain, fallen by the sword, who went down uncircumcised into the nether world, who spread terror in the land of the living, and they bear their shame with those who go down to the Pit. 25 They have made her a bed among the slain with all her multitude, their graves round about her, all of them uncircumcised, slain by the sword; for terror of them was spread in the land of the living, and they bear their shame with those who go down to the Pit; they are placed among the slain.

26 "Me'shech and Tu'bal are there, and all their multitude, their graves round about them, all of them uncircumcised, slain by the sword; for they spread terror in the land of the living. 27 And they do not lie with the fallen mighty men of old who went down to Sheol with their weapons of war, whose swords were laid under their heads, and whose shields are upon their bones; for the terror of the mighty men was in the land of the living. 28 So you shall be broken and lie among the uncircumcised, with those who are slain by the sword.

29 "E'dom is there, her kings and all her princes, who for all their might are laid with those who are slain by the sword; they lie with the uncircumcised, with those who go down to the Pit.

30 "The princes of the north are there, all of them, and all the Sidonians, who have gone down in shame with the slain, for all the terror which they caused by their might; they lie uncircumcised with those who are slain by the sword, and bear their shame with those who go down to the Pit.

31 "When Pharaoh sees them, he will comfort himself for all his multitude, Pharaoh and all his army, slain by the sword, says the Lord GOD. 32 For he spread terror in the land of the living; therefore he shall be laid among the uncircumcised, with those who are slain by the sword, Pharaoh and all his multitude, says the Lord GOD."

SIRACH 19

A workman who is a drunkard will not
become rich;
he who despises small things will fail
little by little.
2 Wine and women lead intelligent men astray,
and the man who consorts with harlots is
very reckless.
3 Decay and worms will inherit him,
and the reckless soul will be snatched away.

4 One who trusts others too quickly
is lightminded,
and one who sins does wrong to himself.
5 One who rejoices in wickedness will
be condemned,
6 and for one who hates gossip evil
is lessened.
7 Never repeat a conversation,
and you will lose nothing at all.
8 With friend or foe do not report it,
and unless it would be a sin for you, do
not disclose it;

[9]for some one has heard you and watched you,
and when the time comes he will hate you.
[10]Have you heard a word? Let it die with you.
Be brave! It will not make
you burst!
[11]With such a word a fool will suffer pangs
like a woman in labor
with a child.
[12]Like an arrow stuck in the flesh of the thigh,
so is a word inside a fool.

2 TIMOTHY 1

Paul, an apostle of Christ Jesus by the will of God according to the promise of the life which is in Christ Jesus,

[2]To Timothy, my beloved child:

Grace, mercy, and peace from God the
Father and Christ Jesus our Lord.

[3]I thank God whom I serve with a clear
conscience, as did my fathers, when I remember you constantly in my prayers.
[4]As I remember your tears, I long night
and day to see you, that I may be filled
with joy. [5]I am reminded of your sincere
faith, a faith that dwelt first in your
grandmother Lois and your mother
Eunice and now, I am sure, dwells in you.
[6]For this reason I remind you to rekindle
the gift of God that is within you through
the laying on of my hands; [7]for God did
not give us a spirit of timidity but a spirit
of power and love and self-control.

[8]Do not be ashamed then of testifying
to our Lord, nor of me his prisoner, but
take your share of suffering for the gospel
in the power of God, [9]who saved us and
called us with a holy calling, not in virtue
of our works but in virtue of his own
purpose and the grace which he gave us
in Christ Jesus ages ago, [10]and now has
manifested through the appearing of our
Savior Christ Jesus, who abolished death
and brought life and immortality to light
through the gospel. [11]For this gospel I
was appointed a preacher and apostle and
teacher, [12]and therefore I suffer as I do.
But I am not ashamed, for I know whom
I have believed, and I am sure that he is
able to guard until that Day what has been
entrusted to me. [13]Follow the pattern of
the sound words which you have heard
from me, in the faith and love which are
in Christ Jesus; [14]guard the truth that has
been entrusted to you by the Holy Spirit
who dwells within us.

[15]You are aware that all who are in Asia
turned away from me, and among them
Phy′gelus and Hermog′enes. [16]May the
Lord grant mercy to the household of
One-siph′orus, for he often refreshed me;
he was not ashamed of my chains, [17]but
when he arrived in Rome he searched for
me eagerly and found me—[18]may the Lord
grant him to find mercy from the Lord on
that Day—and you well know all the service
he rendered at Ephesus.

REFLECTION

In today's reading, Sirach gives us some very straightforward advice: "Never repeat a conversation, and you will lose nothing at all. With friend or foe do not report it, and unless it would be a sin for you, do not disclose it" (Sir 19:7–8). We know that the words of Sirach are true and that talking about other people behind their backs is not only harmful to our own spiritual life but also to the person about whom we are speaking. Nevertheless, this command is still very hard to follow. Why is it that we like to talk about other people, often negatively? Perhaps it is a way of making ourselves look better, or a way of complaining, or even a way of appearing "in the know," that is, to appear to be someone who has privileged information. We should examine our conscience before we speak about other people. As Sirach recommends, unless it would be worse to remain silent than to speak, we should remain silent. Sirach even pokes a little fun at us for finding this task difficult: "Be brave! It will not make you burst!" (v. 10). Following St. Paul, let us be ashamed of gossip but not of the Gospel (see 2 Tim 1:8). How often do you find yourself in conversations about people who are not present?

November 1

EZEKIEL 33

The word of the LORD came to
me: [2]"Son of man, speak to your
people and say to them, If I bring
the sword upon a land, and the people of
the land take a man from among them,
and make him their watchman; [3]and
if he sees the sword coming upon the land
and blows the trumpet and warns the people;
[4]then if any one who hears the sound of the
trumpet does not take warning, and the sword
comes and takes him away, his blood shall be
upon his own head. [5]He heard the sound of
the trumpet, and did not take warning; his
blood shall be upon himself. But if he had
taken warning, he would have saved his life.
[6]But if the watchman sees the sword coming
and does not blow the trumpet, so that the
people are not warned, and the sword comes,
and takes any one of them; that man is taken
away in his iniquity, but his blood I will
require at the watchman's hand.

[7]"So you, son of man, I have made a
watchman for the house of Israel; whenever
you hear a word from my mouth, you shall give
them warning from me. [8]If I say to the wicked,
O wicked man, you shall surely die, and you do
not speak to warn the wicked to turn from his
way, that wicked man shall die in his iniquity,
but his blood I will require at your hand. [9]But if
you warn the wicked to turn from his way, and
he does not turn from his way; he shall die in
his iniquity, but you will have saved your life.

[10]"And you, son of man, say to the house of
Israel, Thus have you said: 'Our transgressions
and our sins are upon us, and we waste away
because of them; how then can we live?' [11]Say
to them, As I live, says the Lord GOD, I have
no pleasure in the death of the wicked, but that
the wicked turn from his way and live; turn
back, turn back from your evil ways; for why
will you die, O house of Israel? [12]And you, son
of man, say to your people, The righteousness
of the righteous shall not deliver him when
he transgresses; and as for the wickedness
of the wicked, he shall not fall by it when he
turns from his wickedness; and the righteous
shall not be able to live by his righteousness
when he sins. [13]Though I say to the righteous
that he shall surely live, yet if he trusts in his
righteousness and commits iniquity, none of
his righteous deeds shall be remembered; but
in the iniquity that he has committed he shall
die. [14]Again, though I say to the wicked, 'You
shall surely die,' yet if he turns from his sin and
does what is lawful and right, [15]if the wicked
restores the pledge, gives back what he has
taken by robbery, and walks in the statutes of
life, committing no iniquity; he shall surely live,
he shall not die. [16]None of the sins that
he has committed shall be remembered
against him; he has done what is lawful
and right, he shall surely live.

[17]"Yet your people say, 'The way of the
Lord is not just'; when it is their own way
that is not just. [18]When the righteous turns
from his righteousness, and commits iniquity, he shall die for it. [19]And when the
wicked turns from his wickedness, and
does what is lawful and right, he shall live
by it. [20]Yet you say, 'The way of the Lord
is not just.' O house of Israel, I will judge
each of you according to his ways."

[21]In the twelfth year of our exile, in
the tenth month, on the fifth day of the
month, a man who had escaped from
Jerusalem came to me and said, "The city
has fallen." [22]Now the hand of the LORD
had been upon me the evening before
the fugitive came; and he had opened my
mouth by the time the man came to me in
the morning; so my mouth was opened,
and I was no longer mute.

[23]The word of the LORD came to me:
[24]"Son of man, the inhabitants of these
waste places in the land of Israel keep
saying, 'Abraham was only one man, yet
he got possession of the land; but we
are many; the land is surely given us to
possess.' [25]Therefore say to them, Thus
says the Lord GOD: You eat flesh with the
blood, and lift up your eyes to your idols,
and shed blood; shall you then possess
the land? [26]You resort to the sword, you

commit abominations and each of you defiles his neighbor's wife; shall you then possess the land? 27Say this to them, Thus says the Lord GOD: As I live, surely those who are in the waste places shall fall by the sword; and him that is in the open field I will give to the beasts to be devoured; and those who are in strongholds and in caves shall die by pestilence. 28And I will make the land a desolation and a waste; and her proud might shall come to an end; and the mountains of Israel shall be so desolate that none will pass through. 29Then they will know that I am the LORD, when I have made the land a desolation and a waste because of all their abominations which they have committed.

30"As for you, son of man, your people who talk together about you by the walls and at the doors of the houses, say to one another, each to his brother, 'Come, and hear what the word is that comes forth from the LORD.' 31And they come to you as people come, and they sit before you as my people, and they hear what you say but they will not do it; for with their lips they show much love, but their heart is set on their gain. 32And behold, you are to them like one who sings love songs with a beautiful voice and plays well on an instrument, for they hear what you say, but they will not do it. 33When this comes—and come it will!—then they will know that a prophet has been among them."

34 The word of the LORD came to me: 2"Son of man, prophesy against the shepherds of Israel, prophesy, and say to them, even to the shepherds, Thus says the Lord GOD: Ho, shepherds of Israel who have been feeding yourselves! Should not shepherds feed the sheep? 3You eat the fat, you clothe yourselves with the wool, you slaughter the fatlings; but you do not feed the sheep. 4The weak you have not strengthened, the sick you have not healed, the crippled you have not bound up, the strayed you have not brought back, the lost you have not sought, and with force and harshness you have ruled them. 5So they were scattered, because there was no shepherd; and they became food for all the wild beasts. 6My sheep were scattered, they wandered over all the mountains and on every high hill; my sheep were scattered over all the face of the earth, with none to search or seek for them.

7"Therefore, you shepherds, hear the word of the LORD: 8As I live, says the Lord GOD, because my sheep have become a prey, and my sheep have become food for all the wild beasts, since there was no shepherd; and because my shepherds have not searched for my sheep, but the shepherds have fed themselves, and have not fed my sheep; 9therefore, you shepherds, hear the word of the LORD: 10Thus says the Lord GOD, Behold, I am against the shepherds; and I will require my sheep at their hand, and put a stop to their feeding the sheep; no longer shall the shepherds feed themselves. I will rescue my sheep from their mouths, that they may not be food for them.

11"For thus says the Lord GOD: Behold, I, I myself will search for my sheep, and will seek them out. 12As a shepherd seeks out his flock when some of his sheep have been scattered abroad, so will I seek out my sheep; and I will rescue them from all places where they have been scattered on a day of clouds and thick darkness. 13And I will bring them out from the peoples, and gather them from the countries, and will bring them into their own land; and I will feed them on the mountains of Israel, by the fountains, and in all the inhabited places of the country. 14I will feed them with good pasture, and upon the mountain heights of Israel shall be their pasture; there they shall lie down in good grazing land, and on fat pasture they shall feed on the mountains of Israel. 15I myself will be the shepherd of my sheep, and I will make them lie down, says the Lord GOD. 16I will seek the lost, and I will bring back the strayed, and I will bind up the crippled, and I will strengthen the weak, and the fat and the strong I will watch over; I will feed them in justice.

17"As for you, my flock, thus says the Lord GOD: Behold, I judge between sheep and sheep, rams and he-goats. 18Is it not enough

for you to feed on the good pasture, that you
must tread down with your feet the rest of
your pasture; and to drink of clear water,
that you must foul the rest with your feet?
19 And must my sheep eat what you have
trodden with your feet, and drink what you
have fouled with your feet?
20 "Therefore, thus says the Lord GOD
to them: Behold, I, I myself will judge
between the fat sheep and the lean
sheep. 21 Because you push with side and
shoulder, and thrust at all the weak with
your horns, till you have scattered them
abroad, 22 I will save my flock, they shall no
longer be a prey; and I will judge between
sheep and sheep. 23 And I will set up over
them one shepherd, my servant David,
and he shall feed them: he shall feed them
and be their shepherd. 24 And I, the LORD,
will be their God, and my servant David
shall be prince among them; I, the LORD,
have spoken.
25 "I will make with them a covenant of
peace and banish wild beasts from the
land, so that they may dwell securely in
the wilderness and sleep in the woods.
26 And I will make them and the places
round about my hill a blessing; and I will
send down the showers in their season;
they shall be showers of blessing. 27 And
the trees of the field shall yield their fruit,
and the earth shall yield its increase,
and they shall be secure in their land;
and they shall know that I am the LORD,
when I break the bars of their yoke, and
deliver them from the hand of those who
enslaved them. 28 They shall no more be a
prey to the nations, nor shall the beasts
of the land devour them; they shall dwell
securely, and none shall make them
afraid. 29 And I will provide for them
prosperous plantations so that they shall
no more be consumed with hunger in the
land, and no longer suffer the reproach
of the nations. 30 And they shall know that
I, the LORD their God, am with them,
and that they, the house of Israel, are my
people, says the Lord GOD. 31 And you are
my sheep, the sheep of my pasture, and I
am your God, says the Lord GOD."

SIRACH 19

13 Question a friend, perhaps he did not do it;
but if he did anything, so that he may do
it no more.
14 Question a neighbor, perhaps he did not
say it;
but if he said it, so that he may not say
it again.
15 Question a friend, for often it is slander;
so do not believe everything you hear.
16 A person may make a slip without
intending it.
Who has never sinned with his tongue?
17 Question your neighbor before you
threaten him;
and let the law of the Most High take
its course.

20 All wisdom is the fear of the Lord,
and in all wisdom there is the fulfilment
of the law.
22 But the knowledge of wickedness is
not wisdom,
nor is there prudence where sinners
take counsel.
23 There is a cleverness which is
abominable,
but there is a fool who merely
lacks wisdom.
24 Better is the God-fearing man who
lacks intelligence,
than the highly prudent man who
transgresses the law.
25 There is a cleverness which is scrupulous
but unjust,
and there are people who distort kindness
to gain a verdict.
26 There is a rascal bowed down in mourning,
but inwardly he is full of deceit.
27 He hides his face and pretends not to hear;
but where no one notices, he will
forestall you.
28 And if by lack of strength he is prevented
from sinning,
he will do evil when he finds an
opportunity.
29 A man is known by his appearance,
and a sensible man is known by his face,
when you meet him.

30A man's attire and open-mouthed laughter,
and a man's manner of walking, show
what he is.

2 TIMOTHY 2

**You then, my son, be strong in
the grace that is in Christ Jesus,
2and what you have heard from me before many witnesses entrust to faithful**
men who will be able to teach others also.
3Take your share of suffering as a good
soldier of Christ Jesus. 4No soldier on
service gets entangled in civilian pursuits,
since his aim is to satisfy the one who
enlisted him. 5An athlete is not crowned
unless he competes according to the rules.
6It is the hard-working farmer who ought
to have the first share of the crops. 7Think
over what I say, for the Lord will grant you
understanding in everything.
8Remember Jesus Christ, risen from the
dead, descended from David, as preached
in my gospel, 9the gospel for which I am
suffering and wearing chains like a criminal.
But the word of God is not chained. 10There-
fore I endure everything for the sake of the
elect, that they also may obtain the salvation
which in Christ Jesus goes with eternal
glory. 11The saying is sure:
If we have died with him, we shall also live
with him;
12if we endure, we shall also reign with him;
if we deny him, he also will deny us;
13if we are faithless, he remains faithful—
for he cannot deny himself.

REFLECTION

In Ezekiel and 2 Timothy, we find our spiritual vocation compared to earthly careers: shepherd, soldier, athlete, and farmer. All these professions involve exertion and commitment. They also require patience. A soldier or an athlete must train extensively before even setting foot on the field or in the arena. A shepherd or a farmer must tend his flocks and fields for long hours every day before reaping any reward for the labor. It is this quality of perseverance that St. Paul is highlighting: we should welcome a share of Christ's suffering, and we should endure to the end (see 2 Tm 2:3, 10). Perseverance is also something that has been found wanting in Ezekiel's generation—they are not good shepherds, and they want rewards without any labor. Practicing patience can be difficult in any situation, and in our spiritual lives it can sometimes be the hardest. But even more than an earthly farmer or athlete, we know we will reap the rewards of our labor. Can these images help you to resist the culture of instant gratification and to persevere in your spiritual labor?

November 2

EZEKIEL 35

**The word of the Lord came to
me: 2"Son of man, set your face
against Mount Se′ir, and prophesy
against it, 3and say to it, Thus says the**
Lord God: Behold, I am against you, Mount
Se′ir, and I will stretch out my hand against
you, and I will make you a desolation and
a waste. 4I will lay your cities waste, and
you shall become a desolation; and you
shall know that I am the Lord. 5Because
you cherished perpetual enmity, and gave
over the people of Israel to the power of the
sword at the time of their calamity, at the
time of their final punishment; 6therefore,
as I live, says the Lord God, I will prepare
you for blood, and blood shall pursue you;
because you are guilty of blood, therefore
blood shall pursue you. 7I will make Mount
Se′ir a waste and a desolation; and I will
cut off from it all who come and go. 8And
I will fill your mountains with the slain; on
your hills and in your valleys and in all your
ravines those slain with the sword shall fall.

[9]I will make you a perpetual desolation, and
your cities shall not be inhabited. Then you
will know that I am the LORD.
[10]“Because you said, ‘These two nations
and these two countries shall be mine, and
we will take possession of them,’—although
the LORD was there—[11]therefore, as I live,
says the Lord GOD, I will deal with you
according to the anger and envy which
you showed because of your hatred against
them; and I will make myself known among
you, when I judge you. [12]And you shall know
that I, the LORD, have heard all the revilings
which you uttered against the mountains of
Israel, saying, ‘They are laid desolate, they
are given us to devour.’ [13]And you magnified
yourselves against me with your mouth, and
multiplied your words against me; I heard it.
[14]Thus says the Lord GOD: For the rejoicing
of the whole earth I will make you desolate.
[15]As you rejoiced over the inheritance of the
house of Israel, because it was desolate, so
I will deal with you; you shall be desolate,
Mount Se′ir, and all E′dom, all of it. Then
they will know that I am the LORD.

36 “And you, son of man, prophesy to
the mountains of Israel, and say, O
mountains of Israel, hear the word of the
LORD. [2]Thus says the Lord GOD: Because the
enemy said of you, ‘Aha!’ and, ‘The ancient
heights have become our possession,’
[3]therefore prophesy, and say, Thus says
the Lord GOD: Because, yes, because they
made you desolate, and crushed you from
all sides, so that you became the possession
of the rest of the nations, and you became
the talk and evil gossip of the people;
[4]therefore, O mountains of Israel, hear the
word of the Lord GOD: Thus says the Lord
GOD to the mountains and the hills, the
ravines and the valleys, the desolate wastes
and the deserted cities, which have become
a prey and derision to the rest of the nations
round about; [5]therefore thus says the Lord
GOD: I speak in my hot jealousy against the
rest of the nations, and against all E′dom,
who gave my land to themselves as a
possession with wholehearted joy and utter
contempt, that they might possess it and
plunder it. [6]Therefore prophesy concerning
the land of Israel, and say to the mountains
and hills, to the ravines and valleys, Thus
says the Lord GOD: Behold, I speak in my
jealous wrath, because you have suffered
the reproach of the nations; [7]therefore thus
says the Lord GOD: I swear that the nations
that are round about you shall themselves
suffer reproach.
[8]“But you, O mountains of Israel, shall
shoot forth your branches, and yield your
fruit to my people Israel; for they will soon
come home. [9]For, behold, I am for you, and
I will turn to you, and you shall be tilled
and sown; [10]and I will multiply men upon
you, the whole house of Israel, all of it; the
cities shall be inhabited and the waste places
rebuilt; [11]and I will multiply upon you man
and beast; and they shall increase and be
fruitful; and I will cause you to be inhabited
as in your former times, and will do more
good to you than ever before. Then you will
know that I am the LORD. [12]Yes, I will let
men walk upon you, even my people Israel;
and they shall possess you, and you shall be
their inheritance, and you shall no longer
bereave them of children. [13]Thus says the
Lord GOD: Because men say to you, ‘You
devour men, and you bereave your nation
of children,’ [14]therefore you shall no longer
devour men and no longer bereave your
nation of children, says the Lord GOD; [15]and
I will not let you hear any more the reproach
of the nations, and you shall no longer bear
the disgrace of the peoples and no longer cause your nation to stumble, says the
Lord GOD.”
[16]The word of the LORD came to me:
[17]“Son of man, when the house of Israel
dwelt in their own land, they defiled it by
their ways and their doings; their conduct
before me was like the uncleanness of a
woman in her impurity. [18]So I poured out
my wrath upon them for the blood which
they had shed in the land, for the idols with
which they had defiled it. [19]I scattered them
among the nations, and they were dispersed
through the countries; in accordance with
their conduct and their deeds I judged
them. [20]But when they came to the nations,
wherever they came, they profaned my holy

name, in that men said of them, 'These are the people of the LORD, and yet they had to go out of his land.' 21But I had concern for my holy name, which the house of Israel caused to be profaned among the nations to which they came.

22"Therefore say to the house of Israel, Thus says the Lord GOD: It is not for your sake, O house of Israel, that I am about to act, but for the sake of my holy name, which you have profaned among the nations to which you came. 23And I will vindicate the holiness of my great name, which has been profaned among the nations, and which you have profaned among them; and the nations will know that I am the LORD, says the Lord GOD, when through you I vindicate my holiness before their eyes. 24For I will take you from the nations, and gather you from all the countries, and bring you into your own land. 25I will sprinkle clean water upon you, and you shall be clean from all your uncleannesses, and from all your idols I will cleanse you. 26A new heart I will give you, and a new spirit I will put within you; and I will take out of your flesh the heart of stone and give you a heart of flesh. 27And I will put my spirit within you, and cause you to walk in my statutes and be careful to observe my ordinances. 28You shall dwell in the land which I gave to your fathers; and you shall be my people, and I will be your God. 29And I will deliver you from all your uncleannesses; and I will summon the grain and make it abundant and lay no famine upon you. 30I will make the fruit of the tree and the increase of the field abundant, that you may never again suffer the disgrace of famine among the nations. 31Then you will remember your evil ways, and your deeds that were not good; and you will loathe yourselves for your iniquities and your abominable deeds. 32It is not for your sake that I will act, says the Lord GOD; let that be known to you. Be ashamed and confounded for your ways, O house of Israel.

33"Thus says the Lord GOD: On the day that I cleanse you from all your iniquities, I will cause the cities to be inhabited, and the waste places shall be rebuilt. 34And the land that was desolate shall be tilled, instead of being the desolation that it was in the sight of all who passed by. 35And they will say, 'This land that was desolate has become like the garden of Eden; and the waste and desolate and ruined cities are now inhabited and fortified.' 36Then the nations that are left round about you shall know that I, the LORD, have rebuilt the ruined places, and replanted that which was desolate; I, the LORD, have spoken, and I will do it.

37"Thus says the Lord GOD: This also I will let the house of Israel ask me to do for them: to increase their men like a flock. 38Like the flock for sacrifices, like the flock at Jerusalem during her appointed feasts, so shall the waste cities be filled with flocks of men. Then they will know that I am the LORD."

SIRACH 20

There is a reproof which is not timely;
and there is a man who keeps silent
but is wise.
2How much better it is to reprove than
to stay angry!
And the one who confesses his fault will
be kept from loss.
4Like a eunuch's desire to violate a maiden
is a man who executes judgments
by violence.
5There is one who by keeping silent is
found wise,
while another is detested for being
too talkative.
6There is one who keeps silent because he
has no answer,
while another keeps silent because
he knows when to speak.
7A wise man will be silent until
the right moment,
but a braggart and fool goes beyond the
right moment.
8Whoever uses too many words will
be loathed,
and whoever usurps the right to speak
will be hated.

[9]There may be good fortune for a man
in adversity,
and a windfall may result in a loss.
[10]There is a gift that profits you nothing,
and there is a gift that brings a
double return.
[11]There are losses because of glory,
and there are men who have raised their
heads from humble circumstances.
[12]There is a man who buys much for
a little,
but pays for it seven times over.

[13]The wise man makes himself beloved
through his words,
but the courtesies of fools are wasted.
[14]A fool's gift will profit you nothing,
for he has many eyes instead of one.
[15]He gives little and upbraids much,
he opens his mouth like a herald;
today he lends and tomorrow he
asks it back;
such a one is a hateful man.
[16]A fool will say, "I have no friend,
and there is no gratitude for my
good deeds;
those who eat my bread speak unkindly."
[17]How many will ridicule him, and
how often!

2 TIMOTHY 2

[14]Remind them of this, and charge them before the Lord to avoid disputing about words, which does no good, but only ruins the hearers. [15]Do your best to present yourself to God as one approved, a workman who has no need to be ashamed, rightly handling the word of truth. [16]Avoid such godless chatter, for it will lead people into more and more ungodliness, [17]and their talk will eat its way like gangrene. Among them are Hymenae´us and Phile´tus, [18]who have swerved from the truth by holding that the resurrection is past already. They are upsetting the faith of some. [19]But God's firm foundation stands, bearing this seal: "The Lord knows those who are his," and, "Let every one who names the name of the Lord depart from iniquity."

[20]In a great house there are not only vessels of gold and silver but also of wood and earthenware, and some for noble use, some for ignoble. [21]If any one purifies himself from what is ignoble, then he will be a vessel for noble use, consecrated and useful to the master of the house, ready for any good work. [22]So shun youthful passions and aim at righteousness, faith, love, and peace, along with those who call upon the Lord from a pure heart. [23]Have nothing to do with stupid, senseless controversies; you know that they breed quarrels. [24]And the Lord's servant must not be quarrelsome but kindly to every one, an apt teacher, forbearing, [25]correcting his opponents with gentleness. God may perhaps grant that they will repent and come to know the truth, [26]and they may escape from the snare of the devil, after being captured by him to do his will.

3 But understand this, that in the last days there will come times of stress. [2]For men will be lovers of self, lovers of money, proud, arrogant, abusive, disobedient to their parents, ungrateful, unholy, [3]inhuman, implacable, slanderers, profligates, fierce, haters of good, [4]treacherous, reckless, swollen with conceit, lovers of pleasure rather than lovers of God, [5]holding the form of religion but denying the power of it. Avoid such people. [6]For among them are those who make their way into households and capture weak women, burdened with sins and swayed by various impulses, [7]who will listen to anybody and can never arrive at a knowledge of the truth. [8]As Jan´nes and Jam´bres opposed Moses, so these men also oppose the truth, men of corrupt mind and counterfeit faith; [9]but they will not get very far, for their folly will be plain to all, as was that of those two men.

[10]Now you have observed my teaching, my conduct, my aim in life, my faith, my patience, my love, my steadfastness, [11]my

persecutions, my sufferings, what befell me at Antioch, at Ico′nium, and at Lystra, what persecutions I endured; yet from them all the Lord rescued me. [12]Indeed all who desire to live a godly life in Christ Jesus will be persecuted, [13]while evil men and impostors will go on from bad to worse, deceivers and deceived. [14]But as for you, continue in what you have learned and have firmly believed, knowing from whom you learned it [15]and how from childhood you have been acquainted with the Sacred Writings which are able to instruct you for salvation through faith in Christ Jesus. [16]All Scripture is inspired by God and profitable for teaching, for reproof, for correction, and for training in righteousness, [17]that the man of God may be complete, equipped for every good work.

REFLECTION

Ezekiel 36:16–28 is the last of seven Old Testament passages read at the Easter vigil. These readings tell the story of salvation history, culminating in Christ, the one who died for us and our salvation. So why does God say that he is not acting for the sake of his people but for his own holy name (see Ez 36:22–23)? It cannot be that God's actions are not good for his people, because the people are going to be cleansed of their sin and given a new heart (see vv. 25–26). This passage, however, is a reminder of the radical grace of God. God's saving act is not caused by any merit of ours, but it is done out of love. It was out of love that God tied his reputation on earth (his "name") to the people of Israel and consequently to the Church, not because we deserved his patronage. As Sirach tells us, violence cannot achieve justice (see Sir 20:4), and the violence that is recorded in Ezekiel does not have the final word. Things are put right, in the end, by a completely free and gratuitous act of love on God's part, which was not necessitated by any human deed. When you pray "hallowed be your name" in the Lord's Prayer, do you remember that God, in his love, has entrusted his name and reputation on earth to you?

November 3

EZEKIEL 37

The hand of the LORD was upon me, and he brought me out by the Spirit of the LORD, and set me down in the midst of the valley; it was full of bones. [2]And he led me round among them; and behold, there were very many upon the valley; and behold, they were very dry. [3]And he said to me, "Son of man, can these bones live?" And I answered, "O Lord GOD, you know." [4]Again he said to me, "Prophesy to these bones, and say to them, O dry bones, hear the word of the LORD. [5]Thus says the Lord GOD to these bones: Behold, I will cause breath to enter you, and you shall live. [6]And I will lay sinews upon you, and will cause flesh to come upon you, and cover you with skin, and put breath in you, and you shall live; and you shall know that I am the LORD."

[7]So I prophesied as I was commanded; and as I prophesied, there was a noise, and behold, a rattling; and the bones came together, bone to its bone. [8]And as I looked, there were sinews on them, and flesh had come upon them, and skin had covered them; but there was no spirit in them. [9]Then he said to me, "Prophesy to the spirit, prophesy, son of man, and say to the spirit, Thus says the Lord GOD: Come from the four winds, O spirit, and breathe upon these slain, that they may live." [10]So I prophesied as he commanded me, and the spirit came into them, and they lived, and stood upon their feet, an exceedingly great host.

[11]Then he said to me, "Son of man, these bones are the whole house of Israel. Behold, they say, 'Our bones are dried up, and our hope is lost; we are clean cut off.' [12]Therefore prophesy, and say to them, Thus says the Lord GOD: Behold, I will open your graves, and raise you from your graves, O my people; and I will bring you home into the land of Israel. [13]And you shall know that I am the LORD, when I open your graves, and raise you from your graves, O my people. [14]And I

will put my Spirit within you, and you shall
live, and I will place you in your own land;
then you shall know that I, the LORD, have
spoken, and I have done it, says the LORD."
15 The word of the LORD came to me: 16 "Son
of man, take a stick and write on it, 'For
Judah, and the children of Israel associated
with him'; then take another stick and write
upon it, 'For Joseph (the stick of E´phraim)
and all the house of Israel associated with
him'; 17 and join them together into one
stick, that they may become one in your
hand. 18 And when your people say to you,
'Will you not show us what you mean by
these?' 19 say to them, Thus says the Lord
GOD: Behold, I am about to take the stick
of Joseph (which is in the hand of E´phraim)
and the tribes of Israel associated with him;
and I will join with it the stick of Judah, and
make them one stick, that they may be one
in my hand. 20 When the sticks on which you
write are in your hand before their eyes,
21 then say to them, Thus says the Lord GOD:
Behold, I will take the sons of Israel from
the nations among which they have gone,
and will gather them from all sides, and
bring them to their own land; 22 and I will
make them one nation in the land, upon
the mountains of Israel; and one king shall
be king over them all; and they shall be no
longer two nations, and no longer divided
into two kingdoms. 23 They shall not defile
themselves any more with their idols and
their detestable things, or with any of their
transgressions; but I will save them from all
the backslidings in which they have sinned,
and will cleanse them; and they shall be my
people, and I will be their God.
24 "My servant David shall be king over
them; and they shall all have one shepherd.
They shall follow my ordinances and be careful to observe my statutes. 25 They shall dwell
in the land where your fathers dwelt that
I gave to my servant Jacob; they and their
children and their children's children shall
dwell there for ever; and David my servant
shall be their prince for ever. 26 I will make a
covenant of peace with them; it shall be an
everlasting covenant with them; and I will
bless them and multiply them, and will set my
sanctuary in the midst of them for evermore.
27 My dwelling place shall be with them; and
I will be their God, and they shall be my
people. 28 Then the nations will know that I
the LORD sanctify Israel, when my sanctuary
is in the midst of them for evermore."

38 The word of the LORD came to me:
2 "Son of man, set your face toward
Gog, of the land of Ma´gog, the chief prince
of Me´shech and Tu´bal, and prophesy
against him 3 and say, Thus says the Lord
GOD: Behold, I am against you, O Gog, chief
prince of Me´shech and Tu´bal; 4 and I will
turn you about, and put hooks into your
jaws, and I will bring you forth, and all your
army, horses and horsemen, all of them
clothed in full armor, a great company, all
of them with buckler and shield, wielding
swords; 5 Persia, Cush, and Put are with
them, all of them with shield and helmet;
6 Gomer and all his hordes; Beth″-togar´mah
from the uttermost parts of the north with
all his hordes—many peoples are with you.
7 "Be ready and keep ready, you and all the
hosts that are assembled about you, and be
a guard for them. 8 After many days you will
be mustered; in the latter years you will go
against the land that is restored from war,
the land where people were gathered from
many nations upon the mountains of Israel,
which had been a continual waste; its people
were brought out from the nations and
now dwell securely, all of them. 9 You will
advance, coming on like a storm, you will
be like a cloud covering the land, you and all
your hordes, and many peoples with you.
10 "Thus says the Lord GOD: On that day
thoughts will come into your mind, and you
will devise an evil scheme 11 and say, 'I will go
up against the land of unwalled villages; I will
fall upon the quiet people who dwell securely,
all of them dwelling without walls, and having
no bars or gates'; 12 to seize spoil and carry
off plunder; to assail the waste places which
are now inhabited, and the people who were
gathered from the nations, who have gotten
cattle and goods, who dwell at the center of the
earth. 13 Sheba and De´dan and the merchants
of Tar´shish and all its villages will say to you,
'Have you come to seize spoil? Have you

assembled your hosts to carry off plunder, to
carry away silver and gold, to take away cattle
and goods, to seize great spoil?’
14 “Therefore, son of man, prophesy, and say
to Gog, Thus says the Lord GOD: On that day
when my people Israel are dwelling securely,
you will bestir yourself 15 and come from your
place out of the uttermost parts of the north,
you and many peoples with you, all of them
riding on horses, a great host, a mighty army;
16 you will come up against my people Israel,
like a cloud covering the land. In the latter
days I will bring you against my land, that the
nations may know me, when through you, O
Gog, I vindicate my holiness before their eyes.
17 “Thus says the Lord GOD: Are you he of
whom I spoke in former days by my servants
the prophets of Israel, who in those days
prophesied for years that I would bring you
against them? 18 But on that day, when Gog
shall come against the land of Israel, says the
Lord GOD, my wrath will be roused. 19 For in
my jealousy and in my blazing wrath I declare,
On that day there shall be a great shaking in the
land of Israel; 20 the fish of the sea, and the birds
of the air, and the beasts of the field, and all
creeping things that creep on the ground, and
all the men that are upon the face of the earth,
shall quake at my presence, and the mountains
shall be thrown down, and the cliffs shall fall,
and every wall shall tumble to the ground. 21 I
will summon every kind of terror against
Gog, says the Lord GOD; every man’s sword
will be against his brother. 22 With pestilence
and bloodshed I will enter into judgment
with him; and I will rain upon him and his
hordes and the many peoples that are with
him, torrential rains and hailstones, fire and
brimstone. 23 So I will show my greatness
and my holiness and make myself known
in the eyes of many nations. Then they will
know that I am the LORD.”

SIRACH 20

18 A slip on the pavement is better than
a slip of the tongue;
so the downfall of the wicked will
occur speedily.
19 An ungracious man is like a story told
at the wrong time,
which is continually on the lips of
the ignorant.
20 A proverb from a fool’s lips will be rejected,
for he does not tell it at its proper time.

21 A man may be prevented from sinning by
his poverty,
so when he rests he feels no remorse.
22 A man may lose his life through shame,
or lose it because of his foolish look.
23 A man may for shame make promises
to a friend,
and needlessly make him an enemy.
24 A lie is an ugly blot on a man;
it is continually on the lips of
the ignorant.
25 A thief is preferable to a habitual liar,
but the lot of both is ruin.
26 The disposition of a liar brings disgrace,
and his shame is ever with him.

27 He who speaks wisely will advance himself,
and a sensible man will please
great men.
28 Whoever cultivates the soil will heap up
his harvest,
and whoever pleases great men will atone
for injustice.
29 Presents and gifts blind the eyes of the wise;
like a muzzle on the mouth they
avert reproofs.
30 Hidden wisdom and unseen treasure,
what advantage is there in either
of them?
31 Better is the man who hides his folly
than the man who hides his wisdom.

2 TIMOTHY 4

I charge you in the presence of God and of Christ Jesus who is to judge the living and the dead, and by his appearing and his kingdom: 2 preach
the word, be urgent in season and out of
season, convince, rebuke, and exhort, be

unfailing in patience and in teaching. 3For the time is coming when people will not endure sound teaching, but having itching ears they will accumulate for themselves teachers to suit their own likings, 4and will turn away from listening to the truth and wander into myths. 5As for you, always be steady, endure suffering, do the work of an evangelist, fulfil your ministry.

6For I am already on the point of being sacrificed; the time of my departure has come. 7I have fought the good fight, I have finished the race, I have kept the faith. 8From now on there is laid up for me the crown of righteousness, which the Lord, the righteous judge, will award to me on that Day, and not only to me but also to all who have loved his appearing.

9Do your best to come to me soon. 10For Demas, in love with this present world, has deserted me and gone to Thessaloni′ca; Crescens has gone to Galatia, Titus to Dalmatia. 11Luke alone is with me. Get Mark and bring him with you; for he is very useful in serving me. 12Tych′icus I have sent to Ephesus. 13When you come, bring the cloak that I left with Carpus at Tro′as, also the books, and above all the parchments. 14Alexander the coppersmith did me great harm; the Lord will pay him back for his deeds. 15Beware of him yourself, for he strongly opposed our message. 16At my first defense no one took my part; all deserted me. May it not be charged against them! 17But the Lord stood by me and gave me strength to proclaim the word fully, that all the Gentiles might hear it. So I was rescued from the lion's mouth. 18The Lord will rescue me from every evil and save me for his heavenly kingdom. To him be the glory for ever and ever. Amen.

19Greet Prisca and Aqui′la, and the household of Onesiph′orus. 20Eras′tus remained at Corinth; Troph′imus I left ill at Mile′tus. 21Do your best to come before winter. Eubu′lus sends greetings to you, as do Pudens and Linus and Claudia and all the brethren.

22The Lord be with your spirit. Grace be with you.

REFLECTION

Today, St. Paul tries to instill in us a sense of urgency because a time is coming when people will no longer listen; they will flock to a teacher who says only what pleases them (see 2 Tm 4:3–4). Reading this passage might make us anxious, as Paul's warning seems to describe our own time, a time in which dialogue between people who disagree is disappearing. Let us not despair of our own time or of our fellow brothers and sisters, because many generations have passed between Paul's time and our own in which the Church has been tested and preaching has seemed vain. Let us keep the story from Ezekiel before us as an image of hope because God can renew even a nation that seems completely lifeless and dead (see Ez 37:11). And how is this resurrection achieved? It is through the voice of Ezekiel preaching to a pile of dry bones! Let us not be discouraged, therefore, because however difficult our witness in the world is, we are preaching to the living and not the dead. So until we have finished running our own race (see 2 Tm 4:7), let us be urgent in our ministry as Paul recommends. Do you ever let a sense of defeat discourage you in sharing your faith with others?

November 4

EZEKIEL 39

"And you, son of man, prophesy against Gog, and say, Thus says the Lord GOD: Behold, I am against you, O Gog, chief prince of Me′shech and Tu′bal; 2and I will turn you about and drive you forward, and bring you up from the uttermost parts of the north, and lead you against the mountains of Israel; 3then I will strike your bow from your left hand, and will make your arrows drop out of your right hand. 4You shall fall upon the mountains of Israel, you and all your hordes and the peoples that are with you; I will give you to birds of prey of every sort and to the wild beasts to be devoured. 5You shall fall in the open field; for I have spoken, says the Lord GOD. 6I will send fire on Magog and on those who dwell securely in the islands; and they shall know that I am the LORD.

7"And my holy name I will make known in the midst of my people Israel; and I will not let my holy name be profaned any more; and the nations shall know that I am the LORD, the Holy One in Israel. 8Behold, it is coming and it will be brought about, says the Lord GOD. That is the day of which I have spoken.

9"Then those who dwell in the cities of Israel will go forth and make fires of the weapons and burn them, shields and bucklers, bows and arrows, handpikes and spears, and they will make fires of them for seven years; 10so that they will not need to take wood out of the field or cut down any out of the forests, for they will make their fires of the weapons; they will despoil those who despoiled them, and plunder those who plundered them, says the Lord GOD.

11"On that day I will give to Gog a place for burial in Israel, the Valley of the Travelers east of the sea; it will block the travelers, for there Gog and all his multitude will be buried; it will be called the Valley of Ha′mon-gog. 12For seven months the house of Israel will be burying them, in order to cleanse the land. 13All the people of the land will bury them; and it will redound to their honor on the day that I show my glory, says the Lord GOD. 14They will set apart men to pass through the land continually and bury those remaining upon the face of the land, so as to cleanse it; at the end of seven months they will make their search. 15And when these pass through the land and any one sees a man's bone, then he shall set up a sign by it, till the buriers have buried it in the Valley of Ha′mon-gog. 16(A city Hamo′nah is there also.) Thus shall they cleanse the land.

17"As for you, son of man, thus says the Lord GOD: Speak to the birds of every sort and to all beasts of the field, 'Assemble and come, gather from all sides to the sacrificial feast which I am preparing for you, a great sacrificial feast upon the mountains of Israel, and you shall eat flesh and drink blood. 18You shall eat the flesh of the mighty, and drink the blood of the princes of the earth—of rams, of lambs, and of goats, of bulls, all of them fatlings of Bashan. 19And you shall eat fat till you are filled, and drink blood till you are drunk, at the sacrificial feast which I am preparing for you. 20And you shall be filled at my table with horses and riders, with mighty men and all kinds of warriors,' says the Lord GOD.

21"And I will set my glory among the nations; and all the nations shall see my judgment which I have executed, and my hand which I have laid on them. 22The house of Israel shall know that I am the LORD their God, from that day forward. 23And the nations shall know that the house of Israel went into captivity for their iniquity, because they dealt so treacherously with me that I hid my face from them and gave them into the hand of their adversaries, and they all fell by the sword. 24I dealt with them according to their uncleanness and their transgressions, and hid my face from them.

25"Therefore thus says the Lord GOD: Now I will restore the fortunes of Jacob, and have mercy upon the whole house of Israel; and I will be jealous for my holy name. 26They shall forget their shame, and all the treachery they have practiced against me, when they dwell securely in their land with none to make them afraid, 27when I have brought them back from the peoples and gathered them from their enemies' lands, and through them have vindicated my holiness in the sight of many nations. 28Then they shall know that I am the LORD their God because I sent them into exile among the nations, and then gathered them into their own land. I will leave none of them remaining among the nations any more; 29and I will not hide my face any more from them, when I pour out my Spirit upon the house of Israel, says the Lord GOD."

40 In the twenty-fifth year of our exile,
at the beginning of the year, on the
tenth day of the month, in the fourteenth
year after the city was conquered, on that
very day, the hand of the LORD was upon
me, [2]and brought me in the visions of
God into the land of Israel, and set me
down upon a very high mountain, on
which was a structure like a city opposite
me. [3]When he brought me there, behold,
there was a man, whose appearance was
like bronze, with a line of flax and a
measuring reed in his hand; and he was
standing in the gateway. [4]And the man
said to me, "Son of man, look with your
eyes, and hear with your ears, and set
your mind upon all that I shall show you,
for you were brought here in order that I
might show it to you; declare all that you
see to the house of Israel."

[5]And behold, there was a wall all around
the outside of the temple area, and the
length of the measuring reed in the man's
hand was six long cubits, each being a
cubit and a handbreadth in length; so he
measured the thickness of the wall, one
reed; and the height, one reed. [6]Then he
went into the gateway facing east, going
up its steps, and measured the threshold
of the gate, one reed deep; [7]and the side
rooms, one reed long, and one reed broad;
and the space between the side rooms, five
cubits; and the threshold of the gate by the
vestibule of the gate at the inner end, one
reed. [8]Then he measured the vestibule of
the gateway, eight cubits; [9]and its jambs,
two cubits; and the vestibule of the gate
was at the inner end. [10]And there were
three side rooms on either side of the east
gate; the three were of the same size; and
the jambs on either side were of the same
size. [11]Then he measured the breadth of
the opening of the gateway, ten cubits;
and the breadth of the gateway, thirteen
cubits. [12]There was a barrier before the
side rooms, one cubit on either side; and
the side rooms were six cubits on either
side. [13]Then he measured the gate from
the back of the one side room to the back
of the other, a breadth of five and twenty
cubits, from door to door. [14]He measured
also the vestibule, twenty cubits; and
round about the vestibule of the gateway
was the court. [15]From the front of the gate
at the entrance to the end of the inner
vestibule of the gate was fifty cubits. [16]And
the gateway had windows round about,
narrowing inwards into their jambs in
the side rooms, and likewise the vestibule
had windows round about inside, and on
the jambs were palm trees.

[17]Then he brought me into the outer
court; and behold, there were chambers
and a pavement, round about the court;
thirty chambers fronted on the pavement.
[18]And the pavement ran along the side of
the gates, corresponding to the length of
the gates; this was the lower pavement.
[19]Then he measured the distance from the
inner front of the lower gate to the outer
front of the inner court, a hundred cubits.

Then he went before me to the north,
[20]and behold, there was a gate which faced
toward the north, belonging to the outer
court. He measured its length and its
breadth. [21]Its side rooms, three on either
side, and its jambs and its vestibule were
of the same size as those of the first gate;
its length was fifty cubits, and its breadth
twenty-five cubits. [22]And its windows, its
vestibule, and its palm trees were of the
same size as those of the gate which faced
toward the east; and seven steps led up
to it; and its vestibule was on the inside.
[23]And opposite the gate on the north, as
on the east, was a gate to the inner court;
and he measured from gate to gate, a
hundred cubits.

[24]And he led me toward the south, and
behold, there was a gate on the south; and
he measured its jambs and its vestibule;
they had the same size as the others.
[25]And there were windows round about
in it and in its vestibule, like the windows of
the others; its length was fifty cubits, and its
breadth twenty-five cubits. [26]And there were
seven steps leading up to it, and its vestibule
was on the inside; and it had palm trees on
its jambs, one on either side. [27]And there
was a gate on the south of the inner court;

and he measured from gate to gate toward the south, a hundred cubits.

SIRACH 21

Have you sinned, my son? Do so no more,
but pray about your former sins.
2 Flee from sin as from a snake;
for if you approach sin, it will bite you.
Its teeth are lion's teeth,
and destroy the souls of men.
3 All lawlessness is like a two-edged sword;
there is no healing for its wound.
4 Terror and violence will lay waste riches;
thus the house of the proud will be
laid waste.
5 The prayer of a poor man goes from his lips
to the ears of God,
and his judgment comes speedily.
6 Whoever hates reproof walks in the steps
of the sinner,
but he that fears the Lord will repent
in his heart.
7 He who is mighty in speech is known
from afar;
but the sensible man, when he slips, is
aware of it.
8 A man who builds his house with other
people's money
is like one who gathers stones for his
burial mound.
9 An assembly of the wicked is like tow
gathered together,
and their end is a flame of fire.
10 The way of sinners is smoothly paved
with stones,
but at its end is the pit of Hades.

TITUS 1

Paul, a servant of God and an apostle of Jesus Christ, to further the faith of God's elect and their knowledge of the truth which accords with
godliness, 2 in hope of eternal life which
God, who never lies, promised ages ago
3 and at the proper time manifested in his
word through the preaching with which I
have been entrusted by command of God
our Savior;
4 To Titus, my true child in a common
faith:
Grace and peace from God the Father and
Christ Jesus our Savior.
5 This is why I left you in Crete, that you
might amend what was defective, and
appoint elders in every town as I directed
you, 6 if any man is blameless, the husband of
one wife, and his children are believers and
not open to the charge of debauchery and not
being insubordinate. 7 For a bishop, as God's
steward, must be blameless; he must not be
arrogant or quick-tempered or a drunkard or
violent or greedy for gain, 8 but hospitable, a
lover of goodness, master of himself, upright,
holy, and self-controlled; 9 he must hold firm
to the sure word as taught, so that he may be
able to give instruction in sound doctrine
and also to confute those who contradict
it. 10 For there are many insubordinate men,
empty talkers and deceivers, especially the
circumcision party; 11 they must be silenced,
since they are upsetting whole families by
teaching for base gain what they have no
right to teach. 12 One of themselves, a prophet
of their own, said, "Cretans are always liars,
evil beasts, lazy gluttons." 13 This testimony
is true. Therefore rebuke them sharply, that
they may be sound in the faith, 14 instead of
giving heed to Jewish myths or to commands
of men who reject the truth. 15 To the pure
all things are pure, but to the corrupt and
unbelieving nothing is pure; their very
minds and consciences are corrupted. 16 They
profess to know God, but they deny him by
their deeds; they are detestable, disobedient,
unfit for any good deed.

REFLECTION

In today's readings, St. Paul warns us against hypocrisy. A Christian, especially a teacher or bishop, should live an upright life, he explains, and hypocrisy is the characteristic of false teachers: "They profess to know God, but they deny him by their deeds" (Ti 1:16). It is difficult for anyone to be found completely innocent of the charge of hypocrisy because our deeds often fall short of the good we desire. We try to cultivate in our children, students, and friends good habits that we ourselves might not yet possess. It is not a bad thing to encourage others in virtue, but we should also have a sincere desire and actively work to practice what we preach. If we have sinned, let us flee from it and sin no more (see Sir 21:1). But, after we have repented and have been forgiven, let us not simply forget all of our past struggles and sins. Like the Israelites to whom Ezekiel is prophesying, let us remember our hardships but forget our shame (see Ez 39:23–29). If we listen to Sirach, therefore, we will diligently work toward greater holiness. And, if we listen to Ezekiel, the memory of our struggles will keep us humble, and we will not adopt a holier-than-thou attitude, which is the hallmark of a hypocrite. Do you ever find yourself criticizing someone else for a fault that you yourself have? Who have you criticized in the past that you can encourage today with a word of kindness?

November 5

EZEKIEL 40

28Then he brought me to the
inner court by the south gate,
and he measured the south gate; it was
of the same size as the others; 29Its side
rooms, its jambs, and its vestibule were
of the same size as the others; and there
were windows round about in it and in its
vestibule; its length was fifty cubits, and
its breadth twenty-five cubits. 30And there
were vestibules round about, twenty-five
cubits long and five cubits broad. 31Its
vestibule faced the outer court, and palm
trees were on its jambs, and its stairway
had eight steps.

32Then he brought me to the inner court
on the east side, and he measured the gate;
it was of the same size as the others. 33Its
side rooms, its jambs, and its vestibule were
of the same size as the others; and there
were windows round about in it and in its
vestibule; its length was fifty cubits, and its
breadth twenty-five cubits. 34Its vestibule
faced the outer court, and it had palm trees
on its jambs, one on either side; and its
stairway had eight steps.

35Then he brought me to the north gate,
and he measured it; it had the same size as
the others. 36Its side rooms, its jambs, and its
vestibule were of the same size as the others;
and it had windows round about; its length
was fifty cubits, and its breadth twenty-five
cubits. 37Its vestibule faced the outer court,
and it had palm trees on its jambs, one on
either side; and its stairway had eight steps.

38There was a chamber with its door in
the vestibule of the gate, where the burnt
offering was to be washed. 39And in the
vestibule of the gate were two tables on
either side, on which the burnt offering and
the sin offering and the guilt offering were
to be slaughtered. 40And on the outside of
the vestibule at the entrance of the north
gate were two tables; and on the other side
of the vestibule of the gate were two tables.
41Four tables were on the inside, and four
tables on the outside of the side of the gate,
eight tables, on which the sacrifices were to
be slaughtered. 42And there were also four
tables of hewn stone for the burnt offering,
a cubit and a half long, and a cubit and a
half broad, and one cubit high, on which
the instruments were to be laid with which
the burnt offerings and the sacrifices were
slaughtered. 43And hooks, a handbreadth
long, were fastened round about within.
And on the tables the flesh of the offering
was to be laid.

44Then he brought me from without into
the inner court, and behold, there were two
chambers in the inner court, one at the side
of the north gate facing south, the other at
the side of the south gate facing north. 45And
he said to me, This chamber which faces
south is for the priests who have charge of

the temple, 46and the chamber which faces
north is for the priests who have charge of
the altar; these are the sons of Za´dok, who
alone among the sons of Levi may come near
to the LORD to minister to him. 47And he
measured the court, a hundred cubits long,
and a hundred cubits broad, foursquare;
and the altar was in front of the temple.

48Then he brought me to the vestibule of
the temple and measured the jambs of the
vestibule, five cubits on either side; and the
breadth of the gate was fourteen cubits; and
the sidewalls of the gate were three cubits
on either side. 49The length of the vestibule
was twenty cubits, and the breadth twelve
cubits; and ten steps led up to it; and there
were pillars beside the jambs on either side.

41 Then he brought me to the nave, and
measured the jambs; on each side six
cubits was the breadth of the jambs. 2And
the breadth of the entrance was ten cubits;
and the sidewalls of the entrance were
five cubits on either side; and he measured
the length of the nave forty cubits, and its
breadth, twenty cubits. 3Then he went into
the inner room and measured the jambs of
the entrance, two cubits; and the breadth of
the entrance, six cubits; and the sidewalls of
the entrance, seven cubits. 4And he measured
the length of the room, twenty cubits, and its
breadth, twenty cubits, beyond the nave. And
he said to me, "This is the most holy place."

5Then he measured the wall of the temple,
six cubits thick; and the breadth of the side
chambers, four cubits, round about the
temple. 6And the side chambers were in
three stories, one over another, thirty in each
story. There were offsets all around the wall
of the temple to serve as supports for the
side chambers, so that they should not be
supported by the wall of the temple. 7And
the side chambers became broader as they
rose from story to story, corresponding to
the enlargement of the offset from story to
story round about the temple; on the side
of the temple a stairway led upward, and
thus one went up from the lowest story
to the top story through the middle story.
8I saw also that the temple had a raised
platform round about; the foundations of
the side chambers measured a full reed of
six long cubits. 9The thickness of the outer
wall of the side chambers was five cubits;
and the part of the platform which was left
free was five cubits. Between the platform
of the temple and the 10chambers of the
court was a breadth of twenty cubits round
about the temple on every side. 11And the
doors of the side chambers opened on
the part of the platform that was left free,
one door toward the north, and another
door toward the south; and the breadth of
the part that was left free was five cubits
round about.

12The building that was facing the temple
yard on the west side was seventy cubits
broad; and the wall of the building was five
cubits thick round about, and its length
ninety cubits.

13Then he measured the temple, a hundred
cubits long; and the yard and the building
with its walls, a hundred cubits long; 14also
the breadth of the east front of the temple
and the yard, a hundred cubits.

15Then he measured the length of the
building facing the yard which was at the west
and its walls on either side, a hundred cubits.

The nave of the temple and the inner room
and the outer vestibule 16were paneled and
round about all three had windows with
recessed frames. Over against the threshold
the temple was paneled with wood round
about, from the floor up to the windows (now
the windows were covered), 17to the space
above the door, even to the inner room, and on
the outside. And on all the walls round about
in the inner room and the nave were carved
likenesses 18of cherubim and palm trees, a
palm tree between cherub and cherub. Every
cherub had two faces: 19the face of a man
toward the palm tree on the one side, and
the face of a young lion toward the palm tree
on the other side. They were carved on the
whole temple round about; 20from the floor
to above the door cherubim and palm trees
were carved on the wall.

21The doorposts of the nave were squared;
and in front of the holy place was something
resembling 22an altar of wood, three cubits
high, two cubits long, and two cubits broad; its

corners, its base, and its walls were of wood. He said to me, "This is the table which is before the LORD." [23]The nave and the holy place had each a double door. [24]The doors had two leaves apiece, two swinging leaves for each door. [25]And on the doors of the nave were carved cherubim and palm trees, such as were carved on the walls; and there was a canopy of wood in front of the vestibule outside. [26]And there were recessed windows and palm trees on either side, on the sidewalls of the vestibule.

SIRACH 21

[11]Whoever keeps the law controls
his thoughts,
and wisdom is the fulfilment of
the fear of the Lord.
[12]He who is not clever cannot be taught,
but there is a cleverness which increases
bitterness.
[13]The knowledge of a wise man will increase
like a flood,
and his counsel like a flowing spring.
[14]The mind of a fool is like a
broken jar;
it will hold no knowledge.

[15]When a man of understanding hears a
wise saying,
he will praise it and add to it;
when a reveler hears it, he dislikes it
and casts it behind his back.
[16]A fool's narration is like a burden
on a journey,
but delight will be found in the speech of
the intelligent.
[17]The utterance of a sensible man will
be sought in the assembly,
and they will ponder his words in
their minds.

[18]Like a house that has vanished, so is
wisdom to a fool;
and the knowledge of the ignorant is
unexamined talk.
[19]To a senseless man education is chains
on his feet,
and like manacles on his right hand.
[20]A fool raises his voice when he laughs,
but a clever man smiles quietly.
[21]To a sensible man education is like a
golden ornament,
and like a bracelet on the right arm.

TITUS 2

**But as for you, teach what befits
sound doctrine. [2]Bid the older
men be temperate, serious, sensible, sound
in faith, in love, and in steadfastness. [3]Bid**
the older women likewise to be reverent in
behavior, not to be slanderers or slaves to
drink; they are to teach what is good, [4]and
so train the young women to love their
husbands and children, [5]to be sensible,
chaste, domestic, kind, and submissive to
their husbands, that the word of God may
not be discredited. [6]Likewise urge the
younger men to control themselves. [7]Show
yourself in all respects a model of good
deeds, and in your teaching show integrity,
gravity, [8]and sound speech that cannot be
censured, so that an opponent may be put
to shame, having nothing evil to say of us.
[9]Bid slaves to be submissive to their masters
and to give satisfaction in every respect;
they are not to talk back, [10]nor to pilfer, but
to show entire and true fidelity, so that in
everything they may adorn the doctrine of
God our Savior.

[11]For the grace of God has appeared for
the salvation of all men, [12]training us to
renounce irreligion and worldly passions,
and to live sober, upright, and godly lives
in this world, [13]awaiting our blessed hope,
the appearing of the glory of our great God
and Savior Jesus Christ, [14]who gave himself
for us to redeem us from all iniquity and to
purify for himself a people of his own who
are zealous for good deeds.

[15]Declare these things; exhort and reprove
with all authority. Let no one disregard you.

3 Remind them to be submissive to rulers
and authorities, to be obedient, to be
ready for any honest work, [2]to speak evil
of no one, to avoid quarreling, to be gentle,

and to show perfect courtesy toward all
men. 3For we ourselves were once foolish,
disobedient, led astray, slaves to various
passions and pleasures, passing our days in
malice and envy, hated by men and hating
one another; 4but when the goodness and
loving kindness of God our Savior appeared,
5he saved us, not because of deeds done by
us in righteousness, but in virtue of his own
mercy, by the washing of regeneration and
renewal in the Holy Spirit, 6which he poured
out upon us richly through Jesus Christ our
Savior, 7so that we might be justified by his
grace and become heirs in hope of eternal
life. 8The saying is sure.

I desire you to insist on these things, so
that those who have believed in God may be
careful to apply themselves to good deeds;
these are excellent and profitable to men.
9But avoid stupid controversies, genealogies,
dissensions, and quarrels over the law, for
they are unprofitable and futile. 10As for
a man who is factious, after admonishing
him once or twice, have nothing more to do
with him, 11knowing that such a person is
perverted and sinful; he is self-condemned.
12When I send Ar′temas or Tych′icus
to you, do your best to come to me at
Nicop′olis, for I have decided to spend the
winter there. 13Do your best to speed Ze′nas
the lawyer and Apol′los on their way; see
that they lack nothing. 14And let our people
learn to apply themselves to good deeds, so
as to help cases of urgent need, and not to be
unfruitful.

15All who are with me send greetings to
you. Greet those who love us in the faith.

Grace be with you all.

REFLECTION

In Titus 2–3, St. Paul offers us a type of "household code," which was commonplace in his time. We should be faithful, loving, and temperate, Paul says, and yet obedient to those with higher authority and with greater wisdom. This way of thinking may seem antiquated, and because some of the power structures in our own time are mercifully different from that of the Roman empire, e.g., that of slavery, it can be easy to pass over these words. We, however, can benefit from the wisdom that constructs the household code because this code encourages us to respect and learn from those with greater experience and responsibility. As Sirach tells us, it is only the fool who refuses to hear the words of the wise (see Sir 21:15), and the fool views education as a chain upon him (see v. 19). We must not be too proud to learn from anyone, even those with authority over us whom we might be tempted to undervalue, such as a boss, parent, or teacher. Ezekiel, who is used to proclaiming the very word of God, remains entirely silent throughout his tour of the new Temple in Jerusalem and listens to him who has been given greater authority. Do you ever refuse to listen to a superior simply because you dislike that they have some authority over you?

November 6

EZEKIEL 42

**Then he led me out into the in-
ner court, toward the north, and
he brought me to the chambers
which were opposite the temple yard
and opposite the building on the north.
2The length of the building which was**
on the north side was a hundred cubits,
and the breadth fifty cubits. 3Adjoining
the twenty cubits which belonged to the
inner court, and facing the pavement which
belonged to the outer court, was gallery
against gallery in three stories. 4And before
the chambers was a passage inward, ten
cubits wide and a hundred cubits long,
and their doors were on the north. 5Now
the upper chambers were narrower, for the
galleries took more away from them than
from the lower and middle chambers in the

building. 6For they were in three stories,
and they had no pillars like the pillars of the
outer court; hence the upper chambers were
set back from the ground more than the
lower and the middle ones. 7And there was a
wall outside parallel to the chambers, toward
the outer court, opposite the chambers,
fifty cubits long. 8For the chambers on the
outer court were fifty cubits long, while
those opposite the temple were a hundred
cubits long. 9Below these chambers was an
entrance on the east side, as one enters them
from the outer court, 10where the outside
wall begins.

On the south also, opposite the yard and
opposite the building, there were chambers
11with a passage in front of them; they were
similar to the chambers on the north, of the
same length and breadth, with the same exits
and arrangements and doors. 12And below
the south chambers was an entrance on the
east side, where one enters the passage, and
opposite them was a dividing wall.

13Then he said to me, "The north chambers and the south chambers opposite the
yard are the holy chambers, where the priests
who approach the LORD shall eat the most
holy offerings; there they shall put the most
holy offerings—the cereal offering, the sin
offering, and the guilt offering, for the place
is holy. 14When the priests enter the holy
place, they shall not go out of it into the outer
court without laying there the garments in
which they minister, for these are holy; they
shall put on other garments before they go
near to that which is for the people."

15Now when he had finished measuring
the interior of the temple area, he led me out
by the gate which faced east, and measured
the temple area round about. 16He measured
the east side with the measuring reed, five
hundred cubits by the measuring reed.
17Then he turned and measured the north
side, five hundred cubits by the measuring
reed. 18Then he turned and measured the
south side, five hundred cubits by the
measuring reed. 19Then he turned to the
west side and measured, five hundred cubits
by the measuring reed. 20He measured it
on the four sides. It had a wall around it,
five hundred cubits long and five hundred
cubits broad, to make a separation between
the holy and the common.

43 Afterward he brought me to the gate,
the gate facing east. 2And behold,
the glory of the God of Israel came from
the east; and the sound of his coming was
like the sound of many waters; and the earth
shone with his glory. 3And the vision I saw
was like the vision which I had seen when he
came to destroy the city, and like the vision
which I had seen by the river Che′bar; and I
fell upon my face. 4As the glory of the LORD
entered the temple by the gate facing east,
5the Spirit lifted me up, and brought me into
the inner court; and behold, the glory of the
LORD filled the temple.

6While the man was standing beside
me, I heard one speaking to me out of the
temple; 7and he said to me, "Son of man,
this is the place of my throne and the place
of the soles of my feet, where I will dwell in
the midst of the sons of Israel for ever. And
the house of Israel shall no more defile my
holy name, neither they, nor their kings, by
their harlotry, and by the dead bodies of
their kings, 8by setting their threshold by
my threshold and their doorposts beside
my doorposts, with only a wall between me
and them. They have defiled my holy name
by their abominations which they have
committed, so I have consumed them in my
anger. 9Now let them put away their idolatry
and the dead bodies of their kings far from
me, and I will dwell in their midst for ever.

10"And you, son of man, describe to
the house of Israel the temple and its
appearance and plan, that they may be
ashamed of their iniquities. 11And if they
are ashamed of all that they have done,
portray the temple, its arrangement, its
exits and its entrances, and its whole form;
and make known to them all its ordinances
and all its laws; and write it down in
their sight, so that they may observe and
perform all its laws and all its ordinances.
12This is the law of the temple: the whole
territory round about upon the top of the
mountain shall be most holy. Behold, this
is the law of the temple.

13“These are the dimensions of the altar by cubits (the cubit being a cubit and a handbreadth): its base shall be one cubit high, and one cubit broad, with a rim of one span around its edge. And this shall be the height of the altar: 14from the base on the ground to the lower ledge, two cubits, with a breadth of one cubit; and from the smaller ledge to the larger ledge, four cubits, with a breadth of one cubit; 15and the altar hearth, four cubits; and from the altar hearth projecting upward, four horns, one cubit high. 16The altar hearth shall be square, twelve cubits long by twelve broad. 17The ledge also shall be square, fourteen cubits long by fourteen broad, with a rim around it half a cubit broad, and its base one cubit round about. The steps of the altar shall face east.”

18And he said to me, “Son of man, thus says the Lord GOD: These are the ordinances for the altar: On the day when it is erected for offering burnt offerings upon it and for throwing blood against it, 19you shall give to the Levitical priests of the family of Za′dok, who draw near to me to minister to me, says the Lord GOD, a bull for a sin offering. 20And you shall take some of its blood, and put it on the four horns of the altar, and on the four corners of the ledge, and upon the rim round about; thus you shall cleanse the altar and make atonement for it. 21You shall also take the bull of the sin offering, and it shall be burnt in the appointed place belonging to the temple, outside the sacred area. 22And on the second day you shall offer a he-goat without blemish for a sin offering; and the altar shall be cleansed, as it was cleansed with the bull. 23When you have finished cleansing it, you shall offer a bull without blemish and a ram from the flock without blemish. 24You shall present them before the LORD, and the priests shall sprinkle salt upon them and offer them up as a burnt offering to the LORD. 25For seven days you shall provide daily a goat for a sin offering; also a bull and a ram from the flock, without blemish, shall be provided. 26Seven days shall they make atonement for the altar and purify it, and so consecrate it. 27And when they have completed these days, then from the eighth day onward the priests shall offer upon the altar your burnt offerings and your peace offerings; and I will accept you, says the Lord GOD.”

44 Then he brought me back to the outer gate of the sanctuary, which faces east; and it was shut. 2And he said to me, “This gate shall remain shut; it shall not be opened, and no one shall enter by it; for the LORD, the God of Israel, has entered by it; therefore it shall remain shut. 3Only the prince may sit in it to eat bread before the LORD; he shall enter by way of the vestibule of the gate, and shall go out by the same way.”

4Then he brought me by way of the north gate to the front of the temple; and I looked, and behold, the glory of the LORD filled the temple of the LORD; and I fell upon my face. 5And the LORD said to me, “Son of man, mark well, see with your eyes, and hear with your ears all that I shall tell you concerning all the ordinances of the temple of the LORD and all its laws; and mark well those who may be admitted to the temple and all those who are to be excluded from the sanctuary. 6And say to the rebellious house, to the house of Israel, Thus says the Lord GOD: O house of Israel, let there be an end to all your abominations, 7in admitting foreigners, uncircumcised in heart and flesh, to be in my sanctuary, profaning it, when you offer to me my food, the fat and the blood. You have broken my covenant, in addition to all your abominations. 8And you have not kept charge of my holy things; but you have set foreigners to keep my charge in my sanctuary.

9“Therefore thus says the Lord GOD: No foreigner, uncircumcised in heart and flesh, of all the foreigners who are among the people of Israel, shall enter my sanctuary. 10But the Levites who went far from me, going astray from me after their idols when Israel went astray, shall bear their punishment. 11They shall be ministers in my sanctuary, having oversight at the gates of the temple, and serving in the temple; they shall slay the burnt offering and the sacrifice for the people, and they shall attend on the

people, to serve them. 12Because they
ministered to them before their idols and
became a stumbling block of iniquity to
the house of Israel, therefore I have sworn
concerning them, says the Lord GOD, that
they shall bear their punishment. 13They
shall not come near to me, to serve me as
priest, nor come near any of my sacred
things and the things that are most
sacred; but they shall bear their shame,
because of the abominations which they
have committed. 14Yet I will appoint them
to keep charge of the temple, to do all its
service and all that is to be done in it."

SIRACH 21

22The foot of a fool rushes into a house,
but a man of experience stands
respectfully before it.
23A boor peers into the house from the door,
but a cultivated man remains outside.
24It is ill-mannered for a man to listen
at a door,
and a discreet man is grieved by
the disgrace.
25The lips of strangers will speak of
these things,
but the words of the prudent will be
weighed in the balance.
26The mind of fools is in their mouth,
but the mouth of wise men is in their mind.
27When an ungodly man curses his adversary,
he curses his own soul.
28A whisperer defiles his own soul
and is hated in his neighborhood.

PHILEMON 1

Paul, a prisoner for Christ Jesus, and Timothy our brother,

**To Phile′mon our beloved fellow work-
er 2and Ap′phia our sister and Archip′pus**
our fellow soldier, and the church in your
house:

3Grace to you and peace from God our
Father and the Lord Jesus Christ.

4I thank my God always when I remember
you in my prayers, 5because I hear of your
love and of the faith which you have toward
the Lord Jesus and all the saints, 6and I pray
that the sharing of your faith may promote
the knowledge of all the good that is ours
in Christ. 7For I have derived much joy
and comfort from your love, my brother,
because the hearts of the saints have been
refreshed through you.

8Accordingly, though I am bold enough
in Christ to command you to do what is
required, 9yet for love's sake I prefer to appeal
to you—I, Paul, an ambassador and now a
prisoner also for Christ Jesus—10I appeal
to you for my child, Ones′imus, whose
father I have become in my imprisonment.
11(Formerly he was useless to you, but now
he is indeed useful to you and to me.) 12I am
sending him back to you, sending my very
heart. 13I would have been glad to keep him
with me, in order that he might serve me on
your behalf during my imprisonment for
the gospel; 14but I preferred to do nothing
without your consent in order that your
goodness might not be by compulsion but
of your own free will.

15Perhaps this is why he was parted from
you for a while, that you might have him
back for ever, 16no longer as a slave but more
than a slave, as a beloved brother, especially
to me but how much more to you, both in
the flesh and in the Lord. 17So if you consider
me your partner, receive him as you would
receive me. 18If he has wronged you at all,
or owes you anything, charge that to my
account. 19I, Paul, write this with my own
hand, I will repay it—to say nothing of your
owing me even your own self. 20Yes, brother,
I want some benefit from you in the Lord.
Refresh my heart in Christ.

21Confident of your obedience, I write to
you, knowing that you will do even more
than I say. 22At the same time, prepare a
guest room for me, for I am hoping through
your prayers to be granted to you.

23Ep′aphras, my fellow prisoner in Christ
Jesus, sends greetings to you, 24and so do
Mark, Aristar′chus, Demas, and Luke, my
fellow workers.

[25]The grace of the Lord Jesus Christ be with your spirit.

REFLECTION

During his tour of the Temple complex, Ezekiel sees the glory of the Lord coming into the gate, and God tells him, "This is the place of my throne and the place of the soles of my feet, where I will dwell" (Ez 43:7). Just as God went out to the people in exile in Ezekiel 1, now he is returning to Jerusalem (see v. 3). What does this going and coming of God mean? Isn't God everywhere all the time? The meticulous detail in which the Temple is described heightens this scandalous idea: God is coming to rest in a specific place. Of course, God is all-powerful and is not confined to any space, but God in his mercy has chosen to dwell and be found in particular places for our sake. God made himself visible in the Person of Jesus Christ, and he is truly present in the consecrated bread on our altars. Sometimes the idea that God is everywhere can give us an excuse not to go to church, not to pray, and not to seek God's presence where he has assured us we will find him. Do you think of a church and the Tabernacle as a place where God is truly present?

November 7

EZEKIEL 44

[15]**"But the Levitical priests, the sons of Za′dok, who kept the charge of my sanctuary when the people of Israel went astray from me, shall come**
near to me to minister to me; and they
shall attend on me to offer me the fat and
the blood, says the Lord GOD; [16]they shall
enter my sanctuary, and they shall approach
my table, to minister to me, and they shall
keep my charge. [17]When they enter the
gates of the inner court, they shall wear
linen garments; they shall have nothing of
wool on them, while they minister at the
gates of the inner court, and within. [18]They
shall have linen turbans upon their heads,
and linen breeches upon their loins; they
shall not clothe themselves with anything
that causes sweat. [19]And when they go out
into the outer court to the people, they
shall put off the garments in which they
have been ministering, and lay them in the
holy chambers; and they shall put on other
garments, lest they communicate holiness to
the people with their garments. [20]They shall
not shave their heads or let their locks grow
long; they shall only trim the hair of their
heads. [21]No priest shall drink wine, when he
enters the inner court. [22]They shall not marry
a widow, or a divorced woman, but only a
virgin of the stock of the house of Israel, or a
widow who is the widow of a priest. [23]They
shall teach my people the difference between
the holy and the common, and show them
how to distinguish between the unclean and
the clean. [24]In a controversy they shall act
as judges, and they shall judge it according
to my judgments. They shall keep my
laws and my statutes in all my appointed
feasts, and they shall keep my sabbaths
holy. [25]They shall not defile themselves by
going near to a dead person; however, for
father or mother, for son or daughter, for
brother or unmarried sister they may defile
themselves. [26]After he is defiled, he shall
count for himself seven days, and then he
shall be clean. [27]And on the day that he goes
into the holy place, into the inner court, to
minister in the holy place, he shall offer his
sin offering, says the Lord GOD.

[28]"They shall have no inheritance; I am
their inheritance: and you shall give them no
possession in Israel; I am their possession.
[29]They shall eat the cereal offering, the sin
offering, and the guilt offering; and every
devoted thing in Israel shall be theirs. [30]And
the first of all the first fruits of all kinds,
and every offering of all kinds from all
your offerings, shall belong to the priests;
you shall also give to the priests the first of
your coarse meal, that a blessing may rest
on your house. [31]The priests shall not eat

of anything, whether bird or beast, that has died of itself or is torn.

45 “When you allot the land as a possession, you shall set apart for the Lord a portion of the land as a holy district, twenty-five thousand cubits long and twenty thousand cubits broad; it shall be holy throughout its whole extent. [2]Of this a square plot of five hundred by five hundred cubits shall be for the sanctuary, with fifty cubits for an open space around it. [3]And in the holy district you shall measure off a section twenty-five thousand cubits long and ten thousand broad, in which shall be the sanctuary, the most holy place. [4]It shall be the holy portion of the land; it shall be for the priests, who minister in the sanctuary and approach the Lord to minister to him; and it shall be a place for their houses and a holy place for the sanctuary. [5]Another section, twenty-five thousand cubits long and ten thousand cubits broad, shall be for the Levites who minister at the temple, as their possession for cities to live in.

[6]“Alongside the portion set apart as the holy district you shall assign for the possession of the city an area five thousand cubits broad, and twenty-five thousand cubits long; it shall belong to the whole house of Israel.

[7]“And to the prince shall belong the land on both sides of the holy district and the property of the city, alongside the holy district and the property of the city, on the west and on the east, corresponding in length to one of the tribal portions, and extending from the western to the eastern boundary of the land. [8]It is to be his property in Israel. And my princes shall no more oppress my people; but they shall let the house of Israel have the land according to their tribes.

[9]“Thus says the Lord God: Enough, O princes of Israel! Put away violence and oppression, and execute justice and righteousness; cease your evictions of my people, says the Lord God.

[10]“You shall have just balances, a just ephah, and a just bath. [11]The ephah and the bath shall be of the same measure, the bath containing one tenth of a homer, and the ephah one tenth of a homer; the homer shall be the standard measure. [12]The shekel shall be twenty gerahs; five shekels shall be five shekels, and ten shekels shall be ten shekels, and your mina shall be fifty shekels.

[13]“This is the offering which you shall make: one sixth of an ephah from each homer of wheat, and one sixth of an ephah from each homer of barley, [14]and as the fixed portion of oil, one tenth of a bath from each cor (the cor, like the homer, contains ten baths); [15]and one sheep from every flock of two hundred, from the families of Israel. This is the offering for cereal offerings, burnt offerings, and peace offerings, to make atonement for them, says the Lord God. [16]All the people of the land shall give this offering to the prince in Israel. [17]It shall be the prince's duty to furnish the burnt offerings, cereal offerings, and drink offerings, at the feasts, the new moons, and the sabbaths, all the appointed feasts of the house of Israel: he shall provide the sin offerings, cereal offerings, burnt offerings, and peace offerings, to make atonement for the house of Israel.

[18]“Thus says the Lord God: In the first month, on the first day of the month, you shall take a young bull without blemish, and cleanse the sanctuary. [19]The priest shall take some of the blood of the sin offering and put it on the doorposts of the temple, the four corners of the ledge of the altar, and the posts of the gate of the inner court. [20]You shall do the same on the seventh day of the month for any one who has sinned through error or ignorance; so you shall make atonement for the temple.

[21]“In the first month, on the fourteenth day of the month, you shall celebrate the feast of the passover, and for seven days unleavened bread shall be eaten. [22]On that day the prince shall provide for himself and all the people of the land a young bull for a sin offering. [23]And on the seven days of the festival he shall provide as a burnt offering to the Lord seven young bulls and seven rams without blemish, on each of the seven days; and a he-goat daily for a sin offering. [24]And he shall provide as a cereal offering

an ephah for each bull, an ephah for each ram, and a hin of oil to each ephah. 25 In the seventh month, on the fifteenth day of the month and for the seven days of the feast, he shall make the same provision for sin offerings, burnt offerings, and cereal offerings, and for the oil.

46 "Thus says the Lord GOD: The gate of the inner court that faces east shall be shut on the six working days; but on the sabbath day it shall be opened and on the day of the new moon it shall be opened. 2 The prince shall enter by the vestibule of the gate from without, and shall take his stand by the post of the gate. The priests shall offer his burnt offering and his peace offerings, and he shall worship at the threshold of the gate. Then he shall go out, but the gate shall not be shut until evening. 3 The people of the land shall worship at the entrance of that gate before the LORD on the sabbaths and on the new moons. 4 The burnt offering that the prince offers to the LORD on the sabbath day shall be six lambs without blemish and a ram without blemish; 5 and the cereal offering with the ram shall be an ephah, and the cereal offering with the lambs shall be as much as he is able, together with a hin of oil to each ephah. 6 On the day of the new moon he shall offer a young bull without blemish, and six lambs and a ram, which shall be without blemish; 7 as a cereal offering he shall provide an ephah with the bull and an ephah with the ram, and with the lambs as much as he is able, together with a hin of oil to each ephah. 8 When the prince enters, he shall go in by the vestibule of the gate, and he shall go out by the same way.

9 "When the people of the land come before the LORD at the appointed feasts, he who enters by the north gate to worship shall go out by the south gate; and he who enters by the south gate shall go out by the north gate: no one shall return by way of the gate by which he entered, but each shall go out straight ahead. 10 When they go in, the prince shall go in with them; and when they go out, he shall go out.

11 "At the feasts and the appointed seasons the cereal offering with a young bull shall be an ephah, and with a ram an ephah, and with the lambs as much as one is able to give, together with a hin of oil to an ephah. 12 When the prince provides a freewill offering, either a burnt offering or peace offerings as a freewill offering to the LORD, the gate facing east shall be opened for him; and he shall offer his burnt offering or his peace offerings as he does on the sabbath day. Then he shall go out, and after he has gone out the gate shall be shut.

13 "He shall provide a lamb a year old without blemish for a burnt offering to the LORD daily; morning by morning he shall provide it. 14 And he shall provide a cereal offering with it morning by morning, one sixth of an ephah, and one third of a hin of oil to moisten the flour, as a cereal offering to the LORD; this is the ordinance for the continual burnt offering. 15 Thus the lamb and the meal offering and the oil shall be provided, morning by morning, for a continual burnt offering.

16 "Thus says the Lord GOD: If the prince makes a gift to any of his sons out of his inheritance, it shall belong to his sons, it is their property by inheritance. 17 But if he makes a gift out of his inheritance to one of his servants, it shall be his to the year of liberty; then it shall revert to the prince; only his sons may keep a gift from his inheritance. 18 The prince shall not take any of the inheritance of the people, thrusting them out of their property; he shall give his sons their inheritance out of his own property, so that none of my people shall be dispossessed of his property."

SIRACH 22

The indolent may be compared to a
filthy stone,
and every one hisses at his disgrace.
2 The indolent may be compared to the filth
of dunghills;
any one that picks it up will shake it off
his hand.

3It is a disgrace to be the father of an
undisciplined son,
and the birth of a daughter is a loss.
4A sensible daughter obtains her husband,
but one who acts shamefully brings grief
to her father.
5An impudent daughter disgraces father
and husband,
and will be despised by both.
6Like music in mourning is a tale told at the
wrong time,
but chastising and discipline are wisdom
at all times.

7He who teaches a fool is like one who glues
potsherds together,
or who rouses a sleeper from deep slumber.
8He who tells a story to a fool tells it to a
drowsy man;
and at the end he will say, "What is it?"
11Weep for the dead, for he lacks the light;
and weep for the fool, for he lacks
intelligence;
weep less bitterly for the dead, for he has
attained rest;
but the life of the fool is worse than death.
12Mourning for the dead lasts seven days,
but for a fool or an ungodly man it lasts
all his life.

HEBREWS 1

In many and various ways God spoke of old to our fathers by the prophets; 2but in these last days he has spoken to us by a Son, whom he appointed the heir of all things, through whom also he created the ages. 3He reflects the glory of God and bears the very stamp of his nature, upholding the universe by his word of power. When he had made purification for sins, he sat down at the right hand of the Majesty on high, 4having become as much superior to angels as the name he has obtained is more excellent than theirs.

5For to what angel did God ever say,
"You are my Son,
today I have begotten you"?
Or again,
"I will be to him a father,
and he shall be to me a son"?
6And again, when he brings the first-born into the world, he says,
"Let all God's angels worship him."
7Of the angels he says,
"Who makes his angels winds,
and his servants flames of fire."
8But of the Son he says,
"Your throne, O God, is for ever
and ever,
the righteous scepter is the scepter of
your kingdom.
9You have loved righteousness and
hated lawlessness;
therefore God, your God, has anointed you
with the oil of gladness beyond your
comrades."
10And,
"You, Lord, founded the earth in
the beginning,
and the heavens are the work of
your hands;
11they will perish, but you remain;
they will all grow old like a garment,
12like a cloak you will roll them up,
and they will be changed.
But you are the same,
and your years will never end."
13But to what angel has he ever said,
"Sit at my right hand,
till I make your enemies
a stool for your feet"?
14Are they not all ministering spirits sent forth to serve, for the sake of those who are to obtain salvation?

2 Therefore we must pay the closer
attention to what we have heard, lest
we drift away from it. 2For if the message
declared by angels was valid and every
transgression or disobedience received a
just retribution, 3how shall we escape if
we neglect such a great salvation? It was
declared at first by the Lord, and it was
attested to us by those who heard him,
4while God also bore witness by signs and
wonders and various miracles and by gifts
of the Holy Spirit distributed according to
his own will.

REFLECTION

When we read the priestly instructions found in Ezekiel 44–46, we might be tempted to pass them over quickly and to see in them nothing of importance. But the Book of Hebrews reminds us that the teaching of the prophets is essential—the Son of God is the one who fulfills the prophets' work and words. The prophets prepared God's people to recognize Christ (see Heb 1:1–14). In Hebrews 2, the importance of the Law, delivered by angels, serves to highlight the importance of the teaching of Christ, who is God (see v. 2). Let us not think these Levitical instructions, therefore, are the result of an ancient legalism that shares nothing with our present faith. Just as Ezekiel details priestly clothes only worn for ministering in the Temple, so too our priests wear vestments with symbolic meaning and aesthetic qualities that form part of our worship. Many of us wear our "Sunday best" to attend church, and this is not simply legalistic. These vestments and clothes are a symbol of coming to God with a pure heart and yet without fear (without sweating—see Ez 44:17–18). Do you see the carefully observed traditions in the Mass as simply legalistic, or as a reflection of God's intimate care for us as in his detailed instructions to Ezekiel?

November 8

EZEKIEL 46

[19]Then he brought me through
the entrance, which was at the
side of the gate, to the north row of the
holy chambers for the priests; and there
I saw a place at the extreme western end of
them. [20]And he said to me, "This is the place
where the priests shall boil the guilt offering
and the sin offering, and where they shall
bake the cereal offering, in order not to
bring them out into the outer court and so
communicate holiness to the people."

[21]Then he brought me forth to the outer
court, and led me to the four corners of the
court; and in each corner of the court there
was a court—[22]in the four corners of the
court were small courts, forty cubits long
and thirty broad; the four were of the same
size. [23]On the inside, around each of the four
courts was a row of masonry, with hearths
made at the bottom of the rows round about.
[24]Then he said to me, "These are the kitchens
where those who minister at the temple shall
boil the sacrifices of the people."

47 Then he brought me back to the door
of the temple; and behold, water was
issuing from below the threshold of the
temple toward the east (for the temple faced
east); and the water was flowing down from
below the right side of the threshold of the
temple, south of the altar. [2]Then he brought
me out by way of the north gate, and led
me round on the outside to the outer gate,
that faces toward the east; and the water was
coming out on the right side.

[3]Going on eastward with a line in his
hand, the man measured a thousand cubits,
and then led me through the water; and
it was ankle-deep. [4]Again he measured a
thousand, and led me through the water;
and it was knee-deep. Again he measured a
thousand, and led me through the water; and
it was up to the loins. [5]Again he measured a
thousand, and it was a river that I could not
pass through, for the water had risen; it was
deep enough to swim in, a river that could
not be passed through. [6]And he said to me,
"Son of man, have you seen this?"

Then he led me back along the bank of
the river. [7]As I went back, I saw upon the
bank of the river very many trees on the one
side and on the other. [8]And he said to me,
"This water flows toward the eastern region
and goes down into the Ar′abah; and when
it enters the stagnant waters of the sea, the
water will become fresh. [9]And wherever
the river goes every living creature which
swarms will live, and there will be very
many fish; for this water goes there, that
the waters of the sea may become fresh; so
everything will live where the river goes.
[10]Fishermen will stand beside the sea; from

En-ge′di to En-eg′laim it will be a place
for the spreading of nets; its fish will be of
very many kinds, like the fish of the Great
Sea. 11 But its swamps and marshes will not
become fresh; they are to be left for salt.
12 And on the banks, on both sides of the
river, there will grow all kinds of trees for
food. Their leaves will not wither nor their
fruit fail, but they will bear fresh fruit every
month, because the water for them flows
from the sanctuary. Their fruit will be for
food, and their leaves for healing."

13 Thus says the Lord GOD: "These are the
boundaries by which you shall divide the
land for inheritance among the twelve tribes
of Israel. Joseph shall have two portions.
14 And you shall divide it equally; I swore to
give it to your fathers, and this land shall fall
to you as your inheritance.

15 "This shall be the boundary of the land:
On the north side, from the Great Sea by way
of Heth′lon to the entrance of Ha′math, and
on to Ze′dad, 16 Bero′thah, Sib′raim (which
lies on the border between Damascus
and Ha′math), as far as Hazer-hat′ticon,
which is on the border of Hau′ran. 17 So the
boundary shall run from the sea to Ha′zar-
e′non, which is on the northern border of
Damascus, with the border of Ha′math to
the north. This shall be the north side.

18 "On the east side, the boundary shall run
from Ha′zar-e′non between Hau′ran and
Damascus; along the Jordan between Gilead
and the land of Israel; to the eastern sea and
as far as Ta′mar. This shall be the east side.

19 "On the south side, it shall run from
Ta′mar as far as the waters of Meribath′-
ka′desh, thence along the Brook of Egypt to
the Great Sea. This shall be the south side.

20 "On the west side, the Great Sea shall
be the boundary to a point opposite the
entrance of Ha′math. This shall be the west
side.

21 "So you shall divide this land among
you according to the tribes of Israel. 22 You
shall allot it as an inheritance for yourselves
and for the aliens who reside among you
and have begotten children among you.
They shall be to you as native-born sons
of Israel; with you they shall be allotted an
inheritance among the tribes of Israel. 23 In
whatever tribe the alien resides, there you
shall assign him his inheritance, says the
Lord GOD.

48 "These are the names of the tribes:
Beginning at the northern border,
from the sea by way of Heth′lon to the
entrance of Ha′math, as far as Ha′zar-
e′non (which is on the northern border
of Damascus over against Hamath), and
extending from the east side to the west, Dan,
one portion. 2 Adjoining the territory of Dan,
from the east side to the west, Asher, one
portion. 3 Adjoining the territory of Asher,
from the east side to the west, Naph′tali,
one portion. 4 Adjoining the territory of
Naph′tali, from the east side to the west,
Manas′seh, one portion. 5 Adjoining the
territory of Manas′seh, from the east side to
the west, E′phraim, one portion. 6 Adjoining
the territory of E′phraim, from the east side
to the west, Reuben, one portion. 7 Adjoining
the territory of Reuben, from the east side to
the west, Judah, one portion.

8 "Adjoining the territory of Judah, from
the east side to the west, shall be the portion
which you shall set apart, twenty-five
thousand cubits in breadth, and in length
equal to one of the tribal portions, from
the east side to the west, with the sanctuary
in the midst of it. 9 The portion which you
shall set apart for the LORD shall be twenty-
five thousand cubits in length, and twenty
thousand in breadth. 10 These shall be the
allotments of the holy portion: the priests
shall have an allotment measuring twenty-
five thousand cubits on the northern side,
ten thousand cubits in breadth on the
western side, ten thousand in breadth on
the eastern side, and twenty-five thousand
in length on the southern side, with the
sanctuary of the LORD in the midst of it.
11 This shall be for the consecrated priests,
the sons of Za′dok, who kept my charge,
who did not go astray when the people of
Israel went astray, as the Levites did. 12 And
it shall belong to them as a special portion
from the holy portion of the land, a most
holy place, adjoining the territory of the
Levites. 13 And alongside the territory of the

priests, the Levites shall have an allotment
twenty-five thousand cubits in length and
ten thousand in breadth. The whole length
shall be twenty-five thousand cubits and
the breadth twenty thousand. [14]They shall
not sell or exchange any of it; they shall not
alienate this choice portion of the land, for
it is holy to the LORD.
[15]"The remainder, five thousand cubits in
breadth and twenty-five thousand in length,
shall be for ordinary use for the city, for
dwellings and for open country. In the midst
of it shall be the city; [16]and these shall be its
dimensions: the north side four thousand five
hundred cubits, the south side four thousand
five hundred, the east side four thousand five
hundred, and the west side four thousand five
hundred. [17]And the city shall have open land:
on the north two hundred and fifty cubits, on
the south two hundred and fifty, on the east
two hundred and fifty, and on the west two
hundred and fifty. [18]The remainder of the
length alongside the holy portion shall be ten
thousand cubits to the east, and ten thousand
to the west, and it shall be alongside the holy
portion. Its produce shall be food for the
workers of the city. [19]And the workers of the
city, from all the tribes of Israel, shall till it.
[20]The whole portion which you shall set apart
shall be twenty-five thousand cubits square,
that is, the holy portion together with the
property of the city.
[21]"What remains on both sides of the
holy portion and of the property of the city
shall belong to the prince. Extending from
the twenty-five thousand cubits of the holy
portion to the east border, and westward
from the twenty-five thousand cubits to the
west border, parallel to the tribal portions,
it shall belong to the prince. The holy
portion with the sanctuary of the temple in
its midst, [22]and the property of the Levites
and the property of the city, shall be in the
midst of that which belongs to the prince.
The portion of the prince shall lie between
the territory of Judah and the territory of
Benjamin.
[23]"As for the rest of the tribes: from the
east side to the west, Benjamin, one portion.
[24]Adjoining the territory of Benjamin, from
the east side to the west, Simeon, one portion.
[25]Adjoining the territory of Simeon, from the
east side to the west, Is′sachar, one portion.
[26]Adjoining the territory of Is′sachar, from the
east side to the west, Zeb′ulun, one portion.
[27]Adjoining the territory of Zeb′ulun, from
the east side to the west, Gad, one portion.
[28]And adjoining the territory of Gad to the
south, the boundary shall run from Ta′mar
to the waters of Meribath′-ka′desh, thence
along the Brook of Egypt to the Great Sea.
[29]This is the land which you shall allot as
an inheritance among the tribes of Israel,
and these are their several portions, says the
Lord GOD.
[30]"These shall be the exits of the city:
On the north side, which is to be four
thousand five hundred cubits by measure,
[31]three gates, the gate of Reuben, the gate of
Judah, and the gate of Levi, the gates of the
city being named after the tribes of Israel.
[32]On the east side, which is to be four
thousand five hundred cubits, three gates,
the gate of Joseph, the gate of Benjamin,
and the gate of Dan. [33]On the south side,
which is to be four thousand five hundred
cubits by measure, three gates, the gate of
Simeon, the gate of Is′sachar, and the gate
of Zeb′ulun. [34]On the west side, which is
to be four thousand five hundred cubits,
three gates, the gate of Gad, the gate of
Asher, and the gate of Naph′tali. [35]The
circumference of the city shall be eighteen
thousand cubits. And the name of the city
henceforth shall be, The LORD is there."

SIRACH 22

[13]Do not talk much with a foolish man,
and do not visit an unintelligent man;
guard yourself from him to escape
trouble,
and you will not be soiled when he shakes
himself off;
avoid him and you will find rest,
and you will never be wearied by
his madness.
[14]What is heavier than lead?
And what is its name except "Fool"?

15Sand, salt, and a piece of iron
are easier to bear than a stupid man.

16A wooden beam firmly bonded
into a building
will not be torn loose by
an earthquake;
so the mind firmly fixed on a
reasonable counsel
will not be afraid in a crisis.
17A mind settled on an intelligent thought
is like the stucco decoration on the wall
of a colonnade.
18Fences set on a high place
will not stand firm against the wind;
so a timid heart with a fool's purpose
will not stand firm against any fear.

19A man who pricks an eye will make
tears fall,
and one who pricks the heart makes it
show feeling.
20One who throws a stone at birds scares
them away,
and one who reviles a friend will break
off the friendship.
21Even if you have drawn your sword against
a friend,
do not despair, for a renewal of friendship
is possible.
22If you have opened your mouth against
your friend,
do not worry, for reconciliation
is possible;
but as for reviling, arrogance, disclosure of
secrets, or a treacherous blow—
in these cases any friend will flee.

23Gain the trust of your neighbor in
his poverty,
that you may rejoice with him in
his prosperity;
stand by him in time of affliction,
that you may share with him in
his inheritance.
24The vapor and smoke of the furnace
precede the fire;
so insults precede bloodshed.
25I will not be ashamed to protect a friend,
and I will not hide from him;
26but if some harm should happen to me
because of him,
whoever hears of it will beware of him.

27O that a guard were set over my mouth,
and a seal of prudence upon my lips,
that it may keep me from falling,
so that my tongue may not destroy me!

HEBREWS 2

5For it was not to angels that God subjected the world to come, of which we are speaking. 6It has been testified somewhere,

"What is man that you are mindful of him,
or the son of man, that you care for him?
7You made him for a little while lower than
the angels,
you have crowned him with glory and
honor,
8putting everything in subjection under
his feet."
Now in putting everything in subjection
to him, he left nothing outside his control.
As it is, we do not yet see everything in
subjection to him. 9But we see Jesus, who
for a little while was made lower than the
angels, crowned with glory and honor
because of the suffering of death, so that
by the grace of God he might taste death
for every one.
10For it was fitting that he, for whom
and by whom all things exist, in bringing
many sons to glory, should make the
pioneer of their salvation perfect through
suffering. 11For he who sanctifies and
those who are sanctified have all one
origin. That is why he is not ashamed to
call them brethren, 12saying,
"I will proclaim your name to my brethren,
in the midst of the congregation I will
praise you."
13And again,
"I will put my trust in him."
And again,
"Here am I, and the children God has
given me."

14Since therefore the children share
in flesh and blood, he himself likewise
partook of the same nature, that through
death he might destroy him who has the
power of death, that is, the devil, 15and
deliver all those who through fear of
death were subject to lifelong bondage.
16For surely it is not with angels that he
is concerned but with the descendants of
Abraham. 17Therefore he had to be made
like his brethren in every respect, so that
he might become a merciful and faithful
high priest in the service of God, to make
expiation for the sins of the people. 18For
because he himself has suffered and been
tempted, he is able to help those who are
tempted.

REFLECTION

As Ezekiel tours the Temple grounds, he sees water flowing from the Temple, teeming with life (see Ez 47:2–12). In this water we find an image of the Church, whose love should overflow its visible bounds and touch everything in the world, giving life and quenching thirst. This is a beautiful image, but in practice we often find it difficult to share our life in Christ with those God puts in our daily path. Sirach offers us some wisdom for creating friendships; and our ability to share the love of Christ with others surely depends on our willingness to befriend them. Let us therefore love our neighbors who are poor (see Sir 22:23) and guard our tongues because careless speech is a great danger to any relationship (see v. 27). Above all, if we want our temple to overflow, let us imitate the Lord. Let us imitate him who became like us in our weakness, who became our brother and inhabited our suffering (see Heb 2:10–11). Christ was tempted in order to help us in our temptations, and he tasted death for everyone (see v. 18). Just as Christ died to give us life, so we too must sacrifice to share that life with others. Are you willing to love others as Christ has loved us, regardless of the cost?

November 9

DANIEL 1

**In the third year of the reign
of Jehoi′akim king of Judah,
Nebuchadnez′zar king of Babylon came
to Jerusalem and besieged it. 2And the**
Lord gave Jehoi′akim king of Judah into
his hand, with some of the vessels of the
house of God; and he brought them to the
land of Shi′nar, to the house of his god, and
placed the vessels in the treasury of his god.
3Then the king commanded Ash′penaz, his
chief eunuch, to bring some of the people
of Israel, both of the royal family and of the
nobility, 4youths without blemish, handsome
and skilful in all wisdom, endowed with
knowledge, understanding learning, and
competent to serve in the king's palace, and
to teach them the letters and language of the
Chalde′ans. 5The king assigned them a daily
portion of the rich food which the king ate,
and of the wine which he drank. They were
to be educated for three years, and at the end
of that time they were to stand before the
king. 6Among these were Daniel, Hanani′ah,
Mish′a-el, and Azari′ah of the tribe of
Judah. 7And the chief of the eunuchs gave
them names: Daniel he called Belteshaz′zar,
Hanani′ah he called Shad′rach, Mish′a-el
he called Me′shach, and Azari′ah he called
Abed′nego.

8But Daniel resolved that he would not
defile himself with the king's rich food, or
with the wine which he drank; therefore
he asked the chief of the eunuchs to allow
him not to defile himself. 9And God gave
Daniel favor and compassion in the sight
of the chief of the eunuchs; 10and the chief
of the eunuchs said to Daniel, "I fear lest
my lord the king, who appointed your food
and your drink, should see that you were in
poorer condition than the youths who are of
your own age. So you would endanger my
head with the king." 11Then Daniel said to the
steward whom the chief of the eunuchs had
appointed over Daniel, Hanani′ah, Mish′a-el,

and Azari′ah; 12“Test your servants for ten
days; let us be given vegetables to eat and
water to drink. 13Then let our appearance
and the appearance of the youths who eat
the king's rich food be observed by you, and
according to what you see deal with your
servants.” 14So he listened to them in this
matter, and tested them for ten days. 15At the
end of ten days it was seen that they were
better in appearance and fatter in flesh than
all the youths who ate the king's rich food.
16So the steward took away their rich food
and the wine they were to drink, and gave
them vegetables.

17As for these four youths, God gave them
learning and skill in all letters and wisdom;
and Daniel had understanding in all visions
and dreams. 18At the end of the time, when
the king had commanded that they should be
brought in, the chief of the eunuchs brought
them in before Nebuchadnez′zar. 19And the
king spoke with them, and among them
all none was found like Daniel, Hanani′ah,
Mish′a-el, and Azari′ah; therefore they
stood before the king. 20And in every matter
of wisdom and understanding concerning
which the king inquired of them, he found
them ten times better than all the magicians
and enchanters that were in all his kingdom.
21And Daniel continued until the first year
of King Cyrus.

2 In the second year of the reign of Nebuch-
ad-nez′zar, Nebuchadnezzar had dreams;
and his spirit was troubled, and his sleep left
him. 2Then the king commanded that the
magicians, the enchanters, the sorcerers,
and the Chalde′ans be summoned, to tell
the king his dreams. So they came in and
stood before the king. 3And the king said
to them, “I had a dream, and my spirit is
troubled to know the dream.” 4Then the
Chalde′ans said to the king, “O king, live
for ever! Tell your servants the dream, and
we will show the interpretation.” 5The king
answered the Chalde′ans, “The word from
me is sure: if you do not make known to
me the dream and its interpretation, you
shall be torn limb from limb, and your
houses shall be laid in ruins. 6But if you
show the dream and its interpretation, you
shall receive from me gifts and rewards
and great honor. Therefore show me
the dream and its interpretation.” 7They
answered a second time, “Let the king tell
his servants the dream, and we will show
its interpretation.” 8The king answered, “I
know with certainty that you are trying to
gain time, because you see that the word
from me is sure 9that if you do not make
the dream known to me, there is but one
sentence for you. You have agreed to speak
lying and corrupt words before me till the
times change. Therefore tell me the dream,
and I shall know that you can show me its
interpretation.” 10The Chalde′ans answered
the king, “There is not a man on earth who
can meet the king's demand; for no great
and powerful king has asked such a thing
of any magician or enchanter or Chalde′an.
11The thing that the king asks is difficult,
and none can show it to the king except the
gods, whose dwelling is not with flesh.”

12Because of this the king was angry and
very furious, and commanded that all the
wise men of Babylon be destroyed. 13So the
decree went forth that the wise men were
to be slain, and they sought Daniel and his
companions, to slay them. 14Then Daniel
replied with prudence and discretion to
Ar′ioch, the captain of the king's guard, who
had gone out to slay the wise men of Babylon;
15he said to Ar′ioch, the king's captain, “Why
is the decree of the king so severe?” Then
Arioch made the matter known to Daniel.
16And Daniel went in and besought the king
to appoint him a time, that he might show to
the king the interpretation.

17Then Daniel went to his house and made
the matter known to Hanani′ah, Mish′a-el,
and Azari′ah, his companions, 18and told
them to seek mercy of the God of heaven
concerning this mystery, so that Daniel and
his companions might not perish with the
rest of the wise men of Babylon. 19Then the
mystery was revealed to Daniel in a vision
of the night. Then Daniel blessed the God
of heaven. 20Daniel said:

“Blessed be the name of God for ever
and ever,
to whom belong wisdom and might.

[21]He changes times and seasons;
he removes kings and sets up kings;
he gives wisdom to the wise
and knowledge to those who
have understanding;
[22]he reveals deep and mysterious things;
he knows what is in the darkness,
and the light dwells with him.
[23]To you, O God of my fathers,
I give thanks and praise,
for you have given me wisdom
and strength,
and have now made known to me what
we asked of you,
for you have made known to us the
king's matter."

SIRACH 23

O Lord, Father and Ruler of my life,
do not abandon me to their counsel,
and let me not fall because of them!
[2]O that whips were set over my thoughts,
and the discipline of wisdom over
my mind!
That they may not spare me in my errors,
and that it may not pass by my sins;
[3]in order that my mistakes may not
be multiplied,
and my sins may not abound;
then I will not fall before my adversaries,
and my enemy will not rejoice over me.
[4]O Lord, Father and God of my life,
do not give me haughty eyes,
[5] and remove from me evil desire.
[6]Let neither gluttony nor lust overcome me,
and do not surrender me to a
shameless soul.

[7]Listen, my children, to instruction
concerning speech;
the one who observes it will never
be caught.
[8]The sinner is overtaken through his lips,
the reviler and the arrogant are tripped
by them.
[9]Do not accustom your mouth to oaths,
and do not habitually utter the name of
the Holy One;
[10]for as a servant who is continually
examined under torture
will not lack bruises,
so also the man who always swears and
utters the Name
will not be cleansed from sin.
[11]A man who swears many oaths will be
filled with iniquity,
and the scourge will not leave his house;
if he offends, his sin remains on him,
and if he disregards it, he sins doubly;
if he has sworn needlessly, he will not
be justified,
for his house will be filled with calamities.
[12]There is an utterance which is comparable
to death;
may it never be found in the inheritance
of Jacob!
For all these errors will be far from
the godly,
and they will not wallow in sins.
[13]Do not accustom your mouth to
lewd vulgarity,
for it involves sinful speech.
[14]Remember your father and mother
when you sit among great men;
lest you be forgetful in their presence,
and be deemed a fool on account of
your habits;
then you will wish that you had never
been born,
and you will curse the day of your birth.

HEBREWS 3

**Therefore, holy brethren, who
share in a heavenly call, consider
Jesus, the apostle and high priest of our
confession. [2]He was faithful to him**
who appointed him, just as Moses also was
faithful in God's house. [3]Yet Jesus has been
counted worthy of as much more glory than
Moses as the builder of a house has more
honor than the house. [4](For every house
is built by some one, but the builder of all
things is God.) [5]Now Moses was faithful
in all God's house as a servant, to testify

to the things that were to be spoken later,
[6]but Christ was faithful over God's house as
a son. And we are his house if we hold fast
our confidence and pride in our hope.
[7]Therefore, as the Holy Spirit says,
"Today, when you hear his voice,
[8]do not harden your hearts as in
the rebellion,
on the day of testing in the wilderness,
[9]where your fathers put me to the test
and saw my works for forty years.
[10]Therefore I was provoked with
that generation,
and said, 'They always go astray in
their hearts;
they have not known my ways.'
[11]As I swore in my wrath,
'They shall never enter my rest.'"
[12]Take care, brethren, lest there be in any
of you an evil, unbelieving heart, leading
you to fall away from the living God.
[13]But exhort one another every day, as
long as it is called "today," that none of
you may be hardened by the deceitfulness
of sin. [14]For we share in Christ, if only we
hold our first confidence firm to the end,
[15]while it is said,
"Today, when you hear his voice,
do not harden your hearts as in the
rebellion."
[16]Who were they that heard and yet were
rebellious? Was it not all those who left
Egypt under the leadership of Moses? [17]And
with whom was he provoked forty years?
Was it not with those who sinned, whose
bodies fell in the wilderness? [18]And to whom
did he swear that they should never enter
his rest, but to those who were disobedient?
[19]So we see that they were unable to enter
because of unbelief.

4 Therefore, while the promise of entering
his rest remains, let us fear lest any of
you be judged to have failed to reach it. [2]For
good news came to us just as to them; but the
message which they heard did not benefit
them, because it did not meet with faith in
the hearers. [3]For we who have believed enter
that rest, as he has said,
"As I swore in my wrath,
'They shall never enter my rest,'"
although his works were finished from the
foundation of the world. [4]For he has somewhere spoken of the seventh day in this way,
"And God rested on the seventh day from all
his works." [5]And again in this place he said,
"They shall never enter my rest."
[6]Since therefore it remains for some to
enter it, and those who formerly received
the good news failed to enter because of
disobedience, [7]again he sets a certain day,
"Today," saying through David so long afterward, in the words already quoted,
"Today, when you hear his voice,
do not harden your hearts."
[8]For if Joshua had given them rest, God would
not speak later of another day. [9]So then, there
remains a sabbath rest for the people of God;
[10]for whoever enters God's rest also ceases
from his labors as God did from his.
[11]Let us therefore strive to enter that
rest, that no one fall by the same sort of
disobedience. [12]For the word of God is living
and active, sharper than any two-edged
sword, piercing to the division of soul and
spirit, of joints and marrow, and discerning
the thoughts and intentions of the heart.
[13]And before him no creature is hidden, but
all are open and laid bare to the eyes of him
with whom we have to do.

REFLECTION

Many people are gifted with great physical abilities, but only a few make it to the Olympics and even fewer receive the coveted gold medal. These kinds of accomplishments require dedication, devotion, and a lot of practice. The same goes for the spiritual life. In order to progress in the spiritual life, we must be dedicated and practice. Even if we are given great spiritual gifts, we must put them into use or risk losing them. Daniel gives us a great example. He, along with his three friends, is given the gift of wisdom. When confronted with their first test (a sort of spiritual exercise) of staying obedient to the dietary laws prescribed in the Old Testament, they pass with flying colors. As a result, Daniel grows in wisdom and is gifted further with deeper knowledge and understanding.

Sirach prays, “O that whips were set over my thoughts, and the discipline of wisdom over my mind!” (Sir 23:2). To make any progression in the spiritual life requires effort and practice on our part. The best way to start is by reading, praying with, and putting into action the Word of God, “for the word of God is living and active, sharper than any two-edged sword” (Heb 4:12). The world gives us plenty of opportunities to practice and grow in our spiritual life. How can you exercise your “spiritual body” today?

November 10

DANIEL 2

24Therefore Daniel went in to
Ar′ioch, whom the king had ap-
pointed to destroy the wise men
of Babylon; he went and said thus to
him, “Do not destroy the wise men of
Babylon; bring me in before the king, and I
will show the king the interpretation.”
25Then Ar′ioch brought in Daniel before
the king in haste, and said thus to him: “I
have found among the exiles from Judah a
man who can make known to the king the
interpretation.” 26The king said to Daniel,
whose name was Belteshaz′zar, “Are you
able to make known to me the dream
that I have seen and its interpretation?”
27Daniel answered the king, “No wise men,
enchanters, magicians, or astrologers can
show to the king the mystery which the king
has asked, 28but there is a God in heaven who
reveals mysteries, and he has made known
to King Nebuchadnez′zar what will be in
the latter days. Your dream and the visions
of your head as you lay in bed are these:
29To you, O king, as you lay in bed came
thoughts of what would be hereafter, and he
who reveals mysteries made known to you
what is to be. 30But as for me, not because
of any wisdom that I have more than all the
living has this mystery been revealed to me,
but in order that the interpretation may be
made known to the king, and that you may
know the thoughts of your mind.
31“You saw, O king, and behold, a great
image. This image, mighty and of exceeding
brightness, stood before you, and its
appearance was frightening. 32The head of
this image was of fine gold, its breast and
arms of silver, its belly and thighs of bronze,
33its legs of iron, its feet partly of iron and
partly of clay. 34As you looked, a stone was
cut out by no human hand, and it struck the
image on its feet of iron and clay, and broke
them in pieces; 35then the iron, the clay, the
bronze, the silver, and the gold, all together
were broken in pieces, and became like the
chaff of the summer threshing floors; and
the wind carried them away, so that not
a trace of them could be found. But the
stone that struck the image became a great
mountain and filled the whole earth.
36“This was the dream; now we will tell the
king its interpretation. 37You, O king, the
king of kings, to whom the God of heaven
has given the kingdom, the power, and
the might, and the glory, 38and into whose
hand he has given, wherever they dwell, the
sons of men, the beasts of the field, and the
birds of the air, making you rule over them
all—you are the head of gold. 39After you
shall arise another kingdom inferior to you,
and yet a third kingdom of bronze, which
shall rule over all the earth. 40And there
shall be a fourth kingdom, strong as iron,
because iron breaks to pieces and shatters
all things; and like iron which crushes, it
shall break and crush all these. 41And as
you saw the feet and toes partly of potter’s
clay and partly of iron, it shall be a divided
kingdom; but some of the firmness of iron
shall be in it, just as you saw iron mixed
with the miry clay. 42And as the toes of the
feet were partly iron and partly clay, so the
kingdom shall be partly strong and partly
brittle. 43As you saw the iron mixed with
miry clay, so they will mix with one another
in marriage, but they will not hold together,
just as iron does not mix with clay. 44And in

the days of those kings the God of heaven will set up a kingdom which shall never be destroyed, nor shall its sovereignty be left to another people. It shall break in pieces all these kingdoms and bring them to an end, and it shall stand for ever; 45just as you saw that a stone was cut from a mountain by no human hand, and that it broke in pieces the iron, the bronze, the clay, the silver, and the gold. A great God has made known to the king what shall be hereafter. The dream is certain, and its interpretation sure."

46Then King Nebuchadnez′zar fell upon his face, and did homage to Daniel, and commanded that an offering and incense be offered up to him. 47The king said to Daniel, "Truly, your God is God of gods and Lord of kings, and a revealer of mysteries, for you have been able to reveal this mystery." 48Then the king gave Daniel high honors and many great gifts, and made him ruler over the whole province of Babylon, and chief prefect over all the wise men of Babylon. 49Daniel made request of the king, and he appointed Shad′rach, Me′shach, and Abed′nego over the affairs of the province of Babylon; but Daniel remained at the king's court.

3 King Nebuchadnez′zar made an image of gold, whose height was sixty cubits and its breadth six cubits. He set it up on the plain of Dura, in the province of Babylon. 2Then King Nebuchadnez′zar sent to assemble the satraps, the prefects, and the governors, the counselors, the treasurers, the justices, the magistrates, and all the officials of the provinces to come to the dedication of the image which King Nebuchadnezzar had set up. 3Then the satraps, the prefects, and the governors, the counselors, the treasurers, the justices, the magistrates, and all the officials of the provinces, were assembled for the dedication of the image that King Nebuchadnez′zar had set up; and they stood before the image that Nebuchadnezzar had set up. 4And the herald proclaimed aloud, "You are commanded, O peoples, nations, and languages, 5that when you hear the sound of the horn, pipe, lyre, trigon, harp, bagpipe, and every kind of music, you are to fall down and worship the golden image that King Nebuchadnez′zar has set up; 6and whoever does not fall down and worship shall immediately be cast into a burning fiery furnace." 7Therefore, as soon as all the peoples heard the sound of the horn, pipe, lyre, trigon, harp, bagpipe, and every kind of music, all the peoples, nations, and languages fell down and worshiped the golden image which King Nebuchadnez′zar had set up.

8Therefore at that time certain Chalde′ans came forward and maliciously accused the Jews. 9They said to King Nebuchadnez′zar, "O king, live for ever! 10You, O king, have made a decree, that every man who hears the sound of the horn, pipe, lyre, trigon, harp, bagpipe, and every kind of music, shall fall down and worship the golden image; 11and whoever does not fall down and worship shall be cast into a burning fiery furnace. 12There are certain Jews whom you have appointed over the affairs of the province of Babylon: Shad′rach, Me′shach, and Abed′nego. These men, O king, pay no heed to you; they do not serve your gods or worship the golden image which you have set up."

13Then Nebuchadnez′zar in furious rage commanded that Shad′rach, Me′shach, and Abed′nego be brought. Then they brought these men before the king. 14Nebuchadnez′zar said to them, "Is it true, O Shad′rach, Me′shach, and Abed′nego, that you do not serve my gods or worship the golden image which I have set up? 15Now if you are ready when you hear the sound of the horn, pipe, lyre, trigon, harp, bagpipe, and every kind of music, to fall down and worship the image which I have made, well and good; but if you do not worship, you shall immediately be cast into a burning fiery furnace; and who is the god that will deliver you out of my hands?"

16Shad′rach, Me′shach, and Abed′nego answered the king, "O Nebuchadnez′zar, we have no need to answer you in this matter. 17If it be so, our God whom we serve is able to deliver us from the burning fiery furnace; and he will deliver us out of your hand, O king. 18But if not, be it known to you, O king, that we will not serve your gods or

worship the golden image which you have set up."
[19]Then Nebuchadnez'zar was full of fury, and the expression of his face was changed against Shad'rach, Me'shach, and Abed'nego. He ordered the furnace heated seven times more than it was accustomed to be heated. [20]And he ordered certain mighty men of his army to bind Shad'rach, Me'shach, and Abed'nego, and to cast them into the burning fiery furnace. [21]Then these men were bound in their mantles, their tunics, their hats, and their other garments, and they were cast into the burning fiery furnace. [22]Because the king's order was strict and the furnace very hot, the flame of the fire slew those men who took up Shad'rach, Me'shach, and Abed'nego. [23]And these three men, Shad'rach, Me'shach, and Abed'nego, fell bound into the burning fiery furnace.

SIRACH 23

[15]A man accustomed to using insulting words
will never become disciplined all his days.

[16]Two sorts of men multiply sins,
and a third incurs wrath.
The soul heated like a burning fire
will not be quenched until it is consumed;
a man who commits fornication with his
near of kin
will never cease until the fire burns
him up.
[17]To a fornicator all bread tastes sweet;
he will never cease until he dies.
[18]A man who breaks his marriage vows
says to himself, "Who sees me?
Darkness surrounds me, and the walls
hide me,
and no one sees me. Why should I fear?
The Most High will not take notice of
my sins."
[19]His fear is confined to the eyes of men,
and he does not realize that the eyes of
the Lord
are ten thousand times brighter than
the sun;
they look upon all the ways of men,
and perceive even the hidden places.
[20]Before the universe was created, it was
known to him;
so it was also after it was finished.
[21]This man will be punished in the streets
of the city,
and where he least suspects it, he
will be seized.
[22]So it is with a woman who leaves
her husband
and provides an heir by a stranger.
[23]For first of all, she has disobeyed the law of
the Most High;
second, she has committed an offense
against her husband;
and third, she has committed adultery
through harlotry
and brought forth children by
another man.
[24]She herself will be brought before
the assembly,
and punishment will fall on her children.
[25]Her children will not take root,
and her branches will not bear fruit.
[26]She will leave her memory for a curse,
and her disgrace will not be blotted out.
[27]Those who survive her will recognize
that nothing is better than the fear
of the Lord,
and nothing sweeter than to heed the
commandments of the Lord.

HEBREWS 4

[14]Since then we have a great high priest who has passed through the heavens, Jesus, the Son of God, let us hold fast our confession. [15]For we have
not a high priest who is unable to sympathize with our weaknesses, but one who in every respect has been tempted as we are, yet without sinning. [16]Let us then with confidence draw near to the throne of grace, that we may receive mercy and find grace to help in time of need.

5 For every high priest chosen from among men is appointed to act on behalf of men in relation to God, to offer gifts and sacrifices for sins. [2]He can deal gently with the ignorant and wayward, since he himself

is beset with weakness. 3Because of this he
is bound to offer sacrifice for his own sins
as well as for those of the people. 4And one
does not take the honor upon himself, but
he is called by God, just as Aaron was.
5So also Christ did not exalt himself to be
made a high priest, but was appointed by
him who said to him,
"You are my Son,
today I have begotten you";
6as he says also in another place,
"You are a priest for ever,
according to the order of Melchiz′edek."
7In the days of his flesh, Jesus offered up
prayers and supplications, with loud cries
and tears, to him who was able to save him
from death, and he was heard for his godly
fear. 8Although he was a Son, he learned
obedience through what he suffered; 9and
being made perfect he became the source
of eternal salvation to all who obey him,
10being designated by God a high priest
according to the order of Melchiz′edek.
11About this we have much to say which is
hard to explain, since you have become dull
of hearing. 12For though by this time you
ought to be teachers, you need some one to
teach you again the first principles of God's
word. You need milk, not solid food; 13for
every one who lives on milk is unskilled in
the word of righteousness, for he is a child.
14But solid food is for the mature, for those
who have their faculties trained by practice
to distinguish good from evil.

REFLECTION

Do you need milk or solid food? This is a question we should ask ourselves as it pertains to our spiritual lives, and we should be as honest as possible when answering it. Each person is a unique creation and has his or her own unique circumstances. Each of us starts at a different point, and we all progress in our spiritual lives at different rates, but the one thing we all have in common is sin; we are all sinners. It's part of the human condition to want to hide our weaknesses and sins from others, but it is foolish to think we can hide them from God (see Sir 23:18–19). Hebrews tells us that Jesus Christ sympathizes with our weaknesses even though he himself never sinned (see Heb 4:15). We are encouraged to confess our sins and "draw near to the throne of grace, that we may receive mercy and find grace to help in time of need" (v. 4:16). Confession is a throne of grace. The more frequently we draw close to this throne of grace, the stronger we become and the more we prepare ourselves to move on to solid food in the spiritual life. Does your spiritual life need milk or solid food?

November 11

DANIEL 3*

And they walked about in the midst of the flames, singing hymns to God and blessing the Lord. 2Then Azariah stood and offered this prayer; in the midst of the fire he opened his mouth and said:

3"Blessed are you, O Lord, God of our fathers,
and worthy of praise;
and your name is glorified for ever.
4For you are just in all that you have done to us,
and all your works are true and your
ways right,
and all your judgments are truth.
5You have executed true judgments in all that
you have brought upon us
and upon Jerusalem, the holy city of
our fathers,
for in truth and justice you have brought
all this upon us because of our sins.
6For we have sinfully and lawlessly departed
from you,
and have sinned in all things and have not
obeyed your commandments;
7we have not observed them or
done them,
as you have commanded us that it might
go well with us.

* This section (sixty-eight verses) printed in italics is contained only in the Greek. It is here translated from Theodotion's version.

[8]So all that you have brought upon us,
and all that you have done to us,
you have done in true judgment.
[9]You have given us into the hands of lawless enemies, most hateful rebels,
and to an unjust king, the most wicked in all the world.
[10]And now we cannot open our mouths;
shame and disgrace have befallen your servants and worshipers.
[11]For your name's sake do not give us up utterly,
and do not break your covenant,
[12] *and do not withdraw your mercy from us,*
for the sake of Abraham your beloved
and for the sake of Isaac your servant
and Israel your holy one,
[13]to whom you promised
to make their descendants as many as the stars of heaven
and as the sand on the shore of the sea.
[14]For we, O Lord, have become fewer than any nation,
and are brought low this day in all the world because of our sins.
[15]And at this time there is no prince, or prophet, or leader,
no burnt offering, or sacrifice, or oblation, or incense,
no place to make an offering before you or to find mercy.
[16]Yet with a contrite heart and a humble spirit may we be accepted,
as though it were with burnt offerings of rams and bulls,
and with tens of thousands of fat lambs;
[17] *such may our sacrifice be in your sight this day,*
and may we wholly follow you,
for there will be no shame for those who trust in you.
[18]And now with all our heart we follow you,
we fear you and seek your face.
[19]Do not put us to shame,
but deal with us in your forbearance
and in your abundant mercy.
[20]Deliver us in accordance with your marvelous works,
and give glory to your name, O Lord!
Let all who do harm to your servants be put to shame;
[21]let them be disgraced and deprived of all power and dominion,
and let their strength be broken.
[22]Let them know that you are the Lord, the only God,
glorious over the whole world."

[23]Now the king's servants who threw them
in did not cease feeding the furnace fires
with naphtha, pitch, tow, and brush. [24]And
the flame streamed out above the furnace
forty-nine cubits, [25]and it broke through
and burned those of the Chaldeans whom it
caught about the furnace. [26]But the angel of
the Lord came down into the furnace to be
with Azariah and his companions, and drove
the fiery flame out of the furnace, [27]and made
the midst of the furnace like a moist whistling
wind, so that the fire did not touch them at all
or hurt or trouble them.

[28]Then the three, as with one mouth, praised
and glorified and blessed God in the furnace,
saying:
[29]"Blessed are you, O Lord, God of our fathers,
and to be praised and highly exalted for ever;
[30]And blessed is your glorious, holy name
and to be highly praised and highly exalted for ever;
[31]Blessed are you in the temple of your holy glory
and to be extolled and highly glorified for ever.
[32]Blessed are you, who sit upon cherubim
and look upon the deeps,
and to be praised and highly exalted for ever.
[33]Blessed are you upon the throne of your kingdom
and to be extolled and highly exalted for ever.
[34]Blessed are you in the firmament of heaven
and to be sung and glorified for ever.
[35]"Bless the Lord, all works of the Lord,
sing praise to him and highly exalt him for ever.

36 *Bless the Lord, you heavens,*
sing praise to him and highly exalt him
for ever.
37 *Bless the Lord, you angels of the Lord,*
sing praise to him and highly exalt him
for ever.
38 *Bless the Lord, all waters above*
the heaven,
sing praise to him and highly exalt him
for ever.
39 *Bless the Lord, all powers,*
sing praise to him and highly exalt him
for ever.
40 *Bless the Lord, sun and moon,*
sing praise to him and highly exalt him
for ever.
41 *Bless the Lord, stars of heaven,*
sing praise to him and highly exalt him
for ever.
42 *Bless the Lord, all rain and dew,*
sing praise to him and highly exalt him
for ever.
43 *Bless the Lord, all winds,*
sing praise to him and highly exalt him
for ever.
44 *Bless the Lord, fire and heat,*
sing praise to him and highly exalt him
for ever.
45 *Bless the Lord, winter cold and*
summer heat,
sing praise to him and highly exalt him
for ever.
46 *Bless the Lord, dews and snows,*
sing praise to him and highly exalt him
for ever.
47 *Bless the Lord, nights and days,*
sing praise to him and highly exalt him
for ever.
48 *Bless the Lord, light and darkness,*
sing praise to him and highly exalt him
for ever.
49 *Bless the Lord, ice and cold,*
sing praise to him and highly exalt him
for ever.
50 *Bless the Lord, frosts and snows,*
sing praise to him and highly exalt him
for ever.
51 *Bless the Lord, lightnings and clouds,*
sing praise to him and highly exalt him
for ever.
52 *Let the earth bless the Lord;*
let it sing praise to him and highly exalt
him for ever.
53 *Bless the Lord, mountains and hills,*
sing praise to him and highly exalt him
for ever.
54 *Bless the Lord, all things that grow on*
the earth,
sing praise to him and highly exalt him
for ever.
55 *Bless the Lord, you springs,*
sing praise to him and highly exalt him
for ever.
56 *Bless the Lord, seas and rivers,*
sing praise to him and highly exalt him
for ever.
57 *Bless the Lord, you whales and all creatures*
that move in the waters,
sing praise to him and highly exalt him
for ever.
58 *Bless the Lord, all birds of the air,*
sing praise to him and highly exalt him
for ever.
59 *Bless the Lord, all beasts and cattle,*
sing praise to him and highly exalt him
for ever.
60 *Bless the Lord, you sons of men,*
sing praise to him and highly exalt him
for ever.
61 *Bless the Lord, O Israel,*
sing praise to him and highly exalt him
for ever.
62 *Bless the Lord, you priests of the Lord,*
sing praise to him and highly exalt him
for ever.
63 *Bless the Lord, you servants of the Lord,*
sing praise to him and highly exalt him
for ever.
64 *Bless the Lord, spirits and souls of*
the righteous,
sing praise to him and highly exalt him
for ever.
65 *Bless the Lord, you who are holy and humble*
in heart,
sing praise to him and highly exalt him
for ever.
66 *Bless the Lord, Hananiah, Azariah,*
and Mishael,
sing praise to him and highly exalt him
for ever;

for he has rescued us from Hades and saved
us from the hand of death,
and delivered us from the midst of the
burning fiery furnace;
from the midst of the fire he has delivered us.
67 *Give thanks to the Lord, for he is good,*
for his mercy endures for ever.
68 *Bless him, all who worship the Lord, the*
God of gods,
sing praise to him and give thanks to him,
for his mercy endures for ever."

24 Then King Nebuchadnez′zar was
astonished and rose up in haste. He said
to his counselors, "Did we not cast three
men bound into the fire?" They answered
the king, "True, O king." 25 He answered,
"But I see four men loose, walking in the
midst of the fire, and they are not hurt;
and the appearance of the fourth is like a
son of the gods."

26 Then Nebuchadnez′zar came near
to the door of the burning fiery furnace
and said, "Shad′rach, Me′shach, and
Abed′nego, servants of the Most High
God, come forth, and come here!" Then
Shadrach, Meshach, and Abednego came
out from the fire. 27 And the satraps, the
prefects, the governors, and the king's
counselors gathered together and saw
that the fire had not had any power over
the bodies of those men; the hair of their
heads was not singed, their mantles were
not harmed, and no smell of fire had
come upon them. 28 Nebuchadnez′zar
said, "Blessed be the God of Shad′rach,
Me′shach, and Abed′nego, who has sent
his angel and delivered his servants, who
trusted in him, and set at nothing the
king's command, and yielded up their
bodies rather than serve and worship any
god except their own God. 29 Therefore
I make a decree: Any people, nation, or
language that speaks anything against
the God of Shad′rach, Me′shach, and
Abed′nego shall be torn limb from limb,
and their houses laid in ruins; for there
is no other god who is able to deliver
in this way." 30 Then the king promoted
Shad′rach, Me′shach, and Abed′nego in
the province of Babylon.

SIRACH 24

Wisdom will praise herself and is honored
in God,
and will glory in the midst of her people.
2 In the assembly of the Most High she will
open her mouth,
and in the presence of his host she
will glory.
In the midst of her people she is exalted;
in holy fulness she is admired.
In the multitude of the chosen she
finds praise,
and among the blessed she is blessed,
saying:
3 "I came forth from the mouth of the
Most High,
the first-born before all creatures.
I ordained that an unfailing light
should arise in the heavens,
and I covered the earth like a mist.
4 I dwelt in high places,
and my throne was in a pillar of cloud.
5 Alone I have made the circuit of the vault
of heaven
and have walked in the depths of
the abyss.
6 In the waves of the sea, in the whole earth,
and in every people and nation I have
gotten a possession.
7 Among all these I sought a resting place;
I sought in whose territory I might lodge.

8 "Then the Creator of all things gave me a
commandment,
and the one who created me assigned a
place for my tent.
And he said, 'Make your dwelling in Jacob,
and in Israel receive your inheritance,
and among my chosen put down
your roots.'
9 From eternity, in the beginning, he
created me,
and for eternity I shall not cease to exist.
10 In the holy tabernacle I ministered
before him,
and so I was established in Zion.
11 In the beloved city likewise he gave me a
resting place,
and in Jerusalem was my dominion.

[12]So I took root in an honored people,
in the portion of the Lord, who is
their inheritance,
and my abode was in the full assembly of
the saints.
[13]"I grew tall like a cedar in Lebanon,
and like a cypress on the heights of Hermon.
[14]I grew tall like a palm tree in En-ge′di,
and like rose plants in Jericho;
like a beautiful olive tree in the field,
and like a plane tree I grew tall.
[15]Like cassia and camel's thorn I gave forth
the aroma of spices,
and like choice myrrh I spread a
pleasant odor,
like galbanum, onycha, and stacte,
and like the fragrance of frankincense in
the tabernacle.
[16]Like a terebinth I spread out my branches,
and my branches are glorious and graceful.
[17]Like a vine I caused loveliness to bud,
and my blossoms became glorious and
abundant fruit.*

[19]"Come to me, you who desire me,
and eat your fill of my produce.
[20]For my teaching is sweeter than honey,
and my inheritance sweeter than
the honeycomb,
and my remembrance lasts throughout
all generations.
[21]Those who eat me will hunger for more,
and those who drink me will thirst
for more.
[22]Whoever obeys me will not be put to shame,
and those who work with my help will
not sin."

HEBREWS 6

Therefore let us leave the elementary doctrines of Christ and go on to maturity, not laying again a foundation of repentance from dead
works and of faith toward God, [2]with
instruction about baptisms, the laying on of
hands, the resurrection of the dead, and
eternal judgment. [3]And this we will do if
God permits. [4]For it is impossible to restore
again to repentance those who have once
been enlightened, who have tasted the
heavenly gift, and have become partakers
of the Holy Spirit, [5]and have tasted the
goodness of the word of God and the
powers of the age to come, [6]if they then
commit apostasy, since they crucify the Son
of God on their own account and hold him
up to contempt. [7]For land which has drunk
the rain that often falls upon it, and brings
forth vegetation useful to those for whose
sake it is cultivated, receives a blessing from
God. [8]But if it bears thorns and thistles, it is
worthless and near to being cursed; its end
is to be burned.

[9]Though we speak thus, yet in your case,
beloved, we feel sure of better things that
belong to salvation. [10]For God is not so
unjust as to overlook your work and the love
which you showed for his sake in serving the
saints, as you still do. [11]And we desire each
one of you to show the same earnestness in
realizing the full assurance of hope until the
end, [12]so that you may not be sluggish, but
imitators of those who through faith and
patience inherit the promises.

[13]For when God made a promise to Abraham, since he had no one greater by whom to
swear, he swore by himself, [14]saying, "Surely I
will bless you and multiply you." [15]And thus
Abraham, having patiently endured, obtained
the promise. [16]Men indeed swear by a greater
than themselves, and in all their disputes
an oath is final for confirmation. [17]So when
God desired to show more convincingly to
the heirs of the promise the unchangeable
character of his purpose, he interposed with
an oath, [18]so that through two unchangeable
things, in which it is impossible that God
should prove false, we who have fled for
refuge might have strong encouragement to
seize the hope set before us. [19]We have this
as a sure and steadfast anchor of the soul, a
hope that enters into the inner shrine behind
the curtain, [20]where Jesus has gone as a

* Other authorities add [18]*I am the mother of beautiful love, of fear, of knowledge, and of holy hope: being eternal, I therefore am given to all my children, to those who are named by him.*

forerunner on our behalf, having become a high priest for ever according to the order of Melchiz′edek.

REFLECTION

Sirach gives us a beautiful poem praising wisdom. But this is not just beautiful poetry; it's revelation. Wisdom was given to the people of Israel in the form of the Torah. The word *torah* is most often translated as "law," but it is better understood as "instruction." The Torah was a gift given to Israel to instruct them in how to live in a right relationship with God and all creation. Israel was given the gift of wisdom in her Scriptures. In turn, she was to live out that relationship and, thus, be a light for all the other nations. Wisdom is not a standard developed by man; it has a divine origin: "I came forth from the mouth of the Most High, the first-born before all creatures" (see Sir 24:3). Wisdom is the word that came forth from God and "afterward she appeared upon earth and lived among men" (Bar 3:37). How have you grown in wisdom from reading the Scriptures?

November 12

DANIEL 4

King Nebuchadnez′zar to all peo-
ples, nations, and languages, that
dwell in all the earth: Peace be multiplied
to you! 2It has seemed good to me to show
the signs and wonders that the Most High
God has wrought toward me.

3How great are his signs,
how mighty his wonders!
His kingdom is an everlasting kingdom,
and his dominion is from generation to generation.

4I, Nebuchadnez′zar, was at ease in my
house and prospering in my palace. 5I had
a dream which made me afraid; as I lay in
bed the fancies and the visions of my head
alarmed me. 6Therefore I made a decree
that all the wise men of Babylon should
be brought before me, that they might
make known to me the interpretation
of the dream. 7Then the magicians, the
enchanters, the Chalde′ans, and the
astrologers came in; and I told them the
dream, but they could not make known
to me its interpretation. 8At last Daniel
came in before me—he who was named
Belteshaz′zar after the name of my god,
and in whom is the spirit of the holy
gods—and I told him the dream, saying,
9"O Belteshaz′zar, chief of the magicians,
because I know that the spirit of the
holy gods is in you and that no mystery
is difficult for you, here is the dream
which I saw; tell me its interpretation.
10The visions of my head as I lay in bed
were these: I saw, and behold, a tree in
the midst of the earth; and its height was
great. 11The tree grew and became strong,
and its top reached to heaven, and it was
visible to the end of the whole earth. 12Its
leaves were fair and its fruit abundant,
and in it was food for all. The beasts of
the field found shade under it, and the
birds of the air dwelt in its branches, and
all flesh was fed from it.

13"I saw in the visions of my head as I lay
in bed, and behold, a watcher, a holy one,
came down from heaven. 14He cried aloud
and said thus, 'Hew down the tree and cut
off its branches, strip off its leaves and
scatter its fruit; let the beasts flee from
under it and the birds from its branches.
15But leave the stump of its roots in the
earth, bound with a band of iron and
bronze, amid the tender grass of the field.
Let him be wet with the dew of heaven;
let his lot be with the beasts in the grass
of the earth; 16let his mind be changed
from a man's, and let a beast's mind be
given to him; and let seven times pass
over him. 17The sentence is by the decree
of the watchers, the decision by the word
of the holy ones, to the end that the living
may know that the Most High rules the
kingdom of men, and gives it to whom he

will, and sets over it the lowliest of men.' 18This dream I, King Nebuchadnez'zar, saw. And you, O Belteshaz'zar, declare the interpretation, because all the wise men of my kingdom are not able to make known to me the interpretation, but you are able, for the spirit of the holy gods is in you."

19Then Daniel, whose name was Belteshaz'zar, was dismayed for a moment, and his thoughts alarmed him. The king said, "Belteshazzar, let not the dream or the interpretation alarm you." Belteshazzar answered, "My lord, may the dream be for those who hate you and its interpretation for your enemies! 20The tree you saw, which grew and became strong, so that its top reached to heaven, and it was visible to the end of the whole earth; 21whose leaves were fair and its fruit abundant, and in which was food for all; under which beasts of the field found shade, and in whose branches the birds of the air dwelt—22it is you, O king, who have grown and become strong. Your greatness has grown and reaches to heaven, and your dominion to the ends of the earth. 23And whereas the king saw a watcher, a holy one, coming down from heaven and saying, 'Hew down the tree and destroy it, but leave the stump of its roots in the earth, bound with a band of iron and bronze, in the tender grass of the field; and let him be wet with the dew of heaven; and let his lot be with the beasts of the field, till seven times pass over him'; 24this is the interpretation, O king: It is a decree of the Most High, which has come upon my lord the king, 25that you shall be driven from among men, and your dwelling shall be with the beasts of the field; you shall be made to eat grass like an ox, and you shall be wet with the dew of heaven, and seven times shall pass over you, till you know that the Most High rules the kingdom of men, and gives it to whom he will. 26And as it was commanded to leave the stump of the roots of the tree, your kingdom shall be sure for you from the time that you know that Heaven rules. 27Therefore, O king, let my counsel be acceptable to you; break off your sins by practicing righteousness, and your iniquities by showing mercy to the oppressed, that there may perhaps be a lengthening of your tranquillity."

28All this came upon King Nebuchadnez'zar. 29At the end of twelve months he was walking on the roof of the royal palace of Babylon, 30and the king said, "Is not this great Babylon, which I have built by my mighty power as a royal residence and for the glory of my majesty?" 31While the words were still in the king's mouth, there fell a voice from heaven, "O King Nebuchadnez'zar, to you it is spoken: The kingdom has departed from you, 32and you shall be driven from among men, and your dwelling shall be with the beasts of the field; and you shall be made to eat grass like an ox; and seven times shall pass over you, until you have learned that the Most High rules the kingdom of men and gives it to whom he will." 33Immediately the word was fulfilled upon Nebuchadnez'zar. He was driven from among men, and ate grass like an ox, and his body was wet with the dew of heaven till his hair grew as long as eagles' feathers, and his nails were like birds' claws.

34At the end of the days I, Nebuchadnez'zar, lifted my eyes to heaven, and my reason returned to me, and I blessed the Most High, and praised and honored him who lives for ever;

for his dominion is an everlasting dominion,
  and his kingdom endures from
    generation to generation;
35all the inhabitants of the earth are
    accounted as nothing;
  and he does according to his will in the
    host of heaven
  and among the inhabitants of the earth;
and none can stay his hand
  or say to him, "What have you done?"

36At the same time my reason returned to me; and for the glory of my kingdom, my majesty and splendor returned to me. My counselors and my lords sought me, and I was established in my kingdom,

and still more greatness was added to
me. [37]Now I, Nebuchadnez′zar, praise and
extol and honor the King of heaven; for
all his works are right and his ways are
just; and those who walk in pride he is
able to abase.

SIRACH 24

[23]All this is the book of the covenant of the
Most High God,
the law which Moses commanded us
as an inheritance for the congregations
of Jacob.*
[25]It fills men with wisdom, like
the Pi′shon,
and like the Tigris at the time of the
first fruits.
[26]It makes them full of understanding, like
the Euphrates,
and like the Jordan at harvest time.
[27]It makes instruction shine forth like light,
like the Gi′hon at the time of vintage.
[28]Just as the first man did not know
her perfectly,
the last one has not fathomed her;
[29]for her thought is more abundant than
the sea,
and her counsel deeper than the
great abyss.

[30]I went forth like a canal from a river
and like a water channel into a garden.
[31]I said, "I will water my orchard
and drench my garden plot";
and behold, my canal became a river,
and my river became a sea.
[32]I will again make instruction shine forth
like the dawn,
and I will make it shine afar;
[33]I will again pour out teaching like prophecy,
and leave it to all future generations.
[34]Observe that I have not labored for
myself alone,
but for all who seek instruction.

* Other authorities add [24]*Do not cease to be strong in the Lord, cleave to him so that he may strengthen you; the Lord Almighty alone is God, and besides him there is no savior.*

25 My soul takes pleasure in three
things,
and they are beautiful in the sight of the
Lord and of men:
agreement between brothers, friendship
between neighbors,
and a wife and husband who live
in harmony.
[2]My soul hates three kinds of men,
and I am greatly offended at their life:
a beggar who is proud, a rich man who is
a liar,
and an adulterous old man who lacks
good sense.

[3]You have gathered nothing in your youth;
how then can you find anything in your
old age?
[4]What an attractive thing is judgment in
gray-haired men,
and for the aged to possess good counsel!
[5]How attractive is wisdom in the aged,
and understanding and counsel in
honorable men!
[6]Rich experience is the crown of the aged,
and their boast is the fear of the Lord.

[7]With nine thoughts I have gladdened
my heart,
and a tenth I shall tell with my tongue:
a man rejoicing in his children;
a man who lives to see the downfall of
his foes;
[8]happy is he who lives with an intelligent wife,
and he who has not made a slip with
his tongue,
and he who has not served a man inferior
to himself;
[9]happy is he who has gained good sense,
and he who speaks to attentive listeners.
[10]How great is he who has gained wisdom!
But there is no one superior to him who
fears the Lord.
[11]The fear of the Lord surpasses everything;
to whom shall be likened the one who
holds it fast?**

** Other authorities add [12]*The fear of the Lord is the beginning of love for him, and faith is the beginning of clinging to him.*

HEBREWS 7

For this Melchiz′edek, king of
Salem, priest of the Most High
God, met Abraham returning from the
slaughter of the kings and blessed him;
2and to him Abraham apportioned a tenth
part of everything. He is first, by translation
of his name, king of righteousness, and
then he is also king of Salem, that is, king
of peace. 3He is without father or mother
or genealogy, and has neither beginning of
days nor end of life, but resembling the Son
of God he continues a priest for ever.
4See how great he is! Abraham the patriarch gave him a tithe of the spoils. 5And
those descendants of Levi who receive the
priestly office have a commandment in
the law to take tithes from the people, that
is, from their brethren, though these also
are descended from Abraham. 6But this
man who has not their genealogy received
tithes from Abraham and blessed him who
had the promises. 7It is beyond dispute
that the inferior is blessed by the superior.
8Here tithes are received by mortal men;
there, by one of whom it is testified that
he lives. 9One might even say that Levi
himself, who receives tithes, paid tithes
through Abraham, 10for he was still in the
loins of his ancestor when Melchiz′edek
met him.
11Now if perfection had been attainable
through the Levitical priesthood (for
under it the people received the law),
what further need would there have been
for another priest to arise according to
the order of Melchiz′edek, rather than
one named according to the order of
Aaron? 12For when there is a change in
the priesthood, there is necessarily a
change in the law as well. 13For the one of
whom these things are spoken belonged
to another tribe, from which no one has
ever served at the altar. 14For it is evident
that our Lord was descended from Judah,
and in connection with that tribe Moses
said nothing about priests.
15This becomes even more evident when
another priest arises in the likeness of Mel-
chiz′edek, 16who has become a priest, not
according to a legal requirement concerning
bodily descent but by the power of an indestructible life. 17For it is witnessed of him,
"You are a priest for ever,
according to the order of Melchiz′edek."
18On the one hand, a former commandment
is set aside because of its weakness and
uselessness 19(for the law made nothing
perfect); on the other hand, a better hope is
introduced, through which we draw near to
God.
20And it was not without an oath. 21Those
who formerly became priests took their
office without an oath, but this one was
addressed with an oath,
"The Lord has sworn
and will not change his mind,
'You are a priest for ever.'"
22This makes Jesus the surety of a better
covenant.
23The former priests were many in
number, because they were prevented by
death from continuing in office; 24but he
holds his priesthood permanently, because
he continues for ever. 25Consequently he is
able for all time to save those who draw near
to God through him, since he always lives to
make intercession for them.
26For it was fitting that we should have such
a high priest, holy, blameless, unstained,
separated from sinners, exalted above the
heavens. 27He has no need, like those high
priests, to offer sacrifices daily, first for his
own sins and then for those of the people;
he did this once for all when he offered up
himself. 28Indeed, the law appoints men in
their weakness as high priests, but the word
of the oath, which came later than the law,
appoints a Son who has been made perfect
for ever.

REFLECTION

Pride is a strange thing, and it comes disguised in many forms. For example, we can
be lured into believing that we are responsible for our own salvation, that we can earn

our place in Heaven if we just do all the right things or pray all the right prayers. It's the devil's devious deception. The fact is there is nothing we can do that merits the purely gratuitous gift of our salvation. The story of King Nebuchadnezzar's madness is a skillfully crafted analogy. He is under the illusion that the Kingdom of Babylon came about by his power: "Is not this great Babylon, which I have built by my mighty power as a royal residence and for the glory of my majesty?" (Dn 4:30). Pride deceives the king into confusing himself with God. To misunderstand or reject our place as creature (and therefore, not God) is to be out of touch with reality, to be insane. It is only through humility, which is an antidote of pride, that the king's sanity returns. He praises God and acknowledges his power. The story closes with a powerful admonition for the prideful person: "Those who walk in pride, he is able to abase" (v. 37). Do you sometimes fall into the trap of thinking you are responsible for your own salvation? How can you better rely on God and receive his gift of salvation in all humility?

November 13

DANIEL 5

King Belshaz′zar made a great feast for a thousand of his lords, and drank wine in front of the thousand. [2]Belshaz′zar, when he tasted the wine, commanded that the vessels of gold and of silver which Nebuchadnez′zar his father had taken out of the temple in Jerusalem be brought, that the king and his lords, his wives, and his concubines might drink from them. [3]Then they brought in the golden and silver vessels which had been taken out of the temple, the house of God in Jerusalem; and the king and his lords, his wives, and his concubines drank from them. [4]They drank wine, and praised the gods of gold and silver, bronze, iron, wood, and stone.

[5]Immediately the fingers of a man's hand appeared and wrote on the plaster of the wall of the king's palace, opposite the lampstand; and the king saw the hand as it wrote. [6]Then the king's color changed, and his thoughts alarmed him; his limbs gave way, and his knees knocked together. [7]The king cried aloud to bring in the enchanters, the Chalde′ans, and the astrologers. The king said to the wise men of Babylon, "Whoever reads this writing, and shows me its interpretation, shall be clothed with purple, and have a chain of gold about his neck, and shall be the third ruler in the kingdom." [8]Then all the king's wise men came in, but they could not read the writing or make known to the king the interpretation. [9]Then King Belshaz′zar was greatly alarmed, and his color changed; and his lords were perplexed.

[10]The queen, because of the words of the king and his lords, came into the banqueting hall; and the queen said, "O king, live for ever! Let not your thoughts alarm you or your color change. [11]There is in your kingdom a man in whom is the spirit of the holy gods. In the days of your father light and understanding and wisdom, like the wisdom of the gods, were found in him, and King Nebuchadnez′zar, your father, made him chief of the magicians, enchanters, Chalde′ans, and astrologers, [12]because an excellent spirit, knowledge, and understanding to interpret dreams, explain riddles, and solve problems were found in this Daniel, whom the king named Belteshaz′zar. Now let Daniel be called, and he will show the interpretation."

[13]Then Daniel was brought in before the king. The king said to Daniel, "You are that Daniel, one of the exiles of Judah, whom the king my father brought from Judah. [14]I have heard of you that the spirit of the holy gods is in you, and that light and understanding and excellent wisdom are found in you. [15]Now the wise men, the enchanters, have been brought in before me to read this writing and make known to me its interpretation; but they could not show the interpretation

of the matter. [16]But I have heard that you can give interpretations and solve problems. Now if you can read the writing and make known to me its interpretation, you shall be clothed with purple, and have a chain of gold about your neck, and shall be the third ruler in the kingdom.

[17]Then Daniel answered before the king, "Let your gifts be for yourself, and give your rewards to another; nevertheless I will read the writing to the king and make known to him the interpretation. [18]O king, the Most High God gave Nebuchadnez′zar your father kingship and greatness and glory and majesty; [19]and because of the greatness that he gave him, all peoples, nations, and languages trembled and feared before him; whom he would he slew, and whom he would he kept alive; whom he would he raised up, and whom he would he put down. [20]But when his heart was lifted up and his spirit was hardened so that he dealt proudly, he was deposed from his kingly throne, and his glory was taken from him; [21]he was driven from among men, and his mind was made like that of a beast, and his dwelling was with the wild donkeys; he was fed grass like an ox, and his body was wet with the dew of heaven, until he knew that the Most High God rules the kingdom of men, and sets over it whom he will. [22]And you his son, Belshaz′zar, have not humbled your heart, though you knew all this, [23]but you have lifted up yourself against the Lord of heaven; and the vessels of his house have been brought in before you, and you and your lords, your wives, and your concubines have drunk wine from them; and you have praised the gods of silver and gold, of bronze, iron, wood, and stone, which do not see or hear or know, but the God in whose hand is your breath, and whose are all your ways, you have not honored.

[24]"Then from his presence the hand was sent, and this writing was inscribed. [25]And this is the writing that was inscribed: MENE, MENE, TEKEL, and PARSIN. [26]This is the interpretation of the matter: MENE, God has numbered the days of your kingdom and brought it to an end; [27]TEKEL, you have been weighed in the balances and found wanting; [28]PERES, your kingdom is divided and given to the Medes and Persians."

[29]Then Belshaz′zar commanded, and Daniel was clothed with purple, a chain of gold was put about his neck, and proclamation was made concerning him, that he should be the third ruler in the kingdom.

[30]That very night Belshaz′zar the Chalde′an king was slain. [31]And Dari′us the Mede received the kingdom, being about sixty-two years old.

6 It pleased Dari′us to set over the kingdom a hundred and twenty satraps, to be throughout the whole kingdom; [2]and over them three presidents, of whom Daniel was one, to whom these satraps should give account, so that the king might suffer no loss. [3]Then this Daniel became distinguished above all the other presidents and satraps, because an excellent spirit was in him; and the king planned to set him over the whole kingdom. [4]Then the presidents and the satraps sought to find a ground for complaint against Daniel with regard to the kingdom; but they could find no ground for complaint or any fault, because he was faithful, and no error or fault was found in him. [5]Then these men said, "We shall not find any ground for complaint against this Daniel unless we find it in connection with the law of his God."

[6]Then these presidents and satraps came by agreement to the king and said to him, "O King Dari′us, live for ever! [7]All the presidents of the kingdom, the prefects and the satraps, the counselors and the governors are agreed that the king should establish an ordinance and enforce an interdict, that whoever makes petition to any god or man for thirty days, except to you, O king, shall be cast into the den of lions. [8]Now, O king, establish the interdict and sign the document, so that it cannot be changed, according to the law of the Medes and the Persians, which cannot be revoked." [9]Therefore King Dari′us signed the document and interdict.

[10]When Daniel knew that the document had been signed, he went to his house

where he had windows in his upper
chamber open toward Jerusalem; and he
got down upon his knees three times a
day and prayed and gave thanks before his
God, as he had done previously. 11Then
these men came by agreement and found
Daniel making petition and supplication
before his God. 12Then they came near
and said before the king, concerning the
interdict, "O king! Did you not sign an
interdict, that any man who makes petition
to any god or man within thirty days except
to you, O king, shall be cast into the den
of lions?" The king answered, "The thing
stands fast, according to the law of the
Medes and Persians, which cannot be
revoked." 13Then they answered before the
king, "That Daniel, who is one of the exiles
from Judah, pays no heed to you, O king,
or the interdict you have signed, but makes
his petition three times a day."

14Then the king, when he heard these
words, was much distressed, and set his
mind to deliver Daniel; and he labored till
the sun went down to rescue him. 15Then
these men came by agreement to the king,
and said to the king, "Know, O king, that
it is a law of the Medes and Persians that
no interdict or ordinance which the king
establishes can be changed."

16Then the king commanded, and Daniel
was brought and cast into the den of lions.
The king said to Daniel, "May your God,
whom you serve continually, deliver you!"
17And a stone was brought and laid upon
the mouth of the den, and the king sealed
it with his own signet and with the signet
of his lords, that nothing might be changed
concerning Daniel. 18Then the king went to
his palace, and spent the night fasting; no
diversions were brought to him, and sleep
fled from him.

19Then, at break of day, the king arose and
went in haste to the den of lions. 20When he
came near to the den where Daniel was, he
cried out in a tone of anguish and said to
Daniel, "O Daniel, servant of the living God,
has your God, whom you serve continually,
been able to deliver you from the lions?"
21Then Daniel said to the king, "O king, live
for ever! 22My God sent his angel and shut
the lions' mouths, and they have not hurt
me, because I was found blameless before
him; and also before you, O king, I have done
no wrong." 23Then the king was exceedingly
glad, and commanded that Daniel be taken
up out of the den. So Daniel was taken up
out of the den, and no kind of hurt was
found upon him, because he had trusted in
his God. 24And the king commanded, and
those men who had accused Daniel were
brought and cast into the den of lions—they,
their children, and their wives; and before
they reached the bottom of the den the lions
overpowered them and broke all their bones
in pieces.

25Then King Dari′us wrote to all the
peoples, nations, and languages that dwell
in all the earth: "Peace be multiplied to
you. 26I make a decree, that in all my royal
dominion men tremble and fear before the
God of Daniel,

for he is the living God,
  enduring for ever;
his kingdom shall never be destroyed,
  and his dominion shall be to the end.
27He delivers and rescues,
  he works signs and wonders
  in heaven and on earth,
he who has saved Daniel
  from the power of the lions."

28So this Daniel prospered during the reign
of Dari′us and the reign of Cyrus the Persian.

SIRACH 25

13Any wound, but not a wound of the heart!
  Any wickedness, but not the wickedness
    of a wife!
14Any attack, but not an attack from those
    who hate!
  And any vengeance, but not the
    vengeance of enemies!
15There is no venom worse than a snake's
    venom,
  and no wrath worse than an enemy's wrath.
16I would rather dwell with a lion and a
    dragon
  than dwell with an evil wife.

17The wickedness of a wife changes
her appearance,
and darkens her face like that of a bear.
18Her husband takes his meals among
the neighbors,
and he cannot help sighing bitterly.
19Any iniquity is insignificant compared to
a wife's iniquity;
may a sinner's lot befall her!
20A sandy ascent for the feet of the aged—
such is a garrulous wife for a quiet husband.
21Do not be ensnared by a woman's beauty,
and do not desire a woman for
her possessions.
22There is wrath and impudence and
great disgrace
when a wife supports her husband.
23A dejected mind, a gloomy face,
and a wounded heart are caused by an
evil wife.
Drooping hands and weak knees
are caused by the wife who does not
make her husband happy.
24From a woman sin had its beginning,
and because of her we all die.
25Allow no outlet to water,
and no boldness of speech in an evil wife.
26If she does not go as you direct,
separate her from yourself.

HEBREWS 8

Now the point in what we are saying is this: we have such a high priest, one who is seated at the right hand of the throne of the Majesty
in heaven, 2a minister in the sanctuary and
the true tent which is set up not by man
but by the Lord. 3For every high priest
is appointed to offer gifts and sacrifices;
hence it is necessary for this priest also to
have something to offer. 4Now if he were on
earth, he would not be a priest at all, since
there are priests who offer gifts according to
the law. 5They serve a copy and shadow of
the heavenly sanctuary; for when Moses was
about to erect the tent, he was instructed by
God, saying, "See that you make everything
according to the pattern which was shown
you on the mountain." 6But as it is, Christ
has obtained a ministry which is as much
more excellent than the old as the covenant
he mediates is better, since it is enacted on
better promises. 7For if that first covenant
had been faultless, there would have been
no occasion for a second.

8For he finds fault with them when he says:
"The days will come, says the Lord,
when I will establish a new covenant with
the house of Israel
and with the house of Judah;
9not like the covenant that I made with
their fathers
on the day when I took them by the hand
to lead them out of the land of Egypt;
for they did not continue in my covenant,
and so I paid no heed to them, says the Lord.
10This is the covenant that I will make with
the house of Israel
after those days, says the Lord:
I will put my laws into their minds,
and write them on their hearts,
and I will be their God,
and they shall be my people.
11And they shall not teach every one
his fellow
or every one his brother, saying, 'Know
the Lord,'
for all shall know me,
from the least of them to the greatest.
12For I will be merciful toward
their iniquities,
and I will remember their sins no more."
13In speaking of a new covenant he treats
the first as obsolete. And what is becoming
obsolete and growing old is ready to vanish
away.

REFLECTION

Maybe you've heard the saying "I saw the handwriting on the wall," but didn't know that it finds its origin in a story from Scripture. Even if you didn't know where it came from, you most likely understood the implication: you saw it coming! The prophet Daniel is called by the king of Babylon to translate the meaning of the strange words that appeared on the wall. Unfortunately for the king, it is bad news; the kingdom of Babylon is coming to an end. The good news is not the rise of another kingdom but the certainty that after these kingdoms pass away, God will establish his kingdom, and it will be an everlasting kingdom where God will reign with justice and righteousness forever. The Old Covenant was never meant to be an everlasting covenant. It pointed to the New Covenant that would be fully realized in Christ, a covenant that would not be written on stone tablets but on the heart of every human being. It was meant to prepare us to understand the New Covenant in Christ. The blood of lambs and bulls could never fully atone for the sins of mankind; only the Blood of Christ can wash away our sins and bring us to everlasting life in his eternal Kingdom. Spend some time giving thanks to God for the forgiveness of sins that he has given in the New Covenant, and that he remembers your sin no more (see Heb 8:12).

November 14

DANIEL 7

In the first year of Belshaz′zar king of Babylon, Daniel had a dream and visions of his head as he lay in his bed. Then he wrote down the dream,
and told the sum of the matter. 2Daniel said, "I
saw in my vision by night, and behold, the four
winds of heaven were stirring up the great sea.
3And four great beasts came up out of the sea,
different from one another. 4The first was like
a lion and had eagles' wings. Then as I looked
its wings were plucked off, and it was lifted
up from the ground and made to stand upon
two feet like a man; and the mind of a man
was given to it. 5And behold, another beast, a
second one, like a bear. It was raised up on one
side; it had three ribs in its mouth between its
teeth; and it was told, 'Arise, devour much flesh.'
6After this I looked, and behold, another, like a
leopard, with four wings of a bird on its back;
and the beast had four heads; and dominion
was given to it. 7After this I saw in the night
visions, and behold, a fourth beast, terrifying
and dreadful and exceedingly strong; and it
had great iron teeth; it devoured and broke in
pieces, and stamped the residue with its feet.
It was different from all the beasts that were
before it; and it had ten horns. 8I considered
the horns, and behold, there came up among
them another horn, a little one, before which
three of the first horns were plucked up by the
roots; and behold, in this horn were eyes like
the eyes of a man, and a mouth speaking great
things. 9As I looked,

thrones were placed
  and one that was ancient of days took
    his seat;
his clothing was white as snow,
  and the hair of his head like pure wool;
his throne was fiery flames,
  its wheels were burning fire.
10A stream of fire issued
  and came forth from before him;
a thousand thousands served him,
  and ten thousand times ten thousand
    stood before him;
the court sat in judgment,
  and the books were opened.

11I looked then because of the sound of the
great words which the horn was speaking.
And as I looked, the beast was slain, and its
body destroyed and given over to be burned
with fire. 12As for the rest of the beasts, their
dominion was taken away, but their lives
were prolonged for a season and a time. 13I
saw in the night visions,

and behold, with the clouds of heaven
  there came one like a son of man,
and he came to the Ancient of Days
  and was presented before him.
14And to him was given dominion
  and glory and kingdom,
that all peoples, nations, and languages
  should serve him;
his dominion is an everlasting dominion,
  which shall not pass away,
and his kingdom one
  that shall not be destroyed.

[15]"As for me, Daniel, my spirit within me was
anxious and the visions of my head alarmed
me. [16]I approached one of those who stood
there and asked him the truth concerning all
this. So he told me, and made known to me the
interpretation of the things. [17]"These four great
beasts are four kings who shall arise out of the
earth. [18]But the saints of the Most High shall
receive the kingdom, and possess the kingdom
for ever, for ever and ever.'

[19]"Then I desired to know the truth concerning the fourth beast, which was different
from all the rest, exceedingly terrifying,
with its teeth of iron and claws of bronze;
and which devoured and broke in pieces,
and stamped the residue with its feet; [20]and
concerning the ten horns that were on its
head, and the other horn which came up
and before which three of them fell, the horn
which had eyes and a mouth that spoke
great things, and which seemed greater
than its fellows. [21]As I looked, this horn
made war with the saints, and prevailed
over them, [22]until the Ancient of Days came,
and judgment was given for the saints of the
Most High, and the time came when the
saints received the kingdom.

[23]"Thus he said: 'As for the fourth beast,
there shall be a fourth kingdom on earth,
which shall be different from all the
kingdoms,
and it shall devour the whole earth,
and trample it down, and break it
to pieces.
[24]As for the ten horns,
out of this kingdom
ten kings shall arise,
and another shall arise after them;
he shall be different from the former ones,
and shall put down three kings.
[25]He shall speak words against the Most High,
and shall wear out the saints of the
Most High,
and shall think to change the times
and the law;
and they shall be given into his hand
for a time, two times, and half a time.
[26]But the court shall sit in judgment,
and his dominion shall be taken away,
to be consumed and destroyed to the end.
[27]And the kingdom and the dominion
and the greatness of the kingdoms under
the whole heaven
shall be given to the people of the saints
of the Most High;
their kingdom shall be an everlasting
kingdom,
and all dominions shall serve and
obey them.'

[28]"Here is the end of the matter. As for me,
Daniel, my thoughts greatly alarmed me,
and my color changed; but I kept the matter
in my mind."

SIRACH 26

Happy is the husband of a good wife;
the number of his days will be doubled.
[2]A loyal wife rejoices her husband,
and he will complete his years in peace.
[3]A good wife is a great blessing;
she will be granted among the blessings
of the man who fears the Lord.
[4]Whether rich or poor, his heart is glad,
and at all times his face is cheerful.
[5]Of three things my heart is afraid,
and of a fourth I am frightened:
The slander of a city, the gathering
of a mob,
and false accusation—all these are worse
than death.
[6]There is grief of heart and sorrow when a
wife is envious of a rival,
and a tongue-lashing makes it known
to all.
[7]An evil wife is an ox yoke which chafes;
taking hold of her is like grasping
a scorpion.
[8]There is great anger when a wife is drunken;
she will not hide her shame.
[9]A wife's harlotry shows in her
lustful eyes,
and she is known by her eyelids.
[10]Keep strict watch over a headstrong
daughter,
lest, when she finds liberty, she use it to
her hurt.
[11]Be on guard against her impudent eye,
and do not wonder if she sins against you.

12 As a thirsty wayfarer opens his mouth
and drinks from any water near him,
so will she sit in front of every post
and open her quiver to the arrow.
13 A wife's charm delights her husband,
and her skill puts fat on his bones.
14 A sensible and silent wife is a gift of
the Lord,
and there is nothing so precious as a
disciplined soul.
15 A modest wife adds charm to charm,
and no balance can weigh the value
of a chaste soul.
16 Like the sun rising in the heights of
the Lord,
so is the beauty of a good wife in her
well-ordered home.
17 Like the shining lamp on the holy lampstand,
so is a beautiful face on a stately figure.
18 Like pillars of gold on a base of silver,
so are beautiful feet with a steadfast heart.*
28 At two things my heart is grieved,
and because of a third anger comes
over me:
a warrior in want through poverty,
and intelligent men who are treated
contemptuously;
a man who turns back from righteousness
to sin—
the Lord will prepare him for the sword!

* Other authorities add verses 19–27:
19 My son, keep sound the bloom of your youth,
and do not give your strength to strangers.
20 Seek a fertile field within the whole plain,
and sow it with your own seed, trusting in your fine stock.
21 So your offspring will survive
and, having confidence in their good descent, will grow great.
22 A harlot is regarded as spittle,
and a married woman as a tower of death to her lovers.
23 A godless wife is given as a portion to a lawless man,
but a pious wife is given to the man who fears the Lord.
24 A shameless woman constantly acts disgracefully,
but a modest daughter will even be embarrassed before her husband.
25 A headstrong wife is regarded as a dog,
but one who has a sense of shame will fear the Lord.
26 A wife honoring her husband will seem wise to all,
but if she dishonors him in her pride she will be known to all as ungodly.
Happy is the husband of a good wife;
for the number of his years will be doubled.
27 A loud-voiced and garrulous wife is regarded as a war trumpet for putting the enemy into flight,
and every person like this lives in the anarchy of war.

29 A merchant can hardly keep from
wrongdoing,
and a tradesman will not be declared
innocent of sin.

HEBREWS 9

**Now even the first covenant had
regulations for worship and an
earthly sanctuary. 2 For a tent was prepared, the outer one, in which were the**
lampstand and the table and the bread of
offering; it is called the Holy Place. 3 Behind
the second curtain stood a tent called the
Holy of Holies, 4 having the golden altar of
incense and the ark of the covenant covered
on all sides with gold, which contained
a golden urn holding the manna, and
Aaron's rod that budded, and the tables of
the covenant; 5 above it were the cherubim
of glory overshadowing the mercy seat. Of
these things we cannot now speak in detail.
6 These preparations having thus been
made, the priests go continually into the
outer tent, performing their ritual duties;
7 but into the second only the high priest
goes, and he but once a year, and not
without taking blood which he offers for
himself and for the errors of the people. 8 By
this the Holy Spirit indicates that the way
into the sanctuary is not yet opened as long
as the outer tent is still standing 9 (which is
symbolic for the present age). According
to this arrangement, gifts and sacrifices are
offered which cannot perfect the conscience
of the worshiper, 10 but deal only with food
and drink and various baptisms, regulations
for the body imposed until the time of
reformation.
11 But when Christ appeared as a high
priest of the good things that have come,
then through the greater and more perfect
tent (not made with hands, that is, not of
this creation) 12 he entered once for all into
the Holy Place, taking not the blood of
goats and calves but his own blood, thus
securing an eternal redemption. 13 For if
the sprinkling of defiled persons with the

blood of goats and bulls and with the ashes of a heifer sanctifies for the purification of the flesh, [14]how much more shall the blood of Christ, who through the eternal Spirit offered himself without blemish to God, purify your conscience from dead works to serve the living God.

[15]Therefore he is the mediator of a new covenant, so that those who are called may receive the promised eternal inheritance, since a death has occurred which redeems them from the transgressions under the first covenant. [16]For where a will is involved, the death of the one who made it must be established. [17]For a will takes effect only at death, since it is not in force as long as the one who made it is alive. [18]Hence even the first covenant was not ratified without blood. [19]For when every commandment of the law had been declared by Moses to all the people, he took the blood of calves and goats, with water and scarlet wool and hyssop, and sprinkled both the book itself and all the people, [20]saying, "This is the blood of the covenant which God commanded you." [21]And in the same way he sprinkled with the blood both the tent and all the vessels used in worship. [22]Indeed, under the law almost everything is purified with blood, and without the shedding of blood there is no forgiveness of sins.

[23]Thus it was necessary for the copies of the heavenly things to be purified with these rites, but the heavenly things themselves with better sacrifices than these. [24]For Christ has entered, not into a sanctuary made with hands, a copy of the true one, but into heaven itself, now to appear in the presence of God on our behalf. [25]Nor was it to offer himself repeatedly, as the high priest enters the Holy Place yearly with blood not his own; [26]for then he would have had to suffer repeatedly since the foundation of the world. But as it is, he has appeared once for all at the end of the age to put away sin by the sacrifice of himself. [27]And just as it is appointed for men to die once, and after that comes judgment, [28]so Christ, having been offered once to bear the sins of many, will appear a second time, not to deal with sin but to save those who are eagerly waiting for him.

REFLECTION

Daniel's vision of the Son of Man contains one of the most important prophecies in all of Scripture. Daniel has a vision that one like a "son of man" receives all authority from God to rule his Kingdom, an everlasting kingdom that will never pass away and never be destroyed. This kingdom was established when Jesus became the unblemished lamb sacrificed for the sins of the world, the sacrifice that accomplished once and for all the forgiveness of sins. After his Death and Resurrection, Jesus then ascends to Heaven where he sits at the right hand of God the Father in glory, fulfilling Daniel's vision. We also learn from Daniel that the saints of the Most High will share in the Kingdom and its dominion (see Dn 7:27). The Church is the Kingdom of God on earth and the bride of Christ. As his bride, we should strive to please God like the good wife described in Sirach: "Like the sun rising in the heights of the Lord, so is the beauty of a good wife in her well-ordered home" (Sir 26:16). What are some practical changes that you can make to better please God in your life?

November 15

DANIEL 8

In the third year of the reign of King Belshaz′zar a vision appeared to me, Daniel, after that which appeared to me at the first. [2]And I saw in the vision; and when I saw, I was in Susa the capital, which is in the province of E′lam; and I saw in the vision, and I was at the river U′lai. [3]I raised my eyes and saw, and behold, a ram standing on the bank of the river. It had two horns; and both horns were

high, but one was higher than the other,
and the higher one came up last. [4]I saw the
ram charging westward and northward and
southward; no beast could stand before
him, and there was no one who could rescue
from his power; he did as he pleased and
magnified himself.

[5]As I was considering, behold, a he-goat
came from the west across the face of the
whole earth, without touching the ground;
and the goat had a conspicuous horn
between his eyes. [6]He came to the ram with
the two horns, which I had seen standing
on the bank of the river, and he ran at him
in his mighty wrath. [7]I saw him come close
to the ram, and he was enraged against him
and struck the ram and broke his two horns;
and the ram had no power to stand before
him, but he cast him down to the ground
and trampled upon him; and there was no
one who could rescue the ram from his
power. [8]Then the he-goat magnified himself
exceedingly; but when he was strong, the
great horn was broken, and instead of it
there came up four conspicuous horns
toward the four winds of heaven.

[9]Out of one of them came forth a little
horn, which grew exceedingly great toward
the south, toward the east, and toward the
glorious land. [10]It grew great, even to the
host of heaven; and some of the host of
the stars it cast down to the ground, and
trampled upon them. [11]It magnified itself,
even up to the Prince of the host; and the
continual burnt offering was taken away
from him, and the place of his sanctuary was
overthrown. [12]And the host was given over to
it together with the continual burnt offering
through transgression; and truth was cast
down to the ground, and the horn acted
and prospered. [13]Then I heard a holy one
speaking; and another holy one said to the
one that spoke, "For how long is the vision
concerning the continual burnt offering,
the transgression that makes desolate, and
the giving over of the sanctuary and host to
be trampled under foot?" [14]And he said to
him, "For two thousand and three hundred
evenings and mornings; then the sanctuary
shall be restored to its rightful state."

[15]When I, Daniel, had seen the vision, I
sought to understand it; and behold, there
stood before me one having the appearance
of a man. [16]And I heard a man's voice between
the banks of the U'lai, and it called, "Gabriel,
make this man understand the vision." [17]So
he came near where I stood; and when he
came, I was frightened and fell upon my
face. But he said to me, "Understand, O son
of man, that the vision is for the time of the
end."

[18]As he was speaking to me, I fell into a
deep sleep with my face to the ground; but
he touched me and set me on my feet. [19]He
said, "Behold, I will make known to you what
shall be at the latter end of the indignation;
for it pertains to the appointed time of the
end. [20]As for the ram which you saw with
the two horns, these are the kings of Me'dia
and Persia. [21]And the he-goat is the king of
Greece; and the great horn between his eyes
is the first king. [22]As for the horn that was
broken, in place of which four others arose,
four kingdoms shall arise from his nation,
but not with his power. [23]And at the latter
end of their rule, when the transgressors
have reached their full measure, a king of
bold countenance, one who understands
riddles, shall arise. [24]His power shall be
great, and he shall cause fearful destruction,
and shall succeed in what he does, and
destroy mighty men and the people of the
saints. [25]By his cunning he shall make deceit
prosper under his hand, and in his own
mind he shall magnify himself. Without
warning he shall destroy many; and he
shall even rise up against the Prince of
princes; but, by no human hand, he shall be
broken. [26]The vision of the evenings and the
mornings which has been told is true; but
seal up the vision, for it pertains to many
days hence."

[27]And I, Daniel, was overcome and lay sick
for some days; then I rose and went about
the king's business; but I was appalled by the
vision and did not understand it.

9 In the first year of Dari'us the son of
Ahas'uerus, by birth a Mede, who became
king over the realm of the Chalde'ans—
[2]in the first year of his reign, I, Daniel,

perceived in the books the number of years
which, according to the word of the Lord to
Jeremi´ah the prophet, must pass before the
end of the desolations of Jerusalem, namely,
seventy years.
3Then I turned my face to the Lord God,
seeking him by prayer and supplications
with fasting and sackcloth and ashes. 4I
prayed to the Lord my God and made
confession, saying, "O Lord, the great
and awesome God, who keeps covenant
and merciful love with those who love
him and keep his commandments, 5we
have sinned and done wrong and acted
wickedly and rebelled, turning aside from
your commandments and ordinances;
6we have not listened to your servants the
prophets, who spoke in your name to our
kings, our princes, and our fathers, and to
all the people of the land. 7To you, O Lord,
belongs righteousness, but to us confusion
of face, as at this day, to the men of Judah,
to the inhabitants of Jerusalem, and to all
Israel, those that are near and those that
are far away, in all the lands to which you
have driven them, because of the treachery
which they have committed against you.
8To us, O Lord, belongs confusion of face,
to our kings, to our princes, and to our
fathers, because we have sinned against
you. 9To the Lord our God belong mercy
and forgiveness; because we have rebelled
against him, 10and have not obeyed the
voice of the Lord our God by following his
laws, which he set before us by his servants
the prophets. 11All Israel has transgressed
your law and turned aside, refusing to obey
your voice. And the curse and oath which
are written in the law of Moses the servant
of God have been poured out upon us,
because we have sinned against him. 12He
has confirmed his words, which he spoke
against us and against our rulers who ruled
us, by bringing upon us a great calamity; for
under the whole heaven there has not been
done the like of what has been done against
Jerusalem. 13As it is written in the law of
Moses, all this calamity has come upon us,
yet we have not entreated the favor of the
Lord our God, turning from our iniquities
and giving heed to your truth. 14Therefore
the Lord has kept ready the calamity and
has brought it upon us; for the Lord our
God is righteous in all the works which he
has done, and we have not obeyed his voice.
15And now, O Lord our God, who brought
your people out of the land of Egypt with a
mighty hand, and have made you a name,
as at this day, we have sinned, we have done
wickedly. 16O Lord, according to all your
righteous acts, let your anger and your wrath
turn away from your city Jerusalem, your
holy hill; because for our sins, and for the
iniquities of our fathers, Jerusalem and your
people have become a byword among all
who are round about us. 17Now therefore, O
our God, listen to the prayer of your servant
and to his supplications, and for your own
sake, O Lord, cause your face to shine upon
your sanctuary, which is desolate. 18O my
God, incline your ear and hear; open your
eyes and behold our desolations, and the
city which is called by your name; for we do
not present our supplications before you on
the ground of our righteousness, but on the
ground of your great mercy. 19O Lord, hear;
O Lord, forgive; O Lord, give heed and act;
delay not, for your own sake, O my God,
because your city and your people are called
by your name."

20While I was speaking and praying, confessing my sin and the sin of my people
Israel, and presenting my supplication
before the Lord my God for the holy hill
of my God; 21while I was speaking in prayer,
the man Gabriel, whom I had seen in the
vision at the first, came to me in swift flight
at the time of the evening sacrifice. 22He
came and he said to me, "O Daniel, I have
now come out to give you wisdom and
understanding. 23At the beginning of your
supplications a word went forth, and I have
come to tell it to you, for you are greatly
beloved; therefore consider the word and
understand the vision.

24"Seventy weeks of years are decreed
concerning your people and your holy city,
to finish the transgression, to put an end
to sin, and to atone for iniquity, to bring in
everlasting righteousness, to seal both vision

and prophet, and to anoint a most holy
place. [25]Know therefore and understand
that from the going forth of the word to
restore and build Jerusalem to the coming
of an anointed one, a prince, there shall be
seven weeks. Then for sixty-two weeks it
shall be built again with squares and moat,
but in a troubled time. [26]And after the sixty-
two weeks, an anointed one shall be cut off,
and shall have nothing; and the people of
the prince who is to come shall destroy the
city and the sanctuary. Its end shall come
with a flood, and to the end there shall be
war; desolations are decreed. [27]And he shall
make a strong covenant with many for one
week; and for half of the week he shall cause
sacrifice and offering to cease; and upon the
wing of abominations shall come one who
makes desolate, until the decreed end is
poured out on the desolator."

SIRACH 27

Many have committed sin for a trifle,
and whoever seeks to get rich will avert
his eyes.
[2]As a stake is driven firmly into a fissure
between stones,
so sin is wedged in between selling
and buying.
[3]If a man is not steadfast and zealous in the
fear of the Lord,
his house will be quickly overthrown.

[4]When a sieve is shaken, the refuse remains;
so a man's filth remains in his thoughts.
[5]The kiln tests the potter's vessels;
so the test of just men is in tribulation.
[6]The fruit discloses the cultivation of a tree;
so the expression of a thought discloses
the cultivation of a man's mind.
[7]Do not praise a man before you hear
him speak,
for this is the test of men.

[8]If you pursue justice, you will attain it
and wear it as a glorious robe.
[9]Birds flock with their kind;
so truth returns to those who practice it.
[10]A lion lies in wait for prey;
so does sin for the workers of iniquity.
[11]The talk of the godly man is always wise,
but the fool changes like the moon.
[12]Among stupid people watch for a chance
to leave,
but among thoughtful people stay on.
[13]The talk of fools is offensive,
and their laughter is wantonly sinful.
[14]The talk of men given to swearing makes
one's hair stand on end,
and their quarrels make a man stop
his ears.
[15]The strife of the proud leads to bloodshed,
and their abuse is grievous to hear.

[16]Whoever betrays secrets destroys
confidence,
and he will never find a congenial friend.
[17]Love your friend and keep faith with him;
but if you betray his secrets, do not run
after him.
[18]For as a man destroys his enemy,
so you have destroyed the friendship of
your neighbor.
[19]And as you allow a bird to escape from
your hand,
so you have let your neighbor go, and will
not catch him again.
[20]Do not go after him, for he is too far off,
and has escaped like a gazelle from
a snare.
[21]For a wound may be bandaged,
and there is reconciliation after abuse,
but whoever has betrayed secrets is
without hope.

HEBREWS 10

**For since the law has but a shad-
ow of the good things to come
instead of the true form of these realities,
it can never, by the same sacrifices which**
are continually offered year after year, make
perfect those who draw near. [2]Otherwise,
would they not have ceased to be offered? If
the worshipers had once been cleansed, they

would no longer have any consciousness of sin.
3But in these sacrifices there is a reminder of
sin year after year. 4For it is impossible that the
blood of bulls and goats should take away sins.
5Consequently, when Christ came into the
world, he said,

"Sacrifices and offerings you have not desired,
but a body have you prepared for me;
6in burnt offerings and sin offerings you
have taken no pleasure.
7Then I said, 'Behold, I have come to do
your will, O God,'
as it is written of me in the roll of the book."

8When he said above, "You have neither
desired nor taken pleasure in sacrifices and
offerings and burnt offerings and sin offerings"
(these are offered according to the law), 9then
he added, "Behold, I have come to do your
will." He abolishes the first in order to establish
the second. 10And by that will we have been
sanctified through the offering of the body of
Jesus Christ once for all.

11And every priest stands daily at his service,
offering repeatedly the same sacrifices, which
can never take away sins. 12But when Christ had
offered for all time a single sacrifice for sins, he
sat down at the right hand of God, 13then to
wait until his enemies should be made a stool
for his feet. 14For by a single offering he has
perfected for all time those who are sanctified.
15And the Holy Spirit also bears witness to us;
for after saying,

16"This is the covenant that I will make
with them
after those days, says the Lord:
I will put my laws on their hearts,
and write them on their minds,"
17then he adds,
"I will remember their sins and their
misdeeds no more."

18Where there is forgiveness of these, there
is no longer any offering for sin.

REFLECTION

In this reading, Daniel is reminded of Jeremiah's prophesy that God's people would not return to the Promised Land from exile until seventy years had passed. Recognizing that the period of exile has reached its completion, Daniel turns his face to God in supplication, praying, "O LORD, hear; O LORD, forgive; O LORD, give heed and act" (Dn 9:19). In response to Daniel's earnest prayer, God sends the Archangel Gabriel. God acts, and the return of a remnant of God's people "to restore and build Jerusalem" (v. 25) is soon to begin. Gabriel's next words are a bad-news/good-news combination. The bad news: seventy weeks of years (490 years) are decreed; the sins of God's people were so numerous and grave that seventy years of exile will not be enough to finish the transgressions. The "good news": actually, the wonderful news, is that at the end of the 490 years "an anointed one, a prince" will come and "put an end to sin," "atone for iniquity" and "bring an everlasting righteousness" (vv. 24–25). Gabriel's words to Daniel begin a countdown that explains why messianic expectation was so high around the time of the birth of Jesus. The archangel Gabriel will not appear in Scripture again until the 490 years are completed, at which time he will appear to a humble virgin in Nazareth. God himself will become man to save us from our sins. God is never outdone in his generosity and his mercy.

November 16

DANIEL 10

In the third year of Cyrus king of Persia a word was revealed to Daniel, who was named Belteshaz′zar. And the word was true, and it was a great
conflict. And he understood the word and
had understanding of the vision.
2In those days I, Daniel, was mourning for
three weeks. 3I ate no delicacies, no meat or
wine entered my mouth, nor did I anoint
myself at all, for the full three weeks. 4On
the twenty-fourth day of the first month,

as I was standing on the bank of the great river, that is, the Tigris, 5I lifted up my eyes and looked, and behold, a man clothed in linen, whose loins were belted with gold of U′phaz. 6His body was like beryl, his face like the appearance of lightning, his eyes like flaming torches, his arms and legs like the gleam of burnished bronze, and the sound of his words like the noise of a multitude. 7And I, Daniel, alone saw the vision, for the men who were with me did not see the vision, but a great trembling fell upon them, and they fled to hide themselves. 8So I was left alone and saw this great vision, and no strength was left in me; my radiant appearance was fearfully changed, and I retained no strength. 9Then I heard the sound of his words; and when I heard the sound of his words, I fell on my face in a deep sleep with my face to the ground.

10And behold, a hand touched me and set me trembling on my hands and knees. 11And he said to me, "O Daniel, man greatly beloved, give heed to the words that I speak to you, and stand upright, for now I have been sent to you." While he was speaking this word to me, I stood up trembling. 12Then he said to me, "Fear not, Daniel, for from the first day that you set your mind to understand and humbled yourself before your God, your words have been heard, and I have come because of your words. 13The prince of the kingdom of Persia withstood me twenty-one days; but Michael, one of the chief princes, came to help me, so I left him there with the prince of the kingdom of Persia 14and came to make you understand what is to befall your people in the latter days. For the vision is for days yet to come."

15When he had spoken to me according to these words, I turned my face toward the ground and was speechless. 16And behold, one in the likeness of the sons of men touched my lips; then I opened my mouth and spoke. I said to him who stood before me, "O my lord, by reason of the vision pains have come upon me, and I retain no strength. 17How can my lord's servant talk with my lord? For now no strength remains in me, and no breath is left in me."

18Again one having the appearance of a man touched me and strengthened me. 19And he said, "O man greatly beloved, fear not, peace be with you; be strong and of good courage." And when he spoke to me, I was strengthened and said, "Let my lord speak, for you have strengthened me." 20Then he said, "Do you know why I have come to you? But now I will return to fight against the prince of Persia; and when I am through with him, behold, the prince of Greece will come. 21But I will tell you what is inscribed in the book of truth: there is none who contends by my side against these except Michael, your prince.

11 And as for me, in the first year of Dari′us the Mede, I stood up to confirm and strengthen him.

2"And now I will show you the truth. Behold, three more kings shall arise in Persia; and a fourth shall be far richer than all of them; and when he has become strong through his riches, he shall stir up all against the kingdom of Greece. 3Then a mighty king shall arise, who shall rule with great dominion and do according to his will. 4And when he has arisen, his kingdom shall be broken and divided toward the four winds of heaven, but not to his posterity, nor according to the dominion with which he ruled; for his kingdom shall be plucked up and go to others besides these.

5"Then the king of the south shall be strong, but one of his princes shall be stronger than he and his dominion shall be a great dominion. 6After some years they shall make an alliance, and the daughter of the king of the south shall come to the king of the north to make peace; but she shall not retain the strength of her arm, and he and his offspring shall not endure; but she shall be given up, and her attendants, her child, and he who got possession of her.

7"In those times a branch from her roots shall arise in his place; he shall come against the army and enter the fortress of the king of the north, and he shall deal with them and shall prevail. 8He shall also carry off to Egypt their gods with their molten images and with their precious vessels of silver and

of gold; and for some years he shall refrain
from attacking the king of the north. 9Then
the latter shall come into the realm of the
king of the south but shall return into his
own land.
10"His sons shall wage war and assemble
a multitude of great forces, which shall
come on and overflow and pass through,
and again shall carry the war as far as his
fortress. 11Then the king of the south,
moved with anger, shall come out and fight
with the king of the north; and he shall
raise a great multitude, but it shall be given
into his hand. 12And when the multitude is
taken, his heart shall be exalted, and he shall
cast down tens of thousands, but he shall
not prevail. 13For the king of the north shall
again raise a multitude, greater than the
former; and after some years he shall come
on with a great army and abundant supplies.
14"In those times many shall rise against
the king of the south; and the men of
violence among your own people shall lift
themselves up in order to fulfil the vision;
but they shall fail. 15Then the king of the
north shall come and throw up siegeworks,
and take a well-fortified city. And the forces
of the south shall not stand, or even his
picked troops, for there shall be no strength
to stand. 16But he who comes against him
shall do according to his own will, and none
shall stand before him; and he shall stand in
the glorious land, and all of it shall be in his
power. 17He shall set his face to come with
the strength of his whole kingdom, and
he shall bring terms of peace and perform
them. He shall give him the daughter of
women to destroy the kingdom; but it shall
not stand or be to his advantage. 18Afterward
he shall turn his face to the islands, and shall
take many of them; but a commander shall
put an end to his insolence; indeed he shall
turn his insolence back upon him. 19Then he
shall turn his face back toward the fortresses
of his own land; but he shall stumble and
fall, and shall not be found.
20"Then shall arise in his place one who
shall send an exactor of tribute through
the glory of the kingdom; but within a
few days he shall be broken, neither in
anger nor in battle. 21In his place shall
arise a contemptible person to whom royal
majesty has not been given; he shall come
in without warning and obtain the kingdom
by flatteries. 22Armies shall be utterly swept
away before him and broken, and the prince
of the covenant also. 23And from the time
that an alliance is made with him he shall act
deceitfully; and he shall become strong with
a small people. 24Without warning he shall
come into the richest parts of the province;
and he shall do what neither his fathers nor
his fathers' fathers have done, scattering
among them plunder, spoil, and goods.
He shall devise plans against strongholds,
but only for a time. 25And he shall stir up
his power and his courage against the king
of the south with a great army; and the
king of the south shall wage war with an
exceedingly great and mighty army; but he
shall not stand, for plots shall be devised
against him. 26Even those who eat his rich
food shall be his undoing; his army shall be
swept away, and many shall fall down slain.
27And as for the two kings, their minds shall
be bent on mischief; they shall speak lies at
the same table, but to no avail; for the end
is yet to be at the time appointed. 28And he
shall return to his land with great substance,
but his heart shall be set against the holy
covenant. And he shall work his will, and
return to his own land.
29"At the time appointed he shall return and
come into the south; but it shall not be this
time as it was before. 30For ships of Kittim shall
come against him, and he shall be afraid and
withdraw, and shall turn back and be enraged
and take action against the holy covenant.
He shall turn back and give heed to those
who forsake the holy covenant. 31Forces from
him shall appear and profane the temple and
fortress, and shall take away the continual
burnt offering. And they shall set up the
abomination that makes desolate. 32He shall
seduce with flattery those who violate the
covenant; but the people who know their God
shall stand firm and take action. 33And those
among the people who are wise shall make
many understand, though they shall fall by
sword and flame, by captivity and plunder, for

some days. 34When they fall, they shall receive a little help. And many shall join themselves to them with flattery; 35and some of those who are wise shall fall, to refine and to cleanse them and to make them white, until the time of the end, for it is yet for the time appointed.

36"And the king shall do according to his will; he shall exalt himself and magnify himself above every god, and shall speak astonishing things against the God of gods. He shall prosper till the indignation is accomplished; for what is determined shall be done. 37He shall give no heed to the gods of his fathers, or to the one beloved by women; he shall not give heed to any other god, for he shall magnify himself above all. 38He shall honor the god of fortresses instead of these; a god whom his fathers did not know he shall honor with gold and silver, with precious stones and costly gifts. 39He shall deal with the strongest fortresses by the help of a foreign god; those who acknowledge him he shall magnify with honor. He shall make them rulers over many and shall divide the land for a price."

SIRACH 27

22Whoever winks his eye plans evil deeds,
and no one can keep him from them.
23In your presence his mouth is all sweetness,
and he admires your words;
but later he will twist his speech
and with your own words he will
give offense.
24I have hated many things, but none to be
compared to him;
even the Lord will hate him.
25Whoever throws a stone straight up throws
it on his own head;
and a treacherous blow opens up wounds.
26He who digs a pit will fall into it,
and he who sets a snare will be caught in it.
27If a man does evil, it will roll back upon him,
and he will not know where it came from.
28Mockery and abuse issue from the
proud man,
but vengeance lies in wait for him like
a lion.
29Those who rejoice in the fall of the godly
will be caught in a snare,
and pain will consume them before
their death.

30Anger and wrath, these also are
abominations,
and the sinful man will possess them.

HEBREWS 10

19Therefore, brethren, since we have confidence to enter the sanctuary by the blood of Jesus, 20by the new and living way which he opened for us through the curtain, that is, through his flesh, 21and since we have a great priest over the house of God, 22let us draw near with a true heart in full assurance of faith, with our hearts sprinkled clean from an evil conscience and our bodies washed with pure water. 23Let us hold fast the confession of our hope without wavering, for he who promised is faithful; 24and let us consider how to stir up one another to love and good works, 25not neglecting to meet together, as is the habit of some, but encouraging one another, and all the more as you see the Day drawing near.

26For if we sin deliberately after receiving the knowledge of the truth, there no longer remains a sacrifice for sins, 27but a fearful prospect of judgment, and a fury of fire which will consume the adversaries. 28A man who has violated the law of Moses dies without mercy at the testimony of two or three witnesses. 29How much worse punishment do you think will be deserved by the man who has spurned the Son of God, and profaned the blood of the covenant by which he was sanctified, and outraged the Spirit of grace? 30For we know him who said, "Vengeance is mine, I will repay." And again, "The Lord will judge his people." 31It is a fearful thing to fall into the hands of the living God.

32But recall the former days when, after you were enlightened, you endured a hard

struggle with sufferings, [33]sometimes being
publicly exposed to abuse and affliction,
and sometimes being partners with those
so treated. [34]For you had compassion on
the prisoners, and you joyfully accepted
the plundering of your property, since
you knew that you yourselves had a better
possession and an abiding one. [35]Therefore
do not throw away your confidence, which
has a great reward. [36]For you have need of
endurance, so that you may do the will of
God and receive what is promised.
[37]"For yet a little while,
and the coming one shall come and shall
not tarry;
[38]but my righteous one shall live by faith,
and if he shrinks back,
my soul has no pleasure in him."
[39]But we are not of those who shrink back
and are destroyed, but of those who have
faith and keep their souls.

REFLECTION

The Book of Daniel enlightens our reading of the New Testament in so many ways. But for Daniel, who did not have the fullness of the revelation of Jesus Christ, it must have been a frustrating and frightening experience. We see remarkable prophecy in his visions while he struggles to make sense of them. Daniel is an example of what is expressed in Hebrews 10:38: "My righteous one shall live by faith." There may be times when we don't understand a particular Scripture reading or Church teaching. As Catholics, we are called to live by faith—faith in the Church that Jesus Christ established and faith in the Holy Spirit who guides her. That doesn't mean we shouldn't continue to strive for understanding. Our faith is not a blind faith but a living, reasonable, and accessible faith. As Catholics we are blessed to belong to a body that has millions of members, many of whom were saints. From Sts. Jerome and Augustine to Sts. Catherine of Siena and Thérèse of Lisieux, we are surrounded by a cloud of witnesses whose lives and writings help guide us in our faith. Do you allow the communion of the saints to be a part of your faith life?

November 17

DANIEL 11

[40]**"At the time of the end the king
of the south shall attack him;
but the king of the north shall rush upon
him like a whirlwind, with chariots and**
horsemen, and with many ships; and he
shall come into countries and shall overflow
and pass through. [41]He shall come into the
glorious land. And tens of thousands shall fall,
but these shall be delivered out of his hand:
E′dom and Moab and the main part of the
Am′monites. [42]He shall stretch out his hand
against the countries, and the land of Egypt
shall not escape. [43]He shall become ruler of
the treasures of gold and of silver, and all the
precious things of Egypt; and the Libyans and
the Ethiopians shall follow in his train. [44]But
tidings from the east and the north shall alarm
him, and he shall go forth with great fury to
exterminate and utterly destroy many. [45]And
he shall pitch his palatial tents between the sea
and the glorious holy mountain; yet he shall
come to his end, with none to help him.

12 "At that time shall arise Michael, the
great prince who has charge of your
people. And there shall be a time of trouble,
such as never has been since there was a
nation till that time; but at that time your
people shall be delivered, every one whose
name shall be found written in the book.
[2]And many of those who sleep in the dust of
the earth shall awake, some to everlasting life,
and some to shame and everlasting contempt.
[3]And those who are wise shall shine like the
brightness of the firmament; and those who
turn many to righteousness, like the stars for
ever and ever. [4]But you, Daniel, shut up the
words, and seal the book, until the time of
the end. Many shall run back and forth, and
knowledge shall increase."
[5]Then I Daniel looked, and behold, two
others stood, one on this bank of the stream
and one on that bank of the stream. [6]And I said
to the man clothed in linen, who was above the

waters of the stream, "How long shall it be till the end of these wonders?" 7The man clothed in linen, who was above the waters of the stream, raised his right hand and his left hand toward heaven; and I heard him swear by him who lives for ever that it would be for a time, two times, and half a time; and that when the shattering of the power of the holy people comes to an end all these things would be accomplished. 8I heard, but I did not understand. Then I said, "O my lord, what shall be the issue of these things?" 9He said, "Go your way, Daniel, for the words are shut up and sealed until the time of the end. 10Many shall purify themselves, and make themselves white, and be refined; but the wicked shall do wickedly; and none of the wicked shall understand; but those who are wise shall understand. 11And from the time that the continual burnt offering is taken away, and the abomination that makes desolate is set up, there shall be a thousand two hundred and ninety days. 12Blessed is he who waits and comes to the thousand three hundred and thirty-five days. 13But go your way till the end; and you shall rest, and shall stand in your allotted place at the end of the days."

13 There was a man living in Babylon whose name was Jo′akim. 2And he took a wife named Susanna, the daughter of Hilki′ah, a very beautiful woman and one who feared the Lord. 3Her parents were righteous, and had taught their daughter according to the law of Moses. 4Jo′akim was very rich, and had a spacious garden adjoining his house; and the Jews used to come to him because he was the most honored of them all.

5In that year two elders from the people were appointed as judges. Concerning them the Lord had said: "Iniquity came forth from Babylon, from elders who were judges, who were supposed to govern the people." 6These men were frequently at Jo′akim's house, and all who had suits at law came to them.

7When the people departed at noon, Susanna would go into her husband's garden to walk. 8The two elders used to see her every day, going in and walking about, and they began to desire her. 9And they perverted their minds and turned away their eyes from looking to Heaven or remembering righteous judgments. 10Both were overwhelmed with passion for her, but they did not tell each other of their distress, 11for they were ashamed to disclose their lustful desire to possess her. 12And they watched eagerly, day after day, to see her.

13They said to each other, "Let us go home, for it is mealtime." 14And when they went out, they parted from each other. But turning back, they met again; and when each pressed the other for the reason, they confessed their lust. And then together they arranged for a time when they could find her alone.

15Once, while they were watching for an opportune day, she went in as before with only two maids, and wished to bathe in the garden, for it was very hot. 16And no one was there except the two elders, who had hid themselves and were watching her. 17She said to her maids, "Bring me oil and ointments, and shut the garden doors so that I may bathe." 18They did as she said, shut the garden doors, and went out by the side doors to bring what they had been commanded; and they did not see the elders, because they were hidden.

19When the maids had gone out, the two elders rose and ran to her, and said: 20"Look, the garden doors are shut, no one sees us, and we are in love with you; so give your consent, and lie with us. 21If you refuse, we will testify against you that a young man was with you, and this was why you sent your maids away."

22Susanna sighed deeply, and said, "I am hemmed in on every side. For if I do this thing, it is death for me; and if I do not, I shall not escape your hands. 23I choose not to do it and to fall into your hands, rather than to sin in the sight of the Lord."

24Then Susanna cried out with a loud voice, and the two elders shouted against her. 25And one of them ran and opened the garden doors. 26When the household servants heard the shouting in the garden, they rushed in at the side door to see what had happened to her. 27And when the elders told their tale, the servants were greatly ashamed, for nothing like this had ever been said about Susanna.

28The next day, when the people gathered at the house of her husband Jo′akim, the two

elders came, full of their wicked plot to have
Susanna put to death. 29They said before the
people, "Send for Susanna, the daughter of
Hilki′ah, who is the wife of Jo′akim." 30So they
sent for her. And she came, with her parents,
her children, and all her kindred.

31Now Susanna was a woman of great
refinement, and beautiful in appearance. 32As
she was veiled, the wicked men ordered her
to be unveiled, that they might feed upon her
beauty. 33But her family and friends and all
who saw her wept.

34Then the two elders stood up in the midst of
the people, and laid their hands upon her head.
35And she, weeping, looked up toward heaven,
for her heart trusted in the Lord. 36The elders
said, "As we were walking in the garden alone,
this woman came in with two maids, shut the
garden doors, and dismissed the maids. 37Then
a young man, who had been hidden, came to
her and lay with her. 38We were in a corner of
the garden, and when we saw this wickedness
we ran to them. 39We saw them embracing,
but we could not hold the man, for he was too
strong for us, and he opened the doors and
dashed out. 40So we seized this woman and
asked her who the young man was, but she
would not tell us. These things we testify."

41The assembly believed them, because they
were elders of the people and judges; and they
condemned her to death.

42Then Susanna cried out with a loud voice,
and said, "O eternal God, who discern what is
secret, who are aware of all things before they
come to be, 43you know that these men have
borne false witness against me. And now
I am to die! Yet I have done none of the
things that they have wickedly invented
against me!"

SIRACH 28

He that takes vengeance will suffer
vengeance from the Lord,
and he will firmly establish his sins.
2Forgive your neighbor the wrong he
has done,
and then your sins will be pardoned
when you pray.
3Does a man harbor anger against another,
and yet seek for healing from the Lord?
4Does he have no mercy toward a man like
himself,
and yet pray for his own sins?
5If he himself, being flesh, maintains wrath,
will he then seek forgiveness from God?
Who will make expiation for his sins?
6Remember the end of your life, and cease
from enmity,
remember destruction and death, and be
true to the commandments.
7Remember the commandments, and do
not be angry with your neighbor;
remember the covenant of the Most
High, and overlook ignorance.

8Refrain from strife, and you will lessen sins;
for a man given to anger
will kindle strife,
9and a sinful man will disturb friends
and inject enmity among those who are
at peace.
10In proportion to the fuel for the fire, so
will be the burning,
and in proportion to the obstinacy of
strife will be the burning;
in proportion to the strength of the man
will be his anger,
and in proportion to his wealth he will
heighten his wrath.
11A hasty quarrel kindles fire,
and urgent strife sheds blood.
12If you blow on a spark, it will glow;
if you spit on it, it will be put out;
and both come out of your mouth.

HEBREWS 11

Now faith is the assurance of things hoped for, the conviction of things not seen. 2For by it the men of old received divine approval. 3By faith
we understand that the world was created
by the word of God, so that what is seen was
made out of things which do not appear.

4By faith Abel offered to God a more
acceptable sacrifice than Cain, through
which he received approval as righteous,

God bearing witness by accepting his gifts; he died, but through his faith he is still speaking. 5By faith E´noch was taken up so that he should not see death; and he was not found, because God had taken him. Now before he was taken he was attested as having pleased God. 6And without faith it is impossible to please him. For whoever would draw near to God must believe that he exists and that he rewards those who seek him. 7By faith Noah, being warned by God concerning events as yet unseen, took heed and constructed an ark for the saving of his household; by this he condemned the world and became an heir of the righteousness which comes by faith.

8By faith Abraham obeyed when he was called to go out to a place which he was to receive as an inheritance; and he went out, not knowing where he was to go. 9By faith he sojourned in the land of promise, as in a foreign land, living in tents with Isaac and Jacob, heirs with him of the same promise. 10For he looked forward to the city which has foundations, whose builder and maker is God. 11By faith Sarah herself received power to conceive, even when she was past the age, since she considered him faithful who had promised. 12Therefore from one man, and him as good as dead, were born descendants as many as the stars of heaven and as the innumerable grains of sand by the seashore.

13These all died in faith, not having received what was promised, but having seen it and greeted it from afar, and having acknowledged that they were strangers and exiles on the earth. 14For people who speak thus make it clear that they are seeking a homeland. 15If they had been thinking of that land from which they had gone out, they would have had opportunity to return. 16But as it is, they desire a better country, that is, a heavenly one. Therefore God is not ashamed to be called their God, for he has prepared for them a city.

17By faith Abraham, when he was tested, offered up Isaac, and he who had received the promises was ready to offer up his only-begotten son, 18of whom it was said, "Through Isaac shall your descendants be named." 19He considered that God was able to raise men even from the dead; hence he did receive him back and this was a symbol. 20By faith Isaac invoked future blessings on Jacob and Esau. 21By faith Jacob, when dying, blessed each of the sons of Joseph, bowing in worship over the head of his staff. 22By faith Joseph, at the end of his life, made mention of the exodus of the Israelites and gave directions concerning his burial.

REFLECTION

What would you do if God came to you and told you there was going to be a flood and you had to start building a boat? Or told you to leave home with nothing and go somewhere you had never been before? Would you build? Would you go? It's easy to think that those who have followed God's will in the past had something we don't have, some special knowledge or gift. But the fact is, they didn't. What they did have was faith. "Faith is the assurance of things hoped for, the conviction of things not seen" (Heb 11:1). The truth is that Noah, Abraham, and Moses believed though they had not seen. They had a deep conviction that God was leading them down a path, and though they could not see where they were heading or what was waiting for them at the end, they fully trusted God. Our faith requires the same commitment and trust in God. And we, on this side of the Cross, have an advantage—we have the words and deeds of Jesus, who has revealed the Father. How is God asking you to step out in faith?

November 18

DANIEL 13

44The Lord heard her cry. 45And as she was being led away to be put to death, God aroused the holy spirit of a young lad named Daniel; 46and he

cried with a loud voice, "I am innocent of the blood of this woman."

47 All the people turned to him, and said, "What is this that you have said?" 48 Taking his stand in the midst of them, he said, "Are you such fools, you sons of Israel? Have you condemned a daughter of Israel without examination and without learning the facts? 49 Return to the place of judgment. For these men have borne false witness against her."

50 Then all the people returned in haste. And the elders said to him, "Come, sit among us and inform us, for God has given you that right." 51 And Daniel said to them, "Separate them far from each other, and I will examine them."

52 When they were separated from each other, he summoned one of them and said to him, "You old relic of wicked days, your sins have now come home, which you have committed in the past, 53 pronouncing unjust judgments, condemning the innocent and letting the guilty go free, though the Lord said, 'Do not put to death an innocent and righteous person.' 54 Now then, if you really saw her, tell me this: Under what tree did you see them being intimate with each other?" He answered, "Under a mastic tree." 55 And Daniel said, "Very well! You have lied against your own head, for the angel of God has received the sentence from God and will immediately cut you in two."

56 Then he put him aside, and commanded them to bring the other. And he said to him, "You offspring of Canaan and not of Judah, beauty has deceived you and lust has perverted your heart. 57 This is how you both have been dealing with the daughters of Israel, and they were intimate with you through fear; but a daughter of Judah would not endure your wickedness. 58 Now then, tell me: Under what tree did you catch them being intimate with each other?" He answered, "Under an evergreen oak." 59 And Daniel said to him, "Very well! You also have lied against your own head, for the angel of God is waiting with his sword to saw you in two, that he may destroy you both."

60 Then all the assembly shouted loudly and blessed God, who saves those who hope in him. 61 And they rose against the two elders, for out of their own mouths Daniel had convicted them of bearing false witness; 62 and they did to them as they had wickedly planned to do to their neighbor; acting in accordance with the law of Moses, they put them to death. Thus innocent blood was saved that day.

63 And Hilki'ah and his wife praised God for their daughter Susanna, and so did Jo'akim her husband and all her kindred, because nothing shameful was found in her. 64 And from that day onward Daniel had a great reputation among the people.

14 When King Asty'ages was laid with his fathers, Cyrus the Persian received his kingdom. 2 And Daniel was a companion of the king, and was the most honored of his friends.

3 Now the Babylonians had an idol called Bel, and every day they spent on it twelve bushels of fine flour and forty sheep and fifty gallons of wine. 4 The king revered it and went every day to worship it. But Daniel worshiped his own God.

5 And the king said to him, "Why do you not worship Bel?" He answered, "Because I do not revere man-made idols, but the living God, who created heaven and earth and has dominion over all flesh."

6 The king said to him, "Do you not think that Bel is a living God? Do you not see how much he eats and drinks every day?" 7 Then Daniel laughed, and said, "Do not be deceived, O king; for this is but clay inside and brass outside, and it never ate or drank anything."

8 Then the king was angry, and he called his priests and said to them, "If you do not tell me who is eating these provisions, you shall die. 9 But if you prove that Bel is eating them, Daniel shall die, because he blasphemed against Bel." And Daniel said to the king, "Let it be done as you have said."

10 Now there were seventy priests of Bel, besides their wives and children. And the king went with Daniel into the temple of Bel. 11 And the priests of Bel said, "Behold, we are going outside; you yourself, O king, shall set forth the food and mix and place the wine, and shut the door and seal it with your signet. 12 And when you return in the morning, if you do not find that Bel

has eaten it all, we will die; or else Daniel
will, who is telling lies about us." [13]They
were unconcerned, for beneath the table
they had made a hidden entrance, through
which they used to go in regularly and
consume the provisions. [14]When they had
gone out, the king set forth the food for Bel.
Then Daniel ordered his servants to bring
ashes and they sifted them throughout the
whole temple in the presence of the king
alone. Then they went out, shut the door
and sealed it with the king's signet, and
departed. [15]In the night the priests came
with their wives and children, as they
were accustomed to do, and ate and drank
everything.

[16]Early in the morning the king rose and
came, and Daniel with him. [17]And the king
said, "Are the seals unbroken, Daniel?" He
answered, "They are unbroken, O king." [18]As
soon as the doors were opened, the king
looked at the table, and shouted in a loud voice,
"You are great, O Bel; and with you there is no
deceit, none at all."

[19]Then Daniel laughed, and restrained the
king from going in, and said, "Look at the
floor, and notice whose footsteps these are."
[20]The king said, "I see the footsteps of men and
women and children."

[21]Then the king was enraged, and he seized
the priests and their wives and children; and
they showed him the secret doors through
which they were accustomed to enter and
devour what was on the table. [22]Therefore the
king put them to death, and gave Bel over to
Daniel, who destroyed it and its temple.

[23]There was also a great dragon, which the
Babylonians revered. [24]And the king said
to Daniel, "You cannot deny that this is a
living god; so worship him." [25]Daniel said, "I
will worship the Lord my God, for he is the
living God. [26]But if you, O king, will give me
permission, I will slay the dragon without
sword or club." The king said, "I give you
permission."

[27]Then Daniel took pitch, fat, and hair, and
boiled them together and made cakes, which
he fed to the dragon. The dragon ate them, and
burst open. And Daniel said, "See what you
have been worshiping!"

[28]When the Babylonians heard it, they were
very indignant and conspired against the king,
saying, "The king has become a Jew; he has destroyed Bel, and slain the dragon, and slaughtered the priests." [29]Going to the king, they said,
"Hand Daniel over to us, or else we will kill you
and your household." [30]The king saw that they
were pressing him hard, and under compulsion he handed Daniel over to them.

[31]They threw Daniel into the lions' den, and
he was there for six days. [32]There were seven
lions in the den, and every day they had been
given two human bodies and two sheep; but
these were not given to them now, so that they
might devour Daniel.

[33]Now the prophet Habak′kuk was in Jude′a.
He had boiled pottage and had broken bread
into a bowl, and was going into the field to take
it to the reapers. [34]But the angel of the Lord
said to Habak′kuk, "Take the dinner which
you have to Babylon, to Daniel, in the lions'
den." [35]Habak′kuk said, "Sir, I have never seen
Babylon, and I know nothing about the den."
[36]Then the angel of the Lord took him by the
crown of his head, and lifted him by his hair
and set him down in Babylon, right over the
den, with the rushing sound of the wind itself.

[37]Then Habak′kuk shouted, "Daniel, Daniel!
Take the dinner which God has sent you."
[38]And Daniel said, "You have remembered me,
O God, and have not forsaken those who love
you." [39]So Daniel arose and ate. And the angel
of God immediately returned Habak′kuk to his
own place.

[40]On the seventh day the king came to
mourn for Daniel. When he came to the den
he looked in, and there sat Daniel. [41]And the
king shouted with a loud voice, "You are great,
O Lord God of Daniel, and there is no other
besides you." [42]And he pulled Daniel out, and
threw into the den the men who had attempted
his destruction, and they were devoured
immediately before his eyes.

SIRACH 28

[13]Curse the whisperer and deceiver,
for he has destroyed many who were
at peace.

[14]Slander has shaken many,
and scattered them from nation to nation,
and destroyed strong cities,
and overturned the houses of great men.
[15]Slander has driven away courageous women,
and deprived them of the fruit of their toil.
[16]Whoever pays heed to slander will not
find rest,
nor will he settle down in peace.
[17]The blow of a whip raises a welt,
but a blow of the tongue crushes the bones.
[18]Many have fallen by the edge of the sword,
but not so many as have fallen because of
the tongue.
[19]Happy is the man who is protected from it,
who has not been exposed to its anger,
who has not borne its yoke,
and has not been bound with its chains;
[20]for its yoke is a yoke of iron,
and its chains are chains of bronze;
[21]its death is an evil death,
and Hades is preferable to it.
[22]It will not be master over the godly,
and they will not be burned in its flame.
[23]Those who forsake the Lord will fall into
its power;
it will burn among them and will not be
put out.
It will be sent out against them like a lion;
like a leopard it will mangle them.
[24]See that you fence in your property
with thorns,
lock up your silver and gold,
[25]make balances and scales for your words,
and make a door and a bolt for your mouth.
[26]Beware lest you err with your tongue,
lest you fall before him who lies in wait.

HEBREWS 11

**[23]By faith Moses, when he was
born, was hidden for three months
by his parents, because they saw that the
child was beautiful; and they were not**
afraid of the king's edict. [24]By faith Moses,
when he was grown up, refused to be called the
son of Pharaoh's daughter, [25]choosing rather
to share ill-treatment with the people of God
than to enjoy the fleeting pleasures of sin.
[26]He considered abuse suffered for the Christ
greater wealth than the treasures of Egypt,
for he looked to the reward. [27]By faith he left
Egypt, not being afraid of the anger of the king;
for he endured as seeing him who is invisible.
[28]By faith he kept the Passover and sprinkled
the blood, so that the Destroyer of the first-
born might not touch them.

[29]By faith the people crossed the Red Sea as
if on dry land; but the Egyptians, when they
attempted to do the same, were drowned. [30]By
faith the walls of Jericho fell down after they
had been encircled for seven days. [31]By faith
Rahab the harlot did not perish with those
who were disobedient, because she had given
friendly welcome to the spies.

[32]And what more shall I say? For time would
fail me to tell of Gideon, Barak, Samson,
Jephthah, of David and Samuel and the
prophets—[33]who through faith conquered
kingdoms, enforced justice, received promises,
stopped the mouths of lions, [34]quenched
raging fire, escaped the edge of the sword,
won strength out of weakness, became mighty
in war, put foreign armies to flight. [35]Women
received their dead by resurrection. Some
were tortured, refusing to accept release, that
they might rise again to a better life. [36]Others
suffered mocking and scourging, and even
chains and imprisonment. [37]They were stoned,
they were sawn in two, they were killed with
the sword; they went about in skins of sheep
and goats, destitute, afflicted, ill-treated—[38]of
whom the world was not worthy—wandering
over deserts and mountains, and in dens and
caves of the earth.

[39]And all these, though well attested by their
faith, did not receive what was promised,
[40]since God had foreseen something better for
us, that apart from us they should not be made
perfect.

REFLECTION

Sirach has direct words regarding deception: "Curse the whisperer and deceiver, for he has destroyed many who were at peace" (Sir 28:13) and "many have fallen by the edge of the sword, but not so many as have fallen because of the tongue" (v. 18). We see the truth of these words played out in the final chapters of the Book of Daniel. Susanna's false accusers destroy the peace of Susanna and her family with scandalous accusations, but Daniel intervenes and reveals their falsehood by their own deceitful words. Because of his attempt to reveal the falsehood of the Babylonian idol, Daniel's accusers conspire against him and the king seeks Daniel's destruction, but God, in whom is all truth, protects Daniel, and it is his lying enemies who are devoured in the pit. Jesus describes the devil as a liar and the father of lies (see Jn 8:44), and Sirach warns us against following in his ways. In contrast, Hebrews holds up for us a myriad of examples of those in Israel's history who responded to God in obedience and show us all manner of virtue—honesty, courage, perseverance, etc. We too must choose the way in which we will walk, following falsehood or following the one who is the way, the truth and the life (see Jn 14:6), whose coming these holy men and women foresaw.

November 19

HOSEA 1

The word of the LORD that came to Hose´a the son of Bee´ri, in the days of Uzzi´ah, Jo´tham, A´haz, and Hezeki´ah, kings of Judah, and in the days of Jerobo´am the son of Jo´ash, king of Israel.
[2]When the LORD first spoke through
Hose´a, the LORD said to Hosea, "Go, take
to yourself a wife of harlotry and have
children of harlotry, for the land commits
great harlotry by forsaking the LORD." [3]So
he went and took Gomer the daughter
of Dibla´im, and she conceived and bore
him a son.
[4]And the LORD said to him, "Call his
name Jezre´el; for yet a little while, and
I will punish the house of Je´hu for the
blood of Jezreel, and I will put an end to
the kingdom of the house of Israel. [5]And
on that day, I will break the bow of Israel
in the valley of Jezre´el."
[6]She conceived again and bore a daughter.
And the LORD said to him, "Call her name
Not pitied, for I will no more have pity
on the house of Israel, to forgive them
at all. [7]But I will have pity on the house
of Judah, and I will deliver them by the
LORD their God; I will not deliver them
by bow, nor by sword, nor by war, nor by
horses, nor by horsemen."
[8]When she had weaned Not pitied, she
conceived and bore a son. [9]And the LORD
said, "Call his name Not my people, for you
are not my people and I am not your God."
[10]Yet the number of the people of Israel
shall be like the sand of the sea, which can
be neither measured nor numbered; and in
the place where it was said to them, "You
are not my people," it shall be said to them,
"Sons of the living God." [11]And the people
of Judah and the people of Israel shall be
gathered together, and they shall appoint
for themselves one head; and they shall go
up from the land, for great shall be the day
of Jezre´el.

2 Say to your brother, "My people," and to
your sister, "She has obtained pity."

[2]"Plead with your mother, plead—
for she is not my wife,
and I am not her husband—
that she put away her harlotry from
her face,
and her adultery from between
her breasts;
[3]lest I strip her naked
and make her as in the day she was born,
and make her like a wilderness,
and set her like a parched land,
and slay her with thirst.
[4]Upon her children also I will have no pity,
because they are children of harlotry.
[5]For their mother has played the harlot;
she that conceived them has
acted shamefully.

For she said, 'I will go after my lovers,
who give me my bread and my water,
my wool and my flax, my oil and
my drink.'
6Therefore I will hedge up her way
with thorns;
and I will build a wall against her,
so that she cannot find her paths.
7She shall pursue her lovers,
but not overtake them;
and she shall seek them,
but shall not find them.
Then she shall say, 'I will go
and return to my first husband,
for it was better with me then
than now.'
8And she did not know
that it was I who gave her
the grain, the wine, and the oil,
and who lavished upon her silver
and gold which they used for Ba'al.
9Therefore I will take back
my grain in its time,
and my wine in its season;
and I will take away my wool and
my flax,
which were to cover her nakedness.
10Now I will uncover her lewdness
in the sight of her lovers,
and no one shall rescue her out of
my hand.
11And I will put an end to all her mirth,
her feasts, her new moons,
her sabbaths,
and all her appointed feasts.
12And I will lay waste her vines and
her fig trees,
of which she said,
'These are my hire,
which my lovers have given me.'
I will make them a forest,
and the beasts of the field shall devour
them.
13And I will punish her for the feast days
of the Ba'als
when she burned incense to them
and decked herself with her ring
and jewelry,
and went after her lovers,
and forgot me, says the LORD.

14"Therefore, behold, I will allure her,
and bring her into the wilderness,
and speak tenderly to her.
15And there I will give her her vineyards,
and make the Valley of A'chor a door
of hope.
And there she shall answer as in the days
of her youth,
as at the time when she came out of the
land of Egypt.

16"And in that day, says the LORD, you
will call me, 'My husband,' and no longer
will you call me, 'My Ba'al.' 17For I will
remove the names of the Ba'als from her
mouth, and they shall be mentioned by
name no more. 18And I will make for you
a covenant on that day with the beasts
of the field, the birds of the air, and the
creeping things of the ground; and I will
abolish the bow, the sword, and war from
the land; and I will make you lie down in
safety. 19And I will espouse you for ever; I
will espouse you in righteousness and in
justice, in steadfast love, and in mercy. 20I
will espouse you in faithfulness; and you
shall know the LORD.

21"And in that day, says the LORD,
I will answer the heavens
and they shall answer the earth;
22and the earth shall answer the grain, the
wine, and the oil,
and they shall answer Jezre'el;
23 and I will sow him for myself in the land.
And I will have pity on Not pitied,
and I will say to Not my people, 'You are
my people';
and he shall say 'You are my God.'"

3 And the LORD said to me, "Go again,
love a woman who is beloved of a
paramour and is an adulteress; even as the
LORD loves the people of Israel, though
they turn to other gods and love cakes of
raisins." 2So I bought her for fifteen shekels
of silver and a homer and a lethech of
barley. 3And I said to her, "You must dwell
as mine for many days; you shall not play
the harlot, or belong to another man; so
will I also be to you." 4For the children
of Israel shall dwell many days without
king or prince, without sacrifice or pillar,

without ephod or teraphim. [5]Afterward the
children of Israel shall return and seek the
LORD their God, and David their king; and
they shall come in fear to the LORD and to
his goodness in the latter days.

4 Hear the word of the LORD, O people
of Israel;
for the LORD has a controversy with the
inhabitants of the land.
There is no faithfulness or kindness,
and no knowledge of God in the land;
[2]there is swearing, lying, killing, stealing,
and committing adultery;
they break all bounds and murder
follows murder.
[3]Therefore the land mourns,
and all who dwell in it languish,
and also the beasts of the field,
and the birds of the air;
and even the fish of the sea are
taken away.

[4]Yet let no one contend,
and let none accuse,
for with you is my contention,
O priest.
[5]You shall stumble by day,
the prophet also shall stumble with you
by night;
and I will destroy your mother.
[6]My people are destroyed for lack
of knowledge;
because you have rejected knowledge,
I reject you from being a priest to me.
And since you have forgotten the law of
your God,
I also will forget your children.

[7]The more they increased,
the more they sinned against me;
I will change their glory into shame.
[8]They feed on the sin of my people;
they are greedy for their iniquity.
[9]And it shall be like people, like priest;
I will punish them for their ways,
and repay them for their deeds.
[10]They shall eat, but not be satisfied;
they shall play the harlot, but not multiply;
because they have forsaken the LORD
to cherish harlotry.
[11]Wine and new wine
take away the understanding.
[12]My people inquire of a thing of wood,
and their staff gives them oracles.
For a spirit of harlotry has led them astray,
and they have left their God to play
the harlot.
[13]They sacrifice on the tops of the mountains,
and make offerings upon the hills,
under oak, poplar, and terebinth,
because their shade is good.

Therefore your daughters play the harlot,
and your brides commit adultery.
[14]I will not punish your daughters when
they play the harlot,
nor your brides when they
commit adultery;
for the men themselves go aside
with harlots,
and sacrifice with cult prostitutes,
and a people without understanding shall
come to ruin.

[15]Though you play the harlot, O Israel,
let not Judah become guilty.
Enter not into Gilgal,
nor go up to Beth-a′ven,
and swear not, "As the LORD lives."
[16]Like a stubborn heifer,
Israel is stubborn;
can the LORD now feed them
like a lamb in a broad pasture?

[17]E′phraim is joined to idols,
let him alone.
[18]A band of drunkards, they give themselves
to harlotry;
they love shame more than their glory.
[19]A wind has wrapped them in its wings,
and they shall be ashamed because of
their altars.

SIRACH 29

He that shows mercy will lend to
his neighbor,
and he that strengthens him with his
hand keeps the commandments.

[2]Lend to your neighbor in the time of
his need;
and in turn, repay your neighbor promptly.
[3]Confirm your word and keep faith with him,
and on every occasion you will find what
you need.
[4]Many persons regard a loan as a windfall,
and cause trouble to those who help them.
[5]A man will kiss another's hands until he
gets a loan,
and will lower his voice in speaking of his
neighbor's money;
but at the time for repayment he will delay,
and will pay in words of unconcern,
and will find fault with the time.
[6]If the lender exerts pressure, he will hardly
get back half,
and will regard that as a windfall.
If he does not, the borrower has robbed
him of his money,
and he has needlessly made him his enemy;
he will repay him with curses and
reproaches,
and instead of glory will repay him
with dishonor.
[7]Because of such wickedness, therefore,
many have refused to lend;
they have been afraid of being
defrauded needlessly.

[8]Nevertheless, be patient with a man in
humble circumstances,
and do not make him wait for your alms.
[9]Help a poor man for the commandment's
sake,
and because of his need do not send him
away empty.
[10]Lose your silver for the sake of a brother
or a friend,
and do not let it rust under a stone
and be lost.
[11]Lay up your treasure according to the
commandments of the Most High,
and it will profit you more than gold.
[12]Store up almsgiving in your treasury,
and it will rescue you from all affliction;
[13]more than a mighty shield and more than
a heavy spear,
it will fight on your behalf against
your enemy.

HEBREWS 12

**Therefore, since we are surround-
ed by so great a cloud of witnesses,
let us also lay aside every weight, and sin
which clings so closely, and let us run**
with perseverance the race that is set
before us, [2]looking to Jesus the pioneer
and perfecter of our faith, who for the joy
that was set before him endured the cross,
despising the shame, and is seated at the
right hand of the throne of God.
[3]Consider him who endured from sinners
such hostility against himself, so that you
may not grow weary or fainthearted. [4]In
your struggle against sin you have not yet
resisted to the point of shedding your blood.
[5]And have you forgotten the exhortation
which addresses you as sons?—
"My son, do not regard lightly the discipline
of the Lord,
nor lose courage when you are
punished by him.
[6]For the Lord disciplines him whom
he loves,
and chastises every son whom he receives."
[7]It is for discipline that you have to endure.
God is treating you as sons; for what son is
there whom his father does not discipline?
[8]If you are left without discipline, in which
all have participated, then you are illegitimate children and not sons. [9]Besides this,
we have had earthly fathers to discipline us
and we respected them. Shall we not much
more be subject to the Father of spirits and
live? [10]For they disciplined us for a short
time at their pleasure, but he disciplines us
for our good, that we may share his holiness.
[11]For the moment all discipline seems painful rather than pleasant; later it yields the
peaceful fruit of righteousness to those who
have been trained by it.
[12]Therefore lift your drooping hands and
strengthen your weak knees, [13]and make
straight paths for your feet, so that what is
lame may not be put out of joint but rather be
healed. [14]Strive for peace with all men, and for
the holiness without which no one will see the
Lord. [15]See to it that no one fail to obtain the
grace of God; that no "root of bitterness"

spring up and cause trouble, and by it the
many become defiled; 16that no one be
immoral or irreligious like Esau, who sold
his birthright for a single meal. 17For you
know that afterward, when he desired to
inherit the blessing, he was rejected, for
he found no chance to repent, though he
sought it with tears.

18For you have not come to what may be
touched, a blazing fire, and darkness, and
gloom, and a tempest, 19and the sound of a
trumpet, and a voice whose words made the
hearers entreat that no further messages be
spoken to them. 20For they could not endure
the order that was given, "If even a beast
touches the mountain, it shall be stoned."
21Indeed, so terrifying was the sight that Moses
said, "I tremble with fear." 22But you have come
to Mount Zion and to the city of the living God,
the heavenly Jerusalem, and to innumerable
angels in festal gathering, 23and to the assembly
of the first-born who are enrolled in heaven,
and to a judge who is God of all, and to the
spirits of just men made perfect, 24and to Jesus,
the mediator of a new covenant, and to the
sprinkled blood that speaks more graciously
than the blood of Abel.

25See that you do not refuse him who is
speaking. For if they did not escape when
they refused him who warned them on earth,
much less shall we escape if we reject him who
warns from heaven. 26His voice then shook
the earth; but now he has promised, "Yet once
more I will shake not only the earth but also
the heaven." 27This phrase, "Yet once more,"
indicates the removal of what is shaken, as of
what has been made, in order that what cannot
be shaken may remain. 28Therefore let us be
grateful for receiving a kingdom that cannot be
shaken, and thus let us offer to God acceptable
worship, with reverence and awe; 29for our God
is a consuming fire.

REFLECTION

Many of the Old Testament prophets are called by God to not only speak God's message in words, but also to embody that message in their lives. This is the case with Hosea, who is called by God to speak to Israel about her covenant infidelity. To embody his message, Hosea is called to marry a harlot, Gomer, who, after bearing him three children, runs off after other lovers. When Gomer finally hits rock bottom and realizes the depth of her depravity, Hosea is called to take her back. God made a covenant with Israel at Mt. Sinai: "I will take you for my people, and I will be your God" (Ex 6:7). But God's virgin bride, the people of Israel, broke that covenant by going after foreign gods (idols that were not gods). Despite Israel's adultery, God will take his people back and make them new again. There is no end to God's mercy. God never stops calling us back to himself, no matter what we have done. He even sent us his only begotten Son, who gave his life for our sins. That is the undying love God has for us. Why do you think the prophets chose the metaphor of adultery to describe infidelity to God?

November 20

HOSEA 5

Hear this, O priests!
Give heed, O house of Israel!
Listen, O house of the king!
For the judgment pertains to you;
for you have been a snare at Mizpah,
and a net spread upon Ta′bor.
2And they have made deep the pit of Shittim;
but I will chastise all of them.

3I know E′phraim,
and Israel is not hidden from me;
for now, O Ephraim, you have played
the harlot,
Israel is defiled.
4Their deeds do not permit them
to return to their God.
For the spirit of harlotry is within them,
and they know not the Lord.

[5]The pride of Israel testifies to his face;
E´phraim shall stumble in his guilt;
Judah also shall stumble with them.
[6]With their flocks and herds they shall go
to seek the LORD,
but they will not find him;
he has withdrawn from them.
[7]They have dealt faithlessly with the LORD;
for they have borne alien children.
Now the new moon shall devour them
with their fields.

[8]Blow the horn in Gib´e-ah,
the trumpet in Ra´mah.
Sound the alarm at Beth-a´ven;
tremble, O Benjamin!
[9]E´phraim shall become a desolation
in the day of punishment;
among the tribes of Israel
I declare what is sure.
[10]The princes of Judah have become
like those who remove the landmark;
upon them I will pour out
my wrath like water.
[11]E´phraim is oppressed, crushed in judgment,
because he was determined to go
after vanity.
[12]Therefore I am like a moth to E´phraim,
and like dry rot to the house of Judah.

[13]When E´phraim saw his sickness,
and Judah his wound,
then Ephraim went to Assyria,
and sent to the great king.
But he is not able to cure you
or heal your wound.
[14]For I will be like a lion to E´phraim,
and like a young lion to the house of Judah.
I, even I, will tear and go away,
I will carry off, and none shall rescue.
[15]I will return again to my place,
until they acknowledge their guilt and
seek my face,
and in their distress they seek me, saying,
6 "Come, let us return to the LORD;
for he has torn, that he may heal us;
he has stricken, and he will bind us up.
[2]After two days he will revive us;
on the third day he will raise us up,
that we may live before him.
[3]Let us know, let us press on to know
the LORD;
his going forth is sure as the dawn;
he will come to us as the showers,
as the spring rains that water the earth."
[4]What shall I do with you, O E´phraim?
What shall I do with you, O Judah?
Your love is like a morning cloud,
like the dew that goes early away.
[5]Therefore I have hewn them by the
prophets,
I have slain them by the words of
my mouth,
and my judgment goes forth as the light.

[6]For I desire mercy and not sacrifice,
the knowledge of God, rather than
burnt offerings.

[7]But at Adam they transgressed the covenant;
there they dealt faithlessly with me.
[8]Gilead is a city of evildoers,
tracked with blood.
[9]As robbers lie in wait for a man,
so the priests are banded together;
they murder on the way to She´chem,
yes, they commit villainy.
[10]In the house of Israel I have seen a
horrible thing;
E´phraim's harlotry is there, Israel
is defiled.
[11]For you also, O Judah, a harvest
is appointed.
When I would restore the fortunes of
my people,
7 when I would heal Israel,
the corruption of E´phraim is revealed,
and the wicked deeds of Samar´ia;
for they deal falsely,
the thief breaks in,
and the bandits raid without.
[2]But they do not consider
that I remember all their evil works.
Now their deeds encompass them,
they are before my face.
[3]By their wickedness they make the king glad,
and the princes by their treachery.
[4]They are all adulterers;
they are like a heated oven,

whose baker ceases to stir the fire,
from the kneading of the dough until it
is leavened.
5 On the day of our king the princes
became sick with the heat of wine;
he stretched out his hand with mockers.
6 For like an oven their hearts burn
with intrigue;
all night their anger smolders;
in the morning it blazes like a
flaming fire.
7 All of them are hot as an oven,
and they devour their rulers.
All their kings have fallen;
and none of them calls upon me.

8 E′phraim mixes himself with the peoples;
Ephraim is a cake not turned.
9 Aliens devour his strength,
and he knows it not;
gray hairs are sprinkled upon him,
and he knows it not.
10 The pride of Israel witnesses
against him;
yet they do not return to the
LORD their God,
nor seek him, for all this.

11 E′phraim is like a dove,
silly and without sense,
calling to Egypt, going to Assyria.
12 As they go, I will spread over them my net;
I will bring them down like birds of
the air;
I will chastise them for their
wicked deeds.
13 Woe to them, for they have strayed
from me!
Destruction to them, for they have
rebelled against me!
I would redeem them,
but they speak lies against me.

14 They do not cry to me from the heart,
but they wail upon their beds;
for grain and wine they gash themselves,
they rebel against me.
15 Although I trained and strengthened
their arms,
yet they devise evil against me.
16 They turn to Ba′al;
they are like a treacherous bow,
their princes shall fall by the sword
because of the insolence of
their tongue.
This shall be their derision in the land
of Egypt.

8 Set the trumpet to your lips,
for a vulture is over the house
of the LORD,
because they have broken my covenant,
and transgressed my law.
2 To me they cry,
My God, we Israel know you.
3 Israel has spurned the good;
the enemy shall pursue him.

4 They made kings, but not through me.
They set up princes, but without my
knowledge.
With their silver and gold they
made idols
for their own destruction.
5 I have spurned your calf, O Samar′ia.
My anger burns against them.
How long will it be
till they are pure 6 in Israel?

A workman made it;
it is not God.
The calf of Samar′ia
shall be broken to pieces.

7 For they sow the wind,
and they shall reap the whirlwind.
The standing grain has no heads,
it shall yield no meal;
if it were to yield,
aliens would devour it.
8 Israel is swallowed up;
already they are among the nations
as a useless vessel.
9 For they have gone up to Assyria,
a wild donkey wandering alone;
E′phraim has hired lovers.
10 Though they hire allies among the
nations,
I will soon gather them up.
And they shall cease for a little while
from anointing king and princes.

[11]Because E′phraim has multiplied altars
for sinning,
they have become to him altars
for sinning.
[12]Were I to write for him my laws
by ten thousands,
they would be regarded as a
strange thing.
[13]They love sacrifice;
they sacrifice flesh and eat it;
but the LORD has no delight in them.
Now he will remember their iniquity,
and punish their sins;
they shall return to Egypt.
[14]For Israel has forgotten his Maker,
and built palaces;
and Judah has multiplied fortified cities;
but I will send a fire upon his cities,
and it shall devour his strongholds.

9 Rejoice not, O Israel!
Exult not like the peoples;
for you have played the harlot, forsaking
your God.
You have loved a harlot's hire
upon all threshing floors.
[2]Threshing floor and winevat shall
not feed them,
and the new wine shall fail them.
[3]They shall not remain in the land of the LORD;
but E′phraim shall return to Egypt,
and they shall eat unclean food in Assyria.
[4]They shall not pour libations of wine
to the LORD;
and they shall not please him with
their sacrifices.
Their bread shall be like mourners' bread;
all who eat of it shall be defiled;
for their bread shall be for their hunger only;
it shall not come to the house of the LORD.

[5]What will you do on the day of
appointed festival,
and on the day of the feast of the LORD?
[6]For behold, they are going to Assyria;
Egypt shall gather them,
Memphis shall bury them.
Nettles shall possess their precious things
of silver;
thorns shall be in their tents.
[7]The days of punishment have come,
the days of recompense have come;
Israel shall know it.
The prophet is a fool,
the man of the spirit is mad,
because of your great iniquity
and great hatred.
[8]The prophet is the watchman of E′phraim,
the people of my God,
yet a fowler's snare is on all his ways,
and hatred in the house of his God.
[9]They have deeply corrupted themselves
as in the days of Gib′e-ah:
he will remember their iniquity,
he will punish their sins.

[10]Like grapes in the wilderness,
I found Israel.
Like the first fruit on the fig tree,
in its first season,
I saw your fathers.
But they came to Ba′al-pe′or,
and consecrated themselves to Ba′al,
and became detestable like the thing
they loved.
[11]E′phraim's glory shall fly away like a bird—
no birth, no pregnancy, no conception!
[12]Even if they bring up children,
I will bereave them till none is left.
Woe to them
when I depart from them!
[13]E′phraim's sons, as I have seen, are destined
for a prey;
Ephraim must lead forth his sons
to slaughter.
[14]Give them, O LORD—
what will you give?
Give them a miscarrying womb
and dry breasts.

[15]Every evil of theirs is in Gilgal;
there I began to hate them.
Because of the wickedness of their deeds
I will drive them out of my house.
I will love them no more;
all their princes are rebels.

[16]E′phraim is stricken,
their root is dried up,
they shall bear no fruit.

Even though they bring forth,
I will slay their beloved children.
17My God will cast them off,
because they have not listened to him;
they shall be wanderers among the nations.

SIRACH 29

14A good man will be surety for his neighbor,
but a man who has lost his sense of shame
will fail him.
15Do not forget all the kindness of
your surety,
for he has given his life for you.
16A sinner will overthrow the prosperity
of his surety,
17 and one who does not feel grateful will
abandon his rescuer.
18Being surety has ruined many men who
were prosperous,
and has shaken them like a wave of
the sea;
it has driven men of power into exile,
and they have wandered among
foreign nations.
19The sinner who has fallen into suretyship
and pursues gain will fall into lawsuits.
20Assist your neighbor according to
your ability,
but take heed to yourself lest you fall.

21The essentials for life are water and bread
and clothing and a house to cover
one's nakedness.
22Better is the life of a poor man under
the shelter of his roof
than sumptuous food in another
man's house.
23Be content with little or much.
24It is a miserable life to go from house
to house,
and where you are a stranger you may
not open your mouth;
25you will play the host and provide drink
without being thanked,
and besides this you will hear bitter words:
26"Come here, stranger, prepare the table,
and if you have anything at hand, let me
have it to eat."
27"Give place, stranger, to an honored person;
my brother has come to stay with me; I
need my house."
28These things are hard to bear for a man
who has feeling:
scolding about lodging and the reproach
of the moneylender.

HEBREWS 13

**Let brotherly love continue. 2Do
not neglect to show hospitality to
strangers, for thereby some have entertained angels unawares. 3Remember those**
who are in prison, as though in prison with
them; and those who are ill-treated, since
you also are in the body. 4Let marriage
be held in honor among all, and let the
marriage bed be undefiled; for God will
judge the immoral and adulterous. 5Keep
your life free from love of money, and be
content with what you have; for he has
said, "I will never fail you nor forsake you."
6Hence we can confidently say,

"The Lord is my helper,
I will not be afraid;
what can man do to me?"

7Remember your leaders, those who
spoke to you the word of God; consider
the outcome of their life, and imitate their
faith. 8Jesus Christ is the same yesterday
and today and for ever. 9Do not be led
away by diverse and strange teachings; for
it is well that the heart be strengthened
by grace, not by foods, which have not
benefited their adherents. 10We have an
altar from which those who serve the tent
have no right to eat. 11For the bodies of
those animals whose blood is brought
into the sanctuary by the high priest as
a sacrifice for sin are burned outside the
camp. 12So Jesus also suffered outside
the gate in order to sanctify the people
through his own blood. 13Therefore let us
go forth to him outside the camp, bearing
abuse for him. 14For here we have no
lasting city, but we seek the city which is
to come.

REFLECTION

Marriage is the image *par excellence* used to describe the relationship between God and his people. God uses this nuptial imagery to describe his covenant relationship with Israel in the Old Testament (as seen in Hosea), and that imagery continues to be used in the New Testament to describe the relationship between Christ and his Church. As the Book of Hebrews comes to a close, the importance of marriage is stressed yet again: "Let marriage be held in honor among all, and let the marriage bed be undefiled; for God will judge the immoral and adulterous" (Heb 13:4). These are strong words and a chilling reminder for a world that no longer values marriage and family. We are warned just a few verses later, "Do not be led away by diverse and strange teachings" (v. 9). This is not a coincidence. Satan, the prince of this world, tries to convince us that Scripture is outdated and irrelevant. But we know that "Jesus Christ is the same yesterday and today and for ever" (v. 8). Therefore, have confidence in the divinely inspired Word of God. The fact that God is unchanging means that truth, likewise, is unchanging. Why do you think many in the world think that truth can change with cultural circumstances?

November 21

HOSEA 10

Israel is a luxuriant vine
that yields its fruit.
The more his fruit increased
the more altars he built;
as his country improved
he improved his pillars.
2Their heart is false;
now they must bear their guilt.
The LORD will break down their altars,
and destroy their pillars.
3For now they will say:
"We have no king,
for we fear not the LORD,
and a king, what could he do for us?"
4They utter mere words;
with empty oaths they make covenants;
so judgment springs up like poisonous weeds
in the furrows of the field.
5The inhabitants of Samar′ia tremble
for the calf of Beth-a′ven.
Its people shall mourn for it,
and its idolatrous priests shall wail over it,
over its glory which has departed from it.
6Yes, the thing itself shall be carried
to Assyria,
as tribute to the great king.
E′phraim shall be put to shame,
and Israel shall be ashamed of his idol.

7Samar′ia's king shall perish,
like a chip on the face of the waters.
8The high places of A′ven, the sin of Israel,
shall be destroyed.
Thorn and thistle shall grow up
on their altars;
and they shall say to the mountains, Cover us,
and to the hills, Fall upon us.

9From the days of Gib′e-ah, you have sinned,
O Israel;
there they have continued.
Shall not war overtake them in Gibe-ah?
10I will come against the wayward people to
chastise them;
and nations shall be gathered against them
when they are chastised for their double
iniquity.

11E′phraim was a trained heifer
that loved to thresh,
and I spared her fair neck;
but I will put Ephraim to the yoke,
Judah must plow,
Jacob must harrow for himself.
12Sow for yourselves righteousness,
reap the fruit of mercy;
break up your fallow ground,
for it is the time to seek the LORD,
that he may come and rain salvation
upon you.

[13]You have plowed iniquity,
you have reaped injustice,
you have eaten the fruit of lies.
Because you have trusted in your chariots
and in the multitude of your warriors,
[14]therefore the tumult of war shall arise
among your people,
and all your fortresses shall be destroyed,
as Shal′man destroyed Beth-ar′bel on the
day of battle;
mothers were dashed in pieces with
their children.
[15]Thus it shall be done to you, O house
of Israel,
because of your great wickedness.
In the storm the king of Israel
shall be utterly cut off.

11 When Israel was a child, I loved him,
and out of Egypt I called my son.
[2]The more I called them,
the more they went from me;
they kept sacrificing to the Ba′als,
and burning incense to idols.

[3]Yet it was I who taught E′phraim to walk,
I took them up in my arms;
but they did not know that I healed them.
[4]I led them with cords of compassion,
with the bands of love,
and I became to them as one
who raises an infant to his cheeks,
and I bent down to them and fed them.

[5]They shall return to the land of Egypt,
and Assyria shall be their king,
because they have refused to return to me.
[6]The sword shall rage against their cities,
consume the bars of their gates,
and devour them in their fortresses.
[7]My people are bent on turning away
from me;
so they are appointed to the yoke,
and none shall remove it.

[8]How can I give you up, O E′phraim!
How can I hand you over, O Israel!
How can I make you like Admah!
How can I treat you like Zeboi′im!
My heart recoils within me,
my compassion grows warm and tender.
[9]I will not execute my fierce anger,
I will not again destroy E′phraim;
for I am God and not man,
the Holy One in your midst,
and I will not come to destroy.

[10]They shall go after the Lord,
he will roar like a lion;
yes, he will roar,
and his sons shall come trembling
from the west;
[11]they shall come trembling like birds
from Egypt,
and like doves from the land of Assyria;
and I will return them to their homes,
says the Lord.
[12]E′phraim has encompassed me with lies,
and the house of Israel with deceit;
but Judah is still known by God,
and is faithful to the Holy One.

12 E′phraim herds the wind,
and pursues the east wind all day
long;
they multiply falsehood and violence;
they make a bargain with Assyria,
and oil is carried to Egypt.

[2]The LORD has an indictment against Judah,
and will punish Jacob according to
his ways,
and repay him according to his deeds.
[3]In the womb he took his brother by
the heel,
and in his manhood he strove with God.
[4]He strove with the angel and prevailed,
he wept and sought his favor.
He met God at Bethel,
and there God spoke with him—
[5]the LORD the God of hosts,
the LORD is his name:
[6]"So you, by the help of your God, return,
hold fast to love and justice,
and wait continually for your God."

[7]A trader, in whose hands are false balances,
he loves to oppress.
[8]E′phraim has said, "Ah, but I am rich,
I have gained wealth for myself";
but all his riches can never offset
the guilt he has incurred.

[9]I am the LORD your God
from the land of Egypt;
I will again make you dwell in tents,
as in the days of the appointed feast.

[10]I spoke to the prophets;
it was I who multiplied visions,
and through the prophets gave parables.
[11]If there is iniquity in Gilead
they shall surely come to nothing;
if in Gilgal they sacrifice bulls,
their altars also shall be like stone heaps
on the furrows of the field.
[12](Jacob fled to the land of Ar′am,
there Israel did service for a wife,
and for a wife he herded sheep.)
[13]By a prophet the LORD brought Israel up
from Egypt,
and by a prophet he was preserved.
[14]E′phraim has given bitter provocation;
so his LORD will leave his bloodguilt
upon him,
and will turn back upon him his
reproaches.

13 When E′phraim spoke, men trembled;
he was exalted in Israel;
but he incurred guilt through Ba′al and
died.
[2]And now they sin more and more,
and make for themselves molten images,
idols skilfully made of their silver,
all of them the work of craftsmen.
Sacrifice to these, they say.
Men kiss calves!
[3]Therefore they shall be like the morning mist
or like the dew that goes early away,
like the chaff that swirls from the
threshing floor
or like smoke from a window.

[4]I am the LORD your God
from the land of Egypt;
you know no God but me,
and besides me there is no savior.
[5]It was I who knew you in the wilderness,
in the land of drought;
[6]but when they had fed to the full,
they were filled, and their heart was
lifted up;
therefore they forgot me.
[7]So I will be to them like a lion,
like a leopard I will lurk beside the way.
[8]I will fall upon them like a bear robbed of
her cubs,
I will tear open their breast,
and there I will devour them like a lion,
as a wild beast would tear them.

[9]I will destroy you, O Israel;
who can help you?
[10]Where now is your king, to save you;
where are all your princes, to
defend you—
those of whom you said,
"Give me a king and princes"?
[11]I have given you kings in my anger,
and I have taken them away in my wrath.
[12]The iniquity of E′phraim is bound up,
his sin is kept in store.
[13]The pangs of childbirth come for him,
but he is an unwise son;
for now he does not present himself
at the mouth of the womb.

[14]Shall I ransom them from the power
of Sheol?
Shall I redeem them from Death?
O Death, where are your plagues?
O Sheol, where is your destruction?
Compassion is hidden from my eyes.

[15]Though he may flourish as the reed plant,
the east wind, the wind of the LORD,
shall come,
rising from the wilderness;
and his fountain shall dry up,
his spring shall be parched;
it shall strip his treasury
of every precious thing.
[16]Samar′ia shall bear her guilt,
because she has rebelled against her God;
they shall fall by the sword,
their little ones shall be dashed in pieces,
and their pregnant women ripped open.

14 Return, O Israel, to the LORD your
God,
for you have stumbled because of your
iniquity.
[2]Take with you words
and return to the LORD;

say to him,
"Take away all iniquity;
accept that which is good
and we will render
the fruit of our lips.
3 Assyria shall not save us,
we will not ride upon horses;
and we will say no more, 'Our God,'
to the work of our hands.
In you the orphan finds mercy."

4 I will heal their faithlessness;
I will love them freely,
for my anger has turned from them.
5 I will be as the dew to Israel;
he shall blossom as the lily,
he shall strike root as the poplar;
6 his shoots shall spread out;
his beauty shall be like the olive,
and his fragrance like Lebanon.
7 They shall return and dwell beneath
my shadow,
they shall flourish as a garden;
they shall blossom as the vine,
their fragrance shall be like the wine
of Lebanon.
8 O E´phraim, what have I to do
with idols?
It is I who answer and look after you.
I am like an evergreen cypress,
from me comes your fruit.

9 Whoever is wise, let him understand
these things;
whoever is discerning, let him
know them;
for the ways of the LORD are right,
and the upright walk in them,
but transgressors stumble in them.

SIRACH 30

He who loves his son will whip him often,
in order that he may rejoice at the way he
turns out.
2 He who disciplines his son will profit
by him,
and will boast of him among
acquaintances.
3 He who teaches his son will make his
enemies envious,
and will glory in him in the presence
of friends.
4 The father may die, and yet he is not dead,
for he has left behind him one like himself;
5 while alive he saw and rejoiced,
and when he died he was not grieved;
6 he has left behind him an avenger against
his enemies,
and one to repay the kindness of
his friends.

7 He who spoils his son will bind up
his wounds,
and his feelings will be troubled at
every cry.
8 A horse that is untamed turns out to
be stubborn,
and a son unrestrained turns out to
be wilful.
9 Pamper a child, and he will frighten you;
play with him, and he will give you grief.
10 Do not laugh with him, lest you have
sorrow with him,
and in the end you will gnash your teeth.
11 Give him no authority in his youth,
and do not ignore his errors.
12 Bow down his neck in his youth,
and beat his sides while he is young,
lest he become stubborn and disobey you,
and you have sorrow of soul from him.
13 Discipline your son and take pains
with him,
that you may not be offended by
his shamelessness.

14 Better off is a poor man who is well and
strong in constitution
than a rich man who is severely afflicted
in body.
15 Health and soundness are better than
all gold,
and a robust body than countless riches.
16 There is no wealth better than health
of body,
and there is no gladness above joy
of heart.
17 Death is better than a miserable life,
and eternal rest than chronic sickness.

[18]Good things poured out upon a mouth
that is closed
are like offerings of food placed upon a
grave.
[19]Of what use to an idol is an offering
of fruit?
For it can neither eat nor smell.
So is he who is afflicted by the Lord;
[20]he sees with his eyes and groans,
like a eunuch who embraces a maiden
and groans.

[21]Do not give yourself over to sorrow,
and do not afflict yourself deliberately.
[22]Gladness of heart is the life of man,
and the rejoicing of a man is length of days.
[23]Delight your soul and comfort your heart,
and remove sorrow far from you,
for sorrow has destroyed many,
and there is no profit in it.
[24]Jealousy and anger shorten life,
and anxiety brings on old age too soon.
[25]A man of cheerful and good heart
will give heed to the food he eats.

HEBREWS 13

**[15]Through him then let us con-
tinually offer up a sacrifice of
praise to God, that is, the fruit of lips that
acknowledge his name. [16]Do not neglect**
to do good and to share what you have, for
such sacrifices are pleasing to God.
[17]Obey your leaders and submit to them;
for they are keeping watch over your souls,
as men who will have to give account. Let
them do this joyfully, and not sadly, for that
would be of no advantage to you.
[18]Pray for us, for we are sure that we have
a clear conscience, desiring to act honorably
in all things. [19]I urge you the more earnestly
to do this in order that I may be restored to
you the sooner.
[20]Now may the God of peace who brought
again from the dead our Lord Jesus, the
great shepherd of the sheep, by the blood
of the eternal covenant, [21]equip you with
everything good that you may do his will,
working in you that which is pleasing in
his sight, through Jesus Christ; to whom be
glory for ever and ever. Amen.
[22]I appeal to you, brethren, bear with my
word of exhortation, for I have written to
you briefly. [23]You should understand that
our brother Timothy has been released,
with whom I shall see you if he comes
soon. [24]Greet all your leaders and all the
saints. Those who come from Italy send you
greetings. [25]Grace be with all of you. Amen.

REFLECTION

The benediction at the end of the Book of Hebrews (Heb 13:20–21) gives us some beautiful images of God which we can use for contemplation and prayer. The Lord is the God of peace, who desires us to enter into his rest. He wants us to have peace for our souls and health for our bodies (see Sir 30:16)—the peace of Christ that brings gladness of heart regardless of our current circumstances. Jesus is the great shepherd of his sheep. He refers to himself as the Good Shepherd (see Jn 10:11), who lays down his life for his sheep, binds up the crippled, heals the blind and the deaf, goes after the lost, and feeds his sheep with his own Body. Finally, it was Jesus's Blood that instituted the new and eternal covenant, and his sacrifice, his total gift of self that won for us the forgiveness of sins. All glory has been given to Jesus, the Son of Man who reigns as King over his eternal Kingdom. Blessed are we who belong to the Kingdom of God! Amen! What is your favorite image of Jesus to bring to prayer?

November 22

JOEL 1

The word of the LORD that came to Joel, the son of Pethu′el:

**[2]Hear this, you aged men,
give ear, all inhabitants of the land!**

Has such a thing happened in your days,
or in the days of your fathers?
3 Tell your children of it,
and let your children tell their children,
and their children another generation.

4 What the cutting locust left,
the swarming locust has eaten.
What the swarming locust left,
the hopping locust has eaten,
and what the hopping locust left,
the destroying locust has eaten.

5 Awake, you drunkards, and weep;
and wail, all you drinkers of wine,
because of the sweet wine,
for it is cut off from your mouth.
6 For a nation has come up against my land,
powerful and without number;
its teeth are lions' teeth,
and it has the fangs of a lioness.
7 It has laid waste my vines,
and splintered my fig trees;
it has stripped off their bark and thrown
it down;
their branches are made white.
8 Lament like a virgin clothed with sackcloth
for the bridegroom of her youth.
9 The cereal offering and the drink offering
are cut off
from the house of the LORD.
The priests mourn,
the ministers of the LORD.
10 The fields are laid waste,
the ground mourns;
because the grain is destroyed,
the wine fails,
the oil languishes.

11 Be confounded, O tillers of the soil,
wail, O vinedressers,
for the wheat and the barley;
because the harvest of the field has
perished.
12 The vine withers,
the fig tree languishes.
Pomegranate, palm, and apple,
all the trees of the field are withered;
and gladness fails
from the sons of men.

13 Put on sackcloth and lament, O priests,
wail, O ministers of the altar.
Go in, pass the night in sackcloth,
O ministers of my God!
Because cereal offering and drink offering
are withheld from the house of
your God.

14 Sanctify a fast,
call a solemn assembly.
Gather the elders
and all the inhabitants of the land
to the house of the LORD your God;
and cry to the LORD.

15 Alas for the day!
For the day of the LORD is near,
and as destruction from the Almighty
it comes.
16 Is not the food cut off
before our eyes,
joy and gladness
from the house of our God?

17 The seed shrivels under the clods,
the storehouses are desolate;
the granaries are ruined
because the grain has failed.
18 How the beasts groan!
The herds of cattle are perplexed
because there is no pasture for them;
even the flocks of sheep are dismayed.

19 Unto you, O LORD, I cry.
For fire has devoured
the pastures of the wilderness,
and flame has burned
all the trees of the field.
20 Even the wild beasts cry to you
because the water brooks are dried up,
and fire has devoured
the pastures of the wilderness.

2 Blow the trumpet in Zion;
sound the alarm on my holy
mountain!
Let all the inhabitants of the land tremble,
for the day of the LORD is coming,
it is near,
2 a day of darkness and gloom,
a day of clouds and thick darkness!

Like blackness there is spread upon
the mountains
a great and powerful people;
their like has never been from of old,
nor will be again after them
through the years of all generations.

3 Fire devours before them,
and behind them a flame burns.
The land is like the garden of Eden
before them,
but after them a desolate wilderness,
and nothing escapes them.

4 Their appearance is like the appearance
of horses,
and like war horses they run.
5 As with the rumbling of chariots,
they leap on the tops of the mountains,
like the crackling of a flame of fire
devouring the stubble,
like a powerful army
drawn up for battle.

6 Before them peoples are in anguish,
all faces grow pale.
7 Like warriors they charge,
like soldiers they scale the wall.
They march each on his way,
they do not swerve from their paths.
8 They do not jostle one another,
each marches in his path;
they burst through the weapons
and are not halted.
9 They leap upon the city,
they run upon the walls;
they climb up into the houses,
they enter through the windows like a thief.

10 The earth quakes before them,
the heavens tremble.
The sun and the moon are darkened,
and the stars withdraw their shining.
11 The LORD utters his voice
before his army,
for his host is exceedingly great;
he that executes his word is powerful.
For the day of the LORD is great and
very awesome;
who can endure it?

12 "Yet even now," says the LORD,
"return to me with all your heart,
with fasting, with weeping, and
with mourning;
13 and tear your hearts and not
your garments."
Return to the LORD, your God,
for he is gracious and merciful,
slow to anger, and abounding in mercy,
and repents of evil.
14 Who knows whether he will not turn
and repent,
and leave a blessing behind him,
a cereal offering and a drink offering
for the LORD, your God?

15 Blow the trumpet in Zion;
sanctify a fast;
call a solemn assembly;
16 gather the people.
Sanctify the congregation;
assemble the elders;
gather the children,
even nursing infants.
Let the bridegroom leave his room,
and the bride her chamber.

17 Between the vestibule and the altar
let the priests, the ministers of the,
LORD weep
and say, "Spare your people, O LORD,
and make not your heritage a reproach,
a byword among the nations.
Why should they say among the peoples,
'Where is their God?' "

18 Then the LORD became jealous for his land,
and had pity on his people.
19 The LORD answered and said to his people,
"Behold, I am sending to you
grain, wine, and oil,
and you will be satisfied;
and I will no more make you
a reproach among the nations.

20 "I will remove the northerner far from you,
and drive him into a parched and
desolate land,
his front into the eastern sea,
and his rear into the western sea;

the stench and foul smell of him will rise,
for he has done great things.

[21]"Fear not, O land;
be glad and rejoice,
for the LORD has done great things!
[22]Fear not, you beasts of the field,
for the pastures of the wilderness
are green;
the tree bears its fruit,
the fig tree and vine give their full yield.

[23]"Be glad, O sons of Zion,
and rejoice in the LORD, your God;
for he has given the early rain for
your vindication,
he has poured down for you abundant rain,
the early and the latter rain, as before.

[24]"The threshing floors shall be full of grain,
the vats shall overflow with wine and oil.
[25]I will restore to you the years
which the swarming locust has eaten,
the hopper, the destroyer, and the cutter,
my great army, which I sent among you.

[26]"You shall eat in plenty and be satisfied,
and praise the name of the LORD
your God,
who has dealt wondrously with you.
And my people shall never again be put
to shame.
[27]You shall know that I am in the midst
of Israel,
and that I, the LORD, am your God and
there is none else.
And my people shall never again be put
to shame.

[28]"And it shall come to pass afterward,
that I will pour out my spirit on all flesh;
your sons and your daughters
shall prophesy,
your old men shall dream dreams,
and your young men shall see visions.
[29]Even upon the menservants and
maidservants
in those days, I will pour out my spirit.

[30]"And I will give signs in the heavens and
on the earth, blood and fire and columns of
smoke. [31]The sun shall be turned to darkness,
and the moon to blood, before the great and
awesome day of the LORD comes. [32]And it
shall come to pass that all who call upon the
name of the LORD shall be delivered; for in
Mount Zion and in Jerusalem there shall be
those who escape, as the LORD has said, and
among the survivors shall be those whom
the LORD calls.

3 "For behold, in those days and at that
time, when I restore the fortunes of
Judah and Jerusalem, [2]I will gather all the
nations and bring them down to the valley of
Jehosh′aphat, and I will enter into judgment
with them there, on account of my people and
my heritage Israel, because they have scattered
them among the nations, and have divided up
my land, [3]and have cast lots for my people, and
have given a boy for a harlot, and have sold a
girl for wine, and have drunk it.

[4]"What are you to me, O Tyre and Si′don,
and all the regions of Philis′tia? Are you
paying me back for something? If you are
paying me back, I will repay your deed upon
your own head swiftly and speedily. [5]For you
have taken my silver and my gold, and have
carried my rich treasures into your temples.
[6]You have sold the people of Judah and
Jerusalem to the Greeks, removing them far
from their own border. [7]But now I will stir
them up from the place to which you have
sold them, and I will repay your deed upon
your own head. [8]I will sell your sons and your
daughters into the hand of the sons of Judah,
and they will sell them to the Sabe′ans, to a
nation far off; for the LORD has spoken."

[9]Proclaim this among the nations:
Prepare war,
stir up the mighty men.
Let all the men of war draw near,
let them come up.
[10]Beat your plowshares into swords,
and your pruning hooks into spears;
let the weak say, "I am a warrior."

[11]Hasten and come,
all you nations round about,
gather yourselves there.
Bring down your warriors, O LORD.

12Let the nations bestir themselves,
and come up to the valley of
Jehosh′aphat;
for there I will sit to judge
all the nations round about.

13Put in the sickle,
for the harvest is ripe.
Go in, tread,
for the wine press is full.
The vats overflow,
for their wickedness is great.

14Multitudes, multitudes,
in the valley of decision!
For the day of the LORD is near
in the valley of decision.
15The sun and the moon are darkened,
and the stars withdraw their shining.

16And the LORD roars from Zion,
and utters his voice from Jerusalem,
and the heavens and the earth shake.
But the LORD is a refuge to his people,
a stronghold to the people of Israel.

17"So you shall know that I am the LORD
your God,
who dwell in Zion, my holy mountain.
And Jerusalem shall be holy
and strangers shall never again pass
through it.

18"And in that day
the mountains shall drip sweet wine,
and the hills shall flow with milk,
and all the stream beds of Judah
shall flow with water;
and a fountain shall come forth from the
house of the LORD
and water the valley of Shittim.

19"Egypt shall become a desolation
and E′dom a desolate wilderness,
for the violence done to the people of
Judah,
because they have shed innocent blood
in their land.
20But Judah shall be inhabited for ever,
and Jerusalem to all generations.
21I will avenge their blood, and I will not
clear the guilty,
for the LORD dwells in Zion."

SIRACH 31

Wakefulness over wealth wastes away
one's flesh,
and anxiety about it removes sleep.
2Wakeful anxiety prevents slumber,
and a severe illness carries off sleep.
3The rich man toils as his wealth
accumulates,
and when he rests he fills himself with
his dainties.
4The poor man toils as his livelihood
diminishes,
and when he rests he becomes needy.

5He who loves gold will not be justified,
and he who pursues money will be led
astray by it.
6Many have come to ruin because of gold,
and their destruction has met them face
to face.
7It is a stumbling block to those who are
devoted to it,
and every fool will be taken captive by it.
8Blessed is the rich man who is found
blameless,
and who does not go after gold.
9Who is he? And we will call him blessed,
for he has done wonderful things among
his people.
10Who has been tested by it and been
found perfect?
Let it be for him a ground for boasting.
Who has had the power to transgress and
did not transgress,
and to do evil and did not do it?
11His prosperity will be established,
and the assembly will relate his acts
of charity.

12Are you seated at the table of a great man?
Do not be greedy at it,
and do not say, "There is certainly much
upon it!"

[13]Remember that a greedy eye is a bad thing.
What has been created more greedy than the eye?
Therefore it sheds tears from every face.
[14]Do not reach out your hand for everything you see,
and do not crowd your neighbor at the dish.
[15]Judge your neighbor's feelings by your own,
and in every matter be thoughtful.

JAMES 1

James, a servant of God and of the Lord Jesus Christ,

To the twelve tribes in the Dispersion: Greeting.

[2]Count it all joy, my brethren, when
you meet various trials, [3]for you know that the
testing of your faith produces steadfastness.
[4]And let steadfastness have its full effect, that
you may be perfect and complete, lacking in
nothing.

[5]If any of you lacks wisdom, let him ask God,
who gives to all men generously and without
reproaching, and it will be given him. [6]But let
him ask in faith, with no doubting, for he who
doubts is like a wave of the sea that is driven
and tossed by the wind. [7, 8]For that person
must not suppose that a double-minded man,
unstable in all his ways, will receive anything
from the Lord.

[9]Let the lowly brother boast in his exaltation,
[10]and the rich in his humiliation, because
like the flower of the grass he will pass away.
[11]For the sun rises with its scorching heat and
withers the grass; its flower falls, and its beauty
perishes. So will the rich man fade away in the
midst of his pursuits.

[12]Blessed is the man who endures trial, for
when he has stood the test he will receive
the crown of life which God has promised to
those who love him. [13]Let no one say when he
is tempted, "I am tempted by God"; for God
cannot be tempted with evil and he himself
tempts no one; [14]but each person is tempted
when he is lured and enticed by his own desire.
[15]Then desire when it has conceived gives birth
to sin; and sin when it is full-grown brings
forth death.

[16]Do not be deceived, my beloved brethren.
[17]Every good endowment and every perfect gift
is from above, coming down from the Father
of lights with whom there is no variation or
shadow due to change. [18]Of his own will he
brought us forth by the word of truth that we
should be a kind of first fruits of his creatures.

REFLECTION

While we may not like them at the time, tests and trials help us evaluate our progress and abilities. Whether it is an exam at school, tryouts for a part in a play or an application for a new position at work, such tests reveal our weaknesses and challenge us to up our game. The Letter of James opens by proclaiming that the testing of our faith produces not only steadfastness, but if we let the testing have its full effect, if we learn from it, if we ask God for what we lack and grow in the areas where our faith is weak, such testing moves us toward perfection, toward a more perfect imitation of Jesus Christ our Lord. James also corrects what appears to be a misunderstanding about temptations, making clear that God tempts no one. When we are tempted, we must call on God's grace so that we are like the one of whom Sirach speaks: "Who has had the power to transgress and did not transgress, and to do evil and did not do it" (Sir 31:10). If we are faithful to God's grace in temptation, testing, and trial, a crown of glory awaits us. How can you make better use of God's grace in times of testing?

November 23

AMOS 1

The words of Amos, who was among the shepherds of Teko´a, which he saw concerning Israel in the days of Uzzi´ah king of Judah and in

the days of Jerobo′am the son of Jo′ash, king
of Israel, two years before the earthquake.
2And he said:
"The LORD roars from Zion,
and utters his voice from Jerusalem;
the pastures of the shepherds mourn,
and the top of Carmel withers."

3Thus says the LORD:
"For three transgressions of Damascus,
and for four, I will not revoke
the punishment;
because they have threshed Gilead
with threshing sledges of iron.
4So I will send a fire upon the house
of Haz′ael,
and it shall devour the strongholds
of Benha′dad.
5I will break the bar of Damascus,
and cut off the inhabitants from
Valley of A′ven,
and him that holds the scepter
from Beth-e′den;
and the people of Syria shall go into
exile to Kir,"
says the LORD.

6Thus says the LORD:
"For three transgressions of Gaza,
and for four, I will not revoke
punishment;
because they carried into exile a
whole people
to deliver them up to E′dom.
7So I will send a fire upon the wall
of Gaza,
and it shall devour her strongholds.
8I will cut off the inhabitants
from Ash′dod,
and him that holds the scepter
from Ash′kelon;
I will turn my hand against Ek′ron;
and the remnant of the Philis′tines
shall perish,"
says the Lord GOD.

9Thus says the LORD:
"For three transgressions of Tyre,
and for four, I will not revoke
the punishment;
because they delivered up a whole people
to E′dom,
and did not remember the covenant
of brotherhood.
10So I will send a fire upon the wall of Tyre,
and it shall devour her strongholds."

11Thus says the LORD:
"For three transgressions of E′dom,
and for four, I will not revoke
the punishment;
because he pursued his brother with
the sword,
and cast off all pity,
and his anger tore perpetually,
and he kept his wrath for ever.
12So I will send a fire upon Te′man,
and it shall devour the strongholds
of Bozrah."

13Thus says the LORD:
"For three transgressions of
the Am′monites,
and for four, I will not revoke
the punishment;
because they have ripped up women with
child in Gilead,
that they might enlarge their border.
14So I will kindle a fire in the wall of Rabbah,
and it shall devour her strongholds,
with shouting in the day of battle,
with a tempest in the day of the whirlwind;
15and their king shall go into exile,
he and his princes together,"
says the LORD.

2 Thus says the LORD:
"For three transgressions of Moab,
and for four, I will not revoke
the punishment;
because he burned to lime
the bones of the king of E′dom.
2So I will send a fire upon Moab,
and it shall devour the strongholds
of Ker′ioth,
and Moab shall die amid uproar,
amid shouting and the sound of
the trumpet;
3I will cut off the ruler from its midst,
and will slay all its princes with him,"
says the LORD.

4Thus says the LORD:
"For three transgressions of Judah,
and for four, I will not revoke
the punishment;
because they have rejected the law
of the LORD,
and have not kept his statutes,
but their lies have led them astray,
after which their fathers walked.
5So I will send a fire upon Judah,
and it shall devour the strongholds
of Jerusalem."

6Thus says the LORD:
"For three transgressions of Israel,
and for four, I will not revoke
the punishment;
because they sell the righteous for silver,
and the needy for a pair of shoes—
7they that trample the head of the poor into
the dust of the earth,
and turn aside the way of the afflicted;
a man and his father go in to the
same maiden,
so that my holy name is profaned;
8they lay themselves down beside
every altar
upon garments taken in pledge;
and in the house of their God they drink
the wine of those who have been fined.

9"Yet I destroyed the Am′orite before them,
whose height was like the height of
the cedars,
and who was as strong as the oaks;
I destroyed his fruit above,
and his roots beneath.
10Also I brought you up out of the land
of Egypt,
and led you forty years in the wilderness,
to possess the land of the Am′orite.
11And I raised up some of your sons
for prophets,
and some of your young men for Naz′irites.
Is it not indeed so, O people of Israel?"
says the LORD.

12"But you made the Naz′irites drink wine,
and commanded the prophets,
saying, 'You shall not prophesy.'
13"Behold, I will press you down in
your place,
as a cart full of sheaves presses down.
14Flight shall perish from the swift,
and the strong shall not retain his strength,
nor shall the mighty save his life;
15he who handles the bow shall not stand,
and he who is swift of foot shall not
save himself,
nor shall he who rides the horse save
his life;
16and he who is stout of heart among
the mighty
shall flee away naked in that day,"
says the LORD.

3 Hear this word that the LORD has spoken
against you, O sons of Israel, against the
whole family which I brought up out of the
land of Egypt:
2"You only have I known
of all the families of the earth;
therefore I will punish you
for all your iniquities.

3"Do two walk together,
unless they have made
an appointment?
4Does a lion roar in the forest,
when he has no prey?
Does a young lion cry out from his den,
if he has taken nothing?
5Does a bird fall in a snare on the earth,
when there is no trap for it?
Does a snare spring up from the ground,
when it has taken nothing?
6Is a trumpet blown in a city,
and the people are not afraid?
Does evil befall a city,
unless the LORD has done it?
7Surely the Lord GOD does nothing,
without revealing his secret
to his servants the prophets.
8The lion has roared;
who will not fear?
The Lord GOD has spoken;
who can but prophesy?"

9Proclaim to the strongholds in Assyria,
and to the strongholds in the land
of Egypt,

and say, "Assemble yourselves upon the
mountains of Samar'ia,
and see the great tumults within her,
and the oppressions in her midst."
10"They do not know how to do right," says
the LORD,
"those who store up violence and robbery
in their strongholds."
11Therefore thus says the Lord GOD:
"An adversary shall surround the land,
and bring down your defenses
from you,
and your strongholds shall be plundered."
12Thus says the LORD: "As the shepherd
rescues from the mouth of the lion two legs,
or a piece of an ear, so shall the people of
Israel who dwell in Samar'ia be rescued, with
the corner of a couch and part of a bed."

13"Hear, and testify against the house
of Jacob,"
says the Lord GOD, the God of hosts,
14"that on the day I punish Israel for his
transgressions,
I will punish the altars of Bethel,
and the horns of the altar shall be cut off
and fall to the ground.
15I will strike the winter house with the
summer house;
and the houses of ivory shall perish,
and the great houses shall come to an end,"
says the LORD.

4 "Hear this word, you cows of Bashan,
who are in the mountain of Samar'ia,
who oppress the poor, who crush the needy,
who say to their husbands, 'Bring, that
we may drink!'
2The Lord GOD has sworn by his holiness
that, behold, the days are coming upon you,
when they shall take you away with hooks,
even the last of you with fishhooks.
3And you shall go out through the breaches,
every one straight before her;
and you shall be cast forth into Har'mon,"
says the LORD.

4"Come to Bethel, and transgress;
to Gilgal, and multiply transgression;
bring your sacrifices every morning,
your tithes every three days;
5offer a sacrifice of thanksgiving of that
which is leavened,
and proclaim freewill offerings,
publish them;
for so you love to do, O people of Israel!"
says the Lord GOD.

6"I gave you cleanness of teeth in all
your cities,
and lack of bread in all your places,
yet you did not return to me,"
says the LORD.

7"And I also withheld the rain from you
when there were yet three months to
the harvest;
I would send rain upon one city,
and send no rain upon another city;
one field would be rained upon,
and the field on which it did not
rain withered;
8so two or three cities wandered to one city
to drink water, and were not satisfied;
yet you did not return to me,"
says the LORD.

9"I struck you with blight and mildew;
I laid waste your gardens and your
vineyards;
your fig trees and your olive trees the
locust devoured;
yet you did not return to me,"
says the LORD.

10"I sent among you a pestilence after the
manner of Egypt;
I slew your young men with the sword;
I carried away your horses;
and I made the stench of your camp go
up into your nostrils;
yet you did not return to me,"
says the LORD.

11"I overthrew some of you,
as when God overthrew Sodom
and Gomor'rah,
and you were as a brand plucked out of
the burning;
yet you did not return to me,"
says the LORD.

[12]"Therefore thus I will do to you, O Israel;
because I will do this to you,
prepare to meet your God, O Israel!"

[13]For behold, he who forms the mountains,
and creates the wind,
and declares to man what is his thought;
who makes the morning darkness,
and treads on the heights of the earth—
the LORD, the God of hosts, is his name!

SIRACH 31

[16]Eat like a human being what is set
before you,
and do not chew greedily, lest you
be hated.
[17]Be the first to stop eating, for the sake of
good manners,
and do not be insatiable, lest you
give offense.
[18]If you are seated among many persons,
do not reach out your hand before
they do.

[19]How ample a little is for a well-disciplined
man!
He does not breathe heavily upon
his bed.
[20]Healthy sleep depends on
moderate eating;
he rises early, and feels fit.
The distress of sleeplessness
and of nausea
and colic are with the glutton.
[21]If you are overstuffed with food,
get up in the middle of the meal, and you
will have relief.
[22]Listen to me, my son, and do not
disregard me,
and in the end you will appreciate
my words.
In all your work be industrious,
and no sickness will overtake you.

[23]Men will praise the one who is liberal
with food,
and their testimony to his excellence
is trustworthy.
[24]The city will complain of the one who is
miserly with food,
and their testimony to his miserliness
is accurate.

[25]Do not aim to be valiant over wine,
for wine has destroyed many.
[26]Fire and water prove the temper of steel,
so wine tests hearts in the strife of
the proud.
[27]Wine is like life to men,
if you drink it in moderation.
What is life to a man who is
without wine?
It has been created to make men glad.
[28]Wine drunk in season and temperately
is rejoicing of heart and gladness of soul.
[29]Wine drunk to excess is bitterness of soul,
with provocation and stumbling.
[30]Drunkenness increases the anger of a fool
to his injury,
reducing his strength and
adding wounds.

[31]Do not reprove your neighbor at a banquet
of wine,
and do not despise him in his
merrymaking;
speak no word of reproach to him,
and do not afflict him by making
demands of him.

JAMES 1

**[19]Know this, my beloved breth-
ren. Let every man be quick to
hear, slow to speak, slow to anger, [20]for
the anger of man does not work the**
righteousness of God. [21]Therefore put away
all filthiness and rank growth of wickedness
and receive with meekness the implanted
word, which is able to save your souls.
[22]But be doers of the word, and not
hearers only, deceiving yourselves. [23]For
if any one is a hearer of the word and not
a doer, he is like a man who observes his
natural face in a mirror; [24]for he observes
himself and goes away and at once forgets

what he was like. [25]But he who looks into
the perfect law, the law of liberty, and
perseveres, being no hearer that forgets
but a doer that acts, he shall be blessed in
his doing.
[26]If any one thinks he is religious, and does
not bridle his tongue but deceives his heart,
this man's religion is vain. [27]Religion that
is pure and undefiled before God and the
Father is this: to visit orphans and widows
in their affliction, and to keep oneself
unstained from the world.
2 My brethren, show no partiality as you
hold the faith of our Lord Jesus Christ,
the Lord of glory. [2]For if a man with
gold rings and in fine clothing comes
into your assembly, and a poor man
in shabby clothing also comes in, [3]and
you pay attention to the one who wears
the fine clothing and say, "Have a seat
here, please," while you say to the poor
man, "Stand there," or, "Sit at my feet,"
[4]have you not made distinctions among
yourselves, and become judges with evil
thoughts? [5]Listen, my beloved brethren.
Has not God chosen those who are poor
in the world to be rich in faith and heirs
of the kingdom which he has promised
to those who love him? [6]But you have
dishonored the poor man. Is it not the
rich who oppress you, is it not they who
drag you into court? [7]Is it not they who
blaspheme that honorable name by which
you are called?
[8]If you really fulfil the royal law,
according to the Scripture, "You shall
love your neighbor as yourself," you do
well. [9]But if you show partiality, you
commit sin, and are convicted by the law
as transgressors. [10]For whoever keeps the
whole law but fails in one point has become
guilty of all of it. [11]For he who said, "Do
not commit adultery," said also, "Do not
kill." If you do not commit adultery but do
kill, you have become a transgressor of the
law. [12]So speak and so act as those who are
to be judged under the law of liberty. [13]For
judgment is without mercy to one who
has shown no mercy; yet mercy triumphs
over judgment.

REFLECTION

Reading and listening to God's Word are imperative if we want to follow Jesus Christ, but our encounter with the Word of God should not end there; it should move us to action. As James says, "Be doers of the word, and not hearers only, deceiving yourselves" (Jas 1:22). We would be deceiving ourselves to think that reading Scripture is a purely intellectual exercise. When we encounter Christ in his Word, he fills us with the desire to walk in his footsteps and share the good news of our redemption. While we may not be called to be missionaries in a foreign land, the people we encounter in our daily lives should be able to recognize us as Christians by our actions and attitudes. We are all called to live the joy of the Gospel, to care for widows and orphans, and to share the Good News of Jesus Christ in our particular spheres of influence. And probably the best advice James gives us is to be quick to hear and slow to speak (see v. 19). Like Jesus on the road to Emmaus, we should meet people where they are, but never leave them there. How can you be Christ to someone today?

November 24

AMOS 5

Hear this word which I take up over you in lamentation, O house of Israel:
[2]"Fallen, no more to rise,
is the virgin Israel;
forsaken on her land,
with none to raise her up."

[3]For thus says the Lord God:
"The city that went forth a thousand
shall have a hundred left,
and that which went forth a hundred
shall have ten left
to the house of Israel."

[4]For thus says the LORD to the house
of Israel:
"Seek me and live;
[5] but do not seek Bethel,
and do not enter into Gilgal
or cross over to Be′er-she′ba;
for Gilgal shall surely go into exile,
and Bethel shall come to nothing."

[6]Seek the LORD and live,
lest he break out like fire in the house
of Joseph,
and it devour, with none to quench it
for Bethel,
[7]O you who turn justice to wormwood,
and cast down righteousness to
the earth!

[8]He who made the Pleiades and Orion,
and turns deep darkness into
the morning,
and darkens the day into night,
who calls for the waters of the sea,
and pours them out upon the surface of
the earth,
the LORD is his name,
[9]who makes destruction flash forth against
the strong,
so that destruction comes upon
the fortress.

[10]They hate him who reproves in the gate,
and they abhor him who speaks
the truth.
[11]Therefore because you trample upon
the poor
and take from him exactions of wheat,
you have built houses of hewn stone,
but you shall not dwell in them;
you have planted pleasant vineyards,
but you shall not drink their wine.
[12]For I know how many are your
transgressions,
and how great are your sins—
you who afflict the righteous, who
take a bribe,
and turn aside the needy in the gate.
[13]Therefore he who is prudent will keep
silent in such a time;
for it is an evil time.

[14]Seek good, and not evil,
that you may live;
and so the LORD, the God of hosts, will be
with you,
as you have said.
[15]Hate evil, and love good,
and establish justice in the gate;
it may be that the LORD, the God of hosts,
will be gracious to the remnant of
Joseph.

[16]Therefore thus says the LORD, the God of
hosts, the Lord:
"In all the squares there shall be wailing;
and in all the streets they shall say,
'Alas! alas!'
They shall call the farmers to mourning
and to wailing those who are skilled in
lamentation,
[17]and in all vineyards there shall be wailing,
for I will pass through the midst of you,"
says the LORD.

[18]Woe to you who desire the day of
the LORD!
Why would you have the day of the LORD?
It is darkness, and not light;
[19] as if a man fled from a lion,
and a bear met him;
or went into the house and leaned with his
hand against the wall,
and a serpent bit him.
[20]Is not the day of the LORD darkness, and
not light,
and gloom with no brightness in it?

[21]"I hate, I despise your feasts,
and I take no delight in your
solemn assemblies.
[22]Even though you offer me your burnt
offerings and cereal offerings,
I will not accept them,
and the peace offerings of your fatted beasts
I will not look upon.
[23]Take away from me the noise of your songs;
to the melody of your harps I will
not listen.
[24]But let justice roll down like waters,
and righteousness like an ever-flowing
stream.

[25]"Did you bring to me sacrifices and
offerings the forty years in the wilderness, O
house of Israel? [26]You shall take up Sakkuth
your king, and Kai′wan your star-god, your
images, which you made for yourselves;
[27]therefore I will take you into exile beyond
Damascus," says the LORD, whose name is
the God of hosts.

6 "Woe to those who are at ease in Zion,
and to those who feel secure on the
mountain of Samar′ia,
the notable men of the first of the nations,
to whom the house of Israel come!
[2]Pass over to Cal′neh, and see;
and from there go to Ha′math the great;
then go down to Gath of the Philis′tines.
Are they better than these kingdoms?
Or is their territory greater than your
territory,
[3]O you who put far away the evil day,
and bring near the seat of violence?

[4]"Woe to those who lie upon beds of ivory,
and stretch themselves upon their
couches,
and eat lambs from the flock,
and calves from the midst of the stall;
[5]who sing idle songs to the sound of the harp,
and like David invent for themselves
instruments of music;
[6]who drink wine in bowls,
and anoint themselves with the finest oils,
but are not grieved over the ruin
of Joseph!
[7]Therefore they shall now be the first of
those to go into exile,
and the revelry of those who stretch
themselves shall pass away."

[8]The Lord GOD has sworn by himself
(says the LORD, the God of hosts):
"I abhor the pride of Jacob,
and hate his strongholds;
and I will deliver up the city and all that
is in it."

[9]And if ten men remain in one house, they
shall die. [10]And when a man's kinsman, he
who burns him, shall take him up to bring
the bones out of the house, and shall say to
him who is in the innermost parts of the
house, "Is there still any one with you?" he
shall say, "No"; and he shall say, "Hush! We
must not mention the name of the LORD."

[11]For behold, the LORD commands,
and the great house shall be struck
down into fragments,
and the little house into bits.
[12]Do horses run upon rocks?
Does one plow the sea with oxen?
But you have turned justice into poison
and the fruit of righteousness into
wormwood—
[13]you who rejoice in Lo-de′bar,
who say, "Have we not by our
own strength
taken Karna′im for ourselves?"
[14]"For behold, I will raise up against
you a nation,
O house of Israel," says the LORD,
the God of hosts;
"and they shall oppress you from the
entrance of Ha′math
to the Brook of the Ar′abah."

7 Thus the Lord GOD showed me: behold,
he was forming locusts in the beginning
of the shooting up of the latter growth; and
behold, it was the latter growth after the
king's mowings. [2]When they had finished
eating the grass of the land, I said,
"O Lord GOD, forgive, I beg you!
How can Jacob stand?
He is so small!"
[3]The LORD repented concerning this;
"It shall not be," said the LORD.

[4]Thus the Lord GOD showed me: behold,
the Lord GOD was calling for a judgment by
fire, and it devoured the great deep and was
eating up the land. [5]Then I said,
"O Lord GOD, cease, I beg you!
How can Jacob stand?
He is so small!"
[6]The LORD repented concerning this;
"This also shall not be," said the
Lord GOD.

[7]He showed me: behold, the Lord was
standing beside a wall built with a plumb
line, with a plumb line in his hand. [8]And the
LORD said to me, "Amos, what do you see?"

And I said, "A plumb line." Then the Lord
said,
"Behold, I am setting a plumb line
in the midst of my people Israel;
I will never again pass by them;
9 the high places of Isaac shall be
made desolate,
and the sanctuaries of Israel shall be
laid waste,
and I will rise against the house of
Jerobo′am with the sword."
10 Then Amazi′ah the priest of Bethel sent
to Jerobo′am king of Israel, saying, "Amos
has conspired against you in the midst of
the house of Israel; the land is not able to
bear all his words. 11 For thus Amos has said,
'Jerobo′am shall die by the sword,
and Israel must go into exile away from
his land.' "
12 And Amazi′ah said to Amos, "O seer,
go, flee away to the land of Judah, and eat
bread there, and prophesy there; 13 but never
again prophesy at Bethel, for it is the king's
sanctuary, and it is a temple of the kingdom."
14 Then Amos answered Amazi′ah, "I am
no prophet, nor a prophet's son; but I am a
herdsman, and a dresser of sycamore trees,
15 and the LORD took me from following
the flock, and the LORD said to me, 'Go,
prophesy to my people Israel.'
16 "Now therefore hear the word of the LORD.
You say, 'Do not prophesy against Israel,
and do not preach against the house
of Isaac.'
17 Therefore thus says the LORD:
'Your wife shall be a harlot in the city,
and your sons and your daughters shall
fall by the sword,
and your land shall be parceled out
by line;
you yourself shall die in an unclean land,
and Israel shall surely go into exile away
from its land.' "

SIRACH 32

If they make you master of the feast, do not
exalt yourself;
be among them as one of them;
take good care of them and then be seated;
2 when you have fulfilled your duties, take
your place,
that you may be merry on their account
and receive a wreath for your excellent
leadership.

3 Speak, you who are older, for it is fitting
that you should,
but with accurate knowledge, and do not
interrupt the music.
4 Where there is entertainment, do not pour
out talk;
do not display your cleverness out
of season.
5 A ruby seal in a setting of gold
is a concert of music at a banquet of wine.
6 A seal of emerald in a rich setting of gold
is the melody of music with good wine.

7 Speak, young man, if there is need of you,
but no more than twice, and only if asked.
8 Speak concisely, say much in few words;
be as one who knows and yet holds
his tongue.
9 Among the great do not act as their equal;
and when another is speaking, do
not babble.

10 Lightning speeds before the thunder,
and approval precedes a modest man.
11 Leave in good time and do not be the last;
go home quickly and do not linger.
12 Amuse yourself there, and do what you
have in mind,
but do not sin through proud speech.
13 And for these things bless him who
made you
and satisfies you with his good gifts.

14 He who fears the Lord will accept
his discipline,
and those who rise early to seek him will
find favor.
15 He who seeks the law will be filled with it,
but the hypocrite will stumble at it.
16 Those who fear the Lord will form
true judgments,
and like a light they will kindle
righteous deeds.

17A sinful man will shun reproof,
and will find a decision according to
his liking.

18A man of judgment will not overlook an idea,
and an insolent and proud man will not
cower in fear.
19Do nothing without deliberation;
and when you have acted, do not regret it.
20Do not go on a path full of hazards,
and do not stumble over stony ground.
21Do not be overconfident on a
smooth way,
22 and give good heed to your paths.
23Guard yourself in every act,
for this is the keeping of
the commandments.

24He who believes the law gives heed to the
commandments,
and he who trusts the Lord will not
suffer loss.

JAMES 2

14What does it profit, my brethren, if a man says he has faith but has not works? Can his faith save him? 15If a brother or sister is poorly clothed and in
lack of daily food, 16and one of you says to
them, "Go in peace, be warmed and filled,"
without giving them the things needed for the
body, what does it profit? 17So faith by itself, if it
has no works, is dead.
18But some one will say, "You have faith and
I have works." Show me your faith apart from
your works, and I by my works will show you
my faith. 19You believe that God is one; you do
well. Even the demons believe—and shudder.
20Do you want to be shown, you foolish fellow,
that faith apart from works is barren? 21Was not
Abraham our father justified by works, when
he offered his son Isaac upon the altar? 22You
see that faith was active along with his works,
and faith was completed by works, 23and the
Scripture was fulfilled which says, "Abraham
believed God, and it was reckoned to him as
righteousness"; and he was called the friend of
God. 24You see that a man is justified by works
and not by faith alone. 25And in the same way
was not also Ra'hab the harlot justified by
works when she received the messengers and
sent them out another way? 26For as the body
apart from the spirit is dead, so faith apart from
works is dead.

REFLECTION

The prophet Amos repeatedly tells us the importance of seeking the Lord in order to have life (Am 5:4, 6, 14). Sirach also tells us that "those who rise early to seek him will find favor" (Sir 32:14). The Letter of James directs us to an important way that we can seek and find the Lord. We are told that if we do not help our brother or sister in need, it profits us nothing because "faith by itself, if it has no works, is dead" (Jas 2:17). St. James is reiterating what Jesus said: "As you did it to one of the least of these my brethren, you did it to me" (Mt 25:40). Jesus expresses the importance of this issue by making the point again in the negative: "Truly, I say to you, as you did it not to one of the least of these, you did it not to me" (v. 45). Mother Teresa, St. Teresa of Calcutta, reminds us that we can find God in the distressing disguise of the poor, our neighbors and those in our own families. Every human life is precious because we are made in the image and likeness of God. When we perform these corporal works of mercy—feeding the hungry, sheltering the homeless, visiting the sick, giving alms to the poor, etc.—we are given an opportunity to find the God we seek and to love him. How do you illustrate your faith through the corporal works of mercy?

November 25

AMOS 8

Thus the Lord God showed me: behold, a basket of summer fruit. 2And he said, "Amos, what do you see?" And I said, "A basket of summer fruit." Then the LORD said to me,

"The end has come upon my people Israel;
I will never again pass by them.
3The songs of the temple shall become
wailings in that day,"
says the Lord GOD;
"the dead bodies shall be many;
in every place they shall be cast out
in silence."

4Hear this, you who trample upon the
needy,
and bring the poor of the land to an end,
5saying, "When will the new moon be over,
that we may sell grain?
And the sabbath,
that we may offer wheat for sale,
that we may make the ephah small and
the shekel great,
and deal deceitfully with false balances,
6that we may buy the poor for silver
and the needy for a pair of sandals,
and sell the refuse of the wheat?"

7The LORD has sworn by the pride of Jacob:
"Surely I will never forget any of
their deeds.
8Shall not the land tremble on
this account,
and every one mourn who dwells in it,
and all of it rise like the Nile,
and be tossed about and sink again, like
the Nile of Egypt?"

9"And on that day," says the Lord GOD,
"I will make the sun go down at noon,
and darken the earth in broad daylight.
10I will turn your feasts into mourning,
and all your songs into lamentation;
I will bring sackcloth upon all loins,
and baldness on every head;
I will make it like the mourning for an
only son,
and the end of it like a bitter day.

11"Behold, the days are coming," says the
Lord GOD,
"when I will send a famine on the land;
not a famine of bread, nor a thirst for
water,
but of hearing the words of the LORD.
12They shall wander from sea to sea,
and from north to east;
they shall run back and forth, to seek the
word of the LORD,
but they shall not find it.

13"In that day the fair virgins and the
young men
shall faint for thirst.
14Those who swear by Ash′imah of Samar′ia,
and say, 'As your god lives, O Dan,'
and, 'As the way of Be′er-she′ba lives,'
they shall fall, and never rise again."

9 I saw the LORD standing beside the altar,
and he said:
"Strike the capitals until the
thresholds shake,
and shatter them on the heads
of all the people;
and what are left of them I will slay
with the sword;
not one of them shall flee away,
not one of them shall escape.

2"Though they dig into Sheol,
from there shall my hand take them;
though they climb up to heaven,
from there I will bring them down.
3Though they hide themselves on the top
of Carmel,
from there I will search out and take them;
and though they hide from my sight at the
bottom of the sea,
there I will command the serpent, and it
shall bite them.
4And though they go into captivity before
their enemies,
there I will command the sword, and it
shall slay them;
and I will set my eyes upon them for evil
and not for good."
5The Lord, GOD of hosts,
he who touches the earth and it melts,
and all who dwell in it mourn,
and all of it rises like the Nile,
and sinks again, like the Nile of Egypt;
6who builds his upper chambers in
the heavens,
and founds his vault upon the earth;

who calls for the waters of the sea,
and pours them out upon the surface of the earth—
the LORD is his name.

7"Are you not like the Ethiopians to me,
O people of Israel?" says the LORD.
"Did I not bring up Israel from the land of Egypt,
and the Philis′tines from Caphtor and the Syrians from Kir?
8Behold, the eyes of the Lord GOD are upon the sinful kingdom,
and I will destroy it from the surface of the ground;
except that I will not utterly destroy the house of Jacob,"
says the LORD.

9"For behold, I will command,
and shake the house of Israel among all the nations
as one shakes with a sieve,
but no pebble shall fall upon the earth.
10All the sinners of my people shall die by the sword,
who say, 'Evil shall not overtake or meet us.'

11"In that day I will raise up
the booth of David that is fallen
and repair its breaches,
and raise up its ruins,
and rebuild it as in the days of old;
12that they may possess the remnant of E′dom
and all the nations who are called by my name,"
says the LORD who does this.
13"Behold, the days are coming," says the LORD,
"when the plowman shall overtake the reaper
and the treader of grapes him who sows the seed;
the mountains shall drip sweet wine,
and all the hills shall flow with it.
14I will restore the fortunes of my people Israel,
and they shall rebuild the ruined cities and inhabit them;
they shall plant vineyards and drink their wine,
and they shall make gardens and eat their fruit.
15I will plant them upon their land,
and they shall never again be plucked up
out of the land which I have given them,"
says the LORD your God.

OBADIAH

The vision of Obadi′ah.

Thus says the Lord GOD concerning E′dom:
We have heard tidings from the LORD,
and a messenger has been sent among the nations:
"Rise up! let us rise against her for battle!"
2Behold, I will make you small among the nations,
you shall be utterly despised.
3The pride of your heart has deceived you,
you who live in the clefts of the rock,
whose dwelling is high,
who say in your heart,
"Who will bring me down to the ground?"
4Though you soar aloft like the eagle,
though your nest is set among the stars,
from there I will bring you down,
says the LORD.

5If thieves came to you,
if plunderers by night—
how you have been destroyed!—
would they not steal only enough for themselves?
If grape gatherers came to you,
would they not leave gleanings?
6How Esau has been pillaged,
his treasures sought out!
7All your allies have deceived you,
they have driven you to the border;
your confederates have prevailed against you;
your trusted friends have set a trap under you—
there is no understanding of it.
8Will I not on that day, says the LORD,
destroy the wise men out of E′dom,
and understanding out of Mount Esau?

[9]And your mighty men shall be dismayed,
O Te′man,
so that every man from Mount Esau will
be cut off by slaughter.
[10]For the violence done to your brother Jacob,
shame shall cover you,
and you shall be cut off for ever.
[11]On the day that you stood aloof,
on the day that strangers carried
off his wealth,
and foreigners entered his gates
and cast lots for Jerusalem,
you were like one of them.
[12]But you should not have gloated over the
day of your brother
in the day of his misfortune;
you should not have rejoiced over the
people of Judah
in the day of their ruin;
you should not have boasted
in the day of distress.
[13]You should not have entered the gate
of my people
in the day of his calamity;
you should not have gloated over
his disaster
in the day of his calamity;
you should not have looted his goods
in the day of his calamity.
[14]You should not have stood at the parting
of the ways
to cut off his fugitives;
you should not have delivered up
his survivors
in the day of distress.
[15]For the day of the LORD is near upon all
the nations.
As you have done, it shall be done to you,
your deeds shall return on your
own head.
[16]For as you have drunk upon my
holy mountain,
all the nations round about shall drink;
they shall drink, and stagger,
and shall be as though they had not been.
[17]But in Mount Zion there shall be those
that escape,
and it shall be holy;
and the house of Jacob shall possess their
own possessions.
[18]The house of Jacob shall be a fire,
and the house of Joseph a flame,
and the house of Esau stubble;
they shall burn them and consume them,
and there shall be no survivor to the
house of Esau;
for the LORD has spoken.
[19]Those of the Neg′eb shall possess
Mount Esau,
and those of the Shephe′lah the land of
the Philis′tines;
they shall possess the land of E′phraim and
the land of Samar′ia
and Benjamin shall possess Gilead.
[20]The exiles in Ha′lah who are of the people
of Israel
shall possess Phoeni′cia as far
as Zar′ephath;
and the exiles of Jerusalem who
are in Sephar′ad
shall possess the cities of the Neg′eb.
[21]Saviors shall go up to Mount Zion
to rule Mount Esau;
and the kingdom shall be the LORD's.

SIRACH 33

No evil will befall the man who fears
the Lord,
but in trial he will deliver him again
and again.
[2]A wise man will not hate the law,
but he who is hypocritical about it is like
a boat in a storm.
[3]A man of understanding will trust in
the law;
for him the law is as dependable as an
inquiry by means of Urim.
[4]Prepare what to say, and thus you will
be heard;
bind together your instruction, and make
your answer.
[5]The heart of a fool is like a cart wheel,
and his thoughts like a turning axle.
[6]A stallion is like a mocking friend;
he neighs under every one who sits
on him.

[7]Why is any day better than another,
when all the daylight in the year is
from the sun?
[8]By the Lord's decision they were
distinguished,
and he appointed the different seasons
and feasts;
[9]some of them he exalted and hallowed,
and some of them he made
ordinary days.
[10]All men are from the ground,
and Adam was created of the dust.
[11]In the fulness of his knowledge the Lord
distinguished them
and appointed their different ways;
[12]some of them he blessed and exalted,
and some of them he made holy and
brought near to himself;
but some of them he cursed and
brought low,
and he turned them out of their place.
[13]As clay in the hand of the potter—
for all his ways are as he pleases—
so men are in the hand of him who
made them,
to give them as he decides.

JAMES 3

Let not many of you become teachers, my brethren, for you know that we who teach shall be judged with greater strictness. [2]For we all make
many mistakes, and if any one makes no
mistakes in what he says he is a perfect man,
able to bridle the whole body also. [3]If we
put bits into the mouths of horses that they
may obey us, we guide their whole bodies.
[4]Look at the ships also; though they are so
great and are driven by strong winds, they
are guided by a very small rudder wherever
the will of the pilot directs. [5]So the tongue
is a little member and boasts of great
things. How great a forest is set ablaze by
a small fire!
[6]And the tongue is a fire. The tongue is
an unrighteous world among our members,
staining the whole body, setting on fire the
cycle of nature, and set on fire by hell. [7]For
every kind of beast and bird, of reptile and
sea creature, can be tamed and has been
tamed by mankind, [8]but no human being
can tame the tongue—a restless evil, full of
deadly poison. [9]With it we bless the Lord
and Father, and with it we curse men, who
are made in the likeness of God. [10]From the
same mouth come blessing and cursing. My
brethren, this ought not to be so. [11]Does a
spring pour forth from the same opening
fresh water and brackish? [12]Can a fig tree,
my brethren, yield olives, or a grapevine
figs? No more can salt water yield fresh.
[13]Who is wise and understanding among
you? By his good life let him show his works
in the meekness of wisdom. [14]But if you
have bitter jealousy and selfish ambition in
your hearts, do not boast and be false to the
truth. [15]This wisdom is not such as comes
down from above, but is earthly, unspiritual,
devilish. [16]For where jealousy and selfish
ambition exist, there will be disorder and
every vile practice. [17]But the wisdom from
above is first pure, then peaceable, gentle,
open to reason, full of mercy and good
fruits, without uncertainty or insincerity.
[18]And the harvest of righteousness is sown
in peace by those who make peace.

4 What causes wars, and what causes
fightings among you? Is it not your
passions that are at war in your members?
[2]You desire and do not have; so you kill.
And you covet and cannot obtain; so
you fight and wage war. You do not have,
because you do not ask. [3]You ask and do not
receive, because you ask wrongly, to spend
it on your passions. [4]Unfaithful creatures!
Do you not know that friendship with
the world is enmity with God? Therefore
whoever wishes to be a friend of the world
makes himself an enemy of God. [5]Or do you
suppose it is in vain that the Scripture says,
"He yearns jealously over the spirit which
he has made to dwell in us"? [6]But he gives
more grace; therefore it says, "God opposes
the proud, but gives grace to the humble."
[7]Submit yourselves therefore to God. Resist
the devil and he will flee from you. [8]Draw
near to God and he will draw near to you.

Cleanse your hands, you sinners, and purify
your hearts, you men of double mind. [9]Be
wretched and mourn and weep. Let your
laughter be turned to mourning and your
joy to dejection. [10]Humble yourselves before
the Lord and he will exalt you.

REFLECTION

There are few things that do more damage than words. This is something that every human being can relate to, either as victim or culprit, but most likely both. The gift of speech is a double-edged sword, both a blessing and a curse. That is why St. James spends a fair amount of time describing the dangers of an untamed tongue. He states, in a very matter-of-fact manner, that "no human being can tame the tongue—a restless evil, full of deadly poison" (Jas 3:8). He points out the hypocrisy of blessing God with the same mouth that curses the people he made in his image and likeness. So what are we to do if there is no way to tame the tongue? Do we just give up and give in to this broken part of our human nature? Of course not. God is always calling us to rise above our brokenness, to seek him and his wisdom from above, which is pure, peaceable, gentle, and full of mercy (see v. 8). Practice can make perfect. If we are willing to humble ourselves when we fall, ask God for his grace, and strive anew, we can see progress even if it is slow. What words of kindness can you share with someone today to continue the work of taming your tongue?

November 26

JONAH 1

**Now the word of the LORD came
to Jonah the son of Amit′tai,
saying, [2]"Arise, go to Nin′eveh, that great
city, and cry against it; for their wickedness has come up before me." [3]But Jonah**
rose to flee to Tar′shish from the presence
of the LORD. He went down to Joppa and
found a ship going to Tarshish; so he paid
the fare, and went on board, to go with them
to Tarshish, away from the presence of the
LORD.

[4]But the LORD hurled a great wind upon
the sea, and there was a mighty tempest
on the sea, so that the ship threatened to
break up. [5]Then the mariners were afraid,
and each cried to his god; and they threw
the wares that were in the ship into the sea,
to lighten it for them. But Jonah had gone
down into the inner part of the ship and
had lain down, and was fast asleep. [6]So the
captain came and said to him, "What do you
mean, you sleeper? Arise, call upon your
god! Perhaps the god will give a thought to
us, that we do not perish."

[7]And they said to one another, "Come, let us
cast lots, that we may know on whose account
this evil has come upon us." So they cast lots,
and the lot fell upon Jonah. [8]Then they said
to him, "Tell us on whose account this evil
has come upon us. What is your occupation?
And from where do you come? What is your
country? And of what people are you?" [9]And
he said to them, "I am a Hebrew; and I fear
the LORD, the God of heaven, who made the
sea and the dry land." [10]Then the men were
exceedingly afraid, and said to him, "What is
this that you have done!" For the men knew
that he was fleeing from the presence of the
LORD, because he had told them.

[11]Then they said to him, "What shall
we do to you, that the sea may quiet down
for us?" For the sea grew more and more
tempestuous. [12]He said to them, "Take me up
and throw me into the sea; then the sea will
quiet down for you; for I know it is because
of me that this great tempest has come upon
you." [13]Nevertheless the men rowed hard
to bring the ship back to land, but they
could not, for the sea grew more and more
tempestuous against them. [14]Therefore they
cried to the LORD, "We beg you, O LORD, let
us not perish for this man's life, and lay not
on us innocent blood; for you, O LORD, have
done as it pleased you." [15]So they took up
Jonah and threw him into the sea; and the sea

ceased from its raging. 16Then the men feared
the LORD exceedingly, and they offered a
sacrifice to the LORD and made vows.
17And the LORD appointed a great fish
to swallow up Jonah; and Jonah was in
the belly of the fish three days and three
nights.

2 Then Jonah prayed to the LORD his God
from the belly of the fish, 2saying,

"I called to the LORD, out of my distress,
and he answered me;
out of the belly of Sheol I cried,
and you heard my voice.
3For you cast me into the deep,
into the heart of the seas,
and the flood was round about me;
all your waves and your billows
passed over me.
4Then I said, 'I am cast out
from your presence;
how shall I again look
upon your holy temple?'
5The waters closed in over me,
the deep was round about me;
weeds were wrapped about my head
6 at the roots of the mountains.
I went down to the land
whose bars closed upon me for ever;
yet you brought up my life from the Pit,
O LORD my God.
7When my soul fainted within me,
I remembered the LORD;
and my prayer came to you,
into your holy temple.
8Those who pay regard to vain idols
forsake their true loyalty.
9But I with the voice of thanksgiving
will sacrifice to you;
what I have vowed I will pay.
Deliverance belongs to the LORD!"

10And the LORD spoke to the fish, and it
vomited out Jonah upon the dry land.

3 Then the word of the LORD came to
Jonah the second time, saying, 2"Arise,
go to Nin′eveh, that great city, and proclaim
to it the message that I tell you." 3So Jonah
arose and went to Nin′eveh, according
to the word of the LORD. Now Nineveh
was an exceedingly great city, three days'
journey in breadth. 4Jonah began to go
into the city, going a day's journey. And he
cried, "Yet forty days, and Nin′eveh shall be
overthrown!" 5And the people of Nin′eveh
believed God; they proclaimed a fast, and
put on sackcloth, from the greatest of them
to the least of them.
6Then tidings reached the king of
Nin′eveh, and he arose from his throne,
removed his robe, and covered himself
with sackcloth, and sat in ashes. 7And he
made proclamation and published through
Nin′eveh, "By the decree of the king and
his nobles: Let neither man nor beast, herd
nor flock, taste anything; let them not feed,
or drink water, 8but let man and beast be
covered with sackcloth, and let them cry
mightily to God; yes, let every one turn from
his evil way and from the violence which is
in his hands. 9Who knows, God may yet
repent and turn from his fierce anger, so
that we perish not?"
10When God saw what they did, how they
turned from their evil way, God repented of
the evil which he had said he would do to
them; and he did not do it.

4 But it displeased Jonah exceedingly,
and he was angry. 2And he prayed to
the LORD and said, "I pray you, LORD, is
not this what I said when I was yet in my
country? That is why I made haste to flee to
Tar′shish; for I knew that you are a gracious
God and merciful, slow to anger, and
abounding in mercy, and that you repent of
evil. 3Therefore now, O LORD, take my life
from me, I beg you, for it is better for me to
die than to live." 4And the LORD said, "Do
you do well to be angry?" 5Then Jonah went
out of the city and sat to the east of the city,
and made a booth for himself there. He sat
under it in the shade, till he should see what
would become of the city.
6And the LORD God appointed a plant, and
made it come up over Jonah, that it might be
a shade over his head, to save him from his
discomfort. So Jonah was exceedingly glad
because of the plant. 7But when dawn came
up the next day, God appointed a worm which
attacked the plant, so that it withered. 8When
the sun rose, God appointed a sultry east wind,
and the sun beat upon the head of Jonah so

that he was faint; and he asked that he might
die, and said, "It is better for me to die than to
live." 9But God said to Jonah, "Do you do well
to be angry for the plant?" And he said, "I do
well to be angry, angry enough to die." 10And
the LORD said, "You pity the plant, for which
you did not labor, nor did you make it grow,
which came into being in a night, and perished
in a night. 11And should not I pity Nin′eveh,
that great city, in which there are more than a
hundred and twenty thousand persons who do
not know their right hand from their left, and
also much cattle?"

SIRACH 33

14Good is the opposite of evil,
and life the opposite of death;
so the sinner is the opposite of the godly.
15Look upon all the works of the Most High;
they likewise are in pairs, one the
opposite of the other.
16I was the last on watch;
I was like one who gleans after the
grape-gatherers;
by the blessing of the Lord I excelled,
and like a grape-gatherer I filled my
wine press.
17Consider that I have not labored for
myself alone,
but for all who seek instruction.
18Hear me, you who are great among
the people,
and you leaders of the congregation,
listen.

19To son or wife, to brother or friend,
do not give power over yourself, as long
as you live;
and do not give your property to another,
lest you change your mind and must ask
for it.
20While you are still alive and have breath
in you,
do not let any one take your place.
21For it is better that your children should
ask from you
than that you should look to the hand of
your sons.
22Excel in all that you do;
bring no stain upon your honor.
23At the time when you end the days of
your life,
in the hour of death, distribute
your inheritance.

24Fodder and a stick and burdens for a donkey;
bread and discipline and work for
a servant.
25Set your slave to work, and you will
find rest;
leave his hands idle, and he will
seek liberty.
26Yoke and thong will bow the neck,
and for a wicked servant there are racks
and tortures.
27Put him to work, that he may not be idle,
for idleness teaches much evil.
28Set him to work, as is fitting for him,
and if he does not obey, make his chains
heavy.
29Do not act immoderately toward anybody,
and do nothing without discretion.

30If you have a servant, let him be as yourself,
because you have bought him with blood.
31If you have a servant, treat him as a brother,
for as your own soul you will need him.
If you ill-treat him, and he leaves and
runs away,
which way will you go to seek him?

JAMES 4

**11Do not speak evil against one
another, brethren. He that speaks
evil against a brother or judges his brother,
speaks evil against the law and judges the**
law. But if you judge the law, you are not a
doer of the law but a judge. 12There is one
lawgiver and judge, he who is able to save
and to destroy. But who are you that you
judge your neighbor?
13Come now, you who say, "Today or
tomorrow we will go into such and such
a town and spend a year there and trade
and get gain"; 14whereas you do not know

about tomorrow. What is your life? For you are a mist that appears for a little time and then vanishes. 15Instead you ought to say, "If the Lord wills, we shall live and we shall do this or that." 16As it is, you boast in your arrogance. All such boasting is evil. 17Whoever knows what is right to do and fails to do it, for him it is sin.

5 Come now, you rich, weep and howl for the miseries that are coming upon you. 2Your riches have rotted and your garments are moth-eaten. 3Your gold and silver have rusted, and their rust will be evidence against you and will eat your flesh like fire. You have laid up treasure for the last days. 4Behold, the wages of the laborers who mowed your fields, which you kept back by fraud, cry out; and the cries of the harvesters have reached the ears of the Lord of hosts. 5You have lived on the earth in luxury and in pleasure; you have fattened your hearts in a day of slaughter. 6You have condemned, you have killed the righteous man; he does not resist you.

7Be patient, therefore, brethren, until the coming of the Lord. Behold, the farmer waits for the precious fruit of the earth, being patient over it until it receives the early and the late rain. 8You also be patient. Establish your hearts, for the coming of the Lord is at hand. 9Do not grumble, brethren, against one another, that you may not be judged; behold, the Judge is standing at the doors. 10As an example of suffering and patience, brethren, take the prophets who spoke in the name of the Lord. 11Behold, we call those happy who were steadfast. You have heard of the steadfastness of Job, and you have seen the purpose of the Lord, how the Lord is compassionate and merciful.

12But above all, my brethren, do not swear, either by heaven or by earth or with any other oath, but let your yes be yes and your no be no, that you may not fall under condemnation.

13Is any one among you suffering? Let him pray. Is any cheerful? Let him sing praise. 14Is any among you sick? Let him call for the elders of the Church, and let them pray over him, anointing him with oil in the name of the Lord; 15and the prayer of faith will save the sick man, and the Lord will raise him up; and if he has committed sins, he will be forgiven. 16Therefore confess your sins to one another, and pray for one another, that you may be healed. The prayer of a righteous man has great power in its effects. 17Eli′jah was a man of like nature with ourselves and he prayed fervently that it might not rain, and for three years and six months it did not rain on the earth. 18Then he prayed again and the heaven gave rain, and the earth brought forth its fruit.

19My brethren, if any one among you wanders from the truth and some one brings him back, 20let him know that whoever brings back a sinner from the error of his way will save his soul from death and will cover a multitude of sins.

REFLECTION

When God calls Jonah to preach to the people of Nineveh, Jonah runs away. Why? God was asking Jonah to go to a violent, pagan nation to speak against it for its wickedness—a message that would likely not be well received. But it wasn't just fear of the people's response that drove Jonah to flee. The Ninevites were the enemies of God's people and Jonah really didn't want the Ninevites to repent and be spared God's wrath. Jonah has more pity on a plant that offers him a few hours shade than on the 120,000 residents of Nineveh. God's call to love our enemies is hard. And when those enemies have hurt not just us but our loved ones, it gets even tougher. James reminds us that "the Lord is compassionate and merciful" (Jas 5:11). When we are tempted to run away from our enemies, we need to keep before us Jesus' prayer from the Cross for his enemies: "Father, forgive them; for they know not what they do" (Lk 23:34) and pray for Jesus to share his compassionate heart with us. Who are you keeping God's mercy from by not obeying, like Jonah, God's command to "go"?

November 27

MICAH 1

The word of the Lord that came to Mi′cah of Mo′resheth in the days of Jo′tham, A′haz, and Hezeki′ah, kings of Judah, which he saw concerning Samar′ia and Jerusalem.

2Hear, you peoples, all of you;
listen, O earth, and all that is in it;
and let the Lord God be a witness
against you,
the Lord from his holy temple.
3For behold, the LORD is coming forth out
of his place,
and will come down and tread upon the
high places of the earth.
4And the mountains will melt under him
and the valleys will be cleft,
like wax before the fire,
like waters poured down a steep place.
5All this is for the transgression of Jacob
and for the sins of the house of Israel.
What is the transgression of Jacob?
Is it not Samar′ia?
And what is the sin of the house of Judah?
Is it not Jerusalem?
6Therefore I will make Samar′ia a heap in
the open country,
a place for planting vineyards;
and I will pour down her stones into
the valley,
and uncover her foundations.
7All her images shall be beaten to pieces,
all her hires shall be burned with fire,
and all her idols I will lay waste;
for from the hire of a harlot she
gathered them,
and to the hire of a harlot they shall return.

8For this I will lament and wail;
I will go stripped and naked;
I will make lamentation like the jackals,
and mourning like the ostriches.
9For her wound is incurable;
and it has come to Judah,
it has reached to the gate of my people,
to Jerusalem.
10Tell it not in Gath,
weep not at all;
in Beth″-le-aph′rah
roll yourselves in the dust.
11Pass on your way,
inhabitants of Sha′phir,
in nakedness and shame;
the inhabitants of Za′anan
do not come forth;
the wailing of Beth-e′zel
shall take away from you its
standing place.
12For the inhabitants of Ma′roth
wait anxiously for good,
because evil has come down from the LORD
to the gate of Jerusalem.
13Harness the steeds to the chariots,
inhabitants of La′chish;
you were the beginning of sin
to the daughter of Zion,
for in you were found
the transgressions of Israel.
14Therefore you shall give parting gifts
to Mo′resheth-gath;
the houses of Ach′zib shall be a deceitful
thing
to the kings of Israel.
15I will again bring a conqueror upon you,
inhabitants of Mare′shah;
the glory of Israel
shall come to Adul′lam.
16Make yourselves bald and cut off your hair,
for the children of your delight;
make yourselves as bald as the eagle,
for they shall go from you into exile.

2 Woe to those who devise wickedness
and work evil upon their beds!
When the morning dawns, they perform it,
because it is in the power of their hand.
2They covet fields, and seize them;
and houses, and take them away;
they oppress a man and his house,
a man and his inheritance.
3Therefore thus says the LORD:
Behold, against this family I am
devising evil,
from which you cannot remove your necks;

and you shall not walk haughtily,
for it will be an evil time.
4In that day they shall take up a taunt song
against you,
and wail with bitter lamentation,
and say, "We are utterly ruined;
he changes the portion of my people;
how he removes it from me!
Among our captors he divides our fields."
5Therefore you will have none to cast the
line by lot
in the assembly of the LORD.

6"Do not preach"—thus they preach—
"one should not preach of such things;
disgrace will not overtake us."
7Should this be said, O house of Jacob?
Is the Spirit of the LORD impatient?
Are these his doings?
Do not my words do good
to him who walks uprightly?
8But you rise against my people as
an enemy;
you strip the robe from the peaceful,
from those who pass by trustingly
with no thought of war.
9The women of my people you drive out
from their pleasant houses;
from their young children you take away
my glory for ever.
10Arise and go,
for this is no place to rest;
because of uncleanness that destroys
with a grievous destruction.
11If a man should go about and utter wind
and lies,
saying, "I will preach to you of wine and
strong drink,"
he would be the preacher for this people!

12I will surely gather all of you, O Jacob,
I will gather the remnant of Israel;
I will set them together
like sheep in a fold,
like a flock in its pasture,
a noisy multitude of men.
13He who opens the breach will go up before
them;
they will break through and pass the gate,
going out by it.
Their king will pass on before them,
the LORD at their head.

3 And I said:
Hear, you heads of Jacob
and rulers of the house of Israel!
Is it not for you to know justice?—
2 you who hate the good and love the evil,
who tear the skin from off my people,
and their flesh from off their bones;
3who eat the flesh of my people,
and flay their skin from off them,
and break their bones in pieces,
and chop them up like meat in a kettle,
like flesh in a caldron.

4Then they will cry to the LORD,
but he will not answer them;
he will hide his face from them at
that time,
because they have made their deeds evil.

5Thus says the LORD concerning
the prophets
who lead my people astray,
who cry "Peace"
when they have something to eat,
but declare war against him
who puts nothing into their mouths.
6Therefore it shall be night to you, without
vision,
and darkness to you, without divination.
The sun shall go down upon the prophets,
and the day shall be black over them;
7the seers shall be disgraced,
and the diviners put to shame;
they shall all cover their lips,
for there is no answer from God.
8But as for me, I am filled with power,
with the Spirit of the LORD,
and with justice and might,
to declare to Jacob his transgression
and to Israel his sin.

9Hear this, you heads of the house
of Jacob
and rulers of the house of Israel,
who abhor justice
and pervert all equity,
10who build Zion with blood
and Jerusalem with wrong.

11 Its heads give judgment for a bribe,
its priests teach for hire,
its prophets divine for money;
yet they lean upon the LORD and say,
"Is not the LORD in the midst of us?
No evil shall come upon us."
12 Therefore because of you
Zion shall be plowed as a field;
Jerusalem shall become a heap of ruins,
and the mountain of the house a wooded height.

4 It shall come to pass in the latter days
that the mountain of the house of the LORD
shall be established as the highest of the mountains,
and shall be raised up above the hills;
and peoples shall flow to it,
2 and many nations shall come, and say:
"Come, let us go up to the mountain of the LORD,
to the house of the God of Jacob;
that he may teach us his ways
and we may walk in his paths."
For out of Zion shall go forth the law,
and the word of the LORD from Jerusalem.
3 He shall judge between many peoples,
and shall decide for strong nations afar off;
and they shall beat their swords into plowshares,
and their spears into pruning hooks;
nation shall not lift up sword against nation,
neither shall they learn war any more;
4 but they shall sit every man under his vine
and under his fig tree,
and none shall make them afraid;
for the mouth of the LORD of hosts has spoken.

5 For all the peoples walk
each in the name of its god,
but we will walk in the name of the LORD our God
for ever and ever.

6 In that day, says the LORD,
I will assemble the lame
and gather those who have been driven away,
and those whom I have afflicted;
7 and the lame I will make the remnant;
and those who were cast off, a strong nation;
and the LORD will reign over them in Mount Zion
from this time forth and for evermore.

8 And you, O tower of the flock,
hill of the daughter of Zion,
to you shall it come,
the former dominion shall come,
the kingdom of the daughter of Jerusalem.

9 Now why do you cry aloud?
Is there no king in you?
Has your counselor perished,
that pangs have seized you like a woman in labor?
10 Writhe and groan, O daughter of Zion,
like a woman with labor pains;
for now you shall go forth from the city
and dwell in the open country;
you shall go to Babylon.
There you shall be rescued,
there the LORD will redeem you
from the hand of your enemies.

11 Now many nations
are assembled against you,
saying, "Let her be profaned,
and let our eyes gaze upon Zion."
12 But they do not know
the thoughts of the LORD,
they do not understand his plan,
that he has gathered them as sheaves to the threshing floor.
13 Arise and thresh,
O daughter of Zion,
for I will make your horn iron
and your hoofs bronze;
you shall beat in pieces many peoples,
and shall devote their gain to the LORD,
their wealth to the Lord of the whole earth.

SIRACH 34

A man of no understanding has vain and false hopes,
and dreams give wings to fools.

2 As one who catches at a shadow and
pursues the wind,
so is he who gives heed to dreams.
3 The vision of dreams is this against that,
the likeness of a face confronting a face.
4 From an unclean thing what will be
made clean?
And from something false what will
be true?
5 Divinations and omens and dreams are folly,
and like a woman with labor pains the
mind has fancies.
6 Unless they are sent from the Most High
as a visitation,
do not give your mind to them.
7 For dreams have deceived many,
and those who put their hope in them
have failed.
8 Without such deceptions the law will
be fulfilled,
and wisdom is made perfect in truthful lips.

9 An educated man knows many things,
and one with much experience will speak
with understanding.
10 He that is inexperienced knows few things,
but he that has traveled acquires much
cleverness.
11 I have seen many things in my travels,
and I understand more than I can express.
12 I have often been in danger of death,
but have escaped because of these
experiences.

13 The spirit of those who fear the Lord
will live,
for their hope is in him who saves them.
14 He who fears the Lord will not be timid,
nor play the coward, for he is his hope.
15 Blessed is the soul of the man who fears
the Lord!
To whom does he look? And who is
his support?
16 The eyes of the Lord are upon those
who love him,
a mighty protection and strong support,
a shelter from the hot wind and a shade
from noonday sun,
a guard against stumbling and a defense
against falling.
17 He lifts up the soul and gives light to
the eyes;
he grants healing, life, and blessing.

18 If one sacrifices from what has been
wrongfully obtained, the offeringx
is blemished;
the gifts of the lawless are not acceptable.
19 The Most High is not pleased with the
offerings of the ungodly;
and he is not propitiated for sins by a
multitude of sacrifices.
20 Like one who kills a son before his
father's eyes
is the man who offers a sacrifice from the
property of the poor.
21 The bread of the needy is the life of
the poor;
whoever deprives them of it is a man
of blood.
22 To take away a neighbor's living is to
murder him;
to deprive an employee of his wages is to
shed blood.

23 When one builds and another tears down,
what do they gain but toil?
24 When one prays and another curses,
to whose voice will the Lord listen?
25 If a man washes after touching a dead
body, and touches it again,
what has he gained by his washing?
26 So if a man fasts for his sins,
and goes again and does the same things,
who will listen to his prayer?
And what has he gained by
humbling himself?

---

1 PETER 1

Peter, an apostle of Jesus Christ, To the exiles of the Dispersion in Pontus, Galatia, Cappado′cia, Asia, and Bithyn′ia, 2 chosen and destined by God the Father and sanctified by the Spirit for obedience to Jesus Christ and for sprinkling with his blood:

May grace and peace be multiplied to you.

3 Blessed be the God and Father of our
Lord Jesus Christ! By his great mercy we
have been born anew to a living hope
through the resurrection of Jesus Christ
from the dead, 4 and to an inheritance which
is imperishable, undefiled, and unfading,
kept in heaven for you, 5 who by God's power
are guarded through faith for a salvation
ready to be revealed in the last time. 6 In this
you rejoice, though now for a little while
you may have to suffer various trials, 7 so
that the genuineness of your faith, more
precious than gold which though perishable
is tested by fire, may redound to praise and
glory and honor at the revelation of Jesus
Christ. 8 Without having seen him you love
him; though you do not now see him you
believe in him and rejoice with unutterable
and exalted joy. 9 As the outcome of your
faith you obtain the salvation of your souls.
10 The prophets who prophesied of the
grace that was to be yours searched and inquired about this salvation; 11 they inquired
what person or time was indicated by the
Spirit of Christ within them when predicting
the sufferings of Christ and the subsequent
glory. 12 It was revealed to them that they were
serving not themselves but you, in the things
which have now been announced to you by
those who preached the good news to you
through the Holy Spirit sent from heaven,
things into which angels long to look.

REFLECTION

The prophets, like Micah, looked forward to, and spoke of, "the latter days" (Mi 4:1) when God's kingdom would be established, when nations and peoples would flow to the house of the Lord for instruction, and the lame and afflicted would be gathered together (see Mi 4). The fulfillment that the prophets looked for, St. Peter proclaims as accomplished through the sufferings of Christ and the Good News already being preached to the first Christians. Since the outpouring of the Holy Spirit at Pentecost, Peter himself had preached instruction to men and women of various nations, had personally witnessed the lame walk, and had seen the kingdom established in the hearts of thousands who he and the Apostles baptized. But Peter makes clear that there is more to come: an inheritance awaits us, an inheritance that is "imperishable, undefiled, and unfading, kept in heaven" (1 Pt 1:4). How is God establishing his kingdom in your heart?

November 28

MICAH 5

Now you are walled about with
a wall;
siege is laid against us;
with a rod they strike upon the cheek
the ruler of Israel.

2 But you, O Bethlehem Eph′rathah,
who are little to be among the clans
of Judah,
from you shall come forth for me
one who is to be ruler in Israel,
whose origin is from of old,
from ancient days.
3 Therefore he shall give them up until
the time
when she who has labor pains has
brought forth;
then the rest of his brethren shall return
to the sons of Israel.
4 And he shall stand and feed his flock in the
strength of the Lord,
in the majesty of the name of the Lord
his God.
And they shall dwell secure, for now he
shall be great
to the ends of the earth.

5 And this shall be peace,
when the Assyrian comes into our land
and treads upon our soil,
that we will raise against him seven shepherds
and eight princes of men;

[6]they shall rule the land of Assyria with
the sword,
and the land of Nimrod with the
drawn sword;
and they shall deliver us from the Assyrian
when he comes into our land
and treads within our border.

[7]Then the remnant of Jacob shall be
in the midst of many peoples
like dew from the LORD,
like showers upon the grass,
which do not depend upon men
nor wait for the sons of men.
[8]And the remnant of Jacob shall be among
the nations,
in the midst of many peoples,
like a lion among the beasts of the forest,
like a young lion among the flocks
of sheep,
which, when it goes through, treads down
and tears in pieces, and there is none
to deliver.
[9]Your hand shall be lifted up over your
adversaries,
and all your enemies shall be cut off.

[10]And in that day, says the LORD,
I will cut off your horses from
among you
and will destroy your chariots;
[11]and I will cut off the cities of your land
and throw down all your strongholds;
[12]and I will cut off sorceries from
your hand,
and you shall have no more soothsayers;
[13]and I will cut off your images
and your pillars from among you,
and you shall bow down no more
to the work of your hands;
[14]and I will root out your Ashe′rim from
among you
and destroy your cities.
[15]And in anger and wrath I will execute
vengeance
upon the nations that did not obey.

6 Hear what the LORD says:
Arise, plead your case before the
mountains,
and let the hills hear your voice.
[2]Hear, you mountains, the controversy of
the LORD,
and you enduring foundations of
the earth;
for the LORD has a controversy with
his people,
and he will contend with Israel.

[3]"O my people, what have I done to you?
In what have I wearied you? Answer me!
[4]For I brought you up from the land
of Egypt,
and redeemed you from the house
of bondage;
and I sent before you Moses,
Aaron, and Miriam.
[5]O my people, remember what Balak king of
Moab devised,
and what Balaam the son of Beor
answered him,
and what happened from Shittim to Gilgal,
that you may know the saving acts of
the LORD."

[6]"With what shall I come before the LORD,
and bow myself before God on high?
Shall I come before him with burnt
offerings,
with calves a year old?
[7]Will the LORD be pleased with thousands
of rams,
with ten thousands of rivers of oil?
Shall I give my first-born for my
transgression,
the fruit of my body for the sin of
my soul?"
[8]He has showed you, O man, what is good;
and what does the LORD require of you
but to do justice, and to love kindness,
and to walk humbly with your God?

[9]The voice of the LORD cries to the city—
and it is sound wisdom to fear
your name:
"Hear, O tribe and assembly of the city!
[10] Can I forget the treasures of wickedness
in the house of the wicked,
and the scant measure that is accursed?
[11]Shall I acquit the man with wicked scales
and with a bag of deceitful weights?

12 Your rich men are full of violence;
your inhabitants speak lies,
and their tongue is deceitful in
their mouth.
13 Therefore I have begun to strike you,
making you desolate because of
your sins.
14 You shall eat, but not be satisfied,
and there shall be hunger in your
inward parts;
you shall put away, but not save,
and what you save I will give to
the sword.
15 You shall sow, but not reap;
you shall tread olives, but not anoint
yourselves with oil;
you shall tread grapes, but not drink
wine.
16 For you have kept the statutes of Omri,
and all the works of the house of A'hab;
and you have walked in their counsels;
that I may make you a desolation, and your
inhabitants a hissing;
so you shall bear the scorn of the peoples."

7 Woe is me! For I have become
as when the summer fruit has
been gathered,
as when the vintage has been gleaned:
there is no cluster to eat,
no first-ripe fig which my soul desires.
2 The godly man has perished from
the earth,
and there is none upright among men;
they all lie in wait for blood,
and each hunts his brother with a net.
3 Their hands are upon what is evil, to
do it diligently;
the prince and the judge ask for a bribe,
and the great man utters the evil desire of
his soul;
thus they weave it together.
4 The best of them is like a brier,
the most upright of them a thorn hedge.
The day of their watchmen, of their
punishment, has come;
now their confusion is at hand.
5 Put no trust in a neighbor,
have no confidence in a friend;
guard the doors of your mouth
from her who lies in your bosom;
6 for the son treats the father with contempt,
the daughter rises up against her mother,
the daughter-in-law against her mother-
in-law;
a man's enemies are the men of his
own house.
7 But as for me, I will look to the LORD,
I will wait for the God of my salvation;
my God will hear me.

8 Rejoice not over me, O my enemy;
when I fall, I shall rise;
when I sit in darkness,
the LORD will be a light to me.
9 I will bear the indignation of the LORD
because I have sinned against him,
until he pleads my cause
and executes judgment for me.
He will bring me forth to the light;
I shall behold his deliverance.
10 Then my enemy will see,
and shame will cover her who said
to me,
"Where is the LORD your God?"
My eyes will gloat over her;
now she will be trodden down
like the mire of the streets.

11 A day for the building of your walls!
In that day the boundary shall be
far extended.
12 In that day they will come to you,
from Assyria to Egypt,
and from Egypt to the River,
from sea to sea and from mountain
to mountain.
13 But the earth will be desolate
because of its inhabitants,
for the fruit of their doings.

14 Shepherd your people with your staff,
the flock of your inheritance,
who dwell alone in a forest
in the midst of a garden land;
let them feed in Bashan and Gilead
as in the days of old.

15 As in the days when you came out of the
land of Egypt
I will show them marvelous things.

16 The nations shall see and be ashamed
of all their might;
they shall lay their hands on their
mouths;
their ears shall be deaf;
17 they shall lick the dust like a serpent,
like the crawling things of the earth;
they shall come trembling out of their
strongholds,
they shall turn in dread to the LORD
our God,
and they shall fear because of you.

18 Who is a God like you, pardoning
iniquity
and passing over transgression
for the remnant of his inheritance?
He does not retain his anger for ever
because he delights in mercy.
19 He will again have compassion
upon us,
he will tread our iniquities under foot.
You will cast all our sins
into the depths of the sea.
20 You will show faithfulness to Jacob
and mercy to Abraham,
as you have sworn to our fathers
from the days of old.

SIRACH 35

He who keeps the law makes many offerings;
he who heeds the commandments
sacrifices a peace offering.
2 He who returns a kindness offers fine flour,
and he who gives alms sacrifices a
thank offering.
3 To keep from wickedness is pleasing
to the Lord,
and to forsake unrighteousness
is atonement.
4 Do not appear before the Lord
empty-handed,
5 for all these things are to be done because
of the commandment.
6 The offering of a righteous man anoints
the altar,
and its pleasing odor rises before the
Most High.
7 The sacrifice of a righteous man
is acceptable,
and the memory of it will not
be forgotten.
8 Glorify the Lord generously,
and do not stint the first fruits of
your hands.
9 With every gift show a cheerful face,
and dedicate your tithe with gladness.
10 Give to the Most High as he has given,
and as generously as your hand has found.
11 For the Lord is the one who repays,
and he will repay you sevenfold.

12 Do not offer him a bribe, for he will not
accept it;
and do not trust to an unrighteous
sacrifice;
for the Lord is the judge,
and with him is no partiality.
13 He will not show partiality in the case of a
poor man;
and he will listen to the prayer of one
who is wronged.
14 He will not ignore the supplication of
the fatherless,
nor the widow when she pours out
her story.
15 Do not the tears of the widow run down
her cheek
as she cries out against him who has
caused them to fall?
16 He whose service is pleasing to the Lord
will be accepted,
and his prayer will reach to the clouds.
17 The prayer of the humble pierces
the clouds,
and he will not be consoled until it
reaches the Lord;
he will not desist until the Most High
visits him,
and the just judge executes judgment.
18 And the Lord will not delay,
neither will he be patient with them,
till he crushes the loins of the unmerciful
and repays vengeance on the nations;
till he takes away the multitude of
the insolent,
and breaks the scepters of
the unrighteous;

[19]till he repays man according to his deeds,
and the works of men according to
their devices;
till he judges the case of his people
and makes them rejoice in his mercy.
[20]Mercy is as welcome when he
afflicts them
as clouds of rain in the time of drought.

1 PETER 1

[13]Therefore gird up your minds, be sober, set your hopefully upon the grace that is coming to you at the revelation of Jesus Christ. [14]As obedient
children, do not be conformed to the
passions of your former ignorance, [15]but
as he who called you is holy, be holy
yourselves in all your conduct; [16]since it is
written, "You shall be holy, for I am holy."
[17]And if you invoke as Father him who
judges each one impartially according to
his deeds, conduct yourselves with fear
throughout the time of your exile. [18]You
know that you were ransomed from the
futile ways inherited from your fathers,
not with perishable things such as silver
or gold, [19]but with the precious blood
of Christ, like that of a lamb without
blemish or spot. [20]He was destined before
the foundation of the world but was made
manifest at the end of the times for your
sake. [21]Through him you have confidence
in God, who raised him from the dead
and gave him glory, so that your faith and
hope are in God.

[22]Having purified your souls by your
obedience to the truth for a sincere
love of the brethren, love one another
earnestly from the heart. [23]You have been
born anew, not of perishable seed but
of imperishable, through the living and
abiding word of God; [24]for

"All flesh is like grass
and all its glory like the flower of grass.
The grass withers, and the flower falls,
[25]but the word of the Lord abides for ever."

That word is the good news which was preached to you.

REFLECTION

"You know that you were ransomed . . . with the precious blood of Christ" (1 Pt 1:18–19). It's an incredible truth. The Son of God took on human flesh, suffered and died, pouring out his Blood for each of us, for our salvation—for your salvation. There is nothing we could do to repay such a debt. Nothing. But we rightly desire to express our gratitude. And so St. Peter shows us the way: "As obedient children, do not be conformed to the passions of your former ignorance, but as he who called you is holy, be holy yourselves in all your conduct" (vv. 14–15). All of our good works, the love we show our neighbor, and our praise and thanksgiving to God are but a response of thanksgiving for what God has first done for us. We must not be ungrateful; we should not "appear before the Lord empty-handed" (Sir 35:4). St. Ignatius of Loyola used to end each day by reviewing all the things he should be grateful to God for. Do you make it a habit to recall in gratitude what God has done for you each day?

November 29

NAHUM 1

An oracle concerning Nin′eveh. The book of the vision of Na′hum of El′kosh.

**[2]The LORD is a jealous God and
avenging,
the LORD is avenging and wrathful;**
the LORD takes vengeance on his adversaries
and keeps wrath for his enemies.
[3]The LORD is slow to anger and of great might,
and the LORD will by no means clear
the guilty.

His way is in whirlwind and storm,
and the clouds are the dust of his feet.
[4]He rebukes the sea and makes it dry,
he dries up all the rivers;

Bashan and Carmel wither,
the bloom of Lebanon fades.
5The mountains quake before him,
the hills melt;
the earth is laid waste before him,
the world and all that dwell therein.

6Who can stand before his indignation?
Who can endure the heat of his anger?
His wrath is poured out like fire,
and the rocks are broken asunder by him.
7The LORD is good,
a stronghold in the day of trouble;
he knows those who take refuge
in him.
8But with an overflowing flood
he will make a full end of his
adversaries,
and will pursue his enemies
into darkness.
9What do you plot against the LORD?
He will make a full end;
he will not take vengeance twice
on his foes.
10Like entangled thorns they are consumed,
like dry stubble.
11Did one not come out from you,
who plotted evil against the LORD,
and counseled villainy?

12Thus says the LORD,
"Though they be strong and many,
they will be cut off and pass away.
Though I have afflicted you,
I will afflict you no more.
13And now I will break his yoke
from off you
and will burst your bonds asunder."

14The LORD has given commandment
about you:
"No more shall your name
be perpetuated;
from the house of your gods I will cut off
the graven image and the molten image.
I will make your grave, for you are vile."

15Behold, on the mountains the feet of him
who brings good tidings,
who proclaims peace!
Keep your feasts, O Judah,
fulfil your vows,
for never again shall the wicked come
against you,
he is utterly cut off.

2 The shatterer has come up against you.
Man the ramparts;
watch the road;
gird your loins;
collect all your strength.
2(For the LORD is restoring the majesty
of Jacob
as the majesty of Israel,
for plunderers have stripped them
and ruined their branches.)

3The shield of his mighty men is red,
his soldiers are clothed in scarlet.
The chariots flash like flame
when mustered in array;
the chargers prance.
4The chariots rage in the streets,
they rush back and forth through
the squares;
they gleam like torches,
they dart like lightning.
5The officers are summoned,
they stumble as they go,
they hasten to the wall,
the mantelet is set up.
6The river gates are opened,
the palace is in dismay;
7its mistress is stripped, she is
carried off,
her maidens lamenting,
moaning like doves,
and beating their breasts.
8Nin′eveh is like a pool
whose waters run away.
"Halt! Halt!" they cry;
but none turns back.
9Plunder the silver,
plunder the gold!
There is no end of treasure,
or wealth of every precious thing.
10Desolate! Desolation and ruin!
Hearts faint and knees tremble,
anguish is on all loins,
all faces grow pale!

11 Where is the lions' den,
the cave of the young lions,
where the lion brought his prey,
where his cubs were, with none
to disturb?
12 The lion tore enough for his whelps
and strangled prey for his lionesses;
he filled his caves with prey
and his dens with torn flesh.
13 Behold, I am against you, says the LORD
of hosts, and I will burn your chariots in
smoke, and the sword shall devour your
young lions; I will cut off your prey from
the earth, and the voice of your messengers
shall no more be heard.

3 Woe to the bloody city,
all full of lies and booty—
no end to the plunder!
2 The crack of whip, and rumble of wheel,
galloping horse and bounding chariot!
3 Horsemen charging,
flashing sword and glittering spear,
hosts of slain,
heaps of corpses,
dead bodies without end—
they stumble over the bodies!
4 And all for the countless harlotries
of the harlot,
graceful and of deadly charms,
who betrays nations with her harlotries,
and peoples with her charms.

5 Behold, I am against you,
says the LORD of hosts,
and will lift up your skirts over your face;
and I will let nations look on your nakedness
and kingdoms on your shame.
6 I will throw filth at you
and treat you with contempt,
and make you an object of scorn.
7 And all who look on you will shrink from
you and say,
Wasted is Nin′eveh; who will moan over her?
from where shall I seek comforters for her?

8 Are you better than Thebes
that sat by the Nile,
with water around her,
her rampart a sea,
and water her wall?
9 Ethiopia was her strength,
Egypt too, and that without limit;
Put and the Libyans were her helpers.

10 Yet she was carried away,
she went into captivity;
her little ones were dashed in pieces
at the head of every street;
for her honored men lots were cast,
and all her great men were bound
in chains.
11 You also will be drunken,
you will be dazed;
you will seek
a refuge from the enemy.
12 All your fortresses are like fig trees
with first-ripe figs—
if shaken they fall
into the mouth of the eater.
13 Behold, your troops
are women in your midst.
The gates of your land
are wide open to your foes;
fire has devoured your bars.
14 Draw water for the siege,
strengthen your forts;
go into the clay,
tread the mortar,
take hold of the brick mold!
15 There will the fire devour you,
the sword will cut you off.
It will devour you like the locust.

Multiply yourselves like the locust,
multiply like the grasshopper!
16 You increased your merchants
more than the stars of the heavens.
The locust spreads its wings and flies away.
17 Your princes are like grasshoppers,
your scribes like clouds of locusts
settling on the fences
in a day of cold—
when the sun rises, they fly away;
no one knows where they are.

18 Your shepherds are asleep,
O king of Assyria;
your nobles slumber.
Your people are scattered on the mountains
with none to gather them.

[19]There is no assuaging your hurt,
your wound is grievous.
All who hear the news of you
clap their hands over you.
For upon whom has not come
your unceasing evil?

SIRACH 36

Have mercy upon us, O Lord, the God of all,
and look upon us,
and show us the light of your mercy;
[2] send fear of you upon the nations.
[3]Lift up your hand against foreign nations
and let them see your might.
[4]As in us you have been sanctified
before them,
so in them may you be magnified
before us;
[5]and let them know you, as we have known
that there is no God but you, O Lord.
[6]Show signs anew, and work further wonders;
make your hand and your right
arm glorious.
[7]Rouse your anger and pour out your wrath;
destroy the adversary and wipe out
the enemy.
[8]Hasten the day, and remember the
appointed time,
and let people recount your mighty deeds.
[9]Let him who survives be consumed in the
fiery wrath,
and may those who harm your people
meet destruction.
[10]Crush the heads of the rulers of the enemy,
who say, "There is no one
but ourselves."
[11]Gather all the tribes of Jacob,
and give them their inheritance, as at the
beginning.
[12]Have mercy, O Lord, upon the people
called by your name,
upon Israel, whom you have likened to a
first-born son.
[13]Have pity on the city of your sanctuary,
Jerusalem, the place of your rest.
[14]Fill Zion with the celebration of your
wondrous deeds,
and your temple with your glory.
[15]Bear witness to those whom you created in
the beginning,
and fulfil the prophecies spoken in
your name.
[16]Reward those who wait for you,
and let your prophets be found
trustworthy.
[17]Listen, O Lord, to the prayer of
your servants,
according to the blessing of Aaron for
your people,
and direct us in the way of righteousness,
and all who are on the earth will know
that you are the Lord, the God of the ages.

1 PETER 2

**So put away all malice and all
guile and insincerity and envy
and all slander. [2]Like newborn
infants, long for the pure spiritual
milk, that by it you may grow up to**
salvation; [3]for you have tasted the kindness
of the Lord.
[4]Come to him, to that living stone,
rejected by men but in God's sight chosen
and precious; [5]and like living stones be
yourselves built into a spiritual house, to
be a holy priesthood, to offer spiritual
sacrifices acceptable to God through Jesus
Christ. [6]For it stands in Scripture:
"Behold, I am laying in Zion a stone, a
cornerstone chosen and precious,
and he who believes in him will not be put
to shame."
[7]To you therefore who believe, he is precious,
but for those who do not believe,
"The very stone which the builders rejected
has become the cornerstone,"
[8]and
"A stone that will make men stumble,
a rock that will make them fall";
for they stumble because they disobey the
word, as they were destined to do.
[9]But you are a chosen race, a royal priesthood, a holy nation, God's own people, that you
may declare the wonderful deeds of him who
called you out of darkness into his marvelous

light. 10 Once you were no people but now you are God's people; once you had not received mercy but now you have received mercy.

11 Beloved, I beg you as aliens and exiles to abstain from the passions of the flesh that wage war against your soul. 12 Maintain good conduct among the Gentiles, so that in case they speak against you as wrongdoers, they may see your good deeds and glorify God on the day of visitation.

13 Be subject for the Lord's sake to every human institution, whether it be to the emperor as supreme, 14 or to governors as sent by him to punish those who do wrong and to praise those who do right. 15 For it is God's will that by doing right you should put to silence the ignorance of foolish men. 16 Live as free men, yet without using your freedom as a pretext for evil; but live as servants of God. 17 Honor all men. Love the brotherhood. Fear God. Honor the emperor.

18 Servants, be submissive to your masters with all respect, not only to the kind and gentle but also to the overbearing. 19 For one is approved if, mindful of God, he endures pain while suffering unjustly. 20 For what credit is it, if when you do wrong and are beaten for it you take it patiently? But if when you do right and suffer for it you take it patiently, you have God's approval. 21 For to this you have been called, because Christ also suffered for you, leaving you an example, that you should follow in his steps. 22 He committed no sin; no guile was found on his lips. 23 When he was reviled, he did not revile in return; when he suffered, he did not threaten; but he trusted to him who judges justly. 24 He himself bore our sins in his body on the tree, that we might die to sin and live to righteousness. By his wounds you have been healed. 25 For you were straying like sheep, but have now returned to the Shepherd and Guardian of your souls.

REFLECTION

It can be difficult to make sense of the injustices and suffering we see around us in the world. Why does one person suffer the death of a loved one, another a devastating illness, and yet another some terrible wrongdoing? These are questions that we will never fully understand this side of Heaven. One thing is certain: no one escapes this life without some suffering. Whether our suffering comes by our own hand, the hand of another, or an accidental circumstance, we are called to endure it with patience. There is never a situation that warrants retaliation or vengeance. Christ's suffering provides us with the supreme example. If ever there was an unjust act or undeserved suffering, it was the Passion and Crucifixion of the Son of God, who knew no sin. Yet Jesus never even cursed those who inflicted his pain, let alone sought revenge. He trusted fully in the justice of God and relied on the mercy of God, and he invites us to imitate his example. How can Jesus's example help you persevere in patience in your suffering?

November 30

HABAKKUK 1

The oracle of God which Habak′kuk the prophet saw.

2 O Lord, how long shall I cry for help,
and you will not hear?
Or cry to you "Violence!"
and you will not save?
3 Why do you make me see wrongs
and look upon trouble?
Destruction and violence are before me;
strife and contention arise.
4 So the law is slacked
and justice never goes forth.
For the wicked surround the righteous,
so justice goes forth perverted.
5 Look among the nations, and see;
wonder and be astounded.
For I am doing a work in your days
that you would not believe if told.

[6]For behold, I am rousing the Chalde′ans,
that bitter and hasty nation,
who march through the breadth of
the earth,
to seize habitations not their own.
[7]Dread and fearsome are they;
their justice and dignity proceed
from themselves.
[8]Their horses are swifter than leopards,
more fierce than the evening wolves;
their horsemen press proudly on.
Yes, their horsemen come from afar;
they fly like an eagle swift to devour.
[9]They all come for violence;
terror of them goes before them.
They gather captives like sand.
[10]At kings they scoff,
and of rulers they make sport.
They laugh at every fortress,
for they heap up earth and take it.
[11]Then they sweep by like the wind
and go on,
guilty men, whose own might is their god!
[12]Are you not from everlasting,
O LORD my God, my Holy One?
We shall not die.
O LORD, you have ordained them
as a judgment;
and you, O Rock, have established them
for chastisement.
[13]You who are of purer eyes than to
behold evil
and cannot look on wrong,
why do you look on faithless men,
and are silent when the wicked
swallows up
the man more righteous than he?
[14]For you make men like the fish of the sea,
like crawling things that have no ruler.
[15]He brings all of them up with a hook,
he drags them out with his net,
he gathers them in his seine;
so he rejoices and exults.
[16]Therefore he sacrifices to his net
and burns incense to his seine;
for by them he lives in luxury,
and his food is rich.
[17]Is he then to keep on emptying his net,
and mercilessly slaying nations for ever?

2 I will take my stand to watch,
and station myself on the tower,
and look forth to see what he will say to me,
and what I will answer concerning
my complaint.
[2]And the LORD answered me:
"Write the vision;
make it plain upon tablets,
so he may run who reads it.
[3]For still the vision awaits its time;
it hastens to the end—it will not lie.
If it seem slow, wait for it;
it will surely come, it will not delay.
[4]Behold, he whose soul is not upright in
him shall fail,
but the righteous shall live by his faith.
[5]Moreover, wine is treacherous;
the arrogant man shall not abide.
His greed is as wide as Sheol;
like death he has never enough.
He gathers for himself all nations,
and collects as his own all peoples."

[6]Shall not all these take up their taunt against him, in scoffing derision of him, and say,
"Woe to him who heaps up what is not
his own—
for how long?—
and loads himself with pledges!"
[7]Will not your debtors suddenly arise,
and those awake who will make you
tremble?
Then you will be booty for them.
[8]Because you have plundered many nations,
all the remnant of the peoples shall
plunder you,
for the blood of men and violence to the earth,
to cities and all who dwell therein.

[9]Woe to him who gets evil gain for
his house,
to set his nest on high,
to be safe from the reach of harm!
[10]You have devised shame to your house
by cutting off many peoples;
you have forfeited your life.
[11]For the stone will cry out from the wall,
and the beam from the
woodwork respond.

12Woe to him who builds a town with blood,
and founds a city on iniquity!
13Behold, is it not from the LORD of hosts
that peoples labor only for fire,
and nations weary themselves
for nothing?
14For the earth will be filled
with the knowledge of the glory
of the LORD,
as the waters cover the sea.

15Woe to him who makes his neighbors drink
of the cup of his wrath, and makes
them drunk,
to gaze on their shame!
16You will be sated with contempt instead
of glory.
Drink, yourself, and stagger!
The cup in the LORD's right hand
will come around to you,
and shame will come upon your glory!
17The violence done to Lebanon will
overwhelm you;
the destruction of the beasts will
terrify you,
for the blood of men and violence
to the earth,
to cities and all who dwell therein.

18What profit is an idol
when its maker has shaped it,
a metal image, a teacher of lies?
For the workman trusts in his own creation
when he makes dumb idols!
19Woe to him who says to a wooden thing,
Awake;
to a mute stone, Arise!
Can this give revelation?
Behold, it is overlaid with gold and silver,
and there is no breath at all in it.

20But the LORD is in his holy temple;
let all the earth keep silence before him.

3 A prayer of Habak´kuk the prophet,
according to Shigion´oth.
2O LORD, I have heard the report of you,
and your work, O LORD, I fear.
In the midst of the years renew it;
in the midst of the years make it known;
in wrath remember mercy.
3God came from Te´man,
and the Holy One from Mount Par´an.
His glory covered the heavens,
and the earth was full of his praise. *Selah*
4His brightness was like the light,
rays flashed from his hand;
and there he veiled his power.
5Before him went pestilence,
and plague followed close behind.
6He stood and measured the earth;
he looked and shook the nations;
Then the eternal mountains were scattered,
the everlasting hills sank low.
His ways were as of old.
7I saw the tents of Cush´an in affliction;
the curtains of the land of Mid´ian
trembled.
8Was your wrath against the rivers, O LORD?
Was your anger against the rivers,
or your indignation against the sea,
when you rode upon your horses,
upon your chariot of victory?
9You stripped the sheath from your bow,
and put the arrows to the string. *Selah*
You split the earth with rivers.
10The mountains saw you, and writhed;
the raging waters swept on;
the deep gave forth its voice,
it lifted its hands on high.
11The sun and moon stood still in
their habitation
at the light of your arrows as they sped,
at the flash of your glittering spear.
12You bestrode the earth in fury,
you trampled the nations in anger.
13You went forth for the salvation of
your people,
for the salvation of your anointed.
You crushed the head of the wicked,
laying him bare from thigh to neck. *Selah*
14You pierced with your shafts the head of
his warriors,
who came like a whirlwind to scatter me,
rejoicing as if to devour the poor in secret.
15You trampled the sea with your horses,
the surging of mighty waters.
16I hear, and my body trembles,
my lips quiver at the sound;
rottenness enters into my bones,
my steps totter beneath me.

I will quietly wait for the day of trouble
to come upon people who invade us.

17 Though the fig tree does not blossom,
nor fruit be on the vines,
the produce of the olive fail
and the fields yield no food,
the flock be cut off from the fold
and there be no herd in the stalls,
18 yet I will rejoice in the LORD,
I will joy in the God of my salvation.
19 GOD, the Lord, is my strength;
he makes my feet like deer's feet,
he makes me tread upon my
high places.

To the choirmaster: with stringed instruments.

SIRACH 36

18 The stomach will take any food,
yet one food is better than another.
19 As the palate tastes the kinds of game,
so an intelligent mind detects
false words.
20 A perverse mind will cause grief,
but a man of experience will pay
him back.
21 A woman will accept any man,
but one daughter is better than another.
22 A woman's beauty gladdens
the countenance,
and surpasses every human desire.
23 If kindness and humility mark
her speech,
her husband is not like other men.
24 He who acquires a wife gets his
best possession,
a helper fit for him and a pillar of support.
25 Where there is no fence, the property
will be plundered;
and where there is no wife, a man will
wander about and sigh.
26 For who will trust a nimble robber
that skips from city to city?
So who will trust a man that has
no home,
and lodges wherever night finds him?

1 PETER 3

**Likewise you wives, be submiss-
ive to your husbands, so that
some, though they do not obey the word,
may be won without a word by the be-**
havior of their wives, 2 when they see your
reverent and chaste behavior. 3 Let not yours
be the outward adorning with braiding of
hair, decoration of gold, and wearing of
robes, 4 but let it be the hidden person of the
heart with the imperishable jewel of a gentle
and quiet spirit, which in God's sight is very
precious. 5 So once the holy women who
hoped in God used to adorn themselves and
were submissive to their husbands, 6 as Sarah
obeyed Abraham, calling him lord. And you
are now her children if you do right and let
nothing terrify you.

7 Likewise you husbands, live considerately
with your wives, bestowing honor on the
woman as the weaker sex, since you are
joint heirs of the grace of life, in order that
your prayers may not be hindered.

8 Finally, all of you, have unity of spirit,
sympathy, love of the brethren, a tender
heart and a humble mind. 9 Do not return
evil for evil or reviling for reviling; but on
the contrary bless, for to this you have been
called, that you may obtain a blessing. 10 For
"He that would love life
and see good days,
let him keep his tongue from evil
and his lips from speaking guile;
11 let him turn away from evil and do right;
let him seek peace and pursue it.
12 For the eyes of the Lord are upon the
righteous,
and his ears are open to their prayer.
But the face of the Lord is against those
that do evil."

13 Now who is there to harm you if you are
zealous for what is right? 14 But even if you
do suffer for righteousness' sake, you will be
blessed. Have no fear of them, nor be troubled,
15 but in your hearts reverence Christ as Lord.
Always be prepared to make a defense to any
one who calls you to account for the hope
that is in you, yet do it with gentleness and
reverence; 16 and keep your conscience clear,

so that, when you are abused, those who
revile your good behavior in Christ may be
put to shame. [17]For it is better to suffer for
doing right, if that should be God's will,
than for doing wrong. [18]For Christ also died
for sins once for all, the righteous for the
unrighteous, that he might bring us to God,
being put to death in the flesh but made alive
in the spirit; [19]in which he went and preached
to the spirits in prison, [20]who formerly did
not obey, when God's patience waited in
the days of Noah, during the building of the
ark, in which a few, that is, eight persons,
were saved through water. [21]Baptism, which
corresponds to this, now saves you, not as
a removal of dirt from the body but as an
appeal to God for a clear conscience, through
the resurrection of Jesus Christ, [22]who has
gone into heaven and is at the right hand of
God, with angels, authorities, and powers
subject to him.

4 Since therefore Christ suffered in the
flesh, arm yourselves with the same
thought, for whoever has suffered in the
flesh has ceased from sin, [2]so as to live for
the rest of the time in the flesh no longer by
human passions but by the will of God. [3]Let
the time that is past suffice for doing what the
Gentiles like to do, living in licentiousness,
passions, drunkenness, revels, carousing,
and lawless idolatry. [4]They are surprised
that you do not now join them in the same
wild debauchery, and they abuse you; [5]but
they will give account to him who is ready
to judge the living and the dead. [6]For this
is why the gospel was preached even to the
dead, that though judged in the flesh like
men, they might live in the spirit like God.

[7]The end of all things is at hand; therefore
keep sane and sober for your prayers.
[8]Above all hold unfailing your love for one
another, since love covers a multitude of
sins. [9]Practice hospitality ungrudgingly to
one another. [10]As each has received a gift,
employ it for one another, as good stewards
of God's varied grace: [11]whoever speaks, as
one who utters oracles of God; whoever
renders service, as one who renders it by
the strength which God supplies; in order
that in everything God may be glorified
through Jesus Christ. To him belong glory
and dominion for ever and ever. Amen.

REFLECTION

St. Peter exhorts us, "Always be prepared to make a defense to any one who calls you to account for the hope that is in you"; adding, "yet do it with gentleness and reverence" (1 Pt 3:15). This exhortation demands two things of us. First, we must be formed in the Faith so that we can "make a defense." This means we should make a practice of ongoing study of the Scriptures and the Church's teachings. Second, we should be ready to share what we believe and why we believe it, recognizing that the truth we share must be matched with the charity by which we communicate it. Words are effective tools, but they become even more effective when communicated in charity and paired with deeds. Modeling the love of Christ in word and deed is a more powerful testament than simply providing an intellectual argument. Do you share the Good News of the Gospel in both word and deed?

December 1

ZEPHANIAH 1

The word of the LORD which came to Zephani′ah the son of Cu′shi, son of Gedali′ah, son of Amari′ah, son of Hezeki′ah, in the days of Josi′ah the son of A′mon, king of Judah.

2"I will utterly sweep away everything
from the face of the earth," says the LORD.
3"I will sweep away man and beast;
I will sweep away the birds of the air
and the fish of the sea.
I will overthrow the wicked;
I will cut off mankind
from the face of the earth," says the LORD.
4"I will stretch out my hand against Judah,
and against all the inhabitants of
Jerusalem;
and I will cut off from this place the
remnant of Ba′al
and the name of the idolatrous priests;
5those who bow down on the roofs
to the host of the heavens;
those who bow down and swear to the LORD
and yet swear by Milcom;
6those who have turned back from following
the LORD,
who do not seek the LORD or inquire
of him."

7Be silent before the Lord GOD!
For the day of the LORD is at hand;
the LORD has prepared a sacrifice
and consecrated his guests.
8And on the day of the LORD's sacrifice—
"I will punish the officials and the
king's sons
and all who clothe themselves in
foreign attire.
9On that day I will punish
every one who leaps over the threshold,
and those who fill their master's house
with violence and fraud."

10"On that day," says the LORD,
"a cry will be heard from the Fish Gate,
a wail from the Second Quarter,
a loud crash from the hills.
11Wail, O inhabitants of the Mortar!
For all the traders are no more;
all who weigh out silver are cut off.
12At that time I will search Jerusalem
with lamps,
and I will punish the men
who are thickening on their dregs,
those who say in their hearts,
'The LORD will not do good,
nor will he do ill.'
13Their goods shall be plundered,
and their houses laid waste.
Though they build houses,
they shall not inhabit them;
though they plant vineyards,
they shall not drink wine from them."

14The great day of the LORD is near,
near and hastening fast;
the sound of the day of the LORD is bitter,
the mighty man cries aloud there.
15A day of wrath is that day,
a day of distress and anguish,
a day of ruin and devastation,
a day of darkness and gloom,
a day of clouds and thick darkness,
16 a day of trumpet blast and battle cry
against the fortified cities
and against the lofty battlements.

17I will bring distress on men,
so that they shall walk like the blind,
because they have sinned against the
LORD;
their blood shall be poured out like dust,
and their flesh like dung.
18Neither their silver nor their gold
shall be able to deliver them
on the day of the wrath of the LORD.
In the fire of his jealous wrath,
all the earth shall be consumed;
for a full, yes, sudden end
he will make of all the inhabitants
of the earth.

2 Come together and hold assembly,
O shameless nation,

[2]before you are driven away
like the drifting chaff,
before there comes upon you
the fierce anger of the LORD,
before there comes upon you
the day of the wrath of the LORD.
[3]Seek the LORD, all you humble
of the land,
who do his commands;
seek righteousness, seek humility;
perhaps you may be hidden
on the day of the wrath of the LORD.
[4]For Gaza shall be deserted,
and Ash′kelon shall become a
desolation;
Ash′dod's people shall be driven out
at noon,
and Ek′ron shall be uprooted.
[5]Woe to you inhabitants of the seacoast,
you nation of the Cher′ethites!
The word of the LORD is against you,
O Canaan, land of the Philis′tines;
and I will destroy you till no inhabitant
is left.
[6]And you, O seacoast, shall be pastures,
meadows for shepherds
and folds for flocks.
[7]The seacoast shall become the possession
of the remnant of the house of Judah,
on which they shall pasture,
and in the houses of Ash′kelon
they shall lie down at evening.
For the LORD their God will be mindful
of them
and restore their fortunes.

[8]"I have heard the taunts of Moab
and the revilings of the Am′monites,
how they have taunted my people
and made boasts against their territory.
[9]Therefore, as I live," says the LORD of hosts,
the God of Israel,
"Moab shall become like Sodom,
and the Am′monites like Gomor′rah,
a land possessed by nettles and salt pits,
and a waste for ever.
The remnant of my people shall
plunder them,
and the survivors of my nation shall
possess them."
[10]This shall be their lot in return for
their pride,
because they scoffed and boasted
against the people of the LORD of hosts.
[11]The LORD will be terrifying against them;
yes, he will famish all the gods of
the earth,
and to him shall bow down,
each in its place,
all the lands of the nations.

[12]You also, O Ethiopians,
shall be slain by my sword.
[13]And he will stretch out his hand against
the north,
and destroy Assyria;
and he will make Nin′eveh a desolation,
a dry waste like the desert.
[14]Herds shall lie down in the midst of her,
all the beasts of the field;
the vulture and the hedgehog
shall lodge in her capitals;
the owl shall hoot in the window,
the raven croak on the threshold;
for her cedar work will be laid bare.
[15]This is the exultant city
that dwelt secure,
that said to herself,
"I am and there is none else."
What a desolation she has become,
a lair for wild beasts!
Every one who passes by her
hisses and shakes his fist.

3 Woe to her that is rebellious and defiled,
the oppressing city!
[2]She listens to no voice,
she accepts no correction.
She does not trust in the LORD,
she does not draw near to her God.

[3]Her officials within her
are roaring lions;
her judges are evening wolves
that leave nothing till the morning.
[4]Her prophets are wanton,
faithless men;
her priests profane what is sacred,
they do violence to the law.
[5]The LORD within her is righteous,
he does no wrong;

every morning he shows forth his justice,
each dawn he does not fail;
but the unjust knows no shame.

6"I have cut off nations;
their battlements are in ruins;
I have laid waste their streets
so that none walks in them;
their cities have been made desolate,
without a man, without an inhabitant.
7I said, 'Surely she will fear me,
she will accept correction;
she will not lose sight
of all that I have enjoined upon her.'
But all the more they were eager
to make all their deeds corrupt."

8"Therefore wait for me," says the LORD,
"for the day when I arise as a witness.
For my decision is to gather nations,
to assemble kingdoms,
to pour out upon them my indignation,
all the heat of my anger;
for in the fire of my jealous wrath
all the earth shall be consumed.
9"Yes, at that time I will change the speech
of the peoples
to a pure speech,
that all of them may call on the name of
the LORD
and serve him with one accord.
10From beyond the rivers of Ethiopia
my suppliants, the daughter of my
dispersed ones,
shall bring my offering.

11"On that day you shall not be put to shame
because of the deeds by which you have
rebelled against me;
for then I will remove from your midst
your proudly exultant ones,
and you shall no longer be haughty
in my holy mountain.
12For I will leave in the midst of you
a people humble and lowly.
They shall seek refuge in the name
of the LORD,
13 those who are left in Israel;
they shall do no wrong
and utter no lies,
nor shall there be found in their mouth
a deceitful tongue.
For they shall pasture and lie down,
and none shall make them afraid."

14Sing aloud, O daughter of Zion;
shout, O Israel!
Rejoice and exult with all your heart,
O daughter of Jerusalem!
15The LORD has taken away the judgments
against you,
he has cast out your enemies.
The King of Israel, the LORD, is in
your midst;
you shall fear evil no more.
16On that day it shall be said to Jerusalem:
"Do not fear, O Zion;
let not your hands grow weak.
17The LORD, your God, is in your midst,
a warrior who gives victory;
he will rejoice over you with gladness,
he will renew you in his love;
he will exult over you with loud singing
18as on a day of festival.
"I will remove disaster from you,
so that you will not bear reproach for it.
19Behold, at that time I will deal
with all your oppressors.
And I will save the lame
and gather the outcast,
and I will change their shame into praise
and renown in all the earth.
20At that time I will bring you home,
at the time when I gather you together;
yes, I will make you renowned
and praised
among all the peoples of the earth,
when I restore your fortunes
before your eyes," says the LORD.

SIRACH 37

Every friend will say, "I too am a friend";
but some friends are friends only in name.
2Is it not a grief to the death
when a companion and friend turns
to enmity?
3O evil imagination, why were you formed
to cover the land with deceit?

[4]Some companions rejoice in the happiness
of a friend,
but in time of trouble are against him.
[5]Some companions help a friend for their
stomachs' sake,
and in the face of battle take up the shield.
[6]Do not forget a friend in your heart,
and be not unmindful of him in
your wealth.

[7]Every counselor praises counsel,
but some give counsel in their own interest.
[8]Be wary of a counselor,
and learn first what is his interest—
for he will take thought for himself—
lest he cast the lot against you
[9] and tell you, "Your way is good,"
and then stand aloof to see what will
happen to you.
[10]Do not consult with one who looks at you
suspiciously;
hide your counsel from those who are
jealous of you.
[11]Do not consult with a woman about
her rival
or with a coward about war,
with a merchant about barter
or with a buyer about selling,
with a grudging man about gratitude
or with a merciless man about kindness,
with an idler about any work
or with a man hired for a year about
completing his work,
with a lazy servant about a big task—
pay no attention to these in any matter
of counsel.
[12]But stay constantly with a godly man
whom you know to be a keeper of the
commandments,
whose soul is in accord with your soul,
and who will sorrow with you if you fail.
[13]And establish the counsel of your own
heart,
for no one is more faithful to you than it is.
[14]For a man's soul sometimes keeps him
better informed
than seven watchmen sitting high on a
watchtower.
[15]And besides all this pray to the Most High
that he may direct your way in truth.

1 PETER 4

[12]Beloved, do not be surprised at the fiery ordeal which comes upon you to prove you, as though something strange were happening to you.
[13]But rejoice in so far as you share Christ's
sufferings, that you may also rejoice and
be glad when his glory is revealed. [14]If you
are reproached for the name of Christ,
you are blessed, because the spirit of glory
and of God rests upon you. [15]But let none
of you suffer as a murderer, or a thief, or
a wrongdoer, or a mischief-maker; [16]yet
if one suffers as a Christian, let him not
be ashamed, but under that name let him
glorify God. [17]For the time has come for
judgment to begin with the household of
God; and if it begins with us, what will be
the end of those who do not obey the gospel
of God? [18]And
"If the righteous man is scarcely saved,
where will the impious and sinner appear?"
[19]Therefore let those who suffer according
to God's will do right and entrust their souls
to a faithful Creator.

5 So I exhort the elders among you, as a
fellow elder and a witness of the
sufferings of Christ as well as a partaker
in the glory that is to be revealed. [2]Tend
the flock of God that is your charge,
not by constraint but willingly, not
for shameful gain but eagerly, [3]not as
domineering over those in your charge
but being examples to the flock. [4]And
when the chief Shepherd is manifested
you will obtain the unfading crown of
glory. [5]Likewise you that are younger be
subject to the elders. Clothe yourselves,
all of you, with humility toward one
another, for "God opposes the proud, but
gives grace to the humble."

[6]Humble yourselves therefore under the
mighty hand of God, that in due time he
may exalt you. [7]Cast all your anxieties on
him, for he cares about you. [8]Be sober, be
watchful. Your adversary the devil prowls
around like a roaring lion, seeking some
one to devour. [9]Resist him, firm in your
faith, knowing that the same experience of

suffering is required of your brotherhood
throughout the world. [10]And after you have
suffered a little while, the God of all grace,
who has called you to his eternal glory in
Christ, will himself restore, establish, and
strengthen you. [11]To him be the dominion
for ever and ever. Amen.
[12]By Silva′nus, a faithful brother as I regard
him, I have written briefly to you, exhorting
and declaring that this is the true grace of
God; stand fast in it. [13]She who is at Babylon,
who is likewise chosen, sends you greetings;
and so does my son Mark. [14]Greet one
another with the kiss of love.
Peace to all of you that are in Christ.

REFLECTION

When reading wisdom literature like Sirach, it can be difficult to find the narrative thread or the larger picture as each line moves to a different image or metaphor. However, careful reading often shows that there is an order and larger purpose to the proverbial sayings gathered together. Starting with the theme of friendship, Sirach warns that a counselor may have his own agenda, or, even worse, he may give advice with his best interests rather than yours in mind. Then comes a list of bad sources for counsel, such as seeking advice from a coward about war or a woman about her rival. Read closely and you will see a list of ten bad sources of counsel (see Sir 37:10–11), followed by three good sources of counsel (see vv. 12–15). The three worthy sources move in ascending order of trust: the godly, your own heart, and God. Out of the many voices, know well your true friend and loyal source of counsel. St. Peter warns about a "fiery ordeal" (1 Pt 4:12) from "Babylon," which is code for Rome, the capital of the empire soon to persecute the followers of Christ. The source of the ordeal is the devil, who prowls like a hungry lion looking to devour. Resistance is through "firm faith" that understands suffering is not a sign of God's absence, and that trust will be rewarded by the "unfading crown of glory" (5:4). Do you seek counsel from worthy or unworthy sources?

December 2

HAGGAI 1

**In the second year of Dari′us
the king, in the sixth month,
on the first day of the month,
the word of the LORD came by Hag′gai
the prophet to Zerub′babel the son of
She-al′ti-el, governor of Judah, and to**
Joshua the son of Jehoz′adak, the high
priest, [2]"Thus says the LORD of hosts:
This people say the time has not yet come
to rebuild the house of the LORD." [3]Then
the word of the LORD came by Hag′gai the
prophet, [4]"Is it a time for you yourselves
to dwell in your paneled houses, while
this house lies in ruins? [5]Now therefore
thus says the LORD of hosts: Consider
how you have fared. [6]You have sown
much, and harvested little; you eat, but
you never have enough; you drink, but
you never have your fill; you clothe
yourselves, but no one is warm; and he
who earns wages earns wages to put them
into a bag with holes.
[7]"Thus says the LORD of hosts: Consider
how you have fared. [8]Go up to the hills
and bring wood and build the house,
that I may take pleasure in it and that I
may appear in my glory, says the LORD.
[9]You have looked for much, and behold,
it came to little; and when you brought
it home, I blew it away. Why? says the
LORD of hosts. Because of my house that
lies in ruins, while you busy yourselves
each with his own house. [10]Therefore the
heavens above you have withheld the dew,
and the earth has withheld its produce.
[11]And I have called for a drought upon
the land and the hills, upon the grain, the
new wine, the oil, upon what the ground
brings forth, upon men and cattle, and
upon all their labors."
[12]Then Zerub′babel the son of She-al′ti-
el, and Joshua the son of Jehoz′adak, the
high priest, with all the remnant of the

people, obeyed the voice of the LORD
their God, and the words of Hag′gai the
prophet, as the LORD their God had sent
him; and the people feared before the
LORD. [13]Then Hag′gai, the messenger of
the LORD, spoke to the people with the
LORD's message, "I am with you, says
the LORD." [14]And the LORD stirred up
the spirit of Zerub′babel the son of She-
al′ti-el, governor of Judah, and the spirit
of Joshua the son of Jehoz′adak, the high
priest, and the spirit of all the remnant of
the people; and they came and worked on
the house of the LORD of hosts, their God,
[15]on the twenty-fourth day of the month,
in the sixth month.

2 In the second year of Dari′us the king,
[1]in the seventh month, on the twenty-
first day of the month, the word of the
LORD came by Hag′gai the prophet,
[2]"Speak now to Zerub′babel the son of
She-al′ti-el, governor of Judah, and to
Joshua the son of Jehoz′adak, the high
priest, and to all the remnant of the
people, and say, [3]'Who is left among you
that saw this house in its former glory?
How do you see it now? Is it not in your
sight as nothing? [4]Yet now take courage,
O Zerub′babel, says the LORD; take
courage, O Joshua, son of Jehoz′adak, the
high priest; take courage, all you people
of the land, says the LORD; work, for I
am with you, says the LORD of hosts,
[5]according to the promise that I made you
when you came out of Egypt. My Spirit
abides among you; fear not. [6]For thus
says the LORD of hosts: Once again, in a
little while, I will shake the heavens and
the earth and the sea and the dry land;
[7]and I will shake all nations, so that the
treasures of all nations shall come in, and
I will fill this house with splendor, says
the LORD of hosts. [8]The silver is mine,
and the gold is mine, says the LORD of
hosts. [9]The latter splendor of this house
shall be greater than the former, says the
LORD of hosts; and in this place I will give
prosperity, says the LORD of hosts.' "

[10]On the twenty-fourth day of the ninth
month, in the second year of Dari′us, the
word of the LORD came by Hag′gai the
prophet, [11]"Thus says the LORD of hosts:
Ask the priests to decide this question,
[12]'If one carries holy flesh in the skirt of his
garment, and touches with his skirt bread,
or pottage, or wine, or oil, or any kind of
food, does it become holy?' " The priests
answered, "No." [13]Then said Hag′gai, "If
one who is unclean by contact with a dead
body touches any of these, does it become
unclean?" The priests answered, "It does
become unclean." [14]Then Hag′gai said,
"So is it with this people, and with this
nation before me, says the LORD; and so
with every work of their hands; and what
they offer there is unclean. [15]Please now,
consider what will come to pass from this
day onward. Before a stone was placed
upon a stone in the temple of the LORD,
[16]how did you fare? When one came to
a heap of twenty measures, there were
but ten; when one came to the winevat
to draw fifty measures, there were but
twenty. [17]I struck you and all the products
of your toil with blight and mildew and
hail; yet you did not return to me, says the
LORD. [18]Consider from this day onward,
from the twenty-fourth day of the ninth
month. Since the day that the foundation
of the LORD's temple was laid, consider:
[19]Is the seed yet in the barn? Do the vine,
the fig tree, the pomegranate, and the
olive tree still yield nothing? From this
day on I will bless you."

[20]The word of the LORD came a second
time to Hag′gai on the twenty-fourth day
of the month, [21]"Speak to Zerub′babel,
governor of Judah, saying, I am about to
shake the heavens and the earth, [22]and
to overthrow the throne of kingdoms; I
am about to destroy the strength of the
kingdoms of the nations, and overthrow
the chariots and their riders; and the
horses and their riders shall go down,
every one by the sword of his fellow. [23]On
that day, says the LORD of hosts, I will take
you, O Zerub′babel my servant, the son of
She-al′ti-el, says the LORD, and make you
like a signet ring; for I have chosen you,
says the LORD of hosts."

SIRACH 37

16Reason is the beginning of every work,
and counsel precedes every undertaking.
17As a clue to changes of heart
18 four turns of fortune appear,
good and evil, life and death;
and it is the tongue that continually
rules them.
19A man may be shrewd and the teacher
of many,
and yet be unprofitable to himself.
20A man skilled in words may be hated;
he will be destitute of all food,
21for grace was not given him by the Lord,
since he is lacking in all wisdom.
22A man may be wise to his own advantage,
and the fruits of his understanding may
be trustworthy on his lips.
23A wise man will instruct his own people,
and the fruits of his understanding will
be trustworthy.
24A wise man will have praise heaped
upon him,
and all who see him will call him happy.
25The life of a man is numbered by days,
but the days of Israel are without number.
26He who is wise among his people will
inherit confidence,
and his name will live for ever.

27My son, test your soul while you live;
see what is bad for it and do not give
it that.
28For not everything is good for every one,
and not every person enjoys everything.
29Do not have an insatiable appetite for
any luxury,
and do not give yourself up to food;
30for overeating brings sickness,
and gluttony leads to nausea.
31Many have died of gluttony,
but he who is careful to avoid it prolongs
his life.

38 Honor the physician with the honor due him, according to your need of him,
for the Lord created him;
2for healing comes from the Most High,
and he will receive a gift from the king.
3The skill of the physician lifts up his head,
and in the presence of great men he
is admired.
4The Lord created medicines from the earth,
and a sensible man will not despise them.
5Was not water made sweet with a tree
in order that his power might be known?
6And he gave skill to men
that he might be glorified in his
marvelous works.
7By them he heals and takes away pain;
8 the pharmacist makes of them a
compound.
His works will never be finished;
and from him health is upon the face of
the earth.

2 PETER 1

Simon Peter, a servant and apostle of Jesus Christ,

To those who have obtained a faith of equal standing with ours in the righteousness of our God and Savior Jesus Christ:

2May grace and peace be multiplied to you
in the knowledge of God and of Jesus our
Lord.
3His divine power has granted to us all
things that pertain to life and godliness,
through the knowledge of him who called
us to his own glory and excellence, 4by
which he has granted to us his precious and
very great promises, that through these you
may escape from the corruption that is in
the world because of passion, and become
partakers of the divine nature. 5For this
very reason make every effort to supplement your faith with virtue, and virtue
with knowledge, 6and knowledge with self-
control, and self-control with steadfastness, and steadfastness with godliness, 7and
godliness with brotherly affection, and
brotherly affection with love. 8For if these
things are yours and abound, they keep
you from being ineffective or unfruitful in
the knowledge of our Lord Jesus Christ.
9For whoever lacks these things is blind
and shortsighted and has forgotten that he

was cleansed from his old sins. 10Therefore, brethren, be the more zealous to confirm your call and election, for if you do this you will never fall; 11so there will be richly provided for you an entrance into the eternal kingdom of our Lord and Savior Jesus Christ.

12Therefore I intend always to remind you of these things, though you know them and are established in the truth that you have. 13I think it right, as long as I am in this body, to arouse you by way of reminder, 14since I know that the putting off of my body will be soon, as our Lord Jesus Christ showed me. 15And I will see to it that after my departure you may be able at any time to recall these things.

16For we did not follow cleverly devised myths when we made known to you the power and coming of our Lord Jesus Christ, but we were eyewitnesses of his majesty. 17For when he received honor and glory from God the Father and the voice was borne to him by the Majestic Glory, "This is my beloved Son, with whom I am well pleased," 18we heard this voice borne from heaven, for we were with him on the holy mountain. 19And we have the prophetic word made more sure. You will do well to pay attention to this as to a lamp shining in a dark place, until the day dawns and the morning star rises in your hearts. 20First of all you must understand this, that no prophecy of Scripture is a matter of one's own interpretation, 21because no prophecy ever came by the impulse of man, but men moved by the Holy Spirit spoke from God.

REFLECTION

St. Peter begins his final letter, knowing his martyrdom is imminent, by relaying an urgent summons to holiness. He begins with a reminder of God's great promise, that through faith and grace we can become "partakers of the divine nature" (2 Pt 1:4). Extraordinary. Extravagant. And extraterrestrial glory. How to inherit such promise? Peter tells us "to make every effort to supplement [our] faith with virtue" (v. 5). It starts with faith, but our faith must move us to good works, the habit of which is called a virtue. The habit of telling the truth, honesty. The habit of employing wisdom in action, prudence. Such virtues will "keep you from being ineffective or unfruitful" (v. 8). Next we are to confirm our virtue with growth in knowledge of the Lord (see v. 5). So, the three steps toward partaking in God's divine nature are first, faith; second, habitual good works of virtue; and third, knowledge of God. Peter knows well that this is a good roadmap for participation in Christ, as he reminds us that he is an eyewitness to God's revelation of Jesus's divine nature on the Mount of Transfiguration (see v. 18). This promise is no mere myth devised by men, but a prophetic promise given by the Holy Spirit and Peter's personal testimony to us. Do you make a conscious effort to supplement your faith with the practice of virtue and to confirm your virtue with knowledge, so as to grow in holiness?

December 3

ZECHARIAH 1

In the eighth month, in the second year of Dari′us, the word of the LORD came to Zechari′ah the son of Berechi′ah, son of Iddo, the prophet, saying, 2"The LORD was very angry with your fathers. 3Therefore say to them, Thus says the LORD of hosts: Return to me, says the LORD of hosts, and I will return to you, says the LORD of hosts. 4Be not like your fathers, to whom the former prophets cried out, 'Thus says the LORD of hosts, Return from your evil ways and from your evil deeds.' But they did not hear or heed me, says the LORD. 5Your fathers, where are they? And the prophets, do they live for ever? 6But my words and my statutes, which I commanded my servants the prophets, did they not overtake your fathers? So they repented and said, As the LORD of hosts purposed to deal

with us for our ways and deeds, so has he
dealt with us."
7On the twenty-fourth day of the eleventh
month which is the month of Shebat', in the
second year of Dari'us, the word of the LORD
came to Zechari'ah the son of Berechi'ah,
son of Iddo, the prophet; and Zechariah
said, 8"I saw in the night, and behold, a man
riding upon a red horse! He was standing
among the myrtle trees in the glen; and
behind him were red, sorrel, and white
horses. 9Then I said, 'What are these, my
lord?' The angel who talked with me said to
me, 'I will show you what they are.' 10So the
man who was standing among the myrtle
trees answered, 'These are they whom the
LORD has sent to patrol the earth.' 11And
they answered the angel of the LORD who
was standing among the myrtle trees, 'We
have patrolled the earth, and behold, all the
earth remains at rest.' 12Then the angel of the
LORD said, 'O LORD of hosts, how long will
you have no mercy on Jerusalem and the
cities of Judah, against which you have had
indignation these seventy years?' 13And the
LORD answered gracious and comforting
words to the angel who talked with me.
14So the angel who talked with me said to
me, 'Cry out, Thus says the LORD of hosts:
I am exceedingly jealous for Jerusalem and
for Zion. 15And I am very angry with the
nations that are at ease; for while I was only
a little angry they furthered the disaster.
16Therefore, thus says the LORD, I have
returned to Jerusalem with compassion;
my house shall be built in it, says the LORD
of hosts, and the measuring line shall be
stretched out over Jerusalem. 17Cry again,
Thus says the LORD of hosts: My cities shall
again overflow with prosperity, and the
LORD will again comfort Zion and again
choose Jerusalem.'"
18And I lifted my eyes and saw, and behold,
four horns! 19And I said to the angel who
talked with me, "What are these?" And he
answered me, "These are the horns which
have scattered Judah, Israel, and Jerusalem."
20Then the LORD showed me four smiths.
21And I said, "What are these coming to do?"
He answered, "These are the horns which
scattered Judah, so that no man raised his
head; and these have come to terrify them,
to cast down the horns of the nations who
lifted up their horns against the land of
Judah to scatter it."

2 And I lifted my eyes and saw, and behold,
a man with a measuring line in his hand!
2Then I said, "Where are you going?" And
he said to me, "To measure Jerusalem, to see
what is its breadth and what is its length."
3And behold, the angel who talked with
me came forward, and another angel came
forward to meet him, 4and said to him,
"Run, say to that young man, 'Jerusalem
shall be inhabited as villages without walls,
because of the multitude of men and cattle
in it. 5For I will be to her a wall of fire round
about, says the LORD, and I will be the glory
within her.'"
6Ho! ho! Flee from the land of the north,
says the LORD; for I have spread you abroad
as the four winds of the heavens, says the
LORD. 7Ho! Escape to Zion, you who dwell
with the daughter of Babylon. 8For thus said
the LORD of hosts, after his glory sent me to
the nations who plundered you, for he who
touches you touches the apple of his eye:
9"Behold, I will shake my hand over them,
and they shall become plunder for those
who served them. Then you will know that
the LORD of hosts has sent me. 10Sing and
rejoice, O daughter of Zion; for behold, I
come and I will dwell in the midst of you,
says the LORD. 11And many nations shall
join themselves to the LORD in that day, and
shall be my people; and I will dwell in the
midst of you, and you shall know that the
LORD of hosts has sent me to you. 12And the
LORD will inherit Judah as his portion in the
holy land, and will again choose Jerusalem."
13Be silent, all flesh, before the LORD; for he
has roused himself from his holy dwelling.

3 Then he showed me Joshua the high
priest standing before the angel of the
LORD, and Satan standing at his right hand
to accuse him. 2And the LORD said to Satan,
"The LORD rebuke you, O Satan! The LORD
who has chosen Jerusalem rebuke you! Is
not this a brand plucked from the fire?"
3Now Joshua was standing before the angel,

clothed with filthy garments. 4And the angel
said to those who were standing before him,
"Remove the filthy garments from him."
And to him he said, "Behold, I have taken
your iniquity away from you, and I will
clothe you with rich apparel." 5And I said,
"Let them put a clean turban on his head."
So they put a clean turban on his head and
clothed him with garments; and the angel of
the LORD was standing by.

6And the angel of the LORD enjoined
Joshua, 7"Thus says the LORD of hosts: If you
will walk in my ways and keep my charge,
then you shall rule my house and have charge
of my courts, and I will give you the right of
access among those who are standing here.
8Hear now, O Joshua the high priest, you and
your friends who sit before you, for they are
men of good omen: behold, I will bring my
servant the Branch. 9For behold, upon the
stone which I have set before Joshua, upon a
single stone with seven facets, I will engrave
its inscription, says the LORD of hosts, and I
will remove the guilt of this land in a single
day. 10In that day, says the LORD of hosts,
every one of you will invite his neighbor
under his vine and under his fig tree."

4 And the angel who talked with me came
again, and waked me, like a man that is
wakened out of his sleep. 2And he said to me,
"What do you see?" I said, "I see, and behold,
a lampstand all of gold, with a bowl on the
top of it, and seven lamps on it, with seven
lips on each of the lamps which are on the
top of it. 3And there are two olive trees by it,
one on the right of the bowl and the other on
its left." 4And I said to the angel who talked
with me, "What are these, my lord?" 5Then
the angel who talked with me answered me,
"Do you not know what these are?" I said,
"No, my lord." 6Then he said to me, "This is
the word of the LORD to Zerubʹbabel: Not by
might, nor by power, but by my Spirit, says
the LORD of hosts. 7What are you, O great
mountain? Before Zerubʹbabel you shall
become a plain; and he shall bring forward
the top stone amid shouts of 'Grace, grace to
it!' " 8Moreover the word of the LORD came
to me, saying, 9"The hands of Zerubʹbabel
have laid the foundation of this house; his
hands shall also complete it. Then you will
know that the LORD of hosts has sent me to
you. 10For whoever has despised the day of
small things shall rejoice, and shall see the
plummet in the hand of Zerubʹbabel.

"These seven are the eyes of the LORD,
which range through the whole earth."
11Then I said to him, "What are these two
olive trees on the right and the left of the
lampstand?" 12And a second time I said to
him, "What are these two branches of the
olive trees, which are beside the two golden
pipes from which the oil is poured out?"
13He said to me, "Do you not know what
these are?" I said, "No, my lord." 14Then he
said, "These are the two anointed who stand
by the Lord of the whole earth."

SIRACH 38

9My son, when you are sick do not
be negligent,
but pray to the Lord, and he will heal you.
10Give up your faults and direct your hands
aright,
and cleanse your heart from all sin.
11Offer a sweet-smelling sacrifice, and a
memorial portion of fine flour,
and pour oil on your offering, as much as
you can afford.
12And give the physician his place, for the
Lord created him;
let him not leave you, for there is need
of him.
13There is a time when success lies in the
hands of physicians,
14 for they too will pray to the Lord
that he should grant them success
in diagnosis
and in healing, for the sake of
preserving life.
15He who sins before his Maker,
may he fall into the care of a physician.

16My son, let your tears fall for the dead,
and as one who is suffering grievously
begin the lament.
Lay out his body with the honor due him,
and do not neglect his burial.

[17]Let your weeping be bitter and your
wailing fervent;
observe the mourning according to
his merit,
for one day, or two, to avoid criticism;
then be comforted for your sorrow.
[18]For sorrow results in death,
and sorrow of heart saps one's strength.
[19]In calamity sorrow continues,
and the life of the poor man weighs down
his heart.
[20]Do not give your heart to sorrow;
drive it away, remembering the end of life.
[21]Do not forget, there is no coming back;
you do the dead no good, and you
injure yourself.
[22]"Remember my doom, for yours is like it:
yesterday it was mine, and today it is
yours."
[23]When the dead is at rest, let his
remembrance cease,
and be comforted for him when his spirit
has departed.

2 PETER 2

But false prophets also arose
among the people, just as there
will be false teachers among you, who
will secretly bring in destructive heresies,
even denying the Master who bought them,
bringing upon themselves swift destruction.
[2]And many will follow their licentiousness,
and because of them the way of truth will be
reviled. [3]And in their greed they will exploit
you with false words; from of old their
condemnation has not been idle, and their
destruction has not been asleep.

[4]For if God did not spare the angels when
they sinned, but cast them into hell and
committed them to pits of deepest darkness
to be kept until the judgment; [5]if he did not
spare the ancient world, but preserved Noah,
a herald of righteousness, with seven other
persons, when he brought a flood upon
the world of the ungodly; [6]if by turning the
cities of Sodom and Gomor′rah to ashes he
condemned them to extinction and made
them an example to those who were to be
ungodly; [7]and if he rescued righteous Lot,
greatly distressed by the licentiousness of
the wicked [8](for by what that righteous man
saw and heard as he lived among them, he
was vexed in his righteous soul day after
day with their lawless deeds), [9]then the
Lord knows how to rescue the godly from
trial, and to keep the unrighteous under
punishment until the day of judgment, [10]and
especially those who indulge in the lust of
defiling passion and despise authority.

Bold and wilful, they are not afraid to
revile the glorious ones, [11]whereas angels,
though greater in might and power, do not
pronounce a reviling judgment upon them
before the Lord. [12]But these, like irrational
animals, creatures of instinct, born to be
caught and killed, reviling in matters of
which they are ignorant, will be destroyed in
the same destruction with them, [13]suffering
wrong for their wrongdoing. They count
it pleasure to revel in the daytime. They
are blots and blemishes, reveling in their
dissipation, carousing with you. [14]They
have eyes full of adultery, insatiable for
sin. They entice unsteady souls. They have
hearts trained in greed. Accursed children!
[15]Forsaking the right way they have gone
astray; they have followed the way of
Balaam, the son of Beor, who loved gain
from wrongdoing, [16]but was rebuked for
his own transgression; a speechless donkey
spoke with human voice and restrained the
prophet's madness.

[17]These are waterless springs and mists
driven by a storm; for them the deepest
gloom of darkness has been reserved. [18]For,
uttering loud boasts of folly, they entice with
licentious passions of the flesh men who
have barely escaped from those who live in
error. [19]They promise them freedom, but
they themselves are slaves of corruption;
for whatever overcomes a man, to that he
is enslaved. [20]For if, after they have escaped
the defilements of the world through the
knowledge of our Lord and Savior Jesus
Christ, they are again entangled in them and
overpowered, the last state has become worse
for them than the first. [21]For it would have

been better for them never to have known
the way of righteousness than after knowing
it to turn back from the holy commandment
delivered to them. 22It has happened to them
according to the true proverb, The dog turns
back to his own vomit, and the sow is washed
only to wallow in the mire.

REFLECTION

It is revealed to St. Peter not only that he will soon die for Christ but that a great threat is arising for the Church: "There will be false teachers among you" (2 Pt 2:1). After warning that "many will follow" them, Peter gives us two clues to discerning false teachers: they will permit a licentiousness in following base passions, and they will revile the truth (v. 2). Peter forewarns of this conflict within the Church, between the true and false teachers, so its occurrence will not throw off the faithful, and they will be able to discern the shepherds from the wolves. The faithful need not lose heart, for "the Lord knows how to rescue the godly from trial" (v. 9). The false teachers will "promise them freedom, but they themselves are slaves of corruption; for whatever overcomes a man, to that he is enslaved" (v. 19). Enslaved to passions, they fall back into the paganism of the world but justify it by a new name, claiming such license fits under the banner of Christianity. Peter warns about these false promises, counterfeit to the divine promise with which he began his letter. Why do you think he describes such false promises as "waterless springs" (v. 17)?

December 4

ZECHARIAH 5

**Again I lifted my eyes and saw,
and behold, a flying scroll! 2And
he said to me, "What do you see?" I answered, "I see a flying scroll; its length is**
twenty cubits, and its breadth ten cubits."
3Then he said to me, "This is the curse
that goes out over the face of the whole
land; for every one who steals shall be cut
off henceforth according to it, and every
one who swears falsely shall be cut off
henceforth according to it. 4I will send it
forth, says the LORD of hosts, and it shall
enter the house of the thief, and the house
of him who swears falsely by my name; and
it shall abide in his house and consume it,
both timber and stones."
5Then the angel who talked with me came
forward and said to me, "Lift your eyes,
and see what this is that goes forth." 6And
I said, "What is it?" He said, "This is the
ephah that goes forth." And he said, "This is
their iniquity in all the land." 7And behold,
the leaden cover was lifted, and there was a
woman sitting in the ephah! 8And he said,
"This is Wickedness." And he thrust her
back into the ephah, and thrust down the
leaden weight upon its mouth. 9Then I lifted
my eyes and saw, and behold, two women
coming forward! The wind was in their
wings; they had wings like the wings of a
stork, and they lifted up the ephah between
earth and heaven. 10Then I said to the angel
who talked with me, "Where are they taking
the ephah?" 11He said to me, "To the land
of Shi′nar, to build a house for it; and when
this is prepared, they will set the ephah
down there on its base."
6 And again I lifted my eyes and saw,
and behold, four chariots came out from
between two mountains; and the mountains
were mountains of bronze. 2The first chariot
had red horses, the second black horses, 3the
third white horses, and the fourth chariot
dappled gray horses. 4Then I said to the
angel who talked with me, "What are these,
my lord?" 5And the angel answered me,
"These are going forth to the four winds of
heaven, after presenting themselves before
the LORD of all the earth. 6The chariot with
the black horses goes toward the north
country, the white ones go toward the west
country, and the dappled ones go toward the
south country." 7When the steeds came out,
they were impatient to get off and patrol the

earth. And he said, "Go, patrol the earth."
So they patrolled the earth. 8Then he cried
to me, "Behold, those who go toward the
north country have set my Spirit at rest in
the north country."
9And the word of the LORD came to me:
10"Take from the exiles Hel′dai, Tobi′jah, and
Jedai′ah, who have arrived from Babylon;
and go the same day to the house of Josi′ah,
the son of Zephani′ah. 11Take from them
silver and gold, and make a crown, and
set it upon the head of Joshua, the son of
Jehoz′adak, the high priest; 12and say to
him, 'Thus says the LORD of hosts, "Behold,
the man whose name is the Branch: for he
shall grow up in his place, and he shall build
the temple of the LORD. 13It is he who shall
build the temple of the LORD, and shall bear
royal honor, and shall sit and rule upon his
throne. And there shall be a priest by his
throne, and peaceful understanding shall be
between them both."' 14And the crown shall
be in the temple of the LORD as a reminder
to Hel′dai, Tobi′jah, Jedai′ah, and Josi′ah the
son of Zephani′ah.
15"And those who are far off shall come
and help to build the temple of the LORD;
and you shall know that the LORD of hosts
has sent me to you. And this shall come to
pass, if you will diligently obey the voice of
the LORD your God."

7 In the fourth year of King Dari′us, the
word of the LORD came to Zechari′ah in
the fourth day of the ninth month, which is
Chis′lev. 2Now the people of Bethel had sent
Share′zer and Reg′em-mel′ech and their
men, to entreat the favor of the LORD, 3and
to ask the priests of the house of the LORD
of hosts and the prophets, "Should I mourn
and fast in the fifth month, as I have done
for so many years?" 4Then the word of the
LORD of hosts came to me: 5"Say to all the
people of the land and the priests, When you
fasted and mourned in the fifth month and
in the seventh, for these seventy years, was
it for me that you fasted? 6And when you
eat and when you drink, do you not eat for
yourselves and drink for yourselves? 7When
Jerusalem was inhabited and in prosperity,
with her cities round about her, and the
South and the lowland were inhabited,
were not these the words which the LORD
proclaimed by the former prophets?"
8And the word of the LORD came to
Zechari′ah, saying, 9"Thus says the LORD
of hosts, Render true judgments, show
kindness and mercy each to his brother,
10do not oppress the widow, the fatherless,
the sojourner, or the poor; and let none of
you devise evil against his brother in your
heart." 11But they refused to listen, and
turned a stubborn shoulder, and stopped
their ears that they might not hear. 12They
made their hearts like adamant lest they
should hear the law and the words which
the LORD of hosts had sent by his Spirit
through the former prophets. Therefore
great wrath came from the LORD of hosts.
13"As I called, and they would not hear, so
they called, and I would not hear," says
the LORD of hosts, 14"and I scattered them
with a whirlwind among all the nations
which they had not known. Thus the land
they left was desolate, so that no one went
back and forth, and the pleasant land was
made desolate."

8 And the word of the LORD of hosts came
to me, saying, 2"Thus says the LORD
of hosts: I am jealous for Zion with great
jealousy, and I am jealous for her with
great wrath. 3Thus says the LORD: I will
return to Zion, and will dwell in the midst
of Jerusalem, and Jerusalem shall be called
the faithful city, and the mountain of the
LORD of hosts, the holy mountain. 4Thus
says the LORD of hosts: Old men and old
women shall again sit in the streets of
Jerusalem, each with staff in hand for very
age. 5And the streets of the city shall be full
of boys and girls playing in its streets. 6Thus
says the LORD of hosts: If it is marvelous
in the sight of the remnant of this people
in these days, should it also be marvelous
in my sight, says the LORD of hosts? 7Thus
says the LORD of hosts: Behold, I will save
my people from the east country and from
the west country; 8and I will bring them to
dwell in the midst of Jerusalem; and they
shall be my people and I will be their God,
in faithfulness and in righteousness."

9Thus says the LORD of hosts: "Let your
hands be strong, you who in these days
have been hearing these words from the
mouth of the prophets, since the day that
the foundation of the house of the LORD
of hosts was laid, that the temple might be
built. 10For before those days there was no
wage for man or any wage for beast, neither
was there any safety from the foe for him
who went out or came in; for I set every man
against his fellow. 11But now I will not deal
with the remnant of this people as in the
former days, says the LORD of hosts. 12For
there shall be a sowing of peace; the vine
shall yield its fruit, and the ground shall give
its increase, and the heavens shall give their
dew; and I will cause the remnant of this
people to possess all these things. 13And as
you have been a byword of cursing among
the nations, O house of Judah and house
of Israel, so will I save you and you shall be
a blessing. Fear not, but let your hands be
strong."

14For thus says the LORD of hosts: "As
I planned to do evil to you, when your
fathers provoked me to wrath, and I did not
relent, says the LORD of hosts, 15so again I
have planned in these days to do good to
Jerusalem and to the house of Judah; fear
not. 16These are the things that you shall do:
Speak the truth to one another, render in
your gates judgments that are true and make
for peace, 17do not devise evil in your hearts
against one another, and love no false oath,
for all these things I hate, says the LORD."

18And the word of the LORD of hosts came
to me, saying, 19"Thus says the LORD of hosts:
The fast of the fourth month, and the fast of
the fifth, and the fast of the seventh, and the
fast of the tenth, shall be to the house of Judah
seasons of joy and gladness, and cheerful
feasts; therefore love truth and peace.

20"Thus says the LORD of hosts: Peoples
shall yet come, even the inhabitants of many
cities; 21the inhabitants of one city shall go to
another, saying, 'Let us go at once to entreat
the favor of the LORD, and to seek the LORD
of hosts; I am going.' 22Many peoples and
strong nations shall come to seek the LORD
of hosts in Jerusalem, and to entreat the
favor of the LORD. 23Thus says the LORD
of hosts: In those days ten men from the
nations of every tongue shall take hold of
the robe of a Jew, saying, 'Let us go with you,
for we have heard that God is with you.'"

SIRACH 38

24The wisdom of the scribe depends on the
opportunity of leisure;
and he who has little business may
become wise.
25How can he become wise who handles
the plow,
and who glories in the shaft of a goad,
who drives oxen and is occupied with
their work,
and whose talk is about bulls?
26He sets his heart on plowing furrows,
and he is careful about fodder for
the heifers.
27So too is every craftsman and
master workman
who labors by night as well as by day;
those who cut the signets of seals,
each is diligent in making a great variety;
he sets his heart on painting a lifelike image,
and he is careful to finish his work.
28So too is the smith sitting by the anvil,
intent upon his handiwork in iron;
the breath of the fire melts his flesh,
and he wastes away in the heat of
the furnace;
he inclines his ear to the sound of
the hammer,
and his eyes are on the pattern of
the object.
He sets his heart on finishing his handiwork,
and he is careful to complete its
decoration.
29So too is the potter sitting at his work
and turning the wheel with his feet;
he is always deeply concerned over
his work,
and all his output is by number.
30He moulds the clay with his arm
and makes it pliable with his feet;
he sets his heart to finish the glazing,
and he is careful to clean the furnace.

31 All these rely upon their hands,
and each is skilful in his own work.
32 Without them a city cannot be established,
and men can neither sojourn nor
live there.
33 Yet they are not sought out for the council
of the people,
nor do they attain eminence in the
public assembly.
They do not sit in the judge's seat,
nor do they understand the sentence
of judgment;
they cannot expound discipline
or judgment,
and they are not found using proverbs.
34 But they keep stable the fabric of the world,
and their prayer is in the practice of
their trade.

2 PETER 3

This is now the second letter that I have written to you, beloved, and in both of them I have aroused your sincere mind by way of reminder; [2]**that**
you should remember the predictions of the
holy prophets and the commandment of the
Lord and Savior through your apostles. [3]First
of all you must understand this, that scoffers
will come in the last days with scoffing,
following their own passions [4]and saying,
"Where is the promise of his coming? For ever
since the fathers fell asleep, all things have
continued as they were from the beginning of
creation." [5]They deliberately ignore this fact,
that by the word of God heavens existed long
ago, and an earth formed out of water and by
means of water, [6]through which the world
that then existed was deluged with water and
perished. [7]But by the same word the heavens
and earth that now exist have been stored up
for fire, being kept until the day of judgment
and destruction of ungodly men.

[8]But do not ignore this one fact, beloved, that
with the Lord one day is as a thousand years,
and a thousand years as one day. [9]The Lord
is not slow about his promise as some count
slowness, but is forbearing toward you, not
wishing that any should perish, but that all
should reach repentance. [10]But the day of
the Lord will come like a thief, and then the
heavens will pass away with a loud noise,
and the elements will be dissolved with fire,
and the earth and the works that are upon it
will be burned up.

[11]Since all these things are thus to be
dissolved, what sort of persons ought you to
be in lives of holiness and godliness, [12]waiting
for and hastening the coming of the day of
God, because of which the heavens will be
kindled and dissolved, and the elements
will melt with fire! [13]But according to his
promise we wait for new heavens and a new
earth in which righteousness dwells.

[14]Therefore, beloved, since you wait for
these, be zealous to be found by him without
spot or blemish, and at peace. [15]And count
the forbearance of our Lord as salvation.
So also our beloved brother Paul wrote to
you according to the wisdom given him,
[16]speaking of this as he does in all his letters.
There are some things in them hard to
understand, which the ignorant and unstable
twist to their own destruction, as they do the
other Scriptures. [17]You therefore, beloved,
knowing this beforehand, beware lest you be
carried away with the error of lawless men
and lose your own stability. [18]But grow in the
grace and knowledge of our Lord and Savior
Jesus Christ. To him be the glory both now
and to the day of eternity. Amen.

REFLECTION

A striking twofold pattern in Israel's history is reflected in the prophets: a pattern that moves from judgment to restoration, from plight to promise, and from loss to restoration. Sin leads to exile, but God's mercy returns Israel back home. The prophets bear witness and warning of judgment, whether Amos and Joel about Assyria or Isaiah and Jeremiah about Babylon's conquest; but they also foretell the exile would end in return, and that destruction would lead to rebuilding. St. Peter picks up this biblical pattern by warning about the worldwide judgment with fire that would come on the day of the Lord. Some will question the threat as it is delayed (as did many in the days of the prophets), but it will come like a thief in the night. And in spite of the fiery judgment that will engulf the earth, as the waters in Noah's deluge, there is promise on the other side of the prophetic doom: God will restore once again but this time with a new heaven and earth. Through the crucible of the final judgment, a purified remnant will inherit a new paradise. When you hear Zechariah and Peter, do you hear the promise amidst the threat? And what strikes you most, the hope or the doom? Why?

December 5

An Oracle

ZECHARIAH 9

The word of the LORD is
against the land of
Had′rach
and will rest upon Damascus.
For to the LORD belong the cities of Ar′am,
even as all the tribes of Israel;
2Hamath also, which borders thereon,
Tyre and Si′don, though they are very wise.
3Tyre has built herself a rampart,
and heaped up silver like dust,
and gold like the dirt of the streets.
4But behold, the Lord will strip her of
her possessions
and hurl her wealth into the sea,
and she shall be devoured by fire.

5Ash′kelon shall see it, and be afraid;
Gaza too, and shall writhe in anguish;
Ek′ron also, because its hopes are
confounded.
The king shall perish from Gaza;
Ashkelon shall be uninhabited;
6a mongrel people shall dwell in Ash′dod;
and I will make an end of the pride
of Philis′tia.
7I will take away its blood from its mouth,
and its abominations from between
its teeth;
it too shall be a remnant for our God;
it shall be like a clan in Judah,
and Ek′ron shall be like the Jeb′usites.
8Then I will encamp at my house as a guard,
so that none shall march back and forth;
no oppressor shall again overrun them, for
now I see with my own eyes.
9Rejoice greatly, O daughter of Zion!
Shout aloud, O daughter of Jerusalem!
Behold, your king comes to you;
triumphant and victorious is he,
humble and riding on a donkey,
on a colt the foal of a donkey.
10I will cut off the chariot from E′phraim
and the war horse from Jerusalem;
and the battle bow shall be cut off,
and he shall command peace to
the nations;
his dominion shall be from sea to sea,
and from the River to the ends of
the earth.

11As for you also, because of the blood of my
covenant with you,
I will set your captives free from the
waterless pit.
12Return to your stronghold, O prisoners
of hope;
today I declare that I will restore to
you double.
13For I have bent Judah as my bow;
I have made E′phraim its arrow.
I will brandish your sons, O Zion,
over your sons, O Greece,
and wield you like a warrior's sword.
14Then the LORD will appear over them,
and his arrow go forth like lightning;
the Lord GOD will sound the trumpet,
and march forth in the whirlwinds of
the south.
15The LORD of hosts will protect them,
and they shall devour and tread down
the slingers;
and they shall drink their blood like wine,
and be full like a bowl,
drenched like the corners of the altar.

[16]On that day the LORD their God will
save them
for they are the flock of his people;
for like the jewels of a crown
they shall shine on his land.
[17]Yes, how good and how fair it shall be!
Grain shall make the young men flourish,
and new wine the maidens.

10 Ask rain from the LORD
in the season of the spring rain,
from the LORD who makes the storm clouds,
who gives men showers of rain,
to every one the vegetation in the field.
[2]For the teraphim utter nonsense,
and the diviners see lies;
the dreamers tell false dreams,
and give empty consolation.
Therefore the people wander like sheep;
they are afflicted for want of a
shepherd.

[3]"My anger is hot against the shepherds,
and I will punish the leaders;
for the LORD of hosts cares for his flock, the
house of Judah,
and will make them like his proud steed
in battle.
[4]Out of them shall come the cornerstone,
out of them the tent peg,
out of them the battle bow,
out of them every ruler.
[5]Together they shall be like mighty men
in battle,
trampling the foe in the mud of the streets;
they shall fight because the LORD is
with them,
and they shall confound the riders
on horses.

[6]"I will strengthen the house of Judah,
and I will save the house of Joseph.
I will bring them back because I have
compassion on them,
and they shall be as though I had not
rejected them;
for I am the LORD their God and I will
answer them.
[7]Then E′phraim shall become like a mighty
warrior,
and their hearts shall be glad as with wine.
Their children shall see it and rejoice,
their hearts shall exult in the LORD.

[8]"I will signal for them and gather them in,
for I have redeemed them,
and they shall be as many as of old.
[9]Though I scattered them among the nations,
yet in far countries they shall remember me,
and with their children they shall live
and return.
[10]I will bring them home from the land
of Egypt,
and gather them from Assyria;
and I will bring them to the land of Gilead
and to Lebanon,
till there is no room for them.
[11]They shall pass through the sea of Egypt,
and the waves of the sea shall be struck
down,
and all the depths of the Nile dried up.
The pride of Assyria shall be laid low,
and the scepter of Egypt shall depart.
[12]I will make them strong in the LORD
and they shall glory in his name," says
the LORD.

11 Open your doors, O Lebanon,
that the fire may devour your cedars!
[2]Wail, O cypress, for the cedar has fallen,
for the glorious trees are ruined!
Wail, oaks of Ba′shan,
for the thick forest has been felled!
[3]Listen, the wail of the shepherds,
for their glory is despoiled!
Listen, the roar of the lions,
for the jungle of the Jordan is laid waste!

[4]Thus said the LORD my God: "Become
shepherd of the flock doomed to slaughter.
[5]Those who buy them slay them and go
unpunished; and those who sell them say,
'Blessed be the LORD, I have become rich';
and their own shepherds have no pity on
them. [6]For I will no longer have pity on
the inhabitants of this land, says the LORD.
Behold, I will cause men to fall each into the
hand of his shepherd, and each into the hand
of his king; and they shall crush the earth,
and I will deliver none from their hand."

[7]So I became the shepherd of the
flock doomed to be slain for those who

trafficked in the sheep. And I took two
staffs; one I named Grace, the other I
named Union. And I tended the sheep.
[8]In one month I destroyed the three
shepherds. But I became impatient with
them, and they also detested me. [9]So I
said, "I will not be your shepherd. What
is to die, let it die; what is to be destroyed,
let it be destroyed; and let those that are
left devour the flesh of one another."
[10]And I took my staff Grace, and I broke
it, annulling the covenant which I had
made with all the peoples. [11]So it was
annulled on that day, and the traffickers
in the sheep, who were watching me,
knew that it was the word of the LORD.
[12]Then I said to them, "If it seems right
to you, give me my wages; but if not, keep
them." And they weighed out as my wages
thirty shekels of silver. [13]Then the LORD
said to me, "Cast it into the treasury"—
the lordly price at which I was paid off
by them. So I took the thirty shekels of
silver and cast them into the treasury in
the house of the LORD. [14]Then I broke
my second staff Union, annulling the
brotherhood between Judah and Israel.

[15]Then the LORD said to me, "Take once
more the implements of a worthless shepherd. [16]For behold, I am raising up in the
land a shepherd who does not care for the
perishing, or seek the wandering, or heal
the maimed, or nourish the sound, but
devours the flesh of the fat ones, tearing off
even their hoofs.

[17]Woe to my worthless shepherd,
who deserts the flock!
May the sword strike his arm
and his right eye!
Let his arm be wholly withered,
his right eye utterly blinded!"

SIRACH 39

On the other hand he who devotes himself
to the study of the law of the Most High
will seek out the wisdom of all the
ancients,
and will be concerned with prophecies;
[2]he will preserve the discourse of
notable men
and penetrate the subtleties of parables;
[3]he will seek out the hidden meanings
of proverbs
and be at home with the obscurities
of parables.
[4]He will serve among great men
and appear before rulers;
he will travel through the lands of
foreign nations,
for he tests the good and the evil
among men.
[5]He will set his heart to rise early
to seek the Lord who made him,
and will make supplication before the
Most High;
he will open his mouth in prayer
and make supplication for his sins.

[6]If the great Lord is willing,
he will be filled with the spirit of
understanding;
he will pour forth words of wisdom
and give thanks to the Lord in prayer.
[7]He will direct his counsel and knowledge
rightly,
and meditate on his secrets.
[8]He will reveal instruction in his teaching,
and will glory in the law of the Lord's
covenant.
[9]Many will praise his understanding,
and it will never be blotted out;
his memory will not disappear,
and his name will live through
all generations.
[10]Nations will declare his wisdom,
and the congregation will proclaim
his praise;
[11]if he lives long, he will leave a name greater
than a thousand,
and if he goes to rest, it is enough
for him.

[12]I have yet more to say, which I have
thought upon,
and I am filled, like the moon at the full.
[13]Listen to me, O you holy sons,
and bud like a rose growing by a stream
of water;

14 send forth fragrance like frankincense,
and put forth blossoms like a lily.
Scatter the fragrance, and sing a hymn of praise;
bless the Lord for all his works;
15 ascribe majesty to his name
and give thanks to him with praise,
with songs on your lips, and with lyres;
and this you shall say in thanksgiving:
16 "All things are the works of the Lord, for they are very good,
and whatever he commands will be done in his time."

1 JOHN 1

That which was from the beginning, which we have heard, which we have seen with our eyes, which we have looked upon and touched with our hands, concerning the word of life— 2 the life was made manifest, and we saw it, and testify to it, and proclaim to you the eternal life which was with the Father and was made manifest to us— 3 that which we have seen and heard we proclaim also to you, so that you may have fellowship with us; and our fellowship is with the Father and with his Son Jesus Christ. 4 And we are writing this that our joy may be complete.

5 This is the message we have heard from him and proclaim to you, that God is light and in him is no darkness at all. 6 If we say we have fellowship with him while we walk in darkness, we lie and do not live according to the truth; 7 but if we walk in the light, as he is in the light, we have fellowship with one another, and the blood of Jesus his Son cleanses us from all sin. 8 If we say we have no sin, we deceive ourselves, and the truth is not in us. 9 If we confess our sins, he is faithful and just, and will forgive our sins and cleanse us from all unrighteousness. 10 If we say we have not sinned, we make him a liar, and his word is not in us.

2 My little children, I am writing this to you so that you may not sin; but if any one does sin, we have an advocate with the Father, Jesus Christ the righteous; 2 and he is the expiation for our sins, and not for ours only but also for the sins of the whole world. 3 And by this we may be sure that we know him, if we keep his commandments. 4 He who says "I know him" but disobeys his commandments is a liar, and the truth is not in him; 5 but whoever keeps his word, in him truly love for God is perfected. By this we may be sure that we are in him: 6 he who says he abides in him ought to walk in the same way in which he walked.

7 Beloved, I am writing you no new commandment, but an old commandment which you had from the beginning; the old commandment is the word which you have heard. 8 Yet I am writing you a new commandment, which is true in him and in you, because the darkness is passing away and the true light is already shining. 9 He who says he is in the light and hates his brother is in the darkness still. 10 He who loves his brother abides in the light, and in it there is no cause for stumbling. 11 But he who hates his brother is in the darkness and walks in the darkness, and does not know where he is going, because the darkness has blinded his eyes.

12 I am writing to you, little children, because your sins are forgiven for his sake. 13 I am writing to you, fathers, because you know him who is from the beginning. I am writing to you, young men, because you have overcome the Evil One. I write to you, children, because you know the Father. 14 I write to you, fathers, because you know him who is from the beginning. I write to you, young men, because you are strong, and the word of God abides in you, and you have overcome the Evil One.

15 Do not love the world or the things in the world. If any one loves the world, love for the Father is not in him. 16 For all that is in the world, the lust of the flesh and the lust of the eyes and the pride of life, is not of the Father but is of the world. 17 And the world passes away, and the lust of it; but he who does the will of God abides for ever.

REFLECTION

Sirach gives a beautiful teaching about those who dedicate themselves to meditation on the Word of God Most High. Such people not only seek out wisdom and the hidden meanings of things, but they set their hearts "to rise early, to seek the Lord" who made them (Sir 39:5). Sirach shares a well-practiced wisdom: the heart of those who pray perseveringly often rise early to pray before the noise of the world is stirred up. During this quiet time of the morning, spent beside God's Word, the Lord may well grant them "understanding" (v. 6). Their prayer with God's Word moves to supplication (see v. 5) and then rests finally in thanksgiving (see vv. 14–16). Remember the Psalter's opening image of the righteous one who meditates day and night upon God's Word and is likened to a tree planted by streams (see Psalm 1)? Sirach echoes that image and refines it, saying that the one who prays with God's Word will "bud like a rose growing by a stream of water" and that their "fragrance" will go out to others (vv. 13–14). That rising fragrance is the joy, praise, and thanksgiving that arise from the heart of one planted daily in the garden of God's Word.

December 6

An Oracle

ZECHARIAH 12

The word of the LORD concern-
ing Israel: Thus says the LORD,
who stretched out the heavens and
founded the earth and formed the spirit
of man within him: 2"Behold, I am about to
make Jerusalem a cup of reeling to all the
peoples round about; it will be against Judah
also in the siege against Jerusalem. 3On that
day I will make Jerusalem a heavy stone for
all the peoples; all who lift it shall grievously
hurt themselves. And all the nations of the
earth will come together against it. 4On that
day, says the LORD, I will strike every horse
with panic, and its rider with madness. But
upon the house of Judah I will open my eyes,
when I strike every horse of the peoples
with blindness. 5Then the clans of Judah
shall say to themselves, 'The inhabitants of
Jerusalem have strength through the LORD
of hosts, their God.'
6"On that day I will make the clans of
Judah like a blazing pot in the midst of
wood, like a flaming torch among sheaves;
and they shall devour to the right and to
the left all the peoples round about, while
Jerusalem shall still be inhabited in its place,
in Jerusalem.
7"And the LORD will give victory to the
tents of Judah first, that the glory of the house
of David and the glory of the inhabitants
of Jerusalem may not be exalted over that
of Judah. 8On that day the LORD will put a
shield about the inhabitants of Jerusalem so
that the feeblest among them on that day
shall be like David, and the house of David
shall be like God, like the angel of the LORD,
at their head. 9And on that day I will seek
to destroy all the nations that come against
Jerusalem.
10"And I will pour out on the house of David
and the inhabitants of Jerusalem a spirit of
compassion and supplication, so that, when
they look on him whom they have pierced,
they shall mourn for him, as one mourns for
an only child, and weep bitterly over him,
as one weeps over a first-born. 11On that
day the mourning in Jerusalem will be as
great as the mourning for Ha'dadrim'mon
in the plain of Megid'do. 12The land shall
mourn, each family by itself; the family
of the house of David by itself, and their
wives by themselves; the family of the
house of Nathan by itself, and their wives by
themselves; 13the family of the house of Levi
by itself, and their wives by themselves; the
family of the Shime'ites by itself, and their
wives by themselves; 14and all the families

that are left, each by itself, and their wives
by themselves.

13 On that day there shall be a fountain
opened for the house of David and
the inhabitants of Jerusalem to cleanse them
from sin and uncleanness.

2“And on that day, says the LORD of hosts,
I will cut off the names of the idols from the
land, so that they shall be remembered no
more; and also I will remove from the land
the prophets and the unclean spirit. 3And
if any one again appears as a prophet, his
father and mother who bore him will say to
him, ‘You shall not live, for you speak lies
in the name of the LORD’; and his father
and mother who bore him shall pierce him
through when he prophesies. 4On that day
every prophet will be ashamed of his vision
when he prophesies; he will not put on a
hairy mantle in order to deceive, 5but he will
say, ‘I am no prophet, I am a tiller of the soil;
for the land has been my possession since
my youth.’ 6And if one asks him, ‘What are
these wounds on your back?’ he will say,
‘The wounds I received in the house of my
friends.’ ”

7“Awake, O sword, against my shepherd,
against the man who stands next to me,”
says the LORD of hosts.
“Strike the shepherd, that the sheep may be
scattered;
I will turn my hand against the little ones.
8In the whole land, says the LORD,
two thirds shall be cut off and perish,
and one third shall be left alive.
9And I will put this third into the fire,
and refine them as one refines silver,
and test them as gold is tested.
They will call on my name,
and I will answer them.
I will say, ‘They are my people’;
and they will say, ‘The LORD is my God.’ ”

14 Behold, a day of the LORD is coming,
when the spoil taken from you will
be divided in the midst of you. 2For I will
gather all the nations against Jerusalem to
battle, and the city shall be taken and the
houses plundered and the women ravished;
half of the city shall go into exile, but the
rest of the people shall not be cut off from
the city. 3Then the LORD will go forth and
fight against those nations as when he fights
on a day of battle. 4On that day his feet shall
stand on the Mount of Olives which lies
before Jerusalem on the east; and the Mount
of Olives shall be split in two from east to
west by a very wide valley; so that one half
of the Mount shall withdraw northward,
and the other half southward. 5And the
valley of my mountains shall be stopped up,
for the valley of the mountains shall touch
the side of it; and you shall flee as you fled
from the earthquake in the days of Uzzi′ah
king of Judah. Then the LORD your God will
come, and all the holy ones with him.

6On that day there shall be neither cold
nor frost. 7And there shall be continuous
day (it is known to the LORD), not day and
not night, for at evening time there shall be
light.

8On that day living waters shall flow out
from Jerusalem, half of them to the eastern
sea and half of them to the western sea; it
shall continue in summer as in winter.

9And the LORD will become king over all
the earth; on that day the LORD will be one
and his name one.

10The whole land shall be turned into
a plain from Ge′ba to Rimmon south of
Jerusalem. But Jerusalem shall remain aloft
upon its site from the Gate of Benjamin to
the place of the former gate, to the Corner
Gate, and from the Tower of Hanan′el to
the king’s wine presses. 11And it shall be
inhabited, for there shall be no more curse;
Jerusalem shall dwell in security.

12And this shall be the plague with which
the LORD will strike all the peoples that
wage war against Jerusalem: their flesh
shall rot while they are still on their feet,
their eyes shall rot in their sockets, and
their tongues shall rot in their mouths.
13And on that day a great panic from the
LORD shall fall on them, so that each will
lay hold on the hand of his fellow, and
the hand of the one will be raised against
the hand of the other; 14even Judah will
fight against Jerusalem. And the wealth
of all the nations round about shall be

collected, gold, silver, and garments in
great abundance. 15 And a plague like this
plague shall fall on the horses, the mules,
the camels, the donkeys, and whatever
beasts may be in those camps.
16 Then every one that survives of all the
nations that have come against Jerusalem
shall go up year after year to worship the
King, the LORD of hosts, and to keep the
feast of booths. 17 And if any of the families
of the earth do not go up to Jerusalem to
worship the King, the LORD of hosts, there
will be no rain upon them. 18 And if the
family of Egypt do not go up and present
themselves, then upon them shall come
the plague with which the LORD afflicts the
nations that do not go up to keep the feast
of booths. 19 This shall be the punishment
to Egypt and the punishment to all the
nations that do not go up to keep the feast
of booths.
20 And on that day there shall be inscribed
on the bells of the horses, "Holy to the
LORD." And the pots in the house of the
LORD shall be as the bowls before the altar;
21 and every pot in Jerusalem and Judah shall
be sacred to the LORD of hosts, so that all
who sacrifice may come and take of them
and boil the flesh of the sacrifice in them.
And there shall no longer be a trader in the
house of the LORD of hosts on that day.

SIRACH 39

17 No one can say, "What is this?" "Why
is that?"
for in God's time all things will be
sought after.
At his word the waters stood in a heap,
and the reservoirs of water at the word
of his mouth.
18 At his command whatever pleases him
is done,
and none can limit his saving power.
19 The works of all flesh are before him,
and nothing can be hid from his eyes.
20 From everlasting to everlasting he
beholds them,
and nothing is marvelous to him.
21 No one can say, "What is this?" "Why
is that?"
for everything has been created for
its use.

22 His blessing covers the dry land like a river,
and drenches it like a flood.
23 The nations will incur his wrath,
just as he turns fresh water into salt.
24 To the holy his ways are straight,
just as they are obstacles to the wicked.
25 From the beginning good things were
created for good people,
just as evil things for sinners.
26 Basic to all the needs of man's life
are water and fire and iron and salt
and wheat flour and milk and honey,
the blood of the grape, and oil and
clothing.
27 All these are for good to the godly,
just as they turn into evils for sinners.

28 There are winds that have been created
for vengeance,
and in their anger they scourge heavily;
in the time of consummation they will
pour out their strength
and calm the anger of their Maker.
29 Fire and hail and famine and pestilence,
all these have been created for vengeance;
30 the teeth of wild beasts, and scorpions
and vipers,
and the sword that punishes the ungodly
with destruction;
31 they will rejoice in his commands,
and be made ready on earth for their
service,
and when their times come they will not
transgress his word.

32 Therefore from the beginning I have
been convinced,
and have thought this out and left it
in writing:
33 The works of the Lord are all good,
and he will supply every need in its hour.
34 And no one can say, "This is worse
than that,"
for all things will prove good in
their season.

35So now sing praise with all your heart
and voice,
and bless the name of the Lord.

---

1 JOHN 2

18Children, it is the last hour; and as you have heard that antichrist is coming, so now many antichrists have come; therefore we know that it is the last hour. 19They went out from us, but they were not of us; for if they had been of us, they would have continued with us; but they went out, that it might be plain that they all are not of us. 20But you have been anointed by the Holy One, and you all know. 21I write to you, not because you do not know the truth, but because you know it, and know that no lie is of the truth. 22Who is the liar but he who denies that Jesus is the Christ? This is the antichrist, he who denies the Father and the Son. 23Any one who denies the Son does not have the Father. He who confesses the Son has the Father also. 24Let what you heard from the beginning abide in you. If what you heard from the beginning abides in you, then you will abide in the Son and in the Father. 25And this is what he has promised us, eternal life.

26I write this to you about those who would deceive you; 27but the anointing which you received from him abides in you, and you have no need that any one should teach you; as his anointing teaches you about everything, and is true, and is no lie, just as it has taught you, abide in him.

28And now, little children, abide in him, so that when he appears we may have confidence and not shrink from him in shame at his coming. 29If you know that he is righteous, you may be sure that every one who does right is born of him.

3 See what love the Father has given us, that we should be called children of God; and so we are. The reason why the world does not know us is that it did not know him. 2Beloved, we are God's children now; it does not yet appear what we shall be, but we know that when he appears we shall be like him, for we shall see him as he is. 3And every one who thus hopes in him purifies himself as he is pure.

4Every one who commits sin is guilty of lawlessness; sin is lawlessness. 5You know that he appeared to take away sins, and in him there is no sin. 6Any one who abides in him does not sin; any one who sins has not seen him, nor has he known him. 7Little children, let no one deceive you. He who does right is righteous, as he is righteous. 8He who commits sin is of the devil; for the devil has sinned from the beginning. The reason the Son of God appeared was to destroy the works of the devil. 9Any one born of God does not commit sin; for God's seed abides in him, and he cannot sin because he is born of God. 10By this it may be seen who are the children of God, and who are the children of the devil: whoever does not do right is not of God, nor he who does not love his brother.

REFLECTION

St. John, the beloved disciple of Jesus, writes with warmth and love and yet at the same time, motivated by love, warns his flock about the Antichrist. Indeed, John observes that there are many "antichrists," not just one. What is the fundamental description of an Antichrist? "This is the antichrist, he who denies the Father and the Son" (1 John 2:22). The denial that God is Father and has a Son is fundamental to any antichrist. Interestingly, John moves on from this discussion to remind us how great is the Father's love for us, in that the Father made us sons and daughters by the work of his Son. Counter to antichrists, those who believe in the Father and Son can become themselves children of God. "Beloved, we are God's children now; it does not yet appear what we shall be, but we know that when he appears we shall be like him, for we shall see him as he is" (3:2). Here, in his first letter, John admits that he does not know "what we shall be," but perhaps he does see that later in his visions in the Book of Revelation, when he sees the bride adorned for the wedding feast of the Lamb. Do you live each day in joyful affirmation that God is indeed your Father?

December 7

MALACHI 1

The oracle of the word of the LORD to Israel by Mal′achi.

2"I have loved you," says the LORD. But you say, "How have you loved us?" "Is not Esau Jacob's brother?" says the LORD. "Yet I have loved Jacob 3but I have hated Esau; I have laid waste his hill country and left his heritage to jackals of the desert." 4If E′dom says, "We are shattered but we will rebuild the ruins," the LORD of hosts says, "They may build, but I will tear down, till they are called the wicked country, the people with whom the LORD is angry for ever." 5Your own eyes shall see this, and you shall say, "Great is the LORD, beyond the border of Israel!"

6"A son honors his father, and a servant his master. If then I am a father, where is my honor? And if I am a master, where is my fear? says the LORD of hosts to you, O priests, who despise my name. You say, 'How have we despised your name?' 7By offering polluted food upon my altar. And you say, 'How have we polluted it?' By thinking that the LORD's table may be despised. 8When you offer blind animals in sacrifice, is that no evil? And when you offer those that are lame or sick, is that no evil? Present that to your governor; will he be pleased with you or show you favor? says the LORD of hosts. 9And now entreat the favor of God, that he may be gracious to us. With such a gift from your hand, will he show favor to any of you? says the LORD of hosts. 10Oh, that there were one among you who would shut the doors, that you might not kindle fire upon my altar in vain! I have no pleasure in you, says the LORD of hosts, and I will not accept an offering from your hand. 11For from the rising of the sun to its setting my name is great among the nations, and in every place incense is offered to my name, and a pure offering; for my name is great among the nations, says the LORD of hosts. 12But you profane it when you say that the LORD's table is polluted, and the food for it may be despised. 13'What a weariness this is,' you say, and you sniff at me, says the LORD of hosts. You bring what has been taken by violence or is lame or sick, and this you bring as your offering! Shall I accept that from your hand? says the LORD. 14Cursed be the cheat who has a male in his flock, and vows it, and yet sacrifices to the Lord what is blemished; for I am a great King, says the LORD of hosts, and my name is feared among the nations.

2 "And now, O priests, this command is for you. 2If you will not listen, if you will not lay it to heart to give glory to my name, says the LORD of hosts, then I will send the curse upon you and I will curse your blessings; indeed I have already cursed them, because you do not lay it to heart. 3Behold, I will rebuke your offspring, and spread dung upon your faces, the dung of your offerings, and I will put you out of my presence. 4So shall you know that I have sent this command to you, that my covenant with Levi may hold, says the LORD of hosts. 5My covenant with him was a covenant of life and peace, and I gave them to him, that he might fear; and he feared me, he stood in awe of my name. 6True instruction was in his mouth, and no wrong was found on his lips. He walked with me in peace and uprightness, and he turned many from iniquity. 7For the lips of a priest should guard knowledge, and men should seek instruction from his mouth, for he is the messenger of the LORD of hosts. 8But you have turned aside from the way; you have caused many to stumble by your instruction; you have corrupted the covenant of Levi, says the LORD of hosts, 9and so I make you despised and abased before all the people, inasmuch as you have not kept my ways but have shown partiality in your instruction."

10Have we not all one father? Has not one God created us? Why then are we faithless to one another, profaning the covenant of our fathers? 11Judah has been faithless, and abomination has been committed in Israel and in Jerusalem; for Judah has profaned the sanctuary of the LORD, which he loves, and has married the daughter of a foreign god. [12]May the LORD cut off from the tents of Jacob, for the man who does this, any to witness or answer, or to bring an offering to the LORD of hosts!

[13]And this again you do. You cover the LORD's altar with tears, with weeping and groaning because he no longer regards the offering or accepts it with favor at your hand. [14]You ask, "Why does he not?" Because the LORD was witness to the covenant between you and the wife of your youth, to whom you have been faithless, though she is your companion and your wife by covenant. [15]Has not the one God made and sustained for us the spirit of life? And what does he desire? Godly offspring. So take heed to yourselves, and let none be faithless to the wife of his youth. [16]"For I hate divorce, says the LORD the God of Israel, and covering one's garment with violence, says the LORD of hosts. So take heed to yourselves and do not be faithless."

[17]You have wearied the LORD with your words. Yet you say, "How have we wearied him?" By saying, "Every one who does evil is good in the sight of the LORD, and he delights in them." Or by asking, "Where is the God of justice?"

3 "Behold, I send my messenger to prepare the way before me, and the Lord whom you seek will suddenly come to his temple; the messenger of the covenant in whom you delight, behold, he is coming, says the LORD of hosts. [2]But who can endure the day of his coming, and who can stand when he appears?

"For he is like a refiner's fire and like fullers' soap; [3]he will sit as a refiner and purifier of silver, and he will purify the sons of Levi and refine them like gold and silver, till they present right offerings to the LORD. [4]Then the offering of Judah and Jerusalem will be pleasing to the LORD as in the days of old and as in former years.

[5]"Then I will draw near to you for judgment; I will be a swift witness against the sorcerers, against the adulterers, against those who swear falsely, against those who oppress the hireling in his wages, the widow and the orphan, against those who thrust aside the sojourner, and do not fear me, says the LORD of hosts.

[6]"For I the LORD do not change; therefore you, O sons of Jacob, are not consumed. [7]From the days of your fathers you have turned aside from my statutes and have not kept them. Return to me, and I will return to you, says the LORD of hosts. But you say, 'How shall we return?' [8]Will man rob God? Yet you are robbing me. But you say, 'How are we robbing you?' In your tithes and offerings. [9]You are cursed with a curse, for you are robbing me; the whole nation of you. [10]Bring the full tithes into the storehouse, that there may be food in my house; and thereby put me to the test, says the LORD of hosts, if I will not open the windows of heaven for you and pour down for you an overflowing blessing. [11]I will rebuke the devourer for you, so that it will not destroy the fruits of your soil; and your vine in the field shall not fail to bear, says the LORD of hosts. [12]Then all nations will call you blessed, for you will be a land of delight, says the LORD of hosts.

[13]"Your words have been stout against me, says the LORD. Yet you say, 'How have we spoken against you?' [14]You have said, 'It is vain to serve God. What is the good of our keeping his charge or of walking as in mourning before the LORD of hosts? [15]Henceforth we deem the arrogant blessed; evildoers not only prosper but when they put God to the test they escape.'"

[16]Then those who feared the LORD spoke with one another; the LORD heeded and heard them, and a book of remembrance was written before him of those who feared the LORD and thought on his name. [17]"They shall be mine, says the LORD of hosts, my special possession on the day when I act, and I will spare them as a man spares his son who serves him. [18]Then once more you shall distinguish between the righteous and the wicked, between one who serves God and one who does not serve him.

4 "For behold, the day comes, burning like an oven, when all the arrogant and all evildoers will be stubble; the day that

comes shall burn them up, says the LORD of hosts, so that it will leave them neither root nor branch. 2But for you who fear my name the sun of righteousness shall rise, with healing in its wings. You shall go forth leaping like calves from the stall. 3And you shall tread down the wicked, for they will be ashes under the soles of your feet, on the day when I act, says the LORD of hosts.

4"Remember the law of my servant Moses, the statutes and ordinances that I commanded him at Horeb for all Israel.

5"Behold, I will send you Eli′jah the prophet before the great and awesome day of the LORD comes. 6And he will turn the hearts of fathers to their children and the hearts of children to their fathers, lest I come and strike the land with a curse."

SIRACH 40

Much labor was created for every man,
and a heavy yoke is upon the sons
of Adam,
from the day they come forth from their
mother's womb
till the day they return to the mother
of all.
2Their perplexities and fear of heart—
their anxious thought is the day of death,
3from the man who sits on a splendid throne
to the one who is humbled in dust
and ashes,
4from the man who wears purple and a crown
to the one who is clothed in burlap;
5there is anger and envy and trouble
and unrest,
and fear of death, and fury and strife.
And when one rests upon his bed,
his sleep at night confuses his mind.
6He gets little or no rest,
and afterward in his sleep, as though he
were on watch,
he is troubled by the visions of his mind
like one who has escaped from the
battlefront;
7at the moment of his rescue he wakes up,
and wonders that his fear came to
nothing.
8With all flesh, both man and beast,
and upon sinners seven times more,
9are death and bloodshed and strife
and sword,
calamities, famine and affliction
and plague.
10All these were created for the wicked,
and on their account the flood came.
11All things that are from the earth turn
back to the earth,
and what is from the waters returns to
the sea.

1 JOHN 3

11For this is the message which you have heard from the beginning, that we should love one another, 12and not be like Cain who was of the Evil One and murdered his brother. And why did he murder him? Because his own deeds were evil and his brother's righteous. 13Do not wonder, brethren, that the world hates you. 14We know that we have passed out of death into life, because we love the brethren. He who does not love remains in death. 15Any one who hates his brother is a murderer, and you know that no murderer has eternal life abiding in him. 16By this we know love, that he laid down his life for us; and we ought to lay down our lives for the brethren. 17But if any one has the world's goods and sees his brother in need, yet closes his heart against him, how does God's love abide in him? 18Little children, let us not love in word or speech but in deed and in truth.

19By this we shall know that we are of the truth, and reassure our hearts before him 20whenever our hearts condemn us; for God is greater than our hearts, and he knows everything. 21Beloved, if our hearts do not condemn us, we have confidence before God; 22and we receive from him whatever we ask, because we keep his commandments and do what pleases him. 23And this is his commandment, that we should believe in the name of his Son Jesus Christ and love one another, just as he has commanded us.

24 All who keep his commandments abide in
him, and he in them. And by this we know
that he abides in us, by the Spirit which he
has given us.

4 Beloved, do not believe every spirit, but
test the spirits to see whether they are
of God; for many false prophets have gone
out into the world. 2 By this you know the
Spirit of God: every spirit which confesses
that Jesus Christ has come in the flesh is
of God, 3 and every spirit which does not
confess Jesus is not of God. This is the
spirit of antichrist, of which you heard that
it was coming, and now it is in the world
already. 4 Little children, you are of God,
and have overcome them; for he who is in
you is greater than he who is in the world.
5 They are of the world, therefore what they
say is of the world, and the world listens to
them. 6 We are of God. Whoever knows God
listens to us, and he who is not of God does
not listen to us. By this we know the spirit of
truth and the spirit of error.

REFLECTION

God gives the last of all the Hebrew prophets a formula for the long looked-for renewal of Israel: "He will turn the hearts of fathers to their children and the hearts of children to their fathers" (Mal 4:6). Perhaps this turning of a father's heart to his children will solve the pressing problem with which Malachi began: divorce. Malachi tells us that a messenger of the covenant will come to refine the sons of Levi, and Luke shows us that this messenger is none other than John the Baptist, who goes forth "in the spirit and power of Elijah" (Lk 1:17). John bursts forth like a flame, born of the lineage of his priestly father Zechariah. John does what many priests in his day did not have the courage to do: he condemns Herod's marrying of his brother's divorced wife. The messenger of the covenant defends the sanctity of the marriage covenant and will be beheaded, much like a later saint who also stood for the inviolability of marriage, St. Thomas More, who suffered the same fate. Divorce creates widows and orphans, and yet the turning of a father's heart can lead back to marriage, restoration, and God. Are you doing all that is possible to be a modern-day witness to the sanctity of marriage?

December 8

1 MACCABEES 1

**After Alexander son of Philip,
the Macedonian, who came from
the land of Kittim, had defeated Dari′us, king of the Persians and
the Medes, he succeeded him as king.
(He had previously become king of**
Greece.) 2 He fought many battles, conquered strongholds, and put to death the
kings of the earth. 3 He advanced to the ends
of the earth, and plundered many nations.
When the earth became quiet before him,
he was exalted, and his heart was lifted up.
4 He gathered a very strong army and ruled
over countries, nations, and princes, and
they became tributary to him.

5 After this he fell sick and perceived that
he was dying. 6 So he summoned his most
honored officers, who had been brought
up with him from youth, and divided his
kingdom among them while he was still
alive. 7 And after Alexander had reigned
twelve years, he died.

8 Then his officers began to rule, each in
his own place. 9 They all put on crowns after
his death, and so did their sons after them
for many years; and they caused many evils
on the earth.

10 From them came forth a sinful root,
Anti′ochus Epiph′anes, son of Anti′ochus
the king; he had been a hostage in Rome.
He began to reign in the one hundred and
thirty-seventh year of the kingdom of the
Greeks.

11 In those days lawless men came forth
from Israel, and misled many, saying, "Let
us go and make a covenant with the Gentiles
round about us, for since we separated
from them many evils have come upon us."
12 This proposal pleased them, 13 and some
of the people eagerly went to the king. He
authorized them to observe the ordinances
of the Gentiles. 14 So they built a gymnasium
in Jerusalem, according to Gentile custom,

[15]and removed the marks of circumcision,
and abandoned the holy covenant. They
joined with the Gentiles and sold themselves
to do evil.
[16]When Anti′ochus saw that his kingdom
was established, he determined to become
king of the land of Egypt, that he might
reign over both kingdoms. [17]So he invaded
Egypt with a strong force, with chariots
and elephants and cavalry and with a large
fleet. [18]He engaged Ptol′emy king of Egypt
in battle, and Ptolemy turned and fled
before him, and many were wounded and
fell. [19]And they captured the fortified cities
in the land of Egypt, and he plundered the
land of Egypt.
[20]After subduing Egypt, Anti′ochus
returned in the one hundred and forty-
third year. He went up against Israel and
came to Jerusalem with a strong force.
[21]He arrogantly entered the sanctuary and
took the golden altar, the lampstand for
the light, and all its utensils. [22]He took also
the table for the bread of the Presence, the
cups for drink offerings, the bowls, the
golden censers, the curtain, the crowns,
and the gold decoration on the front of the
temple; he stripped it all off. [23]He took the
silver and the gold, and the costly vessels;
he took also the hidden treasures which he
found. [24]Taking them all, he departed to
his own land.

He committed deeds of murder,
  and spoke with great arrogance.
[25]Israel mourned deeply in every community,
[26] rulers and elders groaned,
maidens and young men became faint,
  the beauty of women faded.
[27]Every bridegroom took up the lament;
  she who sat in the bridal chamber
    was mourning.
[28]Even the land shook for its inhabitants,
  and all the house of Jacob was clothed
    with shame.

[29]Two years later the king sent to the
cities of Judah a chief collector of tribute,
and he came to Jerusalem with a large
force. [30]Deceitfully he spoke peaceable
words to them, and they believed him;
but he suddenly fell upon the city, dealt it
a severe blow, and destroyed many people
of Israel. [31]He plundered the city, burned
it with fire, and tore down its houses and
its surrounding walls. [32]And they took
captive the women and children, and
seized the cattle. [33]Then they fortified the
city of David with a great strong wall and
strong towers, and it became their citadel.
[34]And they stationed there a sinful people,
lawless men. These strengthened their
position; [35]they stored up arms and food,
and collecting the spoils of Jerusalem
they stored them there, and became a
great snare.

[36]It became an ambush against the sanctuary,
  an evil adversary of Israel continually.
[37]On every side of the sanctuary they shed
    innocent blood;
  they even defiled the sanctuary.
[38]Because of them the residents of
    Jerusalem fled;
  she became a dwelling of strangers;
she became strange to her offspring,
  and her children forsook her.
[39]Her sanctuary became desolate as a desert;
  her feasts were turned into mourning,
her sabbaths into a reproach,
  her honor into contempt.
[40]Her dishonor now grew as great as
    her glory;
  her exaltation was turned into mourning.

[41]Then the king wrote to his whole kingdom that all should be one people, [42]and
that each should give up his customs.
[43]All the Gentiles accepted the command
of the king. Many even from Israel gladly adopted his religion; they sacrificed to
idols and profaned the sabbath. [44]And the
king sent letters by messengers to Jerusalem and the cities of Judah; he directed
them to follow customs strange to the
land, [45]to forbid burnt offerings and sacrifices and drink offerings in the sanctuary,
to profane sabbaths and feasts, [46]to defile
the sanctuary and the priests, [47]to build
altars and sacred precincts and shrines
for idols, to sacrifice swine and unclean
animals, [48]and to leave their sons uncircumcised. They were to make themselves
abominable by everything unclean and

profane, 49so that they should forget the
law and change all the ordinances. 50"And
whoever does not obey the command of
the king shall die."
51In such words he wrote to his whole
kingdom. And he appointed inspectors over
all the people and commanded the cities of
Judah to offer sacrifice, city by city. 52Many
of the people, every one who forsook the
law, joined them, and they did evil in the
land; 53they drove Israel into hiding in every
place of refuge they had.
54Now on the fifteenth day of Chis′lev,
in the one hundred and forty-fifth year,
they erected a desolating sacrilege upon
the altar of burnt offering. They also built
altars in the surrounding cities of Judah,
55and burned incense at the doors of the
houses and in the streets. 56The books of the
law which they found they tore to pieces
and burned with fire. 57Where the book of
the covenant was found in the possession
of any one, or if any one adhered to the
law, the decree of the king condemned
him to death. 58They kept using violence
against Israel, against those found month
after month in the cities. 59And on the
twenty-fifth day of the month they offered
sacrifice on the altar which was upon the
altar of burnt offering. 60According to
the decree, they put to death the women
who had their children circumcised, 61and
their families and those who circumcised
them; and they hung the infants from their
mothers' necks.
62But many in Israel stood firm and were
resolved in their hearts not to eat unclean
food. 63They chose to die rather than to
be defiled by food or to profane the holy
covenant; and they did die. 64And very great
wrath came upon Israel.

2 In those days Mattathi′as the son of
John, son of Simeon, a priest of the
sons of Jo′arib, moved from Jerusalem and
settled in Mo′dein. 2He had five sons, John
surnamed Gaddi, 3Simon called Thassi,
4Judas called Mac″cabe′us, 5Elea′zar called
Av′aran, and Jonathan called Ap′phus. 6He
saw the blasphemies being committed in
Judah and Jerusalem, 7and said,

"Alas! Why was I born to see this,
the ruin of my people, the ruin of the
holy city,
and to dwell there when it was given over
to the enemy,
the sanctuary given over to aliens?
8Her temple has become like a man without
honor;
9 her glorious vessels have been carried
into captivity.
Her infants have been killed in her streets,
her youths by the sword of the foe.
10What nation has not inherited her
palaces
and has not seized her spoils?
11All her adornment has been taken away;
no longer free, she has become a slave.
12And behold, our holy place, our beauty,
and our glory have been laid waste;
the Gentiles have profaned it.
13 Why should we live any longer?"
14And Mattathi′as and his sons tore their
clothes, put on sackcloth, and mourned
greatly.
15Then the king's officers who were en-
forcing the apostasy came to the city of
Mo′dein to make them offer sacrifice. 16Many
from Israel came to them; and Mattathi′as and
his sons were assembled. 17Then the king's
officers spoke to Mattathi′as as follows: "You
are a leader, honored and great in this city,
and supported by sons and brothers. 18Now
be the first to come and do what the king
commands, as all the Gentiles and the men
of Judah and those that are left in Jerusalem
have done. Then you and your sons will be
numbered among the friends of the king, and
you and your sons will be honored with silver
and gold and many gifts."
19But Mattathi′as answered and said in
a loud voice: "Even if all the nations that
live under the rule of the king obey him,
and have chosen to do his commandments,
departing each one from the religion of his
fathers, 20yet I and my sons and my brothers
will live by the covenant of our fathers.
21Far be it from us to desert the law and the
ordinances. 22We will not obey the king's
words by turning aside from our religion to
the right hand or to the left."

23When he had finished speaking these words, a Jew came forward in the sight of all to offer sacrifice upon the altar in Mo´dein, according to the king's command. 24When Mattathi´as saw it, he burned with zeal and his heart was stirred. He gave vent to righteous anger; he ran and killed him upon the altar. 25At the same time he killed the king's officer who was forcing them to sacrifice, and he tore down the altar. 26Thus he burned with zeal for the law, as Phin´ehas did against Zimri the son of Sa´lu.

27Then Mattathi´as cried out in the city with a loud voice, saying: "Let every one who is zealous for the law and supports the covenant come out with me!" 28And he and his sons fled to the hills and left all that they had in the city.

29Then many who were seeking righteousness and justice went down to the wilderness to dwell there, 30they, their sons, their wives, and their cattle, because evils pressed heavily upon them. 31And it was reported to the king's officers, and to the troops in Jerusalem the city of David, that men who had rejected the king's command had gone down to the hiding places in the wilderness. 32Many pursued them, and overtook them; they encamped opposite them and prepared for battle against them on the sabbath day. 33And they said to them, "Enough of this! Come out and do what the king commands, and you will live." 34But they said, "We will not come out, nor will we do what the king commands and so profane the sabbath day." 35Then the enemy hastened to attack them. 36But they did not answer them or hurl a stone at them or block up their hiding places, 37for they said, "Let us all die in our innocence; heaven and earth testify for us that you are killing us unjustly." 38So they attacked them on the sabbath, and they died, with their wives and children and cattle, to the number of a thousand persons.

39When Mattathi´as and his friends learned of it, they mourned for them deeply. 40And each said to his neighbor: "If we all do as our brethren have done and refuse to fight with the Gentiles for our lives and for our ordinances, they will quickly destroy us from the earth." 41So they made this decision that day: "Let us fight against every man who comes to attack us on the sabbath day; let us not all die as our brethren died in their hiding places."

SIRACH 40

12All bribery and injustice will be
blotted out,
but good faith will stand for ever.
13The wealth of the unjust will dry up
like a torrent,
and crash like a loud clap of thunder
in a rain.
14A generous man will be made glad;
likewise transgressors will utterly fail.
15The children of the ungodly will not put
forth many branches;
they are unhealthy roots upon sheer rock.
16The reeds by any water or river bank
will be plucked up before any grass.
17Kindness is like a garden of blessings,
and almsgiving endures for ever.

1 JOHN 4

7Beloved, let us love one another; for love is of God, and he who loves is born of God and knows God. 8He who does not love does not know God; for God is love. 9In this the love of God was made manifest among us, that God sent his only-begotten Son into the world, so that we might live through him. 10In this is love, not that we loved God but that he loved us and sent his Son to be the expiation for our sins. 11Beloved, if God so loved us, we also ought to love one another. 12No man has ever seen God; if we love one another, God abides in us and his love is perfected in us.

13By this we know that we abide in him and he in us, because he has given us of

his own Spirit. [14]And we have seen and
testify that the Father has sent his Son
as the Savior of the world. [15]Whoever
confesses that Jesus is the Son of God, God
abides in him, and he in God. [16]So we know
and believe the love God has for us. God
is love, and he who abides in love abides
in God, and God abides in him. [17]In this
is love perfected with us, that we may have
confidence for the day of judgment, because
as he is so are we in this world. [18]There is no
fear in love, but perfect love casts out fear.
For fear has to do with punishment, and he
who fears is not perfected in love. [19]We love,
because he first loved us. [20]If any one says, "I
love God," and hates his brother, he is a liar;
for he who does not love his brother whom
he has seen, cannot love God whom he has
not seen. [21]And this commandment we have
from him, that he who loves God should
love his brother also.

REFLECTION

Sirach contrasts two very different uses of wealth. In the first, an unjust man uses his wealth for bribes and gaining influence. In the other, a generous man uses his wealth, not as a means of power and influence, but for charity. Thus, charitable giving is compared to a garden, perhaps even Eden, and the fruit of almsgiving is everlasting: "Kindness is like a garden of blessings, and almsgiving endures for ever" (Sir 40:17). The beloved disciple, St. John, gives a deep yet simple theology of God: "God is love" (1 John 4:8). This profound insight is proven by the fact that God gave his Son as "expiation for our sins" (v. 10). Given the love God gave to us, even when we did not deserve it—and here is Christianity's unique position on love—we ought to love others even if they don't deserve it. While love is common to all of humanity, Christians believe that we must love those who are undeserving of our love. Thus, John concludes that we cannot love God and hate others. Why does John insist that loving everyone, regardless of their merit, is the normative behavior of all Christians?

December 9

1 MACCABEES 2

**[42]Then there united with them
a company of Hasid′eans, mighty
warriors of Israel, every one who
offered himself willingly for the law. [43]And
all who became fugitives to escape their
troubles joined them and reinforced**
them. [44]They organized an army, and struck
down sinners in their anger and lawless
men in their wrath; the survivors fled to
the Gentiles for safety. [45]And Mattathi′as
and his friends went about and tore down
the altars; [46]they forcibly circumcised all
the uncircumcised boys that they found
within the borders of Israel. [47]They hunted
down the arrogant men, and the work
prospered in their hands. [48]They rescued
the law out of the hands of the Gentiles and
kings, and they never let the sinner gain
the upper hand.

[49]Now the days drew near for Mattathi′as
to die, and he said to his sons: "Arrogance
and reproach have now become strong; it
is a time of ruin and furious anger. [50]Now,
my children, show zeal for the law, and give
your lives for the covenant of our fathers.

[51]"Remember the deeds of the fathers,
which they did in their generations; and
receive great honor and an everlasting
name. [52]Was not Abraham found faithful
when tested, and it was reckoned to him
as righteousness? [53]Joseph in the time of
his distress kept the commandment, and
became lord of Egypt. [54]Phin′ehas our father,
because he was deeply zealous, received the
covenant of everlasting priesthood. [55]Joshua,
because he fulfilled the command, became a
judge in Israel. [56]Caleb, because he testified
in the assembly, received an inheritance in
the land. [57]David, because he was merciful,
inherited the throne of the kingdom for ever.
[58]Eli′jah because of great zeal for the law was
taken up into heaven. [59]Hanani′ah, Azari′ah,
and Mish′a-el believed and were saved from

the flame. 60 Daniel because of his innocence was delivered from the mouth of the lions.

61 "And so observe, from generation to generation, that none who put their trust in him will lack strength. 62 Do not fear the words of a sinner, for his splendor will turn into dung and worms. 63 Today he will be exalted, but tomorrow he will not be found, because he has returned to the dust, and his plans will perish. 64 My children, be courageous and grow strong in the law, for by it you will gain honor.

65 "Now behold, I know that Simeon your brother is wise in counsel; always listen to him; he shall be your father. 66 Judas Mac″cabe′us has been a mighty warrior from his youth; he shall command the army for you and fight the battle against the peoples. 67 You shall rally about you all who observe the law, and avenge the wrong done to your people. 68 Pay back the Gentiles in full, and heed what the law commands."

69 Then he blessed them, and was gathered to his fathers. 70 He died in the one hundred and forty-sixth year and was buried in the tomb of his fathers at Mo′dein. And all Israel mourned for him with great lamentation.

3 Then Judas his son, who was called Mac″cabe′us, took command in his place. 2 All his brothers and all who had joined his father helped him; they gladly fought for Israel.

3 He extended the glory of his people.
Like a giant he put on his breastplate;
he belted on his armor of war and
waged battles,
protecting the host by his sword.
4 He was like a lion in his deeds,
like a lion's cub roaring for prey.
5 He searched out and pursued the lawless;
he burned those who troubled his people.
6 Lawless men shrank back for fear of him;
all the evildoers were confounded;
and deliverance prospered by his hand.
7 He embittered many kings,
but he made Jacob glad by his deeds,
and his memory is blessed for ever.
8 He went through the cities of Judah;
he destroyed the ungodly out of the land;
thus he turned away wrath from Israel.
9 He was renowned to the ends of the earth;
he gathered in those who were perishing.

10 But Apollo′nius gathered together Gentiles and a large force from Samar′ia to fight against Israel. 11 When Judas learned of it, he went out to meet him, and he defeated and killed him. Many were wounded and fell, and the rest fled. 12 Then they seized their spoils; and Judas took the sword of Apollo′nius, and used it in battle the rest of his life.

13 Now when Se′ron, the commander of the Syrian army, heard that Judas had gathered a large company, including a body of faithful men who stayed with him and went out to battle, 14 he said, "I will make a name for myself and win honor in the kingdom. I will make war on Judas and his companions, who scorn the king's command." 15 And again a strong army of ungodly men went up with him to help him, to take vengeance on the sons of Israel.

16 When he approached the ascent of Beth-ho′ron, Judas went out to meet him with a small company. 17 But when they saw the army coming to meet them, they said to Judas, "How can we, few as we are, fight against so great and strong a multitude? And we are faint, for we have eaten nothing today." 18 Judas replied, "It is easy for many to be hemmed in by few, for in the sight of Heaven there is no difference between saving by many or by few. 19 It is not on the size of the army that victory in battle depends, but strength comes from Heaven. 20 They come against us in great pride and lawlessness to destroy us and our wives and our children, and to despoil us; 21 but we fight for our lives and our laws. 22 He himself will crush them before us; as for you, do not be afraid of them."

23 When he finished speaking, he rushed suddenly against Se′ron and his army, and they were crushed before him. 24 They pursued them down the descent of Beth-ho′ron to the plain; eight hundred of them fell, and the rest fled into the land of the Philis′tines. 25 Then Judas and his brothers began to be feared, and terror fell upon the Gentiles round about them. 26 His fame

reached the king, and the Gentiles talked of
the battles of Judas.
27 When king Anti′ochus heard these
reports, he was greatly angered; and he sent
and gathered all the forces of his kingdom,
a very strong army. 28 And he opened his
coffers and gave a year's pay to his forces,
and ordered them to be ready for any need.
29 Then he saw that the money in the treasury
was exhausted, and that the revenues from
the country were small because of the
dissension and disaster which he had caused
in the land by abolishing the laws that had
existed from the earliest days. 30 He feared
that he might not have such funds as he
had before for his expenses and for the gifts
which he used to give more lavishly than
preceding kings. 31 He was greatly perplexed
in mind, and determined to go to Persia and
collect the revenues from those regions and
raise a large fund.
32 He left Lys′ias, a distinguished man of
royal lineage, in charge of the king's affairs
from the river Euphra′tes to the borders
of Egypt. 33 Lys′ias was also to take care
of Anti′ochus his son until he returned.
34 And he turned over to Lys′ias half of his
troops and the elephants, and gave him
orders about all that he wanted done. As
for the residents of Judea and Jerusalem,
35 Lys′ias was to send a force against them
to wipe out and destroy the strength of
Israel and the remnant of Jerusalem; he
was to banish the memory of them from
the place, 36 settle aliens in all their territory,
and distribute their land. 37 Then the king
took the remaining half of his troops and
departed from Antioch his capital in the one
hundred and forty-seventh year. He crossed
the Euphra′tes river and went through the
upper provinces.
38 Lys′ias chose Ptol′emy the son of
Dorym′enes, and Nica′nor and Gor′gias,
mighty men among the friends of the king,
39 and sent with them forty thousand infantry
and seven thousand cavalry to go into the
land of Judah and destroy it, as the king
had commanded. 40 So they departed with
their entire force, and when they arrived
they encamped near Emma′us in the plain.
41 When the traders of the region heard what
was said of them, they took silver and gold
in immense amounts, and shackles, and
went to the camp to get the sons of Israel for
slaves. And forces from Syria and the land of
the Philis′tines joined with them.
42 Now Judas and his brothers saw that
misfortunes had increased and that the forces
were encamped in their territory. They also
learned what the king had commanded to do
to the people to cause their final destruction.
43 But they said to one another, "Let us repair
the destruction of our people, and fight for
our people and the sanctuary." 44 And the
congregation assembled to be ready for battle,
and to pray and ask for mercy and compassion.
45 Jerusalem was uninhabited like
a wilderness;
not one of her children went in or out.
The sanctuary was trampled down,
and the sons of aliens held the citadel;
it was a lodging place for the Gentiles.
Joy was taken from Jacob;
the flute and the harp ceased to play.
46 So they assembled and went to Mizpah,
opposite Jerusalem, because Israel formerly
had a place of prayer in Mizpah. 47 They
fasted that day, put on sackcloth and
sprinkled ashes on their heads, and tore
their clothes. 48 And they opened the book of
the law to inquire into those matters about
which the Gentiles were consulting the
images of their idols. 49 They also brought
the garments of the priesthood and the first
fruits and the tithes, and they stirred up the
Naz′irites who had completed their days;
50 and they cried aloud to Heaven, saying,
"What shall we do with these?
Where shall we take them?
51 Your sanctuary is trampled down
and profaned,
and your priests mourn in humiliation.
52 And behold, the Gentiles are assembled
against us to destroy us;
you know what they plot against us.
53 How will we be able to withstand them,
if you do not help us?"
54 Then they sounded the trumpets and gave
a loud shout. 55 After this Judas appointed
leaders of the people, in charge of thousands

and hundreds and fifties and tens. 56And he
said to those who were building houses, or
were betrothed, or were planting vineyards,
or were fainthearted, that each should return
to his home, according to the law. 57Then
the army marched out and encamped to the
south of Emma′us.
58And Judas said, "Gird yourselves and
be valiant. Be ready early in the morning
to fight with these Gentiles who have assembled against us to destroy us and our
sanctuary. 59It is better for us to die in battle
than to see the misfortunes of our nation
and of the sanctuary. 60But as his will in
heaven may be, so he will do."

27The fear of the Lord is like a garden
of blessing,
and covers a man better than any glory.
28My son, do not lead the life of a beggar;
it is better to die than to beg.
29When a man looks to the table of another,
his existence cannot be considered as life.
He pollutes himself with another man's
food,
but a man who is intelligent and well
instructed guards against that.
30In the mouth of the shameless begging
is sweet,
but in his stomach a fire is kindled.

SIRACH 40

18Life is sweet for the self-reliant and
the worker,
but he who finds treasure is better
off than both.
19Children and the building of a city
establish a man's name,
but a blameless wife is accounted
better than both.
20Wine and music gladden the heart,
but the love of wisdom is better than both.
21The flute and the harp make pleasant
melody,
but a pleasant voice is better than both.
22The eye desires grace and beauty,
but the green shoots of grain more
than both.
23A friend or a companion never meets
one amiss,
but a wife with her husband is better
than both.
24Brothers and help are for a time of trouble,
but almsgiving rescues better than both.
25Gold and silver make the foot stand sure,
but good counsel is esteemed more
than both.
26Riches and strength lift up the heart,
but the fear of the Lord is better
than both.
There is no loss in the fear of the Lord,
and with it there is no need to seek
for help.

1 JOHN 5

Every one who believes that Jesus is the Christ has been born of God, and every one who loves the parent loves the one begotten by him. 2By this we
know that we love the children of God, when
we love God and obey his commandments.
3For this is the love of God, that we keep his
commandments. And his commandments are
not burdensome. 4For whatever is born of God
overcomes the world; and this is the victory
that overcomes the world, our faith. 5Who is it
that overcomes the world but he who believes
that Jesus is the Son of God?
6This is he who came by water and blood,
Jesus Christ, not with the water only but with
the water and the blood. 7And the Spirit is the
witness, because the Spirit is the truth. 8There
are three witnesses, the Spirit, the water, and
the blood; and these three agree. 9If we receive
the testimony of men, the testimony of God is
greater; for this is the testimony of God that
he has borne witness to his Son. 10He who
believes in the Son of God has the testimony
in himself. He who does not believe God has
made him a liar, because he has not believed in
the testimony that God has borne to his Son.
11And this is the testimony, that God gave us
eternal life, and this life is in his Son. 12He who
has the Son has life; he who has not the Son of
God has not life.

13I write this to you who believe in the name of the Son of God, that you may know that you have eternal life. 14And this is the confidence which we have in him, that if we ask anything according to his will he hears us. 15And if we know that he hears us in whatever we ask, we know that we have obtained the requests made of him. 16If any one sees his brother committing what is not a deadly sin, he will ask, and God will give him life for those whose sin is not deadly. There is sin which is deadly; I do not say that one is to pray for that. 17All wrongdoing is sin, but there is sin which is not deadly.

18We know that any one born of God does not sin, but He who was born of God keeps him, and the Evil One does not touch him.

19We know that we are of God, and the whole world is in the power of the Evil One.

20And we know that the Son of God has come and has given us understanding, to know him who is true; and we are in him who is true, in his Son Jesus Christ. This is the true God and eternal life. 21Little children, keep yourselves from idols.

REFLECTION

The sons of Mattathias are legendary heroes in the history of Israel and in the biblical story of Maccabees. But the apple does not fall far from the tree—the sons' rise to greatness is the fruit of their father's investment in their faith. As the cultural crisis sweeps over Israel, it is Mattathias who sparks the Jewish resistance. In the hour of crisis, he gives a remarkable speech telling the grand story, from Abraham to Daniel, of how their ancestors, when tested by tribulation, persevered by faith and courage. He begins with the call to "remember the deeds of the fathers," which means that as a father he is teaching his sons the key stories of Scripture—something that formed their hearts deeply (1 Mc 2:51). At the end of his account of Israel's greatest heroes, he impresses the main point for application in their lives: "And so observe, from generation to generation, that none who put their trust in him will lack strength" (v. 61). Armed with the examples of Israel's faithful heroes, and most immediately their father's living example, the sons of Mattathias will go out against all odds and win renown for themselves and glory for God. How does knowing Scripture's story and plot inform your own story today?

December 10

1 MACCABEES 4

Now Gor′gias took five thousand infantry and a thousand picked cavalry, and this division moved out by night 2to fall upon the camp of the Jews and attack them suddenly. Men from the citadel were his guides. 3But Judas heard of it, and he and his mighty men moved out to attack the king's force in Emma′us 4while the division was still absent from the camp. 5When Gor′gias entered the camp of Judas by night, he found no one there, so he looked for them in the hills, because he said, "These men are fleeing from us."

6At daybreak Judas appeared in the plain with three thousand men, but they did not have armor and swords such as they desired. 7And they saw the camp of the Gentiles, strong and fortified, with cavalry round about it; and these men were trained in war. 8But Judas said to the men who were with him, "Do not fear their numbers or be afraid when they charge. 9Remember how our fathers were saved at the Red Sea, when Pharaoh with his forces pursued them. 10And now let us cry to Heaven, to see whether he will favor us and remember his covenant with our fathers and crush this army before us today. 11Then all the Gentiles will know that there is one who redeems and saves Israel."

12When the foreigners looked up and saw them coming against them, 13they went forth from their camp to battle. Then the men with Judas blew their trumpets 14and engaged in battle. The Gentiles were crushed and fled into the plain, 15and all those in the rear fell by the sword. They pursued them to Gaza′ra, and to the plains of Idume′a, and to Azo′tus and Jam′nia; and three thousand of them fell. 16Then Judas and his force turned back from pursuing them, 17and he said to the people, "Do not be greedy for plunder, for there is a battle before us; 18Gor′gias and his force are

near us in the hills. But stand now against our
enemies and fight them, and afterward seize
the plunder boldly."

19 Just as Judas was finishing this speech,
a detachment appeared, coming out of the
hills. 20 They saw that their army had been
put to flight, and that the Jews were burning
the camp, for the smoke that was seen
showed what had happened. 21 When they
perceived this they were greatly frightened,
and when they also saw the army of Judas
drawn up in the plain for battle, 22 they all
fled into the land of the Philis′tines. 23 Then
Judas returned to plunder the camp, and
they seized much gold and silver, and cloth
dyed blue and sea purple, and great riches.
24 On their return they sang hymns and
praises to Heaven, for he is good, for his
mercy endures for ever. 25 Thus Israel had a
great deliverance that day.

26 Those of the foreigners who escaped went
and reported to Lys′ias all that had happened.
27 When he heard it, he was perplexed and
discouraged, for things had not happened to
Israel as he had intended, nor had they turned
out as the king had commanded him. 28 But the
next year he mustered sixty thousand picked
infantrymen and five thousand cavalry to
subdue them. 29 They came into Idume′a and
encamped at Beth-zur, and Judas met them
with ten thousand men.

30 When he saw that the army was strong,
he prayed, saying, "Blessed are you, O
Savior of Israel, who did crush the attack
of the mighty warrior by the hand of your
servant David, and did give the camp of the
Philis′tines into the hands of Jonathan, the
son of Saul, and of the man who carried
his armor. 31 So do you hem in this army
by the hand of your people Israel, and let
them be ashamed of their troops and their
cavalry. 32 Fill them with cowardice; melt the
boldness of their strength; let them tremble
in their destruction. 33 Strike them down
with the sword of those who love you, and
let all who know your name praise you with
hymns."

34 Then both sides attacked, and there fell
of the army of Lys′ias five thousand men;
they fell in action. 35 And when Lys′ias saw
the rout of his troops and observed the
boldness which inspired those of Judas, and
how ready they were either to live or to die
nobly, he departed to Antioch and enlisted
mercenaries, to invade Judea again with an
even larger army.

36 Then said Judas and his brothers, "Behold, our enemies are crushed; let us go
up to cleanse the sanctuary and dedicate
it." 37 So all the army assembled and they
went up to Mount Zion. 38 And they saw the
sanctuary desolate, the altar profaned, and
the gates burned. In the courts they saw
bushes sprung up as in a thicket, or as on
one of the mountains. They saw also the
chambers of the priests in ruins. 39 Then they
tore their clothes, and mourned with great
lamentation, and sprinkled themselves with
ashes. 40 They fell face down on the ground,
and sounded the signal on the trumpets,
and cried out to Heaven. 41 Then Judas
detailed men to fight against those in the
citadel until he had cleansed the sanctuary.

42 He chose blameless priests devoted to
the law, 43 and they cleansed the sanctuary
and removed the defiled stones to an
unclean place. 44 They deliberated what to
do about the altar of burnt offering, which
had been profaned. 45 And they thought it
best to tear it down, lest it bring reproach
upon them, for the Gentiles had defiled it.
So they tore down the altar, 46 and stored the
stones in a convenient place on the temple
hill until there should come a prophet to
tell what to do with them. 47 Then they took
unhewn stones, as the law directs, and built
a new altar like the former one. 48 They also
rebuilt the sanctuary and the interior of the
temple, and consecrated the courts. 49 They
made new holy vessels, and brought the
lampstand, the altar of incense, and the
table into the temple. 50 Then they burned
incense on the altar and lighted the lamps
on the lampstand, and these gave light in
the temple. 51 They placed the bread on the
table and hung up the curtains. Thus they
finished all the work they had undertaken.

52 Early in the morning on the twenty-fifth
day of the ninth month, which is the month
of Chis′lev, in the one hundred and forty-

eighth year, 53they rose and offered sacrifice,
as the law directs, on the new altar of burnt
offering which they had built. 54At the very
season and on the very day that the Gentiles
had profaned it, it was dedicated with
songs and harps and lutes and cymbals.
55All the people fell on their faces and
worshiped and blessed Heaven, who had
prospered them. 56So they celebrated the
dedication of the altar for eight days, and
offered burnt offerings with gladness; they
offered a sacrifice of deliverance and praise.
57They decorated the front of the temple
with golden crowns and small shields; they
restored the gates and the chambers for the
priests, and furnished them with doors.
58There was very great gladness among the
people, and the reproach of the Gentiles was
removed.

59Then Judas and his brothers and all the
assembly of Israel determined that every
year at that season the days of the dedication
of the altar should be observed with gladness
and joy for eight days, beginning with the
twenty-fifth day of the month of Chis'lev.

60At that time they fortified Mount Zion
with high walls and strong towers round
about, to keep the Gentiles from coming
and trampling them down as they had done
before. 61And he stationed a garrison there
to hold it. He also fortified Beth-zur, so that
the people might have a stronghold that
faced Idume'a.

SIRACH 41

O death, how bitter is the reminder of you
to one who lives at peace among his
possessions,
to a man without distractions, who is
prosperous in everything,
and who still has the vigor to enjoy
his food!
2O death, how welcome is your sentence
to one who is in need and is failing
in strength,
very old and distracted over everything;
to one who is contrary, and has lost
his patience!
3Do not fear the sentence of death;
remember your former days and the end
of life;
this is the decree from the Lord for
all flesh,
4 and how can you reject the good pleasure
of the Most High?
Whether life is for ten or a hundred or a
thousand years,
there is no inquiry about it in Hades.

5The children of sinners are abominable
children,
and they frequent the haunts of the
ungodly.
6The inheritance of the children of sinners
will perish,
and on their posterity will be a perpetual
reproach.
7Children will blame an ungodly father,
for they suffer reproach because of him.
8Woe to you, ungodly men,
who have forsaken the law of the Most
High God!
9When you are born, you are born to a curse;
and when you die, a curse is your lot.
10Whatever is from the dust returns to dust;
so the ungodly go from curse to
destruction.

11The mourning of men is about
their bodies,
but the evil name of sinners will
be blotted out.
12Have regard for your name, since it will
remain for you
longer than a thousand great stores
of gold.
13The days of a good life are numbered,
but a good name endures for ever.

2 JOHN

**The elder to the elect lady and
her children, whom I love in the
truth, and not only I but also all who know
the truth, 2because of the truth which
abides in us and will be with us for ever:**

3Grace, mercy, and peace will be with us,
from God the Father and from Jesus Christ
the Father's Son, in truth and love.
4I rejoiced greatly to find some of your
children following the truth, just as we have
been commanded by the Father. 5And now
I beg you, lady, not as though I were writing
you a new commandment, but the one we
have had from the beginning, that we love one
another. 6And this is love, that we follow his
commandments; this is the commandment, as
you have heard from the beginning, that you
follow love. 7For many deceivers have gone out
into the world, men who will not acknowledge
the coming of Jesus Christ in the flesh; such a
one is the deceiver and the antichrist. 8Look
to yourselves, that you may not lose what you
have worked for, but may win a full reward.
9Any one who goes ahead and does not abide
in the doctrine of Christ does not have God; he
who abides in the doctrine has both the Father
and the Son. 10If any one comes to you and does
not bring this doctrine, do not receive him into
the house or give him any greeting; 11for he
who greets him shares his wicked work.
12Though I have much to write to you, I
would rather not use paper and ink, but I
hope to come to see you and talk with you
face to face, so that our joy may be complete.
13The children of your elect sister greet you.

---

3 JOHN

The elder to the beloved Ga′ius, whom I love in the truth.

**2Beloved, I pray that all may go well
with you and that you may be in health;**
I know that it is well with your soul. 3For
I greatly rejoiced when some of the brethren
arrived and testified to the truth of your life, as
indeed you do follow the truth. 4No greater joy
can I have than this, to hear that my children
follow the truth.
5Beloved, it is a loyal thing you do when you
render any service to the brethren, especially
to strangers, 6who have testified to your love
before the Church. You will do well to send
them on their journey as befits God's service.
7For they have set out for his sake and have
accepted nothing from the heathen. 8So we
ought to support such men, that we may be
fellow workers in the truth.
9I have written something to the Church; but
Diot′rephes, who likes to put himself first,
does not acknowledge my authority. 10So
if I come, I will bring up what he is doing,
accusing me falsely with evil words. And
not content with that, he refuses himself to
welcome the brethren, and also stops those
who want to welcome them and puts them
out of the Church.
11Beloved, do not imitate evil but imitate
good. He who does good is of God; he who
does evil has not seen God. 12Deme′trius has
testimony from every one, and from the truth
itself; I testify to him too, and you know my
testimony is true.
13I had much to write to you, but I would
rather not write with pen and ink; 14I hope
to see you soon, and we will talk together
face to face.
15Peace be to you. The friends greet you.
Greet the friends, every one of them.

REFLECTION

Judas exhorts his men not to fear the greater numbers of their enemies, but rather to "remember how our fathers were saved at the Red Sea, when Pharaoh with his forces pursued them" (1 Mc 4:9). Like his father Mattathias, Judas calls upon a remembrance of God's saving deeds of the past to build trust in the present. Armed with this lively faith, they call upon God, who grants them victory. A memory soaked in Scripture is a memory fertile for faith. In St. John's last two letters, he brings together two key themes that are like arms by which he embraces his readers: the twin themes of truth and love. In his second letter, he extolls the "elect lady," the Church, because her children are "following the truth" (2 Jn 1:4). In his third letter to Gaius, he praises him saying you "follow the truth" (3 Jn 1:3). As deceitful teachers are spreading error, he reminds the faithful that being in the truth keeps us on the path to right loving. How would John react to those today who would divide truth and love, dogma and charity?

December 11

1 MACCABEES 5

**When the Gentiles round about
heard that the altar had been
built and the sanctuary dedicated as it was before, they became very
angry, 2and they determined to destroy
the descendants of Jacob who lived**
among them. So they began to kill and
destroy among the people. 3But Judas made
war on the sons of Esau in Idume′a, at
Ak″rabatte′ne, because they kept lying in
wait for Israel. He dealt them a heavy blow
and humbled them and despoiled them.
4He also remembered the wickedness of
the sons of Bae′an, who were a trap and a
snare to the people and ambushed them on
the highways. 5They were shut up by him
in their towers; and he encamped against
them, vowed their complete destruction,
and burned with fire their towers and
all who were in them. 6Then he crossed
over to attack the Am′monites, where he
found a strong band and many people
with Timothy as their leader. 7He engaged
in many battles with them and they were
crushed before him; he struck them down.
8He also took Ja′zer and its villages; then he
returned to Judea.

9Now the Gentiles in Gilead gathered together against the Israelites who lived in
their territory, and planned to destroy them.
But they fled to the stronghold of Dath′ema,
10and sent to Judas and his brothers a letter
which said, "The Gentiles around us have
gathered together against us to destroy us.
11They are preparing to come and capture
the stronghold to which we have fled, and
Timothy is leading their forces. 12Now
then come and rescue us from their hands,
for many of us have fallen, 13and all our
brethren who were in the land of Tob have
been killed; the enemy have captured their
wives and children and goods, and have
destroyed about a thousand men there."

14While the letter was still being read, behold, other messengers, with their garments
torn, came from Galilee and made a similar
report; 15they said that against them had
gathered together men of Ptolema′is and Tyre
and Si′don, and all Galilee of the Gentiles, "to
annihilate us." 16When Judas and the people
heard these messages, a great assembly was
called to determine what they should do for
their brethren who were in distress and were
being attacked by enemies. 17Then Judas said
to Simon his brother, "Choose your men and
go and rescue your brethren in Galilee; I and
Jonathan my brother will go to Gilead." 18But
he left Joseph, the son of Zechari′ah, and
Azari′ah, a leader of the people, with the rest
of the forces, in Judea to guard it; 19and he
gave them this command, "Take charge of
this people, but do not engage in battle with
the Gentiles until we return." 20Then three
thousand men were assigned to Simon to
go to Galilee, and eight thousand to Judas
for Gilead.

21So Simon went to Galilee and fought
many battles against the Gentiles, and the
Gentiles were crushed before him. 22He
pursued them to the gate of Ptolema′is, and
as many as three thousand of the Gentiles
fell, and he despoiled them. 23Then he took
the Jews of Galilee and Ar′batta, with their
wives and children, and all they possessed,
and led them to Judea with great rejoicing.

24Judas Mac″cabe′us and Jonathan his
brother crossed the Jordan and went three
days' journey into the wilderness. 25They
encountered the Nab″ate′ans, who met
them peaceably and told them all that
had happened to their brethren in Gilead:
26"Many of them have been shut up in
Bozrah and Bo′sor, in Al′ema and Chas′pho,
Ma′ked and Carna′im"—all these cities were
strong and large—27"and some have been
shut up in the other cities of Gilead; the
enemy are getting ready to attack the strongholds tomorrow and take and destroy all
these men in one day."

28Then Judas and his army quickly turned
back by the wilderness road to Bozrah; and
he took the city, and killed every male by the
edge of the sword; then he seized all its spoils

and burned it with fire. 29He departed from
there at night, and they went all the way to
the stronghold of Dath′ema. 30At dawn they
looked up, and behold, a large company, that
could not be counted, carrying ladders and
engines of war to capture the stronghold,
and attacking the Jews within. 31So Judas
saw that the battle had begun and that the
cry of the city went up to Heaven with
trumpets and loud shouts, 32and he said to
the men of his forces, "Fight today for your
brethren!" 33Then he came up behind them
in three companies, who sounded their
trumpets and cried aloud in prayer. 34And
when the army of Timothy realized that it
was Mac″cabe′us, they fled before him, and
he dealt them a heavy blow. As many as
eight thousand of them fell that day.

35Next he turned aside to Al′ema, and
fought against it and took it; and he killed
every male in it, plundered it, and burned it
with fire. 36From there he marched on and
took Chas′pho, Ma′ked, and Bo′sor, and the
other cities of Gilead.

37After these things Timothy gathered
another army and encamped opposite
Ra′phon on the other side of the stream.
38Judas sent men to spy out the camp,
and they reported to him, "All the
Gentiles around us have gathered to him;
it is a very large force. 39They also have
hired Arabs to help them, and they are
encamped across the stream, ready to
come and fight against you." And Judas
went to meet them.

40Now as Judas and his army drew near
to the stream of water, Timothy said to the
officers of his forces, "If he crosses over to
us first, we will not be able to resist him,
for he will surely defeat us. 41But if he
shows fear and camps on the other side
of the river, we will cross over to him and
defeat him." 42When Judas approached
the stream of water, he stationed the
scribes of the people at the stream and
gave them this command, "Permit no
man to encamp, but make them all enter
the battle." 43Then he crossed over against
them first, and the whole army followed
him. All the Gentiles were defeated before
him, and they threw away their arms and
fled into the sacred precincts at Carna′im.
44But he took the city and burned the
sacred precincts with fire, together with
all who were in them. Thus Carna′im was
conquered; they could stand before Judas
no longer.

45Then Judas gathered together all the
Israelites in Gilead, the small and the
great, with their wives and children and
goods, a very large company, to go to the
land of Judah. 46So they came to E′phron.
This was a large and very strong city on
the road, and they could not go round it
to the right or to the left; they had to go
through it. 47But the men of the city shut
them out and blocked up the gates with
stones. 48And Judas sent them this friendly
message, "Let us pass through your land
to get to our land. No one will do you
harm; we will simply pass by on foot." But
they refused to open to him. 49Then Judas
ordered proclamation to be made to the
army that each should encamp where he
was. 50So the men of the forces encamped,
and he fought against the city all that
day and all the night, and the city was
delivered into his hands. 51He destroyed
every male by the edge of the sword, and
razed and plundered the city. Then he
passed through the city over the slain.

52And they crossed the Jordan into
the large plain before Beth-shan. 53And
Judas kept rallying the laggards and
encouraging the people all the way till
he came to the land of Judah. 54So they
went up to Mount Zion with gladness and
joy, and offered burnt offerings, because
not one of them had fallen before they
returned in safety.

55Now while Judas and Jonathan were in
Gilead and Simon his brother was in Galilee
before Ptolema′is, 56Joseph, the son of
Zechari′ah, and Azari′ah, the commanders
of the forces, heard of their brave deeds and
of the heroic war they had fought. 57So they
said, "Let us also make a name for ourselves;
let us go and make war on the Gentiles
around us." 58And they issued orders to
the men of the forces that were with them,

and they marched against Jam′nia. [59]And Gor′gias and his men came out of the city to meet them in battle. [60]Then Joseph and Azari′ah were routed, and were pursued to the borders of Judea; as many as two thousand of the people of Israel fell that day. [61]Thus the people suffered a great rout because, thinking to do a brave deed, they did not listen to Judas and his brothers. [62]But they did not belong to the family of those men through whom deliverance was given to Israel.

[63]The man Judas and his brothers were greatly honored in all Israel and among all the Gentiles, wherever their name was heard. [64]Men gathered to them and praised them.

[65]Then Judas and his brothers went forth and fought the sons of Esau in the land to the south. He struck He′bron and its villages and tore down its strongholds and burned its towers round about. [66]Then he marched off to go into the land of the Philis′tines, and passed through Mar′isa. [67]On that day some priests, who wished to do a brave deed, fell in battle, for they went out to battle unwisely. [68]But Judas turned aside to Azo′tus in the land of the Philis′tines; he tore down their altars, and the graven images of their gods he burned with fire; he plundered the cities and returned to the land of Judah.

SIRACH 41

[14]My children, observe instruction and
be at peace;
hidden wisdom and unseen treasure,
what advantage is there in either of them?
[15]Better is the man who hides his folly
than the man who hides his wisdom.
[16]Therefore show respect for my words:
For it is not good to retain every kind
of shame,
and not everything is confidently
esteemed by every one.

[17]Be ashamed of immorality, before your
father or mother;
and of a lie, before a prince or a ruler;
[18]of a transgression, before a judge
or magistrate;
and of iniquity, before a congregation
or the people;
of unjust dealing, before your partner
or friend;
[19] and of theft, in the place where you live.
Be ashamed before the truth of God and
his covenant.
Be ashamed of selfish behavior at meals,
of surliness in receiving and giving,
[20] and of silence, before those who greet you;
of looking at a woman who is a harlot,
[21] and of rejecting the appeal of a kinsman;
of taking away some one's portion or gift,
and of gazing at another man's wife;
[22]of meddling with his maidservant—
and do not approach her bed;
of abusive words, before friends—
and do not upbraid after making a gift;
[23]of repeating and telling what you hear,
and of revealing secrets.
Then you will show proper shame,
and will find favor with every man.

JUDE

Jude, a servant of Jesus Christ and brother of James,

To those who are called, beloved in God the Father and kept for Jesus Christ:

[2]May mercy, peace, and love be multiplied to you.

[3]Beloved, being very eager to write to you of our common salvation, I found it necessary to write appealing to you to contend for the faith which was once for all delivered to the saints. [4]For admission has been secretly gained by some who long ago were designated for this condemnation, ungodly persons who pervert the grace of our God into licentiousness and deny our only Master and Lord, Jesus Christ.

[5]Now I desire to remind you, though you were once for all fully informed, that he who saved a people out of the land of Egypt, afterward destroyed those who did not believe. [6]And the angels that did not

keep their own position but left their proper dwelling have been kept by him in eternal chains in the deepest darkness until the judgment of the great day; 7just as Sodom and Gomor′rah and the surrounding cities, which likewise acted immorally and indulged in unnatural lust, serve as an example by undergoing a punishment of eternal fire.

8Yet in like manner these men in their dreamings defile the flesh, reject authority, and revile the glorious ones. 9But when the archangel Michael, contending with the devil, disputed about the body of Moses, he did not presume to pronounce a reviling judgment upon him, but said, "The Lord rebuke you." 10But these men revile whatever they do not understand, and by those things that they know by instinct as irrational animals do, they are destroyed. 11Woe to them! For they walk in the way of Cain, and abandon themselves for the sake of gain to Balaam's error, and perish in Ko′rah's rebellion. 12These are blemishes on your love feasts, as they boldly carouse together, looking after themselves; waterless clouds, carried along by winds; fruitless trees in late autumn, twice dead, uprooted; 13wild waves of the sea, casting up the foam of their own shame; wandering stars for whom the deepest darkness has been reserved for ever.

14It was of these also that Enoch in the seventh generation from Adam prophesied, saying, "Behold, the Lord came with myriads of his holy ones, 15to execute judgment on all, and to convict all the ungodly of all their deeds of ungodliness which they have committed in such an ungodly way, and of all the harsh things which ungodly sinners have spoken against him." 16These are grumblers, malcontents, following their own passions, loud-mouthed boasters, flattering people to gain advantage.

17But you must remember, beloved, the predictions of the apostles of our Lord Jesus Christ; 18they said to you, "In the last time there will be scoffers, following their own ungodly passions." 19It is these who set up divisions, worldly people, devoid of the Spirit. 20But you, beloved, build yourselves up on your most holy faith; pray in the Holy Spirit; 21keep yourselves in the love of God; wait for the mercy of our Lord Jesus Christ unto eternal life. 22And convince some, who doubt; 23save some, by snatching them out of the fire; on some have mercy with fear, hating even the garment spotted by the flesh.

24Now to him who is able to keep you from falling and to present you without blemish before the presence of his glory with rejoicing, 25to the only God, our Savior through Jesus Christ our Lord, be glory, majesty, dominion, and authority, before all time and now and for ever. Amen.

REFLECTION

Reading the letter from Jude gives us a glimpse into the life of the early Church. We know of the early zeal, enthusiasm, and heroic lives of many of the early Christians, a number of whom, like Sts. Peter and Paul, give their lives in martyrdom. However, St. Jude addresses the challenge that some who entered the Church continue to live and think like pagans, leading to divisions, confusion, and conflict within the young and vibrant community. Jude gives good advice to those who are earnest in living the Faith so that they do not lose heart. First, he reminds them that such divisions within the Church were predicted at the outset (recall Jesus's parables about the Church that spoke of division between the wheat and the weeds). He exhorts them, and us, not to let this fact work against our faith. Second, Jude recommends three things they must do for themselves: "build yourselves up" in the faith; "keep yourselves in the love of God"; and "wait for the mercy of our Lord" (Jude 1:20–21). Jude also recommends three things they should do regarding others: convince those who have doubts; work to save souls by evangelizing; and be merciful to others in the fear of the Lord (see vv. 22–23). Do you grow discouraged by the challenges faced by the Church? Or do you seek to grow in knowledge of the Faith, keep the love of God, and wait patiently upon the Lord?

December 12

1 MACCABEES 6

King Anti′ochus was going through the upper provinces when he heard that Elyma′is in Persia was a city famed for its wealth in silver and gold. [2]Its temple was very rich, containing golden shields, breastplates, and weapons left there by Alexander, the son of Philip, the Macedonian king who first reigned over the Greeks. [3]So he came and tried to take the city and plunder it, but he could not, because his plan became known to the men of the city [4]and they withstood him in battle. So he fled and in great grief departed from there to return to Babylon.

[5]Then some one came to him in Persia and reported that the armies which had gone into the land of Judah had been routed; [6]that Lys′ias had gone first with a strong force, but had turned and fled before the Jews; that the Jews had grown strong from the arms, supplies, and abundant spoils which they had taken from the armies they had cut down; [7]that they had torn down the abomination which he had erected upon the altar in Jerusalem; and that they had surrounded the sanctuary with high walls as before, and also Beth-zur, his city.

[8]When the king heard this news, he was astounded and badly shaken. He took to his bed and became sick from grief, because things had not turned out for him as he had planned. [9]He lay there for many days, because deep grief continually gripped him, and he concluded that he was dying. [10]So he called all his friends and said to them, "Sleep departs from my eyes and I am downhearted with worry. [11]I said to myself, 'To what distress I have come! And into what a great flood I now am plunged! For I was kind and beloved in my power.' [12]But now I remember the evils I did in Jerusalem. I seized all her vessels of silver and gold; and I sent to destroy the inhabitants of Judah without good reason. [13]I know that it is because of this that these evils have come upon me; and behold, I am perishing of deep grief in a strange land."

[14]Then he called for Philip, one of his friends, and made him ruler over all his kingdom. [15]He gave him the crown and his robe and the signet, that he might guide Anti′ochus his son and bring him up to be king. [16]Thus Anti′ochus the king died there in the one hundred and forty-ninth year. [17]And when Lys′ias learned that the king was dead, he set up Anti′ochus the king's son to reign. Lysias had brought him up as a boy, and he named him Eu′pator.

[18]Now the men in the citadel kept hemming Israel in around the sanctuary. They were trying in every way to harm them and strengthen the Gentiles. [19]So Judas decided to destroy them, and assembled all the people to besiege them. [20]They gathered together and besieged the citadel in the one hundred and fiftieth year; and he built siege towers and other engines of war. [21]But some of the garrison escaped from the siege and some of the ungodly Israelites joined them. [22]They went to the king and said, "How long will you fail to do justice and to avenge our brethren? [23]We were happy to serve your father, to live by what he said and to follow his commands. [24]For this reason the sons of our people besieged the citadel and became hostile to us; moreover, they have put to death as many of us as they have caught, and they have seized our inheritances. [25]And not against us alone have they stretched out their hands, but also against all the lands on their borders. [26]And behold, today they have encamped against the citadel in Jerusalem to take it; they have fortified both the sanctuary and Beth-zur; [27]and unless you quickly prevent them, they will do still greater things, and you will not be able to stop them."

[28]The king was enraged when he heard this. He assembled all his friends, the commanders of his forces and those in authority. [29]And mercenary forces came to him from other kingdoms and from islands of the seas. [30]The number of his

forces was a hundred thousand foot soldiers, twenty thousand horsemen, and thirty-two elephants accustomed to war. [31]They came through Idume'a and encamped against Beth-zur, and for many days they fought and built engines of war; but the Jews sallied out and burned these with fire, and fought manfully.

[32]Then Judas marched away from the citadel and encamped at Beth-zech"ari'ah, opposite the camp of the king. [33]Early in the morning the king rose and took his army by a forced march along the road to Beth-zech"ari'ah, and his troops made ready for battle and sounded their trumpets. [34]They showed the elephants the juice of grapes and mulberries, to arouse them for battle. [35]And they distributed the beasts among the phalanxes; with each elephant they stationed a thousand men armed with coats of mail, and with brass helmets on their heads; and five hundred picked horsemen were assigned to each beast. [36]These took their position beforehand wherever the beast was; wherever it went they went with it, and they never left it. [37]And upon the elephants were wooden towers, strong and covered; they were fastened upon each beast by special harness, and upon each were four armed men who fought from there, and also its Indian driver. [38]The rest of the horsemen were stationed on either side, on the two flanks of the army, to harass the enemy while being themselves protected by the phalanxes. [39]When the sun shone upon the shields of gold and brass, the hills were ablaze with them and gleamed like flaming torches.

[40]Now a part of the king's army was spread out on the high hills, and some troops were on the plain, and they advanced steadily and in good order. [41]All who heard the noise made by their multitude, by the marching of the multitude and the clanking of their arms, trembled, for the army was very large and strong. [42]But Judas and his army advanced to the battle, and six hundred men of the king's army fell. [43]And Elea'zar, called Av'aran, saw that one of the beasts was equipped with royal armor. It was taller than all the others, and he supposed that the king was upon it. [44]So he gave his life to save his people and to win for himself an everlasting name. [45]He courageously ran into the midst of the phalanx to reach it; he killed men right and left, and they parted before him on both sides. [46]He got under the elephant, stabbed it from beneath, and killed it; but it fell to the ground upon him and there he died. [47]And when the Jews saw the royal might and the fierce attack of the forces, they turned away in flight.

[48]The soldiers of the king's army went up to Jerusalem against them, and the king encamped in Judea and at Mount Zion. [49]He made peace with the men of Beth-zur, and they evacuated the city, because they had no provisions there to withstand a siege, since it was a sabbatical year for the land. [50]So the king took Beth-zur and stationed a guard there to hold it. [51]Then he encamped before the sanctuary for many days. He set up siege towers, engines of war to throw fire and stones, machines to shoot arrows, and catapults. [52]The Jews also made engines of war to match theirs, and fought for many days. [53]But they had no food in storage, because it was the seventh year; those who found safety in Judea from the Gentiles had consumed the last of the stores. [54]Few men were left in the sanctuary, because famine had prevailed over the rest and they had been scattered, each to his own place.

[55]Then Lys'ias heard that Philip, whom King Anti'ochus while still living had appointed to bring up Antiochus his son to be king, [56]had returned from Persia and Med'ia with the forces that had gone with the king, and that he was trying to seize control of the government. [57]So he quickly gave orders to depart, and said to the king, to the commanders of the forces, and to the men, "We daily grow weaker, our food supply is scant, the place against which we are fighting is strong, and the affairs of the kingdom press urgently upon us. [58]Now then let us come to terms with these men,

and make peace with them and with all their
nation, 59and agree to let them live by their
laws as they did before; for it was on account
of their laws which we abolished that they
became angry and did all these things."
60The speech pleased the king and the
commanders, and he sent to the Jews an offer
of peace, and they accepted it. 61So the king
and the commanders gave them their oath.
On these conditions the Jews evacuated the
stronghold. 62But when the king entered
Mount Zion and saw what a strong fortress
the place was, he broke the oath he had
sworn and gave orders to tear down the wall
all around. 63Then he departed with haste
and returned to Antioch. He found Philip
in control of the city, but he fought against
him, and took the city by force.

SIRACH 42

Of the following things do not be ashamed,
and do not let partiality lead you to sin:
2of the law of the Most High and his
covenant,
and of rendering judgment to acquit
the ungodly;
3of keeping accounts with a partner or with
traveling companions,
and of dividing the inheritance of friends;
4of accuracy with scales and weights,
and of acquiring much or little;
5of profit from dealing with merchants,
and of much discipline of children,
and of whipping a wicked servant severely.
6Where there is an evil wife, a seal is a
good thing;
and where there are many hands,
lock things up.
7Whatever you deal out, let it be by number
and weight,
and make a record of all that you give out
or take in.
8Do not be ashamed to instruct the stupid
or foolish
or the aged man who quarrels with
the young.
Then you will be truly instructed,
and will be approved before all men.
9A daughter keeps her father secretly wakeful,
and worry over her robs him of sleep;
when she is young, lest she not marry,
or if married, lest she be hated;
10while a virgin, lest she be defiled
or become pregnant in her father's house;
or having a husband, lest she prove
unfaithful,
or, though married, lest she be barren.
11Keep strict watch over a headstrong
daughter,
lest she make you a laughingstock to
your enemies,
a byword in the city and notorious among
the people,
and put you to shame before the great
multitude.

12Do not look upon any one for beauty,
and do not sit in the midst of women;
13for from garments comes the moth,
and from a woman comes woman's
wickedness.
14Better is the wickedness of a man than a
woman who does good;
and it is a woman who brings shame
and disgrace.

REVELATION 1

**The revelation of Jesus Christ,
which God gave him to show to
his servants what must soon take place;
and he made it known by sending his**
angel to his servant John, 2who bore witness
to the word of God and to the testimony of
Jesus Christ, even to all that he saw. 3Blessed
is he who reads aloud the words of the
prophecy, and blessed are those who hear,
and who keep what is written therein; for
the time is near.

4John to the seven churches that are in
Asia:
Grace to you and peace from him who is
and who was and who is to come, and from
the seven spirits who are before his throne,
5and from Jesus Christ the faithful witness,

the first-born of the dead, and the ruler of kings on earth.

To him who loves us and has freed us from our sins by his blood 6and made us a kingdom, priests to his God and Father, to him be glory and dominion for ever and ever. Amen. 7Behold, he is coming with the clouds, and every eye will see him, every one who pierced him; and all tribes of the earth will wail on account of him. Even so. Amen.

8"I am the Alpha and the Omega," says the Lord God, who is and who was and who is to come, the Almighty.

9I John, your brother, who share with you in Jesus the tribulation and the kingdom and the patient endurance, was on the island called Patmos on account of the word of God and the testimony of Jesus. 10I was in the Spirit on the Lord's day, and I heard behind me a loud voice like a trumpet 11saying, "Write what you see in a book and send it to the seven churches, to Ephesus and to Smyrna and to Per′gamum and to Thyati′ra and to Sardis and to Philadelphia and to La-odice′a."

12Then I turned to see the voice that was speaking to me, and on turning I saw seven golden lampstands, 13and in the midst of the lampstands one like a Son of man, clothed with a long robe and with a golden sash across his chest; 14his head and his hair were white as white wool, white as snow; his eyes were like a flame of fire, 15his feet were like burnished bronze, refined as in a furnace, and his voice was like the sound of many waters; 16in his right hand he held seven stars, from his mouth issued a sharp two-edged sword, and his face was like the sun shining in full strength.

17When I saw him, I fell at his feet as though dead. But he laid his right hand upon me, saying, "Fear not, I am the first and the last, 18and the living one; I died, and behold I am alive for evermore, and I have the keys of Death and Hades. 19Now write what you see, what is and what is to take place hereafter. 20As for the mystery of the seven stars which you saw in my right hand, and the seven golden lampstands, the seven stars are the angels of the seven churches and the seven lampstands are the seven churches."

REFLECTION

Jesus, risen in glory, instructs John, the beloved disciple, to write the Book of Revelation "to the seven churches that are in Asia" (Rev 1:4). However, the focus of this revelation does not stop with these seven churches, for as John sees Jesus in glory, the Lord is standing amidst seven lampstands, which represent the Church. Jesus's presence amidst the Church is the first "mystery" (v. 20) we encounter. John introduces himself to those in the Church as their "brother" who shares with them in the "tribulation" and "kingdom," along with sharing in the "patient endurance" (v. 9) that will be important for those faithful to Christ in the midst of the world. Part of what is to be revealed is the suffering that must be endured by the Church, which may be why a special blessing is attached for those who can endure to read and hear this book (v. 3). The seven churches are listed in the order of the Roman postal system for that district, which speaks to the historical accuracy of Revelation. Given the present and future suffering, could the most important part of the revelation be that Jesus is not standing alone but amidst the Church, and that in the end he is seen holding the Church in his hand (see v. 20)? When faced with suffering, do you realize that Christ is there with you?

December 13

1 MACCABEES 7

In the one hundred and fifty-first year Deme′trius the son of Seleu′cus set forth from Rome, sailed with a few men to a city by the sea, and there began to reign. 2As he was entering the royal palace of his fathers, the army seized Anti′ochus and Lys′ias to bring them to him. 3But when this act became known to him, he said, "Do not let me see their faces!" 4So the army killed them, and Deme′trius took his seat upon the throne of his kingdom.

5Then there came to him all the lawless and ungodly men of Israel; they were led by Al′cimus, who wanted to be high priest. 6And they brought to the king this accusation against the people: "Judas and his brothers have destroyed all your friends, and have driven us out of our land. 7Now then send a man whom you trust; let him go and see all the ruin which Judas has brought upon us and upon the land of the king, and let him punish them and all who help them."

8So the king chose Bacchi′des, one of the king's friends, governor of the province Beyond the River; he was a great man in the kingdom and was faithful to the king. 9And he sent him, and with him the ungodly Al′cimus, whom he made high priest; and he commanded him to take vengeance on the sons of Israel. 10So they marched away and came with a large force into the land of Judah; and he sent messengers to Judas and his brothers with peaceable but treacherous words. 11But they paid no attention to their words, for they saw that they had come with a large force.

12Then a group of scribes appeared in a body before Al′cimus and Bacchi′des to ask for just terms. 13The Hasid′eans were first among the sons of Israel to seek peace from them, 14for they said, "A priest of the line of Aaron has come with the army, and he will not harm us." 15And he spoke peaceable words to them and swore this oath to them, "We will not seek to injure you or your friends." 16So they trusted him; but he seized sixty of them and killed them in one day, in accordance with the word which was written,

17"The flesh of your saints and their blood
they poured out round about Jerusalem,
and there was none to bury them."

18Then the fear and dread of them fell upon all the people, for they said, "There is no truth or justice in them, for they have violated the agreement and the oath which they swore."

19Then Bacchi′des departed from Jerusalem and encamped in Beth-za′ith. And he sent and seized many of the men who had deserted to him, and some of the people, and killed them and threw them into the great pit. 20He placed Al′cimus in charge of the country and left with him a force to help him; then Bacchi′des went back to the king.

21Al′cimus strove for the high priesthood, 22and all who were troubling their people joined him. They gained control of the land of Judah and did great damage in Israel. 23And Judas saw all the evil that Al′cimus and those with him had done among the sons of Israel; it was more than the Gentiles had done. 24So Judas went out into all the surrounding parts of Judea, and took vengeance on the men who had deserted, and he prevented those in the city from going out into the country. 25When Al′cimus saw that Judas and those with him had grown strong, and realized that he could not withstand them, he returned to the king and brought wicked charges against them.

26Then the king sent Nica′nor, one of his honored princes, who hated and detested Israel, and he commanded him to destroy the people. 27So Nica′nor came to Jerusalem with a large force, and treacherously sent to Judas and his brothers this peaceable message, 28"Let there be no fighting between me and you; I shall come with a few men to see you face to face in peace." 29So he came to Judas, and they greeted one another peaceably. But the enemy were ready to seize Judas. 30It became known to Judas that Nica′nor had come to him with treacherous intent, and he was afraid of him and would not meet him again. 31When Nica′nor learned that his plan had been disclosed, he went out to meet Judas in battle near Caph″arsal′ama. 32About five hundred men of the army of Nica′nor fell, and the rest fled into the city of David.

33After these events Nica′nor went up to Mount Zion. Some of the priests came out of the sanctuary, and some of the elders of the people, to greet him peaceably and to show him the burnt offering that was being offered for the king. 34But he mocked them and derided them and defiled them and spoke arrogantly, 35and in anger he swore this oath, "Unless Judas and his army are delivered into my hands this time, then if

I return safely I will burn up this house."
And he went out in great anger. 36 Then the
priests went in and stood before the altar
and the temple, and they wept and said,
37 "You chose this house to be called by your
name,
and to be for your people a house of
prayer and supplication.
38 Take vengeance on this man and on
his army,
and let them fall by the sword;
remember their blasphemies,
and let them live no longer."
39 Now Nica′nor went out from Jerusalem
and encamped in Beth-ho′ron, and the
Syrian army joined him. 40 And Judas
encamped in Ad′asa with three thousand
men. Then Judas prayed and said, 41 "When
the messengers from the king spoke
blasphemy, your angel went forth and
struck down one hundred and eighty-five
thousand of the Assyrians. 42 So also crush
this army before us today; let the rest learn
that Nica′nor has spoken wickedly against
your sanctuary, and judge him according
to this wickedness." 43 So the armies met in
battle on the thirteenth day of the month of
Adar′. The army of Nica′nor was crushed,
and he himself was the first to fall in the
battle. 44 When his army saw that Nica′nor
had fallen, they threw down their arms
and fled. 45 The Jews pursued them a day's
journey, from Ad′asa as far as Gaza′ra, and
as they followed kept sounding the battle
call on the trumpets. 46 And men came out
of all the villages of Judea round about,
and they outflanked the enemy and drove
them back to their pursuers, so that they
all fell by the sword; not even one of them
was left. 47 Then the Jews seized the spoils
and the plunder, and they cut off Nica′nor's
head and the right hand which he so
arrogantly stretched out, and brought them
and displayed them just outside Jerusalem.
48 The people rejoiced greatly and celebrated
that day as a day of great gladness. 49 And
they decreed that this day should be
celebrated each year on the thirteenth day
of Adar′. 50 So the land of Judah had rest for
a few days.

8 Now Judas heard of the fame of the
Romans, that they were very strong and
were well-disposed toward all who made
an alliance with them, that they pledged
friendship to those who came to them, 2 and
that they were very strong. Men told him
of their wars and of the brave deeds which
they were doing among the Gauls, how they
had defeated them and forced them to pay
tribute, 3 and what they had done in the
land of Spain to get control of the silver and
gold mines there, 4 and how they had gained
control of the whole region by their planning
and patience, even though the place was
far distant from them. They also subdued
the kings who came against them from the
ends of the earth, until they crushed them
and inflicted great disaster upon them; the
rest paid them tribute every year. 5 Philip,
and Per′seus king of the Macedonians, and
the others who rose up against them, they
crushed in battle and conquered. 6 They
also defeated Anti′ochus the Great, king of
Asia, who went to fight against them with
a hundred and twenty elephants and with
cavalry and chariots and a very large army.
He was crushed by them; 7 they took him
alive and decreed that he and those who
should reign after him should pay a heavy
tribute and give hostages and surrender some
of their best provinces, 8 the country of India
and Med′ia and Lyd′ia. These they took from
him and gave to Eu′menes the king. 9 The
Greeks planned to come and destroy them,
10 but this became known to them, and they
sent a general against the Greeks and attacked
them. Many of them were wounded and fell,
and the Romans took captive their wives and
children; they plundered them, conquered
the land, tore down their strongholds, and
enslaved them to this day. 11 The remaining
kingdoms and islands, as many as ever
opposed them, they destroyed and enslaved;
12 but with their friends and those who rely
on them they have kept friendship. They
have subdued kings far and near, and as
many as have heard of their fame have feared
them. 13 Those whom they wish to help and
to make kings, they make kings, and those
whom they wish they depose; and they have

been greatly exalted. [14]Yet for all this not one of them has put on a crown or worn purple as a mark of pride,[15]but they have built for themselves a senate chamber, and every day three hundred and twenty senators constantly deliberate concerning the people, to govern them well. [16]They trust one man each year to rule over them and to control all their land; they all heed the one man, and there is no envy or jealousy among them.

SIRACH 42

[15]I will now call to mind the works of
the Lord,
and will declare what I have seen.
By the words of the Lord his works
are done,
and in his will, justice is carried out.
[16]The sun looks down on everything
with its light,
and the work of the Lord is full of
his glory.
[17]The Lord has not enabled his holy ones
to recount all his marvelous works,
which the Lord the Almighty has established
that the universe may stand firm in
his glory.
[18]He searches out the abyss, and the
hearts of men,
and considers their crafty devices.
For the Most High knows all that may
be known,
and he looks into the signs of the age.
[19]He declares what has been and what is to be,
and he reveals the tracks of hidden
things.
[20]No thought escapes him,
and not one word is hidden from him.
[21]He has ordained the splendors of
his wisdom,
and he is from everlasting and
to everlasting.
Nothing can be added or taken away,
and he needs no one to be his counselor.
[22]How greatly to be desired are all his works,
and how sparkling they are to see!
[23]All these things live and remain for ever
for every need, and are all obedient.
[24]All things are twofold, one opposite
the other,
and he has made nothing incomplete.
[25]One confirms the good things of the other,
and who can have enough of beholding
his glory?

REVELATION 2

"To the angel of the Church in Ephesus write: 'The words of him who holds the seven stars in his right hand, who walks among the seven golden lampstands.

[2]" 'I know your works, your toil and your
patient endurance, and how you cannot
bear evil men but have tested those who
call themselves apostles but are not, and
found them to be false; [3]I know you are
enduring patiently and bearing up for
my name's sake, and you have not grown
weary. [4]But I have this against you, that
you have abandoned the love you had
at first. [5]Remember then from what you
have fallen, repent and do the works you
did at first. If not, I will come to you and
remove your lampstand from its place,
unless you repent. [6]Yet this you have, you
hate the works of the Nicola´itans, which
I also hate. [7]He who has an ear, let him
hear what the Spirit says to the churches.
To him who conquers I will grant to eat
of the tree of life, which is in the paradise
of God.'

[8]"And to the angel of the Church in
Smyrna write: 'The words of the first and
the last, who died and came to life.

[9]" 'I know your tribulation and your
poverty (but you are rich) and the slander
of those who say that they are Jews and
are not, but are a synagogue of Satan.
[10]Do not fear what you are about to suffer.
Behold, the devil is about to throw some
of you into prison, that you may be tested,
and for ten days you will have tribulation.
Be faithful unto death, and I will give you
the crown of life. [11]He who has an ear,
let him hear what the Spirit says to the

churches. He who conquers shall not be
hurt by the second death.'

12"And to the angel of the Church in
Per′gamum write: 'The words of him who
has the sharp two-edged sword.

13"'I know where you dwell, where Satan's
throne is; you hold fast my name and you
did not deny my faith even in the days
of An′tipas my witness, my faithful one,
who was killed among you, where Satan
dwells. 14But I have a few things against
you: you have some there who hold the
teaching of Balaam, who taught Balak to
put a stumbling block before the sons of
Israel, that they might eat food sacrificed
to idols and practice immorality. 15So you
also have some who hold the teaching of
the Nicola′itans. 16Repent then. If not, I
will come to you soon and war against
them with the sword of my mouth. 17He
who has an ear, let him hear what the
Spirit says to the churches. To him who
conquers I will give some of the hidden
manna, and I will give him a white stone,
with a new name written on the stone
which no one knows except him who
receives it.'

18"And to the angel of the Church in
Thyati′ra write: 'The words of the Son of
God, who has eyes like a flame of fire, and
whose feet are like burnished bronze.

19"'I know your works, your love and
faith and service and patient endurance,
and that your latter works exceed the
first. 20But I have this against you, that
you tolerate the woman Jez′ebel, who
calls herself a prophetess and is teaching
and beguiling my servants to practice
immorality and to eat food sacrificed
to idols. 21I gave her time to repent, but
she refuses to repent of her immorality.
22Behold, I will throw her on a sickbed,
and those who commit adultery with
her I will throw into great tribulation,
unless they repent of her doings; 23and I
will strike her children dead. And all the
churches shall know that I am he who
searches mind and heart, and I will give
to each of you as your works deserve.
24But to the rest of you in Thyati′ra, who
do not hold this teaching, who have not
learned what some call the deep things
of Satan, to you I say, I do not lay upon
you any other burden; 25only hold fast
what you have, until I come. 26He who
conquers and who keeps my works until
the end, I will give him power over the
nations, 27and he shall rule them with
a rod of iron, as when earthen pots are
broken in pieces, even as I myself have
received power from my Father; 28and I
will give him the morning star. 29He who
has an ear, let him hear what the Spirit
says to the churches.'"

REFLECTION

At the outset of Revelation, Jesus is seen amidst the seven lampstands, and chapter 2 begins with Jesus identified as the one "who walks among the seven golden lampstands" (Rev 2:1). This is manifest in the opening words Jesus gives each church: "I know your works" (to Ephesus in v. 2); "I know your tribulation and your poverty" (to Smyrna in v. 9); "I know where you dwell" (to Pergamum in v. 13); "I know your works, your love and faith and service and patient endurance, and that your latter works exceed the first" (to Thyatira in v. 19). From our good works to our suffering and short fallings, Jesus knows the state of the Church and its members. Jesus encourages everyone to "conquer" the challenges they face. He holds out great rewards, all of which come after the resurrection: "to eat of the tree of life" (v. 7); to have the hidden manna and a white stone with one's name signifying heavenly citizenship (see v. 17); and a share in Jesus's triumphant rule. In the face of tribulation and suffering, the response must be faithful endurance, but such patience will be richly rewarded. Conquering is the greatest act of glory in the Roman world, but here conquering is the overcoming of fear, selfishness, worldly indulgence, and passions. In other words, we must conquer ourselves by God's grace, and then we will share in the eternal victory. How odd would it seem to the Romans that "patient endurance" is the virtue most needed to "conquer"?

December 14

1 MACCABEES 8

17So Judas chose Eupol′emus the son of John, son of Ac′cos, and Jason the son of Elea′zar, and sent them to Rome to establish friendship and alliance, 18and to free themselves from the yoke; for they saw that the kingdom of the Greeks was completely enslaving Israel. 19They went to Rome, a very long journey; and they entered the senate chamber and spoke as follows: 20"Judas, who is also called Mac″cabe′us, and his brothers and the people of the Jews have sent us to you to establish alliance and peace with you, that we may be enrolled as your allies and friends." 21The proposal pleased them, 22and this is a copy of the letter which they wrote in reply, on bronze tablets, and sent to Jerusalem to remain with them there as a memorial of peace and alliance:

23"May all go well with the Romans and with the nation of the Jews at sea and on land for ever, and may sword and enemy be far from them. 24If war comes first to Rome or to any of their allies in all their dominion, 25the nation of the Jews shall act as their allies wholeheartedly, as the occasion may indicate to them. 26And to the enemy who makes war they shall not give or supply grain, arms, money, or ships, as Rome has decided; and they shall keep their obligations without receiving any return. 27In the same way, if war comes first to the nation of the Jews, the Romans shall willingly act as their allies, as the occasion may indicate to them. 28And to the enemy allies shall be given no grain, arms, money, or ships, as Rome has decided; and they shall keep these obligations and do so without deceit. 29Thus on these terms the Romans make a treaty with the Jewish people. 30If after these terms are in effect both parties shall determine to add or delete anything, they shall do so at their discretion, and any addition or deletion that they may make shall be valid.

31"And concerning the wrongs which King Deme′trius is doing to them we have written to him as follows, 'Why have you made your yoke heavy upon our friends and allies the Jews? 32If now they appeal again for help against you, we will defend their rights and fight you on sea and on land.' "

9 When Deme′trius heard that Nica′nor and his army had fallen in battle, he sent Bacchi′des and Al′cimus into the land of Judah a second time, and with them the right wing of the army. 2They went by the road which leads to Gilgal and encamped against Mes′aloth in Arbe′la, and they took it and killed many people. 3In the first month of the one hundred and fifty-second year they encamped against Jerusalem; 4then they marched off and went to Bere′a with twenty thousand foot soldiers and two thousand cavalry.

5Now Judas was encamped in El′asa, and with him were three thousand picked men. 6When they saw the huge number of the enemy forces, they were greatly frightened, and many slipped away from the camp, until no more than eight hundred of them were left.

7When Judas saw that his army had slipped away and the battle was imminent, he was crushed in spirit, for he had no time to assemble them. 8He became faint, but he said to those who were left, "Let us rise and go up against our enemies. We may be able to fight them." 9But they tried to dissuade him, saying, "We are not able. Let us rather save our own lives now, and let us come back with our brethren and fight them; we are too few." 10But Judas said, "Far be it from us to do such a thing as to flee from them. If our time has come, let us die bravely for our brethren, and leave no cause to question our honor."

11Then the army of Bacchi′des marched out from the camp and took its stand for the encounter. The cavalry was divided into two companies, and the slingers and the archers went ahead of the army, as did all the chief warriors. 12Bacchi′des was on the right wing. Flanked by the two companies, the phalanx advanced to the sound of the trumpets; and the men with Judas also blew

their trumpets. 13The earth was shaken by
the noise of the armies, and the battle raged
from morning till evening.
14Judas saw that Bacchi´des and the
strength of his army were on the right;
then all the stouthearted men went with
him, 15and they crushed the right wing, and
he pursued them as far as Mount Azo´tus.
16When those on the left wing saw that the
right wing was crushed, they turned and
followed close behind Judas and his men.
17The battle became desperate, and many on
both sides were wounded and fell. 18Judas
also fell, and the rest fled.
19Then Jonathan and Simon took Judas
their brother and buried him in the tomb of
their fathers at Mo´dein, 20and wept for him.
And all Israel made great lamentation for
him; they mourned many days and said,
21"How is the mighty fallen,
the savior of Israel!"
22Now the rest of the acts of Judas, and his
wars and the brave deeds that he did, and
his greatness, have not been recorded, for
they were very many.
23After the death of Judas, the lawless
emerged in all parts of Israel; all the doers
of injustice appeared. 24In those days a very
great famine occurred, and the country
deserted with them to the enemy. 25And
Bacchi´des chose the ungodly and put them
in charge of the country. 26They sought
and searched for the friends of Judas, and
brought them to Bacchi´des, and he took
vengeance on them and made sport of
them. 27Thus there was great distress in
Israel, such as had not been since the time
that prophets ceased to appear among them.
28Then all the friends of Judas assembled
and said to Jonathan, 29"Since the death of
your brother Judas there has been no one
like him to go against our enemies and
Bacchi´des, and to deal with those of our
nation who hate us. 30So now we have chosen
you today to take his place as our ruler and
leader, to fight our battle." 31And Jonathan at
that time accepted the leadership and took
the place of Judas his brother.
32When Bacchi´des learned of this, he tried
to kill him. 33But Jonathan and Simon his
brother and all who were with him heard
of it, and they fled into the wilderness of
Teko´a and camped by the water of the pool
of As´phar. 34Bacchi´des found this out on
the sabbath day, and he with all his army
crossed the Jordan.
35And Jonathan sent his brother as leader
of the multitude and begged the Nab´ate´ans,
who were his friends, for permission to store
with them the great amount of baggage
which they had. 36But the sons of Jam´bri
from Med´eba came out and seized John
and all that he had, and departed with it.
37After these things it was reported to
Jonathan and Simon his brother, "The sons of
Jam´bri are celebrating a great wedding, and are
conducting the bride, a daughter of one of the
great nobles of Canaan, from Nad´abath with
a large escort." 38And they remembered the
blood of John their brother, and went up and
hid under cover of the mountain. 39They raised
their eyes and looked, and saw a tumultuous
procession with much baggage; and the
bridegroom came out with his friends and
his brothers to meet them with tambourines
and musicians and many weapons. 40Then
they rushed upon them from the ambush and
began killing them. Many were wounded and
fell, and the rest fled to the mountain; and
they took all their goods. 41Thus the wedding
was turned into mourning and the voice of
their musicians into a funeral dirge. 42And
when they had fully avenged the blood of
their brother, they returned to the marshes of
the Jordan.
43When Bacchi´des heard of this, he came
with a large force on the sabbath day to the
banks of the Jordan. 44And Jonathan said to
those with him, "Let us rise up now and fight
for our lives, for today things are not as they
were before. 45For look! the battle is in front
of us and behind us; the water of the Jordan
is on this side and on that, with marsh and
thicket; there is no place to turn. 46Cry out
now to Heaven that you may be delivered
from the hands of our enemies." 47So the
battle began, and Jonathan stretched out
his hand to strike Bacchi´des, but he eluded
him and went to the rear. 48Then Jonathan
and the men with him leaped into the

Jordan and swam across to the other side, and the enemy did not cross the Jordan to attack them. 49And about one thousand of Bacchi´des' men fell that day.

SIRACH 43

The pride of the heavenly heights is the clear firmament,
the appearance of heaven in a spectacle of glory.
2The sun, when it appears, making proclamation as it goes forth,
is a marvelous instrument, the work of the Most High.
3At noon it parches the land;
and who can withstand its burning heat?
4A man tending a furnace works in burning heat,
but the sun burns the mountains three times as much;
it breathes out fiery vapors,
and with bright beams it blinds the eyes.
5Great is the Lord who made it;
and at his command it hastens on its course.

6He made the moon also, to serve in its season
to mark the times and to be an everlasting sign.
7From the moon comes the sign for feast days,
a light that wanes when it has reached the full.
8The month is named for the moon,
increasing marvelously in its phases,
an instrument of the hosts on high
shining forth in the firmament of heaven.

9The glory of the stars is the beauty of heaven,
a gleaming array in the heights of the Lord.
10At the command of the Holy One they stand as ordered,
they never relax in their watches.
11Look upon the rainbow, and praise him who made it,
exceedingly beautiful in its brightness.
12It encircles the heaven with its glorious arc;
the hands of the Most High have stretched it out.

REVELATION 3

"And to the angel of the Church in Sardis write: 'The words of him who has the seven spirits of God and the seven stars.

"'I know your works; you have the name of
being alive, and you are dead. 2Awake, and
strengthen what remains and is on the point
of death, for I have not found your works
perfect in the sight of my God. 3Remember
then what you received and heard; keep
that, and repent. If you will not awake, I will
come like a thief, and you will not know at
what hour I will come upon you. 4Yet you
have still a few names in Sardis, people who
have not soiled their garments; and they
shall walk with me in white, for they are
worthy. 5He who conquers shall be clothed
like them in white garments, and I will not
blot his name out of the book of life; I will
confess his name before my Father and
before his angels. 6He who has an ear, let him
hear what the Spirit says to the churches.'

7"And to the angel of the Church in
Philadelphia write: 'The words of the holy
one, the true one, who has the key of David,
who opens and no one shall shut, who shuts
and no one opens.

8"'I know your works. Behold, I have set
before you an open door, which no one is
able to shut; I know that you have but little
power, and yet you have kept my word
and have not denied my name. 9Behold, I
will make those of the synagogue of Satan
who say that they are Jews and are not, but
lie—behold, I will make them come and
bow down before your feet, and learn that
I have loved you. 10Because you have kept
my word of patient endurance, I will keep
you from the hour of trial which is coming
on the whole world, to try those who dwell
upon the earth. 11I am coming soon; hold
fast what you have, so that no one may seize

your crown. 12He who conquers, I will make him a pillar in the temple of my God; never shall he go out of it, and I will write on him the name of my God, and the name of the city of my God, the new Jerusalem which comes down from my God out of heaven, and my own new name. 13He who has an ear, let him hear what the Spirit says to the churches.'

14"And to the angel of the Church in La-odice′a write: 'The words of the Amen, the faithful and true witness, the beginning of God's creation.

15" 'I know your works: you are neither cold nor hot. Would that you were cold or hot! 16So, because you are lukewarm, and neither cold nor hot, I will spew you out of my mouth. 17For you say, I am rich, I have prospered, and I need nothing; not knowing that you are wretched, pitiable, poor, blind, and naked. 18Therefore I counsel you to buy from me gold refined by fire, that you may be rich, and white garments to clothe you and to keep the shame of your nakedness from being seen, and salve to anoint your eyes, that you may see. 19Those whom I love, I reprove and chasten; so be zealous and repent. 20Behold, I stand at the door and knock; if any one hears my voice and opens the door, I will come in to him and eat with him, and he with me. 21He who conquers, I will grant him to sit with me on my throne, as I myself conquered and sat down with my Father on his throne. 22He who has an ear, let him hear what the Spirit says to the churches.' "

REFLECTION

"I know your works," says Jesus to each of the churches addressed in Revelation 3. Indeed, Jesus's evaluation of each church is based on the quality of its works. In other words, this divine evaluation is based on performance. "I have not found your works perfect," he warns those in Sardis, but some have walked in purity and will receive a white garment (see Rev 3:3–5). Those in Philadelphia have done better: "You have kept my word of patient endurance, I will keep you from the hour of trial which is coming on the whole world" (v. 10). He encourages them to "hold fast . . . so that no one may seize [their] crown" (v. 11). Clearly, Christ rewards those who are faithful and filled with deeds of love. Indeed, he will crown them with glory. The Laodiceans, however, are known for their lukewarmness. Their works are tepid and so bland as to be vomited out. Christ seeks a vibrant zeal for good deeds and for love: "Those whom I love, I reprove and chasten; so be zealous and repent" (v. 19). What does Jesus mean by works? These are the deeds of love that we do for Christ. What works do you do for Christ? What would Jesus say to you about the quality of your deeds?

December 15

1 MACCABEES 9

50Bacchi′des then returned to Jerusalem and built strong cities in Judea: the fortress in Jericho, and Emma′us, and Beth-ho′ron, and Beth′el, and Tim′nath, and Phar′athon, and Teph′on, with high walls and gates and bars. 51And he placed garrisons in them to harass Israel. 52He also fortified the city of Beth-zur, and Gaza′ra, and the citadel, and in them he put troops and stores of food. 53And he took the sons of the leading men of the land as hostages and put them under guard in the citadel at Jerusalem.

54In the one hundred and fifty-third year, in the second month, Al′cimus gave orders to tear down the wall of the inner court of the sanctuary. He tore down the work of the prophets! 55But he only began to tear it down, for at that time Al′cimus was stricken and his work was hindered; his mouth was stopped and he was paralyzed, so that he could no longer say a word or give commands concerning his house. 56And Al′cimus died at that time in great agony.

57When Bacchi´des saw that Al´cimus was dead, he returned to the king, and the land of Judah had rest for two years.

58Then all the lawless plotted and said, "See! Jonathan and his men are living in quiet and confidence. So now let us bring Bacchi´des back, and he will capture them all in one night." 59And they went and consulted with him. 60He started to come with a large force, and secretly sent letters to all his allies in Judea, telling them to seize Jonathan and his men; but they were unable to do it, because their plan became known. 61And Jonathan's men seized about fifty of the men of the country who were leaders in this treachery, and killed them.

62Then Jonathan with his men, and Simon, withdrew to Beth-ba´si in the wilderness; he rebuilt the parts of it that had been demolished, and they fortified it. 63When Bacchi´des learned of this, he assembled all his forces, and sent orders to the men of Judea. 64Then he came and encamped against Beth-ba´si; he fought against it for many days and made machines of war.

65But Jonathan left Simon his brother in the city, while he went out into the country; and he went with only a few men. 66He struck down Odomer´a and his brothers and the sons of Pha´siron in their tents. 67Then he began to attack and went into battle with his forces; and Simon and his men sallied out from the city and set fire to the machines of war. 68They fought with Bacchi´des, and he was crushed by them. They distressed him greatly, for his plan and his expedition had been in vain. 69So he was greatly enraged at the lawless men who had counseled him to come into the country, and he killed many of them. Then he decided to depart to his own land.

70When Jonathan learned of this, he sent ambassadors to him to make peace with him and obtain release of the captives. 71He agreed, and did as he said; and he swore to Jonathan that he would not try to harm him as long as he lived. 72He restored to him the captives whom he had formerly taken from the land of Judah; then he turned and departed to his own land, and came no more into their territory. 73Thus the sword ceased from Israel. And Jonathan dwelt in Mich´mash. And Jonathan began to judge the people, and he destroyed the ungodly out of Israel.

10 In the one hundred and sixtieth year Alexander Epiph´anes, the son of Anti´ochus, landed and occupied Ptolema´is. They welcomed him, and there he began to reign. 2When Deme´trius the king heard of it, he assembled a very large army and marched out to meet him in battle. 3And Deme´trius sent Jonathan a letter in peaceable words to honor him; 4for he said, "Let us act first to make peace with him before he makes peace with Alexander against us, 5for he will remember all the wrongs which we did to him and to his brothers and his nation." 6So Deme´trius gave him authority to recruit troops, to equip them with arms, and to become his ally; and he commanded that the hostages in the citadel should be released to him.

7Then Jonathan came to Jerusalem and read the letter in the hearing of all the people and of the men in the citadel. 8They were greatly alarmed when they heard that the king had given him authority to recruit troops. 9But the men in the citadel released the hostages to Jonathan, and he returned them to their parents.

10And Jonathan dwelt in Jerusalem and began to rebuild and restore the city. 11He directed those who were doing the work to build the walls and encircle Mount Zion with squared stones, for better fortification; and they did so.

12Then the foreigners who were in the strongholds that Bacchi´des had built fled; 13each left his place and departed to his own land. 14Only in Beth-zur did some remain who had forsaken the law and the commandments, for it served as a place of refuge.

15Now Alexander the king heard of all the promises which Deme´trius had sent to Jonathan, and men told him of the battles that Jonathan and his brothers had fought, of the brave deeds that they had done, and of the troubles that they had endured. 16So he said, "Shall we find another such man?

Come now, we will make him our friend
and ally." 17And he wrote a letter and sent it
to him, in the following words:
18"King Alexander to his brother Jonathan,
greeting. 19We have heard about you, that
you are a mighty warrior and worthy to be
our friend. 20And so we have appointed you
today to be the high priest of your nation;
you are to be called the king's friend" (and
he sent him a purple robe and a golden
crown) "and you are to take our side and
keep friendship with us."
21So Jonathan put on the holy garments in
the seventh month of the one hundred and
sixtieth year, at the feast of tabernacles, and
he recruited troops and equipped them with
arms in abundance. 22When Deme´trius
heard of these things he was grieved and
said, 23"What is this that we have done?
Alexander has gotten ahead of us in forming
a friendship with the Jews to strengthen
himself. 24I also will write them words of
encouragement and promise them honor
and gifts, that I may have their help." 25So
he sent a message to them in the following
words:
"King Deme´trius to the nation of the
Jews, greeting. 26Since you have kept your
agreement with us and have continued
your friendship with us, and have not sided
with our enemies, we have heard of it and
rejoiced. 27And now continue still to keep
faith with us, and we will repay you with
good for what you do for us. 28We will grant
you many immunities and give you gifts.
29"And now I free you and exempt all the
Jews from payment of tribute and salt tax
and crown levies, 30and instead of collecting
the third of the grain and the half of the fruit
of the trees that I should receive, I release
them from this day and henceforth. I will not
collect them from the land of Judah or from
the three districts added to it from Samar´ia
and Galilee, from this day and for all time.
31And let Jerusalem and her environs, her
tithes and her revenues, be holy and free
from tax. 32I release also my control of the
citadel in Jerusalem and give it to the high
priest, that he may station in it men of his
own choice to guard it. 33And every one of
the Jews taken as a captive from the land of
Judah into any part of my kingdom, I set free
without payment; and let all officials cancel
also the taxes on their cattle.
34"And all the feasts and sabbaths and
new moons and appointed days, and the
three days before a feast and the three after
a feast—let them all be days of immunity
and release for all the Jews who are in my
kingdom. 35No one shall have authority to
exact anything from them or annoy any of
them about any matter.
36"Let Jews be enrolled in the king's forces
to the number of thirty thousand men, and
let the maintenance be given them that is
due to all the forces of the king. 37Let some of
them be stationed in the great strongholds
of the king, and let some of them be put in
positions of trust in the kingdom. Let their
officers and leaders be of their own number,
and let them live by their own laws, just
as the king has commanded in the land of
Judah.
38"As for the three districts that have been
added to Judea from the country of Samar´ia,
let them be so annexed to Judea that they
are considered to be under one ruler and
obey no other authority but the high priest.
39Ptolema´is and the land adjoining it I have
given as a gift to the sanctuary in Jerusalem,
to meet the necessary expenses of the
sanctuary. 40I also grant fifteen thousand
shekels of silver yearly out of the king's
revenues from appropriate places. 41And all
the additional funds which the government
officials have not paid as they did in the
first years, they shall give from now on for
the service of the temple. 42Moreover, the
five thousand shekels of silver which my
officials have received every year from the
income of the services of the temple, this
too is canceled, because it belongs to the
priests who minister there. 43And whoever
takes refuge at the temple in Jerusalem,
or in any of its precincts, because he owes
money to the king or has any debt, let him
be released and receive back all his property
in my kingdom.
44"Let the cost of rebuilding and restoring
the structures of the sanctuary be paid from

the revenues of the king. [45]And let the cost of rebuilding the walls of Jerusalem and fortifying it round about, and the cost of rebuilding the walls in Judea, also be paid from the revenues of the king."

SIRACH 43

[13]By his command he sends the driving snow
and speeds the lightning of his judgment.
[14]Therefore the storehouses are opened,
and the clouds fly forth like birds.
[15]In his majesty he amasses the clouds,
and the hailstones are broken in pieces.
[16]At his appearing the mountains are shaken;
at his will the south wind blows.
[17]The voice of his thunder rebukes the earth;
so do the tempest from the north and the whirlwind.
He scatters the snow like birds flying down,
and its descent is like locusts alighting.
[18]The eye marvels at the beauty of its whiteness,
and the mind is amazed at its falling.
[19]He pours the hoarfrost upon the earth like salt,
and when it freezes, it becomes pointed thorns.
[20]The cold north wind blows,
and ice freezes over the water;
it rests upon every pool of water,
and the water puts it on like a breastplate.
[21]He consumes the mountains and burns up the wilderness,
and withers the tender grass like fire.
[22]A mist quickly heals all things;
when the dew appears, it refreshes from the heat.

REVELATION 4

After this I looked, and behold, in heaven an open door! And the first voice, which I had heard speaking to me like a trumpet, said, "Come up here, and I will show you what must take place after this." [2]At once I was in the Spirit, and behold, a throne stood in heaven, with one seated on the throne! [3]And he who sat there appeared like jasper and carnelian, and round the throne was a rainbow that looked like an emerald. [4]Round the throne were twenty-four thrones, and seated on the thrones were twenty-four elders, clothed in white garments, with golden crowns upon their heads. [5]From the throne issue flashes of lightning, and voices and peals of thunder, and before the throne burn seven torches of fire, which are the seven spirits of God; [6]and before the throne there is as it were a sea of glass, like crystal.

And round the throne, on each side of the throne, are four living creatures, full of eyes in front and behind: [7]the first living creature like a lion, the second living creature like an ox, the third living creature with the face of a man, and the fourth living creature like a flying eagle. [8]And the four living creatures, each of them with six wings, are full of eyes all round and within, and day and night they never cease to sing,

"Holy, holy, holy, is the Lord God Almighty,
who was and is and is to come!"

[9]And whenever the living creatures give glory and honor and thanks to him who is seated on the throne, who lives for ever and ever, [10]the twenty-four elders fall down before him who is seated on the throne and worship him who lives for ever and ever; they cast their crowns before the throne, singing,

[11]"Worthy are you, our Lord and God,
to receive glory and honor and power,
for you created all things,
and by your will they existed and were created."

5 And I saw in the right hand of him who was seated on the throne a scroll written within and on the back, sealed with seven seals; [2]and I saw a strong angel proclaiming with a loud voice, "Who is worthy to open the scroll and break its seals?" [3]And no one in heaven or on earth or under the earth was able to open the scroll or to look into it, [4]and I wept much that no one was found worthy to open the scroll or to look into it. [5]Then one of the elders said to me, "Weep

not; behold, the Lion of the tribe of Judah, the Root of David, has conquered, so that he can open the scroll and its seven seals."
6And between the throne and the four living creatures and among the elders, I saw a Lamb standing, as though it had been slain, with seven horns and with seven eyes, which are the seven spirits of God sent out into all the earth;
7and he went and took the scroll from the right hand of him who was seated on the throne.
8And when he had taken the scroll, the four living creatures and the twenty-four elders fell down before the Lamb, each holding a harp, and with golden bowls full of incense, which are the prayers of the saints;
9and they sang a new song, saying,

"Worthy are you to take the scroll and to
open its seals,
for you were slain and by your blood you
ransomed men for God
from every tribe and tongue and people
and nation,
10and have made them a kingdom and
priests to our God,
and they shall reign on earth."

11Then I looked, and I heard around the throne and the living creatures and the elders the voice of many angels, numbering myriads of myriads and thousands of thousands,
12saying with a loud voice, "Worthy is the Lamb who was slain, to receive power and wealth and wisdom and might and honor and glory and blessing!"
13And I heard every creature in heaven and on earth and under the earth and in the sea, and all therein, saying, "To him who sits upon the throne and to the Lamb be blessing and honor and glory and might for ever and ever!"
14And the four living creatures said, "Amen!" and the elders fell down and worshiped.

REFLECTION

In his words to the last church, Jesus says that those who conquer will sit upon his throne, just as he conquered and sat upon his Father's throne (see Rev 3:21). After exhorting the seven churches to works worthy of following Christ, we turn to the work that God himself has first done, from which all their works flow. Taken up into Heaven, John sees God the Father seated upon his throne, attended by twenty-four elders and the four living creatures, who give him perpetual praise. The one on the throne is "worthy" because he created all things (see 4:11). Next a scroll is seen in his right hand, and no one is found "worthy" to open it, which is tragically sad. Then St. John hears that the "Lion of the tribe of Judah" is worthy and has conquered; he then sees a lamb standing slain, who takes the scroll and opens it, bringing salvation to the world. The meaning of what John saw at the foot of the Cross is now being unveiled. Jesus's death brought redemption and, as the true lamb of God, he is worthy above all to be praised. Jesus has conquered and now sits upon the throne. His work is the ultimate work of love, and all creation joins the alleluia chorus! Do you constantly seek to perform good works worthy of following Christ?

December 16

1 MACCABEES 10

46When Jonathan and the people heard these words, they did not believe or accept them, because they remembered the great wrongs which Deme′trius had done in Israel and how he had greatly oppressed them.
47They favored Alexander, because he had been the first to speak peaceable words to them, and they remained his allies all his days.
48Now Alexander the king assembled large forces and encamped opposite Deme′trius.
49The two kings met in battle, and the army of Deme′trius fled, and Alexander pursued him and defeated them.
50He pressed the battle strongly until the sun set, and Deme′trius fell on that day.
51Then Alexander sent ambassadors to Ptol′emy king of Egypt with the following message:
52"Since I have returned to my

kingdom and have taken my seat on the
throne of my fathers, and established my
rule—for I crushed Deme´trius and gained
control of our country; 53I met him in battle,
and he and his army were crushed by us,
and we have taken our seat on the throne of
his kingdom—54now therefore let us establish
friendship with one another; give me now your
daughter as my wife, and I will become your
son-in-law, and will make gifts to you and to
her in keeping with your position."
55Ptol´emy the king replied and said, "Happy
was the day on which you returned to the land
of your fathers and took your seat on the throne
of their kingdom. 56And now I will do for you
as you wrote, but meet me at Ptolema´is, so that
we may see one another, and I will become
your father-in-law, as you have said."
57So Ptol´emy set out from Egypt, he and
Cleopa´tra his daughter, and came to Ptolema´is
in the one hundred and sixty-second year.
58Alexander the king met him, and Ptol´emy
gave him Cleopa´tra his daughter in marriage,
and celebrated her wedding at Ptolema´is with
great pomp, as kings do.
59Then Alexander the king wrote to
Jonathan to come to meet him. 60So he
went with pomp to Ptolema´is and met the
two kings; he gave them and their friends
silver and gold and many gifts, and found
favor with them. 61A group of pestilent men
from Israel, lawless men, gathered together
against him to accuse him; but the king
paid no attention to them. 62The king gave
orders to take off Jonathan's garments and
to clothe him in purple, and they did so.
63The king also seated him at his side; and
he said to his officers, "Go forth with him
into the middle of the city and proclaim
that no one is to bring charges against
him about any matter, and let no one
annoy him for any reason." 64And when his
accusers saw the honor that was paid him,
in accordance with the proclamation, and
saw him clothed in purple, they all fled.
65Thus the king honored him and enrolled
him among his chief friends, and made
him general and governor of the province.
66And Jonathan returned to Jerusalem in
peace and gladness.
67In the one hundred and sixty-fifth year
Deme´trius the son of Demetrius came from
Crete to the land of his fathers. 68When
Alexander the king heard of it, he was
greatly grieved and returned to Antioch.
69And Deme´trius appointed Apollo´nius the
governor of Coe´le-syr´ia, and he assembled
a large force and encamped against Jam´nia.
Then he sent the following message to
Jonathan the high priest:
70"You are the only one to rise up against
us, and I have become a laughingstock
and reproach because of you. Why do you
assume authority against us in the hill
country? 71If you now have confidence in
your forces, come down to the plain to meet
us, and let us match strength with each
other there, for I have with me the power of
the cities. 72Ask and learn who I am and who
the others are that are helping us. Men will
tell you that you cannot stand before us, for
your fathers were twice put to flight in their
own land. 73And now you will not be able to
withstand my cavalry and such an army in
the plain, where there is no stone or pebble,
or place to flee."
74When Jonathan heard the words of
Apollo´nius, his spirit was aroused. He
chose ten thousand men and set out from
Jerusalem, and Simon his brother met him
to help him. 75He encamped before Joppa,
but the men of the city closed its gates, for
Apollo´nius had a garrison in Joppa. 76So
they fought against it, and the men of the
city became afraid and opened the gates,
and Jonathan gained possession of Joppa.
77When Apollo´nius heard of it, he mustered three thousand cavalry and a large
army, and went to Azo´tus as though he
were going farther. At the same time he
advanced into the plain, for he had a
large troop of cavalry and put confidence
in it. 78Jonathan pursued him to Azo´tus,
and the armies engaged in battle. 79Now
Apollo´nius had secretly left a thousand
cavalry behind them. 80Jonathan learned
that there was an ambush behind him,
for they surrounded his army and shot
arrows at his men from early morning till
late afternoon. 81But his men stood fast,

as Jonathan commanded, and the enemy's
horses grew tired.
82 Then Simon brought forward his force
and engaged the phalanx in battle (for
the cavalry was exhausted); they were
overwhelmed by him and fled, 83 and the
cavalry was dispersed in the plain. They
fled to Azo´tus and entered Beth-da´gon, the
temple of their idol, for safety. 84 But Jonathan
burned Azo´tus and the surrounding towns
and plundered them; and the temple of
Da´gon, and those who had taken refuge
in it he burned with fire. 85 The number
of those who fell by the sword, with those
burned alive, came to eight thousand men.
86 Then Jonathan departed from there and
encamped against Aska´lon, and the men
of the city came out to meet him with great
pomp. 87 And Jonathan and those with him
returned to Jerusalem with much booty.
88 When Alexander the king heard of these
things, he honored Jonathan still more;
89 and he sent to him a golden buckle, such
as it is the custom to give to the kinsmen of
kings. He also gave him Ek´ron and all its
environs as his possession.

11 Then the king of Egypt gathered
great forces, like the sand by the
seashore, and many ships; and he tried to
get possession of Alexander's kingdom by
trickery and add it to his own kingdom. 2 He
set out for Syria with peaceable words, and
the people of the cities opened their gates to
him and went to meet him, for Alexander
the king had commanded them to meet
him, since he was Alexander's father-in-law.
3 But when Ptol´emy entered the cities he
stationed forces as a garrison in each city.
4 When he approached Azo´tus, they
showed him the temple of Da´gon burned
down, and Azo´tus and its suburbs destroyed,
and the corpses lying about, and the charred
bodies of those whom Jonathan had burned
in the war, for they had piled them in heaps
along his route. 5 They also told the king
what Jonathan had done, to throw blame
on him; but the king kept silent. 6 Jonathan
met the king at Joppa with pomp, and they
greeted one another and spent the night
there. 7 And Jonathan went with the king as
far as the river called Eleu´therus; then he
returned to Jerusalem.
8 So King Ptol´emy gained control of the
coastal cities as far as Seleu´cia by the sea,
and he kept devising evil designs against
Alexander. 9 He sent envoys to Deme´trius
the king, saying, "Come, let us make a
covenant with each other, and I will give
you in marriage my daughter who was
Alexander's wife, and you shall reign over
your father's kingdom. 10 For I now regret
that I gave him my daughter, for he has tried
to kill me." 11 He threw blame on Alexander
because he coveted his kingdom. 12 So he
took his daughter away from him and
gave her to Deme´trius. He was estranged
from Alexander, and their enmity became
manifest.
13 Then Ptol´emy entered Antioch and
put on the crown of Asia. Thus he put two
crowns upon his head, the crown of Egypt
and that of Asia. 14 Now Alexander the king
was in Cili´cia at that time, because the
people of that region were in revolt. 15 And
Alexander heard of it and came against him
in battle. Ptol´emy marched out and met him
with a strong force, and put him to flight.
16 So Alexander fled into Arabia to find
protection there, and King Ptol´emy was
exalted. 17 And Zab´diel the Arab cut off the
head of Alexander and sent it to Ptol´emy.
18 But King Ptol´emy died three days later,
and his troops in the strongholds were killed
by the inhabitants of the strongholds. 19 So
Deme´trius became king in the one hundred
and sixty-seventh year.

SIRACH 43

23 By his counsel he stilled the great deep
and planted islands in it.
24 Those who sail the sea tell of its dangers,
and we marvel at what we hear.
25 For in it are strange and marvelous works,
all kinds of living things, and huge
creatures of the sea.
26 Because of him his messenger finds
the way,
and by his word all things hold together.

[27]Though we speak much we cannot reach
the end,
and the sum of our words is: "He is
the all."
[28]Where shall we find strength to praise him?
For he is greater than all his works.
[29]Terrible is the Lord and very great,
and marvelous is his power.
[30]When you praise the Lord, exalt him as
much as you can;
for he will surpass even that.
When you exalt him, put forth all
your strength,
and do not grow weary, for you cannot
praise him enough.
[31]Who has seen him and can describe him?
Or who can extol him as he is?
[32]Many things greater than these lie hidden,
for we have seen but few of his works.
[33]For the Lord has made all things,
and to the godly he has granted wisdom.

REVELATION 6

Now I saw when the Lamb opened one of the seven seals, and I heard one of the four living creatures say, as with a voice of thunder, "Come!"
[2]And I saw, and behold, a white horse,
and its rider had a bow; and a crown was
given to him, and he went out conquering
and to conquer.
[3]When he opened the second seal, I heard
the second living creature say, "Come!"
[4]And out came another horse, bright red; its
rider was permitted to take peace from the
earth, so that men should slay one another;
and he was given a great sword.
[5]When he opened the third seal, I heard
the third living creature say, "Come!" And I
saw, and behold, a black horse, and its rider
had a balance in his hand; [6]and I heard
what seemed to be a voice in the midst of
the four living creatures saying, "A quart of
wheat for a denarius, and three quarts of
barley for a denarius; but do not harm oil
and wine!"
[7]When he opened the fourth seal, I heard
the voice of the fourth living creature say,
"Come!" [8]And I saw, and behold, a pale
horse, and its rider's name was Death, and
Hades followed him; and they were given
power over a fourth of the earth, to kill with
sword and with famine and with pestilence
and by wild beasts of the earth.
[9]When he opened the fifth seal, I saw
under the altar the souls of those who had
been slain for the word of God and for the
witness they had borne; [10]they cried out with
a loud voice, "O Sovereign Lord, holy and
true, how long before you will judge and
avenge our blood on those who dwell upon
the earth?" [11]Then they were each given a
white robe and told to rest a little longer,
until the number of their fellow servants and
their brethren should be complete, who were
to be killed as they themselves had been.
[12]When he opened the sixth seal, I looked,
and behold, there was a great earthquake;
and the sun became black as sackcloth, the
full moon became like blood, [13]and the stars
of the sky fell to the earth as the fig tree
sheds its winter fruit when shaken by a gale;
[14]the sky vanished like a scroll that is rolled
up, and every mountain and island was
removed from its place. [15]Then the kings of
the earth and the great men and the generals
and the rich and the strong, and every one,
slave and free, hid in the caves and among
the rocks of the mountains, [16]calling to the
mountains and rocks, "Fall on us and hide
us from the face of him who is seated on the
throne, and from the wrath of the Lamb;
[17]for the great day of their wrath has come,
and who can stand before it?"

REFLECTION

Today's reading from Sirach is the conclusion of a hymn of praise to God for his creation. Sirach begins his hymn by "call[ing] to mind the works of the Lord" (Sir 42:15), which starts the praise of God's creation that ends with today's reading (the end of Sirach 43) with all that is made in the heavens and upon earth. Sirach comments on the "great deep," that is the sea, which is filled with "strange and marvelous works" (vv. 23–25). The observation of the vast ocean and its multitude of marvels follows the review of the heavens, tracing the wonders of the sun, moon, and stars, and finally the mountains and storms. All of these wonders, however, are surpassed by their maker: "He is greater than all his works" (v. 28). Finally, the hymn concludes with the humble observation that "many things greater than these lie hidden, for we have seen but few of his works. For the Lord has made all things, and to the godly he has granted wisdom" (vv. 32–33). If God's works are astounding, so much more must God be himself. The tradition of prayer is not simply reflecting on God's words, but also, as Sirach shows us here, pondering his works. Both pursuits in prayer lead us to praise God. Do you often marvel at the great wonders of Creation and the even greater wonder of God himself?

December 17

1 MACCABEES 11

**[20]In those days Jonathan assem-
bled the men of Judea to attack
the citadel in Jerusalem, and he
built many engines of war to use against
it. [21]But certain lawless men who hated
their nation went to the king and reported**
to him that Jonathan was besieging the
citadel. [22]When he heard this he was angry,
and as soon as he heard it he set out and
came to Ptolema′is; and he wrote Jonathan
not to continue the siege, but to meet him for a
conference at Ptolemais as quickly as possible.
[23]When Jonathan heard this, he gave orders
to continue the siege; and he chose some of the
elders of Israel and some of the priests, and put
himself in danger, [24]for he went to the king at
Ptolema′is, taking silver and gold and clothing
and numerous other gifts. And he won his
favor. [25]Although certain lawless men of his
nation kept making complaints against him,
[26]the king treated him as his predecessors had
treated him; he exalted him in the presence
of all his friends. [27]He confirmed him in the
high priesthood and in as many other honors
as he had formerly had, and made him to be
regarded as one of his chief friends. [28]Then
Jonathan asked the king to free Judea and
the three districts of Samar′ia from tribute,
and promised him three hundred talents.
[29]The king consented, and wrote a letter to
Jonathan about all these things; its contents
were as follows:
[30]"King Deme′trius to Jonathan his brother
and to the nation of the Jews, greeting. [31]This
copy of the letter which we wrote concerning
you to Las′thenes our kinsman we have written
to you also, so that you may know what it says.
[32]'King Deme′trius to Las′thenes his father,
greeting. [33]To the nation of the Jews, who
are our friends and fulfil their obligations to
us, we have determined to do good, because
of the good will they show toward us. [34]We
have confirmed as their possession both the
territory of Judea and the three districts of
Aphai′rema and Lydda and Rath′amin; the
latter, with all the region bordering them, were
added to Judea from Samar′ia. To all those who
offer sacrifice in Jerusalem, we have granted
release from the royal taxes which the king
formerly received from them each year, from
the crops of the land and the fruit of the trees.
[35]And the other payments henceforth due to us
of the tithes, and the taxes due to us, and the
salt pits and the crown taxes due to us—from
all these we shall grant them release. [36]And not
one of these grants shall be canceled from this
time forth for ever. [37]Now therefore take care
to make a copy of this, and let it be given to
Jonathan and put up in a conspicuous place on
the holy mountain.'"
[38]Now when Deme′trius the king saw that
the land was quiet before him and that there
was no opposition to him, he dismissed all his
troops, each man to his own place, except the
foreign troops which he had recruited from
the islands of the nations. So all the troops
who had served his fathers hated him. [39]Now
Try′pho had formerly been one of Alexander's
supporters. He saw that all the troops were

murmuring against Deme´trius. So he went to Imal´kue the Arab, who was bringing up Anti´ochus, the young son of Alexander, [40]and insistently urged him to hand Anti´ochus over to him, to become king in place of his father. He also reported to Imal´kue what Deme´trius had done and told of the hatred which the troops of Demetrius had for him; and he stayed there many days.

[41]Now Jonathan sent to Deme´trius the king the request that he remove the troops of the citadel from Jerusalem, and the troops in the strongholds; for they kept fighting against Israel. [42]And Deme´trius sent this message to Jonathan, "Not only will I do these things for you and your nation, but I will confer great honor on you and your nation, if I find an opportunity. [43]Now then you will do well to send me men who will help me, for all my troops have revolted." [44]So Jonathan sent three thousand stalwart men to him at Antioch, and when they came to the king, the king rejoiced at their arrival.

[45]Then the men of the city assembled within the city, to the number of a hundred and twenty thousand, and they wanted to kill the king. [46]But the king fled into the palace. Then the men of the city seized the main streets of the city and began to fight. [47]So the king called the Jews to his aid, and they all rallied about him and then spread out through the city; and they killed on that day as many as a hundred thousand men. [48]They set fire to the city and seized much spoil on that day, and they saved the king. [49]When the men of the city saw that the Jews had gained control of the city as they pleased, their courage failed and they cried out to the king with this entreaty, [50]"Grant us peace, and make the Jews stop fighting against us and our city." [51]And they threw down their arms and made peace. So the Jews gained glory in the eyes of the king and of all the people in his kingdom, and they returned to Jerusalem with much spoil.

[52]So Deme´trius the king sat on the throne of his kingdom, and the land was quiet before him. [53]But he broke his word about all that he had promised; and he became estranged from Jonathan and did not repay the favors which Jonathan had done him, but oppressed him greatly.

[54]After this Try´pho returned, and with him the young boy Anti´ochus who began to reign and put on the crown. [55]All the troops that Deme´trius had cast off gathered around him, and they fought against Demetrius, and he fled and was routed. [56]And Try´pho captured the elephants and gained control of Antioch. [57]Then the young Anti´ochus wrote to Jonathan, saying, "I confirm you in the high priesthood and set you over the four districts and make you one of the friends of the king." [58]And he sent him gold plate and a table service, and granted him the right to drink from gold cups and dress in purple and wear a gold buckle. [59]Simon his brother he made governor from the Ladder of Tyre to the borders of Egypt.

[60]Then Jonathan set forth and traveled beyond the river and among the cities, and all the army of Syria gathered to him as allies. When he came to Aska´lon, the people of the city met him and paid him honor. [61]From there he departed to Gaza, but the men of Gaza shut him out. So he besieged it and burned its suburbs with fire and plundered them. [62]Then the people of Gaza pleaded with Jonathan, and he made peace with them, and took the sons of their rulers as hostages and sent them to Jerusalem. And he passed through the country as far as Damascus.

[63]Then Jonathan heard that the officers of Deme´trius had come to Ka´desh in Galilee with a large army, intending to remove him from office. [64]He went to meet them, but left his brother Simon in the country. [65]Simon encamped before Beth-zur and fought against it for many days and hemmed it in. [66]Then they asked him to grant them terms of peace, and he did so. He removed them from there, took possession of the city, and set a garrison over it.

[67]Jonathan and his army encamped by the waters of Gennes´aret. Early in the morning they marched to the plain of Ha´zor, [68]and behold, the army of the foreigners met him in the plain; they had set an ambush against him in the mountains, but they themselves met him face to face. [69]Then the men in ambush emerged from their

places and joined battle. 70All the men with
Jonathan fled; not one of them was left
except Mattathi′as the son of Ab′salom and
Judas the son of Chal′phi, commanders of
the forces of the army. 71Jonathan tore his
garments and put dust on his head, and
prayed. 72Then he turned back to the battle
against the enemy and routed them, and
they fled. 73When his men who were fleeing
saw this, they returned to him and joined
him in the pursuit as far as Ka′desh, to their
camp, and there they encamped. 74As many
as three thousand of the foreigners fell that
day. And Jonathan returned to Jerusalem.

SIRACH 44

Let us now praise famous men,
and our fathers in their generations.
2The Lord apportioned to them great glory,
his majesty from the beginning.
3There were those who ruled in their
kingdoms,
and were men renowned for their power,
giving counsel by their understanding,
and proclaiming prophecies;
4leaders of the people in their deliberations
and in understanding of learning
for the people,
wise in their words of instruction;
5those who composed musical tunes,
and set forth verses in writing;
6rich men furnished with resources,
living peaceably in their habitations—
7all these were honored in their generations,
and were the glory of their times.
8There are some of them who have
left a name,
so that men declare their praise.
9And there are some who have no memorial,
who have perished as though they
had not lived;
they have become as though they had
not been born,
and so have their children after them.
10But these were men of mercy,
whose righteous deeds have not
been forgotten;
11their prosperity will remain with
their descendants,
and their inheritance to their
children's children.
12Their descendants stand by the covenants;
their children also, for their sake.
13Their posterity will continue for ever,
and their glory will not be blotted out.
14Their bodies were buried in peace,
and their name lives to all generations.
15Peoples will declare their wisdom,
and the congregation proclaims
their praise.

16E′noch pleased the Lord, and was
taken up;
he was an example of repentance
to all generations.
17Noah was found perfect and righteous;
in the time of wrath he was taken
in exchange;
therefore a remnant was left to the earth
when the flood came.
18Everlasting covenants were made with him
that all flesh should not be blotted out by
a flood.
19Abraham was the great father of a
multitude of nations,
and no one has been found like him
in glory;
20he kept the law of the Most High,
and was taken into covenant with him;
he established the covenant in his flesh,
and when he was tested he was
found faithful.
21Therefore the Lord assured him by
an oath
that the nations would be blessed through
his posterity;
that he would multiply him like the dust
of the earth,
and exalt his posterity like the stars,
and cause them to inherit from sea to sea
and from the River to the ends of
the earth.
22To Isaac also he gave the same assurance
for the sake of Abraham his father.

23The blessing of all men and the covenant
he made to rest upon the head of Jacob;
he acknowledged him with his blessings,
and gave him his inheritance;
he determined his portions,
and distributed them among twelve
tribes.

REVELATION 7

After this I saw four angels standing at the four corners of the earth, holding back the four winds of the earth, that no wind might blow on earth or sea or against any tree. 2Then I saw another angel ascend from the rising of the sun, with the seal of the living God, and he called with a loud voice to the four angels who had been given power to harm earth and sea, 3saying, "Do not harm the earth or the sea or the trees, till we have sealed the servants of our God upon their foreheads." 4And I heard the number of the sealed, a hundred and forty-four thousand sealed, out of every tribe of the sons of Israel, 5twelve thousand sealed out of the tribe of Judah, twelve thousand of the tribe of Reuben, twelve thousand of the tribe of Gad, 6twelve thousand of the tribe of Asher, twelve thousand of the tribe of Naph′tali, twelve thousand of the tribe of Manas′seh, 7twelve thousand of the tribe of Simeon, twelve thousand of the tribe of Levi, twelve thousand of the tribe of Is′sachar, 8twelve thousand of the tribe of Zeb′ulun, twelve thousand of the tribe of Joseph, twelve thousand sealed out of the tribe of Benjamin.

9After this I looked, and behold, a great multitude which no man could number, from every nation, from all tribes and peoples and tongues, standing before the throne and before the Lamb, clothed in white robes, with palm branches in their hands, 10and crying out with a loud voice, "Salvation belongs to our God who sits upon the throne, and to the Lamb!" 11And all the angels stood round the throne and round the elders and the four living creatures, and they fell on their faces before the throne and worshiped God, 12saying, "Amen! Blessing and glory and wisdom and thanksgiving and honor and power and might be to our God for ever and ever! Amen."

13Then one of the elders addressed me, saying, "Who are these, clothed in white robes, and from where have they come?" 14I said to him, "Sir, you know." And he said to me, "These are they who have come out of the great tribulation; they have washed their robes and made them white in the blood of the Lamb.

15Therefore are they before the throne
of God,
and serve him day and night within
his temple;
and he who sits upon the throne will
shelter them with his presence.
16They shall hunger no more, neither
thirst any more;
the sun shall not strike them, nor any
scorching heat.
17For the Lamb in the midst of the throne
will be their shepherd,
and he will guide them to springs of
living water;
and God will wipe away every tear from
their eyes."

REFLECTION

After describing the splendor of God's works, Sirach moves to a much larger treatment of the glory of the Old Testament saints. There is a nice bookend with Enoch, who is the first named in Sirach 44:16 and then named again in the closing account of the holy ones (see 49:14). Enoch is a rather mysterious character who is assumed into Heaven. He "frames the saints" because he embodies their destiny, which is to be with God in Heaven. This is precisely what John sees in Revelation 7 when he learns that these saints are marked with a seal upon their foreheads (see Rev 7:3). This most likely refers to the origins of the Christian practice of anointing the foreheads of those being baptized with oil in the shape of the cross. Those anointed are saved, and the first group is 144,000 from the Twelve Tribes of Israel. After this symbolic number of those saved from Israel, a "great multitude" that cannot be counted (v. 9) is seen from the rest of the nations. These are the Gentiles who are saved. They all worship God "who sits upon the throne" and "the Lamb" (v. 10). These who endure through the tribulation wash their robes in the blood of the Lamb, which means they died faithful to Christ. Here, the consolation given to us is that those who die for God are "before the throne" (v. 15) and suffer no more, for the Lamb, as their Shepherd, leads them to "living water," an allusion no doubt to Psalm 23. Do you think of the glory of those who die for Christ, or simply the agony of their deaths?

December 18

1 MACCABEES 12

Now when Jonathan saw that
the time was favorable for him,
he chose men and sent them to
Rome to confirm and renew the friend-
ship with them. 2He also sent letters to the
same effect to the Spartans and to other
places. 3So they went to Rome and entered
the senate chamber and said, "Jonathan
the high priest and the Jewish nation have
sent us to renew the former friendship and
alliance with them." 4And the Romans gave
them letters to the people in every place,
asking them to provide for the envoys safe
conduct to the land of Judah.

5This is a copy of the letter which Jonathan
wrote to the Spartans: 6"Jonathan the
high priest, the senate of the nation, the
priests, and the rest of the Jewish people
to their brethren the Spartans, greeting.
7Already in time past a letter was sent to
Oni′as the high priest from A′rius, who
was king among you, stating that you are
our brethren, as the appended copy shows.
8Oni′as welcomed the envoy with honor,
and received the letter, which contained a
clear declaration of alliance and friendship.
9Therefore, though we have no need of these
things, since we have as encouragement
the holy books which are in our hands,
10we have undertaken to send to renew our
brotherhood and friendship with you, so
that we may not become estranged from
you, for considerable time has passed since
you sent your letter to us. 11We therefore
remember you constantly on every occasion,
both in our feasts and on other appropriate
days, at the sacrifices which we offer and
in our prayers, as it is right and proper to
remember brethren. 12And we rejoice in your
glory. 13But as for ourselves, many afflictions
and many wars have encircled us; the kings
round about us have waged war against us.
14We were unwilling to annoy you and our
other allies and friends with these wars, 15for
we have the help which comes from Heaven
for our aid; and we were delivered from our
enemies and our enemies were humbled.
16We therefore have chosen Nume′nius the
son of Anti′ochus and Antip′ater the son of
Jason, and have sent them to Rome to renew
our former friendship and alliance with
them. 17We have commanded them to go
also to you and greet you and deliver to you
this letter from us concerning the renewal of
our brotherhood. 18And now please send us
a reply to this."

19This is a copy of the letter which
they sent to Oni′as: 20"A′rius, king of the
Spartans, to Oni′as the high priest, greeting.
21It has been found in writing concerning
the Spartans and the Jews that they are
brethren and are of the family of Abraham.
22And now that we have learned this, please
write us concerning your welfare; 23we on
our part write to you that your cattle and
your property belong to us, and ours belong
to you. We therefore command that our
envoys report to you accordingly."

24Now Jonathan heard that the commanders of Deme′trius had returned, with a larger
force than before, to wage war against him.
25So he marched away from Jerusalem and
met them in the region of Ha′math, for he
gave them no opportunity to invade his own
country. 26He sent spies to their camp, and

they returned and reported to him that the enemy were being drawn up in formation to fall upon the Jews by night. 27So when the sun set, Jonathan commanded his men to be alert and to keep their arms at hand so as to be ready all night for battle, and he stationed outposts around the camp. 28When the enemy heard that Jonathan and his men were prepared for battle, they were afraid and were terrified at heart; so they kindled fires in their camp and withdrew. 29But Jonathan and his men did not know it until morning, for they saw the fires burning. 30Then Jonathan pursued them, but he did not overtake them, for they had crossed the Eleu′therus river. 31So Jonathan turned aside against the Arabs who are called Zabade′ans and he crushed them and plundered them. 32Then he broke camp and went to Damascus, and marched through all that region.

33Simon also went forth and marched through the country as far as Aska′lon and the neighboring strongholds. He turned aside to Joppa and took it by surprise, 34for he had heard that they were ready to hand over the stronghold to the men whom Deme′trius had sent. And he stationed a garrison there to guard it.

35When Jonathan returned he convened the elders of the people and planned with them to build strongholds in Judea, 36to build the walls of Jerusalem still higher, and to erect a high barrier between the citadel and the city to separate it from the city, in order to isolate it so that its garrison could neither buy nor sell. 37So they gathered together to build up the city; part of the wall on the valley to the east had fallen, and he repaired the section called Chaphen′atha. 38And Simon built Ad′ida in the Shephe′lah; he fortified it and installed gates with bolts.

39Then Try′pho attempted to become king of Asia and put on the crown, and to raise his hand against Anti′ochus the king. 40He feared that Jonathan might not permit him to do so, but might make war on him, so he kept seeking to seize and kill him, and he marched forth and came to Beth-shan. 41Jonathan went out to meet him with forty thousand picked fighting men, and he came to Beth-shan. 42When Try′pho saw that he had come with a large army, he was afraid to raise his hand against him. 43So he received him with honor and commended him to all his friends, and he gave him gifts and commanded his friends and his troops to obey him as they would himself. 44Then he said to Jonathan, "Why have you wearied all these people when we are not at war? 45Dismiss them now to their homes and choose for yourself a few men to stay with you, and come with me to Ptolema′is. I will hand it over to you as well as the other strongholds and the remaining troops and all the officials, and will turn round and go home. For that is why I am here."

46Jonathan trusted him and did as he said; he sent away the troops, and they returned to the land of Judah. 47He kept with himself three thousand men, two thousand of whom he left in Galilee, while a thousand accompanied him. 48But when Jonathan entered Ptolema′is, the men of Ptolemais closed the gates and seized him, and all who had entered with him they killed with the sword.

49Then Try′pho sent troops and cavalry into Galilee and the Great Plain to destroy all Jonathan's soldiers. 50But they realized that Jonathan had been seized and had perished along with his men, and they encouraged one another and kept marching in close formation, ready for battle. 51When their pursuers saw that they would fight for their lives, they turned back. 52So they all reached the land of Judah safely, and they mourned for Jonathan and his companions and were in great fear; and all Israel mourned deeply. 53And all the nations round about them tried to destroy them, for they said, "They have no leader or helper. Now therefore let us make war on them and blot out the memory of them from among men."

SIRACH 45

From his descendants the Lord brought
forth a man of mercy,

who found favor in the sight of all flesh
and was beloved by God and man,
Moses, whose memory is blessed.
2He made him equal in glory to the
holy ones,
and made him great in the fears of
his enemies.
3By his words he caused signs to cease;
the Lord glorified him in the presence
of kings.
He gave him commands for his people,
and showed him part of his glory.
4He sanctified him through faithfulness
and meekness;
he chose him out of all mankind.
5He made him hear his voice,
and led him into the thick darkness,
and gave him the commandments face
to face,
the law of life and knowledge,
to teach Jacob the covenant,
and Israel his judgments.

6He exalted Aaron, the brother of Moses,
a holy man like him, of the tribe of Levi.
7He made an everlasting covenant with him,
and gave him the priesthood of the people.
He blessed him with splendid vestments,
and put a glorious robe upon him.
8He clothed him with superb perfection,
and strengthened him with the symbols
of authority,
the linen breeches, the long robe,
and the ephod.
9And he encircled him with pomegranates,
with very many golden bells round about,
to send forth a sound as he walked,
to make their ringing heard in the temple
as a reminder to the sons of his people;
10with a holy garment, of gold and blue
and purple, the work of an embroiderer;
with the oracle of judgment, U′rim and
Thummim;
11 with twisted scarlet, the work of a
craftsman;
with precious stones engraved like signets,
in a setting of gold, the work of a jeweler,
for a reminder, in engraved letters,
according to the number of the tribes
of Israel;
12with a gold crown upon his turban,
inscribed like a signet with "Holiness,"
a distinction to be prized, the work of
an expert,
the delight of the eyes, richly adorned.
13Before his time there never were such
beautiful things.
No outsider ever put them on,
but only his sons
and his descendants perpetually.
14His sacrifices shall be wholly burned
twice every day continually.
15Moses ordained him,
and anointed him with holy oil;
it was an everlasting covenant for him
and for his descendants all the days
of heaven,
to minister to the Lord and serve as priest
and bless his people in his name.
16He chose him out of all the living
to offer sacrifice to the Lord,
incense and a pleasing odor as a
memorial portion,
to make atonement for the people.
17In his commandments he gave him
authority in statutes and judgments,
to teach Jacob the testimonies,
and to enlighten Israel with his law.
18Outsiders conspired against him,
and envied him in the wilderness,
Da′than and Abi′ram and their men
and the company of Ko′rah, in wrath
and anger.
19The Lord saw it and was not pleased,
and in the wrath of his anger they
were destroyed;
he wrought wonders against them
to consume them in flaming fire.
20He added glory to Aaron
and gave him a heritage;
he allotted to him the first of the first fruits,
he prepared bread of first fruits
in abundance;
21for they eat the sacrifices to the Lord,
which he gave to him and his descendants.
22But in the land of the people he has
no inheritance,
and he has no portion among the people;
for the Lord himself is his portion
and inheritance.

[23]Phin′ehas the son of Elea′zar is the third
in glory,
for he was zealous in the fear of the Lord,
and stood fast, when the people
turned away,
in the ready goodness of his soul,
and made atonement for Israel.
[24]Therefore a covenant of peace was
established with him,
that he should be leader of the sanctuary
and of his people,
that he and his descendants should have
the dignity of the priesthood for ever.
[25]A covenant was also established
with David,
the son of Jesse, of the tribe of Judah:
the heritage of the king is from son to
son only;
so the heritage of Aaron is for
his descendants.
[26]May the Lord grant you wisdom in
your heart
to judge his people in righteousness,
so that their prosperity may not vanish,
and that their glory may endure
throughout their generations.

REVELATION 8

When the Lamb opened the seventh seal, there was silence in heaven for about half an hour. [2]Then I saw the seven angels who stand before God, and seven trumpets were given to them. [3]And another angel
came and stood at the altar with a golden
censer; and he was given much incense to
mingle with the prayers of all the saints
upon the golden altar before the throne;
[4]and the smoke of the incense rose with the
prayers of the saints from the hand of the
angel before God. [5]Then the angel took the
censer and filled it with fire from the altar
and threw it on the earth; and there were
peals of thunder, loud noises, flashes of
lightning, and an earthquake.

[6]Now the seven angels who had the seven
trumpets made ready to blow them.

[7]The first angel blew his trumpet, and there
followed hail and fire, mixed with blood, which
fell on the earth; and a third of the earth was
burnt up, and a third of the trees were burnt up,
and all green grass was burnt up.

[8]The second angel blew his trumpet, and
something like a great mountain, burning
with fire, was thrown into the sea; [9]and a
third of the sea became blood, a third of the
living creatures in the sea died, and a third
of the ships were destroyed.

[10]The third angel blew his trumpet, and
a great star fell from heaven, blazing like a
torch, and it fell on a third of the rivers and
on the fountains of water. [11]The name of the
star is Wormwood. A third of the waters
became wormwood, and many men died of
the water, because it was made bitter.

[12]The fourth angel blew his trumpet, and
a third of the sun was struck, and a third of
the moon, and a third of the stars, so that a
third of their light was darkened; a third of
the day was kept from shining, and likewise
a third of the night.

[13]Then I looked, and I heard an eagle
crying with a loud voice, as it flew in
midheaven, "Woe, woe, woe to those who
dwell on the earth, at the blasts of the other
trumpets which the three angels are about
to blow!"

REFLECTION

Jonathan, the brother of Judas Maccabeus, begins 1 Maccabees 12 in a strong position. Unlike his brother before him, he has a strong army, is able to build new defenses around Jerusalem, and is not hemmed in and constantly on the run. With relative safety, he sends out envoys to make alliances with Rome and others. Surely, now that he and his family are recognized as a legitimate state power, the best way to secure his and Israel's future is to make strong alliances with rising powers like Rome. This is worldly wisdom and a trap. Whenever Israel makes an alliance with a nation, when it seeks security in earthly powers rather than in the Lord, it ends up left to its own devices, which means failure. Israel trusted in Assyria and was conquered by them. Judah welcomed envoys from Babylon and became vassals to them. Jonathan and the Maccabeans were liberated by the Lord and then sought security in political alliances. Inevitably, Israel will end up in the hands of Rome. In Revelation 8 we see the rising smoke of incense symbolizing the prayers of the saints being presented to God (see v. 4). Seven trumpets of judgment follow next, the reverberation of which echoes the sevenfold blowing of trumpets that brought down Jericho, ushering in the conquest of the Promised Land. Could this series of trumpets signify that the downfall of the world in the final judgment is likened to Jericho?

December 19

1 MACCABEES 13

Simon heard that Try´pho had assembled a large army to invade the land of Judah and destroy it, 2and he saw that the people were trembling and fearful. So he went up to Jerusalem, and gathering
the people together 3he encouraged them,
saying to them, "You yourselves know what
great things I and my brothers and the house
of my father have done for the laws and the
sanctuary; you know also the wars and the
difficulties which we have seen. 4By reason
of this all my brothers have perished for
the sake of Israel, and I alone am left. 5And
now, far be it from me to spare my life in any
time of distress, for I am not better than my
brothers. 6But I will avenge my nation and
the sanctuary and your wives and children,
for all the nations have gathered together
out of hatred to destroy us."
7The spirit of the people was rekindled when
they heard these words, 8and they answered
in a loud voice, "You are our leader in place of
Judas and Jonathan your brother. 9Fight our
battles, and all that you say to us we will do."
10So he assembled all the warriors and hastened
to complete the walls of Jerusalem, and he
fortified it on every side. 11He sent Jonathan
the son of Ab´salom to Joppa, and with him a
considerable army; he drove out its occupants
and remained there.
12Then Try´pho departed from Ptolema´is
with a large army to invade the land of Judah,
and Jonathan was with him under guard.
13And Simon encamped in Ad´ida, facing the
plain. 14Try´pho learned that Simon had risen
up in place of Jonathan his brother, and that he
was about to join battle with him, so he sent
envoys to him and said, 15"It is for the money
that Jonathan your brother owed the royal
treasury, in connection with the offices he
held, that we are detaining him. 16Send now a
hundred talents of silver and two of his sons
as hostages, so that when released he will not
revolt against us, and we will release him."
17Simon knew that they were speaking
deceitfully to him, but he sent to get the money
and the sons, lest he arouse great hostility
among the people, who might say, 18"Because
Simon did not send him the money and the
sons, he perished." 19So he sent the sons and the
hundred talents, but Try´pho broke his word
and did not release Jonathan.
20After this Try´pho came to invade the
country and destroy it, and he circled around
by the way to Ado´ra. But Simon and his army
kept marching along opposite him to every
place he went. 21Now the men in the citadel
kept sending envoys to Try´pho urging him
to come to them by way of the wilderness
and to send them food. 22So Try´pho got all
his cavalry ready to go, but that night a very
heavy snow fell, and he did not go because
of the snow. He marched off and went into
the land of Gilead. 23When he approached
Bas´kama, he killed Jonathan, and he was
buried there. 24Then Try´pho turned back
and departed to his own land.
25And Simon sent and took the bones of
Jonathan his brother, and buried him in
Mo´dein, the city of his fathers. 26All Israel
bewailed him with great lamentation, and
mourned for him many days. 27And Simon
built a monument over the tomb of his father

and his brothers; he made it high that it might
be seen, with polished stone at the front and
back. 28He also erected seven pyramids,
opposite one another, for his father and mother
and four brothers. 29And for the pyramids he
devised an elaborate setting, erecting about
them great columns, and upon the columns he
put suits of armor for a permanent memorial,
and beside the suits of armor carved ships, so
that they could be seen by all who sail the sea.
30This is the tomb which he built in Mo´dein; it
remains to this day.

31Try´pho dealt treacherously with the
young king Anti´ochus; he killed him
32and became king in his place, putting on
the crown of Asia; and he brought great
calamity upon the land. 33But Simon built
up the strongholds of Judea and walled
them all around, with high towers and great
walls and gates and bolts, and he stored
food in the strongholds. 34Simon also chose
men and sent them to Deme´trius the king
with a request to grant relief to the country,
for all that Try´pho did was to plunder.
35Deme´trius the king sent him a favorable
reply to this request, and wrote him a letter
as follows, 36"King Deme´trius to Simon,
the high priest and friend of kings, and to
the elders and nation of the Jews, greeting.
37We have received the gold crown and the
palm branch which you sent, and we are
ready to make a general peace with you
and to write to our officials to grant you
release from tribute. 38All the grants that
we have made to you remain valid, and let
the strongholds that you have built be your
possession. 39We pardon any errors and
offenses committed to this day, and cancel
the crown tax which you owe; and whatever
other tax has been collected in Jerusalem
shall be collected no longer. 40And if any
of you are qualified to be enrolled in our
bodyguard, let them be enrolled, and let
there be peace between us."

41In the one hundred and seventieth year
the yoke of the Gentiles was removed from
Israel, 42and the people began to write in their
documents and contracts, "In the first year of
Simon the great high priest and commander
and leader of the Jews."

43In those days Simon encamped against
Gaza´ra and surrounded it with troops. He
made a siege engine, brought it up to the city,
and battered and captured one tower. 44The
men in the siege engine leaped out into the
city, and a great tumult arose in the city. 45The
men in the city, with their wives and children,
went up on the wall with their clothes torn, and
they cried out with a loud voice, asking Simon
to make peace with them; 46they said, "Do
not treat us according to our wicked acts but
according to your mercy." 47So Simon reached
an agreement with them and stopped fighting
against them. But he expelled them from the
city and cleansed the houses in which the idols
were, and then entered it with hymns and
praise. 48He cast out of it all uncleanness, and
settled in it men who observed the law. He also
strengthened its fortifications and built in it a
house for himself.

49The men in the citadel at Jerusalem were
prevented from going out to the country and
back to buy and sell. So they were very hungry,
and many of them perished from famine.
50Then they cried to Simon to make peace
with them, and he did so. But he expelled
them from there and cleansed the citadel from
its pollutions. 51On the twenty-third day of
the second month, in the one hundred and
seventy-first year, the Jews entered it with
praise and palm branches, and with harps
and cymbals and stringed instruments, and
with hymns and songs, because a great
enemy had been crushed and removed
from Israel. 52And Simon decreed that
every year they should celebrate this
day with rejoicing. He strengthened the
fortifications of the temple hill alongside
the citadel, and he and his men dwelt
there. 53And Simon saw that John his son
had reached manhood, so he made him
commander of all the forces, and he dwelt
in Gaza´ra.

SIRACH 46

Joshua the son of Nun was mighty in war,
and was the successor of Moses in
prophesying.

He became, in accordance with his name,
a great savior of God's elect,
to take vengeance on the enemies that rose against them,
so that he might give Israel its inheritance.
2 How glorious he was when he lifted his hands
and stretched out his sword against the cities!
3 Who before him ever stood so firm?
For he waged the wars of the Lord.
4 Was not the sun held back by his hand?
And did not one day become as long as two?
5 He called upon the Most High, the Mighty One,
when enemies pressed him on every side,
6 and the great Lord answered him
with hailstones of mighty power.
He hurled down war upon that nation,
and at the descent of Beth-ho´ron he destroyed those who resisted,
so that the nations might know his armament,
that he was fighting in the sight of the Lord;
for he wholly followed the Mighty One.
7 And in the days of Moses he did a loyal deed,
he and Caleb the son of Jephun´neh:
they withstood the congregation,
restrained the people from sin,
and stilled their wicked murmuring.
8 And these two alone were preserved
out of six hundred thousand people on foot,
to bring them into their inheritance,
into a land flowing with milk and honey.
9 And the Lord gave Caleb strength,
which remained with him to old age,
so that he went up to the hill country,
and his children obtained it for an inheritance;
10 so that all the sons of Israel might see
that it is good to follow the Lord.

11 The judges also, with their respective names,
those whose hearts did not fall into idolatry
and who did not turn away from the Lord—
may their memory be blessed!
12 May their bones revive from where they lie,
and may the name of those who have been honored
live again in their sons!
13 Samuel, beloved by his Lord,
a prophet of the Lord, established the kingdom
and anointed rulers over his people.
14 By the law of the Lord he judged the congregation,
and the Lord watched over Jacob.
15 By his faithfulness he was proved to be a prophet,
and by his words he became known as a trustworthy seer.
16 He called upon the Lord, the Mighty One,
when his enemies pressed him on every side,
and he offered in sacrifice a sucking lamb.
17 Then the Lord thundered from heaven,
and made his voice heard with a mighty sound;
18 and he wiped out the leaders of the people of Tyre
and all the rulers of the Philis´tines.
19 Before the time of his eternal sleep,
Samuel called men to witness before the Lord and his anointed:
"I have not taken any one's property,
not so much as a pair of shoes."
And no man accused him.
20 Even after he had fallen asleep he prophesied
and revealed to the king his death,
and lifted up his voice out of the earth in prophecy,
to blot out the wickedness of the people.

REVELATION 9

And the fifth angel blew his trumpet, and I saw a star fallen from heaven to earth, and he was given the key of the shaft of the bottomless
pit; 2 he opened the shaft of the bottomless
pit, and from the shaft rose smoke like

the smoke of a great furnace, and the sun and the air were darkened with the smoke from the shaft. [3]Then from the smoke came locusts on the earth, and they were given power like the power of scorpions of the earth; [4]they were told not to harm the grass of the earth or any green growth or any tree, but only those of mankind who have not the seal of God upon their foreheads; [5]they were allowed to torture them for five months, but not to kill them, and their torture was like the torture of a scorpion, when it stings a man. [6]And in those days men will seek death and will not find it; they will long to die, and death will fly from them.

[7]In appearance the locusts were like horses arrayed for battle; on their heads were what looked like crowns of gold; their faces were like human faces, [8]their hair like women's hair, and their teeth like lions' teeth; [9]they had scales like iron breastplates, and the noise of their wings was like the noise of many chariots with horses rushing into battle. [10]They have tails like scorpions, and stings, and their power of hurting men for five months lies in their tails. [11]They have as king over them the angel of the bottomless pit; his name in Hebrew is Abad′don, and in Greek he is called Apol′lyon.

[12]The first woe has passed; behold, two woes are still to come.

[13]Then the sixth angel blew his trumpet, and I heard a voice from the four horns of the golden altar before God, [14]saying to the sixth angel who had the trumpet, "Release the four angels who are bound at the great river Euphra′tes." [15]So the four angels were released, who had been held ready for the hour, the day, the month, and the year, to kill a third of mankind. [16]The number of the troops of cavalry was twice ten thousand times ten thousand; I heard their number. [17]And this was how I saw the horses in my vision: the riders wore breastplates the color of fire and of sapphire and of sulphur, and the heads of the horses were like lions' heads, and fire and smoke and sulphur issued from their mouths. [18]By these three plagues a third of mankind was killed, by the fire and smoke and sulphur issuing from their mouths. [19]For the power of the horses is in their mouths and in their tails; their tails are like serpents, with heads, and by means of them they wound.

[20]The rest of mankind, who were not killed by these plagues, did not repent of the works of their hands nor give up worshiping demons and idols of gold and silver and bronze and stone and wood, which cannot either see or hear or walk; [21]nor did they repent of their murders or their sorceries or their immorality or their thefts.

REFLECTION

Sirach describes the valor of Joshua, Caleb, the judges, and Samuel. Starting with Joshua we are told that he "called upon the Most High" when "his enemies pressed him on every side" (Sir 46:5), and that the Lord answered him and fought on his behalf. A parallel account is given for Samuel at the end of our chapter: "He called upon the Lord, the Mighty One, when his enemies pressed him on every side" (v. 16), and the Lord "thundered from heaven . . . and wiped out the leaders of the people of Tyre" and the Philistines. Echoing language woven throughout the Psalms, these faithful men call upon God, and God answers them. Their character compels God to answer their prayers. Joshua "wholly followed the Mighty One" (v. 6), and Samuel was "beloved" of the Lord (v. 13) and "a trustworthy seer" (v. 15), so much so that no one could accuse him of seeking self-gain or exploitation (see v. 19). Their calling out to God marks a life of prayer, and their life of prayer forges strong moral character that puts them "in the sight of the Lord" (v. 6), and thus God answers them. How do these holy men illustrate that it is "good to follow the Lord" (v. 9)?

December 20

1 MACCABEES 14

In the one hundred and seventy-second year Deme′trius the king assembled his forces and marched into Med′ia to secure help, so that he

could make war against Try´pho. [2]When
Ar´saces the king of Persia and Med´ia heard
that Deme´trius had invaded his territory,
he sent one of his commanders to take him
alive. [3]And he went and defeated the army
of Deme´trius, and seized him and took him
to Ar´saces, who put him under guard.

[4]The land had rest all the days of Simon.
He sought the good of his nation;
his rule was pleasing to them,
as was the honor shown him, all his days.
[5]To crown all his honors he took Joppa for
a harbor,
and opened a way to the isles of the sea.
[6]He extended the borders of his nation,
and gained full control of the country.
[7]He gathered a host of captives;
he ruled over Gaza´ra and Beth-zur and
the citadel,
and he removed its uncleanness from it;
and there was none to oppose him.
[8]They tilled their land in peace;
the ground gave its increase,
and the trees of the plains their fruit.
[9]Old men sat in the streets;
they all talked together of good things;
and the youths donned the glories and
garments of war.
[10]He supplied the cities with food,
and furnished them with the means
offense,
till his renown spread to the ends of
the earth.
[11]He established peace in the land,
and Israel rejoiced with great joy.
[12]Each man sat under his vine and his fig tree,
and there was none to make them afraid.
[13]No one was left in the land to fight them,
and the kings were crushed in those days.
[14]He strengthened all the humble of
his people;
he sought out the law,
and did away with every lawless and
wicked man.
[15]He made the sanctuary glorious,
and added to the vessels of the sanctuary.

[16]It was heard in Rome, and as far away
as Sparta, that Jonathan had died, and
they were deeply grieved. [17]When they
heard that Simon his brother had become
high priest in his place, and that he was
ruling over the country and the cities in
it, [18]they wrote to him on bronze tablets
to renew with him the friendship and
alliance which they had established with
Judas and Jonathan his brothers. [19]And
these were read before the assembly in
Jerusalem.

[20]This is a copy of the letter which the
Spartans sent: "The rulers and the city of
the Spartans to Simon the high priest and
to the elders and the priests and the rest of
the Jewish people, our brethren, greeting.
[21]The envoys who were sent to our people
have told us about your glory and honor,
and we rejoiced at their coming. [22]And
what they said we have recorded in our
public decrees, as follows, 'Nume´nius the
son of Anti´ochus and Antip´ater the son
of Jason, envoys of the Jews, have come to
us to renew their friendship with us. [23]It
has pleased our people to receive these
men with honor and to put a copy of their
words in the public archives, so that the
people of the Spartans may have a record
of them. And they have sent a copy of this
to Simon the high priest.' "

[24]After this Simon sent Nume´nius to
Rome with a large gold shield weighing a
thousand minas, to confirm the alliance
with the Romans.

[25]When the people heard these things
they said, "How shall we thank Simon and
his sons? [26]For he and his brothers and the
house of his father have stood firm; they
have fought and repulsed Israel's enemies
and established its freedom." [27]So they
made a record on bronze tablets and put it
upon pillars on Mount Zion.

This is a copy of what they wrote: "On the
eighteenth day of E´lul, in the one hundred
and seventy-second year, which is the
third year of Simon the great high priest,
[28]in Asar´amel, in the great assembly of the
priests and the people and the rulers of the
nation and the elders of the country, the
following was proclaimed to us:

[29]"Since wars often occurred in the
country, Simon the son of Mattathi´as, a
priest of the sons of Jo´arib, and his brothers,

exposed themselves to danger and resisted
the enemies of their nation, in order that
their sanctuary and the law might be
perserved; and they brought great glory to
their nation. 30Jonathan rallied the nation,
and became their high priest, and was
gathered to his people. 31And when their
enemies decided to invade their country
and lay hands on their sanctuary, 32then
Simon rose up and fought for his nation.
He spent great sums of his own money; he
armed the men of his nation's forces and
paid them wages. 33He fortified the cities of
Judea, and Beth-zur on the borders of Judea,
where formerly the arms of the enemy had
been stored, and he placed there a garrison
of Jews. 34He also fortified Joppa, which is by
the sea, and Gaza′ra, which is on the borders
of Azo′tus, where the enemy formerly dwelt.
He settled Jews there, and provided in those
cities whatever was necessary for their
restoration.

35"The people saw Simon's faithfulness
and the glory which he had resolved to win
for his nation, and they made him their
leader and high priest, because he had done
all these things and because of the justice
and loyalty which he had maintained
toward his nation. He sought in every way
to exalt his people. 36And in his days things
prospered in his hands, so that the Gentiles
were put out of the country, as were also
the men in the city of David in Jerusalem,
who had built themselves a citadel from
which they used to sally forth and defile
the environs of the sanctuary and do great
damage to its purity. 37He settled Jews
in it, and fortified it for the safety of the
country and of the city, and built the walls
of Jerusalem higher.

38"In view of these things King Deme′trius
confirmed him in the high priesthood,
39and he made him one of the king's friends
and paid him high honors. 40For he had
heard that the Jews were addressed by the
Romans as friends and allies and brethren,
and that the Romans had received the
envoys of Simon with honor.

41"And the Jews and their priests decided
that Simon should be their leader and
high priest for ever, until a trustworthy
prophet should arise, 42and that he should
be governor over them and that he should
take charge of the sanctuary and appoint
men over its tasks and over the country
and the weapons and the strongholds, and
that he should take charge of the sanctuary,
43and that he should be obeyed by all, and
that all contracts in the country should be
written in his name, and that he should be
clothed in purple and wear gold.

44"And none of the people or priests
shall be permitted to nullify any of
these decisions or to oppose what he
says, or to convene an assembly in the
country without his permission, or to
be clothed in purple or put on a gold
buckle. 45Whoever acts contrary to these
decisions or nullifies any of them shall be
liable to punishment."

46And all the people agreed to grant
Simon the right to act in accord with
these decisions. 47So Simon accepted
and agreed to be high priest, to be
commander and ethnarch of the Jews and
priests, and to be protector of them all.
48And they gave orders to inscribe this
decree upon bronze tablets, to put them
up in a conspicuous place in the precincts
of the sanctuary, 49and to deposit copies
of them in the treasury, so that Simon and
his sons might have them.

SIRACH 47

And after him Nathan rose up
to prophesy in the days of David.
2As the fat is selected from the
peace offering,
so David was selected from
the sons of Israel.
3He played with lions as with young goats,
and with bears as with lambs of
the flock.
4In his youth did he not kill a giant,
and take away reproach from the people,
when he lifted his hand with a stone in
the sling
and struck down the boasting of Goliath?

[5]For he appealed to the Lord, the Most High,
and he gave him strength in his
right hand
to slay a man mighty in war,
to exalt the power of his people.
[6]So they glorified him for his ten thousands,
and praised him for the blessings of
the Lord,
when the glorious diadem was bestowed
upon him.
[7]For he wiped out his enemies on every side,
and annihilated his adversaries
the Philis′tines;
he crushed their power even to this day.
[8]In all that he did he gave thanks
to the Holy One, the Most High, with
ascriptions of glory;
he sang praise with all his heart,
and he loved his Maker.
[9]He placed singers before the altar,
to make sweet melody with
their voices.
[10]He gave beauty to the feasts,
and arranged their times throughout
the year,
while they praised God's holy name,
and the sanctuary resounded from
early morning.
[11]The Lord took away his sins,
and exalted his power for ever;
he gave him the covenant of kings
and a throne of glory in Israel.

[12]After him rose up a wise son
who fared amply because of him;
[13]Solomon reigned in days of peace,
and God gave him rest on every side,
that he might build a house for his name
and prepare a sanctuary to stand for ever.
[14]How wise you became in your youth!
You overflowed like a river with
understanding.
[15]Your soul covered the earth,
and you filled it with parables
and riddles.
[16]Your name reached to far-off islands,
and you were loved for your peace.
[17]For your songs and proverbs and parables,
and for your interpretations, the
countries marveled at you.
[18]In the name of the Lord God,
who is called the God of Israel,
you gathered gold like tin
and amassed silver like lead.
[19]But you laid your loins beside women,
and through your body you were brought
into subjection.
[20]You put stain upon your honor,
and defiled your posterity,
so that you brought wrath upon
your children
and they were grieved at your folly,
[21]so that the sovereignty was divided
and a disobedient kingdom arose out
of E′phraim.
[22]But the Lord will never give up his mercy,
nor cause any of his works
to perish;
he will never blot out the descendants of
his chosen one,
nor destroy the posterity of him who
loved him;
so he gave a remnant to Jacob,
and to David a root of his stock.

[23]Solomon rested with his fathers,
and left behind him one of his sons,
ample in folly and lacking in
understanding,
Rehobo′am, whose policy caused the
people to revolt.
Also Jerobo′am the son of Ne′bat, who
caused Israel to sin
and gave to E′phraim a sinful way.
[24]Their sins became exceedingly many,
so as to remove them from their land.
[25]For they sought out every sort of
wickedness,
till vengeance came upon them.

48 Then the prophet Eli′jah arose like
a fire,
and his word burned like a torch.
[2]He brought a famine upon them,
and by his zeal he made them few in
number.
[3]By the word of the Lord he shut up
the heavens,
and also three times brought
down fire.

4How glorious you were, O Eli′jah, in your
wondrous deeds!
And who has the right to boast which
you have?
5You who raised a corpse from death
and from Hades, by the word of the
Most High;
6who brought kings down to destruction,
and famous men from their beds,
and easily destroyed their dominion;
7who heard rebuke at Sinai
and judgments of vengeance at Horeb;
8who anointed kings to inflict retribution,
and prophets to succeed you.
9You who were taken up by a whirlwind of fire,
in a chariot with horses of fire;
10you who are ready at the appointed time,
it is written,
to calm the wrath of God before it breaks
out in fury,
to turn the heart of the father to the son,
and to restore the tribes of Jacob.
11Blessed are those who saw you,
and those who have fallen asleep in
your love;
for we also shall surely live,
but our name, after death, will not be such.

REVELATION 10

Then I saw another mighty angel coming down from heaven, wrapped in a cloud, with a rainbow over his head, and his face was like the sun, and his legs like pillars of fire. 2He had a little scroll open in his
hand. And he set his right foot on the sea,
and his left foot on the land, 3and called out
with a loud voice, like a lion roaring; when he
called out, the seven thunders sounded. 4And
when the seven thunders had sounded, I was
about to write, but I heard a voice from heaven
saying, "Seal up what the seven thunders have
said, and do not write it down." 5And the angel whom I saw standing on sea and land lifted
up his right hand to heaven 6and swore by him
who lives for ever and ever, who created heav-
en and what is in it, the earth and what is in it,
and the sea and what is in it, that there should
be no more delay, 7but that in the days of the
trumpet call to be sounded by the seventh angel, the mystery of God, as he announced to his
servants the prophets, should be fulfilled.
8Then the voice which I had heard from
heaven spoke to me again, saying, "Go, take the
scroll which is open in the hand of the angel
who is standing on the sea and on the land."
9So I went to the angel and told him to give me
the little scroll; and he said to me, "Take it and
eat; it will be bitter to your stomach, but sweet
as honey in your mouth." 10And I took the little
scroll from the hand of the angel and ate it; it
was sweet as honey in my mouth, but when
I had eaten it my stomach was made bitter.
11And I was told, "You must again prophesy
about many peoples and nations and tongues
and kings."

REFLECTION

In the description of the idyllic peace that dawned upon the Jews in the time of Simon Maccebeus, it says, "Each man sat under his vine and his fig tree, and there was none to make them afraid" (1 Mc 14:12). This image goes back to Solomon's golden age (see 1 Kgs 4:25) and is also used by Sirach to describe the peace Solomon is given: "God gave him rest on every side" (Sir 47:13). The prophets then foretell the future restoration of Israel, when the Messiah comes, as ushering in an era when everyone can sit in peace under their vine and fig tree (see Mi 4:4; Zec 3:10). Peace is a gift from God and, for Israel, lasting peace will come only with the Messiah. This is perhaps why St. John shows us, at the outset of his Gospel, Jesus encountering Nathanael with a reference to him sitting under his fig tree (see Jn 1:48). Throughout Scripture, peace, *shalom*, is a gift that God gives, indeed, almost imposes upon the normal state of human affairs, which is one of almost constant conflict. When in Revelation the angels blow trumpets, or open seals, or throw down bowls, it is not so much that they are causing violent conflict on earth as they are removing the God-imposed grace of peace in response to growing human sin, thus allowing humanity to reap the fruit of its own sowing. Do you agree that violence is rooted in sin, and that peace is bestowed from above?

December 21

1 MACCABEES 15

**Anti´ochus, the son of De-
me´trius the king, sent a letter
from the islands of the sea to
Simon, the priest and ethnarch of the
Jews, and to all the nation; [2]its contents were as follows: "King Anti´ochus**
to Simon the high priest and ethnarch and
to the nation of the Jews, greeting. [3]Where-
as certain pestilent men have gained control of the kingdom of our fathers, and
I intend to lay claim to the kingdom so
that I may restore it as it formerly was,
and have recruited a host of mercenary
troops and have equipped warships, [4]and
intend to make a landing in the country
so that I may proceed against those who
have destroyed our country and those
who have devastated many cities in my
kingdom, [5]now therefore I confirm to
you all the tax remissions that the kings
before me have granted you, and release
from all the other payments from which
they have released you. [6]I permit you to
mint your own coinage as money for your
country, [7]and I grant freedom to Jerusalem and the sanctuary. All the weapons
which you have prepared and the strongholds which you have built and now hold
shall remain yours. [8]Every debt you owe
to the royal treasury and any such future
debts shall be canceled for you from now
on and for all time. [9]When we gain control of our kingdom, we will bestow great
honor upon you and your nation and the
temple, so that your glory will become
manifest in all the earth."

[10]In the one hundred and seventy-fourth
year Anti´ochus set out and invaded the
land of his fathers. All the troops rallied
to him, so that there were few with
Try´pho. [11]Anti´ochus pursued him, and
he came in his flight to Dor, which is by
the sea; [12]for he knew that troubles had
converged upon him, and his troops had
deserted him. [13]So Anti´ochus encamped
against Dor, and with him were a hundred
and twenty thousand warriors and eight
thousand cavalry. [14]He surrounded the
city, and the ships joined battle from the
sea; he pressed the city hard from land
and sea, and permitted no one to leave or
enter it.

[15]Then Nume´nius and his companions
arrived from Rome, with letters to
the kings and countries, in which the
following was written: [16]"Lucius, consul of
the Romans, to King Ptol´emy, greeting.
[17]The envoys of the Jews have come to
us as our friends and allies to renew our
ancient friendship and alliance. They had
been sent by Simon the high priest and by
the people of the Jews, [18]and have brought
a gold shield weighing a thousand minas.
[19]We therefore have decided to write to
the kings and countries that they should
not seek their harm or make war against
them and their cities and their country, or
make alliance with those who war against
them. [20]And it has seemed good to us to
accept the shield from them. [21]Therefore
if any pestilent men have fled to you from
their country, hand them over to Simon
the high priest, that he may punish them
according to their law."

[22]The consul wrote the same thing to
Deme´trius the king and to At´talus and
A´riara´thes and Ar´saces, [23]and to all the
countries, and to Samp´sames, and to the
Spartans, and to De´los, and to Myn´dos,
and to Sic´yon, and to Ca´ria, and to
Sa´mos, and to Pamphyl´ia, and to Ly´cia,
and to Hal´´icarnas´sus, and to Rhodes, and
to Phase´lis, and to Cos, and to Si´de, and
to Ar´adus and Gorty´na and Cni´dus and
Cyprus and Cyre´ne. [24]They also sent a copy
of these things to Simon the high priest.

[25]Anti´ochus the king besieged Dor anew,
continually throwing his forces against it
and making engines of war; and he shut
Try´pho up and kept him from going out
or in. [26]And Simon sent to Anti´ochus two
thousand picked men, to fight for him,
and silver and gold and much military

equipment. [27]But he refused to receive them, and he broke all the agreements he formerly had made with Simon, and became estranged from him. [28]He sent to him Ath´´eno´bius, one of his friends, to confer with him, saying, "You hold control of Joppa and Gaza´ra and the citadel in Jerusalem; they are cities of my kingdom. [29]You have devastated their territory, you have done great damage in the land, and you have taken possession of many places in my kingdom. [30]Now then, hand over the cities which you have seized and the tribute money of the places which you have conquered outside the borders of Judea; [31]or else give me for them five hundred talents of silver, and for the destruction that you have caused and the tribute money of the cities, five hundred talents more. Otherwise we will come and conquer you."

[32]So Ath´´eno´bius the friend of the king came to Jerusalem, and when he saw the splendor of Simon, and the sideboard with its gold and silver plate, and his great magnificence, he was amazed. He reported to him the words of the king, [33]but Simon gave him this reply: "We have neither taken foreign land nor seized foreign property, but only the inheritance of our fathers, which at one time had been unjustly taken by our enemies. [34]Now that we have the opportunity, we are firmly holding the inheritance of our fathers. [35]As for Joppa and Gaza´ra, which you demand, they were causing great damage among the people and to our land; for them we will give you a hundred talents." Ath´´eno´bius did not answer him a word, [36]but returned in wrath to the king and reported to him these words and the splendor of Simon and all that he had seen. And the king was greatly angered.

[37]Now Try´pho embarked on a ship and escaped to Orthosi´a. [38]Then the king made Cendebe´us commander-in-chief of the coastal country, and gave him troops of infantry and cavalry. [39]He commanded him to encamp against Judea, and commanded him to build up Ked´ron and fortify its gates, and to make war on the people; but the king pursued Try´pho. [40]So Cendebe´us came to Jam´nia and began to provoke the people and invade Judea and take the people captive and kill them. [41]He built up Ked´ron and stationed there horsemen and troops, so that they might go out and make raids along the highways of Judea, as the king had ordered him.

16 John went up from Gaza´ra and reported to Simon his father what Cendebe´us had done. [2]And Simon called in his two older sons Judas and John, and said to them: "I and my brothers and the house of my father have fought the wars of Israel from our youth until this day, and things have prospered in our hands so that we have delivered Israel many times. [3]But now I have grown old, and you by His mercy are mature in years. Take my place and my brother's, and go out and fight for our nation, and may the help which comes from Heaven be with you."

[4]So John chose out of the country twenty thousand warriors and horsemen, and they marched against Cendebe´us and camped for the night in Mo´dein. [5]Early in the morning they arose and marched into the plain, and behold, a large force of infantry and horsemen was coming to meet them; and a stream lay between them. [6]Then he and his army lined up against them. And he saw that the soldiers were afraid to cross the stream, so he crossed over first; and when his men saw him, they crossed over after him. [7]Then he divided the army and placed the horsemen in the midst of the infantry, for the cavalry of the enemy were very numerous. [8]And they sounded the trumpets, and Cendebe´us and his army were put to flight, and many of them were wounded and fell; the rest fled into the stronghold. [9]At that time Judas the brother of John was wounded, but John pursued them until Cendebe´us reached Ked´ron, which he had built. [10]They also fled into the towers that were in the fields of Azo´tus, and John burned it with fire, and about two thousand of them fell. And he returned to Judea safely.

11 Now Ptol′emy the son of Abu′bus had
been appointed governor over the plain of
Jericho, and he had much silver and gold,
12 for he was son-in-law of the high priest.
13 His heart was lifted up; he determined
to get control of the country, and made
treacherous plans against Simon and his
sons, to do away with them. 14 Now Simon
was visiting the cities of the country and
attending to their needs, and he went
down to Jericho with Mattathi′as and
Judas his sons, in the one hundred and
seventy-seventh year, in the eleventh
month, which is the month of Shebat′.
15 The son of Abu′bus received them
treacherously in the little stronghold
called Dok, which he had built; he gave
them a great banquet, and hid men there.
16 When Simon and his sons were drunk,
Ptol′emy and his men rose up, took their
weapons, and rushed in against Simon in
the banquet hall, and they killed him and
his two sons and some of his servants. 17 So
he committed an act of great treachery
and returned evil for good.

18 Then Ptol′emy wrote a report about
these things and sent it to the king,
asking him to send troops to aid him
and to turn over to him the cities and the
country. 19 He sent other men to Gaza′ra
to do away with John; he sent letters to
the captains asking them to come to him
so that he might give them silver and
gold and gifts; 20 and he sent other men
to take possession of Jerusalem and the
temple hill. 21 But some one ran ahead and
reported to John at Gaza′ra that his father
and brothers had perished, and that "he
has sent men to kill you also." 22 When he
heard this, he was greatly shocked; and he
seized the men who came to destroy him
and killed them, for he had found out that
they were seeking to destroy him.

23 The rest of the acts of John and his
wars and the brave deeds which he did,
and the building of the walls which he
built, and his achievements, 24 behold,
they are written in the chronicles of his
high priesthood, from the time that he
became high priest after his father.

SIRACH 48

12 It was Eli′jah who covered by
the whirlwind,
and Eli′sha was filled with his spirit;
in all his days he did not tremble before
any ruler,
and no one brought him into subjection.
13 Nothing was too hard for him,
and when he was dead his body
prophesied.
14 As in his life he did wonders,
so in death his deeds were marvelous.

15 For all this the people did not repent,
and they did not forsake their sins,
till they were carried away captive from
their land
and were scattered over all the earth;
the people were left very few in number,
but with rulers from the house of David.
16 Some of them did what was pleasing to God,
but others multiplied sins.

17 Hezeki′ah fortified his city,
and brought water into the midst of it;
he tunneled the sheer rock with iron
and built pools for water.
18 In his days Sennach′erib came up,
and sent the Rab′shakeh;
he lifted up his hand against Zion
and made great boasts in his arrogance.
19 Then their hearts were shaken and their
hands trembled,
and they were in anguish, like women
with labor pains.
20 But they called upon the Lord who
is merciful,
spreading forth their hands toward him;
and the Holy One quickly heard them
from heaven,
and delivered them by the hand of Isaiah.
21 The Lord struck the camp of the Assyrians,
and his angel wiped them out.
22 For Hezeki′ah did what was pleasing to
the Lord,
and he held strongly to the ways of David
his father,
which Isai′ah the prophet commanded,
who was great and faithful in his vision.

[23]In his days the sun went backward,
and he lengthened the life of the king.
[24]By the spirit of might he saw the last things,
and comforted those who mourned
in Zion.
[25]He revealed what was to occur to the
end of time,
and the hidden things before they
came to pass.

REVELATION 11

Then I was given a measuring rod like a staff, and I was told: "Rise and measure the temple of God and the altar and those who worship
there, [2]but do not measure the court outside
the temple; leave that out, for it is given
over to the nations, and they will trample
over the holy city for forty-two months.
[3]And I will grant my two witnesses power
to prophesy for one thousand two hundred
and sixty days, clothed in sackcloth."
[4]These are the two olive trees and the two
lampstands which stand before the Lord
of the earth. [5]And if any one would harm
them, fire pours from their mouth and
consumes their foes; if any one would harm
them, thus he is doomed to be killed. [6]They
have power to shut the sky, that no rain may
fall during the days of their prophesying,
and they have power over the waters to
turn them into blood, and to afflict the
earth with every plague, as often as they
desire. [7]And when they have finished their
testimony, the beast that ascends from the
bottomless pit will make war upon them
and conquer them and kill them, [8]and their
dead bodies will lie in the street of the great
city which is allegorically called Sodom and
Egypt, where their Lord was crucified. [9]For
three days and a half men from the peoples
and tribes and tongues and nations gaze at
their dead bodies and refuse to let them be
placed in a tomb, [10]and those who dwell on
the earth will rejoice over them and make
merry and exchange presents, because
these two prophets had been a torment to
those who dwell on the earth. [11]But after the
three and a half days a breath of life from
God entered them, and they stood up on
their feet, and great fear fell on those who
saw them. [12]Then they heard a loud voice
from heaven saying to them, "Come up
here!" And in the sight of their foes they
went up to heaven in a cloud. [13]And at that
hour there was a great earthquake, and a
tenth of the city fell; seven thousand people
were killed in the earthquake, and the rest
were terrified and gave glory to the God of
heaven.
[14]The second woe has passed; behold, the
third woe is soon to come.
[15]Then the seventh angel blew his trumpet,
and there were loud voices in heaven, saying,
"The kingdom of the world has become the
kingdom of our Lord and of his Christ, and
he shall reign for ever and ever." [16]And the
twenty-four elders who sit on their thrones
before God fell on their faces and worshiped
God, [17]saying,

"We give thanks to you, Lord God
Almighty, who are and who were,
that you have taken your great power and
begun to reign.
[18]The nations raged, but your wrath came,
and the time for the dead to be judged,
for rewarding your servants, the prophets
and saints,
and those who fear your name, both
small and great,
and for destroying the destroyers of the
earth."

[19]Then God's temple in heaven was
opened, and the ark of his covenant was seen
within his temple; and there were flashes of
lightning, loud noises, peals of thunder, an
earthquake, and heavy hail.

REFLECTION

The description of the second woe in Revelation 11 distinguishes two places, both related to the Temple of God. John is told to "measure" the temple but not its outer court (see Rev 11:2). Measuring implies protection, as compared to the outer court which is to be given up to the trampling of the Gentiles. The Temple of God is the heavenly sanctuary John was taken up to in Revelations 4:1, while the outer court is the "great city" with allegorical names (11:8) where Christ died, which means Jerusalem. This prophecy then refers to the destruction of Jerusalem and its Temple by the Romans in 70 AD. With the blowing of the seventh trumpet, we are taken back to the moment of the Lamb's victory (the Cross) where the twenty-four elders and all Heaven worship God (see Rev 5), giving thanks to the Lord God "who are and who were, that you have taken your great power and begun to reign" (11:17). The Death of Christ, and not the beast ascended to "conquer and kill" (v. 7), is ironically the triumph of the Lamb, by means of which he shows what is true conquering. Note that they celebrate Christ as "who are and who were" (v. 17) but no longer "who is to come" (1:8), because in his Birth and Death he has come, which the next chapter takes up in detail.

December 22

2 MACCABEES 1

The Jewish brethren in Jerusalem and those in the land of Judea,
To their Jewish brethren in Egypt,
Greeting, and good peace.
2May God do good to you, and may he
remember his covenant with Abraham and
Isaac and Jacob, his faithful servants. 3May
he give you all a heart to worship him and to
do his will with a strong heart and a willing
spirit. 4May he open your heart to his law
and his commandments, and may he bring
peace. 5May he hear your prayers and be
reconciled to you, and may he not forsake
you in time of evil. 6We are now praying for
you here.
7In the reign of Deme′trius, in the one
hundred and sixty-ninth year, we Jews
wrote to you, in the critical distress which
came upon us in those years after Jason and
his company revolted from the holy land
and the kingdom 8and burned the gate and
shed innocent blood. We begged the Lord
and we were heard, and we offered sacrifice
and cereal offering, and we lighted the
lamps and we set out the loaves. 9And now
see that you keep the feast of booths in the
month of Chis′lev, in the one hundred and
eighty-eighth year.
10Those in Jerusalem and those in Judea
and the senate and Judas,
To Aristob′ulus, who is of the family of the anointed priests, teacher of Ptol′emy the king, and to the Jews in Egypt,
Greeting, and good health.
11Having been saved by God out of grave
dangers we thank him greatly for taking
our side against the king. 12For he drove
out those who fought against the holy city.
13For when the leader reached Persia with a
force that seemed irresistible, they were cut to
pieces in the temple of Nane′a by a deception
employed by the priests of Nanea. 14For under
pretext of intending to marry her, Anti′ochus
came to the place together with his friends, to
secure most of its treasures as a dowry. 15When
the priests of the temple of Nane′a had set out
the treasures and Anti′ochus had come with a
few men inside the wall of the sacred precinct,
they closed the temple as soon as he entered
it. 16Opening the secret door in the ceiling,
they threw stones and struck down the leader
and his men, and dismembered them and cut
off their heads and threw them to the people
outside. 17Blessed in every way be our God,
who has brought judgment upon those who
have behaved impiously.
18Since on the twenty-fifth day of Chis′lev we
shall celebrate the purification of the temple,
we thought it necessary to notify you, in order
that you also may celebrate the feast of booths
and the feast of the fire given when Nehemi′ah,
who built the temple and the altar, offered
sacrifices.
19For when our fathers were being led captive
to Persia, the pious priests of that time took

some of the fire of the altar and secretly hid it in the hollow of a dry cistern, where they took such precautions that the place was unknown to any one. [20]But after many years had passed, when it pleased God, Nehemi′ah, having been commissioned by the king of Persia, sent the descendants of the priests who had hidden the fire to get it. And when they reported to us that they had not found fire but thick liquid, he ordered them to dip it out and bring it. [21]And when the materials for the sacrifices were presented, Nehemi′ah ordered the priests to sprinkle the liquid on the wood and what was laid upon it. [22]When this was done and some time had passed and the sun, which had been clouded over, shone out, a great fire blazed up, so that all marveled. [23]And while the sacrifice was being consumed, the priests offered prayer—the priests and every one. Jonathan led, and the rest responded, as did Nehemi′ah. [24]The prayer was to this effect:

"O Lord, Lord God, Creator of all things, who are awe-inspiring and strong and just and merciful, who alone are King and are kind, [25]who alone are bountiful, who alone are just and almighty and eternal, who rescue Israel from every evil, who chose the fathers and consecrated them, [26]accept this sacrifice on behalf of all your people Israel and preserve your portion and make it holy. [27]Gather together our scattered people, set free those who are slaves among the Gentiles, look upon those who are rejected and despised, and let the Gentiles know that you are our God. [28]Afflict those who oppress and are insolent with pride. [29]Plant your people in your holy place, as Moses said."

[30]Then the priests sang the hymns. [31]And when the materials of the sacrifice were consumed, Nehemi′ah ordered that the liquid that was left should be poured upon large stones. [32]When this was done, a flame blazed up; but when the light from the altar shone back, it went out. [33]When this matter became known, and it was reported to the king of the Persians that, in the place where the exiled priests had hidden the fire, the liquid had appeared with which Nehemi′ah and his associates had burned the materials of the sacrifice, [34]the king investigated the matter, and enclosed the place and made it sacred. [35]And with those persons whom the king favored he exchanged many excellent gifts. [36]Nehemi′ah and his associates called this "nephthar," which means purification, but by most people it is called naphtha.

2 One finds in the records that Jeremi′ah the prophet ordered those who were being deported to take some of the fire, as has been told, [2]and that the prophet after giving them the law instructed those who were being deported not to forget the commandments of the Lord, nor to be led astray in their thoughts upon seeing the gold and silver statues and their adornment. [3]And with other similar words he exhorted them that the law should not depart from their hearts.

[4]It was also in the writing that the prophet, having received an oracle, ordered that the tent and the ark should follow with him, and that he went out to the mountain where Moses had gone up and had seen the inheritance of God. [5]And Jeremi′ah came and found a cave, and he brought there the tent and the ark and the altar of incense, and he sealed up the entrance. [6]Some of those who followed him came up to mark the way, but could not find it. [7]When Jeremi′ah learned of it, he rebuked them and declared: "The place shall be unknown until God gathers his people together again and shows his mercy. [8]And then the Lord will disclose these things, and the glory of the Lord and the cloud will appear, as they were shown in the case of Moses, and as Solomon asked that the place should be specially consecrated."

[9]It was also made clear that being possessed of wisdom Solomon offered sacrifice for the dedication and completion of the temple. [10]Just as Moses prayed to the Lord, and fire came down from heaven and devoured the sacrifices, so also Solomon prayed, and the fire came down and consumed the whole burnt offerings. [11]And Moses said, "They were consumed because the sin offering had not been eaten." [12]Likewise Solomon also kept the eight days.

[13]The same things are reported in the records and in the memoirs of Nehemi′ah, and also that he founded a library and collected the

books about the kings and prophets, and the writings of David, and letters of kings about votive offerings. 14In the same way Judas also collected all the books that had been lost on account of the war which had come upon us, and they are in our possession. 15So if you have need of them, send people to get them for you.
16Since, therefore, we are about to celebrate the purification, we write to you. Will you therefore please keep the days? 17It is God who has saved all his people, and has returned the inheritance to all, and the kingship and priesthood and consecration, 18as he promised through the law. For we have hope in God that he will soon have mercy upon us and will gather us from everywhere under heaven into his holy place, for he has rescued us from great evils and has purified the place.

SIRACH 49

The memory of Josi′ah is like a blending
of incense
prepared by the art of the perfumer;
it is sweet as honey to every mouth,
and like music at a banquet of wine.
2He was led aright in converting
the people,
and took away the abominations
of iniquity.
3He set his heart upon the Lord;
in the days of wicked men he strengthened
godliness.

4Except David and Hezeki′ah and Josi′ah
they all sinned greatly,
for they forsook the law of the Most High;
the kings of Judah came to an end;
5for they gave their power to others,
and their glory to a foreign nation,
6who set fire to the chosen city of
the sanctuary,
and made her streets desolate,
according to the word of Jeremi′ah.
7For they had afflicted him;
yet he had been consecrated in the womb
as prophet,
to pluck up and afflict and destroy,
and likewise to build and to plant.
8It was Ezek′iel who saw the vision of glory
which God showed him above the chariot
of the cherubim.
9For God remembered his enemies
with storm,
and did good to those who directed their
ways rightly.
10May the bones of the twelve prophets
revive from where they lie,
for they comforted the people of Jacob
and delivered them with confident hope.
11How shall we magnify Zerub′babel?
He was like a signet on the right hand,
12 and so was Jesh′ua the son of Jo′zadak;
in their days they built the house
and raised a temple holy to the Lord,
prepared for everlasting glory.
13The memory of Nehemi′ah also is lasting;
he raised for us the walls that had fallen,
and set up the gates and bars
and rebuilt our ruined houses.
14No one like E′noch has been created
on earth,
for he was taken up from the earth.
15And no man like Joseph has been born,
and his bones are cared for.
16Shem and Seth were honored among men,
and Adam above every living being in
the creation.

REVELATION 12

And a great sign appeared in heaven, a woman clothed with the sun, with the moon under her feet, and on her head a crown of twelve stars; 2she was with child and she cried out in her pangs of birth,
in anguish for delivery. 3And another sign appeared in heaven; behold, a great red dragon, with seven heads and ten horns, and seven diadems upon his heads. 4His tail swept down a third of the stars of heaven, and cast them to the earth. And the dragon stood before the woman who was about to

bear a child, that he might devour her child when she brought it forth; 5she brought forth a male child, one who is to rule all the nations with a rod of iron, but her child was caught up to God and to his throne, 6and the woman fled into the wilderness, where she has a place prepared by God, in which to be nourished for one thousand two hundred and sixty days.

7Now war arose in heaven, Michael and his angels fighting against the dragon; and the dragon and his angels fought, 8but they were defeated and there was no longer any place for them in heaven. 9And the great dragon was thrown down, that ancient serpent, who is called the Devil and Satan, the deceiver of the whole world—he was thrown down to the earth, and his angels were thrown down with him. 10And I heard a loud voice in heaven, saying, "Now the salvation and the power and the kingdom of our God and the authority of his Christ have come, for the accuser of our brethren has been thrown down, who accuses them day and night before our God. 11And they have conquered him by the blood of the Lamb and by the word of their testimony, for they loved not their lives even unto death. 12Rejoice then, O heaven and you that dwell therein! But woe to you, O earth and sea, for the devil has come down to you in great wrath, because he knows that his time is short!"

13And when the dragon saw that he had been thrown down to the earth, he pursued the woman who had borne the male child. 14But the woman was given the two wings of the great eagle that she might fly from the serpent into the wilderness, to the place where she is to be nourished for a time, and times, and half a time. 15The serpent poured water like a river out of his mouth after the woman, to sweep her away with the flood. 16But the earth came to the help of the woman, and the earth opened its mouth and swallowed the river which the dragon had poured from his mouth. 17Then the dragon was angry with the woman, and went off to make war on the rest of her offspring, on those who keep the commandments of God and bear testimony to Jesus. And he stood on the sand of the sea.

REFLECTION

Second Maccabees recounts that the Jews observed Hanukkah, the new festival celebrating the purification of the Temple. When Judas Maccabeus purified the Temple in the month of *Chislev*, in the manner of the Feast of Booths, following the Temple's desecration by the Greeks, it became a new Jewish feast day (see 2 Mc 1:9, 18). God's Temple was the place of encounter between Israel and the Lord, and its purification was necessary for God to be present. At the end of Revelation 11, St. John sees the inner sanctuary of the heavenly Temple and the Ark of the Covenant. Then lightning, hail, and thunder obscure his vision (see Rev 11:19). As they clear he sees (starting in chapter 12) a great sign in the heavens. Where the Ark and Temple had stood now stands a woman clothed in glory and with a crown of twelve stars. Who is the woman? She gives birth to the Messiah. Since the Messiah is Jesus, the woman must be Mary. In her extraordinary purity, the virgin mother is the new purified temple in which God dwells. The dragon cannot conquer the woman, and so in rage he goes off to make war on the rest of her offspring. These are not her biological children as with Jesus, but rather her spiritual children, "who keep the commandments of God and bear testimony to Jesus" (12:17). Do you follow this passage and relate to Mary as your spiritual mother? (see Jn 19:27).

December 23

2 MACCABEES 2

19The story of Judas Mac′cabe′us and his brothers, and the purification of the great temple, and the dedication of the altar, 20and further the wars against Anti′ochus Epiph′anes and his son Eu′pator, 21and the appearances which came from heaven to those who strove zealously on behalf of Judaism, so that though few in number they seized the whole land and pursued the barbarian hordes, [22]and recovered the temple famous throughout the world and freed the city and restored the laws that were about to be abolished, while the Lord with great kindness became gracious to them—[23]all this, which has been set forth by Jason of Cyre′ne in five volumes, we shall attempt to condense into a single book. [24]For considering the flood of numbers involved and the difficulty there is for those who wish to enter upon the narratives of history because of the mass of material, [25]we have aimed to please those who wish to read, to make it easy for those who are inclined to memorize, and to profit all readers. [26]For us who have undertaken the toil of abbreviating, it is no light matter but calls for sweat and loss of sleep, [27]just as it is not easy for one who prepares a banquet and seeks the benefit of others. However, to secure the gratitude of many we will gladly endure the uncomfortable toil, [28]leaving the responsibility for exact details to the compiler, while devoting our effort to arriving at the outlines of the condensation. [29]For as the master builder of a new house must be concerned with the whole construction, while the one who undertakes its painting and decoration has to consider only what is suitable for its adornment, such in my judgment is the case with us. [30]It is the duty of the original historian to occupy the ground and to discuss matters from every side and to take trouble with details, [31]but the one who recasts the narrative should be allowed to strive for brevity of expression and to forego exhaustive treatment. [32]At this point therefore let us begin our narrative, adding only so much to what has already been said; for it is foolish to lengthen the preface while cutting short the history itself.

3 While the holy city was inhabited in unbroken peace and the laws were very well observed because of the piety of the high priest Oni′as and his hatred of wickedness, [2]it came about that the kings themselves honored the place and glorified the temple with the finest presents, [3]so that even Seleu′cus, the king of Asia, defrayed from his own revenues all the expenses connected with the service of the sacrifices. [4]But a man named Simon, of the tribe of Benjamin, who had been made captain of the temple, had a disagreement with the high priest about the administration of the city market; [5]and when he could not prevail over Oni′as he went to Apollo′nius of Tarsus, who at that time was governor of Coe′le-syr′ia and Phoeni′cia. [6]He reported to him that the treasury in Jerusalem was full of untold sums of money, so that the amount of the funds could not be reckoned, and that they did not belong to the account of the sacrifices, but that it was possible for them to fall under the control of the king. [7]When Apollo′nius met the king, he told him of the money about which he had been informed. The king chose He′liodo′rus, who was in charge of his affairs, and sent him with commands to effect the removal of the aforesaid money. [8]He′liodo′rus at once set out on his journey, ostensibly to make a tour of inspection of the cities of Coe′le-syr′ia and Phoeni′cia, but in fact to carry out the king's purpose.

[9]When he had arrived at Jerusalem and had been kindly welcomed by the high priest of the city, he told about the disclosure that had been made and stated why he had come, and he inquired whether this really was the situation. [10]The high priest explained that there were some deposits belonging to widows and orphans, [11]and also some money of Hyrca′nus, son of Tobi′as, a man of very prominent position, and that it totaled in all four hundred talents of silver and two hundred of gold. To such an extent the impious Simon had misrepresented the facts. [12]And he said that it was utterly impossible that wrong should be done to those people who had trusted in the holiness of the place and in the sanctity and inviolability of the temple which is honored throughout the whole world. [13]But He′liodo′rus, because of the king's commands which he had, said that this money must in any case be confiscated for the king's treasury. [14]So he set a day and went in to direct the inspection of these funds.

There was no little distress throughout the whole city. [15]The priests prostrated themselves before the altar in their priestly garments and called toward heaven upon him who had given the law about deposits, that he should keep them safe for those who had deposited them.

16To see the appearance of the high priest was to be wounded at heart, for his face and the change in his color disclosed the anguish of his soul. 17For terror and bodily trembling had come over the man, which plainly showed to those who looked at him the pain lodged in his heart. 18People also hurried out of their houses in crowds to make a general supplication because the holy place was about to be brought into contempt. 19Women, clothed with sackcloth under their breasts, thronged the streets. Some of the maidens who were kept indoors ran together to the gates, and some to the walls, while others peered out of the windows. 20And holding up their hands to heaven, they all made entreaty. 21There was something pitiable in the prostration of the whole populace and the anxiety of the high priest in his great anguish.

22While they were calling upon the Almighty Lord that he would keep what had been entrusted safe and secure for those who had entrusted it, 23He´liodo´rus went on with what had been decided. 24But when he arrived at the treasury with his bodyguard, then and there the Sovereign of spirits and of all authority caused so great a manifestation that all who had been so bold as to accompany him were astounded by the power of God, and became faint with terror. 25For there appeared to them a magnificently caparisoned horse, with a rider of frightening mien, and it rushed furiously at He´liodo´rus and struck at him with its front hoofs. Its rider was seen to have armor and weapons of gold. 26Two young men also appeared to him, remarkably strong, gloriously beautiful and splendidly dressed, who stood on each side of him and scourged him continuously, inflicting many blows on him. 27When he suddenly fell to the ground and deep darkness came over him, his men took him up and put him on a stretcher 28and carried him away, this man who had just entered the aforesaid treasury with a great retinue and all his bodyguard but was now unable to help himself; and they recognized clearly the sovereign power of God. 29While he lay prostrate, speechless because of the divine intervention and deprived of any hope of recovery, 30they praised the Lord who had acted marvelously for his own place. And the temple, which a little while before was full of fear and disturbance, was filled with joy and gladness, now that the Almighty Lord had appeared.

31Quickly some of He´liodo´rus' friends asked Oni´as to call upon the Most High and to grant life to one who was lying quite at his last breath. 32And the high priest, fearing that the king might get the notion that some foul play had been perpetrated by the Jews with regard to He´liodo´rus, offered sacrifice for the man's recovery. 33While the high priest was making the offering of atonement, the same young men appeared again to He´liodo´rus dressed in the same clothing, and they stood and said, "Be very grateful to Oni´as the high priest, since for his sake the Lord has granted you your life. 34And see that you, who have been scourged by heaven, report to all men the majestic power of God." Having said this they vanished.

35Then He´liodo´rus offered sacrifice to the Lord and made very great vows to the Savior of his life, and having bidden Oni´as farewell, he marched off with his forces to the king. 36And he bore testimony to all men of the deeds of the supreme God, which he had seen with his own eyes. 37When the king asked He´liodo´rus what sort of person would be suitable to send on another mission to Jerusalem, he replied, 38"If you have any enemy or plotter against your government, send him there, for you will get him back thoroughly scourged, if he escapes at all, for there certainly is about the place some power of God. 39For he who has his dwelling in heaven watches over that place himself and brings it aid, and he strikes and destroys those who come to do it injury." 40This was the outcome of the episode of He´liodo´rus and the protection of the treasury.

SIRACH 50

The leader of his brethren and the pride of
his people
was Simon the high priest, son of Oni´as,

who in his life repaired the house,
and in his time fortified the temple.
2He laid the foundations for the high double walls,
the high retaining walls for the temple enclosure.
3In his days a cistern for water was quarried out,
a reservoir like the sea in circumference.
4He considered how to save his people from ruin,
and fortified the city to withstand a siege.
5How glorious he was when the people gathered round him
as he came out of the inner sanctuary!
6Like the morning star among the clouds,
like the moon when it is full;
7like the sun shining upon the temple of the Most High,
and like the rainbow gleaming in glorious clouds;
8like roses in the days of the first fruits,
like lilies by a spring of water,
like a green shoot on Lebanon on a summer day;
9like fire and incense in the censer,
like a vessel of hammered gold
adorned with all kinds of precious stones;
10like an olive tree putting forth its fruit,
and like a cypress towering in the clouds.
11When he put on his glorious robe
and clothed himself with superb perfection
and went up to the holy altar,
he made the court of the sanctuary glorious.
12And when he received the portions from the hands of the priests,
as he stood by the hearth of the altar
with a garland of brethren around him,
he was like a young cedar on Lebanon;
and they surrounded him like the trunks of palm trees,
13 all the sons of Aaron in their splendor
with the Lord's offering in their hands,
before the whole congregation of Israel.
14Finishing the service at the altars,
and arranging the offering to the Most High, the Almighty,
15he reached out his hand to the cup
and poured a libation of the blood of the grape;
he poured it out at the foot of the altar,
a pleasing odor to the Most High, the King of all.
16Then the sons of Aaron shouted,
they sounded the trumpets of hammered work,
they made a great noise to be heard
for remembrance before the Most High.
17Then all the people together made haste
and fell to the ground upon their faces
to worship their Lord,
the Almighty, God Most High.
18And the singers praised him with their voices
in sweet and full-toned melody.
19And the people besought the Lord Most High
in prayer before him who is merciful,
till the order of worship of the Lord was ended;
so they completed his service.
20Then Simon came down, and lifted up his hands
over the whole congregation of the sons of Israel,
to pronounce the blessing of the Lord with his lips,
and to glory in his name;
21and they bowed down in worship a second time,
to receive the blessing from the Most High.

22And now bless the God of all,
who in every way does great things;
who exalts our days from birth,
and deals with us according to his mercy.
23May he give us gladness of heart,
and grant that peace may be in our days in Israel,
as in the days of old,
24that Israel may believe that the God of mercy is with us
to deliver us in our days!

25With two nations my soul is vexed,
and the third is no nation:

[26]Those who live on Mount Se´ir, and
the Philis´tines,
and the foolish people that dwell
in She´chem.
[27]Instruction in understanding and
knowledge
I have written in this book,
Jesus the son of Si´rach, son of Elea´zar,
of Jerusalem,
who out of his heart poured forth
wisdom.
[28]Blessed is he who concerns himself with
these things,
and he who lays them to heart will
become wise.
[29]For if he does them, he will be strong for
all things,
for the light of the Lord is his path.

REVELATION 13

And I saw a beast rising out of the sea, with ten horns and seven heads, with ten diadems upon its horns and a blasphemous name upon its heads. [2]And the beast that I saw was like a leopard, its feet were like a bear's, and its mouth was like a lion's mouth. And to it the dragon gave his power and his throne and great authority.
[3]One of its heads seemed to have a mortal wound, but its mortal wound was healed, and the whole earth followed the beast with wonder. [4]Men worshiped the dragon, for he had given his authority to the beast, and they worshiped the beast, saying, "Who is like the beast, and who can fight against it?"

[5]And the beast was given a mouth uttering haughty and blasphemous words, and it was allowed to exercise authority for forty-two months; [6]it opened its mouth to utter blasphemies against God, blaspheming his name and his dwelling, that is, those who dwell in heaven. [7]Also it was allowed to make war on the saints and to conquer them. And authority was given it over every tribe and people and tongue and nation,
[8]and all who dwell on earth will worship it, every one whose name has not been written before the foundation of the world in the book of life of the Lamb that was slain. [9]If any one has an ear, let him hear:
[10]If any one is to be taken captive,
to captivity he goes;
if any one slays with the sword,
with the sword must he be slain.
Here is a call for the endurance and faith of the saints.

[11]Then I saw another beast which rose out of the earth; it had two horns like a lamb and it spoke like a dragon. [12]It exercises all the authority of the first beast in its presence, and makes the earth and its inhabitants worship the first beast, whose mortal wound was healed. [13]It works great signs, even making fire come down from heaven to earth in the sight of men; [14]and by the signs which it is allowed to work in the presence of the beast, it deceives those who dwell on earth, bidding them make an image for the beast which was wounded by the sword and yet lived; [15]and it was allowed to give breath to the image of the beast so that the image of the beast should even speak, and to cause those who would not worship the image of the beast to be slain. [16]Also it causes all, both small and great, both rich and poor, both free and slave, to be marked on the right hand or the forehead, [17]so that no one can buy or sell unless he has the mark, that is, the name of the beast or the number of its name. [18]This calls for wisdom: let him who has understanding reckon the number of the beast, for it is a human number, its number is six hundred and sixty-six.

REFLECTION

Sirach describes the high priest Simon leading Israel in worship at the Temple. The splendor of his priestly robes, the glory of the censer made of "hammered gold adorned with all kinds of precious stones" (Sir 50:9), and the rich description of the Temple and its liturgy evoke comparison to the beauty of the sun, the moon, and the stars (see vv. 6–7) and all of God's handiwork in creation. Here Sirach brings his account of wisdom to its crescendo, showing how God's marvelous works of creation and humanity are embodied in the liturgical worship of God's people. This is the culmination of what is good, true, and beautiful as humanity offers the good things of creation back to the Creator in worship. In return, the liturgy ends with the priestly blessing of Aaron (see Nm 6:24–26), where the priest lifts up his hands and pronounces the name of God in blessing over the people (see Sir 50:20–21). It was only the Levitical priest, at the conclusion of the liturgy, who could invoke the holy name. This story illustrates what is so significant about Zechariah being made mute in the Temple due to disbelief, for he cannot pronounce the blessing (see Lk 1:22). Liturgy reflects a marvelous cycle: God gives good things in creation to us, we offer them back in worship, and then God gives us grace and blessing in return. Do you pay attention with gratitude to the blessing God gives you at the end of Mass?

December 24

2 MACCABEES 4

**The previously mentioned Si-
mon, who had informed about
the money against his own country,
slandered Oni'as, saying that it was he**
who had incited He'liodo'rus and had been
the real cause of the misfortune. 2He dared
to designate as a plotter against the government the man who was the benefactor of the
city, the protector of his fellow countrymen,
and a zealot for the laws. 3When his hatred
progressed to such a degree that even murders were committed by one of Simon's approved agents, 4Oni'as recognized that the
rivalry was serious and that Apollo'nius, the
son of Menes'theus and governor of Coe'le-
syr'ia and Phoeni'cia, was intensifying the
malice of Simon. 5So he betook himself to
the king, not accusing his fellow citizens but
having in view the welfare, both public and
private, of all the people. 6For he saw that
without the king's attention public affairs
could not again reach a peaceful settlement,
and that Simon would not stop his folly.
7When Seleu'cus died and Anti'ochus
who was called Epiph'anes succeeded to
the kingdom, Jason the brother of Oni'as
obtained the high priesthood by corruption,
8promising the king at an interview three
hundred and sixty talents of silver and, from
another source of revenue, eighty talents.
9In addition to this he promised to pay
one hundred and fifty more if permission
were given to establish by his authority a
gymnasium and a body of youth for it, and
to enroll the men of Jerusalem as citizens
of Antioch. 10When the king assented and
Jason came to office, he at once shifted his
countrymen over to the Greek way of life.
11He set aside the existing royal concessions
to the Jews, secured through John the father
of Eupol'emus, who went on the mission
to establish friendship and alliance with
the Romans; and he destroyed the lawful
ways of living and introduced new customs
contrary to the law. 12For with alacrity he
founded a gymnasium right under the
citadel, and he induced the noblest of the
young men to wear the Greek hat. 13There
was such an extreme of Hellenization and
increase in the adoption of foreign ways
because of the surpassing wickedness of
Jason, who was ungodly and no high priest,
14that the priests were no longer intent
upon their service at the altar. Despising
the sanctuary and neglecting the sacrifices,
they hastened to take part in the unlawful
proceedings in the wrestling arena after the
call to the discus, 15disdaining the honors
prized by their fathers and putting the
highest value upon Greek forms of prestige.
16For this reason heavy disaster overtook
them, and those whose ways of living they
admired and wished to imitate completely
became their enemies and punished them.
17For it is no light thing to show irreverence

to the divine laws—a fact which later events will make clear.

18When the quadrennial games were being held at Tyre and the king was present, 19the vile Jason sent envoys, chosen as being An′′tio′chian citizens from Jerusalem, to carry three hundred silver drachmas for the sacrifice to Hercules. Those who carried the money, however, thought best not to use it for sacrifice, because that was inappropriate, but to expend it for another purpose. 20So this money was intended by the sender for the sacrifice to Hercules, but by the decision of its carriers it was applied to the construction of triremes.

21When Apollo′nius the son of Menes′theus was sent to Egypt for the coronation of Phil′′ome′tor as king, Anti′ochus learned that Philometor had become hostile to his government, and he took measures for his own security. Therefore upon arriving at Joppa he proceeded to Jerusalem. 22He was welcomed magnificently by Jason and the city, and ushered in with a blaze of torches and with shouts. Then he marched into Phoeni′cia.

23After a period of three years Jason sent Menela′us, the brother of the previously mentioned Simon, to carry the money to the king and to complete the records of essential business. 24But he, when presented to the king, extolled him with an air of authority, and secured the high priesthood for himself, outbidding Jason by three hundred talents of silver. 25After receiving the king's orders he returned, possessing no qualification for the high priesthood, but having the hot temper of a cruel tyrant and the rage of a savage wild beast. 26So Jason, who after supplanting his own brother was supplanted by another man, was driven as a fugitive into the land of Am′mon. 27And Menela′us held the office, but he did not pay regularly any of the money promised to the king. 28When Sos′tratus the captain of the citadel kept requesting payment, for the collection of the revenue was his responsibility, the two of them were summoned by the king on account of this issue. 29Menela′us left his own brother Lysim′achus as deputy in the high priesthood, while Sos′tratus left Cra′tes, the commander of the Cyprian troops.

30While such was the state of affairs, it happened that the people of Tarsus and of Mallus revolted because their cities had been given as a present to Anti′ochis, the king's concubine. 31So the king went hastily to settle the trouble, leaving Andron′icus, a man of high rank, to act as his deputy. 32But Menela′us, thinking he had obtained a suitable opportunity, stole some of the gold vessels of the temple and gave them to Andron′icus; other vessels, as it happened, he had sold to Tyre and the neighboring cities. 33When Oni′as became fully aware of these acts he publicly exposed them, having first withdrawn to a place of sanctuary at Daphne near Antioch. 34Therefore Menela′us, taking Andron′icus aside, urged him to kill Oni′as. Andronicus came to Onias, and resorting to treachery offered him sworn pledges and gave him his right hand, and in spite of his suspicion persuaded Onias to come out from the place of sanctuary; then, with no regard for justice, he immediately put him out of the way. 35For this reason not only Jews, but many also of other nations, were grieved and displeased at the unjust murder of the man. 36When the king returned from the region of Cili′cia, the Jews in the city appealed to him with regard to the unreasonable murder of Oni′as, and the Greeks shared their hatred of the crime. 37Therefore Anti′ochus was grieved at heart and filled with pity, and wept because of the moderation and good conduct of the deceased; 38and inflamed with anger, he immediately stripped off the purple robe from Andron′icus, tore off his garments, and led him about the whole city to that very place where he had committed the outrage against Oni′as, and there he dispatched the bloodthirsty fellow. The Lord thus repaid him with the punishment he deserved.

39When many acts of sacrilege had been committed in the city by Lysim′achus with the connivance of Menela′us, and when report of them had spread abroad, the populace gathered against Lysimachus, because many of the gold vessels had already been stolen. [40]And since the crowds were becoming aroused and filled with anger, Lysim´achus armed about three thousand men and launched an unjust attack, under the leadership of a certain Aura´nus, a man advanced in years and no less advanced in folly. [41]But when the Jews became aware of Lysim´achus' attack, some picked up stones, some blocks of wood, and others took handfuls of the ashes that were lying about, and threw them in wild confusion at Lysimachus and his men. [42]As a result, they wounded many of them, and killed some, and put them all to flight; and the temple robber himself they killed close by the treasury.

[43]Charges were brought against Menela´us about this incident. [44]When the king came to Tyre, three men sent by the senate presented the case before him. [45]But Menela´us, already as good as beaten, promised a substantial bribe to Ptol´emy son of Dorym´enes to win over the king. [46]Therefore Ptol´emy, taking the king aside into a colonnade as if for refreshment, induced the king to change his mind. [47]Menela´us, the cause of all the evil, he acquitted of the charges against him, while he sentenced to death those unfortunate men, who would have been freed uncondemned if they had pleaded even before Scyth´ians. [48]And so those who had spoken for the city and the villages and the holy vessels quickly suffered the unjust penalty. [49]Therefore even the Ty´rians, showing their hatred of the crime, provided magnificently for their funeral. [50]But Menela´us, because of the cupidity of those in power, remained in office, growing in wickedness, having become the chief plotter against his fellow citizens.

SIRACH 51

I will give thanks to you, O Lord and King,
and will praise you as God my Savior.
I give thanks to your name,
2 for you have been my protector
and helper
and have delivered my body from
destruction
and from the snare of a slanderous
tongue,
from lips that utter lies.
Before those who stood by
you were my helper, 3and delivered me,
in the greatness of your mercy and of
your name,
from the gnashings of teeth about to
devour me,
from the hand of those who sought
my life,
from the many afflictions that I endured,
4from choking fire on every side
and from the midst of fire which I did
not kindle,
5from the depths of the belly of Hades,
from an unclean tongue and
lying words—
6 the slander of an unrighteous tongue to
the king.
My soul drew near to death,
and my life was very near to
Hades beneath.
7They surrounded me on every side,
and there was no one to help me;
I looked for the assistance of men,
and there was none.
8Then I remembered your mercy, O Lord,
and your work from of old,
that you deliver those who wait for you
and save them from the hand of
their enemies.
9And I sent up my supplication from
the earth,
and prayed for deliverance from death.
10I appealed to the Lord, the Father of
my lord,
not to forsake me in the days of affliction,
at the time when there is no help against
the proud.
11I will praise your name continually,
and will sing praise with thanksgiving.
My prayer was heard,
12 for you saved me from destruction
and rescued me from an evil plight.
Therefore I will give thanks to you and
praise you,
and I will bless the name of the Lord.

[13]While I was still young, before I went on
my travels,
I sought wisdom openly in my prayer.
[14]Before the temple I asked for her,
and I will search for her to the last.
[15]From blossom to ripening grape
my heart delighted in her;
my foot entered upon the straight path;
from my youth I followed her steps.
[16]I inclined my ear a little and received her,
and I found for myself much instruction.
[17]I made progress therein;
to him who gives wisdom I will
give glory.
[18]For I resolved to live according to wisdom,
and I was zealous for the good;
and I shall never be put to shame.

REVELATION 14

Then I looked, and behold, on
Mount Zion stood the Lamb,
and with him a hundred and
forty-four thousand who had his name
and his Father's name written on their
foreheads. [2]And I heard a voice from
heaven like the sound of many waters and
like the sound of loud thunder; the voice I
heard was like the sound of harpists playing
on their harps, [3]and they sing a new song
before the throne and before the four living
creatures and before the elders. No one
could learn that song except the hundred
and forty-four thousand who had been
redeemed from the earth. [4]It is these who
have not defiled themselves with women,
for they are chaste; it is these who follow
the Lamb wherever he goes; these have been
redeemed from mankind as first fruits for
God and the Lamb, [5]and in their mouth no
lie was found, for they are spotless.
[6]Then I saw another angel flying in
midheaven, with an eternal gospel to
proclaim to those who dwell on earth, to
every nation and tribe and tongue and
people; [7]and he said with a loud voice, "Fear
God and give him glory, for the hour of his
judgment has come; and worship him who
made heaven and earth, the sea and the
fountains of water."
[8]Another angel, a second, followed,
saying, "Fallen, fallen is Babylon the great,
she who made all nations drink the wine of
her impure passion."
[9]And another angel, a third, followed
them, saying with a loud voice, "If any
one worships the beast and its image, and
receives a mark on his forehead or on his
hand, [10]he also shall drink the wine of God's
wrath, poured unmixed into the cup of his
anger, and he shall be tormented with fire
and brimstone in the presence of the holy
angels and in the presence of the Lamb.
[11]And the smoke of their torment goes up
for ever and ever; and they have no rest, day
or night, these worshipers of the beast and
its image, and whoever receives the mark of
its name."
[12]Here is a call for the endurance of the
saints, those who keep the commandments
of God and the faith of Jesus.
[13]And I heard a voice from heaven saying,
"Write this: Blessed are the dead who from
now on die in the Lord." "Blessed indeed,"
says the Spirit, "that they may rest from
their labors, for their deeds follow them!"
[14]Then I looked, and behold, a white cloud,
and seated on the cloud one like a son of
man, with a golden crown on his head, and
a sharp sickle in his hand. [15]And another
angel came out of the temple, calling with
a loud voice to him who sat upon the cloud,
"Put in your sickle, and reap, for the hour to
reap has come, for the harvest of the earth
is fully ripe." [16]So he who sat upon the cloud
swung his sickle on the earth, and the earth
was reaped.
[17]And another angel came out of the
temple in heaven, and he too had a sharp
sickle. [18]Then another angel came out from
the altar, the angel who has power over fire,
and he called with a loud voice to him who
had the sharp sickle, "Put in your sickle, and
gather the clusters of the vine of the earth,
for its grapes are ripe." [19]So the angel swung
his sickle on the earth and gathered the
vintage of the earth, and threw it into the
great wine press of the wrath of God; [20]and

the wine press was trodden outside the city, and blood flowed from the wine press, as high as a horse's bridle, for one thousand six hundred stadia.

15 Then I saw another sign in heaven, great and wonderful, seven angels with seven plagues, which are the last, for with them the wrath of God is ended.
2And I saw what appeared to be a sea of glass mingled with fire, and those who had conquered the beast and its image and the number of its name, standing beside the sea of glass with harps of God in their hands.
3And they sing the song of Moses, the servant of God, and the song of the Lamb, saying,

"Great and wonderful are your deeds,
O Lord God the Almighty!
Just and true are your ways,
O King of the ages!
4Who shall not fear and glorify your name,
O Lord?
For you alone are holy.
All nations shall come and worship you,
for your judgments have been revealed."

5After this I looked, and the temple of the
tent of witness in heaven was opened, 6and
out of the temple came the seven angels with the seven plagues, robed in pure bright linen, and with golden sashes across their
chests. 7And one of the four living creatures gave the seven angels seven golden bowls full of the wrath of God who lives for ever
and ever; 8and the temple was filled with smoke from the glory of God and from his power, and no one could enter the temple until the seven plagues of the seven angels were ended.

REFLECTION

Sirach 50 showed the liturgical worship of Israel, gathered together in the Temple. Liturgy and its corporate worship models for individuals the piety they are to personalize in their own lives. In Sirach 51, our author shows how liturgy is to move us to a deeply personal spirituality. He begins with a personal account of praise and thanksgiving for what God has done in his life. In the liturgy, we give thanks and praise for what God has done for Israel and his people, and in our personal prayer we give thanks and praise for what he has done for us individually. The movement is from Israel to the individual, from liturgy to personal prayer. Sirach's prayer follows a pattern that he personalizes. Psalms of thanksgiving have a threefold pattern: beginning with praise (see Sir 51:1–2), they move to plight (see vv. 3–10), and then end in praise and thanksgiving (see vv. 11–12). We each have our own reasons for gratitude, our own story of plight that moves to praise. The entire Book of Sirach has been tracing the branches of knowledge down to their deep roots, to wisdom. Here, at the end of the book, we are shown that ultimate wisdom is realized when we recognize the reasons in our own lives for gratitude. Do you agree with Sirach that the measure of our wisdom is encompassed by the degree of our gratitude and the depth of our patterns of praise?

December 25

2 MACCABEES 5

About this time An´tiochus made his second invasion of Egypt. 2And it happened that over all the city, for almost forty days, there appeared golden-clad horsemen charging through the air, in companies fully armed with lances and drawn swords—
3troops of horsemen drawn up, attacks and counterattacks made on this side and on that, brandishing of shields, massing of spears, hurling of missiles, the flash of golden trappings, and armor of all sorts. 4Therefore all men prayed that the apparition might prove to have been a good omen.
5When a false rumor arose that An´tiochus was dead, Jason took no less than a thousand men and suddenly made an assault upon

the city. When the troops upon the wall had been forced back and at last the city was being taken, Menela′us took refuge in the citadel. [6]But Jason kept relentlessly slaughtering his fellow citizens, not realizing that success at the cost of one's kindred is the greatest misfortune, but imagining that he was setting up trophies of victory over enemies and not over fellow countrymen. [7]He did not gain control of the government, however; and in the end got only disgrace from his conspiracy, and fled again into the country of the Am′monites. [8]Finally he met a miserable end. Accused before Ar′etas the ruler of the Arabs, fleeing from city to city, pursued by all men, hated as a rebel against the laws, and abhorred as the executioner of his country and his fellow citizens, he was cast ashore in Egypt; [9]and he who had driven many from their own country into exile died in exile, having embarked to go to the Lac′′edaemo′nians in hope of finding protection because of their kinship. [10]He who had cast out many to lie unburied had no one to mourn for him; he had no funeral of any sort and no place in the tomb of his fathers.

[11]When news of what had happened reached the king, he took it to mean that Judea was in revolt. So, raging inwardly, he left Egypt and took the city by storm. [12]And he commanded his soldiers to cut down relentlessly every one they met and to slay those who went into the houses. [13]Then there was killing of young and old, destruction of boys, women, and children, and slaughter of virgins and infants. [14]Within the total of three days eighty thousand were destroyed, forty thousand in hand-to-hand fighting; and as many were sold into slavery as were slain.

[15]Not content with this, Anti′ochus dared to enter the most holy temple in all the world, guided by Menela′us, who had become a traitor both to the laws and to his country. [16]He took the holy vessels with his polluted hands, and swept away with profane hands the votive offerings which other kings had made to enhance the glory and honor of the place. [17]Anti′ochus was elated in spirit, and did not perceive that the Lord was angered for a little while because of the sins of those who dwelt in the city, and that therefore he was disregarding the holy place. [18]But if it had not happened that they were involved in many sins, this man would have been scourged and turned back from his rash act as soon as he came forward, just as He′′liodo′rus was, whom Seleu′cus the king sent to inspect the treasury. [19]But the Lord did not choose the nation for the sake of the holy place, but the place for the sake of the nation. [20]Therefore the place itself shared in the misfortunes that befell the nation and afterward participated in its benefits; and what was forsaken in the wrath of the Almighty was restored again in all its glory when the great Lord became reconciled.

[21]So Anti′ochus carried off eighteen hundred talents from the temple, and hurried away to Antioch, thinking in his arrogance that he could sail on the land and walk on the sea, because his mind was elated. [22]And he left governors to afflict the people: at Jerusalem, Philip, by birth a Phryg′ian and in character more barbarous than the man who appointed him; [23]and at Ger′izim, Andron′icus; and besides these Menela′us, who lorded it over his fellow citizens worse than the others did. In his malice toward the Jewish citizens, [24]Anti′ochus sent Apollo′nius, the captain of the Mysians, with an army of twenty-two thousand, and commanded him to slay all the grown men and to sell the women and boys as slaves. [25]When this man arrived in Jerusalem, he pretended to be peaceably disposed and waited until the holy sabbath day; then, finding the Jews not at work, he ordered his men to parade under arms. [26]He put to the sword all those who came out to see them, then rushed into the city with his armed men and killed great numbers of people.

[27]But Judas Mac′′cabe′us, with about nine others, got away to the wilderness, and kept himself and his companions alive in the mountains as wild animals do; they continued to live on what grew wild, so that they might not share in the defilement.

6 Not long after this, the king sent an
Athenian senator to compel the Jews
to forsake the laws of their fathers and
cease to live by the laws of God, 2and also
to pollute the temple in Jerusalem and call
it the temple of Olympian Zeus, and to call
the one in Ger′izim the temple of Zeus the
Friend of Strangers, as did the people who
dwelt in that place.
3Harsh and utterly grievous was the
onslaught of evil. 4For the temple was
filled with debauchery and reveling by the
Gentiles, who dallied with harlots and had
intercourse with women within the sacred
precincts, and besides brought in things
for sacrifice that were unfit. 5The altar was
covered with abominable offerings which
were forbidden by the laws. 6A man could
neither keep the sabbath, nor observe the
feasts of his fathers, nor so much as confess
himself to be a Jew.
7On the monthly celebration of the king's
birthday, the Jews were taken, under bitter
constraint, to partake of the sacrifices; and
when the feast of Diony′sus came, they
were compelled to walk in the procession in
honor of Dionysus, wearing wreaths of ivy.
8At the suggestion of Ptol′emy a decree was
issued to the neighboring Greek cities, that
they should adopt the same policy toward
the Jews and make them partake of the
sacrifices, 9and should slay those who did
not choose to change over to Greek customs.
One could see, therefore, the misery that had
come upon them. 10For example, two women
were brought in for having circumcised
their children. These women they publicly
paraded about the city, with their babies
hung at their breasts, then hurled them down
headlong from the wall. 11Others who had
assembled in the caves near by, to observe the
seventh day secretly, were betrayed to Philip
and were all burned together, because their
piety kept them from defending themselves,
in view of their regard for that most holy day.
12Now I urge those who read this book
not to be depressed by such calamities, but
to recognize that these punishments were
designed not to destroy but to discipline our
people. 13In fact, not to let the impious alone
for long, but to punish them immediately, is
a sign of great kindness. 14For in the case of
the other nations the Lord waits patiently to
punish them until they have reached the full
measure of their sins; but he does not deal in
this way with us, 15in order that he may not
take vengeance on us afterward when our
sins have reached their height. 16Therefore
he never withdraws his mercy from us.
Though he disciplines us with calamities, he
does not forsake his own people. 17Let what
we have said serve as a reminder; we must
go on briefly with the story.
18Elea′zar, one of the scribes in high
position, a man now advanced in age and
of noble presence, was being forced to open
his mouth to eat swine's flesh. 19But he,
welcoming death with honor rather than
life with pollution, went up to the rack of his
own accord, spitting out the flesh, 20as men
ought to go who have the courage to refuse
things that it is not right to taste, even for
the natural love of life.
21Those who were in charge of that
unlawful sacrifice took the man aside,
because of their long acquaintance with him,
and privately urged him to bring meat of his
own providing, proper for him to use, and
pretend that he was eating the flesh of the
sacrificial meal which had been commanded
by the king, 22so that by doing this he might
be saved from death, and be treated kindly on
account of his old friendship with them. 23But
making a high resolve, worthy of his years
and the dignity of his old age and the gray
hairs which he had reached with distinction
and his excellent life even from childhood,
and moreover according to the holy God-
given law, he declared himself quickly, telling
them to send him to Hades.
24"Such pretense is not worthy of our time of
life," he said, "lest many of the young should
suppose that Elea′zar in his ninetieth year has
gone over to an alien religion, 25and through
my pretense, for the sake of living a brief
moment longer, they should be led astray
because of me, while I defile and disgrace my
old age. 26For even if for the present I should
avoid the punishment of men, yet whether I
live or die I shall not escape the hands of the

Almighty. 27Therefore, by manfully giving up my life now, I will show myself worthy of my old age 28and leave to the young a noble example of how to die a good death willingly and nobly for the revered and holy laws."

When he had said this, he went at once to the rack. 29And those who a little before had acted toward him with good will now changed to ill will, because the words he had uttered were in their opinion sheer madness. 30When he was about to die under the blows, he groaned aloud and said: "It is clear to the Lord in his holy knowledge that, though I might have been saved from death, I am enduring terrible sufferings in my body under this beating, but in my soul I am glad to suffer these things because I fear him."

31So in this way he died, leaving in his death an example of nobility and a memorial of courage, not only to the young but to the great body of his nation.

SIRACH 51

19My soul grappled with wisdom,
and in my conduct I was strict;
I spread out my hands to the heavens,
and lamented my ignorance of her.
20I directed my soul to her,
and through purification I found her.
I gained understanding with her from
the first;
therefore I will not be forsaken.
21My heart was stirred to seek her,
therefore I have gained a good possession.
22The Lord gave me a tongue as my reward,
and I will praise him with it.

23Draw near to me, you who are untaught,
and lodge in my school.
24Why do you say you are lacking in
these things,
and why are your souls very thirsty?
25I opened my mouth and said,
Get these things for yourselves
without money.
26Put your neck under the yoke,
and let your souls receive instruction;
it is to be found close by.
27See with your eyes that I have
labored little
and found for myself much rest.
28Get instruction with a large sum of silver,
and you will gain by it much gold.
29May your soul rejoice in his mercy,
and may you not be put to shame when
you praise him.
30Do your work before the appointed time,
and in God's time he will give you
your reward.

REVELATION 16

Then I heard a loud voice from the temple telling the seven angels, "Go and pour out on the earth the seven bowls of the wrath of God."

2So the first angel went and poured his bowl on the earth, and foul and evil sores came upon the men who bore the mark of the beast and worshiped its image.

3The second angel poured his bowl into the sea, and it became like the blood of a dead man, and every living thing died that was in the sea.

4The third angel poured his bowl into the rivers and the fountains of water, and they became blood. 5And I heard the angel of water say,
"Just are you in these your judgments,
you who are and were, O Holy One.
6For men have shed the blood of saints
and prophets,
and you have given them blood to drink.
It is their due!"
7And I heard the altar cry,
"Yes, Lord God the Almighty,
true and just are your judgments!"

8The fourth angel poured his bowl on the sun, and it was allowed to scorch men with fire; 9men were scorched by the fierce heat, and they cursed the name of God who had power over these plagues, and they did not repent and give him glory.

10The fifth angel poured his bowl on the throne of the beast, and its kingdom was in darkness; men gnawed their tongues in anguish [11]and cursed the God of heaven for their pain and sores, and did not repent of their deeds.

[12]The sixth angel poured his bowl on the great river Euphra′tes, and its water was dried up, to prepare the way for the kings from the east. [13]And I saw, issuing from the mouth of the dragon and from the mouth of the beast and from the mouth of the false prophet, three foul spirits like frogs; [14]for they are demonic spirits, performing signs, who go abroad to the kings of the whole world, to assemble them for battle on the great day of God the Almighty. [15]("Behold, I am coming like a thief! Blessed is he who is awake, keeping his garments that he may not go naked and be seen exposed!") [16]And they assembled them at the place which is called in Hebrew Armaged′don.

[17]The seventh angel poured his bowl into the air, and a great voice came out of the temple, from the throne, saying, "It is done!" [18]And there were flashes of lightning, loud noises, peals of thunder, and a great earthquake such as had never been since men were on the earth, so great was that earthquake. [19]The great city was split into three parts, and the cities of the nations fell, and God remembered great Babylon, to make her drain the cup of the fury of his wrath. [20]And every island fled away, and no mountains were to be found; [21]and great hailstones, heavy as a hundredweight, dropped on men from heaven, till men cursed God for the plague of the hail, so fearful was that plague.

REFLECTION

Maccabees recounts how the Jews were forced, on the birthday of the king, Antiochus, to join in the pagan feasts in his honor and offer sacrifices in homage to him (see 2 Mc 6:7). At that time in history, it was typical for the birthday of a king to be celebrated by everyone in his kingdom. Scripture refers to two other birthday celebrations, both for pagan kings: Pharaoh (see Gn 40:20) and Herod (see Mt 14:6). Along with their birthdays, the anniversary of the first year of a king's reign was also celebrated. Indeed, the years were counted by the years of a king's reign. Thus, dates were marked as the third year of king so-and-so. When a king died and another began to reign, the calendar would revert back to year one, restarting the clock until the death of the king. Such royal accounting of years may seem a relic of the past, but actually it is still very much alive today. In the West and much of the world, the years are counted from the beginning of Jesus Christ's reign, starting with his Birth. The reason the clock has not been reset is that Christ continues to reign. He is the true King and true God; his Birth heralds Good News for the world and marks the calendar with the turning point of all history.

December 26

2 MACCABEES 7

It happened also that seven brothers and their mother were arrested and were being compelled by the king, under torture with whips and cords, to partake of unlawful swine's flesh. [2]One of them, acting as their spokesman, said, "What do you intend to ask and learn from us? For we are ready to die rather than transgress the laws of our fathers."

[3]The king fell into a rage, and gave orders that pans and caldrons be heated. [4]These were heated immediately, and he commanded that the tongue of their spokesman be cut out and that they scalp him and cut off his hands and feet, while the rest of the brothers and the mother looked on. [5]When he was utterly helpless, the king ordered them to take him to the fire, still breathing, and to fry him in a pan. The smoke from the pan spread widely, but the brothers and their mother encouraged one another to die nobly, saying, [6]"'The Lord

God is watching over us and in truth has compassion on us, as Moses declared in his song which bore witness against the people to their faces, when he said, 'And he will have compassion on his servants.' "

7After the first brother had died in this way, they brought forward the second for their sport. They tore off the skin of his head with the hair, and asked him, "Will you eat rather than have your body punished limb by limb?" 8He replied in the language of his fathers, and said to them, "No." Therefore he in turn underwent tortures as the first brother had done. 9And when he was at his last breath, he said, "You accursed wretch, you dismiss us from this present life, but the King of the universe will raise us up to an everlasting renewal of life, because we have died for his laws."

10After him, the third was the victim of their sport. When it was demanded, he quickly put out his tongue and courageously stretched forth his hands, 11and said nobly, "I got these from Heaven, and because of his laws I disdain them, and from him I hope to get them back again." 12As a result the king himself and those with him were astonished at the young man's spirit, for he regarded his sufferings as nothing.

13When he too had died, they maltreated and tortured the fourth in the same way. 14And when he was near death, he said, "One cannot but choose to die at the hands of men and to cherish the hope that God gives of being raised again by him. But for you there will be no resurrection to life!"

15Next they brought forward the fifth and maltreated him. 16But he looked at the king, and said, "Because you have authority among men, mortal though you are, you do what you please. But do not think that God has forsaken our people. 17Keep on, and see how his mighty power will torture you and your descendants!"

18After him they brought forward the sixth. And when he was about to die, he said, "Do not deceive yourself in vain. For we are suffering these things on our own account, because of our sins against our own God. Therefore astounding things have happened. 19But do not think that you will go unpunished for having tried to fight against God!"

20The mother was especially admirable and worthy of honorable memory. Though she saw her seven sons perish within a single day, she bore it with good courage because of her hope in the Lord. 21She encouraged each of them in the language of their fathers. Filled with a noble spirit, she fired her woman's reasoning with a man's courage, and said to them, 22"I do not know how you came into being in my womb. It was not I who gave you life and breath, nor I who set in order the elements within each of you. 23Therefore the Creator of the world, who shaped the beginning of man and devised the origin of all things, will in his mercy give life and breath back to you again, since you now forget yourselves for the sake of his laws."

24Anti′ochus felt that he was being treated with contempt, and he was suspicious of her reproachful tone. The youngest brother being still alive, Antiochus not only appealed to him in words, but promised with oaths that he would make him rich and enviable if he would turn from the ways of his fathers, and that he would take him for his friend and entrust him with public affairs. 25Since the young man would not listen to him at all, the king called the mother to him and urged her to advise the youth to save himself. 26After much urging on his part, she undertook to persuade her son. 27But, leaning close to him, she spoke in their native tongue as follows, deriding the cruel tyrant: "My son, have pity on me. I carried you nine months in my womb, and nursed you for three years, and have reared you and brought you up to this point in your life, and have taken care of you. 28I beg you, my child, to look at the heaven and the earth and see everything that is in them, and recognize that God did not make them out of things that existed. Thus also mankind comes into being. 29Do not fear this butcher, but prove worthy of your brothers. Accept death, so that in God's mercy I may get you back again with your brothers."

30While she was still speaking, the young
man said, "What are you waiting for? I will
not obey the king's command, but I obey the
command of the law that was given to our
fathers through Moses. 31But you, who have
contrived all sorts of evil against the Hebrews,
will certainly not escape the hands of God.
32For we are suffering because of our own sins.
33And if our living Lord is angry for a little
while, to rebuke and discipline us, he will again
be reconciled with his own servants. 34But
you, unholy wretch, you most defiled of all
men, do not be elated in vain and puffed up
by uncertain hopes, when you raise your hand
against the children of heaven. 35You have not
yet escaped the judgment of the almighty, all-
seeing God. 36For our brothers after enduring
a brief suffering have drunk of everflowing
life under God's covenant; but you, by the
judgment of God, will receive just punishment
for your arrogance. 37I, like my brothers, give
up body and life for the laws of our fathers,
appealing to God to show mercy soon to our
nation and by afflictions and plagues to make
you confess that he alone is God, 38and through
me and my brothers to bring to an end the
wrath of the Almighty which has justly fallen
on our whole nation."
39The king fell into a rage, and handled him
worse than the others, being exasperated
at his scorn. 40So he died in his integrity,
putting his whole trust in the Lord.
41Last of all, the mother died, after her sons.
42Let this be enough, then, about the eating
of sacrifices and the extreme tortures.

SONG OF SOLOMON 1

The Song of Songs, which is Solomon's.

2O that you would kiss me with the kisses of
your mouth!
For your love is better than wine,
3 your anointing oils are fragrant,
your name is oil poured out;
therefore the maidens love you.
4Draw me after you, let us make haste.
The king has brought me into
his chambers.
We will exult and rejoice in you;
we will extol your love more than wine;
rightly do they love you.

5I am very dark, but comely,
O daughters of Jerusalem,
like the tents of Ke′dar,
like the curtains of Solomon.
6Do not gaze at me because I am swarthy,
because the sun has scorched me.
My mother's sons were angry with me,
they made me keeper of the vineyards;
but, my own vineyard I have not kept!
7Tell me, you whom my soul loves,
where you pasture your flock,
where you make it lie down at noon;
for why should I be like one who wanders
beside the flocks of your companions?

8If you do not know,
O fairest among women,
follow in the tracks of the flock,
and pasture your kids
beside the shepherds' tents.

9I compare you, my love,
to a mare of Pharaoh's chariots.
10Your cheeks are comely with ornaments,
your neck with strings of jewels.
11We will make you ornaments of gold,
studded with silver.

12While the king was on his couch,
my nard gave forth its fragrance.
13My beloved is to me a bag of myrrh,
that lies between my breasts.
14My beloved is to me a cluster of
henna blossoms
in the vineyards of En-ge′di.

15Behold, you are beautiful, my love;
behold, you are beautiful;
your eyes are doves.
16Behold, you are beautiful, my beloved,
truly lovely.
Our couch is green;
17 the beams of our house are cedar,
our rafters are pine.

2 I am a rose of Sharon,
a lily of the valleys.

[2]As a lily among brambles,
so is my love among maidens.

[3]As an apple tree among the trees of the wood,
so is my beloved among young men.
With great delight I sat in his shadow,
and his fruit was sweet to my taste.
[4]He brought me to the banqueting house,
and his banner over me was love.
[5]Sustain me with raisins,
refresh me with apples;
for I am sick with love.
[6]O that his left hand were under my head,
and that his right hand embraced me!
[7]I adjure you, O daughters of Jerusalem,
by the gazelles or the deer of the field,
that you stir not up nor awaken love
until it please.

[8]The voice of my beloved!
Behold, he comes,
leaping upon the mountains,
bounding over the hills.
[9]My beloved is like a gazelle,
or a young stag.
Behold, there he stands
behind our wall,
gazing in at the windows,
looking through the lattice.
[10]My beloved speaks and says to me:
"Arise, my love, my dove, my fair one,
and come away;
[11]for behold, the winter is past,
the rain is over and gone.
[12]The flowers appear on the earth,
the time of pruning has come,
and the voice of the turtledove
is heard in our land.
[13]The fig tree puts forth its figs,
and the vines are in blossom;
they give forth fragrance.
Arise, my love, my fair one,
and come away.
[14]O my dove, in the clefts of the rock,
in the covert of the cliff,
let me see your face,
let me hear your voice,
for your voice is sweet,
and your face is comely.
[15]Catch us the foxes,
the little foxes,
that spoil the vineyards,
for our vineyards are in blossom."
[16]My beloved is mine and I am his,
he pastures his flock among the lilies.
[17]Until the day breathes
and the shadows flee,
turn, my beloved, be like a gazelle,
or a young stag upon rugged mountains.

REVELATION 17

Then one of the seven angels who had the seven bowls came and said to me, "Come, I will show you the judgment of the great harlot who is seated upon many waters,
[2]with whom the kings of the earth have
committed fornication, and with the wine of whose fornication the dwellers on earth have become drunk."
[3]And he carried me away in the Spirit into a wilderness, and I saw a woman sitting on a scarlet beast which was full of blasphemous names, and it had seven heads and ten horns.
[4]The woman was clothed in purple and scarlet, and adorned with gold and jewels and pearls, holding in her hand a golden cup full of abominations and the impurities of her fornication;
[5]and on her forehead was written a name of mystery: "Babylon the great, mother of harlots and of earth's abominations."
[6]And I saw the woman, drunk with the blood of the saints and the blood of the martyrs of Jesus.

When I saw her I marveled greatly.
[7]But the angel said to me, "Why marvel? I will tell you the mystery of the woman, and of the beast with seven heads and ten horns that carries her.
[8]The beast that you saw was, and is not, and is to ascend from the bottomless pit and go to perdition; and the dwellers on earth whose names have not been written in the book of life from the foundation of the world, will marvel to behold the beast, because it was and is not and is to come.
[9]This calls for a mind with wisdom: the

seven heads are seven hills on which the woman is seated; 10they are also seven kings, five of whom have fallen, one is, the other has not yet come, and when he comes he must remain only a little while. 11As for the beast that was and is not, it is an eighth but it belongs to the seven, and it goes to perdition. 12And the ten horns that you saw are ten kings who have not yet received royal power, but they are to receive authority as kings for one hour, together with the beast. 13These are of one mind and give over their power and authority to the beast; 14they will make war on the Lamb, and the Lamb will conquer them, for he is Lord of lords and King of kings, and those with him are called and chosen and faithful."

15And he said to me, "The waters that you saw, where the harlot is seated, are peoples and multitudes and nations and tongues. 16And the ten horns that you saw, they and the beast will hate the harlot; they will make her desolate and naked, and devour her flesh and burn her up with fire, 17for God has put it into their hearts to carry out his purpose by being of one mind and giving over their royal power to the beast, until the words of God shall be fulfilled. 18And the woman that you saw is the great city which has dominion over the kings of the earth."

REFLECTION

December 26th is the Feast of St. Stephen, the first Christian martyr. Soon the Church will also celebrate the Feast of the Holy Innocents, those precious children who were ruthlessly slaughtered by Herod in his attempt to snuff out the Birth of the Messiah. Mother Church is teaching us in these feasts that death, even for the very young, is only a temporary victory for evil, and far from the last word. The seven brothers who are also innocent and yet cruelly killed in 2 Maccabees 7 illustrates, like the Holy Innocents and St. Stephen, that martyrs may die, but they do not die without hope. The second of the brothers witnesses this hope in his dying words: "You accursed wretch, you dismiss us from this present life, but the King of the universe will raise us up to an everlasting renewal of life, because we have died for his laws" (2 Mc 7:9). Their mother displays the most heroic courage and faith, perhaps in all of the Old Testament. Her maternal wisdom and humility shine forth as a model for any mother who suffers the unspeakable suffering of seeing her child suffer and die: "I do not know how you came into being in my womb. It was not I who gave you life and breath, nor I who set in order the elements within each of you. Therefore, the Creator of the world, who shaped the beginning of man and devised the origin of all things, will in his mercy give life and breath back to you again" (vv. 22–23).

December 27

2 MACCABEES 8

But Judas, who was also called Mac″cabe′us, and his companions secretly entered the villages and summoned their kinsmen and enlisted those who had continued in the Jewish faith, and so they gathered about six thousand men. 2They begged the Lord to look upon the people who were oppressed by all, and to have pity on the temple which had been profaned by ungodly men, 3and to have mercy on the city which was being destroyed and about to be leveled to the ground, and to heed the blood that cried out to him, 4and to remember also the lawless destruction of the innocent babies and the blasphemies committed against his name, and to show his hatred of evil.

5As soon as Mac″cabe′us got his army organized, the Gentiles could not withstand him, for the wrath of the Lord had turned to mercy. 6Coming without warning, he would set fire to towns and villages. He captured strategic positions and put to flight not a few of the enemy. [7]He found the nights most advantageous for such attacks. And talk of his valor spread everywhere.

[8]When Philip saw that the man was gaining ground little by little, and that he was pushing ahead with more frequent successes, he wrote to Ptol´emy, the governor of Coe´le-syr´ia and Phoeni´cia, for aid to the king's government. [9]And Ptol´emy promptly appointed Nica´nor the son of Patro´clus, one of the king's chief friends, and sent him, in command of no fewer than twenty thousand Gentiles of all nations, to wipe out the whole race of Judea. He associated with him Gor´gias, a general and a man of experience in military service. [10]Nica´nor determined to make up for the king the tribute due to the Romans, two thousand talents, by selling the captured Jews into slavery. [11]And he immediately sent to the cities on the seacoast, inviting them to buy Jewish slaves and promising to hand over ninety slaves for a talent, not expecting the judgment from the Almighty that was about to overtake him.

[12]Word came to Judas concerning Nica´nor's invasion; and when he told his companions of the arrival of the army, [13]those who were cowardly and distrustful of God's justice ran off and got away. [14]Others sold all their remaining property, and at the same time begged the Lord to rescue those who had been sold by the ungodly Nica´nor before he ever met them, [15]if not for their own sake, yet for the sake of the covenants made with their fathers, and because he had called them by his holy and glorious name. [16]But Mac″cabe´us gathered his men together, to the number of six thousand, and exhorted them not to be frightened by the enemy and not to fear the great multitude of Gentiles who were wickedly coming against them, but to fight nobly, [17]keeping before their eyes the lawless outrage which the Gentiles had committed against the holy place, and the torture of the derided city, and besides, the overthrow of their ancestral way of life. [18]"For they trust to arms and acts of daring," he said, "but we trust in the Almighty God, who is able with a single nod to strike down those who are coming against us and even the whole world."

[19]Moreover, he told them of the times when help came to their ancestors; both the time of Sennach´erib, when one hundred and eighty-five thousand perished, [20]and the time of the battle with the Galatians that took place in Babylonia, when eight thousand in all went into the affair, with four thousand Macedonians; and when the Macedonians were hard pressed, the eight thousand, by the help that came to them from heaven, destroyed one hundred and twenty thousand and took much booty.

[21]With these words he filled them with good courage and made them ready to die for their laws and their country; then he divided his army into four parts. [22]He appointed his brothers also, Simon and Joseph and Jonathan, each to command a division, putting fifteen hundred men under each. [23]Besides, he appointed Elea´zar to read aloud from the holy book, and gave the watchword, "God's help"; then, leading the first division himself, he joined battle with Nica´nor.

[24]With the Almighty as their ally, they slew more than nine thousand of the enemy, and wounded and disabled most of Nica´nor's army, and forced them all to flee. [25]They captured the money of those who had come to buy them as slaves. After pursuing them for some distance, they were obliged to return because the hour was late. [26]For it was the day before the sabbath, and for that reason they did not continue their pursuit. [27]And when they had collected the arms of the enemy and stripped them of their spoils, they kept the sabbath, giving great praise and thanks to the Lord, who had preserved them for that day and allotted it to them as the beginning of mercy. [28]After the sabbath they gave some of the spoils to those who had been tortured and to the widows and orphans, and distributed the rest among themselves and

their children. 29When they had done this,
they made common supplication and begged
the merciful Lord to be wholly reconciled
with his servants.
30In encounters with the forces of
Timothy and Bacchi′des they killed more
than twenty thousand of them and got
possession of some exceedingly high
strongholds, and they divided very much
plunder, giving to those who had been
tortured and to the orphans and widows,
and also to the aged, shares equal to their
own. 31Collecting the arms of the enemy,
they stored them all carefully in strategic
places, and carried the rest of the spoils to
Jerusalem. 32They killed the commander
of Timothy's forces, a most unholy man,
and one who had greatly troubled the Jews.
33While they were celebrating the victory
in the city of their fathers, they burned
those who had set fire to the sacred gates,
Callis′thenes and some others, who had
fled into one little house; so these received
the proper recompense for their impiety.
34The thrice-accursed Nica′nor, who
had brought the thousand merchants to
buy the Jews, 35having been humbled with
the help of the Lord by opponents whom
he regarded as of the least account, took
off his splendid uniform and made his
way alone like a runaway slave across the
country till he reached Antioch, having
succeeded chiefly in the destruction
of his own army! 36Thus he who had
undertaken to secure tribute for the
Romans by the capture of the people of
Jerusalem proclaimed that the Jews had
a Defender, and that therefore the Jews
were invulnerable, because they followed
the laws ordained by him.

9 About that time, as it happened,
Anti′ochus had retreated in disorder
from the region of Persia. 2For he had
entered the city called Persep′olis, and
attempted to rob the temples and control
the city. Therefore the people rushed to
the rescue with arms, and Anti′ochus and
his men were defeated, with the result
that Antiochus was put to flight by the
inhabitants and beat a shameful retreat.
3While he was in Ecbat′ana, news came
to him of what had happened to Nica′nor
and the forces of Timothy. 4Transported
with rage, he conceived the idea of turning
upon the Jews the injury done by those
who had put him to flight; so he ordered
his charioteer to drive without stopping
until he completed the journey. But the
judgment of heaven rode with him! For in
his arrogance he said, "When I get there I
will make Jerusalem a cemetery of Jews."
5But the all-seeing Lord, the God of
Israel, struck him an incurable and unseen
blow. As soon as he ceased speaking he
was seized with a pain in his bowels for
which there was no relief and with sharp
internal tortures—6and that very justly,
for he had tortured the bowels of others
with many and strange inflictions. 7Yet
he did not in any way stop his insolence,
but was even more filled with arrogance,
breathing fire in his rage against the Jews,
and giving orders to hasten the journey.
And so it came about that he fell out of
his chariot as it was rushing along, and
the fall was so hard as to torture every
limb of his body. 8Thus he who had just
been thinking that he could command
the waves of the sea, in his superhuman
arrogance, and imagining that he could
weigh the high mountains in a balance,
was brought down to earth and carried
in a litter, making the power of God
manifest to all. 9And so the ungodly
man's body swarmed with worms, and
while he was still living in anguish and
pain, his flesh rotted away, and because of
his stench the whole army felt revulsion
at his decay. 10Because of his intolerable
stench no one was able to carry the man
who a little while before had thought that
he could touch the stars of heaven. 11Then
it was that, broken in spirit, he began to
lose much of his arrogance and to come to
his senses under the scourge of God, for
he was tortured with pain every moment.
12And when he could not endure his own
stench, he uttered these words: "It is
right to be subject to God, and no mortal
should think that he is equal to God."

13Then the abominable fellow made a
vow to the Lord, who would no longer
have mercy on him, stating 14that the holy
city, which he was hastening to level to
the ground and to make a cemetery, he
was now declaring to be free; 15and the
Jews, whom he had not considered worth
burying but had planned to throw out
with their children to the beasts, for the
birds to pick, he would make, all of them,
equal to citizens of Athens; 16and the
holy sanctuary, which he had formerly
plundered, he would adorn with the
finest offerings; and the holy vessels he
would give back, all of them, many times
over; and the expenses incurred for the
sacrifices he would provide from his own
revenues; 17and in addition to all this he
also would become a Jew and would visit
every inhabited place to proclaim the
power of God. 18But when his sufferings
did not in any way abate, for the judgment
of God had justly come upon him, he
gave up all hope for himself and wrote to
the Jews the following letter, in the form
of a supplication. This was its content:

19"To his worthy Jewish citizens,
Anti´ochus their king and general sends
hearty greetings and good wishes for
their health and prosperity. 20If you and
your children are well and your affairs
are as you wish, I am glad. As my hope
is in heaven, 21I remember with affection
your esteem and good will. On my way
back from the region of Persia I suffered
an annoying illness, and I have deemed
it necessary to take thought for the
general security of all. 22I do not despair
of my condition, for I have good hope
of recovering from my illness, 23but I
observed that my father, on the occasions
when he made expeditions into the upper
country, appointed his successor, 24so
that, if anything unexpected happened
or any unwelcome news came, the people
throughout the realm would not be
troubled, for they would know to whom
the government was left. 25Moreover,
I understand how the princes along
the borders and the neighbors to my
kingdom keep watching for opportunities
and waiting to see what will happen. So
I have appointed my son Anti´ochus to
be king, whom I have often entrusted
and commended to most of you when I
hastened off to the upper provinces; and
I have written to him what is written
here. 26I therefore urge and beg you to
remember the public and private services
rendered to you and to maintain your
present good will, each of you, toward me
and my son. 27For I am sure that he will
follow my policy and will treat you with
moderation and kindness."

28So the murderer and blasphemer,
having endured the more intense
suffering, such as he had inflicted on
others, came to the end of his life by a
most pitiable fate, among the mountains
in a strange land. 29And Philip, one of
his courtiers, took his body home; then,
fearing the son of Anti´ochus, he betook
himself to Ptol´emy Phil´´ome´tor in
Egypt.

SONG OF SOLOMON 3

Upon my bed by night
I sought him whom my soul loves;
I sought him, but found him not;
I called him, but he gave no answer.
2"I will rise now and go about the city,
in the streets and in the squares;
I will seek him whom my soul loves."
I sought him, but found him not.
3The watchmen found me,
as they went about in the city.
"Have you seen him whom my soul loves?"
4Scarcely had I passed them,
when I found him whom my soul loves.
I held him, and would not let him go
until I had brought him into my
mother's house,
and into the chamber of her that
conceived me.
5I adjure you, O daughters of Jerusalem,
by the gazelles or the deer of the field,
that you stir not up nor awaken love
until it please.

REVELATION 18

After this I saw another angel coming down from heaven, having great authority; and the earth was made bright with his splendor. [2]And he called out with a mighty voice,

"Fallen, fallen is Babylon the great!
It has become a dwelling place of demons,
a haunt of every foul spirit,
a haunt of every foul and hateful bird;
[3]for all nations have drunk the wine of her impure passion,
and the kings of the earth have committed fornication with her,
and the merchants of the earth have grown rich with the wealth of her wantonness."

[4]Then I heard another voice from heaven saying,

"Come out of her, my people,
lest you take part in her sins,
lest you share in her plagues;
[5]for her sins are heaped high as heaven,
and God has remembered her iniquities.
[6]Render to her as she herself has rendered,
and repay her double for her deeds;
mix a double draught for her in the cup she mixed.
[7]As she glorified herself and played the wanton,
so give her a like measure of torment and mourning.
Since in her heart she says, 'A queen I sit,
I am no widow, mourning I shall never see,'
[8]so shall her plagues come in a single day,
pestilence and mourning and famine,
and she shall be burned with fire;
for mighty is the Lord God who judges her."

[9]And the kings of the earth, who committed fornication and were wanton with her, will weep and wail over her when they see the smoke of her burning; [10]they will stand far off, in fear of her torment, and say,

"Alas! alas! you great city,
you mighty city, Babylon!
In one hour has your judgment come."

[11]And the merchants of the earth weep and mourn for her, since no one buys their cargo any more, [12]cargo of gold, silver, jewels and pearls, fine linen, purple, silk and scarlet, all kinds of scented wood, all articles of ivory, all articles of costly wood, bronze, iron and marble, [13]cinnamon, spice, incense, myrrh, frankincense, wine, oil, fine flour and wheat, cattle and sheep, horses and chariots, and slaves, that is, human souls.

[14]"The fruit for which your soul longed has gone from you,
and all your delicacies and your splendor are lost to you, never to be found again!"

[15]The merchants of these wares, who gained wealth from her, will stand far off, in fear of her torment, weeping and mourning aloud,

[16]"Alas, alas, for the great city
that was clothed in fine linen, in purple and scarlet,
adorned with gold, with jewels, and with pearls!
[17]In one hour all this wealth has been laid waste."

And all shipmasters and seafaring men, sailors and all whose trade is on the sea, stood far off [18]and cried out as they saw the smoke of her burning,

"What city was like the great city?"

[19]And they threw dust on their heads, as they wept and mourned, crying out,

"Alas, alas, for the great city
where all who had ships at sea grew rich by her wealth!
In one hour she has been laid waste.
[20]Rejoice over her, O heaven,
O saints and apostles and prophets,
for God has given judgment for you against her!"

[21]Then a mighty angel took up a stone like a great millstone and threw it into the sea, saying,

"So shall Babylon the great city be thrown down with violence,
and shall be found no more;
[22]and the sound of harpists and minstrels, of flute players and trumpeters,
shall be heard in you no more;

and a craftsman of any craft
shall be found in you no more;
and the sound of the millstone
shall be heard in you no more;
23and the light of a lamp
shall shine in you no more;
and the voice of bridegroom and bride
shall be heard in you no more;
for your merchants were the great men
of the earth,
and all nations were deceived by
your sorcery.
24And in her was found the blood of
prophets and of saints,
and of all who have been slain
on earth."

REFLECTION

St. Thomas Aquinas believed that the Song of Solomon was the most profound book of the Old Testament and that the Book of Revelation was the most profound in the New Testament. The Song of Solomon portrays the romance and love of a man and woman, who in Jewish and Christian tradition represent the spousal love that God has for Israel. Revelation climaxes with the wedding feast of the Lamb with the Church. Both books take up the topic of God's intense spousal love for us. The language of desire that the woman speaks for her beloved illustrates this well. She passionately seeks "him whom my soul loves" (see Sg 3:1–4). This echoes the language of love given in Deuteronomy's *Shema*, the prayer *par excellence* in Israel's Scriptures, where we are called to "love the LORD your God with all your heart, and with all your soul" (Dt 6:4). The woman, by employing the language of prayerful love in the *Shema*, models the love of the bride of Christ, the Church, who should always seek to find and please "him whom my soul loves." The power and intimacy of love between a bride and bridegroom, their passionate desiring of each other, are signposts for the love and intimacy each of us is invited to share with God. How can you love God with passion and deep desiring in your heart and soul?

December 28

2 MACCABEES 10

Now Mac″cabe′us and his followers, the Lord leading them on, recovered the temple and the city; 2and they tore down the altars which had been built in the public square by the foreigners, and also
destroyed the sacred precincts. 3They puri-
fied the sanctuary, and made another altar of
sacrifice; then, striking fire out of flint, they
offered sacrifices, after a lapse of two years,
and they burned incense and lighted lamps
and set out the bread of the Presence. 4And
when they had done this, they fell prostrate
and begged the Lord that they might never
again fall into such misfortunes, but that,
if they should ever sin, they might be disciplined by him with forbearance and not
be handed over to blasphemous and barbarous nations. 5It happened that on the
same day on which the sanctuary had been
profaned by the foreigners, the purification of the sanctuary took place, that is, on
the twenty-fifth day of the same month,
which was Chis′lev. 6And they celebrated it for eight days with rejoicing, in the
manner of the feast of booths, remembering how not long before, during the feast
of booths, they had been wandering in the
mountains and caves like wild animals.
7Therefore bearing ivy-wreathed wands
and beautiful branches and also fronds of
palm, they offered hymns of thanksgiving
to him who had given success to the purifying of his own holy place. 8They decreed
by public ordinance and vote that the
whole nation of the Jews should observe
these days every year.
9Such then was the end of Anti′ochus, who
was called Epiph′anes.

10Now we will tell what took place under
Anti′ochus Eu′pator, who was the son of that
ungodly man, and will give a brief summary

of the principal calamities of the wars. [11]This man, when he succeeded to the kingdom, appointed one Lys′ias to have charge of the government and to be chief governor of Coe′le-syr′ia and Phoeni′cia. [12]Ptol′emy, who was called Ma′cron, took the lead in showing justice to the Jews because of the wrong that had been done to them, and attempted to maintain peaceful relations with them. [13]As a result he was accused before Eu′pator by the king's friends. He heard himself called a traitor at every turn, because he had abandoned Cyprus, which Phil″ome′tor had entrusted to him, and had gone over to Anti′ochus Epiph′anes. Unable to command the respect due his office, he took poison and ended his life.

[14]When Gor′gias became governor of the region, he maintained a force of mercenaries, and at every turn kept on warring against the Jews. [15]Besides this, the Idume′ans, who had control of important strongholds, were harassing the Jews; they received those who were banished from Jerusalem, and endeavored to keep up the war. [16]But Mac″cabe′us and his men, after making solemn supplication and begging God to fight on their side, rushed to the strongholds of the Idume′ans. [17]Attacking them vigorously, they gained possession of the places, and beat off all who fought upon the wall, and slew those whom they encountered, killing no fewer than twenty thousand.

[18]When no less than nine thousand took refuge in two very strong towers well equipped to withstand a siege, [19]Mac″cabe′us left Simon and Joseph, and also Zacchae′us and his men, a force sufficient to besiege them; and he himself set off for places where he was more urgently needed. [20]But the men with Simon, who were money-hungry, were bribed by some of those who were in the towers, and on receiving seventy thousand drachmas let some of them slip away. [21]When word of what had happened came to Mac″cabe′us, he gathered the leaders of the people, and accused these men of having sold their brethren for money by setting their enemies free to fight against them. [22]Then he slew these men who had turned traitor, and immediately captured the two towers. [23]Having success at arms in everything he undertook, he destroyed more than twenty thousand in the two strongholds.

[24]Now Timothy, who had been defeated by the Jews before, gathered a tremendous force of mercenaries and collected the cavalry from Asia in no small number. He came on, intending to take Judea by storm. [25]As he drew near, Mac″cabe′us and his men sprinkled dust upon their heads and put on sackcloth, in supplication to God. [26]Falling upon the steps before the altar, they begged him to be gracious to them and to be an enemy to their enemies and an adversary to their adversaries, as the law declares. [27]And rising from their prayer they took up their arms and advanced a considerable distance from the city; and when they came near to the enemy they halted. [28]Just as dawn was breaking, the two armies joined battle, the one having as pledge of success and victory not only their valor but their reliance upon the Lord, while the other made rage their leader in the fight.

[29]When the battle became fierce, there appeared to the enemy from heaven five resplendent men on horses with golden bridles, and they were leading the Jews. [30]Surrounding Mac″cabe′us and protecting him with their own armor and weapons, they kept him from being wounded. And they showered arrows and thunderbolts upon the enemy, so that, confused and blinded, they were thrown into disorder and cut to pieces. [31]Twenty thousand five hundred were slaughtered, besides six hundred horsemen.

[32]Timothy himself fled to a stronghold called Gaza′ra, especially well garrisoned, where Chae′reas was commander. [33]Then Mac″cabe′us and his men were glad, and they besieged the fort for four days. [34]The men within, relying on the strength of the place, blasphemed terribly and hurled out wicked words. [35]But at dawn of the fifth day, twenty young men in the army of Mac″cabe′us, fired with anger because of the blasphemies, bravely stormed the wall and

with savage fury cut down every one they
met. [36]Others who came up in the same way
wheeled around against the defenders and
set fire to the towers; they kindled fires and
burned the blasphemers alive. Others broke
open the gates and let in the rest of the force,
and they occupied the city. [37]They killed
Timothy, who was hidden in a cistern, and
his brother Chae′reas, and Apolloph′anes.
[38]When they had accomplished these things,
with hymns and thanksgivings they blessed
the Lord who shows great kindness to Israel
and gives them the victory.

11 Very soon after this, Lys′ias, the king's
guardian and kinsman, who was in
charge of the government, being vexed at
what had happened, [2]gathered about eighty
thousand men and all his cavalry and came
against the Jews. He intended to make the
city a home for Greeks, [3]and to levy tribute
on the temple as he did on the sacred places
of the other nations, and to put up the high
priesthood for sale every year. [4]He took
no account whatever of the power of God,
but was elated with his ten thousands of
infantry, and his thousands of cavalry, and
his eighty elephants. [5]Invading Judea, he
approached Beth-zur, which was a fortified
place about five leagues from Jerusalem,
and pressed it hard.

[6]When Mac″cabe′us and his men got word
that Lys′ias was besieging the strongholds,
they and all the people, with lamentations
and tears, begged the Lord to send a good
angel to save Israel. [7]Mac″cabe′us himself
was the first to take up arms, and he
urged the others to risk their lives with
him to aid their brethren. Then they
eagerly rushed off together. [8]And there,
while they were still near Jerusalem, a
horseman appeared at their head, clothed
in white and brandishing weapons of
gold. [9]And they all together praised the
merciful God, and were strengthened in
heart, ready to assail not only men but
the wildest beasts or walls of iron. [10]They
advanced in battle order, having their
heavenly ally, for the Lord had mercy
on them. [11]They hurled themselves like
lions against the enemy, and slew eleven
thousand of them and sixteen hundred
horsemen, and forced all the rest to flee.
[12]Most of them got away stripped and
wounded, and Lys′ias himself escaped
by disgraceful flight. [13]And as he was not
without intelligence, he pondered over
the defeat which had befallen him, and
realized that the Hebrews were invincible
because the mighty God fought on their
side. So he sent to them [14]and persuaded
them to settle everything on just terms,
promising that he would persuade the
king, constraining him to be their friend.
[15]Mac″cabe′us, having regard for the
common good, agreed to all that Lys′ias
urged. For the king granted every request
in behalf of the Jews which Maccabeus
delivered to Lysias in writing.

SONG OF SOLOMON 3

[6]What is that coming up from the wilderness,
like a column of smoke,
perfumed with myrrh and frankincense,
with all the fragrant powders of
the merchant?
[7]Behold, it is the litter of Solomon!
About it are sixty mighty men
of the mighty men of Israel,
[8]all belted with swords
and expert in war,
each with his sword at his thigh,
against alarms by night.
[9]King Solomon made himself a palanquin
from the wood of Lebanon.
[10]He made its posts of silver,
its back of gold, its seat of purple;
it was lovingly wrought within
by the daughters of Jerusalem.
[11]Go forth, O daughters of Zion,
and behold King Solomon,
with the crown with which his mother
crowned him
on the day of his wedding,
on the day of the gladness of his heart.

4 Behold, you are beautiful, my love,
behold, you are beautiful!
Your eyes are doves
behind your veil.

Your hair is like a flock of goats,
moving down the slopes of Gilead.
2Your teeth are like a flock of shorn ewes
that have come up from the washing,
all of which bear twins,
and not one among them is bereaved.
3Your lips are like a scarlet thread,
and your mouth is lovely.
Your cheeks are like halves of a pomegranate
behind your veil.
4Your neck is like the tower of David,
built for an arsenal,
whereon hang a thousand bucklers,
all of them shields of warriors.
5Your two breasts are like two fawns,
twins of a gazelle,
that feed among the lilies.
6Until the day breathes
and the shadows flee,
I will hasten to the mountain of myrrh
and the hill of frankincense.
7You are all fair, my love;
there is no flaw in you.
8Come with me from Lebanon, my bride;
come with me from Lebanon.
Depart from the peak of Ama′na,
from the peak of Se′nir and Hermon,
from the dens of lions,
from the mountains of leopards.

9You have ravished my heart, my sister,
my bride,
you have ravished my heart with a glance
of your eyes,
with one jewel of your necklace.
10How sweet is your love, my sister,
my bride!
how much better is your love than wine,
and the fragrance of your oils than
any spice!
11Your lips distil nectar, my bride;
honey and milk are under your tongue;
the scent of your garments is like the
scent of Lebanon.
12A garden locked is my sister, my bride,
a garden locked, a fountain sealed.
13Your shoots are an orchard of
pomegranates
with all choicest fruits,
henna with nard,
14nard and saffron, calamus and cinnamon,
with all trees of frankincense,
myrrh and aloes,
with all chief spices—
15a garden fountain, a well of living water,
and flowing streams from Lebanon.

16Awake, O north wind,
and come, O south wind!
Blow upon my garden,
let its fragrance be wafted abroad.
Let my beloved come to his garden,
and eat its choicest fruits.

REVELATION 19

After this I heard what seemed to be the mighty voice of a great multitude in heaven, crying,

**"Hallelujah! Salvation and glory and
power belong to our God,**
2for his judgments are true and just;
he has judged the great harlot who
corrupted the earth with her
fornication,
and he has avenged on her the blood
of his servants."
3Once more they cried,
"Hallelujah! The smoke from her goes up
for ever and ever."
4And the twenty-four elders and the four
living creatures fell down and worshiped
God who is seated on the throne, saying,
"Amen. Hallelujah!" 5And from the throne
came a voice crying,
"Praise our God, all you his servants,
you who fear him, small and great."
6Then I heard what seemed to be the voice
of a great multitude, like the sound of
many waters and like the sound of mighty
thunderpeals, crying,
"Hallelujah! For the Lord our God the
Almighty reigns.
7Let us rejoice and exult and give him
the glory,
for the marriage of the Lamb has come,
and his Bride has made herself ready;

[8]it was granted her to be clothed with fine
linen, bright and pure"—
for the fine linen is the righteous deeds of
the saints.
[9]And the angel said to me, "Write this:
Blessed are those who are invited to the
marriage supper of the Lamb." And he said
to me, "These are true words of God." [10]Then
I fell down at his feet to worship him, but he
said to me, "You must not do that! I am a
fellow servant with you and your brethren
who hold the testimony of Jesus. Worship
God." For the testimony of Jesus is the spirit
of prophecy.
[11]Then I saw heaven opened, and behold,
a white horse! He who sat upon it is called
Faithful and True, and in righteousness he
judges and makes war. [12]His eyes are like
a flame of fire, and on his head are many
diadems; and he has a name inscribed
which no one knows but himself. [13]He is
clothed in a robe dipped in blood, and the
name by which he is called is The Word of
God. [14]And the armies of heaven, wearing
fine linen, white and pure, followed him
on white horses. [15]From his mouth issues
a sharp sword with which to strike the
nations, and he will rule them with a rod
of iron; he will tread the wine press of the
fury of the wrath of God the Almighty. [16]On
his robe and on his thigh he has a name
inscribed, King of kings and Lord of lords.
[17]Then I saw an angel standing in the sun,
and with a loud voice he called to all the
birds that fly in midheaven, "Come, gather
for the great supper of God, [18]to eat the flesh
of kings, the flesh of captains, the flesh of
mighty men, the flesh of horses and their
riders, and the flesh of all men, both free
and slave, both small and great." [19]And I saw
the beast and the kings of the earth with
their armies gathered to make war against
him who sits upon the horse and against
his army. [20]And the beast was captured, and
with it the false prophet who in its presence
had worked the signs by which he deceived
those who had received the mark of the
beast and those who worshiped its image.
These two were thrown alive into the lake
of fire that burns with brimstone. [21]And the
rest were slain by the sword of him who sits
upon the horse, the sword that issues from
his mouth; and all the birds were gorged
with their flesh.

REFLECTION

At the end of Revelation, and history, there are two significant characters that stand out: the harlot and the bride. They are two distinct representations of the Church. The harlot represents those in the Church who seek the love of the world and are unfaithful to Christ. In the end, she finds the world, represented by the beast, who turns against her despite her fawning love for it. The harlot is condemned and judged by God and destroyed by the beast. The bride, however, represents the Church who is faithful to God. Her love is pure and unsullied by the world. She loves Christ above and in place of worldly loves. Her fidelity is rewarded with a tremendous invitation, to the wedding supper of the Lamb. Every spectacular wedding dress ever worn by any bride is a but a foreshadowing and signpost to this ultimate wedding, where the bride is adorned in stunning white and "'clothed with fine linen, bright and pure'—for the fine linen is the righteous deeds of the saints" (Rev 19:8). What differentiates the harlot from the bride is not that they love, for they are both lovers, but rather who they love. Whom do you love more, the world or God?

December 29

2 MACCABEES 11

**[16]The letter written to the Jews
by Lys´ias was to this effect:**
**"Lysias to the people of the Jews,
greeting. [17]John and Ab´salom, who were**
sent by you, have delivered your signed
communication and have asked about the
matters indicated therein. [18]I have informed

the king of everything that needed to be
brought before him, and he has agreed to
what was possible. 19If you will maintain
your good will toward the government, I
will endeavor for the future to help promote
your welfare. 20And concerning these matters
and their details, I have ordered these men
and my representatives to confer with you.
21Farewell. The one hundred and forty-eighth
year, Di′′oscorin′thius twenty-fourth."
22The king's letter ran thus:
"King Anti′ochus to his brother Lys′ias,
greeting. 23Now that our father has gone on
to the gods, we desire that the subjects of the
kingdom be undisturbed in caring for their
own affairs. 24We have heard that the Jews do
not consent to our father's change to Greek
customs but prefer their own way of living
and ask that their own customs be allowed
them. 25Accordingly, since we choose that
this nation also be free from disturbance,
our decision is that their temple be restored
to them and that they live according to the
customs of their ancestors. 26You will do
well, therefore, to send word to them and
give them pledges of friendship, so that they
may know our policy and be of good cheer
and go on happily in the conduct of their
own affairs."
27To the nation the king's letter was as
follows:
"King Anti′ochus to the senate of the Jews
and to the other Jews, greeting. 28If you are
well, it is as we desire. We also are in good
health. 29Menela′us has informed us that
you wish to return home and look after
your own affairs. 30Therefore those who
go home by the thirtieth day of Xan′thicus
will have our pledge of friendship and full
permission 31for the Jews to enjoy their own
food and laws, just as formerly, and none
of them shall be molested in any way for
what he may have done in ignorance. 32And
I have also sent Menela′us to encourage
you. 33Farewell. The one hundred and forty-
eighth year, Xan′thicus fifteenth."
34The Romans also sent them a letter,
which read thus:
"Quint′us Mem′mius and Titus Ma′nius,
envoys of the Romans, to the people of the
Jews, greeting. 35With regard to what Lys′ias
the kinsman of the king has granted you,
we also give consent. 36But as to the matters
which he decided are to be referred to the
king, as soon as you have considered them,
send some one promptly, so that we may
make proposals appropriate for you. For
we are on our way to Antioch. 37Therefore
make haste and send some men, so that
we may have your judgment. 38Farewell.
The one hundred and forty-eighth year,
Xan′thicus fifteenth."

12 When this agreement had been
reached, Lys′ias returned to the king,
and the Jews went about their farming.
2But some of the governors in various
places, Timothy and Apollo′nius the son
of Gennae′us, as well as Hi′′eron′ymus
and Dem′ophon, and in addition to these
Nica′nor the governor of Cyprus, would not
let them live quietly and in peace. 3And some
men of Joppa did so ungodly a deed as this:
they invited the Jews who lived among them
to embark, with their wives and children, on
boats which they had provided, as though
there were no ill will to the Jews; 4and this
was done by public vote of the city. And
when they accepted, because they wished
to live peaceably and suspected nothing,
the men of Joppa took them out to sea and
drowned them, not less than two hundred.
5When Judas heard of the cruelty visited on
his countrymen, he gave orders to his men
6and, calling upon God the righteous Judge,
attacked the murderers of his brethren. He
set fire to the harbor by night, and burned
the boats, and massacred those who had
taken refuge there. 7Then, because the city's
gates were closed, he withdrew, intending
to come again and root out the whole
community of Joppa. 8But learning that the
men in Jam′nia meant in the same way to
wipe out the Jews who were living among
them, 9he attacked the people of Jam′nia
by night and set fire to the harbor and the
fleet, so that the glow of the light was seen
in Jerusalem, thirty miles distant.
10When they had gone more than a mile
from there, on their march against Timothy,
not less than five thousand Arabs with five

hundred horsemen attacked them. [11]After a hard fight Judas and his men won the victory, by the help of God. The defeated nomads begged Judas to grant them pledges of friendship, promising to give him cattle and to help his people in all other ways. [12]Judas, thinking that they might really be useful in many ways, agreed to make peace with them; and after receiving his pledges they departed to their tents.

[13]He also attacked a certain city which was strongly fortified with earthworks and walls, and inhabited by all sorts of Gentiles. Its name was Cas´pin. [14]And those who were within, relying on the strength of the walls and on their supply of provisions, behaved most insolently toward Judas and his men, railing at them and even blaspheming and saying unholy things. [15]But Judas and his men, calling upon the great Sovereign of the world, who without battering-rams or engines of war overthrew Jericho in the days of Joshua, rushed furiously upon the walls. [16]They took the city by the will of God, and slaughtered untold numbers, so that the adjoining lake, a quarter of a mile wide, appeared to be running over with blood.

[17]When they had gone ninety-five miles from there, they came to Cha´rax, to the Jews who are called Tou´bia´ni. [18]They did not find Timothy in that region, for he had by then departed from the region without accomplishing anything, though in one place he had left a very strong garrison. [19]Dosith´eus and Sosip´ater, who were captains under Mac″cabe´us, marched out and destroyed those whom Timothy had left in the stronghold, more than ten thousand men. [20]But Mac″cabe´us arranged his army in divisions, set men in command of the divisions, and hastened after Timothy, who had with him a hundred and twenty thousand infantry and two thousand five hundred cavalry. [21]When Timothy learned of the approach of Judas, he sent off the women and the children and also the baggage to a place called Carna´im; for that place was hard to besiege and difficult of access because of the narrowness of all the approaches. [22]But when Judas' first division appeared, terror and fear came over the enemy at the manifestation to them of him who sees all things; and they rushed off in flight and were swept on, this way and that, so that often they were injured by their own men and pierced by the points of their swords. [23]And Judas pressed the pursuit with the utmost vigor, putting the sinners to the sword, and destroyed as many as thirty thousand men.

[24]Timothy himself fell into the hands of Dosith´eus and Sosip´ater and their men. With great guile he begged them to let him go in safety, because he held the parents of most of them and the brothers of some and no consideration would be shown them. [25]And when with many words he had confirmed his solemn promise to restore them unharmed, they let him go, for the sake of saving their brethren.

[26]Then Judas marched against Carna´im and the temple of Atar´gatis, and slaughtered twenty-five thousand people. [27]After the rout and destruction of these, he marched also against E´phron, a fortified city where Lys´ias dwelt with multitudes of people of all nationalities. Stalwart young men took their stand before the walls and made a vigorous defense; and great stores of war engines and missiles were there. [28]But the Jews called upon the Sovereign who with power shatters the might of his enemies, and they got the city into their hands, and killed as many as twenty-five thousand of those who were within it.

[29]Setting out from there, they hastened to Scythop´olis, which is seventy-five miles from Jerusalem. [30]But when the Jews who dwelt there bore witness to the good will which the people of Scythop´olis had shown them and their kind treatment of them in times of misfortune, [31]they thanked them and exhorted them to be well disposed to their race in the future also. Then they went up to Jerusalem, as the feast of weeks was close at hand.

[32]After the feast called Pentecost, they hastened against Gor´gias, the governor of Idume´a. [33]And he came out with three thousand infantry and four hundred cavalry. [34]When they joined battle, it happened

that a few of the Jews fell. 35But a certain
Dosith′eus, one of Bace′nor's men, who was
on horseback and was a strong man, caught
hold of Gor′gias, and grasping his cloak was
dragging him off by main strength, wishing
to take the accursed man alive, when one
of the Thracian horsemen bore down upon
him and cut off his arm; so Gorgias escaped
and reached Mar′isa.
36As Es′dris and his men had been fighting
for a long time and were weary, Judas called
upon the Lord to show himself their ally
and leader in the battle. 37In the language
of their fathers he raised the battle cry, with
hymns; then he charged against Gor′gias'
men when they were not expecting it, and
put them to flight.
38Then Judas assembled his army and went
to the city of Adul′lam. As the seventh day
was coming on, they purified themselves
according to the custom, and they kept the
sabbath there.
39On the next day, as by that time it had
become necessary, Judas and his men went
to take up the bodies of the fallen and to
bring them back to lie with their kinsmen in
the sepulchres of their fathers. 40Then under
the tunic of every one of the dead they
found sacred tokens of the idols of Jam′nia,
which the law forbids the Jews to wear.
And it became clear to all that this was why
these men had fallen. 41So they all blessed
the ways of the Lord, the righteous Judge,
who reveals the things that are hidden; 42and
they turned to prayer, begging that the sin
which had been committed might be wholly
blotted out. And the noble Judas exhorted
the people to keep themselves free from
sin, for they had seen with their own eyes
what had happened because of the sin of
those who had fallen. 43He also took up a
collection, man by man, to the amount of
two thousand drachmas of silver, and sent it
to Jerusalem to provide for a sin offering. In
doing this he acted very well and honorably,
taking account of the resurrection. 44For if
he were not expecting that those who had
fallen would rise again, it would have been
superfluous and foolish to pray for the
dead. 45But if he was looking to the splendid
reward that is laid up for those who fall
asleep in godliness, it was a holy and pious
thought. Therefore he made atonement for
the dead, that they might be delivered from
their sin.

SONG OF SOLOMON 5

I come to my garden, my sister, my bride,
I gather my myrrh with my spice,
I eat my honeycomb with my honey,
I drink my wine with my milk.

Eat, O friends, and drink:
  drink deeply, O lovers!
2I slept, but my heart was awake.
Hark! my beloved is knocking.
"Open to me, my sister, my love,
  my dove, my perfect one;
for my head is wet with dew,
  my locks with the drops of the night."
3I had put off my garment,
  how could I put it on?
I had bathed my feet,
  how could I soil them?
4My beloved put his hand to the latch,
  and my heart was thrilled within me.
5I arose to open to my beloved,
  and my hands dripped with myrrh,
my fingers with liquid myrrh,
  upon the handles of the bolt.
6I opened to my beloved,
  but my beloved had turned and gone.
My soul failed me when he spoke.
I sought him, but found him not;
  I called him, but he gave no answer.
7The watchmen found me,
  as they went about in the city;
they beat me, they wounded me,
  they took away my mantle,
  those watchmen of the walls.
8I adjure you, O daughters of Jerusalem,
  if you find my beloved,
that you tell him
  I am sick with love.

9What is your beloved more than
  another beloved,
  O fairest among women?

What is your beloved more than
  another beloved,
  that you thus adjure us?

10 My beloved is all radiant and ruddy,
  distinguished among ten thousand.
11 His head is the finest gold;
  his locks are wavy,
  black as a raven.
12 His eyes are like doves
  beside springs of water,
bathed in milk,
  fitly set.
13 His cheeks are like beds of spices,
  yielding fragrance.
His lips are lilies,
  distilling liquid myrrh.
14 His arms are rounded gold,
  set with jewels.
His body is ivory work,
  encrusted with sapphires.
15 His legs are alabaster columns,
  set upon bases of gold.
His appearance is like Lebanon,
  choice as the cedars.
16 His speech is most sweet,
  and he is altogether desirable.
This is my beloved and this is my friend,
  O daughters of Jerusalem.

REVELATION 20

Then I saw an angel coming
down from heaven, holding
in his hand the key of the
bottomless pit and a great chain. 2 And
he seized the dragon, that ancient
serpent, who is the Devil and Satan,
and bound him for a thousand years, 3 and
threw him into the pit, and shut it and sealed it
over him, that he should deceive the nations no
more, till the thousand years were ended. After
that he must be let out for a little while.
4 Then I saw thrones, and seated on them were
those to whom judgment was committed. Also
I saw the souls of those who had been beheaded
for their testimony to Jesus and for the word
of God, and who had not worshiped the beast
or its image and had not received its mark on
their foreheads or their hands. They came to
life, and reigned with Christ a thousand years.
5 The rest of the dead did not come to life until
the thousand years were ended. This is the
first resurrection. 6 Blessed and holy is he who
shares in the first resurrection! Over such the
second death has no power, but they shall be
priests of God and of Christ, and they shall
reign with him a thousand years.
7 And when the thousand years are ended,
Satan will be released from his prison 8 and will
come out to deceive the nations which are at
the four corners of the earth, that is, Gog and
Ma′gog, to gather them for battle; their number
is like the sand of the sea. 9 And they marched
up over the broad earth and surrounded the
camp of the saints and the beloved city; but
fire came down from heaven and consumed
them, 10 and the devil who had deceived them
was thrown into the lake of fire and brimstone
where the beast and the false prophet were,
and they will be tormented day and night for
ever and ever.
11 Then I saw a great white throne and him
who sat upon it; from his presence earth and
sky fled away, and no place was found for
them. 12 And I saw the dead, great and small,
standing before the throne, and books were
opened. Also another book was opened, which
is the book of life. And the dead were judged
by what was written in the books, by what they
had done. 13 And the sea gave up the dead in
it, Death and Hades gave up the dead in them,
and all were judged by what they had done.
14 Then Death and Hades were thrown into the
lake of fire. This is the second death, the lake
of fire; 15 and if any one's name was not found
written in the book of life, he was thrown into
the lake of fire.

REFLECTION

Judas Maccabeus, after fighting a battle, returns with his soldiers to bury the dead, which is one of the corporal works of mercy. He discovers, however, that each of his fallen soldiers is wearing pagan medals to give them luck. Of course, the opposite happened, as those wearing such idolatrous charms were precisely those who died! Judas then takes up a collection from his survivors to offer sin offerings in the Temple for atonement of the dead. Scripture observes the nobility and charity of praying for the dead: "In doing this he acted very well and honorably, taking account of the resurrection. For if he were not expecting that those who had fallen would rise again, it would have been superfluous and foolish to pray for the dead. But if he was looking to the splendid reward that is laid up for those who fall asleep in godliness, it was a holy and pious thought. Therefore he made atonement for the dead, that they might be delivered from their sin" (2 Mc 12:43–45). Do you act nobly like Judas Maccabeus and pray for the loved ones and friends in your life who have passed away?

December 30

2 MACCABEES 13

In the one hundred and forty-ninth year word came to Judas and his men that Anti′ochus Eu′pator was coming with a great army against Judea, [2]and with him Lys′ias, his guardian, who had charge of the government. Each of them had a Greek force of one hundred and ten thousand infantry, five thousand three hundred cavalry, twenty-two elephants, and three hundred chariots armed with scythes.

[3]Menela′us also joined them and with utter hypocrisy urged Anti′ochus on, not for the sake of his country's welfare, but because he thought that he would be established in office. [4]But the King of kings aroused the anger of Anti′ochus against the scoundrel; and when Lys′ias informed him that this man was to blame for all the trouble, he ordered them to take him to Beroe′a and to put him to death by the method which is the custom in that place. [5]For there is a tower in that place, fifty cubits high, full of ashes, and it has a rim running around it which on all sides inclines precipitously into the ashes. [6]There they all push to destruction any man guilty of sacrilege or notorious for other crimes. [7]By such a fate it came about that Menela′us the lawbreaker died, without even burial in the earth. [8]And this was eminently just; because he had committed many sins against the altar whose fire and ashes were holy, he met his death in ashes.

[9]The king with barbarous arrogance was coming to show the Jews things far worse than those that had been done in his father's time. [10]But when Judas heard of this, he ordered the people to call upon the Lord day and night, now if ever to help those who were on the point of being deprived of the law and their country and the holy temple, [11]and not to let the people who had just begun to revive fall into the hands of the blasphemous Gentiles. [12]When they had all joined in the same petition and had begged the merciful Lord with weeping and fasting and lying prostrate for three days without ceasing, Judas exhorted them and ordered them to stand ready.

[13]After consulting privately with the elders, he determined to march out and decide the matter by the help of God before the king's army could enter Judea and get possession of the city. [14]So, committing the decision to the Creator of the world and exhorting his men to fight nobly to the death for the laws, temple, city, country, and commonwealth, he pitched his camp near Mo′dein. [15]He gave his men the watchword, "God's victory," and with a picked force of the bravest young men, he attacked the king's pavilion at night and slew as many as two thousand men in the camp. He stabbed the leading elephant and its rider. [16]In the end they filled the camp with terror and confusion and withdrew in triumph. [17]This happened, just as day was dawning, because the Lord's help protected him.

18The king, having had a taste of the daring
of the Jews, tried strategy in attacking their
positions. 19He advanced against Beth-zur,
a strong fortress of the Jews, was turned
back, attacked again, and was defeated.
20Judas sent in to the garrison whatever was
necessary. 21But Rhod′ocus, a man from the
ranks of the Jews, gave secret information
to the enemy; he was sought for, caught,
and put in prison. 22The king negotiated a
second time with the people in Beth-zur,
gave pledges, received theirs, withdrew,
attacked Judas and his men, was defeated;
23he got word that Philip, who had been left
in charge of the government, had revolted
in Antioch; he was dismayed, called in
the Jews, yielded and swore to observe all
their rights, settled with them and offered
sacrifice, honored the sanctuary and
showed generosity to the holy place. 24He
received Mac″cabe′us, left Hegemon′ides as
governor from Ptolema′is to Ge′rar, 25and
went to Ptolemais. The people of Ptolema′is
were indignant over the treaty; in fact they
were so angry that they wanted to annul its
terms. 26Lys′ias took the public platform,
made the best possible defense, convinced
them, appeased them, gained their good
will, and set out for Antioch. This is how the
king's attack and withdrawal turned out.

14 Three years later, word came to Judas
and his men that Deme′trius, the
son of Seleu′cus, had sailed into the harbor
of Trip′olis with a strong army and a fleet,
2and had taken possession of the country,
having made away with Anti′ochus and his
guardian Lys′ias.

3Now a certain Al′cimus, who had
formerly been high priest but had wilfully
defiled himself in the times of separation,
realized that there was no way for him to be
safe or to have access again to the holy altar,
4and went to King Deme′trius in about the
one hundred and fifty-first year, presenting
to him a crown of gold and a palm, and
besides these some of the customary olive
branches from the temple. During that day
he kept quiet. 5But he found an opportunity
that furthered his mad purpose when he was
invited by Deme′trius to a meeting of the
council and was asked about the disposition
and intentions of the Jews. He answered:

6"Those of the Jews who are called Hasid′eans,
whose leader is Judas Mac″cabe′us, are
keeping up war and stirring up sedition, and
will not let the kingdom attain tranquillity.
7Therefore I have laid aside my ancestral
glory—I mean the high priesthood—and
have now come here, 8first because I am
genuinely concerned for the interests of the
king, and second because I have regard also
for my fellow citizens. For through the folly
of those whom I have mentioned our whole
nation is now in no small misfortune. 9Since
you are acquainted, O king, with the details
of this matter, deign to take thought for our
country and our hard-pressed nation with
the gracious kindness which you show to all.
10For as long as Judas lives, it is impossible
for the government to find peace."

11When he had said this, the rest of the
king's friends, who were hostile to Judas,
quickly inflamed Deme′trius still more.
12And he immediately chose Nica′nor, who
had been in command of the elephants,
appointed him governor of Judea, and
sent him off 13with orders to kill Judas and
scatter his men, and to set up Al′cimus as
high priest of the greatest temple. 14And
the Gentiles throughout Judea, who had
fled before Judas, flocked to join Nica′nor,
thinking that the misfortunes and calamities
of the Jews would mean prosperity for
themselves.

15When the Jews heard of Nica′nor's
coming and the gathering of the Gentiles,
they sprinkled dust upon their heads and
prayed to him who established his own
people for ever and always upholds his
own heritage by manifesting himself.
16At the command of the leader, they
set out from there immediately and
engaged them in battle at a village called
Des′sau. 17Simon, the brother of Judas,
had encountered Nica′nor, but had been
temporarily checked because of the sudden
consternation created by the enemy.

18Nevertheless Nica′nor, hearing of
the valor of Judas and his men and their
courage in battle for their country, shrank

from deciding the issue by bloodshed.
[19]Therefore he sent Pos″ido′nius and
Theod′otus and Mattathi′as to give and
receive pledges of friendship. [20]When the
terms had been fully considered, and the
leader had informed the people, and it had
appeared that they were of one mind, they
agreed to the covenant. [21]And the leaders
set a day on which to meet by themselves. A
chariot came forward from each army; seats
of honor were set in place; [22]Judas posted
armed men in readiness at key places to
prevent sudden treachery on the part of the
enemy; they held the proper conference.

[23]Nica′nor stayed on in Jerusalem and did
nothing out of the way, but dismissed the
flocks of people that had gathered. [24]And
he kept Judas always in his presence; he was
warmly attached to the man. [25]And he urged
him to marry and have children; so he married,
settled down, and shared the common life.

SONG OF SOLOMON 6

Where has your beloved gone,
O fairest among women?
Where has your beloved turned,
that we may seek him with you?

[2]My beloved has gone down to his garden,
to the beds of spices,
to pasture his flock in the gardens,
and to gather lilies.
[3]I am my beloved's and my beloved is mine;
he pastures his flock among the lilies.

[4]You are beautiful as Tirzah, my love,
comely as Jerusalem,
terrible as an army with banners.
[5]Turn away your eyes from me,
for they disturb me—
Your hair is like a flock of goats,
moving down the slopes of Gilead.
[6]Your teeth are like a flock of ewes,
that have come up from the washing,
all of them bear twins,
not one among them is bereaved.
[7]Your cheeks are like halves of a pomegranate
behind your veil.
[8]There are sixty queens and eighty
concubines,
and maidens without number.
[9]My dove, my perfect one, is only one,
the darling of her mother,
flawless to her that bore her.
The maidens saw her and called her happy;
the queens and concubines also, and they
praised her.
[10]"Who is this that looks forth like the dawn,
fair as the moon, bright as the sun,
terrible as an army with banners?"

[11]I went down to the nut orchard,
to look at the blossoms of the valley,
to see whether the vines had budded,
whether the pomegranates were
in bloom.
[12]Before I was aware, my fancy set me
in a chariot beside my prince.

[13]Return, return, O Shu′lammite,
return, return, that we may look
upon you.

Why should you look upon the Shulammite,
as upon a dance before two armies?

7 How graceful are your feet in sandals,
O queenly maiden!
Your rounded thighs are like jewels,
the work of a master hand.
[2]Your navel is a rounded bowl
that never lacks mixed wine.
Your belly is a heap of wheat,
encircled with lilies.
[3]Your two breasts are like two fawns,
twins of a gazelle.
[4]Your neck is like an ivory tower.
Your eyes are pools in Hesh′bon,
by the gate of Bath-rab′bim.
Your nose is like a tower of Lebanon,
overlooking Damascus.
[5]Your head crowns you like Car′mel,
and your flowing locks are like purple;
a king is held captive in the tresses.

[6]How fair and pleasant you are,
O loved one, delectable maiden!
[7]You are stately as a palm tree,
and your breasts are like its clusters.

8 I say I will climb the palm tree
and lay hold of its branches.
Oh, may your breasts be like clusters
of the vine,
and the scent of your breath like apples,
9 and your kisses like the best wine
that goes down smoothly,
gliding over lips and teeth.

REVELATION 21

**Then I saw a new heaven and a
new earth; for the first heaven
and the first earth had passed
away, and the sea was no more. 2 And
I saw the holy city, new Jerusalem,
coming down out of heaven from**
God, prepared as a bride adorned for her
husband; 3 and I heard a great voice from the
throne saying, "Behold, the dwelling of God
is with men. He will dwell with them, and
they shall be his people, and God himself
will be with them; 4 he will wipe away every
tear from their eyes, and death shall be no
more, neither shall there be mourning nor
crying nor pain any more, for the former
things have passed away."
5 And he who sat upon the throne said,
"Behold, I make all things new." Also he said,
"Write this, for these words are trustworthy
and true." 6 And he said to me, "It is done! I
am the Alpha and the Omega, the beginning
and the end. To the thirsty I will give water
without price from the fountain of the
water of life. 7 He who conquers shall have
this heritage, and I will be his God and he
shall be my son. 8 But as for the cowardly,
the faithless, the polluted, as for murderers,
fornicators, sorcerers, idolaters, and all liars,
their lot shall be in the lake that burns
with fire and brimstone, which is the
second death."
9 Then came one of the seven angels who
had the seven bowls full of the seven last
plagues, and spoke to me, saying, "Come,
I will show you the Bride, the wife of the
Lamb." 10 And in the Spirit he carried me
away to a great, high mountain, and showed
me the holy city Jerusalem coming down
out of heaven from God, 11 having the glory
of God, its radiance like a most rare jewel,
like a jasper, clear as crystal. 12 It had a great,
high wall, with twelve gates, and at the gates
twelve angels, and on the gates the names of
the twelve tribes of the sons of Israel were
inscribed; 13 on the east three gates, on the
north three gates, on the south three gates,
and on the west three gates. 14 And the wall
of the city had twelve foundations, and
on them the twelve names of the twelve
apostles of the Lamb.
15 And he who talked to me had a
measuring rod of gold to measure the
city and its gates and walls. 16 The city
lies foursquare, its length the same as its
breadth; and he measured the city with
his rod, twelve thousand stadia; its length
and breadth and height are equal. 17 He also
measured its wall, a hundred and forty-
four cubits by a man's measure, that is,
an angel's. 18 The wall was built of jasper,
while the city was pure gold, clear as glass.
19 The foundations of the wall of the city
were adorned with every jewel; the first
was jasper, the second sapphire, the third
agate, the fourth emerald, 20 the fifth onyx,
the sixth carnelian, the seventh chrysolite,
the eighth beryl, the ninth topaz, the tenth
chrysoprase, the eleventh jacinth, the
twelfth amethyst. 21 And the twelve gates
were twelve pearls, each of the gates made
of a single pearl, and the street of the city
was pure gold, transparent as glass.
22 And I saw no temple in the city, for
its temple is the Lord God the Almighty
and the Lamb. 23 And the city has no need
of sun or moon to shine upon it, for the
glory of God is its light, and its lamp is the
Lamb. 24 By its light shall the nations walk;
and the kings of the earth shall bring
their glory into it, 25 and its gates shall
never be shut by day—and there shall be
no night there; 26 they shall bring into it
the glory and the honor of the nations.
27 But nothing unclean shall enter it, nor
any one who practices abomination or
falsehood, but only those who are written
in the Lamb's book of life.

REFLECTION

In the second to last scene of Revelation, St. John sees a new heaven and a new earth. Most people miss this detail, and in missing it they misunderstand where much of eternal life is spent. Indeed, much popular imagination is that at the end we will be raptured up to Heaven, leaving behind earth forever. Many may well be surprised at what John sees at the end, Heaven coming down to earth: "And I saw the holy city, new Jerusalem, coming down out of heaven from God, prepared as a bride adorned for her husband" (Rev 21:2). To emphasize this point, God declares "Behold, the dwelling of God is with men" (v. 3). The Second Coming is like the first, God comes to us. The earth matters, and it will remain our home. At the same time, it will be put through a major renovation, as God declares, "Behold, I make all things new" (v. 5). In the renewed earth, there is no place for evil and therefore God "will wipe away every tear from their eyes, and death shall be no more, neither shall there be mourning nor crying nor pain any more, for the former things have passed away" (v. 4). Are these hope-filled words and images imprinted deeply in your imagination and heart?

December 31

2 MACCABEES 14

26But when Al′cimus noticed their good will for one another, he took the covenant that had been made and went to Deme′trius. He told him that Nica′nor was disloyal to the government, for he had appointed that conspirator against the kingdom, Judas, to be his successor. 27The king became excited and, provoked by the false accusations of that depraved man, wrote to Nica′nor, stating that he was displeased with the covenant and commanding him to send Mac″cabe′us to Antioch as a prisoner without delay.

28When this message came to Nica′nor, he was troubled and grieved that he had to annul their agreement when the man had done no wrong. 29Since it was not possible to oppose the king, he watched for an opportunity to accomplish this by a stratagem. 30But Mac″cabe′us, noticing that Nica′nor was more austere in his dealings with him and was meeting him more rudely than had been his custom, concluded that this austerity did not spring from the best motives. So he gathered not a few of his men, and went into hiding from Nicanor.

31When the latter became aware that he had been cleverly outwitted by the man, he went to the great and holy temple while the priests were offering the customary sacrifices, and commanded them to hand the man over. 32And when they declared on oath that they did not know where the man was whom he sought, 33he stretched out his right hand toward the sanctuary, and swore this oath: "If you do not hand Judas over to me as a prisoner, I will level this precinct of God to the ground and tear down the altar, and I will build here a splendid temple to Diony′sus."

34Having said this, he went away. Then the priests stretched forth their hands toward heaven and called upon the constant Defender of our nation, in these words: 35"O Lord of all, who have need of nothing, you were pleased that there be a temple for your habitation among us; 36so now, O holy One, Lord of all holiness, keep undefiled for ever this house that has been so recently purified."

37A certain Ra′zis, one of the elders of Jerusalem, was denounced to Nica′nor as a man who loved his fellow citizens and was very well thought of and for his good will was called father of the Jews. 38For in former times, when there was no mingling with the Gentiles, he had been accused of Judaism, and for Judaism he had with all zeal risked body and life. 39Nica′nor, wishing to exhibit the enmity which he had for the Jews, sent more than five hundred soldiers to arrest him; 40for he thought that by arresting him he would do them an injury. 41When the

troops were about to capture the tower and
were forcing the door of the courtyard, they
ordered that fire be brought and the doors
burned. Being surrounded, Ra′zis fell upon
his own sword, 42preferring to die nobly
rather than to fall into the hands of sinners
and suffer outrages unworthy of his noble
birth. 43But in the heat of the struggle he
did not hit exactly, and the crowd was now
rushing in through the doors. He bravely
ran up on the wall, and manfully threw
himself down into the crowd. 44But as they
quickly drew back, a space opened and
he fell in the middle of the empty space.
45Still alive and aflame with anger, he rose,
and though his blood gushed forth and his
wounds were severe he ran through the
crowd; and standing upon a steep rock,
46with his blood now completely drained
from him, he tore out his entrails, took
them with both hands and hurled them at
the crowd, calling upon the Lord of life and
spirit to give them back to him again. This
was the manner of his death.

15 When Nica′nor heard that Judas and
his men were in the region of Samar′ia,
he made plans to attack them with complete
safety on the day of rest. 2And when the Jews
who were compelled to follow him said, "Do
not destroy so savagely and barbarously, but
show respect for the day which he who sees
all things has honored and hallowed above
other days," 3the thrice-accursed wretch
asked if there were a sovereign in heaven who
had commanded the keeping of the sabbath
day. 4And when they declared, "It is the
living Lord himself, the Sovereign in heaven,
who ordered us to observe the seventh day,"
5he replied, "And I am a sovereign also, on
earth, and I command you to take up arms
and finish the king's business." Nevertheless,
he did not succeed in carrying out his
abominable design.

6This Nica′nor in his utter boastfulness
and arrogance had determined to erect a
public monument of victory over Judas and
his men. 7But Mac′cabe′us did not cease to
trust with all confidence that he would get
help from the Lord. 8And he exhorted his
men not to fear the attack of the Gentiles, but
to keep in mind the former times when help
had come to them from heaven, and now
to look for the victory which the Almighty
would give them. 9Encouraging them from
the law and the prophets, and reminding
them also of the struggles they had won,
he made them the more eager. 10And when
he had aroused their courage, he gave his
orders, at the same time pointing out the
perfidy of the Gentiles and their violation
of oaths. 11He armed each of them not so
much with confidence in shields and spears
as with the inspiration of brave words, and
he cheered them all by relating a dream, a
sort of vision, which was worthy of belief.

12What he saw was this: Oni′as, who had
been high priest, a noble and good man, of
modest bearing and gentle manner, one who
spoke fittingly and had been trained from
childhood in all that belongs to excellence,
was praying with outstretched hands for
the whole body of the Jews. 13Then likewise
a man appeared, distinguished by his gray
hair and dignity, and of marvelous majesty
and authority. 14And Oni′as spoke, saying,
"This is a man who loves the brethren and
prays much for the people and the holy city,
Jeremi′ah, the prophet of God." 15Jeremi′ah
stretched out his right hand and gave to
Judas a golden sword, and as he gave it he
addressed him thus: 16"Take this holy sword,
a gift from God, with which you will strike
down your adversaries."

17Encouraged by the words of Judas, so
noble and so effective in arousing valor and
awaking manliness in the souls of the young,
they determined not to carry on a campaign
but to attack bravely, and to decide the
matter, by fighting hand to hand with all
courage, because the city and the sanctuary
and the temple were in danger. 18Their
concern for wives and children, and also for
brethren and relatives, lay upon them less
heavily; their greatest and first fear was for
the consecrated sanctuary. 19And those who
had to remain in the city were in no little
distress, being anxious over the encounter
in the open country.

20When all were now looking forward
to the coming decision, and the enemy

was already close at hand with their
army drawn up for battle, the elephants
strategically stationed and the cavalry
deployed on the flanks, 21Mac″cabe′us,
perceiving the hosts that were before
him and the varied supply of arms and
the savagery of the elephants, stretched
out his hands toward heaven and called
upon the Lord who works wonders; for
he knew that it is not by arms, but as the
Lord decides, that he gains the victory
for those who deserve it. 22And he called
upon him in these words: "O Lord, you
sent your angel in the time of Hezeki′ah
king of Judea, and he slew fully a hundred
and eighty-five thousand in the camp of
Sennach′erib. 23So now, O Sovereign of
the heavens, send a good angel to carry
terror and trembling before us. 24By the
might of your arm may these blasphemers
who come against your holy people be
struck down." With these words he ended
his prayer.

25Nica′nor and his men advanced with
trumpets and battle songs; 26and Judas
and his men met the enemy in battle with
invocation to God and prayers. 27So, fighting
with their hands and praying to God in their
hearts, they laid low no less than thirty-five
thousand men, and were greatly gladdened
by God's manifestation.

28When the action was over and they
were returning with joy, they recognized
Nica′nor, lying dead, in full armor. 29Then
there was shouting and tumult, and they
blessed the Sovereign Lord in the language
of their fathers. 30And the man who was
ever in body and soul the defender of his
fellow citizens, the man who maintained his
youthful good will toward his countrymen,
ordered them to cut off Nica′nor's head and
arm and carry them to Jerusalem. 31And
when he arrived there and had called his
countrymen together and stationed the
priests before the altar, he sent for those
who were in the citadel. 32He showed them
the vile Nica′nor's head and that profane
man's arm, which had been boastfully
stretched out against the holy house of the
Almighty; 33and he cut out the tongue of the
ungodly Nica′nor and said that he would
give it piecemeal to the birds and hang
up these rewards of his folly opposite the
sanctuary. 34And they all, looking to heaven,
blessed the Lord who had manifested
himself, saying, "Blessed is he who has kept
his own place undefiled." 35And he hung
Nica′nor's head from the citadel, a clear and
conspicuous sign to every one of the help of
the Lord. 36And they all decreed by public
vote never to let this day go unobserved, but
to celebrate the thirteenth day of the twelfth
month—which is called Adar' in the Syrian
language—the day before Mor′decai's day.

37This, then, is how matters turned out
with Nica′nor. And from that time the city
has been in the possession of the Hebrews.
So I too will here end my story. 38If it is well
told and to the point, that is what I myself
desired; if it is poorly done and mediocre,
that was the best I could do. 39For just as it
is harmful to drink wine alone, or, again, to
drink water alone, while wine mixed with
water is sweet and delicious and enhances
one's enjoyment, so also the style of the
story delights the ears of those who read the
work. And here will be the end.

SONG OF SOLOMON 7

10I am my beloved's,
and his desire is for me.
11Come, my beloved,
let us go forth into the fields,
and lodge in the villages;
12let us go out early to the vineyards,
and see whether the vines have budded,
whether the grape blossoms have opened
and the pomegranates are in bloom.
There I will give you my love.
13The mandrakes give forth fragrance,
and over our doors are all choice fruits,
new as well as old,
which I have laid up for you, O my
beloved.

8 O that you were like a brother to me,
that nursed at my mother's breast!
If I met you outside, I would kiss you,
and none would despise me.

[2]I would lead you and bring you
into the house of my mother,
and into the chamber of her that
conceived me.
I would give you spiced wine to drink,
the juice of my pomegranates.
[3]O that his left hand were under my head,
and that his right hand embraced me!
[4]I adjure you, O daughters of Jerusalem,
that you stir not up nor awaken love
until it please.

[5]Who is that coming up from
the wilderness,
leaning upon her beloved?

Under the apple tree I awakened you.
There your mother was in travail with you,
there she who bore you was in travail.
[6]Set me as a seal upon your heart,
as a seal upon your arm;
for love is strong as death,
jealousy is cruel as the grave.
Its flashes are flashes of fire,
a most vehement flame.
[7]Many waters cannot quench love,
neither can floods drown it.
If a man offered for love
all the wealth of his house,
it would be utterly scorned.

[8]We have a little sister,
and she has no breasts.
What shall we do for our sister,
on the day when she is spoken for?
[9]If she is a wall,
we will build upon her a battlement
of silver;
but if she is a door,
we will enclose her with boards
of cedar.
[10]I was a wall,
and my breasts were like towers;
then I was in his eyes
as one who brings peace.

[11]Solomon had a vineyard at Ba′al-ha′mon;
he let out the vineyard to keepers;
each one was to bring for its fruit a
thousand pieces of silver.
[12]My vineyard, my very own, is for myself;
you, O Solomon, may have the thousand,
and the keepers of the fruit two hundred.
[13]O you who dwell in the gardens,
my companions are listening for your
voice;
let me hear it.

[14]Make haste, my beloved,
and be like a gazelle
or a young stag
upon the mountains of spices.

REVELATION 22

Then he showed me the river of the water of life, bright as crystal, flowing from the throne of God and of the Lamb
[2]through the middle of the street of the city; also, on either side of the
river, the tree of life with its twelve kinds of fruit, yielding its fruit each month; and the leaves of the tree were for the healing of the
nations. [3]There shall no more be anything accursed, but the throne of God and of the Lamb shall be in it, and his servants shall
worship him; [4]they shall see his face, and
his name shall be on their foreheads. [5]And
night shall be no more; they need no light of lamp or sun, for the Lord God will be their light, and they shall reign for ever and ever.

[6]And he said to me, "These words are trustworthy and true. And the Lord, the God of the spirits of the prophets, has sent his angel to show his servants what must soon
take place. [7]And behold, I am coming soon."
Blessed is he who keeps the words of the prophecy of this book.

[8]I John am he who heard and saw these things. And when I heard and saw them, I fell down to worship at the feet of the angel
who showed them to me; [9]but he said to me,
"You must not do that! I am a fellow servant with you and your brethren the prophets, and with those who keep the words of this book. Worship God."

10And he said to me, "Do not seal up the
words of the prophecy of this book, for the
time is near. 11Let the evildoer still do evil,
and the filthy still be filthy, and the righteous
still do right, and the holy still be holy."
12"Behold, I am coming soon, bringing
my recompense, to repay every one for
what he has done. 13I am the Alpha and the
Omega, the first and the last, the beginning
and the end."
14Blessed are those who wash their robes,
that they may have the right to the tree of life
and that they may enter the city by the gates.
15Outside are the dogs and sorcerers and
fornicators and murderers and idolaters,
and every one who loves and practices
falsehood.
16"I Jesus have sent my angel to you with
this testimony for the churches. I am the
root and the offspring of David, the bright
morning star."
17The Spirit and the Bride say, "Come."
And let him who hears say, "Come." And
let him who is thirsty come, let him who
desires take the water of life without price.
18I warn every one who hears the words of
the prophecy of this book: if any one adds
to them, God will add to him the plagues
described in this book, 19and if any one
takes away from the words of the book of
this prophecy, God will take away his share
in the tree of life and in the holy city, which
are described in this book.
20He who testifies to these things says,
"Surely I am coming soon." Amen. Come,
Lord Jesus!
21The grace of the Lord Jesus be with all
the saints. Amen.

REFLECTION

The great mystical writer on prayer and love of God, St. John of the Cross, observes that in the twilight of our days the only thing that will matter in all our lives is how we loved. As he lies dying in his bed, he asks his religious brothers to read the Song of Solomon to him. In the last chapter is found perhaps John's favorite image of love, the image of a burning fire about which he composes his famous canticle "The Living Flame of Love." As he prepares to go to the Divine Bridegroom, John hears these words afresh: "For love is strong as death, jealousy is cruel as the grave. Its flashes are flashes of fire, a most vehement flame. Many waters cannot quench love, neither can floods drown it" (Sg 8:6–7). John loves Scripture and reads it as the epic love story that begins with the original honeymoon suite of Eden and ends with the Garden restored and an invitation for us: "The Spirit and the Bride say, 'Come.' And let him who hears say, 'Come.' And let him who is thirsty come, let him who desires take the water of life without price" (Rev 21:17). Reflecting on the twilight of your life, will your love for God resist the floods and thus your lamp stay lit, so you may walk in the light of love to him whom your soul loves?